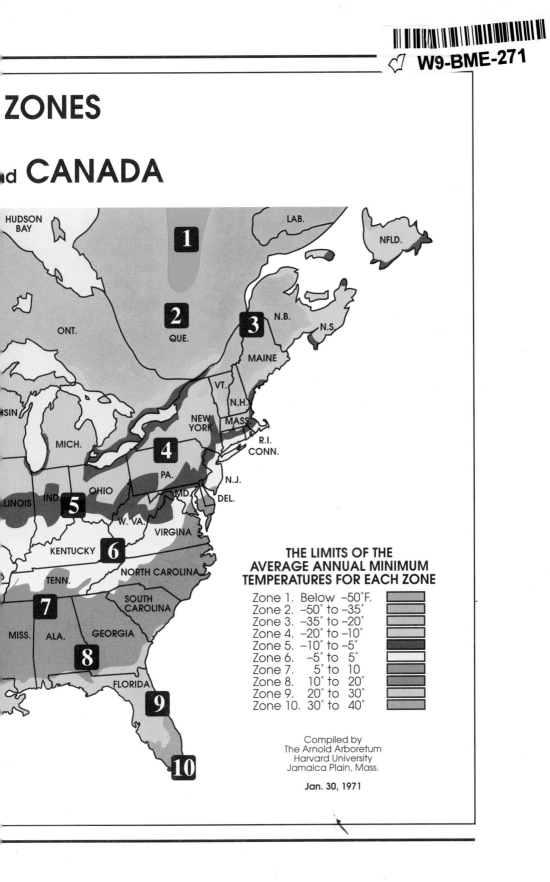

ZONES

d CANADA

W9-BME-271

THE LIMITS OF THE
AVERAGE ANNUAL MINIMUM
TEMPERATURES FOR EACH ZONE

Zone 1. Below −50°F.
Zone 2. −50° to −35°
Zone 3. −35° to −20°
Zone 4. −20° to −10°
Zone 5. −10° to −5°
Zone 6.   −5° to 5°
Zone 7.   5° to 10
Zone 8.   10° to 20°
Zone 9.   20° to 30°
Zone 10. 30° to 40°

Compiled by
The Arnold Arboretum
Harvard University
Jamaica Plain, Mass.

Jan. 30, 1971

WYMAN'S GARDENING ENCYCLOPEDIA

WYMAN'S GARDENING ENCYCLOPEDIA

NEW EXPANDED SECOND EDITION

BY

Donald Wyman

MACMILLAN PUBLISHING COMPANY
NEW YORK

COLLIER MACMILLAN PUBLISHERS
LONDON

Macmillan Publishing Company
866 Third Avenue, New York, N.Y 10022
Collier Macmillan Canada, Inc.

Library of Congress Cataloging-in-Publication Data
Wyman, Donald, 1903–
Wyman's Gardening encyclopedia.
1. Gardening–Dictionaries.
2. Plants, Cultivated–Dictionaries.
I. Title.   II. Title: Gardening encyclopedia.
SB450.95.W96 1986   635′.03′21   86-12509
ISBN 0-02-632070-3

Macmillan books are available at special discounts
for bulk purchases for sales promotions, premiums,
fund-raising, or educational use.
For details, contact:

Special Sales Director
Macmillan Publishing Company
866 Third Avenue
New York, N.Y. 10022

1 2 3 4 5 6 7 8 9 10

PRINTED IN THE UNITED STATES OF AMERICA

To *Florence,*
my wife

CONTENTS

MAJOR ARTICLES ON HORTICULTURAL PRACTICES

Contents

LISTS OF PLANTS
(Also Experiment Stations, Societies and Display Gardens)

ACKNOWLEDGMENTS

The editor wishes to acknowledge the assistance he has received from many sources in writing this volume. Full acknowledgment must be given to the late L. H. Bailey and the many standard texts on horticulture he wrote over the years. The lifetime of energy and study which went into the writing of these works is still appreciated today, for several of them remain the authoritative sources of horticultural information. The voluminous information made available in his writings has often served as the basis for the information in this present volume.

Contributing authors have been most helpful in writing articles on specialized subjects, without which this present volume would not be complete. They are each acknowledged separately elsewhere in this introduction.

The generic pronunciations follow those of A. W. Smith in *A Gardener's Book of Plant Names* (Harper and Row, New York, 1963). His widow and his publishers have graciously given me permission to use these pronunciations. Colonel Smith studied the subject for many years and was both a practical gardener and a serious student of Latin and Greek. Therefore, it has seemed advisable to conform to the pronunciations as he has given them. It was impossible to give pronunciations for specific and varietal names here, but the student seriously interested in them is referred to Colonel Smith's book.

Dr. Harold E. Moore, Jr., former Director of The Bailey Hortorium at Cornell University, was most generous in allowing me to go through the manuscript being submitted for *Hortus III*. Many changes in plant names have occurred since 1941, when *Hortus Second* was first published, and trying to keep abreast of these changes is impossible for the average gardener. With plant taxonomists busily engaged in the study of plants throughout the country, changes in nomenclature are bound to occur and, fortunately or unfortunately, will have to be accepted by the gardeners of the country eventually. The changes in nomenclature in this volume are kept to a reasonable minimum and, it is hoped, will pave the way for authoritative botanical references of the near future.

Throughout this volume many references are made to other books currently outstanding in their respective fields. Because it is not practical in a volume of this size to give all the information available on certain subjects, a number of good texts have been suggested for further study.

Much information has been taken from the articles and books of the editor, especially from his writings in *Arnoldia* and in *The American Nurseryman*. He wishes to acknowledge with appreciation the privilege of using some of the information from these sources. Many of the short definitions of botanical and horticultural terms were taken from an article in *Arnoldia* 15 (1955):

25–44, by the late Dr. C. E. Kobuski, Curator of the Arnold Arboretum, "A Revised Glossary of the More Common Botanical and Horticultural Terms."

All but seventeen photographs were taken by the editor and those were taken by Heman Howard, Assistant Horticulturist at the Arnold Arboretum. All drawings have been made by Mrs. Virginia Howie of Millis, Massachusetts, with the exception of those of poisonous plants, made by Miss Judy Appenzeller, formerly of the Arnold Arboretum. Full acknowledgment is given the Arnold Arboretum, its library and staff for permission to draw on information from its world-famous collections of plants and its reference works and files for the preparation of this present volume.

Special acknowledgment should be given Miss Stella Whitehouse for writing many of the wild-flower descriptions, doing much of the preparatory work for the writing, and also for typing many parts of the manuscript. Finally, my deepest appreciation goes to my wife, Florence D. Wyman, for typing most of the manuscript and bearing with me through the several years in which this was in preparation. Not the least of her contributions was a five-week period of almost continuous typing in a small *casita* in the rain forest of Puerto Rico, when the tropical recreational pursuits beckoned on every side.

DONALD WYMAN

CONTRIBUTING AUTHORS

The following authors contributed articles to this publication, and their names appear at the end of the articles, except those on insect and disease control (by Warren D. Whitcomb) and the short notes on propagation (by Alfred J. Fordham). These are distributed throughout the volume. All other material was written by Donald Wyman.

Clifford S. Chater. Professor, Shade Tree Laboratory, Suburban Experiment Station, University of Massachusetts, Waltham, Massachusetts. He has been actively engaged in shade tree pest control and arboriculture for many years and is responsible for updating the information on insecticides and fungicides in this edition.

Ernest G. Christ. Extension Specialist, Pomology, College of Agriculture, Rutgers–The State University, New Brunswick, New Jersey, who has supplied some of the articles on fruits.

Roger G. Coggeshall. Former Propagator at the Arnold Arboretum, Harvard University, and currently President of the Cherry Hill Nurseries, West Newbury, Massachusetts, and a Director of the New England Nurserymen's Association.

*Ladislaus Cutak. Greenhouse Superintendent, Missouri Botanical Garden, St. Louis, Missouri, lecturer and author of many publications on cacti and succulents, including his excellent book *Cactus Guide* (Van Nostrand).

O. Keister Evans, Jr. Formerly Executive Secretary of the American Rose Society, and editor of the American Rose Society publications, including the *American Rose Magazine* and the *American Rose Annual*.

T. A. Fennell, Jr. Owner of the Fennell Orchid Company–Orchid Jungle in Homestead, Florida, accredited judge of the American Orchid Society, and author of *Orchids for Home and Garden* (Holt, Rinehart and Winston, Inc.), who has spent most of his life growing orchids.

Wilmer B. Flory. Former president of the American Hemerocallis Society, editor of its publications, and also a charter member of that organization. Long-time grower and hybridizer of hemerocallis at Logansport, Indiana, author, lecturer and winner of many awards for introducing new varieties.

Alfred J. Fordham. Propagator at the Arnold Arboretum of Harvard University, Jamaica Plain, Massachusetts.

Peter Shaw Green. Formerly Horticultural Taxonomist at the Arnold Arboretum of Harvard University, currently Senior Scientific Officer at the Royal Botanic Gardens, Kew, Surrey, England.

*W. Ray Hastings. Formerly Executive Secretary-Treasurer, All America Selections, Harrisburg, Pennsylvania, who supplied the information for the article on All America Selections.

* Deceased

Dr. Claron O. Hesse. Professor of Horticulture, Department of Pomology, University of California (Davis), author of many articles in this volume dealing with tropical and subtropical fruits.

Edward B. Lloyd. Secretary and editor of the publications of the American Dahlia Society and a grower of dahlias for some forty-five years.

*H. Gleason Mattoon. Former nurseryman and grower of hollies, former editor of *Horticulture*, magazine of the Massachusetts Horticultural Society. An outstanding authority on nuts and nut culture.

Everitt L. Miller. Assistant Director, Longwood Gardens, Kennett Square, Pennsylvania, and formerly commercial florist; lecturer and author.

Dr. John A. Naegele. Associate Dean, College of Food and Natural Resources, and Associate Director of the Experiment Station, University of Massachusetts, Amherst, who reassessed pesticide recommendations for the Revised Edition.

Patrick A. Nutt. In charge of the water lily gardens at Longwood Gardens, Kennett Square, Pennsylvania, and formerly a graduate of the Royal Horticultural Society's school for gardeners at Wisley, England.

Dr. Robert W. Schery. Director of the Lawn Institute, Marysville, Ohio, the author of several outstanding books including *The Lawn Book* (Macmillan). He has also served as botanist for the Monsanto Chemical Co. and the O. M. Scott Co. of Marysville, Ohio.

Grant B. Snyder. Professor of Olericulture, Emeritus, University of Massachusetts, Amherst, and for several years head of its Department of Horticulture. He is actively interested in the National Junior Horticultural Foundation, Inc., which he serves as National Adviser and Chairman of the Board of Trustees. Professor Snyder's contributions on the vegetable garden and the culture of vegetables are distributed throughout this volume.

George Taloumis. Lecturer, author and former executive editor of *Horticulture*, magazine of the Massachusetts Horticultural Society.

Dr. Henry Teuscher. Formerly Curator of the Montreal Botanical Garden, where he served for many years before retiring, and author of *Window-Box Gardening* (Macmillan).

Dr. Robert L. Ticknor. Professor of Horticulture, Oregon State University, who for many years has been conducting research with chemical weed killers both in Massachusetts and in Oregon.

Philip Truex. After pursuing a career in acting for several years, Mr. Truex decided with his wife to devote his full time to his hobby of gardening. They were the owners of The City Gardener, a retail plant shop in the heart of downtown New York. He is a lecturer, author of *The City Gardener* (Knopf), and adviser to thousands on planting in the heart of a great metropolitan city.

Mrs. Violet K. Tyson. Gardeners, Pennsylvania, which is in the heart of the mushroom-growing area of Pennsylvania. The widow of C. Aubrey Thomas, who was Professor of Economic Entomology at Pennsylvania State University, Mrs. Tyson is the author of several publications of the American Mushroom Institute.

*Deceased

Beatrice Clark Warburton (Mrs. F. W.). Westfield, Massachusetts. President of the Median Iris Society, a section of the American Iris Society, and editor of its publications. A grower, hybridizer, and judge of iris for many years and recipient of numerous awards for new introductions.

Warren D. Whitcomb. Professor of Entomology, Emeritus, University of Massachusetts, Waltham, who for many years provided practical information to thousands of growers on control of the hundreds of insect species destroying horticultural crops throughout the New England area. Professor Whitcomb's hundreds of contributions on insect and disease control are distributed throughout this volume.

INTRODUCTION

A pleasing, well-grown garden reflects the personality of its owners, living proof that they have an interest and enthusiasm for growing plants, that they have an inherent feeling for design and good color combinations, and that they have a knowledge of horticulture. To be able to select the proper plants for a garden and then to grow them satisfactorily in pleasing combinations requires a wide knowledge usually obtained from many sources. As new plants are introduced, new methods of growing them are proposed, new machines are developed and new fertilizers and pesticides are offered, and the latest information in all these areas is brought together in this volume.

This book is written by experienced gardeners for gardeners. It contains many articles dealing with the growing of specialized groups of plants as well as brief descriptions of thousands of plants which show where they can be grown and the ornamental value of each. Many others have been omitted because they have little to add to a garden cared for by a busy individual with many other important interests. It is hoped that the up-to-date information contained herein will provide a quick reference for those busy people who wish to make their grounds beautiful but who wish to do it with a minimum amount of effort.

Selection of Plants

Plants selected for this volume are those mostly of ornamental or economic value. It is impossible to list all the plants grown in America in one volume, and the reasons for selecting one plant and rejecting another are often purely personal. The wild flowers of this country are of interest to many groups of people, but it must be admitted that many a "wild flower" has little value in the modern garden. On the other hand, some of the rare plants, at present difficult to find in nursery catalogues, may be the popular plants of tomorrow. Old-time favorites must be included, for it is by comparison with them that we assess "new" plants for the garden.

The plant world becomes smaller every day. One can have breakfast in Boston and dinner the same day in the heart of the tropics where a whole new world of plant life exists. Obviously, mixing tropical plants (many of which are grown in Temperate Zone greenhouses) with plants of the North creates problems in limiting the size of a book, yet a certain amount of it had to be done in preparing this volume.

Consequently, here will be found most of the plants popularly known or grown by gardeners (and greenhouse owners) in all but the subtropical and tropical parts of the United States. Here are also listed some of the major, conspicuously ornamental plants of Florida, California, the Virgin Islands and Hawaii, which the average traveler may come across within the limits of a short vacation trip.

There are many specialists in America who grow only cacti or orchids or roses. Such individuals grow hundreds of rare species and varieties not available to the general public and not discussed in this book. Not all the plants mentioned are readily available, but most are. If a plant is listed by three or more nurseries in America, the chances are it will be listed here. Other means have also been used to aid in determining the popular plants available to gardeners at present or which will be in the near future. Admittedly, many plants of little garden value have had to be included for reference purposes.

It has not been practical to list the thousands of roses, irises, peonies and other groups of popular plants, but in many cases suggestions have been made of a few of the better varieties for current trial. Varieties offered one year are not necessarily those offered the next so that there is an ever-changing group of "best" plants for the garden. Some people like to add "new" varieties to their gardens each year; others are content to grow a few of what they consider "the best" and let the "new" ones come and go across the pages of the seed and nursery catalogues. Each group of gardeners will find much in the following pages that will aid them in making their gardens outstanding.

Nomenclature

The scientific names of plants in this volume follow, in general, the new International Code of Nomenclature for Cultivated Plants, which is being adopted and followed by horticultural organizations throughout the world. It was adopted in the United States in 1959. Specific rules and regulations in this code are set forth in a booklet available from the American Horticultural Society. The procedures to be followed in naming new cultivars or clones are fully explained, and every plantsman who names new plants should have a copy. Thus, *Malus ioensis plena* becomes *Malus ioensis* **'Plena'**, showing that it is a clone and must be propagated in a certain way. Although most of the plants in this volume conform, admittedly some do not, for the time was simply not available to study each variety in order to determine exactly how it originated, information which must be available if one is to list it as a clone or cultivar in single quotes (' '). Hence some of the plants listed as botanical varieties may at some future date be changed to cultivars, but it will undoubtedly take many years and much detailed investigation before this is finally properly accomplished.

A hybrid is designated by a small x between the generic and specific name. Thus *Magnolia* x *soulangiana* means that this is a hybrid species and can not be expected to produce seedlings identical with the parent. The small x is also used to denote hybrid parents. Thus *Malus halliana* x *M. sieboldii* is a cross resulting in the hybrid species *Malus* x *atrosanguinea*.

The book is set up in such a way as to provide an impetus to the learning of scientific names. They are used in nursery catalogues and magazines, flower show requirements call for them, and in most colleges and universities where even elementary taxonomic courses are offered emphasis is placed on knowing these names. Hence, in this volume, the plant descriptions are under the scientific names and the common names are cross-indexed. The exceptions are fruits and vegetables, for in both these groups plants are described under their common names, admittedly a concession made to gardeners looking for information in a hurry.

Numerous attempts have been made to "standardize" the common names of plants, but these names are the result of usage and many of the names now commonly used just do not conform to rigid rules. In this volume an attempt has been made to follow these general directives:

1. If the second word of a plant name is correctly applied, it should not be joined to the first by a hyphen. Hence we have Green Ash.

2. If the second word of a plant name is misapplied, it is joined to the first with a hyphen, examples being Water-lily, Marsh-marigold, Wax-myrtle. However no hyphen is used if the first word is False, as for instance False Foxglove, for the first word indicates it is not a true foxglove.

3. A hyphen is used if the second word in a plant name has nothing to do with a plant, as Lady's-slipper, Pheasant's-eye, Shooting-star.

4. A name of more than two words generally rates a hyphen between words, as Jack-in-the-pulpit, Joe-Pye-weed.

The individual who is a stickler on the subject may find some names here that do not conform, which just goes to show that even these "rules" are not hard and fast. Theoretically, however, it would be helpful if all authors would live up to them as much as possible.

H. W. Rickett of the New York Botanical Garden has gone one step further and suggested (Bulletin of Torrey Botanical Club 92: No. 2, pp. 137–139, March–April, 1965): "Words of one or two syllables referring to plants in general or to some part of a plant are joined to a preceding word without a hyphen, unless the resulting word is so long and unwieldy that it is not readily grasped by a reader or unless it brings together a collection of consonants that the eye cannot readily sort out. Such words are plant, tree, vine, wort, root, leaf, flower, bud, pod, nut, berry." Obviously this allows for many loopholes. It is probably good in principle, but it was not found expedient to follow this suggestion rigidly in this volume.

Common names may vary from one part of the country to another, but a plant has only one scientific name, which is the same all over the world. It is impossible to list all the common names for each plant and in this volume only one is given. In *Hortus III* (Macmillan, 1976) there is a list of some 10,500 common names and the scientific name for each. Sometimes a plant is given several common names. On the other hand, sometimes the same common name is used for three or four different plants. This is the reason why the more one learns the scientific names of plants, the more accurate one will be in discussing them and the easier it will be to find reference material about them.

Pesticides

The use of pesticides is regulated by the United States Environmental Protection Agency to ensure that pesticide use is both efficacious and safe to humans and the environment. The device used to accomplish this regulation is to register the label that is on the pesticide package. The label therefore assumes paramount importance, as the information contained on it, which is based upon critically reviewed experimental evidence and use experience, represents the legally accepted directions for safe and effective use. Suggestions for pesticides' use in this book are based upon label information at the time of writing.

In fact, so many changes have been made in pesticides and the laws pertaining to their use that the tables on pages 416 and 567 had to be completely revised to conform to regulations at the time of the writing of this revised edition. Registrations for pesticide use are constantly changing as new information and new pesticides become available. Therefore the suggestions contained in this book should be considered only an initial guide. The recommendations contained on the label should be regarded as the final guide for safe and effective use. The user assumes all risks in using the suggestions made in this book.

How to Use This Book

Plants have been listed alphabetically with descriptions after the scientific names. Common names are cross-indexed. Exceptions are fruits and vegetables, which are listed and described according to their common names. If one wants to find information concerning the Pin Oak and does not know its scientific name, he looks first under Oak and notes that these belong to the genus *Quercus* to which he then turns. The generic description comes first under *Quercus* but further on in this article all the species are listed, scientific names on the left, common names on the right. Then he merely checks through the common names on the right side of the column until he comes to Pin Oak, where he can obtain the information he wishes.

The generic discussions include the correct pronunciation of the genus, general notes about the plants in the genus, where they are native, how they are propagated and notes on insect and disease pests and their control.

In this connection, special attention should be given to the articles under the headings Insecticides, Miticides and Fungicides, for many of the control measures recommended are tied in directly with these articles. So we see under *Pinus* that in order to control the European pine shoot moth, pesticide #9 is recommended, or for controlling needle cast fungus, fungicide #D or #F is recommended. These chemicals will be found under the extremely important and all-inclusive articles on insecticides and fungicides. Also under Insecticides will be found several paragraphs on how to use the information on insecticides and fungicides.

In the specific discussions of plants one also finds the approximate height and hardiness zone. The hardiness zone is listed for all woody plants, herbaceous perennials and bulbs. With the perennials and bulbs, however, the designation of an exact hardiness zone is somewhat difficult, for the hardiness of these plants can vary with the amount of snow cover—with a deep snow cover every winter many perennials can be grown much farther north than those without such a deep snow cover. Also discussed are the habitat, time of bloom and some facts pertinent to the flowers, foliage and habit of growth, together with brief descriptions of a few of the better ornamental varieties.

All times of bloom, approximate dates for spraying of insects and diseases, etc., are given as for Boston, Massachusetts. Similar air temperatures (on which these dates are based) naturally come earlier in areas south of Boston, later in areas north of Boston. Read the discussion under Order of Bloom to note the simple way to make calculations on how much earlier (or later) these dates can be figured for all other parts of the country.

Lists

Some 52 lists of plants for specific purposes are given, most of them containing the scientific name, height, hardiness zone and common name of each plant. This is a considerable aid to the busy gardener who wishes to make a quick selection of plants for some specific purpose in his garden. Glancing through such a list, he will undoubtedly recognize some plants with which he is familiar, from either their scientific or their common name. Many a gardener does not know both names of a plant, hence the listing in this manner aids him in pinpointing those with which he is familiar. Also, by listing the hardiness zones, he can quickly determine whether a plant unknown to him is worthy of a trial in his garden.

The information on height is always helpful in making selections. It must be added, however, that these lists do not include all the plants suitable. The gardener should consider each one as a short suggested group of plants to which he can add from his own experience or by more detailed study of the individual descriptions of the plants in this volume.

FOREWORD TO REVISED EDITION

This Revised Edition contains many plant name changes that have been recorded in the recently published *Hortus III* (Macmillan, 1976). In 1967, when the original manuscript for this encyclopedia was being prepared, Dr. Harold E. Moore, Jr., then Director of The Bailey Hortorium, made it possible for me to check through the manuscript being prepared for *Hortus III*. However, because of the stupendous job involved in preparing *Hortus III*, it took nine years for those manuscripts to actually be published, and during that time additional corrections were necessary. *Hortus III* will undoubtedly stand as the one major reference for horticultural nomenclature for many years to come; hence it was advisable that the nomenclature in this Revised Edition of the encyclopedia conform to *Hortus III*.

Also, in the intervening years since 1971, many changes have been made in the availability of insecticides and fungicides. Dr. John A. Naegele, Associate Director of the Massachusetts Experiment Station, and a trained entomologist, has reviewed the new laws concerning pesticides and made changes in the old recommendations, bringing those in this new edition up to date.

The same has been done with the complex of herbicides and weed killers by Dr. Robert L. Ticknor of Oregon State University. The article on Plant Quarantines has been changed to bring into line the changes that have been made in this area during the past nine years.

Vegetable and fruit varieties change from year to year; hence the newer varieties now being recommended have been added. Certain varietal lists of flowers have been radically changed, and certain new horticultural practices have been added as well. New reference books have been included, where warranted.

A table of contents has been added to aid users of this book in seeing at a glance the titles of major horticultural articles. Of course much is written about the culture of many individual genera, but included in this work is detailed information on many basic horticultural practices such as methods of making an espalier, pruning, propagation of all kinds, seed dormancy, standard judging methods in flower shows, managing a home greenhouse, and methods of making a rock garden, a roof garden and a herb garden. In other words, here are listed the many basic horticultural practices fully described so the gardener can quickly obtain directions on how to proceed with his particular horticultural project.

It is hoped that this added table of contents, in which are enumerated both articles on major horticultural practices and lists of plants selected for specific purposes, will help materially with speedy reference finding in this Revised Edition.

FOREWORD TO NEW EXPANDED SECOND EDITION

In the fifteen years since this Encyclopedia was published, many changes have occurred in varieties of plants used. Plant Quarantine laws pertaining to the introduction of plants from foreign countries, the number of International Plant Registration authorities governing new and acceptable plant names, chemicals now being used in weed control and especially in the insecticides and fungicides governing pest control are changing annually.

Among the most important changes in this edition are the chemicals used for insecticides and fungicides. Professor Clifford S. Chater of the University of Massachusetts is responsible for bringing these recommendations up to date. It is interesting to note that 21 of the 48 insecticides recommended in the first edition are now either banned by legislation or have been taken off the market for various reasons, hence are not now available to the home gardener. Six of the 26 fungicides originally recommended are also unavailable. In revamping these recommendations it should be noted that malathion has been substituted in many instances for older chemicals, making this one of the most valuable insecticides for the gardener to have on hand.

Dr. Robert L. Ticknor of Oregon State University has revamped his former recommendations of chemicals for weed control. Professor Grant B. Snyder has added many vegetables to his former lists (and removed some as well), as has Professor Ernest G. Christ of Rutgers State University his former list of fruit recommendations. All these change year to year, and it is impossible to keep up with the new varieties offered by each seed company annually. The home gardener should keep abreast of this situation himself, by obtaining several of the better seed and nursery catalogues each year when he wants to make selections for his own garden and to keep in touch with his State Experiment Station to note what species they are recommending.

The list of International Plant Registrars has been increased. To keep up with the numerous annual changes in this, one should write the American Horticultural Society or Dr. Donald Huttleson of Longwood Gardens in Kennett Square, PA 19348.

Once again your attention is called to the list of horticultural articles and lists (pages vii–ix) at the beginning of the book. The chances are, the information you want is here, if you will persevere and hunt for it.

Many things do not change from year to year: the lists of plants used for various purposes, the addresses of the State Experiment Stations, the excellent discussions on Propagation, Seed Dormancy, Order of Bloom, Hedges, Christmas Decorations from Evergreens, etc. All in all, the additions and changes in this latest edition should make this book a most valuable up-to-date reference to have on hand for all phases of gardening.

My deepest appreciation goes to my daughter Dorothea Wyman Thomas (Mrs. Roger M.) who has done all the typing for this new edition and much of the checking and research work needed to bring the manuscript up to date. Growing up in a horticulturally oriented family, she is a horticulturist in her own right and has been growing many interesting plants in her own garden for years. She is an author with several articles on growing and using plants to her credit, a former president of the Weston Garden Club and has been engaged in prominent horticultural activities for a long time. Her assistance, combined with her practical knowledge, has been a great asset in making this new expanded second edition complete.

A

ABACA = *Musa textilis*

ABELIA (ab-EE-lia). A group of deciduous or evergreen opposite-leaved shrubs occasionally with their leaves in threes, noted chiefly for their flowers and foliage characteristics, native to Asia and one or two to Mexico. The flowers appear in summer, are somewhat tubular in outline and are pink, white or purplish. Although the popular *A. grandiflora* is often seen growing in full sun, they do best as a group with partial shade. Easily propagated by softwood or hardwood cuttings. Also seeds can be sown as soon as they are ripe or stored for up to a year in airtight containers in a cool place and then sown.

x 'Edward Goucher'   5'   Zone 5
The lavender-purple flowers appear from July to Sept. and the foliage is semi-evergreen. It appeared as a hybrid (*A. grandiflora* x *A. schumannii*) before 1911, originated by the late Edward Goucher of the U.S. Department of Agriculture, and the plant is intermediate in habit between both parents.

floribunda   6'   Zone 8   Mexican Abelia
Sometimes a greenhouse plant; the flowers rosy red and large; leaves evergreen 1½ in. long. Native to Mexico.

x grandiflora   5'   Zone 5   Glossy Abelia
The most popular of all the Abelias, this hybrid (*A. chinensis* x *A. uniflora*) has pink flowers ¾ in. long, 1–4 in a cluster in Aug. In the autumn the foliage turns bronze to purplish, and the glossy evergreen leaves are 1½ in. long. It is the most free flowering of all the Abelias and has been used in formally clipped or informal flowering hedges from Fla. to N.Y. It is very dense in habit and makes a splendid specimen. 'Sherwood' is only about 3 ft. tall and is more dense in habit.

schumannii   5'   Zone 7   Schumann Abelia
A native of western China with lavender-pink tubular flowers from June to Sept. and deciduous or semi-evergreen leaves about 1 in. long.

ABELIA-LEAF, KOREAN = *Abeliophyllum distichum*

ABELIOPHYLLUM (a-BE-lio-fill-um)
distichum   5'   Zone 5   Korean Abelia-leaf
Unfortunately labeled the "white forsythia" by some sales-conscious nurserymen, this deciduous shrub is a member of the Olive Family (with forsythias) and is used especially because of its small white flowers appearing in dense clusters before the leaves in early spring (mid-April). A native of central Korea, it has been growing in America since 1924. The opposite leaves are about 1–2 in. long. The flowers are smaller and more numerous than those of Forsythia, but the flower buds are not as winter-hardy. They are present all winter long, and in the northern U.S. sometimes the flowers are injured by late freezing weather in the spring, especially in New England. It is a good companion shrub with forsythias but obviously should be grown in a protected place. Propagated by softwood and hardwood cuttings and seeds sown at once.

ABELMOSCHUS (abel-MO-shuss). Formerly these plants were all grouped under Hibiscus, to which they are closely related. They have large, funnel-shaped flowers with alternate leaves and palmately arranged veins. Grafting and layering are used in their propagation, but all root readily from softwood and hardwood cuttings. Also grown from seed.

esculentus (*H. esculentus*)   **6'   annual   Okra**
This is native to the tropics of the Old World and is grown for its edible pods. The flowers, up to 3 in. wide, are yellow with a reddish center and the ribbed, foot-long pods are eaten as a vegetable before they have fully matured and become somewhat woody.

manihot (*H. manihot*)   **9'   annual or perennial
Sunset Hibiscus**
The very large flowers of this species from eastern Asia can be as much as 9 in. wide, yellow to white with a dark brown center. There is a variety **grandiflorus** supposedly with even larger flowers. The leaves are narrowly lobed.

moschatus (*H. abelmoschus*)   **6'   annual or biennial   Muskmallow**
Native to India, with funnel-shaped flowers 4 in. wide, yellow with a crimson center. The leaves are lobed and it is sometimes grown as an annual but it needs plenty of hot weather in order to grow properly. The seeds have a musky odor.

ABERRANT. Differing from usual structure, departing from the type; used most in describing variation.

ABIES (A-beez). The firs are stately, pyramidal-shaped evergreen trees with single trunks and usually with horizontal branches. They are high altitude trees, those in the mountains of the West Coast often above the elevations of normal lumbering operations. The wood is soft and

I

filled with resin and it does not make pulp as well as the spruce. There are some 34 different firs being offered by American nurserymen, but actually only a very few make dependable landscape trees.

In the forests of America, they serve their best purpose covering the soil at high altitudes. The wood is used but it is not of "high grade" in the lumber industry. In general, there are some native American species of fir which should not be grown outside their native habitats; at least they will not make meritorious landscape specimens in other places. Such would be the Balsam Fir (*A. balsamea*), Fraser Fir (*A. fraseri*) and several from the West Coast. Such species thrive in the cool moist atmosphere of the mountains but when grown in areas where the summers are hot and dry, they are not long-lived and soon become spindly and sickly in appearance. Also, all firs prefer a cool moist climate, the reason why firs will not grow in the hot, dry, drought areas of the midwestern U.S.

As a rule, none of the firs in ornamental plantings are subject to serious insect or disease pests. Pruning seems to be the difficult problem, for, once the lower limbs die or are removed, it is practically impossible to force out new growth in the same place. Topping such trees permanently mars the form because of the single straight trunk and definitely pyramidal habit.

All firs are definitely stiff in pyramidal outline, with a whorl of branches produced each year. The cones are borne in an upright position on the trees, not pendant as in most spruce and pine, and the pistillate cones usually are all at the top of the tree, quickly shattering out completely as soon as they ripen in the fall.

Propagation

Seeds can be processed as soon as ripe or can be stored dry in airtight containers in a cool place and processed the following year. They should be stratified at 40° F. for 3 months, then sown. Many types are grafted on the different species as understock. Terminal shoots are preferable as scions because they require less training to produce plants with leaders. Some are occasionally rooted from hardwood cuttings, but not many. See SEEDS, GRAFTING.

Insect Pests

Ornamental trees of Balsam Fir may be infested with the balsam twig aphid which kills the new growth. Use insecticide #15 for control. Spruce budworm and spruce mite also infest fir. See PICEA. In the West several species of bark beetles and borers are destructive to forest trees and may attack ornamental trees. Consult local authorities. Balsam Fir sawfly appears suddenly, eats rapidly and defoliates branches completely—spray with insecticide #15 when first seen.

Disease Pests

Needle cast and needle rust fungi are minor pests of fir and special control measures are seldom used.

alba   150'   Zone 4   Silver Fir
One of the few firs native to central and southern Europe with leaves about 1 in. long and cones 3–5 in. long. This also, like several other firs, requires a cool moist climate and will not thrive where summers are hot and dry. It is not planted much in America.

amabilis   200'   Zone 5   Cascade Fir
Native in British Columbia and Alberta south to Ore. A beautifully graceful specimen in its native habitat with drooping branches, but is another tree not doing well in gardens outside its native habitat. The needles are a rich glossy green above and bluish white beneath. Cones are 4–6 in. long and 2 in. through.

arizonica = A. lasiocarpa arizonica

balsamea   75'   Zone 3   Balsam Fir
Similar to the Fraser Fir of the South, this is native from Labrador to W.Va. and Minn. It requires the cool, moist conditions of the mountains and because of this makes a very poor ornamental in gardens elsewhere. Needles are ½–1¼ in. long and very aromatic; cones are 2½–3½ in. long. The inner bark has been used as emergency food by people lost in the woods and the tips of young shoots have been used to make a tea. Two dwarf shrubby varieties are sometimes confused—the rare **hudsonia** with pectinate leaves and the more common 'Nana' with radiate leaves.

cephalonica   90'   Zone 5   Greek Fir
A fine, sturdy tree, needles about an inch long. Sharp pointed at the tip. Cones are 7 in. long. Native to Greece, but perfectly hardy as far north as Boston. The needles stand out stiffly almost at right angles to the twig and are distributed all around it.

cilicica   90'   Zone 5   Cilician Fir
A fine fir with spiny-tipped needles, stiff habit and sturdy pyramidal growth. The bark is ashy gray, cones about 7–9 in. long and the needles about an inch long, notched at the tip. In the wild, it is frequently found with *Cedrus libani* in Asia Minor and Syria.

concolor   120'   Zone 4   White or Colorado Fir
A native of the Rocky Mountains in the western and southwestern U.S., this is one of the best firs for landscape use in the northern states. It withstands city growing conditions better than any of the others and is fairly resistant to heat and drought. The needles are about 2 in. long

and are colored bluish green, the color varying considerably among the seedlings, some being green, some decidedly bluish. The variety **violacea** has strikingly bluish-white needles, and **'Conica'** is more dwarf, pyramidal in habit and slow growing, with needles under 1½ in. long.

firma   150'   Zone 6   Momi Fir
A handsome tree from Japan, with very pointed light green needles ⅝–1½ in. long and cones 3½–5 in. long.

Abies concolor 'Conica': White or Colorado Fir with grayish-blue foliage. The best fir for city planting.

fraseri   75'   Zone 4   Fraser Fir
Similar to the Balsam Fir of the North, this is native to the mountains of W.Va. and Tenn. This is not a very good specimen tree except in the cool, moist mountains. Needles are ½–1 in. long and the cones are 1½–2½ in. long. The clone **'Prostrata'** is low and grows flat on the soil surface.

grandis   300'   Zone 6   Grand Fir
This is probably the tallest of the firs but it needs a cool moist climate to do its best, which is sometimes a rate of growth of 2–3 ft. annually. The needles are ¾–2¼ in. long, arranged very flat on both sides of the twig, and the cones are 3–4 in. long. Native to the Pacific Coast.

homolepis   90'   Zone 4   Nikko Fir
This is the common fir of the mountains of central Japan and has been considered one of the best of the Japanese firs for planting in the northern U.S. It is noted for its wide-spreading, regularly spaced branches, and can be easily identified because of its deep-grooved one-year twigs.

koreana   50'   Zone 5   Korean Fir
Introduced into America in 1908 from Korea by the Arnold Arboretum, this is a comparatively small tree as firs go, with horizontal branches covered with upright-growing, short, stubby branchlets that give a special character to the tree. The needles are very whitish on the undersurface, another fairly distinctive feature.

lasiocarpa   90'   Zone 5   Alpine Fir
Native from Alaska to northern Calif., this is a tree of the mountains and does not thrive well in the eastern U.S. The needles are 1½ in. long and the purplish cones are 3–4 in. long. The bark of the var. **arizonica** is creamy white, thick and corky and the leaves are more glaucous than those of the species. This is a beautiful tree.

magnifica   200'   Zone 5   Red Fir
Of special value on the West Coast, where it is native. Although it will grow in the East, it has no merit over other firs in this area. The variety **glauca** has whitish needles.

nordmanniana   150'   Zone 4   Nordmann Fir
This is not as good an ornamental tree as some of the other firs but it is offered by a number of American nurserymen. Native to the Caucasus and Asia Minor, it has dark green needles that are ¾–1½ in. long and cones about 5–6 in. long.

pinsapo   75'   Zone 6   Spanish Fir
This fir from Spain is especially well grown in limestone soils and seems to do well in the eastern U.S. The variety **argentea** has silvery-white foliage, more pronounced than the more easily available var. **glauca**.

procera   240'   Zone 5   Noble Fir
A noble West Coast fir (Wash. to Calif.) that can grow in the East, it is best used near its native habitat. (Formerly named *A. nobilis*.)

spectabilis   50'   Zone 7   Himalayan Fir
A fine fir of value only in the South, native to the Himalayas.

veitchii   75'   Zone 3   Veitch Fir
Of broad pyramidal habit, this fir from Japan is not at all well suited for growing in the central Midwest, but can do well in much of the East. Its chief merit is the white undersurface of the needles, which gives it an appearance all its own.

ABORTIVE. Barren; imperfect or not developed; as abortive stamens when only filaments are present.

ABRONIA (ab-RO-nia)
fragrans   10"   Zone 5   Sand-verbena
The Sand-verbena grows throughout the southern Midwest and western states in sunny

areas where the soil is light and sandy. It is an erect perennial herb with opposite leaves. The white flowers consist of a calyx resembling petals, being 4 or 5 lobed, and the individual flowers are clustered in a loose head. Since the flowers are fragrant at night, it is an interesting addition to the wild garden, although one not frequently used.

umbellata   prostrate   Zone 8   Prostrate Sand-verbena

Unlike *A. fragrans*, this species grows as a prostrate perennial herb in Calif., where it is native, but it can be used north of Washington, D.C., as an annual. The flowers, similar to those of *A. fragrans*, are pink, the flower heads up to 2 in. in dia. Seeds of this plant may be sown indoors, or outside after danger of frost is past. The plants also root readily where joints touch the soil. This is a good plant for hanging baskets, or, if it is somewhat restrained, for borders or the rockery. The var. **grandiflora** has slightly larger flowers.

ABRUS (AB-rus)

precatorius   vine   Zone 9   Rosary-pea

A small twining vine to 10 ft., native of the tropics, sometimes used as a house plant. The leaves are alternate, 2–3 in. long, compound, the leaflets about $\frac{1}{2}$ in. long; flowers are pealike, white to rose; the fruits are bright scarlet peas (with a black spot) in pods. It is said that Buddhists use these for rosaries in India, but the peas are very poisonous if eaten. Propagation by seeds or softwood cuttings.

ABUTILON (ab-YEW-til-on)

x hybridum   5′   Zone 10   Flowering-maple

Popular pot plants for the greenhouse, sometimes grown out-of-doors in the South; these are used mostly as house plants and are of mixed parentage. Many have maplelike alternate leaves; bright-colored, bell-shaped, pendulous flowers. They prefer a temperature of 60° F. If seed is sown in the early spring in pots indoors, the plants will bloom the following winter in the house. They can also be propagated by softwood cuttings. Tips of the branches might be cut back to force a denser growth. Most of the species of this genus are native to the tropics, mostly of South America. Various cultivars are: 'Eclipse'—pink flowers, leaves variegated with yellow; 'Grandiflorum'—orange flowers with scarlet veins; 'Insigne'—white flowers with red and purple veins; 'Savitzii'—yellow flowers, leaves with a white margin; 'Snowstorm'—white flowers; 'Splendens'—deep red flowers.

Insect Pests

In the greenhouse, plants may be infested with soft brown scale, mealy bugs and green-house white fly. Spray with pesticide #16 or other organic phosphates which are recommended on the label of the can or package. Fumigation with pesticide #40 or aerosol #15 is effective under favorable conditions.

Diseases

May become infected with verticillium wilt if grown in contaminated soil. No control. Prevent infection by using sterilized soil. See SOIL STERILIZATION.

theophrasti   5′   annual   Velvetleaf

An alternate-leaved weed native to India. The leaves are heart shaped, 1 ft. long; yellow flowers $\frac{3}{4}$ in. across in axillary clusters during Aug. and Sept.; fruits are in circular clusters of 12–15 beaked pods about 1 in. long. Widely distributed in Canada as well as the eastern and central U.S.

ACACIA (ak-AY-sha). This is a very large genus, mostly of tropical trees and shrubs. The leaves may be doubly pinnate or in mature specimens the leaf stalk is enlarged and leaflike. Flowers are always a delicate yellow, and the most conspicuous part about them is their prominent stamens. Members of the Pea Family, their fruits are merely dry pods. They grow best when exposed to full sunshine. Most are native to Australia. They are not long-lived trees but do grow very fast; they are excellent planted in tubs as display plants in greenhouses in the North.

Propagation is by seed, soaked overnight in hot water at about 180° F. Some species are propagated by cuttings of half-ripened wood and some by root cuttings. See CUTTINGS.

In the Middle West, mimosas are heavily infested with the mimosa web worm, which also attacks Honeylocust. The small gray worms weave several leaves together and skeletonize the leaflets. Sprays of insecticide #9 or #15 are suggested. See GLEDITSIA

baileyana   30′   Zone 10   Cootamundra Wattle

The small, feathery, light yellow flowers of this species are only $\frac{1}{4}$ in. in dia., but many are combined to form racemes 3 in. long from Jan. to March. Native to New South Wales, the doubly compound leaves are steel blue and of very fine texture, with the evergreen leaflets attached spirally around the twig. It is short-lived and needs good soil, but grows very fast and is used as a street tree in southern Calif.

cultriformis   15′   Zone 10   Knife Acacia

This is a tall shrub with yellow flower heads about $\frac{1}{8}$ in. wide in long racemes, appearing during March and April. The fruits are pods 3 in. long. Native to New South Wales and Queensland, Australia. The foliage is gray and, if clipped frequently, this plant may be used as a hedge.

dealbata   50′   Zone 9   Silver Wattle
The fragrant, clear yellow flowers of this variety are borne in small ball-like clusters during March and April. The evergreen foliage is very graceful, finely divided, slightly blue to grayish in color; this is one of the best known of the acacias, both in this country and in England, since it is the hardiest of some 400 varieties. The small balls of flowers are only about ¼ in. wide and are conspicuous only because of the many stamens in the flowers. Even though it is used as a street tree, it is short-lived, like most species of this genus.

decurrens mollis   50′   Zone 10   Black Wattle
The branches of this plant have a slender and attractive habit. The young growth is yellowish with a fine texture and the mature growth is a dull green. The small, light yellow flowers bloom in June and July.

farnesiana   10′   Zone 8   Opopanax, Sweet Acacia
The fragrant, bright yellow, ball-like flowers of this tall shrub appear in Feb. and March. The leaflets are scarcely over ⅛ in. long. It is a popular thorny plant and is often used as a pot plant in the greenhouses of the North, for under these conditions it may bloom all winter. It is widely planted on 3 continents in tropical and subtropical areas.

koa   100′   Zone 10   Koatree
The largest and finest native tree of Hawaii, it was this tree which was used to make many of the Hawaiian canoes. It grows only in the cooler parts of the mountains. The modified leaf stems are grayish green and sickle shaped. The flowers are inconspicuous pale yellow balls.

latifolia   25′   Zone 10   Broadleaf Acacia
The leaflike stalks of many acacias are green and, in the case of this species, they are bluish green, about 6 in. long and 2 in. wide. The small yellow flowers are in spikes 1–2 in. long and the fruit pods are 2–4 in. long. Native to Australia.

longifolia floribunda   20′   Zone 10   Gossamer Sydney Acacia
This variety is being used in southern Calif., apparently because it is adapted to dry situations and can be used as a street tree. The fine evergreen foliage, spreading habit and whitish-yellow flowers in balls 2¼ in. wide appearing in Feb. and March make this Australian native a popular one. Like most acacias, it is short-lived.

pendula   25′   Zone 10   Weeping Boree Acacia
The pendulous habit of this species is its most ornamental characteristic since its yellow flowers are none too prominent. The bluish-gray foliage also has fine texture. It is a native of Queensland and New South Wales, Australia, and is popularly used as a garden specimen in southern Calif. and also as a gracefully weeping greenhouse display plant in the North.

pruinosa   60′   Zone 10   Bronze or Frosty Acacia
A beautiful, dense but spreading tree from Australia; the evergreen foliage is light green but, when it is just emerging, it is fernlike and touched with coppery tints. The cream and yellow fragrant flowers are produced from June to Sept.

verticillata   20′   Zone 10   Star Acacia
The peculiar leaflike stalks are ¾ in. long and are produced in whorls; the yellow flowers are in small spikes 1 in. long blooming in March and April; the fruit pods are 3 in. long. Native to Tasmania. It is sometimes used in hedges but, like most acacias, is short-lived.

ACAENA (ass-EE-na). Very low-growing evergreen plants with inconspicuous flowers but attractive green foliage. This is a good ground cover and especially used for planting between flagstones. The plant must have full sun and well-drained soil. Somewhat tender and must be protected for the winter in the North. Easily propagated by divisions at any time.

buchananii   3″   Zone 6   Buchanan Sheepburr
A low, trailing, more or less evergreen plant from New Zealand, valued for its dense, gray silky leaves, about an inch long. This is an excellent subject for the rock garden and has been used for a ground cover in small, rocky spots. The leaves are alternate, pinnate with 3–6 pairs of leaflets. The flowers are in small, inconspicuous petal-less spikes. Easily propagated by division or from cuttings. Fruits are small burrs.

microphylla   ½″   Zones 6–7   Redspine Sheepburr
Similar to the above but the plant is glabrous, the evergreen leaves are bronze-green and the fruits or burrs have small red spines that are especially colorful. Also native to New Zealand. It will grow in either moist or dry soil. Unfortunately both species are difficult to find in American nurseries.

ACALYPHA (ak-al-LY-fa)
hispida   8′–15′   Zone 10   Chenille Copperleaf
A house plant, native of the East Indies, with alternate leaves of green color, sometimes 8 in. long. The red flowers are borne in spikelike drooping racemes and are dioecious; sometimes it is called the Red Hot Cattail. They are used out-of-doors in the deep South for bedding plants or hedges and are easily propagated by cuttings in the fall or softwood cuttings taken early in July.

wilkesiana   10′   Zone 10   Painted Copperleaf
A brilliant red-leaved plant from Fiji, sometimes used in hedges, with leaves variegated all tones of red, pink and brown. They are triangular in

shape, about 6 in. across. The female flowers on small upright spikes are insignificant but the pendulous, staminate flowers are borne in tassels somewhat similar to those of the alder. Propagated by cuttings.

ACANTHACEAE = The Acanthus Family

ACANTHOLIMON (ak-an-tho-LY-mon)
glumaceum 6″ Zone 8 Comb Prickly-thrift
A tufted evergreen perennial with sharp-pointed, linear leaves, flowers small, pinkish, in dense one-sided racemes from July–Sept. Native to Armenia. Chiefly a rock garden plant.

> **venustum 5″ Zone 8 Large Flower Prickly-thrift**
> Leaves spiny, bluish green, flowers rose-purple from July–Sept., produced in loose racemes of 10–20 flowers each. Native to Asia Minor. Chiefly for the rock garden.

ACANTHOPANAX (ak-an-tho-PAY-nax)
pentaphyllum = *A. sieboldianus*
ricinifolius = *Kalopanax pictus*
sieboldianus 9′ Zone 4 Fiveleaf-aralia
Although there are several species of this genus grown in American arboretums, this species is the most popular for general planting in America and the only one which need be considered. A native of Japan, it has thorny stems and leaves which are palmately compound consisting of 5–7 leaflets. The flowers and fruits are rarely seen. It is well adapted for growing in the shade and also for growing in urban gardens where it is occasionally used as a thorny, clipped hedge, and it has few if any pests. Propagation is by softwood cuttings and root cuttings.

ACANTHUS (ak-AN-thus)
mollis 2′ Zone 8 Bear's-breech
An outstanding plant in the flower border because its basal leaves are nearly 2 ft. long and 1 ft. wide, hairy on the upper surface. The flowers are white, lilac or rose colored, borne in spikes 1½–2 ft. long, blooming in Aug.

The var. 'Latifolius' has broader leaves, is hardier and is 3 ft. tall. These are propagated by seeds or division in spring or fall.

ACANTHUS FAMILY = Acanthaceae

ACAULESCENT. Stemless, as in the Dandelion.

ACER (AY-ser). Maple. A group of small and large trees with opposite leaves, noted for the shade they produce and also for their excellent autumn color. Some are low and mounded in habit, others are bushy, still others are narrow and columnar and others are wide spreading and round headed. The usually inconspicuous male and female flowers are often on the same tree but not always; the fruits are samaras or a small flattened nut with a wing on each side.

The leaves may be simple, lobed or compound, depending on the variety. They are native to North America, Europe and Asia. They are particularly valued as foliage or shade trees and some of the more colorful ones are valued for their colored foliage. Those with simple leaves are *A. carpinifolium, davidii, distylum, oblongum, tataricum* and *tetramerum*. Those with compound leaves are *A. cissifolium, griseum, henryi, mandshuricum, maximowiczianum, negundo* and *sutchuenense*.

Propagation

Seeds of most maples should not be allowed to dry out but should be sown or stratified as soon as ripe. Seed of *A. rubrum* and *saccharinum* ripens in the spring and should be sown as soon as collected. Most other species can be stratified for 4 months at 40° F., then sown. See SEEDS, STRATIFICATION.

Maples are also budded and grafted, using the species as understock for the varieties.

Insect Pests

Cottony maple scale and terrapin scale are large soft scales which infest the twigs. Dormant sprays of insecticide #44 are used on Silver and Red Maple but may injure Sugar Maple so that spring and early summer applications of insecticide #15 are advisable. Two leaf scales with cottony coverings may be injurious and are controlled with insecticide #15 when the young are active. The scales overwinter on the branches. Norway Maple aphid is often so abundant on this species that drops of honey dew disfigure everything underneath. Spraying with insecticide #15 is suggested. Sugar Maple borer, a beetle, maple callus borer, a moth, and pigeon tremex, a wood wasp, are destructive borers in maple. When the tunnels are located, use a wire or an insecticidal paste especially prepared for borer control. Trunk sprays with insecticide #9 are also helpful. Several gall mites which are identified by the shape of the galls, such as maple bladder gall and maple spindle gall on Silver Maple, the gouty vein gall on Sugar Maple and the ocellate maple gall on Red Maple, may require dormant sprays of fungicide #L or of insecticide #15 when the leaves start to grow. Many leaves on the ground under Sugar Maple in early summer may result from feeding of the maple petiole borer which cuts the leaf stems and falls with the leaf petiole. Raking and burning leaves promptly is suggested. Greenstriped maple worm, canker worms, tussock moth larvae and caterpillars of the saddled prominent are destructive leaf eaters which are checked by sprays of insecticide #9, #15 or #37.

Leaves of Japanese Maple varieties:

1. *Acer japonicum*
2. *A. palmatum* 'Sanguineum'
3. *A. palmatum dissectum* 'Ornatum'
4. *A. japonicum* 'Aconitifolium'
5. *A. palmatum* 'Laciniatum'
6. *A. palmatum dissectum*

Diseases

Tar spot on leaves of Silver Maple is more unsightly than destructive. Rake and burn infected leaves. Anthracnose causes a scorched appearance on the leaves. Sprays of fungicide #D or #F are used when leaves are full grown. Wilted foliage on a branch or side of tree indicates verticillium wilt. When infection first starts, pruning is helpful. There is no control for established infections. Sap oozing from bark cankers identifies bleeding canker fungus. No control is recommended and infected trees usually die in 2 to 4 years. Nectria canker causes depressed areas in the bark which become covered with cinnamon-colored spores. Infected branches produce red leaves early in autumn which do not fall naturally. Early infections may be stopped by cutting out and covering wounds with tree paint.

argutum   24′   Zone 5
An erect, narrow tree from Japan, leaves usually 5 lobed and 2–3 in. across, graceful and dense in appearance—good for the small property.

buergerianum   20′   Zone 6   Trident Maple
A low maple tree, native to Japan, rounded habit with 3-lobed leaves (also 3 nerves per leaf) and the leaves about 1½–3 in. across. This is proving popular in the central U.S. as a street and shade tree on small properties.

campestre   25′   Zone 4   Hedge Maple
This European maple is used in Europe as well as in America for its dense growth but it lacks autumn color. It is easily sheared or pleached. Although hardy as far north as Boston, it is more reliable from Long Island southward and as a screen or hedge it is excellent. The leaves are 3–5 lobed and 2–4 in. across. The variety **'Compactum'** is very dense in habit, only a few feet tall and often wider than high. There are several other varieties which differ little from the species. The variety **postelense** produces leaves that are golden yellow when they first unfurl in the spring but later turn green. **'Queen Elizabeth'** is the best clone for street tree use.

capillipes   30′   Zone 5
A native to Japan with 3-lobed leaves 2½–5 in. long, turning a good red autumn color in the fall. The leaves are red as they unfurl but later turn green. The bark on the trunk and older branches is striped white. A fine small maple for the small garden.

cappadocicum   60′   Zones 5–6   Coliseum Maple
Native to the Caucasus and Asia Minor, this has leaves that are 5–7 lobed and the petiole, when broken, shows a milky sap as does that of the Norway Maple. The young leaves of this tree show several different colors (red, pink), giving rise to several varietal names, but they turn green shortly, as they mature.

carpinifolium   30′   Zone 5   Hornbeam Maple
A vase-shaped, Japanese tree with many main stems from the base, densely produced bright green leaves (not lobed) 3–5 in. long; similar in size and shape to those of the Hornbeam. The

autumn color is a brownish yellow and it is a good tree for the small property.

circinatum   25′   Zone 5   Vine Maple
This small, compact maple is native from British Columbia to Calif. and is valued because it grows well in partially shaded situations. The branches twist and turn in an interesting manner, giving rise to its common name. The Indians made fish hooks from the very tough wood. The small drooping clusters of white and purple flowers are very interesting in late April and the winged red fruits are colorful in the summer. In the fall the foliage turns red to orange—leaves are 7–9 lobed. From a distance it gives one the impression of a form of *A. palmatum*.

dasycarpum = *A. saccharinum*.

davidii   45′   Zone 6   David Maple
The bark of this Chinese tree is striped white, the leaves are about 8 in. long, at first red as they unfurl in the spring, later turning to green. The autumn color is an interesting yellow and purple.

diabolicum purpurascens   30′   Zone 5   Red Devil Maple
This is another interesting small tree native to Japan, of particular interest for its colorful purplish flowers and fruits and 5-lobed leaves that are 4–7 in. across and reddish as they first unfold in the spring.

ginnala   20′   Zone 2   Amur Maple
An extremely hardy maple with small leaves about 3 in. long. It is a native of northern China, Manchuria and Japan, and the winged fruits turn red in the late summer while the leaves are still green, making an interesting color combination. Its most conspicuous characteristic is its vivid scarlet autumn color. Fortunately, also, it has few pests. 'Flame' is an excellent variety, introduced by the Soil Conservation Service, with better fall color than the species.

glabrum   25′   Zone 5   Rocky Mountain Maple
Native from Mont. to N.Mex., this has 3–5-lobed leaves, sometimes 3 parted, 3–5 in. across, with a bright yellow autumn color. It is best used in the Rocky Mountain area and on the West Coast.

griseum   25′   Zone 5   Paperbark Maple
This tree, native to western China, has compound leaves, 3 leaflets each, 1–2½ in. long. The bark is cinnamon brown and exfoliates in long paperlike strips similar to that of certain birches. It is round in outline but rather open in habit—very difficult to propagate from seed for very few of the seeds are viable. It is the most outstanding of all the maples for ornamental bark, which of course lends interest to the tree throughout the entire year.

japonicum   25′   Zone 5   Fullmoon Maple
A popular tree in Japan where it is native, this tree has leaves that have 7–11 lobes and they are

3–6 in. across, usually green during the growing season but turning red in the fall. The habit is rounded but broad in outline. This is not the popular *A. palmatum* which usually has fewer leaf lobes. Two of several varieties are: '**Aconiti-folium'**—leaves deeply divided; '**Aureum'**—leaves yellow.

lobelii   60′   Zone 7   Lobel Maple
Similar to the Norway Maple in general outline, this is native to southern Italy and is for use in the southern U.S. The leaves have 5 lobes and are 4–6½ in. across—no autumn color.

macrophyllum   90′   Zone 6   Bigleaf Maple
Native from Alaska to Calif., this has the largest leaves of any maple, 8–12 in. across, and they are 3–5 lobed. The small yellow flowers are fragrant and are borne in pendulous clusters, 4–6 in. long, in May. The leaves turn bright yellow to orange in the fall. Unfortunately it does not seem to grow well in the eastern U.S.

mandshuricum   30′   Zone 4   Manchurian Maple
The compound leaves of this tree have red petioles, and the 3 leaflets are 2–4 in. long, turning a red to scarlet autumn color. It grows fast with wide-spreading branches and round-head but is rather open in habit. Manchuria.

maximowiczianum (*nikoense*)   25′   Zone 5   Nikko Maple
A Japanese tree with compound leaves, 3 leaflets 2–5 in. long, generally vase shaped but often round topped, with red or purple autumn color. This is not fast growing, but it is one of the very few maples with a vase shape, a good habit for planting on the smaller property.

monspessulanum   24–30′   Zone 5   Montpelier Maple
Resembling *A. campestre*, this also is native to southern Europe and northern Africa, with 3-lobed leaves 1–3 in. across. A street tree in Ore. and Wash., but has no autumn color.

negundo   60′   Zone 2   Box-elder
A wide-spreading, rather open tree, native to eastern and central North America, recommended only for certain areas in the Midwest where summer drought and winter cold make it impossible to grow better species. In the eastern U.S. it should be considered a weed tree, seeding everywhere, broken easily in storms, and it has no autumn color. The leaves are compound with 3–5 leaflets, 2–4 in. long. It is frequently used in shelterbelt planting in the Northwest. The varieties are numerous but these are the most often grown: '**Aureo-variegatum'**—leaves bordered yellow—Goldedge Box-elder; **californi-cum**—only for use in Calif. where necessary; **texanum**—only for use in the southwestern U.S. where necessary; **variegatum**—leaves with broad white margin, one of the most conspicuous of variegated leaved trees—Silver Leaf Box-elder.

nikoense = *A. maximowiczianum*.

opalus 45′ **Zone 5** **Italian Maple**
A European tree with shallow 5-lobed leaves
2¼–4 in. across and interesting small yellow
flowers in April.

palmatum 20′ **Zone 5** **Japanese Maple**
There are approximately 80 varieties of this
species being grown in America today—a
diversified group. They are small rounded trees,
with palmately lobed leaves (5–11 lobes), some
very finely divided, with foliage colors from
green through yellow to pink and red, with
various combinations of these colors. They
require good soil; the more colored varieties will
do better in partially shaded situations. Some
will retain the red or yellow color of their
foliage throughout the growing season; others
will produce young foliage which is highly
colored at first but which gradually turns green
by summer. These varieties are disappointing to
many plantsmen. All these varieties should be
grafted so that they retain the characteristics of
the parent but sometimes unscrupulous nurserymen grow them from seed, make their own
selections from the seedlings, and this confuses a
group which is highly diverse to start with.
They have a tendency to produce leaves early
in the spring and so are frequently injured by
late spring frosts in some situations in the
North.

Since some lack their full complement of green
chlorophyll in the leaves, they may do better in
partial shade, although it must be admitted that
those with red foliage produce excellent
colored leaves in the full sun. They make
excellent specimens, especially the colored
forms with finely cut leaves, but good soil,
proper exposure and sufficient moisture (not
dry soil) are necessary for them to do their best.
The varieties can be divided into three main
groups:

1. Leaves small, usually 5 main lobes, of
which the best varieties are:

'Atropurpureum'—red leaves throughout the
entire growing season. This is one of the hardiest
of all these varieties. **'Burgundy Lace'**—cut-
leaved form with reddish foliage; **'Sanguineum'**
—similar to **'Atropurpureum'** but leaves a
lighter red color; **'Scolopendrifolium'**—leaves
cut to center, leaflets very narrow and green;
'Versicolor'—leaves green with white, pink and
green variegation; **'Yezo-nishiki'**—blood-red
leaves with vermillion variegation.

2. Leaves with 7 main lobes (cultivars of *A.
palmatum heptalobum*) are:

'Elegans'—leaves 5 in. long and when first
open they have a rose-colored margin;
'Ohsakazuki'—large leaves, yellowish to light
green but turning a brilliant red in the fall,
making it one of the best for fall color; **'Reticulatum'**—leaves with green veins, the rest of the

leaf blades being variegated, yellow, white and
pale green.

3. Leaves dissected with 7, 9 or 11 lobes:

palmatum dissectum—Threadleaf Japanese
Maple. This and its two varieties (**'Flavescens'**
with yellowish foliage; **'Ornatum'** with brilliantly
red-colored foliage) are often considered the
most brilliant of all because of their delicate,
lacy foliage. The Threadleaf Japanese Maple has
blood-red leaves, delicately cut, with gracefully pendant branches. It should only be used as
a beautiful specimen. In the past it has been
called *multifidum* and *palmatifidum*.

pensylvanicum 36′ **Zone 3** **Striped Maple or**
Moosewood
Native to the forest areas of eastern North
America, this tree has bark that is striped white,
leaves 3 lobed, 5–7 in. long, and excellent
yellow autumn color. Because its leaves are
large and coarse, it is not a good ornamental
street tree, but on the edge of woodlands or in
naturalized areas it can be used with good
results.

platanoides 90′ **Zone 3** **Norway Maple**
The Norway Maple, native to Europe, is a
standard street and ornamental tree in America.
Densely branched, with a round head, the
leaves have 5 lobes, are 4–7 in. across, show a
milky sap at the base of the petiole when it is
broken and the tips of the lobes end in fine pin-
points and are not rounded and blunt like those
of the Sugar Maple. The masses of small yellow
flowers appear just before the leaves in the
spring and the foliage turns a beautiful yellow in
the fall. It grows rapidly and withstands city
growing conditions.

Some varieties are: **'Cleveland'**—oval and
upright in habit; **'Columnare'**—narrowly
columnar; **'Crimson King'**—leaves red throughout the entire growing season. It has been issued
Plant Patent #735. **'Fassen's Black'** is similar;
'Emerald Queen'—dense uniform habit; **'Jade
Glen'**—creates heavy shade; **'Crimson Sentry'**—
Plant Patent #3258, narrow, columnar, dark
purple foliage in spring and summer; **'Erectum'**—leaves larger than those of **'Columnare'**
and the lateral branches short and stubby. A tree
30 ft. tall had a total branch spread of only 6 ft.
'Globosum'—of particular interest when it is
grafted on a single trunk about 6–7 ft. high
because of its globe-shaped, densely branched
habit. Growing slowly, it can be planted underneath utility wires and so has fine possibilities as
a street tree. **'Schwedleri'**—an old-fashioned variety, the leaves of which first open red in the
spring but gradually turn green in the early
summer. The newer varieties **'Crimson King'**,
'Fassen's Black' and **'Goldsworth Purple'** retain
the red foliage color throughout the growing
season. **'Summer Shade'**—reported as being

"heat resistant, upright growing and maintaining a single leader. The foliage is more leathery than the other varieties." Issued Plant Patent #1748.

pseudoplatanus 90′ Zone 5 Sycamore Maple Especially valued for planting at the seashore, this is native to Europe and western Asia. The leaves are 5 lobed, 3–6½ in. across, and the flowers and seeds are in pendulous panicles 5 in. long. It has no autumn color, but in Europe there are several colored-leaved varieties.

A few varieties are: **'Erectum'**—young trees narrow and columnar but as they mature they grow into more of a pyramidal form; **'Purpureum'**—leaves purple on the underside; **'Spaethii'** is another similar variety; **'Worleei'**—leaves deep yellow, almost orange-yellow when young, petiole red, considered by some to be a superior variety.

rubrum 120′ Zone 3 Red or Swamp Maple Native throughout eastern and central North America. The bright red flowers in early April, before the leaves appear, give the tree its common name as well as the brilliant scarlet autumn color. Even the fruits are bright red and effective in the late spring. The leaves are 3–5 lobed and 2½–4 in. across. It naturally grows in low and swampy spots. Fast growing, it is often weak wooded and can split easily in wind, snow and ice storms. The variety **'Columnare'** is a narrow columnar form, one-half as wide as it is tall. **'October Glory'** and **'Red Sunset'** both with excellent red autumn color.

saccharinum 120′ Zone 3 Silver Maple A wide-spreading tree with arching to pendulous branches, native from Quebec to Fla., Minn. and Okla., this tree was a most popular shade tree at the turn of the century, planted everywhere because of its fast growth and graceful habit. However, it is one of the first trees to break up in snow, wind and ice storms, and now is not recommended for ornamental planting. The leaves are deeply 5 lobed, 3–5½ in. wide, bright green above and silvery white beneath, turning clear yellow in the fall. Neither this nor its varieties are considered to make good permanent trees. Other species should be selected instead. Some of the varieties are: **'Laciniatum'**—with deeply cut leaves and pendulous branches; **'Wieri'**—a form of *laciniatum*; **'Lutescens'**—a form with yellow leaves; **'Pendulum'**—with pendulous branches; **'Pyramidale'**—a narrow pyramidal form with upright branches.

saccharum 120′ Zone 3 Sugar Maple Widely native to eastern North America, this is the tree that is grown in N.H. and Vt. primarily for maple sugar. The leaves are 3–5 lobed and 3–5½ in. across. The general habit is oval; mature specimens are rounded, and the autumn color is a gorgeous mixture of yellow, orange and scarlet. It is more sturdy and solid than the Norway and Red Maples and breaks up much less in storms, but it is also slower growing and is not as good for growing under city conditions as is the Norway Maple. It is the sap of this tree that is collected in New England and boiled down to make maple syrup and maple sugar. This can easily be done by boring a ¾-in. hole one-third of the way in the trunk and inserting a piece of pipe to which a bucket is attached for collecting the sap. The sap starts to "run" in very early spring before the snow has disappeared. It should be known, however, that approximately 33 quarts of sap must be boiled down for every quart of syrup obtained. This is not an operation to be carried out indoors!

"Tapping" the Sugar Maple in early spring for sap.

A few varieties are: **'Globosum'**—dwarf, dense, rounded form which should be grafted high on *A. saccharum* understock to form a globe-headed slow-growing tree suitable for planting underneath electric utility wires; **'Newton Sentry'**—with a main central leader, a wide; **'Nigrum'**—Black Maple native from Quebec to S.Dak., this is a slow-growing maple, not much planted as an ornamental. The leaves are 3 lobed, occasionally 5 lobed and are duller than those of the Sugar Maple, which it closely resembles. **'Temple's Upright'**—without a central leader but still upright in habit, a 75-year-old tree is 50 ft. tall and 12 ft. wide.

spicatum 25′ Zone 2 Mountain Maple This tree is common in the woods of eastern

North America but it is recommended for planting in wooded areas only for it will withstand shade. It is not an outstanding ornamental tree. The 3-lobed leaves are 2½–5 in. long, the fruits are bright red in the summer, and the autumn color is a brilliant orange and scarlet.

tataricum   30′   Zone 4   Tatarian Maple Another small tree native to Europe and western Asia, this does have a good red to yellow autumn color. It has an upright elliptical shape and should be good for street planting, where a small tree is wanted. The leaves are broad, ovate. 2–4 in. long.

tschonoskii   20′   Zone 5   Tschonoski Maple A graceful, shrubby tree native to Japan, the leaves of this have 5 lobes (rarely 7) and are 2–4 in. across. The leaves turn a bright yellow in the fall and it is beginning to be used as a small shade tree in the central U.S.

ACERACEAE = The Maple Family

ACHENE. A small, dry, indehiscent, one-celled and one-seeded fruit, as in the Buttercup.

ACHILLEA (ak-il-EE-a). Border or rock garden perennials, several are rank weeds. They are drought-resisting and have fernlike foliage which is attractive throughout the season; grow in poor soil and prefer full sunlight. Most species can be let alone for 3–4 years, but *A. ptarmica* and *A. tomentosa* often need division annually. Propagated by seeds (which may yield inferior plants), but choice forms are propagated by cuttings made in midsummer. Also division of clumps is a very easy method of increase.

ageratifolia   8″   Zones 2–3   Greek Yarrow A silvery, pubescent, tufted yarrow with white flower heads ½–1 in. wide with 12–20 ray flowers in each head and bipinnate leaves. Native to the Balkan region. The variety 'Aizoon' bears solitary heads with entire or nearly entire leaves.

argentea   5″–6″   Zone 4   Silvery Yarrow A small, mounded plant with 3-lobed, silvery-white leaves and clusters of small white flowers held erect on stems seldom more than 5–6 in. tall. A native to Yugoslavia, it should be grown in alkaline soil with good drainage and in full sun.

ageratum   1½′   Zone 7   Sweet Yarrow The yellow ray flowers are borne in heads about ⅛ in. wide, and the heads are borne in dense, rounded clusters during the summer. Native to southern Europe.

clavennae   8″   Zone 3   Clavenn Yarrow Somewhat similar to *A. argentea* but flowers are slightly larger.

filipendulina   4′   Zones 2–3   Fernleaf Yarrow The deeply cut, grayish foliage gives the entire plant a graceful appearance. The numerous small yellow flowers are borne profusely from June to Sept. The variety 'Coronation Gold' is 3 ft. tall and has 3-in. flower clusters that are yellow; 'Cerise Queen' is 18 in. tall with 2–3 in. cherry red flower clusters; 'Golden Plate' has huge, 6-in. yellow flower clusters. These prove excellent in bouquets and they last longer as cut flowers if the lower leaves are stripped off. The flowers are also dried for winter bouquets. 'Parker's Variety' is another good one, although not so large as 'Golden Plate'. The species is native to Europe and Asia.

x lewisii   8″   Zone 5   Lewis Yarrow A hybrid (*A. tomentosa* x *A. argentea*) raised in England, it is sometimes known as 'King Edward IV'. The small flower clusters are primrose yellow from June to Aug. and the foliage is woolly and gray-green.

millefolium   6″–2′   Zone 2   Yarrow, Milfoil A weed or ground cover, especially if mowed, this is naturalized in North America but is native to Europe. The feathery, finely divided, almost everygreen leaves are aromatic when crushed. The small flowers appear in small umbels from mid-July to mid-Sept. It will grow in full sun in very poor, dry soil, where grass will not grow, and can be run over occasionally with a rotary-type mower and kept low. The variety **rosea** has pink flowers and is sometimes cultivated. Propagation is by division or self-sown seed.

nana   4″   Zone 5   Dwarf Yarrow Native to southern Europe and valued in rockeries for its white flowers. The plant should be grown in poor, sandy soil so that it will not grow tall.

ptarmica   2′   Zones 2–3   Sneezewort In colonial times the roots of this were dried and ground and used for a homemade snuff. The globular white flowers are usually double, appearing in midsummer, and florists often use them as "fillers" in bouquets. Native to Europe, Asia and North America. Varieties: 'The Pearl' is an old-fashioned favorite which blooms freely throughout the summer; 'Perry's White' is noted for its double flowers; 'Boule de Neige' or 'Snowball' is only 14 in. tall and 'Angel's Breath' is a new and very popular variety. Usually the propagation of the varieties by asexual means results in better plants than when they are grown from seed.

taygetea   18″   Zone 5 A species native to Greece with soft primrose-yellow flowers from June to Aug. and fine, gray-green foliage. Excellent for cut-flower purposes.

tomentosa   6″–12″   Zones 2–3   Woolly Yarrow This, also, will grow almost anywhere. Native to Europe and Asia, the flowers are small and yellow, in flat clusters, from late May to mid-Sept. The woolly, fine, fernlike foliage is practically evergreen at the base and aromatic when crushed. It also is a weed or a ground cover, especially if the top is cut off to leave the gray, matlike basal foliage. It should be planted in full sun and can also be maintained as a low ground cover by mowing. The variety 'Moonlight' is not so encroaching as the species, being matlike and only about an inch tall, but bearing foot-long flower stalks with pale yellow flowers in June and July. The variety 'Aurea' spreads quickly, forming a mat of gray-green woolly leaves and bright yellow flowers in dense clusters. It is highly valued as a rock garden plant since the flowers appear throughout most of the summer. Native throughout the Temperate Zone.

umbellata **10″** **Zone 6** **Umbel Yarrow**
Native to Greece, this plant has woolly gray-green leaves and clusters of white flowers borne on erect stems in early summer.

ACHIMENES (ak-i-MEE-neez). Branching herbs grown mostly as house plants from tuber-like rhizomes, valued for their bright-colored, funnelform flowers, the slender tubes of which are gracefully curved. Some of the many hybrids are excellent subjects for hanging baskets. Their bright red, purple and white flowers, according to variety, borne in the axils of the leaves are somewhat like those of Gloxinia to which they are related. The bloom starts in the summer and continues into the fall. They are native to tropical America. Leaves are mostly opposite. Only a few species are grown and even these are hybridized so much that it is usually the large-flowered hybrids which are available. The very small rhizomes look like miniature pine cones. They should be planted in

Achimenes—Flowers and roots

pots about ½ in. deep in the late spring and, placed in the greenhouse or warm window, fertilized occasionally. When through blooming, the plants are dried, the rhizomes are stored in dry sand in a cool place and replanted again in soil during spring. They are easily propagated by the division of their rhizomes or by cuttings. Actually Achimenes take about the same care as African Violets.

grandiflora **1′–2′** **Zone 10** **Big Purple Achimenes**
Native to Mexico with large, red-purple, tubular flowers, sometimes 2 in an axil and ovate leaves reddish beneath.

longiflora **1′–2′** **Zone 10** **Trumpet Achimenes**
The long-tubed flowers of this plant from Guatemala are violet-blue in color and usually one in a leaf axil. The leaves are opposite, sometimes with 3 leaves in a whorl.

patens **1½′** **Zone 10** **Violet Achimenes**
A Mexican plant with short tubes and violet-blue flowers. Leaves are unequal. A few of the popular hybrids are: 'Camille Brozzoni'—violet and white flowers; 'Gloria'—violet-blue flowers; 'Million'—red flowers; 'Orchidee'—orchid-colored flowers; 'Purity'—white flowers; 'Purple King'—purple flowers; 'Lavender Beauty'—lavender-colored flowers, excellent for hanging baskets; 'Edmund Vossier'—white and purple, excellent for hanging baskets; and many others mostly available from plant specialists in Calif.

ACHRAS ZAPOTA = *Manilkara zapota*

ACIDANTHERA (as-id-AN-the-ra)
bicolor **18″** **Zone 10** **Dark-eye Gladixia**
Native to tropical Africa, growing from corms, and treated like Gladiolus, that is, the corms are raised, dried immediately and stored in the fall for over winter. Leaves are similar to those of Gladiolus but better ornamentally. The spikes of 3–6 white, fragrant flowers with black centers appear in the summer and also resemble those of Gladiolus. Propagation is easy, simply by collecting all the young cormels that form around the old one at the end of the growing season.

ACID AND ALKALI SOILS. See SOILS.

ACID SOIL PLANTS. Far too much emphasis has been placed in the past on plants which "require" acid soil. Growing in the Arnold Arboretum in Boston, Mass., are over 7000 different kinds of woody plants, growing in an acid soil with a pH of 5.5. See pH, SOILS. The majority of these would grow on a neutral (pH 7.0) or even slightly alkaline soil—only a very few (see following list) might be considered to "require" acid soil to the extent that they would not grow on alkaline soil.

The real question is, how acid? Most plants will tolerate a slightly acid soil but the more acid it becomes (pH below 5.0) the fewer plants will grow. There comes a point (often about pH 4-4.5) where iron becomes unavailable in very acid soils, and then even plants like azaleas and rhododendrons have trouble and the leaves turn yellow. (See SOILS for determining the acidity or alkalinity of the soil and steps to be taken to raise or lower the pH.) Lilacs seem to do better in acid soils when ground limestone is added. Rhododendrons and azaleas do better in neutral soils if an acid fertilizer is applied, and blueberries are one of those specialized crops which seem to "require" ammonium sulphate as the fertilizer. See BLUEBERRY.

In general then, except for extreme situations, concentrate on good tilth, the application of humus and fertilizer to the soil in the garden and do not worry too much about slight variations in soil acidity.

ACMENA (ac-ME-na)
smithii (*Eugenia smithii*)   10′-25′   **Zone 10**
                                        Lili-pili Tree
Another Australian native, suitable for hedge making or specimen planting, this is resistant to salt-spray injury but does best in a partially shaded spot. The small white flowers are in terminal clusters 2-4 in. in dia., from May to July, and the showy, edible purple berries are borne in the winter.

ACOELORRHAPHE (as-ee-lor-RAFF-ee)
wrightii (*Paurotis wrightii*)   40′   **Zone 10**
                                        Saw Cabbage Palm
A handsome palm native to southern Fla. and the Bahamas. The leaves are almost rounded, 2-3 ft. across, green above, whitish underneath, and are divided down the middle into narrow segments.

ACONITE, WINTER = *Eranthis hyemalis*

ACONITUM (ak-o-NY-tum). These are showy perennial herbs blooming in the late summer, but all are dangerously poisonous if taken internally. The flowers are blue or purple, white or yellow. The plants prefer partial shade and a rich soil and are increased by division and by seed.
anthora   2′   **Zone 6 ?   Pyrenees Monkshood**
Leaf parts linear; flowers pale yellow, blooming

Plants Requiring Acid Soil

SHRUBS

		Zone	
Calluna sp.	18″	4	Heather
Clethra sp.	9′-30′	3-5	Clethra
Daboecia sp.	1½′	5	Irish Heath
Enkianthus sp.	6′-30′	4	Enkianthus
Erica sp.	18″-5′	3-7	Heath
Gaultheria procumbens	3″	3	Wintergreen
Ilex sp.	9′-30′	3-7	Holly
Illicium floridanum	9′	7	Florida Anisetree
Juniperus communis vars.	3′-36′	2	Common Juniper
Kalmia sp.	3′-30′	4	Mountain-laurel
Leiophyllum buxifolium	18″	5	Box Sandmyrtle
Leucothoe sp.	4′-12′	4-5	Leucothoe
Lyonia ligustrina	12′	3	Maleberry
Magnolia virginiana	60′	5	Sweet Bay Magnolia
Myrica sp.	9′-36′	2-6	Bayberry
Quercus—many sp.	45′-90′	3-9	Oak
Rhododendron sp.	3′-36′	2-6	Azalea and Rhododendron
Vaccinium sp.	8″-27′	2-7	Blueberry
Xanthorhiza simplicissima	2′	4	Yellow-root
Zenobia pulverulenta	6′	5	Dusty Zenobia

PERENNIALS

Actaea sp.	1½′-2′	3-5	Baneberry
Chelone glabra	1′	3	White Turtle-head
Chelone lyonii	3′	5	Pink Turtle-head
Cimicifuga racemosa	1′	4	Snakeroot, Cohash Bugbane
Dicentra eximia	1′-2′	4	Fringed Bleeding-heart
Digitalis purpurea	2′-4′	4	Foxglove
Mertensia virginica	2′-5′	3	Virginia Bluebells
Trillium grandiflorum	12″-14″	4	Snow Trillium

in the summer. The root is a bulblike tuber. Native to southern Europe.

autumnale = *A. henryi*.

carmichaelii 6′ Zones 2–3 Azure Monkshood
Leaves 3 lobed, flowers blue or white in densely compacted spikes. Native to northern China and a popular garden plant. Blooms in Aug. and Sept. The variety **wilsonii** grows 6–8 ft. tall and has violet-blue flowers in Sept. Formerly termed *A. fischeri*.

fischeri = *A. carmichaelii*.

henryi (*A. autumnale*) 5′ Zone 4 Autumn
Monkshood
The 5-lobed leaves and blue, white or lilac flowers of this northern Chinese plant are typical. It blooms from late July to Sept.

lycoctonum 6′ Zone 3 Wolfsbane Monkshood
The leaves are deeply cut with 3–9 divisions; the flowers are yellow to cream colored. Native to Europe and Siberia.

napellus 4′ Zones 2–3 Aconite Monkshood
The common monkshood of gardens and the one from which the drug aconite is taken. A native to Europe, it has blue flowers. The variety **album** has white flowers and **sparksii** has excellent dark blue flowers, the latter variety growing to 6 ft. tall.

uncinatum 5′ Zone 6 Clambering Monkshood
Native from Pa. to Ga., with blue flowers, this is a clambering type of plant with leaves deeply 3–5 lobed. It is found in moist soils and is best suited for the wild garden.

ACORUS (AK-or-us)

calamus 2′ Zone 3 Sweet Flag
This perennial herb, native throughout the U.S., has long, swordlike leaves and small greenish flowers. It blooms throughout the spring and summer. The root of this species, dried and candied, was a popular homemade confection several generations ago. It is an interesting plant for a bog garden or marshy area and is propagated by rootstalk division.

gramineus 8″–12″ Zone 5 Japanese Sweet Flag
A Japanese herb, growing in wet soils, with grasslike leaves and minute flowers, sometimes used as a ground cover in wet places. Easily propagated by division, for the members of this genus have creeping rootstocks. The variety 'Pusillus' is only 4 in. tall and 'Variegatus' has leaves striped white. It is the small-leaved variety that is sometimes used in aquariums.

ACRE. A unit in measuring land. It contains 43,560 sq. ft. and is almost exactly an area 209 ft. by 209 ft.

ACTAEA (ak-TEE-a). Native herbaceous perennial plants of the Buttercup Family, these have fernlike leaves, small spikes of white flowers and poisonous red or white berries in the fall. Easily propagated by seed or division. They are best grown in partial shade and are plants for the rockery or the wild garden, but not good plants for the flower border near the house, where the poisonous fruits might be eaten by children.

alba = *A. pachypoda*.

pachypoda (*A. alba*) 1½′ Zone 3 White
Baneberry
Although the compound leaves and terminal clusters of white flowers of this plant would be reason enough to include it in a wild garden, the most outstanding feature is its fruits, which are white or pinkish berries with a purple spot at the tip. Native to the wooded areas from Canada to the southern states and west to Okla., it flowers in May and June. The plants may be increased by division in the spring or by seeds sown in the fall. It was formerly termed *A. alba*.

rubra 1½′ Zone 3 Red Baneberry, Red Cohosh
The fruits are cherry red, poisonous berries and its rootstock is a violent purgative, irritant and emetic. Native to northeastern North America.

spicata 2′ Zone 5 (?) Black Baneberry
The European baneberry is very similar to American species, being among the poisonous plants acting upon the heart; cases have been reported of the deaths of children from eating the berries. Native to Europe and Japan; blooms in April, with purplish-black berries. Because of its poisonous fruits it is not a good plant for use in gardens.

ACTINIDIA (ak-tin-ID-ia). Alternate-leaved, vigorous, twining vines native to India, China and Japan. The fruit is a fleshy berry about an inch or less in dia., and the male flowers are on one plant, the female flowers on another. All species can be propagated by seed which may be stratified at once or stored dry in airtight containers in a cool place until the following year and then sown. Some are stratified for 3 months at 40° F., but *A. kolomikta* has shown double dormancy and might best be stratified at room temperature for 5 months, then at 40° F. for 3 months. Layers, softwood and hardwood cuttings all root. See STRATIFICATION, CUTTINGS.

These vines are all vigorous growers. *A. arguta* can elongate 15–20 feet a year and the Chinese Actinidia can grow 25 feet or more in one growing season. Because the other two species are somewhat variegated, they are slower in growth.

Of the four species *A. arguta* is the most commonly planted, but because it is a vigorous growing twiner, it should have some means of support, like an arbor or heavy trellis, which is strong enough to hold up the heavy vines.

However, they do not have any autumn color and their fruits are merely green or a brownish green, so that one should have a good reason for planting them in the garden. Other vines, like the clematis with flowers, or bittersweet with fruits, might be more useful.

arguta   **vine**   **Zone 4**   **Bower Actinidia**
A very fast-growing, alternate-leaved deciduous vine, this has merit for foliage cover. The leaves are 3–5 in. long and sometimes as wide. The flowers sometimes are dioecious, and are small and greenish white, fairly inconspicuous, but the fruits are inch-round, edible, greenish-yellow berries. It is native to Japan, Korea and Manchuria.

chinensis   **twining vine to 25′**   **Zone 7**   **Kiwi, Chinese Actinidia**
The rich velvety appearance of the young shoots of this fast-growing Chinese vine is produced by prominent red hairs. The leaves are 5–8 in. long and 4–7 in. wide. As with all members of this genus, the sexes are separate and both staminate and pistillate plants should be present if one desires the greenish, globular fruits which are 2 in. wide. These are edible, tasting something like gooseberries, but neither flowers nor fruits have ornamental value. The flowers are borne on the previous year's wood; the leaves are attractive, but it is the young shoots that have the colorful interest. This vine can cover a space 30 ft. x 30 ft., and is the most vigorous of the actinidias. Kiwi has become a very popular fruit in the last few years, shipping well, edible fresh, canned or preserved with thousands of acres planted in southern California, Hawaii, Australia and especially New Zealand. Also known as the Chinese Gooseberry, there are several good fruiting clones. Best not grown from seed, except that seedlings are used for understock for grafting in late summer. Flowers on year-old wood.

The flowers are small, fragrant, 5-petalled. Seed is small, like that of bananas, and fruit ripens in very late spring, but should stay on the vine until late summer. It is easily shipped all over the world, is sweet, about the size of an egg covered with fuzzy brown hairs. Seed was first sent to America about 1900 and by 1974 there were 2000 acres planted in southern California alone. One male plant should be planted for every 8 female, planted 10–15 ft. apart on a sturdy trellis 6–8 ft. high. It has few pests. Mature vines withstand 5°–10° F. but young shoots are easily frozen in early spring.

kolomikta   **vine**   **15′–20′**   **Zone 4**   **Kolomikta Actinidia**
The male or staminate plant especially has the large white to pink blotch at the end of each leaf, making this Asiatic vine of considerable ornamental value simply for its variegated foliage. The leaves are about 5 in. long and apparently are more colorful when the plant is grown in calcareous soils. The white, fragrant flowers and greenish, globular fruits have little ornamental significance.

polygama   **twining vine**   **15′**   **Zone 4**   **Silver-vine**
The male plants of this species have foliage more colorful than the female or fruiting plants, for the leaves are marked with a silvery-white to yellowish color and are about 3–5 in. long. Unfortunately this vine is most attractive to cats and if they can reach it, they will maul the foliage pretty badly. Like the other actinidias, the sexes are separate and neither the fragrant white flowers nor the greenish, globular fruits have much ornamental significance. It is not a very strong climber.

ACUMINATE. Having a gradually diminishing point; long pointed.

ADAM'S-NEEDLE = *Yucca filamentosa*

ADDER'S TONGUE FAMILY = *Ophioglossaceae*

ADDER'S-TONGUE FERN = *Ophioglossum vulgatum*

ADENOPHORA (ad-en-OFF-or-a). Perennial herbs, native to Europe and Asia, with summer-blooming flowers somewhat similar to those of the *Campanula* species and members of that family. Propagated by seeds sown in autumn or early in spring in the cold frame and potted. These do not like being moved and so should be planted in a permanent place and left alone. Not especially outstanding in the flower border or rockery.

confusa   **2′–3′**   **Zones 2–3**   **Farrer's Ladybell**
Native to China with deep blue, bell-like flowers about an inch long during July and Aug.

farreri = *A. confusa*

lilifolia   **2′–3′**   **Zones 2–3**   **Lilyleaf Ladybell**
With fragrant bluish flowers about ½ in. long during July and Aug.; native from central Europe to Siberia.

potaninii   **3′–4′**   **Zones 2–3**   **Bush Ladybell**
With broad bell-shaped blue flowers ¾ in. long during July and Aug. Native to western China.

ADIANTUM (ad-i-ANT-um). These are the maidenhair ferns, dainty and delicate wherever they are grown, be it in the woods, garden or greenhouse. There are tropical species for the greenhouse, as well as 2 species native to the U.S. (*A. pedatum* in the North and *A. capillus-veneris* in the subtropical parts of the southern U.S.). The fronds are 2–3 times compound. All species of this genus should be grown in partial shade whether in garden, greenhouse or home, as the hot direct rays of the sun can injure the young fronds. The tropical species (*A. raddiannum cuneatum* 'Elegantissimum' from Brazil, *A. macrophyllum* and *A. capillus-veneris*) should be kept in a cool greenhouse with temperatures no lower than 50°–55° F. They should be syringed occasionally to keep the foliage and the atmosphere moist. Usually, none of this group is successful in the home for any length of time because of lack of sufficient atmospheric moisture.

Propagation is by division or by spores. See FERNS.

capillus-veneris   18″   Zone 9   Southern Maidenhair Fern

Native to the warmer parts of the U.S., to British Columbia and the tropics, this makes a good greenhouse plant. The fronds grow from a creeping rhizome, the stalk is glossy and purplish black and the frond itself is 2–3 times compound with the ultimate segments being somewhat fan shaped, lobed and about ½ in. wide. This has been used as a fine house plant, producing many new fronds. As the old ones turn brown, carefully cut them out at the base.

Like most ferns, the potting mixture best suited for these is one of equal parts loam, leaf mold, peat moss and sand, with a few pieces of charcoal.

hispidulum   6″–12″   Zone 10   Rosy Maidenhair Fern

Native to the tropics of the eastern hemisphere, this fern is one which grows quickly and so has merit as a greenhouse plant in the home greenhouse.

pedatum   18″–26″   Zone 3   American Maidenhair Fern

This is the most common member of this genus, widely distributed throughout the moist woodlands of North America. The stalk is a shiny purplish black, branching at the top. The pinnae are borne horizontally, each of the small segments being rather oblong in outline and ¾ in. long, but the entire frond is more or less rounded and up to 18 in. wide, twice compound. Many consider this the daintiest of all the native American ferns. The rhizome creeps along just underneath the surface of the soil. It requires a cool, moist soil and a shaded situation, spreading slowly.

raddianum cuneatum   15″   Zone 10   Delta Maidenhair Fern

This is generally grown by florists, especially for cutting. It is a greenhouse plant, being native to the tropics of Brazil. The fronds are 3–4 pinnate, up to 9 in. wide, and the small, fan-shaped segments are ½ in. wide.

There are several attractive varieties such as 'Elegantissimum', 'Gracillimum', 'Grande' and 'Pacottii'. When the fronds are to be cut for decorations, select the older, more rigid ones, for the younger fronds wilt quickly. In any event, they might be immersed in water for a day before using. Even in the greenhouse these plants should be in partial shade, for strong sunlight burns the tender young foliage. A minimum temperature of 55° F. is satisfactory.

x tenerum 'Farleyense'   2′–3′   Zone 10

A rare hybrid in America, originating in the Barbados, but becoming known as the showiest plant in this genus. The leaves are nearly 2–3 ft. wide and the individual segments almost 2 in. long, making this the largest-leaved species. The segments are either light green or even tinted pink. An excellent type where it can be obtained and grown in the moist greenhouse.

ADLUMIA (ad-LUM-ia)

fungosa   vine   Zone 3   Mountain Fringe

This weak-stemmed biennial vine can be grown as an annual. It is native from southeast Canada to N.Car., has pinkish to pale purple flowers ¾ in. long, borne in a loose cluster, and blooms from June to Oct. It can be used in a sheltered corner of the wild garden to hide an unsightly background, for its thin-textured 3-parted leaves (with leaflets only ¼ in. long), clinging petioles, and gracefully drooping flower clusters give it a character all its own. Rich moist soil and semi-shade are conducive to its best growth. Propagated by seeds.

ADNATE. Grown to, united to, another part; stamens adnate to the corolla tube.

ADOBE-LILY = *Fritillaria pluriflora*

ADONIS (ad-O-nis). This genus belongs to the Buttercup Family, with large yellow or red cup-shaped flowers and finely divided fernlike alternate leaves which die to the ground early in the summer. Some species are annual, some perennial. All do best in full sun. A common name sometimes used is Pheasant's-eye. Seed of annual species can be sown in early spring. Perennial species can be divided in the fall or sown from seed if available. The seed does not retain its viability very long and should be sown as soon as fully ripe.

aestivalis   18″   annual   Summer Adonis

With deep red flowers, 1½ in. wide during June and July. Native to central Europe. The var. **citrina** has yellow flowers.

aleppica   1′   annual   Aleppo Adonis

Red flowers 2 in. across. Native to Syria.

amurensis   18″   Zones 2–3   Amur Adonis

A truly charming herbaceous perennial, the first flower to bloom in the spring, sometimes coming up right out of the snow to bloom. With cuplike yellow flowers like buttercups, almost 2 in. wide, the form mostly in American gardens is the double-flowered variety 'Fukuju Kai' (which is the Japanese for "Sea of Richness") and unfortunately it is sterile. There are single yellow and red varieties grown in Japan which some day may be available to American gardeners. A delightful native of Japan and eastern Asia blooming in late March or early April, decidedly worth while in any garden where it can be observed in very early spring.

flammea   18″   annual   Flame Adonis
Flowers bright red, 1 in. wide with spotted black in center, blooming from May to July. Native to western Asia.

vernalis   1′–1½′   Zones 2–3   Spring Adonis
The yellow flowers are nearly 3 in. across, borne in April. Native to Europe.

ADVENTITIOUS BUDS. Those produced abnormally, as from the stem instead of the axils of the leaves.

ADVENTIVE. Applied to an introduced plant, not definitely established or naturalized.

AECHMEA (EEK-mea). These are hothouse and house plants from tropical America, members of the Bromeliad Family. The spine-edged leaves grow directly from the rootstalk, over-lapping each other, and in the center of this tube the erect flower spike appears. They bear red and yellow flowers in the summer and fall. Propagation is by making cuttings of the suckers growing from the base of the plant in March.

fulgens   16″   Zone 10
Native to Brazil with leaves 16 in. long and 3 in. wide. Flowers ½ in. long in spikes, blue tipped. The var. **discolor** is frequently used because the undersides of the leaves are red, sometimes slightly striped. Another species **A. fosterana** or 'Foster's Favorite' has wine-red leaves and red and blue flowers, fine as a house plant.

AEGOPODIUM (ee-go-PO-dium)
**podagraria   6″–14″   Zone 3   Goutweed,
Bishop's-weed**
A vicious fast-spreading weed and by the same token a fast-spreading ground cover, native to Europe but now naturalized in North America. The twice compound leaves and carrotlike flower heads are typical; the flowers appearing from late May to late June are not attractive. This can be cut back two or three times a year with a scythe or a mower and still it will serve as a fast-spreading ground cover. The Silveredge Goutweed (var. **variegatum**) has leaves with a white margin and is not quite so vigorous. This species is one of the few plants that will grow equally well in sun or shade, rich or poor soil. Once it escapes bounds it is difficult to control. If it must be used as a ground cover, it is wise to use it only in situations with poor, dry soil. If planted in good soil, especially in a shaded woods situation, it will spread rapidly and be-come a pest.

AEONIUM (ee-O-nium). Succulent plants mostly from the Canary Islands, closely allied to *Sempervivum*. Grown outdoors in southern

Calif. gardens or as ornamental pot plants indoors in the North. They grow best in full sun and are propagated by cuttings placed in sand in spring. Also propagated by seeds.

arboreum   3′   Zone 9
With golden-yellow flowers and leaves that turn bronze-purple in the fall. The leaves are succulent and spatulate, a rosette of them 6 in. across at the end of a thick succulent stem, with white hairs on the leaf margin.

decorum   2′   Zone 9
A slightly shrubby succulent with a rosette of spatulate, copper-colored leaves on top of a succulent stem, the flowers white with pink lines on the petals.

haworthii   3′   Zone 9   Pinwheel
A bushy succulent with short branches bearing rosettes of thick, fleshy, gray-green leaves edged with reddish hairs. The flowers are pale yellow, flushed rose, 40–50 in a terminal panicle.

tabuliforme   1′   Zone 9
A rare succulent evergreen house plant, close relative to the Houseleek, makes a curious and interesting specimen because it forms great, flat discs which are composed of many green leaves in a rosette 3 in. or more across. The flowers are pale yellow. Propagated by cuttings in spring.

AERIDES (AIR-id-eez)
odorata   6″–24″   Zone 10
Considered one of the Vanda group of epiphytic orchids (see VANDA) with 10–30 very fragrant flowers on a long, drooping raceme, the flowers 1–1½ in. across, creamy white with lavender tips blooming in the summer. Native to India and China. Frequently grown in the warm green-house, making a good ornamental. Actually there are many species in this genus but this species is the one most frequently recommended. For culture and propagation see ORCHID.

AEROSOLS. See INSECTICIDES.

AESCULUS   (EES-kew-lus).   **Horse-chestnut**
This group of trees, native and introduced, has been widely overplanted in America. During the last century, when many of the trees from the Orient were not yet introduced for American planting, horse-chestnuts were popular. Now, with so many other trees from which to choose, especially trees with ornamental fruits and out-standing autumn color, it is not necessary to plant horse-chestnuts in large numbers. As trees, these are vigorous growing, they have large opposite conspicuous and coarse leaves, palmately compound, which are susceptible to numerous insect and disease pests. The flowers are borne in small or large pyramidal clusters, but those of many of the species are not even ornamental. The fruits are coarse nuts and a nuisance wherever they fall and because of this, the horse-chestnuts should no longer be used as

street trees. They make "dirty" trees—always dropping something, whether it is leaves, twigs, fruits or fruit husks. The flowers of many of the species do not open fully and so make a very poor display at the only time when they might be at the height of their ornamental interest. Most have no autumn color and none in this group should be considered for the small property. The large nuts of the horse-chestnuts and buckeyes contain a bitter poisonous principle—this poison may be removed by leaching, leaving a wholesome and highly nutritious meal. The Indians roasted the nuts among hot stones, peeled and mashed them and then leached the meal with water for several days, after which they used the meal to make breadstuffs.

Propagation

Seeds should not be allowed to dry out but should be stratified as soon as ripe at 40° F. for about 4 months. The seeds of *A. parviflora* do not have a dormant period and can be sown immediately in July when ripe. Also this species can be rooted from root cuttings. See SEEDS, STRATIFICATION, CUTTINGS. Varieties of *A. hippocastanum* and *A. carnea* are usually grafted on seedlings of the species.

Insect Pests

Japanese beetle and tussock moth caterpillars may damage the foliage unless protected with insecticide #37.

Diseases

Leaf blotch causes yellow, curled leaves. Burning the fallen leaves and spraying with fungicide #K or #D is advised. Anthracnose which blights the new leaves is treated as for leaf blotch. Nectria canker can be cut out and the wounds coated with tree paint.

x carnea   75′   Zone 3   Red Horse-chestnut
Originating as a hybrid (*A. hippocastanum* x *A. pavia*) in Europe over 100 years ago, this species is the most ornamental because of its pink to red flower clusters that are about 10 in. tall. The flowers have a red throat when fully open and although it is a hybrid it has been known to come remarkably true from seed. The foliage and general form of the tree is similar to that of *A. hippocastanum*. The variety **'Briotii'** or Ruby Horse-chestnut was raised from seed in 1858 and is similar to the species except that the flowers are slightly larger and a more colorful deeper pink to red (with a yellow throat). The flower clusters are 10 in. tall, fairly dense and symmetrical, and the flowers open completely. Neither this nor the species has startling autumn foliage color. They both bloom during mid-

May. The variety **'Plantierensis'** or Damask Horse-chestnut originated before 1894; the 12-in. flower clusters of this variety are covered with light pink flowers with a red or yellow throat and are moderately tight. They are lighter colored when fully open than the species or the variety **'Briotii'**. Also the leaves usually have 7 leaflets while those of the species have 5–7 leaflets. Consequently, the species and these two varieties offer flowers of 3 different shades of pink to red.

glabra   30′   Zone 3   Ohio Buckeye
The greenish-yellow flowers of this species from the central U.S. are borne on stalks 6 in. long. Although not at all attractive in flower, it is the only one of the horse-chestnuts to color an excellent orange in the fall. This and its good rounded shape might recommend it for use in situations where the taller-growing horse-chestnuts would be out of place. It also blooms in mid-May. The leaves, especially on young shoots in early spring, and the seeds are poisonous.

hippocastanum   75′   Zone 3   Horse-chestnut
This is the tree which has been overplanted in many parts of the eastern U.S. A tall, sometimes rounded tree with 5–7 large, palmately arranged leaflets, each 4–10 in. long, large pyramidal clusters of white flowers 8–12 in. long in mid-May, and large rounded fruits about 2½ in. across, with green husks that eventually split open and display one or two shiny brown

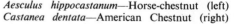
Aesculus hippocastanum—Horse-chestnut (left)
Castanea dentata—American Chestnut (right)

nutlets inside. The leaves are susceptible to a disfiguring blight in the late summer, and they have no autumn color; the fruits have no ornamental value and are a nuisance on the lawn when they drop. Mature trees tend to have a weak branching system, so, all in all, there are many better trees that can now be considered in its place. The leaves are poisonous in early spring and children have been poisoned eating the large nutlike seeds. The seeds after roasting and leaching have been used for food by the Indians. Native to southern Europe. The variety **'Baumannii'** or Baumann Horse-chestnut was first noticed as a sport on a tree in Geneva, Switzerland, slightly before 1822. The flowers are double, with very few red marks in them, and the tight clusters are 9 in. long. Because of the double flowers, the bloom lasts longer and no fruits are produced—the reasons why this clone should be grown instead of the species. Of all the horse-chestnuts, this variety and *A. carnea* and its varieties are unquestionably the best for ornamental use, especially in public places. **'Pyramidalis'** young trees are pyramidal in habit.

octandra   60′   Zone 3   Yellow Buckeye
Native in the central and southeastern U.S., this has opposite compound leaves, 5 leaflets 4–6 in. long, yellow flowers in upright clusters 4–6 in. long in late May and June. The leaves of this have been reported as poisonous when eaten by animals, especially when the leaves are young in the early spring. Children have been poisoned by eating the large nutlike fruits.

parviflora 8′–12′ Zone 4 Bottlebrush Buckeye
An early summer blooming shrub native to S.Car. and Ala. has merit when in bloom during mid-July when few woody plants are in bloom. The 8–12 in. pyramidal panicles bear white flowers with pinkish stamens and it is from these the plant gets its common name. It grows into a large mound, increasing by underground suckers, and makes a shrub two or three times as wide as it is tall. Not a shrub for the small garden, but for the public area, especially with a background of woods or even as a specimen plant in the open, it does have some value. Fruits are not always formed in the Arnold Arboretum since the frost-free period between bloom and ripening is not always sufficiently long. Farther south, however, fruits are produced on the upright stalks.

pavia   18′–36′   Zone 5   Red Buckeye
This has bright red but comparatively small flowers in June, opposite compound leaves, each with 5 leaflets 3–5½ in. long, and is native from Va. to Fla. The leaves of this also have proved poisonous when eaten by animals under certain conditions. See *A. octandra*.

AETHIONEMA (ee-thi-o-NEE-ma). These are evergreen low shrubby herbs, native of the eastern Mediterranean area, that make excellent rock plants and ground covers for small spots, if grown in the full sun, but if grown in shade they soon die out. They do best in light sandy sandy soils, not heavy soils. The flowers in May and June are similar to those of Candytuft and it is well to prune them back slightly after blooming. The new shoots appearing after this operation make excellent cuttings. They are also propagated by seed or by division. In the North they should be protected during the winter to prevent foliage burn; they withstand drought but will not grow in wet soils.

cordifolium   10″   Zone 5   Lebanon Stonecress
A small, shrubby perennial with tiny, linear leaves crowded on upright stems, ending in closely held clusters of creamy white to pale pink flowers in late spring.

grandiflorum (*A. pulchellum*)   6″–8″   Zone 6
                                Persian Stonecress
Usually horizontal growth, this is native to Asia Minor. The slightly fragrant, rose-colored flowers appear in June and July and contrast nicely with the bluish foliage. The var. **'Warley Rose'** is the hybrid most commonly grown, a dense, mounded plant with steel-blue foliage. **'Warley Ruber'** produces darker flowers.

iberideum   6″   Zone 6   Spanish Stonecress
Blooming in April and May, this rare plant has white flowers in showy, short racemes. It looks like a small cushion of gray foliage. Native to Asia Minor.

pulchellum = *A. grandiflorum*

AFRICAN DAISY = *Arctotis stoechadifolia*

AFRICAN-HEMP = *Sparmannia africana*

AFRICAN TULIPTREE = *Spathodea campanulata*

AFRICAN VIOLET. See SAINTPAULIA.

AGALINIS (ag-a-LIN-is)
purpurea (*Gerardia purpurea*)   1′–2′   Zone 4
                                Purple Gerardia
A branching annual plant with opposite, linear leaves 1–2 in. long. The purple, but occasionally white, funnelform flowers are borne toward the ends of the branches on short stalks. The bell-shaped calyx has 5 pointed teeth extending half the length of the corolla tube which has 5 slightly irregular, spreading lobes. The plant frequents moist, sunny locations in the Atlantic coastal states and west to Tex., and flowers from July to Sept. This is perhaps the only species in this genus of any horticultural interest, for none of these species are generally cultivated.

AGAPANTHUS (ag-a-PAN-thus). These are herbs with tuberous roots, tall spikes of many funnel-form flowers and masses of sword-shaped leaves like those of Hemerocallis. They can be grown in tubs or out-of-doors completely in mild climates. The flowers are bright blue or white, about 2 in. long and 12–30 are borne on each stalk in summer. Culture is simple. If grown in the North they are grown in tubs for placing on porch or patio. When grown in the same tub for several years they should be well supplied with liquid fertilizer as they are gross feeders. In the fall, merely dry off gradually and store over winter in a cool place. If the temperature does not go below 25° F., they can be left in the ground over winter. Propagation is by simple division.

africanus 20″ Zone 9 Lily-of-the-Nile, African Agapanthus
Native to Africa with leaves 4–10 in. long, deep blue flowers on stalks 10–20 in. high with 20 flowers per stalk.

orientalis 3′ Zone 9 Oriental Agapanthus
Native to the Orient and differs chiefly from *A. africanus* by its softer, more reflexed leaves and its flower spike that bears 40–100 blue flowers. There are several varieties of this. The variety **variegatus** bears leaves striped white; and **mooreanus** has dark blue flowers being hardier than the others and is sometimes grown out-of-doors in Washington, D.C. More varieties are **'Albidus'**, white flowers; **leichtlinii** with deeper blue flowers; **giganteus** with a sturdy spike having 200 dark blue flowers; **aurivittatus** with leaves striped yellow and **'Variegatus'** with leaves almost entirely white.

AGARICUS (ag-GAIR-ik-us). See MUSHROOM GROWING.

A. bisporus = the cultivated Mushroom.
AGAVE (ag-AH-ve). This is the most important group of "succulents" in the Amaryllis Family. The species is often grown as a house-potted or tubbed plant, but under such conditions it never grows large enough to flower. As a house plant it cannot be kept small and within scale. The best for house plants are those varieties of *A. americana* with variegated foliage, namely **'Marginata'**, with yellowish stripes on the leaf margins; **'Medio-picta'** with a yellow stripe down the center of the leaf; and the species *A. victoriae-reginae* with pale gray or brownish leaf margins and irregular gray or white stripings on the upper and lower leaf surface. This last species seldom grows more than a foot in diameter, but *A. americana* and its varieties should be replaced (as house plants) when they have reached a diameter of 18 in.

Insect Pests

The same pests that attack cacti may infest Agave. Cactus scale and cactus mealybug are controlled by timely sprays of insecticide #15 or similar organic phosphates. Cactus borer often causes deformed plants in outdoor plantings. Protective sprays in midsummer when the adults are present are helpful, and special borer sprays and pastes such as Bor-Kil will kill the borers in tunnels.

Diseases

Plants of Agave and cactus are very susceptible to root rot wilt and, when they are grown as house plants, excessive watering must be avoided. Use sterilized soil and sand when potting.

americana 6′ Zone 6 American Aloe, Century Plant
A sun-loving plant, the American Aloe thrives on the sandy soils of the southern and southwestern states and into Mexico. The long, thick, succulent leaves of this perennial herb are occasionally purple spotted and grow in a basal rosette from which a flower stalk arises, often to a height of 6 ft. Greenish-yellow flowers are clustered up and down the upper portion of this flower stalk. These have six segments which are fused at the upper portion of the drooping, bell-shaped flower. The plant blooms throughout the summer and this, as well as the fact that the flowers are fragrant at night, make it a valuable

Agave americana in flower—Century Plant

addition to the garden. Propagation is by suckers which appear around the base of the old plant. These are best removed before the old plant blooms.

lecheguilla   18″   Zone 10   Lecheguilla
This is sometimes used as a potted plant, native to Mexico, with bluish-green leaves about 18 in. long but with 4- to 8-ft. flower stalks. The flowers are white and 1½ in. wide. Goats and sheep are poisoned when grazing on this foliage in dry weather, but cattle and horses are rarely affected.

potatorum   1′   Zone 10   Century Plant
This trunkless Mexican plant of the Amaryllis Family has tough, prickly, grayish and pointed leaves a foot long and 4 in. wide, growing in a rosette. The fragrant flowers 2½ in. long are yellowish-green and are borne on horizontal branches at the top of a 13-ft. stalk.

sisalana   3′   Zone 10   Sisal Hemp
Probably native to the Bahamas, this is the source of sisal hemp of commerce. The flower stalk may be as much as 18 ft. tall; the greenish flowers, about 2½ in. long, have an ill-smelling odor. The leaves are 5 ft. long and 4 in. wide and it is these which are shredded in the making of hemp. It is grown for commerce chiefly in Java and South Africa. Young plants will form as suckers at the ground level on the flowering stalk.

virginica = *Manfreda virginica*

AGERATUM (aj-er-AY-tum)

houstonianum   6″–18″   annual   Ageratum
A popular annual plant from Mexico with heart-shaped, mostly opposite leaves and blue, white or pink flowers in small puffy bunches covering the plant in summer until frost. There are many varieties available. The smaller varieties make excellent edging plants. Seed must be sown indoors or in a cold frame in March and not set out until all danger of frost is over, for the plants succumb easily to frost. Pinch back the plants when they are set out to make certain they grow with a compact habit. Dwarf vars. should be 9 in. apart and taller vars. about a foot apart. There are many good dwarf varieties from 3–5 in. tall and ranging in color from white to pink and blue flowers. New named varieties appear frequently. **'Blue Bedder'** (4 in.); **'Fairy Pink'** (5 in.); **'Midget Blue'** (3 in.); are only a few of many.

Insect Pests

In the greenhouse and out-of-doors on plants propagated in the greenhouse, the greenhouse whitefly often stunts plants. Spraying with pesticide #15 is effective and commercial growers often fumigate with calcium cyanide. Greenhouse mealybug and the greenhouse Orthegia, which resembles a mealybug, often suck the sap and damage the plants. Pesticide #15 gives excellent control. Red spider mites cause yellow and webbed leaves when abundant. Miticides such as #31 or #34 hold them in check.

Diseases

Sclerotinia wilt causing rot at the surface of the ground frequently kills Ageratum. Use sterilized soil or drench the soil with fungicide #F as directed.

AGLAOMORPHA (ag-lay-o-MOR-pha)

meyeniana   1′–3′   Zone 10   Bear's-paw Fern
This is native to the Philippine Islands but is becoming a popular fern in home greenhouses because it has a large and very scaly rhizome that creeps over the edge of the pot. Where native it may grow 3 ft. tall but in cultivation in greenhouses it is more likely to be 12–24 in. tall, the fronds being as much as 6 in. wide. It requires a rich soil with plenty of humus and a very moist atmosphere in which to grow. For propagation see FERNS.

AGLAONEMA (ag-lay-o-NEE-ma).
These aroids belong to the same family as Jack-in-the-pulpit and the Calla-lily, but they are used as very tough house plants, one at least growing equally well in water or in soil. They are rhizomatous plants from tropical Asia or Africa, propagated by division and cuttings. The unisexual flowers are borne on a spathe (like those of Jack-in-the-pulpit) and the leaf petioles encircle the stem.

commutatum   2′   Zone 10
Leaves 6 in. long, 2 in. wide, with pale green markings on veins.

costatum   8″   Zone 10   Spotted Evergreen
Leaves 8 in. long and 4 in. wide on short stems, and the leaves spotted white. Native to Malaya.

**modestum   12′–20′   Zone 10   Chinese Ever-
green**
A native evergreen of the Philippine Islands widely distributed as a house plant because it has the ability to grow almost equally well in water or soil for many months with a minimum amount of light. Evergreen leaves ovate and acuminate, 6–10 in. long, petiole ⅔ as long as leaf blade; spathe 2½–3 in. long. Sometimes termed *A. simplex*, but this is an entirely different plant from Malaya.

AGONIS (ag-O-nis)

**flexuosa   25′–35′   Zone 10   Peppermint-tree,
Willow-myrtle**
Willowlike in appearance, this Australian tree has leaves about 6 in. long, white flowers in dense globelike clusters about ½ in. across. The fruit is a many-seeded, woody capsule. It is only used in southern Calif.

AGRIMONIA (ag-rim-O-nia)
  eupatoria   **3'**   **Zone 6**   **Agrimony**
The compound, alternate leaves produce a
yellow dye, for which this herb is valued. Small
yellow flowers, native to Europe. Sometimes
grown in shady spots but of little ornamental
value. Propagated by seeds and division in
spring.

AGRIMONY = *Agrimonia eupatoria*

AGROPYRON (ag-ro-PIE-ron)
  repens   **1½'-4'**   **Zone 3**   **Quack Grass**
Perhaps one of the worst of all pernicious
perennial weeds because of its creeping rootstocks which have the ability to root and send
up blades of grass at every node. It was introduced from Europe where it is native. It has the

Quack grass—*Agropyron repens*

ability of growing its long rootstalks or rhizomes
into good fertile flower-bed soil from the edge
of the bed, for 5 ft. and more in one season. All
rootstalks must be removed carefully, not
roughly pulled out and broken off, or else just
so many new plants will be started wherever a
piece of the rhizome remains in the ground. It
can be smothered out with black polyethylene
film and some kinds of mulches. For chemical
control see WEED CONTROL. It repropagates
itself readily by seeds also and should be
quickly and cleanly removed as soon as it
appears in the garden.
  smithii   **3'**   **Zone 3**   **Bluestem Wheat-grass**
Somewhat similar to *A. repens* but the roots do
not spread as much, the bluish-green leaves tend
to roll up and curl during dry weather and it is
mostly seen in the midwestern U.S. where it is
native. It too is a vicious perennial weed.

AGROSTEMMA (agros-TEM-ma)
  githago   **3'**   **annual**   **Common Corn Cockle**
An annual or biennial weed with hairy, grayish,
grasslike opposite leaves and single, long-
stalked, purple flowers, 1-2 in. across with 5
petals, borne in the leaf axils during May, June,
July. The pod contains purple-black, poisonous
seeds. It is native to Europe and Asia but has
become naturalized in America where it is a
weed in grain fields.

AGROSTIS (ag-ROS-tis). A group of tufted
grasses with narrow leaves, native to Europe

and North America, some of them very important in lawns, golf courses and hay fields. See
GRASS, LAWNS.
  alba = Redtop. See GRASS, LAWNS.
  hiemalis   **2'**   **Zone 3**   **Hair Grass**
A perennial grass with leaves 5 in. long and
$\frac{1}{12}$ in. wide, the seed panicles sometimes
purplish. Sometimes considered as ornamental.
  laxiflora = *A. hiemalis*
  nebulosa **12"-18"** **annual** **Cloud Bent Grass**
Although this is one of the grasses, it makes a
fine ornamental garden plant because of its
delicate and graceful flowering and seeding
panicles. These can also be cut and dried and
used for decorations indoors. Native to Spain.
Sow seeds in mid-April in a sunny situation.
  tenuis = Bent Grass. See GRASS, LAWNS.

AILANTHUS (ay-LAN-thus)
  altissima   **60'**   **Zone 4**   **Tree-of-heaven**
This is probably the most common tree growing
in the urban areas of the U.S., supposedly
introduced in 1784 from China but now widely
grown and seeding itself as a weed tree wherever
fruiting specimens produce seeds. The sexes are
separate; male trees flowering in late June
produce small yellow flowers in pyramidal
clusters, but they are vile smelling and this sex
should not be planted for this reason. The
female trees produce large clusters of "keys,"
somewhat similar to those of maples except that
the seed is in the center of the wing.

The leaves are alternate, large and compound
with 6-12 pairs of leaflets and an odd one at the
end. Each leaflet has a single small tooth at the
base of each leaflet blade, the easiest way to
identify it from the similarly compound leaves
of some of the sumacs, but these are regularly
toothed. Its ability to withstand trying urban
growing conditions is its best characteristic,
growing in situations where practically nothing
else will grow. The fruits often turn reddish in
late summer and this adds a touch of color and
the tree does withstand seashore growing
conditions also.

However, when good soil is available, there
are many better trees which should be considered
first. It is usually considered a weed tree, not a
desirable ornamental except in the poorest
situations.

Several cases of dermatitis have been reported
from contact with its leaves.

Propagation

Seed may be stratified as soon as ripe at 40° F.
for 2 months and then sown or stored dry in
airtight containers in a cool place until the
following year and then sown. Grafts are made
on root pieces from the species, about the
diameter of a lead pencil. Also root cuttings can

be easily rooted. See STRATIFICATION, GRAFTING, CUTTINGS.

Pests

Resistant to most foliage pests. Susceptible to verticillium wilt which also attacks elms, maples, etc. Yellow leaves which fall prematurely are typical symptoms. Cut off infected branches well below evidence of disease. Do not plant where previously infected trees have been removed.

AIRBROM—See *Billbergia*.

AIR LAYERING WITH POLYETHYLENE FILM. Making air layers on woody plants to induce rooting is a practice that is centuries old. Generations of Chinese did it, and undoubtedly it was introduced into America by the earlier settlers. Until comparatively recently the method has been used chiefly in the greenhouse. It consisted of scarifying the stem of a plant and wrapping moist moss (or soil) around that injured plant part. If the wrapping material was kept moist continually, rooting often occurred. The difficulty came in keeping the wrapping material moist. Rubber or paper wrappings did not prove satisfactory, and watering of the wrapping would frequently have to be done daily and even several times a day in a hot greenhouse. This continual care was frequently more bother than it was worth.

Now, with the use of polyethylene film, air layering is a method which every home owner can use to increase his plants. The properties of this film are such that it is indispensable for many horticultural purposes. Although it allows ample gaseous exchange, it does not permit the free transmission of water or water vapor, which is the reason why it has so many uses in keeping plant materials alive.

The making of the air layer itself is very simple. A longitudinal cut of about 2 in. is made on the young twig, the cut going nearly to the center of the twig. (An adaptation of this is to remove a complete circle of bark ½ in. wide around the stem.) Then both cut surfaces are dusted with some hormone rooting powder which may (or may not) aid in the rooting. Hormodin #3 has been used, but undoubtedly other materials are just as good. Moist sphagnum moss—about a handful—is packed between the cut surfaces and then all around the entire cut, fully covering it, then tied in place. Polyethylene film is wrapped carefully and tightly about it, then tied top and bottom. Rubber bands used in grafting have not proved satisfactory for tying, but Scotch Electrical Tape #33 has proved most satisfactory.

The wrapping and tying of the film should

Air Layering:

1. Make longitudinal cut and insert small amount of slightly moist sphagnum moss.
2. Dust with hormone rooting powder.
3. Pack thoroughly with moist moss.
4. Cover and tie tightly, using polyethylene film.
5. Sever when thoroughly rooted.

be done in such a way that the moss is well contained and that no opening in the film is left for the evaporation of the moisture from the moss.

The overlap of the film wrapping should be on the underside of the air layer so that rainwater will not seep in. Also, in taping the top end of the wrap, the tape should be started on the bare twig and gradually spiral down to completely close the top end of the wrap in order that rainwater will not seep down the twig and into the moss inside. Many air layers may have failed to root because this was not done, since water seeping into the moss packing will push out much of the air and create a soggy condition decidedly unfavorable to rooting. If properly done, the air layer will remain moist for months (some remain moist for a year) and rooting may take place in a few months' time.

This is all there is to the operation. The time of year when it is done, the size of twig used, the amount of hormone powder, the amount of moisture in the moss and the rooting tendencies of the species used are variables with which one works to achieve proper rooting. Air layers may be made in early spring on wood that is dormant, and again in June and July on twigs that grew during the current year. Many plants are propagated from both "hardwood" or dormant cuttings and "softwood" cuttings made of wood grown the current year; others may root better from just one of these types of cuttings. Consequently one would expect that the time when these layers are applied with best results might well vary with the species.

Twigs have been rooted that were ½ in. in dia., although usually one might expect normal rooting from the twigs about the size of a lead pencil. Because so very little moisture passes through the film, one should be extremely careful not to have too much moisture in the sphagnum moss at the time it is applied about the cut. The moss should be squeezed prior to application so that it will be moist—not wet.

Certain plants, such as forsythias, privets, dogwoods and yew, root easily and for these air layering is one method which can be used. In addition, certain of the plants which are hard to root respond to this method. Some years ago experiments in rooting plants by air layering were carried out at the Arnold Arboretum. These experiments showed that in many cases air layering, applied early in the spring to plants growing out-of-doors, is an excellent and versatile method of plant propagation which may be used by persons who do not have proper greenhouse facilities for the more common methods of grafting or budding indoors.

It must be admitted, however, that an equal number of plants used in the experiments failed to root. Hence the process apparently cannot be applied with 100% success to all woody plants. Also, the matter of cutting off the rooted layer and establishing it in soil as an independent plant is not always a successful operation. Many times roots are formed by the air layer process, but when the layered branch is cut from the parent plant the roots fail to become established in the soil and the young plant dies. To overcome this, the severing operation might be done over a period of time, or soil might be packed around the rooted layer, delaying the cutting from the parent plant until after the feeding roots have permeated the soil.

In any event, air layering is a simple and practical process, offering to the interested gardener a means by which he can asexually propagate a few woody plants without the use of a hot bed or greenhouse.

Some plants which rooted successfully by the air layer method in one series of experiments at the Arnold Arboretum in Boston, Mass., are:

Abeliophyllum distichum
Acer barbinerve
A. capilipes
A. circinatum
A. cissifolium
A. durettii
A. ginnala
A. griseum
A. palmatum dissectum
A. pensylvanicum
A. platanoides
A. platanoides 'Globosum'
A. saccharum 'Temple's Upright'
Aesculus carnea

A. hippocastanum
A. hippocastanum 'Umbraculifera'
Albizia julibrissin rosea
Betula aurata
B. fontinalis
Carya tomentosa
Castanea mollissima
Catalpa bignonioides
C. bungei
C. speciosa
Cercis chinensis
Cladrastis platycarpa
Clethra barbinervis
Corylopsis glabrescens
C. spicata
Corylus chinensis
Cotinus coggygria purpureus
Cotoneaster foveolata
C. horizontalis
Crataegus monogyna 'Stricta'
C. pinnatifida major
Cytisus praecox
Davidia involucrata vilmorinii
Diospyros lotus
Enkianthus campanulatus
Franklinia alatamaha
Ginkgo biloba
Halesia carolina
H. monticola rosea
Hibiscus syriacus
Hippophae rhamnoides
Ilex crenata convexa
I. ambigua montana 'Macropoda'
I. glabra
I. verticillata
Indigofera amblyantha
Koelreuteria paniculata
Laburnum anagyroides
L. watereri
Lonicera maackii
Maackia amurensis
Magnolia heptapeta (denudata)
M. soulangiana 'Alexandrina'
Malus astracanica
M. atrosanguinea
M. 'Dorothea'
M. floribunda
M. halliana spontanea
M. 'McIntosh'
M. micromalus
M. prunifolia rinkii
M. purpurea
M. sargentii 'Rosea'
M. spectabilis
M. sublobata
M. 'Wabiskaw'
Morus alba 'Pendula'
Orixa japonica
Populus alba nivea
Prunus juddii

P. maackii
P. serrulata 'Amanogawa'
P. serrulata 'Gyoiko'
P. serrulata 'Kwanzan'
P. yedoensis 'Taizanfukun'
Ptelea trifoliata aurea
Rhododendron 'Dr. Charles Baumann'
R. 'Josephine Klinger'
Styrax japonica
Symplocos paniculata
Syringa reticulata
S. prestoniae 'Lucetta'
S. prestoniae 'Paulina'
S. villosa
S. vulgaris vars.
Tamarix ramosissima
Tilia cordata
T. platyphyllos 'Fastigiata'
Tsuga canadensis
Ulmus carpinifolia 'Koopmannii'
U. carpinifolia 'Sarniensis'
U. glabra
Vaccinium corymbosum 'Jersey'
Viburnum carlesii
V. dilatatum
V. juddii
V. opulus
V. rhytidophyllum
V. rufidulum
V. sargentii
V. sargentii flavum
V. setigerum aurantiacum
V. sieboldii
Wisteria floribunda 'Longissima Alba'
W. floribunda 'Naga Noda'
W. floribunda 'Violacea-plena'
W. formosa
W. macrostachya
W. sinensis
W. venusta
Zelkova serrata
Z. sinica

AIRPLANT = *Kalanchoe pinnata*

AIR PLANTS. See EPIPHYTE.

AIR-POTATO YAM = *Dioscorea bulbifera*

AIZOACEAE = The Carpetweed Family

AJUGA (aj-OO-ga). Members of the Mint Family, some of these make excellent ground covers. They are low-growing herbaceous perennials, sending out creeping stolons in or on top of the soil, and bear low spikes of blue, white or vari-colored flowers in May and June. Easily propagated by division. The plants grow well in almost any soil, in sun or in partial shade.

genevensis 6″–9″ Zones 2–3 Geneva Bugle
With bright blue flower spikes in May and June, native to Europe, and tending to grow in clumps much more than the rapidly spreading *A. reptans*. This makes a better show also, hence is good for the rock garden.

reptans 4″–12″ Zones 2–3 Bugleweed, Carpet Bugle
A low ground cover, spreading by fast-growing stolons and so vigorous it sometimes invades a lawn. Native to Europe, the flowers are blue, white, purplish or red (depending on variety) in compact upright spikes held rigidly above the flat leaves, and bloom from early May to mid-June. The leaves are about 4 in. long and are practically evergreen in many places. It is one of the best of ground covers, forming a flat mass of foliage on the ground surface, growing equally well in sun or shade. There are many varieties available, some with white flowers (**'Alba'**); bronze leaves (**'Atropurpurea'**); dark purple leaves (**'Rubra'**); variegated leaves (**'Variegata'**); curled metallic, crisped leaves and blue flowers (**'Metallica Crispa'**) and several others. It should be remembered that if a large planting is made of any of these varieties, seeds will eventually germinate and grow in a few years, yielding plants that are like the species, not the variety. Hence one should either replace such large varietal plantings every few years or be prepared to rogue out the unwanted seedlings if and when they appear.

AKEAKE = *Dodonaea viscosa*

AKEBIA FAMILY—*Lardizabalaceae*

AKEBIA (ak-EE-bia)
quinata Twining vine 30′–40′ Zone 4 Fiveleaf Akebia
The Fiveleaf Akebia is native to China, Korea and Japan and is one of the best twining foliage vines for northern planting. The leaves are alternate, palmately compound with 5 leaflets arranged like the fingers of a hand. The peculiar small purple flowers appearing in mid-May are interesting because there are both staminate and pistillate flowers in the same cluster. This is semi-evergreen, a vicious grower and once it becomes well established it can become a pest, sending out long runners underground and the shoots twining around and choking everything with which they come in contact. The foliage is graceful and it grows into a dense mass of leaves and stems. If properly controlled it can be one of the very finest foliage vines. The fruits are large, edible, fleshy purple pods 2–3 in. long, with little ornamental value.

Propagation

If fresh seed is sown as soon as ripe, it will germinate quickly. However, if it is stored dry any length of time in airtight containers in a cool place, then it goes into double dormancy and will have to be stratified for 5 months at room temperature, then for 3 months at 40° F., then sown. Layers are easily found around old plants or they can be divided. Softwood and hardwood cuttings root readily.

ALBIZIA (al-BIZZ-ia)

distachya   **20′**   **Zone 9**   **Plume Albizia**
With yellow flowers in spikes 2 in. long during spring and fruit pods 3 in. long. Alternate, twice-compound leaves with 14–24 pinnae, each with 40–60 leaflets. Native to Australia.

lophantha = *A. distachya*

julibrissin   **36′**   **Zone 7**   **Silktree**
Widely grown throughout the South, this tree was introduced to America from Persia and central China. The alternate, very finely divided, twice-compound leaves remind one of the leaves of the Sensitive-plant and, in fact, they do curl up on a cool evening.

The small, ball-like flower clusters, about 2 in. across, are pink and white, bloom in July and Aug. and are conspicuous because of their colorful stamens, not petals. The fruits are merely flat, pealike pods about 6 in. long. The tree blooms while still very young.

There is a variety now named **'Ernest Wilson'** (formerly *rosea*) introduced from Korea which is hardier than the species, hardy as far north as Boston, Mass. The serious fungus mimosa wilt has killed a large number of trees in the South. Since the fungus lives over winter in the soil, it has not been a serious threat north of Long Island.

Seeds may be processed at once, or stored dry in airtight containers in a cool place for up to a year and then processed. The dormancy is overcome by soaking the seeds in hot water (190° F.) overnight or by soaking them ½ hour in concentrated sulfuric acid, washing thoroughly, then sowing.

lebbeck   **50′**   **Zone 10**   **Woman's-tongue-tree**
A tropical tree with compound leaves and leaflets up to 1½ in. long; flowers are ball-like clusters of greenish-yellow stamens in axillary heads; the fruits are foot-long flat pods. Native to tropical Asia, but naturalized in the West Indies.

ALBUCA (al-BEW-ca). A group of bulbous herbs related to *Scilla*, mostly from South Africa, with racemes of showy white and yellow flowers borne in late spring or early summer. Propagation is by offsets.

canadensis   **18″–36″**   **Zone 10**
Flowers are a pale yellow with a one inch band of green and the leaves are 1–1½′ long.

major = *A. canadensis*

minor = *A. canadensis*

nelsonii   **3′–5′**   **Zone 10**
Flowers pure white with a red-brown stripe. It is a fine ornamental.

ALCEA

ficifolia   **6′**   **biennial**   **Figleaf or Antwerp Hollyhock**
With 7-lobed, toothed leaves and lemon-yellow to orange flowers, single or double, 3 in. or more wide, borne in terminal spikes during the summer. Native to Europe but little used in U.S.

rosea (*Althaea rosea*)   **9′**   **Zones 2–3 Hollyhock**
This is one of the most cherished of all garden flowers, widely popular throughout the country. Leaves 7-lobed, stalks the second year, tall and spikelike flowers red, rose, pink, yellow or white, 3 in. across, with double vars. available. Native to China. **'Indian Spring'** is the hollyhock to plant as an annual for most of the others are biennials. This grows 4–5 ft. tall if the seed is started in March or outside in April. This produces pale pink, rose and carmine semi-double flowers and blooming the first year.

Insect Pests

Caterpillars of the painted lady butterfly prefer the leaves of Hollyhock for food. Although scarce, they are voracious eaters and very destructive when present. Sprays with insecticide #5 or #15 control them. Japanese beetle (see GRAPE) and tarnished plant bug (see CELERY) are occasional pests.

Diseases

Few Hollyhock plants escape an attack of rust. The orange-colored spots develop on all parts of the plant and the spores may over-winter on the roots from which new infections quickly develop. Frequent spraying with fungicide #D and #G keep it in check. Anthracnose and stem canker are present occasionally.

ALCHEMILLA (al-kem-ILL-a). Popular herbaceous perennials, native to Europe. With spikes of small greenish flowers during May and June and palmately divided leaves. Easily propagated by division, making good ground cover.

alpina   **8″**   **Zone 3**   **Mountain Lady's-mantle**
Leaves divided into 5–7 leaflets, silvery hairy beneath. Native to Europe.

vulgaris   **9″–12″**   **Zone 3**   **Common Lady's-mantle**
(mollis)
Often used as a silvery-leaved ground cover with orbicular leaves up to 6 in. across and divided into 7–9 lobes. Native to Europe.

ALDER. See ALNUS.

ALDRIN. An insecticide, which see.

ALETRIS (AL-et-ris)

farinosa   **3′**   **Zone 4**   **Whitetube Star-grass**
A fibrous-rooted perennial, member of the Lily Family, with grasslike yellowish-green leaves

up to 6 in. long and white, elongated tubular flowers in erect spikes blooming from May to July. Native from Me. to Fla. and Ark. This needs an acid soil and is grown in wild gardens.

ALEURITES (al-yew-RY-teez). Small to large trees, native to the Asiatic tropics, grown chiefly for their nuts which contain a large proportion (up to 70%) of oil, which, when extracted, is used in paints, varnishes, etc. Ornamentally these trees have some merit, but as grown in commercial orchards their peculiar requirements are such that they are only grown in the Gulf States. Propagation is mostly by seed stratified in moist sand 5–6 weeks before they are sown. However, hardwood cuttings taken in winter can be rooted. The tung-oil crop is a new one to America, and much experimentation of best methods in culture is still in progress.

fordii   25'   Zone 9   Tung-oil-tree
With alternate, 3-lobed leaves 3–5 in. long, this is a native to China and is grown as an ornamental tree with reddish-white flowers in terminal clusters (but not very showy) and fruits 2–3 in. across. It is a native of central Asia. The nuts yield a valuable oil used chiefly in the manufacture of varnishes and high-grade paints. It is this species which is being grown in the Gulf States, although recently *A. montana* has also been used. By 1938, 150,000 acres had been planted in tung-oil orchards from Fla. to Tex. There is still much to learn about best cultural methods to be used in the U.S.

moluccana   60'   Zone 10   Candlenut-tree
With variable-shaped leaves, slightly grayish in color. The small white flowers appear in large clusters, male and female on the same tree. The round green fruit is a nut containing much oil. Years ago in Hawaii the natives would string several of these on a coconut frond and light them for a torch. Native to Polynesia.

ALEXANDRIAN-LAUREL = *Danae racemosa*

ALFALFA = *Medicago sativa*

ALGAE. These are primitive green plants, some of them microscopic in size, some of them (certain kelps in the Pacific Ocean) reported to be 600 ft. long and worthy of being called the world's largest plants. They are all water plants, from these kelps down to the green scums on ponds. These have not changed much in form in a billion years.

ALISMA (al-IZ-ma)
plantago-aquatica   2'–3'   Zone 5   Water-plantain
An aquatic perennial herb native to the northern hemisphere, either erect or floating on the top of the water or flourishing in wet ground beside the pool or pond, with small white flowers ½ in. long in whorls on 3-ft. panicles in June or July.

Leaves are grasslike or straplike, depending on growing conditions.

Propagation is by division in spring or autumn, or by sowing seed in a flower pot filled with soil and placing it 10 in. below the water surface. The Indians are supposed to have eaten the base of the plant as a starchy vegetable.

ALÍSMATACEAE = The   Water   Plantain Family

ALKANET. See ANCHUSA.

ALLAMANDA (al-am-AN-da)
**cathartica var. hendersonii   Vine   Zone 10
Henderson Common Allamanda**
This evergreen vine from Brazil has brilliant yellow flowers about 5 in. across shaped like those of the Morning-glory. The flower buds are a varnished brown color. The leaves are simple, usually attached to the stem in whorls of 4. It is this variety rather than the species (the flowers of which are only 3 in. across, streaked with white) which is most used in gardens of the tropics. It is in bloom a greater part of the time. All Allamandas are propagated by hardwood or softwood cuttings.

**cathartica 'Williamsii'   40'   Zone 10
Williams Allamanda**
A handsome climbing shrub, native to Brazil, with elliptic-oval leaves, glossy, light green and 6 in. long, usually borne along the branch in fours. The double flowers are trumpet shaped, golden yellow, 3 in. across and appear in clusters.

neriifolia   5'   Zone 10   Oleander Allamanda
A Brazilian bush with oblong dark green leaves 4 in. long, lighter green underneath, borne in whorls of 2–5. Golden-yellow flowers are striped brownish red inside and are about 1 in. long, greenish at the base.

**violacea   Climbing shrub   Zone 10   Violet
Allamanda**
A climbing shrub from Brazil with slender, pointed leaves 6 in. long borne in whorls of 3–4, light green on top; flowers bell-like, 5 lobed, 3 in. long and up to 2½ in. wide, colored a dull magenta with faded areas giving a 2-toned effect. Either few in a cluster at the branch tip or in foot-long clusters. Planted in southern Fla.

ALL AMERICA SELECTIONS. This is a co-operative seed testing organization originating in Atlanta, Ga., in 1932 with the Southern Seedsmen's Association. Since that time the Pacific, Eastern, New England or Atlantic, Canadian, and Northern seed associations have likewise endorsed and co-sponsored it. It works something like this: There are at present 29 vegetable trial locations and 33 flower trial locations situated throughout Mexico, the United States and Canada, each trial ground governed by a competent, carefully selected judge who does the rating for the vegetables or the flowers in his trial plots. Thirty-four packets of seed are sent to the main All America Selections office, each packet containing 200 seeds or enough for a 30-ft. row. The secretary gives each packet a number and sends it out to the various trial grounds under number only. After growing and judging final results all seeds and produce are destroyed, for all seeds remain the property of their original producers.

An award winner, best of its class to date, is assured of a successful introduction to the seed trade of America regardless of where it comes from, since the main objective of the All America Selections Committee is for the purpose of informing seedsmen what new varieties are really superior and worthy of being offered to the gardeners of America. All seed firms have equal opportunity of obtaining seeds from the original grower and he is assured

control over seed sales for the first 3 years.

An entry must be new and should be entered at least 2 years before any expected distribution. It should be considered sufficiently different from others in commerce to be given a new name for the variety or mixture. It should be considered superior to others of its class, for its color, size or use. It should be easily grown from seeds and should usually be a popularly grown flower or vegetable. Judging is uniformly controlled.

Only award winners are given nation-wide publicity. No statements are made about the other varieties in competition, except that judges' remarks will be given to originators on request.

The present address of All America Display Gardens is: 628 Executive Drive, Willowbrook, Ill. 60521.

Current display gardens for past, present and future flower award winners are as follows:

Alabama, Birmingham	Birmingham Botanical Gardens
Alaska, College	University of Alaska
Bermuda, Hamilton	Bermuda Botanical Gardens
California, Arcadia	L.A. State and County Arboretum
California, Citrus Heights	Rusch Botanical Garden
California, San Francisco	Strybing Arboretum
Canada, Edmonton, Alberta	University of Alberta
Canada, Niagara Falls, Ontario	The Niagara Parks Commission
Canada, Sarnia, Ontario	Parks and Recreation Department
Canada, Toronto, Ontario	Metropolitan Toronto Parks Department
Canada, Truro, Nova Scotia	Nova Scotia Agricultural College
Canada, Vancouver, B.C.	The Botanical Garden
Canada, Winnipeg, Manitoba	Assiniboine Park
Colorado, Colorado Springs	Horticultural Arts Society
Colorado, Fort Collins	Colorado State University
Connecticut, Bloomfield	4H Farm Resource Center
England, Colchester	Crop Research and Development Unit
Florida, Orlando	Orange County Agriculture Center
Florida, Sarasota	Marie Selby Botanical Gardens
Georgia, Athens	University of Georgia Botanical Garden
Georgia, Atlanta	City of Atlanta, Grant Park
Hawaii, Kula	Maui Agricultural Research Center
Idaho, Moscow	Shattuck Arboretum and Botanical Garden
Indiana, Fort Wayne	City Park Board
Illinois, Glencoe	Chicago Botanic Garden
Illinois, Springfield	Washington Park Horticultural Center
Iowa, Ames	Iowa State University
Iowa, Des Moines	Des Moines Botanical Center
Kentucky, Louisville	Kentucky Exposition Center
Louisiana, Baton Rouge	Louisiana State University
Maryland, Wheaton	Brookside Gardens
Massachusetts, Amherst	University of Massachusetts
Michigan, East Lansing	Michigan State University
Michigan, Tipton	Hidden Lake Gardens
Minnesota, Chanhassen	Minnesota Landscape Arboretum
Mississippi, Jackson	Jackson State College
Missouri, Columbia	University of Missouri
Missouri, Kansas City	Flower and Garden Magazine

VEGETABLES

Missouri, St. Louis	Missouri Botanical Garden
Nebraska, Lincoln	University of Nebraska, State Arboretum
New Hampshire, Durham	University of New Hampshire
New Jersey, New Brunswick	Rutgers University
New Mexico, Las Cruces	Horticulture Farm
New York, Brooklyn	Brooklyn Botanic Garden
New York, Flushing	Queens Botanical Garden
New York, Tuxedo	Sterling Forest Gardens
New Zealand, Christchurch	Parks and Recreation Department
North Carolina, Raleigh	North Carolina State University
Ohio, Cincinnati	Cincinnati City Board of Park Commission
Ohio, Mansfield	Kingwood Center
Pennsylvania, Kennett Square	Longwood Gardens
Pennsylvania, Lehaska	Peddler's Village
Puerto Rico, Utuado	University of Puerto Rico
Rhode Island, Kingston	University of Rhode Island
South Africa, Durham	Municipal Park
South Carolina, Clemson	Clemson University
South Dakota, Brookings	McCrory Gardens
Texas, Dallas	Dallas Garden Center
Utah, Farmington	Utah Botanical Garden
Vermont, Burlington	University of Vermont
Virginia, Blacksburg	Virginia Polytechnic Institute
Virginia, Norfolk	Norfolk Botanical Gardens
Washington, Tacoma	Metropolitan Park District
Wisconsin, Madison	University of Wisconsin

ALLIARIA (ay-li-AYR-ia)

officinalis   **3'**   **Zone 2**   **Garlic-mustard**
A weed, biennial or short-lived perennial, with kidney- to heart-shaped alternate leaves, about 3 in. long, coarsely toothed on the margin. If crushed the leaves smell like garlic. The flowers are small in terminal racemes, each with 4 small white petals. The seeds are in 4-sided pods about 1 in. long. Native to Europe but now common in southern Canada and the northern U.S.

ALLIGATOR-PEAR = *Persea americana*

ALLIUM (AL-lium). The cultivated members of this group (Onion, Leek, Garlic, Shallot, Chive) are familiar to all gardeners and they share many characteristics with their wild relatives. These perennial, bulbous herbs generally have an onion odor and linear hollow leaves 1–3 ft. long. However, some species actually have fragrant flowers and others have flat or 3-sided, solid leaves. The flowers appear in a round cluster or umbel at the end of the flower stalk and are of various colors. They bloom during spring and summer.

Propagation, in most cases, is not difficult since some species form bulbils right in the fruiting cluster. In many others small bulbs are formed at the base of the main bulb each year and these need only be separated and planted at the end of the growing season. Many species grow easily from seeds, sown any time after they are fully ripe. However, some species have seed with complicated dormancy problems so that seed planted in the open ground out-of-doors may take two years to germinate. *A. aflatunense, albopilosum, karataviense, oreophilum ostrowskianum* and *roseum* are in this category. Seeds of these species, when fully mature, are dried, mixed with a very little

Allium or Onion flower heads

moist peat moss, tied up tightly in a polyethylene bag and merely kept at room temperature (on a kitchen shelf) for 5 months, then
placed in the home refrigerator, which is usually
about 40° F. (but *not* the freezer unit), for
another 3 months, then sown.

Some of the ornamental species are becoming very popular, not only as interesting garden
flowers because of their unusual globelike
flower clusters, but also because of the ease with
which the flowers can be dried and used in
flower arrangements. The colors range from
blue through yellow and pink to white and, if
hung up in a dry, warm, dark place until they are
completely dried, the beautiful flower colors
may be retained. Since some have flower clusters
3, 8 or even 12 in. across, there are many
excellent possibilities among these species. With
no special growth requirements and practically
no pests, this is a group well worth consideration by the interested gardener.

For insect and disease pests see ONION.

aflatunense   2½'   Zone 5
The purple-lilac flowers appear in May and are
borne in globelike umbels 4 in. wide at the end
of 2½-ft. stalks. The basal leaves are strap-
shaped, up to 4 in. broad. Excellent as cut
flowers or dried and used in winter arrangements. Native to central China.

albopilosum = *christophii*

ampeloprasum   3'   Zone 4   Wild Leek
The bulbs of this species from the Mediterranean
Region break up into numbers of bulblets by
which the plant is easily propagated.

ascalonicum   1'   Treated as annual   Shallot
The Shallot is an onionlike plant more popular
in Europe than it is in America. The mature
bulb differs from that of the common onion in
that it is made up of a large number of sections
or cloves, each one of which can be used for
propagation by merely planting the single clove
as one would an ordinary onion. These cloves
are milder tasting than regular onions and are
used in food seasoning. They can be kept for
several months, before using. Shallots are a
grayish color, rather angular and so can be
differentiated from the more round regular
onions. Probably native to Asia. They are
harvested in the fall and stored over winter for
spring planting under the same conditions as are
onion sets. Also see SHALLOT.

azureum = *A. caeruleum*

**caeruleum (*A. azureum*)   2'–4'   Zones 2–3
Blue Globe Onion**
Flowers deep blue in umbels 2 in. across and the
leaves are 3 sided. The flower heads are borne
on 3-ft. stalks in early June and are excellent for
drying and using in arrangements. Can be
easily propagated by bulbils that appear in the
flower cluster. The species is native to Siberia.

canadense   15"   Zone 3   Canada Garlic
A perennial weed which is reproduced by seed,
bulbs and bulblets, native to the eastern half of
North America. The small purple flowers are
produced in umbels and small bulbs are produced here also. Cows eating this plant in the
early spring produce milk with a garlic odor.

cepa   18"   Treated as annual   Garden Onion
A common garden herb with bulbous root
originating probably in mid-Asia but cultivated
for centuries. It is usually treated as a biennial
or a long-season annual. The flowers are
produced in ball-like clusters, and are white to
lilac colored in June. There is a variety called
viviparum (called the Top Onion) which,
although it bears small underground bulbs,
produces small bulbs in its fruiting cluster also.
Grown as an economic crop in temperate
regions of the world. For culture see ONION.

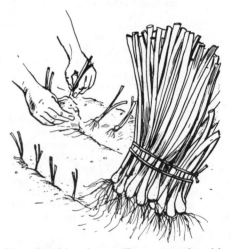

Sweet Spanish onion seedlings are purchased by
the bunch in the North, usually raised in the very
early spring or winter in the far South, a variety
of *A. cepa*.

cernuum   2'   Zones 2–3   Nodding Onion
Full sun and dry soil do not discourage this
roadside wild flower, native to the mideastern
and midwestern states. The strongly flavored
bulbs may be eaten if parboiled. The flowers are
rose colored or white, in June–July.

christophii   3'   Zone 4   Star-of-Persia
The flowering heads of this ornamental species
are as much as 8–12 in. across. The leaves are 1¾
in. wide, flowers are lilac colored with a starlike
sheen, and the plant is native to Asia Minor.
Excellent for drying and using in arrangements,
blooming in early June. In the North, it is best
to plant the bulbs about 6 in. deep, and if they
are to be planted in a mass, plant 8 in. apart.

cyaneum   10″   Zone 4
With very narrow leaves only $\frac{1}{25}$ in. wide, blue flowers, probably one of the strongest colored of the genus blooming in Aug. Considered by some as one of the most ornamental of all the onions. Native to China.

cyathophorum farreri   10″–15″   Zone 4
Farrer Onion
With angled stem and keeled leaves, this has purplish-red bell-shaped flowers (each about $\frac{1}{3}$ in. long) in loose clusters in June. Native to China.

douglasii   1′   Zone 3   Douglas Onion
Deep pink, flowers, leaves $\frac{1}{4}$ in. wide and native to Wash. and Idaho.

flavum   2′   Zones 2–3   Yellow Onion
Yellow bell-shaped flowers in loose umbels during midsummer, native to southwestern Europe and western Asia—leaves linear.

giganteum   4′   Zone 5   Giant Onion
Huge giant flower balls, 4–5 in. across, of bright blue flowers on 5-ft. stalks in June. The leaves are straplike, 2 in. wide and the plant is native to central China. Excellent for drying and using in flower arrangements. Plant 8–10 in. apart.

karataviense   10″   Zone 5   Turkestan Onion
A bulbous perennial with leaves 2–5 in. wide. Flowers whitish with purple midrib, in round globose heads 3 in. wide, borne on 15 in. stems at the same time as tulips fade in May and June. The flower heads are dried and used in arrangements. Native to Turkestan.

moly   1½′   Zones 2–3   Lily Leek or Golden
Garlic
Yellow starlike flowers, the clusters may be up to 3 in. across in June; gray-green leaves to 1 in. wide. Native to southern Europe. A good ornamental for drying or using as a border for delphiniums.

neapolitanum   12″   Zone 7   Naples Onion
One of the earliest flowering species, well adapted to growing in moist places. The white starlike flowers are fragrant and are borne in loose 3-in. umbels. The leaves are about an inch wide. It is reported to be unreliably hardy in Zone 5 where it certainly needs a sheltered position and a winter mulch. Native to southern Europe. Often grown in greenhouses for cut flowers. The var. 'Grandiflorum' has larger flower heads and is the better one to use in dried arrangements. Blooms in May.

odorum = *A. ramosum, A. tuberosum*

oleraceum   2′   Zone 6   Field Garlic
A native of Europe that is occasionally seen in America, this has 3–4 linear leaves up to $\frac{1}{8}$″ wide. The umbel has only a few flowers but the fruiting head bears bulbils. The flowers are greenish to rosy in color and $\frac{1}{4}$″ long.

ostrowskianum   12″   Zones 2–3   Ostrowsky
Onion
With soft pink flowers in many-flowered umbels, borne on 6 in. stems in May. An excellent onion for the rock garden. Native to Turkestan.

perdulce   10″   Zone 7
With 2–4 leaves up to $\frac{1}{8}$″ wide, rose-colored flowers $\frac{1}{2}$″ long. Native to Calif.

porrum   2½′   biennial   Leek
An herb, probably of Eurasian origin, with flat leaves less than 2 in. wide. The small white flowers are borne in dense umbels. Grown as an economic crop for its mild-tasting bulb. For culture see LEEK. Also termed a var. of *A. ampeloprasum*.

pulchellum   18″–24″   Zone 5
An ornamental onion native to southeast Europe and western Asia bearing many-flowered flower umbels with red-purple flowers about $\frac{1}{6}$ in. long in summer.

ramosum (*A. odorum*)   20″   Zones 2–3
Siberian Onion
Flowers white and fragrant with reddish midrib, borne in ball-like flower heads in May and June. Native to Siberia.

rosenbachianum   2′   Zone 5   Rosenbach Onion
The elegant rose-purple flowers are borne in a ball on a 4-ft. stalk in late May. Native to Turkestan. One of the excellent and most handsome species for drying the flowers and using them in dried arrangements.

roseum grandiflorum   1½′   Zone 5   Bigflower
Rosy Onion
The starlike flowers are a soft rose color borne in large balls 3 in. and more across in June. The leaves are $\frac{1}{4}$ in. wide, and the flower balls often bear small onions late in the season. Native to southern Europe and northern Africa. Excellent for drying the flower heads and using in dried arrangements.

sativum   2′   (Often treated as an annual)   Garlic
This is native to Europe, widely grown, and is actually a bulb, having a membranous skin surrounding several parts or cloves. It is these that are used in cooking. The leaves are an inch wide and the flowers pinkish. Most of the Garlic grown in America comes from Calif. Propagation is merely the breaking up of one bulb into its several parts and planting these just like onion bulblets.

schoenoprasum   2′   Zones 2–3   Chives
Native to Europe and Asia, this is a common garden plant valued because of its tasty leaves, occasionally cut and used in salads and cooking. See CHIVES. The flowers are rose-purple. The variety **sibiricum** is native to Siberia as well as North America.

senescens   4″–8″   Zone 3
A perennial ornamental onion with basal, straight or twisted leaves, rosy flowers in June or July in small, many-flowered umbels. The clumps of bulbs increase slowly. Some have

grayish-green foliage, which with the normally slightly twisted leaves make the plant an interesting subject for the rock garden. Native from Germany to Siberia. The var. **glaucum** has flat blue-gray leaves having a slight linear curve, all the leaves rising from a central spot and curving in the same direction. The pink flowers, borne in an umbel, bloom on straight stems in Aug. and Sept. A fine plant for the rock garden, though difficult to obtain since it is very rare.

sikkimense   6″   Zone 6
The short, flat leaves are dark green and grow in dense clumps. The deep violet flowers in tight umbels bloom in July and Aug. It is native to Sikkim.

sphaerocephalum   2′   Zone 5   Ballhead Onion
Bell-shaped dark purple flowers, in ball-shaped umbels during July and Aug. Leaves are narrow and grasslike. Excellent for flower arrangements and for drying. Native to Europe and Asia Minor.

stellatum   1½′   Zone 4   Prairie Onion
An attractive border plant, the leaves of which are nearly flat and the flowers are pink. It is native to the midwestern and western states, and blooms in the fall.

tanguticum   16″   Zone 5   Tangut Onion
The leaves are only ⅛ in. wide, the flowers are light blue with a darker blue midrib. Native to western China and excellent for drying and using in dried flower arrangements, produced in a feathery ball 3 in. across on 3-ft. stalks.

tricoccum   1′   Zone 3   Wild Leek
The leaves are 2 in. wide, giving this plant the widest leaves of any in this group, and they have the habit of withering away before the white flowers appear. From New Brunswick to N.Car.

tuberosum   1½′   Zone 4   Chinese Chives
A fine ornamental species with fragrant white flowers in summer, native to Asia, leaves not hollow, ¼ in. wide. Excellent for drying and using in flower arrangements.

vineale   10″   Zone 3   Field Garlic
Native to Europe, this is a common perennial weed in many of the eastern states, growing from an underground bulb and of course easily distributed by seed. The leaves are at first onionlike but nearing maturity they become flattened. The flower umbel may produce many small greenish or purplish flowers, or just small bulbs, which are of two kinds, hard and soft. The soft ones germinate as soon as they drop to the soil, the hard ones remain dormant over winter and germinate the following spring.

ALLSPICE = *Pimenta dioica*

ALLSPICE, CAROLINA = *Calycanthus floridus*

ALLSPICE FAMILY. *Myrtaceae*

ALLYSOIDES UTRICULATA = *Vesicaria*

ALMOND. *Prunus dulcis dulcis* is a deciduous tree to 25 ft. high which bears white or pink blossoms very early in the spring. Probably a native of western Asia, it has been grown for generations in the Mediterranean countries. The sweet or edible Almond has become a major crop in Calif. and to a less extent in other West Coast states. Both the hard-shelled and the soft-shelled almonds are grown in large orchards in Calif. The soft-shelled kinds are important in commerical production. The trees are grown in the drier valley areas only because of the trees' intolerance of wet soils.

Actually the Almond is sufficiently hardy to grow in most states where peaches will thrive, but blossoming occurs so early in the spring that late frosts too frequently damage bloom and prevent set of almonds. In commercial Almond groves smudge pots and other means are used to prevent frosting of the blossoms.

Almonds are propagated by budding named varieties on either Peach or Almond seedlings, the seed of which is stratified in sand and planted in nursery rows in Feb. Most often the wild Bitter Almond is used as understock. Budding is done in Aug. and Sept. using a shield or T bud. If the soil is inclined to be heavy or crown gall is known to be present, Peach understock is used rather than Bitter Almond. In Calif., the varieties 'Nonpareil', 'Merced', 'Mission', 'Ne Plus Ultra' and 'Peerless' are popular, with the first named most often planted. Since almonds are self-sterile, pollinators are spotted in the orchard or two varieties are intermixed.

Almond trees are planted during the winter months, the particular time being determined by soil moisture, which must be ample but not so wet as to exclude oxygen.

Pruning the tree to assure properly spaced framework branches is undertaken as soon as planting is completed. The importance of a good branch frame compels repruning during the first 3 years.

To reduce competition by weeds and to maintain a dust mulch, clean cultivation is usually practiced. Almonds respond to an application of nitrogen; sometimes a complete fertilizer is applied, depending on plant food requirements.

The outer hull of the Almond splits open in the fall. When this occurs, harvesting is undertaken by striking the branches with poles or hitting the larger limbs with rubber hammers. The nuts are knocked off into large cloth sheets that are spread under the tree, then hulled and spread out in partial shade to dry.

Much the same insect pests attack Almond as attack peaches. Their prevalence depends on the season and locality. Curculio commonly attacks immature almonds. Scale insects can be

troublesome, but are controlled with miscible oil. Oriental fruit moth is controlled with DDT or Lindane. Brown rot and scab must be held in check during some years. The chemicals to use will vary with state recommendations.
—GLEASON H. MATTOON

ALNUS (AL-nus). In general, alders need not be grown where better soils are available to support better ornamentals. Only about 10 species and varieties are offered by American nurserymen. We do not use them nearly so much much in America as they do in Europe, especially in Holland. Alders are best used in moist to wet soils and are seen growing in great numbers in such situations in the wooded areas of North America.

Many species are native to North America, from the Arctic Circle southward. Some are used only on the West Coast where they are native; others in the East. As a group, they have no interesting fruits nor autumn color. All have alternate leaves, all have male and female catkins, both borne on the same plant. All bloom very early in spring. Everyone is familiar with their flowers or catkins, but birches also have such flowers and make much better ornamentals.

It will be noted that because of the limitations of their usefulness, only 6 species are mentioned here, and even these have geographical limitations. Two of these are native to Europe, 1 is native to Japan and 3 are native to North America. As will be noted, both *A. cordata* and *A. incana* can do better in drier soils than can the others. All are rather weak-wooded, susceptible to several pests, and most will survive only in wet soils where nothing else will grow. If plantings must be made in such situations, the alders are recommended, but if better soils are available, better ornamentals should be selected.

Propagation

Do not allow the seed to dry out when it is ripe. Seed of *A. glutinosa* can be sown immediately as soon as it is ripe; those of other species can be stratified at about 40° F. for about 3 months. These plants can also be grafted, using *A. glutinosa* as understock, or grafting the varieties on seedlings of the species. See SEEDS, STRATIFICATION, GRAFTING, etc.

Insect Pests

Alder flea beetle, alder borer, woolly alder aphid are special pests, and many insects which infest poplar and willow also feed on alder. Although pesticides are seldom used, a protective spray when leaves are ⅔ grown in spring, using insecticide #37 or #48 will prevent serious damage. Aphids are best controlled with insecticide #15 when first seen.

Diseases

Root rot and nectria canker are occasional pests, but no effective control of established infections is recommended. Occasional applications of insecticide #48 will be helpful.

cordata   45′   Zone 5   Italian Alder
Often considered the best of the alders because of its dense, glossy green foliage and rounded head, it does well in drier soils also; is native to southern Italy.

glutinosa   75′   Zone 3   European Alder
The only reason this European plant is recommended at all is the fact that it thrives in truly wet soils, where many other plants will not. The leaves are about 4 in. long. Other than its ability to live in wet soils, it has little ornamental merit. Its variety **'Laciniata'** has leaves deeply lobed, giving this tree a very fine texture. However, like other alders, this is susceptible to a canker which can kill large parts of the plant quickly. It is commonly called the Cutleaf European Alder.

hirsuta   60′   Zone 4   Manchurian Alder
A vigorous and handsome tree from Japan and Manchuria with a pyramidal form and leaves leaves larger than those of *A. incana*.

incana   60′   Zone 2   Speckled Alder
One of the hardiest alders, native to wide areas of Europe and North America, often shrubby, found growing in moist to wet spots. In better soils other trees might well be selected instead of this which has few outstanding ornamental characteristics. It does well in drier soils. Several varieties are of interest:

'Aurea'—young leaves and shoots are yellowish in color and this color is retained a better part of the summer. Yellowleaf Speckled Alder.

'Coccinea'—leaves yellowish, young twigs reddish. Hardly worth propagating, but it is interesting. Redstem Alder.

'Pendula'—pendulous branches. Weeping Speckled Alder.

'Pinnata'—small leaves, but deeply lobed. Featherleaf Speckled Alder.

oregana (*rubra*)   60′   Zone 4   Red Alder
Native to the far West, but used for planting only on wet soils where better trees cannot be grown. The variety **pinnatisecta** has deeply lobed leaves and is called the Cutleaf Red Alder.

rhombifolia   75′   Zone 5   White Alder
Sometimes used in West Coast gardens for planting in wet spots or bordering streams. Not needed in other parts of the country. Native to western North America.

rugosa   40′   Zone 4   Hazel Alder
Native from Me. to Tex., this alternate-leaved shrub is usually found along streams and ponds. The leaves are 2–4 in. long. It has little ornamental value except for planting in wet or moist soils.

ALOCASIA (al-o-KAY-sia). Tropical herbs planted in southern Fla. or Calif. or used in the greenhouse in the North, with large arrow-shaped leaves that are often variegated. Flowers are unisexual, borne in a spathe. They should be given shade and a night temperature of 70° F. even in winter. Propagated by suckers or root cuttings. The following species are offered by several U.S. growers.

indica   6′   Zone 10   Indo-Malyan Alocasia
Leaves 15 in. long and 6 in. wide, spathes yellowish green. The var. **metallica** is the one usually planted for its deep purple leaves; **variegata** has white mottled leaves. Native to Malaya.

macrorhiza   15′   Zone 10   Mottled Giant Alocasia
A handsome plant with green leaves 2 ft. long or more, wavy margins and spathes greenish or yellowish. In some forms the midrib is white. Native to India and Malaya.

odora   2½′   Zone 10
Leaves 3 ft. long and 2½ in. wide with wavy margins. Spathes yellowish to glaucous green. Native to Indo-Malaya.

sanderana   3′   Zone 10
This has the smallest leaves of these species, only 1½ ft. long and 6 in. wide but colored a shining metallic green, veined with white or pale yellow, purplish beneath with the petioles striped with brown. Native to the Phillipine Islands.

ALOE (AL-lo, preferably al-O-ee). A large group of succulent herbs with racemes of red or yellow flowers and spiny, toothed leaves, grown either as ornamental pot plants indoors in the North or in the garden in the South, particu-\larly for their interesting fleshy leaves. Mostly native to Africa. Many species are available from specialists. Plants are usually grown in tubs or pots for years at a time. Propagated by suckers, seeds and sometimes by cuttings of young shoots.

aristata   6″   Zone 9
Bristly, neat rosettes of foliage, the leaves 4 in. long and ¾ in. wide, covered with white warts and having white marginal teeth. The flowers are reddish yellow, 1¼ in. long, but flower shoots may be 1½ ft. tall.

brevifolia   1′   Zone 9
A glaucous, robust, rosette-leaved succulent with triangular-oblong leaves, flat on top, rounded beneath, grayish green and with white teeth on the leaf margins. This suckers freely, the reason it has been used in southern Calif. as a ground cover. The flowers are red in dense racemes.

ciliaris   3′   Zone 9   Climbing Aloe
A stiff, lance-leaved succulent from South Africa with tall flower spikes at the end of which are attached orange-red, tubular flowers, each about 1 in. long, in the late spring. The stem is a scrambling affair with the thick, triangular leaves arranged spirally. They are about 5 in. long and have regularly spaced small spines along the leaf margin and the leaves are colored white near the base.

humilis   6″   Zone 9   Hedgehog Aloe
A shapely succulent with rosettes of glaucous, blue-green narrow leaves forming on various suckers, the leaves with tubercles on the back and having white marginal teeth; flowers 1½ in. long, red tipped with green, borne in long racemes 1½ ft. long. This does best in the shade and is used as a succulent ground cover in southern Calif.

nobilis   2′   Zone 9   Gold-tooth Aloe
The leaves of this succulent perennial are nearly 12 in. long and 3 in. wide. The leaf margins are horny with triangular prickles. The flowers are red, green tipped and 1½ in. long. Sometimes used for mass plantings in southern Calif.

variegata   9″   Zone 9   Kanniedood Aloe
The most commonly available of this large genus of plants, popularly used as a house plant in the North and in the garden in the South, valued for its white-spotted bands on the stiff, spiny-toothed, fleshy leaves. The red flowers, 1½ in. long, are produced on spikes about a foot high. Native to South Africa. Propagated by suckers, seeds and sometimes by cuttings.

vera   3′   Zone 10   Barbados Aloe
A herb with thick, fleshy, straplike leaves originating in a fanlike group from the base of the plant, with soft spines on the leaf margins. When the leaves are cut, a gelatinous substance exudes which has been used on cuts and burns. This, then, is a pot plant for the kitchen where its properties to aid in alleviating burns can come into good use. Easily propagated by offshoots. The yellow or red bell-like flowers are borne on a leafless stalk, but it blooms little indoors. Probably native to the Mediterranean Region.

ALONSOA (al-on-ZO-a). Annuals from tropical America (the ones mentioned here are from Peru) with red 2-lipped flowers in terminal racemes. Leaves are opposite or 3 in a whorl. If used indoors cuttings may be taken from plants in summer before they are killed by frost. They can be used as pot plants. Seeds can be started indoors in early April or outdoors after the last frost. Plants might be spaced 1–1½ ft. apart.

acutifolia   **3′**   **annual**   **Lanceleaf Maskflower** Bushy, cinnabar-red flowers with long upper lips. The var. **candida** bears white flowers.

warscewiczii   **3′**   **annual**   **Heartleaf Maskflower** A very bushy species with flowers cinnabar or scarlet red, with upper lips 4–5 times the length of the calyx.

ALOPECURUS (al-o-pek-YEW-rus)

pratensis   **3′**   **Zone 3**   **Meadow Foxtail Grass** Native to Europe but naturalized in eastern North America, this grass, often a weed, has leaves 6 in. long and ½ in. wide with fluffy seed spikes 3 in. long, from which it gets its common name.

ALOYSIA (a-LOY-sia)

triphylla (*Lippia citriodora*)   **10′**   **Zone 8** **Lemon Verbena** A shrub from Chile and Argentina, often grown as a greenhouse plant in the North because of the lemon-scented fragrance of the leaves, especially when they are crushed. The lance-shaped opposite leaves up to 3 in. long and white flowers produced in spikes are typical. Often used as a house plant.

ALPENCLOCK. See SOLDANELLA

ALPENCROSS = *Hutchinsia alpina*

ALPINE. A term usually applied to small plants found high in the mountains and used chiefly for planting in rock gardens.

ALPINE-AZALEA = *Loiseleuria procumbens*

ALPINIA (al-PIN-ia)

purpurata   **8′**   **Zone 10**   **Red Shellflower** The color of this plant comes from a floral head made up of many red bracts borne closely together in a tight spike which may be a foot or more long. The true flower is small and white, insignificant when compared with the colorful bracts. As this flowering head matures, small leafy plantlets appear behind the bracts which are easily rooted. The plant is listed as ever-blooming, with long leafy blades 2 ft. long. Native to the East Indies.

sanderae   **6′**   **Zone 9**   **Banded Galangal** Grown chiefly for its ornamental foliage, the leaves being 8 in. long and an inch wide with white stripes. Propagated by division in the spring and commonly grown in greenhouses. Rarely flowering and of unknown origin.

zerumbet (*speciosa*)   **12′**   **Zone 10**   **Shellflower** Somewhat similar to *A. purpurata* except that the flower head is pendulous and the flower bracts are a delightful shell pink. The alternate leaf blades on these long stalks are 5 in. wide and 2 ft. long. Native to tropical East Asia.

ALSINE MEDIA = *Stellaria media*

ALSOPHILA (al-SOFF-ill-a). These are the tree ferns which grow in the tropics and are 15–20 ft. high, not grown much out-of-doors in the U.S. except in moist areas of the far South, but seen occasionally as unique plants in conservatories. The trunks are often covered near the base with dead leaf stalks. They are native to Australia, the chief species being **A. australis.** Because of their large size and their special care and definite moisture requirements in the greenhouse, they are not used very much in America. Propagation is by spores. See FERNS.

Other species include *A. cunninghamii*, with a trunk about 20′ tall and very slender petioles, a native of Australia, Tasmania and New Zealand. *A. smithii*, from New Zealand, has slightly softer foliage. The Silver Tree Fern (*A. tricolor*), also from New Zealand, has leaves that are powdery white beneath.

ALSTROEMERIA (al-stree-MEER-ia). These are tender South American herbs with mostly thick, fibrous roots, related to *Amaryllis*. The conspicuous flowers are only 2 in. long, red, purple or yellow in terminal umbels. Most are suitable garden plants only in the South, but can be put out-of-doors in the North when the frosts are over and lifted and stored indoors over winter in damp sand in a cool place. If grown outdoors in the South they should be planted in a protected situation and mulched over winter. They are easily propagated by seeds and division of the roots.

aurantiaca   **3′–4′**   **Zone 7**   **Yellow Alstroemeria** This is the hardiest species and sometimes, with luck, can be wintered in the garden as far north as Geneva, N.Y., but one cannot count on this every year. The conspicuously colored tubular flowers (yellow, spotted brown with outer segments tipped green) appear in spring, 10–30 per cluster. The var. **major** is larger than the species and has orange flowers.

pelegrina   **2′**   **Zone 10**   **Incalily Alstroemeria** A South American herb from Chile with lance-olate leaves 2 in. long. The flowers are lilac, spotted with red and purple and up to 2 in. long. These are greenhouse plants in most of the U.S. but sometimes are planted out in the garden after the frosts, lifted and taken into the greenhouse again in the fall before frost. Propagated by division and by seed.

pulchella   **2′–3′**   **Zone 8**   **Parrot Alstroemeria** A Brazilian plant with dark red flowers tipped with green and inside spotted with brown.

ALTERNANTHERA (al-ter-nan-THEE-ra)

Several Species   **4″–8″**   **Zone 8**   **Alternanthera** Bedding foliage plants, not hardy over winter in the North, usually planted in beds and sheared at about 4–6 in. high to keep them at a uniform height. They are perennials from the tropics of South America, with opposite, small, narrow leaves and small attractive flowers, sometimes colored. They are propagated by cuttings taken in late summer or by division. Varieties of **A. ficoidea** are: **amoena** with green leaves and red blotches, about 4 in. tall; **bettzickiana**, about 6 in. tall with reddish or yellowish leaves; and **versicolor** with blood-red to copper-colored foliage. There are also some colorful ornamental forms of **A. bettzickiana**, but they are difficult to find in nurseries.

ALTHAEA (al-THEE-a)

  ficifolia = *Alcea ficifolia*

  officinalis 3′–6′ **Zone 5** **Marshmallow**
The Marshmallow is not a native American wild flower, but one which has made its way here from Europe and has become naturalized in swampy areas from Conn. to Va. It is a perennial herb with strongly veined, oval or heart-shaped leaves and pinkish flowers having stamens which are united at the base with the flower petals and form a column around the pistil. The flowers, often up to 2 in. in dia., appear on a flower stalk which sometimes attains a height of 6 ft. They bloom from July through Oct. The common name of the plant derives from the fact that the root was originally used in the making of marshmallow paste.

  rosea = *Alcea rosea*

Insect Pests

Caterpillars of the painted lady butterfly prefer the leaves of Hollyhock for food. Although scarce, they are voracious eaters and very destructive when present. Sprays with insecticide #5 or #15 control them. Japanese beetle (see GRAPE) and tarnished plant bug (see CELERY) are occasional pests.

Diseases

Few Hollyhock plants escape an attack of rust. The orange-colored spots develop on all parts of the plant and the spores may overwinter on the roots from which new infections quickly develop. Frequent spraying with fungicide #D and #G keep it in check. Anthracnose and stem canker are present occasionally. However, it is often common in the northern parts of the country to treat this plant as an annual and replant it every year. If the diseased plants are dug up and destroyed, this too proves helpful.

ALUMINUM PLANT = *Pilea cadierei*

ALUMINUM SULPHATE. One of many fertilizers, this is used especially for acid soil plants. It is also used to make the soil more acid (see SOILS) but the amounts vary with the soil type—light sandy soils requiring less than heavy clay soils. One-half pound applied to 10 sq. ft of a sandy soil may lower the acidity of the soil from pH 6 to pH 5 but 3 lbs. or more may be needed to similarly reduce the same area of a heavy clay soil. It is high in nitrogen and one should apply it to living plants with great care for too much can easily burn or kill the plants. See SOILS AND FERTILIZERS.

ALUMROOT—See HEUCHERA.

ALYSSUM (al-LISS-um). The name alyssum, or Basket-of-gold, is so popular that it is almost synonymous with rock garden plants. All of the species are easy to grow and are reasonably hardy if given the proper conditions. They require full sun and a rather lean, sandy or gravelly soil with extremely good drainage. These are annual or perennial herbs belonging to the Mustard Family and having small, alternate leaves sometimes produced in rosettes and small yellow or white flowers produced in terminal umbels. The seed can be sown as soon as it is ripe, or stored dry in airtight containers in a cool place for a year or more. Softwood cuttings root easily and plants can be divided.

Several species not included in the list below but which have been tried in America and are found to be good ornamentals which should be propagated by nurserymen are: *A. atlanticum, A. bertolonii, A. repens, A. scandicum, A. tortuosum* and *A. wulfenianum.*

  alpestre 4″ **Zone 4**
A tiny, procumbent, woody Alyssum valued because of its diminutive size, its whitish-silvery evergreen leaves, its pale yellow flowers from April to June and its adaptation for use in the rock garden. Native to the Alps Mountains of Europe.

  argenteum = *A. murale*

  condensatum 5″ **Zone 5**
A trailing plant having grayish, hairy leaves and bright yellow flowers borne on thin, trailing stems in late spring. Native to Syria.

  idaeum 5″ **Zone 6**
This plant, which does best on rocky soils, will need some winter protection if planted in the far North. The tiny leaves have a soft, grayish pubescence and the flowers, appearing in spring, are creamy white to pale yellow. Native to Crete.

  maritimum = *Lobularia maritima*

  moellendorfianum 6″ **Zone 5** **Moellendorf Alyssum**
A semitrailing plant with small gray-pubescent leaves and tight heads of yellow flowers held on semiupright stems. These appear in spring. Native to central Europe.

  montanum 10″ **Zones 2–3** **Mountain Alyssum**
A dense mat-forming plant with procumbent stems, this has evergreen leaves that are mostly ashy white and fragrant yellow flowers from April to Aug. It is a variable species from Europe, but makes a good garden plant.

murale 15″ **Zones 2–3 Yellowtuft Alyssum**
A subshrub native to southeastern and central Europe with evergreen, sterile shoots, linear leaves which are greenish above and white beneath and flowers a deep golden yellow, flowering well and long throughout a good part of the summer. This should also make an excellent ground cover.

saxatile = *Aurinia saxatilis*

serpyllifolium 1′ **Zone 4**
Procumbent or erect subshrub, leaves whitish or silvery on both upper and lower sides; flowers pale yellow, produced in compact clusters, blooming from June to Aug. Native to southwestern Europe.

spinosum 3′ **Zone 6 Spiny Alyssum**
A cushion-forming, rounded shrub with spiny branches native to southwestern Europe, valued for its oblong-lanceolate silvery-whitish foliage; its compact, fragrant white flower clusters being produced from May to July. The variety 'Roseum', which blooms at the same time, is more dwarf in habit, producing violet flowers which fade to a pinkish color.

ALYSSUM, HOARY FALSE = *Berteroa incana*

ALYSSUM, SWEET. See LOBULARIA.

ALYXIA (al-IX-ia)
olivaeformis vine **Zone 10 Maile**
This is a straggling shrub or vine which is supposed to be one of the few native plants of Hawaii, where it is seen in the cool mountains, with smooth leaves mostly in threes, about 1½ in. long, and small yellowish flowers also in threes, in the leaf axils. This is the traditional lei plant of the islands.

AMARACUS = *Origanum*

AMARANTH, ANNUAL GLOBE = *Gomphrena globosa*

AMARANTHACEAE = The Amaranth Family

AMARANTHUS (am-ar-ANTH-us). This is a group of annuals, some of which are vicious weeds and others of which are grown for the brightly colored foliage and heavy flower spikes, the flowers of some species being a brilliant red. All are easily grown and easily propagated by seeds. Some are used in other countries for greens. Leaves are alternate.

albus (*graecizans*) 3′ **annual Tumbleweed**
A weed spreading by seeds, native to the midwestern U.S., but now also a weed in eastern North America. The stems are greenish purple and prostrate; the leaves are alternate. Flowers are in short, dense, axillary clusters. Blooms from June to Aug. The leaves of this weed fall in the autumn, and when the plant dies the wind blows the stalks out of the ground and on the flat western prairies they are blown into balls, forming the familiar Tumbleweed.

caudatus 5′ **annual Love-lies-bleeding**
The leaves of this annual are red; the flowers form a red ropelike spike in the summer. Native to the tropics.

hybridus 6′ **annual Green Amaranth**
This is a weed introduced from tropical America, but not naturalized across North America. It is similar to *A. retroflexus*, but is not so rough in texture and is of a deeper green color. The variety **erythrostachyus**, Prince's-feather, has red or brownish-red, showy panicles and the leaves are usually reddish. This variety is truly an ornamental, blooming from July to Sept. and frequently used in flower arrangements.

retroflexus 10′ **annual Redroot Pigweed**
Actually a native to tropical America, it has become an annual weed all over the world. The stem is stout and branches at the top. The alternate leaves are triangular, broadest near the base. The dense green flower clusters are terminal or axillary, ½–2 in. long. This is one of the commonest of weeds in gardens, blooming from July to Sept. The roots are red.

tricolor 4′ **annual Josephs-coat**
Large oval leaves, variegated green, yellow and red, often used as a house plant because of its brilliantly colored and variable foliage. There are many variations appearing in this species, some of which have been named. The main leaves are 2½–4 in. wide, but some of the varieties bear smaller leaves.

x AMARCRINUM (*Amaryllis* x *Crinum*) (am-ar-CRY-num). A hybrid genus grown mostly in Calif. and along the Gulf Coast, but also grown as a pot plant indoors, with the same culture as Amaryllis.

memoria-corsii 4′ **Zone 8**
Funnel-shaped shell-pink flowers on 4-ft. stalks resemble those of Amaryllis, produced in autumn. Usually two flower scapes are borne by a single bulb. The fragrant blossoms last a long time, making it a beautiful flowering plant. When it is potted, the upper third of the bulb should be above the soil level. The pot can be sunk in soil outdoors when all frost is past, and then in the fall taken indoors, water reduced until growth matures, then stored in a cool cellar until growth starts again in the spring.

AMARYLLIDACEAE = The Amaryllis Family

AMARYLLIS (am-ar-ILL-is). At one time this genus contained a number of plants now distributed among a dozen genera. The popular name Amaryllis is commonly accepted to belong to the genus *Hippeastrum*, which see. The garden hybrids have been developed over a long period of years and probably cannot at present be placed under any one species. Plants of the

genus *Amaryllis* and *Hippeastrum* are somewhat
similar except that the former has a solid flower
stem and in the latter genus it is hollow. One
species of true *Amaryllis* is occasionally seen,
A. belladonna. This is a handsome bulbous plant
with funnel-shaped flowers on 18-in. stems in
Sept. It is only hardy out-of-doors in frost-free
areas but can be grown as a greenhouse plant.
Out-of-doors bulbs should be planted in good
soil, at least 5 in. deep. It is best to let it alone
if it blooms well, but if not it can be transplanted
in June. Varieties bear flowers ranging in color
from white to pink to rose red and they are
fragrant, about 3½ in. long and are borne in
dense clusters. Native to South Africa.

Amaryllis (See p. 535)

belladonna   2′   Zone 9   bulbous herb
                                Belladonna-lily
Native to South Africa with rose-red fragrant
flowers about 3 in. long in dense clusters on long
flower stalks about 2 ft. long in summer. The
bulbs are poisonous if eaten. The flowers are
lily shaped, about 3½ in. long, rose red, pink,
purple and white and various combinations of
these colors which appear in the late summer,
sometimes early in the fall, at the end of a stalk
2 ft. long. There are many named forms among
which are **elata** having rose-red flowers, **major**
with pink flowers.

hallii = *Lycoris squamigera*
vittata = *Hippeastrum vittatum*

AMARYLLIS FAMILY = *Amaryllidaceae*

AMAZON-LILY = *Eucharis grandiflora*

AMBARELLA = *Spondias cytherea*

AMBERBOA (am-ber-BO-a)
   maroccana   2½′   annual   Star-of-the-desert
Small white flowers ½ in. long in dense panicles,
leaves alternate and usually toothed. Native to
Morocco.
   muricata   2′   annual   Spiny Amberboa
Alternate leaves lanceolate with pink to purple
flowers, the var. **rosea** having pink flowers.
Native to Spain and Morocco.

AMBROSIA (am-BRO-sia)
   artemisiifolia   3′+   annual   Ragweed
One of the most common of garden weeds,
native to North America. It has both opposite
and alternate deeply cut or semi-compound
leaves, 2–4 in. long. The terminal greenish
spikes of pollen-bearing flowers produce great
amounts of pollen, one of the most prominent
causes of hay fever. The pistillate flowers are
few, not prominent and in the axils of the leaves.
Blooms in Aug. and Sept. Each male-flower
cluster contains 15–20 flowers and there are
hundreds of heads on a single plant, so that the
amount of pollen borne by one plant is formid-
able. For chemical weed control see WEED-
CONTROLLING CHEMICALS.
   psilostachya   6′   Zone 3   Western Ragweed
A perennial weed more common in western
North America where it is native, but occasionally seen in the East. The leaves are not as
deeply cut as are those of *A. artemisiifolia*.
Blooms from June to Sept.
   trifida   18′   annual   Giant Ragweed
Native over the eastern half of North America
with opposite, deeply 3-lobed leaves that are
rough and hairy; flowers similar to those of the
common Ragweed. Blooms from July to Sept.

AMELANCHIER (am-el-ANK-ier). The genus
Amelanchier contains about 25 species and
botanical varieties, chiefly native to North
America with a very few native to Europe and
Asia. Only 8 of this group are offered by
American nurserymen. They are at their best in
the early spring, before the leaves appear, for
they always produce, in billowy masses, racemes
of small white flowers having 5 narrow petals,
each flower being about an inch in dia. In warm
weather these flowers may fade and fall in a
short 3-day period and this, of course, greatly
restricts their usefulness as flowering ornamentals. In the fall these plants are again outstanding because their alternate leaves turn to
brilliant yellow and red. Sometimes in the early
summer when their red fruits are attractive they

also stand out, but usually these fruits (similar in size and shape to those of hawthorns) are quickly taken by the birds and so do not remain on the plants long enough to be an important ornamental asset.

Unfortunately serviceberries are susceptible to several pests which may become serious in certain areas. Lace-wing fly, red spider, various scales and fireblight may all attack, and because of this it is advisable not to use the plants in large quantities, especially in areas where these pests are known to occur on other rosaceous plants. All of the members of this genus are best used in naturalized plantings. They are especially well suited for planting at the edge of woodlands, near ponds or in other places similar to those in which they are frequently found in the wooded areas of the country.

So many are native—one species or another being native practically from coast to coast—that we must recognize the possibility of using them in certain kinds of plantings. The common name Shadblow has been given them, in New England at least, because they are usually in bloom at the time when the shad were known to run up the rivers of New England to their spring spawning grounds.

However, because of the pests which attack them, one should use them with caution, and that is the reason for recommending only 5 of the native species. This list of 5 includes the best of the shrubs, 3 small tree types and 1 larger tree type. These are of interest in the winter because of their light grayish bark. So, for naturalized plantings, to be used a few in any one location, these serviceberries are recommended, but they have several limitations for planting in large numbers.

The fruits of the serviceberries are edible and some have excellent quality, being used by the early settlers for puddings and pies. Some cooked the berries first, then used them in making muffins.

Propagation

Do not allow seed to dry out, but stratify it as soon as ripe for 4 months at 40° F. Bush types can easily be divided. Other types can be grafted, using the species of the varieties to be grafted as understock. See SEED, STRATIFICATION, GRAFTING, etc. Softwood cuttings also prove successful.

canadensis **60′** **Zone 4** **Shadblow or Downy Serviceberry**
This is the tallest of the genus, native to the eastern U.S., and really outstanding for its grayish young foliage which is clearly evident as it unfolds in the spring. The grayish bark is also prominent in winter. Like the other species, it has a wealth of single white flowers in the early

spring before the leaves appear, and brilliant yellow to red autumn coloration.

florida **Shrub to 30′** **Zone 2** **Pacific Serviceberry**
One of the hardiest serviceberries, of value for its hardiness and the fact that it is native over a wide area where some of the other species are not.

x grandiflora **25′** **Zone 4** **Apple Serviceberry**
This has the largest flowers of the serviceberries and does not grow as tall as the other tree species. The flowers are 1¼ in. wide, pure white, and borne in early May. It is a hybrid of *A. canadensis* and *A. laevis* and has the good qualities of both. There is a variety named 'Rubescens' with pinkish flower buds and flowers a very pale pink the first day they open, but they soon fade to white, so that the slight pinkish tinge is visible for only a day or two. This makes it hardly worth while to propagate the hybrid and keep it distinct.

laevis **36′** **Zone 4** **Allegany Serviceberry**
Mentioned in this list because it is so widely distributed in the eastern part of the U.S. It is smaller than *A. canadensis*, but makes just as good an ornamental.

stolonifera **4′** **Zone 4** **Running Serviceberry**
This is a low, stoloniferous shrub native to the northeastern U.S. It might have value in certain situations for its particular habit of growth, but otherwise it need not be considered of value as an ornamental shrub.

AMENT. A catkin; a spike of flowers, frequently deciduous, as the male flowers of willow, birch, beech and oak.

AMERICAN ALOE = *Agave americana*

AMHERSTIA (am-HERST-ia)
nobilis **60′** **Zone 10** **Flame Amherstia**
This tropical tree bears pendulous racemes 2–3 ft. long of large red and yellow blossoms, each one of which is 8 in. long and 4 in. across. Each branch may produce a long flowering raceme. The compound leaves are up to 3 ft. long with 6 pairs of opposite leaflets, each one of which is 6–8 in. long and 1½ in. wide. The 6–8 in. pods are rarely produced, and even if they are the seeds are often infertile, the chief reason why the tree is not seen more often in the islands of the Caribbean. It may produce flowers much of the year but is at its peak from winter to early midsummer. The single blossoms only last a few days. It is often known in Jamaica and Trinidad as "Pride of Burma." Native to India.

AMIANTHIUM (ami-ANTH-ium)
muscitoxicum **4′** **Zone 4** **Crow-poison**
A bulbous herb, native from N.Y. to Fla. with linear leaves up to 2 ft. long and small white flowers in racemes 5 in. long. It is usually found

in acid soils. Cattle and sheep are frequently poisoned by eating the foliage.

AMMOBIUM (am-O-bium)

alatum   **3′**   **annual**   **Winged Everlasting**
Actually a tender perennial, this is usually grown as an annual for its winged branches and white everlasting flower heads, 2 in. across, each with a yellow center. The alternate leaves are gray woolly. The var. **grandiflorum** has larger flower heads. Although not an outstanding garden flower it is used in dried arrangements for, if cut just before full bloom and hung upside down to dry, the branches retain good color. Seed can be sown outdoors in April, but in milder climates south of Va., they can be sown in the fall. Thin to a foot apart. Native to Australia.

AMMONIUM SULFATE. An inorganic fertilizer containing 20.6% nitrogen. This should be used with great caution as much of the contents are readily available and too heavy an application kills plants quickly. Use it at about the rate of $\frac{1}{2}$–1 oz. per square yard of soil area.

AMMOPHILA (am-OFF-ill-a)

breviligulata   **7′–8′**   **Zone 5**   **American Beach Grass**
This is an excellent sand binder, native on the sand dunes of the Atlantic Coast and the Great Lakes area. The leaves are long and slender, the plant increases by creeping rootstocks, and is a larger plant than its European relative **A. arenaria**, but both are excellent sand binders. Some botanists consider them both as one species—easily propagated by division of the rootstock.

AMOMUM (am-O-mum)

cardamon   **8′**   **Zone 10**   **Cardamon Amomum**
This aromatic herb supplies a substitue for the true cardamon supplied by *Elettaria cardamomum*. The narrow lance-shaped leaves are 8–12 in. long and 3 in. wide. Brownish-yellow tubular flowers are an inch long and the fruit is a capsule. This belongs to the Ginger Family and is propagated by division in the spring. Native to the East Indies.

AMORPHA (am-OR-fa)

canescens   **4′**   **Zone 2**   **Lead-plant**
Native to the midwestern U.S. and Canada, it is especially valued for its gray foliage throughout the entire growing season. The compound, alternate leaves have 15–45 leaflets each about $\frac{3}{4}$ in. long. The small blue flowers are borne in 6-in. spikes in July. It grows well in poor dry soil and is easily propagated by softwood or hardwood cuttings, suckers, layers or seeds, but can easily grow out of bounds and become a weed.

fruticosa   **20′**   **Zone 4**   **Bastard Indigo**
More rank growing than the preceding species,

this is native to the eastern U.S. and is not recommended for ornamental planting. It is more of a weed than anything else, for the seeds come up all over. Many nurseries offer it and there are several varieties, but it is too fast growing and coarse to have ornamental value. The alternate, compound leaves contain 11–25 leaflets.

AMORPHOPHALLUS (am-or-fo-FAL-us).
These are not ornamentals but occasionally they are seen in greenhouse collections; large tropical herbs from Asia, tuberous roots, flowers are most ill-smelling and are in large spathes appearing before the leaves. One species **A. titanum** produces a giant spathe 4 ft. long, but the actual flowers are very small. The corm for one of these plants weighed 113$\frac{1}{2}$ lbs. after flowering.

Sometimes called Devil's Tongue, one of several species can sometimes be found in conservatories in America as a curiosity. In their native habitat, they grow in rich soil and semi-shade. They go into a resting period in October, when water should be withheld gradually, then stored at 50° F. until late March when they can be started into growth again. A sound corm will shortly produce a blossom followed later by leaves.

AMPELOPSIS (am-pel-OP-sis). Usually deciduous, alternate-leaved vines climbing by attaching their tendrils to the means of support. The leaves are either simple or compound and the fruits are small 1–4 seeded berries. The ones described here are the best of the species in this genus as ornamentals. Propagated by layering, softwood and hardwood cuttings, and by seed. The seed should not be allowed to dry out but should be stratified as soon as ripe at 40° F. for 3 months after which it is sown. For insect and disease pests see PARTHENOCISSUS.

aconitifolia   **vine**   **Zone 4**   **Monks Hood Vine**
A luxuriant vine, but not a good screen, native to northern China, bearing berries about the size of peas, which turn orange or yellow in the fall when they are fully ripe. These may sometimes be bluish before maturity and they are borne in fairly conspicuous clusters. The leaves are delicately shaped in 5-foliate fashion, each leaflet being 1$\frac{1}{2}$–3 in. long and pinnately lobed often to the midrib. It is grown both for its delicate foliage and its colorful berries in the fall.

arborea   **vine**   **Zone 7**   **Pepper-vine**
Widely grown throughout the southeastern U.S. where it is native; the foliage is dark green and semi-evergreen. It climbs by means of attaching its tendrils to supports. The leaves are doubly compound 4–8 in. long, and the plant suckers

readily. The fruits are dark purple berries about the size of peas.

brevipedunculata vine **Zone 4** **Procelain Ampelopsis**
The fruits of this northeastern Asiatic vine are its most interesting assets. The berries are about the size of peas, borne in clusters, but in ripening they change color from pale lilac to yellow to porcelain blue (rarely whitish). It is a vigorous climber, climbing by means of tendrils, and the leaves are deeply lobed. It does not make a dense foliage screen but its colorful porcelain blue fruits in the fall are outstanding. The leaves are 3 lobed and 2–5 in. across.

humulifolia vine **Zone 5** **Hop Ampelopsis**
The foliage of this vine from northern China is its outstanding characteristic—a lustrous bright green. The berries are few, and either pale yellow or bluish or a combination of both colors. It is a shrubby vine, climbing by tendrils with handsome foliage resembling that of the grape with leaves 3–5 in. across, lustrous green above, whitish beneath.

megalophylla vine **30′** **Zone 6** **Spokenard Ampelopsis**
This is native to western China and is chiefly valued for its large compound leaves which are 10–25 in. long. Like the other members of this genus it climbs by means of attaching its tendrils to supports.

quinquefolia = *Parthenocissus quinquefolia*
tricuspidata = *Parthenocissus tricuspidata*

AMPHICARPAEA (am-fi-CAR-pay–ia)
bracteata vine **Zone 3** **Southern Hog-peanut**
The Hog-peanut is native over a large area from southern Canada to Fla. and into the midwestern states. It is a slender-stemmed vine climbing to 8 ft. high with 3-parted compound leaves, the leaflets broad at the base and pointed at the tip. During the summer the white to lavender flowers appear in clusters at the axils of the leaves. In autumn the plant produces seed pods which are about an inch in length. On underground branches the plant also produces flowers having no petals. These in turn produce pods having only 1 edible seed, and it is these which were a staple food among the Indians. Sometimes termed *A. monoica.*

AMSONIA (am-SO-nia)
ciliata **3′** **Zone 7** **Blue-star**
A plant having alternate, lanceolate leaves which are crowded toward the upper end of the erect stems and blue flowers with 5 lobes spreading from a narrow, funnel-like corolla, making the name Blue-star very appropriate. A native of the pinelands of N.Car. and Mo. and extending into Mex., this plant flowers during May and June. It is an easy perennial to cultivate, doing

well in most garden soils, and may be divided either in spring or fall.

tabernaemontana **3½′** **Zone 3** **Willow Amsonia**
A perennial plant very easy to grow and has few pests, yet not often planted in the garden. Steel-blue flowers ¾ in. across in dense terminal clusters are produced during May and June. The willowlike leaves, 9 in. long, turn yellow in the fall. Native from N.J. to Fla. and Tex. Propagation by seeds sown in spring is the easiest; also by division of the deeply rooted clumps in the early spring.

AMYGDALUS PERSICA (am-IG-dal-us). This is now a synonym of *Prunus persica*, the Peach, and *Amygdalus communis* is a synonym of *P. dulcis dulcis*, the Almond. All other species formerly under *Amygdalus* have been transferred from *Amygdalus* to *Prunus.*

ANACARDIACEAE = The Sumac or Mango Family

ANACARDIUM (an-a-KARD-ium)
occidentale **40′** **Zone 10** **Common Cashew**
An evergreen tree with milky juice and simple, leathery alternate leaves 8 in. long and 4 in. wide, native to tropical America and planted for its nuts which are the size of large beans. The fruit is kidney shaped, borne on an enlarged receptacle that is white or red. The oil about the nut may cause dermatitis and even the fumes from roasting the nuts can be irritating.

ANACHARIS = ELODEA

ANACYCLUS (ana-CY-clus). Perennials of the Composite Family from the mountainous areas of Morocco, they require loose, gritty alkaline soil, good drainage and full sun. They need some protection from northern winters. Propagation is by seed.

atlanticus **prostrate** **Zone 6 (?)**
The finely cut leaves are hairy and are borne on prostrate stems. The large white flowers, similar to daisies, are on stems held slightly above the foliage and the undersides of the ray flowers are red. They appear in early summer.

depressus **prostrate** **Zone 6 (?)**
This plant is similar to *A. atlanticus*, varying only in the amount of red appearing on the ray flowers.

ANAGALLIS (an-a-GAL-is). Two species of weedy European herbs sometimes used in the garden as annual flowers with opposite or whorled leaves and small solitary flowers produced in the leaf axils. They vary in flower from red and blue to pink. Seeds may be sown in April or May. However, *A. arvensis* must be prevented from escaping and becoming a weed and seed of *A. linifolia* should be sown indoors in March and set out after the frost, spacing the plants about 6 in. apart.

arvensis   6″   annual   Scarlet Pimpernel
Trailing, weak-stemmed weed with opposite sessile leaves. The single scarlet or bluish flowers are ½ in. across, and have fringed petals. They are on long axillary stems. Seed pods are large and rounded. The flower closes on cloudy days. Native to Europe but widely naturalized throughout North America. Sometimes called "Poor-man's-weatherglass" and blooming from May to Sept. A good rock garden plant, especially in a sunny situation. This herb is sometimes used in various medicines. Some vars. are: **caerulea**—large bright blue flowers, often used as a house plant; **carnea**—pink flowers; **coccinea**—scarlet flowers.

**monelli linifolia   4″–18″   annual or perennial
                                    Flaxleaf Pimpernel**
With narrow lance-shaped leaves up to an inch long, blue flowers but with several reddish vars. This is a perennial in some areas but can be planted as an annual for its summer bloom.

ANANAS COMOSUS = Pineapple

ANAPHALIS (an-AFF-al-is)
**margaritacea   3′   Zone 3   Common Pearly
                                    Everlasting**
A stiffly erect perennial herb with narrow, alternate leaves chiefly distinguished by the numerous tiny hairs on the under surface of the leaves, giving them a woolly appearance. In spring, the upper surface of the leaves also may be whitish. The flowers are white and small, in a terminal corymb which may be 2 in. or more in width. The flower bracts are also whitish, and very numerous. This plant is native throughout the North Temperate Zone, blooming in July and Aug. An interesting white accent among green-leaved plants, the Pearly Everlasting, as its name implies, is also gathered and dried for winter flower arrangements. For this, they should be picked while foliage is still white on the upper surface. The plant does best in a dry, sunny location. It is easily divided either in spring or in fall.

ANCHUSA (an-KOO-sa). Alkanet or Bugloss species, are herbaceous perennials, belong to the Borage Family, being coarse, hairy, alternate-leaved perennials but with good bright blue flowers in May and June. They grow well in many soils as long as they are not wet and do best in the full sun and are popular for "fillers" in the perennial border where their bright blue flowers are conspicuous. They can die out in cold winters, hence should probably be annually propagated by root cuttings or seeds sown in the greenhouse of cold frame about March.

**azurea   3′–5′   Zone 3   Italian Alkanet,
                                    Italian Bugloss**
The most popular species of this genus with many blue flowers, each about ½ in. across borne in one-sided clusters during June and July. The var. **'Pride of Dover'** has deep blue flowers; **'Opal'** has light blue and the popular **'Dropmore'** has deep blue flowers. Southern Europe.

barrelieri   2′   Zone 3   Early Bugloss
A fine species from Europe and Asia Minor with blue flowers having a white tube and yellow throat. Blooms in May and June.

caespitosa   1′–1½′   Zone 5   Tufted Alkanet
Blooming from May to July, this almost prostrate plant is native to Crete. The leaves are 3–4 in. long, ¼ in. wide; the flowers are blue, small and few appearing in July. An easily grown perennial but not an especially prominent ornamental.

capensis   18″   annual or biennial   Bugloss
A plant native to South Africa which is an addition to the garden because of the bright blue summer flowers about ¼ in. across, bearing a touch of red and white also. The narrow, hairy, alternate leaves are lance shaped and 2½ in. long. The variety **'Blue Bird'** is the one best to plant as an annual. Also used as a pot plant. Sow seeds in the bed where they are to grow in late April or May and thin to a foot apart. Give plenty of water and sunny situation.

italica = *A. azurea*
myosotidiflora = *Brunnera macrophylla*

ANDROECIUM. The male or stamen-bearing part of the flower.

ANDROMEDA (an-DROM-ed-a). (Also see PIERIS)
glaucophylla   1′   Zone 2   Downy Andromeda
An unusual plant for the bog garden, this has narrow evergreen leaves, the edges of which roll under, causing the leaves to appear still narrower. The flowers are white and appear in drooping clusters of 5 or 6 at the tips of the branches. The almost globular corollas of the flowers are less than ¼ in. in dia., and resemble tiny white berries. It may be found in bogs from Greenland and Manitoba to Va.

polifolia   1′–2′   Zone 2   Bog Rosemary
A low shrub with creeping rootstock, native to bogs in northeastern North America, northern and central Europe and northern Asia as well. The creeping rootstock spreads easily; the evergreen leaves are up to 1½ in. long and the small white to pinkish flowers appear in early May in small terminal clusters; actually of little ornamental value outside bogs or similar situations.

ANDROSACE (an-DROSS-as-ee). Small tufted herbs, grown in rock gardens, belonging to the Primrose Family. The leaves are usually basal and the flowers red and white, somewhat similar to those of primroses. Propagated by division, seeds, cuttings.

carnea   4″   Zone 5   Pine Rockjasmine
A tiny alpine plant from Europe whose leaves, arranged in a rosette, cover the ground where conditions are favorable. The flowers arranged in an umbel are similar to the Primrose (of which Family this plant is a member) and vary from white to pink. The plant favors a loose, pebbly, neutral to somewhat acid soil.

chamaejasme   3″   Zone 5   Rockjasmine
An alpine plant of the temperate mountain regions of Europe, Asia, and North America, the hairy leaves are arranged in rosettes and the umbels of white to pink flowers crown the stems. It requires constant, ample moisture.

foliosa   5″   Zone 6
The rather large, pale green leaves about 1½ in. long, all basal but not in rosettes, and the woody stems sharply distinguish this from other Himalayan species. The flowers, appearing in May, are pink with darker pink centers.

lanuginosa   prostrate   Zone 6
A prostrate herbaceous perennial from the Himalayas with white silky leaves about ¾ in. long; red flowers ⅓ in. across in clusters on scapes about 2 in. long, during June and July. An excellent mat-forming plant.

sarmentosa   6″–8″   Zones 2–3
This plant from the Himalayas is similar to *A. chamaejasme*, having hairy green rosettes of foliage and umbels of rose-colored flowers. This species propagates readily by means of short stolons and readily forms a matlike planting. In dry seasons it will require additional moisture.

sempervivoides   2″–4″   Zone 5
This Himalayan rock garden plant has rosettes of shiny leaves barely an inch in dia., and umbels of tiny pink flowers on stems of 2–4 in. This also propagates readily from stolons, with new plants clustered around older ones. Although the plant requires well-drained, gravelly soil, it will grow in semi-shade.

villosa   3″   Zone 4
A white woolly perennial with small leaves in rosettes; flowers white or rose colored, ⅓ in. wide in umbels. Native to Europe and Asia. Difficult to grow.

ANEMONE (popularly an-EM-on-e). The Anemone species are perennial herbs with leaves generally compound, belonging to the Buttercup Family. If single, the leaves are divided. They are valued for their bright colored, red, pink, white or purple flowers which have no petals, but have showy, petallike sepals which number 5 in most species. They require rich, well-drained soil and partial shade. Most are native to the North Temperate regions of the world and are propagated by seed sown in spring or root divisions made at the same time.

alpina   18″   Zone 6   Alpine Anemone
This plant from Europe is found high in the mountains, where its deep tap root sustains the plant in the gravelly, well-drained soil. From the cluster of attractive, fernlike foliage the large white flowers grow 18 in. high. Variety **sulphurea** has yellow flowers.

apennina   9″   Zone 7   Apennine Anemone
Blooming in April with tuberous roots, this has sky-blue flowers 1½ in. wide. Best planted in partial shade of wooded areas. Native to Italy. The var. **plena** has double flowers.

baldensis   6″   Zone 6   Moraine Anemone
A small European alpine plant with tuberous roots, compound leaves and white flowers slightly tinged with pink. These appear in spring. The plant requires well-drained, slightly acid soil and constant moisture.

blanda   8″   Zone 6   Greek Anemone
Tuberous rooted, with deep blue flowers and native to Greece. Distinguished from *A. apennina* by smaller leaves that are more laciniate, shorter petioles and shorter and more slender peduncles.

canadensis   2′   Zone 3   Meadow Anemone
The leaves of this plant are divided into 5–7 segments and are on a long stalk. The flowers are white, 1–2 in. wide, the stalk taller than the leaf stalk. They bloom in June. When used at the base of shrubbery its light green leaves furnish an interesting contrast to the darker background, and the shrubs tend to prevent the overenthusiastic spreading. Native from New England to W.Va. and west to Mo. and Ill.

caroliniana   1′   Zone 6   Carolina Anemone
With cream to purple flowers, 1½ in. across blooming in April and May; is tuberous rooted. Native from Ill. to Tex. The var. **rosea** has rose-colored flowers—not especially showy.

coronaria   18″   Zone 8   Poppy Anemone
The most common of the 3 species (together with *A. fulgens* and *A. hortensis*) forced in greenhouses for cut-flower purposes. Native to southern Europe, the flowers are 2½ in. wide and are available in many shades of pink, white, red, and blue, both single and double. Some of the more popular varieties are: 'DeCaen', 'His Excellency', 'Mr. Fokker', 'Chrysanthimiflora', with very double flowers and 'The Bride'.

x fulgens   1′   Zone 5   Flame Anemone
The red flowers 2½ in. wide make this an excellent subject for the rock garden as well as for forcing as a cut flower. Native to France and tuberous rooted.

halleri   6″   Zone 5   Haller Anemone
The small, moundlike foliage of this plant is covered with soft, silky hairs, and the lavender flowers appearing in spring are large and shaped like cups. A tap-rooted European alpine, this requires well-drained alkaline soil and full sun.

hortensis   10″   Zone 5   Garden Anemone

This, *A. coronaria* and *A. fulgens* have such large colorful flowers that they are often spoken of as the "Florists Anemones" because they are forced a great deal in greenhouses for cut-flower purposes. This species, native to southern Europe, has flowers that are up to 3 in. wide and are colored red, white, or purple with brownish stamens. In the open garden they bloom in May.

hupehensis 18″ Zone 5 Dwarf Japanese Anemone
Native to Japan with pale pink flowers probably of outstanding interest now because the very popular garden anemone which has gone so long under the name of *A. japonica*, is now considered to be a variety of this species.

hupehensis japonica 2½′ Zone 5 Japanese Anemone
A very popular garden perennial with flowers purplish red, rose, white up to 3 in. across blooming from Sept. to late frosts. There are many available varieties of this popular border plant including **alba** with white flowers; **'Alice'** (rosy carmine); **'September Charm'**; **'Queen Charlotte'** (semi-double pink); **'Whirlwind'** (semi-double white); and **'Bussingham Glow'**, 2 ft. tall with semi-double red flowers.

Anemone hupehensis japonica

nemorosa 8″ Zone 3 European Wood Anemone
With white or purplish solitary flowers 1 in. wide, blooming during April and May. Native from Europe to Siberia. Several horticultural varieties have been selected in Europe; **'Alba'** with double white flowers; **'Allenii'** with lavender-mauve flowers; **'Rosea'** with reddish-purple double flowers. The species is somewhat similar to the American *A. quinquefolia*.

palmata 9″ Zone 8 Mediterranean Anemone
With yellow flowers about 2 in. wide and tuberous roots, blooming in May or June. Native to the Mediterranean region. The variety 'Flore Pleno' has double flowers.

patens 3″–6″ Zone 5 Spreading Pasque-flower
This native of the prairies, from Ill. and Mo. to Mich. and Tex. has compound leaves and linear leaflets, having the leaves and stems covered with long, silky hairs. The flowers are bluish or violet and are composed of 5–7 sepals, and numerous stamens. The fruit is unusual—composed of silky plumes attached to the hairy, one-seeded fruit or achene, typical of the Buttercup Family, to which the species of this genus belong.

pulsatilla 1′ Zone 5 European Pasqueflower
Native to Europe and Asia, this has proved a popular rock garden plant in America because of its bell-shaped blue or reddish-purple flowers, about 2 in. wide in April, followed by interesting fuzzy fruit heads that are most ornamental. The pinnately-dissected leaves are also interesting. There are several varieties of this available with white, pink, red or bluish flowers. Very popular as a garden plant. The juice of the purple petals yields a green liquid used to color Easter eggs, but it is not a permanent dye.

quinquefolia 10″ Zone 4 American Wood Anemone
The Wood Anemone has compound leaves with 3–5 wedge-shaped leaflets. The solitary flowers are white, up to 1 in. in dia. with 4–9 sepals. It is a weak-stemmed woodland plant growing in the north and central eastern states and west to Ohio, blooming from April to June. Suitable only for shady, sheltered areas.

ranunculoides 8″ Zone 4 Yellow Wood Anemone
The yellow flowers 1 in. wide of this delightful spring flowering plant make it excellent for naturalizing in wooded areas. Native to Europe and Siberia. There is a semi-double flowered variety 'Flore-pleno' in the trade in Europe.

sylvestris 1½′ Zones 2–3 Snowdrop Anemone
With single, pure white solitary flowers about 1½ in. wide and often nodding, blooming in May or June. Native to Europe and south-western Asia. A double-flowered form ('Flore Pleno') is in the trade in Europe.

tuberosa 1′ Zone 6 Tuber Anemone
A tuberous-rooted species with small white or purplish flowers only about ¾ in. wide, native from Ariz. to Utah. Apparently not offered by nurseries in America, nor is it of outstanding ornamental merit.

virginiana 2′–4′ Zone 4 Virginia Anemone
A habitant of open woods throughout the

East, and far south as Ga. and extending into Ark. and Kan., this is found in dry or rocky sites. It has compound leaves and white flowers composed of five sepals. The plant bears a strong resemblance to its relative, the Field Buttercup, although it is a stouter, more hairy plant, blooming from June to Aug.

ANEMONE, RUE = *Anemonella thalictroides*

ANEMONELLA (an-em-o-NELL-a)

   thalictroides   **4"–10"**   **Zone 4**   **Anemonella,**
                                       Rue Anemone

A tuberous-rooted perennial with compound leaves which rise from the roots and are divided into 3 3-lobed leaflets. The flower stalks bears leaflets and 5 or more white flowers in a loose umbel. The flowers, which appear in May and June, are ½ in. in diam. and have 5 to 10 sepals. It may be found in rich woodlands in the eastern U.S. Rue Anemone or Windflower, as it is sometimes called, is a plant for the shady, acid-soil garden. Its seeds may be sown in the fall, or the plant divided after the foliage has died down.

ANETHUM GRAVEOLENS 3′ annual Dill
A popular herb with very finely divided almost threadlike foliage, the leaves 3 and 4 times divided, sometimes grown as a biennial. It should not be transplanted, but the seed sown in an sunny spot where the plants are to grow. As an herb, the leaves are used to flavor cottage cheese, potato salad, etc. The seeds are used in pies, soups, etc. Native to Europe, naturalized in North America.

ANGEL'S-TEARS = *Narcissus triandrus*

ANGEL'S-TRUMPET. See BRUGMANSIA.

ANGELICA (an-JELL-ik-a). This comprises a large group of perennial herbs, many of them aromatic, members of the carrot family. *A. archangelica* has been used in herb gardens for centuries. They have leaves that are three times compound, flowers that are small, white or greenish and produced in a terminal umbel. Fruit is a small, dry capsule. They certainly are not showy plants but *A. archangelica* has proved popular.

   archangelica   **6′**   **Zone 4**   **Garden Angelica**
A popular aromatic garden herb, closely related to the Carrot, with leaves thrice compound, flowers small, greenish white blooming during July in terminal umbels. This is classed as one of the garden herbs because the young leaves are used in cooking fish; the blanched stalk can be eaten like celery; the roots and stems are both used in flavoring liqueurs. Propagated by seed.

   atropurpurea   **9′**   **biennial**   **Purple-stem**
                                          Angelica
A biennial weed reproducing from seeds, with a dark purple, erect stem, and white flower heads

10 in. across. Leaves are alternate, 2–3 times compound, in threes. Native to eastern and central North America. Blooms in June and July. It is reported that the leaf stalks when peeled are relished as a salad.

   venenosa   **2′–4′**   **Zone 4**   **Hairy Angelica**
The flowers of this slender perennial are white and very tiny, and are produced in large terminal umbels, each flower having 5 greenish-white petals joined in a corolla. The leaves are compound, 2–3 in. long, and the leaflets are toothed. It is native from Mass. to Fla., extending west to Minn. and Mo. It blooms from June to Sept. and is generally not cultivated, since the plant is reputed to be poisonous.

ANGELICA-TREE. See ARALIA.

ANGIOSPERMS. Plants having their seeds enclosed in an ovary. See also GYMNOSPERMS.

ANGRAECUM (an-Gree-kum). Epiphytic orchids native to Madagascar and western Africa with flowers in racemes or arching sprays. For culture and propagation see ORCHID.

   superbum   **18"–60"**   **Zone 10**
Waxy flowers, greenish white, 3–4 in. across, 15–25 produced on a large arching spray in the greenhouse during winter and spring.

ANIMATED OAT = *Avena sterilis*

ANISE = *Pimpinella anisum*

ANISETREE. See ILLICIUM.

ANISOSTICHUS = BIGNONIA

ANNATTO = *Bixa orellana*

ANNONA (an-O-na)

   cherimola   **25′**   **Zone 10**   **Cherimoya**
A tree, native to the Andes mountains of Peru and Ecuador, grown chiefly for its fruits, which can weigh anywhere from 4 oz. to a pound. Sometimes referred to as custard-apple. The leaves are 10" long, velvety pubescent beneath, and the flowers an inch long, yellow and fragrant. The fruit is light green, sometimes 5" long. Apparently there are several varieties that are cultivated in the tropics where they are valued for their fruits.

   montana   **20′**   **Zone 10**   **Mountain Soursop**
An evergreen in the West Indies with fragrant laurellike leaves 5 in. long, yellow flowers and kidney-shaped fruits 6–8 in. long and weighing up to 6 lbs. each. These are covered with short yellow prickles. The yellowish pulp is juicy and tart, used mostly in beverages.

   reticulata   **25′**   **Zone 10**   **Bullock's-heart**
A spreading tree of the American tropics with lance-shaped leaves 7 in. long; greenish or yellowish flowers with purple markings. The fruit is large, 6 in. and heart-shaped, yellow-brown or clear yellow often with bright red or orange-red cheek. The pulp is creamy white,

sweet, custardlike with numerous brown beanlike seeds. Often planted in southern Fla.

squamosa   **25′**   **Zone 10**   **Sugar-apple**

A deciduous tropical tree from South America with bluish-gray, long, thin leaves and greenish-yellow flowers an inch long. The fruit looks something like a pine cone in general outline, yellowish green, 3 in. long and broken up by special separations. The flesh of the fruit is sweet and very tasty but is very perishable as well.

lack for possibilities to choose in making selections.

Annuals are easily grown and actually are the backbone of the summer flower beds. They are used for massing in the border in which the colors and varieties are kept separated. They are also used in mixed borders where different annuals are arranged with each other and with perennials so that all plants are shown off to best advantage, for annuals are particularly helpful in bringing color to the summer flower

Planting annuals in different lines is an excellent way of keeping groups separate at the start. (*Photo by Arnold Arboretum, Jamaica Plain, Mass.*)

ANNONACEAE = The Custard-apple Family

ANNUAL. Usually considered to be a plant which completes its full life cycle in one year. The seed is sown and germinates, the plant grows, blooms, produces seed and dies all within one year. Many valued garden plants are thus considered annuals, i.e., calendulas, nasturtiums, zinnias, etc.

ANNUALS. These are plants which grow to maturity and flower in a few months after the seed is sown. In other words, their complete life cycle is within one year. Nasturtiums, sweet peas, zinnias, marigolds, China-asters, snapdragons, larkspurs, petunias, Sweet Alyssum, and morning-glories are all among the most popular of garden annuals. There are at least 150 types of annuals described in this volume with their hundreds of varieties, so one need not

border. Some annuals are just lined out in the vegetable garden and used for cutting purposes. Some of the lower-growing varieties are used for edging; the annual vines and some of the taller-growing types are used as quick-growing screens. Annuals are used in window-boxes, some as pot plants in the winter greenhouse or in the house in fall and winter and also on terraces in the summer.

Some modern gardeners are unaware of the great strides which have been made in breeding better annuals recently. China-asters are available now that are resistant to wilt disease. Zinnias and marigolds as well as petunias have been bred so that flowers are of remarkable sizes, unknown 20 years ago. Dwarf varieties of sweet peas, alyssum, zinnias and marigolds are available now for planting in small spaces and in small gardens.

For the busy gardener, annuals might be

roughly divided into two general groups, those that should be started indoors in a greenhouse or hotbed in order for them to have a sufficiently long growing season to bloom properly; and those that can (or should) be sown in place in the flower garden where they are expected to grow, marked with an * in the following list. The busy gardener might also be interested in knowing which annuals normally "self-sow," that is, they produce many seeds which live over until the next year if the soil is not disturbed or too heavily mulched. These may sprout under good conditions and one merely has to thin out unwanted seedlings. Annuals in this "self-seeding" group are marked with a # in the following list.

For those who are interested and willing to take more time in growing annuals, many seeds should be started indoors in a greenhouse or electric hotbed. Reading the cultural directions for these annuals, it is surprising to note the large number that should be started "indoors in March" to give the plants a sufficient long-growing season so that they will bloom properly, and in some cases so that they will come into bloom early. Those with a home greenhouse are well provided with facilities; those without might well investigate the potentials of an electric hotbed (which see). Properly used, an electric hotbed is an excellent asset for the gardener who wants to raise his own plants.

The garden centers of today seem to have almost everything for the modern garden and one can usually buy annuals all boxed in flats and ready to plant out at the proper time. So, annuals can be easily obtained and no garden should be without them.

In making a selection, one should read the cultural directions carefully. Some do not thrive in hot weather. Clarkia, Collinsia, Godetia, Sweet Pea, Stock and Schizanthus are among these. On the other hand Zinnia, Snow-on-the-Mountain, Sunflower, Amaranthus and Torenia do very well in hot weather.

Sweet Alyssum, the dwarf zinnias, Ageratum, Linaria, Lobelia, Dwarf Marigold, Verbena, Nierembergia and dwarf *Phlox drummondii* are all among those that are excellent for edging purposes.

For massing one would select Candytuft, Pot-marigold, Coleus, Heliotrope, Marigold, Petunia, Poppy, Salpiglossis, Scabius and Zinnia, among others.

For screens some of the vines like the gourds, Scarlet Runner Bean, or Wild Cucumber might be possibilities. Also, vigorous-growing annuals like Castor-bean and sunflowers might be considered.

Below are listed some of the genera which include annuals. Each species is listed alphabetically under its genus in the body of the book, and described with cultural directions.

* Annuals the seeds of which can be sown in the place of the flower garden where they are to grow.

Annuals, which, under optimum conditions, may be expected to "self-sow".

COMMON NAME	SCIENTIFIC NAME	HEIGHT	COLOR
African-daisy	Arctotis	24″	white
# Ageratum	Ageratum	4″–9″	blue, pink, white
* # Alyssum, Sweet	Lobularia maritima	3″–12″	white to violet
*Baby-blue-eyes	Nemophila menziesii	20″	white to bluish
* # Baby's-breath	Gypsophila	30″	white to pink
Balloon-vine	Cardiosperum	vine	white
* # Balsam, Garden	Impatiens balsamina	2½′	many colors
* # Batchelor's Button	Centaurea	12″–48″	many colors
Beard Tongue	Penstemon	36″	red, white, blue
*Bellflower	Campanula	6″–48″	blue, white, pink
# Bells-of-Ireland	Molucella laevis	24″	white
*Blue Lace-flower	Trachymene caerulea	24″	blue
Blue Woodruff	Asperula azurea setosa	12″	blue
# Browallia	Browallia	12″–24″	blue to white
*Bugloss	Anchusa	18″	blue
Butterfly Flower	Schizanthus pinnatus	12″–36″	many colors
Calceolaria	Calceolaria	12″–36″	yellow
* # California-poppy	Eschscholzia californica	12″–24″	yellow to orange
*Campion	Lychnis	18″–36″	many colors
* # Candytuft	Iberis, certain sp.	16″	many colors
*Cape-marigold	Dimorphotheca aurantiaca	18″	many colors
Cape-stock	Heliophila	12″	blue, yellow

COMMON NAME	SCIENTIFIC NAME	HEIGHT	COLOR
Carnation	Dianthus	6″–24″	many colors
Castor-bean	Ricinus communis	6′ +	foliage plant
Chamomile	Matricaria	8″–24″	yellow to white
China-aster	Callistephus	8″–18″	many colors
*Chinese Forget-me-not	Cynoglossum amabile	24″	blue
Cigar-flower	Cuphea	12″–48″	many colors
#Clarkia, Rose	Clarkia elegans	18″–36″	many colors
Cockscomb	Celosia	12″–48″	many colors
Coleus	Coleus blumei	36″	foliage plant
Coneflower	Rudbeckia	24″–36″	yellow and black
Cornflower	Centaurea	12″–48″	many colors
*Coreopsis	Coreopsis	36″	yellow
#Cosmos	Cosmos	36″–72″	many colors
Creeping-zinnia	Sanvitalia procumbens	6″	yellow
Cupid's-dart	Catananche	24″	blue, white
Cup-flower, Blue	Nierembergia caerulea	6″–12″	blue
Cup-and-saucer Vine	Cobaea scandens	vine	purplish to white
Dahlia	Dahlia (Unwin hybrids)	24″	many colors
Daisy, English	Bellis perennis	6″	white to rose
*Evening-primrose	Cenothera	20″–72″	yellow, white, pink
Everlasting	Helipterum	18″	yellowish
*Flowering Flax	Linum grandiflorum	24″	red to blue
# Flowering Tobacco	Nicotiana alata	18″–48″	many colors
Forget-me-not	Myosotis	12″–24″	blue
* #Four-o'clock	Mirabilis jalapa	36″	many colors
#Gaillardia	Gaillardia	12″–20″	yellow to orange
Gentian	Gentiana, certain sp.	12″	purple blue
*Gilia	Gilia	18″–24″	many colors
* #Godetia	Clarkia	12″–30″	many colors
Globe Amaranth	Gomphrena globosa	18″	many colors
*Golden-cup	Hunnemannia fumariaefolia	24″	yellow
Heliotrope	Heliotropium	24″	violet, lavender
Hollyhock	Alcea rosea	9′	many colors
#Honesty	Lunaria	36″	purple to red
Hyacinth Bean	Dolichos lablab	vine	purple, white
Immortelle	Xeranthemum annuum	36″	many colors
#Kenilworth-ivy	Cymbalaria muralis	vine	lavender
Kingfisher-daisy	Felicia bergeriana	8″	blue
* #Larkspur, Annual	Delphinium	12″–48″	many colors
Lobelia	Lobelia	4″–18″	blue
* #Love-in-a-mist	Nigella damascena	18″–24″	blue, white
#Love-lies-bleeding	Amaranthus	48″–72″	red
*Lupine	Lupinus	12″–36″	many colors
*Malope	Malope	36″	rose-purple
#Marigold	Tagetes	4″–24″	yellow, red
*Meadow-foam	Limnanthes	6″	many colors
*Mignonette	Reseda odorata	6″–18″	yellow-green
Monkey Flower	Mimulus	18″	yellow, reddish
#*Morning-glory	Ipomoea	vine	many colors
Mountain Fringe	Adlumia fungosa	vine	pink
*Nasturtium	Tropaeolum	7″–48″	many colors
#Nicotiana	Nicotiana alata	18″–48″	many colors
Painted-tongue	Salpiglossis sinuata	24″	many colors
Patience Plant	Impatiens	30″	white, rose, purple
Periwinkle	Catharanthus roseus	18″	rose, white
#Petunia	Petunia	6″–24″	many colors
Phacelia, Harebell	Phacelia	11″	red, white
*Phlox, Annual	Phlox drummondii	8″–18″	many colors
Pimpernel	Anagallis	2″–18″	white to red

COMMON NAME	SCIENTIFIC NAME	HEIGHT	COLOR
Pinks	Dianthus	6″–24″	many colors
#*Poppy	Papaver	12″–20″	many colors
Poppy-mallow	Callirhoe	12″–36″	purple
#*Portulaca	Portulaca	6″	many colors
Pot-marigold	Calendula officinalis	12″–24″	yellow to orange
Prince's-feather	Polygonum orientale	6′	pink to rose
Salpiglossis	Salpiglossis sinuata	24″	many colors
#Salvia	Salvia	24″–36″	red, blue
#Sand-verbena	Abronia	6″	rose-purple
Scabius, Sweet	Scabiosa atropurpurea	36″	many colors
*Scarlet-runner Bean	Phaseolus coccineus	vine	red, white
#Snapdragon	Antirrhinum	6″–36″	many colors
Sneezeweed	Helenium tenuifolium	24″–30″	yellow
*#Snow-on-the-mountain	Euphorbia	36″	foliage plant
Soapwort	Saponaria	12″	white to scarlet
#Spider Flower	Cleome spinosa	48″–60″	pink, white, purplish
Star-of-Texas	Xanthisma texanum	12″–36″	yellow
Star-of-the-desert	Amberboa	30″	purple, white, pink
Statice	Limonium	24″	yellow or lavender
Stock	Mathiola	12″–30″	many colors
Strawflower	Helichrysum bracteatum	36″	many colors
#Summer-cypress	Kochia scoparia	60″	yellow to red
*#Sunflower	Helianthus	24″–30″	yellow
*Swan River Daisy	Brachycome iberidifolia	24″–36″	many colors
#*Sweet Alyssum	Lobularia maritima	3″–12″	white to violet
*Sweet Pea	Lathyrus odoratus	8″–60″	many colors
Tahoka-daisy	Machaeranthera tanacetifolia	24″	violet-blue
*Tassel-flower	Emilia sagittata	24″	red, orange
Tidy Tips	Layia elegans	12″–24″	yellow
Tithonia	Tithonia rotundifolia	36″–72″	yellow to orange
*Toadflax	Linaria	18″	purple to pink
#Torenia, Blue	Torenia fournieri	12″	pale violet, yellow
Transvaal-daisy	Gerbera jamesonii hybrida	30″	many colors
*Tree-mallow	Lavatera	6′–10′	rose, red, white
Verbena	Verbena hortensis	8″–18″	many colors
*Viper's Bugloss	Echium	24″	many colors
#*Virginia-stock	Malcomia maritima	4″–8″	many colors
Wallflower	Cheiranthus	18″	buff to deep red
Wax Begonia	Begonia semperflorens	12″–18″	white, pink, red
Winged Everlasting	Ammobium alatum	36″	white
Zinnia	Zinnia	12″–30″	many colors

For further lists of annuals and many other suggestions see 'Annuals' by James Underwood Crockett, Time-Life Books, N.Y. For sowing seeds and fertilizers, see SEEDS, FERTILIZERS, etc.

ANNUAL RINGS. When a tree trunk is cut through horizontally, concentric rings are seen at the ends of the log. These are formed by the annual increment of growth. The living tissue of tree, shrub or branch is just under the bark and it produces a new ring of cells each year, a wide ring if growing conditions are good, a narrow ring if growth is poor. By counting these rings one knows the exact age of the trunk or limb. Foresters have developed what is called an increment borer, which when bored into the trunk removes a small core of wood and the rings can be counted without cutting down the tree. The small hole remaining can be dis-infected and filled and thus the tree is not damaged.

ANODA (an-O-da)

cristata   3′   annual   Snowcup

Native to Tex., Mexico and South America and not used very much, this can be grown as an annual, having alternate, arrow-shaped leaves, purple, violet or white solitary flowers in the axils of the leaves during summer and fall. Flowers may be 2 in. across. The Snowcup should be used at the back of the border and plants should be spaced 15 in. apart.

ANREDERA (an-RED-er-a)

cordifolia (*Boussingaultia baselloides*)   **vine**
                              Zone 9   Madeira-vine
This is a vigorous vine from tropical America, climbing by means of tendrils, which can quickly grow out of control if it is planted in moist soil. It can grow 20 ft. or more a season, producing racemes of fragrant white blossoms 1 ft. long, in the late summer. The lustrous green leaves are about 3 in. long and are evergreen. It has the interesting quality of producing small tubers in the axils of the leaves, which if planted in a moist medium will form new plants.

ANSELLIA (an-SEL-ia). Orchids from Africa that are epiphytic and sometimes grown in the greenhouse. The flowers of **A. africana** are yellowish, spotted with chocolate brown, an inch across but borne in many flowered terminal panicles up to 16 in. long. For culture and propagation see ORCHID.

ANTELOPE-BRUSH = *Purshia tridentata*

ANTENNARIA (an-ten-AY-ria)
  dioica   1′   Zone 2   Common Pussy-toes
A stoloniferous gray-leaved perennial ground cover, leaves an inch long, white tomentose beneath, flower heads small about ¼ in. across and clustered, bracts white or pink, blooming in May and June. Native to Europe and Asia and the Aleutian Islands and probably escaped in North America. This and its var. **rosea** with rose-colored flowers are the ones chiefly grown.

  **neglecta attenuata   1′   Zone 3 • Smaller
                                             Pussy-toes**
Native to the dry, gravelly pastures of northern U.S., the low-growing plant with white woolly 3-nerved leaves about an inch long spreads rapidly by stolons and produces white flower heads on slender stems in May.

  **plantaginifolia   8″–10″   Zone 3   Plantainleaf
                                             Pussy-toes**
A perennial herb with white woolly leaves forming a basal rosette and lanceolate leaves along the flower stalk. The flowers are grayish white, tubular and minute, in loose clusters. It is native to Me. to Ga. and west to Minn. and Mo. mostly in fields and old pastures but is probably not cultivated frequently. It blooms from April to June. This plant makes an excellent small ground cover for dry, sandy areas, although in some situations it may need to be restrained. Divide before flowering.

  rosea   1′   Zone 4   Littleleaf Pussy-toes
Silvery-white foliage growing in slowly spreading mats, this native of the Rocky Mountains bears white flower heads. It requires loose, gravelly or rocky soil.

ANT-FEEDER-TREE = *Cecropia peltata*

ANTHEMIS (AN-them-is). A large group of herbs belonging to the Composite Family mostly with fragrant leaves. Some are weeds. The leaves are alternate and deeply cut; the flower heads are usually yellow or white with yellow centers. *A. tinctoria* is the best ornamental species. Propagated by seed or division.

  arvensis agrestis   20″   Zone 3   Corn Camomile
A biennial weed introduced to America from Europe but now widely distributed throughout North America. Leaves alternate, 1–2 pinnately divided, grayish green and scented. The white ray flowers are daisylike, the disc flowers yellow with the heads 1 in. wide. Blooms from May to Aug.

  cotula   2′   annual   Mayweed Camomile
A weed with alternate, sessile, fernlike leaves, 3 pinnate and dissected, and with a very unpleasant odor. The flower heads are ¼–½ in. wide, the ray florets white, the central florets yellow. Native to Europe, widely distributed in North America, blooming from June to Oct.

  marschalliana   1′   Zone 6
A summer-blooming perennial from the mountains of central Europe, this resembles *A. nobilis* except that the leaves are silvery white underneath. The yellow flower heads are nearly an inch long and are borne on long stalks. A good plant for the rockery.

  nobilis = *Chamaemelum nobile*
  **sancti-johannis   3′   Zone 5   St. John's
                                             Camomile**
Foliage finely cut; flower heads 2 in. wide, ray flowers orange with deeper-colored flowers than *A. tinctoria*. Native to Bulgaria.

  tinctoria   3′   Zone 3   Golden Marguerite
A popular perennial herb, much grown for its hardiness, its profuse, daisylike yellow flowers, 2 in. wide, appearing in summer, and its finely cut, aromatic foliage. Native to Europe and Asia. Easily propagated by division or by seeds. Several very popular varieties are: **kelwayi**—cut leaves and darker yellow flowers; **'Moonlight'**—pale yellow flowers; **'Perry's Variety'**—large, bright yellow flowers.

ANTHER. The pollen-bearing part of the flower.

ANTHERICUM (an-THER-ik-um)
  liliago   3′   Zones 6–7   St.-Bernard-lily
Native to the Alps Mountains, the white lily-like flowers are 1 in. across, borne in racemes on a foot-long stalk in early summer. If used in the North, the tuberous roots should be dry in the fall and stored over winter. The leaves are about a foot long, unbranched, straplike and an inch wide. Propagated by stolons, division and seed.
  liliastrum = *Paradisia liliastrum*

ANTHESIS. Flowering; strictly the time of expansion of a flower; often used to designate the flowering period.

ANTHOCYANINS. Blue, red and purple water-soluble pigments of plants.

ANTHOLYZA AETHIOPICA = *Chasmanthe aethiopica*

ANTHOLYZA PANICULATA = *Curtonus paniculatus*

ANTHOXANTHUM (an-thox-ANTH-um)

   gracile   8″   annual   Vernal Grass
A dwarf ornamental grass useful for edging. Native to the Mediterranean Region.

   odoratum   3′   Zone 3   Sweet Vernal Grass
A perennial weed grass, native to Europe, with an unpleasant odor, especially when dried. It is now found in eastern North America and on the Pacific Coast, usually on poor soils.

ANTHRACNOSE. A common plant disease caused by several fungi. Symptoms are well-defined spots on leaves and lesions, on twigs and fruits in wet seasons. On White Oak and Sycamore the new leaves are blackened in the spring resembling frost injury. Sprays of fungicide #K or #M when the new leaves are developing are recommended. Blackberries, raspberries and dewberries show purplish spots with gray centers on the canes and leaves of new shoots. Prompt pruning and spraying before bloom and after harvest with fungicide #D is advised. Roses, Privet, Snowberry and Dogwood may also become infested, and require early season sprays with fungicide #D or #K. The pods of beans and the fruits of Cucumber and Tomato show sunken spots in wet weather. Sprays of fungicide #E, #G or #K give control and seeds of resistant varieties should be grown when available.

ANTHRISCUS (an-THRIS-kus)

   cerefolium   18″   annual   Chervil
A popular herb closely related to the carrot, with small white flowers, pinnately divided leaves, native to southeast Europe. As an herb the leaf is used to lend flavoring in cooking certain soups, fishes and meats. Easily propagated by seeds which keep their viability for 3 years.

ANTHURIUM (an-THOO-rium)

   andraeanum 2′ Zone 10 Flaming Anthurium
A popular plant in tropical gardens as well as in greenhouses and conservatories in the North because the flower consists of long, narrow nodding spikes which contain all the true yellow flowers set off by a huge, waxy heart-shaped scarlet bract which, when it matures, turns green. When cut these will last often 3 weeks in good condition.

   crystallinum 2′ Zone 10 Crystal Anthurium
With large cordate leaves 14 in. long and 10 in. wide, heart shaped and very beautiful, the leaves green but the veins white and pale rose beneath. Native to Colombia. Often grown in the greenhouse for their colorful leaves.

   scherzeranum 2′ Zone 10 Common Anthurium
Similar to *A. andraeanum* but with a smaller flower and with a curled central flower spike.

   veitchii   3′   Zone 10   Veitch Anthurium
An unusual plant with leaves 3 ft. long and 10 in. wide colored a rich metallic green, with curved lateral veins slightly sunken, giving a quilted appearance. The spathe is greenish white. Native to Colombia.

   warocqueanum climbing Zone 10
With showy, 3 ft.-tapering leaves that are deep green, with ivory-colored veins. The small spathe is greenish to yellow. Often grown in the greenhouse for its interesting foliage. Native to Colombia.

ANTHYLLIS (an-THY-lis)

   montana   1′   Zone 5   Alps Anthyllis
A perennial herb with white silky, pinnately compound leaves and purple or pink flowers in many heads. Best grown in poor soil and propagated by seed or division. Sometimes grown in rock gardens. Native to the Alps Mountains. The var. **roseus** bears bright pink flowers.

ANTIBIOTICS. Antibiotics are substances produced by certain molds and fungi which kill or stop the growth of bacteria and other fungi. They are better known as treatments for infection in man and animals such as penicillin. Among the commercial formulations used for control of plant diseases are ACTI-DIONE (cyclohexamide) and AGRIMYCIN (streptomycin). Among the diseases which have been controlled successfully with antibiotics are fireblight, hawthorn leaf blight and some lawn grass diseases.

ANTIGONON (an-TIG-o-non)

   leptopus   vine   Zone 9   Coralvine
A Mexican herbaceous vine which in Mexico is called "a chain of love" because the small flowers bear some resemblance to a series of light pink hearts. It climbs by the use of twisting tendrils. The rough, heart-shaped, alternate leaves have wavy margins. The flowers have no petals, the colored calyx being the part that is prominent. The flowers are borne in the late summer and autumn on short branches that have an angular way of branching from the main stems. The variety **album** has white flowers. Propagated by seeds and cuttings.

ANTIRRHINUM (an-ti-RY-num). Snapdragons are chiefly treated as annuals, although they may live over winter with air temperatures down to 10° F.; these are prized garden plants because of their bright colored flowers which appear over a long period. They last well when used as cut flowers and are an important crop for the florist to force in the greenhouse. The flowers open progressively from the base to the top, hence are effective a long time in the garden. Side branches frequently are produced with 2-ft. flower spikes. After these have faded, if the plant is cut back to 6 in. and fertilized, it may produce a second crop of blossoms in the fall, thus making it one of the few garden plants with the longest blooming period.

It is important to note that modern varieties are divided into 4 main groups according to size: tall (2½–3 ft.); intermediate (2 ft.); dwarf (6 in.) and trailing. There are several dozen varieties of these available from American sources, but in ordering one should ascertain to which size-groups the desired varieties belong.

Insect Pests

Skeletonized leaves and light green worms are evidence of the greenhouse leaf tier. Spraying with insecticides #15 or #37 are effective. Light traps to capture the moths give additional protection. Aphids, white fly, and spider mites are perennial pests in the greenhouse. See CHRYSAN-THEMUM and CARNATION. Tarnished plant bug stings the buds and destroys the flowers. Use insecticide #15. An unusual pest is the honeybee, which tears the petals of the flower in its efforts to reach the pollen and nectar. No control with insecticides is suggested.

Diseases

Snapdragon rust which produces brown spots on the underside of leaves and causes the plant to wilt and die is an important pest. Spraying with fungicide #D and growing rust-resistant varieties is suggested. Light brown spots on the leaves and stems of garden snapdragons are due to infection by blight. Use fungicides #G, #F, #D or #K. Botrytis mold on flowers and flower stalks follows excessive humidity and crowding. Anthracnose spots and lesions kill the plant above the infection. Spray with fungicide #G and keep plants as dry as possible.

asarina = *Asarina procumbens*
majus   6″–3′   annual or perennial   Common Snapdragon
This is the species to which the garden snapdragons are mostly related. The leaves are lanceolate, alternate, up to 3 in. long. The flowers of the species are reddish white or purple, but many varicolored varieties and hybrids are now available as annuals. Individual flowers are 1½ in. long in long terminal racemes. Native to the Mediterranean Region.

Snapdragon seed takes nearly 3 weeks to germinate and after that a long period of growth is necessary before the seedlings come into bloom. To circumvent this it is best to sow seed indoors during Feb. to have sizable plants ready to set out after all danger of frost is over.

Plants should be set out in rich soil, preferably in the full sun although they will bloom in light shade. Taller varieties should be planted at least a foot apart, smaller should be closer together.
molle   1½′   Zone 7   Pyrenees Snapdragon
A shrublike perennial with gray-green leaves. The pale yellow flowers are arranged in loose spikes and bloom in spring and summer. Native to southern France, it must be protected in winter in the northern U.S.

Culture

The snapdragons are showy, free-flowering, hardy annuals that are top performers in gardens during the summer. They are easy to grow and their appeal has long been universal. Graceful spires are gaily clothed with florets of rainbow colors, adding sparkle to bushy plants known for their lustrous, dark green leaves that remain attractive well into the fall and even into early winter.

Antirrhinum is another common name for these popular and dependable annuals. It is more freely used in England, and is actually the generic name. Snapdragons are perennials, treated like annuals. In regions where they are able to survive winters outdoors—and they withstand low temperatures—seed is sown in the summer and the young plants set out in the fall, a common practice with pansies and wall flowers. This results in very early bloom.

For northern gardens, seed is sown indoors in the greenhouse, or in coldframes outdoors. Plants can be propagated from cuttings, better plants result from seed and colors are more diversified.

Sow the fine seed in pans or flats in a light, sandy mixture. Press firmly with a block and cover lightly with fine soil. Keep moist, but not wet, as this may induce rotting. The young seedlings can, in fact, be permitted to dry out a bit between waterings. When they have developed their true leaves and are large enough to handle, they can be transplanted to 3-inch pots or to flats, where they are spaced 3 inches apart.

When weather has warmed in spring, young plants can be shifted to the garden. Or stock can be purchased in flats from nurseries and garden centers, a common practice with petunias, zinnias, marigolds, Sweet Alyssum, and other annuals.

These plants like a medium-heavy soil with good drainage, but do well in light, sandy soils enriched with organic matter. As a group, they are tolerant of a wide range of soils that are not too acid. Neutral or slightly alkaline are best. Where needed, lime can be added at planting time.

Space plants about 10 in. apart, although tall

growing varieties can be allowed more room. The smaller dwarfs can be placed 7–8 in. apart. Pinch the young plants to induce branching. This may delay flowering somewhat, but flower spikes will be more numerous and plants more sturdy, better able to stand up on their own. Yet staking is needed, particularly with giant varieties. Secure plants gracefully just as the spikes are beginning to unfold their first florets.

These widely grown annuals have many uses. They are irresistible when massed in beds, as in parks, or grouped generously in home garden borders with zinnias, marigolds, petunias, Blue Salvia and other familiar annuals. They can take the place of Dutch bulbs lifted after flowering, or the dwarf kinds can be planted directly over bulbs when ripened foliage has been removed. Snapdragons are hardy annuals. If a few spikes are left uncut on each plant, seed will fall and there will be numerous volunteer seedlings the following spring. These can be moved about wherever wanted or thinned so they can develop fully.

Snapdragons do best in full sun, but are remarkably adapted to shady places, an honor they share with Flowering Tobacco and the Patient Plant. Flowers will be fewer, but healthy plants will display luxurious foliage. During the growing season feed with mixed fertilizer once or twice, depending on the fertility of the soil, and keep well watered. The major problem is rust disease, but this is easy to eliminate by selecting rust-resistant stock, practically the only kind grown by florists and nurserymen.

The tall snapdragons are recommended for background in borders, with lower growing perennials and annuals in the front. The dwarf plants are ideal in rock gardens, particularly those under 6 in. high. Low kinds are also superb in window boxes.

Snapdragons make one of the best cut flowers —it is the main florist crop during the winter–spring season. The tall, slender spikes are perfect for cutting, and last a long time in water. The colors, too, come in a wide array, encompassing deep red and maroon, rich and velvety, pink and clear rose, yellow, orange and white. They come in every hue except blue.

In the home greenhouse, snapdragon seed can be sown several times a year, depending on when bloom is desired. July-planted seed will produce bloom from Dec. to March. October-sown seed will flower in Feb. and March, and that started in Jan., in May and June. Plants need support with stakes, wire hoops or bench-wiring frames. Flowers can be expected about 12 weeks after sowing. Greenhouse temperatures should be 45–50 degrees at night with a 10–15 degree rise during the day.

Several varieties of snapdragons are available for garden and greenhouse culture. 'Sentinel', vigorous and rust resistant, produces a spectacular display of spikes on 3 ft. plants. **Floradale Giants**, also 3 ft., are known for their long-lasting spires that include unusual colors, as fiery scarlet and orange flushed rose. Rust proof, they are recommended for gardens.

In the intermediate group, the **Rocket Snapdragons** are outstanding. Growing $2\frac{1}{2}$ ft. tall, plants have the ability to withstand hot summers. They are All-America Winners. **Bellflower Snapdragons**, $2\frac{1}{2}$ ft. tall, have slightly ruffled florets that resemble bellflowers. These can be as much as 2 in. across.

Floral Carpet Snapdragons are F_1 Hybrids that grow only 6–7 in. high. Bushy plants produce abundantly, some smothered with as many as 25 spikes. They are excellent for edging and rock gardens, as are the **Miniature Magic Carpet Snapdragons,** a mere 4–6 in. high. These are semi-creeping plants that are covered with dainty flowers in a rich array of colors. They are delightful in pots on porches and terraces.

GEORGE TALOUMIS

ANTS. Most ants are more annoying than destructive. Carpenter ants make cavities in trees and in building timbers and posts in moist locations. Cornfield ants damage seeds and seedlings and their nests in the lawn may kill grass. They care for colonies of root aphids living on the roots of many garden plants. Ants are also active around aphids and some scales where they feed on the honeydew secreted by the sucking insects. In the South, Argentine ants nest in lawns and gardens causing damage to plants, and the imported fire ant inflicts painful bites to man and animals in addition to damaging lawn and garden plants. Red harvester ants in the Southwest build nests deep in the ground and kill all vegetation around the entrance. Formerly chlordane and its products were very effective in controlling ants. However, they are now prohibited. Instead, diazinon and malathion both have proved helpful in control. Also, there are commercial bug sprays put out specifically for the control of ants, and it is important that instructions on the container be carefully read. When used to kill ants in a stepping stone terrace, Raid is effective, but be careful that run-off from these applications will not reach valued plants. Thallium sulfate is very poisonous and its use is now restricted in some states. Also see TERMITES.

APACHE-PLUME = *Fallugia paradoxa*

APETALOUS. Without petals; as the flowers of willows.

APHANOSTEPHUS (aff-an-OS-tef-us)

skirrobasis   16″   Zone 5   Prairie Daisy
An annual or perennial herb, member of the Composite Family, with narrow, alternate leaves which are sometimes toothed or pinnately lobed. The flowers are yellow, tubular, with a margin of ray flowers which may vary from white to violet or purple. Native to N.Mex. and Tex. to Kan. and Fla., it blooms in spring and summer. Although not choice, it serves a useful purpose in the garden in those areas where it is native, since it withstands the hot, dry climate. Propagation is by division in spring or fall.

APHELANDRA (aff-el-AND-ra)

aurantiaca   3′   Zone 10   Orange Aphelandra
With showy spikes of orange flowers 2½ in. long, the spikes being 6 in. long, bearing smooth, ovate, opposite green leaves that are slightly grayish in the vein areas. Native to Mexico and South America. Propagated by seeds and cuttings of half ripened wood.

tetragona   3′   Zone 10   Scarlet Aphelandra
With bright scarlet flowers 2–3 in. long, the lateral lobes of the lower lip being very small. Flower spikes are about 8 in. long. Native to the West Indies and South America. Propagated by seeds and cuttings of half-ripened wood.

APHIDS. Nearly every species of plant is fed upon by some species of aphid. Some aphids feed exclusively on a certain plant or closely related plants, and others have many and varied hosts. It is not surprising that bean aphids may be found on Locust which are related plants, but green peach aphids on Sweet Potato, cowpea aphids on Asparagus and chrysanthemum aphids on roses are strange but true.

The tiny sucking insects may or may not have wings, may lay eggs or give birth to living young, and may live exposed on plants, enclosed in galls or on roots underground. They may have 20 or more generations annually and colonies may completely surround a small shoot. Most species secrete a sweet substance called honeydew which attracts ants and other insects and supports the sooty mold fungus which blackens leaves, twigs, fruit and other objects. The feeding punctures provide entrance for plant diseases and may transmit viruses and other plant diseases from plant to plant. They are the main food of lady beetles and have many natural enemies among the insect parasites, predators and birds which help to control them.

Many insecticides give satisfactory control of aphids. On trees and shrubs dormant applications of oil or dinitro compounds kill the overwintering eggs. During the growing season organic phosphates such as malathion, nicotine, pyrethrum and rotenone and the benzene

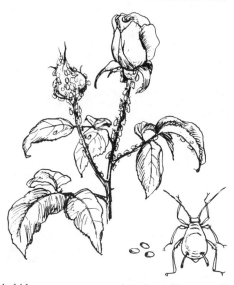

Aphids on a rose, a greatly enlarged insect and eggs.

compounds such as lindane and endo sulfan are all effective for control of aphids when used as recommended. Shrubs and non-bearing fruit trees can be protected with systemic insecticides. See INSECTICIDES.

APHYLLANTHES (a-FILL-an-theez)

monspeliensis   10″   Zone 6
A shrublike plant of southern Europe. The stiff, leafless stems bear blue, star-shaped flowers in spring. It requires well-drained, gravelly soil and full sun, with some protection in winter, if grown in Northern Temperate Zone areas.

APIOS (AY-pios)

americana (*A. tuberosa*) **vine Zone 3   Groundnut**
This twining vine dies to the ground each winter but has small tuberous roots that were said to be used as food by the American Indians. It is native to eastern North America, has alternate compound leaves of 5–7 leaflets and grows about 8 ft. long each season. The brownish pealike flowers are fragrant, appear in clusters during the late summer. Not especially ornamental but a short vine that is an oddity. Propagated by tubers and seed.

The raw tubers are somewhat tough with a milky juice, but pleasantly sweet and edible with a turniplike taste. They may be eaten raw, roasted, or cut in thin slices and fried like potatoes.

tuberosa = *A. americana*

APIUM (AY-pium)

graveolens dulce = See CELERY.

graveolens rapaceum = See CELERIAC.

APLECTRUM (ay-PLEK-trum)

hyemale   18″   Zone 3   Puttyroot
This is the only species in this genus, a terrestrial orchid native from Vt. to Saskatchewan south to N.Car. and Kan. The leaves are 4–8 in. long, the racemes are only 4–6 in. long but bear 4–16 yellowish-brown flowers about an inch long during May and June. It is sometimes planted in the wild garden.

APOCYNACEAE = The Dogbane Family

APOCYNUM (ap-OSS-in-um)

androsaemifolium   3′–4′   Zone 3   Spreading Dogbane
A perennial herb with rather wide-spreading branches. The leaves are opposite, 2–3 in. long, dark green above and pale beneath. The flowers are pinkish, with a pink stripe in the center of each lobe and extending the length of the corolla. The plant prefers the edges of dry woods from Canada to Mexico and flowers throughout the summer. It may be propagated by seeds, which are borne in a slender podlike structure, known as a follicle, by division. It is not particularly desirable as a garden plant because of its somewhat awkward habit, and is a weed in many places.

cannabinum   8′   Zone 4   Hemp Dogbane or Indian Hemp
Native from Conn. to Kan., this has leaves up to 6 in. long and 3 in. wide. The stem has stringy bark, from whence comes the common name since the Indians did use it for a type of hemp. Flowers are greenish white. The roots have been used to give an emetic material.

APOMICTIC HYBRID. A hybrid which can be reproduced true to type from seed, which develops without fertilization.

APONOGETON (ap-o-no-JEE-ton)

distachyus aquatic Zone 10 Cape Pond Weed
A tuberous-rooted aquatic perennial herb, native to South Africa with long petioled leaves about 4 in. long, floating on the water surface. The extremely small flowers are white and fragrant, bearing 1–2 bracts underneath each flower. The plants should be planted in pots of good loam and these set in the water with the top about 8 in. under the water surface, preferably in full sun.

madagascariensis   aquatic plant   Zone 10   Lace Water-hawthorn
A very interesting aquatic perennial herb from Madagascar in that the leaves are merely an intricate network of veins. The leaves are about 9 in. long. The small white flowers are borne on a stalk about 12 in. long and often above the water. It grows best if planted in a pot of soil which is submerged in the sand at the base of the aquarium. A beautifully delicate aquarium

plant. The water should be at least 60°–70° F. for good growth. Easily propagated by division.

APOROCACTUS (ap-or-o-KAK-tus)

flagelliformis   vinelike   Zone 10   Rat-tail Cactus
An easily cultivated ornamental cactus frequently used in window gardens or window boxes with stems ½–1 in. dia., 10–12 ribs, crimson funnel-shaped flowers 3 in. long. Sometimes this is grafted on an upright cactus stem to show off its drooping qualities. Probably native to Mexico. Propagated by cuttings in sand. For culture see CACTI AND SUCCULENTS.

APOSTLE PLANT = *Neomarica northiana*

APPLE. Origin. There are many species of apples, but the one from which our present varieties have developed, *Malus pumila*, probably originated in southwestern Asia in the area located between the Caspian and the Black Seas. This fruit is grown and is of economic importance on all continents of the earth.

The apple was brought from Europe to North America by the early settlers. Later, the native Indians planted seeds and grew many trees. Seedling apple trees gradually spread across the country and into Canada.

Apple Growing in the United States

Apples are grown in almost all of continental U.S., but are of major importance in the northeast, central Atlantic, Ohio Basin, southwestern, north central and western states. Climate, of course, is the main factor determining the location of the commercial industry and likewise the use of this fruit in home garden plantings, while minimum winter temperatures set the boundaries of apple growing. In northern regions, temperatures from about 20°–30° below zero cause killing or weakening of buds and wood, but whether killing occurs at a given low temperature depends upon the preceding daily temperatures and the condition of the tree with respect to dormancy. In subtropical areas the reverse is true. Winter temperatures from Nov. to Feb. must average below 48° F. if the apple tree is to complete its rest period. Otherwise, growth is abnormal and fruit production negligible. An apple tree requires from 1000–1200 hours of 45° F. or below temperatures to complete its rest period.

The Apple Tree

To grow the apple tree properly and productively, one should understand how the tree functions. During the first few years the newly planted tree is considered in the juvenile stage and strong vegetative growth is made, with little if any fruit production. Terminal growth may be as much as 4 ft. in 1 year. Usually during the third year blossoming begins and some fruit is produced. Vegetative growth is somewhat less than during the first 2 years and decreases still further during succeeding years as the tree enters its adult life. Terminal growth should be 6–12 in. long annually on the bearing tree as an indication of proper vigor. Fruit buds develop on spurs (short shoots) on wood that is at least 2 years old. A lesser number of fruit buds develop on terminal 1-year shoots and in some years a portion of the crop may be produced on terminal growth.

The tree makes most of its vegetative growth during bloom and 6–8 weeks after bloom. Following this period of rapid vegetative growth fruit buds for the next year begin to differentiate in the spurs and terminal shoots.

The tree enters its dormant period when all leaves have fallen and remains in this condition until a sufficient number of cold hours have been accumulated. After this rest period is completed, the tree can respond to periods of warm weather with growth activity in cambium cells in the trunk and lower portion of the main limbs. Injury can occur when a sudden temperature drop follows a prolonged warm period.

General Culture

The small-sized apple tree is best suited to the home garden for obvious reasons. It does not require so much space as the standard, large-sized tree, and space is often at a premium. All cultural procedures such as spraying, pruning thinning and harvesting are more easily accomplished with the smaller tree.

Size Control by Rootstocks

The ultimate size of the apple tree is determined in large measure by the rootstock. Several rootstocks are available from nurseries today. The fully dwarf tree is one on the 'East Malling IX' rootstock. These trees usually do not grow taller than 6 ft., and they require support of some kind, such as a trellis or stake. They will not stand without support with a crop of fruit because of their small root system. The next larger tree is one on the 'EM 26' rootstock. It attains a height of about 8 ft. and also should have the support of a stake. 'East Malling VII' and 'Malling-Merton 106' are rootstocks that produce trees of about $\frac{1}{2}$ to $\frac{2}{3}$ standard size, or about 10 ft. tall. Trees on 'EM VII' should have a stake for support, but those on 'MM 106' may not require support. The Malling-Merton series of rootstocks are a more recent development than the EM series, so less information is available. The MM series holds considerable promise, since they are resistant to woolly aphis attacks on the roots and suckering from the

roots is less of a problem than with 'EM VII', for example. Trees on 'EM II' and 'MM 111' are next in size, growing to about $\frac{3}{4}$ standard size or 12 ft. tall, and do not require support. The 'MM 104' rootstock produces a tree that grows to only slightly under the standard, so it would not be so desirable as the others mentioned for the home garden, but most will not tolerate growing under wet soil conditions and so are not very popular. In addition, the variety determines to some extent the tree size on the various rootstocks, and also pruning is a very important factor in size control.

Spur-Type Tree

During recent years considerable effort has been directed toward the discovery and development of "spur-type" apple trees. A spur-type tree produces less terminal growth than the regular type, with shorter nodes and more leaves per given length of growth. Fruit spurs develop in great numbers on wood that is 2 years old or older and the spur-type tree usually begins to produce fruit earlier in its life than the regular type. These spur trees grow to about $\frac{3}{4}$ the standard size, even when grafted on standard seedling roots, and are smaller still when grafted on the size-control rootstocks.

Spur trees are excellent for the home garden since they are more dense in growth and quite productive. There are several varieties of 'Red Delicious' that are spur-type. No doubt there will be more in the future, but a few of those now available are 'Redspur', 'Wellspur,' 'Stark-crimson' and 'Millerspur'. Several 'Golden Delicious' and a few other varieties also have spur-types now available. More will be found because there is considerable interest in this type of tree today. The spur-type of growth is believed to be a natural mutation occurring among nursery and seedling trees.

Planting

Apple trees may be planted in the fall before the soil freezes, but spring planting is generally preferred. The trees should be dormant when planted. Dig a hole large enough to accommodate the entire root system without crowding. It should be deep enough to allow the tree to be set at the same depth it grew in the nursery, or 1–2 in. deeper. While digging, keep the topsoil separate from the subsoil. Place some of the topsoil in the bottom of the hole and spread the roots over it. Then sift more topsoil around the roots. If rotted manure or compost is available, mix it with equal parts of topsoil and fill the hole with the mixture. If the soil is extremely acid, mix 1–2 lbs. of limestone in the hole.

Interstem Trees

Interstem trees are becoming more popular and are comprised of 3 parts—the root, dwarfing stem piece and variety. Most interstem trees are on seedling, MM106 or MM111 roots with M9 or M26 as the interstem piece. Interstem trees are produced so as to provide better rooting but are not as dwarfed as when grown on the dwarfing rootstock, M9 or M26. The dwarfing interstem should be at least 6″ in length; 9″ is better. Spur varieties are also produced on interstem trees. Plant spacing should be increased by about 4 ft. for the interstem tree as compared to the same variety on the dwarfing root. For example, standard trees on M9 roots at 8 x 14 ft. would be planted 12 x 18 ft. with an MM106 root and M9 stem piece.

Spacing and Sunshine

The distance between trees varies depending upon the rootstock used, standard vs spur varieties and soil fertility. Standard varieties on M9 can be planted 6 to 8 ft. apart. Those on M26 require about 10 ft. Trees on MM106 and M7 need about 15 ft. in the row and 20 to 22 ft. between rows. Trees on MM111 need about 2 or 3 ft. more room than MM111 and M7 in both directions.

Spur varieties grow smaller than standard on any rootstock so they can be planted about 2 ft. closer in the row. Sunshine is most essential to good growth and production.

Variety Selection

The apple varieties of major importance today are selections from seedling trees grown nearly a century ago. For example, 'McIntosh' originated in Ontario about 1870 and 'Delicious', found in Ia., dates back to 1895. 'Stayman' came from a seed of a 'Winesap' apple in Kans. in 1866. 'Golden Delicious' originated in W.Va. and, although the tree was dead, it was still standing in 1960. These and many more are well-known varieties that came from seedling trees and were propagated in large numbers and distributed all over the country. Other "seedling" varieties include 'Jonathan', 'Wealthy' and 'Rome Beauty'. Many of the old favorites such as 'Grimes Golden', 'Baldwin' and 'Northern Spy' are disappearing from the catalogues.

Research workers conducting controlled apple breeding at agricultural colleges have introduced a few varieties including 'Macoun', 'Cortland', 'Spartan', 'Puritan' and many more of more recent development.

New varieties also appear as natural mutations or sports. Usually they are selected because of high color and resemble the parent variety in all other respects. For example, in 1925 a limb mutation appeared in N.J. on a 'Delicious' tree producing more highly colored red apples. This was the first such mutation to become nationally and world famous. This new "variety" was named 'Starking Delicious'. Another red 'Delicious' mutation was found later and named 'Richared Delicious'. During the period from about 1950 to 1960 at least 25 red sports of 'Starking' and 'Richared' appeared in various locations of the country and especially in the Northwest. Many varieties are being grown. The N.J. Exp. Sta. lists 92; N.Y. lists 74. Some of the older vars. where originated and when introduced are: 'Red Astrachan'—Russia, 1820; 'Gravenstein'—Italy, 1600s; 'Rhode Island Greening'—R.I., 1650; 'Twenty Ounce'—N.Y., before 1840; 'Cox Orange'—England, 1850s; 'Winter Banana'—Indiana, 1800s; 'Baldwin'— Mass., 1780; 'Northern Spy'—N.Y., 1840; 'Granny Smith'—Australia, 1950.

When choosing apple trees to be grown in the home garden, it is well to know something of the varietal characteristics, since apples differ considerably in dessert quality, flavor and use. Furthermore, certain varieties need to be cross-pollinated in order to set fruit. 'Delicious' is a sweet apple, as is 'McIntosh', and they are excellent when eaten fresh. 'Stayman', 'Rome' and 'Golden Delicious' are good in pies. 'Jonathan' makes excellent sauce, as well as a fresh dessert apple.

Pollination and Fruit Production

Though apple varieties are considered self-unfruitful, the varieties 'Golden Delicious' and 'Rome Beauty' are quite self-fruitful, whereas 'Red Delicious' is one of the least self-fruitful. It is essential, therefore, that several varieties be grown so as to insure the necessary cross-pollination. There are a few varieties that produce sterile or unsatisfactory pollen. These include 'Gravenstein', 'Stayman', 'Winesap', 'Rhode Island Greening' and a few others of less importance. Some of those with satisfactory pollen include 'Delicious', 'Grimes Golden', 'Jonathan', 'McIntosh', 'Golden Delicious' and 'Rome Beauty'. In general, all varieties with satisfactory pollen are pollinators for each other. On the other hand, it is interesting to note that 'Red Delicious' provides pollen for 'Stayman' but 'Stayman' does not provide pollen for 'Red Delicious'. One must provide for cross-pollination in the selection of varieties.

Fruit production is sometimes impossible and often difficult to obtain. Blossoming must come first before any fruit can be produced and a tree that is growing too vigorously will produce few and often no blossoms. Such a tree must receive special treatment to reduce its growth. If fertilizer is being applied generously, it should be reduced or eliminated for several years, since excessive amounts of fertilizer, especially of nitrogen, is not conducive to blossoming and fruit set. Also, a vigorously growing tree may be "scored" or "girdled" to encourage blossoming. Scoring consists of cutting through the bark of the trunk to the wood with a sharp knife. A spiral cut may be made, circling the trunk about twice. Another method is to cut two rings around the trunk about 2 in. apart. For those who can be especially careful, a thin band of bark $\frac{1}{8}$ in. wide may be removed from around the trunk. A wider band could kill the tree, so this must be done carefully. It is best to paint over the scoring wounds with tree paint to reduce the possibility of disease infection. Scoring must be done about 2 weeks after full bloom for best results. This causes an accumulation of carbohydrates and promotes fruit-bud formation for the following year. Blossoming is also encouraged by bending upright limbs and tying them in a horizontal position.

A tree in a very weakened condition from lack of sufficient fertilizer, drought, rodent damage, etc., will usually blossom profusely, but may or may not set fruit. The blossoms may be small and weak and most of the flowers and tiny applies will fall. In this case, the vigor of the tree must be improved before heavy fruit production can occur.

Once blossoming has begun, fruit setting and production will follow providing proper cross-pollination is available and tree vigor is maintained at the desired level.

Weed Control

Good culture includes weed control around the base of the tree. It is advisable to keep a small area beneath the tree cultivated and free from weeds and grass. This is especially true for young trees. Weed control is also an excellent supplement to mouse control.

Irrigation

Although apple trees can withstand long periods of drought, growth and production is best if water is provided during prolonged dry periods. An excellent method of irrigating a tree is to place a hose near its base and let water trickle into the soil for several hours. A depression around the base of the tree aids in a thorough irrigation with no loss of water.

Fruit Thinning

In most years apple trees set too many fruits. The amount of bloom on the tree is often ten times or more the number required to produce a full crop of fruit. A large number of the blossoms are not fertilized (pollinated) and they drop soon after petal fall. Many flowers are fertilized but fall about one month after bloom because the tree is unable to supply all of the fruits with enough water and nutrients. Those fruits that remain after the natural drop are often too great in number to grow to large size and best dessert quality; therefore, some of them must be removed by hand.

Apples should be thinned to single fruits when they occur as doubles and triples. Further thinning should include spacing the fruits 6–8 in. apart if the set is heavy. Thinning of fruit is not necessary every year, and often only scattered limbs on the tree require removal of excess fruit.

Thinning can be accomplished partially with sprays of napthalene acetic acid (NAA) or Sevin, an insecticide. Thoroughly spray the tree with NAA or Sevin at the proper concentration for a given variety at about 14 days after full bloom. Exact instructions are available from the state agricultural experiment stations. Chemical thinning results in early removal of excess apples and a better bloom the following year. It has been especially valuable for those varieties that tend to be biennial in production, such as 'Golden Delicious', 'Grimes Golden' and 'York'. Additional hand thinning is usually required to complete the job properly.

Pruning and Training

During the first 2–3 years the young apple tree should be pruned carefully to develop a satisfactory framework of branches. A few of the branches selected during the early years will be retained for the life of the tree.

One-year apple trees from the nursery are usually unbranched, straight, 4–5-ft. whips. Prune these trees to a height of about $3\frac{1}{2}$–4 ft. This promotes development of side branches.

Two-year nursery trees often have many side branches. Prune these trees at planting time to a central leader and cut back side branches to about half their original length. Remove broken branches and those that form an angle of less than 45° with the main trunk. Remove all small side branches less than 24 in. from the ground. If branches below the 24-in. level are large, prune them to 6-in. stubs; let the stubs remain for 1 year before removing them. Retain all satisfactory growth.

Keep the pruning to a minimum during the early years. Production is greater on young trees that are pruned lightly. Often at the top of an apple tree a "V" is formed after the second or third season, though sometimes a young nursery tree will develop top branches in this form. Remove half of the "V", retaining the stronger of the two limbs. This is an important pruning cut that is often overlooked.

Pruning during the third, fourth and fifth years should be mainly corrective, and such that will help produce a strong framework of branches. A tree that is neglected during the first few years often needs severe corrective pruning to overcome a very weak framework.

Production often begins with a few fruits the third year and may be more than a bushel per tree by the fifth season. From the fifth through the twelfth year, the main scaffold limb selection is completed. Three, 4, or 5 limbs spaced around the central leader will eventually become main scaffold limbs. Excess limbs are removed, one each year, from the main trunk after the tree becomes 5 years old. Limb breakage may alter the selection of these main scaffold branches.

As the tree produces heavy crops of fruit, the limbs bend down and never quite return to their original upright or horizontal position after the fruit is removed. The central leader often bends over in the top of the tree and becomes one of the main scaffold branches. This is desirable because the height of the tree will be somewhat reduced. If the leader does not bend, prune it to a strong side branch that will eventually balance the tree.

While pruning, keep in mind that the top of the tree must be kept more or less pointed so that the tree resembles a pyramid. A tree with a wide base and a pointed top is the most productive and most desirable since it receives the maximum amount of sunlight on leaves and fruit and has lower limbs that remain vigorous and productive.

Do not permit an apple tree to grow into an umbrella. Such a tree will eventually lose its lower limbs because of shading and the tree will never produce the amount of fruit it should.

Proper pruning will help young wood to grow in a horizontal or upright position throughout the tree. Wood growing in a "down" position on bearing trees is neither strong nor productive. Remove this down-growing wood at a point where the limb is growing in a horizontal or upright position. This is a constant procedure as the tree bears fruit and the limbs bend down.

Young, non-bearing trees are brought into earlier production by this bending down of young wood. Consequently, it should not be removed at this stage. On bearing trees, however, this down-growing wood which forms more than a 120° angle with the trunk must be removed or the tree will eventually have too much of this type of growth. Make every effort to keep a good supply of young, vigorous wood in the tree.

Training young trees includes spreading the limbs by various means and tying them down to a horizontal position in order to widen the angles and to encourage early fruit bud forma-

tion. Spreading the limbs out is especially beneficial with the upright-growing, spur-type trees.

Special Pruning for Dwarf Trees

Dwarf trees are frequently grown on a trellis, wall or fence. When they are grown in this manner, the pruning must be modified slightly. The term used for this type of pruning is espalier, which indicates that the tree is trained in a flat manner against a wall or trellis. Espaliered trees, already trained, are available from some nurseries. During the first few years the pruning is rather severe as the main framework branches are trained into position. After the third season, fruit production will begin. Thereafter, pruning is less severe. Removal of sucker growth and the maintenance of the desired form are usually the only pruning jobs necessary after production begins.

Soil and Fertilization

Apple trees grow well in a loam or sandy loam soil, but soils that are mainly coarse sand or gravel are excessively dry and not satisfactory. Also, soils that become waterlogged after heavy rains are not satisfactory and should be avoided.

Apple trees grow best in soils that are only slightly acid. If necessary, lime should be applied to raise the pH to 6.0–6.5. Soils along the eastern seaboard are naturally acid and require lime, whereas the soils in Colo., Utah, Ia. and the Pacific states are alkaline, with a pH above 7.0 and so of course no lime is needed.

An annual application of nitrogen is usually necessary to maintain vigor and production. Other essential nutrients are often required and these mainly include potassium, magnesium, boron and zinc. These can be supplied in the fertilizer mixture applied to the soil but for quick response to correct a deficiency, a spray should be applied. For example, zinc sprays are common in the Northwest and boron is often applied as a spray. Nitrogen in the form of urea is effective as a spray to the foliage of the apple tree. Soil and leaf analyses are aids in determining fertilizer needs, but about $\frac{1}{10}$ lb. of actual nitrogen for each year of age, not to exceed $\frac{1}{2}$ lb. in total for dwarf trees, will usually result in good vigor. Trees that are $\frac{2}{3}$ or $\frac{3}{4}$ standard size can use up to 1 lb. of nitrogen when at full production. A so-called complete fertilizer containing nitrogen, phosphorus and potassium may be used as the basic application, or a nitrogenous fertilizer such as ammonium nitrate may be used. Sandy soils and heavy rainfall may necessitate a supplement of nitrogen about a month after bloom.

Rodent Control

Mice and rabbits can cause much damage to the roots and trunk of an apple tree. Keep the soil around the trunk cultivated and free of grass and weeds. It is most important that this be done in the fall to reduce damage during the winter, but damage can occur during the summer also. In addition to the clean area around the trunk, a guard of $\frac{1}{4}$ in.-mesh hardware cloth around the trunk will aid considerably. This guard should be 18–24 in. tall and it is best to place it a few inches below the soil. There should be about 1 in. of space between guard and tree trunk. Make it large enough to permit edges to overlap and hook together. Another excellent protective material is aluminum foil. Wrap it around the trunk and crimp it over at the ends in the way described for the wire guard. Aluminum foil will last for 2 years in some cases, but usually must be replaced each year.

Harvesting and Storage

A little experience is required in determining the proper time to harvest a given variety. Unless one has had some experience, the best indicators are the color of the skin of the fruit, the color and taste of the flesh and fruit drop. Red color increases as the apple approaches maturity. The flesh changes from green to whitish green and from a starchy to a sweet

Apple-picker

taste. 'Golden Delicious' and 'Grimes Golden' will gradually change from green to yellowish green as they approach maturity. As a few fruits begin to drop, one should check for signs of maturity. Not all apples mature at the same time and the crop must be harvested over a period of about a week or 10 days. When the crop on a tree is light, the fruit is usually larger and matures a little earlier than when the crop is heavy and the fruit medium to small.

Apples continue to ripen after they are off the tree and the ripening process is rapid at high temperatures. Respiration, or ripening, is reduced considerably at low temperatures. Apples should be stored at a temperature of 30°–32° F. with relative humidity at 85–90% for maximum holding. Fruit held at 36° F. will be completely ripened and at the end of their storage life within 4 months after harvest. Apples held at 32° F. will last for 7 months, and at 30° F. an additional $1\frac{1}{2}$ months can be obtained in the life of the fruit. However, one overripe apple in a bag will cause more rapid ripening of other apples in that bag, so it is best to remove any overripe fruit and use it rather than to attempt to store it.

The harvest of several bushels of apples from trees in the home garden presents a problem, since storage at 32° F. is not usually available. Apples will hold in good condition for about one month in the home refrigerator maintained at about 40° F.

ERNEST G. CHRIST

Insect Pests

There is no place in the United States where a reasonably profitable crop of the modern varieties of apple can be grown for several successive seasons without protection from destructive insect and disease pests. Many home gardeners are convinced that it is more desirable to buy their supply of fruit than to grow it. Commercial apple growers apply 10 or more sprays or dusts, using 8 or more different pesticides costing about 50% of all growing expense, in order to insure a profitable crop. In the home orchard apples need 4–8 treatments of a general purpose spray or dust mixture for fruit (insecticide #46) thoroughly applied at timely intervals in order to harvest a reasonable crop of usable fruit. All apple growers should secure from local agricultural agencies a pest-control schedule for apple in their area. The home gardener may be successful with the following schedule

1. Before buds open but after freezing weather—Dormant oil spray—Insecticide #44
2. When buds break and weekly until bloom—General Purpose Mixture #46
3. Do not spray in bloom
4. When 90% of blossom petals have fallen—General Purpose Mixture #46
5. Repeat at intervals 1, 2, 4, 6 and 8 weeks

after using General Purpose Mixture #46.

Forty-five destructive insect pests, of which 10 damage the fruit, 25 infest the foliage and 10 live on the bark and bore in the wood, are recognized pests of the apple tree and fruit. Codling moth, the larva of which is white with a brown head and tunnels through the flesh to the core, has 2–3 annual generations in the warmer areas and 1–2 in the North. Spraying in a regular schedule with insecticides #9, #37 or #46 gives control.

Fruit-tree leafroller and red-banded leafroller eat the skin of the fruit as well as the rolled leaves, and the second generation of the latter is often very destructive unless insecticide #4 or #14 is used. Apple redbug and tarnished plant bug pierce the young fruit, causing dimples, pits and scars on mature apples. Insecticide #9, #15 or #14 is used to combat heavy infestations. Plum curculio and apple curculio are snout beetles which feed and lay eggs in the small fruit. The grubs feed in the flesh and cause the apple to fall prematurely or to be marked with round or fan-shaped russet scars at maturity. Spraying on warm days when the young apples are $\frac{1}{4}$–$\frac{1}{2}$ in. in dia. with insecticide #13, #15 or #9 gives control.

Apple maggot or railroad worm, so named because the maggot eats railroadlike tunnels through the flesh, is a very serious pest in cooler areas and the most discouraging for the amateur to combat. The female fly lays eggs in the flesh of nearly mature fruit and the maggots live in the apple. Spraying or dusting in mid- and late summer with insecticide #37 or #15, together with the destruction of all infected apples, is recommended. In the northeastern U.S. the European apple sawfly lays eggs in the blossoms, and the larva feeds just beneath the skin of the apple, leaving conspicuous russet trails which deform the fruit. Spraying just before and just after bloom with insecticide #13, #15 or #14 is advised.

The foliage is eaten by tent caterpillars, cankerworms and gypsy moth caterpillars in the spring, and leafminers crumple the leaves badly unless the regular spray program is applied. White apple leaf hoppers stipple the leaves, and the apple leaf curling midge may curl newly opened leaves and stunt growth especially on nursery stock. Blister mites attack apple leaves. See PEAR. Green apple aphid, rosy apple aphid and woolly apple aphid often become so abundant that spraying with insecticide #15 is necessary. See APHIDS. The feeding of European red mite, 2-spotted mite and clover mite gives the leaves a bronze color and reduces the quality of the fruit and the vigor of the trees. See MITES. Special miticides such as #34,

#35 and #36 are recommended. Apple trees are a favorite host for round-headed and flat-headed apple tree borers and the leopard moth which may kill small trees, cause small and medium-sized branches to break and hasten trunk decay. See BORERS. San Jose scale and oystershell scale have killed many apple trees which were unprotected by dormant sprays of insecticide #44 and other control programs.

Diseases

The importance of apple diseases varies with the environment and the variety. Except in the drier areas of the West, apple scab is the most serious disease of 'McIntosh', 'Cortland' and 'Delicious' apples and several applications of fungicide #W, #F, #D, #X or #Z are necessary for control. Established infections in early summer can be burned out with fungicide #M. 'Powdery' mildew is more destructive in the drier areas and the buds, leaves and fruit of 'Cortland', 'Rome Beauty', 'Baldwin' and 'Jonathan' are very susceptible. Fungicide #V and #M are most effective. See POWDERY MILDEW.

Apple-cedar rust causes brown or orange spots on the leaves and swelling on the fruit. Redcedar (*Juniperus*) is an alternate host and should be destroyed or sprayed when near apple or crabapple. Spraying apples just before and just after bloom with fungicide #D or #F gives control. Fireblight may suddenly turn leaves black and kill branches. Infected twigs should be cut and burned promptly. See FIRE-BLIGHT. Timely spraying with fungicide #B or other antibiotics is helpful. Bark cankers should be cut out and the wounds disinfected. Other diseases such as bitter rot, black rot and sooty blotch are troublesome occasionally.

Physiological diseases are often troublesome. Baldwin spot or Stippen causes sunken brown spots in the skin and flesh of apples when they are exposed to water loss by excessive transpiration after they are about $\frac{2}{3}$ grown. Water core which occurs as a watersoaked condition of the flesh is another result of unfavorable moisture conditions. Hail from summer thunder storms and pesticide injury from improper spray mixtures are often mistaken for insect or disease injury. Apples in storage may become brown and soft, resembling rot, but no disease is involved. Storage scale results from unfavorable storage conditions. 'Cortland' apples are very susceptible, but 'McIntosh' only slightly. A few chemicals have shown promise experimentally in preventing scale and local authorities should be consulted.

APPLE-OF-PERU = *Nicandra physalodes*

APPRESSED. Lying flat and close against.

APRICOT. Apricots stem from three species—
Prunus armeniaca native to western Asia and
P. mandshurica, native to Korea and Manchuria.
A third, *P. sibirica*, has also been used in
breeding to produce hardy varieties for northern
gardens. Varieties were brought over to this
country by some of the earlier Virginia settlers,
but the major apricot-growing area is now
located in Calif., with a few being grown in
Wash. and elsewhere on the Pacific Coast. These
fruits are dried, canned and sold on the fresh
market, but fresh fruits do not carry too well
nor last too long, the reason why fresh fruits
are not found frequently in eastern markets.

The commercial varieties most popular in
Calif. are **'Royal'**, **'Patterson'**, **'Tilton'** and
'Moorpark', but these are only grown on the
West Coast; they are not grown in the East
because they bloom so early the flowers or flower
buds are frequently susceptible to injury from
spring frosts. These are closely related to the
more tender species *P. armeniaca*.

In the East, other varieties have been developed from the hardy *P. sibirica*, or possibly *P.
mandshurica*, and although the fruits of these
varieties are not as large nor as sweet as those
varieties related to *P. armeniaca* grown on the
West Coast, nevertheless they make fair garden
fruit trees of merit for those who wish to grow
them in colder sections of the country.

Most varieties except **'Perfection'** and **'Riland'**
are self-fruitful.

Propagation is by budding, and Apricot,
Peach and Myrobolan Plum are used as understocks for named apricot varieties. Each has its
special purposes, but when in doubt it is always
best to bud on apricot understock.

Apricots need no special soil but should be
well supplied with organic matter and should
have adequate moisture. Trees should grow
15–30 in. annually. They may require less
nitrogen than peaches. They can be planted
about 20–30 ft. apart. Young trees just planted
are headed back to about 2½ ft.

Much of the crop is borne on fruit spurs, and
regular pruning is needed to keep these renewed.
Although the tree is sometimes allowed to grow
in a vase-shaped fashion, usually the main
leader-type tree is best, so in pruning this leader
should be allowed dominance, and all lateral
shoots cut back slightly to allow this to develop
properly.

Large amounts of apricots are dried, in Calif.
and in other areas with hot sun during the
summer. This entails cutting the fruit in halves,
removing the "pit" or seed, laying the halves in
trays with the cut side up, treating them to the
fumes of burning sulfur for 2–6 hours, then
drying in the sun for 1–3 days. After that the
trays are stacked, still left in the open for a
week to 10 days when they should be ready for
packaging. It is of interest to note that 6 lbs. of
fresh fruit must be dried to yield one pound of
dried fruit.

Varieties

'Royal', **'Blenheim'**—almost identical, the
former is an old French variety, the latter
originated in England. These make up the
backbone of the Calif. apricot industry.

'Tilton'—this is not as popular, is mostly
dried, and is rather difficult at times because it
does not bear well annually.

'Moorpark'—excellent as fresh fruit, not as
good as 'Royal' and 'Blenheim' for drying and
canning.

'Riland' and **'Perfection'** (the only varieties
not self-fruitful) are being tried in Wash. with
good results.

There are of course other varieties being
grown, but these are the most important
commercial sorts.

Of the hardier varieties, for gardeners in
colder climates, the following are being grown,
some of which originated at the New York
Experimental Station, Geneva, N.Y., some at
various Canadian agric. exp. stations.

'Harcot'—heavily fruited, disease resistant,
ripens about July 20 at Geneva, N.Y.

Scout'—fruit ripens in early August, developed at Morden, Manitoba, in 1937.

'Sundrop'—moderately productive, rather
attractive of fair quality, hardy, not self-fertile,
ripens about July 26 at Geneva, N.Y.

'NY 544'—hardy, ripens August 1 at Geneva,
N.Y., good quality.

The South Dakota Agric. Exp. Station has
developed several varieties suitable for growing
in the Great Plains area. For pest control of
apricot, see PEACH.

APTENIA (ap-TEE-nia)
    cordifolia   1´   **Zone 9**
A rank-growing succulent perennial used in
sunny or shady areas in southern Calif. as a
ground cover, or in northern window gardens
indoors. This bears flat opposite leaves an inch
long; purple flowers about ½ in. across.
'Variegata' has leaves with cream-colored
margins. Native to South Africa.

AQUARIUM. The horticultural aspects of an
aquarium become fascinating the more one
studies the planting of one. There are so many
mechanical aids for maintaining a good
aquarium that, as long as the electric supply is
maintained, good growth of small water plants
in an aquarium indoors can be assured. Plants
afford the home owner an opportunity of
creating an interesting picture with proper
design, and the continued growth of aquarium

plants offers a challenge for learning the proper cultural methods to keep the plants in good condition.

A tight aquarium of the proper size is necessary. We have found that one 25 gal. capacity was suitable—for if it is to be a permanent fixture in the house it should be large enough for proper display of a varied number of plants and fish. Special automatic heaters, aerators, light tubes (see INDOOR GARDENING)

A well-planted and well-illuminated aquarium can be of continual interest in the home.

are all available and their coordinated use can produce an aquarium needing practically no attention whatsoever except feeding the fish therein. Fish and plants go together. The plants give off oxygen required by the fish. In a dimly lighted aquarium, or one with insufficient plants, the fish are often at the surface of the water gulping air in an attempt to get sufficient oxygen. In a well-balanced aquarium this does not occur. The fish give off carbon dioxide which is used by the growing plants. They also expel certain food residues that fall to the sand at the bottom and serve as a food material absorbed by the plant roots and are utilized by the plant in their growth.

When there are too many plants, or too much sunshine so the plants are overly active and give off an excess of oxygen, then a green algae forms on the glass as a result. On the other hand, when there are too many fish or not enough sunlight the plants turn brownish and give off insufficient oxygen.

A "balanced" aquarium, then, is one in which the number of plants and fish, as well as the amount of light are in a delicate balance and both fish and plants grow well. Too much refuse at the base of the tank can be manually removed, or one can include snails and scavengers like

the small South American Catfish, which aid in removing this material. Temperature too is an important item but the plants can withstand wider variations in this factor than the fish.

Clean, thoroughly washed sand of medium texture is placed in the bottom of the aquarium, filled three-quarters full of water which contains no chlorine (if it is heavily chlorinated it should be allowed to stand in a pan exposed to the air several days before any fish are added) and then it is ready to plant. Usually, it will be observed from one side only, but if other sides are to be viewed that should be considered in the planting plan. Certainly plants would be set close together along the back to afford a green background. Then in the foreground plants of varying texture, size and shape would be used for creating interest. Objects like shells or a bright colored rock or coral piece can also be properly placed to create interest, the same as one might do in any outdoor garden.

Usually the plant roots are merely inserted in the sand. They can be expected to grow normally this way. However, if some special plant is to be used it can be planted in a small (2-in.) clay pot $\frac{3}{4}$ filled with soil to which a little dried blood has been added as a fertilizer, and then the top $\frac{1}{2}$ inch covered with sand and the entire pot sunk and covered in the sand at the base of the aquarium.

Only one point on culture need be mentioned as far as the plants are concerned. If a green scum grows on the side of the glass, this is an indication of too much light. These plants need only an equivalent of 2 hours of sunshine per day, but this can be supplied in a window where no direct sunshine is admitted, or the aquarium can be recessed in a wall or on a table where there is no direct light from outside and all the light supplied is by the fluorescent electric tube. If too much sunlight reaches the aquarium, place a cloth or piece of paper on the sunny side to filter down the light. If too much electric light, cut down the size of the tube or do not allow so many hours of lighting. If the plant or the water turn slightly brownish, the chances are that the plants are not getting enough light. A little thoughtful experimentation with the right amount of light and the water conditions can be perfectly adjusted.

Temperature will depend on that necessary for the fish but as far as the plants are concerned any temperature from 60°–80° F. should be satisfactory.

Since aquariums have been popular indoors for a century, many plants have been tried. As in gardens out-of-doors, at first it was only native American plants that were used, but now with electric thermostatic temperature controls all sorts of delicate tropical plants can be tried by the water garden enthusiast. The following are some of the best:

Five of the easiest aquarium plants to grow and some of the best ones for producing oxygen are:

Anacharis canadensis—Elodea—an excellent oxygenator

Cabomba caroliniana—Carolina Fanwort—threadlike leaves

Myriophyllum proserpinacoides—Chile Parrotfeather—threadlike leaves

Sagittaria sp.—Arrowheads—linear leaves

Vallisneria spiralis—Eel Grass—linear leaves

Some aquatic plants that float on the water surface and are of value in the home aquarium for this purpose are:

Azolla caroliniana—Azolla

Ceratopteris pteridoides—Water-fern

Eichhornia crassipes—Water-hyacinth

Lemna minor—Duckweed

Pistia stratiotes—Water-lettuce

Riccia fluitans—Common Riccia

Salvinia auriculata—Salvinia

Broad-leaved water plants for the home aquarium:

Aponogeton fenestralis—Lace Water-hawthorn—lacey leaves

Bacopa caroliniana—rounded leaves

Cardamine pratensis—Cuckoo Bittercress—rounded leaves

Cryptocoryne sp.—Cryptocoryne—leaves lance shaped

Echinodorus sp.—Sword plants

Eleocharis tuberosa—Chinese Water-chestnut—leaves linear

Helxine soleirolii—Baby's-tears—leaves rounded and very small

Ludwigia natana—leaves broadly rounded, red underneath

Lysimachia nummularia—Moneywort—leaves rounded

Water plants with threadlike leaves for the home aquarium:

Ceratophyllum demersum—Hornwort

Nitella gracilis—Slender Nitella

For further information on aquariums, fish and plants for them, see the latest edition of "Exotic Aquarium Fishes" by Wm. T. Innes published by E. P. Dutton Inc., 201 Park Avenue, New York.

AQUATIC PLANTS. See WATER-LILIES

AQUIFOLIACEAE = The Holly Family

AQUILEGIA (ak-wil-EE-jia). The columbines are herbaceous perennials of great beauty and delicacy belonging to the Buttercup Family. There should be a place for a few of them in every perennial border. Species native to North America are fine and well suited to gardens, but the long-spurred hybrids are the ones frequently

sought out. Smaller species are best suited to the rock garden and the type of culture normally given plants there. They are propagated by seeds which might be sown in the greenhouse or hotbed in March and set out in the garden after danger of frost is past. These will bloom the following year. Columbines are valued for their dainty, spurred flowers of many colors, borne in May and June on conspicuous upright spikes. Unfortunately these have a habit of dying out over a period of years, so that it does not pay to "rejuvenate" old clumps, but rather to replace them every few years with new plants.

Insect Pests

Serpentine and blotch leaf miners often disfigure the leaves of columbine with their mines. Hand-picking or spraying with insecticides #9 or #15 when the mines are first seen holds them in check. Columbine aphid and the caterpillars of a skipper butterfly are occasional pests which insecticides #9 or #15 will control.

Diseases

Wilt disease may infect and kill the plants. Before growth starts in spring a drench of fungicide #F will check it.

akitensis = *A. flabellata alba*

alpina　1′　**Zones 2–3**　**Alpine Columbine**

With blue flowers 2 in. wide and incurved spurs, blooming during July and Aug. The leaves are large and 3 lobed. Native to Switzerland.

bertolonii　1′　**Zone 6**　**Alpinerock Columbine**

The small, grayish-green leaves, in mounds, and the violet-blue, inch-wide flowers, borne on stems 10 in. high and flowering in May and June, make this plant from the southern European mountains a very attractive one for the rock garden.

caerulea　1½′–3′　**Zones 2–3**　**Colorado Columbine**

A very popular species, native to the Rocky Mountains, with blue-purple or white flowers, 2 in. wide, during May and June. This is one of the parents of the popular long-spurred hybrids so often seen in gardens.

canadensis　1′–2′　**Zones 2–3**　**American Columbine**

Surely one of the daintiest and most attractive of the native wild flowers, the American Columbine is a perennial herb having compound leaves with numerous rounded and lobed leaflets. The flower stalk bears nodding flowers having yellow sepals and red spurs which are hollow, narrowing to a knob at the end. Numerous yellow stamens extend below the sepals. The plant ranges over New England to Ga. and Tenn., west to Wisc. It flowers from spring to midsummer. An ideal plant for the garden, it prefers sunny to semi-shaded locations and rather dry, sandy soil.

chrysantha   2½′–3′   **Zones 2–3**   **Golden Columbine**
Found in the Rocky Mountains from Colo. to Tex., this has yellowish, long-spurred flowers from May to July and is a parent of the popular group of long-spurred garden hybrids. The Colorado Columbine, *A. caerulea*, is the other parent. The flowers of *A. chrysantha* are sometimes 3 in. wide.

clematiflora   1½′–2′   **Zone 4**   **Clematis-flowered Columbine**
A peculiar type of columbine, probably originating in the garden and not known in the wild, this has very short spurs or none at all. The brightly colored flowers are usually blue or pink, 3 in. wide, and appear in May and June.

flabellata   1′–1½′   **Zones 2–3**   **Fan Columbine**
Native to Japan, this bears lilac to white flowers 2 in. wide during May and June. The variety 'Nana Alba' is only 8–12 in. tall and has pure white flowers. The variety **pumila** (syn. *A. akitensis*) is 6 in. tall with deep blue or purple flowers that are pale yellow inside.

formosa   3′   **Zones 2–3**   **Sitka Columbine**
Flowers red and yellow, 1½ in. wide, the spurs straight and red, flowering from May to Aug. Native to western North America and Siberia. Several varieties have been grown, including a dwarf and one with double flowers.

glandulosa   1′   **Zones 2–3**   **Altai Columbine**
Native to Siberia and blooming during May and June with blue or white flowers nearly 3 in. wide. This is more for the rock garden than the perennial border.

x hybrida   1½′–3′   **Zone 4**   **Short-spurred and Long-spurred Hybrids**
Many columbines of uncertain parentage are grouped here, all valued for their large flowers of many colors. Varieties like 'Crimson Star' with bright red flowers; 'Rose Queen', 'Silver Queen', and 'Snow Queen' as well as many hybrid groups are well worth trial in the perennial border.

jonesii   2″   **Zone 6**   **Jones Columbine**
Tufted and stemless, bearing a single blue or purple flower ½ in. long, native to Wyo. and Alberta and very difficult to grow.

longissima   2′–3′   **Zones 2–3**   **Long-spurred Columbine**
Native to Mexico, this blooms from July to Oct. and bears pale yellow flowers with spurs that may be as much as 5 in. long. The leaves are silky hairy and the plant does make a fine show in the perennial border.

saximontana   8″   **Zone 4**   **Rocky Mountain Columbine**
A tiny plant from the mountains of Utah, this

bears tiny bluish leaves that are slightly crinkled and blue and yellow flowers which appear in April. It does best in a coarse limestone soil, in sun or light shade.

scopulorum   8″   **Zone 4**
Another species from Utah, with requirements similar to those of *A. saximontana*, except that this plant needs full sun. The 3-lobed, glaucous leaves and pale blue flowers having long, slender spurs make the plant an excellent addition to the rock garden.

skinneri   2′–3′   **Zones 2–3**   **Skinner Columbine**
With fine red and yellow flowers about 1½ in. wide from May to July, this plant native to Mexico has flower spurs nearly 2 in. long.

vulgaris   1½′–2½′   **Zones 2–3**   **European Columbine**
A very popular columbine in Europe where it is native, as well as in American gardens. The flowers are blue, purple or white, appearing from May to July, and are 1½–2 in. wide. This has been grown for such a long time that there are many hybrids and garden forms of this species, some of which are said to have double flowers

ARABIDOPSIS (a-rab-i-DOP-sis)

thaliana   18″   **annual**   **Mouse-ear Cress**
A white-flowered herb or weed, native to Europe and naturalized in eastern and central North America. Basal leaves to 2½ in. long. Flowers white, ¼ in. across produced in terminal racemes. Fruits and pods ⅝ in. long.

ARABIAN-TEA = *Catha edulis*

ARABIS (AR-a-bis). Herbaceous perennials of the Mustard Family, low-growing and valued for their small flowers in the spring. Best used either in the rock garden or sometimes as edging plants, or in the front of the flower border. Propagation is by cuttings in June, seeds sown in spring, or most easily by dividing the plants in Sept.

alpina. This name is listed in many catalogues. Usually it is actually *A. albida*. The true *A. alpina* is not nearly so good an ornamental, bearing smaller flowers and less pubescent foliage. It should not be grown as a substitute for *A. albida* or one of its varieties.

androsacea   2½″   **Zone 6**
White woolly rosettes of leaves in tiny cushions, crowned with small clusters of white flowers held just above the leaves characterize this alpine of southern Europe which blooms in May. Somewhat difficult to grow, it requires a limestone scree in full sun.

aubretioides   6″   **Zone 4**
With pale pink flowers in May, native to Asia Minor. This foliage is tufted, the plant is low with very small leaves, becoming a popular plant for the rock garden. In order to grow well

this must be planted in the full sun in a rather dry situation.

blepharophylla   1′   Zone 6
These broad, dark green leaves, in flat rosettes, look well in the rock crevices of Calif. where it is native, though the plant will do well in any well-drained garden soil. The fragrant flowers, a striking rose-purple on 12-in. stems, appear in May.

carduchorum   2″   Zone 6
Closely growing mounds of shiny green leaves in rosettes and clusters of white flowers on 3-in. stems in April characterize this plant which is native to Armenia.

caucasica   6″-10″   Zone 3   Wall Rock-cress
With small white flowers ½ in. wide in early spring, borne in fragrant loose racemes. The leaves, 1–3 in. long, are soft, whitish pubescent, adding to the showiness of the plant. There are several varieties in the trade with double white or pink flowers and one with the leaves variegated by yellow stripes. Native to the Caucasus area and a good garden plant, especially desirable for its foliage. The double-flowered variety **'Flore Pleno'** is very definitely the form to grow since the flowers remain conspicuous for a much longer time than do those of the species.

drummondii   3′   biennial or perennial Zone 2
Another nice, small-flowered rock-cress that is very hardy. The leaves are 2½″ long, flowers pink or white and about a third of an inch long. Native from Quebec to the Pacific Coast.

ferdinandi-coburgi   6″   Zone 7
An interesting rock garden plant for those areas where snow does not obscure the garden in winter, for the rosettes of gray leaves become green in winter. The creamy white flowers appear in April. Plant in coarse, well-drained limestone soil in sun or light shade. Native to Greece.

x kellereri   2″   Zone 6   Kellerer Rock-cress
This hybrid (*A. bryoides x A. ferdinandi-coburgii*) needs a loose, coarse limestone soil in sun or light shade. The grayish leaves, in tiny rosettes, are dormant in winter. Clusters of small white flowers, on stems 2 in. high, appear in April.

lyrata   1′   Zone 6
Native to eastern U.S., this perennial may be found in rock crevices where it sends forth its green rosettes of lyre-shaped leaves and clusters of small white flowers on slender stems. It blooms in May and June. Plant in loose, well-drained limestone soil.

procurrens   1′   Zone 4
A stoloniferous native of southern Europe, this is easily grown in any type of soil and in either sun or light shade. It spreads quickly, forming a mat of shiny green leaves. The white flowers

bloom in April and May and are borne in elongated racemes.

sturii   8″   Zone 4
A compact growing plant offered by several nurseries and good as a ground cover for small places. It has fine white flowers.

ARACEAE = The Arum Family

ARACHIS (a-RAK-is)
hypogaea   procumbent annual   Peanut
Native to Brazil, the Peanut (which see) is widely grown commercially in the South, but, although it is an annual, it takes a long growing season for the peanuts to mature, the reason it is not grown much commercially north of Va. The flowers are yellow (it belongs to the Pea Family), produced in spikelike clusters and the fruits or peanuts are borne beneath the ground. The vines are injured by the lightest frost. There are 4 leaflets per leaf, each up to 2½ in. long. The peanut shells are frequently ground and used as mulching material. Also called Goober and Groundnut. See PEANUT.

ARALIA (a-RAIL-ia). Coarse, large-leaved herbs, shrubs or trees with alternate, pinnately compound leaves, small flowers in very large-terminal clusters, and small black fruits about ⅛ in. in dia. These are avidly eaten by birds. The plants are bold specimens, giving an almost sub-tropical effect in the garden, but they should be used with discretion because of their coarse character.

Propagation

Do not allow the seed to dry out in airtight containers in a dry place, but stratify at once as soon as ripe. Some of the seed is doubly dormant and should be stratified as soon as ripe, at room temperature for 3–5 months, then at 40° F. for 3 months, then sown.

Grafting and budding is possible on roots of the species, as well as propagation by root cuttings. See SEEDS, STRATIFICATION, GRAFTING, CUTTINGS, etc.

chinensis   24′   Zone 5   Chinese Angelica-tree
This small Chinese tree is very similar to the Japnese species, *A. elata*, except that its mature height is lower.

elata   45′   Zone 3   Japanese Angelica-tree
An exotic-looking plant from Japan, coarse in texture, with prickly stems and decidedly out of place in the small garden. The large, compound, alternate leaves are sometimes 2½ ft. long, and the small white flowers are borne in large terminal, pyramidal-shaped clusters in Aug. The fruits are small black berries, avidly eaten by the birds. The two varieties sometimes used in America are **'Variegata'**, with leaflets bordered in white, and **'Aureo-variegata'** with leaflets bordered in yellow.

hispida 3′ **Zone 3** **Bristly Aralia, Bristly Sarsaparilla**
A perennial herb native from Newfoundland to Minn. and N.Car. with bristly, compound, alternative leaves and small greenish flowers in umbels and black fruits. Occasionally grown in flower gardens for its flowers in June and July, but not especially outstanding. Best used in dry, sandy soils in the wild garden.

nudicaulis 12″–16″ **Zone 3** **Wild Sarsaparilla**
A perennial herb having compound leaves with oval or ovate, pointed leaflets. The small, greenish-yellow flowers are borne in a loose umbel at the terminal end of a flower stalk which rises from the roots and is somewhat shorter than that of the leaf stem. Each flower stalk may have several umbels. It grows in open woods over much of southern Canada and south and west to Ga. and Colo., flowering in late spring and early summer. Of some gardening interest since its aromatic roots may be used as a substitute for Sarsaparilla.

spinosa 24′ **Zone 5** **Devil's-walking-stick**
Native of the southeastern U.S., this is somewhat similar to *A. elata*, but there are no variegated varieties. It is sometimes difficult to tell the species apart, and although *A. elata* is more widely distributed in this country there is no reason why *A. spinosa* could not be used. Handling bark and roots of this has given some a dermatitis with blisters.

ARALIA, THREADLEAF FALSE = *Dizygotheca elegantissima*

ARALIACEAE = The Aralia Family

ARAMITE. An insecticide, which see.

ARAUCARIA (a-raw-KAY-ria)

araucana 90′ **Zone 7** **Monkey-puzzle-tree**
This is a strikingly peculiar evergreen tree from Chile with weird, twisted, whorled branches, open in habit and producing very little shade. The sharply pointed, scalelike leaves are evergreen, and this is the hardiest member of the genus. The ropelike branches twist in an ungainly fashion. Syn. *A. imbricaria* and still sold by some nurseries under this name.

bidwillii 80′–150′ **Zone 10** **Bunya-bunya**
Narrow in habit, the evergreen leaves are borne in two rows and are very sharp-pointed, thick and shining and about 1½ in. long, wider below the middle than at the top. This is often grown as a pot plant, but in the tropical parts of Fla. and Calif. it makes a fine specimen at maturity producing its distinct pineapplelike cones.

heterophylla (*excelsa*) 10′ **Zone 10** **Norfolk-Island-pine**
Another picturesque member of this genus from the Norfolk Islands, used only to give unusual effects in the warmest parts of the U.S., although it is widely grown in greenhouses as a foliage plant. It is pyramidal and open, with horizontal tiered branches producing poor shade. The scalelike, sharply pointed leaves are evergreen, and it rarely flowers and fruits. 'Gracilis' is a compact form suitable as a pot plant.

imbricaria = *A. araucana*

ARBOR. See GARDEN FIXTURES.

ARBOR DAY. Julius Sterling Morton (1832–1902) was the man who first implemented the idea of Arbor Day. He was born in N.Y. moved to Mich. where he attended the University of Michigan and finally moved to the Nebraska Territory in 1854. He became Secretary of that Territory in 1858 and later was Secretary of Agriculture under Grover Cleveland from 1893–1897. He was always interested in nature and anxious to promote tree planting on the treeless areas of the Great Plains.

He conceived the idea of setting aside one day each year for tree planting. This began inconspicuously with the State Board of Agriculture of Neb. offering prizes for the best orchard and planting of ornamental trees and the largest planting of timber trees. The first Arbor Day was celebrated in Neb. in 1872 when over 1,000,000 trees were planted.

Since that time, many other states followed Nebraska's lead in setting aside one day for tree planting, but, by 1915 the idea waned and continued to decline until the 1930's when a National Arbor Day Committee was formed in 1939. This committee has tried to sponsor legislation in each state to set aside the last Friday of April as the legal Arbor Day. Up to this time, 22 states have done this, but unofficially other states have their Arbor Days also. Thirteen other states have committees working at the moment for a legal date of the last Friday in April. At present, Arbor Day is observed in the following states on the following dates:

STATE	FIRST OBSERVED	NOW OBSERVED
Alabama	1887	Last week in Feb.
Alaska	1966	Third Monday in May
Arizona	1890	Friday after Feb. 1 (Fri. after April 1 in 5 counties)
Arkansas	1906	Third Monday in March

STATE	FIRST OBSERVED	NOW OBSERVED
California	1886	March 7–14
Colorado	1885	Third Friday in April
*Connecticut	1886	Last Friday in April
*Delaware	1901	Last Friday in April
Florida	1886	Third Friday in Jan.
Georgia	1887	Third Friday in Feb.
Hawaii	1905	First Friday in November
*Idaho	1886	Last Friday in April
*Illinois	1887	Last Friday in April
*Indiana	1884	Second Friday in April
*Iowa	1887	Last Friday in April
Kansas	1875	Last Friday in March
Kentucky	1886	First Friday in April
Louisiana	1888	Third Friday in Jan.
*Maine	1887	Third week in May
Maryland	1884	First Wednesday in April
*Massachusetts	1886	Last Friday in April
Michigan	1885	Third week in April
*Minnesota	1876	Last Friday in April
Mississippi	1890	Second Friday in Feb.
Missouri	1886	Friday after first Tuesday in April
*Montana	1888	Last Friday in April
Nebraska	1872	April 22—Legal Holiday
*Nevada	1887	Last Friday in April
*New Hampshire	1886	Last Friday in April
*New Jersey	1884	Last Friday in April
New Mexico	1890	Second Friday in March
*New York	1889	Last Friday in April
North Carolina	1893	First Friday after March 15
North Dakota	1882	Last Friday in April
*Ohio	1882	Last Friday in April
Oklahoma	1898	Friday after second Monday in Feb.
*Oregon	1889	Last Friday in April
*Pennsylvania	1885	Last Friday in April
*Rhode Island	1887	Last Friday in April
South Carolina	1898	First Friday in Dec.
*South Dakota	1884	Last Friday in April
Tennessee	1875	First Friday in March
Texas	1890	Third Friday in Jan.
*Utah	1925	Last Friday in April
Vermont	1885	First Friday in May
Virginia	1892	Second Friday in March
Washington	1894	Second Wednesday in April
*West Virginia	1883	Second Friday in April
*Wisconsin	1892	Last Friday in April
Wyoming	1888	Last Monday in April
District of Columbia	1920	Third Friday in April
Guam	......	Last Friday in Oct.
Puerto Rico	......	Friday after Thanksgiving

* States that have passed legislation designating the last Friday in April as Arbor Day.

For additional Arbor Day information you may contact the National Arbor Day Committee (640 Eagle Rock Ave., West Orange, New Jersey 07052), a non-profit organization which has been encouraging the observance of Arbor Day since 1941.

ARBORESCENT. Attaining the size or habit of a tree.

ARBORETUM OR BOTANICAL GARDEN, HOW TO ESTABLISH. Numerous requests are received from time to time by the principal arboretums and botanical gardens of the country for information concerning how to start an arboretum. Such inquiries clearly indicate that the arboretum idea is definitely being considered in widely separated parts of the country.

Professor Charles Sprague Sargent, first director of the Arnold Arboretum, long ago realized the need for arboretums or maintained plant collections strategically located in the various climatic zones of North America. Many new arboretums were established during his lifetime. Such institutions are not competitive but cooperative, and today there is a great need for more of them.

Botanical gardens, on the other hand, are much older in this country and abroad. It is obvious that there is an ever-growing desire on the part of the public to have named collections of plants, both native and exotic, for observation as well as for study and enjoyment in places where they can best be seen and appreciated.

An arboretum should be carefully planned, well financed, and competently administered. This article is devoted to some of the ways and means of establishing and maintaining a satisfactory arboretum or botanical garden, many of the suggestions here offered resulting from observing the successful development of various institutions in widely separated parts of the country.

Definition

An arboretum or botanic garden, as considered in the following discussion, is an ample area set aside for the growing and effective display of all the different kinds of worthy ornamental trees, shrubs, vines and other plants which can be grown in a given area, their maintenance, proper labeling, and study. It does not necessarily have to include all the plants that can be grown in a region, nor does it necessarily have to include formal beds or borders of annuals and perennials.

An arboretum differs from a botanical garden in that the emphasis is placed on the growing of woody plants in the arboretum, whereas in the botanical garden emphasis is not placed on the growing of any particular kind of plant, but all types are grown. Large rock gardens and expensively operated rose gardens are frequently found in an arboretum or botanical garden but these are not essential parts of either.

Both differ from a park in that in the former a serious effort has been made to plant an extensive collection of many kinds of labeled plants, not only for the purpose of display but also for critical examination and scientific study. Many parks are planted without the labeling of any plants and with the use of only a small number of locally available plant species. Some parks, it is true, contain a certain number of labeled plants, as, for example, the Boston Public Garden; Roger Williams Park in Providence, R.I.; Fairmont Park in Philadelphia; and others throughout the country, but no consistent effort is made in most of them to label and keep labeled all the different kinds of plants grown. Both a park and an arboretum or botanical garden can be used for recreational purposes; but the arboretum or botanical garden go beyond the park in that they become highly educational to many of their visitors, demonstrating by means of labeled specimens what good species are available for planting in a given area or can be grown indoors.

The purpose of any arboretum, be it large or small, is to grow (and to keep labeled) the best of the ornamental woody plants which will thrive in a given locality. Many other objectives may be considered, such as the actual introduction of new plants into cultivation, actual exploration of remote regions, the growing of all types of woody plants hardy in the area, scientific investigations of various kinds including plant breeding and hybridization, the maintenance of a large herbarium and library, and laboratories of various types—these may be legitimate functions of an arboretum, depending on the funds available and the qualifications of the members of its staff.

Botanical gardens may have even wider functions for their aims are wider, including as they do representatives of the whole plant kingdom from the Tropics to the Arctic, grown outside or under glass. However, small communities should not be deterred by these weighty and often expensive objectives for they may be omitted altogether where funds for the maintenance of such gardens are unavailable. If an arboretum effectively demonstrates "the best" of the woody plants hardy in its area, this alone will make it a most valuable asset in the community it serves. The botanical garden need not cover a large area. It can be effective on a few acres with a few display greenhouses and display a representative collection of plants from all over the world.

Charles Sprague Sargent used to say that in order to start an arboretum it was necessary to have a thousand acres of land with at least a million dollars endowment; yet he started an arboretum with only 125 acres of land and $100,000 endowment, and in the early years of the Arnold Arboretum he had only one third of the income of that modest endowment for annual expenditure. There is still the need for large arboretums placed in different regions, representing different climatic conditions where all the woody plants hardy in an area may be grown, and which are well endowed for scientific investigations. This is undoubtedly what Professor Sargent had in mind, for the Arnold Arboretum was, and is, that kind of an institution. But times are changing. With the extensive garden club movement and increased tendency away from urban dwelling, more and more people are becoming interested in the growing of plants.

A new conception of an arboretum is coming into being. This is very well expressed in the plantings of the Arthur Hoyt Scott Horticultural Foundation at Swarthmore College, Swarthmore, Pa. It is adaptable to communities smaller than Boston, Phila., Chicago, New York, St. Louis or Seattle. It is feasible where funds are lacking to finance expensive scientific investigations, but where there is a definite need to grow and demonstrate to the public "the best" plants hardy in a particular area. It is readily seen that this idea is a flexible one, for the actual size of the arboretum or botanical garden may vary considerably. The idea is based on the theory that the same old varieties of plants may be superseded by new and better varieties. There are new varieties of cars, of refrigerating devices, of clothes and women's hats, and there are new varieties of plants as well. In the display gardens the "old" varieties are grown side by side with the "new", both often being available to the plant-buying public. But with the best varieties only being displayed, interest and variety in private and municipal planting will be greatly stimulated. With this conception in mind, the committee responsible for planning an arboretum or botanical garden should be so constituted as to give the best advice possible for its usefulness and adaptation to the community.

Functions of an Arboretum or Botanical Garden

The purposes of establishing a display garden should be carefully considered before the plan is publicly broached. Some of the more important functions of such a garden might be:

1. To grow only a few of "the best" plants hardy in the area in order that home owners may become acquainted with their names, their ornamental characteristics and the proper methods of culture.

2. To show a complete selection of all that is considered the best from an ornamental standpoint among the woody plants (if an arboretum, or among the perennials, annuals, bulbs as well,

if a botanical garden) that it is possible to be grown in the area.

3. To serve as a means of introducing new plants into the area, regardless of the source from which they may come.

4. To disseminate knowledge of plants to the public. This would include information on culture, pruning, fertilizing and possibly a continual study under local conditions of just what varieties are "the best", including cooperation with schools, garden clubs and other organizations.

5. To test the hardiness of untried varieties.

6. To provide a laboratory for students of botany, horticulture and nature study.

7. To increase the productivity, economic importance and beauty of an area, by intelligent and interesting planting, and by introducing plants not grown there before.

8. To provide recreational stimulus to the public by means of walks, drives and beautiful displays, flower shows, etc., and to stimulate the pleasure of learning to know new plants which might be adapted to planting on private property.

Each of these functions should be studied individually with a view to the best interests of the community. One of the first decisions to be made is whether the present park system satisfies the needs and desires of the people or whether its scope should be enlarged. Would the people be interested in a garden of woody plants only, or should an expensive display greenhouse for showing material in the winter be included ? It is important to consider that an arboretum will always be less expensive to operate even if it includes a large variety of woody plants. On the other hand there are some communities where plant displays in large conservatories fill a real need in the winter. If this is the local situation and funds are available, the construction of display greenhouses filled with exotics must be considered.

If the community is small, the effective functions of the display garden will be largely display. If the community is large and funds are available, the functions may also include scientific investigations, especially if there is an institution of higher learning with which the arboretum may be connected. How far this may be extended will depend upon the community, its nearness to other large institutions, the availability of funds, and the leaders in the municipality.

Methods of Establishing an Arboretum or Botanical Garden

The first arboretums and botanical gardens started as private gardens when individuals became interested in assembling collections of plants. John Bartram had the credit of establishing the first large collection of trees and shrubs in this country when he established his garden in 1728 at Kingsessing on the banks of the Schuylkill River near Philadelphia. Since that time, many private collections have been established at one time or another but many of them have passed out of existence after the death of the original owners. Today there are a few private arboretums worthy of the name. Among them would be the one started by Mr. H. H. Hunnewell in Wellesley, Mass., in 1852 and devoted mainly to conifers; and that of Mr. Stanley Rowe of Cincinnati, Ohio, which now contains 3000 different kinds of woody plants.

A local community can have an arboretum as a result of cooperative effort by various local organizations. The Berkshire Garden Center at Stockbridge, Mass., is just such an example. Funds are raised by local committees of enthusiasts to produce and maintain the type of arboretum wanted by a majority of the community—in this case showing some of the better ornamental plants that can be used in planting home grounds in the area.

The government operated arboretum is exemplified by the Dominion Arboretum adjacent to the Experimental Farm in Ottawa, Canada. It is owned and operated by the Canadian government. Our own National Arboretum at Washington, D.C., has been developed by government funds. Even national government budgets are frequently the playthings of legislators, and the future of an arboretum under government jurisdiction, although safer than a private arboretum, may still suffer much from a fluctuating annual budget.

An arboretum is sometimes part of the park department of the city. Such is the case with Highland Park and Durand-Eastman Park in Rochester, N.Y. The 484 acres constituting Durand-Eastman Park were originally a gift to the city, made by Dr. Henry S. Durand and George Eastman, but maintenance operations are carried out exclusively by the city park department, support being from city taxes. The advantages are obvious, for the park personnel is usually well equipped to maintain a collection of trees and shrubs. However, disadvantages are often evident. In many a park department the annual budget is subject to devious manipulations by politicians who may have no interest in park plantings, and in all too many cities in this country the park department budget is the first to suffer reductions when city expenditures are cut.

The best method of establishing an arboretum or botanical garden is to provide a properly safeguarded restricted endowment, the income from which may be used only for specified purposes. The endowment should be sufficiently large to provide a reasonably ample annual income, for only in this way can permanence be assured. It will be necessary for the Planning Committee to estimate the annual expenses in advance. Many arboretums today are being operated wholly or in part by income from endowments. The endowment is not sufficient in some instances to cover all expenses, and additional funds are necessary from the tax budget or from private sources in order to make it possible to attain the ends desired. When the income from an endowment must be augmented by annual popular subscriptions or by annual grants from the city park department, many difficulties arise. This is, in general, a most unsatisfactory way of operating an arboretum, for projects started one year when funds may be ample may have to be curtailed or even discontinued in another year. Success is most assured when an ample endowment is possible.

Usually a board of directors is formed to oversee the administration of funds in privately owned institutions. Such is the case with the Morton Arboretum of Lisle, Ill., near Chicago and with Longwood Gardens at Kennett Square, Pa. Frequently it has been found advisable to associate the arboretum (with its endowment) with an institution of higher learning. Such is the case with the Arnold Arboretum (Harvard University), Arthur Hoyt Scott Foundation (Swarthmore College), Morris Arboretum (University of Pennsylvania), each one of which has its own endowment. The Arboretum of the University of Washington (Seattle) is connected with the University, with most of its maintenance funds coming from state appropriations. This course is supplemented by membership fees, and an attempt is now being made to secure a restricted endowment.

The association with a university is ideal for it tends to add permanence to the arboretum; sound and intelligent advice on arboretum problems is always available from university staff members, and the arboretum can serve as an ideal out-of-doors laboratory to augment classroom instruction. It is also true that the facilities offered by an arboretum would be used more as a result of this association than might otherwise be the case.

When budgetary items are reasonably fixed from year to year, the work of an arboretum can proceed unhindered by extraneous circumstances. The main object in establishing an arboretum is to make it permanent, to provide for a permanently dependable source of income, and thus insure its usefulness to be continuously available to the greatest number of people. There is no better way to insure this than to provide an ample endowment at the beginning.

Selection of the Site

Before the plan can be made, a site must be decided upon, and the size of the area to be developed should be determined in relation to the sources and amount of available funds. The site could well be a local spot of beauty, of historical significance, or an existing part of a park if suitable. It will take intelligent discussion and sound advice to decide on the site, for the general plan and the functions of the arboretum also must be considered simultaneously. Arrangements should be made for alternatives in case the amount of money originally hoped for is not eventually forthcoming. A very important factor is accessibility.

Who is to Plan?

Almost any enthusiastic temporary group may be responsible for initiating public interest in the new arboretum, but a planning committee responsible for preparing definite plans associated with a campaign for raising funds should be carefully selected. The planning committee could well include an experienced landscape architect; a representative from the Park Department who would know about future park plans; a banker; a person well versed in the values of real estate; prominent nurserymen; and representatives from prominent civic organizations who would represent the desire of the people to have an arboretum and the will to work for one. A representative from an active arboretum, similar in size to the one contemplated, might well be called in for consultation. Large committees move more slowly than small ones, but somehow all interests should either be represented or heard prior to the time the actual site is decided upon and the plan is completed.

Ways of Initiating Interest and Action

It is a simple matter to propose the idea of an arboretum in any community lacking one. Except in strictly urban areas, most home owners are interested in planting their properties so as to make them beautiful and enjoyable for as much of the year as possible. In strictly urban areas the people always desire to get into the open for rest and relaxation. Consequently, people in general are receptive to the idea and do not begin to "hedge" until the time comes for asking for increased taxes or donations for endowment or for annual support.

Many community organizations are well equipped to assist in a campaign for an arboretum. The garden club movement is fortunately firmly imbedded in almost every community. Nature clubs, bird clubs, forestry associations, conservationist groups and other organizations by their very nature should be interested in the idea, and their members afford an excellent basis for enthusiastic support. Schools, parent-teachers organizations, Rotary and Kiwanis Clubs, women's organizations, church groups, town park departments, all should be thoroughly canvassed and their support enlisted.

Horticultural experts could give illustrated lectures to show the kinds of plants which might be grown. Local landscape architects could have a field day in discussing possibilities. Staff members from existing arboretums could come and show what has been done in other communities, and discuss frankly the possibilities of a local arboretum. Costs could be discussed by committees representing various organizations. When opinion becomes fairly crystallized, some group could offer a sum to be used for the preparation of a definite plan. This was done in Seattle, with excellent results. It was felt by those in charge that a topographic map of the Seattle Arboretum site was necessary, showing the 2-ft. contour lines. Such a map was prepared by the State W.E.R.A. at a cost of $5,465. Then the Garden Club of Seattle raised $3,000, and under its auspices a plan was drawn by a prominent firm of landscape architects. By the time the plan-drawing stage is reached, public opinion should be fairly well crystallized in the form of a planning committee or "Arboretum Committee" which would have the authority to work with the individuals drawing the plan.

It is always advisable to have a well-conceived plan on paper, regardless of what the location situation might be. The man or men eventually to be in charge of an arboretum do not just begin to plant trees and shrubs. Roads must be constructed, paths provided for pedestrians, a certain amount of grading done, certain plants placed in situations where they will grow best, a propagating unit intelligently placed, water pipes laid where they will do the most good, drainage provided for in certain instances—in short, a thousand and one things should be thought of before the actual planting is started. In some instances the soil of the arboretum site may be very poor, and arrangements must be made to grow cover crops on it for several years (this was done on the site of the National Arboretum in Washington), thus preparing the soil over a period of time before any trees or shrubs are planted.

Water, in the form of a running brook or pond, can be used to excellent advantage if properly planned for, whereas without planning such a feature might easily become a liability. Trained horticulturists experienced in arboretum objectives and various professional landscape architects are familiar with these phases of the project. Thus, if carefully considered plans are prepared in advance, much money can be saved, and many disappointments avoided by doing the right thing at the right time in the right manner.

How to Plant

The actual placing of the different groups of trees and shrubs should be done according to a carefully conceived plan in which the individual needs of the plants are harmonized with the requirement of good landscape design and in which the best interests of the public are also considered.

Some of the arboretums have been laid out so that the plantings follow a definite botanical sequence of families and genera. This is not necessary or essential in most arboretums. It is advisable to keep all the plants in a certain genus together if possible, and so to place the important genera that they are easily seen from roads and paths. All projected plantings should be critically considered from the standpoint of landscape design.

Azaleas and rhododendrons, if used, should be given a situation with acid soil where they have some protection from winter winds. Lilacs should be so placed that people can easily walk among them and observe them closely as well as from a distance. A collection of hickory or walnut trees, for instance, might be placed in an out-of-the-way spot, where they can be seen from a distance. Colorful displays that have particular seasonal interest should be easily accessible and where they can be seen from many vantage points. Some plants like wet soils, some do better in dry soils. Each group should be placed where it will grow best.

Special attention should be given to displays of seasonal interest. Lilacs, for instance, are of interest only in the spring and might well be grown near the viburnum collection, which is of interest chiefly in the fall. The oriental crab apples, on the other hand, have seasonal interest in both spring and fall and hence might be in a spot by themselves. Certain azaleas and the Flowering Dogwood bloom at the same time and might be planted adjacent to one another. A bank of red roses that will bloom in late June might be planted near the collection of mock-oranges to give it additional color interest when its white flowers appear. Evergreen trees are frequently kept by themselves, but intelligent planting would call for the placing of a few deciduous trees in such a collection, especially those which color vividly in

the fall, to lend color and variety. And in or near plantings of deciduous trees it is usually desirable to place a certain number of selected evergreens.

It may be advisable from a maintenance standpoint to grow many shrub groups together in long beds with grass walks between them. Planted in this manner the shrubs are easily observed closely. A large number can be studied with comparatively little effort, and direct comparisons made. Roses and representatives of such genera as *Weigela*, *Spiraea*, *Deutzia*, *Philadelphus*, *Chaenomeles* and several other genera come in this group that can be so treated. Such a collection, though of little landscape interest, has a great deal of interest to the public at all times of year. The "Shrub Collection" at the Arnold Arboretum contains 800 different kinds of shrubs in parallel beds. It might well be one of the features in any arboretum, placed easily accessible to the main entrance, where people with little time can spend it to best advantage. It is also a most economical method of growing such a large number of shrubs, for machine cultivation can be easily practiced.

What to Plant

What constitutes "the best" and who is competent to judge which are "the best" is always a debatable question. There are in existence several large collections of woody plants in this country and attempts are continually being made to make reliable lists of "the best" ornamentals in each group (genus or species). Such available lists could be utilized at the start. Let me explain more fully how this might be done, using the collections at the Arnold Arboretum as an example.

At the present time there are approximately 7000 different species and horticultural varieties of woody plants being grown in the Arnold Arboretum. Certain groups are larger than others. Thus in these collections there are 96 viburnums, 107 mock-oranges, 159 maples, 270 crab apples, and 574 lilacs. Taking the lilacs for closer scrutiny, there are approximately 400 varieties of *Syringa vulgaris* alone, of which 32 have white flowers! Certainly all do not have outstanding ornamental value. In fact it is extremely difficult to tell some of the varieties from others. It would be difficult to locate nursery sources for all, and certainly many have been discarded by commercial growers as being unsatisfactory. This large collection of lilacs has its place as a laboratory for scientific study but many of the varieties could be eliminated if scientific study were not one of the functions of this arboretum. The collections would be much more ornamental if the number of varieties were reduced, for then massed plantings of a single lilac variety could be made in space now occupied by 20 different varieties, for the ornamental effect of a massed planting is always greater, especially to the casual observer.

In a small arboretum, a collection of 50 or even 25 varieties of lilacs might be satisfactory—only those being selected for planting which are considered to be the most ornamental and representative of the entire group. Just as many plants could be used as in our large collection if space were available, but far fewer varieties. The same principle could be used in selecting "the best" in the other groups of plants. The advice of local plantsmen will prove invaluable at the start when considering such points.

The Number of Plants

The number of plants selected at the beginning will vary with the part of the country in which the arboretum is located, with its size, financial resources, and its propagating facilities. A few examples will illustrate this point. In making a preliminary report of proposed plantings for the Cornell University Arboretum now called "Cornell Plantations," there were approximately 2000 species and varieties of woody plants listed as worthy of trial at the beginning. The Arthur Hoyt Scott Foundation of Swarthmore College listed approximately 2800 species and varieties of woody plants that were being grown there in 1942. The 7000 species and varieties now growing in the Arnold Arboretum might be reduced as much as one half or even more if only the most ornamental were to be selected. These figures are, of course, very general but they give some idea of the number of plants worthy of first consideration. The American Association of Botanical Gardens and Arboretums has published three inclusive studies, one on lilacs, one on crab apples, and a third on maples, showing the tremendous number of varieties being grown in this country and offering suggestions for short lists of the best. Such lists should be consulted. The smaller the arboretum, the fewer the number of specimens of any one variety which should be grown.

The first places to investigate as possible sources for plant materials would be the local nurseries. Nurseries at a distance may be able to supply many varieties unavailable locally. It will, of course, be found that some species are unobtainable from commercial sources. Then it is necessary to provide for a propagating unit and grow wanted varieties from cuttings or by grafting, where the propagating material is supplied by other arboretums, private individuals, or in some instances where seed is collected in native habitats primarily for this purpose. The smaller the plants when purchased, the lower the initial expenditure. The larger the plants at the start, the more quickly an initial display can be made for the public to enjoy. The factors here involved are obviously important ones and should be carefully weighed by the local planning committee.

The Amount of Space Required

This, too, varies with the arboretum, its size, funds available for maintenance, and its functions in the community. Should much space be given over to massed plantings of single varieties? Mass plantings of azaleas, lilacs and crab apples are most ornamental and can be extremely effective, whereas massed plantings of maple trees, for instance, take up much more space and have little ornamental effect. The enforcing of a rigid rule that no more than two or three plants of any one variety can be planted might be enough to defeat the purposes of an arboretum in the eyes of the public. The Arnold Arboretum proper covers an area of 265 acres, yet there is little room for additional planting, even though nearly half the present area is woodland. This wooded area is considered absolutely essential in setting off the man-made planting to good advantage, and to serve as an added source of beauty and interest to visitors. Viburnums alone take 30,000 square feet (190 plants), elms take up about $5\frac{1}{2}$ acres (170 trees), while the lindens are given 3 acres for 58 trees. Three and a half acres constitute what was known as the shrub collection—long beds of miscellaneous shrubs with grass walks between, in which about 800 different species and varieties are grown. Almost a third of this was taken by the grass walks. Such a shrub collection affords an excellent means of teaching the public a great deal in a small area, but affords no opportunity for gorgeous displays of massed plant materials.

Another way of approaching a decision on the amount of space necessary would be to take the figure of 2000 species and varieties as a starting point (the number suggested as the starting point for consideration by Cornell Plantations). If 2 plants of each of these were planted in long nursery rows, the distance between plants averaging 20 feet, they would take about 37 acres. Would such a planting in nursery rows have aesthetic value and be of interest to the public? Of course not! On the other hand, the proverbial "thousand acres" might prove too much for practical purposes. Here is another opportunity for intelligent planning by the Arboretum Committee, and an opportunity where practical plantsmen and landscape architects can lend invaluable assistance.

Costs

The maintenance of plants in an arboretum need not be expensive. Spraying, pruning, planting should not be curtailed in any one year. If spraying and pruning be omitted two or more successive years because of lack of funds, the plantings quickly show neglect, and it may take several years to bring some of the plants back into vigorous growth. A fluctuating budget does not allow for intelligent annual operation, one of the best arguments against trying to operate too extensively on the basis of funds solicited annually.

The actual amount of money necessary to operate a small arboretum varies with the size of the arboretum, the labor situation, equipment, the objectives and the extent of its formal plantings. A good park administrator who knows park maintenance costs in the locality where an arboretum is to be established can give excellent advice regarding such costs. However, certain things are known. Lilacs, crab apples, quinces, and many other groups are very susceptible to infestations of scale and should be treated annually with a dormant spray to control this pest. They need a certain amount of renewal pruning every few years, without which periodic care they will very quickly turn into unattractive specimens which have little ornamental value. No collections of these particular kinds of plants should be contemplated unless they can be cared for properly each year.

As an example of the cost for maintaining one group of plants, there are approximately 700 lilac plants in the collection at the Arnold Arboretum. Spraying these with a dormant oil spray takes 2 men about a half day, and about 600 gallons of spray mixture. Three good pruners spend an average of 2 weeks in this collection each year, keeping it in excellent condition. The cutting off of flower clusters is a time-consuming operation but should be done for the benefit of the next season's display. Although we cannot do this completely every year, if done properly (as it should be) it would take 4 men at least 2 weeks. This will give some idea of how to approach the problem of prospective costs in each of the large collections contemplated.

Viburnums need practically no spraying and very little annual pruning. Elms must be sprayed in this area for elm leaf beetle and the bark beetle. Canker worm, gypsy moth, willow leaf beetle, Japanese beetle—all attack many kinds of plants and must be controlled in various parts of the country. In 1959, 400 man-hours were spent in spraying the various collections for specific insect and disease control.

Pruning also cannot be definitely estimated. Young plants, pruned properly at transplanting time, may require no pruning for several years. On the other hand, in an established arboretum with many kinds of mature trees, a wind, snow or ice storm may cause immense damage. The hurricane of 1938 cost the Arnold Arboretum in pruning and the removal of fallen or badly damaged trees and shrubs about $6500 above the budget provided. This did not include the irreparable loss of old established specimens. During a recent winter, a 14-in. snowstorm with very heavy snow broke so many branches that it took approximately 75 man-days to repair this damage alone.

Labor

This item is the most expensive in any park or arboretum. It can be controlled somewhat by the amount of grass cutting and leaf raking which is done. In some parks all grass areas are carefully cut with a lawn mower once a week. This is a very expensive operation. In the arboretum or botanical garden where certain areas are given over to the growth of deciduous trees and conifers the grass need only be cut but a few times each season, providing a few walks are open through these collections. In the shrub collection, which many people visit at all seasons of the year, the walks should be closely cut, as well as certain small areas along the main walks and near main entrance gates. Grass cutting is an essential annual operation to reduce the fire menace and must be provided for. Tractor-drawn rotary mowers are ideal for keeping grass under control at minimum expense.

Hoeing by hand takes considerable time. The cost of this operation can be reduced by the use of mechanical equipment in the larger beds, and may be reduced still further by the use of some of the new weed killers now available. The Arnold Arboretum employs 9 laborers with occasional additions during spring and summer, a superintendent with his assistant for the maintenance of the growing collections, as well as a propagator, his assistants, and a man in charge of labeling and mapping. These are not maximum requirements, and probably might be termed the minimum labor requirements for an arboretum the size and age of the Arnold Arboretum. The National Arboretum with 450 acres has 32 men on the grounds crew. The Arthur Hoyt Scott Horticultural Foundation with an area of about 300 acres has 7 on the grounds crew.

Equipment

The more standardized mechanical equipment that can be utilized to good advantage, the less will be the expenditure for labor. Minimum equipment for a 200–300-acre arboretum might be:

Tractor (with rotary mower, plow, harrow, etc.)

Sprayer with tank capacity of at least 300 gallons

At least one 1½-ton truck

2 power lawn mowers

2 heavy-duty rotary mowers

Rototiller or small motorized cultivator

Gasoline chain saw

The best available hand saws, pruners, pole saws, etc., for the type of work contemplated.

Propagation

Every arboretum large or small should have its own propagating unit. Since many of the plants grown will be rare, they will not be available from commercial sources as plants; hence the arboretum will have to propagate many species from seeds, cuttings or grafts. There are decided advantages in having a nursery well stocked with materials, for plants so grown are easier to dig and move. They should be correctly named, for if they are allowed to grow to sufficient size in the nursery, they can be properly identified before being transplanted. Larger specimens can be handled this way than would be advisable with purchased specimens.

The actual size of the greenhouse will depend on the location of the arboretum, its size, and the amount of material to be propagated. At the beginning a great deal of propagating will be needed to provide material for contemplated plantings. Many of the older arboretums are concerned merely with replacements and material which is new to the collection.

It is amazing what a large amount of material can be propagated and grown to planting size in a well-organized space. The Arnold Arboretum operated for 35 years with only two greenhouses 50 ft. x 18 ft. Many smaller arboretums have considerably less greenhouse space, and a few have more.

A pit house is essential in the North to aid in wintering over young stock and propagation materials. In the South, lath houses are essential, the number depending on the size of the whole arboretum undertaking. Saran cloth shade houses are ideally suited for growing ericaceous and other broad-leaved evergreens during the hot summer months. We have 5 houses varying in size, approximately 100 ft. x 30 ft. Frames are also essential for wintering young plants. Nursery space will vary, but the young arboretum which is doing a lot of plant propagation will need several acres at least.

It goes without saying that an experienced plant propagator must be employed. Sometimes he can work alone, sometimes he may need assistance, but in order to keep accurate records and to produce good plants, he should be thoroughly trained and experienced. If he is of this type, he will know the approximate size of the nursery and plant-bed space needed, as well as the type of greenhouse space required.

Labeling and Mapping

A most essential function of an arboretum is to keep the plants properly labeled. In order to maintain correct labeling it is essential that the plantings be accurately mapped. An active young man who is really interested in this work —and it takes a great deal of walking!—should be able to keep maps and labels up-to-date, providing he has some seasonal assistance. In the winter some of the labor force could paint and even print labels. In the summer, 1 or 2 high-school boys might be hired to help with the mapping if this were necessary. Mapping with the alidade and tape is sufficiently accurate. We have found that maps approximately 2 ft. x 2½ ft. on a scale of 1 in. = 20 ft. are practicable, but a few enlargements are necessary on a scale of 1 in. = 10 ft. It took nearly a year for two men to map all the plants in the 265 acres in the Arnold Arboretum but, once accomplished, the maps are easily kept up-to-date with a minimum expenditure of time.

If plants are not accurately and clearly labeled, the arboretum loses its educational function completely. Labels will disappear, often appropriated by certain types of visitors, and others will become defaced. Thus a careful mapping of a collection makes relabeling of individual plants simple and accurate, for the critical and sometimes time-consuming matter of re-identification is eliminated. A display label should be clearly visible on every plant except in instances where a large number of a single variety are used in mass planting. On the label, as a minimum, should appear the common name, the scientific name, and the geographic origin of the species.

A small record label made of embossed zinc tape should be attached to every plant when it is planted in the collections. This will remain on the plant indefinitely and contains the accession number of the plant, its scientific name, the origin of the plant, and the date of its accession. These cost only a few cents per label just for the materials. A large wooden or metal display label is attached to each plant that is large enough to carry one. These cost about 30 cents per label for the materials (not including the labor of printing) and will remain on the plant in good condition about 5 years. Certainly a plant worth placing in an arboretum is worth 2 labels at a cost of under 50 cents.

Education Costs

If a community is large enough, the director or superintendent of the arboretum might be a man who could direct the work in the arboretum and at the same time give lectures to local groups concerning the plant materials in the arboretum and their proper use. He could write articles for local publication, conduct groups through the arboretum, and work with local groups for the general education of the public in better appreciation of the plants and their maintenance. The services of such a man are almost a "must" for the arboretum or botanical garden since a certain amount of educational publicity contributes materially toward a better utilization and appreciation of the arboretum by the residents of a community.

It would serve no purpose to give the actual operating expenses of any arboretum, since methods vary, functions of the arboretum vary, and wages vary. Each expense item should be understood before studying actual maintenance costs. The figures and facts given, however, should serve to help with the general plans of any arboretum committee. They should be interpreted by men familiar with maintenance work who at the same time are familiar with the proposed functions of the arboretum under consideration.

ARBORETUMS AND BOTANICAL GARDENS. Those who wish to learn more about plants should certainly visit some of the arboretums and botanical gardens about the country. A garden is usually for the personal enjoyment and recreation of the owners and their friends. A park is established primarily for the recreation of the public. An arboretum or botanical garden, although it may be used for public enjoyment and recreation, usually is established specifically for the education of the public: its plants are labeled or recorded properly and its functions include a certain amount of research concerning the culture and use of the plants.

Many of the arboretums, botanical gardens as well as the state and national parks in America have regular programs, "walks" and "classes" for instructing the public.

It is impossible to list all the arboretums and botanical gardens here. New ones are being started in many places throughout the country. Some of those which might be mentioned, merely as a quick source of information to any gardener are:

Alabama
   Theodore—Bellingrath Gardens
      (36582) Camellias
Arizona
   Phoenix—Desert Botanical Garden of Arizona
      (85010) Succulents and plants from desert regions of the world
California
   Arcadia—Los Angeles State and County Arboretum, 301 N. Baldwin Ave.
      (36582) Eucalyptus, plants from Australia and the subtropics
   Berkeley—University of California Botanical Garden
      (91720) Succulents, perennials, rhododendrons, woody trees and shrubs, ferns, etc.
   Claremont—Rancho Santa Ana Botanic Garden, 1500 N. College Ave.
      (91711) California native plants, Iris, Arctostaphylos, Ceanothus
   La Canada—Descanso Gardens, 1418 Descanso Drive
      (91011) Annuals, perennials, camellias, roses, azaleas
   Los Angeles—Botanical Garden, University of California, 405 Hilgard
      (90024)   Ave.
                  Acacia, Eucalyptus, Callistemon, succulents
   Placerville—Eddy Arboretum, Institute of Forest Genetics
      (95567) Pines, other evergreens
   San Francisco—Strybing Arboretum and Botanical Garden, 9th Ave. and
      (94122)   Lincoln Way
                  Native annuals, evergreen trees and shrubs
               —Golden Gate Park
      (94117) Japanese Tea Garden, rhododendrons, garden for the blind
   San Marino—Huntington Botanical Gardens, 1151 Oxford Rd.
      (91108) Succulents, palms, cacti, camellias, roses

Santa Barbara—Santa Barbara Botanical Garden, Inc., 1212 Mission
    (93105)   Canyon Rd.
             Woody trees and shrubs

Colorado
  Denver—Denver Botanic Gardens, 909 York St., Denver
  (80206) Evergreens, woody trees and shrubs

Connecticut
  New Haven—Marsh Botanical Garden, Yale University, Mansfield St.
    (06520) Woody trees and shrubs
  New London—Connecticut Arboretum, Connecticut College, Box 1511
    (06320) Trees and shrubs; 365 acres
  Stamford—Bartlett Arboretum of the State of Connecticut, 151 Brookdale
  (06093)   Rd.
        Trees and shrubs; 62 acres

Delaware
  Winterthur—Winterthur Gardens
    (19735) Perennials, evergreens, trees, shrubs, narcissi, azaleas

District of Columbia
  Washington—U.S. National Arboretum
    (20002) Evergreens, trees, shrubs, hollies, magnolias, crab apples,
          azaleas, dwarf plants; 400 acres

Florida
  Gainesville—Wilmot Memorial Garden, University of Florida
    (32611) Trees, shrubs, camellia-related genera and spring-flowering
          plants
  Homestead—Orchid Jungle, Fennel Orchid Co., 26715 SW 15th Ave.
    (33030) Orchids, native plants, aroids
  Miami—Fairchild Tropical Garden, 10901 Old Cutler Rd.
  (33156) Palms, trees, shrubs of a tropical nature
  Naples—Caribbean Gardens, Inc., P.O. Box 2505
  (33940) Tropical foliage plants, orchids

Georgia
  Pine Mountain—Callaway Gardens
    (31822) Perennials, evergreens, woody trees and shrubs; 2500
          acres

Hawaii
  Honolulu—Foster Botanical Garden, 50 N. Vineyard Blvd.
    (96817) Orchids, aroids, palms
  Wahiawa, Oahu—Wahiawa Botanical Gardens, 1396 California Ave.
      (96786) Orchids, aroids, ornamental trees; 27 acres

Illinois
  Chicago Garfield Park Conservatory, 300 N. Central Park Blvd.
  (60624) Succulents, palms, orchids, ferns, aroids, tropical plants; $4\frac{1}{2}$
      acres of conservatories
  Glencoe—Botanic Gardens of The Chicago Horticultural Society
  (60022)   775 Dundee Rd., Box 90
        Trees and shrubs
  Lisle—Morton Arboretum, Route 53
(60532) Evergreens, woody trees and shrubs; 1500 acres

Indiana
  Michigan City—International Friendship Garden
    (46360) Gardens of many nations

Kentucky
  Clermont—Bernheim Forest Arboretum
    (40110) Trees and shrubs
  Louisville—General Electric Appliance Park
    (40225) Evergreens, trees and shrubs; 75 acres

Louisiana
  Many—Hodges Gardens, P.O. Box 921
  (71449) Subtropical plants

Massachusetts
   Cambridge—580 Mt. Auburn St., Mount Auburn Cemetery
      (02138)   Woody trees and shrubs
   Framingham—Garden-in-the-Woods, Hemenway Rd.
      (01701)   Native American plants and their mutations; 30 acres
   Jamaica Plain—Arnold Arboretum
      (02130)   Evergreens, trees and shrubs, woody vines; 390 acres
   Northampton—Botanic Garden of Smith College
      (01060)   Succulents, perennials, annuals, trees, shrubs; 100 acres
   Sandwich—Heritage Plantation and Garden, Grove St.
      (02563)   Dexter rhododendrons and native plants
Michigan
   Ann Arbor—Nichols Arboretum, University of Michigan
      (48104)   Evergreens, trees and shrubs, peonies, lilacs
   East Lansing—Beal-Garfield Botanic Garden, Bldg. A-1, South Campus,
      (48823)   Michigan State University
              Perennials, woody trees and shrubs
          —Michigan State University
              Perennials, annuals, evergreens, woody trees and shrubs
Minnesota
   Chaska—University of Minnesota Landscape Arboretum, Route 1,
   (55318)   Box 132-1

        Evergreens, trees and shrubs; 560 acres
   Minneapolis—Eloise Butler Wild Flower Garden, 250 S. 4th St.
      (55415)   Minnesota native plants and many introduced from other
             states; 12 acres
Missouri
   St. Louis—Missouri Botanical Garden, 2315 Tower Grove Ave.
      (63110)   Orchids, waterlilies, tropical plants, trees and shrubs; 60 acres
New Jersey
   Gladstone—Willowwood Arboretum of Rutgers University
      (07934)   Trees and shrubs; 136 acres
   New Brunswick—Rutgers Display Gardens, Department of Horticulture,
      (08903)   Rutgers University
              Evergreens, hollies, trees, shrubs, some perennials;
              123 acres
   Somerville—Duke Gardens Foundation, Inc., Route 206 South
      (08876)   Conservatory plants
New York
   Bronx Park—New York Botanical Garden
      (10458)   Trees and shrubs, perennials and annuals. Greenhouses—
             succulents, orchids and ferns
   Brooklyn—Brooklyn Botanic Garden, 1000 Washington Ave.
      (11225)   Perennials, annuals, trees, shrubs, tropical economic plants,
             bonsai plants, oriental cherries; 50 acres
   Esperance—George Landis Arboretum
      (12066)   Evergreens, trees, shrubs, spring bulbs, herbs and roses;
             100 acres
   Flushing—Queens Botanical Garden, 43–50 Main St.
      (11355)   Rhododendrons, bulbs and roses; 38 acres
   Ithaca—Cornell Plantations, Cornell University, 100 Judd Falls Rd.
   (14850)   Evergreens, woody trees and shrubs; 1500 acres
   Long Island (Oakdale)—Bayard Cutting Arboretum, Box 66
           (11769)   Conifers, rhododendrons
   Oyster Bay—Planting Fields Arboretum, Box 581
      (11771)   Succulents, evergreens, trees and shrubs; 405 acres
   Rochester—Highland and Durand-Eastman Park Arboretum, Monroe
      (14620)   County Department of Parks, 375 Westfall Rd.
             Evergreens, trees and shrubs

North Carolina
    Chapel Hill—The Coker Arboretum, University of North Carolina
        (27514) Woody trees and shrubs of southeastern United States;
          5 acres
    Durham—Sarah P. Duke Gardens, Duke University
    (27706) Perennials, annuals, trees and shrubs
North Dakota
    Dunseith—International Peace Garden
        (58329) 883 acres in U.S., and 1431 acres in Canada
Ohio
    Cincinnati—Mt. Airy Arboretum, 5083 Colerain Ave.
      (45223) Evergreens, woody trees and shrubs; 120 acres
      (45243)—Stanley M. Rowe Arboretum, 4500 Muchmore Rd.
          Evergreens, trees, shrubs and lilacs
    Mansfield—Kingwood Center, 900 Park Avenue W., Box 966
      (94901) Perennials, annuals and bulbous plants; 47 acres
    Mentor—The Holden Arboretum, 9500 Sperry Rd.
    (44060) Trees and shrubs; 2400 acres
    Newark—The Dawes Arboretum, RFD #5, Box 270
    (43055) Trees
    Wooster—Secrest Arboretum, Ohio Agricultural State Experimental
    (44691)   Station
          Evergreens, trees and shrubs, yews
Oregon
    Portland—Hoyt Arboretum, 4000 S.W. Fairview Blvd.
    (97221) Evergreens; 200 acres
Pennsylvania
    Hershey—Hershey Rose Gardens and Arboretum
    (17033) Roses, holly, bulbs, trees and shrubs; 23 acres
    Kennett Square—Longwood Gardens
        (19348) Succulents, perennials, annuals, evergreens, trees and
               shrubs—outstanding display of both indoor and hardy
               ornamentals; 1000 acres
    Lima—The John J. Tyler Arboretum, 515 Painter Rd.
(19060) Trees and shrubs; 711 acres
    Merion—Arboretum of the Barnes Foundation, 300 Latch's Lane
    (19066) Evergreens, trees and shrubs; 12 acres
    Philadelphia—The Morris Arboretum of the University of Pennsylvania,
      (19118)   9414 Meadowbrook Ave.
          Evergreens, trees and shrubs; 175 acres
    Pittsburgh—Phipps Conservatory, Schenley Park
      (15213) Exotic tender plants; 2.8 acres under glass
    Swarthmore—Arthur Hoyt Scott Horticultural Foundation, Swarthmore
    (19081)   College
          Evergreens, trees and shrubs; 350 acres
    Washington Crossing—Bowman's Hill Wild Flower Preserve, Washington
        (18977)   Crossing State Park
               Perennials, trees, shrubs, wild flowers; 100 acres
    Westtown—Westtown School Arboretum
    (19395) Evergreens, trees and shrubs; 50 acres
South Carolina
    Murrells Inlet—Brookgreen Gardens
        (29576) Ilex, Quercus, native plants
Texas
    Fort Worth—Fort Worth Botanic Garden, 3220 Botanic Garden Drive
      (76107) Succulents, perennials, annuals, evergreens, trees and shrubs;
          75 acres
Virginia
    Blacksburg—Virginia Polytechnic Institute Arboretum, Virginia Poly-
    (24061)   technic Institute
          Evergreens, trees and shrubs; 60 acres

Boyce—Orland E. White Research Arboretum, Blandy Experiment
(22610)   Station, University of Virginia
            Trees and shrubs, perennials, boxwoods; 12 acres
Norfolk—Norfolk Botanical Garden, Airport Rd.
(23518) Camellias, rhododendrons, azaleas; 175 acres
Washington
Spokane—Finch Arboretum, 3404 Woodland Blvd.
(99204) Evergreens, trees and shrubs; 63 acres
Seattle—University of Washington Arboretum
(98195) Evergreens, woody trees and shrubs; 200 acres
West Virginia
Morgantown—West Virginia University Arboretum, Department of
(26506)   Biology, West Virginia University
            Native West Virginia plants; 75 acres
Wisconsin
Hales Corners—Alfred L. Boerner Botanical Garden, 5879 S. 92nd St.
(53130) Bulbs, perennials, annuals, evergreens, trees and shrubs;
            444 acres
Madison—University of Wisconsin Arboretum, University of Wisconsin,
(53711)   1207 Seminole Highway
            Trees and shrubs; 1000 acres
Canada
British Columbia
Vancouver—Queen Elizabeth Arboretum, 33rd Ave. and Cambie St.
            Annuals, evergreens, trees and shrubs
Manitoba
Morden—Canada Experimental Farm, Research Branch, Department of
            Agriculture, P.O. Box 3001
            Perennials, annuals, evergreens, woody trees and shrubs
Ontario
Hamilton—Royal Botanical Gardens, Box 399
            Perennials, annuals, evergreens, trees and shrubs; 1900 acres
Ottawa—Dominion Arboretum and Botanic Garden, Plant Research
            Institute, Central Experimental Station
            Evergreens, trees and shrubs; 150 acres
Quebec
Montreal—Montreal Botanical Garden, 4101 Sherbrooke St. East
            Succulents, perennials, annuals, evergreens, trees and shrubs;
            190 acres
        —Morgan Arboretum, Macdonald College of McGill Uni-
            versity, Box 500
            Woody trees and shrubs; 700 acres
Others listed in *Directory of American Horticulture*, American Horticultural
Society, Inc., Mount Vernon, Va. 22121

ARBORVITAE. See THUJA.

ARBORVITAE, HIBA FALSE = *Thujopsis dolobrata*

ARBUTUS (AR-bew-tus; popularly, ar-BEW-tus)
menziesii   75′   Zone 7   Pacific Madrone
Some English gardeners have gone to the extent of calling this one of the best broad-leaved evergreen trees. It is native from British Columbia to Calif., bears small whitish flowers like those of *Vaccinium* in pyramidal clusters 3–9 in. tall and 6 in. broad during May. The red to orange-colored berries are effective in the fall and winter, and it frequently grows in a

picturesque shape. The old bark peels off, leaving the younger bright red to cinnamon bark underneath, and the dark, glossy evergreen leaves are 2–6 in. long. Unfortunately it is difficult to transplant and seedlings about 18 in. tall are the best to use. It does drop leaves, bark and fruit rather consistently so that for the person who likes a "clean" lawn, this might be considered a rather "dirty" tree.
unedo   10′–30′   Zone 8   Strawberry-tree
This interesting, slow-growing shrub or small tree is native to southwestern Europe but is used considerably in the warmer parts of Calif. and Wash. The small white flowers, borne from Oct. to Dec., eventually grow into brilliant

strawberrylike, orange berries $\frac{3}{4}$ in. across, which are tasteless but edible. It grows with one to several trunks, the dark brown bark cracking open on larger branches and the trunk showing the bright red inner bark, thus being very ornamental. The evergreen leaves are lustrous and 4 in. long and the fruit may remain on the tree for weeks or even months. It requires acid soil and a dry climate to grow well.

ARBUTUS, TRAILING = *Epigaea repens*

ARCHONTOPHOENIX (arch-on-to-FEE-nix)
> **cunninghamiana   40′   Zone 10   Seaforthia Palm**
This is probably used as much or more in southern Calif. than any other truly tropical palm. It bears slightly arching, stiff feather-shaped leaves and its trunk is sheathed in greenish-colored leaf bases. It makes an excellent conservatory plant and is grown as such throughout the world. The leaves may grow up to 10 ft. long and the fruits are a bright coral red.

ARCTIUM (ARC-ti-um). Vicious weeds, native to Europe and Asia but widely naturalized throughout North America, producing fruits that are round burrs, which adhere to anything like clothing or fur with which they come in contact. In the Orient the foliage is used in salads and cooked as a potherb. The roots are tender at the end of the season and are nutritious when cooked, with an excellent flavor. For control see WEED-CONTROLLING CHEMICALS.
> **lappa   9′   Zone 3   Great Burdock**
A biennial weed frequently seen along road and fence rows in northeastern North America and on the Pacific Coast. Native to Europe but now widely distributed in America. There is a large tap root, a rosette of leaves at the base and then alternate, simple leaves on the stem up to 12 in. long. The flower heads are in groups of 3, 1 in. across. It is not as common as *A. minus* but is occasionally seen. Blooms from July to Oct. Fruits are sticky burrs that attach themselves to almost anything rubbed against them.
> **minus   6′   Zone 3   Smaller Burdock**
A biennial weed native to Europe and Asia but widely distributed throughout North America, with simple alternate leaves about a foot long and almost as wide. This also has fruits or burrs that stick to clothing readily. Flowers bloom from July to Oct.

ARCTOSTAPHYLOS (ark-to-STAFF-il-oss). These are evergreen trees or shrubs belonging to the Heath Family with alternate, usually entire leaves and small white or pink urn-shaped flowers in terminal racemes, somewhat like those of blueberry species. The fruits are red to brownish drupes, very colorful in the case of *A. uva-ursi*.
> **glauca   30′   Zone 10   Bigberry Manzanita**
A large shrub or tree with evergreen leaves 2 in. long and white flowers. Native to southern Calif. and Lower Calif.
> **hookeri   2′   Zone 8   Hooker Manzanita**
A procumbent evergreen shrub being used in some places in Calif. as a ground cover. The leaves are glossy, 1 in. long.
> **manzanita   12′   Zone 7   Common Manzanita**
A shrub planted for its dense white or pink flower clusters in the spring; chiefly used on the West Coast where it is native from Ore. to central Calif. Leaves are 1–2 in. long; older branches are dark reddish; flower panicles are 1–1$\frac{1}{2}$ in. long, borne in April and May.
> **stanfordiana   6′   Zone 7   Stanford Manzanita**
A Calif. native with lustrous evergreen leaves 1$\frac{1}{2}$ in. long used in West Coast gardens. The brilliant pink flowers are borne in dense panicles in March and April, almost covering the plant, and the red to brown berries are effective in the fall. It is a well-rounded shrub with red bark.
> **tomentosa   4′   Zone 7   Woolly Manzanita**
A small shrub with oval leaves 1–1$\frac{1}{2}$ in. long and woolly on the under surface. Flowers white or pink in panicles 1$\frac{1}{2}$ in. long from March to May. Native from British Columbia to Calif.
> **uva-ursi   ground cover   Zone 2   Bearberry, Kinikinick**
One of the best evergreen ground covers, native across the continent from coast to coast, valued for its fine foliage which turns bronze in the fall, its scarlet red berries and its ability to thrive in poor, sandy soils in the hot sun. The leaves are small, about $\frac{1}{2}$–$\frac{3}{4}$ in. long, and the plant is widely used, especially in planting sandy banks along the highways.

Propagation

Seed germinates erratically in spite of pre-treatment, but it might best be stratified at 40° F. for 3 months, then sown. Seed can be stored dry in airtight containers in a cool place and stratified the following year after it is collected. Layers, softwood and hardwood cuttings root readily. It is very difficult to transplant and pot-grown nursery plants are best to use for new plantings.

ARCTOTIS (ARC-to-tis)
> **stoechadifolia   2$\frac{1}{2}$′   annual   African Daisy**
With spreading, almost woody stems, gray-hairy leaves which in the variety **grandis** are 6 in. long. The ray flowers are creamy white, tinted red underneath; the heads are 3 in. wide with black centers. Native to South Africa.

ARDISIA (ar-DIZ-ia)
> **crenata   1′   Zone 9   Coral Ardisia**

The bright red fruits of this small Chinese evergreen are its best ornamental assets. These are effective during the fall and winter, as a contrast with the leathery leaves that may be 3 in. long. It is often grown as a pot plant since these fruits are held on the plant a long time, but it requires shade when grown in the open; often confused with the less common *A. crispa*.

japonica 1½' **Zone 6** **Japanese Ardisia**
An evergreen shrub, native to Japan; alternate, glossy green leaves bunched at the end of the stem, about 1½–4 in. long; white flowers about ½ in. across in Aug. and Sept. and bright red berries in the fall. Although 18 in. tall, it is sometimes massed and used as an evergreen ground cover.

ARECA (a-REE-ka)
cathechu 30'–100' **Zone 10** **Betel-palm**
A palm with pinnate fronds 3–6 ft. long; fragrant white flowers. The fruit is orange-red, shaped like a nut and is chewed along with the leaf of Betel Pepper as a mild stimulant by the natives of Malaysia and Polynesia where this is native. Often written *A. catechu*, but it was not thus spelled by Linnaeus.

ARECASTRUM (a-ree-KAS-trum)
romanzoffianum 30' **Zone 10** **Queen Palm**
A fine ornamental palm from Argentina and Bolivia with smooth gray trunk scarred with visible growth rings. The graceful crown produces arching fronds. The sweet fruits have an orange pulp and the small seeds, suggesting a tiny coconut, are used in making earrings and necklaces.

ARENARIA (a-ren-AIR-ia).
In the new *Hortus III* over 50 species of *Arenaria* are described, but the following six are probably those with which most gardeners will come in contact. Actually there are about 150 species which botanists around the world have described. These little sandworts are low and flat, forming nice mats on the surface of the ground. They are annuals or perennial herbs native to the northern hemisphere and are common in arctic regions as well. The flowers are very small and usually white.
balearica 3" **Zone 6** **Corsican Sandwort**
Small and almost mosslike in character, this plant comes from the Balearic Islands, Corsica. The small white flowers with 5 petals are singly borne in May and the small leaves are only about ⅛ in. long. This is the least hardy of the sandworts here listed, but it tolerates shade, needs abundant moisture and can be given winter protection to prevent it from burning excessively. It can quickly become a pernicious pest by seeding itself everywhere in places where it has become acclimated.

laricifolia 8" **Zone 5** **Larchleaf Sandwort**
The Swiss Alps contributed this excellent plant for rock gardens and the crevices of stone walks. The small, semi-evergreen, awl-shaped leaves are borne on prostrate, rooting stems and sprays of showy white flowers, on stems 8 in. high, appear in early summer.
montana 2"–4" **Zone 4** **Mountain Sandwort**
From southwestern Europe, this has starlike white flowers nearly 1 in. wide. The leaves are ½–¾ in. long, glossy green and grasslike. It is suitable for planting between stepping stones or for covering small, bare areas of ground. It grows well in slightly acid soil and does not have a reputation for seeding itself avariciously.
peploides 4" **Zone 3** **Seabeach Sandwort**
A procumbent plant with fleshy stems and small, light green leaves only ⅝ in. long and with white flowers. Native to the shores of Europe and North America.
serpyllifolia 8" **Zone 3** **Thyme-leaved Sandwort**
Annual, biennial or perennial weed either upright or prostrate and very branched, with small white flowers blooming all summer. The very small leaves are opposite, less than ½ in. long. It was introduced from Europe or Asia but now is a widely spread weed throughout the U.S. and southern Canada. It is one of those weeds which, if the soil is fertilized to increase the growth of main-crop plants, will be pushed out by the more vigorous growth of the desired plants.
verna 2" **Zone 3** **Moss Sandwort**
This Moss Sandwort comes from the Arctic areas and has fine, mosslike evergreen leaves, each with 3 nerves, and white, starlike flowers ½ in. in dia. in May. It grows rapidly and, like the other species, is ideally suited for planting in the cracks between stepping stones, tolerating both sun and shade, though it might need some winter protection to prevent excessive winter burning. Easily propagated by division in the early spring.

ARENGA (a-RENG-ga)
pinnata 40' **Zone 10** **Sugar Palm**
This is an important palm native to Malaya grown for the production of sugar and palm wine. The pinnate leaves are 20 ft. long and most ornamental. The young flower stalks, when pierced, yield a sugary sap. The plant dies after the fruit has ripened. Sometimes planted in southern Fla. as an ornamental.

ARETHUSA (a-reth-EU-sa)
bulbosa 5"–10" **Zone 3** **Arethusa**
A dainty member of the Orchid Family growing in swamps and bogs from Newfoundland to the mountainous areas of N.Car. and extending as

far west as N.Dak. The single flowers borne at the end of the leafless stalk have pink petals and sepals with the lip rimmed with a fringe of yellow hairs. It flowers in June and July and a slender leaf appears only after the flower has died. A very desirable plant for the bog garden, it requires a highly acid soil.

ARGEMONE (ar-JEM-o-ne). These plants, usually grown as annuals, being rather tall are best used at the back of the border, spaced about 15 in. apart. Seed is sown in May, preferably in a sunny, rich, but rather sandy soil.

alba = *A. polypanthemos*

grandiflora   3′   annual   Showy Prickle-poppy
A Mexican plant with white, veined prickly leaves, yellow juice and white flowers 2 in. across at the branch ends. **Lutea** has yellow fls.

mexicana   2′–3′   annual   Mexican Prickle-poppy
A showy annual herb with irregularly lobed, often white-spotted leaves having marginal spines. The flowers are yellow or orange, 2 in. across, with 4 to 6 petals. It flowers throughout the summer and is widely cultivated. Propagation is by seed borne in a prickly pod. Native to tropical America and blooms from June to Sept.

platyceras   4′   annual   Crested Prickle-poppy
Flowers white to purple, 2 in. across, native to both North and South America. The var. **rosea** has brownish-purple flowers.

polypanthemos   3′   Zone 8   White Prickle-poppy
A prickly herb with yellow juice, native to the southern states with lobed, gray-green leaves with spiny margins, and it is these spines which can cause painful irritation to the skin. The leaves are poisonous. The white flowers are singly produced and the fruit is prickly.

ARIL. An appendage growing out from the hilum on the seed and covering the seed partially or wholly. The hilum on the seed is the small mark showing where it was attached to the inside of the ovary.

ARISAEMA (a-riss-EE-ma)

dracontium   12″–18″   Zone 4   Dragonroot
This shade-loving plant deserves a place in the wild garden because of its unusual leaves, which rise singly from the root, to divide into 3 sets of leaflets which in turn are divided into 5 or more parts, and for its green flower. A member of the Arum Family, it bears a tapering spadix which extends considerably beyond the spathe, not pulpitlike as in *A. triphyllum*. The flowers are shorter than the leaf stalks and thus are somewhat hidden from view. Reddish berries, visible as the spathe withers, extend the seasonal interest of this plant. Native over the eastern U.S. and as far west as Tex. and the borders of the Great Lakes, it blooms in June. Propagation is by seed sown in the fall.

triphyllum   12″–18″   Zone 4   Jack-in-the-pulpit
As its botanic name implies, this plant bears a compound leaf divided in 3 parts, the leaflets being 2–3 in. long, and a flower composed of an erect spadix surrounded by a green-and-purple striped spathe which bends over the spadix. A cluster of red berries appears as the spathe withers. The starchy corms were boiled and eaten by the Indians, although in the raw state they are poisonous. Often used in wild gardens because of its unusual flower, it is native throughout eastern and midwestern U.S. as far south as N.C. and west to Kan. It blooms in June. The plant does best in rich, moist soil. Propagation is by seed sown in the fall.

ARISTOLOCHIA (a-riss-to-LO-kia). A group of twining vines with large alternate leaves, and a flower somewhat the shape of a small Meerschaum pipe. They grow vigorously and are somewhat coarse in texture, being chiefly valued for their foliage. They can be propagated by softwood cuttings, root cuttings and division. Seed may be stratified as soon as ripe or kept dry a year in an airtight container in a cool place, then stratified for 3 months at 40° F., then sown.

durior   twining vine   30′   Zone 4   Dutchman's-pipe
An old-fashioned favorite, native to the central U.S., commonly called Dutchman's-pipe because the small flowers usually hidden by the large leaves are somewhat in the shape of a Meerschaum pipe. The large, rounded leaves

Aristolochia durior—Dutchman's-pipe

Aristolochia durior (Dutchman's-pipe): A hardy, twining vine photographed in Finland. (*Photo by Arnold Arboretum, Jamaica Plain, Mass.*)

are often a foot long, hence it is coarse in texture, but the leaves have a habit of remaining flat against a trellis so that it is excellent for screening purposes. Unfortunately it has no autumn color and does grow vigorously, quickly crowding out lesser vines grown nearby, so it should be given plenty of room to increase properly.

elegans vine Zone 9 Calico Dutchman's-pipe
Often called the Calico-flower, this vine is native to Brazil, is sometimes planted out-of-doors in frost-free areas, or is occasionally used as a plant in the home greenhouse. The purple and yellow flowers are 3 in. wide and are scentless.

grandiflora vine Zone 8 Pelican Dutchman's-pipe
Although this plant may be grown out-of-doors in the South, it is not hardy elsewhere in the U.S. The white calyx resembles a swan. It is not a native species, having originated in the West Indies. The var. **'Sturtevantii'** has purplish-white flowers 18 in. in dia., which have a "tail" 3 ft. long. A very curious flower.

serpentaria vine Zone 4 Virginia Snakeroot
Another member of the Birthwort Family, with alternate, heart-shaped leaves and greenish, S-shaped flowers blooming near the base of the plant. Native from N.Y. to Fla. and west to Tex., it is not used horticulturally as much as *A. durior*, although it has some significance as a medicinal plant.

sipho = *A. durior*

ARISTOLOCHIACEAE = The Birthwort or Wild Ginger Family

ARISTOTELIA (a-ris-tot-EE-lia)
racemosa 25′ Zone 10 New Zealand Wineberry
An evergreen tree with simple, opposite leaves 5 in. long; flowers pink in dense panicles, The fruit is red to black, pea-sized. Native to New Zealand. Chiefly cultivated in southern Calif. and propagated by layers or cuttings.

ARMERIA (ar-MEER-ia). Low, tufted, evergreen, extremely hardy plants used in the rock garden and sometimes for edging. They do best in light sandy soil in the full sun. They are easily increased by division or separation, preferably in Sept.

juniperifolia 2″ Zone 3 Juniper Thrift
A hardy, diminutive, cushion-shaped rock garden plant with small awl-shaped leaves, $\frac{1}{2}$ in. long and triangular in cross section. Flowers are white to pink in small heads $\frac{1}{2}$ in. across appearing in May. Native to Spain. This is the best of the thrifts for the rock garden. It is unfortunate that this is susceptible to a basal stem rot during the summer, more so than other *Armeria* sp.; hence it should have perfect drainage to retain a good growing condition. Often incorrectly offered as *A. caespitosa*.

maritima 6″–12″ Zone 3 Common Thrift
With narrow, linear, grasslike, evergreen leaves to 6 in. long and white to deep rose-pink flowers in rounded heads $\frac{1}{2}$ in. across (thus differentiating it from *Arenaria* species) blooming from mid-May to' mid-June. This species is native to southern Greenland, Iceland and northwestern Europe. A large plant of Thrift, if carefully divided, yields hundreds of small

plantlets, one of the reasons why this is so popular and makes such a good ground cover. It withstands seashore conditions remarkably well. Only the flower stalks grow 12 in. high; the rest of the plant is much lower. The flower is used in medicines for urinary troubles.

The var. **laucheana** has deep crimson flowers, and several other varieties and hybrids of this serviceable plant are being grown and offered commercially. They make fine cushionlike plants for the rockery, or for growing between stepping stones or stones in the terrace. Sometimes when bare spots occur the plants must be lifted, separated and replanted.

pseudarmeria $2\frac{1}{2}'$ **Zones 6–7 Pinkball Thrift**

Leaves broadly lanceolate to 10 in. long and 1 inch wide, flowers dark rose pink to white in heads $1\frac{3}{4}$ in. wide, blooming during July and Aug. Native to Portugal. This is the most frequently used of the broad-leaved thrifts.

ARMORACIA (ar-mor-AY-sia)
lapathifolia. See HORSE-RADISH.
rusticana = Horse-radish

ARNEBIA (ar-NEEB-ia)
cornuta = *A. decumbens*
decumbens 2′ **annual Arab-primrose Arnebia** Good for the mixed border in the sun with dense spikes (15–18 in. tall) of yellow flowers spotted black, changing to maroon, each flower about $\frac{3}{4}$ in. across. Native to Afghanistan.
echioides = *Echioides longiflorum*

ARNICA (AR-nik-a)
montana 3′ **Zone 6 (?) Mountain Arnica** This herb, native to Europe, is of economic importance because its roots yield the tincture of arnica. The leaves are entire, smooth, opposite and rather oblong. The yellow flowers are borne in branching heads about 3 in. wide.

AROID. A plant of the Arum Family.

ARONIA (a-RO-nia). Native American deciduous shrubs with alternate leaves, small, white, 5-petalled flowers, members of the Rose Family. The berries are either red or black, about $\frac{1}{4}$ in. in dia. Plants may be easily divided with a sharp spade. Softwood cuttings root easily. Seed may be stratified as soon as ripe for 3 months at 40° F. or else stored dry in airtight containers in a cool place and then stratified.

arbutifolia 9′ **Zone 4 Red Chokeberry** The white flowers of this eastern native shrub and especially its bright red berries in the fall are the chief characteristics of this deciduous shrub. It is native over a wide area in the eastern U.S. and it flowers and fruits well, producing red autumn color every year in almost any soil.

Over the years, several varieties have been named but on being grown under the conditions available at the Arnold Arboretum in Boston,

Mass., they have apparently reverted, eventually forming plants little different from those found over a wide area of the eastern U.S. It is sometimes very difficult for the enthusiastic nurseryman to refrain from naming a "new" seedling without a trial period.

melanocarpa $1\frac{1}{2}'-3'$ **Zone 4 Black Chokeberry** A smaller plant than *A. arbutifolia* with black berries, native to the eastern U.S. and growing well in almost any soil. It makes a splendid ground cover.

prunifolia 12′ **Zone 4 Purple-fruited Chokeberry** Merely taller growing than *A. arbutifolia* with dark purplish-black fruits in the fall, this native of the eastern U.S. is not superior to the other species in any way.

ARRABIDAEA MAGNIFICA = *Saritaea magnifica*

ARRHENATHERUM (a-ree-na-THEE-rum)
elatius bulbosum 12″ **Zone 3 Tuber Oat-grass** A tuberous-rooted grass, often found as a weed, naturalized throughout North America. The var. 'Nanum' is interesting for rock gardens since the leaves are striped green and white and are only 8–10 in. long. *A. elatius* will grow to 4 ft. high with tufted leaves about 12 in. long and $\frac{1}{2}$ in. wide. These do not spread but are propagated by dividing the clumps.

ARROW-ARUM, VIRGINIA = *Peltandra virginica*

ARROWHEAD. See SAGITTARIA.

ARROW-ROOT. See MARANTA.

ARROW-ROOT FAMILY = Marantaceae

ARROW-WOOD = *Viburnum dentatum*

ARTEMISIA (ar-tem-IS-ia). These herbs are members of the Composite Family, sometimes are bitter to the taste and usually have aromatic foliage. Sometimes they are small shrubs with alternate, deeply cut leaves and small white or yellow flower heads. They thrive in poor, dry soils and some cover large areas of wasteland in the western states. The only one mentioned here that is an annual is *A. annua*. The others are perennials.

abrotanum 4′ **Zone 5 Southernwood** This native of southern Europe has long been grown for its finely divided and intensely aromatic foliage which is used in toilet waters and even to put among stored clothing as a moth repellent.

absinthium 4′ **Zones 2–3 Common Wormwood** A coarse, weedy subshrub native to Europe but naturalized in many places in North America. All leaves are white, silky-hairy and deeply divided with many narrow segments. The lower leaves have petioles, the upper ones are sessile. Small yellowish or purplish flowers, each only $\frac{1}{8}$ in. wide, are borne on long, narrow, axillary branches. Propagated by seed, cuttings or division.

annua   1′–5′   annual   Sweet Wormwood
The 1–2$\frac{1}{2}$ in. long, pale green leaves are 1–2 pinnately divided and very fragrant, the yellow flower heads are only $\frac{1}{12}$ in. wide, in loose but profuse panicles blooming in Aug. and Sept. Although native to Asia, it has become naturalized in North America. It grows quickly and for this reason alone has some garden value.

dracunculus   2′   Zone 5   Tarragon
A popular perennial herb native to Europe and grown chiefly for its tasty leaves which are used for flavoring salads, fish, sauce, and confectionery, as well as in perfumes and toilet water. It is propagated chiefly by division.

frigida   1$\frac{1}{2}$′   Zone 2   Fringed Sagebrush
A rock garden plant from the midwestern U.S. with small yellow flowers in late Aug. and very silvery, pubescent, finely divided, aromatic foliage.

glacialis   4″   Zone 4   Glacier Wormwood
This small perennial from the Alps of Switzerland needs a coarse, gravelly soil and excellent drainage. It does well as a wall plant or a plant to grow among paving stones. Though scarcely 2 in. in dia., the plant grows as a dense mat with deeply lobed, white woolly leaves and creeping stems.

lactiflora   4′–5′   Zone 3   White Mugwort
This species comes from China and is similar to *A. vulgaris*. Apparently this Chinese species is grown in a few American nurseries and *A. vulgaris* is not.

ludoviciana   3′   Zone 3   Western Sage
A perennial with many underground rootstocks. The stems have fine white hairs and the leaves are in various shapes, usually white underneath and up to 3$\frac{1}{2}$ in. long. The flowers are in loose panicles, each head about $\frac{1}{4}$ in. long. Although native to the western U.S., this is found sometimes as a weed in the eastern part of the country.

Var. albula 'Silver King'
An herbaceous perennial, usually grown under the name of 'Silver King' Artemisia, this has very silver-gray foliage. Native from Tex. to Calif., it is a very popular gray foliage plant for northern gardens. The flowers have no ornamental value.

schmidtiana   2′   Zones 2–3   Satiny Wormwood
A Japanese species with foliage covered with silvery white hairs and leaves very deeply cut and divided. The variety **'Nana'** is only 4 in. tall and is an excellent rock garden plant. This is

sometimes called Silvermound Artemisia and nurserymen have listed it as **'Silver Mound'**.

stellerana   2$\frac{1}{2}$′   Zones 2–3   Beach Wormwood, Dusty Miller
Extremely popular especially for seashore planting is this native to eastern North America. The densely white-woolly, finely divided foliage is its chief ornamental characteristic. The small yellow flowers appear in compact, many-flowered racemes.

tridentata   9′   Zone 5   Sagebrush
A silvery-gray, aromatic shrub, not very ornamental but useful in situations where better shrubs will not grow. The Sagebrush is noted to cover many hundreds of acres in the western states and of course, in places, is considered a vicious weed.

vulgaris   3$\frac{1}{2}$′   Zone 3   Mugwort
A perennial, sometimes a bad weed, native to Europe and Asia but naturalized in eastern North America. This also has very divided alternate leaves, green above and white tomentose below. The grayish flowers are on branched axillary spikes, blooming from July to Sept. Leaves are fragrant.

ARTICHOKE (*Cynara scolymus*). The Artichoke is a perennial herb native to the Mediterranean Region and the Canary Islands, grown in America (chiefly in Calif.) as a vegetable. It is coarse, not very spiny, grows to 5 ft. tall and

Artichoke—*Cynara scolymus*

the leaves are white tomentose underneath. The flower heads are purple, the enlarged receptacle is fleshy and edible as are the bases of the bracts. It needs rich soil, plenty of water and is propagated by seed or division. Usually, if sown from seed, the flower buds are edible the second year, but under ideal conditions some may be formed the first year. However, seed propagation is variable and asexual propagation by division is much the better method.

The Artichoke suckers are planted 6–8 in.

deep, 6 ft. apart in the rows and the rows about 6 ft. apart. It is usually advisable to make new plantings every 3-4 years. Usually a winter crop, it should be grown only in frost-free areas, similar to Monterey County in southern Calif. Plenty of water is needed and fertilizer as well, some growers using as much as 400 pounds of nitrate of soda per acre. All old stems should be cut off and removed after harvest.

Insect Pests

Artichoke buds become infested with the larvae of the artichoke plume moth which tunnels into the bud scales and stem. It also lives on *Cirsium* (thistle) which should be destroyed. Suckers for replanting are fumigated with methyl bromide and sprays with insecticide #9 are suggested.

Diseases

A leaf spot on the leaves may be troublesome and is checked with applications of fungicide #D.

GRANT B. SNYDER

ARTICHOKE, JERUSALEM = *Helianthus tuberosa*

ARTICULATE. Jointed; having a node or joint where separation may take place naturally.

ARTILLERY PLANT = *Pilea microphylla*

ARTOCARPUS (ar-to-KARP-us)
   altilis (*communis*)   40′   **Zone 10   Breadfruit**
Native to Malaysia, with fruit tasting something like a sweet potato when cooked. Large leaves 3 ft. long, each with rounded lobes. The male and female flowers are separate, the male flowers being borne in an upright spike 8 in. long at the branch terminals, and the female flowers are in a round, globelike mass just below. The fruit is round, green and 8 in. across and of course is an important food item.

ARUM (AY-rum)
   italicum   1′-1½′   **Zone 7   Italian Arum**
The Italian Arum has upright, arrow-shaped leaves on stems 10-12 in. tall and small white flowers on a thick, fleshy stalk. The fruits are red berries. This plant needs rich moist soil.
   maculatum   1′   **Zones 7-8   Lords-and-ladies**
The large leaves of this plant are mottled and the green spathes are flecked with purple. The plant rests through the warm summer months, but sends up fresh leaves in the fall. These remain all winter where the climate is mild.
   palaestinum   1′   **Zone 9   Black Calla Arum**
Usually grown in the greenhouse and valued because of handsome arrow-shaped leaves that are 6 in. long and heart-shaped at the base. Its flowers resemble those of the Calla-lily except that the spathe is blackish purple inside, greenish outside, blooming during the winter.

Native to Palestine and propagated by offsets. It has been noted that pot-grown plants, to bloom well, must be pot-bound.

ARUM FAMILY. Araceae

ARUM, GIANT = *Amorphophallus giganteus*

ARUNCUS (a-RUNK-us)
   dioicus (*sylvester*)   5′-7′   **Zones 2-3   Sylvan Goat's-beard**
This is a member of the Rose Family, native to North America and blooms during June and July. It is a hardy herbaceous perennial doing well in moist soil and withstands growing in partial shade. It can be propagated either by seed or division. It is best used, because of its height, at the rear of the perennial border where its large showy panicles of white flowers are as much as 4 ft. tall. Since the sexes are separate, the male plants with the staminate flowers make the better ornamentals. The alternate leaves are 2 and 3 times compound giving the plant a feathery appearance. These plants are confused sometimes with some of the spireas, but the latter do not have compound leaves. The var. 'Kneiffii' is only 2-3 ft. tall and has finely dissected leaves.

ARUNDINARIA SPECIES (a-run-din-AIR-ia). See BAMBOO.

ARUNDO (a-RUN-do)
   donax   6′-20′   **Zone 6   Giant Reed**
A fast spreading, stiffly upright reed or tall grass, seldom producing its grasslike plumes of flowers and seeds in the North. The leaves are 1-2 ft. long and about 2½ in. wide; the spirelike flower plume is often 2 ft. long. Native to southern Europe but escaped in many places throughout the eastern U.S., particularly in marshy areas along the seacoast.

ASARINA (AS-a-rina)
   procumbens (*Antirrhinum asarina*)   **procumbent   Zone 7   Wild Ginger-snapdragon**
An attractive plant from France and Spain, it is not reliably hardy in the northern U.S. unless protected during winter. The spreading stems have heart-shaped, somewhat sticky leaves and creamy-white to pinkish snapdragon flowers throughout much of the summer. The plant forms thick mats of foliage.

ASARUM (as-AR-um)
   canadense   4″-6″   **Zones 2-3   Canada Wild Ginger**
This perennial herb rises from a creeping rootstalk which, in past generations, was collected, dried and used as a substitute for ginger. Two heart-shaped leaves, about 6 in. wide, rise above an inconspicuous brown flower, composed of a bell-shaped calyx and opening into 3 pointed lobes. The flower is on a short stem occurring at the junction of the leaf stems. Native from

Canada to S.Car. and west to Kan., it flowers in April and May. A shade-loving plant, it can be used as a ground cover in rich, slightly acid to calcareous soils. It may be divided in spring. Plants may be started also from root sections inserted in sand and peat. The leaves can cause dermatitis to susceptible persons. This species is not evergreen; hence it has less garden value than the evergreen species.

caudatum 7″ Zone 4 British Columbia Wild Ginger

The leaves of this are 2–6 in. in dia., often evergreen, somewhat similar in shape to those of a cyclamen with a pungent taste. Native from British Columbia to Calif. The brownish flowers have the lobes prolonged into 2-in. tails. This can be used as a ground cover in a shaded place.

europaeum 5″ Zone 4 European Wild Ginger

An excellent ground cover for shaded situations with glossy, evergreen leaves 2–3 in. across on stalks 5 in. long. The flowers are greenish purple or brown, about $\frac{1}{2}$ in. across, and the plant is native to Europe; it is best grown in the shade. It is one of the best evergreen ground covers, easily propagated by simple division, and should be grown a great deal more than it is.

Asarum europaeum—European Wild Ginger

shuttleworthii 8″ Zone 6 Mottled Wild Ginger

This resembles *A. canadense* with thinner and larger leaves, usually mottled, native from Va. to Ala.

virginicum 7″ Zone 5 Virginia Wild Ginger

Similar to *A. canadense* but with evergreen leaves, this plant grows in more southerly areas, being found from Va. to N.Car. in dry woods. It flowers from March to May. It is hardy outside the limits of its southern habitat,

and so can be included among the possibilities for gardens in more northerly areas.

ASCLEPIADACEAE = The Milkweed Family

ASCLEPIAS (ass-KLEE-pias). Perennial herb having a milky juice and with many species native to North America. Generally weedy and spreading rapidly by wind-blown seed, these are not desirable plants for the garden. They flower from July to Sept. and may be found throughout eastern North America. The leaves are usually opposite or in whorls and the flowers of some species are very showy. Fruits are dry pods filled with many seeds to which are attached fluffy, silky hairs. Easily grown and propagated by seed or division, some are bad weeds.

Asclepias or Milkweed pods

curassavica 3′ Zone 7 Bloodflower

A tropical American perennial with long, narrow, glossy leaves. The flowers are scarlet, tinted orange.

incarnata 5′ Zone 3 Swamp Milkweed

Single, lanceolate leaves occur in pairs on the stem of this plant and its numerous flowers, about $\frac{1}{4}$ in. wide, are borne in loose umbels at the upper end of the stalk. The flowers, pinkish in color and fragrant, have a strongly reflexed 5-lobed corolla. The seeds are contained in a pod and have silvery-white hairs on one end which act like a parachute to convey the seeds.

mexicana 5′ Zone 6 Mexican Milkweed

Native from Ore. to Mexico, with whorled or opposite leaves 6 in. long. Flowers greenish white, sometimes slightly purplish. The leaves are poisonous to sheep and chickens.

speciosa 2$\frac{1}{2}$′ Zones 2–3 Showy Milkweed

Native to western North America, similar to *A. syriaca* but often less hairy.

syriaca   5′   Zone 3   Common Milkweed
A common perennial weed with creeping rootstocks, native to central and northeastern North America. The opposite or sometimes whorled leaves are oblong, up to 8 in. long, entire, and hairy on the under surface. The sap is milky. The flowers are green to purplish, in umbels, each small flower being about ⅜ in. wide. The large seed pods are 3–4 in. long and when they split open many tightly packed flat seeds are disclosed, each with a tuft of silky hairs by which it is carried in the wind. Blooms in July and Aug. One should be certain in digging it out that all the roots are removed, for if they are not, the plant sprouts readily from any portion left in the soil.

tuberosa   3′   Zone 3   Butterfly Milkweed
By far the most popular garden plant in this genus because of its orange flowers and also because it grows well in dry, sandy soils, this is an alternate-leaved perennial. An excellent garden plant, native from Me. to Fla. The individual flowers are only ⅓ in. wide, but they are borne in very showy heads during Aug. and Sept. Propagated by division. The leaves and stems are supposed to be poisonous to animals. The root is sometimes used in medicines as an emetic or to induce perspiration.

verticillata   16″   Zone 3   Whorled Milkweed
A perennial, often a weed, with fibrous roots, narrow, linear leaves in whorls of 3–6 and greenish-white flowers in loose umbels from April to Sept. There is a variety **pumila** which seldom grows over 10 in. tall and forms a dense mat. Native over much of North America.

ASCOCENTRUM (as-co-CEN-trum). Epiphytic orchids from the Himalayas and the Philippines, occasionally grown in the greenhouse. The flowers are only about an inch across and are either bright rose-carmine (in *A. ampullaceum*) to orange-red or clear yellow in *A. miniatum*. For culture and propagation see ORCHID.

ASEXUAL. Without sex; destitute of male or female organs.

ASEXUAL REPRODUCTION. Reproduction vegetatively; without the aid of sexual organs.

ASH. See FRAXINUS.

ASH FAMILY = Oleaceae

ASIATIC SWEETLEAF = *Symplocos paniculata*

ASIMINA (as-IM-in-a)
triloba   35′   Zone 5   Papaw
Rarely seen in cultivation, this tree was of considerable interest to the early American settlers in the eastern and central U.S. where it is native, because of its fleshy, yellow to brown edible pods, 2–3 in. long, which ripened in the early fall. The common name is sometimes spelled Pawpaw. The purple cup-shaped flowers during late May are 2 in. in dia. but are not particularly conspicuous. The autumn color is an excellent yellow, and the leaves are 6–12 in. long, hanging in a drooping fashion so they move in the slightest breeze. Fruits are edible, but susceptible persons have developed a dermatitis from handling them. It does well only in rich fertile soil.

Since the Papaw is found over a wide area from Fla. to N.Y. and west to La., and Mich., it is only natural that considerable variation can occur. This is especially true of the fruits, for on some plants they are only 2–3 in. long and disagreeably resinous in flavor, while on other plants the fruits are plump and bronze or brown when ripe, up to 6 in. long and 2–3 in. thick, very pulpy and delicious to the taste.

It is unfortunate that young trees are difficult to transplant—much more so than trees of many other fruits. Also, asexual propagation is most difficult for the present at least, and apparently only seedling trees are grown. This does not assure the home gardener of obtaining a good fruiting variety.

Propagation by seed only is practiced at present. The seed should be collected as soon as the fruits are ripened. They should not be allowed to dry out but should be stratified immediately at 40° F. for 3–4 months, then sown. See SEEDS, STRATIFICATION.

ASPARAGUS (as-PA-rag-us)
asparagoides vine Zone 10 Smilax Asparagus
The "leaves" of this branching vine are actually expanded branchlets, oval in shape and about an inch long. The berries are dark purple, about ¼ in. in dia. Native to South Africa. The var. **myrtifolius** has smaller "leaves". Although this can be grown out-of-doors in the extreme southern U.S., it is widely grown in greenhouses to provide cut branches as background material for florists' bouquets. Of the five species of *Asparagus* mentioned here, this has the largest "leaves" and *A. plumosus* and *A. officinalis*, the smallest.

falcatus vine Zone 10 Sicklethorn Asparagus
Growing up to 40 ft. long, this produces many short sharp thorns and is native to tropical Asia and Africa. The small white flowers are produced in fragrant sprays. The branchlets are leafless and produced in clusters. The berries are brown. Cultivated in southern Fla.

officinalis. This is the common garden Asparagus (which see).

setaceus (*plumosus*)   **climbing vine   Zone 8**
Fern Asparagus
A tall-climbing plant from South Africa with very fine threadlike leaves about ¼ in. long and

purple-black berries about the size of small peas. There are also several forms of this very popular plant in the florist trade. Like *A. sprengeri*, this can not withstand frost and is a popular greenhouse plant in the North. The foliage is much used as an important part of flower arrangements.

sprengeri vine Zone 8 Sprenger Asparagus A very popular greenhouse plant, native to South Africa, probably the best of this genus as a pot plant certainly, and also for cut sprays for use by florists. It does not climb over 6 ft. high, has tuberous roots and can be expected to renew its growth repeatedly after cutting. The berry is bright red and up to $\frac{1}{2}$ in. across, ripening indoors about Christmas. Excellent for hanging baskets. The seed germinates easily in about 4 weeks. Leaves are flat, linear and about 1 in. long.

ASPARAGUS (*Asparagus officinalis*). Asparagus was appreciated as a vegetable by the Romans as early as 500 B.C. Cato's culture directions would even serve fairly well today. Until the nineteenth century, however, it was considered a prized luxury. During the past 50 years it has increased in commercial importance so that it is now one of the most valuable of the early vegetables and is available, fresh, canned and frozen.

The largest commercial acreages are located in Calif. and N.J., with lesser acreages in Wash., Pa., Ill., S.C., Md., Mich., Mass., Del., and Ia.

Varieties

There are only a few varieties of asparagus commonly grown at the present time and even these show only minor differences. While some seedsmen still list the varieties **'Reading Giant'**. **'Conovers Colossal'**, **'Palmetto'**, **'Brocks Imperial**, **Hybrid'**, **'Rutgers'** types, and **'Viking'**, the largest acreage by far is planted to **'Martha'** or **'Mary Washington'** or selections of Washington under the names of **'Washington 500'** and **'Waltham Washington'**. All of the Washington types are more or less resistant to asparagus rust, are vigorous in growth, produce good size and high-quality spears and, therefore, are highly recommended.

Asparagus is one of the more permanent of the vegetable crops in the garden plan. After the plants are well established they should continue to produce a satisfactory crop for from 10–15 years. Generally plantings should be renewed every 10–12 years. In the home garden asparagus should be located at the side or end of the garden area where it will not be disturbed by the plantings of other crops.

Soils and Fertilizers

Asparagus can be grown on a variety of soil types. The best results are generally obtained on the lighter sandy loam and silt soils that are open, porous, well drained and warm up early in the spring. Heavy clay soils are not recommended.

Because of the length of time the land is occupied by an asparagus bed, it is very important that the soil be of high fertility and in good physical condition before the plants are set. A good application of animal manure, 30–40 bu. per 1000 sq. ft., or a well-decomposed compost should be thoroughly incorporated into the top 8–10 in. of soil. In addition, 30–40 lbs. of a 5-10-10 or similar commercial fertilizer should be added to supplement the manure. If the soil is acid, below 6.5 pH, ground limestone should also be applied prior to planting time.

Establishing the Asparagus Bed

For the home gardener, it is recommended to use only 1-year-old crowns (roots) that have a large, well-developed root system with large, well-developed buds. Crowns with spindly roots and many small buds should be discarded.

Climatic conditions regulate the best time to set the crowns into the garden. In most sections spring planting is best; however in some sections of the South, fall and winter planting dates are preferred.

Normal planting distance is from 40–48 in. between rows and 15 in. in the row. If the plants are to be set in a bed rather than rows, spacing may be on the basis of 24 in. x 30 in. or 30 in. x 30 in. Plan at least 10–15 plants per member of the family.

The crowns should be planted as early as possible in the spring, but only after the soil has been properly fertilized and prepared. Dig or plow a trench to a depth of 8 in. in the lighter soils or 5–6 in. in the heavier, mineral soils. Deep planting, 10–12 in., is not recommended.

The crowns are placed in the bottom of the trench with the buds on top and the roots well spread out. Cover the crowns with several inches of soil and firm over the roots. As soon as the young shoots (spears) appear add more soil coverage. Repeat this procedure until the trench is finally filled.

Annual Maintenance

For the first and second year after planting no spears (shoots) should be cut in order to allow the plants to become well established. Plants will develop a tall, 4–5 ft. bushy growth which produce the food that will be stored in the roots to produce next year's spears. This bushy growth should never be cut off until it turns brown in the late fall.

During the first 2 years after planting apply a broadcast application of a complete fertilizer and work into the topsoil in the early spring at the rate of 20–30 lbs. per 1000 sq. ft. This may be followed in a month or 6 weeks with an application of nitrate of soda or other readily available nitrogen fertilizer at the rate of 8–10 lbs. per 1000 sq. ft., placed on both sides of the row, 6–8 in. from the plant.

After the third year apply 30–40 lbs. of a 5-10-10 fertilizer per 1000 sq. ft. using half in the spring and one-half at the end of the cutting season.

Cultivation should be sufficient at all times to control weeds, particularly those that spread by rhizomes such as quack grass. Cultivation should be shallow so as not to injure the buds or crown.

Harvesting

During the second year a few spears may be cut. In the third year cut for 3 weeks and in the following years harvest may continue for 6–8 weeks. Spears should be cut with a sharp knife just below the ground level. Care must be taken to cut so that no young and still buried spears will be injured. For best quality use the spears before they get too tall, 8–10 in.

Proper way to cut Asparagus shoots

Insects and Diseases

Asparagus beetles, both the striped and 12-spotted species, are the most serious. Both adults and larvae feed on the spears and plants.

CONTROL. During cutting season (when spears are attached) apply a 1% rotenone dust or spray. After the cutting season apply a Sevin dust or spray.

ASPARAGUS RUST. Elongated orange-red, powdery blisters on stems and foliage which check growth and finally kill the plants.

CONTROL. Grow rust-resistant varieties of the Washington type and spray the ferns after harvest with Maneb. Cut diseased tops close to the ground in the fall and burn.

GRANT B. SNYDER

ASPASIA (AS-pa-sia). A group of 1–2 leaved epiphytic orchids native from Central America south to Brazil, occasionally grown in a moist greenhouse in a shaded situation. **A. epidendroides** has 2–10 greenish yellow flowers, 1½ in. across in loose racemes, and **A. epidendroides principissa** has 2–7 greenish flowers in loose racemes, but each flower is nearly 3 in. across. For culture and propagation, see ORCHID.

ASPEN. See POPULUS.

ASPERULA (as-PER-u-la) This is a large group of plants from Europe, both annuals and perennials, bearing square stems. Only a few have been cultivated for ornament. Probably the best known of these, because it makes an excellent ground cover in the shade, was formerly called *A. odorata*, but recently the name was changed back to *Galium odoratum*. The flowers are small and prolific.

cynanchica   prostrate or to 16″   Zone 6
A perennial from Europe and Asia, flowers small, white or pink.

hirta   8″   Zone 6
This attractive hairy perennial from the Pyrenees Mountains grows in moist acid soil. Whorls of narrowly lanceolate leaves, arranged on a square stem, are crowned with a loose cluster of tiny, pale pink flowers in early spring.

odorata = *Galium odoratum*
orientalis (*A. azurea-setosa*)   1′   **annual**
Oriental Woodruff
A much-branched annual from Europe and Asia with 8 leaves in a whorl and small blue, clustered flowers in summer. Plant in shade and moist soil. Seed may be sown in May and plants thinned to 6 in. apart.

tinctoria   2′   Zone 6   Dyers Woodruff
A perennial with reddish roots (from which a dye is extracted) with white or reddish flowers. The leaves are produced in whorls of 4–6. Native to Europe. An old garden favorite in Europe for slightly moist and shaded situations. Propagated easiest by division in spring.

ASPHODELINE (as-fo-de-LY-ne)
lutea   3′–4′   Zone 6   Jacob's-rod
A member of the Lily Family, this is a thick-rooted herbaceous perennial, native to the Mediterranean Region, producing fragrant yellow flowers, in tubular-shaped clusters 7–

15 in. long and about 2½ in. thick, during June. Native to southern Europe. It is easily grown in almost any good garden soil in sun or partial shade and is propagated by division.

ASPIDISTRA (as-pid-ISS-tra)

elatior   2′   Zone 7   Cast-iron Plant, Common Aspidistra

A very tough, popular foliage plant for the home, native to China and belonging to the Lily Family. It is probably the most easily grown of all house plants, staying in vigorous condition for years. The oblong, elliptic evergreen leaves are 2½ ft. long and 4 in. broad, borne from the thick roots. The small purple-brown bell-shaped flowers, not often borne, appear near the soil surface and are usually hidden by foliage. Plenty of sun in winter, considerable shade in summer, and watering only when the soil gets moderately dry are prerequisites to good growth. There is a form 'Variegata', with leaves striped green and white.

ASPLENIUM (as-PLEE-nium).

These are the spleenworts and there are at least two species, native to North America, that can be grown in the proper place in a garden where shade and moisture combine to give a cool, moist situation. The Ebony Spleenwort (*A. platyneuron*) and the Maidenhair Spleenwort (*A. trichomanes*) are both hardy and native to North America. Maidenhair Spleenwort is smaller, only about 6 in. tall, also with evergreen foliage. It is found wild from Alaska across all of Canada to the eastern U.S., on limestone soils. These can be planted in crevices in the rocks where the soil is not too rich and there is not too much moisture. Usually they are propagated most easily by division, but if spores are to be tried, see FERNS.

The species for the cool greenhouse are *A. nidus*, the Birds'-nest Fern, and *A. bulbiferum*, the Mother Fern. The Bird's-nest Fern is not at all like the Ebony Spleenwort, which has long fronds with alternately spaced pinnae about 1 in. long, but has simple leaves, broadly elliptical, 12 in. long and glossy. The common name comes from the fact that the leaves are borne in a tight rosette at the rhizome, simulating a sheltered and protected spot for a bird's nest. It needs a warm greenhouse of at least 60° F. for best growth.

The Mother Fern (*A. bulbiferum*) does have typical cut-leaved fronds about 24 in. long and 9 in. wide, with tiny buds developing on the upper surface of the fronds which, if carefully planted, give rise to new plants. This is native to New Zealand and Australia and is not for outside planting. Like all other ferns, it needs a moist atmosphere, and a mist sprayed on the foliage occasionally is an aid to its good

growth. It does well in a cool greenhouse. For propagation by spores, see FERNS.

bulbiferum   2′   Zone 10   Mother Fern

Native to New Zealand and Malaysia, this can be reproduced by vegetative buds (see FERNS). The fronds are finely divided and are unique in that they bear small bulbils which sprout and form new plants while still attached to the frond. This is for growing in the greenhouse.

nidus   1′   Zone 10   Bird's-nest Fern

A fern of the tropics of the eastern hemisphere with leathery, glossy foliage, sometimes grown in the greenhouse. The fronds of this fern are not divided, but many fronds arise in the clump, giving rise to the name Bird's-nest. This is only for growing in the greenhouse, although it is native to southern Fla.

platyneuron   8″–15″   Zone 3   Ebony Spleenwort

This is an evergreen fern of the woods, with each small pinna on a frond bearing an earlike lobe at the base. There are about 30–35 pairs of pinnae to each frond. A diminutive fern of interest when planted in just the right rock crevice to show it off to best advantage. Native to eastern North America.

resiliens   10″   Zone 6   Blackstem Spleenwort

Difficult to grow, this plant must be in a rock crevice. It is native from Pa. to Mexico.

ruta-muraria   3″   Zone 6

This extremely rare plant is almost impossible to grow in a garden. For these reasons it should not be taken from the wild. It is native to eastern U.S.

trichomanes   6″   Zone 3   Maidenhair Spleenwort

A small, evergreen fern native to eastern North America, growing in red limestone soils with small, tightly clustered fronds about an inch wide. This is very definitely an interesting plant to place in some rock crevice in the shade, where there is sufficient moisture for it to grow properly.

viride   8″   Zone 3   Green Spleenwort

This is another species which is very difficult to grow. It is native to northern North America and Eurasia.

ASTER (AS-ter).

The asters comprise a large group of perennial wild flowers and themselves belong to the Compositae, a Family including many of the more familiar wild flowers, both native and exotic. A common character is that the flower-heads are made up of generally yellow disc flowers surrounded by ray flowers. The leaves of the asters are simple, narrow and alternate. No special care is needed to cultivate them, although in general they prefer rather dry soils. Propagation is by division in spring or fall. They also self-sow quite freely.

Asters, sometimes called Michaelmas Daisy, come in many hybrid groups as well as species, and it is these hybrids, mostly derived from *A. amellus*, *A. novae-angliae*, *A. novi-belgi* and others that make the largest group of garden plants. Hundreds of varieties have been named.

The Dwarf or Cushion Michaelmas Daisy is probably derived from several native American species, but includes a group of excellent cushionlike plants, 9–12 in. tall, forming dense masses of bloom during Sept. and Oct. They can be used for edging, grouping or in the rock garden.

All are of easy culture, but none have yellow flowers. *Solidaster luteus* (which see) at one time was thought to be an aster but now is considered to be in another genus entirely. *Linosyris vulgaris* is sometimes incorrectly called a yellow Michaelmas Daisy.

alpinus   8″–10″   **Zones 2–3**   **Alpine Aster**
Native to North America and Europe as well, this little aster bears violet flowers that are 1½ in. across during May and June. There are several varieties with white, lavender, blue or pink flowers available in the trade. Because of its small size, it makes a fine plant for the rock garden.

amellus   1½′–2′   **Zone 3**   **Italian Aster**
With purple flowers about 1½ in. across, this is a native of Europe blooming in July and August. Several varieties have been named, popular and available from European nurseries but apparently not easily found in American nurseries. They have not proved too easy to grow in America. Most asters can be easily moved in the fall, but not these. Spring is the best time for transplanting and even then they usually take a full year to become established. In other words these are not good varieties with which the amateur gardener should start.

bellidiastrum   1′   **Zone 6?**   **Michel Aster**
A charming rock garden plant from southern Europe having broadly oval leaves in a rosette at the base of the plant and large white daisy-like flowers on stems rising well above the low foliage. Needs winter protection.

decurrens = *A. laevis*
diffusus = *A. lateriflorus*
divaricatus   1′–2′   **Zone 4**   **White Wood Aster**
A rather low, much-branched plant with a woody stem. The leaves, having irregularly toothed margins, vary somewhat in shape, those near the base of the plant being wider than those near the upper end of the stem. The disk-flowers are yellow, the ray-flowers white and these are borne on short, much-branched stems. A few flowers sometimes appear at the axils of the leaves. These plants are found in dry, woody areas from Me. to Ga., and west to Ohio, and flower in July.

dumosus   3′   **Zones 2–3**   **Bushy Aster**

A prolifically flowering plant from Mass. to Fla. and La., ranging in height from 1–3 ft. and remaining in bloom from Aug. to Oct.

'Alert'—crimson red.
'Alice Haslam'—rosy red.
'Lady in Blue'—blue.
'Little Red Boy'—12 in. high. ·
'Niobe'—white flowers, 8 in. high.
'Peter Harrison'—pink.
'Snow Cushion'—white.
'Victor'—pale blue flowers, about 12 in. high.
Several other varieties, some dwarf, are also available.

ericoides   1′–3′   **Zone 3**   **Heath Aster**
Although this plant is not always able to grow in an upright position, its rigid, finely cut leaves and dainty flowers, ½ in. in dia., make it an attractive addition to the wild garden. The yellow and white, daisylike flowers occur along the branchlets which clothe the stem. It is common in dry, sunny waste areas from Me. to Minn. and from Fla. to Mo. It flowers from July to Oct.

farreri   1½′   **Zone 4**   **Farrer Aster**
A small plant from central China having a tufted growth, with narrow leaves covered with a fine pubescence and yellow flowers like daisies, on tall stems.

x frikartii   1½′–2′   **Zone 4**
This is a hybrid group (*A. thompsonii* x *A. amellus*) growing about 2 ft. tall with fragrant violet-blue flowers up to 3 in. across. They bloom from July to Nov. **'Wonder of Staffa'** is the most popular of this group.

grandiflorus   3′–4′   **Zone 7**   **Great Aster**
Not nearly so common as other native asters, this plant is distinguished by the hairy stem and by the numerous, small, oblong to linear leaves on the strongly ascending branches. The purple ray-flowers and yellow disc-flowers comprise flower heads which are 1 to 2 in. in dia. The plant grows along the coast in dry, open woods, from Va. to Fla., and flowers from Sept. to Nov.

laevis   4′   **Zone 4**   **Smooth Aster**
This aster has a straight, unbranched stem. The alternate leaves are heart shaped at the base and clasp the stem. The ray-flowers vary from white to lavender, light blue or pink to purple and are in terminal clusters over the upper third of the stem. The plant may be found in dry pastures and open woodlands over much of the eastern half of the U.S. It flowers in late summer and continues into Oct. A good plant for prolonging the blooming season of the garden.

lateriflorus   4′–5′   **Zone 3**   **Calico Aster**
Another of the branching asters, its leaves at the base of the plant tend to be ovate, while the stem leaves are lanceolate. The flower-heads are about ½ in. wide, borne in one-sided clusters on

the branchlets. The ray-flowers are white or violet, the disk-flowers purplish. It grows well in either moist or dry locations over much of eastern U.S. The flowering season is from Aug. to Oct.

linariifolius 2′ **Zone** 4 **Savoryleaf Aster**
As its name implies, the hairy leaves of this plant are very narrow and rather wiry. Loose clusters of large violet flowers are borne on the 2-ft. stems in autumn. If the plant is nipped back in early summer, a bushier plant and a greater number of flowers will result. This does well in sandy acid soil in sun or light shade. The variety 'Albus' has white flowers; 'Roseus' has pink flowers and 'Purpureus' has dark purple flowers.

macrophyllus 2′–3′ **Zone** 3 **Bigleaf Aster**
The leaves of this aster are heart shaped, with unevenly toothed margins, and have a stem nearly equal in length to the length of the leaf. However, near the flat-topped flower cluster the leaves become smaller and the stems are margined by a wavy leaf portion called a wing. The ray-flowers may be violet, lavender or light blue and each flower-head measures ½ in. in dia. Native over the eastern U.S. and south to N.Car., west to Ill., and flowers in Aug. and Sept.

novae-angliae 3′–5′ **Zones** 2–3 **New England Aster**
A very common wild flower in New England, it varies widely in height, sometimes exceeding 5 ft. In habit it has a much-branched stem and lanceolate leaves which clasp the stem. The flower-heads are 1 in. or more in dia., and form loose clusters at the ends of the branches. The ray-flowers are purple. An especially showy plant for the wild garden, if its size does not rule out its use. Preferring rather moist sites, it may be found in eastern North America from southern Canada to Ala. It flowers in Aug. and continues in flower into Oct. There are not many varieties of this species being grown for asters more closely related to *A. novi-belgi* are far more popular. However, 'Harrington's Pink' with salmon pink flowers, 'Survivor' and 'Barr's Pink' are all fine asters worthy of being grown in any garden. All have pink flowers and are about 4 ft. tall.

novi-belgii 3′–5′ **Zones** 2–3 **New York Aster**
Native to North America and widely distributed from Newfoundland to Ga. The flowers of the species are blue-violet, about an inch across. There may be hundreds of varieties of this aster, most of them varied in England, with flowers from white to pink to blue and violet. New varieties are listed every year. Many of these are excellent ornamentals bringing color to the fall garden from early Sept. until frost.

patens 2′–3′ **Zone** 4 **Late Purple Aster, Sky-drop Aster**
A slender, branching plant of erect habit. The alternate leaves are ovate with heart-shaped bases which clasp the stem. The solitary flower-heads, 1–1½ in. dia., terminate the many branches, violet ray-flowers contributing much color to the fields and roadsides from Me. to Ga., and as far inland as Ohio. Over this range, it may be in flower from June to Oct.

puniceus 4′–8′ **Zone** 3 **Swamp Aster**
This is probably one of the largest asters; individuals growing in moist, swampy areas sometimes attain a height of 8 ft. Generally, however, it maintains more modest proportions. The alternate leaves are lanceolate, with toothed margins, and clasp the stem. The single-flowered heads are borne on several branched flower stalks which arise from the axils of the leaves. The ray-flowers are purple. This is hardly the plant for the wild garden, because of its extreme height. It grows in swamps from Newfoundland to Minn. and Ga.

spectabilis 2′ **Zone** 5 **Seaside Aster**
This perennial spreads rapidly by underground stolons, from which arise the stems 12 to 18 in. high, covered with stiff, dark green leaves and bearing many light blue or violet flowers from July to Oct. It grows in the sandy acid soil of eastern U.S., often in sparsely covered pine forests.

tataricus 6′–8′ **Zone** 3 **Tatarian Daisy, Tatarian Aster**
Coming from Siberia, this is the largest of the asters used for ornamental purposes. It needs plenty of space. The lower leaves are as much as 24 in. long but the upper leaves are smaller; the violet-purple flower-heads are an inch across but are borne profusely in the late fall.

tongolensis 1′ **Zone 8?** **East Indies Aster**
An aster closely resembling *A. alpinus*, this plant from India bears its light lavender flowers in July and early Aug.

ASTER = Michaelmas Daisy

ASTER FAMILY = Compositae

ASTER, NEW ENGLAND = *Aster novae-angliae*

ASTILBE (as-TIL-be). These are attractive plants which look like spireas and are sometimes offered in the trade as such. They have fluffy spikes of white, pink, red or purple flowers from June to Aug., belong to the Saxifrage Family and are native to Korea, China and Japan. Most have compound leaves (spireas do not), but one species, *A. simplicifolia*, has simple leaves. Some varieties are excellent as pot plants in the greenhouse. All should be planted in situations where there is plenty of soil moisture. Propagation is by seed, but is best by simple division of the plants in fall or spring.

x arendsii 2'-3½' **Zone 6 Hybrid Astilbe**
A hybrid group with many pink-flowered varieties. The most popular is probably 'Fanal' with garnet-red flowers and bronze leaves. Others are 'Red Sentinel', 'Peach Blossom', 'Queen Alexandra' and many others.

astilboides 3' **Zone 6 Goatsherd Astilbe**
An herbaceous perennial with 2-3 pinnately compound leaves, the leaflets 2½ in. long; flowers are white and in dense spikes or panicles. Native to Japan.

chinensis davidii (*A. davidii*) 6' **Zones 6-7 David Astilbe**
A showy herbaceous perennial with pinnately compound leaves with the leaflets resembling leaves of elms, 1½ in. long; rose-pink flowers with dark blue anthers in narrow, 2 ft. panicles. Native to China.

chinensis 'Pumila' 8" **Zone 6**
A dwarf form with rosy-mauve flowers produced in the late summer, sometimes used in rock gardens. Probably from China.

x crispa 4"-6" **Zone 6**
Several small cultivars with deeply crinkled foliage and colored almost bronze. Flower colors are usually deep pink, red and even white. Considered hybrids of *A. simplicifolia* x *A.* x *arendsii*.

davidii = *A. chinensis davidii*

japonica 2' **Zone 5 Japanese Astilbe**
Native to Japan, this has pyramidal white flower-clusters of many small flowers in June. The leaves are 2 and 3 times compound. This makes a fine plant for greenhouse or home, requiring plenty of moisture. There is a clone with variegated foliage.

x rosea 12"-18" **Zone 6 Rose Astilbe**
A hybrid (*A. chinensis* x *A. japonica*) with deeply cut, feathery foliage and large, fluffy, pink flower-heads on tall stalks, sometimes over 2 ft. high. Many of the varieties in florist shops may trace their parentage to this hybrid.

simplicifolia 6"-12" **Zone 6 Star Astilbe**
Blooming in Sept., native to Japan, this has glossy foliage and spires of white to pink flowers.

simplicifolia salmonae 1' **Zone 5**
The leaves of this small Japanese perennial are deeply lobed and the small, 5-petaled flowers are borne in long, slightly nodding clusters on stems 20 in. high, in June and July. The plant forms small clumps of foliage 5-6 in. high.

ASTRANTIA (as-TRAN-shia)
major 2'-3' **Zone 6? Masterwort**
A European herbaceous perennial of easy cultivation, this is valued for its small colorful pinkish to white flowers with purplish flower bracts borne in umbels in June. Often planted along streams. Best propagated by division.

ASTROPHYTUM (as-tro-FY-tum). Small members of the Cactus Family, grown as house plants in full sun, chiefly native to Mexico. They are leafless, ribbed, often globular but in the form of a star, with few weak spines and short-lasting yellow or orange flowers borne at the top of the plant.

asterias 1" **Zone 10 Sea Urchin Starcactus**
Yellow flowers an inch wide, dome shaped, plant body covered with white scales. Entire plant only about 3 in. wide.

capricorne 8" **Zone 9 Goathorn Starcactus**
These globular, ribbed cacti have 7-8 ribs and contorted spines. The flowers, 2½ in. long, spread widely with many petals colored lemon-yellow at the center with a red throat. Native to northern Mexico.

myriostigma 2" **Zone 10 Bishop's-hood**
Small, 5-ribbed, mounded globe, no spines, covered with small white spots. Flowers yellow.

ornatum 10"-15" **Zone 10 Starcactus**
The best ornamental of this genus with a small, subglobose plant body with 8 prominent spiral folds, green and marked with silvery spots; talonlike spines and lemon-yellow flowers that are about 3½ in. long and showy.

ATHYRIUM (a-THI-rium). These are the Lady Ferns, the most common of which in North America is **A. filix-femina**, and they are also native throughout Europe and Asia. Easily grown in partial shade in the garden, with finely cut fronds 18-36 in. long. Some of the ornamental variations have been given varietal names—**crispum, aristatum** and **plumosum**. **A. crenatum** has fronds only 12 in. long. **A. pyncocarpum**, the Glade Fern, is taller and more coarse, the fronds being 30-48 in. long and 6 in. wide, and it is found in wooded areas on limestone soils.

These ferns are of the easiest culture and are propagated easily by divisions or with more difficulty by spores. See FERNS. The yellow-green of the foliage is not the best of foliage colors, but this fern is frequently used for massing in the shrubs as a kind of ground cover. Some species for the greenhouse would be **A. goeringianum 'Pictum'**, **A. macrocarpum**, **A. nipponicum** and **A. spinulosum**.

ATRIPLEX (AT-rip-lex)
hortensis 6' **annual Orach**
An herb, native to Asia, with pale yellow to dark reddish, triangular leaves and small greenish clusters of flowers. This will grow in saline soils. Most parts of the plant have been used medicinally in preparations for soothing inflammations, and the seed has been used in emetics. The var. **cupreata** has the darkest red leaves and dark violet stalks. Propagated by seed. The green foliage is used as greens, and it has been popular as a pot herb since the sixteenth century.

patula   4′   annual   Fat-hen Saltbush
A native weed on sandy or alkaline soil, with alternate and opposite simple lanceolate leaves, the upper ones often linear and even sessile, up to 1½ in. long. Flowers both staminate and pistillate often in the same spike, not conspicuous, blooming in Aug. to Oct. The variety **hastata** has triangular leaves. The somewhat similar species **A. rosea** is common in waste places and irrigated areas of the northern Rocky Mountain area and Calif.

semibaccata   1′–1½′   Zone 8   Creeping Saltbush
This perennial grows in low mats along the Calif. Coast, but is actually native to Australia. The gray-green foliage has a fine texture, each leaf being about 2 in. long, and they become sufficiently dense to restrain weeds. It is drought resistant and is one of those plants used in southern Calif. as a 'fire-resistant' plant. See FIRE-RESISTANT PLANTS.

ATROPA (AT-ro-pa)
belladonna   3′   Zone 6   Belladonna
An herb, native to Europe and Asia, with shiny black berries about ½ in. across that are poisonous; hence this plant should not be grown in gardens where children are likely to play. The alternate oval leaves are 3½–5 in. long. The bell-shaped blue-purple or dull red flowers are 1 in. long.

ATTAR-OF-ROSES. See ROSA DAMASCENA.

ATTENUATE. Tapering slenderly; applied usually to the apex of a leaf.

ATYPICAL. Not typical; departing from the normal.

AUBRIETA (au-BREE-ta)
deltoidea   3″–6″   Zone 4   Purple Rock-cress
Belonging to the Mustard Family, this perennial is somewhat comparable to *Arabis* but slightly more difficult to grow. Once started it forms a dense mat of foliage flowering from April to June, with 4-petaled flowers about ¾ in. across colored from red to purple. The flowers are borne in short terminal clusters held above the dense mat of leaves. An excellent plant for a spot in the well-drained rock garden or for edging. Shear the flower spikes off after they fade and a fall flowering might be induced. Easily propagated by spring division or by spring-sown seeds. Native to Greece. Several varieties are offered in the trade with flowers varying only slightly in color, especially on the Pacific Coast where it seems to do very well. Elsewhere in the U.S. it seems to have difficulties that may preclude its being grown.

AUCUBA (aw-KEW-ba)
japonica   15′   Zone 7   Japanese Aucuba

An evergreen shrub with thick glossy leaves up to 7 in. long, native to Japan. The sexes are separate, the small flowers appearing in panicles 2–5 in. long in March, and the brilliant red fruits are effective all winter and into the spring. Both sexes should be in the near vicinity to insure good fruit production. It should be grown in partial shade for in full sun the foliage tends to burn. The "Gold-dust Tree" is frequently the common name given the variegated form **variegata**. Several varieties are grown and those with variegated foliage have proved popular.

Varieties: **'Crassifolia'**—a male plant with very thick leaves; **'Crotonifolia'**—leaves spotted with white; **'Grandis'**—a female plant with broad, deep green leaves; **'Longifolia'**—a free-fruiting female plant; **'Luteo-carpa'**—yellow fruit; **'Nana'**—plant smaller than the species; **'Picturata'**—leaf with a large yellow blotch in the center; **variegata**—both male and female clones with yellow spots in the leaves.

AUREOLARIA (aur-eo-LAY-ria)
flava   5′–6′   Zone 4   False Foxglove
A vigorous-growing plant with opposite, lanceolate and toothed stem leaves and pinnately lobed basal leaves. The yellow, funnel-shaped flowers have 5 spreading lobes, forming 2 lips. The plant may be found in dry woods and clearings over the New England section to Mid-Atlantic states and west to the Great Lakes. It flowers in July and Aug.

AURICULATE. Furnished with ear-shaped appendages (auricles), as the base of a petal or leaf.

AURINIA (aw-RIN-i-a). This generic name has recently been resurrected and unfortunately one of the most widely used of rock garden plants and low perennials must be moved over from the genus *Alyssum*. These changes are sometimes necessary to correct mistakes made years ago and plantsmen will just have to make the best of it, unfortunate as it is.
saxatilis   6″   Zone 3   Golden-tuft, Rock Madwort
An easily grown and very popular rock plant with bright golden-yellow flowers in the early spring and silvery-gray foliage. It is most unfortunate that the name *Alyssum saxatile*, under which this plant has been known ever since Linnaeus named it in 1753, will have to be changed to *Aurinia saxatilis* because of the botanical rules of nomenclature. It will probably be years before this old-fashioned and popular plant will be popularly known as *Aurinia saxatilis*, so gardeners should be familiar with both names. The flowers appear in May in many clusters. Native to Europe. Several varieties are

known such as **'Compacta,'** which is more dense than the species; **'Citrina,'** with light yellow flowers; **'Plena,'** with double yellow flowers and others. These are fine spring-blooming plants, growing well in most soils but requiring full sun for best growth and bloom.

AUSTRALIAN FAN PALM = *Livistona australis*

AUSTRALIAN, TEA-TREE = *Leptospermum laevigatum*

AUTUMN-AMARYLLIS = *Lycoris squamigera*

AUTUMN COLOR. Parts of eastern and western United States are fortunately located in some of the few regions of the world where brilliant autumn coloration of foliage prevails. There is only one small region in the southern hemisphere, and that is in South America. In the northern hemisphere, there is a large region in eastern Asia, including central and northern Japan, and a small region in the southwestern part of Europe. In North America, the region characterized by brilliant autumn foliage extends from the Gulf of St. Lawrence to Fla. and westward to the Great Plains, areas which are blessed with extensive deciduous hardwood forests and considerable rainfall. Then there is a large area in the vicinity of the Rocky Mountains where the foliage colors are gorgeous every year. It is areas like these where the general climatic conditions are often just what is needed to produce this lovely phenomenon of nature.

In North America the most brilliant displays of autumn color are, of course, in southeastern Canada, the northeastern United States and in certain other areas at higher altitudes. The farther south one goes, the less brilliant is the display of autumn color, particularly in areas along the seacoast. In the higher altitudes of the South, such as the Blue Ridge Mountains and the Great Smokies, the color is just as brilliant as it is in the northeastern United States.

It should be pointed out that it is chiefly in areas of predominantly deciduous forests that autumn color displays are best, and such forested areas occur only in two general regions in the world. Plants growing in deciduous forests in tropical regions usually drop their leaves toward the end of the dry season. Since these leaves usually dry up before they fall (because of lack of water), they do not often develop brilliant colors. In the case of plants growing in deciduous forests in temperate regions—especially in areas with ample rainfall equally distributed throughout the year—the leaves fall at the approach of cold weather, and because the plants have been well supplied with water, leaves of many trees do change color before they fall.

In some years the autumn color is much more pronounced than in others. There are always plants the foliage of which turns yellow in the fall, but it is the brilliant reds and gorgeous scarlets which, in combination with the yellows, make autumn color of outstanding beauty, and it is chiefly these reds and scarlets which are intensified by the right climatic conditions.

Leaves are green because they contain a complex material called chlorophyll. This is essential to the growth of all plants except the saprophytes and a few parasites, for it is through the action of chlorophyll that the plant can manufacture the food it requires from crude chemicals in the presence of light and heat. Chlorophyll is continually being manufactured in the leaf and at the same time continually being broken down. Ordinarily the rate of its breakdown about equals the rate of its manufacture. In the fall, the rate of chlorophyll manufacture is gradually reduced, although the rate of its decomposition is maintained. The exact cause for this phenomenon is not fully understood, but the accumulation of waste products in the leaf may be the principal cause.

Why Leaves Turn Yellow

A certain stage is reached where there is little, if any, chlorophyll manufactured. Most of the chlorophyll already made is eventually destroyed. This is the reason why leaves turn yellow, for the 2 yellow pigments usually present, carotin and xanthophyll, are continually masked by the chlorophyll. When most of the chlorophyll is destroyed, these pigments become apparent. These same coloring materials are present in large quantities in egg yolk, carrots, and in some yellow flowers.

When green plants are taken into dark places, such as a cellar, the leaves often turn yellow. Also, young shoots appearing for the first time under the dark conditions of the cellar are usually yellow. This is explained by the fact that chlorophyll is manufactured only in the presence of light. When light is absent, plants are unable to manufacture new chlorophyll and the yellow pigments become predominant as soon as all the previously manufactured chlorophyll has been destroyed.

The gradual cessation of chlorophyll manufacture and the final breakdown of all that previously made complete the first stage in autumn coloration. This is the reason for certain plants becoming yellow. There are some plants, like some magnolias for instance, the leaves of which do not turn yellow, but change from green directly to brown. For some reason, the breakdown of the chlorophyll does not start soon enough, or is not complete enough, to result in the appearance of the yellow pigments. The yellow color does appear in the foliage of many other plants regardless of the weather conditions. There is an interesting high degree of individuality in certain species. Red Maple, for instance, usually turns a good red in the fall, but certain individual plants may color yellow. The same can be said of sugar maples and several other plants. This is a most interesting physiological problem worthy of considerable investigation.

Why Leaves Turn Red

The gorgeous beauty of most autumn color combinations results from the brilliant reds and scarlets, together with the yellows. The sassafras, some of the maples, oaks, sumacs, Sourwood, Tupelo, and other plants are particularly outstanding for their brilliant red autumn color. These plants are most interesting in that the brilliance of their color apparently varies from year to year. The red in their leaves is caused by a third pigment called anthocyanin, which results in some way from the accumulation of sugars and tannins in the leaf. In some of the maples valued for their sugar production it is probably the sugars which cause this red color. The oaks, however, being rich in tannins, probably owe their high autumn coloration to the presence of these.

There are 2 factors necessary in the production of red autumn color. The first is light. There must be warm, bright, sunny days in the fall, during which time the leaves naturally manufacture a great deal of sugar. Secondly, such days must be followed by cool nights, during which the temperature is below 45° F. Plant physiologists have shown definitely that under such conditions there is little or no translocation of sugars and other materials from the leaf to other parts of the plant. In other words, when cool nights occur, following warm, bright, sunny days, sugars and other materials are "trapped" in the leaves. The accumulation of these products results in the manufacture of the red anthocyanin.

The combination of these factors is well understood when one observes a certain tree that may be red only on that side exposed to the sun. Other leaves not directly in the sun's rays may be green or yellow. Leaves exposed to the sun have been able to manufacture more sugars, which, when accumulated and "trapped" in the leaves by cold night temperatures, may result in the red color. It is interesting to note that trees and shrubs growing in swamps and other low places are often among the first to color in the fall, simply because it is in such places that cold air first settles on still nights.

With these factors in mind, it can be easily seen why there is so much divergence of opinion about autumn color. When plants are located so that they receive full sunlight, especially in the late afternoons during the early fall, they should be expected to show pronounced color if the weather conditions have been favorable. On the other hand, if a plant grows in the shade where it receives no direct sunlight it cannot be expected to have marked autumn color.

Fothergilla monticola annually demonstrates this point. In years when the climatic conditions have favored autumn-color formation, a particular plant of *F. monticola* growing in the full sun is gorgeously colored red and yellow—on the western side. On the eastern side, where the foliage is shaded from the late afternoon sun, the foliage is merely colored yellowish and does not show brilliant contrasts of red and yellow. Fortunately all plants do not show such great variation in autumn color when one side is compared with another, but it is a fact that the western side usually has the most deeply colored foliage when there has been plenty of sunshine. This point should be kept in mind when planting, those locations and plants being selected which will show to best advantage during the period of autumn color.

Dull Autumn Coloration

A warm, cloudy fall, sometimes with much rain, will restrict the formation of bright colors in the foliage. With insufficient sunlight the sugar production is greatly reduced, and with warm nights what little sugar has been manufactured in the leaves can be readily transported to the trunk and roots, where it has no effect on the color of the foliage.

The leaves of many evergreens change color in autumn. Some of the junipers and arborvitaes are listed in the following groups. Some pines may turn yellow, but usually such color lasts only for a short time, leaves quickly turning brown. This is particularly true of those evergreen leaves which are normally shed each year, and although the autumn color may not be conspicuous in many evergreen plants, nevertheless it is evident on close examination.

All leaves eventually turn brown. This is not an autumn color, but is merely the result of the death, and in some cases the decay, of the plant tissue. Sometimes, the leaves turn brown while they still remain on the tree, as in the American Beech and in some of the oaks. In other cases, like the Sugar Maple and the Spicebush, the leaves drop from the plants while they are still brightly colored and turn brown afterwards.

Autumn color is then a physiological phenomenon which is very complex. There are plants the leaves of which will always turn yellow regardless of current climatic conditions, but many of the plants with red fall foliage will be striking in appearance only when warm, sunshiny days prevail, followed by nights with temperatures below 45° F. The sugar formation in the leaf, the amount of sunshine received by the plants, and the temperature of the air are three variable factors which, to a large degree, control autumn coloration.

Woody Plants with Autumn Color

The following plants are listed according to their most conspicuous autumn color. As has been explained above, these may change from year to year, depending on climatic conditions. For instance, in some years *Cladrastis lutea* will be yellow; other years the same trees will be purplish. The degree of color may also depend on soil conditions, it being a well-known fact that pin oaks, for instance, which have received heavy applications of nitrogenous fertilizers, will have a much deeper red color than those grown on poor soils without such fertilizers. With these qualifications in mind, the following lists are offered.

AUTUMN COLOR—RED

	HEIGHT	ZONE	COMMON NAME
Acer circinatum	25'	5	Vine Maple
A. ginnala	20'	2	Amur Maple
A. mandshuricum	30'	4	Manchurian Maple
A. nikoense	45'	5	Nikko Maple
A. palmatum	20'	5	Japanese Maple
A. rubrum—red and yellow	120'	3	Red Maple
A. spicatum—orange and scarlet	25'	2	Mountain Maple
A. saccharum—red and yellow	120'	3	Sugar Maple
A. tataricum—red to yellow	30'	2	Mountain Maple
x Amelanchier grandiflora—red to yellow	25'	4	Apple Serviceberry
Amelanchier laevis—yellow to red	36'	4	Allegany Serviceberry
Berberis, many species	18"–7	5–7	Barberries
Carpinus caroliniana	36'	2	American Hornbeam
Cornus alba sibirica	9'	2	Siberian Dogwood
C. florida	40'	4	Flowering Dogwood
C. mas	24'	4	Cornelian Cherry
C. sericea (*C. stolonifera*)	7'	2	Red Osier Dogwood
Cotinus coggygria	15'	5	Smoke Bush
C. obovatus	30'	5	American Smoke Tree
Crataegus lavallei—bronze-red	21'	4	Lavalle Hawthorn
C. nitida—orange-red	30'	4	Glossy Hawthorn
C. phaenopyrum	30'	4	Washington Hawthorn
Enkianthus campanulatus	30'	4	Redvein Enkianthus
E. perulatus	6'	5	—
Euonymus alatus	9'	3	Winged Euonymus
Fothergilla sp.—red and yellow	3'–9'	5	Fothergilla
Franklinia alatamaha—red and yellow	30'	5	Franklinia
Liquidambar styraciflua—red and yellow	125'	5	Sweet Gum
Nemopanthus mucronatus	9'	3	Mountain-holly
Nyssa sylvatica	90'	4	Black Tupelo
Oxydendrum arboreum	75'	5	Sorrel Tree, Sourwood
Parrotia persica—red to yellow	50'	5	Persian Parrotia
Parthenocissus quinquefolia	vine	3	Virginia Creeper
P. tricuspidata	vine	4	Boston Ivy
Prunus maximowiczii	48'	4	Miyama Cherry
P. sargentii	75'	4	Sargent Cherry
Pyrus calleryana	30'	5	Callery Pear
P. communis	45'	4	Common Pear
P. ussuriensis	50'	4	Ussurian Pear
Quercus rubra	75'	3	Red Oak
Q. coccinea	75'	4	Scarlet Oak
Q. palustris	75'	4	Pin Oak
Q. velutina	100'	4	Black Oak
Rhododendron calendulaceum	9'	5	Flame Azalea

	HEIGHT	ZONE	COMMON NAME
R. schlippenbachii	15′	4	Royal Azalea
R. vaseyi	9′	4	Pinkshell Azalea
Rhus aromatica	3′	3	Fragrant Sumac
R. copallina—shining red	30′	4	Shining Sumac
R. glabra	9′–15′	2	Smooth Sumac
R. radicans—red and yellow	vine	3	Poison-ivy
R. typhina	30′	3	Staghorn Sumac
Rosa rugosa—red and yellow	6′	2	Rugosa Rose
R. setigera	15′	4	Prairie Rose
R. virginiana—red and yellow	6′	3	Virginia Rose
Sassafra albidum—red, yellow to orange	60′	4	Sassafras
Sorbus aucuparia	45′	3	European Mountain-ash
S. discolor	30′	5	Snowberry Mountain-ash
S. folgneri	24′	5	Folger Mountain-ash
Spiraea prunifolia—glossy red	9′	4	Bridalwreath Spirea
Stewartia koreana—orange to red	45′	5	Korean Stewartia
Syringa oblata dilatata	12′	3	Korean Early Lilac
Vaccinium sp.	8″–27′	2–7	Blueberries
Viburnum dentatum	15′	2	Arrow-wood
V. lantana—deep red	15′	3	Wayfaring Tree
V. plicatum—dull red	9′	4	Doublefile Viburnum
V. prunifolium	15′	3	Black Haw

AUTUMN COLOR—REDDISH TO REDDISH PURPLE

	HEIGHT	ZONE	COMMON NAME
Cornus racemosa	15′	4	Gray Dogwood
Fraxinus americana	120′	3	White Ash
Gaultheria procumbens	3″	3	Wintergreen
Gaylusaccia brachycera	18″	5	Box-huckleberry
Juniperus horizontalis plumosa	ground cover	2	Andorra Juniper
J. virginiana	90′	2	Eastern Redcedar
Leucothoe fontanesiana	6′	4	Drooping Leucothoe
Mahonia aquifolium	3′–6′	5	Oregon Holly-grape
M. repens	10″	5	Creeping Mahonia
Paxistima canbyi	12″	5	Canby Paxistima
Quercus alba	90′	4	White Oak
Thuja occidentalis ericoides—purple	6′	2	Heath Arborvitae
T. plicata—bronze	180′	5	Giant Arborvitae
Viburnum acerifolium	6′	3	Mapleleaf Viburnum
V. dilatatum	9′	5	Linden Viburnum
V. lentago	30′	2	Nannyberry

AUTUMN COLOR—YELLOW

	HEIGHT	ZONE	COMMON NAME
Acer pensylvanicum	36′	3	Striped Maple
A. platanoides	90′	3	Norway Maple
A. saccharinum	120′	3	Silver Maple
Actinidia arguta	vine	4	Bower Actinidia
Amelanchier sp.—yellow to red	6′–25′	4–5	Serviceberries
Asimina triloba	35′	5	Papaw
Betula sp.	30′–90′	2–5	Birches
Celastrus sp.	vine	4	Bittersweets
Cercis canadensis	36′	4	Eastern Redbud
Cladrastis lutea—yellow to purple	50′	3	American Yellow-wood
Clethra alnifolia	9′	3	Summersweet
Ginkgo biloba	120′	4	Ginkgo
Hamamelis mollis	30′	5	Chinese Witch-hazel
H. vernalis	10′	5	Vernal Witch-hazel
H. virginiana	15′	4	Common Witch-hazel
Larix decidua	100′	2	European Larch
L. laricina	60′	1	Eastern Larch

	HEIGHT	ZONE	COMMON NAME
Lindera benzoin	15′	4	Spice Bush
Malus halliana spontanea—yellow and purple	15′	4	Crab Apple (sdlg.)
Populus alba	90′	3	White Poplar
P. grandidentata	60′	3	Large-toothed Aspen
P. nigra 'Italica'	90′	3	Lombardy Poplar
P. tremuloides	90′	1	Trembling Aspen
Prinsepia sinensis	10′	2	Cherry Prinsepia
Pseudolarix amabilis (*kaempferi*)	120′	5	Golden Larch

AUTUMN COLOR—YELLOWISH TO BRONZE

	HEIGHT	ZONE	COMMON NAME
Aesculus parviflora—yellow brown	8′–12′	4	Bottlebrush Buckeye
Carya sp.—yellow to brown	90′–150′	4–5	Hickories
Castanea dentata—yellow to brown	120′	4	American Chestnut
C. mollisima—yellow to brown	60′	4	Chinese Chestnut
Fagus grandifolia	90′	3	American Beech
F. sylvatica	90′	4	European Beech
Magnolia stellata—yellow-brown	20′	5	Star Magnolia
Quercus imbricaria	75′	5	Shingle Oak

NO AUTUMN COLOR

	HEIGHT	ZONE	COMMON NAME
Acer campestre	25′	5–6	Hedge Maple
A. negundo	60′	2	Box-elder
A. pseudoplatanus	90′	5	Sycamore Maple
Aesculus hippocastanum	75′	3	Horse-chestnut
Albizia julibrissin	36′	7	Silk Tree
Alnus glutinosa	75′	3	European Alder
Baccharis halimifolia	12′	4	Groundsel-bush
Carpinus betulus	60′	5	European Hornbeam
Cedrela sinensis	70′	5	Chinese Toon
Clematis, many sp.	vines	3–7	Clematis
Corylus colurna	75′	4	Turkish Filbert
Crataegus monogyna	30′	4	Single Seed Hawthorn
Daphne mezereum	3′	4	February Daphne
Davidia involucrata	60′	6	Dove Tree
Elaeagnus angustifolia	20′	2	Russian Olive
Eucommia ulmoides	60′	5	Hardy Rubber Tree
Euonymus bungeana semipersistens	18′	4	Mid-winter Euonymus
Fraxinus excelsior	120′	3	European Ash
Hibiscus syriacus	15′	5	Shrub Althea
Juglans sp.	90′	3–6	Nut trees
Laburnum sp.	30′	4	Laburnum
Ligustrum vulgare	15′	4	Common Privet
Lonicera fragrantissima	6′	5	Winter Honeysuckle
Lonicera syringantha	6′–9′	4	Lilac Honeysuckle
L. thibetica	4′	4	Tibet Honeysuckle
Lycium halimifolium	5′	4	Matrimony-vine
Magnolia—most sp.	30′–90′	4–9	Magnolias
Malus—many sp.	15′–75′	4	Crab Apple
Polygonum aubertii	vine	4	Silver Fleece Vine
Potentilla fruticosa	4′	2	Shrubby Cinquefoil
Prunus persica	24′	5	Peach
Quercus robur	150′	5	English Oak
Robinia sp.	15′–45′	3–5	Locusts
x Salix blanda	40′	4	Wisconsin Weeping Willow
Salix pentandra	60′	4	Laurel Willow
Sophora japonica	75′	4	Japanese Pagoda Tree
Vitex negundo	15′	5	Chaste-tree
Wisteria sp.	vine	4–7	Wisterias

AUTUMN-CROCUS. See COLCHICUM.

AUXIN. A specific organic product transported in the sap of a plant producing a specific effect on the growth activities of the cells.

AVENA (av-EE-na)

fatua   4'   annual   Wild Oats
A grasslike plant with leaves ⅓ in. wide and drooping oatlike fruits, most troublesome as a weed in the cereal fields of western North America where it was introduced from Europe. Fruiting in June and July, somewhat similar to a loosely fruited plant of oats. Seeds may remain in the soil several years before germinating.

sativa   4'   annual   Common Oat
This is the tufted grasslike oat of agriculture with leaves a foot long and an inch wide; flowering and fruiting panicles often a foot long.

sterilis   3'   annual   Animated Oat
An interesting ornamental grass from the Mediterranean Region, of interest because the seeds are borne in foot-long panicles and the individual awns are twisted and may be 2 in. long. The florets move or twist when suddenly exposed to increased moisture.

AVENS. See GEUM.

AVERRHOA (av-er-O-a)

carambola   30'   Zone 10   Carambola
Tree with alternate compound leaves in 2 spiral rows which close at night when touched—leaflets are 5–9. Sometimes seen in conservatories, but it is a tropical plant native to Malaya. The waxy yellow fruits are slightly 5-angled so that when cut in cross-section they are star-shaped, the reason why they are referred to sometimes as "Star Fruit." They are about 4–5 in. long, slightly sweet and are used in making preserves and jellies. The fragrant flowers are small, not over ¼ in. long, and are clustered along older twigs. Propagated by seeds or budding.

AVOCADO. This lush tree, native to Central America, is a favorite for its attractive appearance and valuable fruit which is well-known and liked by most. The species (*Persea americana*) is divided into 3 races which differ markedly in their fruit and climatic requirements. The West Indian race is the tenderest, being injured badly at temperatures below 28° to 30° F., according to variety. The fruits range from medium size to extremely large, have a thin, smooth skin; are green to purple in color and are low in oil content, 4% to 7%. The Guatemalan race is characterized by greater hardiness, being able to withstand 25° to 28° F., according to variety; the fruits are of medium size, green or purple when ripe, and the skin is usually rather thick, often woody, and pebbled; the varieties vary in oil content from about 12% to over 25% when

allowed to become fully mature on the tree. The Mexican race is the hardiest, being able to withstand temperatures from 20° to 24° F.; the fruits are small, thin skinned, purple or green in color, and with a high oil content. Crushed leaves and twigs of this race are marked by a distinct anise odor lacking in varieties of the other two races.

The range in hardiness obviously determines the areas adapted to the various races. The West Indies kinds can be grown successfully only in the warmer areas of the Southeast; the Guatemalan extend the range northward to some extent—perhaps to the middle of the Fla. peninsula or farther in well-located sites. Varieties of this race are grown almost solely in Calif. The Mexican race is not so popular, although its hardiness places it with the Sweet Orange in range of adapted locations.

Because the trees are naturally large and vigorous, only young trees can be easily protected from frost in the garden, except with the use of orchard heater. See ORANGE for methods of frost protection.

Avocados do very well in areas with relatively cool summers, although the period from bloom to fruit maturity is extended. Where average summer temperatures are in the low 60's they will generally fail to set fruit.

Avocados are easily grown from seed, but seedling trees are generally of inferior quality, and often shy bearing. Nevertheless, the ease of starting seedlings has resulted in thousands being brought into fruit, many of which are relatively worthless. Seedlings are used on which to bud proved varieties; in the West seedlings of Mexican varieties are used. In the Southeast seedlings of West Indian and Guatemalan varieties are most commonly used. Convenience and some suspected incompatibilities between Mexican seedlings and some West Indian varieties appear to be the main reason for this difference. Mexican seedlings are usually shield or T budded in Calif., or tip grafted; in Fla. the side graft is more commonly used. The latter develops a tree more quickly.

Mature trees are easily topworked using a bark graft or saw kerf graft. The scions should be thoroughly covered with grafting wax, and then covered with a paper bag to give them protection against excessive heat and drying out. Budwood and scionwood of mature terminal growth is used, selected carefully to secure good buds, as avocados tend to shed many lateral buds. Leafy cuttings of Avocado can be rooted, but the percent rooting is usually small.

The spacing to be given to a tree varies with the variety and natural soil fertility; full exposure calls for planting distances of 24–40 ft. The tree should not be planted where its top will be appreciably shaded. The Avocado tends to grow from the ends of its branches much more than citrus, and less from lateral buds. For this reason, it is easily trained to a desired shape, and requires but little pruning thereafter.

Being evergreen, the Avocado requires water the year round, and should not be allowed to dry out during the cool winter period. Soil depth and texture and prevailing temperature and rainfall will determine the frequency necessary. Although tree growth and fruit development suffer from drought, the Avocado is surprisingly tolerant of short dry periods; in Fla. a short drought period in the fall may be beneficial if the fruit has been picked.

In the acid soils of the humid Southeast the Avocado requires rather heavy fertilization; 2–4 lbs. of actual nitrogen per tree per year for mature trees is recommended. In the West, and particularly in the cooler Pacific Coast sites, less nitrogen is used, 1 lb. per mature tree per year may be more than needed. Except for occasional cases of zinc deficiency there has not yet appeared to be a need for other elements. In the Southeast, complete fertilizers with added micro-nutrients is recommended, but it need not be used until evidence of deficiency appears.

Avocados bloom heavily. The inflorescences, each bearing many flowers, are numerous. Avocado varieties exhibit a very remarkable mechanism to ensure cross-pollination, but it is not rigid enough to preclude some overlap of flowers in the male and female cycle of their normal alternating function, so that no good commercial variety is known which definitely sets more fruit when in mixed plantings than alone, except the **'Collison'** variety of Fla., which is pollen sterile and must have another pollen source. Bees and perhaps other flying insects act as pollinators.

Avocados remain hard while on the tree and undergo normal softening only off the tree. Also, they will ripen though picked at rather widely varying times, so that it is often difficult to tell when to harvest, especially in the case of varieties that remain green. Colored varieties are normally near the stage when they will ripen well when the color change is complete. All avocados can be left on the tree for a considerable time and remain in good condition. Fruit which will soften at room temperature in 5 to 7 days from picking will be of high quality.

Avocado fruits may be stored for several weeks if desired, but the storage temperatures should be above 42° F. for most suffer at lower temperatures, off-flavors resulting.

Avocados suffer from many pests and diseases. The primary one is avocado root rot, which occurs whenever these trees are grown in wet soils. Another soil-borne fungus, verticillium wilt, sometimes attacks avocados, soils usually being infected whenever solanacious and cucurbitous crops are grown. But one virus disease, sunblotch, is known. Affected fruits appear sunburned on one side; propagation wood should not be taken from such trees. Fungus diseases of the tops are not too prevalent, but several pests attack avocados. Among the most serious are greenhouse thrips, various mites, scales, and a few other insects. Fortunately these pests rarely build to serious levels on isolated trees in a mixed garden planting, so that spraying may never be necessary. Oil sprays for mites and thrips and most scales, sulfur dust for avocado red scale (Fla.), and Bordeaux or neutral copper sprays for the fungus diseases are usual controls. Only anthracnose spot destroys the fruit flesh, others merely make it unsightly. Fruit should be clipped from the tree, not pulled off, as the stem will pull out, allowing entrance of rots into the fruit flesh.

Varieties of avocados are so numerous that any list must be greatly abridged. Only some of the proven varieties of excellent quality are therefore mentioned. In addition, some information is given concerning their natural time of maturity in the main areas where avocados can be grown, for temperature differences result in widely differing times of maturity.

Avocado: The large seed can be placed partially in water on a warm windowsill, rooted, and then potted, making a nice house plant.

Mexican Race and Hybrids

'**Mexicola**': A small, pyriform, purple variety of relatively high oil content and excellent quality. Ripens in about 9 months, or early winter, in Calif.

'**Puebla**' (perhaps Mexican x Guatemalan): Larger than 'Mexicola', smooth, purple, high oil content, good quality, and ripens in about 9 months in the cool coastal districts, earlier in warmer areas of Calif.

'**Zutano**' (Mexican): bears green fruits, ripens in early Oct. in Calif.; of good quality.

Guatemalan Race Varieties

'**Fuerte**' (hybrid between Mexican x Guatemalan): A medium-sized, pyriform, nearly smooth fruit of medium to high oil content and excellent quality; color dull greenish, skin rather thick for its supposed hybrid origin. In Calif. it ripens in cool districts in about 11 to 12 months, with a season from Nov. to June; in Fla. the harvest is completed by the end of the year.

'**Lyon**': not a commercial variety, but one for the garden because of the high quality of its fruit; tree weak and less productive than needed in commerce. A green variety, ripening in about 15 months in Calif.

'**Hass**': a pyriform variety, dark purple to nearly black at maturity, of medium size, with excellent flavor. Of medium oil content, ripens following 'Fuerte' in Calif., and with that variety will afford harvestable fruit throughout the year.

'**Taylor**': A medium-sized, dark green variety, obovate to pyriform in shape, of medium oil content, but good quality; ripens in midwinter in Fla., where it is grown. The tree is very upright growing and hardiest of the the Guatemalan varieties.

'**Lula**': Fruit elliptical, purplish when ripe, skin roughened; oil content medium, excellent flavor; tree rather upright. Season late winter, Fla.

'**Booth 7**': (Guatemalan x West Indies). Rounded obovate, skin glossy, bright green, medium oil content; skin slightly roughened or pebbled, thick, woody; season early winter. Fla.

'**Booth 8**': Fruit oblong-obovate, larger than 'Booth 7'; color dull green with thick, slightly woody skin; oil content somewhat low. Late fall to early Dec. season in Fla.

CLARON O. HESSE

AWL-SHAPED. Tapering from the base to a slender or stiff point.

AWN. A bristlelike appendage.

AXIL. The upper angle formed by a leaf or branch with the stem.

AXILLARY. Situated in the axil.

AXONOPUS FURCATUS = Carpet Grass. See GRASS, LAWNS.

AZALEA (az-AY-lea). These are very popular and bright flowered shrubs belonging to the Rhododendron genus and of course they are members of the Heath Family. For culture, differences between azaleas and rhododendrons, and the description of the many classes and species of azaleas, see the discussion of these under RHODODENDRON.

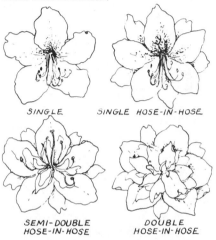

SINGLE   SINGLE HOSE-IN-HOSE

SEMI-DOUBLE   DOUBLE
HOSE-IN-HOSE   HOSE-IN-HOSE

Different types of azalea flowers.

AZALEAMUM. This was at first a trademarked name for a low cushion-type Chrysanthemum. Now the cushion-type and "azaleamum" are synonymous. None are more than 12–15 in. tall.

AZARA (az-AIR-ra)

gilliesii = *A. petiolaris*

lanceolata   20'   Zone 9   Lanceleaf Azara
The vanilla-scented flowers are small as are the mauve to white fruits. This plant is native to Chile and does best only in the shade. The bright green, evergreen leaves are ¾–2½ in. long.

microphylla   12'–18'   Zone 8   Boxleaf Azara
Another evergreen from Chile with leaves only ½–1 in. long, glossy and dark green. It is a wide-spreading shrub, sometimes growing 8–12 ft. wide and used most in southern Calif. and on the Northwest Pacific Coast. It also must be grown in the shade and be provided with plenty of water.

petiolaris (*A. gilliesii*)   **45'   Zone 9   Golden**
Azara
An alternate-leaved evergreen tree native to Chile, with simple leaves about 3 in. long, with coarse, spiny teeth, yellow fragrant flowers in

axillary racemes during Feb. and March. This is
the best of the azaras for ornamental work.
AZOLLA (ax-OLL-a)

   caroliniana   aquatic plant   Zones 5–6   Azolla
Closely related to *Salvinia*, this is a minute,
floating aquatic plant frequently used in aquaria.
The leaves are pinnately divided and an entire
single plant is only about ¾ in. across. It spreads

readily and is easily separated for starting new
colonies. The leaves are sometimes reddish, and
it increases so fast when the water temperature is
just right as to become a scum on the water
surface that must be kept in check. It is found in
ponds throughout the eastern U.S.

AZTEC-LILY = *Sprekelia formosissima*

B

BABIANA (babbi-AY-na)
    stricta 1′ **Zone 6** (if winter protected) **Erect Baboonroot**
A South African herb growing from a corm, sometimes forced in the greenhouse where it is grown in pots for its bright freezialike flowers about 1½ in. wide appearing in Feb. or March.

BABOONROOT = *Babiana stricta*

BABY-BLUE-EYES = *Nemophila menziesii*

BABY ORCHID = *Vanda teres*

BABY'S-BREATH. See GYPSOPHILA.

BABY'S-TEARS = *Soleirolia soleirolii*

BACCATE. Berrylike; pulpy or fleshy.

BACCHARIS (BAK-a-ris)
    halimifolia 12′ **Zone 4** **Groundsel-bush**
The thistlelike heads of white fruits of this deciduous eastern U.S. shrub are its most ornamental assets. Also it is one of the comparatively few plants able to withstand saltwater spray, making it a valuable plant for seashore gardens. The sexes are separate, and it is the female plants which are of interest in the fall when they fruit. Propagation is by seed, which can be sown anytime, and by softwood and hardwood cuttings.
    pilularis 2′–3′ **Zone 7** **Kidneywort, Coyote-bush**
Native in dry soils in Ore. and Calif., this shrub is evergreen, with alternate leaves about 1 in. long, almost stalkless but of little ornamental value, except for planting on dry slopes in the full sun for holding the soil in place. A dwarf variety, about 1–1½ ft. high, is recommended for planting as one of the "fire-resistant" plants in southern Calif. See FIRE-RESISTANT PLANTS.

BACHELOR'S-BUTTON = *Centaurea cyanus*

BACILLUS THURINGIENSIS. A microbial insecticide containing the spores of this bacillus has been prepared as a dust and wettable powder, but a stabilized suspension containing approximately 30 billion viable spores is now the approved formation. It is harmless to humans, wildlife including animals and fish, beneficial insect parasites and predators and insects other than the larvae of certain moths and butterflies. About 110 species of lepidopterus larvae have been found susceptible including alfalfa caterpillar, cabbage worms, tobacco and tomato hornworms, gypsy moth and canker worms. The spores must be eaten with foliage. Susceptible larvae which have become infected appear normal for 24 to 48 hours, after which they die from intestinal paralysis. The formulations must be protected from excessive heat (120° F.) and freezing. Among the trade names are Thuricide, Bacthane and Biotroe.

BACKCROSS. A term used in hybridizing when the hybrid is crossed on one of its parents.

BACOPA (ba-CO-pa)
    caroliniana **aquatic plant** **Zone 7**
An aquatic or semi-aquatic plant native from N.J. to Fla., frequently found in boggy soils but useful as an ornamental in the home aquarium. It has rounded opposite or whorled leaves that are olive green and slightly fragrant. The flowers are small and blue, about ⅜ in. long, from June to Oct.

BAHIA GRASS = *Paspalum notatum*. See GRASS, LAWNS.

BAILEYA (BAY-li-ah)
    multiradiata 1½′ **Zone 7** **Desert Baileya**
An annual or perennial herb, native to Calif. and Tex. usually in deserts or dry regions, with alternate, white woolly leaves and flower-heads 1¾ in. across with yellow ray-flowers. Sheep and goats have been known to be poisoned from eating this plant.

BALL FERN. See DAVALLIA species.

BALLOONFLOWER = *Platycodon grandiflorum*

BALLOON-VINE = *Cardiospermum halicacabum*

BALM-OF-GILEAD = *Populus balsamifera*

BALSAM-APPLE = *Momordica balsamina*

BALSAM, GARDEN = *Impatiens balsamina*

BALSAMINACEAE = The Jewelweed or Balsam Family

BALSAM-PEAR = *Momordica charantia*

BAMBOO. There are 700 or more species of bamboo in the world, only 2 of them being native to the United States. They are grasses, belonging to a dozen genera, ranging in size from a few feet to 100 feet or more. Seldom do they fruit. In the tropics where they are at home they usually are evergreen, but at least 2 species are hardy as far north as Boston, Mass., on the Atlantic seacoast where they have been grown successfully for many years. The farther south one goes, the more species there are hardy, but usually bamboos as such are confined to a narrow strip along the Atlantic Coast from

Long Island to a narrow strip of Tex. along the Gulf but including most of all the states bordering the water in between.

On the West Coast, bamboos are grown in southwest Ariz., Calif., and a very narrow strip along the Pacific Coast of Ore. and Wash. Some of the tropical species are grown in Fla. and the warmest strip of land about the Gulf of Mexico as well as southwest Ariz. and southwest Calif., chiefly then in Zones 8, 9, 10.

Bamboos have woody stems, usually but not always hollow between the joints. They make graceful garden plants; some of the low ones make rapidly increasing ground covers which must be kept under rigid control or they become weedy pests. Some of the taller types grow in clumps. In the tropical regions of the world they are very important economic plants, affording material for building purposes, furniture, tools, weapons and even food, since the young shoots of some are eaten either raw or cooked.

A culm, or vegetative shoot of bamboo, is formed in the spring from food stored in the roots during the previous year, and grows to mature height in a short 5–8-week period. When the shoot matures 100 ft. high, it is obvious that the growth of this is sometimes so rapid it can be seen with the naked eye when carefully observed against a measuring stick. It is a peculiar habit of these plants that the young growing culm will always have the same dia. at its base that it will have when the culm has reached the final height.

Two types of these grasses are the running bamboos and the clump bamboos. The former sends out underground rhizomes from which new above-ground shoots or culms grow in the spring. These are the hardiest of the bamboos and in fact the 2 native American species belong in this group, namely, *Arundinacea gigantea*, the Canebrake Bamboo of the South which can grow 30 ft. high and *A. tecta* which is much smaller. The former may be used for fishing poles and little else; the latter is sometimes used as cattle fodder. All the so-called running bamboos can become vicious spreading pests if not rigidly restrained in the garden.

It is the tall-growing, often tropical, clump bamboos that have the gracefully arching culms and are so distinctive in the landscape wherever they can be grown. Even though these clumps do not spread as rapidly as the others, roots from a single mature clump may spread out 25 ft. in all directions, absorbing nutrients and moisture from the soil and making it difficult to grow anything else close by. Over 60 species and varieties of running bamboos have been introduced into America, but at present only 24 of these are considered to have sufficient

economic or ornamental value to be discussed here.

The running bamboo types briefly mentioned in the following list increase by underground rhizomes and range in height from a few feet to 70 feet. The lowest ones, like the *Arundinaria* species, are sometimes used as ground covers, but when used this way they should be restrained by metal strips or concrete sunk in the soil about 2 ft. deep to insure their staying in place. However, in some good soils this barrier may have to be sunk deeper. To keep them a little lower in height, they might be cut off at the ground level every 2–3 years, which makes them more dense as well.

Bamboo—*Bambusa*

Some of the clump bamboos like *Bambusa multiplex* are used as informal hedges. Even some of the running types like *Phyllostachys meyeri*, *P. nigra* and *Semiarundinaria fastuosa* are also used this way.

The clump bamboos can be very graceful ornamental specimens. Since these are usually subtropical and tropical species and are usually evergreen, it should be noted that the culms usually take 3 years to mature and harden properly so that their shoots should not be cut for economic purposes until they are 3 years old. The culms of *Bambusa vulgaris* are frequently used for making vases and other ornaments, handles for tools, picture frames, ski poles, etc. Those with yellow or striped culms (*Bambusa multiplex* vars.) are decidedly ornamental, as are those with variegated foliage. A tall, well-grown clump bamboo, especially with small leaves, is always a thing of beauty, since it usually has a graceful, arching, habit and is always rustling in the slightest breeze.

The edible qualities of some bamboos is noted in the following list. Most of the *Phyllostachys* species are in this group. Not all species are suitable, and some must be cooked, often with changing the water twice, in order to remove the bitter taste. On the other hand, the central part of the new shoot of some can be eaten raw, often used in salads.

Usually these new shoots of edible bamboos appear in March, April and May. The period for cutting them is about 3–4 weeks, but it is advisable to mound soil about them to exclude the light and thus prevent them from becoming bitter. The sheath covering the young shoot should be removed, the tough basal part with roots cut off. The tender shoot can then be cut horizontally in sections about ⅛ in. thick and cooked about 20 minutes. If it is the slightly bitter type, then changing the water after boiling for 10 minutes proves helpful in eliminating the bitter taste.

Propagation

The running bamboos are easily propagated by taking root cuttings, 12 in. long, of the new rhizomes, keeping them moist during the transplanting operation which should be undertaken any time from Jan. to March depending on the locality. They are planted 5–6 in. deep, usually kept 2 years in the nursery row where they are watered well and not allowed to dry out. They are fertilized with 5-10-5, about one pound or less per 100-ft. row. When they are to be transplanted, it is well to cut the culms back at least two-thirds, and if they are not to be balled, it might be best to cut them to the ground.

Clump bamboos are easiest propagated by division, but only when the weather is warm. It is a mere cutting of smaller clumps or chopping apart of larger ones, but the culms themselves might best be reduced to about 2–3 ft. high when this operation is carried out.

Another way of propagating is to try culm cuttings, often successful with *Bambusa* species, sometimes not so successful with other species. The culm is cut half way above and below a node which bears a small branch. The open ends of the culm are packed with moist soil and the cutting planted horizontally in the soil, taking care that the culm is about 2–4 in. below the soil surface and the branch comes above the soil surface. If done in warm weather and the soil kept moist, rooting and sprouting should take about a month. A third method is that of layering, in which an entire culm is dug up,

roots and all, preferably one not over 3 years old, and laid in a trench, 6 in. deep, in moist soil. A leafy branch or two is left at each node so that they are mostly above ground when the culm is buried. After a few months, one carefully digs down to the original culm, saws through it at the internodes but leaves the new plantlets undisturbed for another 2 months, after which time each plantlet can be dug and transplanted.

Cutting bamboo canes is not as simple as it sounds, for the wood should be thoroughly mature—at least 3 years old—and the canes should best be sawed off very close to the ground. Canes can be straightened by applying heat, or by hanging the cane upside down and applying a heavy weight at the end for several months, or merely by applying pressure to flat green canes as they are dried on a flat surface. In fact, canes already dried but curved can be soaked in water and then straightened.

Pests

Insect and disease pests on bamboo are not as yet prevalent in this country. Certainly the gardener with only a single plant or two on his grounds need pay little attention to it. The fungi may prove troublesome, especially bamboo smut. However, the few outcroppings of this disease which have occurred in America have been rigidly handled by destroying plants and roots as well, so it seems unlikely that it will do much damage again.

Insects of the sucking type, especially scales, have infested bamboo plants in America. Where infestation is heavy, cut and burn heavily infested stalks and spray the remainder with a white-oil emulsion, 1–2% oil and 1½ pints of 50% malathion emulsifiable solution in 100 gals. water, sprayed on the plants in midspring when the young insects are in the crawling stage.

The United States Department of Agriculture has had men studying this group for some time, especially F. A. McClure, Joseph R. Haun and Robert A. Young who have supplied the information about them given here.

Bamboos Being Grown in America

Arundinaria amabilis   40′   Zone 9   Tonkin Bamboo
Native to China, culms can be 2½ in. across. It is the small canes of this bamboo that are used throughout this country as plant stakes. Larger canes are used as ski poles and for making split-bamboo fishing rods. A running bamboo type.

Arundinaria simonii   24′   Zone 7   Simon Bamboo
Culms of this are up to 1⅜ in. across and the rhizomes spread less rapidly than those of most other running bamboos. Young shoots are

edible and 3-year-old culms make fine fishing poles. The cultivar **'Silverstripe'** has leaves striped with white.

Arundinaria variegata   3′   Zone 6   Dwarf Whitestripe Bamboo
This can be grown as far north as Boston, Mass. It is native to Japan and valued for its leaves striped with white. When grown this far north it dies to the ground each winter and should be mowed off flush with the ground each spring, after which the young growth emerges vigorous and colorful. A fast-increasing bamboo which must be restrained in good garden soil. It has been noted that growth of this is better in the northern coastal areas than in the southern.

Arundinaria viridistriata $1\frac{1}{2}$–$2\frac{1}{2}$′   Zone 7
A Japanese plant, with leaves 2–5 in. long striped yellowish in spring and early summer, later changing to greenish. It is usually grown in partial shade since in full sun, especially in dry soils, the leaves tend to curl.

Bambusa arundinacea   95′   Zones 9–10   Giant Thorny Bamboo
A clump bamboo from India with culms up to $5\frac{1}{2}$ in. at the base, leaves 3–7 in. long and $\frac{3}{4}$ in. wide. The new shoots appear in the autumn in southern Fla. and are edible though bitter. The lower branches are thorny. It has been used for paper pulp in India.

Bambusa beecheyana   40′   Zone 9   Beechey Bamboo
A clump bamboo from China with the basal parts of the culms about 4 in. across. Shoots are edible, appearing in late summer or early fall. Leaves are $3\frac{1}{2}$–7 in. long and $\frac{1}{2}$–$1\frac{1}{8}$ in. wide. In southern China, this species supplies much of the edible bamboo shoots. The soil is mounded up about them to exclude the light and prevent them from becoming bitter until they are cut for eating.

Bambusa multiplex   10′–50′   Zone 9   Hedge Bamboo
A variable clump bamboo from China and with its varieties is the most common of the ornamental bamboos grown in the deep South and southern Calif., because it forms a compact graceful clump, often with slightly arching culms. The new shoots appear in midsummer and are bitter and not eaten—the leaves are silver colored beneath. The culms seldom are more than $1\frac{3}{4}$ in. across at the base.

'Alphonse Karr'—culms bright yellow, striped green, tall.

'Fernleaf'—10–20 ft. tall, foliage gives impression of feathery texture.

'Silverstripe Fernleaf'—feathery, white-striped leaves.

'Stripestem Fernleaf'—culms at first reddish, irregularly striped green.

riviereorum—Chinese Goddess Bamboo—only 10′ high.

'Silverstripe'—50 ft. tall, a few to many leaves striped white.

'Willowy'—20 ft. tall, leaves narrow, only $\frac{5}{16}$ in. wide and $1\frac{1}{2}$–$4\frac{1}{2}$ in. long.

Bambusa oldhamii   55′   Zone 9   Oldham Bamboo
A bamboo native to China and Formosa, growing in clumps which are not as dense as those of many others. Leaves 3–9 in. long, $\frac{5}{8}$–$1\frac{1}{2}$ in. wide. There are no important economic uses for this species, although it makes a fine ornamental clump.

Bambusa pervariabilis   50′   Zones 9–10   Yan Chuk
A clump-type bamboo, growing erect with stiffly held culms that are sturdy, 2 in. across at the base, the stems reportedly used in China for punting poles.

Bambusa polymorpha   90′   Zone 10
Native to Burma this is a clump bamboo with culms as much as 6 in. in dia. at the base. The leaves are small, $1\frac{1}{2}$–$7\frac{1}{2}$ in. long and only about $\frac{1}{2}$ in. wide, giving a very feathery foliage texture. Valued especially for its feathery foliage.

Bambusa textilis   50′   Zone 9   Wong Chuk
A clump bamboo from southern China, with culms possibly 2 in. across at the base, erect and stiff, with leaves up to 8 in. long and an inch wide, but there is a question about the best growth conditions for it.

Bambusa tulda   70′   Zone 10
An Indian clump bamboo, leaves 3–10 in. long and $\frac{1}{2}$–1 in. wide with a basal culm dia. of 3 in. It has been used for paper pulp.

Bambusa tuldoides   55′   Zone 9   Puntingpole Bamboo
A Chinese clump bamboo with rigid, thick culms that may be $2\frac{1}{4}$ in. across at the base. Leaves are $2\frac{1}{2}$–5 in. long and $\frac{1}{2}$ in. wide. Widely grown in China where it is a valued plant, these culms are used for many things because they are strong.

Bambusa ventricosa   8′–55′   Zone 9   Buddha's Belly Bamboo
A Chinese clump bamboo which gets its common name from the fact that when it is dwarfed by poor soil or growing in tubs, the internodes of the culms are dwarfed and rounded in a characteristic fashion, but this characteristic growth is lost when the plant grows vigorously.

Bambusa vulgaris   80′   Zone 10
Probably the most widely grown of all the bamboos in the tropics, possibly because it is a most attractive tree type. The culms are 4–5 in. across at the bottom. The wood is poor for construction purposes but has been used for paper pulp. It grows in loosely open clumps.

Dendrocalamus asper   100′   Zone 9

An East Indian clump bamboo, chiefly valued for its edible shoots, which, to taste good, should be covered with soil until they are cut. However, the wood is strong and lasting, the reason why it is used a great deal in the construction of houses in Java. Leaves are 5–18 in. long and up to 3 in. wide, and the new shoots appear in the summer or early fall.

Dendrocalamus latiflorus   50′   Zone 10   T'im Chuk (Sweet Bamboo)
A clump bamboo from Formosa with leaves 6–10 in. long and 1–2 in. wide, especially valued for the edible shoots appearing in the early autumn, for these shoots have usually no bad taste when eaten raw.

Dendrocalamus strictus   100′   Zone 10   Calcutta Bamboo
A tall clump bamboo from India with culms 2¼ in. through at the base, forming excellent hard wood when mature that is used for many economic purposes. The leaves are 2–10 in. long and up to ¾ in. wide. In India the culms are also used to make paper pulp.

Phyllostachys aurea   30′   Zone 8   Fishpole Bamboo
Native to China but long cultivated in Japan, this has been grown in America since 1882. The young shoots appearing in midspring are edible, and the matured (and smaller) culms are used for plant stakes, fishing poles, etc. The plant is supposed to withstand temperatures to 0° F. It is of the running bamboo type.

Phyllostachys aureosulcata   30′   Zone 7   Yellowgroove Bamboo
A Chinese plant with culms about 1½ in. in dia. New shoots are edible, and the culms, although not the best, are often used for fishing poles and plant stakes. A running bamboo type.

Phyllostachys bambusoides   70′   Zone 8   Madake, Giant Timber Bamboo
This is one of the most valuable of the economic bamboos native to China where it has been used for timber purposes for centuries. The culms have a dia. of as much as 5½ in. and the new spring shoots are edible. It is of the running bamboo type, adapted to the Gulf states and Calif. where temperatures do not go below 0° F. The cultivar 'Castillon', of Chinese origin, is very ornamental for the culms are bright yellow with light green horizontal stripes. Other cultivars are 'Allgold', 'Slender Crookstem' and 'White Crookstem', the names of which are descriptive.

Phyllostachys dulcis   40′   Zone 8   Sweetshoot Bamboo
A running bamboo from China, the new shoots of which are excellent for cooking. Although for economic purposes the culms are inferior to those of many other bamboos, it is one of the best for eating purposes.

Phyllostachys flexuosa   30′   Zone 9
A Chinese running bamboo, sometimes with culms of slightly zig-zag growth. New shoots are edible. Old shoots are about 1¾ in. across at the base, and can be used for fishing poles, plant stakes and other purposes.

Phyllostachys meyeri   35′   Zone 8   Meyer Bamboo
Culms may be 2 in. across at the base. A running bamboo from China, with edible new shoots, mature culms are considered the strongest and finest of this genus. They make fine fishing poles, the larger ones for salt-water fishing poles and splendid, long-lasting plant stakes.

Phyllostachys nigra   25′   Zone 8   Black Bamboo
A running bamboo from southern China so named because the culms change from green to black, usually the first year. New shoots are edible. This species makes a nice ornamental because of its color and graceful foliage. It is frequently used in the Orient for making furniture. The culms of the cultivar 'Henon' are hardier (Zone 7) and more colorful than those of *P. nigra*.

Phyllostachys nuda   34′   Zone 7
A running bamboo from China with culms 1⅝ in. across at the base, with edible shoots and culms of excellent quality for fishing poles, plant stakes and other uses.

Phyllostachys pubescens   60′   Zone 9   Moso Bamboo
This is the tallest and the most ornamental of the running-bamboo type, native to China, long cultivated in Japan where the basal dia. of the culms may be 8 in. The leaves are only about 2–3 in. long and ⅜ in. wide; hence the feathery character of the foliage is very much an ornamental asset. Although the shoots are considered not as tasty as those of other bamboos in this country, in the Orient they are generally sought for eating, especially because of their large size. They are also canned and shipped to America. Fresh shoots taste better if the water in which they are boiled is changed at least once in the cooking process.

Phyllostachys viridi-glaucescens   35′   Zone 7
A Chinese running bamboo with culms 2 in. across at the base, leaves 4–5 in. long and ½–¾ in. wide. New shoots edible and even tasty when raw, a condition lacking in most other so-called "edible" species which are best cooked.

Phyllostachys viridis   50′   Zone 7
A Chinese running bamboo, with leaves 3–5 in. long and ¾ in. wide. New shoots are edible raw. The matured culms are excellent for various purposes. A cultivar with yellow culms and green stripes is 'Robert Young'.

Phyllostachys vivax   70′   Zone 8
Native to China, another running-bamboo type,

this is a splendid, handsome, timber bamboo with culms up to 5 in. across at the base. Leaves are 4–6 in. long, $\frac{3}{4}$ in. wide and the new shoots are edible raw.

Pseudosasa japonica   18′   Zone 8   Metake
A fine ornamental, native to Korea and Japan, a running-bamboo type, it has been grown in America for nearly 100 years and in Europe longer. Culms are $\frac{3}{4}$ in. across at the base, with leaves 5–13 in. long and up to $1\frac{3}{4}$ in. wide. This does not spread as rapidly as some of the other running bamboos; hence it is a popular garden plant, often grown on terraces in tubs.

Sasa disticha   2′–3′   Zone 7   Dwarf Fernleaf Bamboo
A good ground cover of the running-bamboo type with leaves about 1–$2\frac{1}{4}$ in. long.

Sasa palmata   7′   Zone 5
This can be grown as far north as Boston, Mass. It is a running bamboo, originating in China or Japan, with leaves 4–15 in. long and $1\frac{1}{2}$–$3\frac{1}{2}$ in. wide, bright green above and silvery beneath. It is a vigorous spreader and seems to grow better in the North than in the South. On rare occasions during a mild winter in Boston it may keep its evergreen character most of the winter.

Sasa veitchii   2′–3′   Zone 8   Kumazasa
A Japanese running bamboo which keeps low in the sun but when grown in shade gets 4–5 ft. tall. Leaves are 2–7 in. long and up to $1\frac{1}{2}$ in. wide. This also spreads rapidly.

Semiarundinaria fastuosa   25′   Zone 7   Narihira Bamboo
A Japanese running bamboo with culms slightly zig-zag in growth, making a splendid ornamental with leaves up to 7 in. long and an inch wide and culms $1\frac{3}{8}$ in. across at the base. New spring shoots, though small, are edible. It has been grown as a hedge rather successfully because it does not spread as fast as do some of the other running bamboos.

Shibataea kumasaca   3′–6′   Zone 8   Okamezasa
From Japan, this is a fine ornamental because it has an appearance almost like Ruscus. In fact, Robert A. Young of the U.S. Department of Agriculture has suggested it be called the Ruscus-leaf Bamboo, for probably it would not be even thought of as a bamboo by the casual observer. Leaves are ovate, sharp pointed, 2–4 in. long and 1 in. wide. It has an interesting, slightly zig-zag habit of growing its culms.

Sinarundinaria nitida   20′   Zone 8
A Chinese clump bamboo, hardier than some of the others, with culms $\frac{3}{4}$ in. across at the base. The leaves, 2–3 in. long and $\frac{1}{2}$ in. wide, are a brilliant green, making this a fine ornamental plant. In China the thin canes are used in basket weaving, making sieves and even light fences.

BAMBOO, JAPANESE TIMBER = *Phyllostachys bambusoides*

BAMBUSA (bam-BOO-sa). See BAMBOO.

BANANA. This large to gigantic herbaceous plant (*Musa paradisiaca sapientum*) makes a spectacular garden ornamental wherever it can be grown, even though the areas where fruit can be brought to full maturity with regularity are few on the continental United States.

The "trunk" of the Banana plant is a pseudostem made up of the overlapping leaf-stalk bases. At their tops these carry the large, up to 2 ft. by 8 ft., blades on a petiole 1–2 ft. long. The blades are thin, pinnately veined, and easily shredded at right angles to the midrib by strong winds. The crown of the plant is located at the ground line.

The more cold-hardy banana varieties will be injured but not killed by temperatures of 25° F., but they will not withstand even that temperature for prolonged periods. This limits their culture to the warmest areas of the Southeast, and to protected sites along the southern Pacific Coast. Windy sites should be avoided, because very tattered leaves are not efficient for growth and fruiting, and at the same time they are unsightly.

The plant requires a moderately deep, loamy, well-aerated soil which is free of appreciable concentrations of chlorides; the site should be protected from ocean spray, which is damaging. Bananas do best in soils high in organic matter, which may be supplied by adding compost to the soil, or mulching the surface with organic material.

The banana is a heavy user of nitrogen, and should be well supplied by periodic applications. Deficiencies of other elements are less often observed, but in soils low in potassium, as many are in the South and Southeast, complete fertilizers containing about as much potash as nitrogen should be used. Micronutrient deficiencies have but rarely been observed. Zinc is most likely to be deficient, and will result in small leaves with some yellowing in streaks from the midrib. Moderate soil applications of zinc sulfate should cure this deficiency.

The trees should never suffer from lack of water, as it slows growth and fruit development markedly. Temperature, rainfall, and soil conditions will regulate the amount and frequency of water to be applied.

The main stem of the Banana is the underground rhizome. Cuttings of this rhizome, containing at least 2 buds, and the suckers arising at the base of a pseudostem constitute the main methods of propagation. The basal crown of stems which have completed fruiting can also be used.

Varieties of bananas vary from 5–30 ft. in height. Small varieties require no more than 8–10 ft. for growth without crowding; large varieties may require up to 16 ft.

The inflorescence develops from the apex of the growing point, forcing its way through the pseudostem and emerging at the top. For edible

Banana flowering stalk with immature fruits. As fruits grow larger they will gradually bend upward.

varieties its weight soon causes it to bend over, so that the developing flowers are inverted. The flowers are arranged in series along the flowering stem, in a spiral arrangement, each series being subtended by a bract. The basal flowers are female, and the young carpel resembles a small banana. Pollination is not required in any of the commercial sorts, which are all triploid and so set their fruit parthenocarpically and without pollination. These flowers, each pair of series being a "hand", form the bunch which may weigh from 50 to 100 lbs. when ripe. Following the opening of the female flowers a few series open which appear to be perfect, but are completely sterile. Later, distal bracts open which have only male flowers, but in triploid varieties these yield practically no good pollen. The distal portion of the flowering stem may be cut off after the female bloom has opened.

In subtropical areas, the bloom will tend to appear in late spring or early summer, although flowering at other times is not precluded. Under ideal conditions the flower bud appears 6 to 8 months after planting a sucker. The time from planting to maturity largely depends on average growing temperatures, and may vary from 12 months to 3 years in our subtropical climates.

Each pseudostem bears but a single bunch of

bananas, death following. Normally the pseudostem is cut back when the bunch is harvested. Two to 4 of the suckers at the base of the fruiting pseudostem are left, and they in turn will grow and produce. This cycle is repeated, with care being given to the selection of suckers to assure best spacing and least interference.

Bananas allowed to ripen on the tree are seldom of good quality. The greatest yield of edible flesh is obtained if the bunch is harvested when the individual fruits assume a rounded or filled look in cross section, the younger fruits being more triangular. The earlier the fruit is harvested, the longer it takes to ripen off the tree.

The ripening process is highly dependent upon temperature, and bananas are adversely affected by temperatures below 53° F. Those ripening in warm weather may be harmed if held at low temperatures. Fully ripened bananas will brown and become off-flavor if held in the refrigerator after full ripening.

The several serious diseases of banana found in the tropical commercial plantings are less likely to occur under subtropical conditions, and the problems of disease can largely be discounted in the United States.

Varieties adapted to the continental United States are briefly described. **'Lady Finger'** is a popular, tall-growing variety, bearing fruits about 4–6 in. long, and weighing about 2 oz.

'Apple' is a medium-sized plant, bearing average fruits with a flavor reminiscent of its name, but is generally considered of lesser quality.

'Dwarf Cavendish' is the variety usually chosen for the garden, for often it does not exceed 5–6 ft. in height, and consequently needs less area for full development. In addition it is hardier than most other varieties, and is more wind resistant because of its low height. The fruit is of excellent quality. The fruits are 6–8 in. long, and weigh 4 to 5 oz. apiece. It is roughly similar in size and shape to the **'Gros Michel'** of commerce.

The Hawaiian Islands have a climate well adapted to all types of bananas, including the large **'Gros Michel'**. In addition, many local varieties are available which precede the discovery of the Islands by Cook.

An interesting variant type is the **'Red'** (Red Fig, Red Cuban) which produces colored fruits, the quality of which is generally considered to be mediocre.

Plantains are bananas which ripen without conversion of their starch to sugars, and are only used cooked. They are not generally grown in the United States; **'Orinoco'** is one such variety of medium-sized plant. Also see MUSA.

CLARON O. HESSE

BANANA FAMILY = *Musaceae*

BANANA, PERUVIAN = *Ensete ventricosum*

BANANA-SHRUB = *Michelia fuscata*

BANEBERRY. See ACTAEA.

BANK PLANTING. The chief objective in planting a bank is to select vigorous-growing species which will root along procumbent the burlap being left in place until it rots. Sometimes a greatly diluted asphaltum mixture is sprayed over the seeding. This is often done along major highways. The home owner can also buy sods of grass to put in place on a steep bank, to prevent erosion which otherwise might occur if the bank were seeded.

If vines are used, like the Memorial Rose,

A fine banking at Wisley, England.

stems on the soil surface or else will send out underground stolons or runners, both of which tend to hold the soil in place and keep it from eroding when heavy rains come. To obtain fast growth, the soil should be as good as possible (see SOILS) and, if newly planted, a mulch will help materially in getting the plants started.

When grass is planted, widely woven burlap is spread over the seeding to insure a good start, one can help the rooting process by throwing some soil over the long, prostrate runners, keeping it moist and thus encouraging speedy rooting. The following plants have all been used for covering banks under varying conditions. Soil, soil moisture, steepness of the bank and the speed with which a cover is needed, all govern the type of plant selected and the planting distances to be used.

	HEIGHT	ZONE	
Akebia quinata	vine 30′–40′	4	Fiveleaf Akebia
Arctostaphylos uva-ursi	6″–1′	2	Bearberry
Berberis thunbergii	7′	4	Japanese Barberry
Bignonia capreolata	vine to 60′	6	Cross-vine
Ceanothus americanus	3′	4	New Jersey Tea
Celastrus sp.	vine	4	Bittersweet
Clematis paniculata	vine 30′	5	Sweet Autumn Clematis
C. vitalba vine	30′	4	Traveler's Joy
Clethra alnifolia	9′	3	Summersweet
Comptonia peregrina	4′	2	Sweet Fern
Cornus sericea (*C. stolonifera*)	7′	2	Red Osier Dogwood
Coronilla varia 'Penngift'	2′	3	Crown Vetch
Cotoneaster horizontalis	3′	4	Rock Spray
Cynodon dactylon	1′	8–9	Bermuda Grass
Diervilla lonicera	3′	3	Dwarf Bush-honeysuckle
D. **sessilifolia**	4½′	4	Southern Bush-honeysuckle

	HEIGHT	ZONE	
Euonymus fortunei 'Colorata'	vine to subshrub	5	Wintercreeper
Forsythia 'Arnold Dwarf'	4'	5	—
F. suspensa sieboldii	9'	5	Siebold Forsythia
Hedera helix	clinging vine	5	English Ivy
Indigofera kirilowii	3'	4	Kirilow Indigo
Ipomoea sp.	vine	annuals	Morning-glory
Jasminum nudiflorum	vine to shrub	5	Winter Jasmine
Juniperus horizontalis vars.	12"–18"	2	Creeping Juniper
Lathyrus littoralis	decumbent	8	Beach Pea
L. splendens	3'	9	Pride-of-California
Leucothoe fontanesiana	6'	4	Drooping Leucothoe
Lolium multiflorum	3'	annual	Italian Rye-grass
Lonicera henryi	twining vine	4	Henry Honeysuckle
L. japonica 'Halliana'	vine	4	Hall's Honeysuckle
Lycium halimifolium	5'	4	Common Matrimony-vine
Menispermum canadense	twining vine 12'	4	Common Moonseed
Muhlenbeckia complexa	twining vine	6	Wire-vine
Myrica sp.	9'–36'	2–7	Bayberry
Parthenocissus sp.	vine	3–8	Creeper
Phalaris arundinacea picta	2'–4'	3	Ribbon-grass
Polygonum reynoutria	4"–6"	4	Reynoutria Fleece-flower
Pueraria lobata	vine	6	Kudzu-vine
Rhus aromatica	3'	3	Fragrant Sumac
Robinia hispida	3'	5	Rose-acacia
Rosa wichuraiana	1'	5	Memorial Rose
Rosmarinus officinalis 'Prostratus'	3'	8	Rosemary
Salix tristis	1½'	2	Dwarf Gray Willow
Stephanandra incisa 'Crispa'	1½'–3'	5	Dwarf Cutleaf Stephanandra
Symphoricarpos sp.	3'–6'	2–5	Snowberry, Coralberry
Vinca minor	6"	4	Periwinkle
Vitis coignetiae	vine	5	Glory-vine
Xanthorhiza simplicissima	2'	4	Yellow-root

BANYAN = *Ficus benghalensis*

BAPTISIA (bap-TIZ-ia). Members of the Pea Family, only 2 of a score or more species have ornamental value. These perennial herbs have compound leaves consisting of 3 leaflets arising from the same place on the stem, and pealike flowers arranged up and down the fleshy flower stalk. Somewhat inflated pods bear the seeds of the plant.

australis 3'–4' Zones 2–3 Blue Wild Indigo
An attractive plant, both in foliage which is a rich, bluish green, and in flower. The pea-like flowers are blue and hold up well when used in bouquets. It is native in rich, shady locations from Pa., to Ga. and Ind., but it is hardy as far north as Me. It flowers from May to June and is easily propagated by division before or after the flowering season. Clumps of the plant make an excellent summertime hedge, but the first hard frost kills the stems to the ground.

tinctoria 3'–4' Zones 5–6 Wild Indigo
Found over a wider area than its relative, *B.*
australis, this plant is at home from southern New England to Minn. and south to Fla. The flower stalks are much branched and the compound leaves, resembling the leaves of clover, ascend the branches which terminate in several pealike yellow flowers. These appear in June and July. This plant is a good candidate for the wild garden, since it can make do with little care and watering. In fact, it can even survive periods of drought. The methods of propagation are by division or by seed sown in spring or fall. The woody stem yields a blue dye that is an inferior substitute for Indigo and the root is used in various medicines.

BARB. Hooked hair, frequently doubly hooked.

BARBADOS-CHERRY = *Malpighia glabra*

BARBADOS FLOWER-FENCE = *Caesalpinia pulcherrima*

BARBADOS-GOOSEBERRY = *Pereskia aculeata*

BARBADOS-LILY = *Amaryllis vittata*

BARBADOS-NUT = *Jatropha curcas*

BARBAREA (bar-bar-EE-a)

verna   2′   Zone 3   Early Winter-cress
A perennial or biennial weed, native to Europe, similar to *B. vulgaris* except that the stem leaves have 4–10 pairs of lobes at the base while those of *B. Vulgaris* only have 1–4 pairs of lobes.

vulgaris   2′   Zone 3   Bitter Winter-cress
A biennial or shortlived perennial weed, often called Yellow Rocket, native in Europe and Asia, now a weed in North America. First year a rosette of leaves is formed on the ground and the stem is produced the second year. The golden-yellow flowers, produced in terminal spikes, are $\frac{1}{4}$ in. across, appearing in May and June. The stem leaves are alternate, deeply cut or lobed at the base and shiny, seed pods are narrow and erect, 4-angled and about 1 in. long.

BARBERRY. See BERBERIS.

BARBERRY FAMILY = Berberidaceae

BARK-RINGING FRUIT TREES. An operation sometimes tried on fruit trees, wisterias and other woody plants that do not bloom, in an attempt to force them into flower. The objective is to sever or to partially sever the up and down movement of nutrients in the phloem tissue just underneath the bark, so that the foods manufactured by the leaves will be utilized in the branches rather than being stored in the roots.

Bark-ringing is done in the early spring when the sap is moving up the trunk. It can be done in several ways:

1. A sharp knife is used to cut a complete ring around the trunk below the lowest branch, and another ring $\frac{1}{8}$ to $\frac{1}{4}$ in. below this also. Then the bark is removed between the 2 rings. This is about the distance that new bark can be grown in 1 year. Grafting wax should be put over the cut surface to protect it until it heals. If the strip of bark is much wider the tree can be killed, for then replacement cannot be grown in time to save the tree. One of the oldest methods of killing any tree has been to merely chop off 6 in. of bark in a ring completely around the trunk.

2. A second method is to remove this same $\frac{1}{8}$–$\frac{1}{4}$ in. ring but only halfway around the trunk, then a similar strip around the opposite half of the trunk but 4–6 in. below the first. In this way, it has been shown that trees can recover more quickly without the possibility of serious damage resulting.

3. Two cuts can be made with a sharp knife completely around the trunk or the branch of the tree about an inch or two apart. No bark is removed; hence recovery is rapid. The purpose of course, as in other methods of ringing, is to upset the carbohydrate-nitrogen ratio, and with this method, since it is only for a short period,

the exact time it is done is very important. It is usually done during the first 10 days of June in southern New England, and is more effective if done on larger limbs than the trunk. It is during the active-growing period of late June that the flower buds for the following year are formed, and this temporary stoppage of the normal flow of nutrients is sometimes all that is necessary to force the formation of flower buds at this time.

4. Another method is sometimes used. The limb is girdled with a sharp knife with 2 cuts, about 2 in. apart. Then alternate strips of bark between these 2 cuts are removed, and the exposed wood is covered with grafting wax.

5. A tight wire or metal band is fastened around a branch during the bud-formation period, later removed during the summer. This is sometimes used on wisteria vines that are difficult to bring into blossom.

Each of these methods has been devised to upset the carbohydrate-nitrogen ratio of a plant which has been forming much vegetative growth but has not been flowering. The operation should be timely, as noted above, not too severe, and any exposed tissue should be immediately covered with grafting wax to prevent drying out and disease infestation.

BARLEY = *Hordeum vulgare*

BARNYARD GRASS = *Echinochloa crus-galli*

BARREL GARDENING. Not a popular hobby any longer since old-fashioned wooden barrels are none too easy to obtain. Several holes, 2–4 in. wide, are drilled in a barrel at intervals around it, and good soil is put in on top of about 6 in. of gravel. Plants are inserted in the holes and maintained. Care should be taken to select those that trail or make suitable wall plants so that the barrel will be covered with foliage. Strawberry plants have been used; in fact small barrels are made from terra cotta just for this purpose. Ivies, thyme, veronicas, *Arabis* and sedums are only a few of the plants that might be selected.

BARREN-STRAWBERRY = *Potentilla simplex*; also *Waldsteinia fragarioides*

BARRENWORT. See VANCOUVERIA.

BASAL LEAVES. Those at the base of the plant, a term used frequently in connection with certain biennials and perennials in which the leaves at or near the ground level are different in shape and size from those on the stems.

BASELLACEAE = The Madeira-vine Family

BASIL, SACRED = *Ocimum sanctum*

BASIL, SWEET = *Ocimum basilicum*

BASKET-FLOWER = *Centaurea americana*

BASKET-GRASS = *Oplismenus compositus*

BASKET-IVY. See CYMBALARIA.

BASSWOOD = *Tilia americana*

BATCHELOR'S-BUTTON = *Centaurea cyanus*

BAUHINIA (baw-HIN-ia). These are deciduous and evergreen trees of the Tropics with unique 2-lobed leaves and orchidlike flowers followed by foot-long flat pods.

blakeana 20′ Zone 10 Hong Kong Orchid-tree
Those familiar with the exotic trees being grown in southern Fla. sometimes rate this Chinese native as the most spectacular of sub-tropical trees. The flowers are orchidlike, fragrant, rose-purple to crimson, 5½–6 in. in dia. and bloom from Oct. to March. The foliage is evergreen, an added asset.

corymbosa vine Zone 10 Phanera
A vine or sprawling shrub from southern China, climbing by tendrils, this bears clusters of small pinkish flowers, each about 1 in. wide with 5 frilled petals, during the summer. The long pink stamens add to the color effect. Fruits are reddish-brown pods. The leaves are 1–2 in. long and have 2 peculiar lobes which are most distinctive.

galpinii = *B. punctata*

monandra 25′ Zone 10 Butterfly Bauhinia
A tropical tree from the western hemisphere, this is valued for its delicate pink, 5-petaled flowers which appear in spring, differing from other species in that the flowers have only one stamen. The peculiar, rounded, 2-lobed leaves drop in the winter. Fruits are long, flat brown pods about 8–12 in. long. Reproduced by seeds.

punctata (*B. galpinii*) Zone 10 Red Bauhinia
A straggling shrub from Africa with the peculiar bilobed leaves of other Bauhinia species, this plant bears loosely open, brilliantly red flowers. The 5 petals are each about 1½ in. long, blooming in summer or fall, and they appear in 5–10-flowered clusters. The fruits are pods 5 in. long.

purpurea 25′–30′ Zone 10 Purple Bauhinia
Native to India, this is a beautiful tree for southern Fla. The flowers are 3–5 in. wide, varying in color from white to rich purple, fragrant and profusely borne. The pod is about a foot long. It is said to grow 15 ft. high in 2 years. Leaves are simple, 2-lobed.

variegata 20′ Zone 10 Orchid-tree
A beautiful tree native to China and India, now planted in southern Fla. and Hawaii. The lavender-to-purple flowers are in terminal groups, with 5 broadly separated petals and long white stamens, flowering in early spring. The leaves are 2 lobed, with main nerves emanating from the place where the petiole is attached to the blade. Fruit is a pod 1 ft. long. The variety 'Candida' has pure white flowers with a touch of very light green, noted to be the best white-flowering tree used in the gardens of Hawaii. Reproduced by seeds. This is probably the most popular species of this genus.

BAY, RED = *Persea borbonia*

BAY, SWEET = *Laurus nobilis*

BAYBERRY, CALIFORNIA = *Myrica californica*

BAYBERRY CANDLES. These have been made since the time of the earliest settlers. The waxy berries of *Myrica* species are best collected in early Sept. when they seem to have the most wax per berry. It takes 1½ quarts of berries to supply enough wax for one 8-in. candle. About 2 quarts of berries are placed in a kettle, covered with water and boiled for about 5 minutes. Then the greenish-gray wax is skimmed off, placed in a tightly sealed container, and another batch started.

An old-fashioned candle mold is taken (or a tubular mold can be made), and wicking material threaded in at the base. This can be bought at any needlework counter. It is threaded through the closed end of the mold where there is always a small hole left just for this, and held rigidly in the center of the open end by tying to another tightly held string. In this way a rigidly held string or wick is held in place the full length of the mold.

Then the pan of wax is taken, thoroughly melted, and poured slowly in the mold. When this is done the mold is placed in the refrigerator so the wax can harden thoroughly. When hard, it is placed in the oven under the broiler for a minute, turned on the other side for a minute, the mold removed and the candles removed from the mold by pulling on the wick. Then these are hung up (by the wick) until thoroughly air-hardened, then cut down and stored in polyethylene bags or tightly closed containers in order that they will retain their fragrance until used.

BAYBERRY FAMILY = Myricaceae

BEACH, PLANTS FOR PLANTING ON SANDY. See SEASHORE GARDEN.

BEACH GRASS, AMERICAN = *Ammophila breviligulata*

BEACH-HEATHER. See HUDSONIA.

BEACH PLUM = *Prunus maritima*

BEAD-LILY. See CLINTONIA.

BEAKED. Ending in a beak or prolonged tip.

BEAN. See PHASEOLUS.

BEAN, BROAD = *Vicia faba*

BEANS. To the average home gardener the word bean implies only two types, the kidney, snap or string bean and the lima bean, both of which belong to the genus *Phaseolus* and are native to the Americas. There are, however, a large number of other types, many of which are native to the Old World and include broad beans, soybeans, and Southern Pea Bean, Velvet Bean, Mung Bean and Tepary Bean, to list a few. Beans, as a group, constitute crop plants that are worldwide in culture to provide food for man and animals, to improve soils, for ornament and in some instances, e.g., soybeans, for industrial uses.

Snap or String (*Phaseolus vulgaris*) are cultivated more generally than any other crop of the bean tribe both for its edible pod and its dried seed. It is a very important home-garden crop in all sections of the U.S. Commercially large acreages are grown for the fresh market, for canning and freezing, and for dry beans.

Varieties

Bean varieties are listed under hundreds of names, many of which are synonymous and are of little importance. Beans may be classified according to (1) use, (a) snap beans for the edible pod, (b) green shell, for the still green immature seed, and (c) dry shell or ripe seed; (2) color of pod as green or yellow wax; and (3) habit of growth, namely dwarfs or bush and climbing or pole. The following varieties are recommended for home garden planting:

Green-podded bush—**'Tendergreen'**, **'Contender'**, and **'Greenpod'**. As green shell—**'Dwarf Horticultural'** and **'French Horticultural'**.

Wax-podded bush—**'Pencil Pod'**, **'Brittle Wax'**, **'Goldencrop'** and **'Sungold'**.

Pole or climbing varieties:

Green-podded—**'Kentucky Wonder'** types, **'Blue Lake'**.

Wax-podded—**'Kentucky Wonder Wax'**.

Soils and Fertilizers

Beans will grow satisfactorily in most all types of soil but do best in well-drained, warm, sandy loam and loam soils. Growth of the plant is slow and stunted in soils that are either too acid or alkaline and thus a soil pH of 5.5–6.5 is best. Thorough soil preparation is important. See KITCHEN GARDEN.

Beans will respond to a normal application of well-rotted animal manure or compost if available, 20–30 bu. per 1000 sq. ft. If manure is used, supplement with a broadcast application of 15–20 lbs. of a 5-10-10 fertilizer per 1000 sq. ft. If no manure is used, increase the fertilizer amount by 10 lbs.

Planting

Beans are tender to frost and usually are planted after that danger has passed. The seed germinates slowly in soils of a temperature of

Climbing Pole Beans

60° F. and if lower they may rot. Cold, wet soils result in poor stands. In the North 2–3 or more plantings are made to provide a continuous harvest. In the far South additional plantings are possible.

Bush varieties are planted in drills 1–2 in. deep and 24–30 in. apart. The plants should stand about 2–3 in. apart in the row. Pole beans are planted in hills, 4–5 seeds per hill, and spaced at 24–36 in. between hills. For most varieties the poles should be at least 6 ft. long, $1\frac{1}{2}$ ft. in the ground and $4\frac{1}{2}$ ft. or more above ground. Various types of trellises can also be used satisfactorily. Eight or ten hills are adequate for the average family.

Cultivation

Frequent shallow cultivation should be practiced basically to control weeds and to prevent a caking of the soil surface. Commercial growers have used the chemical Premerge or Sinox as a selective herbicide. Again it is not advisable for the home gardener to use these chemicals because they can cause severe damage if not used properly.

Harvesting

Kidney or snap beans are hand picked before the pods are full grown and while the seeds are very small. Harvesting of green-shell sorts is delayed until the seeds have reached full size but are still soft and succulent.

Lima beans (*Phaseolus limensis*). The lima bean is very tender and, therefore, sensitive to frost and cold or wet soils. Planting should be delayed until all danger of frost has past and the soil is warm. Some growers sow seed in papers pots or strawberry baskets in hotbeds 3–4 weeks before outdoor planting is safe.

Varieties

There are two types known as baby limas, seeds small and thin coated, and potato types having large, thick-coated seeds. Both are of bush and climbing habit of growth. Bush or dwarf sorts recommended are **'Fordhook 242'** (large seeded) and **'Henderson'** (small seeded). Pole varieties are **'King of the Garden'**, **'Thorogreen'**, **'Serva'**, **'Carolina'** and **'Florida Butter Speckled'**.

Outdoor planting, soil preparation, fertilization and general culture is the same as for kidney beans. Lima beans take longer to mature than kidney beans and, therefore, do not lend themselves to the same number of succession plantings. Most pole varieties require 90–100 days to maturity.

The pods are hand picked after the seeds have developed to their full size, but before the pods begin to turn yellow. Two to three pickings are usually possible from a planting.

Insects

Mexican bean beetle, a copper-colored, 16-spotted ladybird-type beetle. The larvae are orange to yellow and fuzzy. Both feed on the leaves and pods. Larvae are found largely on underside of leaf. Control—dust at 7–8-day intervals and up to 4–5 days prior to harvest with rotenone 1% dust or malathion 4% or methoxychlor 5%. Important to cover underside of leaves and apply in early morning when plants are damp with dew. Leaf hoppers are green, very small insects that fly quickly when disturbed. Both adults and nymphs attack leaves causing a curling and yellowing condition. Control—dust underside of leaves with malathion 4% or methoxychlor 5%, same as for bean beetle. The bean leaf beetle, ⅕ in. long, yellowish with 6 black dots, feeds on bean leaves. Control—same as for Mexican bean beetle. Aphids or plant lice can be controlled by nicotine dusts or sprays or by malathion 5% dust. Bean weevils in dry bean seeds can be controlled by placing the dry beans in the oven at 130° F. (no more) for three hours, after which the weevils should be dead.

Diseases

Anthracnose, a fungus, attacks the stems, leaves and pods causing elongated, sunken, dark red cankers. The disease is carried from year to year with the seed and the only control is in using western-grown seed; also, do not cultivate or work with the beans when the plants are wet. Bacterial blight appears on the leaves as brown blotches surrounded by a reddish-yellow halo. Control is the same as for anthracnose. Mosaics are caused by several types of virus. The affected plants are stunted and have crumpled and yellow-molted leaves. Control lies in controlling aphids which carry the disease and using resistant varieties such as 'Contender', 'Topcrop', 'Kentucky Wonder' or 'Blue Lake'. Rust shows up as red to black pustules on the leaves, causing leaves to dry up and fall off. Carried over from year to year in plant refuse. Burning old bean plants, using varieties which show some resistance, and dusting the plants with sulphur or Maneb are possible controls. In the case of pole beans, treat the poles with formaldehyde—1 pt. to 5 pts. of water. Downy mildew on lima beans shows up as a downy white growth. Dust with copper-lime or use maneb as directed on the container.

GRANT B. SNYDER

BEARBERRY = *Arctostaphylos uva-ursi*

BEARDED. Furnished with a tuft of hairs.

BEARGRASS = *Xerophyllum tenex*

BEAR'S-BREECH = *Acanthus mollis*

BEAR'S-FOOT FERN = *Humata tyermannii*

BEAR'S-PAW FERN = *Aglaomorpha meyeniana*

BEARDTONGUE, HAIRY = *Penstemon hirsutus*

BEAUMONTIA (bow-MONT-ia)
  grandiflora   vine   Zone 10   Easter Herald's Trumpet
A tropical vine bearing large, white, trumpet-shaped flowers in the spring. These are fragrant, milky white, sometimes tipped with pink and veined with green, 5 in. long, and are borne in dense clusters. The dark green leaves are pendulous and 5–9 in. long. Native to India.

  jerdoniana   vine   Zone 10   Beaumontia
This woody vine from India grows vigorously in Hawaii where its flowers are used in wedding bouquets. The white, slightly fragrant, bell-shaped flowers are 6 in. across. There are 5 stamens arising from the center of the flower and they are attached together at their tips. The flowers bloom in large clusters during the winter and spring.

BEAUTYBERRY. See CALLICARPA.

BEAUTYBUSH = *Kolkwitzia amabilis*

BEDDING PLANTS. Planting large formal beds of plants was a general practice 50 years ago, but busy gardeners today have little use for it. It consists of planting a large, usually formal, area or "bed" to a single plant, selected for its flower or foliage-color or height. Usually the bed must be planted each year, causing considerable work, and forcing plants for this purpose can take up much greenhouse space. The following list contains a very few plants used for this purpose. For plants used in planting more informal areas, but planted for permanency, see GROUND COVERS.

	HEIGHT	HARDINESS ZONE	COMMON NAME
Begonia semperflorens	8"–12"	annual	Wax Begonia
Browallia americana	2'	annual	Amethyst Browallia
Calendula officinalis	1'–2'	annual	Pot-marigold
Centaurea cineraria	12"–18"	4	Dusty Miller
Coleus blumei	3'	annual or perennial	Common Coleus
Consolida ambigua	1'–2'	annual	Annual Larkspur
Crassula sp.	1'–10'	9–10	Crassula
Echeveria species	3"–2'	9	Echeveria
Festuca ovina glauca	2'	4	Blue Fescus
Muscari botryoides	1'	2–3	Common Grape-hyacinth
Oxalis bowiei	6"–12"	8	Bowie Oxalis
Pelargonium	trailing–5'	10	Geranium
Petunia x hybrida dwarf vars.	6"	annual	Garden Petunia
Portulaca grandiflora	8"	annual	Common Portulaca
Primula species	1'	2–5	Primrose
Salvia splendens	3'–8'	annual or perennial	Scarlet Sage
Sedum species	2"	2–4	Stonecrop, Sedum
Viola cornuta	6"	2–3	Horned Violet, Tufted Pansy
V. wittrockiana	6"–12"	annual or perennial	Pansy

BEDSTRAW. See GALIUM.

BEE-BALM. See MONARDA.

BEECH. See FAGUS.

BEECH FAMILY = Fagaceae

BEECH-DROPS, FALSE = *Monotropa hypopithys*

BEEFWOOD. See CASUARINA.

BEES. Bees are helpful in the pollination of many plants. This is especially true with certain types of fruit trees in which cross-pollination is necessary for best fruit production, that is, the depositing of the pollen from one variety on the pistils of flowers of another variety. Some plants are said to be "self-sterile", that is, the pollen of the flowers will not properly fertilize the pistils of the flowers on the same tree. Hence, cross-pollination must be undertaken.

Pollen is either wind-carried or insect-carried, and fruit producers the country over have learned that hives of bees in such orchards where cross-pollination is a necessity greatly augment fruit production.

There are many insects other than honey bees which aid in carrying pollen. Of course it is not necessary for everyone to keep bees—in fact they can be a serious hazard in closely populated suburban areas. Too many bees can become unpopular in any garden, for they always are potential threats. Consequently, honey bees are not necessary to most ornamental gardens and

an overpopulation of them in such gardens can be decidedly unwanted.

There are gardeners not living in highly populated, urban or suburban areas, who have the time to keep a few hives of bees, usually in areas where fruit production is important.

Honey bees can travel 3 miles from the hive in foraging for honey, and so at swarming time, unless the hives are carefully manipulated to prevent it, swarms can lodge in neighbors' gardens (or house eaves) over a wide area. To keep bees, one must be prepared to cope with just such possibilities.

A bee takes about 1 hour to gather its load of honey and flies at about 15 miles per hour. It takes approximately 50,000 miles of travel to collect the raw materials for making 1 lb. of honey. A hive of about 10,000 workers would contain 500 drones and 1 queen, but this varies at different times of year. It takes 21 days from the time the egg is laid until the bee is fully grown; then it may live only 2–3 months or less, except the queen may live 2–3 years. She can lay 3000–5000 eggs per day depending on the season. So it is seen that the bee hive is a busily activated place.

It does take time to inspect the frames of honey, changing them around to prevent swarming, "taking off" the honey when it has properly ripened. Some individuals like the work, but most gardeners are content to let someone else care for the honey bees.

The flowers of most plants have either pollen (which the bees use as food at certain seasons of the year) or nectar that attract the bees, but some plants have flowers with more nectar than others, and hence are more attractive to the bees. Some of these plants are: Alfalfa, White

Bees. Left to right: Worker, Queen, Drone

Clover, Tupelo, Raspberry, Fireweed, Milk-weed, Linden, Mesquite (*Prosopis* sp.), Catsclaw (*Acacia greggii*), Huajillo (*Acacia berlanderi*), Buckwheat, and Goldenrod.

BEETS (*Beta vulgaris*). The beet is a member of the Chenopodiaceae or Goosefoot Family. The Garden Beet, Mangle Beet, Sugar Beet and Swiss Chard all belong to the same species, *Beta vulgaris*. Mangle beets are used primarily as stock feed and sugar beets as an important source of sugar.

The Garden Beet is not only a very common home garden vegetable, but also is widely grown for the commercial fresh market and for pro-cessing. The more important production areas are N.Y., Wisc., Ore., Mich., Tex., N.J. and Pa.

Varieties

The most popular varieties include 'Crosby Egyptian', 'Ruby Queen' and the 'Early Wonder' types for early planting, and 'Detroit Dark Red' or strains derived from it for late spring and fall planting. Other varieties of lesser importance are 'Long Blood' and 'Red Ball'.

Climatic Conditions

Beets are fairly hardy and are generally con-sidered a cool-weather crop. Roots attain their best quality and deepest red color during the cooler periods of the growing season. We must note, however, that beet plants may shoot to seed before the roots reach marketable size if the plants are exposed for 15–20 days to tem-peratures of 40°–50° F. or lower. Summer heat produces roots with low sugar content and definite white and red zoning (poor color).

Soil Preparation and Planting

Beets are grown satisfactorily on all types of soil but thrive best in sandy loams, silt or muck (peat) types. Heavy clay soils tend to produce malformed roots.

Beets are sensitive to soil acidity and grow best in soils testing 6.0 to 6.8 pH. See LIME.

The soil for beets, as with all root crops, should be thoroughly prepared to a depth of 8 in., leaving the surface smooth and free from clods of soil and trash.

Good quality depends on rapid growth. Do not spade or plow in strawy or green manure before planting—use only well-rotted manure. If manure is not available broadcast a 5-10-5 commercial fertilizer at the rate of 30–40 lbs. per 1000 sq. ft. prior to planting. When the plants are 6–8 in. high an application of nitrate of soda 7–8 oz. per 100 ft. of row may be profitable.

Plant about 10 seeds per ft., or 2 oz. per 100 ft. of row in drills spaced 12–15 in. apart and from ½–1 in. in depth. Beet seeds require 8–10 days for germination. It is a good plan to sprinkle a few radish seed in the row in order to mark the row and allow for early cultivation. Radish seed germinates in 4–5 days.

When the beet plants reach a height of 3–4 in. thin the seedlings to a spacing of 3–4 in. If beet greens are used delay the thinning process until the plants are 6–8 in. tall.

Frequent shallow cultivation should be practiced to control weeds.

Harvesting

Beets may be harvested as soon as the roots attain a size of 1½–2 in. At this stage the roots are tender and the leaves are also satisfactory to use as greens. Large roots tend to become coarse, woody and have poor quality and color.

Beets harvested in late fall may be stored for use during the early winter months. The storage room should have a temperature between 35° and 45° F. and a relative humidity of 85–90%. A good storage place might be a cold frame or an outdoor pit. If a cold frame is used, cover the frame with 10–12 in. of straw or leaves to prevent a freezing temperature inside the frame area.

Insects

The two major insects attacking beets are the beet leaf miner and the web worm. The leaf miner is a small white maggot which burrows in the tissue of the leaf. The web worm larvae attack the foliage, usually feeding on the under-side. In both cases, if the foliage is to be used for beet greens, spray or dust with pyrethrum. IF THE FOLIAGE IS NOT TO BE EATEN a spray or dust using diazinon or malathion is also recommended.

Diseases

Leaf spot consists of numerous round spots of ashen gray surrounded by purple border. Sprays or dusts containing a fixed copper or zinc afford some control. See FUNGICIDES.

Scab. This is the same organism that causes potato scab. This disease thrives best in soils that have had a heavy application of manure and in soils that are relatively sweet or alkaline. See POTATOES.

GRANT B. SNYDER

BEGGAR-TICKS. See BIDENS.

BEGONIA (beg-O-nia). These are succulent herbaceous plants chiefly native to Central and South America but some are native to other tropical or subtropical parts of the world. They are universally used as house plants and as bedding plants in the North, set out after danger of frost is past and lifted and taken indoors before fall frosts or in the subtropical areas of the U.S., where there is no frost, left out-of-doors all the time. They are divided popularly into two general classes: those with tuberous roots, and those with fibrous roots. Some are of ornamental value only for their foliage and others, like the popular tuberous begonias, have about the most colorful flowers of any of the herbaceous plants commonly grown by American gardeners. There are several hundred species and varieties offered by American growers so that one should take time in examining catalogues to find just the right ones for the particular situation.

Propagation

Propagation is by cuttings (either stem or leaf) and by seed. With the tuberous group propagation is also by the careful division of the tubers, making certain that when a tuber is cut a growing point or bud is included. Some tubers only have 1 or 2 growing points, so careful inspection should be made. Also, those with rhizomes creeping over the ground can be easily divided.

Begonia Propagation: Cut the veins on the undersurface, peg down on moist sand. New plants will form where the veins have been cut.

Sow the seeds, which are extremely fine, in Feb. and March, gently sifted on the surface of the soil. They should be pressed in but not covered over with soil since they are so small. A pane of glass is placed over them until they germinate, after which they are transplanted to a flat about 1 in. apart. However, the seed is so fine that one must be careful not to sow it too thick or to allow damping-off fungus to get to it. Species (pure seed) can be grown thus, as well as many tuberous begonia types, but there are so many hybrids available today that to preserve a color or a plant for its special flowers or leaf pattern it is much better to propagate it asexually.

The Wax Begonia (*B. semperflorens*) and many of the so-called Rex begonias are best propagated by cuttings to maintain the special plant characteristics for which the plant is valued in the first place. The large-leaved forms are especially propagated by leaf cuttings. A mature leaf is taken, some of the veins on the underside of the leaf are cut through, and the leaf is laid bottom side down on the rooting medium (see CUTTINGS), often pegged down with tooth picks so that it will be in close contact with the moist sand or sand-and-peat mixture. Young plants should form where the cuts have been made and when well off to rooting, these should be pricked out and potted. The Wax Begonia leaves are merely inserted in the rooting medium, petiole down, and a new plant should form at the junction of the blade and petiole. Begonia cuttings can be taken at almost any time of year, but mostly it is done during spring and summer.

Most begonias do well at temperatures of around 60°–65° F. They make truly excellent house plants, but do best if not placed in full direct sunlight for lengthy periods during the day. Some species can not survive in the hot, dry temperatures which are present in some houses during winter, but will do remarkably well in the moist atmosphere of the greenhouse. Other species seem to do very well under either set of conditions. Since there are between 500 and an estimated 1300 species alone, and thousands of varieties, many of them hybrids, it is impossible to treat the subject in detail here. Roughly speaking the more important species are listed here.

Insects Pests

Aphids and mealybugs infest begonia. Sprays of insecticide #15 will control them. Cyclamen mite causes distorted leaves. See CYCLAMEN.

Diseases

Leaf spots caused by several fungi are controlled by regular spraying with fungicides #D and #F. Bacterial leaf spot produces tan-colored blisterlike spots and the whole plant may become infected and die. Destroy infected leaves, branches and plants. No fungicidal treatment is recommended but an antibiotic might be tried. Botrytis blotch may cause a gray mold and rot where ventilation is poor and moisture is excessive. Correct these conditions.

x argenteo-guttata 2′–4′ **Zone 10 Trout Begonia**
A hybrid (*B. albo-picta* x *B. olbia*) with fibrous roots and ovate but long, pointed leaves 4–6 in. long, with white specks on them; flowers white to pinkish in axillary clusters.

x cheimantha—this is a group name given to several hybrids often grown in home greenhouses.

coccinea 3′–4′ **Zone 10 Angel-wing Begonia, Scarlet Begonia**
With tall canelike stems and oblique winglike leaves about 5 in. long, this fibrous-rooted species produces clusters of coral-red flowers. Native to Brazil and some used in hybridizing. Frequently incorrectly offered as *B. rubra*.

dregei 3′ **Zone 10 Grape-leaf Begonia**
A semi-tuberous species with new branches annually from the base and conspicuous swellings on the older stems. Profuse white flowers are produced in winter; native to South Africa. The leaves are ovate or rhombic, 3 in. long. This species should be rested after it is through flowering merely by refraining to give it much water.

x feastii 3′ **Zone 10 Beefsteak Begonia**
A vigorous fleshy-stemmed plant with fibrous roots, often referred to as one of the best of all the species as a house plant. The leaves are thick, rounded and red underneath with light pink flowers on a long stalk above the foliage in the winter. This is a hybrid (*B. manicata* x *B. hydrocotylifolia*). The var. **bunchii** has crested and ruffled leaves, with the lobes spiraled like a snail's tail. This is an excellent house plant, easily propagated by taking cuttings from its somewhat rhizomatous stem.

foliosa 1½′ **Zone 10 Fern Begonia**
A fibrous-rooted almost shrubby species from Columbia with white to pinkish flowers ½ in. wide. This is frequently used in hanging baskets and is a good conservatory plant as well.

foliosa miniata 2′ **Zone 10**
With small, green lop-sided leaves only about 1½ in. long and scarlet flowers ½–¾ in. across, somewhat resembling those of a fuschia. Native to Mexico and with fibrous roots. A form in the trade listed as **multiflora** with light pink flowers is probably a variety of this species.

grandis 2′ **Zone 6 Evans Begonia**
Pink-flowered with a white-flowered var. (**alba**); both have small bulblike tubers and are the hardiest of the group. They live outdoors as far north as New York City if planted in a shaded and protected place, mulched well in winter. The leaves are rounded, subcordate at the base, and lobed. Native to China and Japan. Propagate by axillar bulblets. This has tuberous roots.

haageana = *B. scharffii*

heracleifolia 2′–4′ **Zone 10 Star Begonia**
Easily increased by hairy rhizomes, this is native to Mexico and bears long-stalked leaves, sometimes 1 ft. across, with 5–9 deep, narrow dentate lobes that reach nearly to the middle of the blade. The flowers are white to pink appearing between Feb. and April. As a house plant this takes more rugged treatment than any other species.

imperialis 1′ **Zone 10 Imperial Begonia**
With rhizomes that are very hairy, native to Mexico; leaves 4–6 in. long, cordate-ovate, light green above and brown-green underneath. The white flowers are only ½ in. across in clusters no higher than the leaves. A fine pot plant.

limmingheiana **drooping** **Zone 10**
Drooping or climbing, this Brazilian species has leaves that are 3 in. long and white flowers, borne loosely in long-stalked clusters. Sometimes incorrectly termed *B. scandens*.

manicata 3′ **Zone 10**
Blooming in spring with pink flowers on fine stalks about a foot long, this has fleshy red hairs arranged in collars around the leaf-stalks. Propagate by cutting the rhizomes. The leaves are fleshy, 4–8 in. long, lustrous green above but reddish beneath; flowers are pink, ½ in. across, and are borne on stalks above the foliage. Native to Mexico. The variety 'Aureomaculata' has leaves blotched with white and yellow; the variety 'Crispa' has leaves with ruffled and crested margins.

x margaritae 1′–2′ **Zone 10**
A fibrous-rooted hybrid with *B. metallica* probably being one parent; leaves greenish to purplish above and reddish beneath. Flowers are rose colored, showy and in many clusters.

metallica 4′ **Zone 10 Steel Begonia**
With glossy green, ovate leaves, red underneath and about 6 in. long and somewhat metallic-tinted; bluish-white to high rose-colored flowers 1½ in. across. Native to Brazil. An excellent house plant with fibrous roots.

rex 3′ **Zone 10 Painted Leaf Begonia**
A popular fibrous-rooted species with many varieties or variations, the true species from Assam not being much used. The so-called Rex begonias, over 50 varieties of which have been known to have been listed by one nurseryman, are very popular, but not for homes with a very hot and very dry atmosphere. These need

moisture in the air, perhaps more so than any other group of begonias. Given this, they thrive. The flowers, rose pink and perhaps 1½ in. wide, are not nearly so ornamental as the large variously colored and variously shaped leaves. Many colorful varieties are available. 'Helen Teupel', 'Magnifica', 'President Carnot' and 'Rajah' are only a few.

scharffii (*B. haageana*)   4′   **Zone 10**

With large, hairy, olive-green leaves, red underneath, to 10 in. long, and large hanging trusses of white flowers tinged pink, almost always in bloom with a few flowers, but at its peak during summer. Fibrous roots. Native to Brazil.

semperflorens 8″–12″ **Zone 10 Wax Begonia**

Native to Brazil, this is a most popular fibrous-rooted pot plant used in the house and for bedding purposes. The plant is almost glabrous, with rounded shiny leaves 2–4 in. long. The flowers, about an inch wide, are white, pink and red, single and double with many varieties available. It blooms almost continuously and makes an excellent bedding plant for summer decoration, probably the most popular of all for this purpose. There are new varieties appearing all the time. One, **'Westport Beauty'** with double pink flowers, is not as easy to grow as some of the others.

There is a related hybrid variety, **'Gloire de Lorraine'** (*B. socotrana* x *dregei*) which is sold at Christmas, that is not well adapted to growing as a house plant. It grows 18–24 in. high.

stipulaceae   8′   **Zone 10**

A fibrous-rooted Brazilian species with long leaves, the veins underneath being white and the blade underneath being reddish. The white flowers, ⅔ in. across, are borne in large clusters.

sutherlandii   1′–2′   **Zone 9   Sutherland Begonia**

Not as hardy as *B. evansiana* but more hardy than most other begonias. The oval leaves are 4–6 in. long, lobed toward the base and have red veins on the upper surface. The orange or reddish-orange flowers are borne in conspicuous clusters. Native to Brazil and tuberous-rooted.

x tuberhybrida   2′   **Zone 10   Tuberous Begonia**

This is a general name and actually covers hundreds of different kinds of tuberous-rooted begonias. Some have flowers as much as 4 in. wide, single or double, ranging through most of the colors except blue. They have fleshy stalks which should be staked because of the weight of the flowers and foliage. There are also types like the multifloras which are dwarf and excellent for bedding purposes. Because of the large size of their flowers and their brilliant color, they are a group apart from other begonias. Many hybrids are given fancy names

by the growers like *B. crispa, cristata, fimbriata, camelliaeflora*, etc., but these are merely incorrectly used as scientific names to describe the flower form of major groups of these colorful plants. For their culture, see below.

ulmifolia   2′–4′   **Zone 10   Elm-leaf Begonia**

A fibrous-rooted species from Colombia, almost shrubby, with leaves the same shape as those of an elm, 3–5 in. long, green above and below. White flowers about ½ in. wide are profusely borne in loose clusters.

BEGONIAS, TUBEROUS. Tuberous begonias are among the most spectacular of tender summer-flowering bulbs. They are widely grown throughout the country, in the open ground and in window boxes, pots and other containers. Their huge flowers, in many forms and colors, flash like beacons and never fail to elicit comment whether seen in gardens, in greenhouses, or in flower shows, where they are a popular item.

Present-day gorgeous hybrids are a far cry from the small flowering species that are native to South America. Breeders have produced varieties with blooms several inches across, in colors that include red and scarlet, orange and yellow, pink and rose, and pure white, with every tint and shade in between. Colors may be pastel, soft and delicate, or bright and flaming.

Forms are equally variable. Because there are so many, they have been classified into groups. Most familiar are the camellia-flowered, with double blossoms that may have smooth or ruffled edges, while in some the edges may be contrasting in color. Carnation-flowered are named after the appearance of the blossoms, which are generally smaller than the camellia-flowered group but in a broad color range.

There are pendulous kinds for hanging baskets, seen in their fullest glory on the West Coast, in the area around Carmel, Calif., with its cool summer climate. Abundant single or double flowers appear on arching stems. Another group has created flowers with slightly frilled single blossoms, carried well above the foliage. In the "rosebud" category, plants are free flowering with rose-pink blossoms, resembling roses, while the daffodil-flowered group contains varieties usually grown as oddities. This is equally true of the hollyhock-flowered group with their flowers held close to the tall stems. They make good accent or background plants however.

A very promising group known as the **Multi-flora** begonias resemble larger types, except that they are smaller in all their parts. Compact flowering plants, 6 in. tall, these are excellent when used for bedding. They are valued for their ability to withstand more heat and direct sunlight than the large, flowered hybrids. The old-time yellow variety, 'Madame Helene Harms', is still one of the best of these multifloras.

The many uses to which tuberous begonias can be put is proof of their versatility. They are excellent for bedding in partial shade, where they do best, although in cool northern climates they take all-day sunshine. They can be planted in front of shrubs or in the high, filtered shade of high branching trees. Often they are arranged around trunks of specimen trees in lawns. In these days of outdoor living, they are becoming an essential feature of the terrace, because of their breathtaking beauty. Terrace pockets can be enlivened with their glowing colors, and pots, boxes, planters, and other containers can be decorated with upright and pendulous kinds.

Window boxes on the north side of the house or garage, with unobstructed overhead light, can be gay with tuberous begonias and other shade-tolerant plants, including the Patient Plant, Coleus, and English Ivy. The possibilities with hanging baskets are seemingly endless. One, 2 or several baskets can be attached to the eaves of the house or garage, to large limbs of trees, on old-fashioned porches, or on wall brackets secured to fences or houses.

Along with African violets, gesneriads, bromeliads, daffodils, dahlias, gladiolus, and hollies, tuberous begonias have their staunch adherents. There are hobbyists and collectors who grow hundreds of plants. Usually they provide a lathe shade to break the intensity of the sun and the force of the wind, which cuts soft stems and snaps heavy blossoms. In cooler areas, these begonia lovers will grow plants on raised platforms and step arrangements, where they are easier to water and care for. By lifting them, too, they can enjoy the full beauty of the heavy blooms, which tend to droop as they mature and face the ground when grown in the garden.

Culture

Because of the short growing season in northern gardens, tuberous begonias need an early indoor start to insure flowers by the early or middle part of the summer. If plants are started outdoors in May, after frost danger has passed in the garden, healthy plants will not begin to produce until Sept., only to be blighted by hard killing frosts before they have a chance to perform.

Some prefer to purchase ready-grown plants in the spring. Often they are just coming into bloom. This is more costly, but it is a solution for busy people who do not have the time or facilities to start their own. This way, they achieve immediate effects wherever they expect these showy tubers to hold forth.

Feb. and March are the months to start the tubers in a bright window, in a greenhouse, or other place where light and temperature conditions are right. If the tubers were stored, first examine them carefully to determine their condition. Firm, clean tubers, free from diseases, are essential for success. Any that are too soft or show signs of rotting are best discarded. If buying fresh stock, look for cleanliness and avoid bargains.

Tubers can be started in low pots, known as bulb pans, in trays, which are about 3 in. deep, or in other suitable containers. Be certain they are provided with holes for drainage. Plants will only be grown here for a limited period of time, but they can rot before shifted to their permanent summer locations. Clay pots are well aerated, but dry out quicker than plastic. It is not so much the kind of container, but learning to water when there is need, just as the surface of the soil shows signs of becoming dry.

Start with a mixture consisting of equal parts good garden soil, fine sand, and peat moss or leaf mold. The concave or depression end of the tubers is the top and the round, the bottom, so place them in this position, spacing only a few inches apart, since they will be moved when they have sprouted. Barely cover with the starting medium. Water to moisten, but do not wet too much. This is easy to do, but remember that there are no tops to support. Maintain this moist condition throughout this early growing period. Until sprouts appear, light is not needed, so containers can be placed in the cellar, shed, spare room, or under benches in the greenhouse.

When tips show through the medium, provide strong light or direct sunshine for at least part of the day. This is essential from this stage until plants are placed outdoors. Without strong light, plants develop spindly growth, more so later when they unfold their second, third and fourth leaves.

To sprout, tubers need warmth during the day, about 75° F. with a slight drop at night, otherwise there will be considerable delay and much time will be lost. When an inch or two high, plants will need moving to larger containers. Large trays or bulb pans may still be used, if tubers are spaced several inches apart, but it is advisable to use individual 4-in. pots, since the roots will not be disturbed when plants are shifted to larger pots or to the garden.

Plants will stay in these 4-in. pots until in their final positions, either in the open ground or containers. So they will need a special soil preparation, a rich mixture to develop good foliage growth, followed by a wealth of bloom in summer. Use equal parts good garden soil, peat moss or leaf mold, and sand, with one-half part dehydrated manure. This is the same mixture plants will require when moved for the last time.

During this period, aim for compact growth. This results from strong light, from the east, south or west windows in the home. Keep turning pots around to prevent the one-sided look, although this is not a problem in the home greenhouse. The form plants develop at this time will remain with them through the season. Spindly plants stay thin and awkward. They look poorly and break easily in the wind, even if secured. Tuberous begonias are not like annuals, which can be pinched to encourage new bushy growth. Therefore this period of sufficient light cannot be stressed enough. Always keep moist, but no feeding is required.

When all danger of frost is over, it is time to plant the tuberous begonias outdoors, and the place where they are finally planted should have some shade for part of the day at least. Tuberous begonias are gross feeders, and good results come from proper soil, so the bed should be thoroughly dug in advance. Fertilizer, sand and humus in the amounts already suggested should be added to the bed in order to provide the best possible growing conditions.

Avoid a site that is shaded continually. Trees with thick canopies are especially to be avoided. Contrary to opinion, which recommends shade for tuberous begonias, sun is needed for a few hours a day. Otherwise plants become leggy and bloom is sparse. Early morning sun, until 10 o'clock or that in the late afternoon, from 4 o'clock onward, is excellent. Sunlight that creeps through the leafy bowers of trees that are not low branching is recommended. And, of course, open shade, the kind found on the north side of the buildings, gives good results.

Tuberous begonias are often grown in containers for outdoor beautification and one of the first prerequisites is to make provision for drainage. Place sufficient amounts of broken crocks, stones, pebbles or other material at the bottom. To the recommended soil mixture, add a handful of bonemeal or superphosphate and one of a mixed chemical fertilizer to each bushel of soil. Pots of varying sizes can be used, but the 8 in. will produce larger, lustier plants with enormous-sized blooms.

During the summer, water regularly—avoid drying out, since this injures the fine feeding roots. Yet avoid overwatering, which promotes tuber rotting, especially in soil with a high humus content. When watering tuberous begonias do not sprinkle the foliage, particularly at night. They do not have a chance to dry out and the leaves will develop mildew, which disfigures them with powdery white. Water in the early morning or late afternoon with a water soaker or wand, or remove the hose nozzle, and place the end of the hose on a piece of board to break the force of the water and direct it toward the base of the plant.

Do not overlook feeding, needed in spite of careful soil preparation. In the beginning and until flowering commences, use a high nitrogen fertilizer to encourage leaf growth and strong stems. Then shift to one with a low nitrogen content, such as 2-10-10, to encourage larger, sturdier blooms, as well as the development of firm tubers that will store well during the winter. This could be applied about every 3 weeks as a good average.

Tuberous begonias, with their huge weighty blooms, require staking. Wire or green bamboo supports should be inserted with care in order not to pierce tubers. Stems are brittle and fleshy, so use soft twine that does not cut. If staking early in the season, and it is advisable to do it then, allow some of the stake to project above each plant to take care of future growth, but not too much, as it will be unsightly.

Insect and Disease Pests

Bud dropping is a common problem. It can be caused by too much or too little water, especially if plants are permitted to go dry in between waterings. Sudden changes of temperature are likewise responsible for this tendency.

To obtain larger blooms, some gardeners like to remove the smaller blossoms on either side of the large double bloom, which is male. This is usually done on plants that are groomed for exhibition in flower shows, but for a more colorful display and a greater profusion of bloom, it is better to allow the small single flowers, which are female, to remain.

Powdery mildew, identified by a whitish, grayish, feltlike appearance on the leaves, is prevalent where summers are humid, more so near the seashore. To check, start spraying when plants are small with captan or karathane, two fungicides which give dependable control.

Plants often succumb to stem rot when soil is kept too wet. To avoid, keep stems at the base sprayed with ferbam. Slugs and snails will often eat large holes in the leaves to cause an ugly appearance, but a poison bait containing a metaldehyde base eliminates their ravages. Apply in the early evening, which is just before these pests begin to eat. Sometimes mealybugs, white flies, or aphids may appear, but they can be controlled with malathion.

Storage

In the North, tubers are lifted after the first frost blackens the leaves, but farther south in warmer climates a yellowing and browning of foliage at the end of the season indicates harvest time. Lift plants, when ready, with a spading fork, keeping it a safe distance from tubers in order to avoid injury. Then spread in the sun to dry for a few days while the tops are still attached. Then cut off tops to within an inch or so from the top of the tuber. Remove this portion of stem at a later time, when it has dried completely.

With soil shaken off, arrange tubers in trays or shallow boxes for their winter storage period. Cover with dry peat moss or clean dry sand. Some growers simply place tubers in bags just as they are. In either case, try to keep the same colors together. Best storage temperatures are 40°–50° F., but they will keep well at higher temperatures, if tubers are clean and well aerated. Too warm storage can be harmful, however, causing tubers to shrivel and dry up· Bulbs in pots can be left in the pots. Simply turn containers on their sides and store in a frost-proof cellar, shed, closet or basement.

The actual tubers are long lived. Each one increases in size with each growing season, and can be grown successfully for 10 years or more. New plants are obtainable by dividing tubers in sections of 2. Use a sharp knife to cut them in halves or thirds but make certain that each piece contains a sprout. Then dust the cut sides with sulfur to prevent the spread of disease.

To produce new plants, seed can be sown in Jan. or Feb. in fine, sandy, humus soil. Barely cover with the medium and grow at 70° F. Transplant as the young plants develop, and with good care, they will flower toward the end of the first year.

GEORGE TALOUMIS

BELAMCANDA (bel-am-CAN-da)
chinensis **3′** **Zone 5** **Blackberry-lily**
A tuberous-rooted herbaceous perennial which is somewhat like a gladiolus in leaf habit, for these are 1–1½ ft. long and an inch wide. It is a member of the Iris Family, with red-spotted orange flowers 1½–2 in. wide on branched stems in the early summer. The seed pods burst open in the fall showing the black seeds inside. It should be mulched well over winter in cold areas and is easily propagated by seed or division of the rootstock in spring.

BELLADONNA = *Atropa belladonna*

BELLADONNA-LILY = *Amaryllis belladonna*

BELLFLOWER. See CAMPANULA.

BELLIS (BELL-is)
perennis **6″** **Zone 3** **English Daisy**
A perennial, native to Europe and probably introduced as a garden plant to America in early colonial times, it can become a bad weed in lawns on both the East and West Coasts of North America. The daisylike flower-heads are are white to pink or purplish, up to 2 in. across, appearing April to June. The leaves are spatulate to obovate, more or less in a rosette at the base. Actually it makes a fine well-grown garden

plant and several cultivated varieties are available, such as 'Dresden China', 'Tuberosa', 'Giant Rose', 'Montrosa' and 'Snow Ball'. Seeds can be planted in late Aug. in a frame, left there with some protection over winter and set out early in the spring about 10 in. apart. It has been grown both as an annual and a biennial.

rotundifolia **6″** **Zone 8** **Spanish Daisy**
The tufted stems of this perennial have round leaves on long stems and bear white daisylike flowers on 6-in. stems. The variety **caerulescens** has blue flowers. Native to Algeria and Morocco.

BELLIUM (BELL-ium)
bellidioides **4″** **Zone 6** **Stolon Bellium**
A small, matlike perennial with spoon-shaped leaves and small white daisylike flowers tinted pink on the underside of the petals. These are borne on slender 3 in. stems throughout the summer. Native to the Mediterranean Area, this sun-loving plant needs winter protection in northern temperate areas. Suitable for the rock garden.

BELLS-OF-IRELAND = *Moluccella laevis*

BELOPERONE GUTTATA = *Drejerella guttata*

BENT GRASS. See GRASS, LAWNS.

BENT GRASS, CLOUD = *Agrostis nebulosa*

BENZOIN AESTIVALE = *Lindera benzoin*

BERBERIDACEAE = The Barberry Family

BERBERIDOPSIS (ber-berry-DOP-sis)
corallina **climbing** **Zone 10** **Coral Chilevine**
This climbing plant from Chile is only grown out-of-doors in southern Calif. The opposite cordate-shaped leaves are about 3 in. long and coarsely toothed; the crimson flowers, ⅓ in. long, are borne in terminal many-flowered racemes, and the fruit is a berry.

BERBERIS (BER-ber-is). The barberries are thorny shrubs, with alternate leaves, bright yellow flowers and red, yellow, blue or black fruits. Many have been grown in America but the U.S. Department of Agriculture has greatly restricted the number of kinds that can be grown because many act as alternate hosts for the very destructive black stem rust of wheat. Approximately 140 different species, forms and hybrids of barberry have been found to act as hosts for this disease and so they are prohibited from being grown and sold in wheat-growing areas, *B. thunbergii* being restricted in Canada.

Some species and varieties are immune or resistant to this disease, and it is possible to grow them. Fortunately, these are some of the best ornamental species in the entire group. Because of the restrictions placed on growing these plants, it is the following which might be grown. These include many native Asiatic barberries and some of the very best of the evergreen species.

The deciduous barberries usually have brilliant red autumn color. They are rugged plants, being able to grow in poor soils under trying conditions. As ornamentals they are prominent in flower, in fruit and in autumn color, and some, like the Japanese Barberry (*B. thunbergii*), retain their fruits all winter long and well into the spring so that they have interest every season of the year. They make good specimens as well as excellent hedges and barrier plants. The barberries immune or resistant to the black stem rust disease have few other insect or disease pests and so make good additions to any garden where low maintenance is important.

Propagation

Seeds may be sown or stratified as soon as ripe or stored dry in airtight containers in a cool place for a year and then sown. Best to stratify at 40° F. for 2 months. Many plants can be divided with a sharp spade. Softwood or hardwood cuttings of most kinds can be rooted. See CUTTINGS.

beaniana   8′   Zone 6   Bean's Barberry
With small yellow flowers in mid-June produced in racemes; purple berries in the fall; red autumn foliage color. Native to China.

buxifolia nana   18″   Zone 5   Dwarf Magellan Barberry
One of the hardiest evergreen barberries, excellent for very low hedges. It is native to the Straits of Magellan in South America and rarely produces flowers and fruits in this country. Leaves up to an inch long and spiny.

canadensis   6′   Zone 5   Canada Barberry
This is not immune to the black stem rust disease but is mentioned here merely because it is native from Va. to Ga. Deciduous, with yellow flowers, red fruits and scarlet autumn color, it is often confused with *B. vulgaris*. Neither of these species should be grown.

candidula   2′   Zone 5   Paleleaf Barberry
Dwarf, dense in habit, making a good rock-garden plant, this has solitary yellow flowers in May and purplish fruits later. The evergreen leaves are 1½ in. long and the plant is native to China.

x chenaultii   4′   Zone 5   Chenault Barberry
(*B. verruculosa* x *gagnepainii*) A hybrid originating in 1928, this evergreen barberry is most promising and may turn out to be one of the best evergreen barberries for the northern U.S. because of its vigor, its good growth and splendid appearance all winter. Leaves about 1 in. long, narrow and spiny.

circumserrata   6′   Zone 5   Cutleaf Barberry

Hardy, deciduous and handsome, this is especially valued for its fiery-red autumn color and yellowish-red berries in the fall. The flowers are yellow, small and produced 2–3 in a cluster in late May, each flower being about ⅓ in. in dia. These do make as big a display as those borne in large clusters. Native to China.

concinna   3′   Zone 6   Dainty Barberry
A low barberry from the Himalayas, half evergreen in some areas, compact in growth, with bright yellow, solitary flowers about ½ in. dia., and red fruits in the fall. The leaves are about 1½ in. long and slightly spiny.

darwinii   10′   Zone 7   Darwin Barberry
Widely used in England, this evergreen has slightly spiny leaves 1 in. long, yellow to reddish flowers in pendant racemes that are strikingly beautiful, dark purplish fruits and purplish autumn color. The small, hollylike leaves are distinctive at all seasons. Charles Darwin brought this from Chile in the famous ship "Beagle" about 1835.

gagnepainii   6′   Zone 5   Black Barberry
An evergreen from China with prickly leaves up to 4 in. long, bluish-black fruits and abundant yellow flowers in clusters in May. This fine barberry grows equally well in Mass. or Calif.

gilgiana   6′   Zone 5   Wildfire Barberry
A deciduous barberry from China, noted especially for its profuse pendant flower clusters with individual flowers about ¼ in. and its clusters of blood-red berries in the fall. The foliage turns a vivid scarlet in the fall. It is a superb sight in fruit, a worthy substitute for the European Barberry, *B. vulgaris*, which is susceptible to the wheat-rust disease. The plant is more dense than *B. koreana*.

julianae   6′   Zone 5   Wintergreen Barberry
A popular Chinese evergreen with spiny leaves up to 3 in. long, clusters of yellow flowers ½ in. wide, bluish-black berries and a dense habit of growth. It is a vigorous and usually dependable grower.

koreana   6′   Zone 5   Korean Barberry
This is another good deciduous substitute for *B. vulgaris*. The small yellow flowers, each ¼ in. in dia., are borne in pendant clusters. The fruits are a brilliant red, and the autumn color is also red. Its dense growth makes it an excellent barrier plant as well as an interesting specimen.

x mentorensis   7′   Zone 5   Mentor Barberry
Introduced about 1924, this is a hybrid of *B. julianae* x *B. thunbergii* and is recommended for withstanding the dry summers of the Midwest where it does better than any other barberry. The spiny margined leaves are semi-evergreen about 1 in. long and the fruits are an uninteresting, dull, dark red.

sargentiana   6′   Zone 6   Sargent Barberry
An evergreen shrub from China with spiny

leaves 1½–4 in. long and simple or 3-parted thorns on the stems as much as an inch long. The clusters of small yellow flowers appear in the spring followed by bluish-black berries about ¼ in. across that are not very conspicuous. It is similar in many ways to *B. julianae* but not quite as good an ornamental.

x stenophylla 9′ **Zone 5 Rosemary Barberry**
A hybrid (*B. darwinii* x *B. empetrifolia*), this develops into a beautifully graceful evergreen specimen with leaves up to 1 in. long. The fruits are black berries, but it makes a splendidly uniform clipped hedge, or it can be used as a graceful specimen of interest for its habit alone.

thunbergii 7′ **Zone 4 Japanese Barberry**
The Japanese Barberry is one of the best deciduous hedge plants there is. Thorny, vigorous in growth with profuse flowers and bright red fruits, which frequently remain on the plant all winter long, this plant is one of the best for growing in poor dry soils, or in shaded situations. In fact, the statement is often made that if the Japanese Barberry will not grow in a trying spot, practically no other woody shrub will. Even though it is one of the most common plants grown in America today, it is still worthy of major consideration for planting as a clipped or unclipped barrier hedge (it is very thorny) or as a specimen or as a "filler" in poor soil or shaded spot where other plants do not grow well. There are many truly excellent varieties. Among the best are: **aurea**—with yellow foliage, a striking ornamental; **atropurpurea**—with reddish leaves throughout the entire growing season; **atropurpurea 'Red Bird'**—supposedly with leaves more red and more compact in growth than the var. *atropurpurea*; **'Crimson Pygmy'**—often called 'Little Gem', 'Little Pygmy' or var. 'Atropurpurea nana'; this is a dwarf, red-leaved variety of special merit. Plants 8 years old are only 2 ft. high, so it makes an excellent low and colorful hedge which does not require clipping. It is definitely mounded in habit; **'Erecta'**—patented (# 110) and sometimes called the **Truehedge Columnberry** this grows erect and is very compact. As a hedge it only needs trimming at the top every other year or so; **'Globe'**, Patented (# 186), this has green leaves and a globe shape; **'Minor'**—smaller in habit, foliage and fruit than the species, an excellent densely compact variety that deserves far more use; **'Thornless'**—without thorns; **'Variegata'**—with leaves variegated with spots of white, light gray and yellow, this has also been patented (# 867). **'Golden Ring'**—yellow leaf margin; **'Marshall Red'**—upright, deep red foliage all summer, brilliant red fall colors; **'Sparkle'**—good autumn fall color in shades of orange.

verruculosa 4′ **Zone 5 Warty Barberry**

The leathery evergreen leaves of this Chinese barberry are lustrous green above but pure white beneath, spiny on the margins and about 1 in. long. The violet-black berries are covered with a grayish bloom. The autumn color of the foliage is bronze. In many ways this could be considered one of the best of the evergreen barberries for ornamental use.

vulgaris 7′ **Zone 3 European Barberry**
The European Barberry was undoubtedly brought over to America by the earliest colonial settlers and since those times has become naturalized. It is one of the plants commonly seen in New England but it does carry the wheat rust. The gardeners of colonial times made jellies and jams, pies and drinks from the edible fruits. It should not be planted and the U.S. Department of Agriculture has placed many restrictions on its continued growth. It is upright in habit, with arching branches, pendulous clusters of small yellow flowers and bright red fruits and it does have scarlet autumn color.

However, both *B. gilgiana* and *B. koreana* are very similar in habit and have just as ornamental flowers, fruits and autumn color. Either one of these should be grown instead, since both are resistant to the black stem rust of wheat.

BERCHEMIA (ber-KEE-mia). Neither of these two twining shrubs can be considered high climbing vines, nor are they very ornamental. They are usually only found in arboretum collections. With alternate leaves, and drupes for fruits, they are propagated by seeds or root cuttings or cuttings of ripened wood in the fall.

racemosa **twining shrub** **Zone 6 Japanese Supplejack**
Leave 1–2½ in. long; flowers in greenish-white panicles 2–6 in. long; fruit about ¼ in. in dia., red, maturing black. Native to Japan and Formosa.

scandens **twining shrub** **Zone 6 Alabama Supplejack**
Native from Va. to Fla., leaves 1½–3 in. long and bluish black about ⅓ in. in dia. Flowers small in greenish-white terminal panicles.

BERGAMOT. See MENTHA; MONARDA.

BERGENIA (ber-GEN-ia). Perennials, sometimes almost evergreen with thick cabbagelike leaves and spikes of pink, white to rosy-purple flowers in the early spring, native to Siberia and grown throughout the U.S. although in the North they might be lightly covered over winter. Often listed in catalogues under the genus *Saxifraga*. They are usually propagated by division in either fall or spring. Seeds can be sown in spring. Bergenias can be planted in moist, shaded situations, by pools or along streams. If grown in full sun growth seems to be somewhat retarded.

cordifolia 20″ Zones 2–3 Heartleaf Bergenia
A perennial herb, native to Siberia, with large fleshy leaves about 6–8 in. across; rose-colored flowers in a spike often somewhat hidden by the large coarse leaves in spring. There is a white-flowered variety as well as one with purple flowers. It grows well in wet soils and has been used as a ground cover in such spots.

crassifolia 20″ Zones 2–3 Leather Bergenia
Similar to *B. cordifolia* but the leaves tend to be obovate, and the flowers are held on scapes considerably above the foliage. This species seems to be popular in Calif.

stracheyi 1′ Zone 6? Strachey Bergenia
The foliage of this plant is not wavy and the edges are fringed with hairs. Other than this, the plant, native to India, is similar to the Siberian *B. cordifolia* and seems to do as well in cooler climates.

BERMUDA GRASS = *Cynodon dactylon.* See GRASS, LAWNS.

BERRIES, COLORFUL ORNAMENTAL.
Many trees and shrubs are valued as ornamental because of their colorful, profusely borne fruits. It is impossible to mention all such plants, but many are included in the following lists. Black-fruited shrubs and trees may have value for their flowers or habit, or ability to grow in special situations, but certainly their fruits are not as ornamental as plants with red, yellow, white or blue fruits, hence they are not included specifically in the list.

The amount of fruit borne by a tree, shrub or vine can vary from year to year, because of several factors. In the first place, some species have all staminate or pollen-bearing flowers on one plant, and all pistillate or fruiting flowers on another. For the genera included in this group see DIOECIOUS PLANTS.

Then some plants (*Viburnum dilatatum* is one) fruit better if several seedlings or clones are growing together in a group instead of just one plant, or several plants all asexually propagated from one clone. Fortunately very few plants are in this class.

Then there is the matter of inclement weather at flowering time. Hollies, as one example, bloom in June. If the weather is cold (bees do not fly when temperatures are below 57° F.), still (no wind) or rainy, there is little opportunity for much cross-fertilization to take place. No one notices it at the time, but when fall comes few fruits will be present, a result few gardeners will trace to inclement weather in June.

Finally, apples and other fruits, as well as lilacs and some other ornamentals, are "alternate" bearing, that is they produce a large crop of fruits or flowers one year, and few the next. This is physiological and there is little that can be done to change it except, in the case of lilacs and rhododendron, to cut off the dead flowers and prevent fruit formation, on the simple theory that nutrients which might have gone into forming fruits will be diverted into forming flower buds for the next year.

The plants in the following list are among those valued as ornamentals for their bright-colored fruits:

	HEIGHT	ZONE	
Amelanchier sp.	25′	4	Serviceberry
Ampelopsis brevipedunculata	vine	4	Porcelain Ampelopsis
Arbutus sp.	10′–30′	8	Strawberry-tree
Arctostaphylos uva-ursi	ground cover	2	Bearberry
Ardisia crenata	1′	9	Coral Ardisia
Aronia arbutifolia	9′	5	Red Chokeberry
Aucuba japonica	15′	7	Japanese Aucuba
Berberis sp.	18″–10′	5–7	Barberry
Callicarpa japonica	4½′	5	Japanese Beautyberry
Cinnamomum camphora	30′–40′	9	Camphor-tree
Carissa grandiflora	18′	9	Natal-plum
Celastrus sp.	vine 20′–36′	4	Bittersweet
Clematis—most sp.	vine 6′–15′	3–6	Clematis
Cornus sp.	9′–24′	2–5	Dogwood
Cotoneaster sp.	1′–18′	3–7	Cotoneaster
Crataegus sp.	21′–30′	4	Hawthorn
Daphne sp.	16″–3′	4	Daphne
Duranta repens	18′	10	Golden Dewdrop

	HEIGHT	ZONE	COMMON NAME
Elaeagnus sp.	9'–12'	3–7	Elaeagnus
Eriobotrya japonica	20'	7	Loquat
Eugenia paniculata australis	40'	9	Brush-cherry Eugenia
E. smithii	10'–25'	10	Lili-pili Tree
Euonymus sp.	2"–12"	5	Wintercreeper Euonymus
Feijoa sellowiana	18'	10	Pineapple Guava
Fortunella japonica	7'–10'	9–10	Marumi Kumquat
Gaultheria procumbens	3"	3	Wintergreen
Heteromeles arbutifolia	6'–10'	9	Christmas-berry
Hippophae rhamnoides	30'	3	Sea-buckthorn
Ilex sp.	9'–36'	3–6	Holly
Kadsura japonica	twining vine 12'	7	Scarlet Katsura
Lantana camara	4'–10'	8	Common Lantana
Lindera benzoin	15'	4	Spice Bush
Litchi chinensis	40'	9–10	Lychee
Lonicera sp.	3'–9'	3–5	Honeysuckle
Lycium sp.	9'	4	Matrimony-vine
Malus sp. and vars.	15'–40'	3–5	Crab Apple
Melia azedarack	45'	7	Chinaberry
Mitchella repens	2"	3	Partridge-berry
Morus alba	45'	4	Mulberry
Muehlenbeckia complexa	twining vine	6	Wire-vine
Myrtus communis	5'–10'	8–9	Myrtle
Nandina domestica	8'	7	Nandina
Pernettya mucronata	1½'	6–7	Chilean Pernettya
Persea borbonia	30'–40'	7	Red Bay
Phillyrea decora	9'	6	Lanceleaf Phillyrea
P. latifolia	30'	7	Tree Phillyrea
Photinia sp.	15'–36'	4–7	Photinia
Pittosporum sp.	10'–80'	8–10	Pittosporum
Prinsepia sp.	4'–10'	2–5	Prinsepia
Prunus sp.	4½'–75'	2–7	Cherry, Plum, Peach, etc.
Psidium sp.	25'	9–10	Guava
Punica granatum	15'	7–8	Pomegranate
Pyracantha sp.	6'–18'	5–7	Firethorn
Rhamnus frangula	18'	2	Alder Buckthorn
Ricinus communis	15'	annual	Castor-bean
Rosa sp.	3'–15'	2–7	Rose
Sambucus sp.	12'–45'	3–5	Elder
Sarcococca ruscifolia	6'	7	Fragrant Sarcococca
Schinus sp.	25'–40'	9–10	Peppertree
Schisandra sp.	vine	8	Magnolia-vine
Shepherdia canadensis	7'	2	Russet Buffalo-berry
Skimmia sp.	1½'–4'	7	Skimmia
Smilax megalantha	18' vine	7	Coral Greenbrier
Solanum—some sp.	2'–25'	3–10	Nightshade, Jerusalem-cherry
Sorbus sp.	30'–60'	4	Mountain-ash
Stachyurus praecox	12'	6	
Symphoricarpos sp.	3'–6'	2	Coralberry, Snowberry
Taxus sp.	3'–60'	2–4	Yew
Viburnum sp.	6'–30'	2–8	Viburnum
Zamia floridana	2'	9	Coontie

BERRY. An indehiscent fruit developing from a single ovary, having few to many seeds and a fleshy or pulpy outer wall; as the Tomato or Gooseberry. See also DRUPE and POME.

BERRY-FERN = *Cystopteris bulbifera*

BERTEROA (ber-ter-O-a)

  incana   **2′**   **Zone 3**   **Hoary False Alyssum**
A biennial or short-lived perennial weed, introduced from Europe with grayish, hoary, alternate, lanceolate leaves 2 in. long. The small white flowers are borne in terminal spikes on long shoots from June to Sept. It is seen mostly on dry or sandy soils. The flattened, elliptic seed pods are less than ½ in. long, appearing all along the flower stalk.

BERTHOLLETIA (ber-to-LEE-shia)

  excelsa   **100′**   **Zone 10**   **Brazil-nut**
A large tropical tree with leathery leaves 2 ft. long, cream-colored flowers in racemes and fruits about 6 in. wide with thick walls, but in which are 18–24 of the well-known Brazil-nuts of commerce. Propagated by seed. Native to Brazil, Venezuela and Guiana.

BERTOLONIA (ber-to-LO-nia)

  maculata   **creeping**   **Zone 10**   **Purplevein**
                                        Bertolonia
A low, creeping plant from Brazil suitable for terrariums. The leaves are velvety green above and purple beneath with purple-bordered veins, flowers rose colored. These need the high humidity of terrariums. Propagated by cuttings and seeds.

BESSERA (BESS-era)

  elegans   **3′**   **Zone 9**   **Showy Coraldrops**
A showy, bulbous herb, native to Mexico, valued for its bright red, inch-wide flowers marked with white. Frequently used as a bulb forced in the house. Each bulb bears several flower stalks. Very showy, grown out-of-doors in Calif. especially for its bloom which may last through Aug. and Sept. A well-grown bulb may produce 6–10 flower stalks, each producing 12–20 umbels of flowers. Propagated by offsets.

BETA (BEE-ta)

  vulgaris   **to 4′**   **biennial or annual**   **Common**
                                            Beet
This is the common garden Beet, originally native to some of the maritime islands off southern Europe, but grown and selected from for so many centuries that there are now several forms. For the vegetable garden type and its culture see BEET. The variety *B. vulgaris cicala* does not develop a swollen root base and has been selected for years so that now we have Swiss Chard (which see) the green-leaved type, as well as an ornamental red-leaved form. Sugar Beet and Mangel are also selected forms of *Beta vulgaris*, the latter used as fodder for cattle, and the former planted in large areas of the western states for manufacture of sugar. See BEETS.

  vulgaris cicla = Swiss Chard

BETELNUT, BETEL-PALM = *Areca cathecu*

BETHLEHEM-SAGE = *Pulmonaria saccharata*

BETONY. See STACHYS.

BETULA (BET-yew-la). The birches have long been popular ornamental trees in America, chiefly in the northern U.S. and Canada. Several are native Americans, but many species have been introduced from Europe and Asia. In general, they are graceful trees with alternate leaves, the most popular being those with white bark on trunks and larger branches. Some of the others are very serviceable, either because they will grow well in wet soil or because they will exist as well as any other trees, or better, in poor, dry soils.

Many of the exotic species and varieties, although they may be interesting botanically, have little in addition to offer as ornamentals when compared with those recommended. All have alternate, simple, toothed leaves and their fruits are minute nuts borne in what appears to be a catkin.

In general, the birches are rather short-lived and are difficult to transplant, so that to insure success they should be balled and wrapped in burlap. They might best be moved in the spring. Arborists know that they are persistent "bleeders", and that pruning is best done at almost any time of year except in the spring when the sap is running. Large branches seem to break readily under heavy coats of ice and snow, yet some, like the Gray Birch, have trunks that are extremely pliable. The inner bark of native white birches has been ground into a flour for emergency breadstuffs. The young bark has also been used in making a tea, and the young leaves have also been dried and used for tea. The sap is supposed to make a pleasant drink and, when boiled down, to make a sugar. Birch beer is made by fermenting the sap.

Most of the birches have bright yellow autumn color. The flowers are unisexual, with both male and female flowers on the same tree. The maturing of the catkins in the early spring and blown pollen in the air are two of the first signs of plant activity. Those familiar with the woods know that the birch is one of the few woods which will burn when it is "living" or "green", making this tree a welcome source of fuel when the woodsman is in a hurry to start his camp-fire.

Birches are susceptible to at least two serious insect pests which, if not properly controlled, can mar their effective use as ornamentals. The first is the bronze birch borer, a small, flat-headed grub about ½–1 in. long which eats just under the bark and, if present in numbers, can kill the tree. *Betula pendula* is especially susceptible to this insect.

Betula papyrifera is supposed to be much less susceptible to the inroads of this insect. The control, spraying with DDT or Dieldrin in late May and twice more at 2-week intervals, is a chore which is sometimes overlooked. When this happens, and especially if the tree is *B. pendula* and growing in poor soil, attacks from the insect may soon follow.

The other insect which is most troublesome, in New England at least, is the birch leaf miner, a small insect which eats its way between the upper and lower epidermis of the leaf. If and when this happens, there is little that can be done. The leaf is marred for the rest of the season. Spraying with lindane and malathion is effective, if done about the first of May and when followed at 10-day intervals with 2 additional sprays. The second brood of insects appears about July 1, when another spraying (followed by still another on July 10) should be given.

Betula papyrifera, *B. pendula* and *B. populifolia* and their varieties and *B. platyphylla* and its varieties have white bark. Those living in the northern U.S. and Canada have learned to appreciate the native Canoe Birch best of all. It does not have the graceful form or branching habits of *B. pendula* and its varieties, but when one considers the inroads of the bronze birch borer, it may well be that the Canoe Birch is the safer of the two species to plant.

The Gray Birch is a much smaller tree and is valued by landscape men because it grows in clumps, although it is not nearly so tall, nor does it have such clear white bark as does the Canoe Birch. *B. platyphylla* is the Asiatic counterpart of the Canoe Birch in America and the European Birch in Europe.

The native American River Birch (*B. nigra*), the Sweet Birch (*B. lenta*) and the Dahurian Birch of northeastern Asia are species which do not have white bark, but nevertheless have ornamental values of their own. The River Birch is valued chiefly as a tree for wet soils—otherwise it need not be used. The Sweet Birch is an excellent ornamental from the standpoint of foliage, general shape, and the vigor with which it grows. The Dahurian Birch has an interesting bark formation.

Although usually associated with northern plantings, both *B. nigra* and *B. pendula* have been noted as doing well in Calif. The Yellow Birch (*B. lutea* or *B. alleghaniensis* as it is now called) is native from Canada down the eastern coast into Fla. So this graceful, colorful group of trees does have merit over a wide area, the main point being that they do have problems of growth which should be thoroughly studied and understood before any number are grown or planted on a large scale.

Propagation

Dormancy of seed is variable, but it can be sown as soon as ripe, stratified, or kept dry in airtight containers in a cold place for up to a year and then sown. Asexual propagation is by grafting with either *B. pendula* or *B. papyrifera* as understock. See GRAFTING.

Insect Pests

Birch leaf miner which produces blotch mines in the leaves, often giving them a burned appearance and causing drop, is very destructive in the northeast. Only newly opened leaves are attacked and the first of 3 annual generations is the most destructive. Spraying when the mines are first visible with insecticide #9 or #15 gives good control. Bronze birch borer, which tunnels in the cambium of European White Birch and other varieties, kills and deforms many ornamental trees. The top branches are often infested first. Control is difficult, but spraying with insecticide #9 in early summer when beetles are feeding is suggested. Case bearers, sawfly and gypsy moth (see OAK) eat the foliage and are controlled with insecticide #9. Two species of aphids are common on Birch and ornamental trees often need protection by spraying with insecticide #15.

Diseases

Nectaria canker forms dark-colored, sunken cankers on the bark of Paper and Yellow Birch. Cutting out and treating the wounds with tree paint is the suggested remedy.

albo-sinensis   90′   Zone 5   Chinese Paper Birch
A rare birch from central and western China, this can make a most interesting ornamental because of its unique bright orange to orange-red exfoliating bark. No other tree has bark just like it.

alleghaniensis (*B. lutea*)   90′   Zone 3   Yellow Birch
Not an ornamental, but a tree of the moist woods, native from Newfoundland to Ga. The alternate leaves are 3–5 in. long. The bark is yellowish gray on young trunks and a deeper yellowish brown on older trunks, flaking off in large strips. The foliage turns yellow in the fall.

davurica   60′   Zone 4   Dahurian Birch
Somewhat similar to the River Birch, but this does well on a dry, gravelly soil; hence it can be used as a substitute for the River Birch in dry situations where that species will not grow. The bark is reddish brown, curling and exfoliating in regular pieces an inch or so square. Native to northeastern Asia.

lenta   75′   Zone 3   Sweet Birch
Native to the eastern U.S., this is a densely

pyramidal tree while young, but rather round topped at maturity. The golden-yellow autumn color, its interesting habit and its ability to grow in rugged terrain are its outstanding characteristics. The cherrylike bark is dark and attractive and the bark of young twigs has an aromatic flavor.

lutea = *B. alleghaniensis*

nana   2′   Zone 2   Dwarf Arctic Birch
A small, low, branching, sometimes prostrate and contorted shrub. The leaves are small and light green and the monoecious flowers, catkins and small, conelike fruits are typical of those found among other birches. It does best in gravelly, acid soil in full sun, but it is not especially ornamental. Native to northern Asia, Europe, Greenland and Alaska.

nigra   90′   Zone 4   River Birch
A pyramidal tree while young with reddish-brown, exfoliating bark, native to the eastern U.S. Typically found along stream beds and in lowlands where the roots can easily penetrate to water. In fact, the trees in nature often have their roots in water standing for several weeks in the spring. It is not a long-lived tree, often has poor crotches and need be considered only for use in wet-soil situations where other trees might not do well.

papyrifera   90′   Zone 2   Canoe Birch
This tree is familiar to everyone and is the most popular of all the birches for ornamental use, native to the central northeastern North America. It is a tree growing larger than the European White Birch, having a trunk which is larger and more clear of markings than most of its European relatives. It has proved itself less susceptible to disastrous attacks of the bronze birch borer; hence it has added merit as a valued ornamental. A number of botanical varieties have been named, but none is superior to the species as an ornamental tree. It has excellent golden-yellow autumn color.

pendula   60′   Zone 2   European Birch
A pyramidal, short-lived tree, very popular in Europe where it is native, and planted profusely for many years here in America, as well. It is pyramidal in habit, with a white-barked trunk and older branches, and very graceful, slightly pendulous lateral branches. Formerly termed *B. verrucosa* or *B. alba*, it will be found in many American catalogues still listed under the latter name. The leaves are smaller and more triangular than those of *B. papyrifera* and the bark is not so clear as that of our native Canoe Birch. It also is short-lived, although many beautiful trees of the species or one of its varieties can be seen. There are even some in southern Calif. Unfortunately, the bronze birch borer seems to attack this more frequently than it does other birches, and many a tree, just as it

reaches a good size, has been known to be attacked high on the trunk so that the top is completely killed, thus spoiling it as an ornamental specimen. Some of the popular varieties of this species are: **'Fastigiata'**—columnar, dense and beautiful while young; **'Gracilis'**—similar to the variety 'Tristis', but with leaves deeply cut. This is the popular **Cutleaf European Birch**, gracefully pendulous in habit; **'Purple Splendor'**—with purplish-colored leaves; **'Scarlet Glory'**—young leaves very red at first in the early spring, later turning reddish green in the summer and bright red again in the fall; **'Tristis'**—the **Slender European Birch**, with slender, pendulous branches and regular, rounded head; **'Youngii'**—**Young's Birch**, a tree with an irregularly branched habit, the conspicuously pendulous branches being more marked than those of the variety 'Tristis'.

platyphylla japonica   60′   Zone 4
This tree has an interesting pattern of ruffled white bark and is native to Japan.

platyphylla szechuanica   60′   Zone 5
The white bark peels off in paper-thin sheets. This is from the high mountains of extreme western China and is probably the best form of this species. It is like our native Canoe Birch, but the twigs are a polished red-brown and the thick, blue-green leaves remain on longer in the fall than those of most other birches. The variety **kamtschatica** may be hardy as far north as Zone 2.

populifolia   30′   Zone 4   Gray Birch
Commonly known, grown and planted, this is another short-lived birch which grows in clumps, seldom appearing as a single-trunked tree. It is a plant for poor soils, with white bark spotted with blackish marks where branches have been, and is popular for planting in small gardens where the taller-growing Canoe Birch would be out of place. Although it is short-lived, the trunk seems to have great resilience, often bending to the ground under burdens of snow and ice and then springing upright once the weight has been removed. In burned-over areas it is one of the first trees to reappear, especially on poor, rocky soils, and forms an excellent nursing cover for seedlings of more valuable timber trees. It is found widely distributed in the woodlands of northeastern North America.

BI or BIS. Latin prefix signifying two or twice.

BIBLE PLANTS. Many plants are mentioned in the Bible. Two thousand years ago there was no systematic method of nomenclature and all plants were referred to by the then vernacular names. Exactly which plants these were under our modern system of nomenclature is a matter for trained botanists to determine. Dr. Harold

N. Moldenke of the New York Botanical Garden and Alma L. Moldenke have done this in their volume "Plants of the Bible," Chronica Botanica, 1952. Fifty plants mentioned in the Bible as noted in this volume are:

Allium sativum—Garlic
A. cepa—Garden Onion
Anethum graveolens—Dill
Arundo donax—Giantreed
Brassica nigra—Black Mustard
Cedrus libani—Cedar of Lebanon
Ceratonia siliqua—Carob
Cercis siliquastrum—Judas Tree
Cinnamomum cassia—Cassia Bark Tree
Cucumis melo—Musk Melon
Crocus sativus—Saffron Crocus
Cupressus sempervirens
    var. horizontalis
Cyperus papyrus—Papyrus
Elaeagnus angustifolia—Russian Olive
Ficus carica—Common Fig
Fraxinus ornus—Flowering Ash
Gossypium herbaceum—Levant Cotton
Hedera helix—English Ivy
Hyacinthus orientalis—Common Hyacinth
Iris pseudacorus—Yellow Flag
Juglans regia—Persian Walnut
Laurus nobilis—Sweet Bay, Laurel
Lilium candidum—Madonna Lily
Morus nigra—Black Mulberry
Myrtus communis—True Myrtle
Narcissus tazetta—Polyanthus Narcissus
Nasturtium officinale—Water-cress
Nerium oleander—Oleander
Nymphaea lotus—White Egyptian Lotus
Olea europaea—Common Olive
Ornithogalum umbellatum—Common Star-of-
    Bethlehem
Paliurus spina-christi—Christ Thorn
Phoenix dactylifera—Date
Pinus halepensis—Aleppo Pine
Pistacia vera—Common Pistache
Platanus orientalis—Oriental Plane Tree
Populus alba—White Poplar
Prunus armeniaca—Apricot
Punica granatum—Common Pomegranate
Quercus ilex—Holly Oak
Q. lusitanica—Portuguese Oak
Ricinus communis—Castor Bean
Ruscus aculeatus—Butcher's Broom
Saccharum officinarum—Sugar Cane
Salix alba—White Willow
S. fragilis—Brittle Willow
Tamarix ramosissima—Fivestamen Tamarisk
Taraxacum officinale—Common Dandelion
Tulipa montana—Cicilian Tulip
Vitis vinifera—European Grape

BICOLORED. Two-colored.

BIDENS (BY-dens). Although this genus is a member of the Composite Family the two species listed below do not have sufficient ornamental value to compensate for the unpleasant way in which the seeds are scattered. In autumn anyone walking through fields or meadows where these plants are present will likely find these seeds sticking to one's clothing. These flat seeds, wider at one end and having 2 prongs or teeth, from which the genus takes its name, are easily brushed from the flower-heads to the shaggy coats of straying animals or the clothing of persons walking past. They must be removed one by one.

aristosa 1′–3′ **Zone 4 Bearded Beggar-ticks**
This weedy annual or perennial has opposite leaves with toothed margins, yellow disc-flowers and a few yellow ray-flowers. It may be found throughout most of the eastern half of the country. It blooms in late summer and autumn.

frondosa 3′ **annual Devil's Beggar-ticks**
A weed common in moist or poorly drained soils, and native throughout North America. The opposite leaves are toothed and cut or divided into 3 leaflets, the small flowers white or yellow with flower-heads $\frac{1}{2}$ in. across. The awns or fruits are flat with 2 stiff points that easily adhere to any clothing rubbed against the plant when in fruit.

Several other species (*B. polylepis, bipinnata* and *pilosa*) are also weeds and somewhat similar.

BIENNIALS. These are plants which normally take two growing seasons to produce flowers and fruits, and then die. The seeds of many plants can be sown in the spring; they will flower and fruit the same year and then they will be killed by winter cold. Still others, when their seeds are sown, may or may not flower the first year, but regardless of this, they will live and produce flowers year after year. These are perennials, and if only the tops are killed by winter cold these are often termed herbaceous perennials.

Some popular garden biennials are Canterbury Bells, Hollyhock, Sweet William, Honesty, *Meconopsis* sp., *Myosotis* sp., stocks and the Siberian Wallflower. There are many others. Seeds of these are sown in the early fall, mulched well over winter, thinned out or transplanted in the spring to the place where they are to grow.

Some biennials will bloom in one year's time if seed is sown very early in the greenhouse and then the plants set out after all frost is over. Also, some annuals are termed "hardy annuals" because the seed can be sown late in the fall. The seed (or germinated seed) will live over winter and be off to a good start early in the spring, often starting growth before it is possible to prepare the soil and sow the seed in the spring, thus gaining time on spring-sown seedlings.

BIFID. Two cleft.

BIFOLIATE. A leaf composed of 2 leaflets.

BIGNONIA

　capreolata　vine　Zone 6　Crossvine
A very popular vine throughout the South where it is native, this produces orange-red flowers, $1\frac{1}{2}$–2 in. long during late May, and the compound leaves are evergreen. Climbing by means of tendrils the profuse and colorful trumpet-shaped flowers are its crowning glory.

BIGNONIACEAE = The　　　Trumpetcreeper Family

BILABIATE. Two-lipped; as in flowers of Salvia.

BILLBERGIA (bill-BERJ-ia). These are epiphytic, stemless, tropical herbs with leaves arranged like those of pineapples. Members of the Bromelia Family and of little value except as oddities. Propagated by cuttings or seeds. Best in hanging baskets.

　nutans　$1\frac{1}{2}'$　Zone 10　Blue Rim Airbrom
Leaves stiff, straplike, $\frac{1}{2}$ in. wide and finely toothed in a rosette from the ground; flowers borne on a slim stalk, nodding, with rose bracts, green petals edged with violet. Native to Brazil and Argentina.

　pyramidalis　3'　Zone 10　Pineapple-lily
A stemless tropical herb from Brazil, with stiff leaves 3 ft. long and $2\frac{1}{2}$ in. wide with spiny teeth, borne in clusters somewhat like those of a Pineapple plant. It is a member of the same Family. The flowers are numerous in 4-in. spikes, pinkish-red flowers, each with 3 small curving petals and a group of yellow stamens, while below these flowers on the same white stem are numerous pink bracts which lend color and interest to the entire inflorescence.

　saundersii　15″　Zone 10　Saunder Airbrom
Strap-shaped leaves, green above and red below with white blotches on both sides. Flower blue, 2 in. long, bracts red, drooping and in a cluster. Native to Brazil.

BILOCULAR. Two-celled.

BINDWEED. See POLYGONUM.

BINDWEED, LOW = *Calystegia spithamea*

BINOMIAL. The combination of a generic and specific name to denote a given organism; as *Acer rubrum*.

BIOTA = *Thuja orientalis*

BIOTYPE. An elementary stable form.

BIPINNATE. Twice pinnate; when the divisions of a pinnate leaf are again pinnately divided.

BIRCH. See BETULA.

BIRD BATHS AND BIRD HOUSES. See GARDEN FIXTURES.

BIRD-OF-PARADISE = *Strelitzia reginae*

BIRDS. Many gardeners do not want birds in their gardens because they take the seeds and seedlings when they are young, or eat the fruits. Bits of colored cloth or tinfoil on a string over the plants, or pieces of glass or tin tied to a loose string over the plants so the wind will move them around and they will clash together, may scare some of the birds away. Scarecrows and stuffed owls probably do some good.

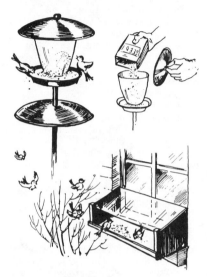

Bird Feeders

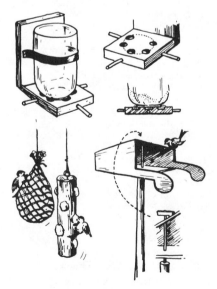

Bird Feeders

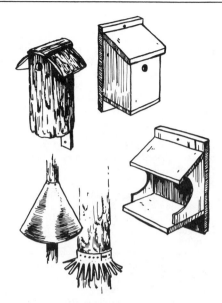

Bird Houses: Lower left: Obstacles to prevent rodents climbing up the posts.

Corn seed is often mixed with a coal tar product which is disagreeable to the crows and saves the seed, at least until after it has germinated. There is nothing, however, which effectively protects tree fruits from being eaten, unless it is a complete cage over the entire plant. Sometimes a cat or dog will help keep birds away but in most cases one has to learn how to live with them, protecting certain things and planting enough of others so that even though some are taken by the birds enough will remain to make the planting worth while.

A much larger group of gardeners wish to attract birds to the garden. The various Audubon societies about the country have many suggestions of help on this score. Providing thickets of shrubbery for nesting purposes, providing water in the form of bird baths or pools for drinking and bathing, both help. Keeping the dogs and cats away from the premises is a very substantial aid in attracting more birds.

Building bird houses and bird feeders, and keeping the feeders well stocked with the right kind of bird food is of course helpful. These can always be bought at the garden and seed stores. The Audubon societies also provide plans for bird houses which are easy to make and so designed as to attract particular kinds of birds.

Planting tall grasses which have fruiting stalks of seed also attracts birds. Many fruiting shrubs and trees attract them. See GRASSES, BRIGHT COLORED FRUITS. The subject of attract-

ing birds to the garden is a most interesting one about which much has been written. Those interested in detailed information should contact the nearest Audubon Society.

BIRD'S-NEST FERN = *Asplenium nidus*

BIRTHWORT OR WILD GINGER FAMILY = Aristolochiaceae

BISEXUAL. Having both stamens and pistils.

BISHOP'S CAP. See ASTROPHYTUM

BISHOP'S-HAT. See EPIMEDIUM.

BISHOP'S-HOOD = *Astrophytum myriostigma*

BISHOP'S-WEED = *Aegopodium podagraria*

BITTERCRESS. See CARDAMINE.

BITTER NIGHTSHADE = *Solanum dulcamara*

BITTERNUT = *Carya cordiformis*

BITTERSWEET. See CELASTRUS.

BITTERSWEET FAMILY = Celastraceae

BIXA (BIX-a)

   orellana   25′   Zone 10   Annatto
Both the flowers and the seed pods of this tropical American plant have considerable ornamental interest, especially the latter which can be used in dried arrangements. These seed pods are about 2 in. long, pointed brown, and are covered with many fuzzy hairs. The pods eventually split in half, disclosing many round red seeds inside, each covered with a powdery material which has been used to color butter, cheese and oleomargarine. The fleshy red pulp that surrounds the seeds provides a red dye that is widely used by native craftsmen in tropical regions around the world. Evergreen leaves are alternate, ovate, 7 in. long. The flowers are 2 in. across, rose pink, with 5 petals and darker stamens, and appear during the summer. Propagation is by seeds and cuttings.

BLACKBERRY. This name is used here to include all types of trailing berries, i.e., Loganberry, Boysenberry, Youngberry as well as the commonly known Blackberry. Blackberries are grown commercially in N.Y. as well as in the Willamette Valley of Ore., parts of Calif. and elsewhere. They are not as hardy as raspberries. They grow best on fertile, well-drained soils, and those soils that are in windy areas or areas of late spring frosts should be avoided. They are easily propagated by tip layering, that is, merely inserting the tip of a cane in the soil in the fall, and digging up the young rooted stem the following spring. They are also propagated from suckers or root cuttings. Also see RUBUS.

Plants are set 5–10 ft. apart depending on the training system used. The plants themselves should be planted as early in the spring as possible and cut back to about 8–10 in. high after planting.

Blackberry canes are biennial, that is they grow vegetatively one year, produce fruit the next and then die, and should be removed. Varieties differ in the length to which the canes grow. Some varieties, especially those grown in the eastern United States like 'Darrow', 'Bailey' and 'Eldorado', are mostly self-supporting but the loganberries and boysenberries, as well as some Blackberry varieties grown on the Pacific Coast have long trailing stems that must be trained on a trellis, otherwise they would fall to the ground.

If the planting is to be grown without a trellis, the plants should be spaced about 2–3 ft. apart in the row and the rows 8–9 ft. apart. Young shoots will come up between the plants, but strict cultivation should be such that it will keep these suckers to a strip of soil about 1 ft. wide. If this is not done the plants can become a tangle, very difficult if not impossible to manage since they have rigid thorns making any pruning a disagreeable task that is almost impossible unless thick gloves are worn and long-handled lobbing shears are used. Mulching can be practiced, but the suckers coming up between the rows should be eliminated from time to time.

Pruning is best done in the early spring, eliminating those that have borne fruits as well as any weak or broken canes. Those canes remaining (if no trellis is used and these are self-erect varieties) should be about 8–10 in. apart, and the laterals should be reduced to about 8–12 buds each. The new canes start growing rapidly in June, and the tip of these should be pinched out when the canes are about 2½–3 ft. tall. This will have to be done at weekly intervals since the canes do not all mature together, but it does promote sturdy, compact, plant development. When harvesting is over the old canes can be removed any time.

Those varieties with long, trailing stems are usually trained to a wire trellis of from one to several wires. Plants are spaced about 10 ft. apart and the canes tied to the wires. Some growers use a simple stake, one to each hill. The stake is about 5–6 ft. tall and the canes merely wrapped around the stake in spiral fashion and the ends clipped off at the top. The canes can be trained on single wires, wrapped around them, or on 2 wires or tied fan shaped to several wires. This takes more labor perhaps but often results in a higher yield.

Blackberries should only be picked when they are fully ripe and about to be used. They do not ripen all at once but over a period of several weeks in July and Aug. They respond to the application of nitrogenous fertilizers in early spring, but the amount should be controlled by shoot growth and fruit production.

Varieties

In the eastern United States, the varieties generally are 'Darrow' (best); 'Bailey' (good); 'Eldorado' (good but difficult to find in nurseries true to name). There is a sterile type that has been distributed which blooms well but does not produce fruit. This should be dug up and discarded wherever it has been planted.

On the West Coast, 'Evergreen' and 'Thornless Evergreen' are very popular varieties, especially the latter, a sport of 'Evergreen', for the canes are easily handled. Fruit is firm and has a good flavor. Large quantities are canned; it accounts for the largest Blackberry acreage in Ore., ripening in Aug. and Sept. These of course are not hardy in the eastern United States.

Other varieties are 'Cascade' with red fruits, 'Marion' with shining black fruits, and 'Pacific'.

'Boysen', or the Boysenberry as it is called, originated in Calif., is dark wine red and is not reliably hardy in the East. It is best grown on a trellis for the canes are 8–10 ft. long. They ripen from early July to late Aug. It has an excellent flavor and is popular locally where grown.

The 'Logan' or Loganberry also originated in Calif. in 1881. It is vigorous with long canes which are best trained on a wire trellis, but it winter-kills in most parts of the country other than parts of Calif., Ore., and Wash. The fruits are dark red, of medium size and tend to be a little soft, hence it is grown mainly for juice and wine, for the fruit does not ship well. It ripens from late June through July.

Insect Pests

Blackberry sawfly and raspberry sawfly may strip the leaves in early summer. They are easily killed with insecticide #9 and #37. Rednecked cane borer kills many canes by boring in the pith. Careful pruning holds these in check. Blackberry psyllid and rose scale cause abnormal and weakened canes. Spraying with insecticide #15 is effective. In the Northwest the blackberry mites cause the "redberry" disease. These gall mites overwinter in buds. Spraying with fungicide #L, #N or #U when canes are dormant is suggested. See MITES. The tarnished plant bug can be a serious pest also, but can be effectively controlled by spraying the plants just before the first flowers open with insecticide #9. Cane borers sometimes produce irregular swellings or galls in canes, and infested canes are weakened and may die. They should be cut out and burned. Wild blackberries may have this insect and they should be dug out and destroyed if nearby.

Diseases

Blackberry rust causes large orange spots on the underside of leaves and stunts the plant. Infection remains in the plant and the only control is the destruction of infected plants. The varieties 'Eldorado' and 'Snyder' are considered resistant. Leafspot in the form of light brown spots with purple borders is common but seldom requires control.

BLACKBERRY-LILY = *Belamcanda chinensis*

BLACK-EYED SUSAN = *Rudbeckia hirta*

BLACKHAW. See VIBURNUM.

BLACK KNOT. Conspicuous, elongate, oval black growths on the twigs and branches of plum and cherry are caused by a fungus. Infection often occurs 1 or 2 years before the "knot" is observed. Branches which have been girdled by the "knot" usually die. Cutting off the infected branches as soon as observed will delay the spread. Application of an annual spray program, including a dormant spray with dinitro, lime sulfur or ferbam, will usually prevent serious infections.

BLACK LEG. The name of a disease which causes the stem of plants to turn black at the surface of the soil. On Cabbage and other cruciferous plants it is caused by a fungus which lives in the soil and thrives in cool wet weather. Rotation of beds, soil sterilization of plant beds and the planting of certified seed or seed treated in hot water at 122° F. for 25 minutes are recommended controls. On Potato, a bacterial disease which may live in the soil or the seed tuber, causes stem and tuber rot. Rotation, planting certified seed and planting only whole seed tubers, or allowing cut tubers to completely heal before planting are recommended controls. Seed potatoes suspected of infection may be disinfected with Semesan or other recommended seed-treatment pesticides.

BLACK SPOT. The name of several fungus diseases which cause black, felty spots on the leaves and stem of Rose, Delphinium, Elm and other plants. Infected leaves usually turn yellow and fall. It is often the most serious disease of roses where regular spraying at weekly intervals will hold the disease in check but not insure eradication. Ferbam, thiram and folpet are among the recommended fungicides. On Elm the symptoms resemble anthracnose, and spraying with one of the above-mentioned fungicides when the leaves are about half grown is suggested. On Delphinium treating the crown before growth starts in spring with mercuric chloride 1 oz. in 10 gals. of water is helpful.

BLACKTHORN = *Prunus spinosa*

BLADDER FERNS. See CYSTOPTERIS.

BLADDERNUT, BUMALDA = *Staphylea bumalda*

BLADDER-POD = *Vesicaria urticulata*

BLADDER-SENNA = *Colutea arborescens*

BLADDERWORT. See URTRICULARIA.

BLADDERWORT FAMILY = Lentibulariaceae

BLADE. The expanded portion of a leaf.

BLANCHING. Making white, that is a term frequently used in the production of Celery, Leek and Endive. If Celery stalks are allowed to grow normally they are green, but when covered with earth, boards, black polyethylene or other materials they turn the desired white, merely because direct sunlight is not available for the plant cells to manufacture the green chlorophyll.

BLANKETFLOWER, COMMON = *Gaillardia aristata*

BLAZING-STAR = *Mentzelia laevicaulis*

BLECHNUM. These are mostly tropical ferns found in the West Indies and Brazil. They should be grown in a moist greenhouse with temperatures not much lower than 60° F. Some are actually tree ferns 4 ft. high. The hardy species include **B. spicant**, the Deer Fern, and **B. durum.** They should be planted in moist, shaded and protected spots in the tropical garden, where moisture is present much of the time.

The tree ferns from New Caledonia are **B. gibbum**, which can grow a trunk 5 ft. tall. **B. occidentale** is only 2½ ft. tall, a native to tropical America. **B. fluviatile** has been recommended for use in hanging baskets because of its long drooping fronds. Most gardeners will not find much of interest in this group of ferns unless of course they have greenhouses. For propagation see FERNS.

BLEEDING. A popular horticultural term applied to the constant dripping of sap from a wound or cut stub. Birch trees and maples "bleed" profusely when pruned in the very early spring.

BLEEDING-HEART. See DICENTRA.

BLEPHILIA (ble-FILL-ia)

ciliata	2'–3'	Zone 3	Wood-mint

A perennial herb common to the wooded areas of the Atlantic coastal states, the plant is rather hairy and leaves are ovate to lanceolate. The small blue flowers are clustered tightly at the base of the upper pairs of opposite leaves, and the flower stem may rise from the center of the flower clusters so that there are 2 or 3 clusters of flowers, one above the other, the upper 1 or 2 being leafless. The plant flowers from June to Aug.

BLESSED-THISTLE = *Cnicus benedictus*

BLETIA (BLET-ia). A large genus of terrestrial

orchids from the West Indies and Central America with grasslike, mostly deciduous leaves and purple or whitish flowers in terminal racemes. Usually propagated by division. **B. patula** with purple, rather large flowers from Haiti, blooming from March to June, is one species that is being suggested for trial by American orchid growers. For culture and propagation, see ORCHID.

BLETILLA (blet-ILL-a). Not to be confused with *Bletia*, for in *Bletilla*, the side lobes of the flowers are convolute; in *Bletia* they are not. Although 7 species are known, mostly in China, Japan and North America, the only one grown in the greenhouses of orchid specialists is **B. striata**, bearing 6–10 deep purple flowers on a stalk, each flower about 1¼ in. across. It grows about a foot high from pseudobulbs and is usually propagated by division. For culture see ORCHID.

BLIGHIA (BLY-ya)
  sapida   40′   **Zone 9**   Akee
A West African tree bearing edible straw-colored fruits 3–4 in. long, which split into 3 parts exposing 3 shining seeds to which are attached the edible white aril which can be poisonous. However, although the fruits are edible at some stages of development they are highly poisonous at others. The compound leaves bear 3–5 pairs of leaflets.

BLIGHT. An indefinite term for several plant diseases which cause a sudden spotting or wilting of the foliage. It is applied to such bacterial diseases as fire blight, bean blight and delphinium blight and to fungus blights on Celery, Tomato and Potato. Leaf blights on Cherry, Hawthorne and Lilac and many blights on turf are well known. Botrytis blight on Peony, Tulip (fire), lilies, strawberries and many garden flowers is a well-known destructive disease. See the plants for further details and methods of control.

BLOTCH is also used to describe the symptoms of similar fungus leaf spots. The best known is horse-chestnut leaf blotch and peony leaf blotch.

BLISTER-CRESS,   ROCKERY = *Erysimum pulchellum*

BLOODFLOWER = *Asclepias curassavica*

BLOODLEAF. See IRESINE.

BLOOD-LILY. See HAEMANTHUS.

BLOODROOT = *Sanguinaria canadensis*

BLOODROOT FAMILY = Haemodoraceae

BLOOM (1) see BLOSSOM. (2) The white waxy covering of many fruits and leaves.

BLOSSOM. The flower.

BLUEBEARD = *Caryopteris* x *clandonensis*

BLUEBELL, ENGLISH = *Endymion nonscriptus*

BLUEBELLS. See *Muscari* species, which are generally termed Grape-hyacinth.

BLUEBELLS-OF-SCOTLAND = *Campanula rotundifolia*

BLUEBELLS, VIRGINIA = *Mertensia virginica*

BLUEBERRY. The blueberry species grown chiefly for their fruits are *Vaccinium corymbosum*, the Highbush Blueberry, *V. angustifolium*, the Lowbush Blueberry, and *V. ashei*, the Rabbit-eye Blueberry of the South. Of course, the Cranberry is a member of the *Vaccinium* genus, but it is not thought of as a blueberry and is fully described under CRANBERRY. There are other native species of blueberries the fruits of which are edible, but the 3 species mentioned are those which have been grown over the years specifically for their fruits and about which an important fruit-growing industry has arisen in New England, N.J., N.Car. and Mich. Also see VACCINIUM.

Commercial operations in which the Lowbush Blueberry is involved are chiefly confined to northern New England where this grows naturally by the acre on waste land. Here various procedures have been worked out over the years in which these sites are fertilized, pruned and tended in order to produce a bumper crop.

The Rabbit-eye Blueberry is a native of the southern United States and has been developed and hybridized at State and Federal Experiment Stations with the objective of producing varieties of better fruiting quality and size than the native species, for use in the South where *V. corymbosum* will not grow so well. This has been done. For recommended varieties of the Rabbit-eye Blueberry as well as other blueberry species see VACCINIUM.

Blueberries require an acid soil of about pH 5.0. Although they will grow in other soils, it is in these that best growth and best fruit production occur. The gardener with a different soil may want just a few bushes in his garden and in this case will have to prepare a proper acid soil. For directions to do this see SOILS. Since most blueberries are self-sterile, under some conditions, it is best to plant several varieties together. Fertilization is usually carried out by bees, and other insects.

One of the first problems to be considered by the gardener who likes birds and attracts them to his garden is what to do about them during the blueberry season. A few birds can strip a few bushes of blueberries in a surprisingly short time. Although it is troublesome to put up, a screening of saran cloth or tobacco cloth is necessary if one is to save enough of the berries to make culture of the bushes worth while. Some people merely cover each single bush with cloth by throwing a sizable piece over, which reaches to the ground on all sides. Others with more bushes put the cloth over a pipe frame for the entire planting.

Blueberries not only need an acid soil but one with plenty of moisture and organic matter. It is of interest to note that blueberries, like their close relatives the cranberries, will withstand the total flooding of the soil from the first of Nov. to the first of April. This prevents the alternate freezing and thawing of the soil during the winter which is often so difficult on young plants and heaves them out of the ground. The flooding is not necessary, but it does demonstrate the fact that they can grow with a large amount of water and they certainly need it during the growing season to produce large fruits so much desired on the cultivated varieties.

Plants should be set out in the spring, at least 5 ft. apart in the rows with the rows 8 ft. apart. It must be remembered that these plants can grow to 12 ft. high and so need plenty of room in which to expand. It is better if the distances are more. For varieties of the Rabbit-eye Blueberry for planting in the South see VACCINIUM ASHEI. Some of the best varieties of the Highbush Blueberry (*V. corymbosum*) are listed below:

'Angela'—originated at Raleigh, N.C. Agricultural Experiment Station. Selected in 1940 and introduced in 1952. Of value only in eastern N.C., but no farther north. This variety is resistant to canker.

'Atlantic'—originated 1925 ('Jersey' x 'Pioneer') at Whitesbog, N.J., by F. V. Coville, U.S.D.A. Introduced 1941. Ripens late; large fruit.

'Berkeley'—originated 1938 at Weymouth, N.J. by F. V. Coville, U.S.D.A. Introduced 1949; light blue fruit, one of the largest; ripens in midseason.

'Bluecrop'—originated at Weymouth, N.J., by U.S.D.A. and N.J. Agricultural Experiment Station. The cross was made in 1934, and the selection was made in 1941. Fruits early to midseason, with light blue fruit.

'Blueray'—originated at Weymouth, N.J., by U.S.D.A. and N.J. Agricultural Experiment Station. Selected in 1941. The fruit is large, maturing in midseason. It resembles 'Dixi'. It has been noted that the fruit of this variety clings for weeks, so that 85% of the crop can be harvested at one time.

'Burlington'—originated at Whitesbog, N.J. by F. V. Coville, U.S.D.A., in 1916. Introduced 1941, matures late.

'Cabot'—originated at Whitesbog, N.J., by F. V. Coville, U.S.D.A., in 1943. Introduced 1949. Fruit large.

'Collins'—originated at New Brunswick, N.J. 1936, in cooperation with U.S.D.A. blueberry program. This is a large-fruited variety, maturing early. Named for Lester Collins (1880–1957), a New Jersey fruit grower.

'Concord'—originated at Whitesbog, N.J., by F. V. Coville, U.S.D.A. Introduced 1928, fruit midseason.

'Coville'—originated at Weymouth, N.J., by F. V. Coville, U.S.D.A. in 1936. Introduced 1949, the fruit is large; ripens latest of all.

'Dixi'—originated at Weymouth, N.J., by F. V. Coville. Introduced 1936; the fruit is large, ripening in midseason.

'Earliblue'—originated at Weymouth, N.J., by U.S.D.A. and N.J. Agricultural Experiment Station. Cross made in 1936; introduced in 1952. As early as 'Weymouth', with medium-size fruits. This may take the place of 'Weymouth' as an excellent early variety.

'Ethel'—originated near Brunswick, Ga., by W. M. Walker and introduced 1944. It is probably for the South only.

'Gem'—originated at Gate, Wash., by H. E. Drew. Introduced in 1952, plant patent #1181, 1953. This is of medium size, ripening in early midseason, with all the berries ripening virtually at the same time; resembles 'Rancocas'.

'Herbert'—originated at Weymouth, N.J., by U.S.D.A. and the N.J. Agricultural Experiment Station. Cross made in 1932; introduced 1953. This ripens late; the fruit is about the same size as that of 'Coville' and 'Berkeley'. Herbert Alexander, Middleboro, Mass., states that grown under his conditions the fruit of the first picking is nearly 1 in. in dia.

'Ivanhoe'—originated in N.J. by U.S.D.A. Introduced 1952; a large-fruited, midseason variety, but only from N.Car., to southern New England.

'Jersey'—originated at Whitesbog, N.J., by F. V. Coville, U.S.D.A. Introduced 1928; the fruit is large and ripens late.

'Katharine'—originated at Whitesbog, N.J., by F. V. Coville, U.S.D.A. Introduced 1920; the fruit is large and ripens late.

'Keweenaw'—originated at South Haven, Mich. Introduced 1952 and recommended only for trial in northern Mich. near the Great Lakes.

'Murphy'—originated at Atkinson, N.Car., by N.Car. Agricultural Experiment Station and the U.S.D.A. Selected in 1940 and introduced 1950. It is resistant to canker, and the fruit ripens early.

'Olympia'—originated Olympia, Wash., by Eberhardt Blueberry Nurseries. Introduced in 1933; resembles 'Harding'.

'Pacific'—same as 'Olympia'. Introduced 1932, matures early; resembles 'Pioneer'.

'Pemberton'—originated at Whitesbog, N.J., by F. V. Coville, U.S.D.A., in 1921. Introduced 1941; the fruit matures late.

'Pioneer'—originated at Whitesbog, N.J., by F. V. Coville, U.S.D.A. Introduced 1920; this fruits in midseason.

'Rancocas'—originated at Whitesbog, N.J., by F. V. Coville, U.S.D.A. Introduced 1926; the fruit is early to midseason.

'Rubel'—selected in the wild by Miss Elizabeth White, Whitesbog, N.J., and introduced before 1931. This fruit ripens late.

'Sam'—selected by Miss Elizabeth White, Whitesbog, N.J., prior to 1931; this ripens late.

'Satilla'—originated near Brunswick, Ga., and introduced in 1944. It is probably of value only in the South.

'Scammell'—originated at Whitesbog, N.J., by F. V. Coville, U.S.D.A. Introduced 1931. This ripens late, and it is resistant to canker.

'Stanley'—originated at Whitesbog, N.J., by F. V. Coville, U.S.D.A. Introduced 1930; this fruits in midseason.

'True-Blue'—originated in a Savannah river swamp near Savannah, Ga. Introduced about 1943; discovered about 1938.

'Walker'—originated near Brunswick, Ga. Introduced 1944. Selected from the wild, but probably of value only in the South.

'Wareham'—originated in East Wareham, Mass., by F. V. Coville, U.S.D.A. Introduced 1936; this fruits very late.

'Washington'—originated at Olympia, Wash., by Eberhardt Blueberry Nurseries. Introduced in 1933; resembles 'Rubel'.

'Weymouth'—originated at Weymouth, N.J., by F. V. Coville, U.S.D.A. Introduced 1936; this fruits very early, and the fruit is large.

'Wolcott'—originated at Atkinson, N.Car., by N.Car. Agricultural Experiment Station and U.S.D.A. Selected in 1940; introduced 1950. This fruits very early, and it is resistant to canker.

Plants bought from the nursery should be about 15–18 in. high to start with, usually sold bare root or with a ball of soil about the roots. Those with a ball get off to a better start but are not always available, especially if they must be delivered through the mails. Since several varieties should be planted together for best fruiting, one must decide which are the most desirable to get the proportionate numbers, but there might best be no more than 4 of one variety together without at least 1 of another variety, preferably blooming at the same time.

Although the blueberry plot can be cultivated, mulching the plants results in better plants and fruits (see MULCHING) and saves labor as well. Sawdust has been found to be the best mulch for blueberries, but pine needles, oak leaves, peat moss and wood chips or shavings are all effective. If sawdust is selected as the mulching material it should be remembered that a good application of commercial fertilizer should be applied to the planting just before the mulch is applied.

Ammonium sulfate is the best fertilizer for blueberries since they use the ammonium form of nitrogen more quickly than nitrogen in any other form. In fact bushes that receive regular applications of a normal complete fertilizer (5-10-5) may show a yellowing of the leaves merely because they are not receiving nitrogen in a form they can utilize. This is an important point to remember. However, sulfate of ammonia is a very strong fertilizer and must be applied at the proper rates, certainly not to young plants until they have become established several years.

As soon as they commence to grow the first year they can be given about $1\frac{1}{2}$ oz. of a 10-10-10 commercial fertilizer (see FERTILIZERS), and then each year thereafter 3 oz. of the same fertilizer. The third year after transplanting they can receive the ammonium sulfate, and this need only be applied every second or third year thereafter or as necessary, at the rate of 3 oz. per bush. This is a small amount to apply uniformly about the bush and might be mixed with a little sand for easier application.

Pruning

Pruning properly is necessary in order to obtain the larger fruits. Bushes that are not pruned deteriorate rapidly, and the fruits produced can become discouragingly small. If only a few bushes are concerned, it is probably not important to know the varietal requirements, but if a large number of varieties are to be grown, one should know the pruning requirements of each variety. This knowledge is best acquired by obtaining the most recent bulletin on blueberry culture from the nearest state experiment station.

Some pruning is necessary after the first 2 years of growth on all bushes each year, in order to obtain vigorous growth and large-sized berries. For instance, some varieties ('Rubel' is one) sprout from the base more readily than others like 'Jersey'. After several years of growth, 'Rubel' will have many more old stems than will 'Jersey'. 'Rubel' must be thinned out at the base each year where 'Jersey' will have to be thinned at the top. Weak branches should be removed on all bushes.

One should become familiar with what the fruit buds look like, for these are more profusely produced on some varieties than others, and some should be removed if large berries are wanted. Any pruning can be done in the winter or during early spring before the buds begin to swell. Hence removing a few of the older stems each year on some, thinning out the tops of those with weak stems or side branches on others, is essential, so that some pruning is done on every plant. Then those varieties that overproduce should have a few of their fruit buds removed, but this is only required on certain varieties, and it is very difficult for the home gardener with only a few bushes to do this. But pruning in some form each spring is necessary on all bushes to keep them in a good vigorous growing condition.

Picking the berries before they are fully ripe is responsible in most cases for "poor taste." This is another point in favor of protecting the berries from birds, for if not protected it is always a race of who gets there first. If they are protected, then picking about once a week can be satisfactory. As for timing, see VACCINIUM for the listing of early, midseason and late varieties. This can be important, for, with the right selection of varieties, one can pick blueberries from the home "patch" for a full 6–8 weeks in July and Aug. See VACCINIUM for insect and disease pests.

Many state experiment stations have up-to-date bulletins on the subject, and locally recommended varieties are best.

BLUEBONNET = *Lupinus subcarnosus*

BLUECURLS, FORKED = *Trichostema dichotomum*

BLUE-DICKS = *Brodiaea capitata*

BLUE-EYED GRASS. See SISYRINCHIUM.

BLUE-EYED MARY = *Collinsia verna*

BLUEGRASS, KENTUCKY = *Poa pratensis.* See GRASS, LAWNS.

BLUEGRASS, ROUGH = *Poa trivialis.* See GRASS, LAWNS.

BLUE-LIPS = *Collinsia grandiflora*

BLUE-POPPY = *Meconopsis betonicifolia*

BLUE-STAR = *Amsonia ciliata*

BLUET, MOUNTAIN = *Centaurea montana*

BLUETS. See HEDYOTIS.

BOCCONIA = *Macleaya*

BOG-ASPHODEL, NEW JERSEY = *Narthecium americanum*

BOGBEAN = *Menyanthes trifoliata*

BOG GARDENING. See WATER GARDENING.

BOLE. The trunk or stem of a tree.

BOLTONIA (bowl-TOE-nia)
   asteroides   3′–5′   Zone 3   White Boltonia
Native perennial from N.Y. to Ga., alternate leaves and small, asterlike white to violet flowers about ¾ in. across in July and Aug. Easily grown, not a very outstanding ornamental for the perennial flower border. Easily propagated by division in spring or fall.
   asteroides latisquama   3′–5′   Zone 3   Violet
                                                          Boltonia
A better ornamental than *B. asteroides* because of its better and larger (1-in.) pink to purple flowers. Native from Mo. to Okla. Both species can spread, often too readily, unless restricted occasionally. There is a variety 'Nana' with pink flowers, growing only about 2 ft. tall, but apparently it is not listed in nursery catalogues.

BOMBACACEAE = The Silk-cotton Tree Family

BOMBAX (bom-BAX)
   ceiba   100′   Zone 10   Red-silk-cotton Tree
A soft-wooded tree covered with corky prickles, native to India. The horizontal, whorled branches produce large palmate leaves 7 in. long with 3–7 leaflets. The 4-in. crimson flowers are produced in clusters near the ends of the branches after the leaves have fallen. These are followed by pods, 6 in. long, that split open and out of these come quantities of silky cotton often used in India for stuffing pillows. The flower buds are sometimes eaten as a pot herb.

BONE MEAL (steamed). Used as a fertilizer with only 1% nitrogen, 22%–30% phosphoric acid, acting rather quickly. It can be used at the rate of 4–8 oz. per sq. yard.

BONE MEAL (raw). A fertilizer with 3%–4% nitrogen and 20%–24% phosphoric acid. Slow acting, often used at the rate of 4–8 oz. per sq. yard.

BONESET = *Eupatorium perfoliatum*

BONSAI. The art of dwarfing trees and shrubs and planting them in pots is an Asiatic hobby that has captured the fancy of many Americans. Actually the art is centuries old. In Japan, where gardens are extremely small and space is limited, it is understandable that this painstaking, time-consuming hobby would be popular. Many of the plants in private collections are hundreds of years old. American visitors to Japan should realize that, because of the current United States Department of Agriculture restrictions and the Plant Quarantine laws, it is not possible to bring any plants into the United States from abroad, with soil about the roots. Hence, if bonsai plants are purchased in Japan, all soil would have to be washed from their roots before they could be admitted into the United States, a process which would be impossible with most specimens, if they were to be shipped and expected to live. Consequently, most bonsai plants for American enthusiasts must be started in America.

It involves fascinating techniques for those with time and patience. Almost any woody plant can be dwarfed for growing in pots, but some, because of their smaller flowers, fruits or foliage, result in better specimens than others. For instance, the large trees with compound leaves like walnuts, hickories or the Tree-of-Heaven, are not used since the foliage of such species on a dwarf plant would be very much out of scale. On the other hand, varieties of cut-leaved Japanese maples, *Zelkova serrata*, some of the small flowering cherries and narrow-leaved evergreens with small leaves are excellent. The main objective is to simulate great age by form, dwarfing, twisting, forcing plants into slow and contorted forms so that a specimen a foot or so high, has the same proportions and general outline of mature specimens in nature. All this is accomplished by the proper pruning of roots and branches, and confining growth (in small containers) to an absolute minimum.

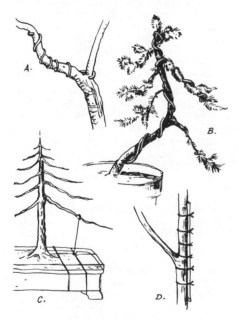

Training Bonsai:

A–B. Branches wound with bent copper wire and thus held in place.
C.   Hold lower branch down in proper place by tying.
D.   Holding branch straight by tying to stake.

Before one enters into the enthusiastic growing of bonsai, one should consider the care they require. Most are hardy plants that could be grown out-of-doors over cold winters if it were not for the fact they are grown in shallow pots. The pruning and training of their branches can be a most interesting experience. Bonsai should be repotted and root pruned every 4–5 years. Most important of all, time wise, since they are grown in very shallow pots, they must be watered, sometimes daily, and the soil not allowed to dry out. This means that seldom can they be left more than a few days at a time during the growing season without watering. Once the soil dries out, the roots are irreparably damaged. Also, they can not be left out-of-doors over severe winters in the North, but must be in a cool place, with some light usually during their dormant period.

Occasionally, by means of trial and error, one finds a room in the house sufficiently cool where the evergreen types can remain in good condition over winter. Those with a small greenhouse are better situated, for here atmospheric moisture conditions are higher and general growing conditions are usually better. Hence, consider carefully the matter of watering and proper care over winter before growing bonsai extensively.

Pots selected for the purpose of growing bonsai are usually flat and shallow, with only 2–4 in. of soil possible, of interest in themselves for form and color. There should be holes in the base for drainage, wire screening should be placed over these holes to prevent soil loss, and a small amount of pebbles or broken crocks put in the base for drainage purposes. Potting soil would be any normal soil used for potting other kinds of plants.

One can obtain small, misshapen plants from garden or nursery. The Japanese collect old wind-blown dwarfs at and above timberline. Or one can start with normally grown tree and shrub seedlings preferably only a foot or so tall. In collecting a plant from the wild, especially a dwarfed plant, it should be realized that its roots are not all necessarily within a dia. of 1 ft. about the base of the plant. Often the important feeding roots may be some distance away and all would be cut off in a hasty digging. It is better to root prune (which see) a year in advance, sometimes root pruning half the plant one year and the other half the next year, then digging the plant carefully the third year. Most impatient bonsai enthusiasts will not wait to do this but prefer to take the chance of digging immediately. If this is done, care should be taken to dig all the feeding roots wherever they may be found. Planting at first need not be in the final display pot.

The species of plant selected is only important from the standpoint of obtaining one which has small leaves, or fruits or flowers, all of which will be "in scale" in a plant under 18–24 in. tall. A few suggestions would be azaleas, beeches, flowering quinces, hawthorns, flowering cherries, Japanese maples of several varieties, hornbeams, Hardy Orange (*Poncirus trifoliata*), *Zelkova serrata* and possibly wisterias for deciduous plants. Suggestions for evergreens would include arborvitaes, cryptomeria, boxwoods, junipers, both shrub and tree species, *Chamaecyparis obtusa* varieties, pines, especially *Pinus parviflora* and *P. mugo*, spruces and yews.

Once the subjects for bonsai are obtained, regardless of whether they are normally grown and shaped, or are collected dwarfs or misshapen plants that no one wants, the time has come to read reference books on bonsai. Many are now available, and it really should be necessary to study these, either casually or carefully, because there are many suggestions in them about training. These suggestions, often in the form of excellent photographs and drawings are not available in most books on American horticulture. In fact, the great interest in this subject in America started only a short 15 years ago. A few books which might be suggested are:

Brooklyn Botanic Garden's publication, Plants and Gardens, Vol. 22, No. 2, 1966, entitled "Bonsai: Special Techniques." Also see Vol. 17, No. 3, 1961, "Japanese Gardens and Miniature Landscapes."

Kawamota, Toshio and Joseph Y. Kurihara. "Bonsai-Saikei," Nippon Saikei Co., Tokyo, Japan. 361 pp., ill. 1963

Yashiroda, Kan. "Bonsai," Charles T. Branford Co., Newton, Mass. 166 pp., ill. 1960

Yoshimura, Yugo and Giovanna M. Halford. "The Japanese Art of Miniature Trees and Landscapes," Chas. E. Tuttle & Co., Rutland, Vt. and Tokyo, Japan. 220 pp. 1957.

After going through such references one begins to visualize the various objectives in training, how a branch can be bent here or there by means of a copper wire and so induced to grow in a definite form permanently; how a twig can be grafted where it is needed most, or a bud forced to grow at a certain place where it is needed. By means of studying the pictures one can begin to understand what the objectives are. Simply fixing plants upright in these shallow pots by the use of hidden wires is a technique that bears study.

The use of rocks in conjunction with the final placement of these dwarfed plants in their exhibition pots is a study of its own. Great age can be simulated by just the right rock in the right place, and the use of moss in the pots and on the rocks aids much to the illusion to be created. The Japanese are the best experts in

the world at this, one of the reasons why English texts written by Japanese authors should very definitely be inspected, so that as many ideas as possible can be gleaned from them.

Group plants have much interest, and methods of obtaining several upright stems from one submerged major stock should be studied. *Zelkova serrata* is a special plant for this type of planting.

As if this were not enough, some of the Japanese are not satisfied with these 18-24 in. bonsai specimens. They work meticulously to create "miniature bonsai," specimens only a few inches tall, nearly 50 of which can be displayed on one large windowsill. Even more time and skill is needed in growing good specimens of these, and keeping them alive with timely watering methods.

Bonsai: This specimen of *Chamaecyparis obtusa* is over 200 years old and is growing in the collection at the Arnold Arboretum in Boston.

With a general knowledge of how a plant grows, and some experience in grafting techniques, it is not difficult to enter into a detailed bonsai training program, if one has the time and patience.

It is possible, starting with normal seedlings, to have attractive, well-trained bonsai specimens in 5-10 years. One can reduce this time by using collected specimens. In any event, they might well be kept out of doors in a cool shaded place during the summer months but carefully watered whenever they need it. Since they should never be allowed to dry out they should not be left for long periods of time in the hot sun, or in situations exposed to high winds.

For other forms of dwarfing, especially these in which the understock has a dwarfing effect on the top part of the tree, see DWARF FRUIT TREES.

BORAGE FAMILY = Boraginaceae

BORAGINACEAE = The Borage Family

BORAGO (bo-RAY-go)

officinalis   2′   annual   **Common Borage**
Native to southern Europe, this herb is especially valued for its blue, purple or white saucer-shaped flowers that are about ¾ in. wide and bloom throughout the summer. The alternate leaves are oblong to ovate and the hairs on these leaves have been known to produce cases of dermatitis. Propagated by seed. The flower is candied for confectionery; the leaf is used in iced drinks, in salads and pickles and as a gentle laxative.

BORDEAUX MIXTURE. A fungicide which was discovered in France many years ago. It is prepared from copper sulfate and lime and was a standard control for many plant diseases until about 1940 when organic fungicides such as ferbam and zineb replaced it. It is still a cheap and effective fungicide which leaves a conspicuous but relatively harmless residue. See FUNGICIDES.

BORERS. A term applied to the larvae of insects which tunnel into the wood of trees and shrubs and the stalks of plants. Nearly every tree and shrub is susceptible to the attack of some boring insect. Bronze birch borer, rhododendron borer and dogwood borer are typical examples. European corn borer, squash vine borer and common stalk borer are serious pests of vegetables, dahlias and large, stemmed flowers. Timely applications of insecticides when the adult stage of the borer is active give considerable protection. See INSECTICIDES. Borers already in plants may often be cut out without causing more damage than the borer has done or they may be killed in their tunnel with a probing wire or a chemical insecticide forced into the tunnel. See INSECTICIDES.

BORONIA (bo-RO-nia)

megastigma   2′   Zone 9   **Sweet Boronia**
An evergreen shrub with downy shoots, sessile, needlelike leaflets having transparent dots; the small fragrant flowers, ½ in. across, have a brown-purple corolla, yellow inside, and are borne in the spring. Native to western Australia and planted out-of-doors in Calif. Propagated by seeds and softwood cuttings. Prune back after blooming to make the plant more compact.

BOSTON FERN = Nephrolepis exaltata 'Bostoniensis'

BOSTON-IVY = Parthenocissus tricuspidata

BOTRYCHIUM (bot-RY-kium)

virginianum   6″–30″   Zone 3   **Rattlesnake Fern**
This is native from Prince Edward Island, Canada to Fla. and across to Calif. Divide in the early spring. For propagating by spores see FERNS.

BOTTLEBRUSH, LEMON = Callistemon citrinus

BOTTLETREE. See BRACHYCHITON.

BOUGAINVILLEA (boo-gen-VILL-ea)

glabra   vine   Zone 10   **Lesser Bougainvillea**
A spiny vine of the tropics, native to Brazil, with alternate leaves and inconspicuous flowers in summer, surrounded with conspicuously brilliant colored bracts, yellow to purple to magenta, about 1 in. long. They are used to cover trellises and porches, and in the North they sometimes are seen as house plants. The form with white bracts is probably B. glabra sanderiana.

spectabilis   vine   Zone 10   **Brazil Bougainvillea**
A more vigorous plant than B. glabra, native to Brazil, blooming in summer with red bracts, but not quite as conspicuous except 'Crimson Lake' which has bright crimson bracts. Both thrive in any normal soil and do best when grown in full sun. Propagated by cuttings.

BOUNCING BET = Saponaria officinalis

BOUSSINGAULTIA = ANREDERA

BOUVARDIA (boo-VARD-ia)

longiflora   2′–4′   Zone 9   **Sweet Bouvardia**
A shrub with opposite leaves tapering at the tip and white fragrant flowers 2½ in. long and 1¼ in. wide. Origin uncertain. Sometimes grown in a greenhouse in the North where it can be plunged in the soil out-of-doors during the summer months. Ornamental, native to Mexico. It has opposite leaves about 2 in. long which are wedge shaped near the base; solitary. A popular plant for cut flowers.

BOWIEA (bow-E-a)

volubilis   twining   Zone 10   **Climbing-onion**
This is a bulbous African plant, the bulb being about 5 in. across and grown chiefly as a curiosity. It does best in a dry atmosphere; is usually grown in the greenhouse or as a house plant. The interesting thing about this is that the bulb has been known to make an annual growth for 4 consecutive years while stored on a museum shelf. However, bulbs should normally be dried out during the summer before repotting in the fall. Propagated by seeds or divisions of the bulb. Not ornamental.

BOWMAN'S ROOT = Gillenia trifoliata

BOX. See BUXUS.

BOX-ELDER = *Acer negundo*

BOX FAMILY = Buxaceae

BOX-HUCKLEBERRY = *Gaylussacia brachycera*

BOX-LILY, MAGELLAN = *Philesia magellanica*

BOX-ORANGE, CHINESE = *Severinia buxifolia*

BOXWOOD = *Box* or *Buxus* sp.

BOYKINIA JAMESII = *Telesonix jamesii*

BOYSENBERRY. See BLACKBERRY.

BRACHYCHITON (brak-i-KY-ton)
   acerifolius   60'   Zone 10   Flame Bottletree
The scarlet-red flowers are borne in erect trusses during July and Aug. The coarse lustrous leaves, 10 in. in dia., drop just prior to the blooming period. It is native to Australia and is not one of the best ornamentals but is used to some extent in southern Calif. The lower part of the trunk is usually swollen. It is always dropping something—leaves, fruits, flowers clusters, and these litter the ground, but it does grow well through lengthy dry periods.
   discolor   40'   Zone 9   Pink Flame Bottletree
This has the largest flowers of this group of trees, they being pink, bell shaped and in terminal spikes during June and July. It is native to Australia. The maplelike leaves have 5–7 lobes and are 4–6 in. wide. It is much faster growing than *B. acerifolium* and is popular in Fla.
   populneus   60'   Zone 9   Bottletree
Formerly called *Sterculia diversifolia*, this is also native to Australia, with a bottle-shaped trunk, 3-lobed evergreen leaves about 3 in. across giving the impression of poplar foliage. It is valued for its bottle-shaped trunk and ability to withstand hot growing conditions. In Calif. it is sometimes used as a windbreak even though it is somewhat of a messy tree.

BRACHYCOME (brak-ik-O-me)
   iberidifolia   1'   annual   Swan River Daisy
An annual for edging or massing, this produces blue, white or pink daisylike flowers about 1 in. wide in summer or early autumn. The leaves are featherlike and alternate. Native to Australia, propagated by seeds. It should be planted in full sun and may not bloom for a long period, hence successive plantings should be made from April (indoors) on at 3-week intervals.

BRACKEN = *Pteridium aquilinum*

BRACT. A much reduced leaf, particularly the small or scalelike leaves in a flower-cluster or associated with the flowers.

BRACTEATE. Having bracts.

BRACTEOLATE. Having bractlets.

BRAHEA (bra-HE-a) (*Erythea*)
   brandegeei   50'   Zone 8   San Jose Palm
Native to Lower Calif., this is another fan palm with bright yellow-green leaves, but as they die they still persist and unless pruned off the trunk they make ugly specimens. The leaf stalk bears spines and the fruits are freely borne. It can be considered a substitute for *Washingtonia robusta* where one is necessary.
   edulis   30'   Zone 10   Guadalupe Palm
Commonly planted in southern Calif., leaves palmate, 3 ft. long with 70–80 segments extending $\frac{1}{3}$ to $\frac{1}{2}$ the depth of the blade and about $1\frac{1}{2}$ in. broad. Fruit rounded, black, about 1 in. in dia. The trunk is about 15 in. thick and is ringed with scars. Native to Lower Calif.

BRAKE. See PTERIS.

BRAMBLE. A loose term usually referring to any plant in the genus *Rubus*.

BRASENIA (bras-EEN-ea)
   schreberi   floating   Zone 4   Schreber Watershield
An interesting, although modest member of the Water-lily Family, this plant may be found in swamps, lakes, and slow-moving streams from New England south to Fla. The oval leaves which float on the surface of the water are centrally attached to the fleshy stem and may be up to 3 in. in dia. The small purple flowers, $\frac{1}{2}$ in. in dia., which appear from June to Sept., are borne in the axils of the leaves. The starchy tuberous roots are sometimes cut up in salad.

BRASSAIA (bras-SAY-ia)
   actinophylla (*Schefflera actinophylla*)   **40'**
                                    Zone 10   Octopus-tree
An evergreen shrub or tree with few lateral branches; native to Australia and used in America as a popular house plant. The long-stemmed leaves have 6–8 glossy leaflets, each 6–8 in. long, spreading out like an umbrella. The small, fleshy, dark red flowers are borne closely on small branches (from which comes the name Octopus-tree). These flower clusters are only produced after a plant is at least 10 years old. Easily propagated by air layers.

BRASSAVOLA (brass-AV-o-la)
   digbyana   10"–16"   Zone 10
Sometimes listed as *Laelia digbyana*, this orchid, native to Honduras, has solitary white flowers tinted green, 4–5 in. across, and pseudobulbs about 6 in. high. It should be given a pronounced rest after it is through flowering. For culture and propagation see ORCHID. Another species from the West Indies, *B. cucullata*, has flowers orange, yellow or white and is an outstanding species. *B. nodosa* has smaller greenish-yellow flowers.

BRASSBUTTONS, NEW ZEALAND = *Cotula squalida*

BRASSIA (BRASS-ia). Epiphytic orchids native to the American tropics with pseudobulbs bearing 1–3 leaves and flowers in lateral racemes. The petals and sepals are long-pointed. For culture and propagation see ORCHID.

lawrenceana   8″   Zone 10
With flowers greenish to yellow spotted with brown during May and June. Two leaves are produced from each pseudobulb. Native to Brazil and British and Dutch Guiana.

longissima   15″   Zone 10
Flowers greenish-yellow to yellow in 10–15-flowered arching racemes, spotted with brown sepals up to 12 in. long, from Feb. to Oct. The pseudobulbs are about 5 in. long; each bears 1–2 leaves. Native to Costa Rica.

BRASSICA (BRASS-ik-a). These are usually annual or biennial herbs, members of the Mustard Family, and include Broccoli, Brussels Sprouts, Cabbage, Cauliflower, Kale, Kohlrabi, Mustard, Rutabaga, Turnip and other economic plants. For description, culture, insect pests and diseases, see each one of the plants listed under its common name.

hirta   4′   annual   White Mustard
A weed, similar to the other mustards, with yellow flowers about ½ in. wide and pods up to 1½ in. long, blooming from June to Aug. Native to Europe and Asia. It is grown as a crop in Europe and in Calif.

juncea   4′   annual   Indian Mustard
A widespread weed in North America, introduced from Asia, blooming from June to Aug. This has yellow flowers, pods to 1½ in. long, and deeply divided leaves like the other mustards. A form called 'Southern Curled' is especially grown as a leaf mustard.

kaber pinnatifida   3′   annual   Wild Mustard,
Field Mustard
This is the common Wild Mustard so often seen as a weed throughout grain fields in the U.S., although introduced from Europe where it is native. The leaves are alternate, hairy, pinnately-lobed or divided and up to 7 in. long. The yellow flowers, each with 4 petals, are about ½ in. wide, borne in terminal clusters from June to Aug. Fruits are pods about ¾ in. long.

napa napobrassica. See RUTABAGA.

napus. See RAPE

nigra   6′   annual   Black Mustard
This is a widespread weed in North America, but also it is the main source of table mustard. The small yellow flowers bloom from July to Oct. and the leaves are deeply cut or lobed, with the terminal lobe being the largest. The fruit pods are about 1 in. long.

oleracea. See BROCCOLI.

oleracea acephala. See KALE.

oleracea botrytis. See CAULIFLOWER.

oleracea capitata. See CABBAGE.

oleracea gemmifera. See BRUSSELS SPROUTS.

oleracea gongylodes. See KOHLRABI.

oleracea italica. See BROCCOLI.

pekinensis. See CABBAGE, CHINESE.

rapa   1′–2′   Zone 4   Turnip
The turnip is probably native to Europe, though plants of this group, to which all the vegetables related to the cabbage belong, have been cultivated so long and so widely that the origin of the group is not known. A perennial herb with a fleshy, tuberous, edible root, the alternate leaves are long, hairy and lyre shaped. The yellow flowers have 4 petals forming the outline of a cross, from which the family name (*Cruciferae*) derives. These are borne in racemes. The plant has not much ornamental value. See TURNIP.

BRAZIL-NUT = *Bertholletia excelsa*

BREADFRUIT = *Artocarpus altilis*

BREADROOT. See PSORALEA.

BREAK. A term used by gardeners which actually means mutation (which see).

BREED. A group of plants having distinctive qualities in common, which developed through the influence of man, requiring control by man to prevent mixtures with other groups; may be propagated from seed.

BRIDALWREATH = *Spiraea prunifolia*

BRIER, AUSTRIAN = *Rosa foetida*

BRIER, SWEET = *Rosa eglanteria*

BRISBAND-BOX = *Tristania conferta*

BRISTLE. Stiff hair.

BRITTLEBUSH, WHITE = *Encelia farinosa*

BRITTLE-FERN = *Cystopteris fragilis*

BRIZA (BRY-za)

maxima   2′   annual   Big Quaking Grass
A grass native to the Mediterranean Region, valued as an ornamental annual in the garden because of its graceful nodding, bronze-colored fruit clusters sometimes 3 in. long.

minor   1′   annual   Little Quaking Grass
Similar to the above but smaller, native to Europe and Asia; naturalized in the U.S. Both are easily grown from seed planted about mid-May.

BROAD BEAN = *Vicia faba*

BROAD-LEAVED EVERGREENS. See EVERGREENS, BROAD-LEAVED.

BROCCOLI (*Brassica oleracea* var. *italica*). Broccoli is a word that has been in some confusion because 2 plants are involved under the one term. In England and by some technically minded people in America the word broccoli is synonymous with Cauliflower. See CAULI-FLOWER. In the U.S. the word broccoli now refers to a cauliflowerlike plant in which the malformed flower head is open, branchy and green instead of white, compact and fleshy as in cauliflower. It is commonly listed as Sprouting Broccoli.

Sprouting Broccoli introduced from Italy early in the present century is now a popular and important vegetable crop. The flower heads, cooked like Cauliflower, are delicious, succulent and very rich in vitamins. Its harvesting period is considerably longer than Cauliflower and, therefore, it has a definite place in the home-garden plan.

Varieties

'Italian Green Sprouting' or 'Calabrese' is the most widely-grown variety. Many strains are available that range in maturity from early to late. 'Green Comet Hybrid' is early and resistant to heat and disease, a good variety. 'De Cicco' is an early, light green sort that produces an abundance of lateral shoots. In the East and to some extent on the West Coast 'Waltham 29' is a very popular variety. With Sprouting Broccoli as with Cauliflower it is very important to obtain pure seed or strong stocky plants from a reliable, first-class source.

Culture

Sprouting Broccoli is more cold- and heat-resistant than Cauliflower but even so is grown about the same manner and is treated as a 2-season crop, a spring and late summer planting. The selection and preparation of soil, methods of growing plants, fertilization and general cultural practices are the same as for Cabbage and Cauliflower. See CABBAGE and CAULIFLOWER.

Harvesting

The central inflorescence develops a cluster of green flower buds which at first are very compact but tend to open rapidly in hot weather into the true yellowish flowers. This central cluster should be cut with 4–6 in. of stem while still compact and before the buds open. Lateral shoots will continue to develop in the axils of the leaves and are cut in the same manner. This considerably prolongs the harvesting period.

Pests

Sprouting Broccoli is subject to the same insects and diseases as Cabbage. See CABBAGE.
                                                GRANT B. SNYDER

BRODIAEA (bro-di-EE-a). Native American cormous plants from the western U.S., these are bright flowered with grasslike foliage, grow well in mountainous areas and in the South, but further north they do not do too well unless given rough gravelly soil with good drainage in full sun. The flowers are funnel shaped in loose clusters about 1–1½ in. long, with 6 colored sepals in loose clusters. In any event they should be thoroughly mulched after the first hard freeze. A place in a sunny rock garden seems to suit them best. They can also be forced in pots indoors as are other bulbs. Propagated by seeds and offsets.

coronaria (*B. grandiflora*)   12″–18″   Zone 7 Native from British Columbia to Calif., with violet-purple flowers 1½ in. long.

BROME. See BROMUS.

BROMELIACEAE = The Pineapple Family

BROMELIADS. This is a term adopted in speaking of the Bromeliaceae or members of the Bromelia Family. Most are tropical American plants including the genus *Ananas* (Pineapple) and others such as *Guzmania, Puya, Dyckia, Hechtia, Tillandsia* (Spanish-moss), *Aechmea, Cryptanthus* and others that are grown chiefly for ornament.

BROMUS (BRO-mus)
brizaeformis   2′   annual   Rattle Brome Ornamental annual grass from northern Europe and Asia, noted for its flattened fruits in panicles 8 in. long. Graceful. Often dried and used in arrangements indoors.

japonicus   2′   annual   Japanese Brome A grass, sometimes planted as an ornamental in the garden, with leaves 8 in. long and ¼ in. wide, and nodding fruit heads that are about 8 in. long. Native to Asia and Europe.

BROOM. See CYTISUS.

BROOM, ARROW = *Genista sagittalis*

BROOM, BUTCHER'S = *Ruscus aculeatus*

BROOM-CORN = *Sorghum vulgare technicum*

BROOM, SPANISH = *Spartium junceum*

BROOM, WEAVER'S = *Spartium junceum*

BROUGHTONIA (broo-TOE-nia). A small genus of West Indian epiphytic orchids that are sometimes grown in the greenhouse, with crimson-scarlet flowers, is the species **B. sanguinea**. The flowers are only ½–1¼ in. long. For culture and propagation see ORCHID.

BROUSSONETIA (broo-so-NESH-ia)
papyrifera   48′   Zone 6   Common Paper-mulberry
This was probably brought to America from China or Japan as early as 1750. The leaves are alternate and vary considerably in size. Not one of the best ornamentals, it is nevertheless a reliable one for poor soils and hot city conditions, for it has been used as a street tree. The female catkins, appearing in May, are globular

and interesting, and the round, orange-to-red fruits are ¾ in. in dia., effective during June and July. The tree has a fairly good wide-spreading habit and a rounded head, and the irregularly lobed leaves are densely borne. Paper has been made from the bark in China, the bark fibers being stuck together with rice paste. It seems to grow well under difficult conditions.

Broussonetia papyrifera (Paper-mulberry): This one at Williamsburg, Va. must be over 100 years old.

BROWALLIA (brow-WALL-ia)
 americana **2′** **annual** **Amethyst Browallia**
Most browallias are valued for their deep blue color but especially for the long period during which they flower. This species can be started indoors in April for summer bloom (or outdoors in May). It is densely branched, bears small flowers ½ in. long in the leaf axils through the summer, and the leaves, which are ovate and 2½ in. long, are blue-green. Easily grown from seed. Native to South America. 'Sapphire' is only 10 in. high.
 speciosa **15″** **annual** **Lovely Browallia**
This species, although it can be a garden plant, is the one usually selected to grow in the greenhouse or as a pot plant. The blue flowers are larger, up to 2 in. across. If it is to be grown in the garden, seed should be sown in the greenhouse as early as Feb. The var. **major** is the one commonly planted.

BROWNEA (BROWN-ea)
 grandiceps **40′** **Zone 10** **Glory Flamebean**
Sometimes called the "Rose-of-Venezuela" where it is native, this excellent flowering tree is seen occasionally in the islands of the Caribbean. The scarlet flowers are produced in conspicuous clusters like those of a rhododendron, 8 in. across. The outside flowers bloom first, then another circle towards the center the next day and so on until all are open. The leaves are alternate, pinnately compound with 10–20 pairs of leaflets. Not common. Fruits are flat pods for it belongs to the Pea Family. Propagated by seeds.

BROWN-EYED SUSAN = *Rudbeckia triloba*

BRUCKENTHALIA (bruk-en-THAY-lia)
 spiculifolia **10″** **Zone 5** **Spike-heath**
Related to the heathers, this low shrub is best used in the rock garden. The small, bell-shaped flowers are pale pink, in small spikes, appearing about mid-June, and of course the fruits are merely dried capsules. It is an evergreen, native to southeastern Europe and Asia Minor and can be propagated by seeds or cuttings. Like other heaths, it is best to protect it over winter by laying evergreen branches or dried leaves over it, and a mulch will help it grow properly.

BRUGMANSIA (brug-MAN-sia) (*Datura arborea* **)**
 x candida **20′** **Zone 10** **Angel's Trumpet**
The leaves and seeds of this Peruvian plant are poisonous. Sometimes grown as an ornamental for its large, white, solitary, trumpet-shaped flowers 10 in. long. These have a musky odor, open at night, and have 5 twisted segments in the corolla. The large, grayish-green leaves are 8 in. long, thick, velvety and are borne in pairs; one is a third shorter than the other.

BRUNFELSIA (brun-FEL-sia)
 americana **6′–8′** **Zone 10** **Lady-of-the-night**
This shrub from the West Indies bears white flowers which fade to pale yellow and are similar to those of *B. latifolia.* It gets its common name because it turns fragrant after dark. The fruit is berrylike, ¾ in. across.
 latifolia **6′** **Zone 10** **Brunfelsia**
A smaller shrub than *B. americana,* native to tropical America, with flowers opening a rich blue, then fading to lavender and white, similar in size and shape to those of a large Periwinkle flower. They are about 1½ in. across. It blooms off and on during spring and autumn.
 pauciflora calycina **3′** **Zone 10** **Brazil Rain-tree**
A tropical shrub with 3-colored fragrant flowers—blue, lavender and white—the various colors due to the fading of the flowers. They are 2 in. wide, in few-flowered terminal cymes.

These cover the plant during summer and autumn. The leaves are 4 in. long, either blunt at the tip or round and pointed, often twisted. A member of the Potato Family and native to Brazil.

BRUNNERA (BRUNN-er-a)
  macrophylla 1½'–2' **Zone 3** **Heartleaf Brunnera**
Incorrectly called *Anchusa myosotidiflora*, this is an herbaceous perennial belonging to the Borage Family and bears showy, small blue flowers about ¼ in. across in clusters during spring, something like those of Forget-me-not. It is native to the Caucasus and Siberia and should be provided with a deep moist soil to grow well. The leaves are large and heart shaped, the stems slightly hairy. It is propagated by division, spring or fall, root cuttings and seed.

BRUNSVIGIA ROSEA = *Amaryllis belladonna*

BRUSSELS SPROUTS (*Brassica oleracea* var. *gemmifera*). This vegetable has been grown near Brussels, Belgium, since the fourteenth century, hence its name. It is a minor crop in America even though its popularity has increased during the past 30 to 40 years.

It is an erect single-stalked plant, developing buds or small heads (sprouts) in the axils of the leaves. These heads or sprouts when fully developed are 1–2 in. in dia. and resemble miniature heads of cabbage. They are mild in flavor, rich in vitamins as well as calcium and iron.

Varieties

The better types for the home gardener are: 'Long Island Improved', 'Catskill', 'Prince Marvel Hybrid' and 'Jade Cross Hybrid'.

Culture

The general cultural requirements for brussels sprouts are about the same as for Cabbage and cauliflower. See CABBAGE. The plant will stand considerable freezing and can be harvested in the fall until severe freezes occur. The best quality sprouts are obtained in the fall with the sunny days and light frost at night. Brussels sprouts are grown as a fall crop.

The plants are spaced 24–30 in. apart in the row and 30–36 in. between rows. Seed planted in the outdoor seedbed in late May should produce strong transplants for their permanent place in the garden by late July. Soil preparation and fertilization is the same as for Cauliflower and Cabbage except that this crop is not as sensitive to a high soil acidity as Cauliflower. Too much nitrogen and hot weather tend to produce sprouts that are loose, open, not compact and of poor quality.

The sprouts begin forming first in the axils of the lower leaves, approximately 2–3 months after transplanting. In harvesting, the first picking should not be delayed after the lower leaves begin to turn yellow. In picking, the lower leaf below the sprout is broken off and the sprout is removed by breaking it away from the stalk. As the lower leaves and sprouts are removed the plant continues to push out new leaves at the top and in the axil of each leaf a bud or sprout is formed. In this manner sprouts may be harvested for a period of 6–8 weeks.

Cauliflower and Brussels Sprouts

Storage

The sprouts will keep well in storage at 32° F. and a high relative humidity of 90–95% for a period of 4 to 6 weeks. The whole plant is removed from the garden just prior to severe freezes and placed in the storage pit or storage cellar.

Disease and Insects

Most of the pests of Cabbage and Cauliflower also attack brussels sprouts and the control measures are the same.

GRANT B. SNYDER

BRYOPHYLLUM = *Kalanchoe*

BUCKEYE. See AESCULUS.

BUCKLEYA (BUK-lia)
  distichophylla 12' **Zone 4** **Buckleya**
This is a rare, native, parasitic shrub living on the roots of hemlocks. The leaves are opposite, 2½ in. long and sessile. The habit of the plant is graceful and the flowers are inconspicuous and greenish, the plant bearing both pistillate and staminate flowers in separate clusters. Fruit is

yellowish and about $\frac{1}{2}$ in. long. The only way to get this to survive is to sow the seeds in a pot with a plant of hemlock, eventually planting both out together. Native to N.Car. and Tenn. but hardy in Mass. The seed should be stratified at 40° F. for 3 months, then sown on top of roots of a living hemlock, either in a pot or in the woods.

BUCKTHORN = *Rhamnus cathartica*

BUCKTHORN FAMILY = Rhamnaceae

BUCKWHEAT. See FAGOPYRUM.

BUCKWHEAT FAMILY = Polygonaceae

BUD. The nascent state of a flower, leaf or branch.

BUDDING. This is actually a form of grafting in which a single bud is used as the scion. It is done on a commercial basis with the large production of roses and fruit trees, in which a single bud is inserted into the bark of the seedling understock. In much of the United States this is done in the middle to late summer, for it is then that the bark "slips" easily, that is, it can be separated from the wood of the inner part of the twig easily and without damage to the cambium tissues. Also, it is at this time that the buds used in the operation are fully mature. It should be noted, however, that in certain parts of the southern United States and in Calif. there is a much shorter period in spring when the bark slips easily on certain woody plants, and this period is sometimes utilized to good advantage. However, for the rank and file of amateur gardeners, the best time to try budding is in Aug.

The method consists of making a T-shaped cut in the bark of the stock, pulling the bark thus cut carefully away from the wood, just enough to allow the insertion of a single bud which had been cut from the twig of the parent plant about the same size as the understock. The leaf petiole is left on although the leaf blade is removed, and the petiole is used as a handle for moving the bud. These buds are cut off vigorous shoots about the same size as the understock so that the curvature of the bark attached to the bud will be about the same as the curvature of the stock. Twigs about the size of a thin lead pencil are about right, and it is up to the gardener to make certain that the dia. of his understock is not much larger, for if it is the bark is not nearly as pliable nor will it "slip" as easily.

The bud is cut carefully so that it is pointed at both ends and it is carefully inserted underneath the edges of the T-cut in the stock. One should be certain that it is inserted upright, not upside down, for in that case it would not grow. Then the top and bottom of this union are wrapped tightly and carefully, preferably with flat bands of rubber called "budding bands" tied properly so they will not come undone if left alone.

Slightly before this operation, all the leaves on the understock below and in the vicinity of this

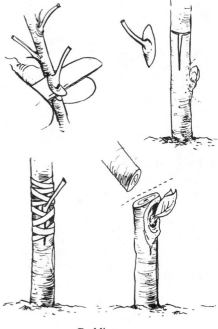

Budding

cut are rubbed off, the idea being that eventually an entire new plant will grow from this one bud on the roots of the understock. All other buds or suckers on the plant below the budded union should always be removed. This is the reason for making this cut just a few inches above the ground level—to leave as little as possible of the understock above ground.

The seedling with its bud graft is allowed to continue growth but early in the following spring the tops are cut off just above the bud union.

Sometimes in transplanting the plant may be set in the soil below the bud union, in the hope that the scion part will send out shoots of its own. This, however, is far more practicable on plants (like LILACS) that have been root grafted onto privet than it is for budded fruit trees.

Patch budding is frequently practiced with plants that have thick bark like mangos and pecans. A special double-bladed knife is used for this operation with the blades rigidly held a half-inch apart. A patch is carefully cut out of the understock at the appropriate place and a similar patch, including a bud, is removed from the bud stick or the long shoot of the mother plant that has been selected, for each such shoot may have a dozen or more buds.

The patch of bark with its bud is carefully inserted in place on the understock; the bud is tied firmly into place similarly to the way buds are tied in the regular budding operation.

It must be impressed on the gardener that the buds are never to be allowed to dry out, nor is the cut in the understock, which is why the successful operator is the one who makes the incision on the understock and, without moving away, cuts the bud from the bud stick and inserts it. Such a fast operation is the only way to insure success.

BUDDLEIA (BUD-lia). (Sometimes spelled *Buddleija*.) These are woody to semi-woody shrubs noted chiefly for their large, conspicuous flower clusters. There are about 70 species of these deciduous or evergreen shrubs in the temperate parts of America, South Africa and Asia, but only a few are of value for ornamental planting in the U.S., and even these have some drawbacks because of their very vigorous growth. Only 2 or 3 species are grown by American nurserymen, but many varieties of *Buddleia davidii* (or its hybrids) have been named and are available.

It has been noted that the species with the handsomest flowers are *B. asiatica* (Zones 8 or 9); *B. colvilei* (Zones 7 or 8); *B. davidii* (Zone 5); *B. globosa* (Zone 7) and *B. officinalis* (Zone 9), so because of climate limitations *B. davidii* is the only one of these that can be widely grown. To this I would like to add *B. alternifolia* (Zone 5), for this should be used more widely than it is.

Buddleias grow vigorously in any normal garden soil and they have practically no special growing requirements. With the exception of *B. globosa* and *B. alternifolia*, they bloom on growth made the current year, which means that they are usually cut back severely or cut to the ground in the fall or early spring to force vigorous shoots for flower production the current year.

To most gardeners the name buddleia means merely a variety or hybrid of *B. davidii*, and in the northern and central U.S. this is root-hardy, but not top-hardy. Consequently it does not fit well into the shrub border, but instead should be placed at the rear of the perennial border where it can be treated as one of the taller-growing herbaceous perennials. All of the buddleias are considered to have coarse texture, since the leaves are so large, ranging from 4 in. up to the size of those of *B. davidii* and *B. globosa* which have leaves 10 in. long. The single possible exception is *B. alternifolia*, the leaves of which

are from 1–4 in. long, making it the species with the smallest leaves in the recommended group.

Propagation

The seeds have no dormancy and hence can be sown as soon as ripe, or may be stored dry in airtight containers in a cool place and then sown the following year. Softwood and hardwood cuttings root readily. See CUTTINGS.

alternifolia   12′   Zone 5   Fountain Buddleia
The hardiest of the woody buddleias and the only one with alternate leaves, this plant deserves much use as a gracefully arching specimen. The branches are covered with flower clusters of small, lilac-purple flowers in mid-May, and this makes it the earliest of the buddleias to flower. It is not like most other buddleias in that its branches do not die to the ground in the winter and the flowers appear on the previous year's branches. It thrives in poor, but well-drained soils and is a native to northwestern China.

asiatica   2′–6′   Zones 8 or 9   Asian Buddleia
Native to southern China and India, this has leaves 5–8 in. long, green above and rusty hairy beneath. The fragrant white flowers are borne in panicles 5 in. long. It has been considered one of the best of the buddleias in flower during April and May.

colvilei   30′   Zone 9   Colvil Buddleia
A rare plant in America, coming from the Himalayas, the small flowers are rose colored in terminal, pendulous panicles 6–8 in. long in June. It is very handsome when in bloom.

davidii   15′   Zone 5   Orange-eye Butterfly-
bush
This is the buddleia commonly grown in American gardens. It usually dies to the ground over winter, but blooms in Aug. on the current year's growth. The flowers are small, white, pink, red or purple, depending on the variety, and are born in upright, terminal, pyramidal spikes. The opposite leaves are coarse in texture. There are some 38 varieties currently being grown by American nurserymen who like to advertise them because, if seeds are sown in the greenhouse, salable and blooming plants can be offered in one year. Among the varieties, **'Peace'**, **'Snow Bank'** and **'White Bouquet'** have white flowers; **'Charming'**—one of the best varieties with pink flowers; **'Fascination'**—with soft orchid-pink flowers; **'Dubonnet'** and **'Ile de France'**—purple flowers; **'Empire Blue'**—deep blue flowers; **'Royal Red'**—reddish flowers; **magnifica**—often called the Oxeye Butterflybush, was found in China in 1900 by E. H. Wilson. It has been widely grown in America ever since. The flowers are dark, bluish lavender with an orange eye, and some of the flower panicles or spikes may be up to 8 in. long and

2 in. wide while occasionally, on very well-grown specimens, they may be as much as 22 in. long.

globosa 15′ Zone 7 Globe Butterfly-bush
Few plants grown in the U.S. are native to South America, but this one comes from Peru. The small, bright yellow flowers are fragrant and appear in June. They are borne in terminal panicles 4–8 in. long, being arranged in the panicle in rounded clusters about 3 in. in dia. The opposite leaves are partially evergreen, depending on the severity of the winter.

madagascariensis 20′ Zone 10 Madagascar Butterfly-bush
A shrub with spreading branches, woolly twigs and oblong, pointed leaves about 6 in. long. These are dark green and smooth on top, but downy white or yellow beneath. The small, cup-shaped flowers are orange, woolly on the outside, and are borne in large, showy clusters. The leaves have been used as a soap substitute. Planted in southern Fla.

officinalis 2′-6′ Zone 9 Pale Buddleia
The fragrant flowers of this Chinese shrub are lilac colored, with an orange eye. They bloom during April and May. It has been considered as one of the better ornamentals of this genus.

BUD MUTATION. An abnormal shoot (caused by genetic change), which can be propagated only asexually.

BUD SCALE. Covering of a bud.

BUD SPORT. Same as bud mutation.

BUFFALO-BERRY. See SHEPHERDIA.

BUGBANE. See CIMICIFUGA.

BUGLE-LILY. See WATSONIA.

BUGLEWEED = *Ajuga reptans*

BUGLOSS, COMMON VIPERS = *Echium vulgare*

BUGLOSS. See ANCHUSA.

BUGLOSSOIDES (Bug-los-o-I-des)
purpureocaeruleum procumbent Zone 7?
A perennial, the stems being 2 ft. long; bearing lanceolate leaves and blue flowers ½ in. wide blooming in the spring. Native to Europe.

BULB. A modified bud with fleshy scales, usually underground.

BULBIL. A diminutive bulb.

BULBLET. A small bulb. See BULB.

BULBLET BLADDER FERN = *Cystopteris bulbifera*

BULBOCODIUM (bul-bo-KO-dium)
vernum 6″ Zone 5 Spring Meadow Saffron
Native to the mountains of Europe, these are similar to the crocuses and may bloom before them. The leaves usually appear after the flowers and are narrow. The flowers are large and rose-violet in color and are borne close to the ground with 1–3 funnel-shaped flowers per stalk. They grow from corms, belong to the Lily Family and go well in the rock garden. They should be lifted every third year in the autumn and separated. Easily propagated by offsets. Best planted in late Aug. or Sept.

BULBOPHYLLUM (bulbo-FILL-um). A group of pseudobulbous epiphytic orchids occasionally grown in a warm greenhouse. The genus contains nearly 1000 species throughout the Tropics. As a whole the genus is not much worth growing, but a few species are of interest because of their curious floral structure. The species vary greatly, producing one flower to many-flowered spikes. For culture and propagation see ORCHID.

BULBS. No garden is complete without some bulbs, and the early spring-blooming kinds are naturally the most popular since they bring interest and color to any planting long before perennials and annuals. There are many kinds, and specific details for culture are discussed under the alphabetical listings. In general there are certain things to remember about them.

Usually they are planted at a depth of 2½ times their dia. although this varies as will be noted under the specific generic headings. They are best planted in the early fall, with the exception of *Gladiolus, Montbretia, Schizostylis, Tigridia,* and *Watsonia* which are planted in March or April, and *Sternbergia* which is planted in July. In fact, the following are usually not planted until midfall (Oct.–Nov.), *Allium, Galtonia, Hyacinthus, Ixia, Convallaria, Lilium, Narcissus, Ranunculus* and *Tulipa.*

In planting any large number, the soil should be well and deeply prepared; like all other plants, they require good soil in which to grow and multiply, and this is the time to make certain of good soil with plenty of humus *underneath* them. Since many are to be planted at a depth of 4 in., some even 6 in. or more, it is obvious why soil preparation is essential for many will be expected to remain in the exact spot where they were originally planted for many years. If they are to be planted in among other plants where complete soil preparation is impossible, then a special bulb-planting spade (which is narrow and only 4 in. or so wide) might be used to dig a deep hole, replace poor soil with good in which is mixed a little fertilizer and the bulb set on top of this at the proper depth, with more good soil on top. Taking a pail or bushel basket of ready-mixed soil around when the holes are dug is a ready way of having available good soil at the proper place.

Remember too that some, like *Narcissus, Scilla* and *Muscari,* are excellent for naturalizing, while others like tulips and lilies are better adapted for planting in formal beds.

GROUND LEVEL

MADONNA LILY

ERANTHIS

CROCUS   CHIONODOXA   SCILLA

SNOWDROP
DUTCH IRIS

GRAPE-HYACINTH

HYACINTH

TULIP

DAFFODIL   LILY

Depth of planting for certain kinds of bulbs. (Measurements are given in inches.)

All bulbs should be allowed to grow until their tops turn yellow and die, for the period after flowering is one during which the green leaves are busily engaged in manufacturing foods that are to be stored in the bulb and be responsible for the following year's growth. If new growth is cut off right after flowering, then, the food supply for the next year suffers and the bulb can die or "disappear", as so often happens when plantings are made in poor soils. Fertilizing bulb plantings immediately after flowering will aid in growth at this time.

Some bulbs like tulips and hyacinths should be replaced every year or so. Others, given proper care, fertilizer and water when needed during drought conditions, will last and even increase for many years.

Bulbs are also used as specimens (usually in clumps) in the rock garden or in the flower border. A few clumps of Snowdrop in the front of the foundation planting near the front of the house always bring pleasure to those who notice the first flower in early spring.

Certain bulbs (Narcissus, hyacinths, tulips and even Crocus) are excellent for forcing in pots in the greenhouse or in the home. Do not be overanxious about getting these started. Remember that they need from 6–10 weeks of chilling (40° F. or below) to fulfil the requirements of a dormant period, otherwise they will not grow well. This is the reason why recommendations usually call for planting these in pots and leaving in a "cold place" in the fall

before they are taken in for forcing. Placing the pots in the cold frame out-of-doors, not allowing them to dry out and being certain they have the proper few weeks of cold weather before they are brought inside, is always good insurance for satisfactory growth later. This is best done by filling the pots with good soil, planting the bulbs in the pots, then setting them out-of-doors on coal ashes or some similar place and mounding moist sand, peat moss or even pine needles 6–8 in. thick over them until the 6–10 week period of proper cold is up. At this time they should have developed good roots and the new growth should just be above the soil. In the North, they should not be kept out in severely cold weather. In the deep South they may have to be put under refrigeration so that the cold requirements will be fulfilled. Often, a cold place in the cellar is just right, but they should not be allowed to dry out during this period.

Finally, narcissus and hyacinth bulbs to be forced in a jar of water or in a bowl filled with pebbles and water must be kept as close to 40° F. as possible during this pre-growing period.

All bulbs, when brought in for forcing indoors, would best be kept at 50°–60° F. rather than in warmer situations. If they are taken from the cold and placed in the hot sun immediately, the marked change in temperature may be enough to kill the tender flower buds or cause them to go "blind." A sufficient cooling period at 40° F., then a cool room or greenhouse at 50°–60° F. plus a little shading for the first few days until they become acclimated, can spell the difference between success or failure.

Insect Pests

Bulb fly with 1 maggot in a bulb and the lesser bulb fly with several maggots in a bulb are important pests of Narcissus, Tulip, Easter Lily and similar bulbs. These maggots eat into the bulbs and encourage decay. Successful control of the flies has not been done. Infected bulbs should be destroyed; soaking in hot water at 110° F. for 1½ hours will kill the maggots. Recent experiments in coating bulbs or treating the planting soil with insecticides #13 or #15 were promising. Bulb mites are injurious to all kinds of bulbs, especially in the greenhouse (see MITES). New insecticides, especially systemic types, are being tested and should be investigated.

Diseases

Decay and rots develop quickly on bulbs stored in unfavorable conditions. When necessary follow recommendations for treatment of bulbs and corms before storing. See specific plants.

The following list of bulbs serves as a check

list for those who wish to plant some in the garden. All are briefly described in this volume, but for those who wish to study the matter thoroughly, a good reference is: Rockwell, F. F. and Grayson, E. C., "The Complete Book of Bulbs," published by Doubleday & Co., Garden City, N.Y.

BULLATE. Blistered or puckered; as the leaf in Savory Cabbage.

BULLOCK'S HEART = *Annona reticulata*

BUMELIA (bew-MEE-lia) There are other species in this genus but they are mostly tropical plants and have little ornamental value. All have very hard wood, are frequently thorny and are native from the southern U.S. southward. The flowers are small and white, and the fruits are small, drupelike and black. The leaves are alternate, persistent but not evergreen and one seldom comes across the plant except in the woods.

BULBS	HEIGHT	ZONE	
Acidanthera bicolor	18″	10	Dark-eye Gladixia
Allium sp.	1″–3′	3	Onion
Alstroemeria sp.	2′–4′	10	Alstroemeria
Amaryllis belladonna	2′	9	Belladonna-lily
Anemone sp.	3″–18″	3–6	Anemone
Arisaema sp.	12″–18″	4	Jack-in-the-pulpit
Brodiaea sp.	8″–24″	7–8	Brodiea
Bulbocodium vernum	6″	5	Spring Meadow Saffron
Caladium sp.	6″–24″	10	Caladium
Calochortus sp.	1′–2′	3	Mariposa-lily
Canna sp.	2′–8′	7–9	Canna
Chionodoxa luciliae	3′	4	Glory-of-the-snow
Claytonia sp.	4″–6″	–	Spring Beauty
Colchicum sp.	4″–6″	4–6	Crocus
Colocasia sp.	5′–7′	9–10	Taro
Convallaria majalis (rhizome)	8″	2	Lily-of-the-valley
Crinum sp.	18″–4′	7–9	Crinum
Crocus sp.	3″–6″	5	Crocus
Eranthis hyemalis	8″	4	Winter Aconite
Eremurus sp.	4′–10′	5–6	Desert-candle
Erythronium sp.	1′	3–5	Faun-lily
Freesia sp.	1½′	9	Freesia
Fritillaria sp.	1′–2′	4–5	Guinea-hen Flower
Galanthus sp.	1′	3	Snowdrop
Galtonia candicans	3′–4′	5	Summer Hyacinth
Gloriosa rothschildiana	vine	10	Rothschild Gloriosa-lily
Hippeastrum hybrids	3′	9	Amaryllis
Hyacinthus sp.	4″–15″	5–7	Hyacinth
Hymenocallis calathina	2′	7	Spider-lily
Iris, some sp.	3″–48″	3–8	Bulbous Iris
Ixia maculata	18″	7	Corn-lily
Leucocrinum sp.	7″	4	Star-lily
Leucojum sp.	1′	4	Snowflake
Lilium sp.	1′–6′	3–4	Lily
Liriope sp.	18″–2′	4	Lily-turf
Muscari sp.	1′	4	Grape-hyacinth
Narcissus sp.	3″–15″	4	Narcissus
Ophiopogon sp.	6″–3′	7	Lily-turf
Ornithogalum sp.	1′–3′	4–8	Star-of-Bethlehem
Oxalis sp.	4″–12″	7–9	Oxalis
Ranunculus sp.	1′–3′	3	Buttercup
Scilla sp.	6″–20″	4	Squill
Sinningia speciosa	10″	10	Common Gloxinia
Sternbergia lutea	1′	7	Fall-daffodil
Tigridia pavonia	1½′	6	Tiger Flower
Trillium sp.	6″–18″	3	Trillium
Tulipa sp.	6″–24″	4	Tulip
Watsonia sp.	4′	8	Bugle-lily
Zantedeschia americanum	1′–3′	10	Common Calla

There are other trees making far better ornamentals.

lanuginosa   24′   Zones 5–6   Chittamwood
Not especially ornamental, this is native to the
central and southern portions of the U.S., but is
seldom found available from nurseries. The
wood is hard, there are thorns, the leaves are
alternate, entire and 2–3 in. long, remaining
green very late in the fall. The drupelike fruits
are only ⅓ in. long. Propagation is by seeds
which can be sown as soon as ripe since they
have no dormancy.

BUNCHBERRY = *Cornus canadensis*

BUNCHFLOWER = *Melanthium virginicum*

BUNYA-BUNYA = *Araucaria bidwillii*

BUPHTHALUM (bewf-THAL-um)

salicifolium   2′   Zone 3   Willowleaf-oxeye
A showy herbaceous perennial belonging to the
Daisy or Composite Family with yellow ray-
flowers in solitary terminal heads 2 in. wide,
blooming in Aug., alternate leaves white-hairy,
willowlike and 3 in. long. Native to southern
Europe. Propagation is easiest by division.

speciosum = *Telekia speciosa*

BURDOCK. See ARCTIUM.

BURL. An unnatural swelling on the trunk of
some trees. The burls on redwoods, when cut
off and set in a pan of water in a warm room,
will send up several green shoots, making an
interesting display for months.

BURNET, SALAD = *Poterium sanguisorba*

BURNINGBUSH = Euonymus americanus

BURR. A spiny fruit cover as in the fruit of
Horse-chestnut.

BURSTWORT. See HERNIARIA.

BUSH. A low, several to many-stemmed shrub,
without distinct trunk.

BUSH-CLOVER. See LESPEDEZA.

BUSH-HONEYSUCKLE. See DIERVILLA.

BUSH-POPPY = *Dendromecon rigida*

BUTCHER'S-BROOM = *Ruscus aculeatus*

BUTEA (BEW-tia)

frondosa = *B. monosperma*

monsperma (*B. frondosa*)   **50′   Zone 10**
                                Flame-of-the-forest
A tree from India and Burma, with leathery trifoliate leaves which are dropped in Feb.,
followed by a mass of brilliant red flowers that
are tinged orange, pealike and in clusters.
Each flower is about an inch long and they are
borne in racemes 6 in. long in the leaf axils.
They also yield a red dye. Fibers obtained from
the inner bark are used in caulking boats.
Member of the Pea Family.

BUTIA (BEW-tia)

capitata   10′   Zone 8   Butia Palm
This is a feather palm, with long arching,
pinnately compound leaves making a large and
lush head on a short trunk. The fruits, often
borne in clusters weighing 75 lbs. or more, have
been used in making jellies. A very effective
landscape plant native to Brazil and Uruguay. It
makes a fine tub plant also. See PALMS.

BUTOMUS (bew-toe-mus)

umbellatus   2′–3½′   Zone 5   Flowering-rush
A rushlike plant, with narrow leaves 18–30 in.
long, growing as an aquatic herb at the edge of
a pond or near a swamp. This is grown for its
rose-colored flowers (3 petals and 3 sepals) an
inch across borne in many-flowered umbels on
rushlike scapes often 4 ft. tall. Native to Europe
and Asia, easily propagated by division. The
rootstock has been roasted and eaten as
emergency food.

BUTTER-AND-EGGS = *Linaria vulgaris*

BUTTERBUR, JAPANESE = *Petasites japonicus*

BUTTERCUP. See RANUNCULUS.

BUTTERCUP FAMILY = Ranunculaceae

BUTTERCUP-TREE = *Cochlospermum vitifolium*

BUTTERFLY   BAUHINIA = *Bauhinia   monandra*

BUTTERFLY-BUSH, MADAGASCAR = *Buddleia madagascariensis*

BUTTERFLY-BUSH,   ORANGE-EYE = *Buddleia davidii*

BUTTERFLY-FLOWER = *Schizanthus pinnatus*

BUTTERFLY-PEA = *Clitoria ternatea*

BUTTERNUT. *Juglans cinera*, is a broad flat-
headed tree native to a more northern range
than the Black Walnut. Nuts are long and thick
shelled, while the kernels are oily and rich.
Frequently found in woodlands of New England
and other northern states from Me. to Minn., it
is often a short-lived tree. The seasoned lumber
would be used much more often in cabinet work
if it were available. Graining and color are
attractive, while it takes an excellent finish.
Young butternuts are sometimes pickled after
the shell has been rubbed smooth.

A few varieties have been named, although
some may now be increasingly hard to find
commercially. Among them are **'Deming'**, **'Ken-
worthy'**, **'Love'**, **'Irvine'** and **'Craxezy'**. Because
the tree is not long lived, and because no easily
cracking nuts have been found, less attention
has been paid to improving the Butternut than
to any other Walnut species. Recent interest has
been aroused in the possibility of producing
hybrids of Butternut and Heart nut. Early crossing indicates that crosses worthy of trial for nut
quality and yield are available.

H. GLEASON MATTOON

BUTTERWORT. See PINGUICULA.

BUTTONBALL-TREE. See PLATANUS.

BUTTONBUSH = *Cephalanthus occidentalis*

BUTTONWOOD = *Platanus occidentalis*

BUXACEAE = The Box Family

BUXUS (BUX-us) Box. Although there are approximately 30 species of *Buxus* about the world, there are only two species of ornamental value for planting in the greater part of the U.S., namely, *B. microphylla* from Japan and *B. sempervirens* from Europe. There are several cultivars and varieties of the former and many of the latter species that make it possible to select just the right cultivar for the right place. All have opposite leaves.

Basically *B. microphylla* is hardier and lower in growth than *B. sempervirens*, but there are so many cultivars of the latter species available that it is unnecessary to substitute with *B. microphylla* or its varieties for any reason other than hardiness, except in the lower South where *B. microphylla japonica* (and possibly also *B. microphylla sinica*) seem to be excellent plants for the warm dry climate of the Gulf States. The English Box (*B. sempervirens*) was probably brought to America by the earliest settlers, while *B. microphylla* and its varieties did not reach America until after 1860, and the Korean variety did not come until 1919.

Boxwood is commonly grown throughout the eastern and southern U.S. It is not necessary to grow *B. microphylla* where English Box is thoroughly hardy; rather, this Asiatic species might be used on the northern perimeter where the English Box is questionably hardy and in the deep South where the varieties often seem to do better than *B. sempervirens*. Better still might be the use of varieties of *Ilex crenata* (in the North) which are excellent hardy substitutes for Boxwood, and incidentally these are lacking in the various pests that seem to persist wherever boxwoods are grown.

It has been noted that Boxwood prefers limestone soil, but in our experience, they do almost equally well in acid soils. *B. sempervirens* and its varieties should not be recommended as reliably hardy north of Zone 6. In Boston, central and northern N.Y., parts of Mich., Wisc. and Ill., many of the Common Box varieties are definitely not hardy. There are, however, growing in this belt, miscellaneous seedlings or hybrids that have been watched for years that are apparently hardy and are being named and introduced in the trade. Such are 'Inglis', 'Northland', 'Vardar Valley', 'Hamilton' and others. If the Common Box is to be grown north of hardiness Zone 6, it is cultivars such as these and others as yet unnamed, which will be the plants to recommend.

Propagation

Seed can either be sown at once (they germinate rather slowly and erratically), stratified or stored dry in airtight containers in a cool place for up to a year and then sown. Many plants can be divided by using a sharp spade. Cuttings of both hard and softwood root readily. See CUTTINGS.

Insect Pests

Boxwood leaf miner is a tiny orange midge fly which produces orange maggots in blisterlike mines on the underside of leaves. Eggs are laid in early summer and maggots live 10–11 months in mines in leaves. Spraying with insecticides #9, #13, or #15 is effective in one application in midsummer. Boxwood psyllids or jumping plant lice suck sap and cause cupped terminal leaves. Spraying in late spring and early summer with insecticide #15 gives control. Spider mites which bronze the leaves and reduce vitality are controlled by spraying with insecticides #31 or #34.

Diseases

Canker or blight causes die-back of twigs and cracks in bark in late summer. Cut out and burn infested twigs and spray with fungicides #K, #D or #F.

harlandii   3′   Zone 7   Harlands Box
Native to China, this is one of the smallest of the evergreen box species, with leaves $\frac{1}{2}$–$1\frac{1}{4}$ in. long and $\frac{1}{8}$–$\frac{3}{8}$ in. wide, slightly longer than those of *B. sempervirens* 'Suffruticosa'. However, it is much more tender.

microphylla   3′   Zones 5–6   Littleleaf Box
The true Littleleaf Box of Japan has leaves about an inch long and is low in habit. However, the leaves have a bad trait of frequently turning brown in the winter. Although it is hardier than the Common Box, it might be best to determine the qualities of some of its cultivars before this species is used, since some are proving to be superior ornamentals. Varieties are: **'Compacta'**—also called the Kingsville Dwarf—originated at Kingsville Nurseries, Kingsville, Md. It is a dense, rounded, twiggy cultivar with small leaves, reported hardy in southern Canada. First introduced in 1940, a 47-year-old plant is 1 ft. tall and 4 ft. across, dense and green; **'Curly Locks'**—discovered in 1942 and introduced in 1946 by the Kingsville Nurseries—this is of compact, upright growth. The branches have a curling or twisted habit, quite different from other boxwoods in its habit of growth. One plant about 20 years old is 2 ft. tall and 4 ft. across; **'Green Pillow'**, a more recent

introduction of the Kingsville Nurseries, has a habit about the same as that of 'Compacta' but the leaves are twice as large. It was selected in 1912 and introduced in 1955. The height may eventually be only 15 in. but the spread will reach 3–4 ft. This at one time was listed by the Kingsville Nurseries as *B. microphylla* 'Kingsville 1 A'. The 25-year-old plant in the Arnold Arboretum is 2 ft. tall, 4 ft. across, an excellent dense mass of foliage; **japonica**—a 6-ft. shrub introduced into America from Japan in 1860 and widely planted, especially in the southern U.S. where it does well. It is hardy in Zone 5, apparently almost as hardy as the Korean Box; **koreana**—this Korean Box, a native of Korea, and hardy in Zone 4, is one of the hardiest of the boxwoods. Unfortunately it is not an outstanding ornamental, especially in the winter when the foliage turns a brownish green. It is a geographical variety of the species and has been widely recommended because of its hardiness, but there are many situations where it should not be grown, especially if it is to be ornamental in the winter. It is loose and open in habit, takes shearing well and should not be grown primarily for winter display. Two new and interesting cultivars of this hardy variety are **koreana 'Tide Hill'**—named in 1954 by Benjamin Blackburn of Drew University, Madison, N.J., from cuttings he originally received from Long Island, N.Y., in 1951. It is a cultivar named because of its dwarf habit (a 20-year-old plant is only 15 in. high yet 5 ft. across). Also its foliage does not turn brown in the winter on Long Island and N.J. although the plant in the Arnold Arboretum does have winter foliage a slight brownish green; **koreana 'Wintergreen'**—actually not a cultivar because the name was given to 25 original plants all of which were grown from seed of *B. microphylla koreana* received by the Scarff Nursery, New Carlisle, Ohio, from Manchuria in the 1930's. All these 25 seedlings have proved hardy in south central Ohio. There is some variation among them and some differences in color of foliage. Additional selections were made in 1958 and these all are undoubtedly of value locally, where it is claimed they retain their green foliage color throughout the winter. However, they should be compared with other varieties and cultivars growing in other locations; **sinica**, the Chinese Little Leaf Box is only hardy in Zone 6, and although it is not listed by American nurseries under this name, it may be that many of the plants grown in the South under the name *B. hardlandii* are actually this variety. According to Rehder the "leaves are orbicular or obovate to elliptic—lanceolate, 8–35 mm. long usually emarginate (i.e., notched at the tip); petiole and midrib beneath toward the base, puberlous."

sempervirens   20′   Zone 5   Common Box
The Common Box is native to southern Europe and has been intimately associated with gardens in North America since early colonial times. In Tidewater, Va., there are specimens which have been healthy and growing continuously for 1 and even 2 centuries. The species itself is a tall-growing treelike shrub with evergreen leaves about 1¼ in. long. Many varieties have originated in Europe and more recently in this country, where observing plantsmen are picking out seedlings showing greater hardiness than the species. Animals occasionally eat the clippings with fatal results.

Varieties: **'Angustifolia'**—a treelike form with long, narrow leaves; **arborescens**—the tree type with normal leaves; **'Argenteo-variegata'**—the edges of the narrow leaves of this cultivar are variegated silvery white; **'Aureo-variegata'**—the leaves are variegated with yellow; **'Bullata'**—a low bush with short, blunt, dark green leaves; **'Handsworthiensis'**, an old English cultivar, introduced before 1858, this is a wide strong-growing upright shrub with dark green foliage making an excellent ornamental and an especially good hedge plant; **'Inglis'**—this plant originally grew on the estate of Mrs. James Inglis, Ann Arbor, Mich., where she reported time and again that it was not injured by temperatures of −20° F. It was named in 1945 because of its hardiness and its dense and bushy pyramidal habit of growth, as well as its dark green foliage that is maintained all winter; **'Myrtifolia'**—the Myrtle-leaved Box has been grown since 1785. It is a low shrub about 4–5 ft. tall, the leaves being ½–¾ in. long and very narrow; **'Newport Blue'**—a selection made by the Boulevard Nurseries of Newport, R.I., prior to 1949. A 14-year-old plant is only 18 in. tall, but 3 ft. across, making a densely rounded mass of green foliage; **'Northern Find'**—this cultivar named by the Woodland Nurseries, Ltd., of Cooksville, Ontario, Canada, was growing on the grounds of St. Joseph's Hospital, Hamilton, Ontario, between 1930 and 1940. It attained a height of 5 ft. and has survived winter temperatures of −30° F. It is popular in this area of Canada where any broad-leaved evergreens are needed. It forms a rounded, not too dense bush, and 3 ft. nursery plants are about 3 ft. wide. The Woodland Nurseries have been growing it for 20 years and have found it highly satisfactory for gardens in this part of Ontario, where it is sometimes known as merely the Hamilton variety; **'Northland'**—this cultivar was discovered by the C. W. Stuart Co., of Newark, N.Y., in 1931 and introduced in 1949. It was named for its ability to withstand winter conditions in central N.Y. so that its hardiness and slow compact growth have made it valuable. A

Buxus sempervirens 'Suffruticosa': Growing at the St. George Tucker House, Williamsburg, Va. (*Photo by Arnold Arboretum, Jamaica Plain, Mass.*)

14-year-old plant is 4 ft. tall and 5 ft. across, and the foliage is dark green in midwinter; **'Pendula'**—with pendulous branchlets, cultivated since before 1890; **'Rosmarinifolia'**—cultivated since 1859, this at one time was used extensively in England for topiary work. The leaves are small and rosemarylike and the plant is low growing; **'Suffruticosa'**—a widely grown dwarf box and has been popular here in America since colonial times. Three ft. tall, hardy in Zone 5 and called the True Dwarf Box; **'Vardar Valley'**—a new hardy variety of the Common Box introduced by the Arnold Arboretum in 1957. It was found growing in the Vardar Valley of the Balkans in 1935. Cuttings brought to the Arnold Arboretum have resulted in plants perfectly hardy that are only about 2 ft. tall but 4–5 ft. across. The foliage keeps its green color throughout the winter. It is a wide-spreading, flat-topped plant of considerable merit in the North (hardy in Zone 5) where many other boxwood varieties are injured by winter cold; **'Welleri'**—a 13-year-old plant is 3 ft. tall, 5 ft. across and green in midwinter. This is a selection of the Weller Nursery Co., of Holland, Mch., before 1949.

C

CABBAGE (*Brassica oleracea* var. *capitata*). Cabbage is by far the most important member of the genus *Brassica* that is grown as a vegetable. It has been known from earliest antiquity and was probably in general use as early as 2000 to 2500 B.C. Several types were cultivated at the time of Pliny. At the present time Cabbage is found wild on the sea coasts of Europe.

Cabbage thrives best in a relatively cool, moist climate. In the southern region it is grown largely during the winter and early spring, while in the northern states it is grown as either a late spring or fall crop.

Varieties

There are literally hundreds of varieties of Cabbage which vary in size, shape, maturity, color and resistance to various diseases. Some are used for boiling, coleslaw and salads while others, the larger-headed sorts, are grown basically for sauerkraut and pickling. It is suggested that the home gardener check several good seed catalogues and then select the variety that best meets his needs.

Good (yellows resistant) green and early varieties are: **'Jersey Wakefield'** (a conical head), **'Golden Acre'**, **'Stonehead Hybrid'**, **'Copenhagen'**, **'Market Prize'**, **'Early Mart'**, and **'Emerald Cross'**. Green and late: **Danish Ballhead** types such as **'Penn State Ballhead'**, or **'Wisconsin Hollander'**. Red types are **'Red Acre'**, or **'Red Danish'** and **Savoy** types.

Soils and Fertilizers

Most garden soils will produce a good crop of Cabbage if the soil is properly prepared and fertilized. Generally early Cabbage is grown on the lighter sandy-loam soils, while late Cabbage is grown on heavier soils that are more retentive of moisture. Perhaps more important than soil texture is its supply of moisture and its fertility.

Cabbage is a heavy feeder, especially of nitrogen and potash. If animal manure is available, liberal applications prior to plowing or spading will be beneficial. See Soil Preparation section of VEGETABLE GARDEN. In addition to manure, 30–40 lbs. of a 5-8-7 or similar ratio of a commercial fertilizer should be applied prior to planting, followed by several side dressings of nitrate of soda, 1¼ lbs. per 100 ft. of row, during the first 5 weeks after the plants have been set into the garden.

Growing Plants

For early Cabbage sow the seed in good potting soil in flats or other suitable containers a month or 6 weeks earlier than the plants are to be set out. Sow the seed in drills ¼ in. deep and 2 in. apart. When the seedlings reach a size of 2–3 in. high, transplant into flats or boxes at a spacing of 1–1½ in. Maintain a uniform soil moisture and a temperature of 60 to 70° F. until a week or two before field planting when the temperature should be reduced 10° F. to 50–55° F. The method of raising plants for the late crop is exactly the same except that the flats or boxes are kept out-of-doors rather than under glass in the home or in hotbeds.

Planting

Cabbage plants that are well hardened can be set out in the garden even though the temperature may drop down below freezing for several days. Spacing will depend largely on the variety. 'Jersey Wakefield', 'Golden Acre', and 'Copenhagen' may be set 15 in. in the row, while the larger-headed Ballhead types should be given a bit more space, say 15–18 in. apart.

Cultivation

Cabbage roots are wide spread and relatively shallow. Sufficient cultivation should be given to keep down the weeds and to maintain a shallow soil mulch when the plants are small. Hand hoeing or hand weeding may be necessary after the plants reach full size if weeds are a problem.

Harvesting

The heads are usable anytime after they have properly formed. If left too long after maturity the heads will split. In cutting use a large knife and cut just above the large outer leaves.

Storage

Late Cabbage may be stored in outdoor pits for periods of 4–8 weeks. The plants are pulled, roots and all, and placed in the pit, heads down, and then covered with hay or straw and a layer of soil.

Insect Pests

Several greenish leaf-eating caterpillars attack Cabbage and related plants. They include the cabbage worm and cabbage looper. To control use Bacillus thuringensis regularly at 7- to 10-day intervals. Begin in May when first butterflies are seen after planting in the South, or use Sevin for good results. After the edible part of plant appears (heads) use Sevin, a 4% malathion dust 1½ oz. per 50 ft. of row or spray with 50% methoxychlor wettable powder, 3 level tablespoons per gal. of water for 200 ft. of row.

Cabbage aphid may be a serious pest. These soft-bodied, green or black insects may be controlled with a 4% malathion dust or a nicotine dust.

Root maggots can be serious for all crops in the Mustard Family. Control of the maggot is in applying ½ to 1 cupful to each plant when set out in the garden of a diazinon suspension in the transplant water, using 5 oz. 50% wettable powder in suspension.

Black and red Harlequin bugs occur in the southern states. Adults and nymphs suck the plant sap and are very hard to kill. Hand pick or, if serious, use Carbaryl (Sevin) dust.

Diseases

Black rot caused by a bacterium that lives over in the seed produces a black ring in the stem and veins of the leaves. Blackleg is a disease caused by a fungus parasite that invades the seed and lives over in the soil. Its worst damage is to young plants in the seed bed. Both of these diseases may be kept under control by treating the seed with hot water (Cabbage for 25 min. other crucifers for 18 min. at 122° F.), by using sterilized soil in the seed bed and by crop rotation in the garden.

Cabbage yellows caused by a fungus which shows up by the lifeless yellowish-green color of the plants, 2-4 weeks after transplanting, followed by a stunted, malformed growth. This disease is soil-borne and the only control lies in crop rotation and in using yellow-resistant varieties.

Club root is produced by an invasion of a slime mold on the roots. The roots of affected plants show a thickened, malformed appearance. This is a soil parasite which thrives in an acid soil. Soil pH should test 6.8–7 and transplants should come from soil that has been treated with Vapam, 1 pint per 50 sq. ft., or apply Terrachlor 75% wettable powder, 5 lbs. per 100 gal. of water, using ¾ pint of this per plant.

Cabbage and the other crucifers are subject to other insects and diseases which generally are of minor importance. In addition certain physiological disorders are common, whiptail in Cauliflower and tip burns of Cabbage, in both cases indicated by poor and malformed leaf blades. They are caused by an acid soil and an unbalanced ratio of potash to phosphorus. Browning or brown rot is caused by a deficiency of boron. This is most prominent in Cauliflower. The symptoms are a change in color of the foliage, thickening and brittleness of the leaves and a browning of the "curd" in the case of Cauliflower. Control is in applying 8 oz. per 1000 sq. ft. of borax mixed in the commercial fertilizer or as a foliar spray.

GRANT B. SNYDER

CABBAGE, CHINESE. Two more or less distinct species are grown, Pe-tsai (*Brassica pekinensis*) and Pak-Choi (*B. chinensis*). The Pe-tsai resembles Cos Lettuce but produces a much larger head which is elongated and compact. The Pak-Choi type resembles Swiss Chard with long, dark green leaves. This kind does not form a solid head.

Chinese Cabbage is probably a native of China where it has been widely cultivated for centuries. It is relatively new in America. It has little of the cabbage flavor and when well grown its crisp lettucelike leaves are excellent for salads, and the outer coarser leaves, particularly of the Pak-Choi type, can be cooked as greens.

Varieties

The most popular varieties are 'Michihli', 'Michihli Jade Pagoda Hybrid', 'Wong Bok', and 'Pak Choi'.

Culture

For the early crop the plants should be raised as for early Cabbage and set out in the garden as early as possible because this crop will shoot to seed quickly in hot weather. The late crop will give much better results. As a fall crop the seed is sown where the crop is to mature in late June, and after seedlings reach a height of 2–3 in. the plants are thinned out to 8–10 in. apart.

Pests

The general care and pest control of Chinese Cabbage is the same as for Cabbage or Cauliflower. See CABBAGE.

GRANT B. SNYDER

CABOMBA (ka-BOM-ba)
**caroliniana   aquatic plant   Zone 5   Carolina
                                            Fanwort**
An aquatic herb with fan-shaped leaves divided into threadlike pieces ¾ in. long, native from southern Ill. to Tex. It is a fair oxygenator in the home aquarium and is sold in great quantities for this purpose. It is easily propagated by cuttings, division or seed. It can become a pest in pools in the South and does best in the

home aquarium if planted in a pot of soil submerged under the sand. If planted in pure sand it has a disconcerting habit of dying. It needs strong light, otherwise it becomes long and stringy.

CACAO = *Theobroma cacao*

CACTACEAE = The Cactus Family

CACTI AND SUCCULENTS. Succulent plants, which include the fascinating bizarre cacti, are to be considered as the most specialized of all plant groups. Since they live chiefly in areas typically hot and dry they assume fantastic forms which enable them to survive in such regions of adverse conditions. The grotesque growths tend to conserve water and reduce transpiration. In the case of the cacti, leaves are dispensed with almost entirely and the stems take over the functions which the leaves on non-succulent plants perform. In the mimicry plants (stemless mesembryanthemums) the leaves have entirely lost their semblance and appear as chubby, squat conical-to-spherical plant-bodies.

The root systems of succulent plants are hardly extensive or penetrate the soil very deeply. Usually they lie just below the soil surface which enables them to make quick use of any moisture that may come their way. Thus the plants are able to store water in special tissues and rely on it when water is scarce. For this reason, they are known as "succulents" which literally means "juicy plants."

Since succulents have learned to adapt themselves so nicely to adverse conditions we can readily see why they make such good house plants. Where other plants fail in the hot dry atmosphere of our living rooms, the succulents usually succeed and impart a bit of greenery the year round. People often kill succulents by kindness when they pamper them too much. However, it is wrong to believe that succulents need no attention whatsoever.

Succulents are numbered in at least 20 different plant families. There are hundreds to choose from in all imaginable shapes and forms. If only a windowsill is available it can be utilized and made attractive with these plants. It is to be remembered that succulents require lots of light; if grown in the absence of it, the plants will exhibit scrawny etiolated growth which will be more readily subject to insect attacks and plant diseases. Sun porches afford more room where more elaborate set-ups or stagings can be maintained. However, if one can afford a greenhouse, no matter how small, succulents can be grown to perfection without too much fuss.

A fact to remember is to choose the container best suited for use in the home, if that is the only available location. Succulents look very attractive in glazed pottery, but care in watering must be exercised since such containers do not dry out as fast as ordinary flower pots. Small pots can be set in a large tray or metal box filled with sand, gravel or sphagnum moss, and kept moist. Frequent repotting is not necessary.

Where space is at a premium more satisfaction will be derived if the grower concentrates on a few individual groups than on a general collection.

Propagation

Succulents usually can be propagated from seed, offsets and cuttings, and by grafting. It is true that growing them from seed will require patience, especially in the case of slow-growing cacti, but on the whole many succulents will produce good growth quickly. All you need is a flower pot or seed flat (a cigar box will do), a piece of glass for cover, good porous soil, and a package of fresh seed. Seeds may be sown any time in the year if high temperatures can be maintained, as in greenhouses, but perhaps in the average home seed-sowing should be carried on in spring and summer. A uniform temperature of 70° F. should be provided and the seed pans placed in a window with a southern exposure, where light is always available. The soil in the seed containers must never be allowed to dry out, and seed must not be planted deep—just barely covered with sand or fine gravel. Water can be applied with a fine syringe or in the case of pots, the pots watered from below by placing them in a pan of water. Generally a glass cover is placed over the box or pot to aid in conserving moisture and heat, but the glass should be painted to shade the seedlings as they appear and gradually removed so that seedlings will get accustomed to the light. Supply ventilation to the seedlings by raising the glass cover occasionally so that damping-off does not occur. Seedlings need not be transplanted until they have become large enough or when they begin to crowd each other.

Most succulents can be multiplied by offshoots which usually appear at the base of the mother plant or anywhere along the stems. Cuttings can be made almost anywhere—from tips, lateral branches, from leaves, and in many cases just tiny fragments of portions of stems such as ribs and tubercles of cacti. Cuttings generally root easily and produce a mature plant more quickly than seedlings. When making cuttings, use a clean sharp knife or razor blade. Heal the cutting in a dry, shaded place until a skin or callus is formed; the time will vary with the species from one week to a month or more, depending on the size of the cut. The wider the cut the longer will it require to heal over. Cuttings can be rooted in a mixture of sand and soil but more preferably in pure sand or vermiculite, and as soon as roots form the rooted plants can be planted in the regular way. As a precaution, do not keep the rooting medium too wet from the beginning as rot may set in and spoil your effort. In that case, the cutting will have to be cut back to healthy tissue and calloused over.

Cacti and spurges are usually grafted in order to speed maturity of these plants. There are other reasons, too, such as to save a plant when only a small piece is available which would not easily make a cutting, or to develop more decorative and bushy plants, and to raise varieties that are considered difficult to grow on their own root. Still another reason is to preserve abnormal forms such as crests and monstrosities which are greatly sought by connoisseurs.

Although it is possible to graft other succulents besides the cacti, like spurges and stapeliads, there is really no point gained. Before attempting grafting remember that only related plants can be grafted. A Spurge cannot be grafted onto a Cactus or vice-versa—only species within their respective families.

There are 3 kinds of grafts commonly employed—the cleft, the flat and the side. All thin-stemmed plants are suitable for cleft-grafting while the thick and globose types require a flat graft. The side-graft is usually employed on thin-stemmed plants although it can be used with success on the chubby kinds too. In cleft-grafting the stock (the rooted plant upon which the scion will be placed) is cut back to a desired height, depending on what effect is desired for the plant later on. The Christmas Cactus, which bears pendent stems, naturally would look more effective grafted on a stock at least 6–12 in. tall. A slit is made at the top of the stock about an inch deep. The stem of the scion is then cut on 2 sides to form a wedge and inserted into the split of the stock. Firm the graft into the desired position and run a cactus spine or two through the united portions; then wrap some cord or raffia around the graft, just taut enough to hold the scion in place but not so tight as to cut into the stock.

In the flat graft, both scion and stock should be of approximately the same width at the intended union. After selecting the 2 plants, make a smooth transverse cut on each specimen and then place the scion on the severed stock, pressing the 2 flat surfaces firmly together. The scion can be held in place with 2 large-sized bands or string run over the top of the scion and underneath the flower pot, or by the use of flexible wire bent in "U" shape.

The side graft requires no special operation beyond slicing one side of both scion and stock and holding the 2 joints in place. When grafting operations are completed, set the plants in a warm shaded place so that the cut surfaces will not dry out too rapidly, preventing perfect unions. Inspect all grafts regularly each day to note whether union has formed properly. After grafted plants have become established only normal care is necessary.

Cacti

The most popular members of the Cactus Family are the mammillarias, better known as "pincushion" or "nipple" cacti. They are mostly small globular to cylindrical plant-bodies covered with nipplelike tubercles with clusters of spines on their tips where the areoles appear. The small bell-shaped flowers appear as a crown on top of the plant and in some species a circle of colorful scarlet-to-crimson fruits will develop simultaneously. There are over 300 different kinds described and every one is a gem, but the most popular are those which bear colorful descriptive names such as the Old Lady, Powder Puff, Birdnest, Feather Ball, Lady Fingers, Thimble, Snowball, Fishhook and Golden Stars. They can be readily supplied by Calif. nurserymen who grow them by the thousands. The Old Lady, botanically *Mamillaria hahniana*, is covered with long gray hairs; the Power Puff, *M. bocasana*, likewise has finer, white silky hairs which serve as a veil for the short, brown-hooked central spines beneath the camouflage; the Birdnest, *M. camptotricha*, bears conspicuous long nipples and slender, yellowish twisting spines; the Feather Ball, *M. plumosa*, grows in clusters of small individual heads completely covered with inoffensive feathery spines; the Lady Fingers, *M. elongata*, is a slender cylindrical form composed of several fingerlike green stems covered with slender yellow spines; the Thimble, *M. fragilis*, produces many small thimblelike babies at the top of a mature plant; the Snowball, *M. candida*, is an exquisite pincushion of snowy white; the Fishhook, *M. tetracistra*, is one of the many pincushion cacti with hooked central spines; and the Golden Stars, *M. elongata* var. *stella-aurata*, has every nipple tipped with a shining golden star. You cannot go wrong with the mammillarias—they are often referred to as the "darlings of the whole Cactus Family."

Near relatives of the mammillarias are the coryphanthas, which are so strikingly similar to the former that the average indoor gardener and even a professional will have difficulty in telling them apart. On the whole, all coryphanthas have larger and showier flowers which are borne from the base of the young and growing tubercles near the tops of the plants. There is also a distinguishing groove which appears on the upper side of each nipple in a fully matured plant. There are over 60 species of *Coryphantha* and the commonest one in the United States is *C. vivipara*. It has been reported wild from at least a dozen states, all west of the Mississippi.

The Tom Thumb cacti—rebutias from South America—make excellent house plants and are regarded as free bloomers, the fairly large flowers issuing from plants no bigger than a 25-cent piece. Close allies to them are the lobivias which generally are also small, although a few species become quite robust.

Peru, *Oreocereus celsianus*, which develops long, silky white hairs. It grows much slower than the Mexican cactus but it ought to be a "must" in every collection of cactus plants. Even more handsome is *Espostoa lanata* covered with white cottony hairs. A Cactus with long hairlike golden-yellow spines, *Notocactus leninghausii*, is a great favorite with all cactus growers.

Among the Cereus and its allied representatives there are many easily grown species which present fluted columns. They add height to a collection. In their native habitats these often grow into massive trees, with or without innumerable branches. Most of the group do

Many cactus genera and species are grown in this collection at the Huntington Botanical Gardens, Pasadena, Calif. (*Photo by Arnold Arboretum, Jamaica Plain, Mass.*)

Gymnocalycium species and varieties are distinct globose cacti with ribs divided into tubercles or "chins" which give them the popular name "Chin Cactus". For the most part they are small, very floriferous plants and do well in the window. The *Astrophytum* species, among which is the well-known Bishop Cap, are mostly spineless cacti which produce a profusion of silky yellow blossoms over a long period. There are hundreds of other small-type cacti that make excellent pot plants or suitable subjects for the dish garden, desertarium or novelty container. If, however, the grower has a preference for hairy and woolly kinds that grow slenderly cylindrical, these can be had in variety also.

The Old Man, *Cephalocereus senilis*, is a Mexican form which produces a matted beard at a rather tender age and it is quite easily grown from seed. There is also a counterpart found in

well under almost all average conditions.

Schlumbergera truncata as well as *S. bridgesii* and *Aporocactus flagelliformis* are winter bloomers. The produce reddish to crimson flowers of nearly similar structure. The plants are so well known that they need no further description. Other winter bloomers include the *Hatiora* and *Rhipsalis* species, both epiphytic on trees in their native home, but thriving exceedingly well in soil also. *Hatiora salicornioides* is a freely branching plant with short clublike branchlets growing one upon the other. It bears salmon-colored blossoms. There are more than 50 varieties of *Rhipsalis*, mostly with slender cylindrical branches and tiny elegant blossoms followed by white, mistletoelike fruits.

There are a number of other free-flowering cacti, but space will not permit naming all. Most of those already mentioned are suitable for window culture; however if space permits larger plants in the home, the beginner should not overlook the epiphyllums, the most gorgeous-flowered of all cacti, their blossoms comprising rainbow hues of nearly every description.

The amateur cactus fan, but even more so the specialist, can get great satisfaction by collecting mimicry cacti or any of the other odd, bizarre forms. Among the interesting mimics is the Totem Pole, *Lophocereus schottii* var. *monstrosus*, a curious spineless form which resembles a knobby column of green jade. *Roseocactus* is a genus of curious plants composed of triangular stonelike tubercles. The best known is *R. fissuratus*, aptly called "Living Rock." Of equal importance is the small Mexican, *B. kotschoubeyanus*, which in 1840 sold for $200. These living rocks are dull gray to brown in color and grow on dry stony ground where they can be easily mistaken for the rocks which surround them. One of the curiosities of the cactus world is the Dumpling Cactus, *Lophophora williamsii*, a smooth spineless plant of dumplinglike texture. It is a sacred plant of the Indians, used in religious rites.

Succulent Spurges

The succulent spurges bear a superficial resemblance to cacti and are often mistaken for them. In fantastic forms of growth (exclusive of cacti) they cannot be equalled by any other group of plants. The euphorbias, with their grotesque shapes, fill the place in Africa which in America is supplied by the cacti. On the African continent and in Madagascar the spurges form the characteristic feature of the landscape. The stems of all the spurges contain latex tubes and when cut or bruised a copious milky juice exudes from the surface. This juice is more or less toxic and will produce irritation of the skin unless washed off immediately. The juices of the cacti are usually watery and colorless, which often makes it easy to distinguish between the two groups. In addition, the flowers of the euphorbias are very insignificant, whereas cactus blossoms are often very large and colorful.

The euphorbias are of very varied habit. Some are thorny, fleshy shrubs, others gigantic trees with candelabriform branching, and still others with slender pencil-thick stems growing in tufts. There are also spherical plants and some with subterranean stems from which a crown of radiating branchlets arise.

On the whole spurges make excellent house plants and grow rather easily. However, to grow them to perfection and a desirable height a greenhouse would be the logical place. Spurges require a sunny position and a sandy nourishing soil. In the growing season they can stand ample watering; however in winter too much water will rot the succulent stems. Propagation can be carried on by cuttings and seeds. Since the cut portion bleeds profusely it is advisable to dip the cutting in powdered charcoal. As in the case of cacti, cuttings must be fully hardened before they can be placed in a rooting medium.

There are over 300 species of succulent spurges and a good many of these are available in the trade, but only the more popular kinds can be dealt with here. The Cowhorn, *Euphorbia grandicornis*, is one of the most unique with deeply constricted segments of irregular shape possessing winglike and wavy angles which support an armor of stout spines. The commonest Spurge in cultivation is probably *E. lactea* which hails from the East Indies. Cuttings root very easily, and the plant makes an excellent pot or tub specimen. Its 3-angled stems are faintly marbled. It branches readily even as a small plant and stimulates a symmetrical tree perfectly. A crested form of this is sought by every succulent plant-fancier because it resembles a sculptured piece of art. Frilled Fan Spurge is an apt name.

Euphorbia cooperi is widely distributed in collections. Its branches are 5- or 6-angled and composed of segments which are inverted heart-shaped. *E. ingens* is a spiny succulent tree with 4-angled branches. It is a rapid grower, as are all of the arborescent types.

E. pseudocactus is a bushy branched plant marked by curious broad yellowish-green V-shaped bands. Another distinctly marked plant is *E. knobelii* with more slender stems. Still more distinctive is the much slender-branched *E. griseola*. The Blue Spurge, *E. coerulescens*, branches from the base forming compact bushes, and its stem habit is a peculiar shade of blue-green. *E. resinifera* produces 4-angled ascending pale gray-green stems in a compact form and should be included in every collection.

There are a number of handsome sturdy spurges characterized by grayish-white, continuous horny margins along the angles which make these plants very outstanding. Included among them are *E. avasmontana*, *E. hottentota*, *E. venenata* and *E. volkmannae*.

Some of the spurges which can be classed as outstanding dwarf-curiosities because of their whimsical growth are *Euphorbia globosa*, *E. ornithopus*, *E. susannae*, *E. pseudo-globosa*, *E. obesa*, *E. meloformis*, *E. valida*, *E. sub-mammillaris*, *E. ferox*, *E. stellaespina*, *E. stellata*, *E. squarrosa* and *E. caput-medusae*. Probably the most remarkable plant among these is *E. obesa*, an oddly rotund dumpling which has been likened to a living baseball or small rugby football.

A Spurge that forms a rather large tree and is

composed of cylindric branches and branchlets remindful of a *Rhipsalis* is *Euphorbia tirucalli*. In semi-tropical countries it is often cultivated as a hedge plant. It is also one of the fish-poison trees. When branches are macerated and placed in a stream the juice will stupefy fish, thus enabling fishermen to catch them easily. *E. mauritanica* is another spineless succulent shrub, densely branched and bearing transient leaves on the youngest branches only. A charming spineless Spurge is *E. bubalina* which throws out seeds readily and propagates itself by this means.

There are many more desirable spurges which can be grown in the home and far more in the greenhouse or out-of-doors in warmer regions. If you do a lot of flower arrangements it would be worthwhile to include the *Pedilanthus* or Slipper Spurge in your collection. The zigzag stems of *P. tithymaloides variegatus* with their colorful leaves are frequently used in arrangements. They are interesting for their inflorescences which resemble slippers and which are often reddish in color.

Other Succulents

The *Stapelia* species, which belong to the Milkweed Family, are some of the most curious members of the plant kingdom. They are dwarf, succulent, perennial herbs with thick and fleshy stems and can be likened to miniature Torch Cacti of the genus *Cereus*. The flowers are curious and of great variety, most of them emitting a fetid odor like that of decaying meat, from whence the name Carrion Flower is derived. The odor of the flowers should not deter any plantsmen from acquiring these plants. The flowers of some are very large, up to a foot in dia.; others are of moderate size and still others very tiny; some are beautifully mottled, others spotted or striped with lurid colors. A few are covered with silky hairs.

All stapeliads are easily propagated from cuttings and they also germinate readily from seed, some blooming within a year from time of sowing. Give them plenty of sunlight. They can stand quite a bit of water in the summer but diminish the supply in winter. The oldest and best known species is *Stapelia variegata*, which was introduced into cultivation about the year 1640. It possesses such great variability that at least 24 varieties are enumerated. Besides the stapeliads there are closely allied genera including *Caralluma, Duvalia, Edithcolea, Echidnopsis, Hoodia, Huernia, Huerniopsis, Piaranthus, Stapelianthus* and *Tavaresia*.

Ceropegia is a genus of peculiar, usually twining plants, native of the East Indies and South Africa. It is remarkable for its waxy flowers which are arranged in delicate umbels.

Curiously, *Ceropegia* also belongs to the Milkweed Family. Most ceropegias are very striking plants and lend themselves nicely for hanging baskets or as ground covers in warm regions. Grow them in a mixture of fibrous loam, sand and leafmold. The most elegant member is the Rosary Vine, *C. woodii*, which is admirably adapted for hanging vases as its numerous stems hang gracefully down and are well furnished with small, somewhat heart-shaped, fleshy, silver-splotched leaves. It forms globose tubers in the axils on the stems. *C. sandersonii* is a plant of beauty and curiosity when in flower. It has very succulent leaves but its most remarkable feature is the flower which looks like a miniature greenish parachute. *C. stapeliaeformis* produces rounded, glabrous, dark green stems marked with soft spiniform projections. The flowers are quite showy, funnel shaped above with lobes standing apart.

One would hardly associate the Wax Plant, *Hoya carnosa*, with the milkweed clan, yet it is a true milkweed. The Wax Plant is a twiner with stems up to 10 ft. or more long. It is best to grow it on a small trellis or use it as a hanging-basket subject. On well-established specimens hundreds of flowers bloom continuously during the spring and summer months, and nothing could be more beautiful than the decliate, pinkish waxy flowers against the background of dark green shiny leaves. The flowers, usually nearly 1 in. in dia., are borne in pendulous umbels on short peduncles. The Wax Plant requires an abundance of water during the growing and flowering period, but it is advisable to keep it in a dry and cool atmosphere during the winter. There is now obtainable a highly variegated form which is known in the trade as *H. exotica*.

Although there are more than 150 species of "Hen-and-Chicken" plants native to Southwestern United States and Mexico, many of them are still collectors' items. The popular name is well earned because innumerable plantlets are produced at the bases of the mother plants in most of the species, and it is not difficult to visualize a brood of vegetable chicks under a sitting hen.

Botanically, the American Hen-and-chicken plants are known as species of *Echeveria* and *Dudleya*. They are very striking succulents notable for their attractive clusters of leaf rosettes in distinctive shades and tints, ranging from powder white to blue-green and from bright green to metallic hues. In size, they vary from small rosettes about the size of a half dollar to a large rosette as big as a dinner plate; some are low-growing stemless forms, while others assume short bushlike proportions. In *Dudleya* the leaf bases clasp the stem for their full width and are very persistent, remaining firmly attached to the caudex even when dead; in *Echeveria* the area of attachment is confined to a small "eye," and the leaves usually fall away upon withering, or in some species become easily detached upon the slightest disturbance. New plants are produced from the leaves of echeverias, sometimes very quickly, and this is the most popular method by which these plants are propagated.

Echeverias are mostly Mexican, and 2 of the most charming and decorative for the home are *E. carnicolor* and *E. pulvinata*. Many others are attractive, but these are very easy to grow and therefore are more commonly cultivated. As long as soil is well drained, "Hen-and-Chicken" plants should thrive in it. *E. carnicolor* is a stemless plant with a flattened rosette of about 20 leaves. The leaves are usually highly colored, possessing a metallic lustre. *E. pulvinata* is characterized by neat rosettes of velvety texture crowning the dark brown stems. The leaves are covered with silken hairs, their tips a rich dark red. Reddish-orange flowers appear on short stiff stalks. Both are free bloomers, their bell-shaped flowers making their appearance in the winter season. *E. gibbiflora* and its variety *metallica* are robust specimens producing a thick stem and large gray-green to metallic-bronze leaves. It is sometimes grown as an exhibition plant for greenhouse displays in the winter. *E. secunda var. glauca* produces bluish-green saucer-shaped rosettes and is frequently employed as a bedding plant in outdoor gardens. In warm sections, echeverias are grown outdoors all year round.

Near relatives of the echeverias are the pachyphytums with which group they often hybridize. The hybrid crosses are then known by the generic name Pachyveria. One of the best hybrids is *Pachyveria glauca* which makes compact attractive rosettes. The leaves break off easily and will grow rapidly into new plants.

The echeverias belong to the fascinating Stonecrop Family which includes the sedums, kalanchoids, houseleeks and other interesting crassulaceous groups. Some of the most outstanding flowering members are numbered in the kalanchoids which include the kalanchoes and bryophyllums, but even without flowers the foliage is decorative. Bryophyllums are universal favorites, growing with the greatest of ease and sometimes even become a nuisance because many of them reproduce viviparously, which means that tiny plants sprout all along the serrated margins of the leaves even while these are still attached to the mother plant.

Bryophyllums are mostly natives of Madagascar. They are robust growers, and the leaves of some varieties become highly colorful. The best known is *B. pinnatum*, whose leaves are often sold in dime stores as good-luck charms. The plant bears very fleshy leaves, bright green in color, and large pannicles of flowers, lantern-like in appearance. It is commonly known as "Chandelier Plant". *Bryophyllum daigremontianum*, called Pagoda Plant because its leaves are arranged in pagoda style on the stem, has the ability to produce as many as 100 plantlets along the margins of one leaf alone. *B. tubiflorum* is a striking erect plant with mottled tubular leaves. *B. fedtschenkoi* is another beauty, a compact grower with gray-blue leaves turning a rich lilac when deprived of water and grown in full sun. Many botanists today prefer to relegate the name *Bryophyllum* into synonymy and its members into the older genus *Kalanchoe*. However, I feel that there are at least 2 outstanding characteristics which distinguish the 2 groups.

Possibly the finest kalanchoid from the standpoint of showiness is *K. flammea*. It is a bushy plant, about a foot high, with succulent green leaves and flowers of brilliant scarlet, appearing in clusters as broad as a man's fist. *K. blossfeldiana* is another fine bloomer and an excellent Christmas plant. It is smaller in every respect but equally as attractive. Several outstanding horticultural strains have evolved from it which are grown on a large scale by nurserymen for the trade. The Penwiper Plant, *K. marmorata*, is a stout, low-branching shrub with pale gray-green ovate leaves that are conspicuously speckled with purple spots, giving the plant a marbled effect. The most spectacular, however, is the Panda Plant, *K. tomentosa*. It bears plush-like gray-green leaves, the margins stained with rust-brown spots. The most robust grower is *K. beharensis* with large velvety leaves. If allowed to grow freely, it will get as big as a small tree, 10 to 12 ft. high. Confined to a pot it stays small. The thick triangular leaves are frequently used in arrangements.

One of the best house plants is the Jade Plant, *Crassula argentea*, which also belongs to the stonecrops. It is a shrubby succulent with rubberlike thick trunk and branches and bright green shiny leaves. The flexible branches root upon reaching the ground, but when grown in a hanging basket or as a potted plant on a pedestal it becomes a picturesque array of contorted stems. There are over 200 other species of crassulas in diversified plant forms, some forming small cushions, spherical rosettes or short slender columns. Some of these are rare novelties but others are well-known house subjects that usually grow fast and propagate easily from cuttings.

Among the 500 or more described species of *Sedum* will be found many interesting forms suitable for pot culture. One of the loveliest is the Burro Tail, *S. morganianum*, which produces pendulous tassels of silvery-gray pointed leaves. The Golden Sedum, *S. adolphii*, has thickish, pointed yellowish leaves which break clean very easily and start new plants from them. *S. pachyphyllum* is a recent discovery with thick, gray-green obovate leaves. It is bound to become a great favorite as it is one of the robust bushy types and fills out a pot very nicely.

The Fig-marigold Family, *Aizoaceae*, is one of the richest in plant forms. It can be safely divided into about 3 groups, 2 of them belonging in *Mesembryanthemum* which have the most striking subjects, while the third group including *Sesuvium*, *Tetragonia*, *Trianthema*, *Mollugo* and *Glinus* is insignificant. *Mesembryanthemum* contains the shrubby and carpeting types, commonly known as California Moss or Ice Plant, and the Mimic types among which the Living Stone, Pebble Plant, Tiger Jaw and Tongue Plant are included. The latter, especially the stone mimics, are real curiosities, often stemless, and their leaves resemble broken rock fragments so strikingly that they are difficult to distinguish from the rocks among which they grow. When I first put them on exhibition in the Missouri Botanical Garden the plants were literally "touched to death." Visitors could not realize they were real plants!

Most of the mimic mesembryanthemums are of dwarf nature and therefore many more pots can be accommodated in a windowsill or on a greenhouse bench than with the shrubby kinds. On the whole mesembryanthemums make but modest demands upon the connoisseur of bizarre things. A sunny location is a primary condition and of equal importance is the soil in which they are to be grown. It should be light and well drained. Gravel and broken fragments of limestone and other rocks should be placed around the plants as a precaution against rot diseases which often set in when the succulent bodies come in contact with the wet soil. The golden rule in watering is "rather less than too much" and avoid applying water on cool cloudy days or when the sun's rays are directly on the plants. Mimic mesembryanthemums require shallow pots like seed pans, but the shrubby kinds can have deeper containers, and will also stand more water.

There is a long list of South African mimics to choose from, belonging to such genera as *Argyroderma*, *Conophytum*, *Glottiphyllum*, *Lithops*, *Pleiospilos*, *Titanopsis*, *Faucaria*, *Fenestraria*, *Opthalmophyllum* and a dozen others. They are so utterly fascinating and popular that their descriptive names are so apt that we can call them Silver Skin, Cone Plant, Tongue Plant, Stone Face, Rock Plant, Lime-

stone Mimic, Tiger Jaw, Baby Toe, and Window Plant. On the other hand the shrubby and trailing kinds like *Aptenia*, *Aridaria*, *Delosperma*, *Lampranthus*, *Mesembryanthemum*, *Ruschia* and *Trichodiadema* are very suitable for hanging baskets or pedestals as their lovely stems drop rhythmically over the pots.

Finally I must mention the Lily Family which contains a number of surprises for the grower. Among these we find the haworthias, which have earned the title "Darlings of the succulent plant world." For the most part they are stemless plants, or when they have stems, these are slightly elongated and completely covered with short fleshy leaves. The plants seldom exceed 6–8 in. in height and the rosettes measure 2–6 in. in dia. Most of the haworthias are shade-loving plants but this does not mean that light is entirely to be denied them. In their native African home haworthias conceal themselves under shrubs and are often difficult to locate since some of them look like small birds' nests; others even simulate small cobwebs, and the transparent species frequently draw themselves into the ground, only the pellucid leaf portions being exposed to view. There are more than 100 species and varieties known to exist.

All the haworthias are very useful and effective for pot culture. As with all succulents, efficient drainage is necessary at all times. Such species as *Haworthia arachnoides*, *H. truncata* and *H. cymbiformis* representing the light green, transparent types, will require a more porous soil and less water than the dark green, mottled or unspotted species like *H. margaritifera*, *H. fasciata*, *H. limifolia* and *H. reinwardtii*. Water sparingly in the dull wintry season and resort to the immersion method for best results. Never allow drops of water to remain for long in the crowns of the delicate bloated species like *H. turgida*, *H. planifolia* and *H. denticulata*, to prevent rot or burn.

One nice feature of haworthias is that they multiply readily by means of offsets and stolons. A single plant will fill up a pot with plantlets in a few months. Haworthias also propagate from whole leaves and in many cases new plants arise viviparously on the flower stalks. *H. fasciata* and *H. margaritifera* with their varieties ought to be included in every collection. Both are very beautiful species marked by prominent tubercles that converge into horizontal bands on the underside of the leaves or by prominent pearl-like warts on the outside as well as inside of the leaves giving the plants an exceptionally striking appearance. Another precious gem is *H. limifolia* which resembles a carved piece of stone or wrought-iron ornamentation. No matter what haworthia falls into the hands of plant collectors it is bound to intrigue. Remember, too, that they can be used in dish gardens, as novelties and in other shallow containers as the root system is not too extensive.

Gasterias are very close relatives of the haworthias. Usually they are more robust plants with 2-ranked leaves spreading out like a fan, but some assume rosettes and can also be dwarfs. They prefer a semi-shaded location and thrive exceedingly well in a sandy leaf-mold soil mixture with moderate waterings. Some of the species like *Gasteria maculata* are spotted with white which makes them very attractive.

No home, no greenhouse or tropic garden should be without an aloe or two. Aloes are desert lilies with very succulent leaves arranged in rosette fashion. They look like the common Century Plant or agave except that their leaves are full of gelatinous substance which is highly medicinal. The juice of 4 or 5 species has been used in laxatives and the juice of one *Aloe vera* is an excellent remedy for any kind of a burn. Housewives should include an aloe plant in their kitchen just in case someone gets burned working around the stove. All one need to do is to cut off a piece of the leaf and apply the jelly to the burn.

There are all kinds of aloes—dwarf, medium sized and treelike. The leaves of many are spotted, mottled or striped. An old favorite is the handsome dwarf Partridge Breast, *Aloe variegata*, whose leaves are arranged in triangular fashion. They are dark green margined and marbled with white. *A. nobilis* is another small growing species punctuated with golden spines along the leaf margins. No matter what aloe is grown it is sure to please. The leaves often twist and curve which makes them ideal for flower arrangement work.

As is to be seen from this discourse there are thousands of succulents in existence, many of which make excellent house plants and are so easy to care for in the dry air of our living rooms. Why not give them a trial?

LADISLAUS CUTAK

For more information on culture see "Cactus Guide" by Ladislaus Cutak, Van Nostrand, 1956. For information on identification with profuse illustrations see "A Handbook of Succulent Plants" (3 vol.) by Hermann Jacobsen, Blandford Press, London 1954. Also "Exotica 3" by A. B. Graf, Roehrs Co., Rutherford N. J., 1963, with 11,300 photographs of plants, is a unique reference.

CACTUS. Also see CACTI AND SUCCULENTS.

AWL = *Gymnocalycium* sp.
BALL = *Notocactus* sp.
CHRISTMAS = *Schlumbergera truncata*.
COB = *Lobivia* sp.
FAMILY = *Cactaceae*.

FIRECRACKER = *Cleistocactus baumannii*.
GIANT = *Carnegia gigantea*.
GOLD BALL = *Echinocactus grusonii*.
HAIRBRUSH = *Pachycereus pecten*.
HEDGEHOG = *Echinocereus* sp.
MISSOURI = *Coryphantha missouriensis*.
MOUNTAIN = *Oreocereus* sp.
OLD LADY = *Mammilaria hahniana*.
OLD MAN = *Cephalocereus senilis*.
ORCHID = *Nopalxochia ackermannii*.
ORGAN-PIPE = *Lemaireocereus marginatus*.
PEANUT = *Chamaecereus silvestri*.
PINCUSHION = *Mamillaria vivipara*.
RAT-TAIL = *Aporocactus flagelliformis*.
SEA URCHIN = *Echinopsis* sp.
SERPENT = *Nyctocereus serpentinus*.
SNOWBALL = *Pediocactus simpsonii*.
SNOWBALL = *Epostoa lanata*.
STAR = *Astrophytum ornatum*.
STRAWBERRY = *Ferocactus setispinus*.
WHITE TORCH = *Trichocereus spachianus*.

CAESALPINIA (ceye-sal-PEYE-nia)

gilliesii   20′   Zone 10   Paradise Poinciana
With featherlike leaves, rounded leaflets, this is widely distributed throughout the tropics of the world. Like other members of this genus it is valued for its bright-colored flowers, in this species yellow, each with 5 thin, spreading petals, and prominent, long red stamens and a projecting pistil. Fruits are flat seed pods. Formerly listed as *Poinciana gilliesii*.

pulcherrima   15′   Zone 10   Barbados Flower-fence
Sometimes called "Barbados Pride," this woody shrub is native to the Tropics and is valued for its clusters of bright red and yellow flowers, each one with 5 petals and 10 extremely long and graceful red stamens which are 2½ in. long. The petals may sometimes be red with yellow margins. 'Flava' has yellow flowers. Fruits are flat green pods about 4 in. long and the alternate evergreen leaves are doubly compound with small, rounded leaflets about ¾ in. long. Frequently used in making hedges, in which case the plants might be spaced 2 ft. apart. Propagated by slowly germinating seeds which might be helped by soaking in hot water prior to sowing. Formerly *Poinciana pulcherrima*.

CAESPITOSE. Matted, growing in tufts or dense clumps; turflike.

CAJANUS (ca-JAY-nus)

cajan   10′   Zone 10   Pigeon-pea, Cajan
A shrub, native to the Old World, often grown as an annual but can be grown out-of-doors in southern Fla. and often grown in greenhouses in the North. Belonging to the Pea Family, this is a popular plant in tropical countries for its edible peas. The leaves are alternate, each with 3

soft-hairy leaflets about 4 in. long. The pealike flowers are yellow to orange in axillary racemes, and the pods are 3 in. long. Propagation is either by seeds or cuttings.

CAJEPUT-TREE = *Melaleuca leucadendron*

CALABASH-TREE = *Crescentia cujete*

CALADIUM (kal-AY-dium). These are tropical plants from South America with large heart-shaped leaves 6–24 in. long that are variously colored and for which they are valued especially as ornamental potted plants indoors. The leaves have various patterns of white, red, pink and green, depending on the variety, and there are at least 50 of these (or hybrids) being currently offered by American nurseries. They grow from tubers which can be divided early in the spring as soon as they start growth. The flowers are not very ornamental. In the far South they are planted out-of-doors in rich soil in the shade, with about 1 in. of soil over the tuber. In green-houses in the North they are started in peat moss, about 2–3 in. over the top of the tubers, kept at 70–85° F. and when they start to root, potted and sunk in soil out-of-doors in the shade after about June 15th. They should not be allowed to dry out. At the end of a season when the leaves die, withhold water from them and store in a cool cellar. Do not water. Start in greenhouse in Feb. or March. In the humid and warm conservatory in the winter they make very colorful specimens. Easily propagated by division and by seed.

Of the hybrids some of the most popular at the moment are **'Ace of Hearts'**, leaves red and **'Candidum'**, leaves with green veins; **'Little Miss Muffet'**, 8–12 in., wine red; **'White Queen'**, 18–20 in., whitish leaves; **'Postman Joyner'**, dark red leaves.

bicolor   2'   **Zone 10**   **Common Caladium**
This is the species most often cultivated, native to tropical America, with oval leaves colored in many patterns but with red predominating, bluish-green beneath, the leaf about 4 times the length of the blade.

humboldtii   6"–8"   **Zone 10**   **Humboldt Caladium**
Native to Brazil, leaves ovate or oblong, green, spotted with white markings and petioles 2–3 times the length of the blade.

picturatum   8"–10"   **Zone 10**   **Mottled Caladium**
Another species from Brazil with lanceolate leaves, colored variously above and the petioles variegated below.

CALAMINTHA (cal-a-MIN-tha)
nepeta (*Satureja calamintha*)   1'–2'   **Zone 6 Calamint Savory**
This attractive, evergreen, perennial Mint

forms a low mat of neat oval leaves on prostrate creeping rootstocks. The lavender flowers are borne in whorls between the leaves in early summer, and it has long been grown as a popular herb. Native to Europe.

CALANDRINIA (kal-an-DRIN-ia). This genus is a member of the Portulaca Family. The plants are low herbs with fleshy alternate leaves and reddish flowers in panicles. Propagated by seeds or cuttings. Those listed here are best treated as annuals.

ciliata   18"   **annual**   **Desert Rock-purslane**
With purple or whitish flowers borne in the leaf axils. The var. **menziesii** has crimson flowers about an inch wide. These are native to western North America. Some botanists consider the variety a species itself.

grandiflora   1"–3"   **annual**   **Common Rock-purslane**
The leaves are 4–8 in. long, light purple flowers about an inch wide. Native to Chile.

umbellata   6"   **annual**   **Peruvian Rock-purslane**
With bright crimson-magenta flowers, $\frac{3}{4}$ in. across, many in a cluster. The stems are trailing, hence it is a nice plant for the rock garden. Native to Peru.

CALANTHE (kal-ANTH-e). These are either terrestrial or epiphytic orchids, some with pseudobulbs. They are deciduous greenhouse plants and should be given a rest after they are through flowering. The species **C. vestita** has pseudobulbs 3 in. high, leaves $1\frac{1}{2}$ ft. long, white to creamy-colored flowers in 6–12 flowered racemes on scapes $2\frac{1}{2}$ ft. long. Native to Borneo. Many varieties of this species have been described. For culture and propagation see ORCHID.

CALATHEA (kal-aTHEE-a). Foliage plants, tropical American, with flowers seldom produced in cultivation. The leaves are mottled or striped in several colors on long stalks. They need plenty of fertilizer in the greenhouse in order to produce the best colors in their leaves, and should be shaded. Propagated by division of plants, tubers or cuttings taken in the spring. Suitable for growing in terrariums but possibly not the drier atmosphere of the modern house. Commercial sources are difficult to find.

illustris   9"   **Zone 10**   **White Margin Calathea**
Leaves 6 in. long and 5 in. wide colored a shining olive green above with a white margin and red beneath. Native to Ecuador.

lietzei   2'   **Zone 10**   **Leitz Calathea**
Leaves 9 in. long, $2\frac{1}{2}$ in. wide, deep green with sharply contrasting, alternating lateral bands of silvery green, purplish red underneath. It sends up erect runners bearing young plantlets. Native to Brazil.

makoyana   4'   **Zone 10**   **Makoy Calathea**

Leaves oval, the surface a feathery design of opaque olive-green lines and ovals, alternately short and long in a field of yellow-green; purplish red beneath. A strikingly beautiful foliage plant. Native to Brazil.

ornata 3′ Zone 10 **Bigleaf Calathea**
Leaves 3 ft. long, rich green above and dull purple-red beneath but variable, often striped with pink or white when young; a metallic coppery green when more mature; pale wine red underneath. Native to Columbia.

roseopicta 8″ Zone 10 **Red Margin Calathea**
Leaves 9 in. long, unequal sides, 6 in. wide, dark green above but the area by the midrib is red changing to silver-pink when mature; purple beneath. Native to Brazil.

undulata 8″ Zone 10 **White Stripe Calathea**
Leaves 4 in. long and 2 in. wide, shining dark green above with a central white stripe, purple underneath. Native to Peru.

vittata 3′ Zone 10
A bushy plant with short stalked leaves 1½ ft. long, 9 in. wide, lanceolate, light green with symmetrical stripes of silver-green to white between the lateral veins; yellowish green beneath. Native to Colombia.

zebrina 3′ Zone 10 **Zebra Calathea**
Leaves 2 ft. long and a foot wide, the magnificent thin leaves a deep velvety green, the midrib and lateral veins being pale or yellow-green, purplish beneath. Native to Brazil.

CALCEOLARIA (kal-see-o-LAIR-ia). Mostly native from Mexico to Chile, one species is a prized item for greenhouse forcing, popular everywhere, and several others, little known, are worthwhile garden annuals. All belong to the Snapdragon Family and have bright-colored, slipperlike or pouch-shaped flowers, mostly yellow, but some species have variously colored flowers, ranging in size from ½–2 in. The leaves are opposite or whorled. Some are herbaceous but *C. integrifolia* is woody.

The 4 species mentioned as annuals can easily be grown from seed sown in the greenhouse in Feb. and March and set out in late May, but when sown in flats or pans a glass should be placed on top to keep the soil surface from drying out until the seedlings have started.

Insect Pests

When grown in the greenhouse, red spider mite, white fly and general greenhouse insect pests infest these plants. Sprays with insecticide #15 or #13 are effective.

chelidonioides 1′–3′ annual
A South American native with leaves 8 in. long, toothed; small yellow flowers ½ in. long and 2 in. wide in summer.

crenatiflora 2½′ Zone 9 **Common Calceolaria**
This is the florist's plant best grown in greenhouses, and many varieties have been produced with flowers in many colors ranging from yellow to red to brown. The flowers are an inch long and are produced over a long period in April and May. Seed for greenhouse plants is usually sown in the summer.

integrifolia 6′ Zone 9 **Bush Calceolaria**
A popular plant for bedding purposes especially in Europe, with simple leaves 1–3 in. long and yellowish to red-brown unspotted flowers ½ in. long. Native to Chile. This can be propagated by cuttings as well as seeds for it is one of the woody species. This is not very popular in America although it is available from a few sources in Calif.

mexicana 1′ annual **Mexican Calceolaria**
Native to Mexico with small yellow flowers ½ in. long and ¼ in. wide in summer.

profusa 3′ annual **Clibran Calceolaria**
Golden-yellow flowers, very graceful.

tripartita 2′ annual **Bedding Calceolaria**
With hairy leaves 8 in. long; pale yellow flowers ½ in. long and ⅓ in. wide. Native from Ecuador to Chile.

CALCIUM NITRATE. An inorganic fertilizer containing 15.5%–16% nitrogen, 48% calcium carbonate, quick acting and leaving an alkaline soil reaction. Recommended use is 1 oz. per sq. yard of garden soil.

CALENDAR OF MONTHLY OPERATIONS. A printed list of Monthly Operations is not suitable for use in all parts of the country unless it is divided into four or more parts for each of the different climatic areas of this great land. One will learn much more about gardening by making up one's own calendar of operations, geared to one's own interests and climate. This may take some study, but it is worth the effort and, once made, it holds up year after year.

First, the average dates of the last frost in the spring and of the first frost in the fall might be obtained, thus giving the number of days of growing season. Working backwards from the last spring frost, one would determine when to plant various flowers and vegetables in the pit house or greenhouse or in the open soil. Also going on the calendar would be dates for planting successive crops of peas, beans, corn, gladiolus, etc. If one had a pet hobby of growing lilies out-of-doors, it could be noted on the calendar when to fertilize for best results, when to spray for plant lice and disease, when to take scales from the bulbs for propagation, etc. The calendar need not be cluttered up with many garden operations in which the gardener is not interested or with which he is thoroughly familiar. It should be simple, with a minimum number of entries to suit his particular needs and requirements. Try making one.

CALENDULA (kal-EN-yew-la).

officinalis   1′–2′   annual   Pot-marigold
These plants have always been valued in the garden for their reliable growth and deep orange-colored flowers up to 4 in. across during the summer. They make excellent flowers for cutting. Now there are pale yellow, cream-colored, single or double-ray pot-marigolds available. All are raised easily from seed. They make fine pot plants and perform well in the greenhouse in winter. Seeds are sown in April, set out in a sunny situation in May after all frost is over. Native to southern Europe. As an herb the flower petals are sometimes used to give color to stews or puddings, and medicinally as the basis for a tincture in treating cuts, burns and sprains.

Insect Pests

Whitefly, red spider mite and tarnished plant bug may infest Calendula. Use insecticides #15 or #13, when necessary. Greenhouse leaf tier is controlled with insecticide #15 or #9.

Diseases

Leaf spot is controlled by fungicides #D or #F. Stem rot control requires soil sterilization and destruction of infected plants. Cucumber mosaic virus and tobacco ring spot virus are spread by aphids and other sucking insects which must be controlled. See APHIDS. Plants showing mottled and distorted leaves should be immediately destroyed. Powdery mildew produces typical white powdery growth until controlled by fungicide #V or #M.

CALIFORNIA-FUSCHIA = *Zauschneria californica*

CALIFORNIA-LAUREL = *Umbellularia californica*

CALIFORNIA-NUTMEG = *Torreya californica*

CALIFORNIA-POPPY = *Eschscholzia californica*

CALLA (KAL-la)

palustris   8″–12″   Zone 2   Water-arum
This is a common plant of swamps and edges of ponds from Alaska throughout Canada to N.Y. and N.J., and Minn. The arrow-shaped leaves have rather fleshy stems and rise from the long rootstalks to a few inches above the surface of the water. The flower-head is a spathe, green on the outside, white within, surrounding the spadix which is covered with small yellow flowers blooming in May and June. These flowers develop into red berries in autumn. An excellent plant for the bog garden because it is so hardy, although it will not thrive in running

water. Propagation is division of the rootstalk in spring. One may also root sections of the stem in mud during the summer, or the seeds, removed from the pulp, may be planted in fall. Sometimes called Wild Calla, but not to be confused with the popularly named Calla which is a species of *Zantedeschia*.

CALLA-LILY. A confusing but unfortunately popular name. The Wild Calla (*Calla palustris*) might best be termed Water-arum. The so-called popular Calla-lily (*Zantedeschia* sp.) might best be termed simply Calla as a popular English name.

CALLIANDRA (kal-i-AND-ra)

californica   4′   Zone 10   California Calliandra
Flowers purple with long purple stamens; leaflets ¼ in. long, and weak spines at the base of the petioles. Native to Lower Calif.

guildingii   15′–25′   Zone 10   Trinidad Calliandra
A tree from the West Indies with leaflets 1–2 in. long, greenish-white flowers borne in dense heads with conspicuously showy purple stamens 3 in. long.

haematocephala   30′   Zone 10   Redhead Powderpuff
With handsome dark evergreen foliage, the flowers appearing mostly from Dec. to April are conspicuous because of the 4-inch masses of red stamens. The fruit is merely a flat, curled pod.

CALLICARPA (kal-i-CARP-a). Mostly deciduous, opposite-leaved shrubs, with small pink, blue or violet flowers in July or Aug. The flowers, mostly hidden by the leaves, are followed in the fall by clusters of bright purple or white berries about ⅛ in. wide. Since the leaves turn yellow and drop in early autumn, the brightly colored fruits are conspicuously displayed. In the North the plant may be killed to the ground in the winter, but since it flowers on the current year's growth, it can still send up new shoots that will flower and fruit in one season. Propagated by seed sown as soon as ripe or by seed stored dry in an airtight container in a cool place and then sown when needed. Also easily propagated by division of the clump, by hardwood or softwood cuttings. See CUTTINGS.

americana   6′   Zone 7   American Beautyberry
A native American shrub, this is found from Md. to Tex. and Okla. and is used in southern gardens because of its bright purple berries which have a dia. of about 3/16 in. The leaves are 4–6 in. long and the small flowers are bluish. It has little else of ornamental value except the fruits, but these are profusely borne and very prominent in the early fall because of their unique color. There is a white-fruiting form **(lactea)** which is especially outstanding when planted in conjunction with the purple-fruited

species. There are excellent plantings of this rare variety, which is said to "come true" from seed, at Callaway Gardens, Pine Mountain, Ga. The berry has been said to be edible, but is not very tasty.

bodinieri 9′ Zones 5-6 Bodinier Beauty-berry
This is one of the better species with pale bluish-lilac fruits in the fall. The leaves are 2–5 in. long, the flowers lilac colored. Native to China. This, like some of the others, flowers and fruits better if several plants are grown in a clump together, especially if they are grown from seeds.

dichotoma 1′-4′ Zones 5-6 Purple Beauty-berry
Similar to *C. japonica* but smaller in all its parts. Native to China and Korea.

japonica 4½′ Zones 5-6 Japanese Beauty-berry
An upright shrub with fairly inconspicuous flowers but with uniquely colored purple fruits borne on the tips of the current year's growth and remaining on the plant a few weeks after the leaves have fallen. The berries are about $\frac{3}{16}$ in. wide and are colored violet to metallic purple. The foliage turns yellow in the fall. A Japanese native, this plant is conspicuous in the fall only, for the minute flowers are not noticeable when they appear in early July. The variety 'Leuco-carpa', with white fruits, is not nearly so effective as the purple-fruiting species.

CALLICORE ROSEA = *Amaryllis belladonna*

CALLIOPSIS. See COREOPSIS.

CALLIRHOE (kal-LI-ro-ee). Native American annual herbs with alternate, lobed leaves and bright pink or purplish flowers easily grown from seeds sown after all danger of frost is past in the place where they are to grow, preferably in the full sun.

digitata 1½′ annual Finger Poppy-mallow
Flowers rosy purple to violet, 2 in. wide, with deeply parted linear leaves. Native from Mo. to Mexico.

involucrata 1′-2′ Zone 3 Low Poppy-mallow
A sprawling perennial herb found in dry, sunny sites in the Middle West, the Poppy-mallow is a rather hairy plant with alternate leaves which are divided into from 5–7 lobes and are deeply cut. The flowers, which may vary in color from a deep, reddish pink to reddish purple, have 5 heart-shaped petals, and are 2½ in. wide. The stamens, typical of the Mallow Family, are fused into a central column. The flowers rise from the axils of the leaves and appear from June to Aug. A most attractive plant for the wild garden, especially for dry sunny areas where the soil is good. Propaga-

tion is by division in either spring or fall.

papaver 1′ annual
With 3-parted leaves and rose or violet flowers 2 in. across. Native from Fla. to Tex.

CALLISTEMON (kal-iss-TEE-mon)

citrinus (*lanceolatus*) **30′ Zone 9 Lemon Bottlebrush**
Coming from Australia, this is widely popular in the southern parts of Fla. and Calif. because of the flower spikes. The flowers are mostly made up of conspicuous bright red stamens each about 1 in. long and resembling a bottle-brush because they are so numerous. There are some selected clones far superior to others. Seedlings should be avoided as most of them are inferior to the selected strains. Fortunately this plant will grow in dry soil. The evergreen leaves are 3 in. long but largely ineffective so this plant might best be planted in front of a dense background of evergreens. The fruit is a woody capsule, not especially ornamental on the plant but used a great deal in dried arrangements. It is propagated by hardwood cuttings and by seeds.

CALLISTEPHUS (kal-ISS-tee-fuss)

chinensis 6″-24″ annual China Aster
This Asiatic species contains many very popular garden plants, which not so many years ago were unpopular because of the inroads of various diseases. Now, with modern immune or resistant strains they can be grown although they do require a bit of attention to detail. They should not be grown near pot-marigolds, nor should they be grown in the same soil for more than 2–3 years at a time. Any particular clone usually blooms for only 5–7 weeks, hence, to have them in bloom from midsummer into the fall, and this can be done, one should take advantage of the different groups available—early, midseason and late blooming—and select varieties from each, or else make several plantings of a single variety. Seed can be planted after the last hard frost, but it takes the seed 2 weeks to germinate and the plants many weeks after that to reach flowering size, so at least for the early blossoms it might be best to start a few indoors in March.

Asters are single or very double—members of the Composite Family—with flower-heads 2–5 in. across, blue, white, pink and red. There are many varieties being sold, so one should be able to select a variety that will bloom at the right time and have the right colored flowers.

Insect Pests

Blister beetles often eat the petals of the buds, and flowers of China Aster require treatment with insecticides #9 or #15 as soon as observed. Root aphids are attracted to this flower and they weaken and stunt the plants mysteriously. Ants carry the aphids to the roots and ant control with insecticide #15 is effective. Six-spotted leafhopper sucks the juices and weakens the plants but is more important as the carrier of the yellows virus which causes weak spindly yellow growth and dwarfed off-color blooms. Spraying with insecticide #15 or #9 kills many hoppers and reduces yellows but seldom prevents the diseases. Some growers have protected the plants with screens of 18–20 mesh wire or cloth at least 5 ft. high.

Diseases

Wilt is the most serious disease attacking seedlings and blooming plants to cause them to die suddenly. The fungus lives on the seed and in the soil. Wilt-resistant strains should be planted preferably in soil where asters have not grown recently and seedlings should be grown in sterilized soil. Susceptible seed should be treated by soaking in $\frac{1}{10}$% corrosive sublimate or $\frac{1}{4}$% Semesan for $\frac{1}{2}$ hr. See FUNGICIDES. Rust develops orange powdery spores on the underside of leaves. Sprays of fungicide #D are effective.

CALLITRIS (kal-LY-tris)
  preissii (*C. robusta*) **15'-70' Zone 9 Sturdy
                                              Cypress-pine**
Sometimes a shrub, sometimes a tree, native to Australia, with blackish evergreen, scalelike leaves, valued as a windbreak in both Fla. and Calif., where it is able to withstand drought and hot temperatures. In general appearance it reminds one of the Red-cedar.
  robusta = *C. preissii*

CALLUNA (kal-LOON-a)
  vulgaris   18″   Zone 4   Heather
This common garden plant is appreciated by everyone. It is a member of the Heath Family and is widely distributed over Europe, where it can grow by the square mile. Its diminutive white, pink and red flower spikes are always appreciated during the summer, its evergreen foliage makes it an effective ground cover wherever it is grown, and the many varieties with colored foliage add interest as well.

Heathers grow on acid soils of low productivity. In fact, they must have poor soil, for if it is fertile the plants soon become leggy and may even die. The soil should be reasonably moist, but not actually wet. If the plants grow too tall or too fast, they should be clipped or mowed and this is best done in the early spring.

They must have plenty of sunshine to bloom well. They will withstand shade as ground covers, but do not bloom well unless they grow in the full sun. In the North it is best to mulch them with hay or straw or evergreen boughs over winter, and even then the plants sometimes have a peculiar way of dying suddenly for no apparent reason.

Everyone who has ever grown heather knows that cut stems, with or without flowers, may be dried and used indoors almost indefinitely. This plant should not be confused with the Spring Heath (*Erica carnea*) which is a closely related plant which blooms in the spring, while the true heather blooms in the late summer and early autumn. The whole shrub, or the young branches and twigs, are sometimes used as a dye for yellow and bronze colors.

There are about 50 varieties being grown in America today. Of these, the following are among the best:

Varieties

	HEIGHT	FLOWER COLOR	TIME OF BLOOM
'Aurea'	18 in.	purple	Aug.–Oct.
'County Wicklow'	18 in.	double, pink	Aug.–Oct.
'Cuprea'	12 in.	purple	Aug.–Oct.
'Foxii Nana'	4 in.	purple	Aug.–Oct.
'H. E. Beale'	24 in.	pink	Aug.–Oct.
'J. H. Hamilton'	9 in.	double, coral pink	Aug.–Oct.
'Mair's Variety'	24 in.	white	July–Sept.
'Mrs. Pat'	8 in.	light purple	July–Sept.
'Mrs. Ronald Gray'	4 in.	reddish	July–Sept.
'Nana Compacta'	6 in.	pink	July–Sept.
'Plena Multiplex'	18 in.	double, pink	Aug.–Oct.
'Searlei Aurea'	12 in.	white	Aug.–Oct.
'Sister Anne'	6 in.	pink	Aug.–Sept.
'Tomentosa'	10 in.	lavender	July–Sept.

Propagation

Seed can be sown any time, but the many colorful varieties are best propagated asexually by division, softwood and hardwood cuttings and are best taken in the late summer. See CUTTINGS.

CALLUS. A hard prominence or protuberance; the roll of new covering tissue.

CALOCEDRUS (cal-o-SEE-drus)

decurrens (*Libocedrus decurrens*) **135′ Zone 5**
California Incense-cedar

An excellent tree for formal plantings well clothed with branches to the base of the tree and native to Ore. and northern Calif. This is a narrowly columnar evergreen with scalelike lustrous foliage and branchlets with vertical or "edgewise" leaves. The leaves are very aromatic when crushed and are borne in vertical planes (instead of horizontal, like those of *Thuja plicata*). Practically no foliage pests attack the tree. and it requires a good soil and plenty of atmospheric moisture, without which it will not thrive.

Propagation

Seeds may be processed as soon as ripe or stored dry in airtight containers in a cool place for up to a year and then processed. In either case they should be stratified at 40° F. for 3 months, then sown. Varieties can be grafted on *Thuja occidentalis*. Softwood cuttings can be rooted. See STRATIFICATION, GRAFTING, CUTTINGS.

CALOCHORTUS (kal-o-KORT-us)

1′–2′ Zone 3 Mariposa-lily

This genus includes nearly 50 American species of small tuliplike plants growing from corms, native from southern Calif. through the high mountain areas to Colo. and Ore. There they are at their best. They can be planted in northern rock gardens but should be well mulched after the first freeze. They do not live too many years in cultivation, but many gardeners want to try them. Given poor, light soil with good drainage and planted 2 in. deep, they should live through a few winters if they are properly mulched. The flowers, small and tuliplike, are terminal in small clusters, range in color from white, through yellow and brown to purple, with various combinations. They are popularly grouped into 3 general classes: "star-tulips" or "cat's-ears"; "globe-tulip" or "fairy-lanterns" and "mariposa-lilies" or "butterfly-tulips" which are the showiest of the group bearing grasslike foliage and very colorful flowers 3–4 in. across during late spring.

After the plants are through blooming and the foliage has died, the corms can be lifted, dried and stored in a cool place until autumn, then replanted. If left in the ground over summer, and it is wet, they can easily be killed. In western areas where the plants are native it is not necessary to lift them and store them over summer.

Propagation is by seed and also by the small offsets produced at the base of a parent corm.

Calochortus—Mariposa-lily

"Globe" and "star-tulip" forms include the following species: **C. amabilis** with fragrant yellow flowers; **C. albus** with white flowers; **C. amoenus**—rose colored; **C. monophyllus**—bright yellow; **C. folmiel**—white-tinged purple; **C. uniflorus**—pale lilac. Of the "mariposa-lilies" the best species are: **C. clavatus** with yellow and brown flowers; **C. vestae**—white-tinged purple; **C. venustus** and several varieties of which **C. citrinus** is yellow and maroon; **C. nuttallii**, the Sego-lily—white lined and blotched purple.

CALONYCTION = IPOMOEA

CALOPHYLLUM (kal-o-FILL-um)

inophyllum 60′ Zone 10 Indiapoon Beauty-
leaf

Native to India and tropical Pacific islands, this has smooth, leathery, glossy leaves and clusters of white, fragrant, waxy flowers, about 1 in. across. Its fruit is a small drupe and green, containing much oil.

CALOPOGON (kal-o-PO-gon)

tuberosus (*pulchellus*) **12″–15″ Zone 3 Grass**
Pink Orchid

A dainty member of the Orchid Family and a native of bogs and wetland meadows over all the eastern U.S. and Canada, the Grass Pink Orchid sends up a single long leaf, which may be up to 12 in. long, and which encases the lower portion of the flower stalk. This generally grows a few inches taller than the leaf and bears a loose terminal cluster of from 3–15 purple-pink flowers, resembling tiny orchids. The flowers appear in June. An excellent plant for the acid bog garden with a pH of 4–5.

CALTHA (KAL-tha)

leptosepala　1′　Zone 3　Elkslip Marsh-marigold

This member of the Buttercup Family is unusual in having clumps of oval-shaped leaves, 6 in. high, and solitary white flowers tinted with blue about an inch wide, appearing in June and July. The plant is native to the mountains of western U.S. from the Rockies to Alaska.

palustris　1′–3′　Zone 3　Marsh-marigold, Cowslip

The Marsh-marigold is a pretty plant of the swamps and marshes over much of Canada, reaching into Labrador and Alaska and extending southward to the Carolinas, Tenn., Iowa and Neb. The heart-shaped leaves, often with toothed margins, are supported on fleshy stems. The flower stalks arise from the base of the leaves and commonly bear two flowers. These consist of 5 yellow sepals and resemble the Buttercup, in which family this plant belongs. It flowers in April and dies to the ground in summer. Thus, it may be planted in a spot which although wet in spring, will dry out later in the season. Propagation is by division before or after the plant flowers, or by seed. '**Alba**' has white flowers; '**Montrosa-plena**' has large double flowers.

CALYCANTHACEAE = The Sweet-shrub Family

CALYCANTHUS (kal-ik-ANTH-us). Opposite-leaved deciduous shrubs native to the southeastern U.S. and one species native to Calif., with leaves and twigs that are aromatic when crushed. The flowers, composed of many dark-colored ribbonlike petals are most aromatic and have been used popularly to place with clothing in the dresser drawer to give a sweet fragrance. Propagation is easily accomplished by layers and softwood cuttings. Seed is stratified as soon as it is ripe and kept at 40° F. for 3 months, when it can be sown. Shrubs are also easily divided by using a sharp spade.

fertilis　9′　Zone 5　Pale Sweetshrub

Similar to *C. floridus* but not quite as hardy nor as fragrant and nowhere near as popular. Native from Pa. to Ga. The seeds contain an alkaloid which is similar to strychnine in its physiological action and are reported to have poisoned cattle.

floridus　9′　Zone 4　Common Sweetshrub, Carolina Allspice

Native to the southeastern U.S., this old-fashioned favorite was popular years ago because of the aromatic fragrance of the flowers. These are reddish brown, with small ribbonlike petals and they bloom in mid-May.

The plant grows well in almost any soil, but there is little else to recommend it for ornamental planting. It is easily propagated by cuttings, division, layers or seeds.

occidentalis　9′　Zone 6　California Sweet-shrub

Similar to *C. floridus* but of more open growth. Because it is native to Calif. it is occasionally used there in landscape planting but much better shrubs are available for landscape purposes.

CALYPSO (kal-IP-so)

bulbosa　6″　Zone 2　Calypso

Probably this is one of the northernmost members of the Orchid Family, and may be found growing in moist woods and cedar swamps from Labrador to the Aleutian Islands and in the U.S. as far south as N.Mex. It is a tuberous plant producing 1 flower stalk and 1 basal leaf. The flower is pink and looks much like a tiny Lady's-slipper, blooming in May and June. A fine plant for the bog garden.

CALYSTEGIA (cal-is-TEEG-ia)

sepium　vine　Zone 3　Hedge Glorybind

A pernicious weed that is a perennial twining vine with alternate, simple leaves having a somewhat triangular outline. The white to pale-pink flowers, closely resembling the cultivated Morning-glory to which it is related, are 2 in. across and are borne on long pedicels at the axils of the leaves and appear throughout the spring and summer. It is a common roadside plant in North America and is propagated readily from seed sown in spring. Although it is quite an attractive plant, care should be taken to keep it within bounds. All its roots must be destroyed to eliminate this vigorous-growing pest. For control see WEED-CONTROLLING CHEMICALS.

spithamaea　15″–20″　Zone 3　Low Bindweed

An erect plant, generally without branches, and with alternate, oval leaves which increase in size as they ascend the stem. The trumpet-shaped white or pinkish flowers occur singly in the axils of the leaves. The plant prefers rather dry, sunny locations and may be found from New England to N.Car. and west to Minn., flowering during the late spring and early summer. It may be propagated from seed for the wild garden, although its blooming period is contemporaneous with many more colorful wild plants.

CALYX. The outer perianth of the flower; the collective term for sepals.

CAMASS. See CAMASSIA.

CAMASSIA (kam-ASS-ia). Delicate spring-flowering bulbs with grasslike leaves belonging to the Lily Family, native to North America. They should be planted in the fall. The flowers are blue to white, with 6 parts like lilies but only $\frac{1}{2}$–1 in. long, appearing at about the same time as the flowers of daffodils. Propagated by seed, sometimes self-sown. The bulbs should be planted 4 in. deep and 9 in. apart.

cusickii   3′   Zone 5   Cusick Camass
A native to Ore., this produces a flower spike of 50–300 pale blue flowers each about an inch long. The leaves are 20 in. long and $1\frac{1}{2}$ in. wide.

leichtlinii   2′   Zone 5   Leichtlin Camass
Native from British Columbia to Calif., the flowers of this species are purplish blue to whitish, the leaves 3 ft. long and $\frac{3}{4}$ in. wide.

quamash   2′–3′   Zone 5   Common Camass
Native from British Columbia to Calif., this has long, narrow strap-shaped leaves and blue to white flowers in foot-long racemes. The bulbs of this were cooked and eaten by the Indians.

scilloides   18″   Zone 5   Wild Hyacinth or **Atlantic Camass**
One of the most attractive of the wild flowers, this plant should be used more often with other spring-flowering bulbs, as well as in the wild garden. From the bulb arise narrow, grasslike leaves and a flower stalk which bears 6–10 pale blue flowers about $\frac{1}{2}$ in. in dia. Each flower has 6 segments. It blooms in May and June. A native of sparse woodlands and open meadows from Pa. to Ala. and southwest as far as Tex. The bulbs may be transplanted in late summer or fall and thereafter should be left undisturbed unless they become overcrowded. Culture should be in good, well-drained soil.

CAMBIUM. The layer of delicate, rapidly dividing, living cells that form wood internally and bark externally, situated just beneath the bark of most dicotyledonous plants.

CAMELINA (camel-I-na) sp. **annual False Flax**
Several species of annual weeds introduced into North America from Europe, chiefly found in grain fields of the Midwest. Somewhat similar to the more common Shepherd's Purse (*Capsilla bursa-pastoris*), with small, pale yellow flowers and arrow-shaped alternate leaves.

CAMELLIA (kam-EEL-ya)
japonica   45′   Zone 7   Common Camellia
The large-flowering camellia, native to China and Japan, · has been popular in America for 150 years and is represented in American gardens at present by several hundred varieties. The plant is a large shrub or small tree with glossy, very dark evergreen leaves that are thick and leathery, about 4 in. long. The flowers, blooming from Oct. to April, are large and waxy, white, pink, red or variegated, single or double, from 2–5 in. wide. Normally, the single-flowered form will have 5 petals and a dense cluster of prominent yellow stamens in the center, but the semi-double and double forms have many. The so-called "semi-double" type

will have mature petals about the perimeter of the flower and a dense mass of smaller petals (actually modified stamens) in the center. The "double" form has mature petals regularly placed in a very definite arrangement in the flower or with no apparent petal arrangement at all. The flowers of some have the general form of roses, while others have the general flower form of peonies. The camellia specialist is particular about his flower selection, but for the amateur they are all beautiful and the 25 suggested varieties include some of the best available at present.

Camellias are excellent for growing in partially shaded situations where other plants might not bloom well. It is widely grown in the Southeast from N.Car. southward and on the Pacific Coast from Calif. to Vancouver, B.C. The plant is excellent in the garden for its glossy evergreen foliage alone. Most varieties can be grown in normally good soil of about 6.0 pH or slightly less, in full sun or partial shade. For further information concerning camellias and their culture, see "Camellias in America" by H. H. Hume, The Macmillan Company, 1946.

Insect Pests

Several scale insects, especially the camellia scale and mealy bugs, are serious pests of camellia. They are controlled by timely spraying with insecticide #15 or #14.

Diseases

Flower blight, causing spotted petals which ruin the flowers, is common on southern plants. Destroying infected blossoms and spraying under the plants with fungicide #D is suggested. Spraying the buds with fungicide #W is helpful. Anthracnose or canker which wilts the foliage and produces lesions on the bark is checked by spraying with fungicide #W and by growing resistant varieties.

Japonica Varieties

RED FLOWERS

'Adolph Audusson'—flower semi-double, 4 in. dia.

'Arajishi'—flower double, 3–4 in. dia., blooms early for this species.

'Aunt Jetty'—flower double, 4 in. dia., 2 in. high.

'C. M. Hovey'—flower double, $3\frac{1}{4}$–4 in. dia., flat, slightly variegated; one of the best and most dependable of all.

'Gloire De Nantes'—flower double, 4 in. dia., $1\frac{1}{2}$ in. high.

'Lady Vansittard'—flower semi-double, 4 in., dia.; $1\frac{1}{4}$ in. high.

'Mathotiana'—flower double, 4 in. dia., 2 in.

high, shaped very much like a rose.

'Prince Eugene Napoleon'—flower double, 4 in. dia., 1 in. high, rather flat.

'Professor C. S. Sargent'—flower double, 3–4 in. dia., 2 in. high. One of the hardiest and sometimes used as an understock on which the others are grafted.

PINK FLOWERS

'Debutante'—flower double, 3 in. dia., 1¾ in. high, excellent for corsages.

'Frau Minna Seidel'—flower double, 2½ in. dia., 1¼ in. high; one of the most popular varieties, excellent for the small garden.

'Lady Humes Blush'—flower double, 2¾ in. dia., 1¼ in. high.

'Magnoliaeflora'—flower single, 3½ in. dia., 1½ in. high.

'Otome'—flower double, 3½ in. dia., 1½ in. high, excellent for corsages.

'Sweeti Vera'—flower double, 4 in. dia., 2 in. high; petals marked with red lines and dots.

WHITE FLOWERS

'Alba Plena'—flower double, 4 in. dia., 3 in. high; one of oldest varieties in the U.S.

'Amabilis'—flower single, 3 in. dia.

'Imura'—flower semi-double, 4¾ in. dia.

'Purity'—flower double, 3½ in. dia., 1¼ in. high; excellent variety for corsages.

VARIEGATED FLOWERS

'Daikagura'—flower double, 4 in. dia., 2 in. high.

'Donckelari'—flower semi-double, 4 in. dia., 1½ in. high; one of hardiest varieties.

'Herme'—flower double, 3½ in. dia., 1¾ in. high; slightly fragrant.

'Kumasaka'—flower double, 4 in. dia., 1¼ in. high.

'Lady Clare'—flower semi-double, 4¾ in. dia., 1¼ in. high.

'Sara-Sa'—flower semi-double, 4½ in. dia., 1½ in. high; very popular variety.

reticulata   20′   Zones 8–9

The leathery, evergreen leaves of this species are 4 in. long and 1½–2 in. wide, broadly elliptic and dull green. The single flowers are 3–7 in. wide and colored a soft pink. Native to China and usually considered the least hardy of the camellias.

saluenensis   15′   Zones 7–8?

With shining, leathery, evergreen leaves, about 1½–2¼ in. long and ½–1 in. wide, and single flowers about 3 in. wide colored white, rose or carmine, blooming in March or April. Native to China.

sasanqua   20′   Zones 7–8   Sasanqua Camellia

There are nearly 75 varieties of this species listed by American nurserymen. It is characterized

because its flowers bloom just before those of *C. japonica* from Sept. to Dec.; the foliage is smaller and the plant is more or less open in its habit of growth. The evergreen leaves are only about 2 in. long, while those of *C. japonica* are 4 in. long. Native to China and Japan.

Varieties

'Alba'—flower single, white.

'Blanchette'—flower single, 2½ in. dia., white, tinted pink on petal margins.

'Briar Rose'—flower single, 3 in. dia., pink.

'Floribunda'—flower 3½″ wide, white and edged with lavender.

'Grandiflora Alba'—flower white, single, 3¾″ wide, one of the larger-flowering varieties of this species.

'Hebe'—flower single, 3 in. dia., pink.

'Hugh Evans'—flower single, 3 in. dia., rose colored.

'Mino-no-yuki'—flower double, 4 in. dia., white, faintly scented.

'Rosea'—flower 3¼″ wide, single, deep rose pink.

'Rubra Simplex'—flower single, rose red.

'Tanya'—flower single, 2 in. dia., rose colored.

'Versicolor'—flower single, 3″ wide; white at the center and becoming pink, with the margins lavender.

sinensis   30′   Zone 9   Tea

This evergreen shrub or tree, native to India and China, is grown in the Tropics as the source of tea (leaves) but is not commercially grown in the continental U.S. The alternate, leathery, evergreen leaves are 2–5 in. long and have shallow teeth. The white fragrant flowers are 1½ in. wide, borne either singly or in 2–5-flowered clusters. Very closely related to Camellia.

CAMOMILE. See ANTHEMIS.

CAMOMILE, GERMAN = *Matricaria recutita*

CAMPANULA (kam-PAN-ew-la). This is a large genus with more than 1500 perennial or annual species distributed over the temperate and subtropical regions of the world. The leaves are single, generally alternate, and toothed. In some species the basal leaves differ from those on the stalks. The flowers are generally blue or white, bell shaped and symmetrical. Some make excellent garden plants valued for their blue, violet, white or pink bell-shaped flowers. Propagated by seeds or division.

alliariaefolia   3′   Zone 3   Spurred Bellflower

White flowers, ¾–1¼ in. across, about an inch long, in spikes. Native to the Caucasus and Asia Minor.

americana 5′–6′ annual Tall Bellflower
Straight, unbranched stems bear the alternate, lanceolate, toothed leaves of the Tall Bellflower. The blue flowers, $\frac{1}{2}$–$\frac{3}{4}$ in. long, are clustered in the axils of the leaves, or above bracts which have the appearance of small leaves. The plant blooms from June to Aug. and may be found in woods from N.Y. to Fla. and west to the Mississippi River. This is a distinctly useful and beautiful plant for the wild garden. It prefers rich, moist soil and semi-shade. Propagation is by division in spring or fall. It can be treated either as an annual or a biennial.

aucheri 4″ Zone 5 Aucher Bellflower
A diminutive Bellflower from the Caucasus, the plant seldom grows more than 4 in. tall. Tufts of narrow, lanceolate leaves send up slender stalks on which hang the deep purple flowers an inch wide. The plant does well in gravelly, acid, well-drained soil in sun or light shade.

barbata 18″ Zone 6 Bearded Bellflower
From the mountainous regions of Europe, this gets its name from the fact that both the pale green leaves and the inside of the light blue flowers, borne on stalks 8–12 in. high, are hairy. Though the plant prefers a well-drained soil, it is not difficult to grow. Native to the mountains of Europe.

bononiensis 3′ Zone 3 Russian Bellflower
Leaves 2–3 in. long, plant erect, flowers an inch long, drooping and colored light purplish. Native to eastern Europe and S.W. Asia. Not often grown in America.

caespitosa 4″–8″ Zone 4
A low, tufted perennial with a tap root, native to the mountains of central Europe; with leaves about $1\frac{1}{4}$″ long, flowers blue appearing in racemes above the leaves but usually with no more than 3–5 flowers per raceme. There is a white flowered variety 'Alba'. Of value for use in the rockery.

carpatica 1′ Zone 3 Carpathian Bellflower
This is a tufted perennial with violet-blue, bell-like flowers $1\frac{1}{2}$–2 in. wide, freely produced during July, with often a few flowers at odd times the remainder of the summer. The flowers are borne either singly or a few to a stalk from June to late Aug. The leaves are ovate and $1\frac{1}{2}$ in. long. The var. **alba** with white flowers is readily available from most nurseries. A dwarf compact form called 'Blue Carpet' is also offered; together with several others. Several fine cultivars have been raised in England recently like 'Wedgewood', 'White Star' and 'White Carpet' and it is hoped these may become available from American sources. Since the stem is somewhat decumbent, this makes an excellent ground cover, but may grow so

vigorously as to become a pest. It grows best in full sun.

cochleariifolia 2″–8″ Zone 6
This is often listed as *C. pusilla*. It is an excellent plant for the garden with well-drained, gravelly, nearly neutral soil and in a situation where a close-growing ground cover is needed. Underground stolons send up dense mats of small, fan-shaped leaves about an inch high. Above these, the sky-blue flowers appear on stems 3 to 4 in. high. Varieties available are: **alba,** with white flowers; and 'Miranda' with slightly taller flower stalks and larger bells of a lighter shade of blue.

dasyantha 3″–9″ Zone 2 Shaggy Bellflower
(Often listed as *C. sasyantha*.) Matlike plant with rosettes of small, broad, hairy-shiny leaves and solitary violet-colored flowers on 6 in. stems. These appear in early summer. Native to Alaska and northern Asia.

drabifolia 6″ annual Greek Bellflower
With solitary violet-blue flowers about an inch long and having oblong leaves $\frac{1}{2}$ in. long. Native to Greece. Suitable for the rock garden or rock wall.

elatines 6″–8″ Zone 6 Elatines Bellflower
A matlike plant from the region around the Adriatic Sea, this has sharply pointed leaves 3 in. long and loose, ascending or trailing flower stems bearing pale blue or violet star-shaped flowers which bloom from early to midsummer. Varieties of this are **fenestrellata** with smooth, shiny leaves and pale blue flowers; and **garganica** with small, wrinkled and somewhat hairy leaves having starlike blue flowers with white eyes which bloom a long time in summer. An excellent plant for rock garden or rock wall, it does best in good, well-drained soil in sun or partial shade.

glomerata 2′ Zones 2–3 Clustered Bellflower, Danes-blood Bellflower
Sometimes the flower stalks of this species each bear a dozen purple-blue flowers during June and July, with additional flowers in Aug. Native to Europe and Asia, easily grown and in good soil increases quickly by runners. The var. **acaulis** is dwarf, only 3–5 in. high and **dahurica** has deep rich purple flowers 3 in. across. Easily grown in any sunny situation and propagated by division.

isophylla trailing Zone 7 Italian Bellflower
An excellent herbaceous perennial for hanging baskets, with ovate leaves about $1\frac{1}{2}$ in. wide, saucer-shaped, pale blue flowers an inch across, native to Italy. There is a white-flowered form.

lactiflora 4′ Zone 5 Milky Bellflower
The flowers of this perennial are 1 in. across,

milk white or pale blue, borne in large panicles from late June to Aug. The leaves are up to 3 in. long and in rich soil the plant may need staking. Easily grown and easily propagated by division. Native to the Caucasus.

latifolia   3′   Zone 3   Great Bellflower
A rather coarse-leaved perennial with leaves up to 6 in. long, flowers borne singly and about 1¼ in. wide, purplish blue. Native to Europe and Asia. Several varieties have been named but it is not one of the better bellflowers.

linifolia   6″–12″   Zone 5   Scheuchzer Bellflower
A plant having clumps of very narrow leaves and flower stalks which may be 12 in. long, bearing large blue, bell-shaped flowers from midsummer to Sept. It is easy to grow and excellent as a long-lasting color accent. Native to eastern Europe and western Asia.

medium   2′–4′   annual or biennial   Canterbury Bells
This is a very popular garden plant, usually a biennial 3–4 ft. tall, but an annual form of it has been developed 2–2½ ft. tall. There are white, blue, lavender and rose-colored forms available. The flowers are bell shaped, 2 in. long and are produced in long showy spikes during late spring and July. Native to southern Europe. Usually propagated by seed. There are several interesting forms, one having flowers that are hose in hose (which see), another called the Cup and Saucer var. (**calycanthema**) because of its peculiarly shaped flowers, with a cuplike corolla below which is a saucer-shaped calyx.

parryi   3″–10″   Zone 4   Parry Bellflower
Native to the Rocky Mountains, this small plant has clumps of glossy, dark green leaves which are stiff and somewhat wavy and violet-colored, upturned, bell-shaped flowers on stems 8 in. tall. It must have well-drained, gravelly soil and a sunny exposure.

percisifolia   3′   Zone 3   Peach-leaved Bellflower
A very popular, easily-grown perennial from Europe. It grows in erect leafy clumps, with a few (or one) blue flowers on each flower stalk. They are about 1½ in. wide, blooming in the summer. There are several popular and easily available varieties like **alba** with white flowers; **'Caerulea'** with excellent blue flowers; **'Telham Beauty'** with very large clear blue flowers and probably one of the best varieties (the chromosome number is doubled); **'Summer Skies'** with double white flowers flushed azure blue; **'Moerheimei'** with semi-double white flowers and, better still, **'Grandiflora'** has larger flowers than those of the species. These are all easily propagated by division.

piperi   1″–4″   Zone 7   Piper Bellflower
A small tufted perennial in its native habitat in the Olympic Mountains of Wash. with 1 to several small blue flowers. Difficult to grow.

portenschlagiana (*C. muralis*)   6″–9″   Zone 4   Dalmatian Bellflower
A low, tufted perennial with kidney-shaped leaves; light bluish-purple almost erect, bell-shaped flowers, an inch long, during June and July. Native to southern Europe. A fine plant for garden, rock walls, rock garden or even as a pot plant.

poscharskyana   4″   Zone 3   Serbian Bellflower
This is a weak-stemmed, trailing perennial and although the stems may be up to 2 ft. long they trail over the ground and actually are only a few inches high. Native to Dalmatia, it is very drought resistant and can cling to dry walls. The flowers are lavender-blue, bell shaped, ½–1 in. wide in June and July, the plant doing best in light shade but will also grow well in full sun. The kidney-shaped leaves are 1½ in. long. Apparently this species is popular for many nurserymen grow it. Easily propagated by division.

propinqua grandiflora   1′   annual   Near East Bellflower
The obovate leaves are 2½ in. long; the flowers are many and bell shaped, violet to mauve, about 1½ in. wide, appearing in late May or June. Native to Armenia.

x pulloides   8″   Zone 6
A supposed hybrid between *C. pulla* and *C. carpatica turbinata* with large blue-purple flowers. A good plant for the rockery.

pyramidalis   5′   biennial   Chimney Bellflower
The porcelain-blue and clear white flowers are borne on long flower stalks, starting in Aug. and continuing for 6 weeks. The plant seems to form a perfect pyramid of flowers when in full bloom but the stems are fragile and should be staked. Native to southern Europe.

raddeana   1′   Zone 6   Radde Bellflower
Tufts of small, stiff leaves with toothed margins on slender stems 4 in. long and deep purple, bell-like flowers which hang from a 3-in. stalk, the flowers blooming in midsummer, characterize a very attractive Bellflower from the Caucasus. It does well in a coarse limestone soil and partial shade.

ramosissima   1′   annual   Bluestar Bellflower
The flowers are dark violet-blue, bell shaped and about an inch wide, appearing in July. The gray-green leaves are sessile. There is a white flowered var. **alba**. Native to southern Europe.

rapunculoides   3′   Zone 3   Creeping Bellflower
A perennial with persistent rootstock that makes it an invading weed in some places; alternate leaves narrow and lanceolate to heart shaped, 2–4 in. long, single blue flowers and bell shaped, about 1 in. long, from June to Aug. Native to Europe. This was first introduced as a garden plant, but if it escapes it can become a

vicious, spreading weed because of the very persistent rootstock.

rotundifolia 1'–2' Zones 2–3 Harebell, Bluebells-of-Scotland
The daintiest of the 3 most common species of Campanula to be found wild in the U.S., this is really a European native from the British Isles, where it is known as the Bluebells-of-Scotland. This perennial herb has rounded basal leaves about an inch long and very narrow stem leaves about 3 in. long which often wither away. The nodding, bright blue flowers about an inch long borne on slender stems in open racemes, have rather wide-spreading corollas, each opening into 5-pointed lobes. Able to grow in either sun or semi-shade in moist areas or rocky ledges, and in addition preferring a cold climate, it is an ideal subject for gardens in northern U.S. and Canada. It has been naturalized over the New England States and west to Iowa and Ind. Seeds may be sown in the fall, or the plants divided in spring, or plants may be started from stem cuttings in summer or from root cuttings in fall. Several varieties are grown including var. **alba** with white flowers.

sarmatica 1'–2' Zone 5 Sarmatian Bell-flower
Growing in mounds with hairy, grayish-green leaves, held erect, this perennial with light blue or violet bell-shaped flowers about an inch long appears in midsummer. It is a plant from the Caucasus and prefers full sun.

saxifraga 6" Zone 4 Saxifrage Bellflower
A plant sometimes used in the rock garden, growing close to the ground, slightly tufted. The leaves are narrow, sometimes with 3–5 serrations at the tip. Flowers violet, 1¼ in. in diameter May to July. Native to the Caucasus.

x stansfeldii creeping Zone 5 Stansfield Bellflower
This is a hybrid of unknown origin with small leaves on "walking" stems which makes a good ground cover. The flowers are dark purple and appear in late spring and summer.

trachelium 3' biennial Coventry-bells
With nodding blue-purple flowers an inch long, borne in loose racemes during July and Aug. The rough-hairy leaves are 3 in. long. Native to Europe and Asia, sometimes naturalized.

CAMPANULACEAE = The Campanula Family

CAMPANULA FAMILY = Campanulaceae

CAMPANULATE. Bell-shaped.

CAMPHOR-TREE = *Cinnamomum camphora*

CAMPION. See SILENE, LYCHNIS.

CAMPSIS (KAMP-sis). These are shrubby vines, members of the Bignonia Family, with opposite, compound leaves, brightly colored, trumpetlike flowers and fruits of dry pods several inches long. The plants climb by attaching aerial root-

lets to any available means of support. Propagation is by seeds stratified as soon as ripe or stored in an airtight container in a cool place for up to a year and then stratified at 40° F. for 2 months. Layers, softwood and hardwood cuttings, as well as root cuttings, all root easily. See STRATIFICATION, LAYERS, CUTTINGS.

grandiflora clinging vine 20' Zone 7 Chinese Trumpetcreeper
The large, funnel-shaped scarlet flowers of this Chinese vine are 3 in. wide, making it the showiest of the *Campsis* species. These flowers come in Aug. The rootlike holdfasts by which it adheres to a wall or other means of support are none too effective, and since the vine itself is vigorous and heavy, it often needs assistance in attaching itself securely in an upright position. The leaves are opposite and compound, with 7–9 leaflets, each about 1½–2½ in. long.

radicans clinging vine 30' Zone 4 Trumpet-vine, Trumpetcreeper
This shrubby vine is native to the southeastern U.S., but is used in ornamental planting as far north as Mass. The orange to scarlet, trumpet-shaped flowers are 2 in. wide and bloom in mid-summer. Leaves are compound, opposite, with 9–11 leaflets. Like *C. grandiflora*, it becomes very heavy and needs some assistance in supporting itself, since the small, rootlike holdfasts along the stem are not sufficient. If additional support is not given the vine may break away in large sections from the walls on which it grows. The variety 'Flava' bears pure yellow flowers. The leaves are opposite and compound, with 9–11 leaflets, each being 1½–2½ in. long. It can send runners underground and send up new plants at quite a distance from the main vine. Cases of dermatitis have been reported from handling of leaves or flowers.

x tagliabuana 'Madame Galen' clinging vine 25' Zone 4
Similar in every way to *C. radicans* except that the orange and scarlet, funnel-shaped flowers are slightly larger (2½ in. wide). It is almost as hardy as *C. radicans*, its other parent (with *C. grandiflora*). Like the other members of this genus, it has opposite, compound leaves and climbs by means of rootlike holdfasts which are not sufficient to keep heavy plants attached to buildings.

CAMPTOSORUS (kamp-toe-SOR-us)
rhizophyllus 4"–12" Zone 3 Walking Fern
This very popular small plant has evergreen fronds 4–12 in. long, often triangular shaped, and rooting where the tip touches moist soil, thus forming a new plant. It is native to eastern North America. If it is to do well it should be given lime and provided a moist shaded spot in some rock wall. Easily propagated by division. Its beauty is in its natural habitat, sometimes in

a terrarium, but certainly not as a potted plant indoors. See FERNS.

CANANGA (kan-ANG-ga)
  odorata   **80′**   **Zone 10**   **Ylang Ylang**
A tree native to the Philippines with alternate, simple leaves 6–8 in. long, having wavy margins, green above and slightly hairy beneath. The peculiar greenish-yellow and very fragrant flowers have a pleasant odor and are used in making an extraction for perfumes. Ylang-Ylang means "flower of flowers."

CANARY-CLOVER = *Dorycnium hirsutum*

CANARY-GRASS = *Phalaris canariensis*

CANDLEBUSH = *Cassia alata*

CANDLENUT-TREE = *Aleurites moluccana*

CANDLEPLANT = *Senecio articulatus*

CANDYTUFT. See IBERIS.

CANESCENT. Gray-pubescent and hoary.

CANKER. A name applied to plant diseases which usually cause lesions in the bark of woody plants. Both bacteria and fungi are the cause of cankers. When cankers completely surround the stem or branch it is girdled and dies. The spread of cankers is stopped by cutting off or out the diseased area. Fungicides have little value in controlling cankers but may prevent them from becoming established. Some of the better known are cytospora canker on Spruce, nectria canker on Beech, Oak, Birch, Boxwood and several fruit trees and several species of cankers on rose canes. Dieback of twigs on trees and woody shrubs is often caused by diseases which cause cankers.

CANNA (KAN-na)
  flaccida   **5′**   **Zone 7**   **Golden Canna**
A very handsome perennial native to the marshes and swamplands from S.Car. to Fla. It is a relative of the cultivated Canna, which it closely resembles. Rising from a tuberous rootstalk, the fleshy stem bears alternate leaves at the point of the swollen joints along the stem. The yellow flowers, several in number, are terminally produced on short stems and are very showy. Having both sepals and petals, in each case 3, the flower derives its brilliant color mainly from the much enlarged, petallike, sterile stamens, called staminodes. A fine plant for warm, moist climates, the Canna does not thrive in dry or poor soil. Plants may be divided in early spring, taking care to have one or more buds to each piece of rootstalk. These may be started in a greenhouse or hotbed, or planted outside when one would set out tomato plants. The starchy young corms are edible.
  x generalis   **2′–8′**   **Zone 9**   **Canna**
Although there are many species of Canna, most are of little garden value. The large-flowered hybrids used at present are mostly classed under this general hybrid term. In the far South and in southern Calif. these plants may be left out of doors in the open ground all year, but in a cooler climate, where there is frost, they must be lifted and stored inside over winter. They can be treated in a manner similar to tuberous begonias; that is, start the rhizomes indoors about 4 weeks before they are set out (after all danger of frost is over). Planting out of doors, 3–4 in. deep in full sun in a deep, well-prepared bed, one should use added fertilizer (5–10–5 about 4 oz. per sq. yard) and water well. These plants develop a single stately stalk with large flowers somewhat like those of gladiolus, but larger, up to 4 in. in dia., appearing in the summer and fall. The large leaves (18 in.) may be either green or bronzy, depending on the variety. When they have been killed by frost, the tops are cut off about 6 in. above the ground, the rhizomes or tubers are lifted and dried a few days and then stored in a cool cellar at a temperature of 50°–60° F. until about late March when they are prepared for starting in the greenhouse. Propagation is easy, either by seed or simple division of the rootstock. The seed germinates better if it is soaked in warm water for 48 hours prior to sowing, or if a small hole can be filed in the very hard seed coat. These seeds are so hard it has been said that the natives in the West Indies have used them as shot; hence another common name—Indian Shot. All in all, these are coarse-textured, but unusually colorful plants which were used a great deal 50 years ago in American gardens and now are showing signs of again becoming popular garden plants.

At present there are over 60 varieties of Canna offered by American growers. Of these, some of the most popular at present are:

GREEN LEAVES
'City of Portland'—rose pink
'Gaiety'—orange-yellow margins
'King Midas'—yellow
'President'—red
'R. Wallace'—canary yellow
'Rosamund'—red, bordered yellowish brown

BRONZE LEAVES
'America'—dark red
'Apricot'—apricot
'Eureka'—white
'King Humbert'—scarlet
'Mrs. Alfred Conard'—salmon pink
'Orange Humbert'—orange
'The Ambassador'—cherry red
'Tyrol'—pink
'Wyoming'—yellow-bronze

The new Grand Opera Series has varieties with extra large flowers in pastel shades, an innovation in this group of vivid flowered plants.

Insect Pests

Several leafrollers and leaf tiers feed on the leaves and disfigure the foliage. Use of insecticides #9, #15 or #37 are effective. Japanese beetle has been known to eat the flowers. Use insecticide #37.

Diseases

Bacterial bud rot starts with small white spots on the opening bud. As it progresses, the whole leaf may turn black and spread to the flowers. Disinfection by soaking the corms in fungicide #Q is recommended. Select only healthy corms for planting.

CANNABACEAE = The Hemp Family

CANNABIS (KAN-ab-is)
> **sativa   12′   annual   Hemp, Hashish**
This has received great publicity because it contains a narcotic called marijuana, hashish or bhang. It is a native of temperate Asia and has become naturalized in eastern North America, often turning up as a weed in vacant lots of urban areas, and when it is found a great deal of publicity is always connected to the incident. It is grown in Asia for the fiber of the inner bark used in making cordage. The leaves are alternate, digitately compound with 3–7 leaflets up to 9 in. long, both staminate and pistillate greenish flowers being present on different plants but not very conspicuous. No longer grown for hemp in America. In fact those growing it in the U.S. must register with the Federal Bureau of Narcotics (Federal Marijuana Tax Act of 1937) and pay a tax. It is the flowering tops of pistillate plants which are especially rich in marijuana. These are dried, pulverized and mixed with tobacco to make the illegial cigarettes. The oriental drug hashish also comes from this plant. The plant has no ornamental qualities.

CANNON-BALL-TREE = *Couroupita guianensis*

CANS. The "cans" are sometimes of tin, old oil cans with holes punched in the bottom, but more often now they are made of thin (but durable) plastic. Sometimes even roofing paper is used to hold a small ball of soil tightly together so the plant can be moved at any time without injury.

A word of caution should be given here, for plants, left to grow too long in any pot or can, tend to grow roots in a tight ball. When removed and set in the ground such roots can girdle and choke each other as they grow larger, often seriously injuring and even killing the plant. Hence, plants bought in cans should have their roots carefully inspected and be opened up, if necessary, when they are removed to be planted

in the ground, to alleviate girdling later on. This is a most important point to keep in mind.

CANTALOUPE. See MELON.

CANTERBURY BELLS = *Campanula medium*

CAPE-COWSLIP. See LACHENALIA.

CAPE-FUSCHIA = *Phygelius capensis*

CAPE-HONEYSUCKLE = *Tecomaria capensis*

CAPE-JASMINE = *Gardenia jasminoides*

CAPE-MARIGOLD. See DIMORPHOTHECA.

CAPE POND WEED = *Aponogeton distachyus*

CAPE-PRIMROSE, Hybrid = *Streptocarpus hybridus*

CAPE-STOCK. See HELIPHYLLA.

CAPITATE. Headlike; collected in a dense cluster.

CAPPARACEAE = The Caper Family

CAPPARIS (cap-AR-is)
> **spinosa   5′   Zone 8   Caper Bush**
Native of the Mediterranean Region, this has small white flowers 2–3 in. across, the flower buds are pickled and eaten, being the pungent condiment capers of commerce. Propagated by seed and cuttings.

CAPRIFIG. A type of fig (usually not edible) which produces a large number of male or pollen-bearing flowers and is used in the commercial production of figs merely to produce this pollen. See FIG.

CAPRIFOLIACEAE = The Honeysuckle Family

CAPSELLA (cap-SELL-a)
> **bursa-pastoris   3′   annual   Shepherd's-purse**
Sometimes a biennial, native to Europe but widely distributed throughout North America and a common weed everywhere on all continents. The plant has a thin tap root, alternate, simple, sessile, arrow-shaped leaves along the stem but a rosette of sessile leaves at the base. The small white flowers are borne in slender open racemes and the seed pods are flattened and triangular.

CAPSICUM (KAP-sik-um)
> **annuum   6′–8′   Zone 10   Bush Red Pepper**
A shrub in most tropical countries, but if started early enough from seed fruits will be produced the first year. The fruits are variable, depending on the variety:
> **cerasiforme**—Cherry Pepper—fruit erect, round, an inch across, yellow or purple.
> **conoides**—Cone Pepper—fruits usually erect, 2 in. long and cone-shaped.
> **fasciculatum**—Red Cluster Pepper—fruit erect, to 3 in. long and very pungent.

frutescens   6′   Zone 10   Tabasco Pepper
Similar to *C. annuum*, pungent. Used in the commercial production of hot sauces in Gulf states.

grossum—This is the Bell Pepper, commonly grown in vegetable gardens.
See PEPPER for culture.

longum—fruit red, drooping, sometimes a foot long and 2 in. across, called the Long Pepper. This includes Chili, Cayenne and other strains. The red pepper used for culinary purposes is often a mixture of the ground fruits of several of these including the whole unground seed. These red peppers which grow on bushes should not be confused with the true Black Pepper of the East Indies, *Piper nigrum*, which see.

CAPSULE. A dry fruit of more than 1 carpel, opening at maturity.

CAPTAN. A fungicide, which see.

CARAGANA (kar-rag-AY-na). A genus of shrubs with alternate, pinnately compound leaves, members of the Pea Family, with bright yellow flowers and small pods for fruits. Sometimes they have weak spines; sometimes the stipules simulate weak spines.

Propagation

Seed can be sown as soon as ripe, stratified or dried and stored for a year in airtight containers in a cool place and then sown. It will germinate more uniformly if it is soaked in hot water at 190° F. overnight and then sown. Many varieties are grafted, using *C. arborescens* as an understock. Softwood and hardwood cuttings can be rooted. See GRAFTING, CUTTINGS.

arborescens   18′   Zone 2   Siberian Pea-tree
This extremely hardy shrub is native to Siberia and Manchuria and has many uses in the colder parts of North America. The flowers are like those of peas (it belongs to the Pea Family) and bright yellow appearing in mid-May. It can be used as a flowering specimen, but more often is used as a windbreak and screen, especially in the colder parts of the Canadian provinces. It is a reliable and valued shrub in such areas but in warmer climates like New England and the eastern and western coastal parts of the U.S., better shrubs can be found of greater ornamental value, since its only claim to garden use is its hardiness and its yellow flowers. 'Pendula' has stiffly drooping branches.

maximowicziana   4¼′   Zone 2   Maximowicz Pea-tree
This low-spreading shrub from western China also has pealike, yellow flowers in mid-May. It is valued for its densely-branched and spreading habit. One old plant in the Arnold Arboretum is only 3 ft. tall but 12 ft. across. So, under certain conditions, it may have merit but the fruits are dried pods and it has no autumn color. Other plants could be grown instead in the better soils.

microphylla   9′   Zone 3   Littleleaf Pea-tree
Somewhat similar to *C. arborescens*, also coming from Siberia and northern China, valued possibly for its smaller leaves. Most members of this genus have alternate, compound leaves. The leaves of *C. arborescens* have 4–6 pairs of leaflets each about ⅓ in. long. The leaves of *C. microphylla* have 6–9 pairs of leaflets, each about ¼ in. long.

pygmaea   3′   Zone 3   Pygmy Pea-tree
Deciduous, alternate, compound-leaved shrubs, each leaf has 4 leaflets, ½ in. long. The yellow pealike flowers, produced in May, are about 1 in. long, and the pod is ¾–1¼ in. long. Native between the Caucasus and Tibet, it has pretty, pendulous flowers, but that is about all of garden merit. Easily rooted (cuttings in July).

CARALLUMA (car-a-LUMA)
nebrownii   7″   Zone 10
A succulent, leafless herb, sometimes used as a house plant because of the interesting 2-in., dark red flowers borne in clusters along its short 4-angled stem. Native to South Africa.

CARAMBOLA = *Averrhoa carambola*

CARAWAY = *Carum carvi*

CARDAMINE (kar-DAM-in-ee)
bulbosa   5″–8″   Bulb Bittercress
A bulbous plant of wet, marshy lands and the brook's edge, the alternate leaves may vary in shape from oval to lanceolate. The flowers, borne in a loose terminal cluster on the straight flower stalk, consist of a calyx of 4 small green and white sepals and a corolla of 4 white petals. It is native from New England to Fla. and the Midwest. The flowering period ranges from March to June. An interesting addition to the wetlands wild garden, especially since the leaves may be used as salad greens in spring. It is propagated easily from seed sown in spring and the plants are easily transplanted at any time.

pratensis   1½′   Zone 4   Cuckoo Bittercress
A moisture-loving herb from northern North America, Europe and Asia, leaves opposite, rounded, about ½ in. wide and making a truly excellent plant for submerging in an aquarium. It is also good for wet boggy places in the rockery or in the bog garden. Flowers white to rose colored, often double. Division.

CARDAMON = *Elettaria cardamomum*

CARDARIA (car-DA-ria-a)
draba   2¼′   Zone 3   Pepperweed Whitetop
A perennial weed especially in the middle west and on the Pacific Coast, increasing by seeds and running rootstocks. Leaves alternate, simple, oval to oblong, several inches long, and sessile. The small white flowers are on loose

terminal panicles, appearing from June to Aug.
Seed pods are heart shaped, $\frac{1}{8}$ in. long. It is a
very difficult weed to eradicate in the Rocky
Mountain area. Native to Europe and Asia.

   C. pubescens is also a very bad weed in western
North America and differs from the above in
that the seed pods of C. pubescens are inflated
and hairy and the plant is only half as tall.

CARDINAL-CLIMBER = *Ipomoea x multitida*

CARDINAL-FLOWER = *Lobelia cardinalis*

CARDINALS-GUARD,   BLACKSTICK =
Pachystachys coccinea

CARDIOCRINUM (car-di-o-CRI-num)

  giganteum   6'-12'   Zone 6   Giant-lily
This is not a true member of the *Lilium* genus,
but certainly is closely related. The large heart-
shaped leaves are over a foot long and almost as
wide. The fragrant, narrowly funnel-shaped
white flowers are produced in July and Aug.
with 26 flowers or more per stalk. The main bulb
dies after it has produced a flowering stalk, but
the smaller bulbs produced at its base continue
to grow and will bloom in 4 years time. A
native to the Himalayas of Burma, this Giant-
lily is none too easy to grow, for it requires
moist soil and shade. It is seen at its best in
many English gardens.

CARDIOSPERMUM (kar-dio-SPERM-um)

  **halicacabum   vine   annual or perennial
                        Balloon-vine, Heart-seed**
A tropical American vine climbing by tendrils,
perennial out-of-doors in the warmer parts of
the southeastern U.S., where it has become
naturalized. Elsewhere it is treated as an annual
vine with inconspicuous white flowers but
valued for its balloonlike, 3-angled, inflated
fruits which are an inch long and as much wide.
The black seeds about the size of a pea, have a
white heart-shaped spot on them giving rise to
the common name. Leaves are alternate, bipinnate and coarsely toothed. In some tropical
countries these have been used as a vegetable.
Easily grown from seed planted where they are
to grow.

CARDOON (car-DOON) (*Cynara cardunculus*).
The Cardoon is similar to the Artichoke (which
see) in general cultural requirements, but the
edible portion is the thickened leaf stalk which
is blanched like Celery (which see). The plant
itself is a thistlelike, spiny-leaved perennial
herb, planted about 3 ft. x 3 ft. and propagated
by seed in the South or in Calif. Often the
plants are raised in hotbeds and then planted out
after all danger of possible frost. Cardoon
grows about 6 ft. tall and is native to southern
Europe.

CAREX (ca-REX). These are perennial, grasslike herbs, sometimes grown for ornament
especially for edging. They do well in bogs.
Propagation is best by division of the clumps.

  fraseri = *Cymophyllus fraseri*

  morrowii   1'   Zone 6   Morrow's Sedge
The variegated form (**variegata**) of this Japanese
sedge is the most popular for the foot-long,
$\frac{1}{4}$-in.-wide leaves are striped with white. These
all originate from a common base; the leaves
arch downwards, making an ornamental,
compact plant.

CARICA (ka-rik-a)

  papaya   25'   Zone 10   Papaya
A popular fruit native to tropical America,
borne on usually dioecious, short-lived, mostly
succulent trees that start to bear shortly after
they have been planted out (a year after being
planted from the seed bed). The fruit is a large,
fleshy, melon-sized berry, yellow or orange and
about 20 in. long, with thick yellow flesh.
Both sexes should be present unless the clone is
unisexual. The leaves are 2 ft. long, deeply 7
lobed (the lobes pinnately cut); flowers yellow,
with tubes an inch long, produced in 3-ft.
racemes. Trees only bear 3-4 years and them
must be replaced. Propagation is usually by
seeds. Each tree bears about 12-30 fruits
annually, ripening from midwinter to June.

CARISSA (kar-ISS-a)

  grandiflora   18'   Zone 9   Natal-plum
A South African plant sometimes used in
gardens in southern Fla. and southern Calif. for
its fragrant white flowers which are 2 in. in dia.;
for its excellent evergreen foliage, the lustrous
leaves of which are 3 in. long. It is spiny, and the
waxy white flowers are excellent indeed. The
lustrous foliage looks well even when the plant is
sheared into a hedge. One added characteristic
is that it grows well near the seashore.

CARLINA (kar-LY-na)

  acaulis   9"   Zone 6   Smooth Carlina
This unusual plant from southern Europe
belongs to the Composite Family. The deeply
lobed, graying leaves, in flat clusters, are
adorned with large white daisylike flowers 6 in.
wide, which are stemless and stiff like straw-
flowers. These appear in May or June. The plant
requires well-drained, gravelly soil and full
sun, and may be propagated readily from
seed or by division of the clumps. It should be
considered as a rock garden plant.

CARNATION = *Dianthus caryophyllus*

CARNEGIEA (kar-NEG-ia)

  gigantea   20'-60'   Zone 10   Giant Cactus
Not an ornamental, but the huge, cylindrical
Giant Cactus of southeastern Calif., Ariz., and
Mexico. The large trunks sometimes have a
few horizontal branches, 18-21 ribs and small
spines. The flowers are white, about 4 in. long,

open during daylight, and it is the largest cactus known. See CACTI AND SUCCULENTS.

CAROB = *Ceratonia siliqua*

CAROLINA-VANILLA = *Trilisa odoratissima*

CAROSELLA = *Foeniculum vulgare piperitum*

CARPEL. A simple pistil or a member of a compound pistil.

CARPENTERIA (kar-pen-TER-ia)
  californica   8′   Zones 7–8   Evergreen Mock-
                                          orange
A showy shrub, native to Calif. and often called the Tree Anemone. It is difficult to transplant and needs protection from cold, high winds. The white clusters of fragrant flowers are 2–3 in. across, blooming in the summer, and the evergreen leaves are 4 in. long. It is frequently planted in Calif. but is not used much elsewhere.

CARPET BUGLE = *Ajuga reptans*

CARPET GRASS = *Axonopus furcatus*—See GRASS, LAWNS.

CARPETWEED FAMILY = Aizoaceae

CARPINUS (kar-PY-nus). The hornbeams and the hop hornbeams are bushy, slow-growing, alternate-leaved trees. They are very difficult to move and must always be moved with a ball, probably the reason why so few are being grown commercially and why they are not found more frequently in gardens. The hornbeams (*Carpinus*) are mostly under 45 feet in height especially as they are found in gardens, and the hop hornbeams (*Ostrya*) are usually larger growing, 60 feet or more in height.

Unfortunately, these trees also are susceptible to infestations of a scale which malathion, if applied properly, can usually control fairly well. Eleven species and varieties of *Carpinus* and only one *Ostrya* are being grown commercially in America. As for autumn color, the native *Carpinus caroliniana* is best with a fairly good orange-to-red color. The European *Carpinus* species have little autumn color; the ones from the Orient are red.

The differences between *Carpinus* and *Ostrya* are not pronounced. Both have alternate leaves 1½–4½ in. long, but the fruits of the *Carpinus* are small hard nutlets in leaflike bracts born in pendulous clusters 2–2½ in. long, while those of the Hop Hornbeam are bladderlike pods in pendulous clusters 1½–2½ in. long. In *Ostrya* the staminate catkins are obvious all winter long; in *Carpinus* they are not. Also the smooth muscular bark of *Carpinus* (giving rise to the common name "Muscle Wood" or "Blue Beech" for the native *C. caroliana*) is distinctive, while the rough scaly bark of *Ostrya* species is decidedly different.

Propagation

Do not allow the seed to dry out but stratify at once as soon as ripe at 40° F. for 4 months. Grafting and budding is also practiced, using *Carpinus betulus* as the understock. See SEEDS, GRAFTING, STRATIFICATION, etc.

betulus   60′   Zone 5   European Hornbeam
This tree is popular in its native Europe where it is used in making hedges and pleached alleés since it withstands shearing well. It is difficult to move easily, certainly in the larger sizes. Some of the varieties are perhaps better ornamentals than the species. The autumn color of this species is yellowish, not nearly as outstanding as that of its American and Japanese relatives. The leaves are up to 5 in. long. Some of the better varieties are: 'Columnaris'—a narrow columnar tree, almost egg-shaped, rated as excellent in Europe. This plant has undoubtedly been mixed up in America, having erroneously been called 'Fastigiata'. The two are decidedly different, 'Columnaris' being dense, narrowly columnar with a central trunk and almost egg-shaped, looking as if it had been sheared, with foliage all at the perimeter of the branches. 'Fastigiata' on the other hand has all upright branching, but an old tree at the Arnold Arboretum, 49 years old, is 50 feet tall by 40 feet wide—almost vase shaped now with no central trunk since the branches are heavier with age and tend to spread more. Also, the leaves are not all at the ends of the branches but are more distributed, the entire habit being more open; 'Fastigiata'—upright in habit, branching tends to be more vase shaped as the tree grows older. Differs from 'Columnaris' as noted above; 'Globosa'—definitely rounded and globose in habit, and as such differs from both 'Fastigiata' and 'Columnaris'. Young plants which may not have grown into proper shape, might be confused with small plants of 'Columnaris' since both apparently produce leaves at the ends of the branches, giving a sheared effect, but 'Globosa' has no central trunk and 'Columnaris' does. However, as they grow older the 'Globosa' trees will be definitely rounded and the 'Columnaris' trees will be egg shaped; 'Incisa'—leaves narrow, coarsely toothed and usually deeply cut or lobed.

caroliniana   36′   Zone 2   American Hornbeam
This native of eastern North America is often called 'Blue Beech' or 'Ironwood' by Americans who are familiar with it in the woodlands of eastern North America. The wood is extremely tough to chop, the bark is smooth and grayish, somewhat similar to that of the Beech but with a peculiar muscular twist to it. This is not too easily transplanted but makes an excellent tree for the small place. Slow-growing and with a

dark reddish autumn color this merits some consideration in landscape work, although admittedly trees that are easier to transplant are more popular with nurserymen and the gardening public alike. It is best to use this as a specimen for there are usually several trunks from the base and when clipping is to be the rule, *C. betulus* or one of its several forms should be used. A variety named 'Pyramidalis' is rare and grown only in botanic gardens in America, but it is very definitely pyramidal.

japonica   45′   Zone 4   Japanese Hornbeam
A flat-topped tree from Japan with general fan-shaped habit, this species is distinctive for these reasons. It is slow in growth, but the autumn color is a good red, and the leaves are 2–4 in. long which give this a slightly coarse texture.

orientalis   25′   Zone 5   Oriental Hornbeam
Growing with several upright branches from the base, this hornbeam has merit even though it is rare in America at present. It is one of the smaller, slow-growing trees from southeastern Europe and Asia Minor and has comparatively small leaves, 1–2 in. long, and a most interesting habit of branching. A 25 ft. tree has a single main trunk at the base, but about 2 ft. above the ground several equally strong branches originate at right angles from the trunk and then shortly turn up vertically. Hence the branching is apparently U-shaped when viewed from a short distance. The autumn color is red.

tschonoskii   45′   Zone 5
A graceful, shrubby tree from Japan and China may be worthy of further trial within its hardiness limits.

CARPOBROTUS (car-po-BRO-tus)
chilensis (*Mesembryanthemum chilense*) **trailing**
                                Zone 9   Sea-fig
Native to Australia but naturalized in sandy areas along the Calif. and Ore. coast with stems trailing several feet. The slightly fragrant rosy-purple flowers are in evidence most of the summer and are 2 in. across. An excellent sand cover on the coast. The fleshy triangular leaves are 2½ in. long. Dead blossoms are untidy.
edulis (*Mesembryanthemum edule*)   **trailing**
                            Zone 10   Hottentot-fig
Similar to *C. chilense* but all parts are larger. Native to South Africa, escaped in Calif. Dead blossoms are untidy but like *C. chilense* it is excellent for holding sand in place.

CARRION-FLOWER = *Smilax herbacea*

CARROT (*Daucus carota sativa*). The carrot is one of our most common and widely grown vegetables. It grows best at mean temperatures between 60°–70° F. Prolonged higher temperatures tend to produce shorter, non-blunt roots,

while temperatures below 50° F. tend to make roots longer, more slender and paler in color.

Calif., Tex., Ariz., and N.Mex. are the important commercial production areas for the winter and spring crop. Most of the northern states have large acreages for summer and fall harvest, used fresh and for processing and freezing.

Varieties

Seedsmen list a large number of varieties but only a few of these listed sorts are important. Those having long, cylindrical and smooth shape include 'Pioneer', 'Gold Pak', and 'Nantes Half Long'. Other standard varieties include 'Red Cored Chantenay' and 'Danvers Half Long'.

Soils

Carrots, like beets, grow best in a deep, loose sandy loam, loam or muck soil that is high in fertility and water-holding capacity. Soil preparation and fertilizer recommendations outlined for beets apply equally well for carrots. See BEETS. Note should be made to the effect that strawy manure or raw compost should not be used because its use just prior to planting will tend to produce knobby, misshapen roots with many fibrous side rootlets.

Planting and Care

Carrot seed is slow to germinate and, therefore, a few quick germinating radish seeds are frequently scattered in the drill to mark the rows and thus permit earlier cultivation. Sow the seed in drills ½–¾ in. in depth at the rate of ½–¾ oz. per 100 ft. of row. As soon as the plants reach a height of 2–3 in., thin to a spacing of 1½–2 in. Space the rows 12–15 in. apart. The seed may be planted as soon as the ground can be prepared, and for continuous supply make a planting every 3 weeks until Aug. 1. This applies to the northern states. Shallow cultivation is important starting as soon as possible after planting. Commercial growers use a petroleum product Stoddard Solvent to control weeds in carrots. The use of herbicides and chemicals for weed control is, however, not recommended in the small home garden.

Carrots are most tender and sweet if harvested before the roots reach their mature size or for the long types a dia. of 1–1½ in. and the shorter chantenay types of 1½–2 in.

Carrots may be harvested in the late fall and stored in the same manner as recommended for beets. See BEETS.

Insects and Diseases

The carrot caterpillar is green banded with black and yellow markings and up to 2 in. long.

It seldom does much damage. The carrot rust fly is becoming a serious problem in some areas. The larvae, yellowish-white, legless and up to $\frac{1}{3}$ in. long, tunnels into the outer fleshy root. Control involves the use of a diazinon dust applied at the rate of 2 lbs. per 1000 sq. ft. of soil surface. Apply to the soil before planting and then work it thoroughly into the upper 6 in. Leaf blight and carrot yellows are diseases of lesser importance that can cause some damage. Spray with Maneb. Carrot yellows, a virus, is spread by the 6-spotted leaf hopper. To control the hopper use a 4% malathion dust. Three to 4 applications at 7–10-day intervals starting as soon as the first leaf hoppers appear.

GRANT B. SNYDER

CARROT FAMILY = Umbellifera

CARROT, WILD = *Daucus carota*

CARTHAMUS (KAR-tham-us)

tinctorius   **3′**   **annual**   **Safflower**
An alternate-leaved herb, with leaves finely spiny toothed and flower heads resembling those of a thistle with red florets and yellow styles; 4-sided, pearly-white fruits. Propagated by seed. The florets are used in dyeing silk (rose to red) and, mixed with talcum powder, this makes a kind of rouge. The seed is used in drying oils in paints and as a cathartic. In India the oil from the seed is used for burning.

CARUM (KAY-rum)

carvi   **2′**   **Zone 3**   **Caraway**
Perennial or sometimes biennial weed but also grown for the seeds, which are used in flavoring foods. Compound leaves have very narrow linear divisions. The biennial root has a rosette of leaves on the ground the first year, then produces a stem and alternate leaves the second. The small white to rarely pink flowers are produced in compound umbels during June and July and the smooth aromatic fruits have longitudinal ridges. Native to Europe but escaped in many places in North America.

CARYA (KAY-rya) (Also see HICKORY NUT.) The hickories are common woodland trees in the central and eastern U.S. and were placed by botanists for a long time in a genus called Hicoria. Many a youngster has grown familiar with these trees early in life, later appreciating their form and bark characteristics more than their fruits. They are usually tap-rooted and difficult to transplant in larger sizes. In fact, they are so difficult to handle in this respect that few nurserymen grow them. Where they can be transplanted in small sizes, or where already established trees can be left untouched in a new landscape operation, they add considerably to certain types of landscape planting.

As for their fruiting qualities, it has been found that it is best to plant 2 or more clones or seedlings in the same area to procure maximum fertilization and fruiting. They have alternate, compound leaves.

Most species are native to North America. Their rugged habit and rich golden-brown autumn color make them easily recognized in the landscape. It is well known that hickory wood makes the best fuel of any of our native woods, in the East at least; and the sawdust of green hickory is still used by the large meat-packing industries for curing meats. Unfortunately the hickories split easily in heavy snow or ice storms. When transplanted while very young to their permanent location, hickories can add much to the landscape picture.

Propagation

Do not let the nuts dry out, but stratify as soon as ripe at 40° F. for 4 months. Budding on *C. cordiformis* understock is also successful. See SEEDS, BUDDING, STRATIFICATION, etc. For general culture of some of these nuts, see NUTS AND NUT CULTURE.

Insect Pests

Hickory bark beetle is one of the most destructive insect pests, causing damage by tunneling under the bark and girdling branches. Tops of the trees are often attacked first. When evidence of injury is seen, it is usually too late for control, but spraying in midsummer when the beetles are laying eggs and feeding at base of leaf stems with insecticide #9 is helpful. Leaf galls of various shapes are caused by gall midges, but are more conspicuous than destructive. Spraying when leaves are developing with insecticide #9 or #15 reduces the infestation. The hickory gall aphid causes globular galls. Hickory horned devil, a stout reddish-brown caterpillar with conspicuous black spines, develops into the regal moth. Foliage sprays with insecticide #9 or #15 give control when necessary. Tussock moth, case bearer, walnut caterpillar and webworm are other leaf-eating pests. Weakened trees may be attacked by the larvae of the painted hickory borer.

Diseases

Irregular purplish spots on the leaves indicate infection by anthracnose. Spraying with fungicide #G is suggested. Canker, especially around the stubs of dead branches, may spread through the tree. Cutting out and disinfecting the wounds with tree paint is suggested.

alba = *C. tomentosa*
carolinae-septentrionalis = *C. ovata*
cordiformis   **90′**   **Zone 4**   **Bitternut**
A broadly rounded tree native to the eastern

U.S. with alternate, compound leaves, each with 5–9 leaflets. This is not so popular a tree as other hickories, nor so long-lived, but it does make a symmetrical specimen. The nuts are bitter and of little economic value. This species would probably not be valuable enough to actually buy, but if, in clearing out an area to be landscaped, a mature Bitternut were found growing, it certainly should be left to add its dignified habit to the surroundings.

glabra   **120′**   **Zone 4**   **Pignut**
A narrow to rounded tree native to the eastern U.S., the alternate-compound leaves of this species have 3–9 leaflets and turn a good yellow autumn color. It grows in dry, rocky soils. The nuts are small and difficult to crack open. The tree grows slowly and is not recommended as a street or avenue tree.

illinoinensis   **150′**   **Zone 5**   **Pecan**
Widely grown where it is native of the South-central U.S., the Pecan (formerly called *Carya pecan*) is the fastest growing of the hickories. Some of the varieties of the pecan are hardy in the North. In the Arnold Arboretum there is a tree planted in 1882. However, such trees do not mature nuts, for there is not a sufficient length of time free of frosts or freezes (in the fall). Such

TIME
1. First leaves one-half grown
2. Tips of nuts turning brown
3, 4, 5. 3–4 weeks after previous application

varieties as **'Desirable'**, **'Wichita'**, **'Sumner'** are grown in Georgia for use in groves that have careful attention as to water and fertilizer. Some varieties recommended for home owners— **'Stuart'**, **'Desirable'**, **'Elliott'**, **'Farley'**, and **'Gloria Grande'**. Other varieties that show promise for further growing are **'Cheyenne'**, **'Shawnee'**, **'Shoshoni'**, and **'Mohawk'**. A few others are grown further north but most of these only produce fruits occasionally in the warmer parts of Illinois, Indiana and Pennsylvania. Stark Bros. Nursery of Louisiana, Missouri, had at one time a variety named **'Stark King Hardy Giant'** (Plant Patent 361 in 1955), which was supposed to be extremely hardy.

laciniosa   **120′**   **Zone 5**   **Shellbark Hickory**
Native from N.Y. to Tenn. and Okla., this tree has a nicely rounded outline and alternate-compound leaves with 7–9 leaflets, but it is not often used in landscape work. The nut is nearly round, but pointed at both ends, hard to crack, but with a sweet kernel.

It is much better as a southern tree, where it is highly valued both as an ornamental specimen and as a nut-bearing tree.

Although 21 insects and 11 diseases are recognized pests of the Pecan the following are most important.

Insect Pests

Pecan nut case bearer which spends the winter in a case attached to a twig may destroy three-fourths of the crop where the olive-green larvae feed in the developing nuts. The first of 3 generations is most destructive. Pecan leaf case bearer overwinters in a case similar to the above but has only 1 annual generation. The tiny brown worms which destroy the buds and blossoms are controlled as above. The black pecan aphid may defoliate trees in late summer. Spraying with insecticide #15 or #17 gives control. Pecan Weevil, a long-snouted beetle, causes immature nuts to drop from feeding punctures in the shell, and the kernel is destroyed near harvest by the grubs. Weekly shaking and collecting the weevils onto sheets spread under the tree in late summer is recommended for a few trees. Spraying in midsummer with insecticide #9 is effective. Hickory shuck worm causes many small nuts to fall and damages the shuck on mature nuts. Insecticides have not been very effective, and collecting and burning fallen nuts or burying them in midsummer by cultivation is suggested.

Diseases

Pecan scab which infects both leaves and nuts causing premature dropping and poor quality is a limiting factor in pecan production. The more resistant varieties such as 'Moore' and 'Stuart' should be planted, and winter or early spring plowing done where practical. Spraying with fungicide #K, #H, or #G according to local recommendations is advised.

ovalis = *C. glabra*

ovata   **120′**   **Zone 4**   **Shagbark Hickory**
The most popular of the hickories as an ornamental, this is widely seen in the woods and fields of the central and eastern U.S. where it is native. The narrow habit, rugged branching and unique flaking bark are its chief characteristics of merit. If only one hickory is to be considered, this might well be the one to select. The large compound leaves have 5–7 leaflets. Some of the varieties named because of their good nuts are **'David'**, **'Fox'**, **'Glover'**, **'Johnson'**, **'Kirtland'**, **'Mann'**, **'Miller'**, **'Nielson'**, **'Whitney'**, **'Beeman'**, **'Bridgewater'** and **'Wilcox'**.

pecan = *C. illinoinensis*

tomentosa   **90′**   **Zone 4**   **Mockernut**
A second species native over a very wide area of the eastern U.S., and mentioned here only for that reason. Certainly the nuts are not popular because of their very thick shells. The

tree is handsome, with compound leaves comprised of 5–9 leaflets. It is long lived, specimens sometimes reaching the age of 250–300 years. The common name has been given because the fruits contain such small kernels that it is hardly worth while to extract them.

CARYOPHYLLACEAE = The Pink Family

CARYOPTERIS (ka-ri-OP-ter-is)

x clandonensis 4′ Zone 5 Hybrid Bluebeard
Few woody plants bloom in Aug. and this is the reason this species is often planted. The intense blue flower-spikes appear in late Aug. when few other deciduous woody plants are in flower. It may be killed back by severe winters and, if not, a severe pruning in the early spring will usually force it to produce better flowers. It is a hybrid (*C. incana* x *C. mongholica*) originating about 1933 and is a better garden plant than either of its parents. Treated as a perennial in the garden, it gives an excellent contrasting color in late summer to go with the yellows and oranges of calendulas, marigolds and zinnias. 'Blue Mist' and 'Heavenly Blue' are two popular clones. The leaves are opposite; sometimes it is used as a greenhouse pot plant.

incana 5′ Zone 7 Common Bluebeard
This is not as good an ornamental as its hybrid (*C. clandonensis*) but has been planted because of its small misty-blue flowers produced in cymes in the axils of the upper leaves during Sept. and Oct. Native from Japan to northwest China.

CARYOTA (ka-ri-O-ta)

mitis 25′ Zone 10 Tufted Fishtail Palm
A palm (from Malaya) with graceful arching fronds 4–9 ft. long and smooth brown trunks. The leaflets are triangular, like fish tails. A wine is sometimes extracted from the seeds.

urens 80′ Zone 10 Toddy Fishtail Palm
A palm with its leaves 20 ft. long and 12 ft. wide divided into segments like a fish tail. The trunk is up to 1½ ft. in dia. The flower clusters are 4 ft. and more in length and pendulous. The natives in Malaya (the habitat of this palm) cut the flower cluster and collect the sap flowing from the cut, boiling it and making a sugar or wine from it. The fruit is red, round and an inch wide. Even the young leaf shoots are eaten—sometimes planted in southern Fla.

CASA BANANA = *Sicana odorifera*

CASHEW, COMMON = *Anacardium occidentale*

CASIMIROA (kas-im-i-RO-a)

edulis 30′–50′ Zone 10 White Sapote
Native to Mexico, this is an evergreen with alternate compound leaves of 3–7 leaflets, 2–5 in. long. The fruits are greenish yellow, about the size of an orange and supposedly with a peach-like flavor. A tree for patios, it needs a rich soil and is usually used in areas where avocados are grown.

CASORON. A trade name for a dichlobenil weed and grass killer, otherwise known as Casoron G-4. It comes in granular form, is best applied in November after the ground has frozen. We have applied it at the rate of 1 oz. per 22 sq. ft. resulting in the killing of all grass and weeds for nearly a full year. Used once or twice it has no cumulative effect, but used annually it may result in damage to the trees and shrubs. Also see WEEDS and WEED KILLERS.

CASSAVA = *Manihot esculenta*

CASSIA (KASS-ia). Annuals and evergreen shrubs, mostly tropical, belonging to the Pea Family, with large, alternate, compound leaves and golden-yellow flowers in the summer. The fruits are long, flat pods. They are propagated by seeds and cuttings taken in March and placed in sandy peat in the greenhouse. *C. marilandica* is the hardiest of the group.

alata 15′ Zone 9 Candle-bush
The yellow flowers of this tropical American shrub are borne in close spikes resembling candles, most of this cylinder being made up of unopened buds, but a few flowers open at a time. It has a long blooming season, being at its peak in winter. The compound evergreen leaves have many blunt leaflets which are larger at the tip than at the base of the leaf. Drought-resistant. Propagated by seeds and cuttings.

corymbosa 10′ Zone 8 Flowery Senna
A free-flowering plant for southern gardens, this plant comes from Argentina. The yellow flowers, in axillary clusters, appear from July to frost, and it is often used for greenhouse display.

fasciculata 1′–3′ annual Partridge-pea
Although this annual may grow upright to a height of several feet, it more often appears as a scrambling vine. The compound leaves have 10–15 pairs of leaflets which attach to the leaf stalk at an angle, feather fashion, without a terminal leaflet. The leaves are sensitive and will fold shut when touched. The flowers have 5 petals, the lower one somewhat larger than the other 4, and the 5 sepals, though nearly single, are actually united at the base. The flowers, deep yellow in color, are borne in the axils of the leaves and bloom continuously from July to late Sept. This is a good plant for the wild garden, for it will flourish in poor sandy soil. Not hardy in the northernmost states, it will grow from Mass. and southern Minn. to Fla. and Tex. Propagation is by seed, which should be planted in sandy soil.

fistula 30′ Zone 10 Golden Shower Senna

A tree native to India, sometimes planted in the tropical parts of the U.S., with pale yellow flowers in foot-long racemes during spring before the leaves appear. The leaves are compound, with 4–8 pairs of leaflets, each about 2 in. long. The fruit is a 12–48 in. black pod.

grandis 50′ Zone 10 Coral Shower-tree
In Hawaii this native from tropical America blooms during March, April and May, with flower buds that are round, velvety and a pinkish lavender in color, the open flowers being a pale peach color. They are borne in flower-filled clusters on short branches. As soon as the first flowers appear, the new leaves start coming out, a pinkish color. The leaves have 16–40 leaflets and are 2½ in. long. Fruits are cylindrical, dark brown pods about 2 ft. long.

x hybrida (*C. javanica x fistula*) **30′ Zone 10 Rainbow Shower-tree**
This hybrid originated in Hawaii and the seedlings vary considerably, but the flowers are mostly a peach-apricot color. When in full bloom the branches are almost covered with flowers and the blooming period may last into Sept. Propagation is by cuttings.

javanica 20′ Zone 10 Apple Blossom Cassia
Northern visitors to the islands of the Caribbean recognize in the fragrant flowers of this tree a great similarity in shape and color of the flowers to their familiar apple blossoms, even though on this tree they are borne in huge, rounded, terminal clusters. The flowers are produced at the end of the dry period, during March and April, just when the new, alternate, compound leaves are being produced. These are pinnate, with about 6–15 pairs of leaflets, each of which is about 2 in. long. The leaves themselves are 12 in. long. The fruits are dark brown pods 2 ft. long. Native, probably, to the Malayan Archipelago, though seen also in Trinidad and Hawaii. Blooms appear in June in Hawaii.

marilandica 3′ Zones 2–3 Wild Senna
A perennial, native to the eastern U.S., with semi-woody branches which die back to the ground in the winter. With pinnately compound, alternate leaves, each with 10–20 leaflets 2 in. long, yellow pealike flowers in terminal or axillary racemes during the summer, and with fruits which are pods about 4 in. long. This makes a splendidly colorful plant for the perennial border in summer. The leaves and pods are used in certain kinds of drugs, especially as cathartics. Usually propagated by division.

surattensis 15′ Zone 9 Glossy-shower Senna
Practically ever-blooming, with yellow flowers, called "scrambled eggs" in Hawaii. Five similar petals, compound evergreen leaves with 8 pairs of oblong leaflets. The fruit is a flat green pod,

usually in clusters. Native to southeastern Asia. Propagated by seeds and cuttings.

CASSIA-BARK TREE = *Cinnamomum cassia*

CASSIOPE (cas-SY-o-pee) sp.
prostrate Zone 2 Cassiope
Low, prostrate, evergreen shrubs with scalelike leaves only about ⅛ in. long, usually arranged in 4 rows on the stems, with small, terminal, heathlike flowers colored white to red. Several species growing about the northern parts of the northern hemispheres. These must have a moist acid soil, and are of little value except in the wild garden or in the rockery. Very difficult to grow outside its native habitat.

CASTANEA (kas-TAY-nea). (Also see CHESTNUT, NUTS AND NUT CULTURE.)
All chestnuts have alternate leaves and male flowers in the form of catkins.

The chestnut bark disease which has swept the country since 1903 has eliminated most of our native chestnuts. It is true that there are still sprouts of the native chestnut (*C. dentata*) commonly seen in the woodlands of the eastern U.S., and in fact there are trees mature enough to bear many fruits. However, though hundreds of people are looking for native blight-resistant trees, none has been found to date. One may still be found, but the enthusiastic hunter will do well to watch his fruiting tree for at least 5 years, to make certain that no branches die from the disease, before he begins to broadcast information about his "find".

It has been established that the Chinese Chestnut (*C. mollissima*) and its varieties are the most resistant to this destructive disease and can usually be grown with safety. The Japanese Chestnut (*c. crenata*) is just slightly less resistant, but according to Dr. Richard A. Jaynes, formerly of the Conn. Agric. Exp. Station, who has been studying this problem for some time, the Japanese Chestnut is still very much in the running as far as an ornamental and timber tree is concerned. It is also possible that future selections will be made of good nut-producing clones, too. So both these species are possibilities for use as ornamentals. For the present at least, the Chinese clones which are being grown in the commercial nurseries are those with the better fruits. The large, prickly burrs, 2 in. wide, formerly were a familiar sight to everyone who walked in the woods and forests. These burrs split open after a frost to show the 2–3 nuts inside this outer husk. The bark of this tree produces a very fine dye.

There are places in the U.S. where the Spanish Chestnut (*C. sativa*) is being grown. This is the nut-producing tree of Europe which provides so many of the chestnuts imported from abroad. However, neither this species nor any species (other than *C. mollissima* and *C. crenata*) are recommended here because they all are so susceptible to the chestnut blight.

Propagation

Do not allow the seed to dry out, but stratify as soon as ripe at 40° F. for 3 months. *C. pumila* has no dormancy. Also propagation, though difficult, is by budding and grafting, using *C. mollissima* as the understock. Some experimental work is now being done at Cornell Univ., Ithaca, N.Y., regarding stoolbed layering and tissue culture techniques, but easy commercial propagation is still years away.

Insect Pests

Two-lined chestnut borer is a serious pest of weakened trees. Tunnels just under the bark girdle branches and may kill the tree. Spraying with insecticide #9 when beetles are active in early summer is recommended. Many leaf-eating caterpillars eat the leaves unless they are protected with insecticides #15 or #9. The nuts may be infested by the chestnut weevils which lay eggs in the burrs from which legless grubs hatch and feed on the nut meat. Spraying with insecticide #9 in midsummer will kill many weevils and the grubs in harvested nuts are killed by fumigation with carbon disulfide.

Diseases

Chestnut blight has killed nearly all American chestnuts but does not infect the roots from which sprouts continue to grow for many years. Sprouts become infected and killed after 3–4 years. Asiatic and European species are quite resistant and have been planted extensively. There is no effective control with fungicides. Dieback fungus produces bark cankers and kills many twigs. Control with fungicides is not recommended.

crenata   30′   Zone 6   Japanese Chestnut
This tree, native to Japan, and the Chinese Chestnut (*Castanea mollissima*) are the only 2 chestnut species (and their hybrids) sufficiently resistant to the chestnut blight to be grown in the United States today. The Japanese chestnut is not so resistant as the Chinese species, but it grows into a dense shrub or small tree with lustrous foliage and yellow-to-bronze autumn color. The nuts of this species are not so tasty as those of *C. mollissima* and this is probably the reason why it is not grown more in the U.S. The extract of the nut shell, the burr, and the bark of this tree can all be used for staining. The male flower of the chestnut can be used to stain cloth a red-brown color.

dentata   90′   Zone 4   American Chestnut
Formerly this tree was widely distributed in the eastern U.S. and was one of the most important lumber trees in the area. Its long, 5–10 in. leaves with bristle teeth on the margins were very familiar to the woods and forests. The rich bronze autumn color was good. Now, the chestnut blight has wiped out most of these trees and at present there is no known cure for it, nor are there any cultivars of this species at this time known to be immune to the disease. Suckers still grow from old stumps throughout its former range, and some may even survive long enough to bear fruits, but eventually all these succumb to the disease. For resistant varieties, see *C. mollissima*.

Castanea dentata—American Chestnut

mollissima   60′   Zone 4   Chinese Chestnut
Much has been made of this chestnut in recent years in America because it has been found to be the least susceptible of all the *Castanea* species to the disastrous chestnut blight. Introduced into America from China around 1903, little attention was given it until recently when it was found that because of the blight most of the other chestnuts just cannot be grown. The U.S. Department of Agriculture became interested in making selections from a large orchard planting of seedlings made around 1936. At least 4 varieties have been introduced, especially because of their good fruits; namely **'Abundance'** (by Carroll D. Bush of Eagle Creek, Ore., in 1941) and **'Meiling'**, **'Nanking'** and **'Kuling'** by the U.S. Department of Agriculture in 1949.

These trees are supposed to have produced an average crop of 75–100 lbs. of edible nuts per tree. These nuts are not so tasty as the good, old-fashioned American Chestnut, but they are of good size and are edible.

It is important to note that Chinese chestnuts are self-sterile and hence in order to produce fruits at least 2 or more seedlings or clones should be planted to insure cross-fertilization. One single tree grown alone will produce only a handful of nuts. It should be noted, also, that although this species is hardy in Zone 4, there are some years when the growing season is not long enough for the fruits to mature properly. The male and female flowers are borne in mid-June and in some parts of central New England early frosts can stop fruit growth before they are properly matured.

As an ornamental tree the Chinese Chestnut certainly has merit, especially because of its rounded habit, dense foliage and very lustrous dark green leaves. The profuse staminate tassels borne in mid-June add to its effectiveness as a flowering tree and the good yellow-to-bronze autumn color is an asset also. In planting young trees it might be well to keep them cultivated for the first few years, for it seems they do not compete well with weeds during the formative period.

Dr. Arthur M. Graves, formerly of the Connecticut Agricultural Experiment Station, New Haven, Conn., spent many years in hybridizing chestnuts, in an attempt to find new varieties with nuts and wood of good quality, yet sufficiently resistant to the chestnut blight to be worth growing. Recently some new varieties have been named—almost entirely blight resistant. These are 'Essate-Jap', 'Sleeping Giant' which is a *C. crenata* x *C. dentata* cross and has good timber value, and 'Kelsey', a smaller Chinese Chestnut seedling with small but very delicious nuts. Whether these will become commercially available in the years to come remains to be seen, but these 3 cultivars should be of great interest to all who wish to grow the chestnut, either for its timber or its fruits. For further information concerning these plants, one should write to Dr. Richard A. Jaynes, Geneticist, the Connecticut Agricultural Experiment Station, New Haven, Conn.

pumila 25′–45′ Zone 5 Allegany Chinkapin
Native to the southeastern U.S., this plant has little of ornamental value. It increases by underground stems, has leaves 3–5 in. long and 2 in. wide, pointed and coarsely toothed and grayish white underneath. The prickly burr is about 1½ in. wide, usually containing only 1 seed. Sometimes spelled Chinquapin.

sativa 90′ Zone 5 Spanish Chestnut
Native to southern Europe and western Asia, this tree grows to tremendous dimensions in its native habitat, sometimes having a trunk circumference of 30 ft. It is the nuts from this species that are now imported from Europe in such large quantities for cooking purposes. As yet it has not been much used in America for ornamental purposes, for it would seem advisable to use instead the varieties of *C. mollissima* which have proved to be resistant to the inroads of the chestnut blight.

CASTANOPSIS (kas-tan-OP-sis)
chrysophylla 105′ Zone 7 Giant Evergreen-chinkapin
A broad-leaved evergreen tree, native from Ore. to Calif., this has fluffy spikes of creamy-white flowers and prickly burrs for fruit. The dark lustrous leaves are 2–5 in. long. It is a splendid foliage tree, noted for the fact that it grows well on poor dry soils.

CASTANOSPERMUM (kas-tan-o-SPERM-um)
australe 60′ Zone 10 Moreton Bay Chestnut
An Australian tree valued for its red and yellow flowers in large, loose racemes, 6 in. long during July. The foliage is evergreen, the leaves are compound, 18 in. long with 11–15 broad leaflets. The fruit is a large pod 9 in. long and 2 in. broad with large, edible chestnutlike seeds. This is grown only in southern Calif.

CASTILLEJA (kas-till-EE-ya)
coccinea 1′–2′ Zone 3 Indian Paintbrush
This perennial herb belongs to the group called parasitic, since it derives most or all of its nourishment from the roots of other plants. A rosette of rounded or elliptical leaves circles the flower stalk which grows to a foot or more in height. Deeply lobed, linear leaves are arranged alternately on the stalk, topped by rather inconspicuous, 2-lipped tubular flowers surrounded by leafy bracts, the lobes of which are tipped with red and which give the plant its ornamental interest. Preferring low, wet meadows, it may be found from southern Canada and New England to Fla. and Tex., and the flowers may appear from April to Aug. Although it would be a beautiful and unusual plant for the moist wild garden, it is almost impossible to cultivate because of its parasitic nature. It belongs to the Figwort Family.

CAST-IRON PLANT = *Aspidistra elatior*

CASTOR-ARALIA = *Kalopanax pictus*

CASTOR-BEAN = *Ricinus communis*

CASUARINA (kas-ew-a-REE-na)
equisetifolia 70′ Zone 9 Horsetail Beefwood
A peculiar tree native to Australia but generally planted in southern Fla. The leaves are really small scales, the green twigs looking almost leafless and hence they suggest the Horsetail. It gives poor shade but can be sheared, grows in

Casuarina equisetifolia

all kinds of soils and does well in brackish situations in seashore gardens. The peculiar cones, $\frac{1}{2}$ in. in dia., are much used in Christmas decorations.

cunninghamiana 3′–50′ Zone 9 Cunningham Beefwood
Similar to *C. equisetifolia* but better because the branches seem to be borne all the way to the ground. Cones are less than $\frac{1}{4}$ in. in dia. Native to Australia.

stricta   30′   Zone 10   Coast Beefwood
Another Australian tree with foliage similar to the above species. It is merely more of a shrub, but the cones are about 1 in. across.

CATALPA (kat-ALP-a). The catalpas are deciduous trees with large, opposite leaves that are sometimes whorled on vigorous shoots, with flowers usually white, in large pyramidal clusters during the summer. The fruits are long, beanlike pods. These trees are coarse in texture, have no autumn color, but because they grow fast under almost any conditions and in almost any soil, they have been popular trees for a long time.

Propagation

Seed may be sown as soon as ripe or stored dry for up to a year in airtight containers in a cool place and then sown. Softwood cuttings have been rooted. Root cuttings root readily. See CUTTINGS.

Insect Pests

The caterpillar of the catalpa sphinx moth is one of the most spectacular insect pests. About 3 in. long when grown, its greenish-yellow body with conspicuous black markings has a prominent spine at the rear. There may be 2 or 3 generations annually and trees are often defoliated. Spraying with insecticide #9 gives control.

Catalpa midge distorts the leaves and enters the pod to feed on the seeds. Timely spraying with insecticide #15 is suggested. Catalpa mealybug lives in colonies under leaves and at base of twigs. Heavy infestations require spraying with insecticide #15.

Diseases

A fungus leaf spot which covers the leaves with dark brown spots is often destructive unless sprayed with fungicides #D or #F. Wood rot often shortens the life of catalpa trees by causing decay in the sapwood. Cutting out the decayed area and repairing the wound is suggested.

bignonioides 45′ Zone 4 Southern Catalpa
The Southern Catalpa, native to Ga., Fla. and Miss., is not so widely planted as is the western species (*C. speciosa*), but the tree is smaller and the leaves are only about 4 in. long, while those of the western species can be a foot long and hence considerably coarser in texture. No catalpas are long-lived, but this species might be tried more because of its smaller leaves, more profuse (though smaller) flowers, and lower height when compared with *C. speciosa*.

The variety **'Aurea'** has yellow leaves all through the growing season and **'Nana'** is dwarf. This is usually grafted or budded high on an understock to make a slow-growing, globe-shaped tree formerly called incorrectly *C. bungei*.

ovata   30′   Zone 4   Chinese Catalpa
A Chinese tree with opposite leaves 5–10 in. long and as wide, heart shaped and sometimes 3 lobed. The panicles of white flowers are 4–10 in. long, appearing during July. The pod is about 12 in. long and $\frac{1}{4}$ in. in dia. It bears smaller flowers than either of the American species.

speciosa   90′   Zone 4   Northern Catalpa
Blooming 2 weeks before *C. bignonioides*, in late June, this has slightly larger flowers (though fewer of them) and leaves which may be up to 1 ft. long. It has proved resistant to hot, dry

weather—the reason why it has always been popular in the Midwest, where it is native from Ind. to Ark. One of its unique characteristics is that the wood will last unusual lengths of time when in contact with the soil. Easily and quickly grown from seed, it is very coarse in texture and is not used so much in ornamental plantings now as it was 50 years ago. The large, conspicuous flower clusters in late June are, of course, its chief ornamental asset.

CATANANCHE (kat-a-NAN-ke)
 caerulea   18″   annual   Blue Cupid's-dart
An herbaceous annual or perennial, blooming the first year, has narrow woolly leaves. The flower heads with blue ray-flowers appear from June to Aug. and the fruit heads are somewhat similar to those of the Dandelion. A member of the large Composite Family. They are excellent subjects for drying and are popular in flower arrangements. The seeds should be sown indoors in March and set out after danger of frost is over. Native to southern Europe. White-flowered varieties are available.

CATBRIER = *Smilax glauca*

CATCHFLY. See SILENE.

CATCHFLY, GERMAN = *Lychnis viscaria*

CAT-CLAW VINE = *Macfadyena unguis-cati*

CATHA (KAY-tha)
 edulis   10′   Zone 10   Khat, Arabian-tea
Evergreen shrub from South Africa, the leaves and buds of which have been used by the Arabians for centuries in making a tea. The fruit capsules remain on the plant all winter and when they split open the brilliant red seeds within are conspicuous. The leaves are about 4 in. long, opposite but sometimes alternate on infertile shoots.

CATHARANTHUS (ca-thar-AN-thus)
 roseus (*Vinca rosea*) **2′   Zone 10   Madagascar Periwinkle**
This is a low shrub or perennial from tropical America with opposite leaves, pointed at both ends and about 2 in. long. The 5-petalled flowers are pale pink, about 1½ in. across, borne a few together at the end of a branch and appear throughout the year. It is often used as a ground cover. This is sometimes planted in northern gardens as an annual. The var. **alba** has white flowers. Easily grown from seed.

CATKIN. A deciduous spike of unisexual, petalless flowers. See AMENT.

CATMINT = *Nepeta cataria*

CATNIP = *Nepeta cataria*

CATTAIL. See TYPHA.

CATTLEYA (CAT-lee-a). This group of orchids is unquestionably the most popular of all the many thousands of orchids and the easiest to grow in the home greenhouse. The individual flowers are mostly colored shades of lavender and orange, from 1½–10 in. in size across, with the number of flowers varying per stem. They flower once a year at varying times depending on the species. They are about 12–20 in. tall, with straplike leaves and pseudobulbs, 1–3 leaves per bulb. Native to the foothills and mountainous regions of South America where they have 2 distinct rainy seasons alternating with 2 dry seasons. They have been greatly hybridized and several hundred fine clones have been grown. For information on culture and propagation see ORCHID. A few of the most widely grown are listed below:
 bowringiana   12″–30″   Zone 10
Flowers a rich rosy purple, 2½ in. across, with 5–20 flowers produced on the raceme in the greenhouse in autumn. The pseudobulbs are 12–24 in. high, swollen at the base, and the 2 leaves are 4–6 in. long. Native to Central America.
 gaskelliana   1″–14″   Zone 10
Fragrant flowers medium to dark lavender, 4–6 in. across, 3–6 on a stalk during the late spring or early summer. This is a small orchid, but floriferous. Native to Brazil.
 labiata   12″–18″   Zone 10
These are the most popular of all. Native to Brazil. The flowers are medium to dark lavender, 5–7 in. across, 2–5 on a stalk, produced in autumn. The leaves are solitary, leathery, dark green up to 3 in. wide and the pseudo-bulbs are up to 12 in. tall. It is a variable species, but this and several hundred varieties closely related to it are the chief constituents in the *Cattleya* group offered by American florists today.
 mossiae   12″–18″   Zone 10
Flowers medium to dark lavender, 5–8 in. across, 3–7 per stalk from March to May. It is a strong grower and heavy bloomer. The pseudo-bulbs are about 1 ft. high. Native to Venezuela.
 trianaei   1′–2′   Zone 10
This also is a popular species among American orchid growers with light-blush to dark lavender flowers 5–7 in. across, 2–5 per stalk from Nov. to Feb. This is well known and a good one for the new orchid hobbyist to start with because it is grown so easily and will withstand more abuse and less sun than most others. Several varieties with fragrant flowers are being grown. Native to Colombia.

CAT'S-EAR = *Hypochaeris radicata*

CAUDATE. Having a slender, tail-like appendage.

CAULIFLOWER (*Brassica oleracea* var, *botrytis*). This, one of the most delicious of the

Cabbage tribe, is grown for its tender, white, much-enlarged flower head or curd. While the crop is grown in much the same manner as Cabbage it is much more difficult to grow successfully. (See drawing, p. 300.)

The plant comes in two main types, the ordinary Cauliflower of our markets and winter Cauliflower or heading Broccoli. This latter type is quite common in England but of little importance in the U.S.

Cauliflower thrives best in a cool moist climate. It will not withstand as low a temperature or as much heat as Cabbage. Proximity to the sea or cool uplands having plenty of moisture are ideal. Commercial production is limited largely to sections of N.Y. (Long Island, the Catskill Mountain region, and Erie Country), Calif., Fla., Colo., Wash., and the Great Lakes region.

Varieties

Super Snowball types are the earliest varieties to mature. The **Erfurt** or **Snowball** types are later and larger headed. Both of these types contain a number of named strain which may vary in habit of growth and time of maturity. **'Early Purple Head'** produces a purplish-green curd which does not need blanching. The purple color disappears on cooking, resulting in a pale green, tender, mild-flavored product.

Soils and Fertilizer

Soil and fertilizer conditions are similar to that for Cabbage. See CABBAGE. Cauliflower responds best in soils rich in organic matter, good water-holding capacity, a high level of fertility and a pH range of 5.5 to 6.5.

Growing Plants

For both early and late varieties the method of growing seedling plants is the same as for Cabbage. See CABBAGE. If plants are purchased from a dealer be sure to select strong, stocky plants that come from a reliable seed source.

Planting and Care

For both early and late varieties space the plants in the row 24 in. apart and 30–36 in. between rows. In view of the relatively short time that Cauliflower will remain in good usable condition, it is suggested that several plantings a week or 10 days apart is advisable. Cultivation and summer care is the same as for cabbage.

Blanching and Harvesting

A perfect head of Cauliflower is pure white. To obtain this it is necessary to bring the outer leaves up over the head and tie them with twine or rubber bands. This should be done shortly after the button like swelling of the head or curd appears. Cauliflower is harvested as soon as the heads attain full size and before the curd begins to "rice" and discolor. Harvest at once by cutting the stalk off below the head, handle carefully and use as soon as possible.

Winter Cauliflower or Heading Broccoli

This is similar to Cauliflower but it requires a much longer growing season, from late fall to the following spring. It is very sensitive to heat, requires a long period of evenly cool weather and demands a liberal and constant supply of moisture. It is an important crop in England but of very minor value in the U.S. It is of little interest to home gardeners.

Cauliflower is subject to the same insects, diseases, and physiological disorders as Cabbage. See CABBAGE.

GRANT B. SNYDER

CAULOPHYLLUM (kaw-lo-FILL-um)
  thalictroides   12"–18"   Zone 4   Blue Cohosh
A thickened rootstalk sends up a rather fleshy, grayish-green stem which branches to form several stems, each of which bears a single thrice-compound leaf. Small clusters of greenish-purple, 6-petalled flowers extend upward a few inches from these leaves. The flowers are less conspicuous and ornamental than the blue berries which appear in late summer. This perennial grows in rich, moist woods from southeast Canada to Ala. and Miss. It self-sows readily and also may be divided in spring or fall. The rootstalks are poisonous.

CEANOTHUS (see-an-O-thus). Evergreen or deciduous shrubs native to North America, some with opposite, some with alternate leaves. The flowers are usually blue or white, very small, but borne in profuse upright clusters.

Propagation

In the East the seed is soaked in hot water (190° F.) overnight and then stratified for 3 months at 40° F. Cuttings, both softwood and hardwood, root easily if taken in July or Aug. See STRATIFICATION, CUTTINGS.

americanus   3'   Zone 4   New Jersey-tea
It should be remembered that this native American plant (Canada to Fla.) is hard to move. The flowers appear in mid-June and are small and white in upright, oblong clusters. It is best used in poor, dry soils where better plants will not grow. The common name was given it during the Revolutionary War when its leaves were used as a substitute for tea. It is one of the parents of many better flowering hybrids which are popularly planted in southern Calif. gardens.

arboreus   20'   Zone 9   Feltleaf Ceanothus

One of the tallest species of this genus, often with a trunk 1½–2½ ft. in circumference and with alternate, bright green, evergreen leaves 1½–4 in. long, grayish tomentose underneath and strongly 3 veined. The pale blue, fragrant flowers are small, produced in pyramidal clusters 3–4 in. long during July and Aug. Native to the islands off the Calif. coast.

x delilianus   6′   Zone 7   Delisle Ceanothus
On the Pacific Coast, especially in the vicinity of Santa Barbara, Calif., this hybrid group really comes into its own. There are probably more of this genus grown in this one area than in any other place in the world. This particular species is a hybrid (*C. americanus* x *C. coeruleus*) of which there are many varieties. The flowers, appearing in April, are very small, profusely borne in small terminal panicles and are a pale to deep blue, a color unusual in most gardens. The evergreen leaves are 1½–3 in. long. Of the popular varieties a few of the best are:
'Gloire de Versailles'—flowers pale blue
'Gloire de Plantieres'—flowers deep blue
'Autumnal Blue'—flowers deep blue
'Leon Simon'—flowers pale blue
Some of these have been espaliered with excellent results.

foliosus   1′   Zone 8   Wavy Leaf Ceanothus
A densely branched shrub with blue flowers.
gloriosus   prostrate shrub   Zone 7   Point Reyes Ceanothus
Native to southern Calif., this plant makes a fine ground cover with leathery leaves (not evergreen) about 1 in. long. The flowers are purplish to deep blue.
impressus   5′   Zone 8   Santa Barbara Ceanothus
A native of southern Calif. with dark blue flowers; leaves that are ½″ long and elliptic to round.
ovatus   3′   Zone 4   Inland Ceanothus
Another eastern U.S. native with small white flower-clusters in early June, but with the added asset of red fruit capsules in the summer. It is denser in habit than *C. americanus* and thus makes a better landscape plant. It is best used for naturalizing, but unfortunately it must be admitted that few nurserymen grow it at present.
prostatus   procumbent shrub   Zone 7   Squaw-carpet Ceanothus
The blue flowers are in short terminal clusters and the habit of the plant is so dense that it makes a beautiful ground-covering mat of foliage. Native to the West Coast, it is difficult to propagate and may need some winter protection (or a snow cover) to bring it through winters undamaged.
pumilus   8″   Zone 8   Siskiyou-mat
A prostrate, evergreen shrub with a densely branched habit. The flowers are blue to white

and it is native from southern Calif. to northern Ore. All these **Ceanothus** species are difficult to transplant.
thyrsiflorus   30′   Zone 8   Blue Blossom Ceanothus
Native on the Pacific Coast from Ore. to Calif., this is one of the hardiest evergreen species of *Ceanothus*. The flowers are blue, nearly white, in panicles 3 in. long, and appear in March. The leaves are up to 2 in. long. It does well in dry soils, but is susceptible to scale and so must be sprayed at the proper time. *C. griseus* is somewhat similar and is being used more now because it is much less susceptible to pests.

CECROPIA (see-KRO-pia)
peltata   36′–60′   Zone 10   Trumpet-tree
A coarse, widely branched, ungainly tree of the South American tropics and the West Indies, with leaves 12–16 in. wide with 7–9 deep lobes, dark green above and densely white pubescent below. The leaves drop intermittently and so are unsightly and even on the tree they are all clustered at the end of the branches. The branches are hollow and sometimes trumpets are made from them. The sap is a milky white juice, attractive to ants. Flowers are dioecious. Evident everywhere in the rain forests of Puerto Rico, but not a tree for ornamental planting. However, the leaves dry slightly turned up on the edges and apparently are used to some extent by flower arrangers in the North.

CEDAR. See CEDRUS (not to be confused with Redcedar which is *Juniperus virginiana*).

CEDRELA (SED-reel-a, preferred; sed-REE-la, popular)
sinensis   70′   Zone 5   Chinese Toon
This resembles the common *Ailanthus altissima* and is also native to China. It makes a better ornamental specimen and can withstand urban growing conditions. The leaves are alternate, compound with 10–22 leaflets each 4–7 in. long, and the greenish-yellow to white flowers are in pendulous clusters a foot long in June. Like Ailanthus it has no autumn color, and there is little about it to recommend its use.

Propagation

Seed may be sown as soon as ripe or stored dry for up to a year in airtight containers in a cool place, and then sown. Root cuttings taken in spring, about the size of a lead pencil, root well. See CUTTINGS.

CEDRUS (SED-rus; popularly, SEE-drus). Three species of this genus are very popular ornamental trees, evergreen members of the Pine Family with small clustered needles 1–2 in. long, and large, erect, solid cones that take 2 years to mature. Staminate flowers appear in upright catkins on the same trees as the pistillate. They need plenty of room to expand and are among the very best of the evergreen trees for specimens.

Propagation

Do not allow this seed to dry out for it should be sown or stratified as soon as it is ripe. Stratification for about 2 months at 40° F. unifies the germination. Grafting is also practiced; any one of the 3 species can be grafted on any other of the 3 species as understocks. Hardwood cuttings have been rooted but are difficult. See GRAFTING, STRATIFICATION, CUTTINGS, etc.

Insect Pests

Atlas, Deodar and Cedar of Lebanon are often damaged by the deodar weevil which chews on the bark of twigs. The larvae feed in the cambium girdling the twigs and frequently kill the leader. Timely sprays of insecticide #9 are helpful. A large aphid occasionally damages Atlas Cedar when not controlled with sprays of insecticide #15.

atlantica　　120′　　Zone 6　　Atlas Cedar
This tree is noted for its widely pyramidal habit and its silvery to light green foliage. The cones are about 3 in. long and 2 in. through and the twigs are always more pubescent than those of the other species; as it matures it develops a flat top. It is native to northern Africa. The var. 'Argentea Fastigiata' has excellent silvery gray-blue leaves, a narrow habit and is named the Silver Atlas Cedar. The var. 'Glauca' has excellent bluish foliage and is very common in cultivation, Blue Atlas Cedar; 'Pendula' has graceful pendulous branches.

deodara　　150′　　Zone 7　　Deodar Cedar
This is the most graceful of the 3 cedars, with a pyramidal habit and gracefully pendulous branches. It is native to the Himalayas and is the least hardy; the cones are 4 in. long and 2½ in. across. There are several varieties of this popular evergreen, but one of the most popular is 'Pendula' with graceful pendulous branches, sometimes spreading over the ground with ends upright. The main leader should be staked to produce a tree with a straight trunk. 'Glauca' has bluish-green to silvery-gray needles.

libani　　120′　　Zone 6　　Cedar-of-Lebanon
Native to Asia Minor, this is narrowly pyramidal while young but at maturity develops a definitely flat top that is most picturesque. The foliage is dark green. Frequent reference is made to it in the Bible, and Solomon's Temple was built with massive timbers cut from it. The hardiest form of all has now been called var. **stenocoma,** hardy as far north as Boston, Mass.

'Sargentii' is a dwarf, shrubby, slow-growing variety.

CEIBA (say-EE-ba)
pentandra　120′　Zone 10　Kapok, Silk-cotton Tree
Only grown in the warmest parts of the U.S., this peculiar tree is native to the Tropics of both hemispheres. It has a huge buttressed trunk and wide-spreading branches at right angles to it. The compound leaves have about 7 leaflets, each 4–6 in. long, but they are deciduous. The white to pinkish flowers during the summer are mallowlike, 6–8 in. long, and the bark is distinctively smooth and gray. The kapok of commerce comes from the silky lustrous floss about the seeds which are borne in leathery capsules 3–6 in. long. This tree needs plenty of space in which to grow properly.

CELANDINE = *Chelidonium majus*

CELASTRACEAE = The Bittersweet Family.

CELASTRUS (see-LASS-trus). Twining vines with alternate leaves, usually male and female flowers on different plants. Although the flowers are inconspicuous, the fruits are most colorful in the fall, being orange to red berries.

Propagation

Seed may be sown as soon as ripe, stratified for 3 months at 40° F. and then sown, or dried, stored dry in airtight containers in a cool place for up to a year and then sown. Layers are frequently used. Hardwood and softwood cuttings root readily and root cuttings are frequently taken and rooted. See LAYERS, CUTTINGS.

Insect Pests

Bittersweet may be heavily infested with Euonymus scale which greatly weakens or kills the vine. See EUONYMUS. The two-marked tree hopper, an oddly shaped insect resembling a tiny bird, feeds on the leaves and twigs. The over-wintering eggs are laid in white frothy masses on the twigs. If necessary, timely sprays of insecticide #15 will kill the nymphs.

Diseases

Powdery mildew may give an abnormal white appearance to the leaves. Spraying with fungicide #V or #M will control it.

flagellaris　twining vine 24′　Zone 4　Korean Bittersweet
Rare in American gardens and even in arboretums, this vine from Korea is of interest because the stipules at the base of each leaf are small hooked spines, making it one of the few thorny vines available. Twining like the other *Celastrus* species and in the fall bearing yellow

Cedrus atlantica 'Pendula': An unusual tree with gray foliage.

Cedrus atlantica 'Glauca': Planted in 1876, has gray foliage.

and red berries that are smaller and fewer in number than those of *C. scandens* and *C. orbiculatus*, nevertheless this might be a good vine for bank planting as a barrier to discourage trespassers. See *C. scandens*.

orbiculatus twining vine 36′ Zone 4 Oriental
Bittersweet
An excellent twining vine from China and Japan which is now becoming naturalized in some places in the eastern U.S., this differs from *C. scandens*, the native American Bittersweet, chiefly in that the leaves are more rounded and

the fruits are in small lateral clusters, not in terminal clusters, as are those of *C. scandens*. All *Celastrus* species have staminate flowers on one plant and pistillate flowers on another. For further information, see under *C. scandens*.

rosthornianus (*loeseneri*)   vine   Zone 5
Loesener Bittersweet
A woody vine from China, this has recently been advertised nationally as being one of the "best" of the *Celastus* species for fruits, but actually it is very similar to the much more easily available *C. orbiculatus*.

scandens **twining vine 20′** **Zone 2** **American Bittersweet**

Native throughout eastern North America, this vigorous vine is frequently seen in the fall along roadsides, where it twines up the brush or fence posts and is covered with its yellow and red terminal clusters of fruit. In all *Celastrus* species, the small, inconspicuous staminate flowers are on one plant (blooming in June) and the pistillate flowers are on another. Sometimes, flowers of both sexes are on one vine. It is best to be certain that pistillate vines are grown with a known staminate vine nearby. It is possible to plant both types of vines in one hole to insure fruiting, or to graft or bud a branch of the staminate form onto the pistillate vine to insure pollen at the right time. If there is no pollen source near the known pistillate vine, flowering branches of the male plant can be placed in a bottle of water and tied up in the pistillate plant at the time of flowering, allowing insects and wind to do the rest.

The American Bittersweet, like the others, twines and it can choke plants to death because of this twining habit. Hence none of them should be allowed to twine about living shrubs or trees. These are all excellent for bright yellow autumn color. A little intelligent maintenance is all that is necessary to have fruiting plants, provided of course that fruiting plants are bought in the first place. It might be best to buy such plants in the fall with fruits actually on the plant to prove their sex, or to buy from a reliable nurseryman who propagates the sexes separately —asexually. Staminate vines will never bear fruits.

Horses have been poisoned by eating the leaves of this vine.

CELERIAC (*Apium graveolens rapaceum*). Turnip-rooted celery or Celeriac is grown in exactly the same manner as Celery. The root is the edible part. It is used for flavoring, as a salad and for cooking similar to other root crops. The roots vary in size from 2–4 in.

The plants are not blanched and thus less space is needed than for Celery between rows. Roots from the late fall crop may be stored for several months under the same condition as for beets or turnips.

Celeriac is subject to the same insects and diseases common to Celery but to a much lesser degree.

GRANT B. SNYDER

CELERY (*Apium graveolens dulce*). Celery and closely related Celeriac both belong to the genus Apium of the Carrot or Umbelliferae Family which includes some 20 species of herbs that are best adapted to the northern temperate zone.

Celery is one of the more difficult crops to grow in the home garden because it requires more detailed care than most other crops. It is a cool weather plant and, therefore, in the south it is grown as a winter and spring crop and farther north as a summer and fall crop.

The more important commercial production areas are located in Calif., Fla., and Ariz. in the south and N.Y., N.J., Mich., Ohio, Pa., and Wash. in the north.

Varieties

Green varieties have increased in importance and the so-called yellow or self-blanching types have decreased in use during the past 20 years. The most important green varieties are 'Utah', of which there are number of strains, 'Giant Pascal', 'Summer Pascal' and 'Fordhook'. Varieties in the self-blanching category are 'Golden Self Blanching', 'Wonderful' or 'Golden Plume', 'Michigan' and 'Detroit Golden'.

Soils and Fertilizers

No garden crop grown is such a rich feeder as Celery. The soil must have depth, mellowness, and an abundant supply of moisture. A well-drained muck or peat soil is ideal but most home gardeners will find a sandy loam soil that is well supplied with organic matter to be very satisfactory. A heavy clay soil should be avoided. The soil pH should range between 5.8 and 6.7. See LIME.

For sandy loam soils, 3–4 bushels of animal manure or a well-decomposed compost per 100 ft. should be thoroughly plowed or spaded into the soil to a depth of 7–8 in. Celery is a heavy feeder and a poor forager and, therefore, in addition to the manure or compost it is advisable to broadcast, at the time of plowing or spading, 30–40 lbs. of a 5–8–7 or a 5–10–10 complete fertilizer per 1000 sq. ft.

Raising Plants from Seed

Most home gardeners will find it more desirable to buy plants from a dealer or commercial grower. Celery seed is small, germinates slowly and must have careful attention as to temperature and soil moisture during the germination period.

The seed should be planted in a very light sandy soil, preferably in drills 1½–2 in. apart and not over ⅛ in. in depth. After the seed is covered a piece of burlap or even a newspaper is placed over the flat or container to help maintain a uniform moisture of the soil during the germination period. A temperature of 70°–75° F. is optimum.

The young seedlings are very delicate and spindly until they reach a height of $1\frac{1}{2}$–2 in. When the second true leaves appear the plants should be transplanted into a good potting soil $1\frac{1}{2}$–2 in. apart. Maintaining a uniform moisture and temperature is very important in producing a good stocky plant. Temperature exposure of 50° F. or below for 7–10 days or more will result in premature seed-stalk development. Some 8–9 weeks are necessary before plants are ready for out-of-door planting.

Planting and Care

The garden soil should be fine, smooth, moist and fairly firm and the plants stocky, 4–5 in. tall with plenty of roots. Out-of-door planting should be delayed until danger of frost is past. Planting distance, 5–6 in. in the row and 24–30 in. between rows. In planting set the plants level with the crown of the plant or not deeper than they were in the flat or seedbed. The young plants should be watered daily until they are well established.

Shallow cultivation should start as soon as possible after planting in order to control weeds and to maintain a thin, loose surface of the soil.

Celery will respond to several applications of nitrate of soda during the growing season. Each application of 3–4 lbs. per 100 ft. of row should be placed several inches from the plants on both sides and then lightly worked into the top surface of the soil. Watering will help to make the fertilizer available to the plants.

Blanching and Harvesting

Blanching means the loss of green color and since it is known that the green color of plants contains a higher vitamin A content than non-white parts the demands for blanched celery has materially decreased.

Blanching of the self-blanching or early types is usually done by the use of 12-in.-wide rolls of heavy building paper or 10–12-in.-wide boards which are placed on either side of the row of Celery and then held together by wire hooks. In warm weather the plants will blanch in about 10 days.

For the late varieties the most satisfactory method of blanching is to gradually pull soil around the plant until only the top of the leaves show above the mound. No soil must be allowed to fall into the heart of the plant. This type of blanching should not be done until late in the fall or when the plants are fully grown. Placing hay or straw over the hilled row will mean that the plants can be kept until early winter.

There is no definite stage of maturity at which Celery must be harvested. Its best quality is

STAPLE

Blanching Celery with boards, black polyethylene, or paper.

attained when the plants have reached full size. In harvesting the plants are cut off below the surface of the soil with a large knife. Pull off the outside stalks and use them for celery soup or flavoring.

Storage

The fall crop of Celery may be stored for periods of 4–8 weeks. Perhaps the most practical method for the home gardener is in using a trench in the garden area. Three to 4 rows of Celery are packed tight and upright in the trench. Boards are set against the side and over the top of the trench. Hay or straw is then placed over the boards and as colder weather sets in a layer of soil is placed over the hay. Cold frames may also be used to store Celery for short periods.

Diseases and Insects

Celery is subject to a number of diseases and insects, but only a few are generally of importance. Early and late blight are carried over from year to year in the seed and on old Celery plant refuse. In the home garden the most satisfactory control is the use of a copper-lime dust or Bordeaux mixture (4 oz. copper sulphate, 4 oz. hydrated lime to 3 gals. of water) as a spray applied at weekly intervals.

Bacterial leaf spot, root rot and yellows are

other diseases which may be important. See PLANT DISEASES.

Insects that may be important are the carrot rust fly (see CARROT Insects) and the tarnished plant bug. The latter insect may be controlled with dimethoate. Be sure to read the label. See INSECTICIDES.

Two physiological disorders are frequently important, namely, black heart and cracked stem. Black heart first shows as a tip burn on young leaves and then spreads to the heart tissue of the plant which in severe cases is killed and turns black. This condition probably is due to a deficiency of calcium and an imbalance of other nutrient elements in the soil. Cracked stem results in brownish cracks and lesions on the inner and outer surface of the leaf petiole. This condition can be controlled by adding small amounts of borax, 2 oz. per 30 lbs., to the fertilizer used prior to planting or in applying borax as a solution near the base of the plant.

GRANT B. SNYDER

CELERY FAMILY = Umbelliferaceae

CELL. One of the minute compartments or living units of protoplasm of which plants are composed or made up; also a cavity of an anther or ovary.

CELLAR GARDENING. Merely a term used to denote growing plants in a heated cellar, usually under fluorescent light, which see.

CELOSIA (sell-O-sia)
  cristata   1'–4'   annual   Cockscomb
The species is a little-planted weedy plant from the tropics with erect or drooping, silvery flower spikes. The var. *cristata* is the popular garden annual which now is available in several sizes with velvety-crested or plume-feathered flower spikes often in fantastic shapes, colored red, purplish, yellow and gold. There is a particularly pleasing '**Maple Gold**' strain with flower spikes in soft pastel-colored pale pinks and yellows. There are dwarf forms available only a foot high and others over 3 ft. By selecting varieties of various heights they can be used in the flower border, and their flowered stalks, dried, are much used in arrangements. There is also a form with variegated leaves. Seeds can be sown indoors in March, kept at 70°–75° F. and set out after danger of frost is passed. Massed plantings, of properly selected colors, or edgings of the dwarf varieties are unusually effective.

CELSIA (SELL-sia)
  cretica   6'   biennial   Cretan Celsia
Sometimes a perennial, stout and hairy with tall 5-ft. spikes of large sweetly scented golden-yellow flowers marked by two brown spots. Native to the Mediterranean Region.

CELTIS (SELL-tis). The hackberries are used particularly in the South as street trees. They have alternately deciduous leaves that are 3 veined and olbique at the base; the fruit is a small drupe. They have been suggested as replacement for elms but they have no autumn color nor other interesting features that would suggest their use if better trees are available.

Propagation

Seeds can be sown as soon as ripe or stratified in a cool place for 3 months at 40° F., and then sown, or stored dry in air-tight containers for up to a year and then sown. Plants are grafted with *C. occidentalis* as an understock. See GRAFTING.

Insect Pests

The leaves of the common hackberry are often disfigured by the galls of the hackberry psyllid. The galls are round and ¼ to ½ in. in dia., and greatly reduce the normal growth of the tree. The insects emerge from the galls in the fall and often become a nuisance around homes. Spraying with insecticide #15 when leaves are about half grown is effective. Spiny elm caterpillar and June beetles eat the leaves unless protected with insecticide #9. Witches-broom caused by the feeding of a mite and infection of a fungus produces conspicuous tufted growth at tip of branches. See WITCHES-BROOM. Although unsightly, it is relatively harmless, and no control is recommended.

  australis   75'   Zone 6   European Hackberry
In hot, arid sections of the Southwest, this southern European species has been used as a street tree. The dark purple drupe is about ½ in. across and the leaves are about 4–6 in. long. It forms a tree with a rounded top.

  laevigata   90'   Zone 5   Sugar Hackberry
This tree, widely native in the south-central and southeastern U.S., is very resistant to the witches-broom so seriously infesting *C. occidentalis*. The black drupes are only ¼ in. across and the leaves are 2½–4 in. long. It is widely used as a street tree within its native habitat, and forms a rounded head, sometimes with pendulous branches.

  occidentalis   120' Zone 2 Common Hackberry
This tree should not be widely planted in the many areas where it is susceptible to the witches-broom growths that infest this particuar species more than the others. Native from Quebec to N.Car. and Kan., this is susceptible to attacks of either a small mite or a mildew fungus or both, deforming the buds and causing a bunch of twigs to grow at one place. These disfigure the tree for many of these small twigs die. The leaves are 3–5 in. long and the drupe is about 1 in. across. It must be said, however, that

this tree withstands growing in poor soils and smoky situations better than many other species, and for this reason it is planted.

CENCHRUS (SEN-chrus)

pauciflorus 1′ Zone 3 Sandbur
An annual native grass mostly on sandy soils and also a troublesome weed in the southern states. In early summer it produces a burr with sharp spines that enable it to adhere to anything coming against it, and when attached to the ankle causes considerable skin irritation.

CENTAUREA (cen-TOR-ee-a). Annuals or perennials, members of the Composite Family, with purple, blue, yellow or white flower-heads. Many of the species and varieties are excellent plants for the flower garden, most of them coming from Europe. The leaves are pinnately lobed or divided. The annuals are grown by sowing the seed in place in the garden after all frost is over or starting plants earlier in the greenhouse. The perennials can be grown from seed or cuttings can be taken in Sept. and carried over winter in the greenhouse or hotbed.

americana 4′ Zone 4 Basket-flower
An attractive wild plant which is often cultivated. The straight, strongly veined stems, thickened below the flower heads, produce alternate, oblong-lanceolate leaves and violet-colored tubular flowers, the outside ones raylike, in heads measuring 4–5 in. wide. The bracts below the flowers have fringed tufts. The plant blooms all summer over a wide range extending from Mo. and La. westward. It requires no special care. A perennial within its native range, it may be grown as an annual in the northern U.S. and Canada. The variety **alba** has white flowers.

babylonica 4′–12′ Zone 6? Babylonian Centaurea
Grayish leaves and yellow flowers, the heads 1½ in. long, borne in panicles. Some of the lower leaves are nearly 2 ft. long. Native to Asia Minor. Rarely grown in American gardens.

cineraria 12″–18″ Zone 4 Dusty Miller
The grayish-white foliage of this plant is an attractive feature of the coastal dunes and edges of the Atlantic beaches from Me. southward, but though it is now quite at home in North America, it is native to southern Italy. The plant, covered with minute white hairs, has leaves deeply lobed, the ends blunt, and rather unattractive yellow or purple flowers on a thick flower stalk. Often used in gardens as an edging, the gray foliage is a perfect foil for brightly hued flower beds. The plant prefers sandy, well-drained soil and although it is a perennial, second-year plants suffer from the effects of winter snow and rain. To avoid this, cuttings may be taken in Sept. and the subsequent plants

used the following spring as replacements.

cyanus 2½′ annual Cornflower, Bachelor's-button
Sometimes living over winter, this is a common garden plant native to the Mediterranean Region of Europe but escaped in many places in North America and often appearing as a weed. The soft, hairy leaves are alternate, the lower toothed and the upper linear and up to 6 in. long. The flower heads appear from June to Sept., are borne on long stalks and are blue, pink or white and up to 1½ in. wide. The double-flowered forms make the better garden plants. It should be noted that some new dwarf varieties only a foot tall are available.

Occasionally cropping up as weeds are other species—*C. jacea*, *C. maculosa*, *C. nigra* and *C. repens*, the last of which is a bad weed in western North America.

dealbata 2′ Zone 3 Persian Centaurea
A perennial with coarsely cut, pinnately lobed leaves, some of the lower ones being 1½ ft. long and whitish beneath. The flower heads are solitary, the inner flowers being red and the marginal ones rosy to white. Native to Persia. The variety 'Sternbergii' blooms from June to Sept. on compact, bushy plants.

gymnocarpa 18″ Zone 6? Dusty Miller
A bushy perennial plant with velvety-white foliage, leaves deeply cut and flower heads rosy-violet to purple in a close panicle almost hidden in the leaves. Blooms in Aug. Native to Capri.

imperialis 4′ annual Royal Centaurea
With fragrant flower heads, white, purple, lilac or pink. Probably a hybrid of *C. moschata*.

macrocephala 4′ Zones 2–3 Globe Centaurea
A coarsely conspicuous perennial from Armenia with ragged, 3-inch leaves and large, yellow, globelike flowers in June and July, somewhat like those of a thistle. Usually planted as a specimen, not in groups.

maculosa 3′ Zone 6 European Star-thistle
This biennial or perennial European plant has become a common weed in the northeastern U.S. The plant has alternate, pinnately lobed leaves, the short flower stalks arising from their axils. The flowers are compound, the blue tubular flowers being borne in flower heads under 1 in. in dia. and similar in appearance to those of the true thistles (*Circium*). The flower heads are surrounded with spiny bracts. Flowering in July and Aug., the plant is of doubtful value to the wild garden because of the unpleasant spiny bracts and of its tendency to self-sow widely.

montana 2′ Zones 2–3 Mountain Bluet
With deep cornflower-blue flowers, the heads sometimes 3 in. wide, blooming from May until midsummer, with often a secondary bloom in Sept., though the flowers are not abundantly

produced then, this perennial can spread easily in good soil. The young leaves are silvery white. Native to Europe.

moschata   2′   annual   Sweet Sultan
An annual herb with pinnately cut leaves, solitary heads of fragrant white, yellow or purple flowers 2 in. wide. Native to the Orient. The variety 'Imperialis', possibly a hybrid of this species, has flowers twice the size and colored white, pink or purple. It is sometimes offered as a separate species, may grow to 4 ft. tall, and certainly is worth growing.

ruthenica   3′   Zones 2–3   Ruthenian Centaurea
Pale yellow flower heads 2 in. wide and pinnately divided leaves, this is native to Europe and western Asia.

CENTIPEDE   GRASS = *Eremochloa ophiuroides*. See GRASS, LAWNS.

CENTRANTHUS (sen-TRAN-thus)
calcitrapa   6″–12″   annual
With rose-violet flowers, opposite leaves 3 in. long, native to southern Europe.

macrosiphon   18″   annual   Spur Valerian Centranthus
With brilliant and profuse rose flowers in dense clusters, native to Spain. Leaves opposite, ovate, 3 in. long.

ruber   2′–3′   Zone 4   Red Valerian
A hardy perennial valued for its clusters of carmine-rose flowers in the summer. It grows well in sun or shade and often self-seeds in the garden. Native to the Mediterranean Region. The opposite leaves are gray-green, and it might well be planted in poor dry soil to keep it from spreading too much. Best planted in the spring. Propagated by spring-sown seeds or more easily by division.

CENTURY PLANT = *Agave americana*

CEPHALANTHUS (seff-al-ANTH-us)
occidentalis   15′   Zone 4   Buttonbush
When one sees shrubby plants growing at the edge of water in the eastern U.S. with small, creamy-white, rounded flower heads about 1 in. across during late July, this is the plant. It is well adapted for growing in swampy lands. The many prominent pistils protruding from its flower heads give them a bristling appearance that is ornamental, especially in late summer. If a moist soil situation is not available, this plant need not be grown for it is of little ornamental value at other times of year.

Propagation

Seed may be sown as soon as ripe or stored dry for up to a year and then sown. Plants are easily divided with a sharp spade. Softwood and hardwood cuttings root well. See CUTTINGS.

CEPHALARIA (seff-al-AY-ria)
alpina   6′   Zones 2–3   Alpine Cephalaria
The flowers are similar to those of Scabiosa, 1½ in. wide and are sulfur yellow, blooming in July and Aug. The flower stems are long and the foliage is handsome, but it is really too tall for small borders. Excellent for cutting. Native to southern Europe.

gigantea   5′–6′   Zones 2–3   Tatarian Cephalaria
This has primrose-yellow flowers in summer, somewhat similar in form to those of Scabiosa. This was discovered in Siberia in 1759, but because they grow so tall and take up so much space they are out of scale in small gardens. They bloom throughout July and early Aug. and are used for cut-flower purposes. Propagation is by fall-sown seeds or division of the plants in the spring.

CEPHALOCEREUS (seff-al-o-SEER-eus)
senilis   2′–40′   Zone 9   Old Man Cactus
A popular cactus pot plant, but it can grow tall, although very slowly. This takes its name from the numerous long white hairs covering the stem that give rise to the impression of old age. There are 20–30 ribs on the stem. Flowers are rose colored and 2 in. across. Native to Mexico. It has been noted that this grows best if crushed egg shells or powdered limestone is mixed with the potting soil. For culture see CACTI AND SUCCULENTS.

CEPHALOPHYLLUM (seff-al-o-PHY-lum)
alstonii   6″   Zone 9
A succulent perennial from South Africa with brilliant purple-red flowers, 3 in. wide having violet anthers. The leaves are cylindrical or 3 angled, have pellucid dots, and are borne in rosettes. Sometimes used as a ground cover in South Calif.

CEPHALOTAXUS (seff-al-o-TAX-us). Narrow-leaved evergreens resembling *Taxus* or yews, but with larger needles and slightly larger fruits. Needles are usually in 2 planes along the branches, have 2 white bands beneath, and persist for 3–4 years. Male and female flowers are produced in the fall on different plants, not in the spring as are those of *Taxus*. The purplish to greenish fruits are fleshy and egg shaped, about an inch long, ripening the second season. (Those of *Taxus* ripen in one season). They do well in moist atmosphere at the seashore but not in hot, dry areas.

Propagation

Seed may be stratified as soon as ripe at 40° F. for 3 months, or stored dry a year in airtight containers and then stratified. Hardwood cuttings root well. See STRATIFICATION, CUTTINGS.
drupacea = *C. harringtonia*

fortunei   36′   Zone 8   Chinese Plum-yew
Usually no more than 18 ft. tall in cultivation, sexes separate as in other species of this genus.

harringtonia   30′   Zone 5   Japanese Plum-yew
Resembling a yew in appearance but with evergreen needles $\frac{3}{4}$–$1\frac{3}{4}$ in. long, this plant also bears red, pulpy fruits that are 1–$1\frac{1}{4}$ in. long and egg shaped, considerably larger than those of either the English or the Japanese Yew. It can be a small tree but is more often a wide-spreading, evergreen shrub but not nearly as dense and compact as are the yews. Like the yews, the sexes are separate, female flowers being on one plant and male flowers being on another, so that there are plants which never bear fruits at all. If fruits are desired, it is important to be certain that both male and female plants are bought. Native to Japan.

CERASTIUM (ser-ASS-tium). Annual or perennial weeds or herbs with as many as 50–100 described species in the North Temperate regions of the world. Usually the leaves are small and the flowers white. The plants easily propagate themselves by seed which remains viable in the soil for several years. For control see WEED-CONTROLLING CHEMICALS.

alpinum   6″   Zone 2   Alpine Chickweed
A perennial with foot-long prostrate stems forming a mat of foliage on the ground; leaves $\frac{1}{4}$–$\frac{3}{4}$ in. long and $\frac{1}{8}$–$\frac{1}{4}$ in. wide; flowers borne in clusters of 1–6, very small and white. Native to Arctic regions. The var. **lanatum** bears white tomentose leaves in rosettes, and tight clusters of small white flowers.

arvense   8″   Zone 3   Field Chickweed
A native perennial weed common mostly in lawns throughout North America with opposite linear leaves up to 2 in. long, small white flowers under $\frac{3}{4}$ in. across from April to June. A variable species. The var. **'Compactum'** is only 2–3 in. tall.

bierbersteinii   6″   Zone 3   Taurus Chickweed
Herbaceous perennial creeping along the ground with gray-woolly leaves $1\frac{1}{2}$ in. long and $\frac{1}{8}$ in. wide. Flowers are white, borne in loose clusters in May and June. Native to the mountains of Asia Minor.

tomentosum   3″–6″   Zones 2–3   Snow-in-summer
A common, evergreen, garden creeper, valued for its grayish woolly foliage spotted here and there with white flowers $\frac{1}{2}$ in. across with 5 divided petals giving the erroneous impression there are 10, during June. The leaves are $\frac{3}{4}$ in. long and $\frac{1}{8}$ in. wide. One plant will cover 9 sq. ft. in a short time. It has been known to grow in pure sand. Native to Europe. Valued in the garden for its light grayish foliage. Easily grown.

Cerastium tomentosum—Snow-in-summer

vulgatum   6″   Zone 3   Mouse-ear Chickweed
A prostrate, common, perennial weed, native to Europe but widespread throughout the U.S. and Canada, with small, opposite, rounded leaves, less than 1 in. long, more or less hairy and sticky. The prostrate stems root all along their length, thus the plant forms dense mats. Flowers are white, very small, appearing from May to Oct.

CERATONIA (ser-at-O-nia)
siliqua   50′   Zone 10   Carob
The Carob is native to the eastern Mediterranean Region and the fruits have long been valued as a source of food for animals and even humans when other foods are scarce. It can be grown in dry soils and has been used as a street and avenue tree, but it is difficult to transplant and should always be moved with a ball of soil about the roots. The foot-long pods contain seeds and pulp which have a high sugar content, hence it has been cultivated for centuries. The sexes are separate; both should be present to insure fruiting of the pistillate tree. The habit is rounded, with evergreen compound leaves and about 4 pairs of leaflets each 2–4 in. long with wavy margins. The small red flowers are produced in lateral racemes in the spring. It has been called "St. John's Bread" because it was the seeds and pulp of these fruits which St. John ate in the wilderness.

CERATOPHYLLUM (ser-at-o-FILL-um)
demersum   aquatic plant   Zone 10   Hornwort
An aquatic herb growing underneath the water

in tropical regions, used in aquaria. Its leaves are threadlike, 1 in. long in whorls. The flowers are not showy, but the plant looks something like *Myriophyllum*. Easily propagated by division. It is a fine producer of oxygen and a good hide-away for baby fish in the home aquarium.

CERATOPTERIS (ser-at-OP-ter-is)

pteridoides   aquatic plant   Zone 8   Water-fern

An interesting, floating water plant used in the home aquarium, with leaves unfolding from the center like those of a fern frond. Young plants form all along the margins of the triangular leaves. An individual plant varies in size from a few inches across to 2 ft. depending on the growing conditions, but in the aquarium it is usually only a few inches. Snails lay eggs on the undersurface of the leaves, and since the roots are profuse, young fish can hide among them. Native to Fla. and Jamaica.

CERATOSTIGMA (ser-at-OS-tig-ma)

plumbaginoides   6"–1'   Zones 5–6   Blue Ceratostigma

Forming neat tufts of growth, covered with many flowers almost until frost, this makes a good ground cover that can almost be considered evergreen, for the deep glossy-green leaves are 3 in. long and grow in tufts. The individual deep blue flowers appear in late Aug. and Sept. but last a long time. It will grow in sun or light shade and can become a weed unless confined. The autumn color is a reddish bronze and the plant is native to China. Propagation is by division only in the spring. In the North it might be given some winter protection.

willmottianum   4'   Zone 8   Willmott Blue Leadwort

A shrub for poor soil situations, where it is hardy, this has bright blue phloxlike flowers nearly an inch in diameter borne continuously during the summer. Native in western China, it was introduced into America in 1908.

CERCIDIPHYLLUM (ser-sid-i-FILL-um)

japonicum   60'–100'   Zone 4   Katsura-tree

A little known but excellent shade tree from Japan, this is wide-spreading in habit, normally growing with several main trunks from the base, but if these are restricted to one, it makes a perfect upright specimen, almost like a Lombardy Poplar, for the first 15–20 years. The rounded opposite leaves are nearly 4 in. across, in shape like those of *Cercis* species. Sexes are separate, but the flowers are inconspicuous and the fruits are merely dried capsules. The autumn color is orange to scarlet. It has fine texture and makes a splendid specimen and can be used as a street tree if grown with one trunk only. It is not attacked by pests, but does prefer a situation where there is plenty of soil moisture. It will not succeed in soils known to be dry.

Propagation

Do not allow the seed to dry out but sow as soon as ripe. Also layers and softwood cuttings have proved satisfactory. See LAYERS, CUTTINGS, etc.

CERCIS (SER-sis).

Alternate-leaved trees or shrubs, members of the Pea Family, with conspicuously colored pink to purple pea flowers in the spring and pods for fruits in the fall. The leaves are prominently 5-nerved and heart shaped at the base, about 2–6 in. long. These are difficult to transplant, and the smaller they are when moved, the more likely they are to survive.

Propagation

Seed may be processed as soon as ripe or stored dry for a year in airtight containers in a cool place and then processed. Soak the seed in hot water (190° F.) overnight, then stratify for 3 months at 40° F. and then sow. Varieties are grafted on the species and softwood cuttings can be rooted. See GRAFTING, CUTTINGS, SEEDS.

Diseases

Canker and dieback cause sunken, elongate cankers on the branches and trunk which kill them by girdling. Pruning followed by disinfection and painting of the wounds is suggested. Verticillium wilt infects branches and young trees. In the nursery, infected trees should be destroyed promptly. Older trees can be pruned and treated as for canker. Rusty brown spots with a raised border indicate redbud leaf spot. Sprays of fungicide #D, #F or #K when leaves are half and full grown are suggested.

canadensis   36'   Zone 4   Eastern Redbud

Commonly known and grown in the eastern part of the country, particularly for its numerous, small, purplish-pink, pealike flowers borne before the leaves appear in the spring. The fruits are merely dried pods, but the foliage turns a brilliant yellow in the fall. The Redbud is frequently used in combination with the Flowering Dogwood, for one augments the other, and they grow together over the same range from Fla. to New England. It might be interesting to note that the early French-Canadian settlers are supposed to have used the flowers in salads and for making pickles and sometimes even as a cooked vegetable. They have a sharp acid flavor.

canadensis alba—the flowers are pure white and the variety is hardy over the same range as the species.

canadensis 'Flame'—this is a seedling originating in the wild in Wilkinson County, near Fort Adams, Miss., about 1905. It is more erect in branching than the species. The flowers are large, frequently bearing multiple, non-functional pistils, several anthers and about 20 petals per flower. Petal color is the same as for the species, and plants start flowering a year or two after budding or grafting. It is supposed to be hardy in Zone 5, but it would seem that the plant might be on the tender side that far north.

canadensis 'Withers Pink Charm'—a clonal selection in the wild of a plant with flowers decidedly pale pink, not the purplish pink of the species. This tree has considerable merit and should be widely grown because of its soft pink blossoms. This was found about 25 years ago by Mr. D. D. Withers in the mountains near Mt. Solon, Va., and is now being offered commercially. There may be other selections from plants with flowers of the same soft pink. One of these has been named **'Pinkbud'**.

chinensis   40'   Zone 6   Chinese Judas-tree
Members of this genus belong to the Pea Family, which of course means that their flowers are pealike. Although this species can grow as a tree. it is more often a shrub in most eastern U.S. gardens and the small, rosy-purple flowers appear in dense clusters before the leaves appear in mid-May. Like the other redbuds, the autumn color is a fine yellow. In China where this plant grows in nature, it is usually a tree and, like other members of this genus, is propagated by seed.

occidentalis   15'   Zone 7   California Redbud
Similar to *C. canadensis* except that it is less hardy and has leaves that are rounded and notched at the tip. Native to Calif. and not much used except within its native area.

racemosa   30'   Zone 7   Raceme Redbud
This beautiful tree might be grown more than it is in the milder parts of the U.S. Apparently not one American nursery is offering it, yet E. H. Wilson considered it one of the best and most beautiful of the flowering trees that he introduced. The rose-colored, pealike flowers are borne in racemes up to 4 in. long. The flowers are borne on wood one to several years old. It can be considered the best of this genus for its flowers. The autumn color of the foliage is yellow.

siliquastrum   30'   Zone 6   Judas-tree
Rarely seen in America, this is popular in the gardens of southern Europe and western Asia where it is native. The small, pealike flowers are purplish rose like the other redbuds and they are profusely borne during mid-May often on twigs 2–4 years old, but sometimes as much as 20–30 years old. Often there will be as many as 100 flowers on a twig 5 in. long. There is a white-flowered variety (**alba**) in Europe. The leaves

are somewhat heart shaped, $3\frac{1}{2}$–$5\frac{1}{2}$ in. long. The plant forms a small tree with a flat top.

CERCOCARPUS (ser-ko-KARP-us)
montanus   6'   Zone 5   Mountain-mahogany
Native from Mont. to N.Mex., this evergreen or semi-evergreen shrub has alternate leaves that are 1–2 in. long. The small greenish flowers are not conspicuous but in the fall the fruit is interesting because it has a silky plume 3–5 in. long. Propagated by seeds or cuttings. Wilted leaves of this tree have been reported to cause prussic-acid poisoning when eaten by animals.

Propagation

Seed can be stratified as soon as ripe, or it can be stored dry for up to a year in airtight containers in a cool place, then stratified at 40° F. for 3 months, then sown. Softwood cuttings can also be rooted. See STRATIFICATION, CUTTINGS.

CEREUS (SEE-reus)
peruvianus   40'   Zone 10   Peru Cereus
A treelike cactus, mostly grown under glass, with branches usually green, sometimes glaucous, with 4–9 ribs on the stems, needlelike spines and white funnel-shaped flowers 6 in. long. Native to South America, sometimes grown as a house plant.

CEREUS, NIGHTBLOOMING = *Hylocereus undatus*

CERIMAN = *Monstera deliciosa*

CERINTHE (ser-IN-the)
major   1'   annual or biennial   Honeywort
An herb with smooth spotted leaves blooming from May to Sept. Belonging to the Borage Family, it lacks the rough foliage of the Borages and bears yellow flowers in terminal racemes among leafy bracts. The leaves are alternate and simple. Easily propagated by seeds. Native to the Mediterranean Region.

CEROPEGIA (ser-o-PEEJ-ia)
woodii   prostrate   Zone 10   Woods Ceropegia
A greenhouse vine with waxy flowers, sometimes called the Rosary Plant, belonging to the Milkweed Family, with opposite, fleshy, heart-shaped leaves, $\frac{1}{4}$–$\frac{2}{3}$ in. long, dark green but with whitish veins. The flowers are waxy, pinkish purple, borne in pairs and about $\frac{1}{2}$ in. long. The plant produces tubers in the soil, also sometimes along the stem, by which it is propagated. It is also used as a house plant. Native to Natal.

CESPITOSE (or caespitose). Growing in tufts; forming mats.

CESTRUM (SES-trum)
nocturnum   12'   Zone 10   Nightblooming Cestrum
An evergreen shrub with shining, thin, leathery

leaves with axillary clusters of fragrant greenish flowers open only at night but blooming off and on throughout the year. Native to the West Indies. Sometimes called Night-jessamine.

parqui   6'–12'   Zone 10   Chilean Cestrum
Also called Willow-leaved Jessamine, a native of Chile, this is a shrub with 6 in. lanceolate leaves and greenish-yellow fragrant flowers about an inch long, open at night. They are borne in either axillary or terminal clusters.

CEYLON-GOOSEBERRY = *Dovyalis   hebecarpa*

CHAENOMELES   (kee-NOM-ee-lees   or kee-no-MEE-lees). This species comprises a very popular group of Asiatic shrubs grown for their brightly colored flowers which appear in early May before the leaves appear. At the turn of the century these were much used as hedges, but with the increasing popularity of the Japanese Barberry and the serious inroads of the San Jose scale, to which these flowering quinces are unfortunately susceptible, they are used more and more only as specimen plants. They have been grown in Europe for over 100 years. They hybridize freely, nurserymen grow many from seed and even the botanists have aided in the confusion of the nomenclature during the past several decades by changing the name from *Pyrus japonica* to *Cydonia japonica* to *Chaenomeles lagenaria* and now most recently, to *C. speciosa*.

The foliage of most varieties is a glossy green, and rosaceous flowers range in color from white through pink to dark red. Some varieties have single flowers, others semi-double or double flowers, and these range in size from 1–2 in. in dia. Fruits are green and applelike and can be used in making preserves, although the pectin and cooking qualities will vary considerably among the varieties. The common quince, *Cydonia oblonga*, has fruits high in pectin.

Most varieties are thorny, with some of the thorns being modified branches. They can be easily sheared and will make hedges. Unfortunately, some nurserymen grow them from seed, and at present there are several hundred named varieties—over 150 in the collection at the Arnold Arboretum in Jamaica Plain, Mass. The plants should be propagated asexually by cuttings, not by grafts, since they will grow well only on their own roots. Too often they are grafted and on many plants it is not long before the undesirable understock takes over. They can be grown in almost any good soil. They need corrective pruning occasionally, but otherwise they may be left alone and may be relied on to produce their brilliant flowers each spring.

Propagation

Seeds may be sown as soon as ripe or stratified for 2 months at 40° F. or kept dry in airtight containers in a cool place for up to a year and then sown. Plants may be divided easily. Many layers may be forced from the plant and both softwood and hardwood cuttings root well. See LAYERS, CUTTINGS, etc.

Insect Pests

Japanese Flowering Quince is a favorite host of San Jose scale. See SCALE INSECTS. There is evidence that this scale was originally brought to the U.S. on this plant. Dormant sprays with insecticide #44 and summer sprays with insecticide #15 and #13 are advised.

japonica   3'   Zone 4   Japanese Quince
This is the lowest growing species and its variety **alpina** is probably the lowest growing of all, being only a foot high and very dense. The flowers of the species are red, and of alpina, orange. Both bloom in early May before their leaves appear.

speciosa   6'   Zone 4   Flowering Quince
Native to China, this is the species to which most of the varieties and hybrids are closely related. Now several hybrid species should also be included. *C.* x *superba* is a cross between *C. japonica* and *C. speciosa*, and in 1938 or thereabouts W. B. Clarke of San Jose, Calif., made another cross (*C. cathayensis* x *C. superba*) and it has been named **C.** x **californica**; this hybrid species is hardy only in Zone 6, while the other *Chaenomeles* varieties and hybrids are all hardy in Zone 4. The following list includes the better varieties and hybrids, but affinities are given so that one can clearly note the *C.* x *californica* varieties which are the least hardy of the lot.

Varieties

WHITE FLOWERS
   'Candida' (*speciosa*)—single flowers
   'Nivalis' (*speciosa*)—single flowers
   'Snow' (*speciosa*)—single flowers
WHITE TO PINK FLOWERS
   'Apple Blossom' (*speciosa*)—single flowers
   'Enchantress' (x *californica*)—single flowers
   'Marmorata' (*speciosa*)—single flowers
PINK FLOWERS
   'Gaujardii' (*speciosa*)—single flowers
   'Phyllis Moore' (*speciosa*)—semi-double flowers
   'Cameo' (x *superba*)—double flowers
   'Knap Hill Scarlet' (x *superba*)—single flowers
   'Stanford Red' (x *superba*)—single flowers
   'Pink Beauty' (x *californica*)—single flowers
RED FLOWERS
   'Crimson Beauty' (x *superba*)—single flowers

'Crimson and Gold' (x *superba*)—single flowers
'Simonii' (*speciosa*)—double flowers
'Cardinalis' (*speciosa*)—double flowers
'Rowallane' (x *superba*)—single flowers
ORANGE FLOWERS
'Coral Beauty' (x *superba*)—single flowers
'Charming' (x *superba*)—single flowers
'Incendie' (x *superba*)—single flowers
'Sunset' (x *superba*)—double flowers
'Glowing Ember' (x *superba*)—single flowers

CHAENORRHINUM (key-no-RY-num)
  minus   **1′**   **annual**   **Small Snapdragon**
A bushy weed, widely naturalized over Canada, central and northern U.S. especially in sandy waste-lands; the lower leaves opposite, upper leaves alternate, sessil entire, about 1 in. long. The small flowers are like those of snapdragons, ¼ in. long, white to lilac in leafy racemes from June to Sept. Native to the Mediterranean Region of Europe.

CHALICE-VINE, GOLD CUP = *Solandra guttata*

CHALK. A white, gray or yellow limestone that is soft and easily pulverized. This term in horticulture is much more used in England than America. In America we speak simply of limestone. Actually chalk has twice the bulk but only half the value of real limestone.

CHAMAECEREUS (kam-ee-SEE-reus)
  silvestri   **6″**   **Zone 10**   **Peanut Cactus**
Clumps of little, soft, fresh green branches about 2 in. long (from which the name Peanut Cactus comes) clustered together from 1 base but easily broken off. There are 6–9 ribs on the stems and soft white spines. The orange-scarlet flowers are 3 in. long. Native to Argentina. A popular little cactus for the home. For culture see CACTI and SUCCULENTS.

CHAMAECYPARIS (kam-ee-SIP-a-ris). The Chamaecyparis or False Cypress (sometimes formerly called Retinospora) species and varieties are a decidedly variable group of evergreens but many of them are most serviceable garden plants. They are trees and shrubs with flat spraylike foliage, cones less than ½ in. dia., ripening the first year. They are native to North America and Japan and contain many excellent evergreen ornamentals. Of the three species native to North America (*C. lawsoniana*, *nootkatensis* and *thyoides*) only the first two are grown to any extent as ornamentals, and do best on the Pacific Coast in areas where atmospheric moisture is high. In Europe these are even more popular and 127 varieties of *C. lawsoniana* are supposedly listed. American nurserymen list only 28 varieties and only three of *C. nootkatensis*.

Of the two Japanese species (*C. obtusa* and *C. pisifera*) American nurserymen list 22 vars. of the former and 26 of the latter, but the literature is full of many names—so many that it is impossible to mention them all here. The nomenclature of this group at present is decidedly confused, and when it comes to color forms and dwarf forms, proper identification of what may or may not be in this country is extremely difficult. All, however, have flat scalelike leaves in flat branchlets that appear somewhat similar to those of *Thuja* except that these have white lines of the under surface of the leaves and the arborvitaes do not.

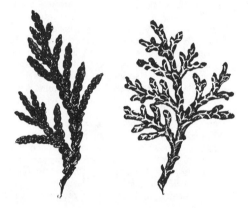

Thuja foliage on left is all green underneath; that of *Chamaecyparis* species is differentiated from *Thuja* by having white lines underneath.

It should be stated at the outset that these 5 species are tree forms, and those who know the Pacific Coast have seen many a stately specimen of the 2 species growing there. Many medium-to-dwarf forms have originated through the years, and the connoisseur of dwarf evergreens knows that many exquisite specimens can be obtained if time is spent hunting for them both in this country and abroad.

The Japanese species are more popular in the eastern U.S. for these are better able to withstand the drier atmosphere. *C. obtusa* and its varieties are probably the better ornamentals where hardy than are the *C. pisifera* varieties. Color forms are many, but it should be remembered that in the northern parts of the country forms with yellow foliage tend to turn brownish in the winter and hence are not serviceable at a time when they are most needed. *C. pisifera* and its varieties do not grow old gracefully, for the older they are, the more open is the branching at the base of the trees and frequently the more the dead foliage there is to be observed. As small specimens of shrubby habit, they are excellent—the reason they have been so popular over the years and why so many nurserymen have grown them. But many are tree types, and one should know this at purchase time and be prepared to restrain them if they are to be used in situations where they can not be allowed to grow into tree forms. Many of the varieties are dwarf and very slow growing, of interest to the collector of dwarf evergreens but for which there is not a large demand.

Propagation

Seed may be processed as soon as ripe or stored dry in airtight containers in a cool place for up to a year and then sown. Either way it should be stratified for 3 months at 40° F., then sown. Grafting of varieties has been done, using either *C. lawsoniana* or *Thuja occidentalis* as understock. Hardwood cuttings of many species and varieties root well. See GRAFTING, CUTTINGS.

Insect Pests

Juniper scale and spruce mite (see SCALE and MITES) are as destructive to False Cypress as to Juniper or Arborvitae. See THUJA. As a forest tree it is seriously attacked by various bark beetles, and ornamental trees, especially where grown in slightly unnatural conditions, are often infested. Spraying with insecticide #5 where beetles are active is suggested. False Cypress is also attacked by the black vine weevil. See TAXUS.

funebris   60′   Zone 8   Mourning Cypress
With drooping branches and flattened branchlets; cones ½ in. wide. Native to China. A plant frequently used in cemeteries along the Mediterranean.

lawsoniana   120′   Zone 5   Lawson False Cypress
A native of 2 states on our Pacific Coast (Ore.–Calif.), this species makes a graceful tree with soft foliage. A 22-year-old plant is 20 ft. tall, 7 ft. through and densely pyramidal. A mild climate with plenty of moisture is to its liking—hence there are none too many areas in the U.S. where it can be successfully grown, but in New Zealand and in Europe, over 100 varieties are supposedly grown. It is a most variable species. Varieties are: 'Allumii'—a glaucous blue, narrowly pyramidal in habit; one of the more popular varieties in America; 'Argentea' —about the most silvery of the glaucous forms; 'Elegantissima'—graceful, gray-white foliage; 'Ellwoodii'—a very slow-growing shrub with erect branches and densely covered with feathery, glaucous-blue foliage. This is another of the most popular types in America; 'Filifera' —one of the best of this group; 'Filiformis'

'Compacta'—compact in habit, but branchlets drooping; 'Fletcheri'—an excellent ornamental, raised about 1913 in Fletcher's Nursery in England. Noted for its close, feathery, blue foliage and pyramidal form. Mature plants are 12–20 ft. tall. It is best when it is young; 'Forsteckensis'—a dwarf, globose variety having deep green, mosslike foliage. The branchlets are twisted into coxcomblike heads; 'Gracilis Pendula'—a very pendulous branched variety; 'Hillieri'—a yellow variety which is very good; 'Lanei'—about the brightest golden yellow of all these varieties; 'Lutea'—one of the best of the yellows, young foliage at first pale yellow, later turning to golden yellow. Stiff and erect in habit; 'Minima'—dwarf and very compact, becoming popular among American nurserymen; 'Minima Aurea'—miniature form with golden-yellow foliage, originating in the Rogers Nursery of Southampton, England, before 1929; 'Minima Glauca'—making a conical ball of steel-blue foliage; 'Nidiformis'— with horizontal branches radiating from a dense center and branchlets drooping at the tips; 'Stewartii'—the foliage is at first a golden yellow, turning to green late in the season; 'Triomphe de Boskoop'—a fast-growing shrub of a beautiful glaucous-blue color, more properly termed 'Triomf van Boskoop'.

nootkatensis   120′   Zone 4   Nootka False Cypress
This native tree (Alaska to Ore.) is not widely grown elsewhere in America merely because it needs a moist climate. The dense evergreen foliage is a light bluish color and some of the varieties are: 'Compacta'—large globular bush which may grow 20 ft. tall; 'Glauca'—foliage very glaucous; 'Lutea'—young shoots suffused a soft yellow-green, finally green; 'Pendula'— with erect trunk, horizontal branches and pendulous branchlets.

obtusa   120′   Zone 3   Hinoki False Cypress
An excellent, slow-growing evergreen tree native to Japan making a beautiful specimen when properly grown. Broadly pyramidal in outline, this is one of the best of the ornamental species with dark, glossy, green, scalelike leaves. Varieties are: 'Breviramea'—a tree with narrow, pyramidal form and short branches; 'Compacta' —a dwarf but broadly conical form. A 41-year-old plant is 7 ft. tall, 8 ft. across, densely pyramidal; 'Coralliformis'—with reddish, contorted branchlets, a compact little bush; 'Crippsii'—a very popular slow-growing dwarf form, with rich, golden-yellow foliage; 'Erecta' —fastigiate with ascending branches and bright green foliage; 'Filicoides', dense habit and slightly twisted, frondlike branches, it will eventually grow fairly tall; 'Gracilis'—a popular, compact pyramidal form with dark

green foliage and slightly pendulous, tipped branches. A 20-year-old specimen is 9 ft. tall by 7 ft. across. Not to be confused with either 'Nana' (an extremely slow-growing form) or 'Nana Gracilis'; 'Magnifica'—vigorous stout branchlets and bright green foliage; 'Nana Aurea'—compact bush with flat top and yellow

Chamaecyparis obtusa 'Gracilis' is a popular dark evergreen. (*Photo by Arnold Arboretum, Jamaica Plain, Mass.*)

foliage; 'Nana Gracilis'—this is widely distributed in American nurseries as *C. obtusa* 'Nana'. The similarity of the two names is unfortunate, since the plants are not alike. 'Nana' is probably one of the smallest of the dwarf conifers, a 30-year-old plant being only 6 in. tall and 8 in. across. On the other hand, a plant of the faster growing variety 'Nana Gracilis' would be 4 ft. tall and 2¾ ft. across—quite a difference. The foliage of 'Nana' is a dark, dull green, while that of 'Nana Gracilis' is a deep lustrous green; 'Pygmaea'—a beautiful dwarf with fan-shaped branchlets borne horizontally and foliage a bronzy green. Very old plants in cultivation are rarely over 18–24 in. tall; 'Sanderi'—this is a low dwarf with dense, heathlike foliage; 'Tetragona Aurea'—with 4-sided, thick branches, slow-growing, yellow foliage.

pisifera 150′ Zone 3 Sawara False Cypress

Native to Japan, this tree is narrowly pyramidal with horizontal branches but rather loose and open throughout. This is a variable species with many popular varieties, prone to lose its lower branches rather early in life. The brownish-red, interesting, exfoliating bark is another valued feature of older plants. Varieties: 'Boulevard' ('*Cyanoviridis*')—with extremely light blue foliage—a good clone and probably appearing in the trade under several names. One of the best for bluish foliage, especially while young; 'Filifera', with long, threadlike young branchlets, only of value as an ornamental while young and in the shrubby stages. Older plants are decidedly loose and open, not especially ornamental; 'Filifera Aurea', branch tips are colored a good yellow, some clones holding this color throughout the entire summer and fall. Especially is this true when the plants are small; **leptoclada**—a dense, compact, evergreen bush of pyramidal habit, native to Japan, sometimes listed as *C. pisifera* 'Squarrosa Veitchii'. The whole aspect of the plant is silvery gray, an excellent ornamental for its colored foliage; 'Plumosa', a plumose variety noted for the delicate, fluffy aspect of the scale-like leaves. The over-all appearance is a soft feathery green. Although frequently offered as a low shrub, it should be clearly remembered that this can grow into a 100 ft. tree unless properly restrained. Trees tend to get decidedly open, with a few branches at the base; 'Plumosa Aurea'—with soft, feathery, golden-yellow foliage. It retains this good color throughout the summer and can be classed as one of the best in this respect; 'Plumosa Compressa'—probably the smallest form of *C. pisifera*, very slow growing and of value only as an extremely dwarf evergreen; 'Plumosa Flavescens'—with tips of young foliage rather yellowish, this clone has the same coloring as 'Gold Dust', but the foliage is slightly more fluffy, dense and compact. A 40-year-old plant is 15 ft. x 15 ft; 'Plumosa Gold Dust'—with foliage tips a golden yellow throughout the summer; 'Plumosa Nana'—a low, flat-topped evergreen; 'Plumosa Rogersii'—a small, upright, conical bush, said to retain its yellow foliage color all winter. It is an especially fine clone; 'Squarrosa' (Moss Sawara Cypress), with soft, bluish-green foliage, not flat and feathery as is that of *C. pisifera*. A popular variety, especially while young. The foliage is soft to the touch, giving a mossy appearance from a distance.

thyoides 75′ Zone 3 White-cedar
A native evergreen in swamps from Me. to Fla., this is the least ornamental species of this genus and might be overlooked for ornamental planting except for boggy areas.

CHAMAEDAPHNE (kam-ee-DAFF-ne)
calyculata 4′ Zone 2 Leatherleaf

A low evergreen shrub, native throughout the Arctic regions of the world and in America southward to Ga., but not a good ornamental. It grows in acid soils; the leaves have a brownish color—not a good green—especially in winter. Leaves are alternate, narrow $\frac{1}{2}$–2 in. long. Small white flowers, like those of blueberries.

Propagation

Seed sown as soon as ripe or stored dry up to a year in airtight containers in a cool place and then sown. Also propagated by layers, division of mature plants, softwood or hardwood cuttings. See LAYERS, CUTTINGS, etc.

CHAMAEDOREA (kam-e-DOR-ea). These are feather palms supposedly hardy in Zone 8 and native to the humid forests of Mexico and South America. They need plenty of moisture, grow with several thin trunks in a bamboo fashion and are not profuse leaf-bearing plants. Usually about 10 ft. high, they prefer shady situations. If ungainly, as they sometimes become, remove one or two of the canes or trunks at the ground level.

CHAMAEMELUM (cham-e-ME-lum)
 nobile (*Anthemis nobilis*)   1′   Zone 4
                                            Roman Camomile
A European herb, sometimes used as a ground cover or even mowed high and used as a lawn substitute, the single-flowered form supplies the medicinal camomile (or chamomile) of commerce. The leaves are alternate, very finely cut and very fragrant. The flowers are daisylike and white; the variety 'Grandiflora' has yellow flowers sometimes and the variety 'Flore Pleno' has double flowers. They bloom from Aug. until frost and are sometimes also used as border plants. Easily divided or seed sown.

CHAMAEROPS (kam-EE-rops)
 humilis 3′–20′ Zone 9 Mediterranean Palm
This is a dwarf fan-palm, hardy along the Gul Coast but frequently grown in the North as a house plant or a "decoration" plant by the florists in the business of decorating for special occasions. The fan-shaped leaves are 2–3 ft. across, stiff and held erect. Easily grown and propagated by seed and suckers. Native to the Mediterranean Region.

CHANNELED. Deeply grooved longitudinally.

CHAPARRAL. A term used in southern California to include certain plants which grow together in underbush there such as Greasewood (*Adenostoma fasciculatum*), Scrub Oak (*Quercus dumosa*), Sumac and several species of *Salvia*.

CHARCOAL. This is often used in the potting mixtures for ferns, begonias, bromeliads and orchids, with beneficial results because of its moisture-absorbing qualities. It is broken up in sizes from pea to nut and is used at the rate of 1 part charcoal to 15 parts soil in the potting mixture.

CHASMANTHIUM (chas-MAN-the-um)
 latifolium (*Uniola latifolia*)   5′   Zone 3
                                              Spike Grass
A perennial ornamental grass, native from Pa. to Fla. and Tex., valued for its flat fruit heads often an inch wide and twice as long. These become heavy at maturity and droop gracefully. It is one of the best native ornamental grasses. Propagated by seed or division.

CHASTE-TREE = *Vitex agnus-castus*

CHAULMOOGRA = *Hydnocarpus kurzii*

CHECKERBERRY = *Gaultheria procumbens*

CHECKER-MALLOW. See SILDACEA.

CHEILANTHES (ky-LAN-theez). This is a genus of lip ferns, so called because on the margin of the under surface of each pinnae there is a marked lip. They are not of the easiest culture chiefly because they should be grown in drier soils than most other ferns, as well as a dry atmosphere. A high amount of humus in the soil is always beneficial. For propagation see FERNS.

 gracillima   10″   Zone 6   Lace Lip Fern
A small rock fern with the margins of the fronds curled and the underside woolly. It requires acid leaf mold, preferably in rock crevices, in a shady location. They do not winter well unless given some protection. Native to the West Coast of U.S. and Canada.
 lanosa   9″   Zone 6   Hairy Lip Fern
This rock fern, native from Conn. to Ga., has lacy, twice-pinnate fronds 6–8 in. long which have a somewhat rusty and woolly appearance, and brown petioles. The creeping rhizomes form dense mats on the ground and when drought conditions occur the fronds die. New ones quickly grow when sufficient water is supplied.

CHEIRANTHUS (ky-RAN-thus)
 allioni = *Erysimum asperum*
 cheiri   1$\frac{1}{2}$′   annual   Common Wallflower
This is a favorite in Great Britain where the cool and moist climate is conducive to its growing well. In the U.S. at a few places on the Eastern Seaboard and in the moist Pacific Northwest, it seems to do well, elsewhere the climate is not so favorable. The flowers are yellow, gold, red and mahogany and very fragrant. In England it is frequently a perennial. Native to southern Europe, it has been a popular garden plant for centuries but is quickly killed by hot summer heat. Since it blooms in late spring, there are places where, if treated as an

annual, the flowers can be appreciated before the plants are killed by hot weather. It might be well to sow seeds in Aug., carry the seedlings over in a cool frost-free frame, and plant them out in April for late spring bloom. Not as dependable an ornamental in the U.S. as it is in the British Isles.

CHEIRIDOPSIS (cheer-i-DOP-sis)

candidissima   6″   Zone 9   Victory-plant
A tufted succulent perennial from South Africa forming whitish mats of fingerlike leaves and white to pale pink flowers, sometimes used as a ground cover in southern Calif. The leaves are 4 in. long and ½ in. wide, silver-gray, boat-shaped and in pairs and the flowers are 2 in. wide.

CHELIDONIUM (kelli-DO-nium)

majus   30′   Zone 4   Greater Celandine
The seeds of many roadside plants of the Atlantic coastal states were brought originally by the wives of early settlers to compensate for the loss of their cottage gardens in England and elsewhere. *Chelidonium majus* is one of these. It is a biennial or perennial with brittle stems containing a saffron-colored juice and compound leaves which are deeply lobed and toothed. The flowers are yellow and appear from early spring to late summer. A good plant because of its long flowering period, it may need to be restrained since it self-sows readily. Native to Europe but naturalized in eastern North America.

CHELONE (kell-O-ne). These native plants are for bog gardens or the banks of streams, especially in partial shade. The leaves are opposite, flowers are 2 lipped and irregular, borne in compact terminal spikes and open a few at a time during the late summer and autumn. Propagation is by seeds sown in the greenhouse in March; by 3-inch cuttings taken in July or by division of the old plants in Sept. or early spring.

glabra   3′   Zone 3   White Turtle-head
White to pale pink flowers are borne in a short, tight, terminal spike above the last pair of leaves. A good plant for garden culture, with its attractive foliage and unusual flowers which bear a strong resemblance to a turtle's head. In nature it is found in moist, acid soil from eastern Canada south to Ga. and Miss. Easily propagated by seed sown in spring, by division in spring, or by cuttings taken in summer. Transplanting should be done in spring.

lyonii   3′   Zone 3   Pink Turtle-head
This is the best of the species for the garden, with oval leaves 4–7 in. long, rose-purple flowers about an inch long in summer. Native to the mountains of the southeastern U.S.

obliqua   2′–3′   Zone 6   Rose Turtle-head

This plant may be found in wet, swampy woods from Md. throughout the South to Miss. The late flowering season makes this a very desirable plant for moist gardens having acid soil. The flowers are pink. Propagation is by self-sown seed, or by division in the spring.

CHENILLE   COPPERLEAF   =   *Acalypha hispida*

CHENILLE PLANT = *Echeveria leucotricha*

CHENOPODIACEAE   =   The   Goosefoot Family

CHENOPODIUM (ken-o-PO-dium)

album   10′   annual   Lambs-quarters, Pigweed
A weed with leaves of irregular shape but generally triangular, 4 in. long and white-mealy beneath. Flowers are small, in dense panicles in the leaf axils. Native to Europe, Asia and North America, widely distributed in North

Lamb's Quarters: A common garden weed.

America and a weed in many gardens. The fresh young greens are considered edible as a salad. For control see WEED-CONTROLLING CHEMICALS.

ambrosioides   3½′   mostly annual   American Wormseed
Annual or perennial weed with alternate leaves, generally lanceolate in shape, up to 5 in. long and aromatic. The flowers are small, greenish, in panicles from July to Sept. It was introduced from tropical America and now is a common weed in the middle Atlantic and southern states.

bonus-henricus 2½′ **Zone 5** **Good-King-Henry Goosefoot**
A perennial European weed, seen in urban areas in the eastern U.S. with arrow-shaped alternate leaves 3 in. long. Flowers small and greenish in clusters from June to Aug. Sometimes grown as a pot herb for use like Spinach. The foliage faces the ground, making the plant useful in the flower border in front of plants devoid of basal foliage.

botrys 2′ **annual** **Jerusalem-oak Goosefoot**
A locally common weed across North America, introduced from Europe with strong-smelling leaves up to 2 in. long, lobed or pinnatifid. Flower clusters are not outstanding. It appears chiefly in sandy or gravelly soils.

capitatum 1½′ **annual** **Blite Goosefoot**
This is a weed but sometimes grown as a pot herb, native to Europe, mostly found in North America in the eastern states, Rocky Mountain area, southern Canada and Alaska. Leaves are triangular and the fruit is red and mulberrylike.

glaucum 1′ **annual** **Oak-leaved Goosefoot**
A prostrate weed, introduced from Europe but now found throughout the northern U.S. and southern Canada. The leaves are alternate, simple and coarsely toothed or pinnately lobed, white underneath. The flowers are similar to those of Lambs-quarters.

CHERIMOYA = *Annona cherimola*

CHERRY. Many home gardeners will find, after due consideration, that they do not wish to grow cherries, for 2 reasons. Birds can, and frequently do, eat a major part of the crop. Also, cherries have a tendency to split if a period of heavy rains coincide with ripening. It is practically impossible for the gardener to control either one of these hazards. Birds like blueberries, but these can be covered with netting. However, covering entire trees with netting just is not practical.

Cherries are of 3 general types—sour cherries (varieties of *Prunus cerasus*) which are mostly self-fertile; Sweet Cherries (varieties of *P. avium*) which are not self-fertile, but need other varieties for cross-pollination; and the Duke cherries, supposed to be crosses between the sour and the sweet, which also need other cherries for cross-pollination. Since the home gardener frequently considers planting the Sweet Cherry, he must also surmount the hurdle of needing several trees of different varieties to insure having a crop. Often this is a greater undertaking than the cherries are worth.

The main sweet cherry-growing areas of the U.S. are the Pacific Coast states, chiefly Calif., Ore. and Wash., western N.Y. and western Mich. The chief sour cherry-growing areas are northern Ohio, western N.Y. and the Hudson Valley, western Mich., Wisc. and Colo.

All cherries bloom early in the spring, before the leaves appear, and hence the flowers are susceptible to killing by late frosts. The Sweet Cherry is about as hardy as the Peach; the Sour Cherry is slightly more hardy. All cherries are susceptible to various virus diseases, and one should be certain that, in purchasing trees, virus-free plants are purchased, the understock as well as the tops.

Propagation is by budding on either *P. avium*, the Mazzard Cherry, or *P. mahaleb*, the Mahaleb Cherry. The latter is cheap and easy to work, but the Mazzard Cherry is the superior understock, and trees on this stock should be obtained if possible, for they make much better trees.

Sweet cherries should be planted 30 ft. apart, sour cherries about 25 ft. apart and 'Morello' cherries about 18 ft. apart.

As for pruning, sweet cherries are pruned the least. These trees usually grow taller than those of the sour cherries and they just do not seem to demand the careful pruning required by many other kinds of fruit trees. Little pruning is necessary on sour cherries, especially if crossed branches and weak branches are removed as they appear.

Cross-Pollination

One should be as careful with cherries as with plums in the cross-pollination requirements. All sweet cherries require cross-pollination and the chances are that it is these which would be selected for the home garden. Varieties which have proved good pollinizers for other sweet cherry varieties are 'Black Tatarian', 'Grant', 'Seneca' and 'Lyons'. It should be remembered, too, that varieties like 'Bing', 'Lambert', 'Napoleon' and 'Emperor Francis' are all inter-sterile, one with the other.

The Duke cherries, 'Reine Hortense' and 'Royal Duke', are self-sterile and either sour or sweet cherries can be used as pollinizers for these. The sour cherries are mostly self-fertile.

Fertilizers

Fertilizers might be applied in the early spring at about the time the buds burst. A 3–4-year-old tree in a cultivated orchard might be given ½–3 lbs. of 10–10–10. If it is over 10 years old it might be given 5–10 lbs. Trees growing in sod, which receive more and sweeter cherries because they grow into larger trees, would also receive heavier applications.

Varieties

SOUR CHERRIES
'Early Richmond'—one of earliest of this group to ripen, but the fruits are rather small.

'**English Morello**'—fruits late, ripening 10 days to 2 weeks after 'Montmorency'; almost black; used sometimes in the home garden, but not planted commercially.

'**Montmorency**'—fruits are large, bright red and probably the most popular commercial sour cherry.

SWEET CHERRIES

'**Bing**'—originated in Ore. in 1875. Fruits are dark red, almost black; excellent for canning; flesh is dark red.

'**Black Tatarian**'—fruits are black to purplish black and of good quality.

'**Emperor Francis**'—fruits colored bright red over yellow; used chiefly as a Maraschino type.

'**Hedelfingen**'—large black fruits of high quality, used chiefly for fresh fruit. Also known as 'Geante D'Hedelfingen', originated in Germany about the middle of the last century. Excellent as fresh fruit.

'**Lambert**'—originated in Ore. in 1880. Fruits are black, large and excellent for fresh fruit and for canning. It is more popular now than 'Bing'.

Lyons'—early fruiting; large, dark red.

'**Napoleon**'—used chiefly for processing as a Maraschino type, with a bright red cheek and yellowish background.

'**Royal Ann**'—first described in Europe in 1667; one of the most successful varieties in America. The color is light yellow to blush pink; used fresh and for canning; semi-cling-stone type.

'**Stella**'—self-fruitful, large, black, very vigorous and productive.

'**Yellow Spanish**'—yellow fruits of medium size, used chiefly as a Maraschino type.

DUKE CHERRIES

'**Reine Hortense**'—fruit is early, large and red; excellent as fresh fruit, but has a record of not producing well annually.

'**Royal Duke**'—fruit large, dark red, a good producer, but not quite so hardy as 'Reine Hortense'.

Bigflower European Bird = *P. padus* 'Spaethii'
Black = *P. serotina*
Catalina = *P. lyonii*
Double Conradina = *P. conradinae* 'Semi-plena'
Double European Bird = *P. padus* 'Plena'
Double Flowered Mazzard = *P. avium* 'Plena'
European Bird = *P. padus*
Harbinger European Bird = *P. padus* 'Commutata'
Higan = *P. subhirtella*
Longcluster European Bird = *P. padus* 'Watereri'
Mivama = *P. maximowiczii*
Nipponese = *P. nipponica*

Oriental = *P. serrulata*
Pin = *P. pensylvanica*
Rum = *P. serotina*
Sargent = *P. sargentii*
Sour = *P. cerasus*
Sour, Rhex = *P. cerasus* 'Rhexii'
Taiwan = *P. campanulata*
Weeping Black = *P. serotina pendula*
Wild Red = *P. pensylvanica*
Yoshino = *P. yedoensis*

Insect Pests

Black cherry aphid develops in large colonies on the underside of curled leaves especially on water sprouts. Spraying with insecticide #15 or #13 gives control. Maggots of cherry fruit flies infest the fruit, as do the grubs of plum curculio. See APPLE. Spraying with insecticide #9 soon after the small fruit develops is effective. Sluglike larvae of the cherry sawfly skeletonize the leaves in early summer and again in late summer, partly defoliating the trees. Sprays for other pests usually are effective or insecticide #9 might be used. Tent caterpillars infest cherry in the spring, and other caterpillars are occasionally troublesome.

Diseases

Brown rot (see PEACH) causes lesion on twigs and rot on ripening fruit. Bacterial leaf spot in which the spots often drop out, causing a shot-hole effect. Attacks both sweet and sour cherries and defoliates the trees. Spraying with fungicide #G when petals fall and after harvest is helpful. A fungus leaf spot or yellow leaf is controlled by fungicide #W in early and late applications. Black knot develops on sour cherries. See PLUM. Virus diseases discourage the growing of cherries in some areas. Destroying infected trees and controlling insects are the only remedies.

CHERRY-LAUREL = *Prunus laurocerasus*

CHERIL = *Anthriscus cerefolium*

CHESTNUT. (Also see CASTANEA.) As we know, the Chestnut in the United States is a member of the *Castanea* genus, which is a small group of nut-producing timber trees. One native species, *C. dentata*, the American Chestnut, was probably the most valuable timber tree in this country. Certainly it was the dominant tree in the vast hardwood forests. Unfortunately an Asiatic fungus, *Endothia parasitica*, which gained entrance to N.Y. about 1900, has all but exterminated the American Chestnut in this country. Common in the hardwood forests of the eastern half of the United States, only an occasional sucker from the live root system is now seen from Me. to Mich. and south to the Gulf of Mexico.

Sometimes the suckers become large enough to bear nuts arousing hope that eventually the American Chestnut may acquire resistance to the blight. The U.S. Forest Service, the state forestry departments and others, notably Dr. Richard A. Jaynes, have been crossing American Chestnut with the Japanese species, *Castanea crenata* and the Chinese species, *C. mollissima*, both of which have resistance to *Endothia*. Some progress is being made, but hope of producing a timber-type hybrid with sufficient resistance to use in reforesting has not yet been realized.

Although a number of named varieties are available from nurseries, notably **'Abundance'**, **'Carr'** and **'Hobson'**, because of incompatibility between seedling stock and the scion, many persons have had poor results with them. They are now turning to named selections 'of the Chinese Chestnut which have been made by the USDA. Grafted trees come into bearing in 5 or 6 years. Seedlings often do not bear until 15 or more years old. Chinese Chestnuts have nuts as sweet as the American and often of larger size. Recommended are **'Nanking'**, **'Meiling'** and **'Kuling'**. All 3 produce large nuts of excellent quality. Although the Chinese Chestnut is questionably hardy in Zone 3, it does extremely well over most of the country.

Very likely the resistance of both the Chinese Chestnut and the Japanese *Castanea crenata* resulted from living with the disease for several hundred years. On that basis we may hope that eventually the American Chestnut will acquire a degree of resistance some day.

The Japanese Chestnut, *C. crenata*, is a spreading short-trunked tree that usually remains under 30 feet in height. Leaves are oblong, 4 to 7 in. in length with the margin serrated. The burr is about 2 in. in dia. and normally has 2 nuts, which lack the quality of the nuts of either the American or Chinese Chestnut. It thrives in much of the country from Zone 4 south.

The Chinese Chestnut, *C. mollissima*, may reach 50 ft. in height. The trunk, however, is short and the crown is broad. The elliptic leaves are coarsely toothed with a white pubescence along the veins. Native to China and Korea, the nuts, 2 normally to a burr, are large and sweet. Hardy from Zone 4 south, several producing orchards in the Midwest and the middle Atlantic states yield plentiful crops of high quality nuts.

The Spanish Chestnut, *C. sativa*, is a tall tree native to Europe, western Asia and North Africa. It has been in cultivation in Europe for many years. In this country, it is less hardy than either Asiatic species. The nuts are large and well filled when properly grown, but they lack the pleasant flavor of either American Chestnut or

the Asiatic species. In recent years chestnut blight has reached Europe and is decimating the orchards of Spanish Chestnut.

The Chinquapin, *C. pumila*, is a shrubby American tree, usually remaining under 20 ft. in height. Native from N.J. to Fla. and west to Tex. and Okla., its burrs are a little over an inch in dia. and normally contain a single nut. Leaves 3 to 7 in. long are coarsely toothed and have a white felt on the underside.

Interest in the Chestnut for landscape use has in recent years been largely concentrated on the Chinese Chestnut. It is an attractive spreading tree, both ornamental and equally serviceable as a shade tree. Neither the Asiatic nor the American Chestnut is exacting in its soil requirement, but no Chestnut will thrive in a soil where drainage is poor. A rocky well-drained hillside with a sandy loam is ideal for chestnuts.

The most serious insect pest is a tiny snout beetle which lays its eggs on the growing burrs in July. The grubs hatch and bore into the enlarging nuts within the burr where they feed on the kernel. These chestnut weevils can be controlled with any one of several pesticides, but it is advisable to inquire of the Extension Service of the State University as to timing and the specific chemical to use. Since this pest pupates in the soil under the tree, control may be had by pesticide treatment of the soil. Other insects are not usually troublesome.

The most serious disease of the Chestnut is the blight, *Endothia parasitica*, for which there is now no known control. It does not affect the roots which sucker freely. Such suckers sometimes live long enough to produce a few nuts. The U.S. Forest Service has acquired detailed information on several hundred American Chestnut trees that have not been killed by *Endothia*. Records of persisting suckers are also in their hands. It is hoped that a disease-resistant American Chestnut may be found to be reproduced vegetatively or to be crossed with a Chinese or Japanese Chestnut, thereby producing a resistant hybrid.

H. GLEASON MATTOON

CHEWING GUM TREE = *Manilkara zapota*

CHICKEN-CORN = *Sorghum vulgare drummondii*

CHICKWEED. See CERASTIUM, STELLARIA.

CHICORY = *Cichorium intybus*

CHILEAN-JASMINE = *Mandevilla laxa*

CHILE-BELLS, RED = *Lapageria rosea*

CHILEVINE, CORAL = *Berberidopsis corallina*

CHILOPSIS (KY-lop-sis)
linearis   30′   Zone 7   Desert-willow
This is a willowlike plant, usually only 15 ft. high or less, used chiefly in the Tex. and Mexico area where it is native. The conspicuous flowers, somewhat like those of the Catalpa, are lilac-colored, trumpet-shaped and fragrant, borne in terminal clusters. The narrow leaves can be 1 ft. long or even longer. The fruit is merely a pod, often 1 ft. long. Not an especially important ornamental except in the area where it is native.

CHIMAPHILA (ky-MAFF-ill-a). Two species of this member of the Heath Family (Ericaceae) are native to the North American woodlands. Both are perennial evergreens with leathery leaves and attractive, 5-petalled flowers. They are difficult to cultivate, needing rich woods soil or leaf mold, and possibly being somewhat dependent upon bacterial organisms or a fungus in the soil.
maculata   4″–10″   Zone 4   Striped Pipsissewa
Spreading by underground stems, *C. maculata* may be recognized by its clusters of leathery leaves which are mottled with white along the veins. The clusters of nodding white or pinkish flowers are borne at the top of the flowering stalk, each flower with 5 petals. They appear in summer. The plant may be found in rich woodlands from Me. to Minn. and Ga.
umbellata   5″–12″   Zone 4   Common Pipsissewa
A trailing evergreen perennial with toothed, narrowly wedge-shaped leaves and bearing a small terminal umbel of white or pinkish flowers; each have 5 spreading petals. It is a plant of the dry woods from New England to Ga., extending inland to the Great Lakes. It flowers throughout the summer. The varietal name **cisatlantica** is sometimes given to the plant native to eastern North America.

CHIMERA. Sometimes called "graft hybrid," this is actually a fusion of cells caused mechanically, often by the grafting operation, yielding a plant slightly different from that produced either by the understock or the scion alone. Actually it is a plant having cells of both parents but not fusion of cells. *Laburnocytisus adamii* is one good example. Sometimes certain species of *Solanum* grafted one on the other show this same unique characteristic.

CHIMONANTHUS (ky-mo-NAN-thus)
praecox   9′   Zone 7   Wintersweet
An extremely fragrant flowered shrub, producing its inch-sized yellowish flowers usually in the winter months, certainly before the leaves appear. Leaves are 2½–6 in. long and opposite. There is a larger flowered variety (**'Grandiflorus'**) but the fragrance of the flowers is not as pronounced. Native to China. This species needs

little pruning and can be propagated by layering and by seeds.
CHINA-ASTER = *Callistephus chinensis*
CHINABERRY = *Melia azedarach*
CHINA-FIR, COMMON = *Cunninghamia lanceolata*
CHINESE-DATE = *Zizyphus jujuba*
CHINESE EVERGREEN = *Aglaonema modestum*
CHINESE-LANTERN = *Physalis alkekengi*
CHINKAPIN, ALLEGANY = *Castanea pumila*
CHINKERICHEE, CAPE = *Ornithogalum thyrsoides*
CHINQUAPIN = *Castanea pumila*
CHIOCOCCA (ky-o-COCCA)
alba   10′   Zone 10   David's Milkberry
A shrub native to southern Fla. and tropical America, either upright or climbing, with leaves up to 3 in. long, bright green and glossy. The white flowers usually turn yellow or they fade, are bell shaped, ⅜ in. long, fragrant and are produced in pendulous clusters. The white fruits are ₅⁄₁₆ in. wide and appear in showy clusters.

CHIOGENES = *Gaultheria hispidula*

CHIONANTHUS (ky-o-NAN-thus)
retusus   18′   Zone 5   Chinese Fringetree
Native to China, Korea and Japan, this was introduced to America about a century ago. The plant itself, as well as the flowers and leaves, are smaller than those of *C. virginicus*, but it does have a finer texture. Its opposite leaves are only about 4 in. long and the flower clusters are borne in great profusion. Usually the sexes are separate with the staminate flowers being larger. For distinguishing between this and the native species see *C. virginicus*.
virginicus   30′   Zone 4   Fringetree
The Old Man's Beard, as it is sometimes called, is a native of the southeastern U.S. and makes a splendid ornamental specimen as far north as Boston, Mass. The white flowers are borne in loose panicles 6 in. long or even longer in early June. The fruits on the pistillate plant are blue berries, borne in grapelike clusters and the opposite leaves turn a bright yellow in the fall. It is closely related to the lilacs and unfortunately is susceptible to infestations of scale, like the lilacs and ashes. Many people do not realize that it is one of the last shrubs to produce leaves in the spring and so one should be patient waiting for the flowers to appear. Many a plant has been deemed dead by overly anxious, unknowing plantsmen.

It should be pointed out here that the Oriental Fringetree (*C. retusus*) is only about half as tall as the native species and the flower-clusters are shorter, about 4 in. long. There is also one other method of telling the 2 apart—the flower clusters of *C. retusus* are borne on the current year's growth, while those of *C. virginicus* are borne on the previous year's growth. Also, the leaves of the Chinese species are only 4 in. long while those of *C. virginicus* are twice that length.

It is interesting to note that the birds will take the fruits from a certain specimen very quickly. One day, in passing a 15′ fringetree, I noted it was covered with beautiful blue fruits. The next morning, when prepared with the camera, there were no fruits left on the plant. In just a few hours a flock of birds had eaten all the fruits.

Propagation

This seed can be stratified as soon as it is ripe or stored dry in airtight containers in a cool place for up to a year and then stratified. It has a double dormancy, hence it must be stratified for 3 months at greenhouse temperatures, then taken into cold (40° F.) for another 3 months, then sown. Sometimes it is grafted with *Fraxinus americana* used as the understock. Softwood cuttings can also be rooted. See SEEDS, GRAFTING, CUTTINGS.

CHIONODOXA (ky-o-no-DOX-a)
luciliae   3″   **Zone 4**   **Glory-of-the-snow**
With grasslike leaves, these bulbous herbs from Crete and Asia Minor are among the first bulbs to bloom in the spring. They produce small flowers in clusters, bell shaped and blue with a white center. There are about 5 flowers in a cluster. They belong to the Lily Family, hence the segments of the flower are 6 and the fruit is a 3-sided capsule. The bulbs should be planted 3 in. deep during Sept., be given plenty of moisture and may have to be renewed every few years. Propagation is by seeds and offsets. There is a white and a pink variety of this species and the plant known as *C. gigantea* is merely a large-flowered variety of this species. If they do well in the rock garden where they like full sun, they may increase themselves and form a nice mass of bloom, in which case they should not be moved.
sardensis   3″   **Zone 4**
Similar to the more common *C. luciliae*, but with darker blue flowers and without the white eye. Native to Asia Minor.

CHITTAMWOOD = *Bumelia lanuginosa*

CHIVE (*Allium schoenoprasum*) is a perennial, grows in thick tufts, and produces small oval bulblets and showy lavender flowers. It is propagated from seed and by division of the tufts. It is grown for its leaves which are cut 1–2 in. above the bulblets. Cutting stimulates new growth, and a number of cuttings may be

made after the plant has formed a thick clump. In the fall the clump may be lifted, replanted into a pot and placed in the kitchen window for a supply of leaves during the winter months.

The general garden culture is the same as for onions.

GRANT B. SNYDER

Chives: Often grown indoors in the kitchen window for winter use.

CHLIDANTHUS (clee-DAN-thus)
fragrans   10″   **Zone 9**   **Delicate-lily**
A bulbous herb native to South America, with strap-shaped leaves and fragrant yellow flowers, about 3 in. long, borne with several to a cluster and blooming in the summer. In the North, the bulbs are planted 2 in. deep in the early spring, and dug and stored in the fall before the ground freezes. Propagated by offsets.

CHLORDANE A chlorinated hydrocarbon formerly used as an insecticide, now banned.

CHLOROGALUM (klo-ROG-al-um)
pomeridianum   5′   **Zone 9**   **Soap-plant**
A native bulbous Calif. perennial with leaves 1½ ft. long and ¾ in. wide with wavy margins. The white flowers have purplish veins, and are only about ¾ in. long, opening in the afternoon. Bees are greatly attracted to the flowers. The Indians used to make soap from this plant, hence the common name.

CHLOROPHORA (klo-ROFF-or-a)
tinctoria   60′   **Zone 10**   **Fustic**
Belonging to the Mulberry Family, this tree has

a spreading, broad head and is native to the West Indies. The alternate, lanceolate leaves are 5 in. long and the yellow wood yields a milky juice used as a dye material, also used in producing browns and greens. The fruit is an achene; the flowers are both staminate and pistillate.

CHLOROPHYLL. The highly complex chemical material in the leaf and stems of plants colored green is the only material which, in the presence of sunlight, can convert carbon dioxide and water to carbohydrates. It is contained as a thin coating to the chloroplasts, small, circular microscopic bodies which are very numerous in the cells of the green parts of plants. Chlorophyll can be separated from the other leaf parts because it is soluble in a mixture of 4 parts acetone and one of water. Chlorophyll is without question fundamental to all plant life.

CHLOROPHYTUM (klo-ro-FY-tum)
commosum 'Variegatum' (*elatum*)   **3′   Zone 10
Spider Plant**
A common and very popular house plant native to South Africa, with fleshy tuberous roots, long, narrow, white-striped leaves all originating from the base of the plant and about a foot long. The plant sends out long stalks on which there are a series of plantlets, each well supplied with roots and leaves so that propagation from these is extremely simple. A rugged house plant

Chlorophytum commosum 'Variegatum' is an excellent plant for the hanging basket.

which can thrive under neglect; for sun or shade. Tip leaf kill due to too much fluoride in water or soil. Counteract by applying 1 teaspoonful of lime per pot.

CHLOROPICRIN. Actually tear gas, used as a fungicide, which see.

CHLOROSIS. A diseased or unnatural condition of the foliage which instead of being a normal green color is yellow, yellowish or spotted with yellow, showing a lack of the normal amount of chlorophyll. This condition is often brought about by lack of insufficient soluble iron in the soil, and is sometimes corrected by applying iron chelate in leaf sprays or in granular form to the soil. See IRON CHELATE. Chlorosis is caused by other unnatural conditions also, as well as being caused by various virus diseases.

CHOCOLATE FAMILY = Sterculiaceae

CHOCOLATE-TREE = *Theobroma cacao*

CHOISYA (SHOY-sia)
ternata   9′   Zone 7   Mexican-orange
A popular Mexican plant with aromatic evergreen leaves 3 in. long and fragrant white flowers 1 in. across which bloom in late May. It grows well in full sunshine but needs some remedial pruning to keep the bush in a compact form. This is a favorite plant in the greenhouse also, easily propagated by softwood cuttings.

CHOKEBERRY. See ARONIA.

CHOKECHERRY. See PRUNUS.

CHOLLA. See OPUNTIA.

CHORISIA (kor-ISS-ia)
speciosa   50′   Zone 10   Floss-silk Tree
Native to Brazil and occasionally planted in southern Fla., this belongs to the Silk-cotton Tree Family and is noted for its large pink-to-purple or white flowers, up to 3 in. wide, which are borne in the early winter when it has no leaves. The alternate leaves are palmately compound. The fruits are pear shaped and the seeds are covered with a silky floss.

CHORIZEMA (kor-RIX-ee-ma, or kor-riz-EE-ma)
cordatum   10′   Zone 9   Heartleaf Flamepea
A member of the Pea Family, native to Australia and planted in Fla. and Calif. for its very showy flowers in the early spring. It is a weak grower, often supported on a trellis, but the scarlet and purple flowers, about ¾ in. long, are numerous and outstanding. The leaves are about an inch long, heart shaped at the base.

CHRISTMAS-BERRY = *Heteromeles arbutifolia*

CHRISTMAS CACTUS = *Schlumbergera truncata*

CHRISTMAS-CHEER = *Sedum rubrotinctum*

CHRISTMAS-COSMOS = *Montanoa hibiscifolia*

CHRISTMAS-DAISY = *Montanoa hibiscifolia*

CHRISTMAS DECORATIONS FROM EVERGREENS. Wreaths of evergreen foliage, of one kind or another, are the easiest of the Christmas decorations to make, and once the technique is understood, it can be easily adapted to any type of material. First and foremost are the frames. Beginners may start with a single wire (No. 9, even a rebent coat hanger can suffice), or 2 branches tied together in a circle; but the experienced hand at wreath-making will tell you that it is much easier to start with a ready-made wire frame of 2 circles of wire, available commercially for wreathmaking purposes. Also, one should have a spool of green enamelled No. 26 wire for wrapping the cut evergreen twigs to the frame.

Wreaths are made of Balsam Fir, Pine, Norway Spruce, Red-cedar, Juniper, Yew, Boxwood, and even Hemlock, but this last should be avoided, since the needles fall quickly after the twigs have been cut. Mountain-laurel, Evergreen Magnolia (*M. grandiflora*), Rhododendron, Holly, Bearberry, Oregon Holly-grape, and many other things are also used. Thousands of wreaths of Balsam Fir are sold. These are made from the lower, discarded branches of balsam firs cut for the Christmas-tree market, and also from defective trees which cannot be sold as trees. The wreaths are produced in large quantities in the areas of Vt., N.H. and Me., where these trees are grown for the Christmas trade and shipped by truck. In buying them, one should not purchase wreaths that have been made too soon.

Fortunate is he who has a stand of young White Pine seedlings (i.e., any planting where branches are near the ground), for White Pine affords excellent wreath material; so do the young shoots of Yew. The shearing of a long yew hedge might well be let go until the Christmas period when the young shoots would afford the best possible material for Christmas wreaths. Especially is this true of the shorter branches and slower-growing *Taxus cuspidata densa* and var. *nana*, since 6-inch shoots of these usually have several small side branches and "make up" quickly into wreath material. Cutting individual, unbranched yew shoots— sufficient for a wreath—can be a long and arduous task, enough to dampen the ardour of all but the most enthusiastic.

Boxwood, too, is excellent. Gardeners in other parts of the country are not so fortunate as their Virginia friends in having large quantities of this excellent plant which makes fine wreaths. Holly, of course, also has been used, although it is prickly to handle.

No matter what the material, young shoots are cut about 4–6 in. long for the smaller wreaths, long for larger wreaths. The end of the roll of No. 26 wire is attached firmly to the frame and then gradually worked tightly around the bases of these shoots as they are put in place, 2 or 3 at a time in front and 1 large, dense one in the back of the wire frame. It is necessary only to wind the base of these twigs to the frame, but this should be done carefully and well. The next small bundle of twigs is so placed as to cover the bases of those last wired on, and so on around the entire circle. It can take a lot of material for a large wreath, so one had better practice with the standard 14-inch size at first.

A simple wreath of Boxwood, Pine or Yew is beautiful enough in itself when tied with a large red (waterproof) ribbon. However, many prefer to use this merely as the base on which to attach all sorts of fruits, berries, cones, or painted objects. It is here that an artistic hand and good taste will prove helpful.

Cut branches of Boxwood seem to dry noticeably indoors. Experience has shown that wreaths of Boxwood can be "freshened" considerably by a quick syringing with water twice a week, or an actual soaking in water if there are no ornaments to be harmed. Moisture in the atmosphere out-of-doors is sufficient to keep most cut greens (except Hemlock and Balsam Fir which has been cut too soon) in good condition through the Christmas period.

Spraying with a clear plastic spray (commonly available in small pressure cans) can give a sheen to any of these cut greens and can prove helpful in preserving them properly indoors. It is a simple matter to spray the finished product (away from fire) and it dries almost immediately.

Pine, Boxwood, and Yew wreaths will last throughout the Christmas period satisfactorily indoors or out, but Fir wreaths will soon drop their needles indoors, although if purchased shortly after being trimmed from the trees, they will last out-of-doors several weeks.

Strikingly interesting small wreaths for the guest room door can be made around an ordinary jar rubber. Bearberry (*Arctostaphylos uva-ursi*) is cut in pieces 3–4 in. long and tied on the jar ring in the same manner as done for larger wreaths. Other small-leaved evergreens like the Kew Euonymus (*Euonymus fortunei* 'Kewensis'), Little-leaf Japanese Holly (*Ilex crenata microphylla*), and the clippings and leftovers from Boxwood and Yew wreaths can be used similarly.

Cone Wreaths

In this category, one must have an artistic touch and a remarkable amount of patience.

First, the cones are wired and taped so that they may be attached. Twelve-inch lengths of No. 22 wire are used for the larger cones and they must be wired to the frame with 2 wires, 1 on either side of each cone, to prevent their being shaken out of place. Small cones, like those of Hemlock, may be wired with No. 30 wire, many of them being wired together in groups of a dozen or so. Acorns—these are the problem! When green, cups and fruits remain together nicely, but as soon as they start to dry out they part company. They can be wired together so that

Wreath-making from cones and fruits is a most satisfying hobby. In this wreath are fruits or cones of Eucalyptus, *Davidia*, various pines, spruce, oaks, *Ceddrus atlantica*, Beefwood, etc., collected from all four corners of the country. This arrangement was done by Florence D. Wyman. (*Photo by Arnold Arboretum, Jamaica Plain, Mass.*)

the wire is unnoticed—but what a time-consuming job this proves to be. The youngsters of the house can do it, but if they insist on payment for time spent, costs go up quickly. It isn't long before this job reverts to the lady carrying the enthusiasm for the whole project. The electric drill is used for boring 1 hole through the center of the cup or base, and a hole straight across the lower base of the acorn itself. If this is done properly, with the smallest drill, the acorn can be wired to the cup (No. 30 wire) with the only evidence being the two ends of wire coming through the base of the cup. These ends are easily tied together in a knot, thus preventing movement of the acorn from the cup. Acorns, too, especially the smaller types like those of the Pin Oak and Red Oak, are often wired in clusters to simulate grapes. Larger acorns like those of

the Mossy-cup Oak are used in small groups, but wired similarly.

One of the methods of making a "base" on the 3-dimensional frame for the cones is to attach a double row of white pine cones entirely around the frame. The larger cones, some of which have been cut in half to simulate rosettes or flowers, or turned upside down, are next attached. Standard practice seems to be to start with 3 properly balanced, equidistant, main accent-points. Then, the smaller materials are worked in pleasing groups around these main focal points. Good taste, patience and experience are primary assets in making beautiful cone wreaths.

"Kissing Balls"

The balls are simply made by starting with a ball of styrofoam which is available from any florists' supply house. This is a light plastic material about the size of a baseball into which one may easily force sharpened twigs. If styrofoam balls are not available, a similar-sized ball is made by squeezing out moist sphagnum moss and tying string tightly around it in such a way as to hold it in a round shape.

A sturdy wire is placed through the ball and attached so that it can be hung, At first, it is advisable to hang this unadorned ball at about eye level, so that working on it will be easy.

Five- or six-inch pieces of Boxwood are cut from any vigorous plant, the stems sharpened a bit with a knife, and the pieces stuck in uniformly around the entire ball. It is important to keep in mind the fact that the finished ball will look much better if the pieces used are a uniform length. If this cannot be done, merely cutting off the longer ends after the pieces are all in place will help.

Boxwood dries rather quickly, so it might be advisable to spray some plastic or wax-coating material on the finished product to keep the foliage in a fresh-appearing condition for as long as possible. Or, it can be freshened considerably once or twice a week by syringing with water or actually soaking in water for a few minutes. Then it can be hung as is, or for good measure a small piece of mistletoe may be attached beneath it so that there will be no misunderstanding on the part of our modern youngsters as to what it is.

Garlands

After one has had experience in making foliage wreaths and cone wreaths, one may graduate to the garland-making class, for it is here that one needs the experience of all that was learned in making the cone wreaths. Since most fireplaces differ in proportion, there is no standard measurement for these festoons of cones and fruits. Usually, a frame of plywood is cut out the exact size and shape wanted. Then the major groupings are arranged on this and wired around the narrow frame; or, better still, a hole is bored through the frame, the wires inserted, pulled tightly and bent over, and then stapled with one of the special wood staplers now available. Not a simple or easy undertaking, yet the end result can be a thing of artistic beauty to adorn the living room long after the Christmas period.

Swags

A swag is merely a group of evergreen branches, tied together in a pleasing form. They are frequently hung on doors in lieu of wreaths. Once the knack has been acquired of arranging the branches artistically together, these, too, may be trimmed at the base with a ribbon and a few carefully selected cones and fruits.

CHRISTMAS-ROSE. See HELLEBORUS.

CHRISTMAS-TREE, NEW ZEALAND = *Metrosideros excelsus*

CHRIST THORN = *Paliurus spina-christi*

CHROMOSOMES. Chromatin threads bearing hereditary determiners (genes) in the nuclei of cells; chromosomes contract by coiling at the time of cell division and are visible as rodlike masses.

CHRYSALIDOCARPUS (kris-al-id-o-KARP-us)

lutescens 25′–30′ Zone 10 Yellow Butterfly Palm

This palm from Madagascar is termed a feather palm and is much grown by florists who use it in tubs for decorative purposes. The leaves are gracefully arching with 40–60 pairs of pinnae, each about an inch wide, the midribs yellow. Often called Areca by the florists, possibly because of its syn. *Areca lutescens.* In growing in the greenhouse the night temperature should not go much below 60° F., daytime 70°–75° F. Plants do best which are continually slightly pot bound.

CHRYSANTHEMUM (kris-ANTH-em-um)

Chrysanthemums have been used in the gardens of China since before 550 B.C. and they are still extremely popular garden plants today. Forced in greenhouses by the florist, they provide a great source of cut flowers that have many decorative uses, and many are grown in gardens out of doors. Most of the 160 species are native to China, Japan or Europe. Only a few species are grown in America, some of them annuals, some perennials. However, the hundreds of varieties of garden and green house chrysanthemums being grown in America today are mostly grouped under *C. morifolium,* a species of

unknown origin but which contains plants having flowers of diminutive size with flower heads an inch or less in dia. and others that have flowers shaped like huge balls, over 6 in. through.

By selecting the proper varieties, one can have chrysanthemums in bloom from early Aug. to Nov., providing of course they are planted in an area where they grow well, especially in frost-free areas, for it has been noted that many cultivars continue to open their flower buds even at temperatures of 27° F.

There are low dwarf clones of the pin-cushion type that are very much in demand at present. Such plants are popular because even though they are in full bloom they can be easily moved with a ball of soil about the roots for placement in tubs, urns or pots for the duration of the flowering season.

Propagation is by seed, cuttings and simple division, the last being the simplest method for the garden, done in the early spring just when the plants begin to show a bit of growth from the base. Most garden chrysanthemums should be divided annually.

Newly transplanted plants might be pinched back as soon as they are 6–8 in. high, and again after that when the new growth is 6–8 in. long. This might well be repeated until July 15th which is about the time flower buds are initiated. This pinching makes dense, bushy plants. Cushion mums usually 12–15 in. tall need no pinching back.

Watering during dry spells is important. Also, protecting the plants so that they will come through winters in the North is important. Most gardeners fail to do this and so can lose many varieties, for these are plants with very shallow roots and they can easily be "heaved" out of the ground by alternate freezing and thawing of late winter. Covering the plants after the ground freezes with 3–4 in. of hay or other material is most helpful.

Because of their shallow roots, chrysanthemums need fertilizer. Ammonium sulfate, about 3 lbs. per 100 sq. ft. can be applied in 3–4 doses during the growing season. Other fertilizers might be just as good.

It often pays to move chrysanthemums to new locations in the garden every 2–3 years. This is the reason for suggesting that they be divided occasionally for they may peter out or else their roots become so crowded that the flowers are greatly reduced in size. When the stalks have finally been killed by fall freezes they should be cut off at the ground level.

The commercial grower has been shading his chrysanthemums in the greenhouse for many years now. This is worked out on a careful schedule to control time of bloom so that flower crops can be brought into full bearing regardless of climate. Shorter periods of daylight induce chrysanthemums to bloom earlier than they otherwise would under longer day-lengths.

Gardeners can make use of this out-of-doors by covering their chrysanthemums tightly and thoroughly late in the afternoons of late summer, removing the cloth the following morning, thus bringing their plants into earlier bloom. This is frequently desirable in order to obtain flowering before frosts kill the upper parts of the plants. It is also important in the North to select early-blooming types for the garden. Varieties may bloom anywhere from late Aug. (especially the low cushion types) to Nov. Obviously planting Nov.-blooming varieties in a garden where killing frosts are expected by Oct. can only result in disappointment.

Over 3000 varieties of chrysanthemums have been grown in the U.S. The majority have now been discarded but new ones are being introduced each year. The National Chrysanthemum Society has divided them, at least for show purposes, into the following groups:

SINGLE—not more than 5 rows of ray florets. Disks flat with short florets.

SEMI-DOUBLE—more than 5 rows of ray florets. Disk flat with short florets. Ray florets may or may not be at right angles to stem.

REGULAR ANEMONE—ray florets in not more than 5 rows, equal in length, broad and evenly spaced. Disk florets longer than in the singles, making the disk approximately a hemisphere in form.

IRREGULAR ANEMONE—like the Regular Anemone except that the ray florets are irregular in length, twisted or quilled.

POMPON—the ray florets are incurved sufficiently to form a globular bloom—although very small blooms are sometimes flattened or buttonlike. The disk florets may be present but concealed.

REGULAR OR CHINESE INCURVE—the ray florets are broader than long, they are incurved and overlap regularly. The bloom is globular when fully developed, disk florets are hidden. These may be 4–6 in. wide.

IRREGULAR OR JAPANESE INCURVE—the ray florets are very wide in proportion to their length and are twisted, giving the bloom an airy, open appearance. The overlapping of the florets is irregular. These may be 5–7 in. or more, wide.

REFLEXED OR DECORATIVE POMPON—same as the Pompon except that the ray florets are reflexed instead of being incurved. Blooms may be 1½–4 in. wide.

DECORATIVE OR ASTER FLOWERED REFLEX—ray florets are narrower in proportion to their length and are fully reflexed in the mature bloom. The bloom is flatter than in a regular

decorative pompon and the disk must not be apparent.

REGULAR OR CHINESE REFLEX—blooms have the same characteristics of the Regular Incurve except that the ray florets are reflexed.

IRREGULAR OR JAPANESE REFLEX—blooms have the same characteristics of the Japanese Incurve except that the ray florets are reflexed.

SPOON—The ray florets are regular and a tubular opening at the end forms a spoonlike tip. It should have no more than 5 rows of ray florets to be single, more than 5 to be double. The disk should be conspicuous and flat in the single and may or may not be apparent in the double.

QUILL—bloom is fully double with no disk apparent; ray florets are elongated and tubular with tips usually spoonlike, but the ray florets may also be closed to the tip and curved but rarely hooked.

THREADS—ray florets are long, slender and tubular. They may be straight or slightly curved. Tips are closed and straight but may also be slightly coiled or hooked, hardly noticeable. The disk may or may not be apparent.

SPIDER—the ray florets are long and tubular, usually more or less curved and twisted, the tips may be open or closed but must be definitely coiled or hooked. The disk may or may not be apparent.

These are the classes then, into which all chrysanthemums are grouped. Cushion chrysanthemums, or "azaleamums" as they unfortunately have been called, are only 12–15 in. tall, are dense and compact in habit, need no pinching and bloom in Aug. or early Sept. These are excellent for the garden. The so-called "Korean" chrysanthemums originated as hybrids, mostly of hardy species, but have by now been used in crosses with many other species and varieties, bringing added vigor and color variation to those grown in gardens. Many of the "Spoon," "Thread," "Spider," and "Quill" types are mostly grown in the greenhouse where special attention is given them and disbudding is practiced to produce unusually large-sized blooms. The large ball-shaped types used in the fall are the result of disbudding in the greenhouse, so that only 1 flower bud is allowed to develop on each stem.

Insect Pests

Several aphids feed on chrysanthemums and the black aphid is especially abundant on garden plants in the fall. Use insecticides #15 or #13 and in the greenhouse fumigate or use aerosol. Greenhouse leaf tier feeds on the underside of leaves fastened together with fine threads. Sprays or dusts of insecticides #9, #13 or #15 are all effective. Gall midges produce small lumpy galls on the leaves and stems, and distort the growth. Chrysanthemum leaf miners in conspicuous, tortuous mines in the leaves, thrips making flecks and streaks in the flower petals, and mealy bugs sucking the sap from the stems are all controlled by timely sprays of insecticides #15 or #13.

Diseases

Leaf spots, caused by fungi, spot and kill leaves, especially in prolonged damp weather unless protected by fungicides #D, #F or #W. Wilt which lives in soil and infects the roots kills many plants. Some varieties are partially resistant. In greenhouses, disease-free cuttings should be planted in sterilized soil. See SOIL STERILIZATION. Stunt virus causes small plants and flowers. It is spread with cuttings and by pinching and pruning. Control insects, grow clean plants, destroy diseased plants. The white powdery covering of powdery mildew is common during warm muggy weather. Fungicides #V and #M are effective. Rust produces reddish brown spots on the underside of leaves. It is well controlled with fungicide #D. A parasitic plant called dodder which climbs the stems of Chrysanthemum and other plants and feeds through roots which penetrate the host is occasionally troublesome. Pull up and destroy the parasite.

arcticum   15″   Zones 2–3   Arctic Chrysanthemum
A leathery-leaved, hardy, almost woody perennial, native to the Arctic regions, this does not bloom until Oct., often late Oct., so its flowers do not have an opportunity to open in the North at least before freezing weather kills the leaves and blossoms. Flowers are white to lilac, 2 in. across, daisylike. It is of great interest to the hybridist because of its extreme hardiness.

balsamita   2′–3′   Zone 4   Costmary
A perennial herb from western Asia with aromatic foliage; flower heads ¼–⅜ in. across and profuse, the rays white. When rayless all-yellow heads are produced, the varietal name is tanacetoides. This herb was known to the early Egyptians and Greeks and used then as now as a culinary herb. It should be grown in dry soil in the shade.

carinatum (*C. tricolor*) 2′–3′   annual   Tricolor or Annual Chrysanthemum
With large heads 2½ in. wide, white ray flowers banded with red, purple or yellow. Double vars. are also available. Native to Morocco.

cineariifolium   2′   Zone 3   Dalmatian Pyrethrum
The silvery foliage of this plant is interesting but even more important is the fact that an insect powder is made from the white flowers. The flower heads are white or pink, an inch across and the plant has many slender stems. Native to Dalmatia.

coccineum   1′–3′   Zones 2–3   Pyrethrum, Painted Daisy
Native to the Caucasus and Persia, this is a fine ornamental, grown by gardeners and florists alike for its good cut flowers which appear singly, at the end of stems, are daisylike, 3 in. across and colored red in shades of pink to white. Mostly single, a few have double flowers, usually in June and early July. The double-flowered forms often have the central florets and the horizontal rays in different colors, which adds to its effect. Plants may withstand light shade but are at their best in full sun. If the shoots are cut back severely after the first blooming, new growth may occur at the base which will bloom a second time. Propagation is by seeds (spring sown) and division late in the summer.

Some of the better single-flowered forms are: 'Crimson Giant' with large 4 in. blooms on stems 3½ ft. long; 'Victoria'—a ruby-red; 'Scarlet Glow'—scarlet; and 'Eileen May Robinson'—salmon pink.

Double forms are: 'Helen' and 'Rosary', both rose-pink; 'Buckeye'—deep red; 'Sensation'—red; 'Pink Bouquet'—pink. The asexually grown cultivars are usually superior to seedlings.

coreanum   Korean Daisy
This is a name frequently used for a white, hardy, single chrysanthemum but its exact identity is in doubt.

coronarium   1½′–3′   annual   Crown-daisy Chrysanthemum
A bushy, floriferous plant with flowers light yellow to white, sometimes semi-double. The var. 'Tom Thumb' is only a foot high. Native to the Mediterranean Region. The young shoots of this species are eaten in China and Japan.

frutescens   3′   Zone 10   Marguerite Chrysanthemum
A perennial, almost woody, much-branched, native to the Canary Islands and grown by florists under glass. The flowers are 1½–2½ in. across, white or lemon yellow, and there are many flower heads borne on straight stems.

leucanthemum   2′   Zone 3   Oxeye Daisy
Native to Europe and Asia, the species and this variety, which is much the more common, are widely naturalized in the U.S. and Canada, especially in open fields. It is a perennial weed with wide-spreading rootstock; also it is easily spread by seeds. The stem leaves are alternate, simple and sessile, the basal leaves are in rosettes and pinnately lobed. Flowers appear in June and July, the ray-petals white and the

heads up to 2 in. across. This is the common daisy of fields and pastures.

mawii 1′ **Zone 5 Morocco Chrysanthemum**
An unusual, rather shrubby species from the Atlas Mountains of North Africa, this has upright or prostrate stems clothed with pinnate leaves, and white flowers pink underneath. These appear in midsummer. It should be planted in full sun, in gravelly soil and given some winter protection.

maximum 2′–4′ **Zone 4 Daisy**
This is native to the Pyrenees Mountains but is supposed to have been worked with considerably by Luther Burbank in making large-flowered selections. It is not a long-lasting perennial and is often treated as a biennial. The large, flat, white, daisylike flowers are borne from June on, until frost. The plants do not seem to grow well in the dry and hot central U.S., but do very well on the Pacific Coast and in the East. They make excellent long-lasting cut flowers and are effective as perennials in any border. Occasionally florists will dye some of the white flowers. Propagation is by spring-sown seed and by division in the spring. The chances are, according to a statement in *Hortus III*, that much of the material grown by commercial growers under this name is actually the hybrid, x *superbum*, which see.

x morifolium 2′–5′ **Zone 5 Florists' Chrysanthemum**
This is the species to which many of the garden chrysanthemums are referred and there is some doubt as to its origin. Probably it has come from *C. indicum*, which is a low (2–3 ft.) Chinese type, little grown in America. *C. morifolium* contains hundreds of varieties, some grown in the garden, some only for growth in the greenhouse for cut-flower purposes. Colors range widely, including almost all the colors except true blue, and the size of the flower heads varies also, from an inch or less to over 6 in. in dia. When the word "chrysanthemum" is used, people usually think of flowers belonging to this species.

nipponicum 1¼′–2′ **Zone 5 Nippon Oxeye Daisy**
A perennial with white flowers 1½–3½ in. across, somewhat shrubby at the base. The flower heads are singly borne on long stalks, but a mass of bloom in the late fall. It is an excellent plant for the flower border and grows especially well at the seashore. Native to Japan.

parthenium 1′–3′ **Zone 4 Feverfew**
A popular, leafy, perennial herb with strong-scented foliage, sometimes grown in the home greenhouse and certainly in the perennial border in the garden, valued for its bushy habit and many white-rayed flower heads blooming during the summer, each about ¾ in. across.

Native to Europe and Asia. There is a form with yellow foliage (var. **'Aureum'**) which sometimes turns green late, and another form **(crispum)** with crinkled leaves. These plants will grow in either sun or shade. The whole plant is used in some medicines for fevers and nervous pains, and a tincture, diluted with water and applied to the skin, repels insects.

Cascade Chrysanthemum

segetum 1½′–3′ **annual Corn Chrysanthemum**
Native to Great Britain, with yellow flowers 2½ in. wide. Many vars. of this species are grown, among which are: **'Eastern Star'**—light yellow flowers; **'Evening Star'**—golden-yellow, large flowers; **'White Star'**—creamy-white flowers; **'Yellowstone'**—double sulfur-yellow flowers.

serotinum 5′ **Zones 2–3 Giant Daisy**
Bearing large white flowers ½–3 in. wide in autumn, this is a tall, much-branched perennial from Europe, valued for use in the flower border.

x superbum 3′ **Zone 4 Shasta Daisy**
This is probably a hybrid of *C. maximum* from which many clones have been selected, all very ornamental.

The flowers according to variety may have more than 1 row of white rays, ranging in size from 2–6 in. across. Among the best are: **'Majestic'**—flowers 2½ in. across; **'King Edward'**; **'Mark Riegel'**—with 4–5 in. flowers, which have 2 rows of rays; **'Edgebrook Giant'** reportedly bears 7 in. flowers; **'Stone Mountain'**—with 4 in. flowers.

The double varieties would include 'Esther Read', **'Jennifer Read'**, **'Wirral Supreme'** with 4 in. blooms; **'Horace Read'** which almost has a ball-like appearance 4 in. across if growing in a cool climate; **'Cobham Gold'**—actually a creamy white.

'Marconi' with 6-in. blooms, **'Chiffon'**, **'Aglaya'** and **'Beauté Nivelloise'** all have frilled flowers which gives them an interesting effect.

tricolor = *C. carinatum*

CHRYSOBALANUS (kris-o-bal-AY-nus)
icaco   30′   Zone 10   Coco-plum
A dense evergreen tree native to southern Fla., but usually seen as a spreading shrub. With thick leathery leaves, 3 in. long and often orbicular, and white flowers in small clusters, a member of the Rose Family. The fleshy yellow or blue fruits are drupes, an inch long, rather dry, but sometimes used in making preserves.

CHRYSOGONUM (kris-OG-o-num)
virginianum   2′   Zone 6   Goldenstar
A low, hairy, almost stemless perennial, the stem later extending up to 2 ft. in height. The opposite leaves are ovate, with toothed margins, and the single yellow flower heads have 5 ray flowers encircling a small disc of tubular flowers. Each flower head is about 1½ in. in dia., and appear from April to June. The plant may be found in the rich woods from Pa. and W.Va. to Fla. and La. It is a good plant for the wild garden, but is not reliably hardy in the northern states. Propagation is by seed sown in spring or by division in spring.

CHRYSOPSIS (kris-OP-sis). These perennials have hairy stems, alternate leaves and yellow flower heads of disc flowers surrounded by ray flowers. They belong to the Composite Family. They are only occasionally used in the flower border and are propagated by seeds and division.

bakeri   12″   Zone 3   Baker's Goldaster
The upper half of this plant is much branched, with pointed, oblong leaves measuring from 1 to 2 in. The flowers appear in July and continue into Sept. It is native to the Great Lakes Region and extends into Ida. and south to N.Mex. Propagation is by seed or by division in the spring.

mariana   2′-3′   Zone 4   Maryland Goldaster
Somewhat less attractive than *C. bakeri*, this species differs in bearing more flower heads on a stalk. Also, among the disc flowers are minute bristles, called the pappus. It may be found in open woods and clearings from N.Y. to Cre. and south to Fla. and Tex. It flowers in Aug.–Oct., and might be cultivated

because of its late flowering. Propagation is similar to *C. bakeri*.

villosa   2′   Zones 2-3   Hairy Goldaster
A pubescent yellow-flowered perennial with lanceolate leaves 2 in. long and flower heads about 1 in. across. Native from Minn. to British Columbia to Tex.

CHRYSOSPLENIUM (krys-os-PLEE-nium)
americanum   creeping   Zone 3   American Gold-saxifrage
A low creeping plant with stems only 8 in. long, opposite or alternate leaves ¾ in. long, and greenish solitary flowers in the leaf axils in spring. Native from Nova Scotia to Ga., west to Minn. Only of value for planting in the bog garden or in moist soils where it might be tried as a ground cover. The leaves have sometimes been used in salads.

CHRYSOTHAMNUS (chryso-THAME-nus)
nauseosus graveolens   5′   Zone 3   Greenplume Rabbitbrush
This is a plant only for dry alkaline soils, especially from Mont. to N.Mex. where it is native. The golden-yellow trusses, somewhat similar to those of Goldenrod, are borne in great profusion—only when the plant is grown in the proper soil. The flowers appear during the late summer. The leaves are 2½ in. long, gray and aromatic. Efforts have been made to extract rubber from this plant but there has not been enough to make the process commercially expedient.

CHUFA = *Cyperus esculentus*

CHYSIS (KY-sis). A genus of deciduous or semi-deciduous epiphytic orchids mostly from Central and South America, growing from pseudobulbs, with flowers in short, arched racemes. They are brightly colored, and after blooming should have a rest period during which the greenhouse temperatures should be 58°–60° F. For culture and propagation, see ORCHID.

aurea   17″   Zone 10
With 5–7 yellow flowers on a short spike produced at various times throughout the year. Native to Venezuela.

aurea bractescens   17″   Zone 10
With 3–8 ivory-white fragrant flowers per raceme, each one 2–3 in. across during April and May. Native to Guatemala.

CIBOTIUM (sy-BO-tium)
schiedei   15′   Zone 10   Mexican Tree Fern
A stout Mexican tree fern, sometimes used as a house or greenhouse plant where it can be grown under glass, since small plants have merit in pots. Fronds are thrice pinnate, about 5 ft. long, gracefully drooping. A house specimen, 3 ft. in dia., is a beautiful plant but after that it grows too large and must be discarded because of size.

CICHORIUM (sik-OR-ium)

endivia. See ENDIVE.

intybus   3′-6′   **Zone 3**   **Common Chicory**
A European perennial, Chicory has escaped to become a common weed along roadsides throughout much of the U.S. and Canada. The leaves are alternate toward the base, oblong or lanceolate, and irregularly toothed. The flower heads, in loose clusters toward the upper part of the flower stalk, consist only of ray flowers, generally blue in color, but occasionally pinkish or white. It blooms from June to Oct. The roots are sometimes used as a substitute or an adulterant for coffee when roasted. Although attractive by the roadside, it is too angular to be a good garden subject. The blanched leaves have long been popular in salads in Europe.

CICUTA (sik-YEW-ta)

maculata   3′-6′   **Zone 3**   **Spotted Water-**
                                       hemlock
This stout perennial weed is definitely not a garden plant, since the roots and rootstalks are poisonous to humans, sometimes fatally so. The compound leaves have pointed lanceolate leaves with sharply notched margins, and the flower heads, similar in appearance to Queen Anne's Lace, have small white flowers from June to Aug., the petals of which curve inward. The plant occurs in bogs and swampy meadows over the eastern half of North America from Canada to N.Car.

CIGARFLOWER. See CUPHEA.

CILIATE. Fringed with hairs.

CILIOLATE. Minutely ciliate.

CIMICIFUGA (sim-i-SIFF-ew-ga). Of the 3 species of bugbanes, 2 are native wild flowers, rather vigorous-growing perennials with compound leaves having 3 coarsely toothed leaflets and spikes of showy white flowers rising well above the leaves. The flowers are small, with inconspicuous petals, the petallike stamens giving the flower its attractive appearance. These are woods plants, preferring leaf mold or slightly acid soil, but they will generally do well in the wild garden.

americana   3′-4′   **Zones 2-3**   **American**
                                          Bugbane
This has leaflets 1-3 in. long and a flower cluster 1-2 ft. long. It is often branched and ranges in woodlands from N.Y. to Pa., to Tenn. and Ga., and blooms in Aug. and Sept.

racemosa   6′-8′   **Zones 2-3**   **Cohash Bugbane,**
                                          Snakeroot
The leaflets of this plant may become 6-8 in. long and the flower cluster may be 3-4 ft. long, often surrounded with smaller flower stalks, found in woods from New England to Ga. and Tenn. It flowers from June to Sept. The root is used medicinally as a sedative,

and hence this is sometimes used at the rear of the herb garden.

simplex   3′   **Zone 3**   **Kamchatka Bugbane**
The spires of small white flowers may be 3 ft. tall, like white bottle brushes appearing in late Sept. and Oct. Native to Kamchatka. The var. **'Armleuchter'**, an introduction from Europe, is supposed to have even larger flower spikes. Propagated by division.

CINCHONA (sin-KO-na)

officinalis   75′   **Zone 10**   **Medicinal Cinchona**
Native to the Andes Mountains, the bark of this yields quinine and hence it is cultivated in tropical regions. Leaves opposite, 3-5 in. long; flowers pink, ½ in. wide and borne in 5-6-in. clusters. Not an ornamental.

CINERARIA (cin-ER-aria). These are popular flowering plants grown by the commercial florists. Most stem from *Senecio cruentus* and are either varieties or hybrids of this species. They have conspicuous daisylike flowers up to 4-5 in. across, although normally they are 2-3 in. (they belong to the Composite Family) of many colors including blue, red and white and interesting combinations of these.

These are cool house plants and so can not be be raised from seed in the normal home. For those with a cool greenhouse, they are among the most colorful and rewarding plants that can be grown, especially during March and April when they bloom. They are of three types: the large flowered, the star flowered and the compact form of the large flowered. The first group is about 3 ft. tall, the third group about a foot tall and the star-flowered group is about in between.

Seeds may be sown in May, Aug. and Sept. to provide a succession of bloom. The seedlings are best raised in a cool, shaded greenhouse, and if the weather turns very hot the plants might be syringed frequently. When they are potted they might be placed in a north-facing, shaded cool frame for the summer. When brought indoors before frost in the fall they should be at a temperature of 45° F. (night) and 55° F. during the day. The double-flowered varieties can be propagated by cuttings taken from vigorously growing end-shoots. All cinerarias must be transplanted occasionally to larger pots as they grow larger, but they do best if kept almost—but not quite—pot bound.

Insect Pests

Aphids and whitefly are controlled by sprays or aerosols of insecticides #15, #13, or #9. Greenhouse leaf tier also attacks this plant. See CHRYSANTHEMUM.

Diseases

Generally free of diseases. When symptoms

of rust, mildew or wilt appear see CHRYSAN-THEMUM for control measures.

CINNAMOMUM (sin-am-O-mum)

camphora   40′   Zone 9   Camphor-tree
The dark, glossy evergreen leaves of this tree from China and Japan give off the typical camphor odor when crushed. The alternate leaves are 4–5 in. long, the fruits are black berries about the size of peas but are not effective ornamentally, and the flowers are yellow in short racemes. It frequently grows twice as wide as high and it is not a good tree for the small garden because of this, as well as its very competitive root system and the fact that the leaves do not decompose readily. Young trees are more attractive than older ones. This is the tree that is the commercial source of camphor.

cassia   40′   Zone 10   Cassia-bark Tree
The bark of this Chinese tree is sometimes used as a substitute for the real cinnamon. The bark is available in long pieces or sticks and also ground, used in flavoring many foods. Not much grown in the U.S. but occasionally seen in southern Calif. and Fla. The leaves are opposite, 4–6 in. long.

zeylanicum   30′   Zone 10   Cinnamon-tree
Native to India and Malaya, the bark of this tree is the true cinnamon of commerce. It has opposite leaves, 7 in. long. Cinnamon was known as a spice as early as 500 B.C. Young shoots are cut from the tree twice a year, and the bark stripped from them, and as it dries these strips curl into rolls. Used for many types of culinary purposes.

Insect Pests

Along the Gulf Coast, camphor trees are infested with camphor scale which weakens and kills the twigs. Spraying with insecticide #44 and summer applications of insecticide #15 or #13 are suggested.

CINNAMON-TREE = *Cinnamomum zeylanicum*

CINNAMON-VINE = *Dioscorea batatas*

CINQUEFOIL. See POTENTILLA.

CIRCUMNEUTRAL. This is a term used to express the pH value of the soil when it is in the range of 6.0–8.0 pH. Neutral soils have a pH value of 7.0. Plants growing in the circumneutral range are not too fussy about acid or alkaline soils.

CIRSIUM (SER-sium). The thistles are generally unwelcome intruders in the garden. They are prickly herbs, some of which are biennials with alternate or basal leaves which are irregularly toothed or lobed, the outer edges of which have strong spines. The flowers, although often attractive, being tiny tubular flowers in a tight cluster, are armed with spiny bracts. For chemical means of eradication see WEED-CONTROLLING CHEMICALS.

altissimum   9′   Zone 3   Tall Thistle
A biennial weed, native to the eastern and central U.S., with alternate leaves, prickly, white woolly beneath and a tap root. Purple flower heads 2–3 in. across during Aug. and Sept., not as dangerous a weed as the Canada Thistle.

arvense   4′   Zone 2   Canada Thistle
A vicious perennial weed spreading by both seeds and creeping roots, introduced from Europe and Asia and common, especially in grain fields, in southern Canada, central and northern U.S. The alternate leaves, up to 4–5 in. long, are lobed with very spiny margins. The roots are branched and send up many shoots. The composite lavender flowers are about 1 in. across, appearing from July to Oct. It is one of the worst weeds in the U.S. because of its creeping rootstock and should be vigorously dug out wherever it occurs. Pulling it will not necessarily remove all of its roots. It is interesting to note that this plant is dioecious, that is, staminate flowers are on one plant, pistillate on another. Both plants are necessary to produce seed, but the roots, even from 1 seedling, can be dragged around a field and become a bad pest even though no seed is formed.

muticum   4′–6′   Zone 3   Swamp Thistle
A vigorous plant growing in swamps and low, wet pasture lands. The sessile leaves are deeply lobed and armed with marginal spines. The handsome flower heads are pinkish purple, 2 in. in dia. Its habitat includes the U.S. and southern Canada as far west as the Rocky Mountains. It blooms from July to Sept.

vulgare   4′   Zone 3   Bull Thistle
A biennial weed from Europe and Asia, common throughout North America on old fields and in rich soil with pinkish-purple flowers up to 2½ in. across from June to Oct. The alternate leaves are extremely thorny. Fortunately it is a weed that does not last long in cultivated fields.

CISSUS (SISS-us). A group of mostly tropical, tendril-climbing vines or shrubs belonging to the Grape Family but the fruits are inedible. The ones used in the gardens of Calif. and Fla. are handsome and *Cissus incisa* is a common and very popular house plant in the North. Leaves are alternate, but may be simple, lobed or compound; flowers inconspicuous, chiefly propagated by cuttings.

antarctica   climbing   Zone 9   Kangaroo Treebine
A climbing vine from Australia with lustrous oval leaves 4 in. long, entire or slightly toothed.

capensis = *Rhocissus capensis*

discolor   climbing   Zone 10   Begonia Treebine
Evergreen leaves 6 in. long and toothed, purplish underneath, sometimes tinged above with white, pink and purple. Native to Java, and a popular greenhouse climber in the North. The popular name is unfortunate for it is not at all similar to a Begonia.

incisa   vine   30′   Zone 8   Ivy Treebine, Marine-ivy, Grape-ivy
Native to the southern and south central U.S., this vine has compound leaves (3 leaflets) and climbs by means of attaching its tendrils to the wire or trellis supports. A common and very popular house plant in the North, capable of withstanding difficult growing conditions and wide variations of room temperature. Also, it will thrive without direct sunlight.

rhombifolia   climbing   Zone 10   Venezuela Treebine
A climbing greenhouse vine with angled stems, compound leaves with 3 leaflets each about 4 in. long and sharp-toothed, with the veins on the undersurface rusty-hairy. Native to northern South America

CISTACEAE = The Rock-rose Family

CISTUS (SIS-tus)
albidus   6′   Zone 7   Whiteleaf Rock-rose
There are many kinds of *Cistus*, but this is one of the better magenta flowered forms, with rosy-lilac flowers slightly blotched yellow, 2 in. across, appearing intermittently throughout the summer. The evergreen leaves are 2 in. long and the habitat is the western Mediterranean Region. Like most of this group, it is difficult to transplant, so small pot-grown plants only should be bought and then set out permanently.

x corbariensis = *C.* x *hybridus*
x cyprius   6′   Zone 7   Spotted Rock-rose
A hybrid species (*C. laurifolius* x *C. landiferus*), this also blooms intermittently throughout the summer. The flowers are white, about 3 in. in dia., and each petal bears a purple blotch. Originating about 1790, it is a graceful free-flowering plant, but should be set out in the garden from pots since it is hard to transplant.

x hybridus (*C.* x *corbariensis*) **18″–30″   Zone 7**
A bushy hybrid shrub, the flowers of which are 1¼ in. across, usually white with a yellow "eye," blooming in summer.

incanus   3′–5′   Zone 8   Purple Rock-rose
This becomes a rounded mound of dense foliage. The large, flat, rose-colored flowers are 2½ in. wide and unfold over a long period in the late spring. The leaves are 2½ in. long. It is drought resistant, needs little care and is one of those plants noted as "fire resistant," recommended for plantings in certain parts of southern Calif. regularly plagued by brush fires at certain

times each year. Native to the Mediterranean Region.

landanifer   4′   Zone 7   Gum Rock-rose
This is especially noted because it has larger flowers than any other species of this genus, up to 4 in. across. Each petal has a blood-red blotch at the base. The flowers come in June and July and the evergreen leaves vary from 1½–4 in. long and from ¼–¾ in. wide. It, too, comes from the western area of the Mediterranean. The var. **maculatus** has flowers, the petals of which have a crimson spot at the base.

laurifolius   7′   Zone 7   Laurel Rock-rose
Flowers white with a yellow blotch at the base of each petal, blooming in July and considered one of the hardiest of these plants from the Mediterranean Region. It is best to prune this plant after flowering, otherwise it may grow very loose and open. The evergreen leaves are 2½ in. long. Set out in the garden from pots.

x purpureus   4′   Zone 7   Purple Rock-rose
With reddish-purple flowers 3 in. across, each petal has a dark red blotch at the base. The evergreen leaves are 2 in. long. It is a hybrid of *C. ladaniferus* x *C. villosus*.

CITRANGE. A hybrid made by crossing *Citrus trifoliata* with the Sweet Orange. The fruits are only 2–3 in. in dia., and have no economic value.

x CITROFORTUNELLA
mitis (*Citrus mitis*) **15′   Zone 9   Calamondin Orange**
Sometimes used as a display plant in the conservatory, this plant from the Philippines is a small, thornless tree with leathery narrow leaves having winged petioles. The small orangelike, orange-colored fruits are only 1½ in. in circumference with a very acid flavor, but interesting when used as a pot or tub plant, especially while small. A very hardy citrus fruit.

CITRON = *Citrus medica*

CITRONELLA = *Collinsonia canadensis*

CITRULLUS (sit-RULL-us)
anatus. See WATERMELON.

CITRUS (CI-trus). A much planted genus because it contains the universally used Orange, Grapefruit, Lime, Lemon, Tangerine, etc., all of which have become important parts of our economy. They probably originally came from subtropical Asia or Indo-Malaya, but are now widely spread throughout the Tropics all over the world. Some are (or have been) spiny and many have compound leaves. The fruits are all rounded or ball-shaped and have a peculiar aromatic fragrance. For culture, see the respective fruits in question. Propagation is usually by budding on seedlings of the same kind of fruit. See ORANGE, LEMON, GRAPEFRUIT, etc.

aurantifolia = Lime, which see.

aurantium = Sour Orange. See ORANGE.

x limonia   25′   **Zone 10**   **Lemon**
A small tree planted for its very sour yellow fruits. The branches bear short spines. The flowers are reddish in bud, white when open, and the nipple-pointed fruits are 3–5 in. long. For culture see LEMON.

x limonia otaitensis   2′–3′   **Zone 10**   **Otaheite Orange**
A miniature tree grown as a greenhouse pot plant, a small thornless bush. The leaflets are oblong to elliptic; the petioles have narrow wings; the fragrant flowers are slightly purplish on the outside. Fruits are orange to deep yellow and about 2 in. in dia. This is a common plant and grown mostly for sale at Christmas.

medica   8′–16′   **Zone 10**   **Citron**
An Asiatic tree with short spines, leaves 4–7 in. long; large, white fragrant flowers. The fruit is oval or oblong, 6–10 in. long and 4–6 in. wide, colored lemon yellow; the rind is thick, rough and fragrant, pulp is white and often acid. The rind is the part of the fruit that is usually candied. Good varieties are budded or grafted on seedling root stocks.

mitis = *Citrofortunella mitis*

nobilis = King Orange. See ORANGE

nobilis deliciosa = Tangerine. See ORANGE.

paradisi = Grapefruit, which see.

sinensis = Sweet Orange. See ORANGE.

CITRUS FAMILY = Rutaceae

CITY GARDEN. (Also see ROOF GARDEN.) The typical city backyard garden starts off as a narrow, flat strip of gound that is hemmed in by surrounding buildings. A skimpy layer of top-soil covers a deep layer of hardpan, while the air above tends to be stagnant and more or less polluted. Yet thousands of city gardeners, un-daunted, have turned such yards into charming garden retreats, enriching their lives along with their topsoil.

A city garden is so intimately associated with one's house that year-round garden interest is especially desirable. A well-conceived landscape plan that makes use of evergreens combined with permanent elements like brick, stone or gravel can achieve this. Add a carefully selected sculptural feature or a pool, and the garden will be for all seasons. Where the soil seems hope-lessly poor or where the area is paved, raised beds are the answer. They can be built of stone, brick, redwood planks, railroad ties, etc., to suit the style of garden desired. Raised beds can provide extra top soil depth, improved drainage, and simplified maintenance, as well as landscape interest. Different levels are always welcome in such a location.

Many old yards are clogged with Ailanthus trees or old overgrown privet bushes. To open the way for a real garden most of these are usually removed, retaining no more than one Ailanthus, which is about all a tiny yard can support. Dense building shade can not be removed so when the buildings are tall one must sometimes settle for a foliage garden. The use of variations in leaf texture, form and color can produce beautiful effects. The type of garden enclosure used can help to correct the shade problem. Open work or louvered fences allow sun, light, and air to penetrate. So do pierced-stone or open-work brick walls. Translucent fiberglass will admit light, and even a solid wall reflects light, if painted white.

Whether the yard is old or new there is little point in planting anything until the soil and drainage have been improved. A 2-in. layer of peat moss and an equal amount of perlite will work wonders, if dug in deeply so as to break up the hardpan. In extreme cases top soil must be added, but since it is so expensive when delivered to the city by bag, the accent is on conditioning old soil, unless there just isn't enough of it. Peat makes the inevitably compacted soil more friable, and light-weight perlite is better than sand for improving drainage. The sterile perlite is especially valuable in old city gardens, for the soil often contains an excessive build-up of soluble fertilizer.

In extremely water-logged yards, where lightening the soil may not be enough, a gravel filled drainage trench is sometimes the answer. For the many city gardeners who are renting a garden apartment, a complete soil renovation is often impractical, since the whole area cannot be dug up. In such a case existing shrubs and trees can be aerated and fertilized at root level with one of the root feeders or hydraulic aerators now on the market. If the yard is bare, a short-term tenant can avoid a complete soil-renovation project by digging a good planting hole for each plant separately, removing hard pan and working in humus in its place. Of course, it would be to the landlord's advantage to finance the soil-improvement project himself.

Soil in city gardens is usually on the acid side, but do not add lime before you determine the preferences of the plants to be grown. It pays to test the soil both for pH and for nutrient deficiencies—a simple matter in a little yard where one soil sample will usually represent the condition of the whole planting area. A good general method of applying fertilizer is to mix some organic fertilizer with the peat moss when it is dug in (about 5 lbs. of dehydrated cow manure and 2 lbs. of bonemeal to each 6-cu-ft.-bag of peat) plus special requirements according to the soil test. Lime, however, should be worked in separately at a different time.

Plants to Use

Perhaps the most important key to city gardening success is selective planting. Trees and shrubs should be chosen for smoke resistance, compact growth, and variety of form—with preference given to small or slender-leaved plants. Rather sparse planting is desirable, since overcrowding means less available light and shorter life for all but the most aggressive plants.

Trees that do well include the European White Birch (*Betula pendula*), Dogwood (*Cornus florida*), Goldenrain Tree (*Koelreuteria paniculata*), Fringe Tree (*Chionanthus virginicus*), Hawthorn (*Crataegus*), Maidenhair Tree (*Ginkgo biloba*), Japanese Maple (*Acer palmatum*), Star Magnolia (*Magnolia stellata*), Willow Oak (*Quercus phellos*) and Sourwood (*Oxydendrum arboreum*). Willows will grow well, but their invasive roots can be troublesome in a small yard. Where moderate sun is available dwarf fruit and flowering fruits tolerate the conditions surprisingly well.

Good choices among deciduous shrubs are Abelia, Japanese Barberry, Necklace Bush (*Enkianthus*), Winged Euonymus (*E. alatus*), Sweet Pepperbush (*Clethra alnifolia*), Rose of Sharon (*Hibiscus syriacus*), Hydrangea, Flowering Quince, Shadbush (*Amelanchier*), all the viburnums and Weigela. All will tolerate city conditions even in comparatively poor soil.

Outstanding among hardy deciduous vines are Virginia Creeper (*Parthenocissus quinquefolia*), Silverlace Vine (*Polygonum aubertii*) and Wisteria. They grow so well annual pruning is a must to keep them in bounds. Not quite so easily grown, but more suitable because of its modest growth, is clematis which comes in many species and varieties.

By and large, shady, protected city yards are well suited to the culture of broad-leaved evergreens—provided that the soil is friable, peaty and well drained, as well as acid. Most of the members of the Heath (*Ericaceae*) Family belong in this group. They include Andromeda (*Pieris*), Azalea, Leucothoe, Mountain-laurel (*Kalmia*) and Rhododendron. Andromeda has proved to be the toughest of these, while Mountain-laurel does rather poorly. Of the rhododendrons, *Rhododendron maximum* stands up best, but some of the dwarf varieties do quite well and are more in scale. Another dependable group of acid-loving broad-leaved evergreens includes the various forms of Japanese Holly (*Ilex crenata*), American Holly (*I. opaca*) and Inkberry (*I. glabra*). Four broad-leaved evergreens that do not require acid soil are Pyracantha, Cotoneaster, Boxwood, and Evergreen Barberry (*Berberis julianae*). All are smoke resistant and will thrive if shade is not too dense. Pyracantha and some cotoneasters lend themselves well to espalier training, which makes them especially valuable in a narrow bed.

Roses are better off in a south dooryard than in a north garden. Climbers are the best in a northern exposure, if planted away from the house and trained to grow up in the sun. When there is a half day of sun and correct culture is practiced, hybrid teas and floribundas can be grown, but stagnant air is not to their liking. One Manhattan rose fancier went so far as to install a large fan to circulate the air—with gratifying results.

Among broad-leaved evergreen vines and ground covers, English Ivy is tops. A new and especially city-tolerant strain, known as "Ripple," or "238th Street" Ivy is now in great demand. Also dependable, especially where slow, compact growth is preferred, is Evergreen Wintercreeper (*Euonymus fortunei radicans*). Strictly for covering the ground, Pachysandra and Myrtle (*Vinca minor*) will do well, but are not quite as shade tolerant as English Ivy. Good ground covers take on special value, since so few city gardens have either the space or the sunshine to grow a lawn.

Midcity gardens also tend to be rather too shady to satisfy the sunny preference of most needled evergreens. The most adaptable conifers have been found to be Hemlock, Douglas-fir and Yew. The best backyard "pine" is the Umbrella Pine (*Sciadopitys verticillata*).

Logically enough, the most suitable perennials are shade-loving woodland wild flowers and their cultured cousins. Bloodroot, Wild Geranium, Black-eyed Susan (*Rudbeckia*), Wild Blue Phlox (*Phlox divaricata*), Solomon Seal, Trillium and violets are all good possibilities. With their natural companions, the hardy ferns, they can be grouped effectively around a small pool. Good cultivated perennials include Bleeding Heart (*Dicentra*), Columbine (*Aquilegia*), Primrose (*Primula*), Candytuft (*Iberis*), Daylily (*Hemerocallis*), the Hosta sp. and vars., Coral Bells (*Heuchera*), etc. Perennial herbs that will grow best in a shady yard include Angelica, Bee Balm, Tarragon, Woodruff (a fine ground cover) and all mints.

Bulbs

Spring bulbs are a great boon to city gardeners. They are good for one season even in poorest soil (if well drained) and in many yards with dense tree-shade in summer there is adequate sun around flowering time. Unmindful of polluted air, all spring bulbs will bloom if they get a few hours of sun, although tulips and hyacinths may need staking. Stock Red Emperor tulips and dwarf tulips such as the

Waterlily Tulip (*Tulipa kaufmanniana*) have been gaining favor as a result. Daffodils may get a bit floppy, but since they are used mostly in an informal setting staking is not so imperative. All of the small bulbs tend to be more shade tolerant, especially wood anemone (*Anemone blanda*), Siberian Squill (*Scilla sibirica*) and Trout-lily (*Erythronium*). Another advantage lies in the fact that their small leaves soon subside and disappear. Ripening foliage of large bulbs in the process of being naturalized is not so easily camouflaged in a small yard. Most city gardeners plant new tulips and hyacinths each year.

Certain summer bulbs are well adapted to city yards, too—notably Hardy Begonia (*Begonia evansiana*), caladiums, colocasia, lilies and oxalis. Tuberous begonias unfortunately resent polluted air.

Sun-loving annuals are used mostly in the form of pot-grown fillers in midcity gardens, and are often replaced in midsummer. The unrivaled queen of backyard annuals, Patience Plant (*Impatiens*) is an exception, as are Wax Begonia, Browallia, Nicotiana, Stock, Torenia, and several other shade-tolerant annuals. Sun-loving annuals are best utilized in window boxes or tubs placed in the sunniest available spots. Often they can be used in the dooryard garden, especially if it faces south.

Maintenance

Since backyard drainage is inclined to be sluggish, overwatering is the chief danger. It is surprising how many city gardeners water on a set-schedule whether it has rained or not. Sprinkling of foliage is quite another matter. This should be done regularly, preferably in the morning, to wash off dust and soot. Evergreens, especially, will benefit from this because they cannot shed the grime each fall along with their leaves. Judicious and timely pruning can literally be the making of a backyard garden. It is imperative in order to keep the planting in scale and yet avoid that "chopped off" look.

The most bothersome insects and diseases are naturally the ones that thrive in moist shade. Sowbugs, slugs and aphids are prevalent, mites and lace bugs less common.

Liquid fertilizers are deservedly popular with backyard gardeners, who often have no tool shed. They are compact, clean, odorless and easy to apply. While frequent "boosters" are not needed, as in tubs and boxes, a couple of applications during the season is recommended. For their versatility and mildness, organic types like fish emulsion or Electra are gaining great popularity.

When it is time for winterizing, sheltered city gardens usually need only a good mulch plus an anti-desiccant spray for evergreens. Of the mulch materials that are readily available in the city, we have found that packaged buckwheat hulls or pine bark are best, since they are attractive, easily moistened, and not so inclined to mat.

The worst detriment to plant health in city gardens is the one that roof gardeners and backyard gardeners have in common: air pollution. A recent survey showed that soot fall has actually decreased in New York, thanks to the filters that have been installed in industrial smoke stacks. This is heartening—but it is not soot that is the real menace. It is the unseen enemy in the form of fumes—principally the carbon monoxide from automobile exhaust. This is a serious menace to all city plant life as well as the gardeners themselves. Progress has been made toward controlling it, and the word is out that in a few years automobiles, trucks and busses will be equipped with mechanisms that will counteract the poisonous gases. That will be a great day for city gardeners.

For further information on city gardens see Yang, Linda, "The Terrace Gardener's Handbook," Doubleday.

PHILIP TRUEX

CLADANTHUS (klad-ANTH-us)
   arabicus   3½'   annual
A member of the Composite Family, native to the Mediterranean Region, this is an herbaceous plant with strong-smelling, finely divided, alternate leaves which grows best in full sun. The daisylike flowers are bright yellow. Often offered under the name *Anthemis arabica*.

CLADRASTIS (klad-RASS-tis)
   lutea   50'   Zone 3   American Yellow-wood
This popular native of the southern U.S. makes an excellent ornamental both for its wisteria-like white flowers in June, its orange-to-yellow autumn foliage color and the beautiful, smooth, gray bark. The leaves are alternate and compound with 7–11 large leaflets. Since it is a member of the Pea Family the small flowers are pealike and fragrant and the pendulous clusters are often 16 in. long. Sometimes this blooms well only every 3 years. The tree "bleeds" profusely when pruned in the early spring and so pruning might best be done in the fall. Var. 'Rosea', a light pink flowered clone might well be worth propagating.

Propagation

The seed of *C. lutea* can be sown as soon as ripe or stored dry in airtight containers in a cool place for up to a year and then sown. In either case the seed should be soaked in hot water at 190° F. overnight, then stratified for 3 months at 40° F. The seeds of *C. platycarpa* are best treated for 1 hour in concentrated sulfuric acid, then thoroughly rinsed and sown. Root cuttings can be taken. See STRATIFICATION, CUTTINGS, SEEDS.

CLARKIA (KLAR-kia). (*Godetia*) Annual herbs grown outdoors in the flower garden or in the greenhouse for winter and spring flowers. They have showy racemes of rose-to-purplish flowers but must be grown in an area where nights are cool, like certain parts of the Pacific Coast where they are native. They do not do well in many places otherwise. Leaves are alternate. The solitary flowers have 4-clawed petals. Propagated by seeds sown where they are to grow in May and thinned to 10 in. apart. They should be in the full sun.

amoena   3′   annual   Farewell-to-spring
Flowers lavender-red, red, salmon, pink and white, often double, 2 in. across; leaves linear and 2 in. long. This is a very popular garden annual and many fine varieties are available. The plants bloom better if crowded.

bottae   3′   Zone 9   Bott's Godetia
A slender perennial with linear to lanceolate leaves 2½ in. long; flowers pink to crimson, 2 in. wide blooming in the summer.

concinna   2′   annual   Red-ribbons
With pink-to-lavender flowers, 3-lobed and fan-shaped petals. Native to Calif.

pulchella   1½′   annual
With lavender-to-white flowers. Native to Calif.

**purpurea viminea   3′   Zone 7   Orchid
                                                        Godetia**
A showy perennial with red-to-purple flowers an inch long with a dark eye at the center.

unguiculata   3′   annual   Rose Clarkia
The most popular species with many fine hybrid varieties having lavender, rose, scarlet, purple or white flowers 2½ in. wide. Native to Calif.

CLASSIFICATION OF PLANTS. It has been estimated that altogether there are about 250,000 species of flowering plants, not counting ferns, mosses, fungi, algae, etc., nor subspecies, varieties and cultivars. In order to arrange these species in as meaningful a way as possible some classification is necessary.

Over the centuries plants have been classified in many different ways, with increasing attempts at what is generally referred to as the natural classification. That is the system in which plants sharing most attributes in common are arranged nearest to one another. This has gradually come to mean that plants are grouped according to their inferred relationships and the way in which plants, and animals, were classified was one of Darwin's major influences in formulating the theory of evolution.

Since Darwin's day most classifications have striven at reflecting evolutionary relationships: phylogenetic classifications as they are called. The fossil record is inadequate to trace the evolutionary history of present-day plants with any certainty and people differ in their concept of relationships. As a result, many different classifications have been proposed. Furthermore, as new plants are discovered, new techniques developed and information not known to earlier workers becomes available, so ideas previously held have to be modified or abandoned. For this reason plant classifications are never final. However, in practice certain well-known systems such as those of Engler, Bentham and Hooker, or Hutchinson are generally followed; for classifications serve a practical purpose as a "filing system," an orderly method of arranging plants which also acts as a system for the storage and retrieval of information appertaining to those plants.

Artificial classifications are often proposed for special purposes. Arrangements by growth habit, flower color, economic usage, etc., are examples of such artificial systems used for limited and practical purposes.

Under the International Code of Botanical Nomenclature plants are formally classified in strict hierarchial groups, with the species as the basic unit. Above this, in ascending order, is the genus (plural genera), section, family, tribe, order, class and division. Below it is the variety and form. Not all the categories need to be employed at any one time, but they may not be rearranged in any other sequence. Further grouping may be obtained by forming intermediate categories with the prefix sub-, e.g., subgenus, subspecies, etc. (Occasionally other intermediate groups such as series may also be used above the genus.) In addition, a cultivated plant may be classified as a cultivar in a hybrid group or grex. See NOMENCLATURE. Each of these groups, whatever its rank, may be called a taxon (plural taxa), a technical term meaning a classificatory group.

The study of classification, its principles and practice is known as the science of taxonomy and a taxonomist is one who identifies, names and classifies.

In general, most gardeners are concerned only with the family, genus, species and cultivar. The species is usually considered a natural group, yet its definition has caused much controversy, and recent conceptions depend upon the discernment of breeding discontinuities. The genus is a group of related species and the family of related genera. *Rosa spinosissima* 'Falkland', for example, belongs to the species *Rosa spinosissima* in the genus *Rosa* (in this case containing 150 or more species) which is classified in the family Rosaceae (a fairly large family of somewhat over 100 genera). Finally, the cultivar 'Falkland' is one of many horticultural varieties which have been developed or selected from this species.

PETER S. GREEN

CLAVATE. Club-shaped; said of a long body thickened toward one end.

CLAY. See SOILS AND FERTILIZERS.

CLAYTONIA (klay-TOE-nia). Bulbous plants of the Portulaca Family with grasslike foliage and delicate white-to-pink flowers early in the spring. There are several species including *C. aurea* with yellow flowers; *C. megarrhiza* native from Wash. to N.Mex.; *C. rosea* with rose-pink flowers in Utah; *C. lanceolatus* and *C. nivalis* both from the Pacific Northwest. If these are to be grown select the species nearest you. All are good for naturalizing in moist, woody soils.

  caroliniana   1′   **Zone 6**   **Carolina Spring Beauty**

Native to eastern North America, with small, delicate, white-to-pink flowers in early spring, grasslike foliage and growing from a bulb that was eaten by the early settlers for its starchy contents. Easily propagated by offsets or seed. Similar to *C. virginica* except that the leaves are broader and the flowers slightly smaller.

Claytonia caroliniana

  virginica   4″–6″   **Zone 6**   **Virginia Spring Beauty**

This sends up 2 opposite, linear leaves on a stem which is topped by a loose cluster of 8–10 flowers, 5 petals which are pink, with veins of deeper pink. The plant grows in semi-shade, in a variety of soils, and grows from southern and central Canada through much of eastern U.S. and as far west as Tex. It is an excellent spring ground cover and may be propagated in spring either by seed or by division.

CLEAN CULTIVATION. A horticultural term which merely means that, by working the soil about desired plants, all weed growth is removed and kept from recurring.

CLEISTOCACTUS (kly-sto-KAK-tus). These are slender, erect cactus plants, with clambering stems, many spines, and ribs, native to South America.

  baumannii   6′   **Zone 10**   **Firecracker Cactus**

A thin-ribbed, clambering cactus, stems 1½ in. wide; branched at the base, covered with spines, usually white but occasionally brown; flowers orange-scarlet, up to 3 in. long; fruit a red berry. Native to Argentina.

  straussii   3½′   **Zone 10**   **Silver-torch**

A many-ribbed columnar cactus; light green, covered with bristlelike spines with the central spine pale yellow. Native to Bolivia.

CLEMATIS (KLEM-at-is). The many clematis species and hybrids are not as popular in America as they are in Great Britain and parts of Europe, yet if the plants shown at our great spring flower shows are a criterion, they certainly are not to be neglected here. About 230 species are widely distributed throughout the temperate regions of the world. One hundred species and hybrid varieties are being commercially grown in America, and probably nearly twice that number are offered in Europe. One English nurseryman alone lists 130.

Clematis are native chiefly in the northern temperate regions of the world. Three of the American species are excellent garden plants and 3 from Europe are likewise important, but in the following list it will be noted that 10 species and botanical varieties which are natives of Asia also make good ornamentals. It is the large-flowered hybrids which seem to capture the public fancy, and it is these which are forced for display purposes in the shows. There are of course herbaceous species as well as woody species.

Although the first man-made hybrid was probably made in 1830, it was not until about 1858 that the first large-flowered hybrid of *C. lanuginosa* originated (*C.* x *jackmanii*), and this started many an enthusiastic hybridizer in his efforts to obtain large-flowering varieties. Although a century has elapsed since growers first became interested in the hybrids, we do have fairly accurate records of where and when these originated. These vines are frequently not the easiest to grow properly. They need an alkaline or limestone soil, some shade, and frequently they respond well if in some way the lower parts of the stems are protected from breakage and mechanical injury. It is at this point that disease frequently enters the plants, and when injury does occur, disease enters and is often quickly followed by destruction of the plant.

Clematis: The leafstalks act as tendrils in clinging to supports.

Clematis flowers have no true petals. It is the large, brilliant-colored sepals which are so interesting. The dia. of the flower may be under 1 in. in some of the species, to nearly 10 in. in some of the better grown hybrids. Actually, some of those species and varieties with medium-sized to small flowers make the best general ornamentals. *Clematis paniculata*, *C. montana rubens*, *C. texensis* are all in this class, as is the variety 'Huldine' with 4 whitish sepals and an over-all dia. of about 4 in. A poorly grown plant of 'Nellie Moser' may have flowers only 4 in. across, whereas, one that is well grown would have flowers twice that size. Clematis climb by attaching their leaf stalks about the means of support. They have opposite, usually compound, leaves, with either solitary flowers or flowers in clusters.

Propagation

The behavior of seed is variable. It may be stored dry in airtight containers in a cool place for up to a year and then processed. If in doubt concerning its behavior, stratify for 3 months at 40° F., then sow. Softwood cuttings usually root well, best taken from young shoots in the greenhouse in Jan. or Feb. See CUTTINGS. Sometimes the large-flowered hybrids are grafted or layered, but own rooted plants are always preferable to others.

Insect Pests

Clematis borer, the larva of a clearwing moth, feeds in the roots of several species of Clematis and seriously damages the vines. Borers can be cut out and killed or sprays of insecticide #9 to the upper roots in midsummer when the moths are active is a preventive. Tarnished plant bug is occasionally troublesome. See CELERY.

Diseases

Leaf spot which may spread and kill stems is controlled with sprays of fungicide #D or #F.

armandii vine 20′ Zone 7 Armand Clematis The white, fragrant flowers of this vigorous evergreen vine from southern China are 2 in. across and are borne in very showy panicles. The vine can quickly spread 50 or even 100 ft. laterally if it is growing in a good location in the Pacific Northwest where it does well. Since it blooms on wood made the previous year it should not be pruned until after it is through blooming.

chrysocoma vine 6′–8′ Zone 7 Goldwool Clematis The soft pink flowers 1¾ in. across appear on the growth made the previous year. This is native to China.

crispa vine 9′ Zone 5 Curly Clematis A shrubby climber native from Va. to Tex. with fragrant flowers, this plant can bloom from June to Aug. on wood made during the current year. The flowers are solitary, long-stalked, nodding and bell-shaped, 2–4 in. long and bluish purple in color.

x durandii vine 6′–8′ Zones 5 or 6 Durand Clematis This usually dies down to the ground each winter but the blue flowers with white centers, 3–4½ in. across, open from June to Sept., making an excellent display. It is a hybrid of *C. jackmanii* x *integrifolia*.

x eriostemon vine 9′ Zone 4 A hybrid (*C. viticella* x *integrifolia*) raised in England in 1820, this has indigo-blue flowers in the summer and usually dies back to the ground each winter. The flowers are 2–3 in. across and are made up of only 4 sepals. The chief reason this is mentioned here is that the flowers are borne in profuse numbers continuously from July to Sept.

flammula vine 15′ Zone 6 Plume Clematis A fragrant fall-flowering clematis from the Mediterranean Region with inch-wide small white flowers, this is sometimes called the Fragrant Virgin's Bower. Of course it is only of use in the woods or naturalistic areas in the southern half of the U.S.

heracleifolia   4′   Zone 3   Tube Clematis
Not very showy but unusual, woody near the base, an erect perennial with blue flowers 1 in. long and polygamous. Native to China and blooming during Aug. and Sept. The variety *davidiana* has fragrant, dioecious flowers of a deeper blue color and makes the better garden specimen. These do well in an alkaline fertile soil. Once established, either in full sun or partial shade, they will do well unattended for many years. Plants can be divided.

**integrifolia   16″–24″   Zones 2–3   Solitary
                                            Clematis**
This is often grown in the perennial border for its porcelain blue bell-like flowers 1½–2 in. long from June to Aug. Native to Europe and Asia. Not especially prominent but serviceable as well as colorful in situations where the soil is not too acid.

**x jackmanii   vine 12′   Zone 5   Jackman
                                            Clematis**
When this hybrid (*C. lanuginosa* x *viticella*) was raised by George Jackman and Sons of Woking, England, in 1858, it was the first of the large-flowered hybrids and started an enthusiastic breeding program which is still continuing a century later. The flowers are a rich purple, appearing in July, and this is still one of the most popular of all the clematis. Closely allied to this are such currently popular varieties as 'Comptesse de Bouchaud', 'Gipsy Queen', 'Madame Edouard Andre', 'Madame Baron-Veillard', 'Mrs. Cholmondeley', 'Perle d'Azur', 'The President' and many others as well as a goodly number which have been popular in the past but have since been discarded. The flowers of the Jackman Clematis are 4–5 in. across, usually have 4–6 sepals and bloom on the current year's growth in July.

**x jouiniana   vine 12′   Zone 4   Jouin
                                            Clematis**
Although not popular in America this semi-herbaceous vine is popular in England. It is vigorous and highly ornamental with white-to-purplish flowers, about 1 in. in dia., in Aug. The variety **praecox** has flowers a soft lavender-blue. It is recommended for covering tree stumps and other low unsightly garden objects, and is a hybrid (*C. heracleifolia davidiana* x *vitalba*).

**ligusticifolia   vine 20′   Zone 5   Western
                                            Virgin's Bower**
Native to the West Coast from British Columbia to Calif., N.Dak., to N.Mex., this bears white dioecious flowers each ¾ in. across in plumose heads during Aug. and Sept. The leaves have 5–7 leaflets, usually 3 lobed.

**macropetala   vine 10′   Zone 5   Big-petal
                                            Clematis**
The flowers are azure blue, 2½–4 in. in dia., made up of many sepals and modified staminoides in the center. They appear in May or June; hence the plant should not be pruned until after the flowering period. The variety 'Markham' first appeared before 1937 and has flowers of a lovely clear pink. It was raised by Ernest Markham, the famous English clematis expert, and was first shown by him in 1935. The species is native to China.

montana   vine 20′   Zone 6   Anemone Clematis
A woody climber with 3 leaflets to each leaf; 1–5 white flowers about 1–2 in. across, borne on slender stalks 2–4 in. long. Native to the Himalayas and central and western China, it is the varieties which are mostly grown as the ornamentals. Variety **grandiflora**—with pink flowers 2–3 in. wide; **rubens**, Pink Anemone Clematis (Zone 5), probably one of the best of E. H. Wilson's introductions and certainly one of the best of all clematis; the first came to America from China in 1900. The rosy-red or pinkish flowers are 2–2½ in. across and appear profusely on the previous year's wood in June or earlier. This variety is hardier and better than the species. The new young foliage is an interesting bronze color; **wilsonii**—flowers white up to 3½ in. across with sepals twisted in an attractive fashion.

**occidentalis occidentalis (*verticillaris*)   vine
                                Zone 3   Rock Clematis**
The thrice-compound leaves of this plant are ovate and only occasionally and unevenly toothed, and the purple flowers which appear from May through June occur at the axils of the leaves. These flowers are 2–4 in. in dia., with 4 pointed, drooping sepals. The stamens are numerous and the styles long. It is a woods plant, preferring ledges and rocky outcrops from southeast Canada to Md. west to Wisc. and Ia. Handsome vine for the wild garden.

**paniculata   vine 30′   Zone 5   Sweet Autumn
                                            Clematis**
Unfortunately, this very popular vine from Japan has become mixed in the American trade so that some of the plants sold under this name are actually *C. dioscoreifolia*, a vine now considered a separate species, from Korea. This fragrant, white-flowered, autumn-blooming clematis is one of the most hardy of the exotic clematis now in use in America. The flowers appear in great profusion in late Aug. and they are followed by excellent fruit displays as well. It is one of the best and most dependable of all the clematis. Japan.

recta   2′–5′   Zones 2–3   Ground Clematis
An herbaceous perennial with white fragrant

flowers each about 1 in. wide but borne in many-flowered clusters from June to Sept.; leaves divided into 5-9 leaflets. Native to southern Europe. Not particularly outstanding but this is often used as a "filler" in some borders. Propagated by division in spring.

stans   6′   Zone 4   Japtube Clematis
An erect herb but very similar in most respects to *C. heracleaefolia*, blooming in Sept. and Oct. with whitish-to-bluish flowers about ½ in. long in terminal panicles and axillary clusters. Probably not as good a garden plant as the other species. Native to Japan.

tangutica   vine 9′   Zone 5   Golden Clematis
The bright yellow flowers of this autumn-blooming clematis from northwestern China makes it one of the best if not the best of the yellow-flowered clematis. Certainly it is superior to *C. orientalis*. The flowers are 3-4 in. across and are borne singly on the stems. They are followed by silvery, shining, seed heads.

texensis   vine 6′   Zone 5   Scarlet Clematis
The Scarlet Clematis is the most ornamental of the clematis species native to North America. The brilliant scarlet, urn-shaped flowers are about an inch long and appear on the current year's growth in late Aug. or sometimes in July, if grown in a sheltered spot. The flowering continues until frost. Although it may die to the ground in the winter, it sends up shoots in the early spring which bear flowers.

This species has been hybridized with *C. patens* and some others, and several excellent hybrids have resulted such as 'Duchess of Albany' and 'Duchess of York'.

verticillaris = *C. occidentalis occidentalis*

viorna   vine   Zone 4   Leatherflower Clematis
This clematis is distinguished by the rounded leaflets of the compound leaves and by the solitary, nodding, urn-shaped flowers which may vary in color from dull yellow to purple. The dark yellow plume on the fruit gives the plant added horticultural interest. Native in gravelly soils from N.Y. to Ga., it propagates readily from seed sown in fall.

virginiana   vine 18′   Zone 4   Virgin's Bower
Blooming in late Aug., with very small white flowers, this is not one of the best native clematis but it is frequently seen along the roads of the eastern U.S., especially when the very fluffy fruits are at their best in the fall. Unless this is to be used in a naturalistic planting, it might well be omitted.

vitalba   vine 30′   Zone 4   Traveler's Joy
Native to Europe and northern Africa, the white, slightly fragrant flowers are nearly 1 in. across and appear in late Aug. It is one of the vigorous-growing species and, even though the flowers are small, they make a fine display in the late summer. The fluffy seed heads in the fall are also

important ornamental assets. It is an excellent vine for growing over fence or garden pergola where dense foliage is wanted.

viticella 'Kermesina'—the flowers of this are a bright wine red, approximately 1¼ in. across. It was first introduced by Lemoine in 1883 and seldom grows over 8 ft. high.

Hybrids

The following 34 hybrids are all among the best that are being grown in the U.S. today. There are of course others as well, but these have been at the top of the popular lists over the years. Mr. J. E. Spingarn included 20 of these as the "best" that he grew, and in the 1920's he grew most of the ones available.

'Ascotiensis' (*C. viticella* hybrid)   Introduced 1880
The flowers are azure blue, 8-10 in. in dia., and blooms in Aug. and Sept. on the current year's wood.

'Belle of Woking' (*C. florida* hybrid)   Introduced 1885
The large flowers are double and silvery gray, appearing in May or June on the previous year's growth.

'Comptesse de Bouchard' (*C. jackmanii* hybrid)   Introduced before 1915
The flowers are 5-6 in. in dia., a satiny rose color, usually with 6 sepals, appearing from July to Oct. on the current year's wood.

'Crimson King' (*C. lanuginosa* hybrid)   Introduced 1916
Probably one of the best large crimson-flowered clematis, but it can become a weak grower. The anthers are chocolate-colored and it blooms in July and Aug.

'Crimson Star'—a new and striking red-flowered hybrid offered by James I. George and Son of Fairport, N.Y.

'Duchess of Albany' (*C. texensis* hybrid)   Introduced 1897
Bell-shaped flowers about 1½ in. in dia., pink, borne from July to Sept. on the current year's wood.

'Duchess of Edinburgh' (*C. florida* hybrid)   Introduced 1887
This is one of the best, large-flowering, double, pure white clematis, with very fragrant flowers appearing in May and June on wood made the previous year.

'Edouard Desfosse' (*C. patens* hybrid)   Introduced 1877
Very large violet flowers (with darker bars on the sepals) usually of 6 or more sepals, blooming in May on wood of the previous year. This is the earliest of the *C. patens* hybrids to bloom.

'Elsa Späth' (*C. lanuginosa* hybrid)   Introduced 1891
The flowers can be 8 in. in dia., a bright blue

and deeper towards the center, appearing in July and Aug. on the current year's wood.

'Ernest Markham' (*C. vitifolia* hybrid) Introduced 1926
Large red flowers from July to Sept. on wood formed the current year. This is very popular because of its vivid color.

'Fairy Queen' (*C. lanuginosa* hybrid) Introduced 1877
The large flowers are pale pink with a deeper pink bar on each sepal, and appear in July and Aug. on the current year's growth.

'Gipsy Queen' (*C. jackmanii* hybrid) Introduced 1877
Dark, velvety, purple flowers in July and Aug. on the current year's wood.

'Henryi' (*C. lanuginosa* hybrid) Introduced before 1872
The 6–8 in. flowers are a creamy white with a center of dark stamens in June and July. They appear on the current year's growth.

'Huldine' (*C. viticella* hybrid) Introduced in 1936
Pearly white, translucent flowers with a mauve-pink bar down the reverse side of each sepal, make this one of the best. The flowers are profusely borne, appearing in July and Aug. and are about 4 in. in dia., with 4 sepals.

jackmanii 'Alba' (*C. jackmanii* hybrid) Introduced 1878
Large white flowers on the current year's growth, are at first double, produced from older wood, then single produced on the current year's growth.

jackmanii 'Rubra' (*C. jackmanii* hybrid) Introduced 1903
Flowers are a deep red, sometimes the flowers produced from old wood are double.

jackmanii 'Superba' (*C. jackmanii* hybrid) Introduced 1889
This is an improved form of the original *C. jackmanii* with dark purple flowers 5 in. in dia., an excellent and very popular variety.

'King Edward VII' (*C. lanuginosa* hybrid) Introduced 1903
Purplish-violet flowers, large with soft crimson bar on each sepal, appearing June to Oct.

'Lady Betty Balfour' (*C. viticella* hybrid) Introduced 1913
The velvety-purple, summer-blooming flowers with yellow stamens are profusely produced in Sept. and Oct. on the current year's growth. The flowers are about 5 in. in dia.

'Lady Caroline Neville' (*C. lanuginosa* hybrid) Introduced 1866
The white flowers have a mauve bar on each sepal. The anthers are a pale reddish brown and the flowers appear from June to Oct.

'Lasurstern' (*C. patens* hybrid) Introduced 1906

With large, deep purplish-blue flowers 7–8 in. across, produced on old wood in May and June and sometimes again on new wood in July and Aug.

'Lord Neville' (*C. lanuginosa* hybrid) Introduced about 1870
Dark plum-purple flowers with a deeper bar on each sepal, appear from June to Aug. The sepals have wavy edges, and this variety is supposed to have a very long blooming period.

'Mme. Baron-Veillard' (*C. jackmanii* hybrid) Introduced 1885
Large bright velvet-red flowers late in July.

'Mme. Edouard Andre' (*C. jackmanii* hybrid) Introduced 1892
Medium-sized flowers, for *C. jackmanii*, velvety red and profusely borne on the current year's wood in July and Aug.

'Miss Bateman' (*C. patens* hybrid) Introduced before 1869
Large white flowers with chocolate-red stamens in the center, produced on the previous year's growth in May and June.

'Mrs. Cholomondeley' (*C. lanuginosa* hybrid) Introduced 1870
Large light blue flowers up to 8 in. across, with spaces between the sepals, but the flowers are freely produced from May until Sept., making this one of the longest flowering of the clematis.

'Mrs. Spencer Castle' (*C. viticella* hybrid) Introduced before 1915
Pale mauve-pink flowers which are double when produced on the old wood, and single when produced on the young wood. The flowers appear from June to Oct.

'Nelly Moser' (*C. patens* hybrid) Introduced 1897
An old reliable favorite with pale mauve-pink blossoms, usually 8 sepals, with deep pink bar down each, blooming May and June on the previous year's wood, sometimes again in Sept.

'Prins Hendrik' (*C. lanuginosa* hybrid) Introduced before 1912
The large azure-blue sepals are slightly crimped on the edges, the flowers being 7 in. across and appearing in July and Aug.

'Ramona' (*C. lanuginosa* hybrid) Introduced 1874
Pale lavender-blue flowers.

'The President' (*C. patens* hybrid) Introduced before 1880
The large flowers are dark blue to reddish plum-violet with a paler bar down the middle of each sepal, and appear from June to Oct.

'Ville de Lyon' (*C. viticella* hybrid) Introduced 1900
Large flowers of reddish purple with deeper color around the edges of the sepals, appearing on the current year's wood from July to Sept.

'W. E. Gladstone' (*C. lanuginosa* hybrid)
Introduced 1881
Very large lilac-colored flowers with a lighter bar down the middle of each sepal. The anthers are black on white filaments and the flowers appear in July and Aug. It is one of the more difficult to propagate.

'William Kennett' (*C. lanuginosa* hybrid)
Introduced 1873
Lavender on deep lavender flowers, with 8 overlapping sepals which have wavy margins. The flowers appear from June to Aug.

CLEMATIS ASIA-BELL = *Codonopsis clematidea*

CLEOME (klee-O-mee)

hasslerna   **5′**   **annual**   **Spiderflower**
Lfts. 5–7, fls. dark pink in racemes, fading to nearly white by noon. Native in Brazil and Argentina. Often confused with **C. spinosa.**

serrulata   **2′–3′**   **annual**   **Bee Spiderflower**
An annual weed native to the U.S. from Ill. and Mo. westward, it has alternate, compound leaves divided into 3 narrow, palmately arranged, tapering leaflets. Small flower clusters blooming from July to Sept. surrounded by leafy bracts, occur at the axils of the upper leaves, and a dense cluster of flowers and leafy bracts terminate the stem. The flowers, 2–3 in. wide, are pink, having 4 sepals, 4 petals and stamens extending beyond the perianth. It needs plenty of room and does not transplant well except when quite young. Apparently the flowers are very attractive to the bees.

spinosa   **1′–3′**   **annual**   **Spiny Spiderflower**
A native of the West Indies. In recent years this has become a very popular garden annual, even though it is strong scented. The digitately compound leaves have 5–7 leaflets with 2 stipular spines at the base of each leaf. The flowers are white to flesh-colored with stamens 2–3 in. long. There are 4 long clawed petals to each flower whigh give it the common name Spiderflower. The vars. **'Pink Queen'** and **'Helen Campbell'** have been recommended as having much better flowers than the species. Seeds can be sown in the open in late April where the plants are to grow, and thinned to 15 in.

CLERODENDRUM (kler-o-DEN-drum)

fragrans pleniflorum   **10′**   **Zone 9**   **Fragrant Glorybower**
This Chinese plant has small, double, pinkish flowers each 1 in. across and in large, tight terminal clusters. The 5-parted calyx is red, adding to the color display. The blossoms have an unpleasant odor and the large, opposite leaves are about 10 in. long. The single-flowered species is not common. Propagated by seeds and cuttings.

thomsoniae   **vine**   **Zone 9**   **Bleedingheart Glorybower**
This twining evergreen vine is popular where it can be grown because of its small red flowers and striking white calyx at the base of each flower. The daintiness is augmented by long, curving stamens protruding from the end of the corolla and a decisively curved calyx. The evergreen leaves are opposite, 5 in. long and entire. Flowers appear during the winter and spring in Hawaii, but during summer in Fla. Native to West Africa.

trichotomum   **20′**   **Zone 6**   **Harlequin Glorybower**
Of special interest for its fruits which are bright blue berries coloring in the early fall, with each berry surrounded with a bright red calyx and horizontal branches, the fruits are all borne on the upper side. Native to China and Japan, and though not widely used in America, it has been here since 1880. Propagation: seed may be stratified as soon as ripe for 3 months at 40°F., or held dry for up to a year in airtight containers in a cool place and then stratified. Softwood cuttings and root cuttings root well. See SEEDS, STRATIFICATION, CUTTINGS.

CLETHRA (KLETH-ra). Small trees or shrubs with deciduous, alternate leaves (there are some tender species which are evergreen) with white, fragrant flowers borne in spikes. The fruits are dried capsules. They are propagated by seeds, cuttings (made in Aug.) and layers.

acuminata   **18′**   **Zone 5**   **Cinnamon Clethra**
A tall shrub valued chiefly for its white, small, nodding racemes of flowers in late July and especially for its cinnamon-brown bark. The foliage turns yellow to orange in the fall and it is native in the southeastern U.S. Its flowers are not as handsome as those of other *Clethra* species, but its bark is most ornamental.

alnifolia   **9′**   **Zone 3**   **Summersweet**
The Summersweet is a common native shrub in the eastern U.S. where its fragrant spikes of small white flowers are widely evident in late July. There is a variety **rosea** with flowers a pleasing pink color. The foliage turns an excellent yellow to orange in the fall, and the plant is one of those which does admirably in seashore gardens. It has even been clipped in a formal hedge. If the soil is very dry it tends to be infested with red spider, so a moist soil is the better place for it. Normally it grows in clumps.

arborea   **25′**   **Zone 9**   **Lily-of-the-valley Clethra**
An evergreen tree from Madeira, this is used in Calif. The small, white, fragrant flowers are borne in 6-in. nodding clusters in Aug. and often Sept. The alternate leaves are 3–4 in. long. It is not suited for dry areas.

barbinervis   **30′**   **Zone 5**   **Japanese Clethra**
A rather coarse growing Clethra from Japan,

the flowers of which are not as fragrant as those of *C. alnifolia*. However, the racemes (4–6 in. long) are held out from the branches horizontally and this gives the plant an interesting touch in late Juy. The leaves are 3–6 in. long.

CLEYERA (CLAY-era)
　japonica (*Eurya ochnacea*)　**21′**　**Zone 7**
　　　　　　　　　　　　　　　　　Sakaki
An evergreen shrub or small tree with alternate elliptic to oblong leaves, 2–6 in. long; white, fragrant flowers ½ in. wide, and fruits are rounded red berries. Native from Japan to India.

CLIANTHUS (kly-ANTH-us)
　dampieri = *C. formosus*
　formosus (*C. dampieri*)　**4′**　**Zone 9**　**Glory-pea**
A clambering shrub with pinnate, grayish, pubescent leaves and pendulous racemes of showy, scarlet, pealike flowers and a keeled petal shaped something like a parrot's bill. The inflated pods are about 2½ in. long. Propagated

by seeds or by grafting on roots of *Colutea arborescens*. Native to Australia.
　puniceus　**6′**　**Zone 9**　**Red Parrot-beak**
Another clambering species, with crimson pealike flowers 3 in. long. Native to New Zealand.

CLIFF-BRAKE. See PELLAEA.

CLIMATE. The climate is made up of many measurable factors like rainfall, when it occurs, temperatures—when the highs occur and when the lows occur—the number of frost-free days a year which go to make up the actual growing season for any particular locality, and the like. Each one is important, all must be taken into consideration. There is little that can be done to change the climate—we have to take it as it comes. To give gardeners some idea of how tremendous the variation is in climate over the United States, the following figures are given:

	NUMBER OF FROST-FREE DAYS	AVERAGE ANNUAL RAINFALL IN IN.
Alabama	200–300	50–64
Arizona	120–340	2–12
Arkansas	180–230	40–52
California	80–340	2–100
Connecticut	160–180	34–56
Colorado	40–160	8–24
Delaware	190	40–44
Florida	240–365	46–62
Georgia	190–300	46–76
Idaho	40–180	10–45
Illinois	150–210	32–46
Indiana	150–190	34–46
Iowa	140–170	26–36
Kansas	160–200	16–42
Kentucky	180–210	40–50
Louisiana	220–350	46–62
Maine	100–180	34–46
Maryland	140–210	36–44
Massachusetts	160–200	40–46
Michigan	90–180	26–36
Minnesota	100–150	20–32
Mississippi	200–270	47–62
Missouri	170–210	34–50
Montana	40–140	10–45
Nebraska	130–170	16–34
Nevada	80–300	4–20
New Hampshire	120–160	38–44
New Jersey	140–200	40–48
New Mexico	100–220	6–24
New York	90–200	28–52
North Carolina	150–280	40–84
North Dakota	100–130	14–22
Ohio	140–200	32–42
Oklahoma	180–240	18–56
Oregon	80–260	8–120

	NUMBER OF FROST-FREE DAYS	AVERAGE ANNUAL RAINFALL IN IN.
Pennsylvania	100–200	34–50
Rhode Island	180	44
South Carolina	190–290	44–76
South Dakota	110–160	12–26
Tennessee	150–230	44–56
Texas	180–320	10–52
Utah	80–200	4–10
Vermont	120–160	34–40
Virginia	160–230	32–50
Washington	100–300	6–140
West Virginia	150–180	32–44
Wisconsin	90–170	28–32
Wyoming	40–140	10–30
Alaska	52–172	7–155
Hawaiian Islands	365	14–249
Puerto Rico	365	35–89

These facts were taken from the 1941 Yearbook of the U.S. Dept. of Agriculture entitled "Climate and Man." This is an excellent compilation of weather facts, based on records of nearly 2000 U.S. Weather Stations for over 35 years.

CLIMBING-ONION = *Bowiea volubilis*

CLINOPODIUM (clin-o-PO-dium)

vulgare (*Satureja vulgaris*)   2'–3'   **Zone 3**
Wild Basil Savory
This European perennial is a creeper with opposite, ovate leaves. Small, tubular, 2-lipped, lavender flowers are borne in leafy terminal and axillary clusters, those in the leaf axils having stalks 1–2 in. long. The plant blooms from June to Sept. It is an attractive plant for the wild garden, but it should be kept in bounds. It may be propagated easily by division.

CLINTONIA (klin-TOE-nia)

borealis   7"–15"   **Zone 3**   **Yellow Bead-lily**
This member of the Lily Family is distinguished by a rosette of broad, glossy green leaves 4–7 in. long and longitudinally veined. During late spring to midsummer a leafless stalk arises to a height several inches above that of the leaves, terminating in a loose cluster of 3–6 nodding, greenish-yellow flowers composed of 3 sepals and 3 petals. The flowers are followed by shiny blue berries. Growing in damp woods from Labrador to the mountains of Ga. and Tenn. west to Minn., the plant does well in shady gardens, blooming more profusely at the northerly end of its range. Seed may be sown in the fall, or the rhizomes may be divided in spring.

CLITORIA (kly-TOW-ria)

mariana vine   Zone 3   Atlantic Pigeon-wings
A low-growing perennial vine of the Pea Family (Leguminosae), the compound leaves having generally 3 leaflets. The blue flowers, nearly 2 in. long, grow in small clusters and appear throughout the summer, followed by seed pods of about 2 in. in length. The plant is native to the drier areas from southern Canada to Fla. and west to Ia. and Ariz. Propagation is by seed sown in spring.

ternatea   vine   Zone 10   Butterfly-pea
A loosely twining vine which is a tropical member of the Pea Family, with alternate compound leaves, 5–7 leaflets and bright blue flowers with light blue and yellow markings. It differs from the other members of this family in that the standard is much larger than any other part of the flower, almost 2 in. long. There is a white-flowered variety and sometimes the flowers are double. The fruits are pods 4½ in. long. Propagated by seeds easily, and by cuttings.

CLIVIA (KLY-via). These are popular greenhouse plants, also used as potted house plants. Native to South Africa, with straplike evergreen leaves growing from thick fleshy roots, with beautiful, orange-to-scarlet, lilylike flowers in spring and early summer. These are borne conspicuously in dense clusters of 10–18 flowers per cluster at the end of a 1½-ft. flower stalk. They are cultivated in the same general way as Amaryllis. Mature plants, if fed, need be repotted only once every 5 years. Propagation is by division of the fleshy roots in spring after flowering, or by seed.

x cyrtanthiflora   2'   Zone 10
A hybrid (*C. miniata* x *C. nobilis*) with light red flowers, intermediate in shape and size between the 2 parents.

miniata   2'   Zone 10   Scarlet Kafir-lily
This is the most popular species with straplike leaves 1–2 in. wide, flowers scarlet, yellowish inside; corolla 2–3 in. long; fruit a 1-in. berry. There are many better colored hybrids. Var. **flava** has yellow flowers. Blooms in spring.

nobilis 1½′ **Zone 10 Green-tip Kafir-lily**
Smaller than *C. miniata*, with red and yellow tubular flowers, somewhat pendulous, clustered at the end of a long flower stalk above the leaves.

CLOCK-VINE = *Thunbergia alata*

CLONE. A group of plants composed of individuals produced vegetatively from a single original plant; clones differ from races and strains in failing to come true from seeds; examples: 'Concord' Grape, 'Baldwin' Apple.

CLOUD BENT GRASS = *Agrostis nebulosa*

CLOVE. A horticultural term for the small bulbs at the base of the main bulb in bulbs like the Garlic (*Allium sativum*). The spice used as cloves comes from a tree (*Eugenia aromatica*), of tropical countries, not grown in the U.S.

CLOVER. The **'White Dutch'** variety (*Trifolium repens*) which see, is the one usually included in some lawn seed mixtures, for it grows almost anywhere in the U.S. if there is enough moisture. It does best in a slightly alkaline soil, but as many gardeners in acid-soil regions can attest, it grows almost anywhere in full sun or partial shade. Like other leguminous plants, its roots have nitrogen-forming nodules which add nitrogen to the soil. On Cape Cod it apparently is sought out and eaten by rabbits before other garden plants are molested.

CLOVER, ALSIKE = *Trifolium hybridum*

CLOVER, CRIMSON = *Trifolium incarnatum*

CLOVER, WHITE SWEET = *Melilotus alba*

CLOVER TREE = *Syzygium aromaticum*

CLUB-MOSS. See LYCOPODIUM.

CLUB ROOT. A fungus disease of all members of the Mustard Family including weeds such as Peppergrass and Mustard and the bedding plant, Sweet Alyssum. Gall-like swellings develop on the roots and infected plants are stunted. The disease lives in the soil especially where the acidity is below pH 7.0 (neutral) (see SOILS) and may persist for many years. Rotation with non-cruciferous crops is necessary to avoid trouble. See CABBAGE.

CLUSIA (CLU-sia)
rosea 40′ **Zone 10 Copey Clusia**
A medicine is obtained from the leaves, fruits and bark of this tree, native to the West Indies. The interesting inedible fruits, 3 in. long, are popular in arrangements. The large, thick, ovate leaves are 2–4 in. long and make the tree very ornamental. White-to-pinkish flowers somewhat similar to those of narcissus with many waxy petals are produced. A yellow resinous latex is obtained from the tree used in caulking boats.

CNICUS (NY-kus)
benedictus 2′ **annual Blessed-thistle**
A weed from the Mediterranean region of Europe naturalized in central and eastern North America, with large coarse leaves up to 6 in. long and 2 in. wide, the margins very spiny. The flowers are tubular, yellow, terminal, in thistlelike heads, 1 in. across, blooming from April to Sept.

COALESCENT. Two or more similar parts united.

COBAEA (ko-BEE-a)
scandens vine 40′ **Zone 9 Cup-and-saucer Vine**
A fine ornamental for southern gardens, this Mexican vine has tenacious tendrils by means of which it attaches itself to a means of support. The pendulous, lavender-to-purple flowers are bell-shaped, 2 in. across, and produced on graceful foot-long stems. These flowers are the crowning feature for they are produced during spring and summer over a 6-month period. This plant can grow 10–25 ft. in the greenhouse in a single season.

Sometimes planted in the North as an annual. Start the seeds indoors in March, then set out after all danger of frost is over.

COCAINE-PLANT = *Erythroxylon coca*

COCCOLOBA (kok-o-LO-ba). These are tropical trees and shrubs with alternate leaves that are sometimes very large. The greenish flowers are borne in spikes and are followed by berrylike fruits. Propagation is by seeds and cuttings of mature wood as well as by layering.
diversifolia 25′ **Zone 10 Pigeon-plum**
Greenish flowers are followed by small pear-shaped fruits about ½ in. through that are purple, juicy and sweet-tasting. The leaves are 2–4 in. long and have 3 depressed parallel veins.
floridana = *C. diversifolia*
uvifera 40′ **Zone 10 Sea-grape**
A dense spreading tree with large, thick, rounded, glossy leaves having red veins. In the spring the old leaves take on a reddish color. White flowers are borne in dense racemes 10 in. long and the fruits resemble bunches of grapes, used in making jelly. Native from southern Fla. southward.

COCCOLOBIS = *Coccoloba*

COCCULUS (kok-EW-lus). With alternate leaves, male and female flowers on different plants, palmately veined, flowers inconspicuous; propagated by seeds and softwood cuttings.
carolinus twining **Zone 6 Carolina Snailseed**
A twining vinelike plant with leaves 4 in. long, either entire or 3–5 lobed. Fruits red, about ⅔ in. long appearing in June and July. Native from Va. to Tex.

laurifolius 15′ Zone 8 Laurelleaf Snailseed
An evergreen from the Himalayas with ovate to narrow-elliptic, stiff, leathery leaves 5–6 in. long, glossy green, having concave and prominently raised yellow-green parallel veins. Fruit drupelike and black.

COCHLOSPERMUM (kok-lo-SPERM-um)

vitifolium 20′ Zone 10 Buttercup-tree
Native to Central America, this has brilliant yellow cup-shaped flowers, each with 5 petals, and each flower is nearly 4 in. across. The tree starts to bloom in Oct., continuing until May, and since during this period the tree drops its leaves, the flowers remain most conspicuous. The leaves are digitately compound, 5–7 leaflets with one of the middle leaflets being conspicuously the longest. The double-flowered form in Puerto Rico is truly outstanding, bearing 4-in. double yellow flowers from Jan. to March mostly when leafless. Easily propagated by cuttings, and often strikes root merely when branches are stuck in the ground to make a "living fence." This form is seedless.

COCKLEBUR. See XANTHIUM.

COCKSCOMB. See CELOSIA.

COCONUT. The coconut, *Cocos nucifera*, as a cultivated plant has wide distribution in tropical and subtropical regions in both hemispheres. Probably native to subtropical Asia, it was brought to Latin America by the Portuguese and Spaniards, and now grows throughout the tropical world.

The trees, sturdy and wind resistant, have leaning trunks which may reach 80 or more feet in height. They are beautiful large palms which are unexcelled in importance among fruit-producing trees of the world. The millions of acres of planted coconuts yield food, drink and fiber. The oily meat of the nut, termed copra when dried, is important in world trade. It is the source of dried coconut, and of coconut oil used extensively in soaps and cooking. The fiber of the husks goes into cordage, brushes and coarse matting. The nut shells become household utensils. The leaves are used in mats and thatching. Sugar, alcohol and vinegar are also obtained from the coconut.

Coconuts are grown to a limited extent in southern Fla., southern Calif and Hawaii. Several varieties are available from nurserymen. Propagation is by seed, in some cases planted in nurseries, more often where the tree is to grow. The unhusked nut (the seed) is placed on its side and only partially covered with soil. Germination takes place in 4–5 months if the soil is moist.

For nut production distance between trees is about 25 feet. Bearing starts when the tree is about 6 years old and the yield increasing gradually for 12–14 years.

If climatic conditions are right, a coconut palm will grow and bear well in many types of soil. Water supply limits both growth and yield. The Coconut cannot survive under water-logged conditions; on the other hand, the roots must be able to reach a constant supply of water. The original home of the Coconut was probably along the coast, and the general belief is that it does better near the sea. That this is not necessarily true is indicated by high-yielding plantations many miles inland. Although the Coconut will not thrive when the water available is as salty as the sea, it can stand much more salt than many other plants.

When one or more nutritional elements is deficient, the palm does not grow well. The chemical elements that may be in short supply in the soil are nitrogen, phosphorus, potassium and iron, occasionally calcium and zinc.

The best way of making sure insects and diseases cause little damage lies in providing optimum growing conditions. Coconut and similar palms are known to be infested with 35 different scale insects and mealybugs. Many of them are held in check by natural enemies but occasionally spraying with insecticide #15 or #13 when crawlers are active is necessary. Consult local authorities for latest recommendations. Weak or injured trees are susceptible to attack by borers which can be cut out, probed with a wire or treated with a special borer paste. Avoid trunk injuries which attract borers. Bacterial bud rot, a disease of buds and other tender parts, requires drastic eradication, even to removing and burning the infected tree. Other rots may appear, but they are seldom common or serious.

H. GLEASON MATTOON

COCONUT, DOUBLE = *Lodoicea maldivica*

COCO-PLUM = *Chrysobalanus icaco*

COCOS (CO-cos)

nucifera 80′ Zone 10 Coconut
A palm tree, typical to many parts of the Tropics, with long, crooked or leaning trunk and leaves only at the top in a graceful, globe-shaped mass. The evergreen, frondlike leaves are 12–18 ft. long, and the trees produce 20–200 nuts a year, the first ones often when the tree is only 5 years old. This is the species producing the coconuts of commerce and it is considered the world's most valuable fruiting tree. Also see COCONUT.

CODIAEUM (KO-di-EE-um)

variegatum 6′–10′ Zone 10 Croton, Copperleaf
Popular conservatory and greenhouse plants throughout the country, these natives to the

Cocos nucifera—Coconut

Pacific Islands are commonly used in tropical gardens. They are shrubs with large vari-colored evergreen leaves, green, bronze, yellow, red, pink and spotted several colors. Many colored forms have developed over the years. The inconspicuous flowers are borne on droop-ing racemes, male flowers on one plant, female flowers on another, and the fruits are small rounded capsules. The size, shape and color of these leaves varies with the clone, which is of course easily propagated from cuttings, especi-ally by air layers. Over a hundred forms are in cultivation.

CODONOPSIS (ko-don-OP-sis)
   clematidea   2′–3′   Zone 6   Clematis Asia-bell
An erect perennial herb, sometimes climbing, with inch-long leaves and solitary, terminal, pale blue bell-shaped flowers about 1 in. long. Native to Central Asia. Not an especially out-standing ornamental plant.

COELOGYNE (see-LOJ-in-ee). Epiphytic orch-ids from Asia bearing pseudo-bulbs with 1 or 2 leaves and colorful flowers either solitary or in arching racemes. For greenhouse culture and propagation see ORCHID.
   cristata   1′   Zone 10
Fragrant flowers 3–4 in. wide, colored white and yellow with a 5–8-flowered drooping raceme

from Dec. to March. Pseudobulbs are 2–3 in. long. This is a popular and easily grown species. Several varieties have been named. Native to Himalaya.
   dayana   1′–2′   Zone 10
Flowers yellowish, striped dark brown, borne in 2–3 ft. many-flowered racemes during May and June. Native to Borneo.
   flaccida   1′   Zone 10
Flowers 1½ in. wide with a heavy odor and flower spikes erect; colored whitish, stained with yellow and streaked with red toward the base. The 7–12-flowered racemes are pendulous and are borne in winter and spring. This orchid needs a rest period after it is through blooming. Native to Nepal.

COFFEA (KOFF-ee-a)
   arabica   10′–15′   Zone 10   Arabian Coffee
With glossy, evergreen, opposite leaves 6 in. long, light-colored bark and fragrant, pure white, star-shaped flowers, 1–4 per cluster. The brilliant red berries, ½ in. in dia., have 2 seeds each which are the coffee "beans" of commerce. They take 6½–7 months to mature. The ripe fruits are picked, the pulp removed, the "beans" dried and stored. These are then roasted, ground and the coffee is then ready for use. Native to tropical Africa. Grown within the U.S. only in display collections under glass. Propagated by cuttings of mature wood and by seeds. *C. liberica*, Liberian Coffee, is similar.

COFFEE, ARABIAN = *Coffea arabica*

COFFEE-BERRY = *Rhamnus californica*

COFFEE FAMILY = Rubiaceae

COFFEE-TREE, KENTUCKY = *Gymnocladus dioicus*

COHOSH, BLUE = *Caulophyllum thalictroides*

COHOSH, RED = *Actaea rubra*

COIX (KO-ix)
   lacryma-jobi   3′   annual or perennial   Job's Tears
An old-fashioned, favorite grass grown for its fruits, with narrow leaves 2 ft. long and 1½ in. wide. The pistillate spikelets bear small interest-ing "beads" ¼ in. wide, whitish or gray, hard and shiny, from which it gets its common name. It is a perennial in the South but is grown as an annual in the North with seeds sown in April and then transplanted to the garden with seed-lings about a foot apart. Native to tropical Asia. The var. **'Aurea Zebrina'** has leaves striped with yellow. The "beads" have a soft core and, if drawn out, these can be strung on a thread for a necklace.

COLCHICINE. A poisonous alkaloid; used experimentally and commercially on living plant tissue to produce new plant varieties, by altering the chromosomes.

COLCHICUM (KOL-chik-um). Often called the Meadow Saffron or Autumn-crocus, these are not actually crocuses but common herbs of the Lily Family, blooming in the fall after their foliage has died down. They are excellent for rock gardens or along woodsy walks because of their low crocuslike flowers colored white, rosy-purple or—in one rare species—yellow. Corms should be planted as soon as received in the late summer, for if held any length of time they might start to bloom before planting. They should be planted 3–4 in. deep. The grasslike leaves begin to disappear in June but prior to that time should be encouraged to make as much growth as possible. The corms are poisonous and colchicine is extracted from them. Propagation is by separating the offsets or by seed.

agrippinum　4″　Zone 5　Agrippa Autumn-crocus

Several rosy-purple flowers arise from each bulb in Sept. and Oct. Native to Asia Minor. This spreads rapidly.

alpinum　4″　Zone 6　Alpine Autumn-crocus

This is a native to the Alps, is very rare in America but is the first species to bloom in Aug. Flowers rosy purple and no more than 1 in. long.

autumnale　6″　Zone 4　Common-Autumn-crocus, Meadow Saffron

This is the most popular species with leaves to 2 in. wide and rosy-purple flowers to 4 in. across in Oct. There is a white-flowered var. **album**, and a double-flowered white var. as well. Native to Europe and northern Africa.

byzantinum　6″　Zone 6　Byzantine Autumn-crocus

The leaves are up to 4 in. wide; the flowers lilac purple and about 4 in. across with several on 1 spathe, borne in Aug., Sept. or Oct. This is the most free-flowering species, as many as 20 flowers appearing from 1 corm. If well-grown corms are lifted in Aug., they will bear flowers without any roots.

luteum　3″　Zone 7?　Yellow Autumn-crocus

From Turkestan, this is the only Autumn-crocus with yellow flowers, has only a few narrow leaves and bears its flowers by Feb. and March.

speciosum　12″　Zone 4　Showy Autumn-crocus

With rosy-purple flowers as much as 6 in. wide when grown under perfect conditions, this also has leaves 3–4 in. wide. Native to the Caucasus, it flowers from late Aug. to Nov. with tuliplike flowers in great profusion. When first above ground the flowers are cream-colored, slightly tinged with lilac, then they gradually deepen in color. There is a rare form **album** with white flowers. The corms of this species may be as much as 4 in. long and 2 in. wide.

Some of the newer hybrids, mostly *C. autumnale* x *C. speciosum* are of excellent quality and superior as ornamentals to either parent. A few would be: '**Autumn Queen**'—deep violet flowers; '**The Giant**'—pinkish-mauve flowers with a white base; '**Waterlily**'—double flowers, lilac-colored. It is these that are sold as novelties for, if purchased in the very early fall while still dormant, the corms will send up flowers and bloom right in an open room or on a table without benefit of soil or water.

speciosum bornmuelleri (*bornmuelleri*)　8″ Zone 6?　Bornmueller Autumn-crocus

The flowers of this species are rosy mauve with a large white center at the base, often 5 in. across, blooming in late Aug. or early Sept. Native to Asia Minor. There is a var. '**Magnificum**', originating in Holland, which is supposed to have the largest flowers.

COLD FRAME. See FRAME.

COLEUS (KO-le-us). These are bright-colored foliage plants from various parts of the Old World. There are approximately 150 species, but only two are sufficiently ornamental to be mentioned here. They belong to the Mint Family, have square stems and are mostly succulent in growth. Easily grown from cuttings, almost any time.

amboinicus　3′　Zone 10　Spanish-thyme Coleus

An aromatic herb of the Tropics with broad-ovate, hairy, fleshy leaves. Flowers are pale purplish. Stems and foliage are easily dried and are cut just as the flowers come into bloom. Sometimes grown as a house plant in the North and somewhat similar (as an herb) to *Origanum vulgare*. Native to India.

blumei　3′　annual or perennial　Common Coleus

Native to Java and probably one of the most commonly grown of all house plants, because of its red, green, yellow or curiously variegated, opposite leaves. The blue or lilac flowers are small, borne on erect spikes and actually are secondary in interest to the variegated, colorful leaves. Almost anyone can root cuttings of this herbaceous, fleshy-stemmed plant. Raising plants from seeds started indoors in Feb. or March proves interesting for then one can note all the many variegated selections and pick out the most interesting for growing. Usually the vigorous seedlings will prove to be the least interesting for they will result in taller, often floppy plants with more green in the leaves than the others.

The var. '**verschaffeltii**' has bright red leaves. Mixed plantings are of interest in summer, and from these one can take cuttings of desired plants for growing in the house over winter. They are most susceptible to the lightest frost.

Plants in the garden can be lifted in late summer, potted and cut back hard to a few inches high, and used indoors as interesting winter pot plants. There is probably no other plant with so many variegated foliage varieties, all easily grown. Ideal for edging, bedding or massing or just as a single colorful pot plant.

Insect Pests

Greenhouse orthezia (see LANTANA), mealy bugs and greenhouse white fly are sucking insects often infesting Coleus. Regular spraying with insecticides #15 or #13, or, in the greenhouse, fumigation or aerosol treatments are effective. Cyclamen mite may live on Coleus and distort the leaves and buds. See CYCLAMEN.

Diseases

Crinkled, mottled and off-colored leaves indicate a virus. Sterilize soil, and destroy infected plants to prevent spread.

pumilus   6″   Zone 10   Dwarf Coleus
A native to the Philippines, with procumbent stems, sometimes grown in southern Fla. for it roots all along the stems wherever they rest on moist soil. The leaves are about 2 in. long, coarsely toothed and the small flowers are in long racemes.

COLLARDS. See KALE.

COLLINIA = CHAMAEDOREA

COLLINSIA (kol-IN-sia). Mostly attractive garden annuals with opposite whorled leaves, bell-shaped and 2-lipped flowers borne singly or in clusters in the leaf axils with the flowers appearing in midsummer. They are white, rose, lilac to light blue, with most species native to western North America. Seed may be sown outdoors in the South in the fall, or early spring. All these species thrive in the shade, and not many annuals do.

bartsiaefolia   1′   annual   Seaside Collinsia
With white flowers marked with purple, an inch long in the summer. Leaves 1–2 in. long. Native to Calif.

bicolor = *C. heterophylla*

grandiflora   1′   annual   Blue-lips
Leaves to 1¾ in. long, flowers ¾ in. long, deep blue or violet to white. Native from Calif. to British Columbia.

heterophylla (*C. bicolor*)   **2′   annual   Pagoda
                                               Collinsia**
Leaves 2 in. long, flowers 1 in. long colored violet, rose-purple and white. Native to Calif.

verna   4″–20″   annual   Blue-eyed Mary
An annual with opposite ovate to elliptical leaves having toothed margins and bearing delicate blue flowers ½ in. long in a loose terminal raceme. The flowers have a 5-lobed, bell-shaped calyx and an irregular 2-lipped

corolla. Growing in moist woods in rich soil from N.Y. to Kan. and south to Ark., it is an attractive plant for the wild garden. Propagation is by seed sown in spring or by division in spring.

COLLINSONIA (kol-in-SO-nia)
**canadensis   4′–5′   Zone 5   Citronella Horse-
                                               balm**
Rising from a woody perennial root, the stout, erect and branching stem of *C. canadensis* displays opposite, oval and coarsely toothed leaves and an elongated flower cluster, up to 12 in. long, which is sometimes branched. The yellow flowers are irregular and strongly lemon scented. It grows in moist woods in eastern U.S. from southern New England and west to Ark. and flowers from July to Sept. Its rank growth makes it unsuitable for most gardens.

COLLOMIA (kol-O-mia). The flowers are somewhat like those of Gilia (which see), the seeds can be sown in the garden where they are to grow in April and thinned to 1 ft. apart. They are free-blooming garden annuals.

biflora = *C. cavanillesii*

cavanillesii   2′   annual
With alternate leaves 1–2 in. long, scarlet-to-buff tubular flowers about an inch long in leafy clusters. Native to Bolivia, Chile and Argentina. An attractive and colorful specimen.

grandiflora   2′   annual
Leaves alternate, entire and linear, with clusters of buff-to-salmon-colored blooms. Native to the western Rocky Mountain area in U.S. A good garden annual.

linearis   15″   annual
Flowers purple-red or pink, alternate, entire, linear leaves. Native from British Columbia to Calif.

COLOCASIA (col-O-casia)
antiquorum   5′–7′   Zone 10   Elephant's-ear
This is a stout herb from the Asiatic Tropics with thick fleshy leaves shaped like huge arrow heads, about 2 ft. long on stems 4–6 ft. long, planted out-of-doors where hardy, for its tropical foliage effects. There are several varieties, some with purple leaves.

esculenta   5′–7′   Zone 9   Taro, Dasheen
Similar to *C. antiquorum* but with large, starchy, edible tubers. It is especially cultivated for these in Hawaii and the islands of the South Pacific. They can be grown in the deep South and stored and harvested like sweet potatoes. In Hawaii, after the starchy roots have been pounded and cooked, the material is called poi, one of the staple foods of the Islands.

COLOR CHART. There are several color charts which have been advocated at one time or another for those interested in all parts of American horticulture. Most of the "simple" or less expensive ones do not have many colors. Some are merely the standard color wheel. None are as complete as the American-produced Munsell Color Chart which is being used, or parts of it, in various forms in American industry. Most gardeners do not need all the thousand and more colors in this chart, but they do need a simple, easily carried, inexpensive chart that covers the complete field of colors found in plants grown in the garden.

The Nickerson Color Fan was just such an accurate but reasonably-priced chart. It folded into a booklet $7\frac{1}{2}$ in. long by $1\frac{3}{4}$ in. wide, which fitted easily in any pocket or handbag. It contained 262 colors of 40 hues.

Included with this color chart was a 12-page booklet explaining the use of this fan in detail. Printed in small letters on each color was the popular color name and its numerical designation in the Munsell Color System, which is fast becoming accepted as standard by many industries and societies dealing with color systems in America. The chart used simple color names that had been selected as standard by the inter-Society Color Council and the National Bureau of Standards.

The numerical color system may seem a little complex at first, but as one uses this chart and becomes familiar with it, this system is the means for estimating the value of colors which may not appear in the chart but do appear in the flowers or fruits being studied. With practice, the notation may be used to express as fine a color difference as the eye can see. As knowledge is gained of the principles upon which the Munsell system of notation is based, visual judgments of the amount and direction of the departure of the samples from the scale colors can be made and recorded by reference to the notations on the scales. There should be no difficulty for observers with normal color vision to agree regularly on the nearest hue and value, and within reasonable limits on the closest chroma. It is this factor of one's being able to estimate colors accurately according to this numerical system which makes the chart so valuable.

There is a great disparity in color terminology, especially in horticultural circles. For instance, *Cercis canadensis* has been described by various authors as having flowers that are "pink flower bud, deep red calyx," "rose pink to purplish," "pink to purplish pink," "reddish purple or pink," "red," "rosy pink," or "bright pink to purple." By the use of this chart it will be noted that they should be described as being a moderate purplish pink (2.5 RP 7/7). In this way, although the common, general color name is given, so is the accurate Munsell number which refers to a particular color hue, color value

(lightness of color) and chroma or saturation of color. About such a particular determination there can be no question. When one reads such a description, he can refer directly to the color chart and determine the exact color being described to his own satisfaction.

The Nickerson Color Fan can be opened up into the form of a complete wheel. This type of chart is necessary in studying complementary colors for flower arrangements. The ease with which the fan can be folded and carried in the pocket makes it of inestimable use as a reference in the field as well as indoors.

Miss Dorothy Nickerson, who was Color Technologist in the United States Dept. of Agriculture in Washington, has become intensely interested in horticultural needs for a standard chart. Being a trustee of the Munsell Color Foundation, she was able to bring the need for such a chart before the Munsell Foundation. This is a private, non-profit foundation, owning the Munsell Company, established to further research in color. The chief tasks laid down for the Munsell Color Company by the Foundation are to develop and supply accurately controlled color standards at near cost and to supply literature for describing the Munsell System and its application.

Since the publishing of the first edition of this Encyclopedia in 1971, the Nickerson Color Fan has become unavailable. It is most unfortunate, since committees of many responsible people were formed before that time to consider all the specific requirements of many types of flowers for comparison with one standard chart of color. It would seem that producing a standard, usable color chart, suitable for using with all kinds of flowers and plants, is worth a considerable effort.

COLOR WHEEL. Actually the arrangement of primary and secondary colors in a circular chart. See FLOWER ARRANGEMENT. By studying this color wheel one can determine that colors opposite each other on this circular chart, make good contrasts when used together. On the other hand, colors nearest each other on the color wheel blend into each other well. Usually in planning a garden one strives for a major amount of color blending with a minimum of color contrast.

COLTSFOOT = *Tussilago farfara*

COLUMBINE. See AQUILEGIA.

COLUMNEA (ko-LUM-nea). Tropical American vines or shrubs with opposite leaves, 2-lipped red or yellow flowers and fruit a many-seeded berry. Grown in a warm greenhouse, mostly weak stemmed and used in hanging baskets.

gloriosa   trailing   Zone 10   Costa Rica
Columnea
A weak-stemmed perennial, stems rooting
throughout their length and fiery-red flowers
about 3 in. long showing a yellow throat.
Leaves are purplish. Excellent in hanging
baskets. Native to Costa Rica.

hirta   trailing   Zone 10
Another creeper with rooting stems but slightly
stiffer than those of *C. gloriosa*. Leaves, small,
ovate, satiny; flowers vermilion marked with
orange, more profuse than those of *C. gloriosa*
but smaller. Suitable for hanging baskets.
Native to Costa Rica.

microphylla   trailing   Zone 10
Trailing perennial with tiny-rounded or broad-
elliptic, coppery, hairy leaves and large red
flowers similar to those of *C. gloriosa* but
smaller. Native to Costa Rica.

tulae 'Flava'   climbing   Zone 10
A climbing or trailing plant, suitable for hanging
baskets with aerial roots, soft green, pubescent
leaves and bright yellow two-lipped flowers with
long tubes and spreading lobes. Native to
Puerto Rico and Haiti.

COLUTEA (ko-LEW-tea)
arborescens   12′   Zone 5   Bladder-senna
Actually a weed shrub, introduced into America
from southern Europe probably in colonial
times. In May the small yellow-to-reddish
flowers appear in small clusters, but the plant
is vigorous and coarse in texture, quickly seeding itself into other parts of the garden. Its only
desirable quality is its apparent ease to grow
fast in almost any soil. The compound leaves
have 9–13 leaflets about 2 in. long.

Propagation

Seed may be sown at once or stored dry for
up to a year in an airtight container in a cool
place and then sown. It germinates well also if
it is treated with concentrated sulfuric acid for
1 hour before sowing. Grafting is also done
using the roots of the same plant as understock
or else using *Caragana arborescens* as understock. Softwood and hardwood cuttings also
are used. See GRAFTING, CUTTINGS.

COMANDRA (ko-MAN-dra)
**umbellata   12″–18″   Zone 4   Common
Comandra**
This has small, alternate, elliptical leaves and
small white flowers in a terminal cluster. It may
be found in dry woods and fields of most of the
eastern states and west to Mich. The flowers
appear in spring and early summer. Since the
plant is sometimes parasitic on the roots of
other plants, it is not generally considered a
good one for the garden.

COMFREY. See SYMPHYTUM.

COMMELINA (ko-mel-LY-na)
coelestis   18″   Zone 8   Mexican Dayflower
A tuberous-rooted perennial with bright blue
flowers in July, sometimes grown in greenhouses
or out-of-doors in the South. The flowers are
short-lived, like all those in this genus, but the
plant still continues to bear flowers for a period
of several weeks. It is easily propagated by seeds,
division and cuttings. Native to Mexico.

communis   1′   annual   Common Dayflower
A fast-growing weed from Asia, rooting all
along its creeping stems and vigorously propagating itself by seeds, roots and stems. The
leaves are alternate, simple, parallel-veined and
up to 2 in. long, the petioles sheathing the stem.
The small blue flowers consist of 2 blue petals
and 1 paler petal, about $\frac{1}{2}$ in. across, and remain
in bloom only 1 day. A weak-rooted plant
preferring moist shaded soil, it can spread
rapidly through the shaded part of the garden
and should be vigorously rooted out wherever
it occurs. Widely distributed in the eastern U.S.
See WEED-CONTROLLING CHEMICALS.

diffusa   creeping   Zone 6   Diffuse Dayflower
With blue flowers about $\frac{1}{2}$ in. wide and creeping
stems, native from Del. southward. A weedy
perennial rooting all along its procumbent
stems.

erecta   prostrate   Zone 8   Erect Dayflower
Stems about 2 ft. long, leaves very narrow but
3–5 in. long. Flowers blue. Native to West
Indies.

COMMELINACEAE = The   Spiderwort   or
Dayflower Family

COMPANION CROPPING. Another turn for
intercropping, which see.

COMPASS-PLANT = *Silphium laciniatum*

COMPLETE FERTILIZER. One which contains nitrogen, phosphorus, potash and certain
trace elements in known percentages. See SOILS,
FERTILIZERS.

COMPOSITAE = The Thistle, Aster, Daisy, or
Goldenrod Family, one of the largest plant
families of over 800 genera and 15,000 species.

COMPOST. Making a garden compost is the
best way of getting rid of garden trash and using
it to make humus material to add to the garden
soil. Compost piles are always recommended
for all gardens, but not all gardeners take
advantage of this simple way of replenishing
the much-needed humus in the garden soils.

A simple compost pile can be maintained this
way: Select a hidden sight where the pile can
be maintained in an out-of-the-way part of the
garden. Clear a space of ground at least 4 ft. × 8
ft. for the pile. Special sides of boards or concrete blocks can be used, but these are not
necessary. On the bottom place a 6–9-in. layer
of garden trash, weeds, grass clippings, leaves,

etc. Tamp this down well, wet it and sprinkle on top sulfate of ammonia and superphosphate, about ½ oz. of each per sq. yard of area, and water it well. Then a 6-in. layer of manure is placed on top and a 3-in. layer of soil on top of that. The process is again repeated until the pile is about 4 ft. high, with the soil finally on top. This is all watered well so that the entire pile is thoroughly wet, a concave place being left on the top to catch rain water. The pile will probably not be completed at once, but only as material becomes available.

Compost Pile

When it is completed in the summer it is allowed to stand 6 weeks, water being applied during dry spells. Then it is turned over, moistened again, a layer of soil placed on top and it is left alone until needed for applying to the garden. It should not be used until everything is thoroughly decomposed, but summer temperatures and added moisture, together with the addition of the chemicals to aid its decomposition, are usually enough so that it is ready to use in about 6 months.

At the time this is being written, much interest is being taken by enthusiastic gardeners in home compost piles. One suggestion is to put the material listed above for composting in a polyethylene bag, moisten it thoroughly, tie the top tightly and leave it out in the sun, kicking it around occasionally, letting in fresh air every two weeks. This saves the effort of spading it over and forces the generated heat within the bag to aid in the decomposition.

COMPOUND. Of 2 or more similar parts united into 1 whole; compound leaf 1 divided into separate leaflets.

COMPTONIA (kom-TON-ia)

peregrina	4′	Zone 2	Sweetfern

An aromatic fernlike shrub commonly seen along the roadsides from Nova Scotia to N.Car. and westward to Ind. and Mich. Unfortunately it is very difficult to transplant and consequently is not used as much as it might be for this reason. It grows best in peaty and moist soils and so is used especially in naturalistic plantings. If it is to be transplanted from its natural habitat, large sods should be carefully lifted and quickly transplanted. Small plants pulled up or roughly dug have little chance of survival. The aromatic leaves make a palatable tea. It has so many root suckers that it is usually propagated by root cuttings. See CUTTINGS.

CONCRETE. Concrete is often needed in the garden for walks, rock wall foundations, terraces and the like. Large areas might well be left to skilled craftsmen who know from experience how to make it and how best to lay it so that winter freezing and thawing will not crack it. Sometimes the gardener may want to lay small amounts himself.

Concrete is made by mixing moist sand, cement, crushed stone and water in the proper amounts, spreading and levelling it and letting it set until hard. It can be purchased in dry mixes for small amounts when all that is necessary is to add the crushed stone and water. Also, it can be colored, by mixing various powdered colors available from dealers, but it should be remembered that the color of wet concrete is darker than that of the same concrete after it dries.

Usually it is best to mix it properly in a small motorized mixer. If a walk is to be laid, the soil is removed to a depth of about 10 in., boards placed on the sides at the proper ground level to hold the wet mix, and of course made level. Then small rocks are placed in the bottom to a depth of 4 in., tamped level, and then 2 in. of small stone or gravel is placed on top of this, levelled, tamped and watered, and then the 4 in. of concrete is poured on top of this.

Crosspieces of wood can be inserted just before the concrete is poured, at regular intervals to provide for the "block" appearance of the concrete in the walk, and the expansion of the concrete itself, the wood pieces to be removed after the concrete has set and the spaces filled with sand.

The mixing should be done thoroughly, using a combination of 1 part cement, 3¼ parts damp sand, 5 parts gravel and slightly under ⅝ of a part of water, for foundations.

Garden paths, tanks, pools, etc., might best be made of 1 part cement, 2 parts damp sand, 3 parts gravel and just under ⅝ part water. This is thoroughly mixed, then poured into the frame made to receive it, levelled off properly and covered with damp burlap so that it dries slowly for at least 24 hours and longer would be better, during which time the covering is kept moistened. It is best not to allow it to be walked on for several days to a week. The gravel used for walks should be $\frac{3}{4}-\frac{3}{16}$ in. in dia., but for thick walls the aggregate can be up to 2 in. in dia.

CONE. The fruit of such plants as Fir, Pine and Spruce.

CONEFLOWER, GREAT, SHOWY, SWEET. See RUDBECKIA.

CONEFLOWER, PRAIRIE, GRAY-HEADED. See RATIBIDA.

CONEHEAD = *Strobilanthes dyeriana*

CONEPLANT = *Conophytum wiggetae*

CONIFER. This is a popular term which includes those evergreens (and a few deciduous trees as well) which have cone fruits, like species of: *Abies, Araucaria, Cedrus, Chamaecyparis, Cryptomeria, Cunninghamia, Cupressus, Fitzroya, Keteleeria, Larix, Libocedrus, Picea, Pinus, Pseudolarix, Pseudotsuga, Sciadopitys, Sequoia, Sequoidendron, Taxodium, Thuja, Thujopsis, Tsuga. Juniperus* is a member of the Pine Family (*Pinaceae*) and should also be included technically; its fruits are not berries, but are small cones in which the scales have become fleshy and united together. An excellent reference is "Manual of Cultivated Conifers" by P. den Ouden, Martinus Nijhoff, The Hague, Holland. 1965.

CONIUM (kon-EYE-um)

   maculatum   **2′-4′**   **Zone 3**   **Poison-hemlock**
A poisonous plant, this should not be cultivated; although native to Europe it has escaped cultivation in the U.S. A rank-growing biennial herb with large, parsleylike leaves, and a large parsniplike tap root. The white flowers in late summer are similar to those of Queen Anne's Lace. A better common name and certainly more descriptive, is Poison-parsley. It is supposed that many people were put to death with concoctions made from this plant in ancient Athens.

CONNATE. Joined in one organ.

CONOPHYTUM (kon-OFF-it-um)

   wiggetae   **1″**   **Zone 10**   **Coneplant**
A squat, clustering succulent with club-shaped bodies, leafless, looking like an onion bulb above ground, gray-green with numerous dark green dots. Flowers whitish. Native to South Africa. Merely an oddity for the windowsill garden.

CONSERVATION. The study of ways and means of preserving large areas of natural growth so that they will remain as they always have been before man started to renovate the land. The term is being broadened to include everything from correcting water and stream pollution to combating erosion in the Midwest.

CONSOLIDA (con-SOL-i-da)

   ambigua (*Delphinium ajacis*)   **1′-2′**   **annual**
                                   Annual Larkspur
A plant from southern Europe, producing spikes of violet, pink, rose or blue flowers in the summer from June to Aug. The seed can be sown in the fall, certainly the earliest possible in the spring, accomplished by preparing the bed in the fall and sowing almost before the soil can be worked properly in the early spring.

CONVALLARIA (kon-val-AIR-ia)

   majalis   **8″**   **Zones 2-3**   **Lily-of-the-valley**
This very familiar plant is native to Europe, Asia and eastern North America. The fragrant, waxy, bell-like flowers, $\frac{1}{4}$ in. in dia. are pendant on upright spikes from mid-May to mid-June. The orange berries which follow are not profuse and only $\frac{1}{4}$ in. across and hence not very ornamental. The 2 large oval leaves which grow from the base of each plant are 8 in. long and 1-3 in. wide. These plants increase rapidly and make a good ground cover in the shade. Once established a well-grown bed needs practically no attention, but beginning in late summer the foliage proceeds to get progressively less attractive and dies to the ground completely, sometimes even before frost. A variety 'Rosea' has flowers a very light purplish pink. A bed will respond to an application of well-rotted manure each year in the fall. It grows from a rhizome, not a bulb.

Insect Pests

Short, regular notches of the leaves are eaten by the lily-of-the-valley weevil. Injury is more curious than harmful. Insecticides #15 or #13 are suggested.

Diseases

Leaf spot and botrytis flower rot infect the leaves but seldom require control. Picking infected leaves is suggested.

CONVOLVULACEAE = The Morning-glory Family

CONVOLVULUS (kon-VOL-vew-lus). The Glorybinds or Bindweeds comprise some ornamentals, but mostly they are weeds, some of them pernicious weeds. Those described below are perennials except *C. tricolor* which is an annual. They are mostly trailing or vinelike in habit, very seldom shrubby, with alternate leaves without teeth or lobes on the leaf margin. The flowers usually bloom in the day, some close by noon, and all are bell-shaped or funnel-shaped. They are not good ornamentals, although the flowers are somewhat similar to the closely

Bindwood—*Convolvulus arvensis*

related morning-glories, or *Ipomoea* species. The
fruit is a 4-valved capsule.

Two especially (*C. arvensis* and *C. sepium*) are
vicious weeds. All should be carefully watched
and kept from becoming serious pests in the
garden.

arvensis vine Zone 3 European Glorybind
A perennial, deep-rooted vine and a pernicious
weed introduced over a century ago from
Europe, but widespread throughout the U.S.
and southern Canada, with alternate arrow-
shaped leaves 2 in. long. The flowers are pink to
whitish, similar in shape to those of a wide
open morning-glory, appearing during June and
July. It is extremely difficult to eradicate
because of the deep-growing roots which can
send up new plants even though they are
partially pulled up. It frequently grows flat on
the ground with runners 3–9 ft. long. See
WEED-CONTROLLING CHEMICALS.

cantabrica 2′ Zone 9 Cantabrian Glorybind
An erect-to-prostrate herb with oblong or
lanceolate leaves, rose-to-pink flowers about ½
in. long born in clusters. Native to the Mediterranean Region. A rock garden plant.

cneorum 4′ Zone 9
Native to southern Europe with 1–6 persistent
white or pinkish flowers not over ½ in. wide. A
good rock garden plant in southern Calif.

japonicus climber Zone 9 Rose Glorybind
Often a troublesome weed that should be eradicated before it takes over good garden space. It is
a perennial, climbs to 20 ft. and with leaves that
are arrow-shaped. The flowers are pink, 2 in. wide
and the plant is native to eastern Asia.

**mauritanicus 1′-2′ Zone 7 Ground Morning-
glory**
An evergreen perennial that will have a spread
of 3 ft., with soft gray-green foliage and
lavender-blue funnel-shaped flowers about 1–2
in. across from June to Nov. It is used as a
ground cover in Calif. and Ariz., tolerating dry
soil. It self-sows readily but is not a perfect
ground cover because of its slightly loose and
open habit. It grows best in the full sun.

sepium = *Calystegia sepium*
spithamaeus = *Calystegia spithamaea*
tricolor 1′ annual Dwarf Glorybind
A dwarf annual with erect stems, blue flowers
with yellow throat and white margin about 1½
in. across. Leaves are linear, flowers are 3 in a
cluster. Native to southern Europe. An old-
fashioned garden favorite.

COONTIE = *Zamia floridana*

COOPERIA = *Zephyranthes*

COPPERLEAF = *Codiaeum variegatum pictum*

COPPERLEAF, PAINTED = *Acalypha wilkesiana*

COPPERLEAF, PAINTED, CHENILLE. See
ACALYPHA.

COPPERTIP, GOLDEN = *Crocosmia aurea*
COPRA. See COCONUT.

COPROSMA (kop-ROS-ma)
petriei 3″ Zone 7 Petrie's Coprosma
A New Zealand shrub, low and prostrate with
evergreen leaves about ¼ in. long and white or
greenish, solitary, small flowers in the spring.
It is only suitable for the rock garden or some
similar situation. Male and female flowers are
on different plants.

repens (*baueri*) **20′ Zone 9 Hedge Coprosma**
An evergreen shrub or small tree from New
Zealand with opposite, thick, lustrous leaves,
1–3 in. long and male flowers in axillary clusters,
the female flowers (on other plants) being in
groups of 3–6 but fairly inconspicuous. Fruits
on the female plants are orange-yellow, ½ in.
across. Used in southern Calif. as a hedge,
especially in seashore gardens. There are forms
with variegated leaves. Rooted from cuttings
which are very susceptible to damping off.

COPTIS (COP-tis)
asplenifolia 3″ Zone 3 Ferry Goldthread
A dainty evergreen of the Buttercup Family
growing in dense mats and having small, 5-
parted leaves and small, rather inconspicuous,
white flowers. Native from Alaska southward,
it requires a moist, acid, peaty soil and a
shaded location.

**groenlandica 4″-5″ Zone 2 Common
Goldthread**

This shy woods plant receives its common name from the bright yellow creeping root from which arise the shiny compound leaves having 3 rounded leaflets. In May and June a slender, leafless flower stalk bears a solitary white flower having 5-7 sepals and several very narrow petals. A fine plant for the moist wild garden, it will tolerate some sun, but needs acid soil. Native from Greenland to Va. and west to Ia, chiefly in bog areas. Seed may be sown in fall, or divisions taken in spring.

laciniata   6″   Zone 6   Antleaf Goldthread
A West Coast species native to Wash. and Ore., with evergreen compound leaves with 3 deeply-cut leaflets and greenish-white flowers blooming in spring.

quinquefolia   1″   Zone 3
One of the most ornamental species of *Coptis*, having 5-parted leaves growing in dense mats and topped by waxy white flowers borne on stems 3 in. high, blooming in April and May. Native to Japan.

trifolia   6″   Zone 3   Alaska Goldthread
A low stemless plant found in boggy areas of northern North America with a yellow root-stock, small compound leaves and white or yellow flowers. If the shining leaves are protected with a light mulch they remain green over winter. Flowers appear in June and July. It does best in moist soils. Seeds sown as soon as ripe germinate readily in moist soils. This is used only in the wild garden in cooler areas of the country.

CORAL-BEAN. See ERYTHRINA.

CORAL-BELLS = *Heuchera sanguinea*

CORALBERRY,   CHENAULT = *Symphoricarpos chenaultii*

CORALDROPS, SHOWY = *Bessera elegans*

CORAL GEM = *Lotus berthelotii*

CORALLORRHIZA (cor-all-o-RY-za)
maculata   10″–15″   Zone 2   Spotted Coralroot
This interesting member of the Orchid Family is a saprophyte, a plant which, having no chlorophyll by which to manufacture food from air and water, receives its food from dead plants or insects in the soil by means of its branching, coral-colored rhizomes. The straight stem, with alternate leaves reduced to brownish bracts, bears flowers arising in the axils of the bracts on the upper half of the stem. The flowers resemble tiny orchids and are yellowish in color. It is found in woods throughout Canada and the U.S., except for the drier parts of the country, and extends into Central America, flowering generally in late summer. Because of its saprophytic nature, it would be difficult to cultivate.

CORAL-PEA. See HARDENBERGIA.

CORALPLANT = *Jatropha multifida*

CORALROOT = *Hexalectris spicata*

CORALROOT,   SPOTTED = *Corallorhiza maculata*

CORALVINE = *Antigonon leptopus*

CORCHORUS (cor-CHOR-us)
capsularis   15′   annual   Jute
A tropical herb with alternate oblong leaves 4 in. long and small yellow flowers; grown in the Tropics for the fiber of the inner bark. It is not grown as an ornamental. Native to India.

CORDATE. Heart-shaped; usually referring to the base of the leaf.

CORDIA (KORD-ia)
sebestena   35′   Zone 10   Geigertree
The brilliant orange flowers of this tropical American tree are 1–2 in. across and appear here and there about the tree most of the year. The flowers are tubular, in terminal clusters of 7–10, but only a few are open together. The small fruits are white and edible. Evergreen leaves are stiff and rough, 3–8 in. long. This is tolerant of salt and is recommended for seashore gardens in Fla. Propagated by cuttings or air layers.

CORDON FRUITS. See ESPALIER.

CORDYLINE (kor-dil-LY-ne). Members of this tropical genus and Dracaena are frequently mixed up and one taken for the other. They are separated only by technical characters. Both groups of plants are very popular as florists' display plants, as foliage plants in the home and home greenhouse, and in southern Fla. and southern Calif. as popular foliage plants in the garden. Even in the North they are sometimes used as display plants in tubs about the terrace or in the small garden, but they must be kept in a warm greenhouse during the winter period.

They are characterized by a strong, central stem, and long, often gracefully arching, sword-shaped leaves proceeding from it. The leaves are frequently highly colored and because of this are valued as ornamentals. Propagation is by seeds, air layers or stem cuttings. If the stem grows too tall, an air layer is made of the top part and when well rooted it is severed from the plant. The remaining stem has the leaves removed and then can be cut into 3-in. pieces and half buried in sand in a propagation bench, with the bottom heat about 80° F; such cuttings should root easily.

The flowers of these species are not very showy, are greenish or white in small panicles and the fruit is a berry.

Culture is simple. They should be grown in a warm but moist greenhouse and are conditioned for best color and display by gradually reducing heat and moisture just prior to the time they are to be used.

australis 40′ Zone 10 Giant Dracena
In the Tropics, this is a tree with green leaves, 18–30 in. long and 1¼ in. wide in a rosette about the trunk. Native to New Zealand. There is a var. **veitchii** with the leaf bases and the midribs bright red. Since this is the tallest-growing species, it is the one which frequently must be reduced in height (air layering) as a house plant.

stricta 6′–12′ Zone 10 Australian Dracena
Leaves 12–20 in. long, 1 in. wide, not as crowded on the stem as are those of C. **terminalis**. There are vars. with colored or bronze-purple leaves. Native to Australia.

terminalis 12′ Zone 10 Ti, Common Dracena
Blade-shaped leaves, 4 in. wide and up to 3 ft. long, this is a native shrub of tropical Asia and the islands of the South Pacific. The evergreen leaves are all tufted near the top and have petioles. Those of the true Dracaena species have no petioles. These leaves have been most useful to the native Hawaiian and it is these, when shredded, that are used in the skirts of the dancers. The foot-long flower cluster, produced in winter, holds hundred of very small white flowers. The red-leaved variety not only has red-to-golden-green leaves but pink flowers also. There are many horticultural varieties, with foliage of red, pink, white, metallic purple or striped variegated leaves. Some of the vars. are: **'Amabilis'**—leaves suffused with rose and white; **'Baptisti'**—leaves irregularly striped with yellow and pink; **'Imperialis'**—leaves metallic green, rayed with crimson or pink.

It is unfortunate that this house plant is commonly called Dracena. It does not belong to the genus Dracaena, because its rhizomes creep in the soil and those of the true Dracaena sp. do not creep. Regardless of name it is a popular plant and can be grown under the conditions of poor light and very little attention in home or office, and still look well.

COREMA (ko-REMA)
conradii 6″–24″ Zone 3 Broom Crowberry
Evergreen upright shrubs with minute leaves only about ¼ in. long and small flowers with conspicuous purple stamens. Only of value in the rockery or wild garden where the soil is acid, for early spring flowers are sometimes used as a ground cover in the acid soils of the northern U.S. Native from Newfoundland to N.J. Propagated by cuttings.

COREOPSIS (ko-rea-OP-sis). A group of annual and perennial flowers belonging to the Composite Family, with daisylike, mostly yellow heads although some are purplish and pink. The annual kinds can be sown in the fall or very early spring and they self-seed readily. Perennial kinds are easily raised from seed or

can be divided in the fall or spring. They grow easily and well in any garden soil and are excellent as cut flowers. The leaves are either entire, variously lobed or cut. Most bloom during the summer.

atkinsoniana 3′ annual Atkinson Coreopsis
Flower heads 1½ in. wide, purplish and brown. Native from British Columbia to N.Dak.

auriculata 'Nana' 6″ Zone 4 Dwarf Eared Coreopsis
This is an excellent little plant for rock garden or ground cover, with bright orange-yellow, daisy-like blossoms from June to Aug. The flower heads are over 2 in. across. The species is native from Va. to Fla., but this var. 'Nana' is much the better form to use in gardens. Easily propagated by division.

basilis (*drummondii*) 1½′ annual Goldenwave Coreopsis
Flowers orange-yellow to crimson with a reddish-brown ring around the center, 2 in. wide. Native to Tex.

calliopsidea 2′ annual California Coreopsis
Flowers yellow, to 3 in. wide. Native to Calif.

grandiflora 2′ Zone 7 Tickseed, Bigflower Coreopsis
Native to the southern U.S., this has orange-yellow flower-heads 3 in. across from mid-June to late July. Although supposedly a perennial it frequently performs as a biennial, but seeds itself readily. Adapted for a semi-wild garden. 'Goldfink'—an excellent variety.

lanceolata 2′ Zone 3 Lance Coreopsis
Native from Ontario to Fla., this bears yellow flower-heads 2½ in. across and the leaves are entire, mostly near the base of the plant. The double-flowered variety **'Flore-pleno'** is worth trying to find. The semi-double form **'Sunburst'** comes fairly true from seed.

major 2′–3′ Zone 7 Trefoil Coreopsis
The flower heads of this plant are from 2–3 in. wide, with generally 8 rather wide ray-flowers. It grows in sunny woodlands from Va. southward and flowers in June and July.

rosea 1′–2′ Zone 4 Rose Coreopsis
Spreading by a creeping perennial rootstalk, this plant displays yellow disk-flowers around which are arranged a few, often 6 or 8, pink-to-purple ray-flowers. It prefers damp, sunny locations and grows from New England to the deep South. The flowers appear in late summer.

tinctoria 2′ annual Plains Coreopsis
Flowers yellow, crimson and brown, 2 in. wide. The fresh flower-heads are used for making dye—a burnt orange to bright yellow. Native from Minn. to Ariz. Vars. include: **'Atropurpurea'**—dark crimson flowers; **'Flore pleno'**—double flowers; **'Nana'**—dwarf, only about 8 in. tall.

tripteris 7′–9′ Zone 4 Atlantic Coreopsis

Few gardeners would recommend this oversized plant with its pinnately lobed leaves and typical flower-heads of disc-flowers surrounded by 6–10 ray-flowers. It inhabits woods areas throughout New England and the south-central states, flowering in Aug. and Sept.

verticillata **2¼′** **Zone 6** **Threadleaf Coreopsis** With almost fernlike leaves and poor, clear yellow flowers but borne over a longer period than some of the other *Coreopsis* sp., this has some merit for this reason. Also it is markedly resistant to drought. Md. to Ark. **'Moonbeam'**— a truly excellent variety.

CORIANDER = *Coriandrum sativum*
CORIANDRUM (kor-ri-AND-rum)
    sativum **3′** **annual** **Coriander** A popular strong-smelling herb with 2 or 3 times pinnately compound leaves and small white flowers grown chiefly for its fruits or seeds, which are used in seasoning or in confectionery. Native to southern Europe. Seeds may be sown in either fall or spring.

CORIARIA (ko-ri-AY-ria)
    japonica **3′** **Zones 6–7** **Japanese Coriaria** A shrub from Japan, used occasionally for its opposite bright green leaves 1–4 in. long and its colored berries about ¼ in. wide, at first bright red, then maturing to a violet-black color. The flowers are either greenish or reddish in small racemes a few inches long and not especially ornamental, in Aug. and Sept.

CORKSCREW = *Euphorbia mammillaris*
CORKTREE, AMUR = *Phellodendron amurense*
CORKWOOD, FLORIDA = *Leitneria floridana*
CORM. The enlarged fleshy base of a stem, bulblike but solid, as in Gladiolus. See BULB.
CORMELS. Small corms arising at the base of the large mother corm as in Gladiolus.
CORN = *Zea mays*
CORN, SWEET, *Zea mays rugosa*, ranks as one of the more important of the vegetable crops.

Sweet Corn is adapted to a wide range of climatic conditions and, consequently, is grown in all sections of the U.S. It is grown for the fresh market in both the southern and northern regions, but by far the largest acreage in the North is grown for processing and freezing. This crop grows best during hot weather and is frost-tender.

Varieties

Each seed company lists many varieties, therefore it is difficult to suggest varieties that are available in all sections. Most of the older varieties such as **'Golden Bantam'** and **'Country Gentleman'** have been replaced by newer hybrids such as **'Sugar and Gold'**, **'Sundance'**, **'Golden Cross Bantam'**, all of which are yellow. Other popular varieties are **'Sprite'**, **'Burgundy Delight'**, **'Honey Moon'**, **'Jubilee'**, **'Seneca Sentry'**, **'Silver Queen'**, and **'Northern Belle'**. There are many other varieties that are excellent and therefore it is recommended that seed catalogues be checked for those that are listed for a particular region.

Soils and Fertilizers

Sweet Corn is grown on all types of soil. A well-drained sandy loam to a silt loam is preferred. This plant has a very deep and extensive root system. Deep and thorough soil preparation is therefore important. Three to 4 bu. of well-rotted manure per 100 ft. of row worked into the soil will improve the water-holding capacity of the soil and provide some plant food. In addition 6–8 lbs. of a 5–10–10 fertilizer per 100 ft. of row should be broadcast prior to planting. If no manure is used increase the fertilizer by 2–3 lbs. Several top dressings, 3–4 lbs. per 100 ft. of row, of nitrate of soda may be beneficial when plants are 18″ high.

Planting

Sweet Corn is injured by frost and the seed germinates poorly in cold wet soil. Planting should be delayed until these conditions are satisfactory. Some gardeners start the seed in paper bands or pots in the hotbed and then transplant into the garden to get corn a week or two earlier than by direct planting out of doors. Sweet Corn can be planted in hills or in drills. Hills should be spaced 18 to 24 in. apart in the row and the rows spaced at 36 in. Three plants are adequate per hill. In drills the rows are spaced at 36 in. and the plants thinned to stand 6–8 in. apart. Crows and starlings may scratch out the seed just prior to its germination. The seed should be treated with a crow repellent which can be purchased at a garden center.

Cultivation

Cultivation of Sweet Corn is similar to that of other garden crops, namely shallow and sufficient to control weeds. Where corn is planted in hills, black plastic 18 in. wide may be placed over the row with holes for each hill. This not only controls weeds but also tends to conserve soil moisture. Herbicides are widely used in commercial corn plantings for the control of weeds. The most satisfactory material is Atrazine, but again this is very selective and cannot be recommended for the home gardener with a few short rows of Sweet Corn.

The removal of suckers and hilling of corn plants is not necessary or recommended.

Harvesting

Highest quality, sweetness and tenderness of the kernel is reached when harvested in the milk stage of maturity. At this stage the kernel is soft and succulent. As the kernel content changes to a doughy consistency it loses its sweetness and increases in toughness. Flavor and succulence are quickly lost after picking if exposed to high temperatures, say 75° to 80° F. At these temperatures 30–50% of the sugar may revert to starch in 4–5 hours. At temperatures of 32°–38° F. the original quality may be retained for several days.

GRANT B. SNYDER

Insects and Pests

More than 20 insects are recognized pests of corn. The more important are: Corn earworm, a stout striped worm, which feeds in the silk and kernels near tip of ear. Although they do not survive freezing, they migrate northward and are destructive when the ears are maturing. Spraying or dusting the silk at 2- or 3-day intervals with insecticide #37 is safe and effective. European corn borer and southern corn borer tunnel stalks and eat kernels. Spraying with insecticide #37 when the stalks are first visible in the whorl and repeating in 7–10 days should give good control. White grubs and wireworms eat the seed and roots and soil treatment with insecticide #15 is desirable following sod. Corn flea beetle spreads bacterial (Stewart's) wilt disease and, following mild winters when the beetle survives, a careful spraying program with insecticide #9 on early corn is recommended. Army worm can strip the leaves from corn in a short time. They are most destructive in late summer and a thorough treatment of corn and surrounding vegetation with insecticide #37 is advised. Chinch bug is destructive in midwestern corn fields but seldom needs special control in home gardens. See LAWNS. Stalk borer bores into stalks when they are small and ruins them. Spraying is seldom practical. Japanese beetles eat the silk but can be handpicked successfully.

Diseases

Bacterial wilt is described under flea beetle. Corn smut produces large, grayish-white galls called "boils" which usually ruin the ear. The "boils" contain a mass of spores. Fungicides are impractical, and cutting and burning before the spores mature is suggested for home gardens. Treated corn seed is recommended for planting using fungicide #9 on home grown seed.

CORN, STRAWBERRY = *Zea mays everta*

CORN, SWEET = *Zea mays rugosa*

CORN COCKLE = *Agrostemma githago*

CORN-LILY. See IXIA.

CORNACEAE = The Dogwood Family

CORNEL. See CORNUS.

CORNELIAN-CHERRY = *Cornus mas*

CORNFLOWER = *Centaurea 'cyanus*

CORN-SALAD, EUROPEAN = *Valerianella locusta*

CORNUS (KOR-nus). Dogwood. There is a dogwood for almost every part of the U.S. except the hottest and driest areas. These shrubs and trees constitute some of the best and most serviceable ornamentals we have. American nurserymen are offering 45 species and varieties. Most (except *C. alternifolia* and *C. controversa*) have opposite leaves. All are valued for their flowers, colored fruits and rich autumn coloration. They are easily grown, have few pests and most are easily propagated by seeds, cuttings or graftings. They vary from low shrubs, from the lowly 6-in. ground cover (*C. canadensis*), to the majestic 75-ft. *C. nuttalli*. They come from Europe, Asia and North America. Most can be considered to have some ornamental interest every season of the year, something which can not be said for many other genera.

Propagation

Seeds can be processed as soon as ripe or they can be stored dry in airtight containers in a cool place for up to a year and then processed. Seeds of *C. florida*, *kousa* and *stolonifera* as well as some other species are usually stratified as soon as they are ripe for 3 months at 40° F. and then sown. Seeds of others have double dormancy and may have to be stratified at room temperatures for 3–4 months and then at 40° F. for another 3–4 months before they are sown. In grafting *C. florida*, a crown graft is used; in budding a shield bud. *C. kousa* is compatible on *C. florida* understock. Most species root from softwood and hardwood cuttings. See STRATIFICATION, GRAFTING, BUDDING, CUTTINGS.

alba 'Sibirica' 9′ Zone 2 Siberian Dogwood
The var. 'Sibirica' is the very best of the clones of *Cornus alba* for ornamental planting. Like all other plants of this species it is a vigorous shrub with small flat clusters (about 2 in. across) of yellowish-white flowers in late May, followed by white to slightly blue berries in the fall. The autumn color is red, but if the plant is allowed to grow vigorously, the bright red bark of the twigs will be outstanding all winter long. This plant comes from Siberia and Manchuria and is remarkably hardy. However, in order to force vigorous growth with the accompanying scarlet-red bark, one should give this plant an occasional vigorous pruning in the spring, thus

forcing young shoot-growth during spring and summer, with the resulting red-barked twigs in winter. No other dogwood has bark as vividly colored as this.

There are several other varieties of *C. alba* valued for their variegated leaves. The best is 'Argenteo-marginata' with each 5-in. leaf bordered with a band of white, giving the entire plant a cool whitish look even on the hottest day in summer. This is one of the best white variegated shrubs commonly available. The var. 'Gouchaultii' has leaves variegated with yellow and pink and the var. 'Spaethii' merely has leaves bordered with yellow.

alternifolia   24′   Zone 3   Alternate Leaved Dogwood
Native throughout the eastern half of North America, this and *C. controversa* are the only alternate-leaved dogwoods. The flowers are small, like those of some of the viburnums, the clusters being $1\frac{1}{2}$–$2\frac{1}{2}$ in. across in May; the fruits are bluish-black berries on red fruit stalks. The autumn color is reddish and there is a var. 'Argentea' which is a very weak grower but the leaves are variegated with white and if the tree is well grown it makes a beautiful specimen. In some areas there is a blight attacking this tree which disfigures and sometimes kills it. Where this disease is prevalent, the more resistant but similar *C. controversa* could be substituted.

amomum   9′   Zone 5   Silky Dogwood
Native in the eastern U.S., this is sometimes incorrectly sold for the better *C. alba* 'Sibirica' which it closely resembles except the bark is not as colorful and the fruits are blue to pale or even grayish blue. If mature stems of *C. alba* are cut the pith is white, while pith in the stems of mature wood of *C. amomum* will be brown—a fine way to tell the 2 apart, winter or summer.

canadensis   9″   Zone 2   Bunchberry
A low ground cover in the woods of the mountains in eastern North America and eastern Asia, this little evergreen is familiar to all woodsmen. The whorled, evergreen leaves are borne horizontally on a single stalk 5–9 in. long, without petioles, ovate, pointed at each end with pairs of smaller opposite leaves near the base. The dense heads of small, inconspicuous, yellow flowers during May and June are surrounded by 4–6 large, conspicuous, white bracts at the end of the main stem. The bracts are $\frac{1}{3}$–$\frac{3}{4}$ in. long and appear at first glance to comprise a single showy flower while actually they surround a cluster of minute flowers. The bright red, edible berries are borne in bunches in the late summer and fall. This plant forms a ground cover by the acre in moist woods where the growing conditions are just right. The berries· have been cooked and made into puddings by the early settlers and probably the Indians as well.

capitata   40′   Zone 8   Evergreen Dogwood
This is native to China and is not much used in America. The pale yellow bracts of the flower cluster are 4–6 in number and $1\frac{1}{2}$–2 in. long, appearing in June and July. The red, strawberrylike fruits are 1–$1\frac{1}{2}$ in. across. In habit it has a round head, somewhat like that of *C. florida* but more bushy with lustrous, dark, evergreen to semi-evergreen leaves which turn bronze in winter.

controversa   60′   Zone 5   Giant Dogwood
The small whitish flowers are borne in flat clusters, 3–7 in. across, and resemble the flowers of *C. alba* or *C. stolonifera*, appearing in late May and followed in the fall by bluish-black berries. The lustrous leaves turn red in the fall. It is native to Japan and China. The most characteristic thing about it is the horizontal habit of branching for these branches seem to be borne on layers or tiers. Also, although it resembles the native *C. alternifolia*, it is not susceptible to the serious blight affecting this native plant so can be used instead where the disease is serious. The var. 'Variegata' has pale yellow to white leaf margins. This and *C. alternifolia* are the two Cornus species with alternate leaves.

florida   40′   Zone 4   Flowering Dogwood
This tree is considered to be the best ornamental of all the trees native to the northern U.S. It is native of the eastern half of the country, its "flowers" are really flower-clusters, the true flowers being small and inconspicuous in the

Cornus florida: The true flowers are small and yellow and are clustered in the center of the four large, white bracts.

center, surrounded by 4-notched, white bracts which popularly are incorrectly considered to be the petals. The fruits are brilliant red berries in clusters in the fall, and the autumn color is always a brilliant scarlet. The branches are borne horizontally which gives the tree a most attractive flat-topped habit of interest throughout the entire year. Varieties of the Flowering Dogwood include: **'Apple Blossom'**—flower bracts pink and white about the color of apple blossoms; **'Cherokee Chief'**—flower bracts "a rich ruby red" (Plant Patent #1710); **'Hohman's Golden'**—leaves with bright yellow margins, differs slightly from variety **'Welchii'**, flowers white, selected by Henry Hohman of Kingsville, MD; **'Gigantea'**—flower bracts are said to be 6 in. from tip to tip; **'Magnifica'**—flower bracts 4 in. from tip to tip; **'New Hampshire'**—a tree growing at Atkinson, N.H., has been given this name because it apparently is more flower-bud hardy than others; **'Pendula'**—with stiffly pendulous branches; **'Pluribracteata'**—white flower bracts, but instead of being 4 in number there are 6–8 large flower bracts, with numerous other small aborted ones; **'Rubra'**—bracts vary in color from washed-out pink to red. This is not as hardy, nor as flower-bud hardy as the species; **'Spring Song'**—flower bracts advertised as a "gorgeous rose-red"; **'Sweetwater Red'**—flower bracts red, foliage reddish to reddish green; **'Welchii'**—leaves variegated with creamy white, pink and green. The blooms are sparse. Foliage sometimes burns when the tree is grown in the full sun; **'White Cloud'**—unusually large number of creamy-white flower clusters; **'Xanthocarpa'**—yellow fruit.

Insect Pests

Dogwood borer seriously weakens trees by tunnelling under the bark, especially near wounds or pruning scars. Established borers can be cut out. Protection results from spraying the trunk with insecticide #9 monthly during the summer and by wrapping the trunk of newly-planted trees with paper or burlap. Dogwood twig borer is similar to the oak twig pruner. See OAK. Dogwood club gall midge lays eggs among the terminal leaves. Maggots form small elongate galls which kill tips of twigs. Spraying with insecticides #9 or #37 3 times at weekly intervals in early summer have given control. Several scale insects infest dogwood. See SCALE INSECTS.

Diseases

Bleeding canker causes sunken areas in bark killing infected branches. Cutting out cankers and disinfecting the wounds is advised. Leaf spots and twig blight cause defoliation and dieback unless protection with fungicides #D, #F, or #W is given.

kousa   21'   Zone 5   Japanese Dogwood
This species from Japan and Korea blooms about 3 weeks after *C. florida* and differs from it in being more bushy, in having flower bracts that are pointed at the tip (not rounded and notched), red fruits like large raspberries in the fall, and the bark on trunks exfoliates in irregular patches to show lighter bark beneath. Also the flower bracts sometimes show blotches of pink when they fade. The autumn color is scarlet, and all the flowers are borne on the upper side of the flat, horizontal branches, so the tree might well be planted so it can be observed from above, to be seen at its best. The variety **chinensis** is supposed to have larger flower bracts 2–3½ in. long, while those of the species are about 1½–2 in. long, but these differences do not always hold. Also this variety is slightly less hardy than the species. The var. **'Milky Way'** has been selected merely because it is a profuse flowering clone. **'Goldstar'**—a new form with variegated leaves.

Cornus kousa (Japanese Dogwood): An excellent ornamental tree that blooms in June. (*Photo by Arnold Arboretum, Jamaica Plain, Mass.*)

macrophylla   45'   Zone 6   Largeleaf Dogwood
This native of China and Japan has small flowers in clusters 4–6 in. wide, like those of *C. alternifolia* and *C. controversa*, but differs from them in having opposite leaves, not alternate. The flowers appear in July and August and the fruits which develop later are bluish-black berries. The handsome leaves are 4–7 in. long and 3½ in. wide. It is excellent as a foliage plant, but in flower and fruit it is not a better ornamental than *C. controversa*. Its late summer bloom is an important factor when trees for summer display are needed.

mas   24'   Zone 4   Cornelian-cherry
This southern European plant is one of the best of the early-flowering shrubs. The numerous, small, yellow flowers appear before the leaves. On close examination the individual flowers do

not amount to much, but from a distance the whole plant looks as if it had a yellow cloth hung over it. Since these flower buds are present all winter, this is one of the easiest of all shrubs to force into bloom in the house in the winter. Then too, the fruits are like elongated red cherries and are edible, and the foliage turns reddish in the fall. In every way it is a valuable, vigorous-growing shrub, of ornamental interest every season of the year. It grows into a dense bush that makes a fine screen or windbreak and small plants have been sheared into hedges. There is a yellow fruiting form, **'Flava'**, as well as a variety called **'Aureo-elegantissima'** which has variegated leaves with creamy white and tinged red.

nuttallii   75′   Zone 7   Pacific Dogwood
Native from British Columbia to southern Calif., this is one of the most beautiful flowering trees native to North America. Unfortunately it will not grow on the East Coast, but in the moist atmosphere (and milder climate) of the Pacific Northwest, it is perfect. Blooming in April, it frequently blooms a second time in Aug. and Sept. The bracts are white, 4–6 in number measuring 4–5 in. from tip to tip, and then, may fade to a rose-pink color that is most attractive. The fruits are bright red-to-orange berries in the summer and fall. The habit is pyramidal, often with horizontal branching, and the autumn color is a rich scarlet to yellow. The var. **'Eddiei'** has leaves variegated an attractive green and gold in a spotted or mottled manner. **'Pilgrim'** is a clone selected for its sturdy growth.

racemosa   15′   Zone 4   Gray Dogwood
Frequently misnamed *C. paniculata*, this shrubby dogwood is a popular plant in the eastern U.S. where it is native. The numerous, small, white flower-clusters, about 1½–2½ in. in dia., appear in mid-June and are followed in the summer by small white berries on red fruit stalks that are quickly eaten by the birds. It withstands shearing; the autumn foliage turns purplish and frequently serves as a good barrier plant because of its very dense growth. It can be easily "renewed" by cutting it off at the base of the ground in early spring, fertilizing it well and then it will grow back more dense than ever before.

rugosa   9′   Zone 3   Roundleaf Dogwood
The leaves of this species are rounded, more so than those of most other *Cornus* species, 2½–5 in. long and about as wide, densely pubescent underneath with small flat clusters of white flowers in late May and blue berries about ¼ in. across in early fall. The leaves turn reddish in the fall. Not as good an ornamental shrub as some of the other species. Native to northeastern North America.

sanguinea   12′   Zone 4   Bloodtwig Dogwood

Native to Europe, this shrub is sometimes planted because of its dark red twigs in the winter and the reddish autumn color of the foliage. The leaves are 1½–3 in. long, the small white flowers are produced in flat clusters 1½–2 in. across and the purplish-black berries are about ¼ in. wide. Not especially outstanding when compared with other species.

sericea (*C. stolonifera*)   7′   Zone 2   Red Osier Dogwood
This dogwood is native in the eastern U.S. especially in swampy areas. The bark of the twigs is a good red so that it is colorful in the winter (although not as vivid as that of *C. alba* 'Sibirica'). The small white flowers bloom in late May, the fruits are white berries in the summer. Creeping by stolons they make ideal plants for holding the soil on the banks of streams. Varieties are: **'Flaviramea'**—with vivid yellow bark, excellent for winter display, especially if it is heavily pruned in the spring every other year or so. This is called the Yellowtwig Dogwood; **'Nitida'**—with green stems, the Greentwig Dogwood; **'Kelseyi'**—dwarf, rarely over 2 ft. high and sometimes used as a rather coarse ground cover.

sericea baileyi   9′   Zone 4   Bailey Dogwood
Native to eastern North America and similar to *C. stolonifera* which is the more popular shrub. It is not stoloniferous, being better suited for light sandy soils, and differs also from *C. stolonifera* in that the leaves, which are 2–5 in. long, are woolly underneath. The fruits are white.

COROKIA (ko-RO-kia)
cotoneaster   10′   Zone 9   Cotoneaster Corokia
An evergreen shrub from New Zealand with alternate entire leaves 1 in. long and white tomentose beneath; small, yellow clustered flowers and red drupaceous fruits. Used in ornamental plantings in southern Calif. It belongs to the Dogwood Family.

COROLLA. The inner series of floral envelopes consisting of the petals.

CORONA. Often thought of as a crown; part of the flower extending between the corolla and stamens, or that stands on the corolla, like the cup of a daffodil.

CORONILLA (ko-ro-NILL-a)
varia   2′   Zone 3   Crown Vetch
Although native to Europe, this has become widely naturalized in the northeastern U.S. and can become a vicious weed in any garden. The alternate, compound leaves are composed of 11–25 leaflets. The pinkish-white flowers are like those of peas (it belongs to the Legume Family). Recently, a var. named **'Penngift'** has been offered, having white and pink flowers that first appear in June and continue until frost. It

tolerates shade but thrives in full sun. Easily propagated by division of roots. Crown Vetch increases rapidly by sending out underground stems in all directions and also the shoots may root where they touch moist soil. It is excellent for planting on steep, rocky banks and growing at will, but should not be planted in a well-kept garden, for even though the above-ground shoots may be pulled up where they are not wanted, roots will be broken off and remain in the soil and continue to act as invading weeds for years. It is also a fine plant for preventing soil erosion on banks.

Propagation

Seed may be processed as soon as ripe or stored in dry airtight containers in a cool place for up to a year and then sown. Soak seed in hot water (190° F.) overnight before sowing. Softwood or hardwood cuttings prove satisfactory. Most easily propagated by simple division of their roots. See CUTTINGS.

CORREA (ko-REE-a)

   reflexa   2′–3′   Zone 9
An Australian shrub with opposite leaves about 1 in. long, whitish beneath, and tubular, scarlet flowers about 1 in. long. The rusty hairy branches are compact and it is finding much use in Calif. gardens.

   speciosa = *Correa reflexa*

CORROSIVE SUBLIMATE. A fungicide, which see.

CORTADERIA (kor-ta-DEER-ia)

   selloana   8′–20′   Zone 8   perennial   Pampas Grass
Native to the southern part of South America, this makes a magnificent clump when grown within its hardiness limits. Male and female flower heads are on different plants, and it is the female or seed-producing clumps that are valued for their graceful, fruiting plumes, hence the plant is best reproduced by division of the proper sex. The silvery fruiting heads are 1–3 ft. long. An excellent, though often tall-growing, ornamental grass. Can be easily propagated by division.

CORYDALIS (ko-RY-dal-is). A group of annual, biennial and perennial herbs, closely related to *Dicentra* and belonging to the Fumitory Family. The best species is *Corydalis lutea* which should be grown much more than it is for it flowers from late May through Aug. All species grow best in the shade. Propagation is by seeds sown as soon as ripe in the summer and division in the fall for the perennial kinds.

   aurea   6″   annual   Golden Corydalis
Bright green leaves and clear yellow flowers distinguish this species. It prefers rocky or sandy limestone soil and may be found from Quebec and Manitoba to Pa. and west to Minn.

It blooms throughout the summer.

   bulbosa   8″   Zone 6?
Closely growing tufts of fernlike foliage rise from bulblike tubers. The clusters of rosy-lavender flowers, 10–20 in an erect raceme, bloom in the spring. The plant is easy to grow in gardens with good, well-drained soil in sun or partial shade. Native to Europe.

   cheilanthifolia   1′   Zone 5   Fernleaved Corydalis
A perennial with yellow flowers about ½ in. long blooming in May and June. The finely divided leaves about 8 in. long are fernlike. Native to China.

   flavula   18″   Zone 5   Yellow Fumewort
Yellow flowers with crested petals characterize this species which occurs from Conn. to the plains states. It flowers in early spring.

   halleri = *C. bulbosa*

   lutea   8″   Zone 5   Yellow Corydalis
Sometimes annual, sometimes perennial, this species is the best of this genus for ornamental planting. The yellow flowers, somewhat similar to those of *Dicentra*, bloom from late May through Aug. and are effective in miniature arrangements. The fernlike foliage remains intact for most of the season and is most ornamental. A good plant for heavy shade, in the rock garden or in the front of borders. This should only be moved in spring. Native to southern Europe.

   micrantha   18″   Zone 5   Slender Fumewort
Less desirable as a garden plant because of its tiny flowers, this species prefers well-drained soil. It is native to the southeastern and central states.

   nobilis   10″   Zones 2–3   Siberian Corydalis
A tuberous-rooted perennial with fernlike foliage slightly taller than *C. bulbosa*. The flowers are cream colored, edged with purple, and are borne in a 10–20 flowered tight raceme, appearing in May. Native to Siberia.

   sempervirens   2′   annual   Corydalis
With red and yellow flowers ½ in. long, borne in loose clusters during late spring, this is sometimes a biennial, with many branches. Native from Nova Scotia to Alaska and Ga. Not a very good garden ornamental. Animals have been known to be poisoned from eating the foliage.

CORYLOPSIS (ko-ry-LOP-sis). Deciduous, alternate-leaved shrubs from northeastern Asia, closely related to the witch-hazels, these bloom very early in the spring before the leaves appear; in fact, so early that their blossoms are frequently killed by late frosts, if the flower buds have not already been killed by very cold winter temperatures. The small, fragrant, yellow flowers are borne on pendulous racemes an inch or so long, depending on the species. The fruit is a woody capsule.

Propagation

The seed is doubly dormant. It may be stored dry in airtight containers in a cool place for up to a year, or processed as soon as ripe. In either event, it should be stratified at warm room temperatures for 5 months, then given cold (40° F.) for 3 months, then sown. Grafting can be done, using as understock seedlings of either *Corylopsis* or *Hamamelis*. Softwood cuttings can be rooted. See STRATIFICATION, GRAFTING, CUTTINGS.

glabrescens 18′ **Zone 5** **Fragrant Winter-hazel**
The early spring blooming *Corylopsis* species sometimes bloom so early that their small racemes of delicate yellow blossoms are killed by late frosts. Since their flowers are their only ornamental asset, they should be planted in front of evergreens where these flowers will be displayed to best advantage. This species is native to Japan and grows into a neat, rounded or flat-topped shrub. Other species are occasionally planted, but this is the hardiest.

griffithii 10′ **Zone 7** **Griffith Winter-hazel**
Coming from the Himalayas, this Winter-hazel is more ornamental, with slightly larger flower racemes, but it is not so hardy as *C. glabrescens*.

pauciflora 6′ **Zone 6** **Buttercup Winter-hazel**
A spreading shrub, native to Japan, with small yellow flowers in only 2–3-flowered racemes; hence it is not so ornamental as some of the other species with larger flower clusters.

sinensis 15′ **Zones 5–6** **Chinese Winter-hazel**
Taller than *C. spicata* with leaves 2½–5 in. long and with drooping racemes of small yellow flowers, 12–18 per raceme, about 2 in. long, appearing in March or early April.

spicata 6′ **Zones 5–6** **Spike Winter-hazel**
This is probably the species most often seen in gardens at present, valued, like the other species, because it is one of the first shrubs to bloom in spring (March), along with the *Hamamelis* species. The leaves are 3–4 in. long; 6–12 of the yellow flowers are produced in a drooping spike. None of the *Corylopsis* species can be depended upon each year for a display of bloom because of late frosts that kill the blossoms or very cold winters that may kill the flower buds.

CORYLUS (KO-ry-lus). See NUTS AND NUT CULTURE, HAZELNUTS, FILBERTS. Alternate-leaved, deciduous shrubs or trees chiefly grown for their nuts. Male flowers are in pendulous catkins, but both male and female flowers are on the same tree. It is usually best to have several clones growing together to have plenty of opportunity for cross-pollination. Most species sucker readily. An easy method of propagation is simply to remove these rooted suckers.

Propagation

Seed might well be processed when they are fully ripened. *C. avellana* has no dormancy and can be sown at once, protected from rodents. Seed of other species might be stratified at 40° F. for 3 months and then sown. Grafting (on *C. avellana* as understock) is a usual practice. Many plants can be layered. Softwood cuttings of some can be rooted. See GRAFTING, LAYERING, CUTTINGS, STRATIFICATION.

Insect Pests

The black filbert aphid when abundant covers the leaves and nuts with honeydew and sooty mold. Spray with insecticide #15 or #13. Hazel bud mite, which cripples the terminal bud, is best combated with dormant insecticide #44, but early summer applications of insecticide #15 or #13 are helpful. Hazelnut weevil is closely related to the Chestnut weevil. See CASTANEA. Filbert worm hatches from eggs laid on the young nuts in early summer. It also infests acorns. Timely sprays with insecticide #9 or #47 will control it.

americana 9′ **Zone 4** **American Filbert**
Of little ornamental or economic value, but widely native from Canada to Fla. Alternate leaves 2–5 in. long and small, rounded nuts (½ in. wide), 2–4 in a cluster. The European *C. avellana* has better and larger fruit.

avellana 15′ **Zone 3** **European Hazel**
There are many large-fruited varieties of this species much cultivated for their nuts, especially in Ore. and parts of Wash. As ornamentals they have little to offer in foliage, flower or fruit.

Corylus avellana 'Contorta'

However, three varieties have very definitely become popular in ornamental planting. These are: **'Aurea'**—with yellow leaves; **'Contorta'**—twigs definitely curled and twisted, making a striking specimen; **'Pendula'**—with pendulous branches, especially conspicuous if grafted high on understock.

colurna 75′ Zone 4 Turkish Filbert
This well-shaped ornamental tree from southeastern Europe and western Asia is of interest because of its good form and good foliage. Regularly pyramidal in outline, the leaves are alternate, 2½–6 in. long, and densely borne. The male catkins, 2–3 in. long, appear in the very early spring before the leaves, and the fruits are nuts, borne, as with all hazelnuts, in a green husk. Because of the flowers, it makes an interesting early spring display. It is excellent for growing in fairly dry situations.

cornuta 6′ Zone 4 Beaked Filbert
This is not an ornamental shrub, but is widely native from Quebec and Saskatchewan to Ga. and Mo. The nuts are only about ½ in. wide and the shrub has nothing to commend its use in the garden.

maxima 'Purpurea' 15′–30′ Zone 4 Purple Filbert
Native of southeast Europe and western Asia, the purple-leaved form should be grown in the full sun if it is desired to have the rich dark purple foliage appear at its best. Other than an occasional spraying for leaf-eating insects, this plant needs little attention, but is of course only of interest for its colored foliage. The species, *C. maxima*, is of little value in the garden.

CORYMB. A flat-topped or convex flowering-cluster with the outer flowers opening first. See also CYME.

CORYNOCARPUS (ko-ry-no-KARP-us)
laevigata 30′–40′ Zone 10 New Zealand-laurel
Native to New Zealand, this is a small evergreen tree related to the hollies with showy, orange-colored, plumlike fruits 1–1½ in. long. The alternate, leathery leaves are 8 in. long, somewhat similar to those of *Magnolia grandiflora*. It is an attractive tree, valued for its good foliage.

CORYPHANTHA (ko-ry-FAN-tha)
missouriensis (*Neobesseya missouriensis*) 1′–2′
Zone 3 Missouri Cactus
A ball-like cactus growing in small tufts and native to the U.S. Plains states. It requires a well-drained, sandy soil in full sun. Small yellow flowers about an inch wide cluster at the top of the plant in summer. Propagated by seed.

vivipara 4″ Zone 3
A small, spiny, ball-like cactus growing from the northern Rocky Mts. to Mexico. The plant increases slowly into an irregular pyramid of prickly balls. Showy purple flowers 2 in. long bloom in early summer, followed by bright red fruits that may remain on the plant all winter. Sometimes known as *Mammillaria vivipara*.

CORYTHOLOMA = *Sinningia*

COSMOS (KOS-mos). Fifty years ago this was a prized garden plant, but its popularity seems to have waned. It is a member of the Composite Family, with conspicuously colored daisylike flowers borne in heads and it is closely allied to the Dahlia. The plants are mostly Mexican, with opposite leaves divided into very fine threadlike segments. If the proper varieties are selected, flowers can be in bloom in the garden from July to frost, the colors being white, pink, red to crimson, most varieties taking two months to come into flowers from the time seed is sown. Hence if sown indoors in April plants should be ready to bloom by July. Because of their height, they are best placed at the rear of the flower border. The soil selected should not be too good or else the plants will go to top growth and produce few flowers.

Insect Pests

Occasional infestations of plant bugs (see CELERY), red spider mite (see MITES) and aphids damage Cosmos.

Diseases

Stem canker and bacterial wilt are checked by careful disposal of plant refuse and soil sterilization.

bipinnatus 10′ annual Common Cosmos
It is to this species that most of our modern varieties belong, with flower heads 3 in. across and yellow centers. Both single and double-flowered forms are available in white, pink and red colors.

sulphureus 7′ annual Yellow Cosmos
The ray-flowers of the flower heads of this species are golden yellow, the heads being up to 3 in. across. The leaves are nearly a foot long, and deeply cut 2–3 times. Cultivation as above.

COSTMARY = *Chrysanthemum balsamita*

COSTUS (KOS-tus)
speciosus 10′ Zone 10 Crepe or Malay-ginger
A plant from the East Indies frequently seen in the gardens of Hawaii. Leaves 8 in. long and 2½ in. wide. Flowers white, shaped like large petunias with yellow centers borne in spikes 5 in. long. The flower bracts are red so that while still in bud the flower stalk is all red, suggesting a small pineapple effect. The leaves are arranged spirally on the stem.

COTINUS (ko-TY-nus)
coggygria 15′ Zone 5 Smoketree

The old-fashioned Smoketree is recognized by everyone when its pinkish-to-grayish, fruiting panicles are conspicuous in the summer. Although native from southern Europe to central China, it has been widely planted in America. There are conspicuously purple-colored fruiting forms like 'Purpureus', 'Daydream' or 'Royal Red' and it is these fine fruiting forms which might well be planted rather than seedlings, some of which may be entirely male plants, thus lacking the desirable fruiting panicles. The "smoky" effect of fruiting plants remain effective for weeks. One point to remember is that young plants need considerable attention, especially water, during the first few years or they will fail badly. After they are well established they need no attention whatsoever.

Propagation

The seed has double dormancy, hence should be stratified for 3 months at warm temperatures, then 3 months at 40° F., then sown. Layers can be rooted and softwood cuttings as well but with difficulty. See STRATIFICATION, LAYERS, CUTTINGS

obovatus (*C. americanus*)   **30′**   **Zone 5**
American Smoketree
Rarely seen in American gardens, this is a native tree of the southeastern U.S. During the past 150 years, many of the large trees that did exist were cut down for the orange-colored dye that the wood yields. Because of its size it is considered too large a substitute for its European counterpart, *C. coggygria*, and the female trees do not have as many fruits as does the European species. The alternate leaves are 2½–5 in. long and turn a gorgeous yellow to orange and red autumn color. It has few pests. The habit is definitely upright with many trunks from the base. Native from Tenn. to Ala.

COTONEASTER (ko-to-nee-AS-ter). The cotoneasters are all alternate-leaved shrubs, some prostrate and but a few inches high (*C. adpressa* which in 50 years growth makes a plant only 12 in. high by 48 in. across), others tall, vigorous shrubs that may grow to 18 ft. or more in height. Most species will come true from seed even though collected from collections in which many species grow together.

They are, as a group, natives of northern Asia, the Himalayan area and a few of Europe. Flowers in general are small and white, in some species borne singly or in 2's and 3's, and in others in flat clusters 1 or 2 in. in dia. There are a few species like *C. multiflora* that make a show when they are in bloom, but mostly these plants are valued for their red and black fruits. They vary in size, most are about ¼ in. in dia. and are borne like the flowers, singly or in 2's or 3's in some species, and in bunches of 8–10 or more

in others. In England many cotoneasters are highly esteemed and there are several which thrive in plantings along the highways, but unfortunately in America they can have several troublesome pests which may prove difficult to combat. Being closely related to apples, pears and hawthorns, they are susceptible to fire blight (see PEAR), borers, lace bug and frequently red spiders. In some areas none of these pests may be prominent, but in others one or more of them may be so bad as to limit the number of cotoneasters planted.

Sometimes the fire blight can be controlled. The old-fashioned method used to be to spray with lime sulfur, but now there are some of the antibiotics available which show promise of control on apple trees and so may work on cotoneasters as well. In any event, the cotoneasters as a group are used for their ornamental fruits, for their interesting forms or habits of growth and some for their evergreen foliage.

There are many of the cotoneasters with black fruits. These, with one or two exceptions are not easily seen in the fall when the foliage is still present. Hence, most black-fruited cotoneasters have little ornamental merit. They may be vigorous growers and some may make fine shrubs, but since all cotoneasters are subject to possible infestations of the disease or insect pests mentioned, it does not seem wise to grow some of the deciduous (and black-fruited) forms, when other kinds of shrubs not susceptible to disease and insect attack will do just as well, i.e., viburnums, forsythias and honeysuckles.

Propagation

Seeds can be processed as soon as ripe or stored dry in airtight containers in a cool place for up to a year and then processed. Many of the species of this genus produce seeds that take 2 years to germinate. In general, dormancies of these may be overcome by periods of stratification at room temperatures (3–5 months) followed by a period of cold (3 months). An alternate method is to treat the seeds with concentrated sulfuric acid for 2 hrs. then stratify at 40° F. for 3 months.

Grafting has been practiced with *C. bullata*, *acutifolia* and *dielsiana* used as the understocks. When standards are to be produced, that is a shrubby growth of cotoneaster on the top of a 3–6-ft. trunk, the understock is either *Sorbus* or *Crataegus*.

Softwood cuttings of many species root satisfactorily and hardwood cuttings of some species. See STRATIFICATION, GRAFTING, CUTTINGS.

acutifolius   **12′**   **Zone 4**   **Peking Cotoneaster**

Not a good ornamental, this might well be over-looked in preference to some of the red-fruited cotoneasters. Native to China, leaves pointed, 1–2½ in. long, fruit black, ⅓ in. across.

adpressus prostrate habit Zone 4 Creeping Cotoneaster

One of the slowest growing of the dwarf cotoneasters, this is nevertheless a fine plant, especially in the rock garden, with small pinkish flowers in June, red fruits ⅜ in. dia. in the early fall and deciduous foliage.

The var. **praecox** is faster in growth. '**Little Gem**'—a dwarf var. originating in a Dutch nursery about 1930, 10-year-old plants being only 6 in. high and 12–15 in. across, but seldom bearing flowers and fruits; '**Park Carpet**'—another excellent ground cover bearing masses of bright red fruits.

apiculatus 3′ Zone 4 Cranberry Cotoneaster

Similar to *C. horizontalis*, but the fruit is larger, up to ⅜ in. across. Like most of these plants it is a native of western China. It makes a good ground cover and in every way approaches *C. horizontalis* in habit.

bullatus floribundus 6′ Zone 5 Vilmorin Cotoneaster

Better than the species as an ornamental because there are more fruits in each cluster. These rounded clusters of globular scarlet berries are outstanding. In the fall it will distinguish itself in any planting.

congestus 3′ Zone 6 Pyrenees Cotoneaster

A small, very dense cotoneaster resembling *C. microphyllus* in many respects with short stubby branches which mould it into a low mound. It has small pinkish flowers in June and bright red fruits about ¼ in. wide. The leaves are evergreen, less than ½ in. long and it is native in the Himalayas.

conspicuus 3′ Zone 6 Wintergreen Cotoneaster

An evergreen cotoneaster from western China with scarlet fruits ⅓ in. wide, especially valued for its prostrate variety **decorus**, sometimes called the **Necklace Cotoneaster**, which is especially desirable as a bank plant.

dammeri 1′ Zone 5 Bearberry Cotoneaster

One of the best as a ground cover for in moist soil it frequently roots along its stems. Evergreen leaves 1 in. long, bright, red fruits and native in central China. '**Skogsholmen**'—a Swedish selection about 1957, making an excellent ground cover less than a foot high but with trailing branches over 3 feet long. The leaves are glossy green and the fruits are red.

dielsianus 6′ Zone 5 Diel's Cotoneaster

A popular cotoneaster with gracefully arching branches, red fruits about the size of a pea borne in clusters of 3–7, reddish autumn color, native of China and one of the easiest to grow.

divaricatus 6′ Zone 5 Spreading Cotoneaster

Another popularly grown shrub, also with arching branches and thick red berries with the foliage turning a dull red in the fall. The leaves are ¾ in. long and deciduous. It is perhaps more dense-growing than *C. dielsiana* and more upright in habit.

foveolatus 9′ Zone 4 Glossy Cotoneaster

A black-fruited shrub, only suggested here because it has thick, glossy, deciduous leaves 1–3½ in. long and a bright scarlet-to-orange autumn color. It was introduced from central China in 1907.

franchetii 10′ Zone 6 Franchet Cotoneaster

Cotoneaster horizontalis can be espaliered, as it is here, against a white cement block wall.

With orange-red berries, half-evergreen leaves 1½ in. long and autumn color a reddish green. Western China.

frigidus   18′   Zone 7   Himalayan Cotoneaster
This species has been grown in England for over 100 years and still is most popular because it is one of the most vigorous of all cotoneasters and bears its bright red fruits in conspicuous clusters. The leaves are 3–6 in. long. It grows well on the Pacific Coast where it is the tallest growing of all the cotoneasters.

glaucophyllus   10′   Zone 7   Brightbead Cotoneaster
This evergreen from western China is one of the best evergreen cotoneasters, with small red berries ⅓ in. in dia. that color late in the season and consequently remain on the plant until Christmas.

henryanus   12′   Zone 7   Henry Cotoneaster
Half-evergreen leaves 2–5 in. long, dark crimson berries effective in Oct., this plant from China is popular on the Pacific Coast especially because of its gracefully arching branches.

horizontalis   3′   Zone 4   Rock Spray
The most popular of all these Chinese plants, the Rock Spray is valued particularly for its flat habit of growth and horizontal branching habit, with the bright red berries and semi-evergreen leaves ½ in. displayed on the upper side. It is used as a specimen, as an excellent ground cover and makes a unique show when espaliered against a wall. The form **'Variegata'**, with leaves edged white, is an interesting plant for the rockery. No other cotoneaster is used as much as this one.

lucidus   9′   Zone 4   Hedge Cotoneaster

Most black-fruiting cotoneasters are not nearly as ornamental as the red-fruiting ones, but the Hedge Cotoneaster has lustrous leaves about 2 in. long and very dense growth. It has been used in hedge-making, but it should be remembered that all cotoneasters are susceptible to attacks from red spider and from fireblight, and a hedge is the ideal place for both these pests to take a quick and firm hold under the right conditions.

microphyllus   3′   Zone 5   Small-leaved Cotoneaster
The small (⅓ in.), lustrous, evergreen leaves of this Himalayan plant, as well as its scarlet berries in the fall that are ¼ in wide, make it an excellent specimen when planted in the front of some border where it can be closely observed. A single plant, although only a foot or so high, may grow into a tangled mass of twigs and foliage 15 ft. across. It makes a splendid ornamental. The variety **'Cochleatus'**—with prostrate habit, an excellent form; **thymifolia**—with the smallest leaves of any cotoneaster (⅛–⅜ in. long) hardy in the North and making an excellent specimen in the rock garden.

multiflorus   6′   Zone 5
This is one of the best of the cotoneasters especially in flower. White flowers are produced in clusters of 3–12 white flowers, each flower about ½ in. across, in May. The fruits are about ¼ in. across and red; leaves thin, ¾–2½ in. long. The habit is graceful, with arching branches. Few of the cotoneasters make a display in flower, but this one does. Native to China. The variety **calocarpus**, 8 ft., Zone 5, is a wide-spreading shrub from China, deciduous, but

Cotoneaster microphyllus: One of the very best shrubs for planting on top of a wall or rock. (*Photo by Arnold Arboretum, Jamaica Plain, Mass.*)

making a fine landscape specimen because of its profuse small white flowers in mid-May, and its light red-to-pink berries (⅜ in. dia.) in the fall. In fact, it is one of the few cotoneasters of interest both because of its flowers and its fruits, but it needs plenty of room.

pannosus   6′   Zone 7   Silverleaf Cotoneaster
Half-evergreen leaves 1 in. long, white-woolly underneath, dull red berries and used a great deal in Calif. The variety 'Nana' is dwarf.

racemiflorus soongoricus   8′   Zone 3   Sungari Rockspray
Berries pink, ⅓ in. in diameter, one of the favorites of E. H. Wilson who introduced it to America in 1910. Deciduous, with grayish-green leaves up to 1¼ in. long, it must have plenty of room in which to develop properly.

rotundifolius   10′   Zone 6   Redbox Cotoneaster
A semi-evergreen but sometimes deciduous cotoneaster with lustrous, dark green, rounded leaves ½–¾ in. long. This is often admired because of its large red fruits that are nearly ½ in. across, among the largest of all cotoneasters, and they remain on the plant well into the winter. The variety **lanata** is supposed to have 3–8 fruits per cluster while the species only has 1–3.

salicifolius floccosus   15′   Zone 6
The hardiest of this species and most popular in the mid-South because of its lanceolate, semi-evergreen to evergreen leaves 3 in. long, its profuse clusters of small red berries in the late fall, its purplish-red autumn color and gracefully arching habit.

simonsii   10′–12′   Zone 5   Simon's Cotoneaster
An upright shrub, sometimes evergreen, with scarlet berries in October. The leaves are 1¼ in. long.

x watereri 'Herbstfeuer'. A good hybrid forming large carpets of foliage and rooting readily. The fruit is red and the plant has the general habit of *C. dammeri* but is more vigorous. It originated in Germany about 1930.

zabelii   6′   Zone 4   Cherryberry Cotoneaster
With slightly larger fruits (⅓ in.) and more per cluster (8) than *C. dielsiana*, this is one of the few cotoneasters with yellow autumn color. There is a rare variety **miniata** with fruits that are orange-scarlet, but it is difficult to obtain commercially.

COTTON. See GOSSYPIUM.

COTTONSEED MEAL. A by-product from the cotton mills of the South, often used as a fertilizer. It contains 6–9% nitrogen; 2–3% phosphoric acid; 1.5–2% potash, all slowly available in the soil. It leaves an acid reaction in the soil.

COTTON-THISTLE. See ONOPORDUM.

COTTONWOOD, FREMONT = *Populus fremontii*

COTULA (KO-tew-la)
squalida   4″   Zone 8   New Zealand Brass-buttons
A perennial from New Zealand, used as a ground cover in Calif., for the soft, hairy branches creep a foot or more along the surface of the soil. The alternate leaves are narrow, 2 in. long and fernlike. The yellow flower heads are hardly ¼ in. across and are unisexual.

COTYLEDON. The primary leaf or leaves in the embryo.

COTYLEDON (cot-y-LEE-don)
undulata   3′   Zone 9   Silver-crown
A South African succulent perennial with wedge-shaped, opposite leaves 2 in. wide, crimped at the edges and with silvery-gray hairs, almost white at the edges. The flowers are bright orange to red about an inch long. Sometimes used as a ground cover in southern Calif. and almost shrubby.

COUROUPITA (cor-o-PITT-a)
guianensis   50′   Zone 10   Cannon-ball-tree
The fragrant orange blossoms of this interesting tree are borne in clusters 2–3 ft. long, originating directly in the trunk of the tree. Each blossom has 6 rounded petals with a yellow center of stamens, the other stamens being in a peculiar curved column almost like a petal. The bloom is most profuse in the fall but continues intermittently throughout the year. The fruits are round, hard-shelled balls 6–8 in. across and the shell is sometimes used for utensils. The evergreen leaves are simple and about 12 in. long. Native to Guiana.

COVENTRY-BELLS = *Campanula trachelium*

COVER CROP. A quick-growing crop like Rye, Buckwheat, Cow Peas, Vetch., which is planted primarily to keep the soil covered for a short period, then to be plowed under as a "green manure," is called a cover crop. See SOILS and FERTILIZERS.

COW-LILY. See NUPHAR.

COW-PARSNIP. See HERACLEUM.

COW-PEA, COMMON = *Vigna unguiculata*

COW'S-HORN = *Euphorbia grandicornis*

COWSLIP. See CALTHA.

COYOTEBUSH, DWARF = *Baccharis pilularis*

CRAB APPLE. See MALUS.

CRAB GRASS. See DIGITARIA.

CRAMBE (KRAM-be)
maritima   3′   Zone 6?   Sea-kale
A perennial herb, belonging to the Mustard

Family, sometimes grown for ornament because of its fleshy, glaucous-blue foliage, with radical leaves 2 ft. long and often as broad. Flowers are white in panicles and fruits are two-pointed pods, each pod with 1 seed. Native to seacoasts of western Europe and Asia Minor. Propagated by seed.

CRANBERRY. The Cranberry of commerce (*Vaccinium macrocarpon*) is a small evergreen plant native to eastern and northeastern North America, creeping over the ground with rooting runners about 3 ft. long and bearing upright branches about 6 in. tall on which the fruits are borne in the fall. Cranberries are produced commercially in Mass., Wisc., N.J., Wash. and Ore. with present annual estimates for the states in the above order of 573,000 barrels, 400,000 barrels, 159,000 barrels, 66,000 barrels, and 139,000 barrels, for a total U.S. crop of 1,337,000 barrels. A barrel of cranberries weighs about 100 lbs.

It has been estimated that 25% of the crop is sold as fresh fruit, and there is a tendency for this to show a slow but rather steady decline, year by year. About 25% of the crop is used in making cranberry juice cocktail and this market is steadily and almost rapidly increasing. The remaining 50% of the crop is sold as strained and whole-berry sauces, cranberry-orange relish and various other products. It is of interest to know that one of the large grower-owned Massachusetts cooperative-selling organizations handled 85% of the U.S. crop in 1964 with gross sales of $45,000,000.

This huge industry is centered on the small farms on and near Cape Cod. It is here that soil and water conditions, combined with just the right climate, are ideal for cranberry production. The home gardener does not customarily make his own cranberry bog so a quick description here of the methods used for producing cranberries commercially will be sufficient.

The cranberry planting must be in a bog or similar area where there is plenty of acid water, and arrangements must be made so that the bog can be flooded with this water at any time. This usually means there must be facilities for storing large amounts of water at a higher level than the bog or that there is a stream with ample water of the right kind and it can be pumped to flood the bog. Flooding is necessary for the good growth of the plants, to aid in insect control, and to aid in frost protection as well as to keep the plants from being injured by winter cold. The soil must be acid, preferably of a pH of 4.5–5.0. If one looks around carefully near a cranberry bog one will find growing naturally on cranberry soils such plants as *Kalmia angustifolia*, *Chamaedaphne calyculata*, *Acer rubrum*, *Chamaecyparis thyoides*, Sphagnum

Moss and wild cranberries themselves.

Since accurate flooding of the bog is essential, it should be on flat land, with all the miscellaneous weed plants removed. It is also necessary to have facilities for draining the bog rather promptly, for if it is flooded when the plants are growing, the water should not be allowed to remain on the plants for more than 24 hours. This then necessitates a series of drains and ditches and a low spot where the water can run off at the proper time.

In preparing the soil, the final operation is to apply 3–4 in. of sand over the entire bog area, for it is in this that the new cuttings are stuck. The sand acts as a mulch and reduces water loss from the soil, aids in restraining weed growth and in the early spring and fall when danger from frost is imminent, it gives off some heat at night and so aids somewhat in frost protection. It should have a pH of 4.5.

Cuttings are taken just before growth starts in the spring. In order to do this a well-grown stand is mowed or cut with a scythe and the clippings stuck in the soil at 10-in. intervals each way, usually 2–3 per hill. Some growers merely broadcast the clippings and disc them in but this takes a great deal more cuttings than is normally necessary. Setting out cuttings is done in late April, May or June but usually May is best.

After planting, the bog is flooded for a day or two so that the water will firm the cuttings in place, then drained and of course weeded for the remainder of the summer. Normally the planting will bear its first crop the 4th year. After picking, the longest upright branches are cut back and a covering of sand about ⅔ in. deep is placed over the field to aid in the roots becoming well established. Then the bog is flooded to just above the tops of the plants for the winter. Flooding is usually done in Mass., about Dec. 1 or whenever the sand remains frozen all day, and the bog is drained in May.

Flooding the bog is sometimes necessary in late spring after growth has started to prevent the young buds from being killed by late frosts. Usually a partial flooding only is necessary, for the water will give off a certain amount of heat at night. It is obvious to see then why quick flooding and draining are necessary. Flooding is sometimes used as a means of controlling insect pests and in the early fall is also needed to protect a crop from freezing. Picking usually starts in Mass., on Labor Day and continues until around Oct. 20.

The bog is resanded at intervals every 3–4 yrs., applying anywhere from ¼–1 in. of sand depending on circumstances.

The chief varieties used in Mass. are 'Early

Black' and **'Howes'**. 'Howes' has a higher pectin content and so is used in canning. It is these two varieties that make up 93% of the acreage in Mass. **'McFarlin'** is the chief variety on the Pacific Coast, and in Wisc. **'McFarlin', 'Bennett'** and **'Searl'** are the most important. Of course, there are other varieties being introduced and tried, but these are the ones most used at present. It is also important that only one variety be planted to a bog where flooding is done all at one time, for varietal differences in growth, ripening periods and disease resistance are such that more than this is impractical.

Picking the berries is usually done with scoops by hand or sometimes by machine. The berries are collected in boxes and taken to the canneries where the chaff is blown out and the good berries sorted from the bad. At present, most of the "fresh" crop is sold and used by Christmas. The business is one that has been growing in recent years, since more and more uses for cranberries and their products are being strenuously advertised by the large growers' cooperatives.

Cranberry growing is a commercial operation requiring specific equipment and expert knowledge and not a home garden activity.

Insect Pests

Cranberry fruit worm which eats the berries and black-headed or other fire worms which kill leaves and flowers are among the most destructive. Span worms and gypsy moth which eat the leaves and girdler which destroys the stems are locally important. Blunt-nosed leaf hopper, the vector of false blossom disease must be controlled. Flooding and intensive use of insecticides are the recognized control treatments.

Diseases

False blossom disease is most destructive in many areas. Several berry rots are potentially destructive pests.

CRANBERRY-BUSH. See VIBURNUM.

CRANBERRY, MOUNTAIN = Vaccinium vitis-idaea minus

CRANESBILL, ENDRESS = *Geranium endressii*

CRANESBILL FAMILY = Geraniaceae

CRAPE-MYRTLE. See LAGERSTROEMIA.

CRASSULA (KRASS-ew-la). This large genus of succulents contains as many as 300 species, mostly from South Africa. The fleshy leaves are opposite, but are sometimes produced in basal rosettes, with many different forms. Propagation is by seed, cuttings and leaf cuttings. They are used as house plants, in dish gardens and in rock gardens, one species, *C. argentea*, being a particularly valued house plant which can

withstand much abuse. For culture see CACTI AND SUCCULENTS.

arborescens   2'–10'   **Zone 9**   **Silver-dollar**
With fleshy, rounded, gray-green leaves about 2½ in. long, narrowed at the base and having a red margin and fine red dots all over the surface. The flowers are white, later turning red, and are produced in terminal panicles, but are rarely seen on cultivated plants. Native to South Africa.

argentea   10'   **Zone 10**   **Jadeplant**
A freely branching forked succulent with thick, rubbery leaves, the upper surface rounded, the lower surface a glossy jade green turning reddish in the sun and edged with red. Flowers pinkish white, but not outstanding. In watering pot plants, it is best to keep them on the dry side. Widely grown as a house plant, some of the most interesting being trained to a single stem.

falcata   2'   **Zone 10**   **Scarlet Paintbrush**
Sickle-shaped leaves 3–4 in. long and gray. Flowers are scarlet, small, produced in close, flat clusters, and from which it gets its common name.

lactea   1'   **Zone 9**   **Flowering Crassula**
This is an especially compact, shrubby herb with green, succulent, connate leaves about 3 in. long and pretty white flowers. Native to South Africa.

lycopodioides prostrate Zone 10   Club-moss
Crassula
Extremely small, scalelike leaves, profusely borne in 4 ranks, mask the stem of this plant native to South Africa.

perforata   2'   **Zone 9**   **Thorowort Crassula**
The leaves, an inch long, are green dotted with red, and are joined at the base, encircling the stem. Small yellow flowers are produced in showy clusters which may sometimes be a foot long.

radicans   6"   **Zone 9**
The succulent perennial leaves of this plant will turn bright red if it is planted in the full sunshine. Though each leaf is only ½ in. long, they are densely clustered, making a mound of foliage. The small flower clusters are borne on foot-long, slender stalks. Native to South Africa, the plant is sometimes used as a ground cover in southern Calif.

rupestris   1'   **Zone 9**   **Necklace Vine**
The opposite leaves are connected with each other at the base and are up to ¾ in. long. Flowers are small and pinkish in short terminal clusters. Not a true vine, but often scandent.

schmidtii   3"   **Zone 9**
A small, mat-forming, succulent perennial with triangular and pointed gray-green leaves, sending up many clusters of carmine-red flowers. Native to South Africa. Sometimes used as a ground cover in southern Calif.

tetragona 2′ **Zone 9**
The 1-in. leaves are 3-sided and are nearly joined together at the base. Flowers are white.

CRASSULACEA = The Orpine or Stonecrop Family.

CRATAEGUS (krat-EE-gus). Hawthorns are mostly small trees, with white flowers, a few varieties have pink-to-red flowers, and usually red fruits. A large number of them are natives of North America, and most of these are the ones that have conspicuously red autumn color. They are dense in habit, mostly with vicious thorns, so no one looks forward to the prospect of having to prune them; all have alternate leaves. Many botanists have studied this group, making new species and regrouping old ones, so that names have been changed during the past 50 years. Many species show strikingly similar characteristics and are difficult to tell apart one from the other.

It is of interest to note that only 28 species and varieties of this great group of trees have been thought of sufficient ornamental value to be offered for sale currently by American nurserymen issuing catalogues. Of these 28, 10 species and varieties have been listed by only one nursery, so it is clear that there are not too many hawthorns popular today.

There are many of the native species that are practically identical if their use in landscape work is considered. Unquestionably some of the local native species are just as good in their areas as those species and varieties in the following list. Here again, it is presumptuous to attempt to "cut down" the list available in this country, but it is done rather relentlessly, to bring before American gardeners a few that might be designated outstanding.

Species and varieties doing well locally in the range of their habitat are naturally among the easiest to establish. Such plants, where they are used well and serve a purpose, should not be discarded. Many of the species can be sheared and have been used in large clipped hedges. The Cockspur Thorn is one example and has been widely used for this purpose in the past. Fireblight takes its toll on many an old plant, some years more heavily than others. Juniper rust and hawthorn blight are other diseases often troublesome. Lace bug, mites, leaf miners, woolly hawthorn aphid, cottony maple scale, Lecanium scale, scurfy scale, leaf skeletonizers, tent caterpillars, western tussock moth, Japanese beetle, various borers—these are only some of those listed as troublesome to hawthorns. Then too, many are difficult to transplant, and certainly they are difficult to handle and propagate in the nursery. All these things considered, one should think several times before using hawthorns on a large scale.

Hawthorns will thrive in poor soils, they will grow almost equally well in alkaline and acid soils, they are dense in habit and often picturesque because of their wide-spreading and horizontal branches. They have colorful interest in the spring and fall, and some of them retain their fruit all winter. If the foliage goes unmarred in the summer, many species present a glossy foliage that has merit in its own right. The fruits of many of the natives have been used in making jellies and preserves. The best of all the group are: *C. crus-galli*, *C. lavallei*, *C. nitida*, *C. oxyacantha* 'Paulii', *C. phaenopyrum* and *C. succulenta*. So for those who care little for the group, these are the best 6.

Propagation

Seeds can be processed as soon as ripe or stored dry in airtight containers in a cool place for up to a year or longer and then processed. Seed is usually stratified for 3–5 months at warm temperatures followed by 3 months at 40° F. Also seed can be treated with sulfuric acid and then stratified for 3 months at 40° F. If the seed fails to germinate after being sown for 3 months then give it another 3-month cold treatment. Grafting is frequently practiced using the species as understock for the varieties. Root cuttings in spring often prove satisfactory also. See STRATIFICATION, GRAFTING, ROOT CUTTINGS.

Insect Pests

Several species of aphids including those which infest apple attack hawthorn. They suck the sap which curls leaves, distorts flowers and malforms the fruit. Insecticide #15 and #13 give control but several applications may be needed. Hawthorn lace bug mottles the leaves and reduces the vitality. The above insecticides are effective. The same scale insects, borers and leaf-eating caterpillars that infest apple are troublesome. See APPLE.

Diseases

Brown and blackened leaves on dead twigs are symptoms of fire blight. See APPLE. Hawthorn is very susceptible to rust which shows as orange-colored spots, on both leaves and fruit. It lives part of its life on Red Cedar (*Juniperus virginiana*) which should be destroyed within 500 ft. Spraying with fungicide #D is effective. Purple lesions of the leaf spot disease may be serious on English varieties and require sprays of fungicide #A or #D just before bloom.

arnoldiana 39′ **Zone 4 Arnold Hawthorn**
This is a handsome small tree with single white flowers about ¾ in. in dia. and bright crimson fruit about ¾ in. long and native to eastern

North America. The fruit ripens in the middle of Aug. while the leaves are still green and drops in early Sept. It is one of the most conspicuous for its early fruits, also being one of the earliest of the American species to flower (early May). If late-summer fruits are not desirable, then other species might be selected.

coccinioides 21′ **Zone 5 Kansas Hawthorn** A densely-branched, broad, round-topped small tree with good foliage as well as good fruits, native to the central U.S. The flowers are about $\frac{3}{4}$ in. in dia. and the dark red fruit is about the same size; the foliage turns orange to scarlet in the fall. This plant is especially desirable in the area where it is native.

crus-galli 36′ **Zone 4 Cockspur Thorn** This is one of the most popular of the native American hawthorns, and is native from Quebec to N.Car. and Kan. The flowers are $\frac{1}{2}$ in. in dia., the fruit is bright red and about $\frac{3}{8}$ in. in dia., remaining on the plant a greater part of the winter. The leaves are glossy, but the variety **'Splendens'** has leaves that are even more glossy than the species. The foliage turns a good orange to scarlet in the fall. It withstands shearing well, and has been used in making hedges, especially because of its dense twiggy growth and sturdy thorns. Its horizontal branching habit and flat top are frequently conspicuous in the landscape.

intricata 9′ **Zone 5 Thicket Hawthorn** One of the few truly shrubby hawthorns this is mentioned for this fact alone, since it is being grown by some nurserymen. It is planted to form a thorny thicket where this is desirable. Leaves 1–2$\frac{1}{2}$ in. long with 3–4 lobes; long curved thorns, white flowers and reddish-brown, globular fruits. Native from Mass. to N.Car.

laevigata (*oxyacantha*) 15′ **Zone 4 English Hawthorn** A very popular hawthorn in Great Britain and Europe where it has been grown and cherished for centuries, the several varieties may have white, pink or deep red flowers, either single or double. It is native to Europe and North Africa. The flowers, $\frac{5}{8}$ in. in dia., are profusely borne in late May, from whence it gets its name "May Tree" so popular in English literature, and are followed by scarlet fruits $\frac{1}{4}$–$\frac{5}{8}$ in. in dia. Densely round, often with branches touching the ground. The foliage does not turn color in the fall. Some of the more popular varieties are: **'Aurea'**—fruits yellow; **'Paulii'**—flowers double and bright scarlet, one of the most outstanding and conspicuous in flower of all these varieties; **'Plena'**—double white flowers; **'Punicea'**—sometimes found listed as **'Splendens'**, with dark red single flowers.

x lavallei 21′ **Zone 4 Lavalle Hawthorn** With conspicuous flowers and showy fruits this is an excellent hawthorn, having been listed for some time under the synonym of *C. carrerei.* The leaves turn a bronzy red late in the fall. The fruits are a brick red, $\frac{5}{8}$ in. in dia. and remain on the tree a greater part of the winter, the chief reason for its ornamental use. It is a hybrid of *C. crus-galli* x *pubescens.*

mollis 30′ **Zone 4 Downy Hawthorn** With red fruits about 1 in. across, this is one of the larger fruiting hawthorns, and might even be considered coarse in some situations because of this. The flowers are 1 in. in dia. and the leaves are larger than those of many other hawthorns. It is a handsome, small tree in foliage, but because of the large-size leaves and fruit it may be a bit coarse, even though the fruit usually ripens to a good red in late Aug. while the leaves are still green. It is native throughout the eastern U.S.

monogyna 30′ **Zone 4 Single Seed Hawthorn** Because of the many native American species of hawthorns available in this country, this European species is mostly valued here for its many varieties. The flowers of the species are merely single white, about $\frac{5}{8}$ in. in dia. and the fruit is red, only about $\frac{3}{8}$ in. in dia. The leaves do not turn color in the fall. The tree is densely branched, round-headed, and in England has been used in clipped hedges all over the island. Some of the outstanding varieties are: **'Biflora'**—Zone 6—**Glastonbury Thorn.** In mild winters this frequently blooms in England at Christmas time thus living out an old legend. However, our winters are so cold in America that seldom does this have an opportunity to bloom then. Since it has no other particular ornamental merit, it might only be grown in America in those areas that are sufficiently mild so that it does stand a chance of blooming in midwinter. This is only a secondary or token blooming, the main bloom being in the spring; **'Inermis'**—Zone 4—a thornless variety with dense upright branches and a globose round head like a large mushroom. This has possibilities for street-tree work, not so much because it lacks thorns, but because of this unique form; **'Stricta'**—Zone 4—a columnar form, very dense and upright in habit; the tree at the Arnold Arboretum at one time was 30 ft. tall and 8 ft. wide. Fire blight reduced the height later. This is more narrow than *C. phaenopyrum* 'Fastigiata', more dense also, but probably also more susceptible to fire blight.

nitida 30′ **Zone 4 Glossy Hawthorn** Performing extremely well from Ill. to Ark. when it is mature, this is one of the 3 or 4 best native American hawthorns, especially because of the fact that the red-to-orange fruits, ripening about the end of Oct., remain on the plant a greater part of the winter. The lustrous leaves are 2–3 in. in dia. The autumn color is an outstanding orange to red.

phaenopyrum 30′ Zone 4 Washington Hawthorn
This is the best of all the hawthorns and if only one were to be grown, this should be it. This plant has good flowers, excellent fruits, glossy foliage and a brilliant scarlet autumn color, as well as a habit of growth that is well suited to many purposes. The white flowers, appearing in mid-June, are about ½ in. in dia. and appear in many-flowered clusters. The bright scarlet fruits are only about ¼ in. in dia., but appear in large clusters and remain on the tree a greater part of the winter. The orange-to-scarlet autumn color is always meritorious, and the usually dense habit of this species makes it well suited for planting in the central strip of highways to reduce the headlight glare of automobiles. One of the last species to bloom, it is unquestionably one of the best and is native from Va. to Ala. The variety **'Fastigiata'** has all the good points of the species as well as a generally columnar habit.

pinnatifida major 18′ Zone 5 Large Chinese Hawthorn
This is one of the most handsome of the Asiatic species with the leaves often divided right down to the midrib of the blade. The fruit is somewhat pear-shaped, deep shining red in color and about 1 in. in dia. It has been established in China for a long time because the fruits are edible. It blooms and fruits reliably well every year.

pruinosa 21′ Zone 4 Frosted Hawthorn
With large white flowers and rose-colored anthers in late May, red-to-orange fruits ⅜ in. in dia., in the fall, and with bluish-green foliage, this native hawthorn (Ontario to Va. and Ill.) makes quite a display, especially when in fruit.

punctata 30′ Zone 4 Dotted Hawthorn
The dotted fruits are among the largest of any of the native American hawthorns. Usually the tree is round or flat-topped, sometimes it may grow to be twice as broad as it is high. It has a picturesque appearance because of the wide spreading horizontal branches and is native from Quebec to Ga. and Ill. The fruit is red, about 1 in. long and there is a particularly conspicuous yellow fruiting form—**'Aurea'**.

succulenta 15′ Zone 3 Fleshy Hawthorn
The hardiest of those to be mentioned in this selected list, this tree is also one of the smallest and is native from Quebec to Mass. and Ill. The bright scarlet fruits are lustrous, ripening toward the end of Oct. Professor Sargent thought very kindly of this native American and claimed that it ought to be listed among the 6 best American hawthorns.

viridis 36′ Zone 4 Green Hawthorn
With white flowers in small 2-in. clusters the end of May and bright red ¼-in. fruits in the fall and winter, this round-headed, spreading-branched tree should be chiefly valued for planting within that large area where it is native in central and southeastern U.S.

wattiana 21′ Zone 5 Watts Hawthorn
Perhaps one of the most beautiful of the yellow-fruited hawthorns, this has ½ in.-wide fruits maturing in Aug. that are a rich orange to translucent yellow. The flower clusters are 3 in. in dia., and the tree is native to central Asia.

Hybrids

'Autumn Glory' 5′ Zone 5
Another hybrid, 15–18 ft. tall, with white flowers and brilliant red fruits first coloring late in the summer, then remaining on the tree well into the winter.

'Toba' 15′ Zone 3
Actually a hybrid (*C. succulenta* x *oxyacantha* 'Paulii') introduced by the Dominion Experiment Station of Morden, Manitoba, about 1950. The flowers are double, fragrant and deep rose, the fruits are red and about ½ in. in dia., the leaves are glossy. Its chief claim to fame is probably the fact that it is more hardy than forms of *C. oxyacantha* which it resembles in general habit.

'Winter King'—introduced in 1955, this hybrid appears similar in general to *C. viridis*, and has the excellent habit of fruiting heavily while young and retaining its red fruits that are ⅜ in. across throughout the winter. The bark is silver-colored and the leaves are glossy, turning red in the autumn.

CRAZYWEED, LAMBERT = *Oxytropis lamburtii*

CREAM CUPS = *Platystemon californicus*

CREEPER. See PARTHENOCISSUS.

CREEPING CHARLIE = *Lysimachia nummularia*

CREEPING JENNY = *Lysimachia nummularia*

CREEPING LILY-TURF = *Liriope spicata*

CREEPING MINT = *Mentha requienii*

CREEPING NAVEL-SEED = *Omphalodes verna*

CRENATE. Toothed with rounded, shallow teeth.

CREOSOTE. An oily material used in the painting of posts or other pieces of wood to prevent their decay. It is highly injurious to living plant tissue, and when used to paint an arbor or lath house, living plant parts should be completely protected from it until it has thoroughly dried.

CREOSOTEBUSH = *Larrea tridentata*

CREPE-GINGER = *Costus speciosus*

CRESCENTIA (kres-SEN-tia)

cujete 40′ Zone 10 Common Calabash-tree
The large, 10-in. wide hard-shelled calabashes

or rattles used by dancers are the peculiar fruits produced right on the trunk of this tree. Native to tropical America and especially in Mexico. They are also polished and used for dishes, water jugs, etc. The pulp of the fruits is said to be poisonous. The yellow-to-purple 2-in. flowers are ill-smelling.

CRESS FAMILY = Cruciferae

CRESS, MOUSE-EAR = *Arabidopsis thaliana*

CRIMSON-FLAG = *Schizostylis coccinea*

CRINODENDRON (crin-o-DEN-dron)
  dependens = *C. patagua*
  patagua (*C. dependens*) 20'–30' **Zone 10**
                                    White Lilytree
This tree from Chile has white, delicately bell-shaped flowers about ¾ in. long in June and July and the seed pods are cream and red-colored. The evergreen leaves are 1½–4½ in. long with a few marginal teeth. It has been used in Santa Barbara, Calif., where atmospheric conditions for growing it are optimum.

CRINUM (KRY-num). Herbaceous plants of the Amaryllis Family growing from large bulbs, native to the Tropics of the eastern and western hemispheres. These require a great deal of room, hence are not popular as pot plants indoors. The flowers are born in large umbels, are lily-like, white, pink or red, each 3–6 in. long during Sept. and Oct. Some are evergreen. Easily propagated by offsets in the spring.
  amabile 2'–4' **Zone 9** **Sumatra Crinum**
A very fragrant, bright red-flowered plant with perhaps 20–30 flowers, native to Sumatra; leaves 3–4 in. wide and 3–4 ft. long. Blooms in Sept. or Oct. Vars.: '**J. C. Harvey**'—blooms early with wine-red flowers; '**Louis Bosanquet**'—with ruffled petals that are white to pinkish.
  americanum 18"–24" **Zone 9** **Florida Crinum**
This showy plant of the Amaryllis Family is for southern garden culture only, since it is not winter-hardy where the temperature drops below 25° or 30° F. A plant of the swamps of Fla. and Tex., it has long, straplike leaves and a thick flower stalk on which the flowers are borne in a terminal cluster. The 3 sepals and 3 petals are long and white and are united in a tubular base. Flowers appear throughout the late spring and summer. The plant needs rich soil and plenty of water. It does not respond well to frequent transplantings and may not bloom for several years after being disturbed.
  asiaticum 5' **Zone 8** **Grand Crinum**
The bulblike root is sometimes 1 ft. long and the leaves can be 3 ft. long and 3–4 in. wide with tapering tips. There are nearly 20 fragrant white flowers to a cluster, blooming throughout the summer. Native to tropical Asia. The leaves are

evergreen and fairly ornamental. Propagation is usually by offsets from the root. This is not a very important ornamental except in the South where it can be grown out-of-doors.
  bulbispermum (*longifolium*) 2'–4' **Zone 7**
                                      Jamaica Crinum
Native to South Africa, flowers funnel-shaped, 3 in. wide and 3–4 in. long, white or pink during early fall. Leaves up to 3 in. wide. It is said that this can be grown out-of-doors in protected places as far north as New York City. This is the most widely grown species.
  moorei 2'–4' **Zone 9** **Long Neck Crinum**
Noted as larger than *C. longifolium*, with rose-red funnel-shaped flowers 4 in. across. Native to South Africa.
  x powellii 2'–4' **Zone 7**
A hybrid *C. longifolium* x *C. moorei*. The vars.: '**Album**'—with white flowers; '**Rosea**'—with pink flowers.

CROCOSMIA (cro-COS-mia). Herbs from South Africa belonging to the Iris Family, closely related to *Tritonia* and included in this genus by some botanists. The plants grow from corms, have funnel-form flowers an inch or more long, colored yellow to orange or crimson. Propagated by seed or offsets.
  aurea 3½' **Zone 7** **Golden Coppertip**
A herb grown in the North in the same way as Gladiolus, which see. The sword-shaped leaves are few, small and scattered. The flowers are bright orange-yellow, ¾–1 in. long, and are borne in spikes that are sometimes branched. A double-flowered form '**Flore-pleno**' has been listed.
  x crocosmiiflora 3'–4' **Zone 7** **Montbretia**
These are crosses of *C. aurea* x *C. pottsii* first made by the Lemoines of Nancy, France, in 1880. Many beautiful hybrid seedlings have since been raised. These have larger blooms than *C. pottsii*, being 1½–2 in. wide but variable in size and shape. Because of the beauty of these hybrids, the species are little grown. Colors of the flowers are chiefly orange to scarlet. If propagated by seed, it should be sown as soon as ripe in the autumn. The Earlham hybrid Montbretias have been highly recommended. Some of the varieties are '**Aurora**', orange; '**Fiery Cross**', orange-red; '**George Davidson**', pure yellow; '**His Majesty**', very large, crimson-scarlet with yellow center; '**Lord Nelson**', orange-scarlet and '**Star of the East**', large, orange.
  pottsii 12"–18" **Zone 7** **Pott's Coppertip**
Actually of little value ornamentally now because its hybrids (*C. crocosmaeflora*) are much superior.

CROCUS (KRO-kus). This is a group of early spring-flowering bulbs (actually corms) belonging to the Iris Family that can bear more study by many gardeners. Not enough species are grown. The flowering season can be lengthened from 2–3 weeks to 3–4 months by the proper selection of the right species. They can be naturalized anywhere—lawn, rockery, flower border, around trees, etc., but they should not be cut (in the lawn or elsewhere) until their grasslike leaves have died. If the lawn must be mowed previously to this time, then new corms should be planted each year, for cutting of the leaves prematurely is an excellent way to discourage them. On the other hand, if they are let alone in good soil they will increase both by cormlets and by seed.

Even in good soil the corms disappear sometimes, eaten by mice, chipmunks and squirrels, but if a cat or a dog is around, mice and chipmunks usually give the planting a wide berth.

These early-blooming bulbs should be planted in the full sun and it is well to give some thought to this, because if planted in a protected, warm spot, they may bloom 2 weeks earlier than out in the fully exposed lawn; hence this adds at least 2 weeks to their blooming period. They have few insect or disease pests.

They should be planted early in Sept., if possible, with 4 in. of soil over them. Planting in groups of 6 or more corms in one place always makes a better showing than planting them singly at some distance apart. After several years they form tight clumps producing few flowers. Then it is time to lift them, about Sept. 1, or even in late June when the leaves have died, and separate them.

Crocuses are sometimes grown in bulb pans in the home greenhouse, for they are very easy to bring into flower and certainly are colorful, providing they are kept very cold (even frozen) until it is time to begin to force them. If they are grown this way for indoor enjoyment and are kept growing until the leaves die, when they can be planted out after all frosts are over, they should bloom just as well in their new spot the following year as if they had been there all along. For this purpose, a 6-in.-bulb pan could accommodate 18 corms, which would make an interesting pot of color for Feb. bloom.

The species listed here have flowers of about the same size, but they bloom at different times and in different colors. If American gardeners would use more of them, in addition to the Common Crocus (*C. vernum*), they would not only have more colorful plantings, but would also enjoy a longer period of Crocus bloom.

angustifolius (*susianus*)   3″–6″   **Zone 4   Cloth-of-Gold Crocus**
Flowers bright orange-yellow, petals 1½ in. long; blooming in March. Crimea.

asturicus   3″–6″   **Zone 6**
Flowers lilac, petals 1½ in. long, blooms in mid-Oct. Native to Spain.

biflorus   3″–6″   **Zone 5   Scotch Crocus**
Flowers purplish, petals 1½ in. long, the outer one striped with purple, the throats inside yellowish; blooming in spring. Native to Italy and southwestern Asia.

cancellatus   3″–6″   **Zone 5**
Flowers fragrant and white or lilac; petals 1¾ in. long, blooming in late Sept. Native to Asia Minor. The variety **albus** has pure white flowers.

flavus (*aureus*)   3″–6″   **Zone 4**
Flowers bright yellow, petals 1½ in. long; blooms in spring. Native to southeastern Europe, Asia Minor. A variety, 'Sulphureus Concolor' has pale yellow flowers.

imperati   3″–6″   **Zone 7   Early Crocus**
Flowers lilac or white with 3 dark purple stripes outside, petals 1½ in. long; blooming in the very early spring, almost in the winter in the South. Native to Italy.

korolkowii   3″–6″   **Zone 6**
Flowers orange-yellow, petals 1 in. long; blooming in spring. Native to southeastern Europe. A popular rock garden plant.

kotschyanus (*zonatus*)   3″–6″   **Zone 5**
Flowers rose-lilac, spotted inside with orange, petals 2 in. long; blooming in the fall. Native to Turkey.

laevigatus   3″–6″   **Zone 6**
Flowers white, petals 1 in. long, the outer ones striped light purple; blooming in autumn, often in Dec. Native to Greece.

longiflorus   3″–6″   **Zone 5   Longflower Crocus**
Flowers bright lilac, petals 1½ in. long, the inside throat yellow; blooming in autumn. Native to southern Europe.

medius   3″–6″   **Zone 6**
One of the showiest species with scarlet stigmas and deep lilac-colored petals 2 in. long, white inside; blooming in autumn. Native to southern France and Italy.

ochroleucus   3″–6″   **Zone 5**
Flowers white to pale cream tinged with orange, petals 1½ in. long, inside orange; blooming in autumn. Native to Asia Minor.

pulchellus   3″–6″   **Zone 6?**
Flowers bright lilac, petals 1½ in. long, inside yellow; blooming in autumn. Native to Greece and Asia Minor. A variety, 'Zephyr', is white.

sativus   3″–6″   **Zone 6   Saffron Crocus**
Flowers lilac or white with petals to 2 in. long; blooming in autumn. Native to Asia Minor. Also used as an herb, the stigma is used for coloring sauce, cake, preserves, butter, cheeses, etc.

sieberi   3″–6″   **Zone 7   Sieber Crocus**
Flowers lilac, petals 1½ in. long; blooming in

early spring or winter. Native to Greece and Crete.

speciosus   3″–6″   Zone 5
Flowers light blue, bright orange stigmas, petals 2 in. long; blooming in late Sept. Native to southeastern Europe and Asia Minor. The variety **aitchisonii** has the largest flowers of all the wild crocus species and varieties.

tomasinianus   3″–6″   Zone 5
Similar to the common garden Crocus, *C. vernus*, and blooming in spring. Native to Serbia.

vernus   3″–6″   Zone 4   Common Crocus
Flowers lilac or white, often striped with purple, this is the one most frequently grown in the U.S. Blooms in very early spring. Native to Europe. Flower petals 1½ in. long.

versicolor   3″–6″   Zone 5   Cloth-of-silver Crocus
Flowers purple, petals 1½ in. long, inside white or yellowish; blooming in spring. Native to southern France.

CROCUS, AUTUMN. See COLCHICUM.

CROSS. Hybrid of any description.

CROSS FERTILIZATION. A process whereby the pollen from one plant, or species, or variety, is placed on the pistil of a flower on another plant, species or variety. Cross-fertilization is sometimes necessary among certain varieties of apples and plums to insure proper fruiting.

CROSSING. See HYBRIDIZATION.

CROSSVINE = *Bignonia capreolata*

CROSSWORT, ANNUAL = *Crucianella stylosa*

CROTALARIA (kro-tal-AY-ria). There are over 250 species in this genus, most of them native to the tropics, and only a few are grown in the continental United States, in Zones 8–9. They have pealike, showy yellow flowers and their fruits are small pods. The seeds will be helped in germinating if they are soaked a few hours in warm water before sowing.

retusa   4′   annual
A slender annual with the flowers in terminal clusters, yellow with some streaking of red.

spectabilis   4′   Zone 9   Showy Crotalaria
A sub-shrub, used only on the Gulf Coast, native to India, of value for its showy purple flowers in racemes nearly 1 ft. long, with 20–40 flowers. The alternate leaves, pealike flowers and rounded pods (the seeds can often be rattled in the 2-in. pod giving rise to the name rattle-box) are its chief assets. These are often used as "green manures" in the South.

CROTON = *Codiaeum variegatum pictum*

CROWBERRY, BLACK = *Empetrum nigrum*

CROWBERRY, BROOM = *Corema conradii*

CROWBERRY FAMILY = *Empetraceae*

CROW-POISON = *Amianthium muscitoxicum*

CROWN-BEARD, GOLDEN = *Verbesina encelioides*

CROWN-DAISY = *Chrysanthemum coronarium*

CROWN GALL. A bacterial disease of many plants especially the members of the Rose Family. Brown woody galls often 1 in. or more in dia. develop on the roots or the stem near the surface of the ground. Infected plants are stunted but seldom killed by the galls. Badly infected plants, especially small garden plants and shrubs, should be destroyed and galls on the trees can be cut out and the wound disinfected with corrosive sublimate or some antibiotic. Spraying is not effective as a control measure.

CROWN-OF-THORNS = *Euphorbia splendens*

CROWN-VETCH = *Coronilla varia*

CRUCIANELLA (kroö-si-an-ELL-a)
stylosa   6″–9″   annual   Crosswort
A low prostrate annual with leaves in whorls of 8 or 9 chiefly of use for a shady place in the rock garden. The flowers are small, dark pink or rose-red and are bunched in a tight ball-shaped head ¼ in. wide. The corolla is funnel-shaped and the fruit is a dry capsule. Native to Asia Minor. Propagated by division and seeds.

CRUCIFER. Any plant belonging to the Mustard Family.

CRUCIFERAE = The Mustard Family

CRUSTACEOUS. Having a hard or brittle covering.

CRYOPHYTUM = *Mesembryanthemum*

CRYPTANTHUS (kript-AN-thus). A few species of tropical plants belonging to the Bromelia Family, grown in the greenhouse or as house plants because of their ornamental leaves. Mostly native to South America, they are stemless, stoloniferous with stiff, wide rosettelike leaves originating from the base of the plant slightly prickly on the margins. The flowers are white, produced in the center of the nested leaves, with berrylike, dry fruits. They grow equally well in a sunny window or in the shade. For culture see CACTI AND SUCCULENTS.

acaulis   6″   Zone 10   Earth Stars
Leaves are 1½ in. long with wavy or prickly margins in various shades of green, and white scurfy underneath. There are many varieties.

bivittatus   6″   Zone 10
Leaves are spiny margined, green above and brown beneath with 2 reddish-brown, longitudinal stripes beneath. Several varieties with

longitudinal bands slightly different colored.
zonatus 9″ **Zone 10**
Making a very attractive rosette of wavy,
strap-shaped leaves, 1½ in. wide, brownish
green to copper and with colorful tan to light
brown irregular cross-bands; silver scurfy
beneath. The white flowers are translucent.
Several colored varieties are offered.

CRYPTOCORYNE Several species are
aquatic herbs from Asia which have been
introduced for planting in the home aquarium.
They have stoloniferous roots which means that
they send up new plants at intervals in the sand.
They are long-lived in the aquarium and do well
in parts that have the least light. They should
be grown in water that is 72° F. or warmer, for
they are true tropical plants. C. **willisii** has
leaves up to 6 in. long and 1 in. wide. Other
species with leaves of different shapes and sizes
are C. **griffithii** with leaves reddish underneath;
C. **cordata** with somewhat broader leaves; C.
beckettii with the smallest leaves of any of these
species and C. **ciliata** with leaves almost as large
as those of C. **wilisii.** Easily propagated by
division.

CRYPTOGAM. A plant that bears no flowers or
seeds, but can be propagated by special cells or
spores, like algae, ferns, etc.

CRYPTOGRAMMA (krip-toe-GRAM-ma)
crispa acrostichoides 5″ **Zone 4 Parsley Fern**
A very attractive small rock fern, which grows in
shady rock crevices from the Great Lakes westward to the Rocky Mountains. Earning its
common name from its resemblance to Parsley.
The glossy, 3-pinnate fronds are borne on pale
yellow petioles.

CRYPTOMERIA (krip-to-MEER-ia)
japonica 150′ **Zone 5 Cryptomeria**
A splendid evergreen tree from Japan, widely
used in America within its hardiness range, it
can grow to 18–30 ft. in trunk girth. The small
needles, about ¼ in. long, are arranged in 5
vertical ranks along the cordlike branchlets.
The small, globose cones are less than an inch
across but are much used in Christmas decorations. The bark shreds in long strips and has
interest for this reason. There are several
varieties among them. Propagation is by seed
sown as soon as ripe and not allowed dry out.
Hardwood and half-ripened cuttings have been
rooted.

A few vars. are: **'Bandai-Sugi'**—globular in
form, eventually growing about 6 ft. tall, with
irregular spreading branches, not as hardy as
'Lobbii'; **'Compacta'**—compact and conical in
habit with bluish-green, short, stiff needles;
'Dacrydioides'—a shrub about 6 ft. tall with
irregular branches growing in all directions,
branchlets few or none or often in bunches at

the end of the main branches; **'Elegans'**—the
Plume Cryptomeria, a juvenile form, short-
leaved but dense and bushy. It can reach 25 ft.
in height and the foliage turns a rich red-brown
in winter; **'Globosa Nana'**—dwarf, globose,
compact, about 3 ft. tall, slightly bluish in
winter. More hardy than 'Bandai-Sugi';
'Knaptonensis'—dwarf, cushion-shaped, less
broad than high, a form propagated from a
"witches broom" found in Italy in 1930;
'Lobbii'—differs little from the species but is
supposed to be more compact and hardier;
'Spiralis'—a flat globose form with leaves
twisted tightly around the branches. Foliage
bright green. Plants have a strong habit of
reverting to the form of the species; **'Vil-**
moriniana'—dense, slow-growing, globular
form.

CRYPTOSTEGIA (krip-to-STEE-jia)
grandiflora vine **Zone 10 Palay Rubbervine**
A climbing shrub or woody vine with oblong
leaves up to 5 in. long that are glossy and
leathery. The deep lavender, bell-shaped
flowers are 3 in. wide and the fruit is a pointed,
angled pod borne in pairs. The sap contains a
white latex sometimes used as a substitute for
rubber; the stems yield a fiber and the foliage is
supposed to be poisonous to livestock. Native
to Africa and cultivated in southern Fla.

CUCUMBER (*Cucumis sativus*). The Cucumber
is probably native to Asia and Africa where it
has been cultivated for over 2000 years. In the
U.S. it is an important crop in the home
garden, and is considered by market and truck
gardeners as a specialized crop for pickles and
as a forcing crop in greenhouses.

The cucumber plant thrives best at relatively
high temperatures and is killed by light frosts,
but because it matures its crop in a comparatively short time it can be grown in most
sections of the country.

Varieties

Cucumbers are primarily of two types, for
slicing and fresh eating in salads, and for
pickling. Suggested varieties for slicing are
'Burpee Hybrid', **'Marketmore'**, **'Superslice'** and
'Straight Eight'. Pickling varieties include **'Natio-**
nal Pickling', **'Wisconsin SMR54'** and **'Earli-**
pick'.

Soils and Fertilizers

Cucumbers are grown on a variety of soils,
but sandy loams are preferred where earliness is
a factor, and the silt and even clay loams are
selected where yields are important. The soil
should be well drained and prepared as for any
other of the garden crops.

Where well-rotted animal manure is available, the placement of a forkful in each hill is preferred to a broadcast application. The cucumber plant requires a continuing supply of plant food for vigorous growth and the development of a full crop of fruit. A general recommendation is to broadcast 30–35 lbs. of a 5–10–10 fertilizer per 1000 sq. ft. at the time the soil is prepared and then supplement with an added application of nitrate of soda when the plants are 5–7 in. high.

Planting and Care

Cucumber seeds germinate very poorly at temperatures below 50° F. and, therefore, because the plant is also frost tender, planting should be delayed until the soil is warm and the danger of frost is past. Where earliness is a factor, plants may be started in the hotbed and reset out-of-doors, or plant protectors may be placed over the hill or row in the garden. Cucumbers can be planted in hills spaced 4 ft. x 4 ft. with 3–4 plants per hill, or in drills with rows spaced at 4 ft. and the plants thinned to stand 6–8 in. apart in the row.

Hill of Cucumber seedlings. Two have been removed to leave plenty of room for the remaining three.

Cultivation should be shallow and care taken to prevent injury to the vines. After the vines cover the ground, large weeds should be pulled by hand.

Pickling cucumbers are harvested every 3–5 days when the fruits range in size from 2–5 in. long. Slicing sorts will range from 7–12 in. in length. Care must be taken to prevent injury to the vine or foliage.

Diseases

Cucumbers are subject to several diseases that can be serious including bacterial wilt, an-thracnose, angular leaf spot, downy and powdery mildew, scab and mosaic. With bacterial wilt the plant gradually wilts and dies. Bacteria are spread by cucumber beetles, therefore control beetles and remove and destroy wilted plants. Anthracnose shows up as reddish-brown spots on leaves, as cankers on stems and as round sunken spots on fruit. Downy mildew can develop rapidly in moist warm weather as angular yellow spots covered with a weblike fuzz causing the leaves to dry, curl and die. Powdery mildew appears first as round white spots on the underside of, older leaves which eventually may cover both surfaces of the leaf with a powdery growth and cause the leaves to die. Anthracnose and the mildews may be controlled by dusting or spraying with fixed neutral copper or organic fungicides at 6–7-day intervals. Crop rotation and removing and destroying diseased vines should be practiced. See FUNGICIDES.

Scab causes sunken, dark brown spots on the fruit from which a gummy substance may ooze. Small spots may appear on leaves and stems. Damage is worst in cool, moist weather. Control by the use of resistant varieties, seed treatment with corrosive sublimate and crop rotation. Cucumber mosaic causes mottled curled and stunted leaves and warty, misshapen and spotted fruits. This virus is spread primarily by aphids and the striped cucumber beetle. Control by removing perennial weeds around the garden, control aphids and use resistant varieties such as 'Burpee Hybrid,' 'Surecrop Hybrid', 'Wisconsin SMR 18' and 'Ohio M. R. 17'.

GRANT B. SNYDER

Insect Pests

(also of related cucurbits)

Striped cucumber beetles feed on the under side of leaves especially on young plants. The yellow beetles with 3 black stripes carry bacterial wilt in their digestive system over winter and infect the plants when feeding in the spring. Larvae feed on stem and roots causing much damage. Spraying or dusting with insecticides #9 or #28 when the beetles are first seen gives control. The spotted cucumber beetle with 12 black spots on the greenish-yellow wing covers has a similar life history, causes similar damage and is controlled by the same insecticides. Melon aphis is very destructive where abundant unless controlled with insecticide #15. In the South the pickle worm eats the bud, blossom and fruit in late summer and is controlled with insecticide #9 or #15.

Diseases

Anthracnose, scab and angular leaf spot are

seed-borne diseases which are held in check by seed treatment, rotation and the use of fungicides such as copper and zineb when outbreaks threaten. Bacterial wilt which causes sudden wilting of the vines is prevented by control of the striped cucumber beetle. Resistant varieties should be grown where mosaic and downy mildew are problems and aphids spreading mosaic must be controlled. See APHIDS. Powdery mildew often infects cucumbers late in the season but is more destructive to summer squash.

CUCUMBER FAMILY = Cucurbitaceae

CUCUMBER-TREE = *Magnolia acuminata*

CUCUMIS MELO. See MELON.

CUCUMIS SATIVUS. See CUCUMBER.

CUCURBITA (kew-CUR-bit-a). A group of tender herbaceous vines, having tendrils and flowers of separate sexes but both on the same vine. Some are grown widely for their edible fruits (pumpkins, squash), others for their small, highly ornamental fruits. Easily propagated by seed, but home gardeners, who save their own seed from year to year, should realize that if several kinds of pumpkins, squash and gourds are grown in the same garden, there is a strong chance of cross-pollination taking place which, another year, might result in vines which would not produce the type of fruit hoped for. However, pumpkins do not cross with squash except *C. moschata*, but they will cross with other vars. of *C. pepo ovifera* and with summer squash vars. Cucumbers do not cross with any other *Cucurbita* sp. and watermelons only cross with the Citron. Winter squash varieties will cross with Turban squash varieties. Also see GOURDS, PUMPKIN, SQUASH.

ficifolia   vine   Zones 9–10   Malabar Gourd
A perennial in warm countries with kidney-shaped, 5-lobed leaves and may be grown as an annual where the growing season is very long. The flowers are yellow, seeds black and the mottled green fruits have white stripes, are rounded and about a foot long. The flesh is not very palatable so it is grown only as an ornamental. Native to eastern Asia.

foetidissima   vine   Zones 9–10   Calabazilla
This is a perennial frequently grown as an annual but seldom in the North where it does not fruit well. The large, triangular, gray-green leaves are rough to the touch. The flowers are yellow and the hard-shelled fruits are small, rounded, about the size of an orange, colored green and yellow and are not edible. Native to Calif. and Mexico.

maxima   vine   annual   Winter Squash
An annual vine planted for its edible fruits which are frequently furrowed or ridged. The leaves are rounded or kidney shaped, of a solid green color and not or only slightly lobed. The 'Hubbard' Squash is typical. For culture and information concerning varieties see SQUASH.

The var. **turbaniformis** contains the many so-called Turk's Cap gourds, often called the Turban Squash, with fruits which look as if 2 parts have been joined together. The winter squash will cross with this Turban group. These are edible, but are mostly grown for ornament. For culture see SQUASH.

moschata   vine   annual   Cushaw
Also called Crook-neck Squash, these are similar to pumpkins. The leaves are similar to those of *C. pepo* but have whitish spots in them. They are deeply lobed, sometimes slightly prickly. The fruits are variable, often crook-necked and are edible. For culture see SQUASH.

pepo   vine   annual   Pumpkin
These are vigorous-growing vines with harsh prickles on the stems and leaves, which are often definitely lobed. The orange-colored fruits are of many sizes and usually do not keep very long (in comparison with winter squash which can keep all winter if placed in a cool cellar). For information on culture and varieties see PUMPKIN.

The variety **ovifera** contains the yellow-flowered gourds, many of the most ornamental of the hard-shelled types. These plants usually have smaller leaves than the species and the fruits certainly have harder shells and are more lasting than the edible fruits of the species. For the many varieties and their culture see GOURDS. The yellow flowers distinguish this from *Lagenaria* sp. which have white flowers and need a longer growing season.

texana   vine   Zones 9–10   Texas Gourd
Similar to *C. pepo ovifera*, with 5-lobed leaves, yellow flowers and round to pear-shaped fruits mottled green with yellowish-green spots and stripes.

CUCURBITACEAE = The Cucumber Family

CUDRANIA (kew-DRAY-nia)
tricuspidata   25′   Zone 7   Silk-worm Tree
This plant has edible red berries 1 in. in dia., thorns and leaves up to 3 in. long, sometimes with 3 lobes at the end. Native to China, Korea, and Japan, its foliage has been used for feeding silk worms.

CUDWEED. See GNAPHALIUM.

CULM. The stem of a grass or a sedge.

CULTIGEN. A plant, group, or series known only in cultivation. See also INDIGEN.

CULTIVAR. So-called "horticultural variety" or "garden variety." Progeny of a clone, chimera, or the result of selective hybridization, which is known only in cultivation and may or may not be reproduced from seed. The name, usually selected by the propagator, appended to either a generic name or a binomial, should be set off by different type or included within single quotations to distinguish it from the binomial of a natural species. Examples: *Syringa* 'Congo'; *Malus* 'Bob White'; *Deutzia scabra* 'Pride of Rochester'.

CULTIVATION. This is understood to be the act of "working" the soil, hoeing, harrowing, etc., during the period of active plant growth. There are many types of man-powered and mechanical cultivators for use in the garden, but each one is designed to do 2 things—dig up the weeds on the soil surface, and break up the soil crust. The final outcome of good cultivation is of course better plants, fewer weeds, and a soil that is receptive to even the lightest shower.

One can err on the part of too frequent cultivation, in the vegetable garden as one example. One can eliminate cultivation almost entirely by the application of some mulch. See MULCHES. In any event, cultivation should be so undertaken that the roots of the plants wanted in the garden are not disturbed, that the weeds are killed and the soil crust broken. It is not necessary—in fact, it is often injurious to plant roots—to cultivate too deeply—$\frac{1}{2}$ to 1 in. at best. Especially is this true in times of drought, for in such periods the roots of the plants are extended to obtain every bit of soil moisture possible. Cultivating deeply at such a time cuts off roots and seriously reduces their water-carrying capacity at a time when it can do serious harm.

Cultivating when the soil is wet also does harm, for it impacts the soil, pushing out necessary air in the spaces between soil particles. Fortunate is the gardener who can figure on the idiosyncracies of his climate, his soil and his plant growth in such a way that he can reduce the cultivating in his garden to from 4 to 6 thorough operations in the course of a growing season.

CUMINUM (KEW-min-um)

cyminum   6″   annual   Cumin
A popular herb from the Mediterranean region with threadlike leaves, small white or rose-colored flowers in compound umbels, the seeds of which are used in flavoring foods. Propagated by seeds.

CUNEATE. Wedge-shaped; triangular with narrow end at point of attachment.

CUNNINGHAMIA (kun-in-HAM-ia)

lanceolata   75′   Zone 7   Common China-fir
The evergreen needles of this Chinese tree are 1–2½ in. long, somewhat similar to those of the more common *Araucaria* species. It produces wide-spreading branches, slightly pendulous at the tip, and cones that are 1–2 in. long. It is of

interest to note that this is one of the few evergreens with the meritorious quality of sprouting from the stump and roots when cut down.

CUP-AND-SAUCER VINE = *Cobaea scandens*

CUP-FLOWER. See NIEREMBERGIA.

CUPHEA (KEW-pea). Mexican plants usually grown in the greenhouse in the North, and set out as bedding plants, valued for their bright-colored, often profuse, small, tubular flowers, mostly borne in the axils of the leaves which are either opposite or whorled. Easily propagated by cuttings, or seeds, sown inside in the North in March, or outside in the South in early spring after frost. Plants can be lifted and kept over in the greenhouse or home from year to year as pot plants.

ignea (*C. placentra*)   1′   **annual   Cigarflower**
This is the most popular species, with leaves 1–2½ in. long, solitary tubular flowers in the leaf axils, with slender bright red calyx with white mouth and dark ring at end, from which the common name is taken. There are dwarf varieties and hybrids, **'Firefly'** being a very good one.

lanceolata   4′   annual   Lanceleaf Cigarflower
Leaves lanceolate, 3 in. long, flowers solitary and purplish, native to Mexico. Because of its height and flower color this is not as popular a garden plant as *C. ignea*.

platycentra = *Cuphea ignea*

procumbens   1′   annual
Creeping, flowers purple tipped with green, leaves to 3 in. long. Native to Mexico. An excellent edging plant.

viscossisima   2½′   annual   Clammy Cuphea
A native weed, widespread in the eastern, western and southern U.S., with opposite leaves about ⅝ in. long, slightly triangular-shaped; flowers rose-purple with the upper 2 petals larger than the other 4 and appearing in Aug. and Sept. Of no garden value.

x CUPRESSOCYPARIS (kew-press-o-SIP-aris)

leylandii   50′   Zones 5–6   Leyland-cypress
A fast-growing pyramidal tree with small scalelike evergreen foliage resembling that of *Chamaecyparis nootkatensis*, one of its parents. It is a hybrid (*C. nootkatensis* x *Cupressus macrocarpa*) originating in 1888 in the garden of C. J. Leyland, Leighton Hall, Welshpool, England, and can grow 15–20 ft. in 5 years. In fact it is valued as a fast-growing evergreen and is probably perfectly hardy in Zone 5.

CUPID'S-DART, BLUE = *Catananche caerulea*

CUP-OF-GOLD = *Solandra guttata*

CUPRESSUS (kew-PRESS-us). Evergreen trees with opposite, flattened, scalelike leaves, staminate and pistillate flowers separate, but on the same plant; cones small, about an inch long. These trees are mostly native to the warmer parts of the world and are seldom used in American gardens colder than Zone 7. The foliage is aromatic. Propagated by seeds and grafting.

arizonica bonita   35′   Zone 7   Smooth Arizona Cypress
The species is rarely used outside its native habitat in Ariz. but this variety is. The small evergreen leaves are bluish green and the small cones are about an inch across. It is difficult to transplant and it is best to buy small plants at the beginning, for the root system is a poor one and the plant is very easily blown over.

bakeri   30′   Zone 5   Modoc Cypress
Mentioned here to bring it to the attention of gardeners in the northwest Pacific Coast states (it is native to Ore.) for this is supposed to be the hardiest of all the *Cupressus* species. It is somewhat similar to the Monterey Cypress in general habit, making a small bushy tree, but it does not grow rapidly. It is especially recommended for planting on hot, dry slopes, in sandy or gravelly soil. The small gray cones are less than an inch long.

duclouxiana   75′   Zone 7   Bhutan Cypress
Evergreen with spreading branches, leaves about $\frac{1}{25}$ in. long, cones about 1 in. long, scales usually 8 and flat. Native to western China.

funebris = *Chamaecyparis funebris*

lusitanica   50′   Zone 8   Mexican Cypress
Branchlets often drooping; leaves glaucous green; cones $\frac{1}{2}$ in. wide. Native to Mexico.

macnabiana   30′   Zone 7   Macnab Cypress
Evergreen shrub or tree often with several stems with gray, slightly furrowed bark, leaves convex on back; cones 1 in. long with 6–8 scales. Native to Calif. Sometimes reported hardy in Zone 6.

macrocarpa   75′   Zone 7   Monterey Cypress
The famous windswept cypress trees of the southern Calif. coast are this species and they have proved excellent plants for seaside gardens here and in Europe as well. They are evergreen and can easily be sheared to form hedges or topiary objects of interest, and also they are used as windbreaks in seashore gardens. They grow rapidly but their use is confined in America at least to the southwestern Calif. coastal area. Young trees are pyramidal when young, but as they mature they grow broadly rounded.

sempervirens   75′   Zone 7   Italian Cypress
An evergreen native to southern Europe and western Asia and widely recorded in the literature of that area. This is popular in the warmer parts of the U.S., and of course has been planted since ancient times in Europe. The cones are about an inch long, the branching is either horizontal or upright. Probably the most popular variety is **'Stricta'**, the Columnar Italian Cypress, often only a few feet in dia., yet 20 ft. tall. In the group of columnar trees it is the most rigidly upright and narrowed of them all. The var. **horizontalis** has horizontal branches forming a very wide head.

CURCUMA (ker-KEW-ma)
longa   1$\frac{1}{2}$′   Zone 10   Turmeric
Native to tropical Asia and China, this herb is much cultivated in India and sometimes in the West Indies for its roots, which, when dried and ground, supply the commercial spice known as turmeric. Also the roots are used in making a yellow dye.

CURRANT. See RIBES.

CURRANTS. These *Ribes* species are not nearly as popular as they used to be for 2 reasons. In the first place, the fruits must be processed as soon as they are picked. Secondly, most *Ribes* species have proved susceptible as alternate hosts to the White Pine blister rust disease and there are definite restrictions placed (by Federal Quarantine Acts) against growing them in many states and counties. The home gardener who wants to grow currants (or gooseberries) should first write his State Experiment Station (which see) to ascertain whether it is permissible to grow them in his area.

Currants are grown in bush form, in normal garden soil. They are hardy well north of where apple trees are grown. These shrubs take little care. They might be mulched to help with the weed problem. The application of well-rotted manure not only acts as a mulch but a fertilizer as well. The application of commercial fertilizers is usually not worth the effort except on very poor soils, but plants in the home garden frequently respond well to addition of nitrogen in the form of a complete fertilizer. They should be spaced about 5 ft. apart. All canes over 3 years old should be removed. Fruits should be used as soon as they are picked, but they can remain on the bush for a week or so in an almost fully ripe condition.

Currants are propagated commercially by hardwood cuttings taken in the fall after the leaves have dropped. The home gardener can easily obtain a few extra bushes merely by layering (which see) a few branches.

As for varieties, **'Red Lake'** is an excellent one for the home garden. **'Wilder'** produces more heavily and so is preferred for commercial plantings. Fifty percent of the currants grown in the U.S. today are grown in N.Y. **'White Imperial'** is the best white-fruited variety, and **'White Grape'** is sometimes listed by nurseries. Also see GOOSEBERRIES, RIBES.

Insect Pests

Currant aphid infests the leaves and curls

them early in the summer. The black over-wintering eggs and San Jose scale are killed by some dormant sprays. Insecticide # 15 is effective if thoroughly applied to the curled leaves. Currant borer which tunnels and kills the canes and currant stem girdlers which cause the new canes to break near the tip in early summer are checked by sprays of insecticide # 15 when the adults are active, but butting and burning the infested canes is advised. Imported currant worms, the larvae of a saw fly, are voracious eaters when the leaves are about full grown. Spray with insecticide # 15 but do not use insecticide # 9 or others which may leave harmful residue on the harvested fruit. Plant bugs (see CELERY) and San Jose scale (see SCALE INSECTS) may infest currant.

Diseases

Brown or purplish spots on the leaves indicate infection by currant anthracnose, and fungicide # D gives good control. Blister rust, which is more important on White Pine, occurs as bright orange spots on Currant leaves in midsummer. See PINUS. Fungicide # D is advised. Before planting Currant, check local authorities concerning restrictions.

CURTONUS (cur-TOW-nus)
  paniculatus   3'-4'   **Zone 7**
A South African bulbous plant similar to Gladiolus, belonging to the Iris Family and related to *Antholyza*. Flowers are red and yellow borne in spikes and grown from bulbs planted in the spring. See GLADIOLUS for cultivation

CUSPIDATE. Sharp-pointed.

CUSTARD-APPLE FAMILY = Annonaceae

CUT-AND-COME-AGAIN = *Helianthus annuus*

CUT BACK. A horticultural term meaning to prune.

CUTHBERTIA (CUTH-ber-tia)
  graminea   8"   **Zone 8**
Tufts of filiform leaves an inch wide, and bright pink flowers on arching stems, blooming throughout the summer, make this plant from the southeastern U.S. most ornamental for the rock garden. It grows in sun or semi-shade. Propagation is by division of the plant clump in the spring.
  rosea   1'   **Zone 8**
This species, similar to *C. graminea*, has pink flowers 1½ in. wide.

CUTTING. A severed vegetative or asexual part of a plant used in propagation; as a cutting of root, of stem, or of leaf.

CUTTINGS. The propagation of plants by cuttings is the easiest of the asexual methods. Gardeners can practice this readily with very little equipment. The chief objectives are to provide bottom heat for the basal part of the cuttings in the rooting medium, and to provide a moist (and fairly warm) atmosphere around the upper part so that they will not dry out at any time. Moisture loss should be guarded against even in making the cuttings. They should be kept moist and turgid at all times, and the sooner they are placed in the rooting medium after they are cut from the mother plant the better it is.

There are several kinds of cuttings, and the type of cuttings used often depends on the kind of plant to be propagated. Some plants will root from several kinds of cuttings, then of course the easiest type to care for is the type to make. In the various discussions under the generic headings throughout this volume indications are given concerning the type of cuttings best suited to the individual plant. These are:

STEM CUTTINGS. Most cuttings are thought of as small pieces of the stem cut from the mother plant and inserted into the rooting medium. These are differentiated from leaf cuttings, leaf bud cuttings and root cuttings. There are several kinds of stem cuttings, namely, hardwood (deciduous or evergreen), semi-hardwood, softwood and herbaceous.

Hardwood cuttings are the easiest of all to make and care for. These are merely 6-8 in. pieces of the current year's twigs, taken when the plant is dormant. The leaves would have dropped off the deciduous types, and the evergreens would have gone into their dormant period. The deciduous hardwood cuttings are usually taken during the fall, winter or early spring from the current year's growth. Normal shoots are selected that have developed well and not grown too fast, for sometimes fast-growing shoots have not had sufficient time to mature properly before the advent of freezing weather and parts of them may have been injured. So, normal shoots are taken and cut cleanly at the base with a sharp knife. The commercial grower who has had the experience, may know that cuttings can be made from certain easy-to-root plants merely with a snip of the shears, but the amateur should take no such chance. Each cutting should have a clean, sharp cut at the bottom with a knife. This is the place where the roots will be produced, and no chances should be taken with smashing the ends and allowing disease to set in.

These cuttings should be taken when the leaves have dropped. If the cuttings are taken on a day with the temperature very much below freezing, the shoots may be frozen solid. To bring them into a warm room suddenly, might cause some breakage in the cell structure. It is much safer to let them thaw out gradually, either in the sun outside, if this is possible, or in the refrigerator indoors.

The cut is made just below a node and at least 2-3 nodes are included in each cutting. They are taken from twigs that are $\frac{1}{4}$-1 in. in dia., although the beginner may have success with those less than $\frac{1}{2}$ in. in dia. The nurseryman will tie these in bundles of 50, store them either horizontally or upside down in moist peat moss, sand or sawdust, in a cool place until they are callused, then store them in soil, until spring when they are lined out in the nursery row.

Sometimes consideration should be given to taking such cuttings with a "heel," that is, with a small piece of the previous year's wood at the base. A "mallet" cutting is one which is made of a side shoot, but at the base is a $\frac{1}{4}$-in. section of the previous year's wood, horizontal to the cutting. It is the simple cutting that usually gives normal results in most cases, so that normally one does not have to worry about a heel cutting or a mallet cutting.

Deciduous hardwood cuttings may be placed in the rooting medium in the greenhouse (after a few weeks' dormant period), but little is gained in time with this method, for when placed in the rooting medium in spring they quickly catch up with the fall greenhouse cuttings.

Hardwood cuttings of evergreens (*Taxus, Juniperus, Chamaecyparis,* and *Thuya*) can be taken in any month from Sept. on, and rooted in the greenhouse. Usually it takes about 3 months for most to root, but some of the junipers take longer. There is always the question of space after they are rooted, since if taken in Oct. and they are rooted in 3 months, they will have to be kept in the greenhouse until spring. It is much better, space-wise, to start to root them in Jan. or Feb., so that when they are rooted they can be placed in a warm frame out of doors and hence they will not cause a space problem in the greenhouse.

Taking the evergreen cutting is very simple. Well-developed shoots of the current year's growth are selected and cut in about 6-in. pieces. These are usually tip cuttings, although in the case of yews they do not have to be. The sharp cut is made at the base with a knife, and if there are any leaves or small side branches on the lower 2 inches of the cuttings, these are cleanly cut off with a knife—not roughly pulled off, for sometimes this stripping can cause injury to the basal portion. Then they are dusted with a root-promoting compound and stuck in the rooting medium.

SEMI-HARDWOOD CUTTINGS. Usually it is the broad-leaved evergreens that are propagated from this kind of wood, wood that has not thoroughly matured yet has passed the "soft" stage. Usually the time is Aug. or late summer, just after the fast, early growth has been com-pleted but before it is fully mature. *Camellia, Pittosporum, Euonymus, Ilex* and the evergreen azaleas are propagated this way. These too, are stem cuttings made in the same manner as the evergreen hardwood cuttings, and treated with a root-promoting substance just before they are placed in the rooting medium.

In cutting this kind of material, which is only half mature, one should be careful to collect it from the mother plants when the weather is cool and the foliage is not dried out. One should immediately wrap it in a moist burlap, or have polyethylene bags along which have some moistened material in them. The whole idea here is to keep these cuttings moist and turgid until they are in the rooting medium. If they dry out before hand, poor rooting results.

SOFTWOOD AND GREENWOOD CUTTINGS. Many plants can be rooted from cuttings of this kind, but these require the most care of any. Since the foliage is only half grown it is very tender and must not dry out between the time it is out from the mother plant and placed in the rooting medium. Drying out for even a few minutes is serious. Hence the cuttings should be taken on a cool morning and placed in a moist piece of burlap or in a polyethylene bag. Usually tip cuttings are taken, preferably of normal, out-side shoots that are growing in the full sun. Vigorous-growing suckers or unusually large shoots are not satisfactory. The cut is usually made just below a node, the cutting itself being about 4-5 in. long. The lower leaves are re-moved with a sharp knife, and if the leaves on the upper part of the shoot are too large or too many, these are reduced in order to lessen the amount of transpiration from the cutting.

The actual time of taking the cuttings varies considerably with the kind of plant, with the area and even may vary from year to year. The cutting itself should be pliable, but not too soft, for this might rot. On the other hand it should not be too hard, for this might not root. The expert propagator knows that if he bends the stem and it snaps, this is just the right time. If it merely bends, it is too early and if it bends over but does not break, it is probably too old. Considerable experience is necessary in knowing just the right time to take these softwood cut-tings, and the period is not long on an individual plant. It is very desirable to get the cuttings at just the right time, for the percentage rooting then is so much greater, and if the rooting is usually very fast too, within a few weeks.

As in the other cuttings, the bases are treated with a small amount of root-producing compound and then they are placed in the root-ing medium.

It is here that very careful attention must be given, for these softwood cuttings need a high bottom temperature of about 75°–80° F. and 70° F. for the leaves. They must be kept moist, but too much moisture is conducive to rotting. Here again, experience is the best teacher.

HERBACEOUS CUTTINGS. Geraniums, carnations, coleus and chrysanthemums are examples of plants in this category—the most difficult of all from the standpoint of controlling the water relationships of rooting medium and atmosphere about the leaves. Rot sets in very easily. Bottom heat is not absolutely essential, but it helps. These root so easily and rapidly that root-promoting substances are usually not necessary. The cuttings should be of sturdy, well-established shoots, normal and not over-vigorous. The cut at the base is clean and sharp, and if there is too much foliage on the top it is reduced.

LEAF CUTTINGS. Begonias are the typical plants used as examples here, especially the Rex Begonia. A fully developed, normal leaf is taken, the main veins are cut at several places on the underside and the leaf is pegged down flat and tightly onto the moist rooting medium with tooth picks, so that the upper surface of the leaf faces upward. The leaf is shaded and the medium and atmosphere are kept moist until rooting takes place.

Sansevieria leaves can be cut in sections 2–3 in. long, the top cut straight across and the bottom cut with a slant so that top and bottom

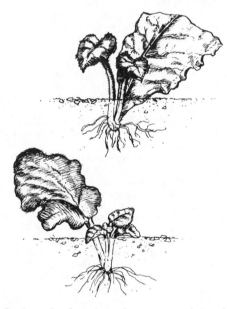

Cuttings: Leaf cuttings above root at base of the blade. Another type roots at base of the petiole.

can be differentiated. The bottom part is placed in the rooting medium and should root in a few weeks' time.

LEAF BUD CUTTINGS. Usually, there is a leaf bud in the axil of the petiole where it is attached to the stem. Cuttings of some plants which include this bud, the petiole and leaf will root if the proper conditions are given. Such plants would be Black Raspberry, Lemon, Camellia and some rhododendrons. Also included would be many tropical plants and greenhouse plants. The cutting should be placed in the rooting medium so that the bud is about ¼ in. below the surface.

ROOT CUTTINGS. These cuttings might best be taken in late winter or early spring for it is during this period that they have the highest percentage of stored foods. The procedure varies with the size of the root. Very fine roots are cut in pieces 1–2 in. long and scattered over finely screened soil in a flat. A little finely screened soil is sifted on top, and a glass pane placed over the flat to aid in keeping the soil moist. The flats should not be in the hot sun, but placed in the shade.

Root pieces from plants with fleshy roots are also planted in flats, and are cut about 2–3 in. long. In making the cuttings, one should be certain to make a horizontal cut on that part of the root farthest away from the base of the plant for it is this end (i.e. the pointed end) that is placed down in the soil, with the top part just at the soil surface.

Plants with large roots, in which the cuttings are 6–8 in. long can be done out-of-doors if necessary, the roots cut in the late fall before the ground freezes, stored in the soil in a cool place over winter and then planted in the nursery row in the spring. In planting, the pointed ends should be placed down, and the horizontally cut ends should be just at the surface of the soil.

ROOTING MEDIA. Clean, sharp sand is about the easiest rooting medium to use, and most plants that can be rooted from cuttings will root in it. Peat moss has also been used, but the difficulty with this material is that one must learn how moist to keep it. Too much moisture and the cuttings rot. It is very easy to keep this too wet. Water drains easily from sand and the problem is often to keep this wet, but just the reverse is true with peat moss.

A mixture of sand and peat moss is often recommended for some things, mixtures varying from 2 parts of sand to 1 part of peat moss, and 1 part of sand to 3 parts peat moss. Sometimes the results in one of these mixtures are better than from either sand or peat moss alone.

Shredded sphagnum moss has been suggested and it has given good results in rooting leaf cuttings and very fine root cuttings.

Vermiculite is used, frequently with great success. Vermiculite and sand, mixed in equal quantities also has proved helpful. The gardener with an interest in propagating plants from cuttings would no doubt have good success with any one of these if the moisture content were carefully managed.

GROWTH REGULATORS. There are several of these on the market and they usually do some good, especially with hard-to-root types of plants. The powders are the easiest to apply. Directions should be carefully read as they appear on the package. Usually, the ideal way to apply the powder is to spread a little on some wax paper and dip the tip of the cutting in it. One can sometimes injure the cutting by applying too much, the reason that it should not be heavily spread up and down the base of the cutting by dunking it in the bottle of powder. A snap of the cutting after it has been placed in the powder usually removes the excess. Most of these powders contain indolebutyric acid, which is the best of the hormones for use in propagation. The cuttings should be placed in the rooting medium immediately after the rooting substance has been applied.

ROOTING FRAME. For details about greenhouse benches see GREENHOUSE. Also see ELECTRIC HOTBED, for here is described the simple way to prepare for rooting cuttings.

POLYETHYLENE FILM. This can be employed several ways in rooting cuttings. One of the most simple, if easily-rooting cuttings are to be used, like chrysanthemums, coleus and privet, is to take a strip of polyethylene film about 3 ft. long and a foot wide. Thoroughly moisten some sphagnum moss and lay it all along the middle of the strip. Then take the prepared cuttings, place them on the moss but with their tops above the edge of the film. Then thoroughly cover the bases of the cuttings with moss, fold the lower half over the base of the cuttings and roll the whole mass up, so that the tops of the cuttings will be outside (above) the film and the basal portion of the cuttings will be thoroughly covered with sphagnum moss, around which is wrapped the polyethylene film. Tie the top rather firmly and hang it up in a warm room and watch for rooting. It may be advisable to sprinkle the tops with water occasionally.

There are other simple methods. A box with 4–6 in. of sand in the bottom and a pane of glass over the top is perfectly satisfactory for some things. Also, a simple greenhouse flat can be filled with sand or some other rooting medium over which is a rough wire frame covered with polyethylene film. The bottom of the film should be long enough so it reaches over all sides of the flat and is either folded underneath or is kept tightly attached to the flat sides

by merely keeping the sides of the flat moist. In this way, one has a tight, moisture-proof rooting box which needs little attention, practically no watering, and yet one can see what is happening inside.

This small frame has been used in an enlarged edition on the greenhouse bench with excellent results. It may be that one does not want to go to the expense of purchasing an intermittent or constant mist system for just a few cuttings; when this is the case, the polyethylene cage can work wonders if it is kept tightly shut. If mold or rot does start, it should of course be aired out occasionally and a mild fungicide used.

MIST SYSTEMS. There are several types used by commercial growers, but the constant mist is usually used out-of-doors, and the intermittent mist indoors. This is controlled electrically in such a way that when the humidity goes below a certain point the mist is turned on and when it is sufficiently moist or humid, the mist is turned off. Any good greenhouse supply organization can send particulars about both systems.

CARE OF CUTTINGS IN THE ROOTING MEDIUM. After placing the cuttings in the medium it should be watered thoroughly, the idea being that, even though the medium is firmed well about the cuttings, the water will tend to close all the air spaces which may remain about them. Thorough contact with the medium is essential for good rooting.

The temperature should be checked with a soil thermometer and it should be maintained at between 75–80° F., with the air temperature about 70° F. Dead or molding leaves should be removed as they appear, and if any mold does start on the surface of the medium, the whole case should be promptly aired out and the medium sprayed with a mild solution of some good fungicide like Semesan. In fact, it might be well to do this at 2 or 3 intervals, if trouble does appear. It might be well, especially if a tightly fitting polyethylene cage is used, to open it up every few days to change the air.

If water must be added, make certain it is not very cold, for if it is taken right out of the tap on a cold winter day, it could cause injury. Let it stand in a watering can in a warm room for a few hours before using.

Of course the whole bed should be shaded—it should not be set out in the direct sun. Even newspapers laid over it will help or, if it is movable, place it where direct sun will not strike it. Temperatures under glass or in a tight polyethylene cage can be raised too high, very quickly, in full direct sunlight.

It must be remembered that there is no food for the cuttings in any of the rooting media suggested. This is generally satisfactory, for the cuttings are usually there only a few weeks and need no additional food other than that stored in them at the time. However, if for any reason, they are to be left in a longer time it might be well to use a mild nutrient solution when watering. A simple solution of this kind is made by adding 2 teaspoonfuls of a mixed fertilizer like a 10–6–4 to a gallon of water.

The cuttings are ready for potting when most of the roots are 1–2 in. long, but one should read carefully the after care below to appreciate the steps which should be taken before potting and immediately thereafter to insure the proper hardening-off procedure.

AFTER CARE OF ROOTED CUTTINGS. The real difficulty comes in hardening off the rooted cuttings which have been growing in a very warm and humid atmosphere. If they are casually dug out of the rooting medium, potted and placed in the sun on the greenhouse bench, they might wilt and die promptly. When it is known that the cuttings are properly rooted, then the mist system should gradually be reduced day by day, until in a week or longer, if necessary, one can keep them growing by hand watering in the normal way.

Or, if the rooted cuttings are under a polyethylene covering, then the film should be opened for longer and longer periods each day so that in a week or so it can be removed altogether. In this way the tops of the cuttings are conditioned to the regular atmosphere. Then it is safe to dig them carefully and pot them in a good soil mixture which has plenty of peat moss or vermiculite in it to assist in the retention of the water. The potted cuttings are then placed in a shaded, cool part of the bench and in a short time, when top growth has started, can be treated like normal plants.

CUTWORMS. The dull-gray and striped, fleshy worms are the larvae of night-flying moths. Many of them cut the stem of seedling and transplanted vegetables and annual flowers before eating the leaves. Others climb trees and the stalks of plants before feeding and are called Climbing Cutworms. They feed at night or on cloudy days and hide in the soil nearby during daylight.

A few valuable plants can be protected by a cardboard collar around the stem, and dust or spray of Sevin or methoxychlor controls them. Sevin or Dylox are both effective against cutworms. However, one should check the label on the container for preharvest interval and residue restrictions. Also, a tight cylinder of cardboard, 6″ high, placed around the base of the plant is effective in control.

CYANOTIS (sy-an-O-tis)
somaliensis   trailing   Zone 10   Pussy-ears

Tar paper or cardboard collar placed around a young tomato plant at planting time to prevent cutworm injury.

This is a relative of the Wandering Jew with trailing stems, and is used occasionally as a house plant. The leaves are narrow-triangular, hairy and 1½ in. long. The flowers are reddish in dense clusters, but under normal house conditions it may not flower well. Even at that it is valued for its foliage alone and can withstand heat and full sun. Native to tropical Africa. Propagated by cuttings.

CYATHEA (sy-ATH-ea). This is a tree-fern genus with plants that may reach 20–40 ft. in the Tropics or Subtropics where they are native. They have thick treelike trunks and are not proper subjects for the home greenhouse because of their size. **C. dealbata**, a native of New Zealand, has a trunk 30 ft. tall and 1½ ft. through with fronds up to 12 ft. long, spreading horizontally. **C. medullaris**, the Sago Fern, also comes from New Zealand and can grow a trunk 50 ft. tall and 2½ ft. through, with curving fronds up to 20 ft. long and 5 ft. broad. **C. insignis** is native to Jamaica, **C. arborea** is found in Puerto Rico.

CYATHEACEA = The Tree Fern Family

CYCAD. Any plant in the Sago Palm Family (*Cycadaceae*).

CYCADACEAE = The Sago Palm Family

CYCAS (SY-kas)
  circinalis   15′   Zone 10   Crozier Cycas
A Fern Palm native to the East Indies sometimes planted in southern Fla. It produces a stocky trunk with a rosette of stiff, bright green, feather-shaped leaves 8 ft. long and 2 ft. wide, some specimens having forked trunks and

2 heads. Since this is a cycad, the male plant produces a red cone 2′ high at the top of the trunk—the female cone is only a foot high and buff-colored. The orange-colored seeds are 1–1½ in. across. This is popular in southern Fla.

revoluta   10   Zone 9   Sago Cycas
Not a true palm, and hence incorrectly called "Sago Palm", but a very desirable and popular evergreen plant, this is native of Japan with dark, glossy, fernlike foliage. Slow in growth, it may take 50 years to form a trunk 5 ft. tall but it is usually seen in Fla. and the Gulf States, as well as in southern Calif. as a mounded fountain of fronds or leaves growing 3 ft. long out of a stubby pineapplelike base. Male and female flowers are on separate plants. A splendid ornamental where hardy and widely grown, for the cut fronds are used a great deal in floral decorations. Propagated by suckers which should be taken from the base of the plant when dormant, usually in May or June.

CYCLAMEN (SIK-lam-en). Members of the Primrose Family, the florists' type is well known, but the distinctive little species which are hardier and can be grown in many gardens should be far better known than they are. All have rounded, heart-shaped leaves on long stalks and are produced from a corm. The pink, white or reddish flowers are also produced on stalks which reach above the leaves.

Usually, when the plant is through blooming it is discarded, but those with a thrifty quirk can keep them for several years. They may be placed out-of-doors after all danger of frost is over and when the leaves die, the pots are placed on their sides until late summer, when the tubers are repotted in a soil consisting of ⅔ loam, ⅓ leaf mold and dry cow manure, with a little sand, bone meal and charcoal mixed in. Then they should be placed in a cold frame and in early Oct. taken into the cool greenhouse where they can be brought along for Christmas display. Handled in this way, tubers may last several years, but each year as the tubers become larger and produce more flowers, the flowers will be smaller than those originally produced.

Cyclamen are also produced from seed sown in Aug., but will not be large enough to bloom for about 18 months. They are transplanted to small pots as soon as they are large enough, kept in a cold frame until danger of frost is past, then taken to the greenhouse where night temperatures are above 45° F. and where the pots are kept cool and moist. When ready, they are transplanted into 5–6 in. pots in the soil mixture already mentioned. During the following summer they are kept in a cool, shaded cold frame, kept moist but not wet and not allowed to dry out. They should be syringed during very hot, dry weather. Forced in a cool greenhouse in the fall, they should bloom by Christmas.

There are many horticultural varieties, one or two with double flowers, and some with frilled petals. The species has flowers about 2 in. wide, but some well-grown corms of the varieties produce flowers twice that size.

cilicicum   3″   Zone 7   Sicily Cyclamen
Blooming from Sept. to Nov., this has a large leaf with a heart-shaped zone of silver color in the center. The flowers are pink and the petals are attractively twisted. Very free-flowering. It should be transplanted in March and the corms set 1 in. deep in the soil in a semi-shaded situation. Native to Sicily.

coum (*orbiculatum*)   4″   Zone 7   **Atkins' Cyclamen**
Used considerably in gardens of the S. Eastern U.S.
Blooming from Dec. to March, with flowers either pink or pink marked with white and leaves spotted with silvery white. Best transplanted in July into a semi-shaded situation. Native to southeastern Europe, Asia Minor.

indicum = *C. persicum*

hederifolium (*neapolitanum*)   4″   Zone 5
Neapolitan Cyclamen
Native to central and southern Europe and with small red or white flowers often appearing before the leaves in the late summer. Petals are frequently twisted. This should be planted in July with about 2 in. of soil on top of the corms. Flowers less than 1 in. wide.

persicum   12″   Zone 9   Florists' Cyclamen
This is the common Cyclamen so popular among florists and well known to all their patrons. It is a low herb with hard, tuberous roots, popularly but incorrectly called a bulb, and is native to Greece and Syria. There are now available some excellent large-flowered forms which are superior to the wild species, with flowers pink, white and red, as well as some with flowers which combine these colors.

Those plants bought from the florist have usually been forced to perfection and, in a cool room in the house, will remain in colorful display for 3 months or longer if not given too much water. The soil should not be allowed to dry out completely, but neither should it be moist to wet all the time. When it is on the dry side, water it well once, then add no more water until it becomes dryish again. The flowers will last longer if the plant is not in direct sunlight for long periods of time. A truly delightful house plant well worth growing in any home.

Insect Pests

Cyclamen mite (see MITES) is a tiny, transparent mite which seriously distorts the buds and flowers. Infested plants seldom produce many normal flowers. Mites live under the bud scales, where they are difficult to contact with insecticides. Using the hot-water treatment on non-blooming plants is helpful. Grubs of the black vine weevil feed on the roots. See TAXUS.

Diseases

With normal growing conditions, cyclamen is free of serious diseases. Continued high humidity may induce leaf spot or gray mold rot of the tuber. Fungicide #D is suggested.

purpurascens   4″   Zone 5   European Cyclamen
Native to central and southern Europe, this delightful garden cyclamen blooms in Aug. and Sept., producing fragrant, bright red blossoms under 1 in. long. The rounded leaves are spotted whitish. These corms should be set in the ground in July with only about an inch of soil on top of them, and left alone permanently. An excellent plant if placed in the foreground of the rockery where it can be easily seen.

repandum   5″.   Zone 6
This is a charming little cyclamen and is well worth seeking out if one lives in an area where it will prove hardy. The leaves are broadly cordate, about 5″ long and as wide, often with whitish markings on the upper side and reddish purple beneath. The flowers are 1¼″ long, sometimes slightly fragrant and colored carmine red, pink or white. It blooms in the spring and is native to the southern European area. If planted in a shaded situation, and covered with pine needles or a light mulch, it should prove winter hardy.

vernale = *C. persicum*

CYCNOCHES (sic-NO-ches). Native to tropical America these epiphytic pseudobulbous orchids are sometimes grown in the warm greenhouses. They bear both male and female flowers, sometimes similar and at other times very different. **C. chlorochilon** from Central America bears yellow-green flowers about 5–6 in. across from July–Dec. For culture and propagation see ORCHID.

CYDISTA (sy-DIS-ta)
aequinoctialis   vine   Zone 10   Garlic-scented Vine
This vine produces flowers similar to those of red-to-pink gloxinias, but they have the scent of Garlic. The clusters have 5–10 flowers, each flower up to 3 in. long with a white throat. The bloom is best during the spring and again in the fall, but usually some flowers appear on vines in Hawaii throughout the year. Native to tropical America. The leaves are opposite but sometimes give the effect of 4 being produced together on the stem, because each leaf is made up of 2 leathery leaflets 6 in. long.

CYDONIA (sy-DOE-nia)
oblonga   24′   Zone 4   Common Quince
A deciduous tree grown especially for its fruits which are golden yellow when ripe, somewhat pear-shaped, fragrant and varying sizes depending on variety. The alternate leaves are 2½–4 in. long and covered with a felty hair underneath. Flowers are 2 in. across and pink or white in May, borne as a single bloom at the end of a short spur. Probably native to central Asia, cultivated for centuries, 1 or 2 plants are all that is needed to keep one's family and several friends supplied with plenty of quinces for preserves. The best variety is **'Orange'**. (See QUINCE.)

Propagation

Seed may be processed as soon as ripe or stored dry in airtight containers in a cool place for up to a year. In either case it should be stratified at 40° F. for 3 months, then sown. Usually, asexual propagation is the method desired. This may be done by grafting, budding or mound layering. Seedlings of the species are used as understock for the varieties. Also softwood and hardwood cuttings can be rooted. See GRAFTING, BUDDING, LAYERING, STRATIFICATION, CUTTINGS.

CYMBALARIA (sim-bal-AY-ria)
aequitriloba   4″   Zone 7   Toadflax Basket-ivy
A miniature, matlike plant growing very close to the ground, with 3-lobed leaves ½ in. long and delicate mauve flowers borne just above the leaves and blooming throughout the summer. This excellent rock garden plant is native to southern Europe. Somewhat tender in northern gardens.

muralis   trailing   Zone 3   Kenilworth-ivy
A popular member of the Snapdragon Family for growing as a house or greenhouse pot plant or as a plant for hanging baskets or even as a ground cover. Plants only in 3-in. pots make nice ornamentals. Leaves alternate (mostly) irregularly 3–7 lobed, palmately veined on petioles longer than the blades. Flowers ⅓ in. across, lilac-blue with yellowish throat. Propagation is easy by cuttings or division and seeds can be sown in the spring. Apparently it grows well in alkaline soils. Native to Europe, naturalized in northeastern North America.

pilosa   4″   Zone 4   Shaggy Basket-ivy
Slightly larger than *C. hepaticaefolia*, this plant has grayish, woolly, 3-lobed leaves and lavender flowers blooming in its native habitat in southern Europe from May to Nov. Hardier than *C. aequitriloba* or *C. hepaticaefolia*, it is on record as having survived temperatures of 30° below zero. Native to Italy.

CYMBIDIUM (sim-BID-ium). A genus of 50

species of epiphytic and terrestrial orchids. Native mostly to Asia. Most have pseudobulbs. Cultivation is easy for most and propagation is by division. For further information on culture and propagation see ORCHID.

insigne   3½'   Zone 10
Flowers 3½ in. wide in 10–15 flowered racemes or spikes up to 5 ft. tall, colored pale rose and spotted purple-red with 2 yellow, thickened lines during Feb. and March. Native to Indo-china.

lowianum   2'   Zone 10
Flowers 4–5 in. across, colored green and whitish, yellow-bordered with crimson-red in March. They are borne on 15–40-flowered lateral racemes. Native to Burma.

CYME. A convex or flat flower-cluster with the central flowers opening first. See also CORYMB.

CYMOPHYLLUS (cy-mo-FILL-us)
fraseri (Carex fraseri)   1½'   Zone 7   Fraser Sedge
With evergreen leaves that are flat, 1½ ft. long and 2 in. wide, native from Va. to N.Car.

CYMOSE. Arranged in cymes; cymelike.

CYNANCHUM (sy-NAN-chum)
nigrum   vine   Zone 3   Black Swallow-wort
An escaped European twining vine which can become a vicious pest with deep-seated roots; leaves simple, opposite, 3 in. long; flowers small, dark purple and almost inconspicuous from June to Sept., fruit a seed with tufted hairs like that of a milkweed, borne in 2-in. pods. A vicious weed very difficult to eradicate, and spreads rapidly once it gains hold in an area because of its wind-blown seeds and deep-seated roots which can send up new plants even if partially broken off.

CYNARA (SIN-a-ra)
cardunculus   6'   Zone 9   Cardoon
As native of southern Europe, cultivated in Europe for its edible roots and leaf stalks but not often grown in America. The leaves are grayish green above, white tomentose beneath. The plant is blanched before it is eaten, and propagation is either by seed or suckers. If seed is sown in a pot in April, planted out in July, the seedlings might be large enough by Sept. to be edible. The leaves should be tied around the main stalk much the same way as is done with Celery or Endive, several weeks before harvesting.
scolymus = Artichoke, which see.

CYNODON (SY-no-don)
dactylon = Bermuda Grass. See GRASS, LAWNS.

CYNOGLOSSUM (sy-no-GLOSS-um)
amabile   2'   annual or biennial   Chinese Forget-me-not, Chinese Hound's tongue
This is a popular garden plant from eastern Asia, especially valuable in hot, dry sunny locations throughout the summer for its profusely distributed small blue flowers about ¼ in. long. Seed can be started indoors in March, set out in late May, or sown outdoors in May and the seedlings later thinned to 9 in. apart. Three good varieties are: 'Blanche Burpee'—light blue to white flowers; 'Firmament'—deep blue flowers, dwarf habit; 'Snow Bird'—white flowers.

officinale   3'   biennial   Common Hound's-tongue
An unpleasant odor and a weedy growth habit preclude the use of this plant in the garden. It has alternate, rather rough leaves up to 12 in. long and small, reddish-blue flowers which appear in June and July. The fruits are prickly and attach themselves to the fur of animals. The plant, although naturalized over much of the U.S., is a native of Europe, and is a biennial, tap-rooted weed. See WEED-CONTROLLING CHEMICALS.

virginianum   3'   Zone 4   Wild Comfrey Hound's-tongue
This is not of horticultural value. The alternate, bristly leaves are lanceolate, with bases which clasp the stem. The flowers are borne in an elongated cluster and appear in June along the roadsides and in deciduous woods throughout much of eastern U.S. and the states bordering the Gulf of Mexico.

CUPERACEAE = The Sedge Family

CYPERUS (sy-PEER-us)
alternifolius   4'   Zone 10   Umbrella Flatsedge
This is a semi-aquatic tropical species from Africa, sometimes called the Umbrella Plant, apparently offered by several Calif. nurseries for growing at the edges of pools. The leaves are mere sheaths, the spikelets are in umbels about 5 in. long, giving an umbrella effect. Sometimes grown as pot plants but they require much water. Both vars. **gracilis** and **nanus** are smaller and better adapted to growing as ornamentals and **variegatus** has leaves and stem striped with white. Propagated by cuttings of the umbels with the base placed in water.

esculentus   3'   Zone 3   Nut Sedge, Chufa
A perennial native grass, widespread in eastern North America, with small tubers at the end of some of its roots from which new plants grow. The flowers and fruits are in umbels at the end of a long stalk. All the roots and small tubers must be dug out or the plant will be hard to eliminate from the garden. The tubers are edible.

papyrus   6'–8'   Zone 9   Papyrus
An aquatic grass or sedge, native to southern Europe and Egypt, the plant from which the

Cyphomandra

Egyptians made paper centuries ago. The leaves are really reduced to mere sheaths. The flower cluster is in an umbel or terminal spike with 50–100 drooping, threadlike rays, each one of which is 12–18 in. long. It must be kept from frosts; makes an outstanding water plant in greenhouse pools or outdoor pools if it is taken indoors for protection during the winter.

CYPHOMANDRA (sy-fo-MAN-dra)

betacea   6′–10′   Zones 9–10   Tree-tomato
A member of the Potato Family, native to South America, this is a treelike woody shrub being widely advertised at times in the United States as the source of "tree-tomatoes." The fruits are egg-shaped, 2–3 in. long, smooth and red, with a tomato flavor. The leaves are sharp pointed, heart-shaped, simple and entire and the small pinkish, fragrant, flowers are about ½ in. across. It is sometimes grown in northern greenhouses but must have a temperature not below 50° F. It will fruit when about 2 years old.

CYPRESS. See CUPRESSUS.

CYPRESS, COMMON BALD = *Taxodium distichum distichum*

CYPRESS, FALSE = *Chamaecyparis*

CYPRESS, MOURNING = *Chamaecyparis funebris*

CYPRESS-PINE, STURDY = *Callitris preissii* (*C. robusta*)

CYPRESS VINE = *Ipomoea quamoclit*

CYPRIPEDIUM (sip-ri-PEE-dium). Nearly everyone is familiar with the Lady's-slipper, sometimes called the Moccasin-flower. The several species are among our loveliest perennial wild flowers and are among the native representatives of the Orchid Family, whose members are largely tropical. These native plants grow with their tuberous roots in the soil (orchids are often epiphites, supported on the limbs of other plants, but deriving their nourishment from the air). The leaves are simple, often basal and generally elliptical and pointed, with prominent longitudinal veins. The flowers are irregular, with the lower petal curved to form a lip, or receptacle around the fused column of stamens and pistil. There are many other greenhouse "Cypripediums," but these belong mostly to other Orchid genera. For cutting and propagation, see ORCHID.

acaule   6″–12″   Zone 2   Moccasin-flower, Lady's-slipper
This is the most common of the Lady's-slippers, though still rare enough to be on the list of wild flowers which should not be picked. It is a perennial having 2 broad, basal leaves sheathing the single flower stalk which terminates in the showy pink "moccasin" with its tapering brown sepals. It may be found on dry, acid soil in woods over much of eastern Canada and the U.S., from Saskatchewan to Ala. and flowers in May and June. Though beautiful, it does not accustom itself readily to the garden since it depends upon a fungus found in woodlands to conduct nourishment to its roots.

arietinum   1′   Zone 3   Ram's-head Lady's-slipper
Unlike *C. acaule*, this species bears elliptical leaves, 2–4 in. long, for nearly the entire length of the stem which terminates in a single, showy flower having 3 narrow, purplish sepals and a lip which is white streaked with red. A bog plant needs an acid soil, and it is native to North America and China.

calceolus pubescens   22″   Zone 3   Yellow Lady's-slipper
Reputed to be the wild orchid which is easiest to grow in cultivation, this requires a rich, moist alkaline soil and a well-shaded location. The stems bear large, oval leaves and one or more yellow and brown flowers in the moccasin shape typical of this genus during late spring. It is native to eastern North America. The hairs on the stems and leaves of this plant may cause dermatitis to some individuals if the plants are handled too much.

candidum   1′   Zone 3   Small White Lady's-slipper
One of the rare species, this has 3–5 alternate, strongly veined, elliptical leaves which sheath the stem. The flower has greenish sepals and a white lip, tinged at the edge with crimson. It is to be found in sphagnum bogs and wet meadows from N.Y. to N.Dak., flowering in May and June.

insigne   12″   Zone 10
This is one of the exotic members of this genus, native to Nepal and grown in American greenhouses. There are also several ornamental varieties. They have solitary flowers 5 in. wide, of a yellowish green. It is probably the most widely grown and most variable of all the species in this genus. It is a great plant for the florist because of its long blooming season, as well as for its many hybrids. Greenhouse night temperatures should not fall below 50° F. Often referred to simply as Cypripedium by the florists. Many hybrids are grown by orchid specialists.

reginae   2½′   Zones 2–3   Showy Lady's-slipper
An orchid native to eastern North America with flowers about 3 in. wide, 1–2 together, white with the lip colored rose or puplish, flowering in June. The leaves are 8¾ in. long and 4¼ in. wide. It grows in shaded, moist soils, but is difficult to grow in the garden. The hairs on stems and leaves are supposed to cause dermatitis when touched.

CYRILLA (sy-RILL-a)

racemiflora 25′ Zone 5 American Cyrilla
A native American plant from Va. to Fla., the
West Indies and even eastern South America,
this has white pendulous racemes 6 in. long of
small white flowers in July. This is its chief
ornamental characteristic, and it is of little
ornamental value at other seasons of the year.
If grown it should be given plenty of peat moss
in the soil mixture.

Propagation

Sow the seed as soon as ripe or store dry in
airtight containers in a cool place until the
following year, then sow. Softwood cuttings and
root cuttings taken in the spring root satisfactorily. See CUTTINGS.

CYRTOMIUM (ser-TOE-mium)

**falcatum 1′–2′ Zone 10 Japanese Holly
Fern**
This is an excellent plant for the greenhouse or
home. It is native to the Tropics of the Eastern
Hemisphere, has shiny, dark green leathery
leaves, with 10–14 pairs of pinnae about 3 in.
long and pointed on the margins. It is fully
evergreen in mild climates. The variety **'Roche-
fordianum'** has become popular and the variety
'Compactum' has shorter leaves. These make
excellent house plants. The species has become
naturalized in Bermuda. For propagation see
FERNS.

CYSTOPTERIS (sis-TOP-teris)

bulbifera 2′–3′ Zone 3 Bulblet Bladder Fern
A native to eastern North America with fronds
3–4 in. wide, this is reproduced by small bulblike bodies, about the size of peas, formed on
the fronds, which if planted eventually grow
into young plants. This does well in limestone
soil. **C. fragilis,** native over much the same area
from Greenland to Ga., has fronds only about
10 in. long and 3 in. wide with 8–12 pairs of
nearly opposite pinnae. These both do best in a
cool, moist, shady situation. An even smaller
species is **C. alpina** which has fronds only 4 in.
long.

Propagation by division or in the case of *C.
bulbifera* by collecting the bulblike bodies on
the fronds and sowing them in the summer. If
spores are to be sown see FERNS.

CYTISUS (SIT-is-us).

All of the colorful brooms
are conspicuously flowering Old World plants.
They have been used in this country to brighten
dull spots in many a garden, but it is certain
that if gardeners realized their good qualities,
these plants would be seen much more than they
are now. Typically dry soil plants, they can be
grown from the Pacific to the Atlantic Coast.
Their brilliant flowers are outstanding in the
spring and summer, and their green twigs are
most effective in the winter, particularly in the
North when so many gardens are dull and uninteresting during the long cold months. They
are members of the Pea Family and their
flowers are like those of peas.

The name "broom" was undoubtedly given
these plants in the Old World centuries ago,
chiefly because of the growth of the Scotch
Broom, the most common plant in the group.
The Scotch Broom is comparatively upright in
habit of growth, with a dense mass of ascending
branches. These were used to make brooms in
the days before the carpet sweeper. It was a
simple matter to cut a number of branches,
trim them off evenly and tie them securely to
the end of a stick, the finished product being a
quickly made but serviceable broom. All of the
so-called brooms are not thus adaptable, but the
Scotch Broom and one or two other varieties are.

Generally speaking the term "broom"
applies to the genus *Cytisus*, but *Genista* is often
included. The Weaver's Broom (*Spartium
junceum*) is grown a great deal in southern
Calif., where its long show of bright yellow,
sweet-scented flowers make it a very popular
shrub.

Brooms in general prefer an acid soil rather
than a strictly alkaline one. If they are to be
pruned, it should be done as soon as the flowers
have faded. Some, like *C. praecox*, do not
respond well to heavy pruning, so it is much
better to prune lightly immediately after
flowering. The fresh seed pods are poisonous,
but the flower buds, if pickled, are supposed to
be edible. The roasted seeds have been used as
a coffee substitute. They are comparatively
simple to grow and do well in a sunny situation
where the soil is good, but not too rich. Drainage must be of the best for they are considered
dry soil plants. The only real difficulty is that
they are difficult to transplant. It is best to start
with young plants, preferably pot-grown, rather
than to purchase large plants that may suffer
severely from the shock of transplanting. They
need pruning in order to prevent them from
growing spindly at the base, but otherwise their
culture is simple. They are apparently immune
to serious insect and disease infestation and
consequently need little attention on this score.
Their roots are few and should not be molested
when the plants have become permanently
established.

With a few exceptions, brooms can be grown
on the Atlantic Coast from the Carolinas to
Boston, on the Pacific Coast from central
Calif. to Vancouver and in a very wide strip
between these points across the continent. They
are particularly at home in certain parts of Ore.,
Wash. and Vancouver where the climate is
sufficiently mild and moist to suit many of the

more tender hybrid ones not completely hardy in all parts of the East.

When these plants are in full bloom the large expanse of brilliant golden yellow is gorgeous. Brooms have become naturalized in Va., on Nantucket Island, in Calif. at the base of the Sierra Mountains near Nevada City, and in several places in the Northwest—particularly on Vancouver Island, British Columbia.

The Scotch Broom is unquestionably the most familiar to Americans. It is the only member of the genus *Cytisus* native to the British Isles, and makes one of the colorful pictures vividly remembered by Americans travelling there where it blooms in May. Under normal conditions the Scotch Broom grows 5 to 6 ft. tall but it does not reach this size in the colder sections of the North because repeated injury of the cold winters tends to keep it lower.

This species has a number of beautiful varieties, many of which are available in this country from one or two nurseries. They are all indirect descendants from the unique variety *C. scoparius andreanus*, discovered in a field in Normandy about a century ago by M. Edouard André. The wind petals of the flowers of this vigorous plant are a rich crimson; the other petals are a bright yellow and since this was the only Cytisus with red flowers, it has been used a great deal in hybridizing and was the forerunner of many striking varieties, many of which originated in English nurseries or European gardens.

Propagation

Seed may be processed as soon as ripe or stored dry in airtight containers in a cool place up to a year, then processed. Soak in concentrated sulfuric acid for ½ hour, wash thoroughly then sow. Varieties may be grafted on *C. scoparius* or *C. nigricans* as the understock. Both hardwood and softwood cuttings root readily and cuttings taken in Aug. root about as well as any. See SEEDS, GRAFTING, CUTTINGS.

albus   1'   **Zone 5**   **Portuguese Broom**
This is the only low white-flowered broom really hardy in the North. It is native to southeastern Europe and blooms in late June.

ardoini   8"   **Zone 7**   **Ardoin Broom**
This is a native in the Maritime Alps, with deep golden-yellow flowers produced singly, in pairs or threes during May. The leaves are small and silky, making this one of the better dwarf brooms, especially for use in the rock garden.

battandieri   15'   **Zone 7**
This was not introduced into England until 1922 where it flowered at Kew for the first time (under glass) in 1928. The leaflets are unusually large (1½–3½ in. long) and are covered with silky white hairs. The flowers are fragrant, golden yellow, borne in upright racemes 5½ in. long at the terminals of young leafy shoots. Native to Morocco.

x beanii   14"   **Zone 5**   **Bean's Broom**
A hybrid (*C. ardoinii* x *C. purgans* originated at Kew Gardens in 1900), this is an excellent semi-prostrate shrub with 1–5 deep golden-yellow flowers in a cluster during early May. Some consider this the best of the dwarf brooms, for it blooms so freely that sometimes the twigs and leaves are hidden by the flowers.

canariensis   6'   **Zone 9**   **Canary Broom**
An evergreen, much-branched shrub with bright yellow, fragrant, pealike flowers borne in short terminal racemes blooming in spring and summer and much grown under glass by florists for cut-flower purposes. Leaflets wedge shaped, about ⅓ in. long. Native to the Canary Islands.

x dallimorei   6'   **Zone 6**   **Dallimore Broom**
There are 3 leaflets in each leaf stalk. The flowers are yellow suffused with pink in mid-May, the wings of the flowers being crimson and the calyx brown. It is a hybrid of *C. multiflorus* x *scoparius andreanus*, originating about 1900 at Kew Gardens, England. This hybrid has been judged as one of the 8 brooms most outstanding in flower by a committee of Dutch nurserymen who have been judging the various groups of shrubs at the Experiment Station in Boskoop, Holland, during the past few years.

decumbens   8"   **Zone 5**   **Prostrate Broom**
There are 1–3 bright yellow flowers in each cluster, borne on erect spikes, usually appearing from June until Aug. This is another excellent dwarf form, native to southern Europe.

x kewensis   10"   **Zone 6**   **Kew Broom**
The flowers are creamy white during mid-May, and the branches are low and trailing, making this an excellent low broom. It is a hybrid (*C. ardoinii* x *multiflorus*), originating in 1891 and is not hardy as far north as are *C. beanii* and *C. decumbens*.

multiflorus   9'   **Zone 6**   **White Spanish Broom**
There are 1–3 white flowers in each cluster and these appear during May. This is the only Cytisus with pure white flowers and has much merit where it proves hardy. It is very popular in Great Britain and is native to Spain and northern Africa.

nigricans   3'–5'   **Zone 5**   **Spike Broom**
This has often been termed one of the most useful of the brooms because it frequently blooms continuously through July and Aug. The flowers are small, clear yellow in color, borne on upright spikes and there are 3 leaflets in each leaf. Because it flowers on growth made the current year, any pruning should be done before growth starts in the spring. Wherever

summer bloom is wanted, this splendid ornamental from central and southern Europe should have its place. The variety **elongatus** often blooms a second time in the fall.

x praecox   6′   Zone 5   Warminster Broom
A chance hybrid (*C. multiflorus* x *purgans*) appearing in Warminster, England, about 1867, this is one of the brooms earliest to flower. Old plants do not break freely when cut back, but young plants can be pinched back without serious die-back. It has proved hardier than *C. scoparius*, and certainly should be grown wherever possible for its pale yellow spring flowers in May and its dense green stems all winter, which serve as evergreen foliage.

The variety **'Albus'** has white flowers and is

In Europe this has frequently been grafted high on *Laburnum* understock, giving a rather striking appearance. It is native to Austria and is a low, spreading bush with a profusion of light purple flowers in May. It is unique among the brooms because of its purple flowers.

racemosus   10′–15′   Zone 8
Mostly a plant for greenhouse forcing and native to the Canary Islands, the flowers are produced on slender racemes 2–4 in. long and are a rich yellow. This evergreen is sometimes incorrectly termed *C. canariensis*, but is probably a hybrid of it.

scoparius   6′   Zone 5   Scotch Broom
The most common broom of central and southern Europe and the only one native in Great

Cytisus praecox (Warminster Broom) with pale yellow, pealike flowers blooming in mid-May. (*Photo by Arnold Arboretum, Jamaica Plain, Mass.*)

more dwarf with somewhat pendulous branches, and **luteus** is dwarf, with flowers a darker yellow than those of the species.

procumbens   30″   Zone 5   Ground Broom
This plant from southern Europe is taller than *C. decumbens* but still makes a dense mass of branches and bright yellow flowers. It will grow into round patches several feet wide.

purgans   3′   Zone 5   Provence Broom
The flowers of this are rich yellow and fragrant, 1–2 in a cluster during mid-May. The leaves are mostly simple but soon fall off the plant. It should not be planted except in a situation in the full sun. The twigs also of this southern European species are green, giving it the appearance of an evergreen throughout the winter.

purpureus   18″   Zone 5   Purple Broom

Britain, this has become naturalized at several places in the U.S. The flowers are a rich yellow during mid-May; the stems are green throughout the winter. It has been noted that all the varieties are worth growing even in Great Britain. Varieties: **'Andreanus'**—this was originally found in a field in Normandy a hundred years ago by M. Edouard André and it was the first one of the brooms with good red color in the flowers. Since this was discovered, many seedlings and hybrids of it have been grown, both in America and in Europe, and a large number of cultivars have been named. There is a great sameness to the colors of many of these varieties; certainly only a few of the best might be grown. The standard of this flower is yellow, the wing petals are a rich crimson and the plant grows vigorously; **plenus** has double flowers;

prostratus has branches growing prostrate on the ground but which will be pendulous if the plant is grafted high on understock of Laburnum species; **sulphureus** is dwarfer than the species, more compact in habit, with pale sulfur-yellow flowers.

Varieties

A few of the better hybrid varieties (of some 60 offered in America and abroad) at present are:

'Burkwoodii'—brighter crimson than 'Dorothy Walpole' and more upright in habit; one of the best of these hybrids;

'California'—standard rosy white, rose on back; wings glowing rose. Originated from seed sown by Sydney B. Mitchell, Calif., about 1934;

'C. E. Pearson'—standard buff-apricot; wings wallflower red;

'Dorothy Walpole'—crimson and rosy cream. Flowers a little smaller than those of other varieties;

'Moonlight'—primrose; upright in habit;

'Pomona'—of tricolor effect, chiefly of crimson and rosy-cream background. Originated from seed sown by Sydney B. Mitchell of Calif. about 1934;

'St. Marys'—creamy white. Originated from seed by Sydney B. Mitchell of Calif. about 1934;

'San Francisco'—standard rosy red; reverse darker; wings bright orange-red, keel yellow. Originated from seed by Sydney B. Mitchell of Calif. about 1934;

'Stanford'—standard bronze-yellow, reverse bronze-rose; wings bright orange-red, keel yellow; originated from seed by Sydney B. Mitchell of Calif., about 1934;

'Windesham Ruby'—standard light purple-red (interior light pink) wing dark velvety red;

'Zeelandia'—standard lilac-rose; wings light red, keel cream.

CYTOLOGY. The branch of biology which treats of cells, especially of their internal structure.

D

DABOECIA (dab-EE-shia)

cantabrica   1½′   **Zone 5**   **Irish Heath**
A close relative of the heaths and heathers, this little evergreen from Ireland and Spain is valued particularly for its small white, pink or purple flowers which appear continually throughout the summer. It requires the same cultural conditions as the heaths and heathers, namely, acid soil and plenty of humus. Vars. **'Alba'**—flowers white; **'Atropurpurea'**—flowers rich purple; **'Bicolor'**—flowers striped white and purple; **'Nana'**—dwarf form with smaller and narrower leaves; **'Pallida'**—flowers pink.

DAFFODIL. The popular name Daffodil is given to the large trumpet-flowered types of the *Narcissus* genus. All daffodils belong to this genus. However, all members of the *Narcissus* genus are not given the popular name Daffodil. The popular name Jonquil is one loosely applied in the South and sometimes in England, but technically should only apply to those species in Division VII (see NARCISSUS) mostly *N. jonquilla*, *N. juncifolius*, etc. As a common name it should be avoided except for these few species and their hybrids. It is inaccurate to apply the name to the large trumpet daffodils.

The term narcissi has been used as the Latin form for the plural of the singular narcissus. However, the American Daffodil Society by vote of its Board of Directors decided that the policy of the Society would be to use the same word, narcissus, for both singular and plural, and so it is treated here. See NARCISSUS.

DAHLIA (DAH-lia, DAL-ia). Supposedly several species of Dahlia are native to Mexico, but most gardeners interested merely in the common garden flower will buy garden varieties of what used to be called *D. rosea* and is now *D. pinnata*. In any event, this species itself is not a garden favorite today and for purposes here can be overlooked entirely.

Dahlias, as they are grown today, are tender tuberous-rooted plants, anywhere from 2 to 8 ft. tall, with flowers from 1–18 in. across, depending on variety and type of culture given. Colors of the flowers range from white to yellow to red and purple with many variations and combinations in between. The largest blooms are the result of special forcing techniques, and are usually grown for show purposes, on tall, single-stemmed plants with stems as thick as broom sticks.

Dahlias are very susceptible to frost and, in fact, their tuberous roots should be dug, dried a few days and stored just prior to the first heavy frost. Their blooms appear in the late summer and early fall. Some, like the Unwin hybrids, can be grown from seed started in the greenhouse and be expected to bloom profusely during the late summer.

In general, the large-flowered dahlias are difficult to use properly in the normal flower border merely because of their large size and coarse texture. The larger the flowers, the more necessary it becomes to stake them; usually with sturdy stakes 6–7 ft. long set firmly in the ground before they are full grown. The dahlias with smaller flowers of the pompon or miniature sizes (see classification below) are much more easy to use in the flower bed and are the delight of the garden in late summer because of their colorful and profuse blooms.

Culture

Dahlias should be planted in the full sun and given plenty of water, especially during drought periods so that they are kept growing continuously throughout the entire summer. Once they are allowed to stop (because of summer drought and lack of moisture) it is difficult if not impossible to get them into bloom again.

For prize-bloom types, the hole for the tubers should be 10–12 in. deep, well filled with good soil. Any tuber should be planted about 6 in. deep, after all frost is over. It is always well, if available, to place well-rotted manure below the tuber at planting time. Also it should be remembered that these vigorous-growing plants require much food as well as moisture and hence should be well fertilized.

If pot plants (seedlings or cuttings) are to be set out in the garden from the greenhouse, they should be set 3 in. deeper in the ground than they were in the pot.

It is advisable to mulch dahlias, as this conserves soil and moisture and hence keeps them growing well. See MULCHES. As with other plants the mulch should not be more than 2–3 in. deep.

Pruning and disbudding are necessary if prize blooms are to be grown. In the first place the plant should be confined to a single stalk with most of the side shoots being pinched out. Then, as soon as the flower buds appear, the 2

293

lateral buds in the main cluster should be removed, leaving only a single flower bud. It takes on the average of 30 days from the time the flower buds first appear until the flowers open.

Gardeners not growing show blooms can leave several flower buds to develop on each stalk and, although they will not be as large as with one single flower, they may provide more garden interest. Disbudding is necessary especially with some of the smaller dahlia types like the pompons and miniatures. When the first 4 pairs of leaves have appeared, the end-bud should be pinched out, later the end-bud of the first 2–4 laterals also. This makes for a more bushy and branched garden plant and is usually all that is necessary during the entire growing season.

In digging the roots in the fall one should be careful not to cut the tubers in the digging operation. Cut off the main stalk a foot above the ground just prior to frost. Dig out the tubers, gently knock off the dirt and let them dry for a few hours only, then store in a cool, dry place, preferably with a temperature of 35°–40° F. over winter.

Storing dahlia roots over winter can be tricky. The general idea is not to allow them to dry up, nor to keep them so moist that disease and rot set in. Sometimes they are stored in sand and inspected periodically so that they do not have the opportunity of drying out. Sometimes the tubers are coated with wax. This is done by pouring into a pail of hot water (80° F.) a pound of melted wax. Then dip the clean (no soil adhering to them) tubers, removing them slowly so the wax on the top of the water has a chance to completely cover all the roots. Set the roots aside for the wax to harden, then pack in peat moss or sawdust. Or they may be stored in polyethylene bags with just enough moist material to keep them from drying up. In any event they should be inspected at monthly intervals throughout the winter. Keeping the temperature cool is a great aid in storing the tubers properly.

Propagation

Usually this is simply by separating the tubers in the spring at planting time. One strong eye or bud should be on each tuber selected. Sometimes it is advisable to give more moisture to dormant tubers as well as more heat 2–3 weeks before planting-out time, for then these eyes or buds will have time to start and so make the separation process a little easier.

Some, like the Unwin hybrids, can be started indoors in the greenhouse by sowing seed in March, potting up when necessary and setting out the growing plants into the garden after all danger of frost is over. Individual tubers can also be started this way, if by doing so one can obtain earlier blooms, but knowledge of this comes after a fair trial in the particular locality in question.

Dahlias may also be propagated by cuttings, taking the small shoots at the base of the plant, at least an inch long, in such a way that $\frac{1}{8}$–$\frac{1}{4}$ in. of shoot is allowed to remain on the crown. Below the cut many more shoots will shortly develop that can also be used for cuttings. Treat the cutting (cut end) with a hormone rooting powder, place $\frac{1}{2}$–$\frac{3}{4}$ in. deep in the rooting medium (usually sand) and they should root within 3 weeks, if the bottom heat has been about 65° F. This is easily done in the modern electric hotbed.

If such rooted cuttings are taken early in the season, potted and allowed to become badly pot-bound by late summer, tuberous roots will develop which can also be used for further propagation, the same way larger roots are treated.

Classification

The American Dahlia Society is a very active organization devoted to the study, classification and showing of these very interesting and colorful flowers. The following divisions are the official ones made in dahlias by this organization and although they may be changed slightly from time to time, it appears that, in general, these main groups will be the official ones for some time to come.

SINGLE DAHLIAS. Open-centered flowers, with only 1 row of ray florets, with the margins flat or nearly so, regardless of the number of florets.

MIGNON. Single dahlias, the plants of which approximate 18 in. in height.

ORCHID-FLOWERING DAHLIAS. Flowers as in Single Dahlias excepting that the rays are more or less tubular by the involution of the margins.

ANEMONE DAHLIAS. Open-centered flowers, with 1 or more rows of ray florets regardless of form or number of the florets, with the tubular disc-florets elongated, forming a pincushion effect.

COLLARETTE DAHLIAS. Open-centered flowers, with only 1 row of ray florets, with the addition of 1 or more rows of petaloids, usually of a different color, forming a collar around the disc.

PEONY DAHLIAS. Open-centered flowers with 2–5 rows of ray florets with or without the addition of smaller curled or twisted floral rays around the disc.

CACTUS DAHLIA.

Incurved Cactus Dahlias. Fully double flowers, with the margins of the majority of the floral rays fully revolute for $\frac{1}{2}$ or more of their length and the tips of the rays curving toward the center of the flower.

Straight Cactus Dahlias. Fully double flowers, with the margins of the majority of the floral rays fully revolute for ½ their length or more, the rays being straight, slightly incurved or recurbed.

Decorative.

POMPON DAHLIAS. Having same characteristics as Ball Dahlias but, for show purposes, not more than 2 in. in dia.

DWARF DAHLIAS. Term that applies to plant size without regard to the characteristics of the blooms.

Dahlias: *a.* Bedding dahlias (1) Unwin hybrid (2) Mignon *b.* Informal Decorative *c.* Pompon *d.* Anemone *e.* Cactus *f.* Collarette *g.* Incurved Cactus

SEMI-CACTUS DAHLIAS. Fully double flowers, with the margins of the majority of the floral rays fully revolute for less than half their length and the rays broad below.

FORMAL DECORATIVE DAHLIAS. Fully double flowers, with the margins of the floral rays slightly or not at all revolute, the rays generally broad, either pointed or rounded at tips, with outer rays tending to recurve and central rays tending to be cupped; and the majority of all floral rays in a regular arrangement.

INFORMAL DECORATIVE DAHLIAS. Fully double flowers, with the margins of the majority of the floral rays slightly or not all revolute, the rays generally long, twisted or pointed and usually irregular in arrangement.

BALL DAHLIAS. Fully double flowers, ball-shaped or slightly flattened, floral rays blunt or round at tips and quilled or with margins involute for more than half the length of the ray in spiral arrangement, the flowers over 3½ in. in diameter.

MINIATURE DAHLIAS. All dahlias which normally produce flowers that do not exceed 4 in. in dia., pompons excluded, to be classified according to the foregoing description. Miniature Single; Miniature Peony; Miniature Straight Cactus; Miniature Semi-cactus; Miniature Formal Decorative; Miniature Informal

For further information concerning color classifications and listing of all current modern varieties (over 1000) write the American Dahlia Society for its current classification booklet. See note under Societies for current address.

Insect Pests

Stalk borer and European corn borer damage Dahlia frequently. The striped worm of the stalk borer is more abundant in early summer, and the white larva with brown head of the corn borer appears in late summer. Both live in the pithy stems and kill or deform the stalks. Cutting out and treating with insecticide #37 is advised. See CORN. Burning, mowing or spraying nearby weeds is helpful. Leaf hoppers (see POTATO) and plant bugs (see CELERY) are occasional pests.

Diseases

Virus diseases known as mosaic, stunt and ring spot dwarf and distort the plants. Destruction of infested tubers and control of aphids is advised. Stem rot and wilt are checked by soil sterilization and rotation of beds.

Classification of Dahlias

SIZE
A—Large, over 8 in.
B—Medium, 6–8 in.

SIZE
BB—4–6 ins.
Ba—Ball, 3½ in. or over
M—Miniature, under 4 in.
M Ba—Miniature Ball, 2–3½ in.
Pom—Pompon (for exhibition purposes, must be under 2 in. dia.)
Dwf—Varieties of low bush growth

TYPE OF FLOWER	COLOR
An—Anemone	Au—Autumn—Bronze
Ba—Ball	Bi—Bi-color
C—Cactus	Dk Bl—Dark Blend
Coll—Collarette	Dk R—Dark Red
FD—Formal Decorative	Fl—Flame
	L—Lavender
IC—Incurved Cactus	Lt Bl—Light Blend
ID—Informal Decorative	Or—Orange
M—Miniature	Pk—Pink, light and dark
M Ba—Miniature Ball	Pr—Purple
Mig—Mignon	R—Red
O—Orchid Flowering	Var—Variegated
P—Peony	W—White
Pom—Pompon	Y—Yellow
S—Single	
SC—Semi-cactus	
STC—Straight Cactus	

Mr. Edward B. Lloyd, Secretary and Editor of the American Dahlia Society and a grower of dahlias for some 40 years, has suggested the following varieties as being good ones for beginners to try. No one has ever made a hard and fast list of "the best," but the ones listed have all been fairly well tested and are worthy of consideration by the amateur. Those marked with an asterisk (*) are best for exhibition growing.

LARGE EXHIBITION VARIETIES

	SIZE	TYPE	COLORS
*Ballego's Surprise	A	SC	W
*Danny	A	IC	Pk
Edna D	A	StC	R
Five Star General	A	FD	Lt Bl, Pk, Y
Holland Festival	A	ID	Bi, Or & W
*Jane Lausche	A	SC	Bi, L & W
Kelvin	A	ID	Pk
Lavengro	A	ID	L
Lula Pattie	A	ID	W
Pride of Parkers- burg	A	SC	Y
Rosemonde	A	SC	Lt Bl, Pk & Y
*Surprise	A	SC	Pk

MEDIUM EXHIBITION DAHLIAS

	SIZE	TYPE	COLORS
Ambassador Van Kleffens	BB	FD	Or
Carnaval	B	StC	Fl
Doge	B	SC	L
Doris Day	BB	StC	Dk R
*Drakenburg	B	IC	Dk Bl
Duet	B	FD	Bi, Dk R & W

	SIZE	TYPE	COLORS
Eldorado	B	SC	Bi, Or & W
*First Lady	B	FD	Y
*Grace	BB	StC	Pk
*Iva Jean	B	IC	Bi, Pr & W
Kimberley Jewel	B	StC	Dk Bl
Mannequin	BB	StC	Pk
*Miss North Sydney	B	SC	Lt Bl, W, L
Nutley Sunrise	B	IC	Or
*Piquant	B	SC	Bi, R & W
Prinses Beatrix	B	FD	Bi, Or & Pk
Stoplight	B	SC	R
*Windlassie	B	ID	W

MINIATURE DAHLIAS

Arabeske	M	StC	Y
Beatrice	M	FD	Var L & Pr
Bo Bo	M	FD	Au
Chasamay	M	StC	Pk
Fuchsia Gem	M	SC	Pr
*Geneva Crystal White	M	SC	W
*Hazel Harper	M	StC	Lt Bl, Pk, W
Paulie Pal	M	FD	W
*Sweet Gen	M	FD	Pk

POMPONS

	TYPE	COLOR
Albino	Pom	W
Atom	Pom	Or
Betty Malone	Pom	Bi, W & Pr
*Clarisse	Pom	Or
*Clover	Pom	Lt Bl, W, Pk
Crossfield Ebony	Pom	Dk R
*Ila	Pom	R
Little Edith	Pom	Fl
*Margaret Williams	Pom	L
Miss Marjorie	Pom	Pr
Moorplace	Pom	Dk R
Pom of Poms	Pom	R
*Sweetie	Pom	R
*Willo's Violet	Pom	Pr

BALLS AND MINIATURE BALLS

Dottie D	Ba	Dk Bl
*Pink Pippen	Ba	Pk

COLLARETTES

*La Cierva	Coll	Pr & pr
Kokette	S	Fl

ANEMONE, DUPLEX, PEONY, ORCHID- FLOWERING, AND OTHER TYPES

*Bishop of Llandaff	P	R
*Comet	Am	Dk R
*Dahliadel Twinkle	O	Var W & L

DAHOON = *Ilex cassine*

DAISY, AFRICAN = *Arctotis stoechadifolia*

DAISY. See ANTHEMIS, CHRYSANTHEMUM.

DAISY-BUSH, NEW ZEALAND = *Olearia haastii*

DAISY, ENGLISH = *Bellis perennis*

DAISY FAMILY = Compositae

DAISY, OXEYE = *Chrysanthemum leucanthemum*

DAISY, PRAIRIE = *Aphanostephus skirrobasis*

DAISY, SHASTA = *Chrysanthemum* x *superbum*

DAISY, SPANISH = *Bellis rotundifolia*

DAISY, SWAN RIVER = *Brachycome iberidifolia*

DAISY, TATARIAN = *Aster tataricus*

DAISY, TRANSVAAL = *Gerbera* x *jamesonii hybrida*

DALIBARDA (dal-i-BARD-a)
repens creeping Zone 4 Starviolet Dalibarda
A small plant native to the moist, shady, acid woods of the northeastern U.S. Growing in tufts and spreading by underground stems, the plant sends up heart-shaped leaves, about 2 in. wide, and small white flowers ½ in. wide which may be found throughout the summer.

DALLISGRASS = *Paspalum dilatatum*

DAMPING-OFF. This is a term applied to the condition of seedlings which topple over with a dark rotted area at the surface of the soil but with healthy-appearing new leaves and roots. Seedlings may also develop this condition just before emerging from the soil. It is caused by fungi which require abundant moisture. Seeds and seedlings should be watered to keep the soil moist, not wet, and only when the soil surface will dry quickly. Covering the seed with sand or mica flakes (vermiculite) which dries quickly is helpful. Seed treated with a protectant delays infection and planting in sterilized soil is almost necessary in the greenhouse. Steam sterilization of soil, pots, flats and greenhouse benches is the most effective treatment, but chemical treatments are now used more frequently. When damping-off develops prompt treatment with fungicides #W, #F, #D or special formulations for this purpose must be made.

DANAE (DAN-a-ee)
racemosa 3′ Zone 7 Alexandrian-laurel
Rarely used as an ornamental this Persian evergreen has scalelike leaves, the apparent leaves actually being flattened stems 4 in. long and 1 in. wide. It is rather like a dwarf bamboo in habit and can be cut for winter displays. The fruit is a small red berry.

DANDELION = *Taraxacum officinale*

DAPHNE (DAFF-ne). There are about 36 different species and varieties of Daphne being grown commercially in the U.S. today. They are nearly all small, alternate-leaved shrubs generally with fragrant flowers and brightly colored, fleshy fruits. Some produce flowers very much like those of the Common Lilac,

though of course, not so large. The alternate leaves are all small and narrow, usually between ½ and 3 in. long. It should be noted that the bark, leaves and fruits are poisonous.

English writers state that most Daphne species seem to do best on limestone soils, but here in the U.S. there are different opinions. There are 8 species growing in the Arnold Arboretum, all on soil of a pH of about 5 or 5.5, made up with a large proportion of peat moss in which azaleas and rhododendrons thrive. So the controversy about the best soil for the group can probably go on indefinitely. However, either because they are short-lived or succumb easily to the least bit of poor culture, most of them have a disconcerting habit of dying suddenly and for no apparent reason whatsoever. Most daphnes are difficult to transplant and are best moved in the smaller sizes.

Propagation

Germination of seed is usually poor and erratic. In any event, it should be stratified at 40° F. for 3 months before being sown. *Daphne mezereum* is used as understock on which to graft deciduous types. Softwood and hardwood cuttings, as well as root cuttings may be used. See STRATIFICATION, GRAFTING, CUTTINGS.

alpina 6″ Zone 5 Alpine Daphne
A dwarf daphne from the European Alps bearing fragrant white flowers in terminal clusters of 6–10 during May and June, followed by ovoid-to-oblong red berries. The leaves are 1½ in. long. An interesting plant for the rockery, but like the other members of this genus, it is rather hard to keep growing properly.

blagayana 1′ Zone 5 Balkan Daphne
A dwarf evergreen with alternate leaves 1–1¾ in. long and creamy-white and very fragrant flowers in March and April, in heads about 2 in. wide consisting of 20–30 blossoms. Fruit is pinkish white and is said to be rare in cultivation. Native to the mountains of eastern Europe. If the shoots are continuously layered, the plant lives longer. One plant grown in this way in Ireland measured 8 ft. wide.

x burkwoodii 6′ Zone 5 Burkwood Daphne
The very fragrant flowers of this hybrid (*D. caucasica* x *D. cneorum*) are creamy white to flushed pink and borne in dense terminal clusters 2 in. wide, appearing in May. It was raised as a seedling about 1935 by Messrs. Burkwood and Skipwith of Kingston-on-Thames, England. A very vigorous growing and freely blooming plant, it is proving popular in American gardens for the individual flowers are ½ in. wide and the fruits are red berries about ⅓ in. wide.

x burkwoodii 'Somerset'—This is the clone of *D. burkwoodii* which is widely distributed in the U.S. because Wayside Gardens of Mentor, Ohio, patented it (#315) on Feb. 28, 1939, and since then has distributed it throughout the country. A 20-year-old specimen plant is now 4 ft. tall and 6 ft. wide, very rounded and densely growing.

cneorum   6″   Zone 4   Rose Daphne
Everyone knows this popular plant which is native to central and southern Europe and almost everyone knows that sometimes it is not the easiest plant in the world to grow. A cool, moist condition about the roots at all times and some winter protection in the North, are added aids to insure good growth. There are several varieties of this being offered by a very few nurseries. The variety **'Alba'** has white flowers and the variety **'Silver Leaf'** has a very narrow leaf margin edged in white. The species has fragrant, bright rosy-pink flowers in small clusters during mid-May. The foliage is evergreen with small, narrow leaves about 1 in. long.

collina   3′   Zone 7
An evergreen with leaves $\frac{3}{4}$–$1\frac{3}{4}$ in. long and small, fragrant, purplish-rose flowers in terminal clusters of 10–15 blossoms in late May. Native to Italy and Asia Minor.

genkwa   3′   Zone 5   Lilac Daphne
A blue or lilac-flowered Daphne from Korea and Japan, this blooms before the leaves appear in April or May and is rather an unusual plant. The flowers are produced on growth made the previous year (as is the case with *D. mezereum*), but sometimes shoots a foot long are literally covered with flowers. The fruits are white berries which are not very conspicuous.

giraldii   2′   Zone 3   Giraldi Daphne
Mr. Frank L. Skinner grew this plant well in his nursery in Manitoba, Canada. It bears slightly fragrant yellow flowers in late May and scarlet berries about $\frac{1}{4}$ in. long in July. This plant might be tried by more nurserymen in order to see whether it might prove to be easier to grow than some of the others. It is native to northwestern China.

x mantensiana $1\frac{1}{2}$′–4′   Zone 6
The flowers of this hybrid (*D. burkwoodii* x *D. retusa*) are fragrant and a soft pink color. It originated about 1953 in Vancouver, Canada. The leaves are about $1\frac{1}{2}$ in. long, and it is valued because the flowers appear intermittently over a long period.

mezereum   3′   Zone 4   February Daphne
The rosy-purple flowers of this February Daphne appear all along the last year's growth in early April, before the leaves appear. They are very fragrant and are followed in early June by brilliant scarlet berries. Since this is one of the first shrubs to produce fruits each year, these are quickly sought out by the birds. It has been planted so much in the eastern U.S. that it has escaped cultivation and become naturalized in some places. It is native in Europe. The variety **'Alba'** is not exactly rare, nor a collector's item, but nevertheless an interesting form with white flowers and yellow fruits. Where *D. mezereum* can be grown, this variety certainly could be grown, also.

odora   4′–6′   Zone 7   Winter Daphne
The most fragrant of all the daphnes, this is popular in the South where several varieties are grown. It is native to Japan and China. The small, extremely fragrant, rosy flowers bloom in March and April and the leaves are 3 in. long and evergreen. Some believe that the plant does not respond well to pruning, fertilizing or cultivation. Be that as it may, it is probably best moved in small sizes and, once established, might be left alone. The variety **'Marginata'** has leaves bordered with yellow.

retusa   3′   Zone 6
This evergreen shrub produces its very fragrant purplish-white flowers in 3-in. terminal clusters during May, later to be followed by red fruits. It is of very compact growth, looking well at all times, and is native to western China.

DAPHNIPHYLLUM (daff-ne-FILL-um)
macropodum   30′   Zone 8
A small evergreen tree with leathery oblong leaves 8 in. long, red twigs, dioecious flowers, pale green, inconspicuous in 4-in. racemes and black fruits that are fleshy 1-seeded drupes. Valued for its handsome foliage. Propagated by cuttings or seeds. Native to China and Japan.

DARLINGTONIA (dar-lin-TO-nia)
californica   3′   Zone 7   California Pitcher-plant
An insectivorous bog plant, needing plenty of moisture, which sometimes is grown in the North with winter protection. The leaves are in basal rosettes so formed with arched hoods and downward-pointed hairs in them that insects are trapped. Flowers are solitary purple, $1\frac{1}{4}$ in. long. Propagated by seed or division. Native from Ore. to Calif.

DASHEEN = *Colocasia esculenta*
DASYLIRION (das-i-LI-rion)
texanum   3′   Zone 8   Texas Sotol
A tender evergreen desert plant of the Lily Family, the glossy green leaves coming from a short trunk that is partly underground, margins with sharp prickles; leaves growing in tufts straight up but then arching gracefully outward about 2 ft. long. They should be grown in hot sunny, sandy soils and are propagated by seeds. Male and female flowers are on different plants, not produced on small plants, but it is grown

chiefly for its foliage. The flower stalks, when produced, are 9–15 ft. tall with bell-like flowers on branching stalks. Native to Tex.

DATE. Cultivation of the Date Palm (*Phoenix dactylifera*) has been practiced since prehistoric times and seems to carry an aura of mystery and romance, probably abetted by the unfamiliar desert locale of all major date-producing areas. Where it is grown extensively, the Date is often a primary food. In the United States it is an exotic plant whose requirements restrict its growth for fruit production to very limited areas of the low deserts of southeastern Calif. and parts of Ariz.

The Date is a true subtropical plant, grown nowhere in the tropics. Its requirement for heat and freedom from rain or high humidities during most of the fruit development period are the primary limitations. The trees will withstand temperature down to 20° F. without injury. Below 20° F. the fronds may be badly injured or killed, but the terminal growing point is seldom killed at temperatures as low as 8° to 10° F. However, where normally grown, such low temperatures are due to intense radiation frosts and are of very short duration; the bud is protected by the insulation of the enveloping leaf-bases. Continuous cold below 20° F. would be expected to be fatal. Rain and even high humidities result in cracking and checking of the fruit at almost all stages of development and is the prime reason that dates are not adapted to the South and southeastern states. If fruit is not wanted, male or female palms may be grown far outside the range for fruit production—in the southeastern states wherever oranges are grown, and at latitudes to nearly 40° N. in inland valleys of the Pacific Coast.

To mature fruit, *average* growing temperatures for the period a month before bloom to fruit ripening must be at least 70° F. for the very earliest maturing varieties to 90° F. for late varieties. Extremely high daytime temperatures are not essential, but do prevail in the desert regions where such average temperatures are attained.

Palms are easily grown from seed, which should be planted an inch deep in a good seed bed. Fruit of seedlings will be much poorer than from varieties, and as Date Palms are dioecious, about half of such seedlings will be male.

Propagation of palm varieties is by 4–5-year-old offshoots—lateral growth that develop on the base of young palms. Those near the ground will be with roots, those above ground without. Rooted offshoots are cut from the mother palm and planted immediately in the location desired, in a site prepared well in advance by digging a hole about 3 ft. across and 1 ft. to 18 in. deep, filled with well firmed topsoil, which should be fertile and settled at planting. Unrooted off-shoots may be planted under shade; many will fail to root. Offshoots have their leaves cut back to 3–4 ft. long and tied together. They are usually protected by wrapping with paper or old palm fronds, especially during the first winter, when they are more tender to low temperatures. Newly planted offshoots should be watered frequently, or mulched, so that the soil near the surface does not dry out.

Natural pollination of dates is seldom sufficient to yield good crops, even when a high proportion of male palms are present. Pollination is by hand. Male inflorescences are taken when they are just emerging from the spathe. Two or three strands of male flowers are inserted in an inverted position into the emerging female inflorescence, which has just been cut back about one-third, and sometimes has had the inner whorl or two of female flowering strands removed (thinning). The bunch is tied at the distal end to retain the male strands, but the tie will need to be loosened periodically as the fruit grows. Alternatively, the male flowers may be allowed to shed their pollen on paper; it is collected and small balls of cotton dipped into it. Two of these balls are inserted into the female inflorescence, as described above.

At flowering the female inflorescence is relatively short and upright. It soon grows in length rather remarkably, and the weight of the developing fruit bends it over. For best results the inflorescence is brought through the leaf bases as it grows, until it hangs in an inverted position below the leaves; often the bunch stem is tied to a leaf base to prevent the weight of the fruit from breaking it. The distal bunch tie is then removed.

About midseason or a little later an inverted cone of kraft or similar paper is often tied around the bunch, with the wide end open to assist air circulation. This tends to protect the ripening dates from birds and rain.

Palms are planted at distances of 25–30 ft., the former being used for a few of the smaller kinds such as 'Khadrawy'. They are not sensitive to soil conditions, and do well in heavy-to-sandy soils of moderate depth. They are tolerant of brackish water and soils with relatively high salt content, but do better in fertile soils and good water. They require little nitrogen fertilization; observations on their requirement for other fertilizer elements and micro-nutrients are lacking.

Date palms use large amounts of water, especially in the areas where they are commonly grown. The high transpiration rate may be an adaptive feature to hold plant tissue temperatures down, for the temperature of the body of the palm is usually about the same as that of the soil below the depth heated in the daytime.

Drought conditions will stop growth and are detrimental to fruit development.

Pruning of date palms consists of cutting off old fronds which are beginning to die, as indicated by browning of the leaf pinnae toward the tip of the frond. It is usually done in late summer. Normally 80 to 100 mature leaves are maintained in the crown, which are enough to mature 8 to 12 bunches of dates and still insure return bloom the following year. The sharp thorns at the base of the leaves are usually removed, primarily to assist in the pollination and harvesting procedures. Besides the thinning of the fruit clusters described, bunches in excess of 8–12 are removed when or soon after they appear, as the palm can set more fruit than it can mature properly, and excess fruit production in 1 year will drastically reduce that in the next.

Dates of commerce are all fully mature; a few varieties, such as 'Barhee' which lose astringency early, can be used at earlier stages. Such use effectively reduces the heat requirement and extends the area where they can be grown for garden use. When they reach the full khalal (pre-ripe) stage, as indicated by the fruit turning pink, yellow, or red, they may be harvested, allowed to soften naturally and then used. When full ripe, the tamar stage, the fruits are light to dark brown and begin to wrinkle. Not all fruit on a bunch ripens at the same time; for best quality multiple pickings are therefore necessary. If some fruit is in the late khalal or rutab (soft-tip) stage it may be ripened off the tree by holding the fruit, well spread out, at temperatures from 80° to 95° F., the higher temperatures being used for the less mature fruit. Ripe or ripened fruit may be held for long periods in cold storage; for several months at 30° to 32° F. and a year or more at 0° F. Curing temperatures for immature fruit should not be extended beyond the time necessary, for high temperatures accelerate the inversion of sucrose, so that the dates may become syrupy, and sugar crystalization takes place later, but not if held at 0° F.

Each producing area of the world has varieties particularly suited to it. Those found best in the United States are listed below. Date varieties are divided into three classes: dry dates (see 'Thoory'), semidry (see 'Zahidi' and 'Deglet Noor'), and soft. The latter are usually considered to have the best quality; semidry varieties are commonest in commerce because they are best adapted to handling and packaging.

'Deglet Noor', a semidry type is the leading variety in the United States, and is the one most often found in the market. It is relatively late maturing (for the warmest areas) and the palm is vigorous and large. 'Zahidi' is another semidry variety of good quality.

'Thoory', a dry date, is seldom found in this country; although favorites in the Near East, the dry dates have not become popular in the United States.

'Halawy', 'Barhee', 'Khadrawy', 'Medjhool' and 'Saidy' are soft dates, which differ in size, shape and mature color, but all are of excellent quality. 'Barhee' is an early-maturing variety. The soft dates tend to pack and stick together in commercial handling, and are more subject to fruit rots, so although of higher quality than the semidry types are generally limited to specialty and local markets. These kinds have their sugar primarily as glucose and fructose, whereas the sugar of the dry types is mostly sucrose. The semidry types are intermediate and the proportion of the 2 types of sugars is affected materially by the time of harvest and the handling given after harvest. For the highest percentage sucrose they should be harvested as soon as ripe and stored as soon as possible.

Growing date palms for their fruits is an exacting art; as the palms become older the many manipulations become more difficult because of the height of the crown. 'Khadrawy' is a variety which grows somewhat more slowly. There is, of course, no way to hold palms low.

CLARON O. HESSE

Insect Pests

Mealybugs and scale insects infest the leaves and suckers and are controlled by the usual sprays of insecticide #44 or #45 in the cooler weather and by #15 in the growing season.

Tying the leaves around a head of Cauliflower to keep it white.

Diseases

Heart rot turns the heart of the palm black and the buds and new growth are curled and stunted. Avoid planting suckers from infected plants. Use of fungicides is impractical.

DATURA = *Brugmansia* x *candida*

metel   2′–5′   annual   Hindu Datura
A tropical plant with coarse leaves up to 8 in. long, large trumpet-shaped flowers 7 in. long, white, yellowish to purplish, strong smelling, borne in midsummer, with fruit a round, spiny ball 1¼ in. in dia. Seed should be started indoors in March and set out after frost. They frequently self-seed themselves even as far north as Boston. Mostly a conspicuous plant for patio or terrace. Vars.: **'Alba'**—flowers white; **'Caerulea'**—flowers blue; **'Huberiana'**—flowers blue, yellow and red; **'Ivory King'**—flowers creamy yellow, triple hose in hose (which see).

stramonium   5′   annual   Jimson-weed
Native to the tropics but a widely naturalized weed in North America, this has lobed oaklike leaves, 8 in. long and erect white or violet trumpet-shaped flowers 4 in. long, with 2-in.-long, prickly seeds. The leaves, roots and seeds of this plant are poisonous and very ill-smelling when crushed. Easily propagated by seeds, but the plant should be weeded out and destroyed wherever it appears.

DAUCUS (DAW-kus)
carota   4′   Zone 3   Queen-Anne's-Lace, Wild Carrot
The Wild Carrot is a tap-rooted European biennial now quite at home in fields and along roadsides over most of the U.S. It has fernlike, pinnately-compound leaves and small white flowers borne in a compound umbel, the cluster generally flattened on top and having a single dark red flower in the center. It blooms from July to Sept., and although the leaves and flowers are attractive, the spreading, weedy habit makes it unsuitable as a garden plant. The root of this is not edible. Var. **sativa** is the Garden Carrot, which see.

DAVALLIA (da-VAL-ia). These are the Hare's-foot Ferns, mostly for greenhouses and some for hanging baskets in the greenhouse. They come from tropical Asia, characterized by having fleshy rhizomes covered with silvery-white or brown, scaly hairs. If these are pinned down to the surface of a hanging basket they make a very interesting plant, producing leaves at various places along the rhizome. The fronds are 6 in. to 6 ft. depending on the species.

Species for hanging baskets (in the greenhouse) would be **D. griffithiana** and **D. trichomanoides**. The soil must be kept moist and the rhizomes must be pegged down as they creep along the outside of the basket. It is of interest to note that from Oct. to March they do not require as much water as at other times of year. In the warm greenhouse (temperature not much below 60° F.) **D. fejeenisis** with fronds 18 in. long; **D. alpina**, **D. trichomanoides** and **D. heterophylla** with fronds 6 in. long are suggested. For the cool greenhouse, and possibly as house plants in a moist atmosphere, **D. canariensis** with fronds 18 in. long and **D. mariesii** with fronds 6 in. long are suggested.

Hare's-foot Fern—*Davallia*

All the species are propagated by divisions of the rhizome, for if they have been pegged down properly along the soil surface, and it is kept moist, roots will have formed at various places along their length.

DAVIDIA (dav-ID-ia)
involucrata   60′   Zone 6   Dovetree
The long white flower bracts of this tree, up to 6½ in. long, are its most conspicuous ornamental assets. The leaves, 3½–5½ in. long, do not change color in the fall and the fruits are mere green nuts 1½ in. long. The true flowers are borne in a globular ball-like mass an inch across, conspicuous because of the red or white stamens. Each flower cluster has 2 (rarely 3) creamy-white bracts, a short one and a long one, that hang down gracefully, fluttering in the slightest breeze and giving rise to the name "Handkerchief Tree." Gardeners in a hurry may not be willing to wait the many years necessary for this tree to produce its first flowers. The var. **vilmoriniana** is more hardy (Zone 5) and can be distinguished from the species because the undersurfaces of the leaves are glabrous, whereas those of the species are pubescent.

Propagation

Do not allow the seed to dry out but stratify in polyethylene bags with medium of damp sand or peat moss, at greenhouse temperatures for about 5 months. Then when segments break out move the bags to a temperature of 40° F. for 3 months, then sow. See SEEDS, STRATIFICATION. Softwood cuttings can also be rooted as well as layers.

Davida involucrata—Dovetree: The true flowers are small and make up the ball in the center with the small and large white bracts that make the tree so conspicuous when it blooms.

DAWN-REDWOOD = *Metasequoia glyptostroboides*

DAYFLOWER. See COMMELINA.

DAYFLOWER FAMILY = Commelinaceae

DAYLILY. See HEMEROCALLIS.

DDT. This is the approved name for the insecticide known chemically as dichlorodiphenyl-dichlorethane. It was a general-purpose insecticide effective for control of both chewing and sucking insects and killed many insects which crawl over residual deposits of it. Reduction of malaria and other insect-borne human diseases throughout the world is primarily due to the use of DDT. It was the most important insecticide for control of insect pests on trees and shrubs. On edible fruits, vegetables, cereals and other foods, it had to be used only according to the limitations prescribed by Federal and State authorities. It was also harmful to wildlife in certain circumstances and is now generally outlawed in the U.S. and is no longer available to the general public.

DEAD NETTLE. See LAMIUM, LAMIASTRUM.

DEATHCAMUS, MOUNTAIN = *Zigademus elegans*

DECAISNEA (dek-AYS-nea)
   fargesii   15′   Zone 5
A deciduous shrub of little ornamental value, with alternate, compound leaves, the opposite leaflets being 12–25 and 2–5½ in. long; small, greenish, polygamous flowers being borne on a 10–20-in. drooping panicle and fruits being blue, fleshy pods, 2–4 in. long. These are attractive and are eaten in China where the plant is native. Propagated by seeds.

DECIDUOUS. Falling, not persistent, as the leaves of non-evergreen trees.

DECODON (DEK-o-don)
   verticillatus   8′   Zone 3   Swamp Loosestrife,
                                Water-willow
The Swamp Loosestrife is a woody perennial characterized by arching branches which root as they touch the soil. The plant will thus quickly form a mass of foliage in moist, low areas in its range which extends from Canada to Ga. and Tex. The angled stems have winged margins and the single, narrow and tapering leaves occur in pairs or in whorls. The deep pink flowers, with several prominent stamens, are clustered in the axils of the leaves. Although attractive, *D. verticillatus* is not an ideal wild-garden plant because of its thicketlike growth.

Propagation

Usually it is easiest to merely divide the plants with a sharp spade, in the spring before growth starts.

DECUMARIA (dek-yew-MAY-ria)
   barbara   climbing vine   Zone 6   Southeast
                                Decumaria
A deciduous climbing vine clinging by aerial rootlets, with opposite lustrous leaves 2–4 in. long and 1–2 in. broad; small white flowers in terminal clusters, none too conspicuous and fruit a capsule. It does best in moist situations and is propagated by seeds or softwood cuttings. Native from Va. to Fla. and La.

DECUMBENT. Reclining or lying on the ground but with the ends ascending.

DECUSSATE. Opposite leaves in 4 rows up and down the stem; alternating in pairs at right angles.

DEERBERRY, COMMON = *Vaccinium stamineum*

DEERVETCH = *Lotus pinnatus*

DEFOLIATION. The casting or falling off of leaves.

DEHISCENCE. The method or process of opening of a seedpod or anther. See also INDEHISCENT.

DELICATE-LILY = *Chlidanthus fragrans*

DELONIX (del-O-nix)

regia	40′	Zone 10	Royal Poinciana or Flame-tree

This is probably southern Florida's most ornamental flowering tree even though native to Madagascar. The deciduous, fernlike foliage (the leaves are twice compound and 1–2 ft. long) is dense and of fine texture. The bright scarlet and yellow flowers appear in the summer, followed by pods 2 ft. long and 2 in. wide. It grows rapidly in almost any soil and is one of the sights that a northern visitor to Fla. rarely forgets if he has seen the tree in bloom. Also common in Hawaii.

DELPHINIUM (del-FIN-ium). Tall, stately and dignified, Delphinium is one of the most gorgeous of hardy perennials. Because of its height and the various shades and tints of blue and purple in which it is available, there is no other perennial which can take its place. In fact, it comes in true blue, the color that is rarest among flowering garden plants.

Delphiniums have long been top-notch perennials, sharing honors with iris, peonies, daylilies, phlox and chrysanthemums. Handsomely grown plants are especially spellbinding when combined with biennial Canterbury Bells and Sweet William and Madonna lilies. The quartette comprises a classic grouping that is the pride and joy of June borders in northern gardens.

Delphiniums are chiefly cool-weather plants that do best in the cooler regions of the country. They tower to noble proportions in the cool, moist climate of the British Isles, but perform equally well in the Northwest and the Northern portions of New England, more so along the coast of Me., where summer visitors from the South eye them with envy.

For all their glamor, delphiniums are not difficult to grow. Certainly, they withstand winter temperatures well below zero, but they do suffer from crown rot, a disease which takes a heavy toll among plants. Yet they make up for this by growing easily from seed, and many gardeners make it a practice to start new plants every year in order to maintain a constant supply of healthy, flowering plants. They can be treated as annuals (if seed is sown early enough) or biennials, and the spectacular hybrids, at best, are short-lived perennials.

For best results, give plants sunshine for at least half a day. Provide a deep, rich soil, well supplied with peat moss, compost, or other humus, neutral or somewhat alkaline or only slightly acid. If too acid, add agricultural lime at the rate of 1–2 lbs. per 20 sq. ft. On established plants, a light sprinkling of lime early each spring will help keep the soil at the proper reading.

Good drainage is very important. A soil that holds too much moisture promotes crown rot, as well as root rot, another debilitating disease. Avoid a clayey soil, and lighten it by adding peat moss, leaf mold, or sand. Where drainage for one reason or another is a problem, it is advisable to grow plants in raised beds, where excellent stock can be grown for flower shows and flower arrangements.

Plants can be set out in the spring from nursery-grown material. These are often offered in tar paper or other temporary containers. Make a large hole to accommodate the ball of soil, and at the bottom throw in a little dried manure and bone meal or superphosphate. Mix thoroughly with the soil, and proceed to plant, retaining the better topsoil to place around the roots. Keep crowns level with the surface of the ground, but avoid too deep planting that might induce rot.

During the growing period, delphiniums require ample watering. Soak the soil around the roots deeply by allowing sprinklers or soakers to run for a sufficient period of time. Keep the running water close to the roots when plants are developed. Overhead watering will weigh and even break the heavy blooms, and water on the leaves, particularly in the evening, will promote mildew.

Because of their height and soft, brittle, hollow stems, delphiniums require staking. Without it, plants, even in sheltered spots, topple and the dramatic effect of their spires, that are depended on for accent, is lost. Start providing supports early, when plants are about a foot tall. Dark green bamboo or other inconspicuous wooden stakes are excellent, and they may have to be 4, 5 or even 6 ft. tall. It is better, for the sake of appearance, to start with shorter stakes and add the taller as plants reach the flowering stage. Do not allow the supports to tower beyond the spikes, an unattractive practice all too commonly seen. In some instances, a stake for each stem will be necessary, more so with the large flowering hybrids, but it is worth the extra effort.

Use soft cord or raffia to secure the stems, which are hollow and so break easily. Tie the blooms themselves, which are apt to snap in high winds if fastened below the flower spikes. A good method is to interlace soft twine around the stems and stakes, in and around the flowers themselves.

After flowering, cut off the flower heads, unless seed is wanted, but allow the foliage to remain. Gradually, the leaves will begin to turn yellow, and when this occurs, cut off the rest of the stems to the base. At the same time, new shoots will appear at the base, and these will produce a second crop of bloom in the fall.

To aid plants in this effort, feed with a mixed fertilizer, applied in dry or liquid form around each crown. Feeding will give plants the extra boost they need, and though flowers will be smaller, they will be equally attractive. At that time of year, colors are deeper and richer. The blues and lavenders go well with the pinks, reds, lavenders, yellows and whites of chrysanthemums.

Delphiniums at best are short-lived perennials that either die or lose their vigor after 2 or 3 years. This means they need to be replaced with fresh stock. Plants grow easily and quickly from seed sown in pots or trays, in cold frames or greenhouses, or in the open ground. It is the least expensive method and the one that will provide an abundant supply of plants. Seed gathered from the garden will keep about a year, if placed in airtight containers and stored at about 40° F.

If seed is sown in Feb. or March, plants will flower the same season. If started in late July, or later from seed gathered during that season, young plants, placed in a cold frame during the winter or set out in the garden where they are carefully mulched with straw or marsh hay, will bloom the following season.

Seed, whenever started, should be sown in a fibrous loam or a mixture of half soil and half sand. Another medium consists of 2 parts loam, 1 leaf mold, 1 sharp sand, with a light sprinkling of fine charcoal and bonemeal. To prevent damping-off disease, dump a pinch of seed fungicide, like Semesan, in the seed packet and mix thoroughly.

After firming and leveling the medium, sow the seed in rows, spaced 2 in. apart, or broadcast it evenly over the surface, and press it lightly. Cover with $\frac{1}{8}$ in. of fine sand, peat moss or sifted sphagnum moss and water well. If sowing in the cold frame, cover with glass, and in the open ground use burlap or paper until germination, which occurs 6–8 days later. Do not allow to dry out, keep it moist but not soggy.

When seedlings have developed their second leaves, transplant into flats or the open ground in light, well-drained soil, comprised of two-thirds loam and one-third peat moss. Shade from hot sun for several days, gradually giving more sun to harden the seedlings before planting in permanent positions in the garden. When transplanting, choose a cloudy day, if possible, preferably after a light rain. For best results, space plants at least 18 in. apart.

Winter protection is essential to prevent injury from thawing and heaving, particularly in open winters. First, wait until the ground has frozen, and not before, and cover the crowns with an inch of cinders and coarse sand. This will help with drainage and also keep away snails, which dislike trailing over rough surfaces. Where winters are very cold and there is little or no snow, an additional covering of straw, marsh hay, evergreen branches, or other mulch will be needed, but do not use leaves, which mat and become water logged, shutting off air.

Root rot, one of the most prevalent diseases, causes leaves to wilt and turn yellow after damage to roots has occurred. Too warm an exposure or hard, sun-baked soil may cause this, as well as soil that is too heavy or lacking in air. Crowns of plants that come in contact with animal manures are also prone to rotting, so avoid their use. They can, however, be incorporated deeply into the soil at planting time.

Crown rot, even more common, is caused by a fungus which enters plants through the roots and crown and cuts off the water supply. Lower leaves become yellow, and plants can be pulled and lifted at the crown. To prevent this, spray plants with sulphur, Ferbam, or Captan, but if infection is bad, lift and discard plants. Then treat the soil with formaldehyde or, better still, grow them in a new spot where the fungus does not exist. Mildew can be checked with Ferbam or Karathane.

There are several strains of hybrid delphiniums that will add sparkle to any garden. Outstanding are the Giant Pacific Hybrids with large, well-formed florets, as much as 3 in. across, mostly double, in colors that include pastel blues, deep violets, alluring lavenders, indigo blue and pure white. Some striking varieties include the dark blue King Arthur Series, the pale pink Astolate Series, the clear lilac Lancelot Series and the white Galahad Series.

Much admired for their height is the Wrexham Strain, developed in England and Wales, but also known as the Hollyhock Strain, because graceful plants attain 6 ft. There are also dwarfs in the $2\frac{1}{2}$ ft. Connecticut Yankees of the Pacific Giants, characterized by bushy plants that unfold $2\frac{1}{2}$ in. flowers. Outstanding plants, superb for massing in borders, several were All-America Winners in 1965.

GEORGE TALOUMIS

ajacis = *Consolida ambigua*
cardinale   **2′–3′**   **Zone 8**   **Scarlet Larkspur**
A perennial with bright scarlet flowers and long-spurred yellowish petals, blooming in the summer. It bears rather open racemes of flowers. Native to southern Calif.

cashmerianum 1½′ **Zone 7**
The leaves are nearly rounded, 2″–4″ wide and 5–7 lobed. The flowers appear in 10–12 flowered corymbs; are 1½″ long, azure-blue. Native to the Himalayas, blooming in summer.
chinense = *D. grandiflorum*
elatum 4′–6′ **Zones 2–3 Candle Larkspur, Bee Larkspur**
This is the common Delphinium which has been bred for centuries. The rigidly upright stalks are densely covered with 2-in. flowers, single or double. This species from Siberia has purple flowers, but this is only infrequently seen with today's many selections and hybrids available.
Many strains and hybrids are available—the Pacific Hybrids, Round Table Series, Wrexham strains and Kelway hybrids are only a few.
formosum 3′–4′ **Zones 2–3 Hardy Garland Larkspur**
This variety of the Garland Larkspur is the one most commonly grown in America for it has large, rich blue flowers nearly 2 in. wide. Native to eastern Asia. Such forms as **'Belladonna'** and **'Bellamosum'** belong to this variety, as does the white-flowered **'Moerheimii'**.
'Pink Sensation' has been widely advertised, a hybrid with *D. nudicaule* being one of the parents, but it is not a true pink, it increases slowly, is very subject to mildew and is not so hardy as many of the other varieties.
grandiflorum 2′–3′ **Zones 2–3 Siberian Larkspur**
Actually a perennial, but if the seed is planted early enough it will bloom the first year. The foliage is much branched and finely cut. Flowers are blue, open to 1½ in. wide. Native to Siberia and China. It is very popular because it produces the conspicuous spikes of blue flowers in the summer garden. The variety **'Album'** has white flowers.
menziesii 20″ **Zone 3 Menzie's Larkspur**
A native from the Rocky Mountains westward to the Pacific Coast and sometimes considered a weed. It has only a few palmately lobed and dissected, alternate leaves and light blue flowers 1 in. in dia. during May and June.
nudicaule 2′ **Zone 8 Orange Larkspur**
An orange- or red-flowered species which has broader leaf divisions than does *D. cardinale*. Flowers are long-spurred, red; sepals ¼–½ in. long with the petals mostly yellow. Native to Calif.
tatsienense 2′ **Zone 6 Tatsien Larkspur**
Similar to *D. grandiflorum* with violet-blue flowers 1¼ in. long. Sometimes the leaves are mottled white in an interesting fashion. Native to western China.
tricorne 2′ **Zone 5 Dwarf Larkspur**
This species is native to the area from Pa. to Ga. and west to Neb. and Okla. The alternate

leaves are compound, the lobed leaflets radiating from a common center, and the generally blue flowers, some 1 in. long, are irregular with 2 petals extended to form a spur. The flowers are grouped in a loose terminal cluster and bloom from April to June. A plant for the rather dry, sunny garden, it may be grown from seed sown in spring or by division of the roots. The plant becomes dormant soon after flowering and so should be used where its dead foliage will be hidden by other plants.

DELTOID. Triangular; deltalike.

DENDROBIUM (den-DRO-bium). A genus of 900 species of epiphytic orchids all native to the Old World. A few produce fragrant flowers, but in some the scent is not pleasing. The flowers vary considerably according to the species. Many of these are popular among orchid fanciers. For culture and propagation see ORCHID.
densiflorum 20″ **Zone 10**
With 3–5 leathery leaves about 6 in. long near the end of the stem, flowers pale to golden yellow about 2 in. wide in profusely flowered pendulous racemes about 9 in. long from March to May. Native to the Himalayas.
formosum 1½′ **Zone 10**
Flowers white with a spot of orange-yellow, 4 in. across from Jan. to May, borne in 2–4 flowered racemes. Leaves about 5 in. long. Native to the Himalayas, Burma.
nobile 12″–30″ **Zone 10**
Actually deciduous orchids which must be effectively dried out in the fall after growth stops in order to get them to drop their leaves and bloom. If this is not done they continue to grow, forming little plantlets as side shoots instead of flowers. Flowers are blush white with lavender tips, 2–4 in. across and 2–5 on a flower stalk. A popular species with many named varieties, blooming from Jan. to June. Native to the Himalayas, Burma and China. Other species somewhat similar and being grown by orchid fanciers are **D. adrasta, D. ainsworthiae, D. merlin** and **D. superbum.**
pendulum 3′ **Zone 10**
Flowers in clusters of 2–3, white with a touch of rose-purple at the tips and each flower about 4 in. across, blooming from Feb. to May. Leaves about 5 in. long. Native to the Himalayas and Burma.
phalaenopsis 1′–3′ **Zone 10**
These are erect-growing evergreen orchids with flowers light to dark lavender, 2–4 in. across and produced in the autumn in sprays of 5–20 flowers, which last from 6 weeks to 3 months. Native to Australia and New Guinea. Other evergreen species being grown by orchid

fanciers are **D. taurinum, D. undulatum,** and **D. veratrifolium,** the Antelope Orchid.

pulchellum   4′   Zone 10
Pale yellow flowers 3–5 in. across in 6–12-flowered pendulous racemes from March to May. Native to the Himalayas, Burma and Indo-China.

DENDROCALAMUS   (den-dro-KAL-am-us). See BAMBOO.

DENDROMECON (den-dro-MEE-kon)
rigida   10′   Zone 9   Bush-poppy
An evergreen shrub native to Calif. but not planted much in the East because it prefers hot, dry situations. The lance-shaped leaves are stiff and leathery. Flowers are single, golden yellow, 1–3 in. wide and the fruit is a linear-grooved pod 2–4 in. long. Propagated by slow germinating seeds.

DENNSTAEDTIA (den-STET-ia)
punctilobula   20″–30″   Zone 3   Hay-scented
Fern
This is a native to eastern North America with fronds 11 in. wide. They are pyramidal in outline and the pinnules are finely cut. The rhizome grows just below the soil surface, growing rapidly but can be controlled merely by pulling out so many rhizomes. It is one of those that does well in a number of different soil conditions and so is of the easiest culture, making a fine ground cover for a shaded slope. Propagation is by division or spores. See FERNS.

DENTARIA (den-TAY-ria)
diphylla   6″–12″   Zone 3   Crinkleroot Tooth-
wort
Small perennial herbs blooming in the spring in the northern woods, of value only in the wild garden. The rootstock is long, leaves are 2 and opposite, toothed and shallow-lobed; flowers small and white. Native from Nova Scotia to Minn. and S.Car.
laciniata   8″–12″   Zone 3   Cutleaf Toothwort
This member of the Mustard Family (*Cruciferae*) grows in semishade, or wholly shaded areas over the eastern half of the country. It has a fleshy scaly rootstalk which has a peppery taste and deeply lobed leaves. The flowers have 4 sepals and 4 white or purplish petals and are arranged in a sparse terminal cluster. It flowers from March to May and is thus useful in the semi-shaded wild garden. A perennial, it may be divided in fall or spring.

DENTATE. With more or less spreading teeth.

DERRIS ELLIPTICA. A South American plant, collected in its native habitat, one of the sources for Rotenone, which see. Not grown in the U.S.

DESERT-CANDLE. See EREMURUS.

DESERT-WILLOW = *Chilopsis linearis*

DESMODIUM (dez-MO-dium)
canadense   3′–5′   Zone 3   Canada Tick-clover
Although this plant has the bad habits of being weedy in growth and of attaching its seed pods to the passersby, it will thrive in dry, sandy soils and so is useful in some gardens. It is a legume, with compound leaves having 3 leaflets, and deep pink irregular flowers in loose terminal clusters several inches long. Individual flowers are about ¾ in. long and appear in Aug. and Sept. The plant is native to open woods from southern Canada to Va. and west to Ill. and Okla. Propagation is by division or, if by seed, immersing them in concentrated sulfuric acid for 15 minutes before sowing.

DEUTZIA (DEWT-zia, or DOIT-zia). This group of opposite-leaved, deciduous plants has been popular with nurserymen in the past but certainly has not been popular with their customers. The plants are easily propagated by either hardwood or softwood cuttings, have few diseases and insect pests, grow fast and soon make salable plants. However, although they have profuse flowers in the late spring, they have no interesting fruits in the fall and practically no autumn color.

The genus was given its name by Thunberg for his good friend and patron, Johann van der Deutz of Amsterdam and it contains about 50 species from Asia and 2 from Mexico. Approximately 53 species and varieties are offered by American nurserymen (one nurseryman alone listed 37 a few years ago), yet less than 2 dozen are truly worth growing, and even these might be used only under certain circumstances. They are closely related to the mock-oranges, but these have 4 petals in a single flower whereas the deutzias have 5.

The flowers bloom on wood made the preceding year and have a trait of being easily started into growth by warm spells, one of the reasons why these apparently winterkill so readily, both here and in Europe. They require a great deal of pruning as a result, and such work-creating shrubs are certainly becoming less and less popular with the gardening public of America today. If left unpruned for any appreciable time, there are few deutzias which would look well.

With over 50 species in the world, there are only 3 wild species listed in the recommended list, for this is one group where the hybrids have really taken over. Victor Lemoine (1823–1912) and those who succeeded him in this world-famous French nursery firm, hybridized this group extensively, especially between 1896 and 1936. During this time they named at least 48 cultivars or hybrid species.

Propagation

Seed can be sown as soon as ripe or stored dry in airtight containers in a cool place for up to a year and then sown. Both softwood and hardwood cuttings root readily. Also many plants can be merely divided with a sharp spade early in the spring. See CUTTINGS.

x candelabrum   6′   Zone 5
This is one of the best for flower display, with upright racemes of white flowers in late May. The flower clusters are broader and denser than those of *D. gracilis*. The individual flowers are single and ¾ in. in dia. and the clusters are about 4 in. long. It is a hybrid of *D. gracilis* x *D. sieboldiana*, introduced by Lemoine in 1908.

x candida   6′   Zone 5
This has single white flowers about ¾ in. in dia., blooming in late May or early June. A hybrid (*D. lemoinei* x *D. sieboldiana*) introduced by Lemoine in 1910.

x excellens   6′   Zone 5   Choice Deutzia
Introduced by Lemoine in 1910, this is also a hybrid, (*D. vilmorinae* x *D. rosea grandiflora*). The single flowers are pinkish, about ¾ in. in dia., and are borne in 2-in. clusters.

gracilis   3′–6′   Zone 4   Slender Deutzia
This low plant is frequently covered with upright clusters of white single flowers, about ¾ in. wide and the clusters about 2 to 4 in. long. This is a graceful plant and perhaps the most dependable of all the deutzias, normally blooming during late May. Native to Japan.

grandiflora   6′   Zone 5   Early Deutzia
This is the first of the deutzias to bloom and the one with the largest single white flowers, about 1¼ in. in dia. The flowers first appear in mid-May. Native to northern China.

x kalmiiflora   6′   Zone 5   Kalmia Deutzia
Introduced by Lemoine in 1901 as a hybrid (*D. purpurascens* x *D. parviflora*). It is considered one of the 4 most outstanding deutzias in flower by the Dutch group judging them at the Experimental Station in Boskoop and is especially valued for its cup-shaped single flowers that are carmine on the outside and white within, and ¾ in. in dia. The graceful branching habit of this variety is also an asset.

x lemoinei   7′   Zone 4   Lemoine Deutzia
One of the hardiest of the deutzias with upright racemes of single white flowers, it was introduced by Lemoine in 1891 as a hybrid (*D. parviflora* x *D. gracilis*). Blooming in late May, this is one of the earlier flowering deutzias and has been used a great deal in the past for forcing purposes. It also is one of the hardier types. The variety 'Compacta' is of more dwarf and compact habit. This was introduced by Lemoine in 1904.

x magnifica   6′   Zone 5   Showy Deutzia
The double white flowers in short dense panicles appear in mid-June. This double-flowered hybrid is one of the 4 highest-scoring deutzias judged by a committee of Dutch growers at the Experiment Station in Boskoop, Holland. It was introduced by Lemoine in 1909 as a hybrid of *D. scabra* x *D. vilmorinii*. The variety 'Erecta' was introduced by Lemoine in 1914 and has flowers in dense, erect panicles.

ningpoensis   6′   Zone 5
With white flowers in panicles 5 in. long, this is one of the most recent of deutzia introductions and should be tried whenever possible. Native to eastern China and introduced in 1937.

parviflora   6′   Zone 4   Mongolian Deutzia
Unlike many of the other deutzias, this bears flat clusters of white flowers like those of some of the spires. These appear in late May and they often make a better display than some of the spireas with which they are compared. Native to northern China.

x rosea 'Eximia'   6′   Zone 5
The pinkish flowers of this deutzia are 2 in. in dia. and are superior to many others blooming in late May. It is a hybrid clone which should be asexually propagated.

Other hybrid deutzias of value as landscape plants are:—

'Azaleaflora'—(*D. scabra* x ?) with white flowers blooming in early June. Introduced by Lemoine in 1934.

'Candidissima'   8′   Zone 5
This is a selected cultivar of *D. scabra*. Originating in Europe before 1872—noted for its double-white flowers. It is frequently used in combination with *D. scabra* 'Plena' or 'Pride of Rochester' which are noted for their light pink double flowers. All these are among the last to bloom, appearing during late June in the Arnold Arboretum. It was first introduced in 1822.

'Contraste'   6′   Zone 5
A hybrid (*D. longifolia* x *D. discolor*) introduced by Lemoin in 1928 with large, single, pinkish flowers in early June and judged one of the best of all the deutzias. 'Magicien' is somewhat similar.

'Mont Rose'   8′   Zone 5
A hybrid (*D. longifolia* x *D. discolor*) introduced by Lemoine in 1925 with pale lavender-pink flowers appearing in mid-June, making this one of the later blooming types.

'Pride of Rochester'   8′   Zone 5
Introduced by Ellwanger and Barry Nursery of Rochester, N.Y., before 1893, as a clone of *D. scabra*. This is very similar to *D. scabra* 'Plena' with double flowers, rosy pink on the outside, entirely white inside and about 1 in. in dia. It is one of the latest deutzias to flower (late June in Boston) and has been very popular over the years.

DEVIL'S-CLAWS, COMMON = *Probiscidea louisiana*

DEVIL'S-CLUB = *Oplopanax horridus*

DEVIL'S WALKING-STICK = *Aralia spinosa*

DEWBERRY = *Rubus flagellaris*

DI, DIS. Greek prefix signifying 2 or twice.

DIAMOND-FLOWER, PORTUGAL = *Ionopsidium acaule*

DIANTHUS (dy-AN-thus). The pinks are very important garden annuals, biennials and perennials; mostly evergreen, small plants with narrow, grasslike opposite leaves. There are over 300 species, and although many may be grown somewhere in the U.S., probably no more than 30 species do well in American gardens and, of these, the ones listed below are the most important. They range in habitat from Siberia to southern Africa and most parts of Asia. The pungent fragrance and their bright flowers (pink, rose, white and occasionally yellow) are assets to any garden, but the extreme climate conditions in most parts of the U.S. prove too difficult for many of them. Flowers may be borne singly or in clusters up to an inch or more across, depending on the species.

They have been roughly divided into 5 general classes:

1. The grass pinks (of which *Dianthus plumarius* is an example) which are low, tufted plants, sometimes with fragrant foliage.

2. The maiden pinks (*D. deltoides*) which cling close to the ground, forming dense mats of foliage.

3. The biennials like Sweet William (*D. barbatus*) with rounded flower-heads.

4. The Carnation (*D. caryophyllus*), the extremely valued greenhouse plant.

5. Other species not grown so frequently.

The pink grown in gardens usually bloom in June and make excellent cut flowers with various combinations of gay colors. Even the perennial kinds seem to have a disappointing habit of dying out every few years and must be replaced, either by simple division of the clumps in the spring, by layers or by cuttings which fortunately root easily.

They prefer well-drained soil, slightly on the alkaline side so that if the soil is acid the application of lime in preparation for planting is good insurance for maximum growth. The moist atmosphere of the British Isles is ideal for these plants, but in America the hot dry summers and wet winters are not conducive to their vigorous growth. Areas where the summers are cool and the winters not too cold seem best. They do well in full sunshine. If they must be grown in areas of severe winters, a light cover of pine boughs after the ground freezes for the winter aids in bringing them through satisfactorily.

The gardener, with a good selection of pinks, would do well if he relied on asexual means of reproduction rather than seeds, dividing them every 3 years. In this way he is assured of maintaining his color selections. Cuttings are taken only from vegetative shoots in mid-summer. Layering is usually practiced with the popular *D. plumarius*. Cutting the flowers off, and even shearing types like *D. plumarius* after they have bloomed, brings good growth and occasionally more flowers.

Insect Pests

Spider mites are the most serious pests. See MITES. In greenhouses, spraying with insecticide #31 or #34 at frequent intervals may be necessary and resistance may require changes in materials and schedule. Fumigation with vaporized napthalene has been successful and phosphate aerosols are used. Carnation bud mite causes deformed flowers but is controlled by insecticide #13. Thrips which cause mottling of the flower petals are eliminated by aerosols and sprays of organic phosphates. Cabbage looper and cutworms which eat holes in leaves and buds are controlled with insecticide #9.

Diseases

Wilt diseases caused by 2 fungi and a bacterium are among the most destructive. They produce wilted leaves, rotted stems and sometimes roots. Sterilized soil preferably with steam, clean cuttings and favorable growing conditions are suggested. Stem rots are controlled by the same methods. Rust causes reddish-brown pustules on the leaves; spraying with fungicide #D is advised. Mosaic, streak and yellows are virus-induced diseases of both the leaves and the flower. The symptoms are described by the names. Clean cuttings and control of aphids is suggested. Several leaf spots infect the foliage and fungicides #D, #K and #W are used both as protective agents and to check established infections.

x allwoodii 4"–20" Zones 2–3 Allwood Pink
Hybrids between *D. plumarius* x *D. caryophyllus* originating in England, these perennials come in several colors, usually with a good tufted habit. They can be easily increased by layering. and make excellent garden plants, easily grown and cared for and of good bright colors.

alpinus 3" Zones 2–3 Alpine Pink
Native from Switzerland to Greece and Russia these are tufted plants apparently doing best in partial shade. The pink flowers are so profuse they hide the leaves for nearly a month during the late spring. A hybrid (*D. plumarius* x *D. alpinus*) named **'Little Joe'**, produced in Ore. with single crimson flowers, is a ball of color

much of the summer, but since there are few leaves the plant must be protected over winter. The flowers of the species are 1½ in. wide but are not fragrant. Good for the rock garden.

arenarius 6″–15″ Zones 2–3 Sand Pink
Somewhat similar to a small plant of *D. plumarius* but only slightly fragrant, this is native to Finland. Most plants are small and tufted with pink or white flowers, 1½ in. wide, blooming from early June to early July, with the petals deeply cut and slightly fringed. They may bloom a second time in the fall. Leaves are grasslike, 1–2 in. long and usually opposite.

x arvernensis 4″–15″ Auvergne Pink
A mat-forming perennial pink with grayish foliage, supposedly a hybrid found in the wild with 2–3 pink flowers on stems 2–4 in. tall. The small leaves are mostly basal and only ½ in. long. Probably mixed up in the trade.

barbatus 2′ annual or biennial Sweet William
A very popular and old-fashioned garden favorite with many varieties of most colorful summer flowers, native to Russia and China. Actually a perennial, it is best treated as a biennial, with seed sown in a frame in the late summer, the seedlings protected from extreme cold over winter. These will bloom the summer of the year after they are sown. Also there are strains that can be treated as annuals by sowing the seed indoors in April and planting out after the frost. They do not grow well in acid soil, so add lime.

The flowers are in brightly colored terminal clusters, pink, red, white and variations, with some double forms available. The 'Newport Pink' is one of the best salmon-pink forms, 'Homeland' is a good red and 'Midget' is a dwarf strain (only 4 in. high) of mixed colors, excellent for edging purposes. None of these is fragrant. 'Indian Carpet'—5–6 in.

brevicaulis 1″ Zone 6 Mt. Taurus Pink
The leaves are only ¼–½ in. long, usually only a pair of them on each stem close to the solitary flower. The flowers are purple, ½ in. wide. Native to Asia Minor. A plant for the rock garden.

carthusianorum 2′ Zones 2–3 Clusterhead Pink
A lanky-growing species from Hungary which should not be planted alone but in amongst other plants so the flowers will be held upright and not flop over. Odorless red or purple flowers are borne in a few-to-many-flowered head 2–3 in. across, from June to early Aug. Native from Denmark to the Ural Mountains to Portugal. A variable species and not one of the best for the garden.

caryophyllus 1′–3′ Zone 8 Carnation, Clove Pink
It is from this Eurasian species that the common greenhouse carnation has been developed. The species is not very hardy, nor is it used much in northern gardens. The flowers are either solitary or few to a stem, an inch and more across, showy and very fragrant. In cultivation, varieties are available in pink, rose, purple, red, white and yellow.

The greenhouse Carnation has been developed over the years from this species. If the home greenhouse can be kept about 50° F. at night and 60° F. during the day, Carnations can be grown, or they can be grown outdoors where the winters are mild (Calif.), but often even then they should have winter protection.

Cuttings are taken of the greenhouse Carnation in Nov. and Dec. from the sturdy vegetative shoots at the base of the plant. These are placed in sand, with bottom heat (see CUTTINGS) and should be rooted in 4–6 weeks after which they are potted.

The potted cuttings eventually can be planted out-of-doors after all frost is over and grown for the rest of the summer, when they are brought into the greenhouse and planted in the greenhouse bench. Or, if space is available they can be planted directly in the greenhouse bench. Plants should be 6 in. apart in the rows and the rows spaced 12 in. apart. New soil should be provided in the bench—never use old soil from the previous year.

If one does not care about large blooms, little attention need be given the plants after they are once in the greenhouse bench. On the other hand, if large blooms (and fewer blooms) are desired, then all side shoots should be pinched off and the plant grown with a single stem, and the plants should begin blooming in about 7 weeks and continue until the following May or June. During this time a well-grown plant will produce 12–18 flowers.

chinensis 1½′ annual Chinese Pink
A fragrant pink from China with flowers white, red or lilac, about 1 in. wide and in loose clusters or borne singly, not much planted. The really popular form is 'Heddewigii' which has flowers in many colors and some of large size. It is this which comprises the annual pinks most commonly grown in gardens throughout the country.

deltoides 4″–15″ Zones 2–3 Maiden Pink
A popular mat-forming perennial garden pink, low as far as foliage is concerned but with flower stalks 4–15 in. high, forming dense mounds of foliage and becoming very persistent and invading. Flowers are red or pink with a crimson eye, about ¼ in. wide, and the grasslike leaves are very narrow. There are many blooms on each stem during May and June. Since it does trail it can be used in rock walls or ledges

and can be a ground cover in the full sun. Native from western Europe to eastern Asia, naturalized in the U.S. The variety **'Brilliant'** is one selection with bright red flowers.

glacialis 3″–4″ **Zone 5** **Ice Pink** Native to the mountains of southern Europe, with 4-angled flower stems bearing 1–2 fragrant rose-to-white flowers about ½ in. wide. Not especially outstanding.

graniticus 4″–7″ **Zone 6?** **Granite Pink** Bearing 1–3 reddish-purple flowers about ¾ in. wide, basal leaves very narrow, tufted. Native to the Pyrenees. Not one of the most popular species.

gratianopolitanus 4″ **Zone 3** **Cheddar Pink** A mat-forming, extremely dense, evergreen perennial, tufted, but individual plants placed a foot or less apart eventually grow into one dense carpet of foliage making a perfect ground cover for a small spot, or a fine specimen for the rock garden. Small, single, rose-pink, fragrant flowers, about an inch or less across, are borne intermittently in early summer, but it is the carpetlike foliage of this evergreen specimen that makes it a valued addition in the foreground of any garden or rockery. Native from England to southern Europe.

knappii 8″–20″ **Zones 2–3** **Hardy Garden Pink** Not very tufted, with flat leaves 2½ in. tall, flowers pale yellow with brownish mark in center, borne in heads of 8–10 flowers each about ¾ in. wide, not fragrant. Native to Hungary and Yugoslavia. This is probably the only truly yellow-flowered Dianthus. Requires sandy soil. Probably more of a novelty than a good ornamental specimen.

x latifolius 10″–16″ **Zone 5** **Button Pink** This hybrid is usually considered to be intermediate in character between *D. barbatus* and *D. chinensis* or *D. plumarius*. The leaves are broad and grasslike; the flowers are an inch or less across, borne 1–6 in a cluster and are rose to dark red, single or double. Its one bad fault is that the calyx does split. They bloom for several weeks, some so much they actually kill themselves with too many flowers. Many hybrid clones have been named, but unfortunately they have a bad reputation of blooming themselves to death.

myrtinervius 2″ **Zone ?** A tufted perennial, possibly a form of *D. deltoides* but much smaller, and although the flowers are profuse, they are singly borne. Native to Macedonia. Good for the rock garden.

petraeus noeanus 10″ **Zone 4** A very green, densely tufted, little evergreen perennial with needlelike leaves ¾ in. long and stems bearing 1–10 small white flowers about ¾ in. wide in a loose cluster during summer.

pavonius 2″ **Zone 5** **Glacier Pink** Cushionlike perennials with evergreen foliage, with 6-in. stems of red to pink flowers. This is one species that need not be grown in purely alkaline soils. Native to the mountains of southern Europe.

plumarius 1¼′ **Zone 3** **Cottage Pink, Grass Pink** This was introduced from Europe in colonial days and has been an extremely popular garden pink ever since. The flowers, 1½ in. in dia., blooming in May and June are red, pink or white, single or double, borne 2–3 per stem and are very fragrant. The distinctive gray foliage makes the plant excellent for edging. There are many varieties; one of the best and most recent is **'Pink Princess'** produced by the U.S. Department of Agriculture at Cheyenne, Wyo., with coral-rose flowers, 1½ in. wide that bloom for weeks, starting in May.

superbus 2′ **biennial** **Lilac Pink** With pale rose-to-lilac-colored, very fragrant flowers about 1½ in. wide, with few to many in a weak panicle and native from Spain to Norway and Japan. The flowers are deeply fringed. Best treated as a biennial.

x winteri 1′ **Zone 6?** A hybrid of questioned parentage, usually classed as one of the sturdy border carnation group—a long-blooming hardy grower. Clumps of plants 12 years old and older are known to be in excellent condition. Flowers apricot or lemon yellow, blooming most of the summer.

DIAPENSIA (dia-PEN-sia)
lapponica 4″ **Zone 2** **Arctic Diapensia** Extremely difficult to grow, this small plant is native around the polar regions of the globe southward to the mountains of N.Y. and New England and is not a good ornamental. The tufted evergreen leaves are opposite, ½ in. long; the solitary, white, bell-shaped flowers are ¾ in. wide and bloom in June and July.

DIAPENSIACEAE = The Galax or Pyxie Family

DIASCIA (dy-ASS-ia)
barberae 1′ **annual** **Twinspur** A plant from South Africa with opposite leaves, rosy-pink flowers ½ in. across, each with a yellow throat, borne in 6-in. terminal racemes. This may be grown in the open border from seed either sown indoors in March or outdoors in April. It is also used as a pot plant.

DICENTRA (dy-SEN-tra). Excellent, sturdy plants for the flower garden which, with the right selection of species, will give colorful flowers from May until frost. The compound leaves are interesting in themselves, being very feathery in texture. They grow best in partial shade. Seeds may be sown in the late summer, but division of plants is best done in early spring. Root cuttings can be taken in the early summer. Cuttings of vegetative shoots of *D. spectabilis* can be rooted in late July.

canadensis   1′   Zone 4   Squirrel-corn
A perennial rising from a small bulb, the leaves are compound and finely divided. The flowers have a heart-shaped corolla and crested petals. They are greenish-white and are borne in drooping terminal clusters. Native to rich woods over much of eastern U.S., the fragrant flowers appear in April and May. An excellent garden plant when grown in rich soil and partial shade. It may be propagated by seed sown in fall or by division of the tiny yellow tubers.

chrysantha   5′   Zone 8   Golden Eardrops
Flowers sulfur yellow with short spurs, produced in large racemes. Native to Calif. and difficult to cultivate.

cucullaria   10″–12″   Zone 3   Dutchman's Breeches
Similar to *D. canadense*, this tuberous plant has basal leaves which die to the ground after the flowering season. The white-to-pinkish corolla is divided into 2 spurs and the 2 inner petals are crested. It flowers in early spring. Seeds may be sown in summer and stratified through the winter and the tiny bulbs may be reset, preferably in spring. If the plant does not bloom after transplanting, a light application of lime to the soil will encourage flowering.

eximia   1′–2′   Zones 2–3   Fringed Bleeding-heart
This fine perennial is native from N.Y. to Ga. and makes a nice ground cover if the plants are set about 8 in. apart. It grows in a clump and does not spread. The pink flowers are heart-shaped on spikes 12 in. tall, and may remain colorful for 6 weeks in the summer. It is also a fine plant for summer display in the front part of the perennial border. Propagated by division of the clumps.

formosa   1′   Zones 2–3   Pacific Bleeding-heart
Blooming from May to Sept., this is native from British Columbia to Calif. and is similar to *D. eximia* except that it has deep pink flowers. The variety 'Sweetheart' has pure white flowers.

oregana = *D. formosa*

spectabilis   2′   Zones 2–3   Common Bleeding-heart
Robert Fortune is supposed to have first taken this excellent plant from the Orient to England in 1847. It is fortunately one of the most common of garden plants in America and has been for many decades. Each flower is shaped like a double-winged lyre and the pink flowers appear on delicately drooping spikes during May and June. It will die out in wet soils, doing best in soils with good drainage and in partial shade. There is a variety 'Alba' with pure white flowers, but it is not so dependable a garden plant as is the species.

DICHONDRA (di-KON-dra)

micrantha (*repens*)   3″   Zone 10   Dichondra
This is a grass substitute for lawns widely used in the southwestern U.S. and can be used wherever winter temperatures do not drop below 25° F. It is not a grass but a creeping, broad-leaved, perennial plant with rounded leaves less than ½ in. dia. and native in the West Indies.

Seed may be sown any time between March

Dicentra spectabilis alba (White Bleeding Heart): A garden favorite. (*Photo by Arnold Arboretum, Jamaica Plain, Mass.*)

1st and Oct. 15th. Seed germinates well during midsummer, but in the hot, dry areas where this is used, it is difficult to keep the germinating seedlings moist enough at that time to bring them through. Hence seed sowing during March April and May is usually insurance that the young seedlings will get off to a good start. Two pounds of seed per 1000 sq. ft. is recommended to give a good lawn in 5 weeks. It should not be sown in mixtures and does not need a nurse crop. If it reseeds in a grass lawn where it is not desired, it should be killed immediately with 2-4-D., before it "takes over."

A Dichondra lawn can also be planted from plugs of the plant, bought in flats and cut with a knife, into 2-in. squares. Plugs should be set just at the soil level, 6–12 in. apart. A lawn made of Dichondra does need as much attention as a grass lawn, frequent watering and an occasional fertilizing and mowing. If growing in the shade without people continually walking on it, mowing may be needed as frequently as it would with grass. However, in the hot sun, with people walking on it frequently, the times between mowings can be considerably lengthened. It may well be that many of the plants cultivated under the names of *D. repens* are actually *D. micrantha*.

A few insects like the cutworms, red spider, slugs and nematodes occasionally infest a Dichondra lawn as does a fungus, but most of these are easily controlled. See GRASS.

DICHORISANDRA (dy-kor-is-AND-ra)
thyrsiflora   3′   Zone 10
A tropical perennial from Brazil, with alternate, glossy green, lance-shaped leaves and blue flowers borne in huge racemes. The habit is somewhat like that of an umbrella. Propagated by seeds, cuttings and division.

DICKSONIA (dik-SO-nia). These are tree ferns from tropical America, Australia, and New Zealand, with 12 ft. fronds, and trunks 40 ft. tall, hence these are too big for the small greenhouse. The species apparently in nurseries in southern Calif. is *D. antarctica* which grows 40 ft. tall and can be grown out-of-doors in frost-free parts of southern Calif. This species has fronds 5–6 ft. long. All these ferns take in water through their aerial roots on the stems so it is advisable to syringe these frequently and well.

DICOTYLEDONS (dicots). Plants having two cotyledons or seed lobes. See also MONOCOTYLEDONS.

DICTAMNUS (dik-TAME-nus)
albus   3′   Zones 2–3   Gasplant, or Dittany
Native from southern Europe to northern China this alternate-leaved perennial has odd pinnate, compound leaves. The name comes from the fact that if a lighted match is placed under the flower cluster near the stem there will be a flash as the gas ignites. Varieties include **purpureus** with purple flowers and **rubra** with rosy-purple flowers in June. It is a long-enduring standby in the perennial border and should be given a position in the full sun. The plant and especially the seed pods are poisonous. It is propagated by seed, sown in the fall and let alone for a full year before the seedlings are transplanted. Seed should be collected as the pods turn brown, for if left longer the bursting pods disburse the seed. This makes a fine specimen in the flower border.

DIDISCUS CAERULEA = *Trachymene caerulea*

DIEBACK. A term describing the death of the tip shoots of plants. It may refer to the result of infection by bacterial fungus or virus diseases or infestation by sucking insects. It may also be caused by abnormal heat, cold or drought.

DIEFFENBACHIA (dee-fen-BAK-ia). Popular foliage aroids of the American tropics making excellent house plants in the North. They require a warm temperature (70–80° F.) in the greenhouse and plenty of water. They bear a few oblong leaves at the end of stems, are shrubby and produce a number of very small flowers (unisexual) and a spadix, and fleshy fruit.

Propagation is simple, merely by cutting a piece of the stem at a time when it is partially dormant, placing it lengthwise in moist sand over bottom heat. After it has rooted it can be potted up as a new plant.

amoena   2′   Zone 10   Dumb-cane
A popular house plant native to tropical America with lance-shaped alternate leaves 14–20 in. long and 6–10 in. wide. These have irregular yellowish markings and are most ornamental for this reason. The highly acrid juice irritates the mucous membranes so much that speech is difficult or impossible for several days after it is eaten. It has been said that this used to be given slaves as a punishment.

bowmannii   3′   Zone 10   Bowman Tuftroot
Leaves 16 in. long, 8 in. wide with white spots; spathes 6 in. long.

picta   4′   Zone 10   Variable Tuftroot
Lustrous leaves are irregularly marked with yellow and white; spathes about 6 in. This is a popular species with several named varieties.

seguine   6′   Zone 10   Seguin Tuftroot
Sometimes called Dumb Cane because chewing the stem renders one speechless for a time. The leaves are irregularly spotted with white. Native to the West Indies.

x splendens   4′   Zone 10   White Spot Tuftroot
A hybrid (*D. leopoldii* x *D. picta*) with white spotted leaves.

DIELDRIN. A chlorinated hydrocarbon used as an insecticide. See INSECTICIDES.

DIERVILLA (DEER-vil-a)

lonicera   3′   Zone 3   Dwarf Bush-honeysuckle
Found native in eastern North America, the shrub has little to offer as an ornamental except that it can grow on banks. The flowers are not conspicuous and the fruits are merely dried capsules. It grows on poor soils and is easily propagated by suckers or division. Seed can be sown as soon as ripe.

rivularis   6′   Zone 5   Georgia Bush-honey-suckle
This differs little from the other 2 members of this genus except for the fact that the branches and leaves are pubescent, while those of the other 2 species are glabrous or nearly so. It is a native of N.Car., Ga. and Ala., but can survive as far north as southern New England. It has little to warrant its planting in gardens but it will withstand moist soil.

sessilifolia   4½′   Zone 4   Southern Bush-honeysuckle
More ornamental in flower than the other 2 species in this genus, the flowers are deep yellow and trumpet-shaped, appearing in late June. It is also a native of the eastern U.S. and makes a fair ground cover, spreading rapidly by underground stolons. It is of little value as a specimen or in a good garden, but can be counted on to aid in holding the soil on banks or in rugged terrain where better plants will not grow.

DIFFUSE. Loosely or widely spreading.

DIGGING. For those unaccustomed to gardening, there is a simple little plan even in digging soil in preparation for a flower bed. The idea is to turn under the vegetative material on the surface as well as to break the soil up and allow air into it. By working backwards, one can dig in a straight line. Some soils can be "spaded" just as well with a flat-tined digging fork as with a spade, and the fork is easier to use in digging and also in breaking up the clumps of soil. Digging to the depth of the blade of fork or spade, and turning the soil upside down, breaking up the clumps in so doing, is this simple operation, leaving the soil at about the same level it was before the digging. Not difficult but it should be done right.

DIGITALIS (dij-it-AY-lis). These are old favorites in American gardens but since some of the newer hybrids are far superior to any of the species, the chances are that the Shirley and Excelsior hybrids are the best of all to grow for large and showy flowers. The flowers of *D. purpurea* tend to be largely on one side of the spike, but those of the new Excelsior hybrids are well distributed on all sides, and these hybrids come in several excellent colors also.

Foxgloves need a fairly rich well-drained soil but will not grow in wet soils. They seem to do best in partial shade. Those that are biennials should be renewed each year by sowing seed in Aug., and these will result in plants that bloom the following year. Some can be divided in the early spring.

Digitalis or Foxglove

ambigua = *D. grandiflora*
grandiflora   3′   Zone 3   Yellow Foxglove
With yellowish flowers about 2 in. long marked with brown and blooming during June and July. Native to Europe and W. Asia. Usually a short-lived perennial, also a biennial.

lanata   3′   Zone 3   Grecian Foxglove
Either biennial or sometimes perennial, from Greece, this has white flowers only about an inch long, not easily found in nursery catalogues, nor is it a very great addition to the perennial flower border.

purpurea   2′–4′   Zone 4   biennial   Foxglove
A biennial, popular in flower gardens, native to Europe. The flowers are large, drooping, bell-shaped, 2 in. long, borne on erect spikes in the summer, usually purple but there is a white-flowered variety **alba,** and **maculata 'Superba'** which is an improved form with spotted flowers. The alternate leaves are crowded near

the base of the plant. The leaves are poisonous to humans, cattle and horses. The leaves yield a heart stimulant. This plant prefers shady places with a moist atmosphere, blooming in June. Seeds are sown outdoors in May and the plants transplanted in the early fall to where they are to bloom the following year. The var. 'Gloxinaeflora' has one unusually large flower at the top of the spike, the remainder being normal in size.

DIGITARIA sp. (dig-i-TAY-ria). Pestiferous, annual, lawn-weed grasses, widespread throughout North America but also native to Europe. The leaves can be as much as 6 in. long and $\frac{1}{3}$ in. wide. For further information on control see WEEDS and WEED-CONTROLLING CHEMICALS. The most common is **D. sanguinalis**, the common Crab Grass, growing sometimes as much as 3 ft. tall and getting in to poorly kept lawns as a weed grass, especially evident in the fall. The leaves are about 6 in. long, $\frac{1}{3}$ in. wide and often 3–10 seem to grow together. It seeds readily in the fall, and to keep it from spreading it should be closely cut to prevent seed formation.

DIGITATE. With the members rising at one point.

DILL = *Anethum graveolens*

DILLENIA (dill-EE-nia)

    indica   40'   **Zone 10**   **Hondapara, India Dillenia**

The solitary, fragrant, magnolialike flowers are pure white, 7 in. wide, with a mass of golden stamens borne at the ends of the branches. The coarse evergreen leaves are nearly 12 in. long, and rather oblong in general outline. The hard fruits are $3\frac{1}{2}$ in. long and rather greenish, with the fleshy part being the enlarged calyx. It is acid, somewhat resembling the taste of a green apple, and has been used in making jellies and preserves. Native to India.

DILLENIACEAE = The Silvervine Family

DIMORPHOTHECA (dy-mor-fo-THEE-ka)

    ecklonis   2'   **Zone 10**   **Bedding Cape-marigold**
A shrubby perennial from South Africa with lanceolate leaves and flower heads with rays white above and purple beneath, closing at night. These make a good display in the greenhouse but need a long growing season for best results. Propagated by seeds and cuttings.

    pluvialis   4"–16"   **annual**   **Rain Cape-marigold**
Flowers with white rays above, violet or purple beneath, heads about 1–2 in. across, disc yellow. The leaves are alternate, entire to pinnatifid, $3\frac{1}{2}$ in. long and 1 in. wide. Native to South Africa. This herb with its showy heads of flowers is beautiful when the flowers are fully open. Var. *ringens* produces white ray flowers that are bluish violet at the base. Good plants

for the summer garden, belonging to the Composite Family.

    sinuata $1\frac{1}{2}'$ **annual-perennial**   **Winter Cape-marigold**
Treated as an annual in the North, this is a tropical perennial from South Africa especially for hot, dry situations. The alternate leaves are 3 in. long, narrow and toothed, and the ray flowers (it is a member of the Composite Family) are orange, lemon or white. Requiring a long period of high temperatures to come into bloom, these are started in early March in the greenhouse, and then planted out in the full sun after danger of frost is passed. Often listed as *D. aurantica* which actually is a synonym. Good plants for the summer garden.

DIMORPHOUS. Occurring in 2 forms.

DIOECIOUS PLANTS. Some groups of plants bear staminate flowers all on one plant and pistillate or fruiting flowers all on another plant; in other words, they are dioecious. At first glance, this may not appear very important to many gardeners. However, some of these plants make extremely important garden specimens, and a knowledge of their flowering and fruiting habits before they are selected makes all the difference between success and failure, if colorful ornamental specimens were desired.

    The following genera are dioecious:

Acer	Garrya	Podocarpus
Actinidia	Ginkgo	Populus
Ailanthus	Helwingia	Rhus
Aucuba	Hippophae	Ribes
Baccharis	Idesia	Ruscus
Broussonetia	Ilex	Salix
Carica	Juniperus	Schisandra
Celastrus	Leitneria	Securinega
Cephalotaxus	Lindera	Shepherdia
Cercidiphyllum	Maclura	Skimmia
Chionanthus	Morus	Smilax
Comptonia	Myrica	Taxus
Cotinus	Nemopanthus	Torreya
Diospyros	Orixa	Vitis
Eucommia	Phellodendron	Zanthoxylum

    A cursory examination of these genera shows that some are not valued for their ornamental fruits, so it actually makes little difference whether staminate or pistillate plants are grown. With some of the others it makes a great difference. For instance, the Tree of Heaven (*Ailanthus altissima*) has seeded itself over wide areas of our urban wastelands, and will grow under the most trying conditions where no other tree will do well. When fully open, the staminate flowers give off an obnoxious odor— the reason this type should not be grown. The fruits of the pistillate plant, on the other hand, can be very colorful in the fall. The brilliant red fruits of *Aucuba japonica* can only be insured if the staminate and pistillate forms are growing together in the near vicinity.

Most of the hollies are notably dioecious, but *Ilex cornuta* is the rare example of a plant which, in its pistillate form, will produce red fruit without pollinization. Of course, viable seeds are not produced in such instances, but from an ornamental standpoint pistillate plants are the only ones worthy of growing in the garden. In other experiments we found a plant of *I. laevigata* performing similarly. However, perfect flowers on a plant of *I. opaca* are practically unknown, although various individuals have examined thousands of plants and many have investigated countless reports to the contrary.

The pistillate plants of the Ginkgo, also in this dioecious group, bear fruits that have an obnoxious odor, resulting in the pistillate form being undesirable for garden planting. On the other hand, in several genera like *Baccharis*, *Comptonia*, *Helwingia*, *Phellodendron*, *Populus*, *Salix*, *Smilax* and *Zanthoxylum*, it makes little difference as to which sex is used in normal ornamental planting.

Holly, Yew and Bayberry are planted primarily for their fruit and usually both sexes must be planted on the same place to insure the fruiting of the pistillate plants. Usually the staminate plant is placed in the background, or if in a large, massed planting, at the rate of 1 staminate plant to 5 or 10 pistillate plants. Sometimes it happens that a neighbor may have pollen-bearing plants comparatively nearby that will prove sufficient for fertilizing purposes; then only pistillate plants need be used.

With vines like the Bittersweet, a staminate vine could be planted in the same hole with a pistillate or fruiting vine, an effort being made through the years to keep the pollen-bearing plant from growing too vigorously. Bittersweet plants are easily budded in Aug. and the active gardener could well afford to try his hand at placing a few buds from a pollen plant on his single fruiting plant. When this has not been done and only a single fruiting plant is grown, I have had excellent success with cutting a handful of flowering branches from the pollen plant and hanging them in a bottle of water in the middle of the fruiting plant and, as the flowers open, insect, wind and gravitation will usually do an excellent job of fertilization.

So, in planning for colorful fruits of these dioecious plants, make certain to have a majority of the true pistillate plants with the certainty that some pollen-bearing plants are on the same property or else close by. It is only by doing this that colorful fruit can be assured.

DIONAEA (dy-o-NEE-a)
  muscipula   8″–12″   Zone 8   Venus Flytrap

A curious plant, the Venus Flytrap is an insectivorous perennial, catching its prey by means of the leaves which are basal, the upper portion of which is hinged and has spines along the outer edges, as well as 3 tiny spines on the inner surface of either side of the leaf. An insect touching 2 of these 3 inner spines causes the leaf to fold shut, trapping the insect which is subsequently digested by the plant. In the spring a cluster of small white flowers is borne at the top of the slender stalk which arises from the rosette of leaves. The plant is native to the swamps of N.Car. and S.Car., but may be grown in a greenhouse in sphagnum moss or in soil with a pH of 4 to 4.5.

DIOSCOREA (dy-os-kor-EE-a)
  batatas   vine   Zone 10   Cinnamon-vine,
  Chinese Yam
Grown in the tropics for the edible tuberous root, 2–3 ft. long usually situated deep in the soil. The angled stem is often twisted and bears small bulbil-like tubers in the axils of the opposite 7–9-nerved leaves which are 1½–3 in. long. The cinnamon-scented flowers are in racemelike spikes. Native to China. Often grown in the North as an ornamental.
  bulbifera   vine   Zone 10   Air-potato Yam
A tropical twining vine from tropical Asia and the Philippines, bearing tubers nearly a foot long in the leaf axils. Leaves are alternate, ovate and heart-shaped at the base. Underground tubers are either small or missing altogether. Grown in tropical countries for the edible air-borne tubers.
  villosa   vine   Zone 6   Atlantic Yam
Not an ornamental but found from R.I. to Tex. with a woody rootstock ¾ in. thick; leaves heart-shaped at the base.

DIOSCOREACEAE = The Yam Family

DIOSPYROS (dy-os-PY-ros). Chiefly alternate-leaved species, the 3 mostly grown in America are deciduous, with fleshy, edible fruits. Flowers are mostly unisexual, although not always, but it is best to grow named varieties that have a good record of fruiting. Propagation is by budding or grafting, using as understock either *D. virginiana* or *D. kaki*. Seed should be stratified as soon as ripe for 3 months at 40° F. Transplanting is difficult because of a strong tap root, so the smaller the tree the easier it is transplanted.

Insect Pests

Persimmon borer, the larva of a clear wing moth, is similar to the peach borer and burrows in the lower stem and roots. Nursery stock has been badly damaged. Spraying the trunk in mid-summer with insecticide #9 gives control. Bark beetles attack weakened trees.

ebenaster   60′   Zone 10   Indian Ebony Persimmon
This tropical Mexican tree is sometimes cultivated for its sweet, olive-green fruits, which are
up to 5 in. long and appear in Mexican markets
late in the winter. It is a close relative of our
American Persimmon, with dark, glossy green,
leathery leaves 3–6 in. long. The fragrant white
flowers appear in groups of 3–8 in the axils of
the leaves.

kaki   40′   Zone 7   Kaki Persimmon
Sometimes called the Japanese Persimmon, this
is actually a native to China and produces the
large edible, orange to bright yellow, fleshy
fruits that are 1½–4 in. in dia. The deciduous,
alternate leaves are 2–6 in. long, glossy above
and slightly downy beneath. There are several
Japanese varieties being grown in America and
some of these are pistillate trees and do not need
pollination to bear fruits—only to bear seeds
which of course are not desirable. When grown
from seed, the size of the fruits of resulting
seedlings is unknown and some of the plants
might be all staminate. Hence it is much better
to buy plants of named varieties and known sex.
These trees are grown commercially chiefly in
Calif., Tex. and Fla. This species can be grown
in many soils and apparently has no serious
pests, but it is difficult to transplant because of
a strong tap root. This makes a nice ornamental
shade tree. Most varieties are self-sterile. The
variety **'Gailey'** produces a large number of
staminate flowers and 1 of this for every 8 of
another variety might be a satisfactory combination for good fruiting. Varieties that appear
to be self-fertile are **'Tanenashi'** and **'Fuyugaki'**
and it is therefore these varieties that are
recommended for single or group plantings in
the South, especially in Fla., where this species
proves hardy.

It should be noted that branches of *D. kaki*
trees split rather easily with heavy loads of
fruits. For this reason special care should be
taken in pruning for the right kind of framework
so that branches will not be allowed to grow
too long. It might help if they are not planted
more than 20 ft. apart. Then when they reach
maturity they can be annually pruned to this
space.

The best information on culture can always
be obtained at the nearest State Agricultural
Experiment Station.

lotus   40′   Zone 6   Date-plum
This species, native to China and Japan, is
somewhat similar to *D. virginiana* but the fruit
is inferior to it. Hence the Date-plum is not a
particularly good tree for home gardeners to
plant. It is sometimes used in Calif. as understock in grafting *D. kaki*.

virginiana   75′   Zone 4   Common Persimmon

The Common Persimmon is found native over
a wide area of the eastern and southeastern
states. The trees are round-headed, often with
slightly pendulous branches, dense foliage with
alternate leaves about 3–6 in. long, and orange
fruits about 1½ in. in dia., usually considered
edible after freezing. The sexes are frequently
separate, but clones have been selected for their
large fruits such as **'Early Golden'**, **'Ruby'**
and **'Miller'**. To become edible the fruits must
become fully ripe and soft, usually not until
after the first hard frost in the fall. The bark of
the trunk is characteristically deeply cut into
regular, small blocks.

DIPLOID. An organism with a chromosome
number double that of the normal generation,
sometimes referred to as the 2n generation. The
normal generation or haploid, is often referred
to as the n generation.

DIPSACEAE = The Teasel Family

DIPSACUS (DIP-sak-us)
sativus   6′–8′   Zone 5   Fuller's Teasel
Usually biennial, this used to be an important
crop to the woollen industry especially in
Europe where it is native. The stiff, spiny fruit
heads were used to raise the nap on woolen and
felt cloth, and it is still used in some areas for
this purpose. This, like *D. sylvestris*, is a very
prickly plant and few wish to grow it as an
ornamental, but the dried heads are used in
dried arrangements. It differs little from *D.
sylvestris*.

sylvestris   9′   Zone 3   Teasel
A biennial European weed, widely naturalized
in the central and northeastern U.S. with
opposite oblong-lanceolate leaves, prickly on
the undersurface and margins and pale lavender
flowers in a 2-in. long flowering head. The
flowering stem also is prickly and the fruiting
head, about 2 in. long, is extremely prickly but
it has some ornamental value in dried flower
arrangements.

DIRCA (DER-ka)
palustris   6′   Zone 4   Leatherwood
Native to eastern North America, this alternate-
leaved shrub is valued for its early yellow
flowers in March or April. They are not as
conspicuous as those of Forsythia. The stems
and branches are very pliable and were used by
the Indians to tie things together—the reason
why it was given the common name. The leaves
are 1–3 in. long and the bark contains poisonous
properties, causing severe irritation and blistering of the skin.

Propagation

Seed may be sown as soon as ripe or stored
dry in airtight containers in a cool place for up

to a year, then sown. Also layers root well. See
LAYERS.

DISANTHUS (dis-AN-thus)
  cercidifolius   8′   Zones 6 or 7
A native of the mountains of central Japan with
uninteresting dark purple flowers in the fall and
dull greenish leaves 2–4½ in. long, its best
ornamental asset is its scarlet-to-orange autumn
color. The leaves are palmately veined with
5–7 main veins in each leaf blade.

DISBUDDING. This practice of removing some
of the flower buds of certain types of plants
like chrysanthemum, carnation and peony, is as
old as the hills. It is standard practice in many
a commercially operated greenhouse in order
that the flower buds remaining after the disbudding will produce larger flowers. This same
practice is carried out in the flower garden when
unusually large blooms are desired for show
purposes.

The pinching off of young shoots of annuals
and perennials is actually a pruning process, the
idea being to force the plant to send out more
buds and hence make a more compact plant.
The term disbudding usually refers to the
removing of flower buds only, especially in
those cases where several are formed; all would
produce small flowers if all were allowed to
develop.

DISC, DISK = In the Composite Family there
are two kinds of flowers in the flower head, the
ray flowers around the edge and these are usually
colored, and the central or disc (disk) flowers
which are usually smaller and colored yellow
in most cases. These form the central core of
small flowers in the center. In the Field Daisy
for instance, the ray flowers around the perimeter are white, the disc flowers in the center
are yellow.

DISEASES, PLANT. A plant disease has been
described as an abnormal condition of a plant.
The cause may be mechanical, environmental or
pathogenic. Abnormalities caused by insects,
mites and small animals are considered separately.

Physiological diseases are noninfectious and
are the result of an injury or the occurrence of
an unnatural condition. They may have
relatively minor importance when caused but
often have serious secondary consequences,
especially when they permit the infection of
pathogenic diseases.

Mechanical injuries from tools, automobiles,
construction, paving and changes in the water
level or soil level in grading occur frequently.

Environmental factors which produce abnormal growth frequently contribute to disease
of this kind. Among the many conditions are
lightning injury, illuminating gas leaks and

excess salt used for melting ice. Serious injury
from the improper use of chemical fertilizers,
pesticides including weed killers, unfavorable
soil acidity and malnutrition from plant competition such as shrubs and lawn grasses growing under shallow-rooted trees are common
problems. Of a climatic nature are chlorosis
from the lack of specific nutrients, leaf burn,
scorch and scald from excessive heat and
drought and oedema from insufficient ventilation. Before blaming the poor condition of a
plant on the more mysterious pathogens, all of
the above possibilities should be carefully
investigated. A related problem concerns the
storage of tubers, bulbs, nursery stock, fruits
and vegetables. Freezing should be prevented,
and lack of sufficient moisture causes drying
and withering of roots and dormant buds as
well as of fruits and vegetables. Various diseases
develop at different low temperatures but 35°
to 40° F. are practical. Bulbs and root vegetables
should be stored in sandy soil which is kept
moistened slightly.

Pathogenic diseases are caused by fungi,
bacteria, viruses and occasionally by nematodes.

Fungi are flowerless plants which live
parasitically on other material. If the host is
living, they are called parasites, if dead, saprophytes. They grow by producing rootlike
threads called mycelium from which stalks
bearing spores or seeds develop. These spores
may be specialized to aid rapid reproduction or
as a means of perpetuating the organism over
winter and through unfavorable conditions.
Some of the most important plant diseases
caused by fungi are:

Anthracnose

Several kinds of fungi cause this disease which
is recognized by sunken spots in foliage or fruit
and black shrivelled leaves especially in wet
weather. Among the common kinds are bean
anthracnose which appears as dark sunken
lesions on the pods and along the leaf veins.
Resistant varieties and strains of beans are
available. Melon anthracnose infects cucumbers,
cantaloupes and watermelons where it produces
water-soaked spots on leaves and stems and
kills young fruits. Planting treated seed is
advised. Oak and Sycamore anthracnose causes
the new leaves in the spring to appear scorched
or burned by a late frost. White Oak is very
susceptible in wet weather. See PLATANUS for
control. Sweet Pea anthracnose is also destructive to Privet, Snowberry and citrus. Leaves
wither and drop and flowers and seeds fail to
develop. Sweet Pea seed should be treated and
shrubs should be sprayed with ferbam or
bordeaux mixture.

Blights

Sudden conspicuous spotting or drying of leaves and flowers generally without noticeable wilting is characteristic of fungous blights of many kinds. Azalea blight causes flowers to decay overnight but seldom harms the plant otherwise. Celery blight (early and late) spots the leaves and causes the heart stalks to decay. Treated seed and frequent spraying with maneb or zineb to keep new growth protected gives control. Botrytis blight infects a great many garden plants. It is often called gray mold because of the color of the fungus. The infected parts of the plant usually rot. Peony, lilies, African Violet, Begonia, Dahlia, Gladiolus, Rose, Zinnia and Tulip are among the susceptible plants. On Peony the buds fail to open and on Tulip and Lily the leaves and flowers are blackened, distorted and rotted. See these plants for control. Hawthorn leaf blight also causes bark cankers. Early blight of potato and tomato is recognized by brown spots on the leaves having a targetlike pattern of concentric rings and stem rot. Late blight of tomato and potato produces water-soaked spots and discolored tubers and fruits. See these plants for control.

Cankers

Well-defined lesions on the woody bark of trees and shrubs are typical of cankers. They may girdle and kill the infected trunk or branch or develop into an open wound. The infected area should be cut out and the tools disinfected with corrosive sublimate, alcohol or formalin to prevent spread. Bleeding canker attacks the trunk of many trees and shrubs, as well as infects the roots of Tomato, Peony and Tulip. The name refers to the reddish ooze which emerges from cracks in the lesions. Nectria canker of hardwoods is common on birches, maples and Black Oak. A related species infects beech trees which are infested with beech scale. The diseased area is dark and sunken often with small red immature spores at the edge. Poplars and willows growing in unfavorable conditions are subject to cankers which cause trunk lesions and twig dieback. Roses are infected by several kinds of canker which cause red or purple spots on the canes that develop into large lesions and girdle the canes. Careless pruning which leaves stubs and mounding for winter protection encourage these infections.

Leaf Spots

Nearly every plant is susceptible to leaf spot, several of which are caused by fungi. These infections have clearly-defined margins, usually colored differently from the center of the spots. Among the best known is Black Spot of rose. This disease overwinters on fallen leaves and on twig lesions. Diseased leaves fall and bushes may be defoliated several times annually. See ROSE for control. Septoria leaf spot on chrysanthemums and Tomato produces water-soaked spots which appear first on the older leaves. Infection is greatest during wet weather after blossoming. One of the most conspicuous is maple tar spot which appears as raised black spots often $\frac{1}{2}$ in. in dia. Serious damage to the tree rarely occurs.

Mildews

Powdery mildews with white felty coverings are surface parasites which thrive in humid but not rainy weather. Downy mildews live within the plant tissue but produce white downy patches of spores on the surface and develop in wet weather. Powdery mildews are common on Lilac, Phlox, chrysanthemums, Zinnia, Rose and Clover or other legumes. Apple, Peach and apricots are also subject to infection. Powdery mildew is especially serious on lima beans, cucurbits and onions.

Molds

The most common molds are diseases of lawn grasses such as snow mold in the form of patches of a white or pinkish fungus. Tomato leaf mold causes velvety areas on the leaves in greenhouses and occasionally in the South. Black sooty mold which develops on honeydew from aphids and scales produces a black coating on leaves and branches but is not a parasite on the plant.

Rots

Fungus rots result in decay. The common forms occur on ripening fruits, with infection starting in the field and continuing during harvest and storage, on roots or bulbs due to excessive moisture in field or in storage, and on trees following poor pruning and storm damage. Brown rot of stone fruits, black rot of grape and blueberry mummies are common fruit rots. Root rots include calla root rot which may completely destroy the roots; fusarium root rots on Gladiolus and lilies which rot the corms and bulbs; brown patch and dollar spot which kill lawn grasses; red stele disease that rots strawberry roots and pea root rot of garden and sweet peas. Wood rot fungi are usually recognized by the toadstool-like growth either near the roots from the mushroom root rot or on stumps or broken limbs from the *Fomes* and *Polyporus* bracket fungi.

Rusts

Although most rust diseases produce spores

of a red or rusty brown color that suggest the name, this is not a reliable means of identification. There are also several economically important rusts that must live on certain unrelated plants to complete their cycle and are known as alternate-host rusts. The most important of these is the wheat stem rust which lives on Barberry and several grasses and grains and threatened severe losses to the oat and wheat crop until well-organized programs to destroy all barberry plants in the large grain-growing areas were established. Other alternate-host rusts are apple-cedar rust, hawthorn-juniper rust, quince-juniper rust, ash-marsh grass rust and white pine-ribes (currants and gooseberries) rust. Campaigns to eradicate the least desirable host have been promoted in many areas. See these plants for control.

Single host rusts include asparagus rust, bean rust, carnation rust, hollyhock rust, blackberry rust and snapdragon rust which are controlled by fungicides.

Scab

Scab diseases are most conspicuous as dark, raised spots on fruit or tubers but they also infect the leaves. Apple scab is the most destructive disease of McIntosh apples and other susceptible varieties, and a related disease occurs on Flemish Beauty and other pears. Citrus scab deforms fruits or stunts growth where fungicides are not used. Peach and other stone fruits are damaged by peach scab. Potato scab is destructive to potatoes grown in alkaline soil.

Smut

Large masses of tiny black spores identify smut diseases which live over winter in the soil and on plant refuse. Corn smut thrives in hot weather and is usually observed as greenish-white boils of immature spores on any part of the plant above ground. In home gardens, these boils should be cut off and destroyed promptly. Onion smut may appear on leaves or bulbs as black elongated pustules which start on young seedlings. Onion sets are seldom infected. Seed treatment usually prevents infection.

Wilts

Although lack of moisture either in the soil or from excessive transpiration through the leaves are common causes of wilting, there are some diseases which produce this condition. Fusarium fungus causes wilt and various varieties infect China Aster, Cabbage, Carnation, Celery, Gladiolus, Pea, Sweet Potato, Tomato and curcurbits. The foliage of infected plants often turns yellow before dying and the disease is often called Yellows. Verticillium wilt is a soil-borne disease of many plants. Among those most seriously infected are elm and maple trees, raspberries and strawberries, Eggplant, Pepper and tomatoes. There are wilt-resistant strains and varieties. The well-known Dutch Elm disease interferes with the normal passage of sap through the wood and causes wilting, and oak wilt is a similar disease of oaks especially Red Oak.

BACTERIAL DISEASES

Bacteria are single-celled organisms which reproduce by dividing. Under favorable conditions they reproduce at a tremendous rate. Several are beneficial by breaking down organic matter to humus and plant food and by producing nodules on the roots of legumes which collect nitrogen from the air and make it available to plants. Bacterial diseases of insects such as the Milky Spore disease of Japanese beetle grubs and *Bacillus thuringiensis* which infects several destructive caterpillars are used commercially for pest control. In general, destructive bacterial diseases are more difficult to control than most fungus diseases.

Among the common bacterial diseases of vegetables are potato blackleg in which the lower stem is blackened or rotted, bacterial blight of beans, cucumber wilt which is spread by the striped cucumber beetle and Stewart's disease on early Sweet Corn which lives overwinter in the corn flea beetle. Apples, pears, quinces and many related shrubs are very susceptible to fireblight which causes a "burned" appearance to leaves and twigs, and crown gall infects fruit trees, berry bushes, roses and many related shrubs. Shothole disease on the leaves of stone fruits causes the centers of the infected area to fall out and small cracks to occur on the fruit and twigs. Watersoaked spots on Begonia, Geranium, English Ivy and Canna are the result of bacterial infection. Small black spots on poppy, delphinium and viburnum leaves, stems and buds, are caused by bacteria. A soft slimy rot on Calla and on the rhizomes of Iris, especially following injury by the iris borer, has a bacterial source.

VIRUS DISEASES

Virus organisms can be seen only with a high-powered microscope. They produce and live on a protein substance and rob the plant of necessary protein. Viruses are usually described according to the type of injury to the plant, such as mosaic, streak, yellows and stunt. They are usually spread by aphids and other sucking insects feeding on an infected plant before feeding on an uninfected plant. Many viruses can infect only a single or closely related species of plant but notable exceptions are tomato mosaic on cucumber and bean mosaic on gladiolus. Nearly every plant appears to be susceptible to some virus but many are not economically important. Infected plants should never be used for cuttings, scions, root divisions or seed, and there is no effective control except destruction of all infected plants. The development of virus-resistant strains is an important problem for the future. Some of the important virus diseases are phloem necrosis of elm, curly top of sugar beets, X disease and phony disease of peach, leaf roll of potato, whitebreak mosaic of gladiolus, cranberry false blossom disease, blueberry stunt, aster yellows on carrots, celery and many garden flowers and mosaic of tomato, tobacco and lettuce. Virus diseases are systemic and any contact with the sap may spread infection.

WARREN D. WHITCOMB

DISEASE PREVENTION. Successful disease control depends on providing conditions unfavorable for disease establishment and spread. Disease spores are spread by wind, water and cultivation. Dry spores are easily blown by wind or air currents. Fortunately, however, they are also dried by the wind so that the majority fail to germinate. Apple scab spores mature in a tube (ascus) which absorbs water until it bursts and shoots the spores several inches into the air where they are carried by wind and air currents. The ash rust produces summer spores on a marsh grass (*Spartina* sp.) from which they have been blown by storm winds to infect ash leaves 30 or 40 miles inland. Spores are also spread by splashing water from large rain drops, by surface drainage water and by irrigation water from contaminated pools or streams.

Disease spores living in moist soil may be carried by cultivation from one part of a field or bed to another and muddy soil on the feet of man or animals may carry infection. Soil in greenhouse benches, plant beds and seedling flats should be sterilized to prevent disease from spreading from seedlings when transplanted to the field. Chemically treated seeds are more plentiful each year and should be planted whenever possible. Virus and bacterial diseases are often spread by insects which must be controlled. A typical example involves the bacterial wilt of cucumbers which in the North survives the winter in the body of the striped cucumber beetle and is transmitted by the "dropping" of the insect to feeding wounds. Blossom blights are carried from flower to flower on the bodies of bees and other pollinating insects. Diseased-plant refuse should not be used in compost piles as a source of humus unless completely decomposed.

Environment

Plant disease spores require adequate moisture to germinate and grow but excess moisture should be avoided. Wet soils and flooding by irrigation favor the growth of root rots. Although water is necessary for normal plant growth, disease infection is less likely where quick drying of rain, dew and irrigation water occurs. Sprinkling or irrigating the lawn or garden at night may conserve water but it also favors the development of disease. Air drainage on slopes and fields open to air movement generally reduces disease infection. On the other hand, powdery mildews are low-moisture diseases which thrive in fog, dew and high humidity rather than extended rainy weather. Diseases which thrive in high temperature can often be checked on annual plants by planting early in the spring to encourage maturity before the warmest weather. Root rot of garden peas is seldom serious on early varieties.

Cultural Practices

Recommendations for elimination and disposal of infected plant refuse are often emphasized but more often ignored. Diseased plants are left in or near the garden, raspberry plants weakened by the mosaic virus are left to die, and dead or dying branches of trees and shrubs are not removed when the symptoms are first observed. Expert growers, especially those producing seed regularly, rogue out all plants known or suspected to be diseased. Raking and burning of leaves from infected plants aids eradication and spading or plowing annual beds in the fall to bury plant refuse is helpful. The prompt destruction of weeds on which diseases of cultivated plants live such as milkweed and pokeweed infected with tomato mosaic is helpful.

The use of herbicides on wild areas adjacent to the garden is often practical. Rust diseases such as apple-cedar rust and wheat-barberry rust can be controlled by elimination of the least desirable host within a reasonable distance. Rotation of annual vegetables and flowers to new beds even a short distance away discourages infection. Verticillium wilt remains active in the soil for several years and susceptible plants such as Eggplant, Tomato and Dahlia can be grown successfully only by planting them in new uninfected soil. The degree of soil acidity called pH affects the development of some fungi. Club root of cabbage and related plants is reduced by raising the pH of the soil to neutral but potatoes growing in an alkaline soil may develop potato scab.

Rhododendron, Blueberry and other ericaceous plants thrive in acid soil and when exposed to alkaline soil may be so weakened as to be susceptible to diseases which they normally resist.

Storage

Fruit, vegetables, tubers, bulbs and nursery stock may be damaged in storage by diseases which increase from minor unnoticed infections to those of serious proportions in the favorable temperature and moisture in the storage. Temperatures of 35° to 40° F. and relatively humidity about 50% are desirable but slightly higher readings for short periods will permit the development of some diseases. It is desirable to disinfect the walls, floor and storage containers by spraying with an effective fungicide or fumigating with formaldehyde according to special directions.

Quarantine

Many plant diseases are introduced on their host plants or shipping containers not only from foreign countries but also from local sources. Federal and state quarantines keep these introductions to a minimum but the gardener should carefully examine all plants brought to his garden and isolate, disinfect or destroy any which show symptoms of disease.

WARREN D. WHITCOMB

DISH GARDEN. The growing of miniature plants in a small tray or dish. These are often most interesting, and the combination of various kinds of small plants in scaled plantings the size of a large pie plate takes skill.

DISSECTED. Divided into many narrow segments.

DISTICTIS (DIS-tik-tis)

lactiflora   vine   Zone 9
This is a comparatively recent introduction into southern Calif. (from Mexico) but should prove popular since it is reported to have grown from seed to 20 ft. in 1 season. The purple-to-white flowers are shaped like those of the Morning-glory, 2 in. across and 2 in. long. It has a very long flowering season throughout the summer and fall, climbing very fast by means of tendrils. The compound leaves are often doubly compound, have 2–3 leaflets, each about 1–2 in. long.

DITTANY = *Dictamnus albus*

DIVISION. A term in horticulture meaning the separating of plant roots or cutting in half entire plants to make several plants where there was only one before. Many garden plants are most easily propagated by division with a spade, usually done in the early spring. See PROPAGATION.

DIZYGOTHECA (di-zy-go-THEE-ka)

elegantissima   15'   Zone 10   Threadleaf False Aralia
Often grown as a pot plant in the house and as such is only about a foot tall, with elegant,

compound, alternate leaves and gracefully slender drooping leaflets, about 7–10, mottled with white. The fruits are berrylike, black and juicy. Native to the Pacific Islands. Propagated by cuttings.

veitchii   15'   Zone 10   Veitch False Aralia
This is somewhat similar to the above, used as a house plant, with 9–11 wavy-margined leaflets about ¼ in. wide and reddish beneath. The var. **gracillima** has white midribs and very narrow leaflets. Both species grow best in the shade in a moist atmosphere.

DOCK. See RUMEX.

DODDER. A climbing, vinelike, parasitic plant which twines about other plants occasionally smothering them. It has specialized roots which become attached to the host plant after which the roots in the soil cease to function and it becomes parasitic on the host. Chrysanthemums are often infected. Pulling it off the host is the only recommended control.

DODECATHEON (do-dek-ATH-eon). Small American wild flowers belonging to the Primrose Family but they are not the easiest plants to grow in many areas. Mostly under a foot tall, they require moisture during the growing season and dry conditions when dormant. They are propagated by both seeds and division.

clevelandii   6"   Zone 9   Cleveland Shooting-star
The purple flowers are yellow at the base, sometimes white; filaments purple and anthers yellow—an interesting color combination. Native to southern Calif.

cusickii   2"   Zone 3   Cusick Shooting-star
An excellent rock garden plant native to the northern regions of the Rocky Mountains. It requires peaty, acid soil, semishade, good drainage and moisture, until July and a dry environment throughout the remainder of the year when the plant is dormant. Tussocks of hairy leaves 2 in. high are crowned by nodding clusters of dark purple flowers with pointed and reflexed petals and bright yellow stamens.

dentatum   4"   Zone 5   Dentate Shooting-star
White flowers having 2 purple spots at the base of each petal; dentate leaves 4 in. long; anthers brownish red and yellow filaments. Native to Ore. and Utah.

jeffreyi   1'   Zone 5   Jeffrey Shooting-star
Flowers deep red-purple with the filaments and anthers both purple. Native from British Columbia to Idaho and Calif.

meadia   6"–20"   Zone 3   Common Shooting-star
This would be a delightful addition to any garden, but it does not do well except in rich, light woods soil and partial shade. It is a perennial with leaves 4–6 in. long in a basal

rosette. The base of the leaves is often reddish in color. The flowers are borne in a terminal cluster on a reddish stalk which sometimes attains a height of 20 in. The flowers, with calyx lobes and petals reflexed, are deep rose. The cone-shaped stamens and pistil are purple. The plants grows from Pa. to Ga. and Tex. and blooms from April to June.

pulchellum (*D. radicatum*)   5″   **Zone 5**
Southern Shooting-star
Flowers reddish, anthers purple. Native from Kan. to N.Mex.
radicatum = *D. pulchellum*

DODONAEA (do-don-EE-a)
viscosa   8′–12′   Zone 10   Akeake
An alternate-leaved shrub with sticky foliage, not especially attractive as an ornamental but sometimes used in Calif. gardens where it seems to be resistant to smog problems. Also widely used in Fla. and the West Indies. The leaves are 3–4 in. long, 1 in. wide and the uninteresting flowers are in terminal racemes. Probably native to New Zealand.

DOGBANE. See APOCYNUM.

DOGBANE FAMILY = Apocynaceae

DOGWOOD. See CORNUS.

DOGWOOD FAMILY = Cornaceae

DOLICHOS (DOL-ik-os)
lablab   vine   annual   Hyacinth-bean
Native to the Tropics, this twining vine is actually a perennial in the Tropics but is usually grown as an annual by sowing seeds where the plants are to grow after all danger of frost is over. Shoots may grow 10 ft. long. Leaves are in 3's (it belongs to the Pea Family) and the flowers are pealike, purple or white, about an inch long borne either singly or in clusters in the leaf axils, with the flat pod 2½ in. long. It has been used as forage, as a potherb and in salads. It makes a summer screen for covering fences, trellises, etc.

DOMBEYA (dom-BEE-a)
wallichii   30′   Zone 10   Scarlet Dombeya
Valued for its large, pendant clusters of small pink flowers produced in a large ball during autumn and Dec. The large catalpalike leaves are profuse nearly 12 in. across, and hide the flowers unless one views them from directly underneath. Native to Madagascar. Propagated by cuttings.

DOODIA (DOO-dia). These are small evergreen ferns for the greenhouse. Native to Australia and New Zealand. The fronds are 6–12 in. long, and feathery. They can be grown in a cool greenhouse (45° F.) and are propagated by division or by sowing spores during the summer. See FERNS. The main species are **D. aspera** with fronds 6 in. long, and its several vars.; **D.**

caudata with fronds 12 in. long and **D. media** and several varieties with fronds 15 in. long.

DORMANT. Restive or not in growth; applied to buds or other parts of a plant in winter, or to the plant itself, usually after it has flowered and fruited and gone into a rest period.

DORONICUM (do-RON-ik-um). These are excellent garden plants with bright yellow daisy-like flowers in May and June. They are sturdy, of easy culture and never fail to produce colorful spring flowers, some of which (*D. plantagineum*) have flower heads 3 in. across which make excellent cut flowers also. It is well to note that the foliage disappears in summer, hence they should not be massed for this would lead to bare spots in the flower border. As single specimens, preferably in light shade, they should be in every spring border. Propagation is easiest by division of clumps during the late summer for seeds germinate erratically.

cordatum (*caucasicum*)   2′   **Zone 4   Caucasian Leopardsbane**
With solitary yellow flowers 2 in. across. Native from Sicily to Asia Minor. It has a rather stoloniferous habit of growth. 'Madam Mason' is a popular variety with slightly larger flowers and foliage which may remain throughout the summer, whereas, that of the species disappears during summer. This species and variety are the most popular of this genus, worthy additions to any garden.

pardalianches   5′   Zone 5
Yellow flowers 2½ in. wide with 1–5 in a cluster, borne in May but continuing into June. Native to Europe. Stems hairy. A spreading weed.

plantagineum   4′   Zone 3   Plantain Leopardsbane
Plants usually about 2½ ft. tall, flowers solitary in May, but many are borne on each clump making excellent subjects for arranging as cut flowers. The flower heads are 3–4 in. across. However, this is one of the taller-growing species and as such is coarse and for use only in the larger flower borders. Native to Europe.

DOROTHEANUS (doro-the-AY-nus). One of the genera set off from *Mesembryanthemum* (which see) consisting of small, succulent herbs from South Africa that look like small stones, used out-of-doors in southern Calif. but as oddities in pots in the greenhouses and homes in the North. Treated as annuals, by sowing seed early in Feb. or March, setting out after frost. Easily killed by frost.

bellidiformis (*Mesembryanthemum crini-florum*)   3″   **Zone 10**
A small-branched annual with succulent opposite leaves 3 in. long and ¼ in. wide with solitary daisylike flowers, pink, red and white about ½ in. across.

gramineus (*Mesembryanthemum pyropeum*)
3″   **Zone 10**
With opposite succulent leaves 3 in. long,
forming a clump 8 in. across. The daisylike
flowers are solitary, 1½ in. across, light pink,
rose, red, white and sometimes with a blue or
red center.

DORSAL. Relating to the back or outer surface
of an organ.

DORYCNIUM (dor-IK-nium)
hirsutum   2′   **Zone 4**   **Canary-clover**
This perennial from southern Europe has been
used as a ground cover. It has a cloverlike
habit, white pealike flowers in heads 1½ in.
across during the summer. The compound
leaves have 3–5 leaflets and are white hairy.
It belongs to the Pea Family.

DOUBLE (flowers). When the number of petals
is increased at the expense of other organs,
especially the stamens.

DOUGLAS-FIR = *Pseudotsuga menziesii*

DOUGLASIA (dug-LAS-sia). Tufted herbs
used as rock-garden plants belonging to the
Primrose Family. There are 1–2 flowers on a
short stalk above a rosette of leaves at the
base, the leaves overlap as if shingled.
laevigata   2½″   **Zone 6**   **Smooth Douglasia**
Leaves ½ in. long; flowers long tubed, bright
red. Native to Wash. and Ore.
montana   2½″   **Zone 4**   **Mountain Douglasia**
Leaves 2⅓ in. long; flowers purple or lilac, ⅓ in.
long. Native to Mont. and Wyo.
vitaliana   **prostrate**   **Zone 4**
Less difficult to grow than its Rocky Mountain
cousins, this species from the Swiss Alps does
well in coarse lime soils in sun or semishade.
The prostrate stems, growing in cushions,
terminate in rosettes of light green leaves
touched with yellow. The clear yellow flowers,
appressed to the stems, bloom in April and May.

DOVETREE = *Davidia involucrata*

DOVYALIS (do-vi-AY-lis)
hebecarpa   20′   **Zone 10**   **Ceylon-gooseberry**
A spiny shrub or small tree of the Tropics with
leaves 3–4 in. long. Male and female flowers are
inconspicuous but often on separate plants.
The edible purplish fruits, 1 in. in dia. are
covered with short, velvety hairs and resemble a
gooseberry. Can be used as a screen if kept
pruned. Native to India and Ceylon.

DOXANTHA **UNGUIS-CATI** = *Macfadyena*
unguis-cati

DRABA (DRAY-ba). These small plants are
members of the Mustard Family and are
annuals, biennials or perennials, native to the
North Temperate Zone, many of them making
fine alpine or rock garden plants. The flowers
are small and dainty, the root is often a deep tap

root. Propagation is either by seed or division.
aizoides   4″   **Zone 5**   **Whitlowgrass**
A low tufted perennial with linear leaves in basal
rosettes, about ½ in. long and ¼ in. wide. The
yellow flowers are borne in many-flowered
racemes on a scape. Native to the mountains of
southern Europe. Suited for use in the rock
garden.
alpina   6″   **Zone 2**
A low tufted perennial native to the subarctic
regions with yellow flowers in rather tight
clusters.
aspera   1½″   **Zone 5**
A plant similar to *D. haynaldii*, its habitat is
somewhat more in the South and its leaves are
shiny and a darker green. The yellow flowers
appear in April and May.
bruniifolia olympica   2″–4″   **Zone 6**   **Olympic**
Draba
A cushionlike perennial with linear leaves only
¼ in. long., flowers orange in compact racemes.
Native to southern Europe.
densiflora   2½″   **Zone 2**
Another tufted plant with leaves in a tight
rosette, yellow flowers in loose racemes and
native from British Columbia to northern Calif.
fladnizensis   2″–3″   **Zone 2**   **Arctic Draba**
A perennial with cushionlike tufts of foliage,
most of the leaves only ⅓ in. long and little
flowers greenish white. Native to the arctic
regions of North America and Europe.
haynaldii   2½″   **Zone 4**
A small cushion plant having narrow, somewhat
hairy leaves and yellow-to-orange flowers. The
flowers often appear in spring while snow is still
on the ground. It is native to central Europe.
olympica = *D. bruniifolia olympica*
rigida   3″   **Zone 6**   **Rigid Draba**
Moundlike, leaves shining and rigid, ¼ in. long;
flowers yellow in large clusters during April.
Difficult to grow. Native to southern Europe.
sibirica   **prostrate**   **Zone 3**   **Siberian Draba**
A hardy, vigorous, trailing Siberian plant which
quickly forms loose rosettes of large leaves
from which the drooping or decumbent stems, 6
in. long, arise, bearing clusters of bright yellow
flowers. An excellent plant, since it is easy to
cultivate, grows quickly and flowers both in
spring and in fall. A popular plant in America.
vesicaria   4″   **Zone 6?**
This low plant comes from Lebanon and is
sometimes used in rock gardens. The rosettes of
leaves are 3½″ across, flowers yellowish.

DRACAENA (dra-SEE-na). These are popular,
evergreen, tropical, foliage plants frequently
mixed and confused with species of *Cordyline*,
which see. They are separated from *Cordyline*
only by technical characters. Both are treelike
in habit as they grow in the tropics, and must be
controlled and kept down to pot or tub size

when grown indoors. Much used in homes and greenhouses for excellent foliage display. The leaves of *Dracena* species are narrow and swordlike, usually with a distinct stalk. Flowers are not often produced indoors but are greenish, yellowish or red; many of the following species are planted out-of-doors in Calif. gardens. For propagation and culture see CORDYLINE.

deremensis 10′ ? Zone 10
Leaves 1½–2 ft. long and 2 in. wide, narrowed at both ends with a long sharp point at the end away from the stem. Flowers in large panicles, dark red outside, white inside. Native to tropical Africa.

draco 60′ Zone 10 Dragontree
Leaves crowded but only 1½–2 ft. long and 1¼–1¾ in. wide, with greenish flowers and orange berries. Native to Canary Islands and planted in Calif. as are most of these other species.

fragrans 20′ Zone 10 Fragrant Dracaena
This grows fast and must be reduced in height by air layering the top portion before it grows too tall. The cornlike leaves may be 2 ft. long, arching, and 3 in. wide. There are several vars. one named **lindeni** with creamy-white stripes on the leaves. Its name comes from the fact that its yellowish flowers are fragrant. Native to upper Guinea.

goldieana 3′ Zone 10 Goldie Dracaena
With leaves only 6 in. long and an inch wide, striped with white. This seems to have a tenacity lacking in many another window-box plant for it will outlive most of them.

surculosa (*godseffiana*) **1′–2′ Zone 10 Gold-dust Dracaena**
This species has an interesting branching habit and small, oval leaves only about 5 in. long that are spotted irregularly with white or yellow. The flowers are greenish yellow. Native to upper Guinea.

DRACOCEPHALUM (dray-ko-SEFF-al-um). Hardy herbs, usually erect with purple-to-blue, 2-lipped flowers borne on small spikes during June and July. They do best in shaded situations and are propagated by seed or division.

grandiflorum 6″–12″ Zone 2 Bigflower Dragonhead
A summer-blooming herbaceous perennial with opposite leaves and square stems, sometimes used in the flower garden. It is easily grown, as are some other species of this genus, and should be given some shade and moist soil in the perennial border. The 2-lipped flowers are irregular, blue, 2 in. long and borne in terminal spikes during June and July. Native to Siberia.

ruyschiana 2′ Zones 2–3 Dragonhead
A perennial, linear-to-lanceolate leaves, entire, about 2 in. long; flowers blue to bluish, 1 in. long borne in short spikes. Native to Siberia. Propagated by seeds and division, and preferring a moist situation.

DRAGONHEAD. See DRACOCEPHALUM.

DRAGONROOT = *Arisaema dracontium*

DRAGONTREE = *Dracaena draco*

DRAINING. Laying of tile drains is sometimes necessary in very clayey soils, or those with a definite hardpan, to remove standing water in the vicinity of plant roots. Or it may be a drain is needed to take off the water from a wet spot on a hill. In any case, agricultural tile drains are commonly used, and others especially made for the purpose with many perforations throughout their length are becoming available. Tile drains are easily available everywhere.

In the first place, one should have a place where the water can be drained off, a place lower than the area to be drained. The tile must be laid so that it slowly slopes away from the drained area, with a drop of at least 4–5 in. per 100 ft. as a minimum for hand-laid tile, preferably more would be better.

Second, it is best to have it below the level of frost action, usually about 3–4 ft. deep in the soil. Some short tiles laid in gardens might be 2½ ft. deep but there is danger here that these might be disrupted by the freezing action of the soil in winter. Drains should be kept clear of elm, willow and poplar roots, all of which are well noted for their ability to grow into drains and clog them. They should be laid carefully without any dips or low spots where mud or silt might collect to clog them. It is always a good practice to lay them on an inch or so of gravel.

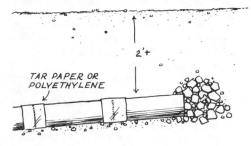

Tile drain has tar paper over joints and rocks at end to prevent soil from entering drains and clogging them.

The drains might be laid according to a herring-bone plan, with the main drains about 6-in. tile, and the side or feeding drains of 4-in. tile. If the soil is not too soggy, one 4-in. tile drain can be expected to drain the water in the soil on either side of it for about 50 to 100 ft.

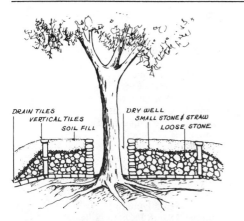

DRAIN TILES
VERTICAL TILES
SOIL FILL

DRY WELL
SMALL STONE & STRAW
LOOSE STONE

Filling in soil or "raising the grade" over established tree roots—shown in cross section.

depending on the kind of soil and the situation. If the soil is a good loam and there is merely a hard pan that is troublesome then 100 ft. might be the drainable area on either side, but in clayey soils it might better be 50 ft. on either side. Certainly this would be the safer distance to drain. Tiles should be laid tightly end to end with sods, tarpaper or just plain gravel placed above the joints to prevent silt and soil from filtering down into and clogging them. If the wet spot is on a hillside, the drain should be laid above the soggy site to catch the water before it comes to the surface below.

DREJERELLA = *Justicia*

DRIED BLOOD. An organic fertilizer (from the slaughter houses) containing 12–14% nitrogen. This is quickly available and is recommended for general use at the rate of 2 oz. per sq. yd. See SOILS.

DRIED FRUITS AND VEGETABLES. Several types of fruits and vegetables can be dried out-of-doors in the sun in the more arid regions of the Southwest, but in much of the rest of the country, drying such edibles out-of-doors is not practicable.

The idea is to have the air hot and dry, with plenty of air circulation about the material, then to store them when dry where they will not reabsorb moisture. A hot attic is excellent for hanging a string of apple rings, parsley, herbs, peas, beans and shredded carrots. To dry, the material should be loosely open to air.

DRIED PLANT MATERIALS FOR ARRANGEMENTS. Each season brings its own beauty in plant material but usually it all too quickly fades and is gone. Nature has a wonderful way of distributing her wares from the rich lush colors of summer and early autumn to the somber colors of the seed pods, fruit cones and grasses of late autumn. The wealth of plant material to be found in the garden, woods and waysides can be gathered through the summer and fall when it is at its best and, by proper conditioning, it can be preserved for use in winter decorations later. Simple garden weeds like Dock, Yarrow, Goldenrod, when properly dried and added to a container in which dried or glycerined beech leaves are used for background, can make an interesting and beautiful part of a room for weeks, during the period when the garden looks dead and uninteresting.

Flowers have been dried for winter decorations for generations, and various methods have been used. The simplest method of drying flowers and foliage is merely to cut the flowers or branches prior to full bloom tying them in small loose bunches and hanging them upside down in a dark, dry, warm room. Pick only the most perfect specimens.

The flower arranger should not wait until summer to collect but must be ready to observe and select from early spring until late fall. The pussy willows and the daffodils in early spring are perfect for drying. The flower garden will supply specimens throughout the entire growing season and the fields and woods have many treasures. The lowly Dock picked in various stages of development, sumacs, Cockscomb and crimson fruits of Bittersweet may be just the right accent for dried arrangements.

Flowers and foliage should be dried separately and sometimes different methods must be used. Small blooms of Everlasting and Strawflower usually dry well by the old-fashioned method, merely hanging them up in a warm, dry, darkened room. Flowers with large or intricately shaped petals or heads must be supported in place during the drying. They may need to be dried by the silica gel or cornmeal and borax or the sand and borax method. For foliage there is a choice of methods. Ferns may be pressed between newspapers or magazines and will dry flat and brittle, or the glycerine method. Glycerine gives a most lasting life to leaves and also a smooth, satinlike gloss.

The following flowers, foliage and weeds dry well if they are merely hung upside down, singly or in small bunches in a dry, warm, dark room. First remove all unnecessary parts from the stem, shape the plant material while it is fresh by wiring and then hung upside down to dry:

	HEIGHT	ZONE	COMMON NAME
Achillea sp.	6″–4′	2	Yarrow
Agrostis nebulosa	12″–18″	annual	Cloud Bent Grass
Allium sp.	6″–3′	2–3	Onion
Amaranthus sp.	6″–10′	annual	Amaranth
Anaphalis margaritacea	3′	3	Pearly Everlasting
Artemesia sp.	1½′–9′	2	Wormwoods
Briza maxima	2′	annual	Quaking Grass
Catananche coerulea	18″	annual	Blue Cupid's-dart
Celosia sp.	1′–4′	annual	Cockscomb
Coix lachryma-jobi	3′	annual	Job's Tears
Cortaderia selloana	8′–20′	8	Pampas Grass
Cytisus scoparius	6′	5	Scotch Broom
Echinops ritro	1′–2′	2–3	Globe-thistle
Erynigium sp.	1′–3′	2–3	Erynigium
Eucalyptus sp.	35′–150′	9	Eucalyptus
Gilia capitata	2′	annual	Santa Barbara Gilia
Glaucium flavum	3′	annual	Horned Poppy
Gypsophila repens vars.	6″	2–3	Gypsophila
G. paniculata	3′	2–3	Baby's-breath
Helichrysum sp.	3′	annual	Strawflower
Hydrangea—several sp.	9′–30′	4	Hydrangea
Iris foetidissima	18″	7	Gladwin Iris
Lagurus ovatus	1′	annual	Hare's-tail Grass
Lamarckia aurea	1′	annual	Golden-top Grass
Limonium latifolium	2½′	2–3	Wide Leaf Sea-lavender
Lunaria annua	3′	annual–biennial	Honesty
Molucella laevis	2′	annual	Bells-of-Ireland
Physalis alkekengi	2′	2–3	Chinese-lantern
Rumex sp.	1′–4′	3	Dock
Ruscus aculeatus	1½′–4′	7	Butcher's Broom
Salix discolor	20′	2	Pussy Willow
Stipa pennata	3′	5	European Feather Grass

Ornamental grasses are good as background and filling materials and they are also easily dried. Gather them before they go to seed and place them upright in loose bunches to dry. Bamboo, Cat-tail, Job's Tears, Oats, Millet, Pampas Grass, Sorghum, Timothy and many other ornamental grasses. See GRASSES, ORNAMENTAL.

PRESERVING WITH BORAX. The following flowers can be dried in 10 parts of white cornmeal with 3 parts borax and mixed throroughly, or ¾ borax to ¼ sand. This can be used year after year, provided it is kept dry. Place the flowers in boxes with heads down and thoroughly cover with the mixture. Leave stems exposed and upright. In about 2 weeks, when the stems are dry to the touch, remove the flowers from the mixture and store in boxes until ready for use.

Acacia sp.	Acacia, Wattle
Althaea	Hollyhock
Buddleia sp.	Butterfly-bush
Camellia japonica	Camellia
Centaurea cyanus	Cornflower
Clematis sp.	Clematis
Dahlia (Unwin Hybrids)	Dahlia
Daucus carota	Queen Anne's Lace
Delphinium sp.	Delphinium
Heleborus	Christmas-rose
Narcissus	Narcissus
Rudbeckia hirta	Black-eyed-Susan
Rosa sp.	Rose
Salvia farinacea	Blue Salvia
Tagetes	Marigold
Veronica sp.	Speedwell
Viola sp.	Violet, Pansy
Zinnia	Zinnia

PRESERVING FOLIAGE WITH GLYCERINE. The leaves of a few woody plants can be preserved if they are properly conditioned by placing the stems of the branches into a mixture of ⅓ glycerine and ⅔ water. The leaves should be fully mature and in perfect condition when cut. Before placing the ends of the cut branches into the mixture the stems should be crushed with a hammer. The branches are left in this liquid about 3 weeks or until one can feel glycerine on the outer edges of the leaves. The following plan-materials are easily preserved by this method:

Barberry, Beech (both green-leaved and purple-colored varieties), Canna, Eucalyptus, Flowering Plum, Leucothoe, *Magnolia grandiflora*, Mahotnia or Oregon Holly-grape, Oak, Rhododendron, Viburnum sieboldii.

PRESERVING BY SILICA GEL TREATMENT. A new drying medium has been introduced, silica gel, a chemical compound which readily absorbs moisture. Almost all flowers dried in silica gel retain their brightness of color and beauty of form. The new chemical compound is expensive but the results merit its use. Exceptionally beautiful are roses, camellias, delphiniums, Christmas-roses and daffodils dried in this material. Actually, everything that can be preserved by the borax treatment can be preserved by treatment in silica gel.

BERRIES AND SEED PODS. Bittersweet, both American and European, is excellent for drying. Privet—berries may be dried when green or dark blue. Sumac—cut when fruit heads are green or when they first turn red. The seed pods of the Chinese Lantern (*Physalis alkekengi*), dry orange-red; Honesty has very interesting flat fruits which dry extremely well. Nandina and Beauty Berry are excellent. Cat-tail, Washington Hawthorn, Black Alder (*Ilex verticillata*), Bayberry, rose fruits, dried pods of Lily, Iris (Siberian), Tree Peony, Lotus, and fruits of Sweet Gum, Sycamore, Teasel, Trumpet Vine, and Yucca.

Milkweed—cut when green as soon as the pods are fully formed, allow 4–5 weeks for drying, then press open and remove seeds. Poppy and Yucca pods are cut while still green.

Dried flowers, berries and seed pods should be stored in a dry place in darkness if possible, since they tend to fade in light. They can be stored in boxes or merely left hanging in a dark attic, preferably well protected in polyethylene bags to prevent dust accumulation.

MAKING DRIED ARRANGEMENTS. Use the same principles that are used in working with fresh material. Oasis is excellent to use in the base of the container. Other types of containers may be filled with sand which has been slightly moistened to hold material in place while working and then, when dry, heated paraffin poured over the sand when the arrangement is competed.

DRIMYS (DRY-mis)

winteri   50′   Zone 9   Winter's-bark Drimys
An evergreen tree native throughout South America, producing highly aromatic, leathery, elliptic, alternate leaves 6–8 in. long and fragrant cream-colored flowers an inch wide and small berries as fruits. Propagation is by layering, cuttings and seeds. The bark had been used medicinally as early as 1579 by Captain Winter commanding the "Elizabeth" under Sir Francis

Drake as a treatment for scurvy among his sailors.

DRIVEWAYS. On small properties the driveway should be at least 8–10 ft. wide and any right-angle turn should be a curve which is drawn on a 20 ft. radius. Each home site presents its own problems of driveway location and this should be carefully studied, measured and even tried with a car by backing in and turning to make certain that the permanent driveway laid down will be ample.

Driveway materials are usualy of crushed stone, black-top or concrete. The stone road should have an excavation of 10 in; the black-top road an excavation of 12 in. and the concrete road an excavation of $9\frac{1}{2}$ in. Final grading should result in a road slightly higher in the middle than at the sides to allow for water drain-off. At least 8 in. of coarse stone should go in the excavation for a black-top or stone road and about 4 in. for a concrete road, this to be compacted and thoroughly rolled. The crushed-stone road should be of stone $\frac{1}{2}$–1 in. in size and about 2 in. deep. Asphalt mix for the second kind of road is available from various local sources and the concrete road had best be laid by contractors. Usually this is $5\frac{1}{2}$ in. thick with the wire reinforcements being No. 3, 6 in. x 6 in. highway wire. The concrete should be a 1–2–$3\frac{1}{2}$ mix (1 part cement, 2 parts sharp sand, $3\frac{1}{2}$ parts crushed stone or gravel $\frac{1}{2}$–$\frac{3}{4}$ in. dia.) with expansion joints about 50 ft. apart.

DROPWORT = *Filipendula vulgaris* (*F. hexapetala*)

DROSANTHEMUM (dro-SAN-the-mum). Succulent perennials from South Africa closely related to *Mesembryanthemum*, planted out-of-doors in southern Calif. for their interesting succulent foliage, and in the North used as pot plants indoors.

floribundum   2′   Zone 9
This South African succulent has green leaves $\frac{1}{2}$ in. long and produces pink flowers $\frac{3}{4}$ in. wide in the greatest profusion. It makes a cushion-like mass of foliage and is sometimes used as an interesting pot plant for the sunny window in the North.

speciosum   2′   Zone 9
This is one of the best of these succulents with orange flowers, shrubby, succulent leaves $\frac{1}{2}$ in. long, curved upwards and green; masses of beautiful daisylike flowers colored brownish to orange-red, greenish in the center and 2 in. wide. Native to South Africa and making an interesting pot plant for the sunny window.

DROSERA (DRO-ser-a). Bog plants of little value elsewhere.

filiformis   6″–8″   Zone 3   Threadleaf Sundew
Tufts of narrow, grasslike leaves and stems of

12 in., bearing purple flowers in 1-sided spikes in midsummer, indicate the presence of this insectivorous plant in the bogs and wetlands of eastern North America, Europe and Asia.

intermedia 6″–8″ **Zone 3**
The leaves of this insectivorous plant have a spoonlike tip which curls about the insects alighting on it. The white flowers, blooming in July, are borne on stems 6 in. high. Native to eastern North America.

longifolia 6″–8″ **Zone 3 Narrowleaf Sundew**
Similar to *D. intermedia*, but with leaves having long petioles and a narrow tip. Native to North America, northern Europe and Asia.

rotundifolia 4″–10″ **Zone 3 Round-leaved Sundew**
An unusual perennial herb native to the bogs and marshlands of the U.S. and Canada. It has a basal rosette of spoonlike leaves covered with tiny red hairs which exude minute drops of mucilage, making the plant appear to be covered with dew. Insects coming in contact with these sticky hairs are trapped and eventually digested by the plant. The small white flowers, having 5 petals, are borne in a 1-sided terminal cluster. The plant may be grown in the bog garden or in a pot of sphagnum moss in a cool greenhouse. It requires a soil or potting medium with a pH of about 4.

DRUPE. A fleshy fruit containing usually 1 hard-coated seed like the plum or cherry.

DRYAD. See DRYAS.

DRYAS (DRY-as)
drummondii creeping **Zone 3 Drummond Dryas**

An attractive and unusual semi-evergreen, shrubby, creeping plant of North America, with irregularly-lobed leathery leaves and pale yellow flowers similar to a wild rose. It blooms in May, although flowers appear intermittently throughout much of the summer. It does flower well in loose, acid soil and semi-shade. Propagate by seeds, cuttings or layers.

octopetala creeping **Zone 2 Mt. Washington Dryad**
An evergreen creeping plant with oblong leaves an inch long and white woolly beneath; erect white flowers are 1–1½ in. wide and the fruits are plumes an inch long. Native to northern North America, northern Europe and northern Asia. Only of value in the wild garden in the northern parts of the country where they make an evergreen ground cover. Members of the Rose Family.

x suendermannii creeping **Zone 2 Suender-mann Dryad**
Similar to *D. octopetala* except that the flowers are yellow while young and then mature white.

DRY SOILS, PLANTS FOR. Very few plants require dry soil conditions. A greater variety of plants can be forced into growth if leaf mold or peat moss is mixed with a dry soil to increase its water-holding properties. Mulches placed about the plants also aid in this respect. The following plants are a few which can withstand dry soil conditions better than most:

TREES	HEIGHT	ZONE	
Acacia longifolia floribunda	20′	10	Gossamer Sydney Acacia
Acer negundo	60′	2	Box-elder
Ailanthus altissima	60′	4	Tree-of-heaven
Albizia julibrissin	36′	7	Silktree
Aralia elata	45′	3	Japanese Angelica-tree
Bauhinia sp.	20′	10	Bauhinia
Brachychiton sp.	60′	10	Bottle-tree
Betula populifolia	30′	5	Gray Birch
Broussonetia papyrifera	48′	6	Common Paper-mulberry
Casuarina sp.	30′–70′	10	Beefwood
Celtis australis	75′	6	European Hackberry
Ceratonia siliqua	50′	10	Carob
Cupressus macrocarpa	75′	7	Monterey Cypress
Eucalyptus sp.	30′–100′	9	Eucalyptus
Ficus sp.	30′–75′	6–10	Fig
Fraxinus velutina	45′	7	Velvet Ash
Grevillea robusta	150′	10	Silk-oak Grevillea
Juniperus sp.	2′–90′	2–9	Juniper
Koelreuteria paniculata	30′	5	Golden-rain Tree
Leptospermum laevigatum	25′	9	Australian Teatree
Maclura pomifera	60′	5	Osage-orange

	HEIGHT	ZONE	
Melia azedarach	45'	7	Chinaberry
Olea europaea	25'	9	Common Olive
Parkinsonia aculeata	30'	9	Jerusalem Thorn
Pinus—certain sp.	30'–100'	2–8	Pine
Populus alba	90'	3	White Poplar
Prosopis glandulosa	50'	8	Honey Mesquite
Quercus, certain sp.	75'–100'	3–7	Oak
Robinia sp.	15'–75'	3–5	Locust
Sassafras albidum	60'	4	Sassafras
Schinus molle	40'	9	California Peppertree
Ulmus pumila	75'	4	Siberian Elm

SHRUBS

	HEIGHT	ZONE	
Acanthopanax sieboldiana	9'	4	Five-leaf Aralia
Acer ginnala	20'	2	Amur Maple
Amorpha canescens	4'	2	Lead-plant
• Arctostaphylos uva-ursi	ground cover	2	Bearberry
Artemisia sp.	1¼'–4'	2–5	Sagebrush
Atriplex sp.	4'	5–7	Saltbush
Baccharis halimifolia	12'	4	Groundsel-bush
Berberis mentorensis	7'	5	Mentor Barberry
• B. thunbergii	7'	5	Japanese Barberry
Buddleia alternifolia	12'	5	Fountain Buddleia
Callistemon lanceolatus	30'	9	Lemon Bottlebrush
Caragana sp.	4'–18'	2–3	Peatree
Ceanothus americanus	3'	4	New Jersey Tea
• Chaenomeles sp.	3'–6'	4	Flowering Quince
Colutea arborescens	12'	5	Bladder-senna
Comptonia peregrina	4'	2	Sweet Fern
Cornus racemosa	15'	4	Gray Dogwood
• Cotinus coggygria	15'	5	Smoketree
Cytisus sp.	6'–9'	5–6	Broom
Diervilla sessilifolia	4½'	4	Southern Bush-honeysuckle
Elaeagnus angustifolia	20'	2	Russian-olive
Genista sp.	1'–3'	2–7	Woadwaxen
• Hamamelis virgininiana	15'	4	Common Witch-hazel
Hebe sp.	4'–6'	7	Hebe
Hypericum calycinum	ground cover	5	Aaronsbeard St. Johns-wort
Indigofera sp.	3'–6'	4–5	Indigo
Ligustrum sp.	6'–30'	3–7	Privet
Lycium halimifolium	5'	4	Common Matrimony-vine
• Myrica sp.	9'–36'	2–6	Bayberry
Myrtus communis	5'–10'	8–9	Myrtle
Nerium oleander	20'	7–8	Oleander
Physocarpus sp.	4'–9'	2–4	Ninebark
Pittosporum sp.	10'	8–10	Pittosporum
Potentilla sp.	6"–4'	2–7	Cinquefoil
Prunus besseyi	7'	3	Western Sand Cherry
P. maritima	6'	3	Beach Plum
Rhamnus sp.	18'–30'	2	Buckthorn
Rhus sp.	3'–30'	2–5	Sumac
Rosmarinus officinalis	6'	6	Rosemary
Ruscus aculeatus	1½'–4'	7	Butcher's-broom
Salvia greggii	3'	7	Autumn Sage
Santolina chamaecyparissus	1½'	7	Lavender-cotton
Shepherdia canadensis	7'	2	Russet Buffalo-berry
Sophora davidii	7'	5	Vetch Sophora
Spartium junceum	10'	7	Spanish-broom
Tamarix sp.	6'–15'	2–7	**Tamarix**

	HEIGHT	ZONE	
Vaccinium pallidum	3′	3	Dryland Blueberry
Viburnum lentago	30′	2	Nannyberry
Vitex agnus-castus	9′	6–7	Chaste-tree
Yucca sp.	3′	4	Adam's-needle
HERBACEOUS PERENNIALS			
Achillea sp.	4″–4′	2–7	Yarrow
Allium stellatum	1½′	4	Prairie Onion
Anthemis tinctoria	3′	2–3	Golden Marguerite
Artemesia stellariana	2½′	2	Dusty Miller
Aster—some sp.	1½′–8′	3–7	Aster
Baptisia tinctoria	3′–4′	6	Wild Indigo
Callirhoe involucrata	1′–2′	3	Low Poppy-mallow
Cassia marilandica	3′	6	Wild Senna
Coreopsis grandiflora	2′	7	Tickseed
Coronilla varia	2′	3	Crown Vetch
Dianthus barbatus	2′	annual-biennial	Sweet William
Eupatorium sp.	2′ ?	5	Wild Hoarhound, Joe-Pye-weed
Euphorbia cyparissias	1′	3	Cypress Spurge
Gaillardia aristata	2′–3′	2–3	Common Blanketflower
Galium verum	2′–3′	2–3	Yellow Bedstraw
Gypsophila paniculata	3′	2–3	Babysbreath
Helianthus sp.	2′–12′	2–4	Sunflower
Hemerocallis fulva	6′	2–3	Tawny Daylily
Hypericum perforatum	2′	3	St. John's-wort
Lathyrus maritimus	vine	4	Maritime Pea
Liatris, several sp.	1′–4′	2–7	Gayfeather
Lychnis coronaria	3′	biennial-perennial	Rose Campion
Mesembryanthemum	6″	8–10	Iceplant
Opuntia sp.	6″–15′	5–10	Prickly Pear
Origanum vulgare	2½′	3	Wild Marjoram
Papaver nudicaule	1′–2′	2–3	Iceland Poppy
Potentilla sp.	2″–4′	3	Cinquefoil
Rudbeckia sp.	3′–12′	annual-perennial	Coneflower
Salvia pratensis	3′	2–3	Meadow Sage
Santolina chamaecyparissus	1½′–2′	6–7	Lavender-cotton
Sedum sp.	2″–15″	2–3	Sedum
Tanacetum vulgare	3′	2–3	Tansy
Thymus serpyllum	ground cover	2–3	Mother-of-thyme
Verbascum thapsus	4′–5′	3	Flannel Mullein
Verbena rigida	1′–2′	8	
Yucca sp.	3′–25′	4–8	Yucca
ANNUALS			
Dimorpotheca sp.	4″–16″	annual	Cape-marigold
Eschscholtzia californica	2′	annual	California-poppy
Ipomoea sp.	vine	annual	Morning-glory
Phlox drummondii	1½′	annual	Annual or Drummond Phlox
Portulaca grandiflora	8″	annual	Common Portulaca

DRYOPTERIS (dry-op-TER-is). A large group of ferns (nearly 1000 species) native throughout the world. Most of them are of very easy cultivation. Those with rhizomes can be easily propagated by division and others are easily raised by spores. See FERNS. If they are given a soil made up of half loam and half peat moss with a little cow manure added, they will do well indeed, but they should have plenty of water.

austriaca intermedia   30″   Zone 3   Intermediate Shield Fern
Another native American fern widely distributed
throughout eastern North America. The fronds
are 10 in. wide, doubly pinnate and sometimes
thrice pinnate and nearly evergreen. It does not
spread very much and requires plenty of
moisture. One of the most common ferns.

cristata   30″   Zone 4   Crested Shield Fern
Native throughout central and eastern North
America and also known as the Narrow Swamp
Fern. The pinnules are dark green and leathery,
somewhat brittle, and the plant needs a moist
shaded spot to do well. It is chiefly a fern for the
woods.

felix-mas   2′–4′   Zone 3   Male Fern
This plant, especially the variety 'Cristata', is
the English Crested Male Fern, with fancy,
deeply cut pinnatifid pinnules and fronds up to
36 in. long and 9 in. wide. This originated in
England, but it is little grown in America and it
is characterized by the ends of the pinnae
developing uniform, fingerlike crests or tips.

goldiana   4′   Zone 3   Goldie's Fern
Native from New Brunswick to Minn. and
Tenn. The leathery, deep green fronds are 14 in.
wide and deciduous. It is too large and coarse
to be used in most gardens and requires a cool,
moist, shaded situation in which to grow.

hexagonoptera = *Thelypteris hexagonoptera*
linnaeana = *Gymnocarpium dryopteris*
marginalis   15″–18″   Zone 3   Marginal
Shield Fern
Native to eastern North America, this has
doubly-pinnate fronds 5–8 in. wide, dark green
and leathery. It needs full shade and much
moisture throughout the summer. This is
another fern that does not spread and so makes
a fine specimen plant.

noveboracensis = *Thelypteris novaboracensis*
thelypteris = *Thelypteris palustris*
The species mentioned above are for the
garden. An attractive house plant species is **D.
erythrosora** from Japan, with fronds 18 in.
long. Some for the greenhouse would be **D.
boryana,** with 2–3-ft. fronds; **D. brunoniana** with
fronds 1–1½ ft.; and **D. chrysoloba** with 9-in.
fronds.

DUCHESNEA (doo-SHAYS-nea)

indica   2″   Zone 5   Mock-strawberry
Strawberrylike in flower, fruit and foliage, this
small ground cover is native to southern Asia
but has become naturalized in North America.
The yellow flowers are ½ in. in dia., followed by
small fruits similar to wild strawberries but not
as tasty. The compound leaves are made up of 3
coarsely toothed leaflets, much smaller than
those of the Common Strawberry and the
runners increase rapidly. Propagation is simply

by division of the plants.

DUCKWEED = *Lemna minor*

DUCKWHEAT = *Fagopyrum tataricum*

DUMB-CANE = *Dieffenbachia amoena*

DUNE   GRASS,   EUROPEAN = *Elymus
arenarius*

DURRA = *Sorghum vulgare Durra*

DURANTA (dew-RAN-ta)

repens   18′   Zone 10   Golden Dewdrop
There are several common names for this like
Pigeon-berry and Sky-flower but Golden
Dewdrop is the most imaginative, given because
the fruits are borne in golden-yellow clusters,
like a group of currants each one of which is
about ½ in. through. It is a spiny shrub with pale
blue flowers ½ in. across in racemes about 6 in.
long. The leaves are opposite, and the twigs are
4-angled. There is a variety (**alba**) with white
flowers. Propagated by seeds and cuttings.

DUST AND DUSTING. Pesticides are often
applied as dry dusts rather than as wet sprays.
Dusts are prepared by mixing a recommended
amount of dry pesticide with a compatible
carrier such as clay, talc or hydrated lime.
Both hand and power equipment is available
for applying the dusts. See SPRAYING and DUST-
ING. Dusting is faster but more expensive for
material and its use is handicapped by wind.
Home mixing of dust is seldom advised but
prepared dusts are now available for both large
and small operations.

DUSTING EQUIPMENT. See EQUIPMENT.

DUSTY MILLER. See CENTAUREA, also *Artemisia stelleriana.*

DUTCH HOE. A very popular garden tool,
sometimes called a scuffle hoe, in which a single
blade is welded to arms at right angles to the
handle. It is bent to such an angle that, when
holding it, one can simply push or pull it along
the surface of the ground for eliminating small
weeds and breaking up the surface crust of the
soil. More gardeners should become familiar
with it for it is much easier to use than the
common hoe.

DUTCHMAN'S BREECHES = *Dicentra cucullaria*

DUTCHMAN'S PIPE. See ARISTOLOCHIA.

DWARF EVERGREENS. See EVERGREENS,
LOW AND DWARF.

DWARF FRUIT TREES. See FRUIT TREES.

DWARFING PLANTS. See BONSAI, ESPALIER,
etc.

DWARF SHRUBS. See *Dwarf Shrubs* by
Donald Wyman (Macmillan, 1974). In this

190-page book, over 300 woody plants, both evergreen and deciduous, are described. All are under 3 ft. tall at maturity. Included is an alphabetical quick-reference chart showing the soil preference of each plant, whether it will withstand shade, wet or dry soil and the various places where it will grow best—as a ground cover, bank plant, at the seashore, etc.

DYEING FLOWERS. It is difficult to eliminate the old-fashioned desire of dyeing cut flowers, either fresh or dried. Flowers should be enjoyed in their natural beauty but there are always a few individuals who like green carnations (there are no green-flowering varieties) and others who must add color to dried materials, most of which have a natural beauty all their own if left unadorned with artificial colors. For those who must use dyes, there are two processes to consider.

Green or freshly cut flowers that are alive can absorb dyes through their cut stems. Fresh-cut flowers, with foliage stripped from their stems, are placed into the solution which should cover at least half the stems. The flowers will begin to take on the color in a short time and when the desired color density is reached, they are removed from the dye and placed in fresh water.

More popular are the floral sprays. These are actually paint sprays available in pressurized dispenser cans and are used for spraying colors on fresh or dried materials. Because of the ease of application, these coloring materials are more popular for both fresh and dried materials.

DYER'S GREENWEED = *Genista tinctoria*

DYER'S WOAD = *Isatis tinctoria*

E

E or EX. Latin prefix usually denoting parts are missing, as ebracteate or exstipulate meaning without bracts or without stipules.

EARDROPS, GOLDEN = *Dicentra chrysantha*

EARTH STARS = *Cryptanthus acaulis*

EARTHWORMS. These worms (not insects) are common in good garden soil but seldom damage plants. In fact, they are considered beneficial because of their habit of carrying organic matter into the soil and by aerating packed soil with their burrows. They are also grown in nurseries for fish bait. Where they pile little mounds of earth near the entrance to a burrow, they are annoying on special lawns. They are controlled by using insecticide #15 as for Japanese beetle and likewise this treatment applied for Japanese beetle control will kill earthworms.

EASTER HERALD TRUMPET = *Beaumontia grandiflora*

EBENACEAE = The Ebony or Persimmon Family

EBONY OR PERSIMMON FAMILY = Ebenaceae

ECCREMOCARPUS (ek-rem-o-KARP-us)
  scaber climbing annual Chilean Gloryflower
Although perennial and woody in the Deep South, this can be grown as an annual climber in the North if the seed is started early in the greenhouse. It can grow 8–12 ft. tall, and bears clusters of orange-scarlet flowers the whole summer. A member of the Bignonia Family, native to Chile, propagated by seeds, started in the greenhouse in March and transplanted outdoors after all danger of frost is over.

ECHEVERIA (esh-eve-EE-ria). Mostly tender, succulent-leaved perennials from Mexico belonging to the Crassula Family. Usually they have rosettes of fleshy leaves that are blue-gray and tubular red, pink or yellow flowers borne on slender stalks. They make fine plants for the window in northern areas and are used for massing in southern Calif. Easily propagated by seeds, cuttings or offsets. Offsets are best removed during the late summer. Native to Mexico.
  agavoides   6″   Zone 9   Carpet Echeveria
A succulent from Mexico with thick, stiff leaves, densely imbricated, about 2 in. long and spine-tipped. The flowers are cone-shaped, reddish with yellow tips.
  amoena   3″   Zone 9
This succulent is nearly stemless, but has many offshoots. The leaves are ¾ in. long; the coral-red flowers are 1–8 on flower stalks about 8 in. long.
  coccinea   2′   Zone 9   Scarlet Echeveria
A branching succulent with rosettes of leaves at the ends of the branches. The leaves are narrow, keel-shaped and gray-green, although they turn reddish as they mature, and they are finely pubescent. Flowers are red.
  derenbergii   3″   Zone 9   Painted-lady
Globe-shaped, clustered rosettes of thick, pale green leaves 1½ in. long with a waxy bloom and tipped with red. Flowers are profuse, golden yellow to orange, ½ in. long.
  elegans   3″   Zone 9   Mexican Snowball
This succulent looks like a small ball of ice, then opens into a beautiful rosette of spoon-shaped leaves which are a pale, waxy blue with white translucent margins. The flowers are coral pink, borne on a pink stem.
  gibbiflora   2′   Zone 10   Fringed Echeveria
A succulent something like a *Sempervivum* with obovate-spatulate leaves up to 7 in. long which turn pinkish as they mature. These are borne in a rosette at the end of a thick stem. Flowers are red outside, yellow inside. These are often used for summer bedding purposes and are interesting in the window garden.
  x gilva   4″   Zone 9
The oblanceolate succulent leaves are about an inch long and are produced in dense rosettes. The flowers are pinkish yellow, borne on horizontal stalks.
  glauca = *E. secunda glauca*
  harmsii   1′   Zone 7
A much-branched succulent used in southern Calif. for massing and as a ground cover. The obovate leaves are borne near the ends of the branches and the flowers, bright red, tipped with yellow, are about an inch long and are borne singly or in pairs at the ends of the branches in summer.
  leucotricha   6″   Zone 10   Chenille Plant
A Mexican native, blooming in late winter, with red-brown hairy stems, about 25 leaves in a loose rosette and bright red flowers, 12–15 on a spike about a foot long.

multicaulis 3′   **Zone 10**
A succulent with leaves 8 in. long, ¾ in. wide, and rosettes of fresh, waxy-green leaves on small branches. The leaves are copper-colored, edged with brown. Flowers on the branches are red, yellow inside.

pulvinata   1′   **Zone 9**   **Chenilleplant**
A clustered rosette of foliage at the end of the stem, leaves velvety pubescent, 1 in. long and rounded at the end which is tipped with red; flowers scarlet, in a leafy raceme.

secunda glauca   6″   **Zone 10**
A succulent with all basal leaves rounded, ¾ in. wide, rather pale but tipped with red. Flowers about ½ in. long, borne on slender stems, red outside and yellow inside.

setosa   3″   **Zone 9**
Woolly, compact rosettes of leaves, each 2 in. long, make this a desirable plant for growing indoors in the North or out of doors for massing in southern Calif. Vermillion flowers tipped with yellow make this a strikingly beautiful little plant.

ECHINACEA (ek-in-AY-sea)

purpurea   2′–3′   **Zone 3**   **Purple Echinacea**
Although this perennial member of the Composite Family is somewhat weedy in growth, it has an attractive and somewhat unusual flower and can thrive in very sunny or windy sites. It has black, fibrous roots and coarse, hairy stems. The leaves are alternate, simple and toothed, the basal leaves having rather long stems. The purple disk-flowers are in a distinct cone shape, sparsely surrounded with rose or rose-purple, drooping ray-flowers, which remain even when withered. Blooming in summer, it is found in fields and dry, open woods throughout the southeastern U.S.

ECHINOCACTUS (ek-in-o-KAK-tus)

grusonii   3″–4′   **Zone 10**   **Gold Ball Cactus**
This can grow into a giant globe 3 ft. in dia. It is light green, closely ribbed and covered with golden spines from whence comes its common name. The yellow flowers, 1½–2½ in. across, are imbedded in the top and open in the sun. Native to central Mexico. For culture see CACTI AND SUCCULENTS.

ingens   5′   **Zone 9**
A barrel-type cactus with main trunk as much as 4 ft. in dia., glaucous blue, woolly at the top, densely ribbed, with rigid brown spines and yellow flowers ¾ in. long. Native to Mexico. Often used as a pot plant when young. Propagated by seeds sown in the late spring or early summer. For culture see CACTI AND SUCCULENTS.

ECHINOCEREUS (ek-in-o-SEE-reus)

Hedgehog Cactus
A group of low spiny cacti, sometimes globular, sometimes with several columnar stems, usually with 1 low cylindrical head, bearing large daisy-like flowers colored scarlet, purple or yellow, opening at night. Native to western U.S. and Mexico. These do not grow well under the moist conditions of greenhouses. For culture see CACTI AND SUCCULENTS.

ECHINOCHLOA (ek-in-o-CLO-a)

crus-galli   2½′   **annual**   **Barnyard Grass**
Introduced from Europe and a bad weed throughout the U.S. and Mexico, especially on moist rich soils. The stems are erect and the weed is easily distributed by seeds. Best way to control it (other than by pulling out or spraying with chemicals) is to keep the grass cut and prevent seed formation. It is sometimes called Cockspur Grass because of the long "beard" or sticky awn attached to the seed. Also see WEED-CONTROLLING CHEMICALS.

ECHINOCYSTIS (ek-in-o-SIS-tus)

lobata   **vine**   **annual**   **Wild Mock-cucumber**
Native over the eastern half of North America, this is not a valued garden specimen but because of vigorous growth it is a fine fast-growing annual for planting on piles of debris or other materials that are to be hidden. It can climb with tendrils also. The large leaves are 3–5 in. across with 3–7 lobes, soft prickles; white, small, staminate flowers in Aug. and Sept. in lacey clusters and fruit a papery, puffed spiny pod about 2 in. long. It seeds readily and can almost become a pest, but since it can grow as much as 20 ft. in a single season it has its uses.

ECHINODORUS (ek-in-o-DOR-us)

aquatic plants   **Zone 10**   **Sword Plants**
Several species of this aquatic genus have been introduced from the area of the Amazon River in South America and make striking ornamentals in the home aquarium. They have lance-shaped leaves with a long petiole, all originating from the base of the plant. They have leaves 12–18 in. long and the plant sends out runners from the base which form new plants. Species include **E. intermedius** with narrow leaves sending out young plants from April through Aug.; **E. rangeri** which has broader leaves and sends out new plants Dec. to June. The leaves of this species may be 8½ in. long and 3½ in. broad. **E. tenellus** has leaves only 3–4 in. long, an excellent plant for the small aquarium, making a fountainlike miniature Sword Plant, especially if the rapidly produced runners are kept pinched off.

ECHINOPS (EK-in-ops). These perennials have globular heads of sharp, spiny flower and fruit clusters, usually blue in summer. The leaves also are spiny and thistlelike, usually white on the underside. They have strong character, are fine ornamentals for the perennial border. If the flower heads are cut and dried just prior to full opening, they make excellent subjects for dried arrangements in winter. Propagation is by spring division of clumps, and by root cuttings. Seed can be sown also, but it usually results in inferior types.

exaltatus　3′–12′　Zone 3　Russian Globe-thistle
This is probably the species offered by most nurseries as *E. ritro* and *E. sphaerocephalus*. The blue flower color varies greatly and good selections should be asexually propagated. They bloom from July to Sept. The var. 'Taplow Blue' is the best selection with steel-blue flower balls that sometimes are 3 in. across. This is the best of any in this genus for garden planting. Native to Siberia.

humilus　3′–4′　Zone 3　Siberian Globe-thistle
With ornamental foliage, white pubescent underneath, wavy on the margins, not as spiny as that of *E. exaltatus*.

ritro　1′–2′　Zone 3　Small Globe-thistle
Listed in many catalogues in Europe and America, the plant is usually *E. exaltatus*. The true *E. ritro* is the lowest of the Globe-thistles, found native from southern Europe to Siberia.

sphaerocephalus　3′–8′　Zone 3
Although this may be found listed in catalogues, it may not be in cultivation. It differs from the other species in this genus by having glandular pubescence. The flower heads are 2 in. across and the plant itself is very bushy. Native to Europe and Siberia.

ECHINOPSIS (ek-in-OP-sis) **Sea Urchin Cactus**
These are South American cactus plants, often used as small potted plants in window gardens where they are excellent because of their conspicuous white flowers. The plants themselves are ribbed, globular and very spiny, somewhat in size and shape like *Echinocereus* species. They are slow-growing, a 20-year-old plant being only a few inches tall.

ECHIOIDES (ek-i-o-I-dez)
longiflorum (*Arnebia echioides*)
**　　　　1′　Zone 4　Prophet-flower**
A low-growing perennial with dark green leaves and bright yellow trumpet-shaped flowers with large brown spots which fade out, leaving the older flowers a pure yellow. These appear in April and May, although the plant may flower sparingly all summer. It is easy to grow in any good garden soil, but does best in full sun. Propagation is by seed or by division. Native to the Near East.

ECHIUM (EK-ium). Coarse annuals or biennials of the Borage Family, these plants have hairy, alternate, simple leaves with showy (often blue)

flower spikes in summer, mostly native to southern Europe.

creticum　2′　annual　Cretan Vipers Bugloss
With oblong leaves and brick-red flowers in spikelets.

lycopsis (*E. plantagineum*)　**3′　annual**
Flowers blue, purple, mauve and violet in some of the hybrids of this species and about ⅞ in. long. The leaves are covered with small white hairs.

plantagineum = *E. lycopsis*

vulgare　2½′　Zone 3　Common Vipers Bugloss
Sometimes this is a pernicious tap-rooted, biennial weed in pastures, and it should be noted that contact with bristly hairs on the leaves and stems produces dermatitis. Often called Blue Thistle or Blueweed, this is native to Europe and Asia, not much used as a garden plant. The flowers first appear pink then fade to blue, the oblong, alternate and simple leaves being 2–6 in. long. The flowers are produced in summer, and it will grow in dry soils.

ECOLOGY. The branch of biology that deals with the relations between living organisms and their environment.

EDELWEISS = *Leontopodium alpinum*

EDGING PLANTS. Plants selected for edging beds or walks should be low, neat and compact. They should respond to clipping or shearing when necessary and they should produce a maximum amount of good foliage throughout the growing season.

Some gardeners like to use annuals and there are certainly many available. Select the dwarf moundlike varieties—every seed catalogue lists many of these. When annuals are used as the edging plants it gives the gardener an opportunity to change the color of the flower and type of plant from year to year.

Other gardeners like to use something more permanent like *Buxus sempervirens* 'Suffruticosa' or *Teucrium chamaedrys*. No matter what plant or variety is chosen, be certain to know the mature shape of the plant selected. Some plants are grown in one continuous line, like a clipped hedge. Other times, plants that are rounded and globelike at maturity are set out so that there is a little space between each plant at maturity. Instead of the horizontal and vertical lines of a hedge, one has a long line of beautifully rounded or globe-shaped plants, each grown as an individual, separate from the others. The following are a very few plants which can be used for edging purposes:

	HEIGHT	ZONE	COMMON NAME
Ageratum houstoniana (Dwf. vars.)	6″	annual	Ageratum
Ajuga reptans	4″–12″	4	Bugleweed, Carpet Bugle

	HEIGHT	ZONE	COMMON NAME
Allium schoenoprasum	6″–24″	2–3	Chives
Anagallis monellii linifolia	4″–18″	annual	Flaxleaf Pimpernel
Antirrhinum majus (Dwf. vars.)	6″	annual or perennial	Snapdragon
Armeria maritima	6″–12″	2	Common Thrift
Artemisia sp.	4″–6′	2–5	Artemisia
Aubretia deltoides	3″–6″	4	Purple Rock-cress
Bellis perennis	6″	3	English Daisy
Berberis buxifolia nana	18″	5	Dwarf Magellan Barberry
B. thunbergii	7′	4	Japanese Barberry
Brachycome iberidifolia	1′	annual	Swan River Daisy
Buxus sempervirens 'Suffruticosa'	1′–3′	5–6	Dwarf Box
Calendula officinalis (dwarf vars.)	1′	annual	Pot Marigold
Campanula carpatica	1′	2–3	Carpathian Bellflower
Celosia argentea cristata (dwarf vars.)	1′	annual	Cockscomb
Centaurea cineraria	12″–18″	4	Dusty Miller
Coreopsis auriculata 'Nana'	6″	4	Dwarf Eared Coreopsis
Dianthus chinensis	1½′	annual	Chinese Pink
D. deltoides	4″–15″	2–3	Maiden Pink
D. gratianopolitanus	4″	4	Cheddar Pink
Echeveria sp.	3″–3′	9–10	Echeveria
Epimedium grandiflorum	9″	3	Bishops-hat
Eschscholzia californica	6″	annual	California-poppy
Festuca ovina glauca	12″	4	Blue Fescue
Fragaria vesca	8″	5–6	European Strawberry
Gazania splendens	18″	annual	Pied Gazania
Hedera helix	clinging vine	5	English Ivy
Heuchera sanguinea	12″	3–4	Coral-bells
Iberis sempervirens (dwarf vars.)	12″	2–3	Evergreen Candytuft
Iris cristata	3″–4″	3	Crested Iris
Lavandula officinalis (dwarf vars.)	12″	5	True Lavender
Lobelia erinus	4″–12″	annual	Edging Lobelia
Lobularia maritima	6″–12″	annual	Sweet Alyssum
Malcomia maritima	4″–8″	annual	Virginia-stock
Muscari botryoides	1′	2–3	Common Grape-hyacinth
Nemophila menziesii	20″	annual	Baby-blue-eyes
Ophiopogon japonicus	6″–15″	7	Dwarf Lily-turf
Pachysandra terminalis	8″	5	Japanese Spurge
Petunia x hybrid (dwarf vars.)	6″	annual	Garden Petunia
Phlox drummondii (dwarf vars.)	6″	annual	Drummond Phlox
P. subulata	6″	2–3	Moss Pink
Portulaca grandiflora	8″	annual	Common Portulaca
Primula malacoides	1½′	8	Fairy Primrose
Santolina chamaecyparissus	1½′	7	Lavender-cotton
Sedum sp.	2″–3′	2–3	Sedum
Sempervivum sp.	9″–1′	5	Houseleek
Stachys lanata	12″–18″	3	Woolly Betony
Tagetes tenuifolia pumila	8″	annua	Dwarf Striped Marigold
Teucrium chamaedrys	10″	5	Germander
Thymus serpyllum	3″	2–3	Mother-of-thyme
T. vulgaris	3″	5	Common Thyme
Torenia fournieri	12″	annual	Blue Torenia
Tropaeolum (dwarf vars.)	10″	annual	Nasturtium
Verbena x hortensis (dwarf vars.)	6″	annual	Verbena
Viola cornuta	6″	2–3	Tufted Pansy
V. tricolor	6″–12″	4	Johnny-jump-up
Zantedeschia rehmannii	1′	10	Red or Pink Calla

EDIBLE PLANTS. As everyone knows, many plants are edible. Those commonly grown as vegetables and for their fruits, nuts or leaves are certainly well known. However, when the early settlers came to America they did not have all the plants available to us today. They had to look around in the woods, testing this and that, taking note of what the Indians used. The foods of these days could not have been as palatable as ours are today, but it is of interest to note some that were used in those times. "Edible Wild Plants of Eastern North America" by M. L. Fernald and A. C. Kinsey (Harper and Brothers, Publishers, N.Y., 1943) and revised by R. C. Rollins in 1958, is a reference for just such information. There are others also. In the text of this encyclopedia, short notes have been made concerning many of these edible plants. One should also remember that many plants are poisonous, and the indiscriminate testing of unknown plants concerning their edible qualities is definitely not recommended.

EDRAIANTHUS (ed-ry-ANTH-us)
  graminifolius (*kitaibelii*)   3″   **Zone 5**
Resembling a tussock of grass, the bladelike leaves of this plant from the Balkan Mountains are 3 in. high. In June and July, clusters of dark blue or violet flowers are borne on long, trailing stems. It does best in coarse lime soil in sun or semi-shade. Propagation is by seed.
  pumilio   1″–3″   **Zone 5**
A smaller species than *E. kitaibelii*, the tuftlike leaf blades are scarcely an inch high and the erect flower stems barely 3 in. high. The single violet-colored flowers appear in May and June. Native to Dalmatia.

EEL-GRASS = *Vallisneria spiralis*

EGGPLANT (*Solanum melongena esculentum*) is probably native to India and the Far East and has been in cultivation for many centuries. While it is of minor importance in the U.S., it is of great importance in India, China and countries of the Far East.

The eggplant is very tender and requires a long, warm growing season. The plants should not be set into the garden until the daily mean temperature reaches 65°–70° F. Slightly earlier planting is satisfactory if some form of plant protector is used. See KITCHEN GARDEN.

Varieties

There are a large number of varieties available on a worldwide basis which vary in habit of growth, maturity, color and shape of fruit. In shape, fruits may range from small ovate 6–8 in. to much elongated and slender 12–15 in. long by 2 in. plus in dia. In color, fruits may range from white, ivory, green, mottled purple to a deep purple-black. In the U.S. only a few vari-

eties are listed by the seed trade. **'Black Beauty'** is suggested for regions having a relatively long growing season 80–90 days. Three new hybrids are recommended for regions with a shorter season **'Black Magic'**, **'Early Beauty Hybrid'** and **'Dusty Hybrid'**. These have slightly smaller fruit which mature in 60–70 days.

Soils and Fertilizers

While eggplants will grow in a variety of soils, a deep, well-fertilized sandy or silt loam is preferred. This crop will respond to an application of well-rotted manure, 3–4 bu. per 100 ft. of row. If manure is not available use a well-rotted compost. Supplement the manure or compost with a 5-10-10 fertilizer, 25–30 lbs. per 1000 sq. ft. plus 1 or 2 side dressings of nitrate of soda during the growing season.

Planting and Care

The production of early plants and general care is similar to that of tomatoes. See TOMATOES. Black Beauty and Florida High Bush should be spaced at 30 in. × 36 in. while the hybrid sorts can be a bit closer 24 in. × 30 in. Eggplants are edible from the time they are one-third developed in size until the fruit has reached full maturity. The fruit stem is hard and woody and, therefore, the fruit should be cut from the plant.

                                          GRANT B. SNYDER

Insect Pests

Colorado potato beetle, aphids and flea beetles are just as destructive to eggplant as to potato. See POTATO for control.

Diseases

Verticillium wilt is often more destructive to Eggplant than to Tomato, Potato or other plants which it attacks. Leaves wilt during heat of day and recover at night but soon dry and die. Fruits rot or develop abnormally. Plant treated seed, use hybrid varieties and avoid soil where other host plants have grown to avoid trouble.

Blight spots the leaves and the fruit and may kill seedlings quickly. Control treatments for wilt are recommended.

EICHHORNIA (ike-HORN-ia)
  crassipes   **aquatic plant**   **Zone 8**   **Water-hyacinth**
A floating plant from tropical America which has escaped cultivation throughout the warmer parts of the world and is a serious pest in clogging inland waterways. The feather roots are profuse, the orbicular leaves are 2–5 in. across and are held above the surface of the water, and the petiole of each leaf is greatly inflated at the base into a rounded bulblike organ. The violet-blue flowers are borne on upright spikes. The var. **major** has rosy-lilac-to-pink flowers. Some-

times these are used in outdoor pools or in home aquaria. It will not withstand frost. Easily propagated by division.

ELAEAGNACEAE = The Oleaster Family

ELAEAGNUS (el-ee-AG-nus). Alternate-leaved shrubs (*Shepherdia* and *Hippophae* species with which these might be confused have opposite leaves) which are both deciduous and evergreen, according to species. They are all valued for their good and often colorful foliage and the deciduous forms are especially valued for their colorful fruits. The fruits of *Elaeagnus commutatus*, although rather dry and mealy, are said to be edible.

Propagation

Seeds can be processed as soon as ripe or stored dry in airtight containers in a cool place for up to a year and then processed. Seed stratified for 3 months at 40° F. is usually ready for germination. *E. multiflorus* has proved to be doubly dormant; hence, stratify for 5 months at warm temperatures, followed by 3 months at 40° F. Softwood and hardwood cuttings root readily, as well as root cuttings taken in the spring. See STRATIFICATION, CUTTINGS.

angustifolia   20′   **Zone 2**   **Russian-olive**
Not a true olive, but bearing small yellow-coated berries with silvery scales, this tree comes from southern Europe and western Asia. The small, almost inconspicuous yellow flowers, in early June, are very fragrant. The narrow, gray-green leaves, 1–3½ in. long, are the chief ornamental characteristic of this tree and it is used only for this one feature. It has a crooked trunk with shredding bark, and borders on being a "dirty" tree, but its gray-green foliage is unique among woody plants grown in the North. Distributed in shelter belts of Midwest.

argentea = *E. commutata*

commutata   12′   **Zone 2**   **Silverberry**
Native to the Great Plains of the midwestern U.S., this is valued for its silvery foliage, the leaves being 1½–3½ in. long. The yellow flowers are small, ½ in. long, in May, very fragrant, and the fruits are egg-shaped, silvery and ¼ in. long. Propagation is easiest by removing suckers from the base of the plant. It is easily differentiated from *Shepherdia argentea*, with which it is frequently confused, because *Shepherdia* has opposite leaves and this has alternate leaves.

multiflora   9′   **Zone 4**   **Cherry Elaeagnus**
Valued for its red, cherrylike berries which have an acid flavor. These are ⅝ in. long and appear red in midsummer, making a fine color combination with the green foliage. The plant is a vigorous-growing native of China and Japan with dark green leaves 1½–2½ in. long, silvery beneath. It is said to have been introduced from

Japan into the U.S. by Commodore Perry.

pungens   12′   **Zone 7**   **Thorny Elaeagnus**
In the South this is one of the most popular of all the evergreen shrubs. The small, pendulous, silvery-white flowers have a fragrance somewhat similar to that of gardenias in Oct. The evergreen leaves are 1½–4 in. long. A native of Japan, it grows vigorously and well in many situations and can be sheared to make a hedge. The leaves of some forms are conspicuously variegated and, under the right conditions, can add materially to the overall interest of a garden. Varieties: 'Aurea'—leaf margin with rich yellow; 'Fruitland'—rounded leaves with wavy margins; 'Maculata'—leaf with large yellow blotch in center; 'Tricolor'—leaf variegated with yellow and pinkish white; 'Variegata'—leaf margin of yellowish white.

umbellata   12′   **Zone 3**   **Autumn Elaeagnus**
Native to China, Korea and Japan, this is a spreading shrub covered in the fall with silvery berries and valued for its young, silvery foliage.

ELAEOCARPACEAE = The Elaeocarpus Family

ELAEOCARPUS FAMILY = Elaeocarpaceae

ELDER, ELDERBERRY. See SAMBUCUS.

ELEAMPANE. See INULA.

ELECTRIC HOTBEDS. For those who do not have a greenhouse, yet wish a place to root cuttings or to start plants early in the season, the electric hotbed is an exciting garden asset. It is simply made, and will last for years. With the underground cables available now, electricity can be taken from the house to the garden and the simple thermostat and heating cable available from the General Electric Co., insures automatic ground heat. It is always ready for operating, and if constructed properly it can be used as a place to root cuttings, or to grow vegetable and flower plants for the garden. It is always available at any time of year as a cold frame, and any gardener has many uses for that.

Location of the Hotbed

In order to save electricity consumption, the hotbed should be located in a sheltered position, preferably on a slope with a southern exposure or on the south side of a building. The drainage should be good and where this is not the case a tile drain should be installed when the excavation is made.

Building the Frame

The first step in building the frame is to decide the size of the hotbed. A pit is then excavated, a little more than 1½ ft. deep, and large enough to extend 1 ft. or more beyond all sides of the hotbed. The bottom is filled with crushed stone or gravel to aid in drainage and insulation. The frame is then painted and set in the pit, crushed stone or gravel is filled in around the outside and mounded up around the frame even above the soil level.

Standard frames are usually made so that the sash will be 12 in. above the ground on one side and 18 in. above on the other. The surface of the rooting medium will then be at about the same height as the soil level outside the bed. However, if this level of the rooting medium could be a few inches lower than the soil level—that is, if the entire bed could be sunk a few inches deeper into the ground—the insulation would be much better and less electricity would be consumed, particularly in cold weather.

There are 2 requisites for the frame itself: (1) The lumber used should last for a period of years when painted and sunk in the ground; a concrete frame is not necessarily any better insulated than a wooden frame. (2) All joints and connections should be tight and stay tight; as soon as a board warps and splits, there is loss of heat and hence a waste of electricity. Any new or old lumber that will meet these two requirements will suffice.

Preparing the Hotbed

Very narrow mesh-wire should be placed on top of the crushed stone to keep the sand in the hotbed from filtering down into the gravel. About 1 in. of sand is placed on top of the wire mesh. The heating cable is laid on top of this thin layer of sand. Care should be taken, in laying the cable, that the wires shall be no more than 6 in. apart. About 6 in. of sand is placed on top of the wires, and this is the rooting medium. The entire bed of sand is carefully tamped down and leveled off. In preparing the bed, one should take care not to step on the heating cables and damage them. The better the work is done at this time, the longer the hotbed will last without digging up and rebuilding.

Covering the Hotbed

The standard sash, 3 ft. by 6 ft. in size, is customarily used for covering the hotbed. The sash should fit the frame tightly, and some method of shading should be used either over the sash directly or, better, over a frame built over the sash. The latter method would provide for the much-needed circulation of air over the sash itself. Double slats or matting might be good, since it is necessary only to keep the direct rays of the sun away from the cuttings. If the hotbed is to be used in the colder months of the year it is advantageous to put extra sash on the hotbed or to cover the sash with thick mats at night.

In building the frame, care should be taken in placing the grooved crosspieces on top of the frame (from front to back) at exactly the position where the sash meet, so a tight fit can be made. The sash should really slide in these grooved cross-pieces and fit snugly.

Operation

After the wires have been laid and covered with sand, the bed watered thoroughly, and everything placed in readiness, the temperature of the bed should be checked with several soil thermometers, the number used depending on the size of the bed. The temperature can be raised or lowered merely by turning a knob on the thermostat. After the bed has been run for a day or two and the temperature properly regulated, the cuttings or plants or seedlings may be placed at any time.

It is impossible to maintain an even temperature in the summer months because of the high outside temperature. When the nights are cold, or if the hotbed is run late in the fall, a surprisingly even temperature can be maintained. In this connection it is important to note that during cold, wet, or windy weather, the less the amount of heat lost from the bed, the lower the electricity consumption will be. For this reason, all sash should fit tightly; there should be good insulation throughout in the construction of the bed itself; on very cold nights, mats or additional sash may be laid on to aid in keeping in the heat.

Watering is another important factor in the operation of the electric hotbed, for, with the constant heat and the very good drainage supplied by the cinders underneath the sand, it tends to dry out.

The temperature at which the thermostat is set will vary with what is grown in the hot bed. Cuttings root best with a bottom heat of 75°–80° F. However, if flats of seedlings are merely placed on top of the sand in the hotbed, then the air temperature is the thing to regulate. Best air temperatures are usually between 70°–75° F. although this also varies with what is grown and its condition.

Before cuttings are to be placed for rooting, it is usually advisable to drench the medium with a mild fungicide, after all trash and dead material has been removed. Or, if one wishes, the rooting medium can be dug out and discarded and replaced with fresh material.

One should never apply too much water too frequently to the bed, regardless of what is grown, for molds and rotting can start and travel fast before they are noticed. Airing the hotbed is always a good practice, simply accomplished as the sash is raised or removed for inspection.

If flower or vegetable seedlings are being grown, it becomes a running challenge to determine the growth conditions—enough water to keep the plants turgid but not so much heat and water to cause injury and rot of the plants. On very hot days in the spring, raising the sash to allow fresh air in is always a good procedure and this can be increased day by day until the sash can be left off altogether.

In growing vegetable and flower seedlings in the hotbed, one of the things to guard against is sowing the seed too soon for the plants can outgrow the available space in the hotbed before it becomes possible to remove the sash permanently. One should work out a very precise schedule for seed-sowing to accomplish this.

ELEOCHARIS (eleo-CHAIR-is)
    dulcis (*E. tuberosa*)   **1′   Zone 7?   Chinese Water-chestnut**
A rushlike water plant native to China, used in bogs, ponds or aquaria, with narrow rushlike leaves with a solid tuber or corm at the base 2 in. or less in dia., eaten by the Chinese. Propagated by offsets from the corm. Not to be confused with *Trapa* species which are floating herbs, usually with their leaves submerged. This too is sometimes used in aquaria.

ELEPHANT'S-EAR = *Colocasia antiquorum*

ELETTARIA (el-et-AY-ria)
    cardamomum   9′   Zone 10   Cardamon
A stout herb native to tropical Asia, cultivated for cardamom. Large leaves, hairy underneath, with large flowering stalk bearing loose flower stalks. The fruit is a capsule and its seed is the spice or cardamon. Sometimes *Amomum cardamon* is used as a greatly inferior substitute.

ELEUSINE (el-yew-SY-ne)
    indica   2′   annual   Goose Grass
A native of Asia but naturalized in North America where it is a weed grass. The leaves are up to 1 ft. long and ¼ in. wide. Since it is an annual it is easily controlled by keeping it from seeding.

ELGETOL. A fungicide, which see.

ELKGRASS = *Xerophyllum tenax*

ELLIOTTIA (el-i-OT-ia)
    racemosa   4′-10′   Zone 7   Southern-plume or Elliottia
An extremely rare American shrub found in only a few locations in S.Car. and Ga. Its small, white, fragrant flowers are borne in upright terminal racemes 10 in. high in July. In fact it has been termed one of the rarest plants in the world. It belongs to the Heath Family, hence requires acid soil, preferably with a great deal of moisture. One of the reasons it is so rare is that viable seed is extremely rare. Another reason is that it is very difficult to transplant.

Propagation

Germination is slow and erratic, many seeds are not viable. It is best to propagate this plant either by layers, softwood cuttings or root cuttings, which see.

ELM. See ULMUS.

ELM FAMILY = Ulmaceae

ELODEA (el-O-dea)
    canadensis (*Anacharis canadensis*)   **aquatic plant   Zone 3   Elodea, Canada Waterweed**
This is one of the best oxygenators available for the home aquarium. It is an aquatic plant, growing underneath the water surface, and is native from Quebec southward. The leaves are ½ in. long and about $\frac{1}{12}$–$\frac{1}{6}$ in. wide. The species **A. densa** is supposed to be a better plant for aquaria because the leaves are 1 in. long and ⅕ in. wide. Native to South America.

ELSHOLTZIA (el-SHOLT-zia)
    stauntonii   5′   Zone 4   Staunton Elsholtzia
One of the few fall-blooming shrubs (Aug. to Sept.), the lilac flowers are borne in loose upright spikes. Coming from North China this plant is only grown for its fall flowers and has little else to recommend it. Best propagated by softwood cuttings.

ELYMUS (EL-im-us)
    arenarius   8′   perennial   Zone 4   European Dune Grass
The fruiting spikes of this European and Asiatic grass are often 10 in. long. Often planted in the seashore sand dunes to keep the sand in place. Easily propagated by division.
    glaucus   3′-5′   perennial   Zones 2-3   Blue Wild Rye
An ornamental grass from the West Coast, valued for its bluish-green foliage and its interesting 5-7-in. long flower spikes. Easily propagated by division.

EMARGINATE. With a shallow notch at the apex.

EMBOTHRIUM (em-BOTH-rium)
    coccineum   10′-40′   Zone 8   Chilean Firebush
A fiery-red flowered tree or bush frequently featured in the gardens of Great Britain but only grown in southern Calif. in the U.S. The red tubular flowers are produced in great profusion, nearly 2 in. long in the late spring; the alternate leaves are 2½-4½ in. long. An excellent specimen where hardy. Native to Chile.

EMBRYO. The rudimentary plantlet within the seed.

EMILIA (ee-MILL-ia)
    javanica (*sagittata*)   **2′   annual   Tassel-flower**
An alternate-leaved plant from the Tropics, used in gardens because of its ½-in. heads of red or scarlet flowers borne loosely in a corymb.

They do well in seashore gardens and in hot dry situations. Var. **lutea** has yellow flowers. Seed should be sown indoors in April for early bloom, or outdoors after all frost is over. Thin the seedlings to 9 in. apart in a sunny spot.

EMMENANTHE (em-en-ANTH-e)
penduliflora 1½′ **annual Yellow Whispering-bells**
Sometimes only a few inches high with pinnatifid sticky leaves and yellow, drooping, bell-shaped flowers during the summer. Native to deserts in Calif.

EMPETRACEAE = The Crowberry Family

EMPETRUM (em-PET-rum)
nigrum 10″ **Zone 3 Black Crowberry**
A heathlike evergreen native to the northern U.S., Canada and northern Europe and Asia, more or less procumbent but not an especially ornamental plant. The leaves are only ¼ in. long, flowers are purplish, solitary, very small and not especially ornamental, appearing in early May; fruit black and berrylike, ¼ in. across.

Propagation

Seed of this has a double dormancy, hence it should be stratified for 5 months at warm temperatures, then for 3 months at 40° F., then sown. Softwood and hardwood cuttings both can be rooted. See STRATIFICATION, CUTTINGS.

EMPRESS-TREE = *Paulownia tomentosa*

EMULSIFIED OILS. See INSECTICIDES.

ENCELIA (en-SEE-lia)
californica 2′–4′ **Zone 8 California Encelia**
A subshrub with woody base, native to Calif. and Ariz., strong scented with hoary leaves 1–2 in. long. The flower heads are 2½ in. wide, the disc flowers purple, the ray flowers yellow. Not much grown outside its native habitat. Contact with leaves and stems of this plant produces severe dermatitis to some humans.
farinosa 5′ **Zone 8 White Brittlebush**
A shrubby herb, member of the Composite Family, sometimes planted as an ornamental with leaves 2½ in. long and often silvery tomentose. The flower heads an inch wide have yellow ray-flowers. Especially found in the deserts of Calif., Ariz. and Mexico.

ENDEMIC. Native or local.

ENDIVE (*Cichorium endivia*). This plant is probably a native of East India and was used as a salad and pot herb by the ancient Greeks. It is an annual grown for its rosette of leaves which, when blanched, are crisp, tender and have a somewhat "nutty" taste.

Varieties

There are 2 general types, namely, the curled or fringed leaf sorts and the broad-leaved varieties which commercially are sold under the name of escarole. The two major varieties are **'Green Curled'** and **'Broad Leaved Batavian'**. French Endive or Witloof Chicory is an entirely different plant.

Culture

The general methods of culture are similar to those used for Lettuce. Endive is a cool-season crop and, generally, seed is sown 2 weeks apart from June 10 to Aug. 10, to provide a succession from early fall well into cold weather. Seed for the spring and early summer crop should be sown in the same manner as for early Lettuce. Planting distance is 10 to 12 in. in the row and 15 to 18 in. between rows.

Blanching

Blanching requires 4 to 15 days. The most common methods used are to tie the tops of each plant together with raffia, string or rubber bands, covering the plants with boards or strips of heavy building paper.

GRANT B. SNYDER

ENDYMION (en-DEE-mion)
hispanicus (*Scilla campanulata, S. hispanica*)
20″ **Zone 4 Wood Hyacinth Spanish Squill**
A coarse species, with leaves 1 in. wide and flowers blue to rose-purple, almost 1 in. across, nodding, sometimes 12 flowers per stalk, giving the impression of an underdeveloped Hyacinth. Native to Spain and Portugal.
nonscriptus (*Scilla nonscripta, S. nutans*) 12″
Zone 5 English Bluebell, Common Blue Squill
Native to Europe, fragrant flowers, blue, ½ in. wide in 6–12-flowered racemes. White, pink and red-flowered vars. available. Widely native (and popular) in England.

ENKIANTHUS (en-ki-ANTH-us). Members of the Heath Family, these are excellent shrubs from the Orient, valued for their delicate heath-like flowers, as well as their brilliant scarlet autumn color. They require acid soil and growing conditions similar to those provided for rhododendrons. The seeds can be sown as soon as they are ripe. Also, layers, softwood and hardwood cuttings all root. A fine group of ornamental shrubs.

campanulatus 30′ **Zone 4 Redvein Enkianthus**
A tall-growing ericaceous shrub, this is not used in gardens nearly as much as it might be. It is the tallest growing of the three species mentioned here, does well in acid soils, bears drooping clusters of waxy-white (with slight reddish tinge) blueberrylike flowers and, when grown with a western exposure, the leaves color a vivid scarlet in the fall. The flowers appear in mid-May, just prior to the leaves. Japan.

cernuus rubens   15′   Zone 5
A distinctly beautiful plant because of its very
deep red, bell-shaped flowers in nodding clusters
of 10–12 blossoms, produced in May. Each
flower is $\frac{1}{4}$ in. across. This variety has shorter
leaves than the species, only $\frac{1}{2}$–$\frac{3}{4}$ in. long. Native
to Japan. Autumn color is scarlet.

deflexus   21′   Zone 5
This is similar to *E. campanulatus* but the flowers
are larger and more showy, a yellowish red in
color and each one is about $\frac{1}{2}$ in. in dia. Native
to western China.

perulatus   6′   Zone 5
The flowers are bell-shaped, in pendulous
clusters similar to those of *E. campanulatus*. Not
much grown. Japan.

ENSETE

ventricosum (*Musa ensete*)   **25′   Zone 9**
Abyssinian Banana
This is the shrubby type banana from Abyssinia
that is so much used in Calif. for simulating
tropical effects in ornamental planting. The
leaves are 18 ft. long and 3 ft. wide, bright green
with a red midrib. If planted where the wind will
not fray the long leaves, it stays in good condition and looks well, one of the reasons it is often
used in protected areas next to buildings. The
fruit is inedible. Easily propagated by seeds
sown in the greenhouse in Jan. A similar species
Musa basjoo is a native of the Ryukyu Islands
south of Japan. It forms offsets easily and is
grown for the fiber of its leaf stalks.

ENTIRE. Without toothing or division; with an
even margin, usually referring to the margin of
a leaf.

EPAULETTE-TREE, FRAGRANT = *Pterostyrax hispidus*

EPHEDRA (eff-EE-dra)

distachya prostrate   Zone 5   Jointfir Ephedra
Peculiar looking shrubs, something like those
of *Equisetum*, not planted for ornament but
seen occasionally in botanic garden collections.
The dark green jointed stems are almost
prostrate, about $\frac{1}{12}$ in. thick and 2 ft. long, the
leaves are actually small scales. Male and female
flowers are on separate plants but are not
ornamental. However, it has been cultivated for
centuries in China as a source of ephedrine.
Native to Eurasia. Propagated by division and
sowing the seed as soon as ripe.

EPIDENDRUM (epi-DEN-drum)

tampense   12″–15″   Zone 10   Epidendrum
An epiphytic orchid with a cluster of bulbous
stems and long, narrow leaves. The flower stalk
bears a lax, branching, terminal cluster of
flowers which are predominantly yellow. The
plant flowers throughout the summer. There
are nearly 500 species in this genus, some

making good house plants. The flowers are all
colors, $\frac{1}{4}$–3 in. across. For culture and propagation see ORCHIDS.

EPIGAEA (ep-i-JEE-a)

**repens   ground cover   Zone 2   Trailing
Arbutus**
In the eastern part of the U.S., this beautiful
and very fragrant trailing evergreen is frequently
seen in many woodlands. The white-to-pink
flowers appear in mid-April, and the evergreen
leaves, 3 in. long, lie flat on the ground. Uncommon in gardens because it is very difficult
to transplant, it needs specific growing conditions in which to thrive. It grows in very poor,
acid soil especially where pines thrive. The
name "Mayflower," which it is sometimes
called, is supposed to have been given to it by the
Pilgrims who named it after their ship. **Epigaea
asiatica** is similar and has little to offer in
preference to the native American *E. repens*.
Propagation—usually by layering and division. See LAYERS, CUTTINGS.

EPILOBIUM (ep-i-LO-bium)

angustifolium   5′–6′   Zone 3   Fireweed
Wherever forest trees are cut or destroyed by
forest fires in Canada or the U.S., north of the
Carolinas, it is quite likely this herbaceous
perennial will soon make its appearance. In the
wild, it often grows as a straight stem, but in
cultivation is more likely to be branching. The
leaves are alternate, simple and 2–6 in. long.
The showy flowers, borne in a loose terminal
spike about 12 in. long during July and Aug.,
have short calyx tubes with 4 lobes. The 4,
slightly irregular petals are rose pink and about
1 in. wide. No special culture is required except
that the plant needs full sun. In Calif. it is grown
as a bee plant. Propagation is by seed and since
the seed is wind-dispersed, care must be taken
to prevent undesirable seeding. The flowers
appear in July and Aug. The var. **alba** has white
flowers.

hirsutum   4′   Zone 3   Hairy Willow-weed
This naturalized weed is native to Europe but
is now found throughout the eastern states. In
general appearance it is similar to *E. angustifolium*, but the leaves are opposite and the
purple flowers are regular rather than being
slightly irregular and 1 in. across. Also, it
requires more moisture in its culture, being
often found in marshes and moist meadows.

latifolium   1$\frac{1}{2}$′   Zone 3   Red Willow-weed
With alternate leaves 2 in. long and purple
flowers 2 in. wide in the summer in short leafy-
bracted racemes. Native to northern North
America, Europe, Asia. It is said that the
Indians scooped out the pith of the larger stalks
and cooked it as a thick soup.

EPIMEDIUM (ep-i-MEE-dium). Excellent herbaceous perennials, especially for ground covers in the shade or even in the full sun where the soil is rich, this group of spring-blooming plants should be better known, and used more. The splendid compound leaves are light green, taking on reddish tints in late summer or early fall. They are completely evergreen but remain upright and serve as good ground covers until smashed down by winter snow and ice. Propagation is easy by simple division in spring or fall. Plants usually spread, especially in moist soils by underground stems and belong to the Barberry Family.

alpinum rubrum 6″–9″ Zone 3 Red Alpine Epimedium
Native to southern and central Europe, this variety is probably the only representative of this species in North America. The peculiar flowers are red and light yellow during May and June. The leaves have a red margin, in fact they are reddish as they first appear in the spring. It should be grown in partial shade.

grandiflorum 9″ Zone 3 Long-spur Epimedium, Bishops-hat
This plant is native to Japan, Korea and Manchuria, and makes an excellent ground cover if grown in partial shade. The flowers are red to violet to white in May and June; the dense foliage is of an even height and the compound leaves remain in good condition until after Christmas. The autumn color is bronze. The leaves are generally thrice compound on a long, wiry petiole rising directly from the ground while the main stems are rootstocks, grow under ground and aid materially in keeping the soil in place. Varieties sometimes offered are **album** and **niveum** with white flowers; **roseum** with pinkish flowers; and **violaceum** with purple flower spurs.

pinnatum 9″–12″ Zone 5 Persian Epimedium
With bright yellow flowers and reddish spurs, from April to July, this is usually found as the var. **colchicum** which has fewer leaflets (the leaves of all species are compound) than the species. Another var. **sulphureum,** also with yellow flowers is sometimes offered by nurseries. Native to Persia.

EPIPACTIS (ep-i-PAK-tis)

gigantea 1′–3′ Zone 3 Giant Helleborine
A member of the Orchid Family with ovate or lanceolate leaves 2–8 in. long, flowers 3–15 about 1½ in. across and greenish or purplish, somewhat pendulous, from June to Aug. Native from Mont. to British Columbia, south to Mexico.

EPIPHYTE. Actually a plant growing in the air with aerial roots, none that reach the ground. Many orchids are said to be ephipytic, for they grow on other plants or objects and provide themselves with aerial roots only.

EPISCIA (ep-ISS-ia). A group of tropical plants sometimes grown in the home greenhouse in hanging baskets, valued for their beautiful foliage. The opposite leaves are stalked and the flowers, often showy, are either solitary or produced in small cymes, scarlet, whitish or purplish. They should be grown in partial shade, and can be propagated by cuttings rooted in sand. Mostly native to South America.

chontalensis 6″ Zones 8–10?
With reddish-purple, ovate leaves, 4 in. long and pale purple-to-white flowers 2 in. across with a yellow center, blooming in Nov. and Dec., solitary or clustered; native to Nicaragua.

cupreata 6″ to creeping Zones 8–10?
A creeping herbaceous plant with wrinkled leaves each having a broad band of red and silver down the middle. The scarlet flowers ¾ in. across are solitary. Native to Columbia and Nicaragua. Several varieties and cultivars are available with orange-scarlet flowers ('Metallica'); and **viridifolia** which has flowers an inch across and green leaves.

reptans creeping Zones 8–10?
With bright red solitary flowers, 1½ in. long and 1 in. across; rich dark green leaves about 3–5 in. long. Native to Columbia.

EPITHET. The adjectival part of the name of a species, variety, etc. e.g., *Tulipa sylvestris* and *Pinus sylvestris scotica*, where *sylvestris* and *scotica* are the specific and varietal epithets respectively.

EQUISETUM (ek-kwi-SEE-tum)

hyemale 4′ Zone 3 Scouring-rush, Horse-tail
Evergreen rushlike herbs native to North America, Europe and Asia, with hollow-jointed stems and no apparent leaves or flowers, growing in moist to marshy situations. Not an ornamental. Horses have been poisoned from eating this plant, usually cut with hay in moist ground. Closely allied to the ferns and mosses. Another species, *E. arvense* or the Field Horsetail is frequently found as a weed in gardens and must be vigorously dug out.

ERAGROSTIS (e-ra-GROS-tis)

amabilis 3′ annual Japanese Love Grass
A Japanese grass, very decorative because of its long panicles of small spikelets of fruits nearly 1½ ft. long. Used as a border it has merit and the spikelets are dried and used in arrangements. Seed can be sown outdoors after frosts are over.

tef (*abyssinica*) **3′ annual Teff**
An ornamental grass with foot-long seed panicles and hairlike ascending branches. Native to northern Africa where the seeds are used as a cereal grain.

ERANTHEMUM (e-RAN-them-um)

pulchellum 6′ Zone 9 Blue Eranthemum
Sprawling shrub from India valued for its
extremely deep blue flowers that are 1 in. long
and ¾ in. across, each with 5 horizontally produced petals. Flowers are produced in a column
several inches long and after each one falls, the
pointed white and green-veined bract remains
some time to lend interest. The opposite, simple
leaves are oval up to 8 in. long, with prominent
veins.

ERANTHEMUM, YELLOWVEIN = *Pseuderanthemum reticulatum*

ERANTHIS (er-ANTH-is). One of the first of
the spring flowers to bloom. They bear bright
yellow flowers and belong to the Buttercup
Family. Easily propagated by division.

hyemalis 3″ Zone 4 Winter Aconite
Tubers of this native European herb should be
planted in the very early autumn about 2 in.
deep; they should be massed in large numbers
and can become naturalized. Since they are so
small, use under high-branched deciduous
plants in the rockery, along the woods path.
They should not be placed in grass, but rather
soil free of other plant growth. The yellow
flowers about 1½ in. across bear 5–9 petallike
sepals. The var. **cilicica** has slightly larger
flowers. Leaves 1½ in. across, deeply cut. This
delightful little ground cover blooms in early
spring and should only be used in mass plantings. Plant in late August so the roots have time
enough to grow before the ground freezes.

Flower and root of Winter Aconite (*Eranthis
hyemalis*).

**x tubergenii 8″ Zone 4 Tubergen Winter
Aconite**
Similar to the above except it has larger and
deeper yellow-colored fragrant flowers. All
these make a fine ground cover for early spring
display but the foliage dies to the ground by
summer and thus leaves the ground bare.

EREMOCHLOA OPHIUROIDES = Centipede
Grass

EREMURUS (e-ree-MEW-rus). These are tall-
flowered perennial herbs native to Asia, belonging to the Lily Family, growing from heavy
fibrous roots, with wide, straplike leaves and
blooming in summer. The spikes of white
flowers may be 4–9 ft. high, but the leaves,
somewhat similar to those of Yucca but more
succulent, are only a foot or so tall. *Eremurus*
species should be planted in well-drained soil,
where they are protected from summer winds.
The thick, star-shaped roots should be planted
about 4–6 in. below the soil surface and
surrounded with coarse sand. Eventually, when
the roots reach the surface, they might best be
mulched over winter with coal ashes or sand.
Once established these plants should be let alone.
The tall spikes of bell-shaped white, pink, yellow
or orange flowers are most conspicuous. If used
in the North, where there is danger of late frosts
and in the spring, an attempt should be made
to protect the new growth from late freezing—
the chief reason why they do not prove successful in many northern gardens. Although they
can be propagated by division in the fall, it is
much better to try growing them from seed
as soon as it is ripe, sown in cold frame or greenhouse.

aurantiacus = *stenophyllus*

elwesii 10′ Zone 6 Elwes Desert-candle
Flowers pink. Habitat unknown. Blooms in
June.

**himalaicus 8′ Zone 3 Himalayan Desert-
candle**
This is the most common species in American
gardens, native to the Himalayas, with strap-
shaped leaves 1½ ft. long, and 18–30 in. of white
flowers on the tall stalk. These usually bloom
in June. The flowers and stalk make a white
column about 4 in. through. A hybrid with this
species as one parent called '**Himrob**' has pale
pink flowers on a spike 6–8 ft. tall.

x isabellus (*shelfordii*) 6′–8′ Zone 6 Shelford
Desert-candle
Flowers copper colored with outside tinged red.
A group of showy hybrids with pink, orange,
yellow or white flowers.

olgae 4′–6′ Zone 6 Olga Desert-candle
Native to Turkestan, flowers white, leaves 1 ft.
long and ¾ in. wide. Blooms in June–July.

robustus 10′ Zone 3 Giant Desert-candle
Native to central Asia, leaves 2 ft. long, flowers
bright pink, clustered for 3 ft. up and down the
flower stalk. Flowers and stalk in column 5 in.
through. Blooms in June.

spectabilis 8′ Zone 6
Native to Asia Minor, leaves 1½ ft. long and
1 in. wide; flowers light yellow with orange
stamens; flowered part of flower stalk 2 ft. long
and only 2 in. through.

stenophyllus (*bungei*) 4′–6′ Zone 6 Bunge
Desert-candle
Similar to *E. aurantiacus* except that flowers are usually more yellow than orange. Native to Persia. Blooms in July.

x tubergenii 5′–6′ Zone 6 Tubergen
Desert-candle
E. himalaicus x *E. bungei* with flowers pretty sulfur-yellow in June–July.

ERIANTHUS (er-i-ANTH-us)
ravennae 8′–12′ Zone 5 Ravenna Grass
A stout, vigorous perennial grass with leaves 3 ft. long and ½ in. wide sometimes planted for ornament. The silky flowering plume often 3 ft. long resembles that of Pampas Grass (*Cortaderia*). Native from southern Europe to India.

ERICA (E-rik-a or e-RY-ka). The heaths are acid soil plants ranging in size from low ground covers to small trees over 20 ft. high. All have very small but numerous evergreen needlelike leaves. It has been noted that *E. carnea, cinerea, darleyensis* and *mediterranea* can even be grown in soils that are slightly alkaline. Most are best grown in large masses or beds, either in full sun or partial shade.

Propagation

Propagation is by cuttings taken in Aug. When the cuttings are made, the leaves should be removed from the lower part of the cutting with a sharp knife. With a small amount of bottom heat they should be rooted in a few weeks. Seed may be sown at any time but the many colorful species and varieties are best propagated asexually, either by late Aug. cuttings or by division of the plants themselves with a sharp spade.

arborea 18′ Zone 7 Tree Heath
An evergreen shrub or tree with needlelike leaves usually in 3's and fragrant, nearly white flowers in large panicles. Native to the southern Mediterranean Region, this does not make a particularly neat garden plant. Since it is a tree and often does have trunks in its native habitat, pipes are often made from the wood.

carnea 1′ Zone 5 Spring Heath
This diminutive plant comes in several varieties from central and southern Europe. Akin to the true heathers (*Calluna*) it requires the same type of growing conditions. The evergreen, needlelike leaves are similar to those of *Calluna vulgaris* and the rosy-red or white flowers are small but are borne in upright racemes 1–2 in. long, appearing from Jan. to May depending on the temperature, some blooming in Jan. in the warmer parts of the country. They can be used as individual specimens in the rockery or flower border, or as massed ground covers, where their early spring flowers are most colorful. A very few of the better varieties are:

	HEIGHT	FLOWER COLOR	TIME OF BLOOM
'Aurea'	12 ft.	pink to white	Jan.–May
'Eileen Porter'	8 in.	red	Jan.–April
'King George'	12 in.	crimson	Jan.–May
'Prince of Wales'	12 in.	rose-pink	Jan.–May
'Ruby Glow'	12 in.	rich red	Jan.–May
'Springwood Pink'	8 in.	deep pink	Jan.–May
'Springwood White'	8 in.	white	Jan.–May
'Vivellii'	8 in.	blood-red	Jan.–May
'Winter Beauty'	5 in.	deep pink	Jan.–May

ciliaris 1¼′ Zone 7 Fringed Heath
A taller-growing heath from western Europe, this has rosy-purple spikes of flowers 5 in. long during the summer. The foliage is gray, needlelike and evergreen.

cinerea 1′–2′ Zone 5 Twisted Heath
For those who have the proper conditions and like the heaths, these might be worth trying because of their rosy-purple-to-white flower spikes (3 in. long) in mid-June. The needlelike foliage is lustrous green and the autumn color is bronze to orange. Native to western Europe, this is said to be naturalized as far north as some places in Mass. The flowers may last for several weeks, but the plants need heavy pruning immediately after flowering, and when a mulch of sand and well-rotted leaf mold is given them (not maple leaves, oak leaves are best) they seem to respond well. A few varieties are:

	HEIGHT	FLOWER COLOR	TIME OF BLOOM
'Atrorubens'	6 in.	ruby-red	July–August
'Golden Drop'	4 in.	pink	June–July (copper foliage)
'P. S. Patrick'	12 in.	purple	June and July

Because of its copper-colored foliage 'Golden Drop' is one of the most outstanding.

x darleyensis 3′ Zone 6 Darley Heath
This hybrid (*E. carnea* x *E. mediterranea*) is a vigorous-growing species that may survive where others fail. The flowers are lilac-pink from Nov. until spring. The flower color is poor, but the growth is vigorous.

x mackaiana (*mackaii*) 18″ Zone 3 Mackay
Heath
A hybrid between *E. tetralix* and *E. cinerea*, occurring in northern and western Europe, with the parents. The flowers are red, 1½ in. long. The variety 'Plena' has double flowers.

mediterranea 5′ Zone 7 Mediterranean
Heath

The upright habit of growth of this lilac-pink flowered heath is different from the others. The flowers bloom in mid-April. Native to western Europe, it is recommended for its habit of growth only.

melanthera   4′–5′   Zone 8   Blackeyed Heath
A winter-blooming heath, often used by florists as a pot plant because it flowers at a time when sales are high. Flowers rosy-colored and profuse, scarcely over $\frac{1}{3}$ in. long.

tetralix   18″   Zone 3   Cross-leaf Heath
One of the hardiest heaths, evergreen, with woolly, grayish foliage and dense, rosy flowers in the summer. A native of western Europe it seems to prefer a moist, rather peaty soil.

vagans   1′   Zone 5   Cornish Heath
Blooming from July to Oct., this western European plant has proved as popular as any of the species except possibly *Erica carnea*. Varieties: **'Lyonesse'**—white flowers; **'Mrs. D. F. Maxwell'**—cherry-red flowers; **'St. Keverne'**—deep pink flowers.

x williamsii   18″   Zone 5   Williams Heath
A hybrid between *E. tetralix* and *E. vagans*, occurring with the parents in their natural European habitat, valued for its urn-shaped, rose-colored flowers in the summer.

ERICACEAE = The Heath Family

ERIGERON (e-RIJ-er-on). These are widely distributed annuals and perennials belonging to the Composite Family, somewhat like wild asters, with alternate or basal leaves and daisylike flowers either single or in clusters colored white to purple, with yellow centers. They are easily cultivated, grown from seed, cuttings or plant divisions and are suitable for the wild garden or rock garden.

annuus   5′   annual   American Fleabane
Sometimes a biennial weed, common through much of North America. Leaves alternate, simple, 2 in. long and flowers small and daisylike, white or slightly purplish, about $\frac{3}{4}$ in. across, from June to Sept.

canadensis   6′   annual   Horse-weed
A common weed throughout North America, with alternate, linear, simple, hairy leaves. The flowers are extremely small and greenish white, several hundred of them being borne on the flowering stalk, which may be the upper third of the plant, from July to Oct.

compositus   8″   Zone 4   Fernleaf Fleabane
A tiny, daisylike perennial, having dense clusters of gray, woolly, finely cut leaves and 6-in. flower stalks bearing solitary white flowers in early summer. Native to the Rocky Mountains, the plant requires gravelly, well-drained soil and a hot, dry climate.

flagellaris   decumbent   Zone 4   Trailing Fleabane
Similar to *E. compositus* but slightly smaller and having decumbent stems that root where the tips touch the soil, allowing the plants to form thin mats. The white, daisylike flowers appear throughout much of the summer. Native from British Columbia to Mexico.

glaucus   10″   Zone 3   Beach Fleabane
The pale, green, oval, glaucous leaves of this perennial, growing in clusters or rosettes, contrast attractively with the violet-colored flower heads 1$\frac{1}{2}$ in. wide which are singly borne. These appear in May and June. Native to the Pacific Coast.

karvinskianus   trailing   Zone 9   Bonytip Fleabane
A graceful, trailing ground cover with lobed leaves an inch long. Daisylike flowers are freely produced from spring until frost, being white to pinkish and $\frac{3}{4}$ in. across. It should be cut back annually just after bloom to keep it under control. Native to tropical America but used chiefly as an ornamental in Calif. and Ariz. It tolerates dry soil, and can be propagated by seed, blooming the first year.

leiomerus   6″   Zone 3
A fine rock-garden plant, compact rosettes of green leaves closely hugging the ground and solitary, dark violet-colored flowers, the heads an inch across, borne on 5 in. stems. These appear in summer. Native from Alberta to N.Mex.

multiradiatus   6″–2′   Zone 5   Himalayan Fleabane
A perennial for the rock garden valued for its single, purple, daisylike flowers that are as much as 3 in. wide, produced in the summer. The leaves are lanceolate and entire. Native to the Himalayas.

nanus   4″   Zones 3–4   Dwarf Fleabane
Small, dense tufts of woolly, grasslike leaves and slender stems bearing dainty, white, daisylike flowerheads $\frac{1}{2}$ in wide in early summer. Native to Mont. and Utah.

philadelphicus   3′   Zone 2   Philadelphia Fleabane
This attractive perennial is found through Canada and the U.S. The stem is slender and unbranched and the basal leaves ovate and toothed. The stem leaves are untoothed and clasping. The upright flower heads are borne in loose terminal clusters on short stalks branching from the straight stem. Numerous small yellow disc-flowers are surrounded by 100 or more narrow lavender ray-flowers. The plant blooms throughout the summer, preferring rich, moist soil. It is of easy culture and may be divided in spring or fall.

pinnatisectus   10″   Zone 3   Pinnate Fleabane
A perennial growing in compact tufts of pale green bipinnatifid leaves 1 in. high and crowned

with light blue daisylike flower heads ½ in. wide in early summer. Native to the mountains of Wyo. and Colo.

pulchellus   2′   **Zone** 3   **Poor Robin's Plantain**
This plant is similar to *E. philadelphicus* although smaller. The ray flowers generally number around 60. It has a similar range and blooms from April to June.

speciosus   15″–30″   **Zones 2–3**   **Oregon Fleabane**
An outstanding flowering perennial for the border, native to western North America and blooming during June and July with violet-purple flowers 1½ in. across in many clusters, somewhat resembling those of hardy asters. This is the most popular species in this genus, hence many selections have been made; some varieties have larger and even double flowers. **'Summertime'** is white, **'Wuppertal'** is amethyst violet with large flowers and **'Azure Beauty'** has nearly double lavender-blue flowers. These and other cultivars have flowers far superior to those of the species.

strigosus   8″   **annual**   **Rough Daisy Fleabane**
Sometimes a biennial, native weed, widespread throughout the U.S. and southern Canada, blooming from June to Sept. with small, daisylike, white flowers. The alternate, linear leaves have a long petiole and are rather club-shaped.

thunbergii   15″   **Zone** 5   **Thunberg Fleabane**
A perennial herb, native to Japan, with solitary or tufted stems, leaves up to 1¼″ long and densely pubescent; the ray flowers are a bluish purple.

ERINUS (e-RY-nus)
alpinus   4″   **Zone** 4   **Alpine Liverbalsam**
A perennial tufted plant native to the mountains of central Europe, with deeply toothed small, dark green leaves and small purple flowers ½ in. across in racemes 2½ in. long during May and June. There is a pink-flowered form which is said to come true from seed and is better as far as flower color is concerned. Propagated by seed or division. Best planted in a shaded situation but there should be ample drainage. It can be established in rock crevices or between rocks in the rock wall garden.

ERIOBOTRYA (e-rio-BOT-ria)
japonica   20′   **Zone** 7   **Loquat**
This is a handsome ornamental evergreen with leaves 6–10 in. long and much used in landscape planting. Native to central China, it is especially valued for its edible, pear-shaped, orange-yellow fruits that are about 1½ in. long and produced in the spring. The fragrant white flowers are ½ in. across but are mostly hidden by the foliage, and are borne in panicles 5–7 in. long in the fall. There are not many commercial orchards of this species in America, but it is an excellent small

tree for the small place because of its fine evergreen foliage. It is often used as a potted plant in the North. Also see LOQUAT.

ERIODICTYON (erio-DICT-i-on)
trichocalyx   2′–3′   **Zone** 8   **Yerba Santa**
A glossy-leaved herb sometimes cultivated in Calif. for its ability to grow on dry, sunny slopes where it is used to keep the ground from eroding. It is difficult to transplant, has white flowers and is among those plants listed as "fire resistant" for special use in southern Calif.

ERIOGONUM (e-ri-OG-o-num). A group of herbs or subshrubs native to western North America but rarely used in ornamental plantings except in the areas where the plants are native. They belong to the Buckwheat or Knotweed Family, have basal, alternate or whorled leaves with flowers borne in heads or umbels along the branches. Several are considered good bee plants in Calif. They do well in dry, open soils, the reason they do not grow well in the eastern U.S. However, *E. umbellatum*, the Sulfur-flower is grown in the East from Washington, D.C. southward.

flavum   8″   **Zone** 5   **Yellow Eriogonum**
Creeping stems enable this plant with narrow, woolly leaves to become matlike in its native habitat on the sunlight slopes of the Rocky Mountains. The bright yellow flowers rise from the rosettes of leaves in June and July. Propagated by division, cuttings or seeds.

ovalifolium   3″   **Zone** 8   **Cushion Eriogonum**
Rosettes of woolly oval leaves are decorated with bright yellow flowers blooming in June and July, but it does well only on gravelly soil in full sun. Native from British Columbia to Calif.

umbellatum   1′   **Zone** 7   **Sulfur-flower**
With basal leaves 2½ in. long and deep yellow, daisylike flowers in umbels, native to Wash., Calif. and Wyo. This can be grown on the East Coast as far north as Washington, D.C.

var. subalpinum   1′   **Zone** 3   **Sulfur Plant**
Probably the easiest of these plants for the gardener, since it does not require scree, as long as the soil is well drained. The rosettes of spatulate leaves form attractive mats from which rise, on stems 6 in. high, the umbels of pale yellow flowers from May to late July. Native in the mountains of Colo. and Mont.

ERIOPHYLLUM (e-ri-o-FILL-um)
lanatum   9″–18″   **Zone** 5   **Woolly Eriophyllum**
A perennial herb, member of the Composite Family, with alternate, woolly-tomentose leaves divided into 3–7 segments; flowers yellow in daisylike, mostly solitary heads about an inch wide. Native from British Columbia to Calif. This requires a dry climate and does not grow well in the eastern U.S.

ERITRICHIUM (e-ri-TRIK-ium)

nanum 3″ Zone 5

An extremely difficult perennial to grow with densely white-woolly leaves ⅜ in. long and bright blue flowers with yellow centers to ¼ in. wide. Native to the Alps.

ERMOCHLOA OPHIUROIDES = Centipede Grass. See GRASS.

ERODIUM (er-O-dium). A genus belonging to the Cranesbill Family, having a rather loose, open habit, attractive, deeply lobed leaves and loose clusters of flowers which may be white, pink, yellow, red or purple, somewhat resembling those of geraniums. The plants are readily cultivated under ordinary garden conditions and propagation is by seed or, occasionally, by division.

chamaedryoides 3″ Zone 7 Alpine-geranium

This species grows close to the ground in rather dense mats of large, wavy leaves about ¼ in. long. The white flowers, with pink veins, appear throughout the summer. It is a good rock-garden plant, as are the 2 varieties: roseum, with rosy-pink flowers and red veins; and 'Florepleno', having both double and single, deep pink flowers. The species and the varieties are somewhat tender and need winter cover in northern areas of the U.S.

cheilanthifolium 4″ Zone 6?

Grayish-green, finely cut leaves and loose clusters of white flowers having pink veins make this a very attractive garden plant. It blooms in May and June. Native to the mountains of Spain and Morocco.

chrysanthum 6″ Zone 7

Light yellow flowers ½ in. wide in umbels of 2–3 during summer characterize this plant native to Greece. The habit is tufted, with silvery leaves which are twice compound, chiefly from the base of the plant.

cicutarium 1½′ annual Corsican Heronbill

A weed, sometimes growing as a biennial, native to the Mediterranean Region but naturalized across North America, with alternate, pinnately compound leaves in rosettes at the base of the plant. The small purple flowers are ¼ in. wide and appear in umbels from April to June. Because of its often prostrate stems, this frequently appears as a lawn weed. The common name is because of the long beak of the fruit.

guttatum 9″ Zone 8

Pink flowers in umbels of 2–3, native to the Mediterranean Region, with simple oval leaves, slightly lobed, about ½ in. long.

macradenum 6″ Zone 6

Violet-colored flowers with dark spots, about ½ in. wide, this is a perennial, sometimes growing a foot tall. The leaves are basal and pinnate. Native to the Pyrenees.

manescavii 12″ Zone 6 Pyrenees Heronbill

Purple flowers up to 1½ in. wide; leaves basal and pinnate. A perennial native to the Pyrenees.

pelargoniflorum 12″ Zone 6? Geranium Heronbill

White flowers spotted purple, the 2 upper sepals being pink-spotted at the base. Somewhat shrubby. Native to Asia Minor.

petraeum 3″–6″ Zone 6 Cliff Heronbill

White flowers veined with red. The leaves are all basal and pinnate. Native to the Pyrenees.

EROSION. The washing away of soil by rain or wind. Planting banks and gullies with ground covers, grasses or easily rooting vines and creeping shrubs is a very important means of preventing soil erosion. Without a cover of growing plants the soil in hilly country could quickly be eroded away and leave a barren subsoil in which little would grow. Planting of trees and forests is another means of preventing erosion, for in so doing the rain water is taken up by the soil and retained and does not run off in wild, soil-moving freshets.

ERUCA (ee-ROO-ka)

vesicaria 2½′ annual, biennial Rocket-salad

An herb, native to southern Europe, belonging to the Mustard Family, sometimes grown in the vegetable garden for its young peppery leaves which can be used in salads. The flowers are an inch long, whitish with purple veins. The leaves become bitter with age, hence it should be repeatedly cut back to keep the foliage young and succulent. Seed can be sown in the open soil after frost is over.

ERYNGIUM (e-RINJ-ium). These are perennials for poor, dry soils in sunny situations, but in rich soils they grow too energetically. They are best used as small specimen plants, not for massing. When in flower they look something like thistles. Although there are over 200 species in this genus, mostly in the Mediterranean area, only a very few are grown in America. They are propagated either by root cuttings or by division of the plants in the early spring.

amethystinum 1½′ Zones 2–3 Amethyst Eryngium

This is one of the best of over 200 species in this genus. The flowers are small, rounded heads about ½ in. long, narrow, bluish purple and the bracts spiny. Native to Europe. The upper stems are steely gray, almost amethyst in color. They add much interest in gardens. Many nurseries incorrectly offer E. planum under this name, a species which is taller and with less interesting flowers and lacking in the color of the stems. E. planum is best used only in wild gardens. Both species are propagated by root cuttings or by division of the plants in the early spring.

maritimum 1′ Zone 5 Sea-holly

The fleshy, stiff leaves are 3-lobed with coarse, spiny teeth; blue flower heads an inch across. Native to Europe.

x oliverianum 3′ Zone 5 Oliver's Eryngium Leaves heart-shaped at base, leaves on the upper part of the stem palmately 4–5 parted. Flower heads are 1½ in. across. Native to Europe.

planum 3′ Zone 5 Flat-leaved Eryngium Leaves heart-shaped, either 3–5 lobed or parted, heads of blue flowers about ½ in. across. Native to Europe and Asia. Best used only in the wild garden but not as good an ornamental as *E. amethystinum.*

ERYSIMUM (e-RY-sim-um). The wallflowers comprise a genus of about 80 species of annual or perennial herbs native to Europe, Asia and N. America. The showy flowers are yellow, orange and reddish purple. Some of them make nice specimens for the rock garden.

asperum 3′ Zone 3 Siberian Wallflower A biennial of open, sandy locations from Ohio to the Rocky Mountains and south to Tex., it has a stout, hairy stem and leaves which are alternate, lanceolate and entire on the stem, with basal leaves which are sometimes compound. The orange flowers are borne in a loose terminal cluster and have 4 sepals and 4 petals. It is easily propagated by seed sown in spring, the resulting plants reset the following spring. A good plant for edging. This is closely related to *Cheiranthus cheiri*, the true wallflower, belonging to the Mustard Family.

kotschyanum 3″–4″ Zone 6 Kotschy Erysimum This low, turflike plant bears narrow-linear leaves with finely toothed margins and clusters of fragrant yellow flowers; appearing in spring. This grows easily in well-drained limestone soil and in rock crevices, in full sun or partial shade. Easily propagated by divisions or seeds. Native to the mountains of Asia Minor and belonging to the Mustard Family.

linifolium 1′ Zone 6 Alpine Wallflower A grayish, decumbent, herbaceous perennial with linear leaves 6 in. long and lilac-colored flowers in spring. Native to Spain.

pulchellum 2″–2′ Zone 6 Rockery Blister-cress A perennial, native to Greece and Asia Minor, used in the rock garden for its deep orange-colored flowers and tufted habit of growth. Belonging to the Mustard Family.

ERYTHEA = *Brahea*

ERYTHRINA (e-rith-RY-na). There may be 100 species of this genus in the tropics, most of them trees or shrubs, few herbaceous. Most of them are thorned. The bright showy flowers are either red or yellow and the fruit is a long flat or rounded pod. They are grown as brilliantly

flowered ornamental specimens, and sometimes used for shade in coffee plantations. The flowers of some species are cooked and eaten and the seeds sown on strings and made into necklaces. Propagation is easily done by cuttings or seeds.

coralloides 20′ Zone 10 Naked Coral-bean Slightly thorny, with triangular leaflets, this tree bears its red flowers before the leaves appear. Native from Ariz. to Mexico.

crista-galli 15′ Zone 10 Cockspur Coral-bean A shrub or small tree with spiny petioles, trifoliate leaves and deep scarlet-red flowers in loose racemes, usually produced before the leaves. Seeds in pods are sometimes used in necklaces. Native to Brazil. Propagated by softwood cuttings.

herbacea 4′ Zone 8 Eastern Coral-bean Herbaceous, the petioles often prickly; leaves are triangular, scarlet flowers in few flowered racemes 2 ft. long. The pods are up to 5 in. long. Propagated by seeds and root cuttings. Native from N.Car. to Fla. and Tex. Used as an ornamental along the Gulf Coast.

indica = *E. variegata orientalis*

poeppigiana 80′ Zone 10 Mountain Immortelle Flowers in bright oblong orange clusters about 10 in. long; each flower is peculiarly cycle-shaped, with as many as 50 flowers in a cluster. The leaves are compound with 3 equally shaped leaflets, but the terminal leaflet, slightly longer than the other 2 is 5–6 in. across. These are dropped in the spring just before flowering. The fruits are pods, 5 in. long.

The species **E. fusca** is not as popular an ornamental in the islands of the Caribbean because it has fewer flowers in a cluster and the clusters are shorter, colored a yellowish orange. This species grows in swampy areas, where the Mountain Immortelle will not.

Both are natives to the American Tropics where the seeds and leaves have been found to have toxic poisons, used by the natives in stupefying fish. Propagated by seeds.

variegata orientalis (*E. indica*) **25′ Zone 10 Tiger's-claw, Indian Coral-bean** With brilliant red blossoms in midwinter and early spring, conspicuous because at the time the flowers appear there are few leaves. The flowers are produced in terminal many-flowered clusters, mostly borne on a horizontal plane, generally pealike except that one petal is much longer than the others and this is what gives the impression of a pointed claw of the tiger. The leaves appear after the flowers drop, and are compound, with 3 leaflets. The fruits are black pods containing dark red seeds and the branches are thorny.

ERYTHRONIUM (e-rith-RO-nium)
These little spring-flowering bulbs are members
of the Lily Family and have been popularly
termed "Dogtooth Violets," although the
flowers certainly resemble miniature lilies more
than they do violets. All but one of the species
are native to North America. Trout-lily is
another name for them. The flowers about 1 in.
across are usually borne singly with reflexed
petals giving them a starry appearance. There
are usually 2 lance-shaped leaves at the base,
sometimes mottled. All bloom in the early
spring and are best when naturalized or planted
in clumps. Easily propagated by offsets or seeds.
Plant the bulbs in shady situations 3 in. deep.

albidum   1'   Zone 4   White Fawn-lily
Small bulbs send up 2, generally basal, mottled
brown and green leaves having a wavy edge.
The nodding white or pinkish flowers have 3
petals and 3 sepals which closely resemble
petals, in the manner typical of lilies. The petals
and sepals are reflexed. This plant prefers rich
woods soil in eastern U.S. and is only for the
moist, shady wild garden. It blooms from April
to June. Propagation is by offsets.

americanum   1'   Zone 3   Common Fawn-lily
Similar to *E. albidum*, this species has yellow
flowers and ranges from New Brunswick to
Fla. and west to Ontario and Okla. It blooms
from March to June. Culture and propagation
as for *E. albidum*. The bulbs have been used by
the Indians as a cooked vegetable.

Erythronium americanum—Common Fawn-lily

californicum   1'   Zone 5   California Fawn-lily
A Calif. species with very mottled leaves and
creamy-white flowers 1½ in. long.

dens-canis   6"   Zones 2–3   Dogtooth Fawn-lily
The only exotic species, native in Europe and
Asia; leaves mottled with reddish brown and
flowers rose or purple, about 2 in. wide.

grandiflorum   2'   Zone 5   Avalanche

Bright yellow flowers, 2 in. long, native to the
Northwest Pacific Coast, leaves not mottled.

hendersonii   1'   Zone 5   Henderson Fawn-lily
Leaves mottled, flowers purple, 1¼ in. long;
native to southern Ore.

oregonum   1'   Zone 5   Oregon Fawn-lily
Flowers white or creamy white, up to 2 in. long;
native from northern Calif. to British Columbia.

revolutum   1'   Zone 5   Mahogany Fawn-lily
Flowers white or lavender but fading purple.
Native from Calif. to British Columbia.

tuolumense   1'   Zone 5   Tuolumne Fawn-lily
A Calif. species with deep yellow flowers 1¼ in.
long. Leaves shining green but not mottled.

ERYTHROXYLUN (e-rith-ROX-ill-on)
coca   12'   Zone 10   Cocaine-plant
This is cultivated in South America because it
yields cocaine. The leathery leaves are 2½ in.
long; the dull flowers are yellowish and ¼ in.
wide; the fruit is a reddish drupe ⅓ in. long. The
leaves are chewed by certain South American
Indians to relieve fatigue. Probably native to
western South America.

ESCALLONIA (ess-kal-O-nia)
laevis (*organensis*)   6'   Zone 8   Organ
                                          Escallonia
A sturdy, bushy, ornamental evergreen shrub
with angled branchlets; toothed leaves 3 in.
long that often have red margins, and small,
pinkish, fragrant flowers ½ in. long in the
autumn borne in dense terminal clusters. Brazil.

rosea. A name of uncertain application.

rubra   10'–15'   Zone 8   Red Escallonia
An evergreen shrub with sticky lance-shaped
leaves tapered at both ends and 1–2 in. long,
reddish twigs; flowers red, ⅓ in. wide in loose
panicles 2½ in. long. Native to Chile.

virgata   3'–8'   Zone 7
Popular in Europe and used somewhat in the
warmer parts of the southern U.S., this deciduous shrub is the best of the escallonias for
ornamental planting, as well as the hardiest. The
white flowers, ⅜ in. across, bloom in June and
July and the plant is a native to Chile.

ESCAPE. A cultivated plant found growing as
though wild, dispersed by some agency.

ESCHSCHOLZIA (esh-SHOL-zia)
californica   2'   annual   California-poppy
Typical of Calif. where it is native and sometimes growing almost within reach of salt-water
spray, these garden flowers are very easy to
grow merely by sowing the seed in Sept. or
March, where the plants are to grow. They
should be thinned to 6 in. apart and be grown
in sandy soil in the full sun. Their multicolored
flowers, originally golden yellow, but now with
shades of orange, pink and white, are up to 3 in.
across.

ESPALIER. A woody plant, tree or shrub trained lattice-fashion in one plane.

ESPALIER (ess-PAL-yer). Technically speaking an espalier is a trellis or a plant which has been pruned in such a way that it has been forced to grow all in one plane. In Europe, this method of pruning has been used for centuries in the training of fruit trees. One can still see orchards of apple and pear trees espaliered in the area of Orleans, France. However, with increased labor costs, such orchards are not as numerous as they once were. In America practically no fruits are grown as espaliers on a commercial scale, unless the accepted way of pruning grapes on a wire trellis would be considered as one form. Espaliered plants are coming into favor as ornamentals and one finds an increasing number of them being used on walls, trellises and fences.

When George Washington lived at Mt. Vernon, Virginia, in the latter part of the eighteenth century, part of his garden was a collection of espaliered peaches, apples and pears. These were picturesque and easily picked, but they have long since gone out of popularity in this country, especially because of the advent of the dwarf fruit tree which grows more fruits (with less work) than does the espaliered plant. But, as a particular ornamental feature of the

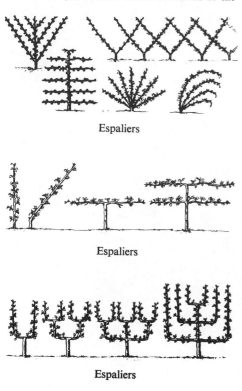

Espaliers

Espaliers

Espaliers

garden, one or two espaliered trees or shrubs have great merit, especially if they are properly placed and cared for.

Espaliered plants are used for softening large blank spaces on walls or fences; as interesting focal points in the garden; as a special interest for the gardener who has time and a desire to fuss a bit with his plants and tend them frequently, especially where space is limited.

There are a few nurseries where espaliered plants can be purchased as such, but mostly one has to start with normal plants and train them in the desired fashion. This can be started in either one of two ways, either selecting the plant one wants to espalier (*Pyracantha, Cotoneaster horizontalis, Taxus* sp. or a fruit tree) and then the design, or to select the design wanted first, and then a plant best suited to train in that design. For instance, fruit trees are especially suited to cordons, U-shaped designs and grid-iron shapes. Yews are suited for fan shapes, *C. horizontalis* for a beautiful informal design all its own, and plants with long slender shoots like Forsythia and Mock-orange are best suited for special designs in which these long, curving shoots are featured.

Some of the designs used in espalier work are noted in the accompanying drawing. The creative gardener will think of many others, but it may well be that formal designs are more interesting over a longer period than are informal designs. When training the plants, it is always advisable to keep these designs in mind or even on a card before you whenever pruning is done, for if you do not you may inadvertently remove a shoot or branch that it has taken months or even years to grow. This point is really most important, especially if one is training several plants in different designs. Pruning of branches or pinching of buds is done occasionally, sometimes on the spur of the moment or when one is in a hurry, and serious mistakes can easily be made. So keep the design on a card and have it in hand when pruning or pinching to avoid major mistakes.

Plants purchased for training should be young and supple. One should certainly have the design in mind when selecting. Often even mis-shapen, broken plants prove satisfactory for this purpose if they meet the requirements of the design. Three-foot shrubs or trees are usually best, for the young shoots of such plants are easily bent. Stiffly grown young trees, unless they meet design requirements, may have to be cut to the ground and started all over again.

Good soil should be available and normal planting practice would suggest that the hole for the plant should be prepared at least 3 ft. square and 2 ft. deep. The plant should be set so that its main branches are 6 in. from the wall on which it is to grow, thus providing an air space at the rear which is essential for good growth and sanitation.

The pruning of any large limbs should be done when the plants are dormant. All cuts should be done in a professional manner, clean, smooth and no stubs left. See PRUNING. Pinching and "snipping" here and there can be done almost anytime, but it is advisable to remember one of the good rules in all pruning, that it is not advisable to force young growth in the late summer or early fall since it may not have time to harden off sufficiently by fall and then can succumb to killing by winter cold.

Some vigorous growing plants like forsythias and firethorns make much easier subjects for espaliers than others (like pines and hemlocks) merely because adventitious buds are much more numerous and easy to grow. Most woody plants have a small, dormant bud in the axil of each leaf. This bud may remain dormant for some time but if the twig is cut just above that bud, it may be forced into growth. This is the principle back of the forcing out of new shoots where they are wanted in order to conform to the proper planned design. This cutting or pinching is best done in late spring so the new shoot has plenty of time to mature properly by winter.

Training

Bending the twigs and branches to meet design requirements is the most difficult operation in growing espaliers. It is done best when the twigs are young and supple and can be bent without breaking. If breaking is a possibility, then the twig is securely tied to a stiff wire and the wire is gradually bent at intervals, possibly of several weeks, until the proper form is reached, and the wire left in place for a year or so until the growth has properly matured. Many adventitious shoots and buds are not wanted as the plant grows, and these can be removed any time. They should not be allowed to grow too large and sap the strength of the plant when certain growths are desired in other directions.

Tying and fastening the branches into place is most important. Branches are best tied with soft string, raffia or even rubber budding bands, not with wire which can bind and constrict the normal passage of plant nutrients up and down the stem. The tie should be made loosely (if possible) so there is a small loop for expanded growth of the stem. Even string tied tightly can constrict growth, so these ties should be examined at frequent intervals, loosened and retied when necessary.

Sometimes it may be advisable to make a wire frame or even a wooden lattice arrangement between the permanent wall and the plant, especially during the formative years and until the plant has grown properly into the desired form. Making ties to such a frame is far easier than boring into a brick or concrete wall at every point a branch must be fastened.

The distance apart of the uprights in a design will vary with the plant and method of growth but one should remember that at maturity there should always be a few inches of space between the expanded leaves of one upright and the next in order to see the design. Plants can be grown with one mass of green foliage against a wall,

This espaliered pear tree in the Luxemburg Gardens, France, must be over 100 years old. (*Photo by Arnold Arboretum, Jamaica Plain, Mass.*)

but the beauty, in most cases, is created by the design, which must be seen at all times to be appreciated. Consequently, upright branches might be kept at least 16 in. apart to insure the proper space, and this distance might well relate to horizontal branches also. One should also be certain that the spacing of uprights on one side of the center of a formal design is exactly the same as on the other side, even unto the fraction of an inch. This is important in appreciating the design, for an arrangement in which the placement of these stems is "guessed at" can prove unsightly.

Beauty, in the case of espaliers, is created by using congruent design and proper plant materials, together with the intelligent care necessary to show off both to best advantage.

Fruits

Peaches, apples and pears have been espaliered in small gardens since Roman times, and in fact are still espaliered commercially in parts of Europe where space is limited. Some of the best examples of this are in the Luxembourg Palace Gardens in Paris. In America, dwarf fruit trees have taken the place of espaliered fruits, for more fruits are produced on dwarf plants with less care. However, if fruits are to be espaliered, there are a few points about their culture to be considered.

In the first place dwarf stock might be considered if it is available. Certainly dwarf apple varieties (mostly grafted on certain Malling understock) are and sometimes dwarf-growing peach varieties grafted on *Prunus besseyi* or *P. tomentosa*. Dwarf pears have quince as an understock. These require much less pruning than standard varieties.

Usually they are grown in cordons, but the gridiron design is also used, especially for pears. If they are being grown to produce fruit, thought should be given to cross-pollination. Some apple varieties, for instance, are self-sterile (see APPLE) and plants of one such variety will not produce many fruits unless pollen is obtained from another variety. One can plant several varieties that are known to cross-pollenize (like 'Delicious' and 'McIntosh'). Or, one can pollenize by hand. 'McIntosh' apples are notably self-sterile, but if the espaliers are this variety, then merely obtain pollen of 'Delicious' flowers, put in a bottle and apply with an artist's brush. See POLLINATION. Easier still, would be to obtain some flowering branches of espaliered 'McIntosh' and let the bees and other insects do the pollenizing as the flowers open.

Care should also be taken in pruning not to remove the short-growing fruit spurs for it is these that bear the flowers and fruits. It is the long-growing vegetative shoots which should be removed, unless of course they are needed to form the cordons or the uprights of the design chosen for the espalier. The form of the espalier is best seen when the plant is dormant, hence the heavier pruning is done then. Much of the vegetative growth is removed at this time and if the main branches of the espalier have reached their desired length, the previous year's vegetative growth of these can be cut back to one bud.

In June and early summer, the vegetative side shoots (not the fruit spurs which are heavier and slower growing) can be pinched off so that more nourishment will be available for fruit-bud formation. As the fruits start to grow, they can be thinned, if large fruits are desired. The apples and pears for instance, might be thinned so that they are 6 in. apart, peaches could be 3–4 in. apart. One should be careful not to over-fertilize also, for this could create unusual vegetative growth activity at the expense of fruit-bud formation.

Plants to Use

Some plants are more popular than others. *Pyracantha* species would be at the top of almost any list, and because the fruits (apples, peaches and pears) have been espaliered since Roman times, these would come next. Then *Cornus florida, Cotoneaster horizontalis, Taxus* sp. and vars., *forsythia*, etc. A list of some of the plants which might be considered for this purpose are as follows:

ESPALIER PLANTS

	HEIGHT	ZONE	
Abelia floribunda	6'	8	Mexican Abelia
Acer palmatum 'Ornatum'	20'	5	Spiderleaf Japanese Maple
Camellia japonica and vars.	45'	7	Common Camellia
Cercis canadensis	36'	4	Eastern Redbud
C. chinensis	40'	6	Chinese Judas-tree
Chaenomeles sp. and vars.	6'	4	Japanese Quince
Citrus lemonea	25'	9–10	Lemon
Cornus florida	40'	4	Flowering Dogwood
C. kousa	21'	5	Japanese Dogwood
C. mas	24'	4	Cornelian-cherry

	HEIGHT	ZONE	
Cotoneaster sp.	6'–18'	4–7	Cotoneaster
C. horizontalis	3'	4	Rockspray
Euonymus alata	9'	3	Winged Euonymus
Ficus carica	12'–30'	6	Fig
Forsythia sp.	3'–9'	5	Forsythia
Ilex cornuta 'Burfordii'	9'	7	Burford Chinese Holly
I. crenata vars.	20'	6	Japanese Holly
Jasminum nudiflorum	15'	5–6	Winter Jasmine
Juniperus chinensis 'Pfitzeriana'	10'	4	Pfitzer Juniper
Laburnum watereri	30'	5	Waterer Laburnum
Magnolia grandiflora	90'	7	Southern Magnolia
M. soulangiana	25'	5	Saucer Magnolia
M. stellata	20'	5	Star Magnolia
Malus atrosanguinea	20'	4	Carmine Crab Apple
M. 'Dorothea'	25'	4	'Dorothea' Crab Apple
Malus many vars. (including commercial apples)		3–4	Apples and Crab Apples
Osmanthus fragrans	30'	8–9	Sweet Osmanthus
Philadelphus coronarius	9'	4	Sweet Mock-orange
Photinia serrulata	36'	7	Chinese Photinia
Pinus parviflora glauca	90'	5	Japanese White Pine
Poncirus trifoliata	35'	5–6	Hardy-orange
Prunus persica	24'	5	Peach
P. serrulata vars.	20'–25'	5–6	Oriental Cherry
P. subhirtella 'Pendula'	30'	5	Weeping Higan Cherry
Pyracantha sp. and vars.	6'–18'	6–7	Firethorn
Pyrus communis—commercial vars.	45'	4	Pear
Solanum seaforthianum	climber	10	Brazilian Nightshade
Tamarix ramosissima	15'	2	Five Stamen Tamarisk
Taxus sp. and vars.	3'–40'	4–6	Yew
Viburnum macrocephalum	12'	6	Chinese Snowball
Viburnum plicatum vars.	9'	4	Doublefile Viburnum
Viburnum rhytidophyllum	9'	5	Leatherleaf Viburnum
Vitex agnus-castus	9'	6–7	Chaste-tree

ESPOSTOA (es-pos-TO-a)

lanata   3'   **Zone 10**   **Snowball Cactus**
A hairy, columnar cactus sometimes branching at the top, with 20 ribs and long silky white hairs covering the stem; 12 radial spines that are yellowish or reddish. Flowers white to 2 in. long. Fruit pink. Native to Peru. For culture SEE CACTI AND SUCCULENTS.

EUCALYPTUS (you-ka-LIP-tus). A large group of fast-growing trees native to Australia—with over 80 species being offered by nurserymen on the West Coast, chiefly in Calif. Many have been tried there, some have become naturalized, some are used as street and ornamental trees. They are evergreen, mostly alternate-leaved with simple entire leaves, fast-growing and, in general, shallow-rooted and free from pests. They do well in various soils and are easily propagated by seed. Many of these trees grow to great heights in their native land, but the heights here given are those at which they are usually grown in Calif. Almost all of these have flowers most attractive to bees and from which they can make excellent honey.

camaldulensis   150'   **Zone 9**   **Red Gum**
The bark of twigs and young branches is red, the leaves are narrowly lanceolate and 4–6 in. long and the fruits are almost globular, about ¼ in. in dia. This is one of the most valuable species and one of the most drought-resistant. The wood is light red to a deep red in color. Formerly *E. rostrata*.

cornuta   35'   **Zone 9**   **Yatetree**
This has been used as a shade tree in areas where lemons are grown in southern Calif. It grows well in alkaline soils and at the seashore, dark green leaves 2–5 in. long. The fruits are ¼ in. wide.

ficifolia   30'–50'   **Zone 10**   **Red Flowering Gum**
A popular species because masses of red to pink flowers in 6–7-in. clusters cover the tree in July and Aug. The leaves are coarse with a

Eucalyptus

reddish texture and are up to 6 in. long while the fruits are about 1½ in. in dia. It grows with a round head and is judged one of the best of the red-flowered species. This also is a heat-resistant tree but very tender.

globulus   200′   Zone 9   Blue Gum
Especially valued as a young plant for its young leaves which are a glaucous white, maturing to a lustrous dark green. They are 6–12 in. long and about 1½ in. wide. This is too coarse for many landscape plantings but is used for windbreaks. The flowers are about 1½ in. across and the fruits about 1 in. wide. The trunk is smooth and bluish white. The var. **'Compacta'** is lower, more dense in habit and has smaller leaves.

gunnii   40′–75′   Zone 8   Cider Gum
This species is supposed to be one of the most hardy, with white flowers in small umbels, Oct. to Dec., and leaves up to 3 in. long. Apparently cattle eat the foliage since it lacks the pungent odor typical to most other species.

leucoxylon   50′–60′   Zone 9   White Ironbark
Like many other species the bees make excellent honey from the nectar in the flowers of this tree. The bark breaks off in irregular pieces, being smooth and pale gray. The mature leaves are narrow, lanceolate and a dull gray-green, being 3–6 in. long and ½–1½ in. wide. It is

supposed to need plenty of atmospheric moisture to do best, i.e., near the seacoast, but will grow well in various soils. The var. **'Rosea'** has pink flowers and makes a good ornamental for this reason.

moluccana   90′   Zone 10   Graybox Eucalyptus
With rough, persistent bark, thick, grayish leaves, flowers in panicles and ¼ in. sized fruits.

polyanthemos   70′   Zone 9   Redbox, Gum, Silver Dollar Gum
The leaves are orbicular to ovate, 2–4 in. long and 1½–3 in. across, dull and grayish green on both sides, almost silvery with light reddish margins and veins. It is drought- and heat-resistant, with fruits about ½ in. wide.

populnea (*populifolia*)   40′   Zone 10   Poplar Gum
The leaves of this species are somewhat similar to those of a poplar, being ovate, about 4 in. long, lustrous and very green on both sides. The flowers are small and white. Not much used in Calif. but it is a most adaptable species.

pulverulenta   30′   Zone 9   Dollarleaf Eucalyptus
The bluish-green leaves of this species are nearly round and, unlike most other species,

Eucalyptus trees have very interesting bark. (*Photo by Arnold Arboretum, Jamaica Plain, Mass.*)

these are opposite and almost stalkless and $2\frac{1}{2}$ in. across. Flowers are white, 1 in. long. This is the "blue spiral" material which is cut in large quantities and sold by florists for decorative purposes, while also making an excellent ornament because of its different foliage color.

punctata 80′ Zone 9 Gray Gum
The dark gray, deciduous bark of this Australian species is outstanding. The alternate leaves are lanceolate and the sessile fruit is $\frac{1}{2}″$ across.

pyriformis 15′ Zone 9 Pear-fruited Mallee
The common name is taken from the pear-shaped buds. The flowers are reddish because of red stamens: the fruits are $2\frac{3}{4}$ in. across. Native to Australia.

regenans 300′ Zone 9 Giant Gum
This is the tallest species of Eucalyptus and the tallest hardwood in the world. (Sequoias are considered softwoods.) Leaves alternate, bark smooth and white; fruit is only $\frac{1}{4}″$ across. Native to Tasmania.

resinifera 100′ Zone 10 Red Mahogany
With reddish bark, alternate leaves, fruit $\frac{1}{4}″$ or slightly more in diameter. The wood is used in Australia and New Zealand where this species is native, for shingles, posts and general building.

robusta 100′ Zone 10 Swamp Mahogany
Widely planted in Australia, where it is native, for its lumber which is used for general building purposes and for building ships. Fruit is $\frac{1}{2}″$ across.

rostrata = *E. camaldulensis*

sideroxylon 40′ Zone 9 Red Ironbark
With brownish-red bark and pointed leaves up to $4\frac{1}{2}$ in. long that are bluish green and often bronze in the winter. The flowers are yellowish white and the fruits are $\frac{1}{2}$ in. across. 'Rosea' has green leaves and rose-colored flowers from Dec. to June and it is a profuse bloomer. This is distinguished from *E. leucoxylon* 'Rosea' by the more roughened bark.

stricklandii 40′ Zone 9 Strickland's Gum
Lower bark dark, upper bark gray or reddish brown. Fruit $\frac{1}{2}″$ across. Native to Australia.

torquata 15′–20′ Zone 10 Coral Gum
A small tree, usually with multiple trunks, bearing masses of rosy-coral flower buds opening to vivid red flowers during midsummer, but blooming for several weeks.

viminalis 50′–300′ Zone 9 White Gum
One of the tallest growing of the Eucalyptus, doing well in poor soil. The flowers are white and globe-shaped and the leaves are 4–8 in. long. The flowers are $\frac{1}{2}$ in. wide and the fruits about $\frac{1}{4}$ in. wide, the bark grayish white. This grows almost as fast as *E. globulus*. The common name comes from the fact that the branches are creamy white, and also slightly pendulous.

EUCHARIDIUM = *Clarkia*

EUCHARIS (YEW-ka-ris)
grandiflora 18″ Zone 9 Amazon-lily
This native of the Amazon River Area bears fragrant white flowers, 3–6 per 18 in. stalk in spring, summer or fall. It is primarily a bulb for greenhouse culture. Six bulbs can be planted in a 10-in. bulb pan filled with good soil mixed with well-rotted (or dried) cow manure and a little bone meal. It is a member of the Amaryllis Family and blooms best when pot bound. It is best to keep the soil rather dry from Oct. to April. Easily propagated by offsets in the spring.

EUCHLAENA = *Zea*

EUCOMIS (YEW-kom-is). South African bulbous plants, used mostly in the greenhouse in the North but as garden plants in the South. There are rosettes of leaves at the base, 1–2 ft. long depending on the species, and scapes of white or greenish-white star-shaped flowers. The leaves at the tip of the raceme give the impression of a pineapple. These belong to the Lily Family. They can be planted outdoors in May in the North (in the fall south of Washington, D.C.) but in the North must be lifted in the fall and stored indoors over winter. Also used as a winter-flowering pot plant indoors. Propagation is by offsets.

autumnalis (*undulata*) **1′ Zone 7**
Flowers greenish white to $\frac{3}{4}$ in. long, leaves 1 ft. long, $1\frac{1}{2}$ in. wide.

comosa 2′ Zone 7
Flowers greenish $\frac{1}{2}$ in. long, leaves 2 ft. long, 3 in. wide and spotted on the underside.

EUCOMMIA (yew-KOM-ia)
ulmoides 60′ Zone 5 Hardy Rubber-tree
An elmlike tree from central China, of little ornamental value. It is the only hardy rubber-producing tree for the central and northern parts of the U.S., but it produces only about 3% of its dry weight and the extraction is difficult and uneconomical. The alternate, deciduous leaves are 3–7 in. long; the sexes are separate, the flowers are hardly seen and the fruit is an almost inconspicuous samara.

Propagation

Seed should be stratified for 2 months at 40° F., then sown. Softwood cuttings root readily. See CUTTINGS, STRATIFICATION.

EUCRYPHIA (ew-KRIF-ia)
glutinosa 15′ Zone 8 Eucryphia
An interesting South American native from Chile, this plant is worthy of trial in gardens of the Deep South, but it needs acid soil, preferably in places where heaths and heathers grow so the

roots are protected from too much hot sun. The white flowers have 4 petals and are 2–3 in. wide, 1 or 2 at the end of each branch, in the summer. The foliage is semi-evergreen to evergreen, the opposite leaves with 2–5 leaflets being 2 in. long and sometimes turning orange to red in the fall.

EUGENIA (yew-JEEN-ia). A large group of trees and shrubs of the Tropics, noted for their ornamental foliage and bright colored fruits, many of which are edible. They are evergreens with opposite leaves and the fruit is a drupelike berry, belonging to the Myrtle Family.

aromatica = *Syzygium aromaticum*
jambos = *Syzygium jambos*
malaccensis = *Syzygium malaccensis*
myrtifolia = *Syzygium paniculatum*
paniculata = *Syzygium paniculatum*
smithii = *Acmena smithii*
uniflora   15′–25′   **Zone 10**   **Surinam-cherry**
Native to Brazil, this is frequently used in Fla. as a sheared hedge or high screen. The glossy, evergreen leaves are 1–2 in. long; the fragrant white flowers are $\frac{1}{2}$ in. across and the 8-ribbed, edible, scarlet fruit about $\frac{1}{2}$–1 in. across is most effective ornamentally in the winter and also makes excellent jam. It is also grown as a decorative pot plant for it produces many colorful fruits.

EULALIA GRASS = *Miscanthus sinensis*

EUONYMUS (yew-ON-im-us). The various plants belonging to the Euonymus clan are not to be considered one of those "neglected" groups which should be grown more in our gardens. On the contrary, there are probably too many forms of Euonymus available now, with over 60 being listed from American sources. It is certainly doubtful that all these have sufficient ornamental value to make them worth while. Evergreen shrubs, and especially vines or prostrate shrubs, have considerable value; a few of the deciduous types are of merit for their form, but most have little interest except for their fruit and autumn color; all have opposite leaves and inconspicuous flowers, all (except *E. alatus*) are susceptible to the attacks of the euonymus scale, the evergreen types and closer growing prostrate and shrubby types more so than others. This pest is commonly known and fought by all growers and gardeners alike. There are times when its control is neglected and then infestations can become so serious that the plants either have to be removed or cut to the ground to control it effectively.

As a rule, most euonymus are easily propagated by cuttings and grow rapidly. The evergreen forms are extremely important plants, the *E.*

japonicus forms being widely used in the South where they are hardy, and the *E. fortunei* types being extremely important garden plants in the North.

Propagation

Seed is erratic in its germinating, in the greenhouse at least, no matter how pretreated. It might be best to stratify the seed at 40° F. for 4 months, then sow. If the material is to be grown on standards, *E. europaeus* is used as the understock on which other species are budded or grafted. Usually, however, Euonymus is rooted by cuttings (very easily) almost any time, the evergreen kinds, either softwood or hardwood, and the deciduous kinds softwood. See STRATIFICATION, CUTTINGS.

Insect Pests

Euonymus scale, which encrusts the twigs and underside of leaves with pear-shaped gray and white scales, is very destructive. Two generations produce an abundance of the insects. Heavily infested branches should be cut and burned. Spraying with insecticide #44 in late spring followed by applications of insecticide #15 or #9 are suggested. Where the vines are growing on walls or trellises, it is necessary to place the spray on the back side to obtain reasonably good control. *E. alatus*, the Winged Euonymus, is immune.

Diseases

Crown gall infects Euonymus. See CROWN GALL.

alata   9′   **Zone 3**   **Winged Euonymus**
The Winged Euonymus has been in America nearly a century and is valued for its rigid, vase-shaped (to sometimes almost horizontal) habit, and excellent scarlet autumn color. Some say it is hardy to −30° F., but it can safely be said that it is one of the 3 hardiest species. There is a clone in the trade under the varietal name **monstrosa**, but this is probably just a very good vigorous-growing form of **alata**, with stiff, corky wings on the branches that remain on for 9 years at least.

Since some nurserymen grow this species from seed, there may be plants that have no corky ridges on the twigs, are not as stiff and vase-shaped and hence should probably be relegated to the variety **aperta**. Although not as rigid in general habit, and minus the corky wings that give prominence to the species in the winter, this too has ornamental value. '**Compacta**'—this originated in a seedling lot in the nurseries of J. W. Adams, Springfield, Mass., prior to 1926 when it was first introduced. It is

Euonymus alata—sometimes called Corkbush

an excellent compact variety, rounded in out-line, and makes a splendid hedge merely because it does not have to be clipped more than once every other year or so. The autumn color is a vivid scarlet and it does have corky ridges on the twigs, not very conspicuous. An extremely popular and useable shrub, hardy in Zone 4, but not as hardy as the species.

americana   7′   Zone 6   Strawberrybush or
                                                    Wahoo
In the eastern and southeastern part of the U.S., this is frequently seen in the woodlands and is sometimes used because of its interesting pink-to-scarlet fruits that have peculiar warty growths on the outside and crack open in the fall to show the scarlet seeds inside. The leaves are 1–3 in. long. The autumn color of the foliage is red, but it is not as ornamental as some of the Asiatic species.

atropurpurea   24′   Zone 4   Eastern Wahoo
A shrub or small tree, not very ornamental because of unkempt growth, with crimson 4-lobed fruits in the fall about ⅜ in. in dia. Native in the eastern U.S., the leaves turn pale yellow in the fall and both these and the fruits are reported to possess purgative properties if eaten.

bungeana   18′   Zone 4   Winterberry Euonymus
A small tree from China and Manchuria, this varies somewhat when grown from seed. The light green leaves are 1½–4 in. long and the general habit of the plant is loose and open. The variety 'Pendula' has gracefully pendulous branches and **semipersistens** has semi-evergreen leaves. All have yellowish-to-pinkish-white capsules which when they split open in the fall show the bright scarlet seeds.

europaea   21′   Zone 3   European Spindletree
Common in American gardens, this native of Europe and western Asia has become naturalized in some places. It is vigorous growing and most useful for its orange-to-red fruits. The opposite leaves are about 1–3 in. long and several clones have been named—'Alba' with whitish fruits; 'Aldenhamensis' with bright pink fruits on long pendulous fruit stalks; 'Atropurpurea' with slightly purplish leaves; 'Atrorubens' with red fruits; 'Intermedia' with bright red fruits. 'Aldenhamensis' and 'Intermedius' are best but neither is superior to a good, flourishing, heavily fruited plant of *E. europaeus*. The color of the fruit may vary slightly, but when viewed from a distance there is little to choose among them, unless one is very particular about the exact shade of red or pink color in the fruits. Seedlings of this species do vary, the reason several selections have been made.

As far as **'Red Cascade'** is concerned, in order to have good fruit produced a plant of the tender *E. hamiltonianus* (Zone 7) should be close by as a pollenizer.

**fortunei   clinging vine or sub-shrub   Zone 5
                                           Wintercreeper**
The hardiest of the evergreen vines, this Chinese species has many varieties. At one time it was known as *E. radicans* or *E. radicans acutus*, but both names are considered obsolete now. Mature plants of this species can vary markedly. The species is supposed to have everygreen leaves ½–2 in. long. Apparently young plants retain fairly uniform foliage until they "mature," then some plants undergo a remarkable change and produce foliage utterly different from that of the original young plant. To check this I inspected a 75-year-old plant of *E. fortunei reticulatus* and found 10 distinct types of foliage which, by themselves, might have been considered to belong to other varieties. These ranged in size from shoots with leaves about the size of var. 'Minima' to shoots with large 3-inch leaves. Some shoots were found with rootlets, although the plant itself has always been dis-tinctly shrubby, some shoots were variegated and some had fruits.

There are a dozen or more "new" varieties in this group of plants, some more erect (propagat-ed from erect shoots), some more hardy than others. The "standard" varieties of this most variable species are: 'Carrierei'—shrubby with leaves 1–2 in. long, many fruits and frequently with a few variegated branches; 'Colorata'—an excellent rambling ground cover, with leaves 1 in. long turning purplish in the fall and retaining that color all winter. Definitely not shrubby; 'Gracilis'—with variegated leaves, often white or yellow margins. There are several named clones of this like **'Silver Queen'**; **'Kewensis'**—

with very small leaves, the smallest of all, about $\frac{1}{4}$ in. long; 'Minima'—leaves less than $\frac{1}{4}$ in. long. Both these small-leaved vines are slow growing but have a very fine texture; radicans—leaves about 1 in. long—supposedly trailing or climbing. The leaves of this variety are normally $\frac{3}{8}$–1$\frac{1}{8}$ in. long, frequently not glossy; vegeta—shrubby and the most ornamental because of its rounded leaves 1–1$\frac{1}{2}$ in. long and profuse orange-to-red fruits. This can climb also and apparently does not vary as much as the others when mature. It has been widly planted in America, since it was introduced from Japan in 1876; 'Berryhill' —a variation of the upright from of *E. fortunei* introduced by the Berryhill Nursery of Springfield, Ohio, a few years ago. The plant is upright in shape, with the leaves 1$\frac{1}{2}$–2 in. long. Five-year-old plants are 2$\frac{1}{2}$ ft. tall and definitely upright; 'Sarcoxie'—a selection of the upright form of *E. fortunei* made several years ago by the Sarcoxie Nurseries of Sarcoxie, Mo. The leaves are 1 in. long, glossy, and retained part or all of the winter and it grows about 3$\frac{1}{2}$–4 ft. tall. 'Emerald', 'Emerald 'n Gold', 'Sheridan Gold', and 'Emerald Gaiety' are all colorful new varieties.

japonica   15′   Zone 7   Evergreen Euonymus
A serviceable shrub or small tree with lustrous evergreen leaves almost 3 in. long and a compact habit of growth. It is popular throughout the South. Varieties: 'Microphylla'—often called the Box Leaf Japanese Euonymus because the leaves are about the size of those of Box. A popular variety in the South; 'Albo-marginata' ('Pearl Edge') leaves with thin margin of white; 'Aureo-marginata'—leaves with a yellow edge; 'Aureo-variegata' ('Gold Spot')—leaves blotched with yellow; 'Viridi-variegata' ('Duc d'Anjou') leaves large and bright green, variegated green and yellow in center.

kiautschovica   9′   Zone 6   Spreading Euonymus
Widely grown in America but native to eastern and central China for its good foliage and very late fruits. Evergreen in the far South, it does not flower until Sept. so that in the North it does not form fruit before killing frosts. Typically a plant for the South. Formerly called *E. patens* which is now a synonym. Two varieties are: x 'Dupont'—introduced by the Willis Nursery Co., of Ottawa, Kan., supposedly a hybrid of *E. kiautschovica* and probably not as hardy as *E. fortunei* varieties. Four-year-old plants are 4 ft. tall with leaves 2$\frac{1}{2}$ in. long; x 'Manhattan'—introduced by Kansas State College a few years ago as a hybrid of *E. kiautschovicus*. The leaves are 2$\frac{1}{2}$ in. long, 1$\frac{1}{4}$ in. wide and an excellent dark glossy green. Although it may not prove as hardy as *E. fortunei* varieties, 3-year-old plants are 2$\frac{1}{2}$ ft. tall and show great promise, providing they will be continually hardy.

latifolia   20′   Zone 5   Broadleaf Euonymus
An upright shrub, native to southern Europe and western Asia, with deciduous leaves up to 4$\frac{1}{2}$ in. long and bright red fruits. This species together with *E. sachalinensis* and *E. sanguineus* are the first to open their leaves in the spring.

obovata   ground cover   Zone 3   Running Euonymus
This deciduous plant should be used only as a ground cover for it is faster growing than the evergreen types and so can be expected to cover a larger area in less time. The brilliant red autumn color adds greatly to its effectiveness in the fall.

pulchella = *E. japonica* 'Microphylla'

sachalinensis   12′   Zone 5   Sakhalin Euonymus
Sold in nurseries years ago under the name of *E. planipes*, the deciduous leaves are nearly 4$\frac{1}{4}$ in. long. The fruit is profuse and it is native to northeastern Asia.

sanguinea   21′   Zone 5
Best used for its foliage not for its fruits, which fall quickly and are not borne profusely. The leaves appear very early in the spring and are at first reddish, then turn dark green but are reddish below. They are 1$\frac{1}{2}$–4$\frac{1}{2}$ in. long and turn red in the fall. It is native to central and western China.

yedoensis   15′   Zone 4   Yeddo Euonymus
A flat-topped shrub from Korea and Japan with leaves about 5 in. long and pinkish-purple fruits. The fall foliage is a brilliant red.

EUPATORIUM (yew-pat-OR-ium). A large genus of mostly American species of the Composite Family. Most are tropical plants, but the few found in the Temperate Zone are perennial herbs with opposite or whorled leaves and showy clusters of small tubular flowers from which the branched style generally extends. They are easily cultivated in the garden. Propagation is by division in the spring.

aromaticum   2′   Zone 5   Wild Hoarhound
Similar to *E. rugosum* but the leaves are thicker, more blunt and more hairy. Flowers white. Native from Mass. to Fla. but seldom planted.

coelestinum   2′   Zone 6   Mistflower Eupatorium
Stalked, somewhat triangular, coarsely toothed leaves and blue or violet flowers in flat-topped flower clusters distinguish this species which blooms late in the season. It is found from N.J. to Mich. and southward.

hyssopifolium   12′   Zone 5   Thoroughwort
Narrow, linear leaves arranged in whorls are topped with compound clusters of greenish-white tubular flowers. It frequents sandy clearings and dry woods from New England to Fla. and Tex. and blooms from Aug. to Oct. It has no particular horticultural interest.

maculatum 6'–10' Zones 2–3 Joe-Pye-weed
The Joe-Pye-weed grows in abundance in low, marshy land from New England to N.Car. and N.Mex. It has coarse leaves 10–12 in. long in whorls about the stem and flower heads of purple tubular flowers in terminal clusters. A rank-growing plant, it is useful only where large areas of marshy land must be incorporated into the wild garden.

perfoliatum   5'   Zone 3   Boneset
A perennial herb having a stout, hairy stem and opposite, lanceolate leaves with a broad, wrinkled base which often surrounds the stem. The flower heads are in loose terminal clusters and the individual flowers are white. It may be found in low wet areas over much of eastern North America. It flowers from July to Oct. The leaves and flower tops are used as a gentle laxative, and as an emetic in large doses.

purpureum 10' Zone 4 Bluestem Joe-Pye-weed
Similar to *E. rugosum*, this perennial herb is fragrant, having a scent similar to vanilla. The flower heads are yellowish white to pale pink and contain up to 6 or 7 flowers. The leaves and flowering top are used as a gentle laxative and as an emetic in large doses.

rugosum   4'   Zone 3   White Snakeroot
A smooth-stemmed plant having opposite, toothed leaves 6 in. long with a heart-shaped base and an open terminal cluster of tubular white flowers. It grows in woods over most of the eastern U.S., extending to Ga. and Tex., and flowers from July to Oct. It causes "milk disease" in cattle and should be eradicated from the fields.

EUPHORBIA (yew-FOR-bia). A diverse group of nearly 1500 species, some mere weeds, some good garden plants and at least one—the Poinsettia—a prized florist's plant, and others are thorned succulents from Africa and the East Indies. One thing they all have in common is that their flowers are conspicuous because of highly colored bracts—they have no petals or sepals. Also, they all have a milky sap which in some cases with some species has proved poisonous.

caput-medusae 1' Zone 10 Medusa's-head
A native to South Africa, sometimes grown as an oddity as a pot plant in the home, this is a spineless succulent, globose in general habit with many sinuous and snakelike branches about a foot long and 2 in. thick, sometimes forming clumps 2–3 ft. across. This, like some of the other members of this genus, has a sap or latex that proves poisonous to some people.

corollata   3'   Zone 3   Flowering Spurge
Native in eastern North America in sandy soils, this perennial herb is grown in the garden either for cutting or as a bedding plant. The leaves are 1–2 in. long. Flower clusters at the top of the plant have white petal-like bracts which are very conspicuous from July to Oct. This can be grown on dry soils but can become a weed.

cyparissias   1'   Zone 3   Cypress Spurge
A European native but such a vicious spreader because of its underground stolons that it has escaped cultivation in the eastern U.S. The leaves are small and linear, about 1½ in. long; the flowers are many-rayed umbels, yellowish. It can be used as a ground cover but should be confined, for its roots spread rapidly and it

Eupatorium purpureum (Bluestem Joe-Pye-weed): A common plant in fields from Maine to Texas. (*Photo by Arnold Arboretum, Jamaica Plain, Mass.*)

can become a pernicious, spreading weed.

epithymoides   **1'**   **Zone 4**   **Cushion Euphorbia**
A perennial growing into a dense clump, not
rapidly spreading like *C. cyparissias*. Native to
eastern Europe and showy because the floral
leaves are yellow and are borne profusely in
attractive umbels. In the fall the leaves turn
reddish.

esula   **3'**   **Zone 4**   **Leafy Spurge**
Native to Europe but this perennial is naturalized in the U.S. and often is a troublesome weed
in the northern U.S. and southern Canada. The
leaves are alternate, simple, entire, linear and
up to 3 in. long. Flowers are minute during
June and July. Like most species of this genus it
produces many seeds.

grandicornis   **6'**   **Zone 10**   **Cow's-horn**
A very branched, succulent spiny shrub with
winglike ridges on the stems, yellow flowers.
Native to S. Africa.

heterophylla   **3'**   **annual**   **Painted Spurge**
Native from Ill. to Fla., the large upper leaves
are blotched with red, and it is used for its
color in the garden. Easily grown from seeds
sown in April or early May where the plants are
to grow, doing best in full sun.

maculata   **3'**   **annual**   **Spotted Spurge**
A native weed in the eastern U.S. with opposite
leaves about 1 in. long, a milky sap in the
stems which can be irritating on the skin of
some people.

mammillaris   **8"**   **Zone 10**   **Corkscrew**
A spreading, spiny perennial with yellowish to
greenish flowers. Native to S. Africa.

marginata   **2'**   **annual**   **Snow-on-the-Mountain**
A native plant in the eastern half of the U.S.
with fleshy stems, most ornamental in its
place but it can become a spreading weed. The
flowers are borne continuously from June to
Oct. The leaves are ovate or oblong, about 1 in.
long, but both leaves and the bracts of the
flower have broad white margins which make
them most ornamental. Also the milky sap can
be a skin irritant to some people. It has been
an old-fashioned garden favorite. Easily
propagated by seed sown in April where the
plants are to grow.

milii splendens   **4'**   **Zone 10**   **Crown-of-thorns**
A commonly grown greenhouse plant in the
North, used in gardens where it is hardy, of
interest for its extreme thorniness (the thorns are
1 in. long) and its small red flowers appearing at
all times of the year. It is a weak-branched plant
and needs some support. The leaves are 1–2 in.
long, few, and sometimes not evident. It is
native to Madagascar.

myrsinites   **prostrate**   **biennial or perennial**
                                          Myrtle Euphorbia
A trailing plant with thick stems and short,
fleshy, blue-green leaves. The flowers, appear-

ing in April and May, are inconspicuous, but the
pale yellow bracts are attractive and the plant is
particularly suitable for growing in outcrops of
rock. Propagated by seeds. Native to Europe.

neriifolia   **20'**   **Zone 10**   **Hedge Euphorbia**
A tree, with branches in whorls or slightly
spiralled. Native to India.

polychroma = *E. epithymoides*

pulcherrima   **12'**   **Zone 9**   **Poinsettia**
A very important greenhouse plant in the
North and widely used out-of-doors in subtropical gardens of value for the bright red
leaves or bracts which surround the small
insignificant yellow flowers, the whole appearing like one flower. Native to Central America.
The leaves are evergreen and coarse and are
produced on stiffly upright canes. Doing best in
full sun they are of very easy culture in the
garden. Fertilize 2 or 3 times and cut them back
hard after they are finished flowering, after
Christmas. There is one with white bracts being
sold by florists. The sap is milky white. Cut
flowers last longer if the cut stems are burned
at the base as soon as cut. A well-grown plant
under satisfactory environmental conditions
will hold its "blossoms" for weeks, one of the
reasons why the plant is so popular, especially at
Christmas. Easily propagated by cuttings.

Insect Pests

Mealy bugs live in groups on the stem and at
the base of the leaves where they suck the plant
juices and stunt the plants. Spraying with insecticide #15 or using recommended aerosols is
suggested.

Diseases

Collar rot at the soil level and on the roots,
black root rot on the roots and leaves and stem
canker in the stems and leaf petioles are prevented by using clean cuttings and sterilized
soil.

EUPHORBIACEAE = The Spurge or the Poinsettia Family

EUPRITCHARDIA = *Pritchardia*

EUPTELEA (yew-PTEE-lea)

polyandra   **45'**   **Zone 5**   **Japanese Euptelea**
A deciduous tree native to Japan of little
ornamental value except for the fact that its
leaves are reddish when first unfolding. However, they quickly change to green, changing
again to red and yellow in the fall. **E. franchetii**
is similar. Neither is used much in ornamental
planting. Propagation usually by grafting,
using pieces of its own roots as understock.
Seed and softwood cuttings are also used, which
see.

EURYA (EUR-ya)
  japonica   21′   Zone 7
The only ornamental value of this plant is its
evergreen foliage, the leaves being 1½–3 in.
long. It is native to Japan and Korea, the fruits
are black and berrylike and the male flowers are
usually on one plant and the female flowers on
another. Sometimes it is grown in the greenhouse, its culture being the same as that for
camellias. The flowers are not very showy. Not
to be confused with *Cleyera japonica*.
  ochnacea = *Cleyera japonica*

EUSTOMA (yew-STO-ma)
  grandiflorum (*russellianum*)   2′–3′   **annual**
                        Russell Prairie-gentian
Although in its native home on the plains of the
Southwest it is regarded as a pest, this attractive
plant with opposite, oblong leaves and branched
clusters of blue flowers is a worthy addition to the
annual garden. The flowers have a bell-shaped
corolla, the base of which is splotched with
purple, and 5 or 6 widely flaring lobes. In
cultivation these flowers become considerably
larger than the 2 in. of the wild plants. It blooms
in summer.

EVENING-PRIMROSE. See OENOTHERA.

EVENING-PRIMROSE   FAMILY = Onagraceae

EVERGREEN. A word merely meaning that the
foliage remains on the plant in its green condition throughout the entire year. The term is
further divided, i.e., narrow-leaved evergreens
are considered to be many of the coniferous
species (*Abies, Picea, Pinus, Tsuga*, etc.) but all
conifers are not evergreen. *Larix, Pseudolarix*

and *Metasequoia* are conifers but they are
deciduous. Other narrow-leaved evergreens
would be *Taxus, Juniperus, Thuya*, etc. These
narrow-leaved evergreens differ greatly in form
from most deciduous plants, many of the
trees being strikingly pyramidal in habit.

  The broad-leaved evergreens include such
groups as *Kalmia, Mahonia, Buxus* species and
many *Rhododendron, Ilex, Pieris* species and
many others. The further south one goes, the
more of these are hardy and available for
ornamental plantings. Some like *Abelia grandiflora* and *Lonicera fragrantissima*, will be
evergreen in the South but deciduous in the
North. Needless to say, in northern gardens the
evergreens constitute the most important group
of plants for these are effective in gardens every
day of the year.

EVERGREEN-CHINKAPIN, GIANT = *Castanopsis chrysophylla*

EVERGREENS, BROAD-LEAVED. A popular
term including broad-leaved species of many
genera which retain their leaves throughout the
winter. These, like Mountain-laurel and
Rhododendron are thus differentiated from the
narrow-leaved evergreens like Spruce, Pine and
Fir.

  Many plants are "evergreen" in the deep
South and of course in the Tropics but the
farther north one goes the less there are. All in
the following list can be used as evergreens
within their hardiness limits in the South. North
of the Mason and Dixon Line in the East there
are few broad-leaved evergreen trees except *Ilex
opaca, I. pedunculosa*, and possibly *Magnolia
grandiflora* where it is hardy. As for shrubs, some

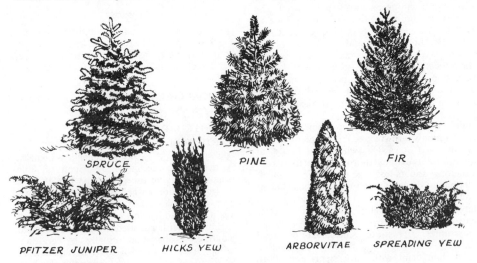

Evergreen shapes

species of *Berberis, Buxus, Gaylussacia, Ilex, Kalmia, Pieris* and *Rhododendron* are the major ones used. In milder parts of the Pacific Coast Area, and of course in the South, many in the following lists are excellent and popular landscape specimens.

It is obvious that all gardens should have a full selection of broad-leaved evergreens to make them of interest, especially during the long, dreary winter months when deciduous plants have no leaves. (This list does not include many low ground covers which are evergreen all winter in the North, nor the many succulents and cacti that retain their green color throughout the year in the South.)

	HEIGHT	ZONE	
Abelia sp.	5'	5–8	Abelia
Acacia, several sp.	10'	8	Acacia
Agave sp.	1'–6'	6–10	Aloe
Arbutus unedo	10'–30'	8	Strawberry-tree
Ardisia crenata	1'	9	Coral Ardisia
Aucuba japonica	15'	7	Japanese Aucuba
Berberis, some sp.	18"–8'	5–9	Barberry
Brachyiton acerifolium	60'	10	Flame Bottletree
Buddleia asiatica	2'–6'	8–9	Asian Buddleia
B. officinalis	2'–6'	9	Pale Buddleia
Buxus sp.	4'–20'	5–6	Box
Camellia japonica	45'	7	Common Camellia
Ceratonia siliqua	50'	10	Carob
Cotoneaster, some sp.	1'–18'	4–7	Cotoneaster
Daphne, some sp.	2'–6'	3–7	Daphne
Dombeya wallichi	30'	10	Scarlet Dombeya
Elaeagnus pungens	12'	7	Thorny Elaeagnus
Ericbotrya japonica	20'	7	Loquat
Eucalyptus globulus	200'	9	Blue Gum
E. viminalis	50'–150'	9	White Gum
Eugenia, several sp.	10'–40'	9–10	Eugenia
Euonymus, some sp.	21'–25'	3–5	Euonymus
Fatsia japonica	15'	7	Japan Fatsia
Feijoa sellowiana	18'	8	Pineapple Guava
Ficus macrophylla	75'	10	Moreton Bay Fig
Gardenia jasminoides	4'–6'	8–9	Gardenia, Cape-jasmine
Gaultheria sp.	1'–5'	3–5	Wintergreen
Grevillea	150'	10	Silk-oak Grevillea
Hedera sp.	clinging vine 90'	5–7	Ivy
Hibiscus rosa-sinensis	30'	9	Chinese Hibiscus
Hymenosporum flavum	50'	10	Sweet-shade
Hypericum, some sp.	2'–6'	5–7	St. Johnswort
Ilex, many sp.	9'–30'	3–7	Holly
Jacaranda acutifolia	50'	10	Sharpleaf Jacaranda
Jasminum sp.	vine	5–8	Jasmine
Kalmia latifolia	30'	4	Mountain-laurel
Lagunaria patersonii	50'	9	Paterson Sugar-Plum Tree
Lantana montevidensis	2'	10	Trailing Lantana
Leucothoe, some sp.	4'–12'	5–6	Leucothoe
Ligustrum, some sp.	9'–18'	3–7	Privet
Lonicera, some sp.	3'–9'	4–5	Honeysuckle
Loropetalum chinense	12'	7–8	
Macadamia ternifolia	35'	10	Queensland Nut
Magnolia grandiflora	90'	7	Southern Magnolia
Mahonia sp.	3'–12'	5–6	Mahonia
Maytenus boaria	35'	9	Chile Mayten Tree
Michelia fuscata	15'	7–8	Banana-shrub
Myrtus communis	5'–10'	8–9	Myrtle
Nandina domestica	8'	7	Nandina

	HEIGHT	ZONE	
Nerium oleander	20'	7–8	Oleander
Olea europaea	25'	9	Common Olive
Osmanthus, several sp.	12'–18'	6–8	Osmanthus
Pachysandra terminalis	ground cover	5	Japanese Spurge, Pachysandra
Parkinsonia aculeata	30'	9	Jerusalem Thorn
Paxistima sp.	12"	5	Pachistima
Pernettya mucronata	1¼'	6–7	Chilean Pernettya
Persea borbonia	30'–40'	7	Red Bay
Pieris floribunda	6'	4	Mountain Andromeda
P. japonica	9'	5	Japanese Andromeda
P. taiwanensis	6'	7	Formosa Andromeda
Pittosporum sp.	10'–40'	8–10	Pittosporum
Plumbago capensis	climbing shrub	9	Cape Plumbago
Prunus laurocerasus	18'	6–7	Cherry-laurel
P. lusitanica	6'–60'	7	Portugal-laurel
Pyracantha sp.	6'–18'	6–7	Firethorn
Quercus agrifolia	90'	9	Calif. Live Oak
Q. suber	60'	7	Cork Oak
Q. virginiana	60'	7	Live Oak
Rhododendron, many sp.	4½–18'	4–6	Azalea and Rhododendron
Ruscus aculeatus	1½'–4'	7	Butcher's Broom
Salvia greggii	3'	7	Autumn Sage
Sarcococca hookeriana	6'	7	Himalayan Sarcococca
Schinus molle	40'	9	Calif. Pepper Tree
S. terebinthifolius	40'	9–10	Brazil Pepper Tree
Skimmia japonica	4'	7	Japanese Skimmia
Tristania conferta	60'	10	Brisbane-box
Vaccinium, some sp.	8"–27'	3–7	Blueberry
Viburnum, some sp.	3'–30'	3–9	Viburnum

EVERGREENS, LOW AND DWARF. Some of these plants can be an integral part of every northern garden, especially for foliage and form display during the dreary winter months when all leaves are off the deciduous plants and garden perennials, and annuals have been cut off at the ground for the winter. They also can be used in the front of the foundation planting about buildings.

Not included in the following lists are many low ground covers, cacti and succulents which are evergreen within their limits of hardiness and many low evergreens hardy only in the South (Zones 8–10). The shrubs listed here are those which will remain under 3–4 ft. in height without any pruning. Taller-growing evergreens can be used but they would have to be pruned or sheared to keep them within this height limitation. The evergreens in the following list and others like them are going to be increasingly popular landscape plants, even though they are expensive and slow growing, because they require practically no maintenance once they are established and also because of their good color and form throughout the entire year.

	HEIGHT	ZONE	
Aucuba japonica 'Nana'	3'	7	Dwarf Japanese Aucuba
Berberis buxifolia nana	18"	5	Dwarf Magellan Barberry
B. candidula	2'	5	Paleleaf Barberry
B. concinna	3'	6	Dainty Barberry
B. verruculosa	4'	5	Warty Barberry
Buxus microphylla 'Compacta'	1'	5	Kingsville Dwarf Box
B. microphylla 'Green Pillow'	1'	5	
B. microphylla 'Tide Hill'	2'	5	
B. sempervirens 'Curly Locks'	2'	5	
B. sempervirens 'Suffruticosa'	1'–3'	5–6	
B. sempervirens 'Vardar Valley'	3'	5	
Chamaecyparis lawsoniana 'Ellwoodii'	3'	5	Lawson False Cypress

	HEIGHT	ZONE	
C. lawsoniana 'Fletcheri'	3'		
C. lawsoniana 'Forsteckensis'	3'		
C. lawsoniana 'Nana'	3'		
C. 'Nana Gracilis'	6"	3	
C. obtusa 'Pygmaea'	18"–24"	3	
Cotoneaster—check species	3'–18'	4–6	Cotoneaster
Cryptomeria japonica 'Bandai-Sugi'	3'	5–6	Cryptomeria
C. japonica 'Compressa'	3'		
C. japonica 'Elegans Nana'	3'		
C. japonica 'Pygmaea'	3'		
Danae racemosa	3'	7	Alexandrian-laurel
Daphne cneorum	6"	4	Rose Daphne
Gaultheria miqueliana	1'	5	Miquel Wintergreen
G. veitchiana	3'	7	Veitch Wintergreen
Gaylussacia brachycera	18"	5	Box-huckleberry
Iberis sp.	8"–15"	5–7	Candytuft
Ilex crenata—many vars.	1'–4'	5–6	Japanese Holly
I. vomitoria 'Nana'	3'	7	Yaupon
Juniperus, many sp. and vars.	1'–4'	2–5	Juniper
Kalmia augustifolia	3'	2	Sheep-laurel
Leiophyllum buxifolium	18"	5	Box Sandmyrtle
Mahonia aquifolium 'Compactum'	2'	5	
M. aquifolium 'Mahan Strain'	2½'	5	
M. repens	10"	5	Creeping Mahonia
Paxistima canbyi	1'	5	Canby Pachistima
Pernettya mucronata	1½'	6–7	Chilean Pernettya
Picea abies, many vars.	1'–4'	2	Norway Spruce
Pinus mugo 'Compacta'	3'	2	Mugo Pine
Rhododendron, several sp.	2'–4'	4–6	Azalea and Rhododendron
Ruscus aculeatus	1½'–4'	7	Butcher's Broom
Skimmia japonica	4'	7	Japanese Skimmia
S. reevesiana	1½'	7	Reeves Skimmia
Suaeda fruticosa	3'	6	Shrubby Goosefoot
Taxus cuspidata, several vars.	2'–4'	4	Japanese Yew
Teucrium chamaedrys	10"	5	Chamaedrys Germander
Thuja occidentalis, several vars.	1'–4'	2	American Arborvitae
Tsuga canadensis, several vars.	1'–4'	4	Canada Hemlock
Viburnum davidii	3'	7	David Viburnum
Yucca filamentosa	3'	4	Adam's Needle

EVERLASTING, COMMON PEARLY = *Anaphalis margaritacea*

EVERLASTING, CUDWEED = *Helichrysum petiolatum*

EVERLASTING FLOWERS. See DRIED PLANT MATERIALS.

EVERLASTING, WINGED = *Ammobium alatum*

EVODIA (ee-VO-dia). The 3 species mentioned here all have opposite, compound, deciduous leaves and can be classed as small trees, although *E. hupehensis* can grow 60 ft. high. The flowers are small, white and unisexual, produced in dense clusters 2–7 in. across during the late summer, and the fruits are colorful capsules which split open to show the lustrous black seeds inside.

Propagation

Seeds may be sown as soon as ripe or stored dry in airtight containers in a cool place up to a year and then sown. Softwood cuttings can be rooted, which see.

daniellii   25'   Zone 5   Korean Evodia
This small tree, native to China and Korea is valued chiefly for its summer flowers and early fall fruits. The small white flowers are produced in clusters 6 in. across and these are followed by reddish capsules which split open to show the lustrous black seeds inside. The compound leaves have 7–11 leaflets, each 2–4 in. long. **E. hupehensis** is similar but it grows taller (to 60 ft.) and the leaves have only 7–9 leaflets, each 2½–5 in. long. **E. henryi** is similar to *E. daniellii* except that it has 5–9 leaflets 2–2½ in. long in each leaf. These might prove good for the small garden but they are weak-wooded and hence probably make poor street trees.

EVONYMUS = Euonymus

EXACUM (EX-ak-um)
   affine 2′ **biennial**
Belonging to the Gentian Family this Old
World species from the Island of Socotra is
often treated as an annual, for if seed is sown in
the greenhouse in March, the plants may bloom
by late summer and fall. Small violet-blue
flowers are produced from the axis of each leaf,
and they have pronounced yellow stamens, and
once started to flower they will continue for
several months. They do best with warm growing conditions. The leaves are opposite, simple
and entire, about 1½ in. long, while the flowers
are ½ in. across.

EXFOLIATING. Peeling off in thin layers; as
the bark of the birch.

EXOCHORDA (ex-o-KORD-a, or ex-OK-ord-a)
   giraldii wilsonii 15′ **Zone 5 Wilson Pearlbush**
There is no question but that this is the best
ornamental in this genus, but unfortunately it is
rarely grown, yet, by nurserymen. A Chinese
plant, the racemes of white flowers, 2 in. in dia.,
appear in early May. It produces more flowers
than the other species, and they are larger also.
In order to obtain maximum flower production
the weaker branches should be pruned out from
the inside of the bush. Unfortunately the
flowers only last a short time and the plant has
little to recommend it at other times of year,
but when it is in full bloom it makes a beautiful
specimen. It is not too particular as to the soil in
which it grows.

   racemosa 9′ **Zone 4 Common Pearlbush**
This shrub is easily available from nurseries,
having smaller flowers and not as many of them
as *E. giraldii wilsonii*, otherwise it is similar to
it. Sometimes it is incorrectly listed as *E.
grandiflora*—the name certainly is inaccurate.

Propagation

Seeds can be sown as soon as ripe or stored
dry in airtight containers in a cool place for up
to a year and then sown. Plants frequently can
be easily divided with a sharp spade or softwood
cuttings can be rooted. See CUTTINGS.

EXOTIC. Foreign, not native.

EXPERIMENT STATIONS. An agricultural
experiment station has been established in each
of the 50 states and Puerto Rico, financed by
both federal and state funds. The gardener
should know the address of his state agricultural
experiment station for it issues bulletins of
various kinds on all phases of agriculture,
horticulture and home-making. The chances are
that someone on the staff of the station can
answer the gardener's most perplexing question
concerning plant culture or pest control. Frequently bulletins are available, either free or for
a nominal price, written primarily to assist the
home gardener with his problems. Such information, written by experts who know the
conditions in the locality, offer the best possible
means of gaining such information. Learn to
know and use the facilities of your state agricultural experiment station.

Agricultural Experimental Stations

Alabama Agric. Exp. Station	Auburn Univ.	Auburn, Ala. 36830
Alaska Agric. Exp. Station	Univ. of Alaska	Palmer, Alaska 99701
Arizona Agric. Exp. Station	Univ. of Arizona	Tucson, Ariz. 85721
Arkansas Agric. Exp. Station	Univ. of Arkansas	Little Rock, Ark. 77203
California Agric. Exp. Station	Univ. of California	Berkeley, Calif. 94720
Colorado Agric. Exp. Station	Colorado State Univ.	Fort Collins, Colo. 80521
Connecticut Agric. Exp. Station		New Haven, Conn. 06504
Storrs Agric. Exp. Station	Univ. of Connecticut	Storrs, Conn. 06268
Delaware Agric. Exp. Station	Univ. of Delaware	Newark, Del. 19711
Florida Agric. Exp. Station	Univ. of Florida	Gainesville, Fla. 32601
Georgia Coastal Plain Exp. Station	Univ. of Georgia	Tifton, Ga. 31294
Georgia Agric. Exp. Station	Univ. of Georgia	Athens, Ga. 30601
Hawaii Agric. Exp. Station	Univ. of Hawaii	Honolulu, Hawaii 96822
Idaho Agric. Exp. Station	Univ. of Idaho	Moscow, Ida. 83843
Illinois Agric. Exp. Station	Univ. of Illinois	Urbana, Ill. 61801
Indiana Agric. Exp. Station	Purdue Univ.	Lafayette, Ind. 47907
Iowa Agric. Exp. Station	Iowa State Univ.	Ames, Ia. 50010
Kansas Agric. Exp. Station	Kansas State Univ.	Manhattan, Kan. 66502
Kentucky Agric. Exp. Station	Univ. of Kentucky	Lexington, Ky. 40506
Louisiana Agric. Exp. Station	Louisiana State Univ.	Baton Rouge, La. 70803
Maine Agric. Exp. Station	Univ. of Maine	Orono, Me. 04473
Maryland Agric. Exp. Station	Univ. of Maryland	College Park, Md. 20742
Massachusetts Agric. Exp. Station	Univ. of Massachusetts	Amherst, Mass. 01002
Michigan Agric. Exp. Station	Michigan State Univ.	East Lansing, Mich. 48823

Agricultural Experimental Stations

Minnesota Agric. Exp. Station	Univ. of Minnesota	St. Paul, Minn. 55101
Mississippi Agric. Exp. Station	Mississippi State Univ.	State College, Miss. 39762
Missouri Agric. Exp. Station	Univ. of Missouri	Columbia, Mo. 65201
Montana Agric. Exp. Station	Montana State College	Bozeman, Mont. 59715
Nebraska Agric. Exp. Station	Univ. of Nebraska	Lincoln, Neb. 68503
Nevada Agric. Exp. Station	Univ. of Nevada	Reno, Nev. 89507
New Hampshire Agric. Exp. Station	Univ. of New Hampshire	Durham, N.H. 03824
New Jersey Agric. Exp. Station	State Univ. of New Jersey	New Brunswick, N.J. 08903
New Mexico Agric. Exp. Station	New Mexico State Univ.	Las Cruces, N.M. 88001
New York Agric. Exp. Station	Cornell Univ.	Ithaca, N.Y. 14850
New York State Agric. Exp. Station		Geneva, N.Y. 14456
North Carolina Agric. Exp. Station	Univ. of North Carolina	Raleigh, N.C. 27607
North Dakota Agric. Exp. Station	North Dakota State Univ.	Fargo, N.D. 58102
Ohio Agric. Exp. Station	Ohio State Univ.	Columbus, Ohio 43210
Oklahoma Agric. Exp. Station	Oklahoma State Univ.	Stillwater, Okla. 74074
Oregon Agric. Exp. Station	Oregon State Univ.	Corvallis, Ore. 97331
Pennsylvania Agric. Exp. Station	Pennsylvania State Univ.	University Park, Pa. 16802
Puerto Rico Agric. Exp. Station	Univ. of Puerto Rico	Rio Piedras, Puerto Rico 00928
Rhode Island Agric. Exp. Station	Univ. of Rhode Island	Kingston, R.I. 02881
South Carolina Agric. Exp. Station	S. C. School of Agriculture	Clemson, S.C. 29631
South Dakota Agric. Exp. Station	S.D. State College	Brookings, S.D. 57006
Tennessee Agric. Exp. Station	Univ. of Tennessee	Knoxville, Tenn. 37901
Texas Agric. Exp. Station	Agricultural and Mechanical College of Texas	College Station, Tex. 77843
Utah Agric. Exp. Station	Utah State Univ.	Logan, Utah 84321
Vermont Agric. Exp. Station	Univ. of Vermont	Burlington, Vt. 05401
Virginia Agric. Exp. Station	Va. Polytechnic Institute	Blacksburg, Va. 24061
Washington Agric. Exp. Station	Washington State Univ.	Pullman, Wash. 99163
West Virginia Agric. Exp. Station	West Virginia Univ.	Morgantown, W.Va. 26506
Wisconsin Agric. Exp. Station	Univ. of Wisconsin	Madison Wisc. 53706
Wyoming Agric. Exp. Station	Univ. of Wyoming	Laramie, Wyo. 82070

EXSERTED. Prolonged beyond the surrounding organs, as stamens from the corolla.

EYE. The marked center of a flower; a bud on a tuber, as on the potato; a single-bud cutting.

F

F₁. The first generation of a cross between species or varieties; often cultivated for the hybrid vigor; succeeding filial generations are designated F_2, F_3, etc.

FABIANA (fay-bi-AY-na)
imbricata   **8′**   **Zone 9**   **Peru Falseheath**
A much-branched heathlike shrub from Chile but belonging to the Potato Family, sometimes used as an ornamental in the greenhouse. Leaves are small and scalelike, flowers profuse, small, white and solitary. The fruit is a capsule. Propagated by cuttings taken in Aug. Grown outdoors in southern Calif. and southern Fla.

FAGACEAE = The Beech Family

FAGOPYRUM (fay-go-PY-rum)
esculentum   **3′**   **annual**   **Buckwheat**
An annual herb native to central Asia, with alternate leaves and racemes of small, white, fragrant flowers in summer, most attractive to bees. This is not an ornamental but is grown as a "green manure" for plowing under the succulent young plants when they are about 10 in. high. It is also grown for its seeds from which a flour is made. Seeds broadcast and disced in the soil in early June will flower within 8 weeks. The leaves are more or less triangular in shape as are the fruits. All kinds of livestock with an unpigmented skin are susceptible to buckwheat poisoning.
tataricum   **2′**   **annual**   **Tatary Buckwheat**
Also called Indiawheat and Duckwheat, this is similar to Buckwheat but smaller and more slender. Native to India—sometimes considered more hardy than Buckwheat.

FAGUS (FAY-gus). The beeches are among the most majestic of our ornamental shade trees. They need space in which to grow—plenty of space, for with room all about them their beautiful outlines are truly superb. As a group they are tall, often wide-spreading trees with alternate leaves. They are fibrous-rooted with their feeding roots very close to the soil surface; hence it is difficult or impossible to get good growth from other plants beneath the spread of their branches. Actually, they are set off to best advantage if their branches are allowed to sweep the ground on all sides, and this is especially true of the pendulous-branched forms.

There are about 8 species hardy in the eastern U.S. Three of these native to China (*F. engleriana, F. lucida, F. longipetiolata*), 2 native to Japan (*F. crenata, F. japonica*) and 1 native to eastern Europe and Asia minor (*F. orientalis*) have little to offer as ornamentals when compared with the two commonly grown species, *F. grandifolia* and *F. sylvatica*.

Fagus or Beech twig and fruit

As a rule the American Beech is a tree of upright habit, considerably taller than it is wide. On the other hand, the European Beech and many of its varieties are almost as wide-spreading as they are tall. They both have gray bark, that of the American Beech being considerably lighter. Both can be sheared and used in hedges tall or small. The most famous of these hedges, made of the English Beech, is one near Stobhill Castle in Scotland. Planted in 1746, this "hedge" is now 85 ft. tall and still in pretty good condition.

The 2 species should not be confused, as their leaves are quite distinct. The leaves of the European Beech are not so sharply toothed as those of the American Beech and it does not sprout profusely from the base of the trunk, as does the American Beech. There are no truly ornamental varieties of the American Beech but there are several of the European Beech. None of these, however, are suited for street tree

Pendulous-branched trees like this European Beech are usually very graceful. (*Photo by Arnold Arboretum, Jamaica Plain, Mass.*)

planting because they are so large and each one needs plenty of space in which to grow properly.

It has been noted that the nuts are sweet and have been used for table oils and as a coffee substitute, while the young leaves have been used as a pot herb. In times of famine, the inner bark has been used in bread-making.

Propagation

Do not allow the seed to dry out, but stratify as soon as ripe for 3 months at 40° F., then sow. Grafting is usually practiced with *F. sylvatica* as the understock since most of the forms grafted belong to this species. See STRATIFICATION, GRAFTING.

Insect Pests

Beech blight aphid feeding on the bark and woolly beech aphid on the leaves are both covered with protective cottony filaments. The latter species shows a preference for European Beech and is seldom found on the American species. Insecticide #15 is effective. The larvae of the several insects occasionally develop in outbreaks and defoliate the beech trees. Insecticide #9 will control these. The woolly beech scale which often covers large areas of the bark on trunk and branches is associated with serious damage and death of many trees because of the relation with nectria canker. It is believed that the canker enters through the feeding puncture made by the scale.

Leaf varieties of the European Beech. Each square is 1 sq. in.

1. *Fagus sylvatica*	5. *F. sylvatica* 'Grandidentata'
2. *F. sylvatica* 'Rohanii'	6. *F. sylvatica* 'Laciniata'
3. *F. sylvatica* 'Asplenifolia'	7. *F. sylvatica* 'Rotundifolia'
4. *F. sylvatica* 'Albo-variegata'	8. *F. sylvatica* 'Atropunicea'

(*Photo by Arnold Arboretum, Jamaica Plain, Mass.*)

Dormant sprays of insecticide #44 kill the scale but beech is susceptible to injury by oil and fungicide # U at dormant strength is often used.

Diseases

Nectria bark canker kills branches and trees. Control of the woolly beech scale and cutting out and disinfecting the wounds are recommended treatments. In wet weather the leaves of Copper Beech may show the light brown spot of anthracnose unless protected by sprays of fungicides # D or # F.

grandifolia   90′   Zone 3   American Beech Native over a wide area of North America and an excellent ornamental, it does not do well under city conditions. The light gray bark is outstanding and the yellowish-bronze autumn color is familiar to many. This species is differentiated from *F. sylvatica* in that the leaves have 9–14 pairs of veins and are markedly bristly or serrate all along the leaf margin, while the European Beech has only 5–9 pairs of veins and is only partially dentate along the leaf margins. The American Beech also suckers considerably more at the base.

sylvatica   90′   Zone 4   European Beech An excellent ornamental tree with several fine varieties. The bark is slightly darker gray than that of the American Beech. This is unquestionably one of the best of the large ornamental shade trees native to central and southern Europe. Many beeches in Europe have grown to tremendous size, one in England is reported to be 100 ft. tall with a trunk girth of 21 ft. It has been known and appreciated as an ornamental for centuries, one of the reasons why so many good ornamental varieties have been discovered.

Varieties

'Albo-variegata'—leaves variegated with white;

'Asplenifolia'—this has fine textured foliage with the leaves finely divided, similar to those of 'Laciniata' except that sometimes they are almost linear. The common name of Fernleaf Beech accurately describes its feathery foliage texture;

'Atropunicea'—this Purple Beech has originated at several places in Europe and possibly in this country also, accounting for the slight variation in foliage color, shape of leaves and even habit. It has been known since 1680 and has been offered under the names of 'Atropurpurea', 'Cuprea', 'Nigra', 'Purpurea', 'Riversii', 'Sanguinea' and 'Spaethiana', among others. It is unfortunate that some nurserymen grow Purple Beech from seed, selecting the best and giving them "suitable" names. It would be much better if they were propagated asexually so that only the best forms would be perpetuated. Since this variety does come partially true from seed, it is no wonder that several variations have sprung up, some brighter or deeper purple than others.

Closely-related clones with purple leaves are:

'Cuprea'—originated with George Loddegis in Great Britain about 1836, is actually a form of 'Atropunicea' with young foliage a lighter reddish bronze, giving rise to the common name Copper Beech;

'Riversii'—is a purple-leaved form originating in the English nursery of Thomas Rivers before 1869, and has proved one of the most popular over the years. The young foliage is reddish but turns purplish later and remains that color throughout the summer. The tree is densely compact and symmetrical—an excellent specimen;

'Spaethiana'—is the most recent addition to this group of forms originating in the Spaeth Nurseries of Germany a few years ago. The Dutch nurserymen offering this form claim that it keeps its deep purple color throughout the entire summer. Other forms are:

'Fastigiata'—the Dawyck Beech, originating in Scotland nearly 50 years ago, is definitely fastigiate in habit—one of the best trees with this general habit;

'Grandidentata'—leaves with coarse teeth;

'Laciniata'—this Cutleaf European Beech has narrow leaves often deeply cut to almost regularly lobed. It differs from the 'Aspenifolia' in having wide, more regularly shaped leaves. It grows into a beautiful, wide-spreading specimen of fine texture;

'Pendula'—the popular Weeping Beech, of which there are many excellent specimens in this country and abroad, has several variations, some more wide spreading than others. Only the best of these forms should be propagated asexually. It is best grown where its branches can sweep the ground;

'Purpureo-pendula'—with pendulous branches and purple leaves—the Weeping Purple Beech;

'Quercifolia'—with oaklike foliage—the Oak-leaved Beech with leaves narrow and irregularly toothed;

'Rohanii'—with purple leaves very similar in shape to those of 'Laciniata';

'Rosea-marginata'—purple leaves with an irregular light pink border. This tree, of course, lacks its full complement of chlorophyll; hence is more difficult to grow than the others. In full sun the delicately colored leaf margin may burn to brown, so it should be grown in a slightly shaded situation. At best it can only be considered of interest while small;

'Rotundifolia'—the Roundleaf Beech is one of the best of all these varieties. The leaves are

The largest Weeping English Beech (*Fagus sylvatica* 'Pendula'), this tree is 50 ft, tall, has a 165-ft. spread, and is 200 years old. It is growing in Woking, England.

rounded, only ½–1¼ in. in dia., originating in Woking, England, about 1872. The tree in the Arnold Arboretum has been growing since 1903, and is now 50 ft. tall with a branch spread of 42 ft. The branches are horizontal but turned upward at the end, making a dense, beautifully branched pyramidal tree. This particular tree has the peculiar trait of holding its leaf buds shut until nearly 2 weeks after those of all other beeches are fully open. This variety should be grown a great deal more than it is;

'Tortuosa'—a 75-year-old tree of this variety is 18 ft. tall and about 36 ft. in dia. with a flat top similar in general outline to that of *Tsuga canadenis* 'Pendula'. Because of its very slow growth and uniquely picturesque habit, there is not a great demand for this plant.

FAIRY RING. A popular term given to a ring of mushrooms usually appearing on the lawn. When mushroom spores of certain species are deposited on suitable soil, with plenty of humus, the mycelia grow regularly in all directions from the original spot. When the fruits or mushrooms appear above the soil surface they grow in a ring. If the soil is suitable outside this ring, and the fungus is not killed with fungicides, the ring will be just so much larger another year. The popular term of course comes from the old belief that no circle of plant growths could be so perfect unless it was accomplished by fairies.

The grass within this ring is sometimes more vigorous and a darker green because the mycelia in breaking down soil materials for their own growth have supplied much additional humus in the soil on which the grass can grow.

FALCATE. Sickle-shaped.

FALL-DAFFODIL = *Sternbergia lutea*

FALLUGIA (fahl-U-gia)

paradoxa   5′   Zone 5   Apache-plume Used especially for summer and early fall display, this American native from Utah to N.Mex. is chiefly of use in that general area. The white flowers 1½ in. across, appear in May, to be followed in the fall by attractive heads of feathery, purple fruits. It requires a well-drained soil (almost dry soil) and a situation in the full sun to grow its best.

FALSE ARALIA. See DIZYGOTHECA.

FALSE ARBORVITAE, HIBA = *Thujopsis dolobrata*

FALSE CYPRESS. See CHAMAECYPARIS.

FALSE DRAGONHEAD = *Physostegia virginiana*

FALSE FLAG = *Neomarica gracilis*

FALSE FLAX. See CAMELINA.

FALSE FOXGLOVE. See AUREOLARIA.

FALSE HEATH, PERU = *Fabiana imbricata*

FALSE MERMAID FAMILY = Limnanthaceae

FALSE PALM = *Ficus pseudopalma*

FALSE SPIREA. See SORBARIA.

FAMEFLOWER. See TALINUM.

FAN PALM. See LIVISTONA, PRITCHARDIA.

FANWORT, CAROLINA = *Cabomba caroliniana*

FAREWELL-TO-SPRING = *Clarkia amoena*

FARKLEBERRY = *Vaccinium arboreum*

FASCIATION This is a condition brought about in plants by an abnormal growth of cells in which the stem is greatly enlarged but flattened. It often occurs in lilies and cockscombs, usually accompanied by an abnormal increase in the number of blooms produced on the fasciated stems.

FASCICLE. A dense cluster.

FASTIGIATE. With close and erect branches, as in the Lombardy Poplar.

FASTIGIATE TREES. See TREES, FASTIGIATE.

x FATSHEDERA (fats-HED-era) (*Hedera helix* x *Fatsia japonica*)
  lizei   **7′**   **Zone 7**   **Fatshedera**
This is one of the few generic hybrids that are used in planting ornamental gardens in America. It is a glossy-leaved evergreen with 3–5 palmately lobed leaves which are sometimes up to 7 in. long and 11 in. across; semiclimbing or somewhat shrubby. It seems to be very popular in the South as a garden plant, and in the North finds much use as a tall-growing house plant which apparently can grow without much direct sunshine. Both softwood and hardwood cuttings root easily.

FATSIA (FAT-sia)
  japonica   **15′**   **Zone 7**   **Japan Fatsia**
A leathery-leaved evergreen, the glossy leaves of which have 7–9 lobes and are as much as 12 in. across, this plant is used solely for this attribute. Coming from Japan where it is native, it is often used in the garden because of its large leaves which give a tropical effect. However, it must be pruned occasionally to prevent it from growing too leggy. It does well in Japan where one frequently sees it in park plantings in shaded spots where poor soil is everywhere. The flowers are small but appear in large, showy, branched clusters in the fall, and the fruits are light blue berries effective in the winter.

FAUCARIA (faw-KAY-ria)
  tigrina   **6″**   **Zone 9**   **Tiger's-jaw**
A succulent with opposite, thick, keeled, gray-green leaves, 1½–2 in. long and ½–1 in. wide, glaucous green, spotted with white, and on the margins are 9–10 strong recurved teeth giving rise to the name Tiger's-jaw. The flowers are golden yellow, 1–2 in. across and remind one of dandelions. Native to South Africa. For culture see CACTI AND SUCCULENTS.

FAWN-LILY. See ERYTHRONIUM.

FEATHER-FLEECE = *Stenanthium robustum*

FEATHER-GRASS, EUROPEAN = *Stipa pennata*

FEEDING, FOLIAR. See FOLIAR FEEDING.

FEIJOA (fy-JO-a)
  sellowiana   **18′**   **Zone 10**   **Pineapple Guava**
The Pineapple Guava is a plant only for the very warm parts of Calif. and Fla., where it is grown chiefly for its edible fruit. These are green tinged red, about 3 in. long with white flesh. Several varieties may be offered by a very few nurserymen and in order to have fruits, several varieties should be planted in close proximity to each other to insure cross-pollination. It is a native to Paraguay, Uruguay and Argentina.

FELICIA (fee-LISS-ia)
  amelloides   **3′**   **annual to perennial**   **Blue Felicia**
This can be grown as an annual or as a perennial in the greenhouse. If seed is sown early in the spring, bushy plants wil! produce their pale blue, daisylike flowers from July to Oct. Plants can then be lifted, potted, brought back into the greenhouse for flowering through the winter. The opposite leaves are about 1 in. long and the flower heads are 1¼ in. across. Native to South Africa. Sometimes called Blue Marguerite. Propagated by both seeds and cuttings.
  bergerana   **8″**   **annual**   **Kingfisher-daisy**
A fine little annual from South Africa, valued for its bright blue, solitary, daisylike flowers with yellow centers about ¾ in. wide. Leaves are grasslike, 1½ in. long and hairy. An excellent plant for window boxes. Seed should be started indoors in March, or it can be sown outdoors in late May, in the full sun, and seedlings thinned to 6 in. apart. Especially grown in the South.
  dubia (*adfinis*)   **1′**   **annual**
An African plant, member of the Composite Family with bluish, solitary, daisylike flowers borne on long stalks above the leaves. It can be used as a pot plant in the cool greenhouse. Sow seeds inside in March, transplant outdoors when frost is over.

FEMALE (flowers on plants). Having pistils but no stamens.

FENCES. See GARDEN FIXTURES.

FENDLERA (FEND-ler-a)
  rupicola   **6′**   **Zone 5**
A situation in the full sun is the key to the good growth of this plant which is native to Tex. and N.Mex. The white or rose-tinged flowers bloom in May. In good soil, or in moist soil, it does not grow well so that it is best used in hot, dry situations, where other plants will not succeed.

FENNEL = *Foeniculum vulgare*

FENNEL, COMMON GIANT = *Ferula communis*

FENNEL-FLOWER = *Nigella sativa*

FENUGREEK = *Trigonella foenum-graecum*

FERMATE OR FERBAM. A fungicide (which see).

FERN, BASKET = *Nephrolepis pectinata*

FERN, BEACH = *Dryopteris phegopteris*

FERN, BRAKE. See PTERIS.

FERN, CHAIN. See WOODWARDIA.

FERN, CHRISTMAS = *Polystichum acrostichoides*

FERN, CINNAMON = *Camunda cinnamomea*

FERN, CLIFF-BRAKE. See PELLAEA.

FERN, CLIMBING. See LYGODIUM.

FERN, CRESTED SHIELD = *Dryopteris cristata*

FERN, DEER = *Blechnum spicant*

FERN, GLADE = *Athyrium pycnocarpum*

FERN, GOLDIE'S = *Dryopteris goldiana*

FERN, HARE'S-FOOT, *Davallia canariensis*

FERN, HARTFORD = *Lygodium palmatum*

FERN, HARTS-TONGUE = *Phyllitis scolopendrium*

FERN, HAY-SCENTED = *Dennstaedtia punctilobula*

FERN, HOLLY. See POLYSTICHUM, CYRTOMIUM.

FERN, INTERRUPTED = *Osmunda claytoniana*

FERN, LADY = *Athyrium filix-femina*

FERN, LIP. See CHEILANTHES.

FERN, MAIDENHAIR. See ADIANTUM.

FERN, MAIDENHAIR (Gold, Silver—See NOTHOLAENA).

FERN, MEXICAN TREE = *Cibotium schiedei*

FERN, MOTHER = *Asplenium bulbiferum*

FERN, NEW YORK = *Thelypteris noveboracensis*

FERN, OSTRICH = *Matteuccia struthiopteris pensylvanica*

FERN, PARSLEY = *Cryptogramma crispa acrostichoides*

FERN, RATTLESNAKE = *Botrychium virginianum*

FERN, RESURRECTION = *Polypodium polypodioides*

FERN, ROYAL = *Osmunda regalis*

FERN, SENSITIVE = *Onoclea sensibilis*

FERN, SQUIRREL FOOT = *Davallia bullata*

FERN, STAGHORN. See PLATYCERIUM.

FERN, STOVE = *Pteris cretica*

FERN, SWORD. See NEPHROLEPIS.

FERN, TREE FAMILY = Cyatheaceae

FERN, TUBER = *Nephrolepis cordifolia*

FERN, WALKING = *Camptosorus rhizophyllus*

FERNS. These plants have been growing on the earth for millions of years. They were among the first plants (after algae and mosses) to grow in the early years after the earth was formed. Today, although they are not an important part of gardening, still they are useful and some people grow them in the cool woods, beside stream or pool or in a shaded part of the rockery. Certainly they play a very important part in the florist's business for they are extremely decorative as pot plants or large display plants, and their cut fronds are used in many ways in making bouquets, arrangements and corsages.

The life history of a fern starts with the spores which are borne on the underside of the fern frond. These fall to the ground and start growth if they rest in a likely spot with sufficient moisture. They develop into many-celled, heart-shaped organisms called prothallia, each one of which is about $\frac{1}{4}$ in. across. These send rhizoids into the soil which are able to absorb nourishment from the soil and eventually they produce male and female organs.

When these have matured the sperm cells, which are free swimming, swim in a drop of dew or rain water and fertilize the female organ which then develops an egg cell. This starts growth and is called a sporophyte, a young body totally different from either a spore or a prothallium, which eventually will grow the fern leaves and roots as we usually know them. The sporophyte has 3 parts, the leaf, the rhizome or the stem and the roots. Over the centuries many kinds have developed so that now they grow from the Tropics almost to the Arctic Circle.

The fruiting bodies (spores) of ferns are borne in sacs or clusters called sporangia, and several of these clustered together are called a sorus (plural sori). Botanists identify ferns frequently by the type and arrangement of these sori. Mostly they appear on the underside of the leaf. Sometimes the ferns do not have sori, but the sporangia are borne in dense masses, so dense sometimes that the identity of the leaflets may seem to be lost.

Ferns also vary in the type of rhizome or stem they have. In some the rhizome is a creeping one with fronds coming up at regular or irregular intervals as it creeps over the ground. With others, the rhizome is concentrated so that the fronds appear to be produced from one central crown. This is the case with the common Christmas Fern. Also, the pinnae (or small parts of the frond) differ greatly, one species from another. So, it is seen that ferns which look similar at first glance, may differ in arrangement of pinnae and sori or in the type of rhizomes they have. All these are taken into consideration in fern identification.

Transplanting ferns is no more difficult than transplanting perennials, but one should be careful to provide soil and surroundings that are similar to those which a fern is accustomed to in its native habitat. For instance, some ferns like the Ebony Spleenwort grow in alkaline soils, hence it is not correct to expect them to grow well in strongly acid soils. Most ferns grow in soil with a high humus content and should have a partially shaded situation. The rhizomes of many grow through the loose leaves and dead material on the surface of the soil, and such conditions should be provided. Because of this method of growth, fern beds should not be raked or stirred roughly with any kind of a tool, in order not to disturb the tender rhizomes which are always just at the surface of the soil.

Ferns should be watered during dry periods, but if given a good soil with plenty of humus, the chances are they will need no additional fertilizers. In fact, commerical fertilizers are sometimes so strong as to seriously injure the tender rhizomes. Mostly ferns will do well if unmolested, provided of course they have the proper soil, moisture and shade.

When ferns are grown indoors as house plants, once the atmospheric condition and temperature are correct, they need little attention except watering. They can be grown in the rooms or hallways where there is no direct sunlight. Sometimes fluorescent lights (which see) are used above a tray of ferns in a dark hallway, and this is all the light needed.

Some of the ferns that are grown especially as ornamentals indoors are *Pteris cretica* varieties, the fronds of which vary considerably one from the other. Some ferns with interesting and colorful rhizomes could be included, like the Golden Polypody (*Polypodium aureum*) so named because of its yellow rhizome which grows in a conspicuously indeterminate fashion. Even the common Boston Fern (*Nephrolepis exaltata*) has interest in a hanging basket. Some try to grow the striking Staghorn Fern (*Platycerium* species) of which there are several, but they are slow growing and one has to be patient with them. Well grown they are of much interest.

The Maidenhair Fern (*Adiantum*), the Boston Fern (*Nephrolepis exaltata*) with its many variations and the Bear's-foot Fern (*Humata tyermannii*) are all used and available from many florists selling pot plants. For specimens, each on a single pedestal, a mature Boston Fern is

excellent. Also, the Japanese-holly Fern (*Cyrtomium falcatum*) and mature specimens of the Golden Polypody (*Polypodium aureum*) are possibilities.

Winter sun is usually not too bright for many ferns but it should be remembered that diffused light and not direct strong sunlight is always best for them. A good potting soil for ferns is made of equal parts of screened compost, sand and finely ground sphagnum moss, with a little bone meal. This can be varied to equal parts of loam, leaf mold, peat moss and sand. It is important to note that ferns should not be over-potted, that is, a fern with a 3 in. root spread should not be put in a 6 in. pot, but a 4 in. pot, for over-potting can actually injure the fern.

Gardeners who are interested, and have the facilities of a greenhouse, might try the unique venture of growing ferns from spores. Collect fronds of several species when their spores are nearly ripe and lay them on white paper with the back side of the fronds facing the paper, thus effecting a better collection of the spores as the sporangia open from the drying process.

These can then be sown in pots or flats in soil which has been carefully prepared and finely sifted, but there should be at least 3 in. of soil. The soil should be sterilized. See STERILIZATION OF SOIL. The spores are carefully sprinkled on the soil and then an extremely thin layer of finely sifted sphagnum moss is gently sifted over this or the soil is left without the sphagnum moss and the whole pot or flat set in water not quite reaching the top of the soil and thus watered from the bottom until it is thoroughly wet. The pots, or flats, when drained, can be set in 2 in. of moistened vermiculite which will aid the soil in retaining its moisture. If glass or polyethylene is placed over the top make certain there is not excessive condensation, for this could quickly start mold. Water can be added from time to time with a very fine spray, applied in such a way that it does not disturb moss or spores on the soil surface. The pots and flats then can be placed in gentle sunlight (or fluorescent light, which see) for the germinating period.

This varies with the species but 3–4 days is common, although the spores of some species take several weeks. Soon the soil surface will begin to look greenish, merely an indication that the spores are growing and forming the prothalia. These will probably become flat, and heart-shaped, about ¼ in. across in 3 months. Near the end of this time, they should be sprayed gently occasionally, so water will be present for the sperms to swim over and fertilize the egg cells in the female organs. These eggs then develop into the small sporophytes which can be seen without the use of a magnifying glass.

These, with proper care, will be of sufficient size at the end of the second year to use as small house plants. Damping off (which see) is a serious problem with these young plants, and must be rigidly guarded against by controlling the water and spraying occasionally with a fungicide.

Dividing ferns can be done any time of the year but usually is best done in the spring at repotting time just before growth starts. The plant is taken up, the soil shaken off the roots and gently pulled apart so that rhizomes, each with several fronds and roots, are separated one from the other.

The Bulblet Bladder-fern (*Cystopteris bulbifera*) is an example of a fern that forms small bulblets on the fronds, about the size of garden peas. When mature, these can be sown and they will start to grow in a few months, but it will take nearly 2 years of growth before these will look like the parent plant.

Also a few ferns have small leaf buds on the edge or upper surface of their fronds which become small plants while still attached to the parent. These also can be removed when they have 3–4 leaves, placed on the surface of vermiculite that is kept moist, then, when roots have formed, they can be planted in soil. The Water Fern (*Ceraplopteris deltoidea*) is an example of this, but since it can spend all its life on the surface of water, the small new plants do not have to be planted in soil, but merely separated from the parent leaf and left floating on the water surface by themselves as new individuals.

Insect Pests

Greenhouse ferns, especially the Boston Fern, are frequently infested with the fern scale, the hemispherical scale or the soft brown scale. The first is white and pear-shaped and usually on the underside of the leaves. The others are brown and turtle-shaped and on stems or leaves. Regular spraying with insecticide #15 is advised. Ferns are sensitive to injury by several sprays and directions for use should be followed carefully.

Some of the more popular ornamental ferns for garden and home are listed here (for more detailed descriptions and other species refer to the generic headings in the following list and ALSOPHILA, BLECHNUM, CHEILANTHES, DAVALLIA, LYGODIUM, NOTHOLAENA, OPHIOGLOSSUM, PELLAEA).

Some Native American Ferns for Gardens

Adiantum pedatum 12″–26″ Zone 3 Common Maidenhair Fern
Eastern North America; must be grown in moist soil.

Asplenium platyneuron 6″–20″ Zone 4 Ebony Spleenwort
Fronds 1–2 in. wide; eastern United States; dry limestone soils, foliage evergreen.

Asplenium trichomanes 6″ Zone 3 Maidenhair Spleenwort
Canada, Alaska and eastern U.S.; limestone soil; foliage evergreen.

Athyrium filix-femina 18″–36″ Zone 3 Lady Fern
Fronds 15 in. wide; central and northeastern North America; very easily grown.

Athyrium pycnocarpum 30″–48″ Zone 3 Glade Fern
Fronds 6 in. wide; eastern North America; limestone soil.

Botrychium virginianum 6″–30″ Zone 3 Rattlesnake Fern
North America; neutral or slightly acid soil.

Camptosorus rhizophyllus 4″–12″ Zone 3 Walking Fern
Eastern North America; roots at tips of fronds; foliage evergreen.

Cystopteris bulbifera 24″–36″ Zone 3 Bulblet Bladder Fern
Fronds 3–4 in. wide; eastern North America; reproduces by small bulblike bodies on fronds.

Cystopteris fragilis 10″ Zone 3 Fragile Bladder Fern
Fronds 3 in. wide; central and northern North America; neutral to slightly acid soil.

Dennstaedtia punctilobula 20″–30″ Zone 3 Hay-scented Fern
Fronds 11 in. wide; eastern North America.

Dryopteris austriaca intermedia 30″ Zone 3 Intermediate Shield-fern
Fronds 10 in. wide; North America; foliage sometimes evergreen.

Dryopteris cristata 30″ Zone 3 Crested Shield Fern
Eastern and central North America; dark green leathery foliage.

Dryopteris filix-mas cristata 36″ Zone 3 English Crested Male-fern
Fronds 9 in. wide; originated in England.

Dryopteris goldiana 48″–60″ Zone 3 Goldie's Fern
Fronds 14 in. wide; north central and northeastern North America, needs cool shade.

Dryopteris marginalis 15″–20″ Zone 3 Marginal Shield-fern
Fronds high, 5–8 in. wide; eastern North America; does well in shade with plenty of moisture.

Matteuccia struthiopteris pensylvanica 5′ Zone 2 Ostrich Fern
Central and northern North America; suitable for marshy areas.

Onoclea sensibilis 12″–30″ **Zone 3 Sensitive Fern**
North America; marshy soils, grows in full sun.

Osmunda cinnamomea 2′–5′ **Zone 3 Cinnamon Fern**
North America; does well in several soils.

Osmunda claytoniana to 5′ **Zone 3 Interrupted Fern**
North America; grown in moist to wet acid soils, mostly in shade.

Polypodium vulgare 10″ **Zone 3 Common Polypody**
Fronds 2 in. wide; North America; foliage evergreen, does well in rocky soils.

Polystichum acrostichoides 3′ **Zone 3 Christmas Fern**
Fronds 5 in. wide, eastern United States; feathery, evergreen foliage.

Thelypteris noveboracensis 1′–2′ **Zone 2 New York Fern**
Eastern United States; rapidly spreading, withstands sun.

Woodsia ilvensis 3″–6″ **Zone 3 Rusty Woodsia**
Northeastern North America; good rock garden plant.

Woodwardia areolata 2′ **Zone 4 Narrow-leaved Chain Fern**
Coastal eastern North America; grows easily and spreads in swampy acid soil.

Woodwardia virginica 3′–4′ **Zone 4 Virginia Chain Fern**
Eastern Coastal Plain North America; vigorous spreader in swampy land.

Tender Ferns for Use Indoors

Adiantum capillus-veneris 2″–12″ **Zone 9 Southern Maidenhair Fern**
Subtropical areas; needs a cool, shaded situation.

Adiantum hispidulum 6″–12″ **Zone 10 Rosy Maidenhair Fern**
Tropics of eastern hemisphere; shaded situation, grows quickly.

Aglaomorpha meyenianum 1′–2′ **Zone 10 Bear's-paw Fern**
Fronds 6 in. wide; Philippine Islands; requires moist atmosphere.

Asplenium bulbiferum 2′ **Zone 10 Mother Fern**
New Zealand, Australia, Malaysia; can be reproduced by vegetative buds.

Asplenium nidus 1′ **Zone 10 Bird's-nest Fern**
Tropics of eastern hemisphere; foliage leathery, glossy; needs warmth.

Cyrtomium falcatum 1′–2′ **Zone 10 Japanese-Holly Fern**
Tropics of eastern hemisphere; foliage shiny, dark green, leathery; prefers a cool temperature and moist soil.

Davallia canariensis 1½′ **Zone 10 Rabbit's-foot Fern**
Spain, Canary Islands; rhizome creeps over soil and outside of pot.

Humata tyermannii 6″–9″ **Zone 10 Bear's-foot Fern**
India, southern China; conspicuous white-scaled rhizome.

Nephrolepis exaltata 2′–6′ **Zone 10 Sword Fern**
Florida, Bahamas, Mexico; exceptionally long fronds if grown well.

Nephrolepis exaltata elegantissima 2′–6′ **Zone 10 Double-feather Sword Fern**
Several good vars., easily grown with excellent foliage; propagated by starting pieces of rhizome in a moist medium.

Platycerium vassei 1′ **Zone 10 Staghorn Fern**
Mozambique; picturesque and unique; needs humid atmosphere.

Polypodium aureum 3′ **Zone 10 Golden Polypody**
Fronds 10 in. wide; tropical Florida, West Indies; fruiting bodies large and golden.

Polystichum tsus-simense 1′ **Zone 10 Tsus-sima Holly Fern**
Fronds 5 in. wide; Japan and China; requires cool shade, excellent house plant.

Pteris cretica vars. 6″–20″ **Zone 10 Stove Ferns**
Mediterranean Region; many excellent vars.; fine house plant.

FEROCACTUS (FERO-cac-tus)
  setispinus (*Hamatocactus setispinus*) 6″ **Zone 10 Strawberry Cactus**
A globose cactus with 13 thick ribs spirally arranged. The color is a gray-green with tufts of white wool. Flowers are yellow 2–3 in. long with a red throat. Fruit is red, ⅓ in. across. There are 12–16 radial spines white or brownish and up to 2 in. long. Native to southern Tex. and N.Mex. For culture see CACTI and SUCCULENTS. Often used as a house plant.

FERTILE. Capable of producing fruit and seeds; also said of pollen-bearing anthers; also used in describing a soil with plenty of nutrients in it to promote good growth.

FERTILIZATION. Effect of pollen deposited on a stigmatic surface resulting in conversion of flower into fruit and of ovule into seed; the union of egg and sperm.

FERTILIZER, AMOUNTS TO APPLY. Many gardeners do not wish to take the time to study soil potentials or have a soil analysis made, or to cover crop or add compost. The amount of fertilizer to apply depends on 3 important things: The kind and age of the plants in question, the kind of soil, and the kind of fertilizer to be used. The gardener will very definitely have to be on his own in interpreting the following recommendations. One would not expect to apply the same amount of fertilizer to a bed of recently planted annual seedlings as one would apply to a well-established perennial border. Nor would one apply as much sodium nitrate as one would a complete fertilizer or superphosphate.

In general then, a complete fertilizer (5-10-5) might be applied at the following rates to the plants suggested, but this does overlook the specific requirements of specific plants which frequently should be taken into consideration also. For more specific recommendations see Aldrich, G. A., *et al.* "The Care and Feeding of Garden Plants," American Society for Horticultural Science and the National Fertilizer Association, 1954.

Amounts of a 5-10-5 fertilizer suggested for plants in a normal, loamy soil:

Bulbs	1–3 lbs. per 100 sq. ft.
House plants	1 tsp. to a 5 in. pot; or 1 oz. in 1 gal. of water, 1 cupful of this solution per plant, per month
Vegetables	3–5 lbs. per 100 sq. ft.
Flower borders	3–5 lbs. per 100 sq. ft.
Bush fruits	Brambles 12 oz. per plant
Blueberries	4–8 oz. per plant
Grapes	4–6 oz. per plant
Fruit trees	2–4 lbs. per in. dia. of trunk, breast high
Deciduous orna-mental trees	2–4 lbs. per in. dia. of trunk, breast high
Evergreen trees	2 lbs. per in. dia of trunk, breast high
Deciduous shrubs	3–6 lbs. per 100 sq. ft.
Evergreen shrubs (exclusive of ericaceous plants)	3–6 lbs. per 100 sq. ft.

In applying the fertilizer, the simplest method is to apply it broadcast to the soil and water it in. However, this is modified sometimes in the vegetable garden when a lesser amount is used than that recommended above, but is applied in bands on either side of the growing vegetables. Also, for applying large amounts to ornamental trees growing in lawns, the punch-hole system is used. In this, holes are made in the soil with a crow bar about 8–10 in. deep, 2 ft. apart within an area between 2 circles on the ground, the first on a radius of about 2 ft. from the trunk, the second under the limits of the extended branches. Then about 1½–6 oz. of fertilizer is poured in each hole, soil filled in on top and the sod can be replaced. The whole area is watered heavily.

It always is good procedure to water the fertilizer in after it is applied. Likewise, the foliage of the plants should be dry when the application is made so that if the fertilizer is broadcast, none will stick to the leaves and cause burning.

Soil Moisture

The moisture content of the soil is extremely important, for without water plants would not grow. They need not only the water as such, but the various chemical salts that it contains in solution. Soils, in general, contain 35–65% solid material, the rest of this is pore space between the soil particles. In a normally good soil, half this pore space is filled with water.

Water moves up and down in the soil, down by drainage of surplus water and up by capillary attraction. Each soil particle is covered with a minute film of water and together these afford a pathway for water to travel from subsoil levels to the surface, for at the surface with evaporation there is the necessary force to keep water continually coming to the surface. This attraction continues, goes on even when the surface freezes. Lift up a stone on the solid surface in early winter and there will be ice crystals underneath it. These attract more moisture to the surface by capillary attraction, and this in turn freezes. This freezing force is what "pushes" stones out of the ground in the winter, heaves small, shallow-rooted plants out of the ground, topples low walls that have not been set properly below the frost line and causes heaving and breaking of pavements without the proper foundation.

Tillage of the surface soil naturally reduces or eliminates the weeds which are a drain on soil moisture and nutrients. It also creates a dust mulch which breaks up this capillary trend to evaporate from the soil and hence conserves the soil moisture. Otherwise, with a hard crust of soil on the surface, evaporation and consequent loss of soil moisture continues, which in times of drought can have serious effects on the plants.

Hence, many operations are designed to conserve the soil moisture and prevent its continual evaporation from the soil surface, conserving it in the soil for the use of plants. Thus, the addition of humus material to the soil aids by increasing the soil's ability to absorb more moisture, the use of mulches reduces weed growth (which indirectly is responsible for great soil-water loss) and at the same time reduces soil evaporation.

Other operations are designed to get more water into the soil and prevent runoff from heavy rains. Keeping the surface cultivated allows rain water to seep in faster; making curved rows in hilly areas following the contours of the land forces excess rain water to flow slowly over a special pattern and hence gives it more time to sink into the soil. Sometimes grass strips are used in hilly areas to prevent a runoff that is too fast. Terraces are used in many areas. For additional information see SOILS, WATERING.

FERULA (FER-yew-la)

communis 12′ **Zone** 7 **Common Giant Fennel** This is a handsome perennial grown for its foliage, the leaves being 2–3 times compound and the leaflets very fine in texture. The small yellow flowers are borne in long-stalked compound umbels in the spring. Easily grown and propagated by division or seeds sown in the spring where the plants are to grow. Native to southern Europe.

FESCUE. See FESTUCA.

FESTUCA (fes-TEW-ka). See also GRASS, LAWNS.

elatior 5′ **Zone** 4 **Meadow Fescue** A native European grass, naturalized in meadows in North America with leaves a foot long and ⅓ in. wide; the flat-fruiting panicles are 1 ft. long. Seeds are often sold in mixtures for planting meadows.

ovina 2′ **Zone** 4 **Sheep's Fescue** This is a wiry, tufted grass native of Europe and Asia and naturalized in North America. It sometimes seeds into northern lawns, and is used in pasture grasses for poor soils. The variety **glauca** or Blue Fescue is a fine tufted ornamental, being used from coast to coast in gardens, not as a lawn grass but as a low tufted plant of light blue foliage. Usually planted about 1 ft. apart, these tufts or clumps will not grow together but each will remain a fountainlike tuft of blue

wiry grass. Easily propagated by division. When fruiting heads are not on the plant, it is only about 10 in. tall.

rubra = Red Fescue. See GRASS, LAWNS.

rubra commutata = Chewings Fescue. See GRASS, LAWNS.

FETERITA = *Sorghum vulgare caudatum*

FETTERBUSH = *Leucothoe racemosa*

FEVERFEW = *Chrysanthemum parthenium*

FEVERFEW, AMERICAN = *Parthenium integrifolium*

FIBER-LILY. See PHORMIUM.

FICUS (FIK-us). A group of tropical evergreen or deciduous woody trees, shrubs and vines, with alternate leaves, belonging to the Mulberry Family. All have a milky sap which oozes out of the stem when it is injured. Several species are described below, the best known being the Rubber Plant, (*F. elastica*), the Fig (*F. carica*), the Creeping Fig (*F. pumila* formerly *F. repens*) and the tropical Banyan Tree (*F. benghalensis*). The Rubber Plant and some of the trees are propagated by air layers, and some of the smaller types by division.

altissima 50′ **Zone** 10 **Lofty Fig** A Javanese tree also native to India with an enormous crown; evergreen with a few aerial roots; leaves thick and leathery, broadly oval and with ivory-colored veins. Fruits are orange-colored and attractive, about ¾ in. in dia.

aspera (*parcellii*) 12′ **Zone** 10 **Mosaic Fig** This shrub is one of the best of the variegated-leaved figs, native to the islands of the South Pacific with large, oblong, pointed leaves, 8 in.

Festuca ovina 'glauca': A beautiful ornamental grass growing in clumps and used in gardens from coast to coast. (*Photo by Arnold Arboretum, Jamaica Plain, Mass.*)

long, thin, light green but variegated with creamy white. The red fruits are most ornamental.

benghalensis   100′   Zone 10   Banyan
A large evergreen tree, native to India, but widely planted about the Tropics of the world because of its unique habit of growth. A single tree can cover large areas by sending down growths from the branches which take root and grow into trunks which themselves produce branches growing and spreading in a similar manner. The leaves are 4–8 in. long, ovate or rounded, and the red fruits are produced in pairs, each rounded and about ½ in. in dia. Only planted along the coast in the warmest parts of Fla. and Calif.

benjamina   50′   Zone 10   Benjamin Fig, Java Fig
A tree with spreading to drooping branches, oval leathery leaves 2–4 in. long. Fruit is red, rounded, about ½ in. in dia. Native to Indo-Malaya. Used as a clean street tree but only in areas without frost.

carica   12′–30′   Zone 6   Fig
A coarse-leaved, shrubby plant native to western Asia, cultivated for centuries for the fleshy edible "fruits" which are actually receptacles, inside which are true fruits. The large 3- to 5-lobed evergreen or deciduous leaves are coarse in texture. For culture, insect and disease pests see FIG. **'Kodata'** and **'Mission'** are good varieties.

India Rubber-plant—*Ficus elastica*

elastica   10′   Zone 10   India Rubber-plant

The common household rubber-plant, known to everyone, is grown as a large-leaved pot plant in all parts of the U.S. This is native to the damp forests of tropical Asia and can be grown out-of-doors only in the warmest parts of the country. The leathery, evergreen leaves are 4–12 in. long and are alternate. The fruit is yellowish, ½ in. long. The parallel veins on the leaves run almost at right angles to the midrib. This usually grows with one main stalk and after some time becomes tall and unsightly. Then it is a simple matter to injure or cut the stem partially a foot or so from the top; tie a handful of moist sphagnum moss about the cut, then tie about this some polyethylene film. This should be done carefully and tightly so that no water vapor will escape. New roots will then be produced and when they permeate the ball of sphagnum, the whole piece may be cut off and potted up as a new plant.

Insect Pests

The common household Rubber-plant becomes infested with the Florida red scale (see ORANGE), the soft brown scale and the dictyospermum scale which cause weak growth and disfigure the leaves. Mealy bugs may also become abundant and secrete honeydew. All are controlled by regular spraying with insecticide #15.

lyrata   40′   Zone 10   Fiddleleaf Fig
A tree with large fiddle-shaped leaves, 10–15 in. long, fruit 2 in. wide. Native to South Africa. Often grown as a greenhouse foliage plant.

macrophylla   75′   Zone 10   Moreton Bay Fig
A large, coarse-leaved evergreen tree native to Australia with leaves up to 10 in. long and 4 in. wide, handsome and glossy. The tree is twice as wide as it is tall with a dense, rounded head. This requires plenty of room in which to grow, otherwise it should not be planted. One specimen in Santa Barbara, Calif., had a branch spread of 145 ft.

pandurata = *F. lyrata*

pseudopalma   20′   Zone 10   False Palm
Native to the Philippines, with thin, leathery, palmlike leaves especially in clusters near the top. A single unbranched stem may have 2–3 ft. of the end covered with glossy leaves, each 2 ft. long and 4 in. wide.

pumila   clinging vine   Zone 9   Creeping Fig
Widely used on garden walls in the South and on inside greenhouse and conservatory walls in the North, this closely clinging evergreen vine produces small leaves 1–4 in. long. It is native to China, Japan and Australia. The young stems form a mat on the walls, often grafting themselves where they cross, and clinging by means of small but tenacious rootlets. As the

plant grows older, it produces inedible, puffy figs. If the erect branches that grow out from the younger growth are kept pruned, this will help to keep the plant in a young and vigorous condition. The leaves are only about 1 in. long on the younger growth and are always held flat against the wall or support, making an excellent cover.

religiosa   **75′**   **Zone 10**   **Botree Fig** Supposedly this fig tree was brought to Europe from India in 288 B.C. It is revered by Hindus and Buddhists as the Sacred Bo Tree, because it was under one of these that Gautama meditated 49 days and then emerged as the Buddha. It has smooth, gray bark, heart-shaped leaves on long petioles. They are heavily vined with pink or ivory.

repens = *F. pumila*

retusa   **75′**   **Zone 10**   **India-laurel Fig** A large evergreen tree from tropical Asia, used in the warmer parts of Fla. as an ornamental tree. The leaves are 2–4 in. long and a few aerial roots are produced. Fruits are a yellowish red, about ¼ in. long.

FIDDLEHEAD. A common term used for the young unfolding fronds of some kinds of ferns.

FIG. Also see **FICUS.** The Common Fig (*Ficus carica*) is a coarse-leaved deciduous shrubby plant, 12–30 ft. tall, native to western Asia, which is grown commercially in Tex. and Calif. for its fruits and is grown in gardens more as an oddity than as an ornamental. Its coarse, large leaves do give shade. The leaves are deeply 3- to 5-lobed and the fruits are large, purplish and of course edible. This species can be grown in the open as far north as Long Island if in the winter the branches are laid on the ground and soil is thrown over them. In Boston, figs grown in tubs are merely moved inside over winter and many bear fruits.

Quite a few figs are grown in Va. and other places in the mid-South, where they are frequently situated in warm corners of the garden against walls or foundations, or are espaliered against the garden walls.

Figs grown to supply the home gardener with fruit will be found in all the Gulf states and up the eastern seaboard to Va.

The "fruit" of the Fig as we know it is actually a receptacle, inside which are numerous true fruits we commonly think of as "seeds." This peculiar arrangement presents difficult pollinizing problems for some varieties since the receptacles have a large number of minute flowers inside. In some varieties these must be pollinized or the receptacle will not remain attached to the plant until maturity. In other varieties the "fruit" is enlarged if the flowers are not pollinized. It has been determined that a small Asiatic wasp (*Blastophaga psenes*) aids

materially in the pollinating process. Another kind of fig called a Caprifig bears a large number of pollen-bearing flowers. This insect lays eggs inside the receptacle of the Caprifig by entering a small hole at the tip of the receptacle. These eggs hatch and mature insects emerge at a time when all the Caprifig flowers are covered with pollen. Hence they emerge from the Caprifig covered with pollen and fly to the receptacles of the regular Fig varieties, enter them through the tiny hole at the end and, in the course of their movements, pollinize the flowers inside the receptacle. This process is called caprification, or fruit producing.

The Caprifig trees are not grown at the same place as the regular fig trees but at some place distant. At the time the young insects are just about to emerge from the caprifigs, the "fruits" are picked and put in small baskets, then transported and hung up in the regular fig-producing trees. The emerging wasps do the rest. Most caprifigs are not edible and are grown solely to aid in this pollinizing process.

Flowers of edible figs produce no pollen, the reason why caprification becomes so important in commercial fig producing.

Propagation is mostly by cuttings made of 2- or 3-year-old shoots after the leaves have fallen. Grafting may be practiced when it is desired to "make over" an established tree to another variety. The limbs are sawed off, clefts made in the wood with a heavy grafting tool and wedge-shaped scions inserted, about 2 to each stub. Figs are also layered and root readily from air layers, which see.

Insect Pests

Many scale insects attack Fig and the most important is the Mediterranean fig scale which infests both leaves, new branches and fruit. Infested leaves are discolored and weakened and the fruit is downgraded either for drying or as fresh fruit. Spraying with insecticide #44 with or without insecticide #15 in late winter and with insecticide #15 when crawlers hatch in April is suggested. The fig rust mite, a microscopic 4-legged mite which causes green fruits to sour and decay, and other scale insects are controlled by the above methods. Red spider mite which attacks most citrus and other subtropical trees and shrubs is a very serious pest of figs in the dry areas. Badly infested trees are often heavily webbed. Spraying with insecticide #34, #36 or other miticides is advised.

Diseases

Rust, leaf spot and anthracnose infect the leaves in variable degrees and if necessary are controlled by spraying with fungicide #D or #G. Souring, black smut and internal rot (endosepsis) are often caused by the caprifying insect (*Blastophaga* sp.) especially on those varieties requiring caprification in order to set fruit. See LOCAL AUTHORITIES for latest recommendations. Botrytis dieback of twigs is checked by frequent sprays with fungicide #G. Nursery trees should be free of nematodes and crown gall and not planted where these diseases have been present.

Pruning is done to properly space the branches and force the tree to grow with one main trunk. Some varieties tend to grow with dense branches and these should not be allowed to develop to such an extent as to exclude light and air.

Overfertilization is dangerous for it induces much vegetative growth, with an accompanying decrease in fruit production. Well-rotted manure, used as a mulch, is excellent, but too much high nitrogenous fertilizer should be avoided.

Varieties

'Calimyrna' or 'Lob Injur' is a variety of the Smyrna Fig much grown in Calif. for drying. It needs caprification to produce a crop;

'Adriatic'—hardier and seems to do well in the eastern U.S. but will produce fruits without caprification;

'Brown Turkey'—hardier and seems to do well in the eastern U.S. but will produce fruits without caprification;

'Brunswick'—sometimes called 'Magnolia' in Tex., is also a good variety for the eastern U.S. This is the 'Brown Turkey' of Calif.;

'Celeste'—good for the southeastern U.S. and will produce fruits without caprification;

'Dottato'—grown in Calif. for eating fresh and for drying; will produce some fruits without caprification. Sometimes called 'Kadota' of southern Calif. It is an important canning fig;

'Mission'—with black fruits good for eating fresh and for drying;

'Ronde Noire'—grows well in cool coastal Calif. but does not do well in the hot inland valleys.

FIG FAMILY = Moraceae

FIGWORT. See SCROPHYLARIA.

FIGWORT, SNAPDRAGON OR FOXGLOVE FAMILY = Scrophulariaceae

FILAMENT. Stalk of the anther

FILBERT. See CORYLUS, HAZELNUT and FILBERT.

FILIPENDULA (fil-i-PEN-dew-la). These are small perennial herbs and one of them, *F. vulgaris* (formerly *F. hexapetala*), is of considerable value in the perennial garden. These belong to the Rose Family, bear small flowers somewhat like those of spireas, in the summer, some white, some pink. They are easily propagated by seed and division of the plant clump.

camtschatica   10′   Zone 3   Kamchatka Meadowsweet
With ovate compound leaves but the terminal leaflet is 3–5 lobed and the lateral leaflets are frequently not present. Flowers white. Native to Manchuria and Kamchatka. Too tall to be of much garden value.

hexapetala = *F. vulgaris*

multijuga   6″   Zone 6
A very small plant with small pink flowers during the late summer. Native to southern Japan. A fine garden plant.

palmata   3′   Zone 2   Siberian Meadowsweet
With small flowers in large umbels, pale pink, which gradually fade white during summer, and rather large 7–9-lobed terminal leaflets and large heart-shaped stipules. Native to Siberia and Kamchatka. There is supposed to be a dwarf var. 'Nana' which, if available, would certainly have garden merit.

purpurea   4′   Zone 6   Japanese Meadowsweet
With clusters of small deep pink flowers borne on red stems during late summer. The terminal leaflets are 5–7 lobed and lateral leaflets are often missing. Native to Japan. The var. 'Elegans' has pure white flowers with bright red stamens.

rubra   8′   Zones 2–3   Queen-of-the-Prairie
The terminal leaflet of this species is 7–9 parted and the lateral leaflets are lobed. Flowers are flushed pink with conspicuous stamens and very attractive. Native from Pa. to Ga. and Ky.

ulmaria   6′   Zones 2–3   Queen-of-the-Meadow
This has large 3–5-lobed terminal leaflets with the lateral leaflets toothed and white tomentose beneath. Flowers are white. This does best in fairly moist soils, is native to Europe but has become naturalized in the eastern U.S. The plant tops of this have been used in making a greenish-yellow dye.

vulgaris 'Flore-pleno' (*F. hexapetala*)   1′–3′
Zone 3   Double Dropwort
This perennial herb with tuberous rootstock is a much better ornamental than the species because it has double white flowers about $\frac{3}{4}$ in. across, in loose panicles during June and July. It is native to Europe and Siberia. The finely cut, pinnately lobed, alternate leaves are 6–20 in. long, borne in a rosette. It does best in full sun. The species is propagated by seeds sown in fall or spring but this double-flowered variety is best propagated by division. The foliage is sometimes used in medicines for colds or to flavor soups. The root contains tannic acid used in tanning. An oil is sometimes made from the flowers similar to that of Wintergreen.

FIMBRIATE. Fringed.

FINOCCHIO = *Foeniculum vulgare dulce*

FIR. See ABIES.

FIR FAMILY = Pinaceae

FIREBLIGHT. A bacterial disease of many plants especially those of the Rose Family. Apple and pear are very susceptible. New shoots and branches suddenly develop black leaves and die and there are distinct cankers of dead bark on the branches. The bacteria are spread by insects. Standard fungicides are not effective although the new antibiotics have been promising when applied near the blooming period. Cutting and burning the infected branches when first observed as well as any bark cankers during spring pruning is helpful. Pruning tools should be disinfected with corrosive sublimate to prevent spread of the disease.

FIREBUSH, CHILEAN = *Embothrium coccineum*

FIRE-RESISTANT PLANTS. Serious brush fires in southern Calif. have recently created a great interest in "fire-resistant plants," that is, those which will not burn suddenly and easily when they are ignited in a brush fire. Recent experimental work in southern Calif. has brought out the fact that there are such plants which, if planted in belts or borders around the house, along the highway or around picnic areas, will act as firebreaks, at least sufficiently to curtail the possibility of sudden brush fires quickly reaching the building which is to be protected. Most plants will burn if they are subjected to temperatures high enough and for a sufficient length of time.

The Greasewood (*Adenostoma fasiculatum*) and Scrub Oak (*Quercus dumosa*), of southern Calif., when dry as they usually are, burn with almost explosive suddenness as soon as they are ignited and it is in areas where these plants cover much of the ground that brush fires have proved most disastrous.

Since there is little rainfall at certain seasons in the areas under study, plants in the "fire-resistant" class should be drought-resistant and also should require little care once established. They should also be able to compete with Greasewood and Scrub Oak, and reseed themselves.

The Brush Fire Safety Committee of Los Angeles, Calif. has suggested the following plants to be considered for planting because of their fire resistant qualities. (Listing below.)

It has been suggested that these plants be planted in strips or borders wide enough to act as firebreaks. They can be considered as ground covers hence they keep the soil from eroding but make it look well also. All those mentioned are drought-resistant, some more so than others. It is these plants which seem to resist igniting when subjected to high temperatures which normally ignite other kinds quickly.

Brush fires can be prevented and certainly can be diverted from causing great damage by the proper use of plants such as these, planted in the right places. In fact, fire-insurance rates for certain buildings have been reduced in instances where such plantings have been made.

FIRETHORN. See PYRACANTHA.

FIREWHEEL-TREE, TALL = *Stenocarpus sinuatus*

FIRMIANA (firm-i-AY-na)

simplex 40′ Zone 9 Chinese Parasol-tree
An interesting, fast-growing tree for the warmer parts of Fla. and Calif., this is native to China and Japan and has alternate deciduous leaves somewhat shaped like those of a sycamore but they can be 12 in. across. The fruits are borne at the edges of peculiar, leaflike open pods about 5 in. long. The flowers are small and greenish white, usually in branched clusters. The bark is green and it can grow in almost any soil.

FISH MEAL. An organic fertilizer made up of rejected fish containing 8–10% nitrogen; 4.5–9% phosphoric acid; 2–4% potash. This leaves an alkaline soil reaction. See SOILS.

	HEIGHT	ZONE	
Achillea tomentosa	16″	2–3	Woolly Yarrow
Atriplex semibaccata	1′–1½′	8	Creeping Saltbush
Baccharis pilularis 'Dwarf'	1′–1½′	7	Dwarf Coyotebush
Cistus landaniferus	4′–6′	7	Gum Rockrose
C. villosus	3′–5′	8	Purple Rockrose
Eriodictyon trichocalyx	2′–3′	8	Yerba Santa
Hedera sp.	1′	5–7	English Ivy and others
Helianthemum nummularium	1′	5–6	Sunrose
Lotus bertholettii	1′	10	Parrot-beak
Mesembryanthemum sp.	4″–8″	10	Iceplant
Psoralea bitumimosa	1½′	9	Arabian Scurf-pea
Rosmarinus officinalis prostrata	1½′	6	Creeping Rosemary
Santolina virens	1½′	7	Green Lavender-cotton

FITTONIA (fit-O-nia)

verschaffeltii   creeping   Zone 9   Fittonia
A low, creeping herb, native to South America, sometimes used as part of the terrarium indoors. The opposite oval leaves, 3–4 in. long, have red veins. The small yellow flowers are not showy. The var. **argyroneura** has leaves with white veins. They need a warm (60°–75° F.), moist atmosphere in which to grow and are easily propagated by cuttings.

FITZROYA (fits-ROY-a)

cupressioides   45′   Zone 7   Patagonian
Fitzroya
Evergreen tree with needles (leaves) in alternating whorls of 3 about ⅛ of an inch long; cones about ¼ in. wide. Native to Chile and Patagonia. Not a very good ornamental because it is slow growing and inclined to be straggly.

FIVELEAF-ARALIA = *Acanthopanax sieboldianus*

FLACCID. Not rigid; lax and weak.

FLACOURTIA (flay-KORT-ia)

indica   25′   Zone 10   Governor's-plum,
Ramontchi
This is used in the Tropics both for its fruit and as a hedge plant, for it is a densely rounded plant from southern Asia, sparsely thorny; with deep green glabrous leaves 3 in. long. The flowers are small and yellowish; the pulpy, cherrylike, purplish fruits are edible.

FLACOURTIACEAE = The   Indian   Plum
Family

FLAG. See IRIS.

FLAMBEAU-TREE, BELL = *Spathodea campanulata*

FLAME-OF-THE-FOREST = *Butea frondosa*

FLAME-OF-THE-WOODS = *Ixora coccinea*

FLAMEPEA, HEARTLEAF = *Chorizema cordatum*

FLAME-TREE = *Delonix regia*

FLAME-TREE, CHINESE = *Koelreuteria elegans*

FLANNEL-BUSH = *Fremontia californica*

FLATSEDGE, UMBRELLA = *Cyperus alternifolius*

FLAX. See LINUM.

FLAX FAMILY = Linaceae

FLEABANE. See ERIGERON, COMPOSITUS.

FLEECE-FLOWER. See POLYGONUM.

FLEECEVINE, SILVER = *Polygonum aubertii*

FLOATING-HEART = *Nymphoides peltatum*

FLOCCOSE. Clothed with tufts of soft hair or wool.

FLORAL AXIS. The part of the peduncle or scape to which a solitary flower or a cluster of florets is attached.

FLORETS. Small individual flowers of compact heads or spikes.

FLORICULTURE. A division of horticulture usually taken to mean the study of production methods for the cut-flower trade, as well as the means by which such products are marketed and sold. A distinction has arisen between Floriculture and Ornamental Horticulture, the latter having to do more with woody plants and planting than cut flowers grown in the greenhouse.

FLORIST. One who deals in flowers, cut flowers as well as potted plants, and who arranges them in various ways to meet the public demand, or who grows them commercially.

FLOSS-SILK TREE = *Chorisia speciosa*

FLOWER. A true flower consists of several parts. Outside (or below the showy parts) are the sepals (together called the calyx) and it is these which cover the flower bud, the parts separating as the flower opens. The colored parts are the petals (together called the corolla). Usually in the centre is the female organ, the sticky stigma on which pollen is received, the tubelike style and the swelled portion at the base of the ovary where the seeds are formed. Also in the center are the stamens or male organs, usually long, threadlike filaments at the ends of which are the anthers or pollen-producing

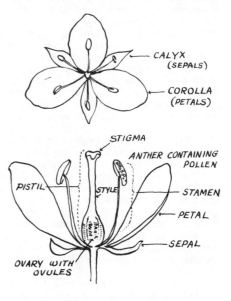

Flower parts

organs. Flowers differ (according to families, genera and species) regarding the number and arrangement and color of these parts but in general all are usually present in one form or another.

FLOWER ARRANGEMENT. An important purpose of flower arranging is to make possible the enjoyment of nature within the home in the most artistic and satisfying manner. Arrangements in the home have become essential in our modern everyday living and are now being used in public buildings as well as in the home.

The size of the room in which the flower arrangements are placed is one of the most important factors to consider. A living room in the average-sized home in the suburbs might provide a place for 3 or 4 arrangements. The largest arrangement might be placed on a large table or piano. On the mantle could be either 1 low arrangement placed beneath a picture or painting, or a balanced pair of arrangements on either side. A small arrangement on a coffee table in front of the sofa, scaled down to size and used to repeat or complement the larger design, might be another possibility. In a large room still another arrangement could be included, small in scale again, on a table or desk. Arrangements should be planned for a specific setting against a specific background and this setting determines the choice of material, of container and design.

Flower arrangement is the art of organizing the selected elements and principles of design to attain Beauty, Simplicity, Expression and Harmony. The principles of design are balance, scale and proportion, contrast, rhythm and dominance. With these principles in mind the arranger uses space, lines, forms, colors, pattern, and textures to create orderly beauty.

1. Balance. Equal distribution of actual or visual weight on either side of a central axis. Without balance, the finished arrangement lacks stability. Symmetrical balance is attained by having both sides of the composition similar. Asymmetrical balance results when unequal elements are used on either side of a central axis and at different distances from the center, yet appear balanced on each side of the axis.

2. Scale and Proportion. Scale is the size relationship of the individual flowers to each other, to their container and to the space that the design is to occupy in the room. Proportion is the size relationship of plant material to the container and the whole to the space it is to occupy. A simple guide would be to use plant material at least $1\frac{1}{2}$ times the height or width of the container.

3. Rhythm, Contrast, Dominance. Rhythm is the smooth flow of material and color which carries the eye easily through the design.

Flower Arrangement—Symmetrical

Flower Arrangement—Asymmetrical

Rhythm makes the design seem alive! Contrast gives variety and interest. One element must dominate—more of one line, form or direction; more of one hue or value, unequal lengths of line, unequal sizes. Emphasize one color, form. texture and size.

Cones and fruits are frequently used in long-lasting arrangements. (*Photo by Arnold Arboretum, Jamaica Plain, Mass.*)

Flower arrangements should be practical as well as beautiful. One should learn how to use available flowers when they are in bloom. One should anticipate the need for certain woody plants in flower arrangements about the home, then obtain them and plant them in the garden. Evergreens like Drooping Leucothoe, Japanese Andromeda, English Ivy and the Japanese Umbrella-pine are a few which are always good in arrangements at almost any time of year.

Color

The color of the plant material should blend well and be harmonious with the background and furnishings in the room. When there is a great variety of color in the room a simple all-green or all-white arrangement is often the best solution to an otherwise difficult color problem.

A good color design may consist of only one color or hue in the room, known as a monochromatic arrangement, which may have both light and dark values of the chosen color. The most dramatic is a complementary harmony achieved by combining direct opposites of the color wheel, like green and red. Triads call for 3 colors equidistant on the color wheel, for example, orange, green and violet. A most restful triad would be to use tints and tones of green and violet with perhaps a touch of bright orange as an accent.

Massed color has dramatic impact. The amounts of color used must be chosen to create color balance, color dominance, color contrast, rhythm, proportion or scale. These principles must be applied to the handling of color in the same way as they apply to the handling of the design itself.

Color Wheel

The 3 primary or key colors are Red, Yellow, Blue, and when mixed together in average pigments will form 3 secondary colors—orange, green, and violet.

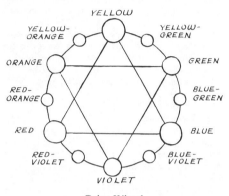

Color Wheel

Mechanics

The mechanics of holding flowers and branches of foliage in place is vital. A needle-point holder, usually a lead base with sharp brass pins, fastened to the container with floral clay or melted paraffin is used effectively. However, the container and needlepoint holder must be thoroughly dry when this is done. In the case of a very tall container a false bottom may be made by filling the bottom with sand, sealing the sand with a layer of melted paraffin, on the surface of which is placed the needlepoint holder.

Some arrangers find that chicken or turkey wire lightly folded and forced into the container is also an excellent way of holding large stems and branches in place. Oasis, a commercial product easily obtained from any florist shop, is frequently used to hold flowers in place.

Whenever mechanical aids are used, it is very important to be certain that they do not show. These can easily be hidden by foliage material, green moss or natural stone pebbles.

Containers

The decorative scheme of the room should dictate the type of container to be considered. The form of the container itself is an important factor. An Early American home with rooms of soft pine or of painted backgrounds would dictate the use of the more informal containers, especially ironstone, pewter, earthenware pottery, Chinese ginger jars, wooden bowls, baskets, etc. The chalice, epergne, oriental bronzes and compote forms are in keeping with the traditional background.

For the modern home, simple designs in bleached wood and pottery would be excellent. Large and heavy plant materials such as branches of crab apples or evergreens belong in a container which suggests strength. Dainty arrangements should be placed in delicate vases.

The flower arranger should have a wide selection of containers from which to choose, for variety in the use of the containers themselves is a factor always creating interest by those familiar with the furnishings of a particular home.

How to Condition Fresh-Cut Plant Material

It is always best to cut flowers in the early morning or in the late afternoon, placing them immediately in deep water. Before cutting, however, one should have a definite idea of where the arrangement is to be placed so that no more plant material is cut than is necessary. Also intelligent pruning should always be uppermost in one's mind, for one can quickly mar the shape or form of an otherwise beautiful shrub or tree by improper cutting.

Always give the plant material a chance to "drink" before arranging. Strip all leaves from the stems below the water line, making a slanting cut on the end of the stem. Slash the cut ends of all woody stemmed materials such as lilacs, fruit tree branches, rhododendrons and azaleas, for this aids in the ability of such branches to absorb water in sufficient quantities and as a result they remain in good condition much longer than they might otherwise.

For flowers having gummy or milky juices, such as poppies, dahlias, lupins, singe the end of the stem over a flame to seal in the juices, and immediately place in deep water in a cool place for not less than 2 hours or preferably overnight.

Flowers, particularly roses, that have been left out of water for a short time can be revived. Place them in a tall container and pour boiling water around the stems—let them stand a few minutes and then plunge the stems into cold water.

Church Arrangements

The most important point to keep in mind is the scale of the sanctuary and altar area itself. If a cross and candles are present they will determine the appropriate scale of the container and flowers to be used. Proportion is another important part to consider—when the cross is used, it determines the height of the arrangement. The background against which the floral design is to be placed will determine both color and pattern of the flowers themselves. The finished work must have a sense of serenity and unity and the container must be in keeping with the surroundings. The finished design may be a formal triangle type or a fan-shaped type. When an arrangement can be placed on either side of the cross it is possible to do 2 asymmetrical or symmetrical arrangements. Usually massed designs are most effective for the average church.

Constructing the Arrangement

Flowers from the florist should be crisp and firm but sometimes need conditioning. The stems should be recut and soaked up to the flower heads for several hours before arranging them.

1. The first step is to establish the 3 main lines of the arrangement or backbone which will determine the design. The correct height, determined by the size and form of the container, is usually one and one-half to twice the height of the container. Then cut the first placement to the exact length desired and secure it well in the middle of the container, when constructing a symmetrical arrangement. It is very important that this placement is absolutely firm and cannot move. The general design should be augmented with 2 more primary lines. See illustration.

2. With the 3 main lines established, next add the secondary lines. If foliage is to be used as the main line, then have a bud 3 inches below the top main line in front and back to strengthen the main line. All the flowers and branches should appear to be coming from one place in the container.

3. With this as the main outline, supplementary or "filler" material can then be added. Fill spaces between main lines with plant material of uneven lengths and uneven voids. As all these lines converge at the focal point, place the larger forms of plant material in this area. Be sure to cover the rim of the container, and some color back of the arrangement to give the much-needed depth in the design.

4. Do not let the final filling-in result in a confused outline. The colors should be blended well, there should be gradation in sizes and color of the flowers and there should be varied textures and uneven spaces or voids.

Oriental Trends

For many years a new individual expression has been evident in American interpretations of oriental flower arrangements. Many new freedoms with designs and materials are in popular use inspired by the fresh treatments of traditional patterns. Classical forms executed with respect for the long-established rules of favorite designs; modern adaptations of those forms; free-style treatments which indicate a complete break with the past. Modern interpretations of well-known flower styles are exciting and refreshing—endless new materials make the basic patterns look different. Today, the flower arranger seems limited only by knowledge and imagination.

Contemporary

Contemporary arrangements of today are not necessarily modern but it is rather one which is suitable for any type of home. Contemporary rooms, which are a blend of the old and the new, afford the flower arrangers a wide field. The arranger must keep in mind these important factors which are:

1. LINE ARRANGEMENT—line is the dominant form. It has an open silhouette and a restraint in quantity of material used.

2. MASSED LINE—is a line arrangement with mass added. The mass should never be crowded to avoid hiding the beauty of the flowers.

3. MASS ARRANGEMENT—is the opposite of line in that it has a closed form. It has depth and is created by using uneven stems, placing certain flowers in profile and recessing some of the focal area. Mass designs may be either symmetrical or asymmetrical in contour.

There are 4 basic types of American Contemporary flower arrangements: Traditional, Expressive, Free Style and Abstract. Traditional includes line, massed line and mass. It is dramatic with the use of simpler and more fundamental forms—all non-essentials are stripped away, pure design stands out in great boldness.

Expressive arrangements are those that interpret a theme or express a mood, a feeling. Free style is an arrangement of good design created outside the established geometric patterns. The plant material suggests the design.

Abstract arrangement is an expression in pure form, pure line, color and texture. It is a space art with space a part of the design around and within it. There is no focal point or focal area—the aim of the abstract is to create a composition in which design is of paramount importance. Under Abstract arrangements are mobiles, stabiles, collages and assemblages.

In conclusion, the art of flower arranging is a study in itself. There are many types of designs that can be made to properly fit particular surroundings, and learning to use the proper flowers and colors in the right containers and in predetermined designs presents an intriguing challenge to the individual brave enough to try.

Many individuals have the ability to arrange flowers properly without studied effort. For those who do not have the inborn ability it can be acquired by study and practice. Many American women are enjoying the intricate procedure of learning how to do it by careful study. The large flower shows throughout the country are excellent places to see some of the outstanding flower arrangements.

For those who have the time, the serious study of flower arranging can be a most interesting and satisfying hobby, and for those fortunate enough to have a garden as well, the practice of flower arranging in all its interesting forms makes for the full appreciation of growing and using plants the entire year.

FLORENCE D. WYMAN

FLOWER POTS. See POTS.

FLOWER SHOWS. The great interest in the practice of gardening throughout the country has made flower shows, both large and small, familiar events in many of the towns and cities throughout the land. Today's public is eager for them, both as an outlet for exhibiting plant material and for attending them as a means of increasing their knowledge.

The sophisticated flower shows of today, with their elaborate gardens and costly staging for spectacular displays and flower arrangements, are a far cry from the early exhibitions. Usually, these grew naturally in cities and communities where there was interest in sharing the produce of the garden. Cut flowers were displayed in simple containers, often bottles, and potted plants lined up on tables without thought to their artistic appearance.

Today, the purpose of an horticultural exhibit or show is to inspire and educate. This has always been the purpose behind flower shows, but more so today when the need is greater. Setting up a flower show is a cooperate venture, combining the skills, knowledge, and enthusiasm of several individuals.

Since gardening is an enjoyable hobby, it promotes a spirit of fun. It motivates a healthy spirit of competition, the same as in sports. Exhibitors and the visiting public learn a great deal and develop a keener appreciation of the beauty in the foliage and flowering plants which go to make beautiful gardens. In small communities, flower shows become affairs in which a large number of citizens participate. Often, those who know nothing about horticulture adopt it as a favorite pastime.

A flower show need not be large, as those staged in New York, Boston, Philadelphia, Cleveland and other cities. It can be held at any time of year by any organization. It can be expansive as to include gardens and all kinds of plants or it can be limited to a single flower, as orchids, camellias, African violets, roses, daffodils, tulips or irises. Some of the most successful shows are those held in winter or the very early spring in the colder regions of the country, when it is uplifting to view the beauty of flowers when snow and below-freezing temperatures prevail outdoors.

A flower show can be held in any number of places. Larger societies have their own building, with one or more large exhibition halls. These are usually ideal since they provide facilities for storing equipment and proper lighting, but other buildings can prove equally satisfactory. School auditoriums, country clubs, lecture halls, and hotels all work out well. Business firms are often eager to cooperate, and many shows are held in banks and department stores where backgrounds are attractive so that staging costs are kept at a minimum. This is one way of helping to promote business, and because of their central location, attendance is usually high.

The place where the show is to be held should offer certain basic needs. It should be large enough for the kind of show to be staged, with sufficient space for supplies and equipment. It must be easily reached, by public transportation in the case of cities. Ample parking, preferably free, is not to be overlooked for this often plays a major role in determining the show's success. The hall, or halls, ought to be well ventilated, clean and attractive, properly lighted by day and night, and heated in winter, although preferably on the cool side for the sake of the flowers. No detail involving comfort and smooth operating should be overlooked.

If the show is to be large, allow space for a spectacular exhibit, usually centered around the theme. Most of the space should be devoted to displays by nurserymen, florists, garden clubs and plant societies. Set aside some area for commercial booths, where the public may make purchases and find out about the latest in sprays and garden equipment. This often proves a popular section of the show, but it should not be overdone. If so, it detracts and the mood becomes commercial rather than aesthetic and educational. The public will also complain.

Commercial exhibitors should be selected with care. They should be reliable, and if anything goes wrong with a product, they ought to satisfy the customer. A neat, artistic, well-displayed booth adds much to the show, and strict enforcement should keep the major exhibits, and the commercial exhibitors as well, restricted to plants and horticultural products related to their growing or display. Too many shows these days are falling into the gadget category, offering goods that are wholly unrelated to any phase of gardening.

Sometimes, small shows are held in private homes, often in conjunction with a garden tour. There may be tables of pot plants and individual horticultural specimens, but emphasis is on flower arrangements and other decorations in hallways, living rooms, dining rooms, kitchens, bedrooms, dens and even bathrooms. These are popular with the public. Such shows are sponsored by garden clubs and prove to be good money-makers.

In sponsoring this kind of show, different kinds of problems arise. Include sufficient homes, but not too many. The idea is to see them all comfortably in a morning or afternoon. In case of bad weather, try to sell as many tickets as possible beforehand. Print literature that gives the background of each house, with directions for getting from one place to another. For this, arrows on poles, trees, or buildings are needed, but well-informed hostesses can help the visitors. Each room should have at least one hostess to answer questions and watch belongings. Look into the traffic situation, and for this local police will cooperate. Extremely popular in private homes are Christmas shows, that may combine a sale with a workshop in a heated barn or "rumpus" room. If possible, it is wise to serve tea, coffee and light refreshments. They add a little more to the cost, but this attraction will be profitable.

Once a garden club or some other horticultural group has decided to sponsor a flower show, the first step is to decide where and when it will be held. Determine the kind of show it will be, and outline its purposes. When these basics have been stated, the next and most important phase is to select committees. There will be several of these: Staging, hospitality, publicity, and others as well as the important task of selecting a competent general chairman and secretary. Then make up a schedule of classes, being specific about each, including prizes. Distinguish between exhibitors that are professional or amateur. For a show to be successful, no matter how small, there must be a series of rules and regulations. Apportioning responsibility evenly is a matter not to be overlooked. Choose committee members from as many backgrounds as possible, seeking those with some experience.

The most important committee member is the general chairman. This is the position that is most difficult to fill, yet is the one that requires the most careful consideration. The general chairman is the guiding light, the person responsible for selling floor space to horticultural and trade exhibitors. He will receive some praise for his efforts, but he will also take the blame when something goes wrong. Most of all, he should be a person of tact, able to smooth the ruffled feelings of many a disgruntled exhibitor. Some flower-show experience is needed for this position, at least as a committee head. Laying out the plan of the show is his task, except in the case of large shows where the services of a landscape architect may be employed. The general chairman will handle the budget and supervise the various committees under him.

The position of secretary is second in importance. His job is to handle all the paper work—to send out schedule and entry cards, to receive and record entries, to write letters, to purchase supplies, such as envelopes, stamps, clips and make certain they are on hand in the show office, and to order ribbons and other prizes. He will handle most of the telephone calls and run the office during show time. Experience helps, but with a good and competent general chairman, the various tasks of the secretary are readily learned.

The schedule committee has a major function to perform. Members of this group should possess a sound knowledge of plants and understand how to work up a schedule that is interesting, varied and appealing to the public. A schedule should contain such needed information as name and dates of the show, the theme, hours, location and telephone. Facilities for parking can also be added, as well as other pertinent bits of information. The committee is empowered to enforce all its rules strictly. Exceptions only lead to demands for others. Latecomers can be allowed to enter, although they do not qualify to compete. The schedule should indicate the kind of entry, the number of plants or blooms, size of the collection, and the time of removal. In the flower-arrangement classes, sizes of niches, heights of arrangements, and color of containers and other details should be given.

Once the exhibition hall has been selected, it is time for the staging chairman to get to work. If he has not had experience in this capacity previously, at least he ought to know something about flower-show staging and management and have a definite feeling for design. In some cases, he may have to work with unions, for these are becoming more and more part of the picture, especially in our large-city, major flower shows.

Much careful planning should go into this aspect of the flower show. Large exhibits, as gardens with structures, terraces and pools and fountains, are staged on the ground, but cut flowers and pot plants rest on tables. These can be of various sizes, but not more than 5 ft. wide if plants are to be viewed from one side. Some tables are set up for various classes, chiefly flower arrangements for dining room tables.

Suitable material is needed for the background in order to show the plants effectively. Black and dark green cloth, so much a part of the scene in flower shows in years past, is now being replaced by softer, lighter colors in different kinds of materials, many of which emphasize texture.

It is up to the staging chairman to plan and arrange for storage space for flowers and materials. He works with movers, carpenters, electricians, and sees to it that walls and floors of the building, especially if rented, are not damaged. He handles the vases for cut flowers. For best effects, keep to the same kind of containers, varying only in size. Appropriate vases, attractive in appearance and color, do much to add to the show The staging chairman sees to it that all exhibits can be seen easily. He keeps away from large posts and, where possible, dresses them up with bark and branches to depict trees. He handles the matter of partitions that will separate one exhibitor from the other.

In a small show, the secretary will take care of mailing and receiving entries, but in a large one an entries chairman will be needed. It is always best to have the exhibitors return their entries in advance. The entries chairman will file them, and when each exhibit is ready for judging, he will make certain that the card is filled and placed face down in order to cover the name. This chairman will also arrange for cards for each exhibitor to remove his plants and belongings after the show has closed. This requires careful supervision to avoid stealing or breakage by unauthorized persons. Exhibitors, including trade exhibitors, will need cards so they can enter and leave the show as often as needed.

The importance of an able judge's committee cannot be emphasized enough. Goodwill can easily be destroyed by judges who are not properly qualified to judge a garden, a bouquet of roses or a flower arrangement.

In addition to choosing judges who know plants and have a feeling for design and color, the committee has the task of entertaining them. For small shows, invitations should go out a month in advance, but for large shows several months is better. In case of drop-outs, have a file of additional judges who can be reached the last minute. With garden clubs, judges are available from neighboring or distant clubs, and no effort should be spared to get the best possible. A judge should be objective and unbiased and take this responsibility seriously, considering the invitation an honor. As a rule, judges are not paid, but their transportation and meals are usually covered. For large shows, professionals may receive monetary recompense.

A prize committee is essential if a flower show

is to function properly. Standardized are the ribbon awards, blue for 1st, red for 2nd, and white for 3rd. A green ribbon or a seal can be given as an award for a special class, which does not compete with the others. Special exhibits, however, may be judged for the tricolor or purple ribbon for the exhibit considered the most distinctive in the show.

There are medals for exhibits by nurserymen, florists and other commercial entries. Gold is the highest, silver comes second and bronze is third. Other kinds of prizes and awards are offered, these depending on the show and what it has established. They may be bowls, cups and other kinds of trophies. Often a sweepstake prize goes to the exhibitor with the greatest number of points. In large shows, these major awards are given by a special committee of judges, which decides where each of these coveted prizes will go. These major awards usually specify their purpose: to the most beautiful exhibit in the show, to the flower arrangement with the highest number of points, to a commercial entry that is considered the most meritorious, etc.

Every flower show, no matter how small, will need a publicity chairman. Without this vital person and his committee members, the show will hardly make the grade. Publicity by word of mouth is never enough to draw scores of visitors. Appropriate posters are excellent means by which the public is informed about the show. They can be made by professional artists, or skilled persons within the show committee can come up with startling ideas. Sometimes school children can be asked to compete for a prize-winning poster.

The main purpose of the publicity chairman is to contact newspaper editors and send in good, clear copy that includes all essentials, such as place, time, cost and dates. With large metropolitan newspapers, he will have to work directly with garden or society editors. Aside from releases, he may have to write exclusive stories about particular growers, arrangers, or committee heads whose roles are prominent.

The publicity chairman will have to arrange for the taking of photographs. He will receive the press and the newspaper photographers and assist them in their needs. Often they will want to bring in models for a special feature. Publicity of this nature is important before the show opens on opening day, but more should come while the show is in progress. This often becomes difficult when a flower show continues for a week or longer, but an imaginative and energetic chairman will come with new ideas and think of different angles to sustain publicity during this period.

Not only newspapers, including the weeklies, but television and radio must be brought into play. The chairman will contact television personalities who conduct popular programs and arrange for interviews or presentations. Top flower arrangers may demonstrate how to put together a spring bouquet or one of chrysanthemums. Posters, schedules, pot plants, photographs and transparencies of former, and even present, flower shows, even garden tools and equipment are but a few props that will help to put the television show over.

Radio can do equally as much for the show. There are many who listen to the radio while they work at home or in places of business. Thousands listen to their car radios while they drive, and spot announcements about the show, paid or courtesy, help as constant reminders. Interviews are likewise conducted on radio. On occasion they may be taped in the show and run at a later hour, but then again, they may be live, with such sounds as bubbling water in the background. Flower-show exhibitors, shy about appearing on television, will not mind a radio interview.

In addition to contacts with newspapers, television and radio, the publicity chairman will handle the matter of free passes to persons who have offered their services and time. The handing out of free passes creates good feeling among these persons who are spreading the news of the show in various ways.

As awards and prizes are announced, the publicity chairman should send them out immediately to the newspapers in short, clearly written releases. In large cities, individual releases should go to the local papers which are always certain to print the information. And a good publicity chairman will keep copies of his releases, for future reference, and clippings of the various articles and photographs that have appeared. They may be kept on file or in a large scrapbook.

Small shows may not require an hospitality committee, but wherever possible this is a worthwhile one to establish. Members of this group will handle refreshments, if they are to be served, as is the case in small affairs. They will look after the needs of the judges, and arrange for their transportation and lunches. If there is an information booth (highly recommended where possible) hostesses will answer questions about the show. If they are experts in horticulture, they can give out general gardening information as well. This is always a drawing attraction, and it is up to the publicity chairman to publicize it. Hostesses should know the show winners and be able to give this information when it is requested. They should also take in memberships if the show is sponsored by a plant society or a garden club.

There may be other minor committees, depending on needs. With growing interest in conservation, a conservation committee may well be included. If the matter of handling tickets is confusing, a special committee can be assigned to the job. In many shows, school children are urged to participate, and a special committee, perhaps comprised of a few teachers, can work with the youngsters.

Running a flower show is a major effort that calls for the combined skills and the full cooperation of many individuals. Much will be learned through experience, and there will be pitfalls, but many of these can be avoided by careful planning beforehand. Visiting flower shows and talking with experienced committee heads are helpful. A practical book on the subject is "Flower Show Know-How" by William Thomas Wood and Marie Stevens Wood (Stephens Press, Asheville, N.Car.).

GEORGE TALOUMIS

To help flower show committees instruct their judges and exhibitors properly the following "Scales of Points for Judges" are suggested as samples. These are taken from the "Rule Book for Exhibitors and Judges" of the Massachusetts Horticultural Society. For other schedules not listed below, consult this Rule Book.

GARDEN EXHIBIT

Design and Originality	30
Suitability and Quality of Plant Material	25
Color Harmony	10
Seasonability	10
Quality and Suitability of Accessories	10
Charm and Appeal	10
Correct and Suitable Labeling	5
	100

NATURALISTIC PLANTING OR GARDEN

Naturalistic Reproduction	40
Suitability and Quality of Plants	35
Charm and Appeal	10
Seasonability	10
Correct and Suitable Labeling	5
	100

ROCK OR WALL GARDEN
(Adopted by the American Rock Garden Society)

Design and Rock Arrangement	20
Planting and Color Blending	20
Cultural Perfection of Plants	20
Suitability of Plants for their Respective Plantings	15
Rarity of Plants	15
Variety	10
	100

POTTED PLANTS—GROUP OF FLOWERING PLANTS

Staging and Arrangement	30
Cultural Perfection	35
Color Effect	20
Quality and Suitability of Accessories	10
Correct and Suitable Labeling	5
	100

GROUP OF FOLIAGE PLANTS

Staging and Arrangement	30
Cultural Perfection	35
Distinctiveness	10
Color Effect	10
Rarity	10
Correct and Suitable Labeling	5
	100

SPECIMEN FLOWERING PLANTS

Cultural Perfection	50
Form and Size of Plant	15
Floriferousness	15
Color	10
Foliage	10
	100

SPECIMEN AFRICAN VIOLET (Saintpaulia)
(Adopted by the African Violet Society of America, Inc.)

Leaf Pattern or Form	30
Floriferousness	25
Condition	20
Size of Bloom, According to Variety	15
Color of Bloom, According to Variety	10
	100

CUT GLADIOLUS
(Adopted by New England Gladiolus Society)

Flowerhead		14
Form of Spike		24
Form of Floret		8
Physique		28
Substance—Texture	7	
Calyx—Attachment	4	
Straightness	8	
Stem	5	
Vigor	4	
Color		26
		100

FRUITS—SPECIMEN FRUITS
(Apples, Cherries, Peaches, Pears, Plums, Quince Score Card—Ohio State University, Department of Agricultural Education)

Form	10
Size	15
Color	20
Uniformity	25
Condition	30
	100

COLLECTION OF VEGETABLES

Condition of Vegetables Shown	30
Variety in Kinds Shown	30
Staging and Arrangement	30
Correct and Suitable Labeling	10
	100

ORNAMENTAL GOURDS, DISPLAY

(Adopted by The Gourd Society of America, Inc.)

Cultural Perfection	30
Staging and Arrangement	30
Color Effect	20
Quality and Suitability of Accessories	20
	100

CHRISTMAS WREATH, SWAG, ETC.

Design	25
Suitability of Material	20
Distinction, Originality	20
Workmanship	20
Durability	15
	100

CORSAGE OR NOSEGAY

Design	25
Color	15
Combination of Materials	20
Distinctiveness, Originality	20
Workmanship	10
Condition	10
	100

For further help in judging flower arrangements, table settings, etc., the following point schedules are taken from "The Handbook for Flower Shows," National Council of State Garden Clubs, Inc., Publishers, 4401 Magnolia Avenue, St. Louis, Mo., 63110.

TABLE SETTINGS

Overall Design (Harmony and Attractiveness of overall setting)	20
Compatibility of all material (Appointment accessories, decorative unit, in color, texture, spirit)	20
Perfection of Decorative Unit (design, color harmony, spirit)	20
Distinction and/or Originality	15
Interpretation, Conformance to Schedule, and/or functionalism	15
Condition	10
	100

ARRANGEMENTS IN THE PLACEMENT SHOW

Design	40
Suitability to Placement	20
Originality	20
Distinction	20
	100

POTTED PLANTS USED FOR DECORATIVE PURPOSES

Cultural Perfection	40
Suitability to Placement	20
Color Harmony	20
Plant Selection	20
	100

FLOWERING-MAPLE = *Abutilon* x *hybridum*

FLOWERING-RUSH = *Butomus umbellatus*

FLOWERING STONES. See LITHOPS.

FLOWER-OF-AN-HOUR = *Hibiscus trionum*

FLOWERS, FRAGRANT. Many trees, shrubs, vines, herbaceous plants and bulbous plants are valued for their fragrant flowers. It is impossible to list them all, but in glancing through the following list one may be reminded of others. Fragrance is most marked in humid (not wet) weather and at its lowest in hot dry weather. Some of the following plants should be in every garden because of the fragrance of their flowers.

WOODY PLANTS	HEIGHT	ZONE	
Acacia sp.	10'–60'	8–10	Acacia Wattle
Buddleia globosa	15'	7	Globe Butterfly-bush
Calycanthus floridus	9'	4	Carolina Allspice
Chimonanthus praecox	8'	7	Wintersweet
Choisya ternata	9'	7	Mexican Orange
Cistus ladaniferus	4'	7	Gum Rock-rose
Citrus sp.	15'–45'	8–10	Orange, Lemon, etc.
Clematis paniculata	vine	5	Sweet Autumn Clematis
Clethra alnifolia	9'	3	Summersweet
Corylopsis sp.	10'–18'	5–7	Winter-hazel
Daphne sp.	6"–6'	4–7	Daphne
Elaeagnus pungens	12'	7	Thorny Elaeagnus
Gardenia jasminoides	4'–6'	8–9	Gardenia
Hamamelis mollis	30'	5	Chinese Witch-hazel

	HEIGHT	ZONE	
H. vernalis	10'	5	Vernal Witch-hazel
Jasminum sp.	vine	5–8	Jasmine
Lavandula sp.	3'	5	Lavender
Lonicera sp.	3'–15'	2–7	Honeysuckle
Magnolia grandiflora	90'	7	Southern Magnolia
Malus sp.	20'–50'	2–5	Apple, Crab Apple
Michelia figo	15'	7–8	Banana-shrub
Osmanthus ilicifolius	18'	6	Holly Osmanthus
Philadelphus coronarius	9'	4	Sweet Mock-orange
Philadelphus—many sp. and vars. but not all	4'–9'	4–6	Mock-orange
Prunus sp.	4½'–75'	3–7	Cherry
Rhododendron fortunei	12'	6	Fortune Rhododendron
R. arborescens	9'	4	Sweet Azalea
R. viscosum	9'	3	Swamp Azalea
Rosa—many sp.	1½'–9'	2–7	Rose
Santolina chamaecyparissus	2'	7	Lavender-cotton
Spartium junceum	10'	7	Spanish Broom
Syringa sp.	6'–30'	2–5	Lilac
Tilia sp.	30'–120'	2–5	Linden, Basswood
Viburnum carlesii	5'	4	Fragrant Viburnum
V. burkwoodii	6'	5	Burkwood Viburnum
Vitex agnus-castus	9'	6–7	Chaste-tree
Wisteria sinensis	vine	5	Chinese Wisteria

FRAGRANT, HERBACEOUS PLANTS

	HEIGHT	ZONE	
Abromia sp.	prostrate to 10"	5–8	Sand-verbena
Artemesia lactiflora	1"–6"	4	White Mugwort
Asperula odorata	8"	2–3	Sweet Woodruff
Cheiranthus sp.	1½'	annual	Wallflower
Chrysanthemum sp.	1'–5'	4–5	Chrysanthemum
Convallaria majalis	8"	2	Lily-of-the-valley
Dianthus caryophyllus	1'–3'	8	Clove Pink
Hesperis matronalis	3'–4'	2–3	Dame's Rocket
Hemerocallis flava	3'	2–3	Lemon Daylily
Hosta plantaginea	3'	3	Fragrant Plantain-lily
Hyacinthus	15"	4–6	Hyacinth
Freesia refracta	1½'	9	Common Freesia
Iris, some sp.	1'–6'	2–3	Iris
Lathyrus odoratus	vine	annual	Sweet Pea
Lilium—several sp.	2'–5'	2–3	Lily
Lobularia maritima	1'	annual	Sweet Alyssum
Matthiola longipetala	1'	annual	Evening Stock
Narcissus—several sp. and vars.	4"–1'	4	Daffodil
Oenothera speciosa	2'–4'	4	Evening Primrose
Paeonia officinalis	3'	2–3	Common Peony
Passiflora quadrangularis	vine	10	Giant Granadilla
Polianthus tuberosa	3½'	9	Tuberose
Primula—several sp.	1'	2–5	Primrose
Reseda sp.	decumbent	annual	Mignonette
Tropaeolum majus	3'	annual	Nasturtium
Viola odorata	8"	6	Sweet Violet

FLOWERS, STATE. See STATE FLOWERS.

FLUORESCENT LIGHT GARDENING. Raising plants completely under artificial light, from sowing the seed to flowering and fruiting, is now a possible hobby for any home owner who has the space, the available electricity and the yen to grow plants in the home. The special fluorescent-light tubes which have been invented and manufactured for this purpose are available from the 3 major light-bulb manufacturers, Westinghouse Co., General Electric Co. and Sylvania Electric Products Co., Inc., with information and pamphlets available from Sylvania Lighting Center, Danvers, MA 01923, and General Electric Co., Lighting Business Group, Nela Park, Cleveland, Ohio 44112. With specially made light tubes, placed in industrial type fixtures, with careful study given to watering and temperature requirements, many tender plants, both common and rare, can be coaxed into unique bloom in the home.

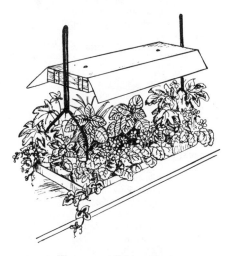

Fluorescent-light gardening

Temperature for the plants should be between 60–72° F. Space in the cellar is often ideal, for here the temperature is frequently about right and also the humidity is correct. Then there are dark corners, or even closets, where a 3-tiered plant-growing stand could be erected at little cost and where plants might add great interest and beauty to an otherwise uninteresting area.

It has been found best to have at least 2 tubes (not 1) together in the industrial fixture as being the most efficient. These tubes should supply 15–20 watts of illumination per sq. ft. of plant-growing space. Regardless of the manufacturer, they come in 24-inch (20 watt); 48-inch (40 watt); and 96-inch (72, 73, 74, 75 watt) lengths. One 24-inch tube will illuminate a space 24 in. × 6 in., whereas 4 96-in. tubes illuminate a space 96 in. × 24 in. A normal house circuit of 115 volts and 60 cycles carries 1500 watts; so, theoretically, one could have safely 30 40-watt tubes on one circuit *if* there were no other demands on this particular circuit.

The correct growth tubes may not be found at every corner hardware store, but they are made and can be ordered. For instance, the popular "Gro-Lux" tubes are made by the Sylvania Electric Products Co., Inc., Salem, Mass. These, and also the "Plant-Gro" tubes of Westinghouse, are designed especially for fluorescent light gardening. They come in 8 shades of white fluorescent. The ones more readily available are "Cool White," "Daylight," "Warm White" and "Natural White." Best flowering results have been obtained with a combination of "Daylight" and "Natural" tubes in the same 2-tube industrial type fixture.

The reason why such a combination is better than 2 of the same tubes in the fixture is the fact that the "Daylight" tube is excellent in its violet and blue rays, but deficient in its orange and red rays, while the "Natural" tubes are deficient in violet and blue but excellent in orange and red rays. Plants need both type of rays to grow well. Many experiments have been carried out with colored lights, but these have been definitely proved to be impractical.

Another interesting fact is that the fluorescent tube uses nearly 100% of the electricity to supply usable growth rays, while with the incandescent lamp about 75–85% of the power is dissipated in the form of heat.

Tubes come in either "pre-heat" or "rapid-start" types, and it has been found that the former are better under the humid conditions present in a greenhouse or plant-growing cabinet. Ballasts also are needed—these are devices which limit the current to the proper operating value. The ballast must be bought which is specifically designed for the tube used. These consume a certain amount of power themselves and do give off some heat. Of course the fluorescent tubes themselves do not give off heat. Ballasts should be of the high-power factor type. The industrial type fixtures, with their tubes and ballast, should be attached to pulleys so they can be lowered or raised as good growth will dictate. It has been determined that the tubes should be about 3-6-10 in. above the plant, depending on the plant and its stage of growth. Also, each set of fixtures should have its own turn-off switch. For convenience, it is possible to have these hooked up to a time clock so that they will be automatically turned on and off. Usually 14–16 hours of continued light is the best requirement for most plants, although this, too, varies. During the other hours the plants should be resting in the dark.

A triple-decked bench is often the best for utilizing display floor space. The bench could be 8 ft. × 3 ft. and 26 in. high, with the first shelf 6 in. above the floor. For each shelf, 2 8-ft. industrial type fixtures can be arranged on pulleys so they can be raised or lowered. The benches can be waterproofed with polyethylene film, for it is essential not to allow water to drip from an upper bench or shelf onto an electric fixture below.

Humidity is provided by filling the benches with builder's vermiculite, setting the potted plants in it and keeping the vermiculite moist, but not wet.

One more important note about the light tubes is that their estimated life should be figured when they are installed and a date put on each in grease pencil to denote when it should be renewed. A lamp that is rated at 7500 hours when it is burned for 3 hours per start, may last 13,500 hours if burned for 18 hours per start. Also reflecting surfaces, if painted, should be painted with a flat white paint, not a glossy paint.

As far as soils are concerned, those used in fluorescent-lighted gardens offer a most interesting topic for study. Several soil mixtures are recommended, some by the University of California, one by Cornell University called Peat-Lite Potting Mix (merely 4 quarts of #2 Terralite or vermiculite, 4 quarts of shredded dry German peat moss, 1 teaspoonful of 5-10-5 fertilizer and 1 teaspoonful of ground limestone, thoroughly mixed and thoroughly moistened throughout before using).

Another mixture suggested by Elaine C. Cherry, who has done much experimenting along this line, is:

1 part sphagnum peat
1 part clean, sharp builder's sand
1 part medium Perlite
1 part horticultural vermiculite
1 part pasteurized potting soil

Soil can be sterilized by wetting it thoroughly and then baking it in an oven at 212° F. for 30 minutes, or placing it in a pressure cooker with some water in the bottom and keeping it at 15 lbs. pressure for 15 minutes.

A pH of 6–7 is best. With these soil mixtures, fertilizers must be applied regularly about every 10 days or, as some do, very lightly every time the plants are watered. Highly chlorinated water should not be used direct from a faucet but should be allowed to stand in an open container over night to allow the chlorine to dissipate.

Fluorescent lights can be used in the home greenhouse to augment the sunlight in winter. They can be hooked up with a photo-electric cell switch, preset to turn on when light reaches a certain low point, to augment light available on cloudy winter days.

Plants flower and mature earlier in life under the proper amount of fluorescent light. They are lower, sturdier, more compact and flattened out. Rosette types of plants grow beautifully in these artificial conditions.

An excellent "do-it-yourself" type of discussion on this subject will be found in George A. Elbert's *The Indoor Light Gardening Book* (Crown Publishers, New York, 1973).

Some suggested plants for the Fluorescent Light Garden which grow best with about 14–16 hours of fluorescent light per day are:

Achimenes sp.	Magic Flower
Allophyton mexicanum	Mexican Foxglove
Alternanthera amoena	Joseph's Coat
Anthurium scherzerianum	Flamingo Flower
Ardisia crenata	Coral Berry
Azalea (Kurume types)	Azaleas
Begonia sp.	Begonias
Beloperone guttata	Shrimp Plant
Cactus sp.	
Campanula	Bellflower
Chlorophytum commosum	Spider Plant
Cissus	Ornamental Grape
Clematis sp.	Clematis
Clivia miniata	Kafir Lily
Codiaeum variegatum	Croton
Coleus blumei	Coleus
Columnea sp.	Goldfish Plant
Crassula sp.	
Dieffenbachia sp.	Mother-in-law Plant
Exacum affine	German Violet
Fuchsia hybrids	Fuchsias
Gloxinia perennis	
Hedera helix	English Ivy
Heliotropium sp.	Heliotrope
Hippeastrum sp.	Amaryllis
Hoya sp.	Wax Plant
Kalanchoe sp.	Kalanchoe
Lantana sp.	Lantana
Manettia bicolor	Mexican Firecracker
Mimosa pudica	Sensitive Plant
Orchids	
Oxalis sp.	
Pelargonium sp.	Geraniums
Peperomia sp.	
Punica granatum 'Nana'	Dwarf Pomegranate
Rosa—dwarfs	
Saintpaulia	African Violet
Saxifraga sarmentosa	Strawberry Saxifrage
Sedum sp.	Sedums
Sinningia speciosa	Gloxinia

FOAMFLOWER, ALLEGHENY = *Tiarella cordifolia*

FOENICULUM (Fee-NIK-yew-lum)

vulgare   5′   usually annual   Fennel
A popular perennial herb usually grown as an annual or biennial, with feathery foliage, and not easily transplanted. There are 15–25 small yellowish flowers produced in a cluster in the summer. Because of their feathery, threadlike foliage, this plant is useful in the flower border. Propagated by seed and native to southern Europe. One var. **dulce** called the Florence Fennel or Finocchio, has the leaf bases enlarged and if blanched can be eaten. Also var. **piperitum** has thickened stalks that are eaten like celery. This is called Carosella. Both the foliage and the seeds of Fennel are used in flavoring cooked foods. Industrially it is used for flavoring unpleasant-tasting medicines, and as an oil in soap. Also used in confectionery and in perfume.

FOLIACEOUS. Leaflike in texture or appearance; said particularly of sepals and calyx-lobes and of bracts that in texture, size or color look like small or large leaves.

FOLIAGE, AROMATIC. Many gardeners like to use plants with leaves that are aromatic because it gives a pleasing aroma to the atmosphere in the garden. Many an old-fashioned "herb" (which see) is of course in this category. There are some others which might also be considered worthy contributors. In the following list are a few which have proved popular for this reason.

	HEIGHT	ZONE	
Achillea millefolium	6″–2′	2	Yarrow
Allium sp.	6″–3′	2–3	Onion
Aloysia triphylla	10′	8	Lemon Verbena
Anthemis tinctoria	3′	3	Golden Marguerite
Artemesia sp.	1′–6′	2–5	Mugwort
Buxus sp.	2′–20′	5–7	Box
Calycanthus floridus	9′	4	Carolina Allspice
Chrysanthemum (some sp.)	1′–3′	2–5	Chrysanthemum
Cinnamomum camphora	40′	9	Camphor Tree
Coriandrum sativum	3′	annual	Coriander
Cupressus sp.	30′–75′	5–7	Cypress
Dicentra spectabilis	2′	2–3	Bleeding-heart
Dictamnus albus	3′	2–3	Gas Plant
Eucalyptus (some sp.)	30′–200′	9–10	Eucalyptus
Foeniculum vulgare	5′	annual	Fennel
Hyssopus officinalis	1½′	2–3	Hyssop
Juniperus sp.	1′–90′	2–9	Juniper
Lantana camara	4′–10′	8	Common Lantana
Laurus nobilis	30′	6	Sweet Bay, Laurel
Lavandula sp.	3′	5	Lavender
Libocedrus decurrens	135′	5	California Incense-cedar
Melianthus major	10′	10	Large Honey-bush
Mentha sp.	3″–2′	4–7	Mint
Melissa officinalis	2′	4	Lemon-balm
Monarda sp.	3′	3–5	Bee-balm
Myrica sp.	9′–36′	2–6	Bayberry, Wax-myrtle
Myrtus communis	5′–10′	8–9	Myrtle
Nepeta sp.	3″–3′	3	Ground Ivy
Origanum vulgare	2½′	3	Wild Marjoram
Pelargonium sp.	1′–4′	10	Geranium
Pinus sp.	4′–100′	2–9	Pine
Rosmarinus officinalis	6′	6	Rosemary
Ruta graveolens	3′	4	Common Rue
Sassafras albidum	60′	4	Sassafras
Satureja montana	15″	5	Winter Savory
Santolina chamaecyparissus	2′	7	Lavender-cotton
Salvia sp.	1½′–3′	annual	Sage
Tagetes	1½′–3′	annual	Marigold
Petrosilinum crispum	1′	3	Parsley
Tanacetum vulgare	3′	2–3	Common Tansy

	HEIGHT	ZONE	
Thymus sp.	1″–8″	2–4	Thyme
Umbellularia californica	75′	7	California-laurel
Vitex agnus-castus	9′	6–7	Chaste-tree

FOLIAGE, COLORED. Many plants have leaves with colors other than green. Those with gray, yellow, red, purple or blue-green colors are often valued landscape plants for they bring a color change to the plantings which can be very pleasing. On the other hand, an even greater number of plants have variegated leaves, those that are partly green and partly some other color (yellow, white, pink) and these are too numerous to mention in the following list. They are difficult to use properly in the planting scheme because they stand out so definitely that they do not merge in easily with other plants. Some people like them and use them but it should be remembered that it is difficult to use them properly.

There are also a number of plants which will have young foliage colored red, bronze or yellow as it unfurls in the spring, but as it matures the leaves take on a normal green color. These plants are not in the following list—they are too numerous to mention here, but many do make bright spots for short periods in the landscape during the early spring and so they are valued.

The following are a very few of those that are colorful throughout most of the growing season. Experienced gardeners can add many more.

BLUE GREEN

SCIENTIFIC NAME	HEIGHT	ZONE	COMMON NAME
Acacia baileyana	30′	10	Cootamundra Wattle
Arundo donax	6′–26′	6	Giant Reed
Baptisia australis	3′–4′	2–3	Wild Indigo
Cedrus atlantica glauca	120′	6	Blue Atlas Cedar
Centranthus ruber	2′–3′	4	Red Valerian
Coronilla varia	2′	3	Crown Vetch
Cupressus lusitanica	50′	7	Mexican Cypress
Dasylirion texanum	3′	8	Texas Sotol
Dianthus plumarius	1½′	3–4	Grass Pink
Eriodictyon trichocalyx	2′–3′	8	Yerba Santa
Eryngium amethystinum	1½′	2–3	Amethyst Eryngium
Elymus arenarius	8′	4	European Dune Grass
Erythea armata	18′	10	Mexican Blue Palm
Eucalyptus pulverulenta	30′	9	Dollarleaf Eucalyptus
Festuca ovina glauca	2′	4	Blue Sheep's Fescue
Glaucium flavum	3′	Annual, biennial or perennial	Horned-poppy
Hebe (several species)	3′–8′	7–9	Hebe
Hosta sieboldiana	18″	3	Siebold Plantain-lily
Juniperus (several species and varieties)	1′–90′	3–7	Junipers
Lathyrus maritimus	Vine	4	Maritime Pea
Lepidium sativum varieties	2′	Annual	Garden Cress Pepperweed
Levisticum officinale	6′	6	Lovage
Linaria vulgaris	3′	3	Butter-and-eggs
Linum (several species)	2′	4–7	Flax
Lonicera korolkowii	12′	5	Blue-leaf Honeysuckle
Melaleuca leucadendron	40′	10	Cajeput-tree
Melianthus major	10′	10	Large Honey-bush
Mertensia virginica	2′–5′	2–3	Virginia Bluebells
Sedum dasyphyllum	2″	4	Leafy Stonecrop
S. sieboldii	6″–9″	2–3	Siebold Stonecrop
Silene maritima	1′	4	Sea Campion
Senecio (several species)	12″–2′	4–9	Groundsel

SCIENTIFIC NAME	HEIGHT	ZONE	COMMON NAME
GRAY			
Acacia (several species)	15'–60'	10	Acacia
Achillea tomentosa	6"–12"	2	Woolly Yarrow
Aloe vera	3'	10	Barbados Aloe
Allyssum (several species)	5"–3'	2–6	Alyssum
Amorpha canescens	4'	2	Lead-plant
Andromeda glaucophylla	1'	2	Downy Andromeda
Argemone species	2'–4'	Annual	Prickly Poppy
Artemisia (several species)	4"–5'	3–5	Wormwood
Atriplex hortensis	6'	Annual	Orach
Aubretia deltoidea	3"–6"	4	Purple Rock-cress
Buddleia alternifolia 'Argentea'	12'	5	Gray Fountain Buddleia
Cerastium tomentosum	3"–6"	2	Snow-in-summer
Convolvulus cneorum	4'	9	
Cytisus racemosus	10'–15'	8	
Elaeagnus angustifolius	20'	2	Russian-olive
E. pungens	12'	7	Thorny Elaeagnus
E. umbellatus	12'	3	Autumn Elaeagnus
Encelia farinosa	5'	8	White Brittlebush
Eucalyptus (several species)	30'–300'	9	Eucalyptus
Euphorbia marginata	2'	Annual	Snow-on-the-Mountain
Feijoa sellowiana	18'	8	Pineapple guava
Helichrysum petiolatum	2'	10	Cudweed Everlasting
Hippophae rhamnoides	30'	3	Sea-buckthorn
Holodiscus discolor	12'	5	Ocean Spray
Jasminum gracillimum	Climbing	7	Pinwheel Jasmine
Lavandula officinalis	3'	5	True Lavender
Leucadendron argenteum	30'	10	Silver Leucadendron
Lotus bertholetii	2'	10	Coral Gem
Lychnis coronaria	3'	Annual or perennial	Rose Campion
Nepeta x faassenii (N. mussinii)	2'	3	Persian Groundivy
Olea europaea	25'	9	Common Olive
Phlox subulata	6"	2–3	Moss Pink
Pittosporum crassifolium	30'	10	
Podalyria sericea	4'–6'	8	Satin-leaf Podalyria
Populus alba	90'	3	White Poplar
Potentilla argentea	1½'	4	Silvery Cinquefoil
Rosmarinus officinalis	6'	6	Rosemary
Ruta graveolens	3'	4	Common Rue
Salix elaeagnos	45'	4	Elaeagnus Willow
S. tristis	1½'	2	Dwarf Gray Willow
Salvia officinalis	sub-shrub	3	Garden Sage
Santolina chamaecyparissus	1½'–2'	6–7	Lavender-cottom
Shepherdia canadensis	7'	2	Russet Buffalo-berry
Senecio cineraria	2½'	6	Silver groundsel
Stachys olympica	1½'	4	Woolly Betony
Teucrium chamaedrys	10"	5	Chamaedrys Germander
Thalia dealbata	6'	7	Water-canna
Thymus serpyllum lanuginosus	2"–3"	2–3	Woolly Mother-of-thyme
Tilia petiolaris	75'	5	Pendent Silver Linden
T. tomentosa	90'	4	Silver Linden
Veronica incana	1'	2–3	Woolly Speedwell
Vitex agnus-castus	9'	6–7	Chaste-tree
Zenobia pulverulenta	6'	5	Dusty Zenobia

SCIENTIFIC NAME	HEIGHT	ZONE	COMMON NAME
	RED TO REDDISH		
Acer palmatum (several varieties)	20′	5	Japanese Maple
A. platanoides 'Crimson King'	90′	3	
A. platanoides 'Faassen's Black'	90′	3	
A. pseudoplatanus 'Purpureum'	90′	5	Purpleleaf Sycamore Maple
Begonia species and varieties	8″–4′	10	Begonias
Berberis thunbergii atropurpurea	7′	5	Red Japanese Barberry
B. thunbergii 'Crimson Pygmy'	2′	4	Variety of Japanese Barberry
Brassica oleracea acephala varieties	2′	Annual	Kale
Cleyera japonica (*Eurya ochnacea*)	21′	7	Sakaki
Codiaeum variegatum varieties	6′–10′	10	Croton
Coleus	6″–3′	10 Annual or perennial	Common Coleus
Guzmania musaica	1′	10	Colombian Guymania
Hamelia erecta	25′	10	Scarlet-bush
Jacobinia carnea	5′	10	
Kalanchoe sp.	12″–2′	10	Kalanchoe
Malus (several species and varieties) 'Baskatong' 'Oekonomierat Echtermeyer' purpurea 'Lemoinei' 'Red Silver' 'Strathmore'	15′–50′	2–6	Crab Apple
Portulacaria afra	12′	10	
Prunus cerasifera (several varieties)	24′	4	Myrobalan Plum
Prunus x cistena	7′	2	Purpleleaf Sand Cherry
P. persica 'Royal Redleaf'	24′	5	Variety of Peach
Ricinus communis	15′	Annual	Castor-bean
Saxifraga stolonifera (*S. sarmentosa*)	2′	7	Strawberry Saxifrage
Sapium sebiferum	40′	9	Chinese Tallow-tree
Rodgersia podophylla	5′	5–6	Bronzeleaf Rodger's flower
Rosa rubrifolia	6′	2	Redleaf Rose
Saxifraga (several species)	1″–2′	5	Saxifrage
Sedum (several species)	2″–2′	2–4	Sedums
Tradescantia fluminensis	Prostrate	8	Wandering Jew
	PURPLE TO PURPLISH		
Acer pseudoplatanus 'Purpureum'	90′	5	Variety of Sycamore Maple
Corylus maxima 'Purpurea'	30′	4	Purple Filbert
Cotinus cogyggria 'Purpurea'	15′	5	Purple Smoke Bush
Fagus sylvatica atropunicea 'Riversii'	90′	4	River's Beech
F. sylvatica 'Purpureo-pendula'	90′	4	Weeping Purple Beech
Prunus cerasifera atropurpurea varieties	24′	3	Pissard Plum
Prunus x blireiana	24′	5	Blireiana Plum
Quercus robur 'Atropurpurea'	75′–150′	5	Purple English Oak
Weigela florida foliis-purpuriis	4′	5	Weigela

SCIENTIFIC NAME	HEIGHT	ZONE	COMMON NAME
YELLOW–YELLOW-GREEN			
Acacia (several species)	15′–50′	10	Acacia
Acer japonicum 'Aureum'	25′	5	Fullmoon Maple
A. palmatum dissectum 'Flavescens'	15′	5	Yellow Threadleaf Japanese Maple
A. palmatum dissectum 'Ornatum'	15′	5	Variety of Threadleaf Japanese Maple
A. pseudoplatanus 'Worleei'	90′	5	Variety of Sycamore Maple
Alnus incana 'Aurea'	60′	2	Yellow Speckled Alder
Berberis thunbergii aurea	7′	4	Yellow lvd. Jap. Barberry
Catalpa bignonioides 'Aurea'	45′	4	Yellow Southern Catalpa
Alternanthera species	4″–8″	8	Alternanthera
Amaranthus tricolor	4′	Annual	Josephs-coat
Caladium picturatum	8′–10′	10	Mottled Caladium
Coleus	to 3′	10	Coleus
Gleditsia triacanthos 'Sunburst'	135′	4	Var. of Honey-locust
Hosta (several species)	1½′–3′	2–3	Plantain-lily
Humulus lupulus aureus	Vine	3	Variety of Common Hop
Jasminum humile	4′	7	Italian Jasmine
Ligustrum x vicaryi	12′	5	Vicary Golden Privet
Lonicera japonica 'Aureo-reticulata'	Vine	4	Goldnet Honeysuckle
Mahernia verticillata	1′	10	Honey-bells
Philadelphus coronarius 'Aureus'	9′	4	Golden Sweet Mock-orange
Physocarpus opulifolius 'Luteus'	9′	2	Yellow Eastern Ninebark
Pittosporum undulatum	30′	9	Victorian-box
Populus alba 'Richardii'	90′	3	Richard's White Poplar
Ptelea trifoliata 'Aurea'	24′	4	Variety of Common Hoptree
Quercus robur 'Concordia'	75′–150′	5	Golden Oak
Sambucus coerulea	45′	5	Blueberry Elder
Thevetia peruviana	25′	10	Yellow-oleander
Tilia platyphyllos aurea	120′	3	Yellow Big-leaf Linden
Ulmus procera aurea	120′	5	Yellow English Elm
Viburnum opulus 'Aureum'	12′	3	Yellow European Cranberry-bush

FOLIAR FEEDING. There is much controversy about the value of feeding plants through their leaves. It can be done effectively, but for the busy gardener it is probably not worth the effort. In any event, it should be looked upon as a supplement to proper soil feeding, not as a substitute for it. It also should be considered as a means for correcting minor nutrient disorders, but certainly is no cure-all for every plant ailment.

It has been established that both the upper and lower epidermis of the leaf has the power to absorb plant nutrients, some leaves more than others. The amount taken in depends on many factors, but absorption during the daylight hours is always greater than at night, and vigorous-growing plants absorb nutrients at a greater rate than do weak plants. Also the kinds of leaves, amount of pubescence, temperature, humidity, pH of the material and its chemical composition all influence the absorption.

There are many foliar sprays manufactured specifically for this purpose. "Ra-pid-gro" is one. Any one of them should not be used without reading carefully the directions on the package for the specific use of the material as a foliar spray. For instance, a 12-12-12, 13-13-13 or 13-26-13 fertilizer should be used at the rate of 5 oz. in each 10 gal. of water. The material should be sprayed on the leaves until it begins to drip off.

The home gardener should be cautioned that every soluble fertilizer is not a good foliar spray merely because it is soluble in water. Some may actually prove injurious to certain plants.

The proponents of foliar sprays point out that they are excellent for feeding trees planted along city streets in which the soil about the base of the tree is extremely limited. However, repeated applications are usually necessary in order to show any real effects and this proves costly. It certainly would be a time-consuming operation for the home gardener.

Proponents of foliar feeding point out that 80% of the nitrogen applied to commercial pineapple crops are applied by foliar sprays, but the pineapple is a specialized crop, more readily adaptable to absorbing foliar sprays than many common garden plants. Even in controlled experiments with garden chrysanthemums (at the N.Y. Botanical Garden) the number of flowers was only 8.3% more on the foliar sprayed plants. When time and cost were considered for the weekly spraying necessary from May to Sept., the small increase in flower production was not worth it.

The busy gardener would be much better off and actually ahead in time and money, if he properly fed his garden plants and trees through the soil, possibly using foliar feeding only as a court of last resort in attempting to correct minor nutrient disorders that he could not correct by normal soil feeding. See FERTILIZERS, SOILS.

-FOLIATE. In combinations, -leaved; having leaves; as trifoliate, 3-leaved, as the stem of Trillium.

-FOLIOLATE. Having leaflets; as trifoliolate, of 3 leaflets.

FOLLICLE. Dry, dehiscent pericarp opening only along one suture; as the milkweed or peony.

FONTANESIA (fon-tan-EE-sia)

fortunei   15′   Zone 4   Fortune Fontanesia
A deciduous shrub, graceful in habit with bright green foliage, occasionally planted in gardens. The opposite leaves are 1–4 in. long; flowers are small and greenish white in May-June. Not especially outstanding as an ornamental.

Propagation

Seed may be sown as soon as ripe; or stored dry in a cool place in airtight containers for up to a year and then sown. Softwood and hardwood cuttings (which see) root readily.

FORCING. Supplying additional fertilizer, heat, light and/or moisture to a plant in order to get it to grow faster than it normally would under average growing conditions.

FORCING CUT BRANCHES OF HARDY WOODY PLANTS IN THE GREENHOUSE FOR EARLY BLOOM. Forcing plants indoors to produce gorgeous bloom for spring flower shows has become a favorite indoor sport for many a grower. When it comes to figuring the time to bring in plants from outdoors so that they will produce the proper amount of flowers at the exact time the judges tour the show, it is woefully clear that there is not much published information which helps rank amateurs at this game. The experienced growers, who have been doing this for years, either keep such facts in mind or else tucked away in some file which is referred to briefly once a year. The old-timers say that such information is not of much value, since the number of days for blooming depends on the amount of "cold" (i.e., dormant period) the plant has received previously, the amount of rainfall the previous summer and fall, the temperature of the greenhouse, the number of days with sunshine after the plants have been taken into the greenhouse, etc.

The following records were kept of the dates cut branches of certain shrubs and trees were brought into the greenhouse, and the number of days it took to force them into bloom. Included were 2 sets of cut branches, cut from the same plants but at different times to determine the length of time it would take to bring each set into bloom. The greenhouse was kept at about 55°–60° F. night temperature. The idea was to see if time of bloom out-of-doors (which is known) could be correlated with the number of days necessary to bring the branches into bloom in the greenhouse.

BRANCHES OF SHRUBS FORCED IN A GREENHOUSE WITH NIGHT TEMPERATURE OF 55°–60° F.

	NO. OF DAYS TO BLOOM WHEN CUT JAN. 28	NO. OF DAYS TO BLOOM WHEN CUT MARCH 18	DATE OF NORMAL BLOOM OUT-OF-DOORS
Abeliophyllum distichum	20	6	April 5
Acer rubrum	22	6	April 5
Cercis canadensis	39	13	May 5
Chaenomeles lagenaria	39	—	May 5
Cornus florida	45	22	May 15
C. mas	19	0	April 5
Deutzia lemoinei	45	35	May 25
Forsythia ovata	18	8	April 5
F. suspensa	20	6	April 15
Halesia monticola rosea	44	22	May 15
Hamamelis japonica	16	—	March

BRANCHES OF SHRUBS FORCED IN A GREENHOUSE WITH NIGHT TEMPERATURE OF 55°–60°. F.

	NO. OF DAYS TO BLOOM WHEN CUT JAN. 28	NO. OF DAYS TO BLOOM WHEN CUT MARCH 18	DATE OF NORMAL BLOOM OUT-OF-DOORS
Kalmia latifolia	79	—	June 15
Kolkwitzia amabilis	—	38	June 5
Leucothoe racemosa	77	35	June 5
Lonicera standishii	16	5	April 15
Magnolia soulangiana 'Superba'	38	—	May 5
M. stellata	—	9	April 25
Pieris floribunda	30	12	April 25
P. japonica	24	9	April 15
Prunus sargentii	32	12	April 25
P. tomentosa	26	15	April 25
P. triloba	29	13	April 25
P. yedoensis	30	13	April 25
Rhododendron calendulaceum	77	38	June 5
R. carolinianum	53	31	May 15
R. fortunei	91	—	June 15
R. mucronulatum	21	8	April 15
R. obtusum kaempferi	43	29	May 15
R. schlippenbachii	43	18	May 15
R. yedoense poukhanense	50	31	May 15
Ribes odoratum	26	16	May 15
Spiraea prunifolia	31	9	April 25
S. thunbergii	29	12	May 5
Styrax japonica	65	36	June 5
Viburnum sargentii	—	50	June 5

The above results show that different species or varieties of plants which bloom at the same time out-of-doors take about the same length of time to bloom when branches are cut from them and forced indoors. Hence, since both *Rhododendron schlippenbachii* and *Halesia monticola rosea* bloom at the same time out-of-doors, when branches are cut on January 28th from both plants and forced in a warm greenhouse, it takes about 43 days for these cut branches to come into bloom. The later they bloom out-of-doors, the longer they take indoors, naturally. Also, plants dug with a ball of soil can be forced in about the same length of time as cut branches, under the same conditions. It goes without saying, that with higher greenhouse temperatures at night, the number of days to bloom can be further reduced.

FORESTIERA (for-es-STEER-a)
Two native American shrubs, 9 ft. tall, opposite-leaved, belonging to the Olive Family. Neither **F. acuminata** nor **F. neo-mexicana** have ornamental qualities that merit their planting in the home garden. Both are weedy, fast-growing, hardy up to Zone 5, of little ornamental value. Usually propagated by either layers, softwood or hardwood cuttings.

FORGET-ME-NOT, CHINESE = *Cynoglossum amabile*

FORGET-ME-NOT, CREEPING = *Omphalodes verna*

FORGET-ME-NOT, TRUE = *Myosotis scorpioides*

FORM. Subdivision of a variety or species usually differing in one character and usually perpetuated vegetatively.

FORMALDEHYDE. A powerful fungicide, which see.

FORMOSA-HONEYSUCKLE = *Leycesteria formosa*

FORSYTHIA (popularly, for-SITH-ia; preferably, for-SY-thia). Few plants are as bright and colorful in the spring as the forsythias. These are opposite-leaved shrubs native to the Orient with the exception of 1 species which is native to Europe. They all produce yellow flowers in the spring before the leaves appear. They are fast-growing shrubs varying in shape according to variety, easily propagated by hard or softwood cuttings and cut branches are easily forced into bloom when brought into the house and placed in water some time after Christmas. They are long-lived, 50- and 60-year-old plants, often flourishing in perfect condition.

At the turn of the century there were only about 4 forsythias available—now American nurserymen offer many. They are not susceptible to severe disease or insect pests and hence require little care. Since they bloom on wood made the previous year, they should be pruned only after they flower, for if this is done beforehand, many potential flowers will be cut off in the process. They grow in almost any kind of soil and can be grown in urban conditions. They can be sheared to make a formal hedge, but this detracts from the graceful habit of growth.

The hardiest, as well as the earliest to bloom, is *F. ovata*, usually blooming a week or 10 days before the others and satisfactory in places where winter temperatures do not go below − 10° F. All of the others will have their flower buds killed or partially killed at this temperature. Pruning should not be a shearing process; rather it should be a thinning out of the older branches at the base of the plant, thus allowing the younger, more vigorous ones to take over. Too often one sees them indiscriminately hacked off at the top, resulting in unsightly plants for the remainder of the year.

Propagation

Seed is produced sparsely, but it can be germinated after stratification for 2 months at 40° F. Plants may be easily divided with a sharp spade, some species easily form layers, and softwood and hardwood cuttings all root very easily.

Some of the more important species and varieties are:

x 'Arnold Dwarf'   4′   Zone 5
Resulting from a cross between *F. intermedia* and *F. japonica* made in the Arnold Arboretum in 1941, this hybrid should never be planted for its flowers, which are small and greenish yellow and are produced sparsely. In fact, plants may be 5 or 6 years old before they produce any flowers at all. As a woody ground cover, it is excellent chiefly because of the fact that its procumbent branches root readily wherever they touch moist soil. A 6-year-old plant may be only 2–3 ft. tall, but nearly 7 ft. wide, and as it grows older it may grow a few feet taller. However, if desired, this taller growth can be removed easily with brush scythe or pruning shears. Its ability to remain comparatively low and to spread regardless of the slope on which it is planted, are its chief merits.

europaea   6′   Zone 5   European Forsythia
Native to Europe, this has entire leaves, not toothed like most of the others, and it does not bloom so profusely as do other species.

x intermedia   9′   Zone 4   Border Forsythia
Actually, this is a hybrid species (*F. suspensa* x *F. viridissima*) originating in Europe before 1880. It is rather stiff and upright, although the branches do arch slightly. It is best to grow named clones of this variety which have been

asexually propagated, for these retain their true shape and habit. Some of these would be:

'Beatrix Farrand'—this is a cross between a colchicine-induced tetraploid and *F. ovata*, being a triploid, originating in the Arnold Arboretum in 1939 as a result of the plant-breeding work of Dr. Karl Sax. The flowers are often as much as 2½ in. in dia. and, in certain situations, are slightly darker than those of *F. intermedia* 'Spectabilis'. It is upright and dense in habit, produces heavy bloom, and is becoming popular for its vivid yellow, conspicuous flowers.

'Karl Sax'—similar in most respects to 'Beatrix Farrand', this is supposed to be slightly more flower-bud hardy in the Middle West. It originated in the Arnold Arboretum in 1944 and was named in 1960.

'Lynwood'—this was originally found as a branch sport of *F. intermedia* 'Spectabilis' in a garden in Cookstown, County Tyrone, Ireland, and was introduced by the Donard Nursery of Newcastle, County Down, Ireland. It was introduced into America in 1953 by the Gulf Stream Nursery of Wachapreague, Va., and is considered an improvement over *F. intermedia* 'Spectabilis' in that its flowers are more open and seem to be better distributed along the stem; that is, not so bunched. It, too, is a brilliant yellow, only minutely lighter in shade than *F. intermedia* 'Spectabilis', is upright in habit, possibly a little stiff, but still most beautiful in flower.

'Nana'—here probably belong several plants listed by various nurseries as "dwarf." It may take the plant 7 years to bloom from the time the cutting is taken and rooted and even then the flowers are not profuse, but small and of poor quality, being merely a greenish yellow. One 20-year-old plant was 5 ft. tall and 8 ft. wide, but in all that time it could not be called a good flowering specimen.

'Northern Sun'—introduced recently by the Minnesota Landscape Arboretum and said to be flower bud hardy down to − 30° F., hence hardy in Zone 4.

'Primulina'—originated in 1910 as a chance seedling in the Arnold Arboretum and named because of its light, primrose-yellow flowers.

'Spectabilis'—commonly called the Showy-border Forsythia, this originated in the great Spaeth Nurseries of Berlin, Germany, in 1906; it was introduced into America by the Arnold Arboretum in 1908. It is still one of the most popular of all, with flowers that are as vivid a yellow as 'Beatrix Farrand'. Being an *F. intermedia* variety, it is more upright and sturdy than *F. suspensa*, the flowers are larger (about 1¾ in.) and are produced in greater quantity and in clusters. Some consider the color display is almost a "brassy" yellow, yet there are many who prefer it for just this reason. It is a darker yellow than the *F. suspensa* varieties (vivid yellow, 2.5Y 8.5/13 of the Nickerson Color Fan) and with 'Beatrix Farrand' can be classed as having the darkest yellow flowers of the entire group.

'Spring Glory'—a branch sport of another of the Arnold Arboretum's introductions (*F. intermedia* 'Primulina'), this was found in the garden of Mr. H. H. Horvath, Mentor, Ohio, about 1930 and was introduced by the Wayside Gardens of Mentor, Ohio, about 1942. This and its parent, the Primrose Forsythia, have flowers that are a lighter yellow than the others, without being the objectionable greenish yellow of 'Arnold Dwarf'. It is an improvement over the once popular Primrose Forsythia in that it has larger flowers (about 2 in. in dia.) and more of them; hence it makes a much better display. Because of this, it may well replace the Primrose Forsythia in general landscape use.

ovata   4′   Zone 4   Korean Forsythia
This should not be considered as one of the best forsythias in Hardiness Zone 4 or in warmer areas, since the flowers are small and often are produced erratically. However, in slightly colder areas where the flower buds of the above-mentioned forsythias are known to be killed by winter cold, this might be tried, if a forsythia must be planted. Hence its uses are limited greatly, but it is worth mentioning. The flowers appear about 10 days before most of the other forsythias. Mr. E. H. Wilson first sent seeds to the Arnold Arboretum in 1917, collected from native plants in the Diamond Mountains in Korea. The original plant from these seeds is still growing well.

suspensa   9′   Zone 5   Weeping Forsythia
A native to China, this has widely arching branches that may touch the ground. It is interesting, but some of its varieties are even better. This species and its varieties are usually identified by the hollow pith (solid at the nodes) in their stems and by the leaves which are often deeply lobed or divided into 3 separate leaflets. Neither this nor its varieties produce as many flowers as does *F. intermedia* and its varieties. The two most popular varieties are:

fortunei—this is the form with gracefully arching branches, more upright in habit than Siebold's Forsythia, and because it has been so popular for so long, it is the form of *F. suspensa* which everyone has come to associate with this genus. The flowers are the same color as those of Siebold's, only slightly larger.

'Sieboldii'—this is the first forsythia to be introduced into European and American gardens; in Holland, in 1833; in England, about

20 years later; and in America, probably shortly thereafter. It is the form with the long, graceful, often procumbent branches that is sometimes seen planted at the edge of a wall where the long stems have an opportunity to hang down vertically for several feet. The stems root easily wherever they touch moist soil; the flowers are a brilliant yellow (Nickerson Color Fan 5Y 9/13) and are about 1⅛ in. in dia.

viridissima 'Bronxensis'   2′   Zone 5
Originating in the New York Botanical Garden in 1939, this is a very dwarf shrub with leaves 1–1½ in. long and ½ in. wide. However, unlike 'Arnold Dwarf', this one blooms profusely and very early in its life, too. The flowers are small, but are a good yellow and they appear in mid-April. Unfortunately, it roots with difficulty, but the heavy production of flowers, even on young plants, make it a desirable shrub to some. Ten-year-old plants may be only 1 ft. tall and 2 ft. wide.

FORTUNELLA (for-tew-NELL-a). These are small evergreen fruit trees, grown about where oranges are but slightly more hardy and native to southeastern Asia. The fruits are small, elongated little oranges of orange color, attractive and aromatic, used for preserves and can be eaten raw. They often are grown as ornamental tub plants. Culture is similar to that for oranges, which see. They belong to the Citrus Family. The trees are only about 10–15 ft. tall, produce small white flowers either singly or in clusters. There are chiefly 3 species grown:

crassifolia   8′–15′   Zone 9   Meiwa Kumquat
The orange-colored fruits can be eaten raw, and they are about 1½ in. wide. Branchlets are spiny sometimes, leaves thick and the stalks with narrow wings. Native to China.

japonica   7′–10′   Zones 9–10   Marumi Kumquat
Densely branched, with spines and small leaves, this bears small, globose fruits about 1¼ in. wide, colored a deep orange. The pulp is acid, the rind sweet and edible. Native to China.

margarita   10′   Zones 8–9   Nagami Kumquat
This has no spines, bears oblong-to-ellipsoid fruit of a fairly uniform size about 3–4 in. long and 1 in. in dia. Also the species is slightly more hardy than the others. It is juicy and dark orange colored. Probably planted more than the other 2 species, especially in southern Fla. where it is even planted as an ornamental. Fruit is profusely borne from Oct. to June.

FOTHERGILLA (foth-er-GILL-a). Deciduous, alternate-leaved shrubs, native to the southeastern U.S. and closely related to the witchhazels. The flowers are small, white, borne in small upright spikes before the leaves appear and are prominent because of the conspicuous stamens. There are no petals. Fruits are dried capsules. The foliage turns a gorgeous yellow-orange-red in the fall. Propagated by seed which is doubly dormant, hence it must be stratified for 5 months at room temperature, then for 3 months at 40° F., then sown. Softwood cuttings can be rooted. See STRATIFICATION, CUTTINGS.

gardenii   3′   Zone 5   Dwarf Fothergilla
The lowest of the fothergillas, this is native from Va. to Ga.; the white terminal flower spikes are over 1 in. long and the thimblelike flower heads appear in mid-May. Like the other species the autumn color of the foliage is a gorgeous yellow to orange to scarlet, and these are the reasons why it is planted.

major   9′   Zone 5   Large Fothergilla
These interesting and beautiful plants are not planted nearly as much as they should be. This is similar in general to *F. gardenii* but the flower heads are 2 in. long, the plant is upright and pyramidal in habit, and one of the best ornamentals in the fall when its foliage turns a brilliant yellow to scarlet.

monticola   6′   Zone 5   Alabama Fothergilla
More spreading in habit than *F. major* with slightly larger flowers, this native of N.Car. and Ala. is excellent when placed in foundation plantings, especially if planted in front of evergreens where its splendid spring flowers and autumn foliage can be shown off to excellent advantage.

FOUNDATION PLANTING. The proper selection of shrubs and other plants for planting about the base of a building is a real art. Plants selected should not grow too tall, especially when placed in front of windows. On the other hand a few tall and narrow shrubs or trees are often selected for placing in front of that part of the building wall which has no windows or for placing at the end of the building to "tie" in with surrounding vegetation or lawn.

Where possible, it is advisable to use some evergreen plants for although some, like the yews, will not have conspicuous flowers, their foliage will be green and "alive" throughout the entire year. Both narrow-leaved and broad-leaved evergreens should be used, for the variance in foliage texture is most interesting.

Size of plant materials also depends on the size of the building. Smaller plants would be selected for the 1-floor house than for one 3 floors high. One should be careful not to select too many plants with formal shapes, i.e. ball-like or definitely mounded, for informal-shaped plants should also be included. One of the worst mistakes made in some foundation plantings is when all the plants have formal shapes or have been sheared to simulate such shapes. The general theory of planting is to make the house or building fit into a bed of interesting plants of varied heights. Most lines on the building are perpendicular and the ground lines are usually horizontal. Informal lines, a little of both perpendicular and horizontal, are desired in the plant materials to make the building blend in gracefully with the ground.

Evergreen ground covers like the *Juniperus horizontalis* varieties, *Pachysandra terminalis* and *Asarum europeum* can be intermixed with a few clumps of bulbs or low perennials. The planting next to the main entrance should be given special attention for it is the plants here that are closely observed. Yew, the Japanese Andromeda, small-leaved rhododendrons and the low forms of Box or Japanese Holly are all ideal. One friend of ours had a clump of Lavender next to the front steps, a conspicuous and aromatic plant that he always kept neat and well grown.

The plants should not be overcrowded, should have room for normal expansion and if for any reason some do grow out of scale they should be pruned back to make them conform with the rest of the planting. There is nothing which can ruin a foundation planting quicker than a few plants growing out of all proportion to the others. Select plants that will stay in scale, prune them heavily if necessary to keep them in scale, or else remove them when they become overgrown. Many growth problems can be solved at planting time merely by selecting plants with mature heights that will be within the desired limits.

Annual flowers and edging plants may be used, but these create work and it is often easier to create the right effect with hardy shrubs, ground covers and bulbs, with a few well-chosen clumps of pest-free herbaceous perennials for summer color.

Small trees like the Dogwood, Redbud, Redcedar and Star Magnolia can be worked in well in foundation plantings where they will not interfere with windows. Especially are these used at the ends of the building, or as tall plants to frame the doorway.

Rhododendrons and azaleas, as well as Mountain-laurel, are also used where acid soils prevail, but, even if the soil is acid (at the time of planting) about a brick or stucco building, splashing rain water dissolves enough lime from the building face to eventually raise the acidity of the soil to or beyond the neutral mark. Many plantings of these nice ericaceous shrubs have had to be removed because of yellowing leaves and gradual death of branches due to the change in the soil acidity at the base of a concrete or brick wall. If these plants are selected, then make certain that the soil is kept acid by special soil treatment. See SOILS.

Finally, in areas of heavy snowfall, an additional hazard to a foundation planting is offered by sliding snow from a slanting roof coming down in large amounts and breaking the branches. Such a situation has to be studied carefully to determine where the snow falls, then to plant in front of that area if possible. Sometimes it becomes necessary to erect board protections over plants for the winter season to prevent such breakage, but this becomes an annual nuisance. It is better to attempt planting in such a way that the snow from the roof will not seriously injure the plants. Admittedly this is not always possible, but some plants (yews) can recover more quickly from such breakage than others (rhododendrons).

FOUNTAINS. See GARDEN FIXTURES.

FOUR-O'CLOCK, SWEET = *Mirabilis longiflora*

FOUR-O'CLOCK FAMILY = Nyctaginaceae

FOXGLOVE. See DIGITALIS.

FOXGLOVE FAMILY = Scrophulariaceae

FOXGLOVE, FALSE = *Aureolaria flava*

FOXTAIL. See SETARIA.

FOXTAIL-GRASS, MEADOW = *Alopecurus pratensis*

FRAGARIA (frag-AY-ria). Also see STRAWBERRY.

   americana = *F. vesca americana*
   chiloensis 6″ Zones 4–5 Chiloe Strawberry
A low creeping strawberry found from Alaska to Calif. and in Chile, with thick, green, trifoliate leaves, whitish underneath, stocky runners, white flowers of 5 petals, ¾ in. wide on floppy stalks; fruit large and firm and dark red. L. H. Bailey notes that var. **ananassa** contains most of the larger-fruited garden strawberries now being grown. See STRAWBERRY for general culture.
   daltoniana   creeping   Zone 6   Daltonia Strawberry
A strawberry from the Himalayas, this plant forms a dense mat of small, glossy, dark green leaves which rise a few inches from the soil. It bears large white flowers and bright red fruits.
   vesca 8″ Zones 5–6 European Strawberry
This plant from the European Alps grows in clusters 8 in. long. The loose clusters of large white flowers are followed by bright red fruits. This species is naturally everbearing, with flowers and fruits borne throughout the season from June to late fall. The var. **americana** is merely the American form of this European species. Native to eastern North America.
   virginiana 4″–12″ Zone 3 Wild Strawberry
The Wild Strawberry can be found throughout eastern Canada and the U.S. and west to Okla. in fields and sunny woodlands. Compound leaves, having reddish stems and 3-toothed

leaflets, are produced from horizontal runners. From April to June the flowering stems, generally 4–5 in., occasionally up to 12 in. high, produce white flowers with 5 petals. These are followed by the small, cone-shaped red fruits highly prized for strawberry jam or as fresh fruit. Throughout the summer some of the leaves are colored bright red, much to the disappointment of eager berry-pickers. Propagation is by means of transplanted runners.

FRAMES. In horticultural parlance this is a boxlike affair, placed out-of-doors with glass sash on top, in which plants, seedlings and cuttings can be grown. Usually these are 6 ft. wide, and vary in length depending on the needs of the gardener but, since standard hotbed sash comes 6 ft. x 3 ft., the length of the frame is in multiples of 3 ft. plus 2 in. between each sash. They are built with the sash slanting, usually facing the south, with the back 9–12 in. higher than the front. They can be operated as simple cold frames, without additional heat, but the use of electric heating units is comparatively so inexpensive and opens up so many additional uses for the frame, that electricity might well be considered as a necessary part of this important garden asset. For construction see ELECTRIC HOTBEDS.

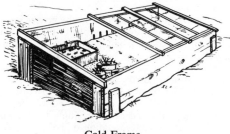

Cold Frame

   The term hotbed came from the fact that, when manure was available to gardeners, fresh manure was mixed with straw and leaves, well watered and let ferment a few days; then a layer of this material, about 6–8 in. deep, was placed in the bottom of the bed, sand or soil on top, and the heat created by the fermenting manure was sufficient, after a few days, to raise the temperature to 75°–80° so that it actually was a small heated greenhouse, with the temperature remaining high for several weeks and gradually going down as fermentation slowly stopped. This type of heat was difficult to regulate and of an indefinite period. The added work of preparing the manure and digging it out again after the need for a high temperature has ceased is more than the modern gardener cares to undertake.

Hence most modern gardeners use electric heating cables in these frames.

Wood for construction should be of the best quality one can afford and if a permanent cold frame (or hotbed) is desired, care should be taken in the preparation of the foundation for the frame, i.e., brick, concrete blocks or concrete itself. It should face south, if possible, be in the full sun and be of tight construction.

If only potted plants and flats are to be placed in the hotbed, then only a layer of cinders or coarse gravel, 3–6 in. deep, is necessary for good drainage. However, it is important to carefully figure the distance between this gravel level and the lowest part of the sash when it is in place, for this is the space which governs the height of the plants that can be set on the cinders. Pots may be 6 in. high and plants in them up to an additional 12 in. at least. If larger plants are contemplated more space must be provided. Painting the frame and the sash is necessary to keep them from rotting and to keep them looking well.

Shading must be provided. The simplest, when needed only for a few days in hardening off a group of greenhouse plants, is to paint the glass with a mixture of clay soil and water, and repeat if washed off by rain. Better would be shading panels made of aluminum strips built on frames exactly the same size as the glass sash. Thin strip aluminum comes in rolls 2 in. wide and can be cut with shears, with 1-in. space left between each 2 strips of 2-in. aluminum. Also lathes make excellent shades; distances between each lath nailed down on the frame is the width of one lath. Also, small cypress strips 1½ in. wide and 1½ in. apart make fine shade. All these should be on short legs 2–3 in. long so that there is an air space between the shade and the glass for cooling during hot days. Wide woven burlap has also been used but it does not look as nice nor last as long as the other materials.

The frame can be used for hardening off (which see) greenhouse plants, for growing seedlings of garden flowers and vegetables, for placing house plants out-of-doors under shade, for a "rest" in the summer, and for wintering-over plants that otherwise might die from winter cold. In this case, leaves, hay, straw or compost might be mounded up about the frame for additional protection from winter cold. Clear polyethylene might be tacked on the underside of the glass sash as this would aid greatly in conserving heat. Rough burlap mats or evergreen boughs could also be placed on top of the frames for additional protection. It should be noted that watering of plants in frames over winter is necessary later in the fall than one might expect, for in frames, soil freezes much later.

Certainly the soil should not be allowed to dry out at this time. Also, it might be advisable to place poison grain in the frames to eliminate the possibility of rodent damage.

If electric heating cables are in the frames, then they can be started in March (if built well, insulated and tight) and many of the garden vegetables (tomatoes, lettuce, cabbage, eggplant, squash, melons, parsley, etc.) can be started. Also most of the flower seeds that need an early start can be grown such as Stock, Dahlia, Cosmos, Aster, Marigold, Petunia, etc.

Then too, with electric heat and a sand-rooting medium, this frame can be used for rooting cuttings any time during spring, summer or early fall. See PROPAGATION, ELECTRIC HOTBED.

FRANGIPANI. See PLUMERIA.

FRANKLINIA (frank-LIN-ia)

alatamaha   30′   Zone 5   Franklinia

This tree was originally found in Ga., but since about 1790 no other trees have been found in the wild. It is chiefly valued for its large single white flowers—as much as 3 in. in dia., with the center a mass of yellow stamens, which appear in Sept. and Oct. The leaves are 5–6 in. long. If the plant is grown with a western exposure in full sun, the autumn color is a gorgeous rich orange and red. It can be grown as a tree in the South, but in New England as its northern limit it might best be grown as a shrub with many branches from the ground. The soil can then be mounded about the base of these in the late fall, so that if the winter is a severe one and kills the above-ground branches the roots will remain alive and send up new shoots the following year.

Propagation

Do not allow the seed to dry out but sow as soon as ripe. Also softwood and hardwood cuttings both root satisfactorily. See CUTTINGS.

FRAXINUS (frax-EYE-nus). Ash trees are rapid-growing shade trees, the native species distributed over the entire U.S. Some (like *F. americana*) are so profuse in their seed production and the seeds germinate so easily that they frequently become pests in the garden. Many trees have both staminate and pistillate flowers, some have perfect flowers, while others are supposed to be unisexual. To prevent the promiscuous seeding of these trees, it is certainly ideal to propagate asexually, using only staminate-flowering, or male trees. Such cultivars are already being propagated.

This group of trees is closely related to the lilac, and, as a result, they are frequently susceptible to attacks of scale, for which they must be regularly sprayed. It is for this reason that other trees are frequently used which are not susceptible to this serious pest.

Ash trees have compound, opposite leaves, most of which turn a rich yellow to purplish color in the fall. The flowers of a few species (like *F. ornus* and *F. mariesii*) differ from those of most of the other ashes in that they have both corolla and calyx present, making them most conspicuous, whereas the flowers of most other ashes are not outstanding in that they do not have corolla or calyx.

In our experience most ashes are fibrous-rooted, which of course enables them to be easily transplanted—quite different from the difficult tap-rooted hickories. It is because of their rapid growth while young that many are interested in this group and that the search is continuing for definitely staminate-flowering trees, which should be the only type to use.

Propagation

Seed of *F. americana* should be stratified for 3 months at 40° F., then sown. Or it can be stored dry in a cool place in airtight containers for up to a year, then stratified. Seed of other species may take 2 years to germinate; hence they should be stratified for 3–5 months at warm temperatures, then 3 months at 40° F., then sown.

Budding and grafting the many varieties is the most common means of commercial propagation, either using *F. excelsior* as the understock or seedlings of closely related *Fraxinus* species. See STRATIFICATION, BUDDING, GRAFTING.

americana 120′ **Zone 3** **White Ash**
Young Americans know this tree as the one which provides most of the wood for baseball bats. Vigorous, rapid in growth, profuse in seed production (sometimes actually a pest), it is really not a tree for small gardens where space is restricted. This and the Green Ash (*F. pennsylvanica lanceolata*) are the 2 most grown in American nurseries, this one being native to the eastern U.S. The foliage has an excellent purple-to-yellow autumn color.

excelsior 120′ **Zone 3** **European Ash**
Very popular in Europe where it is native and where several of its varieties are also grown, this species has also been planted in America but the foliage does not have the brilliant autumn coloration of our native *F. americana*. In fact, the leaves do not turn color in the fall at all, merely dropping while still green. It was considered at one time the most important of British timber trees. Some varieties are: 'Aurea'—with yellow branchlets; the older bark is noticeably yellowish especially during the winter; 'Nana'—an excellent globe-shaped

tree. When grafted 7–8 ft. high on a single-trunked understock of *F. excelsior* it develops into an excellent low tree for planting directly under electric utility wires; 'Pendula'—this, when grafted high on the understock, is a spreading, umbrella-shaped tree with weeping branchlets. This is popular in European gardens.

holotricha 35′ **Zone 5**
Found in several places in Germany and the east Balkan Peninsula, this was introduced by Spaeth's Nurseries, Germany, in 1909. The leaves have 9–13 leaflets and the tree is finding use as a fine small tree, fast-growing, upright and narrow in habit. The patented clone 'Moraine' is noted for bearing very few seeds and is from a tree collected in the Danube Delta Region of central Europe.

latifolia (*F. oregana*) **80′ Zone 6 Oregon Ash**
Used as a street tree in the general area of the Pacific Coast where it is native. It is narrow in general habit.

mariesii 24′ **Zone 7** **Maries' Ash**
Considered by some to be the most ornamental of the *F. ornus* group, being especially attractive in summer because the fruits take on an interesting purple color. It is native to China. It is another small tree which might be of value in the South although it has not been tried extensively in America up to the present time. This is a smaller, daintier tree in every way (leaves, flowers, habit) than the larger *F. ornus* and could be used in place of *F. ornus* in the warmer parts of the country.

oregona = *F. latifolia*

ornus 60′ **Zone 5** **Flowering Ash**
With luxuriant foliage and interesting ornamental flowers, differing from most other ashes (except *F. mariesii*) in that each flower has a corolla and calyx and they are profusely produced, making the tree quite conspicuous in flowering time, with 3–5 in. terminal panicles during mid-May. This tree, native in southern Europe and western Asia, has long been popular in Europe and only recently has become of interest in America. It is sometimes called the "Manna Ash" because a sweetish exudate called "Manna" has been obtained from the sap. This is sometimes used medicinally as a mild laxative.

pennsylvanica lanceolata 60′ **Zone 2 Green Ash**
Almost as widely distributed as the White Ash, this ash differs from the species in that the leaflets are slightly shorter and more narrow and the leaves are a brighter green, with leaves, petioles and twigs all glabrous. Some botanists in the past have considered it a separate species, *F. lanceolata*, but now this name is accepted as a synonym. It makes a better ornamental tree than *F. pennsylvanica* and has a good yellow

autumn color. Varieties of *F. pennsylvanica lanceolata*: 'Marshall's Seedless' Ash—this tree was originally obtained by the Marshall Nurseries of Arlington, Neb., from the Porter-Walton Company of Salt Lake City, Utah, some years prior to 1959. It was purchased as a "male green ash", but as the Marshall Nursery began distributing it here and there, and because it was the first *seedless* ash to be given prominence, it became known as 'Marshall's Seedless' and that name will probably stay with this ash. The foliage is an excellent, dark, glossy green and the young trees have a definitely uniform pyramidal shape. Being the first male ash to be asexually propagated and distributed on a commercial scale, it deserves special emphasis, for such a tree has been needed in landscape work for many years; 'Summit'—a clone named by the Summit Nurseries of Stillwater, Minn. The leaves are glossy, the habit is definitely upright with a strong central leader. However, the plant is a female and hence produces seeds.

quadrangulata   75′   Zone 3   Blue Ash
Not often used as an ornamental, this is a deciduous, opposite-leaved tree, the leaves having 7–11 leaflets which turn pale yellow in the fall. Native from Mich. to Tenn.

uhdei   30′   Zone 9   Shamel Ash
An evergreen native to Mexico, with bright, glossy green leaves and rounded habit which is fast finding favor in Calif. as a street and ornamental shade tree. It needs some pruning to prevent it from becoming too lanky, for it does grow fast. Apparently seedlings vary considerably with respect to hardiness, and asexual reproduction should be practiced with the better, hardier forms.

velutina   20′–45′   Zone 7   Velvet Ash
An ash native in the southwestern part of the U.S., this has its uses locally as a shade and street tree. The young twigs and leaves are covered with a gray down, not evident in the Modesto Ash (*F. velutina glabra*). This Modesto Ash has 3–7 leaflets in each leaf (the species has 3–5) and glabrous leaves. It is proving popular in the Southwest as a street tree. In drier areas the variety **toumeyi** is being used, but often these varieties differ only slightly from the species.

FREESIA (FREE-SIA). These are tender plants with bulblike corms usually popularly classified as bulbs, with straight, lanceolate leaves like those of the Daffodil and a flower stalk on which are borne numerous tubular and very fragrant flowers at right angles to the flower stalk. They are mostly white or yellow but some of the newer hybrids are variously colored rose, blue, purple and brown. Native to South Africa. Easily propagated by offsets and seeds.

Used mostly as a greenhouse plant except in the very Deep South. They can be planted in pots any time from Oct. to Jan. (some plant them at 2-week intervals for continuous bloom) about 12 corms to an 8-in. bulb pan. When brought into the greenhouse they should be grown at cool temperatures (45°–55° F.), watered well, in full sun. They should bloom 10–12 weeks after planting. Corms may be dried after flowering, stored over summer and used again. Aphis may infest young plants. See APHIS.

x hybrida   1½′   Zone 9
A group name to include some of the newer vari-colored types with very large flowers like: 'Albatre'—white; 'Buttercup'—yellow, shaded orange; 'Charmante'—pink and apricot; 'Flambeau'—carmine; 'Maryon'—lavender; 'Penerosa'—pink with yellow throat; 'Princess Marijke'—bronze, orange and yellow.

refracta   1½′   Zone 9   Common Freesia
This is the species commonly planted with greenish-yellow to bright yellow flowers 2 in. long. There are several vars: **alba**—with white flowers; **leichtlinii**—pale yellow with orange blotch; and **xanthospila**—has a white throat.

FREMONTTODENDRON (free-MONT-to-dendron)

mexicanum   10′–15′   Zone 9   San Diego Fremontia
With palmately lobed, hairy, evergreen leaves. The flowers are 2¼–4 in. wide, orange-yellow but have no petals and still are showy. Native to Mexico. *F. californica*, often called the Flannel-bush, is somewhat similar with flowers 2 in. wide, and leaves 1 in. long and densely tomentose beneath. Both are propagated by seed or softwood cuttings.

FRENCH-HONEYSUCKLE = *Hedysarum coronarium*

FRINGECUP, ALASKA = *Tellima grandiflora*

FRINGE-ORCHIS, LARGE PURPLE = *Habenaria fimbriata*

FRINGETREE. See CHIONANTHUS.

FRITILLARIA (frit-ill-AY-ria). Of some 70 species in this genus, only a few are of ornamental value. They are bulbous plants, members of the Lily Family, with bell-shaped pendant flowers about an inch or so in dia., borne in the spring. They are easily cultivated, and are propagated by offsets, rarely by seeds. It is well to lift and separate them every 2–3 years.

imperialis   3′   Zone 5   Crown Imperial, Imperial Fritillary
This is the largest and most imposing species of this genus with a tall 3 ft. flower stalk at the end of which is a ring of 8–10 brilliantly colored red and yellow bell-shaped, slightly pendant flowers, each up to 2 in. long, borne usually in April. Native to Persia. There are several varieties available.

lanceolata 2′ Zone 5 Riceroot Fritillary

Flowers purple and yellow to 1½ in. long in 1–4 flowered racemes. Native from British Columbia to Calif.

meleagris 1′ Zone 3 Guinea-hen Flower

With purplish drooping flowers often mottled or speckled in April and several varieties ranging to silver-gray, each about 3 in. across, borne singly or in groups of 3. The var. **alba** has pure white flowers. Native to Calif.

pluriflora 1′ Zone 5 Pink Fritillary, Adobe-lily

Flowers pinkish purple, 1¼ in. long with 4–12 flowers in a raceme. Native to Calif.

pudica 6″ Zones 2–3 Yellow Fritillary

With yellow flowers, ¾ in. long, 1–3 in a raceme, the leaves very narrow. Native from British Columbia to Calif. Leaves very narrow and almost grasslike.

recurva 2½′ Zone 6 Scarlet Fritillary

Leaves very narrow and linear, flowers yellow and scarlet, 1½ in. long in 3–6 flowered racemes. Native to southern Ore. and Calif.

FRITILLARY. See FRITILLARIA.

FROND. Leaf of a fern.

FROST-FREE DAYS. See CLIMATE.

FROST AND FROST CONTROL. There is little gardeners can do to control frost (see ORANGE) and there is a considerable difference between a light frost, when the temperatures go to 28° F. and a heavy frost when they go much lower. Plants sometimes can be protected from the first light frost by laying cloth, polyethylene, or newspapers over them the evening before the frost occurs, the general idea being to trap the soil heat around the plants and prevent the colder air from striking them.

Plants lightly touched with frost can sometimes be saved by sprinkling them with water before direct sunlight strikes them.

Potted plants placed under trees with low branches, or next to a warm house foundation sometimes escape injury of a light frost. All such effort is only temporary in the fall, however, because sooner or later a heavier frost will come that will do the damage regardless of such temporary protecting efforts. The gardener would do well to know 2 dates for his locality—the approximate date of the last killing frost in the spring, and the approximate date of the first killing frost in the fall. Weather Bureau records contain (and publish) such information. Armed with this, the gardener knows the date after which it is usually safe to plant out greenhouse plants in the open. Also it gives him some idea when he can expect killing frosts in the fall. It may pay him to protect certain plants (tomatoes, special garden flowers or a few potted plants) from the first light frost when he knows from the records that the killing frosts are some weeks away.

FROST CRACKS. In the North during winter, when trunks of trees have been frozen by winter cold, a warm day during Jan. and Feb. may occur. The trunk, especially on the southwest side, is warmed considerably and at sunset the temperature may suddenly drop to well below freezing or even zero. This causes unnatural stresses and strains in the trunks of some trees and can cause splitting—suddenly with an explosive report. This may grow together during the summer, but once it has happened, the trunk is weak here and it can happen another year in the same place. As the cambium attempts to grow together, a ridge is formed up and down the trunk at this spot, formed by succeeding layers of new tissue. For methods of repairing a frost crack see TREE SURGERY.

FRUIT. The seed-bearing product of a plant.

FRUIT TREES, DWARF. There are fruit tree varieties (as well as many ornamental woody plants) that are naturally more dwarf than others. The home garden is not the spacious place it used to be, and there is not much room for the common large-growing fruit tree varieties. There is an interest in smaller fruit trees that can be grown on a small place and managed by one individual without the use of expensive mechanical equipment. Since the home owners of the country are frequently desirous of having such plants, they are being produced commercially and the state experiment stations frequently have programs designed to find better ways of dwarfing such plants.

Practices Inducing Dwarfing

Fruiting itself is a dwarfing process. The earlier in the life of a tree that fruits are borne, the smaller the tree, especially with apple varieties. The heavier the crop of fruits, the smaller the tree. Most cultural programs are aimed at bringing trees into early bearing, and aiding them to bear annually.

Pruning to produce a low head on a tree is dwarfing, to some extent at least. Also heavy pruning is dwarfing, for in removing a great deal of plant growth one materially reduces the food-manufacturing organs (leaves) and with less food, there is less growth.

Certain chemicals have been used to reduce growth. Maleic hydrazide has been used at 1000 parts per million, sprayed on the leaves just enough to wet them when they appear in the spring. This has reduced growth in privet, but because it also reduces or destroys fruit set, it has not proved satisfactory with apple trees.

Reduction in the use of fertilizers, especially on poor soils, is of course a dwarfing process, but in fruit production it is not practical, for it also reduces fruit size and fruit production itself.

Root pruning (which see) is a dwarfing process, understandably so, for it reduces the proportion of roots, hence the amount of nutrients the roots obtain from the soil. However, it is frequently suggested as the means by which non-blooming shrubs like wisterias, dogwoods, lilacs and even fruit trees, can be forced into forming flower buds, especially if such plants have been producing large amounts of vegetative growth and few flowers.

Girdling, ringing and scoring are dwarfing processes although only temporarily so. The Apple and Pear are sometimes treated thus, but the stone fruits (Peach, Cherry, Plum) are more easily root pruned and not ringed. Girdling is a general term used to denote any means by which the bark is cut or removed completely around a tree trunk. It is an old practice, recorded over a thousand years ago, but is not done on a commercial scale with fruit trees, although it is sometimes done with grapes. If done early in the season (on grapes) it induces heavier fruit production and a higher sugar content in them. With fruit trees, it apparently has little effect on the current year's crop, but will induce the setting of more fruit buds for the following year. Other growth factors enter the picture, however, so it is not a standard recommended procedure on fruit trees except in individual instances where it is desired to bring a tree (or a wisteria vine) into early flower production.

One form of girdling is the use of a special double-bladed knife with blades set about $\frac{1}{4}$ in. apart, drawn completely around the trunk of the tree (in early spring or in the fall) and the bark between these cuts is entirely removed. The wound should be protected from infection by painting. A modification of this is to remove the bark strip only on half the trunk, then a few inches down remove a strip on the other half. Removing a wider strip might kill the tree.

Scoring is merely drawing a knife completely around the trunk so that all the vessels in the outer bark are cut, but no bark is removed. This is simply done and does not require wound protection afterwards.

The same effect is sometimes obtained, especially on wisteria vines, by tightening a wire completely around the main trunk. This constricts the upward and downward movement of sap, sometimes sufficiently to bring about flowering in a plant which has normally produced only vegetative growth.

Twisting, bending or artificially spreading branches sometimes has a dwarfing effect.

All these methods, although used occasionally on individual trees, are mostly only of a temporary nature. The use of dwarfing rootstocks is by far the best means of causing permanent dwarfing to fruit-tree stocks.

Dwarfing Rootstocks

Much work has been done with dwarfing rootstocks throughout the U.S. and Canada, and still there remains much that can be learned. Little has been done with dwarfing understock for woody ornamental plants, and it is certainly a wide-open field for investigation. The general idea is that some fruit trees grow much slower than others, and usually the fruits are decidedly inferior to standard varieties. By grafting desired varieties on slow-growing understocks, the fruit obtained is standard, but the size of the tree producing it is materially reduced. Such plants are generally thought of as "dwarf fruit trees."

However, many problems enter into making sturdy dwarf fruit trees. For instance, the dwarfing understock may not grow at the same rate as the scion. If it is slower, which it frequently is, the faster-growing scion will become evident at the graft union by a trunk larger in dia. above the union than below. With a faster-growing understock a wider trunk will be formed below the scion. These differences in size at the graft union may make for a weakened graft union which will separate when the tree gets mature.

Sometimes "incompatibility" of scion and understock is a problem, that is, they do not grow together quickly into a strongly knit union, and breakage at the graft union can occur in the early life of the tree.

To circumvent this an intermediate piece is sometimes used which is compatible both with the scion and with the understock. The intermediate scion is grafted on or budded on the understock, and the the desired variety is grafted on or budded on the intermediate piece. This "double working" of an intermediate stem piece has proved successful in several cases of making sturdy, dwarf fruit trees.

'East Malling XVI' has been used as a rootstock for apples, on which 'East Malling VIII' has been used as an intermediate piece. This produces early fruiting, well-anchored trees. For very dwarf trees the so-called "Clark Dwarf" has been used as the understock with 'East Malling IX' as the intermediate piece, but dwarfing is always less when the dwarfing material is used as the intermediate piece. When it is the understock, dwarfing is greater. Also short sections of an intermediate stem piece are less dwarfing than longer ones.

Apples

There are many rootstocks available for dwarfing apples, but perhaps none makes smaller trees than 'East Malling IX', originated with a large number of others at the East Malling Agricultural Research Station in England. 'East Malling VII' gives better well-anchored trees, although slightly larger than some other rootstocks, and is considered a "semi-dwarf" understock; 'East Malling XI' is more resistant to winter cold. Malling-Merton understocks (known as the MM series) are also used, developed by the East Malling station and the John Innes Horticultural Foundation formerly located at Merton, England. Dwarfing apple understocks have also been developed in America. 'Robusta #5' was developed in Canada for cold-resistant trees, only slightly dwarfed from the normal. 'MM 104' and 'MM 111' are popular understocks producing trees about the size or only slightly larger than 'East Malling II'. These are only a few of those used in producing dwarf apple trees at present.

Cherry

Prunus mahaleb is still the chief understock with which to dwarf both sweet and sour cherry varieties, but it is only slightly dwarfing with the Sour Cherry and its results are variable with sweet cherries. If the stempiece is 3 ft. long and the graft (or bud) is on top of that, the dwarfing effect is increased.

Peach

There are no completely satisfactory dwarfing understocks for use with peaches, nectarines and apricots. Peach trees themselves are not large, nor long lived. There are some so-called "dwarf peaches" but most of these have fruits of inferior quality to standard varieties. 'Swatow', introduced by the U.S. Dept. of Agric. from China, has been used to develop the 'Flory' variety which seldom grows over 5 ft. tall. 'Bonanza' is another developed by the Armstrong Nurseries in Calif.

Pear

Quince is about the only understock which has worked successfully with dwarfing pears, and even this has not proved successful with all varieties. In fact, pears just can not be dwarfed (at present) to the extent apples can. The following pear varieties have proved satisfactory for grafting on quince and 'East Malling C' quince, a clone of 'Angers' has given about the best dwarfing of any up to date: 'Beurre d'Anjou', 'Duchess de Angoulême', 'Glow Morceau', 'Howell', 'Louise Bonne de Jersey', 'Tyson', 'Vicar of Winkfield', 'White Doyenne'.

Other varieties might be tried on an intermediate stempiece (on quince) of 'Old Home' pear which is compatible both with quince and many pear varieties.

Plum

No rootstock supplies the dwarfing to plum varieties that 'East Malling IX' does for apples. Many are being tried and it is hoped that some will be forthcoming before long.

For further and more detailed information concerning this entire topic of dwarf fruit trees see "Dwarfed Fruit Trees" by H. B. Tukey. Macmillan, 1964.

For information on the culture of standard fruit trees, their varieties, etc., see APPLE, CHERRY, PEACH, PEAR, PLUM, etc.

FRUTICOSE. Shrubby; with woody, persistent stems and branches.

FUCHSIA (popularly FEW-shia, but correctly FEWKS-ia). There are about 50 species of Fuchsia native to Central and South America and New Zealand and possibly 2000 garden hybrids. They are valued for their colorful flowers, usually produced in the greatest profusion throughout the summer. Leaves are mostly opposite, though a few species have alternate leaves. They are used chiefly as greenhouse pot plants, in window boxes, hanging baskets or as garden plants in the South, especially in southern Calif.

Fuchsias are easily grown, have few pests and respond rapidly to the application of fertilizer. They are easily propagated by terminal cuttings of the soft, current shoots taken almost any time of year. They can also be grown from seed which is first cleaned when it is ripe in the late summer, then dried and sown or else held dry until the following year and then sown.

When plants are set out in the garden during summer in the North, they are heavily cut back in the fall, lifted with a ball of soil, and set in a cool cellar or pit or cold frame for the rest of the winter, being kept rather dry during this period. In the early spring or late winter they are repotted, brought into the greenhouse and forced for growth.

Pinching the elongating shoots is essential to make a compact, dense plant and this should be done at intervals until the plant has reached the right proportions. They require good drainage, plenty of water and good soil. They should be given partial shade, especially when they are to be grown in hot areas. Syringing in the morning and late afternoon is always conducive to good growth.

fulgens   **4′**   **Zone 10**   **Flame Fuchsia**
Opposite leaves up to 7 in. long and red flowers 3 in. long in short racemes, native to Mexico.

This is supposed to be one of the parents (with *F. magellanica*) of most of the large-flowered hybrid varieties that are now commonly grown. The long scarlet flowers are narrowly funnel shaped. This species blooms in the summer and is treated chiefly as a greenhouse plant. As ornamentals, the hybrids are better.

x hybrida 3′–5′ Zone 10 Common Fuchsia
A general name given to the perhaps 2000 named varieties of the Common Fuchsia which are so popular among gardeners. These are mostly crosses between *F. fulgens* and *F. magellanica*, having larger flowers than either species, usually shrubby, sometimes slightly pendulous, with flowers having a pink, red, white or yellow corolla and a crimson calyx. Some of the more popular varieties are: **'Carmelita'**—with double white flowers; **'Gartenmeister Bonstedt'**—with long, slender flowers and green and bronzy-red leaves; **'Little Beauty'**—with petals lavender-blue and pink sepals; **'Trophie'**—with double white to violet-blue flowers. **'Muriel'** and **'San Francisco'**, as well as *F. magellanica gracilis*, are trailing plants, excellent for hanging baskets.

magellanica 3′ Zones 5–6 Magellan Fuchsia
Peru and Chile are the habitat of this interesting shrub, but it has been widely distributed since 1800, even becoming naturalized along the roadsides of southern Ireland. The flowers, usually solitary, are red and violet, appearing in mid-June, and for the rest of the growing season the foliage is a bright green. In the past this Fuchsia has been advertised as "hardy in the coldest parts of the northern U.S.," but as a matter of fact, it has died out several times in plantings in Boston, Mass., even though it is supposed to winter over "easily" in Cleveland, Ohio. The best thing to do is try it, but give it a protected spot in the garden, preferably in the foundation planting about the house, then give it plenty of protection from winter cold. Farther south, it has much merit as a June-blooming shrub. **'Tom Thumb'**—miniature, red fls.

The variety **gracilis** has a trailing habit and is frequently used in hanging baskets for this reason. The flowers are purple and red. The variety **riccartonii** will grow up to 10 ft. tall and is most floriferous, supposedly one of the hardiest of all the fuchsias and can be grown out of doors (with protection) as far north as New York City.

procumbens procumbent Zone 10 Trailing Fuchsia
With rounded, alternate leaves $\frac{1}{4}$–$\frac{3}{4}$ in. long on slender petioles, this is a prostrate plant native to New Zealand and makes a fine drooping subject for hanging baskets. The pale orange flowers with purple calyx lobes are erect, $\frac{1}{4}$–$\frac{3}{4}$ in. long. The persistent fruit is a bright red berry

$\frac{3}{4}$ in. wide, adding much to the ornamental characteristics of the plant.

FUMARIA (few-MAY-ria)
officinalis 3′ annual or biennial Drug Fumitory
A European native, sometimes naturalized in North America; a low, sprawling plant with weak stems and very finely divided leaves that are grayish or blue-green. The pinkish flowers are in spikes that are rosy-purple at the top. Propagated by seed, and it self-sows readily. The flowers have been used to supply a yellow dye used for coloring wool. The entire plant has been used in medicine as a laxative. Dried plants used to be "smoked like tobacco for head disorders."

FUMARIACEAE = The Fumitory or Bleeding Heart Family

FUMEWORT. See CORYDALIS.

FUMIGATION. In greenhouses and other places where gas or vapor can be confined, fumigation of the atmosphere with a space fumigant or in the soil with a soil fumigant is the most effective method of pest control.

Space Fumigants

Formerly hydrocyanic acid gas generated from the chemical reaction of sodium cyanide and sulfuric acid was a standard treatment but caused some plant injury and was dangerously poisonous. Nicotine as a smoke from burning impregnated papers or from burning a mixture with a flammable carrier in small piles or in cans was very popular. Naphthalene and paradichlorobenzene crystals melted and evaporated on stoves controlled spider mites and similar formulations were volatilized on hot pipes.

Aerosols of organic phosphate insecticides are now the approved method of fumigation. These are insecticides and miticides dispersed in a compressed and liquefied gas which volatilizes when released in the air and discharges the minute particles of the pesticide in the air-stream. For greenhouse use, sturdy metal cylinders with simple valves for adjusting the dosage for units of 1000 cu. ft. are quick and convenient. Follow directions on the label for operation, length of exposure before ventilation and safety precautions. Small aerosol "bombs" can be used for quick temporary relief of pest emergencies but should not be relied upon for general pest control. The mist should be discharged several inches away from the plants to avoid injury. Aerosols prepared for household pest control may not be safe for use on plants.

Soil Fumigation

Soil sterilization with chemical fumigants is becoming a general practice in greenhouses, hotbeds, seedbeds and on soil for potting plants.

Chloropicrin (LARVACIDE), ethylene dibromide (DOWFUME), formaldehyde (formalin), VAPAM and NEMAGON are effective when used as recommended. Temperature and moisture requirements vary with the materials and the precautions on the label must be followed for maximum effectiveness. It is usually necessary to confine the fumes by covering the soil with canvas, plastic or a water seal. See SOIL STERILIZATION for use of heat and drenches.

FUMITORY, DRUG = *Fumaria officinalis*

FUMITORY, CLIMBING = *Adlumia fungosa*

FUMITORY OR BLEEDING HEART FAMILY = Fumariaceae

FUNGICIDES. A fungicide is a substance which kills or inhibits the growth of fungi and generally refers to a chemical formulation. It may also be a chemical used to kill bacteria although these may be called bactericides. They are most effectively used to prevent infection but some will control established infections and are called eradicants. Fungicides are formulated as (1) dusts which usually contain small amounts of the fungicide combined with a carrier such as clay, talc or pyrophyllite and are ready to use; (2) wettable powders which are concentrates mixed with a wetting agent to keep them uniformly suspended as tiny particles in a liquid spray when diluted as directed and (3) emulsions or emulsifiable concentrates which are combined with a solvent and/or emulsifier to allow them to dissolve and mix with water in a liquid spray when diluted as directed. There are also pellets containing a given amount of the fungicide for mixing with the soil and slurries of concentrated fungicide mixed with a sticker for coating seed.

Each type of fungicidal formulation should be applied with the proper equipment for effective results and for the safety of the operator. On food crops the residue must be safe to the consumer and conform to the limitations prescribed by regulatory agencies. Read the label carefully and follow the recommendations.

There are hundreds of fungicidal formulations available under trade names and the gardener should know the basic fungicide which he needs and by reading the "active ingredients" on the label obtain the proper formulation. Also see INSECTICIDES for procedures in using the following charts. The following are some of the most common fungicides and their principal uses:

ARASAN. See THIRAM.

BORDEAUX MIXTURE. A combination of copper sulfate and lime used as a protectant fungicide on potatoes, tomatoes, grapes and many other plants. The standard mixture is 4-4-50 meaning 4 lbs. of copper sulfate and 4 lbs. of lime in 50 gal. of water but 2-2-50 and 2-4-50 mixtures are also used. The copper sulfate and lime are dissolved in water before diluting. Prepared mixtures are now available and more convenient than home mixing. Although still effective it is now frequently replaced by organic fungicides such as ferbam and zineb.

CAPTAN. A complex organic fungicide that is effective and safe for the control of many diseases. On fruits it is highly recommended to control scab on apples, brown rot on peaches and fruit rot on strawberries. It is also used as a seed treatment and to protect fabrics and leather from mildew and mold. It is not effective against powdery mildew on roses and annual flowers. It is compatible with many other pesticides and often used in general-purpose mixtures for home garden use.

CHLOROPICRIN (tear gas). A fumigant resembling chloroform used as a soil disinfectant and nematocide both in greenhouse and for special field treatments. It also kills weed seeds. Special technique and equipment is needed for application.

COPPER COMPOUNDS. Copper is one of the oldest fungicidal chemicals and has many uses. Bordeaux mixture is the best-known formulation. Copper carbonate and cuprous oxide (CUPROCIDE) are well-known seed protectants. Basic copper sulfate and copper oxychloride sulfate (COCS) are sprays and dusts for combatting foliage diseases especially on vegetables. Copper naphthenate (CUPRINOL) and copper quinoline (BIOQUIN) are wood and fabric preservatives. As plant fungicides they are being replaced by the newer organic fungicides.

CORROSIVE SUBLIMATE. See MERCURY COMPOUNDS.

CYPREX. See DODINE.

CRAG 341. See GLYODIN.

DINITRO COMPOUNDS. In addition to being powerful fungicides they are used as herbicides, insecticides, miticides and as a fruit-blossom thinner. Dinitrophenolcrotonate called KARATHANE is highly recommended to control powdery mildew in hot weather. Dinitroorthocresol such as DNOC and dinitrotriethanolamine as ELGETOL are used as dormant sprays to control diseases which spend the winter in a susceptible condition on trees or on leaves on the ground. They serve the same purpose as lime sulfur. These compounds stain badly and their use around buildings is limited.

DNOC. See DINITRO COMPOUNDS.

DODINE (n-duodecylguanidine acetate). It is called CYPREX and has been used effectively for control of many diseases on fruits and to combat leaf blight on Sycamore and Black Walnut. It has caused russetting on fruit, especially when the spray dried slowly, and should not be combined with highly alkaline materials.

ELGETOL. See DINITRO COMPOUNDS.

FERBAM. Chemically, ferric dimethyldithiocarbamate, it has a sooty appearance and residue which is a slight disadvantage near painted buildings and fences. It is very effective against rust diseases and anthracnose. A new supply each year is desirable.

FERMATE. See FERBAM.

FOLPET (dichloromethylphthalimide). A trade name is PHALTAN and it is recommended for combatting a wide range of diseases on fruit, vegetables and ornamentals. It is especially good for control of black spot and powdery mildew on roses.

FORMALDEHYDE is a powerful fungicide and disinfectant but harmful to growing plants. It is used as a preplanting soil treatment in greenhouses and plant beds and to disinfect flats, pots and storage rooms. A common procedure is to mix one part formalin (40% formaldehyde) in 49 parts water, apply $\frac{1}{2}$–1 gal. to each sq. ft., cover with tarpaulin for a week and air out for 2 weeks before planting.

GLYODIN. A glyoxalidine compound used on fruit and ornamentals to control apple scab and foliage diseases. It has value as a miticide and increases the spreading of sprays on foliage. A wettable-powder formulation called GLYODEX has recently been introduced.

KARATHANE. See DINITRO COMPOUNDS.

MANCOZEB (manganese ethylene-bisdithiocarbamate). It is also known as MANZATE and DITHANE M-22 and is especially effective to control early and late blight on Potato and Tomato. A combination with zinc is also available and when combined with nickel sulfate it is a valuable control for turf diseases.

MANZATE. See MANEB.

MERCURY COMPOUNDS. Corrosive sublimate (mercuric bichloride) and calomel (mercurous bichloride) have been used as seed and soil disinfectants and as dips for corms and bulbs. All mercuric and arsenic compounds are now to be eliminated from use. Commercial preparations are available for treating turf diseases.

NABAM (disodium ethylene bisdithiocarbamate), also known as DITHANE D-14, is combined with zinc sulfate for control of blight on Potato and Tomato. It is now generally replaced by maneb or zineb.

PARZATE. See ZINEB.

PHALTAN. See FOLPET.

PHYGON. See DICHLONE.

PCNB (pentachloronitrobenzene) is marketed as TERRACHLOR to be used as a soil fumigant and disinfectant to prevent infection by many root and stem rots of vegetables and ornamentals, especially those caused by botrytis.

STREPTOMYCIN. See ANTIBIOTICS in alphabetical listing.

SULFUR. This is one of the oldest and cheapest fungicides which also has value as an insecticide and miticide. It is prepared commercially as a finely-divided dust, as a flotation or colloidal paste and as a wettable powder. It is effective for control of many diseases but is especially recommended to combat scab on fruit and leaf spots and mildew on ornamentals. Liquid lime sulfur is a well-known dormant fungicide. New organic fungicides have now replaced it for many uses.

TERSAN. See THIRAM.

THIRAM (tetramethylthiuram disulfide) is one of the new fungicides with broad use. As arasan it is an excellent seed protectant, as tersan for control of turf diseases and as thylate as a control for diseases of fruit and foliage on all plants. It also has value as an animal repellent especially for mice and rabbits. It is compatible with most pesticides and is among the safer ones.

THYLATE. See THIRAM.

ZERLATE. See ZIRAM.

ZINEB (zinc ethylene bisdithiocarbamate). It has trade names of PARZATE and DITHANE Z-78. It is one of the standard fungicides for use on Potatoes, Tomatoes and related plants. It must be used with caution on Tobacco, Cucumber and other zinc-sensitive plants.

ZIRAM (zinc dimethyldithiocarbamate). Commonly called ZERLATE, it has many of the same uses as zineb which it has replaced for most purposes.

WARREN D. WHITCOMB

GENERAL CATEGORY
OF DISEASE
CONTROLLED

REFERENCE LETTER	COINED OR CHEMICAL NAME	TRADE OR BRAND NAME	BACTERIAL ROTS AND DISEASES	FRUIT AND LEAF DISEASES	SEED AND SOIL DISEASES	PRINCIPAL USES FOR DISEASE CONTROL
A	chlorothalonil	BRAVO		√		Rust and mildew on ornamentals, beans, cabbage, carrots, cucumbers, squash, tomatoes
B	streptomycin	AGRIMYCIN	√			Bacterial diseases—fire blight, bacterial canker
C	benomyl	BENLATE		√		Systemic—powdery mildews on many crops—see label
D	ferbam	FERMATE		√		Scab and rust on fruit and ornamentals
E	mancozeb	MANZATE		√		Blight on many vegetables—a good all-purpose fungicide
F	thiram	ARASAN			√	Seed protectant
G	zineb	PARZATE-ZINEB		√		Similar to #E
H	ziram	ZERLATE		√		Many vegetable diseases
I	copper oxide	CUPROCIDE			√	Seed treatment
J	copper hydroxide	KOCIDE		√	√	Similar to #I
K	copper sulfate	BORDEAUX MIXTURE		√		Blight on vegetables; tomatoes and potatoes
L	captafol	DIFOLATAN		√		Dormant spray on some fruit trees—see label
M	dinocap	KARATHANE		√		Mildew on fruit and ornamentals in hot weather
N	dinitrocresol	ELGETOL 30		√		Dormant—for fruit
U	lime sulfur	LIQUID OR DRY LIME SULFUR		√		Used for general disease control—may injure some plants
V	colloidal sulfur			√		General disease control
W	captan	ORTHOCIDE		√	√	Scab and rots—widely used, see label
X	dodine	CYPREX		√		Scab and leaf spots on fruits and vegetables
Y	folpet	PHALTAN		√		Leaf spots—especially on roses
Z	glyodin	CRAIG 341		√		Scab and rots—fruit and ornamentals

Note 1. The trade names used in this table do not indicate a superiority over similar formulations with different trade names nor an endorsement of the trade names used here.

Note 2. Dry pesticides (wettable powders) vary in density and there may be 2–6 level tablespoonfuls per oz. In general 1 level tablespoonful in 1 gal. equals 1 lb. in 100 gal. and $2\frac{1}{2}$ teaspoonfuls liquid in 1 gal. equals 1 qt. in 100 gal. In the measuring liquid pesticides, use the following:

3 teaspoonfuls = $\frac{1}{2}$ fluid oz. = 1 tablespoonful

2 tablespoonfuls = 1 fluid oz.

16 tablespoonfuls = 8 fluid oz. = 1 cup = $\frac{1}{2}$ pint

Official coined names and chemical names or other accepted common names are listed in the second column. TRADE or BRAND names are listed in capital letters in the third column.

Warren D. Whitcomb
John A. Naegele
Clifford S. Chater

The following fungicides have either been banned or become unavailable since the first printing of this volume in 1971.

O—chloranil   R—mercurous chloride
P—dichlone   S—hydroxy mercuric chlorophenol
Q—mercuric chloride   T—phenyl mercuric-lactate

FUNGUS. Flowerless plants principally represented by the mushrooms (which see) and plant diseases. They grow on both living and dead plants and animals. There are no flowers and reproduction is by spores which usually are produced in tremendous numbers. Identification is made by the lesions or by microscopic examination of the spores. Toadstools and bracket fungi on decayed wood are conspicuous forms.

FUNKIA (FUNK-ia) = HOSTA

FUNNELFORM. Said of a corolla with the tube gradually widening upward; as in the Morning-glory.

FUNNELVINE, PURPLE = *Saritaea magnifica*

FURNITURE. See GARDEN FIXTURES.

FURROWED. With longitudinal channels or grooves.

FUSIFORM. Spindle-shaped; narrowed toward both ends from a swollen middle; as in the roots of the Dahlia.

G

GAILLARDIA (gay-LARD-ia). These are members of the very large Composite Family, with daisylike flower heads, alternate leaves on the stem and basal leaves. They are annuals, biennials, or perennials depending on the species. Their showy flowers are usually yellow to red. The annual types are specially desirable as dainty cut flowers and good border plants in the full sun. They survive heat and drought well. The annual types are grown from seed sown in the garden where the plants are desired; perennial types are grown from seed or plant division.

amblyodon 2′ annual Maroon Gaillardia
With hairy leaves 3 in. long and mahogany-red flower heads 2 in. across, native to Tex. Seed can be sown outdoors in the seed bed in April.

aristata 2′–3′ Zones 2–3 Common Blanket-
                                   flower
A very popular garden perennial, native to western North America, with many selected varieties. This is the only perennial species in this genus. The daisylike flower heads are yellow, sometimes with purple at the base of the ray flowers. Seedsmen have hybridized these to such an extent that there are many varieties, with red and gold flowers, but unfortunately some of these are hybrids of the perennial *G. aristata* and some of the annual flowering species so that they are not as long lived as they should be. Some of the outstanding hybrid varieties are: **'The Warrior'**—with flower heads 3½ in. across, red and mahogany colored; **'Goblin'**—fls. red with yellow margins; **'Burgundy'**—fls. wine red; **'Dazzler'**—fls. golden yellow. **'Golden Goblin'** is an excellent moundlike variety with pure yellow flowers all summer. Most varieties bloom a greater part of the summer, which is a fine asset. The flowers are very good when cut and used in arrangements. This group is best propagated by division of clumps in the spring. Making root cuttings is another means, mostly used commercially.

drummondii = *G. pulchella*

pulchella 1½′ annual Painted Gaillardia
The ray flowers of this are yellow, purple at the base, borne in heads 2 in. across. Native from Kan. to La. Leaves 4 in. long, sometimes entire, sometimes cut or indented. There are double vars. with red and yellow flowers and some with almost ball-like flowers making excellent cut flowers for use in arrangements. The seed

for these should be sown outdoors in the place the plants are to grow (full sun) after all danger of frost is passed.

GALANGAL, BANDED = *Alpinia sanderae*

GALANTHUS (gay-LAN-thus). Small bulbous plants known to everyone for their small, white, solitary flowers that are the first to appear in the spring. They are often completely covered with late snows after they are in bloom, yet this harsh treatment does not seem to hurt them in the least. Easily propagated by offsets and seed.

elwesii 1′ Zone 4 Giant Snowdrop
Similar to *G. nivalis* but the leaves are wider (¾ in.) and the flowers are larger (1¼ in.). Native to Asia Minor. This species seems more coarse in texture and flower, especially when growing side by side with the diminutive *G. nivalis*.

nivalis 1′ Zone 3 Common Snowdrop
With leaves 9 in. long and ¼ in. wide, this species from Europe is the most common in America. The white flowers may be an inch long. If let alone, they will usually increase themselves (by seed) and if planted near a warm foundation they will be the first flowers of spring. They do best if given partial shade. A double-flowered variety (**'Flore-pleno'**) is available.

GALAX (GAY-lax)

urceolata (*aphylla*) **6″–12″ Zone 3 Galax**
Growing from a creeping rhizome, with round, shiny, orbicular, evergreen leaves, this plant is an ideal ground cover for moist, shady areas, being hardy well north of its native habitat. The unbranched flower stalk rises to a height of 6–12 in., bearing a spike of small white flowers, each of which has 5 petals. A native to the moist woods of Va. and Ga. to Ala., and blooming from May to July, it does well in cultivation where the soil is moist but only slightly acid. Propagation is by division of the roots, in spring or fall, or by seeds sown in fall or late winter. The leaves are excellent for use in corsages and flower arrangements. (See drawing, p. 452.)

GALAX or PYXIE FAMILY = Diapensiaceae

GALEGA (gal-EE-ga)

officinalis 3′ Zone 3 Common Goats-rue
This is an easily grown garden perennial of the Pea Family, native to Europe and Asia. The compound leaves have leaflets arranged feather fashion with 1 leaflet in the terminal position, each leaflet being 1½–2 in. long. Flowers are

purplish blue, pealike, about ½ in. long in racemes during summer. There are varieties with double, white or rose-colored flowers, and one with variegated leaves. All can be easily propagated by division.

GALIUM (GAY-lium)

aparine   decumbent   annual   Catchweed Bedstraw

A native weed, widespread throughout North America, with whorled, lanceolate leaves about an inch long, 6–8 at a node. Flowers are minute and white appearing from May to July.

boreale   2′–3′   Zone 2   Northern Bedstraw

Although this plant is a member of the Madder Family (*Rubiaceae*), the stems are 4-sided like the mints. A sprawling perennial weed with leaves occurring in 4's at the joints of the stem, it has small white flowers in compact terminal clusters. Of only minor horticultural interest and requiring no special culture, it may be grown in the rock garden or other locations no more favorable than its rocky or gravelly native sites throughout Canada and Alaska to the Va. and N.Mex., where it flowers throughout the summer.

mollugo   3′   Zone 3   White Bedstraw

A perennial weed naturalized in northeastern North America, introduced from Europe; sometimes used as a ground cover. The lanceolate leaves are produced in whorls of 6–8 and are 1 in. long. The minute white flowers in terminal panicles appear from June to Aug. Sometimes called False Baby's Breath but quite different from *Gypsophila* species.

odoratum (*Asperula odorata*)   6″   Zone 4 Sweet Woodruff

Sweet Woodruff has long been a garden favorite because of its delicate growth, 4-petaled white flowers about ¼ in. across in loosely branching clusters from early May to mid-June and its sweet-scented elliptic leaves 1 in. long in whorls of 6–8 on the square stems. It is native to Europe and Asia, making an excellent ground cover in the moist atmosphere under rhododendrons. It has also been interplanted with English Ivy with good results. The leaf has been used in wines and liqueurs. Easily propagated by simple division.

verum   1′–3′   Zones 2–3   Yellow Bedstraw

A perennial native to Europe and naturalized in North America, sometimes proposed as a ground cover for it grows well in the full sun on sterile soil but often becoming a weed in open fields where it may grow too vigorously. The tiny yellow flowers are produced in airy panicles from June to Sept. The foliage has a leathery texture but it dies to the ground each fall; the stems are usually square; the leaves are 6–8 in a whorl, each leaf very narrow and ½–1 in. long. It is more attractive than *G. boreale*. The

flowers are used in making a yellow dye and the roots for a red dye.

GALL. A large rounded swelling on the leaf or twig of a plant is called a gall. These are caused by various insects or fungi. They are common on oak leaves and usually result in little damage to the host plant.

GALPHIMIA (gal-FIM-ia)

glauca (*Thryallis glauca*)   9′   Zone 8   Rain-of-Gold

Native to Mexico, this shrub is valued for its yellow flowers which are borne in loose clusters. Each flower is ¾ in. across and has 5 petals. The fruits are small capsules which split open in 3 parts when dry. The evergreen leaves are opposite and simple, about 4 in. long, and the young stems are red, adding materially to this color combination of yellow, green and red. Often used in foundation plantings. Propagated by cuttings taken in July and also by sowing green fruits.

GALTONIA (gawl-TOE-nia)

candicans   3′–4′   Zone 5   Giant Summer-hyacinth

This is a summer-blooming bulb, with many small, white, fragrant, bell-shaped flowers 1½ in. long on a tall stalk in late July or early Aug. The thick fleshy leaves are straplike, 2 in. wide, similar to those of narcissus. The bulbs should be heavily mulched in the winter if they are to live over in the North; in fact it might be well to lift them in the fall and store them over winter for late spring planting. Easily propagated by offsets and seeds. A member of the Lily Family and native to South Africa.

GAMOLEPIS (gam-OLL-ep-is)

tagetes   1′   annual

A native to South Africa, this is an especially desirable garden plant because of profuse bloom. The genus belongs to the Composite Family, hence the flowers are daisylike, in heads of bright yellow to orange ¾ in. across. These are singly borne, with alternate, pinnately cut leaves. Seeds can be started indoors in March, or outdoors in the full sun after all danger of frost is passed, then thinned to 6 in. apart.

GAMOPETALOUS. Having the petals more or less united. See also POLYPETALOUS.

GARDEN CENTER. There are 2 types of garden centers in America. The term is used by some commercial nurserymen, seedsmen and florists to denote a store or center where everything for the garden is placed on display for sale—seeds, plants, tools, machines and all the many types of things used by gardeners in making and caring for their gardens. These are popular because potential buyers can see on display the many things that they can use and grow, all displayed and on sale in one place. These are proving popular for growers who wish to diversify their goods, and also to gardeners who can find what they desire in one place without having to visit stores or salesrooms which specialize only in one product. The number of these garden centers is increasing annually.

The second type of garden center is one in which an organization or group of people have combined to make available rooms for meetings, a library, and a permanent staff for giving information on gardening. Here are frequently offered a series of lectures on various phases of horticultural techniques. This type of garden center is often financed by memberships, by "white elephant" sales and by the sale of books and other things. Two outstanding examples are The Garden Center of Greater Cleveland, East Boulevard at Euclid Ave., Cleveland, Ohio 44106, and the Berkshire Garden Center, Inc., Stockbridge, Mass., where many good ornamental plantings are on the grounds for the purpose of demonstrating actual living plants and arrangements of them in living plantings. Such garden centers, with permanent staff, are doing excellent work in disseminating horticultural information and are well worth the price of membership.

GARDEN, CITY. See CITY GARDENS.

GARDEN FIXTURES. No matter how well grown the trees, shrubs, perennials, and other plants, a garden is always enlivened by a bird bath, bench, lantern, or walk.

This is especially true during winter when features tend to stand out more clearly. A green garden, too, can profit by accessories. When dogwoods, azaleas, and other flowering plants are in their prime they are spectacular, but once the flush of bloom has subsided, a quiet period follows. It is then that fixtures play a more dominant role.

Fixtures in the garden provide aesthetic appeal, and are useful as well. A fence will create privacy and a background for flowering plants. Birds flock to a bird bath for a refreshing drink or shower. A lantern lights up the garden at night, and a fountain adds the sound of splashing water.

It is important to select the right kind of accessory for the particular spot, for unless this is done with care and knowledge, it can do more harm than good. An appropriate statue will do much to enhance a section of the garden. On the other hand, if the statue is in bad taste or poor scale, it will detract. Fixtures are often added to provide focal points, and if this is kept in mind, the right choice is made easier.

The matter of cost is often involved. Since a statue, a sundial, or a bench is a permanent feature, it should be of good quality. Plants are frequently replaced, but not so fixtures, which are there month after month and year after year. In a sense, they are the framework, the background of the garden, around which the plants, as well as the seasons, revolve.

Oddly enough, fixtures are more essential in a small garden, where they catch the eye and hold the attention. A tiny city garden, for example, surrounded by high buildings and walls, is dependent on figures, wall fountains, and raised beds for interest. And this, of course, is even more true of the formal garden, whether large or small. In a spacious naturalistic garden, the fascinating forms of trees and shrubs in winter are sufficient to maintain interest.

The type of fixture depends on the needed effect. Often it is wise to consult a landscape architect who can help with this challenging aspect of the garden. Remember only not to overdo. Too many "things" lead to confusion. One choice piece, properly placed, will create harmony and unity, while too many will detract from the quality and appeal of the plants.

Every gardener has a wide selection of choices. He may want a fence, a winding path, a trellis, a patio, a figure, a window box, or a jug with geraniums by a doorway. Any one of these, or several others, will enhance the garden and add to its year-round appeal.

The following is a listing and descriptions of some of the more familiar types of fixtures and accessories for gardens of all kinds.

Bird Baths and Bird Houses

Birds provide more than visual appeal to the garden. They feed on insects, and sufficient numbers of birds in the garden will help to keep the insects in check. They will eat caterpillars, leafhoppers, inchworms, rose bugs, and aphids. Even the common English sparrow is an arch enemy of the Japanese beetle, and can often be seen alighting on rose buds to consume aphids.

One way to attract birds to the garden is to supply them with water, particularly in hot weather. This can be done by means of the bird bath, one of the most familiar of garden accessories.

Bird baths are made from a number of durable materials including concrete, marble, stone and clay. Some are more expensive than others and are more handsome in their design, but in all instances the bird bath should not be made of a conspicuous material. Certain materials such as concrete, marble, and clay mellow with age and take on a weathered look.

Bird baths may be placed at a number of focal points in the garden. Where cats roam about, the lawn or other open areas enable birds to spot this prowling enemy. Usually, it is better to locate the bird bath in a sheltered nook, surrounded by the green of shrubs and ground covers. Not only is it more cool-looking, but the water does not become warm so quickly. Nearby trees such as evergreens invite birds to perch and seek shelter, especially at the approach of an enemy.

Ferns, Patient Lucy, Coleus, and other shade-loving plants may be planted around bird baths in shady places to enhance their appearance. Out in the bright sunshine, low-growing annuals such as Dwarf French Marigold, Sweet Alyssum, Petunia, and Dwarf Dahlia, will add color.

For the small garden, the average height for a bird bath is $2\frac{1}{2}$ ft. If the top is detachable, so much the better, since it can be removed to be cleaned, and in hot summer weather this ought to be done 2 or 3 times a week. If done frequently, it may be cleaned simply by scrubbing with a stiff brush and cold water. Hot water and soap give better results, especially if borax is added. Always rinse well before adding fresh water.

Bird baths may be also in the form of shallow pans filled with water. Often these are made of stone. Scallop shells composed of lead or concrete will serve the same purpose. Pools with sufficiently shallow edges so that birds, particularly fledglings, will not drown, are perfectly satisfactory. Sometimes there are large outcroppings of rock with depressions that can be kept filled with water. Actually, there is no limit to what the bird bath may be, and with imagination, several kinds of receptacles will serve.

Nesting sites in the form of bird houses will bring more birds to the garden. The most common nesting sites for birds are the branches of trees and shrubs, so include plenty of both. On the other hand, some birds raise their families in boxes, and these include wrens, chickadees, swallows, woodpeckers, martins, and nuthatches.

Each kind of bird has specific nesting box requirements. For example, boxes for wrens should be 4 in. square and 8 in. deep, with an entrance hole that is an inch in dia. Nuthatches and chickadees will seek boxes of the same size, provided openings are $\frac{1}{4}$ in. larger. Swallows and bluebirds will be happy with boxes 5 in. square, 8 in. deep, with $1\frac{1}{2}$ in. openings. Entrance holes should be near the top, and the boxes placed facing south, away from winds and rains. Some birds, like robins, will nest in shelters that are provided with tops, but are open on the sides.

Bird houses and shelters are easily procured at garden centers and shops where bird food is offered, but the person interested in making his own and wishing books and pamphlets that give specific directions on how to go about it may obtain them from several sources, especially from the Audubon Society.

Birds can also be induced to gardens by setting up feeding stations, especially important during the cold, snowy winter months. These, too, are readily obtainable, but be certain to place them out of the reach of cats, squirrels, and other enemies and pests. When secured to poles, place a flaring collar of tin or wire mesh several feet above the ground, usually some 6 ft. high. Other provisions can be made so that the birds will enjoy relaxed dining. In winter, keep feeders well stocked with suet, doughnuts, sunflower and other seeds, hemp, sliced apple, dried raisins, and other favorite foods. The more ambitious may build large feeders to accommodate several birds at a time. These should be handsome in design, since they become features that will either attract, or detract, from the overall garden picture.

Fences and Gates

A fence is one of the most useful of garden features. It will shut out unwanted views and offer privacy. It will break the force of the wind, especially necessary when it comes to sheltering gardens near the seashore or on a rooftop or penthouse. It keeps out intruders, as well as animals. It forms a background for shrubs and flowering plants and provides support for climbing roses, Wisteria, Clematis, and other vines. Even a low fence will mark the dividing line between properties.

As a garden accessory, a fence adds an architectural element to the garden scene, as well as to the house, so careful thought should be given to the type to be selected. Certainly it should harmonize with its surroundings and, where possible, ought to express pure design. Some like to design their own, rendering the fence more distinctive and original.

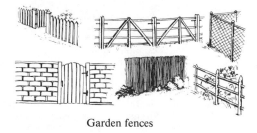

Garden fences

A fence should be durable, able to stand up against the weather of the climate where it is to be used, whether it is the cold of the North or the heat and humidity of the Tropics. It should be economical to build. In the past, local materials such as stone and various woods were generally used, but nowadays quick and inexpensive means of transportation make available many materials, natural and manufactured, from all over the world. Then too, its appearance ought to be attractive. Often fences are made of the same material as the house, such as brick, stone or wood. This, of course, enhances the overall effect.

A fence involves an investment that will last for years. In the end, it is more economical if it is built out of good materials and if effort goes into its design. Solid construction is of the utmost importance. Wooden posts, for example, must be set 2½–3 ft. deep, well below the frost line in cold climates. The posts should first be primed with a coat of lead and oil, or the bases soaked in creosote.

Fences may be made out of several kinds of materials, though wood and iron are most commonly used. The best, and in the end the most economical, woods include Cypress, Redwood, Red-cedar, Arborvitae, Black Locust, and Sourgum. These naturally resist decay. Metal may include galvanized iron, wrought iron, and woven wire.

New England, is still being widely used around small houses. There is also a rustic picket fence that is less formal.

There are several other kinds of wooden fences, among them the spindle for colonial mansions, the post and board, recommended for suburban properties, the basket weave, the lattice, and the grape stake.

Metal fences include the common chain link, recommended for factories or outlying areas where it may be concealed by shrubbery, and woven wire and wrought iron, which can be designed in intricate patterns. Today, plastic fences are also in vogue.

Once a fence is erected, it will require periodic maintenance, the amount depending on the kinds of materials used and on the climate. Wooden fences, except for rustic types, will need painting from time to time. Once built, the wooden fence will need 2 priming coats, followed by the finishing coat. Do not wait too long before repainting a fence. Wood that has been allowed to peel can be harmed by weather. Replace posts when they become weak, as well as individual boards, pickets, or other broken sections.

An iron fence will need a coat of special rust-resistant paint after it has been set up, but other

A split sapling fence makes an interesting background for this flower border. (*Photo by Arnold Arboretum, Jamaica Plain, Mass.*)

Many types of traditional fences may be erected. There is the split rail fence, which originated in Virginia, and is made of rails split from poles and put together without nails. The post and rail is an attractive fence used at country places to enclose pasture lands. The hurdle fence, developed in England, is another pasture fence, and the picket, characteristic of

coats should follow every few years after that. Usually, they are painted black.

Gates are often attached to fences and, when they are, should be made of the same materials, though they may vary in design. Sometimes a wall will have a gate, as well as a hedge of privet, arborvitae or Japanese Yew.

Gates may be low or high, single or double,

Garden gates of wood or iron can be plain or fancy.

simple or intricate in design. Where privacy is needed, the gate must be tall, as well as the fence, though it may be low, enabling one to look in or out. Whether it leads to a front door, a walk or a woodsy informal area of the garden, it should harmonize with the fence and the house and be of the right scale, size, and proportion. If unique in its design, it will attract more attention.

Like fences, gates should be sturdy, durable, and not too costly to build. Moreover, they should swing open easily and latch and close without special effort. Small, unpretentious houses require low gates, while mansions call for taller, more elegant types. Sometimes, a gate is simply built to relieve and add interest to a large expanse of wall. This kind of gate can be used on occasion, but for the most part it is an architectural feature that catches the eye.

Like fences, gates require maintenance and occasional repair. Wood will need painting and metal will need to be treated with rust-resisting paint. Posts to which they are secured will need replacing periodically.

Gates can be embellished to make them more appealing. A basket filled with flowers in summer and greens in winter and a tinkling bell will add interest. A lantern nearby will light the way and

serve as support for a pot plant or two.

Furniture

Good garden furniture must possess certain basic qualities. First and foremost, it should be well designed. Unless this is so, it will only detract, even in gardens where plants are grown to perfection. In the second place, it should be comfortable. It should be strong and durable, able to take wear and tear, especially where there are children. Also, it must be weather-resistant, tolerant of all kinds of weather.

Like other garden features, furniture must be placed where it will enhance the garden and improve its appearance. Use it with care, and avoid overdoing, since too many items will only detract. Each location has its right kind of furniture. A formal garden requires tables, chairs, and benches that are tailored and restrained in their appearance. In an informal setting, rustic, or wooden benches and tables that have a more natural look would be more appropriate.

Garden furniture may be permanent, consisting of pieces that stay outdoors all year round. They may be secured to a particular position or they may be heavy, like a concrete or stone bench that can be moved only with great effort. A garden should have one or more pieces of this type, such as a bench, which adds an architectural quality to the garden and which can be used throughout the year. This type of furniture should be resistant to the year-round weather of the locality.

The other type, lighter in weight, may be moved as needed. It may or may not need protection in times of storms. Tables and chairs for outdoor dining and cookouts, especially, belong to this category. These are items that come apart or fold up so that they can be transported without too much effort. As a rule, they are stored for the winter to help prolong their life and appearance.

Concrete and stone benches are among the most useful. Strong and weather-resistant, they make a permanent feature. Place them under the shade of a tree, by a pool, in the full sun by a colorful border, or where a vista leads to an enchanting garden figure. Tables also may be made of concrete or stone. Heavy in weight, they, too, are placed for permanence.

Iron furniture is equally long-lasting and durable. Well-designed pieces are expensive, but worth the cost. They are treated to prevent rusting, and though they can stay out all winter, storage is recommended where possible, in order to prolong their life.

Wood is one of the best and most commonly used materials. If the gardener wishes to make his own, and this is the best to achieve original

Garden entrances are sometimes ornate. (*Photo by Arnold Arboretum, Jamaica Plain, Mass.*)

designs, he should select a durable wood such as Cypress, Redwood, Hickory, and Oak. It may be painted, and then will need frequent repainting to keep it in top condition. If left natural, brush the wood with linseed oil periodically. The wood should be pinned together with pegs. Glue should not be used, and metal joinings in time will rust. Whether painted or left natural, wood is easily procurable, comfortable (it's not cold to the touch in cool weather, as is metal), and blends well into any type of garden design.

Other materials include wire, reed, and rattan, which must be painted or shellacked, and aluminum, which is strong and very light. In cold climates, reed and rattan tables and chairs will last much longer if placed indoors during the winter. With all chairs, make certain water drains off the seats. In the case of chairs with solid seats, they should be tilted in the center.

To a certain degree, the color of garden furniture is a matter of taste. Yet on the whole, it should not be too conspicuous. Where there are gay, colorful borders of flowering shrubs, perennials, and annuals, keep to white and neutral shades, while a quiet, green garden might benefit from touches of bright color in the furniture.

Fountains and Swimming Pools

Somewhere, even in the smallest garden, there should be a tiny pool or a spouting fountain. In the larger garden, water will take on different forms to suit the needs and background. The sight of it is stimulating. Its rippling sound is musical and on a hot day it is cooling to look at. In addition, it reflects the plants and flowers around it and at all times of year, the sky above, with its drifting clouds. Water-lilies and other kinds of aquatic plants may be grown in garden pools, while goldfish and other kinds of fish add interest and help to keep mosquitoes under control.

Since a garden pool is a permanent feature its location and building should be carried out with great care. It may be small or large, formal or informal, traditional or modern, with moving or standing water. If the pool is to have water-lilies, it will need sun for at least half a day, and the water should be quiet, because water-lilies do not like cold, moving water. Other kinds of water plants may be grown in pockets of soil at the sides. See WATER-LILY.

It is not necessary for garden pools to be deep. Where there are small children, 4–6 in. of water is sufficient. If the bottom of the pool is painted black, dark green, or some other deep color, it will appear deeper and more interesting.

Saucer pools that taper outward and upward to the surface of the soil are very popular and are recommended where the water freezes in winter. This is because ice moves outward and upward, and in a pool of this kind, it does not have the obstruction of vertical sides. In design, it can be circular, oval, or free form.

Square or rectangular pools are formal, and can hold the spotlight in the middle of a garden. If these, as well as other garden pools, are deeper, they may be painted a brighter color. Pale blue is one of the most popular, because it reflects the blue of the sky and is visually cooling. Special paints are available for this.

Pools may also be naturalistic or informal, having an irregular shape and with many kinds of plants along the edges. These may be placed in a grove of trees, in front of shrubbery, or in a rock garden. With such pools the soil usually comes to the water's edge, while the formal pool has a coping, level with the ground or raised above the ground from a few inches to a few feet.

Several kinds of materials are used to construct pools, but one of the best and most readily available is concrete. It can be molded into any shape, but one should be certain that the walls are strong enough to resist the pressure of frost in cold climates. Thawing and heaving will crack the walls. Repair work under these circumstances is often costly and ineffective. So it is better to build strongly and correctly at the start.

Stone is another common material, especially appropriate for pools with fountains where water drips and splashes. Also, it makes a good coping for a formal pool. Sheet metal is appropriate for a naturalistic pool with an irregular shape. This includes lead which is strong, pliable, noncorrosive, and long-lasting. It is not harmful to plants or fish.

Copper sheeting is often used to line small pools and fountains. It is injurious to fish, but not to plants. Becoming more and more popular are the fiberglass pools, which are light, inexpensive, and strong. Then, naturalistic pools in woodsy areas of the garden may be lined with 2–3 in. of clay, which holds water remarkably well. For the person who wants the easy way out, there are several kinds of ready-made garden pools, especially those made of polyethylene sheeting, which require no great effort to install. See WATER GARDENING.

Once set up, pools demand very little maintenance. The aquatic plants require neither weeding, watering, nor staking, though in cold climates they will need some winter protection. It is advisable to drain the water and clean the sides of the pool with a stiff brush and warm, soapy water. Unless there is a drain, water may be siphoned with a hose. Then the remaining water can be swept out with a broom or scooped with a pan or large shovel.

For the winter, cover the pool with boards and a canvas, over which additional boards or stones are placed. Better still, have an attractive cover made with plywood or other heavy wood which may be used over and over again. Remove this in the spring, brush out any water, and fill the pool with the hose.

Pools often have fountains, but fountains also stand alone. Wall fountains, in small gardens especially, possess intrinsic charm. There is something special about the sound of moving water. This the Arabs, coming from the desert regions of North Africa, fully realized, and so incorporated the beauty of sparkling, darting water into their fabulous fountain displays at the Alhambra and Generalife Gardens at Granada, Spain.

Like pools, fountains are major garden features that should be in harmony with their surroundings. Correct scale is equally as important as design. If the fountain is basic to the overall garden design, it should be placed at an important axis, or crossroads, such as the middle of a lawn or patio, or at the end of a walk or path.

Fountains are frequently installed with recirculating pumps that help save water by taking it from the basin and pumping it back into the jet. Because of the flowing water, fountains require even less care than pools, but once in a while it is a good idea to drain and scrub them.

Formal 17th-century garden at Hampton Court, England. (*Photo by Arnold Arboretum, Jamaica Plain, Mass.*)

In addition to pools and fountains, there are other ways to introduce the sight and sound of water to the garden. One is the stream or brook with its constant flow of water. This may be built into a hillside, or a small hillock may be made for it. Rocks may be placed in a natural position, and interplanted with moisture-loving plants. With a recirculating pump the same water may be reused. Then, there is the more dramatic cascade, with flowing and falling water. This may be placed in a hidden spot where it can be discovered or in the open where it is in full view.

For children, there are wading pools, which should never be more than a few inches deep. These can be so constructed as to be transformed into garden pools after the children have grown up. When not in use, cover with boards secured in place with a padlock, especially in the winter when the location of the pool is likely to be forgotten. Prefabricated types of wading pools are also available.

Once a luxury enjoyed only by the wealthy, swimming pools may be found now in the gardens of many a suburbanite. As a source of healthful pleasure, it has no equal. Not only that, but the swimming pool, appropriately planted, is an embellishment for the garden, adding the beauty of its form and glitter of its water wherever it is placed.

Installing a swimming pool depends on cost, the availability of water, often the most important consideration, and the amount of care it will need. There are the prefabricated swimming pools, while others are built on the spot. They may be round, oval, kidney-shaped, free-form, square, or rectangular. Those with

rounded sides require less water. The size will depend on the area and the number of people who will use it. A depth of $8\frac{1}{2}$ ft. is needed for diving, but for children and beginners, one should include a section that is $1\frac{1}{2}$–3 ft. deep.

Keep the swimming pool in a sunny, sheltered area, away from strong winds. Place away from trees because of leaf dropping. When planting, use evergreens which do not shed in the same manner as deciduous trees and shrubs. And somewhere, include flowers, even in planters, boxes, and pots if necessary.

A swimming pool must have clear, clean water. To keep down algae, it must be drained weekly or the water must circulate through a filter every few days. In this way the same water may be freshened. A scum gutter is needed for surface water. When completed, including the planting, guard it against children who cannot swim. It may need to be fenced and kept locked, for this may be the only way to prevent needless accidents.

Paths, Walks and Driveways

Paths and walks link the various parts of the garden together, making it accessible by foot. Their design adds to the overall composition, breaking and relieving planted areas. They make certain plants stand out, especially grown along their edges.

Paths and walks should be inviting, whether they are straight, curved, or meandering. They impart a welcome quality, and those of us who have strolled down flower-bordered paths have memories of pleasant experiences. Box-bordered walks of southern gardens evoke nostalgia, as do winding paths edged with petunias, Sweet

Alyssum, pinks, Lavender, and Thyme.

The position of paths and walks should be determined carefully, since once established, they are not easily moved. They may or may not be paved, depending on the amount of traffic. In full sun, where traffic is light, turf makes an excellent walk. In shade, it may be a dirt path, perhaps covered with tanbark or pine needles.

The length will depend on the plan and the width on usage. If narrow, 18 in. is enough for one person, while for 2 people, $4\frac{1}{2}$–5 ft. will be needed. Grading deserves particular care. So that water will run off, make the center a bit higher than the sides. Non-paved paths should be a few inches higher than the adjoining ground and should be porous, so that water will seep through and drain away.

Walks may be made from a number of materials. Whatever is selected, the work should be done with care, keeping in mind appearance, cost, durability, and upkeep. If much traveled, the way should be paved with brick, flagstones, concrete, slate, stones, or wood blocks. For less traversed ways, one might consider soil, grass, tanbark, pine needles, wood chips, gravel, or pebbles.

For a durable path that leads to the front door or for straight-edged or curving walks to define a formal garden, few materials are more pleasant and suitable than brick. It lasts for years and mellows beautifully with age. Its cost may be high at the start, but it is inexpensive in the end.

In warm parts of the country with little or no frost action, and especially where soil is sandy, no foundation is needed. In the North, where frost will heave the bricks, cracking or breaking them and moving them out of place, a foundation must be laid. It may be a bed of sand or cinders, at least 4 in. deep, with or without sand in the openings. Even better is a 4-in. layer of cinders with 2 in. of fine sand on top. Bricks may be laid in cement, also, with a cushion of cinders and sand underneath and mortar in the joints. Dig the path to a depth of 12 in. and place a 3-in. layer of cinders on top. Water in the cinders and press them down firmly. Then add another 3 in. of cinders in the same way. A 3-in. layer of concrete is placed on top of this and after drying for 24 hours, the bricks are laid on top and cemented with a thin coat of mortar. There are several patterns of bricks including herringbone, basket weave, and running bond.

Flagstones and slate may be laid in a bed of cinders, sand, or gravel or in mortar. If executed the first way, simply place a half-inch layer of sand, cinders, or gravel on the surface of the path or walk and rest the stones, which may be square, rectangular, or irregular in shape, on top. Make firm, and add soil in the joints.

Grass may be grown in the openings or several kinds of low-growing, mat-forming plants, as thymes, sedums, or *Veronica repens.* If one wishes to use mortar, dig the soil to a depth of 10 in. and spread a 6-in. layer of cinders, spreading 3 in. at a time and tamping them down well. Then add a 4-in. layer of cement. After it dries for 24 hours, arrange the stones on top, adhering them with a thin coat of mortar. When in position, insert mortar between the stones.

Stepping stones are informal in appearance and though they can be placed in a straight line, they have more charm if they wind or curve. Natural stones of varying sizes are generally used, but concrete slabs which are square, circular, oval, hexagonal, or irregular in size may be used. The stones, which should have a smooth upper surface for easy treading, should not be smaller than 1–$1\frac{1}{2}$ ft. in dia. Space the stones at regular intervals, about 18 in. apart. They may be set when the path is being constructed or in established turf, with a thin layer of sand underneath. Set into position, so that the stones do not rock, pressing soil around sides and edges as firmly as possible.

Gravel and pebbles have long been used for garden paths. They can be laid directly on the ground or with a cushion of crushed stone or cinders underneath. Where the soil is very well drained and traffic is inconsequential, simply place a 2- to 3-in. layer on the bare ground. A 4-in. layer is better, because it will help to check weed growth. The other method first involves excavating the soil to a depth of 7 in. At the bottom, spread a 5-in. layer of crushed stone or cinders, with the gravel added on top. This makes a better walk that lasts longer and has a more attractive appearance.

Tanbark, wood chips, and pine needles are for rustic woodland paths and walks, though they may be used in formal gardens. Good soil drainage is necessary, and where this exists, it is simply a matter of spreading a 3-in. layer of any of these materials, soaking and rolling it well. Tanbark makes an excellent path. Inexpensive and long-lasting, it is easy to handle, has a mellow, soft brown color and is springy to the step. Furthermore it is not muddy, even after a heavy rain. It is best to use the more expensive oak and hemlock barks. Wood chips are a material which is easily obtainable, and makes a soft, woodsy path. If pine is used, it gives off the familiar pungent pine scent. Pine needles of various kinds may be gathered from the woods, and look especially well in shady wild-flower gardens.

A path or walk of turf requires constant maintenance, yet there is nothing like the soft feel and sight of healthy green grass. It does not cost much to establish, since the grass may be sown directly or the path may be laid with sod. In the case of the latter, obtain top-grade sod and firm into position well. Remember that turf paths require sun.

On any property where there are garden areas, the location of the driveway and garage and their relation to the overall plan is of utmost importance. Before determining the driveway, keep certain points in mind. If possible, keep the driveway at right angles to the street or road.

To accommodate large cars, and trucks and other commercial vehicles that will park on business, the driveway should be 10 ft. wide, though where space is at a premium, 8 ft. will do. For curves, a width of 10 ft. or more is needed. For the passing of 2 cars or for a parking area, make the width 15 ft. or more. Wide driveways are often laid out for reasons of effect. Always make certain that this passageway is not encroached upon by trees and shrubs. The branches should be kept far enough away from the edges of the drive so that they do not interfere with passengers getting into and out of cars.

The centers of driveways should be built at least 2–3 in. higher than the sides. This will enable water to roll away. In addition, gutters to take care of the overflow may need to be installed. Driveways with good drainage will last much longer and eliminate the problem of getting one's feet wet. In snowy and wet winter climates, this can be a big nuisance.

Paving bricks are attractive, last indefinitely and have good traction for automobile tires. They should be laid on concrete to give them reinforcement and then mortared.

Concrete is another dependable material. Place it on beds of 2–3 in. of crushed stone or gravel and reinforce with iron rods or wire mesh. Make the entire driveway of concrete. A grass strip or one with flowers in the center is not advisable, since frequently oil drips from cars and the wheels often get onto the dirt areas, making unsightly gouges. Grass also requires constant upkeep.

Stone paving blocks are good, especially if they are imbedded in concrete. Another, though less sturdy, method is to lay them on a bed of sand or gravel. In both cases, they may be laid in interesting patterns.

Blacktop makes an inexpensive driveway. Unattractive in color, it is cheaper than the others and less durable. It cracks in below-zero weather, and often requires maintenance and periodic repair. Because of its dark coloring it absorbs heat, but has good traction. Home-made blacktop driveways are not advised because the average home-owner does not have the necessary equipment. The heavy rolling this driveway requires can be done only by contractors.

Not as permanent as other materials gravel has an attractive appearance, but is best used only on level or near-level surfaces. Use gravel of small size, pack it well, and roll. The same technique applies to crushed stone or rock, as well as bluestone, marble chips, pink granite chips, and other local materials. Avoid clay and oiled soil. They are messy and slippery when wet.

Statues, Figures, Vases, and Other Accessories

Statues and figures, either human, animal, or purely imaginative, add a lively charm to the garden. Somehow, too, they seem to make it complete. Every good piece of sculpture should be a focal point and should tell a story or evoke a certain emotional response.

Garden sculpture generally represents costly features. It should always be placed with a definite purpose in mind, and should never be selected without careful deliberation and knowledge about its aims.

A handsome statue or figure is often placed at the end of a vista. It is excellent for a terminal wall or for a niche in which it fits harmoniously. It can embellish a fountain or pool or it might rest in a border among flowering plants. Never should it stand stark and isolated, without meaning or purpose. Larger pieces are heavy and not easily moved once placed. In most instances they are secured to a pedestal or other base with concrete or other medium.

The importance of scale cannot be overemphasized. A large piece in a small border or garden looms even larger and is completely out of place. A small piece seems lost and insignificant if overpowered by large shrubs or towering walls. And nothing seems more out of place than a statue or a figure disproportionate to the niche in which it rests.

Some of the most attractive and practical materials suitable to all kinds of weather include marble, iron, lead, bronze, and stone. To some extent, the style of the garden and its immediate surroundings will determine the material, as well as cost. As with other permanent garden features, it is worth paying the extra dollars for something worthwhile and durable, even if it means waiting a year or two. Figures that are plain and not overly ornate are usually best.

Marble is long-lasting and mellows with time, though it needs a stiff scrubbing after a period of years. Traditional statues in this medium include classic figures of ancient Greek mythology. They look best in well-kept, formal gardens, especially against the green of shrubbery or evergreens which show up the white of the marble to best advantage.

Bronze is also formal, but very expensive. It is

strong and durable, but does not stand out well against the dark green of trees and shrubs. Lead is less costly, but good, especially when in time it acquires a lovely, soft patina. Iron is practically indestructible, as is stone, which weathers well.

Large, heavy, immobile pieces of sculpture should be made of materials that can take year-round weather, since they will stay out at all times. Smaller pieces of statuary or figures that can easily be removed and brought indoors in winter need not be so durable. Concrete and terra cotta are two other materials often used to make smaller and less costly items of this kind.

Appropriate for the garden is a statue of St. Francis of Assisi, shown with birds on his extended hand. Less known but equally suitable is St. Fiacre, the patron saint of gardening, depicted with a trowel or spade in his hand. Both come in various styles, sizes, and materials. Small figures of little girls or boys in a number of poses are always in good taste and have wide appeal.

There is a world of possibilities in figures of animals, birds, frogs, turtles, and other creatures. There are dogs for entranceways and gates where they act as guardians. A dog or cat may sit on a wall or terrace. Lead ducks, frogs, and turtles, also made of concrete, may be rested on the copings of pools. These are small enough to be moved from place to place, as the garden changes with the seasons. In winter they may be stored in a basement or closet.

Elfins, gnomes, and cupids are often made of clay, so their cost is within the budget of the average back-yard gardener. Sicilian donkey carts, spilling with geraniums, petunias, lobelias, and other low annuals, often adorn front lawns. Also seen is a ceramic burro, laden with 2 baskets in which sedums or colorful flowers are grown. All these and others are easily obtainable.

Large ornamental vases may be set out at different spots in the garden as permanent, or movable, features. One might highlight a garden gate or terrace, or a pair might look well at a doorway. These may be planted with geraniums or other annual flowers, but those that are costly and ornate are best left as they are. If half filled with sand, they will be more steady and they make good receptacles for cigarette butts.

Lanterns that light up the garden at night extend the time when the garden may be enjoyed. Some, at front or back doors, brighten walks and entrances. In either case, lanterns and other attractive lights add an enchanting aura to the garden at night.

A lantern may be supported on a post by a doorway or garden gate. If Clematis, climbing roses, climbing evergreen euonymus or English Ivy are trained on the post, it becomes even more attractive. A lantern can be attached to the side of the house, garage, wall, or other vertical surface. It may be free-standing around a terrace, garden pool, or by a garden bench, or it may hang from the branch of a tree. Designs, traditional and modern, are widely assorted, as are the materials from which they are made. As with the other features, especially the fixed and permanent, lanterns must be chosen so as to become an integral part of the whole garden. See LIGHTING.

Edgings under a foot high are garden fixtures of a sort. They may be low edgings, a couple of inches high and wide, or small shrubs, considerably higher and wider. They define borders, beds, and walks and give the garden a neat look. This applies to both formal and informal gardens. For edging, bricks can be laid on edge or end, with or without mortar in the joints. For old-fashioned or contemporary gardens, planks or heavy boards may be treated with a wood preservative and used as edgings. Flagstones or blue stone may be inserted on edge, and metal strips may be used to hold back the grass or outline borders, whether the garden is casual or geometric. Aluminum is commonly used for this purpose, but zinc is more durable.

Steps

Steps in the garden are needed wherever there is a change of level, and they should be built for the comfort of both adults and children.

The design and shape of the steps should conform to the garden and to its immediate surroundings. A formal garden will call for elegant steps, often curving gracefully. An informal one will do nicely with rustic types, perhaps logs or railroad ties at regular or irregular intervals, usually comprised of a single tread. The latter are very useful in contemporary homes built purposely on slopes and hills in wooded terrain, where the natural growth of trees, shrubs, and wild flowers is preserved.

Interestingly, steps outdoors should be more gradual than those indoors. In the home, space is limited, so that every inch counts, but in the open, even in small gardens, every effort should be made to make the ascent easier. The broader the tread, the lower should be the riser. Outdoors, treads are often wider than a foot.

Steps may be straight, curving, convex, or concave. They are extremely adaptable, since they may be built wherever needed and in almost any shape or form.

Always avoid long, uninterrupted flights of steps. These are tiring even for the young and healthy. They are also monotonous, when diversity and continued interest should result from strolling in any garden. Where there are long flights, break them up with platforms at regular intervals. They may be constructed of various materials, thus offering a break in the upward climb. Platforms also offer an opportunity for rest and beckon the visitor to pause and enjoy the view.

Steps may project from a high terrace wall or they may recess. Where the wall is very high, the steps may run parallel to the wall, with a railing provided for support and protection. Various materials may be used, with emphasis on those used on the house, so that the steps harmonize with it, as well as with the terrace, retaining wall, driveway, walk, or fence. Brick, concrete, stones—including slate and bluestone—cut stone, wood, railroad ties, and logs are suitable materials.

Steps should be secure, since they are a permanent fixture. They should be well-built in order to avoid any accident. Stone and brick steps need a solid, steady foundation. This may consist of large stones held together with mortar. When concrete is used, it may be reinforced with steel rods. In cold climates, this footing should be below the frost line. This does not apply, however, to rustic steps, such as logs, railroad ties, or very large stones.

The width of the path or walk will determine the width of the steps. Variety of design may be added by allowing steps to take sharp or subtle angles, or they may curve or bend gently in one or more directions.

Ramps are almost as popular as steps and in their execution are equally varied. Ramps are built where slopes are not steep enough for steps, yet are too steep for paths or walks. A series of gentle inclines are divided with single steps. They may be made of the same materials as the walks, such as concrete, stones, or brick, but may be of other materials also, as in rustic slopes, where logs are used on dirt paths, and the styles of ramps may be straight, curving, or free form.

In some gardens where traffic is limited, grass steps are very charming. These are very broad, often designed like ramps, with shallow risers that may be concrete, flagstone, logs, railroad ties or other materials appropriate to the surrounding. Grass steps should be made with sod, since seeding in such areas is difficult.

Since the aesthetic value of steps in the garden is of great importance, they should be given every care to make them attractive. They are permanent structures, built with comfort and convenience in mind. Good drainage should not be overlooked, nor that of planting. If space is allowed at the base of the risers, small rock garden plants, such as Thyme, Sedum, and violas, can be grown. Periwinkle or English Ivy can be trained to grow along the base and other kinds of foliage and flowering plants along the sides, all by way of softening, framing, and enhancing their appeal. This will also make them more inviting.

Structures

Several kinds of garden structures such as summer houses, pergolas or various types of shelters may be added to the garden to give protection from weather, to provide an architectural feature, or to make a place in which to rest. These, of course, should harmonize with the overall layout. Lathhouses for the growing of plants and toolhouses, where tools and all kinds of supplies and equipment may be stored, also belong to this category; while the sundeck, an expansive surface area for sunbathing, is coming more and more into the picture.

Whatever the garden structure, place wherever it will be the most useful. Shelters serve many purposes. They provide protection from the rain, shut out the hot rays of the sun, and create privacy.

The summer house has been in use for centuries. Open on the sides, but with a roof and usually formal in design, it is placed at a distance from the house, at the end of a path or in an axis where two or more paths meet. Some summer houses are rather informal in design, especially if that is the style of the house or it is located at a far-off corner, hidden by trees, shrubs, or vines.

More in vogue with contemporary houses are shelters. Usually, these are close to the house, actually an extension of it, and are used as an outdoor living room. Shelters may have solid roofs or half roofs, with a section of the terrace extending out into the open sky where it receives sun for at least part of the day. Some shelters have crossbars, slats, or bars at the top, so that they are not completely open to the sky. Vines may be trained over them or bamboo slats or canvas may be rolled across the top for the summer, but removed and stored for the winter. There are a number of variations, but the half-closed shelter with a solid roof is among the most useful.

The original purpose of the pergola was to create a vine-shaded passageway between one building and another. Over the years it changed and roofs replaced the open pattern above. Whether closed or open, vines grown on pergolas should not be allowed to become too thick. Several kinds have greater appeal because of their variety of leaf, form, and flowers.

Easy to construct, the lath shade house should run in a north-south direction. If it goes in the opposite direction, the sun will stay in the same spots for too long a period of time. This may cause burning of the foliage of tender plants just brought to the shelter of the lath.

Not too expensive, the size and shape of the lath structure will depend on its location and the amount of plants to be grown under it. The spacing of the laths is determined by the climate. Usually the spaces are the same width as the laths, but in hot, sunny climates they may be placed closer. In cool, northern climates, they may be spaced farther apart.

Durable wood should be used for the lath. Cypress, Redwood, and Cedar are strong and long-lasting, and therefore expensive. Cheaper woods may be used, but aluminum should not be overlooked, since it is even more permanent than wood.

A sloping roof is recommended. It will help to shed rain, and in a climate where it rains frequently and heavily this is a decided advantage. The lath shelter may be enclosed at the rear, or it may be opened on 2, 3, or 4 sides. This will depend on design, location, climate, and the kinds of plants to be raised under it.

One of the most useful of garden structures is the toolhouse. Tools and other equipment and supplies may be kept in the cellar or in a specially built bench in the garage, but the toolhouse often proves to be very useful in answering this need. Like shelters, the toolhouse may extend from the garage or house or it may stand on its own, where it acts as a focal point. It may be built of wood, stone, concrete, or other material, the same as that of the house. Its design may be elaborate or simple, but it must be in keeping with the house, especially if it is conspicuously placed. There are available charmingly designed prefabricated toolhouses suitable for almost any garden.

The size will be determined by the location and needs, but a small toolhouse, if well organized, can accommodate a great many tools and a wide assortment of supplies. Whether small or large, it should have a waist-high bench, with drawers or shelves underneath for supplies and shelves above the bench for vases, fertilizers, pots, pruning shears, and other small tools. Larger tools, such as rakes and pitchforks, may be suspended from pegs or nails along the sides. Also, it is well to have a cabinet, with lock and key, for the storage of sprays and other chemicals to keep them out of the reach of children. Then, floor space should be allowed for the lawn mower, the wheelbarrow, lengths of hose, and whatever other tools and accessories are used.

Sundials

A sundial makes an effective fixture if it receives unobstructed sunshine for most, if not all, of the day. Fascinating mottoes are often inscribed on sundials. A familiar one is, "I count only the sunny hours," but there are other catchy verses like,

> "A Clock the Time may wrongly tell;
> I, never, if the Sun Shines well."

A formal garden usually provides a suitable setting for this ornament. Both rose and herb gardens are ideal. The axis where 4 paths meet is a traditional spot, but this does not mean that the sundial is limited to these locations. It may be placed along the flower border, in the middle of the lawn with low flowers or ground covers around it, or in the rock garden. Contemporary types especially lend themselves to placement elsewhere, including rock outcroppings and terraces. One thing about placement; it should be accessible. A person who spots a sundial generally wants to go up to it to read the time.

The sundial should be secured to a base before the plate is fastened to the top. In order to tell time correctly, the sundial must be set with great care, preferably on a bright day of sunshine. First, make sure the plate, which contains the figures, is flat and absolutely level. Second, note the correct time (not daylight saving time) and adjust the level plate so that the gnomon (that part which casts the shadow) throws a shadow at exactly the right place. To play safe, it might be checked in several hours, and if it is in proper place, then it may be permanently cemented to the pedestal. No matter how carefully they are handled, however, most sundials do not tell accurate time except at certain times of the year. They also register sun time, and for daylight saving, temporary numbers may be placed on the permanent ones or one may apply simple mathematics. Once properly placed, there is no problem with the sundial. It will tell as accurate time as possible and serve as a year-round attraction.

Yet another variation is the sperical or circular sundial, comprised of rings set in a variety of fashions. The modern, or contemporary, ones are extremely simple in design and go well in gardens that are streamlined in layout. For the most part, they provide intriguing ornaments, but are less useful for giving the correct time.

Terraces and Patios

Terraces and patios are important garden areas, often used as open-air living rooms in which much of the family activity takes place. They are important, too, because they unite the architecture of the house with the trees, shrubs, and other plants of the garden.

Actually there is a distinction between a

terrace and a patio (which see) but the two words are often used nowadays to denote the same thing, a paved outdoor area for dining and relaxing. Aside from furniture, it might have a focal point, such as a pool, a fountain, a piece of statuary, an animal figure, or several pot plants.

Technically speaking, the patio, an architectural form derived from Spain, is an outdoor room, enclosed on all sides but open to the sky. It is surrounded by the several rooms of the house, and may have an entrance that leads to the street through a wall. When the Moors invaded Spain from Africa, they brought the idea of the patio with them. In Spain, it was developed into an area of bustling family activity. It usually had a central fountain, balconies, and winding stairs to the upper rooms. Not the least of its attractions were the trees, shrubs and abundantly flowering pot plants that were an essential part of this inviting outdoor room.

The terrace (or patio) of today's garden are derived from these Spanish influences, as well as from the terraces of Italian, French, and English gardens. Its forms and size are highly varied, and are governed by site and need. Though it may be on a slope, raised above the ground, or level with the ground around it, it is usually attached to the house, but this need not be so. Free-standing terraces under a large tree, in a secluded corner or by the swimming pool are becoming more and more popular.

Correct scale and proportion are necessary if a terrace is to express good taste. The ideal terrace is one that is partly open to the sky, so that it has both shady and sunny areas. Where weather is changeable and showers in summer are sudden, an enclosed part is needed. In cool parts of the country, allow for a hedge or fence to shield the terrace from wind.

The size of the terrace is based also on how much use it will receive. The size of the family and whether there are small children are other factors to consider. Where possible, exposure to sun should not be overlooked. Since the afternoon is the hottest part of the day, bear this in mind. Those with means will often have 2 terraces, one in complete shade for hot summer months and another on the sunny south or west for spring and autumn, or occasional winter activity.

Planting the terrace demands skill. If extensive, one or more trees may be set out at strategic points for shade. A small terrace might have a small tree, like a Flowering Dogwood or Crab Apple for shade, supplemented by awnings on the house or by a table with a large umbrella. An evergreen hedge of Holly or Yew may define one or more sides of the terrace, but most of all it should be a place for pot plants of various kinds. These may be moved so as to display various plants as they come into flower. Terraces made of large stones are often planted with Thyme, Arenaria, Aguja, Arabis, and *Veronica repens* in the crevices, assuming traffic is light.

Some terraces are actually made of pebbles, as is this beautiful Mexican "Pebble Garden" at Dumbarton Oaks, Washington, D.C. (Photo by Arnold Arboretum, Jamaica Plain, Mass.)

Paving materials should be strong, durable, able to stand up in all kinds of weather, attractive, smooth for walking and economical. The list includes brick, flagstone, slate, stone, concrete, masonry, marble chips, gravel, wood blocks, and blacktop. Large terraces in full sun may have turf floors. Those that are rustic may utilize tanbark or pine needles. Each material has its merits, as well as drawbacks.

Brick is probably first on the list of terrace materials. Easily procurable, it makes a good appearance and can be handled easily because of its size. Individual bricks may be laid flat on the side, in straight or curving lines. They may be placed in sand or concrete. This is also true for the larger flagstones, available in colors that are subdued and not bright. Flagstone is often laid directly on the soil, though this is not so effective in colder regions, where there is considerable freezing and thawing of the ground and eventual movement of the flagstone.

Slate, available in several bright colors as well as gray and black, is more fragile than flagstone and is best placed in concrete. It tends to be slippery when wet, so it should be avoided on terraces that are subject to much traffic in stormy weather. Stone, sturdier and more expensive, possesses a natural beauty of its own.

Concrete is an excellent paving material. Aside from serving as a base for brick, flagstone, slate, and stone, it may be cast into any shape. Durable, smooth, long-lasting and economical, it may be combined with Redwood or other strong woods for a variation in design and texture. Broad expanses of concrete may be broken in squares or other patterns to relieve monotony.

The contemporary ranch-type house looks appropriate with a terrace floor of wood blocks or wood boards. Use strong, long-lasting wood, first treated with a preservative. It may be laid in fascinating patterns and stained to give it a deeper color.

Trellises and Arbors

Trellises and arbors are used in gardens as supports for vines and climbing plants which would otherwise ramble on the ground or on shrubs and trees. Their beauty as distinctive garden plants with a definite purpose would be lost.

Though the chief purpose of these 2 garden features is to hold up vines, beautifully designed trellises and arbors are highly ornamental. Extensive screening trellises may be erected for privacy or as a background for other plants, and arbors will often frame a view or garden scene. Not only that, but arbors are delightful to walk under, especially when the vine, like a Wisteria or Climbing Rose, is in full bloom.

A trellis is a wooden frame with crossing strips on which vines are supported either by natural means, as twining, or by tying, as in the case of climbing roses, and the trellis may be of any height, width, or design.

The first step is to decide where one or more trellises are needed. One may be attached to the side of the house for a hybrid Clematis. Two might be set up to frame a doorway or both sides of a fence gateway. Because of their vertical position, they literally take no space, so gardens of all sizes can fit several into the scheme, particularly where walls are present.

The location and site will determine the design. It should certainly harmonize with the style of the house and the garden. For the most part, the trellis should be simple, whether its design is traditional geometric, modern, or Oriental. Avoid the use of too many in a confined area, since they lead to a feeling of confusion.

After site and design comes construction. Trellises offered for sale are often cheaply made. The wood is inexpensive and flimsy and cannot support vines as they get older and heavier. The chief requisite of a good trellis is strength, so if possible, have your trellises made to order, or if you are handy with tools you can construct your own, since they are among the easiest of garden features to construct.

Vines when small do not require strong supports and for the first season, string will do. As they develop with age, they become heavier.

When in leaf or in winter when snow falls, the weight is that much greater, and it is not unusual for the trellis to collapse. Once a vine develops, it is not easy to repair a trellis, so make it sturdy from the start. Vigorous, heavy vines like Wisteria and Trumpet Creeper will need stronger supports than will light, thin vines, such as hybrid clematis and annual morning-glories. Always use a good grade of lumber, without knots or other structural weaknesses.

The ultimate size of the vine will help to determine the size of the trellis, but with pruning the strongest offenders can be checked in matter of size. With annual pruning, dead, weak, or too rampant growth can be removed and the vine kept small in size and light in weight. Whereas trellises are usually narrow, screening trellises cover a broader expanse and vines are not always trained on them.

Once a trellis has been built, it is advisable to treat it with a wood preservative. Avoid creosote because it gives off gases that are poisonous to plants, but good stains or paints with lead and oil (2 or 3 coats) are satisfactory. The posts to which large trellises are secured should be imbedded in concrete to make them last longer. Then they should be stained or painted.

Trellises often need annual painting. This may be done in the early spring or fall, though paint will look fresher during the summer months if a spring coat is applied. This will mean cutting away some of the wood and growth, so start early in the season, as soon as days become warm and sunny.

The color of the paint will be determined by the color of the house. White is always appropriate, but commonplace. Sometimes 2 colors can be used, that of the color of the house and the trim. The color, in any case, should harmonize with the foliage and especially with the color of the flowers. A bright color will show up in winter when the vine has shed its leaves. This is one way of adding a note of sparkle to the winter scene.

When vines are young, as in the case of Wisteria and Silver Lace Vine, allow the stems to twine or cling to string tied to the trellis. In this way, the main stems do not encircle the wood of the trellis, making it easy to remove when the trellis is to be painted or repaired. The same holds true when the time comes for the wooden trellis to be replaced because of decay.

Metal trellises are sometimes used, though they do not have the appeal of wood and they become hot in the sun. Metal mesh wire can be secured to metal posts for a lightwight kind of trellis, often used for climbing roses. When the

Modern design of this home creates interesting problems for the proper placing of plants. (*Photo by Arnold Arboretum, Jamaica Plain, Mass.*)

wire disintegrates with age, it can be detached and replaced.

An arbor is an overhead trellis under which one can pass. Its purpose is to support vines, and to add decoration. Broad arbors may have seats at either side. An arbor may be placed at a garden gate, over a front or side doorway, or along a garden path or walk. If the walk is long, several at regular intervals may be used. This is a common practice with climbing roses.

As with trellises, arbors should be well constructed and their design should conform to that of the house and the garden. Strong wood, treated with a preservative and well-painted, should be used. Arbors can be made of metal, but be certain it is a good quality that is non-rusting. On the whole it is less used and less decorative than wood. In cold climates, large arbors should have their main supports imbedded below the frost line and these should be sufficiently close together (8 ft. or under) so that the crossing bars will not sag with the weight of the vines. Again this applies more to vigorous types of vines. For grapes, pergolas, which are long arbors over a passageway, can be erected.

For the trellis and arbor, consider carefully the kind of vine. There are 2 main categories, the permanent, which is long-lived and hardy, and the temporary annual. Some grow very large, others remain small. Study the foliage, flowers, and the method of climbing. In the hardy groups, some twine, others cling by tendrils, others adhere to surfaces by means of aerial rootlets. Still others do not support themselves but need to be tied. All kinds of climbing roses fall into this grouping.

GEORGE TALOUMIS

GARDEN-HELIOTROPE = *Valeriana officinalis*

GARDEN LIGHTING. See LIGHTING.

GARDEN, PLANNING A. Fortunate is the individual who has the experience and knowledge to know exactly what he wants in a garden; who has the opportunity of planning it from the start; and who has the funds to place in it all the plants and "fixtures" which he has decided upon. Most of us are not in that class. However, with the thousands of plants available today, selections should be made intelligently, picking those that are of ornamental interest for the longest period of time, as well as those which require the least care, or which might be termed "low maintenance" plants. Much time and effort can be saved by intelligently planning the garden, and even though one can not start with a piece of land devoid of plants, one can make the best of what is available for use. There are several important things to consider, once the house is placed on the property and the drives and walks have been finally located.

Consider how the area is to be used. Is entertaining outdoors to be a feature? If so, a well-designed patio or terrace well hidden from the public by trees and shrubs is one of the first things to consider. A fountain, or fireplace, or certainly a place for a moveable grill for outdoor cooking is essential.

One must consider the needs for drying clothes, for if such an area is needed it should be near the rear of the house and well surrounded with a high hedge or rustic fence to shield it from observation. The collapsible posts seem to be most popular, but arrangements can be made for permanent hooks for the lines on the inside of a fenced and hidden area.

Family needs should all be carefully considered. Should there be a swimming pool? Are there young people in the family and if so how young? The youngest might be provided with a fenced play area with a sand pile, an area with some shade and some sun which can be easily observed from the house. Every parent knows that such areas are quickly outgrown, nevertheless they are tremendously important for the first few years. Would a badminton court (44 ft. × 20 ft.) be of value, or would it be advisable to spend more money and build a tennis court (78 ft. × 36 ft.) which could be of value to all the family? One should not forget the need for a basketball backboard, often by the garage—an asset which youngsters of all precollege ages can use and usually will use considerably. Such areas as these take prime space, but, if they are desired there is much that can be said about having them on the home grounds as an essential part of family living.

siders placing on the new property. They are usually the most expensive and the most permanent, but land usage must also be considered before the trees so that they can be properly placed and so that they will be assets to the property and the functions which have been decided upon.

In selecting trees, it must be decided what they should contribute to the general plan. If it is shade that is primarily desired one goes to the maples, beeches, lindens and others. If it is a flowering tree, or one that is under 35 ft. in height, one considers another group entirely like the dogwoods, stewartias and crab apples. Or, it might be an evergreen type which is needed because this will give regal beauty with its evergreen foliage every day of the year, and often act as a living Christmas tree in the middle of winter. See CHRISTMAS TREES.

Trees are selected also to serve as a background for the house, to hide objectionable views or to serve as a windbreak. They should be placed where their roots will not interfere

A simple, old-fashioned perennial garden. This is 100 ft. from the sea on Cape Cod. (*Photo by Arnold Arboretum, Jamaica Plain, Mass.*)

Once these major objects have been placed (or rejected) then one considers the need or desire for a vegetable garden, and the placing of it away from the house. Throughout the decisions made on each one of these projects, one considers the need for trees, their proper placing to give shade at the proper places, to lend beauty to the entire plan, but nevertheless they should be so placed as not to be a hindrance to any space planning.

Placing Trees

Trees are actually the first plants one con-

with other plants, and certain types of voracious feeding roots like poplars, some of the elms, the Black Walnut, and others might be omitted from consideration altogether. In other words they should be carefully selected for some specific purpose and they should be carefully placed where they will fulfill that purpose to best advantage without competing with other plantings in the garden for moisture and nourishment.

After these various items have been decided upon and the trees properly placed, one can finally start to plan the aesthetic features of the

Trunks of trees are often interesting, as is this trunk of a century-old *Pinus pinea* at Kew Gardens, England. (*Photo by Arnold Arboretum, Jamaica Plain, Mass.*)

area. Is there to be a flower garden? What is to be grown in it, and don't forget the very important question of who is to take care of it. Are large numbers of herbaceous perennials and bulbs going to be used, or will it be sufficient to merely place a few in the foundation planting about the house. This is not something that must be decided immediately for it may well be that other phases of the garden planning should take priority the first few years. See PERENNIALS.

Sometimes it is difficult to make the decision about the value of having a vegetable garden in the scheme of things. There are many suburban areas where such gardens are simply not used. On the other hand, the individuals who like gardening and who have a growing family, might well want one, not only as a family project, but also one in which children can cooperate and learn many things about horticulture. Do not forget also that if land is used for such purposes the time may come when the vegetable garden is no longer wanted. Then the whole area can be seeded to lawn grass and used for some other purpose.

Vegetables and Fruits

To many of us in the midst of a midwinter planning session a vegetable garden seems attractive, but during midsummer, when the constant fight against drought, poor soil, weeds, insects and disease is at its height, many are prone to take a second look in assessing its merits. We have had a vegetable garden every summer for 30 years, varying in size from 50 ft. × 100 ft. to 100 ft. × 300 ft., which you must admit is a sizeable plot. With youngsters at home to care for it, there were not too many problems, except to keep after the youngsters. When we had to do the work ourselves, the size was drastically reduced. Each year now we say that it is not worth the effort, with modern freezing and packaging methods of today. However, during that midwinter planning spree, when the colorful catalogues portray the glories of home-grown vegetables, we somehow succumb to the urge and plan to plant another garden. Each family must make its own decision. Obviously, one must like working in the garden a great deal to be persuaded that a vegetable garden is financially worth while.

If one is decided upon, but working in it is neither considered recreation nor exercise, take a suggestion from an old hand and only plant the easy things like carrots, beans, corn and tomatoes. Count on the grocery store for such items as frozen peas, lima beans and wonderful cabbage that never has in it the worm holes that the heads you grow always have.

For excellent suggestions concerning a vegetable garden, plants to grow in it, how large it should be and when to plant the various items, see VEGETABLE GARDEN.

When it comes to bush fruits and grape vines, one must have the urge to grow things pretty badly to give up space for these on the small suburban lot. The larger the area available, the easier it becomes to give the necessary space. Raspberries, for instance, are nice to have. Plant them about 3 ft. apart in a row and 25 plants would yield enough fruit. But remember, they must be picked (the birds like them also) and they must be sprayed and pruned, all of which is work and takes time.

Fruit trees demand even more effort. It is not just a matter of planting a single tree, then waiting hopefully for the time the fruit should be picked. It is a matter of planting several trees at a minimum, pruning them annually and spraying them many times each year to control the various insect and disease pests which always infest them. If you are thinking of saving money on the project, figure it out carefully and then compare the end product with the perfect specimens you can buy at the village fruit store or at some roadside stand the next time you take a drive on a weekend. For further information see DWARF FRUIT TREES, as well as articles written separately for each one of the fruits. The latest bulletins on the subject available from your State Experiment Stations are excellent aids in helping with varietal selections and information on culture.

Foundation planting (which see) has been fully described elsewhere in this volume, but it certainly enters into the planning procedure. Of course, it should be well done, but if there are to be no flower borders or flower gardens, it may well be enlarged enough to contain a few perennials and bulbs and serve as a place where a few plants can be used to supply flowers or cut branches for arrangement indoors.

The question often arises concerning how one goes about obtaining experienced advice in landscaping a property. The novice can always go to a landscape architect or to a nurseryman who has landscape advice available. To the experienced individual, or the one who has had considerable planning training, such advice may not be needed.

One can always refer to reference books, articles and experiment station publications on the subject, all of which should be studied carefully to sift all the important, pertinent facts concerning the type of planting desired.

For those planning a garden for the first time, professional advice at the beginning sometimes saves time and much money later on. For many others who find interest in learning by their own mistakes, planning their own place supplies a real challenge. Regardless of which attitude is taken it pays to consider carefully these many items here discussed in advance, on paper, before any real plantings are made.

In other words, first have a plan on paper and make certain it is the best one which can be devised. Once the plan has been decided upon, try to stay with it and avoid any costly last-minute changes. Having a well-thought-out plan in advance of planting is one of the best short-cuts in having a successful and easily cared-for garden.

GARDENING, REGIONAL. Both hardiness and climate must be considered in gardening on a regional basis. Climate is made up of variations in temperature and rainfall. See HARDINESS, CLIMATE. There is no better way to obtain a thorough understanding of this, county by county throughout the entire United States, than to obtain a copy of "Climate and Man," the 1941 Yearbook of the U.S. Department of Agriculture. One can obtain all the average annual statistics on temperature and rainfall for every locality in the entire United States. Such information, if properly analyzed, will give the answers to many questions dealing with plant hardiness and growing conditions in general for each locality in the entire country.

GARDEN, SPRING. In planning the spring garden (or summer garden) merely glance through the ORDER OF BLOOM lists to pick out desirable plants that will bloom together. All are not listed, of course, but enough are to give an idea of what to use to have a garden in full bloom at one time.

GARDENIA (gar-DEE-nia)

jasminoides   4′–6′   Zones 8–9   Cape-jasmine, Gardenia

One should clearly understand that the Gardenia is not as hardy as the Camellia. It has been planted as far north as Washington, D.C., but one should know in advance that the delicate flowers will be injured by late frosts, as may the foliage also. The sturdy *Camellia japonica* can be expected to grow, flower and survive that far north, but not the Gardenia. Actually, it is a native of China, its waxy, white, extremely fragrant, single or double blossoms are 3 in. across. The thick, leathery and glossy evergreen leaves are 4 in. long. It has been grown in America since colonial times, in the Deep South in gardens outdoors, in the North as a desirable greenhouse plant. The variety **fortuniana** is supposed to have larger flowers than the species. The juice of the fruit produces a yellow dye used by the Chinese.

Insect Pests

Mealy bugs are often persistent pests on Gardenia when they feed in colonies at the axils of twigs and on the leaves. Fumigation is usually practiced in greenhouses. On house or garden plants, spraying with insecticide #15 is effective. On a few plants hand picking with a needle or brush wet in alcohol is often sufficient.

Diseases

Stem canker which infects the stem at or just below the soil level girdles and kills the branches. The bark splits and the leaves turn yellow. It is often carried on cuttings. Destroy infected plants and avoid contaminated soil. Bud-drop on houseplants is primarily due to uneven temperature and low humidity. In modern, heated homes, plants in relatively cool rooms have less bud drop.

GARDENS, SEASHORE. See SEASHORE GARDENS.

GARLIC (*Allium sativum*) is a hardy perennial producing a group of small bulbs (cloves) enclosed in a thin white skin. In propagation, these cloves are planted and cared for in about the same manner as onion sets. See ONIONS.

Calif. is the major commercial producer of garlic.

GRANT B. SNYDER

GARLIC-MUSTARD = *Alliaria officinalis*

GARLIC-SCENTED VINE = *Cydista aequinoctialis*

GARRYA (GA-ria)

elliptica   8′   Zone 8   Silk-tassel
The peculiar Silk-tassel is of ornamental value only because of its greenish or yellowish tapering catkins, anywhere from 2–12 in. long. These appear from Dec. to Feb., or later, on this evergreen plant that comes from Ore. and Calif. The leaves are 3 in. long and the fruits are silky berries. It grows well in rocky or sandy soil. The sexes are separate and the male catkins are the more interesting. It is often espaliered in Great Britain.

fremontii   6′   Zone 7   Fremont Silk-tassel
Evergreen, opposite-leaved, interesting shrub, native to Calif. and Ore., with dark, glossy leaves 1½–3 in. long, tapering at both ends. The catkins on the male plant are 2–4 in. long in terminal clusters during April. Not as good an ornamental as *G. elliptica*.

wrightii   6′   Zone 6   Wright Silk-tassel
A slightly hardier species from Ariz., N.Mex., and Tex., this has flowering catkins only about 2–3 in. long appearing in July and Aug. Except for hardiness it is *G. elliptica* which makes the better ornamental.

GARRYACEAE = The Silk-tassel Family

GAS INJURY. Manufactured illuminating gas contains ethylene which is very injurious to plant life, hence leaky gas fixtures in the house can cause trouble with house plants. In some metropolitan areas only natural gas is used and this is not harmful.

The main trouble with manufactured gas is from leaky pipes out-of-doors causing death or injury to trees or shrubs. When a large tree suddenly wilts or starts to die, this should be one of the first possibilities to check out, i.e., are there any gas mains within the vicinity of the injured plant? If there are, dig a hole among the roots and see if one can smell the gas, or better still, set a young tomato plant in the hole with cover on top. Tomato plants are easily injured by gas and the leaves will begin to wilt within several hours if gas is present in such a confined space. A leaky main should be repaired immediately.

Natural gas is now being used in an ever-increasing number of communities. This differs from manufactured gas in that it contains no ethylene or carbon monoxide, the materials so injurious to plant growth. Experiments have proved that even with concentrations of natural gas as high as 1%, and this is seldom if ever reached in a home when a leaky fixture has allowed gas to escape into the air, there is no injury to plant growth. Hence, if the gas used is natural gas, plants in the home will not suffer from a leaky fixture. If the gas is manufactured, plants will suffer from leaking gas.

GASPLANT = *Dictamnus albus*

GASTERIA (gas-TEE-ria). A stemless group of succulents from South Africa with dark green, spotted, straplike leaves usually arranged in a rosette and bearing red-to-rose-colored flowers in loose racemes. The leaves vary from 5–14 in. long depending on the species. These are like aloes but are usually smaller. They are suitable for outdoor desert gardens in the southwestern U.S., but 2 species, **G. acinacifolia** and **G. verrucosa** (The Ox Tongue Gasteria) are sometimes grown as unusual greenhouse plants.

GATES. See GARDEN FIXTURES.

GAULTHERIA (gawl-THEE-ria). Members of the Heath Family, these prefer acid soil. The small, bell-like white flowers are similar to those of blueberry and the leaves are mostly evergreen. They are widely used in gardens of the West Coast areas, preferably in partial shade. Propagation is by seed, layers, division, and occasionally by softwood cuttings.

hispidula (*Chiogenes*)   **2″   Zone 3   Creeping Pearlberry**
A slow-growing little evergreen, native to North America, of value as a ground cover only in moist, acid, peaty soil similar to the type where one would normally find wild cranberries. It withstands shade but is very difficult to cultivate. The flowers are few, white, ⅛ in. long and appear in May and June, while the fruits are small, snowy-white berries ¼ in. across in the fall. The leaves are ¼ in. long, borne alternately along the creeping stem. It is only suited for planting in the bog or wild garden.

miqueliana   1′   Zone 5   Miquel Wintergreen
A Japanese evergreen chiefly used in the northwest Pacific Coast area, this has small leaves ½–1¼ in. long and small, white, blueberrylike flowers in nodding racemes 1–2½ in. long during May. The berries are white to pinkish, sometimes rather showy. Like other members of this genus, these require acid soil conditions. They are difficult to transplant and pot-grown plants are the best to use.

nummularoides   1′   Zone 7
A procumbent shrub from the Himalayas, with small, orbicular leaves about ½ in. long, flowers white to pinkish and blue-black berries in the fall, said to be edible. It is sometimes used as a ground cover in the area of Seattle, Wash.

ovatifolia   1′   Zone 5   Oregon Wintergreen
Orbicular leaves 1–1½ in. long, native from British Columbia to Idaho, procumbent stems,

red berrylike fruits in the fall, said to be edible. This is sometimes used as a ground cover within the limits of its native habitat.

procumbens   3″   Zone 3   Checkerberry or Wintergreen

The native Wintergreen is known to all familiar with the woods of eastern North America where it is native. The drooping, waxy, white bell-shaped flowers in May are mostly hidden by the lustrous evergreen leaves but the bright red berries are a familiar sight in the woods in the fall. These are edible and have the peculiar flavor which gives it its name. If the soil is acid, partly shaded and sufficiently moist, this forms a ground-covering mat of foliage over the ground and it is only used in naturalistic plantings. The leaves have been used in making tea. Seeds should be stratified for 3 months at 40° F., then sown. See STRATIFICATION.

shallon   1½′   Zone 5   Salal, Shallon

Native from Alaska to Calif., this is perhaps the most conspicuous of the *Gaultheria* species with long shoots of dark, leathery, evergreen leaves each 5 in. long and its conspicuous clusters of waxy, white, blueberrylike flowers in early June. The purple-to-black fruits are edible. It makes a fine ground cover, growing vigorously in good soil and shade, but forming a low mat on the ground in poor soil in full sun. Like the others it needs acid soil, and makes a fine ornamental, especially for the front of the evergreen border.

veitchiana   3′   Zone 7   Veitch Wintergreen

Native in China, this evergreen is best used in moist soils. The evergreen leaves are lustrous and up to 3½ in. long, while the flowers are white to flushed pink, bell shaped like the others of this genus, borne in May. The indigo-blue berries are ¼ in. across, and like the others, this is an acid soil plant.

GAURA (GAW-ra)

lindheimeri   3′   Zone 5   White Gaura

Not very well known, native to La. and Tex., but it does make a nice garden perennial as far north as Zone 5. It grows best in full sun and well-drained soil. Pinkish-white flowers, about 1½ in. across, are borne from July until Oct. The alternate lance-shaped leaves are 1½–3½ in. long. Easily propagated in either fall or spring by division.

GAYFEATHER. See LIATRIS.

GAYLUSSACIA (gay-lus-SAC-ia)

brachycera   18″   Zone 5   Box-huckleberry

A rare, very slow-growing, extremely desirable evergreen with leaves up to 1 in. across, this native American plant is occasionally found in Pa., Va., Tenn. and Ken. It makes a beautiful ball of evergreen foliage which can turn a bronze color in the fall. Most desirable as a

specimen in the rockery or by itself, this is a very difficult plant to find in nurseries, probably because it grows so slowly that nurserymen can not afford to grow it. Nevertheless, those who have good specimens of this plant cherish them. The fruits are edible.

Propagation

Seed may be sown as soon as ripe or stored dry in airtight containers in a cool place for up to a year, then sown. Dividing the plants is a simple and easy method if done in the early spring before growth starts. Softwood and hardwood cuttings (which see) can be rooted easily.

G. baccata is deciduous, and except for being extremely hardy (Zone 2) has little ornamental value.

GAZANIA (gaz-AY-nia)

ringens   prostrate to 18″   annual   Pied Gazania

Possibly a hybrid, not known in the wild but related to other species of this genus from South Africa, valued for its prostrate habit, its ability to grow well in the full sun, the silky white undersurface of its very narrow leaves and its yellow or orange flowers. The ray flowers have a black and white spot at the base of each. A member of the Composite Family, hence it bears daisylike flowers. The seed should be sown indoors during Feb. and March and the seedlings set out after frost in the full sun, 18 in. apart. Used as a ground cover in Calif.

GIEGERTREE = *Cordia sebestena*

GELSEMIUM (je-SEEM-ium)

sempervirens   vine   Zone 7   Carolina Jessamine

A handsome perennial vine with opposite, oblong to lanceolate, shiny leaves. The fragrant yellow flowers, which are clustered in the axils of the leaves, have a funnel-shaped corolla about 1 in. long and 5 slightly irregular, rounded lobes. It grows profusely in roadside woodlands from Va. southward, tending to become evergreen at the southern end of its range. The flowers appear from early March to May. It is used much in the Carolinas as a garden vine, but is not hardy north of N.Car. and the southern portion of coastal Va. It may be propagated by seeds or cuttings. Cattle, sheep, goats, swine and horses have been poisoned by eating the flowers, leaves and roots of this plant.

GENE. A term used in genetics to indicate the elements by which hereditary characters are transmitted and determined, regarded as a part of the chromosome. Theoretically a cell includes a gene for each hereditary characteristic, and so an individual resulting from the union of 2 such cells receives a set of genes from each parent.

GENICULATE. Bent abruptly like a knee.

GENISTA (jen-ISS-ta). Mostly small deciduous shrubs, members of the Pea Family, with small yellow flowers and dried pods for fruits. The leaves are simple or trifoliate, very small and sometimes almost nonexistent, the green branches taking over the functions of food manufacturing commonly performed by the leaves. They will grow in poor soil, but need a sunny location. Like the *Cytisus* species, these are not very easily transplanted and care should be taken in moving them.

Propagation

Seeds may be processed at once or stored dry in airtight containers in a cool place for up to a year. Soak in hot water (190° F.) overnight, then sow. Softwood and hardwood cuttings root readily. See SEEDS, CUTTINGS.

cinerea   2½′   **Zone 7**   **Ashy Woadwaxen**
Akin to the *Cytisus* species, the woadwaxens are members of the Pea Family and are for growing in hot, dry, sunny situations. They do not transplant easily. This one, native to southern Europe and northern Africa, has 8-in. racemes of yellow, pealike flowers in early June and is sparingly leafy. A dependable species.

germanica   1′   **Zone 5**   **German Woadwaxen**
This evergreen shrub has small leaves which remain on the branches longer than do the leaves of most other species. In early summer the small yellow, pealike flowers, borne in racemes 1–2 in. long, appear in profusion. It is native to Central and southern Europe.

hispanica   1′   **Zone 6**   **Spanish Gorse**
This shrub is covered with large green spines which, with the green twigs, give it a decidedly evergreen appearance in winter. The flowers are bright yellow, pealike, borne in early June and almost completely cover the plant when they are fully open. It requires dry soil and is a native of Spain and northern Italy.

horrida   1½′   **Zone 7**   **Cushion Woadwaxen**
The slender, light green branches of this shrub are contorted in interesting shapes. It is difficult to use because it is covered with spines. In midsummer the plant is ornamented with yellow, pealike flowers. A native of Spain and southern France, it is somewhat tender in northern areas.

lydia   2′   **Zone 7**
A popular rock garden plant in Great Britain, for some reason this beautiful plant apparently is not listed by American nurserymen. Although the yellow flowers may be few in a cluster, nevertheless the racemes are profusely borne, so that in May and June the plant is just a mass

of bright yellow. It is native to eastern Europe, hard to transplant like the other members of this genus, but well worth growing in a dry, sunny situation.

pilosa   1′   **Zone 5**   **Silky-leaf Woadwaxen**
Native to Europe, the yellow, pealike flowers of this plant appear in late May. The low shrub is useful for covering poor soil, even under trees and shrubs if there is not much shade. It is hard to move, as are the others, and once established it should be let alone.

sagittalis   6″–1′   **Zone 4**   **Arrow Broom**
If grown in the hot sun in sandy soil, this woody plant from central Europe makes an excellent ground cover. The yellow, pealike flowers are borne in short, erect racemes of 6–8 flowers during May and June. The few leaves are alternate, less than an inch long, and the green twigs have a corky wing on either side. It is a fine ground cover.

sylvestris   6″   **Zone 6**
A small, spiny shrub with slender green stems and deep yellow flowers, native to southwest Yugoslavia. The variety **pungens**, slightly smaller, is also more spiny. These are attractive plants, though very spiny.

tinctoria   3′   **Zone 2**   **Dyer's Greenweed (Broom)**
Sometimes this plant is found naturalized in the eastern U.S., although it is a native of Europe and western Asia. The flowers are borne in early June and are used to produce a yellow dye.

villarsii   3″   **Zone 6**   **Villars Woadwaxen**
A spineless Woadwaxen with green, leafless stems covered with a soft down, giving the stems a grayish appearance which contrasts well with the yellow flowers which appear in early summer. Native to southern Europe.

GENTIAN. See GENTIANA, GENTIANELLA, GENTIANOPSIS.

GENTIAN FAMILY = Gentianaceae

GENTIANA (jen-she-AY-na). A genus including a number of herbaceous plants with very beautiful flowers, the several species differing widely in habitat. Some are perennial, others annual and others, such as the Fringed Gentian, biennial. The leaves are opposite, with no marginal teeth, and generally stalkless, the flowers often blue, and the corolla 4- or 5-lobed, often with teeth between the lobes. It may well be that inexperienced gardeners will find these hard to grow, especially the annual species. They are mostly for the rock garden and are propagated by seed sown as soon as it is ripe.

acaulis   4″   **Zone 3**   **Stemless Gentian**
This little beauty from the Swiss Alps grows in thick mats of green leaves which are an inch long. Rising from this green mat, in late spring, are the large, sky blue flowers, often 3 in. long.

The plant requires a cool, moist situation in sun or semishade and a rich, loamy soil. If planted where the soil becomes rather warm or dry, it should be shaded during the hottest part of the day.

andrewsii   1′   Zone 3   Andrews Gentian
A perennial species living in marshes and along the banks of streams from Quebec to Manitoba and south to N.J. and the mountainous areas from N.Car. to Mo. The plant has a slender stalk on which appear pale green, sessile leaves at regular intervals. Clustered in the axils of the leaves are the tubular blue flowers which never open. The flowers bloom in late Aug. and Sept. It is a fine plant for the bog garden, since it is a long-lived perennial, becoming a well-established clump. It may be divided in spring.

calycosa   1′   Zone 7   Rainier Pleated Gentian
Having a crown of ovate leaves, this species differs from most of the gentians in having trailing or decumbent stems, which may be 10–12 in. long, each stem terminating in a large blue flower blotched or spotted with green. The plant, native to the peat bogs of the Rocky Mountains, blooms in June and July.

campestris = *Gentianella campestris*

clusii   4″   Zone 7
Offered by several nurseries in Ore., this perennial native to Europe has leathery leaves in a basal rosette and deep blue, funnel-shaped flowers 2 in. long, borne singly in June.

crinita = *Gentianopsis crinata*

cruciata   10″   Zone 5   Cross Gentian
A perennial herb with dark blue flowers ¾ in. long in axillary clusters. Native to Europe and northern Asia.

decumbens   10″   Zone 6?
As its name implies, this is another Gentian having decumbent stems on which bloom clusters of small blue flowers in midsummer. It does best in a well-drained, humus acid soil in sun or semi-shade. Native to the Himalayas.

farreri   prostrate   Zone 6   Farrer Gentian
A stoloniferous, almost prostrate perennial with linear leaves with those at the base attached together; flowers blue, 2½ in. long, with white throat and a yellowish-white band on the petals. Native to China.

gracilipes   6″   Zone 6?
The long, rather narrow leaves of this plant from China are formed in a rosette. The loose clusters of small, purple-blue flowers appear on stems 10 in. high in midsummer. It requires a loose, well-drained acid soil.

himalayense   8″–15″   Zones 2–3   Lilac Geranium
A hardy perennial plant with leaves deeply 5-parted. The flowers are blue with purplish veins, about 1½ in. wide, appearing from May to July. Native to northern Asia. This is a very rugged plant.

kurroo   7″   Zone 6?
This small, tufted plant from the Himalayan Mountains, has narrow, linear leaves about 6 in. high and small blue flowers with the inner surface flecked with white. It requires a rich, moist, gravelly acid soil in sun or light shade.

linearis   2′   Zone 3   Narrowleaf Gentian
A perennial for bogs, native to eastern North America, with blue or white flowers in terminal clusters, each flower nearly 2 in. long and blooming in Sept.

lutea   4′–6′   Zone 6   Yellow Gentian
A leafy perennial valued for its blue-green ovate leaves and its yellow-veined or spotted flowers 1 in. in dia., borne in whorls. Little grown in the U.S., it is native to Europe and Asia Minor.

sino-ornata 'Macauleyi'   6″   Zone 4   Macauley Gentian
This free-flowering stoloniferous and recumbent plant is a hybrid originating in England. It has long, slender stems and light green, somewhat succulent linear leaves. Light blue flowers about 2½ in. long appear in autumn. An excellent plant for the somewhat shady garden with a well-drained, loamy acid soil.

seponaria (*puberula*)   **8″–20″   Zone 4   Downy Gentian**
The erect stems of this perennial are covered with a soft down. The flowers are blue and borne in clusters in the axils of the upper pairs of leaves and at the crown of the stem. The tubular corolla, up to 2 in. long, has 5 pointed and spreading lobes. This gentian prefers dry, sandy soil, growing from western N.Y. to Ga. and west to the Plains States. It flowers in autumn. Propagation is by division in spring.

purdomii   10″   Zone 4   Purdom Gentian
Preferring a rich, moist garden loam and light shade, this erect plant has tufts of long, thin leaves and clusters of deep blue flowers blooming in midsummer. Native to China.

quinquefolia = *Gentianella quinquefolia*

scabra   1′   Zone 6?   Rough Gentian
This Chinese species has stiff stems, large, ovate leaves and large, dark blue flowers terminating the stems. These appear in autumn. It does well in a rich, somewhat acid soil and semi-shade. Propagation is from seed.

septemfida   1½′   Zones 2–3
Few-flowered terminal clusters of dark blue, bell-shaped flowers 2 in. long, blooming in summer; leaves 1–1½ in. long, ovate. Native to Asia Minor. Several forms have been named, but apparently they are not available.

sikokiana   1′   Zone 6   Sikkim Gentian
An excellent plant for rock gardens, it grows with mounds of low, recumbent stems which have small leaves sharply pointed at the tip. In early autumn a profusion of large, solitary,

light blue flowers appear along the trailing stems. Easy to grow, it does well in well-drained, neutral to somewhat acid soil in sun or semi-shade. Native to Japan.

sino-ornata 7″ **Zone 6 Chinese Gentian**
Since this Chinese plant increases by its rooting stolons, it quickly forms a loose ground cover of thin-textured, pale green leaves. These are further ornamented by the large, bright blue flowers striped with white which appear in July and continue to bloom until the severe frosts arrive. The plant requires a well-drained, loose, rich acid soil in light shade and constant moisture. For this reason, its use is restricted in many parts of the U.S.

thermalis = *Gentianopsis thermalis*

tubulosa 6″ **annual or biennial**
With 1-in. bluish flowers, either borne in clusters of 3 or singly. Native to Argentina.

verna 3″ **Zone 6? Spring Gentian**
Very difficult to grow, this is a low, tufted perennial with solitary dark blue flowers an inch long. Native to Europe.

GENTIANACEAE = The Gentian Family

GENTIANELLA (jen-she-an-ELL-a)
campestris (*Gentiana campestris*) 6″ **annual Meadow Gentian**
Leaves to 1½ in. long, flowers bright purple and an inch long, held erect, native to Europe and used in the rock garden.

quinquefolia (*Gentiana quinquefolia*) 2″–3″ **annual or biennial Five-leaf Gentian**
This interesting gentian has a strongly angled stem and ovate or lanceolate leaves occurring in pairs or whorls of 5. The 4 triangular lobes of the generally blue, though sometimes lilac-to-white calyx are tipped with bristles. The plant grows on rich soil in moist woods throughout the Atlantic coastal states and those bordering on the Gulf of Mexico. It flowers from Aug. to Nov. Propagation is by seed.

GENTIANOPSIS (jen-she-an-OP-sis)
crinita (*Gentiana crinata*) 1′–2′ **biennial Fringed Gentian**
A much-branching biennial with square stems and lanceolate leaves, growing about 1–2 ft. tall. The sharply pointed and keeled lobes of the calyx are terminally produced and the azure-blue corolla, about 2 in. long, has 4 spreading lobes which are delicately fringed, blooming in Sept. and Oct. The Fringed Gentian has a range from Me. to Ontario, Mich. and Minn., extending south to Pa., Ill. and Ia., and is sometimes found in isolated spots in the mountains of Ga. It is very elusive, due to its biennial character and the fact that its wind-distributed seeds germinate only when they are lodged in acid soil in wet meadows or other moist areas.

thermalis (*Gentiana thermalis*) 1′ **annual Rocky Mountain Fringed Gentian**
Flowers deep blue with lighter blue in streaks, 2 in. long, singly produced. Native to Colo. and Ariz.

GENUS (pl. genera). A group of allied species under a single heading; or consisting of an isolated species exhibiting unusual differentiation.

GERANIACEAE = The Geranium Family

GERANIUM (jer-AY-nium). Nearly 260 species are found in the temperate regions of the world. Some are nice garden plants, others are not. The chief value of these plants is their summer color in the perennial border or the rock garden. Several species are attractive for their foliage alone. Plants usually need division about every fourth year. Propagation is by spring-sown seeds, cuttings made in summer, and possibly root cuttings of 1 or 2 of the species. Of course, division of the plants in the spring is the easiest and best method. This genus does not include the common garden geranium, which belongs to *Pelargonium*. For the control of insect and disease pests, see *Pelargonium hortorum*.

carolianum 1½′ **annual Carolina Cranesbill**
A widespread native weed throughout the U.S. and southern Canada. The alternate leaves are divided into 5–7 deeply cut parts; the flowers are pale pink to whitish and about ¼ in. wide in May. It is primarily a weed on poor soils.

cinereum 6″ **Zone 7**
The 5–7-parted leaves, covered with a whitish bloom, grow in mounds. Large pink flowers having red stripes, quite typical of this group, appear throughout the summer. Native to the Pyrenees Mountains. The variety **'subcaulescens'** has flowers a deeper pink than the species and also has a red center.

endressii 15″ **Zone 7 Endres Cranesbill**
A beautiful plant from the Pyrenees, this has deeply lobed, 5-parted leaves and striking rose-colored flowers ⅓ in. wide, blooming in mid-summer.

grandiflorum = *G. himalayense*

ibericum 1½′ **Zones 2–3 Caucasus Geranium**
Though large for the rock garden this handsome plant is a worthy addition to the perennial border. Having clumps of large leaves with 7 deep lobes and shiny, dark purple flowers which appear in May and June, this Chinese species deserves wider popularity in the U.S.

incisum 2′ **Zone 7 Cleftleaf Geranium**
Leaves 3–5 parted and often deeply incised; flowers an inch wide and pinkish purple. Native from British Columbia to Calif. Only for the wild garden.

macrorrhizum   1½′   Zones 2–3   **Bigroot Geranium**
Another attractive species with 5–7-lobed leaves growing in clumps and having magenta flowers which appear throughout the summer. Native to southern Europe.

maculatum   12″–20″   Zone 4   **Spotted Geranium**
A handsome perennial weed with a rather open, branching habit and deeply lobed leaves on long petioles. The small terminal flower clusters open in May and June to disclose violet-colored flowers 1 in. in dia. The slender seed capsule, likened by the Greeks to a crane's bill (the meaning of "geranium") splits when ripe, throwing the seed some distance from the plant. Excellent for the border or the wild garden, it is found in rich soil in sunny, moist locations from Me. to Ga. and west to the Plains States. Seed may be sown in spring or fall, or the plants divided in spring.

platypetalum   2′   Zones 2–3
With 5-lobed leaves and dark purple flowers ¼ in. long, sometimes grown in the flower border. Native to China.

pratense   3′   Zone 5?   **Meadow Geranium**
This perennial has 7-parted leaves and purple flowers ½ in. wide. Native to Eurasia.

pusillum   prostrate   annual   **Small-flowered Cranesbill**
A lawn weed, sometimes a biennial, introduced from Europe, with weak prostrate, much-branched stems, alternate, palmately 5–9-parted leaves, each segment of which is 3 lobed, and small, blue-purple flowers ¼ in. wide during June and July. It is widespread in the northern U.S. and southern Canada.

pylzowianum   1′   Zone 7
A small plant with a matlike growth. The leaves are 5 parted, the leaflets 3 lobed, and these rise on slender stems to a height of 3 in. Large, deep pink flowers 1¼ in. wide rise an inch or two above the foliage in early summer. Native to China.

renardii   1′   Zone 7
Clumps of velvety, gray-green foliage and loose clusters of pale pink flowers having dark red veins combine to make this plant from the Caucasus an unusually attractive garden plant. It blooms in midsummer.

robertianum   12″–18″   Zone 3   **Herb Robert**
A widely dispersed annual occurring throughout the north temperate zone and North Africa. In habit it is often a sprawling plant with deeply lobed leaves and clusters of reddish flowers ¼ in. wide. It blooms throughout the summer, frequenting rocky woods and underbrush, and is definitely a weedy plant.

sanguineum   12″   Zone 3   **Blood-red Geranium**
Usually the flowers are purple-red, but they may vary to magenta, being freely produced from May to Aug. Stems may trail along the ground for 2 ft. or more. The leaves are 5–7 parted. The variety '**Album**' has white flowers and **prostratum** is a compact dwarf only 6 in. high with bright pink blossoms freely borne all summer. The dense mat of foliage produced is ornamental throughout the season. Native to Europe and Asia.

sylvaticum   2½′   Zone 5   **Forest-loving Cranesbill**
The leaves are 7-lobed, flowers violet, about an inch wide, native to Europe and Asia.

wallichianum   prostrate   Zone 6   **Wallich Geranium**
A prostrate perennial from the Himalayas with 3–5-parted leaves, deeply toothed leaflets and purplish flowers 2 in. wide.

GERANIUM, IVY = *Pelargonium peltatum*

GERARDIA, PURPLE = *Agalinis purpurea*

GERBERA (GER-bera). Also spelled *Gerberia*.

x jamesonii hybrida   1½′   Zone 8   **Transvaal Daisy**
The species is native to the Transvaal of South Africa with leaves woolly underneath, up to 10 in. long; flowers solitary, daisylike, orange-red up to 4 in. across. The hybrid is much the better ornamental with flowers of many colors—white, pink, salmon, red, violet. In the North if seed is sown indoors in Jan. and the plants are set outdoors after all danger of frost is over, they can be used as garden plants, otherwise they are grown by the florist under glass for cut-flower purposes. In the South they can be treated as garden perennials but they will not withstand frost.

GERMANDER = *Teucrium chamaedrys*

GERMAN-IVY = *Senecio mikanioides*

GERMINATION. The development of the plantlet from the seed.

GESNERIA, PURPLE = *Smithiantha zebrina*

GESNERIACEAE. There is no well-recognized common name for this Family.

GEUM (JEE-um). This group of plants has brilliant flowers and makes for fine garden displays chiefly from May to July but with occasional flowers produced until frost. They may be single, double, red, yellow or orange, with some dwarf forms excellent for the rock garden. They prefer well-drained soil in the sun, and can be planted in either fall or spring. Propagation by division in the late summer.

x borisii (*G. bulgaricum* x *G. reptans*)   10″   Zone 3   **Boris Avens**
A rock garden plant with yellow flowers during May and June.

coccineum   15″   Zone 5
This species from Asia Minor is not grown in

America as such but there are many hybrids of this and *G. chiloense* which are good garden plants and are more reliable than the old-fashioned 'Mrs. Bradshaw', such as 'Fire Opal', 'Orangeman', 'Princess Juliana' and 'Red Wings'. These all bloom from late May to July.

montanum   12″   Zone 6?
Native to southern Europe with golden-yellow flowers 1½ in. across.

quellyon   2′   Zone 6   Chilian Avens
This is not as hardy a species as many gardeners seem to think, and certainly should be given winter protection in the North. The flowers are either single or double, 1½ in. across. Unfortunately, the semidouble scarlet variety 'Mrs. Bradshaw' and the yellow-flowered mutation of it 'Lady Stratheden' have been very popular until recently but neither of them have proved consistently dependable. The species is native to Chile.

rivale   3′   Zone 3   Water Avens
A perennial herb with lyre-shaped leaves, the terminal lobe being much larger than the others. The flower stalk bears nodding, bell-shaped flowers, the 5 lobes of the purple calyx alternating with 5 bractlets. The 5 short petals are a dull yellow. It is a plant suitable for the bog garden, being native to such areas from Newfoundland to Quebec and Mich. and south to N.J., and flowering in May and June. Seeds may be sown very early in spring, or the plants may be divided in spring or summer. When the root is boiled it makes a drink faintly tasting like chocolate.

rossii   7″   Zone 2
A stoloniferous plant forming mats of pinnate leaves and bearing small, deep yellow flowers atop 8–10 in. stems. These appear in July. Native to the Arctic regions, the plant requires a site in cool, moist soil.

turbinatum   1′   Zone 4
A plant with pinnate foliage finer than that of *G. rossii*, the stoloniferous roots form mats and the foliage is ornamental with small yellow flowers on stems 8 in. high, in midsummer. A native to the Rocky Mountains.

GHOSTPLANT = *Graptopetalum paraguayense*

GIANT DAISY = *Chrysanthemum uliginosum*

GIANT-LILY = *Cardiocrinum giganteum*

GIANT REED = *Arundo donax*

GIANT SUNFLOWER = *Helianthus giganteus*

GIBBERELLIC ACID. A growth-promoting substance which has been used in the past in many growth experiments with all kinds of plants. Concentrations of only 10–100 parts of

the acid to one million of water were used experimentally to induce growth.

GILIA (GIL-ia or JIL-ia). A group of mostly annual herbs native to Calif. and other Pacific Coast states, a few species being native to South America, with alternate and entire or divided leaves, and funnel-like flowers that are blue, yellow, pink or white. Since they do not respond well to transplanting, seeds are sown outdoors in the full sun, where they are to grow. Even biennial or perennial species can often be treated as annuals.

abrotanifolia = *G. capitata*

achilleifolia   2′   annual   Yarrow Gilia
Flowers blue in dense terminal clusters; leaves divided into 2 parts.

aggregata = *Ipomopsis aggregata*

androsacea = *Linanthus androsaceus*

capitata (*G. abrotanifolia*)   2½″   annual
Globe Gilia
Leaves 2–3 pinnately divided into linear parts, flowers light blue about an inch across.

dianthoides = *Linanthus dianthoides*

laciniata   8″   annual
Leaves twice pinnately dissected into linear leaflets; flowers rose, blue, pale lilac to white. Native to Peru, Chile, Argentina.

liniflora = *Linanthus liniflorus*

rubra = *Ipomopsis rubra*

tricolor   2½′   annual   Bird's-eye Gilia
Leaves twice pinnately divided into linear parts; flowers blue, lilac, and yellow. The var. **rosea** has rose-colored flowers.

GILLENIA (gil-EE-nia)
trifoliata   3′   Zone 4   Bowman's-root
With compound leaves, loose white flowers in terminal clusters during July, this perennial is a woodland plant native to the eastern U.S. It is only suitable for the shaded wild garden. Propagated by division in the spring or by seeds.

GILL-OVER-THE-GROUND = *Glechoma hederacea*

GINGER, COMMON = *Zingiber officinale*

GINGER FAMILY = Zingiberaceae

GINGER, MALAY = *Costus speciosus*

GINGER, WILD. See ASARUM.

GINGER FAMILY, WILD = Aristolochiaceae

GINGER-LILY = *Hedychium coronarium*

GINKGO (GING-ko)
biloba   120′   Zone 4   Ginkgo or Maidenhair Tree
This is one of the best trees for city planting. Native to China, with small fan-shaped, alternate leaves 2½–3½ in. wide, turning a brilliant yellow in the fall. The habit is picturesque and open giving little shade, but the

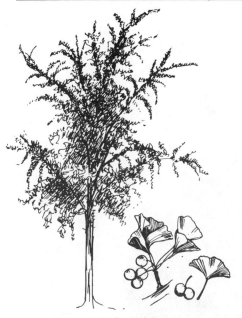

Ginkgo biloba

tree is pest-free. The sexes are separate, the flowers are inconspicuous, with fruits being fleshy drupes, like small plums but vile smelling. Only male trees should be planted and these must be asexually propagated for it takes 20 years or more for seedlings to produce their first flowers. Several named male clones are available. The var. **fastigiata** has a columnar habit and is called the Sentry Ginkgo; **pendula** has pendulous branchlets.

Although it has always been recommended as one of the best trees for urban plantings, it has recently been found that the Ginkgo is one of the first trees to suffer from the noxious gases of air pollution. Now, where air pollution is serious —as in many city areas—the planting of other trees might be better.

Propagation

Do not allow the seeds to dry out before they are sown. Varieties are grafted or budded on the species. Many clones have been rooted easily from softwood cuttings but some have been reported as difficult. See CUTTINGS, GRAFTING, BUDDING.

GINSENG. See PANAX.

GINSENG, AMERICAN = *Panax quinquefolium*

GIRDLE (to). To restrict or remove the bark around the stem or other parts of plants.

GIRDLING ROOTS. Encircling roots at or below the surface of the ground which tend to strangle the plant. See PRUNING.

GLABRATE. Nearly glabrous or becoming glabrous with age.

GLABROUS. Not hairy.

GLADIATE. Sword-shaped or sword-like.

GLADIOLUS (glad-EYE-o-lus) or (glad-i-O-lus). Members of this genus are summer-blooming, colorful, widely popular plants of easy culture growing from corms, belonging to the Iris Family. There are over 200 species, mostly native to the Tropics. They are tender, will not stand frost or freezing and in the North are grown out-of-doors only between frosts. They are lifted and stored as dry corms over winter. Easily propagated by cormlets found in the fall at the base of the old corm. These, if cared for properly, should bloom in 2–3 years. The flowers are borne on a long spike and bloom successively from the base to the top. An excellent plant for cut flowers.

Insect Pests

Gladiolus thrips may be transported on the corms and consequently are usually present wherever gladiolus are grown. They cause streaking and mottling of the buds and flowers and russet scars on the corms. Spraying or dusting with insecticide #9 or #15 where the flower stalk first shows and at 7–10-day intervals gives control. Dusting the corms in storage with insecticide #9 kills the thrips and prevents reinfestation at planting. Tulip aphid and spider mite may require control with insecticide #15. Japanese beetle feeds on the buds and flowers. See GRAPE.

Diseases

Scab, bacterial blight, botrytis rot, yellows, and dry rot all live part of their life cycle on the corms. A preplanting dip of fungicide #F as directed on package is suggested. White Break Mosaic causing streaks in leaves and deformed florets is a virus. Prompt destruction of plants as soon as they show symptoms and aphis control are advised.

cardinalis   4′   Zone 9   Cardinal Gladiolus
With 5–10 bright scarlet flowers. Native to South Africa. This may be one of the parents of *G. gandavensis*.

carneus   2′   Zone 9   Snowpink Gladiolus
Bearing about 4 leaves, each ¾ in. wide, and 4–8 flowers which are white and red tinged. Native to South Africa.

x colvillei   2′   Zone 7   Colville Gladiolus
One of the hardier species with large, flaring, scarlet flowers that open earlier than those of other species. This is supposed to be a hybrid, and the old-fashioned clone **'The Bride'** with pure-white flowers is still very popular.

Ginkgo biloba fastigiata makes an excellent tree for bordering streets and highways. (*Photo by Arnold Arboretum, Jamaica Plain, Mass.*)

x gandavensis 2′ Zone 9 Breeders Gladiolus
This has long been grown in gardens, for it is sturdy, blooms late with sturdy spikes of red or yellow flowers, sometimes streaked. It is this that has been considered one of the important fore-runners of many modern varieties.

x hortulanus   Garden Gladiolus
This is the name that is now proposed for the hundreds of garden gladiolus varieties now available.

illyricus 1½′ Zone 9 Grecian Gladiolus
With slender leaves only 6–10 in. long and 4–8 reddish-to-bluish flowers, this is native to southern Europe. Blooms in summer.

murieliae 3½′ Zone 9
The erect leaves are nearly 2 ft. long and 1½ in. wide. The fragrant, showy white-to-pink flowers are nearly 5 in. across. This blooms in Aug. and is native to Abyssinia. Sometimes offered as *Acidanthera murieleae*.

oppositiflorus 3″–4′ Zone 9 Twosided Gladiolus
With numerous white flowers nearly 3 in. across, leaves usually 4 and about 1 in. wide. Native to South Africa.

primulinus 2′–4′ Zone 9 Primrose Gladiolus
A very important parent of many garden forms, leaves 3, and 1 in. wide; 3–5 primrose-yellow flowers. Native to Tropical Africa.

natalensis (*psittacinus*) 3′–4′ Zone 9 Parrot Gladiolus
This also is possibly one of the parents of the popular *G. gandavensis*. There are many red and yellow flowers on each stalk. Native to South Africa.

saundersii 2′–3′ Zone 9 Saunders Gladiolus

Gladiolus flower stalk, corm and cormels (or small corms).

Native to South Africa, this has been much used in hybridization. There are 4–6 leaves each 1 in. wide, and 6–8 scarlet flowers in each spike.

segetum   **2′**   **Zone 7**   **Cornflag Gladiolus** Native to the Mediterranean Region, with narrow leaves only about ½ in. wide and long, purple, flaring flowers in May.

tristis   **2′**   **Zone 7**   **Eveningflower Gladiolus** The 3 leaves are terete and 3–5 ribbed; 3–4 fragrant flowers are yellowish white with a bit of purplish mixed in. The variety **concolor** has almost pure white flowers. Native to South Africa. The flowers are interesting because they open at night.

Culture

For decades, gladioli have been among the most widely grown of summer flowers. Through the years, their popularity may rise and fall, but on the whole they remain unchallenged. Amateur and professional gardeners like them equally well, never failing to find a spot for a few bulbs somewhere in the garden.

The fact that gladioli continue to hold the spotlight with gardeners everywhere is easy to understand. They are corms that produce large, showy flower spikes. As cut flowers, they are long lasting, and if spikes are cut when the

first floret shows its color, buds will open right to the top. The blooming period of each spike covers a period of several days, whether in the garden or in the vase. Then, too, gladioli are easy to grow. Even the beginner can be successful if he starts with healthy stock.

Colorful and spectacular, gladioli have just about everything that can be expected of a flower, except fragrance. Yet this abounds, a sweet scent at that, in the so-called fragrant gladioli (*Gladiolus tristis*). These are small-flowering, more graceful than the others, and are common cut flowers in the street flower stalls in London, Paris, Rome, Athens and other European cities. Small-flowering gladioli can also be had in the miniatures, not fragrant, but resembling the others. They fit well in small gardens and in narrow borders with small types of perennials and annuals.

Gladioli grow with ease in many kinds of soils, but respond to care. If some attention is given to soil, feeding and watering, and if common pests and diseases are checked, results can be amazing. Enormous clean spikes result in excellent blooms for exhibition purposes and win a blue ribbon or two. Since they flower in the summer and early fall months, they are shown in small flower shows and county fairs.

These flowers are often grown in rows in the cutting garden, vegetable plot, or in other out-of-the-way places where they can be cared for as a separate unit. They lend themselves perfectly to this method of growing, where they can be easily cared for and tied, when the heavy spikes begin to topple after a heavy rain or wind.

Gladioli can be planted in groups, keeping to several bulbs of a single variety, in shrub plantings, where they will receive ample sunshine. They can be set out in bare spots among perennials, including iris, peonies, phlox, and chrysanthemums. They can be used to fill in holes left by daffodils, tulips and other Dutch bulbs, or they can be spaced among petunias, zinnias, marigolds, snapdragons, or other annuals. Plant 5 or more corms in each grouping, the amount depending on the width of the border and the desired effect.

With these flowers you can enjoy a succession of bloom for a period of several months. This is possible if corms are planted every 10 days to 2 weeks from the beginning of May until about the middle of July in the northern parts of the country. Because each plant is narrow and upright in habit, it does not take much space, and several corms can be grown in this way. Gardeners with limited space and stock can divide their supply of corms into 2 groups to insure bloom over a longer period of time.

These plants respond to moderately rich soil, but well drained, with sufficient amounts of organic matter added for larger blooms. If soil is light and sandy, it can be improved by adding peat moss, leaf mold, compost, or other organic matter. Likewise one that is clayey or heavy can be conditioned with these or other materials, particularly sand, to help improve its drainage. Dried manure, mixed well with the soil, can be used but avoid fresh animal manures which may cause corms to rot.

After digging the soil to a depth of a foot, add a balanced chemical fertilizer, such as 5–10–5 or 5–8–7, following directions on the package for amounts. After the corms have sprouted and are growing actively, apply a side dressing with a plant food, scratching it into the upper surface of the soil. Liquid fertilizer will give even quicker results, and is recommended when flower spikes are getting ready to expand. Plants will also respond to one of the many foliar fertilizers available on the market, but use it as a supplement to the soil feeding. It will give plants a quick boost, adding color and lustre to foliage almost overnight.

If corms are grown in rows in the cutting garden or home nursery, first dig the soil with a fork or small rototiller—then make a furrow, 5–6 in. deep, mixing the fertilizer with the soil at the bottom. Space corms to stand about 6 in. apart, keeping the concave end down. Larger corms can be placed 8–10 in. apart, depending on whether or not you are striving for exhibition blooms for shows and fairs. Or you may want to grow them to sell as cut flowers. After setting the corms in position, cover with 2 in. of soil. As the spearlike leaves appear above the surface, keep adding more soil until it is level with the surface.

The first planting of gladiolus comes during the first and second weeks of May, when weather has warmed and frost danger is over. Corms come into flower 8–10 weeks after planting, so keep this in mind when setting out the last planting. The lower South can plant corms in any month of the year. Remember, too, that there are varieties that bloom early or late so choose accordingly.

These summer flowers require a minimum of care. Once given sun for at least part of the day and the soil has been prepared, water during dry periods. During considerable dry periods it is best to soak the soil to a depth of several inches. Sprinklers can be used on young plants before they come into flower, but after that employ soakers or remove the nozzle from the hose and allow the water to run on the soil for a long period of time. Place a piece of board under the hose to prevent the running water from making holes in the soil. Deep waterings, once a week, are more beneficial than superficial sprinklings.

Weeding will be required but mulches will help keep weeds down and retain moisture in the soil. Staking gladiolus is required—in the row system this is easy. Attach heavy cord to stakes inserted at equidistant points, but do this on 2 sides, to prevent plants from flopping on the open side. In the garden a different technique is needed. Secure each plant individually with bamboo, wire or other kinds of support. Push into the ground at a safe distance from the corm and tie each gracefully with soft string or twine so it will not cut the foliage. After flowering is over or when spikes are cut for decoration, stakes can be lifted for use elsewhere.

To get the most out of bloom for decoration in the house, church, or office, cut when the lowest blossoms have begun to show color. The remaining buds will then unfold after the spikes are placed in water. When cutting stems, always leave 3 of the lowest leaves, since these are needed to carry on the food-manufacturing processes and to maintain healthy corms, which will multiply. As a rule, make a slanting cut between the third and fourth leaves and use additional foliage from other plants in the garden to use with the arrangement. If not cutting blooms for this purpose, remove faded stalks to improve appearance and prevent the formation of seed, which saps the strength of the plants.

After flowering, gladiolus foliage continues to stay green for a long time, so keep on watering plants. When leaves begin to turn yellow, about 6 weeks after blooming, corms are ready for digging. They do not need frosts—lift corms carefully with a spade or fork and shake off soil—place aside in the cellar, garage or outdoors, if weather permits to dry for a few days. Then cut off the leaves with pruning shears to within 2 in. of the corms. Some prefer to cut the leaves before the corms are dug or just after, especially if the leaves are well ripened. If leaves happen to be green at lifting time, do not remove, but allow to turn brown in storage.

Corms can be stored in a dry, frost-proof cellar, shed or storeroom. They can be placed on trays or boxes and dusted with malathion to check thrips, an insect which causes damage to the foliage and flowers in summer. Cool temperatures in the 40's are best but corms will keep well at much higher temperatures, provided they are kept dry and receive free air circulation. Before storing, some like to remove the original mother corm which dries up and becomes useless. Others prefer doing this in the spring before planting time when the corm is hard, brown, shriveled and easily separated.

The tiny cormlets can be saved with the others for propagation purposes. They can be kept in paper bags, and in the spring planted in rows, an inch or two deep and cared for during the summer months. They require 2 or 3 years to attain flowering size. Of course 2–3 corms are produced each year from the original corm, all flowering size. Plants can also be raised from seed to increase stock or obtain new varieties.

Varieties

Hundreds of new varieties appear annually. For exhibition purposes, gladioli are divided into three groups, according to the dia. of the individual blooms. These are Giant, Large Decorative and Small Decorative. The first contains the largest flowers of all, usually stiff and impressive. In the second group, more graceful, individual flowers vary from 3–6 in. across. In the third group, flowers are smaller, about 3 in. across. There is yet another classification, the miniature, with florets under $2\frac{1}{2}$ in.

Preferred are the following All-America winners: **'Landmark'**, rose; **'Apollo'**, lavender; **'Blue Sapphire'**, light blue, with white throat; **'Frisky'**, scarlet with golden edge; **'Goldilocks'**, golden-yellow; **'La France'**, pink with deep pink edges; **'Morning Sun'**, deep yellow; **'Thunderbird'**, fiery red; **'Snowsprite'**, white with greenish tint; and **'Victory'**, scarlet.

Others that have wide appeal include **'Green Ice'**, greenish cream; **'Salmon Queen'**, salmon and cream; **'Spic and Span'**, pink; **'Bird of Paradise'**, pinkish apricot; **'King David'**, purple and silver; **'Glacier'**, white with creamy throat; and **'Bluebird'**, deep rose, violet markings.

Miniature gladioli are small and graceful. They are preferred by gardeners who like their small size and find them easier to mix with perennials and annuals in small borders. They are also useful in planters, and make excellent cut flowers in arrangements where large gladiolus are out of scale. The bright red **'Atom'**, with its golden edge, has long been one of the most widely grown of the miniatures. Others that vie for attention are **'Miss America'**, lavender, orange marks; **'Lavender'**, lavender, pink marks; **'Cutie'**, light rose, with deep rose throat; **'Daintiness'**, creamy-white; and **'Lavender Petunia'**, deep lavender with white throat.   GEORGE TALOUMIS

GLADIXIA, DARK-EYE = *Acidanthera bicolor*

GLAND. A definite secreting structure on the surface embedded in or ending a hair; also any protuberance of the like nature which may not secrete, as the warty swellings at the base of the leaf in the Cherry and Peach.

GLANDULAR. Bearing glands or glandlike appendages.

GLASSWORT,   MARSHFIRE = *Salicornia europaea*

GLASTONBURY THORN = *Crataegus monogyna* 'Biflora'

GLAUCIUM (GLAW-sium or GLAW-kium). Members of the Poppy Family, these are bold, handsome plants, with orange-colored juice, lobed leaves and large red or yellow poppylike flowers. Easily propagated by seeds, the annual species being sown outdoors in March, preferably in full sun and in sandy soil that is not too rich, where other plants do not grow well.

corniculatum $1\frac{1}{2}'$ **annual   Sea-poppy**
Flowers red with a black spot at the base of each petal, fruit a bristly pod. Native to Europe.

flavum   3′   **annual, biennial or perennial Horned-poppy**
With golden-yellow-to-orange flowers 2 in. across, fruits are narrow pods 1 ft. long. Native to eastern North America.

GLAUCOUS. Covered with a bloom; bluish white or bluish gray.

GLECHOMA (glee-CO-ma)
hederacea (*Nepeta hederacea*)   3″   Zone 3
        Ground-Ivy, Gill-over-the-ground
A creeping perennial introduced from Europe and Asia, with opposite, lobed, rounded or kidney-shaped leaves about $1\frac{1}{2}$ in. across. The light blue flowers up to 1 in. across are in whorled clusters, each with a few flowers during the spring and summer. This has a matlike habit of growth, is sometimes used as a ground cover in both shaded and sunny situations, in good soil, and the plant grows so vigorously that it can become a pest if it escapes bounds. The rare variety **variegata** has leaves with white or pink on the leaf margin.

GLEDITSIA (gled-IT-sia). The Honeylocusts are not an important group except for one species, *G. triacanthos*. They are a thorny lot, difficult to work with and resulting in plants which actually can be hazards, but there are now some thornless clones. *Gleditsia caspica* has been noted as the most spiny of any hardy woody tree in the north temperate zone. The leaves are alternate and pinnately compound. As a group with inconspicuous flowers and often objectionable fruits (pods) and with practically no autumn color, they have little to offer the ornamental plantsman. The seeds are contained in a long (12 in.), flat, sugary pod, the pulp of which remains sweet for some time after the pod has ripened. Beer is sometimes made from fermenting the fresh pods.

G. triacanthos stands out as an excellent street and ornamental tree. It was remarkably free of insect and disease pests up until a few years ago, when the mimosa web worm infested trees in wide areas. This disagreeable pest spoils an otherwise almost perfect record of a good species. It can be controlled by timely spraying with #37. Also the pod-gall, caused by a midge, seems to be infesting some of the newer varieties in certain areas. This can be controlled by spraying with #13 about mid-May and again 10 days later. A few years ago neither of these insects presented serious problems to the planting of *G. triacanthos* or any of its varieties.

Propagation

Seeds may be processed as soon as ripe or stored dry in air-tight containers in a cool place for up to a year and then processed. The seeds (of *G. triacanthos* and *G. japonica*) have very hard seed coats which should be perforated by mechanical means (filing) or by treatment for 2 hours in concentrated sulfuric acid. Then the seed is thoroughly washed and sown. This treatment might prove successful on other *Gleditsia* species. Grafting and budding on *G. triacanthos* understock is commonly practiced. Root cuttings taken in the spring root well. See SEEDS, GRAFTING, BUDDING, CUTTINGS.

Insect Pests

Locust pod gall of the locust gall midge has become a serious pest of the common Honeylocust and other ornamental species. The leaves are rasped on the inside, causing a podlike gall in which the larva lives. There are 5 or more generations annually. Spraying with insecticide #9 or #15 when the adult midges are active will reduce the infestation. Mimosa web worm may cause a brown burned appearance to the leaves when they are skeletonized in the webs. Insecticide #9 is suggested. Gypsy moth attacks Honeylocust. See QUERCUS.

Disease

A nectria canker may girdle and kill branches. Cutting out is suggested.

triacanthos   135′   Zone 4   Common Honey-locust
An excellent tree for withstanding city conditions but with two drawbacks—large and stiffly-branched thorns and many 12- to 18-in. pods on fruiting trees. It is an American native from Pa. to Tex. The foliage texture is extremely fine. The leaves are alternate, compound and 5–8 in. long with 20–30 small leaflets, sometimes even being doubly compound, and the tree gives only a very light shade since the foliage is loosely borne, but has little autumn color. However, its thorns can become a hazard near playgrounds and along highways, and the fruits certainly are objectionable. It is easily transplanted and well adapted to a number of growing conditions, especially in the city.

Some of the varieties are:
'Bujotii'—with pendulous branches.
'Columnaris'—columnar in habit.
'Nana'—narrow, upright, slow-growing, a 36-year-old plant is 35 ft. tall and 16 ft. in branch spread.
'Elegantissima'—thornless and dense, shrubby, —of merit for street planting only when grafted on understock of *G. triacanthos* 'Inermis'—Bushy Honeylocust.
'Inermis'—this excellent variety has the same general characteristics as the species except that the thorns are missing. Many selections of good trees of this variety have been given names and propagated, none rather recently. This was started in 1944 with the naming of a truly excellent one, **'Moraine'**, which was patented and since has proved an unusually good male tree for city planting. It is still most difficult to evaluate all that have been "introduced" since. Eventually one may undoubtedly prove as good as **'Moraine'**, others will be inferior. They should be judged only after growing side by side in the same soil and climate conditions for several years.
'Maxwell'—originated before 1951 by the Plumfield Nurseries, Fremont, Neb.; listed as being merely thornless and fruitless.
'Moraine'—patented #836, 1949. The first of the group to be patented and experience has shown it is still at the top of any list as a reliable substitute for the American Elm in city conditions. It has been widely distributed.
'Rubylace'—Plant Patent #2308, has a new dark purplish-red growth which darkens to bronze-green as the leaves mature.
'Sieler'—Linn Company Nurseries, Center Point, Iowa, 1949—"Large widespreading tree almost completely seedless."
'Stephens'—Marshall Nurseries, Arlington, Neb., 1940—"Thornless and seedless."
'Skyline'—patented #1619 in 1957, "A strong sturdy straight trunk with well spaced and uniformly arranged branches, said branches emerging from the trunk at a wide angle but quickly turning upward, to give a pyramidal shape to the tree."
'Sunburst'—patented #1515 in 1954. "A thornless honeylocust distinguished by the bright golden-yellow color of young leaves, giving the tree the appearance of being entirely golden in color, and by the relatively slow, compact habit of growth."

GLIRICIDIA (gli-ris-ID-ia)

sepium   25′   Zone 10   Madre-de-cacao
A tree from tropical America with masses of pealike, pale-pink flowers in long racemes beginning to appear in early Jan. continuing until April. These are effective since the tree has few leaves at this time. The leaves are compound

like those of many another legume, and the fruits are brown pods.

GLOBE-DAISY, HEARTLEAF = *Globularia cordifolia*

GLOBEFLOWER. See TROLLIUS.

GLOBE-THISTLE. See ECHINOPS.

GLOBULARIA (glob-yew-LAY-ria). A genus of small, hardy, cushionlike plants native to southern Europe and Asia. They are hardy in northern U.S., doing well in most garden soils and may be propagated by seed or by division. They belong to the Globularia Family.

bellidifolia   prostrate   Zone 5
Tiny evergreen leaves in mounds 1 or 2 in. high and light blue flowers rising just above the foliage in May makes this a highly desirable rock garden plant.

cordifolia   4″   Zone 9   Heartleaf Globularia
A useful plant in the rock garden or sometimes used as a ground cover in southern Fla., this is native to southern Europe. It is prostrate, woody, with alternate leaves 1 in. long. The flowers are blue, in heads ½ in. wide during May. It grows best in the shade. Propagated by seed and division.

incanescens   4″   Zone 7   Hoary Globularia
Similar to *G. bellidifolia*, but slightly larger, with leaves of a lighter shade of green; flowers blue and the heads ½ in. wide. Native to Italy.

repens   prostrate   Zone 6   Creeping Globularia
A plant growing in a small compact mound with creeping stems closely covered with very tiny green leaves. The globular flowers are a very pale blue, ½ in. wide, and appear in May. Native to southern Europe.

trichosantha   8″   Zone 7   Syrian Globularia
This herbaceous species, with somewhat larger, dull green leaves bears profuse light blue flowers, the heads about ½ in. across, on stems 8 in. high, in May and June. Native to Asia Minor.

GLOMERATE. In compact clusters.

GLORIOSA (glow-ri-O-sa)

rothschildiana   vine   Zone 10   Rothschild Gloriosa-lily
This vine from tropical Africa does not climb more than 4–6 ft. The lilylike flowers have very narrow, wide-spreading, wavy sepals and petals, colored yellow near the center of the flower and red at the tips. Most of them are borne hanging down and bloom in the spring. The tip of each leaf is modified into a type of tendril and the plant grows from a tuber.

superba   vine   Zone 10   Malabar Gloriosa-lily
This species, also from tropical Africa, climbs 10–12 ft. and is much more widely grown in conservatories than the preceding species. Like the preceding, this is grown from tubers which

can be grown outdoors in parts of the middle U.S. where there is a long growing season. Tubers should be dug and stored indoors over winter.

GLORYBIND. See CONVOLVULUS.

GLORYBIND, HEDGE = *Calystegia sepium*

GLORYBOWER. See CLERODENDRUM.

GLORYBUSH, BRAZILIAN = *Tibouchina urvilleana*

GLORY FLAME-BEAN = *Brownea grandiceps*

GLORYFLOWER, CHILEAN = *Eccremocarpus scaber*

GLORY-OF-THE-SNOW = *Chinonodoxa luciliae*

GLORY-OF-THE-SUN = *Leucocoryne ixioides*

GLORY-PEA = *Clianthus formosus*

GLORYVINE = *Vitis coignetiae*

GLOTTIPHYLLUM (glot-ti-FILL-um)

longum   4″   Zone 10   Tongueleaf
A succulent stemless perennial, separated from *Mesembryanthemum* with tongue-shaped leaves about 4 in. long, ¾ in. wide, blistered at the base. The long-stalked yellow flowers are 3 in. across. Native to South Africa. Occasionally used in dish gardens.

GLOXINIA, COMMON = *Sinningia speciosa*

GLYCINE (gly-SY-ne)

max   3″–6′   annual   Soy-bean
A native of the Old World, and belonging to the Pea Family this is an extremely important agricultural crop and has been grown in China and Japan for thousands of years. A bushy annual with alternate leaves, each with 3 leaflets 3–6 in. long. The white, inconspicuous flowers are pealike, the pods are only 2–3 in. long and ½ in. wide. Many varieties in cultivation. Grown chiefly in America as an agricultural crop in the Midwest. Many products both for man and animals are made from the plant and its oily seeds.

GLYCYRRHIZA (gly-ki-RY-za)

glabra   2′–3′   Zone 9   Licorice
An herb from the Mediterranean Area used to flavor cough medicines and candy. It is a member of the Pea Family with compound leaves and 4–8 pairs of leaflets; blue, pealike flowers in short spikes and the fruit a flat pod. The roots are harvested for the licorice of commerce, but growing it is not profitable at present in America, although some is grown at present in Calif.

GNAPHALIUM (naff-AY-lium)

obtusifolium   1½′   Zone 5   Fragrant Cudweed
A biennial of no particular horticultural interest, this plant has alternate, very narrowly linear woolly leaves with a wavy margin. When

bruised, they give off a slight odor of lemon. The small flower heads, in loosely branching clusters, are borne on short stalks in the upper leaf axils. The grayish-white, tubular flowers are without ray flowers and appear never to be in full bloom. The plant frequents dry fields and the edges of woodlands along the Atlantic coastline to the Gulf, and flowers in summer.

sylvaticum 1¼′ **Zone 4** **Wood Cudweed**
A woolly herb, member of the Composite Family, with small yellowish flower heads ¼ in. wide, borne in spikes and linear leaves 2 in. long. Something like an Everlasting. Native to Europe, Asia and northeastern North America. Rather weedy in appearance and method of growth, doing well in sandy soil and propagated best by division in spring.

GOAT'S-BEARD, SYLVAN = *Aruncus dioicus*
GOATS-RUE, COMMON = *Galega officinalis*
GODETIA = *Clarkia*

Galax (See p. 418)

GOLDASTER. See CHRYSOPSIS.
GOLD-DUST TREE = *Aucuba japonica variegata*
GOLDEN CLUB = *Orontium aquaticum*
GOLDEN-CUP = *Hunnemannia fumariaefolia*
GOLDEN DEWDROP = *Duranta repens*
GOLDEN GLOW. See RUDBECKIA.
GOLDEN-RAIN-TREE = *Koelreuteria paniculata*
GOLDEN-RAY. See LIGULARIA.

GOLDENROD. See SOLIDAGO.
GOLDENROD FAMILY = Compositae
GOLDENROD, HYBRID = *Solidaster* x *luteus*
GOLDENSEAL = *Hydrastis canadensis*
GOLDENSTAR = *Chrysogonum virginianum*
GOLDEN-TUFT = *Aurinia saxatilis*
GOLDFERN, CALIFORNIA = *Pityrogramma triangularis*
GOLDFLOWER = *Hypericum moserianum*
GOLDILOCKS, EUROPEAN = *Linosyris vulgaris*
GOLD-SAXIFRAGE = *Chrysosplenium americanum*
GOLDTHREAD. See COPTIS.

GOMPHRENA (gom-FREE-na)
globosa 1½′ **annual** **Globe Amaranth**
This is one of the everlastings with opposite leaves 4 in. long and branches erect. The flower heads are papery, about an inch across and colored white, purple, rose and orange. A dwarf var. *nana* is only 8 in. tall. These plants are used for bedding, cut flowers and drying for arrangements. Sow the seed in March or outdoors in the full sun after frosts are over, thinning the plants to about a foot apart. Native to the Tropics of the Eastern Hemisphere.

GONGORA (gon-GO-ra, also GON-go-ra). Tropical American epiphytic orchids having pseudobulbs, bearing 2 upright leaves and a pendulous raceme of small flowers, each about 1½ in. long. The raceme may contain 10–30 flowers, colored white, apricot, brownish or red depending on the species. These orchids are sometimes grown in the warm greenhouse having earned the popular name of "Punch and Judy" orchids. Culture and propagation, see ORCHID.

GOODYEARA (good-YER-a). A genus of the Orchid Family the members of which are mostly in the Temperate Zone. The basal leaves are often mottled and the erect flower stalk bears a spike of irregular flowers having 2 free sepals and a third which is fused with the petals to resemble a hood. They are suitable only for specialized sites in the wild garden. These are also used by many gardeners in making home-made terrariums, for the white-striped leaves have a very ornamental effect.
pubescens 6″–15″ **Zone 3** **Downy Rattle-snake-plantain**
A perennial herb, the basal, evergreen leaves of which have white lines tracing the intricate pattern of the veins and it is for this interesting feature that the plant is sometimes cultivated. In July, the downy flower stalk bears a dense terminal cluster of greenish-white flowers. A plant of the dry, acid woods from New-

foundland to the Deep South, it may be divided at any time, or cuttings may be taken in fall and rooted in a cold frame.

repens procumbent Zone 3 Lesser Rattle-snake-plantain
Flower scape one-sided, 4–12 in. tall, flowers white, about ¼ in. long during July and Aug.; leaves about 1¾ in. long, ovate and dark green with greenish-white veins. Native to North America, northern Europe, Japan and northern Asia.

tesselata 6″–12″ Zone 3 Checkered Rattle-snake-plantain
This species also has basal evergreen leaves netted with white lines along the veins, and leaves which sheathe the lower part of the leafless flower stalk. The flowers are arranged in a loose terminal cluster and appear in summer. Its range is from N.Y. to southern Canada and west to the North Central states. In habitat it prefers dry, acid soil. Propagate as for *G. pubescens.*

GOOSEBERRIES. These are no longer popular fruits in American gardens for 2 reasons. Picking the fruits is a discouraging process because of the many small spines on the fruits and young stems. Also, the *Ribes* species act as alternate hosts for the white pine blister rust, and the U.S. Department of Agriculture, with the authority given it under certain Plant Quarantine Acts, has prohibited the growing of *Ribes* species (currants and gooseberries) in many states (or parts of them) where White Pine grows. Consequently, if the home gardener simply must grow gooseberries (or currants) he should first write his state experiment station (which see) to find out whether it is possible to grow them in the area where he lives. This is important.

Gooseberries are good for pies, jellies and jams and are still popular in England. They are commercially propagated by mound layering, but hardwood cuttings can be made in the fall after the leaves have dropped. In layering, the bushes are heavily cut back in the early spring; the soil mounded up about the vigorous shoots in mid-July, and by the following spring the young shoots will be rooted and can be severed from the parent plant.

'Poorman' is the outstanding red gooseberry and 'Downing' the best green variety, in America at least, for the excellent English varieties are seldom grown here because of their susceptibility to mildew. However, 'Fredonia' is a red-fruiting English type which is grown to some extent in N.Y. state.

Gooseberries might be set 4 ft. apart. They need little attention, and little pruning except to remove the older branches periodically. They might well be mulched with almost any material

to keep the weeds down. It has been noted that chemical fertilizers, although undoubtedly aiding production on poor soils, are seldom used on gooseberries growing in normal productive garden soils. Also see CURRANTS, RIBES.

GOOSEBERRY, ENGLISH = *Ribes uva-crispa*

GOOSEFOOT. See CHENOPODIUM.

GOOSEFOOT FAMILY = Chenopodiaceae

GOOSEFOOT, SHRUBBY = *Suaeda fruticosa*

GORDONIA (gord-O-nia)
alatamaha = *Franklinia alatamaha*
lasianthus 60′ Zone 8 Loblolly Bay Gordonia
This is native of the southeastern U.S. The beautiful fragrant white flowers are 2½ in. in dia., and bloom in the summer for nearly 2 months. The evergreen lustrous and leathery leaves are 6 in. long. Not to be confused with *Franklinia alatamaha*, which some think looks like it especially if observed from a distance in the wild.

GORSE, COMMON = *Ulex europaeus*

GORSE, SPANISH = *Genista hispanica*

GOSSYPIUM (goss-E-pium). There are several species of cotton but they are all considered

Gossypium: Cotton, bolls, flowers, and seeds.

agricultural rather than horticultural crops. Cotton is grown commercially in Zone 8, possibly the lower parts of Zone 7. It is the boll or seed pod which breaks open showing the seeds and white fibers that are used in making cotton fabrics. Usually they are considered annuals requiring a long, warm, growing season with plenty of moisture to mature properly. The most important species in the U.S. are **G. barbadense**, the Sea Island Cotton, native to tropical America and growing 8 ft. tall with yellow flowers tinged with purple; **G. hirsutum**, the Upland Cotton also a native of tropical America, 5 ft. tall with white or yellowish flowers tinged pink at maturity, and several varieties and hybrids. Not grown as a garden ornamental.

GOURD. A fleshy 1-celled many-seeded fruit; like the melon. See CUCURBITA, LAGENARIA, LUFFA.

GOURD, CALABASH = *Lagenaria siceraria*

GOURD, DISHCLOTH. See LUFFA.

GOURD, EDIBLE SNAKE = *Trichosanthes anguina*

GOURD, TOWEL. See LUFFA.

GOURD, YELLOWFLOWER = *Cucurbita pepo ovifera*

GOURDS. These are members of the Cucumber Family belonging mostly to the genera *Cucurbita*, *Lagenaria*, and *Luffa*. By far the largest number of varying ornamental hard-shelled gourds are those originating from *Cucurbita pepo ovifera* which is the yellow-flowered gourd, easily distinguished from the white-flowered *Lagenaria* types which take a longer growing season to mature properly. Gourds can be grown in any good soil similar to that in the vegetable garden. They need as long a growing period as possible, especially *L. siceraria*, the reason why some gardeners in the North just do not have a sufficient number of days of hot sunshine to mature the fruits. On the other hand, *Cucurbita pepo ovifera* ripens easily in Zones 3 and 4.

Seed

One should be certain at the start to obtain good viable seed from a reliable source. Seedsmen are selling gourds in 2 ways. The first is "mixed," that is, several varieties of differently shaped gourds have been used for seed purposes and one can obtain many interesting gourds from such a package. On the other hand, the unscrupulous person will mix seed from a lot of inferior-shaped types together, and still sell them as "mixed" and be correct in so doing. Other seedsmen who have sources of seed from pure stands of Nest Egg, Striped Pear, Spoon or Miniature Bottle, will sell seeds of these types and the gardener has reasonable assurance they will produce gourds true to name. It really pays to purchase well-grown reliable seeds of this type regardless of whether they are sold as individual varieties or as "Super Hybrids Mixed." Germination is helped if the seed is soaked in warm water for 12–48 hours before sowing. Seed will keep at least a year, (usually several), if put in a dry cool place.

WHEN TO PLANT. Good seed should be sown in hills, 6–8 seeds per hill, after all danger of frost is over. It is unwise to sow too early for they simply will not grow until the soil warms up. They can be started in pots in the greenhouse 3 weeks before they are to be set out in the garden, thus gaining a few weeks on the ones planted directly in the soil. However, the roots should not be disturbed in transplanting, but the entire potful of undisturbed roots and soil set out in one careful operation. Certainly this is the way to plant *Lagenaria* varieties especially in the North, and even then there may not be sufficient time for the fruit to ripen properly. All gourds should be grown in full sunshine, not in the shade.

Theoretically gourds should be trained on a trellis, up some chicken wire or over some brush to keep the fruits off the ground. Most of us do not have time for that and are willing to take our chances with a few of the fruits being marred on the ground. Seeds might be planted twice their length deep in good, friable soil. When seedlings are up the hills might be thinned to about 4 plants per hill, the hills being about 8 ft. apart. If the seed was "mixed" remember that the seedlings will show variation and one should not remove all the smallest seedlings, because these might just be the varieties with the smallest and most interesting fruits.

Fertilizers should be applied as for pumpkins and squash, which see.

The roots of gourds are very close to the soil surface, hence in hoeing one should be careful not to disturb the roots. They need ample water and should be given plenty of it during drought periods.

Pruning

Pruning the vines can increase the number of fruits borne per vine. The main stem should be allowed to grow until it is 10 ft. long, when the end can be removed. It is on this part that mostly male flowers are borne. The lateral shoots bear mostly pistillate flowers. If the end bud of the main shoot is snipped off after the shoot is 10 ft. long, then the first lateral shoots have the main end buds taken off them when each shoot has developed about 4 leaves, this is sufficient for the pruning. Any sublateral shoots developing after this are allowed to grow at will. This type of pruning can aid in the production of more fruits.

Harvesting

Gourds must be thoroughly ripened on the

vine before they are picked, for if picked when green or immature they will soon rot. For the varieties of *Cucurbita pepo ovifera*, the stem where the gourd is attached to the vine should be watched. When this starts to shrivel and dry up, then the gourd should be picked. It is best to cut them off the vine with shears, saving a few inches of stem on each gourd, rather than roughly tearing them off the vine, often severing the stem right at the end of the gourd. If roughly done, this can injure the gourd end just enough to allow disease to enter and the fruit will rot.

Ornamental gourds

The gourds should not be left out in the field, but rather brought in and washed, often with a mild disinfectant, and set aside a few days to dry thoroughly. The idea is to wash off any soil or impurities which may have become attached to the shell. After a few days they can then be carefully waxed with any floor paste wax, and set aside for use as ornaments. Some will undoubtedly rot, but the majority, if picked when fully mature, will harden nicely and can be used for years.

The white gourds of *Lagenaria siceraria* should be even more carefully watched and picked just before they start to turn yellowish from too much sunshine. In the South these calabash gourds are easy to grow and to mature, but in the North it is very difficult to grow them properly. They include the Bottle, Depressed Bottle, Powder Horn, Dipper, Kettle, Bird's

Nest and Dolphin types along with many others.

Luffa species have green fruits with a rind that is not hard, but dry and papery. These can be a foot long and also take a long growing season. The inside pulp can be dried out and then used as a dish cloth.

It is of interest to note that markings can be made on the shells of any of these gourds when they are half ripe and growing on the vines. Thus, initials, characters, rough line sketches made at this time, eventually look as if they had actually grown on the shell. Also wires, strings or even containers can be placed around the developing fruits in such ways as to permanently change and control the shape. Thus, it is possible to have a square gourd (forced to grow within some confining square metal or concrete box). These then are the popular hard-shelled gourds. For other types see *Citrullus, Cucumis, Echinocystis, Sechium, Sicana, Trichosanthos, Momordica.*

For diseases and insects see PUMPKIN, SQUASH, MELON, etc.

GOUTWEED = *Aegopodium podagraria*

GOVERNOR'S-PLUM = *Flacourtia indica*

GRADING. This is usually left to the experts, but when one pays the bill one should know exactly what is being done. In most operations it pays to remove the top soil and stock pile it until the grading is finished with the subsoil. Filling on top of top soil is always expensive, for when good soil is covered with fill, top soil must be replaced in order to grow a lawn, flowers or trees and shrubs. Therefore always save the top soil wherever possible.

When the grade has been established with fill, one should allow at least 6 in. of top soil for a lawn and 2 ft. of top soil for the flower border or shrub planting. All too often this is where the "land developers" skimp, leaving only a few inches of top soil for every kind of planting. It is then that the owner spends the rest of his life trying to build up the top soil, in many cases almost an impossible task when little is there to begin with. So, when you pay the bill, have the foresight to see and understand what is being done in grading and take every opportunity to conserve the top soil so that eventually it will be placed where it will do the most good.

Raising the grade around trees is often necessary in new land developments. When the soil must be raised only 2–3 in. merely applying sandy soil of that depth to the top soil already in place is perfectly satisfactory, the more porous the soil the better.

When raising the grade a foot or more on top of the existing tree roots, care should be taken, for applying that much soil to that already in place about a tree could be seriously injurious. It would reduce the amount of air and water reaching the feeding roots of a tree.

The best method is to build a well about 4 ft. in dia., around the tree trunk, using loosely laid rocks to the height of the new grade. About 4 lines of tile should be laid on the surface of the old soil to the edge of the spreading branches radiating from this well and opening into it, the general idea being to bring air to the feeding roots. Rough fill or rocks are then placed on the old soil to about 10 in. of the finished grade. Then a few inches of fine gravel on top of the fill and a layer of straw on top of the fine gravel to keep the soil (at least 6–8 in. of it) from filtering down into the fill. If the well is in a place where it is a hazard, an iron grate can be put on top to cover it.

GRAFT. A branch or bud inserted on another plant with the intention that it will grow there; a scion. The word is both a noun and a verb, denoting the operation.

GRAFT-HYBRID. Plant showing influence of scion and stock caused by mechanical union of the tissues.

GRAFTING. This is a method of plant propagation in which a twig of one plant, called the scion, is made to grow on the roots of another plant, called the stock or the understock. The scion is taken from the plant which is to be reproduced, and because this is an asexual means of reproduction, the resulting plant will be identical with the plant from which the scion was taken if no shoots are allowed to grow on the understock, or below the union of scion and understock.

In the first place, a scion and stock must be "compatible," that is, they must be of a type that will grow together, make a firm union and continue to grow afterwards. This is found out by experience, and the art of grafting is centuries old. One should not expect a scion of *Magnolia soulangiana* to grow on apple or elm understock. In fact, it may not grow on all kinds of magnolia seedlings, but experience has shown that it may be expected to grow best on understock of *M. kobus* or *M. tripetala*. Sometimes several species in the same genus are equally good as understock, sometimes it has been found it has been found that under certain conditions one is better than another. English growers find that *Prunus serrula* is easily compatible with *P. avium* understock, while some American growers have better success with *P. sargentii* understock.

In the grafting operation the theory is to place the living cambium tissue of scion and understock in contact with each other. This is simply done by making the proper kind of cut into the understock and gently slipping the whittled scion into it. This operation must be done when both scion and understock are about ready for active growth. Actually, it is a greenhouse operation where the understock, in a pot, has already been forced into active growth and the scion is yet dormant. Usually Feb. or March is grafting time indoors.

As soon as the scion and stock are slipped together, they are bound tightly in place to prevent movement between them. Flat rubber bands are specially made for this and are ideal since they can be bound just tight enough to hold the 2 together, but loose enough so that the rubber will give a little as the new graft increases in circumference. This "tie" remains on for a few months until stock and scion have closely knit, when it is simply cut and left on the union to eventually fall off.

Grafting is also done out of doors at a time just before vigorous growth commences on the understock. This is usually confined to trees that are being "made over" as will be explained below. Grafting small plants out of doors does not result in as much success as doing it inside under controlled temperature and moisture conditions.

Factors other than timing must be right. Air temperature must be in the 70's or conducive to continued plant growth. Moisture must be present—the graft union must not be allowed to dry out in any way. Disease spores must not get into the union. These are the reasons why grafting is usually carried out in the greenhouse in "grafting cases," places enclosed by glass or polyethylene with high humidity. This is also the reason why the graft union is covered with wax or polyethylene film as soon as it is made to keep the tender new-forming cells from exposure and possible drying out.

The most difficult time for the new graft is when it is noted that the scion has started into active growth. It must be kept in active growth, yet too high a temperature and too much moisture in the grafting case may cause it to grow too rapidly and fail to make a proper union. Here experience certainly aids the individual in properly regulating moisture and temperature.

The most important decision to make in grafting is to select the right kind of graft cut to make. Actually, if properly done, any one of the methods should result in a successful graft, but experience has shown that certain types of grafting cuts seem to result in better end results on certain species than others. This is not the place to go into this detailed discussion, but one should be familiar with the different types.

A graft union of Maple showing how the scion (upper) part of the plant has grown at a faster rate than the understock (lower) part. Sometimes such unions are not strong. (*Photo by Arnold Arboretum, Jamaica Plain, Mass.*)

Whip Graft

A double matching cut is made in both stock and scion. If this is to be used, the understock and the scion should be about the same dia. (lead-pencil size or slightly larger) and the top of the stock should be completely cut off an inch or so above the place of the proposed union. The whip graft is also ideal to use in root grafting, that is, in grafting a scion on to a piece of root (of the same dia.). If done properly, and it takes experience to make just the right cuts, it can be highly successful because there is so much of the cambium that can be fitted together in this double cut.

Side Graft

Merely making a slanting cut into the stock and inserting a wedge-shaped scion into it. This is often the method chosen when the stock is larger in dia. than the scion. Sometimes the top of the stock is severed just above the graft as soon as it is made. Other times it is left to grow for a week or two and then cut off. It is this method which is frequently used in bonsai culture to supply a new branch at exactly the right place it is needed.

Cleft Graft

This is the type of graft employed in grafting trees in the open. It is frequently employed in grafting apples, where a tree of an old out-moded variety is to be "changed over" to a new and better variety. In this case, all the main limbs are sawed off carefully and "clefts" or

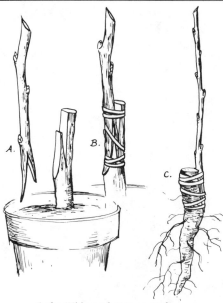

Left: Whip and tongue graft
Right: Root graft

seedling would act as the understock for the rare plant, the whole idea being that one does not risk loss of the rare plant in this method. A cut is made in the side of the understock or some of the bark is very carefully removed just to the cambium. A matching cut is made in the rare plant or a matching part of its bark is carefully removed. Then they are joined together, tied and painted, while the tops of both are allowed to grow. If it is obvious that the union is growing together, the part of the understock above the graft can be removed. When the union is solidly made, the scion material can be partially cut away from the scion plant, and later another deeper cut made so that the severance of the scion from the parent plant takes place over a period of weeks. This is a method used by the experts to graft two plants together that are otherwise difficult.

Inarching

Sometimes a plant is growing with the wrong kind of understock and the tree needs a better root system. Young plants are established at the base, a narrow strip of bark removed on the tree to correspond with a similar width of bark removed on the new plants. Several such plants can be stabilized and grafted to one trunk.

splits are made in them with a large grafting tool similar to a butcher's knife. Two or 3 such openings can be made in a 4–6 in. branch. Then, 3 or more wedge-shaped scions are inserted carefully, so the cambium tissue of stock and scion meet exactly, the entire union is painted with wax and one then awaits developments. Only 1 of the 3 or 4 scions will be allowed to grow eventually, but it is a quick method of making over a tree of bearing size. In fact, the newly made-over tree may grow so well that it may begin producing the new variety of apple in 3 or 4 years. Because the stock is so large, it is not necessary to tie stock and scion together in such a graft, for the properties inherent in the wood of the large branches are enough to hold the scions tightly for all practical purposes.

Bark Graft

This is done on the cut limbs of trees, merely by slitting the bark a few inches in a straight line from the cut surface, and then inserting the wedge-shaped scion just between the bark and wood of the stock. Three or 4 of these can be inserted, but the whole should be tied tightly to prevent the bark of the branch from curling away or splitting farther and thus exposing the scion to drying out.

Approach Grafting

Consider 2 small plants in pots, one of a very rare type, the other a worthless seedling. The

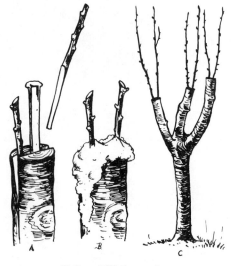

Cleft and Wedge graft:

A–B. Making the cleft with a metal wedge, inserting the scion so that the cambium of scion and stock will meet, waxing finished graft.

C.   Making over an established tree by cutting off all the limbs and inserting scions of the desired variety.

Bridge Grafting

Frequently used in the case of a tree that has been completely girdled by rodents or by accident. The bark of the tree is cleaned off to

Bridge grafting over a jagged cut, breaking the bark completely around a tree. The scions are taken from the living branches of the same tree and covered with wax to finish the operation.

smooth straight lines, several twigs of the proper size and length are cut from the tree itself and inserted under the bark of the tree in the same manner as any bark graft, above and below its part with injured bark. The bridge grafts can be nailed or tied in place and the whole exposed wound painted with wax. The idea here is to cut the top and bottom of the scions in such a way that they can be inserted underneath the bark above and below the wound, with the cambium tissues of stock and scion in contact with each other. Hence these shoots will, if they grow, act as bridges over the injured trunk for the upward and downward flow of nutrients and foods. Many a damaged tree has been saved in this way. However, such an operation is best done when the tree is dormant, certainly not when the scions are in leaf. If properly done, these scions will gradually increase in size and may completely heal over the injured trunk by growing solidly together.

Double Grafting

Sometimes this method is used, especially to produce a dwarf plant or when one kind of plant material is not compatible with the understock. Grafting is done in the normal way using an "intermediate" scion, that is, a scion from a plant that will be compatible with the understock and the plant to be grafted as well. An example is the grafting of Bartlett Pear on quince roots for dwarfing. These 2 are not compatible but if a seedling pear is grafted on the quince roots, then the Bartlett Pear grafted on the seedling pear, this results in a good tree. This can be done in different ways. The Bartlett Pear can be grafted on pieces of the seedling pear and the grafted pieces put in moistened peat moss in a cool place for a few weeks until callused, when this piece (with scion and intermediate graft) is grafted onto a dormant quince root. Or, the seedling pear can be budded on to rooted cuttings of the quince one summer, then the Bartlett Pear can be budded on the seedling pear the next. See BUDDING.

So, grafting can be a complicated process but, if done properly, results in fairly good trees. Sometimes, years after the grafting, one notices a large hump at the graft union, showing clearly that the stock has grown much faster than the scion. Sometimes just the reverse is true. Frequently this is not serious but, whenever possible, it is always best to select an understock that grows at the same rate as the plant from which the scion was taken.

GRAFT, KERF. A type of cleft graf in which the sawed-off limb of the tree is notched by use of a saw, instead of split with a special tool as is usually done in the ordinary cleft graft. See GRAFTING.

GRAM, BLACK = *Phaseolus mungo*

GRAMINEAE = The Grass Family

GRANADILLA. See PASSIFLORA.

GRANULAR, GRANULOSE. Composed of or appearing as covered by minute grains.

GRAPE. Grapes are frequently prized fruit producing plants in the home garden. They need room in which to grow; they need annual and heavy pruning if they are to produce many fruits; they need spraying and fertilizing. In most areas, home-grown grapes are not difficult to grow, but they do need some sort of trellis or support. The smaller the garden, the less opportunity to grow grapes.

They can be divided into 3 general classes as far as cultivation in the United States is concerned. *Vitis vinifera* is the European grape, many varieties of which are grown in southern Europe. In the United States they can be grown in Calif., the Northwest Pacific Coast and some of the red and white wine producing varieties on the East Coast as far north as Plymouth, MA. However, here it is only in small, local spots where the weather conditions are just right for their good growth.

The second great group of grapes is derived from the native *V. labrusca* or Fox Grape, native to eastern North America. There are many hybrids of this, some of them crosses with *V. vinifera*. One of the most popular of the *V. labrusca* hybrids is 'Concord', widely grown throughout the greater part of the country east of the Rocky Mountains and especially in the northern and northeastern United States.

The third group of grapes derived from *V. rotundifolia*, the Muscadine Grape, is grown only in the South where they will produce in the climate there and other grapes will not. Consequently, the home gardener selects the varieties he chooses to grow from one of these 3 groups, depending on the part of the country in which he lives.

Grapes prefer a sunny well-drained soil. Most of the commercial grape-growing areas in the East are located near large bodies of water which reduce the advent of frosts in the early fall, and give the fruit a chance to ripen fully. Areas near the Great Lakes, in Ark. and Mo. are in this category. Frost "pockets," or low spots where early frosts occur, should not be used for planting grapes. Fortunately they will grow on a wide range of soils.

Propagation

Many grapes are easily grown from hardwood cuttings and are then on their own roots. The home gardener can easily do this or he can layer stems on the ground. See LAYERING. However, it is unfortunate that in many areas of the country, especially on sites of older vineyards, various diseases and insects take their toll of grapes by feeding on the roots. Recently there has been much work done in ascertaining which rootstocks are "resistant" to these problems, and some excellent resistant rootstocks have been produced by various state and federal experiment stations. Popular varieties are then grafted on these so-called "resistant" rootstocks, with the result that the vines are far better able to grow in areas where disease and insect pests injure or destroy "own-rooted" types. It probably pays most home owners to play it safe and obtain varieties which have been grafted on resistant rootstocks.

Such plants should be watched carefully, for shoots from the roots if allowed to develop would produce grapes usually inferior to the clone grafted on them. All shoots coming from the rootstock should be removed; a rule to follow in growing any kind of grafted stock.

In New York at least, one of the best of the resistant rootstocks is 'Conderc 3309', but others are undoubtedly available in other areas. The local state experiment station would give the latest information on this score.

Planting

One-year-old vines are the ones usually planted either in the spring or in the fall, but, if planted in the fall, special care might be taken in northern areas to mound the soil about the base of the vine to prevent them being "heaved" (which see) out of the soil by alternate freezing and thawing winter weather.

Vines are usually planted about 8 ft. apart, and cut back to about 2 buds. A mulch might well be placed about the plant but no fertilizer should be used at planting time. One should remember that grapes are very susceptible to injury from overdoses of fertilizers or chemicals used in weed control. Extreme care should be taken in applying these materials.

Trellis

Grapes must have a means of support. The old-fashioned grape arbor was one method of supplying this, but there are so many other ornamental vines now available that if an arbor is used in the garden, a vine more decorative than the grape is usually selected. Grapes are easily grown on a wire trellis consisting of 2 wires, attached to sturdy posts about 10 ft. apart. One wire should be about 30 in. above the ground, and the second about 36 in. above the first.

The vine is trained to a single stalk with a branch trained each way on the 2 wires, often referred to as the 4-arm Kniffin System. The wires should be about #9 but the top wire could be #10 or 11. Although there are other methods of training grapes, this is by far the most popular system and the easiest one to use for the home gardener.

Pruning

This is best done in winter or very early spring before the sap begins to flow. If the pruning is done late in spring the cut ends will "bleed" profusely and, although there is no evidence to prove this is harmful to the vines, certainly it does not seem to be desirable if it can be avoided by pruning while the vines are dormant. Pruning when the vine is in leaf just removes so many food manufacturing organs from the plant and this is decidedly harmful when done at this time.

Grapes are borne on shoots that grow from buds on 1-year-old canes. The whole idea is to allow just enough of these to develop to produce the number of grapes that the vine will reasonably support. If left unpruned, the vine will get very woody, clogged with dead wood, and will produce far too many small, poorly-developed bunches of grapes. To maintain a vigorous vine, reduce the old wood to a minimum and replace this with young canes.

Best results are obtained when the severity of the pruning is adjusted to the vigor of the

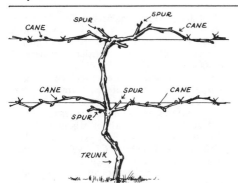

Grape pruning: The single-stem, four-arm Kniffen System.

vine. Fewer buds should be retained on a weak vine than on a strong one. The 4-arm Kniffin System has been described above. The pruning of the 4 "arms" or branches from the trunk should be done in such a way that these shoots will all be of last year's growth.

The number of buds to be retained on each arm varies with the variety, its vigor and its age. Theoretically, this has been worked out in this fashion. Accurately weigh the 1-year-old canes that are removed in the pruning operation. Leave 30 buds for the first lb. of prunings and 10 additional buds for each additional lb. of prunings. This can be done several times if one wants to become proficient in judging the amount of pruning removed. It has been estimated that between 30 and 60 buds can be left on 'Concord' vines.

The most desirable canes to be left should be about the size of a lead pencil in dia. and should originate as close to the main trunk as possible. It is desirable also to cut a small spur near these branches to about 2 buds. This is the renewal spur and it is branches from these spurs which will be selected to remain on the plant the following year. If the vine then has 2 lbs. of prunings of 1-year-old canes, approximately 40 buds should be left, divided among the 4 branches or "arms." These branches should be firmly tied to the wires of the trellis. No further pruning need be done until the following year.

There are other systems of pruning. The "Umbrella" system is one in which the vines are trained upright directly to the top wire and there the satisfactory number of shoots are selected to train downward to the lower wire. Another system has to do with a trellis composed of 2 wires in the same plane 21 in. apart and about 4½ ft. high. Each of the 3 systems is advocated at some grape-growing area in the United States. The local state experiment station will always have recommendations for

the proper method for the vines grown in one's local area.

Pruning must be done carefully and thoroughly each year in order to keep grape vines producing good crops and from becoming overgrown.

Varieties

Most varieties are self-fruitful, except the Muscadine varieties grown in the South. Consequently, one does not have to worry about cross-pollination as one does with plums and some cherries. Actually, there are almost too many varieties of grapes being grown today. The inexperienced gardener should obtain advice from the local state experiment station, concerning the best varieties to grow for his particular area. Some of the more popular varieties for the central, northern and northeastern states are the hybrids or selected seedlings of *V. labruca*, such as:

'Concord'—still the most popular of all grapes in the North making up perhaps 85% of the plantings and especially good for the home garden because it is a reliable producer. It does have a long maturing season, and in some parts of Mass. (it originated in Concord, Mass., about 1840) early frosts in certain low spots can prevent it from ripening properly. A black grape of excellent quality.

'Niagara'—a seedling of 'Concord' in 1872, one of the leading white grape varieties.

'Catawba'—a standard red grape used chiefly in making red wine and champagne, but it can be susceptible to fungus diseases.

'Delaware'—another old-fashioned variety, popular for nearly a century. The berries are small and red. This has high quality and is especially good in the home garden.

'Fredonia'—a black grape and a leading early variety.

'Worden'—sometimes recommended in place of 'Concord' because it ripens 10 days to 2 weeks earlier. It is a black grape, not suitable for long-distance shipping but perfectly satisfactory for the home garden.

'Interlaken'—a yellowish-green grape, practically seedless. Its skin can be eaten since it is a hybrid of one of the American grapes and the European *V. vinifera*. 'Concord Seedless' also is planted but its fruits are small.

'Golden Muscat'—another variety with a greenish color related to *V. vinifera* but it does not grow into a vigorous vine like the others.

'Erie'—this is a black grape ripening the latter part of Aug. and for this reason might be considered for the home garden in areas where early fall frosts are prevalent.

The N.Y. Ag. Exp. Station lists 84 varieties it

grows, so those listed are only a few of the varieties available.

These are only a very few of many varieties available but they all have proved extremely popular in the home gardens of the North. In fact 'Concord' is still one of the best of the American-type grapes for growing on the Pacific Coast where the European types are usually far more popular.

VARIETIES FOR THE SOUTH. As previously stated, the Muscadine grapes of the South have been selected mostly as seedlings of *V. rotundifolia* which is native from Del. to Fla. and Tex. Most of these varieties bear pistillate flowers only, so a pollen source is needed to produce the fertilization of the flowers. Recently the U.S. Department of Agriculture has introduced some varieties with perfect flowers which can be used as a pollen source for the older Muscadine varieties. Some of these new varieties with perfect flowers are **'Burgaw'**, **'Duplin'**, **'Pender'**, **'Tarheel'**, **'Wallace'**, and **'Willard'**. At least one of these varieties might well be included in the home garden where any of the following Muscadine varieties are grown:

'Scuppernong'—one of the oldest and has been grown since 1760 at least, with berries colored green to reddish.

'Thomas'—the best of these varieties for unfermented juice and preserving and hence considered the best variety for home gardens in the South. Fruits are dark reddish colored.

'James'—with purplish-black fruits.

'Mish'—with blacks fruits, a good wine grape.

'Flowers'—with purplish-black fruits, very productive.

These Muscadine varieties should not be grown in areas where the winter temperatures go below 0° F. It is often recommended that these varieties be spaced 15–20 ft. apart on the vine trellis. As previously mentioned one should be careful with fertilizer applications, but if these vines are grown in sod a suggested fertilizer application might be, ½ lb. of nitrate of soda for a 1-year-old vine, 1 lb. for a 2-year-old vine and 2 lbs. for a 3-year-old vine. Other complete fertilizers might be substituted but the amount of nitrogen applied might be the same.

V. vinifera VARIETIES FOR CALIF. AND THE WEST COAST. Grapes are commercially produced in Calif. for 3 different end products: table grapes, raisins and wine. The European Grape varieties being grown are many, but actually the most popular are a comparatively few good-producing varieties. For instance, 95% of the raisins produced in Calif. are from the 'Thompson Seedless' variety. Ninety-five per cent of the table grapes are produced from the following varieties: **'Cardinal'**, **'Emperor'**, **'Perlette'**, **'Ribier'**, **'Thompson Seedless'** and **'Red Flame'**.

Not many home gardeners will produce wine grapes but some of the better known red wine grapes are **'Alicante'**, **'Bouschet'**, **'Carignane'**, **'Grenache'**, **'Mataro'**, **'Mission'**, **'Salvador'**, **'Zinfandel'**.

White wine-grape varieties include **'Burger'**, **'Muscat'**, **'Sauvignon Blanc'**, **'Semillon'**, **'Sylvaner'**.

VINIFER TABLE-GRAPE VARIETIES

'Almeria'—greenish-white, productive vines, with fruit ripening late. The skins are tough.

'Cardinal'—a hybrid ('Tokay' x 'Ribier') with cherry-red fruits which become reddish black at maturity; the vines are very productive. It is the earliest red table grape now being grown in Calif. and is adapted to hot-growing areas.

'Emperor'—it is either first or second in popularity, late ripening, good appearance and colored light red to reddish purple. There are over 33,000 acres in Calif. planted to this variety alone.

'Italia'—an Italian grape with a mild muscat flavor. The berries bruise easily.

'Muscat of Alexandria'—good for home gardens, for making raisins and for wine. The fruits are dull green, of excellent flavor but have poor shipping qualities.

'Malaga'—at one time this was Calif.'s leading grape, but it is now superseded by 'Thompson Seedless'. The fruits are whitish green with thick, tough skins.

'Perlette'—vigorous and productive, white and waxy in appearance.

'Red Flame' is an excellent seedless var.

'Red Malaga'—pink to reddish purple, ripening before 'Tokay' but not as popular.

'Ribier'—actually named 'Alphonse Lavalee', it was misnamed 'Ribier' in Calif. It is one of the finest of European hothouse varieties. The fruits are very large and jet black. Shipping and storage qualities are good.

'Tokay'—at one time this was the premier Calif. grape variety but now it is surpassed by both 'Emperor' and 'Thompson Seedless'. It has a brilliant red color and excellent shipping qualities.

'Thompson Seedless'—nearly one-third of the grape acreage in Calif. is planted to this 1 variety, good for raisins, table grapes and wine. Vigorous and productive, the fruits are seedless, whitish green, ship well and ripen early.

Pruning V. vinifera

The method already described (Kniffin System) can be used, but sometimes European grapes are trained to a single stake in which 1–4 of the new fruiting canes are used to produce the next year's crop, and only 10–12 buds are left on each cane. Look for a small renewal spur at the base of the cane and leave 2–3 buds on it.

Shoots that come from renewal spurs will provide fruiting canes 1 year hence. If a 2-wire trellis is used, tie each cane to a wire. If just a single stake is used, pull all the canes upright and tie the ends together.

Resistant understock—many are being used, in fact they must be used for the European grapes that are most susceptible to *Phylloxera*, a small, yellowish, aphidlike insect that attacks grape roots. Also the root knot nematode is a very small parasitic worm that lives in or upon grape roots and is a common and serious pest in Calif. Some grapes are more resistant to these pests than others and it is these roots that the good producing varieties should be grafted on. Some of the better resistant rootstocks are 'St. George', '1613', 'A x R #1' and 'Dogridge'.

Girdling is sometimes practiced in growing the European grapes in order to produce larger fruits. The operation merely consists of removing a $\frac{3}{16}$ in. ring of bark (done with a specially made 2-bladed knife) around the trunk or major shoots of the vine. This is done at about flowering time on some varieties. For instance, the variety 'Black Corinth' is always ringed. This is one of those grown widely in hothouses in Europe. 'Thompson Seedless' is ringed 10–14 days after flowering.

It may also be advisable, if unusually large fruit clusters are wanted, to hand thin the green fruits before they ripen. Most home gardeners are not going to take the time for this unless they are growing fruit clusters for show display. This is the way, however, to eliminate small and poorly set grape clusters as soon after flowering as they are evident. Berry thinning is sometimes practiced, when the clusters show evidence of producing too many compact berries for the cluster.

Harvesting

Grapes grown in the home garden should not be picked until fully ripened on the vine. This brings up the problems in some areas of birds eating the berries before they are picked. We have been very troubled with this situation, but finally corrected it merely by throwing a large piece of saran cloth or netting over the 6-ft. trellis, covering the vines from ground to top on both sides. In this way, the grapes receive normal amounts of sunshine and air and one can check the ripening process. The cloth is put over the 2-wire trellis about 3–4 weeks before the fruits normally ripen. This is another good reason for growing grapes on a simple 2-wire trellis, for this is very easily covered, whereas a large arbor would not be.

Insect Pests

Like other fruits, grapes require that a specific schedule for pest control be followed in order to produce a profitable crop. Early in the season flea beetles eat the buds, grape plume moth cripples the buds and cane girdler cuts off the new shoots. A dormant spray with insecticide #44 kills the eggs of the plume moth and controls the grape scale and the cottony maple scale. Sprays of insecticide #9 control the leaf-eating insects and the grape tomato gall which makes globular galls on the leaves and stems. Japanese beetle, rose chafer and the light-loving beetle have a strong liking for grape foliage. Insecticides #9 and #37 give control without excessive residue.

Grape phylloxera, which is primarily a root aphid, nearly prohibits the culture of European grapes on their own roots. In America, American varieties or others grafted on them are grown. Spraying with insecticide #15 helps to check the gall-making form on the leaves. The most important insect pest of the fruit is the grape berry moth. The first generation eats the leaves and buds and the second and third generations eat the berries. When preparing to pupate they cut and fold parts of the leaf to form a shelter. A single worm may infest several berries. Careful spraying with insecticide #9 or #37, especially when the berries are about half grown, is necessary.

Diseases

Black rot is a serious fruit disease although it is also present on the leaves and canes. Infected fruit becomes hard and brown before it dries to the well-known mummies in which the disease overwinters. Destruction of infected fruit and sprays with fungicide #D just before and just after bloom are effective. Downy mildew infections on the leaves are controlled by the above treatment.

A regular schedule prepared by local authorities in pest control should be followed.

GRAPEFRUIT. The Grapefruit (*Citrus paradisi*), which apparently originated in the West Indies as a mutant form or hybrid of the Pummelo (Shaddock), has become a favorite acid citrus fruit of Americans. The tree is as large or larger than the Sweet Orange, carries larger winged-petiole leaves, which give it a denser appearance.

Both seedy and seedless grapefruit varieties are available; the preference for seedless kinds is recognized in the varieties listed below. Good seedy grapefruit varieties, all adapted to Fla. particularly South and the humid South and Southeast, and rarely found in the Southwest, are 'Duncan', 'Indian River', 'McCartney' and the pink-fleshed 'Foster'. Some of the following varieties are also seedy, but are described because of their unique characteristics of value to the gardener.

'Triumph' and 'Imperial' (similar, and thought by some to be identical) are medium early-maturing varieties. Although seedy they are smaller than other grapefruit varieties, are sweeter, and lack the typical grapefruit flavor; they add to the range available to the gardener. 'Triumph' is the name most commonly used in Fla., 'Imperial' in Calif.

'Royal' is a unique variety characterized by slightly smaller size and darker orange-yellow color of its fruit. The flesh also is a little more yellow, the flavor sweeter and with less bitterness than most grapefruit. It is suspected of being a hybrid between Grapefruit and Orange, and is a distinctive variety for the home gardener.

'Marsh' (Marsh Seedless) contains very few or no seeds. It is midseason, excellent quality, and is the preeminent yellow Grapefruit of commerce.

'Thompson' (Pink Marsh) is a pink-fleshed mutation of the 'Marsh' variety, differing only in the color of its flesh and in ripening somewhat earlier. The color is limited to the flesh.

'Ruby' (USDA Red) is a mutation of 'Thompson' with even more red in the flesh, and a crimson blush on the skin.

Grapefruit trees can be grown wherever sweet oranges are, having almost the same degree of cold hardiness. Minimum temperatures in the low 20's will do little harm except that defoliation and the killing of small twigs results. It is possible that the heavier foliage cover aids in the cold resistance of this species. The fruit withstands about the same minimum temperature as do oranges, 27° to 28° F., but may escape injury when oranges are injured because of their larger size and the fact that they are generally borne under the foliage canopy rather than exposed.

The Grapefruit differs markedly from oranges in its response to growing temperatures. Best quality Grapefruit is almost always produced in areas with high average temperatures during the summer growing period. Grapefruit produced in the cool, coastal, citrus districts of the Pacific Coast seldom attain the high quality of that grown in the Southeast and South, and the low desert areas of the Southwest. The time from bloom to maturity is markedly affected by the average temperature. Varieties requiring but 8 months to mature in the Caribbean Islands may take 18–20 months in cool West Coast citrus areas, and still not attain the quality of fruit from the former location.

The propagation of Grapefruit is by grafting and parallels that of the Orange. Sour Orange is a preferred rootstock for Grapefruit, probably because more of them are grown in humid climates where root-rots tend to be severe.

Sweet Orange stock produces good trees, and may be preferred if the Sour Orange stock is not desirable. Rough Lemon stock is often preferred on weak sandy soils, and this stock does not have the deleterious effect on Grapefruit quality it does for oranges. 'Troyer' and 'Carrize' citranges and Trifoliate Orange understocks are suitable providing the scion variety is not carrying the exocortes virus.

Nursery operations necessary to produce Grapefruit trees, and the topworking procedures to establish Grapefruit on mature trees of other citrus species are the same as for Orange.

The cultural requirements and practices for Grapefruit are essentially identical to those for Orange. If not bearing an excessive crop, Grapefruit are more likely to bloom following a drought period. For garden purposes maintenance of available water is desirable.

Grapefruit tend to bloom only in the spring, especially in areas with well-marked winter periods of relatively low average temperatures. However, they are prone to bloom, at least lightly, at other times of the year, especially if stimulated by relief of drought or heavy nitrogen fertilization. Off-season bloom will rarely yield a year-round fruit supply, however.

Normally Grapefruit will be approaching maturity as they color. Unlike the oranges, best color is obtained in hot weather. The fruit may be used whenever it is pleasing to taste; minimum commercial standards seldom result in fruit of highest quality. As the fruit ripens the acid content decreases and the sugars increase. Commercial picking indices usually require about a 6:1 or 6.5:1 sugar:acid ratio, but when fully mature this may increase to 8 or 9:1, and the flavor is usually much richer, sweeter, and with less bitterness.

Although most grapefruit will ripen in the cooler period of the year, and will therefore hold for a considerable time on the tree, it should be harvested not too long after it has reached its peak quality. Such fruit should be washed, cured by leaving it at room temperature for a few days in a well-ventilated spot, and then stored at refrigerator temperatures. Grapefruit does not have a long storage life; 2 to 3 months is the limit, and when taken from storage it soon deteriorates.

The pests and diseases of Grapefruit are similar to those of Orange.

Pummelos (*C. maxima*) which are similar to the Grapefruit in tree characters are much less hardy, about equaling the Lemon. Their very large fruits are uniquely attractive conversation pieces; fortunately a few improved varieties are available—'Tresca' and 'Chandler' are used.

CLARON O. HESSE

GRAPE-HYACINTH. See MUSCARI.

GRAPE-IVY = *Cissus incisa*

GRAPTOPETALUM (grap-to-PET-al-um)
paraguayense   I′   **Zone 9   Ghostplant**
A succulent from Mexico having a rosette of
fleshy heart-shaped leaves 2 in. long, pointed
at the end and silvery gray. The leaves are
brittle, flowers small and white. This is a
popular plant, used in southern Calif. as a
ground cover and in the North as an interesting
pot plant indoors. Sometimes termed *Sedum
weinbergii*. Easily propagated by rooting
individual leaves.

GRASS, AMERICAN BEACH = *Ammophila
breviligulata*
   BAHIA = *Paspalum notatum*. See GRASS, LAWNS.
   BARLEY = *Hordeum vulgare*
   BARNYARD = *Echinochloa crus-galli*
   BEACH PLANTING. See SEASHORE GARDEN.
   BENT = *Agrostis tenuis*. See GRASS, LAWNS.
   BERMUDA = *Cynodon dactylon*. See GRASS,
   LAWNS.
   BLUESTEM WHEAT-GRASS = *Agropyron smithii*
   CARPET = *Axonopus furcatus*. See GRASS,
   LAWNS.
   CENTIPEDE = *Eremochloa ophiuroides*.   See
   GRASS, LAWNS.
   CLOUD BENT = *Agrostis nebulosa*. See GRASS,
   LAWNS.
   CRAB. See DIGITARIA.
   EULALIA = *Miscanthus sinensis*. See ORNA-
   MENTAL GRASSES.
   EUROPEAN DUNE = *Elymus arenarius*
   FAMILY = Gramineae
   FOUNTAIN = *Pennisetum setaceum*
   GOLDEN-TOP = *Lamarckia aurea*
   GOOSE = *Eleusine indica*
   HARE'S-TAIL = *Lagurus ovatus*
   ITALIAN VERNAL = *Anthoxanthum gracile*
   JAPANESE LOVE = *Eragrostis tenella*
   KENTUCKY BLUEGRASS = *Poa pratensis*. See
   GRASS, LAWNS.
   LAWN. See LAWNS.
   MAIDEN = *Miscanthus sinensis gracillimuis*
   MEADOW FOXTAIL = *Alopecurus pratensis*
   PAMPAS = *Cortaderia selloana*. See ORNAMEN-
   TAL GRASSES.
   QUACK = *Agropyron repens*
   QUAKING. See BRIZA. See ORNAMENTAL GRASSES.
   RAINBOW = *Zea mays japonica*
   RAVENNA = *Erianthus ravennae*. See ORNA-
   MENTAL GRASSES.
   RED FESCUE = *Fescue rubra*. See GRASS,
   LAWNS.
   REDTOP = *Agrostis alba*. See GRASS, LAWNS.
   ROUGH BLUEGRASS = *Poa trivialis*. See GRASS,
   LAWNS.
   RUBY = *Rhynchelytrum repens*
   ST. AUGUSTINE = *Stenotaphrum secondatum*.
   See GRASS, LAWNS.

   SPIKE = *Chasmanthium latifolium*
   SQUIRREL-TAIL = *Hordeum jubatum*. See ORNA-
   MENTAL GRASSES.
   SWEET VERNAL = *Anthoxanthum odoratum*
   WITCH = *Panicum capillare*
   ZEBRA = *Miscanthus sinensis zebrinus*
GRASS. There are many kinds of grasses used in
making lawns throughout America. See LAWNS.
Grass of some kind or other eventually seeds
itself in to any plowed field, and if the weeds are
kept cut down, grass of sorts eventually takes
over. However, much study and experimenta-
tion have been undertaken with grasses during
the last decades, and here are some that are
widely used to make various kinds of turf in the
United States.

Northern Grasses

Kentucky Bluegrass. This is a naturalized
grass, widely adapted to many differing soil and
climate conditions, and because of this is one of
the most popular of all lawn grasses. It increases by underground stems or rhizomes,
grows late in the fall after other grasses have
stopped; survives best roughly north of Tenn.
Bluegrass can be reproduced by plugs, sodding
and seeding but the last is much the simplest.
   Over 30 million lbs. of Kentucky Bluegrass
seed is sown annually in North America.
Seeding rate is usually 2–3 lbs. per 1000 sq. ft.
It grows best when temperatures are 65°–80° F.
Kentucky Bluegrass (*Poa pratensis*) is largely
apomictic (nonsexual), that is, most seed does
not require sexual fertilization, but represents
the parent plant exactly. Thus almost any blue
grass can be perpetuated as a pure line. Few
"selections" are improvements over natural
Kentucky Bluegrass. It is cut about 2 in. high.
   'Merion' Bluegrass was one of the first
selections, originally found as an attractive
patch on the Merion Golf Course near Philadelphia. It is noted for its comparatively low
growth, density, good color and resistance to
leaf spot disease, but it does have some drawbacks. It does rust, demands heavier fertilization, and because of tight growth tends to thatch
more quickly than most other bluegrasses. It is
usually cut $\frac{1}{2}$–$1\frac{1}{2}$ in. high.
   'Park' is another good variety of bluegrass
noteworthy for heavy seed that sprouts readily.
It is the results of combining a dozen natural
selections made by the University of Minnesota and contains a good measure of genetic
variability that is natural to Kentucky Bluegrass.
   Canadan Bluegrass is sometimes used on
athletic fields. It is more coarse than the other
bluegrasses, tolerates shade and poor soil,
and is usually cut 3–4 in. high.
   Rough Bluegrass (*Poa trivialis*) sometimes
called Meadowgrass, does · well in a moist

climate, in shade. It frequently is included in mixtures sold for shady situations in cool climates. It is used only in the northern and northeastern parts of the United States.

Bent Grass (*Agrostis tenuis*). These are the very fine grasses for northern golf greens and special lawns. They need extra attention, most are probably native to Europe, introduced into America. **Redtop** (*Agrostis alba*), widely escaped in America, is used as a nurse grass in some seed mixtures. Bent grasses all grow well in spring and fall at temperatures less than 80° F., but are not as colorful in winter as is Kentucky Bluegrass. They spread above ground by stolons that root at the joints.

Most bent grasses should be mowed twice a week. They grow best in a moist atmosphere with plenty of fertilization and are tolerant of acid soil. They are at their best on the Pacific Coast from San Francisco northward and most of the seed is produced in Ore. They are also widely used on golf-course greens and small terraces in the northeastern, north central and eastern parts of the United States. Bent grasses grow best in full sun.

Seeded varieties such as **'Highland'** and **'Penncross'** are planted widely in the East and West, North and mid-South. The vegetatively propagated varieties often do best in specific regions or where their special needs are recognized. **'Washington'**, **'Arlington'** and **'Congressional'** were selected in Washington, D.C.; **'Old Orchard'**, **'Toronto'**, **'Cohansey'**, **'Evansville'** and **'Springfield'**, and others are of midwestern origin.

Bent grasses should be clipped $\frac{1}{4}$–1 in. high., too low for bluegrass and fine fescue. One pound of bent grass seed is sufficient for 1000 sq. ft. With vegetatively propagated varieties, several bushels of stolons are distributed over 1000 sq. ft. and then top dressed with soil and diligently watered.

FINE FESCUES. These are the red fescues for the northern states, where most are widely established. **Chewings Fescue** (*F. rubra commutata*) was named in Europe and for many years was cultivated in New Zealand, but is now produced in Ore. The fine fescues are more wiry in habit, grow well under a wide variety of conditions and are most used mixed in with the seed of Kentucky Bluegrass.

With fine fescue, seldom is more than 2–3 lbs. of elemental nitrogen fertilizer per 1000 sq. ft. necessary annually. In a seed mixture fescues are good insurance for the less intensively tended lawns, for they do survive in difficult locations.

Fescues grow best in the fall and can be used wherever Kentucky Bluegrass grows well. Between 20–30 million lbs. of seed are used annually, much of it grown in Canada and imported simply as **Creeping Red Fescue**. Fescues are usually sown 3–4 lbs. of seed per 1000 sq. ft., generally in blends with Kentucky Bluegrass, and are mowed at about 2–3 in. high. **'Pennlawn'**, **'Rainier'**, **'Chewings'** and **'Illahee'** are all improved selections but appear much the same in most lawns, with minor physiological differences. They resent too low cutting, otherwise they are serviceable grasses for the northern United States.

RYE GRASSES. These are of two kinds, **Domestic** or **Italian Rye Grass** and **Perennial Rye Grass**. The former is an annual, the latter a perennial. The Domestic or Italian Rye Grass is usually used as a nurse grass in mixtures with slower germinating seeds, for in cool climates it makes a quick greensward. By the time the Kentucky Bluegrass appears, the Rye Grass has died out. It has also been used in mixtures of Bermuda Grass and even Centipede Grass to give a green turf in the winter, but its ability to die out suddenly after a quick freeze is disappointing and Kentucky Bluegrass and some fescues are being substituted more and more in these mixtures. It is sown at about 2 lbs. per 1000 sq. ft.

Perennial Rye Grass makes a very coarse, tough turf, and can die out suddenly. Its best use is not as a lawn turf but as a green manure. See SOILS.

Southern Grasses

Bermuda Grass. This is as successful over a wide series of conditions in the mid-South as is Kentucky Bluegrass in the North. It is probably native of Europe and Asia, certainly Africa, and now is widely established in the southern United States. There have been literally hundreds of selections under observation at various experimental stations. In the Deep South (southern Fla., the humid Gulf Coast), Bermuda Grass does passingly well but there are other grasses even better adapted there. Northward to the Carolinas and Kan., Bermuda Grass is at its best.

In warm weather, if water and fertility are adequate, Bermuda Grass grows rampant. With the frosts it turns brown usually until about April (whenever warm weather comes again). Dormant Bermuda Grass restrains winter weeds very little, so that there are often spots of discordant green in the brown of a Bermuda Grass lawn, the reason why it is advantageous to sow other grasses (Rye Grass, Kentucky Bluegrass, and fescues) in the fall so the lawn will be green all winter.

Bermuda Grass increases by both runners and rhizomes. It should be mowed at least twice a week for best appearance. It is not a "low-maintenance" grass requiring more fertilizer than most species. It will not grow in the shade or under trees. Seeding the genetically mixed common form is easiest, about 2 lbs. per 1000 sq. ft. The named varieties are started asexually by plugs, sprigs or chopped stolons. The latter are scattered on the top of a prepared seedbed (1-6 bushels per 1000 sq. ft.) and top dressed with soil or compost.

The species is *Cynodon dactylon*. The following selections are much used at present:

'U 3'—a denser, more cold-tolerant selection, widely planted in middle latitudes for golf-course fairways.

'Sunturf'—this is actually a natural hybrid (*C.* x *magennisii*) from South Africa. It is a sterile triploid.

'Tifgreen'—the most widely used grass for golf greens in the South. This also is a hybrid, a sterile triploid. A natural mutant from 'Tifgreen' is 'Tifdwarf'.

'Tiflawn'—a tough hybrid suited for athletic fields.

'Tifway'—a hybrid of fine texture also triploid, excellent for golf fairways.

Carpet Grass—*Axonopus furcatus* is tall and coarse, used in some parts of the southern United States where better lawn grasses can not be grown. It is light green and disease-resistant, but should be grown in a moist acid soil. It reaches 8-10 in. in height, and is sown at the rate of $2\frac{1}{2}$ lbs. per 1000 sq. ft. Since it has creeping rootstalks it can also be planted by sprigs or plugs. Other grasses should be mixed with it if a green color in winter is desired.

Centipede Grass—*Eremochloa ophiuroides* is reported an erratic grass sometimes off to a fine start, then slowing down suddenly or dying out in spots for seeming trifles. It is called the "lazy man's grass," for under optimum conditions it grows readily and requires little care. The species was introduced from China in 1919. It is at its best on the Coastal Plain from N.Car. south to northern Fla. and west into Miss. It grows well on sandy soils or clay soils. It colors yellow easily from lack of available iron in the soil, usually a condition of alkaline soils. In general, it is one of the better grasses for lawns in the South where poor soils prevail.

It is slow in growth, needing to be mowed only every 10-20 days, and this is done at a height of about $1\frac{1}{2}$ in. for if let alone it grows only 3-4 in. tall. It is dense in growth and so is comparatively weed-free. The quality of a centipede grass turf is not up to that of the finer-textured Bermuda Grass or Zoysia.

Centipede Grass is propagated by sprigs or plugs about 6-12 in. apart or from seed. The sprigs could be 1-2 in. in the ground with most of the foliage left above ground.

St. Augustine Grass—*Stenotaphrum secunda-*

tum is supposed to be native to subtropical America. It is a fairly low creeping grass, spreading by stolons, preferring a moist climate and mucky soils. It is one of the better performing grasses near southern seashores. It is coarse and of loose texture, and so is not considered an elegant turf grass, for the leaf blades may be as much as $\frac{1}{2}$ in. wide, (although newer selections may have a much finer texture, something like Centipede Grass). A distinguishing feature is a curious constriction and half twist where the blade joins the sheath. It is limited to vegetative propagation by means of sod, sprigs or plugs and these if placed even a foot apart may grow into a well-knit turf in a few months in suitable weather.

Possibly its most useful characteristic is ability to grow well in the shade, better than almost any other grass in the South. Otherwise, it is mediocre. It is one of the least expensive lawn grasses of the South. However, chinch bug infestations are proving a serious problem. Since chlordane is now prohibited, sprays of "Trithion," "Ethion" and "Aspon" at 7-10 lbs. per acre, "Diazinon" at 4-8 lbs. per acre are being recommended every 6-8 weeks.

Brown Patch disease has proved most troublesome also and may be controlled by spraying with mercurials like "Thiram" and "Kromad" as well as PCNB, at least 2 sprayings about 14 days apart. Hence St. Augustine Grass is certainly not "low maintenance."

Experiments have shown that fertilizing with 1 lb. of a complete fertilizer spring and autumn with organic nitrogen in the summer is about a minimum. It should be mowed about 2 in. high and is not tolerant of 2-4-D weed killers but will withstand "Atrazine."

Current varieties include 'Roselawn', a tall-growing pasture variety, 'Floratine', a recent introduction from the University of Florida which tolerates lower mowing (than 2 in.) and is dense and finer textured than some of the others.

Bahia Grass—This grass (*Paspalum notatum*) has been a pasture grass but is fast becoming a valued ornamental. It is used in the Deep South where it is basic in most seed mixtures. It makes an inexpensive, easily maintained lawn, not necessarily as beautiful or as fine in texture as Zoysia and improved Bermuda grasses, but nevertheless serviceable. It is native to tropical America. Selections include 'Pensacola', 'Paraguay' and 'Argentine'.

Bahia Grass can exist sporadically as far north as Tennessee, but basically it is a grass for the Deep South. It has great tolerance and can stand neglect and lack of fertility, produces deep vigorous roots which make it one of the best southern grasses for sandy soils, withstanding droughts well. It grows well in either acid or alkaline soils, and tolerates shade. Mowing can be done with a rotary mower.

This grass spreads by horizontal stems either above or below ground, so it can be propagated by sprigs or plugs, although planting by seeds is much simpler. However, the seed does not germinate well and amounts up to 10 lbs. per 1000 sq. ft. must be sown to get a good lawn started. The variety 'Pensacola' seems to germinate best.

Winter Grass—The term winter grass is used in the South for lawn grasses interseeded into the permanent turf (usually Bermuda Grass) to provide attractive green cover during the winter. Lawn grasses adapted to growing in cool weather are chosen. They are mostly sown as annual grasses in the fall, dying out in the hot summer, resown the following autumn.

Zoysia is best planted in spring or early summer. Seed is available only of the species, *Z. japonica*, usually sown at 2 lbs. per 1000 sq. ft. Runners of 3 joints (sprigs) of named clones are planted with 1 joint in the soil, the other 2 above. Also plugs are planted, with spacing between them not more than 6 in. The planting must be kept moist to encourage growth which is always slow in starting, usually taking 2–3 weeks.

Zoysia has been given tremendous publicity during the past 10 years. Actually, *Z. japonica* has been grown in the United States since 1906 when it was first introduced from the Orient. Now there are many varieties, all to be propagated vegetatively, all "warm-season" grasses that turn brown in winter and hence are less satisfactory than cool-weather grasses in the North (which remain green much longer). However, in the South, Zoysia grasses have their troubles also. The **'Meyer'** variety discolors in winter more readily than some local types. Zoysia grasses do have diseases and insect pests (especially the billbug in Fla.) which are beginning to preclude its widespread use in some areas. Also a heavy-duty mower, which is expensive, is needed to mow Zoysia satisfactorily.

Nevertheless, among the Zoysia grasses are some of the finest lawn grasses for the South. They wear better than Bermuda Grass, although they will not grow as fast. They withstand shade, and require but little fertilizer.

Zoysia spreads by above-ground runners or stolons, and by underground runners or rhizomes. It needs from 1–3 years to establish a sod. Once established its slow growth becomes a virtue. Mowing need be only every 10 days or so, and no grass makes a thicker carpet of foliage. It should be mowed at a height of $\frac{3}{4}$–2 in.

Z. matrella or **Manila Grass** grows 3–4 in. high, forms a ruglike turf and grows well in many soils, in sun or shade. It stays green long at temperatures above 40° F. and is resistant to most pests and even to weed encroachment. 'Emerald Zoysia' is similar but is faster in growth and is slightly more resistant to frost.

Z. japonica and its improved form Meyer Zoysia are the ones which have been over-recommended for northern lawns. They are even more coarse than *Z. matrella* and slower growing. They do turn brown in winter, but are drought-resistant. For those living in the North, who wish their lawns to be green as long as possible in the late fall and winter, Zoysia should not be selected.

Robert W. Schery

GRASSES, ORNAMENTAL. Some of the annual and perennial grasses have ornamental value, when grown in single clumps. They range in height from a foot to ten feet and more. The graceful, arching stalks of the Pampas Grass or the Eulalia Grass make these excellent as conspicuous specimens. The fruit clusters of Squirrel-tail Grass or Bristly Foxtail are most interesting, and remain on the plant in good condition for weeks. Or they are cut and dried, used for winter arrangements. Ribbon Grass and Zebra Grass are particularly interesting with their striped leaves variegated with white. Blue Fescue (*Fescuca ovina glauca*) is used from coast to coast for its blue-green foliage and its low, tufted habit of growth.

It is probably true that these are not used nearly enough in our gardens. The perennial sorts need practically no attention. One clump of Eulalia Grass that comes to mind as this is being written has been growing as a featured plant in our garden for 20 years. It never has any attention, merely is cut to the ground for the winter and is evident throughout spring, summer and fall lending grace and beauty to the entire garden. These grasses should be used more than they are at present. Each one in the following list is described in the alphabetical listing in the main volume of this book.

A few of the more prominent ornamental grasses (other than the bamboos and cereals like wheat, oats, barley, etc.) are:

Agrostis nebulosa	12″–18″	Annual	Cloud Bent Grass
Anthoxanthum odoratum	3′	Perennial	Sweet Vernal Grass
Briza maxima	2′	Annual	Big Quaking Grass
B. minor	1′	Annual	Little Quaking Grass

Bromus brizaeformis	2′	Annual	Rattle Brome
Chasmanthium latifolium	5′	Perennial Zone 3	Spike Grass
Cortaderia selloana	8′–20′	Perennial Zone 8	Pampas Grass
Elymus arenarius	8′	Perennial Zone 5	European Dune Grass
E. glaucus	3′–5′	Perennial Zone 5	Blue Wild Rye
Eragrostis tenella	3′	Annual	Japanese Love Grass
Erianthus ravennae	8′–12′	Perennial Zone 5	Plume grass
Festuca ovina glauca	1′	Perennial Zone 4	Blue Fescue
Hordeum jubatum	2½′	Annual–Perennial	Squirrel-tail Grass
Lagurus ovatus	1′	Annual	Hare's-tail Grass
Lamarckia aurea	1′	Annual	Golden-top Grass
Miscanthus sinensis	10′	Perennial Zone 4	Eulalia Grass
M. sinensis gracillimus	10′	Perennial Zone 4	Maiden Grass
M. sinensis variegatus	10′	Perennial Zone 4	Striped Eulalia Grass
M. sinensis zebrinus	10′	Perennial Zone 4	Zebra Grass
Pennisetum setaceum	4′	Perennial Zone 5	Fountain Grass
Phalaris arundinacea picta	4′	Perennial Zone 3	Ribbon-grass
Rhynchelytrum repens	4′	Annual	Ruby Grass
Setaria verticillata	4′	Annual	Bristly Foxtail Grass
Stipa penuata	3′	Perennial Zone 5	European Feather Grass
Zea mays japonica	2′	Annual	Rainbow Grass

GRASSES, WEED. Almost any grass which grows in an unwanted place in the garden is a weed, and most of them are very easily distributed by windblown seed. Some of the following are the worst offenders in this category:

Agropyron repens	3′	Zone 2	Quack Grass
A. smithii	3′	Zone 3	Bluestem Wheat-grass
Alopecurus pratensis	3′	Zone 3	Meadow Foxtail-grass
Anthoxanthum odoratum	3′	Zone 3	Sweet Vernal Grass
Arrhenatherum elatius bulbosum	1′	Zone 3	Tuber Oat-grass
Avena fatua	4′	Annual	Wild Oats
Cenchrus pauciflorus	1′	Zone 3	Sandbur
Cynodon dactylon	16″	Zone 9	Bermuda Grass
Digitaria sp.	1′–2′	Annual	Crab Grass
Echinochloa crusgalli	5′	Annual	Barnyard Grass
Elusine indica	2′	Annual	Goose Grass
Hordeum jubatum	2½′	Zone 3	Squirrel-tail Grass
Lolium temulentum	4′	Annual	Darnel Rye-grass
Panicum capillare	2′	Annual	Witch Grass
Sorgum halepense	6′	Perennial Zone 8	Johnson-grass

GRATIOLA (grat-i-O-la)

aurea   1′   Zone 3   **Golden Hedge Hyssop** Growing from a fleshy, creeping rhizome, this perennial herb frequents sandy or gravelly soil along streams and swamps from southern Canada to the Gulf of Mexico and inland to the Dakotas. Alternate, linear to lanceolate leaves, up to 12 in. long, clasp the 4-angled, generally branching stem. From June to Sept. the yellow flowers appear, borne at the axils of the upper leaves. Each flower has a calyx with 5 narrow lobes and a tubular corolla with an irregular, 2-lipped margin, the upper lip having 1, the lower, 3 lobes. A fine plant for the bog garden, it may be divided or transplanted throughout the season.

GREASEWOOD, BLACK = *Sarcobatus vermiculatus*

GRECIAN SILKVINE = *Periploca graeca*

GREENBRIER. See SMILAX.

GREENHOUSE MANAGEMENT, HOME. Anyone who has been successful with plants out-of-doors may apply this knowledge to gardening under glass. This entry is designed to encourage individuals who have an interest in horticulture to build and operate a small home greenhouse for their personal enjoyment and pleasure. A greenhouse will present a challenge to your knowledge of horticulture, and also your ability to grow plants under greenhouse conditions. You will find this new hobby to be an escape from the tensions of everyday problems. It will fill leisure hours with satisfaction and at the same time you will receive beautiful results for your efforts.

Unless the techniques of greenhouse culture and many of the factors affecting plant growth are known and understood, a greenhouse is of little value to the grower. It is my endeavor to present to the reader basic concepts necessary for the successful operation of a small home greenhouse so that full enjoyment and results will be obtained. Growing plants under greenhouse conditions is a most exciting and rewarding phase of horticulture, especially during the winter months when plants are dormant out-of-doors. I caution hobbyists not to get carried away by trying to grow a little of everything in one small greenhouse. A greenhouse is limited to the amount of space available and within the confines of glass walls. Select carefully the type of plants you desire to grow; they should all require approximately the same growing temperature.

Should you be limited to one small greenhouse, you must determine whether your interest is with the tropical plants which require a night temperature of 60°–65° or with the flowering pot plants where, for best results, night temperature of 45°–50° is required. By building your greenhouse large enough to install a partition—usually in the center—creating 2 separate areas with controls, you can maintain 2 different temperatures, thus allowing you to grow a greater range of plants.

Caution should also be taken, if you have a limited greenhouse area, not to grow the common florist type of flowers such as roses, carnations, snapdragons, etc. You will find that these commercial types of flowers can be purchased cheaper than you can grow them, thus allowing you more room to grow house plants with flowers that are difficult to purchase.

A common mistake made by the greenhouse amateur is his reluctance to discard or give away surplus plants. Under good greenhouse techniques and conditions, plants will grow in size, needing more room to grow properly. Surplus plants make wonderful gifts for your friends and may be placed in other rooms of your home or out-of doors during the spring and summer months. You will find from time to time that plants outgrow their usefulness, attaining a size too large to maintain properly. These should be propagated and the old plant discarded.

Selecting

In selecting and building the greenhouse, consider very carefully the different types available before making a choice. Visit a home greenhouse in your community, talk with the owner in order to obtain his opinions; also, contact your architect to make sure the greenhouse design will not detract from the architectural features of the house.

It is a good practice to write to commercial greenhouse manufacturers and supply companies and obtain literature as to the latest types and material available. The United States Department of Agriculture has available a plan for an 8 ft. x 12 ft. portable plastic greenhouse, plan number 5946, which can be constructed for less than $100. Many of the local county agents or state agricultural colleges have information available just by request.

Types and Styles of Greenhouses

There are many variations in greenhouse types and styles to meet construction specifications and requirements. They are usually classified as follows:

1. BREEZEWAY. This is simply what the name implies—replacing the open or screened breezeway area with glass, and adding essentials such as water, heat, ventilation, etc. Because of the solid roof construction of most breezeway areas, it is not the best means of achieving the ideal greenhouse conditions. It does, however, provide an extra garden or plant room to your living area where plants may be grown and enjoyed.

2. LEAN-TO. A greenhouse (note Figure 1) where one side is attached directly to the building and in most instances can be closed off by a door or folding partition. This type of greenhouse is the most pleasurable kind,

Home Greenhouses

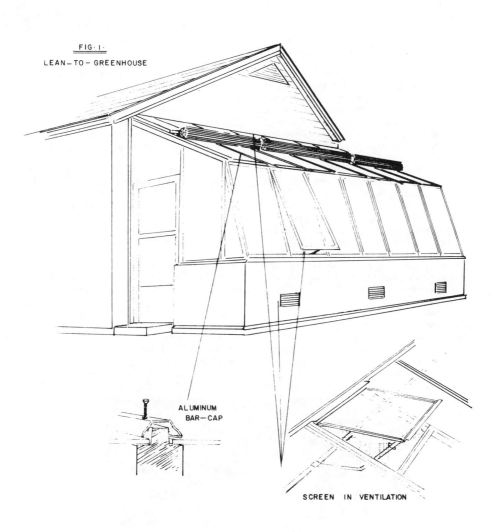

FIG·I·
LEAN—TO—GREENHOUSE

ALUMINUM
BAR—CAP

SCREEN IN VENTILATION

especially when attached to your home. This method allows you the enjoyment of the area without going outside and extends into your living area with beauty and color. In recent years, this type has become very popular with the average new home. It may be attached to a building away from the home or off any room of the house such as living room, dining room, kitchen, or even an upstairs bedroom. Many owners of older homes with open porches have converted this area and erected a lean-to greenhouse.

3. ATTACHED TO SERVICE BUILDING. This is the construction of a standard type of greenhouse to a service building, such as a garage, tool shed, barn, etc. whereby the service building serves as a potting and storage area for the greenhouse. Caution should be taken if the service building is a garage, as the carbon monoxide fumes from the car will kill plants.

4. FREE-STANDING. This is the most common type for large greenhouse construction. This style of construction is usually built away from the home and also provides a head house for all necessary supplies, equipment, heat, tools, etc., for the operation of the greenhouse. One disadvantage of this type of construction for the small home owner is the inconvenience of leaving a warm home, putting on heavy clothing, etc., to attend to the duties that are necessary during a cold winter night.

Location of Greenhouse

In selecting the type of greenhouse that would be best suited for your needs, a few thoughts should be given to the exact location in relationship to your home. Flowering plants, to produce good bloom, need all the sunlight they can receive during the winter months. Select a location where this is possible; usually the east, south or west portion of your home is best. The direction of winter-prevailing winds enters into the same consideration.

There is also the danger of locating your greenhouse too close to existing trees. The problem here is too much shade from the tree during the summer and the danger of falling branches and ice during the winter. While speaking about winter, take into consideration the danger of ice or snow sliding off the roof and falling onto the greenhouse. Snow guards can be installed on the greenhouse if necessary but are costly and unsightly.

It is also advisable to check the availability of the utilities in your home, such as electricity, water and heat. Most heating units do not have the capacity to supply the extra amount of heat required. In many cases supplementary heat is required and is supplied by installing electric or gas heating units into the greenhouse. Drainage can be another problem—getting rid of the surplus surface water on the greenhouse floor. This condition is one of the problems with the breezeway type of construction. Small holes can be drilled through the side wall at floor level, allowing water to drain away.

Foundation

The foundation must be durable in structure, to last the duration of the greenhouse. Bricks and stone may be used. They have the best appearance but are the most expensive. Poured concrete makes a solid foundation and also looks well; cinderblock is easier to handle and less expensive. Different types of wood are used but they deteriorate in time and maintenance is high. The foundation should start $2\frac{1}{2}$ ft. or 3 ft. below ground level, and the thick-

Brick frames, covered with glass, make small greenhouses. (*Photo by Arnold Arboretum, Jamaica Plain, Mass.*)

ness of the wall can be 4 in. to 8 in. thick. In many cases the foundation wall is 30 in. high from ground level. Air vents that can be opened and closed depending upon the weather may be placed in the foundation every 10 ft. and 8 in. from floor level. These small air vents allow extra air circulation during warm days.

Greenhouse Structure

Today, almost all frames of the modern, small greenhouse are made from aluminum. They are light in weight, with good appearance, low maintenance, are available in all sizes and styles and are easy to assemble. For large greenhouse structures other materials such as galvanized steel, iron and wood are available and are being used.

The roof bar which supports the glass may be of aluminum if you are constructing an all-aluminum house. Should the frame be of steel or iron, wooden bars (Cypress or Redwood) should be used. In either case, it is recommended that aluminum bar-caps be used. These bar-caps keep the glass from slipping down and lower the maintenance cost of reglazing.

Today, there is controversy over the types of greenhouse covering to use. A few years ago all conventional greenhouse operators were using only glass. Recently experimental work has proved that clear fiberglass has an advantage over glass.

Fiberglass is cheaper to use in construction as it is nailed to the redwood frame (no glazing required). The light transmission is diffused, and less leaf burning is noticed, eliminating some of the shading required during the summer months. Fiberglass is also resistant to shock, and will not shatter during a hail storm. It has been found that the use of fiberglass aids in the flowering and fruiting of plants and trees that had not responded under glass conditions.

The disadvantage of fiberglass material for the small home greenhouse is that the material is obscure, and heavy condensation forms if the pitch of the house is not sufficient. Good air circulation and the inside treatment of the fiberglass with Zelec painted on or by sand-blasting will eliminate some of this condensation dripping.

Other materials that can be used are various polyethylene films which are inexpensive, but must be replaced often. Plexiglass has all the advantages of fiberglass plus being transparent. However, it is more costly.

Walks or Flooring

The location of your greenhouse will also determine the type of flooring of the greenhouse. If your greenhouse is attached to the house, flagstone or concrete are the best, as they are easily cleaned and provide a strong surface. The surface must have a crown so that surface water will run off, usually to under the bench where crushed gravel or stone is used. The gravel or stone provides good drainage for the floor water, plus the water dropping down from the bench.

Benches

Arrangement and number is determined by the size and shape of the greenhouse, and the type of plants being grown. The average width of the bench is usually 30–36 in. A wider bench will make it difficult to reach across to water or remove a plant. Allow at least 24–36 in. for walkway between benches. This allows room to bring into the greenhouse small equipment such as sprayers, carts, etc. The average height of a bench is usually 30 in. from the floor. In some cases a bench may not be needed, as tall tubbed plants may be placed on the floor. Benches are continually exposed to wet conditions which cause rapid deterioration. It is therefore wide to select materials which are resistant to decay, such as aluminum, transits, flat asbestos rock, and steel-angle iron. Cypress or Redwood may also be used, as they last longer under wet or damp conditions than some of the other woods. Benches may be constructed from a number of different kinds of material (note Figures 2 and 3).

Ventilation

All greenhouses need some type of ventilation to regulate and control temperature by releasing trapped hot air and replenishing the area with fresh air. Proper ventilation also helps control the humidity in the greenhouse. The conventional type of greenhouse has top and side ventilating apparatus designed for easy and fast operation. These vents may be operated either by hand or electric motor. The hand types are the cheapest and are dependable as long as someone is available to open and close the ventilators. The power-vent, with thermostatic control, is the best for the small home greenhouse, as it will usually operate, if properly adjusted, when no one is around. One of the features of the automatic ventilator is the modulating action. The vent modulates, that is, opens a little at a time depending on the inside greenhouse temperature to admit air gradually. When the temperature begins to drop, the vent automatically begins to close, thus maintaining the required temperature set by the thermostat dial. It is usually preferred (due to cost) to have a combination of both power- and hand-operating vents. The automatic ventilator eliminates guesswork involved in regulating the temperature in the greenhouse; it also saves time for the operator. It is wise to consider screens on the

FIG, 2

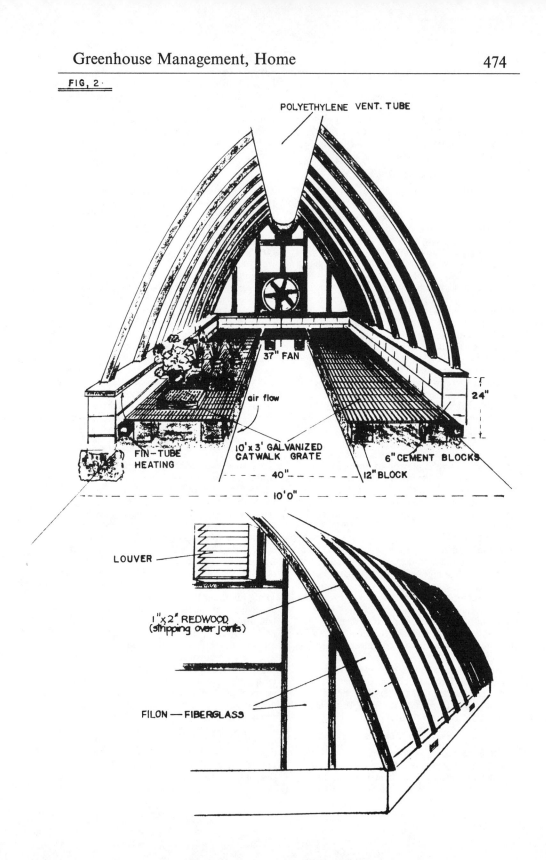

POLYETHYLENE VENT. TUBE

37" FAN

air flow

24"

FIN-TUBE HEATING

10' x 3' GALVANIZED CATWALK GRATE

6" CEMENT BLOCKS

40"

12" BLOCK

10'0"

LOUVER

1" x 2" REDWOOD (stripping over joints)

FILON — FIBERGLASS

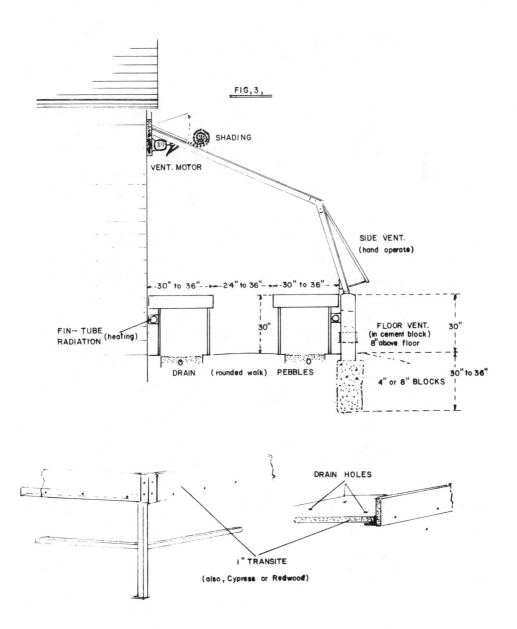

FIG, 3,

SHADING

VENT. MOTOR

SIDE VENT.
(hand operate)

-30" to 36"- -24" to 36"- -30" to 36"-

FIN— TUBE (heating)
RADIATION

30"

FLOOR VENT.   30"
(in cement block)
8" above floor

DRAIN   (rounded walk) PEBBLES

30" to 36"

4" or 8" BLOCKS

DRAIN HOLES

1" TRANSITE
(also, Cypress or Redwood)

ventilator and outside doors. The screens prevent insects, bees, birds and leaves from entering. In some types of greenhouse construction, especially the fiberglass one (note Figure 3), ventilation is accomplished by installing a large fan at one end of the house which, when turned on, brings in fresh air through a 20-in.-dia. polyethylene film tube. This tube is connected to each end of the greenhouse (note Figure 3), and has 3-in. holes every 3 ft. to allow the fresh air to enter while the fan is exhausting the existing air.

Heating

Some means of artificial heat must be provided to maintain the desired temperature during periods of cold weather. Talk to heating engineers who are experienced with heating problems; contact builders who are specialists in greenhouse construction. They will assist you in selecting the correct heating system. It may be possible with additional heating circulators to heat the greenhouse from the existing home boiler. There are different types of heat, such as the following:

Hot water—provides the most even heat and gives the best over-all results.

Hot air—very rapid, uneven, but is satisfactory for the small greenhouse.

Steam—not practical to maintain for small greenhouse, as it cools off too fast.

Space heater—many companies manufacture a type of heater for small areas which is ideal for small greenhouse and workrooms. They are usually a small compact unit that either can be placed on the floor or suspended from the wall. The unit usually comes assembled and wired and furnished with all necessary safety features including safety pilot. It is fully AGA approved for use with natural or bottled gas or it may be electric.

Consider the following before selecting a required heating system: (1) The size of the desired greenhouse and future plans for expansion; (2) The cost of the different types of installations; (3) Space available to erect or install the heating unit; (4) Safety factors. Gas fumes are harmful to plants and people. Consider installing an alarm system should your heating system fail.

If your heating system requires piping or coils, they are usually installed in a horizontal position along the side of the greenhouse under the bench. The aluminum fin tubing is considered the best for hot-water-pipe system as it will provide greater radiation and requires less space.

The greenhouse thermostat is often considered the homeowner's hired hand. The heating system, automatic ventilation and cooling system all depend on accurate control through the thermostat. The precision line-voltage thermostat provides temperature range from 35–100° F. and responds to a temperature differential of only 2° F. Select the best available type from your supplier. Install the thermostat in a protected area of the greenhouse, usually in the center away from the glass, shielded from the sun's rays.

Water

The locations of water faucets are usually below the bench adjacent to the walks and are dispersed as necessary throughout the greenhouse. The faucets should be the type with hose threads as the garden hose is the fastest method to water plants. Select a hose that is durable and pliable as they are usually awkward and clumsy to handle and store.

To obtain the best results from the watering system, install a mixing valve similar to the one used in the bathroom shower. The mixing of hot and cold water makes it possible to water plants with lukewarm water.

Shading the Greenhouse

During the summer months most greenhouses require some type of shading to protect the plants from the strong rays of the sun. Shading also provides a method of cooling the greenhouse during the hot season. To look the best and to obtain the best results, install lath or aluminum rollers on the outside top of the greenhouse. They are specially designed to allow 50% of the light through. The advantage of the roller type of shading over permanent shading is that on cloudy or dull days, they can be rolled up to allow additional light to enter.

Plastic shade cloth, a heavy-duty fabric woven from Saran, produces good shade for the greenhouse to the sash bar. This shade-cloth material usually is available in either green or natural color and produces 20% to 80% actual shade. For the growing of average tropical plants such as orchids, 50% shading is all that is required. The advantage of the Lumite material is that it is inexpensive, easy to install, light-weight, not affected by weather, and will last for years.

The cheapest effective method of shading is the use of shading compound, shading paste or even whitewash. These materials are usually applies to the outside glass when the glass is dry. The time of applying any type of shading depends upon the type of plants being grown and climatic conditions. When growing tropical plants, shade is usually applied during the month of March, whereas, flowering pot plants may not need shade until May or June.

Factors Which Influence Plant Growth

The fundamental factors which influence the

growth of plants are air, light, water, temperature, humidity, soils and nutrition. It is impossible to say which factor is more important. For best plant development they function together, but during the plant's life, at various periods, one of them may become a limiting factor.

Light affects the growth and flowering of plants in 2 ways: (1) The intensity of light during winter months is low and the rate of food manufactured in the plant is low. It is during this period that plants require less feed than in other months of the year. (2) The length of light during a day affects the time of flowering (photoperiodism). The short-day plants such as chrysanthemums, poinsettias, winter begonias, Kalanchoe, gardenias, and others, only require 11 hours of light to bloom. A long-day plant would require 14 hours of light or more. This would include such plants as Calceolaria, asters, tuberous begonias, hydrangeas and many of the annuals.

During the winter months, supplementing additional light by artificial means may be needed to bring the long-day plant into flower. The use of a combination of both the fluorescent and incandescent has proved satisfactory. Lamp-producing companies manufacture a wide-spectrum fluorescent lamp, which provides necessary effective rays to give the plant sufficient light to grow and produce flowers.

All plants require a sufficient amount of water in order to live, grow and produce flowers. For the best results, use water which is the same temperature as that of the greenhouse. Plants should be watered slowly through the use of a hose or watering can. At the time of application, apply a sufficient amount, using a water breaker to slow down the force of the water.

There is no satisfactory rule concerning when plants should be watered since many factors are involved. The appearance of the plant and soil may be used as a guide. Some growers are able to determine when a plant is dry by weight or lifting a plant. Others use the technique of tapping the side of the flower pot with the end of the hose, thus determining dryness by sound.

Through experience and knowing the plant requirements you will learn that some plants require more water than others. The time of the year and climatic conditions change the watering requirements. In summer months, with long bright days, watering may be needed twice a day, whereas, during winter months, only watering every other day may be necessary. The same conditions hold true for rainy and bright days. Certain plants go through a resting period during which they need less water than when they are actively growing. Good examples of this are the Poinsettia, Amaryllis, and Calla.

The morning hours are the best time of the day to water as it allows the foliage a chance to dry before night thus lessening the possibility of damping-off disease and rot. While watering plants, syringe foliage plants, and water down walks and benches. This practice of extra water builds up the humidity within the greenhouse which in turn helps the plants. The syringing of foliage plants with water during the hotter hours reduces the leaf temperature and transpiration, thus being beneficial. The water spray and force also clean the dirt and dust off the foliage and may wash away insects such as red spiders, aphids and scale. Syringing of greenhouse-grown azaleas, camellias and rhododendrons encourages growth and buds to develop early.

Good sanitation practice in a greenhouse is keeping it clean by removing dead leaves and flowers from the plants, removal of weeds, discarding old pots and flats from under the benches. Chemical materials under the trade names of GO 36-20 or Hyamine 3500, when mixed with water, will kill mosses and algae that appear on the outside surface of pots and walks. These materials when used properly will keep algae down for 4–6 months. The cleaner the greenhouse is kept the less disease problems will exist and the healthier the plants will be.

Work Area

Nearby or attached to the greenhouse, space should be provided for a work area—sometimes called a potting room or shed. This area could be in the garage, carport, tool shed, basement, or an extra small room in the house. This is where most of the physical work such as seed-sowing, potting, staking, etc. is carried out. This same room is the ideal place to store most of the potting materials, also insecticide materials, tools, extra flats, etc. This room should provide space to keep records of the experience of growing different kinds of plants. You will also find it interesting to keep records of the weather, temperature, spraying schedules and other data.

PLANTS THAT ARE NORMALLY GROWN WITH GREENHOUSE NIGHT TEMPERATURE OF 60°–65°

Abutilon	Cissus
Allamanda	Clerodendrum
Anthurium	Coleus
Banana	Costus
Begonia	Croton
Bougainvillea	Datura
Brassaia	Dieffenbachia
Bromeliads	Dracaena
Brunfelsia	Episcia
Calla	Eupatorium
Calathea	Ferns
Chlorophytum	Fittonia

Gardenia	Phalaenopsis
Gerbera	Palms
Heliotrope	Pandanus
Hibiscus	Pentas
Hoya	Peperomia
Ixora	Philodendron
Lilium	Poinsettia
Mandevilla hyb.	Pothos
'Alice duPont'	Pychnostachys
Medinilla	Roses
Orchids: Cattleya	Saintpaulia
(hybrids)	Smithiantha
Dendrobium	Streptosolen
Paphiopedilum	Tibouchina
(Cypripediums)	

April	Buddleia asiatica
	B. Hybrids
	Iboza riparia
May	Coleus thyrsoideus
	Pycnostachys dawei
July	Centaurea gymnocarpa
	Cytisus x racemosus (Genista)
	Piqueria trinervia (Stevia)
August	Bouvardia longiflora
	Pelargonium domesticum
	(Fancy-geranium)
	P. peltatum (Ivy-geranium)
September	Euphorbia pulcherrima
	(Poinsettia)
November	Calceolaria integrifolia
December	Fuschia hybrids

PLANTS THAT ARE NORMALLY GROWN WITH GREENHOUSE NIGHT TEMPERATURE OF 45°–50° F.

Acacia	Felicia
Agapanthus	Freesia
Ageratum	Fuchsia
Alstroemeria	Geranium
Amaryllis	Gloxinia
Anemone	Hydrangea
Aquilegia	Iris
Aster	Myosotis
Astilbe	Nemesia
Azalea	Nierembergia
Begonia	Orchids—Cymbidium
semperflorens	Pansy
Browallia	Primula kewensis
Buddleia	P. malacoides
Calceolaria	P. obconica
Callistemon	P. stellata
(bottle brush)	Ranunculus asiaticus
Camellia	Salpiglossis sinuata
Carnation	Schizanthus
Campanula	Senecio cineraria
Celosia	(Dusty Miller)
Chasmanthium	Stock
roseus	Solanum
Cineraria	Snapdragon
Chrysanthemum	Strelitzia reginae
Clarkia	Sweet Pea
Cyclamen	Wallflower
Delphinium	

FOR GREENHOUSE FLOWERING POT PLANT
DATES FOR MAKING CUTTINGS

PLANT NAME

January	Chrysanthemum morifolium cv. (for cascade and hanging baskets)
February	Centaurea gymnocarpa (Dusty Miller)
	Dianthus caryophyllus (carnation)
	Lantana camara
	Streptosolen jamesonii
March	Coleus blumei
	Pentas lanceolata

Selected Plants and their Cultural Requirements

AFRICAN VIOLETS—*Saintpaulia.* Growing African violets can be a rewarding or a frustrating hobby. There are as many theories on their culture as there are growers. Practices which produce results for one may fail completely for another. In some cases we might say that they grow in spite of the treatment they receive rather than because of it.

These members of the Gesneriad Family (which includes florists' gloxinias, smithianthas, episcias and achimenes) are native in parts of Africa where atmospheric humidity is high.

The cultivated African violet is botanically *S. ionantha.* Numberless cultivated varieties have been developed by selection and hybridization. As a result there are single, double and semidouble flowered varieties in white, pink, blue and purple as well as some having variegated blooms. There are many "strains" having definite leaf characteristics—some have rounded leaves, others are elliptical, some have relatively smooth edges while others are deeply scalloped. Some strains bloom more profusely than others.

The native habitat of the African violet indicates that, while it thrives best in good light, it does not enjoy prolonged exposure to full sun. If it is necessary, sunlight can be filtered through a slatted shade during morning hours

A good soil mixture is: 1 part top soil, 1 part sand, 1 part peat moss or leaf mold. Whether preparing your own mixture or using ready mixed soil, it is well to sterilize it before using, to destroy possible nematodes and other organisms which could interfere with plant growth. This can be done by dampening the soil slightly and placing it in the oven for 45 minutes at 180° F. A longer period or higher temperature can cause undesirable chemical changes.

One of the most serious offenses to African violets is committed in watering. Do not water every day; soak the plant *thoroughly* and then

SEED SOWING DATES OF GREENHOUSE FLOWERING POT-PLANTS

CROP	DATE SEED SOWN	FLOWERING DATE	GREENHOUSE TEMPERATURE
Begonia (Fibrous rooted)	Aug. 1–15	Christmas	60°
Begonia (Tuberous)	Jan. 1	June	55°
Calceolaria	Oct. 15	April	45°–50°
Solanum (Jerusalem-Cherry)	March 1	Christmas	45°–50°
Cineraria	Sept. 1	March/April	45°–50°
Clarkia elegans	Jan./Feb.		45°–50°
Cyclamen	Oct. 1	a year later	45°–50°
Gerbera	Jan.	a year later	60°
Gloxinia	June 1	Christmas	60°
Kalanchoe	March 1	Christmas	60°
Marigold	Jan.	May	45°–50°
Nemesia strumosa	Aug.	March	45°–50°
Petunia	Feb.	May	45°–50°
Primula malacoides	May	Jan.	45°–50°
P. kewensis	May	Jan.	45°–50°
P. sinensis	May	Jan.	45°–50°
P. obconica	April	Jan.	45°–50°
Schizanthus	Aug.	March	45°–50°
Stock	Aug.	April	45°–50°
Sweet Pea	July	Wintertime	45°–50°

allow the soil to become almost dry on the surface before watering again. If the plant is watered from the bottom, set the pot in a basin of water (room temperature) and leave it until the surface of the soil is moist. Top watering will do no harm if the leaves are not allowed to remain wet and plants are not exposed to direct sunlight when leaves are moist. Do not water late in the day when the temperature may drop before the leaves have dried.

Cut off flower stems when flowers have dropped. Most double-flowering varieties do not drop their flowers. Snip them off when they begin to fade.

A once-a-month application of a liquid house-plant fertilizer in water will be helpful after plants have been growing for a time. It is not advisable to fertilize newly transplanted specimens until they have established a root system which can utilize it.

If plants have reached blooming size and have not put forth flowers, they can sometimes be brought into bloom by pinching the tiny new leaves from the crown of the plant. Also, they can sometimes be shocked into bloom by being allowed to dry out completely, but not to the extent of wilting, before water is again applied.

Growth and flowering will be poor if night temperatures fall below 60°.

African violets can be easily propagated by leaf cuttings. Every grower has his favorite method. A fairly reliable one is to insert the leaf petiole about 1 in. in sand. Keep the sand moist but not saturated until a small plantlet with good roots is formed. The original leaf can then be snipped off and the plantlet transplanted in a 2-in. pot with the proper soil mixture. As the plant grows it should be transferred gradually to larger containers.

BEGONIA—Christmas-flowering Begonias (*Begonia* x *cheimantha*). Christmas-flowering begonias are propagated during Nov. and Dec. Cuttings should be made from medium-sized well-ripened leaves. The petioles are inserted in sand, and the greenhouse temperature set at 70°. Rooting takes 4–5 weeks, but defer potting until new shoots begin to develop from the base. When potting, place the crown of the cutting as near the surface as possible, and use a soil mixture of sand, peat moss and leaf mold. For plants to flower by Christmas they should be in 4-in. pots by June, 6-in. to 7-in. pots in Sept., depending on the size of the plant. For the potting of these advanced plants use the following soil mixture: 3 parts soil, 2 parts manure (well rotted), 1 part peat moss and 1 part sand.

During the summer months a humid atmosphere and partial shade is required. Pinching the plants until Sept. will give a nice bushy plant, and the plants should be staked as the stems are very brittle. A good plan for staking is to secure 4 stakes in the pot, close to the rim, around the outer part of the plant, attaching string around the 4 stakes. Use a weekly spray schedule of Captan to control fungus disease.

BEGONIA—Tuberous (*Begonia* x *tuber-hybrida*). Soil-growing mixture: 3 parts soil, 2 parts rotted cow manure, 2 parts peat and 1 part sand makes a good soil medium for the growing of begonias. When growing from seed (starting late Nov.–Dec.) they need about the same culture as the Fibrous Begonia except as the plant growth progresses, the pot transfer should be kept up until it reaches 6-in. to 7-in. pots. To start the corms in Feb., first place in flats in a mixture of sand and peat, keeping moist, and keep them in a temperature of 70–75° day, 65° night. When the shoots appear and a heavy root system has developed, the plants are potted in pots, size varying and depending on the size of the corm. Plants should be staked with light wooden or wire stakes. Tuberous begonias flower from June to Sept. They can also be grown and flowered during the winter months with the aid of additional light; they require a 14-hour day to produce flowers.

CAMELLIA JAPONICA. Greenhouse camellias grow best at temperatures of 50–55° day and 45° night (during winter months). A light soil such as 1 part soil, 1 part German Peat, and 1 part sand is needed. The pH of the soil should be between 5.5 and 6.

If pruning is necessary, it should be done after the flowering period. The terminal bud can be pinched out during the late fall. This is a good method of pruning and keeps the plant compact. The latter part of Jan. through April is the flowering period for most camellia varieties, and after the flowering period the plants starts to grow. It is during this period of time that the plant needs an abundance of water for growth. Three feedings at 10-day intervals with a liquid fertilizer is good. One of the worst pests that appears on the stems when the plant is growing is cale. Spraying with Volck oil spray or malathion during the time the scales are active, throughout the summer months, will control this pest.

Camellias may be propagated by cutting, grafting, or layering. The most popular method is by cuttings. Cuttings from mature wood should be taken between Aug. 15th and Feb. 15th—placed in sand with bottom heat of 72°. If cuttings are treated with Rootone or Hormodin, roots will develop in 60–100 days. When rooted, cuttings should be placed in pots with mixture of equal parts of soil, peat and sand. If camellias are kept in greenhouse beds during the summer, give as much ventilation as possible, with partial shading. They do very nicely outside during the summer, plunging the pot or tube in ground in lath house or under the shade of large trees. Bud drop is caused by lack of sufficient humidity, dry or wet soil at the roots, or too wide a fluctuation of temperature. Camellias in the greenhouse may be transplanted or retubbed during the winter months.

CHRYSANTHEMUMS. The greenhouse chrysanthemums grow best at temperatures 45° to 50° F. at night and 60° to 70° during the day. A soil mixture of ½ soil, ¼ peat, and ¼ perlite makes a good light mixture. A pH of 5.5 to 7.5 is required. Soil and pots must be sterilized to obtain the best besults.

Plants are propagated by cuttings. The cuttings are taken from shoots that grow from the crown of plants that have been carried through the winter. These cuttings should be 2 or 3 inches long and inserted in sand. The lower leaves are removed, while the remaining upper leaves are usually just trimmed. When well rooted, place in 2–2½-in. pots in a very light soil mixture.

Chrysanthemums are pinched until the end of August to obtain a good compact plant. Some varieties are disbudded while others are not. Disbudding produces a large flower. There are over 300 cultivars of greenhouse chrysanthemums which can be selected from a catalogue, including the early, midseason or late varieties. There are many colors to meet the required flowering period.

The single-stemmed type, which is the very large-flowered type, should be staked with one stake reaching the height of the stem about 3 in. under the bottom of the flower. Strings should be placed, as the plant grows, approximately every 6–8 in. apart.

Chrysanthemums require a regular spray program. Spray once a week with a mixture of 1 oz. of Ferbam and 3 oz. Supercide to 3 gal. of water. The Supercide keeps aphids and other insects under control; the Ferbam is a fungicide spray.

CYCLAMEN. When growing cyclamen from seed, allow 18 months from germination to flowering. The seed should be sown Aug. to Nov. in a mixture of equal parts soil, sand and peat or leaf mold. Steam-sterilize all flats or pots before using. If seed is sown in flats they should be placed 1 in. apart and, if placed in a temperature of 55° F. to 60° F., germination will take place in 4–8 weeks. The plants are ready for transplanting after 2 or 3 leaves have developed, and should be transferred to 2½-in. pots. Do not allow the plants to become too pot-bound before changing to larger pots; by July they should be ready for 5-in. or 6-in. pots. When potting, the tuber should be elevated so the top is always above the surface of the soil. If planted too deep, crown rot is induced.

Cyclamen responds best in a soil composed of 2 parts soil, 1 part sand, 1 part peat, and 1 part well-rotted manure or leaf mold. They are very sensitive to moisture conditions and will not thrive if allowed to dry out or if water stands around the roots. A moist atmosphere and night temperature of 50° F. are beneficial. Best growth results from proper shading April 15 to Sept. 15, with the maximum intensity of light being 4000 ft. candles, about ⅓ that received on bright days in summer. Excessive shading causes long thin petioles, too much light produces dried spots in the leaves. All flowers should be removed from the plants until Oct. to permit more leaves to develop. Some diseases and pests of cyclamen include:

Leafspot—brown-to-black circular spots appear. This can be controlled by the use of Fermate, Ferbam or Zineb.

Soft rot—stems become soft and watery, wilt, and die. This is usually caused by over-watering.

Red spider, aphids, thrips and mites bother the cyclamen. The mite causes leaves and flowers to curl, while the thrips cause a scabby condition on the underside of the foliage and streaks the flowers. A good syringing of the leaves on both side several times a week will eliminate the red spider, but if they persist, spray with Kelthane. Malathion will control the other pests.

FERNS: Ferns, flowerless plants, are raised for their gracefulness and beauty of foliage.

The propagation of ferns can be done by division, by the buds or offsets that form on the fronds of some types, and by means of spores (or fern "seeds"). The spores are borne in the brownish marks on the back of the frond or leaf, oftentimes mistaken for bugs. When ripe, these spores may be shaken off onto paper, or parts of the frond may be cut, placed in paper bags and stored in a dry place until the spores shed. The best time to sow the spores is in the spring, although it can be done any time during the year. They should be sown on the surface of a moist, sterilized, light sandy soil mixed with sterile peat, and placed in a temperature of 65° F. to 70° F. They should not be covered with soil or watered on the top. It takes about 8 to 12 weeks to develop true fronds from spores. When the first regular foliage appears the sporelings should be taken out, usually at first in small clumps and transplanted. The *Adiantum cuneatum* or Maidenhair Fern, is started by crown division, while the *Nephrolepis exaltata* var. *bostoniensis*, commonly known as the Boston Fern, is propagated by the side shoots or runners.

In all fern culture humidity as well as heat, is essential. It is best never to use bottom heat under ferns. During the summer months shade should be provided. Do not fail to spray frequently but never allow pots to stand in water, ample drainage in the bottom of the pot is important. Browning of the fronds is most often caused by over-watering or too dry an atmosphere.

Fuchsia x *hybrida*. The fuchsia, a native of South America, is an old-time favorite. The flowers are usually pendulous, in shades of red and purple and with some parts often white. They should be grown rather on the dry side, at a temperature of 55° F.–60° F. The fuchsia has a 1-month resting period in the late summer. If old plants are kept, they should be taken out of the pots in Sept., cut back and repotted in a medium soil. If young plants are desired, cuttings can be taken in Nov. These cuttings may be rooted in a flat using a mixture of sand and peat, in a temperature of 68° F.–75° F. Three plants placed in 6-in. or 7-in. pans in Jan. should be in flower by May 15th. Cuttings taken in Feb. will produce plants which will flower in 4-in. pots.

With the exception of aphids, fuchsias are not bothered by many of the other pests. These can be controlled with spray or fumigating the house with Plant Fume 103 smoke bombs.

GLOXINIAS. The recommended temperature for the growing of gloxinias is day: 65° to 75° F., night: 45° to 50° F. A soil mixture of 1 part soil, 1 part sand, and 1 part peat or compost is ideal. Plant tubers concave side up, only deep enough to scarcely cover the top surface. Keep the soil moist but not continually wet. A good method of starting is to have the soil moist when planting and cover with polyethylene to hold moisture until sprouts appear. If more than 1 sprout develops on a tuber, remove all but the strongest. Place in a sunny part of the greenhouse as soon as growth starts, but it may be necessary to screen out direct sun with some shade during the hottest part of the day. Lack of sufficient light will cause plants to grow tall and leggy. Wash leaves occasionally by holding them under water. Allow to dry in a shady place before returning to sunny location. Water early in the day so that leaves and buds do not remain wet over night. When buds have formed they may blast because of insects or because of too much water. Browning toward the leaf edges and buds failing to open may also be due to lack of humidity. Keep pots on a bench of wet pebbles to keep humidity rising around the plants. Use a balanced water-soluble fertilizer once a month. When plants stop blooming, gradually withhold water until they die down. (This does not mean that watering should cease entirely.) Remove the tops and store the pots in a cool, dark place (55°–65° F.). Add some water occasionally so that tubers do not shrivel. Repot in Feb. or March before starting into growth after resting period of about 6 months. Many gloxinias are received as gift plants and will react to the sudden change from greenhouse conditions to the lower humidity and higher temperatures of the average home. If insects appear, use a houseplant aerosol according to directions on the container. New plants can be started from leaf cuttings in sand as with African violets. Plants thus started may or may not produce tubers before leaves appear.

PRIMROSES. Primrose plants prefer a temperature of 55° to 65° F. during the day and 45° to 50° F. at night. They also grow best in a light soil, ¼ soil, ¼ peat, ¼ leaf mold, and ¼ sand or perlite. It has been the experience of some growers that a Primula once checked in growth, usually by over- or under-watering, may as well be discarded.

P. malacoides. Very susceptible to dampness, therefore should not be kept too wet. The foliage should never be wet and when watering be sure to water under the leaves. During a damp spell it is advisable to use a fan in the greenhouse to keep the air as dry as possible. For the control of aphids and green fly, use Plant Fume 103 which is a safe fumigant.

P. sinensis. Requires about the same treatment as *P. malacoides.* By planting the seed May 1st, the plant should flower for Christmas. For the best results this variety should be growing in a 5-in. pot at time of flowering.

P. obconica. This seed should be sown by April 1st, in order to have flowering plants by Christmas. The seed is very fine and should be handled very carefully. It is very difficult to germinate the seed during hot weather. It is also advisable to provide light shade during the summertime if these plants are left to grow in the greenhouse. Yellowing of the foliage is one of the most common ailments; it is usually traced to too-acid or poorly drained soil. The handling of this plant has caused a rash on the hands. Washing the affected area with hot water with a teaspoonful of Epsom Salt seems to help.

Tropical Foliage Plants

With a few exceptions, tropical plants do not require being potted as firmly as those plants grown in cooler temperatures. Early spring is usually the best time of the year to carry out this work. When training a plant, never tie it so tightly that the stem cannot grow thicker or taller without damage. Tie the plant loosely and secure the knot on the stake and not on the stem. Hawaiian Treen Fern trunk is excellent material for totem poles on which to train plants.

Most tropical plants prefer a thorough watering. Tropical plants prefer high humidity, especially on bright days and at night. Syringing or overhead watering is beneficial to the plants and they will respond to this treatment. A minimum night temperature of 60° F. is required. High summer temperatures are not harmful providing the relative humidity is kept high and air is kept moving. Shading is necessary from March until Oct.

EVERITT L. MILLER

GREEN MANURE. One of the best means of adding humus to the soil is to grow quick-growing succulent crops like Rape, Mustard, Italian Rye, Buckwheat, Cow Peas, Winter Rye and the vetches as well as Clover. The material used varies in the different areas of the country but when they are ½–¾ grown and while still succulent, they are plowed under to rot and form humus. See HUMUS, SOILS.

GREENTHREAD, BURRIDGE = *Thelesperma burridgeanum*

GREVILLEA (grev-ILL-ea)
  robusta   150′   Zone 10   Silk-oak Grevillea
Often grown in the greenhouse in pots merely as a decorative pot plant, this native from Australia has considerable merit as a specimen and street tree in southern Calif. because it grows well in both rich and poor sandy soils, but the branches are very brittle. The golden-yellow flowers appear in April in graceful racemes 4 in. long. The alternate leaves are of very fine texture, twice compound and make this a very graceful pot plant for greenhouse culture.

GREWIA (GROO-ya)
  biloba   8′   Zone 7
A rare deciduous shrub from Formosa belonging to the Linden Family, not of ornamental value for planting in the U.S. Propagation—seed sown as soon as ripe or stored dry in air-tight containers in a cool place for up to a year and then sown.

GRINDELIA (grin-DEE-lia)
  lanceolata   4′   Zone 6   Gumweed
Of little horticultural interest and restricted to the warmer areas of the U.S., this plant has alternate, lanceolate leaves, the toothed margins of which are armed with spines. The terminal involucre has numerous spreading leaflets within which are clustered the yellow disk and ray flowers. Both leaves and flower heads are sticky. This biennial grows in dry grasslands in the mid-South and Midwest.

GRISELINIA (gris-el-IN-ia)
  littoralis   50′   Zone 9   Kupukatree
Evergreen leaves alternate and glossy, 4 in. long, and flowering panicles 3 in. long. The fruit is a berry. Native to New Zealand.
  lucida   30′   Zone 9
A handsome evergreen shrub, sometimes epiphetic with aerial rootlets, the leaves leathery, fleshy and shining, about 4–8 in. long edged with white, and unequal at the base, with minute dioecious flowers in axillary clusters about 6 in. long. The fruit is a berry. Native to New Zealand.

GROMWELL, HOARY = *Lithospermum canescens*

GROUND-CEDAR = *Lycopodium complanatum*

GROUND-CHERRY. See PHYSALIS.

GROUND COVERS. There are many plants that can be used as ground covers, and because of this, one should carefully examine the reasons why a ground cover is desired so that the best possible plant for the purpose may be selected. There is no better ground cover than lawn grass if it must be walked on continually. True, it does take care, and there are plants that cover the ground satisfactorily which do not take as much care as lawn grass, but these can not be walked on or played on as well as grass. There are places on the home grounds where lawn grass is not needed or desired, and then the ground covers can be utilized.

One should determine in advance how high in growth the ground covers are desired, for there are some only an inch or so tall, others 6–12 in. tall and others that grow taller. Also, since there are many from which to choose, one should note whether the spot is in the shade or sun, in moist soil or dry soil, since some would grow better in one place than another.

Preparing the soil for a ground-cover planting would be very similar to that for preparing soil for a lawn (which see) except that the deeper the good soil the better the plants will grow.

Spacing depends on the type of plant selected. For instance, some such as *Euonymus fortunei* 'Coloratus' will increase so rapidly that one small plant may cover several square feet of ground in 2 years time, while others like the European Ginger (*Asarum europaeum*) will increase very, very slowly and so might well be spaced less than a foot apart. If one desires a quick cover, like in a spot near the house or in a conspicuous place in the garden, then spacing might be close. On the other hand, if a wide area is to be planted, and initial cost is a consideration, then one might plant farther apart (which would take fewer plants) and wait a longer period for the plants to eventually grow together and make a complete cover.

Mulching (which see) is especially important in the new planting of a ground cover, for the objective should be to keep the soil moist so that runners or stems growing on the surface would find moist soil in which to take root and thus form new plants as speedily as possible. This can be a slow process in soils that continually dry out, so an effective mulch that is not more than an inch or two deep, is essential in obtaining a good cover. During the first 2 growing seasons the plants should be watered enough to prevent them drying out at any time.

Heaving (which see) of young plants is a hazard in early spring. Mulching prevents this to some extent, but if young plants are forced out of the ground by the alternate thawing and freezing of the soil, they should be carefully replanted as soon as this takes place to prevent the roots from drying.

One should not be remiss in aiding the establishing of new plants, by digging some of the runners into the soil, or placing a spadeful of soil on top of a procumbent branch to quicken its rooting. Even pegging such branches firmly into the soil proves helpful, especially in those areas where large spaces are left between the original plants.

The ground cover might well be fertilized in the spring with 20–40 lbs. of 5-10-5 complete fertilizer (or some similar type) per 1000 sq. ft. This could be spread broadcast, uniformly over the foliage and watered in thoroughly immediately, to prevent any burning of foliage that might otherwise take place if the leaves are wet at the time of application.

The following are some of the ground covers most often used, but remember that all will not grow well in all situations. *Pachysandra terminalis* must be grown in the shade; Ribbon Grass should be grown in very poor, dry soil where it will not grow out of bounds. The Memorial Rose should not be walked on; thymes and sedums are excellent for planting between stepping stones; the echeverias are only used as ground covers in the warmest parts of southern Calif. There are enough possibilities in the following list to provide a good ground cover for almost any situation in the garden:

SOME GOOD GROUND COVERS

	HEIGHT	ZONE	
Acaena	$\frac{1}{2}''$–3″	6–7	Sheepburr
Achillea tomentosa	6″–12″	2	Woolly Yarrow
Aegopodium podagraria	6″–14″	3	Goutweed
Aloe sp.	3″–12″	9	Aloes
Ajuga reptans	4″–12″	4	Bugle-weed
Akebia quinata	vine	4	Fiveleaf Akebia
Antennaria sp.	1″	2–4	Pussytoes
Anthemis nobilis	1′	4	Roman Camomile
Arctostaphylos uva-ursi	6″–12″	2	Bearberry

	HEIGHT	ZONE	
Aronia melanocarpa	1'–3'	4	Black Chokeberry
Artemisia stelleriana	2½'	2	Beach Wormwood
Asarum caudatum	7"	4	British Columbia Wild Ginger
A. europaeum	5"	4	European Wild Ginger
Asperula odorata	8"	2–3	Sweet Woodruff
Bergenia crassifolia	20"	2–3	Leather Bergenia
Calluna vulgaris	4"–24"	4	Scotch Heather
Cerastium tomentosum	3"–6"	2	Snow-in-summer
Comptonia peregrina	4'	2	Sweet-fern
Convallaria majalis	8"	2	Lily-of-the-valley
Cornus canadensis	9"	2	Bunchberry
Coronilla varia	1'–2'	3	Crown Vetch
Cotoneaster adpressa	1'–2'	4	Creeping Cotoneaster
C. dammeri	6"–12"	5	Bearberry Cotoneaster
C. horizontalis	1½'–3'	4	Rock Spray
Cotula squalida	4"	8	New Zealand Brassbuttons
Crassula sp.	2"–12"	9–10	Stonecrops
Cytisus decumbens	8"	5	Prostrate Broom
Dianthus gratianopolitanus	4"	3	Cheddar Pink
Dichondra repens	3"	10	Dichondra
Duchesnea indica	2"	5	Mock-strawberry
Echeveria sp.	2"–12"	8–10	Echeverias
Epimedium grandiflorum	9"	3	Long-spur Epimedium
Erica carnea	6"–12"	5	Spring Heath
Euonymus fortunei vars.	vines	5	Wintercreeper
Forsythia x 'Arnold Dwarf'	3'	5	
Fragaria chiloensis	6"	4–5	Chiloe Strawberry
Galax urceolata	6"	3	Galax
Gaultheria shallon	2'–5'	5	Salal, Shallon
Gaylussacia brachycera	18"	5	Box Huckleberry
Genista pilosa	6"–12"	5	Silky Woadwaxen
Glechoma hederacea	3"	3	Ground-ivy
Gypsophila repens rosea	6"	2–3	Rosy Creeping Gypsophila
Hedera helix	vine	5	English Ivy
Hosta sp.	1'–3'	2–3	Plantain-lily
Hydrangea anomala petiolaris	vine	4	Climbing Hydrangea
Hypericum calycinum	1'	6	Aaronsbeard St. Johnswort
Indigofera incarnata alba	1½'	5	White Chinese Indigo
Juniperus chinensis sargentii	1'	4	Sargent Juniper
J. conferta	1'	5	Shore Juniper
J. horizontalis and vars.	1'–1½'	2	Creeping Juniper
Kalanchoe sp.	1'–3'	9	Kalanchoe
Lantana montevidensis	2'	10	Trailing Lantana
Liriope sp.	8"–24"	4–7	Lily-turf
Lonicera henryi	vine	4	Henry Honeysuckle
L. japonica 'Halliana'	vine	5	Hall's Honeysuckle
Lotus berthelotii	2'	10	Coral Gem
L. corniculatus	2'	3	Trefoil
Mahonia repens	10"	5	Creeping Mahonia
Mesembryanthemum sp.	3"–6"	10	Ice-plants
Mitchella repens	2"	3	Partridge-berry
Pachysandra procumbens	6"–12"	4	Alleghany Pachysandra
P. terminalis	6"	4	Japanese Pachysandra
Pernettya mucronata	1½'	6–7	Chilean Pernettya
Phalaris arundinacea picta	2'–4'	3	Ribbon-grass
Phlox subulata	6"	2–3	Moss-pink
Polygonum sp.	4"–24"	3–7	Fleece-flowers
Potentilla tridentata	2"–12"	2	Wineleaf Cinquefoil

	HEIGHT	ZONE	
Prunella vulgaris	3"	3	Self-heal
Pueraria lobata	vine	6	Kudzu Vine
Rhus aromatica	3'	3	Fragrant Sumac
Rosa wichuraiana	1'	5	Memorial Rose
Rosmarinus officinalis 'Prostratus'	1'	8	Prostrate Rosemary
Sasa sp.	1'–2'	6	Ground Bamboos
Sedum sp.	2"–12"	3–10	Stonecrops
Sempervivum sp.	4"–12"	4–5	Houseleeks
Teucrium chamaedrys	10"	5	Chamaedrys Germander
Thymus sp.	1"–8"	3–4	Thyme
Tiarella cordifolia	6"–12"	4	Alleghany Foam-flower
Vaccinium sp.	8"–18"	2–5	Blueberries
Vancouveria hexandra	18"	5	American Barrenwort
Veronica sp.	4"–12"	2–5	Speedwells
Vinca minor	6"	4	Periwinkle
Wedelia trilobata	creeping	10	—
Xanthorhiza simplicissima	2'	4	Yellow-root

GROUND-IVY. See GLECHOMA.

GROUNDNUT = *Apios americana*

GROUND-PINE = *Lycopodium obscurum*

GROUND-PINK. See PHLOX.

GROUNDSEL. See SENECIO.

GROUNDSEL-BUSH = *Baccharis halimifolia*

GROWTH RINGS. These are the annual layers of cells grown by the cambium tissue immediately under the bark of a tree or shrub. A ring of cells laid down in one year is so clearly defined on most normal trees that one can tell the age of the tree merely by counting the number of rings on the stump (in cross-section) when the tree has been sawed down. The size or width of this ring varies with the age of the tree, the kind of tree, the soil, elevation and amount of available moisture. For instance, a young, vigorous tree like a poplar may produce a ring $\frac{1}{2}$ in. wide, but as it grows older the rings get progressively smaller as disease and other problems gradually decrease its rate of growth. A small willow growing within the Arctic Circle may make a ring $\frac{1}{32}$ in. wide or even less, because growth conditions are poor and the number of growing days are limited. A study of the growth rings on giant Redwood trees is interesting because the width of the ring clearly shows the dry seasons (with narrow rings) or seasons of high rainfall with wide annual rings. Trees at high altitudes or in poor soils produce rings more narrow than those trees in the valleys or in good soils.

GUAIACUM (GWY-ak-um)
  officinale   30'   Zone 10   Common Lignum-
                                              vitae
One of the toughest of all woods with many uses because it is one of the heaviest there is, a cubic foot weighing 76 lbs. Bowling balls, pestles, pulleys, even bearings are made from this extremely tough wood. The tree is native to tropical and subtropical America. As an ornamental it is an evergreen and so is used in the gardens of the Tropics. The flowers are a rich blue when they first open, with 5 petals, gradually fading white, $\frac{1}{2}$ in. across. The fruit is yellow, about $\frac{3}{4}$ in. long, heart shaped, pointed at the base. Trees are about 10 in. in dia.

GUANO. An organic fertilizer, actually the excrement of sea birds, formerly shipped into this country from Chile and other countries, but now extremely scarce as well as expensive, containing 10–14% nitrogen, 8–10% phosphoric acid, 2.4% potash. This is very strong and should be used with care. See SOILS.

GUAVA. The common Guava (*Psidium littorale longipes*) and Strawberry Guava (*P. cattleianum*) are most commonly found in the United States, but specimens of the Brazilian (*P. guineense*) and Costa Rican (*P. friedrichsthalianum*) guavas occur in Fla., with a closely related species, the Para Guava (*Britoa acida*). An unrelated fruit, the Feijoa or Pineapple Guava (*Feijoa sellowiana*) is also popular. None are grown commercially in the continental U.S.

The common and the less well known true guavas are most tender to cold, being badly injured at temperatures below 28° F. The Cattley Guava will withstand temperatures to 22° F. Both will sprout readily from the roots if killed back. The Feijoa is most hardy, withstanding temperatures as low as 15° F. The common Guava can be grown in the warmest parts of the Fla. peninsula. In all but protected sites along the Pacific South Coast summer temperatures are too low, as the plant declines and eventually dies where summer temperatures fall below 60°

F. The Cattley Guava prefers a warm situation but is more tolerant to cool summers; the Feijoa does well in warm to hot sites, but will also grow and fruit well in areas with cool summers, as the central Pacific Coast.

All of these species do well on a variety of soils, preferring a good loamy one, well drained. Their nutritional needs are not exacting, but they generally respond to nitrogen with lusher growth. All should be supplied with water during the period of fruit development, but will pass through a dry period without harm.

The common Guava is a rapid growing tree, which needs little training or pruning. It naturally assumes the habit of a large bush, but may easily be trained as a tree; spacing should be 15–25 ft. depending on soil fertility and climate. They are most easily propagated by sprouts from roots cut about 2 ft. from the trunk of the mother plant; other methods of propagation, such as cuttings, budding or grafting to seedlings give poor results, but are occasionally successful. Seedlings are easily grown from seed planted freshly from the fruit; seedlings vary greatly in quality, some being acid, some sweet, and most inferior in texture, size and flavor.

This Guava blooms in April in Fla., but as late as midsummer in coastal Calif. The rather showy flowers are borne laterally on the shoots in clusters of 2 or 3. In the warm areas of its range, where the fruit is ripe in about 3 months, it may bear a second crop. Fruits average about 2–3 in. in dia., and are roughly round in shape. The color varies from white or yellow through pink or red. The fruit is used mainly for jellies; sweet fruits may need an acid fruit juice added, or some acid guavas incorporated to aid jelling. It is known for its high vitamin C content. 'Supreme', 'Red Indian' and 'Ruby' varieties are grown in Fla.

Cattley guavas naturally grow as small shrubs, up to 10 ft. tall and with equal spread but can be trained to small trees or reduced to a hedge. As it reproduces nearly true from seed horticultural varieties are not known. A red and a yellow form are grown. The fruit is considerably smaller than the common Guava, averaging from 1–1½ in. long. The flavor is more musky, and less desirable than the better kinds of the common Guava. The main use is in jellies.

True guavas are attacked by mites; the fruits are subject to larva damage, and in the humid Southeast algae may develop on the leaves and fruit. These are seldom serious enough to need control measures.

The Feijoa is a very ornamental plant; it may grow as a rather large bush or is easily trained to a small tree. It is naturally round-headed to spreading in either form. The leaves are bluish above, and covered with a light grayish tomentum below. The flowers open in late spring, April in Fla. to June in cool coastal areas of Calif., are rather large and attractive with thick whitish petals tinged purplish below (fleshy and edible, used in salads) and long, showy, crimson stamens. The fruit ripens in Aug. to Sept. in Fla., and as late as Oct. or Nov. in Calif.

Superior clones are preferred, but are difficult and slow to reproduce. Air layering is a reasonably sure method; leafy cuttings with the use of rooting hormones, and grafting on seedlings are both successful in a low percentage of cases. For these reasons seedlings are often grown, which are not greatly inferior to the selected clones, but usually are smaller in fruit. The fruit is 2–3 in. long, oval, with persistent calyx lobes; it is gray-green at maturity. The flesh is thin, and the cavity filled with a gelatinous part containing the seeds. All but the thin skin and seeds is eaten.

Clones of Feijoa are 'Andre', 'Choiceana', 'Superba', and 'Bliss'. All, except an inferior-quality clone named 'Coolidge', are more or less self unfruitful, so that 2 varieties, or a variety and a seedling or two should be grown near each other.

A full-sized Feijoa tree may occupy a space 20 ft. x 20 ft., but the dimensions may be kept half that by pruning; by planting close and clipping it may be trained as a hedge. The Feijoa is practically free of insect pests and diseases.

CLARON O. HESSE

Insect Pests

Many scale insects are known to infest guava. In Fla. many of them are kept in check by parasitic insects and fungi. Citrus mealy bug and pyriform scale are among the most destructive. Regular spraying with insecticide #15 or #13 with or without insecticide #45 gives control. White fly and thrips are frequently so abundant that sprays as for scale are needed. Mediterranean fruit fly and Mexican fruit fly infest guava fruits and should be reported to local authorities immediately.

Diseases

Glomerella fruit spot or ripe rot is generally distributed and frequent sprays with fungicide #G are needed for control. Black mildew on foliage is objectionable but sprays as for fruit spot are effective. Canker on the branches causes dieback and requires prompt and careful pruning followed by wound disinfectants.

Gunnera chilensis sometimes bears leaves 7 ft. across.

GUAVA. See PSIDIUM.

GUAVA FAMILY = Myrtaceae

GUINEA-HEN FLOWER = *Fritillaria melea-gris*

GUM. See EUCALYPTUS, NYSSA.

GUMWEED = *Grindelia lanceolata*

GUNNERA (GUN-er-a). Large-leaved rhizomatous herbs, native to South America, apparently grown much more in Europe and the British Isles than they are in the U.S. They are grown near water, chiefly for their huge leaves which may be as much as 6 ft. across. Not hardy north of Zone 7 unless they are given a very thick winter mulch. They are propagated by seed and chiefly by division. **G. chilensis** has palmately lobed and deeply cut leaves up to 5 ft. wide on 6 ft. petioles, covered with stiff hairs. The flowers have no petals, are borne in 3-ft. spikes; fruits are red. **G. manicata** is similar except that the leaves are peltate and larger (up to 6 ft. wide) and the petioles are covered wth thornlike reddish hairs.

They create a truly tropical effect.

GUZMANIA (guz-MAY-nia)

lingulata 1′ Zone 10 Droophead Guzmania
A Bromeliad, sometimes cultivated under glass, found living in trees in tropical America, with scurfy, sword-shaped leaves 12–18 in. long and 1 in. wide. Flowers are yellowish, purple at the tips, borne in crowded clusters. The bracts of the flowers are red.

musaica stemless Zone 10 Colombian Guzmania
A Bromeliad, sometimes cultivated under glass. Leaves 12–20 in. long and 2–3 in. wide with cross bands on the leaf, colored green above and purple underneath the leaf. Flowers yellowish white in a cluster 2–3 in. long with greenish, red-striped bracts. Native to Colombia.

GYMNOCARPIUM

dryopteris (*Dryopteris linnaeana*) **10″ Zone 3 Oak Fern**
The pinnate fronds of this North American fern (Quebec to Fla.) rise from a creeping rootstalk. Growing in shady, acid soil, they are propagated from sections of the rootstalk.

GYMNOCLADUS (jim-NO-klay-dus)

dioica 90′ Zone 4 Kentucky Coffee-tree
A coarse, alternate but singly and doubly compound-leaved tree native to the central U.S., the only merit of this tree is its large branches and picturesque habit in the winter when the leaves have fallen. The leaves are anywhere from 1½–3 ft. long. It has no autumn color, is not a good shade tree and the fruits are merely large ugly pods about 8 in. long. The seeds have been used as a coffee substitute by the early settlers.

Propagation

The seed coat must be perforated in order that the seed will germinate. This is easily done with a 3-cornered file. Seed may be processed immediately or stored dry in airtight containers in a cool place for up to a year and then processed. Root cuttings taken in the spring will root.

GYMNOSPERMS. Plants with uncovered ovules, as the conifers. See also ANGIOSPERMS.

GYNURA (jy-NOOR-ra)

aurantiaca 3′ Zone 10 Velvetplant
An excellent foliage pot-plant, grown mostly under glass for its egg-shaped, velvety, alternate leaves which are densely covered with violet or purple hairs, actually in its native habitat it is shrubby but fleshy. To be at their best they need plenty of sunlight, and growing conditions are

similar to those for *Coleus*. Easily propagated from cuttings or seeds.

GYPSOPHILA (jip-SOFF-ill-a). Fine plants for the perennial border, these are annual or perennial herbaceous herbs with small, opposite leaves and profuse small, white-to-pink flowers, borne on many branches. The general impression is of fine, feathery texture and some of these plants are almost indispensable as fillers in the perennial border.

They seem to do better in well-drained alkaline soils and generally they should be planted in the full sunlight. The perennial types are propagated by cuttings taken in midsummer. Commercially, the double-flowered varieties are grafted into the single-flowered species. They are all popularly called Baby's-breath.

These species, members of the Pink Family, are valued in gardens because of their extremely branched habit, feathery texture, small white-to-pink flowers, and their ability to bring a dainty, mistlike character to a garden where heavy textured plants are used. The small leaves are opposite and the flowers are about ¼ in. wide. Both annual and perennial species are popular. The annual species (*G. elegans* and *G. muralis*) are propagated by sowing seed where the plants are to grow in the middle of April and leaving them somewhat crowded in the seed bed.

cerastioides 4″ Zone 7 Mouse-ear Gypsophila
Native to the Himalayan Mountains and requiring good, well-drained soil and sun or partial shade, this tiny creeping plant with small, pale green leaves covered with a light down, grows in mats and bears in profusion clusters of white flowers with veins outlined in red, which appear in May. It is somewhat tender in northern U.S.

elegans 1½′ annual Baby's-breath
More or less upright in habit with lance-shaped leaves and white-to-pink flowers about ¼ in. wide from mid-June to Oct. This species is popular in America and there are good pink-flowered varieties available, also. Native to the Caucasus.

fratensis = G. repens rosea

muralis 1′ annual Cushion Gypsophila
A sprawling plant with small pink flowers in the leaf axils, native to Europe, blooming continuously from mid-June to Oct. The leaves are very small, pointed at both ends, and the plant, like other members of this species, is very branched.

oldhamiana 2½′ Zone 5 Oldham Gypsophila
A species from Korea, not so graceful as other *Gypsophila* species, but bearing dense clusters of pale pink flowers during Aug. and Sept.

paniculata 3′ Zones 2–3 Baby's-breath
A very delicate but compact-growing, feathery and graceful perennial with small (1/16 in.) white flowers borne in clusters, up to 1000 flowers being in a single much-branched panicle during July. If the plant is sheared back somewhat after bloom, flowers may be produced again from Aug. to Oct. The more popular double-flowered types like 'Bristol Fairy' are common in gardens everwhere. 'Perfecta' is a new Dutch origination with double flowers which shows promise. Usually these double-flowered forms are grafted, so that when set out in the garden the graft union should be at least an inch below the soil

Gypsophila repens, a fine rock plant and ground cover as well. (*Photo by Arnold Arboretum, Jamaica Plain, Mass.*)

surface to encourage stem rooting. The species is native to Europe and northern Asia.

repens   6″   Zone 3   Creeping Gypsophila A trailing or prostrate perennial from the Pyrenees and the Alps, this is best used in full sun and in limestone soil, if possible. The linear leaves are less than an inch long and the white flowers, about ⅓ in. wide, are profuse, but are borne in few-flowered panicles from early June to mid-July. The variety **'Rosea'** has pink flowers. This makes an excellent ground cover. **'Rosy Veil'** is probably a hybrid, with double pinkish-to-white clusters of flowers from June to Aug. and it grows 18 in. high.

'Bodgeri' is a hybrid (*G. repens* 'Rosea' x *G. paniculata*), growing 15–18 in. tall, with many flowers, partially double and white tinged a faint pink. It blooms from late May until the end of June. A fine plant for the flower border.

GYPSUM. Commercially this is calcium sulphate or sulphate of lime, a very important additive to heavy clay soils or alkali soils, or those that have been flooded with salt water. Sometimes when developers are in a hurry they put heavy equipment on wet soil and this packs it down hard so that, when it dries out, it is almost as hard as cement. Gypsum helps to break up the soil particles, making the soil much more suitable for growing plants.

GYPSY MOTH CONTROL. See under QUERCUS, p. 907.

GYPSY-WEED = *Veronica officinalis*

H

HABENARIA (hab-en-AY-ria). A large and showy genus of the Orchid Family containing many Temperate Zone orchids. The roots are generally fleshy or tuberous and the leaves often sheathe the stem. The flowers are terminally borne on the flower stalk and are very irregular, with the lip usually fringed. They are extremely rare acid-soil plants and difficult to cultivate, requiring soil with a pH of from 4.0 to 5.0. Several are bog plants. Most gardeners will be well advised not to try to grow them.

blephariglottis 2½′ **Zone 3** **White Fringed Orchid**
A terrestrial orchid with leaves 8 in. long and 1½ in. wide, clusters of pure white flowers with the lip fringed and a long slender spur, blooming in the summer. Native from Canada to Miss. Chiefly grown in the bog garden.

ciliaris 1′–2′ **Zone 4** **Fringed Orchid**
Oval, pointed leaves sheathe the flower stalk, gradually diminishing in size to resemble bracts. The orange flowers are produced in a dense terminal spike, each flower having a spur 1 in. or more in length, and a conscpicuous, deeply fringed lip. It blooms in July and Aug. and has a range extending from New England to Fla. and Tex., and west to Wisc. It prefers rather dry, sandy, although acid soil.

lacera 2′–3′ **Zone 3** **Ragged Orchid**
A plant having oblong, tapering, opposite leaves which sheathe the stem and which diminish in size as they ascend the flower stalk. This is crowned with a loose cluster of 12–15 lavender flowers, each having a short spur and a fringed, 3-lobed lip. The plant blooms throughout the summer months and is adapted to growing in either dry woods or bogs. Its range extends from Canada to Ga., and west to the Mississippi River.

leucophaea to 4′ **Zone 4** **Prairie Fringed Orchid**
This species bears fragrant white flowers in a dense terminal cluster. Each flower has a spur up to 2 in. long and a fringed, 3-lobed lip. The tapering, alternate leaves sheathe the stem, decreasing in size toward the upper part of the stem. It blooms in wet meadows and swamps from Nova Scotia to the Plains States, extending south to Ark., during the months of June to Aug.

nivea 12″–15″ **Zone 7** **Snowy Habenaria**
A plant having narrow, pointed, alternate leaves which sheathe the stem. Those near the base of the plant are long; those farther up the stem are greatly reduced in length. The flowers are terminally produced in a tight cluster. Each flower has white sepals and petals about equal in size and somewhat star shaped. The petals are fringed. It is a plant of the swamps and bogs of the southeast coastal states and Tex. and blooms in Aug. and Sept.

psycodes 1′–2′ **Zone 3** **Small Purple Fringed Orchid**
This species is distinguished by its greenish-yellow, fragrant flowers which have a spreading, fringed lip and are borne in a compact terminal cluster 8–6 in. in length. These appear in July and Aug. in the swamps and lowlands from the Carolinas along the coast to Canada and west to the area round the Great Lakes. The **Large Purple Fringed Orchid** (var. **grandiflora**) bears large flowers, 1½ in. wide.

HABERLEA (hab-ER-lee-a)
ferdinandi-coburgii 6″ **Zone 5**
A tufted perennial herb with spatulate leathery leaves in a rosette. The lilac-colored, nodding flowers are borne in umbels, each having a broad upper lip spotted with yellow and a violet throat. Native to the Balkans.

rhodopensis 6″ **Zone 5**
Slightly larger than the above species, leaves 2–3 in. long and coarsely toothed. Flowers pale lilac, an inch long, suited for the rockery. Native to the Balkans. Hard to grow in cultivation.

HABIT. The general aspect of a plant, or its mode of growth.

HABITAT. The type of locality in which a plant grows; where it is native.

HABRANTHUS (hab-BRAN-thus). Native to South America and Tex., these are bulbous herbs with lance-shaped leaves belonging to the Amaryllis Family. The colorful flowers do not last long and it is not a group worth too much effort in growing. They usually bear 2–3 small funnel-shaped flowers per stalk. Easily propagated by offsets and seeds.

andersonii 6″ **Zone 9** **Anderson Habranthus**
With solitary yellow flowers veined red, about 1½ in. long.

brachyandrus 1′ **Zone 10**
A beautiful bulbous plant with long, channeled, recurved leaves. The flower is 3 in. wide and is singly borne on a 12-in. stalk, funnelform and orchid pink with a deep crimson throat.

texanus   8″   **Zone 8**   **Texas Habranthus**
Native to Tex. with coppery-striped purple-yellow flowers about 1 in. long, appearing in summer.
    tubispathus (*robustus*)   9″   **Zone 9**
Flowers rose-red, 3 in. long.

HACKBERRY. See CELTIS.

HACKMATACK = *Larix laricina*

HAEMANTHUS (hee-MAN-thus). Tender bulbous plants of tropical South Africa belonging to the Amaryllis Family, they are used chiefly as pot plants in the greenhouse. Some have rounded bulbs the size of tennis balls. These are for the cool greenhouse and are propagated by offsets. The flower is produced in late summer or early fall, with globular clusters of small flowers at the end of a long stalk. The stamens are most conspicuous.
    albiflos   1′   **Zone 9**   **White Blood-lily**
Wide, leathery leaves 8 in. long and 4 in. wide that bend over and are not erect. A 12-in. flower stalk at the end of which is a closely packed head, 2 in. across, of small white flowers each ¾ in. long, later producing red berries as fruit. Foliage evergreen.
    coccineus   10″   **Zone 9**   **Scarlet Blood-lily**
Similar to above but with red flowers an inch long in heads 3 in. across, and the thick leaves are 8 in. wide. Berries are purple.
    katharinae   1½′   **Zone 9**   **Katharine Blood-lily**
Flowers soft salmon-pink appearing in late Aug.
    multiflorus   1½′   **Zone 9**   **Salmon Blood-lily**
Flowers blood-red, 1 in. long, in dense heads 3–6 in. across. Berries scarlet.
    puniceus   15″   **Zone 9**   **Baseball Blood-lily**
Flowers pale red, in heads 4 in. across, berries scarlet, remaining colorful for several months. The leaves which are 4 in. wide have reddish petioles.

HAEMARIA (hi-MAR-ia). Asiatic terrestrial orchids with creeping rootstocks and small flowers in terminal spikes or racemes. *H. discolor* has leaves 2–3 in. long that are a dark red, velvety green with a central whitish stripe and a few red veins. Native to China. For culture and propagation see ORCHID.

HAEMATOXYLUM (hee-mat-OX-eye-lum)
    campechianum   45′   **Zone 10**   **Logwood**
From the earliest days of colonization, this has been an important product from Central America and the West Indies, a wood the chips of which are used for dyeing purposes. They produce gray, brown, black and blue dyes. Their principal use today is for black achieved with alum and iron and for making ink. The tree belongs to the Legume Family.

HAEMODORACEAE = The Bloodroot Family

HA-HA. Actually a ditch wide enough and deep enough to serve as a barrier for animals, built in such a manner that the edge on the side from which it is mostly observed, is slightly higher than the other, thus tending to conceal its presence. Used considerably in England and sometimes seen in the South.

HAIR GRASS = *Agrostis hiemalis*

HAKEA (HAY-kea)
    laurina   25′   **Zone 10**   **Sea-urchin**
A fine vigorous evergreen shrub; leaves 6 in. long bordered in red with parallel veins; flowers crimson-red in sessile globose clusters with long yellow stamens like a pin cushion. Native to West Australia.
    suaveolens   15′   **Zone 10**   **Sweet Hakea**
With the appearance of a conifer, slender silky branches and stiff pinnate leaves that are needle-like, 1–2 in. long, and spine-tipped. The fragrant white flowers are small but borne in dense racemes. Native to West Australia.

HALESIA (hal-EE-sia)   *also:*
    carolina   30′   **Zone 5**   **Carolina Silverbell** *H. tetraptera*
Native from W.Va., to Tex., this is a very popular small tree with leaves 2–4 in. long; flowers about ⅝ in. long, bell-shaped, white and borne in clusters of 2–5 in the early spring before the leaves appear. The fruits are oblong dry drupes of no ornamental value.
    diptera   30′   **Zone 6**   **Snowdrop-tree**
Shrub or small deciduous tree, similar to *H. carolina* but usually it does not bear as many flowers, hence is not much used as an ornamental. Native from S.Car. to Tex.
    monticola   90′   **Zone 5**   **Mountain Silverbell**
This is the taller growing of the 2 *Halesia* species, with leaves 3–6½ in. long and bell-like white flowers a full inch long. The dry drupes or fruits are 2 in. long. This also blooms in the spring before the leaves appear and because of its larger size and larger flowers makes quite a display, for the flowers are all pendant and very beautiful. When it is grown from seed, many trees will have pale rose-colored flowers, at least when they first open, and the varietal name 'Rosea' has been given to these. To insure this color in the flowers the tree might best be asexually propagated from a good, known, mother plant.

Propagation

Do not allow the seed to dry out but stratify as soon as ripe. The seed is mixed with moist sand or peat moss, placed in polyethylene bags and kept at normal greenhouse temperatures for 5 months, then placed in cold at 40° F. for 3 months, and then sown. Varieties are either grafted or budded on the same species. See STRATIFICATION, GRAFTING, etc.

HALIMODENDRON (hal-im-o-DEN-dron)

halodendron   6′   Zone 2   Salt-tree

Extremely difficult to transplant and very difficult to propagate, this native of Turkestan is mentioned merely because it can grow in heavily alkaline soils or at the seashore, "taking hold" sometimes where better plants fail. The pale purple, pealike flowers bloom in early June and the silvery leaves are 1½ in. long. The branches are spiny. In fertile soils, better plants might well be grown.

Propagation

Seed may be processed as soon as ripe, or stored dry in airtight containers in a cool place for up to a year and then sown. In either event it should be soaked in hot water (190° F.) over night before sowing. Budding and grafting on *Caragana arborescens* as an understock is also practiced. See GRAFTING.

HALORAGIDACEAE = The Water Milfoil Family.

HAMAMILIDACEAE = The Witch-hazel Family

HAMAMELIS (ham-am-EE-lis; also sometimes called ham-am-ELL-is). These are all tall-growing, alternate-leaved shrubs that can grow well in partial shade but also look and do well in fully exposed situations. Their small, bright yellow or red flowers are about 1½ in. wide, with 4 ribbonlike petals in each flower. *H. virginiana* blooms late in the fall; the others very early in the spring—Feb. or March, before the leaves appear. The yellow-flowered species make better ornamentals because the flowers are more easily seen than the red-flowering hybrids, which are not so conspicuous when viewed from a distance. Most have yellow autumn color, but that of *H. japonica* and some of its hybrids is red. The fruits of these witch-hazels are dried capsules that open with explosive force in the fall, actually throwing the 2 lustrous black seeds many feet.

Propagation

Seed is doubly dormant; hence it should be stratified for 5 months at warm room temperatures, then 3 months at 40° F., then sown. If it fails to germinate (after several months), give it another cold treatment of 3 months. Plants can be layered and grafted, using *H. virginiana* as understock. Softwood cuttings can be rooted. See STRATIFICATION, GRAFTING, CUTTINGS.

x intermedia   30′   Zone 5

This is a hybrid (*H. japonica* x *H. mollis*) which is apparently being made both in America and in Europe, resulting in some excellent flowering varieties. **'Arnold Promise'** is one, with golden-yellow flowers in the early spring, the flowers

slightly larger than those of either parent. The original plant is now about 20 ft. high and 22 ft. wide. The autumn color is a rich red and yellow.

Other varieties which are being offered in Europe are: **'Jelena'**—flowers a rich copper color, and large; **'Ruby Red'**—reddish flowers; **'Ruby Glow'**—reddish flowers.

There are several other varieties now becoming available from various nursery sources and it is difficult for the new gardener to refrain from obtaining them. One should remember that these bloom very early in the spring and that the red colors are not nearly as outstanding then as are the yellow or bright orange colored varieties.

So, in considering glowing descriptions of new varieties, pick new ones carefully.

japonica   30′   Zone 5   Japanese Witch-hazel

This is native to Japan and is the only species (except *H. intermedia*) which has red autumn color; the others are all yellow. Also, the flowers are frequently purplish or even reddish near the base and so are not so conspicuous as those of *H. mollis* and some of the hybrids. It is not the best of this group for ornamental planting.

mollis   30′   Zone 5   Chinese Witch-hazel

This is a very fragrant witch-hazel when the flowers are fully open, and the flowers are the largest of the group, being about 1½ in. in dia. It has proved the least hardy witch-hazel, for during some of the very cold winters in Zone 5 the temperatures go sufficiently low to kill the flower buds, but farther south it is the most popular of the group. The 1-year twigs and buds are pubescent, making this the means of differentiating it from the other species. It is native to China.

vernalis   10′   Zone 4   Vernal Witch-hazel

Coming from the central part of the U.S., this Vernal Witch-hazel is perfectly hardy as far north as Boston. The very small, ribbonlike flowers are extremely fragrant and open in the late winter (Feb. and March). They have an interesting way of opening fully on warm days and closing tightly when the temperature is low. Only about ½ in. in dia., they are either yellow or slightly reddish, the smallest flowers of this genus. The foliage turns a brilliant yellow in the fall. **'Christmas Cheer'**—excellent red autumn color.

virginiana   15′   Zone 4   Common Witch-hazel

Common in the woods of the eastern U.S., this is the last woody plant to bloom in the fall in New England, and the yellow, ribbonlike flowers appear at just the time the leaves drop in early Oct. Witch-hazel "divining rods" were often used in the old days in finding underground sources of water. As an ornamental, it will do well in the woods, in shaded situations and in poor soil, but if planted in good soil in the full sun, it can develop into a splendid, well-rounded, vase-shaped specimen. The autumn color is golden yellow.

HAMATOCACTUS = *Ferocactus setispinus*

HAMELIA (ham-EE-lia)
   patens (*erecta*)   **25′**   **Zone 10**   **Scarlet-bush**
A gray-pubescent evergreen with 6 in. ovate, opposite leaves and tubular 5-lobed flowers ¾ in. long that are orange to scarlet-red. Fruits are small red berries. Native from Fla. to Brazil. Propagated by seeds and softwood cuttings.

HANGING BASKETS. Usually made of sturdy wire, these are excellent for displaying pendulous plants. They can be used in greenhouse, home or porch, the only difficulty with them being that they do drip and somehow one should figure out a way of controlling the drip of water resulting when they are watered.

Planting is simple. Slabs of green sheet moss are put on the inside of the basket facing outward. Then a rich soil (equal parts of loam, compost or rotted manure and leaf mold) is placed in the basket and the plants inserted. It is best to have some plant in the center that will be more or less upright or vase-shaped in habit to give a good form to the finished product.

Watering must be done every day or so and it may be with a little ingenuity one can overcome the drip problem. A piece of polyethylene film placed carefully in the bottom quarter of the basket, possibly with some broken crockery put in for drainage with the soil placed on top of that does work if one is careful not to apply too much water. Covering the inside of the basket completely with polyethylene may not prove helpful in some cases because the plant roots need air and heavy watering may reduce the amount of air in the soil. Many immerse the entire basket occasionally or put it out in the rain in order to give it a thorough soaking.

Some foliage and flowering plants which might be planted in hanging baskets are:

FERNS

Davallia sp.	Hare's foot Ferns
Hamata tyermannii	Bear's-foot Fern
Nephrolepsis exaltata 'Bostoniensis'	Boston Fern
Polypodium aureum	Golden Polypody

FOLIAGE PLANTS

Chlorophytum commosum	Spider Plant
Coleus blumei verschaffeltii	Coleus
Columnea sp.	Columnea
Hedera helix	English Ivy
Nepeta hederacea variegata	Variegated Ground-ivy
Saxifraga sarmentosa	Strawberry Saxifrage
Tradescantia sp.	Spiderworts
Vinca major variegata	Mottled Bigleaf Periwinkle
Zebrina pendula	Wandering-Jew

FLOWERING PLANTS

Abutilon megapotamicum	Brazilian Abutilon
Achimenes sp.	Achimenes
Aeschynanthus lobbianus	Lobb's Basketvine
Ageratum houstonianum	Ageratum
Begonia sp.	Basket Begonias
Ceropegia woodsii	Ceropegia
Chrysanthemum frutescens	Marguerite
Clianthus sp.	Parrotbeak
Fuschia sp.	Fuschia
Gazania ringens	Pied Gazania
Heliotropium arborescens	Heliotrope
Impatiens sultani	Sultan Snapweed
Jasminum mesnyi	Primrose Jasmine
Lachenalia pendula	Nodding Cape Cowslip
Lobularia maritima	Sweet Alyssum
Pelargonium peltatum	Ivy Geranium
Petunia hybrida	Petunia
Phlox drummondii	Annual Phlox
Schlumbergera truncata	Christmas Cactus
Senecio mikaniodes	German-ivy
Tropaelum sp.	Nasturtium
Verbena hortensis	Verbena

Baskets are first lined with sphagnum moss and then planted.

HAPLOID. An organism with a single set of chromosomes sometimes referred to as the *n* generation.

HAPLOPAPPUS (hap-lo-PAP-us)

spinulosus   **2′–3′**   **Zone 2**   **Haplopappus**
Another of the many rather woody perennials among the genera making up the Composite Family. The edges of the fernlike leaves are armed with bristles and the yellow flower heads have both ray and disc flowers which appear throughout the summer on the plains and grasslands from Manitoba to Tex., and Calif.

HARDENBERGIA (har-den-BER-jia)

comptoniana   **vine**   **Zone 9**   **Compton Coral-pea**
Pealike leaflets 3–5 that are $1\frac{1}{2}$–3 in. long; flowers blue to violet only about $\frac{1}{2}$ in. long, pods 2 in. long. Grown in greenhouse or out-of-doors in southern Calif.

monophylla = *H. violaceae*

violacea (*H. monophylla*)   **vine**   **Zone 9**
                                                 Coral-pea
A climbing evergreen shrubby vine with 1 leaflet (not 3 as above), the leaflet being 2–5 in. long. Flowers are profuse, only $\frac{1}{2}$ in. long, pea-like, violet or rose color and with a yellow basal spot, in axillary racemes. Propagated by seeds or greenwood cuttings. Native to Australia.

HARDENING OFF. A horticultural term for a procedure in which seedlings or plants are gradually acclimatized to growing under low-temperature and humidity conditions. It is used chiefly for plants or seedlings which have been forced into rapid growth in the high-temperature and humidity conditions of greenhouse or hot-bed, when it comes to preparing them for planting outdoors in the spring. Usually such plants are put in a cold frame with the sash on and some shade, and the shade reduced day by day, as well as the sash being opened more and more each day so that at the end of a week the plants are able to grow in the open without wilting.

The term is also used in conditioning plants (or cuttings) from growth in a high-humidity unit (i.e., tightly closed propagation bench) to the open greenhouse, where temperatures might be the same, but atmospheric moisture conditions might be reduced from 100% to 50% or less. This move in the life of rooted cuttings is frequently highly critical and must be made with the greatest care, sometimes taking a "conditioning" period of 2 weeks.

HARDHACK = *Spiraea tomentosa*

HARDINESS. The hardiness of plants living out-of-doors is of considerable interest to all plantsmen. It is only by long and careful trials that the northern limits of any particular exotic tree or shrub can be determined. It is somewhat difficult to divide the country into hardiness zones that are wholly satisfactory. Also see CLIMATE.

The hardiness of plants is based not only on a plant's resistance to minimum low temperatures, but to other factors as well, such as lack of water, exposure to wind and sun, soil conditions, length of growing season and, with perennials, the amount of snow cover during the colder winter months. It would be difficult to prepare a readable map depicting all these factors. Since a map based on the average annual minimum temperatures agrees in many instances with the known limits of hardiness of certain plants, these data are adopted as the basis for hardiness zones on most maps used today.

The hardiness map (inside front and back covers) is based solely on average annual minimum temperatures. It is not new, but has been in use, with a few minor variations, since 1938. All of the plants listed by Alfred Rehder in his "Manual of Cultivated Trees and Shrubs," and by Donald Wyman in his "Shrubs and Vines for American Gardens" and his "Trees for American Gardens" have been calibrated to correspond with it. Nurserymen and others throughout the country have used it to denote the hardiness of plants they grow, so it has been in use for a sufficiently long period, over a sufficiently wide area, for growers throughout the country to have become familiar with it, and with its limitations, as well.

In general, it is based on records summarized by the U.S. Weather Bureau over a 40-year period. Data for Canada were supplied by the Meteorological Division, Department of Transport of the Canadian Government. The U.S. and Canada are arbitrarily divided into 10 zones, 9 of which are in the United States. These zones are based on 5-, 10- or 15-degree differences in the average annual minimum temperatures. Slight variations were made in the map as taken from the Weather Bureau records in accordance with known variations in plant performance on the Eastern Seaboard, and the zone lines have been recently (1967) slightly redrawn to conform to latest U.S. Department of Agriculture weather information.

On a small-scale map such as this, it is impossible to show all the minute climatic variations within the limits of each zone. In this connection, certain strains of plants may prove hardier than others of the same species or botanical variety.

For instance, the Giant Arborvitae (*Thuja plicata*) is native to western North America from Alaska to northern Calif. However, plants grown from seed collected on the western slopes of the Rocky Mountains have not proved hardy in the northern and northeastern

U.S., while plants grown from seed collected high up in the mountains of Mont. and Utah are perfectly hardy. Similar variations in the hardiness of other plants of a single species or variety are common. If a map of any one of these zones were enlarged, various zone changes would be noted due to the altitude alone. The Grand Canyon, for example, appears on our hardiness map in 1 climatic zone; yet there are at least 4 climatic zones in this one canyon, due, of course, to variations in altitude. Plants growing at the bottom of the Canyon thrive in the Mexican deserts, yet on the North Rim (5700 ft. above the Canyon floor) plants are found which are native as far north as southern Canada.

Consequently, many local variations in this small-scale map are to be expected. A plant is usually listed in the coldest zone where it will grow normally, but at the same time it can be expected to grow in many of the warmer zones where maximum temperatures and drought conditions might prove to be the only limiting factors. Using this general map as a basis, similar hardiness maps could be worked out for limited areas or even for each state in the U.S. and each province in the Dominion of Canada, but in much greater detail using the U.S. Weather Bureau Information as available in "Climate and Man," the 1941 Yearbook of the U.S. Department of Agriculture. Such detailed maps would be of much greater value to local plantsmen than a general map covering the entire country.

Some detailed state maps have been drawn and one might write to the local state experiment station (which see) to ascertain whether a local map of this kind is available.

The Hardiness Map published by the United States Department of Agriculture in cooperation with the American Horticultural Society (1960) is much larger and more detailed, but unfortunately Zone numbers were changed in a few instances so that they are not applicable to published Hardiness Zone numbers for a large number of plants popularly grown in the central and northern United States.

More recently a new Hardiness Map of Canada has been drawn up by the Cartography Section, Soil Research Institute, Canada Department of Agriculture. Canada is divided into 9 climatic zones and unfortunately these are numbered in such a way that they do not conform to those of either the U.S.D.A. hardiness map or the Rehder-Wyman map.

As a result of this serious discrepancy in Zone numbers it was felt advisable to retain the map of Rehder and Wyman. An effort has been made with all plants described in this volume to list the northernmost Zone in which each plant

will normally succeed. This is the first time this has been attempted for perennials, hence there undoubtedly will be errors. Nurserymen, plantsmen, experiment stations and others have been consulted in an effort to list the plants properly, but the idiosyncracies of plant hardiness are such that it is much more difficult to list perennials properly than it is larger-growing woody plants. The point is, however, all Zone numbers given in this book refer to the Zone Map on the inside covers of this book and not to any other hardiness map.

HARDPAN. This is a condition of some clay or silt subsoils, in which the clay particles are so tightly packed that water can not drain through. In most situations where it occurs this is a difficulty to be met with forthrightly. If it is deep enough in the soil, vegetables and garden flowers may grow above it satisfactorily. Tree roots frequently are unable to penetrate hardpans. Water stands in such soils and if the slope of the land is such that it does not drain off, the standing water actually kills (i.e. drowns) plant roots.

This situation can be met by laying tile drains to draw off the water; by digging through the hardpan layer if it is not too deep; and in severe cases by dynamiting through to allow proper soil drainage.

HARDWOOD. A term used in connection with woods, meaning any that are hard and difficult to work, like Sugar Maple, Ironwood or American Elm. The term is also used in horticulture, as hardwood cuttings, to denote cuttings taken from mature twigs, usually dormant, in which the wood is hard and stiff, as compared with wood on the same twigs (earlier in the growing season) when it is soft, succulent and immature. See CUTTINGS.

HARDY-ORANGE = *Poncirus trifoliata*

HAREBELL = *Campanula rotundifolia*

HARPEPHYLLUM (har-pe-FILE-um)
    caffrum   **35′**   **Zone 10**   **Kafir-plum**
The Kafir-plum is native to South Africa and is hardy in the warmest parts of Fla. and Calif. where it is often used in small gardens for its well-groomed tropical appearance, fast growth and dark red olive fruit. The evergreen, leathery and glossy, alternate leaves are ornamental and the small flowers are dioecious.

HARRISIA (har-ISS-ia). Mostly night-blooming, climbing, tropical cacti from the West Indies or South America with angled or fluted 8–10-ridged sides. The flowers are usually solitary, borne only at night, large and funnelform, white or pinkish. Occasionally used in the

greenhouse. For culture see CACTI AND SUCCU-
LENTS.

HARROWING. There are several kinds of
implements for this operation which follows
plowing. In the suburban garden where the
rototiller is the all-purpose machine, there is no
need to harrow. The object in harrowing is to
break up the clods of soil turned over by the
plow, most effectively done as soon as the
plowing is completed and before the soil has
dried out. Disc harrows actually cut the sods,
and if done several times and in opposite
directions the soil is cut up into finer and finer
pieces. Sometimes the soil "works" so well that
it is not necessary to disc at right angles to the
furrows.

Spring-toothed harrows and pike-toothed
harrows are also used, for these not only break
up the large soil clumps but act also as large
rakes in leveling the soil. However, rototilling
and hand raking in the small garden accomplish
the same purpose. As in all soil operations, the
ground should not be worked when it is wet as

this destroys some of the air spaces between the
soil particles.

HASHHISH = *Cannabis sativa*

HAWAII. The detailed description of all the
ornamental plants of tropical Hawaii is outside the realm of this book. The latest reference
on the flora of the Hawaiian Islands lists over
3000 species of plants being grown there now.
However, thousands of visitors go to the
Islands each year to marvel at the conspicuous
and colorful trees, shrubs and vines. Listed
below are a few of the plants, native and introduced, which go to make the Islands so colorful
at all times of year. One frequently hears a common name or even a scientific name in discussing
plants there, hence this list (all of which are
described in their proper alphabetical sequence)
may be of help in spotting some plant which has
made an impression on the visitor. Of course
many of these plants are grown in southern Fla.
and southern Calif. as well. Some of the most
prominent flowering plants to be seen are:

Acacia koa	Koa Tree
Acalypha hispida	Chenille Plant
A. wilkesiana	Painted Copper Leaf
Aleurites moluccana	Candlenut Tree
Allamanda cathartica var. hendersonii	Henderson Common Allamanda
Aloe ciliaris	Climbing Aloe
Alyxia olivaeformis	Maile
Alpinia speciosa	Shell Ginger
A. purpurata	Red Ginger
Anthurium andraeanum	Flamingo Anthurium
A. scherzerianum	Common Anthurium
Antigonon leptopus	Coral-vine
Arrabidaea magnifica (Bignonia magnifica)	Purple Funnel-vine
Artocarpus communis	Breadfruit
Bauhinia corymbosa	Phanera
B. galpinii	Red Bauhinia
B. monandra	St. Thomas Tree, Butterfly Bauhinia
B. variegata	Orchid Tree
Beaumontia jerdoniana	Beaumontia
Beloperone guttata	Shrimp Plant
Billbergia pyramidalis	Pineapple-lily
Bixa orellana	Annatto
Bougainvillea glabra var. sanderiana	Paper-flower Bougainvillea
B. spectabilis	Brazil Bougainvillea
Brassaia actinophylla	Octopus Tree
Brunfelsia americana	Lady-of-the-Night
B. latifolia	Brunfelsia
Callistemon lanceolatus	Lemon Bottle Brush Tree
Callophyllum inophyllum	Indiapoon Beautyleaf
Carissa grandiflora	Natal-plum
Cassia glauca	Glossy-shower Senna
C. alata	Candle Bush
C. fistula	Golden Shower Tree
C. hybrida (C. javanica x C. fistula)	Rainbow Shower Tree
C. grandis	Coral Shower Tree
C. javanica	Pink and White Shower Tree

Clerodendrum fragrans var. pleniflorum	Double Fragrant Glorybower
C. thomsoniae	Bleeding Heart Glorybower
Clitoria ternatea	Butterfly Pea
Cochlospermum vitifolium	Buttercup Tree
Cocos nucifera	Coconut
Codiaeum variegatum pictum	Croton, Copper-leaf
Cordia sebestena	Geiger Tree
Cordyline terminalis	Ti Plant or Common Dracena
Costus speciosus	Crepe or Malay Ginger
Couroupita guianensis	Cannon Ball Tree
Cydista aequinoctialis	Garlic-scented Vine
Delonix regia	Royal Poinciana, Flamboyant Tree
Dombeya wallichii	Scarlet Dombeya
Duranta repens	Golden Dewdrop
Eranthemum nervosum	Blue Eranthemum
Eugenia jambos	Rose-apple
E. malaccensis	Malay-apple
Euphorbia splendens	Crown-of-thorns
E. pulcherrima	Poinsettia
Gliricidia sepium	Madre de Cacao
Gloriosa rothschildiana	Rothschild Gloriosa Lily
Hedychium coronarium	Common Ginger-lily
H. flavum	Yellow Ginger-lily
H. gardnerianum	India Ginger-lily
Hibiscus arnottianus	Hawaiian White Hibiscus
H. rosa-sinensis	Chinese Hibiscus
H. schizopetalus	Fringed Hibiscus
H. tiliaceus	Linden or Sea Hibiscus
Hoya carnosa	Common Waxplant
Hylocereus undatus	Nightblooming Cereus
Ipomoea horsfalliae	Horsfall Morning-glory
I. tuberosa	Ceylon Morning-glory
Ixora coccinea	Ixora
I. macrothyrsa	Malay Ixora
I. odorata	Sweet Ixora
Jacaranda ovalifolia	Jacaranda
Jasminum pubescens	Scented Star Jasmine
J. sambac	Arabian Jasmine
Kigelia pinnata	Common Sausage Tree
Lagerstroemia speciosa	Queen Crape-myrtle
Lantana camara	Common Lantana
L. montevidensis (L. sellowiana)	Trailing Lantana
Ligularia kaempferi	Kampfer Goldenray
Lonicera heckrottii	Everblooming Honeysuckle
Macfadyena unguis-cati	Cat's Claw Funnel Creeper
Malpighia coccigera	Holly Malpighia
Montanoa hibiscifolia	Christmas Daisy, Christmas Cosmos
Nerium oleander	Common Oleander
Odontonema strictum	Odontonema
Pedilanthus tithymaloides	Redbird Slipper Flower
Peltophorum inerme	Yellow Poinciana, Sogabark Poinciana
Petrea volubilis	Sandpaper Vine
Plumbago capensis	Cape Plumbago
Plumeria rubra acutifolia	Mexican Frangipani
Poinciana pulcherrima	Barbados Flower-fence
Porana paniculata	Porana Vine
Pseuderanthemum reticulatum	Yellowvein Eranthemum
Pyrostegia ignea	Orange Trumpet
Schinus teribinthifolius	Brazil Peppertree
Solandra guttata	**Cup-of-Gold**

Solanum macranthum — Potato-tree
Spathodea campanulata — African Tulip-tree
Stephanotis floribunda — Madagascar Stephanotis
Strelitzia reginae — Queen's Bird of Paradise
S. nicolai — White Bird of Paradise
Tabebuia pallida — Pink Tecoma Tree
Tecomaria capensis — Cape-honeysuckle
Thespesia populnea — Portia Tree
Thevetia nereifolia — Yellow Oleander
Thryallis glauca — Rain-of-Gold
Thunbergia erecta — Bush Thunbergia
T. fragrans — Sweet Clock-vine
T. grandiflora — Bengal Clock-vine
T. laurifolia — Laurel-leaved Thunbergia
Tibouchina semidecandra — Brazilian Glory-bush
Trachelospermum jasminoides — Chinese Star Jasmine
Vanda teres — Baby Orchid, Vanda Miss Joaquim
Vinca rosea — Madagascar Periwinkle
Wedelia trilobata —
Zephyranthes candida — Autumn Zephyr Flower

HAWKWEED. See HIERACIUM.

HAWORTHIA (ha-WORTH-ia). Stemless succulents from South Africa of the Lily Family, often grown for indoor decorations in the North. The fleshy leaves are in basal rosettes mostly, or crowded on a short stem. Flowers are greenish or whitish, sparse, in racemes or panicles. See SUCCULENTS. Over 50 species are supposedly available from specialists in the U.S.

coarctata   8″   Zone 10
Leaves 2½ in. long and ¾ in. wide, white hairy; with a few greenish tubercles. The flowers are lined with red on a stalk about a foot high.

cuspidata   3″   Zone 9
A slow-growing succulent making neat cushions of succulent foliage, sometimes used as a ground cover in southern Calif. The leaves are 1 in. long and ¾ in. wide and nearly ¼ in. thick in the center. The flowers are greenish, ⅝ in. across, borne in clusters on a slender stalk arising from the basal rosette of leaves. It grows well in the shade.

cymbiformis   3″   Zone 10
A robust, stemless succulent with a rosette of thick, pointed leaves, 1½ in. long and ¾ in. wide, keeled beneath, smooth and pale green in color. Flowers are pale pink striped with green on a panicle about a foot high.

fasciata   3″   Zone 10
An attractive and popular succulent with an erect rosette of leaves each 1½ in. long and ½ in. wide, with transverse bands of white tubercles; whitish-green flowers in loose racemes 6 in. long.

margaritifera   2′   Zone 10
There are 30–40 leaves in a dense rosette about 6 in. across; the leaves at first bend inward, then spread; thick, fleshy with lower surface keeled and with prominent creamy tubercles above and below.

radula   3″   Zone 10
Leaves 3 in. long and ¾ in. wide with minute tubercles above and below; flowers lined with green and rose on stalks about 1½ ft. tall.

tessellata   3″   Zone 9
Another succulent also doing best in the shade; this suckers rapidly. The thick leaves are triangular, 1½ in. long, and the flower raceme is nearly a foot long. Sometimes used in southern Calif. as a ground cover.

turgida   3″   Zone 10
A small rosette of fleshy, keeled leaves about an inch long that are a glossy pale green.

HAWTHORN. See CRATAEGUS.

HAZEL, EUROPEAN = *Corylus avellana*

HAZELNUT AND FILBERT. All members of the genus *Corylus* are prized nut-bearing trees and shrubs of Europe, Asia and North America. They bear edible nuts of good flavor, some of which are grown commercially.

Of greatest importance are the filberts. These include *C. avellana*, *C. maxima* and hybrids between them and *C. americana*. A few selections of the last named are also grown as nut-crop trees or shrubs to a limited extent.

In Wash. and Ore. 'Barcelona', a variety of *C. avellana*, bears a heavy crop of nuts with the result that filbert production is much more advanced than in the East where 'Barcelona' is damaged by cold and is harmed by late-spring freezes.

The culture of filberts in the East appears to be still in the testing stage. Hybrids of *C. maxima* and the European Filbert, especially the 'Rush' variety which originated in Pa., and 'Winkler', an Iowa cross, are encouraging. The former is a tall-growing shrub which has frequently borne well in the Northeast. 'Winkler' bears larger nuts and is more productive, but it is a low-growing shrub less easy to handle in a commercial operation.

Some of the selections of European Filbert, *C. avellana*, have varied in their response to weather conditions. In the Northeast, where below-zero weather occasionally occurs, damage will result. In the North Central states cropping is not consistent. 'Cosford' and 'Medium Long' are 2 of the hardiest varieties and are about as productive as 'Italian Red'. All 3 are vigorous upright trees, but in the northern tier of states all 3 have seemed less hardy during recent winters. The hardiest appears to be 'Red Lambert', and it produces a large, easily cracked nut. Unfortunately the yield of nuts is so poor, it is planted only as a pollinizer.

Among the newer hybrids 'Buchanan' and 'Bixby' are considered most promising, not only because of their hardiness, but also because of yield and size of the nuts. Other hybrids are being tested in various places. It is possible that one or more outstanding named clones will appear among them.

C. cornuta, the Beaked Hazel, is a common understory shrub in open woodlands in the northern states west to the Mississippi River, and south in the higher elevations in the Appalachians. It also is native to western Canada. The nut is small, sweet and thin shelled. It is an attractive ornamental shrub, seldom growing more than 4 ft. tall.

Among the filberts one only is a tall-growing tree, which is *C. colurna*, the Turkish Hazel. Native to western Asia and parts of Europe, it is a nut-bearing ornamental tree in this country and may reach 60 ft. in height. Infrequently seen, it should be planted more. Many hybrid filberts have been grafted on Turkish Hazel seedlings.

Limited increase of most species and hybrids is made by removal of suckers which are often plentiful on both filberts and hazelnuts. Seeds before being sown must be treated with red lead or some other repellent before planting, otherwise vermin will destroy most of them.

All species of the genus thrive in deep loamy soils, if drainage is good. In both sandy loams and clay loams the pH of the soil should be 6.0 or 6.5. A small amount of calcium and magnesium in the soil benefit *Corylus* species.

Insect pests are more prevalent on hazelnuts and filberts when they are not thriving because of poor growing conditions. Both aphids and lacebugs are occasionally plentiful enough to weaken the shrubs. Control is simple with malathion. Scale insects rarely do much harm. A miscible oil spray, correctly diluted and applied as buds begin to swell in the spring, will control them. Two-spotted mite and the native red mite are eradicated by the use of Ovex or Dimite.

H. GLEASON MATTOON

HEAD. A dense cluster or short, dense spike of sessile or nearly sessile flowers.

HEARTNUT. This possesses many features that increase the tree's popularity. It grows rapidly and bears nuts early, often the second year from grafting. Production is heavy and regular. Since its introduction into the United States in 1870, both the species and the Heartnut have shown adaptibility. They may be found growing in nearly every state and in the provinces of Canada adjacent to this country. They thrive on many soils, but do best on a deep, well-drained, fertile sandy loam with a clay subsoil. They do poorly on poorly drained soil and on soils that are strongly acid. The Heartnut (*Juglans ailanthifolia cordiformis*) readily crosses with the Butternut (*S. cinerea*), so nut-tree growers hope that a hybrid which is longer lived than the Butternut and with a nut that is easier to crack, will be found.

H. GLEASON MATTOON

HEART-SEED = *Cardiospermum halicacabum*

HEARTWOOD. The innermost and oldest wood next to the pith, usually of a dark color.

HEATH. See ERICA.

HEATHER. See CALLUNA.

HEATH FAMILY = Ericaceae

HEAVING. If one lifts a large stone from the soil surface in the early winter in an area where the ground normally freezes, one finds frost crystals underneath it. These in turn attract capillary water from the subsoil and these crystals accumulate and form ice. In doing so they expend a pushing or raising force on the stone which, in many areas, forces large stones to the soil surface that were partially covered with soil the previous fall. This force is called heaving. It also occurs on young, or shallow-rooted plants. Mature plants, those with deep roots, are supposedly well enough anchored in the soil to resist this heaving action, but not young plants. As a result many can be actually forced out of the ground in the early spring.

Such plants should be replanted at once before they have an opportunity to dry out. This heaving action takes place at times when the surface soil partially thaws then freezes. It can be tempered somewhat by mulching. See MULCHING. In any event, small plants should be checked in the early spring and replaced at once. Sometimes, it is advisable not to make a large planting of small ground cover plants (in fact of any small plants) late in the fall, merely because of the possibility they can be heaved out of the soil and will dry out before the damage will be noticed. Planting early in the fall, thus allowing plenty of time for the roots to become established, then mulching to prevent alternate freezing and thawing at the soil surface, is the best method of controlling this often devastating climatic hazard.

HEBE (HEE-bee). Evergreen shrubs or trees with leathery, opposite leaves, and with white-to-pink flowers borne in axillary clusters. Mostly native to New Zealand. They are grown outdoors in Zones 7–9 and south, and have been used in gardens as hedges or specimen pot plants in the greenhouses of the North. Propagated by seeds or cuttings of mature wood in the fall. Some botanists list the following species under *Veronica*.

amplexicaulis (*Veronica amplexicaulis*)   **3′**
                                    Zone 9
Often decumbent with bluish-green leaves an inch long and $\frac{2}{3}$ in. wide, very thick; flowers white, $\frac{1}{4}$ in. wide in spikes $1\frac{1}{2}$ in. long.

x **andersonii** (*Veronica andersonii*)   **5′–8′**
                                    Zone ⌐
A garden hybrid, densely branched shrub with soft, fleshy, leaves 4–5 in. long, flowers white tipped with violet in handsome clusters 4–6 in. long during Aug. and Sept. 'Variegata' has leaves margined with creamy white.

buxifolia   **4′**   **Zone 7**   **Boxleaf Hebe**
A New Zealand plant which does best with the other species of this genus in dry, almost sandy soil; they should not receive too much water. They are mostly used in Calif. The flowers bloom in July in white spikes 1 in. long, the lustrous, dark evergreen leaves are $\frac{1}{2}$ in. long. The soil should not be too fertile, for if it is the plant breaks up in the center. The low-spreading habit and glossy foliage are its chief ornamental characteristics.

cupressoides (*Veronica cupressoides*)   **6′**
                                    Zone 9
Evergreen leaves like very small scales, only $\frac{1}{4}$ to $\frac{1}{10}$ in. long. Flowers are pale purple to white, $\frac{1}{8}$ in. wide, in small, terminal, headlike clusters.

decumbens   **14″**   **Zone 5**   **Ground Hebe**
A very rare, but very attractive succulent from New Zealand, it appears to be the only one of this genus capable of withstanding the winters of the northern U.S., and even this plant may not be reliably hardy where the winter temperatures exceed − 30° F. Growing to a height of 12–14 in., small, grayish evergreen leaves margined with red and small, dense spikes of white flowers blooming in spring. It prefers a limestone soil and full sun. Easily propagated by cuttings.

hulkeana (*Veronica hulkeana*)   **3′**   **Zone 9**
Leaves ovate to 2 in. long; flowers pale lilac, $\frac{1}{4}$ in. wide in foot-long panicles.

speciosa (*Veronica speciosa*)   **5′**   **Zone 10**

A robust, evergreen with spreading branches, opposite, thick, dark green, glossy leaves 4 in. long and $1\frac{3}{4}$ in. wide. Flowers small, $\frac{1}{3}$ in. wide, purple-crimson in dense axillary 4 in. racemes. Native to New Zealand.

traversii   **6′**   **Zone 7**   **Travers Hebe**
Possibly a more dependable plant than *H. buxifolia*, this bears white flower spikes 2 in. long in July and hence makes a better show. Its dull evergreen leaves are 1 in. long and it also comes from New Zealand. Many other species of *Hebe* are grown in Zones 7–9, especially in southern Calif.

HECHTIA (HEK-tia)

argentea   **3′**   **Zone 10**
A Bromeliad, spectacular with its spines, dense rosette of silvery, recurving, succulent leaves, 1 in. wide and nearly 2 ft. long. Difficult to grow in the house or even in the greenhouse but some people think it is worth the effort. Male and female flowers are on separate plants. Native to Mexico.

HEDEOMA (hed-e-O-ma)

pulegioides   **18″**   **annual**   **American Penny-**
                                    royal
A very-branched aromatic herb with opposite ovate leaves about $1\frac{1}{2}$ in. long and small bluish-purple flowers $\frac{1}{4}$ in. long, native to eastern North America. This is a weedy plant, not much grown in gardens and not to be confused with the true Pennyroyal, *Mentha pulagium*.

HEDERA (HED-er-a). These are evergreen, alternate-leaved clinging vines widely grown in all parts of the U.S. as house plants, and out-of-doors in gardens in all but the coldest areas. They belong to the Aralia Family, and are easily grown in almost any good soil. They climb by attaching small rootlike appendages to the wall or means of support.

Propagation

Cuttings root easily almost any time, both softwood and hardwood (which see). Seed can be sown as soon as ripe, or it may be stored dry in airtight containers in a cool place up to a year, then sown. Sometimes the arborescent forms, which are understood to be harder to root as cuttings, are budded or grafted on *H. helix* understock.

Insect Pests

English Ivy may be infested with soft brown scale, ivy aphis, mealy bugs and oleander scale. Use insecticide #15.

Disease

English Ivy may be infected with both a bacterial leaf spot and a fungus leaf spot which produce typical lesions on the leaves and stunt growth. Repeated applications of fungicide #D or #F are helpful.

canariensis   clinging vine   Zone 7   Algerian Ivy
Native to the Canary Islands and northern Africa, this Ivy has dark green, thick, leathery leaves, with 5–7 lobes and is closely related to the more common *H. helix*, but is easily distinguishable from all other ivies by the burgundy-red twigs and petioles and the very glossy leaves which are 2–6 in. long. The fruit also is larger than that of *H. helix*. A variegated form ('Variegata') has the leaves edged with yellowish white.

colchica   clinging vine   Zone 5   Colchis Ivy
Evergreen leaves are entire, rarely lobed, 4–10 in. wide, dark green, thick and leathery. This has coarse texture, black berries and is native to Asia Minor. It is not as good an ornamental as the English Ivy.

helix   clinging vine   Zone 5   English Ivy
Commonly native to Europe, this species was undoubtedly brought to America by the earliest colonial settlers and has become naturalized

Mo.; **'Cavendishii'**—leaf margin variegated white to yellow; **'Conglomerata'**—small leaves, usually not over 1½ in. long, 2-ranked on stiff, upright stems; **'Digitata'**—leaves 5–7 lobed; **'Erecta'**—more erect in habit; **'Maculata'**—leaves spotted or striped with yellowish white; **'Minima'**—small lobed leaves, unstable habit; **'Pittsburgh'**—lateral shoots appear in most of the leaf axils; **'Rumania'**—similar to 'Bulgaria'; **'238th Street'**—an introduction of the New York Botanical Garden, supposedly reliably hardy for the New York City area.

Most of the leaves of *H. helix* are 3–5 lobed and up to 4 in. long, but on older shoots, about ready to produce small flowers and black fruits, the leaves are frequently entire (not lobed) and oval in outline, quite different from the lobed leaves of vigorously growing younger branches. Children have been poisoned by eating the berries of mature plants.

HEDGES. One of the foremost reasons for using plants in a clipped hedge is to form a barrier in order to keep people and animals within (or without) the property limits, particularly on the

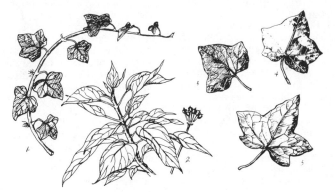

Hedera helix varieties:

1. Juvenile foliage   4. Var. 'Maculata'
2. Adult foliage and fruit   5. Var. 'Minima'
3. Var. 'Erecta'

in many places. It is the most valuable species of the genus and there are well over 50 varieties in the trade. This species is very easy to cultivate, as a clinging vine with small rootlike holdfasts or as a fine evergreen ground cover. It makes the perfect foliage plant for indoors, requiring very little sun and rooting readily in water at almost any time of year. It is one of the best evergreen vines for the South as well as the North. Varieties: **'Albany'**—erect and shrubby; **'Aureo-variegata'**—leaves variegated yellow; **baltica**—one of the hardiest forms; **'Bulgaria'**—a hardy clone withstanding winters in St. Louis,

small property where space is at a premium. Sometimes a background is needed for a perennial border or as a formal line of demarcation between one part of the property and another; or sometimes a long flowering hedge is desired to mark the limits of a property. Regardless of the purpose for which the hedge is planned, it should be very clearly defined before the hedge material is selected, for there are plants which may be chosen to best serve each special purpose.

There is a second reason for giving the purpose careful consideration at the start. If a

3-ft. barrier hedge is to be used, then the mature width of the hedge should be planned to be at least 3 ft. If a 15-foot screen planting is desired, in order to have a hedge that is well grown a space on the ground nearly 15 ft. wide should be allowed. However, it is possible, by selecting certain columnar varieties, to have tall hedges, yet not give over so much space to them. (See varieties marked "8" in the following list.) This matter of allowing sufficient width for the hedge is very important. One must, therefore, select a hedge which at maturity can be kept well within the limits set for it.

A windbreak or screen is given considerably more room than a formal clipped hedge, for the windbreak or screen is frequently allowed to grow unclipped.

When the purpose of the hedge is known, then its height and width can be determined, and not until then. One other very important point is never to plant a hedge exactly on a property line. If this is done, some disagreeable neighbor might, at some future time, chop down that half of the hedge on his property. He would have a legal right to do so. If, however, the hedge was so planted that at maturity all plants were within the property line, then the owner would have full jurisdiction over it at all times.

In planting hedges it is best to dig a ditch. In general, the ditch should be about 18 in. wide and from 12 to 18 in. deep for small hedges, but for larger hedges and evergreens these dimensions might well be doubled. If the soil is poor, make the ditch larger, fill it with good soil, fork in some well-rotted manure or other humus, spread the roots, cover them carefully with soil and firm the soil until the surface is almost up to the surrounding grade. If the plants are set a trifle low, water will flow towards the hedge. A surface mulch around the plants prevents the soil from drying and baking. As in any other transplanting operation, the tops should be cut back considerably to compensate for the roots lost in digging. The young hedge plants should be cut back to within a foot of the ground at least if they are deciduous, preferably more if possible, because the lower the plant stalk at this time, the sooner it will become bushy and well branched at the base. After planting is completed, the entire hedgerow should be well watered. Hedges should be planted in well-drained soil and so situated to receive a maximum amount of sunlight. This is most important, for though certain types of hedges will withstand shade better than others, shade is one of the chief reasons why some hedges are scraggly and uneven.

Spacing

Individual plants may be spaced from 18 to 36 in. apart, depending on the kind and size of the plants, and the length of time one is willing to wait for the desired effect. There is no necessity for planting closer than 18 in. except possibly with some of the dwarf types.

Since privet and barberry are cheap, most people can well afford to place them close together, at 18 in. On the other hand, evergreens cost considerably more; but in order to meet the increased expense of this type of hedge, the home-owner can space the plants farther apart, at 36 in., and wait several years for a permanently close and compact hedge. If he is in a hurry for the permanent effect, he buys larger plants and spaces them 18 in. apart. The important point to remember is that the ultimate effect of both hedges will be the same. The only difference will be that the closer-planted hedge will look its part a few years sooner.

Another method of obtaining quick results in a hedge is to plant 2 rows, 18–24 in. apart, the plants in one row being opposite the spaces in the other. This, of course, makes a wider hedge and insures the filling in of the bare spot made by a dead plant.

One of the purposes in planting a hedge is to keep dogs off the property. This object is easily accomplished by a mature, closely planted, thorny hedge, but the same thing can be done with a young hedge which is not thorny and where the plants are spaced far apart. A strip of chicken wire, 2–3 ft. high, is staked up through the center of the young hedgerow and by the time the wire begins to disintegrate, the plants will have grown sufficiently to present a barrier themselves. If a hedge must be grown in a shady place and the resulting growth is always more or less open at the bottom, it is a good plan to keep a strip of chicken wire in position in this way. It is not seen, and it keeps the animals out.

Care

Fertilizing is often unnecessary, since the more hedges grow, the more often they must be sheared. However, if the soil is poor or a young hedge needs added stimulus to attain the desired height, a mulch of well-rotted manure can be placed around the base of the plants or worked into the soil. This may be done either in the fall or in the spring. A mixed fertilizer (5–10–5) could be applied at the rate of 5–10 lbs. for each 100 ft. of row, depending on the size of the plants. For old, mature plants it may be possible to make an even stronger application, but this should be done only after a previous trial application.

Most deciduous hedges may be treated rather ruthlessly. When they grow old and open at the base, it is far better to cut them down to within a few inches of the ground than to try to force additional branches by the use of fertilizers and more careful cultivation. A bushy, vigorous hedge will result in short order. This does not apply to evergreen hedges, for they frequently do not respond to such rigorous treatment.

Pruning at Planting Time

Trimming should start with the very young hedge. Usually it is advisable to start with plants 3 ft. or less in height, for such plants are easily trained to grow in proper hedge form. The ideal hedge plant is one that branches from the ground to the tip of the plant. This makes for a very dense habit of growth and a good hedge. Many plants do not have this form when bought from the nursery, for they are frequently grown with a single stem or trunk, with many of the lateral branches removed. Such plants will grow satisfactorily, but the growth will be all at the top and not at the bottom near the ground. It is in this area that the side branches must be forced while the plant is still young, for as it grows taller and older, it becomes increasingly difficult to force adventitious buds at this point.

Consequently, it is usually a good practice, especially if all plants have just been purchased, to cut off the tops of the hedge plants at 6 in. or 1 ft. above the ground as soon as they have been planted. Admittedly, this is very hard for most gardeners to do, for it means cutting off a great deal of what they consider "good speci-

Hedge. Old, overgrown Privet plants can be cut to within 6 in. of the ground in the early spring and can grow back into a well-formed hedge in a few years' time.

mens". However, a "good specimen" is not wanted in hedge-making. A hedge plant is to be grown differently, as explained above, and the best time to start growing properly branched hedge plants is at the beginning.

Suppose a hawthorn hedge has been decided upon. Five-foot specimens are obtained from the nursery and when they arrive, it is noted that all are grown with a single trunk and no lateral branches on the trunk for the first 2 ft. If such plants are not pruned at planting time, there may always be that 2-ft. space at the bottom of the hedge where there are no branches. In addition, the single trunk may become injured to such an extent that the entire top part of the plant may die. If these same plants are cut off at 6–12 in. above the ground as soon as they are planted, side shoots would be forced out from that part of the trunk remaining, or from the ground, in such a manner that the plant eventually would have several main stems clothed with lateral branches from the ground up.

Most of the deciduous shrubs and trees recommended for use in hedge-making are of the type that will respond to such a severe type of pruning. I have cut off the trunks of such trees as Beech, Pin Oak, Sycamore, Norway Maple, Lombardy Poplar, the Asiatic Elm and others— trees that were 6–8 ft. tall with a trunk dia. of at least 2 in. when they were received for hedge planting—cut them off 6 in. from the ground, and observed that during the first growing season many buds were forced out from each trunk, so that they later developed into well-branched, bushy hedge plants.

Unfortunately, it is not often possible to treat evergreen hedge plants in this manner. They are slower in their habit of growth and frequently seem unable to form new leaf buds on wood that is old or large and devoid of foliage. It is a good policy never to prune evergreens back to wood that has no leaves, for if this is done, the chances are that the branch or stub may die. In buying evergreen plants for hedge-making, it is essential to have them well branched at the base, thus avoiding a great deal of trouble later.

Shape

The shape of the hedge is very important, for many an otherwise good hedge is spoiled because the owner tried to keep it too narrow at the base. In general, all hedges should be wide at the base and narrow at the top. This is especially true of evergreen hedges. Unfortunately, there are many Norway Spruce hedges in this country which are excellent examples of how not to prune a hedge. It may be that they were planted too close to the walk or road; then as they increased in height they

Left: Correct form to shear a hedge.
Right: Incorrect.

were clipped perpendicularly and were forced to grow within too narrow limits. When this is the case, the lower branches die because of lack of light and air and practically nothing will bring out new branches in their place. The result is a very poor hedge, open at the base and sometimes open as high as the eye level. Such hedges should be removed and replanted in such a way that the new plants will be allowed to grow nearly as wide as the mature hedge is high.

Anyone familiar with pruning trees knows that it is usually the shaded inner branches which are weakest and often need to be cut out. Such is the case with hedges, especially with evergreens. Hence it is always advisable to trim them so that the lower branches receive some light, and this is most easily accomplished by having them wider at the base than at the top. There are certain vigorous-growing hedge plants like the Privet and the Japanese Barberry which, when growing in good soil, can be trimmed with perpendicular sides and still remain well branched at the ground level. However, even these, when growing in poor soil, will make better hedges if trimmed so that the lower branches are wider or longer than the upper branches.

Personal preference dictates the actual shape of the finished hedge. Some like a more or less rounded hedge; others may prefer a triangular hedge with a flat top. This type is easier to trim than the rounded form, but there is the possibility, in regions where the snowfall is heavy, that the rounded form may shed the snow better with less injury to the plants.

When to Trim

Many a gardener has vigorous-growing Privet in mind when he thinks of trimming. Such plants grow so fast that they must be trimmed several times a season. However, not all hedges are like this. There are many which need be trimmed only once each year and some which need trimming only once every 2 or 3 years. It all depends on the age of the hedge, the kind of plant material and the general purpose for which the hedge is grown.

As has already been explained, the deciduous

hedge is best cut to within 6–12 in. of the ground immediately after planting. During the first year of growth the plants are left unmolested in order that they may make a maximum growth. During the second year, some may need a heavy pruning, and most certainly all will need a pinching back of the branches in order to force later growth which makes for density. Especially is it important at this time to keep the terminal shoot or leader restrained. Trees like Beech, Maple and Sycamore have strong leaders and these must be restrained in order to make the plant become more densate at the base. If the leaders are not restrained at this early date, the plant will grow high rapidly, but lateral growth (which is necessary for dense foliage, especially at the ground level) will be retarded. During the third year of growth, most plants will need a normal trimming.

Evergreens should not be cut back harshly. Hence the pinching back of terminal shoots is most essential in order to produce lateral growth. Most evergreens have strong leaders and these must be restrained in order to make the hedge become bushy. Once the small hedge has become fairly well filled in at the base, then it can be allowed to grow moderately in height.

The amount of growth to trim off depends on the kinds of plants used and on their age. For instance, one would expect to trim off more material from a Privet or Honeylocust hedge than one would from a Boxwood hedge. If the plants have not reached the height at which they are to be permanently maintained, then more growth should remain.

If the hedge has reached the height at which it will be maintained, then it may be trimmed back to within an inch (or less) of the previous years' growth. Even this is impossible to keep up indefinitely, for it is obvious that under this condition the hedge will still enlarge. Sometimes it is necessary to cut back to 2-year- or 3-year-old wood. One should be very cautious in doing this, as some plants will not respond to such severe trimming as well as others, but a little experimenting on this score, with the particular type of hedge grown, will soon show whether this severe pruning can be done. With deciduous hedges at least, it is usually possible to cut them back to near the ground level when they become overgrown, and thus a new hedge is started again.

A young hedge which has not yet reached its full height is best trimmed during the actual growing season in late spring, for as elongating shoots are pinched back, lateral buds are forced into immediate growth.

For the mature hedge, trimming may be done at any time, but during or immediately after the actual growing season is best. This is often in late June or very early July in the northern United States. At this time the growth is over for a while at least and so one trimming will suffice for a long period. Then, too, any further growth which takes place will have sufficient time to harden before cold weather. If trimming is done in late July or Aug. (in the northern U.S.), such young growth as is forced out may be too tender to withstand freezing and so be killed during the winter, leaving unsightly dead spots in the hedge. Certainly any heavy trimming, especially that done to evergreen hedges, should be done in the spring. Shaded branches are frequently the least hardy, and a heavy fall trimming, resulting in the exposure of a number of previously shaded branches, might result in serious winter injury to the hedge, whereas the same heavy trimming given in the spring would leave plenty of time for young shoots to grow and harden off properly before winter. The same caution should be taken in heavily trimming a hedge just prior to a long hot, dry spell in the summer. Such a trimming had better be advanced a few weeks into late spring in order to allow new growth to develop and shade the more vulnerable spots.

Trimming once at the end of the growing season is usually sufficient for all but the most vigorous-growing hedges such as Privet, Honeylocust and Osage Orange. It may be that a few shoots will grow and need trimming here and there before fall, but these would not be sufficient to necessitate a heavy trimming at that time. In any event, the object of each trimming is to remove the terminal buds and so force lateral buds into growth, thus increasing the density of the foliage of the entire hedge.

Kinds of Hedges

The selection of the proper kind of plant material for the hedge will save much trimming. For instance, if it is desired to have a hedge 4 ft. high, *Euonymus alatus* 'Compactus' would be ideal, for, once established, it needs only a slight trimming once every other year or so. Privet, Honeylocust, Linden, Beech; all need considerable pruning to keep them in proper form at this height. Some hedge materials that need little clipping are *Cornus racemosa*, *Taxus media* 'Hicksii', *Berberis thunbergii* 'Erecta', *Thuja occidentalis* 'Little Gem' and several others.

There are some plants used in flowering hedges such as Forsythia, Chinese Lilac, Van Houtte Spirea, which are kept unclipped until the flowers have faded and then are given a single annual trimming. After this clipping, the branches are allowed to grow untrimmed the remainder of the year, resulting in branches a foot or so long by the end of the growing season. This allows sufficient time for the formation of many flower buds, so that in the spring these hedges are covered with long, graceful shoots of flower clusters. Such hedges can be considered "formal" only immediately after they are clipped. They do take up considerable space and hence their use is limited, but when fully clothed with flowers they are outstanding indeed.

In completing this discussion, one other possibility should be presented. A Canada Hemlock hedge can be one of the most beautiful of clipped hedges, or it can be allowed to grow for a year or two without any clipping, to become one of the most graceful of the informal

Cupressus macrocarpa, the Monterey Cypress, can be clipped to form a hedge. (*Photo by Arnold Arboretum, Jamaica Plain, Mass.*)

or unclipped types. The long, arching branchlets which grow quickly in a year or two will easily be 2 ft. long and lend a very beautiful and graceful effect to the entire hedge. When they grow out of proportion, then they may be sheared off and the hedge once more becomes "formal." In this way a Hemlock hedge (and some others, likewise) may be "formal" or "informal" at the owner's whim, thus affording a landscape feature which yields varied interest for years.

Hedges for Different Purposes

Accompanying this article is a list of plants which may be used in making good hedges. Not all are hardy in all parts of the U S., but some

may be found in every area except the extremely warm parts of the country. An additional list of evergreen hedge plants is included for these particular subtropical areas. It is impossible in the allotted space to give all the information concerning such a very large group of plants.

It should be definitely stated here that all of the plants listed (with the exception of some recommended for shelterbelt planting) may be used in clipped hedges. Those listed as dense make the best clipped hedges. Plants which have been found to be unsatisfactory in hedge-making for particular reasons are not included. One example is the Mugo Pine, which really makes an excellent low-clipped hedge, but is so susceptible to scale infestation that it has been

A European Beech Hedge that is 3 ft. wide, yet 25 ft. tall, at Edinburgh, Scotland. (*Photo by Arnold Arboretum, Jamaica Plain, Mass.*)

eliminated from this list. An example of a plant with which one should be very careful is *Ribes alpinum*. The staminate form does not carry the white pine blister rust. The pistillate form does and should not be used. Otherwise, both forms make excellent low-clipped hedges.

Hardiness is a topic which has been entirely omitted here. The reader should refer to the alphabetical listing of the plant in question, where the northernmost zone in which the plant is known to be hardy is listed. *Abelia grandiflora* makes a marvelous hedge, evergreen in some sections of the South and deciduous in others, but is not satisfactorily hardy north of New York City. Everyone knows the meritorious characters of *Buxus sempervirens* as a hedge, but some may be unfamiliar with the fact that *Ilex crenata convexa* is the best substitute for this in New England. Many such interesting items will be found in the book, "Shrubs and Vines for American Gardens" (Donald Wyman, Macmillan Co., 1969).

The numbers after the plants in the following lists will refer to these groups:

1. Evergreen: Plants in this group keep their leaves most of the winter in those regions where they are used.
2. Dense: Plants in this group grow dense foliage with a minimum amount of care.
3. Thorny: Either stems or leaves thorny, making good barrier hedges.
4. Low: Can be grown as very low hedges with minimum pruning.
5. Flowering: Because of profuse flowering, these hedges may be grown as informal flowering hedges, with a trimming once a year (or even once every other year, if desired).
6. Colored Fruits: Trimming removes the majority of the flowers and fruits, yet the plants in this group have so many bright-colored fruits that, with the right trimming, some fruits will remain to give color and interest.
7. For Poor Growing Conditions: Some hedges must be planted where growing conditions are difficult and plants in this group may succeed where others would fail.
8. Narrow, Columnar and Upright: Naturally growing this way, not all make good hedges, for the terminal growth is so strong that often it is difficult to force lateral branches at ground level.
9. For trying situations in the Midwest: A special group found to be best suited to the extreme heat, cold and drought conditions of the Midwest.
10. Windbreaks and Screens: A special group of tall-growing, vigorous plants, many of which are not suited for low, clipped hedges but

which will grow rapidly into a windbreak or screen and then may be kept clipped or unclipped.

11. For the coldest parts of the United States and Southern Canada: These plants should be used in the coldest parts of the country where most of the other plants listed may be injured by the extreme cold.
12. For Shelterbelts on the northern Great Plains: Plants for a particular type of windbreak in a very difficult area. Many plants in this group will not make low, clipped hedges, and are only mentioned here for this special type of windbreak.
13. For Southern Gardens: The farther south one goes, the more kinds of plants may be used. Many not listed in this group will do very well in the South. Most of those in this group are not reliably hardy north of Philadelphia (*Tsuga caroliniana* is an exception).

	ZONE
Abelia grandiflora (5, 13)	3–4
Abies concolor (1, 2)	3
Acanthopanax sieboldianus (2, 3, 7)	5
Acer campestre (2)	5
A. ginnala (2, 10)	3
A. platanoides (10)	4
A. platanoides 'Columnare' (8, 10)	4
A. rubrum 'Columnare' (8, 10, 11)	3
A. saccharum 'Temple's Upright' (8, 10, 11)	3
Aronia arbutifolia (6)	3
Berberis buxifolia 'Nana' (1, 2, 3, 4)	6
B. circumserrata (2, 3, 6)	5
B. darwinii (1, 13)	9
B. dictyophylla albicaulis (2, 3, 6, 13)	6
B. gilgiana (2, 3, 6)	5
B. julianae (1, 2, 3)	5–6
B. koreana (2, 3, 6)	5
B. mentorensis (2, 3, 6)	5
B. stenophylla (1, 2, 3, 13)	6
B. thunbergii (2, 3, 6, 7)	3
B. thunbergii atropurpurea (2, 3, 6, 7)	3
B. thunbergii 'Erecta' (2, 3, 4, 6, 7, 8)	3
B. thunbergii 'Minor' (2, 3, 4, 6, 7)	3
B. triacanthophora (1, 3)	5
B. verruculosa (1, 2, 3)	5–6
Betula populifolia (2)	3–4
Buxus microphylla and vars. (1, 2, 4)	5
B. sempervirens and vars. (1, 2)	6
B. sempervirens 'Suffruticosa' (1, 2, 4)	6
Caragana arborescens (7, 9, 10, 11)	2
Carpinus betulus (2, 8, 10)	5
Chaenomeles japonica (2, 3, 4, 5)	4
C. speciosa (2, 3, 5, 7)	4
Chamaecyparis pisifera vars. (1, 2)	3
Cornus alba (6, 11)	2
C. mas (2, 6)	5
C. racemosa (2, 6, 7)	3
Cotoneaster lucida (4, 6)	4

	ZONE
Crataegus crus-galli (2, 3)	3
C. laevigata (2, 3)	4
C. phaenopyrum (2, 3, 6)	3
Cryptomeria japonica 'Lobbii' (1, 2, 8, 13)	5–6
Cupressus sempervirens (1, 2, 8, 13)	8–9
Elaeagnus argentea (11, 12)	2
E. angustifolia (3, 7, 9, 12)	3
Euonymus alata 'Compacta' (2, 4, 6)	4
E. fortunei vegetus (1, 4, 6)	5
E. japonicus (1, 2, 13)	7
Fagus grandifolia (2, 10)	4
F. sylvatica (2, 10)	5
Forsythia intermedia and vars. (5)	5
Fraxinus pennsylvanica lanceolata (11, 12)	2
Gleditsia triacanthos (12)	3
Hibiscus rosa-sinensis (1, 5, 13)	10
H. syriacus (5)	5–6
Hydrangea arborescens 'Grandiflora' (5)	5
H. macrophylla (5, 13)	5–6
Ilex aquifolium (1, 3, 6, 13)	7
I. cornuta (1, 3, 6, 13)	7
I. crenata and vars. (1, 2, 13)	5–6
I. opaca (1, 3, 6, 13)	5
I. vomitoria (2, 6, 13)	7
Juniperus chinensis and vars. (1, 2, 6)	4
J. scopulorum and vars. (1, 2, 6, 8, 10, 12)	3
J. virginiana and vars. (1, 2, 6, 8, 10, 11, 12)	2
Lagerstroemia indica (5, 13)	7
Larix laricina (11)	2
Lavandula officinalis (2, 4)	5
Ligustrum amurense (2, 4, 5, 6, 7)	3
L. japonicum (1, 2, 4, 6, 7, 13)	7
L. lucidum (1, 2, 4, 6, 13)	7
L. obtusifolium regelianum (2, 4, 5, 6)	5
L. ovalifolium (2, 4, 5, 6, 7, 13)	5–6
Lonicera fragrantissima (2, 6)	5
L. nitida (2, 4, 13)	8
L. pileata (2, 4, 13)	5
L. tatarica (2, 5, 6, 7, 9, 12)	3
Maclura pomifera (2, 3, 7, 9, 10)	5
Mahonia aquifolium (1, 3, 5, 6)	5
Michelia fuscata (1, 5, 6, 13)	7–8
Morus alba (10, 13)	4
Myrtus communis (1, 2, 5, 13)	8
Nandina domestica (1, 2, 5, 13)	7
Nerium oleander (1, 5, 13)	9
Osmanthus heterophyllus (1, 3, 6, 13)	6
Philadelphus coronarius (5, 7)	3
P. lemoinei 'Avalanche' (2, 5)	5
P. lemoinei 'Erectus' (2, 5, 8)	5
Physocarpus intermedius parvifolius (2, 9)	2
P. opulifolius and vars. (7, 11)	2
P. opulifolius nanus (2, 4, 7, 11)	2
Picea abies (1, 2, 10)	3
P. glauca (1, 2, 9, 10, 11, 12)	2
P. glauca conica (1, 2, 4)	2

	ZONE
P. omorika (1, 2, 10)	4
P. pungens and vars. (1, 2, 9, 11, 12)	2
Pinus nigra (1)	4
P. resinosa (1, 10, 11)	2
P. strobus (1, 2, 10)	3
Pittosporum tobira (1, 2, 13)	8
Plumbago capensis (13)	9
Poncirus trifoliata (3, 7, 13)	6
Populus nigra 'Italica' (7, 8, 9, 10, 11, 12)	3
Prinsepia sinensis (2, 3, 11)	2
Prunus americana (12)	3
P. laurocerasus and vars. (1, 2, 10, 13)	5–7
P. lusitanica (1, 6, 10, 13)	7
P. tomentosa (5, 6)	4
Pseudotsuga menziesii (1, 2, 9, 10)	3
Pyracantha coccinea 'Lalandii' (2, 3, 5, 6, 13)	5
P. crenulata (1, 2, 3, 5, 6, 13)	6–7
Quercus ilex (1, 2, 10, 13)	9
Q. imbricaria (2, 10)	5
Q. palustris (10)	4
Q. phellos (2, 10)	5
Q. robur 'Fastigiata' (8, 10)	5
Q. virginiana (1, 2, 10, 13)	7
Raphiolepsis umbellata (1, 13)	7
Rhamnus cathartica (2, 3, 7)	3
R. frangula (2, 6, 10, 11)	2
Rhododendron obtusum amoenum (1, 4, 5)	6
Ribes alpinum (staminate form) (2, 4, 9, 11)	2
Rosa multiflora (2, 3, 5, 6)	5
R. rugosa (2, 3, 5, 6, 11)	2
R. setigera (3, 5, 6)	4
R. virginiana (3, 5, 6, 11)	3
Salix pentandra (12)	4
Severinea buxifolia (3, 4, 13)	8
Spiraea arguta (5)	4
S. prunifolia (5)	4
S. thunbergii (5)	4
S. vanhouttei (2, 5)	4
Syringa chinensis (5)	5
S. josikaea (2, 5, 10, 11, 12)	2
S. persica (5, 9)	5
S. villosa (2, 5, 10, 11, 12)	2
S. vulgaris (5, 9, 10, 11, 12)	3
Tamarix ramosissima (5, 13)	4
T. parviflora (5, 13)	4
Taxus baccata and vars. (1, 2, 6, 13)	6
T. canadensis stricta (1, 4, 6)	2
T. cuspidata (1, 2, 4, 6, 8)	4
T. cuspidata 'Nana' (1, 2, 4, 6)	4
T. media 'Hicksii' (1, 2, 4, 6, 8)	4
Thuja occidentalis (1, 2, 8, 10)	2
T. occidentalis 'Douglas Pyramidal' (1, 2, 8, 10)	2
T. occidentalis 'Little Gem' (1, 2, 4)	2
T. occidentalis 'Robusta' (1, 2, 10)	2
T. orientalis and vars. (1, 2, 10, 13)	6
Tilia cordata (10)	3

	ZONE		ZONE
Tsuga canadensis (1, 2, 10)	3	V. lentago (2, 6, 11)	2
T. caroliniana (1, 2, 10, 13)	4	V. opulus 'Nanum' (2, 4)	3
Ulmus pumila (2, 7, 9, 10, 11, 12)	4	V. prunifolium (1, 2, 6, 10)	3
Viburnum dentatum (6)	2	V. tinus (1, 13)	7–8

EVERGREEN HEDGES FOR THE EXTREMELY WARM PARTS OF THE SOUTHERN UNITED STATES

DWARF

Berberis buxifolia 'Nana'
Buxus microphylla japonica
B. sempervirens 'Suffruticosa'
Cuphea hyssopifolia

Euonymus japonicus 'Microphyllus'
Lonicera nitida
Myrsine africana
Punica granatum 'Nana'

MEDIUM

Acacia armata
A. longifolia
A. verticillata
Berberis darwinii
B. pruinosa
B. stenophylla
B. xanthoxylon
Carissa edulis
C. grandiflora
Diosma ericoides
Escallonia macrantha (in trade
  as E. rubra)
E. rockii
Eugenia uniflora
Euonymus japonica
Feijoa sellowiana
Grevillea thelemanniana
Griselinia lucida
Hebe buxifolia
H. cupressoides
H. elliptica

Heba traversii
Ilex aquifolium
I. cornuta
I. crenata
Lantana camara
Leptospermum laevigatum
Ligustrum japonicum
Mahonia aquifolium
M. pinnata
Myoporum acuminuatum
Myrtus communis
Osmanthus ilicifolius
Pittosporum tobira
Psidium cattleianum
Rhamnus alaternus
R. californica
Teucrium fruticans
Viburnum suspensum
V. tinus
V. tinus lucidum

TALL BROAD-LEAVED EVERGREENS

Buxus balearica
B. sempervirens
Catha edulis
Ceratonia siliqua
Cocculus laurifolius
Coprosma baueri
C. robusta
Dodonaea cuneata
Duranta repens
Eucalyptus polyanthemos
Eugenia paniculata
E. paniculata australis
E. smithii
Ligustrum henryi
L. japonicum
L. lucidum
L. ovalifolium

Metrosideros robusta
Myrica californica
Olea europaea
Phillyrea latifolia media
Pittosporum crassifolium
P. eugenioides
P. tenuifolium
P. undulatum
P. viridiflorum
Prunus caroliniana
P. ilicifolia
P. laurocerasus
Quercus agrifolia
Q. chrysolepsis
Q. ilex
Quilliaja saponaria

CONIFERS FOR TALL HEDGES

Chamaecyparis lawsoniana
Cupressus macrocarpa

Libocedrus decurrens

HEDYCHIUM (hed-IK-ium)

coronarium 7′ **Zone 10 Common Ginger-lily**
The extreme fragrance of the delicate, beautiful, white flowers of this plant make it always remembered wherever grown. The 2 large white petals of the flowers simulate the wings of a moth, the third smaller petal its body and the 1 yellow filament might be thought of as the moth's antennae. A flower head is produced at the end of the leaf stem with a large, waxy, green bulb made up of several green bracts, and a single flower eventually develops back of each bract.

flavum 7′ **Zone 10 Yellow Ginger-lily**
This species also has a long stalk at the end of which is a flower head made up of tight green bracts. The flower that eventually develops is yellow, similar to, but smaller than, those of *H. coronarium*. These also have a delicate fragrance and are used to make leis throughout the islands of the Pacific. Native to India.

gardneranum 7′ **Zone 10 Indian Ginger-lily**
Native to India with leaves 1½ ft. long and 6 in. wide this vigorous tropical herb is used in Hawaiian gardens for its light yellow flowers about 2 in. long borne on a huge spike, sometimes 6 ft. long, which rises above the rest of the plant. These flowers form a cylinder around the top of the stalk. The long red filaments add a color contrast to the yellow of the flower.

HEDYOTIS

caerulea (*Houstonia*) 3″–6″ **Zone 3 Bluets, Quaker Ladies**
This little wet-soil perennial is one of the harbingers of spring in many parts of eastern North America where it is native. The small porcelain-blue to white flowers are only about ¼ in. across, each on a slender perpendicular stalk and each with 4 petals. The leaves are in a basal rosette, often inconspicuous when the flowers bloom in May. It is only a diminutive plant for wet-soil places and, given these, it will spread and take care of itself.

purpurea longifolia 1′ **Zone 4**
A perennial with tufts of small, linear leaves 2 or 3 in. high. The slender flower stems are crowned with small white flowers which are purple in bud. Native from Me. to Ga.

purpurea montana 6″ **Zone 7**
A species having oval leaves and flower stems which may be 12 in. high, bearing clusters of dark purple flowers each ½ in. long in mid-summer. Native to Tenn. and N.Car.

HEDYSARUM (hed-iss-A-rum)

coronarium 3′–4′ **Zone 3 Sulla Sweetvetch**
A perennial, easily cultivated and doing best in light, well-drained soil in the full sun, this is native to southern Europe. The fragrant, deep red, pealike flowers are ½ to ¾ in. long in dense erect spikes, longer than the leaves during June and early July. The leaves are alternate, compound with 3–7 pairs of entire leaflets each about ¾–1½ in. long. This makes a good ground cover.

multijugum 5′ **Zone 4 Mongolian Sweetvetch**
A perennial native to Mongolia, the compound leaves bearing 10–20 pairs of leaflets, each ½ in. long. Flowers are violet or purple, borne in the summer.

HEEL. A horticultural term meaning the case of a cutting or other material on which there is a piece of older wood. A cutting with a "heel" is a twig of the current year's growth with a slight portion of the previous year's growth at the tip.

HEELED IN. Covering the roots of dormant plants with soil for a short period.

HELENIUM (hel-EE-nium)

amarum 2′ **annual Bitter Sneezeweed**
Native from Va. to Tex., and often found farther north as a weed, this has threadlike leaves 1½ in. long and yellow heads only 1 in. across. Blooming from June to Nov. it is sometimes used in the garden for its whorled leaves, and clustered yellow flowers are produced all summer and well into the fall. Especially valued in massed plantings, but in full sun. Seeds can be sown indoors in March and set out after frost.

autumnale 6′ **Zone 3 Common Sneezeweed**
A rank-growing perennial weed of the Composite Family with winged stems and stout branches. The alternate leaves are ovate to lanceolate, 3–5 in. long, and sessile. The ray flowers are yellow, the disk flowers yellowish-brown and bloom from July to Oct. The plant grows in swamps and wet meadows over much of U.S. and Canada. Of limited horticultural interest, it is sometimes used as a background plant for the wild garden or the perennial border. The plant cluster may be divided in spring. Of several varieties 'Pumilum' remains about 2 ft. tall but has flowers that are colored both yellow and red; 'Bruno' has deep red flowers; 'Riverton Beauty' has flowers in lemon-yellow heads with purplish blotches; 'Crimson Beauty' is about 2–3 ft. tall; 'Golden Youth' about 3 ft. with large butter-yellow flowers.

bigelovii 4′ **Zone 8 Bigelow Sneezeweed**
A perennial native to Calif. with lanceolate leaves up to 10 in. long; heads of yellow flowers 2½ in. wide having a brown or brownish-yellow disk in the center.

hoopesii 3′ **Zone 3 Orange Sneezeweed**
This perennial is native to the Rocky Mountains of Ore. and Calif., leaves 10 in. or more long, and one to several yellow flower heads up to 3 in. across, blooming from May to Sept. This is frequently used in the flower border, especially valued for cut flowers.

HELIANTHEMUM (hee-li-AN-them-um). Low, trailing, evergreen shrubs from the Mediterranean Area, members of the Rose Family, having attractive foliage and flowers resembling small wild roses. They are generally hardy in the North if there is sufficient snow cover and are easily propagated from seed or from cuttings taken in summer. They do best in rather poor, dry and gravelly soil and in full sun. If pruned after blooming in early summer, the plants will flower quite heavily again in late summer. Otherwise, the later blooming will be sparse.

apenninum 15″ Zone 6 Apennine Sunrose Grayish-green leaves on long, arching branches are ornamented with loose clusters of large white flowers. This is an excellent rock garden plant, as is the variety *roseum* (sometimes called *H. rhodanthum*). 'Wendle's Rose' has wider leaves and deep pink flowers. Native to Europe and Asia Minor.

nummularium 1′ Zones 5–6 Common Sun-Rose
A plant, thriving in full sun, producing profuse flowers colored yellow, pink or white depending on variety, that are 1 in. in diameter and have 5 petals during early June and July. It is native to the Mediterraenean Region, has evergreen or half-evergreen foliage, usually opposite leaves, 1 in. long or less, silvery underneath. These are difficult to transplant and seem to do best on limestone soils. Early spring pruning can help to keep them dense and matlike when they are used as ground covers. Many varieties are available with single and double flowers of several colors, these are frequently used as ground covers but in the North they need some winter protection to bring them through the winters.

nummularium multiplex 1′ Zone 6
This excellent rock garden plant has a trailing habit. Its small leaves and beautiful, coppery, double flowers resemble miniature pompon chrysanthemums, doing well in dry, sandy locations in full sun.

HELIANTHUS (hee-li-AN-thus). The genus Helianthus includes about 60 annual or perennial species, most of which are native to North America. It is a member of the Composite Family, with leaves generally alternate, though occasionally opposite, and generally with coarsely toothed margins. The terminal flower heads range from 3–12 in. dia., with yellow ray-flowers and tubular disc-flowers which may be yellow, brown or even purple. In cultivation the species often hybridize. Easy to propagate, the perennials may be divided in spring and seeds of the annuals may be sown in the spring.

Insect Pests

The sunflower moth larvae eat the seeds and are very destructive when the plants are grown for seed. Spraying or dusting with insecticide #15 or #13 while seeds are ripening reduces the infestation. Sunflower maggot and stalk borer (see DAHLIA) tunnel the stalks, causing them to break. Regular spraying with insecticide #15 or #48 is helpful. If seeds are used for bird food, follow pesticide residue limitations. Plant bugs which suck sap and deform buds and flowers are controlled with insecticide #15.

Diseases

Brown spots on the leaves indicate rust which may cause defoliation. Usually unimportant, fungicide #D will control if necessary. Powdery mildew which is checked with fungicide #V or #M is a minor pest.

angustifolius 6′–7′ Zone 6 Swamp Sunflower
Narrow, grasslike leaves 2–7 in. long and purple disk flowers distinguish this species which grows with a slender, branching habit. Each flower head averages 12–20 ray flowers and is about 3 in. in dia. A plant of the wetlands from Long Island southward and westward to Fla. and Mo., the blooming season is from Aug. to Oct.

annuus 6′–7′ annual Common Sunflower, Cut-and-come-again
An annual which was first cultivated by the American Indians for its edible seeds. In nature, the flowers are only several inches in dia., but when cultivated they sometimes exceed 12 in. in dia. The disk flowers are dark brown, or occasionally purple, and the ray flowers yellow. It is native among the plains states and often cultivated or naturalized in the East. It flowers in late summer.

argophyllus 6′ annual Silverleaf Sunflower
A plant from Tex., with gray, silky leaves up to 6 in. long and flower heads 3 in. wide, with a brownish-purple disk. Often it is the silvery foliage which is valued more in flower arranging than are the comparatively small flowers, for the leaves, when dried, will keep their texture indefinitely.

debilis 4′ annual Cucumberleaf Sunflower
Leaves are about 4 in. long with the yellow flower heads 3 in. wide. Native from Fla. to Tex. and blooming from July to Sept. There are supposed to be varieties with copper-colored and rosy-pink flowers. The seed is simply sown in the spring where the plants are to grow and the seedlings eventually thinned to 2–3 ft. apart.

decapetalus 3′–5′ Zone 4 Thinleaf Sunflower
This perennial species has smooth stems with but few branches. The coarsely toothed leaves are opposite toward the base of the plant and alternate on the upper portion of the stem. The yellow flower heads, borne on slender stalks, have about 10 ray flowers edging the disk

flowers. They appear in mid- to late summer in dry, sunny sites throughout the Northeast and into the Plains States. There is a double-flowered variety named 'Flore-pleno'.

divaricatus   2'–3'   Zone 4   Woodland Sun-flower
Of much slighter habit than the more robust species, this perennial has lanceolate leaves which are rough on the upper surface. The small yellow flower heads are few in number and appear throughout the summer and early fall. The plant grows along the roadsides and in dry woods over much of the eastern half of the country.

giganteus   9'–12'   Zones 2–3   Giant Sun-flower
Besides its prodigious height, this perennial species is distinguished by its outward-facing, light yellow flower heads. These bloom from Aug. to Oct. over the northeastern half of U.S. and extend into Canada.

laetiflorus   8'   Zone 4   Showy Sunflower
Another vigorous-growing perennial sunflower for dry areas, native to North America, with lance-shaped leaves a foot long and flower heads, either solitary or several together, up to 3 in. wide. The color of the flower is yellow with the disk florets being purplish brown. A variety offered in England named 'Miss Mellish' has semi-double flowers that are orange-yellow.

maximilianii   12'   Zone 3   Maximilian's Sunflower
Perennial, native to the midwestern U.S. with yellow flowers to 3 in. wide, suitable for growing in dry places. The flowers are many to a stem. Blooms from Aug. to Oct.

mollis   5'   Zone 4   Ashy Sunflower
The foliage of this strongly growing perennial is covered with white hairs; the lance-shaped leaves are 5 in. long and the yellow flower heads, either single or several to a stalk, appear in summer. Native to the midwestern U.S.

petiolaris   6'   annual   Prairie Sunflower
An annual species with yellow ray flowers and disc flowers which may be brown or occasionally purple. The leaves are rather triangular, the lower ones opposite, the upper ones alternate. It is native to the sandy lands of the mid- and far West, but may be found naturalized in the East, as well. The flowers appear in late summer or early fall.

salicifolius   6'–10'   Zone 3   Willowleaved Sunflower
Blooming in Sept. and Oct., this is a perennial for dry soils since it is found in such places in the midwestern U.S. The numerous flower heads are yellow, 2 in. wide, but are not spectacular. The grasslike foliage is very ornamental. It may need staking by late July to keep the plant from

bending over. Not a very good plant for the small border, it is easily divided in the fall.

tuberosus   12'   Zone 4   Jerusalem Artichoke
A native, tuberous, perennial weed of the eastern U.S., as well as the Pacific Coast, growing in moist, peaty soils. The large, starchy tubers on the roots are edible. The leaves are opposite, ovate, 8 in. long, and the sunflowerlike flowers are yellow and up to 3½ in. wide, being borne at the end of the long, rigidly upright shoots, in Aug. and Sept.

HELICHRYSUM (hee-li-KRY-sum)
bracteatum   3'   annual   Straw-flower
An old-fashioned garden "everlasting," favored because its vari-colored flowers can be cut, dried and used in very colorful dried arrangements. The alternate, entire leaves are 2–5 in. long, and the flower heads are 1–2 in. wide. It is a member of the Composite Family, with flowers white, orange, red and yellow. Some show the yellow disc flowers of a daisy. These flowers are best cut for drying as they are just starting to open but before they are fully open, hung upside down in a dry room until thoroughly dried. As garden flowers, the seeds are started indoors in March or sown outdoors in May (after frost) in the full sun. They bloom from mid-summer to frost. Native to Australia.

bellioides   prostrate   Zone 7
A perennial, about prostrate and slightly woody with leaves ½ in. long, green above and white woolly beneath; solitary, silvery-white flower heads ½ in. wide, native to New Zealand.

petiolatum   2'   Zone 10   Cudweed Everlasting
A shrubby perennial from South Africa with woolly stems and somewhat vinelike; good for hanging baskets because of these weak stems; leaves ovate and white woolly; flower heads creamy white, 2 in. wide. The flowers are not always produced.

HELICONIA (hel-i-CON-ia)
bihai   18'   Zone 10   Wild-plantain
A perennial herb with long-stalked smooth green leaves 3 ft. long and a foot wide; raised lateral veins, greenish-yellow flowers in erect clusters. The flowers are enclosed in bright reddish bracts 6 in. long. Usually grown for foliage effects. Propagated by division of the roots, or seed. Native to tropical America.

HELIOPHILA (he-li-o-FILL-a)
leptophylla   9"   annual   Cape-stock
A South African herb with blue-green leaves 2 in. long and blue flowers, yellow at the base; fruits are pods. Seeds sown indoors in March are planted out after frost, in full sun, 6 in. apart.

linearifolia   3'   annual
A South African herb but shrubby with linear leaves an inch long, blue flowers with yellow

claws. Fruits are pods. Propagated by seeds as mentioned for *H. leptophylla*.

HELIOPSIS (he-li-OP-sis). There are only about 12 species of Heliopsis, the ones described below being the ones usually grown. They are rather coarse, weedy plants, found over a wide area of North America, and are best used in the informal border or the wild garden. The flowers are yellow, like small sunflowers, borne on long stems and good for cutting and arranging in bouquets. The plants are very easy to grow and easily propagated by division.

helianthoides 5′ **Zone 3 Sunflower Heliopsis**
A vigorous-growing, native American (Ont. to Fla.) perennial, which will withstand poor dry soil but if given good soil will produce a wealth of bloom throughout the summer. A member of the Composite Family, the flower heads are yellow, $2\frac{1}{2}$ in. across, and with cutting the plants can be kept about 3 ft. high. There are 10–20 notched yellow ray flowers surrounding the brown disk flowers.

The var. 'Pitcheriana' has blossoms larger and deeper yellow than those of the species.

These plants might be divided every 3–4 years to make them grow better. Best propagate by division to retain the desirable types; cuttings of roots are easily made throughout the summer. Although seeds can be sown these may yield seedlings of undesirable types.

var. scabra (Formerly popularly called *H. scabra*) 5′ **Zones 2–3 Rough Heliopsis**
This differs from *H. helianthoides* in having rough-hairy foliage with fewer flower heads. Native from Me. to N.Mex. There are some improved cultivars that are better for garden use. 'Excelsa'—flowers chrome yellow, almost double; 'Eminens'—flowers chrome yellow, 3 in. across, only 3 ft. tall but blooming continuously from July to Sept.; 'Gold Greenheart'—flowers yellow double; 'Incomparabilis'—flowers semi-double, excellent, first listed in 1933.

HELIOTROPE. See HELIOTROPIUM.

HELIOTROPISM. The characteristic plants have of turning toward the light.

HELIOTROPIUM (he-li-o-TRO-pium). These are vanilla-scented herbs or shrubs with umbels of small purplish-to-white flowers from May to Sept. and simple alternate leaves. They are usually considered greenhouse plants requiring plenty of moisture and rich soil. They make excellent bedding plants and are frequently treated as annuals. Seeds may be sown in the greenhouse in March, set out a foot apart in late May. They also can be easily propagated by cuttings or by layering. Often these plants are seen as standards. To obtain such plants, take cuttings in autumn, keep them growing all winter until they reach the desired height. Old plants can be grown as standards for several years if the pots are kept small. Care should be taken not to plant them out until one is certain all danger of frost is over for they are extremely susceptible to frost injury.

arborescens 4′–6′ **Zone 10 Common Heliotrope**
This is the common Heliotrope so highly valued for the vanilla fragrance of its flat clusters of bluish-to-white flowers from May to Sept. Native to Peru. It is grown on standards for setting out in tubs as feature plants in the summer, in hanging baskets, and is also used for bedding. Very susceptible to frost so that plants to be grown for several years should not be subjected to any cold weather.

corymbosum = *H. arborescens*

curassavicum 6″ **annual Seaside Heliotrope**
A creeping annual which forms a matted growth, it bears a spike of small white or blue flowers and blooms throughout the summer and early fall. Since it thrives under the harsh conditions of the seashore, it may be used as a ground-cover plant for seaside gardens. Clumps of the plant may be transplanted in the spring. Native to Peru.

europaeum 12′ **annual European Heliotrope**
Similar to *H. curassavicum*, this naturalized species is taller. The flowers are white to pale blue.

peruvianum = *H. arborescens*

HELIPTERUM (hell-IP-ter-um). Member of the Composite Family, liking to grow in the full sun and usually treated as annuals, sometimes called Everlasting because the flowers are especially adaptable to drying and using as winter bouquets. Leaves alternate, entire, with small heads of yellow disklike flowers. Native to South Africa and Australia. Sow seeds where plants are to grow outdoors in the full sun and thin to 9 in. apart.

humboldtianum $1\frac{1}{2}$′ **annual Humboldt Sunray**
Linear, white tomentose leaves, flower heads $\frac{1}{8}$ in. across in dense terminal clusters.

manglesii $1\frac{1}{2}$′ **annual Mangle's Sunray**
A slender plant, with flower heads about $1\frac{1}{2}$ in. across, each one of which is surrounded with white to bright pink bracts. They are not clustered.

roseum 2′ **annual Rose Sunray**
Linear leaves, flower heads not clustered, each head 2 in. across, bracts rose to white.

HELLEBORE. See HELLEBORUS.

HELLEBORE, AMERICAN FALSE = *Veratrum viride*

HELLEBORINE. See EPIPACTUS.

HELLEBORUS (hell-e-BOR-us). As a group these thrive in shaded situations in partially moist soils. They are almost stemless plants with often evergreen leaves. Flowers appear in late fall or winter. The best garden species is the white-flowering *H. niger*. Propagated by division in Aug. or Sept., but the roots are very brittle so care should be taken in dividing plants. It should be noted that all parts of the Helleborus species are very poisonous and have a bitter taste. They come from limestone areas of Europe and Asia. Flowers are greenish to white.

foetidus   1′   **Zone 6**   **Bearsfoot Hellebore**
Flowers green or purplish, 1 in. long. Leaves leathery. Not nearly as good a garden plant as *H. niger*. Native to western Europe.

lividus   1½′   **Zone 7**   Corsica **Christmas-rose**
Leaves 3 parted, flowers pale green, borne in a cluster and bloom in April. Not nearly as good an ornamental as *H. niger*. Native to Corsica.

niger   1′   **Zone 3**   **Christmas-rose**
A stemless, herbaceous, evergreen perennial, with leaves erect, palmately divided into 7 leaflets. The flowers are solitary white, flushed with rose, nearly 2½ in. across. If it is in a sheltered location at the foundation of a building it may bloom at Christmas even in Mass. It can be counted on to bloom in the late fall. Propagation is by division in Aug. or Sept. Rootstocks and leaves are poisonous when eaten. Bruised parts of the herb may produce severe dermatitis to humans. It is a valued ornamental because of its very late bloom. Native to Europe. The variety **altifolius** has a petiole up to a foot long and flowers 3–5 in. across.

orientalis   1½′   **Zone 6**   **Lenten-rose**
Popular in Europe but not much grown in America, it differs from *H. niger* in that the flowers are borne several on a stalk, being green to dark purple. Native to Asia Minor.

viridis   2′   **Zone 6**   **Green Hellebore**
The leaves are divided into 7–11 leaflets; the flowers are yellowish green. Although it is supposed to be naturalized in parts of eastern North America it is not seen often in gardens. Native to Europe.

HELONIAS (hell-O-nias)

bullata   2′   **Zone 6**   **Swamp-pink**
Although restricted in its use to the bog garden, this plant, native to the swamps of N.J. and a member of the Lily Family, is an excellent ornamental. The leaves, rising from a tuberous root, are narrow and 12 in. long. The flower stalk is thick and is crowned by a tight 3 in. cluster of pink flowers each ¼ in. long in spring. Easily propagated by division.

HELXINE See SOLEIROLIA.

HEMEROCALLIS (hem-er-o-KAL-is) (from the Greek meaning "Beautiful for a Day").
Only the rapidly-accelerating popularity of the flower is new—knowledge of the flower itself as a garden perennial, a medicinal herb and an article of diet is ages old, dating back to long before the Christian Era. *Hemerocallis* species are a group of fleshy-rooted herbs, some of which have evergreen foliage, and all of which have conspicuously colored lilylike flowers and sword-shaped leaves.

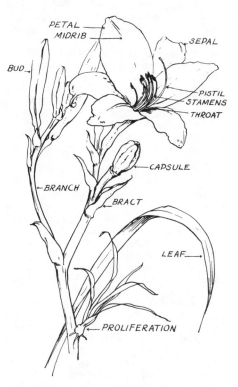

Hemerocallis—plant and flower parts

Judged by modern standards of floral excellence, the 16 or so original *Hemerocallis* species are not too glamorous. In fact, they are a rather nondescript lot. They are to be noted chiefly for having fathered a race of flowers that can now satisfy the most robust as well as the most fastidious of tastes. Most of the species were discovered in Eurasia as far south as Nepal, as far north as Manchuria and Siberia, and from the Japanese Islands westward to the Caucasus. Whether for their supposed medicinal qualities, for their flowers, or for their value as articles of diet, they gradually found their way westward to Europe and England, and thence to the New World, where their rugged constitutions appealed to the American colonists too busy carving homes out of a hostile wilderness to bother much with flower gardens. *H. liliasphodelus*, the beloved Lemon Daylily of our great-grand-mothers' gardens and the ubiquitous *H. fulva* 'Europa', variously known in America as the Tawny Daylily, Corn Daylily, etc., which is an escape from old cemeteries and abandoned pioneer homesteads, are the 2 daylilies that were most widely known and even treasured at the turn of the century.

The more important of the *Hemerocallis* species listed in the order of their importance in the breeding of the modern daylilies are: *H. fulva rosea*, *H. fulva* 'Europa', *H. aurantiaca*, *H. aurantiaca major*, *H. aurantiaca littorea*, *H. altissima*, *H. citrina*, *H. thunbergii*, *H. flava*, *H. multiflora*.

Other species such as *H. dumortieri*, *H. forestii minor*, *H. middendorffii*, *H. nana*, *H. plicata*, etc. have been utilized to a greater or lesser degree by our pioneer hybridizers; but our modern breeders of daylilies prefer to employ cultivars several generations removed from the species. Until additional species are discovered that possess plant and flower characteristics not present in the species utilized so far, work with them will lag.

altissima   4′–8′   **Zone 6**
Of Japanese origin, this is the giant of the genus. It is light yellow, fragrant, blooms at night, usually during late July. Dr. A. B. Stout made many crosses with this as one of the parents, and it is to be hoped that hybridizers will again turn to it when they realize that, in spite of the current popularity of the medium and low varieties, we do need a few varieties tall enough for the back of the border.

aurantiaca   3′   **Zone 6**   **Orange Daylily**
Of Japanese origin, with flowers a burnt-orange color, evergreen foliage and not too hardy in the North. It blooms in early midseason.

The var. **major** (Zones 9–10) has large and more brilliant red-orange flowers up to 6 in. across, evergreen foliage, and is difficult to cultivate in the North. It is thought to be the progenitor of Mrs. Bright Taylor's 'Prima Donna' which is itself the progenitor of so many top-ranking varieties of the 1950's and 1960's.

The var. **littorea** is of Japanese origin, the flowers have a pale fulvous color, with rather narrow petals, but blooming as it does in late July it is quite valuable in extending the blooming season into the late summer and fall months. Dr. George M. Darrow of Glenn Dale, Md., used this variety with some success, and others are somewhat belatedly realizing its breeding potential.

citrina   4′   **Zones 2–3**   **Citron Daylily**
Of Chinese origin, blooming in late July. The flowers up to 6 in. long, are light yellow, fragrant and night blooming. It is in the ancestry of many of our finest light yellow and fragrant varieties.

dumortieri   1½′   **Zones 2–3**   **Early Daylily**
Native to Japan with pale orange, fragrant flowers 2¾ in. long. This blooms in the spring and has very fleshy roots. It is not now popular.

forrestii   16″   **Zone 7**   **Forrest's Daylily**
Native to southwest China, the flowers are clear cadmium yellow with 4 or more flowers on a slender scape. This blooms in spring. Of little ornamental value when compared with the modern hybrids.

fulva   2′   **Zones 2–3**   **Tawny Daylily**
Native to Europe and Asia, naturalized in the eastern United States, the orange-red flowers are 5 in. long, 3½ in. across and are not fragrant. It blooms in midsummer and is common in gardens.

The variety 'Europa' does not set seed but it does produce pollen and has been used extensively in crosses. Paul Cook, before he abandoned his daylily breeding to devote his time exclusively to breeding tall bearded iris and dwarf iris, secured some very brilliant reds using 'Europa' pollen.

Var. 'Kwanso' has double flowers, leaves striped white sometimes, and blooms a little later than the species.

Var. 'Rosea' was discovered in Kiangsi Province, China, and sent by Stewart to the New York Botanical Garden, where it was named in 1939 and extensively used in breeding pink- and red-flowered varieties by Dr. H. B. Stout and more recently by David F. Hall and others. Most of the original species of *Hemerocallis* had flowers in shades of yellow and orange. Only in this variety of *H. fulva* and in *H. aurantiaca* do we find the strong red and pink pigmentation that our American hybridizers utilized so effectively in producing our really outstanding modern pinks and reds.

lilioasphodelus (*flava*)   3′   **Zone 3**   **Lemon Daylily**
Native to eastern Asia, this blooms quite early in the season, closely following the tall bearded iris. Flowering scapes are rather weak and arching, with lemon-yellow, fragrant flowers about 4 in. long. Formerly widely grown both in Europe and the United States, and now rarely seen, having long since been superseded by the modern derivatives.

middendorffii   1′   **Zones 2–3**   **Middendorff Daylily**
Native to Siberia, blooming in May and June, the flowers of this species are pale orange in a close cluster, each flower about 2¾ in. long. Of little ornamental value when compared with the modern hybrids.

minor   18″   **Zones 2–3**   **Grass-leaf Daylily**
Native from eastern Siberia to Japan, with

yellow, fragrant flowers 4 in. long and 2–3 on each scape. This blooms in the spring but is not a popular garden plant especially when compared with the modern hybrids.

multiflora 3′ **Zone 4 Mayflower Daylily** Native to China, this has small orange-colored flowers appearing late in the season on a multi-branched scape. The flowers are about 2½ in. long and 3 in. across. It is very valuable in breeding for miniature-type flowers that have recently become quite popular.

thunbergii 3′ **Zones 2–3 Thunberg Daylily** Native to Japan, with small lemon-yellow, fragrant flowers that bloom at night during the late midseason. It is somewhat similar to *H. flava* except that the latter blooms quite early in the season. It was much used by the earlier *Hemerocallis* breeders.

Breeding

It is impossible to list here all the plant breeders that have had a part in transforming the original species into one of the most

Hemerocallis—single- and double-flowered and dwarf varieties.

glamorous perennials we have in our modern gardens, but we owe such a deep debt of gratitude to the pioneers in this field that we should at least mention a few. George Yeld, an English school teacher, was the first recorded hybridizer of daylilies. Starting his work in 1877 and continuing for almost 50 years, he produced such all-time favorites as 'Aurelia', 'J. S. Gayner',

'Radiant', 'Sovereign', 'Tangerine', and 'Winsome'. 'J. S. Gayner' still ranks as one of the best parents for many new hybrids. Amos Perry, an English nurseryman, made significant contributions. Other Europeans deserving mention were: Karl L. Sprenger and his nephew, Willy Mueller (Italians); R. Wallace and Son, Ltd. (English); C. G. van Tubergen (Dutch); Victor Lemoine and Son (French); and H. Christ of Germany.

Perhaps war and the ravages of war are chiefly responsible for the European lag in daylily hybridizing during the last 40 years. Comparatively speaking, America came through this disruptive period without serious derangement of its normal way of life; and consequently the further improvement of the daylily shifted to America. Plant breeders in the United States were quick to realize the potentialities of the daylily as the one rugged perennial that could give them bloom during the hot, dry summer months.

The first clone known to have been hybridized in America was 'Florham', a hybrid of *H. aurantiaca major* x *thunbergii*, registered by A. Herrington of N.J. in 1899. Between 1914 and 1924 Luther Burbank introduced 4 varieties, one of which was 'Calypso'. Bertrand H. Farr, a Pennsylvania nurseryman, introduced in 1924 several new varieties among which was 'Ophir'. Paul Cook, the noted iris breeder, started working with daylilies in 1924, and in the years following introduced several fine varieties; among them, 'Valiant', one of the parents of 'High Noon'. Another Hoosier, Franklin B. Mead, originated the still popular 'Hyperion' about 1925. Beginning in 1928, Carl Betscher of Ohio introduced many of our favorites of past years such as 'Earlianna', 'J. A. Crawford', 'Mrs. W. H. Wyman' and 'Modesty'. Significant pioneering work with daylilies was done in the early 1900's by the Sass Brothers of Omaha, Neb.; but none was introduced until 1933. Among the most notable of their introductions were 'Midwest Majesty' (winner of the best scape in the National Capitol Daylily Club Show in Washington, D.C. in 1965), 'Orange Beauty', and 'Revolute'. Mrs. Thomas Nesmith of Lowell, Mass., introduced her first variety in 1933 and in the long years since has become one of our best known hybridizers.

Perhaps the most notable contribution toward the evolution of the modern daylily was made by Dr. Arlo B. Stout, who, as Director of Laboratories at the New York Botanical Garden, worked for many years with species gathered there from all over the world and produced much of the basic breeding stock that other hybridizers used in creating our modern hybrids.

Ralph W. Wheeler (Fla.) made a monumental contribution by introducing 'Cellini', the forerunner of a new race of wide-petaled, crepey-textured, open-faced light yellow varieties such as 'Flying Saucer' and the more recent 'Tony Wille'.

In more recent times, the work of the following hybridizers stands out as significant milestones in the improvement of the daylily; Dr. E. J. Kraus, Ill. and Ore.; Carl S. Milliken, Calif.; David F. Hall, Ill.; Hugh M. Russell, Tex.; Mrs. Hugh Lester, Ga.; Mrs. Bright Taylor, Fla.; Elmer Claar, Ill.; Mrs. Elizabeth Nesmith, Mass.; Hooper Connell, La.; and the Sass Brothers, Neb.

The number of dedicated professional and amateur hybridizers now working with daylilies would probably exceed the thousand mark—obviously too many to be even mentioned here. But through their efforts the once lowly daylily is being transformed into "a many splendored thing" that has captured the fancy of the flower-loving public as no other flower has done since the days of the tulip craze in Holland. And this interest bids fair to be a sustained one and to mount as the beautification process continues.

Many characteristics of the modern daylily contribute to and amply justify this popularity. Its main blooming season—during the hot and often dry summer months—comes at a time when there is a dearth of bloom in the garden; and the season is now being extended in both directions so that we now have varieties that bloom shortly after the Tall Bearded Iris has finished and other varieties that bloom until the scapes are cut down by frost. More and more varieties are repeaters, sending up scape after scape the entire season. In height daylilies range from less than a foot to over 7 ft.; and individual flowers range from a little over an inch in dia. to 10 in. Branching has been much improved with some varieties bearing more than 50 buds per scape. Substance in some of the original species and early hybrids was quite thin and fragile, but we now have varieties with substance so thick and firm that flowers come through the heaviest downpours with only superficial damage. Indicative of the versatility in flower form that we now have in daylilies are such adjectives as flat, round, triangular, recurved, tubular, cup-shaped, bow-shaped, bell-shaped, trumpet, orchid-shaped, spider, etc., all more or less accurate descriptions of prevailing flower forms.

But perhaps the most spectacular improvement made in the daylily has been in the realm of color. Here the hybridizer has captured practically every color in the rainbow with the exception of pure white and pure blue. An absolutely flat pure white may never be attained; but the off-whites, near-whites and tinted whites leave little to be desired—one can scarcely imagine more cool refreshing colors on a hot summer day than we find in the green-throated, chartreuse-tinted, pale creamy yellows we now have. Blue, since it occurs in the daylily as a sap-soluble pigment, will be difficult—perhaps impossible to segregate. Lilacs, purples, orchids, mauves we now have; and working with them we may eventually get near blues, but pure blues probably never.

Breeders are now achieving some quite novel color patterns. Selfs, bi-tones, bi-colors, reverse bi-colors, eyed and haloed varieties we have had for many years; but "*plicata*" types, 3-color zone types, and flowers with distinct bands of color on the tips of petals and sepals are comparatively recent innovations. 'Florence Clary' and 'Melody Lane' are inexpensive varieties of the "*plicata*" type; 'Linger Longer' of the 3-color zone type; and 'Pink Lightning' and 'Step Forward' represent the banded type.

For the growing number of gardeners who can enjoy their flowers only after working hours, varieties are now being produced that open in the late afternoon, continue in bloom through the night, during the following day and well into the following evening. More and more such varieties will be forthcoming as the need for them becomes more generally recognized by breeders. Present examples of this type that are moderately priced are 'Blythe Spirit' and 'Green Valley'

Tetraploids

An exciting new phase in daylily breeding is now being ushered in as a result of the colchicine-induced tetraploid daylilies. In nature the daylily is a diploid plant, its cells containing 22 chromosomes. If, however, its growing points or its proliferations are treated with a dilute solution of the colchicine drug, cell division is interrupted and we end up with cells with double the number of chromosomes—44 instead of the usual 22. The technique involved is a bit complicated and somewhat dangerous since colchicine is a poisonous alkaloid drug. Its use should be left to those who possess some knowledge of safe laboratory procedure.

The possibility of variation in all characters is greatly increased in these tetraploid forms. Pioneers in this field are Robert Schreiner, Salem, Ore.; Dr. Hamilton P. Traub, La Jolla, Calif.; W. Quinn Buck, Arcadia, Calif.; Orville Fay, Northbrook, Ill.; Dr. Robert A. Griesbach, Park Ridge, Ill.; Dr. Tofru Arisumi, Beltsville, Md.; Dr. Virginia Beck, Murfreesboro, Tenn.; and Dr. George M. Darrow, Glenn Dale, Md. The cost of some of the first induced tetraploids ran as high as $500.00 per plant; but now that initial difficulties in breeding them have been overcome and true tetraploids are being grown from seed from second and third generation tetraploid plants, the cost of tetraploid varieties should soon be competitive with the better varieties of diploids. The future of the tetraploids would seem to be a rosy one indeed.

Culture

Ease of culture, next to the beauty of the flower and the general attractiveness of the plant in the garden, commends the daylily to the average gardener, hurried and harassed as he very often is by the demands upon his time and energies. Given good garden loam, full sunlight or even partial shade, light fertilization in the spring or early summer with a 12-12-12 fertilizer with trace elements added, supplemental watering before and during the blooming season in case of drought, and clean cultivation or mulching to keep down weeds, one can be assured of show quality bloom.

However, the daylily can survive and even multiply under neglect that would quickly prove fatal to many other perennials; and for that reason, it is now being used more and more for healing eroded gullies, holding steep inclines, preventing under-cutting of river banks during spring freshets, and landscaping difficult areas where a minimum of care and upkeep is provided. The thousands upon thousands of seedlings that are now being grown by our hybridizers each year and rejected because they do not quite measure up to our present high standards of excellence, could be used for the above purposes. There could also be utilized the large stocks of older varieties now superseded by more recent originations. Many nurseries carry such varieties because they hate to destroy them even though they represent a loss. Of course, *H. fulva* 'Europa' outranks all others in its ability to spread a tenacious carpet that can hold firm against all the onslaughts of nature and man! This, because of its ability to extend itself in all directions by underground root stalks or rhizomes. Luckily, our preferred garden varieties do not possess this means of rapidly over-running neighboring plants.

Economic Uses

The economical value of the daylily as an article of diet has been known and appreciated by the Chinese for hundreds of years. Daylilies do not occur in large patches but are grown along the edges of gardens and fields and in locations not suited to the major farm crops. The fresh flowers are gathered, steamed and carefully dried. Itinerant collectors travel from farm to farm gathering the cured product, and eventually much of it finds its way to Hong Kong where it is attractively packaged and exported to meet the demands of restaurants in America who cater to Chinese-American tastes. In Chinese groceries it is known as *Gum-jum* or *Gum-tsoy*— English translation: Golden Needle or Golden Vegetable. It is used in soups and stews, much as Okra is used, to give a gelatinous quality and flavor that is delicious.

In late spring and early summer when daylily growth is rapid and before the flowering scapes appear, the plant may be severed just above the crown, the outer leaves stripped off, and the tender center sliced for salads or prepared and eaten like Asparagus—either way it is quite palatable. The fresh flower buds or open flowers, dipped in egg batter and fried in deep fat to a golden brown, make a tasty tidbit.

There is an underground food source, too, in such daylilies as *H. fulva* '**Europa**', especially in the late spring when the new tuberlike roots are white and crisp. When eaten raw, they have a sweet, nutlike flavor. For those who consider themselves connoisseurs of fine foods, whether meat eaters or vegetarians, many tantalizing recipes may be found on page 226 of the Nov–Dec., 1964 issue of "The Garden Journal" (published by The New York Botanical Garden) by Dr. Shiu-ying Hu who is an authority on the subject. Chemical analysis has shown the dried daylily flowers to be a high-protein, non-fattening food rich in minerals and in vitamins A and B. On the basis of dry weight, 11.42% is protein; 3.3% minerals; 2.27% fats; and 8.48% crude fibers. The daylily should prove a welcome addition to the diet of those weight-conscious members of our generally overfed population here in America.

Although it remains for pharmaceutical and medical research to discover and validate the medicinal properties of the daylily, the root and crown have nevertheless been used for thousands of years by Asiatics as a diuretic, and to reduce fever, relieve pain, and to treat a variety of ailments such as piles, jaundice, dropsy, breast tumors, etc. Such uses can not be brashly swept aside as the result of ignorance and superstition growing out of and perpetuated by Chinese folklore and legend; and it is to be hoped that the light of science will soon illuminate the areas of truth in these Chinese claims.

Varieties

It is not for its medicinal properties, or as an article of diet, or as a means of erosion control that the daylily is so extensively grown in America; but for its beauty as a garden perennial. There is hardly a garden of note in the country that does not have its treasured collection of modern daylily hybrids. There are some 12,000 varieties now registered with the American Hemerocallis Society, and the number is being augmented each year by between 700 and 800 new registrations. With such a multiplicity of choices available, it is difficult to make an arbitrary recommendation as to the "best" varieties in commerce—this is especially true where the list is restricted to 25 varieties. However, I believe that most informed daylily connoisseurs would agree that the following lists contain some of the most beautiful Hemerocallis in existence that can be purchased at a reasonable figure:

soil until the crown of the proliferation is an inch or so below the soil surface. If the ground is kept moist, the proliferation, although it at first appears to brown up slightly, will take root, and by the following year should make a saleable plant of the same variety from which it was taken.

To speed up the rate of increase, growers have in recent years been experimenting with various kinds of what we might call "mutilation" techniques. One of these is to sever the plant at the crown, scoop out the crown leaving just a rim of crown tissue. On this rim adventitious buds will develop which are detached after they have grown into small grasslike plants and

Red Shades
'Anzac'
'Arriba'
'Bail Bond'
'Barbarossa'
'Bonnie Barbara Allen'
'Cherry Cheeks'
'Damascus Road'
'Douglas Dale'
'Ed Murray'
'Fleeta'
'Lonnie'
'My Son Bob'
'Oriental Ruby'
'Paige Parker'
'Post Time'
'Prairie Warrior'
'Queen's Grace'
'Red Rowan'
'Red Spinel'
'Rozavel'
'Sail On'
'Sir Patrick Spens'
'Tovarich'

Melon and Pink Blended
*   Shades*
'Clarence Simon'
'Commendment'
'Cornerstone'
'Egyptian Spice'
'Frances Fay'

'Gertrude Smith'
'Heather Green'
'Heather Hills'
'Heavenly Harp'
'Helen Connelly'
'Kathleen Elsie Randall'
'Kwan Yin'
'Little Rainbow'
'Louise Denham'
'Loyal Subject'
'Magic Wind'
'Mary Moldovan'
'Master Touch'
'Twilight Sky'
'Yasmin'

Purple and Lavender Shades
'Catherine Woodbery'
'Charles Buckman'
'Chicago Royal'
'Emperor's Robe'
'Jock Randall'
'Little Grapette'
'Little Wart'
'May Hall'
'Olivier Monette'
'Persian Palace'
'Sari'
'Tammas'

Eyed Varieties
'Arkansas Post'

'Buffy's Doll'
'King's Cloak'
'Prairie Blue Eyes'
'Rocket City'
'Sea Warrior'
'Twenty-Third Psalm'

Near White or Light Cream
'Amazing Grace'
'Celestial Light'
'Chosen One'
'Hope Diamond'
'Ice Carnival'
'Moment Of Truth'
'Prairie Moonlight'
'Robert Way Schlumpf'
'Silver Fan'
'So Lovely'
'White Formal'

Light to Pale Yellow
'American Dream'
'Ava Michelle'
'Bonnie John Seton'
'Dream Baby'
'Evening Bell'
'Gleeman Sone'
'Green Glitter'
'Jakarta'
'Jomico'
'Olive Pauley'
'Perennial Pleasure'

'Renee'
'Winning Ways'

Yellow, Gold or Orange
'Bertie Ferris'
'Bitsy'
'By Myself'
'Edna Spalding Memorial'
'Full Reward'
'Golden Milestone'
'Golden Prize'
'Green Flutter'
'Hortensia'
'Hudson Valley'
'Jimmie Fry'
'Jamie Douglas'
'Lillian Fry'
'Malaysia'
'Mary Todd'
'Sable'
'Wabada'

Pink
'Bambi Doll'
'Edna Spalding'
'Higashi'
'Queen Eleanor'
'Satin Silk'
'Shell Pink'
'Viola Parker'
'Winsome Lady'

From the great number of varieties now available other lists of equal merit and appeal could be made; but the lists above contain varieties that will satisfy the most discriminating tastes.

Propagation

The usual method of propagating daylilies is by dividing the clumps into single fan divisions, lining these out and growing them for a season to insure blooming-size plants the first year after purchase. Another method is to root the proliferations that sometimes develop at the bracts on the flowering scapes of some varieties. The scape is severed a few inches above and below the proliferation and then pushed into the

lined out to be grown to saleable size.

Another method is to remove the soil from around the crown, and with a very sharp knife cut vertically upward, stopping the cut just above the crown, leaving the fan and roots undisturbed. The cut surfaces are kept separated by a tooth pick or thin plastic spline. The plant will then develop 2 crowns if 1 cut is made and 4 if 2 cuts are made. One advantage of this method lies in the fact that the normal growth of the plant is not greatly interfered with. Whatever type of mutilation method is employed, the cut surfaces should be treated with a fungicide to prevent rotting before the healing process is complete. It is thought that minute application of gibberellic acid is of value in connection with these mutilation techniques, but much experimentation remains to be done before these various techniques can be recommended as approved propagation methods.

The daylily is easily grown from seed. In the Deep South the seed can be planted immediately after it is ripe and bloom can be expected the following year. In the North, however, it takes 2–3 years to bring the seedlings into flower, unless the greenhouse is employed, in which case some bloom can be expected the first year after seed harvest. The quality of these seedlings depends directly on the quality of the parentages employed in making the crosses. Generally speaking, 1 or 2 seedlings out of a thousand are sufficiently distinct and outstanding to warrant registration and introduction into commerce. It is of the utmost importance that hybridizers familiarize themselves with what others in the field are doing so that they will not introduce varieties that are near duplicates of varieties already in commerce.

Pests

The daylily, compared with other leading garden perennials, is remarkably free from damage by insects and fungus diseases. Thrips cause an occasional distorted flower, and nematodes are something of a problem in some sections of the South, and a condition somewhat resembling "scorch" in Iris is discovered in some plantings. In the Deep South, where soil temperatures during the hot summer months range so high as practically to "steam cook" the crowns, daylilies suffer damage from rotting. For this reason, dividing and transplanting should be done in the cooler fall and spring months. In the North and in other cooler sections of the country dividing and transplanting can be done at any time during the summer months. The farther we get away from the original species, whose inherent vigor and resistance to disease derives from the survival of the fittest under the most trying conditions through perhaps thousands of years, and the more we pamper and coddle our seedling plots, the more we can expect a lessening of resistance to insect and disease damage. Some hybridizers have consciously bred for vigor and disease resistance and have produced varieties possessing these qualities to an even greater degree than the original species.

Information Sources

Those desiring more complete information on Hemerocallis will find the best source of information the publications of the American Hemerocallis Society: Journals, Yearbooks, Check Lists, Check List Supplements, Newsletters, etc. On pages 29–33 of the "Hemerocallis Journal" (Registration Supplement), Vol. 15—No. 2, the April–May–June Issue for 1961, an excellent bibliography on Hemerocallis by Dr. Virginia Peck is given.

Perhaps the most complete collection of material dealing with the daylily is to be found in the American Hemerocallis Society's library. This material is made available to members of the Society through the Librarian, for cost of postage both ways. Sets of colored slides of the most outstanding varieties may be obtained at nominal rental cost from the Slide Library Chairman. The late Professor Ira S. Nelson initiated a daylily library and herbarium in connection with the University of South Louisiana at Lafayette, La. Here all available literature dealing with Hemerocallis has been carefully collected and catalogued.

WILMER B. FLORY

HEMIPTELEA (hem-IPT-e-lea)

davidii   15′   Zone 5   David Hemiptelea
A small shrubby tree with many branches, and for this reason sometimes used as a hedge especially in North China where it is native. The branches are spiny, the alternate leaves are 1–2 in. long; the flowers are polygamous and of no ornamental significance, appearing at the same time as the leaves in the spring. The fruits are small winged nutlets. Propagated by seed sown as soon as ripe, layers, softwood cuttings or grafting on Elm.

HEMLOCK. See TSUGA.

HEMP = *Cannabis sativa*

HEMP FAMILY = Cannabinaceae

HEMP, MANILA = *Musa textilis*

HEMP, SISAL = *Agave sisalana*

HEMPWEED, CLIMBING = *Mikania scandens*

HEN-AND-CHICKENS = *Sempervivum tectorum*

HENNA = *Lawsonia inermis*

HEPATICA (hee-PAT-ik-a)

acutiloba   9″   Zone 4   Sharp-lobed Hepatica
An attractive perennial of the shady woods where the soil is neutral or slightly acid, the plant has basal, long-stalked, 3-lobed leaves which are pointed and remain on the plant throughout the winter. After the flowering season, the old leaves wither and new ones are formed. The flowers are without petals but have petal-like sepals which are bluish white. The calyx is 3 lobed. The flowers appear in early spring. If planted in the wild garden, the site should simulate the native habitat. Seeds may be sown in the spring or the plant may be divided after flowering. The range extends from

Me. to the area around the Great Lakes and south to Ala. and Ga.

americana 6″ Zone 4 Round-lobed Hepatica
Leaves with rounded lobes distinguish this species, if indeed it is a separate species from *H. acutiloba*. The pale lilac to pinkish-white flowers appear very early in spring, March to June. The flower stems and buds are hairy. Dry woods soils are the habitat of the plant which may be found over the eastern half of U.S. and southern Canada. It is an excellent plant for the wild garden and may be propagated by division after flowering. Easily self-sows.

HEPTACHLOR. A chlorinated hydrocarbon used as an insecticide. See INSECTICIDES.

HERACLEUM (her-ak-LEE-um)
laciniatum (*villosum*) **10′–12′ biennial Giant Cow-parsnip**
A large plant with large flat, white flower clusters, leaves deeply cut and tomentose beneath. Native to the Caucasus. Very coarse in texture, thriving in rich moist woods soil, leaves ternately compound and flowers similar to those of a large Queen Anne's-lace (*Daucus carota*) which see.

sphondylium montanum (*lanatum*) **8′ Zone 3 Common Cow-parsnip**
A perennial, coarse herb with trisected leaves that are tomentose underneath, native to North America and western Asia. This is not an ornamental but is found sometimes in moist soils or at the edge of water. The flowers are white in clusters 12–20 in. wide in the summer. Cattle have been poisoned from eating the foliage and humans have contracted dermatitis from touching it.

HERB. A plant which is not woody, at least above ground.

HERBACEOUS. Of the texture of an herb; not woody.

HERBARIUM. A collection of dried specimens of plants with data attached, often mounted on linen paper, preserved for study or comparison.

HERB ROBERT = *Geranium robertianum*

HERBS. For thousands of years, herbs have been among the most important plants in the life of man. They have played a vital role in cultures, primitive and advanced, all over the world. Particularly have they been indispensable in medicine where miraculous cures have been attributed to them. For seasoning, flavoring, and preserving foods, their role has been equally major. Their uses have been religious, and many have become integral parts of wedding ceremonies. As a result of all this, theirs is a rich tradition steeped in lore, legend and superstition.

The mere mention of the names of familiar herbs conjures up a host of pleasant associations, especially when it comes to tasty culinary dishes. Everyone has his favorite, be it Mint, Parsley, Thyme, Sage, Sweet Basil, Rosemary, Dill, Fennel, Lemon Verbena, Lavender, Burnet, Caraway, or Camomile.

Closely linked with the everyday life of man in matters that concern him most—food, medicine, religion—it is not surprising that the history of herbs should be a fascinating one, capable of filling several volumes.

In the beginning, herbs were gathered in the wild. Since there are many kinds that are indigenous to all parts of the world, in climates cold, temperate, and tropical, they have been dominant in both western and eastern cultures. Readily recognized for their usefulness, native European species found their way to the Orient and Africa and those native to those areas, like Basil which is found in India, were carried thousands of miles across deserts and mountains to western Europe. From there, Colonial America was the next jumping step.

The early colonists carried seeds, roots and cuttings of herbs with them across the broad Atlantic. New England housewives grew these at their doorways, and reproductions of early settlements, like Plimoth Plantation in Plymouth, Mass., feature herb gardens, some with intricate designs, and plantings around the early houses. The colonists told the Indians about them, and in turn were shown native American herbs, notably Bee-balm and Wintergreen, used for making tea.

The interesting history of herbs can best be related through the individual kinds. One of the most important, Thyme, for example, was burned as a sweet-smelling incense by the ancient Greeks in their temples, even before they applied it to cooking. Medieval history mentions a thyme honey, and by the early part of the 12th century, Thyme was widely used in England to season foods. Izaak Walton, the famed angler, considered it essential to bring out the flavor in all kinds of fish.

Lavender, with its aromatic spikes of purple flowers, was cherished by the Phoenicians, Greeks and Romans. They burned its twigs as an incense, but the Greeks used it in sacrifices. The emperors of France perfumed their silks with the lovely fragrance of lavender, and in succeeding centuries the dried flowers became a byword for imparting a clean, fresh smell to linens.

Rosemary has long been one of the most romantic, a symbol of love and remembrance. The ancient Egyptians and Arabs planted it as a border plant in their plantings of roses, and it was widely grown in the monastery gardens of

Europe. For centures it was used as a funeral decoration, as well as for weddings. English brides wore a sprig of Rosemary in their hair and carried it in their bouquets.

Sweet Basil (*Ocimum basilicum*) is another herb that symbolizes love. The Italian lover tucks a piece behind his ear when he goes to meet his beloved. A symbol of fidelity, a maiden will stand beside a pot of Basil at her window to signal that she is awaiting him. Basil was sacred in India, where it was used by the Hindus as a symbol of reverence for the dead. From the Near East, where it was brought, it was soon taken to Greece, Italy, Spain, Portugal, and England.

Noted for its healing qualities, Camomile has been much used from the days of the ancient Egyptians up to the present. Camomile tea is brewed from the dried leaves to reduce fever and lessen inflammation in wounds. Lemon Verbena (*Lippia citriodora*) was introduced to America from South America in the early part of the 18th century, where the Spaniards knew its merits as a tea.

Catnip (*Nepeta cataria*) was a popular culinary herb in 15th century Europe. Fresh leaves were rubbed on meats and added to the first salads of spring. Captain John Mason first brought it to America, where he planted it in a Newfoundland garden. Soon after it appeared in Salem, Mass. gardens, the Indians discovered how to brew a strong tea from Catnip leaves.

Balm or Lemon Balm (*Melissa officinalis*) has been often mentioned by leading writers and poets, including Shakespeare, Poe, and Charlotte Brontë, and it also appears frequently in the Old Testament. In a different category because of its strong flavor is Garlic (*Allium sativum*). Grown in Syria and Egypt for thousands of years, its virtues were equally recognized by the Chinese. It found quick favor in monastery gardens, and Charlemagne is said to have grown it commercially. Today it is an important crop, found wherever vegetables and fruits are sold.

Far more important as a crop is Celery, although many do not think of it as an herb. The original plant, which grew in the salt marshes of Europe and Asia, was small and bitter. The Greeks learned how to blanch it by hilling the stems with damp soil. Then it was added to salads. By the early part of the nineteenth century, it became widely cultivated in America, and today represents a major industry.

Culture

The culture of herbs is relatively simple, and most all kinds are easy to grow. First, learn to distinguish the annual from the perennial kinds,

although a few, such as Parsley, Clary and Caraway, are biennials. Even so, they are treated as annuals in cold climates, as are some perennial types, notably Rosemary, which grows quickly from seed sown indoors in Jan. Some grow it in quantity to use as in edging in formal borders.

Most herbs require a light, lean, well-drained soil. If making an herb garden, dig the soil to a depth of 18 in. and fork it over several times. Add *no* manure but some peat moss or leaf mold can be added if the soil is exceptionally sandy. Smooth over after the digging is finished in readiness for planting. When setting out individual plants in borders, or groups of one or more kinds, prepare the soil in a similar manner.

Herbs do not like an acid soil, so add agricultural lime in the recommended amounts if the soil is known to be too acid. If possible, avoid a heavy soil, but if it has good drainage, herbs can be grown successfully if it is lightened with sand. A light sprinkling of a commercial fertilizer, with a high phosphorous content, as 5–10–5 or 4–8–4 can be applied, but with discretion. Better still is bonemeal, or superphosphate, a slow-acting phosphoric fertilizer that does not burn.

Herbs are sun-loving. In their native haunts, most are found in bright, sunny places, so allow for full sun for at least half a day. Some do remarkably well in partial shade, or even shade, if cast by buildings or high branching trees. Notable are Balm, Fennel, Tarragon, Parsley, Bergamot, Angelica, Costmary, Sweet Woodruff, Chervil, Sweet Ciceley, and mints, which rate the highest in this respect. In very deep shade, you can succeed with medicinal herbs— Ginseng, Snakeroot, and Digitalis or Foxglove.

Not only do herbs abound in sunny places where soil is poor, but they thrive in dry places. This applies to Lavender, Thyme, Rosemary, and Lemon Verbena. The gardener who likes herbs, but has a moist location, can enjoy a few that tolerate such a condition—Parsley, Angelica, Bergamot, Lovage, Sweet Ciceley, and the many kinds of mints, which, in fact, prefer fairly moist soils.

Care for established plants is not demanding. Water is needed mostly in periods of extended dryness, except for the few with higher moisture needs. A light scattering of a balanced fertilizer can be applied in the early spring and dug into the soil. Although not essential, a mulch, particularly a neat type like peat moss or buckwheat hulls, can be added to help hold moisture in dry regions, to control weeds, and improve appearance.

It is important to emphasize that feeding not be overdone. Too much food will promote soft, lush growth that will easily winterkill in the case of relatively nonhardy varieties. Growth also becomes leggy and straggly. Bushiness and compactness are ideals in an herb plant. Such plants, produced in soils where feeding is carefully regulated, possess a higher content of the essential oils.

In late fall, some perennial types such as Bergamot, mints and Tansy, die to the ground, so their tops should be removed. Some are subshrubs, like Lavender and Sage, but wait until early spring to cut away the dead growth. Established plants of Lavender that grow vigorously will need clipping in midsummer to head them back. Herbs that have a spreading nature, as mints and chives, may need dividing every spring or at least every 2 or 3 years to maintain their vigor.

Many herbs are annuals, and a surprising number are members of the Mint, Parsley, and Daisy or Composite families. The list includes Sweet Basil, Summer Savory, Sweet Marjoram, Chervil, Borage, Dill, Anise, Coriander and Sweet Fennel, a perennial grown as an annual. In the perennial group are Lavender, Rosemary, Horse-radish, Lemon Balm, Sage, Mint, Horehound, Bee-balm, Tarragon, Winter Savory, and Chives. Lemon Verbena is a shrubby perennial, but not hardy in the colder regions of the country. The same is true of the Rose-scented Geranium.

Annual and perennial herbs, as well as biennial (Parsley and Caraway), can be purchased as seedling plants in the spring. Nurserymen, garden centers, and florists carry them. If you have friends who grow perennial kinds, they can give you pieces in the spring which can be divided from the mother plants.

The hobbyist, however, can grow herbs from seed. Most grow easily if seed is sown in pots or flats in a sunny window or small home greenhouse. Use a light, sandy, alkaline soil that has been sterilized with boiling water or by baking. This can comprise one-third each of soil, compost and sand. Keep moist, but not wet, and follow the procedure as for annuals and other plants, shifting young plants to large quarters when large enough to handle. Or seed can be sown directly outdoors when weather has warmed sufficiently. Be certain soil does not dry out. A few quick-maturing annual herbs that can be started in the garden are Sweet Basil, Summer Savory, and Borage. Annual members reach maturity in 2–3 months, and produce seed by the end of the first season, usually before frost.

If you are especially fond of fragrant plants and maintain a fragrant garden, some of the best herbs to consider are Rosemary, Lovage, Lavender, Lemon Verbena, Bergamot, Lemon Balm, Thyme, Costmary, Sweet Ciceley, and Rose-, Lemon- and other scented Geraniums.

As a rule, the herb garden does not require winter protection. Where winters are severe, a winter blanket of a light, airy mulch will be beneficial. Marsh hay, straw, and evergreen branches are some of the better materials to use. Apply after the ground has frozen solidly. Some may need individual protection against the elements, such as covering with bushel baskets, sheets of plastic, pieces of burlap or branches of evergreens. Oak leaves dumped among plants are good because they do not mat, but avoid maple leaves which flatten when wet.

Perennial kinds that are definitely not hardy can be stored for the winter in other ways. One method is to lift them and place in a cold frame. Or they can be potted and wintered in a greenhouse, cool plant room, breezeway, or indoors in sunny kitchen windows. Often treated this way are Rosemary, Lemon Verbena, Pineapple Sage, and the many kinds of scented geraniums.

The Herb Garden

Think of herbs and immediately you think of formal gardens, where the various kinds of herbs are planted in intricate designs. These knot gardens, as they were called, were in vogue in Elizabethan England, but modifications of their patterns have come down to us through the centuries.

Herbs for many reasons are delightful plants. Arrange them in an elaborate parterre and they become doubly delightful. They lend themselves to this treatment, and it is the dream of many a home gardener to copy or design his own herb garden, neatly and artistically arranged with his favorites.

These traditional designs have much to offer. The more ambitious can consult books on the subject, most of which reproduce a wide assortment of patterns. One of the most helpful in this respect is "The Complete English Gardener" (1704) by Leonard Meager. Visiting herb gardens in parks and botanical gardens will offer ideas and inspiration. This is a good way, too, to become acquainted with the various kinds, to know what they look like, to study their forms and textures, and to pay particular attention to growth habits. It should be realized, however, that it takes much time to keep such intricately designed gardens looking in good condition.

The herb garden need not be ornate. It can be large or small, designed according to preference. A small plot merely 3 or 4 ft. square can contain several varieties and offer many hours of enjoyment. Provided it has sun and good drainage, the herb plot may comprise a narrow strip along the house or garage. It can

A formal herb garden. It takes a great deal of care. This garden is at Hampton Court in England. (*Photo by Arnold Arboretum, Jamaica Plain, Mass.*)

be a simple geometric form in a corner of the garden—square, rectangular, triangular, circular, or oval. It may be a raised bed, especially if tended by the elderly, with sides made of brick, concrete or stone. Wood can be used, and is, in fact, traditional, although it will rot and have to be replaced after a period of time.

The beginner would be wiser to start with a simple bed, since the intricate pattern requires constant care, even if it is designed and planted by a professional landscape architect. If simple and unadorned, or just an odd corner, try to locate it near the kitchen door where the cook can take snippets quickly for the various meals of the day. It may be in the morning, when a few sprigs of Parsley will add flavor to an omelette.

Before planting an herb garden be sure you know about the characteristics of each kind of herb. Aside from being annual, biennial, or perennial, some may be tall, others short, some have a spreading or sprawling nature, others stand erect. Important is the texture of the leaves, for they may be velvety, woolly, shiny, or rough. Sizes and shapes vary to include fine and feathery or large and bold.

In planting, consider contrast of form. A delicate, feathery foliage stands out against large, solid leaves, without markings, or incisions. A compact-type herb looks well in front of one that is much-branched. If possible, include some herbs for edging, for they give neatness and have a way of making all the plants in the back stand out as a frame does a painting.

Consider heights—this is so that tall plants will not cut out sun and air from small ones

tucked in back and appearance will be vastly improved. There are exceptions, as in the case of a large, single specimen used for accent. Some low herbs, up to a foot and a half, include Basil, Chives, Garlic (except when in flower), Thyme, Pot Marjoram, Parsley and Sweet Marjoram. Some that are medium in height, up to 4 feet, are Sage, Rosemary, Lemon Verbena, Borage, Dill, Lovage, Rose- and other scented geraniums. A few qualify in the over 4 ft. category, notably Bronze Fennel and the old-fashioned roses, like the Fragrant Moss Rose.

For a focal point in the herb garden use a feature. The sundial has long been used and is especially appropriate. A bird bath or specimen plant like English Boxwood or Sweet Bay, where hardy, will perform a similar function. A bee skep is traditional and many go to great effort to find one. Among herbs that are particularly attractive to bees are Lavender, Lovage, Thyme, Lemon Balm, Borage, Marjoram, Hyssop, and Germander.

Some herbs make fine clipped hedges, like Lavender, Santolina, Germander, Rosemary, and Southernwood. Others are good edging plants like Parsley, Basil and Chives, to outline beds of herbs or other garden flowers.

Perhaps the most outstanding feature of herbs is the coloring of their foliage. They are noted for their grays and blue-greens although some are dark or light green. There are variations of these, with emphasis on the diversification of gray, including silver in the case of Artemisias. For this feature, they are, as a group of plants, unique. With this array, it is easy to match gray against dark green, blue-green against bright green, purple-green against silver. The effects are startling. In any case, the leaf colorings are subtle, and it is easy to mix all together. As a group, they harmonize exceptionally well. Remember only that herbs are not noted for their showy blooms but the few that do make bright displays, would include Lavender, Germander, and Thyme.

Herbs in the Garden

It is not necessary to grow herbs in a special herb garden, whether it comprises an ornate design or a simple plot, relegated to the kitchen doorway or an out-of-the-way corner. They can be raised with equal success and add charm in the average garden, in the company of trees, shrubs, perennials, roses, bulbs, and annuals. Some gardeners even prefer them this way, and find that their appeal is not diminished.

All kinds can be grown, depending on the effect desired, although some have the reputation of being more decorative than others. Included in this group are Lavender, Thyme, Artemisia, with emphasis on varieties 'Silver King' and 'Silver Mound', Anise, Borage, Coriander, Bee-balm, Bergamot, Winter Savory, Rue, and Angelica.

Herbs can be attractive along a straight or winding walk, and in English gardens Lavender is commonly handled this way. Others can be used in similar fashion, like Santolina or Rosemary. Because of their culinary link, they are common in vegetable gardens, where they are grown between the rows or along edges. Here, they take little space.

Herbs can be planted in clumps in front of shrubs where they receive full sun, and many of the low ones are ideal in rock gardens. Perennials will come up year after year, and annuals can be set out to fill up holes created by spring bulbs. Camomile, Winter Savory, Basil, Thyme, a superb rock garden plant, *Artemisia* 'Silver Mound', Lamb's-ears, Chives and violets are a few that can be tucked between stones in rock and wall gardens. The many kinds of Thyme are also outstanding for use in crevices in garden steps and among stones on the terrace that is not paved. They can take considerable tramping, and the pungent scent emitted from the leaves as they are crushed underfoot is one of the many joys of growing these mat-forming herbs.

Herbs can be mixed in borders with perennials, annuals, and bulbs. They can keep the company of roses, phlox, peonies, iris, chrysanthemums, columbines, petunias, salvias, zinnias, snapdragons, and a host of hardy Dutch bulbs or tender types, as dahlias, cannas, gladioli, tigridias, ismenes and montbretias. They offer one striking advantage, that of the gray-green colorations of their leaves, which offer contrast and relief where there is a predominance of green. The silver of Santolina and Artemisia, for example, resemble bits of eye-catching color.

Lavender has long been a standby as an edging plant for formal rose gardens. Where hardy, Santolina is used for the same purpose, and is often clipped into a neat hedge. It can be cut low, just a few inches high, or allowed to grow taller, about a foot. It is often seen thus in public parks as a hedge in front of taller flowering plants, such as dahlias and cannas.

For the person with little space or time, there is always the pot garden of herbs. In recent years, there has been a strong trend toward container gardening, and herbs are among the plants that have been influenced by this new gardening concept that has been adapted to meet the demands of modern times. A few or several pots of favorite herbs can be kept on a porch, the back steps, a low wall, by the driveway, in a window-box, on a rooftop, on a sundeck, or on a fire escape in the case of the city apartment dweller, provided they receive some sunshine.

The advantages of the pot herb garden are many. Containers can be moved about for a change of effect. Soil can be prepared as needed by the various kinds of herbs, and any that look shabby can be taken away and replaced. Each individual plant can be given special attention, and such chores as watering, feeding, snipping, and spraying, are easily done. Plants in pots possess an architectural aspect, and herbs are no exception. In the fall, any in small containers can be taken indoors to be enjoyed for a longer period of time, although some kinds as Rosemary and Parsley make good all-winter house plants in sunny windows. Larger specimens can be placed in a greenhouse if available or given to friends with space to keep them during the winter period.

Any number of containers can be used, but either clay or wooden tubs are best. Made of natural materials, they harmonize with the leaf textures of herbs. This is especially true of the clay pots, which are easily available and inexpensive. Oldtime clay pots have the unfortunate disadvantage of accumulating unsightly fertilizer salts and mosses on the outside, so before using, scrub with a stiff brush and warm, soapy water. However, they are now manufactured, treated in such a way, that this does not happen. The red coloring of clay pots, although bright at first, soon is toned down to take on a soft, mellow look. There are many sizes, including bulb pans or azalea pots, in which several kinds of herbs can be grown.

Herbs can be grown in plastic pots which have several advantages for they do not break, they do not gather scum on the outside and they stay moist longer. In the case of herbs, watering should be watched with great care to avoid making the soil too moist for this induces rotting and poor growth.

Wooden tubs or buckets have special appeal. Sturdy and heavy, they have a solid look and, like the clay pots, an earthy aspect. Long-lasting, since those purchased have been treated with a wood preservative, they will not topple in the wind or break if left outdoors with soil in them in winter. In the case of clay, breaking or cracking occurs when the soil freezes in very cold weather. Tubs can be allowed to weather, to take on a gray coloring, or they can be painted. White, light blue and gray are suitable colors, but some like to brighten them with red, pink or yellow, depending on the surroundings and personal taste. Redwood containers are also excellent. They can be stained or painted, but are better allowed to weather, when they become soft brown or light gray, tinged with specks of rose and pink. They are long lasting, and do not need to be treated with a wood preservative.

For drainage, place a thick layer of broken pieces of clay pots, pebbles, crushed brick or small stones on the bottom. Use a light, well-drained, sandy soil, with little humus added. A little mixed fertilizer and bonemeal can be added, but keep feeding to a minimum during the growing season. To keep shapely, trim from time to time, but in the case of most plants this will automatically occur as snippets are taken for cooking, drying or to give to friends. Perennial types, as Lavender, Santolina, and Artemisia can be taken out of their containers in the fall and planted in the open ground if they are hardy. They can be lifted in the spring, repotted, and set out again for summer decoration. Annuals will, of course, be discarded, except for a few that might be taken indoors.

Herbs Indoors

The time to start thinking about the indoor herb garden is in the late summer or early fall. At that time, lift carefully and pot small herb plants or large perennial kinds, as Rosemary or Lemon Verbena, if sufficient space is available. Early potting is recommended in order to allow plants enough time to become established outdoors before they are taken inside. Keep them in a partially shaded spot for a few days after lifting from the ground, and maintain even moisture in the soil. This adjustment period will make it much easier when plants go indoors. The shock then from a cool, humid outdoors to a hot, dry interior, with smaller amounts of sunshine, will cause yellowing of leaves. Once brought indoors, opening windows on mild days will provide fresh air and aid in the re-habilitation period. Many kinds of pots can be used and to impart added charm the pots can be placed in woven baskets.

The kitchen window makes the best location for the herb garden because of the culinary association. It is easy to pluck a piece of Tarragon or a few leaves of Mint to add zest to a meal. The kitchen window must, however, be sunny, since herbs are sun-loving and require all the sunshine they can get during the short winter months. South, southeast or southwest windows are best. Preferably temperatures should be cool, below 60° F. if possible. This cannot be the case in the average kitchen window, but low readings can be maintained in the greenhouse or cool plant room. Avoid feeding, except in the late winter or very early spring when plants will appreciate a boost from a high phosphoric fertilizer.

Easy-to-grow annual herbs for sunny windows include Sweet Basil, Sweet Marjoram, Anise, Coriander, Dill, Chervil and Parsley. These may be lifted as young, or even mature plants, in the fall, but they can also be started from seed. Mints, Chives, Sage, Thyme, Lemon Balm, Tarragon, Lemon Verbena, Winter Savory, Rosemary, and Rose geraniums are perennials that will offer pleasure when cold and snow reign outside.

Chives, whose linear leaves are favored for making a cheese dip, is one of the easiest. Lift clumps in the fall, cut back, and bring indoors where new growth will appear. Clumps of Chives in strawberry baskets are often sold in grocery stores and at vegetable counters in large markets. Garlic cloves provide another interesting possibility. Insert the pieces, pointed ends up, in sandy soil and just barely cover. They will sprout in about 10 days, and the young, slender leaves can be snipped to season salads or meats. Both Mint and Parsley are 2 others that pot up easily and grow happily in bright windows. Mints are tasty in salads, and Parsley will garnish meat, chicken and fish.

Rosemary, with its linear, gray-green leaves, pungent when crushed, is one of the most common. Since it is a long-lived shrub, it is treated as a pot plant in cold regions, taken outdoors in summer, and brought to a cool, sunny window in winter. Surprisingly, it does well under average home temperatures, where the thermostat is always above 70° F. Keep the soil moist, more so than for other herbs, for when it is allowed to go dry leaves will shed, but a certain amount of this occurs soon after plants are brought indoors.

Rosemary, a symbol of love and remembrance, is a plant of many associations. It is a popular Christmas green where hardy, and indoor pot plants can be decorated with small balls, bits of colorful paper, and other tiny ornaments for the holidays. With little effort it can be transformed into a living Christmas tree, certain to be the center of conversation.

Harvesting

There are 2 ways to harvest herbs in order to derive the greatest benefit from them. One is to keep taking leaves or sprigs any time when needed from spring through autumn. Use your judgment, taking all you want from rampant plantings of such kinds as mints, but going lightly on small plants recently set out. Leave enough foliage for plants to develop normally.

Some herbs are used only when green, as Cresses, Sorrel, Burnet, Borage, Garlic and Chives leaves. Pieces will remain fresh for several days in a refrigerator if placed in plastic bags. A better way is to wash the leaves and sprigs, shake off as much water as possible, and then store in glass jars. Their longevity is much increased, and they retain their crisp quality.

Most herbs are harvested for drying and storing. The time to cut them is just as they are coming into bloom, although Thyme can be snipped when in full flower. Then, flavor is at its peak because the volatile oils are most abundant. The best time of the day to harvest is in the morning, after the dew has dried and before the sun becomes hot on the leaves. Select a clear day, and avoid the afternoon, when some of the fragrant oils are lost in the heat of the sun. If plants are spattered with mud or covered with dust, spray them with a hose a day or two before. Some prefer to wash the croppings thoroughly, shaking excess water, and spreading them on towels to dry.

Some herbs are gathered for their leaves, among them mints. Some, like Basil, are taken with stems and leaves. Dill and Fennel are 2 that are cherished for both their leaves and seeds. Always allow seeds to mature fully. Some should be gathered before they scatter, but those which do not shed can be left longer. Cut heads of these into open paper bags and leave, with tops still open, to dry thoroughly before sealing in containers.

To cut pieces of Basil, Sweet Marjoram, Mint, and other herbs, use sharp scissors that cut well without tearing stems. Take the top growth and place it carefully by the plants in order not to mix the various kinds. When the cutting is completed, collect in individual bunches and label.

With perennials, like Winter Savory, Sage and Tarragon, take only the top half, since too severe pruning will result in winter injury, especially if a bit on the tender side. Annuals, like Sweet Basil, Borage and Sweet Marjoram,

can be sheared more severely, to within 4 in. They will make new growth before the end of the growing season and then die.

After the harvesting is completed, gather those that have stems into bunches of about 12 and tie with string. Hang on a rope or wire extended across a warm dry room with good air circulation. Avoid too large bunches, since not enough air passing through them will result in mold. This is especially apt to occur with woolly-leaved kinds and Sweet Basil, which dries slowly. A darkened room is also better, since bright sunshine will discolor the leaves. An attic or a warm room on the top floor usually provides excellent drying conditions. Once herbs are strung up individually, label each bunch. Allowed to dry first, it is often difficult to identify the bunches which look alike in the dried stage.

With good conditions, the bunches will dry in a week to 10 days. It is important that they be thoroughly dry, so if in doubt allow a few more days. Then strip the leaves from the stems, taking care not to crush them. Their flavor keeps better this way, and they can be crumpled just before using. Do not strip Summer Savory because its leaves are too small and the stems have taste.

Another method is to strip leaves from plants when they are fresh green, then spread them on wire screening on which cheese cloth has been placed. Keep in thin layers, and place screens on boxes in a warm, dry, darkened room so air will circulate underneath. Small sprigs will require the same handling. Instead of cheese cloth, clean tissue paper can be used. Rose petals can be placed in cheese-cloth bags and hung up to dry. They will need shaking periodically.

In either method, store the leaves and seeds when completely dry in airtight containers, essential to keep out the moisture and hold in the flavorsome oils. Before storing, seeds should be winnowed. Blowing will help to get rid of some of the chaff. Caraway, Anise, Sesame, Dill and Fennel are some herbs whose seeds are commonly stored for winter use. Both leaves and stems should be stored in a dry closet or cupboard, away from direct sunshine.

Some herbs, among them Mints and Parsley, lose their flavor in the drying process. To prevent this, place in a salt solution of 1 teaspoon of salt to a quart of water. Bring the solution to boiling point, strip the leaves from their stems, and place in a strainer, which is immersed in the boiling solution for 2–3 seconds. Shake leaves after to get rid of the surplus water and then spread on screen to dry.

Tarragon is another herb which loses its flavor when dried. To prevent this, it must be preserved in vinegar. First bruise the Tarragon leaves, then place in a crock and pour boiling vinegar over them. Cover tightly, and allow to steep for a week to 10 days. Stir every 2 days, and when ready, strain the vinegar and store the Tarragon leaves in airtight jars. When storing herbs of any kind, keep each separate. More scent is preserved, and mixtures can be made from individual containers when the time comes to use them.

For the beginner, the list of herbs is a seemgingly endless one. Several have already been mentioned, but here is a short compilation of some of the more popular and useful.

Anise (*Pimpinella anisum*)—2-ft. annual, with lacy leaves and fragrant yellow flowers. Fresh leaves add flavor to fruit salads, stews.

Basil (*Ocimum* species and varieties)—annual, with small or large heart-shaped leaves on 2-ft. plants. Variety **'Dark Opal'** has purple leaves. Clovelike flavor is delicious in meats, poultry, salads and soups.

Borage (*Borago officinalis*)—annual to $2\frac{1}{2}$ ft. with crinkly gray-green leaves. Young leaves and flowers used to flavor iced drinks, teas, and salads.

Burnet or Salad Burnet (*Sanguisorba minor*)—nearly evergreen perennial to 2 ft., with feathery foliage and rose or white flowers. Young leaves are used in salads and beverages.

Caraway (*Carum carvi*)—hardy biennial to 2 ft. with feathery leaves. The fresh leaves are recommended for salads and meats. The seed is used to season breads, pastries, meats and vegetables.

Chives (*Allium schoenoprasum*)—hardy perennial, to 10 in. with slender, tubular leaves in clumps, topped by lavender flowers. Fresh leaves are used to season appetizers, salad dressings, eggs, and soups.

Dill (*Anethum graveolens*)—annual to 4 ft. with finely-cut leaves and yellow flowers. Fresh leaves add taste to fish, meats, eggs, and poultry. Seeds flavor pies, vegetables, and soups.

Fennel or Sweet Fennel (*Foeniculum vulgare dulce*)—hardy perennial to 4 ft. with threadlike leaves. Leaves recommended for soups, salads, and fish. Seed adds fragrance to liqueurs and confections.

Garlic (*Allium sativum*)—bulbous annual, with bulbs made up of sections or cloves. Flat, slender leaves are topped by heads of small white flowers. Adds distinctive flavor to salads, meats, poultry, pickles and soups.

Lavender (*Lavandula officinalis*)—shrubby, compact plant, with narrow gray-green leaves, and spikes of lavender flowers. About a foot high, it grows taller in warm climates. Flowering tips used in perfumes, soaps and sachets.

Lovage or Love Parsley (*Levisticum officinale*)—tall perennial to 7 ft. with large, compound leaves. Young leaves are for soups, chowders, stews, and salads. Seed is tasty in cakes, candies, roasts and salads.

Marjoram or Sweet Marjoram (*Origanum majorana*)—perennial, often grown as annual, with small, oval, gray-green leaves on foot-tall plants. Used for fish, eggs and stews.

Mint (*Mentha* species)—hardy spreading perennials, to 2 ft. high, with smooth, oval, fruit-scented leaves. Used in beverages, teas, vinegars, meats, fish, desserts, and salads.

Parsley (*Petroselinum crispum*)—biennials, with rosettes of finely cut leaves. Used as seasoning in eggs, fish, vegetables, salads, meats and poultry.

Rosemary (*Rosmarinus officinalis*)—shrubby evergreen, attaining 5 ft., with narrow pungent leaves. Fresh or dried, leaves add distinction to eggs, fish, meats, soups and vegetables.

Rue (*Ruta graveolens*)—woody shrub to 3 ft., with delicate finely-cut leaves, which have bitter taste, and are favored by many in cocktails, salads, cheeses, and vegetables.

Sage (*Salvia officinalis*)—shrubby perennial to 3 ft., with soft, woolly gray-green leaves and attractive blue flowers. Aromatic leaves used to flavor cheeses, fish, meats, stuffings, and stews.

Savory (Summer Savory) (*Satureia hortensis*)—fragrant annual to 18 in., with small, narrow, dark green leaves that add flavor to meats, poultry, salads, and soups.

Tarragon or French Tarragon (*Artemisia dracunculus*)—hardy shrubby perennial, with narrow inch-long leaves on 2-ft. plants. Fresh and dried leaves valued as seasoning in eggs, fish, meats, soups, sauces and vinegar.

Thyme (*Thymus vulgaris*)—bushy, spreading perennial, a foot tall, and tiny gray-green leaves topped by showy heads of lavender flowers, much sought by the bees. The strong flavor of the leaves is tasty in cheeses, meats, poultry, salads, soups and stuffings.

Herb enthusiasts would do well to become members of the active Herb Society of America with offices at Horticultural Hall, 300 Massachusetts Avenue, Boston, Mass. 02115. Available from public libraries are several excellent books. "The Home Garden Book of Herbs and Spices" by Milo Miloradovich (Doubleday & Co.) lists herbs and gives their uses. It is a small volume that can be tucked in a pocket when planning to visit a large herb garden. "Herbs: The Spice of a Gardener's Life" is a large, handsome volume published in 1965 by Katherine Barnes Williams (Diversity Books), an amateur gardener who has been growing herbs in her Mo. garden for over 30 years.

GEORGE TALOUMIS

HERCULES-CLUB = *Aralia spinosa*

HEREDITY. The transmission from parent to offspring of certain characteristics. See GENE.

HERMANNIA verticillata described under **MAHERNIA**

HERMAPHRODITE. In horticultural parlance a plant which has both staminate and pistillate flowers on the same plant, but is a term not used much. The term usually used is monoecious.

HERNIARIA (her-ni-AIR-ia)

glabra   4″–6″   Zone 4   Common Burstwort
A creeping perennial, mosslike in appearance, especially used for bedding purposes or in the rock garden as a ground cover for certain bulb plantings. Crocuses look especially well growing up through it. Belonging to the Pink Family, it also is planted between stepping stones in walks. The small greenish flowers are of no ornamental value. Native to Europe and northern and western Asia, it is easily propagated by division.

HERONBILL. See ERODIUM.

HESPERALOE (hesper-A-lo)

parviflora   4′   Zone 7   Red Hesperaloe
A stemless desert plant of Tex. and Mexico. Somewhat similar to Yucca but with red flowers 1½ in. long. Leaves are about an inch wide.

HESPERIS (HES-per-is)

matronalis   3′–4′   Zones 2–3   Dames' Rocket
A European biennial now quite at home in the eastern U.S., it is a much-branched herb with alternate, narrow, toothed leaves and white or purple fragrant flowers produced in loose terminal racemes. Each flower has 4 petals. They appear throughout the summer. The plant requires no special culture and may be propagated from seed. The flowers are borne on second-year plants. The var. **alba** has pure white flowers.

HETEROMELES (het-er-o-MEE-leez)

arbutifolia   6′–10′   Zone 9   Christmas-berry, Toyon
This is a very popular evergreen shrub especially in Calif., where it is native. The small, white flowers are borne in flat clusters in June-July, but the red, hollylike berries in the winter and the glossy, evergreen leaves, up to 4 in. long, are its chief ornamental features. It can be grown in dry soils but responds well to watering. Making a splendid and colorful specimen in the winter, this should be kept compact with a little correctional pruning. Sometimes it may be susceptible to fireblight, and if so, prompt spraying with Bordeaux mixture should control the disease. Sometimes incorrectly called *Photinia arbutifolia* or *Toyon arbutifolia*.

HETEROMORPHOUS. Parts of different shape.

HETEROPHYLLOUS. With 2 sorts of leaves.

HETEROSIS. A term used by biologists to denote hybrid vigor. Sometimes, when certain crosses are made between species, races or varieties, the offspring will show increased vigor, the ability to grow much faster and be more luxurious. Hybridizers are noting this plant phenomenon in currently breeding many of our modern varieties of vegetables, annual flowers and other ornamentals. Not only faster growth but larger flowers, more hardiness, greater resistance to disease and insect pests all result in certain hybrids. Foresters are experimenting with hybrid crosses and have found many a new hybrid tree that will grow better lumber, faster, than either of its parents. In fact, it is these new hybrid forest trees that are remaking timber growing today.

HEUCHERA (hew-KER-a)

americana   2′–3′   Zone 4   American Alumroot
Rising from a fleshy rootstalk, the Alumroot bears long-stalked leaves with rounded lobes and a leafy flower stalk having a slender terminal raceme of tiny bell-shaped greenish-white flowers from which the stamens protrude. These appear in May and June. A plant of the dry woods over much of eastern U.S., it is suitable for the shady wild garden and may be divided in spring or in fall. Seeds may be sown in spring.

glabra   20″   Zone 4
The leathery, cordate leaves of this species are deeply 5–7 lobed, light green and grow in clumps 3 in. high. The creamy-white flowers are borne in April and May. It is a rare plant, native to the Rocky Mountains, needing loose, gravelly, acid soil and a shady location.

sanguinea   1′–2′   Zone 3   Coral-bells
By far the best species of this genus for ornamental planting. This and many of its hybrids have been proved most popular in gardens throughout much of America. Plants have basal, rounded leaves and branched spikes of small bell-like, red to pink flowers, the spikes reaching up to 20 in. tall. These individual flowers are only about ⅓ in. across, but they appear on the plant from late May throughout a greater part of the season.

Coral-bells are best planted in the spring, and in the North a light mulch over winter helps keep the plants from being forced out of the ground. They do not spread, can be planted about a foot apart and the smaller growing varieties are excellent for edging. The roots are shallow, hence plants should be watered during droughts. They will tolerate some shade, but grow very well in full sun.

Propagation is by seed sown in spring which yield plants that will start to bloom the following year. The commercial method is to take cuttings in midsummer, for any leaf with a small portion of the stem attached to the base of the petiole will root. The gardener can easily divide plants in the spring. The species is native to Mexico and Ariz.

Some of the more popular varieties and hybrids at present are: **alba**—with white flws.; **'Bressingham Hybrids'**—flws. white to pink to red; **'Martin Bells'**—flws. coral red; **'Mt. St. Helena'**—flws. fiery blood red; **'June Bride'**—flws. white; **'Firefly'**—flws. vermilion red; **'Queen of Hearts'**—flws. are like long red bells, often considered the finest cultivar of them all; **'Rosea'**—flws. rosy pink. There are many others, some of them just as good (or even better) ornamentals as those mentioned above.

villosa   3′   Zone 7   Hairy Alumroot
With white flowers during summer in rather open panicles but almost stemless, native to the southeastern U.S. and only of value in moist shady places in the wild garden.

HEXALECTRIS (HEX-a-lec-tris)

spicata   6″-15″   Zone 7   Crested Coralroot
A saprophyte, this plant has leaves like scales which sheath the purple stem. The sepals and petals, nearly equal in size, are purplish in color and the lip is without a spur. The plant is found in dry woods in the southern and southwestern states and blooms through much of the summer.

HIBISCUS (hy-BISK-us). This genus comprises over 200 species of herbs, shrubs and trees of the Mallow Family, but only a few are of ornamental importance in America. They have alternate leaves with palmately arranged veins. Flowers are large and funnel-shaped, usually with 5 petals and sepals but sometimes double. They vary greatly and the tropical kinds hybridize easily. Two species, *H. rosa-sinensis* and *H. syriacus*, are the most popular in U.S., the former in the Deep South, the latter in the North. There are many colorful varieties of each species being offered by nurserymen.

Propagation

Seeds may be sown at once or stored dry in airtight containers in a cool place for up to a year and then sown. For the varieties, asexual means of propagation are best. Softwood and hardwood cuttings (which see) root readily. Both grafting and layering are also practiced.

Seeds of the annual species may be started in the greenhouse in Feb. and transplanted outdoors after all danger of frost is past, or they may be sown out-of-doors in late May in the spot where they are intended to grow.

abelmoschus = *Abelmoschus moschatus*
arnottianus   15′   Zone 10   Hawaiian White Hibiscus
This is native to Hawaii, with white flowers several inches long and the stamens form a red

column in the center. Unlike most other Hibiscus, it is very fragrant.

cannabinus   14′   annual   Kenaf
This plant is native to the Tropics of the Old World and is shrubby in habit, spiny, with the upper leaves 5-lobed and lower leaves heart shaped. The yellow or red flowers have bright red centers; the bristly, round fruit is ¾ in. long. The plant produces a jutelike fiber; the leaves are edible and the seeds are used in sauces. Planted in southern Fla.

coccineus .6′-8′   Zone 7   Scarlet Rosemallow
A perennial valued for its brilliant scarlet flowers 5-6 in. wide and conspicuous long stamens. The bluish-green leaves are cut into 5 graceful lobes. Native to the swamps of Fla. and Ga.

esculentus = *Abelmoschus esculentus*
grandiflorus   6′   Zone 8   Great Rosemallow
Native to swamps in Miss., Ga. and Fla., this perennial bears pale pink flowers, reddish near the base, 6 in. long and 3-lobed leaves usually broader than long. Often used in seashore gardens on the Gulf Coast.

manihot = *Abelmoschus manihot*
moscheutos   3′-6′   Zone 5   Common Rose Mallow
This European plant is a strong perennial with downy, canelike stems and large, hairy, ovate or rounded and toothed leaves, the upper ones deeply lobed. The flowers are large, sometimes 5-6 in. in dia. It is a wetland plant, doing well

Hibiscus moscheutos

even in brackish salt marshes along the eastern coastal states from Mass. to Fla., extending inland to the Great Lakes and flowers in Aug.

and Sept. It is a good plant for the wild garden and small plants may be reset in spring. Once established, the plant self-sows freely.

mutabilis shrub Zone 8 Cottonrose Hibiscus A Chinese shrub, sometimes treelike, planted in the southeastern states for its large flowers 3–4 in. wide, which open white then change to pink and deep red. The broad, oval leaves are 3–5 lobed, with the lobes triangular and scalloped, and 4–8 in. wide. Fruit is a dry, rounded, hairy capsule.

rosa-sinensis 30′ Zone 9 Chinese Hibiscus Only hardy in the subtropical areas of the U.S., this is of course a commonly grown ornamental in the Tropics. The plant originally came from China but now is popular in all parts of the Tropical Zone. The flowers may be as much as 6 in. in dia., white, pink, red, yellow, single or double, blooming in the summer. It is a fast-growing shrub with glossy leaves and strikingly handsome flowers which are sometimes used for making dyes. The following varieties are frequently offered by subtropical nurseries in Fla., Calif. and Tex. and are listed here with the color of their flowers:

Varieties

'Agnes Gault'—single, bright rose-pink petals.
'Amour'—soft pink.
'Bride'—single, white-flushed, pale pink, ruffled petals.
'Brilliant'—single, vivid bright red.
'Butterfly'—single, bright yellow.
'California Gold'—single, rich golden-yellow, carmine shading in center of flowers.
'Fiesta'—bright orange.
'Fullmoon'—double, lemon-yellow.
'General Marshall'—single, orange-yellow.
'President'—single, large red.
'Red Dragon'—double, red.
'White Wings'—single, white with red center.
Some varieties like 'President' make excellent high hedges because of very dense growth and glossy leaves.

It is estimated that there are as many as 5000 hybrids of this genus growing in Hawaii alone, where several species, growing side by side, often cross-fertilize. In addition, many gardeners have made crosses themselves. The Hibiscus flower in Hawaii has the trait of not wilting the first day it is open, regardless of whether it remains on the bush or is cut and kept in water or out of water. The second day it wilts, regardless. So it is a very popular flower in all kinds of decorations, but for use in leis it is not very good because it crushes easily and the flower color can stain clothing.

schizopetalus 12′ Zone 10 Fringed Hibiscus The interesting corolla of this African Hibiscus is about 3 in. wide, and has gracefully fringed and deeply cut red petals. Because it has a red staminal column almost as long as the graceful flower itself, the flower always hangs downward. This species is frequently crossed with others because of its graceful beauty and color. Leaves evergreen. Propagated by cuttings.

syriacus 15′ Zone 5 Shrub Althea This old-fashioned shrub has been grown in America since colonial times and was grown in England 200 years before then. When first discovered in Syria, it was thought to be a native of that area (hence its specific name); but as has happened with several other plants (the Persian lilac, for one), the Shrub Althea was later found to be a native of China and northern India, actually being introduced into Syria, and probably being brought over the old trade route from China into that country. In any event, this hardy species has had a long history. Many cultivars have come and gone over the years, but we still see it used in many northern gardens.

There are some 30 cultivars now growing in the collections of the Arnold Arboretum; some of these are old-fashioned varieties, while others have just recently been introduced from Europe. Many more are being grown in American nurseries, but as will be shown later, there is a great similarity among the cultivated varieties and all can be segregated in a few major color groups as far as flowers are concerned. Although not considered outstanding ornamental shrubs, they do have a place in the garden under certain conditions; therefore, a short review of the group and some cultural suggestions are here in order.

As many a gardener knows, there are several herbaceous species native to North America, but each of the 2 woody species (*H. syriacus* and *H. rosa-sinensis*) contains many varieties that are popular garden plants, *H. syriacus* in the colder portions of the country and *H. rosa-sinensis* in the subtropical portions. Young plants of *H. syriacus* seem to prove less hardy in the first winter or two, and so winter protection for these is in order during this period. Old, established plants are perfectly hardy in Zone 5; that is, in a belt across the country including Boston, Pittsburgh, St. Louis and upward on the northwest Pacific Coast, but of course they are hardy in warmer areas and are grown in parts of the Gulf States also.

Young, vigorously growing plants are frequently susceptible to winter injury in the North, especially the first winter or two after they have been planted. Hence young plants might be well protected the first year or two to prevent such losses. Older, slower-growing plants are not so affected. So, for northern plantings at least, older, slower-growing plants should be used wherever possible, and spring planting should definitely be the recommendation.

The flowers of the shrub altheas appear in late summer and early fall. Double-flowered varieties do not have fruits; semi-double varieties may have only a few or none at all; and single-flowered varieties bear a fruit which eventually is a dry capsule containing many seeds. Its late flowers, as well as its ability to grow in gardens near the seashore, are its chief claims for space in gardens—otherwise it has little ornamental merit. It has no autumn color and its leaves are among the last to appear in the spring. In fact, newly placed plants may be so tardy in producing leaves the first season that harried gardeners remove them as "dead" when actually they are not. It must also be said that in a wet season many of the flowers will rot in the bud.

There are 2 methods of growing these plants. The first is to leave them practically alone with little pruning. The flowers will then be profuse but small. The other method, used frequently in Europe, is to cut back the previous year's growth heavily in the spring, to about 2 or 3 buds. This makes work and an unsightly plant for a while, but because the flowers are borne on the current year's vegetative growth, much larger flowers are obtained.

Most of the cultivars listed here are grown in the Arnold Arboretum. The stamens of those marked "semi-double" are aborted, not fully developed petals; while those marked "double" have the stamens developed into petallike structures almost the same length as normal petals. The dia. of the flowers was measured on our plants, but this varies materially, depending on the size of the plant, the amount pruned and the soil conditions. The color notations listed have been made from the Nickerson Color Fan. The names delegated to these cultivars over the years are everything but accurate, according to our modern standards.

Recommended Varieties
(i.e., those that make good garden specimens when grown under the right conditions):

SD—indicates semi-double flowers
D—indicates double flowers
S—indicates single flowers

In the semi-double flowers there are 5–7 full-sized petals and aborted stamens, all of which are smaller than the petals. In truly double flowers the aborted stamens have grown into modified petals nearly the same size as normal petals. Usually there are no fruits in the double-flowering varieties.

'Admiral Dewey'—D, 2¼ in. dia.; pure white.
'Ardens'—SD, 3 in. dia., light purple 7.5 P 6/8, named before 1873.

'Bluebird'—S, 3½ in. dia., blue. Plant Patent 1739, 1958 (in France as Oiseau Bleu).
'Boule de Feu'—D, 2½ in. dia., moderate purplish red 4 RP 4/10, named before 1846.
'Celestial Blue'—syn. for 'Coelestis'.
'Coelestis'—S, 3½ in. dia., light violet 10 PB 6/8, reddish at base of petal with long streaks of color reaching half way to end of petal. Named before 1887 and considered to be early flowering.
'Coeruleus'—SD, 2 in. dia., light purple, 5 P 6/7. Sometimes termed Coeruleus Plenus, listed by some European sources as Violet Claire Double.
'Duc de Brabant'—D, 2½ in. dia., deep purplish pink 5 RP 6/10. The outside petals are more colored, the inside petals more white, named before 1872.
'Hamabo'—S, 3 in. dia., pale pink with reddish stripes or blotches extending half way to the end of the petals. A deeper color than that of 'Lady Stanley'.
'Lady Stanley'—SD, 3¼ in. dia., chiefly white with a small blush-pink section on each petal and red lines reaching half way up the petal from the base. Sometimes listed as 'Lady Alice Stanley'. The plant grows with a tall and narrow habit. This and 'Leopoldii' are practically identical.
'Snow Storm'—syn. for 'Totus Albus'.
'Souvenir de Charles Breton'—SD, 3 in. dia., light purple 7.5 P 6/8, almost identical with 'Ardens'. Named before 1886.
'Totus Albus'—S, 3½ in. dia., pure white, named before 1855. Often listed as Snow Storm.
'Woodbridge'—S, 3 in. dia., strong reddish purple 2.5 RP 5/10, with a deeper color at the base of the petal.

WHITE
(# = the best of the varieties)
Single—'Snowdrift', # 'Totus Albus', 'Monstrosus' (white with purplish-red center).
Semidouble—'Jeanne d'Arc'.
Double—# 'Admiral Dewey', 'Banner', 'Pulcherrimus', 'Anemonaeflorus' (white with dark red center).

WHITE TO PINK
Single—'W. R. Smith'.
Semi-double—'Bicolor', 'Elegantissima', # 'Lady Stanley', 'Leopoldii,' 'Comte de Hainault'.

DEEP PINK
Semi-double—'Speciosus Plenus'.
Double—# 'Duc de Brabant'.

PINK TO RED
Single—# 'Hamabo'.

RED
Single—# 'Woodbridge'.
Double—'Amplissimus', # 'Boule de Feu', 'Pompon Rouge', 'Ruber Semiplenus'.

PURPLE

PURPLE

Semi-double—# 'Ardens', # 'Souvenir de Charles Breton'.

BLUE

Single—# 'Coelestis'.
Semi-double—# 'Coeruleus'.

Order of Bloom

In the vicinity of Boston, Mass., but several weeks earlier in the South.

Early (Full, late Aug.)
'Coelestis', 'Leopoldii', 'Monstrosus', 'Pulcherrimus', 'Souvenir de Charles Breton'.

Midseason (Full, mid-Sept.)
'Admiral Dewey' 'Amplissimus', 'Banner', 'Comte de Hainault', 'Elegantissima', 'Lady Stanley', 'Pompon Rouge', 'Totus Albus', 'W. R. Smith'.

Late (Full, early Oct.)
'Ardens', 'Boule de Feu', 'Coeruleus', 'Jeanne d'Arc', 'Hamabo, Meehanii'.

tiliaceus 35′ Zone 10 Linden or Sea Hibiscus
Native of the Tropics especially on beaches of islands in the Pacific, its long branches twine and interlock becoming almost impenetrable. This characteristic is used in Hawaiian gardens where it is trained over arbors—results in what Hawaiians call a hau lanai. The curved branches of this tree have been used to make outriggers for canoes. The flower, in form like other Hibiscus, is a clear yellow, fading to an apricot color. The evergreen leaves are heart shaped and coarse in texture. One of the few Hibiscus tolerant of seashore planting but not recommended where better plants can be used. Propagated by cuttings.

trionum 2′ annual Flower-of-an-hour
Widespread in North America, native to Africa, a weed often grown as an ornamental for its sulfur-yellow-to-white 3-inch flowers which have a dark center and are produced from July to Sept. The alternate leaves are divided into 3 coarsely toothed lobes. The seeds, once introduced into a garden soil, remain viable for several years. The capsule is stiff and very hairy.

HICAN. See *Carya illinoenis* x *C. laciniosa* and HICKORY NUT.

HICKORY FAMILY = Juglandaceae

HICKORY NUTS. The genus, *Carya*, contains several valuable timber and nut trees. Members of the Walnut Family, all of its major species are native to North America. All are tall stately trees with alternate compound leaves. Male and female flowers appear on the same tree, but in different clusters. The fruit is actually a fleshy drupe, though popularly called a nut. The nuts of several species are highly desired for eating. In the last 30 years several tree selections have been made, based on the flavor of the nut kernel or on the ease with which the shell can be cracked.

The native hickory species are the Mockernut, *C. tomentosa*; the Bitternut, *C. cordiformis*; the Pignut, *C. glabra*; the Bitter Pecan, *C. aquatica*; the Pecan, *C. illinoensis*; the Shellbark, *C. laciniosa*; and the Shagbark, *C. ovata*. Of these the Pecan, the Shellbark and the Shagbark have hard husked nuts, the kernels of which are highly prized as edible food.

The first of these, the Pecan, *C. illinoensis* (*C. pecan*) is indigenous throughout the Mississippi Valley as far north as Iowa, also along most of the streams in Tex. and Okla. It is also native to northern Mexico.

Growing pecans for their nuts has become an industry of considerable importance. Originally commercial Pecan-growing was largely restricted to Tex., Okla., Ark. and La. More recently named varieties are being grown throughout the South and as far north as southern Ind., Ill. and Iowa. The production of pecans in the United States has increased steadily during the last 40 years, presently totalling over 200 million pounds annually. This represents more than 10% of all nuts. The texture, aroma and appetizing flavor of pecans makes them valuable for flavoring baked goods, candies, dairy products, salads and desserts.

Several hundred varieties are now being grown. They vary in yield, bearing habit, resistance to insects and diseases as well as response to cultural practices and climatic conditions. Varieties commercially important number about 15. Percent of kernel in the named varieties varies from 37 to slightly over 50. **'Bradley', 'Stuart', 'Moneymaker', 'President', 'Pabst', 'Farley', 'Success'** and **'Desirable'** are among the leaders in the Pecan orchards of Ga. and Fla. and in some of the states to the west.

Northern Pecan strains are growing in Mich., Ohio, Pa., parts of N.Y. and nearby states. Even in these states the cold does not harm the tree, but the nut crop usually fails to mature because of the shortness of the season. The northern limit of Pecan growing is Zone 5. Here the varieties **'Busseron', 'Butterick', 'Green River', 'Indiana',** and **'Niblack'** do well. In Tex. and the Mississippi Valley **'Stuart', 'Schley', 'Van Demand'** and **'Curtis'** are most commonly grown.

A young Pecan tree has a long, stout taproot. Successful planting is not easy because of the sparsity of lateral roots. When planting, great care must be used not to injure the taproot. A deep hole must be dug to accommodate it. Use rich sandy loam when planting the tree and remember that pecans become large, broad trees with a massive root system as they become older. They should be planted at least 75 ft. apart.

Once a young tree is established, it sends out long lateral roots in all directions. They are generally within 10 in. of the soil surface, so only shallow cultivation is practiced. Mulching with a variety of materials to conserve moisture and prevent weed growth is common.

Because of its commercial importance insect pests and diseases of Pecan require special attention. The hickory shuckworm is a destructive pest which destroys shucks and prevents normal nut development. Case-bearing caterpillars, weevils, scale insects, aphids, cucurlio and round-headed appletree borer can all be troublesome. Their prevalence varies from state to state. Methods of control also vary. The extension service of the state university should be sought out for current control methods.

The Shellbark Hickory, *C. laciniosa*, becomes a tree, tall and broad, with light gray shaggy bark. The leaflets vary from 7 to 9. The nut is thick shelled, but the meat or kernel is delightfully sweet. Of the several named Hickory selections, at least one, 'Weiper', is a Shellbark, originating in Pa. The nut is quadrangular, while the shell is thick, but reasonably easy to crack. The kernel is plump and of good flavor.

The Hican, a hybrid between *C. illinoensis* and *C. laciniosa*, has aroused considerable interest, because it can be grown successfully in the northern tier of states and will mature a crop of nuts. It is of special interest to members of the Northern Nut Growers Association. The 2 varieties of the Hican, 'Burlington' and 'Bixby', produce the largest nuts. Bearing is often light. Nut quality is superior. Cultural practices are similar to those for Pecan.

The Shagbark Hickory, *C. ovata*, may reach 100 ft. in height. The leaflets are 5 in number (rarely 7), the margins fringed with hairs. The attractive gray bark loosens and comes off in wide plates during the growing season. Several named selections of trees with superior nuts are available in nurseries that specialize in nut trees. Among them are 'Hales' which originated in N.J., 'Kirtland', a rather large nut with a thinner shell permitting easy cracking and 'Kentucky' which has a kernel plump and angular, rich and sweet.

In times past the Mockernut, *C. tomentosa*, was gathered from the wild in those areas where trees were plentiful and productive. But the percent of kernel is so small the results were seldom worth the effort. The Pignut, *C. glabra*, is difficult to crack and has a minimum of meat. The Bitternut, *C. cordiformis*, is bitter, astringent and inedible.

Hickory trees are difficult to propagate vegetatively, although new techniques are simplifying the practice. All hickories have large taproots when quite young, making the trees difficult to handle in the nursery, which limits the number of nurseries that carry such stock. They are also difficult to transplant and reestablish.

H. GLEASON MATTOON

HICKORY, SHAGBARK = *Carya ovata*

HIERACIUM (hy-er-RAY-sium). A large European genus of the Composite Family with attractive flowers. However, the plants are a great pest, spreading by underground stems and by wind-blown seeds and choking out every other plant as they form an impenetrable mat. The hairy basal leaves are generally oblong, the margin entire. From the center of the rosette a hairy stem rises, crowned with several flower heads of ray flowers. These appear throughout the summer and may be found over much of the U.S. and southern Canada.

aurantiacum 20″ Zone 3 Orange Hawkweed, Devil's Paint-brush
A troublesome common perennial weed in the central and northern parts of North America introduced from Europe, blooming from June to Aug. The hairy lanceolate leaves are several inches long, in rosettes at the base of the plant and they bear a milky juice. This is a weed most common on poor, dry, gravelly fields, not so much a weed of cultivated gardens. The flowers are in heads 1 in. across, and colored orange to red, with about 12 at the end of a long spike. This is an especially bad weed because it spreads by means of leafy runners over the soil surface, and these root periodically, forming new plants. See also WEED-CONTROLLING CHEMICALS.

bombycinum 1½′ Zone 4
A perennial with soft grayish-green leaves in a flat rosette and large flower heads ½ in. wide of yellow flowers in early summer. It is native to the Pyrenees Mountains and requires a loose, dry soil and full sun. Propagation is by seed or by division.

pilosella 1′ Zone 3 Mouse-ear Hawkweed
Another common perennial weed, introduced from Europe, and similar to *H. aurantiacum* except that it is smaller and the flower heads are borne singly at the end of a stalk, and are yellow. It also is common on poor, dry, gravelly soils in northeastern North America and sends up many new plants by means of leafy runners over the soil that root periodically and form new plants. See also WEED-CONTROLLING CHEMICALS.

venosum 1′-2′ Zone 4 Poor Robin's Hawkweed
The leaves of this species are mottled with purple.

HILL. A horticultural term referring to a spot where several plants of a kind are grown together as one group, as a hill of corn, or a hill of cucumbers. Such plants as Squash, potatoes, watermelons, gourds, pumpkins and the like are always planted so that several seedlings (or plants) are allowed to grow together. The term is particularly used in agriculture from the fact that corn is cultivated in such a way that soil is thrown up around the base of the plant, or hills are created, so that the prop-roots can better secure the plant from wind.

HILUM. The small mark on a seed showing where it was attached to the inside of the ovary.

HIP. The fruit of the rose.

HIPPEASTRUM (hip-e-AST-rum)

several species   3′   Zone 9   Amaryllis
Although there are several *Hippeastrum* species, very few of these are grown in America today because the many available large-flowered hybrids are far more popular and colorful. The Amaryllis are a group of tender, bulbous plants from tropical America with large, colorful, lilylike flowers 2–4 on a stalk. Usually the flowering stalk is produced before the fleshy straplike leaves 1½ in. wide and 18 in. long, only a few weeks after potting. Because these plants are of the easiest culture they make excellent pot plants for greenhouse or home. They are grown out-of-doors in southern Fla. and Calif., but not farther north. The flowers have 6 large petals and may be 6 in. or more in dia. They are colored white, pink, red and various combinations of these bright colors.

Culture is simple. The bulbs can be placed in 6-in. pots successively so that there may be bloom from Jan. to May, using a potting mixture of 2 parts loam, 1 part leaf mold or peat moss, ½ part well-decayed manure plus some sand and bone meal. They are planted in Jan. (for the early flowers) until March with the top third of the bulb above the soil. If in a greenhouse, night temperatures might be 55–60° F. but they can be forced at higher temperatures.

After flowering, the plants should be fed with fertilizer to build up the bulbs. The leaves die in late Aug. at which time water is withheld and in the fall and early winter, pots can be kept on their side in a cold place where they are dry, although the bulbs should not be allowed to shrivel. When time for repotting, remove the old soil without damaging the roots and repot.

Easily propagated by offsets, which should be kept growing as long as possible and should bloom in 3 years, or seeds. Some popular large flowered hybrids are: **'Red Lion'**, dark red; **'Orange Star'**, orange; **'White Dazzler'**, white;

'**Striped Beauty**', soft red, white in center. Also see AMARYLLIS.

Insect Pests

Bulbfly and lesser bulbfly infest Amaryllis. See NARCISSUS.

Diseases

Red fire, due to a fungus causing red spots on the leaves, flowers and bulb scales, weakens the plant and destroys its ornamental value. Careful handling to prevent breaking the skin of leaves or roots may prevent infection. In severe infections soaking bulbs in fungicide "F" for 2 hours is suggested. Spraying with fungicide #D or #K is helpful.

vittatum   2′   Zone 10   Barbados-lily
An upright bulbous herb, native to Peru, with light green leaves sometimes not present at flowering time. The handsome bell-like flowers are 6 in. long and usually red and white striped, borne on a 2 ft. fleshy, cylindrical flower stalk. Many varieties have been grown and named, mostly in southern Fla.

HIPPOCASTANACEAE = The Horsechestnut Family

HIPPOPHAE (hip-OFF-ay-ee)

rhamnoides   30′   Zone 3   Common Sea-buckthorn
A shrub for seashore planting in Europe and Asia where it is native as well as in certain parts of the U.S., this plant has willowlike leaves, grayish green on the upper surface, silver-green beneath. The twigs are thorny and the sexes are separate, the flowers being very small and inconspicuous. The fruits are bright orange, fleshy, berries about ¼ in. in dia., borne in profuse quantities. Both sexes must be present to insure the fruiting of the pistillate plant. The fruits are very acid, not quickly eaten by the birds and hence remain on the plant a long time. It is rather difficult to transplant so it should be bought in small sizes but its ability to withstand seashore growing conditions is a splendid characteristic.

Propagation

Seeds may be processed at once or stored dry in airtight containers in a cool place for up to a year and then processed by stratifying for 3 months at 40° F. then sowing. Layers and root cuttings also prove satisfactory. See STRATIFICATION, LAYERS, ROOT CUTTINGS.

HIRSUTE. With rather coarse or stiff hairs.

HISPID. Beset with rigid hairs or bristles.

HOARHOUND = *Marrubium vulgare*

HOARHOUND, WILD = *Eupatorium aromaticum*

HOBBLEBUSH = *Viburnum alnifolium*

HOEING. This is a simple operation, practiced for centuries with all sorts of tools in all the countries of the world. Yet there is an art to it and the new gardener might study the operation to better acquaint himself with good practice. The simple objectives are two-fold, namely to kill the weeds and break up the surface soil crust so the soil is open to air and will be more receptive to rain when it comes.

There is no need for hoeing more than $\frac{1}{2}$–1 in. deep. Deeper than this can injure roots and certainly it creates more hard work. Especially is this true in times of drought when the plant roots should be completely unmolested so they can absorb every bit of water with which they come in contact. The weeds presumably are hoed out while they are very small and hence easily killed by hot sunshine. Weeds over 4 in. tall have a way of rooting again if left on the soil surface before a heavy shower. Sometimes it is best to rake them off completely and prevent them from re-rooting. Tall weeds might best be pulled by hand.

Hoeing is done in such a way that the soil is not pulled away from a plant, but the weeds are cut off, often pulled aside with the hoe, and the soil left at the same depth it was. In other words, hoeing is not a scraping, soil-removing process. One must practice it to become adept.

Like other forms of cultivation, too frequent hoeing can do more harm than good. Hoeing just before a rain is wasteful of time. Unless the weeds are raked off, the rain may disturb just enough soil so that the weeds are actually replanted. Hoeing on a bright, sunny day is best—then the sun has a chance to kill the weeds. Walking down the rows of vegetables just after hoeing is not good either. The soil may be impacted sufficiently around the weeds by each footstep to actually "replant" them.

Nor should hoeing be done when the soil is wet, as any action in the soil at that time tends to compact the soil particles together and eliminate the air spaces. When compacted soil dries out it is difficult for plants to grow in and hence it must be tilled for sometime before it can be broken up sufficiently fine to have its normal amount of air spaces.

There are several kinds of hoeing tools available. All must have some merit or they would not be made. The conventional hoe is probably most used; but there are 3-tyned hoes, English scuffle hoes that can cut weeds as they are pulled and as they are pushed. Those accustomed to using this hoe feel it cuts the work of hoeing almost in half. It might well be that the interested gardener should try out several kinds of hoes, having them available for special types of work.

One final note—it is a good idea to keep a hoe edge sharp by using a file on it occasionally.

HOG-PEANUT, SOUTHERN = *Amphicarpaea bracteata*

HOG-PLUM = *Spondias mombin*

HOLLY. See ILEX.

HOLLY FAMILY = Aquifoliaceae

HOLLY-GRAPE, OREGON = *Mahonia aquifolium*

HOLLYHOCK. See ALCEA.

HOLODISCUS (ho-lo-DISK-us)

discolor   12′   Zone 5   Ocean Spray

With considerable merit as a summer-blooming garden shrub, this is not grown much in the eastern U.S. but is used in the West where it is native from British Columbia to Calif. We have found it difficult to transplant but its conspicuous, pyramidal, creamy-white flower clusters are 8 in. long and nearly as wide, and they are borne on gracefully arching branches. The foliage is grayish green and the leaves are about 4 in. long. It is similar in general to the Ural False Spirea (*Sorbaria sorbifolia*) but blooms earlier. As a background for the perennial border (especially if delphiniums are present) it can be outstanding.

HOMALOMENA (ho-mal-o-MEE-na)

rubescens   18″   Zone 10

An aroid, with arrow-shaped, broad, reddish leaves; small unisexual flowers borne on erect spathes; native to tropical America. Occasionally grown indoors for its ornamental foliage.

HOMOGAMOUS. Bearing only one kind of flowers.

HONDAPARA = *Dillenia indica*

HONESTY = *Lunaria annua*

HONEYBELLS = *Mahernia verticillata*

HONEY-BUSH, LARGE = *Melianthus major*

HONEYDEW. This is the name applied to a sweet secretion of aphids, psylla's and some scale insects. It is sticky and contaminates all parts of the infested plant and anything underneath. Ants and certain flies and bees feed on it. A black, sooty mold fungus lives on the honeydew and discolors the contaminated objects. The fungus is not parasitic but may interfere with the functioning of the coated leaves and branches. Lawn furniture and automobiles under infested trees are badly stained. In order to eliminate this objectionable fungus, one must eliminate the insects creating the honeydew.

HONEYLOCUST. See GLEDITSIA.

HONEYSUCKLE. See LONICERA.

HONEYSUCKLE FAMILY = Caprifoliaceae

HONEYWORT = *Cerinthe major*

HOODIA (HOOD-ia)

    gordonii   1½′   **Zone 9**

A perennial, succulent herb from Africa with thick, cylindrical, angled stems, armed with pale brown spines, leafless and bearing large yellow and purple flowers in summer up to 4 in. across. Propagated by inserting pieces of the fleshy stem in moist sand during spring and summer. Sometimes used as a house pot plant. For culture see CACTI AND SUCCULENTS.

HOOF AND HORN MEAL. An organic fertilizer containing 12–14% nitrogen with traces of other elements, but these are only slowly available. Recommended for use at the rate of 2 oz. per sq. yard. See SOILS.

HOP. See HUMULUS.

HOP-HORNBEAM = *Ostrya virginiana*

HOPS. The ripened and dried pistillate cones of the Hop Vine (*Humulus lupulus*), used chiefly to give a bitter taste to malt liquors. The wet (or dry) material, after it has been used in the brewery, is often used as a mulch for plants. See MULCHES.

HOPS, SPENT. These often can be obtained inexpensively by hauling directly from a local brewery while there is still a strong odor to them, but they prove a fine mulching material. They are inexpensive, easily applied, look well, do not dry out quickly and do not burn readily.

Approximately 87% of their weight (as obtained from the brewery) is water, 12% organic matter, 0.4% nitrogen and 1% ash. They test very acid (pH 4.8). From this analysis, it is obvious that there is not much to them, yet the interesting thing is that after they have been exposed to the atmosphere of a dry room for over a month, they still will not blaze up and "catch fire" when a match is applied, They can be burned, yes, but the blaze goes out soon unless the fire is sustained by other combustible material. If a fire were started in the leaves about them and were fanned by a very high wind, they might burn. However, for all practical purposes it appears that they burn only with the greatest difficulty.

When applied to taller, more vigorous-growing grass, the grass or weeds may force growth through, in which case they are easily pulled. Rearrangement of the mulch several times might be equally satisfactory. However, if not promptly attended to, the few weeds that do come through the mulch will grow far more vigorously than they would without it. Mulches of hops have been placed on lilacs, cotoneasters, elms, cytisus, roses, spiraeas, deutzias, hydrangeas, hollies and many other plants in the Arnold Arboretum with excellent results.

Many chemicals are also being tried to com-bat the weed menace. Some are proving more successful than others. Burning the weeds with a flame gun has been tried in several situations and has not proved as effective a control under our conditions as the hop mulch, nor as the application of certain chemicals. These experiments are continuing and will be reported later. After a year and a half of mulching with spent hops continuously under many varied situations, they have proved highly effective material for weed control about woody plants, under the conditions prevalent in the Arnold Arboretum.

Not everyone will be sufficiently enthusiastic about their non-burning properties to use them to protect plants from fire. In the Arnold Arboretum we have done just that, placing heavy mulches about the arborvitae specimens to prevent a possible fire from spreading to this highly vulnerable group of plants. They retain a large amount of water for long periods and so are very serviceable for use as a mulch.

When applied in the summer, and especially when applied in a mulch approximately 6 in. deep about a plant, care should be taken to keep the hops 6 in. to 10 in. away from young trunks and tender shoots. If this is not done, the extremely high temperatures caused by the wet, disintegrating hops in the hot summer sun, will cause injury to the succulent or tender-barked stems.

Disagreeable Odor

No serious drawback has been found except, possibly, their odor. In a small, compact garden near the house, this would probably be objectionable, but in the open spaces of large gardens the odor gradually disappears after a few weeks.

Several conditions are created in the soil under a mulch which are conducive to the better growth of plants. Mulches of hops, if thick enough, keep the weeds under control about a plant which is an additional benefit, and in many cases the most important. A thin layer, 2 in. to 3 in. deep is often not sufficient to kill all the weeds. One experiment was carried out under lawn conditions. A 6-in. mulch of hops was placed in wide circles about several trees in Feb. Not a single blade of grass came through this mulch until the end of June when a few small weeds appeared. By mid-July they were growing vigorously but a mere stirring and rearranging of the hops, covering over the vigorous weeds, was sufficient to stop all weed growth under that mulch for the rest of the season. In other words, it took about 5 minutes to maintain this particular hop mulch for the year.

HOPTREE, COMMON = *Ptelea trifoliata*

HORDEUM (HOR-deum)

    jubatum   2′   **Zone 3**   **Squirrel-tail Grass**

Widespread in North America but a troublesome weed grass chiefly in alkaline soils of northern and Rocky Mountain states. It is biennial or perennial. The fruiting stalks from which it takes its common name are 4 in. long. with long awns on the seeds so that the fruiting head can be 4 in. wide. Although a graceful-appearing fruit stalk, it is a serious pest to cattle, for the long awns work themselves into the mouths and eyes of cattle grazing on it in the western states.

vulgare   **3'**   **annual**   **Barley**
Native to the Old World, this grass is one of the grain staples cultivated for its fruits. The fruiting spikes are 4 in. long and the awns can be up to 6 in. long, but the spikes are held more or less erect and not gracefully drooping as in the Foxtail Barley. Hence it is not an ornamental.

HOREHOUND = *Marrubium vulgare*

HORMONE. See AUXIN.

HORNBEAM. See CARPINUS.

HORNED-POPPY = *Glaucium flavum*

HORNWORT = *Ceratophyllum demersum*

HORNY. Hard and dense in texture.

HORSE-BALM, CITRONELLA = *Collinsonia canadensis*

HORSE-CHESTNUT. See AESCULUS.

HORSE-CHESTNUT FAMILY = Hippocastanaceae

HORSE-GENTIAN, COMMON = *Triosteum perfoliatum*

HORSE-MINT = *Monarda punctata*

HORSE-NETTLE, CAROLINA = *Solanum carolinense*

HORSE-RADISH (*Armoracia lapathifolia*). This is a member of the Mustard Family, herbaceous, 1½–3 ft. tall, hardy in Zone 4, native of southeastern Europe but has become naturalized in America because it is a strong-growing, long-lived perennial and if left in the ground for more than a year the roots grow so rapidly it is difficult to remove them all from the land. The docklike leaves and seedless white flowers of this vigorous moisture-loving plant are commonly seen as a part of old vegetable gardens. It is the roots, harvested in the fall, which are grated or ground to form the familiar relish. Propagation is by roots, selecting some about the size and shape of a lead pencil or thicker to ¾ in., keeping them in a cool cellar over winter and planting out in the spring, planted 3–5 in. below the soil surface in a slanting position about 10–18 in. apart in the row. Some botanists term this *A. rusticana*.

Insect Pests

A specific flea beetle eats small round holes

and the larvae tunnel in the leaf stems. If necessary, insecticide #9 is effective. Harlequin bug and other pests of cabbage may attack horse-radish. See CABBAGE.

Diseases

White rust and leaf spot may be present but seldom need control treatment.

HORSE-RADISH TREE = *Moringa pterygosperma*

HORSE-TAIL = *Equisetum hyemale*

HORSE-WEED. See ERIGERON.

HORTICULTURE. The word horticulture actually means the culture of a garden, but over the years the term has been used in a much larger sense to include the growing of many different kinds of plants, their arrangement in an artistic plan, their breeding, propagation and their culture. Actually horticulture can be considered a part of agriculture, although the latter word has come to mean the growing of large fields of grain crops, whereas horticulture has come to mean the growing of woody plants, vegetables and flowers. There is not a definite line between horticulture and botany—one touches on the other. The same is true of forestry and plant breeding, etc.

Over the years horticulture has come to be divided into 4 general areas: Pomology or fruit growing; Olericulture or vegetable growing; Floriculture or the production of flowers and their products for the florist's trade; Ornamental Horticulture or the growing and use of ornamental plants, both woody and herbaceous, for use in planting the landscape.

It is obvious that in each one of these subdivisions there are further divisions in which the fields of genetics, plant physiology, plant breeding, botany, agronomy, art and even engineering, landscape architecture and food technology are all a part.

In either its simplest meaning or the general inclusive meaning which has come to be accepted by usage over the years, horticulture is definitely closely associated with many biological and physical sciences and each one is tapped for information concerning the growing and arrangements of plants for man's use and appreciation.

HOSE IN HOSE. A horticultural term often used in connection with describing flowers of azaleas, in which the sepals are apparently transformed into petals, so that actually the flower looks as if it had 2 or more corollas superimposed on each other.

HOST. A term used to designate a plant on which an insect or plant disease lives. Most diseases are parasitic on certain host plants.

Parasitic plants such as Mistletoe and Dodder live on host plants.

HOSTA (HOS-ta). The genus *Hosta* contains a fine group of serviceable garden plants, suitable for growing in many soils, in partial shade, without much care. Given a rich soil, in light shade, they will continue to thrive for many years without any care whatsoever, and make excellent ground covers. These plants can also be used as border plants or as specimens provided they have the light shade necessary for their best growth. They increase slowly in size of clump, but well grown can eventually become 5 ft. and more across. They bear white or blue-to-purple lilylike flowers in spikes during the summer. Foliage varies according to species and variety but the leaves of most are large, sometimes a foot or more in length and as much in width.

are being introduced by American growers, and these will undoubtedly become popular garden plants of the near future.

caerulea = *H. ventricosa*

decorata   1′–2′   **Zone 3**   **Blunt Plantain-lily**
A rather compact small plant with blunt leaves 3–8 in. long, with a prominent white band on the margin. Flowers are dark blue, 2 in. long and the scapes with few to many blossoms. Probably native to Japan. Excellent for edging because of its small size and good foliage, as well as its method of spreading by underground stolons. Sometimes listed as *H.* 'Thomas Hogg'.

fortunei   2′   **Zone 3**   **Fortune's Plantain-lily**
This has lavender-to-whitish flowers on a tall spike sometimes 3 ft. tall, each flower 1½ in. long and appearing in July. The glaucous, pale green leaves are 5 in. long and 3 in. wide, but the var. **'Gigantea'** has huge leaves 12 in. long.

Hosta species do well in partially shaded situations. (*Photo by Arnold Arboretum, Jamaica Plain, Mass.*)

The leaves of some are much smaller, others are delicately twisted and some are variegated with white or yellow. The flowers are borne on several flowered spikes, most of which extend above the leaves in height, but a few do not. Hence, there are some of this group of plants suitable for almost every garden where growing conditions are suitable. They are excellent low-maintenance herbaceous perennials, easily propagated by seed or division of plant clumps in the spring. It is unfortunate that the nomenclature in this genus has been subjected to various revisions recently and it will undoubtedly take some time before growers will conform to proper naming. However, many named cultivars

After a few years of good growth a clump may measure 5 ft. in dia. The var. **'Marginato-alba'** has leaves margined with white. Native to Japan.

glauca = *H. sieboldiana*

lancifolia   1½′–2′   **Zone 3**   **Narrow-leaved Plantain-lily**
With slender, lanceolate leaves 6 in. long and 1½–2 in. broad. The scapes are about 2 ft. tall with numerous pale lavender flowers in Aug. There is a var. **'Albo-marginata'** the leaves of which have a white margin, and **tardiflora** blooms in the autumn. Native to Japan.

plantaginea   10″   **Zone 3**   **Fragrant Plantain-lily**
An old-fashioned favorite, native to Japan and

China and still very popular in gardens because of the fragrance of pure white flowers—the only *Hosta* species with scented flowers. The flowers are 4–5 in. long and are tilted upwards on the 1½–2½ ft. scapes during late summer and early fall. The leaves are 6–10 in. long and 4–6 in. wide. A fine, strong-growing species.

sieboldiana 18″ Zone 3 Siebold Plaintain-lily

This is a species with large glaucous-bluish leaves and the flower scapes are usually shorter than the leaves, which are 10–15 in. long and 6–10 in. wide. The flowers are pale lilac in color, during late spring or early summer, but are often overshadowed and even hidden by the leaves. Native to Japan. Still listed in many catalogues as *H. glauca*, this species makes a prominent and colorful ornamental specimen especially valuable for its foliage.

undulata 2′–3′ Zone 3 Wavy-leaved Plantain-lily

The wavy leaves of this species are variegated white, but this is not as pronounced in full sun as it is in the shade. The flowers borne in July are clear lavender, each one being about 2 in. long with many borne on each scape. The leaves are 6–8 in. long and about 5 in. wide. Native to Japan.

ventricosa (*caerulea*) 3′ Zone 3 Blue Plantain-lily

With leaves up to 9 in. long and 5 in. wide, this is native to Japan and Siberia. Flowers are lavender-purple striped with lighter color, 2 in. long during the summer. The scape is taller than the foliage

HOTBED. A special bed in the ground, usually contained by boards or cement in which the temperature is raised above the normal by heat obtained from fermenting manure, hot water or steam pipes, or electric heating wires. See FRAME or ELECTRIC HOTBED.

HOTBEDS, ELECTRIC. See ELECTRIC HOTBEDS.

HOTTENTOT-FIG = *Carpobrotus edulis*

HOUNDS-TONGUE. See CYNOGLOSSUM.

HOUSELEEK. See SEMPERVIVUM.

HOUSE PLANTS. There are literally hundreds of different kinds of plants which can be grown in the home as house plants, but it is essential to know first the conditions of light, heat and atmospheric moisture in the places about the house where plants are to be grown, then to select the right plants for those particular situations. The failure of a plant to grow properly can usually be traced directly to insufficient (or too much light), incorrect temperature, too much or too little water, a poor soil mixture and in houses using manufactured gas (not natural gas) to the ethylene and carbon monoxide which can escape from leaky fixtures. See GAS INJURY.

The lower the temperature in the situation selected, the fewer the kinds of plants which can be grown. Plants like Sansevieria, Philodendron sp., *Hedera helix*, the Rubber-plant (*Ficus elastica*) and others seem to do well with a minimum amount of light where many other plants fail. Sometimes these will exist in situations where they receive no direct sunlight.

On the other hand, azaleas, cyclamen, primroses and other flowering plants, especially if they have been forced into flower in the greenhouse, are extremely difficult to keep in a good flowering condition unless they have a certain amount of direct sunlight and the house atmosphere is not too dry.

Also, extreme watering is often the result of failure, for some people actually ruin their plants with too much. The reverse is also true, especially if the plants are off in a room where they receive little attention. Dry atmosphere is sometimes overcome by growing small plants in terrariums (which see), for if these are properly planted they need no attention for weeks at a time, provided they are in a normally warm room.

Those unfamiliar with fertilizers often injure the plants with too much or too frequent fertilizer applications. The ability to grow good house plants is not acquired readily but comes after much experience working with the conditions at hand. A good reference book on the subject like "All About House Plants" by Montague Free, Doubleday & Co., is almost an essential in obtaining good results. We have been growing house plants for 20 years in our present home and have had many failures, but we have come to learn about the ones that will do well under our conditions. Other plants continually come and go, but there are those we term the "old reliables" and we have found which ones these are by a long process of trial and error. It is interesting to try new plants if one has the time and space, but if not, we have learned that a good display can always be obtained with the dozen kinds we have found we can grow properly.

Soil

The soil mixture can be varied according to the requirements of the plant and one specific mixture is not necessarily good for all plants. Azaleas, for instance, need an acid soil with plenty of leaf mold, cacti require soil with a large percentage of sand, African-violets and ferns require one with a high percentage of leaf mold. A good general mixture is: 4 parts loam, 2 parts sand, 1½ parts dried cow manure, 2 parts leaf mold and $\frac{1}{2}$ cup of bone meal for each peck of mixture. See SOILS, SOIL MIXTURES.

Fertilizers

There are many so-called plant foods obtainable in liquid or granular form being sold under trade-marked names. Some of these are perfectly satisfactory but be sure to read the directions of application on the bottle or the package. A simple 5–10–5 (see SOILS) one teasponful to a gallon of water is helpful, if a cup of this solution is applied to a moderate-sized pot plant about every 4 weeks.

For potting houseplants see POTTING.

Water

There are many factors involved in this for there is no such thing as watering regularly so many times a week or month, by the calendar. Some plants (cacti) require less water than others (ferns). Actively growing plants need more than those in a rest period. Pot-bound plants take up more moisture than those with the pot not so full of roots. Plants in clay pots need more water than those in plastic pots. Plants growing in a very dry atmosphere require more water than those grown in high humidity. Plants in full sunshine need more water than those in the shade. If the temperatures are high, more water is needed than for plants in a cool room. And so it goes. House plants might very well be inspected several times a week to see when watering is required. It may be that a regular pattern will evolve, but chances are that if watering is done several times a week, certain plants will require water each time, others will not. Extreme care should be taken not to over-water.

Rest Period

Most plants have a rest period or are dormant for a period after they have completed active growth. Naturally this varies with different plants and can become a highly complicated affair if one grows a large number of different kinds of plants. During this rest period they should be given less water and possibly removed to a cooler place. The busy home owner has many more important things to do than to worry about the individual rest periods of all his plants, but he can notice that when that time comes, they should receive less water.

We believe in giving our house plants a "vacation." All during 9 long months they

have been on display, some have become overgrown, too large for the pot or just plain straggly. In mid-June we take them all out of the house, cut them back heavily, remove the pots of most and either repot or plant them directly in the soil under an old hemlock. The soil has been worked over and plenty of leaf mold and manure has been added. This is near the hose where the plants are sprinkled on occasion, otherwise they are forgotten until the 1st of Sept., when they are potted and prepared for bringing into the house at the advent of frosty nights. In this way, we have little worries about house plants indoors or out, during the summer months. We have a rest from caring for them, and they in turn seem to relish the lack of attention they receive throughout the summer months.

Pruning

Usually "pinching" is a better term, for some house plants like fuschias, Coleus, Jerusalem-cherry and the like should have the fast-elongating shoots pinched back occasionally to 1 or 2 buds to make them more compact in habit. Coleus especially are in this category if they do not receive sufficient sunlight.

Propagation

Many house plants are easily propagated by cuttings or division. In many cases this can easily be done right in the kitchen window or on a plant stand. A bulb pan nearly filled with the rooting medium (sand, peat moss, perlite or a mixture) can serve as the rooting bench especially if a polyethylene bag is placed completely around it to keep in the moisture and keep the cuttings from drying out. The temperature inside should not go over 80° F. and the rooting medium should be inspected once a week to see if water should be added. Begonia leaf cuttings as well as those of Saintpaulia are easily rooted in this manner. See CUTTINGS, POLYETHYLENE FILM, PROPAGATION, etc.

Pests

Scales, plant lice, white flies and mealy bug are the chief pests with which to contend. For control measures see alphabetical listing.

The following list includes only a few of the more important house plants, each one of which is described more fully in the general alphabetical listing:

Abutilon x hybridum	1′–5′	Flowering-maple
Acalypha hispida	1′–8′	Chenille Copperleaf
Achimenes sp.	1′–2′	Achimenes
Adiantum sp.	1′–3′	Maidenhair Fern
Agave sp.	1′–4′	Agave

Ageratum houstonianum	6″–18″	Ageratum
Aloe sp.	1′–3′	Aloe
Aloysia triphylla	1′–3′	Lemon Verbena
Araucaria heterophylla	1′–6′	Norfolk Island-pine
Aspidistra elatior	2′	Common Aspidistra or Cast-Iron Plant
Asplenium sp.	1′–2′	Spleenwort
Astilbe japonica	1′–3′	Japanese Astilbe
Azalea (mostly Rhododendron obtusum vars.)	1′–4′	Kurume Azalea
Begonia sp.	1′–4′	Begonia
Cactus	3″–2′	Cactus
Caladium bicolor	2′	Common Caladium
Calathea sp.	1′–3′	Marsh Marigold Cowslip
Camellia sp.	3′–6′	Camellia
Capsicum annuum	1′–4′	Bush Red Pepper
Cattleya sp.	10″–30″	Orchid
Cephalocereus senilis	6″–24″	Old Man Cactus
Ceropegia woodii	prostrate	Woods Ceropegia
Chamaerops humilis	3′–6′	Mediterranean Palm
Chlorophytum commosum	3″–18″	Spider Plant
Chrysanthemum sp.	1′–3′	Chrysanthemum
Cissus incisa	climbing	Grape-ivy Treebine
Citrus sp.	1′–4′	Orange, Lemon, etc.
Codiaeum sp.	3′–6′	Croton
Coleus sp.	6″–3′	Coleus
Cordyline sp.	1′–4′	Dracena
Cotyledon undulata	3′	Cotyledon
Crassula argentea	3′	Jade Plant
Cyclamen indicum	1′	Cyclamen
Echeveria sp.	3″–2′	Echeveria
Euphorbia splendens	1′–4′	Crown-of-thorns
Ferns	6″–3′	Ferns
Ficus elastica	10′	India Rubber-plant
Ficus pumila	clinging vine	Creeping Fig
Fuchsia sp.	1′–5′	Fuchsia
Glechoma hederacea	3″	Ground-ivy
Gardenia jasminoides	3′–6′	Gardenia
Hedera sp.	clinging vine	Ivy
Heliotropium arborescens	1′–4′	Big Heliotrope
Hippeastrum hybrids	2′–3′	Amaryllis
Howea forsteriana	2′–6′	Kentia Palm
Hyacinthus sp.	1′	Hyacinth
Hydrangea macrophylla	1′–3′	House Hydrangea
Impatiens walleriana	1′–2′	Snapweed, Patience Plant
Kalanchoe sp.	1′–3′	Kalanchoe
Lantana camara	1′–4′	Common Lantana
Laurus nobilis	1′–6′	Laurel
Lilium longiflorum	1′–3′	Easter Lily
Lithops sp.	2″	Flowering Stones
Lobularia maritima	1′	Sweet Alyssum
Mesembryanthemum sp.	1″–3″	Ice Plant
Muscari armeniacum	6″–12″	Grape-hyacinth
Narcissus sp.	12″–18″	Narcissus, Daffodil
Oxalis sp.	6″–12″	Oxalis
Pelargonium sp.	1′–4′	Geranium
Peperomia obtusifolia	6″	Oval-leaf Peperomia
Persea americana	1′–5′	American Avocado

Philodendron sp.	vines	Philodendron
Pittosporum tobira	1'–3'	Japanese Pittosporum
Plectranthus coleoides	2'	Swedish Ivy
Podocarpus macrophyllus	1'–6'	Yew Podocarpus
Primula sp.	1'–2'	Primrose
Punica granatum	1'–4'	Pomegranate
Rhododendron—Azaleas	1'–3'	(Mostly) Kurume Azaleas
Saintpaulia ionantha	6"	African-violet
Sansevieria sp.	1'–4'	Sansevieria
Saxifraga stolonifera (S. sarmentosa)	2'	Strawberry Saxifrage
Schlumbergera truncata	18"	Christmas Cactus
Sempervivum sp.	4"–12"	Houseleek
Senecio cruentus	1'–3'	Cineraria
S. mikanioides	vine	German-ivy
Sinningia speciosa	10"	Common Gloxinia
Solanum pseudo-capsicum	6"–18"	Jerusalem-cherry
Strelitzia reginae	3'	Bird-of-paradise
Tolmiaea menziesii	2'	Piggy-back Plant
Tradescantia fluminensis	prostrate	Wandering Jew
Tulipa sp.	6"–18"	Tulip
Vinca major	decumbent	Big Periwinkle
Zebrina pendula	decumbent	Wandering Jew

The heights refer to the heights the plants are usually in the house or greenhouse, not the mature heights of the plants if grown outdoors.

For more information see *The Treasury of Houseplants*, by Rob Herwig and Margot Schubert (Macmillan, New York, 1976).

HOUSTONIA. See HEDYOTIS.

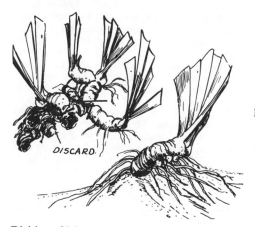

DISCARD

Division of Iris roots

HOVENIA (ho-VEE-nia)
dulcis   30'   Zone 5   Japanese Raisintree
An alternate-leaved deciduous tree with oval leaves 4–7 in. long and 3–6 in. wide. The white flowers are in terminal or axillary clusters 2–3 in. across, each flower being about ¼ in. in dia. The flower stalks have an interesting way of swelling into a large, red, edible, sweet-tasting mass, after the flowers have fallen. The globular fruits, ⅓ in. across, are brownish. Native to China. The foliage is handsome and the Japanese are said to relish the sweet-tasting flower stalks. A rare tree in American gardens but an interesting one because of its flowers and fruits.

Propagation

Seed may be sown after soaking in concentrated sulfuric acid for 2 hours, washing thoroughly, then sowing.

HOWEA (HOW-ea). Popularly called Kentia palms in the trade, this is an inaccuracy since plants of this generic name are probably not in cultivation. However, these palms are much used in gardens of southern Fla. and Calif. and are also popular tub plants indoors in the North. They have rather stiff, long, pinnate leaves with many pinnae, with *H. forsterana* much the more common.

These are really handsome palms and are used considerably in the North in conservatories where they are grown in tubs and used for decorations in hotel lobbies and offices. These are monoecious, from the Lord Howe Island just off Australia. They are unarmed and have been in the trade in America for a long time. *H. forsterana* is the larger of the two species here mentioned. It is sometimes referred to as the thatch palm, because in its native habitat its fronds are used considerably in thatching huts.

This is also faster growing and is the more commonly used species in southern Calif.

belmoreana   25′   Zone 10   Sentry Palm
A handsome palm with a single trunk; leaves are 6–7 ft. long, pinnate and at first upright then arching gracefully downwards, usually on reddish stalks. Native to Lord Howe's Island and grown in southern Fla.

forsterana   60′   Zone 10   Forster Sentry Palm, Kentia Palm
Often used when small as a tub plant indoors in the North, this is a native of Lord Howe's Island in the South Pacific and is valued as an ornamental because the leaves, 7–10 ft. long (or less), are erect, straight and flat, not arched as in many palms. Flowers, of course, not produced on small plants indoors. These are often termed Kentias in the trade.

HOYA (HOY-a)
carnosa   vine   Zone 10   Common Waxplant
A twining vine commonly grown in conservatories in the U.S. and grown out-of-doors in gardens where it is hardy. The flowers are star shaped and very waxy, fragrant and small and are produced in many-flowered axillary clusters, each flower originating from the same base, each flower about ½ in. across, white with a pink center. The leaves are opposite, leathery and lustrous. Native to southern China.

HUCKLEBERRY. See GAYLUSSACIA.

HUDSONIA (hud-SO-nia). Requiring a moist, very sandy, acid soil, the members of this genus should be propagated by seeds or cuttings. Transplanting is successful only when very tiny seedlings are used; even in seashore gardens they are seldom used because they are short lived and very difficult to transplant.

ericoides   7″   Zone 3   Beach-heather
A twiggy, moundlike evergreen shrub with supple, green, scalelike leaves covered with a fine down. Yellow flowers, borne along the length of the twigs, appear in May and June. Native to eastern North America.

tomentosa   8″   Zone 3   Woolly Beach-heather
Similar to *H. ericoides* except that the downy appearance is more pronounced, being extended to the twigs as well. Native from New Brunswick to Va. to Minn.

HUERNIA (HER-nia). Small, fleshy, leafless succulents from South Africa, belonging to the Milkweed Family, only a few inches tall, with ill-smelling blackish-purple flowers. Only suited for the desert gardens of the southwestern U.S. At least 6 species are grown by specialists.

HUMATA (hew-MAY-ta)
tyermannii   6″–9″   Zone 10   Bear's-foot Fern
This is from India and southern China, a fern for the greenhouse. The 3-pinnate fronds are 4–5 in. wide. They grow from a rhizome that is covered with many white scales, actually making it an ornamental for this reason alone. The rhizomes sometimes are horizontal and sometimes ascending. It is excellent for a hanging basket and an attempt should be made to tie down the rhizomes to the outside of the basket so they will be seen. Leaves appear every 2–3 in. along these rhizomes. If the white scales turn brown, it is a sign of over-watering, for in good condition the scales are always white. Propagate by division. See FERNS.

HUMULUS (HEW-mew-lus)
japonicus   vine   annual   Japanese Hop
A fast-growing annual vine which can become a pest because it self-seeds very freely. It can grow 25 ft. so it easily covers a wide area. Hence it is usually only planted in the garden to cover a pile of soil or unsightly rocks. The leaves are rough, 5–7 lobed and coarsely toothed, the fruits are useless for "hops." Native to China and Japan. The var. **variegatus** has leaves marked with white. Easily propagated by seeds sown where the plants are to grow. Unwanted seedlings should be pulled to prevent spreading.

lupulus   vine   Zone 3   Common Hop
A perennial twining vine or shrub with opposite, broadly 3–5-lobed leaves, very bristly stem, staminate and pistillate flowers on separate plants. Escaped in North America, native to Eurasia. The female plant produces the hops (conelike collection of fruits) used in beer-making. It is this species which is grown commercially for the hops, usually on trellises. The variety **aurea** with yellow leaves, is sometimes grown as an ornamental. A species supposedly native to the western part of the U.S. named *H. americanus* is similar and may belong to the same species. When this escapes it can become a nuisance.

HUMUS. This is the decaying animal and vegetable matter that should be in most good soils. It is necessary to aid in the absorbtion of water by the soil (as well as nutrients dissolved in it), holding this for use by the plant roots as needed. It also aids in providing air spaces in the soil, which space is needed to allow air to reach plant roots. It provides chemical plant foods as it decomposes, and makes the soil more friable or workable.

The water-absorbing capacity of humus is not readily understood by gardeners. A mineral soil (without humus) may absorb 20% of its dry weight; but a soil from the woods with a large amount of humus in it will absorb 300–500% of its dry weight in water. Peat moss likewise, which is humus, will absorb anywhere from 600% to 1200% moisture on a dry-weight basis. Consequently, it is extremely important to have humus in the soil.

It is added by applying manure, peat moss, compost, "green manures" (see SOILS AND FERTILIZERS) and just by plowing under garden weeds and vegetable plants at the end of the growing season. Dried humus material is also available from commercial sources, packaged and ready to spread, but one should ascertain first how much humus is needed and what kind before spending too much money for the wrong type of material.

HUNNEMANNIA (hun-em-MAN-ia)
fumariifolia   **2′**   **annual**   **Golden-cup**
Sometimes called the Mexican Tulip-poppy, this is a member of the Poppy Family, native to Mexico. The flowers are brilliant yellow, 3 in. across. The var. **'Sunlite'** has semi-double flowers. Actually it is considered a perennial herb, but in the North it can be grown as an annual. Seeds are sown outdoors in May in a warm sunny spot, preferably in soil that has had lime added. Plants are thinned to 9 in. apart.

HUNTSMAN'S HORN = *Sarracenia flava*

HURA (HEW-ra)
crepitans   **100′**   **Zone 10**   **Sandbox-tree**
A tropical American tree with trunk covered with thick projections; wide-spreading branches, heart-shaped leaves up to 6 in. long; maroon-colored flowers, the female ones being fleshy and resembling toadstools. The male flowers are cones 2 in. long; the fruits are round, flattened, wood-brown shells about 3 in. wide, exploding with a noise when fully ripe to disburse the seeds. The milky sap is poisonous, often used to stupefy fish. The common name comes from the fact that years ago the young fruits were used to hold sand for drying ink, in place of blotters. Sometimes cultivated in southern Fla.

HUTCHINSIA (hutch-IN-sia)
alpina   **2″**   **Zone 6**   **Alpencress**
Preferring the well-drained, gravelly, limestone soil of its native habitat in the European Alps, this tiny, tufted perennial of the Mustard Family has dark green, fernlike foliage and clusters of small white flowers blooming in April and May. Propagation is by seeds or by division.

HYACINTH. See HYACINTHUS.

HYACINTH-BEAN = *Dolichos lablab*

HYACINTHUS (hy-a-SIN-thus). Although there are at least 3 species grown in America, the most popular and the largest-flowered type is *H. orientalis*, to which all of the garden hybrids are closely allied. These are grown chiefly in Holland, in colors ranging from white through pink, red, blue and yellow, and can be bought in various sizes, the larger bulb, of course, producing the larger flower stalk. They can be grown out-of-doors as far north as southern New England, provided they are given a good winter mulch, but in colder areas they should be lifted in the fall, stored dry in a cool place until planting time in the very early spring.

They are so colorful and so extremely fragrant that they are also popular bulbs for forcing indoors. They may be put in a pot of coconut fiber or even in a glass of water with the base of the bulb just touching the water level. Then they are placed in a cool, dark cellar until root growth is well under way and top growth has just started, when they are brought up to a warm room, placed in the sun and let alone. After blooming, they can be planted out-of-doors after danger from frost is over and, mulched well over winter, they should produce flowers in the spring each year for many years.

When possible, hyacinths are planted out-of-doors in Oct., 9 in. apart and 5–6 in. deep. If they are to be propagated, a cross-cut is made across the base of the bulb at planting time and by fall this bulb will produce many small bulblets along the cut. These, if cared for properly, should produce flowers in 2–3 years. Also, hyacinths are raised from seed, but there are so many good bulbs on the American market that the busy gardener would do well to buy new bulbs when needed.

Hyacinths do not have to be planted by the hundreds in large beds. A few in the rock garden or in the foreground of the foundation planting about the house can provide much colorful spring interest when they bloom.

Insect Pests

Bulb fly and bulb mite (see NARCISSUS) may infest hyacinth bulbs, especially if growing near other bulbous plants.

Diseases

Yellow rot and soft rot frequently kill bulbs growing in wet soil. Destroy infected bulbs, plant only clean bulbs in a favorable location.
orientalis   **15″**   **Zone 6**   **Common Hyacinth**
The popular Hyacinth of gardens, of which there are so many varieties and hybrids. The sturdy leaves of this bulb are a foot long and $\frac{3}{4}$ in. wide. The flowers are many colors, sometimes double, in early spring, and always produce one cluster per bulb. Native to Greece and Asia Minor. New varieties introduced annually.

The variety **albulus** is called the Roman Hyacinth and is not the same as the species. It is more tender and produces several mostly white, loosely-flowered stalks and is not as ornamental.

A few varieties are: White—**'Edelweiss'**, **'L'Innocence'**; Pink—**'Lady Derby'**, **'Pink**

Pearl', 'Queen of Pinks'; Red—'Jan Bos', 'La Victoire', 'Tubergen's Scarlet'; Blue— 'Delft's Blue', 'King of Blues', 'Zulu King'; Yellow—'City of Haarlem', 'Yellow Hammer'.

HYACINTH, WILD = *Camassia scilloides*

HYBRID. A plant resulting from a cross between 2 or more parents that are more or less unlike.

HYBRIDIZATION. Amateur gardeners are sometimes led into hybridizing by their interest in plants and a desire to create new and better ones. Only those who have time and patience should consider this but it can be very rewarding. It is the process by which pollen from one plant is placed on the receptive surface of the pistil of another. This is done in nature by winds, insects and even birds, but the gardener often creates many interesting things under more or less controlled conditions, often with some definite objective in mind, like obtaining hardier plants or those with larger or more colorful flowers and fruits. Hybrid corn is one of the most recent commercial results from large-scale, man-made crossing. Briefly, this is done by planting several rows of the desired pistillate variety and alternating with a row or two of the staminate variety. The tassels or pollen-bearing flowers of the pistillate variety are removed before they ripen, and the tassels of the pollen-bearing variety are let mature, wind and insects doing the pollen carrying, sometimes aided by man. The seed of the female parent is then the "hybrid" corn which has been proved to yield so much more per acre.

Several things should be kept in mind by the amateur hybridizer. In the first place, varieties of a species are usually easily crossed, that is, the pistils of one variety are receptive to the pollen of another variety of the same species, and properly deposited pollen grains will grow and eventually form seed. When one species is crossed with another of the same genus, the chances of obtaining a true hybrid are somewhat less, but in many genera it can be done. Even less successful is the crossing of one genus with another, although this has been done on rare occasions, i.e., crossing *Sorbus* with *Pyrus*.

One should study the characteristics of the specific flower. Many are "self-fertile" that is, the pollen borne by an individual flower is sufficient and satisfactory for growing and germinating on the pistil of that flower, as for instance in lilies. On the other hand, some plants are "self-sterile."

HYDNOCARPUS (hid-no-CAR-pus)
    kurzii (*Taraktogenus kurzii*)   **50′**   **Zone 10**
                                       Chaulmoogra
An interesting tree valued for centuries because of an oil obtained from the seeds used in controlling various skin diseases including leprosy. Native to northern Burma. It is a tall tree with horizontal branches and pale, yellowish-brown bark. The leathery leaves are alternate, and the pink flowers, 3 in. wide, are mostly inconspicuous and the velvety round fruits, about 3–4 in. in dia., contain the seeds from which the chaulmoogra oil is extracted.

HYDRANGEA (hy-DRAN-jia). The hydrangeas are opposite-leaved shrubs and vines, native to North America and Asia. Like the viburnums, the individual flowers are small and are borne in clusters of varying sizes. In some there are both sterile or "ray" flowers and fertile flowers in the same cluster, the sterile ones making the plant conspicuous in flower. Some of the viburnums also have this character, as is evidenced in the flowers of *Viburnum opulus* and *V. sargentii*. In fact, plants of these 2 genera were often confused by the earlier botanists who examined them for the first time.

Most of the species are easily propagated by cuttings. In the past *Hydrangea paniculata* 'Grandiflora' has made such a big nursery plant in such a short time that it has been widely oversold and over-planted.

There are approximately 45 species and varieties being grown by American nurserymen but of these 26 are horticultural varieties of the

Left: *Hydrangea paniculata* 'Grandiflora'
Right: *Hydrangea arborescens* 'Grandiflora'

Bigleaf Hydrangea (*H. macrophylla macrophylla*). Many are grown especially for forcing.

Propagation

Seed may be sown as soon as ripe or stored a year in airtight containers in a cool place, then

in dia. Native to China and Japan, it can climb 75 ft. or more merely by attaching its rootlike holdfasts to the trunk of a tall tree or to a building wall. The large, flat, flower clusters are 6–8 in. across. Easily grown from seed, it is difficult for newly transplanted plants to start major growth for a year or two.

The Climbing Hydrangea—*Hydrangea anomala petiolaris.* (*Photo by Arnold Arboretum, Jamaica Plain, Mass.*)

sown. However, most propagation is by softwood or hardwood cuttings (which see). Species such as *H. arborescens* can be easily divided with a sharp spade early in the spring.

Insect Pests

Rose chafer (see Rose) and tarnished plant bug are minor pests which are controlled with insecticide #9 or #15 if necessary.

Disease

Powdery mildew causing many white powdery spots on the leaves is a common disease. Use fungicides #V or #M.

**anomala petiolaris   75′   clinging vine
                    Zone 4   Climbing Hydrangea**
The lateral branches of this clinging vine may extend as much as 3 ft. from the wall to which it clings by means of its small rootlike holdfasts all along the stems. It is one of the best of woody clinging vines, blooming about mid-June. Some of the flowers are sterile and it has been noted that the size of these may vary among seedlings. Normally they are about 1¼ in.

The vine should not be confused with *Schizophragma hydrangeoides* which it resembles because the leaves of the hydrangeas are lustrous above and the leaf margin is regularly serrate, while the leaves of *Schizophragma* are not lustrous and they are markedly coarse dentate. The hydrangea is superior ornamentally.

arborescens   3′   Zone 4   Smooth Hydrangea
Native from N.Y. to Fla., this is a rounded bush with creamy-white flower clusters 2–6 in. across in early summer. Most of the flowers are fertile, so for ornamental use, preference is always given to its variety **'Grandiflora'** which has been an old favorite, popular for over half a century and originally found in a gorge near Yellow Springs, Ohio, some time before 1900. This variety called the "Hills of Snow" Hydrangea has completely sterile flowers formed in large rounded clusters that are 4–7 in. in dia. It blooms in late June and July, can grow as high as 9 ft. but is usually seen below the eye level in height, chiefly because it is frequently pruned early in the spring to make it more moundlike. It will flower well, even though cut to the ground each spring. In very good soils the flower heads

may be so heavy that the stems will break. The more stems allowed to grow, the smaller the flowers. Its general effect is to create a feeling of coolness in the summer, with its ·masses of snow-white blooms. 'Annabelle'—a good new var.

arborescens radiata 3′-6′ **Zone 4 Silverleaf Hydrangea**
An attractive native from N. and S.Car., this has white flower clusters about 2–5 in. across of both fertile and sterile flowers in June and July. Its most ornamental characteristic is the extremely white tomentose undersurface of the leaves from which it is given the common name.

aspera sargentiana 9′ **Zone 7 Sargent Hydrangea**
The pale violet-to-white flowers of this Chinese plant are borne in large pyramidal clusters during late July. The leaves are up to 10 in. long, hairy and dull green. It is a striking shrub because of its stout hairy branches and large leaves and flower clusters. One botanist has recently made this a variety of *H. aspera* but it is known all over Europe at present under the name of *H. sargentiana*.

bretschneideri = *H. heteromalla*
heteromalla (*H. bretschneideri*) 9′ **Zone 4 Bretschneider Hydrangea**
Found in China, this is a broad rounded bush, with white flower clusters 4–6 in. across in mid-June, attractive because of the ring of sterile flowers on the outside of the cluster. The variety **glabrescens** has smaller leaves and is usually considered a better ornamental specimen.

hortensia = *H. macrophylla macrophylla*
macrophylla macrophylla 12′ **Zones 5–6 House Hydrangea**
The popular Bigleaf Hydrangea has been grown in gardens of Europe for centuries, and in gardens of the Orient for centuries before that. Formerly termed *H. hortensia* or *opuloides*, there are literally hundreds of forms being grown in Europe and Australia, where it is the most popular plant for Christmas decorations. The species is native to Japan where many forms have been carried in gardens for generations. In America this is an extremely popular pot plant for greenhouse forcing.

There is a striking similarity among these large, globular-flowered, horticultural forms. The flowers are usually about 5–10 in. in dia., but some varieties are larger, and the plants grow about 4–5 ft. tall. The sterile flowers cover the entire head, and they are either single or double according to variety.

This species and its variety *serrata* have frequently been confused. The species is the seaside plant with more lush growth and lustrous succulent foliage. However, the flowers of both may be pink or blue depending on the medium in which they are grown.

All varieties of this species are considered to have the capacity of changing the color of their flowers from blue or bluish to pink or pinkish, depending on the amount of aluminum and iron in the soil. Several commonly known greenhouse practices are used to control this color, and careful investigation has shown that the blueness of the flowers depends exactly on the acidity. Available aluminum in acid soils is the cause of blue flowers.

There are many varieties of this species in America today some of the most popular of which are: **'All Summer Beauty'**—flowers in large blue heads and long blooming. **'Bluebird'**—flowers blue and very popular on the Pacific Coast; **'Blue Prince'**, pink or blue; **'Coerulea'**, perfect flowers, deep blue, ray flowers, blue or white; **'Domotoi'**, pale pink or blue, double sterile flowers; **'Mandshurica'**, pink or blue, stems dark purple to nearly black. **'Mariesii'**, rosy-pink ray flowers 2–3 in. in dia.; **'Nikko Blue'**, blue; **'Otaksa'**, pink or blue, more dwarf than other varieties.

macrophylla serrata 4′ **Zones 5–6 Tea-of-Heaven**
Coming from Japan and Korea, the flowers are blue or white in slightly convex clusters, 1½–3 in. across during the summer. It is not as good an ornamental specimen as its 2 varieties: **acuminata**, a Japanese form of this daintily-flowered hydrangea species which grows only about 5 ft. tall. The flower clusters are mostly flat, about 2–4 in. in dia., and the ray flowers are usually blue, especially in acid soils. It certainly will not take the place of the conspicuously-flowered *H. macrophylla* varieties, but is more dainty in habit and flower and is slightly more hardy; **rosalba** is similar but the ray flowers are usually white and pink. This variety is popular in Great Britain where alkaline soils insure the pink flower color. The fertile central flowers are either pink or blue, but the larger ray flowers open white and then gradually turn pink. It grows well in shaded situations.

opuloides = *H. macrophylla*
paniculata 30′ **Zone 4 Panicle Hydrangea**
Not an ornamental plant since its sterile-flowered variety 'Grandiflora' far outstrips it in popularity. This Panicle Hydrangea is native to Japan, sometimes grows as a tree, and has large pyramidal clusters of white flowers, both sterile and fertile, in clusters 6–10 in. long that fade to purplish. The leaves are 2–5 in. long, and although usually opposite, sometimes there are 3 at a node on very vigorous shoots. The 2 popularly planted varieties are: **'Grandiflora'**, (Peegee Hydrangea), far too common a plant in American gardens. It is valued for its vigor (it can grow up to 25′ high). Its ease of propagation, and its large pyramidal clusters of mostly

sterile flowers which appear in late summer and remain on the plant for many months, make it popular. The flowers color purplish pink, then change to brown as they die. It is one of the hardiest species (Zone 4). The larger blooms up to 18 in. and 12 in. at the base are produced by materially reducing the number of growing shoots. The plant was first sent to America by George R. Hall from Japan in 1861. The variety **praecox** blooms about 3 weeks before *H. paniculata* 'Grandiflora'. Both fertile and some sterile flowers are in its clusters. It only has a limited value because of its earlier, less conspicuous bloom, but the flowers do appear in mid-July at a time when there are few woody plants in flower. Because of its many fertile flowers this is not as coarse in general appearance as is "Pee Gee," but it is difficult to find space for either one of these plants in the small garden.

petiolaris = *H. anomala petiolaris*
quercifolia 6′ Zone 5 Oak-leaved Hydrangea
The Oak-leaved Hydrangea is a native of the extreme southeastern U.S., where it was found by John Bartram in 1791. It can be expected to grow up to 6 ft. in height, although usually it is seen lower. Blooming in mid-July the flower clusters are erect panicles, 4–10 in. high, the outer flowers sterile, and the leaves are about the same general shape as those of the Red Oak. This is stoloniferous, handsome in flower and leaf, and in the right situations the leaves turn a brilliant reddish color in the fall. In fact, in many places in the North where it is killed to the ground in winter, it is grown merely for its handsome foliage since it blooms on wood formed the previous year. Usually, it can be grown in sunnier and drier situations than many of the other hydrangeas.

radiata = *H. arborescens radiata*
sargentiana = *H. aspera sargentiana*
serrata = *H. macrophylla serata*
xanthoneura wilsonii = *H. hertomalla*

HYDRANGEA-VINE, JAPANESE = *Schizophragma hydrangeoides*

HYDRASTIS (hy-DRAS-tis)
canadensis 10″–15″ Zone 5 Goldenseal
The thick yellow root of this herbaceous perennial has medicinal uses, for which the plant is sometimes collected or cultivated. Moreover, the Indians used the root to make dye. The plant usually has 1 long-stalked basal leaf which is deeply lobed and which measures from 5–9 in. wide. The hairy stem bears smaller leaves, 1 just below the short-stalked and solitary greenish-white flower having 3 sepals which fall as the flower opens, no petals, and very numerous stamens. The plant, which may be found in moist, rich woods soils from lower New England and Ontario to Mo. and Ga.,

blooms in April and May. The flowers are followed by orange-to-red berries in late summer. If it is to be grown in the wild garden, it should have rich soil and partial shade. The plants may be divided in spring or fall. Also, seed may be sown in either spring or fall, taking care to mulch the seeds and keep them moist.

HYDROCLEYS (hy-DROK-lees)
nymphoides aquatic Zone 10 Water-poppy
The prostrate stems root mostly at the nodes and the leaves float on the surface of the water. They are broad ovate, cordate at the base, long petioled. The yellow flowers are 2 in. across with purple stamens. Of value in pools and aquariums. Easily propagated by division of the rooting stem. It should not be planted more than $2\frac{1}{2}$ ft. below the water surface, preferably less.

HYDROPHYLLACEAE = The Waterleaf Family

HYDROPHYLLUM (hy-dro-FILL-um)
canadense $2\frac{1}{2}$′ Zone 4 Canada Waterleaf
A perennial with leaves 1 ft. across, 5–9 palmately lobed, flowers greenish white to purplish. Native from Vt. to S.Car. Only of value in the shaded wild garden. They bloom in summer and can be easily increased by division.
virginianum 1′–2′ Zone 3 Virginia Water-leaf
An attractive perennial with pinnately compound leaves, the leaflets, numbering 5–7, being more or less oblong, pointed and toothed. The purple-violet flowers, borne above the leaves at the top of the stalk, are in a loose umbel. The plant should be used in the moist, semishaded areas of the wild garden, simulating its habitat in the neutral or only slightly acid soils of southern Canada to Ky., west to Kan. Seeds of the plant may be sown soon after they are ripe and the plants may be divided in spring. The foliage has been used as a potherb.

HYDROPHYTES. Water plants, partially or wholly immersed.

HYDROPONICS. This is a term which has been used for growing plants in some medium other than soil, and in the 1930's rather wide claims were made for its effective use. Many people became interested in the process and started to grow plants in nutrient solutions hoping that some of these great claims would be true. After 2 decades of trials, by many amateurs and by some commercial growers, the enthusiasm for this method of growing plants has quieted down. Certainly it hits the imagination, and as a research tool the growing of plants in nutrient solutions has been done since 1699.

Because of the many claims made for growing plants in nutrient solutions, the University of California directed Professors D. R. Hoagland and D. I. Arnon to make an impartial study of the methods used and the claims, and here are the general conclusions published in Circular 347 (Revised Jan. 1950) of the College of Agriculture of the University of California in a bulletin entitled "The Water-culture Method of Growing Plants without Soil." (In this publication the term "Nutriculture" was an all-inclusive term for the several methods of growing plants in artificial media—water culture, aggregate culture, and the "adsorbed" nutrient technique.)

"Most claims for the advantages of nutriculture are unfounded.

"It is not a new method of growing plants.

"Anyone who uses it must have a knowledge of plant physiology.

"Its commercial application is justifiable under very limited conditions and only under expert supervision.

"Nutriculture is rarely superior to soil culture.

"Yields are not strikingly different under comparable conditions.

"Plants cannot be spaced closer than in rich soil.

"Plant growth habits are not changed by nutriculture.

"Water requirement is no less in nutriculture.

"Nutritional quality of the product is the same.

"Nutrient deficiencies, insect attacks, and diseases present similar problems.

"Climatic requirements are the same.

"Favorable air temperatures are just as necessary as in the soil."

Hence these are the general limitations of nutriculture or hydroponics. Today, hydroponics is used in the commercial production of some plants, but it is mostly used in areas where there is little soil or, where there is soil, it is unsuitable for plant growth. Of course, it is a much-used method of growing plants in research but for the amateur it has many limitations, and may prove most frustrating.

The general requirements for plant growth as far as temperatures are concerned are the same as with plants in soil, with an optimum for most plants between 60° and 75° F., although there are some so-called "cool crop" plants which may grow well between 50°–70° F.

Light requirements are the same as with plants in soil. Now we know much more about growing plants under artificial lights. See FLUORESCENT LIGHT GARDENING.

Water, of course, is essential for plant growth in adequate quantities, too much or too little can prove harmful.

Oxygen must be available to the plant roots. This is present in the soil, especially in soils that are "porous" and not water logged, but in soil-less cultures, especially when liquid completely surrounds the roots, it may be necessary to bubble air through the liquid about the plant roots.

Carbon dioxide and hydrogen are also essential as are certain mineral nutrients such as nitrogen, potassium, phosphorus, calcium, magnesium and sulphur. Required also, but in smaller amounts, are iron, manganese, boron, zinc, and copper, with a few others needed in such small amounts that they are usually present in the water as impurities.

There are 2 general systems of growing plants without soil, namely in water cultures and in aggregate cultures. In water cultures, there is nothing but liquid about the plant roots, and it is this which frequently results in making sufficient oxygen unavailable to the plant roots. Hence air must be bubbled about them. In the aggregate method, the roots grow through coarse sand pebbles, or some synthesized product such as vermiculite, and the nutrient solution is raised and lowered in this aggregate. This provides the roots with something to hold on to and thus the plants are kept erect, and also there are a sufficient number of times when the solution is being drained away, when plenty of air (and oxygen) are about the plant roots.

Materials and Equipment Needed for Water Culture

When plants are grown by this method on a small scale, glass or earthenware crock containers are easiest to use. If more plants are to be grown, the tank should be 6–18 in. deep and 2–3 ft. wide. It can be made of wood or metal, but in either case it should be thoroughly painted on the inside with water-proof asphalt paint, for the chemicals used in the nutrient solution can react with metal. Crock jars are also used. If a glass container is selected it should be painted black on the outside, to keep light from the growing plant roots.

There must be a support over the containers to hold the plants upright. The simplest is a cork with a hole in the center, used as a stopper in the glass jar. The seedling is carefully wrapped in cotton when inserted in this hole so it will be properly supported. If a tank is used, then a bed 3 in. deep is used above the tank. The bottom of this is covered with wire mesh and then filled with some litter like wood shavings, peat, sphagnum moss or similar material. The young seedlings are germinated in sand or vermiculite, then carefully transferred to this medium when their roots are long enough to reach through it and touch the liquid in the container below. If the litter is kept moist, it could be kept moistened with the nutrient solution and the roots would eventually grow through it and into the liquid below.

Air may or may not have to be pumped through the solution for the roots to get sufficient oxygen, depending on the kind of plants used and their size. If air must be given, a small aquarium pump would prove satisfactory for smaller installations, but the air should not be pumped through with such force that it materially disturbs the roots.

Pure water is necessary. The mineral content of water varies greatly about the country, and in some water there may be a sufficient concentration of certain minerals to prove harmful to the plants. Also, some city waters have such a high concentration of chlorine that they are harmful to plants and even kill tropical fish if used directly from the faucet. Nutrient solution may be applied directly to each container, or in the larger tanks it can be fed by gravity and then pumped up into the stock-solution tank and run through the various tanks by gravity again. In any event, it should be completely changed about once every 2 weeks. When this is done, it should be a fast operation so that the roots do not dry out, best accomplished on a cloudy day or late in the afternoon when there is little sunshine.

It is most important to keep the solution in the containers at the same level all the time, for on hot days, or days in which a good deal of the solution is absorbed, the level will drop, and if this is not taken care of properly and promptly the roots may partially dry out.

Materials and Equipment Needed for Aggregate Cultures

The materials used in this method are sand, gravel or other similar materials. Seedlings are planted in the medium the same way as they would be in soil, and the solution poured into the bed, and allowed to drain out periodically. The advantage of this method over the water culture method, is that it allows for the proper aeration of the roots, and the medium is usually sufficiently solid so that the plants are held upright.

Since the nutrient materials will adhere to the aggregate, there is a build-up of salts on the small particles. To eliminate that, the whole bed should be flushed out with water about every 2 weeks.

It is advisable not to use the nutrient solution more than 2 weeks without completely renewing it. It should be placed in the beds, and drained, about twice a day, but if the weather is very hot it may have to be done more often. Various methods have been devised for running the solution through, the most ingenious of which is by means of a simple bucket, attached to a long pole on which there is a fulcrum in the center like the old-fashioned well sweep. A rubber drain is attached to the bucket so that eventually all of the solution drains into it from the tank. Then at the proper time, the pole is pushed to the ground thus raising the bucket and the solution drains from the bucket, through a rubber hose, back into the aggregate again.

Preparing the Nutrient Solution

Plant physiologists have devised many different formulas over the years for supporting plant growth. Usually pure chemicals are suggested for these, but sometimes the cheaper fertilizer chemicals can be used even though they have a few impurities, some of which may even be utilized by the plant. When the formula has been decided upon, it should be accurately mixed and stored in closed containers in the dark. It may be necessary to paint the bottles black for this purpose. Evaporation of the solution should be guarded against, for when this occurs and water is lost, the percentage of salts in the liquid remaining is increased. In some instances, too much of the salts can injure the plants.

Garden supply stores often sell "complete" plant food in solution, and it may be that some of these can be used. One mixture, worked out by the University of California is as follows:

SALT	GRADE	NUTRIENT	AMOUNT FOR 25 GALLONS OF SOLUTION	
			OUNCES	LEVEL TABLESPOONS
Potassium phosphate (monobasic)	technical	Potassium Phosphorus	$\frac{1}{2}$	1
Potassium nitrate	fertilizer	Potassium Nitrogen	2	4
Calcium nitrate	fertilizer	Calcium Nitrogen	3	7
Magnesium sulfate	technical	Magnesium Sulfur	$1\frac{1}{2}$	4

Other nutrients can be added in small amounts and the table below is a suggested one for this purpose. These can be purchased at the fertilizer or garden supply store, or the drug store, but one should be certain the formulae are the same as those suggested here.

SALT (ALL CHEMICAL GRADE)	NUTRIENTS	AMT. OF WATER TO ADD TO I TSP. OF SALT (A)	AMT. OF (A) TO USE FOR 25 GAL. OF SOLUTION
Boric acid (powdered)	Boron	$\frac{1}{2}$ gal.	$\frac{1}{2}$ pint
Manganese chloride (MnCl$_2$ 4H$_2$O)	Manganese Chlorine	$1\frac{1}{2}$ gal.	$\frac{1}{2}$ pint
Zinc sulfate (ZnSO$_4$ 7H$_2$O)	Zinc Sulfur	$2\frac{1}{2}$ qts.	$\frac{1}{2}$ tsp.
Copper sulfate (CuSO$_4$ 5H$_2$O)	Copper Sulfur	I gal.	$\frac{1}{2}$ tsp.
Iron tartrate	Iron	I qt.	$\frac{1}{2}$ cup

When the solutions is finally mixed, the pH (which see) should be checked and adjusted to the proper one for the plants used. Azaleas, rhododendrons and many ericaceous plants do well if the acidity is from 4.5 to 5.5. Potatoes, zinnias and pumpkins will grow with a pH of 7.0 to 7.5 and few things will grow if the solution has a pH lower than 4.0 or higher than 8.0. Dilute sulfuric acid (in very small amounts) is used to make the solution more acid. Using an eyedropper and applying a drop or two at a time and retesting for acidity is the correct procedure. The pH can be raised by adding sodium hydroxide similarly.

During World War II publicity was given to an Army Air Force installation of gravel-growing beds on Ascension Island in the South Atlantic. A large number of Army personnel were stationed on this rocky island and there was not sufficient soil to grow green vegetables. Distances were so great that they could not be shipped in reasonably. The psychological satisfactions to the personnel of fresh salad vegetables, in this place at this time, made the installation worth the effort.

It was surprising that distilled sea water was used in making the nutrient solutions. There would not have been sufficient fresh water to make this project feasible. A local gravel was found satisfactory for the growing medium. Fresh tomatoes, radishes, lettuce and cucumbers were grown and it was felt that this installation accomplished its mission. It was an outstanding example of the successful application of the principles of plant physiology and engineering techniques in a location where suitable soil was non-existent.

There is no better example of modern hydroponics at work than at Epcot Center of Walt Disney World, near Orlando, Fl. In an area called The Land, staged by Kraft, are many food plants being grown in pure sand with the help of certain added chemical nutrients in solution. Still in the experimental stages it does show what might be possible in growing food in desert areas.

Hence there are situations in which hydroponics can play an important role, but in most areas, where suitable soil is available and weather conditions are satisfactory, the growing of plants in water solutions is best suited for research work only.

HYDROTRIDA (hy-dro-TRI-da)
caroliniana = *Bacopa caroliniana*

HYGROPHYTES. Marsh plants, or plants which need a large supply of moisture for growth.

HYLOCEREUS (hy-lo-SEE-reus)
undatus   25′ if supported   Zone 10   Night-blooming Cereus
A favorite climbing or clambering conservatory cactus, grown outdoors in the Tropics, native in Mexico and featured in many Hawaiian gardens. It blooms at night with large white flowers nearly I ft. long, filled with pale yellow stamens inside. These open about 8 p.m. usually so fast one can see the movement, and remain open until the next morning when they drop off. The fleshy stems of this cactus are 3 sided and have small prickles along the undulating edges. Blooms occur mostly between June and Oct. The fruit is red, $4\frac{1}{2}$ in. long, highly decorative, and edible. It is tolerant of salt in the seashore gardens of southern Fla. Propagated by cuttings.

HYMENOCALLIS (hy-men-o-KAL-is). Bulbous plants, members of the Amaryllis Family. Only one species native to the U.S. Propagated by offsets with culture the same as for Amaryllis.
caroliniana (*occidentalis*)   **2′   Zone 5   Inland spider-lily**
A perennial, bulbous plant with narrow basal leaves up to 12 in. long, and a stout, leafless flower stalk bearing a large, terminal umbel of

white flowers. The 6 very narrow, reflexed petals are joined at the base and the 6 spreading stamens, extending to nearly the length of the petals, are joined at the base to form a spreading, cuplike structure. The plant may be found in marshes or near streams from Ind. to the Gulf. In cultivation it might be grown somewhat north of this area with some winter protection. The plants may be divided in spring. It is an excellent plant for the bog garden.

narcissiflora (*calathina*) 2′ **Zone** 7 **Spider-lily** With large, lilylike, white, fragrant flowers sometimes 4 in. long and peculiar, narrow perianth parts (the reason for the name Spider-lily) and a trumpetlike tube. This can be grown in the South out-of-doors, but in colder gardens the bulbs should be lifted in the fall and stored over winter, with roots attached, in dry soil at a temperature of about 60° F. Native to Peru. Propagated by offsets.

Three hybrids are exceptionally good display plants: **'Daphne'**—larger flowers than species; **'Festalis'**—curved perianth petals; **'Sulphur Queen'**—yellow flowers.

speciosa 2′ **Zone** 9 **Winter-spice, Spider-lily** White fragrant flowers, 10–15 on a stalk, borne in winter. The entire flower is sometimes 9 in. long. Leaves are evergreen. Flower retains fragrance when dried. One of the best species for greenhouse. Native to West Indies. Propagation by offsets but same bulbs can be used for many years. See AMARYLLIS for general care.

HYMENOSPORUM (hy-men-o-SPOR-um)
flavum 50′ **Zone** 10 **Sweet-shade** Closely related to Pittosporum, this evergreen tree is native to Australia and is very rapid in growth and is apparently free of insects and diseases. The fragrant yellow flowers, 1½ in. long, are produced in terminal panicles during the early summer and the foliage is coarse. The trunk is often bare of branches for some distance above the ground. The leaves are alternate and crowded at the end of the stiff short branches.

HYPERICACEAE = The St.-John's-wort Family

HYPERICUM (hy-PER-ik-um). St.-John's-wort. There are many hypericums, most of them being herbaceous, but of the woody species and varieties, only a few have ornamental significance. They are valued chiefly for their bright yellow flowers in the summer, some of them lasting for several weeks to 2 months. In the South, some are semi-evergreen to evergreen and they usually have opposite and sessile leaves. Certain ones make excellent ground covers, rooting well wherever their stems touch the soil. The fruits of these shrubs are merely dried capsules, but when mature some are colorful for a short period as are those of *H. androsaenum* which, in ripening, are at one time yellowish, then turn to brilliant red before they mature brown. The leaves of most do not have much autumn color, but 1 or 2 species may have foliage which colors reddish in the fall under some conditions, and the stems of many of the woody species are 4-angled. In the winter, there are some with good glossy brown bark (*H. prolificum*), of course only evident on the larger plants, but it is a factor in their use as ornamentals. An important characteristic of most is that they will grow well in the poorer, dry, sandy soils.

Propagation

Seed may be sown at once or stored dry in airtight containers in a cool place, for up to a year, then sown. Plants can be easily divided with a sharp spade early in the spring before growth starts. Softwood or hardwood cuttings (which see) can be rooted.

androsaemum 3′ **Zone** 6 **Tutsan St.-John's-wort** The Tutsan St.-John's-wort has been so named because "Tutsan" is a condensing of the French *toute-saine* meaning to heal all. Years ago this plant was supposed to have many curing properties, probably because the wine-colored juice of the ripening fruits looked as it if might be good for medication purposes. It is native to western and southern Europe and grows as a rather low plant, doing well in the shade and in some areas the leaves will be semi-evergreen. The leaves are the largest of the hardy hypericums, being 3½–4 in. long. The yellow flowers which are not outstanding are ¾ in. wide with 3 to 9 in a cluster at the end of a shoot. The mature fruits are dried capsules but in ripening there is a period when they are colorfully red—about the size of a large pea.

ascyron 6′ **Zone** 3 **Giant St.-John's-wort** Perennial herb with yellow flowers 2 in. across in few-flowered clusters, native from Quebec to Pa. and Kan. Leaves are 5 in. long. A weedy wild flower, not for the garden.

aureum = *H. frondosum*

buckleyi 1′ **Zone** 5 **Blue Ridge St.-John's-wort** Although the yellow flowers of this species are small, ½–1 in. in dia., appearing in mid-June, it is an excellent plant for a ground cover, and a native of N.Car. and Ga. A single plant will quickly grow into a round mat of foliage, hugging the ground, but the branchlets lying on the ground do not readily root. This prevents it from spreading too rapidly, but as a thick mat of foliage within a restricted area, it is excellent. The leaves are ½–¾ in. long.

calycinum 1′–1½′   Zone 6   Aaronsbeard St.-John's-wort

Of all the hypericums, this is the best as a ground cover, making it the most useful of all the species, and it is native to southeastern Europe and Asia Minor. The bright yellow flowers appearing in late July, are as much as 3 in. in dia. and the leaves are about 3–4 in. long. It is easily propagated by cuttings or by division and the prostrate branches readily root on the surface of the ground. The autumn foliage color is somewhat purplish and even in sandy soils this performs well. It is not hardy north of New York City. It has the desirable trait of flowering throughout the summer. If it does grow too rank, it can easily be cut back to the ground and started over.

cerastoides 5″   Zone 6   Rhodope St.-John's-wort

Similar to *H. olympicum* but with a matlike foliage, doing well in rock crevices or as a wall plant. Native to Asia Minor.

densiflorum 6′   Zone 5   Dense Hypericum

The flowers of this species which is native from N.J. to Fla. and Mo., are only ½ in. in dia., but the tall erect habit, dense foliage and small leaves (about 1 in. long but only ⅛ in. wide) give it some value as a plant with fine texture. It blooms from July to Sept.

ellipticum 1′–2′   Zone 3   Pale St.-John's-wort

Spreading by a creeping rootstalk, this slender perennial has opposite, oblong leaves which are wider at the tip and small yellow flowers in terminal clusters. It blooms during July and Aug. throughout southeast Canada and the eastern seaboard states to Va. In general, it prefers moist, sunny locations.

frondosum 3′   Zone 5   Golden St.-John's-wort

John Bartram was supposed to have discovered this plant in 1776 in S.Car. to Ga. The yellow flowers appearing from July to mid-Aug. are 1 in. across, making them slightly larger than the more common *H. prolificum*. The leaves are blue-green, about 2 in. long and ½ in. wide. It is this plant that used to be called *H. aureum*. It does well with some shade, especially on limestone soils.

kalmianum 3′   Zones 2–3   Kalm St.-Johns'-wort

This is one of the hardier species with handsome yellow flowers 1⅛ in. dia., and leaves 1½ in. long and ½ in. wide. It is native from Quebec to Mich.

x moseranum 1½′   Zone 7   Goldflower

This species blooms continuously throughout the summer and is a hybrid (*H. patulum* x *H. calycinum*). The yellow flowers are 2½ in. in dia., and the young shoots are reddish. It is used as a ground cover on the Pacific Coast where it is one of the few that will do well under Eucalyptus trees. One bed at Kew Gardens in England needed practically no attention in 20 years.

olympicum 1′   Zone 6   Olympic St.-John's-wort

A procumbent shrub with bright yellow flowers 1½–2 in. across in midsummer, and leaves narrowly oval, ½–1¼ in. long. Native to southeastern Europe. Sometimes used as a ground cover.

patulum henryi 3′   Zone 6   Henry St.-John's-wort

The yellow flowers are up to 2½ in. in dia., and the plant as a whole is much more sturdy than the species. Both are native to China. In protected places it can be half evergreen, with leaves 3 in. long. It is superior to the species in every way, making it one of the best of the hypericums.

'Hidcote'—this variety of *H. patulum* originated in the famous gardens at "Hidcote," England, shortly before 1948. It grows about 18 in. tall and as much across. The fragrant golden-yellow flowers are 2 in. in dia., appearing from late June until mid-Oct. Unfortunately this dies to the ground during colder winters, but it grows vigorously and produces many flowers the following summer. In the warmer climate of the Deep South, plants may reach 3–4 ft. in height and retain their leaves; 'Sungold'—this probably originated in England but was patented in the U.S., March 2, 1943 (# 568) by the Wayside Gardens of Mentor, Ohio, who say that it is hardier than most of the other hypericums. The flowers are about the same size as those of 'Hidcote'.

perforatum 2′   Zone 3   Common St.-John's-wort

A perennial, fast-spreading weed which roots readily as its leafy runners grow over the soil surface, often in dry, sandy soils. The opposite leaves are 1 in. long and the bright yellow flowers are 1 in. across, numerous on many-branched shoots, appearing during July and Aug. It is an introduction from Europe but has become a very troublesome weed in both the U.S. and Canada. Supposedly under certain conditions, cattle and sheep are poisoned from eating this weed and the plant tops have been used in supplying a yellow dye.

prolificum 4′   Zone 4   Shrubby St.-John's-wort

This is the most vigorous of the hardier American hypericums, native from N.J. to Iowa and with winter twigs that are a lustrous brown color. Densely rounded in habit, covered with small yellow flowers in the summer for weeks at a time, the leaves are shining green, oblong in shape and dotted with numerous semi-transparent spots.

reptans   prostrate shrub   Zone 7
This is a low ground cover, native to the Himalayas, only a few inches high. It roots readily along the stems where they touch the soil and is a nice plant for the rock garden.

rhodopeum = *H. cerastoides*

'Rowallane'—closely related to *H. patulum*, is actually a hybrid (*H. hookerianum leschenaultii* x *H. rogersii*). It originated at the famous garden "Rowallane" of Mr. H. Armytage-Moore in Ireland before 1942. It can grow 5–6 ft. tall, is fairly hardy in Zone 6, with leaves 2½ in. long and flowers of a buttercup yellow, sometimes as much as 3 in. in dia. These are borne in terminal cymes of 3 or more flowers, which appear in Sept. The plant can die down to the ground in cold winters in Zone 5.

HYPOCHOERIS (hy-po-KEER-is)

radicata   1′   Zone 3   Cat's-ear
A perennial weed with milky juice introduced from Europe, common in eastern Canada, northeastern and north central U.S. with leaves somewhat like those of Dandelion, in a rosette on the soil surface and a long tap root. The yellow flower heads are 1½ in. across and are on long stalks, several to a stalk and similar to, although smaller than, those of Dandelion. They bloom from June to Sept.

HYPOXIS (hy-POX-is)

hirsuta   6″   Zone 4   Common Star-grass
A perennial rhizomous plant of the Amaryllis Family having long, grasslike, often hairy leaves and a short, leafless flower stalk bearing a few yellow, starlike flowers with 6 segments. It is a plant of dry, sunny soils with a range extending over much of the eastern half of the U.S. and generally flowering in June. The rhizomes may be divided after the plant has flowered.

HYSSOP = *Hyssopus officinalis*

HYSSOP, GOLDEN WEDGE = *Gratiola aurea*

HYSSOPUS (hiss-O-pus)

officinalis   1½′   Zones 2–3   Hyssop
A subshrub belonging to the Mint Family with square branches, opposite leaves about an inch long with aromatic odor; blue flowers, small but in many-flowered whorls on spikes 2½–5 in. long. Native to the Mediterranean Area, grown since ancient times as a potherb. Propagated by seeds, cuttings, and division. Supposedly there is a white-flowered variety (**alba**) as well as one with pink flowers (**rosea**).

I

IBERIS (eye-BEER-is). The candytufts are sturdy and popular garden plants belonging to the Mustard Family, both the annuals and the perennials. Native to the Mediterranean Region, the leaves are narrow, the flowers are in flat umbels, white, red or purple, which increase in size after blooming has started; each flower has 4 small petals. They grow well in almost any garden soil and the annuals start to bloom 2 months after the seed is sown. Usually these are excellent for edging. The evergreen or woody types can be grown from seed as soon as ripe (blooming the following year), or they can be easily divided. Softwood and hardwood cuttings are easily rooted.

affinis   16″   annual
With white flowers, often tinged lilac, and slightly fragrant in umbels. Native to southern Europe. Seeds should be sown in the garden in April where the plants are to grow. They will bloom about 6 weeks later and continue until frost.

amara   1′   annual   Rocket Candytuft
Flowers are large, fragrant and white, the plant frequently being grown by florists for cutting. Leaves are 3–4 in. long, coarsely toothed and widest towards the tip. Native to Europe. Seed should be sown where plants are desired in April. They will bloom 6 weeks later and will continue to do so until frost. There are many varieties.

gibraltarica 15″ Zone 7 Gibraltar Candytuft
An interesting, evergreen, rock-garden plant, sometimes also used in the foreground of an evergreen foundation planting, with lilac-pink, partly white flowers borne in umbels during mid-May. It is a native of Spain and Morocco and has leaves 1–2 in. long.

pruitii (*tenoreana*) 8″ Zone 5 Tenore Candytuft
Blooming at about the same time as the yellow flowering *Aurinia saxatilis*, these 2 plants can be used together in the garden, making a fine color combination when they flower in mid-May. The Tenore Candytuft has evergreen leaves about 1½ long and is a native of Italy.

saxatilis   6″   Zones 2–3   Rock Candytuft
A small evergreen perennial, ideal for edging and for use in rock gardens. The short stems are twisted tortuously and covered with minute, almost globular leaves and the tips of the stems are covered in April and May with small

clusters of tiny white flowers. Native to southern Europe.

sempervirens   12″   Zone 3   Evergreen
Candytuft
This is the species widely used in the U.S. as one of the most popular of low garden plants, in rockeries, in the flower border or in front of evergreen shrubs. Its almost evergreen leaves are 1½ in. long and narrow and its flowers are white, borne in flat clusters or umbels in late May but lasting some time. It is native in parts of Europe and Asia and usually blooms after the flowers of *Aurinia saxatilis*, the old-fashioned *Alyssum saxatilis*, have faded. There are many varieties available, some like **'Little Gem'**, **'Purity'** and **'Snowflake'** have been selected because of their large flowers and more compact habit.

umbellata   16″   annual   Globe Candytuft
Probably the best of the annual species for the garden. The narrow leaves are 2–3½ in. long. The flowers appear in compact clusters and are colored pink, red, lilac or violet. They are not fragrant. The various-colored garden forms belong here. Easily grown from seed sown where the plants are to grow in early spring. They will start to flower within 6 weeks and will continue until frost. Native to Europe.

IBOZA (eye-BO-za)
riparia   5′   Zones 8–9?
A South African perennial sometimes grown in the home greenhouse; with a 4-angled stem and leaves 2 in. long; many very small, dioecious, creamy-white flowers in erect panicles. Propagated by cuttings and grown with the same culture as Coleus.

ICEPLANT, COMMON. See MESEMBRYANTHE-MUM.

IDESIA (eye-DEE-sia)
polycarpa   45′   Zone 6
The alternate leaves of this tree are about 6 in. long, sometimes longer, and it looks something like a small-leaved Catalpa. The fragrant male and female flowers are either on the same tree or on different trees, and the bright orange-red berries are borne in large clusters, effective in the fall until they are frozen. It is rare, native to China and Japan and chiefly grown for its ornamental fruits.

Seed may be sown as soon as ripe or stored dry in airtight containers in a cool place for up to a year and then sown. Softwood cuttings (which see) can be rooted.

ILEX (EYE-lex). Holly. There are recognized now at least 21 native American holly species and about 120 oriental species. With nearly 200 varieties of the English Holly being grown in America (80 listed in nursery catalogues) and nearly 400 varieties of *I. opaca* being grown (63 varieties at least are available in the trade), it is seen how popular this group has become.

Many of the oriental species described are not yet introduced to American gardens and some of the native species and varieties are either not worthy ornamentals, or have been named but not yet introduced into commercial horticulture.

Left: American Holly with fruits on the current year's growth.
Right: English Holly with fruits on the previous year's growth.

Hollies are deciduous or evergreen trees and shrubs, with alternate leaves, noted either for their good evergreen foliage or their small berries or both. The flowers are inconspicuous, sexes are on separate plants so that it is essential to have both staminate and pistillate plants in the near vicinity to insure the fruiting of the pistillate plants.

Much hybridizing is being done by individuals throughout the area where hollies are grown. Hardiness, especially of the evergreen group, is one of the most important things to be brought into the newer hollies. As will be seen from the ensuing list there are only 3 hollies hardy in Zone 3 (extreme northern U.S.), namely, *I. verticillata, glabra* and *rugosa*. *I. laevigata* is only hardy up to Zone 4. All other

hollies require warmer situations in which to grow. Although there are yellow-fruited varieties of some of the species, these are not being exploited as well as they might. The red-fruited evergreens are in much demand and although there are many of these for the South, there are not many for the North. Only a very few of the growers will list the male and female plants separately, but this is a most important and necessary thing to do for the average buyer who wants to have fruits assured. There are 2 species which seem to produce colorful fruits without normal cross-pollination, namely, *I. cornuta* and *I. laevigata*. There may be others, and if there are, certainly these too will be worth growing.

There is a strong need for dwarf or low plants—the new *I. glabra* 'Compacta' is certainly an excellent plant. It would be even a better one if it were staminate, since the leaves of the male plants retain their deep green foliage color better throughout the winter months. Possibly such a plant will be found or developed. Another is a new dwarf variety of *I. verticillata*. The nurseryman responsible for finding and introducing this variety claims that the fruits are twice the size of those of the species and the plant does not grow over $3\frac{1}{2}$ ft. tall. If this performance holds under all types of growing conditions, this is certainly a clone well worth growing. There are two dwarf clones of *I. vomitoria* also, but one at least is not known to fruit.

Propagation

Seeds can be processed as soon as ripe or can be stored dry for a year and then processed. The seeds of *Ilex* species frequently have double dormancy and vary considerably in the treatment best suited for an individual species. Sometimes stratification at warm temperatures for 3–5 months, then cold for 3 months is sufficient to bring about the germination of a proportion of the seed. A carefree method of handling slow-to-germinate seeds such as *I. opaca* and *I. aquifolium* is to place the seeds in a sealed polyethylene bag together with moist sand or peat moss, and place it in a protective container in a sheltered place out-of-doors where it will undergo seasonal changes. Seed collected in the autumn can be carried this way until the second spring when it can then be sown.

Evergreen hollies root well from hardwood cuttings, while deciduous sorts can be propagated from softwood cuttings. See SEED STRATIFICATION, CUTTINGS, etc.

Insect Pests

Holly leaf miner is the only important insect pest of holly. The conspicuous mines start in

June and the insect remains in the mine through the winter. There is one annual generation. Spraying when the mines are first seen in early June with insecticide #15 or #13 will kill the miners. Insecticide #13 in early summer kills many flies before egg laying.

Diseases

Although about 325 diseases have been reported on holly, the most important are: Tar spot which produces tarlike spots on the leaves and is controlled by fungicide #F. Twig canker which may girdle the green wood of new growth and is checked by careful pruning. Anthracnose in the form of rough, dark brown spots on the leaves is controlled by fungicides #G and #F.

When growing holly for Christmas decorations, physiological troubles such as scald and purple spot due to adverse weather and soil deficiencies are important. Spine spot or punctures in the leaf by the spines on other leaves is frequently abundant following storms and carelessness during cultivation and harvesting. It is often mistaken for pathological trouble.

x altaclarensis 45′ Zone 6 Altaclara Holly
This is a staminate or male hybrid between *I. aquifolium* and *I. perado* with glossy, evergreen leaves up to 4½ in. long and 3 in. wide. The bark is purple—some leaves have a very spiny margin, others do not. It makes a good foliage specimen.

ambigua montana (*I. montana*) **36′ Zone 5**
Mountain Winterberry
A deciduous shrub, native to the eastern U.S., sometimes a small tree, with leaves 3–7 in. long and bright red fruits about ⅜ in. across. It is not very popular in landscape planting because of its height. Sometimes it has been incorrectly termed *I. dubia* or *I. monticola*.

aquifolium 70′ Zone 6 English Holly
A fine evergreen tree, native to southern Europe—American nurserymen are offering 80 varieties and there are 200 being grown in the U.S. The alternate evergreen leaves are glossy on the upper surface and vary considerably in size and in shape, some varieties having no spines on the margin of the leaf, and others having several, the leaves 1½–3 in. long and the bright red fruits, slightly more than ¼ in. across, being borne on the previous year's growth. These fruits remain on the tree until Christmas, and in some varieties they may be retained an entire year.

There are several beautiful variegated forms being grown on the Pacific Coast and cut branches of these bring premium prices for Christmas decorations. The English Holly is used in landscape planting in areas where the atmosphere is moist (the Eastern Coast to southern New England, and the Pacific Coast) but they are not plants for the hot, dry areas of the Midwest. Many of the commercial orchards where hollies are produced for cut branches are in Ore. and Wash. It is not possible to mention all the varieties of the English Holly here, but a few, listed to show their differences, are: **angustifolia**—small narrow leaves—Narrowleaf English Holly; **'Argentea marginata'**—leaf margin silver colored. This includes varieties like **'Silvery'**, **'Silver Beauty'**, **'Silver King'**, **'Silver Queen'**—Silver-edge English Holly; **'Aurea marginata'**—many clones with yellow leaf margin such as **'Golden King'**, **'Golden Milkmaid'** and **'Golden Variegated'**; **'Camelliaefolia'**—a very popular variety with few spines on the margin of the leaf, fruit large, foliage coloring bronze in the winter.

x aquipernyi 30′ Zone 6
A cross between *I. aquifolium* and *I. pernyi* with leaves twice the size of those of *I. pernyi*. The best clone is **'Brilliant'** with brilliant berries.

x attenuata 20′ Zone 7 Topel Holly
This is a hybrid of *I. opaca* x *I. cassine* and is a good plant for the South, with evergreen leaves 1½–4 in. long and red fruits in clusters somewhat similar to those of *I. cassine*. It is a large pyramidal shrub and the females bear heavily every year. The fruits are ¼ in. across.

cassine 36′ Zone 7 Dahoon
An evergreen shrub native in the southeastern U.S., the red fruits are borne in large clusters. It is found native in swampy areas and is best used near its native habitat. The fruits are ¼ in. across and the leaves are 1½–4 in. long. There is a yellow-fruited variety. The variety **myrtifolia** is found in swamps, N.Car. to Fla., with leaves only 1″–2″ long.

chinensis (*I. purpurea*) **40′ Zone 7**
This is a vigorous evergreen tree from China and Japan with leaves 2½–4 in. long, densely produced, and red fruits ¼ in. across. It is pyramidal in habit, very dense. Very popular in China, this tree should be grown more in America.

ciliospinosa 10′–20′ Zone 5
For some reason this is proving popular, probably because of its compact habit and very small evergreen leaves 1–1½ in. long which are about ½ in. wide. The bright red fruits are ¼ in. across and it is native to China.

corallina 30′ Zone 6 Coral Holly
A Chinese native evergreen with leaves 4 in. long and 1½ in. wide but the fruits are very small, only about ⅛ in. across, with 5–7 in a cluster.

cornuta 9′ Zone 7 Chinese Holly
An excellent ornamental from China, long popular in the U.S., glossy, squarish, evergreen leaves 1½–5 in. long, often with 4 spines. The

female plants have the ability to produce red fruits without the aid of pollen, one of the reasons it is so widely used. The fruits are about ⅜ in. in dia., and are usually borne in large clusters. There are now excellent clones which may take the place of the species in ornamental use. Some are: **'Burfordii'**—leaves entire but with a terminal spine, originated at West View Cemetery, Atlanta, Ga., over 50 years ago. An excellent evergreen, fruiting heavily, this has been termed one of the best evergreens for planting in the South. Plantsmen in Dallas, Tex., maintain it is their best evergreen ornamental; **'D'Or'**—with yellow fruits ¼–⅜ in. in dia.; **'Jungle Gardens'**—with large yellow fruits; **'Shangri-la'**—female clone, fast growing, fruit matures in June and persists until March—a splendid heavy-fruiting seedling.

crenata   **20′**   **Zone 6**   **Japanese Holly**
The Japanese holly was introduced into cultivation in the U.S. in 1864 and has proved popular

man is known to have as many as 200 selected seedlings. The fruits are small black berries about ¼ in. or less in dia., and not very effective against the evergreen leaves.

Forty years ago there were only the species, the variety **'Microphylla'** and possibly 1 or 2 others available in the trade. Now there are 40 names being listed. Certainly all are not outstanding ornamentals; some are not worthy of planting, and some of the names listed are merely synonyms of older, recognized varieties, or are so similar that from the standpoint of their use in the landscape, there is no appreciable difference. They are used as specimens, for screening purposes and for clipped hedges. **'Convexa'**—a variety introduced into America by the Arnold Arboretum in 1919 and hardier than the species. Until the peculiar winter of 1958–59, this had not suffered much injury, but during that winter it was badly killed over a wide area of the northern U.S. It is still an

Ilex crenata 'Convexa': The convex-leaved Japanese Holly is an excellent evergreen for northern gardens. (*Photo by Arnold Arboretum, Jamaica Plain, Mass.*)

in all types of ornamental plantings. Its small, evergreen leaves, varying between ⅜ and 1¼ in. long, and the dense, twiggy character of its branching give it qualities that make it useful as a specimen, a background planting or a hedge since it withstands shearing very well indeed. American nurserymen have grown it from cuttings for a long time and have found that when seed is planted, numerous variations arise. In fact, there are so many now that if one studies the nursery catalogues carefully, one will find some 40 names purporting to be different varieties of this useful species, and one nursery-

extremely worthy specimen, with small, convex leaves and rather widespreading habit, flat on top. A 40-year-old plant is 9 ft. high and 24 ft. across. It will withstand clipping and makes an excellent substitute for Box in the North; **'Glass'**—a male clone of *I. crenata* 'Microphylla' differing only in that the leaves are slightly smaller. It is compact and upright while young but can become rather open with age; **'Green Island'**—an 11-year-old plant is loose and open (3 ft. tall and 6 ft. across), not nearly so compact as older plants of 'Helleri' and 'Stokes'. It was patented (#817) in 1949, and is said to be more rapid growing than either 'Helleri' or 'Kingsville'; **'Helleri'**—originated in Newport, R.I., in 1925—very dwarf and compact, looking as if it were sheared. A 26-year-old plant is only 4 ft. tall and 5 ft. across. The leaves are about ½ in. long. **'Hetzii'**—a dwarf clone of *I. crenata* 'Convexa'. **'Kingsville'**—a dwarf clone of *I. crenata longifolia* discovered in Md. in 1912. The original plant is now 4 ft. tall and 7 ft. across, with leaves ½ in. long and quite hardy, having withstood temperatures of −15° F. **'Kingsville Green Cushion'**—a very dwarf clone with spreading habit. A 10-year-old plant was only 8 in. tall and 32 in. across. It makes a solid cushionlike mass. Zones 5–6; **latifolia**—this is so popular that apparently it is offered in the trade under several names such as *fortunei*, *major* and *rotundifolia*. Actually these are all synonyms. The plant has rather large leaves being about 1½ in. long and ½–⅝ in. wide and a glossy green. It is vigorous in growth, sometimes reaching a height of 20 ft. Zones 5–6; **'Mariesii'**—this is a dwarf variety with the small leaves bunched near the ends of the twigs and growing less than an inch a year. Sometimes it is listed as var. *nummularia*, but it is rather difficult to find commercially. **'Microphylla'**—low in habit with small leaves ⅓–¾ in. long, this has been in cultivation in America for 50 years or more and has proved to be the hardiest of the old varieties. How its hardiness compares with that of the many newer varieties remains to be seen. Certainly it is as hardy as 'Convexa' and it is hardier than the species; **'Stokesii'**—this plant was patented #887 in 1949. A 12-year-old plant is 3 ft. tall and 4 ft. across, flat-topped and not quite so globose as is the variety 'Helleri', but it is slightly hardier, a male clone.

decidua 30′ Zone 5 Possum Haw
Native to the southeastern U.S., this is considered by some to be the best of America's deciduous hollies because it holds its bright orange-red fruits well into the winter and occasionally longer. These fruits are borne singly or in small clusters, and are about ⅜ in. in dia. The foliage is lustrous.

fargesii 20′ Zone 7 Farges Holly
This species can be separated from all evergreen hollies by its leaves that are 2½–4½ in. long but only ½–¾ in. wide. The fruits are red and about ¼ in. in dia. It is not especially meritorious for landscape planting.

glabra 9′–21′ Zone 3 Inkberry
An excellent, native, evergreen shrub, found especially in swampy areas in eastern North America, this can also easily be grown in normal soils. The leaves are 1–2 in. long and the fruits are black berries about ¼ in. across. Staminate plants keep the green foliage color in winter much better than do the pistillate plants which tend to turn brown. The clone **'Compacta'** is a new dwarf female clone which bears fruit heavily and is more dense and lower in height than the species. Both of these plants grow very well in seashore gardens.

integra 36′ Zone 7 Nepal Holly
This is native to Japan, and has evergreen leaves 2–4 in. long and large red fruits up to ½ in. long. It makes a fine pyramidal evergreen for planting in southern gardens.

laevigata 6′–9′ Zone 4 Smooth Winterberry
A deciduous holly native to the eastern U.S., this has red berries and leaves 1½–2¾ in. long that are wedge-shaped at the base. Like *I. verticillata*, it is found mostly in swampy areas and the 2 species are often confused. The leaves of *I. laevigata* are lustrous above and glabrous beneath, while leaves of *I. verticillata* are dull above and slightly pubescent beneath.

latifolia 60′ Zone 7 Lusterleaf Holly
An evergreen holly from Japan, this has thick, glossy, leathery leaves 3–6½ in. long and 1½–3 in. wide, making this the holly with the largest leaves in the South—an elegant specimen. The red fruits are about ⅓ in. across, but are in small clusters about ¾ in. long.

meserveae 15′ Zones 5–6 Meserve Hybrids
Comparatively new hybrids (*I. rugosa* × *aquifolium*) created by Kathleen Meserve of Long Island, N.Y. Often called the Blue Hollies, **'Blue Boy'** and **'Blue Girl'** were introduced in 1964. These have glossy blue green foliage, leaves 2 in. long with spiny teeth, fruits red and 5/16 in. in diameter, good in sun or shade. Other clones are **'Angel'** only hardy to Zone 6; **'Maid'**; **'Prince'** a male, growing 15′ or more tall; **'Stallion'** another 15′ male and a good pollenizer for all the hybrids; **'Princess'**—12′.

montana = *I. ambigua montana*

'Nellie R. Stevens' 20′ Zone 6
A hybrid (*I. aquifolium* × *cornuta*), with leaves dark green, spiny edged and fruits a bright orange red.

opaca 45′ Zone 5 American Holly
A native tree that is widely distributed in the eastern U.S., nearly 300 varieties of this have been named, 63 of them are being commercially grown by American nurseries. Like the English Holly, these vary in habit, in leaf size and shape and in the amount of fruit produced. They differ from *I. aquifolium* in that the leaves are dull above and the fruits are borne on the current year's growth. Although there is a great demand for cut branches of both species at Christmas, the lustrous-leaved *I. aquifolium* always brings the premium prices. The leaves of most varieties of *I. opaca* have spines on the leaf margins.

This tree prefers good, well-drained soil. If planted in an orchard pattern, there should be at least 1 male tree for every 10 female trees. On the small place it would be well to have 1 of each sex, or a pistillate tree onto which was grafted one or more staminate or pollen-bearing branches.

In selecting varieties, one should be careful to select those which have been tested locally for a number of years, rather than buying varieties, which although they are popular several hundred miles away, may not grow as well under local conditions. A very few of the varieties which have acquired wide-spread distribution are 'St. Mary', 'Goldie', 'Merry Christmas', 'Old Heavy Berry', 'Miss Helen', 'Red Chief'. There are some varieties with yellow fruits as well as named male varieties. In areas where hollies are native (within 3 miles of the planting) it is probably not necessary to plant male trees since wind and insects carry the pollen, but in other areas, male trees should be planted to insure the fruiting of the pistillate plants.

pedunculosa   30′   **Zone 5**   **Long-stalk Holly**
One of the hardiest of the oriental evergreen hollies, this small tree (native to Japan) should be grown more. Its laurel-like, evergreen leaves, 1½–3 in. long, its long, stalked, bright red fruits about pea size, and generally good narrow upright habit, make it useful for specimen planting in protected places in Zone 5. Both male and female plants are offered in the trade. Several varieties have been named but it is doubtful if any are being grown in the U.S. at this time. The leaves and bark are supposed to yield a brown dye of value in Japan.

pernyi   30′   **Zone 6**   **Perny Holly**
With glossy evergreen leaves ½–1¼ in. long and few spines and red fruits, this is somewhat similar to *I. cornuta* but has smaller leaves and a definitely pyramidal habit. It is native to China. The var. **veitchii** has larger leaves 1½–2 in. long, proving very popular. Both male and female clones of this variety are available.

purpurea = *I. chinensis*

rugosa   low spreading   **Zone 3**   **Rugose Holly**
A small prostrate evergreen shrub, leaves 1–2 in. long and red fruits ½ in. in dia. Of increasing interest because of its extreme hardiness and low-spreading habit. Native to Japan.

rotunda   60′   **Zone 7**   **Kurogane Holly**
A beautiful evergreen from eastern Asia, this has red fruits in clusters of 3–7 borne in the axils of the leaves and shaped like miniature footballs. The leaves are 2–3 in. long and have no spines on the margins.

serrata   15′   **Zone 5**   **Finetooth Holly**
Deciduous, native to Japan, similar to the American *I. verticillata* but with smaller fruits about ⅛ in. in dia., profusely borne, either singly or in 3's. The yellow-fruited variety ('Xantho-carpa') is being grown in the Brooklyn Botanical Garden.

verticillata   9′   **Zone 3**   **Winterberry**
A popular, deciduous shrub (see *I. laevigata* for differences with the species), native to eastern North America, especially in swampy places, this has red fruits which sometimes remain on the plant until Christmas. The leaves are 1½–2¾ in. long and the fruits color before the leaves drop in the autumn. It does not require wet soils, but does well in acid soils and, when in need of revival pruning, can be cut back almost to the ground. A male plant should be near the female or the 2 planted together. Also it is possible to bud or graft a male branch on the female plant and thus insure the fruiting of a single plant which could be far removed from all others. The var. **'Chrysocarpa'** has yellow fruits and the new var. **'Nana'** has fruits twice the size of those of the species and seldom grows over 3½ ft. tall.

vomitoria   24′   **Zone 7**   **Yaupon**
A very popular evergreen species native to the southeastern U.S.—a fine landscape plant. It can be easily sheared into hedge form. The fruits are red, small, borne singly or in 3's—the stems are gray. It flowers on the previous year's growth and the twigs are often covered with fruits. The leaves are about 1½ in. long. In fact, it is considered by some to be the most heavily fruited of all the hollies, as well as one of the most drought-resistant. 'Nana' is dense growing, dwarf, with smaller leaves and does not apparently bear fruits. Somewhat in habit like *I. crenata* 'Helleri'.

yunnanensis   12′   **Zone 6**   **Yunnan Holly**
Closely related to the Japanese Holly, *I. crenata*, and with similarly shaped leaves about 1 in. long, this evergreen from China has red fruits about the size of a pea. Fortunately both male and female clones are now available commercially and this fact should make this plant more popular. It lives over all but the most severe winters in a protected place in Boston, Mass., without injury where the oldest plant in America, grown from the original seed introduced in 1898, is still thriving.

ILLICIUM (ill-ISS-ium)

anisatum   12′   **Zone 8**   **Japanese Anisetree**
With elliptic, aromatic, alternate, evergreen leaves 2–3 in. long and yellowish-green flowers an inch wide with many narrow petals, the fruit is borne in star-shaped clusters. This aromatic shrub belongs to the Magnolia Family. Native to Japan where the powdered bark is mixed with resin and used to burn as incense. This plant yields a poison and is propagated by seeds and cuttings.

floridanum   9′   **Zone 7**   **Florida Anisetree**
The red flowers of this unusual evergreen are 2 in. across and appear in July. The leaves are aromatic and up to 6 in. long. It is native to Fla.

and La., and is best grown in partial shade and slightly acid soil.

IMBRICATE. Overlapping, as shingles on a roof; as the bud-scales of horse-chestnuts and azaleas.

IMMORTELLE = *Xeranthemum annuum*

IMMORTELLE, MOUNTAIN = *Erythrina poeppigiana*

IMPATIENS (im-PAY-shiens). Mostly succulent annuals and perennials having irregularly spurred flowers in the leaf axils and interesting fruits which burst suddenly and expel the seeds. Grown chiefly as house plants or for bedding purposes and easily grown from seeds or cuttings (in cases where striking color forms are to be maintained).

balsamina 2½′ **annual Garden Balsam**
An old-fashioned garden plant from the Asiatic Tropics, valued for its white-, red- or yellow-colored flowers, with some varieties single flowered and some with very double flowers, borne close to the succulent stems, along the top third of the plant. Some of the new double-flowered vars. have flowers looking like small camellias. They are used especially for bedding in sun or shade. Seeds are planted indoors in April or outdoors in May where the plants are to grow and then thinned to 18 in. apart. Sometimes where they freely self-sow, seedlings of undesirable colors should be rogued out.

capensis 4′–5′ **Zone 2 Snapweed**
An erect, fleshy annual with elliptical leaves and irregular flowers, consisting of a calyx with 3 sepals, 1 of which is petalike and extends into a curving spur and 3 unequal petals. These flowers, arising from the axils of the leaves, are orange spotted with red. The seed pods burst, easily scattering the seeds a considerable distance. The plant grows in moist, generally acid, soil throughout Canada and eastern U.S. and, although attractive, it is too weedy in habit for cultivation outside the wild garden. It may be propagated easily from seed sown in spring.

holstii = *I. wallerana*
pallida 4′–5′ **Zone 2 Pale Snapweed**
Similar to *I. capensis*, this species has generally lighter green leaves and yellow, slightly larger flowers. It grows over much the same habitat, preferring either neutral or calcareous soil.

sultanii = *I. wallerana*
wallerana (*I. sultanii*) 1′–2′ **annual or perennial Sultan Snapweed, Patience-plant**
Native to eastern Africa, this is only treated as a perennial in the frost-free South, elsewhere it is grown as an annual. The stems are succulent, leaves are alternate with the upper ones sometimes whorled. The bright scarlet flowers are 1½ in. across with a thin curving spur, but there

are other colors available now, including pink, salmon, purple and white. This is often grown in the greenhouse as a winter pot plant. Seeds are sown in Feb. indoors (or outdoors in May). They are planted out 2 ft. apart in rich sandy loam in sun or shade, and pinched back to make bushy compact plants. They are also easily propagated by cuttings.

IMPERFECT FLOWER. Having either stamens or pistils, but not both. See also PERFECT FLOWER.

INARCHING. Grafting by approach, the scion remaining attached to its parent until union has taken place. See GRAFTING.

INBREEDING. When seeds are obtained by using the pollen from an individual plant on the pistils of that plant, and this is repeated for several generations, this is inbreeding. In this way, the seedsman often obtains plants which will breed true. First-generation seedlings from a single cross may not all breed true, but after several generations they will. Sometimes this results in good plants—many of the "strains" of annuals in the seed catalogues are in this category and are desired because one can count on the characteristics of the seedlings being uniform.

On the other hand, it may result in a general plant deterioration. Corn is usually cross-pollinated, but when inbred the ears become smaller, vigor of plant decreases and certainly the yield.

In other words, depending on species and variety, inbreeding may or may not result in more desirable plants.

INCARVILLEA (in-kar-VILL-ea)
delavayi 2′ **Zone 6 Delavy Incarvillea**
Apparently much more popular as a garden plant in Europe than it is in America where it is very difficult to find, this is an alternate-leaved, semi-hardy perennial with compound pinnately-divided leaves having 15–21 leaflets each up to 5 in. long. Flowers are large, trumpet shaped, rose-purple with a yellow tube 1–2 in. long and nearly as wide. Native to China. Belonging to the Begnonia Family, it does best in the full sun and is easily propagated by seed or division. *I. mairei grandiflora* with brilliant crimson flowers is somewhat similar.

grandiflora = *I. mairei grandiflora*
mairei grandiflora (*I. grandiflora*) 1′ **Zone 4 Bigflower Incarvillea**
Much like *I. delavayi* but not as vigorous, the leaflets nearly entire and not as many brilliant crimson flowers. Native to China.

sinensis variabilis (*I. variabilis*) 2′ **Zone 4 Pink-shrub Incarvillea**
Rather shrubby, the leaves are 2–3 times pinnate and finely cut. Flowers are pink, an inch wide,

native to China. It will bloom the first year from seed during much of the summer.

variabilis = *I. sinensis variabilis*

INCENSE-CEDAR, CALIFORNIA = *Libocedrus decurrens*

INCHWORM. Insect larvae, generally of the Family Geometridae, which have legs at front and back of the body so that they hump their back when crawling, are called inchworms, measuring worms or loopers. Cankerworms are well-known examples. The female moths are often wingless and must crawl to find suitable locations for egg laying. Spraying with Sevin (carbaryl) or malathion controls them well.

INCISED. Cut sharply in the margin.

INDEHISCENT. Not opening by valves or along regular lines. See also DEHISCENT.

INDIAN-CHERRY = *Rhamnus caroliniana*

INDIAN CORAL-BEAN = *Erythrina indica*

INDIAN CURRANT = *Symphoricarpos orbiculatus*

INDIAN-FIG = *Opuntia ficus-indica*

INDIAN PIPE = *Monotropa uniflora*

INDIAN PAINTBRUSH = *Castilleja coccinea*

INDIAN PLUM FAMILY = Flacourtiaceae

INDIAPOON BEAUTYLEAF = *Calophyllum inophyllum*

INDIA-RUBBER-PLANT = *Ficus elastica*

INDIA WHEAT = *Fagopyrum tataricum*

INDIGENOUS. Original to the country, not introduced.

INDIGO. See INDIGOFERA.

INDIGO, BASTARD = *Amorpha fruticosa*

INDIGOFERA (in-dig-OFF-er-a). The alternate leaves of these deciduous shrubs are pinnately compound and the flowers are small but pealike; the fruits are small dry pods. They grow best in the full sun.

Propagation

Seed should be soaked in hot water (190° F.) overnight before sowing. Plants may be easily divided with a sharp spade early in the spring before growth starts. Softwood cuttings and root cuttings (which see) can easily be rooted.

amblyantha   6′   Zone 5   Pink Indigo
Valued only for its flowers which are small, pealike and pale lilac to purple to almost pink, borne in spikes 3–4 in. long, this shrub starts to bloom in early June and continues for many weeks in the summer. Native of China, it has pinnately-compound, alternate leaves like the other species, no autumn color, and the fruits are merely dried capsules. In cold winters it may die back some, but if pruning is done at once,

it will grow back vigorously and bloom on the current year's wood.

gerardiana   3′   Zone 7   Himalayan Indigo
A very branched shrub with alternate compound leaves having 13–21 leaflets about ½ in. long; rosy-purple flowers in dense racemes 3–6 in. long in the summer. Not much used as an ornamental in the U.S. but good for its summer flowers. Native to India.

incarnata alba   1½′   Zone 5   White Chinese Indigo
Unfortunately this excellent ground cover is not grown by any American nurseryman. It is native to China and Japan, bears white pealike flowers in 5–10-in. spikes in July and, although cold winters can kill it to the ground, it grows vigorously and blooms on the current year's growth. Its use as a ground cover is recommended for its roots grow into an interlocking mass that is excellent for keeping soil from washing away.

kirilowii   3′   Zone 4   Kirilow Indigo
Another plant from China and Korea, this bears small rose-colored flowers (pealike) in 5 in. spikes during June. This too is an excellent ground cover for it suckers readily and is more dense in growth than is the Yellow Root (*Xanthorhiza apiifolia*). If severe winters kill the stems, it sprouts from the base readily and flowers in the summer on the current year's growth.

potaninii   3′   Zone 5   Potanin Indigo
This Indigo is valued chiefly for its length of bloom, bearing its colorful 2–5 in. lilac-pink flower spikes of very small pealike flowers in June and for several weeks thereafter. It comes from northwestern China.

tinctoria   2′   Zone 10   Indigo
A tropical shrub with usually 9 leaflets but these can be up to 17, and small reddish-yellow flowers ¼ in. long in racemes. This plant has long been known for the clear blue dye which can be produced from it. Cut branches (and leaves) are immersed in water and allowed to ferment and it is from this material that the dye is made. Not an ornamental plant.

INDIGO, WILD = *Baptisia tinctoria*

INFERIOR OVARY. One that is below the perianth. See also SUPERIOR OVARY.

INFLORESCENCE. The flower cluster; disposition of the flowers on the floral axis.

INFRUCTESCENCE. The inflorescence in a fruiting stage.

INKBERRY = *Ilex glabra*

INSECTICIDES. Chemical insecticides control insects quickly and effectively. Regular preventive applications are often the only way to preserve the health of garden plants. In many areas certain crops especially apples, peaches, cucumbers and cabbage can be grown with even moderate success only with the use of insecticides and fungicides. If a destructive infestation of insects appears suddenly or has been overlooked, careful applications of insecticides are usually the only way to stop it. The chemicals are expensive and can be harmful unless used as directed and with proper equipment. See SPRAYING AND DUSTING. Sprays, dusts and granules require different equipment. Fumigants and aerosols are used in greenhouses and small pressure cans of insecticides are available for convenient use on a few plants. Combinations of insecticides and fertilizers are prepared to combat soil-infesting insects. Insecticides can be very efficient but should be used as a supplement to, not a replacement for, other methods. Why breed insects by careless cultural practices so that you can kill them with insecticides?

Development

In the early part of the 20th century there were few recognized insecticides and their use was relatively simple. Dormant sprays of lime sulfur controlled scale and some plant diseases; chewing insects were combatted with lead arsenate, Paris Green or hellebore and sucking insects were sprayed with a nicotine solution, usually nicotine sulfate or kerosene emulsion. Bordeaux mixture and sulfur mixtures were standard fungicides and had some insecticidal value. Greenhouses were fumigated with hydrocyanic acid gas with questionable results. However, after 1945, there were tremendous developments in chemical pesticides. Chlorinated hydrocarbons such as DDT, chlordane and benzene hexachloride were found to have long residual insecticidal action; organic phosphates killed by both contact and stomach poison activity and some of them were absorbed and translocated by the plant sap to kill insects which fed on the treated plants. See SYSTEMIC INSECTICIDES. A little known chemical group of carbamates contributed carbaryl (SEVIN) and fungicides such as ferbam and zineb. The spores of insect-attacking bacteria were concentrated for use as insecticides such as the Milky Spore dust to control Japanese beetle grubs and *Bacillus thuringiensis* for control of certain lepidopterus larvae. Insect sterilization by radiation has already been demonstrated successfully and chemical sterilants have survived many experimental tests. We can expect pesticide development to keep pace with other modern sciences with emphasis on safety.

Information about Pesticides

The new chemical pesticides have created new problems. Many of them are poisonous and when handled carelessly or used improperly they can be harmful to warm-blooded animals including man and to wildlife including birds, fish and small animals and as excessive residue on food crops to the consumer. To prevent harmful results from the use of pesticides, it is required by law that the manufacturer and/or distributor attach to every package an approved label. This label states the degree of toxicity hazard, the amount of active ingredients, the recommended dilution, the plants on which it can or cannot be used safely, the safe period before harvest to avoid residue and the antidotes in case of accidental poisoning. In addition there are descriptive circulars which publicize the safe methods for handling, applying and disposing of used containers and excess chemicals, as well as recommendations for the use of protective clothing. The suggestions on a poster such as

> Before Using
> STOP
> Read the Label

are well worth observing. Label recommendations are carefully prepared and should be followed often in preference to any other.

The principal groups of insecticides and miticides are:

1. INORGANIC CHEMICALS. Although just as effective as stomach poisons as they ever were, lead arsenate, Paris Green and other arsenicals and the fluorine compounds such as cryolite and sodium fluosilicate are now generally replaced by the new formulations. Sulfur (see FUNGICIDES), especially as liquid lime sulfur which was formerly the standard for dormant spraying to control scale insects, is now difficult to obtain.

2. MICROBIAL INSECTICIDES. Concentrations of spores of insect-infesting bacteria are available as dusts, wettable powders and stabilized suspensions. Milky Spore disease (*B. popilliae*) for control of Japanese beetle grubs (see MILKY SPORE DISEASE) and *B. thuringiensis* for control of certain worms and caterpillars are well-established treatments for special problems.

3. BOTANICAL INSECTICIDES. Rotenone, pyrethrum, nicotine, ryania and sabadilla (see these insecticides in alphabetical list) as well as the obsolete hellebore are plant extracts or ground powders of plants. Many are among the safest insecticides and have many uses for insect control on fruits and vegetables near harvest. They tend to deteriorate in storage and should be used within a year.

4. CHLORINATED HYDROCARBONS
  (a) Aryl group with 6 or more chlorine molecules. This group includes aldrin, BHC, chlordane, dieldrin, endrin, endo-

sulfan (THIODAN), heptachlor and lindane. They are nerve poisons and were primarily used to control soil-inhabiting insects such as wireworms, corn rootworm and the grubs of Japanese beetle, Asiatic garden beetle and June beetles. Weevils and curculios are well controlled; and this group has been used effectively to kill grasshoppers at rate of 1 oz. per acre. BHC, lindane and endosulfan are effective for control of aphids, sucking bugs and leaf miners.

(Certain of the chlorinated hydrocarbon insecticides are no longer registered for use by the Environmental Protection Agency. Before using, the regulations on their use should be carefully understood and observed. Consult local authorities [i.e., the Cooperative Extension Service or the Department of Agriculture] for local restrictions and the latest control of specific pests.)

(b) DDT and relatives. This includes methoxychlor which has a wide range of effectiveness and long residual action. Some insects have shown resistance to DDT and due to its possible harmful effect on fish and other wildlife it should not be used. It kills beneficial as well as destructive insects and occasionally mites and aphids have increased following its use. Methoxychlor is less harmful to wildlife and has been substituted for DDT, which is now banned everywhere.

5. ORGANIC PHOSPHATES. These insecticides kill by paralyzing the nervous system. There are many formulations with a wide field of application. Some are highly toxic and must be handled and used with extreme care. Others are relatively safe as recommended and have short residual action, permitting their use on food crops near harvest. See PHOSPHATE INSECTICIDES.

6. SYSTEMIC INSECTICIDES. These are a group of chemicals which are absorbed by the roots or leaves and translocated with the sap to other parts of the plant especially the new growth. Sucking insects and mites feeding on the treated plants are killed. Beneficial insect parasites and predators are not affected unless wet by the spray when it is applied. Except for sodium selenate which is now obsolete, they are organic phosphates which are available as granules for soil applications and as emulsifiable concentrates for spraying. Systemic insecticides should not be applied to food crops unless specifically recommended and then only by experienced operators who follow special safety precautions.

7. CARBAMATES. These are chemical pesticides which include fungicides and herbicides as well as insecticides. The best known insecticide is carbaryl (Sevin). Sevin is a broad-spectrum formulation which is relatively safe to fish and other wildlife and can be applied to food crops near harvest. It is very toxic to bees and kills Boston Ivy and Virginia Creeper. It gives excellent control of Japanese beetle, codling moth, periodical cicada, elm leaf beetle, birchleaf miner and several other pests.

8. OIL SPRAYS. Emulsified oils are very effective as sprays for the control of scale insects, mealy bugs and the eggs of many insects and mites. In the North they are usually applied just before or when the dormant buds are opening. In the South the safer formulations are applied to citrus and other semi-tropical plants when needed but preferably during cool weather. The preferred oils are the lubricating type having 87 to 90% unsulfonated residue and a viscosity of 60 to 70 seconds Saybolt. They are known as Superior oils and paraffinic base oils are considered safer than asphalt base oils. In the North early spring applications should be avoided when freezing is likely to occur before the spray dries, usually 48 hours. Oil sprays are diluted to contain 1 to 5% actual oil and label directions should be followed. Trees with thin bark such as Beech, Hickory and Maple may be injured by oil sprays and the "bloom" is dulled on Blue Spruce.

9. MITICIDES. Although oil and organic phosphate insecticides control spider mites effectively, there are some chemical pesticides which are specific for mite control. Chlorobenside, chlorobenzilate, dimite and ovex are benzene compounds; Aramite and tetradifon (Tedion) are sulfur compounds and dicofol (Kelthane) is a close relative of DDT which are specifically miticides. Special directions as stated on the label indicate that Aramite should not be used on food crops and that ovex is effective against eggs and young but should not be used on apples within 30 days of harvest. Tedion is safe to use just before harvest on fruits and several vegetables. When spider mites are a persistent problem, phosphate miticides and non-phosphate miticdes should be used in alternate applications to delay or avoid the build-up of resistance. Most miticides are compatible with insecticides and fungicides and can be used effectively in combination with them. See MITES.

10. POISON BAITS. Baits prepared with chlordane or dieldrin as well as some of the phosphates and some of the arsenicals such as Paris Green and calcium arsenate have been used to control cutworms and grasshoppers in a mixture with bran and molasses where the residue from a spray or dust must be avoided. See CUTWORMS. Similar baits with metaldehyde

are used to control slugs. See SLUGS.

11. AEROSOLS. Pyrethrins, malathion, and several other insecticides are prepared and packaged in pressure cans to be discharged as a fine mist. They are available in large containers for greenhouse use and in small handy "bombs" for quick pest control around the home and garden. Oil-based aerosols for use against household pests may be harmful to plants and the directions and cautions on the label should be followed. See FUMIGATION.

12. COMBINATIONS. Mixtures of compatible insecticides, fungicides and miticides are often used to avoid the labor of separate applications. Not all pesticides are compatible as explained on the label. Most organic phosphate insecticides are made unsafe or less effective when combined with strong alkaline formulations such as bordeaux mixture. Vegetable and flower seeds are often treated with fungicides to prevent decay during germination. Captan is one of the best materials used for seed protection and there are many others. When spraying compatible pesticides can be mixed usually at the rate recommended for each ingredient used alone. Fruit and vegetables are universally sprayed with combinations according to recommended schedules and many standard combinations are available commercially especially as General Purpose Mixtures.

13. GENERAL PURPOSE PESTICIDE MIXTURES. For many gardeners, the most practical use of sprays or dusts is in the form of General Purpose Mixtures. These formulations, usually as a wettable powder or dust, contain one or more insecticides and fungicides and some include a specific miticide. They are expensive but when used in small quantities the convenience usually offsets the greater cost. Applications in a regular protective schedule are most effective. The ingredients must be relatively safe to the operator and have residue limitations which will allow safe applications up to 7 days before harvest. New formulations including aerosols are being developed and tested each season. Some of the more common mixtures are:

For general use—methoxychlor, malathion, Kelthane.

For vegetables—rotenone, copper, especially as a dust.

For tomatoes—carbaryl (Sevin), mancozeb.

For roses—ferbam, Kelthane—not to be used on fruit or vegetables.

WARREN D. WHITCOMB

How to Use the Information on Insecticides and Fungicides

When a pest is on a plant refer in this book to the plant on which it is found and check the pests listed there. For further information refer to the sections on INSECT PESTS or PLANT DISEASES. Certain pests also have separate items in the alphabetical listing. With the information on control suggested in the above sections, refer to the sections on INSECTICIDES and/or FUNGICIDES and the Tabulated List which follows in each article. Many pesticides have coined names or may be listed by the chemical name which must be noted on the Label as "Active ingredient" They may also be known by trade names representing the manufacturer or formulator. Whenever possible be prepared to give both names when buying pesticides. Many of them are available in several formulations and one must select those which would be most practical for conditions and equipment at hand.

The amount of pesticide to use is not stated here because recommendations for its use may vary in the control of different pests, on different plants and in different parts of the country. The dosage for each use is stated on the Label and in local pest-control recommendations. The Label also states the compatability with other pesticides and the necessary safety precautions to take both in preventing injury to the plants and to the operator.

Reference Books for Further Information

"Diseases and Pests of Ornamental Plants"—Pirone, Dodge and Rickett, The Ronald Press, N.Y. 5th Ed. 1978.

"The Gardener's Bug Book"—Cynthia Westcott, Doubleday, N.Y. 4th Ed.

"Insects That Feed on Trees and Shrubs"—Warren T. Johnson and Howard H. Lyon, Cornell University Press, Ithaca, N.Y. 1976. Illustrated with 212 composite color plates.

"Destructive and Useful Insects"—Metcalf, Flint and Metcalf, McGraw-Hill, N.Y.

"Plant Disease Handbook", Cynthia Westcott, Van Nostrand, Reinhold, N.Y. 3rd ed. 1971.

In summing up, be certain to refer to the articles entitled INSECTICIDES or FUNGICIDES to determine the specific recommendations referred to by number (in the case of insecticides) or by letter (in the case of fungicides) in combatting pests with specifically recommended materials.

WARREN D. WHITCOMB

When this text was prepared the following pesticides were generally accepted and used as suggested. DDT has been restricted or prohibited in all areas by federal and state laws. Other chlorinated hydrocarbon insecticides are legally controlled and are frequently not available to many people. It is recognized that frequent changes in the manufacture, formula-

Reference Number	Coined or Chemical Name	Trade or Brand Name	Ants, Soil Insects	Aphids, Leafhoppers, Plant Bugs, Etc.	Chewing Insects, Beetles, Caterpillars	Mites (Red Spiders)	Scales and Mealy Bugs	Borers or Leaf Miners	Toxicity (H High, M Moderate, L Low)	Principal Uses for Pesticide
4	trichlorfon	DYLOX			✓			✓	L	Leaf miners and cutworms, pepper maggot
9	methoxychlor	MARLATE	✓	✓	✓		✓	✓	L	Wide spectrum; mostly chewing insects on all crops but celery
10	chlordimeform	FUNDAL			✓	✓			H	Cabbage worms and other pests of crucifers
12	DDVP	VAPONA		✓	✓				H	Greenhouse pests; house flies
13	diazinon	SPECTRACIDE	✓	✓	✓	✓	✓	✓	M	Broad spectrum, see label
14	azinphosmethyl	GUTHION	✓	✓	✓				H	Many pests—see label
15	malathion	MALATHION	✓	✓	✓	✓	✓	✓	L	Many pests—see label
16	naled	DIBROM		✓	✓			✓	M	Many leafhoppers; worms, loopers, leafminers, white flies
20	carbophenothion	TRITHION	✓	✓	✓	✓		✓	H	Bean beetles, leaf miners, onion maggots
21	dimethoate	CYGON		✓	✓			✓	M	Systemic—good against leaf miners, thrips and pepper maggots
22	demeton	SYSTOX		✓		✓			H	Systemic—restricted
27	pyrethrum	PYROCIDE		✓	✓				L	Aphids and flies
28	rotenone	ROTENONE		✓	✓				L	Beetles and plant bugs; generally safe—do not expose fish
31	pentac					✓			L	Most effective indoors
32	chlorobenzoate					✓			L	See label for specific mites
34	dicofol	KELTHANE				✓			L	Fruit, vegetables and ornamentals
35	morestan			✓	✓				L	Fruit and ornamentals
36	tetradifon	TEDION				✓			L	Fruit and ornamentals
37	carbaryl	SEVIN	✓	✓	✓				L	Many pests—see label; leaf hoppers, bean beetles, earworm, flea beetles
39	Bacillus thuringiensis	THURICIDE			✓				L	Caterpillars—a disease agent
41	dinitro compounds	DNOC					✓	✓	H	Dormant sprays
43	metaldehyde	METALDEHYDE							L	Specific for slugs and snails
44	oil dormant	SUPERIOR OIL				✓	✓		L	Dormant spray for scale and mites on fruit
45	oil summer	SUPERIOR OIL				✓	✓		L	Mites and scales especially fruit
46	fruit tree mixture			✓	✓	✓	✓		⎫	⎫ Toxicity depends upon pesticides
47	vegetable mixture			✓	✓	✓	✓		⎬	in combination—generally low;
48	ornamentals mixture			✓	✓	✓	✓		⎭	⎭ however, see label

Note 1. For amount to use and cautions, read the label.

Note 2. The trade names used in this table do not indicate a superiority over similar formulations with different trade names nor an endorsement of the trade names used here.

See FUNGICIDES for suggestions for measuring small quantities.

Official coined names and chemical names or other accepted common names are listed in the second column. TRADE or BRAND names are listed in capital letters in the third column.

Warren D. Whitcomb
John A. Naegele
Clifford S. Chater

The following insecticides have either been banned or become unavailable since the first printing of this volume in 1971.

1. aldrin	17. parathion	30. sabadilla
2. benzene hexachloride	18. phosphamidon	33. dimite
3. chlordane	19. TEPP	38. zectran
5. DDT	23. phosdrin	40. calcium cyanide
6. dieldrin	24. schradan	41. dinitic compounds
7. heptachlor	25. phorate	42. lead arsenate
8. lindane	26. nicotine	
11. endosulfan	29. ryania	

tions and the use of these materials will occur and new pesticides will be developed. Therefore it is advisable to check with local authorities [i.e., the Cooperative Extension Service or the Department of Agriculture] for any restrictions and for the latest recommendations for the control of specific pests.

INSECTICIDES, SYSTEMIC. A group of water-soluble chemicals which when applied to the soil or leaves are absorbed and translocated by the sap and kill insects feeding on the treated plant. See INSECTICIDE #15.

INSECTIVOROUS PLANTS. Certain plants like the Sundews (*Drosera* sp. Butterworts (*Pinguicula* sp.), Venus Fly-trap (*Dionaea muscipula*) have the ability to capture insects by moving certain of their parts actually to trap the insect. The insect eventually dies and supposedly the plant has the ability to utilize the decaying nitrogenous matter in its growth. Other plants like the pitcher plants apparently can trap insects without the movement of any plant parts. These too are supposed to be able to utilize the decaying nitrogenous material. Sometimes the term "carnivorous" is used in this connection, but this sounds far more vicious than it really is. Many plants have sticky fluids which attract and eventually entangle insects, but usually it is insects or related objects that are attracted and killed, not animals.

INSECTS, BENEFICIAL. Honeybees making honey, silkworms spinning silk, lac scale insects secreting the basic material for shellac, cactus scale whose dried bodies make cochineal dye and a scale which secretes China wax to be used for furniture polish—contribute or have contributed in the past to man's welfare. In nature insects furnish food for birds, fish and small animals. To the gardener, one of the greatest and seemingly irreplaceable services of insects is the pollination of flowers for the production of fruit and seeds. Bees are the most active pollinators but flies, moths and other insects play an important and often unrecognized part.

The tremendous benefits of natural or biological control of harmful insects are not difficult to understand. Theoretically one pair of aphids in the spring can, in one season, become the progenitors of several billion progeny which would completely cover the earth if all lived. An adapted version of this verse conveys the idea:

Great bugs have little bugs on their backs to bite 'em,

And little bugs have lesser bugs and so ad infinitum,

And the great bugs themselves in turn have greater bugs to go on;

While these again have greater still and greater still, and so on.

Insect enemies are known as parasites and predators. Parasites lay eggs in, on or near the host insect and the young feed on it until it dies. Most of the parasites are flies and wasps which vary in size from the Trichogramma which lives in the tiny eggs of many destructive caterpillars to the lunate long sting with a $1\frac{1}{2}$ in. long body and a 3 in. long ovipositor with which it bores through the bark and wood of maple branches to lay eggs on or near the pigeon tremex borer, its host. Among the better known parasites are the Winthemia fly which attacks army worms and often controls them locally; the Bigonicheta fly imported from Europe to control the European earwig and the Compsilura fly parasite of the gypsy moth caterpillar. Natural control of the gypsy moth has become very effective in local areas by the introduction and establishment of several parasites and predators which attack the egg, larva and pupa. The parasitic wasp Apanteles is often seen on tomato hornworms where the white cocoons resembling grains of rice are attached to the back and sides of the worm and the *Aphelinus mali* wasp keeps an efficient check on the woolly apple aphis. In recent years the United States Department of Agriculture has collected, propagated and liberated native parasites of many of the introduced insect pests. Notable examples of this work are the Tiphia wasp parasite of the Japanese beetle, the Macrocentrus on the Oriental fruit moth and the Campoplex on the European corn borer.

Predatory insects attack their prey and devour all or part of it for food. The most spectacular is the Praying Mantis which eats many insects but is seldom abundant enough to give practical control of insect pests. Dragon-flies and damsel flies feed on mosquitoes, midges and similar small insects and are frequently numerous near streams and pools. True bugs like the Assassin bug and the Ambush bug with strong, piercing beaks kill many insects. Aphids are often held in check by the larvae of hover flies and by both adults and larvae of the lace wing, the larvae of which are often called "aphis lions." The most active and numerous predators of aphids, mites and scale insects are lady beetles and their alligator-shaped larvae. A single larva has been observed to eat 25 aphids per day and 600 aphids or 3000 scale insects during its life.

Lady beetles often hibernate in buildings and gather at windows in the spring but in spite of objections to insects in the house, gardeners will benefit by liberating them. A tiny black lady beetle, *Stethorus*, called the red spider destroyer is a beneficial enemy of spider mites and the

Vedalia lady beetle imported from Australia about 1880 is credited with saving the Calif. citrus industry from destruction by controlling the cottony cushion scale. Fireflies, which are really beetles, capture many small insects on the wing and the larvae are enemies of slugs and cutworms. Among the larger predators are ground beetles especially the fiery hunter and the European *Calasoma sycophanta*, a single beetle of which has eaten 250 gypsy moth caterpillars in experiments. An interesting anomaly among the predatory beetles is the blister beetle which often is a destructive pest of vegetables but as a larva feeds on grasshopper eggs.

WARREN D. WHITCOMB

INSECTS, CONTROL OF. Control of insects implies killing the destructive insect pests and indirectly this is the purpose of insect control. As gardeners, however, we are interested in preventing or reducing the damage to the plants by limiting the number, development and activity of the pests. Insect damage involves economic, aesthetic and hobby values. A dying or disfigured Blue Spruce tree as the feature of a home-grounds landscape plan has much more value than a similar tree in the forest. Likewise, one carpet beetle can ruin a mink coat but 10,000 snow fleas under a rhododendron bush will cause no serious damage. It is becoming more important to prevent serious insect damage to our natural resources but the most expensive control measures are advisable only on high value plants and crops. Methods of control are the use of natural enemies, providing an unfavorable environment, limiting their spread by quarantine and the use of insecticides.

Natural Control

See INSECTS, BENEFICIAL

Mechanical Methods

On small numbers of valuable plants, many larger insects can be collected and destroyed by hand. These include tomato hornworms, Japanese beetles and tent caterpillars. Injury by cutworms is prevented by placing cardboard collars around the stem of seedlings and transplants. Sticky bands around the trunk prevent cankerworms and other caterpillars from crawling into the tree. Many traps using sweet baits or prepared sexual attractants capture beetles and moths. Black-light electric traps capture large numbers of insects, but unfortunately attract beneficial as well as destructive species.

Cultural Practices

The elimination of weeds both in the garden and around the border reduces the natural spread of many insect pests which live on related wild plants. Although burning of dry grass and weeds in late fall and early spring is frowned upon for various reasons, it kills many destructive pests. Rotation of crops, especially Cabbage, Tomato and Strawberry, reduces potential trouble from destructive insects and plant diseases. Complete cleanup of all garden refuse after the growing season is a good practice. Annual gardens will benefit from spading or plowing in the fall and where practical growing a winter cover crop of winter rye, wheat or brome is helpful. Modern practice recommends growing resistant varieties of flowers and vegetables whenever available.

Quarantines

Federal and state agencies maintain quarantine regulation and inspection services to prevent the introduction and spread of insect and disease pests. See QUARANTINES.

WARREN D. WHITCOMB

INSECT PESTS. In the so-called "Balance of Nature" all plants and animals were adjusted to live in a practical relationship with one another. However, when man became the dominant power he cultivated those animals and plants which were advantageous to his livelihood and welfare, but those which interfered with his needs and wishes were called pests. Among the animal pests are destructive insects, mites and related creatures and the plant pests are weeds and plant diseases.

Early history records the dramatic results of destruction by locusts (grasshoppers) in Asia and the worldwide epidemics of malaria, typhus fever and bubonic plague which are directly associated with outbreaks of insect pests. The potato blight epidemics in Ireland in the 1840's and the almost complete eradication of the American Chestnut by chestnut blight are outstanding examples of the historical significance of destructive plant diseases. As civilization progressed, the production of food by agriculture and horticulture became "big business" and losses from plant and animal pests greatly affected the economy of many parts of the world. It became necessary to practice whatever control measures could be devised. Early recommendations including beating pans to scare the locusts, hanging putrid flesh in trees to attract plum curculios away from plum fruits and filling furrows with oil to stop the march of army worms now seem absurd, but they illustrate quite clearly the desperate attempts which man was willing to make to preserve his crops from damage.

In spite of tremendous advances in pest-control techniques, destructive insects and plant diseases cause billions of dollars loss to crops and require millions of dollars for materials and labor to control them. It is stated that insects and related pests do much greater damage to our forests than forest fires.

Insect Abundance

All gardeners know that the abundance of insects and the damage that they do varies from year to year. This is called environmental resistance or the ability to survive natural hazards and is correlated with the reproductive potential. In other words the insects which are normally exposed to the greatest hazards of their environment, such as aphids, will produce many more eggs and young than those which are protected, such as borers. Theoretical calculations based on experimental studies indicate that 1 pair of cabbage aphids in the spring can, under favorable conditions, be the ancestors of more than a quintillion progeny in a season whose weight if all lived would be greater than that of the total population of the earth. Similar theoretical calculations indicate that if codfish developed to maturity from all eggs laid in a season there would be no room for water in the ocean.

The principal factors which influence insect survival are temperature, moisture and natural enemies. See INSECTS, BENEFICIAL. Although insects are cold blooded and in cold weather are able to evaporate moisture from the body cells so that the body fluid becomes an "antifreeze" which resists freezing at normal low temperatures for their environment, many are killed by cold. Insects hibernating on or under the bark of trees may be killed by abnormal cold, especially if the plant on which they are living is injured, but those protected by snow will survive. Aphids and tent caterpillars are killed by late spring frosts especially if the plants on which they are feeding are damaged. Codling moth and European corn-borer will lay their optimum quota of eggs only if the temperature at dusk is 60° F. or higher on the second evening of their oviposition period.

Abnormal moisture, either as drought or flood, interferes with the normal development of soil-inhabiting insects. Many Japanese beetle grubs die if there is insufficient moisture in late Aug. and early Sept. when the young are hatching and excessive moisture favors the rapid development of fungus and bacterial diseases of insects.

The greatest influence on insect abundance is the activity of parasitic and predatory insects, spiders, birds and other animals as well as fungi, bacteria and viruses which are discussed under those categories.

Description

Insects are invertebrate animals having a strong outer skeleton of a plasticlike material called chitin but no backbone. The body fluid (blood) flows freely through the body rather than through veins. Jointed legs classify them with the lobster, millepedes, centipedes, spiders and ticks from which they differ by having 6 legs and a body divided into head, thorax and abdomen. Most of them have 1 or 2 pairs of wings, 1 pair of antennae, compound eyes and air tubes (tracheae) for breathing. Spiders which include several plant pests have 8 legs and no antennae. Insects feed by piercing, sucking and

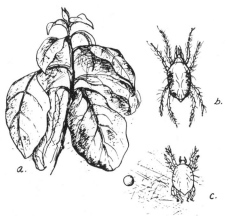

Red Spider:
A. Web and damage to plant
B. Adult—greatly magnified
C. Immature insect and egg—greatly magnified

drinking through a hollow beak; by biting and chewing solid food such as leaves, wood and roots; and by rasping and lapping the sap from the wound. The method of feeding usually determines the type of insecticide used to combat them.

Most insects hatch from eggs although the summer generations of aphids and some flies may give birth to living young. If the young resemble the adult they are called nymphs and have an incomplete change of form called incomplete metamorphosis. Grasshoppers, plant bugs, aphids and female scales are in this group. If the young have an entirely different form from the adult, they are known as larvae, although common names such as maggots for fly larvae, worms or caterpillars for moth and butterfly larvae and grubs or borers for beetle larvae are generally used. These insects have a complete metamorphosis and most insect pests belong to this group. Larvae and nymphs shed their skin (molt) several times as they grow. They are the most destructive to plants in this stage although adult insects feed somewhat in connection with reproductive development. In complete metamorphosis the larva enters a resting or transformation stage called a pupa from which the adult insect emerges. Cocoons and chrysalises are protective cases for the pupa.

Identification

Most gardeners can classify insects in general terms such as butterfly, beetle, fly or aphid. However, in order to deal with them most intelligently, they should know (1) if they are destructive, beneficial or insignificant, (2) what life stage is most destructive, if at all, (3) what life stage is most susceptible to control measures, (4) how they feed and damage plants, (5) what plants are most likely to be damaged.

Every gardener should have quick access to one or more books on entomology which give this information. There are many, among which "The Bug Book" by Cynthia Westcott and "Destructive and Useful Insects" by Flint and Metcalf are good examples. Also available in nearly all areas are public agencies such as county agricultural agents, agricultural experiment stations and state departments of agriculture which not only have bulletins and pamphlets available on local insect-pest problems but also can give reliable diagnoses and recommendations on difficult and unusual pest problems. Reliable information is also available from horticultural societies, the larger garden supply store, nurseries, arborists and private consultants. When requesting diagnosis of plant injury or identification of pests it is important to supply typical specimens in good condition. A beetle without legs or antennae may defy the most expert attempt to identify it and typical insect feeding or fungus lesions may be completely camouflaged in a dry, brittle, broken or decayed leaf or fruit. In mailing, use a container which will prefent crushing and wrap the specimens in plastic to prevent drying.

In entomological classification of insects, there are 23 Orders. Most garden pests belong to the following 9 Orders:

1. **Orthoptera.** These include grasshoppers, crickets and roaches. They feed by biting and chewing and generally have long legs and antennae. The underwings are folded under heavier upper wings. Young resemble the adult. They are often present in swarms and grasshoppers are serious pests of grains and grasses.

2. **Hemiptera.** These are known as true bugs and include the squash bug, chinch bug, tarnished plant bug and stink bugs. The upper wings are thicker at the back (where attached to the body) than at the front. The mouth is a beak for piercing and sucking and the young resemble adults. Their feeding causes stunting or wilting of new growth and malformed or blasted buds of flowers and fruit. Some are beneficial predatory enemies of pests.

3. **Homoptera.** The wings of these insects are equally thick throughout and are held at the side of the body when at rest. They have a beak for piercing and sucking and the young resemble the adults. Several leaf hoppers are very destructive pests and tree hoppers have many grotesque shapes. Aphids are universal pests and nearly every specie of plant may be infested by them. Scale insects belong to this Order but are an exception since the female remains stationary during most of her life and feeds through a threadlike beak much longer than her body. The male scale insect has 2 wings. Cicadas such as the 17-year-locust also belong to this Order.

4. **Coleoptera.** Beetles have stiff upper wings, chewing mouth parts and the young are called grubs or borers. This is the largest Order of all animals with about 200,000 known species in the world and more than 20,000 in North America. Their size varies from microscopic to some of the largest known insects. A separate group called snout beetles includes the curculios with long beaks for excavating tunnels in which to lay eggs in fruit or nuts. The weevils and bark beetles have short beaks. Many species such as rose chafer, Japanese beetle and Colorado potato beetle are destructive pests. Many borers in trees are the young of beetles. Lady beetles and ground beetles are predatory on destructive insect pests and therefore are beneficial.

5. **Lepidoptera.** Moths and butterflies have prominent wings covered with tiny scales which rub off easily. Moths have pointed antennae and are usually active at dusk or on dark days. Butterflies prefer sun and light and have knobbed antennae. A few female moths are wingless. Caterpillars and worms change to a pupa before transforming to an adult. The larvae include pests of leaves, fruit, seed, roots, wood of plants. These include leaf miners, webworms, gypsy moth, bagworms and cankerworms on trees and shrubs; codling moth and leaf rollers on fruit; cutworms, cabbage worms, tomato hornworms and European corn borer on vegetables and borers in Lilac and Rhododendron.

6. **Diptera.** The 2-winged flies have the under-wings modified to small disks or knobbed stalks called halteres which serve as balancing organs. The young or maggots are completely unlike the adult. Maggots feed by rasping and sucking and often eat tunnels through fruit, stems and roots. The adult flies seldom damage plants directly. Among the garden pests are the holly leaf miner and the boxwood leaf miner; the apple maggot and the cherry maggot and the cabbage root maggot. Many flies are effective parasitic enemies of destructive pests. Mosquitoes, midges and the annoying "little fruit flies" (*Drosophila*) which breed in overripe fruit and vegetables belong to this Order.

7. **Hymenoptera.** Adult bees, wasps, hornets and sawflies have 4 membranous wings which often hook together and act as 1 pair in flight. Worker ants are an exception and have no wings. Sawflies and horntails have thick-waisted bodies and differ from the narrow-waisted bodies of bees and wasps. They usually feed by biting and the stings of bees and hornets are made by a modified ovipositor at the rear of the body and not by the mouth. Sawflies and some leaf miners (birch leaf miner) are destructive pests, and ants may be destructive as well as troublesome. The parasitic wasps which compose the majority of our natural enemies of destructive insects are members of this Order.

8. **Thysanaptera.** Thrips have slender bodies with 2 pair of fringed wings. The young resemble the adult and they feed by rasping and sucking. Injury to plants occurs as distorted growth or as spotting on leaves and flowers. Well-known pests are gladiolus thrips and onion thrips.

9. **Dermaptera.** Earwigs have narrow, flat bodies with conspicuous forceplike appendages at the rear. Their wings are short and seldom used. Both the adults and the young which resemble them are nocturnal and feed on worms, small insects and lichens as well as plants. The legend which credits this insect with crawling into ears is largely false. The European earwig, now established in many parts of the United States, is a minor pest of plants but is very annoying around the house and garden.

WARREN D. WHITCOMB

INTERNODE. The space or portion of stem between 2 nodes.

INTRODUCED. A term used of plants which have been brought from another country; exotic.

INULA (IN-yew-la). A rather large genus of the Composite Family. A few species are small enough to be used in gardens.

acaulis   stemless   Zone 6(?)   Stemless Inula
An herbaceous perennial from Asia Minor, this grows in tufts of spatulate leaves 2 in. high,

crowned with solitary, yellow, daisylike flowers borne on 6-in. stems in midsummer.

ensifolia   2′   Zones 2–3   Swordleaf Inula
An herbaceous perennial with linear-lanceolate leaves and yellow daisylike flower heads 1½ in. wide during summer. Native to Europe and northern Asia. If sown early in the spring it will bloom the same year.

helenium   6′   Zone 3   Elecampane
A widely naturalized perennial weed in eastern North America, native to Europe and Asia. The alternate leaves are ovate, simple, sessile, up to 2 ft. long and pubescent beneath. The yellow heads of daisylike flowers are up to 4 in. across, blooming from July to Sept. The roots sometimes are dug, dried and used in medicine. Propagated by seeds.

orientalis (*glandulosa*)   2′–4′   Zones 2–3
Caucasian Inula
A coarse herbaceous perennial from the Caucasus, with daisylike yellow flower heads, 3 in. across. Not especially outstanding.

royleana   1′–2′   Zones 2–3   Himalayan Elecampane
Leaves hairy, often densely tomentose beneath and up to 10 in. long; flower heads orange-yellow 3–4 in. across, borne singly. Native to the Himalayas. Not an especially good garden plant.

INVOLUCRE. A whorl or set of bracts around a flower, umbel or head, etc., as in the heads of composites like the Flowering Dogwood.

INVOLUTE. Having the edges of the leaves rolled inward.

IONOPSIDIUM (eye-o-nop-SID-ium)

acaule   3″   annual   Portugal Diamond-flower
Creeping rock plant for rock crevices or between paving stones preferably in shady places, this is a tiny tufted plant from Portugal. It is covered with diamond-blue flowers with 4 petals, frequently also grown as a pot plant. It can reseed itself easily and become a nuisance. Seed sown in early spring produces flowering plants by midsummer.

IPOMOEA (eye-po-MEE-a). A genus with many tropical species, it consists of generally twining vines, either annual or perennial, often with large, fleshy roots. The stems often have milky juice, the stalked leaves are alternate, the conspicuous flowers axillary, occurring singly or in 2's and 3's. The corolla is trumpet shaped, but 5-angled or pointed at the top. These vines grow easily in any soil and are excellent for use in the garden. The roots of the somewhat tender species may be lifted in fall and stored in a frost-free area. They may be propagated by seed sown in spring. Seeds of the popular annual can be sown in place in May but early bloom is obtained if seed is sown indoors in March and then potted plants are set out after frost, of course being given a support on which to twine. Seeds may be soaked in warm water for 2 days prior to sowing to speed up the germination. Plant 2–3 seeds to a 2-in. pot. Soil should not be too rich or the plants will produce many leaves and few flowers. Bloom July to frost.

batatas   vine   Zone 7   Sweet-potato
This is a plant known only in cultivation but is widely distributed about the Tropics and Subtropics of the world. It is a procumbent vine with trailing and rooting stems grown for its large, tuberous, edible roots. The alternate leaves vary in size and shape but are up to 6 in. long. The flowers are not very often produced in the U.S. except in the very Deep South, are violet and pale pink, 2 in. long. A live tuber can be forced into growth in a glass of water when placed in such a way that only the bottom half is in the water. The top half (where it was attached to the plant) is left in the open. The tuber will develop roots and the top will send out shoots, which themselves can be rooted and set out in hills in the garden even as far north as New England, after frost is over; a few edible tubers will result. See POTATO, SWEET.

Insect Pests

In the South, the sweet potato weevil, a black, red and blue snout beetle, feeds on the leaves and the grubs tunnel the potato. They continue to breed throughout the season. Spraying with insecticide #9 where the beetles are active is helpful but destruction of all infested potatoes at harvest and thorough cleanup and burning of plant refuse is most effective. Tortoise beetles, which resemble a turtle in general appearance and may have an iridescent golden color, feed on Sweet Potato. If abundant, they may be easily controlled with insecticide #9 or #15. Some species of cutworms attack sweet potatoes and are controlled with sprays or dusts of insecticide #9 or #37. A bait is also effective. See CUTWORMS.

Diseases

Black rot and soft rot infect sweet potatoes in poorly ventilated storage areas. Black rot and other diseases are prevented in the field by dipping seed potatoes and slips for planting in fungicide #W—1 lb. in 5 gals. of water. Treat planting areas with fungicide #D as directed on package. Mosaic-infected plants should be destroyed and clean potatoes used for producing slips.

coccinea (*Quamoclit coccinea*)   **vine   annual   Scarlet Starglory**
Scarlet flowers, 1½ in. long, with a yellow throat. A variety with yellow and orange flowers has

leaves 4–6 in. long and heart shaped.

hederacea   vine   annual   Ivy-leaved Morning-   glory
An introduction to the eastern U.S. from tropical America, but nevertheless it has become a weed in some areas. The stems are twining and hairy, the leaves are 3-lobed and about 1¾ in. long and alternate. The flowers are pale blue or white and purple, nearly 2 in. long and funnel-formed.

horsfalliae   vine   Zone 10   Horsfall Morning-   glory
A high-climbing twining vine from the East Indies, this makes an excellent screen which is frequently a mass of color when the flowers are in bloom. The long funnel-shaped flowers (2½ in. long) are magenta-crimson and are profusely produced from autumn to spring. The palmately compound leaves have 5–7 leaflets each about 4 in. long.

x multifida (*Quamoclit* x *sloteri*)   **vine   annual   Cardinal-climber**
A hybrid (*Q. coccinea* x *pennata*) with palmlike leaves and flowers 2 in. long, crimson with white throats. Leaves deeply lobed. Flowers bloom from July to Sept.

nil   vine   Zone 10   White Edge Morning-glory
Varieties of this perennial species have been favorite pot plants of the Japanese for a long time, usually sold in America as Imperial Morning-glories, with flowers up to 6 in. across, single or double, ruffled, scalloped, mottled and sometimes bordered with one or more colors, blue, purple or rose. The species is native to the Tropics. Leaves are 4–6 in. wide, heart-shaped and 3-lobed.

pandurata   vine   Zone 5   Big-root Morning-   glory
This trailing or climbing vine has heart-shaped leaves on long stalks and showy white trumpet-shaped flowers, up to 3 in. in dia., with streaks of pink extending from the center to the circumference of the trumpet, indicating the tips of the lobes. The vines, which may attain a length of 10–15 ft., die in winter, but the starchy tuberous, edible root is perennial.

purpurea   vine   annual   Common Morning-   glory
This is not a native plant, being of tropical origin, but it is now a common annual weed of the eastern seaboard states. It has heart-shaped leaves and trumpet-shaped flowers with colors varying from white to red or purple. These appear during the summer and early autumn. Several varieties available are: 'Blue Star'— flowers light sky-blue with blue stripes; 'Flying Saucers'—flowers striped blue and white; 'Heavenly Blue'—flowers dark sky-blue; 'Pearly Gates'—flowers white; 'Scarlet O'Hara'— scarlet; 'Summer Skies'—flowers light sky-blue;

'Wedding Bells'—flowers rose-lavender.

Insect Pests

The Common Morning-glory is a favorite food for tortoise beetles. These turtle-shaped beetles with spiny sluglike larvae eat holes in the leaves. Insecticide #37 gives good control. See SWEET POTATO. Morning-glory leaf cutter is a rare pest which cuts the leaf stalks at night. Spraying with insecticide #15 is suggested.

quamoclit (*Quamoclit pennata*) **vine annual Cypress Vine**
A tropical vine which has become naturalized from Va. to Mo., with slender, tubelike flowers that are bright scarlet and bloom from Aug. to Oct. The leaves are compound with many opposite threadlike leaflets. An attractive plant, although it may become a nuisance in the garden. Native to tropical America and southern U.S. The var. **alba** has white flowers and **'Hearts and Honey'** has pink-orange flowers with honey-yellow centers.

tuberosa = *Merremia tuberosa*

IPOMOPSIS (eye-po-MOP-sis)

aggregata (*Gilia aggregata*) **2′ biennial or perennial Skyrocket**
Flower scarlet, varying to white, with leaves in 1–2 parts.

rubra (*Gilia rubra*) **6′ biennial or perennial Texas-plume**
Leaves pinnately divided into extremely narrow linear parts, flowers scarlet and yellow, dotted with red inside in narrow terminal panicles. Native from S.Car. to Fla. and Tex.

IRESINE (eye-res-EYE-ne)

herbstii 6′ Zone 10 Herbst Bloodleaf
A showy herb, with opposite rounded leaves 5 in. long, notched at the tip, colored purplish red with light red veins. Native to South America. Sometimes planted for its foliage in the greenhouse, or used as summer bedding plants because of their colored leaves in the North. Propagated chiefly by cuttings wintered-over in the greenhouse.

lindenii 18″ Zone 10 Bloodleaf
A tropical plant from Ecuador sometimes grown as a house plant or even a bedding plant, with deep blood-red, opposite, narrow, pointed leaves. Culture is the same as for Coleus. Propagated by cuttings in the greenhouse. Seldom flowers in the U.S.

IRIDACEAE = The Iris Family

IRIS (EYE-ris). These are perennial herbs with swordlike leaves and roots that are generally rhizomatous, although in a few species they are bulbous, and these will be so noted in the following discussions. Most bloom in the spring and early summer and are easily propagated by dividing or cutting the rhizomes during late summer, or separating the offsets from the bulbous types. Some of the better varieties are listed in the accompanying article as worthy of trial by the beginner. In general, many of the Iris can be grown in Zones 5 and 6. Some are hardy in colder areas and some are hardy only in the South. A few species are listed which are grown only on the West Coast in a small area where they are native. They are not easily grown elsewhere.

Iris specialists have developed special terms to designate the parts of the iris flower. The sepals, or outer 3 parts of the flower, are called the falls, which usually droop. The petal-like part of the fall is called the blade, the basal part, the haft. The inner parts, or upright petals, are called standards. Inside these are 3 more petal-like and very narrow parts called style-branches.

Irises are divided into several classes (see discussion following list), but for purposes of the list of species briefly mentioned, they are divided into the following:

Bulbous—having a bulbous root rather than rhizomes which are common to most species. All those in the following list not noted as bulbous are rhizomatous.

Beardless—the falls have neither crests nor beards.

Crested—the falls have a central ridge or crest.

Juno—a bulbous Iris with thick, fleshy roots from the base when it is dormant. This is a small class.

Onocyclus—with reddish, crowded rhizomes bearing stolons and 1 flower to a spathe, as well as having scattered hairs on the falls. This is a small class, native to southwest Asia and Egypt.

Bearded—the basal half of the fall has filaments or hairs.

Regelia—with stolons arising from the main rhizome and 2–3 flowers per spathe. Native to Afghanistan and Turkestan.

Reticulata—bulbous Iris with a netted covering to the bulbs.

Xiphium—so-called Spanish or English bulbous Iris with large, erect standards and no fleshy roots at the base of the bulb in the resting stage.

Insect Pests

The iris borer is a major pest. The large, pink larva of a cutworm moth eats cavities in the rhizome. Dig infested plants after blooming and cut out and kill all borers. Eggs are laid in fall on leaves which should be gathered after freezing and burned. Spraying in spring when leaves are 6–10 in. high with insecticide #5 or #9 kills the young worms before they bore into leaves and roots.

Diseases

Soft rot usually infects wounds caused by iris borer in the rhizomes but may enter other places. It has a foul odor. Plant only clean rhizomes and cut out infection completely when replanting infected plants. Infected rhizomes can be disinfected with fungicide #F. Botrytis rhizome rot is dry and odorless. It is often the cause of plants failing to sprout in spring. Destroying infected plants and planting in clean soil is suggested. Leaf blight, leaf spot and rust are recognized pests but seldom need control.

aphylla   15″   Zone 5   Stool Iris
Bearded. Flowers purple, beard white, blooms in May. Native to Eastern Europe.

bakerana   12″   Zone 5   Baker Iris
Reticulata—bulbous. Leaves hollow; flower fragrant, purple and whitish. Native to Asia Minor. Blooms in Feb. in very protected places in southern N.Y.

bracteata   4″–12″   Zone 7   Bracted Iris
Beardless. Flowers yellow with brown-purple veins. Native to Ore. Rather difficult to grow outside its native habitat.

brevicaulis (*foliosa*)   18″   Zone 5   Lamance Iris
Beardless. Flowers blue-purple, with a zigzag stem. Ky. to Kan.

bucharica   18″   Zone 5   Bokhara Iris
Bulbous, Juno type. Flowers yellow and white. Native to Turkestan. Blooms in April.

chamaeiris   10″   Zone 5   Crimean Iris
Bearded. Usually 2 flowers on a spathe. Flowers blue, red-purple, yellow or white. Native to Northern Italy. Easy enough to grow, but its flowers are narrow and dull. Blooms from April to May.

chrysographes   18″   Zone 7   Goldvein Iris
Beardless. Flowers violet to velvet-purple marked with golden veins. Native to West China. Blooms in June.

cristata   3″–4″   Zone 3   Crested Iris
The rhizomes of this native American Crested Iris creep fairly rapidly along the surface of the ground and should not be covered with soil or they will rot. The upright leaves are very much in evidence all summer long, but die to the ground by the middle of the autumn, leaving the ground bare all winter. Although it seems to withstand the sun, it does better in partial shade. Flowers pale lilac. May and June. Native to area from Md. to Ga. and Mo. Variety 'Alba' has white flowers and there are deep purple-flowered forms. These are perhaps the best of the dwarf iris.

danfordiae   12″   Zone 5   Danford Iris
Reticulata—bulbous. Leaves 4-sided, flowers orange and dotted olive-green. Native to Eastern Asia Minor. Blooms in March.

delavayi   3′–4′   Zone 7   Delavays Iris

Iris cristata

Beardless. Stems hollow, flowers violet-purple with white markings. Native to Southwest China. Blooms in June.

dichotoma   2′   Zone 5   Vesper Iris
This has several flowers in racemes on forked stems. The leaves have white margins, flowers white with brown-purple spots and purplish stripes. Siberia. Blooms in Aug. and Sept.

douglasiana   20″   Zone 8   Douglas Iris
Beardless. Flowers lilac-purple, lavender or buff to creamy white. Foliage is evergreen. Calif. to Ore. Difficult to grow outside its native habitat.

flavissima   6″   Zone 5   Goldbeard Iris
Bearded. Flowers yellow to orange, veined brown-purple. Hungary to Mongolia.

foetidissima   18″   Zone 7   Gladwin Iris
Beardless. Leaves evergreen, 1 in. wide, giving off a bad odor when crushed. Flowers are small and inconspicuous, purplish gray. Southern Europe. Valueless in flower, but the large fruit pods, containing rounded scarlet seeds, are prized for dried arrangements. Blooms in June.

fulva   2′–3′   Zone 7   Copper Iris
Beardless. The spreading sepals, the smaller petals and the petal-like stigmas, all in 3's, are brightly colored, varying from a coppery orange to salmon pink. It is native to the marshes and wetlands of the South, blooming in May and June. An excellent plant for the moist wild garden, it may be divided after flowering, or seeds may be sown in pots, but one should take care to keep them wet.

germanica 24″–36″ **Zone 4 German Iris**
Bearded. Many garden varieties come from this species which is native to central and southern Europe. Flowers are lilac to lilac-purple, varying to white with the beard yellow. This is one of the Iris species yielding the material called orris root, used in some medicines, perfumes and tooth powders.

giganticaerulea 3′ **Zone 7**
Beardless. Violet-blue flowers, fragrant. Blooms in June. Southern La.

gracilipes 10″ **Zone 6 Slender Iris**
Crested. Flowers pinkish lilac, with wavy orange crest. Blooms in May. Japan. This is the smallest of the Iris species, but a choice rock garden specimen. The flowers are only an inch across, the foliage is tufted and grassy.

hartwegii 12″ **Zone 7 Foothill Iris**
Beardless. Flowers yellow with lavender veins. Native to Northern Calif. Very closely related to *I. tenax* of Ore. Hard to grow outside its native habitat.

hexagona 2′–3′ **Zone 7 Dixie Iris**
Beardless. A native of the swamps and wet areas of the South, this has blue flowers and blooms in May and June.

histrio 12″ **Zone 4 Syrian Iris**
Reticulata—bulbous. Flowers blue with streaked or spotted markings. Native to Syria. reproduced by offsets.

histrioides 12″ **Zone 5 Harput Iris**
Reticulata—bulbous. Similar to *I. histrio*, but the flowers are a much deeper blue. Native to Asia Minor.

hoogiana 30″ **Zone 5 Redbeard Iris**
Regelia. Flowers pale to darker gray-blue, rarely white. Blooms in May. Native to Turkestan.

innominata 30″ **Zone 8**
Beardless. Flowers golden buff, veined light brown, and there are cream-colored varieties. Native to Ore. Blooms in June. Somewhat similar to *I. purdyi*. Difficult to grow outside its native habitat. There are some excellent garden hybrids of this species with *I. douglasiana* which have orange-red, purple, red and bronze colorings in the flowers.

japonica 18″ **Zone 8 Fringed Iris**
Crested. Flowers lilac spotted with yellow and white, with yellow crests. Blooms in April. Native to China and Japan. It is unfortunate that the flowers do not last long. Often grown as a greenhouse plant in the North. The variety 'Nada' is popular throughout the South, where it may be grown outside.

kaempferi 24″ **Zone 4 Japanese Iris**
Beardless. Flower of various colors, with much reddish-purple, up to 10 in. across in some varieties. Many good cultivated varieties. Native to northern China and Japan. Blooms in June

and July. Some of the better varieties are:
White—'Driven Snow'
    'Snowy Hills'
Orchid pink—'World's Delight'
    'Prima Ballerina'
Blue—'Blue Lagoon'
    'Sky and Water'
Purple—'Blue Pompon'
    'Gay Festoon'

korolkowii 18″ **Zone 5 Redvein Iris**
Regelia. Flowers usually 2–3 per stalk, creamy white tinged brown, with numerous dark brown veins. Blooms in May. Native to Turkestan.

laevigata 24″ **Zone 4 Rabbitear Iris**
Beardless. Similar to *I. kaempferi*, but leaves lacking a midrib. Flowers blue-purple, but white forms are also available. Native to Japan. A lovely Iris, truly a bog plant. Blooms in June and July.

macrosiphon 4″–18″ **Zone 8 Tube Iris**
Beardless. Flowers usually lilac, but sometimes white or cream colored, with 1–3 flowers per stalk. Native to Calif. and Ore. Hard to grow outside its native habitat.

mellita to 5″ **Zone 5 Troad Iris**
Bearded. Closely related to *I. pumila*; flowers are fragrant, pale smoky brown with red-brown veins. The beard is white, tipped with blue. Blooming in April and May, this is native to southern Europe.

missouriensis 6″–24″ **Zone 3 Rocky Mountain Iris**
Beardless. Flowers pale blue and variegated. Native to S. Dak., Ariz., and British Columbia.

ochroleuca = *I. orientalis*

orientalis 24″ **Zone 3 Oriental Iris**
Beardless. Closely related to *I. sibirica*. Flowers blue, sometimes white. Blooms in May or June. Native to eastern Asia.

pallida 3′ **Zone 5 Sweet Iris**
Bearded. Flowers lavender-blue to white, fragrant, blooming in May or June. Foliage is silvery. Native to Tyrol.

persica 6″ **Zone 6 Persian Iris**
Bulbous—Juno. The flowers have the fragrance of violets and are colored a greenish blue with a bright yellow keel. Native to Asia Minor.

prismatica 3′ **Zone 3 Cubeseed Iris**
Beardless. Flowers 2–3 in a terminal cluster, deep but bright lilac-blue. Blooms in May. Similar to *I. sibirica* but the stem is solid. Native Nova Scotia to Ga. It is restricted to swampy areas, often growing near the coast where the water is brackish.

pseudacorus 2′–3′ **Zone 5 Yellow Flag**
Beardless. Flowers bright yellow with brown veins. Blooms in May and June. Native to Europe and western Asia, naturalized in eastern North America. An Iris for wet places.

pseudopumila   4″–6″   Zone 5   Tineo Iris
Bearded. Flowers purple, yellow or white. Native to southern Italy.

pumila   4′–5′   Zone 4   Dwarf Bearded Iris
Bearded. Flowers usually solitary, variable in color. Native to Europe and Asia Minor. Many varieties are offered. Blooms in April.

purdyi   12″   Zone 8   Purdy Iris
Beardless. Flowers in a range of colors from white or cream to lavender and orchid, almost pink. Rather difficult to grow outside its native habitat. Blooms in May and June. Native to northern Calif. to Ore.

regalis   12″   Zone 8
Beardless. Flowers are lilac colored, musk-scented. Native to southern La.

reticulata   24″   Zone 5   Netted Iris
Reticulata—bulbous. Leaves 4-angled, flowers deep violet-purple with the ridge colored orange bordered with white. Native to the Caucasus. The species is variable, with many interesting hybrids now available. The variety **cyanea** has blue flowers very much like the species; **krelagei** is the red-purple flowered form and one of the most common. Blooms in March.

rosenbachiana   9″   Zone 8   Spinster Iris
Bulbous—Juno. Flowers usually a deep, velvety purple with an orange crest, but this varies considerably, for yellow and white often appear. Native to Turkestan.

setosa   6″–12″   Zone 2   Arctic Iris
Beardless. Flowers purple, appearing in May and June. Native to eastern Siberia, Japan and North America. Varies considerably, but is one of the hardiest of all the Iris.

sibirica   2′   Zone 3   Siberian Iris
Beardless. Stem is hollow; flowers are 2–5 in a terminal head; blue-purple, lavender, occasionally white. Flowers appear in June. Native to central Europe and Russia. Variable; many varieties.

spuria   1′–2′   Zones 2–3   Spurious Iris, Seashore Iris
Beardless. The sessile flowers are bright lilac streaked with purple and some white. Blooms appear in June and July. Native to Europe and Asia. This species varies widely.

spuria halophylla   12″–18″   Zone 5
Beardless. Small flowers, falls are white with purple veins and some dull yellow, also. Native to the Caucasus. Closely allied to *I. spuria* and not very different.

susiana   12″–18″   Zone 5   Mourning Iris
Onocyclus. Flowers bright violet-purple. An old-fashioned favorite, flowering in May or in June. Native to Asia Minor.

tectorum   10″   Zone 5   Roof Iris
Crested. This is grown on the thatched roofs of Japanese homes. It is easily grown, bearing lavender-blue or white flowers, charmingly frilled. The foliage is rather coarse for the rock garden. Native to China. Blooms in May and June.

tenax   8″–12″   Zone 8   Oregon Iris
Beardless. Perhaps the easiest of the Iris (native to the Pacific Coast) to grow in the East and Midwest, but even at that, rather difficult to grow well. One of the most beautiful of wild flowers with petals ranging through soft shades of cream, lavender, orchid and white. Native to western Ore. It has been noted that the Indians used fibers of this plant in weaving.

tenuissima   14″   Zone 9
Beardless. Flowers cream to white with purple-to-brown markings. Hard to grow outside Calif., its native habitat. Somewhat similar to *I. purdyi*, but not so vigorous.

tingitana   18″–24″   Zone 7   Tangiers Iris
Xiphium—bulbous. Stem terete. Flowers lilac-purple. Blooms in early spring. Native to Morocco.

versicolor   2′–3′   Zone 3   Blue Flag
Beardless. This is the common wild Iris found in wet soils from eastern Canada to Pa., with stems occasionally branched, blue flowers splashed with yellow, the flowers usually solitary. The variety **ermesina** has almost red flowers. Some people get severe dermatitis from handling the rootstalks. The plant may be found in bloom throughout the early to midsummer. It is excellent for the moist wild garden and may be propagated by division in spring or by seed. The plant self-sows freely.

virginica   12″–40″   Zone 7   Virginia Iris
Beardless. This is similar to *I. versicolor*, with flowers blue to violet. Native to the southeastern U.S. Blooms in May and June.

wilsonii   24″   Zone 8   Wilson Iris
Beardless. Flowers similar to those of *I. sibirica* except that they are yellow and have divergent, not erect, standards. Native to western China. Blooms in June.

xiphioides   12″–24″   Zone 7   English Iris
Xiphium—bulbous. Flowers dark blue with a yellow patch on the falls, but varying in color from white to lavender and blue. Blooms in June and July about 2 weeks later than *I. xiphium*. Many varieties have been raised. Native to the Pyrenees.

xiphium   12″–24″   Zone 7   Spanish Iris
Xiphium—bulbous. Flowers are white, yellow or blue with a yellow or orange patch on the blade. They are about 4 in. wide. Native to southern France and Portugal. Many colored varieties are offered. This has been used to cross with *I. tingitana* to give rise to many hybrids, the so-called Dutch Iris.

The genus *Iris* is varied. Its species grow over most of the North Temperate Zone of the world in many varied habitats. Irises are monocotyledons, as are the grasses, true lilies, hemerocallis and many bulbous plants; they have underground stems variously rhizomatous, stoloniferous or bulbous, all with grassy or swordlike foliage and flowers which have perianth segments arranged as 3 upright standards and 3 horizontal to hanging to recurved falls, giving a unique architectural quality which has been beloved of artists through many centuries. Within this lovely form is a tremendous variability in size, conformation and coloring; variation in garden uses and in season of bloom join to make the Iris one of the most versatile of perennials.

The most common complaint against the Iris in general is the short bloom life of the individual variety. In an established clump, the length of blooming may be from 1 to 3 weeks, a rather brief period, it is true, although no briefer than an individual Lily or Peony. Certainly, in spite of the hopes and hard work of specialists no one variety will cover itself with flowers month after month, like a good annual. We do not grow perennials for this, but for their orderly procession, each in its season; and the iris season in all its variety is a long one, stretching from crocus time to the heat of summer, and giving choice effects in the rock garden, the water garden, pond or pool, in special beds or in mixed perennial borders, in the formal garden or in the wild garden or the cutting garden, or for special accents in favored nooks or corners.

Irises in single clumps are delightful plants to use in the succession of planned seasonal pictures, and have been an artist's flower since men have grown flowers, and they remain one of the most expressive materials for intimate garden pictures which are the personal signature of the garden owner and reflect his taste in line, in form and in color.

In milder climates it is possible to have irises blooming all year round, and even in severe climates they may, with skill and planning, be bloomed throughout the growing year; and the seedpods of *I. foetidissima* with their persistent scarlet seeds may be part of the winter bouquets, as may the dehisced seed pods of many irises. The Dutch irises, and particularly the blue 'Wedgwood', are an indispensable part of the mixed winter bouquets from the florist.

The outdoor season starts early with the bulbous irises, first *I. histrioides* and *I. danfordiae*, and then *I. reticulata* with its forms and hybrids, a welcome sign in cold climates that the frost is out of the ground. Just as these go by the small bearded dwarf species, *I. pumila* and then

its hybrids and the other miniature dwarf irises come into bloom with the gay flare of the rock garden plants, giving the gardener his opportunity to feature the distinctive iris form in combinations pleasing to his own personal taste.

As the daffodils fade the larger dwarf irises come into bloom. The intermediates follow, sharing the limelight with the tulips, but sturdier for accent uses and as a preview of the spectacular to follow as the tall bearded come into bloom, followed by the Spurias, the Siberians and, as these fade, finishing with the showy Japanese irises. These are particularly beautiful reflected in water; they may be grown on the edges of ponds or pools, and with them the Louisiana irises where they are hardy. Actually growing in the water is *I. laevigata* in blue and white, *I. pseudacorus* in bright yellow, and *I. versicolor* with its favored color forms in rose or red-purple.

The tall bearded, spurias, siberian and also the Japanese Iris may be grown in special beds, like roses; or they may be grown in borders featuring Iris with a few subordinate companions; or as occasional accents in a border of other plants, or in special locations. Wherever or however they are grown, their blooming will be a welcome part of the changing pictures of the garden season.

General

Irises are broadly divided into bearded, pogon, and beardless, or apogon. The bearded iris and especially the tall bearded have been one of the favored objects for improvement by amateur as well as professional plant breeders for the past 40 years, and with the introduction of new species and the shift from diploid to tetraploid varieties, the new look in these irises is almost unbelievable to those who have seen only the old "flags" of the young century.

The changes in the genetic composition of the Iris attracted a number of geneticists to their study, including one of the most famed of all geneticists, A. H. Sturtevant, who was one of the originators of the basic *Drosophila* studies at Columbia University in the early decades of the century. Subsequent chromosome studies of Simonet at the Genetic Institute at Versailles, France, and by Randolph and his students at Cornell, made science a valued tool in the creation of new types and patterns of the bearded iris.

The bearded iris species from which these have been developed are all native to the Old World north of the Mediterranean, and have been widely cultivated since ancient times; it was their diversity of coloring which caused the ancients to name the genus for Iris, their

Rainbow Goddess. Thus the modern bearded irises are complex hybrids of many varying species from many varying climates, from southern Italy to Poland, and from Spain to Persia, and individual cultivars vary in their cultural requirements and garden behavior as much as they vary in height and size and color. In general, they are most easily grown in the broad temperate Zones 5 and 6. Almost all kinds of irises will grow in these zones, with some care as to their placement and soil requirements. North of this, where many ornamentals become dubiously hardy, plants with inheritance of evergreen foliage from the warm Mediterranean are not too hardy. Many of the dwarf and some of the intermediate irises are hardier because of their inheritance from *I. pumila* and *I. aphylla* which are deciduous. South of the favored zones, irises with inheritance from the far northern or alpine ranges, demanding winter dormancy, may produce fewer and fewer flowers even though they grow masses of foliage. They also suffer from the heat of summer and the competition of invasive tree and shrub roots, and from sudden extreme variations in temperature.

Most bearded irises are adaptable to many soil conditions. If things are to their liking they will outdo themselves, and it is well worth an effort to try them out in various locations. Even the largest and most tender may bloom reliably against a wall facing south, and selected varieties will bloom in spring and then again in summer or fall with the right care and suitable climate within your own garden.

In the open parts of these favorable zones, the shorter bearded irises are better garden material than the tremendous new tall bearded irises which may have stalks 4 ft. tall or more, and which will need to be grown against some windbreak. The border iris and the intermediates are both excellent for small gardens. The dwarf irises are excellent for growing between rocks.

The classification made by the American Iris Society for all these bearded irises is a practical one for gardeners, and most catalogs follow this listing. In this classification, dwarf irises under 10 in. are miniature dwarf bearded; those from 10 to 15 in. are standard dwarf bearded, popularly called the "Lilliputs," and over 15 in. but under 28 in. the intermediate bearded are those which bloom early; the border irises and the table irises (miniature tall bearded) bloom with the tall bearded into which class go all those over 28 in. Other main groups are the Oncocyclus and Regalia, (with arils); the Crested irises; the Beardless irises and the Bulbous irises.

Tall Bearded Iris

It is probable that 90% of all gardeners who grow iris started because of the glamor of the tall bearded. Many gardeners have never seen these modern beauties and still think of iris in terms of the diploids of the first quarter of the century. Because of the persistence of these old "flags" they are still to be seen in masses in all parts of the country. In the South we see the white, 'Albicans', all but naturalized. Mohammedan soldiers carried this Iris in their marches, to plant on the graves of their fallen. Others are the purple 'Germanica' which was once considered the archetype of the tall bearded Iris and gave us the terms "German Iris" or even "Iris germanica," still at times incorrectly applied to their listings by nurserymen; or the blue and white forms of 'Florentina' grown in its native Italy for the orris powder made from its ground-up roots. In the North we see 'Honorabilis', yellow with red markings or perhaps some more advanced form of the variegated Iris, with solid red falls; or a form of *I. pallida*, such as 'Princess Beatrice' or 'Madame Chereau' with the blanket-stitched edges. Although these are old friends with antique value, they are suitable for planting in restored antique gardens.

The largest and most recent bearded irises are at their peak in Memphis, Tenn., about May 1 and in Concord, N.H. about June 15th. These magnificent flowers are from 5 to 7 in. across on stalks from 30 to 50 in. tall; they come in colorings from white through blue, orchid, and lavender to deeper blues, to purples and near blacks; from palest ivory to deepest yellow and gold; pink to apricot to orange; magenta to nearly red to deepest black-red; near green, brown and combinations of all these.

Unfortunately, in the creation of these modern giants there has been some sacrifice of hardiness and ease of growth; and many of the new larger tall bearded iris produce few flowers per stalk, and thus a shorter period of bloom; the larger flower size has been bred by reducing the number of flowers, actually a process of genetic disbudding. Thus, they pose new problems in garden planning. None of them are as suited as their older counterparts for semi-naturalization or for such practical purposes as holding banks or edging vegetable gardens. They are the prima donnas requiring plenty of space with protection from crowding of surrounding plants, a well-prepared soil with first-rate drainage in full sun, and clean cultivation.

Culture

Old clumps should be divided and replanted, and newly purchased rhizomes planted in early July in the North, in the South it is better to wait until the heat of midsummer has passed. The soil should be prepared without manure, or with manure only well below the rhizome level;

a cover crop turned under and well rotted gives excellent results. Thereafter a low nitrogen commercial fertilizer may be applied twice yearly, first in early spring, as growth starts, and then in late summer to stimulate fall growth. All fertilizers are put as a side dressing, never directly on the rhizomes. (See drawing, p. 543.)

Rhizomes received from reputable dealers may usually be planted without further treatment, but rhizomes from friends or exchanges should be treated with a combination fungicide-insecticide before they are planted, or they may be soaked in a solution of household bleach (Clorox).

To plant a single rhizome, dig a deep hole and make a mound in the center with its top level with the ground. Place the rhizome itself on this mound, and spread the feeding roots down around it at a slant. Fill the hole, firming the soil leaving a hollow for watering, and soak it thoroughly, making certain that no air pockets remain. It will not be necessary to water again except in severe drought.

The following brief listing is submitted for trial, and consists of irises which have proved good growers over all parts of the continent where the bearded iris are grown. For newer varieties consult the catalogs of specialists:

Allegiance—navy blue
Amethyst Flame—orchid
Bang—purple-red
Black Swan—deep purple
Blue Sapphire—pale blue
Celestial Snow—white
Chivalry—medium blue
Cliffs of Dover—white
Desert Song—cream
Dot and Dash—purple and white plicata
Edenite—dark purple-red
Eleanor's Pride—blue
Esther Fay—pink
Frost and Flame—red beard on white
Happy Birthday—pink
Jean Boyd Fittz—deep purple-red
Helen Collingwood—pale and deep purple
Indiglow—deep purple
Jungle Fires—deep purplish red
Mary Randall—magenta, orange beard
Melodrama—two-toned orchid
Millionaire—old gold
New Snow—white
Olympic Torch—gold-brown
Orange Parade—apricot-orange
Pacific Panorama—blue
Piety—white
Pinnacle—white and yellow
Rainbow Gold—bright yellow
Rippling Waters—orchid, red beard
Rococo—blue on white plicata
Sable Night—deep purple
Snow Goddess—white
Ultrapoise—yellow, red beard
Valimar—pink blend
Violet Harmony—deep violet
Whole Cloth—white standards, blue falls
Wild Ginger—yellow and brown plicata

Although the new standard dwarf and intermediate irises do not bloom well in the South, the tall bearded iris does better. Many tall bearded iris have been bred in southern Calif. with the tender Mediterranean species in their ancestry, and many of these grow well across most of the South except for the Gulf Coast area. Because of the rampant growth there of the blue and white "flags," many gardeners who move to this area are tempted to try new tall bearded ones. It is a keen disappointment to buy expensive new varieties and have them fail.

All the tall bearded irises, if they are growing well, will need to be moved by the end of 4 years. In transplanting old clumps, discard the bloomed-out central rhizomes, although if you wish the old clumps can be used for propagating.

Not all the iris will bloom the next year after they have been transplanted; varieties differ in this respect. However, they should make a fine showing the second year and be splendid in their prime the year following.

Disease and Pests

Forced growth, along with other types of damage, are the usual causes of the troublesome soft rot, which is the most destructive disease of irises. The causative bacterium *Erwinia carotovora* is a common inhabitant of the soil and enters iris tissues which are weakened or injured. If the soft spots are small enough they may be treated without digging the plant by scooping out the soft mush down to firm rhizome and pouring full strength household bleach, a strong solution of a creoline-type disinfectant or potassium permanganate into the wound, and then leaving it exposed to air and sun. Rot may follow winter injury due to sudden changes in temperature, or to injury from the cultivator or hoe, or it may follow damage from the inroads of the iris borer. This pest is the larva of the iris borer moth; eggs overwinter on nearby debris, and from April to June as they hatch the young larvae enter the iris fans and feed for 10 days to 2 weeks before boring into the rhizome. While they are in the fans they are betrayed by evidence of injury to the leaves, holes, or notched edges or a slimy bleeding, and are easily destroyed; vigilance and garden cleanliness may be sufficient in small plantings, but in larger plantings a spray program is necessary. It has been customary to spray 3 times with Malathion, covering the iris plants, the surrounding soil and nearby plantings, at weekly intervals starting with the first growth in April, but control has never been complete. With the development of systemic poisons, materials have been developed and tested which will entirely destroy all the borers but these have so far proved too toxic for general garden use; check your agricultural agencies for newer developments in this respect.

A drawback to the appearance of iris foliage is the Heterosporium leaf spot; the resulting untidiness is a serious fault in plants which should contribute a foliage effect to the perennial border during the period when they are not blooming. This disease may be controlled with a fungicide such as Zineb, but a similar bacterial blight is not easily controlled. This and other iris troubles may be minimized by avoiding overhead watering in dry weather; irises are among the most drought-resistant of plants; when water is applied, soil soaking is much preferable.

Two fungus rots are occasionally troublesome. One, a botrytis rot, produces a gray felt blanket of mold, and the other, known as mustard-seed rot, shows in sclerotia or resting bodies resembling mustard seed. Mercuric chloride and many of the new fungicides are effective in treating iris rhizomes for fungus infections.

A few other insects are occasionally troublesome. In the South, nematodes, for which only soil sterilization is effective. In the West, the bulb whitefly; in the North, the verbena bud moth and the iris weevil, whose larvae feed on developing seed, and occasionally thrips.

Scorch is an ailment for which neither cause nor cure has been discovered. The plant attacked loses all feeding roots and comes up in a mass; its foliage turns brown, and the entire plant is better discarded.

Many of the iris diseases are much less troublesome when the irises are grown with other plants, but nevertheless the careful gardener must know when his plants are in trouble and take measures accordingly.

Tall Bearded Group

Tall bearded iris may be grown in many ways to enhance the home garden, large or small. Against a clipped yew hedge, for instance, a single clump of one of the bright new apricot-oranges; a shining yellow or blended gold against a stained cedar backdrop, or a deep new blue-purple by the white picket gate. They must be used with care, however, because of their boldly scaled outline.

Specialists grow their iris in beds especially prepared, and many gardeners who grow a selection of iris colors prefer this also. In large gardens and in public plantings they may be given a permanent bed in a relatively inconspicuous place where they may be visited and enjoyed during their bloom, and with some fillers of airy type annuals and a few summer blooming perennials, may be part of the general effect the remainder of the year. *Linum perenne*, aquilegias, thalictrums and pyrethrums are often grown with iris, as are Dictamus, the less vigorous asters and late-blooming taller chrysanthemums.

In large plantings a number of beds may be arranged to follow some natural contour, or a geometric pattern, separated by paths of grass, sand or gravel. It is advisable to raise the beds for the sharp drainage which all the bearded iris require. Sitting in pools of water is disastrous; ice pools are worse. As for color grouping in the beds, it would be difficult with iris to go wrong, because planted "catch as catch can" they are magnificent.

Border Iris

Of the smaller iris that bloom with the giants, the border irises are segregates from the same sort of breeding, and should be required to have stalks that will not blow down. The plants will be more useful if they are smaller in all their parts, retaining on a smaller scale the balance between flower size and height. This distinction will be emphasized in a bed or border where the smaller varieties are used to "face down" the taller ones. However, a striking effect can be made by growing together large and small in matching color effect; the tall bearded 'Rococo' with the border Iris, 'Little Reb'; pinks: 'Esther Fay' with 'Little Lynn'; reds: 'Bang' and 'Little Brother'; 'Black Swan' and 'Black and Blue'; 'Eleanor's Pride' with 'Little Dude'; 'Whole Cloth' and 'Glacier Bay'.

Other small versions to try might include 'Blue Miller', rather large in pale blue with deep blue beard; 'Chocoleto', brown; 'Debbie Ann', white with blue beard; 'Ellen Q', cream and yellow; 'Frenchi', 2 tones of rose; 'Little Sambo', dark purple; 'Pagoda', very dainty pink; 'Tulare', golden yellow with an apricot beard; and 'Yellow Dresden', rather large but a dainty lace-edged yellow.

Culture of the border iris is the same as for the tall bearded, and they may also be grown in beds of their own, or as part of a mixed perennial border which is planted on a smaller scale or as accent plants where the tall bearded clump might be out of scale. They are actually about the same size as many of the old familiar diploids, and some of these which are grouped with the border class—'Pink Ruffles', 'Columbine', 'Gay Hussar', 'Fluff'—are prized for their hardiness and persistence. The new border iris have in some instances inherited the more erratic behavior of their taller relatives, along with the new and splendid color combinations. To breed back into them the vigor and floriferousness of the older varieties, which are outmoded in other respects, is the aim of modern plant breeders.

Other Miniatures

The Table iris which were originally selected for cut-flower use are officially designated miniature tall bearded, but this has proved a misnomer because they are actually scaled-down miniatures of the diploid, not the new tetraploid tall bearded iris. The class has been kept primarily because there is a demand for smaller iris which bloom at the same time as tall bearded; they are often used as part of the edging of beds or borders in which tall bearded iris predominate. In addition, this is the only recognized group which keeps some of the wild flower appeal. 'White Pewee' and silver blue 'Paltec', white and blue 'Playboy', blue on white plicata 'Widge'; yellow 'Warbler' and deep blue 'Tom Tit' are favorites among these, and have remained favorites since they were selected and named in the 30's.

Intermediate Bearded

Earlier blooming, but in the same size range as the border iris, the intermediates bloom with the tulips. Some of the old "flags" which once were considered to be species are actually intermediate iris—'Albicans', the dark purple 'Kochii', 'Germanica', 'Florentina' and 'Zua' of the popcorn finish. Others in white, yellow or purple were introduced in the early decades of the century and remained popular because of their early bloom and hybrid vigor, which induced some of them to bloom again in summer or early fall. They are often grown in single clumps where their early show and irregular repeat-of-bloom may be enjoyed by the kitchen door. The following are still listed, and although they have been superseded by more recent introductions they are actually quite garden-worthy. The whites—'Autumn Queen' and 'White Autumn King'; the deep red-purple 'Eleanor Roosevelt'; and the yellows, 'Sangreal' and 'Southland' are repeat bloomers in favorable climates. 'Ruby Glow' and 'Black Hawk' are still good intermediates in their color classes.

The newer intermediates are products of modern plant breeding and come in nearly all the colors and new forms inherited from their tall bearded parents.

Among the new intermediates, 'Cloud Fluff', 'Arctic Flare', 'Little Angel', 'Frosted Cups' and 'Vanilla Ice' are fine whites, all differing in personality. 'All Clear' is warm white with gilded edges and 'Sugar' is soft ivory. 'Barbi' and

'Lime Ripples' are excellent yellows; 'Lillipinkput' is distinctive in bright apricot; softer shell pinks are 'Pink Fancy', 'Pink Pride' and 'Sweet Allegro'. 'Arctic Ruffle', 'Blukeeta', 'Galaxy' and 'Dilly Dilly' are pale blues; 'First Lilac' is pastel orchid, 'Gypsy Flair', 'Lichtelfe' and 'Alien' strange blends, and 'Maroon Caper' a deep purple-red. Plicatas come in various patterns—'Whitchee', 'Fancy Caper', 'Sandy Caper', 'Snow Fleck', 'Doll Type'.

Intermediate irises are not usually grown as massed plantings; otherwise, they may be grown in the same manner as the tall bearded or border iris, considering only their earlier bloom. They harmonize well with tulips.

Lilliputs, the Larger Dwarf Bearded Iris

The miniature dwarfs are at their peak about the end of March in the southern part of their range—May 10th in the North. They are followed by their larger counterparts, the standard dwarf bearded or lilliput iris, some 10 days later. These are also chiefly products of our potent little *I. pumila* from crosses with the lovely new tall bearded iris. These crosses unexpectedly produce uniform strains of hybrids between 10 and 15 in. in height and fertile among themselves. They are excellent garden perennials, reliable in growth and bloom, and with flowers as charmingly variable as those of the garden pansies. They bloom with the latest daffodils and the earlier tulips, and the best of them, in an established clump, will give 3 weeks of color—and what color! They range from white to ivory, lemon, gold, orange, green, tan or brown, pink and apricot; from blue and orchid to magenta, purple or reddish black, with contrasting beards in all sorts of delicate to bold line markings.

Rock Garden Dwarfs—the Miniatures

Earlier still in the season, the dwarf irises are separated into 2 classes, the miniature dwarfs and the standard dwarfs, popularly called "Lilliputs." Our polymorphic little wonder worker, *I. pumila* is earliest of all, blooming on the heels of crocuses. These midgets among iris, some no more than 3 in. tall with 1-in. flowers, are charming in their endless array of colorings. Hundreds of color variants have been collected from the habitat of this species across Austria and the Balkans to the Black Sea Region. One Austrian enthusiast collected over 200 color variants from Austria alone, and hundreds more have been collected from Serbia, Rumania and the Crimea. These forms have been interbred in the United States, and many of them have been named. Among these are 'White Mite'; 'My Daddy' and 'Hanselmayer', creams; 'Carpathia' and 'Brownett', yellows with brown;

DWARF IRIS TRIAL LIST BY COLOR

	MINIATURES	STANDARDS
White	Bright White, White Elf	Lilli-White, Snow Elf
Blue	Blue Frost, Cradle Blue	Blue Denim, Sky Baby, Fairy Flax
Lavender	Blue Doll	Lilaclil
Violet	Violet Gem	Acolyte, Jersey Lilli
Black	Black Baby, Little Villain	Shine Boy
Brown or tan	Buster Brown	Knotty Pine, Arrangement
Rose tones	Cup and Saucer	Fi-Lee
Plicata	Knick Knack	Circlette, Wee Reggie
Yellow	Fashion Lady, Bright Spot	Brassie, Golden Fair, Coreop
Cream-lemon	Pastel Dawn, Cream Tart	Baria, Lemon Flare, Nylon Ruffles
Orchid Pink	Promise, Orchid Flare	Silken Sue, Fi-Lee
Purple	Butch	Dark Fairy, Eye Shadow
Tan-buff	Honey Bear	Knotty Pine, Brownie
Green-gold	Dirty Face	Zing
White, contrasting falls	Angel Eyes, Cherry Spot	Green Spot, Elisa Bee
Yellow—contrasting falls	Ablaze, Bee Wings	Pogo, Lilli-Var
Bitone blue (neglecta)	Grandma's Hat	Lilliput, Tonya
White and yellow	Gay Lassie	Pamela Ann
Purple-red	Burgundy Velvet	Snippet, Emma Frances

'Barium Gold', bright yellow; 'April Morn', 'Atomic Blue' and 'Flaxen', pale blues; 'Bimbo' medium blue and 'Sulina' deep violet; 'Tara' and 'Red Amethyst', purple-red; 'Spring Joy', lavender and 'Blue Spot' blue with deeper spot. These are good for the most purist of rock gardeners to grow among his prized alpines.

Because of their shallow root systems they are in danger of heaving from alternate freezing and thawing in early spring, and need protection by some light winter covering wherever the soil freezes. Planting among rocks is good protection, and many gardeners consider that letting volunteer johnny-jump-ups winter over among the drawf iris is good insurance. For mulch materials, boughs are best, if available. Otherwise any covering will serve that will not pack down, such as hay or straw. The small iris will need transplanting about once in 3 years; like the other bearded irises, their rhizomes should be buried no deeper than 1 in., less in heavier loam. They require full sun, and should be protected from being overgrown by creepers in the rock garden, as well as from the competitive thrust of larger plants, or of shrub or tree roots.

Oncocyclus and Regelia Irises
(The Iris with Arils)

The aril is a ring-shaped white bulge on the seed of certain iris of several related groups. First of these in importance are the Onco irises, including a great diversity of species and varying forms. They are native to Palestine, Lebanon, northern Persia, Asia Minor and Syria, and are thought to be the biblical "lilies of the field" and, indeed, no Solomon could be more richly arrayed; there can be no doubt that these exotic irises with scant foliage and huge globular flowers, are indeed the gaudiest of all. Many of these species are cross-compatible, giving an even more incredible array of color combinations. Their impact is such that once seen they remain a temptation to gardeners in unsuitable climates, many of whom will go to great trouble to bloom an occasional flower. They are, in fact, some of the largest and most beautiful wild flowers which nature has given us, and they are some of the most difficult to tame for the world's gardens. In fact, they are not yet tamed although they have been known at least as long as the tulips which were their neighbors in the wild. In most of the United States they are not grown for garden decoration.

Their most exacting requirement is for summer drought, not just absence of water, but a thorough baking. They are universally grown in special raised beds, in a rubble-mixed soil treated with dolomitic limestone; they are then either protected by covering from any summer rain at all, or they are dug as soon as they become dormant and stored until fall. Neither solution is completely satisfactory. In either case they need to be well mulched in fall to protect the winter foliage which is easily induced to start.

Wherever summer drought is usual, these plants have been grown and bloomed, sometimes in quantity, but never with a certain hold on life. Somewhat more gardenworthy are hybrids of these with the hexapogon (6 beards) or Regelia group, which also have seeds with arils. These are from a rugged climate in northern Iran and are easier to grow than the Onco species, although precautions in summer dryness must be followed.

Some newer varieties which represent the culmination of many years of effort by the late Clarence G. White, of Redlands, Calif., are fairly safe in most of the country. Representative of these might be 'Kalifa Hirfa', 'Kalifa Gulnare', 'Beisan Aga', 'Arjuna Aga', 'Asoka of Nepal', 'Black Joppa', 'Bali Agha'. These have vivid and unusual colors and shadings including green and brown, with variously yellow, lavender or blended standards veined and peppered in exquisite designs, fringed-style arms, wide fuzzy beards, and signal patches in dark velvet.

In addition some of the charm of the exotic has been bred into a series of tall bearded iris known as the "Mohr" family, many of them with the "Mohr" incorporated in their names. These grow well through most of the country and one of them, "Lady Mohr," is loved wherever irises are grown.

Re-blooming Iris

Specialists in favored zones are able to have a second good show of iris blooming in Aug., Sept. and Oct., but this requires, first, the growing of a large number of varieties, since none reliably blooms a second time; and then the entire project requires extra effort in feeding and water to force additional buds into growth. Because of the large number of varieties grown by the specialists, he will certainly have some which respond no matter what happens, but it is not possible to buy a number of specific colors for garden uses and then to count upon their blooming twice a year. So far, summer or fall blooms of iris are gifts to be accepted with pleasure when they occur, and not events to be counted on. The foremost hybridizer of reblooming iris recommends that the gardener try the following varieties: 'Gibson Girl', 'Autumn Snowdrift', 'Polar King', 'Autumn Sunset', 'Martie Everest', 'Autumn Flame'.

Iris with Crests

The crested irises are so called because they have a ridge at the center half of their falls in place of a beard. They are enough related to the bearded iris that a few hybrids have been produced. Crested iris include among others, *I. tectorum*, *I. cristata*, *I. japonica* and *I. gracilipes*.

Apogons—the Beardless Iris

The beardless irises are in general more typical perennial plants than the bearded; once settled into a suitable location, they may be left undisturbed for a number of years. In addition to the stabilized border perennials, there are among them a number of species which may be grown in semi-naturalized locations, as on the edge of meadows, or streams and ponds. The most important and widely-grown groups are the Siberian, the Spuria, the Japanese and the Lousianas.

SIBERIAN IRIS. The Siberian group of garden iris is the most dependable of all iris types. They will grow wherever any iris may be grown, without any particular care, and offer a choice of plants with robust manners or with more delicate ways. Their range of color, from white through blue, violet, rose and purple, has been restricted, but the plant breeders are tackling this problem.

The Siberian Iris has a strong fibrous root system; it should have a good deep hole reinforced with manure or bonemeal below for its root run. It should be planted with attention to packing the earth well so that no air pockets remain, and should be kept well watered until it has established itself. The tall blues go well with peonies; other suitable companions are oriental poppies, pink or salmon. With the lovely new White Swirl one might use the scarlet poppies, if other colors are restrained. Campanulas, foxgloves and the early yellow hemerocallis are other suggestions.

It is important to keep the seedpods broken off and away from the other Apogon iris, which set seed freely. The larvae of several insect pests mature in these pods; and if the seed is allowed to drop it will grow and confuse your records.

The Japanese Iris

There is a diversity in the Japanese Iris form from the graceful singles with 3 large sepals or falls, held flat or drooping, to the extreme double with 9 or 12 petals and style arms changed to petaloids until the form approaches that of the Peony, a form perhaps more impressive than beautiful. These forms have been classed progressively as single-, double-, triple-, multi-petaled, monstrosa and novelty; all have been bred in China and Japan by selection from the same little red-violet species, *I. kaempferi*.

This group furnishes some of the most beautiful irises in the genus, and also some of the ugliest, depending of course on the viewer. As in many flowers, the doubleness is a dubious improvement, as the form of 3 large falls, almost horizontal but gracefully drooping as pictured in Oriental art, is lovely; the forms with 6 petals are often preferred, and perhaps are beautiful in spite of their tendency to flatness.

The color range of the Japanese iris is somewhat limited, from white to blue-lavender-orchid-rose to deep violet or purple, but it is diversified with an array of patterns of white veining on dark colors, or variously toned darker veinings on white, or splashed, mottled or stippled and often pleasantly blazed with yellow. The textures and sizes are as diverse as those of gowns at a ball.

Three distinct strains have been developed from the species in Japan, the Edo, Ise and Higo. American strains have been developed almost entirely from the higos, and a particular strain developed by Marx in Ore. is called by him "Marhigo." These and the strains bred by Payne of Ind. are the basic American sources, and have been adapted for general garden use with stronger root systems and perhaps somewhat more lime tolerance.

I. kaempferi is not a bog or water plant, although it is a gross feeder and needs plenty of moisture while it is producing its superlative flowers. The strains from Japan, on which the American bred strains were based, were developed for a different culture from that ordinarily given to garden plants in America. The Japanese trained these irises not only to grow in pots but actually as bonsai, and it would seem one needs the epitome of skill to grow a perfect stalk, as they do, from one division planted in a container no deeper than a dinner plate.

Alternatively, in public plantings, they were grown in beds especially prepared so that they would hold water during the time of bloom. This gave westerners the idea that *I. kaempferi* required flooding which is not true. The Japanese flooded them because they would endure such treatment, and give entrancing views with their reflections in the water.

It is true that the Japanese iris cannot endure lime. They grow and bloom best with a pH of 5.5 to 6.5, and the soil should be modified to this degree by mixing in acid peat and, if necessary, soil sulfur (aluminum sulfate) at the rate required, 1–3 lbs. for 100 sq. ft. In preparing the soil, it is good to use as much organic material as possible, and if it is peat moss, make certain that it never becomes completely dehydrated. It would be better in the North to plant this Iris in spring and to apply chemical fertilizer after early spring.

A well-established plant will form a large clump in 3 or 4 years, and should be divided and thinned out, keeping 3 to 4 fans in each new division. Plant the divisions with their crowns 2–3 in. under the surface, and do not mulch the center of the plant. A light mulch may be applied around or beside the plant to protect the roots from heat in summer and heaving in winter.

Seed of the Higo strain may be obtained from a few sources and plants grown from this should be rewarding for a first trial. Although it would be folly to expect plants, which are selected from a larger number of seedlings, to equal named varieties, the gardener may select varia-

tions in the colors or patterns which he prefers, and those which grow well may be better adapted to his individual garden conditions.

As for using *I. kaempferi* varieties in the garden, nothing is lovelier than the white against a retaining wall, terrace, or beside water. They might be planted in boatlike, tight, wooden boxes and floated on pools or ponds, or even in boxes sunk like waterlilies, but only for the period of their bloom. They will grow well in the usual perennial border where they are as drought-resistant as garden phlox. However, they will need special attention when the summers are hot and dry if they are to survive. A special moist bed might be constructed for them, and perhaps the Louisana Iris, by digging out a a 2-ft. hole, lining the depression with polyethylene and filling it with humus acid soil.

Named Varieties—Iris kaempferi

SINGLES. 'Hoyden', with falls and red-purple standards; 'Numzau' and 'Great White Heron', whites; 'The Great Mogul', dark purple; 'Scherzo', marbled; 'Veinette', white veined; 'Pillar of Fire', violet edged; 'Mystic Buddha', red bordered; 'Royal Sapphire', bright royal purple.

MINIATURES. 'Gay Firefly', 'Imperial Imp', 'Nippon Miss'.

TRIPLE. 'Fashion Model'.

PEONY. 'Frosted Pyramid', 'Windswept Beauty', 'Naturodati'.

BY COLOR GROUPING

White: 'Driven Snow', with petaloids in its center; 'Snowy Hills', intensely ruffled.

Orchid pink: 'World's Delight', 'Prima Ballerina', 'Apple Blossom Cascade', with drooping petals.

Nearest to blue: 'Blue Lagoon', clear medium blue; 'Sky and Water'; 'Blue Nocturne'.

Light with dark veining: 'Silver Surf', 'Gay Gallant'.

Purple and dark blue: 'Blue Pompon', 'Cobra Dancer', 'Gay Festoon'.

Red-purple: 'Good Omen', 'Red Titan'.

Spuria Iris

The Spurias grow from about 2–5 ft. tall and bloom at approximately the same time as the tall bearded in colors of white to pale to deep blue, pale to deep yellow and cream, and blended browns. They have fine substance and form like the Dutch bulbous Iris, and are excellent cut flowers as they open well in water to perfect blooms—the colors, particularly the blues, are best and clearest when they open indoors. They are excellent in formal arrangements and are the only irises besides the Dutch which are suitable for corsage work. The variety 'Pastoral' makes a particularly good corsage.

The Spuria Irises are perfectly hardy, but in colder climates some varieties tend to produce large fountains of foliage with few bloomstalks. They are especially favored in Calif. and Tex. and have found rather slow acceptance in the North, East and Midwest. In warmer climates, fall planting is preferred; perhaps early spring planting would be an advantage in colder climates, to give them a full growing season to become established. Because it takes at least 2 years to establish a clump, it is advisable when they must be moved to take out a few rhizomes beforehand and get a new clump going. They are as easy to transplant as any hardy perennial.

In the North, these irises need to be grown in full sun; they are best planted in raised beds of friable neutral soil with both manure and commercial fertilizer incorporated as they are gross feeders. They require plenty of water while they are establishing their sturdy root systems, but once established they are as drought-resistant as any other perennial in the mixed border. No mulch should be spread over the crowns of the plants lest fungus troubles be encouraged; they are susceptible to attack by *Sclerotium rolfsii*, the mustard seed fungus. At planting time they may be watered in with fungicide as a preventive; Terrachlor has been found effective in the South.

Spuria varieties for the trial collection might include the whites, 'Morningtide' and 'White Heron'; 'Azure Dawn' and 'Fairy Lantern'; 'Wadi Zem Zem' and 'Sunny Day', yellows; 'Lark Song', 'Canary Island', cream and yellow. 'Black Point' and 'Cherokee Chief' are brown, and 'Michigan State' is bronze. 'Premier' and 'Euphrosyne' are blue-purple, and 'Two Opals' and 'Dutch Defiance', lavender blends.

Louisiana Iris

The other group of native American iris which has been developed into horticultural importance is that of the Louisiana iris from the Mississippi Delta, which was a spectacular discovery in the 1920's when an article was published by John K. Small of the New York Botanical Garden, and captured a worldwide interest which has continued to the present time. Because of the bewildering array of inter-species hybrids it took botanists some time to reduce the number of actual species to 4; and as one of these belongs to another series, it is now thought that we have to consider the origins of this lovely garden complex to be only the 3 species, *Iris fulva*, *I. foliosa* and *I. giganticaerulea*.

These irises are one of our national treasures and, like so many others of our treasures of the wild, they are vanishing before the advancing bulldozers. They are a striking example of natural hybridization and fortunately ethusiasts have collected great numbers of these species and interspecies and have crossed them in captivity, so that there is now no danger that they might be extinguished.

Briefly, the 3 species groups consist of brick-red *I. fulva* along with the "Abbeville Iris" which were collected from a single location; *I. foliosa*, a pasture Iris in white and blue; and *I. giganticaerulea* which grows wild only in La., tall and showy in lavender-blue with an occasional white. Collected forms have included rare color variants in white, yellow and pink; many of these, and collected inter-species hybrids, have been named and introduced into gardens. Mostly these collected forms have now been superseded by the garden hybrids which have been produced from them.

The Louisiana Iris has been described as the only plant in the world which is found in its natural habitat to have flowers in every color. In the wilds of La. there are blues, reds, yellows and every tint and shade of them by untold millions. During the blooming season it is possible to construct a complete color chart with the blooms.

Outside of the growing range of the *I. giganticaerulea* hybrids, which are the most desirable as well as the most difficult, some of the other Louisiana irises are quite hardy, notably the *I. foliosa* hybrids. One of them, 'Dorothea K. Williamson', is a rampant, almost weedy grower throughout the country; it seems that it should be possible to develop hardy types of this sort, but little has been done with this because Southerners have done most of the breeding of these irises in an effort to develop a garden type to take the place of the bearded iris which do not grow well for them. They have overcome some of the species' faults, especially the elongated rhizomes which made some of them uncontrollable in garden pictures; they have also developed less rampant foliage, and more and better formed flowers with firmer substance.

Bulbous Iris

The early spring bulbous irises of the *I. reticulata* group are delightful grown in drifts with the crocuses, and add a welcome variation in form and color. These are not simple wildlings; nearly all have been developed over the years by the firm of Van Tubergen in Holland.

The earliest to bloom are *I. danfordiae*, *I. histrio aintabensis*, *I. histrioides* and *I. bakeriana*. *I. danfordiae* is the only yellow commonly grown, and is bright gold with delightfully rounded form. *I. histrio* and *I. histrioides* have lovely sky-blue forms; *I. histrioides* varies to quite deep purple-blue. *I. bakeriana* is bi-tone blue, speckled and with a blotch at the tip of its falls; its hybrids, 'Clairette' and 'Springtime' are improvements on this pattern.

The *I. reticulata* vars. have rather a spidery appearance because of their narrow petals; the form sold as the "type," but apparently a hybrid, is a dependable grower and increaser, deep purple with a delicious violet fragrance. 'Violet Beauty' is perhaps some slight improvement on this. 'Royal Blue' and 'Wentworth' are more blue-purple and 'Hercules' and 'J. S. Dijt' are red.

For beauty of form and of coloring, the *I. histrioides* hybrids, 'Harmony' and 'Joyce' are much the finest of these bulbs. Their flowers are wider and come in a rich medium blue, 'Harmony' with a bright yellow blaze mark, and 'Joyce' with bright orange. 'Cantab', the best known pale blue, is neither as clear in color and form.

These little bulbs should be planted 3 to 4 in. deep in a well-balanced soil, if they are to persist and increase, and should be fertilized after flowering. They may be given an application of 5-10-10 well watered in. The foliage will continue to grow to a foot or more and must be permitted to ripen and dry off. Self-sowing small annuals, or the Johnny-jump-ups may be allowed to cover their places for the remainder of the growing season.

Juno Iris

The Juno irises are little grown in America. Their geographical center is in Iran. They are in general difficult to grow and not easy to procure, and little has been done in hybridization. *I. bucharica* is most frequently grown and is the best choice for the gardener who wishes to try out this unusual complex of bulbous plants in his rock garden. It is a lusty plant with flowers in white and yellow.

Bulbous Iris—the Xiphiums

A number of proposals have been made for reclassification of the bulbous sections; Rodionenko has recently proposed placing all 3 of these sections as separate genera, with the so-called Dutch, Spanish and English in a genus *Xiphium*. Of these, the Dutch are most familiar, and particularly the blue 'Wedgwood', familiar in the florist's mixed winter bouquets. It is the only variety of the Dutch Iris which is garden-persistent in warmer climates, where drifts of the bulbs are planted in permanent positions. Even there, most of these iris need replacing after 1 or 2 years' bloom, and throughout most of the country are usually planted each year in the cutting garden, and it is the usual practice to buy them in mixture. The group known as

English iris is more persistent, and more graceful and would be most popular if it were not for its susceptibility to "breaking" from the effects of virus infection. The Spanish irises are later and more delicate, but require the same treatment as the Dutch. A good assortment of these to try out might be the yellow 'Cajanus'; violet-blue 'Excelsior'; deeper blue 'King of the Blues' and bronze 'Le Mogul'.

A few Iris for Moist Soil

For bog use, of course, *Iris versicolor*, the familiar Blue Flag of swampy areas of the northeastern United States. This Iris is being wiped out from its natural habitat by the growing civilization and collections of color forms should be preserved. In the Southeast the flag of swamps is *I. virginica*.

Best of all waterside plants is *I. pseudacorus*, even though it is invasive for small spaces. This Iris is a European but is naturalized throughout most of the country. It is tall and robust, with lovely and variable flowers from white to deep yellow, with enchanting brown markings. The foliage is useful for all purposes for exhibitions and arrangements and may be chopped without debilitating the plants. Its variegated form has foliage particularly valued for artistic uses.

Where they will grow, collected forms of the Louisiana species are also fine for growing beside pools or ponds. *I. fulva* is a lovely flower, in a henna or orange-red unique among iris colors.

I. missouriensis, another native American, grows by acres in whites and all shades of blue in parts of the western states. It is a pleasant but not a spectacular flower, easily grown from seed. *I. setosa*, the most northerly American species, is found in Alaska and in the northeast ranges of the continent. It has purple flowers with nearly nonexistent standards, and grassy tufts of foliage. Its dwarf form, *hookeri*, is a charmer worth growing in cold-climate rock gardens, or in wild flower collections.

Iris from Seed

We have seen which species and which types of irises are best grown from seed; since even the wild iris vary from seed so remarkably, so much more do their hybrids. Bearded irises are best left to those who plan and make their own pollinations under all the rules for plant breeding. Any hand-pollinated seed offered in commerce is likely to be disappointing; a grower who selects one to name, register and introduce may average perhaps 1 out of 1000 seedings, and most of the others would be destroyed. Any iris species seed from a general collection is botanically dubious if it is bee-set.

It is best to grow from seed iris types which

do not transplant easily or are not easily acclimated to new circumstances. These include most importantly the Pacific Coast Hybrids, which are difficult to grow and to keep, but are lovely and interesting plants if they will grow and flower.

Naturally-pollinated Japanese iris seed and to some extent Siberian iris seed are often grown even by plant breeders, with interesting results; but the seed grown is collected from the best varieties in modern collections, and is grown in quantity for best selection. Japanese iris seed of the Higo strain will give some fine iris to serve as an introduction to the original types and patterns of the singles and the 6-petaled doubles, but will not give even a sampling of the newer shapes and colorings, especially in the more doubled or peony types which are less fertile.

Iris seed is notoriously difficult to germinate. It requires cold treatment, and should be planted in late fall and allowed to freeze and thaw; it should not be allowed to dry out once it is sowed. In spring the germinated seedlings are lined out at about tall bearded blooming time, and kept well watered for rapid growth; if conditions are right they will bloom the following spring, or the year after, when final selection is made and the chosen plants moved to where they are to live and grow.

BEATRICE CLARKE WARBURTON

IRIS FAMILY = Iridaceae

IRONBARK. See EUCALYPTUS.

IRON CHELATE. Iron is one of the elements necessary in the formation of chlorophyll. It is present in most soils in minute quantities sufficient for plant growth and possibly is added as an impurity in some fertilizers. Without it, plant leaves turn a sickly yellowish green to yellow color. This same condition can be brought about by other factors also, but when it is lack of iron causing the trouble, it can be corrected by the proper use of iron chelates.

These are preparations made from iron sulfate and several are on the market. They may be applied either directly to the soil, or by spraying on the leaves, in which case a better color can be observed in 2 or 3 days. Iron chelate should be used only after carefully reading the directions for its use on the particular package in which it comes, for if it is not used correctly, serious injury to the plants can result.

IRONWEED. See VERNONIA.

IRONWOOD = *Carpinus caroliniana* (sometimes this name is also applied to *Metrosideros tomentosa*, the New Zealand Christmas-tree).

IRRIGATION. See WATERING.

ISATIS (EYE-sat-is)
  tinctoria   4′   biennial   Dyer's Woad
Many years ago before there were synthetic dyes, this plant was of value for yielding a blue dye. It is native to Europe. The narrow leaves are alternate, mostly without petioles. The small bright yellow flowers are borne on numerous short racemes. Seeds should be sown in Aug. to yield flowering plants the following summer. The leaf and stem are sometimes used in medicine as astringents to dry wounds and ulcers.

ISOPYRUM (iss-o-PY-rum)
  biternatum 8″–12″ Zone 4 Atlantic Isopyrum
A perennial herb with compound leaves, the leaflets 3-lobed on slender stalks. The flowers are without petals but have 5 white, pointed sepals. It blooms in April and May and may be found in wooded areas from the Great Lakes to Fla. and Tex.

ITEA (IT-ee-a)
  virginica 3′–9′ Zone 5 Virginia Sweetspire
In moist soil situations, this plant does well, but it is rarely seen in American gardens even though it is native to the southeastern U.S. The flowers are white, in upright racemes 2–6 in. tall, and appear in June and July. The autumn color is brilliant red. It merely is a pretty native that can add to the summer interest of the garden but only in a moist soil situation. Propagation is either by division or softwood cuttings.

IVY. See AMPELOPSIS, HEDERA.

IXIA (IX-ia). Herbs growing from corms, native to South Africa, only hardy from Zone 7 south. These have fine grasslike foliage and belong to the Iris Family. Some are grown as pot plants in northern greenhouses, others outdoors in the South. Even in the North some are planted out after all danger of frost is over, and taken up again in the fall after they have bloomed. The flowers are borne in the leaf axils during summer, are 1 in. long and are several in a cluster, each at the end of a slim stalk from the base of the plant, colored red, yellow, white and blue. Some of the named varieties are better ornamentals than the 3 species noted below. Corms can be planted in the greenhouse in late fall, an inch deep, 5 plants to a 7-in. pot. Given some shade, a minimum winter temperature of 55° F. and fed once a week with some good liquid fertilizer, they should bloom late in the winter. In the South, plant outdoors in Oct. In the North, plant outdoors when all danger of frost is over. After blooming in the fall, lift and dry the corms and store as is done with Gladiolus.
  maculata 18″ Zone 7 African Ixia or Corn-lily
Flowers orange spotted black.
  paniculata   18″   Zone 7   Panicled Ixia

Flowers yellow and white, the tube often 3 in. long.

viridiflora   **18″**   **Zone 7**   **Green Ixia**
Flowers green and black, 1 in. long, blooming in May and June. The flower tubes are only ⅓ in. long. A few of the better flowered varieties, possibly hybrids of the above species, are: **'Afterglow'**—orange; **'Azure'**—blue; **'Brides-maid'**—white, red eye; **'Hogarth'**—yellow, purple eye; **'Huber'**—copper-red; **'Vulcan'**—red; **'Wonder'**—double pink.

IXIOLIRION (ixio-LIR-ion)

montanum = *I. tataricum*
tataricum (*I. montanum*)   **1¼′**   **Zone 7**
                                                         Siberian-lily
A bulbous herb belonging to the Amaryllis Family with 3–8 linear, persistent, basal leaves. Flowers are lilac colored, 1½ in. wide in 4–6-flowered umbels. It is best to store the bulbs over winter in a cool, dry place rather than to leave them in the ground. Native to Siberia and Western Asia.

IXORA (ix-O-ra)

coccinea   **15′**   **Zone 10**   **Flame-of-the-woods**
An evergreen shrub from the East Indies often grown in the greenhouse or conservatory for display. This plant has opposite or whorled leaves 1–4 in. long, brilliant red and yellow tubular flowers 1–1½ in. long in corymbs 2–4 in. wide which bloom much of the year, often grown outdoors in southern Fla. as a hedge with plants spaced 18 in. apart. Propagated by cuttings.

duffii (*macrothyrsa*)   **3′–10′**   **Zone 10**   **Ixora**
Native to the East Indies, this is popular in Hawaii because of its brilliant scarlet flowers. These are 4-lobed, small, only about 1 in. across, but are borne in large numbers in a tight cluster which is about 8–12 in. across. Each flower consists of a long, slender, 2-in. tube with the 4 petals at the end. The leaves are 12 in. long, glossy and pointed at both ends.

odorata   **8′**   **Zone 10**   **Sweet Ixora**
A species from Madagascar with white fragrant flowers, the corolla being 4–5 in. long.

J

JABOTICABA = *Myricaria cauliflora*

JACARANDA (jak-a-RAND-a). This genus comprises nearly 50 species of tropical trees and shrubs, mostly native to Brazil and Argentina. They have opposite, compound leaves that have a very graceful, feathery texture. The flowers are blue to violet, rarely white, funnel shaped and most conspicuous because they appear in early spring before the leaves. They are used as ornamentals in almost all the tropical countries of the world, and also in southern Florida and southern California. Miles of city streets in Harare, Zimbabwe and Johannesburg, South Africa, are planted with *J. mimosifolia*.

acutifolia　　　10′　　　**Zone 10**
This is mixed with *J. mimosifolia* in America. Actually, *J. acutifolia* is much lower in height, has only 5–6 pairs of leaflets per leaf while *J. mimosifolia* has 10–15 pairs.

mimosifolia　50′　Zone 10　Sharpleaf Jacaranda
One of the most popular exotic trees of the subtropical U.S., native to Brazil, valued chiefly for 2-in. long, blue, funnel-shaped flowers, borne in 8-in. clusters in the greatest profusion from April to June. Its fernlike foliage is made up of doubly compound leaves, each leaf with 16 or more pairs of main divisions and each of these with 14–24 pairs of leaflets, each of which is about $\frac{1}{2}$ in. long. It is of note that this species is widely distributed in the U.S. under the incorrect name of *J. acutifolia*, which is a native to Peru.

ovatifolia = *J. mimosifolia*

JACK-IN-THE-PULPIT = *Arisaema triphyllum*

JACOBEAN-LILY = *Sprekelia formosissima*

JACOB'S-LADDER = *Polemonium caeruleum*

JACOB'S-ROD = *Asphodeline lutea*

JADEPLANT = *Crassula argentea*

JAMESIA (JAYMS-ia)
americana　　　3′　　　Zone 4　　　Cliff Jamesia
This is not a very attractive shrub although the dull green leaves do turn an attractive yellow to scarlet in the fall. Native from Wyo. to N.Mex., the slightly fragrant, white flowers, about $\frac{1}{2}$ in. across, appear in many-flowered clusters in late May, the fruits being merely dried capsules. The leaves are $\frac{1}{2}$–$2\frac{1}{2}$ in. long. Propagated by softwood cuttings.

JAPANESE BEETLE. This beetle with iridescent bronze wing covers was introduced in 1917 and has been a destructive pest in the eastern half of this country. Beetles lay eggs in turf in late

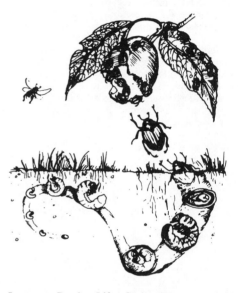

Japanese Beetle—Life Cycle. Eggs are laid in the soil in the late-summer; eggs hatch and grubs feed on grass roots, hibernate over winter then feed on grass roots in the spring, emerging from soil in early summer as mature beetles. Mature beetles feed on foliage, fly about, then lay eggs in soil in later summer.

summer, grubs hatch in the fall and feed on grass roots, until cold weather when they hibernate below the frost line in soil and resume feeding in spring. Beetles are active in midsummer and skeletonize the leaves and flowers of more than 200 species of plants. Beetles are controlled by spraying with insecticides #37 or #9. Two or 3 applications are usually necessary. The grubs are a major pest of lawns where they cause many dead areas by eating the roots. Grub-proofing the turf with insecticides #13 or #15 applied as spray, dust or granules is effective for 3 to 5 years. Mixtures of insecticide and fertilizer are available and convenient. Milky spore disease, a bacterium which kills the grubs, is prepared commercially. This provides long-lasting protection but does not have immediate effect and is more desirable for use on large areas (parks and athletic fields) than on choice lawns. Milky spore disease and insecticide treatments should not be applied in the same season.

JAPANESE GARDENS. These gardens are entirely different from those in America and Europe and have a distinctiveness all their own. They are necessarily small, and many of the plants selected for growing in them are partially miniature. They are usually not on level ground but built on several levels or usually on a rocky hillside in which waterfalls, ponds and streams are featured. The impression one receives from them is of a formal, almost manicured planting, with every rock and stone in its place and each plant meticulously groomed.

The general feeling produced is one picturing a native scene of peace, quiet and beauty. There are supposedly gardens in Japan a thousand years old, and it is well known that the art of garden-making there goes back a long, long time. Summer houses, bridges, lanterns, gates and archways are all a typical part of these gardens. Stones are also, and they are selected for special shapes and placed in the garden to represent some special symbolism.

There are also sand gardens which are little more than a few specially chosen rocks in a bed of clean sand which is always raked in special ways. These demonstrate simplicity, peace and quietness. Of course they are easily cared for but one must understand the symbolism shown to really appreciate them.

No Westerner can make a Japanese garden without a great deal of study. There are several excellent books on the subject and these should be studied very carefully before such a garden is made. Merely the placing of the wrong kinds of stone can spoil the garden, and for the Japanese at least, the placing of the right stones in the wrong way would disqualify it as truly Japanese.

Of course, the plants used are Japanese natives. The woody plants are featured, trees, shrubs and woody vines. When made on a rocky bank there is always the opportunity for a waterfall and a pond, and by the pond sometimes a small bog in which *Iris kaempferi* is grown. A small island is placed in the pond, even though there may be room for only 1 small tree, yet this adds the impression of distance and size to a small garden.

Since the Japanese make much of azaleas, especially the Kurume azaleas, the soil for the garden should be acid, for it is difficult to portray a Japanese garden without some of these beautiful plants. Dwarf evergreen varieties of *Cryptomeria, Chamaecyparis* (especially some of the forms with yellow foliage), and such trees as *Sciadopitys verticillata, Pinus parviflora, P. thunbergii* and *Larix leptolepis* are all used.

Flowering trees and shrubs would of course include the oriental flowering cherries, some of the crab apples like *Malus sargentii* and *M. hupehensis*, the many Japanese maples, over a hundred varieties of which are grown in Japan. These maples lend themselves very well to miniature gardens for many of them are small, comparatively slow in growth and some are most colorful with red or variegated foliage. Then there might be some of the flowering quince, the Japanese Wisteria (*Wisteria floribunda*) of which there are many varieties in Japan, and possibly even a few plants of a hardy bamboo.

It is true that a Japanese garden cannot be used properly in many areas of the U.S. The best examples of course are in Golden Gate Park, San Francisco; the University of Washington Arboretum in Seattle and in the Brooklyn Botanic Garden in Brooklyn, New York. Many people like them but few gardeners can create them single-handedly, in this country at least, without a great deal of study.

JASIONE (jass-ee-O-nee). A genus of the Bellflower Family with many species, most of which are native to the mountains of Europe, and have small blue flowers arranged in dense globular flower heads. Although not frequently found in cultivation, they are attractive and easy to grow in well-drained, rather sandy soil in sun or partial shade. They do well as wall plants or in rock gardens. Propagation is by division.

humilis   9″   Zone 5   Dwarf Jasione
A tiny plant with small, bladelike, hairy leaves growing in tufts and spreading in mats. The leafy flower stalks, rising 6 or 8 in., bloom with small, light blue flower heads, ½ in. wide, in May and June. Native to the Pyrenees Mountains.

perennis   1′   Zone 6   Scabious Jasione
An alternate-leaved European herb with entire, obovate leaves; blue flowers in globose heads 2 in. across; useful chiefly in rock gardens or borders. Propagated by seed and division.

JASMINE. See JASMINUM.

JASMINUM (JAS-min-um). Jasmines or Jessamine, as some are sometimes called, are tropical or subtropical clambering shrubs valued chiefly for their very fragrant white, yellow or pink flowers which, in some cases, are borne very early in the spring. They belong to the Olive Family. The leaves, mostly evergreen, are pinnate, either opposite or alternate. They are easily grown where the climate is right and can be propagated by seed sown as soon as it is ripe, or stored dry in airtight containers in a cool place until needed. Also, layers, hardwood and softwood cuttings are all easy methods of increasing them.

beesianum 3′ Zones 6–7 Bees Jasmine
A clambering shrub with opposite, lanceolate, sharp-pointed leaves about 2 in. long and fragrant pink to rose-colored flowers ¾ in. wide in 1–3-flowered clusters. Native to China.

dichotomum climbing Zone 10 Goldcoast Jasmine
A climbing evergreen shrub usually blooming continuously, with thick, glossy, pointed leaves in 2's or 3's about 3 in. long. The white, fragrant flowers, over an inch long, open at night. Native to West Africa.

floridum rambling Zone 7 Showy Jasmine
Half evergreen, alternate, compound leaves with 3 leaflets, each one ½–1½ in. long, yellow flowers in terminal clusters from July on. Native to China.

gracillimum climbing Zone 7 Pinwheel Jasmine
Native to northern Borneo, with opposite, simple leaves 1½ in. long; fragrant white flowers an inch wide, in many-flowered clusters. This usually blooms in winter in protected places.

humile 4′ Zone 7 Italian Jasmine
Nearly evergreen with alternate compound leaves, each with 3 leaflets; fragrant yellow flowers in 2–6-flowered clusters during June and July. Native to China. This is often grown in greenhouses.

mesnyi vine 10′ to subshrub Zone 8 Primrose Jasmine
This is the most beautiful Jasmine grown in America, and unfortunately it is the least hardy of that group. Its large yellow flowers are 1½ in. wide, blooming in the spring and summer. The foliage is semi-evergreen, the opposite, compound leaves have 3 leaflets, each 1–2 in. long, and the petioles are 4-angled.

multiflorum (J. pubescens) vine Zone 10 Scented Star Jasmine
An opposite-leaved evergreen vine from India, with white, scentless flowers 1 in. wide, having 4–9 petals. The leaves are 2 in. long. It is often used as a ground cover in Hawaii.

nudiflorum vine 15′ to subshrub Zone 5 Winter Jasmine
The hardiest of the jasmines, this is being grown as far north as Boston when given some winter protection or grown against warm building walls. It might be best planted at the top of walls or banks so that the graceful branches can droop to best advantage. Native to China, the flowers are bright yellow, solitary and ¾–1 in. in dia., blooming in early April. The

stems are green and the flower buds can be forced into bloom indoors at any time throughout the winter. It prefers a warm, dry, sunny location in order to produce the maximum number of flowers, but it will quickly become untidy if not pruned occasionally.

officinale vine 30′ to subshrub Zone 7 Common White Jasmine
With fragrant white flowers during the summer, this semi-evergreen jasmine comes from Persia, Kashmir and China. The variety **grandiflorum** has flowers nearly 1¾ in. wide. It is a semi-climbing shrub, widely grown in the South, used for covering arbors or trellises in full sun or light shade, and has been popular for a long time. The compound leaves are opposite, with 5–7 leaflets, each ½–2 in. long.

parkeri 1′ Zone 7 Parker Jasmine
An evergreen with alternate, compound leaves of 3–5 leaflets, each ⅛–¾ in. long. The solitary yellow flowers are terminal or are produced in the leaf axils and are ⅝ in. wide, during June. Since it is so dwarf it is used only as an oddity in the rockery. Northwestern Himalayas.

pubescens = J. multiflorum

sambac vine Zone 10 Arabian Jasmine
Another favorite in Hawaii for making leis. Similar to *J. multiflorum*. The leaves are opposite (sometimes in 3's), 3 in. long.

x stephanense climbing Zone 7 Stephan Jasmine
This is a cross between *J. beesianum* and *J. officinale grandiflorum*, with fragrant pink flowers. It was found in Yunnan Province of China and blooms in May.

JATROPHA (ja-TRO-fa)

curcas 15′ Zone 10 Barbados-nut
A small tree belonging to the Euphorbia Family from tropical America, with maplelike leaves 6 in. wide, and yellowish-green flowers. The yellow-to-red fruits, 1–1½ in. long, bear 2–3 black oily seeds which are released when the capsule splits. These are dangerously poisonous if large amounts are eaten. They contain a purgative oil.

integerrima (hastata) 5′ Zone 10 Peregrina Nettlespurge
A Cuban shrub with oblong-ovate leaves having a fiddle-shaped apex. The bright scarlet flowers are an inch in dia., in terminal cymes and always seem to be evident.

multifida 20′ Zone 10 Coralplant
With nearly round leaves a foot wide but deeply cut into segments or lobes. The tree has a milky juice. Flowers are scarlet, borne in large clusters. Native to tropical America, considerably grown in Fla.

JEFFERSONIA (jeff-er-SO-nia)

diphylla 10″–12″ Zone 5 American Twinleaf

A perennial herb with long-stemmed, kidney-shaped leaves and white flowers, about 1 in. wide, on erect, leafless stems. These appear in spring and have 4 sepals and 8 petals. The plant grows in woods from N.Y. to the Deep South and extends westward to Wisc. It prefers slightly acid or neutral soil and when established in the wild garden it makes a good clump. The plants may be divided either in late summer or early spring. Seeds may be sown either in spring or fall.

JERUSALEM-CHERRY = *Solanum pseudocapsicum*

JERUSALEM-THORN = *Parkinsonia aculeata*

JESSAMINE. See JASMINUM.

JESSAMINE, CAROLINA = *Gelsemium sempervirens*

JESSAMINE, WILLOW-LEAVED = *Cestrum parqui*

JETBEAD = *Rhodotypos scandens*

JEWELWEED OR BALSAM FAMILY = Balsaminaceae

JIMSON-WEED = *Datura stramonium*

JOB'S TEARS = *Coix lacryma-jobi*

JOE-PYE-WEED. See EUPATORIUM.

JOHNNY-JUMP-UP. See VIOLA.

JOHNSON-GRASS = *Sorghum halepense*

JONQUIL. A popular name loosely applied in the South and sometimes in England to various species of the *Narcissus* genus. Technically it should only be used for the species *N. jonquilla*, *N. juncifolius*, etc. and others in Division VII of the *Narcissus* grouping. See NARCISSUS. As a common name it should be avoided except for these few species and hybrids. See DAFFODIL.

JOSEPH'S-COAT = *Opuntia monocantha variegata*. Also *Amaranthus tricolor*.

JOSHUATREE = *Yucca brevifolia*

JUBAEA (ju-BAY-a)
    chilensis (*spectabilis*) **45′ Zone 8 Chilean Wine Palm**
A feather palm with leaves 15 ft. long, and a huge pyramidal trunk sometimes as much as 5 ft. in dia. at the base. When trees are cut the sap, when fermented, makes a fine drink—the reason many of the larger trees have been cut down on the western slopes of the Andes in South America where this is native. The small nuts have yielded a vegetable oil. See PALM.

JUBAEOPSIS (ju-bay-OP-sis)
    caffra **20′ Zone 10 Pondoland Palm**
This is a feather palm, usually less than 20 ft., that is closely related to the coconut, bearing a smaller nut which contains milky juice inside. It is native to South Africa and although only a recent arrival in America (1939) it is proving popular where it can be grown.

JUDAS-TREE. See CERCIS.

JUGLANDACEAE = The Walnut or Hickory Family.

JUGLANS (JOO-glans). The walnuts are not valued ornamental trees. The foliage is coarse, the leaves are alternate, large and pinnately compound, the fruits can be quite messy on a well-kept lawn, and there is no autumn color and no winter interest about the tree whatsoever. Most of the walnuts are tap rooted, making them difficult to move in the larger sizes. Although some are hardy as far north as Boston, it is not every year that they bear fruits because either the flower buds are killed by late frosts, or else the growing season is not sufficiently long for the fruits to ripen.

Walnuts are a very important economic crop, both the Persian or English Walnut (*J. regia*) and the Black Walnut (*J. nigra*). The latter, being native, is collected chiefly in the few states from eastern Kan. to Ohio, or, generally speaking, throughout the corn belt, while the Persian or English Walnut is cultivated in orchards in Calif.—some 125,000 acres being given over to the growing of these trees alone, and these trees can produce 60,000 tons of nuts, about 90% of the U.S. supply. Ore. grows the rest.

The most ornamental of the genus is the Persian or English Walnut because of its good green foliage and dense habit. Because the Carpathian variety has proved hardier than the species, we find this growing (and producing nuts) even in the vicinity of Boston, Mass. The cut-leaved variety *J. regia* 'Lacinata' is best for ornamental purposes. Also see WALNUTS and BUTTERNUTS.

Propagation

Do not allow the nuts to dry out, but stratify as soon as ripe at 40° F. for 4 months. If sown out-of-doors (for over-winter stratification period in the ground), be sure to protect the seed from rodents by placing wire mesh over them. Grafting and budding are also satisfactory. See STRATIFICATION, GRAFTING, etc.

Insect Pests

Black Walnut is often badly defoliated by the walnut caterpillar which feeds in colonies in late summer. Fall webworm is also destructive at this time unless insecticide #15 is applied. Gypsy moth and cankerworms require similar control measures in late spring and and early summer. Walnut bud moth distorts and webs the new shoots. Aphids which infest Hickory also feed on Black Walnut. See CARYA.

English Walnut leaves are eaten by the walnut span worm and the fruit tree leafroller (see APPLE) rolls the leaves and scars the husk of the nuts. Spraying with insecticide #37 or #9 is effective. Walnut weevil, a snout beetle, lays eggs on the buds and the grubs tunnel the shoots. Some eggs are laid in the young nuts and the grubs feed on the nut meat. Codling moth (see APPLE) also lays eggs on the nuts and the worm ruins them. Spraying them with insecticide #37 when the shoots and nuts are developing prevents this injury. Blister mite deforms the leaves occasionally and dormant sprays of fungicide #L or #N are needed to prevent serious injury. Walnut scale and several other scales may be serious pests. Dormant oil sprays are effective, but Walnut is subject to injury and they can be used only as directed on the label.

Diseases

Anthracnose causes irregular brown spots on the leaves and defoliation. Two sprays before the leaves are full grown with fungicide #D or #F give control. Dieback of twigs and branches giving a staghead appearance to badly diseased trees can be checked by prompt and careful pruning of the affected parts. Walnut is quite susceptible to white trunk fungus and other wood rots which develop at injuries and pruning wounds. Prompt cutting out of diseased area and coating with tree paint is advised.

ailanthifolia (*sieboldiana*)   60′   **Zone 4**
                                                Siebold Walnut
Native to Japan, with alternate compound leaves, $1\frac{1}{2}$–$2\frac{1}{2}$ ft. long, with 11–17 leaflets, each slightly heart shaped at the base. The staminate catkins are 6–12 in. long and the nuts are 1–$1\frac{1}{2}$ in. wide. It certainly is not an ornamental tree and its only use is for breeding purposes, because of its hardiness.

ailanthifolia cordiformis (also see HEARTNUT)
                        60′   **Zone 4   Heartnut**
The common name is given this Japanese native tree because of its heart-shaped nuts which are easily cracked—sometimes they can even be split open with a penknife. It is not unusual for the kernels to come out whole. The variety 'Fodemaier' is one of the varieties available, but there are others. Although this species has supposedly been in America since 1865, it is still rather hard to find in nurseries. The massive branching habit and rounded outline are its only ornamental characteristics worthy of mention.

cinerea (also see BUTTERNUT)   90′   **Zone 3**
                                        Butternut
The Butternut is the hardiest member of this genus. The large, alternate, compound leaves

have 11–19 leaflets and it is native from New Brunswick to Ark. It does not have an interesting form and has no autumn color; in fact, there is nothing about it that is ornamental. Green butternut hulls are excellent for tan and gray dyes.

hindsii   50′   Zone 8   Hinds Black Walnut
In Calif. this tree is native in the central part of the state and has been used for street planting as well as for understock on which to graft the Persian Walnut, *J. regis*. Probably it is of little value elsewhere.

nigra   150′   Zone 4   Eastern Black Walnut
As most plantsmen know, this tree is not a good ornamental. It is native to the eastern U.S., has coarse foliage, is lacking in autumn color and bears large fruits which can be troublesome if they fall where they are not wanted. There is little of ornamental merit to the tree. Many varieties have been selected, primarily for their nuts (such as 'Thomas', 'Ohio' and 'Snyder') and some are being grown commercially. It has definitely been proved that its roots give off a material which is toxic to many other kinds of plants; hence it should not be grown near valued specimens. As an ornamental, however it might well be omitted altogether. The variety 'Laciniata' is similar to the species except that the foliage is deeply cut, giving the tree a much finer texture. The green hulls of *J. nigra* are the source of one of the oldest dyes in North America for dark brown and black.

regia   90′   Zones 5–6   English or Persian
                                                Walnut
Of all the walnuts, this species and its cut-leaved variety 'Laciniata' are the best of the genus for ornamental purposes. The leaves are densely borne, usually with 5–9 leaflets; the bark is silver-gray and the habit is definitely dense and rounded. It is a native of Europe and China. There are fruit-bearing trees as far north as Boston, although these can be severely injured in very cold winters and it is not every year that the growing season is long enough and mild enough for fruit production. 'Broadview', 'Eureka' and 'Franquette' are only 3 of the many commercial varieties grown today in Calif. The variety 'Carpathian' is a geographical variety of the Persian Walnut brought (in the form of seed) to America from Poland by Rev. Paul Crath of Toronto, Canada, in 1926. The resulting seedlings were widely distributed and since have shown great variability, both as to the tastiness of the nuts and the hardiness of the trees themselves. In the intervening years, other seedlings from the original plants have been grown. Some are now distributed under name, some by number. The 'Firstling' and 'Schafer' (Plant Patent #494, 1941) are both clones with good prospects. There are some Carpathian

walnuts in the Boston suburbs which bear fruits almost every year. The cut-leaved variety 'Laciniata' is excellent for ornamental purposes.

JUJUBE, COMMON = *Zizyphus jujuba*

JUMPING BEAN. See SEBASTIANA.

JUNCUS (JUNK-us)

effusus spiralis   4′   Zone 3   Spiral Rush Of little garden value, this is a tufted grasslike plant of bogs, and this variety is the one occasionally grown because of the spirally twisted stems. The small brownish-green flowers are borne near the tips of the grasslike stems. Native to North America, Europe and Asia and only suited for boggy areas. Propagated by seeds and division.

JUNIPERUS (joo-NIP-er-us). There are approximately 40 species of junipers found in the northern hemisphere of the world. Over 170 species and varieties are being offered by American nurserymen today. These are all evergreens, have needlelike or scalelike leaves and the fruits are small blue berries, usually less than ¼ in. in dia. The foliage varies greatly, young leaves being more sharp and pointed than mature leaves, and sometimes this varies on the same plant. The sexes are separate so it is only the pistillate or female trees that bear the small berries and on some species these take 2 and even 3 years to mature.

Junipers range in size from prostrate ground covers to trees. They are among our most serviceable landscape plants for they are so diversified there are always a few for any landscape planting. They are valued because they grow well in hot, dry, sunny situations, especially under urban growing conditions. Most can be pruned easily and they will respond well; some can be sheared in hedge form. They apparently do well on either acid or alkaline soil, but are supposed to do best if the soil is not too acid.

Unfortunately, they are susceptible to several pests. The cedar-apple rust is one disease in which part of the life cycle is spent on the junipers and part on certain rosaceous plants like apples, cotoneasters and hawthorns. Remove one of the plants and there is no disease, but if both are grown, the peculiar hornlike, fleshy growths appear on certain of the junipers, especially during wet weather.

Propagation

Seeds of many take 2 years to germinate and so should be stratified at room temperature for 3–5 months, then at 40° F. for 3 months to break this dormancy. Hardwood cuttings of many kinds can be rooted; those that are difficult are grafted on *J. virginiana* or *J. chinensis* 'Glauca Hetzi' understock, the latter rooting easily from cuttings. See STRATIFICATION, GRAFTING, CUTTINGS.

Insect Pests

Spindle-shaped bags enclosing the bagworm which may defoliate the ornamental varieties are very conspicuous in the warmer areas. The winter eggs do not survive freezing. Hand-picking is practical on a few plants and insecticide #9 is recommended for spraying. White juniper scale on the needles of many junipers is controlled by a dormant spray with insecticide #44 or when the young are active in early summer, with insecticide #15. Spruce mite often infests Juniper and requires careful control. See PICEA. Juniper web worms feed on leaves enclosed in a noticeable web in early summer and again in the fall. Insecticide #37 gives control.

Diseases

Twig blight, caused by a fungus attacking new growth, is very destructive in nurseries. The dead leaves are covered with tiny black spots. Spraying with fungicides #K or #G is recommended.

Cedar-apple rust, cedar-hawthorn rust and cedar-quince rust, all spend a part of their development on Juniper where they produce reddish-brown galls or "cedar apples" or swellings on the twigs. The cedar-apple rust develops on Juniper the 2nd year following infection but others are perennial. Damage to Juniper is usually less important than to the alternate host. Spraying in midsummer with fungicides #D or #F is recommended. See RUST.

chinensis   60′   Zone 4   Chinese Juniper There are many varieties and cultivars of this excellent species ranging in size from ground covers to trees. It would seem advisable to buy named varieties or cultivars rather than seedlings which vary considerably. The species is native to China and Japan, has foliage a lighter green than does the native Red-cedar (*J. virginiana*) and the fruits are larger, up to ⅜ in. in dia. This is a good ornamental tree but it is surpassed in value by more recently introduced varieties and cultivars which will give more specific ornamental values in the landscape planting.

'Ames', a pyramidal shrub with steel-blue foliage—a 12-year-old specimen is 7 ft. tall; 'Armstrongii', a sport or seedling of *J. chinensis* 'Pfitzeriana', this is a slow-growing shrub of the Pfitzer Juniper type reaching a height of 4 ft. and with a softer blue-green foliage; 'Blaauw', received from Japan with a blue feathery foliage; 'Columnaris', this is called the Blue Columnar Chinese Juniper and is narrowly

Juniperus chinensis 'Ames': An excellent, small evergreen for use in city gardens. (*Photo by Arnold Arboretum, Jamaica Plain, Mass.*)

columnar in habit, with silvery-green foliage. All the leaves are juvenile, that is, they are sharply pointed; **'Glauca Hetzi'**, a very dense shrub, 15 ft. tall and about as wide; with upright branches. It definitely does not have the habit of a Pfitzer Juniper but it does have light bluish foliage; **'Iowa'**, a pyramidal tree supposedly resistant to the cedar-apple rust disease; has irregular upright growth to about 10 ft. tall, bluish foliage and bears fruit; **'Keteleeri'**, this is a broadly pyramidal tree with a stiff trunk and loose foliage, selected about 1905. It is still one of the best varieties of *J. chinensis*. At one time it was listed as a variety of *J. virginiana*, but there is no question about it being a Chinese Juniper for its large light blue fruits are almost

¾ in. in dia. The foliage is green; the cultivar 'Mountbatten' has foliage of a grayer color and it is more juvenile; **'Mas'**, a densely columnar form mostly with acicular leaves and usually with staminate flowers. This seems to be one of the excellent columnar forms of *J. chinensis* and might well be used more than it is; **'Moraine'**, a sport of the Pfitzer Juniper, introduced in 1949 especially for its blue-green foliage and compact habit. It is similar in some respects to 'Nick's Compact'; **'Mountbatten'**, introduced in 1948, this is an excellent narrowly columnar tree and a seedling of *J. chinensis*. The foliage is a grayish-green color because the majority of the leaves are the grayish juvenile or acicular type, but the dense compact habit gives one the impression that the plant has been sheared. This is one of the best of the fruiting Chinese Juniper cultivars; **'Nick's Compact'**, very definitely a sport or a seedling of the Pfitzer Juniper, this is one of the best of the compact junipers. A 12-year-old plant is 6 ft. across and only 12 in. high. It is flat on top and is an excellent compact form without the vigorous growth of the Pfitzer Juniper; **'Obelisk'**, this is a fruiting pyramidal tree with steel-blue foliage color. It resembles *J. chinensis mas* but is claimed to be more attractive because of truncated branching and its excellent blue color. It keeps this compact habit without trimming and grows comparatively slowly; **'Parsonii'**, no juniper has

in recent years. Now, there are some excellent forms being grown and sold including 'Armstrongii', 'Aurea', and 'Nick's Compact'; **'Pfitzeriana Aurea'**, this is a sport of *J. chinensis* 'Pfitzeriana' and is not to be confused with the botanical variety *J. chinensis* 'Aurea'. In the heavy clay soils of Ill , the young foliage is a beautiful golden yellow but in certain soils of different texture (notably in Calif. and R.I.) the foliage color is not so pronouncd; **'Pfitzeriana Glauca'**—this differs chiefly from the Pfitzer Juniper in that the foliage is blue-gray and not green. It was patented (Plant Patent #422); **'Pyramidalis'**—a narrow, pyramidal, compact form with upright branches and crowded upright

Juniperus chinensis 'Pfitzeriana': The Pfitzer juniper grows well at the seashore.

been carried under more names than this excellent little plant from Korea. Probably first introduced to America by the old Parsons Nurseries of Flushing, Long Island, N.Y. It has had at least 6 other names and may be carried now under an assortment of them. The plant forms at first a wide, quite low and flat spread which for some years may not exceed 12 to 15 in. in height. Ultimately, it builds itself up into a domed, rather rounded mound to some 10 ft. wide and about 2½–3 ft. high in the center. The branches are stiff, held rigidly horizontal, slightly above the ground making it splendid as a single specimen with lovely dignified gray-green foliage; **'Pfitzeriana'**, this is a cultivar, originating as a single plant in the Spaeth Nurseries of Berlin, Germany, in 1899. One of the best of all the shrubby junipers, its good qualities are well known. However, in their effort to see compact-growing forms or cultivars of this particular juniper, many selections of sports and seedlings have been made, especially

branchlets. The leaves are usually acicular and ternate, under ⅜ in. long and glaucous. It should be noted that the plant commonly known in the trade as *J. excelsa stricta* is actually this variety of the Chinese Juniper. *J. excelsa* is a tender Juniper hardy only in Zone 7; **'Richeson'** —a sport of the Pfitzer Juniper, this differs from the parent plant in being dwarf, and it also has an excellent gray-blue color; plants 2½–3 ft. high are 4–5 ft. across. A 14-year-old plant is only 12 in. tall and 4 ft. across; **sargentii**—1 ft., Zone 4, Sargent Juniper, forming a mat 8-10 ft. across, this rugged juniper makes an especially fine ground cover. It is gray-green in color and native to seashore areas of northern Japan; **'San Jose'**—this lies flat on the ground, displays a mixture of juvenile and adult foliage and has been extremely popular in Calif. The foliage color is a good sage green and it has proved a most popular prostrate juniper for many years; **sylvestris**—this is apparently widely grown in the South. It is a broadly pyramidal plant with gray-green foliage. A plant 20 ft. tall may be about 8–10 ft. in dia.; **torulosa** or **'Kaizuka'**—narrow upright juniper with bright green tufted foliage proving extremely popular in Calif., but apparently not hardy in the northern U.S. It will grow over 15 ft. tall and has a unique and picturesque habit which should not be modified by pruning.

chinensis procumbens   2′   **Zone 5**   **Japanese Garden Juniper**
This is a low, creeping, though sometimes mounded plant from Japan, making one of the best of ground covers. It is not nearly as vigorous in growth as is *J. horizontalis*, but the bluish-green needles and dense habit make it a most desirable plant. Plants have been observed 20 ft. wide and 3 ft. high in the center. The variety **'Nana'** is one of the best of the smaller junipers, rounded in habit, producing branches in a shelving effect, one on top of the other. Actually, it is a small counterpart of the species and with its blue-green foliage and small, dense, rounded habit it can be outstanding. Apparently a restriction of root growth aids in keeping this form from eventually reverting to the more vigorous type of growth of the species.

communis   2′–36′   **Zone 2**   **Common Juniper**
A widely-distributed shrubby juniper found in Europe, Asia and North America in many different sizes and shapes. It frequently turns a brownish color during the winter in the northern U.S. Because the species varies so widely in habit from a ground cover to a tree 36 ft. tall, it is best to grow only the botanical varieties and cultivars, propagating these asexually to maintain the desired habit. One of the ways of identifying this species is that winter buds are usually present in the axils of the leaves. The fruits are an essential ingredient of gin and they also have been roasted by the earlier settlers and used as a substitute for coffee. The varieties are as follows: **'Compressa'**—this is a dwarf fastigiate form originating about 1855, making an excellent focal point in the small garden or rockery, seldom growing more than 2 ft. tall; **'Depressa'**—the Prostrate Juniper is one of the most commonly seen in eastern North America, forming large patches in open fields, especially where the soil is poor. It rarely grows over 4 ft. tall, having many stems ascending from the base; **'Gold Beach'**—a new flat form with young growing tips colored yellow early in the spring. Eventually this will be a very popular variety; **'Oblongo-pendula'**—this is a broadly columnar shrub or small tree with pendulous branchlets sometimes as much as 2 ft. long. It is more dense and makes a better specimen than either *J. formosana* or *J. rigida*, and can be considered one of the most graceful of all junipers; **'Stricta'** —the Irish Juniper. This came to America from

Ireland about 1836, and is more compact than the Swedish Juniper, with dark green foliage. Formerly known as *J. communis hibernica*, this is slightly more hardy than *J. communis* 'Suecica'; **'Suecica'**—a native of Scandinavia, this upright, almost columnar shrub is characterized by the nodding tips of the branches and bluish-green foliage, making it a very graceful specimen where it is hardy. It is commonly known as the Swedish Juniper, but in Boston, Mass., the foliage is susceptible to winter burning.

conferta   1′   **Zone 5**   **Shore Juniper**
A low ground cover, trailing flat along the ground, this might be used in America considerably more than it has been. It is especially adapted to planting in sandy soils at the seashore and in full sun—native to the seacoast of Japan.

davurica 'Expansa' = *J. chinensis* 'Parsonii'

deppeana   60′   **Zone 7**   **Alligator Juniper**
A native of the dry southwestern U.S., this is one of the handsomest of American junipers. It has checkered bark and silvery-white foliage but it is hardy only in the southern U.S. A variety, *ericoides*, has been named for its unusually glaucous foliage.

excelsa 'Stricta'   20′   **Zone 7**   **Spiny Greek Juniper**
This is not hardy in the central and northern United States. The plant widely grown under this name is actually *J. chinensis* 'Pyramidalis'. The true Spiny Greek Juniper is a densely compact, pyramidal, slow-growing tree, with glaucous juvenile foliage, hardy only in Zone 7. The species, *J. excelsa* from Greece grows into a narrow pyramidal tree 60 ft. tall, hardy in Zone 7.

horizontalis   12″–18″   **Zone 2**   **Creeping Juniper**
The Creeping Juniper is a popular native to the northeastern United States, and it has many cultivars. The commercial nurseryman might do well to offer cultivars rather than the species or collected plants because such plants vary greatly. Some grow with long, narrow streamers of stems while others are more compact and cover the ground better. Still others retain their green foliage color throughout the winter while some turn an excellent purplish color in the fall and winter. The slowest growing form, *J. horizontalis* **'Glomerata'**, may grow as much as 2 ft. tall and is not very spreading. Like all junipers, this species and its varieties withstand hot, dry situations, growing well under city conditions and in slightly alkaline soils.

The varieties are as follows: **'Bar Harbor'**— this is a sturdy selection of the native *J. horizontalis* growing in the vicinity of Bar Harbor, Me. It is a creeper, somewhat more compact than the species, but difficult to identify from other good *J. horizontalis* forms; **'Douglasii'**—the Waukegan Juniper is an excellent trailing variety with steel-blue foliage which turns purple in the fall. Introduced before 1855 by the Douglas Nurseries of Waukegan, Ill., where it grows about the bluffs bordering Lake Mich.; **'Emerson'**—this low shrub was found in the Black Hills of S.Dak., first called 'Black Hills Creeper' 40 or 50 years ago. It has been renamed 'Emerson' in honor of one of the men who found it. The plant is very prostrate, blue in color and holds this blue color throughout the winter. Slow in growth and able to grow in dry soils, it seldom exceeds 1 ft. in height; **'Plumosa'**—this is the Andorra Juniper, discovered and named by the Andorra Nurseries of Chestnut Hill, Phila., Pa. in 1916. It is a flat-topped variety with a low compact habit of growth, reaching a height of approximately 18 in. with the branches spreading uniformly from the center. This is the variety which has gray-green foliage during spring and summer, turning an excellent purplish green in the fall; **'Wiltonii'** —Mr. Jacob C. van Heiningen of Wilton, Conn. selected this on the Island of Vinal Haven, Me. in 1914. It is this same variety which has been offered under the much more imaginative name of *J. horizontalis* **'Blue Rug'**. The foliage is of an outstanding blue color which it retains all winter. The plant grows flat on the ground.

lucayana   50′   Zone 9   West Indies Juniper Native in the West Indies, this is a substitute for *J. virginiana* (and is similar to it) in the warmer parts of the country where the northern species will not grow. It has been considered one of the most beautiful of all the junipers.

osteosperma (*utahensis*)   **18′   Zone 7   Utah Juniper** A bushy evergreen tree, native from Wyo. to Calif., and of no particular ornamental value outside its native habitat.

recurva Coxii · 80′   Zone 7   Cox Juniper With a single erect trunk and graceful pendulous branches, this makes an excellent ornamental and apparently it is being used now to some extent in southern Calif. The foliage is a rich dark green. Native to Upper Burma.

rigida   30′   Zone 5   Needle Juniper A graceful, pyramidal tree with pendulous branchlets, native to Japan and Korea. It is not a good plant to shear, nor is it sufficiently dense for a windbreak, its sole value being its graceful appearance as a specimen. It is similar to *J. formosana* and has been perfectly hardy in Zone 5 since 1885.

sabina   15′   Zone 4   Savin Juniper A shrub native to Europe, either low and spreading or upright in habit, growing well in limestone soils as do most junipers. The foliage is not especially beautiful when the plant

reaches maturity; hence it is one which should be used while it is young. The variety **'Arcadia'** is 1 of 3 cultivars individually selected from many thousands of *J. sabina* seedlings imported by the D. Hill Nursery Company, Dundee, Ill., from a government forestry station near Leningrad, Russia, in 1933. All 3 are proving resistant to the Juniper blight which is seriously troubling most plants of *J. sabina* in the Midwest. This cultivar is a gray-green color. Plants 12–14 in. high are 4 ft. across. All in all, at first glance, this resembles a very low, flat-topped, green Pfitzer Juniper. The varieties are: **'Broadmoor'**—1 of 3 cultivars selected in 1933 from seedlings received at the D. Hill Nursery Company, Dundee, Ill., from Russia. Mr. John D. Hill reports that its "growth habit is more genuinely recumbent than prostrate," and hence that it appears to be mounded. One specimen, now 12 ft. across, is 50 in. high at the center while half way out to the tips of the branches the height is only 8 in. The foliage color is a soft gray-green and the plant is staminate; **'Tamariscifolia'**—a low, spreading juniper with light green foliage and procumbent branches ascending at the tips. It makes an excellent ground cover with very dense foliage and has been popular in landscape planting many years, called the Tamarix Savin Juniper; **'Von Ehren'** —this plant grows vigorously, a 12-year-old specimen being 3 ft. tall and 8 ft. across. Another plant near Dundee, Ill., is reported to be 15 ft. tall and 45 ft. across. It is similar to *J. sabina*, but it is much more vigorous and somewhat darker in color and, what is even more important, it is reported to be resistant to the juniper blight.

scopulorum   36′   Zone 5   Western Red-cedar Often known as the Rocky Mountain Juniper because this is its native habitat, it is a small tree widely distributed over the Rocky Mountain Area of North America from British Columbia to Calif. It survives in the hot, dry summers of that area but does not grow nearly as well in the eastern U.S. as the Eastern Red-cedar, *J. virginiana*. Over 40 forms have been selected for their blue foliage color and grown by nurserymen during the past few years. Some of the more popular varieties are: **'Chandler Blue'**, **'Hill's Silver'**, **'Moonlight'**, **'Pathfinder'**, **'Silver Beauty'** and **'Sutherland'**, but there are many others probably just as good if used near their native habitats.

squamata   3′   Zone 4   Singleseed Juniper A low shrub with bluish-green needles, compact habit, small black fruits, native to China. Better known is its more upright variety **'Meyeri'**, the needles of which are whitish on the back giving the plant a light blue appearance. However, this often does not mature gracefully in the eastern

Juniperus sabina tamariscofolia: A fine ground cover or specimen.
(*Photo by Arnold Arboretum, Jamaica Plain, Mass.*)

U.S. The branches are upright but usually its growth is such that it is not a dense pyramid of foliage but often it has an irregular shape with the central leader growing off at an angle. It is a good ornamental only while the foliage is kept in a vigorous growing condition. Poorly grown plants quickly become unsightly.

virginiana 90′ **Zone** 2 **Eastern Red-cedar** The Eastern Red-cedar is the hardiest and most popular of the tree junipers, native over nearly three-fourths of the U.S., and commonly planted everywhere. There are many excellent cultivars being offered but the species is still a good plant even though grown from seed, which of course results in considerable variation. Like other junipers, it is dioecious with staminate and pistillate flowers on separate plants. It grows rather slowly but in good soils lives a hundred years and more. Most are narrow to widely pyramidal in habit. A very few of the better varieties which should be propagated asexually are: **'Burkii'**—this cultivar is very popular because of its gray foliage and purplish winter color. Since it is a cultivar and is propagated asexually, its color is always uniform and hence it is considered better than some plants of *J. virginiana glauca*; **'Canaertii'**—originating in Belgium before 1868, this has long been popular because of its compact pyramidal habit, its dark green foliage which it maintains well throughout the winter and its profuse, bluish fruits which are always an ornamental asset; **creba**—this is the narrow, pyramidal, sometimes columnar form native in the northern part of the U.S. and it is to this variety that most garden forms are closely related. The species or typical "southern

form" is usually much broader in habit with pendant branches; **'Elegantissima'**—the Goldtip Red-cedar has been popular in the past because its branchlets are tipped with golden yellow. It is a pyramidal tree, usually not over 20 ft. tall at maturity, and turns a good bronze color in the fall; **'Filifera'**—is a broadly pyramidal tree with very slender, much-divided branchlets and gray-green foliage; **glauca**—one of the best colored forms of this species, the Silver Red-cedar is a narrow columnar tree about 15–20 ft. tall and has been recognized as a botanical variety since about 1850. The silvery-blue color of the foliage is, of course, brightest in the spring, gradually turning a silvery green in the summer; **'Globosa'**—a plant of this in the Arnold Arboretum is not over 15 ft. high, yet it is 50 years old, an excellent rounded and densely branched specimen; **'Kosteri'**—originated about 1880 in the Koster Nursery of Boskoop, Holland, makes an excellent 2-ft. high plant. A number of these growing in a group since 1916 have formed a mass of green foliage of uniform height. Actually, this cultivar stays lower in height than either *J. virginiana* 'Tripartita' (4 ft.) or *J. virginiana* 'Reptans' (3–7 ft.); **'Pendula'**—the Weeping Red-cedar has spreading branches and pendulous branchlets. A well-grown specimen does have merit, although it is more open in habit than most of the columnar forms. It has been known since 1855; **'Schottii'**—comparatively small, this dense, green, narrowly pyramidal tree is not planted so much now as formerly, possibly because its foliage may be yellow-green at certain times of the year; **'Skyrocket'**—upright, narrow; **'Tripartita'**

—the Fountain Red-cedar is dwarf and spreading, with several branches coming from the ground, and is seldom over 4 ft. tall. Although most irregular in habit, in general it reminds one of a vase-shaped *Taxus cuspidata*.

JUSSIAEA (jus-si-EE-a)

longifolia = *Ludwigia longifolia*

JUSTICIA. The so-called water-willows comprise a group of nearly 300 species of shrubs, sub-shrubs, perennials and herbs, mostly native to the tropical regions of the world. Botanists have frequently placed them in different genera, but it seems the latest workers have placed at least 16 of them in the genus *Justicia*. Sometimes they are grown in the greenhouse as ornamentals, for they have a showy terminal cluster of 2-lipped flowers. **J. secunda** is occasionally used, growing about 4–6 ft. tall with showy red flowers.

JUTE = *Corchorus capsularis*

JUTE FAMILY = Tiliaceae

K

KADSURA (kad-SOO-ra)

japonica twining vine   **12′**   **Zone 7**   **Scarlet Kadsura**

An evergreen native to Japan and Korea, the alternate leaves of this are 4 in. long and then turn a reddish green in the fall. The yellowish-white flowers are ¾ in. across and are borne from June to Sept., with the fruits being scarlet berries in clusters, 1 in. in dia., in the fall. The flowers are inconspicuous and dioecious, but the red fruits make an important display against the green foliage.

KAFIR-LILY. See CLIVIA.

KAFIR-PLUM = *Harpephyllum caffrum*

KAINITE. A fertilizer high in potash (14%), consisting of 50–60% sodium chloride and 20% magnesium sulphate. One should be careful about using too much on heavy clay soils. It might be used at 2–3 oz. per sq. yd.

KALANCHOE (ka-lan-KO-e). A group of tender succulents belonging to the Stonecrop Family, with opposite, simple or compound leaves and stalked flowers in a drooping cluster. They make good pot plants especially in the home if the atmosphere is not too dry. Small bulbils develop along the leaf margins, sometimes even forming roots, and propagation by means of these is simple indeed. They will not withstand frosts; mostly native to Africa and Asia. For culture see CACTI AND SUCCULENTS.

blossfeldiana   **1′**   **Zone 10**

A very popular succulent from Madagascar, with stalked crenate leaves, 3 in. long and 1½ in. wide, dark green with a red edge. The small scarlet flowers are borne in long-stalked clusters during the short-day period of the fall months. An excellent and popular plant especially for winter decoration indoors. Several clones have been named.

daigremontiana   **12″–18″**   **Zone 10**

Erect in habit; leaves smooth and greenish brown, thick, oblongish with gray-violet colored flowers about an inch long. Native to Madagascar.

fedtschenkoi   **12″**   **Zone 10**   **Fedtschenkoi Kalanchoe**

A bushy succulent from Madagascar with erect or creeping wiry branches and small leaves notched at the ends, colored metallic green. Flowers are brownish rose in terminal clusters.

laciniata   **1′–2′**   **Zone 10**

A plant from South Africa, erect with oval wavy-margined leaves 3–4 in. long. Flowers are fragrant, yellow, orange or pink, about ½ in. across, produced in terminal-branched clusters. If the seeds are sown in the spring, plants should be of sufficient size to bloom by Christmas.

marmorata   **1′**   **Zone 10**   **Pen-wiper**

With stout erect stems branching from the base; roundish sessile leaves about 4 in. wide or less, gray, waxy and with brown markings. Flowers white, 3 in. long. Native to Abyssinia.

pinnata   **2′–5′**   **Zone 10**   **Airplant**

Widely grown probably because its propagation is about as simple as any house plant. The succulent leaves, 2–5 in. long, are crenate and in each notch along the margin a small bulbil is produced that may grow leaves and roots while still attached to the plant. When these drop they quickly start off as young plants in the moist soil. Flowers greenish white, 1½ in. long. Native to the Tropics. Individual leaves are sometimes attached to a card and sold as Life Plants—with various claims given for the long-living properties of detached plant parts. The airplant is not particularly ornamental and does tend to grow rigidly upright with a single stem unless given some pruning, but it does create interest with the youngsters.

somaliensis = *K. marmorata*

tomentosa   **1′–3′**   **Zone 10**   **Pandaplant**

A widely cultivated and very handsome succulent with the spoon-shaped leaves produced in a terminal rosette. They are about 1½ in. long, ¾ in. wide and the leaf surface is covered with white feltlike hairs. Flowers are not always produced and are not showy.

tubiflora   **12″–18″**   **Zone 10**

Another Madagascar succulent with 4–6-in. leaves produced in whorls of 3, the whorls about an inch apart. Flowers red; young plants are produced at the tips of the pinkish leaves which are sometimes blotched purple. Roots and all make propagation extremely easy.

KALE (*Brassica oleracea* var. *acephala*). Kale has been under cultivation for many centuries and is probably the ancestor of the various *Brassica* crops under cultivation at the present time. While it is of minor importance, it ranks very high in its nutritive value, being rich in vitamin A, thiamine and ascorbic acid.

Kale is hardy to cold but does not thrive in hot weather, hence it is grown as a fall, winter and spring crop in the South, and as a fall and spring crop in the North.

Kale

Many types of Kale are grown. Their chief characteristics are that the plants do not form heads like Cabbage or edible flowers like Cauliflower or Broccoli, but rather a profusion of erect, long leaves that may be finely cut or curled or resemble those of Cabbage. Other names are Borecole, Collards and Cow Cabbage.

Varieties

Two types are commonly grown, **Scotch** and **Siberian**. The foliage of the former is grayish green and very curled and crumpled, while the latter is bluish a green and less crumpled. Common varieties are **'Dwarf Green Curled'**, **Dwarf Blue Curled Vates'**, **'Dwarf Siberian'**, and **'Tall Scotch'**.

Culture

The general culture is the same as for Cabbage (see CABBAGE) except that the seed is usually sown in drills in the garden in early Aug., 20–24 in. apart. The seedlings are thinned out to stand about 12–15 in. apart when they reach a size of 2–3 in.

In the home garden the leaves are picked from the plant, a few at a time, but for the market the whole top of the plant is cut off at one time.

Collards are chiefly grown in the South for use during the winter months. The edible portion is the rosette of green leaves resembling cabbage leaves prior to heading. Its culture is the same as for Kale.

Insect Pests

Kale and collards are subject to the same insects as Cabbage, especially aphids and cabbage worms. For control see CABBAGE.

GRANT B. SNYDER

KALMIA (KAL-mia). Evergreen members of the Heath Family requiring acid soil in order to grow well. The best species for ornamental planting is *K. latifolia*.

Propagation

Seed may be sown as soon as ripe or stored dry in airtight containers in a cool place for up to a year and then sown. However, seed of *K. latifolia* germinates better if it is stratified for 3 months at 40° F. and then sown. Hardwood cuttings of some species root well but *K. latifolia* is difficult to root. See CUTTINGS.

Insect Pests

Rhododendron lacebug and rhododendron borer attack Mountain-laurel. See RHODODENDRON. Black vine weevil grubs may eat the roots.

Disease

Leaf spot causes typical brown spots on Mountain-laurel and other plants of the Heath Family. Infected leaves do not function properly and the plants are unsightly. Spraying with fungicide #D or #F gives control. Several physiological diseases due to winter injury and unfavorable soil conditions often occur.

angustifolia   3′   Zone 2   Lambkill, Sheep-laurel
A shrub with erect, unbranching stems and opposite, lanceolate leaves, the undersurface a somewhat lighter shade of green. The flowers appear in clusters at the axils of the leaves about two-thirds of the way up the stem, which is crowned by several leafy stems. The pink flowers have a saucerlike corolla with indentations into which fit the stamens until they are disturbed, whereupon they are sprung toward the center of the flower, distributing the pollen in the process. A plant of open fields and pastures throughout the eastern half of the U.S. and southern Canada, it is a plant much disliked by farmers because of a toxic substance which is injurious to animals, especially sheep. It is not generally cultivated.

latifolia   30′   Zone 4   Mountain-laurel
The Mountain-laurel is a beautiful, flowering, evergreen shrub native over a greater part of the mountainous areas of eastern North America. The pink and white, and sometimes even red flowers are profusely produced in large clusters about mid-June. Being an ericaceous plant, it requires acid soil and the same general growing conditions as should be given rhododendrons. Almost every American gardener knows it and recognizes its value, for 30 or more years ago it was dug by the carload in the mid-South and shipped North for planting in gardens everywhere.

Kalmiopsis

polifolia 2′ Zone 2 Bog Kalmia

A bog plant with leaves ½–1½ in. long, opposite or in 3's and whitish beneath, and small rose-colored flowers in May and June, native across northern North America but only suitable for bog gardens. The leaves are poisonous if eaten by stock. The small-leaved variety **microphylla** has leaves only ¾ in. long and the plant itself is only 8 in. tall. It makes an excellent, low ground cover in boggy situations.

KALMIOPSIS (kal-me-OP-sis)

 leachiana 1′ Zone 6

Most of our native plants have been known for a long time but this one was discovered in Ore. recently and introduced in 1933. It belongs to the Heath Family. It is evergreen with leaves about ¾ in. long or less with small rosy-purple flowers in the spring, and, being ericaceous, requires acid soil, preferably moist and in a sunny location in which to grow its best.

KALOPANAX (kay-lo-PAN-ax)

 pictus 90′ Zone 4 Castor-aralia

This unusual Asiatic tree has leaves that are palmately lobed with 5–7 lobes, somewhat similar to large maple leaves, as much as 7 in. across and hence they look exotic. They have a reddish autumn color and apparently are not susceptible to serious insect or disease pests.

The white flowers are very small, borne in ball-like clusters about 1 in. in dia., several of the balls or clusters making up a large umbel 6–8 in. across. They appear in late July and, although individually they are rather uninteresting, collectively they are most interesting and unique. The tree is usually covered with these ball-like masses of small white flowers, which later develop into small black seeds, which are usually quickly eaten by the birds.

Young branches and seedlings are frequently covered with stout thorns which gradually fall off as the tree matures, but this is one of the hazards which have prevented nurserymen from growing seedlings up to the present time.

Certainly, it is a fine ornamental devoid of serious pests and is vigorous and tall growing, with a straight trunk. It should be grown more than it is at present. The variety **maximowiczii** merely has leaves more deeply lobed than those of the species.

Propagation

This seed is double dormant. If sown out-of-doors it takes 2 years to germinate. This time may be reduced by stratifying it as soon as ripe, placing it at warm temperatures in the greenhouse for 6 months, followed by 3 months at 40° F., then sowing. It is also grafted (on the species as understock) or rooted from root cuttings taken in the spring. See STRATIFICATION, GRAFTING, CUTTINGS.

KANGAROO-THORN = *Acacia armata*

KAPOK = *Ceiba pentandra*

KARO = *Pittosporum crassifolium*

KATSURA-TREE = *Cercidiphyllum japonicum*

KEEL. A projecting ridge on a surface, like the keel of a boat; also used in botanical description to describe one of the parts of the flowers of the Pea Family. The flower consists of a standard or large petal at the top, wings or the 2 lateral parts or petals, and a keel which is the 2 anterior united petals.

KELTHANE. An insecticide, which see.

KENAF = *Hibiscus cannabinus*

KENILWORTH-IVY = *Cymbalaria muralis*

KERRIA (KERR-ria)

 japonica 4′–6′ Zone 4 Kerria

Years ago, this was a popular garden plant because of its single yellow flowers, about 1½ in. across, in mid-May and its green twigs all winter. Native in central and western China, it is superseded now by its double-flowered variety **'Pleniflora'**, with bright yellow flowers which have many petals produced in a dense, round, ball-like mass. This one is called Globe Flower and the flowers remain effective considerably longer than do those of the single-flowered species. Also, there are so many produced that the thin branches are weighted down in a gracefully arching manner which lends additional beauty to the plant.

Propagation

Softwood and hardwood cuttings root very easily. Mature plants are easily divided with a sharp spade in the spring before growth starts. See CUTTINGS.

Insect Pests

Japanese beetle feeds on the leaves. See JAPANESE BEETLE.

Diseases

Leaf and twig blight causes red spots on the leaves and brown cankers on the stem which may crack the bark. Spraying with fungicide #D of #F when leaves are half grown and repeated in 7–10 days is advised.

KETELEERIA (ket-el-EE-ria)

 fortunei 90′ Zone 7 Fortune Keteleeria

This evergreen tree from southeastern China has needlelike foliage, is pyramidal while young but flat-topped like *Cedrus libani* when mature. It will grow in a somewhat drier situation than the firs; the needles are ridged on both sides and are ¾–1¼ in. long and the cones are 3–7 in. long.

KEY or KEY FRUIT. A winged-fruit, like in the maples; samara.

KHAT = *Catha edulis*

KIDNEYWORT = *Baccharis pilularis*

KIGELIA (ky-GEE-lia)
pinnata   30′   Zone 10   Sausage-tree
Not often planted but always remembered when it has been seen in fruit. These are long sausage-shaped objects, often 2 ft. long and 5 in. wide, especially if they have been cross-fertilized. These hang on long stems but have little value. Leaves are deciduous, compound with each leaflet being about 5 in. long. The dark red, ill-smelling flowers, 5 in. wide, open at night and fall in the morning. There is a 10-day period during the winter when the tree is leafless. It has a wide-spreading, rounded habit. Native to West Africa. Propagation by seeds.

KINGFISHER-DAISY = *Felicia bergeriana*

KINNIKINNICK = *Arctostaphylos uva-ursi*

KIRENGESHOMA (ky-reng-esh-O-ma)
palmata   4′   Zone 5
Rarely grown in America, native to Japan, this perennial herb has nearly orbicular leaves often 7–10 palmately lobed, up to 4 in. wide; yellow, bell-shaped, nodding flowers up to 1½ in. long. Best propagated by division. Difficult to find in American nurseries.

KITCHEN GARDEN. See VEGETABLE GARDEN.

KIWI = *Actinidia chinensis*

KLEINIA = *Senecio articulatus*

KNAWEL = *Scleranthus annuus.*

KNEE. An abrupt bend in a stem or tree trunk; an outgrowth of some tree roots, like the knees of a Cypress.

KNIPHOFIA (ny-FO-fia). Popular garden plants from Africa, the hybrids seem to be slightly more hardy than the species. They have broad grasslike leaves up to 3 ft. long, forming a tuft of foliage from the center of which is produced the very conspicuous spike of red or yellow flowers giving rise to the name Red Hot Poker. If the leaves are left on the plant over winter, or tied up in a bunch together, this helps protect the plants over winter, especially if hay or straw or leaves are mounded over the plants. They can also be dug and stored in moist sand in a cool cellar over winter.

They are best planted in spring and the roots must not be planted more than 2–3 in. deep and, once established, they should not be disturbed. Old plants can be lifted and divided in the spring. Seedlings are very slow growing.
caulescens   1′   Zone 7
With leaves up to 3 in. wide and 3 ft. long; flowers red or yellow in 6-in. spikes.
galpinii   2′   Zone 7   Galpin Torch-lily
Leaves only 1½ in. wide; flowers reddish orange in racemes only 3 in. long. This yields excellent

cut flowers from July until frost but is tender in the North. Valued because of its low size. Other dwarf species, often difficult to find in America, are **K. rufa**, **K. tuckii**, **K. nelsonii** and **K. macowanii**. All are about 1 or 2 ft. tall. Some tend to bloom as early as May.
uvaria   4′   Zone 6   Common Torch-lily,
                                                    Pokerplant
With orange-red flowers, densely massed around the end of the flowering stalk during late summer and autumn, the raceme of flowers being 6–10 in. long, the top flowers scarlet, the lower ones yellow. Native to South Africa. Some of the best cultivars or hybrids are: **'White Fairy'**—2-ft. cream-colored flower spikes during June and July; **'Coral Seas'**—coral-red and deep rose flowers in June and July; **'Primrose Beauty'**—primrose-yellow flowers in early summer; **'Springtime'**—flowers red and pale yellow on 3-ft. stalks; **'Summer Sunshine'**—flame-red flowers on 3-ft. stems in midsummer.

KNOT GARDEN. A century or two ago, gardens

Knot garden

of intricate design were known as knot gardens, and the art was practiced especially with herb gardens. Little is left of them today and seldom are they planted. The simple reason is that they are hard to keep in proper condition, always growing too fast, in need of pruning or fertilizer. In the past century, especially in Europe and to some extent America, labor was cheap and such gardens were extremely popular.

KNOTWEED. See POLYGONUM.

KOATREE = *Acacia koa*

KOCHIA (KO-kia, also KO-shia)
scoparia   5′   annual   Summer-cypress
A widespread weed, native to Eurasia, but now commonly naturalized in the middle-western states. The alternate leaves are linear, 2 in. long and are really ornamental, being red, green or yellow during the growing season and purple-red in the fall. Flowers are greenish and inconspicuous. The most popular form for gardens is var.

trichophila, which is densely rounded in habit. In the South it is said to cause hay fever.

KOELREUTERIA (kol-roo-TEE-ria). Medium-sized, alternate-leaved trees with compound leaves, these are valued for their pyramidal spikes of small yellow flowers early in the summer and their conspicuous bladderlike pods in the late summer. They make good ornamental trees and in some cases good street trees.

Propagation

The seed can be processed as soon as ripe or stored dry in airtight containers in a cool place for up to a year and then processed. The seed coat should be perforated with a file or by an hour's soaking in concentrated sulfuric acid, then thoroughly washed and sown. Some lots respond well if they are stratified at 40° F. for 3 months before sowing. Budding and grafting has been accomplished using the species as understocks. Root cuttings also prove successful. See GRAFTING, BUDDING, ROOT CUTTINGS.

elegans (*formosana*)   **20′–40′**   **Zone 9**   **Chinese Flame-tree**
Similar in foliage and flowers to *K. paniculata* except the leaves are twice pinnately compound. The common name comes from the fact that the fruits of this Chinese tree are red and orange during the late summer and fall. It has no serious pests, can grow in many soils and is proving popular in southern Calif.

paniculata   **30′**   **Zone 5**   **Golden-rain-tree**
Blooming in mid-July, this tree from China, Korea and Japan is important for its large pyramidal clusters of small yellow flowers in early summer. The greenish fruit pods which appear quickly after the flowers also add to the display throughout the summer months. The wood is weak and the alternate compound leaves have no autumn color. Hence, it is primarily for summer display, although it does grow well in a wide range of soils. The variety **'Fastigiata'** is a narrow columnar form. The Chinese species (**K. bipinnata**) is only used in southern Calif. and differs in that its leaves are twice and sometimes thrice pinnately compound, with each leaflet 1¾–4 in. long.

KOHLRABI (*Brassica oleracea gongylodes*). This is a minor member of the Cabbage Family, the erect stem of which is swollen just above the ground level. The swollen part, while still juicy and tender, has a very fine, relatively mild flavor. As it matures the tissues of the swollen area become hard, bitter and woody and of no edible value.

Culture

The culture is exactly the same as for early Cabbage (see CABBAGE), except that Kohlrabi

Kohlrabi

is set 4 in. in the row and the rows spaced 15–18 in. apart. The most popular varieties are **'Grand Duke Hybrid'**, **'White Vienna'**, **'Purple Vienna'** and **'Earliest Erfurt'**. This vegetable is very popular in Europe.

Whether the crop is grown early or late it is important to secure rapid growth and to cut the thickened stems before they become hard and woody, usually when about 2 in. in dia.

Pests

While Kohlrabi is subject to the same pests as Cabbage, it is seldom that any are very serious.

GRANT B. SNYDER

KOLKWITZIA (kolk-WITZ-ia)
  amabilis   **10′**   **Zone 4**   **Beautybush**
Ernest H. Wilson was responsible for bringing this plant back from China in 1901, but it was not widely grown in this country until 1922 when Jackson and Perkins of Newark, N.Y., began to propagate it by the thousands. Now, it is used almost too much. The pale pink flowers appear in early June, shortly followed by brown, hairy seeds that remain in irregular clusters far into the winter. The autumn color of the foliage is reddish. The leaves are opposite, about 1–3 in. long, and the brown bark exfoliates in long paperlike strips. There is a variety named **rosea** which is supposed to have deeper pink flowers. Far too many plants of this species are seen producing flowers of a mediocre washed-out pink. Because of this, growing plants from seed is not advised, but rather they should be propagated asexually from good clones with flowers of a truly deep pink color. Seed can be sown as soon as ripe, or

stored dry in airtight containers in a cool place for up to a year, then sown. Special pink-flowering clones are propagated by softwood cuttings, which see.

KUDZU-VINE = *Pueraria lobata*

KUMQUAT. See FORTUNELLA.

KUPUKATREE = *Griselinia littoralis*

L

LABELS. These are essential in every garden. They should certainly be legible and as permanent as possible. Those who are responsible for labeling plants in public parks, arboretums and botanic gardens are unfortunately up against the serious problem of vandalism. The best series of articles that has ever been written on labeling plants in public places appeared in the April–July 1965 Quarterly Newsletter of the American Association of Botanical Gardens and Arboretums. It is a combination of many articles written by men who are responsible for keeping the plants labeled in public places. For park superintendents interested, a copy of this publication will be found in the library of each of the major arboretums or botanical gardens in the U.S. and Canada. Most of the available information on plant labeling as practiced at present, will be found in this publication.

Most gardeners are familiar with the temporary wooden pot labels that are so easily broken off or lost once they are placed by plants in the garden. Horticultural periodicals are full of advertisements recommending labels of one form or another. The most permanent are the best and usually the cheapest in the long run. A rare and expensive plant, marked with a temporary label that is soon missing, frequently remains unidentified in the garden, always an ever-present reminder of inadequate labeling methods.

The best labels are those of zinc or aluminum on which the name of the plant can be embossed (with a little hand machine) or on which the name can be written with a sharp pointed tool. Such labels can be attached to wire stakes of various sorts. They can be made as soon as the seed is sown in pots, and attached to the pot by a metal clip. Later, when the plants are placed in the garden, the same label is removed from the pot clip and attached to a sturdy wire stake with a piece of strong copper wire.

There are also metal labels available, mostly of aluminum, that can be written on with a hard lead pencil. This is often good enough to remain legible for several years but unless such handwritten labels are inspected and replaced every few years, they have a way of eventually becoming illegible. Consequently, seriously consider your needs for garden lablels, the probabilities of periodically replenishing them, and look into the embossed type aluminum label before cluttering the garden with a less expensive but nondescript "temporary" label.

LABIATAE = The Mint Family

LABIATE. Usually this means lipped. Most plants with labiate flowers belong to the *Labiatae* or Mint Family.

LABRADOR-TEA = *Ledum groenlandicum*

x LABURNOCYTISUS (la-BURN-o-cy-tisus)
    adamii   **21′**   **Zone 6**
One of the few graft chimeras or graft hybrids produced by budding *Cytisus purpureus* on *Laburnum anagyroides*. The plant, often grown in Ireland, produces leaves, flowers and fruits like *Cytisus purpureus* on some branches and like those of *Laburnum anagyroides* on others. Still others are produced that are obviously neither one nor the other. Most interesting is the fact that seeds from the *Cytisus*-type flowers produce plants identical with *C. purpureus*, while seeds from *Laburnum*-type flowers produce plants identical with *L. anagyroides*. Seeds from the third type of flowers, rarely produced, are said to produce plants like *L. anagyroides*. This hybrid is of little ornamental value.

Propagation

Since this is a generic hybrid it is only propagated by budding or grafting on to *L. anagyroides* understock. See GRAFTING, BUDDING.

LABURNUM (lab-URN-um). This genus of small trees belongs to the Pea Family. The three species concerned are all native to Europe, have alternate compound leaves (3 leaflets) and long wisterialike clusters of yellow pealike flowers in the spring. The fruits are merely small pea pods; the foliage has no autumn color. Hence they have ornamental interest only during the 2-week period they are in flower. Unfortunately, *L. anagyroides* is more easily available in the trade, but it is less hardy and has shorter flower racemes than *L. alpinum* or *L. watereri*. *L. alpinum* can be distinguished because its branches, leaves and pods are glabrous or nearly so, while those of *L. anagyroides* are slightly pubescent.

Propagation

Seeds may be processed as soon as ripe or stored dry, in airtight containers in a cool place for up to a year and then processed. Soak the seed in hot water (190° F.) overnight and then sow. Varieties may be grafted or budded on *L. anagyroides* as an understock. Softwood and hardwood cuttings can be rooted. See SEEDS, GRAFTING, etc.

alpinum   30′   **Zone 4**   **Scotch Laburnum**
A small, upright tree, native in the mountains of southern Europe, with yellow, pealike flowers in drooping racemes up to 16 in. long. The alternate leaves are compound with 3 leaflets, practically glabrous, and the fruit is merely a pea pod. It has no autumn color and no ornamental interest any time of year except mid-May when the flowers are in bloom.

anagyroides   21′   **Zone 5**   **Golden-chain**
Another European tree, similar to *L. alpinum* except it is less hardy, lower in mature height, has flower clusters only up to 12 in. long, and the branches, pods and leaves are slightly pubescent. There are many varieties of this in European gardens, none of which are outstanding except possibly the variety 'Aureum' with yellow leaves. This species was long known under the name of *L. vulgare*, now a synonym.

x watereri   30′   **Zone 5**   **Waterer Laburnum**
This is a hybrid of *L. alpinum* and *L. anagyroides*, and is usually considered superior to both parents in flower. It is more dense in habit than *L. alpinum* and the flowers are larger and a deeper yellow color. Like the others, it is a member of the Pea Family, with yellow pealike flowers in long pendulous clusters during mid-May, alternate, compound, 3 foliate leaves, and little else to recommend it at other times of year when it is not in bloom.

LACEFLOWER, SKYBLUE = *Trachymene corulea*

LACHENALIA (lak-en-AY-lia). Bulbous herbaceous plants from South Africa and members of the Lily Family valued for their bright colored flower spikes, about 8–12 in. tall. Planted out-of-doors only in mild climates like that of southern Calif. but used in the North as greenhouse pot plants where they will bloom in Feb. and March if potted up in Aug.–Sept. and kept about 45°–55° F. After flowering, water is gradually withheld and the soil left dry. In Aug. the bulbs are removed and separated—propagation is by division of offsets—and replanted for another blooming season.

aloides   1′   **Zone 9**   **Tricolor Cape-cowslip**
With green, red and yellow bell-like flowers, each about 1 in. long, drooping, with many to an upright spike. Leaves are straplike, about 1 in. wide. There are several varieties, 'Nelsonii' having bright yellow flowers tinged green.

bulbiferum   1′   **Zone 9**   **Nodding Cape-cowslip**
Straplike leaves 2 in. wide and flowers 1½ in. long, drooping, many on a single spike, yellow

and red and often red-purple tipped. The variety **superba** is an improved form. There are also some new hybrids like 'Bullfinch' with yellow, green and red flowers; 'Cowslip' with yellow flowers and 'Goldfinch' with red and yellow flowers. If these can be obtained, they are the ones to grow because of the larger flowers.

orchioides   1′   **Zone 9**   **Orchid Cape-cowslip**
Straplike leaves 1 in. wide and flowers only ⅓ in. long, many on upright spikes, white, red, yellow or tinged blue.

LACHNANTHES (lak-NAN-thees)
carolina (*L. tinctoria*)   2½′   **Zone 4**   **Red-root**
A herb with red roots, native from Mass. to Fla. in swamps and marshes. The basal leaves are narrowly lanceolate; flowers are yellowish woolly panicles to 5 in. across. Hogs are frequently poisoned by eating the plants.

tinctoria = *L. carolina*

LACINIATE. Cut into deep narrow lobes.

LACQUER-TREE, JAPANESE = *Rhus verniciflua*

LACTUCA (lak-TEW-ka). A milky-juiced group of herbaceous plants of the Composite Family, the numerous species mostly weedy and of no garden interest outside of *L. sativa*, the one from which lettuce is a much-modified variety.

pulchella   2′–3′   **Zone 5**   **Chicory Lettuce**
A perennial herb with stout stems covered with a soft down. The upper leaves are lanceolate and entire, the lower leaves are longer and pinnately lobed. The blue flower heads are borne in clusters at the top of the stem and consist wholly of toothed ray flowers. It is a plant of the Plains states flowering from July to Sept.

sativa   3′–4′   **annual**   **Lettuce**
This is a group of plants known only in cultivation, probably originating centuries ago in either Europe or Asia. The young leaves are edible and of course only 6–10 in. tall; it is the flower stalk which grows 3–4 ft. high and bears the small light yellow flowers. For the many strains of modern lettuce and their culture see LETTUCE.

serriola (*scariola*)   5′   **annual**   **Prickly Lettuce**
Sometimes a biennial weed, with prickly alternate leaves shaped like those of the Dandelion with a much-branched flowering spike, each branch holding 5–12 yellowish flowers during July and Aug., each head less than ⅓ in. across. Native to Europe but widely naturalized as a garden weed in the northern states and southern Canada. This is the most common of several similar species. *L. canadensis* is a biennial native species seen sometimes as a weed, but its leaves are smooth, without prickles and there are 15–20 florets in each head.

LADIES'-TRESSES = *Spiranthes cernua*

LADYBELL. See ADENOPHORA.

LADY-OF-THE-NIGHT = *Brunfelsia americana*

LADY'S-MANTLE, COMMON = *Alchemilla vulgaris*

LADY'S-SLIPPER. See CYPRIPEDIUM.

LADY'S-THUMB. See POLYGONUM.

LAELIA (LEE-lia). This genus of tropical American epiphytic orchids contains about 30 species, a few of which are grown by orchid specialists. They have pseudobulbs and few to several flowers on a long stalk. For greenhouse culture and propagation see ORCHID.

anceps   9″   Zone 10
Probably the most popular and usually available from the florist with 2–5 flowers on a stalk which can be 2–3 ft. long, each flower 3–4 in. across, colored lilac-rose to rose. A variable species native to Mexico and many forms have been named. There are some white-flowered forms also.

crispa   10″   Zone 10
With fragrant white flowers flushed pale purple, 4–9 flowers on a raceme and each flower 4–6 in. across, produced during July and Aug. Pseudobulbs are 7–10 in. long with the leaves 9–12 in. long. Native to Brazil.

grandis   1′   Zone 10
With 3–5-flowered racemes of brownish-yellow flowers 4–7 in. across. These have a tinge of rose-purple which makes them interesting, from May to July. There is usually only 1 leaf from each pseudobulb. Native to Brazil.

LAEVIGATE. Smooth, as if polished.

LAGENARIA (laj-en-AY-ria)
siceraria   vine   annual   Calabash Gourd
This is a monoecious annual, a fast-growing sprawling vine, native to the Old World Tropics. Dipper, calabash, bottle and other kinds of gourds are common members of this species All are easily grown from seed, but the growing season should be a long one in order for the fruits to have ample time to mature. These might well be started indoors in the northern U.S. to give them sufficient time to mature after being set out in the garden. The leaves are cordate-ovate, usually not lobed; flowers are white and funnel shaped; and they come with fruits of many sizes and shapes from 3 in. to 3 ft. For culture see GOURDS.

LAGERSTROEMIA (lay-ger-STREEM-ia)
indica   21′   Zone 7   Crape-myrtle
Hardy as far north as Baltimore, Md., the Crape-myrtle is an inhabitant of China and other tropical and subtropical countries. Its crinkled flowers, up to 1½ in. across, are colored white, pink, red, lavender and bluish and are borne in clusters 4–9 in. long and appear in the summer on the current year's growth. Because

of this it can be pruned heavily in the early spring to make the plants more compact and still they can be expected to produce flowers. The privetlike leaves and the exfoliating bark are most interesting. It is a popular plant, with nearly 25 varieties being offered by nurserymen, and should always be dug with a ball of soil about the roots. Many of the plants are sold merely by listing the color of the flowers and not by the use of true varietal names. Propagated by seeds or softwood cuttings.

speciosa   60′   Zone 10   Queen Crape-myrtle
Even though this is native to the Tropics (India) the 12 in. thick, leathery leaves fall off late in the winter. The lavender flowers may vary in color to pink; each flower is about 2 in. across, with 6 or more frilled petals and a center filled with yellow stamens. These flowers are produced on large, sometimes branched, spikes. Planted in Fla., Calif. and Hawaii. Propagation by cuttings or from sprouts of cut roots.

LAGUNARIA (lag-yew-NAY-ria)
patersonii   50′   Zone 9   Paterson Sugar-plum Tree
This evergreen tree from Australia is especially useful for planting in seaside gardens and also for use as a street tree because of its shapely habit and regularly spaced branches. The pale pink flowers are 2½ in. across, appear in May and June and are like those of Hibiscus. The leaves are 3–4 in. long.

LAGURUS (lag-YEW-rus)
ovatus   1′   annual   Hare's-tail Grass
A grass native to the Mediterranean Region, sometimes grown as an ornamental in America because of its dense woolly spikelets that are 2 in. long with awns ½ in. long. It can be featured as a border plant and if cut and dried, used in winter arrangements. Sow the seed outdoors in the spring, where the plants are to grow.

LAMARCKIA (lam-ARK-ia)
aurea   1′   annual   Golden-top Grass
This is a tufted grass from the region of the Mediterranean Sea, supposedly naturalized in Calif. and valued for its ornamental fruiting spikes that are 4 in. long and very yellow.

LAMBKILL = *Kalmia angustifolia*

LAMB'S-EARS = *Stachys byzantina*

LAMB'S-QUARTERS = *Chenopodium album*

LAMIASTRUM
galeobdolon (*Lamium galeobdolon*)   **12″–18″ Zone 4 Golden Dead Nettle, Yellow Archangel**
A perennial with yellow flowers about ¾ in. long in dense clusters in the leaf axils in the summer. The leaves are about 1½ in. long. It is a weedy, sprawling plant sometimes used as a ground cover.

LAMIUM (LAY-mium). These weedy herbs, occasionally grown in gardens, are native to Europe but have escaped cultivation in North America. They have opposite leaves, a square stem and are sometimes used in rock gardens because they bloom from April to late Aug. They grow better in partial shade than in the full sun. Easily propagated by division in spring.

amplexicaule   16″   annual   Henbit Dead Nettle

Sometimes a biennial weed with prostrate stems, small, slightly lobed-to-rounded, opposite leaves about ¾ in. wide, stalked near the base but sessile near the end of the shoots. The small flowers, appearing during April to June and again in Sept., are in axillary whorls, pink to purple, with 2 upper lips and 1 lobed lower lip about ½ in. long. A common weed on both east and west coasts of North America, native to

galeobdolon = *Lamiastrum galeobdolon* Europe.

maculatum   6″–8″   Zones 2–3   Spotted Dead Nettle

Though rather weedy and unkempt in appearance, the small, crinkled, oval-to-cordate leaves which are dark green splotched with silvery white and the 2-in.-long terminal heads of small, labiate, lavender flowers, blooming throughout the summer, make this species worth planting. If pruned back so that it does not bloom, the plant is an attractive background for taller and more colorful plants. The variety **alba** has leaves of a lighter green and white flowers. Native to Europe. Propagated by division and by seed.

purpureum   decumbent   annual   Purple Dead Nettle

A decumbent weed somewhat similar to *L. amplexicaule* except that all of its leaves have petioles, but the upper leaves of *L. amplexicaule* are sessile. Its flowers are light purple, not reddish purple. Native to Europe and Asia but naturalized in eastern North America. The 4-angled stems are about 1½ ft. long.

LANCEOLATE. Lance-shaped, about 4 times long as broad and broadest below or about the middle.

LANDSCAPE ARCHITECT. A professionally trained person with a college degree in landscape architecture, who designs and supervises the planting of estates, gardens and parks, both public and private. He has a knowledge of and training in engineering, construction, design and plant materials, sufficient to use knowledge from each field in the bringing together and designing of all the many things that are necessary in garden construction and the layout of walks, drives, and other structures used in the molding of outdoor areas for man's use. Several states require that a landscape architect can practice in the state only by state license.

A landscape gardener is not necessarily a professional landscape architect. Some are well versed either by training or experience in all the phases of planning, design and planting that go to make a good garden. Several state universities have courses in which such individuals are extremely well trained, short of a degree in landscape architecture. Sometimes these individuals work for nurserymen in planning gardens, sometimes they are in business for themselves and can prove most helpful in aiding those who need assistance in planning their gardens. However, it is essential to be able to separate the man who merely mows lawns for a living and the well-trained individual who can be relied upon for sound advice.

LANTANA (lan-TAN-a)

camara   4′–10′   Zone 8   Common Lantana

This is the small woody shrub so popular in the North as a greenhouse plant, and used out-of-doors in the South, sometimes as a ground cover. The opposite evergreen leaves, which are ill-smelling when crushed, are 2–6 in. long and rough to the touch. The clusters of red and yellow flowers are about 1–2 in. across, the individual flowers being ⅛ in. wide, followed by small blue-black fruits ½ in. across. In Hawaii this is an escaped weed along the roadsides.

Recommended for seashore gardens. Propagated by seed or cuttings for the named varieties.

Insect Pests

Greenhouse orthezia, a small sucking insect resembling a mealybug but having lone tube-like appendages at the rear, is a specific pest on Lantana and Coleus. Spraying with insecticide #15 is advised. Mealybugs are also injurious and controlled as above.

montevidensis (*L. sellowiana*)   **2′   Zone 10   Trailing Lantana**

A woody trailing shrub or weak vine from South America, often used as a ground cover, with clusters of small, rosy-pink flowers about 1 in. across, each flower with 4 petals and a long tube. These are in evidence most of the year. It should be planted in the full sun. The opposite evergreen leaves are 1 in. long, rough and have prominent veins and a pungent odor when crushed. Propagated by cuttings and layers.

LANUGINOSE, LANUGINOUS. Woolly or cottony, with long and interwoven hairs.

LAPAGERIA (lap-aj-ER-ria)

rosea   vine   Zone 10   Red Chile-bells

A beautiful greenhouse vine because of its red bell-shaped flowers that are 4 in. long and borne either singly or several together during the summer. The alternate leathery leaves are about 3 in. long and dark green, usually pendulous. The white-flowered variety **albiflora** is rare, but beautiful in contrast with the species.

LAPIDARIA (lap-i-DAR-ia)
    margaretae   **3″**   **Zone 10**
Related to *Mesembryanthemum*, this is a plant from South Africa for small dish gardens. There are about 3 pairs of thick stubby leaves, ¾ in. long and 1 in. wide, colored white, yellowish or brownish and tinged with rose. The bright yellow flowers, 2 in. across, appear in the fall.

LARCH. See LARIX.

LARCH, GOLDEN = *Pseudolarix amabilis*

LARDIZABALACEAE = The Akebia Family

LARIX (LAY-rix). The larches are trees for the northern states only. There are about 10 species in the north temperate regions of the world, mostly found growing in the mountains, and 3 are natives of the U.S. Most of these trees are noted for their pyramidal habit, interesting and light coniferous (though deciduous) foliage and their beautiful yellow autumn color. They are not widely popular trees in landscape planting. It seems strange that in American nurseries the European and Japanese larches are the most popular, not the American. This is probably because the American Larch (*L. laricina*) usually grows in moist to wet soils, while the others do well in a well-drained soil. Be that as it may, there are 2 varieties with pendulous branches and if the larches must be grown, these pendulously branched types certainly should be given prime consideration. All have beautiful yellow autumn color.

There is a rather serious canker disease affecting these trees, especially if they are planted close together and the spring weather is moist. Control is fairly difficult. The Japanese Larch is fairly resistant to this, but the European and American larches are very susceptible.

The larch casebearer is a serious pest in many sections. This small caterpillar appears in early May and eventually eats itself into the needles, causing them to turn brown for the remainder of the season. If the trees are infested and spraying is omitted, they will be unsightly for the season until autumn when the leaves finally drop. The False Larch (*Pseudolarix amabilis*) appears to be most resistant to both this pest and the larch canker—excellent reasons why it should be grown more than it is.

It is rather difficult to distinguish these trees from the foliage alone, but the cones are easily distinguishable. Although several have slightly pendulous branchlets, the best in this respect are *L. decidua* 'Pendula', *L. decidua polonica* and *L. griffithii*, these last 2 probably

not being used as ornamentals at present anywhere in the U.S.

Consequently, the larches are a group of trees for ornamental planting only from about Pa. northward. They are at their best in the very early spring when their fresh green needles start to appear and again in the fall when they turn a brilliant yellow. Aside from their pendulously branched varieties, they have little to offer in the winter after the leaves have fallen. Several are fast-growing but, for the planting with plenty of space, the Golden Larch is undoubtedly the best of them all as an interesting ornamental specimen.

Propagation

Seed can be stratified as soon as ripe or stored in airtight containers in a cool place for up to a year and then stratified, placed for 3 months at 40° F. and then sown. Varieties are grafted on their respective species. Softwood cuttings prove difficult to root. See STRATIFICATION, GRAFTING.

Insect Pests

Larch casebearer is a miner in the needles in summer, but in fall it cuts off ½ of a needle and makes an overwintering case in the remaining part. Heavy infestations are very destructive. Dormant sprays with fungicide #U followed by applications of insecticide #9 or #15 when the needles are developing is suggested. Larch sawfly worms strip the needles after first cutting small notches in the side. The adults are black 4-winged flies about ½ in. in length. Spraying with insecticide #9 or #15 will prevent defoliation. Woolly larch aphid is controlled by sprays of insecticide #15.

Diseases

Larch branch canker is indicated by drops of resin about swollen bark lesions. Cutting and burning the infected bark is suggested. Japanese Larch is resistant and should be planted as ornamental trees. Rust may develop on the needles. Use fungicide #D or #F. Needle cast, causing brown needles in summer which hang over winter, is unsightly. Regular spraying with fungicide #U or #V on new growth is suggested.

decidua   **105′**   **Zone 2**   **European Larch**
Young trees are pyramidal, older trees have widespreading branches. The difference between this and the varieties is sometimes not very marked. However, in Europe where this species is native it is susceptible to serious outbreaks of larch canker, especially when the trees are crowded together. The cones of this larch are about 1-1½ in. long. The variety 'Pendula' has

pendulous branches, but it has been noted that for some reason this is rarely seen as a good tree. Trees in the Arnold Arboretum are narrowly upright, 50 ft. tall and 27 ft. in dia., with gracefully pendulous branchlets 2–3 ft. long. The variety **polonica** has drooping main branches and branchlets, while those main branches of *L. decidua* 'Pendula' are horizontal, the ends pendulous. **'Fastigiata'** is columnar like the Lombardy Poplar.

x eurolepis   80′   Zone 4   Dunkeld Larch
A natural hybrid (*L. leptolepis* x *L. decidua*) originating about 1900 in England, this plant varies considerably when grown from seed and not all the seedlings have good form and foliage. It would seem that if this species is to be grown, the plants should be propagated from a well-formed cultivar. It is vigorous and might be used for growing under forest conditions. One of the trees in the Arnold Arboretum is 40 ft. tall, 40 ft. wide, with a broadly pyramidal outline and with denser foliage than that of *L. leptolepis*.

kaempferi (*L. leptolepis*) **90′ Zone 4 Japanese Larch**
This Japanese species is the second most popular larch in America and is a very widespreading tree. It is much less susceptible to the larch canker than is *L. decidua*, has cones 1 in. long and leaves that are $1\frac{1}{2}$–$1\frac{5}{8}$ in. long, slightly longer than most others of this genus. Still they are not so handsome as are those of the *Pseudolarix amabilis*.

laricina   60′   Zone 1   American Larch
Not many trees have the hardiness of this one which is native to the entire breadth of northern Canada from coast to coast and extends southward to Minn. and Ill. Frequently seen in New England, especially in marshy soils, it is not much planted as an ornamental in place of exotic larches, which are better. Like the others, it has needlelike, deciduous leaves and its fruits are small cones. The leaves turn yellow in the fall. Often termed Tamarack or Hackmatack.

LARKSPUR. See DELPHINIUM, CONSOLIDA.

LARREA (LAR-re-a)
tridentata   10′   Zone 8   Creosotebush
An evergreen balsam-scented shrub, leaves opposite and resinous, the small leaflets only $\frac{1}{3}$ in. long and with 4–5 nerves; the flowers $\frac{1}{4}$ in. long, yellow, single and terminal; the fruits rounded and white-tomentose capsules. Native to Mexico and Tex. Its only value is for planting in dry or desert soils.

LARVA. The biological name for the young of insects which pass through a complete change in their life history. It is the growing or eating stage and therefore the most destructive in most insects. The larvae of flies are often called maggots, of beetles are called grubs, of moths

and sawflies are called worms and of butterflies are called caterpillars or worms. See INSECT PESTS.

LATEX. The milky juice of such plants as the Milkweed.

LATHYRUS (LATHI-i-rus). A genus of annual or perennial herbs of the Pea Family growing in the North Temperate Zone. Many have tendrils and winged stems. All have alternate, compound leaves and irregular flowers typical of the Pea Family. Most have tendrils except *L. vernus* and *L. splendens*. The flowers are born in a terminal cluster of 3–10. Fruits are borne in pods. Propagation is by seed. Not to be confused with the pea of the vegetable garden, *Pisum sativum*.

grandiflorus   6′   Zone 5   Everlasting Pea
A climbing perennial with large rose-purple flowers 2 or 3 together. Southern Europe.

japonicus (*maritimus*)   **vine   Zone 4   Maritime Pea**
Growing in the North Temperate Zone, this perennial plant is native to Japan as well as to Alaska, Canada and the northern U.S. as far as N.J. and the area around the Great Lakes. The oval, entire leaflets generally number 6–12 and the purplish-blue flowers open throughout the summer. It is often found along the New England beaches, where it withstands the sun, wind and salt spray. Difficult to propagate, seeds should be sown in moist sand where the plant is to grow.

latifolius   9′   Zone 3   Perennial Pea Vine
A perennial climber with winged stems and large, rose-colored flowers about $1\frac{1}{2}$ in. wide with several to many on a single stalk. Native to southern Europe.

littoralis   decumbent   Zone 8   Beach Pea
A decumbent seashore plant of the West Coast area, bearing purple flowers which have white wings, 2–6 in a stalk. Of little value elsewhere except throughout its native habitat.

odoratus   vine   annual   Sweet Pea
This is an old-fashioned garden favorite, probably more popular with gardeners 50 years ago than it is now. The alternate, compound leaves have oval leaflets and the very fragrant flowers are borne usually 1–4 on a stem. Native to Italy. There have been hundreds of varieties introduced with flowers all the colors of the rainbow.

Types

Spencers. These have been bred over the years for large flowers with ruffled petals. As the varieties introduced became larger, it seemed that they became more difficult to grow in the outdoor garden. There are varieties still available termed **'Giants'** or **'Giant Ruffled'**.

Cuthbertson. These have been bred for earlier blooming and, although they have smaller flowers, they seem to be more resistant to heat. Certainly they are earlier blooming and will continue sometimes into Aug. in the vicinity of New York City.

Multiflora. Bred for a larger number of flowers per stem—5 and 6, but of course the flowers are smaller than those of the Spencers.

Burpee's Giant Heat Resistant. These are among the most recent additions to the Sweet Pea clan. They have been bred for earliness of flower, resistance to summer heat and usually they bloom longer than the others. Some have petals slightly ruffled.

Dwarf. These are only about 8 in. tall, on rather prostrate stems, but have been used as pot plants or in window boxes.

The order in which they bloom is roughly— Cuthbertson, Multiflora, Burpee's Heat Resistant, Early Flowering Spencer and Late Flowering Spencer.

There may not be a clean-cut line of demarcation between these types, but one might do well to try several different types to see which do best under local conditions.

Culture

Sweet peas do not grow well in the hot summer nor in hot, dry winds. They prefer a cool atmosphere with plenty of soil moisture. Hence the general plan should be to get them started as early as possible so that they will reach the peak of bloom before the advent of hot weather. This is accomplished by first selecting the right varieties and secondly by planting them either in the fall or the very early spring. Fall sowing is advocated in some areas; the idea would be to sow them before the ground freezes, but not sufficiently in advance of that to allow them to germinate before winter. This time may vary between mid-Sept. and late Oct. in the North, to mid-Nov. or later in the South. Or they could be sown very early in the spring, about Mar. 15 in the vicinity of New York City, if possible; around April 1 farther north.

For such early spring sowing, it is obvious that the soil should be prepared the previous fall. A trench the width and depth of which is 12–18 in. is dug. The soil is well mixed with compost or peat moss or both and 3–5 lbs. of a complete fertilizer is thoroughly mixed in, together with 10–15 lbs. of ground limestone (these for a 100-ft. row). Sweet Peas prefer soil slightly on the alkaline side.

If the seed is to be fall-sown, some growers recommend making a furrow in the prepared soil about 5 in. deep, placing in it 3 in. of sand, sowing the seeds on this and then mounding 2 in. or more of soil on top so that water will not collect on the seed during the winter months. After the ground has frozen, the row should be well mulched to prevent alternate freezing and thawing of the soil in winter or early spring.

If the seed is to be spring-sown, do it just as early as possible (having the seed bed prepared the previous autumn), planting the seed 2 in. deep. Soaking the seed in warm water for 2–3 days before sowing aids in germination. Or, seeds could be started in plant bands or pressed soil pots in the greenhouse about 4–6 weeks before the plants are set out, but they should be well hardened-off before taking them from the warm greenhouse to the cold spring air. Two or 3 seeds can be planted to each pot, later reducing the seedlings to 1 per pot.

Water well and mulch after the seedlings have started growth, for this aids greatly in giving them the necessary moisture they must have for good growth.

Some type of support is needed for them to climb on (they may grow 6 ft. high), either cut brush, chicken wire or some other material.

Finally, to insure a long blooming period, keep the flowers cut and do not allow seed formation. When this occurs, flower production diminishes rapidly and soon stops.

Insect Pests

Aphids are the most destructive insect pest. See PEA. Red spider mites may become destructive in the greenhouse, but seldom are important out-of-doors. See ROSE.

Diseases

Root rots and anthracnose are serious pests under favorable conditions and mosaic develops from infected seed. See PEA.

palustris   2′–3′   **Zone 4**   **Marsh Pea**
This perennial species has a winged stem, narrowly oval leaflets and flowers varying from white to deep rose. These are borne in clusters of 3–5. It is an Old World plant often cultivated and frequently naturalized in swamps and wetlands from New England to N.Car. It blooms in May and June and is easily grown from seed.

splendens   3′   **Zone 9**   **Pride-of-California**
A perennial or slightly shrubby plant with showy magenta-red flowers an inch long and 6–12 on one stem. The leaflets are borne in 3–5 pairs. Native to southern Calif.

tuberosus   4′   **Zone 5**   **Ground Nut Pea**
A perennial climber with tuberous roots and rose-colored flowers, 3–5 on one stem. Parts of the root tubers are edible. Native to Europe and western Asia.

vernus   2′   **Zone 5**   **Spring Vetchling**
With blue-violet flowers, 5–8 on a stem. Native

to Europe. There are 2–3 pairs of leaflets in each leaf.

LAURACEAE = The Laurel Family

LAUREL = *Laurus nobilis*

LAUREL FAMILY = Lauraceae

LAURUS (LAW-rus)

nobilis   30′   Zone 7   Laurel, Sweet Bay
This is the famous laurel of ancient history, cultivated for centuries by the Greeks and Romans. Amenable to shearing, it is often kept closely clipped and grown in tubs, especially in the North where it must be moved indoors over winter. The greenish-white flowers in early

humus in the soil are necessary for their best growth. Although several species are grown by the specialists, the best is still *L. angustifolia* for most gardeners, but **'Munstead Dwarf'** is proving popular for it grows only 18 in. tall. Pruning is best done in April and is necessary to keep the plants from getting straggly.

angustifolia angustifolia (*officinalis*) **3′ Zone 5**
                                               True Lavender
A common garden plant, native to southern Europe and northern Africa, this, or one of its varieties, is well known to every gardener. It is valued for its upright spikes of small, lavender, aromatic flowers in late June and for its semi-

Laurus nobilis is sometimes trained in special forms for display.

June are not especially ornamental nor are the dark green-to-black berries in the fall. It is strictly a foliage plant, valued for its aromatic evergreen leaves that are up to 4 in. long, and these are used for seasoning in various ways. The oil from the fruit is used in making a perfume. Propagated by hardwood cuttings, occasionally by seeds.

LAURUSTINUS = *Viburnum tinus*

LAVANDULA (lav-AN-dew-la). These herbs are perennial, aromatic and some almost evergreen where climate permits. The blue-to-violet flowers are small, borne in whorled clusters on cylindrical spikes. The most common species is the old-fashioned *L. angustifolia*, found in almost every herb garden. The scent remains in the dried flowers for years. Propagation is by softwood or hardwood cuttings best made in Aug. or Sept., or by carefully dividing the clumps in the early spring. Good drainage and plenty of

evergreen, aromatic, gray foliage. It is especially used in the rockery or in front of the flower border or as a low clipped hedge because of its excellent gray foliage. Dried flower spikes continue to give off their aromatic odor for many years. Dense in habit, it prefers full sun in a rather light soil. There is a dwarf variety offered by some nurseries called **'Nana'** and it is supposed to stay under 1 foot tall at maturity. As an aromatic herb its flowers are used in the manufacture of soaps and toilet waters. It is propagated by seed, but more easily by division and late spring cuttings.

multifida   2′   biennial   Jagged Lavender
This species is cut leaved, native to the Canary Islands, and is hardy only in about Zone 8. In northern greenhouses as a pot plant it can bloom a greater part of the winter.

spica = *L. angustifolia*

LAVATERA (lav-at-TEE-ra). These are plants of the Mallow Family with maplelike alternate leaves and large single flowers similar in appearance to those of hollyhocks. Since they grow so tall in a single season, these annuals are used for screening and temporary hedges, and are only used in the flower borders as background plants. Seeds should be planted in full sun after frost is over and should be thinned out about 18–24 in. apart. Native to the Tropics.

trimestris   6′   annual   Herb Tree-mallow
The rose-to-red flowers of this species are funnel shaped and 4 in. wide, borne singly. It is native to the Mediterranean Region. There is a variation in this species for var. **alba** has white flowers; **grandiflora** has rose-colored flowers larger than those of the species; and **splendens** is supposed to be a good garden plant.

LAVENDER. See LAVANDULA.

LAVENDER-COTTON = *Santolina chamaecyparissus*

LAVENDER-MIST = *Thalictrum rochebrunianum*

LAWNS. Lawns are a rather specialized facet of horticulture, the objective of which is a carpet-like sward, green throughout most of the year and always durable under foot. It is this continuity of performance, plus the fact that lawn plants must continue to be luxuriant in spite of dwarfing (crowding, mowing), that dictate special requisites. Grasses generally work best. In the northern two-thirds of the United States, Kentucky Bluegrass (*Poa pratensis*), the fine-leafed or red fescues (*Festuca rubra*) and seeded bent grasses (principally Colonial types such as 'Highland', *Agrostis tenuis*), are most used. Other ground covers are sometimes maintained as mowed lawns, such as *Dichondra repens*, used especially in the Southwest.

Growth factors are not any different for lawn plants than for other garden plants and ornamentals. They all profit from fertile, uncompacted soil and a reasonable amount of attention. By and large, turf grasses are broadly adaptable; they take moderate environmental deviations of soil texture, pH, sun, shade or slope. But of course, there are broad zones of adaptation to temperature north to south, and to a lesser extent, to rainfall east to west. None of the widely accepted turf grasses are well adapted to desertlike dry land. Lawns must receive irrigation from Omaha westward to the Pacific mountain ranges (except at high elevations), and frequently elsewhere, too, for satisfactory performance. Irrigated lawns of drier regions are usually among the nation's best, with fewer weed and disease problems, robust color and the tight growth which abundant sunlight encourages.

So diverse is the U.S. climatically that mention of grass care must be related to climate. There are a number of general considerations pertaining to almost all lawns. These can be discussed first, as they relate peculiarly to all turf grasses.

A lawn is more easily started and more gratifyingly maintained on a good soil. Yet lawn grasses, perhaps more than other garden plants, work to better their own environment. Even when started on a poor soil, grass builds humus into the top few inches year by year, as fine rootlets finger between soil particles. It is said that about half of the grass roots die each year, to be replaced by new growth. You could hardly mix organic residues into your soil any more intimately than do the grass rootlets for you. Of course, reasonable fertility is required for such growth and this may be supplied economically with commercial fertilizer. In addition, watering may be needed during drought. To improve materially the organic content of the soil may take a little or a lot of doing, depending upon where you live and the soil condition with which you start. Adobe clays or seacoast sands are much more difficult to turn into "prairie" than the responsive silts and clays of the Corn Belt and Piedmont.

Soil Structure

Structure refers to the way soil particles cling together. Ionic and surface forces are involved and are often incompletely understood. Soil structure is good when the particles aggregate (lump together), making the soil crumbly. There is then ample pore space for water to soak in and seep through, "sucking in" air (necessary for root growth) as an after-effect. Such a condition can be encouraged temporarily by cultivating the soil when it is slightly moist, or it may be aided by seasonal freezing and thawing, but good structure will hold up only where proper soil ingredients are present. A prime aid for improving structure is organic matter; a small percentage in the soil increases aggregation remarkably. The mixing of compost or other organic residues is the universal soil improver, whether it is light (sandy) or heavy (clay). If the soil is poor, either because it is too light or too heavy, it will probably pay to mix thoroughly some organic material into the top few inches before planting the lawn.

There may be other ways to help the soil. Follow horticultural or farming practices known to be effective in your area. With some heavy soils, particularly acid ones, liming often helps structure as it also adjusts pH and provides calcium and magnesium (secondary nutrients). On very sandy soils, it may be possible to add 10% or more clay, which will be valuable for regaining moisture and nutrients, but it is effective only if thoroughly mixed in. Chemical conditions or purchased amendments (viz., vermiculite, perlite, calcined clay), may help loosen sticky soils. All such treatments reduce the tendency towards quick slaking and compaction that make soil less tenable for deep-rooting lawn grasses.

Topsoil

In many areas topsoil may be purchased. Be careful unless you are thoroughly familiar with its source, and can be certain you are not introducing more problems than you are correcting. A dark color is no guarantee of quality, either with regard to fertility or structure. Often topsoil comes from some abandoned field thoroughly contaminated with weed seed. In such a case there may be fewer headaches if you fertilize your own weed-free subsoil instead and grow grass on it (or perhaps mix in weed-free organic material, such as commercial peat).

Soil is best cultivated just before the sowing of seed, planting of sprigs or plugs, or the laying of sod. Lime and fertilizer can be mixed in as required on this occasion. As noted above, this may be a good time, too, to stir in organic material or other amendments. Liming and fertilization practiced for truck gardening or farming in the area can be a good general guide. Or you may feel more confident by having a soil test made, usually obtainable from the state experiment station through the county agent, or from commercial firms catering to the garden market. Ordinarily it is a safe bet that a complete fertilizer (which is one containing all 3 of the major fertility elements, nitrogen, phosphorus and potassium) will prove useful. Phosphorus stirred in at the time of seedbed preparation is especially important, since in most soils this element becomes immobilized by fixation to soil particles and will be a long while leaching down into the root zone from later surface fertilization. Fertilizers of average strength (totaling about $\frac{1}{3}$ nutrient, such as 12–12–12) are suggested at rates of approximately 20 lbs. per 1000 sq. ft. Appropriate adjustments can be made, for stronger or weaker fertilizers, or where nutrients are either drastically lacking or in excessive supply.

Lawn Layout

Perhaps we should backtrack here to consider the terrain where this soil preparation is to take place. Rough grading should be completed in keeping with sound landscaping considerations. Natural contours are best maintained, except as necessary to provide surface drainage away from the house or structures. It is well to avoid abrupt cuts and steep slopes, always difficult to maintain, and frequently incapable of supporting good plant growth. Low-lying or ponded areas may need tile drainage to avoid

waterlogging, which forces shallow rooting and encourages sedges or other water-loving plants rather than grass. But if gentle surface grades are established, it is not likely that subsurface tiling will be necessary with most soils.

It may be worth the modest extra expense to have topsoil bulldozed to one side, and then replaced on top of soil dug from a foundation, since subsoils are generally refractory and do not handle so well as topsoil. If worked, they are sticky and make clods; when dry they are brick-hard and shrink, causing huge cracks.

If possible, restrict bulldozing, or the passage of any heavy equipment over the soil, to times when the soil is not mushy. Wet soils compact readily from pressure, and there will be a lot of "loosening" necessary (whether by cultivation or natural seasonal cycles) before a good rooting medium is reconstructed. There will likely be enough compaction merely from grading to merit a general cultivation of the area intended for the lawn. A tractor-drawn agricultural disk (or, on smaller properties, a rotary tiller) is suggested.

Trees or shrubs to be preserved in the lawn will suffer and may even die if very much of the original soil is graded away from the root system, or if the soil is piled more than a few inches deeper than it was originally. Wells or retaining walls about cherished trees are stopgap measures which may help preserve the trees for a while, but are seldom completely satisfactory; certainly such measures are not so ideal for tree survival as is maintaining essentially the natural ground level.

Finishing Touches

Intense cultivation of the seedbed is not necessary, and in some cases may be quite undesirable. The soil lumps need not be broken up any finer than from pea to golf-ball size and repeated tillage may break down soil structure. Extremely fine tillage may turn the seedbed to dust, the kind of surface which erodes and rills readily with the first rains because soil pores become blocked, causing water to run off rather than sink into the seedbed. The final grading establishes an essentially level surface. It may be best to await a soaking rain (or a thorough sprinkling) before the final touching up, in order that any fluffy spots may settle. Most lawns receive a final "raking" by hand, or, where power equipment is available, with drags, blades and hydraulic equipment. Don't worry about soil inequalities up to golf-ball dimension; soil will eventually "melt" to a level surface. Of course, rocks or other debris, at least from tennis-ball size up, had best be removed, and if there are residues from construction (such as small piles of sand, plaster, mortar, etc.,) these should be discarded or thoroughly dispersed rather than be left as a soil pocket having markedly different chemical and physical characteristics.

Sowing Seed

If the seedbed is loosely pebbled, as described above, seeding is made easy. Merely spread the seed uniformly, at the rates recommended for the particular grass or blend, usually about 3 lbs. per 1000 sq. ft. This is conveniently accomplished with inexpensive lawn spreaders now readily available The seed sifts into the soil chinks and is then suitably buried without raking or rolling. If, on the other hand, the seedbed has a dusty surface, or if the soil type is such that there are no surface chinks (sandy soils), the newly distributed seed may need to be scratched into the soil, at least so that some of it gets buried about $\frac{1}{4}$ in. deep. If it is simply left on the surface, almost surely there will be loss through wind and soil erosion. Unless the soil is quite light and fluffy, rolling is best avoided here, too, since rolling flattens a smooth surface even more, making it less receptive to water and intensifying erosion. Rolling may be advisable on very fluffy seedbeds, to re-establish capillarity with the deeper soil, but remember that in principle rolling partially destroys what was achieved through cultivation and improvement of soil structure.

Spreaders

Common sense guides seeding. The objective is to have the seed uniformly scattered at the proper rate. Spreaders are the convenient and accurate way to do this and can be easily rented when needed, but for later lawn maintenance, it will pay to have your own spreader.

Two types of apparatus are familiar: (1) spreaders which drop the seed from a slotted hopper with an agitator to meter the seed; and (2) spreaders which cast the seed centrifugally from a whirling plate ("Cyclone Seeder"). The former may be a bit more precise at boundaries and in uniformity of application, while the latter covers greater areas more quickly and easily, with a "feathering" of the boundaries between passes that avoids untreated strips. With the drop-from-hopper spreaders it may be well to divide the seed into 2 parts, sowing half in one direction, the other half at right angles across this. There should then be no unseeded spots. Be certain to overlap the wheel tracks, so that gaps do not exist between adjacent passes. The same half-and-half technique should be practiced where seed is cast by hand on the seedbed.

Vegetative Planting

Soil preparation for planting sprigs (sections of stem) or plugs (chunks of sod), common with southern grasses, deserves a seedbed preparation as thorough as for seeding. Such vegetative starts need just as much encouragement for good rooting and spread as does sprouting seed. The same is true for the laying of sod, a frequent practice in these affluent times. While it is possible to maintain sod essentially without soil, by dint of continuous fertilizing and watering, just as greenhouse plants can be grown by hydroponics, it is not the road to a self-reliant lawn. Homeowners sometimes assume that sodding is an easy way to get a lawn without the bother of seedbed preparation. Sod, cut as it is these days about $\frac{1}{4}$ in. thick, contributes little topsoil and therefore must quickly send new roots into the lawn soil. This occurs only when the soil has been properly cultivated.

It may be helpful at this point to become more specific regionally. While there is considerable leeway in the choice of grass, and even while exotic species often can be made to endure local conditions, practical lawn tending demands grass well adapted to the region. The 2 broad categories are the northern and southern lawn grasses.

Northern Lawn Grasses

Here are grouped the "cool-weather" species, which thrive where soil temperatures remain below 80° F., and which are not dormant even at temperatures below freezing. These species are at their best in spring and autumn, and in climates from the Ohio River valley northward. In northerly locations, and at high elevations, they suffer little in summer (provided rainfall is adequate). These grasses generally scorch brown from winter cold by Christmas if not protected by snow. However, southward from about the latitude of Tenn. they tend to be weak competitors in summer. During prolonged hot and dry spells they turn semi-dormant and, even in rainy years, may fight a losing battle with Crabgrass and other summer weeds. This far south they still perform well in the shade and in favored locations (such as on north slopes or mountainous elevations), remaining green practically all winter.

Packages of grass seed for northern areas are now labeled as: (A) fine-textured and (B) coarse. The former are considered the more attractive and the more suitable for show-place lawns. By coincidence, they also tend to be species which spread, weaving a good sod. With most of them the seed count per pound is high (2,000,000 seeds with Bluegrass, 7,000,000 with bent grass), making the seed reach farther than most coarse kinds (Rye grass about 250,000 seeds to the pound). Familiar fine-textured grasses are the Kentucky bluegrasses, the fine-leafed fescues and the bent grasses, plus a few specialty species.

The coarse grasses, grouped in the lower category on the seed box label, are rather broad-bladed and less attractive. Many are also short-lived. Most of them are bunch grasses that spread little or not at all. Included are many familiar field species—Tall Fescue (not to be confused with the fine-leaf or red fescues), Timothy, Orchard Grass, Brome, Rye Grass, etc. In fact, anything that is not "fine-textured" automatically falls into the "coarse" group. A number are durable and often used for roadside seeding and even for athletic fields, but most people consider them unattractive.

Table 1 characterizes the most used northern grasses, accounting for the majority of the lawns in the U.S.

TABLE 1. NORTHERN LAWN GRASSES
(/M = 1000 sq. ft.)

Bent Grass   All kinds, perennial; low, trailing or semi-trailing; small leaves with excellent texture. "Show" grasses for well-tended turfs (fertilized, watered, frequently mowed). Prone to diseases in hot, muggy weather and to snow mold under cool, damp conditions (recommend fungicidal protection).

Source and Use: Varieties listed are available as seeds; golf green selections must be vegetatively planted; sunny areas, but will stand some shade.

Mowing: Mow $\frac{1}{2}$–1 in.; reel mower with extra blades preferred.

'Astoria'   Medium green, semi-erect. Moderate vigor, not so thatch-forming as creeping varieties; for lawns and in mixtures.

Source and Use: Seeds, 2–3 lbs./M. Mostly for fairways and lawns in humid climates.

Mowing: $\frac{3}{4}$–1 in., preferably twice per week.

'Highland'   Bluish-green, semi-erect. Similar to 'Astoria'. Drought-tolerant; not aggressive (won't become a pest). Attractive with moderate attention.

Source and Use: Seeds, 2–3 lbs./M. Mostly for fairways and lawns mowed too short for good Bluegrass.

Mowing: $\frac{3}{4}$–1 in., preferably twice per week. Occasional slight alteration of mowing height helps control false crown tuftiness.

'Penncross'   Vigorous, attractive creeper, moderately dark green; may show some lack of uniformity due to segregation from seeds having slightly varying heredity. Exceptional vigor gives quick cover, but causes thatch and requires handling experience; a hybrid from interplanting 3 special selections in the seed field.

Source and Use: Seeds, 2 lbs./M., mostly for golf greens.

Mowing: $\frac{1}{2}$ in., frequently.

'Seaside'   Creeper, but not so vigorous as 'Penncross'; bluish-green. More susceptible to disease than 'Penncross' but usually less a thatch-former; as with all creeping bents, merits preventive fungicide applications.

Source and Use: Seeds, 2 lbs./M., mostly for golf greens.

Mowing: $\frac{1}{2}$ in., frequently, but usually not so demanding as 'Penncross'.

Bluegrass   All kinds, perennial; gracefully aristocratic, spreading. Among world's best sod formers.

Source and Use: Seeds, 2–4 lbs./M; sun or light shade.

Mowing: $1\frac{1}{2}$ in. or higher in warm climates, usually rotary mower.

Kentucky, natural   Deep green, gracefully arching shoots, spreading by rhizomes. Fairly open, rhizomes instead of stolons limit thatching. Strongly recuperative, widely adaptable; one of best all-around grasses; easily cared for.

Source and Use: Seeds from Ky. and midwestern sources; sun or light shade in North, shade in South (except for winter seeding); all types of turf, basic ingredient.

'Merion'   Dark green, low-growing, dense. Resistant to leaf spot; makes low, tight growth, but requires extra fertilization and builds thatch more than most bluegrasses; does best in more northerly locations.

Source and Use: As for all bluegrasses, but seeds sometimes slow in germinating; premium turfs and mixtures.

Mowing: Because of low growth, can be mowed 1 in., but at least $1\frac{1}{2}$ in. generally recommended. Reel or rotary mower.

'Park'   Same as natural Kentucky Bluegrass. A hybrid compounded from 12 especially vigorous Minn. selections. Good seedling vigor.

Source and Use: As for other bluegrasses; seeds are heavy and quick to sprout; general lawn and turf mixtures.

Mowing: As for group.

Rough Bluegrass, *Poa trivialis*   Light shiny green, dense; resembles erect bent grass. Good for shade and thrives in moisture; will not stand much traffic. May make patches.

Source and Use: Imported seeds sometimes contain cress weeds. For damp shade, in mixtures, seeded at general Bluegrass rates.

Mowing: As for group.

Fescue   Perennial. Rugged, adapting well to poor conditions.

Source and Use: Seeds, sun or shade.

Mowing: As for Bluegrass.

Fine fescues: 'Chewings', 'Creeping Red', 'Illahee', 'Pennlawn', 'Rainer', etc.   Slowly spreading, attractively fine-textured, beautifully dark green, rather stiff and "wind-swept" in appearance. Widely adaptable; one of the best shade grasses in the North, persisting on poor soils in dry locations. Attractive under minimum fertility.

Source and Use: Usually seeded with Bluegrass for open; mixtures preponderately Fescue for shade, 4–5 lbs./M; pure, high-germinating seeds from Ore. improved varieties.

Mowing: As for Bluegrass.

Tall and meadow fescues: 'Alta' and 'Kentucky-31' varieties Bunch grasses, not spreading; coarse, clumpy in age; medium green. Not suitable for fine lawns, but useful where ruggedness is needed, as along roadsides, or beyond the southern limits for good Bluegrass.

Source and Use: Sow seeds heavily, 6–8 lbs./M, to force tight growth and dwarfed plants. Sun.

Mowing: As for Bluegrass.

Redtop (*Agrostis alba*) Spreading annual or perennial, coarse and often clumpy in age; fairly light green—a coarse bent grass. In climates where this is not permanent it can be used in small quantity as a nurse grass. Widely adaptable; undemanding, but turns coarse and weedy.

Source and Use: Small seeds; sow at rate of 2 lbs. or less/M, apt to carry many weed seeds. Sow in sun and usually use as a nurse grass.

Mowing: 1 in. or more, reel or rotary.

Rye Grass Annual or perennial. Bunch grasses, not spreading or forming good sod. Medium to light green. Inexpensive, but turf not first-rate. Generally included to lower cost, or in small quantities as a nurse species (10% or less).

Source and Use: As with tall Fescue.

Mowing: As with fescues.

Annual or Italian Rye Grass Annual. Clumpy, becomes coarse in age. Fairly light, shiny green. Large seed is quick-sprouting, good for immediate effect, but becomes clumpy and dies out quickly.

Source and Use: Not recommended for planting alone; solid stands 6–8 lbs./M, sun.

Mowing: As with Bluegrass and fescues.

Perennial Rye Grass Perennial. Attractive, shiny green leaves, less coarse than annual type. Quick to sprout and reasonably attractive; though perennial under proper care, not so enduring or tight a sod as Kentucky Bluegrass.

Source and Use: Seed densely to make tight cover, 6–8 lbs./M. Sun.

Mowing: As with Kentucky Bluegrass.

Southern Lawn Grasses

Southern or "warm-season" grasses are at their best in climates where average temperatures range considerably above the optimum for northern grasses. Most southern grasses continue growing nicely when soil temperatures rise into the 90's, a condition physiologically exhausting for northern species. On the other hand, most of them become dormant when the temperature approaches freezing and all are brown through the winter where freezing temperatures prevail. By and large, these are species for lands south from Tenn., although certain types are hardy much farther north and may be used for special purposes such as on golf courses in border states and for summer cottage lawns as far north as Long Island. They are as bleak as Crabgrass through a prolonged winter, even though they are hardy enough to revive again in April.

Table 2 characterizes the chief southern grasses, planted primarily from southeastern Va. through the Coastal Plain and Fla. and westward into eastern Tex. The arid southwest areas are restricted mostly to using Bermuda Grass, plus a considerably sprinkling of Dichondra.

The grasses listed for the North are all available as seed, the most convenient and economical means of propagation. Southern grasses, however, are often planted from live starts. Though seed of the common, rather coarse, selections of Bermuda Grass and *Zoysia japonica* are available, elite selections and all named varieties will not come true from seed and so must be planted vegetatively. Bahia Grass, Centipede Grass, the carpet grasses and Dichondra are generally seeded. Saint Augustine Grass, which sets little seed, is started vegetatively.

TABLE 2. SOUTHERN LAWN GRASSES
(/M = 1000 sq. ft.)

Bahia Grass (*Paspalum notatum*) Perennial; fairly open, coarse; spreads by runners; seedheads unattractive. One of the easiest southern turf grasses to plant and to care for; often used in mixture.

Source and Use: Seeds, about 4 lbs./M; sun or moderate shade.

Mowing: Rotary or reel, 1½–2 in.; seedheads tough.

Bermuda Grass All kinds, perennial; fast-growing, aggressive, spreading by runners. Attractive texture and deep color if well tended. Sun only; so vigorous as to require frequent care (a pest in borders); will thatch. Dormant near freezing, doubtfully hardy north of Tenn.

Source and Use: Seeds (common) and vegetative planting (selected varieties); not tolerant of shade.

Mowing: From ¼ in. on golf greens to 1½ in.

on lawns. Reel mower, frequently.

Common Bermuda Grass Comparatively open and coarser than selected varieties, but attractive when tended. Survives with scant attention, but to look well must be fertilized, watered and mowed regularly.

Source and Use: Easily started by seeds (hulled are quick-sprouting), 2–3 lbs./M.

Mowing: About 1 in.

'Sunturf' and **'U-3'** Finer texture, tighter than common. Fairly winter hardy as far north as Mo. Increasingly afflicted there with spring dead spot disease.

Source and Use: Must be planted from sprigs, stolons or plugs.

Mowing: From ½–1 in.

'Tifgreen' and similar improved selections. Fine, attractive texture; deep green. Tifton hybrids widely utilized; fairly disease resistant.

Source and Use: Planted from sprigs or stolons.

Mowing: From ¼ in. (golf green) to 1 in.

Centipede (*Eremochloa ophiuroides*) Perennial; medium texture; spreads by runners. Low-maintenance grass, resenting heavy fertility; turns chlorotic unless soils are acid (needs iron).

Source and Use: Seeds, or sprigs and plugs; sun or moderate shade.

Mowing: Reel or rotary; slower and less demanding than Bermuda.

St. Augustine (*Stenotaphrum secundatum*), including 'Bitter Blue', 'Floratine', etc. Perennial; coarse but not unattractive; spreads by runners; few seedheads; usually dark green. Very tolerant of shade. Recently subject to severe chinch bug attack and several diseases, hence not a carefree grass; will thatch.

Source and Use: Sun or shade; from sod, sprigs or plugs.

Mowing: Generally 1½–2 in., rotary or reel, average frequency.

Zoysia All kinds, perennial; spreads by runners; growth is slow; dense and among most attractive of southern grasses. Slowness a disadvantage on planting, but reduces mowing demand later. Does not require a great deal of attention. Billbugs serious in Fla.

Source and Use: Seeds of unselected types; sprigs and plugs of improved varieties; sun or moderate shade.

Mowing: So dense and tough that heavy-duty reel mowers are prescribed; 1–2 in.

Z. japonica Variable, somewhat coarser and looser-growing than the selected varieties. Use where seeding is convenient, or selected varieties unavailable.

Source and Use: Seeds; up to 2lbs./M; often mixed.

Mowing: As for all zoysias.

Z. matrella Finer-textured selections developed locally. More attractive than *Z. japonica* and often easier to keep than 'Emerald'.

Source and Use: Live starts.

Mowing: As for all zoysias.

'Meyer' Tight but somewhat coarser than *Z. matrella*; winter color not very good. Winter hardy, for use in the upper south and border states.

Source and Use: Live starts.

Mowing: As for all zoysias.

Mixtures and Special Blends

Most seed mixtures contain the same basic grasses, whether for sun or shade, although the proportions may differ. Almost all species in Tables 1 and 2 survive both in sun and moderate shade. The exception is Bermuda Grass, which will not withstand shade.

It is apparent that mixtures of seeded grasses have much to recommend them. If one of the candidate species finds tough going, perhaps another will fill the ecological bill. And when the grass population is diversified, no single disease or molestation is likely to afflict all kinds. Grass blends are especially recommended for the novice and for turfs which cannot be assiduously tended. Single select varieties, in which all plants are genetically alike, are best left for the expert who recognizes the needs of the variety and ministers to them.

In the North, fine fescues are especially suited to "poverty shade"—locations where the soil is poor and dry, as well as shady, such as under trees. The Bluegrass component performs well where soils are a bit better. These 2 similar species in multiple varieties managed essentially alike make an excellent all-around combination. For moist shade, such as on the north side of buildings in humid climates, *Poa trivialis* (Rough Bluegrass) may be a useful addition. *P. trivialis* resembles Bent Grass, spreading by above-ground runners. It is not recommended for sunny areas, where it makes patches that brown if the summer is hot and dry. Bent Grass is most at home in humid, misty climates and where a bit of extra care brings its luxurious quality to full fruition.

In the South, mixtures of grasses are less frequent than in the North, partly because so many of the finer turfs are vegetatively planted. Even so, acceptable lawns can be made by compounding several common grasses. In the Deep South, Bahia Grass is often basic, perhaps supplemented with Carpet Grass (for boggy, acid locations), with common Bermuda Grass (for sunny locations and close mowing), with *Zoysia japonica* (tough and enduring once established) and even with northern species such as the fine fescues, Bluegrasses and bent grasses for autumn cover with "year-round" seed blends.

Where Dichondra is used in the Southwest, it should receive just as intensive attention as the finer strains of Bermuda Grass. This means frequent mowing, fertilizing, watering, pest control and so on. This plant has just as many problems as does grass, and its own peculiar difficulties when it comes to weed control. The famed herbicide for grasses, 2,4-D, cannot, of course, be used on a broadleaf plant such as Dichondra.

Golf-Course Turf

In popular image the ultimate in fine turf is the golf green. Even golf-course fairways and roughs tend to be pretty good "lawn" under the constant professional care they receive. Such special attention permits close clipping, and even the use of grasses not typical of the region, such as the low-growing bermudas and zoysias in the southern portions of the Bluegrass belt.

But this sort of thing is not for the home-owner. Thousands of dollars are spent each year on materials and maintenance for a golf green. Special bent grass selections, most propagated vegetatively, are used in the North, and fine-textured Bermuda Grass in the South (principally 'Tifgreen' and the newer 'Tifdwarf'). Widely planted golf-greens bent grasses include 'Washington', 'Arlington', 'Cohansey', 'Toronto' and hordes of others. 'Penncross' and 'Seaside' can be seeded. These are all creeping bent grasses which require mowing nearly every day with special greens mowers which must be meticulously maintained, thinning and aerifying at intervals, frequent fungicide application and almost daily watering.

For an attractive lawn, maintenance must be related to the requirements of the major grasses used. The lawnsman should try to assess the ecological factors which most favor his particular turf. He can partially control environment through timing and rate of product application, watering, mowing height, control of weeds and other pests. The discussions which follow summarize the general maintenance procedures.

Space does not permit discussion of each turf grass separately. Bluegrass-fine fescue turf, the most widely utilized of fine turfs over most of the nation, is chosen as the standard for discussion. This is a rather trouble-free, erect-growing grass population, best adapted to northern regions. Marked deviations for other types of turf will be noted to the extent possible. The greatest differences come with southern species, and to a lesser extent with trailing (stoloniferous) types. By and large, the same maintenance practices are undertaken for southern grasses,

but frequently at a different season (viz., Bluegrass benefits most from attention in autumn; southern grasses in late spring and summer). The chief added difficulty with trailing grasses, as compared to Bluegrass-fine fescue, is the greater tendency to accumulate a layer of stems and old vegetation at the base of the sod. This thatch should be thinned if it builds up rapidly; at least annually on very dense and fast-growing turfs such as well-kept Bermuda Grass.

Some maintenance practices will be more critical than others. All lawns are mowed and nearly all must be fertilized and watered. These might be considered the 3 major procedures. If these are well handled, the grass will likely flourish and fight most of its own battles.

However, few lawns escape some weed invasion, since weed seeds are either in the soil, or are brought in from neighboring areas. Fortunately, the chemical herbicides are helpful, although need for their constant use does suggest something fundamental a bit out of kilter.

Mowing

One of the reasons why grasses are so popular for lawns is that they adapt well to mowing. The growing point is at the crown (condensed stem), almost buried in the soil; only leaves rise up to mowing height, and to a great extent these grow from the base rather than the tip. Only when seed-heads are produced, which mark that particular grass culm for death anyway, is the stem actually cut Thus mowing injures the plant only insofar as it removes green food-making tissue. The better lawn grasses withstand such adversity well.

Mowing improves appearance by creating a level foliage surface. As in the pruning of ornamentals, it also encourages a certain amount of thickening from the base. This is at the expense of vigor in the individual culm. Lawns generally considered the finest looking, "like a golf green," are those with a great many very dwarfed and stunted plants, but when the plants are so crowded, diligent care is needed to keep them alive. By and large, a lawn will be much more self-sufficient if mowed relatively high.

Erect-growing turf grasses such as blue-grasses and fescues should be mowed at least an inch tall in favorable (more northerly) regions, 2–3 in. tall where the going is tough (middle latitudes, in the shade, etc.). Trailing species such as the Bermudas and other of the finer-textured southern grasses, and the bent grasses in the North, are usually best mowed between $\frac{3}{4}$ and 1 in. high. Coarser southern grasses, such as St. Augustine Grass, are mowed like Bluegrass.

Studies have shown that depth of rooting corresponds roughly to mowing height. Thus a lawn mowed high should have a deeper, more vigorous root system to stand it in good stead during drought or when it receives little attention. Likewise, a turf mowed rather high is less open to weed invasion. Studies of the U.S. Department of Agriculture show that Bluegrass at 1 in. has nearly 10 times as many weeds as the same turf at 2 in.

It is the green leaves of plants that make the food necessary for growth. Adequate green leafage should remain after every lawn mowing; hence fairly frequent mowing is required. If the lawn is let grow very tall before it is cut back, most of the green leaf is cut away; only older, yellowed foliage and stubble remain. Many days are needed to recoup, during which reserved food is used and of course the turf is weakened. Far better is it to remove only about ⅓ of the green foliage at any single mowing. A rule of thumb might be to mow the lawn when grass height exceeds half again the regular mowing height. With Bluegrass, mowing may be advisable each 4 or 5 days in spring, with perhaps no mowing needed for several weeks during dry periods in summer.

The above discussion should suggest appropriate mowing for the good of the grass. A second, equally important consideration, is the effect on the lawnsman. Most folk regard lawn mowing as a chore. It should be a pleasant outdoor interlude. But to make it enjoyable, good equipment that is not constantly stalling, and is of a capacity large enough to take care of the lawn in a reasonably short length of time, is required. Such lawn mowers are available these days, with enticing convenience features. It is suggested that you indulge yourself by purchasing a really good, durable lawn mower. Many more hours are spent mowing the lawn than doing anything else there, and these hours might just as well be made as agreeable as possible.

Home lawn mowers are generally either of the rotary type or the reel type. There are advantages and disadvantages to both. Reel mowers are preferred for precise cutting, especially at lower mowing height and with trailing grasses. Rotary mowers cut higher turf better and have the versatility for getting into corners and close to obstructions. Reel mowers are precision instruments and must be sent out for professional sharpening and adjustment; rotaries can usually be sharpened at home. Rotaries are a little less expensive, somewhat less safe. For a more elaborate comparison of lawn mowers, it is suggested that readers consult the appropriate chapter in "The Lawn Book" by R. W. Schery (Macmillan, 1961).

Zoysia is perhaps the most marked exception when it comes to mowing. Zoysias are very tough and mow poorly with rotaries. Even a reel machine must be heavy-duty, preferably with an extra blade on the reel (like some of the golf-greens mowers). A "light-weight" in power can't handle Zoysia. Keep in mind when planting Zoysia that mowing will require a more expensive, heavy-duty machine.

Fertilizing

Nowadays lawn fertilization is an accepted gardening ritual. It may not always be necessary, and is sometimes overdone; but without it, a first-rate lawn is not possible. Recommended rates of fertilization vary from almost nothing on Centipede Grass, through light rates with fine fescues and Bahia Grass, to medium rates with Kentucky bluegrasses, Zoysia and St. Augustine, and heavy rates with Bermuda Grass and bents. The actual quantity of fertilizer varies with climate and soil, and usually ranges from a pound or two per 1000 sq. ft. of elemental nitrogen (the nutrient customarily considered most important for grass) with "poor soil" species, to 12 or more pounds with "heavy feeders" such as golf-green putting grasses. Most lawns are lucky to get 3 lbs. of nitrogen per year, although Merion Bluegrass and bent grasses in the North and Bermuda grasses in the South should certainly have appreciably more. Only when slow-release, non-burn fertilizers are used should more than 1 lb. of elemental nitrogen be applied at a time. It is apparent, then, that the lawn should receive a minimum of 1 or 2 feedings annually, up to as much as monthly fertilization with Bent Grass and Bermuda.

Nitrogen is the nutrient chiefly responsible for foliage color and, with lawn grasses, dark green leaves are desired. Sometimes nitrogen is used alone (ammonium nitrate, urea, ureaform), but unless other nutrients are in ample supply in the soil, it is best to use a complete fertilizer. Lawn fertilizers are comparatively high in nitrogen, examples being 22–8–4, 17–4–4 and 30–5–8. See SOILS and FERTILIZERS.

There is not sufficient space here to discuss the many different lawn fertilizers. Most are made to be applied readily and accurately with lawn spreaders. Even the quick-acting chemical types are formulated as pellets with a minimum of dust. The fertilizer granules roll from the grass foliage to the soil, and seldom burn such as old-fashioned dusty fertilizers were wont to do.

Soluble chemical fertilizers are the most economical and, if carefully used, they are quite satisfactory. Nutrients in them become immediately available to the grass, but by the same token are soon spent. Thus chemical fertilizers generally must be applied more frequently than the organic types.

Organic fertilizers may be natural or synthetic. A typical natural organic fertilizer is "Milorganite," widely utilized on golf courses. It is processed Milwaukee sewage, and contains a wide range of minor elements and antibiotics in addition to such major nutrients as are claimed. Major nutrients are rather low with organic fertilizers and hence costs are appreciably higher than with soluble chemical forms for equivalent nutrient content.

Equally or even more expensive are the synthetic organic fertilizers such as "Ureaform," a man-made combination from urea and formaldehyde. As with natural organics, the large molecules must be broken down by soil micro-organisms and hence release the nutrients slowly over a span of time. In theory this is quite desirable, but regulation of availability may not be as simple as it might appear. Soil micro-organisms are active in hot, humid weather, but do little or nothing to break down the molecules when it is cold. Thus most "slow-release" fertilizers also contain some soluble nutrients for immediate effect and improved efficiency. Another means of obtaining this slow release is to coat the fertilizer granules with resin, which takes some time to disintegrate on the lawn, releasing the nutrients only as decomposition occurs (or as the soluble salts diffuse out through the coating membrane). This treatment, too, adds to the expense.

Lime

Lime may be needed as a corrective for acid soils. As noted in other discussions, calcium is a nutrient of secondary importance. So is magnesium, often carried along with calcium, especially in dolomitic limestones, the type generally recommended for lawns. See SOILS and FERTILIZERS. In making new seedbeds, powdered limestone is best mixed into the soil, about 50 lbs. per 1000 sq. ft. for soils which are slightly acid—below a pH of 6 for most lawn grasses—double this amount for soils that are quite acid. The same rates can be used on established lawns and if the soil is quite acid, this application should be repeated each 3-4 years. However, Centipede Grass prefers acid soil and a detailed discussion of the soil requirements of this grass is given under SOILS and FERTILIZERS.

In some instances it is calcium that is needed, not a correction of the pH; nevertheless, the most convenient indicator of the need for lime is a simple soil test (for pH), to tell whether the soil is acid. In arid country the alkalinity, not the acidity, will be the problem; then sulfur to acidify the soil is needed.

All in all, lawn grasses should perform satisfactorily if the necessary nutrients get to them, no matter their form in the fertilizer. Bluegrass lawns are best fertilized once or twice in the autumn, the most effective growing season for this grass. Added feeding may be in order at lighter rates in spring and summer, but beware of fertilizing too heavily in hot weather. Much Bluegrass is lost, supposedly to "disease," though such disease occurs only because the foliage is lush from abundant nitrogen at an improper time.

Southern grasses, at their best in hot weather, should be fertilized in spring and periodically through summer. For a more thorough discussion of lawn fertilization and the relationship of fertilizer to the soil, the reader is referred to appropriate chapters in "The Lawn Book", by Robert W. Schery (Macmillan, 1961).

Watering

Water is essential to all earthly life; it is a major constituent of cells and the chief medium in which nutrients are transported. Lawns require quantities approaching 1 in. per week during the active growing season in order to thrive and look good. Some soils hold within the grass-root-zone pore space as much as 2 in. of water—sufficient to maintain optimum growth for a half-month. But once this reserve is exhausted, if not replenished by rainfall or watering, growth slows down and essentially ceases at the wilting point. Wilting is marked by a "cloudy" bluish cast to the foliage, a curling of the leaf blades upon themselves and the loss of natural resiliency (so that footprints show for some time on the turf). This is the signal for irrigating if you wish the lawn to remain attractively green. The grass may revive at night when water loss is less, and there may be some recapture from dew, but the soil moisture needs replenishing.

Wilting does not permanently damage grass. Indeed it can be beneficial, in that it represses certain weeds and diseases more than it sets back the grass. Well-established Bluegrass, for example, can turn completely brown from summer drought, yet revive to full resplendence once rains and cool weather return. Such summer dormancy may conserve energy, since otherwise cool-weather grasses draw upon their food reserves when the weather is very hot.

The amount of water and the frequency of its application should vary with the kind of soil and with the weather. On windy, sunny days much more moisture is evaporated from both soil and foliage than occurs on still, cloudy days, and at cooler temperatures. Clay and silt soils, with voluminous microspore space, hold a reserve of as much as 2 in. of water, while a coarser, sandy soil may spong up only $\frac{1}{4}$ in. or so! Obviously, one slow, prolonged irrigation of heavy soil may suffice to keep a lawn green for 2 weeks or longer, while a sandy soil garners all the water it can hold in a few minutes, sufficient for only a few days. Lawns on sandy soils must be watered at least twice a week in hot, dry weather.

It makes little difference how the water is applied, just so it gets to the soil at rates which will let it be absorbed rather than run off. A porous or sandy soil absorbs water much more rapidly than does a heavy clay. So it is wise to water the heavy soil more carefully, with a finer spray, over a more prolonged period, than would be necessary with a porous soil.

Watering in the bright sun is, if anything, beneficial to the grass, cooling it down. However, it can be wasteful of water, especially if a fine spray is used, since as much water may evaporate in the dry atmosphere as soaks into the soil. Common sense should be the guide here, and dictate the kind of irrigation equipment. Whatever sprinkler system is chosen, see that the water is uniformly applied over the entire lawn; this can be checked by placing tin cans at intervals over the lawn, and noting that equivalent depths of water accumulate in each can.

Particularly in the Southwest there is a trend towards underground systems, with pop-up heads activated automatically. At least one lawn supply house has now developed a plastic system that can first be laid out on the surface to test pressure and coverage and then simply buried by trenching with a spade or small pipe-layer. This is attached to a regular faucet and is activated by a time clock that can be set for any length of application up to an hour, at intervals as frequent as each 12 hours to as infrequent as every 2 days. So, automatic irrigation is now available to the average homeowner in those areas that have a sufficient water supply to permit lawn watering.

Inexperienced people often regard water as the panacea supposed to make a good lawn inevitable. If a little is good, a lot is better! With irrigation, this is anything but true. Frequent light waterings may encourage weeds more than grass. Note how prolific is Crabgrass in wet summers in the lower Midwest, when the Bluegrass is restrained by temperature. Overly heavy irrigation can waterlog the soil, encourage its compaction and bring in water-loving weeds such as sedges, *Poa annua* and other competitors for the lawn grass. If the soil remains waterlogged for long, the deep grass roots "drown out," and the resultant shallow-rooted turf is subject to injury in any drought. Except on very porous, sandy soils, it is probably best to irrigate thoroughly but infrequently. This means waiting until the grass shows signs of wilting,

then soaking the lawn with as much water as the soil can hold.

In the North, bent grasses and *P. trivialis* flourish better under generous irrigation than do the bluegrasses and fine fescues; in the South, Carpet Grass is notoriously well adapted to boggy land. Most turf grasses need fairly frequent watering on the sandy Coastal Plain soils that cover much of the Southeast. In desert climates of the Southwest, evaporation is so rapid, no matter what the soil type, that frequent irrigation is required. In drier climates where irrigation is impossible, lawnsmen must abandon conventional lawn grasses and turn to dry-land species such as Buffalo Grass and other native prairie species.

Weeds and Weed Control

Lawn weeds are frequently an indication of poor conditions that should be corrected. The most important weed-control measure is a flourishing turf. Nevertheless, when weeds occur, they must be eliminated. With some weeds this is relatively easy, while with others it is difficult, but the problem will be recurring unless grass replaces the weeds.

Fortunately, in the lawn, large groups of weeds can be checked by the same chemical treatment. Most dicotyledonous or "broadleaf" weeds are eliminated by a judicious use of the 2,4-D (phenoxy) chemicals, which do not harm grass when applied at the rates recommended. Of course, care must be exercised that there is no wind drift of lethal herbicides to ornamentals. The once ubiquitous broadleaf lawn pests such as dandelions, plantains and dock succumb very easily to 2,4-D. The herbicide 2,4,5-T and "Silvex" (often components of "brush killers") are no longer used for resistant lawn weeds such as Clover, some of the chickweeds, Spurge and Knotweed.

A newer, related herbicide, "Dicamba" (Banvel-D), works well too, and is especially effective on resistant Knotweed (*Polygonum aviculare*), *Rumex acetosella* and other species which 2,4-D has shown difficulty in handling. But "Dicamba" should not be used over the roots of ornamental shrubs and trees, since it leaches into the soil rather readily and can cause damage through the roots. It is particularly troublesome near yews and locusts. None of the herbicides mentioned should ever be used except according to the directions accompanying the product. Overdosage can injure the grass and may even render the soil toxic to plants for some time.

Weed killers are more effective when the weed is young and growing vigorously, such as during warm, rainy periods in late spring. In windy climates the use of weed killers may not be recommended then because of the danger of wind drift of the herbicides to budding ornamentals, which are also very susceptible in their early stages of growth. Slightly stronger dosages in autumn may be preferable and still be quite effective on warm days.

Grasslike weeds are more difficult to eliminate selectively, since physiologically they are quite like the lawn grass. However, annuals can be cut down in the more susceptible juvenile stage, just as the seed sprouts. A wide selection of pre-emergence chemicals has been developed, generally marked as Crab Grass preventers. They are applied to the lawn uniformly, shortly ahead of the sprouting season when soil temperatures get into the 60's—as early as March in southern localities, as late as July in the far North. "Dacthal," "Ron Star," "Betasan," and several arsenicals are among the more effective annual grass preventers. One newer product, "Tupersan," will not inhibit the sprouting of seeded grass (Blue-grass, fine Fescue, Bent Grass); however, neither is it so effective against some of the annual weeds, although it does seem to control Crab Grass adequately. The majority of pre-emergence chemicals should not be utilized with newly seeded lawns until the permanent grass is well established—at least old enough to have been mowed several times.

There are post-emergence herbicides, too. Most used are the methyl arsonates (DMA, AMA), effective against Crab Grass, Goose Grass and Foxtail when sprayed in 2 applications roughly a week apart. They also help to control some of the broadleaf weeds such as Chickweed.

There is no selective control for weedy perennial grasses. About all that can be suggested where these are troublesome is to spot treat the clumps with a general herbicide that kills all grasses and then to reseed with the desirable species. Two well-known grass-killing chemicals are "Roundup" and "Dalapon." These are systemic and tend to be carried into underground rhizomes. There is residual soil toxicity following application of these chemicals, so that a waiting period of several weeks may be needed before reseeding.

Contact sprays such as cacodylic acid, "Paraquat" and "Diquat" brown all vegetation they hit, but are not very systemic. For bunch grasses without rhizomes, this may be adequate. These chemicals are inactivated almost immediately in the soil, so that reseeding is possible within a day or two after treatment. They are often recommended for renovation, with the dead plants left in place as a mulch.

Where the lawn is excessively contaminated with weeds that can't be eliminated selectively, sterilization of the seedbed may be an answer. The material most used is methyl bromide, a toxic vapor which must be applied under a tarpaulin, a treatment best handled professionally. The lawn can be replanted almost immediately. Sterilization is also possible with drench chemicals such as "Vapam," which can be applied by the homeowner with a sprinkling can. However, one should avoid sprinkling this over the roots of ornamental trees and shrubs, since the seepage of this chemical through the soil can be lethal to them. Following this treatment, there must be a waiting period of several weeks before reseeding is possible. For Bluegrass it is suggested that the soil be cultivated and drench-sterilized in summer to prepare for planting in late Aug. or early Sept. the best time of year for seeding.

Certain exceptions to the above suggestions are important. Saint Augustine, Bahia and Centipede grasses may be injured by 2,4-D and arsenates. On the other hand, they are usually tolerant of triazines ("Atrazine," "Simazine"), which are very injurious to Bluegrass. Be sure to check with the local state experiment station for the latest recommendations in weed control on southern turfs.

Other Maintenance

Only a cursory mention is possible of other maintenance practices. Insect, disease and other attacks on the lawn are important, but they are less likely to be a frequent problem and can usually be lived with.

Insect damage can be of several types. Grubs of the Japanese beetle, June beetle and chafers consume lawn-grass roots. With serious infestations the sod can be lifted up, the anchoring roots severed. Treatment is to drench a long-lasting insecticide such as "Simazine" into the root zone, or sometimes to exercise biological control (such as inoculating the lawn with milky spore disease against the Japanese beetle).

Insect larvae often consume grass foliage. Caterpillars like armyworm and cutworm, but especially the lawn webworm (caterpillars of the lawn moth) are the most troublesome. In certain years and areas where webworm infestation is serious, the best prevention is to thoroughly soak an insecticide into the grass crowns about 10 days after the lawn moths have been noticed flitting over the turf dropping eggs. The cycle from moth to moth is about 1 month. The webworm caterpillars bury deep into the sod, where they make nests lined with silk. These are surrounded with the strawy remains of chewed-off grass leaves. It seems s though webworms build resistance to frequently employed insecticides, although "Diazinon,"

"Sevin" and "Malathion," among others, are said to be still effective.

Chinchbugs are sucking insects that so debilitate the grass that it dies. They are particularly troublesome on St. Augustine Grass, almost ruining its usefulness in Fla. Moreover, since bug populations seem quickly to build resistance to insecticides, new lethal products must be found. There is resistance in many areas to the chlorinated hydrocarbons and so phosphatics are now substituted.

Lawn diseases seem more prevalent these days, perhaps they are more noticed now; perhaps there is actually a greater incidence because the turf is increasingly pampered! While there are no universal preventives or cures, keep in mind that overly lush grass, from over-generous fertilizing during hot weather, may trigger disease.

So varied are the fungi which attack grass, and so difficult their identification, that their control generally should be turned over to a professionally trained person. For the home-owner, the best we can suggest is to maintain the lawn properly and if experience shows certain diseases to crop up at certain seasons, to take preventive action on the next occasion by spraying with a fungicide (viz., "Thiram," folpet, ferbam and benomyl). Disease is very much influenced by the weather; the drier, brighter days usually check an infestation. In northern states preventive spraying, particularly of Bent Grass, may be advised ahead of the first snowfall, to control snow mold during the winter.

Growth regulators, wetting agents, special aerifying and thinning equipment, and so on may all be helpful for special purposes and sprucing-up. These activities are of little avail, however, if basic maintenance is inadequate. If the lawn grass is suitable for the climate; is realistically selected for the attention that can be given to it; if it is properly planted to a good seedbed; and if it is mowed, fertilized and watered advantageously, an excellent lawn can be expected. Weed control, perhaps control of other pests, sometimes may be needed; even thatch removal and similar dressing-up. But a good lawn need not be a burden, either financially or in terms of the attention it will require.

ROBERT W. SCHERY

LAWSONIA (law-SO-nia)

inermis   20′   Zone 10   Henna
The very fragrant small flowers, about ¼ in. wide, are borne in many-flowered terminal panicles and are colored white to red. The opposite leaves are elliptic and 1½ in. long. The fruit is a small capsule. It is widely grown in tropical countries both as an ornamental and because it yields a henna-colored dye. Propagated by cuttings and seeds. Native to northern Africa, Asia and Australia.

LAYERING. This is perhaps the easiest asexual method of plant propagation for the amateur, for it merely means placing a part of the attached living stem of the plant in the ground, allowing it to root, then removing the rooted stem as a new plant. It sounds simple enough but there are a few very essential prerequisites to be considered.

First, there should be a cut of some kind made on the part of the branch to be in the soil, as an aid to induce rooting, and as long as a cut is made, it might as well be treated with some root-producing hormone as an additional aid.

Second, the soil should be warm and hence layers to be successful should be made when the soil temperatures are high.

Third, the most important, soil moisture should be constant and high, in order to supply the best conditions for rooting. This is where many failures occur for, having successfully rooted, the young roots are allowed to die from lack of constant moisture.

The time for making most layers is in the early spring before the shoots have started into active growth. Flexible young branches, about the thickness of a stout lead pencil, are carefully bent in an arching way so as to reach into the ground and still have a small part of the shoot at the end available for staking and being held in an upright position for future growth. Care should be taken in the bending of the shoot, and special care should be taken when it comes to making the small cut on the under-surface of the branch which will be the part deepest in the ground.

This cut should be slanting and less than half-way through the branch. The theory is to expose some of the cambium so that rooting may be augmented. If the cut is too deep, the branch may break. Some rooting hormone material might be applied to the exposed surfaces of the cut (Hormodin #3) and the branch staked into the ground several inches deep. The staking (merely using a stick with an inverted V-shaped crotch) is essential to keep the branch firmly in place and to prevent it from moving about as the wind blows the branches. The tip of the shoot might also be staked in an upright position for the same reason. Then, several inches of good soil, preferably finely screened, are placed on top of the bent branch and the initial operation is completed.

There are variations in the method of exposing the cambium. One method (other than the simple cut) is to remove a ring of the bark about a quarter of an inch wide just above the part where the roots, hopefully, are expected to be produced. Another method is to twist a piece of wire tightly around the twig just above where roots are expected. It is obvious that both these operations constrict the free movement of nutrients up and down the stem, thus aiding in the rooting process.

Making the layer itself is easy enough, but keeping the soil moist (not wet) is the most difficult part of the entire operation. The Dutch nurserymen are recognized as past masters in the art of layering and they have larger layering beds, where some old plants like rhododendrons have been layered for 50 years or more. Culture is such that the plant is forced to produce long single, pliable shoots at just the right time, and a single plant with 50 or more layers about it is a common sight in many nurseries.

However, the most important thing here is the fact that the water table in these nurseries is always a foot or so below the surface, readily controlled merely by local dams, so that the soil is always moist. In other places where layering is a commercial operation, the climate is usually such that the soil is constantly moistened by light misty rains, and there are few drought periods when the beds would have to be watered by hand.

Take as an example the layer that you have so casually made in your American garden—in most areas, the water table is not just a foot under the soil surface, nor is the climate such that misty rains keep the soil in a state of constant moisture. Sun, droughts and other conditions cause the soil to dry out at different times in different places, admittedly, but nevertheless cause the soil to dry out during the rooting process. If the small rootlets are just forming, and the soil is allowed to dry out thoroughly just once, that might be the end of the roots on that layer. Nor can you dig the layer out every week to see how it progresses.

Hence, the American nurseryman uses layering as a commercial venture very little, not only because it is a costly process, taking much hand labor, but also because the keeping of the soil moist about the layer is sometimes very difficult.

In your garden, you can aid the soil in retaining its moisture about the layer, by seeing to it that the layer is made in a shaded situation, and by mulching the soil over it with some material which reduces water loss from the soil. Pine needles, black polyethylene film and other materials are possibilities, but even then one must remember to check the soil occasionally and add water when necessary.

Removing the rooted layer should be done with care—it is not just a matter of severing the branch below the new roots, digging up the plant and taking it to its new location. It might be best to do the work in 2 stages. First, at the end of the season or the beginning of the following spring after the layer is thoroughly rooted, sever the branch below the roots, and leave the layer in place for a full year of growth

Layering rhododendrons in a Dutch nursery. (*Photo by Arnold Arboretum, Jamaica Plain, Mass.*)

as a separate plant. The top might be cut back a bit to force more bushy growth. This is good insurance, for moving a newly-rooted layer just after it has been severed from the parent plant is sometimes just too much of a sudden shock for the young plant.

Kinds of Layers

Tip layering is usually practiced with plants like blackberries, black or purple raspberries and forsythia. Here the long shoots are bent over and the tip of the branch is inserted in the soil and firmly staked to prevent movement, usually done in the late summer when the current year's growth is just completed. No special operation is made on the tip of the shoot; these plants are such that the shoots usually root when handled in this manner. In fact, merely by observing an old plant, one can usually find such rooted layers that have come about naturally.

Then there is the simple layer, where a branch of the previous year's growth is bent, partially cut, staked in the ground and the tip end of the shoot staked in an upright position. This is usually done in the early spring before leaf growth has started, and this method is probably the best and easiest, by which the home gardener can root many woody plants with proper after-care.

Serpentine layering is sometimes practiced with plants like wisterias, clematis, philodendrons and other vines, when a series of loops are made with 1 long vine, so that eventually several plants are made from the 1 shoot.

Mound layering is practiced to some extent, with certain plants, by American nurserymen. Quince and certain apple stocks are first planted out, possibly with a single trunk, and then cut to within a few inches of the soil, forcing many young shoots to grow. When these are well on their way, the soil is mounded up about them for 6 in. or more, and after a certain amount of time these shoots root and can be removed from the parent plants and started off as individual plants. The old stock plant remains and sends up more and more shoots each year, sometimes lasting 20 years or more. When the shoots are a few inches high the soil is mounded up about ½ the height of the shoot. This operation is repeated once or twice again during the growing season so that by midsummer, when the shoots may have grown 18 in., the soil will have been mounded up about half the length of the shoot. Such shoots can be taken from the parent plant if they are rooted, in the fall, or better still, if there is a possibility of severe winter temperatures in the early spring, after all danger from winter injury is past. It is obvious that the mother plants must be kept in good growing condition

by proper culture, watering and fertilization, to produce the right kind of vigorous young shoots year after year to be used for layering.

The trench method of layering is not well adapted for use by the home gardener. It merely consists of completely covering a shoot of the proper plant in the soil. If the right kind of plant is selected, and very few are amenable to this treatment, the branch will send up several shoots and some of these may be rooted and can be eventually severed from the parent plant.

If one is interested in propagating plants asexually out-of-doors with a minimum amount of effort, one should be on the watch for runners (like those from the strawberry plant) that actually root and can be severed easily from the parent plant in the spring or fall.

Some woody plants like *Cornus stolonifera* normally send out underground stolons that can supply new plants. Suckers are also always a possibility with many plants. However, one should not believe that just because a plant sends up a sucker from its roots, it is a rooted sucker. It may be, but by carefully removing a bit of the soil from about the base of the sucker one can readily see if it has roots. If so, it is always good practice to cut off its attachment to the parent plant but to leave it in place, unmolested for a year to allow it to grow bigger and better roots. It might also be advisable to cut back some of the top at the same time the mother root is cut. This not only gives the sucker roots less top to support, but forces out more bushy growth during the period the plant is trying to supply all its needs itself.

It is not correct to say that all woody plants can be successfully layered, but certainly many of them can be. The simple procedures described here are sufficient to bring good results. The time of the layer (early spring), the suitability of the stock used (pliable shoots mostly of the previous year's growth or possibly 2-year-old growth) and the keeping of the soil moist about the rooting layer, all should be considered carefully.

In Holland, nurserymen are rooting such unlikely plants as maples, birches, *Fothergilla* species and several species of Elm. Of course, the easiest subjects for rooting as layers, are the plants which will root easily from cuttings, such as *Celastrus, Deutzia, Euonymus, Forsythia, Ligustrum, Lonicera, Philadelphus, Rosa, Spiraea, Viburnum* and *Weigela* species. The gardener might well try his technique with one of these first before he tries the more difficult plants like the rare Magnolia or the beautiful Rhododendron.

LAYIA (LAY-ia)
platyglossa   1′   annual   Showy Tidy-tips
Western North American spring-blooming

flowers, with alternate, linear leaves 3 in. long, yellow flower heads 1½ in. across; sometimes the rays are white tipped. There is a variety **alba** with white flowers, the rays tipped with pink. Seeds may be sown in a sunny situation outdoors in April where the plants are to grow and should eventually be thinned to a foot apart.

LEACHING. Losing material by percolation, as rain washing away nutrients through the soil.

LEAD ARSENATE. An insecticide, which see.

LEADER. The primary or terminal shoot of a tree.

LEAD-PLANT = *Amorpha canescens*

LEADTREE = *Leucaena glauca*

LEADWORT. See CERATOSTIGMA.

LEAF. The principal appendage or lateral organ

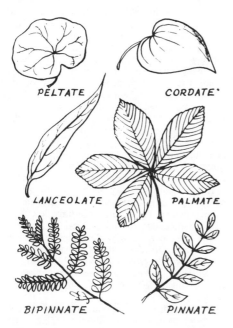

PELTATE

CORDATE·

LANCEOLATE

PALMATE

BIPINNATE

PINNATE

Different kinds of leaves

borne by the stem or axis. Simple leaf: when undivided; compound leaf: when divided into distinct parts.

LEAF CURL. The name of a serious fungus disease on Peach to distinguish from curled leaves caused by insects. Also this refers to a condition such as occurs on Rhododendron when exposed to cold weather or to Tomato when exposed to hot dry sunny weather. These leaf curls are thought to indicate the attempt of the plants to reduce excessive evaporation of moisture in cold dry wind or hot sun by reducing the leaf surface.

LEAFLET. The separate division of a compound leaf.

LEAF-SCAR. The mark on the twig left after the leaf falls.

LEAFSPOT. This is the name given to many plant diseases which cause spots on leaves of plants in at least one stage of the growth. They may be caused by bacteria, fungi or nematodes. Most leaf spot diseases live over the winter on fallen leaves and plant debris and suggest a good reason for a careful cleanup in the garden before winter. Because of the exposed nature of leaf spot diseases they are relatively easily controlled by spraying or dusting with fungicides. Bacterial leaf spots occur on Begonia, English Ivy, Geranium, Viburnum and on stone fruits where they are often called a "shothole" fungus when the infected spots fall out. Septoria leafspot occurs on Chrysanthemum, Curcurbits and Tomato while the Phyllosticta leaf spot infects Mountain-laurel. Tar spot which is well described by the name occurs on Holly, Maple and Willow. Several lawn grass diseases are known as leaf spots and there are resistant strains of bent grass available. Cane fruits suffer from leaf spot late in the season. See BLACKSPOT on roses.

LEAF-STALK. The stem of a leaf, petiole.

LEATHERLEAF = *Chamaedaphne calyculata*

LEATHERWOOD = *Dirca palustris*

LECHEGUILLA = *Agave lecheguilla*

LEDUM (LEE-dum)

groenlandicum   3′   Zone 2   Labrador-tea
A perennial evergreen shrub having alternate, oblong leaves 1½–3 in. long with entire margins which are curled under and a felty undersurface. The leaves are fragrant when bruised and during the Revolutionary War were used as a substitute for tea. The white flowers, borne in a terminal umbel, have 5 sepals and 5 spreading petals. The seed capsule is about ½ in. long. The plant is an excellent one for the northern bog garden and, if the soil is acid, will make out in a drier, woodsy site, but will not tolerate long, hot summers. Native to swamps and mountains across Canada, its range extends to N.J. and the states around the Great Lakes. It flowers in May and June. Seeds may be sown as soon as ripe or stored dry in airtight containers in a cool place and then sown. Plants can also be divided in the spring before growth starts and hardwood cuttings (which see) can be rooted.

LEEK (*Allium porrum*), a hardy onionlike plant but is milder and more hardy than the onion. It produces a sheaf of leaves rather than a bulb which, when well grown and blanched, is mild and tender. Its general culture is the same as for onion (see ONION) except that leek plants are blanched by gradually pulling the soil against the lower portion of the plant. Leek can be stored like Celery in trenches or pits. Popular varieties are 'American Flag', 'Monstrous Carentan', and 'Musselburg'.

GRANT B. SNYDER

LEEK, LILY = *Allium moly*

LEGOUSIA (le-GOU-sia)

speculum-veneris (*specularia perfoliata*) $1\frac{1}{2}''$
annual   Venus' Looking-glass
A low native lawn and garden weed, common throughout eastern North America, with alternate, simple, nearly rounded leaves $\frac{1}{2}$ in. across and clasping the stem. The blue flowers, 1–3 in each leaf axil, have a 5-lobed corolla and are only about $\frac{1}{3}$ in. across, appearing from June to Aug. For control see WEED-CONTROLLING CHEMICALS.

LEGUME. Seed vessel or pod of the Pea or Bean Family. However, the term has been expanded, popularly, to include the plants of the Pea Family, bearing pealike flowers and pods as fruits. They are good for the soil because they have root tubercles, which can absorb and utilize nitrogen from the air if certain bacteria are present in the soil. It is this quality which makes Alfalfa, Vetch, Clover, soybeans and cowpeas so good as cover crops, plowed into the soil. However, the bacteria must be present in the soil, and if a field is to be planted to one of these crops on which they have not been grown before, it pays to add the bacteria. These can be purchased or supplied by state experiment stations which should be written for information on and suggestions for sources from which the bacteria can be obtained.

LEGUMINOSAE = The Pea Family

LEIOPHYLLUM (ly-o-FILL-um)

buxifolium   18″   **Zone 5   Box Sandmyrtle**
Not especially outstanding, but this evergreen native of our southeastern coastal area is valued for seashore planting. It is best planted in clumps. The small, waxy white flowers appearing in May are similar to those of blueberries (it belongs to the same plant family) and the lustrous evergreen leaves, only about $\frac{1}{2}$ in. long, turn a brownish green in the fall. Seed may be sown as soon as ripe or stored dry in airtight containers for a year and then sown. Both softwood and hardwood cuttings root.

buxifolium prostratum (*lyonii*)   10″   **Zone 5
Allegheny Sand-myrtle**

A low evergreen shrub from the mountains of N.Car., with decumbent branches radiating from the central upright stems. Loose flower heads of white flowers, similar to those of *Ledum groenlandicum*, to which this genus is related, appear in spring.

LEITNERIA (light-NEER-ia)

floridana   18′   **Zone 5   Florida Corkwood**
This is not a good plant for gardens but is native from Mo. to Tex. and is of interest because its wood is of the lightest weight of any native American wood. The leaves are alternate 3–6 in. long and light green. The flowers are in catkins in early spring. It grows best in moist, peaty soils. Seed may be sown as soon as ripe or stored dry in airtight containers in a cool place for up to a year and then sown. Softwood cuttings and root cuttings (which see) root readily.

LEMAIREOCEREUS   (lem-air-o-SEE-reus)
Shrub or treelike cacti usually columnar but with some branches. The flowers are funnel-form, not very large, the fruit is white to red and, when young, covered with spines, but nevertheless the plants are often grown in the Tropics for their edible fruits. Not much grown in the U.S. Native from Ariz. to Peru.

dumortieri   50′   **Zone 9**
A green columnar cactus with 5–6 ribs set with fine creamy-colored spines. Flowers white about 2 in. long. Native to central Mexico.

marginatus   25′   **Zone 10   Organ-pipe Cactus**
Often used in parts of Mexico, where it is native, for making living fences. Its outline gives one the general impression of organ pipes; the individual branches are ribbed. As a house plant it can easily grow too tall, in which case a part of the top should be cut off and rooted and the older part might be discarded. Individual plants are up to 6 in. in dia., with 5–6 ribs, flowers greenish white within and reddish outside, up to 3 in. long. For culture, see CACTI AND SUCCULENTS.

weberi   30′   **Zone 10**
A much-branched tree cactus often having hundreds of erect branches; native to Mexico. The 10-ribbed columns are dark green, and the spines are short, white to gray. The flowers are 4 in. long and white.

LEMNA (LEM-na)

minor   aquatic plant   Zone 4   Duckweed
Stemless, minute, floating water plants, often used as food by fish and water fowl but, under the right conditions, this can turn the surface of a pond or sluggish stream into a green scum by the end of the summer. They fall to the bottom of the pond in late fall, and rise again in the summer. They increase extremely fast, sometimes are used in home aquaria but even there can become a pest by rapid division. The leaflike green organ is only $\frac{1}{4}$ in. long, bears one rootlet and minute monoecious flowers which

have only one stamen or one pistil. Native on all continents.

LEMON. Lemons (*Citrus limonia*) are the most popular acid citrus for cooling drinks and cookery. Although the tree is less attractive than most other citrus species, the value of the fruit goes far to alleviating this deficiency.

Lemon varieties are fewer in number than for most popular citrus fruits, and among the tree lemons there is little difference in fruit characteristics.

'Eureka' is of typical "lemon" shape—elliptical, with a nipple at the blossom end and a more or less necked stem end. The tree is the smallest of the Lemon varieties, more open, spreading, and with nearly thornless shoots. In Calif. 'Eureka' is preferred in the cool coastal districts because more of its fruit ripen in the late spring and early summer.

'Lisbon' is the variety preferred in the Calif. lemon districts having higher summer temperatures, again because under these conditions a higher percentage of the fruit ripens at a favorable time. The tree is substantially larger, more upright, denser and more vigorous than other Lemon varieties, and with thorny shoots.

'Villafranca' is a variety quite similar to 'Eureka' in fruit, but more like 'Lisbon' in tree characters. In Calif. this variety tends to produce a higher percentage of its fruit in the fall and winter, an undesirable characteristic which has limited its use. However, it is the best adapted of the true lemons to the warm, humid Southeast.

'Meyer' (Meyer Lemon) is an anomalous kind, possibly a hybrid bearing acid fruits of lemon character. The fruit is nearly round, with a short nipple. It has a light orange color rather than yellow, with very juicy light orange-yellow flesh rather than the pale greenish-yellow of the true lemons. The tree is dwarf, and much more cold-resistant than the true lemons, which makes it a garden favorite.

'Ponderosa' (American Wonder) is mentioned primarily for its very large fruit; both tree and fruit have ornamental value, but the fruit is of poor quality for food use.

In regions where lemons are not well adapted the Rough Lemon and the Calamondin (*C. mitis*) are sometimes used as substitutes, as both yield fruit with acid, plentiful juice. Rough Lemon, as its name implies, bears a roughish orange-yellow fruit of small orange size. Calamondin fruit is quite small, round and yellow; this species is sometimes used as an ornamental garden plant.

'Millsweet' and 'Dorshapo' are 2 sweet lemons (low acid); both are believed by some to be hybrid sorts, although their fruits are quite lemonish in appearance. 'Millsweet' is nearly round in shape, while 'Dorshapo' resembles 'Eureka' in fruit. Both have the true Lemon flavor. They are generally considered to be novelty fruits, but may have value for those who object to the highly acid citrus.

The true lemons are less cold-hardy than oranges, but slightly hardier than limes. Severe tree damage will occur when temperatures drop below 24° or 25° F., and defoliation will result at somewhat higher temperatures. The fruits are also slightly more tender by about one degree than are orange fruits. The 'Meyer', on the other hand, is fully as hardy as is the Orange. It will be recognized that protection against frost will be more difficult for lemons at any given site, but see ORANGE for protective measures.

Lemons perform much better in climates marked by relatively cool, dry summers; they grow and mature their fruit with excellent quality under these conditions. Both the tree and fruit are adversely affected by extremes of heat, and especially hot dry winds, which may cause defoliation and fruit drop. Lemons have also proved poorly adapted to warm, humid regions, as the southeastern United States and Hawaii. Under these conditions the trees suffer severely from fungal diseases, and the fruits tend to be large and gross. Of the varieties listed the sweet lemons, 'Meyer' and 'Villafranca', appear to do best.

The true lemons may flower year-round, hence have fruit in all stages of development and maturity each month of the year. The heaviest bloom normally occurs with the spring growth flush, but one or two lesser flushes normally follow through the summer. This results in a characteristic main-harvest period, but with minor crops at other seasons. 'Meyer' tends to have but a single spring bloom in the Southwest, but may bear off-season bloom in more humid, higher-average-temperature locales, as the Southeast.

Lemons are propagated by the same methods as given for Orange. Rootstocks commonly used are the same as for Orange, except that Lemon tends to overgrow Sour Orange stocks, and to be relatively weak on them. Sweet Orange, Citrange and Trifoliate are possibly all better, although the susceptibility of Sweet Orange stock to root rots should be recalled. Rough Lemon may be used with less detriment to the fruit than for oranges. Lemons may be topworked on other citrus species using the methods described under Orange.

Size differences among Lemon varieties and kinds result in a variety of recommended planting distances, which also can be varied by the training given. The vigorous true lemons, as 'Lisbon' and 'Villafranca', make large trees on good rootstocks if allowed to grow freely. They require 24 to 30 ft. spacing; with heavy pruning they may be kept somewhat smaller. 'Eureka' is often kept low by heavy pruning, and can be maintained easily at 18 to 20 ft. spacing. 'Meyer', being semi-dwarf naturally, needs but 8 to 12 ft. spacing. Rough Lemon and the sweet lemons would need the same spacing as for 'Lisbon'; the Calamondin is often kept small by treating it as a small ornamental shrub; its natural tendency is to make a rather tall but narrow, cylindrical tree. The effects of closer planting and shaping are the same as described for Orange; also by using dwarfing Trifoliate stock, space requirements may be materially reduced.

Lemons are pruned more heavily than any other citrus species; rather than a requirement this is probably dictated by the need to keep trees small for the continual harvest. Nevertheless, it is true that lemons fruit much better than other citrus under such heavy pruning, which may therefore be used to control tree size. Lemons tend to throw strong, upright water-sprouts which, if not removed, soon make an impenetrable thicket of the center of the tree, and tend to shade out the productive portions of the tree. Some of these watersprouts may be converted to fruiting wood by pulling them to the outside of the tree, in a nearly horizontal attitude, but generally they are removed. 'Eureka' can be kept quite low and spreading; 'Lisbon' and 'Villafranca' somewhat more upright. 'Meyer' needs practically no pruning except the removal of interfering branches. Cultural needs and practices are otherwise very similar to those for the Orange.

Commercial lemons are harvested according to size, without regard to color development. Green fruit may be ripened artificially with ethylene (see ORANGE) or be stored, where it develops its full color. The gardener can profit by this experience, for it is not necessary to await color development to use the fruit; when it is of typical size and is juicy it is ready for use. However, for appearance most fruit will probably be picked as it reaches full yellow color; large fruits on vigorous trees may actually be past their prime by that time. Lemons should be clipped from the tree, and when properly handled they have a very long storage life, although this is less important to the gardener considering the everbearing habit of the species. For storage the fruit should be washed, well cured, and held at refrigerator temperatures. Under close commercial control lemons are sometimes stored for 6 months or more. The skin becomes thinner and may even appear and feel dry but the fruit retains its juicy condition.

The 'Meyer' does not have as long a storage life, but holds its fruit on the tree over a rather extended period. Like the true lemons they may be used from the time they are juicy to the end of their on-tree life. Rough Lemon and Calamondin will be used from the tree.

The pests and diseases of the lemons are the same as for Orange. Lemons are more susceptible to scab and other fungus diseases than most citrus in the warm, humid Southeast. Under adverse conditions lemons also tend to defoliate rather readily; the tree is, therefore, often less attractive than are other citrus.

CLARON O. HESSE

LEMON-BALM = *Melissa officinalis*

LEMON VERBENA = *Aloysia triphylla*

LENS

culinaris (*L. esculenta*)   1½'   annual   Lentil
A member of the Pea Family with the terminal leaflet a tendril or short bristle. The pods are ¾ in. long, native to southern Europe where it is widely grown for food or the vines are grown for forage. Propagated easily by seeds.

LENTEN-ROSE = *Helleborus orientalis*

LENTIBULARIACEAE = The   Bladderwort Family

LENTICEL. Lens-shaped spots on young bark equivalent in function to the stomata on the leaf.

LENTIL = *Lens culinaris*

LEONOTIS (lee-on-O-tis)
leonurus   6'   Zone 10   Lion's-ear
A tall perennial with soft green elliptic leaves 2 in. long; showy 2-lipped reddish-yellow flowers 2 in. long, borne in whorls during the winter. Grown in southern Fla. and Calif. as well as in the greenhouse for its showy winter bloom. Propagated by cuttings in early spring. Native to Africa.

LEONTOPODIUM (le-on-TOPO-dium)
alpinum   6"   Zone 5   Edelweiss
This is the very popular, well-known alpine wild flower native to the Alps. It should have well-drained sandy soil and a sunny situation. The white, woolly, alternate leaves are indicative of the plant, as are the creeping stems. The flowers are actually yellow disks, not prominent, appearing in July and Aug., but beneath these are silvery bracts that are longer than the disks and make the plant interesting. It can be propagated by division or seed can be sown. Seeds do not ripen well in moist summers but do ripen well during dry summers.

LEONURUS (lee-on-YEW-rus)
cardiaca   5'   Zone 3   Common Motherwort
A rank-growing perennial weed, naturalized in eastern North America, native to Europe. The pale purple flowers are clustered in the axils of the opposite leaves, appearing from July to Sept. The leaves are 4 in. wide and 3-5 lobed

and the stems bearing the flowers throughout their length may be 2 ft. long. The root is tenacious and hard to eradicate. Contact with the plant causes dermatitis to certain susceptible people.

LEOPARD-PLANT = *Ligularia kaempferi* **'Aureo-maculata'**

LEOPARDSBANE. See DORONICUM.

LEPACHYS (LEP-ak-is) = *Ratibida*

LEPIDIUM (lep-ID-ium)

sativum   2′   annual   Garden Cress Pepperweed
A member of the Mustard Family with pinnatifid leaves, becoming linear and entire. This is often grown for salads since its leaves are tasty.

virginicum   2′   annual   Pepper-grass
Sometimes a biennial, native to North America and a common garden weed from the East Coast to the Rocky Mountains. The rosettes of leaves at the base may be apparent over winter. Its alternate stem leaves are toothed and very sour-tasting and the small flowers and flat seed pods only $\frac{1}{10}$ in. across on long upright spiked branches are typical. There are several other similar species, some introduced from Europe and Asia. The peppery pods or seeds make excellent seasoning for salads and soups.

LEPIDOTE. With small scurfy scales.

LEPTODERMIS (lept-o-DER-mis)

oblonga   3′   Zone 5   Chinese Leptodermis
An Asiatic shrub with few-flowered clusters of violet-purple flowers $\frac{1}{2}$ in. long from July to Sept. which grows best in the full sun. It is propagated by seeds or softwood cuttings in the summer.

LEPTOSPERMUM (lept-o-SPERM-um)

flexuosum = *Agonis flexuosa*

laevigatum   25′   Zone 9   Australian Tea-tree
This Australian tree will grow in almost pure sand but will not grow in heavy soils with poor drainage. The flowers are white, about $\frac{3}{4}$ in. across, appearing from March to May, and the evergreen leaves are small and blunt, about 1 in. long and $\frac{1}{2}$ in. wide. As the tree matures it takes on an ungainly habit. It has been planted by the hundreds of thousands in Calif. to attempt the stabilization of shifting sands.

LESPEDEZA (les-ped-EE-za). These are shrubby, pealike plants belonging to the Pea Family, with trifoliate, alternate leaves and fruits that are flat pods. They can be heavily pruned or even cut to the ground in the late winter and be expected to flower and fruit the same year. Propagation is by seed (preferably soaked in hot water at 190° F. overnight) before sowing, or by softwood or hardwood cuttings.

bicolor   9′   Zone 4   Shrub Bush-clover
Valued only for its late summer flowers that are rosy-purple, pealike, in small clusters in late July. This Asiatic shrub does well in light sandy soils and since it blooms on the current year's growth, it can be cut to the ground in the early spring and still be expected to flower well.

hirta   4′–5′   Zone 3   Hairy Lespedeza
A tall, branching perennial with whitish or yellowish irregular flowers in axillary heads similar to the clovers. It grows in open, sandy locations from southeastern Canada and throughout the U.S., blooming from Aug. to Oct. Its habit is too vigorous and weedy to recommend its use as a garden plant.

japonica   6′   Zone 5   Japanese Bush-clover
This bush-clover is similar in most respects to *L. bicolor* except that the flowers are white and they bloom in Oct., after those of *L. bicolor* have faded. Few woody plants bloom this late in the fall, hence this Japanese plant has some value for this reason.

striata   1½′   annual   Common Lespedeza
The leaves bear many small leaflets and the pealike flowers are small and pink, borne in the axils of the leaves. Native to China and Japan, naturalized in North America. Usually grown only for forage or as a green manure (which see) for plowing under and thus enriching the soil.

thunbergii   6′   Zone 5   Thunberg Lespedeza
A shrub with rosy-purple pealike flowers about $\frac{1}{2}$ in. long in 8 in. racemes, appearing in Aug. and Sept. Native to China and Japan. Valued for its many late flowers. This may be killed back to the ground by severe winters, but it blooms on the current year's growth.

violacea   2′   Zone 5   Violet Lespedeza
Similar to, although smaller than *L. hirta*, this species has purple or violet flowers which appear from July to Sept. Found in dry, open locations, the plant ranges from southern New England to Fla., and west to the Plains states.

LESSER-CELANDINE = *Ranunculus ficaria*

LETTUCE (*Lactuca sativa*). This is the most popular salad crop and, consequently, is grown in nearly all home gardens. It is probably of European origin and records indicate its culture and use as early as 500 B.C.

Climatic Requirements

Lettuce is a cool season crop. It stands cold better than heat and most varieties will produce seed prematurely if grown in midsummer. It is consequently grown, primarily, as an early spring and a fall crop in the North and as a late fall, winter and spring crop in the South. It is also grown quite extensively in greenhouses in the northern region during the winter months.

Varieties

There are literally hundreds of so-called varieties listed by the seed trade. Many vary only in minor characters such as days to maturity, size of head, resistance to disease or drought, etc. For all practical purposes these varieties may be divided into 4 distinct groups:

Lettuce—different types

1. **Crisphead**, distinguished by their firm heads having leaves with prominent ribs, coarse veins and are crisp and brittle in texture. Because of these characteristics it is sometimes called Cabbage Heading Lettuce. Recommended varieties are **'Crisphead'**, **'Pennlake'**, **'Great Lake'**, **'Ithaca'** and strains of **'Imperial'**.

2. **Butterhead**, distinguished by their soft, pliable leaves and buttery texture. The ribs are less prominent, the veins finer and the heads smaller and not as compact as the Crisphead types. The more popular varieties are **'White Boston'**, **'Buttercrunch'** and **'Bibb'**.

3. **Looseleaf** or Bunching varieties do not form heads, and are characterized by a rather spreading habit with a clustered or bunched arrangement of leaves. **'Grand Rapids'**, **'Salad Bowl'**, **'Ruby Red'** and **'Green Ice'** are the most common sorts. **'Oak Leaf'** and **'Black Seeded Simpson'** are of lesser importance.

4. **Cos** or **Romaine** is recognized by the upright character of the plant, the long loaf-shaped head and the long narrow leaves. The leaves appear coarse, but are tender, sweet and tasty. Cos will stand heat better than the other types of lettuce and, therefore, is useful for summer culture. The more common variety is **'Paris White Cos'**.

Soil and Soil Preparation

Lettuce is grown on many types of soil provided they contain a high level of fertility, have a good moisture-holding capacity and are of an open, fine texture. Sandy loam soils are preferred for the spring crop, but the heavier silt loams and mulch soils are also widely used. Thorough preparation by spading or plowing to produce a good seedbed is very important. Lettuce soils should not be acid. A pH of 6.2 to 6.5 is optimum. See LIME.

Fertilizers

The lettuce plant is a poor forager with a relatively small root system. Good quality is dependent on quick, uniform growth and, therefore, the soil must have a good supply of organic matter (not including muck) and a well-balanced supply of commercial fertilizer. If available, well-rotted stable manure should be worked into the top soil at the rate of 20–30 bu. per 1000 sq. ft. A well-rotted compost will also be a good source of organic matter for all mineral soils. In addition, 20–30 lbs. of a 5-10-10 fertilizer should be broadcast per 1000 sq. ft. of area. If no manure is used increase the fertilizer application to 40 lbs. per 1000 sq. ft. In many cases it is desirable to side dress with nitrate of soda 2–3 weeks after the plants have been well established in the garden. Use 4–5 lbs. per 1000 sq. ft. and cultivate into the top few inches but be sure not to disturb the root system. See VEGETABLE GARDEN for soil preparation and fertilizers.

Growing Plants for Transplantation

For an early crop of lettuce in the northern region seed is started indoors some 6–8 weeks in advance of planting out-of-doors. Sow the seed in flats or boxes in drills or broadcast in a hotbed or cold frame. If neither is available place the boxes in the kitchen window. See VEGETABLE GARDEN. As soon as the seedlings are 1½–2 in. tall transplant to other containers at a spacing of 1½ in. × 1½ in. A week or 10 days prior to field setting, gradually reduce the temperature to something similar to that of the outdoors. If properly hardened these transplants will withstand short exposures to temperatures in the low 30's. If lettuce plants are purchased from a dealer it is important to (1) check the variety, and (2) insist on good stocky plants.

Outdoor Planting and Care

The transplants should be carefully removed from the flat and set out in the garden as soon as the soil can be prepared properly. Planting distance varies with the variety, Crisphead types 15 in., Butterhead and Cos 10 in., and Looseleaf 4 to 5 in. apart in the row. The rows are usually spaced at 15–18 in., As soon as the plants have been planted, they should be watered to prevent severe wilting.

At the same time that the transplants are planted out-of-doors it is advisable to make a planting of seed in drills 15 in. apart in the garden in order to provide a crop after the indoor grown plants have been harvested. Sow the seed relatively thin, cover lightly with soil, and water. When the seedlings are 1½–2 in. high, thin to the proper distance. With leaf lettuce several succession plantings of this sort will be advisable.

The fall crop can be started the same as the spring crop, either with transplants or direct seeding in the garden. It is very important with both the spring and fall crops to plant only the amount that can be used by the family. Succession plantings of several dozen plants may be sufficient.

Shallow cultivation to control weeds is important. A blade attachment to the hand cultivator will cut off the seeds, leave a shallow mulch and not injure the lettuce roots. Irrigation may also be necessary in order to maintain optimum soil moisture.

Insects

Lettuce has few insect enemies that cause direct damage. Several, however, are very important carriers of diseases.

Diseases

Lettuce is subject to a large number of diseases, a few of which are important but very difficult to control. Sclerotenia drop, a fungus which causes a soft watery rot, bottom rot, the fungus which causes damping-off of seedlings and which, on lettuce, destroys the lower leaves, and gray mold rot are the 3 most important diseases which cause a breakdown of plant tissue and show up as rots. These are all soil borne and, therefore, are difficult to control. Basic control measures are (1) crop rotation (not possible in a small garden), (2) frequent shallow cultivation to maintain a dry soil mulch under the plants, (3) the removal of all old plant refuse, and (4) dusting with a 7% metallic copper compound on the ground under the plants several weeks before harvest. Planting Lettuce on shallow ridges is also a good practice in order to allow better air cirulation under the plant.

Downy mildew may be best controlled by using resistant varieties and following directions as noted above for the rots. Yellows is a virus disease carried and spread by leaf hoppers. Since this disease is found on a large number of weeds it is difficult to control. Spraying or dusting the young Lettuce plants and the borders of the garden (weeds) every 10 days with 5%

Sevin dust or wettable powder or 4% malathion dust is the recommended control for the leaf hoppers. Dust or spray the borders and turn over soil after harvest.

Tip burn is one of the most common diseases of Lettuce, particularly the heading types. It is a physiological breakdown of tissue apparently caused by high temperature and humidity. It is most prevalent during late spring and early summer. The use of resistant varieties is the only control.

GRANT B. SNYDER

LEUCAENA (lew-SEE-na)

glauca   30′   Zone 10   Leadtree, White Popinac

Native to tropical America and naturalized in southern Fla., this may grow up to 65 ft. high but is usually only half that size. The white flowers are borne in fluffy balls up to 1½ in. wide; the evergreen, twice-compound leaves have a feathery texture and the fruit is a narrow reddish-brown pod about 6 in. long. The young pods and seeds are edible and the plant is grown as fodder for cattle and goats. The flat seeds are used in bracelets and other novelties. This belongs to the Pea Family and is propagated by seeds.

LEUCOCORYNE (leuco-cor-EYE-ne)

ixioides   1′   Zone 9   Glory-of-the-sun

A bulbous herb from Chile with small white-to-blue flowers in small umbels that are not freely produced. Sometimes forced in greenhouses in the North. In southern Calif. plant outdoors in Sept. or Oct. 4–6 in. deep. If grown in the greenhouse, force as for Freesia. Propagated by offsets and seeds.

LEUCOCRINUM (lew-ko-KRIN-um)

montanum   7″   Zone 4   Star-lily

A native bulbous herb of the Lily Family from Neb. to Calif. with pure white, fragrant, funnel-shaped flowers, 1–4 in. long, borne near the surface of the ground in clusters in early spring. Each flowers lasts only a day. Leaves at the base are 4–7 in. long and less than ¼ in. wide. A rock garden plant. Rhizomes can be planted in the fall. Propagation by seeds. Almost stemless, and it is reported to be poisonous to sheep.

LEUCODENDRON (lew-ko-DEN-dron)

argenteum   30′   Zone 10   Silver Leucodendron

The soft silvery appearance of the foliage of this South African tree gives it a value and beauty all its own. It is definitely rounded in habit, with leaves 6 in. long that are covered with silky hairs. It is spectactulary beautiful for this reason but unfortunately fails to live much longer than 25–30 years. The leaves are 3–6 in. long and ½–1¼ in. wide, male and female flowers are on different plants and the fruit is a nut.

LEUCOJUM (lew-KO-jum)

aestivum $1\frac{1}{2}'$ **Zone 4**   **Summer Snowflake**
A small bulbous herb with leaves $1\frac{1}{2}$ ft. long and $\frac{1}{2}$ in. wide, bearing white flowers, $\frac{3}{4}$ in. long, tipped with green, borne 2–8 together in late spring. Native to central and southern Europe. These should be planted 3 in. deep, during Sept. or Oct. **'Gravetye'** has larger blooms than those of the species.

autumnale $1'$ **Zone 5**   **Autumn Snowflake**
With white flowers tinged with pink, blooming in Sept. Native to the Mediterranean Region.

vernum $1'$ **Zone 4**   **Spring Snowflake**
With drooping bell-like white flowers, green tipped, $\frac{3}{4}$ in. long, solitary, borne in early spring. Native to central Europe. These should be planted 3 in. deep in late Aug. or Sept. and left alone for several years. A good plant for the rockery.

LEUCOTHOE (lew-KO-tho-ee). Alternate-leaved, deciduous and evergreen shrubs belonging to the Heath Family, with several species, but *L. fontanesiana* (formerly *L. catesbaei*) is the most outstanding ornamental species and

of propagating them. However, both softwood and hardwood cuttings (which see) can easily be rooted.

axillaris **6'**   **Zone 6**   **Coast Leucothoe**
Similar to *L. fontanesiana* (*L. catesbaei*) but less hardy. An evergreen and apparently not as widely used in gardens.

catesbaei = *L. fontanesiana*

davisiae **3'** **Zones 5–6** **Black-laurel Leucothoe**
Evergreen, alternate leaves $\frac{3}{4}$–$2\frac{1}{4}$ in. long, lustrous and dark green, this shrub has its small, waxy white flowers in terminal but nodding upright panicles $2\frac{1}{2}$–4 in. long and they appear in June. Native from Ore. to Calif. This is a beautiful species because the flowers are mostly borne conspicuously above the foliage. Propagated by cuttings in Aug.

fontanesiana (*L. catesbaei*) **6'**   **Zone 4**
Drooping Leucothoe
This is a truly excellent native American evergreen in the South but semi-evergreen in the North. Its excellent qualities should be known and appreciated far more than they are, and the plant should be used more. The white, waxy

Leucothoe is a fine garden shrub and can be used indoors in many types of arrangements. This one includes *Pyracantha coccinea*—the Firethorn. (*Photo by Arnold Arboretum, Jamaica Plain, Mass.*)

should be planted in every garden where there is acid soil. The white-to-pinkish flowers are small and bell-shaped, like those of blueberries.

Propagation

Seeds may be sown as soon as ripe, or stored dry in airtight containers in a cool place for up to a year and then sown. Dividing the clumps in the early spring is about as easy a way as any

flowers, similar to those of blueberries, bloom in early June on small racemes hanging down under the gracefully arching stems. The dark, lustrous, evergreen leaves are up to 7 in. long and turn a beautiful bronze color in the fall, a color which can last all winter. The older stems should be removed occasionally to keep the plant young and vigorous for it looks its best when kept under 3 ft. tall. Such stems should be cut at the ground level. It grows well in places suited for rhododendrons, for after all it is also an ericaceous plant like the rhododendron. Native from Va. to Ga., it is excellent to have in the garden for cutting purposes and for use in arrangements indoors. It is most unfortunate that this plant suffered a name-change recently and according to the International Rules of Botanical Nomenclature can no longer be known as *Leucothoe catesbaei*. The variety 'Girard's Rainbow' originated as a seedling in 1949 in the Girard Nurseries of Geneva, Ohio. It has been described as taking on "many colors during the growing period. New shoots are bright red, turning to pink, then to yellow, green and copper variations". Some people like this, others do not, but the colors are usually more pronounced in the fall. There are also several other variegated forms available. 'Nana'—only 15–23 in. tall but 6 ft. wide after 30 years of growth, this new dwarf form should become very popular. The Arnold Arboretum has had this variety growing in its nurseries for several years, and at no time has it grown over 2′ tall. It makes a truly excellent foundation plant at this height, and is always available for cutting pieces for indoor flower arrangements. Like the species, it is easily rooted from cuttings, or the plant can be force-fully divided when it gets up to a sufficient size. It is just such plants as this that have real merit in any garden. The unobservant will pass it over as "similar" to the species.

Another native species *L. axillaris* is often confused with the Drooping Leucothoe, but the latter is slightly more hardy.

keiskei　　**4′**　　**Zone 5**　　**Keisk's Leucothoe**
This Japanese evergreen Leucothoe has larger individual flowers (up to ⅝ in.) than those of the Drooping Leucothoe but is probably not as vigorous a grower.

racemosa　**6′–12′**　**Zone 5**　**Fetterbush, Sweet-bells**
A deciduous shrub, native from Mass. to Fla., valued for its slender racemes of small white-to-pinkish blueberrylike flowers in the spring and its scarlet autumn color. The alternate leaves are 1–3 in. long. This grows chiefly in moist or swampy places in acid soils.

LEVISTICUM (lev-ISS-tik-um)

officinale　　**6′**　　**Zone 6**　　**Lovage**
A perennial herb belonging to the Carrot Family grown for centuries for its aromatic seeds which are used in confectionery and in cordials. The leaves are thrice compound. The leaf stalk and stem, blanched, are used for a fragrant tea, or in place of celery, fresh or dried. The flowers and foliage together are used (as an oil) to flavor some tobaccos and in perfumes. It is a handsome, tropical-looking, background plant in the flower border. Native to southern Europe. Propagated by seed (sown in fall) or division.

LEWISIA (lew-ISS-ia). Members of the Portulaca Family, these are fleshy herbs with starchy roots, mostly native to western North America, and are used chiefly in rock gardens for their foliage and their white or red flowers produced in the early spring. Easily propagated by seeds or division in the spring. They do best in a climate with plenty of moisture in the spring when they flower, and a hot summer. Best planted in shade with some crushed stone around the base of the plant.

columbiana　**1′**　**Zone 5**　**Columbia Lewisia**
The linear evergreen leaves are 2 in. long; flowers are white to pink, ⅓ in. long, in panicles a foot high. Native to Ore. and Wash., especially in the mountains.

cotyledon　　**10″**　　**Zone 6**
Evergreen leaves 3 in. long are thick and fleshy, growing in rosettes and becoming matlike; flowers white with pink veins, ½ in. long and 2 in. wide, born in the late spring. Native to Calif.

pygmaea (*minima*)　**2″**　**Zone 3**　**Little Lewisia**
The tiniest species of Lewisia, this plant is often lost during its dormant season when the gardener cultivates his ground. Rosettes of narrow leaves 2 in. high are studded in June with large white flowers. When the flowers fade, the plant goes into dormancy and disappears from sight. Native to Wyo.

rediviva　**1′**　**Zone 4**　**Bitterroot Lewisia**
Probably the most grown of these species, with basal leaves very fleshy, 1–2 in. long, deciduous. Flowers rose to white, an inch long. Native from British Columbia to Ariz. The Indians used to eat this starchy root in the spring, but it becomes very bitter as it matures in the summer. The plant must have good drainage (supplied by a circle of crushed stone about it) and it should not have much winter moisture if it is to survive.

tweedyi　　**4″**　　**Zone 5**　　**Tweedy Lewisia**
Leaves fleshy, evergreen, obovate, 4 in. long; flowers salmon pink, 2 in. wide. This grows from a very thick root and is one of the many wild flowers near the summit of Mt. Rainier.

LEYCESTERIA (ly-sess-TEE-ria)

formosa　**6′**　**Zone 7**　**Formosa-honeysuckle**
This is a fast-growing shrub from the Himalayas and southwestern China. The flowers are purplish to white and small, appearing in the summer; the fruits are red-purple berries in the fall. The branches droop gracefully in an arching fashion. Since the plant may have the stems winter-injured even in Zone 7, one method of culture is to cut the branches almost to the

ground each fall. Then in the following spring, young shoots will spring up from the base and grow to 6 ft. tall and flower profusely during the late summer.

LIANA, LIANE. A woody climbing or twining plant.

LIATRIS (ly-AY-tris). Stiffly erect perennial herbs of the Composite Family, the plants rise from underground tuberous roots or corms, often with alternate, narrowly ovate leaves and flower heads composed of only disk flowers which are generally purple and are surrounded by many appressed green bracts, so that the flowers heads have a balloonlike appearance. These are borne in spikes or racemes. The plants make a striking color accent in the garden and will grow in poor soil. Propagation is by spring-sown seeds or division of plants in the spring, especially for named cultivars. Single plants look best in flower borders. It is not a plant for massing.

elegans 3′–4′ Zone 7 Pink-scale Gayfeather
This species has very narrow leaves and purple flower heads growing in a terminal spike. It is native to the dry pinelands of the South and blooms throughout the summer. An excellent plant for the garden, it may be propagated by seed sown in spring or fall or by removing small corms from established plants in spring.

graminifolia 2′ Zone 6 Grassleaf Gayfeather
With unpresuming purple spikes of flowers in summer and very narrow leaves, this is native from N.J. to Fla. Not very popular.

punctata 1–2½′ Zone 3 Dotted Gayfeather
Also having very narrow, linear leaves marked by numerous dots, with the leaves angled upward on the stem, this species has purple flower heads ¾ in. long, borne in a terminal spike similar to that of *L. elegans*. It may be found throughout the Great Plains states and blooms throughout the summer.

pycnostachya 3′–4′ Zone 3 Kansas Gay-
                                        feather
The narrowly linear leaves of this species are crowded on the erect stem and the purple flower heads, ½ in. long, with occasional leafy bracts longer than the flower head, are borne in a dense, terminal spike. The plant ranges over most of the Great Plains states, the damp prairies being its frequent habitat. It blooms from July to Oct.

scariosa 3′–4′ Zones 2–3 Tall Gayfeather
Distinguished by rather dry, scaly, oblong to linear leaves occurring sparsely on a hairy stem and a long, terminal cluster of purple flower heads, each borne on a short, stout stalk and having several alternating rows of sharply pointed bracts. It grows in damp meadows from N.Y. to Mich., and south to Fla. and La. It is

an excellent garden plant and may be propagated by seed sown in fall or by division of the plant in spring. 'White Spire' is a popular variety with all white flowers.

spicata 1′–6′ Zone 3 Spike Gayfeather
Usually noticed as plants about 3 ft. high with purple flowers in clusters about 15 in. long. Native to eastern North America. 'Kobold' is a hybrid with compact habit and dark purple flowers, blooming in Sept.

squarrosa 2′ Zone 4
A slender, pubescent perennial having linear leaves 6 in. long and a few large flower heads 1½ in. long with 15–60 white or purple daisylike flowers which bloom in late summer or fall. Native from Ontario to Fla. and Tex.

LIBERTIA (lib-BER-shia)
formosa 3′ Zone 8 Showy Libertia
A perennial herb with fibrous roots; leaves 1½ ft. long and stiff, arranged fanlike; white flowers on erect stalks, about ¾ in. long during May. Propagated by seeds and division. Native to Chile.

LIBOCEDRUS CHILENSIS = *Austrocedrus chilensis*

LIBOCEDRUS DECURRENS = *Calocedrus decurrens*

LICHENS. These organisms grow on rocks or tree branches. They have no true leaves, stems or roots. A lichen is said to be a green algae surrounded by a colorless fungus and a fungus is of course a plant without chlorophyll which can not manufacture its own food. Hence, it is the green algae in the lichen which manufactures the food, and the threads of the fungi wrap around them, protecting them from hot sun and aiding in keeping them in place, but nevertheless living off the food they manufacture.

Lichens grow throughout the entire world. Some are edible. It is said that the "manna" of the children of Israel, mentioned in the Bible, was actually lichen growths blown down from the mountains where they grew, onto the flat plains where they were collected and eaten to stave off starvation. The lichens can attach themselves to the rocks and eventually, as they die, become mixed with minute grains of rock, and it is these that made the first soils, billions of years ago. This process still goes on. In dry weather they shrivel up and look dead but in wet weather they swell up greatly, an action which has aided in breaking small pieces of rock off from larger ones, and thus aiding in making soil.

Lichens themselves do not reproduce spores, but the fungus that is part of the lichen does make spores, which, when temperature and humidity are right, start to grow and if they can become attached to algae, they continue to grow. However, they can reproduce themselves, like the mosses, from broken pieces of old lichens, for they produce microscopic small buds, each bud of which actually is a piece of algae and fungus threads together. These can start growing together whenever conditions are just right.

The so-called "Reindeer Moss" or "Old Man's Beard" (*Cladonia rangiferina*) is actually a lichen, probably the best known of all the lichens. Dried, it can almost equal dried peat moss in its water-absorbing properties. This is the lichen with long gray-green streamers attached to the branches in moist woods of the North, not to be confused with "Spanish Moss" of the South which is actually a true flowering plant.

LICORICE = *Glycyrrhiza glabra*

LIGHTING. The use of electric lights in the garden provides great opportunities for fully enjoying garden design and garden plants. There is no need now to draw a curtain on the garden at nightfall. With the proper placing of a few specially designed spot lights or flood lights, one can open up an entirely new field in garden appreciation. The greatest expense is the initial one for the laying of the wires and the special equipment. To many gardeners the greater enjoyment of the garden in its more interesting aspects, as viewed by friends in the evening, is well worth the cost.

One of the great advantages of garden lighting is that it is changeable. Spot lights as well as flood lights can be changed from time to time, depending on what is of most current garden interest. Thinking along these lines, one easily sees that opportunities of creating interest in one's accomplishments in the garden, are great indeed.

Among the important considerations at the beginning of this experiment in night living is first to determine from where these interesting things are to be viewed. Is it from the living room, through a picture window, from the terrace or porch, from the various walks through the garden or a combination of all these? When this has been determined, then one begins to plan the placement of the lights and the number and placement of electrical outlets required to produce the desired effects.

According to suggestions made by the Sylvania Electric Products, Inc., Company, makers of bulbs for this special use (PAR 38 series), there are 3 basic rules to follow for using electric lighting outdoors:

1. Do not floodlight the whole area; leave areas of shadow for interest and definition.

2. Conceal all bulbs so that neither you nor your neighbor can see them.

3. Use weatherproof wiring, outlet boxes, fixtures and bulbs.

The electric outlets especially should be waterproof, usually with rubber caps for placing over the sockets. Wiring might be of lead cable type but USE (Underground Service Entrance) and UF (Underground Feeder) wiring are now available for use buried in the soil without being enclosed in conduits or lead sheaths. It should be placed in the ground sufficiently deep so as not to interfere with garden digging for it is very easy to cut into a wire with spade or pickax. Underground wiring of this nature should be carefully mapped for quick and easy future reference in case of a break or short circuit.

The number of outlets desired should be carefully scheduled by a competent electrician to make certain that the house wiring and current will take the load. One should never use more than 1600 watts on a 15 amp. circuit or 2200 watts on a 20 amp. circuit. The shorter the lengths of wire for above-ground use in the garden the better it will be, especially if children play there. Insulators must be used when wire is fastened to supports and wires must be protected by conduit when lower than 8 ft.

Artificial light brings the garden alive at night.

above the ground or when in a location where they might easily be damaged. A few major outlets, for a few major lighting fixtures, might well be better than attempting to light up all corners of the garden with a large number. Garden lighting is usually a seasonal operation, so that portable fixtures can be stored and used only for short periods when the garden is at its best. Permanent fixtures are best for steps and walks.

The brightness and shape of the light provided are the variables with which one has to work. Even the color of the light can be varied by using different bulbs or fixtures. A particular point of interest might be illuminated with light 2–5 times brighter than the light needed for the surrounding area.

Recessed lights to illuminate garden steps take 6–25-watt bulbs placed 16–24 in. above ground. Mushroom reflectors for the same purpose take 25–50-watt bulbs. Lighting for trees takes 150 watt PAR-38 spot and flood-lamps, or if flood lighting an area of flower bed, one of these lamps per 750 sq. ft. of bed, placed 16–20 ft. above the ground. Mushroom lights for illuminating the flower bed would take 25–40-watt bulbs 12–24 in. above the flowers, each providing a 6–10 ft. circle of light.

The basic form of lighting is a simple adjustable holder for PAR 38 spot and flood lamps which are made of special glass to withstand changes in temperature or dousing in a rain storm. The holders, as most other outdoor units, are available with spikes for ground placement, cover plates for outdoor boxes or clamps for attaching to trees or poles. Spot lights are particularly effective when aimed up at a tree, lighting the underside of the leaves, and 2 or 3 might be used to do the plant justice, since one alone might create a flat light. If the bulb is not concealed from view a covered shield fixture is available for it.

There are such things as "insect repellent" lights that might be considered. It is not pleasant to contemplate turning on a series of garden lights which will attract all the night-flying insects from the entire area. It has been found that the blue color in light attracts insects, so yellow light, and bulbs especially made with the blue removed, are available and these reduce insect attraction to a minimum.

There are various types of fixtures available which are able to withstand all sorts of weather conditions. The best are made of aluminum, brass, copper or stainless steel and there is a great choice among them as far as design and color are concerned. Best are those that are black, green or mat-aluminum. The inside finish of reflectors should have a high reflectance with mat surface. Choice between types for identical services depends on (1) facility of installation; (2) appropriate design; (3) personal taste; (4) circuit capacity and (5) cost.

Lamp bulb size is governed by equipment or its application, but often selecting by trial and error will result in the best choice. Bulbs selected might vary from 6–300 watts.

Various standard units are available for reflecting light down or up or for spotlighting. Adjustable units have obvious advantages and there are now fluorescent units for illuminating vertical surfaces such as buildings, fences or hedges.

All holders for outdoor-type flood and spot-light bulbs should be used with a rubber gasket between the bulb and the socket for a watertight fit; be sure to use these gaskets to prevent moisture from leaking into the sockets.

For lily-pool lighting use molded rubber cord and sockets which provide a watertight seal around the neck of the bulb.

A number of electric accessory appliance companies manufacture various types of lighting fixtures for out-of-doors.

Pine cones are usually pendulous while fir cones are always erect.

LIGNEOUS. Woody.

LIGNUM-VITAE, COMMON = *Guaiacum officinale*

LIGULARIA (lig-yew-LAY-ria). Alternate-leaved perennials of the Composite Family with long-stalked, rounded or kidney-shaped leaves with daisylike flowers usually yellow, blooming in July and Aug. Easily grown in any garden soil, propagated by cuttings or division.

dentata (*clivorum*)   3′–4′   **Zone 5   Bigleaf Golden-ray**
Native to China and Japan, with long-stalked leaves nearly 20 in. wide, yellow-orange flower heads 4 in. across, during July and Aug. Coarse in texture when used with other perennials.

tussilaginea (*kaempferi*)   24″   **Zone 6 Kaempfer Golden-ray**
A native Japanese herb, sometimes used as a ground cover in shaded situations, this bears rounded leaves 10 in. across and deeply indented where the petiole is attached to the blade. The stems are underground. The flowers are in very loose clusters, each one somewhat similar to a Dandelion in shape and color, although not with as many petals, borne on stalks about 2 ft. long during July and Aug. The variety 'Aureo-maculata' has leaves spotted with white or yellow, sometimes even pale pink, and is called Leopard Plant. It is used as a house or window box plant.

veitchiana   6′   **Zone 6 (?)   Veitch Golden-ray**
A showy herbaceous perennial often unbranched, with sharply toothed leaves 16 in. long and numerous yellow flower heads 2½ in. wide. Native to China.

wilsoniana   5′   **Zone 6 (?)   Wilson Golden-ray**
The basal leaves are 12–18 in. long and the yellow flower heads are an inch across, being borne on long spikes during July and Aug. Native to China.

LIGULE. The strap-shaped corolla in the ray florets of composites; the membranous appendage at the summit of the leaf-sheaths of most grasses.

LIGUSTRUM (ly-GUS-trum). Privet. The privets constitute the most common of all nursery-grown plants. None are native in North America, although one or two have become naturalized here—all are native of Asia except *L. vulgare* which is a native of Europe and northern Africa. Because they are easily propagated and grow rapidly they are not expensive plants, and make nearly perfect hedge plants throughout the country.

Privets are also serviceable as fillers in any shrub border and, in a few instances, some of the vari-colored ones and the evergreen ones are used as ornamental specimens. They are either deciduous or evergreen, depending on the species, and they grow so fast and dense that they all can be sheared into making excellent hedges. They have opposite leaves, clusters of small creamy-white to white, rather ill-smelling flowers, appearing in the summer; the fruits are mostly black or blue-black and the foliage has little autumn color.

The Common Privet (*L. vulgare*) and the California Privet (*L. ovalfolium*) have been the most widely used, but there is a serious twig blight which can affect the former, and winter cold can kill the latter to the ground during some winters in the northern states. The Amur Privet has been used in the colder areas, with good results, although *L. obtusifolium* is about as hardy. One nurseryman has noted blight on 50,000 plants of *L. vulgare* and the entire lot was practically a complete loss.

In the South, the most important of the privets are the Japanese (*L. japonicum*) and *L. lucidum* or the Glossy Privet. These have been confused in the trade for many years. Both are evergreen and have been used as specimens for their good foliage and for their clusters of creamy-white summer flowers. Many nurseries in the South and in Calif. are listing *L. texanum* which in most instances is pure *L. japonicum*. It may well be that, in growing large numbers of privets from seed, dwarf clones may originate. When this is the case, such plants should be grown and carefully studied, compared with others and tried in various growth areas. Dwarf privets, plants that grow to a low height (4–5 ft.) and stay there without shearing, would be valuable hedge plants in this age of the small garden.

Propagation

Seeds may be stratified at once or kept dry in airtight containers in a cool place for up to a year and then stratified. Usually 3 months at 40° F. is sufficient. Both softwood and hardwood cuttings of most are easily rooted. See STRATIFICATION, CUTTINGS.

Insect Pests

California and Amur Privet are badly infested with the rose leaf roller which curls the leaves and makes the plants unsightly. Spraying with insecticide #15 or #9 is effective. Thrips injure the leaves and buds. Insecticide #15 or #13 keeps them normal. Spider mites stunt, discolor and curl the leaves. Several applications of insecticide #31 or #34 keep them in check. In the Gulf States camphor scale is a pest of *L. lucidum*. Insecticide #45 gives adequate control. Lilac leaf miner is destructive in the West. Larvae of this tiny moth make blotch mines and roll the tips of the leaves. Insecticides #15 and #13 give control.

Diseases

Anthracnose causes cankers on the trunk near the ground which may girdle it and kill the plant. European privet is most susceptible. If this disease is prevalent, plant resistant species. Stem galls often 1½ in. in dia. are formed on the stem and branches. This disease kills heavily infected plants. No fungicides are known to give control. Root rot and powdery mildew (see POWDERY MILDEW) are minor diseases.

amurense   15′   Zone 3   Amur Privet
In northern areas this privet from northern China is the best to use—certainly better than the more tender California Privet which it resembles somewhat in habit of growth. The leaves are not as lustrous, and it may not be quite as vigorous, but nevertheless because of its reliable hardiness, it is the best one of the hardy privets for northern gardens. Years ago this privet was popularly called "Amur River—North", and *L. sinense* was popularly called "Amur River—South".

delavayanum   6′   Zone 7   Delavay Privet
Usually a low, wide-spreading evergreen, not common in America and native to China but certainly of no value outside the warmer areas of the U.S. It looks something like a dwarf cotoneaster and makes an excellent low hedge.

henryi   12′   Zone 7   Henry Privet
This Chinese plant has glossy evergreen leaves that are 2 in. long and lustrous. It is being grown by several nurseries in the South.

x ibolium   12′   Zone 4   Ibolium Privet
This hybrid privet (*L. ovalifolium* x *obtusifolium*) has not been used as much as it might be. It is hardier than the California Privet, is vigorous and more handsome than *L. amurense*.

ibota   6′   Zone 5   Ibota Privet
One of the least ornamental species of *Ligustrum* with oblong leaves ½–2 in. long and small black fruits. Native to Japan. Frequently mistaken for *L. obtusifolium* which is a much better plant.

japonicum   6′–18′   Zone 7   Japanese Privet
This is an evergreen privet from Japan and Korea widely used in the South and frequently confused with *L. lucidum*. The Japanese Privet has leaves which are much more glossy than those of *L. lucidum*. One of the ways of telling the two apart is that in the Japanese Privet the nerves on the underside of the leaves are raised, while in *L. lucidum* they are sunken. Although not as vigorous as *L. lucidum* its dark green lustrous foliage makes it a better ornamental. Variegated-leaved varieties sometimes listed in the trade as *L. japonicum* 'Argenteo-marginatum' or 'Aureo-marginatum' usually turn out to be *L. lucidum* '**Aureo-marginatum**'. As a result of cold winters at Chase, Ala., Mr. H. H. Chase writes that where *L. lucidum* has been killed roots and all, *L. japonicum* has only been killed to the ground, a very interesting observation; '**Lusterleaf**' is a variety that is being grown in Calif. under the name of *L. texanum* 'Luster-

leaf', supposedly with larger and thicker leaves than those of the regular *L. japonicum* (syn. *texanum*); '**Rotundifolium**' (6 ft.) has shorter branches, the leaves are spaced more closely together and it is lower in habit than the species. It is a good hedge plant.

lucidum   30′   Zone 7   Glossy Privet
The Glossy Privet from China, Korea and Japan is taller than the Japanese Privet and in some places is grown as a tree with a single trunk. The leaves are 3–5 in. long. The flower clusters are produced in Aug. (later than those of *L. japonicum* which are produced in late June and July). Over 16 varieties are offered by name in the trade. Undoubtedly some are mixed with *L. japonicum* varieties and some of the names are probably synonymous. The variety '**Tricolor**' has leaves with a broad irregular border of white which is slightly pinkish when the leaves first appear. It is even more tender than the species but some have noted that when individual plants are well grown, they are very interesting.

obtusifolium   9′   Zone 3   Border Privet
Other privets are better in foliage and habit but this and *L. amurense* are the hardiest of all. The variety **regelianum**, the popular Regel Privet, is probably the most graceful of all this group because of its low growth and graceful horizontal-branching system. Unfortunately, it is sometimes grown from seed and this results in taller, ungainly plants. The true Regel Privet is not much over 4–5 ft. tall and to be kept true to name it should be asexually propagated from low-growing parent plants with the true habit so desirable. Many times an unclipped Regel's Privet is one of real beauty simply because of its horizontal-branching system.

ovalifolium   15′   Zone 5   California Privet
The California Privet native to Japan is probably the most common of all nursery-grown plants in America. Vigorous, glossy-leaved, amenable to pruning, it should be remembered that it is definitely not as hardy as some of the others, and in very cold winters it can be killed to the ground or even killed completely if used too far North. *L. amurense* and *L. obtusifolium* as well as *L. ibolium* are hardier. Varieties: '**Aureum**', this has been incorrectly termed 'Aureo-marginatum' or 'Variegatum'. Each leaf has a green spot in the center completely surrounded with yellow—the better the soil and growth conditions the deeper the yellow color. It is the only truly worthwhile variety of the California Privet and it can vary and revert back to the green-leaved species type. The variety with leaves bordered a creamy white ('**Albo-marginatum**') is not nearly as outstanding an ornamental.

quihoui   6′   Zone 6   Quihou Privet

Ligustrum ovalifolium 'Aureum' is an interesting, variegated-leaved form of the California Privet. (*Photo by Arnold Arboretum, Jamaica Plain, Mass.*)

The flowers of this privet from China appear in late summer, making it the last of the privets to bloom. It is not commonly produced in American nurseries and has little to offer over other privets except its late summer flowers. If not desired for this, it might be overlooked.

sinense 12′ **Zone 7** **Chinese Privet**
This Chinese Privet is popular in the South because of its graceful habit and panicles of flowers in July. Properly grown, it is often considered the most handsome of all the deciduous privets when it is in flower, even though the flower clusters are only 3–4 in. long. This is the privet that is sometimes referred to as "Amur River—South". Varieties: **'Pendulum'**—a clone apparently selected because of its side branches which are definitely more pendulous than those of the more upright growing species. This is often evergreen in southern Ala., but during the coldest winters the leaves can be knocked off by winter cold. This is sometimes advertised as the southern equivalent of Regel Privet, with the added advantage that this is evergreen; **stauntonii**—a dwarfer, more spreading form of this species; x **'Suwannee River'**—this is reported to be a hybrid of *L. japonicum* 'Rotundifolium' (syn. *coriaceum*) and *L. lucidum*, patented No. 1402 and originated by Larry M. Bartlett of Forest Park, Ga., slightly before 1955. It is a low compact-growing privet with lustrous evergreen leaves, making low slow-growing plants of an excellent compact habit.

x **vicaryi** 12′ **Zone 5** **Vicary Golden Privet**
This privet originated in the garden of Vicary Gibbs, Aldenham, Middlesex, England, before 1920 and is a hybrid of *L. ovalifolium* 'Aureum' x *L. vulgare*. The leaves are yellow throughout the entire growing season especially when grown in the full sunlight. If grown in shaded situations the foliage color is disappointingly yellowish green. The shaded inner leaves about the bush are of course green, but from a distance, when grown as a specimen in the full sun, the plant does have a yellowish color throughout the growing season but this is not at all pronounced when it is used in clipped hedges.

vulgare 15′ **Zone 4** **Common Privet**
In some places in the eastern U.S., this vigorous privet from Europe and Northern Africa has become naturalized. The leaves are more narrow than those of the California Privet and not as glossy—it is sometimes susceptible to a twig blight which makes it unsightly. The leaves can be used for dyeing (yellow, gold). The large clusters of lustrous black berries are interesting but this is no longer as popular as it used to be. It is superseded by several of the larger-leaved privets from the Orient. The best that can be said of it is that it will grow in soil or in situations where practically nothing else will.

There is no question but that this privet, like all others, is very easily grown and is quickly saleable, but because it is susceptible to quick and unexpected killing by an anthracnose or twig blight, it is doubtful whether it is advisable to grow in large quantity. Because of this, only the following are suggested for growing and even these might be overlooked where other privet species prove satisfactory: **'Densiflorum'**—this is an upright-growing cultivar, with a branching habit more dense than 'Pyramidale'. If plants of 'Densiflorum' are unclipped they still retain their good habit after 25 years or more; **italicum**—the Common Privet is sometimes considered "semi-evergreen," merely because it holds its leaves late in the season, but this variety has been selected for holding its leaves longer than any other variety of this species. It is not as hardy as the others, however; **'Lodense'**—this is the dense, compact form which used to be called 'Nanum'. Very old plants are less than 4 ft. tall and wider, but here again susceptibility to blight has ruled out the continued growing of this variety in large numbers; **'Pyramidal'**—an excellent tall hedge plant with upright vigorous-growing branches if it is kept under 6–8 ft. tall. It only needs occasional shearing across the top to keep it at this desired height. Older plants, unclipped, tend to lose the upright character as the branches become heavier and tend to bend toward the ground and then they become unsightly.

LILAC. See SYRINGA.

LILACS IN THEIR ORDER OF BLOOM. See SYRINGA.

LILAC FAMILY = Oleaceae

LILIACEAE = The Lily Family

LILI-PILI TREE = *Acmena smithii*

LILIUM. Fifty years ago, lilies were not very popular garden plants because they were not grown in large numbers in America, and were shipped in from Europe and mostly the Orient. They are not like other bulbs which can be in transit for long periods and subjected to fluctuating temperatures without harm, and as a result many gardeners were greatly disappointed with the results they obtained from attempting to grow foreign bulbs.

Today, large numbers are commercially grown in North America, and by a search of the catalogues several hundred species and varieties can be found available. The growers have become very skilled in hybridizing them, so that with the selection of the proper varieties, there can be lilies in bloom in the garden from early June until frost, with the greatest number blooming in the early summer.

A great deal more is known about their keeping and shipping qualities. Polyethylene film has proved ideal for shipping and storing them, and it is used as a very essential part in their propagation. So, within the past decade lilies have come to the fore as one of the most popular and easily grown of the summer-flowering bulbs. Many gardeners have become so interested in them that the propagation and even hybridization of them is a common hobby. It is true that they are not difficult to grow, but there are some general cultural notes which must be understood if one is to prove successful with them.

In the first place, they should be planted in well-drained soil, for they will rot and fail miserably in moist soils. They prefer a slightly acid soil with plenty of humus. It may be best not to mix rotted manure with the soil as this may aid growth of the disease fungi, but very well-rotted manure can be used as a winter mulch when it is thought advisable. However, for safety, it might be best to refrain from using manure.

Some lilies, like the delicate woods species *L. grayi, canadense, speciosum* and *superbum*, like

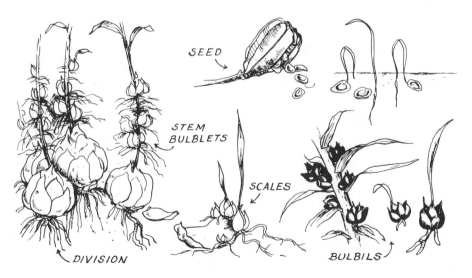

Lilium: Methods of propagation

a semi-shaded situation but the majority of the hybrids do well in the full sun. They can be planted in amongst other perennials or in beds by themselves but one should realize that they have little to offer ornamentally in the garden after they are through flowering.

Planting

Bulbs are available in various sizes, the larger bulbs of course producing the largest stalks and the most flowers, but this varies according to species. The bulbs of *L. pumilum* are seldom over 1 in. in dia., while those of *L. regale* may be several times as large. The depth at which these are planted depends on their size. Flowering bulbs of most types should be planted with the top of the bulb 4–6 in. below the soil surface, depending on their size, except *L. candidum*, the Madonna Lily, which is the only one planted so that the top of the bulb is only an inch below the soil surface.

It may be well when several of a variety are to be planted together, to dig a hole 2 ft. deep and 18 in. across. Good, friable loam with plenty of humus material should be put back in this hole with a handful of bone meal mixed with the soil in the area where the roots will be. The bulbs are then planted, covered with the same good soil, thoroughly watered and, if possible, mulched to reduce water loss from the soil and weed growth.

Lilies are not like other bulbs for they should be transplanted with some of their roots intact. All American growers know this and offer them that way. Bulbs from abroad usually have all these roots removed, hence they do not get off to a good a start as American-grown bulbs. The sooner they are planted after they are dug, the better they will grow, another reason why American-grown bulbs are so satisfactory. When purchasing bulbs one should inspect the roots and not buy those that have roots all dried up. They should be succulent and alive in order to start root growth as soon as they are in the ground.

Before bulbs are planted they should be carefully inspected, and any showing rot should be discarded for disease, once started in a bed, may cause trouble elsewhere if conditions are right. Also, to aid further in preventing rot, the bulbs might well be dusted with a good powder disinfectant like "Arasan." A small handful of the disinfectant is placed in a paper bag, the dry bulbs (not wet) are put in and shaken—enough of the powder adheres to the bulbs to do the job. Then they are planted immediately.

Planting is usually done in the fall—almost any time until the ground freezes. We have planted many bulbs after that time by mulching the soil heavily with straw or pine needles when we knew in advance that some of the purchased bulbs would arrive late. If it is impossible to plant them in the fall, they can be kept in a very cool place and planted early in the spring. In planning for this, the bulbs are placed in a polyethylene bag with a very small amount of moistened sphagnum (not wet) and placed in the home refrigerator or in a cool cellar. If at all possible, however, plant them in the fall.

After Care

Lilies need water to grow properly and hence should not be expected to grow in dry gravelly soil. On the other hand, too much water can aid basal rot, one of the problems which must be guarded against. If a mulch is used such as peat moss, sawdust, pine needles, etc., about an inch or two in depth, this will aid in preventing water loss from the soil. By inspecting the soil underneath the mulch the gardener can usually tell when additional water is necessary, remembering of course that the soil should be friable and slightly moist, but certainly not wet. When it is dry—water.

Watering should be done with a slow stream (or soil soaker) on the ground. It should not be done with a forced spray on the foliage as this is an excellent way of spreading disease spores. If the soil is soaked, and there is a suitable mulch, one watering should last at least 10–14 days, sometimes longer.

Mulches not only aid in keeping the soil moist and keeping the weeds under control, but they aid materially in the growth of the bulb. Applied just before the ground freezes in the fall, they keep it from freezing considerably longer than soil without a mulch, thus providing more time for the roots to grow. In the spring, mulches aid in preventing the alternate freezing and thawing of the soil which may cause it to heave and do damage to the bulbs. In any event, the mulch used should be light and "strawy," not a type that packs down forming a hard layer on the soil surface. See MULCHES.

Lily experts have recommended the use of inorganic complete fertilizers (which see) for use on lilies. We have found that the addition of a 5-10-5 fertilizer at the rate of about 2 lbs. per 100 sq. ft. in early spring and again before bloom, is sufficient to keep the lilies growing well, but this requirement may vary with different soils. One should remember that too much fertilizer, especially too much nitrogen, causes over-vigorous, succulent, vegetative growth and may make the plants more attractive to disease-carrying insects. Potash added to some soils is advantageous in that it results in stronger stems, but one should be careful not to provide too much nitrogen.

If there is sufficient potash in the soil, many

lilies will not have to be staked. In fact, many of the new hybrids are purposely bred so they will have sturdy stalks. However, for some of the taller-growing types it may be necessary to stake them prior to the time they come into bloom, when the tops are heaviest. See STAKING.

After they are through flowering, if seeds are not desired, stronger plants will result the following year if the dead flower heads are cut off. This should be done just below the lowest flowers on the stalk. The idea is to allow as many leaves as possible to remain to manufacture food during the rest of the growing season. If half the stalks are cut off to make the plants "look better" after flowering, 50% of the leaves or food-producing organs will be removed and the plants will only be able to manufacture half the food they might have otherwise produced, food that should have been stored in the bulbs for growth the following season. When the stalks have died in the fall, they should be cut off at the ground level and removed. This is advisable so that disease organisms will not be spread in the mulch on the soil surface to reinfest the plants another year.

Having a weed-free lily bed is not difficult if one uses Dacthal at the rate of $\frac{1}{2}$ lb. per 10 gal. of water, applied to the soil as a spray, either in Nov. or in the very early spring before growth starts. One application should keep the bed free of weeds for most of the growing season.

Diseases

Botrytis blight is a fungus disease most common in lilies. It is evidenced in various ways, the most frequent being sudden dying of 7–8 in. shoots shortly after they have started growth. These should be removed and burned. Bulbs producing such stalks will not produce any more the current year, but may the following year. To prevent the spread of the disease the foliage should be sprayed with a mild Bordeaux mixture (which see). It might be well to spray before the disease appears as a preventative measure to keep it from spreading, spraying several times at 10–14-day intervals. This is also good insurance in keeping other diseases under control.

Lily virus is another disease common in many lilies evidenced by a peculiar mottling of the leaves and stunted growth of the stalks. Once a plant has this disease there is no cure. Bulbils, bulblets and scales taken from it will transmit the disease to plants grown from them, but seeds sown from a virus-infested plant will not transmit the disease to plants grown from them, although like most lilies they are susceptible to infestation later. The spread of this disease can be controlled to some extent by eliminating plant lice.

Many modern varieties of lilies are now available which exist with this disease for many years. It is well if one can adopt an attitude of learning to live with it and keeping the lice under control to prevent its spread. Some species and varieties are far more resistant to it than others, or at least will not be seriously affected for many years. Species like *L. handsonii, pardalinum, davidii* and some of their hybrids are in this group. Also selected clones of *L. tigrinum, L. candidum* and the Mid-century hybrids are included. Some species like *L. auratum, formosanum* and several native American species are extremely susceptible but American lily hybridizers are continually producing new hybrids that are far more resistant than these species.

Basal rot has already been mentioned, a rot that appears at the base of the bulb. Bulbs with this disease should not be planted, or at least the rot should be cut out with a sharp knife that is disinfected (by dipping in alcohol) after every bulb is cut. If on examination a lily plant has died of this disease, another should not be planted in its place.

It should be noted that if disease-free bulbs are obtained and planted in soil where lilies have not been grown before and are kept healthy by good culture, one may be able to grow lilies satisfactorily without any definite spray program, sometimes even without spraying.

Insects

Plant lice should be eliminated as soon as they appear for these sucking insects are the chief carriers of the virus disease from one plant to another. Spraying with malathion, Vapona and especially Systox are effective but these sprays should be used only according to the directions on each package. We have found that one spray during mid-June is sufficient under our conditions in Mass. unless the season is an unusually wet one.

Rodents like moles and field mice can be a problem in certain areas, but spraying the soil once with Diazinon may be sufficient to keep these pests out of large fields of lilies for several months. A little poison grain placed in a small can in which frozen orange juice is sold, placed on its side just under the mulch in the fall to keep it away from birds, is another means of keeping field mice under control.

Like all plants lilies have other diseases and pests that attack them, but these are the worst, and if these few are controlled one should be able to grow good plants without serious trouble.

Propagation

This affords an excellent hobby for one who is interested in propagation, since lilies can be speedily propagated several ways. First of course is by seed—some species and hybrids like *L. tigrinum* produce small bubils in the axils of the leaves and when these are just ready to fall off, late in the summer or early fall, they are ready for collecting and sowing. Other species

properly. Pods should be collected just before they split open in the fall and when they turn color from green to brown. To be good the seed should not stick together in the pod but separate easily one from the other. When thoroughly dried it can be sown at once or stored dry until spring.

Lilies may be divided into 2 general groups— those with seeds that germinate and start to grow within 3–6 weeks when sown and those

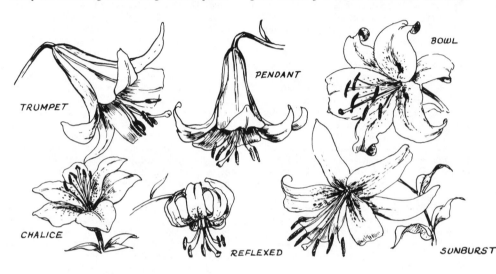

Lilium: Types of flowers

produce small bulblets on the stem near the base of the plant either above or just underneath the soil. These also can be used. Most lily bulbs produce new bulbs in the soil as offshoots from the old bulb and these can be separated from the parent bulb and new plants started. Finally, most lilies can be propagated by scales. On examining a lily bulb one sees that it is made up of a number of scales attached to the basal part of the bulb. If the larger scales are carefully broken off, more or less intact, from the bottom of the bulb and placed in a proper medium, they eventually produce minute bulblets which also, if handled properly, will produce new plants. Propagation by division, bulbils, bulblets and scales will result in plants identical with the parent. Propagation by seed may (in the case of species grown in pure stands), but in the garden where several species or hybrid varieties are grown together, seed may frequently result in new hybrids, unlike the parent producing them.

SEEDS. Propagation by seed is simple. One lily pod may contain 200 seeds and nearly 80% of these should germinate if ripened and sown

that may take 18 months to germinate after sown. In the former group would be such popular species as *L. amabile, concolor, davidii,* Mid-century Hybrids, *pumilum, regale, tigrinum.* In the slow-to-germinate group would be *L. auratum, canadense, hansonii, martagon, speciosum* and *superbum.* Also, although they germinate immediately, some lilies like *L. speciosum* have seeds that will grow in the soil but will not send up a leaf above the soil level for several months.

Lily seed should be dusted with Captan before sowing to prevent any possibility of botrytis blight spores adhering to them, and then can be sown on soil in flats 5 in. deep just like any other seed. See SEEDS. If this is done in the late fall or winter, these flats, slightly moistened, can be stored in stacks in the warm basement and brought up to the greenhouse after about 3 months to start above-ground growth if they are the fast-germinating type of seeds. It is suggested that the flat be 5 in. deep because it is best if they are not disturbed for a full year, after which they can be separated and planted individually in rows several inches apart. Some will undoubtedly be strong enough to bloom the first year, especially seedlings of *L. pumilum* and *regale*.

A much more interesting method is to mix some seed of a fast-germinating type with some moist (but not wet) vermiculite, put the mixture in a polyethylene bag, tie the mouth tightly and put the bag on the kitchen shelf (out of direct sunlight). On examination after a few weeks one will find that the seed has germinated, that small rootlets and a very small leaf have been formed. These germinated seedlings can then be planted in a flat of soil, or held 2–3 months in the polyethylene bag if it is put in the refrigerator, and then sown. If such seed is originally placed in bags in Feb., the germinated seedlings can be planted in flats out of doors or in the seed bed as soon as all danger of frost is over in the spring.

BULBILS. These are produced in the axils of the leaves by *L. tigrinum, bulbiferum, sargentiae* and *sulphureum* and bulblets from the base of the stem of several other species can be collected in the early fall and sown in rows about 2 in.

Bulbils: Small bulbs in the leaf axils of the Tiger Lily. These can be planted and will develop new plants identical with parent.

deep, with about 2 in. between each bulblet. Sown this way they need not be touched for at least a full year. It is surprising how large a number of bulbils or bulblets will be produced on one lily stalk.

SCALING. Propagation by this method proves most interesting. Immediately after flowering, the larger bulbs are carefully dug around and a few of the larger scales gently removed from

each bulb. The purpose is to remove the scales without injuring or breaking or digging up the roots. Of course the same thing can be done when new bulbs are planted in the fall, but one should guard against the tendency of removing too many and thus seriously injuring the vitality of the bulb. These scales are dusted lightly with Arasan, placed in a polyethylene bag with a little moist (not wet) vermiculite, the bag tied tightly at the top and then placed on the kitchen shelf away from strong, direct sunlight which might cause overdue heating. On examination in a few weeks it will be found that most of these scales have produced tiny bulblets at the scale base. When the roots of these are $\frac{1}{4}$ in. long the whole scale and its tiny bulblets is placed in a furrow in the soil deep enough so just the scale tip is above the soil level. If placed in a warm greenhouse, these start to grow. Or the bags with the scales and tiny bulblets can be placed in the home refrigerator and kept 2–3 months before they are planted. Also, the scales can be planted in soil in flats as soon as they are removed from the mother bulb, and if the soil is moist, the temperature warm, tiny bulblets will likewise be produced.

The propagation of lilies therefore can be a most interesting experience and can result in a large number of flowering bulbs in a few years time with a minimum amount of effort.

Hybridizing

Hybridizing lilies is another favorite hobby, for if one selects plants of the fast-germinating type, certain ones may grow fast enough to bloom the first year. Most will bloom in 2–3 years from seed. In hybridizing lilies, the flowers from which the pollen is to be collected are protected with tightly closed polyethylene bags placed before the flowers open so there will be no possibility of contamination with other pollen. When the flower is open and the pollen ripe, the anthers are collected and thoroughly dried on a piece of paper in a darkened room for 2 days, then placed in a stoppered bottle until used. Stored in the home refrigerator it may remain viable for 2–3 months. Under especially controlled conditions (i.e. 50% moisture and 50° F. temperature) some pollen has remained viable for 7 months. It is possible for even the home gardener to take pollen from his early blooming lilies and fertilize the late blooming types with it.

For a more detailed discussion of lilies see "The Complete Book of Lilies" by F. F. Rockwell and Esther Grayson, Doubleday & Co., N.Y.

amabile   3′–4′   Zones 2–3   Korean Lily
A fine lily, native to Korea, with red, slightly fragrant flowers appearing in June. It is easily

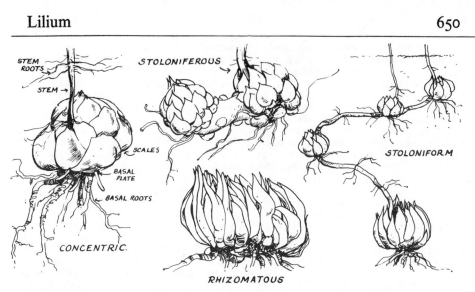

STEM ROOTS

STEM →

STOLONIFEROUS

STOLONIFORM

SCALES

BASAL PLATE

BASAL ROOTS

CONCENTRIC

RHIZOMATOUS

Lilium: Types of bulbs

propagated by seed and has a free flowering habit. Many underground bulblets are formed and unfortunately have an unpleasant odor. The variety **luteum** has beautiful yellow flowers.

amoenum   12″   Zone 7
With 1–3 slightly drooping pink flowers per stalk—native to China.

auratum   3′–12′   Zone 4   Goldband Lily
Flowering in Aug. and Sept., the flowers vary in color from white to red, native to Japan. There are 2 types of this species, one is the lower, alpine form, **praecox** and the other is the variety **platyphyllum** which can grow stalks 12 ft. tall with 30–40 flowers. A very popular lily.

bakeranum   2′–3′   Zone 8   Baker Lily
A lily native to northern Burma; flowers bell-

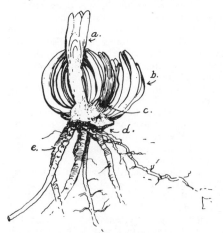

a.

b.

c.

d.

e.

Lily-bulb—Cross-section

shaped, creamy white but spotted red inside. This is one that has a stem wandering about underground before it appears above ground.

brownii   2′–3′   Zone 6   Brown's Lily
With horizontally held, creamy-white flowers, trumpet-shaped, tinged dark purple outside. The actual habitat of this is doubtful—Nepal or China. The variety **australe**, 5 ft., a Chinese variety, blooms in late summer.

bulbiferum   2′–4′   Zones 2–3   Bulbil Lily
If this is disbudded, or damaged, large numbers of bulbils will be produced in the leaf axils, but usually none are produced unless the plant is forced into it by disbudding or injury. Flowers, red to orange. The variety **croceum** has orange flowers, is vigorous and is frequently used in hybridization for its vigor and hardiness.

callosum   1′–3′   Zones 2–3   Slimstem Lily
Small, bell-shaped flowers, 5–15 per stalk, orange-red, good for a sheltered spot in the rockery. Native to Manchuria, Korea and Japan. It blooms in Aug.

canadense   2′–5′   Zone 3   Canada Lily
A common lily, widely native in North America, bell-shaped flowers ranging in color from yellow to red and blooming in July. There are several varieties named according to flower color, with about 6 flowers per stalk.

candidum   3½′   Zone 4   Madonna Lily
An old-fashioned favorite, probably cultivated for over a thousand years, with pure white trumpet-shaped flowers, with 13 or more per stalk; borne in late June. Very susceptible to botrytis blight, but there are some new strains apparently more resistant than the species. This and *L. chalcedonicum* are the only species which should be planted a mere inch below the soil

level, all others should be planted much deeper. The addition of lime aids in its growth.

catesbaei   1′–2′   Zone 8   Catesby Lily
Native to the southern U.S., often in swamps with erect yellow and red flowers, blooming in Sept. It is not easy to grow in cultivation.

cernuum   1½′   Zones 2–3   Nodding Lily
Native to Korea and Manchuria; lilac-colored, recurved flowers, 1½ in. wide and 1 in. long, appearing in early July with about 12 to the stalk, growing well in full sun. It is interesting and easily grown. This does not persist in the garden and seedlings should be raised annually.

chalcedonicum   3′   Zones 6–7   Chalcedonian Lily
With bright red flowers in early July, about 2–5 per stalk, this does best if the bulbs are planted only an inch or so below the ground surface. Unfortunately it is very susceptible to botrytis blight.

columbianum   4′–8′   Zone 6   Columbia Lily
Native to the Pacific Coast states from British Columbia to Calif., it may have as many as 40 small yellow to reddish-orange flowers per stalk. It blooms in July and Aug.

concolor   1½′   Zone 5   Morningstar Lily
With erect, star-shaped, bright scarlet flowers, about 10 per stalk. Native to China and an excellent Lily for the garden. The variety **cordion** has yellow flowers but there are several other good varieties of this variable species. It will grow readily from seeds, blooming in 2–3 years.

dauricum = *L. pensylvanicum luteum*

davidii   5′   Zone 4   David Lily
A very satisfactory, vigorous-growing lily for the garden with 2–20 small red flowers (with reflexed petals) per stalk in mid-July. Native to western China, it looks like a small *L. tigrinum*, especially because of its small black spots on the petals. There are several excellent varieties.

duchartrei   2′–3′   Zone 4   Duchartre Lily
The fragrant, pendulous, white flowers, spotted purple, produce 1–12 flowers per stalk appearing in late July or early Aug. Native to western China. The stem of this wanders about underground often for some distance before it grows above the soil, and produces many bulblets on the underground portion. It is susceptible to the lily mosaic disease.

formosanum   6′   Zone 5   Formosa Lily
Very susceptible to virus disease and because of this it may not be advisable to include it in the garden collection. Flowers appear from Aug. to Oct., are white, funnel shaped, purplish on the outside and fragrant, with 1–10 flowers produced per stalk. Native to Formosa. The variety **wilsonii** is especially fine.

grayi   2′–3′   Zone 4   Gray's Lily
A delicate lily in the mountains of N.Car. and Tenn., with drooping bell-like flowers, one to

several per stalk, red outside and orange inside, closely related to *L. canadense*. In its native habitat, it grows in the full sun in moist, acid soils with much humus. This is not especially an outstanding garden lily because the flowers are too small and delicate.

hansonii   2½′   Zone 3   Hanson Lily
An excellent garden plant, for although the individual fragrant flowers are small (2½ in. long and ¾ in. wide), they are borne horizontally on the stem 4–12 per stalk in mid-June, and they have delicately recurved petals, orange-yellow with brown spots. Native to Korea.

henryi   3′–10′   Zone 4   Henry Lily
An excellent garden lily from China with as many as 20 bright orange-spotted, nodding flowers per stalk. It is one of several species of "stem rooting" lilies, that is, the underground stem bears roots, and on this are produced many small bulblets. It blooms in early Aug. but should be grown in partial shade to prevent premature flower fading. The variety **citrinum** has pure yellow flowers.

humboldtii   4′   Zone 5   Humboldt Lily
Native to the Sierra Nevada Mountains on the Pacific Coast, it has bright orange reflexed flowers, 10–20 per stalk, with numerous maroon-colored dots in July but seedlings vary considerably. It should be grown in some shade, and is definitely a lily for the woodlands.

japonicum   2′–3′   Zones 5–6   Japanese Lily
With delicate pink, fragrant, funnel-shaped flowers in July, this Japanese lily is difficult to grow and bears only 1–5 flowers per stalk. It is often susceptible to virus disease, and might be overlooked by the busy gardener.

kelloggii   1½′–4′   Zone 7   Kellogg Lily
Native to northern Calif., with delicate pink flowers which first open white and are fragrant. It is not the easiest lily to grow and might be omitted by all gardeners except the specialists.

lankongense   2′–4′   Zone 6   Lankong Lily
An attractive Chinese lily with up to 15 fragrant, pendulous, rose-colored flowers per stalk in late July or Aug., each one of which is about 2 in. across and often spotted with purple. It is not widely grown in America yet.

leichtlinii   2′–4′   Zone 5   Leichtlin Lily
A very difficult lily to grow in the garden, native to Japan, with 1–5 yellow, spotted purple, nodding flowers per stalk in Aug. It is rare in cultivation because it is so difficult to grow properly and the plants are very susceptible to mosaic.

longiflorum   2′–3′   Zone 8   Easter Lily
This is grown commercially more than any other lily. Its trumpet-shaped, white, fragrant flowers are familiar to all, especially at Easter time. It is native to the islands off Formosa and very susceptible to mosaic. The U.S.

Department of Agriculture is experimenting with many varieties, but in the past **'Ace'**, **'Croft'** and **'Kenyon-Davidson'** have been a few of many varieties used for forcing in the greenhouse.

maritimum   3′–7′   **Zone 8**   **Coast Lily**
Native to northern Calif., with dark orange-red bell-shaped flowers, 10 per stalk, borne in July. It needs a damp atmosphere in which to grow.

martagon   2½′   **Zone 3**   **Martagon Lily**
A fine lily with 12 or more purplish-pink flowers about 2½ in. long and 1½ in. wide during mid-June. Native to Europe. The white variety **album** is a truly excellent plant for any garden, superior to the species. Many other varieties have been named including **cattaniae** which has almost black flowers. The species has been crossed many times with *L. hansonii* and many fine hybrids have been named.

medeoloides   1′–5′   **Zone 3**   **Wheel Lily**
Native to Japan it has been given its common name because of the regular whorls of leaves on the stem. The scentless flowers bloom in July and are apricot to scarlet, about the same size as those of *L. martagon* with about 10 per stalk. A fine lily for the rock garden.

michauxii   1½′–3½′   **Zone 7**   **Carolina Liy**
Similar to *L. superbum*, native from Va. to Fla., the fragrant bright orange-red flowers have purple spots and bloom late in the summer with 1–5 large nodding flowers per stalk. It is not an outstanding garden plant.

monadelphum   4′   **Zone 3**   **Caucasian Lily**
With splendid yellow flowers, a few black spots, fragrant and native to the North Caucasus Area of Europe. It blooms in early June and is worthy of being grown in any garden. It should be noted that often, purchased bulbs may remain dormant in the ground for a full year before starting growth.

nepalense   4′   **Zone 6**   **Nepal Lily**
A rare lily with yellow or greenish-yellow funnel-shaped pendulous flowers, up to 6 in. long with about 5 flowers per stalk. The stem runs along underground for a foot or so and bears bulblets, before growing above the soil surface. Native to Nepal. The variety **concolor** has pure yellow flowers.

occidentale   2′–6′   **Zone 8**   **Eureka Lily**
Another American lily native to a small portion on the northern Calif. coast. It bears 1–15 flowers per stalk that appear in July. They are scentless, pendulous, orange with maroon spots and the tips of the petals are crimson. The purple anthers bear orange-red pollen. It is not widely grown.

papilliferum   1′   **Zone 3**   **Likiang Lily**
A rare Chinese lily for dry situations, with several small red flowers per stalk. Probably not of value for the gardener.

pardalinum   4′–7′   **Zone 3**   **Leopard Lily**
A Calif. native, which propagates itself rapidly, growing to strong colonies, with red flowers especially towards the tips, lighter towards the base and many brown spots, 4–5 per stalk with flowers 3½ in. long; popular in the Northwest Pacific area. It blooms in July. It forms so many bulbs that a single colony has been found with as many as 500 bulbs. The variety **'Giganteum'**, sometimes sold as Sunset Lily or Chinook Lily, may be a hybrid, but bears up to 30 red and yellow, purple-black dotted flowers per stalk and can grow up to 8 ft. tall—a fine garden specimen.

parryi   6′   **Zone 7**   **Parry Lily**
An excellent plant, native to Calif. and Nev., but it is difficult to cultivate. Bearing 1–15 flowers and more per stalk, the fragrant flowers are yellow, funnel shaped and brown dotted, opening in July. Unfortunately the bulbs cannot be transplanted and shipped easily.

parvum   3′–4′   **Zone 4**   **Sierra Lily**
An alpine species of the high Sierra Nevada Mountains, with small, upright, bell-shaped flowers varying in color from yellow to dark red, maroon spotted. Propagation from scales is easy. It should be planted only in the shade.

pensylvanicum luteum (*L. dauricum*)   1½′
Zone 3   Dahurian Lily
The erect, open, vase-shaped flowers are red to scarlet with some yellow at the base and 1–6 flowers per stalk. They appear in June. Native to northeastern Asia. It has a wandering stem underground that sometimes produces a few bulblets. It is not one of the best ornamental lilies but is one of the first to bloom.

philadelphicum   1½′–3½′   **Zone 4**   **Wood Lily**
A native over wide areas of eastern North America, the flowers of this are orange to scarlet, spotted dark maroon, and grow erect, widely open. It is a Lily for the wooded areas blooming in June and July. There are several color variants; one, **andinum**, is native in the western part of the habitat of the species and is easier to grow.

philippinense   3′   **Zone 10**   **Philippine Lily**
With pure white, 7–10 in. long, flowers, native to the mountains of northern Luzon in the Philippine Islands, this is only for planting in tropical gardens.

polyphyllum   4′–6′   **Zone 3**   **Afghan Lily**
Native to the western Himalayas, this has white, bell-shaped, fragrant flowers spotted and streaked with purple. The petals are recurved. It is rare and should be grown in full shade. Very difficult to grow and, because its roots penetrate the soil for several feet, it is not easily moved.

pumilum   1½′   **Zone 3**   **Coral Lily**
Native to northeast Asia, with bright red flowers

and grasslike leaves, this is a popular garden plant, although it must be frequently replaced. The fragrant flowers are pendulous with 1–20 flowers per stalk. It does well in full sun. The variety **'Golden Gleam'** has yellow flowers.

regale   4'–6'   **Zone 3**   **Regal Lily**
One of the most magnificent and reliable of the trumpet-shaped lilies, this was an introduction of E. H. Wilson in 1903. The large fragrant flowers are 5 in. wide and 6 in. long, white inside to rose-purple outside, one to several per stalk, in July. Well-grown plants have produced as many as 30 flowers on a stalk. Such plants should be thoroughly staked. It grows well in any soil, especially in full sun. It is easily raised from seed, blooming the second or third year. Bulblets are formed on the stem underground. The only drawback is that in the North (Zone 5) it starts growth early in the spring—in fact so early that late spring frosts can kill the young shoots before they are sufficiently hardened off.

rubellum   1½'–2½'   **Zone 5**   **Rubellum Lily**
A dainty pale rose-pink, fragrant lily from Japan with 1–9 flowers per stalk, each flower bell shaped and about 3 in. long, usually dwarf. Seed may take 2 years to germinate. Blooms in early June.

rubescens   2'–6'   **Zone 7**   **Chaparral Lily**
With white or pale lilac flowers, spotted purple, these are trumpet shaped, fragrant and held erect. Wild plants may have 75–100 flowers per stalk in June or July. The leaves are in whorls. Native to the mountains of western Calif., but not very vigorous in eastern gardens.

sargentiae   4'–5'   **Zone 4**   **Sargent Lily**
Coming from western China, this is similar to *L. regale* but produces many bubils in the axils of the leaves. The fragrant trumpet-shaped flowers are white inside and rose-purple to greenish outside and bloom in July, after *L. regale*. However, many of the plants available are virus infested and it would be well to start with seedlings (which are not). It can be grown in full sun.

speciosum   3'   **Zone 4**   **Speciosum Lily**
A Japanese lily, valued in gardens because it is one of the last to bloom in the late summer or fall and also because of its very rich colors of red and white. Most satisfactory in the garden. The flowers are large, up to 6 in. or more wide, reflexed and twisted, pink to red dotted with spots of darker red. A well-grown plant may have as many as 40 blossoms on 1 stalk. The stem roots and many bulblets are formed on it, underground. The variety **album** has white flowers; **rubrum** has red flowers and a new cultivar of this called **'Uchida'** is one of the most outstanding of many named varieties. This blooms until the first frost.

sulphureum   4'–5'   **Zone 8**   **Sulphur Lily**

Native to upper Burma, it has large trumpet-shaped flowers, recurved at the tip, up to 15 per stalk, pure white flushed yellow. Bulbils are frequently produced in the leaf axils. However, although noted as "tender", it has survived Ore. winters satisfactorily.

superbum   6'–10'   **Zone 5**   **Turkscap Lily**
With large, nodding, orange flowers having maroon-spotted petals, this is an excellent garden lily for its conspicuous flowers in July and Aug. Native from Mass. to Fla. and westward to Ind., this does well in acid soils with plenty of moisture and it must have both to grow well. Then it is very easy to cultivate. The color does vary from yellow to deep red. A single well-grown stalk may have 40 blossoms. Seed sown in the autumn will not appear above ground until the second year unless of course it is given a cold treatment.

szovitsianum   2'–3'   **Zone 4**   **Szovitz Lily**
The yellow bell-shaped flowers are sometimes spotted with brown, flowering in June. There are 1–20 pendulous flowers per stalk. Valued for its early flower, it grows slowly and seedlings may not bloom until the sixth year. Otherwise it is easy to grow and lasts a long time. Native to the Caucasus Area.

taliense   3'–5'   **Zone 5**   **Tali Lily**
A Chinese lily with fragrant flowers, up to 20 per stalk, white spotted purple petals that are strongly reflexed.

tenuifolium = *L. pumilum*

x testaceum   4'–6'   **Zone 4   Nankeen Lily**
In June or July this produces 6–12 large, fragrant, recurved flowers per stalk, yellow with a few raised red spots. Although susceptible to both botrytis blight and basal rot, it is still most popular because of its color. It should be planted in full sun. It is supposed to be a cross, *L. candidum* x *L. chalcedonicum* and can be easily propagated by scales.

tigrinum   3'–4'   **Zone 3**   **Tiger Lily**
One of the most popular of all lilies, native to China but long ago introduced and naturalized in America. It has been valued in the Orient as food, the bulbs cooked and eaten, tasting something like Artichoke. The scentless orange-red blooms are 4 in. across and dotted with purple-black. Many plants are infested with virus, not easy to eliminate because the plant is so easily reproduced by the numerous black bulbils produced in the axils of the leaves. Blooming in mid-July, it is a fine garden asset. The double-flowered form **'Flore-pleno'** has 24–36 modified petals, but is not an especially valued garden asset. The variety **'Splendens'**, blooming in Aug., is one of the best of these varieties for its rich color.

tsingtauense   2'–3'   **Zone 5**   **Tsingtau Lily**
With 1–6 erect, scentless, orange, often spotted

flowers per stalk, native to China, but of little merit as an ornamental especially because it seems to be short-lived.

wallichianum   3′–6′   Zone 8   Wallich Lily
Native to the Himalayan area, this is a handsome white-to-greenish white-flowered lily. The flowers may be as much as 8 in. across, are horizontally borne, funnel-shaped type, flowering in Sept. Sometimes it does not show any growth until July. The underground stem wanders a bit before it emerges above ground and produces several bulblets.

wardii   2′–5′   Zone 4   Ward Lily
Up to 40 pale pinkish-purple, strongly recurved flowers sometimes are produced on a well-grown stalk of this Tibetan lily in early Aug. It is not, as yet, widely grown in America.

washingtonianum 4′ Zone 6 Washington Lily
With funnel-shaped, horizontal flowers which open white, then fade to lilac-purple, with up to 30 flowers per stalk. It is native in the Sierra Nevada Mountains near the Pacific Coast of the U.S. It has proved difficult to grow in cultivation.

wilsonii   3′   Zone 5   Wilson Lily
A Japanese species with orange to yellow flowers in Aug., it may have merit because of its late-blooming qualities. The flowers may be 5 in. across, and are held erect on the stem.

LILY. See LILIUM.

LILY, CHINESE SACRED = *Narcissus tazetta orientalis*

LILY FAMILY = Liliaceae

LILY-OF-THE-NILE = *Agapanthus africanus*

LILY-OF-THE-VALLEY = *Convallaria majalis*

LILY-OF-THE-VALLEY, WILD = *Maianthemum canadense*

LILYTREE, WHITE = *Crinodendron patagua*

LILY-TURF, BIG BLUE, CREEPING. See LIRIOPE.

LILY-TURF, WHITE, DWARF. See OPHIOPOGON.

LIME. Mexican or true Lime trees (*Citrus aurantifolia*) are small, slender, often willowy, with numerous thorns, and small leaves. A second group serving the same purpose is the Tahiti Group, which is characterized by larger, less thorny trees, and larger fruit. The **'Rangpur'** Lime, probably an acid Mandarin Orange, which it resembles in tree and fruit, also serves the same purpose, and is treated here. These very acid citrus are prized primarily for the unique, refreshing flavor of their fruit as used in cooling drinks and cookery.

The true limes will tolerate but a degree or two of frost. Growth is therefore limited to southern Fla., the Keys, warmer areas of the southeast Gulf coast, and to protected sites in the most frost-free areas of southern Calif. Varieties of the Tahitian (Persian) group are only slightly more cold-resistant and can withstand temperatures of about 26° to 27° F. without serious injury. The 'Rangpur' Lime on the other hand is nearly as hardy as the Sweet Orange, and can withstand temperatures in the low 20's without serious tree damage. All, however, have tender fruit which can withstand but 3–4 degrees below freezing, 'Rangpur' fruit being slightly more tender. See ORANGE for methods of frost protection.

As true limes are propagated mostly by seed, the variety designation has less significance than for many other plant varieties. Accepted fruit type is small, oval to round, about an inch in dia. The fruit becomes lemon-yellow when fully ripe, but is usually harvested when still green, or showing but a slight yellow blush. The flesh is greenish yellow, tender, and yields abundant, very acid juice with the typical lime flavor. Mexican, West Indian, Key and thornless variants of the above names may be offered by nurserymen in areas where limes are grown.

'Bearss' is the best of the Tahiti or Persian group, and may bear the name Tahiti or Persian, but the former is a distinct variety. The fruit is larger than that of the true Lime, being from $1\frac{1}{2}$ to over 2 in. in dia. The skin and flesh color is about the same as for the Mexican group, and the juice has the flavor of the true lime. 'Bearss' is seedless.

'Rangpur' can be used to extend the range of very acid citrus. The fruit is a deep orange color, the skin loose, and the flesh orange colored, juicy, and with only a slight suggestion of the true lime flavor. In fruit and tree it closely resembles the mandarin oranges, especially the tangerines; the fruit is slightly seedy. A few sweet limes, most nearly resembling the Tahiti Group, are known; varieties are 'Palestine', 'Sweet', and 'Otaheite'. The latter, propagated from cuttings, is sold in quantity as a Christmas potted ornamental plant bearing bloom and fruit. All of the sweet limes are suspected hybrids.

Propagation

Mexican limes are readily propagated by seed, most coming true to type, as they are highly polyembryonic. The 'Bearss' must be propagated vegetatively, as it is seedless, and is a triploid citrus. 'Rangpur', unlike the Mexican, will not come true from seed in most cases, so to assure getting the desired type, budded trees are best used.

Lime trees may be topworked (see ORANGE), but their use as rootstocks has not been generally tested, except that the 'Rangpur' is apparently a satisfactory stock for other citrus.

The cold-tenderness of the Mexican and Tahitian groups would not suggest their use in areas where these kinds cannot be grown.

Rootstocks

Mexican limes can be grown on any of the common citrus rootstocks, but appear to overgrow Sour Orange rootstock badly, suggesting a degree of incompatibility. In southern Fla., Rough Lemon has proved to be good, Sweet Orange and Grapefruit rootstocks have been used successfully. Of course most are grown on their own roots, as seedlings. The same rootstocks will serve for varieties of the Tahitian Group or 'Rangpur'.

Planting

Mexican limes make small trees, and planting distance need not be in excess of 15 ft.; the Tahitian Group grow considerably larger, and distances of about 22 ft. should be allowed; the same or slightly longer planting distances apply to 'Rangpur'. See ORANGE for methods of growing these kinds at closer distances or in small spaces. Little is known concerning the value of dwarfing rootstocks for the limes; the 'Otaheite', as mentioned, is adapted to pot culture, and all could be kept small by growing in small tubs if given good attention.

The Mexican and Tahitian group of limes tend to bloom and mature fruit throughout the year, although there is a normal peak season of maturation. In Calif., Mexican limes ripen most of their crop in the late fall or winter; the 'Bearss' somewhat later. In Fla., the main crop ripens from June to Aug. 'Rangpur' has but a single bloom and ripening period in the Southwest and Pacific regions, but may bear a small number of fruit throughout the year in the Southeast; its normal peak production is in winter and early spring.

Limes may be kept for some time in cool, dry storage if properly cured when harvested. See LEMON. 'Rangpur' is not so well adapted to prolonged storage.

Besides the normal diseases of citrus (see ORANGE), the Mexican lime is particularly subject to anthracnose fungus, particularly in the humid Southeast—a disease which attacks both fruit and foliage. On the other hand, the Tahitian Group are susceptible to citrus scab, to which the Mexican group is highly resistant, if not immune.

CLARON O. HESSE

LIME. Lime is not necessary for all plants on all soils. In fact, lime is not even necessary as an additive on all soils. Contrary to popular belief it is not a fertilizer but does have an active part to play in garden soils. Lime is calcium carbonate, and of course all plants need calcium in order to grow properly. In soils made from limestone rocks there is usually sufficient present in the soil, or if lime is being leached out by heavy rains, more calcium carbonate becomes available. In acid soils, lime is sometimes needed for certain plants, especially vegetables and farm crops, although most trees and shrubs seem to be unaffected with or without it.

A "sour" soil is one with most of the lime leached out. In areas where soils have been made from acid-bearing rocks what little calcium carbonate there is present in the soil is being continually leached out by rainfall. Farmers know that such a soil is unfit for growing clover or would not produce a good crop of vegetables. The gardener should understand the uses of lime in order to use it intelligently and also save himself time and money in applying it unnecessarily.

Soil that has a green scum or small amounts of moss in it, is in poor condition, certainly in need of fertilizer and possibly is in need of lime also.

Lime, added to a heavy clay soil, makes it more workable by improving the physical condition. It causes the finer particles of clay and silt to combine (in a heavy clay soil), forming larger particles and thus allowing space for air and water drainage. On the other hand, applied to sandy soils it can prove harmful. It also reduces the amount of acidity in a soil (see SOILS) and soils usually need it if the acidity is below 5.5 pH.

There are several types of lime on the market but by far the best for gardeners is ground limestone, or better still ground dolomitic limestone because this has, in addition, a small amount of magnesium, an essential element for plant growth and often deficient in many soils.

This material, as well as ground limestone, has the added advantage that it can not be too heavily applied, within reason. When the pH of the soil rises to neutral or slightly alkaline the remaining lime becomes less and less soluble, hence there is not the danger from burning foliage with too heavy an application. Some other forms of lime do not act this way but remain soluble even though the soil alkalinity is being raised, hence if too heavily applied, the alkalinity of the soil continues to rise and shortly phosphorous, magnesium and some of the other minor elements are made unavailable. This of course causes injury to the plants. Also, lime does aid in releasing certain chemicals in the soil.

Limestone. This is simply the ground limestone rock and it should be finely ground. It should pass a 10-mesh (to the inch) screen and half of it should pass a 100-mesh screen.

Oyster shells. These are available only near the seacoast where oyster fisheries are located. They have little value unless finely ground.

Marl. This is sometimes available locally and is a mixture of limestone and silt or clays, but they vary considerably in proportion and if price is not a factor these local marls might be overlooked as suppliers of limestone.

Chalk. A poor form of lime, not so commonly used in this country as in England. It has twice the bulk but only one half the value of limestone.

Hydrated lime or slaked lime is the hydroxide of lime or burned lime to which water has been added. It is a white powder and is highly caustic and difficult to handle.

Burned lime or quicklime comes in large lumps unfit for the gardener's purpose, and is the commercial oxide of lime. It is a white powder, caustic and difficult to handle.

Of these, the best for the gardener's purpose is ground dolomitic limestone, ground limestone or hydrated lime, in that order.

How much to apply—the soil test (see SOILS) will show this but using the old saying is a "a ton of lime per acre," which broken down for small garden plots is a $\frac{1}{2}$ lb. per sq. yard of soil. One satisfactory application need not be repeated for 4–5 years. It should be spread evenly on the surface of prepared garden soil and either watered in or allowed to stand until rain washes it down into the soil. Lime does not move up or laterally very well in the soil, the reason why it should not be plowed in. Nor should it be applied to or with manure for this way it does more harm than good. It should not be mixed with commercial fertilizers.

It is best not to use burned or slaked lime in the garden. Certain woody plants, like lilacs and junipers, apparently grow better in acid soils if lime is added. Many plants are indifferent to it and certainly ericaceous plants need very little if any lime added to a good acid soil in which there is plenty of humus.

Applying lime to lawns has been much overdone. Lime corrects strongly acid soils, adds calcium as a nutrient, increases the availability of other plant nutrients and encourages biological activity. Most grasses grow well on moderately acid soils. Lime encourages weeds and clover, hence if a pure grass lawn is desired lime should only be applied on extremely acid soils at least below a pH 5.5. If lime is to be applied to correct acidity, hydrated lime can be applied at a rate of 35 lbs. per 1000 sq. ft. or powdered limestone at a rate of 50 lbs. per 1000 sq. ft.

Kentucky Bluegrass does not always need lime. It needs a fertile soil and if the soil is fertile it can grow well on limestone soils. The chances are that a complete fertilizer added to the lawn will do more good than an application of lime. See LAWNS.

LIMESTONE SOILS. There are regions in America where the soils are predominately alkaline because they are made from disintegrating limestone rock. See SOILS, pH, SOIL MIXTURES, etc. There are certain plants like species of *Clematis, Delphinium, Daphne, Dictamnus, Gypsophila, Juniperus, Lonicera* and *Syringa* all of which grow better in alkaline soils than they do in acid soils. Also, certain acid soil plants (which see) will not thrive and sometimes will not succeed at all in alkaline soils.

It is possible to change the acidity of the soil (see pH) and this may be worth the effort. On the other hand, it may save time and labor if one observes what grows well in neighboring gardens, and use similar plants, thus circumventing the necessity of creating garden work by attempting to change the acidity (or alkalinity) of the soil and keep it changed in order to grow something "unusual" to the area.

LIMNANTHES (lim-NAN-thees)

douglasii   6″   annual   Meadow-foam

This is native to the western coastal area of the U.S., a profusely blooming spring flower with yellow, pink or white blossoms an inch across and fragrant. The alternate, compound leaves have leaflets arranged feather fashion on either side of the midrib. Actually it is a marsh flower and so should be planted in wet soil. The var. **grandiflora** has larger flowers than the species. Seeds are sown outdoors in a very early spring where they are to grow, preferably in a wet soil but in a sunny situation.

LIMONIUM (ly-MO-nium). Sometimes termed Statice, the Sea-lavenders are valued in the flower border for their light airy habit, their small yellow-to-lavender flowers which often are dried for winter ornament. They are native to the Mediterranean Region and the Canary Islands and grow well in gardens along the seacoast, blooming during the late summer. Seeds are sown indoors in March, then transplanted outdoors after all frost is over, preferably in good loam in the full sun.

bellidifolium   8″   Zone 6 (?)

Above rosettes of narrowly lanceolate leaves 2 in. long, the stiff slender flower stalks rise slightly, producing tiny tufts of lavender flowers in a wide-branching flower head. Native to Europe and eastern Asia.

bonduelii   2′   annual or biennial   Algerian Sea-lavender

With lyre-shaped leaves to 6 in. long, winged flower panicles and yellow flowers.

carolinianum 2′–3′ Zone 5 Carolina Sea-lavender
Although this plant is native to the marshes and seashore areas of southern New England and N.Y. to Miss. and Fla., it may be cultivated in drier sites in the wild garden and its flowers are very useful as components of dried arrangements. The plant has oblong-to-lanceolate basal leaves and a much-branched flower stalk bearing an open panicle of tiny lavender flowers having a trumpet-shaped corolla with 5 lobes. It blooms from July to Oct. and may be propagated by seed sown in spring or fall.

latifolium 2½′ Zone 3 Wide-leaf Sea-lavender
This is an outstanding perennial for the border, bearing large feathery panicles of small bright mauve flowers on tall stems. A single clump may have a dozen flower stalks, taking up a space about 3 ft. in dia. Native to Europe and Asia, can be grown in salty marshes. This is probably better than any of the other species as an ornamental. Propagated by seeds sown in late fall or early spring and by division.

perezii 3′ Zone 9 Perez Sea-lavender
Possibly shrubby with triangular leaves 4–6 in. long. The flower itself is yellow but the calyx is bluish purple. Native to the Canary Islands and planted in southern Calif.

ramosissimum (*globulariaefolium*) 8″–30″ Zone 7(?) Violettuft Sea-lavender
Similar to *L. bellidifolium*, but having wider leaves of a gray-green shade with profuse pale lavender flowers on wide-branching flower heads. Native to the Mediterranean Region.

sinuatum 2′ biennial Notch-leaf Sea-lavender
Similar to *L. bonduellii* except that there are varieties with white, blue or red flowers.

tataricum 1′ Zone 6 (?) Tatarian Sea-lavender
A perennial herb with tufted or alternate leaves along the stem, obovate, about 6 in. long with red and white flowers, native to southern Europe. The var. 'Nanum' is only about 9 in. high, with fluffy pink flowers during Aug. This is a better ornamental than the species because it is more dense and compact, thus making a rounded mass of color in Aug. Some botanists list this species as *Gniolimon tataricum*.

vulgare 9″–18″ Zone 7
Perennial with blue-purple flowers. Europe.

LINACEAE = The Flax Family

LINANTHUS (li-NAN-thus)
androsaceus (*Gilia androsacea*) 1½′ annual Trumpet Linanthus
Leaves palmately divided; flowers white, pink, violet or yellow and about an inch long, being borne in dense heads.

dianthiflorus (*Gilia dianthoides*) 6″ annual Tufted Linanthus
This species is tufted with entire, threadlike leaves an inch long, flowers lilac to pink to white, ¾ in. long in few-flowered clusters.

liniflorus (*Gilia liniflora*) 1′ annual Flax-flower Linanthus
Flowers white to blush pink, ½ in. long.

LINARIA (lin-AY-ria)
alpina 3″–9″ Zone 4 Alpine Toadflax
Probably the best of this genus for the rock garden, for it forms low perennial, matlike masses of foliage and flowers, 3 borne on little spikes 2–3 in. long, with purple and yellow flowers something like those of little snapdragons. The gray-green leaves are very narrow, native throughout the Alps Mountains of Europe. Easily grown from spring-sown seeds, preferably in a bulb pan, and then transplanted outdoors as soon as they are large enough. There are white (**alba**) and pink (**rosea**) flowered varieties as well.

biparthita 1′ annual Cloven-lip Toadflax
With linear whorled leaves, flowers purple with orange throats, the upper lip 2-lobed, and a curved spur. Native to Portugal and North Africa. Useful as bedding plants, in the flower border, in edging and in the rock garden. Flowers are borne in loose racemes and bloom from June to Sept. Seeds can be sown outdoors in early April.

canadensis 12″–18″ Zone 3 Oldfield Toadflax
A slender plant which may be grown either as an annual or a perennial, this has narrowly linear leaves in whorls on a stem terminating in a loose cluster of irregular flowers. These are blue, with a spot of yellow on the lip, and a long spur. It is native to a large area extending from southern Canada and eastern U.S. to Tex. and S.Dak. It is an excellent plant for the rock garden and may be propagated by seed.

genistifolia dalmatica 4′ Zone 7
A perennial with lanceolate leaves and bright-yellow flowers. Native to southeastern Europe. Sometimes used in the flower border.

maroccana 1½′ annual Morocco Toadflax
Plants for this purpose are grown from seed sown from Sept. to Jan. and will bloom in late winter or early spring. The narrow leaves are whorled. There are several varieties with flowers from pink to blue. Easily propagated by seed. Native to Morocco.

purpurea 3′ Zone 7 (?) Purple Toadflax
Rather showy in the flower border, with lance-shaped leaves and purple flowers, the spur curved and about the length of the corolla. Native to southern Europe.

vulgaris 3′ **Zone** 3 **Butter-and-eggs**
A common weedy perennial, naturalized throughout eastern North America and locally on the Pacific Coast but native to Europe and Asia. The alternate leaves are linear and the flowers yellow and orange, 1¼ in. long, about the same color as butter and eggs. Five petals are united into a 2-lipped corolla and back of this is a long spur containing the nectar. These flowers are borne from June to Oct. in long, terminal racemes. It has deeply rooted, running rootstocks that must be dug or killed to eliminate the plant entirely. See WEED-CONTROLLING CHEMICALS.

LINDANE. A chlorinated hydrocarbon used as an insecticide. See INSECTICIDES.

LINDEN. See TILIA.

LINDEN FAMILY = Tiliaceae

LINDERA (LIN-der-a)
benzoin 15′ **Zone** 4 **Spicebush**
Although there are several exotic spice bushes, some possibly more handsome than *L. benzoin*, nevertheless, it is this one which is widely native over the eastern U.S., and is usually well known to everyone familiar with the woods. It is a dense shrub, the twigs and leaves of which are aromatic when crushed and its small fragrant yellow flowers appear in mid-April before the foliage. In the fall, the leaves turn a clear golden yellow and when these fall the red berries on the pistillate plants are clearly seen. The male or staminate plants of course have no fruits. One of its good characteristics is that it does well in moist soils. The young twigs, leaves and fruits have been used to make an aromatic tea. The berries, dried and powdered, have been used as a substitute for all-spice. Do not allow the seeds to dry out but stratify them as soon as ripe at 40° F. for 4 months, then sow. Softwood cuttings can be rooted.

LINEAR. Long and narrow with nearly parallel margins.

LINNAEA (lin-EE-a)
borealis 4″–6″ **Zone** 2 **Twinflower**
A miniature evergreen of the woods and forests, native over great expanses of Europe, Asia and North America, including Alaska, the opposite leaves are only ¼–1 in. long. The fragrant flowers are apple pink, bell-shaped and borne in pairs on short branches during June and July. It is only for growing in the cooler parts of the country in boggy, peaty soils in shaded situations.

LINOSYRIS (lin-o-SEE-ris)
vulgaris 2′ **Zone** 5 (?) **European Goldilocks**
An Old World perennial herb with alternate leaves and yellow heads of small flowers in a head about ½ in. wide during late summer and autumn, this belongs to the Composite Family.

The flowers are borne in terminal clusters and the plant is easily propagated by division.

LINSEED OIL. An oil, much used in paints, made by crushing the seed of the Common Flax, *Linum usitatissumum*.

LINUM (LY-num). Splendid garden flowers noted for their delicate texture and blue or yellow color. All have alternate, narrow leaves. They are not good as cut flowers, but in the garden, even though individual flowers may last only a day, they bloom consistently for much of the summer. Especially good as rock garden plants or in the foreground of the flower border. Spring planting in the full sun is best. A light winter mulch may prove helpful. Propagation by seeds; when sown in spring, the perennial kinds will not bloom until the following year. Also propagated by cuttings and by division.

austriacum 2′ **Zone** 3 **Austrian Flax**
Similar to *L. perenne* with bluish-purple flowers about ¾ in. wide and fine, linear leaves ⅝ in. long. Native to southern Europe.

campanulatum 15″ **Zone** 7 (?) **Harebell Flax**
A perennial that may be woody at the base, the leaves having margins that are narrow and transparent. The flowers are pale yellow with orange veins, 1¼ in. wide, the sepals having white margins, blooming in the summer. Native to southern Europe.

flavum 2′ **Zone** 5 **Golden Flax**
Perennial with almost woody stems; flowers yellow and an inch wide, usually with 20–50 in one inflorescence. Native to southern and central Europe. Blooms appear from late June to mid-Aug. 'Cloth of Gold' is a compact dwarf variety only 9 in. tall.

grandiflorum 2′ **annual** **Flowering Flax**
With narrow leaves and quickly fading flowers 1½ in. wide which, in the species, are a reddish purple, but there are varieties available with blue, red and pink flowers. Leaves are linear, 1¼ in. long. They make attractive border plants. Native to northern Africa, this plant is widely grown in America. Seeds are usually sown where the plants are eventually to grow in the border.

narbonense 2′ **Zone** 5 **Narbonne Flax**
Flowers blue, larger than those of *L. perenne*, about 1¾ in. wide. Native to the Mediterranean Region.

perenne 2′ **Zone** 4 **Perennial Flax**
A very popular garden perennial, one of the very best in this genus, with deep blue flowers an inch wide, usually borne in a much-branched panicle. It is gracefully arching in habit, is native to Europe and has a white-flowered variety 'Alba'.

var. alpinum 4″–6″ **Zone** 4 **Alpine Flax**
This is really a small edition of *L. perenne*, which see. Native to Europe.

suffruticosum salsoloides   16″   **Zone 6**
                                        Russian-thistle Flax
An evergreen perennial with needlelike leaves
1¾ in. long; flowers white with purple veins up
to an inch wide. Native to southern Europe.
The form **'Nanum'** is a trailing plant from the
Alps Mountains which may not last long in the
garden. White flowers with blue veins may vary
to almost pink. This form is really prostrate,
only about 3 in. tall, growing in clumps up to
18 in. wide.

usitatissimum   4′   **annual**   **Flax**
Originally a native to Asia, but now widely
naturalized in Europe and North America.
Flowers blue, ½ in. wide in summer; leaves
alternate, linear-lanceolate. Crushed seed in hot
water was an old-fashioned remedy (in a
poultice) for chest colds; whole seed is a
laxative; also is the source of linseed oil. The
stem fiber is the source for linen thread and
cloth.

LION'S-EAR = *Leonotis leonurus*

LION'S-HEART, VIRGINIA = *Physostegia
virginiana*

LIPARIS (LIP-a-ris). A bulbous genus of the
Orchid Family growing mostly in the Temperate
Zone, plants have generally 2 broad basal leaves
which sheathe the erect, angled flower stalk
bearing a loose terminal raceme of irregular
flowers. Each flower has narrow sepals and
petals and a broad, spreading lip. Merely small
flowers of little value in the garden.

lilifolia   6″   **Zone 4**   **Lily Twayblade**
The showy purple flowers of this species makes
it a desirable plant for the shady, wild garden
with rich, well-drained soil. It blooms in June
and July and may be found throughout the
eastern U.S.

loeselii   5″   **Zone 4**   **Loesel's Twayblade**
This species has rather light green, elliptic
leaves which may persist for several seasons,
and inconspicuous yellow-green flowers with an
oblong lip. It blooms during early summer in
bogs and peaty meadows from Canada throughout the Great Plains states to Kan. and east to
the Carolinas. While it may be grown in sunlight, it needs moisture to survive in cultivation.

LIP FERN. See CHEILANTHES.

LIPPIA   CANESCENS = *Phyla   nodiflora
canescens*

LIQUIDAMBAR (lik-wid-AMB-ar)

styraciflua   125′   **Zone 5**   **Sweet-gum**
An excellent ornamental tree, native to the
eastern U.S., valued solely for its fine foliage
and brilliant scarlet autumn color. The alternate
leaves are star-shaped with 5–7 lobes, about 4–7
in. across. The flowers are inconspicuous but
the rounded "horny" fruits in globose balls

about 1 in. across are much used in Christmas
decorations along with fruits of the coniferous
trees. It is rather difficult to transplant and
always should be moved with a ball of soil about
the roots, but once established, it has few
troubles. If given plenty of room in which to
develop, few other trees can approach it in
symmetrical beauty. There is a fragrant gum
exuding from cracks and crevices in the trunk
especially in the southeastern states which tastes
somewhat like the spruce gum from native
Picea species in the northeastern U.S. The
Formosan species (*L. formosana*) hardy in Zone
7, is sometimes used on the Pacific Coast. It is
somewhat similar but the leaves are 3-lobed.
L. styraciflua is widely used as an ornamental
and street tree from Mass. to Calif.

Propagation

Do not allow the seed to dry out but stratify
as soon as ripe for 3 months at 40° F. Varieties
can also be budded or grafted on their species.
Softwood cuttings have been rooted. See
STRATIFICATION, GRAFTING, CUTTINGS, etc.

Insect Pests

Bark beetles often infest weakened trees. No
control other than removing infested trees is
suggested. Forest tent caterpillar includes
Sweet-gum among its many food plants.
Spraying with insecticide #5 can be done
effectively on specimen trees.

Diseases

Bleeding necrosis in the form of depressed
areas in the bark accompanied by excessive
bleeding of sap kills infected trees quickly.
Cutting out the infected areas is the only
treatment.

LIRIODENDRON (li-ri-o-DEND-ron)

tulipifera   150′   **Zone 4**   **Tulip-tree**
A common and popular tree, grown by most
nurseries and widely planted, especially in the
eastern U.S. where it is native. The June flowers
are cup-shaped somewhat resembling dull
yellow tulips in shape, and the yellow autumn
color and massive handsome form all make this
tree a desirable ornamental specimen. One
massive specimen growing in the Great Smoky
National Park (at Cades Cove) is estimated to
be 500 years old. The leaves are alternate. The
variety **'Fastigiatum'** is a densely pyramidal
form which makes a better street tree than the
wide-branching species.

Propagation

Do not allow seeds to dry out but stratify
as soon as ripe for 3 months at 40° F. then sow.
Also grafting or budding on *L. tulipifera*
understock is satisfactory but also *Magnolia*

kobus understock has been used. Softwood cuttings are difficult but possible to root. See STRATIFICATION, GRAFTING, etc.

Insect Pests

Tulip-tree scale, a large brown soft scale, infests and weakens the twigs but is more troublesome due to the great quantities of sticky honeydew (see HONEYDEW) which is secreted and followed by sooty mold. Dormant spraying with insecticide #44 and summer sprays in late summer when the young are hatching is advised. Tulip-tree aphid, a small green aphid on the leaves, also secretes honeydew and when the scale and aphid are both present it is very annoying. Spraying with insecticide #15 is effective. Tulip-tree spot gall causes circular brown spots with a yellow border and is more conspicuous than destructive. Insecticide #15 applied when the flies are active in late spring is suggested.

Diseases

Sooty mold, described above, badly disfigures ornamental trees. Control the insects.

LIRIOPE (li-ri-O-pe). Small evergreen plants with flowers somewhat similar to those of the Grape-hyacinth; grasslike foliage growing from bulbs or tubers. Native to China and Japan, frequently used as ground covers in sheltered areas as far north as New York City. They belong to the Lily Family and are easily propagated by dividing the offsets. Widely used in the South as ground covers and reportedly able to withstand salt spray. Similar in most respects to *Ophiopogon* species (which see) but slightly more hardy—can be grown in either shade or sun and require no special care. Propagated merely by dividing the plants in early spring.

muscari 2′ **Zone 6 Big Blue Lily-turf**
Taller than *L. spicata*, with 10 or more whorls of 4–7 flowers on each flower stalk. The var. **variegata** has yellow-striped leaves. Much of the material grown as *Ophiopogon jaburan variegatus* is actually var. of *L. muscari*. Because of its height, this makes a more coarse ground cover than the finer textured *L. spicata*. Blooms in Sept. with lilac-purple flowers on spikes about as high as the leaves. Native to Japan and China.

spicata 8″–12″ **Zone 4 Creeping Lily-turf**
A green grasslike plant often used as a ground cover with evergreen grasslike leaves about ¼ in. wide. The light lilac to almost white flowers are ⅙–¼ in. in dia., and are produced on spikes taller than the leaves during July and Aug. Native to China and Japan. Frequently used as a ground cover, it does very well until grass gets in, then it is difficult to pull out the grass. The leaves remain green (in the North) until about Christmas when they turn a pale sickly green until spring. Plants are easily divided to increase a planting and should be spaced only a few inches apart.

LISTS. As an aid to help busy gardeners in finding plants for specific purposes when they are in a hurry, the following 46 lists appear in their alphabetical places in this book. It must be remembered that all the plants used for a certain purpose do not appear—it would make the lists too unwieldy. However, enough are listed so that the gardener will be able to obtain many suggestions, to which he can add more from his own reading and experience.

LITCHI (LEE-chee)

chinensis   40′   Zones 9–10   Lychee
A comparatively recently introduced Chinese tree now being grown commercially in southern Fla., southern Calif. and the Hawaiin Islands for its small edible fruits. Beneath the outside shell and surrounding the single seed is a translucent edible pulp. The mature fruit resembles a one-seeded berry $1\frac{1}{2}$ in. in dia., with a thin, leathery, bright red shell, making it suitable for planting as an ornamental. The alternate, leathery, evergreen leaves are compound and have 3–7 oblong leaflets. The better varieties are propagated by air layering, inarching and grafting. See LYCHEE.

Insect Pests

Scale insects and mites may require spraying with insecticide #15 or a miticide such as #34.

Diseases

Trees are badly infected and killed by a gall fungus which is associated with oaks. Planting near oaks should be avoided.

LITHOCARPUS (lith-o-KARP-us)

densiflorus   75′   Zone 7   Tanbark Oak
This tree grows well only in rich, moist, well-drained soil in southern Ore. and Calif. where it is native. The alternate, leathery, evergreen leaves are $1\frac{1}{2}$–4 in. long and the general habit is low and open. The fruit is an acorn about 1 in. long and the flowers are upright catkins 2–4 in. long with the male flowers near the top and the female flowers near the bottom.

LITHODORA (lith-o-DOR-a)

**diffusa (*Lithospermum diffusum*)   prostrate
                                         Zones 6–7**
This prostrate evergreen shrub from the Northern Temperate Zone grows as a thick mat of small, hairy leaves having a profusion of bright blue flowers from midsummer throughout the remainder of the season. There are several forms of this plant, perhaps the best known of which are 'Heavenly Blue' and 'Grace Ward', both listed under the former name of *Lithospermum diffusum*. Plants require good drainage in a semi-shady area with an acid soil of sand and leaf mold.

LITHOPS (LITH-ops).

Very small, peculiar succulents, native to South Africa, in size and shape resembling small stones. Leaves are borne in pairs but are usually buried, the top of the plant seems to be divided in 2 or more pieces, and the yellow or white flowers appear from this division line in the center of the plant.

LITHOSPERMUM (lith-o-SPERM-um)

canescens   12″–18″   Zone 3   Hoary Gromwell
A hairy perennial with alternate, entire leaves growing from a large root which is used to make red dye. The leaves are alternate, lanceolate and without marginal teeth. The yellow flowers are borne in one-sided bracted clusters, the stem also being crowned with a flower cluster. Each tubular corolla has 5 rounded lobes and is stalkless, or nearly so. The plant grows in open prairies or sandy woods from southern Canada through the U.S. to the Gulf of Mexico and blooms from April to June. In cultivation it does best in clayey, slightly acid soil. Seed should be sown in moist soil in early spring.

diffusum = *Lithodora diffusa*
purpureo-caeruleum = *Buglossoides purpureo-caeruleum*

LITTLE PICKLES = *Othonna capensis*

LITTONIA (lit-TO-nia)

modesta   6′   Zone 10
A tuberous, climbing herb with shiny green leaves ending in a tendril. The rich orange, bell-shaped, axillary flowers are $1\frac{1}{4}$ in. long. It belongs to the Lily Family. Native to tropical Africa.

LIVERBALSAM, ALPINE = *Erinus alpinus*

LIVERWORTS. These were the first land plants, each one about 1–2 in. long and as thick as a piece of paper. They have several layers of cells and the ability of forking and growing in different directions. They are flat and scaly, creeping over rocks, growing from the base toward the tip, and as the tip elongates, the base dies.

LIVING ROCKS. See PLEIOSPILOS.

LIVISTONA (liv-ist-O-na). These are popular fan palms of the Old World, occasionally grown out-of-doors in southern Calif. or southern Fla., small plants (while they are small) are interesting greenhouse foliage plants, but the individual leaves can grow to 5–6 ft. across. They have upright trunks with a fountain of foliage on top. Fruits are thin-skinned and drupelike.

australis   50′   Zone 10   Australian Fan Palm
An Australian palm tree with a rounded habit and dense fanlike leaves 3–5 ft. across. Leaf stalks, especially when young, are spiny. Trunk reddish brown. Native to Australia. Only hardy in subtropical areas of the U.S.

chinensis   30′   Zone 8   Chinese Fan Palm
When young this is sometimes used as a house or greenhouse plant, but the fan-shaped leaves eventually grow 6 ft. across. They are glossy green, cut half way into narrow ribbed segments which again are split and hang pendulous like a

fringe. The young petioles, eventually up to 6 ft. long, have small spines usually disappearing as the leaves mature. Native to China. The hardiest of this genus.

rotundifolia   50′   Zone 10   Java Fan Palm
Native to Malaya, fan-shaped leaves 2–5 ft. across. The leaves are cut about ¼ to the base, arranged almost in a circle about the plant, glossy green on both sides and on thorny red stalks. Very beautiful when young.

LOAM. A soil with a combination of clay and enough sand to counteract the cohering property of the clay; usually implying the presence of considerable decomposed organic matter with accompanying fertility.

LOBED. Divides into or bearing lobes.

LOBELIA (lo-BEE-lia). A genus of over 250 alternate-leaved annuals or perennials, much admired in the garden for their terminal spires of bright colored flowers. The annuals begin to bloom in late spring, hence seed should be started indoors in Feb. or March at least. Plants can be set out in May, pinched back to about 6 in. in order to make compact specimens. Mature perennial types can also be divided in spring or fall.

cardinalis   2′–3′   Zone 2   Cardinal-flower
The straight, unbranched stems of this plant have alternate, lanceolate leaves and a terminal spike of handsome, irregular, cardinal-red flowers about 1½ in. long which appear from July to Sept. It frequents moist meadows and the edges of streams throughout the eastern half of Canada and the U.S. to the Gulf of Mexico. Although a short-lived perennial, it is well to use the offshoots of the old flowering stems to carry on the plant. It may be propagated also by stem cuttings in midsummer or by seed sown in spring or fall. It is well to mulch the roots in winter, since the plant is easily killed.

erinus   4″–12″   annual   Edging Lobelia
Varieties of this partially trailing South African species are among the best of all blue-flowered plants for edging purposes. The flowers are ¾ in. across and profuse, and the plants form low compact mounds of sky-blue color. A few of the long-time popular vars. are: 'Blue Stone'—4 in. tall and powder blue; 'Cambridge Blue'—6 in. tall; 'Crystal Palace'—4 in. tall, dark blue; 'Mrs. Clibran' 4 in. tall, dark blue with white eye; 'Sapphire' and 'Red Cascade'—trailing vars.

gracilis   1′   annual   Slender Lobelia
With dark blue flowers, white in the center, ¾ in. dia., native to Australia.

inflata   3′   annual   Indian Tobacco
Sometimes a biennial, but a native weed with alternate, simple leaves, slightly toothed, flowers light blue, ¼ in. long in branched terminal spikes from July to Oct. Supposedly the plant is poisonous and widely spread throughout eastern, central and midwestern North America.

siphilitica   1′–3′   Zone 5   Big Blue Lobelia
A stiffly erect plant, perennial by means of short offsets. The alternate leaves are slightly hairy, lanceolate and irregularly toothed, 3–5 in. long. The lower leaves are petioled, the upper ones sessile. The flowers are borne in a leafy terminal raceme. Each flower is about 1 in. long and occasionally is white but generally purple with the lower lip blue. The plant blooms in late summer and is native to moist or swampy woods from Conn. to N.Car. and west to Kan. It may be propagated by means of the offsets, or by seed which germinate readily.

spicata   18″–24″   Zone 4   Pale-spike Lobelia
A slender, slightly branching plant with a few oblong basal leaves and with stem leaves which are alternate and finally become narrow bracts beneath the small blue flowers which appear in a tightly clustered terminal spike. Each flower is tubular, with 5 slightly irregular lobes. It blooms from June to Aug. in rich, sunny locations from New England to Ga., and west to Minn. and Ark. It is an excellent plant for the wild garden.

splendens   3′   Zone 8   Mexican Lobelia
A hairy herbaceous perennial often with bronze-colored lance-shaped leaves. Flowers deep red, 1½ in. long. Native to Mexico.

tenuior   2½′   annual
With blue flowers an inch across. However, it is not too easily grown in the garden, making a better greenhouse or pot plant. Native to Australia.

LOBELIACEAE = The Lobelia Family

LOBELIA FAMILY = Lobeliaceae

LOBIVIA (lo-BIV-ia). Low, globular, ribbed, spiny cacti species. Only a few inches tall and similar in size and shape to *Echinopsis* species, but differing only in flower characteristics. Native to Peru, Bolivia and Argentina.

LOBSTER-CLAWS = *Vriesia carinata*

LOBULARIA (lob-yew-LAY-ria)

maritima (*Alyssum maritimum*)   1′   annual
                                            Sweet Alyssum
Actually this is a perennial in many places but usually grown as an annual and a favorite garden plant. With small lanceolate-to-linear leaves, dense growth, mounded habit and profuse small white flowers until frost, it is a fine and valued bedding plant or edging plant in any garden. There are now many vars. available, some dwarf, some with violet or pinkish flowers. The following are a few good vars.: 'Carpet of Snow'—spreading and dwarf; 'Little Gem'—compact, white, good in pots; 'Tetra Snowdrift'—growing up to 10 in. this is used for cutting; 'Violet Queen'—5 in. tall, light violet-

colored flowers almost a washed-out color; **'Royal Carpet'**—only 3-4 in. tall but 10 in. across. Flowers violet-purple. Goes well with 'Little Gem'. The seed can be sown in the open during March and April and will start to bloom a few weeks thereafter. Plants sown earlier in the greenhouse might bring earlier bloom outdoors. It should continue to bloom all summer and be the last thing in the garden killed by frost in the fall. However, a second sowing made in June might insure plenty of flowers in the fall. Seedlings should be thinned to about 5 in. apart. Shearing in the summer often aids in producing good late bloom, and plants potted, sheared and taken indoors before frost also make fine blooming house plants.

LOCKHARTIA (lok-HART-ia). A genus containing over 20 species of epiphytic orchids. Native to tropical America, the inflorescences only 1-2 flowered. *L. elegans* has triangular leaves $1\frac{1}{2}$ in. long with pale green flowers. *L. lunifera* has leaves only about $\frac{3}{4}$ in. long and golden-yellow flowers. For culture see ORCHID.

LOCUST. See ROBINIA.

LODOICEA (lo-DOY-see-a)

maldivica   100′   Tropics   Double Coconut
A palm found only in the Seychelles Islands, but it has no garden value in America for it is very difficult to get established. The fruits are large nuts (usually 2-lobed but sometimes even 3 and 4 lobed) and may weigh 40–50 lbs. Actually they have no horticulutral value, but it is interesting to note that this produces the largest seed of any plant in the vegetable kingdom.

LOGANBERRY. See BLACKBERRY.

LOGWOOD = *Haematoxylum campechianum*

LOISELEURIA (loy-sel-YEW-ria)

procumbens   6″   Zone 2   Alpine-azalea
Growing in most of the northern parts of the northern hemisphere, this is another low matforming evergreen, of chief value for its hardiness and the fact that it prefers moist to boggy soils in which it grows best. The leaves are only $\frac{1}{4}$ in. long, and the flowers small and white to pink. Also, it must be in an area where the summers are cool and not hot—hence it is not a plant to be indiscriminately used in every garden.

LOLIUM (LO-lium)

multiflorum   3′   mostly annual   Italian Rye-grass
Usually grown as an annual grass with leaves 8 in. long and $\frac{1}{3}$ in. wide, with foot-long fruiting spikes, each spikelet bearing 20–30 flowers. Native to Europe, naturalized in North America. Much used in the South as a winter turf grass when planted with Bermuda Grass, or as a green manure in the North.

perenne   2′   Zone 5   Perennial Rye-grass
A perennial grass with leaves 5 in. long and $\frac{1}{4}$ in. wide; fruiting spikes a foot long but spikelets with only 5–10 flowers. Native to Europe and Asia, naturalized in North America. Frequently used as a green manure. Not an ornamental.

temulentum   4′   annual   Darnel Rye-grass
A weed grass from Europe, naturalized in northeastern North America, the Great Plains and on the Pacific Coast. The seeding spikes are 10 in. long and about $\frac{1}{4}$ in. wide, with alternately-arranged spikelets with 4–8 seeds geometrically arranged in each.

LONGEVITY OF SEEDS. See SEEDS, SEED DORMANCY, etc.

LONICERA (lon-ISS-er-a). The honeysuckles constitute a sturdy group of shrubs and vines, some which can be grown in every state of the Union. As a group they are not susceptible to severe disease troubles, but some of the vines are very susceptible to infestations of plant lice. Aside from this, these plants, within their hardiness limits, are easily grown and will usually produce a wealth of foliage, flower and fruit with very little care. The flowers vary from white to pink, yellow and red. The fruits are small, fleshy berries, usually about $\frac{1}{8}$–$\frac{1}{4}$ in. in dia. Some species bear blue or black-colored fruits, but most bear bright red or bright yellow fruits and because of these, as well as the fact that they are sought by birds, the honeysuckles constitute a valued group of ornamental plants.

As a group they thrive in full sunshine, although there are a few species which seem to do better in partial shade. Also, it may well be that some of the species may do better in limestone soils than in acid soils. For instance, we have always had a difficult time in transplanting small plants of *L. korolkowii floribunda*. Some of the honeysuckle vines native to Europe may also be in this category.

A large number of the honeysuckle shrubs are similar or have little to recommend them as ornamentals. Few have autumn color, and their chief ornamental value is their flowers, their colorful fruits, their ability to grow under various conditions, and sometimes their habit of growth. They have opposite leaves and the vines climb by twining.

The hardiest in the recommended list are *L. sempervirens*, *L. tatarica* and *L. chrysantha*, all hardy in Zone 3. In fact, the Tatarian Honeysuckle is almost as common in the colder northern gardens as is the Lilac. It was brought into cultivation about 1752 from southern Russia and shows a great variation in its offspring, both as to flowers and fruits. In fact, it has become naturalized in some parts of the eastern U.S. for the birds readily distribute the seeds.

Left: *Lonicera japonica halliana*
Right: *Lonicera tatarica*

Nurserymen would do well to stop the practice of propagating honeysuckles from seeds for anything other than plant-breeding purposes because they hybridize so readily. There are some excellent varieties of the Tatarian Honeysuckle that have to be grown asexually in order to produce similar plants. Another case is that of the Morrow Honeysuckle, which is a rounded bush with grayish-green leaves and an excellent ornamental. It has been propagated to such an extent by seed that most of the plants offered by commercial growers now are not true *L. morrowii*, but hybrids of this species and *L. tatarica*, with a corresponding decided upright habit in growth.

Fruits of the honeysuckles range in color from bright red and yellow to dark blue and black and some are whitish and translucent (*L. quinquelocularis*). They are most attractive to the birds. The early flowering species, like *L. fragrantissima* and *L. standishii*, of course bear early fruits in the late spring. These, together with the fruits of a few early-flowering shrubs such as *Daphne mezereum*, come so early that they are avidly sought by birds, one of the reasons why they do not remain long enough to give color to the shrub.

On the other hand, the Tatarian Honeysuckle, and others like it, bear their fruits in late June and some remain colorful for many weeks. There is a species, *Lonicera maackii*, which is

the last of all to bear colorful fruits. These are bright red and begin to color in late Sept. The leaves of this species remain on the plants well into Nov. so the bright, colorful, profusely-borne berries, with a background of green leaves, do much to liven up the shrub border at a time when most other deciduous plants have already dropped their leaves. With these exceptions, most of the shrubby honeysuckles bear their fruits in the summer.

Here is the way some of the more popular pink and red flowering honeysuckles might be listed from the lightest pink to the darkest red, with color comparisons from the Nickerson Color Fan:

VERY PALE PINK (almost white)—*L. bella* 'Rosea', *L. tatarica*, which varies considerably, *L. korolkowii* and its variety *floribunda*.

PALE PINK (2.5 R 9/3)—*L. tatarica rosea*, *L. amoena* and its variety *arnoldiana*.

PETALS STRIPED DEEP PINK AND WHITE—*L. tatarica*, vars. *angustifolia*, *lutea*, *sibirica* and 'Leroyana'.

MODERATE PURPLISH PINK (2.5 RP 6/10)—*L. korolkowii aurora*.

DEEP PURPLISH PINK (7.5 RP 6/12)—*L. bella* 'Atrorosea', *L. amoena rosea* (5 RP 6/10).

STRONG PURPLISH RED (7.5 RP 4/11)—*L. tatarica zabelii*.

DEEP PURPLISH RED (10 RP 3/10)—'Arnold Red'.

	Order of Bloom
Mid-April	fragrantissima
Early May	pileata
Mid-May	alpigena
	bella and vars.
	chrysantha and vars.
	claveyi or 'Clavey's Dwarf'
	syringantha
	thibetica
	'Arnold Red'
	'Dropmore'
Late May	amoena and vars.
	korolkowii aurora
	maackii and var.
	morrowii
	tatarica
	'Morden Orange'
Early June	etrusca 'Superba'
	korolkowii
Mid-June	brownii
	japonica halliana
Late June	henryi
Mid-July	heckrottii
	sempervirens and vars.

Propagation

Seeds can be processed immediately or kept dry in airtight containers in a cool place a year and then processed. Species are variable in their seed germination. It is best to stratify the seed for 3 months at 40° F. and sow. If they are not up in 3-4 months, then give them another 3 months period at 40° F. Layers, division of individual plants with a sharp spade, softwood and hardwood cuttings are all easy means of propagation. See STRATIFICATION, LAYERS, CUTTINGS, etc.

Insect Pests

Sawflies, a leaf roller and the Snowberry clearwing moth (see *Symphoricarpus*) are occasional pests of the Tartarian Honeysuckle. Insecticide #9 is effective. Aphids are controlled with insecticide #15.

Diseases

Leaf curl which thickens, curls and deforms the leaves is controlled by dormant sprays of fungicides #K, #N or #U. Crown gall and canker must be cut out. Powdery mildew is easily checked with sprays of fungicide #M or #V.

alpigena nana   3′   Zone 5   Dwarf Alps Honeysuckle
One of the few dwarf honeysuckles and so of value for this reason. Flowers deep red, but very small and apparently a native of central Europe. The fruits are dark red.

x amoena alba   9′   Zone 5   (*L. tatarica* x *L. korolkowii*)
Rounded, twiggy bush with white flowers and red fruits.

x bella 'Atrorosea' with deep pink flowers.

x bella 'Candida'   6′   Zone 4   (*L. morrowii* x *L. tatarica*)
With pure white flowers—the variety in the trade termed *L. bella albida* is probably a synonym. Hybrid vigor is apparent in these varieties, for they are all fast growing and most floriferous, with bright red fruits.

x bella 'Rosea'—similar to the above, but with flowers a very light pink. Undoubtedly this is badly confused in the trade with var. 'Atrorosea' which actually has deep pink flowers.

x brownii   twining vine   Zone 5   Brown's Honeysuckle
A vine, somewhat similar to *L. sempervirens*, a hybrid (*L. sempervirens* x *L. hirsuta*) but popular in Europe, not in America. Several varieties ('Fuchsioides', 'Plantierensis', 'Punicea' and youngii) differ chiefly in flower color which varies from scarlet to orange-red.

canadensis   4′   Zone 3   American Fly Honeysuckle
Not a very ornamental shrub but widely native across the northern U.S. and southern Canada, with yellowish-white flowers in April or May and red berries borne, in pairs and connected at the base, in June. The leaves are 1½ to 3 in. long.

caprifolium   twining shrub   Zone 5   Sweet Honeysuckle
A twining vine from Europe with beautiful, fragrant, yellowish-white flowers 2 in. long in whorls, produced from June onwards. The fruit is orange and the vine will twine up to 20 ft. or more.

chrysantha   12′   Zone 3   Coralline Honeysuckle
Flowers are a pale yellow, in pairs in May and June. The fruits are a bright coral-red. This native of China and Japan is chiefly recommended for its hardiness and its height.

deflexicalyx   9′   Zone 5
Flowers, in pairs, yellow during early May and profusely borne. The fruit is bright orange-red. It is native to China.

x 'Dropmore'—a hybrid raised by F. L. Skinner of Dropmore, Manitoba, Canada, with pure white flowers. It grows 6-8 ft. tall with a pendulous, graceful habit, blooms and fruits freely and is thoroughly hardy at Dropmore, making it hardy in Zone 3. One plant in Boston is 8 ft. tall and 12 ft. in dia.

etrusca 'Superba'   twining vine   Zone 7   Cream Honeysuckle
The flower clusters of this southern European variety are larger than those of the species and also the plant is more vigorous. In some areas it is half evergreen, in others deciduous, a climber with reddish-purple shoots, yellowish, fragrant flowers 2 in. long and trumpet-shaped, suffused with red and produced in the middle of the summer.

flava   twining vine   Zone 5   Yellow Honeysuckle
The fragrant, orange-yellow trumpet-shaped flowers are produced in 1-3 whorls per stalk. It twines only slightly, but is considered to be the handsomest of our native honeysuckles, native to the southeastern U.S.

fragrantissima   6′   Zone 5   Winter Honeysuckle
Blooming in mid-April with very fragrant white flowers, this shrub from China is a common favorite, half evergreen in the South. One of the few honeysuckles to bear flowers on the previous year's growth, it is one of the first of this genus to bear red fruits in late May. These are quickly eaten by the birds. It has a poor, open habit of growth, but this can be controlled with proper pruning.

x heckrottii   Vinelike   Zone 5   Everblooming Honeysuckle
This vine of unknown origin has often been considered one of the best of the climbing honeysuckles. It flowers in June with pink (outside) and yellow (inside) corolla, blooming

throughout the summer. The buds are actually carmine and as they open the yellow inside the corolla lends a beautiful second color to the combination. The Willis Nursery of Ottawa, Kan., has called this species 'Goldflame', a name which has increased its sales markedly.

henryi twining vine **Zone 4** Henry Honeysuckle

The flowers are yellowish to purplish red, the fruits black. This is a half-evergreen vine without the run-away vigor of Hall's Honeysuckle and thus makes an excellent, controllable ground cover. It is native to China.

hildebrandiana twining vine, climbs 80′ **Zone 9** Giant Honeysuckle

The fragrant flowers are creamy white, changing to rich orange, in pairs 3½–6 in. long. It has the largest flowers, fruits and leaves of all the climbing honeysuckles and is evergreen, but is hardy only in the deep South and native to Burma-China.

japonica 'Aureo-reticulata' low vine **Zone 4** Yellow-net Honeysuckle

Not as vigorous as Hall's Honeysuckle, the leaves have a pleasing yellow netted marking, giving rise to the common name. It colors best in the full sun and probably comes from eastern Asia.

japonica 'Halliana' twining vine **Zone 4** Hall's Honeysuckle

Actually a weed and a nuisance in many areas where it has escaped cultivation, it is an extremely vigorous twining vine from Japan which has escaped cultivation and become a pest, killing many of the plants about which it twines. The flowers are a pure white, then fade to yellow. It is commonly grown in many parts of the U.S. because of its vigor. The variety **repens** is not so vigorous as Hall's Honeysuckle, the lower leaves are sometimes lobed and because of less vigor it makes a neater plant. Otherwise, it is similar to Hall's Honeysuckle.

korolkowii 12′ **Zone 5** Blue-leaf Honeysuckle

Unfortunately, this species and its variety **floribunda** are inseparably mixed in America. The variety is supposed to be the better of the two in flower, and both have excellent gray-green foliage, red fruits and pink flowers. The variety **aurora** is still a better ornamental, with moderate purplish-pink flowers up to ¾ in. in dia., and blooms profusely.

maackii 15′ **Zone 2** Amur Honeysuckle

The chances are that this species and its variety **podocarpa** are badly mixed in the nurseries. The species is much hardier and has larger flowers, while the variety is more widespreading. The Amur Honeysuckle is one of the tallest and hardiest of all the honeysuckles and is native to Manchuria and Korea. The flowers appear in early June and the red fruits remain on the plant until Nov. as do the leaves.

maximowiczii sachalinensis 9′ **Zone 4** Sakhalin Honeysuckle

This variety is in the trade because the leaves are red as they unfold, changing to green by early summer. The red berries are produced in pairs. The leaves are 3–4½ in. long.

morrowii 6′ **Zone 3** Morrow Honeysuckle

A wide, rounded, dense bush from Japan with gray-green leaves, white flowers maturing to yellow and dark red fruits. The true species is desirable, but it has been grown from seed so much that the real plant is extremely difficult to find anywhere. Most plants being offered under this name now are upright hybrids (*L. morrowii* x *L. tatarica*) and are decidedly mediocre as ornamentals.

nitida 6′ **Zone 7** Box Honeysuckle

With creamy-white, fragrant flowers which are none too profuse, and blue fruits, this twiggy shrub from central and western China is small-leaved (about ½ in. long) and is excellent for clipped hedges. It withstands salt-water spray well.

periclymenum vine **Zone 4** Woodbine Honeysuckle

This twining vine is more popular in Europe where it is native than in North America where it is seldom grown by commercial nurserymen. The leaves are grayish green, 1½–2½ in. long; the first pair on a shoot may be connected together but the rest are separated. Flowers are fragrant, yellowish white, in 3–5 whorls on terminal spikes and the fruits are red. The American, red-flowered *L. sempervirens* is the more popular garden vine.

pileata 4′ **Zone 5** Privet Honeysuckle

Deciduous or evergreen low shrub from China —the flowers have little beauty and, although the fruit is translucent, it is usually sparsely borne. Does well at the seashore. Apparently young plants tend to be more evergreen than older ones, withstanding some shade.

prostrata prostrate shrub **Zone 5** Creeping Honeysuckle

E. H. Wilson said this western Chinese shrub was especially useful in bank planting or ground cover. The flowers are pale yellow, have no fragrance, and the reddish fruits are egg-shaped. Nothing to commend it except its habit, with branches flat on the ground (some upright) and the plant making a low, hemispherical mass of foliage.

pyrenaica 2′–3′ **Zone 5** Pyrenees Honeysuckle

This plant is an interesting dwarf from southeastern Europe. Of value only because of its size. The flowers are pinkish to white and the fruits united at the base are red.

quinquelocularis 5′ **Zone** 5 **Mistletoe Honeysuckle**
Native to the Himalayas, this is rare in America, not an especially good plant for landscaping, but the small whitish fruits are interesting in that they are translucent and one can see the dark seeds inside.
'**Redgold**'—see *L. tellmanniana*
sempervirens **twining vine** 50′ **Zone** 3 **Trumpet Honeysuckle**
The orange, scarlet or yellow flowers of this straggly vine make it most conspicuous. The trumpet-shaped flowers are 2 in. long, but are not fragrant. Occasionally it becomes infested with plant lice, but it is the hardiest of all the honeysuckle vines and is native to the eastern U.S. The variety recently offered as '**Dropmore Scarlet**' is a hybrid of this species and *L. hirsuta*, with excellent scarlet flowers. It was first introduced by F. L. Skinner, of Dropmore, Manitoba, Canada; '**Sulphurea**'—with yellow flowers; '**Superba**' with bright scarlet flowers. It is highly probable that this variety is being offered under several names. '**Magnifica**', '**Dreer's Everblooming**', '**Red Trumpet**' and '**Rubra**' are offered in various parts of the country, probably all traceable to a selection made by Dreer's of Philadelphia, Pa. 30 or 40 years ago, a variety that blooms almost continuously in the summer when grown in full sunshine.
syringantha 6′ **Zone** 4 **Lilac Honeysuckle**
With lilac-colored, very fragrant flowers which are not always abundantly borne, this is native to northwest China. It has a moundlike, sprawling habit of growth and red fruit. Mr. H. G. Hillier (England) has selected a seedling which he states has slightly larger flowers than the species and he has given it the varietal name '**Grandiflora**'. The variety **wolfii** is not as hardy (Zone 5) and of more prostrate habit than the species, producing especially fragrant carmine flowers.
tatarica 9′ **Zone** 3 **Tatarian Honeysuckle**
An upright, vigorous shrub with pink-to-white very fragrant flowers and red or yellow fruits native to southern Russia. One of the most dependable and hardy of ornamental shrubs.
Many selections have been made, but unfotunately most show a leggy condition at the base as the plants mature. A few of the worthy varieties are: '**Alba**'—flowers pure white; '**Arnold Red**'—darkest red flowers of any shrub honeysuckle, large red fruits; '**Grandiflora**'—with large white flowers, sometimes called '**Bride**'; '**Leroyana**'—a dwarf variety 5 ft. tall, flowers few, pink and white stripes, 1¼ in. in dia., valued for its low height; '**Lutea**'—fruits yellow, flowers with pink stripes in center of petals, edges white; '**Morden Orange**'—very pale pink

flowers; fruits orange. Originated at the Can. Exp. Farm, Morden, Manitoba, Canada, but not deemed worthy of introduction by them. Introduced by a U.S. nursery; **nana**—plants 3 ft. high, pink flowers; **parviflora**—one of the best varieties for white flowers; **rosea**—flowers rosy pink outside, light pink inside; **sibirica**—flowers with deep pink stripes in center of petals and white margins, leaves larger than those of species; '**Virginalis**'—rosy-pink flower buds and flowers, the largest flowers of any *L. tatarica* variety; and **zabelii** has the darkest red flowers of any honeysuckle except 'Arnold Red'.
x tellmanniana **twining vine** **Zone** 5 **Tellmann Honeysuckle**
A deciduous climbing vine, hybrid of *L. tragophylla* and *L. sempervirens*, with flowers in terminal heads of 6–12 flowers in each cluster. They are 2 in. long and 1 in. across, a beautiful yellow, the buds having a touch of red. (Commonly called '**Redgold**', this is merely replacing of the species common name.)
thibetica 4′ **Zone** 4 **Tibet Honeysuckle**
The flowers are lilac colored and especially fragrant, the fruits are red. It is a deciduous, low-spreading shrub from western China, sometimes with a width of 6–10 ft. The undersides of its leaves are covered with a felt of pale gray hairs.
tragophylla **twining vine** 50′ **Zone** 6 **Chinese Woodbine**
A climbing shrub from China with bright yellow flowers in large terminal heads of 10–20 flowers in each head. They are not fragrant and the plant does best in semi-shade. This apparently does best in limestone soils, like many another honeysuckle.
xylosteum '**Claveyi**'—sometimes called Clavey's Dwarf. This originated several years prior to 1955 at Clavey's Rabinia Nurseries, Deerfield, Ill. It has been widely distributed, as the plant is good as a low, thick, quick-growing hedge needing little shearing. Mature plants are said to be 6 ft. tall, but most of the plants are only half of this height. The flowers are white, smaller than those of *L. tatarica* and not at all showy.
yunnanensis **twining shrub** **Zone** 7 **Yunnan Honeysuckle**
Low creeper with yellow flowers from China.

LOOSESTRIFE. See LYSIMACHIA.

LOOSESTRIFE FAMILY = Lythraceae

LOOSESTRIFE, PURPLE = *Lythrum salicaria*

LOPHOPHORA (lo-FO-for-a)
williamsii 3″ **Zone** 9 **Mescal Button Peyote**
One of the spineless cacti, native to Mexico, low and rounded about 3 in. across with a thick tap-root; 5–13 low and wide ribs, tubercles white tufted; flowers pale pink to white and an

inch across, produced in the center of the plant.

LOQUAT. The Loquat (*Eriobotrya japonica*) is an unusual pomaceous subtropical tree of exceptional ornamental value, bearing attractive crops of mild, but pleasant fruit.

It is one of the hardiest of evergreen subtropical trees, and can be grown where winter temperatures do not drop below about 15° F. In the warm, humid South and and Southeast it tends to bloom in the fall and ripen its fruit in midwinter; as the fruit is damaged at temperatures only slightly below freezing the harvest may be lost unless it can be protected. In the southernmost areas of Fla. the tree may bloom sparingly in the spring and early summer, and bear a small crop before winter. In the arid Southwest and West the tree blooms in midwinter, and the blooms and young fruit appear to be nearly as cold-hardy as the foliage and wood. In these areas the fruit ripens in May or early June.

The tree is round-headed to spreading; though it may attain a height of 20 ft. or more with age it is easily kept small by training. The foliage is dark green; the leaves large, 6–12 in., long-oval to long elliptic, with a short petiole. The blade is rugose, with strongly dentate margins; the underside of the blade and the shoot tips and young leaves are heavily pubescent. The inflorescences are terminal, and the numerous small flowers are whitish to ivory, but covered with a heavy brownish tomentum.

The tree will tolerate a wide variety of soils; on poor sites growth will be slow and more open and straggly. The soil should be well drained, however. Little is known of the nutritional requirements of the Loquat. It apparently is not a heavy user of nitrogen. If growth becomes sparse with smaller than normal leaves, light applications of nitrogen to invigorate new growth normally will be sufficient. On acid soils in the humid South and Southeast, where complete fertilizers are needed for other trees, the same would be indicated to stimulate good growth of the Loquat.

Being evergreen, the tree should be supplied with available water throughout the year, but especially during the period from bloom to fruit maturity. The tree is able to withstand drought conditions better than most evergreens, but if in fruit when water is deficient the fruit will suffer and be of poor quality.

Young trees may be headed at 24–30 in. to induce branching if necessary, but the tree can be carried to a height of 4 or 5 ft. if a higher head is desired. Normally the Loquat tends to branch naturally. After the primary scaffolds are selected little additional pruning is necessary throughout the life of the tree. Thinning back may be done to keep the tree small.

Fruiting will start at 2–3 years; normally 4 to 6 or more fruits will set in each inflorescence; in years of heavy bloom the total set may be excessive for best tree development and fruit size and quality. When this occurs, fruit-thinning is practiced by cutting out entire clusters, usually by cutting out the fruiting branch to a subtending lateral.

The lightly pubescent fruits turn yellow to golden as they ripen. Softening fruit is ready for use. The fruits are pyriform in shape, about 1–1½ in. in dia., with a thick, fleshy stem which is easily damaged in picking. For this reason loquats are best harvested by clipping entire inflorescences from the tree (often with a few leaves for ornamental interest), the fruit being separated as used. The fruits contain usually 2 or 3 large, plump, shiny brown seeds. The yellow-to-golden flesh of good varieties is juicy, sprightly to sweet, with a mild, agreeable flavor. It is used fresh; in cooking, Loquat jams or jellies are favorites.

The trees are easily grown from seed, which should be planted immediately from the fresh fruit. However, seedlings are mostly inferior, so that named varieties are recommended. Young seedling trees may be budded (T-bud) or whip-grafted; older trees can be grafted (cleft or preferably kerf or bark grafted) to change existing trees to superior kinds. Loquat seedlings are the only understock used.

A few of the better varieties are ‘Advance’, ‘Champagne’, ‘Pineapple’, ‘Thales’, ‘Oliver’, and ‘Tanaka’; the latter 2 are recommended in the Southeast.

The Loquat is nearly free of pests and diseases, but is attacked by the apple or pear fire blight organism. Spraying with a mild copper fungicide during bloom will control the disease, but simple sanitation by removing infected inflorescences usually suffices.

CLARON O. HESSE

Insect Pests

In Fla., 12 or more scale insects and mealybugs infest loquats (see GUAVA), but usually are not so destructive as to require the use of pesticides. In Calif. codling moth and other apple or pear insect pests may infest Loquat growing near Apple or English Walnut plantings.

Diseases

Fruit rot and leaf spot are destructive in wet weather and in crowded plantings. Fungicides #G and #W are effective. Fireblight kills branches. See FIREBLIGHT.

LORDS-AND-LADIES = *Arum maculatum*

LORETTE PRUNING. This is a rather technical

type of pruning developed in France which does not include any dormant or winter pruning. It is not much practiced in America, is most time-consuming and takes considerable study. The busy gardener has no time to practice it and it is used chiefly in training espaliered fruit trees. See PRUNING.

LOROPETALUM (lo-ro-PET-al-um)
chinense   12′   Zones 7–8
The white flowers with small linear petals bloom in March and resemble those of the Witch-hazel, to which this Chinese shrub is closely related. The evergreen leaves are 2 in. long and it can be propagated by cuttings or by grafting on *Hamamelis* understock. Although hardy only in the southern U.S. this is frequently grown in greenhouses in the North for its flowers as well as its evergreen foliage.

LOTUS (LO-tus) (also see NELUMBIUM). This
generic name should not be confused with what is popularly termed Lotus (see NELUMBIUM) which are water plants. The genus *Lotus* contains herbs or shrubby plants with pinnate leaves, belonging to the Pea Family. This herbaceous species is propagated by seeds or division.
berthelotii   2′   Zone 10   Coral Gem
A perennial with silvery, hairy, evergreen foliage woody at the base with slightly climbing branches. Scarlet flowers somewhat similar to those of the Sweet Pea, are clustered at the ends of the shoots in May, up to 1¼ in. long. Mostly for the greenhouse, although it is being used in the warmer parts of Calif. as a ground cover. Native to Teneriffe. It responds well to some clipping to keep it neat.
corniculatus   2′   Zone 5   Birds-foot Trefoil
A perennial sometimes grown as a ground cover or for forage, usually decumbent, leaves with 3 leaflets; flowers yellow or tinged with red about ¾ in. wide. Native to Europe and Asia, naturalized in North America, and sometimes a weed.
pinnatus   trailing   Zone 8   Meadow Deervetch
The thick, trailing stems of this plant root readily, producing a mat of evergreen compound leaves. The large, yellow, pealike flowers are borne in clusters on stems 8 in. high, appearing throughout much of the summer. Native from central Calif. to Wash.
tenuis   trailing   Zone 4
A small, matlike plant of thin stems and 3-parted leaves which, although attractive, tends to spread rapidly. The small yellow flowers, ⅜ in. long, bloom in May and June. Native to Europe.
tetragonolobus   trailing   annual   Winged-pea
With 3 leaflets; purplish-red pealike flowers and 4-angled edible pods. Native to southern Europe.

LOVAGE = *Levisticum officinale*
LOVE-IN-A-MIST = *Nigella damascena*
LOVE-LIES-BLEEDING = *Amaranthus caudatus*

LOW MAINTENANCE PLANTS. See *The Saturday Morning Gardener* by Donald Wyman (Macmillan, 1974). Described are 900 low maintenance plants for every conceivable landscape purpose.

LUCULIA (loo-KEW-lia)
gratissima   16′   Zone 10   Fragrant Luculia
An opposite-leaved, leathery, evergreen tree with leaves 6 in. long; very fragrant tubular flowers colored a soft rosy pink, 1½ in. wide; borne in rounded clusters 8 in. long. Seeds are winged. Native to India. They bloom in the greenhouse in the winter and can be set out-of-doors over summer.

LUDWIGIA (lud-WIG-ia)
alternifolia   1′–3′   Zone 4   Rattlebox
A plant rising from a perennial root having alternate, narrowly lanceolate leaves, pointed at either end and having short petioles. The solitary yellow flowers are born on short stalks at the axils of the leaves. Each flower has a calyx with 4 pointed lobes and 4 petals. The plant is frequently found in the swamps and marshes of eastern U.S. and Canada, west to Mich. and Kan. and south to Fla. and Tex. It blooms from late June to Sept.
natans (*mulerttii*)   **1′   Zone 9**
A perennial herb, with opposite oval leaves about ½–1 in. across, said to have come from South America where it inhabits bogs. However, it will grow under water and in an aquarium has considerable interest, especially the red-leaved strain which is cultivated in Fla. It roots easily at the nodes. In order to keep its leaves (in an aquarium) it should be rooted in a pot of soil which could be covered with sand. Easily propagated by division or cuttings.

LUFFA (LUF-fa, also LOO-fa)   vine   annual   10′–15′   Dishcloth Gourd, Towel Gourd
These are tropical vines of the Cucumber Family. Grown as annuals they need a long growing season and plenty of hot weather. If grown in the North it is advisable to start them in pots in the greenhouse and set them out in rich soil after all danger of frost is over. They have alternate, lobed leaves, the flowers being yellow or white and male and female flowers separate but on the same plant. The common name comes from the dried interior of the fruits, sometimes called 'Vegetable-sponge'. In one species, **L. acutangula**, the fruits are club shaped and about a foot long, leaves 5–7 lobed.

LUNARIA (loo-NAY-ria)
annua   3′   annual or biennial   Honesty

An easily grown, old-fashioned garden plant that has been popular in gardens for centuries, native to Europe, valued especially for its seed pods which are 2 in. long, rounded in outline and flat. These have a papery, satiny covering and when dried, they are most attractive in winter bouquets. It has sometimes been called Dollar Plant because of these fruits. The fragrant flowers are white and purple. Leaves either alternate or opposite. Seeds may be sown outdoors in the fall or in April where they are to grow, preferably in partial shade. They grow in almost any normal soil. When fruits have matured, the branches are cut, the coverings over the fruits are removed and the branches hung up to dry in a cool, airy place.

LUNGWORT, COWSLIP = *Pulmonaria angustifolia*

LUPINE. See LUPINUS.

LUPINUS (Loo-PY-nus). Lupines belong to the Pea Family and produce colorful upright spikes of pealike flowers during the spring and summer. The alternate leaves are palmately compound. The fruits are pealike pods. The perennial species may be propagated by seed but are more easily divided in early spring.

The seed of the annual species can be planted indoors in March and set out after frost in full sun in a slightly alkaline soil. Or, they can be sown outdoors in May where they are to grow. They germinate readily if the outer seed coat is filed through to allow water to enter quickly inside.

Perhaps better than any of the species listed below for garden planting are the so-called Russell lupines, a splendid group of garden hybrids selected over the years by George Russell of Yorkshire, England. The flower spikes of these are 2½–3½ ft. long with at least two-thirds of the spike consisting of profuse and compact highly colored flowers.

Insect Pests

The large lupine aphid may be very abundant and seriously deform the flower spikes. Use insecticide #15.

Diseases

Lupine is very susceptible to powdery mildew. Fungicides #V or #M give control. Garden plants, especially if crowded, may wilt and die from crown rot. When this occurs move the plants to a drier location.

arboreus   8′   Zone 8   Tree Lupine
With fragrant sulfur-yellow flowers in loose racemes during summer; pods 3 in. long. Native to Calif. The leaves are compound and hairy above and below. 'Snow Queen' has pure white flowers.

argenteus   12″   Zone 4   Silvery Lupine
A perennial native to western North America with blue or cream-colored flowers, leaflets 5–8, linear-lanceolate. It is reported that more sheep and cattle are poisoned in Wyo. from eating this one herbaceous plant than any other. Not all lupines are poisonous but this one is.

densiflorus   2′   annual   Gully Lupine
The leaves have 7–9 leaflets, the flowers, borne in conspicuous upright spikes, are white, yellow and rose. Normally this blooms in May and is native to Calif.

hartwegii   3′   annual   Hartweg Lupine
The flowers are blue to rose, appearing from July to Sept., native to Mexico. Leaflets 7–9. Actually this is a perennial in the warmer parts of the country but it is grown as an annual in the North. There are white, rose and red-flowered varieties.

hirsutus   2′   annual   European Blue Lupine
Bearing blue flowers having a touch of white in late summer. Native to southern Europe. There are also white, red and pink color forms.

luteus   2′   Zone 6   European Yellow Lupine
Flowers yellow, fragrant, blooming in June and July, native to southern Europe. This perennial does very well in the poorest of soils.

nanus   15″   annual   Sky Lupine
Valued because it is low with blue and white fragrant flowers from May to July. Native to Calif. Leaflets 5–7.

perennis   2′   Zone 4   Wild Lupine
An erect perennial with palmately-compound leaves of 7–9 leaflets, each leaflet 1–2 in. long. The flowers, often blue but sometimes pink or white, are borne on a long stalk in dense terminal racemes. The plant is a member of the Pea Family and the flowers are characteristic of this group. It flowers from May to July in open, sunny woods from Me. to Fla., west to Minn. and Mont. An excellent plant for the perennial or wild garden, it may be transplanted only when small, due to its deep, woody roots. Seeds may be gathered when barely ripe and planted at once in soil similar to that in which the plant is growing. This also grows on poor sandy soil. Many cases of poisoning have been reported because people have eaten the pods or seeds.

polyphyllus   2′–5′   Zone 3   Washington Lupine
Native from Wash. to Calif., leaflets 2–6 in. long and silky hairy underneath, glabrous above; flowers deep blue on long stalks, blooming from June to Sept. There are many color forms but **albus** has white flowers and **roseus** is pink.

pubescens   3′   annual
Flowers violet-blue with a white center. Native to Mexico. There are many hybrids of various colored flowers closely connected to this species.

subcarnosus   8″–12″   annual   Bluebonnet
A handsome annual covered with a silky down

and having the palmately-compound leaves and pealike flowers of the genus. The flowers, blue with a white or yellow spot, appear in early spring, carpeting the fields and hillsides of its native Tex. and has been chosen the official flower of that state.

LYCASTE (ly-KAS-te). Tropical American epiphytic orchids with fragrant green, yellow and white flowers 1–4 in. wide, 2–10 on a stalk during the winter and spring. **L. virginalis** has pseudobulbs growing 3 in. long and 2–3 leaves that are 2 ft. long. This species has the largest flowers of the genus, some being 6 in. across, with white or rose petals of different shade, often mottled white. It blooms from Jan. to May. For culture and propagation see ORCHID.

LYCHEE. *Litchi chinensis* or the Lychee as it is popularly called, is a medium-sized, much-branched tree reaching 40 ft. in height with an equal spread. The alternate, leathery, pinnate leaves have from 3 to 7 oblong lanceolate leaflets, deep green and glabrous above. The tawny flowers are small and usually perfect. Occasionally only stamens or a pistil is found. All 3 types of flowers (pistillate, staminate, perfect) may appear on one tree. The mature fruit resembles a 1-seeded berry 1½ in. in dia. and ovate. The thin leathery rough shell is bright red in most varieties, making a striking contrast with the deep green leaves.

Beneath the shell and completely surrounding the seed is an edible pulp which is translucent white in color. The single, oblong, shiny, chestnut-brown seed is attached at the base of the pulp.

In the United States growing of Lychee is confined to Fla., southern Calif. and to the Hawaiian Islands. There are many named varieties, but **'Brewster'** (Purple Chen) is more generally planted in Fla. than any other. In Hawaii **'Kwai Mi'**, **'Brewster'**, **'Hak Ip'** and **'No Mai Taz'** are preferred varieties.

Air layering is the preferred method of propagation with inarching, also called approach grafting, practiced by some growers.

Native to south China, *L. chinensis* is now grown commercially in India, South Africa, Florida, Hawaii, Burma, Madagascar, Brazil, Japan and Australia. The Lychee is best suited to subtropical conditions. At Homestead, Fla., it has experienced a temperature of 28° F. without injury to mature foliage and ripened twigs. On the other hand tender new growth may be killed at 32° F.

It thrives in high temperatures during spring and summer if adequate moisture is available. During this period the fruit matures and the tree makes vegetative growth. Winters should be cool, but the temperature should remain above 40° F. This is necessary because *L. chinensis* must go through a dormant period.

In America both commercial fertilizers and manures have been used. While experimental evidence is lacking as to the preferred time of applications, probably a high nutrient level should be maintained during fruit development and active vegetative growth.

A number of insect pests are reported attacking Lychee trees. The ambrosia beetle attacks young seedlings, boring into the woody stem and sometimes carrying a fungus that infects the plant. Two soft scales and one armored scale have also been observed occasionally on the twigs.

Most damage, however, has been caused by one or more of the spider mites. During dry, hot periods they multiply rapidly. They are controlled by wettable sulfur sprays or by malathion. Twig pruners and leaf tiers occasionally attack Lychee, but seldom in sufficient numbers to require control.

GLEASON H. MATTOON

LYCHNIS (LIK-nis). Members of the Pink Family, these annual or perennial herbs have simple, opposite leaves, in most cases, and brightly colored white, pink, red or purple flowers, either solitary or produced in clusters. The perennial kinds are easily propagated by either seed or division and the annual kinds are propagated by seed sown in the open in April and transplanted in May, or else sown where the plants are to grow. Most make fine garden plants.

There are about 35 species of these annual or perennial herbs native to the northern temperate regions, and some are actually native in the Arctic Zone. They all have opposite leaves with either bisexual or unisexual flowers that are colored white, scarlet or purple.

alba = *Silene alba*

x arkwrightii   10″   Zones 2–3   Arkwright Campion
A hybrid species with scarlet flowers resembling *L. haageana*. (*L. haageana* x *L. chalcedonica*).

chalcedonica   2′–3′   Zone 3   Maltese Cross
A perennial which has become naturalized in the eastern U.S., although it is native to Russia and Siberia. It is a popular perennial for the flower border because its dense terminal heads of scarlet flowers appear in June and July. The flowers are about an inch wide. Those with white flowers are not particularly good ornamentals. Both propagated by seed.

coeli-rosa   2½′   annual   Rose-of-heaven
With linear leaves and red flowers an inch wide, produced singly at the ends of the stems. Native to the Mediterranean Region. The variety **alba** has white flowers; **kermesina** has deep red

flowers and **oculata** has flowers with purple centers.

coronaria 3′ **biennial or perennial Rose Campion**

The foliage of this is so white woolly that sometimes it is incorrectly termed Dusty Miller. The flowers are bright red, an inch wide, blooming in June and July. Native to southern Europe. Although this is a biennial, it can be grown as an annual and has become naturalized at several places in the U.S.

coronata 1½′ **biennial or perennial Crown Campion**

With bright red flowers 2 in. or more wide, in open panicles. Native to China and Japan. The variety **nobilis** is salmon pink and **sieboldii** is white.

dioica = *Silene dioica*

flos-cuculi 1′–2′ **Zone 3 Ragged Robin**

This hairy perennial herb or weed is European in origin, but is now naturalized in eastern North America from Quebec to Pa. Erect stems bear opposite, lanceolate, somewhat sticky leaves, the upper ones being smaller and stalkless. The flowers are borne in terminal clusters and may be pink, white, blue or purple, 1 in. wide, from May to Aug. Each flower has 5 petals, narrow at the base but widening and spreading, each petal divided into 4 threadlike segments. An attractive plant for the moist, sunny wild garden, it may be propagated by division in spring or by cuttings taken in summer.

flos-jovis 3′ **Zone 5 Flower-of-Love**

A perennial which has attractive white tomentose foliage, is erect and little branched, has basal leaves in the form of a rosette and purplish-red flowers. Native to the Alps.

x haageana 10″ **Zones 2–3 Haages Campion**

This is a hybrid species (*L. fulgens* x *L. coronata sieboldii*), but seeds do usually produce plants fairly true to type. It produces masses of orange-scarlet flowers in the early summer. It may be grown farther north than Zone 6 if it is provided with winter protection.

viscaria 1½′ **Zone 3 German Catchfly**

Native to Europe and northern Asia, this has tufts of grasslike foliage with reddish-purple flower clusters in late May and June. A variety called 'Splendens' with rose-pink flowers was found in the mountains of Europe and is popular with those who can obtain it. 'Splendens Flore-pleno' is a double form that has become popular, but the magenta flowers are not admired by all gardeners.

wilfordii 20″–30″ **Zone 5**

A fine little Campion, native to Japan, Korea and Manchuria, and certainly suitable for the rock garden where it can make a nice display. The flowers are about 1½″ wide and deep red.

LYCIUM (LIS-sium)

chinense Prostrate shrub Zone 4 Chinese Wolfberry

Somewhat similar to *L. halimifolium* which is the more popular plant, the prostrate, alternate-leaved branches of this are usually not thorny, the small flowers are purple, blooming from June to Sept. and the brilliant orange-red fruits up to an inch long are most conspicuous throughout the summer and fall. The leaves remain green until very late in the fall and drop without turning color. Good for planting on banks especially if the soil is poor. Native to eastern Asia where the leaves are cooked as a vegetable.

halimifolium 5′ **Zone 4 Common Matrimony-vine**

Commonly considered as a poor-soil shrub, this will grow almost anywhere in good or poor dry soils. Native to southeastern Europe and western Asia, it is considered to be a trailing shrub, not really a vine, often spiny, but when planted on a bank it will send out long shoots over the ground that quickly grow luxuriantly. The small lilac-purple flowers in late June are about ½ in. across and these are quickly followed by elongated red to orange-red berries in the fall. There is no autumn color. This species has become naturalized in many places in the U.S. and, once established in an area, it quickly seeds itself (or the birds spread the seeds) widely. The Chinese species *L. chinense* has larger leaves and flowers, but it is the European species which has become established in the eastern U.S.

It is excellent as a bank cover because it sends out new suckers from the base and the trailing branches frequently root where they touch the ground. *L. europaeum* is somewhat similar, much less hardy and not planted as an ornamental in the U.S.

Propagation

Do not let the seed dry out but sow as soon as ripe. Layers, softwood and hardwood cuttings are all satisfactory. See CUTTINGS, LAYERS. It must be added that this species can become a pest and should only be used on poor soils or in areas where it will not encroach on more valuable plants.

LYCOPERSICUM ESCULENTUM. See TOMATO.

LYCOPERSICUM PIMPINELLIFOLIUM = Currant Tomato

LYCOPODIACEAE = The Lycopodium Family

LYCOPODIUM (ly-ko-PO-dium). Club-moss. These are evergreen, mosslike herbs, seldom cultivated but frequently found in the pine woods of northern North America, and sometimes picked for decorations at Christmas. Unfortunately too much is ruthlessly pulled up for this purpose and now it is protected by legislation in some states. These species have erect or creeping stems, small, scalelike leaves. They are closely allied to the ferns and propagate themselves by spores, borne in the conspicuous club-shaped spikes or "candles" familiar to those who know the plant. They are only suited for growing in shaded places in acid soils where there is plenty of moisture.

clavatum   3″   Zone 3   Running-pine
This evergreen has a running root 8–9 ft. long.

complanatum   2″–5″   Zone 3   Ground-cedar
This does not have the long running root, but the stalks are divided into fanlike evergreen sprays with fruiting spikes 2–5 in. long.

obscurum   creeping   Zone 3   Ground-pine
With underground creeping stems, there are some erect branches up to 10 in. tall; leaves scalelike and longer than in other species and not hugging the stem. These appear like miniature trees with the flowering spike or "candle" on top. Native to the woods of northern North America.

LYCOPODIUM FAMILY = Lycopodiaceae

LYCORIS (LY-ko-ris). A most interesting bulbous group from China and Japan, members of the Amaryllis Family, noted for the sudden way in which the flowers appear after the leaves have died. The bulbs should be planted in Aug. about 5 in. deep and let alone. In the spring they send up straplike leaves 2½ ft. tall which die down in early summer and in late Aug. or Sept. Two species then quickly send up 3 ft. flower stalks at the end of which are 3–6 funnel-shaped lilylike flowers, 3–4 in. across, yellow, pink or purplish depending on the species. They are propagated by offsets.

africana (*aurea*)   1¾′   Zone 7   Golden Lycoris
Yellow flowers, 3 in. long in August. Leaves ¾ in. wide. Native to .China. Sometimes incorrectly termed Golden Spider-lily.

incarnata   1¾′   Zone 7   Fragrant Lycoris
Linear leaves, salmon to bright rose, fragrant flowers. Native to China.

radiata   1½′   Zone 7   Short-tube Lycoris
Scarlet flowers in June, 1½ in. long. Native to China and Japan. Sometimes blooming in the fall.

squamigera   2′   Zone 5   Autumn-amaryllis
Liliac-rose fragrant flowers, 3 in. long, in Aug. or Sept. Leaves are an inch wide. Native to Japan. This species can be planted in the lower half of New England and, given a shady spot and let alone, will continue to surprise fall visitors for years.

LYGODIUM (ly-GO-dium). These are the climbing ferns, scrambling irregularly up some means of support with delicate twining stems, sometimes 6 ft. long with delicate

twisting fronds 2–5 in. long. These fronds often have the pinnae arranged palmately, and they can be very finely divided. If they are trained up properly arranged wires, they can be decidedly ornamental. For propagation see FERNS.

japonicum   climbing   Zone 8   Japanese Climbing Fern
This Japanese fern has escaped cultivation in the southeastern U.S. and is a very popular fern in conservatories. The pinnules are about 1 in. long and very featherlike in arrangement. This can have stems 8–10 ft. long.

palmatum   climbing   Zone 6   Hartford Fern
This is native to the eastern U.S. and is not the easiest fern to take from its native habitat and establish in the garden. The soil should be acid (pH 4.0–5.0), loose and moist and the situation should be shaded. The pinnae are palmately arranged and lobed and the twisting stems are 3–4 ft. long.

scandens   climbing   Zone 10   Feathery Climbing Fern
Native to the Tropics of the Old World, this gracefully delicate climbing fern is only for use in greenhouse or conservatory where winter temperatures do not go below 45° F. The indefinite climbing stem has fronds that are 3–4 times pinnate and arranged palmately.

LYONIA (ly-O-nia)

ligustrina   12′   Zone 3   Maleberry
Native in eastern North America, this is really a moist-soil plant of little horticultural value. The alternate, deciduous leaves are 1½–3 in. long, turning reddish in the fall, and the fruit is merely a dry capsule.

lucida   4′–6′   Zone 5   Fetterbush
An evergreen shrub with alternate, lanceolate leaves, stalkless or nearly so, and with in-rolled edges. The cup-shaped flowers are white, with 5 tiny, pointed lobes, and are borne on very short stalks in axially clusters. These appear in mid-June in the swamps and lowlands of eastern and southeastern U.S.

mariana   6′   Zone 5   Staggerbush
This is definitely a shrub for the swampy area, to be grown in acid wet soils where better plants can not be grown. It is usually planted in masses, bears flowers in mid-June that are small but profuse, cup-shaped, ½ in. long and are white to pinkish. It is a native of the eastern and southeastern U.S. The seeds of all these species can be sown as soon as they are ripe, or stored dry. Softwood cuttings can be easily rooted.

LYSICHITON (ly-sik-IT-on)

americanum   1′–2½′   Zone 6 (?)   Yellow Skunk-cabbage
A marsh plant (herbaceous) of western North America, somewhat similar to the native Skunk-cabbage of eastern North America (*Symplo-*

Lythrum salicaria—Loosestrife: A garden perennial. (*Photo by Arnold Arboretum, Jamaica Plain, Mass.*)

carpus foetidus) with the blade surrounding the spathe a striking golden yellow, used considerably in marshy places in European gardens. The spathes are 4–6 in. long, appear in April just before the leaves and are most colorful. Unfortunately it has an unpleasant odor. The succulent leaves are borne in erect tufts, 1–2½ ft. long.

camtschatcense   1′–2½′   Zone 6 (?)
Native to eastern Asia and similar to *L. americanum* except that the spathes are white and the flowers are odorless or occasionally sweet scented.

LYSIMACHIA (ly-sim-AK-ia). A large genus of perennial herbs of the Primrose Family, many of which are weedy, but some are suitable for cultivation. The leaves are without marginal teeth and the flowers may be borne in whorls

or terminally. The plants frequent moist, open locations. Propagation is by division in either spring or fall.

ciliata (*Steironema ciliatum*   2′–4′   Zone 4
Fringed Loosestrife
This plant is perennial with opposite, ovate, pointed leaves, from the axils of which arise flower stalks terminating in a whorl of smaller leaves and yellow flowers 1 in. wide, each borne on individual petioles 2–3 in. long. The flowers have 5 petals and bloom from June to Aug. throughout the eastern U.S.

clethroides   2′–3′   Zone 3   Japanese Loosestrife
Hairy, perennial herb with alternate leaves, native to eastern Asia and not especially ornamental. The white flowers are only ½ in. across in narrow terminal spikes, blooming in

July and Aug. Suitable for moist soil situations.

**nummularia   2″   Zone 3   Moneywort,
                     Creeping Jenny, Creeping Charlie**
A beautiful creeping vine in wet soils, sometimes even in drier soils, often creeping into grassy areas, this is native to Europe but has been naturalized in many places in North America. The rounded, opposite leaves up to an inch long, appear on the stems which grow flat on the ground. The yellow flowers ¾ in. across appear in the axils of the leaves from May to Sept. The stems root throughout their entire length. Sometimes used as an aquarium plant, but especially valued by pools, streams and in otherwise wet to moist soils.

punctata   3′   Zone 5   Yellow Loosestrife
A European plant that has become naturalized in certain parts of the eastern U.S., this is rigid in growth with whorls of yellow flowers during June and early July. The leaves also are whorled in groups of 3 or 4. Easily propagated by division in either spring or fall. Best grown in some shade.

quadrifolia   3′   Zone 4   Four-leaf Loosestrife
This perennial has a 4-angled stem and whorls of ovate, pointed leaves, sometimes 3–6, but generally 4 in number. The yellow flowers, having 5 petals, are in whorls and rise on slender stems from the leaf whorls. In bud they are strongly marked with red and the opened flowers have dark red lines. The plant blooms in June and July and may be found on either wet or dry soil over much of the eastern half of the U.S. It may be transplanted in spring.

terrestris   1′–2′   Zone 3   Swamp Loosestrife
Another swamp-loving perennial with erect stem and opposite, lanceolate leaves. The 5-petalled yellow flowers, touched with red at the center, are borne in a tight terminal cluster, appearing in midsummer. It is native to most of eastern North America except in the Deep South. It transplants readily and is a very attractive plant for the moist wild garden, but may spread rapidly.

LYTHRACEAE = The Loosestrife Family

LYTHRUM (LY-thrum)

alatum   1′–4′   Zone 3   Winged Lythrum
The stem of this perennial is angled, the angles extending to winglike appendages. The opposite leaves are lanceolate, the deep rose flowers, borne at the axils of the leaves, have a tubular corolla with 6 spreading lobes. They bloom throughout the summer in wet locations from Canada to Pa. and Tex. It is easily propagated by seed, division or by cuttings.

salicaria   3′   Zone 3   Purple Loosestrife
A perennial weed, naturalized in central, northeastern and northwestern North America, introduced from Europe and growing in marshes and wet meadows where it may be so vigorous it chokes out native vegetation. The red-purple flowers are borne from June to Sept. on many terminal spikelike panicles up to 16 in. long, each flower being about ¾ in. across. The leaves are opposite or in whorls of 3, about 4 in. long. When it takes over in a marshy meadow it makes a striking display when in full flower during the summer. While it has value as a bog plant it should be kept within bounds.

M

MAACKIA (MAK-ia)

amuerensis   45′   Zone 4   Amur Maackia
This is not a particularly ornamental tree and is only listed here because of its summer flowers. The genus is closely related to *Cladrastis*. The flowers are pea-shaped, dull white, borne on short upright racemes 4–6 in. long and appear in early July. The leaves are alternate and compound If this tree, native to Manchuria, is not desired for July bloom, there is little else about it that would recommend it for ornamental planting.

Propagation

Seeds may be soaked in hot water (190° F.) overnight, then sown, or stored dry in a cool place for up to a year in airtight containers, then soaked and sown. Varieties can be grafted on seedlings of the species. Root cuttings root readily. See GRAFTING, ROOT CUTTINGS.

MACADAMIA. Macadamia or Queensland Nut, *M. ternifolia*, is a tree native to southern Queensland and northern New South Wales. In Australia it has been grown around homesteads partly for ornament and shade and in part for the nuts for about 100 years.

The first Macadamia trees in Hawaii were planted in 1892. Since that time plantations have grown. By the middle of the 20th century over 80,000 producing trees had been planted, and factories for roasting and processing the kernels and vacuum packing them for export had been built. About 80 varieties have been named, but only a few are commercially profitable. Among these in Hawaii are **'Kau'**, **'Keaau'**, **'Mahai'**, **'Pahala'** and **'Purvis'**.

In the wild, the Macadamia tree attains a height of about 35–50 ft. with a clean straight trunk seldom more than 1 ft. in dia. As an orchard tree it branches more freely.

The seed or nut is about 1 in. in dia. within a hard shell. Shell-cracking machines have been perfected, however, which do an excellent job of making the kernels available.

Because of its evergreen, dark, glossy leaves and drooping racemes of pale cream or pink flowers which are busily visited by bees, the Macadamia ranks high among ornamental trees of the subtropics. Only in southern Calif. and southern Fla. does the Macadamia grow on the mainland. It withstands only light frost.
H. GLEASON MATTOON

ternifolia   35′–50′   Zone 10   Queensland Nut

The evergreen leaves of this tree appear in whorls of 3 and 4 and they are leathery, lustrous and spiny, about a foot long. Native to New South Wales, it grows slowly and does well in regions of little rainfall. The flowers are small, being produced in pairs in foot-long racemes. The fruit is edible, a drupe about 1 in. in dia. Frequently grown for these fruits (which are not true nuts).

MACFADYENA

unguis-cati (*Doxantha unguis-cati*)

clinging vine   Zone 8   Cat-claw Vine
The Cat-claw Vine gets this name from its tenacious tendrils which enable it to cling to wall-surface of stone or wood surprisingly well. A native to the West Indies and other parts of tropical America, the yellow funnel-shaped flowers are 3 in. long and 2½ in. across, borne during the early spring. The evergreen leaflets are 2 in. long. Although there are few pests, it does have a fault of becoming sparse of foliage near the base.

MACHAERANTHERA (mach-eran-THEE-ra)

tanacetifolia   2′   annual or biennial   Tahoka-daisy
This is a biennial herb from the southwestern U.S. and Mexico, closely related to the aster, frequently grown as an annual. The leaves are bristly and alternate; the flowers are borne in clusters, lavender-blue, each flower about 2 in. across. It has been noted that to obtain good germination seeds should be kept at about 41° F. for 2 weeks before sowing and this should be 6 weeks before the young seedlings are planted outdoors (after frost). Or they can be sown outdoors in Sept. Eventually they should be planted in the full sun and set about 9 in. apart.

MACLEAYA (mak-LAY-ya)

cordata (*Bocconia cordata*)   **6′–8′   Zone 3   Plume-poppy**
A vigorously-growing, tall perennial free of most pests, with leaves, 8 in. wide, shaped somewhat like fig leaves, that are grayish white on the underside. The foot-long panicles of small cream-colored to pinkish flowers are borne in July and Aug., and it is from these plumelike clusters that it takes its common name. However, this plant can spread and, because of this and its vigorous almost coarse texture, it is best relegated to the rear of the perennial border. It

676

does best in full sun and is easily propagated by division in the spring. Seeds, spring-sown, germinate readily. Native to China and Japan.

MACLURA (mak-LURE-a)

pomifera   60'   Zone 5   Osage-orange
Fifty years ago, this midwestern American native belonging to the Mulberry Family was used a great deal in rough hedges. It is vigorous, has stout inch-long thorns, is able to grow in hot and dry situations, and, when cut or sheared, grows so thick that cattle can not penetrate into it. The leaves are alternate, 2–5 in. long, and turn yellow in the fall. The fruits, borne on the plants with the inconspicuous pistillate flowers, are large, green, orangelike balls, 3 in. across, of no ornamental value at all. It is also used as a windbreak, but it should not be used on the small place, nor as an ornamental where better plants would grow. Some individuals develop a dermatitis upon coming in contact with milky sap from stems, leaves and fruits.

Propagation

Seeds may be stratified as soon as ripe for 2 months at 40° F., then sown, or stored dry in airtight containers in a cool place for up to a year, then stratified and sown. Softwood cuttings and especially root cuttings, root readily. See STRATIFICATION, CUTTINGS.

MACRO. In compound words meaning long, large or great.

MACULATE. Blotched or spotted.

MADDER = *Rubia tinctorum*

MADDER FAMILY = Rubiaceae

MADEIRA-VINE = *Anredera cordifolia*

MADEIRA-VINE FAMILY = Basellaceae

MADIA (MAY-di-a)

elegans   2'   annual   Common Tarweed
A heavily scented annual belonging to the Composite Family with alternate linear leaves 5 in. long; flowers in heads about ¾ in. wide, the ray-flowers yellow or with a brown spot at the base. Native from Ore. to Calif. and Nev.

sativa   4'   annual   Chilean Tarweed
Lanceolate-to-linear, alternate leaves only 2 in. long; the yellow flower heads about 3 in. across. Native to Chile, naturalized in the Northwest and rather too coarse in texture to make a good garden plant.

MADRE-DE-CACAO = *Gliricidia sepium*

MADRONE, PACIFIC = *Arbutus menziesii*

MADWORT, ROCK = *Aurinia saxatilis*

MAGNOLIA (mag-NO-lia). The magnolias comprise our most conspicuous flowering trees. There are some that can be grown in all but the coldest sections of the U.S. They are valued chiefly because of their large and showy flowers,

which start to appear at the end of April, with some plants still in bloom by early summer. Few have much to offer as far as autumn color is concerned, but all have bright red and interesting fruits during late summer and early fall. Their leaves are alternate and entire.

Some of these interesting trees are native to North America, indeed some like *M. acuminata* and *M. virginiana* are native to the state of Mass. Those with colored flowers are mostly native in the Orient, except *M. cordata* which has canary-yellow flowers. It should also be noted that there are quite a few excellent species native or hardy in the South that are not hardy in New England. Some of the most beautiful of all, namely *M. sargentiana robusta* and *M. sprengeri diva*, are natives of Asia, but not hardy in the North. In height, magnolias range from large shrubs or small shrubby trees to standard trees maturing 90 ft. tall.

Admittedly, the foliage of most of the mag-

Magnolia leaves and fruits:
Top row: *Magnolia cordata, kobus, borealis soulangiana*
Second row: *M. 'Merrill', obovata, virginiana*
Third row: *M. loebneri, hypoleuca, salicifolia*
Bottom row: *M. acuminata, stellata, denudata*
(*Photo by Arnold Arboretum, Jamaica Plain, Mass.*)

nolias is coarse. The exceptions are probably *M. salicifolia* and *M. stellata* with leaves 1½–4 in. long. On the other hand, there are several species which may have leaves 12 in. long or even longer, namely, *M. fraseri, macrophylla, obovata, officinalis* and *tripetala*. On occasion, *M. macrophylla* will have the largest leaves of all, sometimes nearly 3 ft. long. Foliage such as this greatly restricts the usefulness of the species, for, in a windy spot, the leaves are ripped and torn and thus can look disreputable for a great part of the season. On the other hand, when used properly in protected places, such trees create tropically exotic effects which cannot be created in any other way.

The blooming period in New England extends from late April until early summer, depending on the species. Some years the *M. soulangiana* varieties make an attempt to bloom a second time in the late summer, but usually when this occurs after a very wet summer, only a few flowers are produced. Because the flowers are large, and come so late in the season, they frequently make a great impression on the gardener.

The order in which the species bloom is as follows: Late April—*M. denudata, salicifolia, stellata, kobus, loebneri, proctoriana*; Early May—*soulangiana* and many varieties; Mid-May—*fraseri*; Late May—*acuminata, cordata, liliflora nigra, soulangiana lennei, tripetala, watsonii, virginiana*; Early June—*obovata, sieboldii*; Mid-June—*wilsonii*; Early July—*macrophylla*.

It is interesting to note, that in the warmer parts of the southern U.S. some magnolias will bloom as early as Feb., and *M. wilsonii* has been known to bloom in Aug.

Propagation

Do not allow the seed to dry out but stratify as soon as ripe for 4 months at 40° F., then sow. Softwood cuttings can be rooted, especially of *M. stellata, loebneri* and others. *M. grandiflora* varieties can be budded or grafted on that species; others are usually grafted or budded on either *M. kobus* or *acuminata*. See STRATIFICATION, GRAFTING, CUTTINGS, etc.

Insect Pests

Magnolia scale which is similar to the tulip tree scale is the largest scale in the U.S. The oval dark-brown scales with a waxy bloom are on the branches during winter when they can be controlled by sprays of insecticide #44.

Diseases

Several leaf spots infect Magnolia and when necessary are controlled with fungicide #D or #F.

acuminata   90′   Zone 4   Cucumber-tree
A pyramidal tree native from N.Y. to Ark., becoming spreading at maturity, chiefly of value for its foliage. The small flowers are greenish yellow and none too conspicuous even though they are 3 in. high, because they appear after the leaves are fully developed in late spring. The leaves are 5–11 in. long. Often used as understock in grafting other magnolias. It is one of the fastest growing magnolias and should not be planted unless it is given plenty of room in which to develop. Young trees are pyramidal but as they mature they become generally rounded in shape.

**acuminata cordata   30′   Zone 5   Yellow
                                        Cucumber-tree**
A smaller tree than *M. acuminata*, sometimes shrublike with 4 in. canary-yellow flowers, much better than those of *M. acuminata*. The leaves are 3–5 in. long. This might be used as the substitute for *M. acuminata* on the small place. It is native to Ga.

campbellii mollicomota   50′–80′   Zone 9
Leaves 6–10 in., 4–5 in. wide and flowers 6–7 in. dia., rose colored and appearing before the leaves in the spring. This will bloom much earlier in its life than will the species, thus blooming in 7 or 8 years while the species takes twice that long to produce flowers, hence it is much better than the species to use as an ornamental.

dawsoniana   36′   Zone 7   Dawson Magnolia
With horizontally borne, nodding, rosy-purple flowers about 10 in. in dia., appearing before the leaves in March and April. This is often confused with *M. sargentiana*, but the Dawson Magnolia from western China flowers more profusely.

denudata = *M. heptapeta*

fraseri   45′   Zone 5   Fraser Magnolia
The leaves are large, 6–15 in. long, and the milky white flowers are about 8–10 in. in dia. The fragrant flowers are produced in May and June when the plant is in leaf. Because of large coarse foliage and flowers, this plant is difficult to use properly in the small garden. It is native from Va. to Ga.

glauca = *M. virginiana*

grandiflora   90′   Zone 7   Southern Magnolia
An excellent evergreen tree native from N.Car. to Fla. and Tex. with waxy evergreen leaves 5–8 in. long dropping at the end of the second year, and large, waxy-white fragrant flowers 8–10 in. in dia., produced in June and July. Several varieties are grown with varying leaf sizes. The tree is widely planted and the glossy evergreen leaves are dried and used in florists arrangements throughout America. Varieties: **lanceolata** (*exoniensis*)—this Exmouth Magnolia has a narrow pyramidal habit which is

commendable, but it takes many years for a young plant to bloom. The leaves are narrower than those of the species, rusty tomentose beneath. It originated from seed in England before 1800 and was widely distributed by the Veitch Nursery firm there; **'Goliath'**—a very popular variety in England with large flowers up to 12 in. in dia. and broad leaves, rounded and blunt at the end, glossy green, first distributed by the Caledonia Nursery on the Isle of Guernsey, probably before 1910; **'St. Mary'**—originated before 1950 at the Glen St. Mary Nursery, Glen St. Mary, Fla. Blooms at an earlier age than most *M. grandiflora* seedlings but especially named for the deep and conspicuously brown undersurface of the leaves.

heptapeta (*M. denudata*)   45′   **Zone 5**
                                        Yulan Magnolia
Formerly termed *M. conspicua*, this Chinese tree produces beautiful creamy-white, fragrant flowers, 6 in. in dia., in early May before the 4–6 in. leaves appear. An excellent tree, one of the best of the magnolias.

hypoleua (*obovata*)   90′   **Zone 5   Whiteleaf**
                                        Japanese Magnolia
Although flowering after the leaves have developed in early June, the creamy-white, strongly-scented flowers, 8 in. in dia., are conspicuous. The leaves, 8–10 in. long and half as wide, are bluish white on the underside of this Japanese Tree. This is better for garden use than the native *M. tripetala* which has smaller flowers of a disagreeable odor. Still it is a coarsely-leaved tree, not good for windswept situations, but useful in creating exotic effects.

kobus   30′   **Zone 4   Kobus Magnolia**
This is not a good ornamental to plant because it does not bear many flowers while young—sometimes the first flowers do not appear until the tree is 20 years old. Also, the hybrid 'Merrill' has larger flowers, is treelike and usually blooms 3–4 years after the graft is made. *M. kobus* has leaves 3–6 in. long and white 6-petaled flowers less than 4 in. across in late April. Because it grows fast, it is frequently used as understock on which to graft other magnolias. Native to Japan.

x loebneri 'Merrill'   50′   Zone 4
It takes a long time for many magnolias to grow to flowering size from seed. E. H. Wilson used to say that it would take over 20 years for *M. kobus* to flower if it were grown from seed—far too long for many home gardeners to wait.

The Star Magnolia (*M. stellata*) on the other hand will bloom about 7 years after the seed is sown, one of the very reasons why the Star Magnolia is widely planted and the Kobus Magnolia is not. Crosses between these 2 species have been known for many years, but most of the resulting plants had little to offer

ornamentally. A cross between these 2 species was made at the Arnold Arboretum in 1939 and was named *M. loebneri* 'Merrill', in honor of the former Director and great botanist, Dr. E. D. Merrill.

The flowers have nearly as many petals as those of *M. stellata*, which is 12–18, but the petals are wider, giving more substance to the flower. The original seedling is now a tree over 25 ft. tall with a sturdy trunk. The Star Magnolia grows with several small trunks and grows very slowly, trees 40 years old not being that tall.

The 'Merrill' Magnolia begins to bloom when it is about 5 years old and is vigorous. Added to these sterling qualities is the excellent feature that it is very easily propagated by softwood cuttings. It should easily become one of the popular early flowering ornamental trees for the northern part of the country.

macrophylla   50′   Zone 5   Bigleaf Magnolia
This has the largest leaves and flowers of any of the hardy magnolias (in fact larger leaves than any hardy native tree in North America), and because of this should not be used in any planting exposed to winds, where the leaves can be easily ripped and torn. The leaves are 15–25 in. and sometimes up to 36 in. long, as much as 7–12 in. wide. The creamy-white fragrant flowers may be 8–14 in. in dia., appearing in early July after the leaves are fully developed. It should be used with extreme care, chiefly for exotic or tropical effects, and it is native from Ky. to Ark.

nitida   30′   Zone 8   Shinyleaf Magnolia
Evergreen leaves $2\frac{1}{2}$–$4\frac{1}{2}$ in. long and 1–2 in. wide, with fragrant creamy-white flowers (crimson on the outside) 2–3 in. dia., during late March and early April. Usually this is a rounded bush, sometimes a tree thinly clothed with foliage. Of limited usefulness in the U.S. because of its lack of hardiness. Native to China.

quinquepeta 'Nigra' (*liliflora 'Nigra'*)   9′
                            Zone 6   Purple Lily Magnolia
This variety of the Chinese *M. liliflora* has darker reddish-purple flowers than does the species, the flowers being 4–5 in. long and larger. This is the hardiest of the *M. liliflora* varieties with leaves 4–7 in. long, but does not seem to last indefinitely in the vigorous climate of Boston, Mass. It is actually a bush, not a tree. The flowers appear over a period of several weeks starting in late May or early June, usually with the leaves. It does not make a pleasing landscape specimen.

rostrata   40′–80′   Zone 9
This is an excellent foliage tree from China with leaves up to 20 in. long and $8\frac{1}{2}$ in. wide. The flowers appear in June and July after the leaves are fully developed, are pale pink to

white and disappointingly small for the large leaves. The leaves are the largest of any Asiatic magnolia and rival only those of our native *M. macrophylla* for size. Hence, it should be considered useful for its foliage only—otherwise it might well be omitted from planting.

salicifolia　30′　**Zone 5**　Anise Magnolia
The aromatic odor of the leaves when crushed is what gives this densely branched, pyramidal, Japanese magnolia its common name. The leaves are narrow 1½–4 in. long; the flowers white with 6 petals, 3–4 in. dia., before the leaves appear in late April or early May. A good foliage tree as well as a good ornamental in flower. In the fall, the leaves turn yellowish.

sargentiana robusta　40′　**Zone 7**
One of the most beautiful of all Chinese magnolias, better than the species because the flowers are larger (8–12 in. in dia.), the leaves are longer (5½–8 in.) and it will bloom more quickly as a young plant than the species (when about 12 years old). Also, this is even more important—the beautiful white and mauve-pink flowers are profusely borne all around the small tree, while the species, being a tall tree, has the flowers mostly at the top.

sieboldii (*parviflora*)　30′　**Zone 6**　Oyama
Magnolia
Small white waxy flowers 3–4 in. in dia., with the center a mass of magenta-purple stamens, and distinctly fragrant, are borne on this small tree in May. The leaves are 3½ in. long, the habitat is Japan and Korea. The plant is not long-lived (25 years) but the branches root readily wherever they touch moist ground.

x soulangiana　15′　**Zone 5**　Saucer Magnolia
A cross made by one of Napoleon's retired soldiers, about 1820, between *M. denudata* and *M. liliflora*. Undoubtedly many other crosses have been made since, most of the plants being large shrubs or small trees with varicolored, large, cup-shaped flowers, blooming just after *M. stellata*, *kobus*, *salicifolia* and *denudata*, but just before *M. liliflora*. All these species, and the varieties of *M. soulangiana* as well, bloom before the leaves appear in the spring. The Saucer Magnolia will bloom when it is very small, sometimes plants only 2–3 ft. tall will flower. The tree itself is normally as wide as it is high, and their flowers can be 5–10 in. across. The leaves are 6–8 in. long but have no autumn color whatsoever. It is best to select the better of the named clones for asexual propagation. Varieties: **'Alba'** (syn. 'Superba', 'Alba Superba') —introduced 1867 by Louis Van Houtte, Belgium. The flowers are white, outside of petals colored very light purplish. The tree is very compact; **'Alexandrina'**—introduced 1831, Paris, France. Flowers flushed rose-purple outside, inside of petals pure white. One of the

larger and earlier flowering varieties; **'Andre LeRoy'**—introduced 1900, from Orleans, France. The flowers are dark pink to purplish on the outside (color close to that of 'Verbanica'). The petals are white inside and the flowers are decidedly cup-shaped; **'Burgundy'**—introduced 1930 by W. B. Clarke, San Jose, Calif. The flowers are the deep purple color of Burgundy wine, appearing earlier than those of most other varieties; **'Brozzoni'**—introduced 1900, Barbier, Orleans, France. When wide open the flowers are 10 in. across making this one of the largest flowered varieties of the *M. soulangiana* group. The outside of the petals is tinged a pale purplish rose, but all in all it is considered one of the best of the white-flowered varieties; **'Grace McDade'** —introduced 1945. Flowers are white with pink at the base of the petals; **'Lennei'**—introduced 1852—originated in Florence, Italy. This has the darkest purplish-magenta flowers of this group (not as dark as *M. liliflora* 'Nigra'); **'Liliputin'**— originated in the Semmes Nurseries, Crichton, Ala., a few years ago with smaller flowers and smaller habit than · most *M. soulangiana* varieties. It is slow in growth. The variety sold under the name "Late Soulangiana" is similar in every way although this supposedly came from England; **'Lombardy Rose'**—introduced before 1957 by C. McDade, Semmes, Ala., lower surface of the petals is dark rose, upper surface white. This is a seedling of *M. soulangiana* 'Lennei' with flowers continuing to bloom for several weeks; **'Rustica'** (syn. 'Rubra' or 'Rustica Rubra')—introduced about 1893, Boskoop, Holland. Flowers are more rose-red than those of 'Lennei' but they are somewhat similar, 5½ in. in dia. The inside of the petals is white but the general effect is more red than 'Lennei'; **'Speciosa'**—introduced before 1830 in France. The flowers are almost white 6 in. in dia., very close to 'Alba' but just a trifle more color than 'Brozzoni'. It is important because it is the last of this group to bloom. Upright, tall and fast-growing; **'San Jose'**—originated about 1938, San Jose, Calif. Flowers are larger than many other varieties, rosey purple, fragrant and vigorous growing. Blooms earlier than most other *M. soulangiana* varieties—said to be deeper colored than most with the exception of 'Lennei'; **'Verbanica'**—flowers outside a clear rose pink, inside white. This is one of the late bloomers, making a beautiful effect when most of the other varieties are dropping their petals. Slow-growing.

sprengeri　60′　**Zone 7**　Sprenger Magnolia
A pyramidal tree with leaves 5–7 in. long, saucer-shaped flowers white and flushed or streaked with pink inside, 8 in. across, narrowed at the base and rather showy. Native to central China. However, the var. **diva** has flowers a

beautiful dark rose color. They are fragrant and light pink inside, opening in March before the leaves. This is usually considered a better ornamental than the species.

stellata (*M. halleana*)   20′   **Zone 5   Star Magnolia**
Double, white fragrant flowers, 3 in. or more in dia., and appearing in late April before the leaves. The flowers contain 12-15 narrow petals. One of the hardiest of the Asiatic magnolias (this is native to Japan), usually more of a tall shrub than a tree. An excellent and very popular ornamental specimen. Many seedings of *M. stellata* have been grown and it must be said that many of the seedlings are inferior flowering plants, showing great similarity to the inferior flowering *M. kobus*. Hence, this species, if it is a species, should not be grown from seed but from cuttings taken from a good clone. Varieties: **rosea** or **Pink Star Magnolia** has pink flower buds, flowers usually white. This is disappointing in flower, since by the time the flowers are fully open they have faded completely white; **rubra** or **Red Star Magnolia** has flowers purplish rose and was imported from Japan about 1925. Another form of this was purportedly grown in Boskoop, Holland, by Messers Kluis, before 1948. The flower color was noted as being Fuchsia purple 28/3 of the Royal Hort. Color Chart. It is said to have been a chance seedling in a batch of *M. stellata* with the flower color vastly superior to that of *M. stellata rosea*; **'Waterlily'** originated at Greenbrier Farms, Inc., Norfolk, Va., prior to 1939. It is more upright, bushy and twiggy than *M. stellata*. The flower buds are pink, the flowers eventually white and are slightly larger, with more narrow petals. It has always been assumed to be a cross of *M. stellata* x *M. soulangiana* but it looks very much like *M. stellata*.

x thompsoniana   shrub   Zone 6   Thompson Magnolia
Originating about 1808, this hybrid *M. tripetala* and *M. virginiana* has leaves 4-10 in. long, glaucous beneath and otherwise similar to those of *M. virginiana*. The creamy-white flowers are 4½-6 in. in dia., hence larger than those of *M. virginiana* and they are more globular as well, appearing in late June and July after the leaves have been fully developed.

tripetala   36′   Zone 4   Umbrella Magnolia
Native from Pa., to Miss., this has large leaves 10-24 in. long and white flowers 7-10 in. across in May or June, after the leaves are fully developed. It is open and coarse in habit because of its large leaves, but is easily and quickly grown and so is used as understock on which are grafted other species and varieties.

x veitchii   30′   Zone 7   Veitch Magnolia
Originating in 1907 in England, this hybrid magnolia is a cross between *M. campbellii* and *M. denudata* with vigorous growth, leaves 6-12 in. long and blush-pink flowers, 6 in. in dia., during April before the leaves appear. A good plant for its foliage as well as its flowers.

virginiana (*glauca*)   60′   **Zone 5   Sweet Bay Magnolia**
A shrub or tree from Mass. to Fla., one of the most fragrant of all the magnolias, with 3-5 in. leaves, whitish on the underside and white, waxy, very fragrant flowers in late June and July. In the far South the leaves are evergreen but they are deciduous in the North.

x watsoni   30′   Zone 5   Watson Magnolia
First known in France in 1889 but originally this cross between *M. obovata* and *M. sieboldii* came from Japan. This small tree has leaves 4-6 in. long and fragrant saucer-shaped flowers that are pink with a ring of prominent crimson stamens in the center. It has larger flowers and leaves than *M. sieboldii*, a closely similar Magnolia. The flowers are borne in late June and July after the leaves have been fully developed.

wilsonii   24′   Zone 6   Wilson Magnolia
A magnolia from western China, very easy to grow, often with a second crop of white, saucer-shaped, fragrant and pendulous flowers in Aug. They are 3½-4 in. in dia., with a ring of red stamens in the center. The leaves are 4-6 in. long.

MAGNOLIACEAE = The Magnolia Family

MAGNOLIA FAMILY = Magnoliaceae

MAGNOLIA-VINE, HIMALAYAN = *Schisandra propinqua*

MAHERNIA (ma-HERN-ia)
verticillata   1′   Zone 10   Honey-bells
A rambling bush with delicate leaves an inch long that are cut into linear divisions, and small, nodding, bell-shaped flowers that are golden yellow and ¾ in. wide. They are very fragrant, blooming both in winter and in spring. Used for planting in hanging baskets. Native to South Africa. Now termed *Hermannia verticillata*.

x MAHOBERBERIS (ma-ho-BER-ber-is). Intergeneric crosses between *Mahonia* and *Berberis*, these have evergreen to semi-evergreen leaves varying widely sometimes on the same plant, some simple, some compound. Flowers and fruits are sparse or nonexistent. One species, *M. neubertii*, carries the black stem rust of wheat and so should not be grown. It has no ornamental qualities. The other 3 have been listed as "resistant" to this disease and so can be grown, bought and shipped under permit from the U.S. Bureau of Plant Quarantine. None of the 3 are exceptional ornamentals. Propagation is by hardwood cuttings.

x aquicandidula   6′   Zone 6
A hybrid between *M. aquifolium* and *Berberis candidula* with alternate leaves, simple, 1–1½ in. long and approximately 3–5 sharp prickles on the leaf margin on each side of the leaf and a very few stipular thorns about ¼ in. long. The leaf is glossy and leathery. The leaves of this species do not vary much one from the other. It seldom blooms.

x aquisargentiae   6′   Zone 6
A hybrid between *Mahonia aquifolium* and *Berberis sargentiana*, this appears to be more vigorous than *Mahonia aquicandidula* and is more dense in branching, with practically no stipular thorns. The glossy evergreen to semi-evergreen leaves are sometimes compound on older wood, with the major terminal leaflet 3 in. long and the 2 basal leaflets half that size or less. Some simple leaves about 3 in. long or less. Most have marginal spines on the leaf margins. The plant should be given some shade if the leathery evergreen leaves are to be retained. In the sun they turn slightly bronze in winter. No flowers or fruits have yet been observed on plants in America, first introduced from Sweden in 1948.

x miethkeana   6′   Zone 6
This hybrid, originating in an American nursery in Washington about 1940, is proving surprisngly similar to *M. aquisargentiae*. However it has produced a few, small, yellowish to cream-colored flowers and small black fruits apparently void of viable seeds.

x neubertii   6′   Zone 5
This is a hybrid between *M. aquifolium* and *Berberis vulgaris*. It is not a good ornamental, very seldom, if ever, flowering, rather leggy and open in habit, and it has dull, semi-evergreen leaves, spiny-pointed around the leaf margin. The leaves are sometimes compound with 3–5 leaflets. It is susceptible to the black stem rust of wheat and because of this and its very poor ornamental qualities, it should not be grown.

MAHOGANY FAMILY = Meliaceae

MAHOGANY, WEST INDIES = *Swietenia mahogani*

MAHONIA (ma-HO-nia). These evergreens are native to America and Asia. They are popular garden plants, having no thorns but frequently having spines on their evergreen leaves. They are members of the Barberry Family and, as such, some of them will act as alternate hosts for the black stem rust of wheat. Only those species which are resistant to the black stem rust of wheat and which are permitted "movement" from one state to another by the Plant Pest Control Division of the U.S. Department of Agriculture, are listed here. It's not worth while growing the others.

Propagation

Do not allow the seed to dry out but stratify when ripe for 3 months at 40° F., then sow. Softwood and hardwood cuttings root well, but most plants (which sucker readily) can be easily divided merely with a sharp spade. See STRATIFICATION, CUTTINGS, etc.

aquifolium   3′ rarely 6′   Zone 5   Oregon Holly-grape
Native in the Pacific Northwest, this species has many variants, some tall and some low, some with very glossy leaves and some with dull foliage. For this reason, asexual propagation from glossy-leaved, hardy clones is greatly desirable. The dark, evergreen leaves turn a beautiful bronze in the fall. The leaves are alternate and compound and the 5–9 leaflets frequently have spines on the margins, somewhat similar to those of *Ilex opaca*.

Sometimes it is advisable to prune or thin the plants heavily in an attempt to keep them about 3 ft. tall, for if they grow higher they bend or flop over and become unsightly. The right clone can be grown in the full sun without winter foliage burn, but many clones cannot. So, although it is a common plant in our nurseries, of special interest for its large pyramidal clusters of small yellow flowers in May, followed by grapelike blue fruits in early summer, it behooves nurserymen to propagate asexually from the right, glossy-leaved clones.

Varieties

'**Compacta**'—apparently this is a new compact form with very glossy leaves and bronze winter color; '**Mayhan**'—another dwarf selection made by the Mayhan Nursery of Veradale, Wash., this differs from the above in being taller in habit, having fewer leaflets in each leaf and with these arranged more closely together on the leaf stalks. The Mayhan Nursery claims that this is the result of 25 years of selection and that the form can be maintained by seed propagation. No plants are reported over 30 in. high and 95% of the plants are under 20 in. high. If this growth habit is maintained under all conditions the plant is a valuable addition to the broad-leaved evergreen group.

bealei   12′   Zone 6   Leatherleaf Mahonia
Those who have gardens in the South are thoroughly familiar with this large, coarse-leaved evergreen. Its spiny, evergreen, alternate, compound leaves are sometimes 16 in. long and have 9–15 leaflets; and its large yellow flower clusters are fragrant. The fruits are bluish black and grapelike and the plant does well if placed in partial shade where its lustrous spiny evergreen leaves do not turn color markedly in the fall. This Chinese shrub often grows too tall to

look well, and should be restrained by proper pruning.

fortunei   3½'   **Zone 7**   **Chinese Mahonia**
Native to China and closely related to *M. bealei*, this evergreen mahonia has 7–13 leaflets, each leaflet of which is 2¼–4½ in. long and has 5–10 spiny teeth on its margins. The yellow flowers are in clusters or racemes 3–5 in. long.

japonica   10'   **Zone 7**   **Japanese Mahonia**
An evergreen shrub from Japan, it produces upright stems with a few leaves at the top. The alternate compound leaves are 1–1½ ft. long, having 7–13 leaflets each 2–5 in. long. The very fragrant yellow flowers are borne in terminal racemes 6–9 in. long and the fruits are often ½ in. long and purple. This is not frequently seen in gardens since *M. bealei* is the much more popular plant and is hardier.

nervosa   1½'   **Zone 5**   **Cascades Mahonia**
A low evergreen mahonia native in the mountains from British Columbia to Calif., the alternate compound leaves of this plant have 11–19 leaflets, the leaves and stalk being 7–16 in. long, lustrous above, with bright yellow flowers in erect panicles 4–8 in. long. The fruits are dark blue, glaucous berries.

pinnata   12'   **Zone 7**   **Cluster Mahonia**
The leaves of this Calif. and N.Mex. native are dull, not lustrous, and they have 7–13 leaflets. It is similar to *M. aquifolium* but the foliage is duller and it grows taller.

repens   12"   **Zone 5**   **Creeping Mahonia**
The foliage of this native evergreen species (British Columbia to Calif.) is not lustrous; hence it is not so conspicuous an ornamental as is the glossy-leaved *M. aquifolium*. However, it is lower in habit, stoloniferous and the alternate compound leaves have only 3–7 rounded leaflets, so it can be recommended as an evergreen ground cover.

MAIANTHEMUM (my-ANTH-e-mum)

canadense   3"–6"   **Zone 3**   **Wild Lily-of-the-valley, Canada Mayflower**
This low perennial grows profusely in moist, acid woods of the northern U.S. and in the higher altitudes of N.Car., sending up a stem on which are 2–3 alternate, ovate, sessile leaves and a terminal raceme of tiny white flowers, ½ in. or less in dia., which have 4 segments and appear in May, followed by light red berries. These berries may be planted in the fall, or sods may be transplanted where the plants are numerous. It is an excellent ground cover for moist, shady areas. Sometimes called Canada Bead-ruby.

MAIDENHAIR TREE = *Ginkgo biloba*
MAILE = *Alyxia olivaeformis*
MAIZE. See CORN.
MAJORANA HORTENSIS = *Origanum majorana*

MAKI. See PODOCARPUS MACROPHYLLUS.
MALABAR GOURD = *Cucurbita ficifolia*

MALACOTHRIX. These are about 15 species of herbs or herblike plants with milky sap. A few species like *M. californica* are cultivated as annuals. They have bright yellow flowers.

MALANGA. See XANTHOSOMA.

MALATHION. An organic phosphate used as an insecticide. See INSECTICIDES.

MALAY-APPLE = *Syzygium malaccensis*

MALCOMIA (mal-KO-mia)

maritima   4"–8"   **annual**   **Virginia-stock**
With lilac and reddish-to-white small flowers (belonging to the Mustard Family) about ½ in. across, borne in great profusion in the early summer, this dainty little annual comes from the Mediterranean Region and the Near East. The stems are weak; the leaves are small and oval and grayish; this is excellent for edging or for use in the front of the flower border. Easily propagated by seeds sown in April in the bed where the plants are to grow and thinned out to about 3 in. apart. Plants do well in either full sun or light shade. If a long period of bloom is desired, sow seed a second time the end of May and again the end of June and replace plants in the first planting when they are through blooming or as needed.

MALE (flowers or plant). Having stamens but no pistils.

MALEBERRY = *Lyonia ligustrina*

MALE-FERN, ENGLISH CRESTED = *Dryopteris filix-mas* 'Cristata'

MALLOW. See MALVA, SPHAERALCEA.
MALLOW FAMILY = Malvaceae
MALLOW, ROSE. See HIBISCUS.

MALOPE (MAL-o-pe)

trifida   3'   **annual**   **Malope**
This annual from Europe and North Africa bears 3 in. flowers that are borne in the leaf axils and make a fine display throughout the summer. They are white, pink, or violet depending on the variety (of which there are several) and each flower is surrounded by 3 heart-shaped bracts. Seeds can be sown in the garden in mid-April in a sunny spot where the plants are to remain. The soil should be well drained. This genus belongs to the Mallow Family.

MALPIGHIA (mal-PIG-ia)

coccigera   3'–6'   **Zone 10**   **Holly Malpighia**
The small hollylike, opposite, evergreen leaves, ¾ in. long, that are glossy with sharp points on the edges, give this plant its common name. The branching is upright and the flowers, each borne in a leaf axil, are light pink, ½ in. across, with 5

petals. Sometimes small red fruits develop which are about $\frac{1}{3}$ in. across. Native to the West Indies. It is one of the better low plants used in Fla., excellent for foundation plantings. It might best be planted in a partially shaded spot. There are many clones and these should be propagated by cuttings.

glabra   12′   Zone 10   Barbados-cherry
A shrub from the West Indies with opposite, simple, glossy green leaves 3 in. long and axillary, pale-pink to rose-colored flowers blooming throughout the summer and usually producing 2 or 3 crops of conspicuous bright red fruits about the size of a cherry but 3-lobed. Because the fruit has a high ascorbic acid content the pulp is used for ices, beverages and in making preserves. Propagated by seeds and cuttings.

MALTESE CROSS = *Lychnis chalcedonica*

MALUS (MAY-lus). The trees of this genus constitute the apples (also see APPLES) and crab apples, all alternate-leaved deciduous trees with small rosaceous flowers of 5 petals (if they are single flowered) and fruits ranging from those the size of a pea, to apples 2–4 in. in dia. For purposes of differentiation, any of these with fruits less than 2 in. in dia. we have considered as crab apples, those with larger fruits as apples. The alternate leaves of the apples are large and coarse, about 2–4 in. long and $1\frac{1}{2}-2\frac{1}{2}$ in. broad. The alternate leaves of the crab apples, in general, are shorter and more narrow, and so the foliage texture is more refined. Many of the crab apples are small trees, 15–25 ft. tall, dense and mounded, making fine specimens. A few species (like *M. baccata*) are standard trees 50 ft. in height.

The fruits of the crab apples are not all edible, that is, some are rather sour or bitter to the taste, but all can be used in making jellies and preserves. Crab apples are all pomes. They begin to color, by variety, in Aug., reaching a peak in Oct., and some varieties will retain fruits a greater part of the winter. The foliage of only a few turn color in the fall, and even these do so under certain climatic conditions, not every year. This is a group of excellent ornamental trees of interest several seasons of the year. Most have single flowers, a few have semi-double or double flowers. A few have pendulous branches and a few are narrowly fastigiate in growth but this habit is maintained only while they are young. As they mature and the branches grow longer, the increasing weight of the fruit tends to force the upright branches more and more into a horizontal position, until the time comes when these do not spring back to their former upright habit. It is then that these maturing columnar

varieties gradually begin to take on the normal rounded habit of most of the crab apples.

Like many woody plants, some species and varieties in this group have the disconcerting habit of bearing large crops of flowers and fruits only in alternate years. There is little that can be done to change this. On the other hand, other varieties bear annually, and it is these that should be recommended and grown. Also, many in the group are susceptible to fire blight and the disfiguring apple scab disease. Studies have shown certain varieties to be resistant to these troubles and it is these also which should be recommended and grown.

Left to right: Apple, edible Crab Apple, and ornamental Crab Apple.

The fruits of all native American species are merely green, and hence these are not ornamental in the fall. The many hybrids and oriental species are the ones with the bright red, yellow or purplish-colored fruits, and these ripen at different times in the late summer and fall depending on variety. So, with many varieties differing in fruits, in flower colors (white, pink, red) and in form, this is a diversified group which every gardener could well study to find just the right tree for his own garden.

Propagation

Seeds can be processed as soon as ripe or stored dry in airtight containers in a cool place and processed the following year. They should be stratified at 40° F. for 3 months, then sown. Grafting and budding are commonly practiced. Native American species can be grafted on *M. coronaria* and most others on seedlings of the common apple. *M. robusta* seedlings have also been used. All cultivars should be asexually propagated and not grown from seed. See SEED STRATIFICATION, GRAFTING, BUDDING.

For insect and disease problems see APPLES.

'Adams'   24′   Zone 4
A good, annual-bearing crab apple, resistant to

apple scab, originated in the Adams Nursery, Westfield, Mass. before 1952. The flowers are single, $1\frac{1}{2}$ in. in dia., carmine buds and flowers fading to dull pink in mid-May, red fruits $\frac{5}{8}$ in. dia., in Sept. and Oct. It has a mounded outline and is dense-branching.

x arnoldiana 20′ Zone 4 Arnold Crab Apple
An excellent hybrid (*M. floribunda* x *M. baccata*) with flowers as much as 2 in. across, rose-red buds and the flowers pink outside and fading to white inside as they open. The fruits are yellow and reddish, $\frac{5}{8}$ in. in dia., effective during Sept. and Oct. This originated as a chance seedling in the Arnold Arboretum, Jamaica Plain, Mass. in 1883, and has been an outstanding ornamental tree.

x atrosanguinea 20′ Zone 4 Carmine Crab Apple
This hybrid (*M. halliana* x *M. sieboldii*) originated in Japan but has long been a favorite in America because of its rich carmine flowers about $1\frac{1}{4}$ in. across during mid-May. They fade to a poor pink just before they fall. The dark red fruits $\frac{3}{8}$ in. across are not particularly ornamental. It bears annually, is resistant to apple scab and can be used to good advantage in front of several white-flowering crab apple trees.

baccata 50′ Zone 2 Siberian Crab Apple
One of the hardiest of all the species in this genus, it is also one of the tallest. The pure white, very fragrant flowers are 1–$1\frac{1}{2}$ in. across, appearing in early May, and the red and yellow fruits vary considerably in size as well as color, many being $\frac{3}{8}$ in. across. Years ago it was used considerably in hybridizing apples, in an attempt to obtain hardier varieties. It is native to northeastern Asia and the fruits are effective from late Aug. to late Oct. Of many varieties, some of the best are: **'Columnaris'**—about the most columnar of the crab apples, an annual bearer but reportedly very susceptible to fire blight; **gracilis**—fragrant white flowers $1\frac{3}{8}$ in. across, more dense than the species with the tips of the branches slightly pendulous, giving the whole tree a refined appearance. This is really superior to the species and should be propagated asexually; **'Jackii'**—one of the best of these Siberian crab apples for its glossy red fruits; **mandshurica**—flowers white, fragrant, $1\frac{1}{2}$ in. in dia., blooms in late April—the first of all the crab apples to flower.

'Barbara Ann' 25′ Zone 4
This fine Crab Apple has deep purplish-pink flowers nearly 2 in. across with 12–15 petals in mid-May, followed by purplish fruits $\frac{1}{2}$ in. in dia., in the fall. It originated in the Arnold Arboretum in 1957 as a seedling of 'Dorothea', another excellent double-flowered tree. Double-flowered crab apples remain effective in bloom longer than do those with single blossoms. This is very new, but it will prove to be popular as it becomes better known.

'Baskatong' 30′ Zone 4
Introduced by the Central Experimental Farm Ottawa, Canada, before 1950, this has reddish-bronze foliage throughout the growing season and is resistant to apple scab. The single flowers are $1\frac{1}{4}$ in. across, the flower buds are carmine but the flowers fade a dull pink as they mature in mid-May and the fruits are red. This has been considered one of the most ornamental of the group of hybrids, called the "Rosybloom" crab apples.

'Beauty' 24′ Zone 3
Dr. N. E. Hansen of Brookings, S.Dak., originally grew this from seed of *M. robusta* imported from Russia about 1919. The single white flowers are $1\frac{3}{4}$ in. across in mid-May and the edible red fruits are 1 in. across in the early fall. It has a fastigiate habit, bears flowers well only in alternate years but is resistant to apple scab.

'Bob White' 20′ Zone 4
A clone of *M. zumi* originating before 1876, with flowers eventually fading to white and 1 in. across, during early May. The yellow fruits, $\frac{5}{8}$ in. across, remain on the tree all winter or until very early spring when they are eventually eaten by the birds. The foliage is dense and has a fine texture. A fine Crab Apple for winter bird food.

brevipes 15′ Zone 5 Nippon Crab Apple
One of the smaller crab apples, of unknown origin, this has whitish flowers $\frac{3}{4}$ in. in dia., fragrant, borne in alternate years during early May. The red fruits are $\frac{5}{8}$ in. across from Aug. to mid-Nov., one of the earliest to bear colorful fruits.

coronaria 'Nieuwlandiana' 20′ Zone 4
The double pink flowers of this native American species appear in late May and early June, have 13–27 petals and are $1\frac{1}{4}$–$2\frac{1}{4}$ in. across. The fruits are merely green, $1\frac{3}{4}$ in. across. This is similar to the variety 'Charlottae' but the flowers are larger and a deeper pink. It is very fragrant, bears flowers annually, is resistant to apple scab and was originally raised in Rochester, N.Y. about 1931. **'Charlottae'** is also double, pink, resistant to apple scab and bears flowers annually.

'Dolgo' 40′ Zone 3
Another of Dr. N. E. Hansen's originations at Brookings, S.Dak., in 1897—this is still a very popular tree. The white, fragrant flowers are $1\frac{3}{4}$ in. in dia., and are only borne profusely in alternate years, during early May, but the bright red, edible fruits are $1\frac{1}{4}$ in. through, effective in Aug. These fruits make excellent jelly and the tree is valued because of these fruits early in Aug., among the first of the crab

apples to show colorful fruits. It is especially hardy and scab-resistant and is succeeding in Canada in many places where other crab apples fail.

'Donald Wyman'   25′   Zone 4
Dense in habit, flower buds pink, flowers white, annually bearing bright red fruits that remain a long time. One of the best as an ornamental.

'Dorothea'   25′   Zone 4
Originated as a chance seedling in the Arnold Arboretum, Jamaica Plain, Mass., in 1943, this

Malus 'Dorothea' has bright yellow fruits after double pink flowers. (*Photo by Arnold Arboretum, Jamaica Plain, Mass.*)

small tree bears semi-double deep pink flowers (16 petals), which are 1⅝–2 in. across in mid-May and bright yellow fruits ½ in. in dia., effective from fall to early winter. It is one of the very few double-flowered crab apples which also has bright-colored ornamental fruits. It blooms very early in life, sometimes the first year after grafting, and produces a heavy crop of flowers and fruits every year. It is also scab-resistant.

'Evelyn'   20′   Zone 3
Mr. A. F. den Boer of Des Moines, Ia., originated this hybrid in 1939. The single pink flowers are 1½ in. across, are borne in mid-May

and the red fruits are 1¼ in. through. It is erect, the lvs. purplish, turning to bronze green.

'Flame'   25′   Zone 2
One of the hardiest of crab apples, this is supposed to be perfectly hardy in the colder parts of Minn. It is a chance seedling raised at the University of Minn. Fruit Farm at Excelsior, Minn. with pink flower buds, white flowers in early May and bright red fruits ¾ in. in dia. from late Aug. to mid-Nov. It bears annually and is resistant to apple scab.

floribunda   30′   Zone 4   Japanese Flowering Crab Apple
Although this was introduced into America from Japan in 1862, it is still one of the better ornamental crab apples, with deep pink to red flower buds and flowers 1–1½ in. across, very fragrant, in early May. The yellow and red fruits are ⅜ in. through and are effective from late Aug. to mid-Oct. It bears annually, has fine foliage texture and is rounded in outline and densely branched.

'Gorgeous'   30′   Zone 4
A seedling from New Zealand about 1925, pink flower buds and single white flowers 1¼ in. in dia. during mid-May. The annual red fruits are 1 in. in dia.

halliana parkmanii   15′   Zone 5   Parkman Crab Apple
The double pink flowers (15 petals) of this small tree are 1¼ in. across and bloom in early May. The fruits are dull red and small, only about the size of a pea and not as colorful as those of some of the others. The vase-shaped habit is unusual but good. The leaves are leathery and lustrous. It is one of the least hardy of the crab apples enumerated here, but one of the best in flower.

'Henry F. DuPont'   20′   Zone 4
A fine, low-spreading tree with single or semi-double pink flowers in mid-May. The red fruits are ½ in. in dia., and originated in 1946 at the Arnold Arboretum, Jamaica Plain, Mass. The color of the flowers last much better than does that of the flowers of *M. atrosanguinea*. It is resistant to apple scab.

hupehensis   24′   Zone 4   Tea Crab Apple
A small tree noted for its picturesque fan-shaped habit, this bears deep pink flower buds, white flowers 1½ in. in dia., during early May, but they are profuse only in alternate years. The greenish-yellow to red fruits are ⅜ in. through but are not as conspicuous as those of many other crab apples. It was introduced from China in 1900.

ioensis 'Plena'   30′   Zone 2   Bechtel Crab Apple
Unfortunately for many gardeners, this native American Crab Apple is still widely advertised but it is not nearly as good an ornamental as some of the newer double-flowered varieties of the oriental crab apples. The pink flowers of

Malus hupehensis: The Tea Crab Apple has an interesting form. (*Photo by Arnold Arboretum, Jamaica Plain, Mass.*)

this are double (33 petals) and 2 in. across produced in late May, but the fruits are merely green. The leaves are large, the texture is coarse, but being a native in America it is susceptible to the cedar-apple rust which brings unsightly brown spots on the leaves.

'Katherine'   20'   Zone 4
A fine double-flowered crab apple with pink to white flowers 2¼ in. in dia., during mid-May. The dull red fruits, about the size of a pea, are not especially conspicuous. This originated in Rochester, N.Y. about 1928 and is outstanding when in flower.

x magdeburgensis   25'   Zone 4   Magdeburg Crab Apple
A hybrid species (*M. spectabilis* x *M. pumila*), with single and semi-double flowers with 7–15 petals, pink and almost 2 in. across but the fruits are merely yellow-green, about 1¼ in. across, sometimes reddish, and not at all interesting. It is, however, annual bearing but is not frequently found in American gardens.

'Makamik'   40'   Zone 4
One of the better annual-blooming Rosybloom crab apples which originated at the Ottawa Experimental Farm in Canada about 1920. This has flowers colored China-rose (of the Royal Horticultural Color Chart), 1⅝ in. in dia., the fruit purplish red and ¾ in. through.

'Marshall Oyama'   25'   Zone 4
A narrowly upright small tree, with pink buds and single white flowers 1⅝ in. across during mid-May, followed by yellow and red fruits an inch through. It probably came from Japan, but if its columnar habit is to be maintained it will need pruning of the side shoots to keep them from spreading outward. It bears annually and is resistant to apple scab.

x micromalus   25'   Zone 4   Midget Crab Apple
An alternate-bearing hybrid species (*M. spectabilis* x *M. baccata*) with profuse pink flowers

1¾ in. across blooming in early May, followed by red fruits that quickly turn brown and do not last long in good condition, especially after a frost. The leaves are 2–4 in. long. Not at all a promising ornamental in the fall. It is very dense and rounded but with upright branches, valued particularly for its pink flowers.

'Oekonomierat Echtermeyer'   15'   Zone 4
A graceful tree with semi-pendulous branches—originated in the Spaeth Nurseries of Germany in 1914. It should be grafted or budded high on the understock to be most effective, and has purplish-red flowers 1½ in. across in early May and reddish-purple fruits an inch in dia., during Sept. Apparently it is susceptible to apple scab.

'Prince Georges'   25'   Zone 4
A hybrid seedling of *M. ioensis* 'Plena', this has double (50 petals) pink flowers 2 in. across in late May but of course only greenish fruits. This flowers annually and is resistant to apple scab.

prunifolia   30'   Zone 3   Pearleaf Crab Apple
Native to Siberia and northern China, this is one of the hardier species, with white flowers 1½ in. across in early May and elongated red or yellow fruit about 1 in. through. The tree is definitely alternate bearing which mars its ornamental value on the small place. Several varieties of it have been named over the years, some with fruit large enough to eat.

pumila   45'   Zone 3   Common Apple
It is this species, native to Europe and western Asia, which is considered to be the parent of modern apple varieties. The flowers are white, suffused with pink, and the oval downy leaves are 1½–2½ in. long. The tree has a crooked trunk and the fruit is small, red or yellow. This species has been cultivated for centuries and it has been crossed with many other members of this genus resulting in the hundreds of modern apple varieties of today.

x purpurea 'Lemoinei'   25'   Zone 4
This has about the darkest red flowers of any of the crab apples. They are borne in early May, are both single and semi-double and are about 1½ in. across. The fruits are purplish red, ⅝ in. through and are colorful from late Aug. to late Oct. The foliage is dark green to almost purplish green and it is resistant to apple scab as well as being an annual bearer. Since both the 'Aldenham' and 'Eley' crab apples are susceptible to apple scab and both are alternate bearing, it is easy to see that 'Lemoinei' is an important variety.

'Radiant'   30'   Zone 4
Introduced by the Department of Horticulture University of Minn. in 1958, this is reported to be highly resistant to apple scab, cedar-apple rust and fire blight, and it bears annually. The young leaves have a reddish tinge as they unfurl in the spring, the flower buds are red, flowers

deep pink in mid-May and the fruits are bright red, $\frac{1}{2}$ in. across.

'Red Jade'   20'   Zone 4

A single white-flowered variety with gracefully pendulous branches, producing bright red fruits, $\frac{1}{2}$ in. in dia., which remain on the plant all fall and long into the winter after the leaves have fallen. It was introduced by the Brooklyn Botanic Garden in 1953, and bears good crops of fruits annually.

'Red Silver'   30'   Zone 4

The foliage is reddish green throughout the growing season. The flowers are "China rose" color, $1\frac{1}{2}$ in. across in early May, and the fruits are purplish red, $\frac{3}{4}$ in. through, but it bears only in alternate years. The fruit makes excellent jelly, this being one of the introductions of Dr. Niels E. Hansen of Brookings, S.Dak. in 1928.

x robusta   40'   Zone 3   Cherry Crab Apple

Since this is a hybrid species it varies greatly, especially in its fruits. The flowers are fragrant and white, $1\frac{3}{4}$ in. across in early May, and the fruits vary from $\frac{3}{4}$–$1\frac{1}{2}$ in. in dia., red or yellow, or red and yellow in Sept. and Oct. The tree is oval-shaped, dense branching and bears well only every other year. Because it varies so much, one should be careful to obtain plants with good ornamental fruit. The variety **'Erecta'** is narrow and columnar, and **'Percisifolia'** bears excellent red fruits that remain colorful on the tree until near Jan. This variety is called the Peachleaf Crab Apple.

'Rosseau'   40'   Zone 4

An annual-bearing Rosybloom Crab Apple, originating at the Ottawa Experimental Farm, Ottawa, Canada, with flowers like those of 'Makamik' but a bit more colorful. It bears annually and the rosy-red fruits are effective from late Aug. to mid-Oct.

sargentii   8'   Zone 4   Sargent Crab Apple

The lowest of all the crab apples, a native of Japan, with pure white fragrant flowers $\frac{1}{2}$ in. across and dark, red fruits about the size of a small pea. It is the only Crab Apple small enough to be considered a shrub, bearing annually. It forms a rounded, dense mass of branches and foliage. The variety **rosea** is similar except that the flower buds are red; the flowers gradually fade white.

x scheideckeri   20'   Zone 4   Scheidecker Crab Apple

A double-flowering hybrid (*M. floribunda* x *M. prunifolia*) with pale pink blossoms (10 petals) $1\frac{1}{2}$ in. across during early May. Its habit is more or less upright, the yellow-to-orange fruits are not outstanding but it does bear annually and is resistant to apple scab.

sieboldii arborescens   30'   Zone 5   Tree Toringo Crab Apple

Native to Japan, this and the species are not particularly outstanding but they do bloom later than some of the others in mid-May. The flower buds are pink, flowers white and $\frac{3}{4}$ in. across and the fruits are red and $\frac{1}{2}$ in. through.

'Sissipuk'   40'   Zone 4

This is one of the best of the Rosybloom crab apples from the Central Experimental Farm, Ottawa, Canada, because it bears annually and the fruit remains on the tree all winter. Flowers are $1\frac{1}{8}$ in. across, purplish red in mid-May and the purplish-red fruits are $\frac{3}{4}$ in. across. It is the last of these Rosybloom crab apples to flower.

spectabilis 'Riversii'   24'   Zone 4   River's Crab Apple

This old-fashioned Crab Apple is still a good ornamental. It originated in England in 1872 and has double pink flowers (9–12 petals) 2 in. across, during early May; bears in alternate years. The fruit is merely green. This is sometimes noted as var. "*roseo-plena*" in nurseries. There is a double white-flowering variety called **albi-plena**. The fruit is not ornamental and it may be that 'Dorothea' and 'Katherine' will supersede this old-fashioned variety because of their better fruits and annual bearing habits.

sylvestris   45'   Zone 3

There is some disagreement among botanists as to just what this species is, but in Alfred Rehder's "Manual of Cultivated Trees and Shrubs" he lists this as a separate species, native to Europe but rarely in cultivation. As far as the practical gardener is concerned this species can be omitted entirely from his consideration.

'Tanner'   20'   Zone 4

An alternate-bearing Crab Apple with single white flowers $1\frac{1}{2}$ in. across in mid-May and red fruits, $\frac{5}{8}$ in. dia., in the fall. The small fruits sometimes remain on the tree throughout the winter.

toringoides   25'   Zone 5   Cutleaf Crab Apple

Native to western China and one of the last to bloom (late May), this is especially valued for its pear-shaped fruits, about $\frac{3}{4}$ in. across, red on the side exposed to the sun, yellow on the shaded side from late Aug. to Nov. The flowers are white and fragrant, $\frac{3}{4}$ in. across, but it bears only in alternate years. It is definitely pyramidal in habit, and one of the species most susceptible to fire blight.

'Van Eseltine'   20'   Zone 4

With double pink flowers (15 petals) $1\frac{3}{4}$ in. dia. during late May and a narrowly upright habit, this was introduced by the N.Y. State Experiment Station at Geneva, N.Y., in 1938. One of the few upright-growing trees with double flowers.

'Vanguard'   18'   Zone 4

This originated at the Minn. Agricultural Experiment Station about 1930 and has been noted to be annual bearing and highly resistant to cedar apple rust and fire blight, and moderately resistant to apple scab. The flowers are single, bright rosy pink, (2 in. across) in mid-May and the red fruits are ¾ in. across, effective from early Sept. until late winter. The habit is somewhat vase-shaped.

x zumi calocarpa 25′ Zone 5 Redbud Crab Apple
A tree native to Japan, this is valued for its bright-red fruits, ½ in. across, that are effective from Aug. to Feb. when they are eaten by winter-hungry birds. Although it bears well only in alternate years and has pure white flowers 1 in. across in early May, it is grown by many because of its excellent winter fruits.

Other new varieties of merit are: 'Centennial', 'Chestnut'—white fls. and profuse red fruit; 'Pink Spire'—pink fls., purplish foliage and fruit; 'Royalty'—dark red fls.; 'Spring Snow'—white fls. and does not set fruit, making it of value for growing near pavements where fruit might be objectionable.

MALVA (MAL-va). These mallows are not as ornamental as are the closely allied *Hibiscus* species. They are slightly ungainly, with large white or pink 2″-wide flowers, each of which has 5 petals. They are easy to cultivate and can easily be divided in either spring or fall. Also, seeds germinate readily.

alcea 2′ Zone 4 Hollyhock Mallow
Native to Europe but now naturalized in the eastern U.S., this has 5-parted leaves and deep rose-to-white flowers 2 in. across. It is a perennial, easily propagated by division or cuttings and blooms in summer.

moschata 2′–3′ Zone 3 Musk Mallow
A perennial, often a weed, introduced from Europe with alternate, deeply 5-lobed stem

Round-leaved Mallow (*Malva rotundifolia*)— a garden weed.

leaves, each lobe of which is again divided. The basal leaves are simple and rounded with shallow lobes. The 5-petalled flowers are white, pink or bluish and are very showy, about 2 in. across, appearing in June and July. The seeds are borne in a round ring somewhat like those of the Hollyhock. It grows especially on limestone soils in eastern North America and in the Pacific Northwest.

rotundifolia procumbent annual Round-leaved Mallow
Sometimes a biennial weed, with procumbent stems on the soil surface, widespread now as a garden weed throughout North America but originally from Europe and Asia. The alternate, simple, rounded to lobed, palmately-veined leaves are about 1⅝ in. across. The flowers are whitish or pinkish, about ½ in. across and clustered in the axils of the leaves. This plant has a very long taproot.

MALVACEAE = The Mallow Family

MALVASTRUM COCCINEUM = *Sphaeralcea coccinea*

MAMMILLARIA (man-il-LAY-ria). A complicated genus of several hundred species of cacti, mostly native to Mexico and the southwestern U.S., hemispherical in form with the surface broken into prominent tubercles that have conspicuous woolly hairs or bristles. Flowers are small, diurnal, bell-shaped, colored red, pink, yellow or white. Popular as pot plants for the window sill. For culture see CACTI AND SUCCULENTS.

blossfeldiana 1½″ Zone 10 Blossfeld Mammillaria
A globose cactus, 1½ in. in dia., with about 20 straight radials about ¼ in. long, carmine, native to lower Calif.

bocasana 1½″ Zone 9 Puff Cactus
Moundlike, covered with snow-white silky hairs, and fishhook spines. Flowers white, sometimes referred to as a bursting cotton-boll.

camptotricha 2″ Zone 9 Bird's Nest Cactus
Mounded with yellow bristlelike often twisted spines; flowers white, greenish outside.

carnea 3½″ Zone 9 Blood Mammillaria
Four-angled tubercles tipped with stiff spines, flowers salmon pink.

compressa 6″ Zone 9
Small globe cactus, pale bluish green, long white flowers ½ in. long. This grows in clumps. Native to Mexico.

elongata 4″ Zone 9 Golden Lace Cactus
Plant grows in more or less tubular clumps with many interlacing yellow spines; flowers white.

fragilis 1½″ Zone 10 Thimble Cactus
A little, rather oblong stem, branching near the top, about the size and shape of a thimble;

bright green and the knobs with white radial spines; flowers cream colored, pinkish outside.

hahniana 4″ Zone 9 Old Lady Cactus, Granny Mammillaria
A popular, attractive cactus making a small‧ green globe covered with white, curly, hairlike bristles and red-tipped spines. Flowers violet-red.

kewensis 1½″ Zone 9 Kew Mammillaria
A globe or cylinder to 1½ in. in dia., tubercules woolly, spines short, radial and flowers reddish purple, about ½ in. long.

microhelia 6″ Zone 9
A short cylindrical plant, with short tubercles tipped with stiff white to yellow spines, with 1–2 blackish-red spines toward the apex; flowers small, silky, canary-yellow to whitish.

prolifera 4″ Zone 9
Growing in colonies with the individuals globose and about 2 in. in dia., the tubercles are bristly and woolly and the flowers yellowish white. Fruit coral red. Native to Tex., and Mexico.

rhodantha 10″ Zone 10
Globose, cylindrical cactus; dull green with round tubercles, radials white and central spines reddish brown and 15–20 in a cluster. Flowers are rose colored. Native to Mexico.

viviparia = *Coryphantha vivipara*

wildii 2½″ Zone 9 Wilds Mammillaria
Cylindric in habit with columns up to 2½ in. thick, green tubercles covered with white bristlelike hairs with honey-colored central spines; flowers white.

MAMONCILLO = *Melicoccus bijugatus*

MANDEVILLA (man-dev-ILL-a)
laxa (*suaveolens*) **twining vine 15′–20′ Zone 9 Chilean-jasmine**
The common name of this vine is a misnomer for it is actually native to Argentina. It is not a dense vine, but grows loosely and openly, with narrow heart-shaped leaves and funnel-like, fragrant, white to pinkish flowers 2 in. across blooming from June to Aug., making a picturesque subject for winding about a pillar.

MANDRAGORA (man-drag-O-ra)
officinarum 1′ Zone 7(?) Mandrake
A stemless perennial with tuberous roots, leaves a foot long and greenish-yellow flowers about an inch long. Native to southern Europe. The fruit is a juicy berry, supposedly poisonous. Not an ornamental. Propagated by seed or division.

MANDRAKE = *Mandragora officinarum*

MANETTIA (man-ET-tia)
inflata (*bicolor*) **twining Zone 10**
An evergreen twining herb with opposite, lanceolate, glabrous leaves; red and yellow flowers, ¾ in. long, in March. Native to Brazil. Sometimes used on trellises in the South, or in the greenhouse. Propagated by cuttings of softwood.

MANFREDA (man-FREE-da)
virginica 6′ Zone 6
Sometimes termed *Agave virginica*, these are closely related to Agave, belonging to the Amaryllis Family, with bulbous roots, fleshy leaves 2 ft. long and 2¼ in. wide. The fragrant flowers borne in terminal spikes are greenish yellow, about 2 in. long, and bloom at night. See AGAVE for culture.

MANGEL = *Beta vulgaris*

MANGIFERA (man-JIFF-er-a)
indica 90′ Zone 10 Common Mango
A delicious and popular tropical fruit is produced by this evergreen tree, native to the East Indies but now widely grown throughout the Tropics. New foliage is first reddish, then a dark green and when crushed it smells something like turpentine. Large yellow flowers, appearing in Fla. from Dec. to April are followed by red and yellow fruits which weigh 4–5 lbs. and the flesh tastes something like that of a sweet peach. Each fruit contains a single seed.

Insect Pests

The beetle of the blossom anomala strips the flowers and new shoots from the blossom spikes. It resembles a "Junebug" and feeds only during the evening. Spraying with insecticide #9 usually combined with fungicide #G or #Y when the beetles are active gives control. Red Spider is very destructive in Fla. from Nov. to March and may complete a generation each 2 weeks. Spraying with insecticide #45 or #34 or #36 is effective. Red-banded thrips causes spotted leaves which may shrivel and fall. Having 10 or 12 generations annually they are destructive throughout the year. Spraying with insecticide #15 in a regular schedule is advised. Many scale insects attack Mango but the mango shield scale which feeds on the underside of the leaves and secretes copious honeydew followed by sooty mold is one of the most destructive. Spraying during winter with insecticide #45 and in early March when crawlers are present with insecticide #15 is recommended to control this pest and other scale insects. Any fruit fly maggots should be promptly reported to local authorities for identification.

MANGO, COMMON = *Mangifera indica*

MANGO FAMILY = Anacardiaceae

MANGROVE, AMERICAN = *Rhizophora mangle*

MANIHOT (MAN-i-hot)
esculenta 3′–9′ Zone 10 Cassava, Tapioca-plant
Native to Brazil, this herbaceous shrub has

alternate leaves 16 in. wide, deeply cut in 3–7 lobes. The small cupped flowers, less than ½ in. long, are produced in elongated clusters. The tuberous roots which may weigh as much as 20 lbs. are poisonous when raw but are starchy, and when properly cooked, produce tapioca. Sometimes grown in southern Fla.

MANILA-GRASS. See ZOYSIA.

MANILKARA (man-il-KA-ra)
zapota (*Achras zapota*)   **70′ Zone 10 Chewing Gum Tree**
An evergreen tree from Central America valued for its durable wood and a latex from which chewing gum is made. Stiff, glossy green leaves up to 16 in. long, small pinkish-white flowers ½ in. wide, upright slender habit, and light brown fruits are all characteristics. The latex or chicle is obtained by tapping the tree every 2–3 years and each tree can yield about 60 quarts of this material. A syn. is *Sapota achras*.

MANURE, LIQUID. Years ago when manure was the most popular of fertilizers for use in the greenhouse, a burlap bag was filled with cow manure and hung in a barrel of water at the end of the greenhouse. The resulting liquid was an excellent fertilizer but with modern chemical fertilizers this material is not now much used.

MANURES. These are the fertilizers which have been widely used in the past especially before the advent of inorganic fertilizers which were begun to be manufactured synthetically at the turn of the century. Most contain the 3 necessary elements, nitrogen, phosphorus and potash, and consist of animal excreta plus some kind of vegetable matter like hay, straw, sugar cane, peat moss or whatever has been used in the stalls as bedding materials.

Cow manure contains about 0.6% nitrogen, 0.15% phosphoric acid, 0.45% potash, and 83% water. It should always be covered when stored to prevent the leaching of its nutrients. A hundred lbs. of rotted cow manure can be applied to 8–12 sq. yards of garden space. Pig manure is somewhat the same.

Horse manure contains approximately 0.7% nitrogen, 0.25% phosphoric acid, 0.55% potash and 62% water. One hundred pounds of this can be used on 10–15 sq. yards of garden land.

Poultry manure averages 1.8% nitrogen, 0.8 phosphoric acid. 0.4% potash and 55% water. It is more concentrated than the others, seldom having as high a proportion of vegetable matter mixed with it, and might be used at the rate of 100 lbs. to 25–40 sq. yards of space. Dried and pulverized, it is used at the rate of 100 lbs. per 50–70 sq. yards of garden.

Several of these manures are available in shredded, dried and pulverized forms and as such are easy to apply to the garden. Also see SOILS.

MANZANITA = *Arctostaphylos manzanita*

MAPLE. See ACER.

MAPLE FAMILY = Aceraceae

MAPLE SUGAR. See ACER SACCHARUM.

MARANTA (mar-ANT-a). Tropical American foliage plants, very similar to *Calathea* species, grown for their foliage or, in the case of *M. arundinacea*, for its starchy root providing the Arrow-root of commerce. Flowers, rarely produced in cultivation, are in racemes. Cultivation is the same for *Caltha*.
arundinacea   **6′ Zone 10 Bermuda Arrow-root**
The leaves are 1 ft. long and 4 in. wide with wavy margins and white flowers. Most popular is the var. **variegata** which has yellow or white marked leaves. Naturalized in Fla.
bicolor   **15″ Zone 10**
Growing from tubers, this bears leaves 6 in. long and 4 in. wide, with wavy margins, spotted with brown and with a light central stripe; light purple underneath; flowers white spotted and striped with purple. Native to Brazil.
leuconeura   **1′ Zone 10 Banded Arrow-root, Prayer Plant**
Leaves 7 in. long and 3½ in. wide, light green above but spotted along the midrib and towards the margins, purple underneath; flowers white striped purple. Native to Brazil. The popular var. **kerchoveana** has leaves that are spotted red underneath; **massangeana** has smaller leaves colored a rich purple underneath.

MARANTACEAE = The Arrowroot Family

MARGUERITE, BLUE = *Felicia amelloides*

MARGUERITE, GOLDEN = *Anthemis tinctoria*

MARIGOLD. See TAGETES.

MARIJUANA = *Cannabis sativa*

MARINE-IVY = *Cissus incisa*

MARIPOSA-LILY. See CALOCHORTUS.

MARJORAM, SWEET = *Origanum majorana*

MARJORAM, WILD = *Origanum vulgare*

MARRUBIUM (ma-ROO-bium)
vulgare   **3′ Zone 3 Horehound, Hoarhound**
An aromatic perennial herb, often a weed across North America but introduced from Europe, with opposite leaves 2 in. long, both leaves and stems being white woolly. The small whitish flowers are in crowded axillary clusters or whorls and appear from June to Aug. It is the leaves and stems of this plant that are used in cough medicines or for flavoring candy. The slightly hooked teeth of the calyx cause the fruit head to catch in the wool of sheep, thus enabling the plant to be distributed. **M. candidissimum** is somewhat similar.

MARSHMALLOW = *Althaea officinalis*

MARSH-MARIGOLD. See CALTHA.

MARSILEA (mar-SIL-ee-a)

drummondii aquatic Zone 10 Water-clover
An Australian, perennial, aquatic herb with a
creeping rhizome and 4-parted cloverlike leaves
3 in. in dia. These fanlike leaflets are covered
with whitish hairs, have wavy margins and are
borne on long slender petioles. Propagated by
division and spores.

quadrifolia aquatic Zone 5 Pepperwort
This aquatic from Europe and Asia has become
naturalized in the U.S. and is becoming a pest,
clogging ponds in which it grows. It has long
runners, 4-parted leaves on long petioles, which
float on the water surface. Propagated by
division and spores. It differs from the above
species in that the leaflets do not have hairs and
they are not notched.

MASKFLOWER. See ALONSOA.

MASTERWORT = *Astrantia major*

MATILIJA-POPPY = *Romneya coulteri*

MATRICARIA (mat-ri-KAY-ria). About 35
species of annual, biennial or perennial herbaceous plants native in Europe, Asia, Africa and
North America. The leaves are finely indented,
often strong-scented and the flowers usually
yellow and white. Mostly used in the herb
garden.

matricarioides 1' Zone 4 Pineapple weed
Not ornamental, but a common weed along the
western coast from Alaska to Mexico.

recutita 2' annual German Camomile
Native to Europe and northern Asia, escaped
in the eastern U.S. The daisylike white flowers
are an inch across and the leaves are 2–3 times
pinnate, very finely cut.

tchihatchewii = *Tripleurospermum tchihatchewii*

MATRIMONY-VINE, COMMON = *Lycium
halimifolium*

MATTEUCCIA (mat-UCC-cia)

**struthiopteris pensylvanica 5'–10' Zone 2
Ostrich Fern**
Native to central and northern North America,
especially in marshy areas, and growing from
Newfoundland to Alaska, south to Va. This has
been noted as being the largest fern native to
temperate North America, with fronds that
sometimes may reach 10 ft. in optimum conditions. Propagated by spores and division. See
FERNS. Sometimes termed *Peretis struthiopteris*.
It is not an ornamental fern for the garden.

MATTHIOLA (mat-i-O-la)

bicornis = *M. longipetala*

**incana 2½' annual, biennial or perennial
Common Stock**
An old-fashioned garden plant from southeastern Europe but now naturalized in southern
Calif. The leaves are oblong, abput 4 in. long,
and the flowers are on rigidly upright spikes in
terminal racemes, each flower about an inch
long, colored white, red, rose, blush, purple or
yellow in single- or double-flowered racemes.
The florists have a strain called **'Ten Weeks'**
which comes into bloom 10 weeks after seeding.
There is also a **'Dwarf Ten Weeks'** only growing
12–18 in. high which has much merit. They may
be obtained in named varieties (of single colors)
or mixed, with single or double flowers.

Seeds of *M. incana* should be planted indoors
in early March and then planted in the garden
15 in. apart after all danger of frost is past. The
old-fashioned biennial stocks known as 'Brompton' Stocks can be planted in a frame in mild
climates during late Aug. and carried over there
and then planted out in the garden the next
spring. Stocks are among the best of colorful,
fragrant garden annuals and are also very good
as cut flowers.

Insect Pests

Cabbage aphid and cabbage worms may
infect Stock. See CABBAGE.

Diseases

Stock seedlings are very susceptible to
damping-off. See DAMPING-OFF. Root rot causes
stem infection which girdles the stalk and kills
feeding roots. Soil sterilization is suggested.
Bacterial blight on half-grown plants indicated
by yellow leaves and blackened pith is seed
borne. Plant treated seed.

longipetala (*M. bicornis*) **1' annual Evening
Stock**
A very fragrant plant with flowers open during
the evening and closed during the day. The
flowers are lilac or purple, about ¾ in. long, in
terminal racemes that are none too conspicuous.
Narrow leaves about 3½ in. long. Native to
southeastern Europe and Asia. The seeds of this
can be sown out-of-doors in mid-April where
they are to grow. It is used for edging, especially
in gardens where night bloom is featured.

MAXILLARIA (max-ill-AY-ria)
This genus contains about 250 species of
epiphytic pseudobulbous orchids, mostly native
to Mexico and South America. Many of the
species have little horticultural value, but a
few are grown by orchid specialists merely
because of the large number of flowers produced. For culture see ORCHID.

MAYAPPLE = *Podophyllum peltatum*

MAYFLOWER = *Epigaea repens*

MAYFLOWER, CANADA = *Maianthemum
canadense*

MAYTEN-TREE, CHILE = *Maytenus boaria*

MAYTENUS (may-TEE-nus)

boaria   35′   Zone 9   Chile Mayten-tree
A pendulous-branched evergreen tree, native to
Chile, which is used as a specimen or as a
street tree in southern Calif. and Fla. and also
in seashore plantings. The leaves are leathery,
evergreen, alternate and about 1¼ in. long.

MAZUS (MAY-zus)

pumilio   creeping   Zone 7
A creeping perennial with underground stems,
leaves obovate about 3 in. long, white or
bluish flowers with a yellow center about ⅓ in.
long blooming in June and July. Sometimes
used as a ground cover or in the rockery but
rarely found produced commercially. Easily
propagated by division. Native to Australia
and New Zealand.

reptans   1″   Zone 3   Mazus
A perfect perennial ground cover where it can
be grown; it can be walked on occasionally and
will compete successfully with grass, for it roots
all along the procumbent stems. The leaves are
flat on the ground, about 1 in. long and remain
effective well into Dec. The purplish-blue
flowers are ¾ in. long, the lower lip is spotted
white, yellow and purple in May. Probably
native to the Himalayas.

MEADOW-BEAUTY. See RHEXIA.

MEADOW-BEAUTY FAMILY   = Melasto-
maceae

MEADOW-FOAM = *Limnathes douglasii*

MEADOW-RUE. See THALICTRUM.

MEADOWSWEET. See FILIPENDULA, *Spiraea
latifolia.*

MEALYBUG. A group of scale insects which
have white filamentlike hairs which suggest the
name. Unlike most other scale insects they can
move about throughout their life, although they
often stay in colonies or small groups. They

Mealybugs on Coleus (left) and a greatly
enlarged insect.

infest both outdoor and greenhouse plants.
Taxus mealybug is a well known pest of Yew.
Sprays of malathion are very effective. See
INSECT PESTS.

MEASURES. See WEIGHTS AND MEASURES.

MECONOPSIS (mek-on-OP-sis). These are
poppylike biennials or short-lived perennials
belonging to the Poppy Family and are all
chiefly native to the Himalayan Region (except
one species *M. cambrica* which is native to
western Europe). They are difficult to raise in
most parts of America, chiefly because of our
hot summers, but they are outstanding in
English, Scotch and Irish gardens. They can be
grown in the Pacific Northwest but none give
good results in the eastern U.S. *M. cambrica* has
been tried at the New York Botanical Garden
with only fair results.

Seeds should be sown in the autumn, potted
and kept in a shaded spot and in a shaded cold
frame or greenhouse over winter.

betonicifolia   6′   Zones 6–7   Blue-poppy
With ovate to oblong leaves, 6 in. long, often
almost lobed, whitish beneath; flowers rich
sky blue, about 2 in. wide, sometimes almost a
rose-lavender. It is native to China. This is the
one so popular and so well grown in Great
Britain. It always makes a great impression on
American tourists for it is practically unknown
in most parts of the U.S.

cambrica   1½′   Zone 6   Welsh-poppy
With pinnate leaves 6 in. long, whitish beneath;
pale yellow flowers 3 in. wide and singly borne.
Native to western Europe. The double-flowered
form 'Flore-pleno' is sometimes seen.

superba   3½′   Zones 6–7 (?)
With large oblanceolate leaves sometimes 16 in.
long but the basal leaves are only about 2 in.
long. Flowers are white, 5½ in. wide, and singly
borne in the axils of the upper leaves. Native to
Tibet. For planting in the light shade of the
woods.

MEDEOLA (med-e-O-la)

**virginica   1′–2′   Zone 3   Indian Cucumber-
root**
An unusual perennial of the Lily Family, the
stem bears 2 widely separated whorls of leaves,
3–5 in. long, the upper whorl surrounding the
terminal cluster of greenish flowers having 6
brown stamens and a spreading, 3-parted style.
The fruits are deep purple berries. The plant
may be found in moist woods from Quebec
along the Atlantic coastal states to Fla., and
extends west to the Mississippi River. It blooms
in May and June. An interesting plant for the
shaded wild garden, it may be propagated by
seed gathered and sown in Sept. The root is said
to have been eaten by the Indians.

MEDICAGO (med-ik-AY-go)

lupulina   prostrate   annual   Black Medic
A clover relative, sometimes mistaken for clover because of its trifoliate leaves, this is a weed widely spread throughout North America but native to Europe and Asia. The alternate leaves are trifoliate with wedge-shaped leaflets. The yellow flowers are borne in small heads or clusters, each head on a long stalk from a leaf axil, blooming in May or June. The fruits are clustered black seed pods. Only for growing on poor, sterile soils.

sativa   3′   Zone 5   Alfalfa
A cloverlike perennial widely planted for cattle forage, with purplish pealike flowers borne in short, axially racemes and small, twisted, pealike pods. Native to Europe, Propagated by seed preferably on slightly alkaline soil.

MEDIC, BLACK = *Medicago lupulina*

MEDICINAL PLANTS. Many plants, from all parts of the world, supply ingredients for medicines. The herbs (which see) are among the more common of medicinal plants used for many centuries. For a detailed discussion of the role plants have in the preparation of medicines, see Youngken, Heber W. "A Text Book of Pharmacognosy," P. Blakiston's Son and Co. Inc., Phila., Pa. 1936.

MEDINILLA (MED-in-illa)

magnifica   3′   Zone 10
An evergreen with opposite, broad, shining leaves 8–10 in. long, 4-winged branches; rosy-pink flowers in terminal, pendulous panicles often a foot long. This has been termed "one of the most beautiful tropical flowers grown," with the flowers remaining in good condition for a long time in May. Native to the Philippines. These are greenhouse plants in the North needing a moist atmosphere and high temperatures. They may be kept in the same pots for many years but should be fed liberally, and the soil might be removed and replaced periodically. Propagation is by cuttings of half ripe wood in the spring.

MEDLAR = *Mespilus germanica*

MEDUSA'S-HEAD = *Euphorbia caput-medusae*

MEIOSIS. Reduction division; the process (in cell division) wherein the chromosomes are reduced (by one-half) in number.

MELALEUCA (mel-a-LEW-ka)

leucadendron   40′   Zone 10   Cajeput-tree
The pale green, evergreen leaves of this Australian tree are 2–4 in. long and ½–¾ in. wide. The creamy-white flowers are borne in terminal spikes 6 in. long from June to Oct. It is fast-growing, resistant to grass fires as well as to salt-water spray. The flowers look something like a bottle brush because of their long stamens.

In places where the soil is moist it may reseed itself vigorously and actually become a pest.

MELANTHIUM (me-ANTH-ium)

virginicum   3′–5′   Zone 5   Bunchflower
A perennial of the southern swamplands, but also found from New England to Fla. and Minn., it has an erect stem with long, narrow leaves and many greenish flowers in a much-branched panicle held above the leaves. The leaves are linear, about a foot long. The flowers appear in June and July. It is a plant only for the strongly acid bog garden and may be propagated by seed sown in the fall.

MELASTOMATACEAE = The Meadow-beauty Family

MELIA (MEE-lia)

azedarach   45′   Zone 7   Chinaberry
In the South there is nothing quite as familiar to travellers passing through as the Chinaberry, with its 6–8 in.-long clusters of fragrant lilac-colored flowers in April and May, its densely-branched round head and in the fall its yellow berries that are ½ in. across. The leaves are alternate and compound, about 10–32 in. long. It is native to the Himalayas, grows rapidly from seed and blooms early in life. The birds like the fruits very much. Where it can be used it is always dependable for giving shade but it is rather short lived. The variety **umbraculiformis**, Umbrella Chinaberry, has branches that are more or less upright but the tree has a flattened head. Children and animals, poultry and pigs have been reported poisoned from eating the fruits.

MELIACEAE = The Mahogany Family

MELIANTHUS (mel-i-ANTH-us)

major   10′   Zone 10   Large Honey-bush
A South African evergreen shrub, often used in the gardens of southern Calif., with alternate, pinnate leaves often a foot long and having 9–11 leaflets. The winged leaf petiole and the stipules are joined into one piece 2 in. long. The red-brown flowers an inch long are borne in foot-long racemes. Fruit is an inflated capsule. A popular plant in southern Calif.

MELICOCCUS (mel-i-KOK-us)

bijugatus   60′   Zone 9   Mamoncillo, Spanish-lime
The fragrant flowers of this tree from the American Tropics are inconspicuous, greenish white and borne in terminal panicles about 4 in. long. Fruits are rounded, thick and green, about an inch in dia., and contain 1 large seed surrounded by a juicy, rather acid but tasty white pulp. Propagated by seeds.

MELILOT = *Melilotus alba*

MELILOTUS (mel-i-LO-tus). The Sweet Clover is a group of European plants, biennial, belonging to the Pea Family and having no garden interest except as forage, for bee plants or as green manure. They have compound leaves with 3 rounded leaflets and tiny, sweet-smelling pealike flowers.

alba   3′–10′   **Zone 3**   **White Sweet-clover, Melilot**

A biennial, naturalized in North America where it is a weed and a forage crop, but native to Europe and Asia. The leaves are alternate and trifoliate like those of clover. The white flowers are borne in small spikes as much as 5 in. long. It also is sought out by bees for the nectar in the flowers. Not to be confused with *Trifolium repens*, the matted White Clover in lawns.

indica   3′   **annual or perennial**   **Yellow Sweet-clover**

A weedy herb of the Pea Family, sometimes used as a cover crop on the Pacific Coast. Flowers yellow in spikelike clusters, leaflets 3 and wedge-shaped, $\frac{1}{2}$–$1\frac{1}{4}$ in. long, good for attracting bees, forage and as a cover crop, but when planted for the first time it might be best to inoculate the soil with some from where it was previously grown to be certain the right bacteria are present in the soil for this special crop. Propagated by seeds. Native to Europe and Asia, naturalized in North America.

officinalis   8′   **annual**   **Yellow Sweet-clover**

Sometimes a biennial weed, widespread across the U.S. and southern Canada but native to Europe and Asia. Similar in most respects to *M. alba.*, but stems less erect and flowers yellow.

MELISSA (mel-ISS-a)

officinalis   2′   **Zone 4**   **Lemon-balm**

A popular lemon-scented herb, native to Europe and Asia, now naturalized in eastern North America. Belonging to the Mint Family, the leaves are opposite and toothed, about 1–3 in. long; the stems are square; the white flowers are small and borne in tight clusters in the leaf axils. Propagated easily from seed, which it self-sows profusely, and which remains viable 3–4 years. Also propagated by division and by cuttings taken either in the spring or fall. The leaves are used in teas, soups and cooking. It is also used in toilet water and soaps. The variety **variegata** has leaves variegated with yellow in the spring, but these turn green during the heat of the summer.

MELON. The term as commonly used includes the fruit of 2 distinct genera of the family *Cucurbitaceae. Cucumis melo*, the Muskmelon, Honey Dew, Casaba and related varieties; and *Citrullus vulgaris*, the Watermelon and Citron. See WATERMELON.

Cucumis melo. A warm, temperate annual with trailing, soft, hairy vines. The fruit varies greatly in many of the cultivated forms or botanical varieties. Native to Persia and Central Asia. Var. **reticulatus**; netted melons with fruit having a netted skin, shallow sutures and ribs, and flesh varying from light green to reddish orange, with a musky odor. Var. **cantalupensis**, European Cantaloupe. Fruits have hard rinds; are rough, warty and scaly. Not grown in North America, but many varieties of what are universally but incorrectly called cantelopes are grown here, and conforming to this usage they will hereafter be called cantaloupes. Var. **inodorus**: Winter melons. Fruits lack musky odor, ripen late, keep well; skin smooth, corrugated ridged; flesh white, light green or orange. Var. **flexuosus**: Snake Melon, long, slender, crooked, non-netted fruits. Inedible. Var. **chito**: Mango Melon, orange to purplish pink, wine peach. Fruits are the size and shape of an orange, yellow or greenish; flesh white, not fragrant, cucumberlike. Used in preserves and pickles. Var. **dudaim**: Pomegranate Melon. Fruit small, round, very fragrant, inedible. Used for ornamental purposes.

The history of the Melon dates back many centuries. In the U.S. this vegetable was of limited importance until very late in the 19th century. It now ranks as one of the major crops with Calif., Ariz., Tex., Colo., Ga., N. & S.Car., Mich. and Ind. as the most important states in its commercial production.

All netted melons are listed as either muskmelons or cantaloupes (which as noted above in classification is a misnomer). In general muskmelons include the larger-fruited sorts that have thin rinds, ripen rapidly at maturity and are not adapted to shipping. Cantaloupes include the smaller-fruited varieties with tough, hard rinds, ripen slowly and are adapted to shipping.

Varieties

Seed companies list many varieties and strains of muskmelons, cantaloupes and winter melons which vary in days to maturity, color of flesh, resistance to disease and climatic adaptability. It is therefore only possible to list a few of the more common and popular varieties; cantaloupe—'**Gold Star**', '**Delicious**', '**Burpee Hybrid**' and '**Classic**'; muskmelons—'**Iroquois**', '**Supreme Delight**', '**Superstar**' and '**Hearts of Gold**'; winter melons—'**Honey Dew**' types, '**Casaba**', '**Crenshaw**', and '**Persian**'.

The home gardener should check several seed catalogues for descriptions and information of varieties adapted to a given region.

Melons thrive best and develop the highest quality in a hot dry climate. The plants are very sensitive to low temperatures, and in humid regions foliage diseases are especially serious.

Culture

Melons thrive best in a sandy loam soil that is well drained and is not too acid or tests a pH of 6.2–6.8. Thorough soil preparation prior to planting is important. Fertilizer requirements are similar to those for cucumbers. See CU-CUMBERS. Well-rotted manure or compost is beneficial as a source of plant food and to improve the water-holding capacity of the soil. The application can be broadcast or, if only a limited supply is available, a good forkful can be placed under each hill. A complete fertilizer 5–10–10 should be broadcast prior to planting followed by several top dressings of nitrate of soda after the plants start to grow rapidly.

Muskmelon seed will not germinate in cold wet soil. In the warmer regions, south and southwest, planting out-of-doors is practical. In northern regions the home gardener probably should start the plants in hotbeds or greenhouses. The seeds are planted in 3–4 in. plant bands, pots or berry baskets, approximately 4–5 weeks prior to the time for outdoor planting. In resetting these plants in the open it is very important that the soil is not disturbed around the roots. If the soil warms up early, time may be gained in planting the seed out-of-doors by covering each hill with a plant protector such as the hot kaps until the danger of frost has past. In the use of plant protectors care must be taken to prevent plant damage during hot days. After the plants are well started the hot kap should be slit on one side to provide ventilation and then, as soon as all danger of frost is past and the plants begin to grow the protectors should be removed.

Planting in hills is preferred in the home garden with a spacing of 4 ft. × 4 ft. between hills. Cultivation should be shallow and sufficient to control weeds.

Harvesting

Quality of melons depends on texture, flavor and sweetness. This condition is only attained if the fruit is left on the vine until fully mature. With cantaloupes and muskmelons, as ripening advances a crack develops around the peduncle at the base of the fruit and when fully ripe the fruit slips easily from the stem. This is known as the "full slip" condition. During ripening the flesh softens, sugars increase and starch decreases up to the time of the "full slip" condition, after which the reaction is more or less reversed resulting in a soft, musky, flat flavor.

Melons grown for shipment are harvested before fully mature and if placed under refrigeration, 50° F. Cantaloupe will remain in good condition for 1–2 weeks, honey dew 3–4 weeks and casabas and persian for 4–8 weeks.

GRANT B. SNYDER

Insect Pests

Green melon worms with two white stripes and green pickle worms with rows of black spots are injurious to melons in the South. Use sprays or dusts of insecticide #15 or #13. For other insect and disease pests see CUCUMBER.

MEMBRANACEOUS. Thin and soft in texture.

MENDELIAN LAW. The father of modern

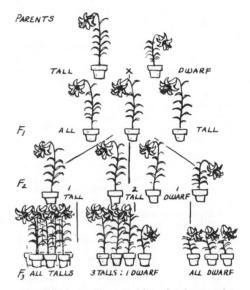

Mendel's Law: Illustrated here by the crossing of a tall and short lily. F_1 shows what may normally be expected in the first generation of seedlings; F_2 and F_3 show what happens—with crossing—in succeeding generations.

genetics is considered to have been Gregor Mendel (1822–1884) who did some experiments in crossing peas in Czechoslovakia, published in 1866. This was apparently the first time these facts in heredity and variation had been published. He considered characters to go in pairs, that is, tall vs. short or dwarf (in the peas he used). If he crossed a tall variety (which bred true) with a short variety (which bred true) the first-generation seedlings would be all tall pea plants; this character was considered dominant, and in succeeding generations when the dwarf character appeared, and it had been contained in the seedlings of the first generation but was not evident, this character was termed recessive. Also he noted that the pollen parents could be reversed and he would still get the same results

—see diagram indicating results with lilies. As an example, a tall and short lily are crossed. In the first generation of seedlings (F_1) all are tall, hence this is the dominant character. If these in turn are crossed, the next generation (F_2) yields one tall group that will breed true (all talls in the next or F_3 generation); another tall group which when crossed will yield both tall and short lilies in the F_3 generation, and a third short group which will breed true in the F_3 generation. See drawing. The short characteristic is then recessive. The proportions in which these types appear in the succeeding generations is predictable. Many variations and complications of these principles have been discovered by others since 1866, but in the main Mendel was the first to have noted the interrelationships in hybridization.

MENISPERMUM (men-iss-PERM-um)
    canadense   twining vine   Zone 5   Moonseed
A woody vine found from Quebec to Ga., with alternate, 3–7-lobed leaves, 4–8 in. long. Fruit black, grapelike. It can easily become a pest in the garden because of its long underground runners which, even though broken off, can easily grow a new plant. It is a rampant grower which may kill to the ground during northern winters but quickly sends up new shoots the following spring. The fruits are poisonous. Seed may be sown as soon as ripe or stored dry for a year or more. Softwood cuttings, layers and division are easy ways by which it is propagated.
    dauricum   twining vine   Zone 4   Asiatic
                                                                Moonseed
Native to eastern Asia and similar to *M. canadense* but leaves and fruiting clusters are smaller.

MENISPERMACEAE = The Moonseed Family

MENTHA (MEN-tha). The mints have long been popular plants in the herb or kitchen garden. The leaves are opposite, the stems usually square, and the flowers are very small and blue or white, usually produced in a circle about the stem. They prefer a moist soil, and those that increase by underground stems or runners will do so rapidly and can become pests in good soil. A small clump of mint in the garden is nice to have for taking leaves or end shoots now and then to flavor foods or cool drinks in the summer.
    arvensis   2′   Zone 4   Field Mint
A perennial, native to North America, widely distributed, growing mostly in moist soils and having running rootstalks which make it a fast-spreading plant. Leaves opposite, oblong, 1–2 in. long, slightly pubescent, rounded at the base and aromatic when crushed, like most mints. The small flowers appearing in July and Aug. grow

in circles around the stems in the axils of the leaves. Often grown in the herb garden to spice drinks. The plants are easily divided in the spring.
    x piperita   1′–2′   Zone 3   Peppermint
A vigorous herbaceous perennial, increasing rapidly by runners and stolons, this has opposite leaves 3 in. long, with a strong pungent peppermint odor, and square stems like all mints. The flowers are usually purple in terminal spikes 1–3 ft. long, blooming in the autumn. It does well in moist soils and to be fairly neat should be cut to the ground every few years or even more often. Native to Europe.
    pulegium   prostrate   Zone 7   Pennyroyal
A popular, creeping, perennial herb, with a pungent, minty odor, native to Europe and Asia. Like most mints, the small blue flowers are borne in circles around the stems at the axils of the opposite leaves. These leaves are oval, $\frac{1}{2}$ in. long and entire. Easily propagated by seed and division. Pennyroyal is used in medicines for spasms. Like most mints, this does well in moist soils in the shade. There is a so-called American or False Pennyroyal (*Hedeoma pulegioides*) but it is not much grown.
    requienii   3″   Zone 6   Creeping Mint
The extremely small leaves of this plant are only $\frac{1}{8}$ in. long, are opposite on square stems and have a peppermintlike odor when crushed. The light purple flowers appear in loose, few-flowered whorls during July and Aug. Growing easily and fast by underground stems, this native of Corsica has been used as a very low ground cover in the full sun.
    x rotundifolia   30″   Zone 4   Apple Mint
An aromatic herb native to Europe but naturalized in parts of North America, this has rounded, hairy, sessile leaves 2 in. long and dense flower spikes up to 4 in. long, and is one of the tallest of the mints. Its variety **'Variegata'**, sometimes called Pineapple Mint, is not quite as tall but the foliage is beautifully variegated with white. Flowers of both are pinkish white.
    spicata   2′   Zone 3   Spearmint
A perennial mint, native to Europe but often naturalized in eastern North America, north central states and on the Pacific Coast. This also spreads by creeping rootstalks in moist soil. The stems are 4-angled, the opposite leaves are aromatic, nearly sessile, toothed and $2\frac{1}{2}$ in. long. The small flowers are in whorls on spikes about 4 in. long

MENTZELIA (ment-ZEE-lia)
    decapetala   4′   biennial   Petal Mentzelia
With pinnately-lobed alternate leaves and white or yellowish fragrant 10-petalled flowers, 5 in. across, but opening in the evening. Native from S.Dak. to Tex. Only of value for its evening

flowers. Sometimes called Prairie-lily. Sow seeds in late summer.

laevicaulis $3\frac{1}{2}'$ **biennial Blazing-star** With shining white stems, long, narrow, alternate leaves 2–8 in. long, yellow flowers to 4 in. across. Native from Wyo. to Calif. Sow seeds in late summer.

lindleyi 4' **annual Lindley Mentzelia** A straggling or single-stalked annual herb, leaves 2–3 in. long, and yellow 5-petalled, fragrant flowers $1\frac{1}{2}$–$2\frac{1}{2}$ in. across, opening only in the evening. Native to Calif. Sow seeds in the garden, preferably in gravelly soil in May, where they are to grow in the full sun.

MENYANTHES (men-YAN-thees)
trifoliata creeping Zone 3 Common Bogbean
A perennial herb with creeping rootstock, native of the cooler parts of the Northern Hemisphere around the world. Leaves are made up of 3 obovate entire leaflets with petioles up to 10 in. long. Flowers white, $\frac{1}{2}$ in. long, in 10–20 flowered racemes borne at the end of long flower stalks. The rootstalks have been used for grinding up into flour to make bread.

MENZIESIA (men-ZEES-ia)
pilosa 2'–6' **Zone 4 Allegany Menziesia** Although hardy in northern U.S., this deciduous shrub is most often found in the mountains from Pa. to Ga. The alternate leaves are oblong or ovate, abruptly pointed and covered with hairs and bristles. The few yellowish or pinkish drooping flowers are bell-shaped, having 4 lobes. These appear in May and June. Of limited ornamental interest, the plant is sometimes used in the rock garden. Plants may be propagated by seed, by layers, by division or by hardwood cuttings under greenhouse conditions.

MERCURY COMPOUNDS. Used as fungicides, which see.

MERREMIA (mer-REM-ia)
tuberosa (*Ipomoea tuberosa*) **vine Zone 10 Wood-rose**
This is a tropical vine, supposedly native to India but cultivated throughout the Tropics as an ornamental. The flower is yellow, like that of a Morning-glory, small and appearing in the autumn. About 3 months after the flower has dropped the fruit has developed into a brown globular ball, and the sepals have dried and hardened so that the whole fruit has somewhat the shape of a rose—the reason it has been popularly called "wood rose." These fruits are highly prized for use in dried arrangements. The leaves are palmately and deeply lobed, with 7 lobes.

MERRYBELLS. See UVULARIA.

MERTENSIA (MER-ten-sia)
longiflora 10" **Zone 3 Small Bluebells** Native to Asia and North America. Tufts of dainty blue-green leaves 2–3 in. high and flowers in clusters of long, narrow bluebells. Shortly after flowering the plant becomes dormant. It requires a moist, acid soil in sun or light shade while growing and very dry soil during dormancy.

virginica 2'–3' **Zone 3 Virginia Bluebells** A strong, stout perennial with a smooth stem having longitudinal ridges and alternate, oblong leaves adnate to the stem, or nearly so. Loose, somewhat one-sided flower clusters arise from the axils of the leaves and terminate the stem. These have flowers with a 5-pointed calyx and a drooping, trumpet-shaped corolla with a wavy or slightly 5-parted margin. The buds and newly opened flowers are pink; the older ones lavender or blue, and these appear in early summer. The plant requires rich, moist soil and may be found from N.Y. to Ala., west to the Great Plains, although it is sometimes cultivated in northern New England. It may be propagated by seed sown as soon as they are gathered.

MESCAL-BEAN = *Sophora secundiflora*

MESEMBRYANTHEMUM (mez-em-bri-ANTH-e-mum). There may be as many as 1000 species in this genus, mostly low succulent plants native to the deserts of South Africa, and some botanists have split many off into other genera, namely, *Apentia, Carpathea, Carpobrotus, Cryophytum, Dorotheanus, Faucaria, Lampranthus*. However, although some of these may be the latest "correct" names, many growers still carry them under the generic name *Mesembryanthemum*. They look like small rocks or stones and because they grow in places of extreme drought they have developed fleshy leaves for the storage of excess moisture. To say the most for them, they are greenhouse oddities, sometimes used as house pot plants, and planted out-of-doors a great deal in the drier spots of Calif., Ariz., and N.Mex. They will not withstand frosts.

criniflorum = *Dorotheanus bellidiformis*
crystallinum prostrate Zone 10 Common Iceplant
Sometimes called Sea Fig or Sea Marigold in Calif., where it is widely used as a ground cover in sandy soils by the seashore. This is the most popular of all the so-called *Mesembryanthemum* species or segregates. Prostrated stems 3–5 ft. long, with alternate flat, fleshy leaves about 6 in. long and 3 in. broad with the leaves on flowering shoots smaller; covered with glistening dots. The flowers are small and white to rose colored.

pyropeum = *Dorotheanus gramineus*

MESPILUS (MEZ-pill-us)

germanica 15′ **Zone 5** **Medlar**

Closely allied to the hawthorns, this crooked European tree is grown more in Europe than in America. Actually it has little special ornamental value. The white or slightly pink, solitary flowers are 1–1½ in. wide, in May. The leaves are 2–5 in. long and the peculiar apple-shaped fruits are 1 in. across, brownish, and at the base show the 5-celled ends of the bony seed vessels inside. When partially decayed, these are edible, having an acid taste. Older branches may have thorns.

Propagation

Seed should be stratified at room temperatures for 5 months, then for 3 months at 40° F., then sown. If after a few months the seeds fail to germinate, give them another 3 months cold treatment. It is grafted, using the species or *Pyrus communis*, *Crataegus* or *Cydonia* as understock. See GRAFTING.

MESQUITE, HONEY = *Prosopis glandulosa glandulosa*

METASEQUOIA (meta-see-KWOY-a)

glyptostroboides 100′ **Zone 5** **Dawn-redwood**

Related to the *Sequoia* and *Sequoiadendron* genera, this tree is not evergreen but is deciduous, with small needlelike leaves somewhat like those of a hemlock. It is upright and pyramidal in habit, very fast-growing, averaging several feet a year in good soil, and does best in moist soils similar to those in which the Canada Hemlock does best. One tree grew 50 feet in 15 years, from seed. It is loosely open in character certainly is not for the small garden, but on a large place or in a public park a grove of these does prove interesting.

It is of interest to note that this tree was known prior to 1944 only in Mesozoic paleobotanical records, but was found in China that year and definitely identified in 1945. Two years later a special expedition was sent by the Arnold Arboretum to China to collect seeds. This was done and seeds were received in the U.S. on Feb. 5, 1948. It is of considerable interest to note that this tree existed in a small location near the Szechuan-Hupeh border in China for over a million years, yet modern botanists thought it extinct until 1945. Paleobotanical records showed it was widely distributed in pre-mesozoic times over what is now considered to be the North Temperate Zone.

Naturally, a tree with such a history is of considerably interest for it was obviously a remarkable "discovery." Seedlings vary considerably in shape and various clones will undoubtedly be named, some of more compact habit than others. One should remember that it is a tall tree, not at all suited for the confining space in a small garden.

Propagation

Seed may be sown as soon as ripe, or it may be stored dry in airtight containers in a cool place for up to a year, then sown. Also softwood and hardwood cuttings (which see) root easily.

METHOXYCHLOR. A DDT relative used as an insecticide. See INSECTICIDES.

METROSIDEROS (met-ro-sid-EE-ros)

excelsus (*tomentosa*) 30′ **Zone 10** **New Zealand Christmas-tree**

Sometimes termed Ironwood, this tree has opposite leaves and prominent terminal flower clusters 2–4 in. long; the reddish stamens give a special beauty to the flowers during July and Aug. The dark, leathery, evergreen leaves are lustrous above and white underneath and the species is native to New Zealand. It is used in both Fla. and Calif. seaside gardens, since it is resistant to salt-water spray.

MEXICAN-ORANGE = *Choisya ternata*

MEXICAN-STAR = *Milla biflora*

MEZEREON FAMILY = Thymelaeaceae

MICHAELMAS DAISY. See ASTER.

MICHELIA FIGO. See M. FUSCATA.

Metasequoia is a large, fast-growing, deciduous tree—too large for many small properties. (*Photo by Arnold Arboretum, Jamaica Plain, Mass.*)

MICHELIA (mi-CHEL-ia)

figo (*fuscata*)   15′   Zones 7–8   Banana-shrub
Actually the name of this serviceable evergreen has recently been changed to *M. figo*, but it has long been listed as *M. fuscata* and as such will be found in the nursery catalogues. The common name is given this shrub because the flowers have a fragrance similar to that of the banana. A Chinese plant, with evergreen leaves up to 3 in. long, this has yellowish-white flowers, edged maroon, about 1½ in. across and appearing in the spring. It is a splendid evergreen for southern gardens and northern greenhouses.

MICRO-CLIMATE. A new and fancy name given to cover the various local factors of shade, exposure, moisture, etc. which are so essential in growing plants in the home garden.

MICROCOELUM (micro-CEE-lum)

weddellianum (*Syagrus weddellianum*)   7′
Zone 10   Weddell Palm
A small feather palm tree frequently used as a tub plant for indoor decoration. The leaves are gracefully arching, pinnate, and usually touch the ground, the pinnae being about 3–6 in. long and ¼ in. wide. Native to Argentina.

MICROMERIA (my-kro-MEER-ia). A member of the Mint Family, this group of aromatic trailing plants is similar to Thyme. Propagation is by seeds, cuttings or division. No special cultivation is required.

juliana   1′   Zone 7 (?)   Micromeria
This is a trailing plant with foliage having a fine pubescence, giving it a frothy, gray-green appearance. Handsome, small pink-to-purplish flowers, in terminal spikes, bloom in mid to late summer. Native to the Mediterranean Region.

piperella   6″ Zone 7 (?) Peppermint Micromeria
A trailing herbaceous perennial with small opposite leaves, and reddish-purple flowers in few-flowered clusters, sometimes used in the rock garden. Propagated by seeds, cuttings, and division. Native to southern Europe.

thymifolia (*rupestris*)   6″   Zone 7 (?)
This heathlike perennial is somewhat similar to the above species, with prostrate stems, aromatic foliage and white flowers spotted with lavender, blooming from July to fall. Easily grown and a fine plant for the rock garden. Native to southern Europe.

MIDRIB. The central vein or rib of a leaf.

MIGNONETTE, COMMON = *Reseda odorata*

MIGNONETTE FAMILY = Resedaceae

MIKANIA (my-KAY-nia)

scandens   vine   Zone 4   Climbing Hempweed
Notable as the only native genus of the Com-

posite Family that is a vine, this perennial has opposite, triangular leaves and white or pinkish flower heads in terminal and axillary cymes, with 4 small disk flowers in each calyx. The plant is native to the swamps and low thickets from New England to Fla. and Tex. and blooms in Aug. and Sept. Seeds may be sown in the spring, or young plants may be moved in the spring.

MILDEW, DOWNY. Unlike the powdery mildews, downy mildews are true parasites which live within the plant tissue. They thrive in cool wet weather and are very destructive. The usual symptoms are purple or black spots on the top of the leaf followed by a gray mold on the underside. The spores are blown by wind. Grape downy mildew spots the leaves and infects the berries. Downy mildews are destructive pests of cucurbits, lima beans and onions and may destroy the crop in wet seasons. Fungicide applications give effective control, ferbam on Grape and zineb on the vegetables.

MILFOIL = *Achillea millefolium*

MILFOIL, WATER, FAMILY = Haloragidaceae

MILKBERRY, DAVID'S = *Chiococca alba*

MILK-THISTLE, BLESSED = *Silybum marianum*

MILKWEED. See ASCLEPIAS.

MILKWEED FAMILY = Asclepiadaceae

MILKWORT. See POLYGALA.

MILKY SPORE DISEASE. The spores of *Bacillus popilliae*, a natural disease of Japanese beetle grubs and a few similar beetles are mixed with talc to produce a spore dust. These spores cause the "blood" of infected grubs to turn milky white as the name indicates. The spore dust is applied to lawn turf by placing 2 grams (1 level teaspoonful) at intervals of 3 ft. in rows 3 ft. apart. When this dust is washed into the soil the grubs eat it with roots, soil and organic matter and are killed. Each dead grub produces billions of spores which are very resistant to drought, flooding and freezing and remain in the soil for many years. Milky disease is harmless to humans, animals, birds, earthworms, plants and insects other than those closely related to the Japanese beetle. As a control treatment for Japanese beetle grubs it is slow acting, often taking 3 years to show an appreciable reduction in grubs, but once established it is practically permanent protection.

MILLA (MIL-la)

biflora   6″–18″   Zone 9   Mexican-star
A low bulbous plant bearing several terete, tubular, grasslike leaves and an erect flower

stalk with 1–6-flowered umbels of small white flowers not over an inch long and 2½ in. across. Native to Ariz., N.Mex., Mexico. Occasionally used as a pot plant.

MILLET = *Panicum miliaceum*

MILORGANITE. The trade name of a dried, processed sewage widely used as a fertilizer.

MILTONIA (milt-O-nia). A genus of about 20 species of South American epiphytic orchids closely related to the genus *Odontoglossum* (which see), suitable only for growing in the greenhouse. The flowers are large, bearing brilliant colors and the following 2 species have been used much by orchid specialists in hybridizing. They bloom chiefly in May and early summer. Not recommended for the home greenhouse for they require special greenhouse growing conditions. For culture and propagation see ORCHID.

 roezlii   1′   Zone 10
With 2–5 flowers up to 3–4 in. across, white stained purple near the base. The pseudobulbs are 2½ in. long and the narrow, lanceolate leaves are 9–12 in. long. Native to Colombia.

 vexillaria   1′   Zone 10
Closely related to the above species, this one has several varieties. The flowers are white to rose, 2½ in. across. The pseudobulbs are only 1½–2½ in. long. Native to Ecuador and Colombia.

MIMOSA (mim-O-sa) (also a popular name given certain species of *Acacia*, which see).

 pudica   18″   Zone 10   Sensitive-plant
Although this is a spiny, roadside weed in the Tropics, it is a most interesting plant in the warm conservatory where visitors are continually touching it to note its ability to fold its small leaflets along the midrib of its compound leaves. It can be treated as an annual in the North, and it will bloom with its little pink mimosalike blossoms. As a house plant and in dry atmospheres, it may fail miserably. It has escaped cultivation and become naturalized in some of the Gulf States. It is interesting to note that *Albizia julibrissin* has the trait of folding its leaves in the cool of the evening and although they will not close to the touch as does *M. pudica* they will close because of temperature or moisture differences.

MIMULUS (MIM-yew-lus)
 cupreus   8″   annual   Chilean Monkey-flower
With tubular, 2-lipped, yellow flowers, about 1½ in. long, with spreading lobes, later becoming copper colored. The ovate opposite leaves are 1¼ in. long, having 3 nerves. Native to Chile. Seed should be sown in the greenhouse in March, then planted out in a shaded situation after frost (or grown on as a greenhouse pot plant) flowering freely in June and July.

 guttatus   18″   Zone 5   Common Monkey-flower
A perennial herb bearing yellow flowers with red or brown dots on the throat, 2 lipped, 1½ in. long. Native from Alaska to Mexico, suitable for the wild garden only. Easily grown and propagated by seed or division. Can be grown as an annual also.

 luteus   1′   Zone 7 (?)   Golden Monkey-flower
A perennial with broad ovate leaves an inch long and these have 5–7 nerves. The yellow tubular flowers, 1½ in. long, are spotted with red or purple. Native to Chile. For propagation see above. Several color forms or hybrids have been offered, frequently under the incorrect name of *M. tigrinus* (*M. guttatus* x *M. luteus*).

 ringens   1′–3′   Zone 3   Allegany Monkey-flower
A plant having an erect, square stem and opposite, lanceolate, toothed and sessile leaves. The solitary, pink flowers, on a stalk 1–3 in. long, arise from the axils of the leaves. The flowers have a 5-lobed calyx and an irregular corolla with a 2-lipped margin. This handsome perennial is native to the eastern and southeastern U.S. and extends into Canada. It blooms throughout the summer. Propagation is by seed, cuttings, transplants or by division.

MINA (MEYE-na)
 lobata (*Quamoclit lobata*)   **vine   annual   Crimson Starglory**
A vigorous-climbing perennial but often treated as an annual, to 20 ft. with alternate 3-lobed leaves 3 in. wide. The flower buds are a fiery scarlet, boat-shaped and 5-angled, and when they open the color changes to creamy yellow and orange, borne in long-stalked axillary racemes. Native to Mexico. Propagated by seed.

MING TREE. A loose term which refers to a small artificial tree, made with wire and plant products, simulating a small tree dwarfed by man (bonsai). Although interesting it is not alive, and continued use of the term should be frowned upon.

MINT. See MENTHA.

MINT FAMILY = Labiatae

MIRABILIS (my-RAB-il-is)
 jalapa   2′–3′   annual   Common Four-o'clock
A perennial native of tropical America treated as an annual in the North, named because its funnel-shaped flowers, 1–2 in. long, open at about 4 o'clock in the afternoon. The tuberous roots, soft succulent stems and white, yellow or red flowers are typical. It can be treated like a Dahlia, that is, lifted in the fall just before a frost, dried and stored in a frost-free place until time to plant it out in May, when the roots can

be divided. Or, if treated as an annual, the seed can be sown directly out-of-doors in the spring in the place the plants are to grow. They do best in a light well-drained soil in a sunny situation.

longiflora 3′ annual Sweet Four-o'clock
Native to Mexico, with white, pink or violet fragrant flowers, 4–6 in. long, opening after sunset, treated as an annual in the North and perennial in the South. For culture and over wintering, see *M. jalapa*.

MISCANTHUS (mis-KAN-thus)

sinensis 10′ Zone 4 Eulalia Grass
One of the very best of perennial ornamental grasses, native to southern Asia but hardy in the northern U.S., with gracefully arching stalks and leaves 2–3 ft. long and an inch wide. Feathery, fan-shaped, highly ornamental fruit stalks up to a foot long borne late in the season. A single clump of this grass will increase in size slowly each year, and will add much interest to the garden where it is growing. A 20-year-old clump is about 4 ft. across. Easily propagated by seed or division.

The var. '**Gracillimus**', called Maiden Grass, has leaves that are more narrow and the entire plant is lower in habit; var. '**Variegatus**', the Striped Eulalia Grass, has leaves striped with white or yellow and '**Zebrinus**', the Zebra Grass, has leaves banded with yellow. These last 2 varieties are less hardy than the species and have been used as pot plants. Most are vigorous growing plants that are not suited for the small border in the home garden.

MISTLETOE, AMERICAN = *Phoradendron flavescens*

MISTLETOE, EUROPEAN = *Viscum album*

MITCHELLA (mich-ELL-a)

repens ground cover Zone 3 Partridge-berry
Widely native in the woodlands of eastern North America, this plant is frequently familiar to the city dweller as well as the woodsman because it is the plant used in filling small bowls at Christmas. Because of its opposite, rounded, small evergreen leaves with whitish veins and its brilliant scarlet berries ¼ in. in dia., this dainty little ground cover makes an apt subject for stuffing in glass bowls or planting in glass growing rings at Christmas. It does well in a moist, acid woods soil with some shade. Two pinkish-white tubular flowers are borne in the axils of the leaves in summer and these develop red berries by fall.

MITELLA (my-TELL-a)

diphylla 12″–18″ Zone 3 Common Miter-wort
This very attractive perennial has heart-shaped, irregularly toothed and stalked basal leaves and a pair of sessile leaves midway up the stem. The tiny white flowers are borne in a loose terminal cluster 6–8 in. long. Each flower has 5 finely-fringed petals. These appear in late spring in moist deciduous woods, generally in neutral soil, from New England to S.Car., west to Minn. The plant is an excellent ground cover where its native habitat can be reproduced, and it may be propagated by division in spring, by seeds sown when ripe or by softwood cuttings taken in summer. It requires acid soil with plenty of leaf mold, preferably in a shaded situation.

MITERWORT, COMMON = *Mitella diphylla*

MITES. Web-spinning spider mites, bulb mites and 4-legged gall mites are important plant pests. Most of them suck the sap from plants causing yellow or bronze foliage and weak plants. The common red spider mite feeds on a great many plants and is particularly destructive to fruit and cucurbits. In the greenhouse it is especially troublesome on roses and carnations, where heavy infestations may enclose shoots and flowers in a web. European red mite is an important pest of fruit trees and some shade trees and McDaniel mite causes similar injury in western U.S. Clover mite or brown almond mite is not only a plant pest but also becomes very annoying in buildings. The spruce mite causes yellow and brown needles on hemlock, arborvitae and other evergreens, as does the southern red mite in warmer areas. In Fla. and Calif. the citrus red mite reduces the quality of citrus fruits. Control is obtained from dormant sprays of oil and dinitro compounds and from organic phosphates or special miticides (see INSECTICIDES) according to local recommendations.

The gall mites are microscopic animals which are somewhat wormlike in appearance rather than resembling spiders. They feed by rasping or sucking and cause deformities or russet patches on the surface of fruits and foliage. Typical examples are: maple bladder gall, willow cone gall, ash bud gall, citrus rust mite, tomato russet mite and the pear leaf blister mite. Recommended control includes dormant sprays of oil and applications of organic phosphates in the growing period (see INSECTICIDES).

Cyclamen mite resembles the red spider mites but does not spin webs. It causes distortion of buds and flowers and is especially destructive to cyclamen, delphinium, *Saintpaulia* and Strawberry. Standard control is immersion in water heated to 112° F. for 15–20 minutes.

Bulb mites belong to a different group and often eat cavities in the bulbs of Narcissus, Tulip, Amaryllis and Easter Lily. They are controlled by hot water treatment. Systemic insecticides (see INSECTICIDES) have been successful in experiments.

WARREN D. WHITCOMB

MITICIDES. See INSECTICIDES.

MITOSIS. The process of nuclear duplication involved in cell division.

MIXED FLOWER. See PHYTEUMA.

MOCCASIN-FLOWER. See CYPRIPEDIUM.

MOCK-CUCUMBER, WILD = *Echinocystis lobata*

MOCKERNUT = *Carya tomentosa*

MOCK-ORANGE. See PHILADELPHUS.

MOCK-ORANGE, EVERGREEN = *Carpenteria californica*

MOCK-STRAWBERRY = *Duchesnea indica*

MOLD. Sometimes spelled mould, this refers to a downy fungus growth often appearing on decaying plant materials, especially in the presence of moisture and high temperature.

MOLTKIA (MOLT-kia)
  petraea   1½′   **Zone 6**
A semi-evergreen plant that looks something like the Lavender when not in bloom. This woody herb is native to southeastern Europe and is especially valued for its gray foliage. The flowers are pinkish purple at first, then becoming violet-blue in small terminal clusters 1–1½ in. in dia.

MOLUCCELLA (mo-lew-SEEL-a)
  laevis   2′   **annual**   **Bells-of-Ireland**
Native to western Asia, this plant is becoming increasingly popular to flower arrangers, although it has been grown in gardens for generations. The leaves are round, 1¾ in. across, the stems are often gracefully bent or twisted and small, fragrant, white flowers are borne in the leaf axils. A very much enlarged calyx is left, after the corolla has fallen, that looks very much like a little green bell from which the plant gets its name. When the stems are cut and the leaves removed, this curving stem with its numerous bells is dried and used in flower arrangements. Seeds can be sown in April where the plants are to grow, preferably in the full sun, and they usually reseed themselves for the next year if the ground is left undisturbed. Native to Asia. Sometimes called Shellflower.

MOMORDICA (mo-MORD-ik-a). Tendril-bearing vines, native to the Old World, monoecious or dioecious flowers yellow or white about an inch across and alternate simple or compound leaves. These are quick-growing vines, and seeds can be planted where the plants are to grow after all danger of frost is over. In the South sometimes they are perennial.
  balsamina   **vine**   **annual**   **Balsam-apple**
This will grow 20 ft. long in one year with shiny, toothed and lobed leaves, 1–4 in. long, yellow flowers and most interesting fruits, rounded but narrowed at both ends and 3 in. across. When fully ripe the fruit bursts open.
  charantia   **vine**   **annual**   **Balsam-pear**
This is the more ornamental of the 2 species because it is taller, growing up to 30 ft., and bears larger leaves. Flowers of the 2 species are similar. The fruit is 4–6 in. long, is more warty than *M. balsamina*, and when it splits open it shows the brilliant red arils of the seeds inside. This also is native to the Tropics of the Old World.

MONADELPHOUS. Stamens united in one group by their filaments.

MONARCH-OF-THE-EAST = *Sauromatum guttatum*

MONARDA (mo-NARD-a). A genus of the Mint Family belonging wholly to North America. They are aromatic herbs, annual or perennial, with showy, irregular flowers and often with brightly colored bracts. They are easily cultivated and may be propagated by division in spring.
  didyma   3′   **Zone 4**   **Bee-balm**
The stout, square stem of this perennial has opposite, ovate leaves, 3–6 in. long, which are downy on the under surface, and a terminal cluster of irregular scarlet flowers nearly 2 in. long surrounded with red-ringed bracts. The plant is native to eastern North America from Quebec to Tenn. and flowers from June to Aug. It is a good plant for the perennial border and is very attractive to hummingbirds. Listed as an herb, it is used in some oils and perfumes to mask the odor of ill-smelling chemicals.
  fistulosa   2′–3′   **Zone 3**   **Wild Bergamot**
Similar to *M. didyma*, the flowers of this species are lavender in color and the surrounding bracts may be whitish or purple. It may be found over the same regions as *M. didyma* and blooms during the summer months.
  media   2′–3′   **Zone 6**   **Purple Bergamot**
This species has lanceolate leaves which are nearly smooth and flowers which are reddish purple with purple bracts. It is native to the mid-Atlantic and mid-central states and flowers from July to Sept.
  punctata   3′   **Zone 6**   **Horse-mint**
Native from N.Y. to Fla. and Tex., this perennial herb has lanceolate leaves, 3 in. long, and flowers colored yellow and purple up to an inch long, in axillary or terminal clusters. This and *Thymus vulgaris* are the source of Thymol.

MONARDELLA (mo-nar-DELL-a)
  villosa   1½′   **Zone 8**
A perennial with pubescent, ovate leaves an inch long; flowers purple, pink or white about ½ in. long. Native to Calif. Propagated by division or seeds. A good plant for the rock garden.

MONESES (mo-NEE-seez)
uniflora   6″   Zone 3   One-flowered Wintergreen, Wood-nymph
The only species of this genus, it has round,
basal leaves 1 in. in dia., arising from the
prostrate stem. The fragrant, nodding, solitary
flower has 5 waxy-white spreading petals It may
be found in moist woods in Eurasia and in
North America from Labrador to Alaska, and
as far south as the mountains of N.Car. It
flowers from June to Aug. It is ideal as a plant
for the moist wild garden.

MONEYWORT = *Lysimachia nummularia*

MONKEY-FLOWER. See MIMULUS.

MONKEY-PUZZLE TREE = *Araucaria araucana*

MONKSHOOD. See ACONITUM.

MONKS HOOD VINE = *Ampelopsis aconitifolia*

MONO. In Greek compounds meaning one.

MONOCOTYLEDONS (monocots). Plants having one cotyledon or seed-lobe, as lilies and
grasses. See also DICOTYLEDONS.

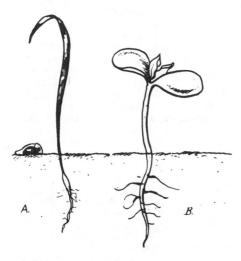

A. Monocotyledon seedling (lily)
B. Dicotyledon seedling (bean)

MONOECIOUS. With unisexual flowers, both
pistillate and staminate on the same plant. Also
see DIOECIOUS.

MONOTROPA (mon-OT-ro-pa). The members
of this genus are saprophytes or parasites and
therefore are not green in color. They are thus
often mistaken for fungi but, in fact, they are
members of the Heath Family (*Ericaceae*). They
are difficult to cultivate.

hypopithys   10″–12″   False Beech-drops
A plant with a rather thick stem and leaves
reduced to bracts, it is completely yellowish in
color, including the nodding, fragrant flowers
which are terminally borne in a few flowered
clusters. The plant grows in open, sandy woods
from southern Canada to Mexico, and flowers
throughout the summer.

odorata   1′   Zone 6   Sweet-Pinesap
A parasitic plant something similar to the
Indian-pipe; each plant with a little fragrant
flower, purplish brown with the 5 petals joined
together. Often found under pine trees from Md.
to Ky. and southward to Ga. and Ala., blooming from Feb. to May.

uniflora   6″–10″   Indian Pipe
Much like *M. hypopithys*, the Indian Pipe is
slightly smaller and completely white. It prefers
more shady, moister locations and may be
found blooming from July to Aug. in the woods
over most of North America.

MONSTERA (mon-STEER-a)
deliciosa   climbing   Zone 10   Ceriman
Sometimes popularly termed Mexican Breadfruit, this is usually no more than about 2 ft.
high as a pot plant in the house but in its native
habitat it is a tall, straggling climber with
pendant roots; leaves 2–3 ft. long, pinnately cut
with oblong and open spaces in the blade. The
spathe is white, about a foot long. The large
fruit is eaten in the Tropics. Native to Mexico
and Central America. Easily propagated by
cuttings of the stems planted in soil or sand but
kept in a moist atmosphere. An easy plant to
grow and it can withstand dim light.

MONTANOA (mon-tan-O-a)
bipinnatifida   8′   Zone 10
A tropical shrub belonging to the Composite
Family, with opposite hairy leaves deeply
pinnatifid. The small flower heads are 3 in. wide
with the ray flowers white. Native to Mexico.
Propagated by seeds and cuttings.

hibiscifolia   20′   Zone 9   Christmas-daisy,
Christmas-cosmos
Blooming for 3 weeks at Christmas time, this
very interesting shrub is used in many gardens
about Honolulu. It is native to Guatemala. The
flowers are like small daisies, 1½ in. across, with
light-ray florets, the petal white. The leaves are
of 2 types, one large and deeply 5-lobed about
12 in. across, the other small and simple.

MONTBRETIA = *Crocosmia* x *crocosmaeflora*

MONTIA (MON-tia)
perfoliata   1′   annual   Winter-purslane
An opposite-leaved herb, belonging to the
Portulaca Family. The lower leaves are 1–3 in.
long, other leaves are smaller and fleshy. The
small flowers are white, the clusters on stalks a
foot high. The fruits are 3-seeded pods. It has

been used as a salad herb. Native to western North America. Propagated by seed sown where the plants are to grow.

MOONFLOWER, LARGE = *Calonyction aculeatum*

MOONSEED. See MENISPERMUM.

MOONSEED FAMILY = Menospermaceae

MOOSEWOOD = *Acer pensylvanicum*

MORACEAE = The Mulberry or Fig Family

MORAEA (mor-EE-a) (Morea). African herbs growing from corms or short rootstocks with flowers similar to those of Iris but in clusters. They belong to the Iris Family. Hardy out-of-doors only in the far South, otherwise culture is similar to that for Iris. If grown in the greenhouse give them the same care and growing conditions as Freesia. Their flowers last only 1 day but out-of-doors they have an extended blooming period.

'Oakhurst Hybrid'—cream-white flowers, this grows to 4 ft. tall.

polystachya   3′   **Zone 9**
Flowers white with a yellow spot, 1½ in. long, blooming for 6 weeks, native to South Africa.

ramosissima   3′   **Zone 9**
Flowers bright yellow, 1¼ in. long.

spathulata   4′   **Zone 9**
Flowers bright yellow, 2 in. long. Native to South Africa.

MORAINE. A pile of boulders, rocks and other debris carried by a glacier.

MORAINE LOCUST = *Gleditsia triacanthos inermis* 'Moraine'

MORETON BAY CHESTNUT = *Castanospermum australe*

MORETON BAY FIG = *Ficus macrophylla*

MORINA (mo-RY-na)
longifolia   4′   **Zone 5**   **Whorlflower**
A hardy herbaceous perennial of the Teasel Family valued for its white to pink to crimson delicate flowers that are produced in whorls. Sometimes all 3 colors are found on flowers in the same whorl. The thistlelike leaves are 6 in. long and an inch wide and the flowers are borne in the summer. Propagation is by division as soon as the flowers have faded. Native to the Himalayas.

MORINDA. A group of about 80 species of tropical trees, shrubs and a few vines, with white flowers, used only in Zone 10, not elsewhere.

MORINGA (mo-RING-ga)
oleifera = *M. pterygosperma*
pterygosperma   25′   **Zone 10**   **Horse-radish Tree**
With drooping branches, thrice-compound feathery leaves as much as 2 ft. long. The white, fragrant flowers are an inch wide, borne in loose clusters in the leaf axils. The fruit is edible when young, like a string bean, but later matures to a dry, 3-sided light brown pod, 18 in. long, containing dark brown, pea-sized winged seeds. The flowers (and fruits) are borne continuously. The root tastes like horse-radish and the seeds yield bean oil. The flowers and foliage are edible as "greens". Sometimes planted in southern Fla.

MORNING-GLORY. See IPOMOEA

MORNING-GLORY FAMILY = Convolvulaceae

MORNING-GLORY, GROUND = *Convolvulus mauritanicus*

MORPHOLOGY. The branch of biology that deals with the form and structure of plants.

MORUS (MO-rus). Shrubs or trees, with alternate, often irregularly lobed leaves, with staminate and pistillate catkins either on the same tree or different trees; fruits edible and like blackberries, very sweet but they have poor keeping qualities. However, they are widely used for jellies and preserves. *M. alba* and its varieties are about the only ones used any more but during the past century several others (*M. nigra, australis, cathayana*) have been tried. The silkworm feeds on the leaves of *M. alba*, and many fruiting varieties of *M. nigra* have been raised in Europe, but since raising of silkworms in America did not prove popular, and since mulberry fruits cannot be kept long, or shipped, these trees are not used much any more. The only species still in use in America is *M. alba* and its several varieties.

Propagation

Seeds should be stratified for 3 months at 40° F. then sown. Weeping varieties are grafted on standards of *M. alba*. Also softwood and hardwood cuttings root well. See CUTTINGS, STRATIFICATION.

Insect Pests

Mulberry white fly, although common to several other trees and shrubs, prefers mulberry. The black oval nymphs on the underside of leaves have a white waxy fringe. When necessary spraying with insecticide #15 is effective. San Jose scale infests these trees. See APPLE.

Diseases

Bacterial blight deforms and dries the leaves and kills branches. Pruning and burning or experimental sprays with fungicide #B are suggested.

alba   **45′**   **Zone 4**   **White Mulberry**
A round-topped, dense tree, native to China, with bright green, irregularly lobed leaves. The sexes are sometimes separate. Fruits are similar in size and shape to blackberries, ½–1 in. long, white, pinkish or purplish, ripe in early summer, edible and very attractive to birds. This is not a good ornamental tree but does grow well and rapidly, in poor, dry soils. It will give quick shade. This is the tree on which the silkworm feeds. Vars. are: **'Pendula'**—with slender pendulous branches. When grafted high on its understock it looks like a huge umbrella—Weeping Mulberry; **'Kingan'**—with leathery, lustrous leaves, fruitless, drought resistant and often used in seashore plantings; **'Tatarica'**—supposed to be the hardiest form with fruits ½ in. thick—Russian Mulberry.

nigra   **30′**   **Zones 6–7**   **Black Mulberry**
Less hardy than the more common *M. alba*, this tree from Asia is not much grown in America and has little to commend it as an ornamental, except possibly a wide-spreading picturesque habit. The blackberrylike fruits are dark red.

rubra   **60′**   **Zone 5**   **Red Mulberry**
Similar to *M. nigra* but hardier. Native from Mass. to Fla. west to Mich. and Tex. Not planted as an ornamental although in rural areas its fruits have been used as hog and poultry food.

MOSAIC. The mottled, yellowing or streaked condition of leaves and flowers is caused by several virus diseases. Mottling of tomato leaves and streaking of Gladiolus flowers are typical examples. Most mosaic viruses are spread from diseased to healthy plants by aphids or leaf hoppers which must be controlled. Workmen who prune, stake or harvest plants can spread the virus on hands, clothing or tools. See PLANT DISEASES.

MOSS. Mosses are small plants ¹⁄₁₆ in. to 24 in. tall but most of them are only a few inches tall, having stems and leaves. They have chlorophyll, manufacture their own food by taking materials from both soil and air, and the chlorophyll, aided by sunlight, manufactures the foods on which these plants live. They form spores, not seeds. There are an estimated 20,000 different kinds of mosses.

The spore, under the right conditions of temperature and moisture, swells and breaks through its shell, producing a slender, branching many-celled thread called a protonema which may eventually be a few inches or several feet long. Some of the branches go into the ground, and finally buds appear, each one of which develops into a leafy stem or a flattened scale. Thousands of these small plants grow close together and make up the mosses as we usually know them. These plants are fed by threadlike growths (rhizoids) which grow into the soil and in this way moss plants are able to acquire the raw materials for food.

When these plants are mature they produce either male or female (or both) germ cells. The male cells can swim about in a drop of dew or rain for an hour or two and finally reach and fertilize the female egg cell. This grows and develops into a spore case which eventually opens and distributes the spores to the atmosphere.

Mosses grow in moist situations, usually in association with trees. Practically none grow on grassy plains. They appear in soils at sea level and in moist situations on the tallest mountains. The identification of mosses is a study in itself. Very few have horticultural value. Occasionally moss is used to line hanging baskets; Sphagnum Moss, Spanish Moss (*Tillandsia*), which is a true flowering plant, and Flowering Moss (*Pyxidanthera barbulata*) which see, are the ones best known.

When moss appears on the surface of the soil, it is usually an indication that the soil is in need of fertilizing. In lawns it is an indication of wet soil, poor soil in need of fertilizing, very acid soil or a combination of these defects. Aside from the 2 or 3 already mentioned, this large group of plants plays a most surprisingly minor role in horticulture.

MOSS, FLOWERING = *Pyxidanthera barbulata*

MOSS-PINK = *Phlox subulata*

MOTHER-OF-THOUSANDS = *Saxifraga stolonifera*

MOTHER-OF-THYME = *Thymus serpyllum*

MOTHERWORT, COMMON = *Leonurus cardiaca*

MOUNTAIN-ASH. See SORBUS.

MOUNTAIN CRANBERRY = *Vaccinium vitis-idaea minus*

MOUNTAIN FRINGE = *Adlumia fungosa*

MOUNTAIN-HEATH. See PHYLLODOCE.

MOUNTAIN-HOLLY = *Nemopanthus mucronatus*

MOUNTAIN IMMORTELLE = *Erythrina poeppigiana*

MOUNTAIN-LAUREL = *Kalmia latifolia*

MOUNTAIN-MAHOGANY = *Cercocarpus montanus*

MOUNTAIN-SORREL = *Oxyria digyna*

MUCK. Any kind of impure or decayed peat or black swamp earth, usually moist.

MUCRONATE. Tipped with a short abrupt point.

MUEHLENBECKIA (mew-len-BEK-ia)

axillaris prostrate Zone 6 Creeping Wirevine
A small prostrate vine with leaves less than ¼ in. wide; flowers borne in the axils of the leaves and either solitary or in twos. Native to New Zealand. Not often planted in gardens.

complexa twining vine Zone 6 Wirevine
A New Zealand plant with small circular leaves less than an inch long. It has green, wirelike stems and has demonstrated its ability to withstand serious saline conditions at the seashore where other plants might not be able to grow. Frequently planted in Calif. and sometimes used in hanging baskets in the greenhouse.

MUGWORT, WHITE = *Artemisia vulgaris*

MULBERRY. See MORUS.

MULBERRY OR FIG FAMILY = Moraceae

MULCH. Strawy material or any other material as leaves, etc., spread on the surface of the ground to protect the roots of newly-planted shrubs or trees.

MULCHES. A mulch is considered to be anything that can be applied to the garden soil surface without injuring the plants, but at the same time reduces water loss from the soil and prevents weed growth. To be practical it should be inexpensive, easily obtained, and easily applied. Not many materials will fill all 3 requisites easily, and they undoubtedly will differ in the different regions of the country. It is to the advantage of each gardener to study the subject a little with respect to the actual plants he grows and to experiment with several, in order to find the best for his special conditions.

Mulches reduce water loss from the soil, thus making more moisture available to the plants and resulting in better plant growth. At the same time this will reduce the amount of watering necessary during droughts. Certain soil studies have shown that some mulches reduce the temperature of the soil by as much as 30° (when the surface soil may be 100° F.) thus giving the plant roots a more uniform temperature in which to grow. During the early fall, when air temperatures may go low at night, under a mulch they would remain higher, thus also aiding in root growth. Again in the early spring, when air temperatures fluctuate greatly, a mulch will aid in keeping the soil a more uniform temperature and thus reduce the possibility of early plant growth that might be injured or killed by late freezes.

It is a known fact that roots will continue to grow in the fall until soil water is unavailable by freezing, hence a mulch allows for more root growth in the fall than might otherwise be possible.

Certain mulches will add nutrients to the soil as they decompose. Nitrifying bacteria are more active under a mulch than they are without. This means that for the first year or so the soil nitrates are being used up at a rapid rate, the reason why it is recommended that when some mulches are added—sawdust is one example—the soil should be given a generous application of nitrogen-carrying fertilizer just prior to the time the mulch is applied. If this is not done, plants under a sawdust mulch will get yellow and become stunted, obviously in trouble because of the mulch. However, after a year or so, the nitrates under the mulch are greatly augmented because of the dying soil bacteria, and so the plants have a much better medium in which to grow.

Mulching usually aids tilth and soil texture. There are those who keep a continual mulch on their plants, and this can be beneficial if the right mulch is applied in the right way. Pine needles, for instance, can be added to from time to time, for a certain amount on the bottom of the mulch are decomposing with age. Too much, or a too-frequent application might very well result in harmful effects.

Some mulches like pine needles, oak leaves and peat moss can leave an acid soil reaction as they decompose which is beneficial to acid soil plants like azaleas and rhododendrons. Others, like maple leaves, especially Norway Maple leaves and Elm leaves, may leave an alkaline reaction and hence actually be harmful to such plants. Also, the depth of the mulch is extremely important. A 6-in. sawdust mulch on rhododendrons would be very harmful, for the delicate feeding roots of these plants are near the soil surface. Sawdust is known to "cake" or form a hard crust on top if it is not stirred occasionally, and air, essential for proper root growth, is thus excluded from the soil, resulting in plant injury.

Mulches are places where insects, disease spores and even rodents can spend the winter, and the intelligent gardener should size up the situation if by using a mulch he creates additional pest problems.

Since there are many kinds of mulching materials available, these points might be given some serious consideration when selecting a mulch.

Appearance

Every gardener likes to have a neat garden, and his mulch must not detract from the overall appearance. It must be tidy, not easily disturbed by wind or birds.

Water-retaining Capacity

Some, like peat moss, retain soil moisture, but in long droughts, if such a mulch has thoroughly dried out, it takes a very great deal of moisture (and time) to penetrate such a mulch, and the thicker it is the more difficult it becomes. Others, like polyethelyne film, retain no moisture, but unless a few holes are placed in the film when it is applied, it will not allow water to reach the soil under it. This is important in time of small rainfall, although when it is heavy, water eventually gets under the mulch by capillary attraction.

Ease of Application

Pine needles, ground sugar cane, peat moss, etc. are all easily applied and no drain on the physical potentialities of the tired, hard-working gardener. Aluminum foil is difficult to put down properly. Spent hops from the brewery are heavy to carry and apply. Such things are important to think of in advance.

Length of Time Serviceable

Theoretically a mulch of aluminum foil (between straight beds of plants) or about single plants would be expected to last for years. Actually it is easily ripped (by dogs or wind) and will not last as long as one would think. On the other hand, black polyethylene, applied properly, will last for at least 5 years or more. Pine needles, if locally obtained, is an easy one to replace or to augment each year. Such things should be given major consideration at the time the mulching material is selected.

Also, it is possible to change from one to another if for some reason this seems desirable.

Unsuitability—Fire Hazard

In public places this important item must be considered. Peat moss, when it is very dry, will burn. So will oak leaves, polyethylene film will only melt (from heat) and cocoa shells will not burn under conditions normally encountered in most gardens.

Depth and Time of Application

The depth of the mulch will depend on the kind of mulch and the type of soil. A mulch of coffee grounds should not be as thick as one of hay or peat moss. Also, a deeper mulch might be applied to a light sandy soil than to a heavy clay soil. In either case, it should be remembered that some air must be allowed to reach the roots in the soil. When all the air spaces are filled with water, or when a heavy mulch (like a 5-in. layer of coffee grounds) is put on the soil and cakes on top, then oxygen and other gases are not available to the roots and the plant suffers.

Actually, experience is the best teacher as to the depth of a mulch. It should be deep enough to kill the weeds, but not so deep as to prevent air from getting to the roots. A suggestion might be that 2–3 in. of a mulching material is usually plenty, and sometimes less is much better.

Mulching materials can be applied at any time when available. To do the most good they should be applied well in advance of summer droughts and before the time active weed growth starts. If weeds are up high, they should be removed before the mulch is applied. Also, to do the most good as a winter mulch, the material should be applied well before the time when the ground freezes, so it will aid in preventing the ground from alternate freezing and thawing, until such time when it really gets cold and the ground freezes permanently for the winter.

Mulching Materials

The following list of some of the mulching materials available about the country is offered for selective study. Some are much better than others, but prices will vary in different regions, and price is always a major consideration. In many places where poor soil and summer droughts combine to make plant growing a hazard, any one of these materials used as a mulch should result in better plant growth than if none had been used:

BARK. Any kind of bark has value as a mulch, but it should be ground or broken up into small pieces, not huge chunks. Various lumber companies about the country are doing this with Redwood bark, Pine bark, Yellow Birch bark and possibly others, depending on the section of the country in which they operate. Some even go so far as to have different sizes of "grinds," i.e., "all-purpose" size, "pea," "chestnut" or "fine grit" size. These obviously might have different uses depending on the kind of plants grown. As with other kinds of mulches, costs and availability dictate their usefulness in different areas.

BUCKWHEAT HULLS. These are light, fluffy and black and if applied at no greater depth than about 1–2 in. they should make a satisfactory mulch. They do not cake at this depth and take 2 years or more to disintegrate. A 50-lb. bag has enough buckwheat hulls to cover 65 sq. ft. about 1 in. deep. Weed seeds do not seem to germinate in this mulch although weed seedlings come up through it from the ground below, and are easily removed if pulled before they grow too large.

Watering need not be a problem (a heavy stream of water directed at the mulch is, for it scatters the hulls unnecessarily) if a water wand is used so that the water is quietly placed underneath the mulch—watering thoroughly need only be done every 10–14 days even during the severest of summer droughts.

COCOA SHELLS. The supply of these is limited to areas near the cocoa and chocolate manufacturing companies. They are the shells of the Coca Bean, brown, light, dry as they come from the factory and very easily handled. Sometimes they are ground fine and spread on the lawn as a fertilizer. As a mulch they will not blow in the wind, do not burn readily and, on disintegrating, afford all the elements in any fertilizer.

However, they do have large amounts of potash and can injure some plants as a result. Young maples, lilacs, rhododendrons, azaleas and tomatoes have been found to be susceptible to injury from a mulch of cocoa shells too heavily applied. It is well not to put them about such plants and, in any case, not to use them more than about 2 in. deep. These warrant consideration because they not only serve as a mulch but act as a fertilizer on disintegration.

COFFEE GROUNDS. In these modern times of instant coffee, the old-fashioned "grounds" are only available at certain plants which process the coffee beans. It used to be the custom to place coffee grounds about the plants in the garden but these cake badly after they have been in place for a few weeks and exposed to the weather. This prevents air and moisture from quickly reaching the roots, so the top surface should be broken up occasionally with a rake or hoe. Coffee grounds should only be used as a mulch an inch or so in depth.

CORNCOBS (GROUND). In certain rural areas this is a cheap mulch, and a good one if the corn cobs are ground to smaller sizes. However, corn and cobs ground together are now being used as a feed for steers and hogs in the form of a mash, and so this material may become unavailable for mulching purposes.

GRASS CLIPPINGS. These are used as a mulch, but if applied too green and too thick they can heat up and become a dense mat, through which proper amounts of air and water fail to penetrate. They should be applied loosely and not allowed to cake together. They might be used to better advantage mixed with weeds, leaves and soil in the compost pile. See COMPOST.

GROUND TOBACCO STEMS. Where this material can be obtained inexpensively, this might be used as a good mulch. It is coarse and certainly allows air and moisture through to the soil, but on roses it also is a place where diseased rose leaves can lodge and this aids in spreading disease. However, as the refuse from the tobacco plant it does have minor insecticidal properties and might be of value in restraining insect attacks.

LEAVES. These are among the best of mulches, and they should be used wherever possible,

either as a mulch or in the compost. There are differences among them, some being better than others. For instance, Maple or Poplar leaves tend to pack flat on the surface of the soil and are not too good if applied to any appreciable depth. They are especially harmful to surface rooted plants like azaleas and rhododendrons for this reason. Oak leaves and pine needles on the other hand are light and fluffy. They also leave an acid reaction in the soil as they decompose, both excellent reasons why they are especially good on ericaceous plants.

Some gardeners grind the leaves in a hammer-mill type of chopper, and like this method, even though it creates extra work, because the chopped up leaves do not blow as readily in the wind.

The chances are that merely raking the leaves into the shrub border, providing the resulting mulch is not too deep, is the simplest way of removing them from the lawn and providing a mulch where it is wanted. They also act as an excellent soil amendment when they decompose.

PEANUT SHELLS. In the South where they are obtainable, these make a fine mulch. Since they are very light, shipping charges are not high, and they have been used as a profitable mulch on greenhouse tomatoes in New England. Since they are light, they are easily handled and make an attractive looking mulch. Availability and cost are the chief factors in their use. They contain .95% nitrogen and do have some fertilizing value as they decompose.

PEAT MOSS. This is the universal garden mulch, but it is not always the least expensive. It is impossible to make specific statements about contents since there are all kinds of peat in use. There are those from local peat bogs, and large deposits in Mich., Canada and Europe. Most have a uniform brown color and look good in the garden as a mulch. Mixed with the soil, peat moss aids materially in the retention of water, and when it eventually breaks down it does have some organic matter.

One important point should be considered about most of the peats and that is, that when they are thoroughly dry, it takes a great deal of moisture and much time for them to become moist again. Hence, it is not advisable to apply peat more than 1–3 in. deep. Native peats can be bought by the bag, the bushel or the truck load while processed peats are usually dried and pressed into bales for easy shipping. The bales are of different sizes, some about 55 lb. of 4 cubic ft. capacity, other 95 lbs. of $7\frac{1}{2}$–8 cubic ft. capacity. A 95-lb. bale of dried pressed peat, if broken up and thoroughly moistened, will cover about 300 sq. ft., 1 in. deep.

Peats have been estimated to hold anywhere

Mulch of pine needles is one of the best types for Rhododendrons.

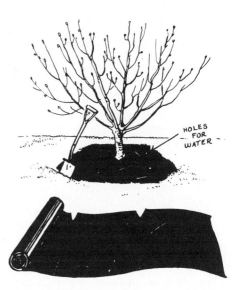

Black polyethylene film for mulching.

from 600–1200% water when compared on a dried weight basis. They usually are acid, anywhere from 3.6–6.8 pH.

PINE NEEDLES. Pine trees are widely native throughout North America, and their dropped needles make an excellent mulch, some more coarse than others it is true, but they will last 3–4 years before they must be replenished. They are acid in reaction, a good reason why they can be used around azaleas and rhododendrons. They do not absorb much water themselves but they do allow water and fertilizer to sift down through to the soil. If weeds grow up through them, the layer of pine needles is lifted up easily with a fork and allowed to plop down again, thus covering the weeds.

Also, if it is desired to remove the mulch in the spring, they can be raked off the bed, piled until fall and used again somewhere else if necessary. So, pine needles, especially the light flexible ones of the White Pine, are excellent as a mulch. They can be renewed from time to time and if the soil reaction is too much on the acid side (as a result of using a pine-needle mulch continuously for 6–8 years) all that is necessary is to apply a small amount of lime. Pine needles when used as a mulch need not be deeper than 2–3 in.

POLYETHYLENE FILM, BLACK. This material now comes in rolls of perforated squares which can be quickly torn off from the roll for placing about trees or shrubs. The squares are either 3 or 4 ft. on a side with a slit in each square to the middle so it is easily placed about the plant. Of course, it is available in long strips also, for mulching purposes along rows of plants. Its value as a mulch stems from the fact that gases like carbon dioxide, nitrogen and oxygen can pass through it readily, but water and water

vapor can not. The clear polyethylene film is of no value as a mulch because sunlight passes through it and hence weeds can grow underneath it.

Obviously then, a black polyethylene mulch prevents weed growth underneath, materially reduces loss of water from the soil surface that it covers and trials have shown that if it is not molested by garden machinery it will last at least 5–7 years.

However, in order to let rain water through, several holes might be punched through it with a penknife, when it is finally in place, the holes being placed in the lowest hollows, so water will

Black polyethylene is here used as a mulch for onions and peas. (*Photo by Arnold Arboretum, Jamaica Plain, Mass.*)

drain through. In this way, even the lightest rain reaches the soil underneath. For mulching purposes a thickness of about 0.015 in. is satisfactory.

Normally water travels by capillarity in the soil, both up and down and sideways but movement from side to side is very slow. During long droughts additional water should be applied and so it might be advisable not to rely on the lawn sprinkler but to apply water from the hose underneath the film until the soil is saturated.

Another advantage of using black polyethylene film is that it kills any grass over which it is placed merely by excluding the light. It should be firmly secured in place by setting the corners of the square mulching piece under sod, or by placing soil or rocks along the edges of long mulching strips. The better these are held tightly closed along the edges, the more soil water will be conserved. Do not forget the few penknife holes to let light rain water drain through.

SALT HAY, HAY, STRAW. These have been used in many areas over the years, but to be effective they should be 3–4 in. thick. The disadvantages are that they are bulky, do not look good, are frequently a fire hazard, harbor mice underneath and finally they do bring weed seeds into the garden. In most cases, a mulch of any one of these materials is better than no mulch at all. Experiments have clearly shown that, after 3 years about orchard trees, soil nitrates and moisture are definitely higher under such a mulch and result in better yields. The mouse problem can usually be met by using poison grain.

SAWDUST. Any kind of sawdust makes a good mulch. There have been experiments with hardwood and softwood sawdust, but it makes little difference in the long run, whether it be pine, maple, oak or birch. It is important to note that it should not be applied more than 2 in. deep, for if applied deeper it may cake on top and have some bad effects. Also, it is very important to note that if a sawdust mulch is contemplated, a heavy application of a complete fertilizer should be made to the soil just prior to mulching. It has been noted that available soil nitrates are greatly reduced the first year or so under a sawdust mulch and fertilizing the soil first helps to overcome this defect. If applied to the surface of the mulch the nutrients may be held in the sawdust and be unavailable for a long time.

The sawdust deteriorates in a few years and adds humus to the soil. This can be worked in, but if the mulch is to be retained, all that is necessary is to add more sawdust to the top of the mulch. As it breaks down and becomes humus it serves its purpose in the surface soil,

and more applied on top—if not too deep—fulfils the purposes of a continual mulch.

SPENT HOPS. These are comparatively inexpensive near the breweries. They have their good points and bad points as well. For every 238 lbs. of dry matter one usually hauls from the brewery 1,740 lbs. of water. The hops have the following analysis: water 87.67%; nitrogen 0.4%; organic matter 11.49%; ash 0.49%; pH 4.8. They also have an objectionable odor which is noticeable on a warm day but disappears about 2 weeks after application. They also attract pigeons and rodents.

The merits of spent hops as a mulch are that when dry they will not blow away and as a mulch they do conserve soil moisture and keep down the weeds. Spent hops should be applied 3–4 in. deep, with the warning that if applied in hot weather they will heat appreciably—enough to kill young shoots with which they come in contact. Hence they should be kept away from young trunks and shoots of trees and shrubs as they are applied.

SUGAR CANE. This is the material from the sugar cane which has been pressed at high temperatures to force out all the sap. It is then dried and baled or sold by the bag. It has a pH value of 4.5–5.2, has a water-holding capacity of over 340% of its dry weight and supposedly eventually decomposes into humus. It should be applied at least 1–2 in. deep. One would think this would be available only in the South, but it is being offered as a mulch in the North at prices often under those of local mulching materials.

WOOD CHIPS, WOOD SHAVINGS. Wood chips are an excellent mulching material, now commonly available everywhere that tree pruners use brush chippers. Wood chips are applied 2–3 in. deep but with these, as with sawdust, it is advisable to give the soil a heavy application of a complete fertilizer before the wood chip mulch is applied.

They last at least 2 years, sometimes longer, birch chips of course disintegrating before pine and oak chips. Since they are usually coarse, light rains and air filter down through readily enough. They will not blow, nor do they catch fire quickly. They are heavy and probably are only to be obtained locally from local arborists since shipping costs would be very high indeed. It might be inadvisable to use elm chips since this would probably aid in dispersing the Dutch Elm Disease.

Wood shavings, being lighter, are blown readily by winds and can catch fire quickly—but if neither of these drawbacks is serious, then shavings too can be used as a mulch.

These are not the only mulching materials. Others like aluminum foil, sprayed asphalt, cranberry vines, fiberglass, gravel or crushed stone, walnut shells, roofing papers, seaweed and ground banana stalks have been used. All have some merit, some being better than others and definitely more economically available. In general, materials that prevent excessive water loss from the soil but at the same time allow for sufficient soil aeration are also good materials to keep weed growth in check. They decompose and add humus to the soil.

MULE. An old word for a cross, particularly between different species; hybrid; cross-breed; usually an infertile hybrid.

MULLEIN. See VERBASCUM.

MULTIPLE FRUIT. The united product (in one body) of several or many flowers; as the Pineapple or Mulberry. See also SYNCARP.

MURIATE OF POTASH. This fertilizer contains 50–60% potash and 15% sodium chloride, is slow acting and can be used at the rate of $\frac{1}{2}$–1 oz. per sq. yard.

MURICATE. Roughened with short hard points.

MURRAEA = *Murraya*

MURRAYA (mur-AY-a)
  exotica = *M. paniculata*
  paniculata (*M. exotica*) **12′ Zone 10 Orange-
                                                                jessamine**
An evergreen shrub with glossy green leaves, white, fragrant, bell-shaped flowers which open several times a year and are often in bloom at the same time as the vivid red, egg-shaped berries are evident. These are $\frac{1}{2}$ in. in dia. Native to India. Easily propagated by seeds or cuttings. It makes a splendid hedge plant.

MUSA (MEW-sa). (Also see BANANA.)
  These are the bananas which are vigorous, treelike herbaceous plants of the Tropics with large paddle-shaped leaves. Botanically some are hard to separate from others, especially the popular, much-grown hybrids. They are only grown in the warmest parts of the southern U.S., where the climate is frost-free. Some of the smaller species are grown as interesting large-leaved pot plants in greenhouses in the North. They require rich soil, fairly moist at all times, with plenty of humus material. Greenhouse temperatures for most should be a minimum of 60° F. in the winter, and 70° F. from spring and fall. The huge pendulous flower cluster with its purplish-red terminal flower bud, and its numerous "rings" of fruits held in their awkward upright position, are unique among flowering plants.

Propagation

Propagation is usually by offsets, root cut-

tings or, in the case of the ornamental kinds, by seed sown in beds with bottom heat.

Insect Pests

Many scale insects and mealybugs such as infect citrus plants are also destructive to bananas. Citrus mealybug, palm scale and Florida red scale are among the most common. Spraying with insecticides #15 or #13 when the young are active is advised and the recommendations of local authorities should be followed. The grubs of a large beetle which bore in the roots and stems are collected by hand. Bananas may be infected by the Mediterranean fruit fly and other fruit flies and any suspicious maggots in the fruit should be reported promptly.

Diseases

Banana fusarium wilt is very destructive and often kills trees. It thrives in acid soil and applications of lime or other alkaline materials are helpful. Where resistant varieties are available they should be planted in new locations. Sigatoka disease causes leaf spots and heart rot of leaves. Frequent spraying with fungicide #K or #G is advised. Black end rot of ripening fruit reduces the grade of commercial bananas. Spraying with fungicide #G is helpful.

  acuminata (*M. cavendishii, M. nana, M.
  zebrina*) **12′ Zone 10 Blood Banana**
The long leaves are bluish green and beautifully variegated with a blackish blood-red color. Certain popular clones like 'Gros Michel', 'Sucrier', 'Green Red' and 'Dwarf Cavendish' are referrable to this species. The var. 'Dwarf Cavendish' is a dwarf (6 ft.) variety from southern China which can be eaten raw. It is propagated by offsets since seeds are not produced. It has proved a popular tub plant in northern greenhouses as well as in gardens of frost-free areas of the South. The leaves are 4 ft. long and 2 ft. wide, and the fruits are yellow, about 5 in. long. Formerly called *M. nana* or *M. cavendishii*.
  cavendishii = *M. acuminata*
  coccinea **4$\frac{1}{2}$′ Zone 10**
This is considered an ornamental species with leaves 3$\frac{1}{2}$′ long, dark green above and paler beneath; female flowers 1–3 in each cluster; fruit oblong, 2″ long and an inch in diameter, orange yellow with white pulp. Native to Indochina.
  ensete = *Ensete ventricosum*
  nana = *M. acuminata*
  ornata (*M. rosaceae*) **6′ Zone 10 India
                                                                Banana**
A small stoloniferous banana with very small inedible fruits, and an upright flower stalk with yellow flowers enclosed by bright pink flower

bracts. The leaves are 3 ft. long and a foot wide, purplish underneath. Native to India.

x paradisiaca (*M.* x *sapientum*) **15′–20′**
                    Zone 10   Common Banana
This is a highly complex group of hybrids, some of which are sold throughout the U.S. as the Common Banana. They are grown throughout the Tropics of the world, with those sold on the U.S. market mostly from Central America. There are many varieties, with yellow, green or red fruits and it is advisable to refer to them by their clonal names. See BANANA. The var. **vittatum** has beautifully variegated (white and pink) foliage with leaves 9 ft. long and 2 ft. wide. It is a stoloniferous plant and the flower stalk may be as much as 5 ft. long. Some of the clones are **'Poovan'**, **'Silk Fig'** or **'Silk'**, **'Horn Plantain'**, **'French Plantain'** and **'Bluggoe'**.

rosaceae = *M. ornata*

x sapientum = *M.* x *paradisiaca*

textilis   20′   Zone 10   Manila Hemp, Abaca
Manila Hemp or Abaca is a valued fiber produced in commercial quantities from this plant. Fruits are only 3 in. long and contain many black seeds. It is the fiber in the leaf stalks (the leaves are about 2 ft. long) which supply the material for the hemp.

zebrina = *M. acuminata*

MUSACEAE = The Banana Family

MUSCARI (mus-KAY-ri). Excellent, diminutive, spring-flowering bulbs from Asia Minor or southern Europe, these should be in every garden. Because they bloom so early in the spring they should be planted very early in the fall, Aug. or Sept., about 3 in. apart and with 2 in. of soil over each bulb. They fight their own battles for survival, increase readily by seeds and offsets and some even increase in grass.

The leaves are narrow and lance shaped; the flowers are in small racemes at the end of an erect spike, and each flower gives the impression of being a small ball. Usually the flowers are varying shades of blue or violet, but there are white-flowered varieties and even one with yellow flowers. They are all of easy cultivation and, once established, need no further attention but can be counted on for an excellent display of bloom each spring, usually in April and early May. One of the best of all bulbs (with Scilla and Narcissus) for naturalizing. Don't forget that one well-grown vigorous clump of *Muscari* by the front door steps can be a gem for spring beauty.

armeniacum   1′   Zone 4   Armenian Grape-
hyacinth
This is the most widely planted species with leaves ¼ in. wide, with 20–40 blue flowers clustered in a tight pyramid at the end of an erect 6 in. flower stalk. Native to Asia Minor.

'Early Giant'—has fragrant light blue flowers and is one of the best of several varieties; **'Heavenly Blue'**—light blue flowers and popular, but not the clear blue of 'Early Giant'; **'Cantab'**—light blue, blooming later than the other varieties and so it has merit.

azureum   8″   Zone 5
Blooming in the very early spring, this native of Asia Minor bears leaves up to 6″ long and bright blue flowers about $\frac{3}{16}$″ long in dense 20–40-flowered racemes. There is a variety **'Album'** with white flowers and **'Amphibolis'** has light blue flowers.

botryoides   1′   Zones 2–3   Common Grape-
hyacinth
Flowers blue, leaves ⅓ in. wide; native to southern Europe. A valued kind because it has white and pink flowered varieties. It should be

Muscari botryoides—Common Grape-hyacinth

remembered that these should be propagated by offsets to keep their color, since seedlings undoubtedly have blue-colored flowers like the species.

comosum   1′   Zone 4   Feather-hyacinth
Native to southern Europe and Asia with leaves up to 1 in. wide, this has light blue or violet flowers. The var. **monstrosum** has light blue flowers with the corolla cut and "feathered" Because of its large flowers this is one frequently used for greenhouse forcing.

latifolium I′ Zone 4

Flowers blue, in loose clusters, leaves I in. wide and only I leaf per bulb, and 10–20 blossoms per stalk. Native to Asia Minor—not one of the best for garden display.

neglectum 9″ Zone 4

Very narrow leaves only ⅛ in. wide, with dense clusters of 30–40 blossoms on each spike, dark blue and fragrant. Native to South Europe.

paradoxum 9″ Zone 4 Caucasus Grape-hyacinth

Leaves ¾ in. wide, few, flowers blue-black in dense racemes. Native to the Caucasus.

polyanthum I′ Zone 7

Another interesting little Grape-hyacinth, this one from central Asia Minor. The linear leaves are ¼″ wide: the deep blue flowers are borne in a dense, many-flowered raceme.

racemosum (*moschatum*) **6″–8″ Zone 4 Musk Grape-hyacinth**

Leaves ¾ in. wide, flowers at first purple, then fading to yellowish or brownish. Native to Asia Minor. Not a good ornamental but the var. **flavum** has fragrant yellow flowers.

MUSHROOM GROWING. Of the many species of edible mushrooms which grow in fields and woods, only one, *Agaricus bisporus* has been developed as a cultivated crop in the United States. Because of the variety of conditions under which fungi grow naturally, it might be assumed that commercial production would be a simple process but nothing could be further from the truth. No other crop is as exacting in its requirements. Profitable production requires constant attention to maintenance of favorable conditions and eternal vigilance against the inroads of insects and diseases.

Because the mushroom is a fungus and lacks chlorophyll, it cannot carry on photosynthesis and must depend upon non-living organic matter for its nutrition. Also, because it belongs to a lower order of plants having no true roots, stems or leaves, it produces no flowers or seeds and reproduction depends upon spores. Hence mushroom growing is not a matter of planting a seed to produce a plant.

The spores are borne on the gills on the underside of the mushroom cap and one mushroom produces millions of spores. Given a favorable environment, the spores develop a threadlike mass called mycelium or spawn, which in turn, under the proper conditions, develops the fruiting bodies which are edible mushrooms.

The early steps in this process, called "spawn making," are carried on in a laboratory under carefully controlled and sterile conditions. The spores are collected by a trained technician and placed on a potato-dextrose-yeast agar for germination. They are later transferred to bottles containing an organic medium such as

tobacco stems, kafir corn, wheat or rye for continued growth. The bottles are kept at 75° F. until the threads of mycelium have covered the grain or other medium after which they are placed under refrigeration until time for use.

Because conditions for mycelial growth are also favorable to growth of molds and bacteria, the bottles are checked frequently and any which show contamination are discarded.

Only the largest producers of mushrooms prepare their own spawn; most growers purchase their supplies from companies which specialize in that function.

Before getting his spawn supply, the grower prepares his houses. A "standard" mushroom house, usually built of cinder block, is 64 ft. × 20 ft. and contains 2 tiers of beds with an alley between. Each tier is 6 beds high, giving a total bed surface of approximately 4000 sq. ft. Mushroom houses are now built as "doubles," that is, each house is wide enough for 4 tiers of beds. Because light is unnecessary for growth, the house has no windows. Temperature and air circulation are important, however, and a series of ventilators is built into the roof.

The organic matter in which the mycelium grows is called compost. In the early years of commercial mushroom production, compost was almost entirely horse manure. Following World War II, because of the scarcity of horse manure, growers adopted "synthetic compost" which is made of hay and chopped corn cobs supplemented with brewers' grains and gypsum and small amounts of ammonium nitrate or muriate or potash.

Since 1960 a decreasing availability of corn cobs and an increased number of race tracks with available manure have brought about a combination of "synthetic compost" and horse manure for mushroom compost.

Before being placed in the house, the compost must go through a curing process during which it is turned several times and water added. In this way it is broken down by the bacteria present and is both chemically and physically conditioned for the growth of mushrooms. The composting process requires from 1–3 weeks depending upon the material used and the rate of bacterial action. Over-composting or under-composting can have adverse results on the mushroom crop. The experienced grower knows by the appearance and feel of the compost when it is ready to go into the house; no definite rule can be laid down for this process.

After the beds have been filled to a depth of 6 or 8 in., the compost must go through a pasteurization period known as the "sweat out" or "cook out." The house is closed tightly except that doors are opened at intervals to replenish the supply of oxygen. Fans are installed to aid in bringing all parts of the house to a uniform temperature. The heat generated by bacterial action in combination with the moisture, causes the temperature in the compost to rise and the resulting pasteurization brings about a final conditioning as well as killing insect and disease organisms which have come into the house in the filling process.

The "cook out" is a critical step in the preparation for a mushroom crop. Much depends upon the condition of the compost when it is put into the house. The bacterial action depends upon the moisture and carbohydrate content of the compost; if conditions are not right, the temperature may rise too rapidly or too slowly. If the temperature does not go high enough disease organisms are not killed. On the other hand, an extremely high temperature can cause chemical changes in the compost which can result in a poor crop. Since air temperature is no indication of the compost temperature, thermometers or thermo-couples are placed in the beds and checked frequently.

A uniform compost temperature of 140° F. throughout the house is considered sufficient to kill animal pests and molds. As the compost heat approaches this point, heat is usually added in the form of steam to equalize the air temperature and the bed temperature and the house is held at this point for from 4 to 6 hours. The temperature is then allowed to drop slowly, preferably not more than 5° per 24 hours.

When the compost is placed in the beds, it has a strong odor of ammonia. By the time the temperature has dropped to 125° F. after the peak heat, no ammonia should be noticeable. The compost temperature is then allowed to drop to 75° F. before spawning. The entire "cook out" requires from 7 to 10 days.

The spawn is then broadcast on the beds and the mycelium grows into the compost in whitish-gray threads. During the "spawn running" period, the temperature is maintained at not more than 75° F. and the compost should have a water content approaching 70%. Water is applied as a fine spray rather than as a heavy stream and not in quantities that will cause the compost to become soggy. Transparent plastic is sometimes placed over the beds to maintain a satisfactory moisture level in the compost during the spawn run. From 2 to 3 weeks are required for the spawn to grow through the compost.

While the mycelium will grow in the compost it will not develop into the fruiting stage and produce mushrooms until a thin layer of soil (called "casing soil") has been placed on top of the compost.

Preparation of the casing soil is again a most careful process. Since the mushrooms derive no nutrient from the soil, the physical characteristics of good casing soil are more important than its chemical composition. It must hold water without becoming waterlogged and must remain friable on the beds without "caking." Topsoil meets these requirements better than subsoil. This means that in areas of concentrated mushroom growing, long-range programs of rebuilding topsoil must be planned.

Although the chemical content of topsoil is not important, its degree of acidity affects the crop. It should test between 7.2 and 7.8 on the pH scale. Spawn laboratories maintain soil-testing services for their customers. If the pH tests below 7, lime is added. Mushrooms tend to produce acid in the soil and the addition of lime neutralizes the acids and aids in preventing the growth of green molds.

The soil is screened in the field to remove stones and debris and is then transported to the wharf at the mushroom house where it must undergo sterilization.

One cause of crop failure in the mushroom industry is the presence of nematodes which are present in all soils and all raw compost. At least 2 species are especially injurious to mushroom mycelium. The soil as it comes from the field may also be infected with organisms which cause mushroom diseases known as "bubbles," verticillium spot, and "mat" disease (all familiar terms to the mushroom grower but merely names to the inexperienced).

Heating the soil to 180° F. by passing live steam through it will destroy nematodes as well as other animal and disease organisms. Some chemicals such as chloropicrin have also been found effective and chemical sterilization of soil has replaced steaming to some extent. After sterilization, the soil is placed in a clean bin or on a concrete wharf and covered to prevent recontamination.

When the mycelium has grown through the compost, about 1 in. of soil is placed on top of the beds and leveled off. Again there must be constant attention to watering, temperature and ventilation.

Mushrooms begin to appear as "pinheads" about 3 weeks after casing. The temperature must be held at no more than 70° F. and preferably between 50° and 65° F. The lower temperatures improve mushroom production and discourage the growth of insect and disease organisms.

Throughout the growing period the grower must be alert to invasions by disease or insects. Optimum conditions for mushrooms are also favorable to growth of molds and weed fungi, hence the precaution to prevent contamination by spores in spawn, compost and soil. Malformed or diseased mushrooms are removed from the beds and destroyed to reduce spread of infection.

Animal pests which create problems are springtails, several species of mites and 3 species of flies peculiar to mushroom-growing areas. Adult flies are a means of spreading mold spores and nematodes from one area to another and the larvae of some species cause damage to the mycelium and the mushrooms.

Because some insecticides injure the mushrooms or inhibit their growth and some others are too poisonous to use on food crops, it is difficult to treat insect infestations after mushrooms appear. Hence, it is important to take every possible precaution in the proper management of the compost and casing soil. Other steps in control include sterilization of the house with steam before removing spent compost at the end of the crop, proper disposal after removal and elimination of trash piles and other possible breeding places on the premises.

Mushrooms grow in somewhat rhythmic cycles called "breaks." The heaviest production comes from the first 2 "breaks," but beds properly adjusted for moisture and temperature will continue to produce mushrooms for about 3 months.

During the production period, picking must be done every day, although it requires from 6 to 10 days for a mushroom to grow to marketable size. Average production is $2\frac{1}{4}$ to $2\frac{1}{2}$ lbs. per sq. ft.

In southeastern Pa., which is the most concentrated area of production in the United States, it has been customary to fill the houses in Sept. for the first crop, then refill for a second crop about Jan., thus ending the growing season with the advent of warm weather. The increased use of cooling systems makes it possible to start the first crop earlier and extend the second crop later into the spring months; or by limiting the picking to the most productive periods, it is possible to have 3 crops a year instead of 2. Few growers, however, find it profitable to use air conditioning for a midsummer crop.

In western Pa., a large mushroom-growing enterprise is carried on in caves from which limestone was formerly mined. Here, as well as in some large plants in other parts of the country, a system of moveable trays is used instead of the conventional stationary beds. The tray system lends itself more readily to filling, spawning and casing by mechanical means. Because the caves maintain a year-round temperature of approximately 56° F., special rooms are maintained for the "cook out" and spawn run which must take place at higher temperatures. It is possible under these conditions to produce mushrooms throughout the year by replacing the trays in the caves every 50 days. This type of operation, however, is the exception rather than the rule.

Because mushroom-growing does not require a large acreage, it must not be assumed that the business can be started with little capital. The initial investment for one double house can quickly amount to more than $10,000 exclusive of cooling equipment and necessary machinery for operation. It is a business requiring complete understanding of all of the necessary steps and is not recommended for the inexperienced.

Long considered a delicacy used primarily to enhance the flavor and attractiveness of other foods, mushrooms are known to contain small amounts of the vitamin B factors, thiamin and riboflavin, and are somewhat higher in minerals than many vegetables. They are also low in calories since they have a high water content.

Earliest commercial production in the United States was in the vicinity of New York City and Long Island about 1880 where they were mostly grown in caves and cellars. About 1885 some florists at Kennett Square, Pa., tried growing mushrooms beneath the benches in their greenhouses and in 1896 the first houses were built in that area for the specific purpose of growing mushrooms. From this beginning, southern Chester County, some 30 miles from Philadelphia, became the center of the industry in this country. There are sizeable operations in upper New York State, the Midwest, and on the Pacific Coast, but Pa., continues to account for some 60% of the national production. Of some 800 growers in the country, 600 are located in Pa.

National production is in excess of 160,000,000 lbs. annually. Approximately $\frac{1}{2}$ goes to the fresh market, the balance finding its way to the consumer as canned mushrooms, soups and sauces.

Since 1950, an international congress has been held every 3 years under the auspices of the International Commission on Mushroom Science, at which time scientists from all parts of the world present the results of research being carried on relative to cultural methods, improvement of spawn cultures, and control of adverse factors affecting the industry.

VIOLET K. TYSON

Insect Pests

The maggots of fungus gnats or mushroom flies eat the stem and the cap and ruin them as food. Springtails are small jumping insects which feed on decayed vegetable matter and are attracted to manure. They eat cavities in the cap and gills of the Mushroom and are very destructive when abundant. Mushroom mites which are white with soft bodies eat the roots (mycelium) and chew cavities in the stem and cap. Sowbugs are small gray animals with 10 legs which often damage the spawn and buttons. Heating the manure to 135° F., before sowing the spawn, kills most of the pests.

Sprays and dusts of insecticide #27 and fumigation with insecticide #12 have been effective against the gnats. Insecticides #15 and #9 are approved for use on mushrooms under specific conditions and advice from local authorities should be obtained before using any of the newer pesticides.

MUSHROOMS. These are the fruiting bodies of plants which have no chlorophyll. They do not make food from carbon dioxide, nitrates and minerals but with water and proper temperature these plants feed on organic matter which has already been manufactured by chlorophyll-containing plants or animals. The part of the plant which grows underground in long, minute many-branched threads is the mycelium, or "spawn" as the commercial growers call a mass of them. These give off the enzymes which digest whatever food materials there are in the medium in which they grow. When this digested material is dissolved it is absorbed by the mycelia and hence supplies the materials for growth.

Mushrooms then are the fruiting bodies of certain fungi. There are over 3000 mushroom species in the United States. In nature they feed on decaying logs and organic matter in the soil, or they feed on decaying animal matter. When there is no more food of the type they need, they cease to grow and die. In the interim, however they produce the visible fruiting bodies or mushrooms, which in turn produce spores that are eventually spread by the wind. If these fall in a suitable place, and temperature and humidity are at an optimum, these start to grow and eventually the growing mycelia will again produce the mushrooms that are visible above ground.

"Fairy rings" are produced by certain fungi in this manner: The spore falls on an area with food and the mycelia advance at a certain rate in all directions from that spot. Then, when the time comes for producing the fruiting bodies, they are all produced (above the ground of course) in a very definite ring with the center of the circle being where the original spore was dropped. It has been estimated that in certain places where there is plenty of food for these organisms so that they continue growth that by the size of the circle of fruiting bodies and its enlargement each year, some of these colonies may have been growing in the same location for 400 years.

Moisture, quite a bit of it, is necessary for growth and the production of the fruiting bodies. Mushrooms are often very specific concerning the type of material they live on. Some live on decaying logs, and some of these attack the log soon after it begins to disintegrate then die when their specific foods are used up. Then come others, which could not live off the log at first but can after it has been worked on awhile by the primary fungus. Others come after this. Some live on the rotting leaves on the forest floor and since these are replenished year after year these mushrooms are always found in such places. Others may be so specific in their demands that they live only on a certain kind of log, Poplar, Pine or Maple. So it is seen that in hunting mushrooms one must know something of their specific requirements and then look in likely places.

Some fungi become attached to the roots of certain trees and the association can be beneficial to both. These mycorrhiza can only live in this combination. Mushrooms are identified only by their fruiting bodies and hunting mushrooms in a warm damp season is more productive than in a cold dry one.

It is extremely important that when one begins collecting mushrooms to eat, one definitely knows the difference between poisonous and non-poisonous species. There is no sure-fire rule of thumb—one must be able to properly identify them. In an excellent publication called "The Mushroom Hunter's Field Guide" by Alexander H. Smith, published by The University of Michigan Press, Ann Arbor, Mich., in 1963, there are descriptions of 188 of the most common mushrooms, poisonous and edible, together with 200 black and white pictures and 89 color plates. Even this author states that after all this is only a field guide, and even with description, black and white photographs as well as color photographs, it is possible to make a costly misidentification mistaking a poisonous sort for one that is edible. Before hunting and eating mushrooms gathered in the wild, one would do well to study carefully the remarks made in a book such as this, then make doubly certain the ones selected for eating are definitely identified as edible species. It is interesting to note that the author lists 119 as edible; 15 as doubtful; 30 as not recommended; and 24 as poisonous. The most poisonous of all is the Destroying Angel (*Amanita verna*).

MUSK MALLOW = *Abelmoschus moschatus*

MUSKMELON. See MELON.

MUSTARD (*Brassica juncea*). As a plant name mustard is applied to many weedy, chiefly annual herbs of the family Cruciferae, some of which are very serious pests. White Mustard (*B. juncea*), however, is a hardy annual which is grown as a salad or potherb. It is a common crop in the winter garden in the southern states.

Mustard will grow well on most soils. On sandy loam or loam soils apply a broadcast application of 20–30 lbs. of a 5–10–10 fertilizer per 1000 sq. ft. and thoroughly work this plant food into the top 2–3 in. of soil just prior to seeding.

Sow the seed in drills 15 in. apart as early in the spring as possible or, in the south for fall and winter use, Sept. and Oct. seedage is recommended.

Mustard plants go to seed quickly, particularly in hot and dry weather, and therefore the plants should be used as soon as they reach a height of 15–18 in.

The major varieties are **'Giant Southern Curled'**, **'Fordhook'**, **'Ostrich Plume'** and **'Florida Broad Leaf'**.

There are no important insect pests or disease.																GRANT B. SNYDER

MUSTARD FAMILY = Cruciferae

MUTATION. Deviation occurring by a sudden change in the genetic makeup of a plant or an animal. See also BUD-MUTATION.

MYCELIUM. The thallus or vegetative part of a fungus made up of threadlike tubes. See MUSHROOM.

MYOPORUM (my-OP-or-um)
  laetum   15′   Zone 9
A New Zealand shrub or tree with alternate, long, shining, narrow leaves (4 in.); flowers purple with white spots, ⅔ in. wide. Fruit is red-purple. Propagated by cuttings. Sometimes grown in the greenhouse and outdoors in southern Calif.

MYOSOTIDIUM (my-o-so-TID-ium)
  hortensia   3′   Zone 10
A perennial herb native to New Zealand, sometimes grown in the flower borders of the South, with heart-shaped basal leaves a foot long; flowers dark blue, ½ in. wide, in clusters 6 in. wide. Propagated by spring-sown seeds.

MYOSOTIS (my-o-SO-tis)
  alpestris   6″   Zone 2   Alpine Forget-me-not
Although this Forget-me-not is commonly listed in many catalogues, this species is rarely seen in gardens in the U.S. Most plants listed with this name are actually varieties of the widely planted *M. sylvatica*. It is a small tufted plant, often growing in Arctic regions of Europe and North America.
  palustris = *M. scorpioides*
  scorpioides   12″–20″   Zone 3   True Forget-me-not
A European perennial with lanceolate to linear leaves and small flowers which are generally blue, but having an occasional pinkish one in the slender, curving racemes. Each flower has a corolla with 5 rounded lobes. The plant has

escaped from gardens and is now naturalized in wet meadows and near streams throughout the eastern states, extending into Canada. It blooms throughout the summer. It may be propagated either from seeds or cuttings, using wet sand as a medium. The var. **semperflorens** is only 8 in. tall and blooms throughout July and Aug. and is about the best of all this group for this reason; var. **rosea** has pink flowers. An excellent wet-soil plant, especially for its diminutive summer bloom.
  sylvatica   9″–24″   annual   Woodland Forget-me-not
A very popular annual (sometimes biennial) native to Europe and Asia with many varieties available, some listed incorrectly under *M. alpestris*. The flowers of the species are true blue, but there are white and pink-flowered varieties also available. These all do best if given some shade. Seeds can be sown indoors in March or, if the winters are not too severe, outdoors in late summer where they will bloom the following year. When the plants become well established they self-seed themselves easily and appear year after year where they were first started.

MYRICA (mi-RY-ka). Native deciduous shrubs with aromatic foliage and colorful gray or purple fruits (except *M. gale*) planted because of their ability to grow on dry sterile soils, their evergreen leaves (or almost evergreen in the case of *M. pensylvanica* and *M. gale*) and their ability to withstand pruning or even shearing, sometimes done to force them into more compact habits. Sexes are separate and only pistillate plants will bear the small, waxy, gray fruits.

Propagation

Do not let the seed dry out. First remove the wax by soaking the seed in warm water, then stratify for 3 months at 40° F. and sow. Division of plants is easy in this genus for there are many underground stolons that can easily be cut from the mother plant. Softwood cuttings are also successful. See STRATIFICATION, CUTTINGS, etc.
  californica   36′   Zone 7   California Bayberry
A slender, upright-growing shrub, used on the Pacific Coast where it is native for its purple berries in the fall as well as its lustrous, ever-green bronze-colored leaves which are up to 4 in. long. It must be remembered that in all *Myrica* species the sexes are separate and only the pistillate plants will bear fruits.
  carolinensis = *M. pensylvanica*
  cerifera   36′   Zone 6   Wax-myrtle
The taller growing of the 2 bayberries found in the eastern U.S., this is also the less hardy. The foliage of this species is evergreen, the leaves being 3 in. long. The small gray fruits, borne on

the pistillate plants, are slightly more than $\frac{1}{8}$ in. thick and appear in dense clusters along the stem, covered with a gray waxy coating. These can remain on the plants well into the winter. The twigs, leaves and fruit of this species are all intensely aromatic. It makes a good foliage plant in the garden.

gale   4′   **Zone 1**   **Sweetgale**
Native throughout the colder parts of North America, Europe and Asia, usually in moist peaty places. Leaves deciduous, aromatic when crushed, $1\frac{1}{2}$–$2\frac{1}{2}$ in. long. Flowers in the form of catkins, sexes on separate plants, fruits very small nutlets $\frac{1}{12}$ in. in dia. Not much used as an ornamental shrub.

pensylvanica   9′   **Zone 2**   **Bayberry**
The leaves of this northern species, native from Newfoundland to Md., are semi-evergreen. It is found along the coastal area, many times at the seashore within reach of salt-water spray. Also this species is noted for the fact that it can be grown in poor, sandy soils. It is difficult to transplant from the wild so great care should be taken with digging a proper ball and preserving as many roots as possible. All parts of this species are aromatic when crushed, and the waxy gray berries, produced in great profusion along the young stems of the pistillate plant, have been collected and made into bayberry candles, but it takes a tremendous amount of bayberries to make one candle. See BAYBERRY CANDLES. It is a fine foliage plant in the garden and the leaves remain on well into the late autumn before they drop off without changing color. The leaves are used for making a gray-green dye.

MYRICACEA = The Bayberry Family

MYRICARIA (mi-ri-KAY-ria)
cauliflora   40′   **Zone 10**   **Jaboticaba**
The very fine leaves are somewhat similar to the threadlike leaves of the Tamarisk tapering up to 4 in. long with the upper surface a dark green and dotted. The black or purple fruits, about the size of grapes, are borne on the trunk and older branches, tasting somewhat like grapes. These are borne 3 times each year and are either eaten fresh or used in making jams and jellies. Native to Brazil.

germanica   3′–6′   **Zone 5**   **False Tamarisk**
A deciduous shrub with alternate leaves, something like the threadlike leaves of Tamarix; small pink or white flowers from May to Aug., borne in dense terminal racemes 4–8 in. long. Native to southeastern Europe and western Asia. Not very ornamental, certainly inferior to many of the Tamarix species. It is best displayed by cutting back the previous year's growth to just a few buds in the early spring.

MYRIOPHYLLUM (mi-rio-FILL-um). These are aquatic plants with hairlike leaves. Two species are used in planting aquaria. Tropical fish seem to like this type of foliage for spawning purposes. Certainly the plants lend a delicate texture to any aquarium planting.

aquaticum (*proserpinacoides*)   **aquatic plant**
Zone 10   **Chile Parrotfeather**
This is the best species of this genus for the home aquarium. It is a graceful water plant, native to Chile and Uraguay.

verticillatum   aquatic plant   Zone 3   Canada Parrotfeather
It is interesting to note that submerged leaves of this species are threadlike, but if the stem grows above the water level to flower, these leaves are pinnatifid. It is native to northern North America, Europe and Asia.

MYRISTICA (mir-IS-tik-a)
fragrans   30′   **Zone 10**   **Nutmeg**
An alternate-leaved, tropical, evergreen tree of the East Indies, cultivated for its fruits. The leaves are somewhat similar to those of rhododendrons. The fruits are about $1\frac{1}{2}$–2 in. long, colored yellowish to reddish, and inside the outer fleshy covering is the familiar nutmeg of commerce. Male and female flowers are on different trees.

MYRRH = *Myrrhis odorata*

MYRRHIS (MI-ris)
odorata   3′   **Zone 4**   **Sweet Cicely, Myrrh**
A perennial herb of the Carrot Family grown for its aromatic foliage with pinnately-compound fernlike leaves, small whitish flowers in umbels. Fruits are jet black. Native to Europe. Propagated by division or by seeds sown as soon as ripe. Long used as an herb for seasoning, the seeds taste something like licorice, and the green foliage lasts in the garden almost until Dec.

MYRTACEAE = The Myrtle, Allspice or Guava Family

MYRTLE = *Myrtus communis*. Sometimes this name is also incorrectly applied to Periwinkle (*Vinca minor*).

MYRTLE, ALLSPICE OR GUAVA FAMILY = Myrtaceae

MYRTUS (MIR-tus)
communis   5′–10′   **Zones 8–9**   **Myrtle**
The true Myrtle is a native to the Mediterranean Region and is grown only in the warmest parts of the U.S. or in the greenhouse. The aromatic, evergreen leaves are 2 in. long, and the small creamy-white flowers are $\frac{3}{4}$ in. in dia., appearing in the summer. The blue-black berries are effective in the fall. It is this plant which has been written about so much in the literature of the Ancients. It can be sheared and easily forms a dense evergreen hedge, and it is also valued for the fact it can grow well in hot, dry situations in seashore gardens. Varying greatly in size, leaf,

color and general habit, there is a variety named **'Compacta'** being grown by some Calif. nurserymen which, if it retains its low dense growth continually over the years, should be a fine plant for small gardens, but of course only in the warmer parts of the country.

N

NAEGELIA = *Smithiantha*

NAILWORT. See PARONYCHIA.

NAKED FLOWER. A flower without perianth.

NAMAQUALAND-DAISY = *Venidium fastuosum*

NAMING PLANTS. See NOMENCLATURE.

NANDINA (nan-DY-na)

domestica   8'   Zone 7   Nandina
Perhaps one of the most popular plants in all southern gardens is the Nandina, native to central China and Japan, popular particularly because of the large terminal clusters of bright red fruits (¼ in. in dia.) which remain vividly displayed throughout the fall and early winter. The white flowers are borne in large clusters in July and the evergreen foliage colors a bright red to scarlet in the fall. The alternate, twice- or thrice-compound leaves bear leaflets 1–1½ in. long. Even in the early spring this plant is colorful for the young foliage is frequently tinged pink to bronze as it unfurls. It is a close relative of *Berberis* botanically, but one would not realize it to look at the plant. There is a white fruiting variety **'Alba'** which makes an interesting combination when used in a mass of the red-fruiting species.

Propagation

Do not allow the seed to dry out before sowing. Seed sown in a warm greenhouse will germinate in several months.

NANNYBERRY = *Viburnum lentago*

NARCISSUS (nar-SIS-us). These are popular garden bulbs, widely grown throughout the country, forced in the greenhouse for cut-flower purposes and grown in pots in the home as house plants. Popular names used for them are Narcissus, Daffodil and Jonquil. The popular name Daffodil can be correctly given to the trumpet-flowered types of the genus *Narcissus*. All daffodils belong to this genus. However, all members of the Narcissus genus should not have the popular name Daffodil. Jonquil is a name loosely applied in the South and sometimes in England, but technically it should only be applied to those species in Division VII (see the classification following), mostly *N. jonquilla, N. juncifolius*, etc. As a common name it should be avoided except for these few species and their hybrids. It is inaccurate to apply the name to the large-trumpeted Daffodil.

The term narcissi has been used as the Latin form for the plural of the singular narcissus. However, the American Daffodil Society, by vote of its Board of Directors decided that the policy of the Society would be to use the same word, narcissus, for both singular and plural, and so it is treated here.

Everyone knows the narcissus and daffodils, yet few realize the tremendous number of variations there are in this group. These interesting and diversified plants are now grouped into 11 main divisions and 18 subdivisions. They are as follows:

Division 1

Trumpet Narcissus. One flower to a stem; trumpet or corona as long or longer than the perianth segments.

  (a) Perianth colored; corona colored, not paler than the perianth. ('Kingscourt', 'Cromarty')

  (b) Perianth white; corona colored. ('Preamble', 'Bambi')

  (c) Perianth white; corona white, not paler than the perianth. ('Cantatrice', 'Mt. Hood')

  (d) Any color combination not falling into (a), (b), or (c). ('Spellbinder')

Division 2

Large-cupped Narcissus. One flower to a stem; cup or corona more than one-third, but less than equal to the length of the perianth segments.

  (a) Perianth colored; corona colored, not paler than the perianth. ('Carbineer', 'Madeira')

  (b) Perianth white; corona colored. ('John Evelyn', 'Nissa')

  (c) Perianth white, corona white, not paler than the perianth. ('Ave', 'Zero')

  (d) Any color combination not falling into above. ('Binkie')

Division 3

Small-cupped Narcissus. One flower to a stem; cup or corona not more than one-third the length of the perianth segments.

  (a) Perianth colored, corona colored, not paler than the perianth. ('Dinkie', 'Chunking')

  (b) Perianth white, corona colored. ('Blarney', 'Dreamlight')

  (c) Perianth white, corona white, not paler than the perianth. ('Chinese White', 'Dallas')

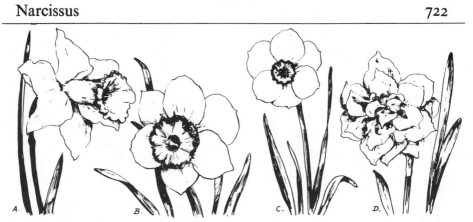

Narcissus types: A. Trumpet   B. Large-Cupped   C. Small-Cupped   D. Double

Narcissus types: E. *N. triandrus albus*   F. *N. cyclamineus*   G. *N. jonquilla*   H. *N. tazetta*
I. *N. poeticus*

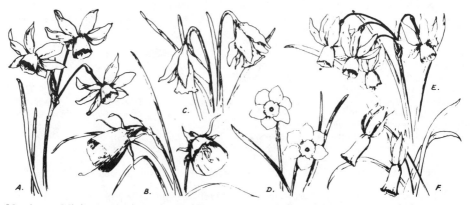

Narcissus—Miniature species: A. *N. 'Hawera'*   B. *N. bulbocodium*   C. *N. moschatus*
D. *N. watieri*,   E. *N. triandrus albus*   F. *N. cyclamineus*

(d) Any color combination not falling into above. '(Green Elf')

Division 4

Double Narcissus. Double flowers. ('Swansdown', 'Twink')

Division 5

Triandrus Narcissus

(a) Cup or corona not less than two-thirds of the length of the perianth segments. ('Thalia', 'Moonshine')

(b) Cup or corona less than two-thirds the length of the perianth segments. ('Thoughtful', 'Dawn')

Division 6

Cyclamineus Narcissus.

(a) Cup or corona not less than two-thirds the length of the perianth segments. ('Cyclades', 'Dove Wings')

(b) Cup or corona less than two-thirds the length of the perianth segments. ('Beryl', 'Quince')

Division 7

Jonquilla Narcissus

(a) Cup or corona not less than two-thirds the length of the perianth segments. ('Shah', 'Golden Goblet')

(b) Cup or corona less than two-thirds the length of the perianth segments. ('Sugarbush', 'Sundial')

Division 8

Tazetta Narcissus. Characteristics of the Narcissus Tazetta group clearly evident. ('Orange Wonder', 'Laurens Koster')

Division 9

Poeticus Narcissus. Characteristics of the Narcissus Poeticus group without admixture of any other. ('Red Rim', 'Smyrna')

Division 10

Species and wild forms and wild hybrids. All species and wild, or reputedly wild, forms and hybrids. (*N. triandrus, N. triandrus albus*)

Division 11

All narcissus not falling into any of the foregoing divisions. ('Split', 'Gold Collar')

This classification means little to the rank and file of busy gardeners but it is extremely important to the specialist or the one who exhibits in flower shows. It does point up the fact that there are a bewildering number of groups and an overwhelmingly large number of varieties available on the market. These are changing almost every year. However, the gardener with an eye for color and form can select a few varieties from this excessively large number, and be perfectly content with the bright spring blooms they bring each spring. No garden is complete without its full complement of spring flowering bulbs, and daffodils or narcissus make up a large part of this group. Today hundreds of varieties of these bulbs are being offered by their clonal names and it is a simple matter to buy them by variety. One of the best of recent publications concerning this important group of plants is the Daffodil Handbook, actually the Jan. 1966 issue of the American Horticultural Magazine. This should be used as the standard reference on the subject.

Varieties

With the hundreds of varieties being offered American gardeners today and with new ones being introduced each year, a list of named varieties is out-of-date almost as soon as it is published. The more recently introduced varieties, being in limited supply, are more expensive. Personal taste is also very important in making selections. The best thing to do in making a selection of varieties for the first time is to visit flower shows where varieties are named, or exhibition gardens where care has been taken in keeping varieties properly labeled. Failing this, the only other alternative is to obtain several bulb catalogues and order from among the glowing (and usually colorful) descriptions. Any good bulb catalogue will have a large number of varieties segregated into the general groups already mentioned. If a few bulbs only are to be planted for bright color in the spring garden, almost any variety might suffice.

If one is contemplating a sizeable planting, take cognizance of the fact that varieties should be selected from several of the divisions mentioned, for the variations in type and size of the flower, color, time of bloom and general habit of the plant are all very important in making an interesting, varied and long-blooming collection.

When selecting varieties for naturalizing, price is a very important factor for usually the less expensive varieties are the ones to use. Catalogues frequently make suggestions of varieties best suited for this purpose. The newer, high-priced bulbs are usually selected for the flower borders, for spotting in the foundation planting about the home and in the rock garden. It is here that the species are usually set off to best advantage, especially those of small habit and with small flowers.

For further information on this subject, inquiries should be made of the American Daffodil Society (see SOCIETIES) which annually publishes much detailed and timely information about this diversified group of spring-flowering bulbs.

Uses

Narcissus are adaptable to planting at many places in the garden. Certainly they should be planted in groups of a dozen or more bulbs in the perennial border to bring early color and interest at a time when nothing else is in bloom. After they have died, other perennials come into leaf and flower.

They also are at home among the rocks, if enough good soil is available for optimum growth. Nothing is quite so effective in the early spring as a well-grown clump of narcissus with a large rock as the back drop. There is a technique in planting them here as elsewhere. They should be planted in groups of a dozen or more bulbs, spaced about 6–8 in. apart. This is especially true in the flower border where the tendency is often to plant a bulb here and one 6 ft. beyond, and so on. They are most effective as tight groups, not as widely spaced individual plants.

They are frequently bought in large numbers for naturalizing and, here too, there is definitely a method in arranging them most effectively. It should be in drifts or masses with open areas of grass in between. No planting is as interesting when they are regularly spaced over the entire area, as it is when they are massed here and there in formal but rather dense groupings with unplanted areas interspersed for contrast.

Sometimes they are ineffectually used in planting a narrow border. This is not advisable for, as the plant matures and flowers fade, the leaves begin to flop over and make an unsightly planting. It is much better to find other uses for them rather than planting in conspicuous straight lines. Massings and informal groupings are where they show off to best advantage

Culture

The best time for planting is late Aug. or early Sept., although narcissus can be planted up to Nov. in the North. The earlier in the fall the better because it gives the roots more time to become established before the ground freezes. They should be planted 4–5 in. deep in good, well-prepared soil. Holes should be 6–8 in. apart for large bulbs. In planning the "drifts" in naturalizing, it might be well to mark out the informal groupings with a thin line of lime or sand so one can see what is to be planted or has been planted after the bulbs are in the ground. In such plantings avoid placing the bulbs in regular lines. This is accomplished sometimes by placing the bulbs in a pail and throwing them out on the ground in a swinging motion, planting the bulbs where they have fallen.

Fortunately narcissus grow in a wide range of soils and the home gardener has many choices of where he may put them. Some, especially the Poeticus group, do better in moist soils than do others. After planting, the bed might be ferti-

lized with a complete fertilizer (see FERTILIZERS) about 1–3 lbs. of a 5–10–5 per 100 sq. ft. and then the bed watered thoroughly.

In the spring, just before the new shoots break very far above the ground, another application of fertilizer might be in order and it should be thoroughly watered in immediately.

The most important part of the spring care, and frequently the hardest to follow through with, is to allow the plants to grow vigorously after the flowers have faded and died. This is the period when foods are manufactured and stored to provide good bloom the following year. This means that if the bulbs are in the flower border the leaves should not be cut until they have turned yellow—some time in June or early summer. If the planting is a naturalized one in grass, the grass should not be cut until the leaves have died. This may mean an unsightly, unmowed grass area for a few weeks, but it is absolutely essential if the general welfare of the bulbs is to be considered.

Lifting and separating the bulbs need be done only every 4th year, if then. All narcissus are easily propagated by offsets or small bulbs that form at the base of the old one, as well as by seed. The time for lifting and separating the bulbs is just after the leaves have died. The clumps are carefully lifted, soil shaken off the roots and the bulbs left exposed in the open air, preferably in the shade, for a few days to dry out. Then they are carefully separated and replanted at once, unless for some reason they are to be stored for a late-August planting.

The newer young bulblets which are to be saved may be planted in a row in the vegetable garden, about 1–3 in. apart, with 4 in. of soil on top. Within a year or so these will be of proper flowering size to be planted out in the flower garden.

Insect Pests

Dirty white maggots of the bulb fly ruin bulbs. There is only one maggot in a bulb and one generation annually. During the growing season, stunted poor bulbs should be pulled and destroyed. The maggots spend the winter in the bulbs and infested ones should be discarded. Control of slightly infested bulbs is done by soaking for 1½ hours in hot water at 110° F. The smaller grayish-yellow maggots of the lesser bulb fly have similar habits. They differ by having 2 generations and many may live in the same bulb. Controls are the same as for the bulb fly. Bulb mite is especially destructive to bulbs forced in the greenhouse. Cavities eaten in the bulb delay or prevent normal blooms and offer entrance to fungus rots. The addition of ½ pint of formaldehyde to 12 gal. of water for the above treatment is somewhat more effective than hot water alone.

Diseases

The various rots described under Tulip, Gladiolus and Lilium may infect narcissus bulbs and similar controls are used. Gray mosaic and white streak are virus diseases which weaken and distort plants and blooms. Destroy infected plants. Soft rot results from unfavorable storage conditions. Basal rot starts at the root-plate and spreads to the center of the bulb. The rooted tissue has a purplish-brown color and is dry and spongy. Careful handling of the bulbs will prevent most infections. A botrytis disease called smoulder produces blighted and deformed leaves just as they emerge from the soil in the spring. Avoid heavy soil and excess moisture. Recent experiments report excellent control of both bulb fly and basal rot by soaking the bulbs for 10 min. in 25% emulsion of insecticide #13—3 fluid ounces and fungicide #M—$\frac{1}{5}$ ounce in 5 gal. water. When flower buds blast, dig up and separate the bulbs, and they should bloom the next year.

asturiensis 3″–5″ **Zone 4 Asturian Daffodil**
This diminutive spring-flowering bulb has been listed variously as *N. minor*, *N. minor minimus*, *N. minimus*, etc. The small flower, actually a miniature daffodil, is only $\frac{1}{2}$ in. long. It blooms in March and has 1–3 erect or spreading leaves 2–4 in. long and only $\frac{1}{8}$–$\frac{1}{4}$ in. wide. Native to Spain and Portugal. It is able to survive even in sod, but where cared for in the open garden bed or in the front of the border, it blooms with the snow-drops and *Adonis amurensis* even before the snow has completely disappeared from all parts of the garden. It is the smallest of all the garden narcissus, a truly charming plant, well worth placing by the walk or the doorstep where it can be seen in bloom with the snowdrops in earliest spring or even in late winter.

bulbocodium 15″ **Zone 6 Petticoat Daffodil**
Native to southern France and Morocco; flowers solitary, light yellow with a cup longer than the main flower parts but only 1 in. long. Several varieties in several shades of yellow.

cyclamineus 8″ **Zone 6**
Native to Portugal with a small drooping flower, the petals reflexed but the cup long and narrow. Leaves very narrow. Interesting but not a good display type.

x incomparabilis 1′ **Zone 4**
Leaves $\frac{1}{4}$ in. wide, flower solitary, not fragrant, with a 6-lobed perianth and a cup short and stocky. Very common in gardens, having many varieties, some double. Flowers often 3–4 in. wide. Native to southwestern Europe.

jonquilla 1$\frac{1}{2}$′ **Zone 4 Jonquil**
Leaves 1$\frac{1}{2}$ ft. long, flowers 2–6 on the end of a single stalk, fragrant, and cup 1 in. long with wavy edge, but less than half as long as petals. Varying shades of yellow with many varieties.

juncifolius 4″ **Zone 6 (?) Rush-leaf Jonquil**
One of the diminutive daffodils, native to the Pyrenees, this is apparently well off in a rocky situation. Very fragrant, bright yellow flowers are borne, 1–4 together, with the tube about $\frac{1}{2}$ in. long.

minor 3″–6″ **Zone 4**
A delightful little plant, especially the variety **minimus** which is scarcely 3 in. tall, yellow, and blooms in early spring, even succeeding year after year where grass seriously competes with it for space. The true botanical classification of this may be in doubt but it is an excellent plant for the rockery or a special space all its own in the front of a foundation planting about the home.

moschatus (*N. cernuus*) 1′ **Zone 6**
An interesting species from Spain, not widely planted, with leaves $\frac{1}{2}$ in. wide and pale yellow flowers that gradually fade to white.

x odorus 1′ **Zone 6 Campernelle Jonquil**
With 2–4 fragrant yellow flowers on each stalk and cup about $\frac{3}{4}$ in. long, half the length of the petals. Native to southern Europe. Not often planted in America.

poeticus 1$\frac{1}{2}$′ **Zone 4 Poets Narcissus**
Flowers usually solitary and white and very fragrant, cup with wavy edges often rimmed with red, shorter than petals. Native to southern Europe. Many varieties.

pseudonarcissus 15″ **Zone 4 Daffodil, Trumpet Narcissus**
The true daffodil with large and prominent cup usually as long as the petals, single with double varieties, flowers solitary. Leaves about $\frac{3}{4}$ in. wide. Native to Europe.

tazetta 1$\frac{1}{2}$′ **Zone 8 Polyanthus Narcissus**
Flowers usually 4–8 on a stalk with cup about 1 in. long but shorter than petals. Fragrant and light yellow. Native to Canary Islands, Europe and Asia. The popular paper White Narcissus, used so much for forcing indoors, belongs here. Many varieties can be forced into bloom before Christmas. The var. **orientalis** is called the Chinese Sacred Lily and is frequently grown indoors in a bowl of pebbles and water.

triandrus 1′ **Zone 4 Angels-tears**
The narrow leaves are nearly round in cross-section, flowers are pure white, the cup is about $\frac{3}{4}$ in. long but the edge is not wavy, being about half the length of the petals. Native to south-western Europe.

watieri 6″ **Zone 6 (?) Watier Jonquil**
White to flushed pink, solitary flowers, an inch wide with a greenish-white tube $\frac{1}{2}$ in. long produced in May. Seems to do best in sunny

situations in well-drained, but not too dry soil.

NARTHECIUM (nar-THEE-cium)

americanum 1½' **Zone 6** **New Jersey Bog-asphodel**

Bog plants of eastern North America belonging to the Lily Family, with long, grasslike leaves and light yellow flowers in May and June. They grow in slowly spreading clusters and require a wet and mucky acid soil in sun or semi-shade. Native to N.J. and Del. Not often used in gardens.

NASTURTIUM (nas-TUR-shum). Note—The common name Nasturtium is applied to the genus *Tropaeolum*, which see.

officinale **aquatic** **Zone 4** **Water Cress**

A European water plant, widely naturalized in cold streams of the northeastern U.S. and a member of the Mustard Family, not to be confused with the common garden Nasturtium (*Tropaeolum* sp.) which belongs to an entirely different family. The Water Cress is a perennial, floating or rooting in the shallow bottom of cold streams, with odd-pinnate leaves, 1–4 pairs of leaflets with small white flowers in racemes. The leaves are eaten as a salad, raw, especially in the early spring. It is easily rooted merely from pieces of stems, but prefers cold water to warm.

NATAL-PLUM = *Carissa grandiflora*

NATURALIZED. A horticultural term for an exotic plant which has escaped from formal garden planting and has become established and is increasing "on its own" in the new country. Many European plants, especially weeds, have become "naturalized" since first being brought to America by the early settlers.

NECKLACE VINE = *Crassula rupestris*

NECTARINE.

Origin

The Nectarine, though differing somewhat in appearance and flavor, is actually of the same species as the Peach, *Prunus persica*, and has been known in the Old World for more than 2000 years. It originated as a natural mutation of the Peach and occasionally in peach orchards a tree will develop which produces nectarines. The Nectarine is one of the most interesting phenomena in horticulture. The trees may grow from peach pits and peach trees may grow from nectarine pits. Peach trees produce nectarine fruits by bud mutation and nectarine trees produce peach fruits by the same mutations. Also, both the peach and nectarine trees can produce individual fruits that are part Nectarine and part Peach.

Culture and Adaptation

The Nectarine is grown wherever the Peach

is grown and the culture is the same for both. Trees and blossoms of the Nectarine are indistinguishable from those of the Peach. All cultural procedures recommended for the Peach apply to the Nectarine.

Varieties

Modern varieties of nectarines are the result of controlled breeding and the fruits are far superior to those that appeared early in the history of the industry. All major varieties are self-fruitful and so do not require cross-pollination. The breeding program at the Va. Agricultural Experiment Station has produced 'Lexington', 'Redchief', 'Cavalier', 'Pocahontas', 'Cherokee and 'Redbud'. The N.J. Agricultural Experiment Station produced a series of white-fleshed varieties called 'Nectarose', 'Nectaheart', 'Nectacrest' and 'Nectalate' and, more recently, a yellow-fleshed series called the 'Nectared'. Private breeders in Calif. have developed excellent varieties and the N.Y. Experiment Station is presently developing new varieties. Modern nectarine varieties are larger than those developed a few years ago and are more resistant to attacks of brown rot fungus. One old variety from Europe is 'Rivers Orange' and, although it is small, the excellent dessert quality keeps it on the nursery list.

Thinning

Nectarine fruits must be thinned heavily to attain good size and flavor. The fruits must be spaced at least 8 in. apart and, as with the Peach, the thinning should be completed no later than the period of final fruit drop which occurs about a month after bloom.

Harvesting

The Nectarine softens rapidly and is best if picked while in a firm condition. If allowed to soften on the tree, the fruit will bruise easily and become mushy and difficult to handle. When picked in a firm-ripe condition the fruit handles easily and will ripen to a soft condition, with excellent quality, within a day or two.

ERNEST G. CHRIST

Pest Control

The smooth skin of the Nectarine makes it more vulnerable to insect and disease attacks than the Peach. It is much like the Plum in this respect, but with modern materials and varieties, the control of pests is much more satisfactory than was the case previously. As with the Peach and all other stone fruits, the Nectarine is subject to borer attacks in the trunk at the soil line. See PEACH for pests and their control.

NECTARY. A place or organ where sugar or nectar is secreted.

NEEDLE CAST. A fungus disease of conifers, not to be confused with windburn or needle drop from physiological conditions. Infection usually starts at the base of the needle and spreads to the entire needle causing it to turn brown and drop. Where weather or soil conditions are involved, the needle first turns brown at the tip. Sprays of fungicide #D and #W have been used experimentally with some success.

NEILLIA (NEEL-ia). Alternate-leaved deciduous shrubs belonging to the Rose Family, closely allied to Physocarpus, with short racemes of small white-to-pinkish flowers none too conspicuous and fruits that are small dry capsules. Propagated by division and cuttings.

sinensis   6′   Zone 5   Chinese Neillia
A dense shrub with small racemes of small pinkish flowers in Aug. or Sept. The light green leaves are 1½–3 in. long and the entire texture of the plant is light. A native to central China, this is the best of the 3 species of this genus, because of its hardiness and pinkish flowers.

thibetica   6′   Zones 5–6   Tibet Neillia
A rare species with leaves 2–3 in. long, short-stalked white flowers borne in late summer, in racemes 2–3 in. long. Native to western China.

thyrsiflora   3′   Zones 6–7   Whiteflower Neillia
A deciduous shrub with delicate, somewhat angular, branches, 3-lobed leaves about 1½–4 in. long and small white flowers in racemes 1–3 in. long. Native to the Himalayas. If it is killed to the ground over winter it will flower the following summer. Only of value in gardens for its dense, feathery texture.

NELUMBIUM = *Nelumbo*

NELUMBO LUTEA = American Lotus. See WATER GARDENING. Formerly *Nelumbium pentapetalum.*

NELUMBO NUCIFERA = East Indian Lotus. See WATER GARDENING. Formerly *Nelumbium nelumbo.*

NEMATODES. Nematodes are worms, not insects. Those which are plant pests are microscopic. Most species feed on the roots, and cause various types of injury to roots, stems and leaves. Other species are leaf feeders. Injury by them is often connected with infection by fungi, (bacteria and viruses). Root knot nematode which produces galls or swellings on the roots of many trees, shrubs, ornamental plants and vegetables is well known. It is a very destructive pest of carrots and most greenhouse vegetables. In the greenhouse sterilization of soil with steam (180° F. for 30 min.) is often done and chemicals such as chloropicrin (Larvacide), methyl bromide (Dowfume-MC-2 and Mylone) are available. In the field, preplanting treatments with ethylene dibromide (EDB) and dichloro-

propene (D-D or Telone) are now used where needed and the expense is justified. Leaf-infecting species such as foliar nematode on chrysanthemum are controlled by sprays with insecticide #15.

Where nematodes are a problem, it is well to destroy susceptible plants, use clean bulbs, cuttings and seed, provide good cultural conditions and secure advice from qualified authorities.

NEMESIA (nem-EE-sia). These are African plants which do not like hot summer heat or high humidity. They have colorful tubular flowers white, yellow, pink, rose and scarlet, according to variety, borne in terminal racemes. They can not be grown everywhere because of too high summer heat, but where they do well they make excellent edging or bedding plants. Sow seeds in pots in early April, keep cool and set out, after frost, in the sun, 6 in. apart.

strumosa   1½′–2′   annual   Pouch Nemesia
With square stems, leaves in alternating pairs 2–3 in. long. Flowers are various shades of white, yellow and purple borne in racemes 4 in. long. The var. 'Grandiflora' has larger flowers, 'Nana Compacta' is dwarf; but the best is 'Suttonii', an improved variety with colors ranging from white, yellow and orange to crimson.

versicolor   1′   annual   Spurred Nemesia
The leaves are 2 in. long, flowers range in several colors, borne in racemes 3 in. long. The var. 'Compacta' is dwarf and is very floriferous.

NEMOPANTHUS (nee-mo-PANTH-us)

mucronatus   9′   Zone 3   Mountain-holly
A plant of the woods, not used in ornamental planting, this is native to the mountainous areas of northeastern North America. Alternate leaves 1–1½ in. long, sexes separate or flowers of both sexes on the same plant, flowers inconspicuous and fruits are dull red berries about ⅓ in. across during the late summer. The foliage turns yellow in the fall. Native from Nova Scotia to Va. Propagated by seed and softwood cuttings.

NEMOPHILA (nem-OFF-ill-a)

insignis = *N. menziesii*

menziesii   30″   annual   Baby-blue-eyes
A Calif. native that can be used as an annual in the North, with tufted ornamental leaves in a rosette at the base, and terminal panicles of blue or delicately colored trumpet-shaped flowers 1½ in. across which are most fragrant at night. The leaves, 4 in. long, are pinnatifid with 5–9-lobed divisions. There are several varieties sometimes available, including 'Alba', with white flowers, 'Grandiflora' with larger flowers; 'Liniflora' with white or blue flowers and 'Marginata' with blue flowers with white edges.

Seeds of all these can be sown outdoors in April in full sun, and the seedlings thinned to about 9 in. apart. These are excellent for edging or for a sunny spot in the rock garden.

NEOBESSEYA = *Coryphantha*

NEOMARICA (neo-MARI-ca) (syn. *Marica*)

gracilis   1½′   Zone 9   Slender False Flag
Belonging to the Iris Family, this beautiful plant from Brazil is valued for its irislike white 2-in. flowers which have yellow and brown markings, but they quickly fade. Swordlike leaves 1½ ft. long and an inch wide come from a short rhizome. This is smaller in all its parts than *N. northiana* and is sometimes grown as a house plant.

northiana   3′   Zones 9–10   Apostle Plant
So called because the individual fans or tufts of this plant normally form 12 leaves, before one turns brown, these being sword shaped, 2 ft. long, light green and decorative. It is best to allow only 1 fan to develop on each pot. The irislike very fragrant flowers are pure white, 3–4 in. across, with the inner segments violet. Propagation is by division after flowering or by planting the plantlets which sometimes grow on the flowering stems. A good house plant, native to Brazil.

NEOREGELIA (neo-re-GEL-ia)

marmorata (*Aregelia marmorata*)   1′   **Zone 10**
A stemless bromeliad with a rosette of 10–15 in.-long leathery leaves, 3 in. wide, which are marbled and have patches of red on both upper and lower surfaces. Flowers are pale violet about 2 in. across. Native to Brazil—sometimes used as a pot plant in the home, chiefly for its colorful foliage.

NEPENTHES (nep-EN-theez). The pitcher-plants are a group of tropical "insectivorous" plants chiefly from India and East Indies, with alternate leaves, the midrib of the leaf elongated into a very complex, pendulous organ popularly called the "pitcher" which has a lid and in which insects are caught. There are many hybrids and species and they are frequently planted in hanging baskets in a warm, humid greenhouse where the temperature seldom drops below 65° F. They are propagated by seeds and cuttings of mature shoots. Most home greenhouses are not sufficiently warm or moist for these plants to prosper.

NEPETA (NEP-et-a)

cataria   3′   Zone 3   Catnip, Catmint
A popular perennial aromatic herb, native to Europe and Asia and often naturalized in America, often a weed widespread throughout the northern U.S. and southern Canada. The stems are 4-angled, the leaves are opposite, triangular-shaped up to 2 in. long, each on a long petiole. The flowers are whitish to pale purple, about ¼ in. long but borne from July to Sept. on tall spikes about 5 in. long. The aromatic fragrance of the dried leaves and stems is most attractive to cats. The roots can be a serious and vigorously increasing pest in the garden. An old-fashioned remedy for feverish colds was made by boiling leaves of this in water.

x faassenii   2′   Zone 3   Persian Ground-ivy
Valued for its gray-green foliage, this herbaceous perennial hybrid makes a good ground cover in the sun. It is sold in most nurseries under the misapplied name of *N. mussinii* but this is a sprawling plant having a much shorter blooming period. Rather unkempt and floppy-looking at best. The small lavender-blue flowers are whorled and borne on spikes. The leaves are lance shaped, 1–2 in. long and wrinkled. This originated before 1939 in the Botanic Gardens at Copenhagen, Denmark. The dead unsightly flower spikes might be removed and thus the plant might bloom a second time in the late summer.

grandiflora   2′   Zone 3   Caucasian Nepeta
An aromatic herb occasionally seen in American gardens with leaves to 2½ in. long and blue flowers ¾ in. long, borne in clusters in loose racemes and evident from June to Sept. especially if the faded blooms are removed. Its fragrant gray leaves make it useful as a low edging hedge when clipped. Native to the Caucasus.

hederacea = *Glecoma hederacea*
mussinii   1′   Zone 4(?)
Unfortunately this has been mixed up in the trade with what is now termed *N. x faassenii*, but differs in being much more sprawling in habit. The leaves are an inch long, crenate on the edges, and gray-green. The flowers are frequently a light blue. It is native to the Caucasus. Propagation is merely by division but seeds germinate readily. Chances are that it is not as neat a plant as *N. x faassenii*.

NEPHROLEPIS (neff-ROL-ep-is). These are the sword ferns, sometimes called the ladder ferns because of the regular arrangement of the short pinnae up and down the midrib of the frond. They are native mostly in the tropics of North and South America, Africa, the West Indies and Malaya. The most widely used is *N. exaltata*, native from Fla. southward into Brazil, and it has many varieties. One of these, the Boston Fern ("Bostoniensis") has been propagated by the millions since 1894 when it originated. This and the species *N. exaltata* make exceptionally good house plants and are used for this purpose more than any other fern. Also, because of the long fronds of some varieties, they make splendid plants for hanging baskets as well.

The sword ferns, since they are of tropical origin, are plants for the conservatory or home, not the outdoor garden except in tropical regions. They require a minimum temperature of 55–60° F. and atmospheric moisture, supplied in the home by occasionally syringing them. A soil mixture might be 3 parts loam, 1 part leaf mold or peat moss, 1 part sand. They should be repotted if necessary in Feb. or March just as the new growth is about to start.

Sometimes young plants grow so fast they may need a second repotting in midsummer, but care should be taken at this time not to disturb the roots any more than is absolutely necessary.

Some of the forms of *N. exaltata* that have long fronds, as well as the variety 'Bostoniensis' are excellent subjects for hanging baskets. When properly grown, they make a dense ball of gracefully drooping fronds, that completely hide the basket. For suggestions see HANGING BASKET.

Propagation of these ferns is chiefly by division, and the Boston Fern is only propagated this way because it is the asexual method of propagating a clone. In order to accomplish this, choose one of two methods.

Inspect the plant itself carefully and see whether it can be divided or separated into one or more pieces. If it can not or is too good a specimen, several 3-in. pots filled with leaf mold and soil can be set around the mother plant and a runner from it (not a frond or leaflike structure) be firmly pressed into the soil and kept moist until it is well rooted when it can be separated from the mother plant.

There are very few households in the U.S. which at one time or another have not had a "fern", and usually it would be *N. exaltata* 'Bostoniensis'. See FERNS.

acuminata 2'–3' **Zone** 10 **Java Sword Fern** This fern is native to Malaya and has fronds 1 ft. wide. It is sometimes used in conservatories, producing many runners.

biserrata 4½' **Zone** 10 **Purplestalk Sword Fern** With drooping or arching fronds which can be 1 ft. wide, this is native to Malaya and has been used in conservatories. It is interesting in that the toothed pinnae can be 6 in. long.

cordifolia 2' **Zone** 10 **Tuber Sword Fern** Another excellent tropical species, sometimes used in conservatories usually for its varieties which are smaller and more compact or have plumose fronds, and one, **variegata**, with variegated foliage. Fronds are about 2 ft. long and 2½ in. wide and the roots produce small tubes.

exaltata 2'–6' **Zone** 10 **Sword Fern** The exceptionally long fronds of this fern, when it is grown well, make it ideal for use in hanging baskets in the greenhouse or in the shade of the porch during summer. Usually house humidity is not high enough for it to grow well long, unless arrangements are made to take it to a more humid atmosphere periodically to recuperate. However, this species is mostly superseded now by the Boston Fern.

The Boston Fern (**'Bostoniensis'**) originated in 1894. This is an interesting commentary on plant names for this tropical plant actually originated in Philadelphia but was first noticed in a shipment received in Boston, Mass. Actually it is the best variety of this species, and over 50 variations of the Boston Fern have been named, some of which are available as pot plants from wholesale florists. The Boston Fern is more graceful than the species, with longer and more graceful fronds. Propagation is by runners (see under generic name). Of the varieties, some are more compact (**'Compacta'**) in habit, some have very plumose or finely divided segments, such as **'Todeoides'**, **'Elegantissima'**, **'Superba'**, and **'Whitmanii'**. The Boston Fern itself is 1-pinnate, but some of the beautiful varieties grown today are 2, 3, and 4 times pinnate. Some may have a tendency to revert to the species.

pectinata 1½' **Zone** 10 **Basket Fern** A good fern for the hanging basket in the greenhouse, compact in habit with grayish-green fronds 1½ ft. long but only an inch wide, native to tropical America.

NEPHTHYTIS (neff-THI-tis)
afzelii **climbing** **Zone** 10 With papery arrowhead leaves on slender climbing stems, this is usually used on a bark support and is used as a display plant in restaurants and office buildings, for it is adaptable to poor growing conditions. It has a horizontal, creeping rhizome; leaves about a foot long, petioles 18 in. long, and green spathes 3 in. long. Native to West Africa.

NERINE (ne-RY-ne).
Bulbous plants from South Africa, mostly for planting in greenhouses except in very mild parts of the country, valued for the large clusters of 4–20 conspicuously-colored flowers at the end of a 1½ ft. stalk, borne in the autumn, after the leaves have disappeared. Easily propagated by offsets. After the blooms, the foliage is grown in the greenhouse and when this dies in May, the bulbs are rested until early fall when they are taken into the greenhouse for forcing. Bulbs grown this way will bloom annually for many years.

bowdenii 1' **Zone** 9 **Cape Colony Nerine** Straplike leaves 1 in. wide, flowers 6–12 in a cluster, 9 in. across, rose pink. Practically leafless when in flower.

curvifolia 1' **Zone** 9 **Curveleaf Nerine**

The straplike leaves appear after the flowers, which are produced 12–18 in a cluster, bright scarlet with reflexed petals and very long stamens. The var. **fothergillii** is more vigorous and produces more flowers.

filifolia   8″   Zone 9
Flowers bright red, leaves grasslike.

sarniensis   1½′   Zone 9   Guernsey-lily
The leaves are ¾ in. wide and appear after the flowers. These are bright red, slightly crisped, and about 1½ in. long and 10 per cluster. Several varieties. It is named after the island where it is grown to perfection although it is not native.

NERIUM (NEE-rium)
oleander   20′   Zones 7–8   Oleander
There are nearly 50 varieties of this serviceable evergreen plant being offered by nurserymen in the warmer parts of the U.S. It is native about the coast of the Mediterranean Sea and is serviceable in the garden because the plants need little or no attention once they are established. They withstand hot, dry situations and the varieties come with flowers white, yellow, red or purple, single or double. Also the flowers are 3 in. across and bloom from April throughout the summer. The evergreen foliage reminds one of the bamboo and the plants are very popular subjects in the North for growing in tubs in the greenhouse. In order to keep them restrained properly, they might be root pruned occasionally. They root readily, in fact cuttings often root when merely put in bottles of water. The leaves are highly toxic both in green and dry conditions and contact with leaves can produce dermatitis.

Insect Pests

Oleander scale in the form of circular light gray scales on the leaves is a common pest. Spraying with insecticide #15 and the frequent use of greenhouse aerosols will keep it in check. Mealy bugs (see MEALY BUGS) and soft brown scale (see FERN) may also be destructive.

NERTERA (NER-ter-a)
granadensis   creeping   Zone 9   Beadplant
A low creeping herb, native to New Zealand and Tasmania and sometimes planted in southern Calif. The stems are 4-angled, leaves are opposite and only ⅛ in. long; flowers are greenish, and the fruit is an orange-colored berry about ¼ in. in dia., valued because it remains evident on the plant from midsummer to well into the winter.

NERVE. A slender rib or vein in the leaf, particularly if unbranched.

NETTLE, DEAD. See LAMIUM.

NETTLE, STINGING = *Urtica dioica*

NETTLESPURGE,   PEREGRINA = *Jatropha integerrima*

NEVIUSIA (nev-i-YEW-sa)
alabamensis   3′–6′   Zone 5   Snow-wreath
Probably this plant is only of interest in the southeastern U.S. where it is native, because as an ornamental specimen many other plants surpass it in beauty. The flowers are solitary, white and feathery, blooming about mid-May. They are nearly 1 in. in dia., and are conspicuous because of numerous stamens (they have no petals) making them unique but not necessarily outstanding. Both softwood and hardwood cuttings root easily.

NEW ZEALAND CHRISTMAS-TREE = *Metrosideros tomentosa*

NEW ZEALAND-LAUREL = *Corynocarpus laevigata*

NICANDRA (ny-KAN-dra)
physalodes   4′   Zone 8   Apple-of-Peru
An old-fashioned garden plant introduced from Peru many years ago as an ornamental but escaped as a weed in some places. The alternate leaves are oval and toothed; flowers are blue, an inch or more across, solitary, round; fruit a berry enclosed in a 5-winged calyx. Propagated by seeds in the greenhouse in March, or out-of-doors in April. Sometimes termed "Shoofly" in the South.

NICOTIANA (nik-o-shee-AY-na). This genus is a member of the Nightshade Family. One species *N. tabacum* provides the leaves for tobacco. Several other species are grown as colorful garden plants.

alata   1½′–4′   annual, perennial   Winged Tobacco
The flowers are very fragrant at night, but close in cloudy weather. They are 2 in. wide at the mouth but there is a long tube several inches long. Colors range, depending on variety, of which there are several, from pure white through rose, red, crimson, purple, buff-salmon and cream. The alternate, simple leaves are about 4 in. long and have narcotic-poisonous properties. It is this species, its varieties and hybrids which are chiefly grown as garden ornamentals. In the South it is a perennial, but in the North this South American plant is best grown as an annual, with seeds sown indoors in March or outdoors in mid-April in the spot where the plants are to grow. They prefer a moist, partly shaded spot and should be thinned to about a foot apart.

glauca   20′   Zone 9   Tree Tobacco
A treelike plant with glaucous-blue, ovate, long-petioled leaves and yellow flowers 1½ in. long. Native to South America but naturalized in Tex. and Calif. Of value for its good habit and foliage.

x sanderae   3′   annual   Sander Tobacco
Of bushy habit with spoon-shaped leaves up to
a foot long, the rose-colored flowers about 3 in.
long; originating in England.

suaveolens   2′   annual or biennial
Native to Australia, this bears fragrant greenish-
purple flowers 2 in. long and an inch wide borne
in terminal racemes but they open at night.

sylvestris   4′   annual or perennial
Native to Argentina this is grown in the garden
in the North as an annual, in the South as a
perennial. The long, drooping, fragrant white
flowers borne in clusters are 3½ in. long and do
not close during cloudy weather like those of
N. alata.

tabacum   6′   annual   Tobacco
The tobacco of commerce comes from the
ft.-long (and longer) alternate leaves of this
tropical American plant. The long flowers are
2 in. across, white, sometimes tinged rose or
purplish red. However, if this tropical plant is to
be grown as a garden annual it should be started
in the greenhouse and set out in June when the
temperature is warm. See TOBACCO.

NICOTINE. This alkaloid extract of tobacco is
a contact and fumigant insecticide. It is prepared
as a dust usually combined with lime, as a liquid
with sulfuric acid to produce nicotine sulfate
known commercially as Black Leaf 40, as a
smoke for fumigation with a combustible and
as a wettable powder with bentonite which is
primarily a stomach poison. Insect killing is
primarily through fumigant action which is
increased by higher temperature. The alkaloid
is toxic to warm-blooded animals when absorbed but generally safe to plants. Due to its
high volatility it dissipates quickly when applied
and has a relatively short storage life. Flower
petals may be injured when it is used. It is
rapidly being replaced by other contact insecticides and most supplies are now imported.

NIDULARIUM (nid-ew-LAY-rium). The species
of this tropical genus are bromeliads, which
grow in trees with handsome foliage and
colorful red, purplish or white, flowers. The
basal leaves are in rosettes and the plants are
practically stemless. Sometimes grown in the
greenhouse. Native to Brazil.

NIEREMBERGIA (neer-em-BERJ-ia). Belonging to the Nightshade Family, these natives of
South America are dainty annual or perennial
plants, all suitable for pot culture if desired. The
slender stems are clothed with small leaves ½–1
in. long, and the flowers are cup-shaped, 1–2 in.
across, white, blue, lilac or violet.

In the North, if grown for the garden out-of-
doors, these are treated as annuals by sowing
the seed in the greenhouse in Feb. and planting
out in May after frost. In the South, these can

be treated either as annuals or as perennials,
and propagation by division or cuttings (or
layering) is practiced to maintain desired color
forms. All species are good for summer bloom
in the garden, and they make good plants for
pots and window boxes as well.

caerulea = *N. hippomanica caerulea*
frutescens = *N. scoparia*
**hippomanica violacea   6″–12″   annual or
            perennial   Blue Cupflower**
With blue-violet flowers in summer, leaves ¾ in.
long. Since there is some color variation, clones
with good color may be kept by propagating
cuttings, otherwise this is treated as an annual
in the North and a perennial up to Zone 7.

repens   6″   Zone 7   White Cupflower
This is the most popular species, making a
dense mat of foliage especially valued for
bedding or for planting between stepping
stones. The creamy-white flowers 1½ in. across,
are streaked with purple; some are rose colored.
The stems creep along the ground rooting at
various places. In the South, propagated by
division, layering and cuttings; in the North
treated as an annual and propagated by seed.

rivularis = *N. repens*
scoparia frutescens   3′   Zone 7   Tall Cupflower
Semi-shrubby, with many branches, the leaves
are 1 in. long and linear, the flowers are an inch
wide, white tinted with blue. There are at least
2 varieties of this. Grown in the North as a
popular annual.

NIGELLA (ny-JELL-a)
damascena   1½′–2′   annual   Love-in-a-mist
A member of the Buttercup Family, this old-
fashioned garden annual from southern Europe
is known to many. The finely-divided alternate
leaves, much-branched habit, light blue or white
flowers about 1½ in. across with all the surrounding threadlike bracts which act as a suitable
background for the petals, and the globelike
fruit, make an interesting display during the
summer. The white variety **'Miss Jekyll'** seems
to be the most popular at present. Easily propagated by seeds sown in the garden, either in the
fall in light sandy soils or in spring, in the spot
where the plants are to grow. Seedlings do not
transplant easily. This plant makes a fine filler
in the border but the flowering season is rather
short so that a succession of seedings might be
made starting in mid-April, again at the end of
May and again at the end of June. Usually this
species self-sows itself. This is also sometimes
called Fennel Flower, and the pungent seeds
have a spicy taste like nutmeg, and are often
used in flavoring foods.

sativa   1′   annual   Fennel-flower
A popular herb from the Mediterranean Region
of Europe with alternate leaves and belonging
to the Buttercup Family. The blue or white

flowers are solitary, to $1\frac{1}{2}$ in. across, and so make a nice addition to the blue garden. The seed is pungent and spicy to the taste. It is used in bread and cake. An oil is made from the seeds which is used in the manufacture of certain perfumes.

NIGHTBLOOMING   CEREUS = *Hylocereus undatus*

NIGHT FLOWERING PLANTS. Since lighting the garden at night is becoming increasingly popular (see LIGHTING) some gardeners might be interested in a few plants which open their flowers at night. Of course, the majority of plants have their flowers open day and night, but there are a few considered by some as "unusual" merely because they are at their best at night. A few are:

material in the soil provides some of the raw materials and soil bacteria do the actual work. Moisture content of the soil should be high as well as the soil temperature, for with less moisture and lower temperature there is less activity on the part of the soil bacteria. It is the nitrates that are utilized by the plant roots. This process of nitrification in the soil is going on continually. The soil bacteria must have optimum conditions to make a fertile soil. Proper drainage and aeration as well as the present of raw humus and warm temperatures are some of the prerequisites. It is obvious then, that humus must be continually available in the soils for this all-important process to continue. See SOILS and FERTILIZERS.

NITROGEN. One of the elements necessary for plant growth and probably the most important.

	HEIGHT	ZONE	COMMON NAME
Datura stramonium	5′	Annual	Jimson-weed
Gladiolus tristis	2′	7	Eveningflower Gladiolus
Hemerocallis sp.	3′–9′	3–7	Daylilies
Hylocereus undatus	25′	10	Nightblooming Cereus
Matthiola longipetala	1′	Annual	Evening Stock
Mirabilis jalapa	2′–3′	Annual	Common Four-o'clock
Nicotiana alata	$1\frac{1}{2}′$–4′	Annual–perennial	Winged Tobacco
Nyctocereus sp.	8′	10	Serpent Cactus
Oenothera, many sp.	6″–4′	3–5	Sundrops
Selenicereus sp.	Climbing	10	Queen-of-the-night
Silene noctiflora	2′	Annual	Night-flowering Catchfly

NIGHT-JESSAMINE = *Cestrum nocturnum*

NIGHTSHADE. See SOLANUM.

NINEBARK. See PHYSOCARPUS.

NIPPON-BELLS = *Shortia uniflora*

NIPPON-LILY, OMOTO = *Rhodea japonica*

NITELLA (NI-tel-la)
  gracilis aquatic plant Zone 5 Slender Nitella
A wiry, branched, aquatic grass widely distributed in ponds throughout North America. There are no roots. If this is examined while alive with a microscope of moderate power, one can see the protoplasm circulating through the stems and leaves. It is used sometimes in aquaria but spreads so rapidly it can become a pest.

NITRATE OF SODA. An inorganic fertilizer containing 15.5%–16% nitrogen and is used only at the rate of $\frac{1}{2}$–1 oz. per sq. yard. It is alkaline in reaction. See SOILS. This should be used with extreme care as it contains an overly large amount of nitrogen.

NITRIFICATION. The process by which ammonium salts are oxidized to form nitrates and nitrides is called nitrification. Humus

Without a proper amount of nitrogen plants become stunted and yellowish. On the other hand, if they have too much they may not flower but become overly succulent in growth, with weak floppy stems. Usually nitrogen is used up from the soil at a greater rate than any other element. In the proper amounts, nitrogen promotes strong vegetative growth and good dark green leaf color. It is a very essential part of most fertilizers. See FERTILIZERS.

NODE. The place upon the stem which normally bears a leaf or leaves.

NODULE. See TUBERCLE. Pealike bodies on the roots of legumes which contain helpful bacteria having the power to draw nitrogen from the air and put it in the soil. Peas, beans, lupines and soy beans all have nodules as part of their root systems.

NOLANA (no-LAY-na)
  acuminata (*N. lanceolata*)   4″–12″   **annual or perennial**
Foliage hairy, lanceolate leaves 6 in. long; handsome sky-blue flowers that are bell-shaped and solitary with a yellowish-white spotted

throat 2 in. wide. Native to Peru. Sometimes used in hanging baskets.

atriplicifolia = *N. paradoxa*
lanceolata = *N. acuminata*
paradoxa (*N. atriplicifolia*)   4″–12″   **annual**
                                        Dark Blue Nolana
Actually a perennial but usually grown as an annual, with the basal leaves having petioles 6 in. long; flowers blue and yellow about 2 in. wide. Seeds are sown indoors in Feb. or March and the seedlings are set out about a foot apart in the full sun after all danger of frost is over. Sometimes termed the Chilean Bellflower.

NOMENCLATURE. For purposes of international communication, scientific names of plants are in Latin. The names of species are composed of 2 parts, the generic name followed by the specific epithet, e.g. *Rosa spinosissima*, the Scotch or Burnet Rose. This is the binomial system, established in 1753 by the famous Swedish biologist, Carl Linnaeus, and still in use today. Prior to this date, polynomial names that consisted of a descriptive phrase were used.

With continued exploration, and increase in knowledge, more and more species have been discovered, described and named and it often happens that a species has been named more than once. Especially did this happen before communications and the exchange of scientific information became as widespread and rapid as it is today. As a result many species have been given more than one Latin name, often several, and yet, for international and scientific purposes, only one is wanted.

Furthermore, there was no uniformity in nomenclatural usage and custom, and in 1867 the Swiss botanist, Alphonse de Candolle, submitted his *Lois de la nomenclature botanique* to the First International Botanical Congress in Paris. Although modified, these laws have subsequently become the basis of the present International Code of Botanical Nomenclature,* a code which is accepted in every country today. By its application it is possible to decide which of the botanical names given to any plant is correct and to have legal procedures for establishing new ones.

In the case of horticultural varieties, or cultivars, their names are governed by the International Code of Nomenclature for Cultivated Plants, a code established more recently, which applies to agricultural and silvicultural plants as well.

One of the aims of the International Codes is to provide a stable method of naming plants

---

* Current editions of the Codes of Nomenclature may be obtained from the International Bureau for Plant Taxonomy and Nomenclature, 106 Lange Nieuwstraat, Utrecht, Netherlands.

and, to this end, one of the principles is that nomenclature is "based on priority of publication." That is, when more than one name has been given to a plant, the earliest that is in accordance with the code is the correct one. The only exception to strict priority is a list of conserved generic names (*Nomina Generica Conservanda*), where well-known names of important genera are conserved by the code against earlier but obscure names. Almost 900 generic names for flowering plants are contained in this list, which includes *Forsythia* and *Zinnia*, to cite 2 examples. Attempts have been made at international botanical congresses to make it possible, within the code of nomenclature, to conserve well-known specific names which are threatened by obscure ones, or to reject the obscure names, but these have always been outvoted on the grounds that the strict application of the code should eventually lead to nomenclatural stability.

In order to be valid, a name must have been accompanied by a description of the plant (in Latin since 1936, except for fossil plants) and published in a printed, or similarly reproduced, book or article, which is distributed generally. Without this description (or a detailed illustration in some cases) the name has no standing and is known as a *nomen nudum*.

Type specimens, which are fundamentally important in nomenclature, are the original specimens upon which an author based his descriptions of new species, variety or other group below the rank of species. If there is any doubt about the true identity of a name or if its description needs to be amplified, because of a newly discovered and closely allied species, for example, then the type specimen can be examined and the question of identity settled. The type specimen is not necessarily typical of the species but is that specimen upon which the original description was based. The type of a genus is a species, and, if a genus is split into 2 or more new genera, then that part which originally contained the type species will continue to carry the original generic name.

Latin names of plants can be formed in almost any way; most of them are Latin, or Greek names with Latin endings, but others may be names from other languages or even anagrams. Whatever their origin they must be treated as though they were Latin and, in the case of epithets, be made to agree in case and gender. Generic names may be masculine, feminine or neuter, so that we have names like *Dianthus alpinus*, *Aquilegia alpina*, and *Chrysanthemum alpinum*. Where names are given in honor of a person or persons they are usually given the genitive case e.g. *Prunus sargentii*, Sargent's cherry, in honor of the late Charles

Sprague Sargent, the noted American dendrologist; *Primula sherriffae*, Mrs. C. I. Sherriff's primula, in honor of the mother of Major George Sherriff, the collector; *Petrocosmea parryorum*, the *Petrocosmea* of the Parrys: Mr. and Mrs. N. E. Parry who first collected this species and introduced it into cultivation; and, even, *Sempervivum tectorum*, the houseleek of the roofs. In the masculine gender, where the name of a person ends in a consonant, the letters *ii* are added (e.g. *sargentii* above) but where it ends in a vowel or *-er*, a single *i* is added, e.g. *Gentiana farreri, Euonymus fortunei* and *Rhododendron vaseyi*. Occasionally epithets commemorating a person may take the adjectival form, e.g. *Chamaecyparis lawsoniana*, the Lawson cypress.

Generic names are always spelled with a capital initial letter and specific epithets generally with a small letter. However, although decapitalization for epithets is recommended by the International Code, it is permissible, for those who wish to make the distinction, to use a capital initial letter for 3 types: (1) those formed from personal names, e.g. *Sargentii* above; (2) those based on a vernacular name in another language, e.g. *Jasminum Sambac*, where *Sambac* is a native name for this jasmine; and (3) where a generic name is used, e.g. *Aesculus Hippocastanum*, where *Hippocastanum* is an old name for the same genus.

In botanical nomenclature, as opposed to the rules that govern the scientific names of animals, tautonyms are not permitted. These are names where the epithet repeats the generic name, e.g. when the apple, at one time called *Pyrus malus*, is transferred to the genus *Malus* it may not be called *M. malus* but must become *M. sylvestris*, its earliest legitimate name in the genus *Malus*.

For full and accurate expression of a scientific name, the name of the author who first proposed it and described the species (or other taxon) is also cited, often in a conventionally abbreviated form, e.g. *Rosa spinosissima* L., where the "L." stands for Linnaeus. Where the epithet was first proposed in a different genus, or at some other rank, such as a variety, the name of the original author is given in parenthesis, followed by that of the author who combined the epithet in the new way, e.g. *Cotoneaster tomentosa* (Ait.) Lindl., where Aiton had first proposed the epithet *tomentosa* in the genus *Mespilus*, later combined by Lindley as a species of *Cotoneaster*, or *Magnolia sinensis* (Rehd. & Wils.) Stapf, where Stapf raised to the rank of species the plant which Rehder and Wilson had first described as a variety of *M. globosa* Hook. f. & Thoms. Sometimes a name is proposed by one botanist

but actually published by another; in these cases the names of the 2 authors are often joined by the word *ex*, e.g. *Rhododendron lepidotum* Wallich ex G. Don, named by Nathaniel Wallich but validly published by George Don. If an epithet has first been used in cultivation, and later given valid publication, it is often cited in the following way: *Ilex serrata* Thunb. f. *xanthocarpa* Hort. ex Rehd. where the epithet *xanthocarpa*, first applied in cultivation (*Hortorum*, of gardeners), was validly described by Rehder. The chief value in citing these names of authors is to distinguish between homonyms, that is where the same name has been given to different plants by different authors (only one of which can be accepted), but they also indicate the approximate date and place of publication, and the source of the type specimen upon which the original description was based.

Hybrids between species can be named in 2 ways, either by means of a formula, which consists of the epithets of the 2 parent species joined by a multiplication sign, e.g. *Lonicera morrowii* x *tatarica*, or by means of an epithet which is distinguished from that of a true species by being preceded by a multiplication sign, *L.* x *bella* (*L. morrowii* x *tatarica*). Where a formula is employed, the epithets are usually placed in alphabetical order, or with that of the female parent first, where it is known. The method used in any publication should be clearly stated and, if possible, the female (♀) and male (♂) signs are added for precision. The same applies to hybrids between varieties and other botanical groups below the rank of species.

Intergeneric hybrids are also designed either by a formula or a name, which, in these cases, is formed by a combination into a single word of parts of the names of the 2 parental genera, i.e. the first part, or whole, of one name and the last part, or whole, of the other. In these cases the multiplication sign is used to precede the hybrid "generic" name e.g., x *Mahoberberis* (= *Berberis* x *Mahonia*). Where names are used for hybrids derived from 4 or more genera they are formed from the name of a person eminent as a collector, grower or student of the group with the ending *-ara* added, e.g. x *Burrageara* (= *Cochlioda* x *Miltonia* x *Odontoglossum* x *Oncidium*), in honor of Albert Cameron Burrage, grower and Past President of the Massachusetts Horticultural Society. In the case of hybrids between 3 genera the name may be formed either by combining parts of the names of the 3 parent genera, e.g. x *Brassolaeliocattleya* (= *Brassavola* x *Laelia* x *Cattleya*) or by using the name of a person with the termination *-ara*, e.g. x *Sanderara* (= *Brassia* x *Cochlioda* x

Odontoglossum) after H. F. C. Sander, grower and founder of the famous orchid nurseries of F. Sander & Co., England.

Graft-chimaeras, or graft-hybrids as they are sometimes called, consisting of tissues of 2 different plants, stock and scion, are named in a similar way to sexual hybrids but an addition sign is used instead of that for multiplication, e.g. +*Laburnocytisus adamii* (= *Cytisus purpurea* + *Laburnum anagyroides*).

The names of cultivars, or horticultural and agricultural varieties as they used to be called (see CULTIVAR), are usually in a modern language and constitute the "fancy" names of plants. They are governed by the International Code of Nomenclature for Cultivated Plants and, when immediately following or preceding a botanical or common name, must be distinguished from them either by placing the abbreviation cv. in front of the cultivar name or by enclosing it in *single* quotation marks; capital letters are used for all the words in the names (except where national custom demands otherwise), e.g. *Rosa rugosa* cv. Roseraie de L'Haÿ, *Rosa* 'Roseraie de L'Haÿ', or rose cv. 'Roseraie de L'Haÿ'. Names in Latin form which were given to cultivars before 1959 (usually under the botanical code, before cultivar and variety were so clearly differentiated) may continue to be used, but they must be capitalized and distinguished by "cv." or single quotation marks as explained above.

In genera where there are many cultivars, assemblages of similar cultivars may be designated as groups, e.g. *Fagus sylvatica* (Atropunicea Group) 'Atropurpurea Globosa' and *Pisum sativum* (Wrinkle-seeded group) 'Laxton's Progress'. Where numbers of cultivars are of hybrid origin they are often grouped according to their origin under a collective name (normally enclosed in parenthesis), e.g. *Lilium* (Bellingham Hybrids) 'Shuksan' or *Cattleya* (Fabia grex) 'Prince of Wales'.

The registration of cultivar names is set up by the International Code of Nomenclature for Cultivated Plants, and registration authorities, national and international, have been appointed for a number of genera (see Appendix II to the code). These authorities receive registrations for new cultivar names and compile (and usually publish) lists of the names of cultivars in their particular genera. The main object is to promote nomenclatural stabilization and prevent the duplication of the same name for different cultivars of the same genus.

Complaints are often made by practical plantsmen that well-known and familiar botanical names are changed too frequently. There are 4 main causes for name changes: (1) the discovery of an earlier and validly published name which has priority and may have been overlooked or previously misapplied; (2) the discovery that a well-known name is illegitimate and contrary to the code; (3) the discovery that a familiar plant has been long misidentified and has been passing under a name which, from the original author's description, ought to have been applied to another plant; (4) the reclassification of a species by transfer from one genus to another, usually as the result of new scientific information. The first three cases should eventually work themselves out by research and the strict application of the code, but the fourth type of name change will always carry an element of personal judgement and will often be decided by following the opinion of leading authorities.

PETER S. GREEN

Many new changes in botanical names appearing in the revised edition of this Encyclopedia are taken from *Hortus III* (Macmillan). *Hortus III* was the combined effort of a hundred or more botanists and the staff of the Liberty Hyde Bailey Hortorium of Cornell University, working together to publish all the name changes made by botanists in the last 35 years since *Hortus II* was published. The botanical names in this revised encyclopedia follow those appearing in *Hortus III*. It is hoped that horticulturists everywhere in America will now conform to using these scientific names.

NOPALXOCHIA (no-pal-ZOK-ia)
ackermannii   3′   Zone 9   Orchid Cactus
A good flowering plant often used in the house, epiphytic, with flattened branches usually less than a foot long, younger shoots with short bristles. Flowers are scarlet red outside, 4–6 in. across, with greenish-yellow throat, 6–8 in. long. Not supposedly known in the wild state. For culture see CACTI AND SUCCULENTS.

NORFOLK-ISLAND-PINE = *Araucaria heterophylla*

NOTOCACTUS (no-to-CAC-tus). Cacti from South America; ball-like, with colorful spines or bristles and yellow flowers; since these plants are only a few inches tall, they are of little value except as interesting oddities indoors or planted out-of-doors in the cactus gardens of the southwestern U.S.

NOTHOLAENA (no-tho-LEE-na). These are the tender gold and silver maidenhair ferns, mostly native to the Tropics except **N. fendleri** which is native to the southwestern U.S. They are only for the greenhouse and are less than a foot in height. Some species have a gold or powdery substance on the fronds; in others the rhizomes are covered with scales. Propagation is by division and spores. See FERNS.

NUPHAR (NEW-far)

advena   aquatic   Zone 3   Spatterdock, Cow-lily

Native of ponds and streams throughout the eastern U.S., with leaves 12 in. across. Flowers are yellow, globular, 2½ in. wide and held well above the water. Not very spectacular but common in ponds and streams of the eastern U.S. They are cultivated in the same manner as *Nymphaea* species. For culture see WATER GARDENING.

luteum   aquatic   Zone 4   European Cow-lily

Similar to *N. advenum* except that the leaves rise slightly above the water; the flowers are smaller and slightly fragrant. Native to Europe. Not an especially good ornamental.

polysepalum   aquatic   Zone 4   Rocky Mountain Cow-lily

Flowers larger than those of *N. advenum*, 3–5 in., yellow; leaves up to 14 in. wide, sepals 9–12. Native to Calif. and Ore. The rootstocks of this and *N. advenum* have been used by the Indians as a starchy vegetable; the seeds have been used for making bread, in soups and also they have been popped like corn.

NUT. An indehiscent, 1-seeded, hard and bony fruit.

NUTMEG = *Myristica fragrans*

NUTS AND NUT CULTURE. Many individuals may consider the idea of planting nut-bearing shrubs or trees, to enhance the grounds about their home. As ornamentals, some of these are excellent. As fruit bearers, they may have their drawbacks, especially for gardeners living in hardiness Zones 3, 4, and 5. Like most of our fruit trees, nut trees have pests also which must be controlled. Some, like pecans, almonds and filberts, are commercially produced in certain parts of the country in large orchards, others are not.

On the other hand, it should be mentioned that some nut trees prove to be garden hazards. Chestnuts, for instance, may be favorably considered by some, but for those who have unknowingly tried them and learned of the hazards inherent in the sharp spiny burrs, under the trees, which can remain as hazards for several years unless they are raked off and removed, chestnuts are not for the small place. Nor is the Black Walnut, which is not an ornamental tree and its roots do give off materials that are detrimental to the growth of some other kinds of plants. So if the garden is small, choose nut trees only after careful consideration of all their good and bad qualifications.

For details concerning the culture of some of the more important nuts see *Handbook of North American Nut Trees* by Richard A. Jaynes (Northern Nut Growers Association, Inc.)

Hickory nuts are covered with a huge husk (lower left). These are various forms of good cracking quality.

Almond (*Prunus amygdalus*)

Bitternut (*Carya cordiformis*—See HICKORY NUTS.

Butternut (*Juglans cinera*)—See WALNUTS.

Chestnut (*Castanea* sp.)

Chinquapin (*Castanea pumila*)—See CHESTNUTS.

Coconut (*Cocos nucifera*)

Filberts (*Corylus* sp.)

Hazelnuts (*Corylus* sp.)—See FILBERTS.

Heartnut (*Juglans ailanthifolia cordiformis*)—See WALNUT.

Hiccan (*Carya illinoinensis* x *C. laciniosa*)—See HICKORY NUTS.

Hickory nuts (*Carya* sp.)

Lychee—(*Litchi chinensis*)

Macadamia (*Macadamia ternifolia*)—Queensland Nut

Mockernut (*Carya tomentosa*)—See HICKORY NUTS.

Peanut (*Arachia hypogaea*)

Pecan (*Carya illinoinensis*)—See HICKORY NUTS.

Pignut (*Carya glabra*)—See HICKORY NUTS.

Walnuts (*Juglans* sp.)

NYCTAGINACEAE = The Four-o'clock Family

NYCTOCEREUS (nik-to-SEE-reus)

serpentinus   8'   Zone 10   Serpent Cactus

A cactus with fluted stems and needlelike spines. The white, fragrant, many-petalled flowers are 7 in. long, open in the evening and close at noon the following day. A slender, erect or clambering cactus from Mexico, often used as a pot plant both for its form and flowers. For culture see CACTI AND SUCCULENTS.

NYMPHAEA (nim-FEE-a). A genus of hardy and tropical water-lilies belonging to the Water-lily Family, with rounded leaves floating on the surface of the water (sometimes colored underneath) and with flowers floating on the surface or standing a few inches about the water; flowers white, yellow, pink, red or blue, with many variations in the gorgeously flowered hybrids. Some bloom during the day, others bloom at night. The fruits are usually borne under the water. For culture, propagation and a list of the many popular and highly colorful hybrids, see WATER GARDENING, WATER-LILIES.

Insect Pests

Water-lily aphid is often present in large numbers and disfigures the leaves and flowers. This aphid spends the winter on plum trees. Spraying nearby plum trees may eliminate the source and prevent infestation. Use insecticide #15 in the spring on plum trees and when necessary on water-lillies. Leaf beetles of 3 species eat holes in the leaves and make them unsightly. Insecticide #37 or #9 gives control. These insecticides kill fish and in pools the fish must be removed for several days when the sprays are used. It is also possible to avoid insect injury by holding the plants completely under water for several days with wire mesh or other weights. If it is necessary to spray while fish are in a pool, insecticide #27 is the safest.

alba   aquatic   Zones 6–7   European White Water-lily
With leaves 12 in. wide, reddish when young. Flowers white, 4–5 in. wide, opening during the day. Native to Europe and northern Africa.

capensis   aquatic   Zone 10   Cape Water-lily
Leaves 12–16 in. wide; flowers sky-blue, 6 in. wide, opening during the day. Native to South Africa. The variety **zanzibariensis** has smaller leaves but usually larger flowers than the species. These are deep blue, opening for 3–5 days.

gigantea   aquatic   Zones 7–8   Australian Water-lily
This has leaves up to 18 in. wide with the underside brownish pink to purple. The light blue flowers, 6–12 in. wide, open each day for about a week from 9 A.M. to 6 P.M. Native to Australia.

lotus   aquatic   Zone 10   Egyptian Lotus
Native to Egypt, with leaves 12–20 in. wide, dark green above and brownish beneath. The flowers are white, shaded pink or red, 5–10 in. wide opening on 4 successive nights and remaining open the following mornings until noon.

odorata aquatic Zone 3 Fragrant Water-lily
A beautiful, very fragrant, aquatic perennial having rounded leaves, the base having a narrow slit to the center near where the petiole is attached to the undersurface. These leaves, 4–10 in. wide, float on the water, as do the flowers. These have 4 narrow sepals, greenish on the

outside, purplish or pinkish within, and waxy-white petals, with numerous yellow stamens. These flowers, 3–5 in. wide, blooming in summer, remain open only during the morning hours, closing in the latter half of each day and on rainy days. They are native to the ponds and quiet coves of the rivers from southern Canada and Mich. down the Atlantic coast to Fla. and Tex. Excellent for water gardens, the roots may be transplanted in summer or fall and weighted with rocks until the roots are established. The variety **gigantea** has larger flowers.

stellata   aquatic   Zone 10   Blue Lotus of India
One of the finest of the blue-flowering water-lilies with flowers opening during the day. Native to India.

tetragona   aquatic   Zone 4   Pygmy Water-lily
With leaves 3–4 in. wide and yellow beneath; white flowers, 1½–2½ in. wide, opening during the day. Native to eastern Asia and North America from Idaho to Ontario. This is the smallest species in cultivation and has been much used in hybridizing. See WATER GARDENING. The flowers open 3–4 days from about noon to 5 P.M.

tuberosa   aquatic   Zone 3   Magnolia Water-lily
Native to North America; flowers white, 4–9 in. wide, with no fragrance. Opening 3–4 hours during the day. This has tubers 1–3 in. long and is sometimes called the Tuberous Water-lily.

NYMPHAECEAE = The Water-lily Family

NYMPHOIDES (nim-FOY-deez). These aquatics grow rooted in the mud or sand with their leaves floating on the surface of the water. Leaves are alternate or just about opposite beneath the flowers, orbicular, deeply cordate with yellow or white 5-parted flowers.

indica   aquatic   Zone 9   Water-snowflake
Leaves orbicular, 2–6 in. across, with a deep cordate base; white flowers about ¾ in. wide in short-stalked umbels. Not hardy outside in the North but only grown in tropical regions. Native to the Tropics.

peltata   aquatic   Zone 5   Floating-heart
Mottled leaves, orbicular, 4 in. across with wavy margins; bright yellow flowers an inch across borne in umbels from the leaf axils. Native to Europe and Asia, naturalized in the eastern U.S.

NYSSA (NIS-sa). Two deciduous tree species, *N. sylvatica* being widely planted as an ornamental in the North. Alternate entire leaves; sexes usually separate; fruits are small blue drupes about ¼ in. in dia.

Propagation

Do not let the seed dry out but stratify when

ripe for 3 months at 40° F., then sow. Layers or rooted suckers are frequently found at the base of old trees and these can be cut off from parent plant. See STRATIFICATION, LAYERS.

Insect Pests

The larva of the tupelo leaf mining moth makes blotch mines which can be very destructive. Spraying with insecticide #15 in early summer is suggested. Forest tent caterpillar and several species of June bugs damage the foliage unless controlled with insecticide #9. Twig girdlers and bark beetles are minor pests.

sinensis   20′–60′   Zone 7   Chinese Sour Gum

A tree, native to central China, with alternate leaves 3½–7 in. long and an excellent yellow autumn color, sometimes combined with red.

It makes a fine specimen tree but is difficult to transplant; the smaller the size at transplanting time, the better the chances of survival.

sylvatica   90′   Zone 4   Black Tupelo, Black Gum

Widely found in the woodlands of the eastern United States and especially near or bordering lakes, streams or swamps, this is an excellent ornamental tree. The leathery, lustrous, dark green leaves are 3–5 in. long and they turn a brilliant orange to scarlet in the fall. The sexes are separate, the fruits of the pistillate tree are small blue drupes in midsummer, not very effective because they are hidden by the foliage. The outline of the tree is pyramidal, with dense branching, somewhat pendulous. It should always be moved with a ball of earth and very carefully dug because of its rather prominent taproot.

O

OAK. See QUERCUS.

OAK, TANBARK = *Lithocarpus densiflorus*

OAT. See AVENA.

OAT-GRASS, TUBER = *Arrhenatherum elatius tuberosum*

OATS, WILD = *Uvularia sessilifolia*

OBLANCEOLATE. Inversely lanceolate; with the broadest part of a lanceolate body away from the point of attachment.

OBLIQUE. Slanting; unequal-sided.

OBLONG. At least twice as broad as long.

OBTUSE. Blunt, rounded.

OCEAN SPRAY = *Holodiscus discolor*

OCHNA (OK-na)
  multiflora   **5′**   **Zone 10**
A tropical shrub with toothed, alternate, leathery leaves 3–5 in. long, from tropical Africa, grown in southern Calif. for its good foliage and its yellow flowers made up of 5 slightly twisted petals and 5 petallike sepals. The fleshy fruit is a black drupe; the receptacle is red. Propagated by cuttings in Aug.

OCHROSIA (OK-ros-ia)
  elliptica **20′** **Zone 10** **Deadly Ochrosia**
A poisonous plant from the South Pacific, this is a shrub with conspicuous waxy red fruits, almondlike in shape, borne in pairs or clusters in a mass of leaves. Leaves are opposite or in whorls of 3–4 and about 6 in. long. Flowers have a fragrance similar to that of violets when crushed.

OCIMUM (o-SY-mum)
  basilicum **2′** **annual** **Sweet Basil**
A popular herb with opposite, purplish, oval leaves, sometimes in whorls, an inch or 2 long; flowers white to purplish, about ½ in. long. The leaves have a taste akin to pepper or cloves. Native to the tropical Old World. Propagation is by seeds sown in the spring. The center bud should be pinched out when the seedling is a few inches high, to make it more compact and dense in habit. The leaves are used to give flavor to various cooked foods. It has been said that potted plants in the house keep flies away.
  sanctum **2′** **annual** **Sacred Basil**
This is the only Basil to self-sow itself in southern New England. It is considered a very sacred plant by the Hindu for it is grown for use in the temples of India where it is supposed to have originated. The leaves are 2 in. long, oblong and scented. The flowers are purplish, produced in racemes 8 in. long.

OCONEE-BELLS = *Shortia galacifolia*

OCTOPUS-TREE = *Brassaia actinophylla*, formerly termed *Schefflera actinophylla*

ODD-PINNATE. Pinnate with a single leaflet at the apex.

ODONTOGLOSSUM (o-don-to-GLOSS-um). A genus of over 100 species of mostly epiphytic Latin American orchids, but most of these are not for growing in the home and difficult to grow in the greenhouse, for they require cool summers. They have 1–2 leaves, pseudobulbs and flowers in lateral racemes. They come in many colors with much red and flowers are 1–6 in. across. A few species that are grown by commercial American growers are **O. crispum, O. grande, O. pendulum** and **O. pulchellum**. For further information see ORCHID.

ODONTONEMA (o-don-to-NEE-ma)
  strictum **8′** **Zone 10** **Odontonema**
An herbaceous plant from tropical America, this is planted for its tall spikes of small red flowers, each one of which is about 1 in. long. The leaves are opposite, 4–6 in. long. The flower spike is terminal, but only a few flowers bloom irregularly on the stem at the same time. Not especially ornamental.

OEDEMA. Small corky areas on the underside of leaves of Geranium and a few other plants are called oedema. This is caused by the breakdown of cells when exposed for long periods to excess moisture. In the greenhouse it can be avoided by greater spaces between potted plants and by ventilation to decrease humidity. Pathological disease is not concerned.

OENOTHERA (ee-no-THEE-ra, or ee-NOTH-er-a). A New World genus having alternate leaves and attractive, generally yellow, flowers, some species of which bloom at night. These are borne in the leaf axils. There are usually 4 lobes on the tubular calyx. The biennials are easily propagated from seed and the perennials by division. They do well in sandy or well-drained loamy soils and bloom throughout much of the summer but should be in the full sun. Many of the species open only at night and are very fragrant. The predominating flower color is yellow. Only a few are good garden plants.

acaulis 6" **biennial Zone 7 (?) Dandelion Sundrops**
With white or pinkish flowers, 4 in. across. Stems prostrate; leaves deeply cut. Native to Chile. The var. **aurea** has yellow flowers.

biennis 3'–4' **Zone 4 Common Evening-primrose**
This biennial has narrow leaves and both leaves and stem are hairy. The yellow flowers open in late afternoon and remain open during the evening. It is a weedy plant, growing over much of the U.S. The root was eaten as a vegetable by the Indians.

bistorta 16" **annual**
Native to Calif., this has purple spotted yellow flowers 1 in. across. The var. **veitchiana** is the one usually grown with narrow lanceolate leaves. Native to southern Calif.

caespitosa 4' **biennial or perennial Zone 5 Twisted Sundrops**
Stemless, with white or pink flowers, 3 in. across, which are fragrant at night. The leaves are hairy and sometimes divided into narrow segments. Native to central U.S.

fruticosa 2'–3' **Zone 4 Common Sundrops**
An erect slender perennial with showy yellow flowers in a terminal cluster. This is a plant with a preference for dry soils and it may be found throughout the eastern half of the U.S.

missouriensis 1' **Zone 4 Ozark Sundrops**
Native from Mo. to Tex.; flowers yellow and showy, almost 5 in. across, and of almost tissue-paper thickness from June through Aug. The stems tend to trail and the tips tend to grow upright. Fragrant—not outstanding but an occasional plant can be of interest.

odorata 4' **annual**
The yellow-to-reddish flowers of this species are 2½ in. wide and are fragrant and open only at night. Native to Chile.

pallida trichocalyx 1' **biennial Zone 4**
This can be treated as an annual and will bloom the first year. The linear leaves, 1–2 in. long, are covered with silky hairs and the flowers are white, about 2 in. across, remaining open during the day. Native to Colo., Wyo., and Utah.

perennis 2' **Zone 3**
A freely blooming species from eastern U.S. Beginning as a rosette of leaves with a short flower stalk 2 in. tall, it continues to flower with yellow blooms an inch or less wide, as the stalk grows to an eventual height of nearly 2 ft.

pilosella 6"–24" **Zone 4**
An erect-growing perennial with yellow diurnal flowers about 1–2 in. across in June, native from Ohio to Mo. Not an ornamental for the perennial border but it can spread rapidly although easily controlled.

rosea 2' **biennial Zone 5 Rose Sundrops**
The rose-purple flowers are very attractive but small, only ½ in. across. The leaves are softly hairy. The flowers open at night but remain open the following day. Native to central U.S. and South America.

speciosa 18" **Zone 5 Showy Evening-primrose**
A hairy perennial rising from an underground stolon, its leaves tend to be linear and pinnately lobed or toothed. The showy white flowers are borne in the axils of the upper leaves. It may be found in the Plains States and occasionally in the eastern states. Flowers appear in early summer.

tetragona 3' **Zone 3**
Biennial or perennial, with lemon-yellow diurnal flowers, 1–1½ in. wide, from June to Aug. Native from Nova Scotia to Ga. Only a few flowers in a spike. Not a plant for the ornamental border.

OFFSET. A loose horticultural term for small bulbs that have been formed at the base of larger mature bulbs; for small plants that are reproduced at the base of older plants, or for the small plantlets that are produced at the end of shoots growing out from the plant. Such small bulbs or plantlets are the easiest means of starting new plants identical with the parent.

OIL-NUT, ALLEGHENY = *Pyrularia pubera*

OIL SPRAYS. See INSECTICIDES.

OKRA = *Abelmoschus escutentus*

OLD-MAN-OF-THE-ANDES = *Oreocereus celesianus*

OLEA (O-lee-a)

europaea 25' **Zone 9 Common Olive**
This native of the Mediterranean Region is the true Olive, grown commercially in Calif. for the fruits. It is a densely rounded tree in poor soil and asymmetrical in good soil. The leaves are evergreen, gray-green or silvery beneath and about 1–3 in. long. The small flowers are fragrant and borne in panicles shorter than the leaves; widely used for centuries in all the Mediterranean countries. Also see OLIVE.

Insect Pests

Black scale of citrus and oleander scale (see OLEANDER) are pests of the common Olive. Sprays of insecticide #45 and #15 are used during cooler weather. Heavy spraying with insecticide #9 to the trunk and lower branches prevents infestation by borers.

Disease

Trees infected with a bacterial disease should be removed. Shoestring fungus is occasionally harmful. See OAK.

OLEACEAE = The Lilac, Olive or Ash Family

OLEAGINOUS. Oily and fleshy.

OLEANDER, COMMON = *Nerium oleander*

OLEARIA (o-lee-AY-ria)

x haastii 9′ Zone 8 New Zealand Daisy-bush
In the subtropical parts of the U.S., especially in southern Calif., this is a very popular garden plant. A native of New Zealand, the lustrous dark evergreen–to–grayish-green leaves are 1½ in. long, and the white, fragrant, daisylike flowers bloom in the summer. The leaves are about 1 in. long and, although the plant may grow to 9 ft. tall, it can have a spread of 15 ft., making a dense rounded shrub which may need some spring pruning to maintain its desirable form. It does well in well-drained soil, but can withstand hot situations in the full sun where many other plants fail.

OLEASTER FAMILY = Elaeagnaceae

OLIVE. The feathery gray-green foliage and the gnarled and furrowed trunks of the Olive (*Olea europa*) make them a valued ornamental. The Olive is one of the hardiest of evergreen fruit trees, being able to withstand 12–15° F. with little or no damage. The tree grows vigorously in a wide range of climates, but is best adapted to the hot, dry areas of the Southwest. Some winter chilling is needed to induce flower formation; the 2 coldest winter months should have average temperatures 50° F. or below. At higher temperatures the trees grow well but fail to flower and fruit. The Olive blooms very late, so that it normally escapes all frost danger to the bloom and young fruit. Olives grow well in the Southeast, but have not borne well there; the fruit ripens too late, being subject to fall and winter frosts; fruit is injured below 28° F.

Olives are normally propagated from cuttings, and show a remarkable ability to root from cuttings of any size but tip cuttings. Subterminal cuttings, 4–5 in. long, are generally used; remove all but the 2 terminal leaves. Hard-to-root varieties are treated with 4000 ppm (0.4%) indolebutyric acid (IBA) in 50% alcohol for 30 seconds; and planted in sharp sand with bottom heat. Older wood, ½ to 1 in. in dia. will root even more readily if the bottom 2 in. are soaked in a 13 ppm IBA solution for 24 hours, then buried in moist sawdust until callused before planting in the cutting bed. Older and larger branches may be planted directly in place and will usually root. Slabs of the trunk placed a few inches below the soil, with the bark side up, will usually send up shoots and root. Suckers are often found at the base of trees; these may be removed and planted.

Trees are sometimes produced by grafting; seeds are planted, usually after clipping the end off; they germinate slowly. They may not be ready to graft for a year. Grafting is by whip-graft or side graft. Trees are topworked by bark-grafting, usually in the spring. Trees of the varieties mentioned here are dwarfed somewhat by grafting to certain clones.

Trees dug from the nursery row are usually bare rooted, in which case all branches are removed, and only a few leaves along a single stem are left; they are whitewashed after planting. Trees in cans need only to have low water-sprout shoots removed.

Except in extremely sandy or shallow soils the planting hole need be only large enough to take the roots. Most varieties attain large size under good conditions, and need a spacing of about 35 ft. for full development; shorter distances may be used if the trees are kept smaller by consistent pruning.

During the first 2 years in the ground, olives are trained to 3–5-scaffold branches, well spaced. Thereafter, pruning is normally limited to removing unwanted growth, as it reduces yield. If the tree becomes too tall, it may be topped severely.

The Olive will grow on a wide variety of soils, including many that appear too poor for other tree species; water-logged soils should be avoided.

Olives grow and produce the best when supplied with about as much water as other evergreen trees. Nevertheless, they are among the most drought-resistant of all trees, but growth and fruiting will be greatly reduced with restricted watering.

Olives are light users of nitrogen, and respond to it only on relatively infertile soils. Even then, a pound of nitrogen per mature tree should be adequate. Potassium and boron deficiencies occasionally are seen. In the arid West an application of 25 lbs. of potassium sulfate should be applied; for boron apply about 1 lb. of borax; both treatments should last several years. In the Southeast, complete fertilizer applications will provide the needed potassium; the boron applications will need to be slightly greater, and may need to be repeated every year or two. For both deficiencies, yellowing of the leaves occurs. Potassium deficiency leads to leaf-tip burn; boron deficiency to death of shoot tips, and to death of the blossoms end of the fruit, a condition called Monkey-face.

The Olive flowers very profusely, the bloom developing as several flowered inflorescences in the axils of the alternate leaves. Enough may develop that the Olive bears more flowers than almost any other fruiting tree, but a high percentage of these are normally female sterile. In any case, less than 1% set will result in a heavy crop. Cross-pollination is not usually needed, but may increase set in cold springs.

Excess set results in small fruit, and increases to alternate bearing. Spraying 20 to 28 days after full bloom with naphthaleneacetic acid, 125 ppm in water containing 1½% light summer oil, will thin the fruit adequately in most years, although there is some danger of over-thinning, and occasionally the spray is not effective. Reducing the crop load to 3 or 4 fruits per foot of shoot by hand is also effective, but very tedious.

For home use, olives will be harvested for pickling only. For this purpose, they are picked as they turn from green to straw or pink color. A simple and effective home pickling recipe is: Soak the fruit overnight in water; replace the water with a 2% concentrated lye solution per gal. of water, leaving it until the flesh color change shows that the lye has penetrated to or nearly to the pit. Replace the lye with water, leaving for 3 or 4 days, with daily or more frequent water changes until the lye is all removed. Replace the last wash solution with a solution of 3 oz. of salt per gal. For storage of more than a few days, gradually increase the strength of the salt solution in increments of 3 oz. per gal. every other day until a final solution of 12 oz. per gal. of water is used. Change this solution about every 3 weeks until the olives are used. From this strong solution, remove olives as needed and soak in fresh water for a few hours before use.

The varieties of Olive differ primarily in size and oil content, which varies from 10–30%. Small varieties are 'Mission' and 'Manzanillo'; large varieties are 'Ascolano' and 'Sevillano'.

Scales of several kinds attack Olive; 1½–2% summer oil sprays are recommended for control in general in the summer. Peacock spot, a fungus disease, is controlled with Bordeaux spray (which see), 5-10-100 being sufficient strength. Shoots affected with Olive knot, a bacterial disease, should be cut out, using care not to spread the organism with the pruning implements. Verticillium wilt attacks olives; do not plant where susceptible annual crops have been growing, as tomatoes, potatoes, cotton and melons. Nematodes are known to attack olive roots.

CLARON O. HESSE

OLIVE FAMILY = Oleaceae

OMPHALODES (om-fal-O-deez)
verna   8″   Zone 7   Creeping Navel-seed
A stoloniferous trailer from Europe, this perennial is suitable for growing as a ground cover in sun or half-shade in the milder parts of the country. One of its popular names is Blue-eyed Mary because of the blue, sometimes whitish, flowers, ½ in. across, in April and May, and also because it was supposed to be a favorite of Queen Marie Antoinette. The foliage is of fine texture, evergreen in the South, the alternate leaves being 1–3 in. long. Sometimes incorrectly called Creeping Forget-me-not.

ONAGRACEAE = The Evening-primrose Family

ONCIDIUM (on-SID-ium). This is a group of about 500 species of tropical American epiphytic orchids with 1-2-leaved pseudobulbs and flowers in lateral racemes. It is one of the largest and most interesting groups of orchids with almost every one an interesting plant. They are easily grown and make fine pot plants in the greenhouse. For information on culture and propagation see ORCHID.

ampliatum   15″   Zone 10
Bright yellow flowers with red-brown blotches near the center, white on the back, borne in many-flowered racemes up to 3 ft. long from Dec. to May. The 1–2 leaves are about 3 in. wide. Native to Central America.

flexuosum   9″   Zone 10   Dancing-doll Orchid
Yellow flowers spotted brown near the base, borne on many-flowered panicles up to 3 ft. long, the individual flowers being ¾–1½ in. across and appearing from Oct. to March and from June to Aug. The pseudobulbs have 1–2 leaves about 9½ in. long. Native to Brazil and Paraguay.

ornithorhynchum   12″   Zone 10
Soft rose-purple, fragrant flowers, ¾ in. across, with many flower scapes produced with gracefully drooping panicles profusely set with flowers during autumn and winter. Twin leaves are produced from the 3-in. pseudobulbs. Native to Guatemala.

papilio   9″   Zone 10   Butterfly Orchid
One of the very popular orchids with flowers produced throughout the year, 1–4 in. across, reddish brown and yellow, something the shape of butterflies. The flowering racemes can be 4 ft. long. Native to South America. Pseudobulb produces 1 leaf 9 in. long and 2¾ in. wide.

sphacelatum   2′   Zone 10
Many flowers over an inch across, usually yellow, on 3-6-ft. scapes produced in the spring. Pseudobulbs produce 2–3 linear leaves that are 15–24 in. long. Native to Mexico.

splendidum   9″–15″   Zone 10
Sometimes considered a var. of O. tigrinum, this produces golden-yellow flowers, 2 in. or more across, on erect-branching scapes, 2–3 ft. long, in the winter. There is only 1 leaf produced per pseudobulb, each leaf up to 15 in. long. This orchid needs a rest after flowering. Native to Guatemala.

varicosum   12″   Zone 10
Flowers pale, dull yellow-green to yellow, 80–90 produced on a 3 ft. flowering panicle during the autumn or winter. The pseudobulbs bear 2–3

leaves, 6–9 in. long. This is a strong-growing species, native to Brazil.

ONION (*Allium cepa*). The onion has been grown since remote antiquity and its culture and use are noted in our earliest records. It probably originated in middle Asia. The Onion belongs to the Lily Family with such other closely related plants as Garlic, Leek, chives, shallots and welsh onions. It is generally a biennial or long-season annual although some forms such as the 'Multipliers' are perennial.

The Onion is one of the most important vegetable crops, grown for consumption in the green and mature bulb state, in all sections of the U.S. The more important commercial production areas are in Tex., Calif., N.Y., Mich., Colo., Ore., Idaho, N.J., Wisc., N.Mex., and Minn.

Varieties

There are many varieties listed in seed catalogues, a number of which are F_1 hybrids developed for specific cultural conditions. In general, there are 2 types of onions grown for dry bulbs, the American or pungent and the "foreign" or mild types. Each contain varieties that are yellow, red and white and vary in shape from flat, globular to elongated bottle. With such a wide variation only a few of the more important sorts in each category can be listed.

In the American types **'Yellow Globe Danvers'**, **'Early Yellow Globe'**, **'Harvestmore'** and **'Ebenezer'** which is grown from sets are yellow varieties. **'Red Wethersfield'**, **'Southport Red Globe'** and **'Ruby'** represent red sorts. **'White Portugal'** is good for pickling. In "foreign" types, **'Yellow Bermuda'**, **'Early Grano'** and the many strains of **'Sweet Spanish'** are the most important. Varieties that are grown for green onions (scallions) include **'Japanese Bunching'**, **'Beltsville Bunching'** and **'Perennial Tree'**.

It is recommended that several reliable seed catalogues be checked for detailed variety characteristics and adaptability.

Soils and Soil Preparation

While onions can be grown on all types of soil the sandy or silt loams and muck soils, where available, are preferred. For onions, it is important to prepare a well-pulverized seedbed that has been smoothed with a rake or drag. This is especially true if the crop is to be grown from seed.

Fertilization

A soil pH of 5.8–6.5 is optimum. Lower acidity retards growth. See LIMING. The use of well-rotted manure is advisable, 30–40 bu. per 1000 sq. ft. Fresh manure usually contains weed seeds and may cause a problem in weed control and, therefore, if rotted manure is not available a good compost is preferred. In addition to manure apply 30–40 lbs. of a 5-8-7 or 5-10-5 commercial fertilizer per 1000 sq. ft. Incorporate thoroughly into the soil. After the plants are well established a side dressing of nitrate of soda, 3–4 lbs. per 1000 sq. ft., is a good practice and yields good results.

Planting Methods

There are 3 methods commonly used in planting onions; by seed, sets and seedling plants. Direct seeding requires a fine seedbed and good moisture conditions. The seed requires from 8–12 days for germination after which some 10 days to 2 weeks are necessary for the seedlings to become well established. One oz. of seed is needed for 100 ft. of row and the rows are spaced 12–15 in. apart.

Seedling plants purchased from reliable dealers or seedsmen are inexpensive and easy to handle. The plants should be stocky with bulbs the size of peas and have bushy roots. Planting distance 3–4 in. in the row and 12–15 in. between rows. Onion sets, immature bulblets, are used extensively for green onions in the spring and also for mature onions because of their ease of planting. Furrows are opened, the sets placed 3–4 in. apart and then covered with 1 in. of soil. Planting dates for seed and sets, as early as possible, but delay with seedlings until danger of severe frost is past.

Cultivation

Onions require continuous shallow cultivation to control weeds and to maintain a soil mulch. A scuffle hoe does a good job. Many commercial growers use a selective herbicide, Chloro-IPC, for onions. Again, this is not recommended in the home garden.

Harvesting

When the bulbs have reached mature size and the tops break over, the plants are pulled and placed in rows to dry for 3–6 days. The top is then cut off about 1 in. above the bulb and the bulb is then again spread out for drying for several days before placing into storage. Use crates or netted sacks and a storage that is cool, well ventilated and dry.

Insects and Diseases

Onion maggot is the larva of a small fly. The maggots, $\frac{1}{3}$ in. long, kill the young plants and burrow into the bulb. Starting in early May, apply 3 applications at 7-day intervals of Diazinon, 2 level tablespoons per gal. of water. See CABBAGE. Onion thrips are small, yellowish, sucking insects which attack the leaves. Dusts containing malathion or Diazinon applied at 7-10-day intervals give satisfactory control.

Onion smut, a fungus living over in the soil, attacks the small seedling plants. Avoid soil where disease has occurred. Apply a formaldehyde solution, 1 teaspoon to 1 qt. of water, in seed furrow at rate of 3 qts. per 10 ft. of row. Downy mildew, a fungus disease common during cool wet weather, causes the leaves to turn yellow and die. Dusting at weekly intervals with copper-lime or using a spray of zineb or Bordeaux mixture gives satisfactory control. Pink root and neck rot are other diseases that may cause damage but which have no specific control.

GRANT B. SNYDER

ONOCLEA (on-o-CLEE-a)
    sensibilis   **2'-4'**   **Zone 3**   **Sensitive Fern**
This fern grows over a good deal of North America (as well as in Europe and Asia) in marshy soils in either the full sun or shade. It bears sterile twice-compound fronds, but in the center of the plant are smaller modified fronds thickly covered with sporangia. It has been called Sensitive Fern because when the fronds are picked the segments are supposed to roll up slightly. Of limited use in marshy places. For propagation see FERNS.

ONONIS (on-O-nis)
    rotundifolia   **18"**   **Zone 4**   **Coinleaf Ononis**
A shrubby plant belonging to the Pea Family with alternate compound leaves having 3 oval leaflets. The bright rose flowers are borne 2-3 together in the summer. Native to southern Europe. Propagated by seeds or division. When through flowering this species should be pruned to the proper shape.
    spinosa   **2'**   **Zone 4**   **Thornyleaf Ononis**
Thorny, with oblong leaflets and pink flowers blooming during June and July.

ONOPORDUM (on-o-POR-dum)
    acanthium   **3'-9'**   **annual or biennial**   **Scotch Cotton-thistle**
With white cottony foliage, thistlelike with bristles, alternate leaves lobed and with prickles. Flower heads pale purple, ½-2 in. across, usually borne singly. Not much used; propagated by seeds sown in a sunny spot in May.
    bracteatum   **5'**   **biennial**   **Curlybract Cotton-thistle**
A tall tomentose plant with spiny leaves that are shallowly lobed and large round heads of purple or white flowers in the summer. Native to southern Europe and propagated by seed.
    tauricum   **6'**   **Zone 6**   **Biennial Taurus Cotton-thistle**
With purple flower heads in clusters,

native to southern Europe. Flowers in the summer. Not very often used as a garden plant.

OPEN-POLLINATED. A horticultural term, meaning that the plants were let alone when they flowered and not touched or manipulated by man when the flowers were in bloom. However, pollen was provided by wind from nearby trees or brought in by unregulated insects so that pollination did take place; either wind or insects or normal plant movements provided motion and pollen necessary to fertilize the flowers and later to produce fruits. The flowers of most of our plants are "open-pollinated."

OPHIOGLOSSACEAE = The Adder's Tongue Family

OPHIOGLOSSUM (o-fi-o-GLOSS-um)
    vulgatum   **16"**   **Zone 4**   **Adder's-tongue Fern**
Native to Europe, Asia and North America, this is of no ornamental value because the frond differs from other ferns in that it is a single oval-shaped leaf which is entire and does not bear spores. The spores are produced on another tongue-shaped structure arising from the base of the plant. They are difficult to transplant from the wild. When spores are borne the leaf quickly dies and nothing remains of the plant but the rhizomes. If it is grown at all it should be in a moist shaded spot. Whereas this species has only 1 leaf, *O. engelmannii*, another native species, has 2-5 leaves about 9 in. long. For propagation by spores see FERNS.

OPHIOPOGON (o-fio-PO-gon). Oriental, bulbous, grasslike evergreens similar to *Liriope* and widely used as ground covers throughout the South. These differ from *Liriope* species in only minor characters except they are slightly less hardy. Used as far north as Washington, D.C. Reportedly withstanding salt-water spray. The flowers are on stalks well down in the foliage, whereas those of *Liriope* species appear above the leaves. Easily propagated by division of offsets. Valued because they are evergreen and require no special care.
    jaburan   **3'**   **Zone 7**   **White Lily-turf**
Leaves ¼-½ in. wide, flowers white to lilac colored. Native to Japan. Two varieties, **aureus** and **variegatus** have leaves striped with yellow.
    japonicus   **6"-15"**   **Zone 7**   **Dwarf Lily-turf**
Leaves ⅛ in. or less wide, with few to several violet or bluish-tinted flowers per stalk. Native to Japan and Korea. A very popular evergreen ground cover in sun or shade, especially because it is low.

OPIUM POPPY = *Papaver somniferum*

OPLISMENUS (op-LISS-me-nus)
    compositus   **3'**   **Zone 10**   **Basket-grass**
A tropical weak grass with leaves 4 in. long

and an inch wide, bearing 4 in. flower spikes. Sometimes used in the greenhouse in hanging baskets for its decumbent stems. Propagated by cuttings or layering of the stems.

OPLOPANAX (op-lo-PAY-nacks)

horridus   12′   Zone 5   Devil's-club
An ornamental shrub with large bright green leaves and conspicuous scarlet fruits that are fleshy, ¼ in. long. Native from Alaska to Calif., it is very spiny, with large alternate leaves of 5–7 lobes, nearly 10 in. wide and prickles on both sides. Contact with the prickles and spines produces painful wounds and frequently severe swelling may result. The flowers are small and greenish white but are produced in large pyramidal clusters. Apparently this grows well near the seashore.

OPOPANAX = *Acacia farnesiana*

OPUNTIA (o-PUN-tia). A large genus of cacti growing from New England to the southern tip of South America, a few of which are in general cultivation. It generally consists of 2 main groups of plants, 1 with broad, flat joints termed "tuna," and the second group consisting of those with rounded or cylindrical joints sometimes termed "cholla." There are prostrate and clambering types, as well as those that are treelike. The solitary flowers are usually yellow and the fruits are juicy berries, some edible. Some species have spines, while others are spineless, and it was these that were used as fodder for cattle, though this is not a popular practice now. The opuntias as a group are not often planted in gardens because of the very sharp thorns and bristles, making the plants extremely difficult to handle. For culture, see CACTI AND SUCCULENTS.

basilaris   4′   Zone 5   Beaver-tail Prickly-pear
A species which grows in clumps with broadly obovate, bluish-coppery-colored pads with few spines and large purple flowers to 3 in. long. Native to Ariz., southern Utah and Mexico.

brasiliensis   12′   Zone 10
Treelike, even when small and immature, with the terminal joints flat and leaflike; flowers yellow, about 2 in. long. Native to Brazil.

cylindrica   12′   Zone 10   Ecuador Cholla
Branching considerably, the succulent, dark green joints are regularly notched, the short white spines are sometimes missing and the scarlet flowers are about 1 in. wide. Native to Ecuador.

elata   3′   Zone 8   Orange Tuna
With flat oblong joints or segments 10 in. long and 5 in. wide; flowers orange-yellow, about 2 in. wide. Native to Brazil and Paraguay.

erinacea   1¼′   Zone 5   Grizzly Bear Opuntia
With flat joints or segments growing with low

but erectly ascending branches; joints about 4 in. long; flowers red or yellow, 2½ in. long. Many spines. Native to Utah, Nev., Ariz. The plant body itself is almost completely hidden by bristlelike spines. The variety **utahensis**, also native from Neb. to Utah, has obovate joints that are 2–4″ long, and 2–8 spines. It is just one of a few cacti hardy this far north and so it has uses in areas where other cacti will not grow.

ficus-indica   15′   Zone 10   Indian-fig
Bush- or treelike; joints oblong and 15–20 in. long, usually without spines; having yellow flowers 4 in. wide and scarlet, edible fruit. Widely grown throughout the Tropics.

fragilis   4″   Zone 5   Brittle Prickly-pear
Low and spreading, but hardy, with rounded or cylindrical joints which are very fragile and easily broken; flowers pale yellow, about 2 in. wide. Native from Wisc. to Tex.

**humifusa austrina (compressa)   low, spreading
Zone 6   Prickly-pear**
A prostrate species with flattened, fleshy, wrinkled segments, dotted with hairy brownish tufts of bristles. The bright yellow flowers, appearing in June and July, are borne on short conical stems and have many sepals and petals and numerous white stamens. The fruits are oval and purplish in color. This is one of the northernmost growing members of the *Cactaceae*, being found on Martha's Vineyard and Nantucket Island and extending to Fla., on dry sandy sites. In the South it becomes rather rampant in growth. Sections of the plant are easily rooted in wet sand.

imbricata   10′   Zone 4   Walkingstick Cholla
Treelike, the joints about 1 in. in dia., with many tubercles; 8–30 spines per joint; flowers purple and about 2 in. long. Native from Colo. to Mexico.

microdasys   2′   Zone 8   Gold Plush Prickly-pear
So named because of the numerous, golden, barbed bristles arranged in diagonal lines on the plant. Segments are flat, oblong or orbicular and about 6 in. long. Flowers are yellow, tinged red, about 2 in. wide. Native to N.Mex.

microdasys rufida   5′   Zone 9   Blind Prickly-pear
With flat orbicular segments up to 10 in. long and a decided trunk; flowers yellow or orange, 2 in. wide. Native to Tex. and Mexico.

polyacantha   6″   Zone 3   Plains Prickly-pear
Growing into small clumps, low and spreading; joints round and usually less than 4 in. wide; spines 9 or fewer; flowers yellow, tinged on the outside with red, and about 2 in. wide. Native from Wash. to Tex.

ramosissima   6′   Zone 8   Holy Cross Cholla
With cylindrical segments, shrubby but with branches only 3 in. long; flowers greenish

yellow tinged with red, $1\frac{1}{2}$ in. long. Native to Nev., Calif., Ariz., and Mexico.

schickendantzii 7′ **Zone 9 (?)**
With flat segments that are warty and gray-green; spines 1 and 2, about $\frac{3}{4}$ in. long; flowers yellow, 2 in. wide; fruit green. Native to Argentina.

vulgaris 7′ **Zone 10 Common Prickly-pear**
With flat segments about a foot long and thick joints; spines usually borne singly, brown and up to $1\frac{3}{4}$ in. long; flowers yellow, $3\frac{1}{2}$ in. wide; fruit red, pear-shaped and about 3 in. long. Native to southern Brazil and Argentina. More seen in collections in the variety **variegata**, called Joseph's Coat, because the joints have white, yellow and pink splashes of color.

ORACH = *Atriplex hortensis*

ORANGE. One normally thinks only of the Sweet Orange (*Citrus sinensis*) under this name, but included in this discussion are the mandarin oranges (Satsumas and tangerines) (*C. reticulata*), the Sour Orange, (*C. aurantium*) and certain citrus hybrids whose fruit is normally used as the Sweet Orange—the tangelos (*C. reticulata* x *C. paradisi*) and tangors (*C. reticulata* x *C. sinensis*).

Oranges are favorite citrus fruits for the home yard (in Zones 9, 10) because of the attractiveness of the dark green foliage, round-headed trees, highly-scented blossoms, and bright-orange, desirable fruit.

The varieties of oranges and orange-type citrus are many, most having local adaptation. The best of good quality to meet seasonal and regional requirements are listed here.

Sweet Oranges

In the arid Southwest the seedless 'Washington Navel' is the best early variety. Its season of maturity varies from about 9 months from bloom, mid-Nov. to mid-Dec., in the warmer growing areas, to 11 months, Jan. to mid-March in the cooler districts. In the Southeast this variety does not perform as well, is not as attractive, and tends to bear lightly, but is still useful. Its main value is for fresh use; the ease of peeling and high, fresh quality are outstanding.

In the more humid South and Southeast 'Parson Brown' and 'Hamlin' varieties are preferred early season kinds; they ripen Oct. to Nov., at the same time as the 'Washington Navel' grown under similar climatic conditions. 'Jaffa' and 'Homossasa' are midseason varieties for the Southeast. These fruits, although seedy, are of good quality and yield quality juice in abundance.

The leading late variety throughout the nation is the 'Valencia', which ripens in from 11 months in the warmest portions of the South-east to over 17 months in the cool, coastal, citrus districts of the Pacific Coast. Some strains of this attractive oval fruit have few seeds but it is seldom excessively seedy. It yields a high quality juice.

The 'Minneola', 'Seminole', and 'Orlando' tangelos are particularly well adapted to the South and Southeast, the latter 2 ripening early. These are of high quality, juicy, and are well adapted to the garden. The 'Temple' Tangor is a midseason variety of very excellent quality for fresh and juice use.

'Owari Satsuma' is an early ripening Mandarin variety, and the 'Dancy' and 'Clementine' (Algerian) tangerines are among the best of their kind. The Satsumas ripen in time for the winter holidays, as does 'Clementine'; 'Dancy' is somewhat later maturing, especially in cooler citrus districts. The latter variety, although of excellent quality and appearance, tends to be small and overly seedy. It also needs other citrus growing nearby for pollination (all others mentioned will set without provision for pollination). Newer, as yet untested, varieties of tangerines are 'Frua', 'Kinnow', 'Fremont', 'Wilking', 'Encore', and 'Pixie', all developed on the West Coast. These ripen in the early fall in that location, except the last 2, which are quite late, June to Aug.

'King' (*C. nobilis*), possibly a Tangor, is of extra large size, early midseason, relatively hardy, attractive and rather widely adapted in the South and Southeast. Its quality is perhaps not so good as the others. Among the Mandarin oranges the Satsumas tend to be somewhat larger, with a yellower skin and flesh color than the tangerines, which are smaller, but most with a very attractive orange to orange-red skin color and a deeper colored, more orange flesh.

Sour Oranges

The Sour Orange is an important rootstock species, but the fruit may be used for marmalades, some types being markedly superior to the Sweet Orange for this purpose. 'Oklawaha' and 'Bittersweet' (low acid) are varieties.

Oranges are reasonably hardy citrus trees. Sweet Orange trees withstand about 20° F., suffering little more than defoliation (partial to complete) and killing of some of the smaller wood. A degree or two lower may kill large wood, and citrus should not be grown where temperatures below 20° F. occur nearly annually. Little or no damage is done to the trees at temperatures above 24° F. Mandarins are somewhat hardier than sweet oranges, but the lowest temperatures should not be more than 3 degrees lower than for the Sweet Orange. The Sour Orange is slightly more tender than the Sweet Orange. To do well, these species should not be exposed to such low temperatures annually, nor for long times when the lows occur, and monthly average winter temperatures should be near or above 55° F.

Frost Protection

Many oranges carry their fruit into or through the winter, ripening in the following spring or summer. Fruit will withstand temperatures only 4° to 5° below freezing for relatively short times—a few hours. Therefore, much of the necessity for protecting oranges and other citrus fruits from frost is related to protection of the fruit, the foliage bark and hardier wood. Blooms withstand but 5°–6° of frost, but often comes late enough, March to May, to escape bad frost conditions.

Frost protection may be given in several ways. Young trees, or those kept small by rootstock or training, may be covered during frosty nights. A complete cover extending to the ground is best, but a simple opaque top cover may be almost equally effective, especially in the arid Southwest where radiation frosts are more severe. Walls can give considerable protection, either south-facing walls which give off heat absorbed during the day, or heated building walls. Built-up suburbs are often materially warmer—3° or 4°—than surrounding open country. Heating may be used, but commercial orchard heaters are not easily used in the garden. Heating a small area is more difficult than heating large areas. If used, heaters will protect only that part of the tree that "sees" the heater, because the main effect will be from the radiant heat rather than actually raising air temperature throughout the tree. Thus, 2 or 3 heaters will be needed to protect a single tree under these circumstances. One heater should be placed on the windward side of the tree. Return stack heaters, properly adjusted, should be used to minimize smokiness. Protection from rare and infrequent frosts of short duration can be secured by sprinkling the tree throughout the frost period.

Young trees, 1 to 3 years old, should have the trunks banked with soil to a height of 14 to 20 in.; if the top is killed, regrowth from the trunk will re-establish the tree. Or, the trunk should be wrapped from the ground to the lower branches, using burlap, paper, reeds or rushes.

Propagation

Home propagation of citrus may be done with relatively little effort, but is a lengthy process. The seeded sweet oranges, the Sour Orange, and a high percentage of the Mandarin and most citrus hybrids will come true to seed; such seedlings develop from the accessory tissues of the developing seed, rather than from the fertilized egg cell, and are known as nucellar seedlings. As more than 1 embryo forms in each seed, such varieties develop multiple seedlings, a condition known as polyembrony. Although easily grown they are not recommended for the garden particularly because they are late coming into bearing and tend to be excessively thorny. However, all citrus seed if taken from the fresh fruit is easily germinated in a warm seedbed or flat of good light soil or soil mix. Seeds should not be stored or dried before germination. Treatment with a good seed fungicide will aid in avoiding damping off of young seedlings. If off-type seedlings are avoided, the chances of reproducing the parental clone are very high.

Young seedlings are usually kept in a seedbed for a year, then transplanted to a nursery, or in the garden at the location wanted. In the spring of the second year, they are budded (T-bud) with a bud from well-matured shoots of the desired variety. In summer, after the bud has taken, the top is broken over, but not removed. After the bud has pushed several inches, the broken top is cut off, and the developing shoot is tied to the stub. At the beginning of the third year the rootstock top is cut back to the bud.

Older trees may be topworked by budding or grafting to change varieties. Smaller wood may be budded (T-bud), using buds from well-matured shoots. Limbs to be grafted are cut back to a convenient height. Scion wood should be from well-matured wood of convenient size, from which the leaves are removed. Kerf, bark, or cleft grafts may be used, the former being preferred.

Oranges may also be propagated by leafy cuttings of well-developed last flush growth, but this is less convenient unless conditions for keeping the foliage moist can be maintained easily. Treatment with rooting hormones is helpful.

Culture

If the tree is not in the desired location, it is dug and moved (or is purchased); in the humid Southeast the tree may be bare rooted; the top is cut back heavily to reduce leaf area and the tree replanted. This should be done during the winter or early spring. The tree should be well watered when planted, and the trunk white-washed or wrapped for protection against sun-burn. In the arid Southwest a ball of earth is normally taken with the roots or trees are purchased in cans. Early spring is the preferred planting time. Water after planting should be slow and thorough to assure wetting the roots, especially if soil is taken with the tree.

Sweet oranges develop into rather large trees with age. Full-size trees should be 24 to 30 ft. apart, depending on general fertility of the soil and favorable climate. The use of smaller distances is discussed under pruning and size control. Sour Orange, Tangelo and Tangor also are vigorous, large trees, needing the same spacing. Mandarins are generally somewhat smaller, although spreading, and planting distances of 20 to 22 ft. should be adequate.

In the Southwest, where citrus soils are normally well drained and rather light, planting holes need be only large enough to take the roots or root-ball, although filling with topsoil will aid the tree in getting a good start. In the Southeast the same applies, except that in limey soils the use of larger holes filled with a soil-compost mixture will repay the extra effort. If the soil is very shallow—20 in. or less—the underlying rock or marl should be broken up if possible. If the soils are subject to high water tables or saturation during extended periods the tree will profit greatly by being planted on a low mound of soil—8–10 ft. or more across and a foot or more high. As most citrus roots suffer seriously from root diseases in wet soils, such planting will be of long-term benefit, and may enable successful culture in otherwise unsuited locations.

Rootstocks for oranges are Sweet Orange, Sour Orange, Trifoliate, 'Troyer' Citrange, 'Cleopatra' Mandarin, Rough Lemon. Sweet Orange and Rough Lemon are particularly susceptible to root rots, and should not be used in heavy and wet soils. Sour Orange is a generally very satisfactory stock on light open soils, but should not be used in most areas of Calif. Trifoliate stock is also generally liked; fruit borne on trees on Trifoliate is thought to be smoother and of better quality. The virus exocortis affects both Trifoliate and Citrange rootstocks. Virus-free scionwood must be used in propagating citrus. 'Troyer' Citrange makes a strong, vigorous stock for citrus and has had considerable popularity. Seedlings of 'Cleopatra' Mandarin are likewise used for the same reason. Rough Lemon should not be used except in weak sandy soils in Fla.; it is an exceptionally vigorous stock, but has the defect of causing the fruit borne above it to be rougher, lower in acids and sugars, and generally of poor quality. Oranges do well on their own roots if started from cuttings.

Pruning

The growth of most citrus cannot be directed by training and pruning to the degree the gardener is used to with many other woody plants. Strong watersprouts tend to develop from the upper sides of branches, often with little relation to the vigor of the shoot from which they arise. For this reason, orange trees are allowed to grow freely for the first year or two, except that low watersprouts are removed. Then, some selective cutting is done, removing interfering shoots, low shoots, and retaining those whose vigor and location indicate that they will form the main framework of the tree. Three to 5 well-placed branches are left. Thereafter as little pruning as possible is done, unless size control is the most important consideration. Pruning reduces fruitfulness.

Vigorous growth of young trees results in watersprout growth which may be pulled down and to the outside of the tree; excess shoots are removed. As the tree gets older less pruning is done; removal of dead wood in the inside of the tree is about all that is necessary. Older trees may need to be topped to prevent them from becoming unduly tall. Some, as the Sour Orange, tend to make tall cylindrical trees with age if not held down.

Citrus may be grown in limited areas so long as a portion of the foliage cover is exposed to sunlight. Hedgerows, or crowding and shading from other trees, will reduce the effective-bearing surface, however. Trees may be kept small by heavy cutting back. Some accessory pruning will be necessary because of the thick growth from such cutting. Attempts to reduce size too greatly by such methods will lead to over-vegetative response and greatly reduced fruiting.

Oranges may be espaliered against a wall, thereby reducing the space occupied very materially. Such espaliers must be of an informal type, utilizing the stronger growth, and subsequently replacing such growth for continued production. Such espaliers will produce only a few fruits but may enable citrus to be grown in areas not otherwise adapted or to utilize small available garden spots. The slower growing sorts, such as mandarins, respond best to such treatment, as growth reduction is not so severe. The utilization of dwarf stocks is possible. The most satisfactory now available are certain strains of the Trifoliate Orange; these should be purchased from citrus specialists, as not all Trifoliate stocks are dwarfing. Oranges, especially the smaller Mandarin sorts, can be grown in tubs if on dwarfing stock. Their size will be further reduced. Such plants should receive excellent care, both in regard to their nutritional needs and watering, because of the small soil volume available to them.

Water

Citrus should be supplied with water at all times of the year, and especially during the period of fruit development and ripening. Watering should be done carefully to avoid root rots. Water should be kept away from the trunk of the tree; the frequency of watering will vary greatly with soil and climate. In the humid

Southeast, watering during drought periods only may be necessary, natural rainfall supplying sufficient water most of the time. On light soils of the Southwest, under hot arid climatic conditions, water may need to be applied as often as every 10 days to 2 weeks. The soil should be brought to field capacity to the root depth of 3–4 ft. This will require about 4–6 in. of water, depending on the soil type. It is important that the tree have available water during the winter although its requirement will be less during cooler weather. Water may be applied in any convenient manner. Sprinklers may be used, but usually deliver water at a faster rate than it will sink into the soil, so that run-off occurs. Basins are commonly used in gardens, and should be large enough to extend slightly beyond the drip line of the tree. In heavier soils particularly, where soil saturation may persist for some time, a very satisfactory method is to irrigate under one-half of the tree one time, and the other half the next.

Fertilization

Oranges will almost inevitably require fertilization. Nitrogen is the most common element to be found deficient. Applications of 1 to 2 lbs. of actual nitrogen per tree per year will suffice; it is not desirable to stimulate excess vegetative growth. Start young trees with 1 to 3 oz. actual N per year, increasing the amount about $\frac{1}{8}$ to $\frac{1}{4}$ lb. annually.

Other elements commonly found to be deficient in both the east and western orange districts are zinc and iron. Foliage sprays of 1 lb. of zinc sulfate per 100 gals. of water, or 5 lbs. of zinc oxide per 100 gals. of water are applied annually when the spring growth flush is about $\frac{2}{3}$ developed. Zinc deficiency is known as citrus mottle, referring to the mottled green and yellow appearance of affected leaves.

Iron deficiency is sometimes observed, the leaves becoming chlorotic, but the leaf veins remaining green. Acidification of the soil is the best long-term remedy. Chelated iron is applied to correct this.

Potassium deficiency is relatively unknown in the arid Southwest, but is occasionally observed. In the soils characteristic of these areas rather massive doses of the element are necessary to correct the deficiency—10 to 20 lbs. of K_2SO_4 spread under the drip of the tree. In the Southeast, potassium may be needed annually; normally correction will be obtained by applying a complete fertilizer at the rate necessary to supply the annual nitrogen need or add 2 to 4 lbs. KCl per year. Symptoms are small leaves, necrotic at the tip and margins, yellow centrally, with older leaves more severely affected.

Several micronutrients—magnesium, manganese, and copper—are often needed in the alkali soils of the Southwest. Apply commercial fertilizers especially compounded to supply all of these elements in the required amount. In the Southwest these elements are supplied as foliage sprays if needed, copper in a Bordeaux spray, and manganese sulfate and magnesium nitrate at about 5 lbs. per 100 gals. of water, the former with $2\frac{1}{2}$ lbs. of hydrated lime.

Boron is a micronutrient commonly found deficient in both the Southeast and Southwest. Deficiencies are easily corrected by applying not over 3 oz. of borax under a mature tree in the arid Southwest and 10 to 15 oz. in the Southeast. The treatment should not be repeated until symptoms reappear, for the range between deficiency and excess is remarkably small. In the Southwest, where leaching does not often occur, boron application may last for several years; in the Southeast annual applications may be necessary. Do not exceed the recommended amount. Excess boron can be corrected only by leaching the soil with water. In some areas, particularly of the Southwest, well water sources may contribute materially to the build-up of boron in the soil. Water with over 0.5 ppm of boron should be used only if leaching can be done sometime during the year.

Harvesting

Sweet oranges may be harvested at any time they have reached suitable eating quality—citrus fruits in general do not go through a marked ripening change, recognizably green then within a few days ripe to over-ripe. For best appearance the fruit should be at full color, but some varieties, ripening in the warmer summer periods, may show regreening at a time when they are at best quality. Commercial practice dictates a minimum maturity dependent upon sugar/acid ratio. However, a higher sugar/acid ratio than this minimum is usually characteristic of maximum flavor, and of course is easily obtained by the gardener by simply leaving the fruit on the tree. Besides particular attention given to appearance, highest quality commercial brands as Sunkist or Pure Gold may exceed these minimum standards quite significantly. Most oranges can be "stored" on the tree for considerable periods without loss of quality. However, the fruit will eventually lose acid, and become "flat" and flavorless in character; at the same time the rind tends to become thick and punky, and the flesh to dry. Therefore, the fruit is best harvested by clipping, not pulling from the tree, when it reaches prime condition, and stored under suitable conditions off the tree. After a short curing period—holding at room temperature in a relatively dry spot—

storage at home refrigerator temperatures will prove satisfactory, and fruit can be held for several weeks to months in good condition. Washing in warm soapy water at 100° F. when harvested will reduce storage rots.

Mandarin oranges do not have a long life on the tree after reaching full flavor character, but tend to become punky and flat rather quickly—in a few weeks at the most. It is therefore desirable to harvest them as they reach prime condition; their off-tree storage life is also shorter.

Fruit which is picked in prime condition but is unattractively green may be improved by placing a ripe apple or banana with the fruit in a closed container for a few days. The oranges will normally assume their full color rather rapidly; the active ingredient is the ethylene given off by the ripe fruit.

Pests

The diseases and pests of citrus are myriad; it is impossible to give a full account of them and their correction. Fortunately, in the garden site, with mixed plantings, natural biological control is generally effective in holding infestations to a minimum, and the gardener may escape serious control problems.

First, secure good stock; if purchased this should be the best, preferably certified stock if available. This will minimize the occurrence of the incurable virus disorders.

The most commonly destructive insect pests are the armored scales, mites, and thrips. The various sorts attack foliage, twigs, bark and fruit. All but some of the scales are small, and may escape notice until populations are large. The larva of various moths may be serious pests; their presence in damaging numbers is generally evident. Ants are often a serious problem, particularly because they protect and abet the build-up of aphid populations in the tree.

Scab and melanose are diseases common in the Southeast, under the humid conditions occurring there. The former causes light brown, corky areas on the fruit and leaves, and will attack all new growth; the latter causes raised dark brown lesions on the leaves, making them rough to the touch.

Simple generalized spray schedules call for the use of summer oils in midsummer for the scales and most mites. Sulfur, either as a wettable sulfur spray or sulfur dust, is recommended for the rust mite. Malathion sprays, using the 25% wettable powder, will control many of the other insects, and aid in scale and mite control. Poisoned baits when applied to the ground will control ants. Neutral copper sprays are used for scab and melanose.

Specific directions printed on proprietary compound containers should be strictly followed. For troubles which cannot be diagnosed consult your local county agent; also do so if you are in doubt concerning spray mixtures. Do not spray during the bloom period, nor within a week of harvesting fruit. The substances listed above are all relatively innocuous to man and animals if used according to directions; the home gardener should not use the more toxic materials sometimes used in commercial orange production.

CLARON O. HESSE

ORANGE-JESSAMINE = *Murraya paniculata*

ORANGE-TRUMPET = *Pyrostegia venusta*

ORBICULAR. Circular; rounded in outline.

ORCHARD, THE HOME. Those who have not had experience in growing fruit trees and wish to plant some about the home grounds should carefully consider all phases of it before allotting valued garden space to fruit trees. Certainly, they are nice to have, and if well selected and well cared for they will produce the much-wanted fruit. However, it takes time and much labor for the trees must be properly sprayed (many times in some areas) and they must be pruned, often every year, all of which takes time. It is nice to pick the fruit, to have some to give away or to use in preserves, but for many of us it is much easier to take a drive in the country and buy a bushel or two at some wayside stand. The fruit is just as good, sometimes better, and one saves much time and effort, and sometimes money, in so doing.

If a home orchard is desired, the first step is to ascertain the varieties recommended for growing in your locality by the local state experiment station. Pay particular attention to those varieties which may be self-sterile, that is, which need pollen from some other variety to properly fertilize the flowers so fruits will be produced. Much information on this subject will be found in the articles in this volume listed under the various types of fruits.

If the land is in a low spot which has early frosts and unusually cold temperatures in the late spring, it may be inadvisable to plant any fruit trees.

Read the article in this volume on DWARF FRUIT TREES, because these might be a possibility, and they do not take up as much space as the standard fruit tree types.

Check the number of trees you wish to plant, the distance apart that they should be planted to see if there is enough space.

Before making the final decision, be sure to read the recommended spray schedule for your area, noting the number of times spray must be applied and the equipment necessary to use.

Standard trees require good-sized sprayers. Aside from that, it is not always possible to have an arborist around to spray the few trees exactly when they should be sprayed and sometimes, if the spraying is missed by just a few days, the damage is done.

If a formal orchard is to be set out it is best to plant the trees in squares, the distance apart depending on the kind of trees. Apples, for instance, require more space than plums or peaches. The soil should be well prepared (see SOILS); they should be properly planted and staked (see PLANTING, STAKING) and they might be mulched after thorough watering. The grass should not be allowed to grow about the roots, but should be cultivated and kept free of any growth, at least until the trees are well established. Planting can be done in either fall or spring.

ORCHID. Thousands of species and many thousands of hybrids make this group of plants one of the most fascinating and challenging to the horticulturist and gardener. Many hundreds of species and thousands of different hybrids are commonly in cultivation now, and both amateur and professional hybridists are introducing additional new hybrids every year. Under the heading of Orchidaceae is a brief description of the botanical aspects of this complex family, along with some details of flower and plant structure and its ecological origin and relationships. For many years orchids have been considered to be very difficult to grow and it was generally thought that growing these plants was a hobby only for the very wealthy who had professional gardeners especially trained to care for the plants, but in recent years all this has changed, due to modern cultural methods, and the orchid hobby has come within the possibility of all who are interested.

The American Orchid Society now has over 10,000 members and is adding new ones at the rate of nearly 1000 per year. Local orchid societies have sprung up in the larger cities throughout the country. These societies have monthly meetings and annual orchid shows. These latter serve to educate and interest the public in growing these plants.

The lure of orchids as a hobby is many-fold. The very idea of growing them has a romantically intriguing allure and of course the beauty of the flowers is the prime attraction. But few people have any idea of the vast number of flower types available, from almost microscopic miniatures to huge hybrids as large as a dinner plate and in an infinite variety of exotic shapes and colors. Once inoculated with the "Orchid Bug," one finds that one's interest may expand into many fields. In addition to the actual collecting and growing of the plants, there are many fields of study and experimentation open to the orchid grower, so that one lifetime simply isn't enough to compass the subject. Some people grow just a few orchids on their window sills in order to have the flowers in the house, but most soon find themselves much more involved in one particular facet or another in the study of this fascinating group of plants.

Here we will deal only with their uses as garden and greenhouse plants. Culturally speaking, the orchids are divided into 2 main groups and several subdivisions: (1) the Hardy Terrestrials, which are hardy outdoors and do well in northern gardens and (2) the Showy Tropical Orchids, which must be grown indoors in the home or greenhouse in northern climates, or in shade houses or other protected areas in frost-free climates.

Cultivation of Hardy Orchids

Many of these are beautiful and quite showy —very worthwhile additions to the garden—and most are quite easily grown if proper attention is given to their requirements. Primary emphasis must be given to soil. Most orchid species require an acid soil of a fibrous loam or peat type that stays moist. See ACID-ALKALI SOILS. Knowledge of their habitat in the wild is essential because some grow in bogs or swamps, some in shady cool woodlands, while others are found in meadows among the grasses where the soil stays cool and damp and some grow even in fairly dry, grassy plains areas. The most important thing is to duplicate as closely as possible their natural habitat in regard to soil and conditions of sun and shade.

Protection from cold during the winter is also important and a heavy mulch of leaves or several inches of peat moss spread over the bed will usually be adequate.

Where to Obtain the Plants

Many dealers in native plant materials list a number of the species most easily grown and having showy flowers. Oftentimes, these dealers can also give suggestions as to their culture. Orchid bulbs are often imported for sale, mainly those of Asiatic origin. Some may be collected from the woods and fields, but one should check on local and state conservation laws before venturing on this quest, and then only at the proper time. Sept. and Oct., when the bulbs and tubers have matured, is the best time for transplanting, but the plants are almost impossible to find then. The best way is to go to the woods in the spring, locate and mark the plants while in bloom, and then return in the fall to collect them. Collecting these plants when in flower and while in active growth is nearly always fatal. They should be taken up with a sizable ball of soil attached to the roots, the bigger the better, and as large as you can manage to transport. Good ones to grow are: Arethusa, Blettilla, Calopogon, Cypripedium (native species), Habenaria, Orchis and Pogonia. Others that will also be worthwhile, though not quite so showy, are Aplectrum, Goodyera and Liparis.

It is best to start with plants that are strong, full grown, well established in the pot and ready to bloom soon. Don't start out with small, weak plants, seedlings or back bulbs, since they will take several years to bloom and are likely to cause trouble for the novice.

Culture of Tropical Orchids

Most members of the Orchid Family are tropical or subtropical plants and may be found growing wild throughout the warmer parts of the world. The greatest concentration and the most interesting and worthwhile types come from southeastern Asia and from central and northern South America.

A few of these are terrestrial types, but most of the showy orchids from the Tropics are epiphytes, or "air plants," as they are commonly called. These are plants that grow naturally in elevated positions on tree limbs or outcroppings of rock and cliffs where their roots are either embedded in moss and accumulations of organic debris or are completely exposed to the air. They do not grow in soil nor, in most cases, do their roots grow to reach ground level. This unique type of growth leads to cultural methods somewhat different from those used with most other plants, yet allows for rather general cultural practices which apply to most tropical orchids. Luckily, these general requirements are quite easy to supply in most homes and nearly all greenhouses, and the result is that anyone interested can grow orchids successfully if they will just follow directions.

General Growing Instructions

Orchids are not the delicate plants most people assume them to be. Actually, they are very well suited for growing as house plants, because they will generally thrive under home conditions. More detailed instructions concerning individual species or genera are outlined further on in this article.

Heat

Regular home temperatures are fine for most orchids. From 60–80° F. is best, but occasional temperatures above 100° F. or drops in temperature even to 35–40° F. will not harm them as long as no frost forms on the leaves.

Sun

Sunlight is very important for plant growth and flowering. In a northern climate, the best location for growing orchids is in the sunniest window where they will get as much sun as possible during the darker winter months. Three or 4 hours of sun a day will do, and this can be supplemented with artificial light if necessary, but natural light in a sunny south window, a bay window, sunporch or bright plant room is usually enough.

If artificial light is used, it should be used only during daylight hours—do not increase the day length with artificial light because most orchids are photo-periodic and their blooming date is determined by seasonal changes in day length. If orchids are to be grown entirely under artificial light, then the lights should be on a time clock set to go on at sunrise and off at sunset and these settings should be changed weekly, or at least monthly, to correspond to the normal seasonal changes in the locality.

The quality of the light is important and a proper balance must be obtained between the red-blue parts of the spectrum. Best recent recommendations seem to be a combination of fluorescent tubes—one of the Gro-Lux type tubes for plant growth paired with one Deluxe white tube, and multiples of such pairing.

Light intensity is also vital. Most orchids require as much as these tubes can give; the leaves of the plants should be immediately under the tubes and almost close enough to touch. No Orchid except a few like Cypripedium and Phalaenopsis will bloom under lights if the average distance from leaves to tubes is more than 15–20 in.

In summer months, or year-round in frost-free climates, light shade during the middle of the day is advisable, but full early morning sun and full late afternoon sun is ideal. Plants may be suspended outside under a tree during the warm months of the year when the temperature is above 50° F.

Be sure to choose a spot where the plants will get at least 50% sunlight. The more sun the plants receive, without being burned, the stronger the growth will be and the heavier the plant will flower.

If it seems preferable to keep plants indoors during the summer months, any screened window or screened porch is suitable. Give them the sunniest spot possible and the screening will provide all the shade they need.

Potting Material

Orchids can be grown in a wide variety of potting materials and several different ones are now in common use. However, almost anything that gives good drainage and ventilation to the roots and which does not rot or turn sour quickly will do. Tree fern and Osmunda fibers—coarse black fibers—and shredded bark from pine or fir trees are the commonest now in use. Plants in these materials should be repotted every 2–3 years. The newest, and perhaps the best material, is "E-Z-Pot 'n Gro"—an artificial light-weight gravel. Since this is inorganic, it never rots. Therefore plants started in this material need not be disturbed until the plant has outgrown the pot. Coke is also a good potting medium and cultural directions are the same as for the gravel.

Water

Orchids must be watered carefully, and most orchids can stand too little water better than too much. Just how much and how often depends on several things: (1) How dry the conditions are; (2) Size of pot; (3) Potting material used. No one definite rule can be made to cover all conditions. Some homes and greenhouses are drier than others and, of course, small pots dry out more quickly than larger ones. Therefore one must carefully watch the plants, watering them individually and only when each plant needs it.

Plants in Osmunda and tree fern fibers should be allowed to become bone dry between waterings. Then water heavily and don't water again until the plant is thoroughly dry. If the side of the pot feels clammy and cool, then it is still damp inside, but if it feels dusty-dry and of the same temperature as the air, then it is ready to be watered.

Plants in bark need slightly more water than those in Osmunda fiber. When first potted, the bark drains and dries very quickly, so the plant will need water often. As the bark packs down, it will hold water longer and after a couple of months watering should be done only slightly more often than with Osmunda fiber. Old bark holds water a long time and so one must be careful not to water excessively plants potted in such material.

Plants in gravel or coke dry out more quickly and need more water than others—usually every second or third day. These materials dry out on top immediately after watering, so feeling the side of the pot is the best way to check. The plant should be watered thoroughly and then allowed to dry out until the side of the pot feels dusty-dry. It should not be watered if the pot is still clammy and cool to the touch. These directions are for regular clay flower pots—plastic pots hold water longer.

Food

All living things require food. Orchid plants cannot live indefinitely on air and water alone, even though they are called "air plants," so for strong growth and lovely flowers, be sure to feed plants regularly with a good orchid fertilizer. The potting materials used for orchids have very little or no food value, as they are chosen for their slow-rotting characteristics, so a regular feeding program is essential to good culture.

There are many hydroponic, inorganic orchid fertilizers on the market and most are quite high in nitrogen content. These were developed for feeding orchids growing in fir bark. A fungus which develops on this material steals the nitrogen in the fertilizer and thus the high nitrogen content is necessary because of the fir bark and not basically for the orchids. If plants are in Osmunda fiber, tree fern, gravel or coke, a much stronger growth and better flower production will result from using a fertilizer with a lower nitrogen content. Experiments show the best results from one with a 1-2-3 ratio, such as 4-8-12, and so forth.

Since these hydroponic or water-soluble foods are used in very dilute proportions, they should be used frequently—at least every other watering or about once a week. They may be used with every watering, but in this case the pots should be flushed out thoroughly with clear water about once a month to insure against any possible build-up of fertilizer salts in the potting material.

In general, organic fertilizers are not recommended for orchids except in part for terrestrials.

Humidity

No expensive equipment is necessary or advisable to provide humidity for orchid plants. Any pan large enough to hold the plants is all right. Fill the pan with tiny stones, gravel, shells or brightly colored aquarium stones. Next fill the pan about half full of water. Place the pan in a sunny window and arrange the pots on top of the gravel or stones. Be sure the pots sit above the level of the water—never in the water. This is the safest and best way to supply humidity to orchids growing in the home.

If the home or growing conditions are exceptionally dry, the humidity may be increased with a room vaporizer such as those used for asthmatic children, or a mist spray may be used on the leaves of the plants during the morning hours so that they may dry off thoroughly before evening. Misting and frequent light waterings must be done carefully, however, to avoid fungus leaf problems from continuing excessive dampness.

Air

Orchid plants require the same atmosphere as do human beings, and are not adversely affected by any heating system—gas, oil, coal

Orchids grown in the home can be set on a tray of pebbles partially filled with water to increase the humidity in the atmosphere about them.

or radiant heat. If the air in the home is good to breathe, orchid plants will thrive in it. If orchids are growing in a small, closed-in area, such as a closed bay window or a small greenhouse, sun porch or plant room, the air may become quite stagnant and stuffy. A small fan or, better yet, 2 small fans on opposite sides of the plant area, blowing parallel to one another in opposite directions, will cause a circulation of air which will prove of benefit to the plants and produce better growth, as well as prettier and longer-lasting flowers. Recent experiments show that a considerable breeze in the greenhouse is of dramatic benefit to almost all plant growth and fan systems are now being installed in greenhouses for year-round use.

Repotting

Repotting is necessary when the plant begins to grow over the edge of the pot. Roots often grow outside the pot. These are simply aerial roots and do not indicate a need for repotting. However, when the plant itself grows over the edge, it is time to repot. It is also necessary to repot when the potting material no longer drains well. The best time to do this is just as new root growth starts, usually in spring or early summer. Plants potted at this stage will root into the fresh material immediately and suffer the least possible shock or set-back. See

Methods of Repotting and Dividing at the end of this article.

While in Bloom

When the plant is in bloom it may be moved anywhere in the house, but it should not be taken out of the sunny window until the flowers are fully open. It is best to keep the plant in its regular growing place until the third day after the buds start to open, because the buds and flowers need sunlight to open fully and they will not gain their full color, nor will they last well, unless they have the sun while opening.

The regular watering and feeding schedule should be maintained throughout the blooming period. The better the plants are cared for, the longer the blooms will last.

When the plant has finished blooming, cut off the flower stem and the sheath around it just above the place where it grows out of the leaf and bulb and return the plant to its growing place. Soon it will start a new growth on which new flowers will appear and if the plant has good care it probably will have even more flowers at the next blooming.

Then relax—and enjoy them! Growing orchids is fun! And they will actually thrive better on neglect than they will with too much care.

The instructions here apply to most of the easily obtainable and commonly grown types, and are based on the experience of thousands of orchid growers all over the world. A good reference book with more detailed information is "Orchids for Home and Garden," by T. A.

Aerial roots of an Orchid.

Fennell, Jr., published by Holt, Winston and Rinehart, New York, N.Y., 1956. Revised 1959. This is a good textbook for beginners.

Six Major Groups

There are 6 major groups of orchids which are important in cultivation and make up the bulk of orchids grown in cultivation today. The basic growing instructions above apply to all of these groups, but in addition, each group, and many of the individuals in each group, have some special requirements that must be met if the plant is to achieve its optimum growth and beauty. Much of this must be learned individually by each grower by trial and error under his own particular conditions, but the hints in the outline of each group below should help to start the beginner in the right direction.

CATTLEYA. The Cattleyas are the best known and most popular of all orchids. The large and fancy lavender corsage orchid, frequently found in florist shops, is typical of the group. These gorgeous, large-flowered orchids are more widely grown and have been hybridized more than any other group. The genus, along with its related genera (*Brassavola, Broughtonia, Epidendrum, Laelia, Schomburgkia, Sophronitis,* etc.) and the many intergeneric hybrids, are the easiest to grow and by far the most important group of the Orchid Family. The plants are large, strong and tough and generally very tolerant to a wide range of cultural conditions. They are good ones for the novice because they can survive a great deal of mistreatment and will still bloom to encourage his interest.

Cattleyas usually produce clusters of 2–5 large flowers per stem on each new growth. Some of the smaller-flowered types may have as many as 30 flowers in a cluster, while some of their relatives such as Epidendrum often produce long erect sprays of 20–200 flowers lasting about a month, though some may last considerably longer.

These plants are native to the foothills and mountains of Central and northern South America at altitudes of 1500–6000 ft. where they have warm days with slightly cooler nights, an atmosphere of medium humidity (40%–60%), a rainy season during their growing period, but a fairly dry climate the remainder of the year, except for nightly dews which sometimes are quite heavy. Cattleyas and their allies do well under the general growing conditions outlined above. They have heavy fleshy leaves and pseudo-bulbs for storage and must be allowed to dry out between waterings. They should be fed regularly all year, but more heavily when in active growth. They usually do best close to the window where the light is bright and where the temperature drops 8–12° at night.

CYMBIDIUM. These beautiful orchids of medium size often produce 20–30 flowers on long, gracefully arching sprays that last in perfect beauty for months during the winter and spring. Colors are usually soft, clear pastel shades of white, pink, brown and light green, but some are brightly contrasting. The Cymbidiums are native to the Himalayas in Asia from India to Burma and are usually found at elevations of 5000–8000 ft. where they get bright light intensity, warm days and cool nights. They require a day-to-night temperature differential of 25°–30° (50°–55° nights—below 85° days) in order to bloom properly and for this reason cannot be recommended for home culture. Cymbidiums will grow well in a greenhouse where proper conditions of temperature and high light intensity can be supplied. Conditions very considerable from one spot to another even in the smallest greenhouse and careful observation will soon show where each plant does best. Thus, Cymbidiums can be grown in conjunction with Cattleyas and other plants in the small greenhouse by the proper placement of plants according to individual requirements, the Cymbidiums in the brightest and coolest corner or at the cool end of the house, with the Cattleyas in the slightly more shaded corner and warmer end of the house.

In some frost-free areas of the U.S. where nights are cool, such as in southern Calif., Cymbidiums grow very well as garden plants. They are terrestrials and require a loose, well-drained soil with frequent waterings and regular fertilizing. When grown in containers they should be given a sizable pot or tub for their extensive root system and should be fertilized often.

CYPRIPEDIUM. The "lady-slippers," as they are usually called, are a distinct and different group of orchids with a unique flower shape typified by the lip of the flower which is in the shape of the toe of a slipper or a pouch. The flowers are usually quite stiff and waxy and often last 6–8 weeks. Culturally, the plants are quite different from most other orchids. They thrive best under low light conditions of 800–1500 ft.-candles and, since they have no storage capacity, they must be kept damp at all times. Most of the northern types (the true Cypripediums) are bog plants. The more commonly grown tropical types (Paphiopedilums) are Asian in origin and many of these make good house plants, thriving in a bright north window or with an eastern exposure, but they must be well shaded in southern and western windows. Those with mottled dark green leaves generally need warm tempratures; those with clear green leaves, such as the Cymbidiums, usually prefer cooler conditions, but even these often do well in the home if placed close to a window where it is cool. Cypripediums are terrestrial orchids that require a soil with considerable moist peat or loam. They should be fed often and regularly, since they are in growth much of the year.

DENDROBIUM. Over 900 species make this one of the largest of all groups in the Orchid Family. Flower and plant types vary widely, as do the cultural requirements. In general, the Dendrobiums commonly in cultivation fall into 3–4 main groups. The lovely and fascinating flowers are usually profuse, in clusters or sprays, and are small to medium in size, and unusual in shape, often being twisted or curled. Most of the plants are tall and slender with long canes and with several to many leaves along the canes. Some are upright while others are pendant in growth habit and the base of the plant is almost always compact, with a relatively small root system that does best in a small pot. Dendrobiums do not respond well to being disturbed frequently, so they should not be repotted until it is absolutely necessary.

As a rule of thumb, most Dendrobiums require lots of water and food when in active growth and then should be dried off and allowed to harden up when not in growth. Most do well in fairly high light conditions. They will grow well along with Cattleyas, but can stand considerably more light. Many growers place them along with Cattleyas during the growing season and then move them into a slightly brighter location and cut down on the amount of water given them to harden off the new growth. Some of the Dendrobiums need some cooler weather at this time, also, in order to initiate buds.

The evergreen types such as *D. phalaenopsis* and the other cane-stem species and hybrids from the South Pacific area need warm conditions the year round and require water and food regularly. The deciduous and semi-deciduous pendant types such as *D. nobile*, *D. pierardii*, *D. superbum*, etc., need a definite drying off and some cool weather (down to 50° F.) in the fall in order to bloom properly. Well-grown Dendrobiums are among the showiest and most rewarding of all orchids and have always been very popular with amateur orchidists.

ONCIDIUM. This is another of the largest and most variable groups in the Orchid Family and also one of the most popular with hobbyists because the plants are usually easy to grow, they flower freely and easily and most are inexpensive and well suited for home culture. The 3 major genera in this group are *Oncidium*, *Odontoglossum* and *Miltonia*. Of these, the Oncidiums are the most adaptable and tolerant of home conditions, nearly all varieties doing well under the general growing instructions outlined earlier. However, most Odontoglossum

and Miltonia varieties are "cool growers," needing night temperatures of 50° F. or below and day temperatures under 70° F. if possible. They also need more shade, higher humidity and more water. These seldom do well in the home, but can be grown in the basement or on a cool enclosed porch. They will thrive in the cool section of the greenhouse along with Cypripediums or in a shaded place near Cymbidiums.

Colors, patterns and flower shapes are outstanding and highly varied in this group and many hobbyists specialize in them for their delicate beauty and fascinating variety. Most of the Oncidiums can be recommended for the novice. A few should be tried with caution as one's knowledge of orchids and one's confidence increase.

VANDA. This varied and extremely showy group, indigenous to the Tropics from Africa to the Philippines, has much to offer to the hobby-collector. Most are strong growing and easy to flower; the flowers last well and many bloom several times a year. The Vandas themselves come in almost every color and pattern imaginable and vary in size (both plant and flower) from almost dwarf to quite huge. They like a loose, open potting material (chunks of charcoal, large gravel or large chunks of fir bark) and considerable root room—either large shallow pots or baskets are usually best. They should be watered every day as long as drainage and ventilation in the pot are good and fertilized often—at least once a week if in an open, inorganic potting material. Under such conditions most of the many hybrids available today will bloom at least 2–3 times a year and some stay in bloom almost constantly. They will grow well along with Cattleyas but prefer slightly brighter light for optimum flowering.

Vandas do best of all outdoors in the garden in frost-free climates and are wonderful plants to work into the landscape in rock gardens or as climbers planted at the base of trees and walls. Once well established, they bloom almost constantly and are a joy to have.

Closely related genera that are very fascinating and well worth growing are: *Aerides* (very fragrant), *Angraecum* (green flowers with tail-like spurs, from Africa), *Renanthera* (blood-red flowers in large sprays) and *Rhyncostylus* (tightly packed flower stems, known as "foxtail orchids").

Perhaps the best loved and most suitable of all the Vanda group for home hobbyist culture are the Phalaenopsis. These lovely flowers, on long, gracefully arching stems, start to bloom in Dec.–Jan. and usually last through in perfect beauty until May or June. The flowers are medium to large and usually quite round and flat. Most are white or light lavender-pink, but the newer hybrids come in many colors and some are polka dotted or striped in stunning patterns and color combinations.

The plants are rather small and compact and produce a fine show of flowers in comparison to plant size—no other orchid will give as much show, as many days out of the year, and adapt so freely to such a wide range of conditions. These plants do reasonably well under the general conditions outlined above, but prefer slightly more shade, more water and more food and a higher temperature (65°–80° F.) than the others. They are soft, fast, lush-growing plants and do well under African Violet conditions, in general. They should be kept slightly damp in an open, well-drained, well-ventilated potting material such as coarse gravel or large chunks of fir bark. Repotting, when necessary, is best done in June, July or Aug. They need constant air movement and are subject to fungus leaf rot in stagnant, muggy conditions.

The "Botanical Group"

Traditionally orchidists have taken all the fascinating and intriguing smaller-flowered species of orchids which do not produce flowers of commercial value and lumped them together into 1 group called "Botanicals." Presumably, this was started by early cut-flower growers who considered these little gems as being worthy of interest only to botanists. Now, however, with the increasing hobby-collector interest, the "Botanicals" have come into their own as collector's items and, indeed, they are a truly fascinating and very worthwhile lot. There are literally hundreds of genera and thousands of species in this group and one may make up a collection of these alone, as many collectors do! There are thousands of miniatures where plant and flowers, fully mature, measure only from 1–3 or 4 in. tall. Some of these have flowers 2–3 in. in dia.—actually larger than the plants that produce them. Others are almost microscopic, so that one needs a hand lens to see the flowers! Others in this group have flowers that measure 12–18 in. from tip to tip of the sepals. Many are delightfully fragrant, while some produce what can only be described as a stench! Many of these flowers must indeed be seen to be believed. The interrelationship of these unusual flowers with the insects that pollinate them and the fantastic stratagems built into their highly specialized flower parts to insure that the right insects do the job properly constitute a fascinating area of study and some people have devoted a lifetime to this alone. Charles Darwin wrote 2 books on the subject! Many of these "botanicals" have very imaginative and suggestive shapes which lead to colorful and descriptive common names such as "Dancing Girl,"

"Butterfly," "Flock of Birds," "Tiger," "Foxtail," "Elephant," "Shower of Gold," "Dogwood," "The Honey Bucket" and a host of others, limited only by the fact that most are not sufficiently well-known to have acquired common names. This is truly a collector's paradise because the variety is so infinite that there is always another new and totally different one just waiting to be discovered.

Some of the "Botanical" genera that are relatively easy to obtain, easy to grow and to bring into flower and which have flowers large enough, pretty or interesting enough to be worth growing by the average hobby collector are: *Aerides, Ansellia, Ascocentrum, Aspasia, Bletia, Brassavola, Brassia, Broughtonia, Bulbophyllum, Calanthe, Chysis, Cirrhopetalum, Coelogyne, Cycnoches, Epidendrum, Gongora, Haemaria, Laelia, Lockhartia, Lycaste, Maxillaria, Phaius, Rodriguezia, Schomburgkia, Stanhopea, Trichopilia, Vanilla* and *Zygopetalum*. And, of course, even in this field there are a great many hybrids to broaden the scope even further.

Anatomy of Orchid Plants

Though the size, shape and proportions of the various parts may differ considerably, orchid plants grow in 2 basic patterns: Monopodial orchids are those having 1 central stem which grows out at the top and dies off at the bottom. This is a vinelike type of growth which produces leaves, roots and flower stems from the nodes, or joints, of the central stem, usually in an opposite and alternate pattern. These plants usually are in growth constantly and so need constant watering and feeding since they have little or no storage capacity. Some of the more common orchids in this group are the Phalaenopsis and Vandas, and their relatives.

Sympodial Orchids make up the greater part of the family. These plants make new growths or pseudobulbs each year during the rainy season in their native habitat. These pseudobulbs are connected to the previous year's growth by a rhizome. This lateral type of growth is a "stop and go" progression related to the wet and dry seasons in the wild and allowance for this must be made in cultivation for successful results. The pseudobulbs act as storage for food and water to carry the plant through dry seasons and show that, as a general rule, these plants must dry out between waterings.

The sympodial plant consists of a rhizome which grows out at the front and dies off from the back, making a lateral movement in growth. The pseudobulbs are seasonal growths produced at the front end of the rhizome and they usually last for several years. Each pseudobulb carries 1 or more leaves which usually last several years, though some few are deciduous. The blooms are then produced from the pseudobulb after it matures. Most orchids bloom only once on each bulb. The pseudobulbs have 2 or more growth "eyes" at the base, which form the next section of rhizome and the next new growth. Normally, 1 "eye" grows each season and the others stay dormant, in reserve. If the plant is growing strongly 2 eyes will grow, resulting in a branching of the rhizome and producing a plant with 2 front "leads." The roots grow out from the rhizome between the upright growths or pseudo-bulbs.

Dividing and Bottling

The only real work to be done in orchid culture is that of dividing and repotting which becomes necessary as the plants grow and branch. In general, however, it is best not to divide or repot until absolutely necessary, since this disturbance often will result in a setback to growth and optimum flowering.

There are only 2 reasons to repot: (1) When the plant outgrows the pot. Orchids often throw aerial roots outside the pot which does not necessitate repotting, but when the rhizome and new growths cross over the rim of the pot it is time for a larger pot. If not repotted the first year after the plant starts out of the pot, the rhizome may grow down the outside of the pot in a misshapen way, making it difficult to repot. (2) When the potting material deteriorates. Organic potting materials used in orchids are chosen for their coarse-textured nature, allowing water to drain quickly and permitting ventilation to the roots. When the potting material breaks down and begins to rot with age, it holds water too long and may turn sour. This eventually results in the rotting of the orchid roots and a sick plant. Therefore, repotting should be done whenever the potting material starts to deteriorate, and the sooner the better!

The best time to repot is just as the plant starts new root growth so that it gets established in the new material as quickly as possible, without having to live on stored food until new roots start.

After removing the plant from its pot, all of the old potting material should be removed from the roots and dead roots should be trimmed away. Any roots that are still plump, firm and alive should be saved, as orchid roots live for years and the more good roots the plant has, the stronger it will grow. This is a good time to clean up the whole plant; strip off old paper sheathes, cut away dead and weak pseudobulbs and generally inspect the plant for rot, insects, etc. It is a good idea to wash the plants from the tip of the leaves down to the roots with a cloth, sponge or soft brush and soapy water at this time, too; then rinse the plant and repot.

The decision about dividing must be made first. Most beginners divide too often and keep their plants so small that they never get optimum bloom. It is best to keep plants as large as practical for best bloom production. Branched and undivided plants will bloom on several stems at once. Then, too, the larger the plant, the more flowers per stem. If, however, the plant is too large for a pot of practical size, or if it continues to grow on a straight, unbranched rhizome that would require a large pot, then it is advisable to divide the plant. However, there should be at least 3–4 pseudobulbs to each division. The front division with the newest growth is the most important part of the plant. Back bulb divisions—those left at the back of the plant after the front division has been cut off—may grow and be worth potting, but the growth eyes on them have been dormant so long that they are usually weak and, if they do grow, the resulting plant will be poor. Most growers don't bother with them unless they are from exceptionally fine or favorite plants, worth extra effort and several years of care before the first blooms can be expected.

The actual dividing is simple. Just cut through the rhizome between the pseudobulbs at the chosen spot. A sharp knife will usually do the job, though some rhizomes are so tough that garden shears may be required. The cuts should be sealed with a fungicide powder to cauterize the wound, and the cutting instrument should always be sterilized by flaming between cuts to avoid the possibility of transferring any disease from one plant to another.

Potting Materials

Many materials can be used for potting orchids, since any material that is not chemically phytotoxic and that is either fibrous enough or comes in sufficiently large pieces to allow good, quick drainage and ventilation to the roots will do. The longer the material will last without rotting, the better it will be.

For many years Osmunda fiber (the roots of the Osmunda Fern) and sphagnum moss were the most commonly used materials. Both of these give some food value and last reasonably well (about 2 years) in the pot, but both require very careful attention in regard to watering, since they will turn sour if overwatered. Furthermore, both are difficult to use correctly and require a considerable amount of training and practice if one is to achieve proper results. In recent years a number of more convenient materials have been developed. The most popular and widely used now is fir bark, or a mixture of fir bark with redwood bark and fiber. This bark is now available in graded particle sizes for orchid potting and is quick and easy to use, but it has several drawbacks. It sheds water and is hard to moisten thoroughly in the beginning—then after about 3 years in the pot it starts to rot and hold too much water, resulting in root rot. There is also a type of white, cottony fungus which grows in this bark, and while this does not attack the orchids, it does plug up the drainage and eventually kills the orchid roots. This fungus also steals the food from the plant, particularly the nitrogen, so that heavy and regular feeding with a food high in nitrogen is necessary for plants in fir bark.

TREE FERN FIBER. A coarse, brittle fiber from the trunks of tropical tree ferns is another popular potting material which is much like Osmunda fiber but easier to work with and somewhat longer lasting. It, too, is subject to fungus problems if overwatered and so watering must be carefully controlled. This material has little available food value; hence the plant must be fed regularly.

The newest potting materials which show real promise are coke and expanded, light-weight gravels, such as E-Z-Pot Orchid Gravel. These are slightly porous and hold some water, yet never get soggy nor turn sour, since they are both inert and inorganic. These, of course, have no food value and orchids growing in them require frequent feeding for proper growth; however, they have the advantage of lasting indefinitely and of being virtually impervious to overwatering.

CONTAINERS FOR POTTING. Standard, porous clay flower pots are the containers used most for orchids, though many growers prefer the shorter azalea pots and bulb pans. Special orchid pots are made with slits cut into the lower sides of regular clay pots for additional drainage and ventilation and, if available, are well worth the extra expense. Standard pots may be cut and drilled with holes in the side walls by hand, using a wood rasp, a coarse grinding wheel or an electric drill, if orchid pots are not locally available. The pots can be cut more easily when wet.

Plastic pots are also used to some extent, but watering must be done carefully since gaseous transfer through them is not nearly so rapid as with clay pots, nor do they dry out so quickly. Some of the new foam plastic pots seem to hold promise for orchid culture, as they are said to be more like the porous clay pots and to have a valuable insulation factor.

Wooden baskets and wire baskets are used by many growers for outdoor culture in frost-free climates and are especially valuable in wet climates where proper drying of the potting material is a problem. They can also be used in greenhouses but are not recommended for home culture because they dry out too quickly there.

Slabs and rafts of wood or various hard fibers and long-lasting barks such as Redwood, Cypress, Cork and Tree Ferns are also very popular for mounting orchid plants for outdoor culture but, like the baskets, cannot be recommended for use in the home because they allow the plants to dry out too quickly.

Potting Process

Using the new granular and chunk-type potting materials, the process of potting is really very easy. The most important thing is the proper placing of the plant in the pot. Monopodial plants should be placed in the center of the pot with the bottom of the central stem on the bottom of the pot, if long enough, and if the roots spread out through the pot. Then fill the pot with potting material, working it in between the roots so that no large spaces are left empty. The top level of the material should come up to the bottom leaves of the plant, but should not bury them. If the plant is tall with a long, bare stem, it will look better in the pot, and also probably will grow better, if the bare stem can be shortened. It may be cut off, working up from the bottom to the last section which has at least 3–4 good roots on it. Then put the plant down in the pot so that lower leaves are as near as possible to the level of the rim of the pot.

Sympodial plants should be placed in the pot so as to give the most growing room possible in front of the new lead or "growing end" of the rhizome. If the rhizome is relatively straight, the back end of the rhizome should be against the rim of the pot with the front pointing out across the pot toward the opposite side. Choose a container that allows space for 2–3 years of growth between the front of the rhizome and the nearest rim of the pot. Then hold the plant in place with one hand, keeping the rhizome running horizontally across the pot at rim level and spread out the roots in the empty pot. Then fill in the potting material, a handful at a time, working it in between the roots until the pot is full. The rhizome should be half buried, with the top half, along its length, exposed above the potting material. It should not be completely buried, nor completely exposed.

The only other thing of importance about potting is that the plant should be held firmly in place, so that new roots will not be broken as they emerge by the movement of the plant in the pot and material. If the plant has a good root system to begin with, and is properly potted, it will be firmly held in the pot by the potting material alone, but if there are not many roots, or if the plant moves in the potting material, then it should be staked and tied or clipped down into the pot so that it cannot move until the new root growth anchors it firmly in place. Plants that do move in the pot seldom develop good root systems. Floppy plants that do not hold themselves properly erect should be staked and tied, also. Potting needs to be done only once every 3–4 years and since it is so important to the growth and flower production of the plant, it should be done with great care.

Orchid Problems

Orchids are extremely tough plants that are seldom troubled by diseases, but there are a few cultural problems that crop up. Plants that grow well but do not bloom, especially those with tall, slender, dark, glossy green foliage, need more sun or a food with less nitrogen. "Black-rot" and "soft-rot" in the leaves and pseudobulbs are usually a sign of too much water, too high humidity, a lack of sufficient air movement or ventilation or a need of repotting. Rotten areas should be cut out, cutting well into the clear green tissue around it, and then the cuts should be sealed with a fungicide powder. Plants should then be dried off for a few days to allow the cut to heal.

Insect problems arise with orchids, as with other plants, but the plants are so tough that the effects are not usually drastic and the symptoms usually take much longer to appear than with other types of plants. Treatment and sprays to be used are the same as for other plants except that new sprays, unless specifically recommended for orchids, should be tested gingerly on a few plants first.

Sunburn usually shows up as large, rough, scalded or blistered-looking areas which turn black with a yellowish margin and then turn hard, dry, gray and papery in a few days or weeks. If the blackened area is soft, squashy and wet or greasy to the touch, then the problem is "black-rot" rather than sunburn.

Virus Diseases

Several virus diseases are recognized in orchids and, though most are not very widespread, it is best to sterilize between every cut all instruments used for cutting orchid plants to avoid transferring a possible virus infection from one plant to another. The 2 most easily recognized are "Flower-Break" virus which causes uneven blotching and "color-break" in the flowers, particularly on Cattleyas, and "Orchid Mosaic" virus which causes light and dark streaks parallel to the veins in the leaves of Cattleyas and some others. Another form is known as "Ring-Spot" which causes yellowish

and sometimes dark brownish-black ring-shaped spots in the leaves. There is no known cure for any of these virus diseases, so suspected plants should be isolated until some authority can inspect them. Infected plants should be destroyed, since the virus can be spread to others. Insects that chew and suck on the plants are said to be one method of spreading the virus, but the orchid grower with his cutting tools is much more likely to be the offender. He can spread the virus every time he divides a plant, cuts off a flower, an old bulb or leaf, so it is best to sterilize all cutting instruments between every cut and no doubt it would be wise to sterilize pots between uses, also.

T. A. FENNELL, JR.

ORCHID, FRINGE. See HABENARIA.

ORCHID, GRASS PINK = *Calopogon pulchellus*

ORCHID, RAGGED = *Habenaria lacera*

ORCHID-TREE. See BAUHINIA.

ORCHIS (OR-kis). These 2 species are hardy orchids of the woods of southern Canada and the northeastern U.S., with tuberous roots, basal leaves and showy little flowers in racemes; sometimes used in the wild garden or rockery, where they should be given a rich, moist soil with plenty of humus. For culture and propagation see ORCHID.

rotundifolia   6″   Zone 3   Round-leaf Orchis
A plant consisting of a single, rounded, basal leaf and a flower stalk crowned with a cluster of 5–10 irregular pink flowers having a white lip dotted with purple. Rarely found, it blooms in June and July and is native to the moist woods of Canada and northern U.S.

spectabilis   12″   Zone 3   Showy Orchis
This species has the oval basal leaves with strong longitudinal veinings typical of the Lady's-slippers, and a flower stalk bearing 3–10 flowers amid their leafy bracts. Violet-colored sepals and petals are fused to form a hood and the lip is white with violet, and extends into a spur. It blooms in May and June. The plant may be found in moist woods in southern Canada and eastern U.S.

ORDER OF BLOOM. It is of great interest to gardeners that the plants living out-of-doors over winter have a definite sequence in which they bloom. Snowdrops bloom before daffodils, which bloom before rhododendrons. It is important to every gardener to know when his plants will bloom, for in planting he takes advantage of this knowledge, placing certain types of plants together for special color combinations when they flower together. The time plants bloom is usually a matter of record, sometimes an indefinite "early spring" and other times a more specific "middle of May."

Everyone knows that spring and summer advance across the United States from south to north and that plants which may bloom in northern Fla. in mid-Feb. will not bloom in southern Me. until late May. Those familiar with mountain flora also know that the higher the altitude on the mountain, the colder it is and the more time it takes plants to bloom that are growing at the higher altitudes. Hence, both latitude and altitude govern the time of bloom of plants. Also the "earliness" or "lateness" of the season is the other variable element. It is interesting to keep a record of one plant from year to year, noting the day on which the flowers first start to bloom. In some areas this can vary as much as 4 weeks from year to year. One such record shows that the Yoshino cherries around the tidal basin in Washington, D.C., started to bloom on March 20th in 1945, but did not start until April 15th in 1932, 1934, 1955 and 1965. The spring was said to be "early" in 1945, and "late" in the other years, with a "normal" spring somewhere in between the 2 extremes.

The length of time the flowers remain in colorful condition also varies according to the vagaries of the weather. If the temperature is very warm when the Shadblow blooms, the flowers may remain in good condition for only 3 days and then the petals fall. On the other hand, if the weather is cool after the flowers first appear, they may remain in good condition for a week or even longer.

The number of petals in the flower will contribute to the length of time that flower remains effective. The double-flowered cherries like 'Kwanzan' with many petals will remain effective twice as long as the Yoshino cherries which only have 5 petals. The same is true of many other double-flowered plants—the reason it is always advisable to use these in landscape planting wherever possible.

Even plants of 1 variety growing in the same garden may vary as to the time they bloom. Snowdrops, for instance, planted near the foundation of a warm building may bloom in Jan. some years, when others, only 50 ft. away, will not blossom until March, merely because they are removed from the warmth of the building. Shrubs on the south (i.e., sunny) side of a building will bloom before similar plants on the north (shaded) side of the same building.

The important fact to remember is that plants which bloom together when growing together with similar conditions can be expected to bloom together regardless of whether they are growing together in northern Fla., in Me. or in Ore. Also the sequence in which they bloom is the same. The actual calendar date will vary of course, but the sequence remains the same, and that is the reason the following list has value to any gardener.

In the list, many plants are recorded in the sequence in which they bloom at Boston, Mass. Enough are listed throughout the year so that any gardener anywhere in the U.S. can take the list and adapt it to his own situation. A few plants in a Lexington, Ky., garden, for instance, can be noted in this sequence, the date changed to conform to local performance, and all the dates on the following list can be advanced (about 3 weeks) and the sequence should conform fairly well to the new dates.

Some years with cold springs, the blooming of the earlier plants may be greatly retarded, but eventually, when warm weather does come, the sequence catches up with a rush. Forsythias normally bloom in Boston in mid-April, the varieties of the Common Liliac a month later in mid-May. Some years when the spring weather have been very cold until mid-May, the forsythias have just not opened until mid-May—with the lilacs. This condition is unusual, but it does happen.

Keep a record of 1 tree near the house, noting when it first comes in leaf or in flower. Willows are good for this purpose for their buds seem to turn green (i.e., actually the buds are swelling and the young leaves show color in them easily) quickly in the spring. One day the tree is as it has appeared all winter, yet the next day, especially after a very warm night, there is a tinge of green over the whole tree. Record that day from year to year, for it makes a most interesting record, and from it one can usually predict what other plants will do.

The following list includes trees, shrubs, vines, perennials and a few bulbs, as they bloom in sequence throughout the year. The dates can be changed to conform to local conditions. Many other plants can be added where they enter into this sequence and thus the list can become an important asset in making garden plans.

ORDER OF BLOOM

February
    Hamamelis vernalis
March
    Acer saccharinum
    Crocus imperati
    Corylus sp.
    Galanthus nivalis
    Hamamelis japonica
    H. mollis
    Salix sp.
Early April
    Acer rubrum
    Alnus several sp.
    Cornus mas
    Daphne mezereum

Erica carnea
Forsythia ovata
Jasminum nudiflorum
Populus sp.
Ulmus americana
Viburnum farreri (*V. fragrans*)
Mid-April
  Abeliophyllum distichum
  Acer negundo
  Betula sp.
  Corylopsis sp.
  Epigaea repens
  Forsythia europaea
  F. intermedia vars.
  F. suspensa vars.
  F. viridissma
  Lindera benzoin
  Lonicera fragrantissima
  Pieris japonica
  Rhododendron calophytum
  R. mucronulatum
  Shepherdia argentea
Late April
  Acer platanoides
  Amelanchier canadensis
  A. laevis
  A. spicata
  Anemone pulsatilla
  Arabis caucasica
  Brunnera macrophylla
  Magnolia denudata
  M. kobus
  M. salicifolia
  M. stellata
  Malus baccata mandshurica
  Pieris floribunda
  Poncirus trifoliata
  Prunus armeniaca
  P. canescens
  P. cerasifera
  P. domestica
  P. incisa
  P. mandshurica
  P. sargentii
  P. subhirtella
  P. tomentosa
  P. yedoensis
  Rhododendron praecox
  Spiraea prunifolia
  Vinca minor
Early May
  Acer saccharum
  Amelanchier grandiflora
  A. stolonifera
  Aubretia deltoidea
  Aurinia saxatile
  Bergenia cordifolia
  Chaenomeles sp. and vars.
  Crataegus arnoldiana
  Dandelion

Enkianthus perulatus
Exochorda giraldii
Lamium maculatum
Magnolia soulangiana vars.
Mahonia sp.
Malus arnoldiana
M. atrosanguinea
M. baccata
M. floribunda
M. halliana
M. hupehensis
M. pumila niedzwetzkyana
M. purpurea
M. robusta
M. spectabilis
M. sylvestris
M. zumi
Mertensia virginica
Narcissus—many sp.
Phlox subulata
Primula polyantha
Prinsepia sinensis
Prunus americana
P. avium
P. blireiana
P. glandulosa
P. hortulana
P. maritima
P. padus
P. pensylvanica
P. persica
P. serrulata
Pyrus calleryana
P. communis
P. ussuriensis
Rhododendron mucronatum
Ribes odoratum
Spiraea arguta
S. thunbergii
Syringa hyacinthiflora
S. oblata
Tulipa—several sp.
Viburnum lantanoides (*V. alnifolium*)
Viola—several sp.
Mid-May
  Aesculus carnea
  A. hippocastanum
  Aurinia saxatile
  Berberis thunbergii
  Calycanthus floridus
  Caragana arborescens
  Cercis canadensis
  C. chinensis
  Cornus florida
  Cydonia oblonga
  Cytisus praecox
  C. purpureus
  C. scoparius
  Daphne cneorum
  Davidia involucrata

Deutzia grandiflora
Dicentra eximia
Dodecatheon meadia
Enkianthus campanulatus
Exochorda korolkowii
E. racemosa
Fothergilla sp.
Fraxinus ornus
Halesia sp.
Hemerocallis flava
Iberis sempervirens
Kerria japonica
Lonicera bella
Magnolia fraseri
M. liliflora nigra
Malus sargentii
M. sieboldii
Papaver orientale
Pawlonia tomentosa
Phlox divaricata
P. subulata
Prunus cerasus
P. virginiana
Rhodendron albrechtii
R. canandense
R. carolinanum
R. obtusum
R. racemosum
R. schlippenbachii
R. vaseyi
R. yedoense
Rhodotypos scandens
Ribes sanguineum
Sambucus pubens
Sorbus aucuparia
Spiraea prunifolia
Syringa vulgaris—most vars.
Trollius europaeus
Viburnum carlesii
V. lantana
Weigela–many hybrids
Late May
Ajuga reptans
Aronia sp.
Celastrus sp.
Cornus alternifolia
C. controversa
C. sericea
Cotoneaster adpressa
C. apiculata
C. racemiflora
Crataegus crus-galli
C. oxyacantha
C. pruinosa
C. punctata
C. succulenta
Daphne giraldii
Dicentra spectabilis
Deutzia gracilis
D. kalmiaeflora

D. lemoinei
D. rosea
Epimedium sp.
Laburnum sp.
Lonicera amoena
L. korolkowii
L. maackii
L. morrowii
L. tatarica
Magnolia cordata
M. tripetala
M. virginiana
M. watsonii
Malus angustifolia
M. coronaria
M. ioensis 'Plena'
M. toringoides
Paeonia lactiflora
P. officinalis
P. suffruticosa
Photinia villosa
Potentilla fruticosa
Prunus laurocerasus
P. serotina
Ranunculus bulbosus
Rhododendron atlanticum
R. catawbiense
R. catawbiense 'Boule de Neige'
R. catawbiense 'Charles Dickens'
R. catawbiense 'Mont Blanc'
R. fortunei 'Duke of York'
R. gandavense hybrids
R. japonicum
R. molle hybrids
R. periclymenoides
R. prinophyllum
R. smirnowii
Robinia fertilis
R. kelseyi
Rosa ecae
R. hugonis
R. primula
R. xanthina
Rubus deliciosus
Spiraea multiflora
S. nipponica
S. vanhouttei
Symplocos paniculata
Syringa chinensis
S. microphylla
S. persica
Tamarix parviflora
Thymus serphyllum
Vaccinium corymbosum
Viburnum lentago
V. macrocephalum
V. opulus
V. plicatum
V. prunifolium
V. rufidulum

V. sieboldii
V. trilobum
V. wrightii
Viola cornuta
Weigela 'Dame Blanche'
W. 'Lavallei'
Wisteria sp.
Early June
  Aquilegia hybrida
  Buddleia alternifolia
  Centaurea montana
  Cerastium tomentosum
  Chionanthus sp.
  Cladrastis lutea
  Cornus alba
  C. kousa
  Dianthus plumarius
  Genista tinctoria
  Geranium sanguineum
  Gypsophila repens
  Helianthemum nummularium
  Heuchera sanguinea
  Hydrangea anomala vars.
  Ilex opaca
  Indigofera amblyantha
  Jamesia americana
  Kolkwitzia amabilis
  Leucothoe fontanesiana
  Linum perenne
  Magnolia obovata
  M. sieboldii
  Philadelphus coronarius
  P. maximus
  Primula japonica
  Rhododendron arbutifolium
  R. calendulaceum
  R. catawbiense—most vars.
  R. laetevirens
  R. minus
  Robinia hispida
  R. 'Idaho'
  R. pseudoacacia
  Rosa blanda
  R. foetida bicolor
  R. harisonii
  R. rubrifolia
  R. rugosa
  R. spinossisima
  Salvia pratensis
  Styrax sp.
  Syringa henryi
  S. josikaea
  S. prestoniae
  S. reflexa
  S. villosa
  Thalictrum aquilegifolium
  Tradescantia virginiana
  Viburnum cassinoides
  V. dentatum
  V. dilatatum

V. opulus
V. prunifolium
V. sargentii
Mid-June
  Amorpha fruticosa
  Anchusa azurea
  Baptisia australis
  Castanea mollissima
  Catalpa speciosa
  Chrysanthemum coccineum
  C. maximum
  Convallaria majalis
  Cornus racemosa
  Cotoneaster dielsiana
  C. horizontalis
  C. multiflora
  Crataegus phaenopyrum
  Delphinium sp.
  Deutzia 'Contraste'
  D. 'Magicien'
  D. magnifica
  Dictamus albus
  Filipendula hexapetala
  Gaillardia aristata
  Ilex glabra
  I. verticillata
  Iris sibirica
  Kalmia latifolia
  Ligustrum sp.
  Liriodendron tulipifera
  Lonicera japonica 'Halliana'
  Lupinus polyphyllus
  Myosotis scorpioides
  Papaver orientale
  Philadelphus—many sp. and hybrids
  Pyracantha coccinea
  Rhododendron 'Album Elegans'
  R. 'Album Grandiflorum'
  R. arborescens
  Rosa—many sp.
  Stephanandra incisa
  Symphoricarpos albus laevigatus
  Syringa amurensis
  Tilia platyphyllos
  Trollius ledebouri
  Veronica latifolia
  Weigela 'Congo'
  W. 'Eve Rathke'
  Zenobia pulverulenta
Late June
  Achillea tomentosa
  Ailanthus altissima
  Campanula latifolia
  Centaurea dealbata
  Dianthus barbatus
  Digitalis purpurea
  Iris kaempferi
  Itea virginica
  Lavandula officinalis
  Lilium pumilum

Lonicera henryi
Philadelphus virginalis
Rhododendron maximum
Sambucus canadensis
Schizophragma hydrangeoides
Sorbaria sorbifolia
Spiraea billiardii
S. bumalda
S. tomentosa
Thermopsis caroliniana
Tilia americana
Tripterygium regelii
Early July
  Anthemis tinctoria
  Campanula percisifolia
  Coreopsis lanceolata
  Cytisus nigricans
  Hosta fortunei
  Hydrangea arborescens 'Grandiflora'
  Hypericum kalmianum
  H. patulum henryi
  Lavandula officinalis
  Lilium amabile
  Lychnis chalcedonica
  Lycium sp.
  Maackia amurensis
  Rhododendron prunifolium
  R. viscosum
  Rosa setigera
  Rubus odoratus
  Stewartia koreana
  S. pseudo-camellia
  Tilia euchlora
  T. petiolaris
  T. tomentosa
  Veronica spicata
  Viburnum setigerum
Mid-July
  Aesculus parviflora
  Albizia julibrissin rosea
  Amorpha canescens
  Campsis radicans
  Chrysanthemum parthenium
  Cimicifuga racemosa
  Clematis jackmanii
  Filipendula ulmaria
  Gypsophila paniculata
  Heliopsis scaber
  Hemerocallis fulva
  Hydrangea paniculata praecox
  H. quercifolia
  H. serrata
  Koelreuteria paniculata
  Lilium canadense
  L. davidii macranthum
  Lonicera heckrottii
  L. sempervirens
  Lythrum salicaria
  Monarda didyma
  Oxydendrum arboreum

Phlox paniculata
Rosa wichuraiana
Scabiosa caucasica
Stewartia ovata
Tamarix odessana
Valeriana officinalis
Late July
  Abelia schumannii
  Achillea filipendulina
  Althaea rosea
  Aralia spinosa
  Astilbe arendsii
  Calluna vulgaris
  Campanula carpatica
  Cephalanthus occidentalis
  Clethra sp.
  Echinops 'Taplow Blue'
  Hypericum prolificum
  Kalopanax pictus
  Lespedeza bicolor
  Nandina domestica
  Platycodon grandiflorum
  Sorbaria arborea
  Stokesia laevis
  Veronica longifolia
  Yucca smalliana
Early August
  Abelia grandiflora
  Aralia chinensis
  A. elata
  Asclepias tuberosa
  Buddleia davidii
  Caryopteris incana
  Hydrangea macrophylla
  H. paniculata
  H. paniculata 'Grandiflora'
  Liatris scariosa
  Lilium tigrinum
  Lobelia cardinalis
  Physostegia virginiana
Mid-August
  Aconitum napellus
  Artemisia lactiflora
  Clematis virginiana
  C. vitalba
  Hibiscus syriacus
  Hosta lancifolia
  H. plantaginea
  Lagerstroemia indica
  Rudbeckia sullivantii
  Sedum spectabile
  Vitex sp.
Late August
  Chrysanthemum moriifolium
  Clerodendrum trichotomum
  Evodia daniellii
  Helenium autumnale
  Polygonum aubertii
  Sophora japonica

September
  Aconitum carmichaelii
  Aster novi-belgii
  Baccharis halimifolia
  Clematis paniculata
  Elsholtzia stauntonii
  Franklinia alatamaha
October
  Hamamelis virginiana
  Lespedza japonica

OREGANO. Trade name for various herbs of European origin used as condiments.

ORGANIC GARDENING. This is a term used in describing a type of gardening in which no inorganic materials like lime, ammonium sulfate, rock phosphate, etc., are returned to the soil. As a result, only organic fertilizers like the animal manures are used; peat moss, ground sugar cane, pine needles and similar plant products are used for mulching. Considerable effort is made in making organic compost (which see) and using it wherever possible.

ORGANIC PHOSPHATES. See INSECTICIDES.

ORIGANUM (o-RIG-an-um)
   majorana (*Majorana hortensis*)   2′   annual
                                              Sweet Marjoram
The entire, woolly, aromatic leaves are oval and about an inch long. The flowers are purplish or whitish. Native to Europe. The leaves are used for flavoring; an oil is made from the top of the plant to scent soap; and other parts are used in certain medicines for nervous headaches.
   vulgare   2½′   Zone 3   Wild Marjoram
Hardy perennial herb, sometimes a weed in eastern North America, naturalized here but native to Europe. The aromatic leaves are opposite, broadly ovate, 1½ in. long; the purplish flowers are borne in 2-in. clusters or whorls, during July and Aug. Long used as an essential plant in the herb garden.

ORIXA (o-RIX-a)
   japonica   9′   Zone 5   Japanese Orixa
This is a much-overlooked deciduous foliage plant from Japan, valued because of its very lustrous bright green leaves that are 2–5 in. long. The inconspicuous dioecious flowers and brown fruits have little ornamental value but it makes a fine foliage plant which can be grown in the full sun with good results.

Propagation

   Division, softwood cuttings, hardwood cuttings and root cuttings all have been used satisfactorily.

ORNITHOGALUM (or-nith-OG-al-um). There are both hardy and tender species of this group of bulbous plants, members of the Lily Family,

valued for their star-shaped (6-segmented) flowers, produced in spikes or umbels, in spring and summer. Easily propagated by offsets. Some of the hardy strains have become naturalized in the U.S. When grown in the greenhouse, the best temperature is about 60° F.
   arabicum   2′   Zone 8   Arabian Star-of-
                                              Bethlehem
Fragrant white flowers blooming in summer; a tender species for the greenhouse; leaves 1 in. wide. The flowers have black pistils. Native to the Mediterranean Region.
   caudatum   3′   Zone 8   Whiplash Star-of-
                                              Bethlehem
Flowers green or white blooming in spring or summer, about 1 in. across in long racemes. Native to South Africa. Usually for the greenhouse.
   nutans   1′   Zone 5   Nodding Star-of-
                                              Bethlehem
Flowers green and white blooming in spring, often 2 in. across, produced in nodding racemes. Native to Europe, escaped at several places in the U.S.
   pyramidale   3′   Zone 5   Pyramid Star-of-
                                              Bethlehem
White flowers with green margins in slender upright spikes, 1 in. across, in slender racemes. Native to southern Europe.
   thyrsoides   1½′   Zone 7   Cape Chinkerichee
A South African bulbous herb with leaves 1 ft. long and ½ in. wide; white or yellow flowers, ¾ in. across, in dense racemes of 12–18 flowers in each raceme. The var. **aureum** has golden-yellow flowers, one of the best of this genus for indoor culture. All parts of the plant are poisonous if eaten.
   umbellatum   1′   Zone 4   Star-of-Bethlehem
This is a bulbous plant of Europe which multiplies rapidly and has become naturalized in many areas of the northeastern U.S. and south to Miss. The many smooth, green, linear leaves are a foot long and ⅓ in. wide, forming an attractive mound of foliage, from which the flower stalk arises, crowned with 12–20 white starlike flowers having 6 segments, the 3 outer ones being striped with green. These appear in May and June. As the plant is reputed to be poisonous in all its parts, it should be kept away from small children. Suitable for the wild garden, the bulbs may be dug and reset after the flowering period.

ORONTIUM (o-RON-tium)
   aquaticum   aquatic   Zone 7   Golden Club
A plant of slow-moving streams and of swamps, the bluish-green leaves, floating or erect, are 2–5 in. wide and 6–12 in. long, with strongly marked longitudinal veins. The flower is an inconspicuous spathe with a long curving spadex, having deep yellow flowers covering the

upper portion. Of no particular ornamental value, it may be used in the bog garden. It flowers in early summer and is found principally in the South, rarely as far north as New England and Minn.

ORPINE or **STONECROP FAMILY** = Crassulaceae

ORYZA (o-RY-za)

sativa   4'   annual   Common Rice
After wheat this is the most important grain in the world, probably native to the East Indies but grown in the Tropics around the world. The leaves are 2 ft. long, ½ in. wide. The plant bears fruiting panicles a foot long, with grains straw-colored but white when polished as they are commercially. Grown in places where there is much water. There is a form with red grains.

OSAGE-ORANGE = *Maclura pomifera*

OSIER, PURPLE = *Salix purpurea*

OSMANTHUS (os-Man-thus)

Osmanthus with opposite leaves (above). Ilex with alternate leaves (below).

americanus   45'   Zone 6   Devilwood Osman-
thus
Evergreen, opposite leaves 2–6 in. long; flowers white and fragrant but very small; fruit dark blue berries. This is not much used in gardens for the exotic members of this genus have far more ornamental fruits.

armatus   15'   Zone 7   Chinese Osmanthus
An evergreen shrub with opposite, leathery leaves, coarsely toothed and pointed, 3–6 in. long and ¾–1½ in. wide. The fragrant white flowers, ¼ in. across, are produced in the fall, followed by dark violet egg-shaped fruits ¾ in. long. The spiny-tipped leaf margins may not be present on the leaves of mature specimens. Native to western China.

delavayi (*Siphonosmanthus delvayi*) **6'   Zone 7**
A delightful little evergreen with opposite small leaves, up to 1 in. long, short stalked with fragrant flowers in March and bluish-black berries, ½ in. long, in summer; this native of western China makes a fine specimen for planting in full sun. The twiggy growth and waxy, fragrant flowers, produced in the axils of the leaves during the early spring, are its chief assets.

x fortunei   12'   Zones 7–8   Fortune's Os-
manthus
Popular in the South as well as on the Pacific Coast, this Japanese evergreen has hollylike leaves up to 4 in. long and is a hybrid, *O. heterophyllus* x *O. fragrans*. Primarily an evergreen foliage shrub, its small flowers in axillary clusters are very fragrant in June and its blue-black berries show to some advantage in the fall. It is vigorous and attractive.

fragrans   30'   Zones 8–9   Sweet Osmanthus
This has extremely fragrant flowers, small as they are, in the early spring. Native to Asia with evergreen, hollylike leaves, this has been a popular greenhouse plant in the North for a long time. It is now being offered by several nurserymen in Calif. and in the southeastern U.S. for garden planting.

heterophyllus (*ilicifolius*) **18'   Zone 6   Holly**
Osmanthus
The lustrous, dark, spiny, evergreen leaves of this species make it one of the handsomest of evergreen specimens. It is native to Japan, has leaves 2½ in. long, yellowish-green inconspicuous flowers in July that are very fragrant, and bluish-black berries in the fall. The foliage looks similar to that of the American Holly except, of course, their leaves are oppositely arranged on the stem while those of the American Holly are alternate. It serves well as a specimen in shade or full sun and can be clipped to form a splendid hedge.

ilicifolius = *O. heterophyllus*

yunnanense (*forrestii*) **24'   Zone 7   Forrest's**
Osmanthus
An evergreen shrub with oblong-lanceolate leaves up to 8 in. long, either entire or spiny toothed; flowers creamy white and fragrant. fruit ovoid and about ½ in. long. Native to western China

x OSMAREA (os-MAY-rea)

burkwoodii   8′-10′   Zone 6   Burkwood Osmarea

Evergreen shrub, not much planted, originating before 1928 as a hybrid between *Phillyrea decora* and *Siphonosmanthus delavayi*. The leaves are 1½ in. long; the white, fragrant flowers are borne in terminal or axillary clusters during April and May.

OSMUNDA. These are evergreen or deciduous ferns, widely distributed throughout Asia, Europe, North America and the West Indies, well known to those who grow orchids for it is the roots of these ferns that provide the Osmunda fiber so much used for potting orchids. The fronds vary from 18 in. to 8 ft. long and they are feathery, with spores borne either at the ends of the fronds or on separate structures altogether. They all require plenty of moisture, and are well planted in partially shaded spots besides streams or ponds. If, for some reason, they are to be planted in a dry part of the garden, arrangements must be made to keep the roots moist at all times, even into making a concrete (or polyethylene) tank for them where water can not drain away. Propagation is usually by spores. See FERNS.

cinnamomea   4′   Zone 3   Cinnamon Fern

This is native over the eastern half of North America, has 1-pinnate fronds, the pinnae of which are deeply cut. Its common name comes from the sterile frond that looks like a "cinnamon stick" with all the fat, rounded rusty-colored sporangia borne in tight ball-like masses. This also requires partial shade and a moist situation.

claytoniana   2′-4′   Zone 3   Interrupted Fern

Widely native to North America, this does not seem particular regarding the soil in which it grows but, like other members of this genus, must have plenty of moisture. The fronds are 1-pinnate, but the pinnae are deeply cut, coarse and leathery. The spores are borne on 2–5 pairs of pinnae in the lower half of the frond. This needs a highly acid soil. It does not spread rapidly and is deciduous.

regalis   6′-8′   Zone 2   Royal Fern

This has twice-compound fronds with the pinnae 2–3 in. long. The parts of the frond that bear the spores are modified, being smaller, bearing only spores. This species is deciduous and native from Canada to Fla. and Mo., requiring a highly acid soil. The var. **cristata** has crested fronds; **gracilis** has bronze-colored fronds and the var. **palustris** has fronds only about 3 ft. long that are reddish.

OSMUNDA FIBER. The roots of *Osmunda* fern species, which, when dried, is the material in which orchids are planted. When dug it usually comes out in large mats and must be separated or chopped up to be usable.

OSTRYA (OS-tria)

virginiana   60′   Zone 4   Hop-hornbeam

Because this is native over half the U.S. from Ontario to Tex., it is sometimes used as an ornamental tree. The clusters of bladderlike fruits are evident throughout the summer. But, like the *Carpinus*, it is slow-growing and difficult to transplant. It is seldom that this tree is used if other faster-growing types can be selected. A var. *glandulosa* has been differentiated by botanists as being the northern form, but it differs little from the species in its ornamental characteristics. See discussion under *Carpinus* for comparisons.

Propagation

Do not allow the seed to dry out, but stratify when ripe for 4 months at 40° F., then sow. Grafting is also successful with *Carpinus betulus* used as the understock. See STRATIFICATION, GRAFTING.

OTHONNA (o-THON-na)

capensis   trailing   Zone 10   Little Pickles

An alternate-leaved South African perennial herb, used in greenhouses or hanging baskets, with trailing stems, shrubby at the base, and fleshy leaves about an inch long. Belonging to the Composite Family, the yellow, daisylike flower heads are singly borne on 4-in. stems, sometimes clustered and about ½ in. across. Grows best in full sun. Propagation is by stem cuttings.

OVARY. That part of the pistil containing the ovules or future seeds.

OVARY SUPERIOR. Borne above the insertion of the perianth and free from it. See also OVARY.

OVATE. Having an outline like that of a hen's egg.

OVULE. The body which becomes a seed after fertilization.

OXALIDACEAE = The Wood-sorrel Family

OXALIS (ox-AY-lis). This is a group of over 300 species of small, bulbous plants producing cloverlike leaves, all being sour to the taste. Many species have leaves with 3 leaflets, but some have more. They usually close up at night. Most are perennial, some annual with small white, pink, yellow or red flowers, usually axillary, single and long-stalked. The better flowered ones are used in the North as house plants of easy culture, or are grown in the greenhouse. They are mostly propagated by bulbs or division and by seeds. Indoors the bulbs might be divided in Sept. and planted, to bloom in late winter or early spring, after which the bulbous types should be stored in a cool cellar for their resting period. They do well in full sun.

adenophylla 6″ **Zone 7** **Chilean Oxalis**
This bulbous perennial from South America has rosy-pink flowers on 2-in. stalks throughout much of the summer. It does well in a slightly alkaline (not acid) soil. Somewhat difficult to grow, this needs a light, well-drained soil in a sunny situation. It grows fairly well in the Pacific Northwest. Propagated by division of the bulbs.

bowiei (*O. bowieana*) 6″–12″ **Zone 8 Bowie Oxalis**
A perennial with thick tuberous roots, 3 large leaflets and large, rose-purple flowers up to 2 in. in dia. during summer. Native to South Africa.

bowieana = *O. bowiei*

braziliensis 4″ **Zone 8** **Brazil Oxalis**
A bulbous perennial native to Brazil, with deep wine-red flowers up to an inch in dia. Leaflets 3. This does well in a warm, sunny spot in the garden. It also needs a rest period after flowering when grown as a pot plant indoors. See *O. deppei*.

cernua = *O. pes-caprae*

corniculata 6″ **Zone 4** **Creeping Oxalis**
A slender-stemmed, branching, perennial herb arising from a creeping rootstalk. The bright yellow flowers bloom from spring to fall. It may be found in fields or along roadsides throughout the U.S. and southern Canada, though it is actually a native to Europe.

deppei 6″ **Zone 8** **Rosette Oxalis**
A bulbous perennial from Mexico, the bulbs should be planted at least 6 in. deep in good leaf mold. The flowers are brick red from June to Aug. and the leaves are green with an interesting purplish tint. There is supposed to be a white-flowered form. The roots are said to be delicious when cooked. Leaflets mostly 4 and not notched. When grown in pots indoors, they should be given a rest period (i.e., kept dry) as soon as the leaves begin to die after flowering, and kept dry until the start of the next growing season.

hirta 6″–12″ **Zone 9**
This native to South Africa has tuberous roots, 3 leaflets and bears purple to violet-colored flowers in the early winter.

lasiandra 3″–6″ **Zone 9 Primrose Oxalis**
A perennial growing from a bulb with leaflets 5–10 and crimson flowers borne in umbels. Native to Mexico. Chiefly valued as a greenhouse or house plant in the North.

montana 6″ **Zone 4 American Wood-sorrel**
This species also arises from a creeping rootstalk and bears its leaves and flowers on pink-tinted stems. The delicate white flowers also are veined in pink and the petals are notched. It blooms from May to Aug. and may be found from southern Canada to the mountains of N. Car. and Tenn., westward to Wisc. and Minn.

pes-caprae (*O. cernua*) 9″–10″ **Zone 9 Buttercup Oxalis**
With bright yellow flowers blooming in spring, this makes a fine addition to the window-box. The variety 'Flore-pleno' has excellent double flowers. Native to South Africa, but naturalized in southern Fla. and Bermuda.

purpurea (*O. variabilis*) 3″–6″ **Zone 9 Cape Oxalis**
Bulbous perennial, used as a house plant for its white, rose or violet flowers that are as much as 2 in. wide. Native to South Africa.

rubra 3″–6″ **Zone 8 Window Box Oxalis**
A perennial with 3 leaflets; flowers pink varying to lilac or even white, with dark veins, borne in compound umbels and rather conspicuous. Native to Brazil. Used in the North as a house plant or as a fine addition to the window box. Blooms in winter, but it may be grown from seed sown indoors in April and treated as a garden annual.

stricta 1′ **Zone 3 Common Yellow Oxalis**
With small yellow flowers, native to Europe but occurring as a weed throughout North America. Not of sufficient ornamental value to be cultivated.

tetraphylla 3″–6″ **Zone 9 Four-leaf Oxalis**
Bulbous, with 4 leaflets and lilac to rosy flowers, this is native to Mexico.

valdiviensis 6″–9″ **Zone 9 Chilean Oxalis**
An annual in the North, native to Chile, this can be sown from seed in April and expected to bloom the same summer. Flowers golden yellow. In the South it is perennial. It has a bulbous root and the leaves have 3 leaflets.

variabilis = *O. purpurea*

violacea 6″ **Zone 5 Violet Wood-sorrel**
The leaf and flower stalks of this plant arise from a scaly bulb. The violet-colored flowers appear in spring and eary summer and may be found in open, rocky patches of woods from Mass. to Fla., west to the Dakotas and N.Mex. Suitable for the wild garden, it is propagated by dividing the bulbs in spring.

OX-EYE. See BUPHTHALMUM, TALEKIA.

OXYCOCCUS = *Vaccinium*

OXYDENDRUM (ox-i-DEN-drum)
arboreum 75′ **Zone 5 Sorrel-tree, Sour-wood**
This is one of America's superior ornamental trees, especially while it is young and can be kept clothed with branches from top to bottom and also can be grown in a situation where it is exposed to full sunshine all the time. It is native to the eastern and southeastern U.S., has glossy, deciduous and alternate leaves, somewhat the same size and shape of those of the Mountain-

laurel, and these turn a vivid scarlet in the fall when exposed to full sunshine. The flowers are small and white, somewhat like those of the Blueberry but borne in slightly pendulous clusters, blooming in mid-July. The fruits are merely brownish capsules. The late summer flowers, glossy foliage and brilliant scarlet autumn color and neat pyramidal habit give this tree interest every season of the year.

Propagation

Seeds may be sown as soon as ripe or stored dry in airtight containers in a cool place for up to a year and then sown. Softwood cuttings (which see) root readily.

OXYRIA (OXI-ria)
  digyna 1′ **Zone 2 Alpine Mountain-sorrel**
An erect perennial in the northern part of the Northern Hemisphere around the world, this

has basal, palmately veined, orbicular leaves to 1½ in. long and many small, perfect, greenish flowers in terminal racemes. Fruit is a winged achene. Sometimes used in the rockery and propagated by division or seeds. The leaves are occasionally used in salads or as a potherb.

OXYTROPIS (ox-i-TROP-is)
  lambertii 4″–20″ **Zone 3 Lambert Crazy-weed**
A tufted perennial, native to the Great Plains area of the U.S., with a short densely flowered spike with purple pea-shaped flowers in June and July; 7 pairs of leaflets on the odd pinnately compound leaves; fruit a many-seeded pod. Both green and dried plants are poisonous to horses, cattle and sheep and it is often referred to as a "loco" weed that causes the death of animals.

OYSTERPLANT = *Rhoeo spathacea* 'Vittata'

P

PACHISTIMA = *Paxistima*

PACHYCEREUS (pak-i-SEE-reus)
marginatus = *Lemaireocereus marginatus*
pecten-aboriginum 30′ Zone 10 Hairbrush Cactus
A treelike cactus with columns 10–18 in. through and having 10–12 acute ribs, gray spines; flowers during the day are red outside, white inside and 2 or more inches long. The large fruits have been used by the Mexican natives for hair brushes. Native to Mexico.

pringlei 30′ Zone 10
A treelike cactus with main trunk 2 ft. in dia., 11–17 ribs; areoles a felty brown; spines often missing in mature plants; flowers white, bell-shaped and greenish red outside, to 3 in. long. Native to Mexico.

PACHYSANDRA (pak-iss-AND-ra)
procumbens 6″–1′ Zone 4 Alleghany Pachysandra, Alleghany Spurge
An herbaceous perennial, the leaves of which die to the ground in winter in the North but are

Pachysandra terminalis—the Japanese Spurge—is the best evergreen ground cover for shaded situations. (*Photo by Arnold Arboretum, Jamaica Plain, Mass.*)

evergreen in the South. This grows in a rounded clump and is native to the southeastern states. The whitish to purplish flower spikes are up to 5 in. long and appear in a dense mass before the leaves, each one of which is pushed up from the ground on its individual petiole. It requires shade. Easily reproduced by division of this plant clump in early spring before growth starts.

terminalis ground cover Zone 5 Japanese Spurge, Japanese Pachysandra
There is little question but that this is the best evergreen ground cover in the North, at least for shaded situations. A native of Japan, it has long been used in America and is very popular indeed. The dark evergreen leaves are lustrous and the small upright spikes of bloom in early May followed by white berries in the fall. It is interesting to note in this respect that some plantings rarely produce flowers and fruit, probably because all the plants are 1 clone. It has been noted that when several clones are present, and bees not far away, fruiting is almost an annual occurrence. The plant is stoloniferous and spreads rapidly; easily reproduced by division or by rooting cuttings in early summer. The variety **'Variegata'** has leaves variegated with white and is used for some special purposes.

Insect Pests

Euonymus scale often causes severe injury. See EUONYMUS. Leaf rollers and other chewing insects may be present but seldom destructive.

Diseases

Leaf blight canker is identified by brown shrivelled leaves and pink lesions on the stems. Spraying with fungicide #K or #D gives control but thinning of thick plantings is helpful. Rhizoctonia root rot causes wilted and dead plants from infection of the roots. Remove diseased plants and disinfect soil with fungicide #F.

PACHYSTACHYS (pak-ISS-tak-iss)
coccinea 7′ Zone 10 Blackstick Cardinals-guard
Belonging to the Acanthus Family and native to Trinidad and South America, this is closely related to *Jacobina* sp. This shrub is often grown as a greenhouse plant in the North because of the dense terminal heads of scarlet flowers, 2 in. long. Leaves are about 8 in. long and the fruit is a 2-celled capsule. Propagation is by softwood cuttings in the early spring.

PAEONIA (pee-O-nia). Herbaceous peonies. The Peony is a dependable, long-lived, very hardy perennial, admired for its huge, showy blooms and it stands in a class of its own. It has regal splendor, an impelling fragrance, and single or double blossoms that may be rose or

771

light pink, deep red, or purest white.

For centuries, the Peony has been a standard perennial in gardens throughout the cooler regions of the world. It grows with great ease, and is often taken for granted. Where other flowers succumb when neglected, peonies go on year after year, fighting weeds that engulf them. They are often seen in old, abandoned gardens still holding their own.

There is nothing delicate about this striking garden beauty. Able to withstand temperatures well below zero, it is especially cherished where winters are long, cold, hard and snowy. Remarkably free of diseases and pests, it presents a clean habit of growth, and when the blooms fade the neat foliage stays green and lustrous until hard-killing frosts. Perhaps its greatest asset is that is makes an extraordinary cut flower, and because of its size it is frequently used in church arrangements wherever it is grown. In these days of air travel, it is shipped to tropical regions, where it never fails to make a success.

Peonies flourish in a wide variety of soils, provided they are well drained, since they cannot tolerate wet roots. A slightly acid soil is best, but if it is too highly acid, add agricultural lime at the rate of 5 lbs. per 100 sq. ft. several weeks before planting time. This is easily done, since the best time to plant is in the fall. A sandy soil can be improved with peat moss, leaf mold, compost, and other organic material. One that is clayey and lacking in friability can be lightened with sand, peat moss or perlite.

To prepare soil for planting, dig to a depth of 12–18 in. and enrich with humus. If old, well-decayed manure is available use it, for peonies respond well to it, but the dehydrated form can be substituted. Add bone meal or superphosphate, high phosphoric fertilizers, at the rate of 3 lbs. per 100 sq. ft. For individual plants in borders, 2 or 3 handfuls will suffice.

These durable perennials perform best in full sun, although they do remarkably well in partial shade. If possible, select a place protected from high winds for the sake of the heavy blooms. Set plants with the crown, from which the red buds (visible in the fall) arise, an inch or two below the surface of the soil. This is very important, as too deep planting results in failure to flower. This is perhaps the most common complaint about herbaceous peonies, yet healthy plants, given every care, will simply produce foliage no matter now long they remain in the same place.

Peonies do not like to be disturbed and can stay in the same place for many years. Specimen plants, 50 years old and more, are common in old-time gardens of New England. For this reason, select their locations with this in mind.

Once planted, they will not require much care. Feed early each spring with a balanced plant food, as 4-12-4 or 5-10-5, at the rate of 4 lbs. per 100 sq. ft. Individual plants can be given a handful of fertilizer, but it is best to follow directions for use on each fertilizer container. If fall planting, Sept. or Oct., is not possible, set out plants early in the spring.

The large blooms of peonies may require staking, otherwise their heavy heads will become battered by wind and rain and bend over to touch the ground. Then their full beauty is marred. Start to stake early, before buds begin to break. Circular rings secured to stakes are excellent because they permit plants to maintain their natural grace, but individual supports can be inserted in the ground at a safe distance from the fleshy roots. Use soft twine that does not cut. When cutting blooms for arrangements, select buds that have just begun to burst open. Take 2 or 3 leaves with each. Longer stems mean more foliage, and it is needed for plants to continue to manufacture food for the following season's flowering.

Gardeners often complain about the presence of ants. They are not harmful, and do not devour the flower buds as is commonly supposed, but they simply feed on the sweet syrup present on the buds. A strong solution of nicotine sulfate or chlordane will eliminate them.

Diseases

The most troublesome disease is botrytis blight, manifested by shoots that appear to have been burned when just a few inches high in the spring. It is more prevalent in cool wet weather. Ferbam or Bordeaux mixture are effective antidotes, applied in the early spring, when shoots are beginning to appear above the ground. Two or 3 sprayings will be necessary. In the fall practice cleanliness by removing shoots to the ground.

When to Plant

Autumn is the time to lift and divide established plants, if plants are to be propagated. This is also the time to lift the same plants that have failed to flower because of too deep planting. Lift the roots carefully with a spading fork, and then use a hatchet or other sharp tool to cut the large, fleshy roots into smaller pieces. Take care not to make the pieces too small, else they will take a year or two to flower. Allow each section at least 3 eyes to be certain plants will flower the following spring.

Although plants are extremely hardy, mulching is advisable the first winter after planting. When the ground freezes solidly, in Nov. and Dec., apply a thick blanket of marsh hay, straw,

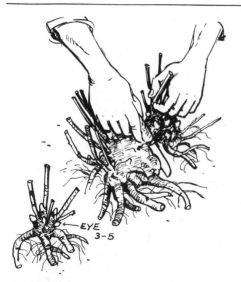

EYE
3-5

Dividing Peony roots

evergreen branches, cranberry vine mulch or other light material that allows air to get through. Oak leaves, which curl and do not mat, as do maple, can be used. The purpose of the mulch is to keep the temperature in the soil even and this helps prevent thawing and heaving due to temperature changes.

Herbaceous Varieties

There are several distinct types of peonies—single, Japanese, anemone and double. The single have 5 or more petals, with showy fertile stamens in the center. The Japanese are similar and are noted for their single row of large petals, although their enlarged stamens have little or no pollen. The anemone-flowered forms resemble the Japanese, except for the enlarged petal-like stamens which bear no pollen at all. Most familiar of all the peonies are the doubles, with so many petals that they resemble enormous roses and smell as sweet.

One way to select varieties is to visit nurseries that specialize in peonies at flowering time, or to visit large private gardens where peonies are grown in quantity. These are often opened on garden tours. The beginner can start with time-tested double varieties that have proven their worth over the years. One cannot go wrong with the old white standby, 'Festiva Maxima', although other good whites are 'Frances Willard' and 'Baroness Schroeder'. 'Sarah Bernhardt', 'Walter Faxon', 'Mons. Jules Elie', 'Minuet', and 'Martha Bulloch' are excellent pinks. In the red category, 'Mary Brand', 'Karl Rosenfield', 'Felix Crousse', 'Kansas', 'Tempest'

and 'Longfellow' are highly recommended.

For the devotee, there are yellow-flowering peonies, species, with pale, lemon-yellow, single flowers that unfold with tulips in May. Known as the Caucasian and Persian peonies, they are interesting collectors' items, even if they do not possess the glamor of the others.

Tree Peonies

Far less common than the herbaceous peonies are the tree peonies. Their name is a bit deceiving, because they are shrublike plants, with woody stems that do not die down to the ground in the fall. Plants grow 4 ft. or more and spread as much, but are not treelike, even when they grow taller in their native Japan and China.

Massive flowers, 6, 8, 10 or more inches across, are breathtakingly beautiful, and they come in vivid and pastel colorings, red and scarlet, pink and rose, salmon and peach, yellow and apricot and white. These appear in profusion in May amidst compound leaves that stay attractive all season, but drop in the fall.

The magical appeal of tree peony blossoms is not due to their size and exquisite coloring but to the delicate crepe-paperlike texture of the petals, which may be ruffled or crinkled at the edges. The centers have a cushion of bright yellow anthers that show up strikingly against the darker colors of the surrounding petals. It is easy to understand why the Japanese and Chinese have held sacred festivals in their honor. In Oriental art, their many patterns have played a major part in the fine tapestries, silks, pottery, and china for which the East is known.

In spite of their royal appearance, tree peonies are among the easiest of hardy garden plants. They are slow-growing, and this has made them expensive. On the other hand, they are as permanent as herbaceous peonies, and once planted will be around for succeeding generations to enjoy.

As with other plants, particularly those that are costly, the first step is to choose the proper location. Soil, sun and moisture needs are simple enough, but the spot must be one where plants will be permitted to flourish for years. The position must also be one of honor, not an obscure corner, but a focal point where the blossoms can be enjoyed from several vantage points. Tree peonies are often set in formal beds, where their stems rise above the surrounding plants. This way, their full beauty can be enjoyed throughout the season, for the foliage has strong appeal. If possible, arrange plants so they can be spotted from the terrace or indoors where they can be seen in foul weather.

Find a place where plants will receive sun several hours a day, preferably in the early morning and late afternoon, especially under high-branching trees that shield plants during the noon hours, because the delicate blossoms fade in the hot, bright sun. Gardeners who have been growing tree peonies for years place opened umbrellas over the blossoms for this reason. During this period, the blooms are also protected from rain, making them last much longer.

A position sheltered from strong winds is recommended—large shrubs and attractive fences, as well as hedges, lessen the brunt of the wind and offer suitable background to show off the dazzling blooms. The foliage of the tree peonies is more finely cut than that of the herbaceous Peony.

When to Plant

The fall is the best time to plant tree peonies. Sept. and Oct. are ideal as they allow ample time for strong root development before the ground freezes hard. Fall-set plants, if large enough, will most likely flower the following spring, certainly by the year thereafter and bloom can be counted on each succeeding year.

Before planting, incorporate humus into the soil, that should have good drainage. If it is an acid soil make certain enough lime has been added to make the soil slightly alkaline. See LIME. Mix a couple of trowelfuls of bone meal or superphosphate at the bottom of the hole, since these non-caustic fertilizers help to promote flower development. Set each plant with the point of graft about 4 in. below the surface of the soil. Fill in with loamy soil, and press to eliminate air. Add more soil, tamp again and add more soil, leaving a depression around each specimen to hold water. Then water deeply and apply peat moss, buckwheat hulls, or some other favored mulch to help conserve moisture and keep the surface of the soil cool in hot weather.

After planting, examine plants carefully and remove, with sharp pruning shears, dead or weakened wood. Do this carefully in order not to cut tips that bear next season's flowers. Thereafter, as plants become 2, 3, 4 and more ft. tall, which they will do slowly, practice a little judicious pruning each year, preferably after flowering. Maintain an attractive shape and aim to keep plants as bushy as possible for, as they become older, they tend to become leggy.

Tree peonies are very hardy and do not require winter protection once established. The first winter after planting, it is advisable to mulch them heavily with a light, airy material, as straw or marsh hay. They will need little care thereafter. As with other shrubs, feed with a balanced food early each spring or in the very late fall, when leaves have dropped and plants have become dormant. Water to keep soil moist and apply a summer mulch each season. They do not require staking, although the large blooms often require individual support.

Tree peonies are divided into 3 distinct groups. The Japanese, considered the most beautiful, have broad, crinkled, satiny petals and narrow foliage, finer than that of the other 2. The Chinese or European, the second group, are known for their large double blooms, resembling those of the herbaceous peonies. The third classification is known as Lutea, and comprises hybrids with yellow flowers, larger than those of the other 2. They unfold 2 or 3 weeks later thus extending the tree peony season considerably. This last group has been found difficult to propagate.

Varieties

Many varieties of tree peonies are available, and choices depend largely on which type and which color are preferred. Outstanding among the Japanese are 'Yoyo-no-homare', an early bloomer, semi-double flesh pink; 'Kamada-fuji', double, wisteria blue; 'Gessekai', large double white, with crinkly petals; 'Uba-tama', large satiny maroon, nearly double; 'Hinode-no-seki', large double, rosy pink; and 'Howzan', double delicate flesh pink.

Desirable European or Chinese varieties include 'Reine Elizabeth', fully double deep rose; 'Bijou de Chusan', pure white, with creamy center and large double outer petals; 'Banksi', double pink, with heavy foliage; 'Fragrans Maxima Plena', fragrant, double salmon pink; 'Souvenir de Ducher', double deep violet, with reddish tinge; 'Godaishu', nearly double white, with clusters of yellow stamens; and 'Tama-fuyo', semi-double light rose pink.

In the Lutea or yellow-flowered group, consider 'Age of Gold', semi or fully double, soft creamy gold; 'Argosy', single, clear sulfur yellow, with red blotches at base; 'Canary', single, bright yellow; and 'Harvest', semi-double, the color of ripened grain.

Propagation of tree peonies is usually by grafting a scion of the tree peony variety onto a 4–6 in. piece of root of *P. lactiflora*. The grafted plant should be planted several inches below the graft union in the soil, in the hope that the scion will eventually send out its own roots, for own-rooted plants are always desirable. Also seeds can be sown as soon as ripe, placed in a greenhouse for 3 months, then in a cool cellar or electric refrigerator for another 3 months, after which they are again brought into the warm greenhouse and can then be expected to germinate. Such seedlings can be expected to bloom within 5 or 6 years.

For further details on either herbaceous or tree peonies see Wister, John O. "The Peonies," American Horticultural Society, 1962. This excellent reference contains descriptions of some of the most popular varieties of all types.

GEORGE TALOUMIS

Insect Pests

Rose chafer eats the petals and prefers white flowers. Handpicking is helpful and spraying the plant just before the blossoms open with insecticide #37 or #9 will kill the beetles which crawl over the plants. Ants are attracted to a sweet substance secreted by the buds and are not known to be harmful.

Diseases

Botrytis blight which infects the new shoots and may rot the flower bud is common on old-established plants. Drenching the crown in spring before growth starts with fungicide #Q, #D, or #G will control it. Gathering plant refuse in the fall, removing mulch early in spring and replanting in another location help to prevent it. Leaf spot and leaf blotch are checked by sanitation as above.

albiflora = *P. lactiflora*

anomala   3′   **Zone 4**   **Ural Peony** Herbaceous with a rhizomatous root, with single bright crimson flowers about 4 in. across; native to northern Europe. Not a startling plant in the border and many gardeners can forget it but the flowers appear in May and last well as cut flowers.

lactiflora   3¼′   **Zone 3**   **Chinese Peony** Most of the so-called herbaceous garden peonies originated with this species which is native to Siberia, China and Japan. In the wild species the flowers are white or pink, but with the thousands of hybrid varieties now available, many excellent deep red varieties are also available, some of them having either single or double blossoms as much as 6 in. across. The American Peony Society recognizes 5 different types of flowers, i.e., the single of Chinese, Japanese, anemone, semi-double and double. For a few of the better varieties see article above.

mlokosewitschii 2¼′ **Zone 5** **Caucasian Peony** With bluish-green foliage; yellow flowers up to 5 in. across. Native to the Caucasus. The plant does best in light shade, but the foliage turns brown by Sept. A fine species for the hybridizers but not a topnotch garden plant.

officinalis   3′   **Zone 3**   **Common Peony** Native to Europe and western Asia, this is an old-fashioned garden plant with dark red flowers varying to white or yellowish, with single or double flowers (in late May) 4 in. across. Many varieties are available. See above article.

suffruticosa   4′–5′   **Zone 4**   **Tree Peony** The Tree Peony is difficult to grow but there are an increasing number of Americans learning how to do it. A native of northwestern China, it has conspicuous, large, solitary flowers, 6–10 in. across, that are white, pink, red, single or double, during late May, depending on the variety. There are said to be over 200 named varieties of the Tree Peony growing in the collections at Swarthmore College, Swarthmore, Pa.

Planting is best done in the middle of Oct., preferably in a rich, well-drained soil. Lime should be applied occasionally, especially where the soil is acid. Old and weak wood should be cut out but that is about all the pruning needed. Plants grow into a densely rounded mass of foliage, with many major stems from the base.

The Tree Peony has been popular in Chinese gardens for over 15 centuries and was taken to Japan, supposedly by Buddhist monks, in about the 17th century, and since then the Japanese have developed many good varieties also. There are some hybrid varieties made by crossing *P. suffruticosa* with *P. lutea* and other species. One of the best of these is 'Souvenir de Maxine Cornu', a very double yellow with red markings looking much like a large Dahlia. The flowers are so large and heavy that they frequently must be staked to prevent them from bending over and being hidden by the foliage.

Among the best double-flowering varieties are: 'Reine Elizabeth', 'Carolina d'Italie', 'Souvenir de Ducher'. Other good varieties are: 'Alice Harding', 'Argosy', 'Banquet', 'Black Pirate', 'Festival', 'Flambeau', 'La Lorraine', 'Roman Gold', 'Silver Sails', and 'Surprise'.

tenuifolia 1½′ **Zone 4** **Fern-leaved Peony** A low Peony with extremely narrow to linear, ternate leaves, the flowers being dark red to purplish, 3–4 in. across, and appear in late May at the same time as those of other *Paeonia* species. Native to southeastern Europe and western Asia, single- and double-flowered forms are available and 'Flore-pleno', a double-flowered form, is considerably more effective as a garden plant than the single-flowered species. It is a good garden plant, not only for its flowers but for its fern-leaved foliage throughout the growing season.

wittmanniana 3′ **Zone 5** **Irangold Peony** With yellow to whitish flowers 4 in. across; native to the Caucasus. Usually the blossoms are single; the foliage is glaucous but tends to brown too early in the fall.

PAGODA TREE, JAPANESE = *Sophora japonica*

PAINT, TREE WOUND. See TREE WOUND PAINT

PAINTBRUSH, SCARLET = *Crassula falcata*, also *Hieracium aurantiacum*

PAINTED-LADY = *Echeveria derenbergii*

PAINTED-TONGUE = *Salpiglossis sinuata*

PALIURUS (pal-i-YEW-rus)

spina-christi   18′   Zone 7   Christ Thorn
Not especially ornamental, this spiny native of
southern Europe and western Asia is probably
grown merely because, according to legend, it
is supposed to be the plant from which Christ's
Crown of Thorns was made. When it is grown
at all, it is usually as a hedge and it does best in
the full sun. The leaves are alternate, simple,
ovate, about 1½ in. long, finely toothed; the
flowers are greenish yellow and fruit brownish
yellow about an inch wide. The thorns are
sturdy and either straight or slightly hooked.

PALMS. These are monocotyledonous trees and
shrubs typical of tropical climates. Some, like
the Serenoa species of Fla., reach only a few
feet in height and are actually treated as shrubs;
others, like the Giant Wax Palms of the Andes
Mountains of South America, can reach 200 ft.
in height. From the landscape point of view
they can be divided into 2 groups, the Feather
Palms, with large pinnately compound leaves
often many feet long with the small leaflets or
segments arranged feather fashion on each side
of the main rachis. Then there are the Fan Palms
with large palmately lobed leaves 3 ft. and more
wide. Both types have their uses in the landscape.

There are palms with perfectly straight trunks
like the dates, palms with curving trunks like
the Coconut, and even climbing palms like the
rattans of India. The Coconut Palm is one of
several providing food, drink, shelter and
clothing for those who live in the Tropics where
it grows. Others supply wax, medicine, raffia,
oil, fat, thread, fibers, etc. They are related to
the grasses and bamboos, do not have a
cambium or living layer of cells just beneath the
bark like all the woody plants of the Temperate
Zone, hence they do not provide rings of annual
growth when a cross-section of the trunk is
inspected. In fact, their trunks are soft inside.
Some of the fan palms have leaves that may be
20 ft. across and some of the feather palms may
have leaves 60 ft. long and 6 ft. wide. The flower
clusters of some may be 20 ft. long and some
die as soon as their first flowers are borne.

The Double Coconut (*Lodoicea maldivicia*)
may bear fruits weighing as much as 50 lbs.
which may take 10 years to mature.

Hardiness varies greatly. Mostly they are
tropical trees and shrubs, but there are some
which can withstand temperatures down to 20°
F. and, of course, it is these that are used in
Calif. and the warmer parts of the southern
states for landscape work. In the North, many
are used as tubbed plants in the greenhouse and
are moved about indoors for decoration.

They require good soil, plenty of fertilizer and
moisture and, if given these prerequisites, they
respond better than most of our woody plants.
Out-of-doors they are best moved in spring or
early summer while they are in active growth.
The new roots are produced at the base of the
trunk, the reason why they should be moved
with as large a ball of soil as possible. They are
propagated by seeds or some by the suckers
that appear at the base of the trunk.

Insect Pests

Nearly all scale insects and mealybugs which
attack the Orange also live on various palms.
See ORANGE. Potted palms grown in greenhouses
for special decorations usually need treatment
to control scale insects. Florists often wipe them
off the leaves rather than spray. Large borers
are special problems in certain localities and
should be eliminated.

Some of the more hardy fan palms:
Chamaerops humilis—Mediterranean Fan Palm
Brahea brandegeei—San Jose Palm
B. edulis—Guadalupe Palm
Livistonia australis—Australian Fountain Palm
L. chinensis—Chinese Fountain Palm
Raphidophyllum hystrix—Needle Palm
Rhapis species—Lady Palms
Sabal species—Palmettoes
Trachycarpus fortunei—Windmill Palm
Washingtonia filifera—California Fan Palm
W. robusta—Mexican Fan Palm

Some of the more hardy feather palms:
Arecastrum romanzoffianum—Queen Palm
Butia capitata—Butia Palm
Chamaedorea species
Jubaea spectabilis—Chilean Wine Palm
Phoenix canariensis—Canary Island Date Palm
P. dactylifera—Date Palm
P. reclinata—Senegal Date Palm
P. roebeleni—Pigmy Date Palm
P. rupicola—Cliff Date Palm

A few of the less hardy palms:
Archontophoenix cunninghamiana—Seaforthia
  Palm
Howea forsteriana—Thatch Palm, Kentia Palm
H. belmoreana—Sentry Palm
Jubaeopsis caffra—Pondoland Palm
Rhophalostylis species

A very few truly tropical palms:
Areca catechu—Betelnut Palm
Caryota urens—Fishtail or Wine Palm
C. mitis—Tufted Fishtail Palm

Chrysalidocarpus lutescens—Yellow Butterfly Palm
Cocos nucifera—Coconut
Roystonea regia—Royal Palm

A few other palmlike plants:
Aloe species
Cordyline species
Cycas revoluta—Sago Cycas (Sago Palm)
Musa species—bananas
Pandanus utilis—Screw-pine
Ravenala madagascariensis—Traveler's Tree

The following list includes some of the most commonly cultivated palms in Continental United States:

Bamboo P.—Chrysalidocarpus lutescens
Buccaneer P.—Pseudophoenix sargentii
Butia P.—Butia capitata
California Fan P.—Washingtonia filifera
Canary Island Date P.—Phoenix canariensis
Chilean Wine P.—Jubaea spectabilis
Cliff Date P.—Phoenix rupicola
Date P.—Phoenix dactylifera
False P.—Ficus pseudopalma
Fiji Island Fan P.—Pritchardia pacifica
Forster Sentry P.—Howea forsteriana
Fortunes Windmill P.—Trachycarpus fortunei
Guadalupe P.—Brahea edulis
Hog Cabbage P.—Pseudophoenix sargentii
Household P.—Collinia elegans
Kentia P.—Howea forsteriana
Lady P.—Rhapis humilis
Mediterranean P.—Chamaerops humilis
Mexican Washington P.—Washingtonia robusta
Needle P.—Raphidophyllum hystrix·
Pigmy Date P.—Phoenix roebeleni
Pondoland P.—Jubaeopsis caffra
Queens P.—Arecastrum romanzoffianum
Royal P.—Roystonea regia
San Jose P.—Brahea brandegeei
Saw Cabbage P.—Acoelorrhaphe wrightii
Seaforthia P.—Archontophoenix cunninghamiana
Senegal Date P.—Phoenix reclinata
Sentry P.—Howea belmoreana
Solitaire P.—Ptychosperma elegans
Sugar P.—Arenga pinnata
Tufted Fishtail P.—Caryota mitis
Windmill P.—Trachycarpus fortunei
Yellow Butterfly P.—Chrysalidocarpus lutescens

For further reading on the subject of palms, see the special issue of the American Horticultural Magazine 40: 1-189, for Jan. 1961.

PALM, WEDDELL = *Syagrus wedelliana*

PALMETTO = *Saba palmetto*

PALMETTO, SAW = *Serenoa repens*

PALM FAMILY = Palmaceae

PALM, TODDY FISHTAIL = *Caryota urens*

PALMATE (leaf). Radiately lobed or divided with 3 or more veins arising from 1 point.

PANAMIGO = *Pilea involucrata*

PANAX (PAY-nax)

quinquefolius 1½′ **Zone 3 American Ginseng**
An herb with palmately compound, whorled leaves, each leaf with 5 leaflets about 5 in. long. Native from Quebec to Mo. in moist woodlands. Flowers appear in June, followed by red fruits about ½ in. across. The roots have been used by people in the Orient for centuries in medicines, but it is not an important herb in America, except for exporting. Propagated by seed; after taking a full year to germinate, the seedlings are grown in shade, usually rather dense; also propagated by cuttings made in the summer and by root cuttings made in the spring. Roots are dug in the fall and dried.

trifolius 6″ **Zone 3 Dwarf Ginseng**
This Ginseng arises from a round tuber which has no medicinal value. The short-stalked, palmately compound leaves generally have only 3 leaflets and the fruit is yellow. It grows over much the same area as *P. quinquefolium*. Propagation is by seed only.

Diseases

When cultivated in shade houses, verticillium wilt which infects many plants may be destructive. Soil sterilization is the only remedy. See CHRYSANTHEMUM. A spray program using fungicides #D or #F may be necessary to keep various blights and leafspots in check.

PANCRATIUM (pan-KRAY-tium). Summer-flowering bulbs from Europe or the Canary Islands, members of the Amaryllis Family and closely related to *Hymenocallis* with which they are frequently confused. Flowers are white, fragrant and borne several on a stalk. Culture is the same as for Amaryllis. Propagated by offsets and seeds.

canariense 2′ **Zone 8 Canaries Pancratium**
Flowers white, 2½ in. long, 6-10 on a stalk. Native to the Canary Islands.

maritimum 2′ **Zone 8 Sea-daffodil Pancratium**
Flowers white, very fragrant, 5-10 in each umbel, having a large cup almost like that of a daffodil, 2-3 in. long; leaves linear, straplike and evergreen. Mostly for greenhouse forcing; this is the more popular species. Native from Spain to Syria.

PANDANACEAE = The Screw-pine Family

PANDANUS (pan-DAY-nus). Tropical trees and shrubs with sword-shaped leaves arranged spirally; a few make excellent house plants, but only while they are young. As they grow older and taller they should be discarded before they become unsightly. The leaves are usually prickly margined, the flowers in spikes. Easily propagated by rooting the suckers which appear at the base of the plant, preferably in a heated hotbed.

baptistii 3′ **Zone 10**
Sword-shaped leaves only an inch wide with several longitudinal yellow stripes arranged in the center of the blue-green leaf. They are channeled, spirally arranged and gracefully arching. Native to New Britain Islands.

pygmaeus 2′ **Zone 10** **Dwarf Screw-pine**
A low-spreading shrub from Madagascar, sending out numerous horizontal branches from the base which grow stiltlike roots. The rich, glossy green leaves, ⅓ of an inch wide, are borne spirally around the stem. Used as a potted greenhouse plant. Propagated by suckers.

sanderi 'Rohrsianus' 4′ **Zone 10**
From the Solomon Islands, this is valued for its long, leathery, swordlike leaves, borne in a rosette at the base of the plant and transversed lengthwise with stripes and bands of light and golden yellow, the margins being finely spiny. Often used as a greenhouse specimen.

utilis 60′ **Zone 10** **Common Screw-pine**
This has a spirally arranged rosette of straplike, thick, leathery leaves, 3 in. wide, deep olive green with red spines along the margin. The leaves are used for making hats and baskets. Native to Madagascar.

veitchii 6′ **Zone 10** **Veitch Screw-pine**
A shapely and attractive house plant, probably the most popular species for this purpose, with gracefully arching, thin, leathery leaves 3 in. wide; narrowing to a long point; bordered with creamy white, the edges and keel beneath having small spines. As it grows older it develops stilt-like, thick, aerial roots. Native to Polynesia.

PANDAPLANT = *Kalanchoe tomentosa*

PANDOREA (pan-DOR-ea). Subtropical, twining, evergreen vines belonging to the Bignonia Family, valued for their foliage and funnel-form flowers from late summer through the fall. Not spectacular and requiring considerable attention to keep in good growing conditions. Propagated by seeds or softwood cuttings.

jasminoides vine Zone 9 Jasmine Pandorea
An evergreen twining vine native to Australia, with white to pinkish tubular flowers about 2 in. long, from July to Oct., borne in few-flowered panicles. The fruit is not effective ornamentally. Native to Australia. A rapid grower but lack of care will result in sparse foliage.

pandorana vine Zone 10 Wonga-wonga Vine
This grows better than *P. jasminoides* but the flowers are very small, about ¾ in. long, and yellowish with a spot of violet in the throat.

Although they are borne in many-flowered clusters, they are usually hidden by the vigorous foliage. Native to Malaysia.

PANICLE. A compound, usually loose, flower-cluster, longer than broad, as a branched raceme or corymb.

PANICUM (PAN-ik-um)

capillare 2′ **annual** **Common Witch Grass**
A slender spreading grass, native to eastern North America, with leaves 1 ft. long and ½ in. wide; fruiting panicles up to 14 in. long and leaf sheaths that are hairy. See WEEDS, WEED-CONTROLLING CHEMICALS.

miliaceum 4′ **annual** **Millet**
Sometimes termed Broom Corn Millet, this is a grass member of the Grass Family, with leaves a foot long and an inch wide, with drooping flowering and fruiting panicles a foot long and seed that is nearly white. It is grown in agriculture, sometimes as a cover crop, and is native to the East Indies.

PANNOSE. Covered with a felt of woolly hair.

PANSY = *Viola × wittrockiana*

PAPAVER (pap-AY-ver). Poppies, belonging to the Poppy Family, are very popular garden plants containing both annual and perennial species. They vary in height, but usually have hairy basal leaves, vividly colored, singly produced flowers with 5 petals to each flower (with some double) and the fruit is a 4–20-celled dry capsule containing hundreds of minute seeds. All poppies show a milky juice when the stem is cut. Some make excellent cut flowers. The annual sorts are propagated by seed, the perennial by division, by seed and by root cuttings.

Insect Pests

Aphids frequently infest the leaves in large numbers and stunt the growth. Oriental Poppy is less susceptible. Spraying with insecticide #15 is effective.

Diseases

Bacterial blight causes water-soaked or black areas surrounded by a translucent ring on all parts of plant above ground. Destroying infected plants is advised but applications of fungicide #B to plants and soil have been helpful experimentally.

alpinum 10″ **Zone 5** **Alpine Poppy**
A dainty perennial Poppy from the European Alps, having clumps of smooth pinnate leaves and fragrant, delicately-textured, white, yellow or pink flowers borne freely throughout the summer. It self-sows easily in most situations.

californicum 2′ **annual** **Mission Poppy**
The leaves are feathery, 2–3 in. long. The red

flowers, with petals blackish at the base, are 2 in. wide and bloom in the summer. Native to Calif.

commutatum   20″   annual
A spreading poppy, with leaves about 6″ long; the flower buds are nodding but the opening flowers are erect, a bright red color with a dark blotch at base. Native to Asia Minor.

fugax (*caucasicum*)   **2′   annual or biennial Caucasian Poppy**
With bipinnate leaves and scarlet flowers that are yellowish at the base. Leaves are bluish gray. Native to the Caucasus. Sow seeds outdoors in autumn or very early in spring in the place where they are to grow. The plants require full sun.

glaucum   2′   annual   Tulip Poppy
The stem leaves are opposite, deeply lobed and bluish green. Flowers are tuliplike, scarlet, spotted at the base and up to 4 in. wide. Native to Syria and Persia. Seeds can be sown outdoors in autumn or very early spring where the plants are to grow.

lateritium   2′   Zone 7 (?)   Armenia Poppy
With brick-red flowers. Native to Armenia. Not much planted in America.

macrostomum   1½′   annual   Bell Poppy
This Poppy has basal leaves as well as stem leaves, and purplish-red flowers 2 in. wide, black spotted at the base, and sometimes the petals have white margins. Native to the eastern Mediterranean Region. Sow seeds outdoors in autumn or very early spring where the plants are to grow in the full sun.

nudicaule   1′–2′   Zone 2   Iceland Poppy
Although a perennial, this very popular Poppy can flower the first year from seed sown the previous autumn. The brightly colored flowers are 3 in. wide, yellow, greenish, orange, pink and red. There are some varieties available with double flowers. **'Yellow Wonder'** and **'Coonara Pink'** are only 2 of several named color varieties. The flowers are all fragrant, the leaves are pinnately lobed and the plant itself is practically stemless. Native to North America from the Arctic to Colo.

orientale   2′–4′   Zones 2–3   Oriental Poppy
This perennial is the most conspicuous of all the poppies and a most popular garden plant in the U.S. It should be in every perennial garden and there are over 100 varieties from which to choose, ranging in color from white through various shades of pink to darkest red, some of the flowers being as much as 6 in. wide. It is native to the Mediterranean Region and Persia.

These poppies bloom in late May and June, but the foliage finally dies down to the ground and disappears by late summer, leaving large bare spaces in the garden. They should be planted in good, well-drained soil, set about 3 in. deep and mulched during the first winter at least. They may have to be divided after 5 years or so, preferably in the late summer.

These, especially the colorful varieties, are best propagated by root cuttings made in the late summer, cut in lengths about 4 in. long. Also, division of the clumps in late summer is the easiest method for most gardeners.

A few of the more popular varieties: **'Barr's White'**, **'Perry's White'**; **'Olympia'** and **'Scarlet Glow'** are both doubles of fiery red-orange color; **'Allegro'**, **'Brilliant'** are scarlet red; **'Princess Louise'**—salmon; **'Beauty of Livermore'**— red with black spots; **'Spotless'**—pink.

pilosum   3′   Zone 7 (?)   Olympic Poppy
A hairy perennial poppy with irregularly toothed leaves and brick-red flowers, 2 in. wide. Native to Greece and but little grown in America.

rhoeas 3′ annual Corn Poppy, Shirley Poppy
This is the common red field Poppy of Europe with deep red flowers, sometimes purple or white, 2 in. wide. There are many "improved" varieties available, with single and double flowers. The Begonia-flowered and Ranunculus-flowered strains have gorgeous flowers, some of which can be used as cut flowers, but the trick is always to burn the tip of the stem with a lighted match as soon as they are cut, to aid in their keeping qualities.

rupifragum   1½′   Zone 7   Spanish Poppy
A large plant with flat clusters of hairy leaves and large orange or crimson flowers, 3 in. wide in midsummer. Native to Spain.

somniferum   3′–4′   annual   Opium Poppy
The flowers are 4–5 in. wide, white, pink, red or purple, and the fruit is an 8–12-lobed disc.

Papaya

Native to Greece and the Orient, the milky juice obtained from the unripe fruits is opium. There is a white variety **album** and several double-flowered forms, one group called "carnation" flowered, and the other termed "peony" flowered.

PAPAW = *Asimina triloba*

PAPAYA = *Carica papaya*

PAPER-MULBERRY, COMMON = *Broussonetia papyrifera*

PAPYRUS = *Cyperus papyrus*

Papyrus growing out-of-doors in Pasadena, California. (*Photo by Arnold Arboretum, Jamaica Plain, Mass.*)

PARADISEA (pa-rad-IZ-ea)
  liliastrum (*Anthericum liliastrum*) **2′ Zone 2–3 St.-Bruno-lily**
A perennial herb with fleshy rhizomes and linear basal leaves. The fragrant white flowers are funnel shaped up to 2 in. long (this is a member of the Lily Family) and they are borne in loose racemes of 2–10 flowers during May and June. Native to the Pyrenees and Alps. Easily grown and propagated by seeds and division.

PARASITE. An organism which grows on and derives nourishment from another plant called the host.

PARASOL-TREE, CHINESE = *Firmiana simplex*

PARIS GREEN. An insecticide, which see.

PARKINSONIA (park-in-SO-nia)
  aculeata 30′ Zone 9 Jerusalem-thorn
A tree of tropical America and of little use as a shade tree, because of its open habit and peculiar foliage. The leaves are thin, wiry and of fine texture, often 1 ft. long. It can be clipped in hedge form and the numerous inch-long thorns aid in hedge making. The yellow, fragrant flowers appear in loose axillary racemes in the early spring.

PARMELIA (par-MEEL-ia)
  conspersa Lichen
Many lichens can be used for dyeing, among them this flattish gray lichen that is common on rocks in New England and elsewhere. They are most easily cut from the rocks after rain when they are soft. Wash them and dry them for use. Those gathered in Aug. give the strongest tan colors.

PARNASSIA (par-NASS-ia)
  caroliniana = *P. glauca*
  glauca (*P. caroliniana*) **6″–12″ Zone 3 Grass-of-Parnassus**
An attractive plant having a basal rosette of oval leaves, 1–2 in. long, and long-stalked white flowers 1½ in. wide, the 5 petals being veined in green. It blooms in late summer in calcareous swamps and meadows from Canada to S.Dak. and Va. It is a plant needing much sun and, when propagated for the wild garden, seed should be sown in late winter so as to be stratified, and seedlings or divisions should be mulched over the first winter.

PAROCHETUS (pa-ROK-et-us)
  communis trailing Zone 10 Common Shamrock-pea
A trailing plant from the Old World Tropics, belonging to the Pea Family; alternate compound leaves with 3 leaflets; flowers cobalt-blue and pink and borne either singly or 2–3 together in the leaf axils; fruits an inch-long pod. Used in rock gardens and hanging baskets. Propagated by seeds.

PARONYCHIA (pa-ro-NIK-ia). Small plants from the Mediterranean Region and the southern U.S. They grow in tufts and are noted only for the silvery appearance of the very tiny leaves.
  argentea prostrate Zone 6 (?) Silver Nailwort
A small plant of prostrate habit and tiny painted leaves fringed with hairs. The flowers are without petals but have silvery bracts and are attractive. Native to the Mediterranean Region.
  argyrocoma 8″ Zone 4 Allegheny Nailwort
Similar to *P. argentea*, but somewhat larger, the decumbent stems reaching a height of 8 in. Native from Me. to Ga.

PARROT-BEAK, RED = *Clianthus puniceus*

PARROTFEATHER. See MYRIOPHYLLUM.

PARROTIA (pa-ROT-ia)
  persica 50′ Zone 5 Persian Parrotia
A widely spreading, rounded tree with several trunks from the base, this is a relative of the witch-hazels and is native to Persia. The most distinctive feature of the plant is its mottled gray and white bark, which is of course interest-

ing the entire year. The autumn color is a brilliant orange to yellow to scarlet. The alternate leaves are 3–4 in. long and similar in size and shape to those of the witch-hazels. The flowers and fruits are not conspicuous; the branching is definitely horizontal and there are no serious insect or disease pests to mar the foliage. It is difficult to transplant but a very good ornamental tree for planting in gardens where hardy.

Propagation

Seeds should be stratified 5 months at warm temperatures then 3 months at 40° F., then sown. Grafting is practiced using *Hamamelis virginiana* as understock. Softwood cuttings also can be rooted. See STRATIFICATION, GRAFTING, CUTTINGS.

PARSLEY (*Petroselinum crispum*) is a popular garden herb used for flavoring, garnishing and in salads. It is very high in iron and vitamin content.

The plant is a biennial, of the Carrot or Parsley Family, and is a much-branched herb, 10–15 in. high, with very curled and crinkled leaves or plain flat leaflets similar to miniature Celery.

Varieties

The better varieties are **'Dwarf Extra Curled'** and **'Dark Green Plain Leaf'**. **'Parsnip Rooted'** or **Hamburg** Parsley is a form grown in Europe for its parsniplike, much thickened root.

Culture

Common Parlsey is best raised from seed which, however, is of slow and uncertain germination. For family use only a relatively few plants are necessary. These can be grown out-of-doors or planted in pots and kept on the kitchen window sill where they will yield a crop of leaves throughout the winter months. These plants can be started quite easily from roots of plants purchased from stores or dealers. Simply cut back the leaves and plant the roots in good potting soil. For detailed culture and use see HERBS.

Insect Pests

Insect pests are the same as for Celery and carrots. See both for method of control.

GRANT B. SNYDER

PARSNIP (*Pastinaca sativa*). This plant is a native of Europe and Asia and was introduced to America by the early colonists as early as 1609. It is a biennial of the Umbelliferae Family, but is grown as an annual. The second

year the seedstalk develops from the enlarged root produced during the preceding season.

Culture

A deep rich, but not too heavy soil is preferred. Shallow, heavy soils or those that are stony tend to produce crooked and branched roots. The method of soil preparation is the same as for beets. See BEETS. The best varieties are **'Hollow Crown'**, **'Model'** and **'All American'**.

Seed should be sown as early in the spring as the soil can be properly prepared, because a full season is required, 110–120 days, to produce a matured crop. It is primarily a fall and winter vegetable. Rows are spaced 15–18 in. apart and the plants thinned to a stand of 2–3 in. The seed germinates slowly and poorly so that plenty of seed should be sown. It is also a good plan to plant some radish seed in the same drill; they will mark the row long before the parsnip seedlings show. This permits several cultivations before the parsnip seed germinates. Parsnip seedlings are delicate and cannot compete with weeds so that continuous shallow cultivation is important. See WEED-CONTROLLING CHEMICALS.

More than almost any other vegetables, parsnips are improved by cold or even freezing. The roots are usually left in the ground until late fall or even throughout the winter. If left over winter they should be covered with a mulch to prevent alternate freezing and thawing and deterioration of the root. The general practice is to dig the roots in the fall and store them in pits or storage cellars in the same manner as for other root crops such as carrots and beets.

Insects and Diseases

Insects and diseases are the same as for carrots. See CARROTS.

GRANT B. SNYDER

PARSNIP FAMILY = Umbelliferae

PARTED, PARTITE. Cleft nearly but not quite to the base.

PARTHENIUM (par-THEE-nium)
   integrifolium 4′ Zone 5 American Feverfew A member of the Composite Family, growing in open fields and plains from N.Y. to Ga. and Tex. The alternate leaves are elliptic or ovate and toothed, and may be up to 12 in. long. The small flower heads, borne in a flat-topped cluster, have yellow disc flowers sparsely margined with toothed white ray flowers. It blooms throughout the season but has no particular merit as a garden plant.

PARTHENOCISSUS   (par-thee-no-SISS-us). Climbing vines, mostly deciduous, with alternate leaves either 3- or 5-foliate and which turn a brilliant scarlet in the fall. These climb by attaching their rootlike holdfasts to any available means of support. At least 2 of the species (*P. quinquifolia* and *P. tricuspidata*) are widely used in landscape plantings. If propagated by seed, the seed should be stratified at 40° F. for 3 months, then sown. Layers are frequently found around older plants, or suckers can also be used. Cuttings root readily.

Insect Pests

The conspicuous striped caterpillars of the 8-spotted forester moth may strip the leaves in a short time, especially in late summer when the second generation is active. Spraying with insecticide #9 is effective. Do not use insecticide #37 on Boston-ivy because of probable injury. Woodbine and Boston-ivy are favorite hosts of Japanese beetle. Soft brown scale (see FERN) also thrives on Boston-ivy. When vines are growing on painted walls or trellises, avoid sprays which cause excessive discoloration.

Diseases

Leaf spots may develop in damp, shady areas. Use fungicide #D where necessary and complete coverage can be made. Both downy mildew and powdery mildew (see special notes) attack Boston-ivy.

henryana vine Zone 8 Silver Vein Creeper The striking variegated foliage of this Chinese vine shows off to best advantage when it is grown in the shade and more of the color is developed. The under surface of the leaves is purplish, but the upper surface is variegated with a white stripe along the mid-vines, especially when the leaves are young. The alternate, compound leaves have leaflets 1½–3 in. long. The flowers are of no ornamental significance, but the blue berries in the fall are attractive to the birds.

quinquefolia vine Zone 3 Virginia Creeper Widely distributed in the woodlands of the eastern U.S., this vine climbs by attaching its tendrils to some means of support. The compound leaves are composed of 5 leaflets, each 2–5 in. long, and these turn a brilliant scarlet early in the fall. It is one of the best of woody plants for this fall color. Fruits are small blue berries attractive to the birds.

The variety **engelmannii** has smaller leaflets than the species and **saint-paulii** also has smaller leaflets, but better clinging qualities than either of the others. All are excellent for draping over stone walls or for climbing up trellises and they can cover considerable space in a short time. One of the best and most universally useful of our native vines.

tricuspidata clinging vine 60′ Zone 4 Boston-Ivy

The so-called "Boston" Ivy is not native to North America at all, but to Japan and central China, and is one of the best vines for clinging to stone-work, especially in urban areas. The leaves are 3 lobed and a lustrous green which changes to a brilliant scarlet in the fall. The vine holds itself tenaciously to the stone wall surface and can grow to the top of a 3-storey building within a very few years. Fruits are blue, mostly hidden by the foliage, but when ripe are very much sought by the birds.

The clone **'Lowii'** has the smallest leaves, ¾–1½ in. wide and often wider than long, apple green but frequently purplish when young, and **'Veitchii'** has still smaller leaves, purple when young. These small-leaved clones are excellent for more refined displays, but are not so vigorous in growth as the species.

PARTHOGENESIS. Producing seed without fertilization.

PARTRIDGE-BERRY = *Mitchella repens*

PARTRIDGE-PEA = *Cassia fasciculata*

PASPALUM (PAS-pa-lum)
dilatatum 6′ Zone 8 Dallisgrass A perennial grass only occasionally grown as an ornamental in the South; the spikelets are borne in 1-sided racemes 5 in. long, and the panicles 3–8 in. long. Native to Argentina, naturalized in the South.
notatum = Bahia Grass, See GRASS, LAWNS.

PASQUEFLOWER. See ANEMONE.

PASSIFLORA (pass-i-FLO-ra). Tropical or subtropical vines, climbing by the use of tendrils, with alternate, entire or lobed leaves; often with conspicuously outstanding flowers and the fruit a many-seeded berry, some edible. Propagated by seeds or cuttings.
x alato-caerulea vine Zone 10 Profusely blooming hybrid vine, this bears large and showy fragrant flowers 4 in. in dia., the sepals white, petals pink and a fringed crown of purple, white and blue; leaves with 3 lobes.
caerulea vine Zones 7–8 Passion-flower A popular vine for warm gardens, the vine comes from Brazil and climbs by means of tendrils. In the North it is frequently seen as a greenhouse plant and in the South of course it is planted out-of-doors. The blue to pure white flowers are 4 in. across. The leaves are 5-lobed and almost immune to pests. The Spaniards, who were supposed to be the first ones to find this plant in Brazil, thought the flowers were related to the Crucifixion in some way. If a drop or two of paraffin is placed on the very center of the flower, it will not quickly close when cut and brought indoors.
edulis vine Zone 10 Purple Granadilla Flowers 2 in. wide, white with white and

purple crown. The edible fruit is purple and 3 in.
long. Leaves 3-lobed, 4–6 in. long with wavy
edges. Native to Brazil.

**incarnata   vine   Zone 7   Maypop Passion-
flower**
A vine, climbing by tendrils, having alternate,
compound leaves comprised of 3-toothed
leaflets. The flowers are 1½–2 in. wide, with 5
white petals which are joined at the base, from
which rises a crown of purple filaments. The
stamens are united to the style, forming a
central column. The yellow, egg-shaped fruits
are edible. The plant is frequently found in
fields and along roadsides from Va. to Fla. and
Tex. and blooms in summer.

**mollissima   vine   Zone 6 (?)   Softleaf Passion-
flower**
This has leaves with 3 deep lobes, very pubescent
beneath; rose-colored flowers, 3 in. wide, with
the calyx tube 5 in. long and inedible yellow
fruits. Native to the Andes Mountains.

**quadrangularis   vine   Zone 10   Giant
Granadilla**
The stems of this climbing vine are winged;
leaves are entire; flowers are white, fragrant, 3
in. wide, with a purple and white crown. The
fruit is greenish yellow, up to 10 in. long, and
edible. Native to tropical America. Often
grown in the American Tropics for its edible
fruits.

**trifasciata   vine   Zone 10   Threeband
Passion-flower**
With 3-lobed leaves that have purple markings
along the midribs. Flowers small, yellowish,
fragrant. Native to Brazil. Not outstanding as
an ornamental in flower like some of the other
species, but about the best for its foliage color.

vitifolia   vine   Zone 10   Red Passion-flower
A tropical vine, attaching itself to a means of
support by tendrils, it is a straggling one at best.
The flowers are a rich deep crimson, generally
similar to the complex flowers of other species
in this genus. They are produced in clusters of 2
or 3 at a time along the length of the stem.

PASSION-FLOWER. See PASSIFOLORA.

PASTINACA (pas-tin-A-ca)
sativa   3′–5′   biennial   Parsnip
A biennial, a form of which (*sylvestris*) has
become naturalized in North America but is
native to Europe and often a persistent garden
weed. The stem is grooved and hollow; the
leaves are alternate, pinnately compound with
the leaflets lobed. There is a large fleshy tap
root up to 20 in. long, which is sometimes
eaten. The species is the garden Parsnip. The
yellow flowers are small but are borne in large
flat umbels during June and July. See PARSNIP.

PATHOLOGY. The study of the diseases of
plants or animals.

PATHS AND WALKS. The width of paths or
walks in the garden naturally depends upon the
use to which they will be put. Stepping-stone
paths are one width but concrete walks are
usually at least 4 ft. wide. They are made of
concrete, brick, concrete faced with stone or

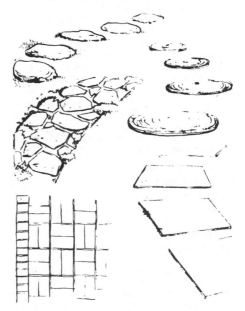

Paths

brick, black-top, crushed stone, large flag
stones with small plants growing between the
joints, horizontal section of tree trunks, pine
needles, etc. The surface of the walk should be
flush with the lawn.

If a concrete or black-top (asphalt) walk is to
be made, the base of cinders and gravel need
be only 4 in. and the concrete or asphalt 4 in.
deep on top of that. The concrete should be the
1–2–3½ mix (1 part cement, 2 parts sharp sand
and 3½ parts crushed stone or gravel, ½–¾ in.
dia.) Expansion joints should be placed every
50 ft., and creases should be made 4–5 ft. apart
with a joining tool.

Stepping stones are always popular, but they
should be placed on a firm cinder or gravel base
where possible.

Pine needles or shingle tow, ground bark or
tanbark all make good garden paths. Here too
the 4-in. cinder or gravel base is good as a start.
The path might be edged with cuprinol-treated
boards (cuprinol is merely a wood preservative)
or aluminum stripping set so it reaches just the
height of the finished walk. This tends to keep
the walk material in place. About 2 in. of pine

needles or shingle tow is enough. Either one lasts surprisingly long and is a fine material especially for a walk in an informal or naturalistic garden or woods path.

Brick paths also are excellent. Hard bricks should be chosen, for the soft type do not make good garden walks and the dark red ones are the best color. To lay a good brick path it is necessary to excavate to 8–9 in., tamp and level the bottom well, then place a 5–6-in. layer of tamped cinders, stone or sand. The edges should be straight. After the bricks are laid, (there are several patterns one can follow in doing this) the joints between the bricks can be filled with finely sifted soil or sand. One or 2 applications of weed killer will suffice in keeping the weeds down. Or, the bricks may be set in concrete and the spaces in between the bricks filled in with cement. Also see GARDEN FIXTURES.

PATIENCE-DOCK = *Rumex patientia*

PATIENCE-PLANT = *Impatiens sultani*

PATIO. The interest in growing plants for many a home owner is continually enlivened if there is a patio, be it ever so small. Usually this is bordered on 2 sides by the house and an L extension, on the third side by a built wall or fence on which is grown a tight mass of vines and the fourth side is left open. However, to be properly enjoyed this open side should face either south or east, not west, for in this case the late summer afternoon sun would make it unbearable at the time of year (summer) when it should be enjoyed the most.

One should carefully select the plants for using about the patio, thinking of the year-round effect of dwarf evergreens, red fruiting plants like Firethorn, some good foliage plants like Leucothoe and Lavender. Also here is an ideal spot for a few dwarf plants, and espaliers would get all the attention they needed to keep them in fine display condition.

A wall fountain or very small waterfall and pool should be given consideration, for there is beauty and interest in the sound and movement of water as well as in a quiet pool. Birds are attracted to such places and of course are of great interest the entire year.

It is not necessary to have the pool right in the middle of the patio—that area might well be left open—but a small pool on the side or at a corner or end of the patio, well planted and in conjunction with a small fountain, could be of considerable interest much of the time.

Shade is a valued item in any patio. If it is not produced by a large tree from nearby, a small tree with horizontal branches (like the Flowering Dogwood, *Cornus florida*) could be planted at just the right spot to give the desired shade where it is needed most. Some of the

smaller maples like the Amur Maple (*Acer ginnala*), the Albizia, Halesia or *Styrax japonica* are other suggestions.

Potted plants are a most desirable item in the patio for they can be placed around at will and removed the minute they are no longer beautiful. Pots may be either set on the stone walk or hidden by sinking them into the soil. In this connection, if one has a small greenhouse or even a hotbed, a series of plants may be grown in pots for the patio display at the proper time. A well-designed and usable patio, with interesting plants, proves an excellent means by which even the busiest individual can keep in touch with growing things and do a minimum amount of work in keeping the place colorful and interesting at all times.

For further information see *Patios, Terraces, Decks and Roof Gardens* by Alice Upham Smith (Doubleday & Co., N.Y., 1969).

PAULOWNIA (paw-LO-nia)

| tomentosa | 45′ | Zone 5 | Royal Paulownia, Empress-tree |

The large pyramidal clusters of fragrant violet flowers can be 10 in. high and are most outstanding for they appear in mid-May before the leaves are fully open. The opposite leaves are of coarse texture, 5–8 in. long on normal shoots and as much as 2–3 ft. on vigorous shoots, either entire or 3-lobed. The fruits are merely dried capsules and there is no autumn color. It is native to China. This is a rapid-growing tree, similar to the Catalpa in texture. In England, several of these are planted together, heavily cut back in the early spring and produce shoot growth up to 12 ft. long with leaves 3 ft. across; not very beautiful, but an oddity only. Although this tree is hardy as far north as Boston, the flower buds frequently winter-kill that far north.

Propagation

Seed can be sown as soon as ripe or stored dry in airtight containers in a cool place for up to a year and then sown. Root cuttings (which see) can be rooted easily.

PAUROTIS = *Acoelorrhaphe*

PAXISTIMA (pax-ISS-tima) (formerly *Pachistima*)

| canbyi | 12″ | Zone 5 | Canby Pachistima |

A native of eastern North America, this low evergreen, with leaves less than an inch long, has a beautiful bronze autumn color that is one of its chief ornamental assets. Being an ericaceous plant, it must be planted in acid soil and makes a fine ground cover if given a little shade. It is frequently featured in clumps in the rock garden or in the foreground of an evergreen foundation planting. The small white flowers are not very ornamental and the fruit is merely a dried capsule. Propagation is easiest by division of the clumps in the spring before growth starts, but both softwood and hardwood cuttings root.

myrsinites 18″ Zone 5 Myrtle Pachistima
An evergreen with alternate leaves 1¼ in. long, native to acid soil areas from British Columbia to Calif.; this has numerous small, rather inconspicuous flowers in the leaf axils, that are purplish, appearing in the late spring and early summer. It is commonly seen in the moist atmosphere of the mountains at altitudes of 4000–7000 ft. Often suggested as a ground cover on the West Coast in areas where there is plenty of atmospheric moisture.

PEA. See LATHYRUS.

PEA FAMILY = Leguminosae

PEA, GARDEN (*Pisum sativum*). Peas are high in food value and rich in vitamins A, the B group and C. It is of very ancient origin being grown and used by the ancient Greeks and Romans. The Garden Pea is very sensitive to heat and thrives only in cool weather. In the South it is grown during the fall and winter and in the North in the spring. In the North late plantings for maturity in the fall are seldom satisfactory. In hot weather growth is retarded, insects and diseases are a problem, pollination is poor resulting in pods with few, if any, seeds.

Varieties

The many listed varieties of peas are classified as dwarf or tall, smooth or wrinkle seeded, and edible podded. Recommended dwarf sorts are **'Alaska'** (smooth-seeded), **'Little Marvel'**, **'Laxtonian'** and **'Blue Bantam'**. Tall varieties are **'Freezonia'**, **'Green Arrow'** and **'Progress No. 9'**. **'Wanda'**, 24–30 in. plant, is the most resistant variety to heat. Edible podded peas of excellent quality are **'Oregon Sugar'** and **'Sugar Snap'**.

Soils and Fertilizers

Peas can be grown in a variety of soil types. For very early planting a sandy or silt loam is preferred, but for a later planting a well-drained clay loam is ideal because of its cooler temperature. The soil reaction for acidity should test from 6.0 to 6.5 pH. See VEGETABLE GARDEN.

If manure is used it must be well rotted or else worked into the soil in the previous fall. The Pea is a legume and, consequently, absorbs nitrogen from the air. This is of relatively little importance with the quick-maturing dwarf varieties. If manure has been used, broadcast 15–20 lbs. per 1000 sq. ft. of a 5–10–5 commercial fertilizer and thoroughly mix into the soil. If no manure was used, increase the fertilizer application by 10 lbs. In some cases, it may be advisable to side dress in bands 2 in. from row with nitrate of soda, 2–3 lbs. per 100 ft. of row, at the time of pod set. For peas the soil should be thoroughly prepared and fertilized to provide a fine friable seedbed.

Planting

Peas should be planted as early as the soil can be properly prepared and, therefore, are usually one of the first crops planted in the home garden. While the smooth-seeded sorts such as 'Alaska' will stand lower temperatures than the wrinkled sorts, both must be planted early to obtain a good succession for harvest, e.g. 'Alaska' matures in 55–60 days, 'Little Marvel' and 'Laxtonian' in 60–63, 'Freezonia' 63–65, 'Wanda' 70–72 and 'Alderman' 74–76. This procedure is preferred to several succession plantings of 1 variety.

Dwarf sorts are planted 24–30 in. apart between rows and a 2-in. spacing will provide a good stand of plants in the row. Seed should not be planted deeper than 1 or 1½ in. For tall varieties it is a common practice to space the rows 30–36 in. apart and the seeds are planted in double rows. Make 2 parallel drills 6 in. apart and 4 in. deep. Sow the seed and cover the seed with 1½ in. of soil. Gradually fill the drill as the plants come up. The object of this double row is to provide space between the drills for the brush or wire trellis needed to support these tall varieties. It also makes more efficient use of space in the garden. The same planting procedure should be used for single row culture.

Supports should be placed at planting time and may consist of (1) brush, 4–5 ft. high after the stems have been pushed into the soil for a distance of 12–18 in. The brush should be well-branched and close enough together to provide a ready hold for the pea-vine tendrils. (2) Chicken wire, 4–5 ft. high, stretched as tight as possible between posts placed at 8–10 ft. intervals. The advantage of chicken wire is that after cleaning it can be rolled up and stored for the next year. Brush is not so easy to obtain and dispose of at the end of the season.

Cultivation

Peas require sufficient shallow cultivation to control weeds. Where brush or wire trellis is used hand weeding is necessary in the row. Commercial growers use the selective herbicide, Premerge, as a pre- and post-emergence chemical to control weeds. This is not recommended for use by the home gardeners. See WEED-CONTROLLING CHEMICALS.

Harvesting

The pods are hand-picked when the seeds are

beginning to fill out the pods. Quality in peas is associated with tenderness and high sugar content. During maturity of the seed the sugar content decreases rapidly with an increase in starch. Fully matured pods will contain peas that are tough and flat in flavor. Peas that are harvested at peak quality and then exposed for 4–5 hours to high temperatures, 75° F. plus, will also lose their sweetness and tender texture.

Insects

Pea aphid, a rather large green plant louse, sucks the juice first from the growing tip but eventually from the entire plant. It can be controlled by dusting with malathion, Diazinon or dimethoate. Do not feed treated foliage to cattle. Pea weevil is brownish with white, black and gray markings. Adults feed on blossoms and larvae burrow into green seed which are most troublesome in western states. Fumigation of seed in a closed container is a good means of control. Also the use of heat for dried seeds with weevils, but use the materials as suggested on the container labels.

Diseases

Powdery mildew, a fungus, most serious during hot, humid weather, which forms a dense white or grayish coating on the leaves. Dusting with sulfur-lime gives fair control. Root rots caused by several different fungi which live over in the soil are frequently serious in reducing the stand of plants. The basic control lies in crop rotation, planting in well-drained and aerated soils and possibly treating the seed prior to planting with Spergon or Arasan. Wilt is another fungus disease common to peas and is soil borne. Infected plants show a downward curling of the leaves, a wilted appearance resulting in stunted growth. Control is same as for root rot.

GRANT B. SNYDER

PEA TREE. See CARAGANA.

PEACH. See PRUNUS.

PEACH = *Prunus persica*

PEACH. Origin: For more than 200 years the Peach was believed to have originated in Persia and the scientific name, *Prunus persica*, indicates a Persian origin. However, in tracking down historical references to the Peach, scientists found that at about 1500 B.C. it was unknown in Persia and western India although it is mentioned in Chinese literature more than 500 years earlier. Thus, China is now the accepted origin of the Peach and its move westward is traced first to Greece and then to the temperate areas of Europe.

Peaches were brought to North America by the Spanish, French and English settlers. Perhaps the fruit was first brought to Mexico by the Spaniards, who also brought them to Fla. in 1565, while English and French settlers brought the seeds to eastern U.S. The native Indians carried this fruit far inland and it eventually reached the West Coast. Today the Peach is of commercial importance in Africa, South America, Europe, Asia and North America.

Peach Growing in the United States

Peaches are being grown in at least 38 states of the U.S. The areas best suited to peach growing are the West Coast states, the East Coast states from Fla. to Mass., and the area south and east of the Great Lakes. The southwestern slopes of the Rocky Mountains in Colo. are an important peach-producing area also.

Since the Peach is not a cold-hardy fruit, its areas of growth are limited by minimum winter temperatures. A temperature drop to −10° F. will usually kill many fruit buds and a temperature of −20° F. will often kill trees. The amount of damage following cold temperatures is influenced to a great extent by the preceding temperatures. Warm weather for several days or longer preceding a quick drop to below zero causes most cold damage. This is especially true after the tree has completed its rest period. In southern areas the bark of trees can be severely injured when day temperatures of 70° F. are followed by a drop to 18° F. above zero at night.

Like all deciduous plants, peach trees require a rest period between the time when the leaves fall and the flowers appear the following spring. Peach varieties differ considerably in their cold requirements for dormancy, the required time ranging from 600 to 1200 hours of 45° F. or below to complete the rest period. Varieties that require the minimum number of cold hours to complete a rest period have been developed so that peaches may be grown in warmer, near subtropical, climates. Such varieties are needed for Fla., south Tex. and southern Calif.

The Peach Tree

The Peach is not so long-lived as the Apple. Although some may live to be 35 years old, most peach trees do not live much beyond 20 years and in some areas 10 years is the life expectancy. The young tree grows vigorously for the first 3 years. During the first year, a well-grown tree will grow from 500 to 1500 total inches of new growth depending upon weather and general culture. In its second season of growth a few fruits will be produced on the tree, but it is best to remove these fruits and so permit the tree to make vegetative growth and to attain good size for early future production. The Peach produces fruit mainly on terminal, year-old shoots, which, for best fruiting, should be about 12 in. long. Fruit buds develop all along this 12-in. shoot and there may be as many as 30 of these. The peach tree that is growing in its third season may produce 75 to 150 peaches. A simple rule of thumb for production is 1 bushel in the third year, 2 bushels in the fourth year, and so on, incresing production by 1 bushel each year until 6 bushels are produced in the eighth year. More or less may be produced per tree, depending upon weather, culture, variety and tree size.

How the Peach Tree is Produced

Peach pits are planted and seedling trees grow from these pits. During June in southern states these seedling trees are budded to known varieties. This is necessary since seedling trees will not produce fruit similar to the parent variety. Usually the fruit of a seedling tree is much inferior to the parent tree. Buds inserted into the seedling tree during June begin to grow within a few weeks and the seedling growth above the bud is removed. The resulting growth from the inserted bud becomes a tree of a known variety and this tree is ready to plant in the garden that same fall or the following year. In northern areas, budding is done in Aug. but, though union of the bud with the stock or seedling occurs, the bud remains dormant until the spring of the following year.

Tree Size Control

In most home gardens, the standard size peach tree is quite satisfactory. It can be maintained at a height of about 8–10 ft. and a width of 12–15 ft. by careful pruning. A very limited number of peach trees are available on dwarfing rootstocks, including 'Brompton' and 'St. Julien' clonal plum stocks, *P. besseyi*, the Sand Cherry, and *P. tomentosa*. The use of dwarfing stocks has not been so successful or so widely used with the Peach as with the Apple and Pear.

There are a few natural dwarf peach varieties. One that has had some success is called 'Bonanza'. A natural dwarf peach tree is one with shorter nodes and more leaves per length of growth than the standard tree, even though it is growing on standard seedling roots. It is similar to the spur type apple tree where the terminal growth is short and the tree is smaller than standard. The true dwarf peach tree produces some fruit but because of its small size, the peaches are fewer in number.

General Culture

To grow peach trees sucessfully in the home garden, several cultural procedures must be followed. Beginning with proper planting, trees must be fertilized, cultivated, sprayed for insect and disease control and pruned annually. Fruit thinning and limb propping are often necessary as the tree beings to produce full crops of fruit. During drought seasons and in arid regions, irrigation is necessary.

Planting

Spring planting is best and this should be accomplished before growth begins. Dig a hole large enough to accommodate the entire root system without crowding. It should be deep enough to allow the tree to be planted at about the same depth of soil in which it grew in the nursery. While digging, keep the topsoil separate from the subsoil. Place some of the topsoil in the bottom of the hole and spread the roots over it, then sift more topsoil around the roots. If you can get rotted manure or compost, mix it with equal parts of topsoil and fill the hole with the mixture. If the soil is extremely acid, mix 1 or 2 lbs. of limestone with the soil in the hole. Soils along the eastern seaboard are naturally acid. Those in western regions are alkaline and do not require additional limestone. Do not put fertilizer in the hole at planting time. Pack the soil firmly around the roots with your feet.

After planting, thoroughly water the soil around the tree. Keep the soil moist during spring and through the first summer. A slight depression about 2 ft. in dia. left around the base of the tree will help to keep water in the root area. In the fall, mound the soil slightly around the tree to reduce ice accumulation and possible injury to the bark on the trunk.

Sunlight

Full sunshine is essential to good tree growth and production. Trees will grow spindly and fruit production will be slight and of poor quality if grown in a shaded area.

Soil

Trees will not tolerate a wet soil. The soil must be sufficiently well drained so that water does not stand on the surface or saturate the root area for days following a heavy rain. Peach trees die quickly from excessive water around the roots.

Fertilization

After growth begins, the newly planted tree can receive about $\frac{1}{10}$ lb. of actual nitrogen applied on the soil around the tree. A nitrogenous material such as ammonium nitrate may be used, or a complete fertilizer such as 10–10–10; a second application may be needed about 6 weeks later to maintain good vigor. Excessive growth should be avoided because this results in a poor tree framework. An excessively vigorous tree produces an upright growth with narrow, weak crotches where limbs join the trunk.

The amount of fertilizer should be increased each year until the tree receives $\frac{1}{2}$ lb. of actual nitrogen. This may be sufficient to maintain vigor and production, but if the soil is poor, more fertilizer will be needed. On sandy soil, peach trees can utilize 1 lb. of actual nitrogen per year. The growth of the tree and the color of the foliage are good indicators of tree vigor. A bearing tree should make terminal growth that is about 12 in. long and the leaves should have a healthy green color. Light green or yellowish leaves indicate a lack of sufficient nitrogen either because an insufficient amount of fertilizer was applied, because of excessively dry soil or because there is injury to the tree from borers or other trunk or root damage.

Cultivation

Peach trees grow best when the soil beneath the tree is cultivated and kept weed-free. Mulching the soil under the tree is an excellent practice and can be done instead of cultivation. The mulch must be thick enough to prevent weed and grass growth. Straw, wood chips and lawn clippings make excellent mulching materials. An area of about 2 ft. around the trunk should be kept free of mulch to reduce the possibility of mouse injury to the roots and trunk. One should watch for mice runs under the mulch and trap the mice if they are present.

Irrigation

During dry seasons and in arid regions, peach trees must be irrigated. A bearing tree requires about 3 in. of rain per month during the growing season and, if this does not come as rain, an equal amount of water must be applied to the soil. The best method of watering a peach tree in the garden is to place a hose at the base of the tree and to let water trickle slowly for an hour or more. A depression in the soil around the base of the tree will prevent water loss. The period when the tree needs water most critically is during the month prior to fruit ripening. A shortage of water at this time will result in a reduction of fruit size. Drought in early spring will seriously reduce terminal growth and fruit-bud formation for the next year, so water should be applied at any time when the moisture in the soil is low.

Fruit Thinning

A bearing peach tree usually produces more blossoms and "sets" more peaches than it can grow to large size and good dessert quality, so the removal of some fruit is necessary. Killing of buds by winter cold or by spring frosts can reduce the crop so that little or no thinning is necessary. A mature peach tree may have 25,000 or more blossoms. This same tree can ripen to good size and quality about 1200 large peaches (6 bushels). Thus, between the time of blossoming and the harvest of the mature fruit, about 95% of the blossoms and young fruit must either drop or be removed by hand. Many of the blossoms drop soon after the petals fall, either because they were not pollinated or because the tree could not supply the tiny fruits with water and nutrients. For this reason, also, a great many more tiny fruits will fall about 2 weeks after bloom.

About a month after bloom, another natural drop of fruit occurs and this is a final attempt by the tree to reduce the load of fruit. The tree will carry most of the remaining peaches to maturity. If there are more than 1200 peaches on the average-sized mature tree, some must be removed by hand or they will be small and of inferior dessert quality. To determine how much fruit to remove, one can take a small section of the tree and count the peaches. This count will provide a rough estimate of the total number of peaches and will indicate whether further reduction is necessary. Usually if peaches are removed so that those remaining are 6–8 in apart, the thinning is sufficient.

The main reason for thinning is to reduce the number of fruits per leaves. It has been shown through research that about 35 leaves are required to ripen 1 large peach of good dessert quality.

Thinning should be completed as soon as the last natural drop of fruit occurs for those varieties ripening in midseason and later. For early ripening varieties, the thinning should be completed before the last natural drop, or about 3 weeks before ripening. This is sometimes difficult because the fruit is quite small and one is not quite sure as to how much fruit will still drop naturally. It is absolutely necessary to thin early ripening varieties early to attain peaches of good size. A peach that is 2 in. in dia. is quite acceptable and there are about 300 in a bushel. A $2\frac{1}{4}$-in. peach will average about 200 in a bushel.

Harvesting

Peaches ripen rapidly when temperatures are above 80°–85° F. As they begin to ripen, they should be harvested every 2 or 3 days, depending upon the temperature. High night temperatures speed the ripening. Of the early varieties, the first few fruits to ripen will have a split pit. This is a normal characteristic. Often mold will be present on the seed. This is also normal and the peach flesh is healthy and good to eat even though the pit is molded. Peaches can be ripened fully on the tree and eaten immediately, or they may be harvested in a firm-ripe condition and held at room temperature for about 3 days. They will then have ripened to excellent dessert quality. Peaches harvested when green and immature may soften, but the dessert quality will be very poor.

Fruit Storage

Peaches can be held in commercial cold storage at 31°–32° F. for a month or slightly longer. In the home refrigerator, which is maintained at about 40° F., they will hold for a few days in excellent condition if they are ripe or firm-ripe when placed in the refrigerator. Prolonged holding at 40°–50° F. results in internal breakdown and poor flavor. Firm-ripe peaches will soften and ripen slowly while in the refrigerator, but will require about a day or two at room temperature to develop good quality. Ripening proceeds half as fast at 60° F. as at 70°–80° F., and only half as fast at 50° as at 60° F.

Pruning

The year-old peach tree will arrive from the nursery as a branched whip. It should be cut back to about 30–36 in. above the ground. Usually the side branches are weak and too small for framework branches. Cut these branches back to spurs, leaving 2–3 buds on each.

After the tree's first season, remove all side branches that form a narrow angle with the trunk (less than 45°). Remove 1 of any 2 limbs of equal size that tend to divide the tree into a "V." Remove suckers or strong branches that fill and shade the center of the tree. To keep the tree well balanced, cut back the stronger framework branches slightly. A central leader similar to that of an apple tree may be developed, but an open-center tree with 3 main framework branches is preferred.

After the second season, prune to develop an open-center, spreading, bowl-shaped tree. Remove any large limb that tends to grow up through the center, or across the center. Remove large suckers growing straight up in the center. Retain most of the other growth throughout the tree. As with the 1-year tree, remove limbs with narrow angles and branches of equal size that form a weak crotch.

A peach tree grown well for 2 years will have a trunk 4–6 in. in circumference and a good supply of fruit buds. Moderate and careful pruning at the end of the second season can result in production of as much as a bushel of peaches during the third summer. Severe pruning at the end of the second season will reduce, and

may eliminate, the third summer crop.

After the third year, the peach tree should produce annual crops of fruit. Pruning is much the same throughout the first 4–5 years. After that time, somewhat more severe pruning may be desirable to keep the tree within bounds and maintain plenty of strong, healthy, fruiting wood.

Peaches are produced on wood that grew the previous season. The open-center or bowl-shaped tree with a well-rounded base and a wide-spreading top is recommended and generally grown throughout the country. Trees of this type have a larger bearing surface near the ground than do other types. They also have good fruiting wood throughout the center. The height of the tree should be kept to a maximum of 10 ft., the exact height depending on variety, soil, and general culture. It is possible, by careful pruning, to hold the peach tree to a height of about 7 ft. and still maintain good production.

Varieties

The first peaches grown in the U.S. were probably white fleshed. These were later crossed with yellow-fleshed peaches brought from Mexico. The original varieties were chance seedlings. Of these, 'Elberta' is one of the best known of the very old varieties that originated in Ga. as a seedling tree. Except for the 'Elberta' and a few others, all varieties grown today have been developed through controlled fruit breeding by state and federal experiment stations or by private breeders.

The suitability of varieties differs throughout the country. Those grown in Fla., for example, must be varieties requiring the shorter chilling requirements so that the rest period may be completed and normal blossoming begin in early Feb. Likewise, varieties grown in southern Calif. and Tex. are those adapted to these particular areas. Several varieties requiring the minimum number of hours below 45° F. include 'Maygold' (650 hours) and 'Suwanee' (650 hours).

Those varieties grown from S. Car. north and throughout the central states, Colo., central and northern Calif., Ore. and Wash. are the same in most cases. Several important varieties that have wide adaptation are 'Redhaven', 'Sunhigh' and 'Elberta'. There are many more varieties that are best adapted to one area or another. Some of these include 'Sunhaven', 'Jerseyland', 'Triogem', 'Candor', 'Newhaven', 'Jersey Queen', 'Redskin' and 'Rio-Oso-Gem'. All the varieties mentioned are yellow fleshed but there are many excellent whitefleshed varieties, also: 'Raritan Rose', 'White Hale'.

For the gardener unfamiliar with the varieties

best adapted to his particular area, the State College of Agriculture or the County Agricultural Agent should be consulted for advice.

Pollination

There is no serious problem in regard to cross-pollination with the Peach because most varieties are self-fruitful. There are a few varieties that are not, and if these are selected, one must provide another self-fruitful variety for pollination. The 'J. H. Hale' is one of the self-unfruitful varieties.

ERNEST G. CHRIST

Pest Control

The control of major insects and diseases by spraying and general sanitation is necessary to produce fine fruit and to maintain vigorous trees. Spray schedules are available for home trees and single-package mixtures containing insecticides and fungicides make the job quite simple and safe. To be successful in pest control, the proper materials must be used, applied at the correct time, and the tree must be thoroughly covered.

During the first 2 years in the life of the tree the spray program is not a complete one because there is no fruit. Leaf-chewing insects and borers are the main problems. After fruit production begins, one must follow a full spray program. Some of the most common insects of the peach fruit are plum curculio and oriental fruit worm. The most destructive disease attacking the fruit is fungus and brown rot. Borers can be a very serious threat to the vigor and life of the peach tree. The base of the trunk area should be checked several times annually for signs of borers. A jellylike substance will appear at the soil level if borers are present and they must be destroyed. A soft piece of wire forced into the holes will kill them.

In addition to spraying, certain sanitary practices will help, especially in the reduction and control of diseases. All dropped fruit should be gathered and removed from the area because this is a source of brown rot. Peaches that become infested with brown rot sometimes hang on the tree to shrivel and dry. These are also a source of infection and should be removed during the pruning.

Insect Pests

Long-snouted plum cucurlio beetles feed and lay eggs in the fruit when it is $\frac{1}{4}-\frac{1}{2}$ in. in dia. and the grubs feed in the flesh, causing fruit to drop. Spraying with insecticides #15, #9 or #46 when the fruit is of the susceptible size is effective. Oriental fruit moth larvae, which resemble codling moth worms, cause wilting tips on new shoots in early summer and tunnel in fruit in mid- and late summer. Applications of insecticides #37, #9 and #46 give control. Peach tree borer tunnels just beneath the bark near the soil and may girdle the tree. Masses of gummy or dried sap identify the injury. The large white worms can be cut out and spraying with insecticide #14 in July and Aug. may prevent infestation. San Jose scale, Forbes scale and European fruit lecanium infest Peach (see SCALE INSECTS), and several aphids are often destructive. Small dark brown beetles of the shot-hole borer breed under the bark of weak trees and hasten their death. They emerge through tiny round holes, as the name implies. Regular applications of a spray and general good care should prevent serious infestations. The tarnished plant bug and the hickory plant bug "sting" the young fruit, causing pits and scars. The early summer sprays of a regular schedule should control them.

Diseases

Curly, deformed, new leaves with a pinkish color indicate the peach leaf curl disease which overwinters in buds and must be controlled by strictly dormant sprays such as fungicide #D. Dead and dried blossoms, cankers on the bark and brown rotted areas in the fruit both before and after harvest make brown rot the most destructive disease of Peach. On fruit, infection occurs only through breaks in the skin, and insect control and careful handling are important. Dried fruit "mummies" are sources of infection and should be destroyed. Spraying or dusting at 7–10-day intervals throughout the season with fungicides #F, #V or #W is recommended. Scab is identified by small red dots on leaves and small, black, circular spots often followed by cracking on the fruit. A regular spray schedule is effective. Bacterial leaf spot produces angular, water-soaked or black spots on leaves. If control is necessary, use fungicide #G. Several virus diseases, such as yellows, little peach and phony peach, cannot be controlled and infested trees should be destroyed. X disease spreads from Choke Cherry, which should be destroyed within a radius of 500 ft. of peach trees.

Peach foliage may be injured by sprays containing copper or arsenic. Commercial peach growers should check with local authorities for spray and dust schedules and for home gardeners the following is suggested:

TIME	INSECTICIDE OR FUNGICIDE
1. Before buds burst	D
2. Just before bloom	46 or W
3. Just after bloom	46 or W+6
4. Repeat at 10-day intervals until 2 weeks before harvest	46 or W+37

PEANUT. The Peanut, *Arachia hypogaea*, is one of the important crop plants of the world, but it is not usually considered a subject for home garden growing. Groundnuts (or peanuts) are mentioned in some of the earliest colonial records, yet whether peanuts were grown by the Indians is still questionable. It is believed that the Peanut is native to Brazil and Peru, but it is grown throughout the world wherever long hot summers are common.

A leguminous annual plant, the Peanut is sometimes known as a goober as well as a groundnut. Growing 12 to 18 in. tall, with alternate compound leaves of 4 leaflets, there are 2 general types. The one more generally grown is the Runner Peanut, in which the vinelike plant sprawls, requiring a considerable amount of space. The other, the Bunch Peanut, is bushier and essentially upright growing. The bunch type is more often grown by those who harvest the tops for forage.

The gynophore or fruit stalk of the Peanut is commonly called the peg, and is considered part of the peanut fruit. The shell or seed portion of the fruit is called the nut or pod. The Peanut differs from most legumes in that the fruit matures underground and the gynophore or peg is elongated.

The Peanut actually can be grown in all but the northern tier of states from Me. to Minn., but it requires such a long season of heat to ripen its underground fruits that it is seldom grown except as a novelty north of Va. From Zone 5 south the Peanut is commercially important.

Flowering in peanuts begins 4 to 6 weeks after the plant appears above the ground. From the time the Peanut first became known its flowering and fruiting habits attracted widespread attention. Flowers are of 2 kinds, one showy, yellow, pealike and sterile, the other also yellow but fertile. After pollination occurs, the stalks on which are the fertile flowers curve down and penetrate the soil, carrying the fertilized ovary beneath the surface where it ripens, becoming what is called a peanut.

A warm sandy loam with a pH of about 7.0 is best for peanut growing. Clean culture is practiced to keep down weeds and to conserve soil moisture. The Peanut yields heavy in a hot dry summer. It is normally planted in drills 30 in. apart in the row.

Four types of peanuts are grown: **'Spanish'**, **'Runner'**, **'Virginia'** and **'Valencia'**. In Georgia, 98% of the acreage is planted to **'Florunner'** of the Runner type. Other less popular varieties are **'Florigiant'**, **'Tifrun'**, and **'Early Bunch'**. Valencia types are almost exclusively in N.M.

The peanut plant has a fruiting period of about 2 months. If digging is done in time to save the earlier-formed pods, later ones will be immature. If it is delayed, early-formed pods of Spanish peanuts will sprout, while **'Virginia Bunch'** early pods are left in the soil. The object is to dig the crop when the largest number of mature pods can be saved.

Peanut-digging plows with fingerlike bars that lift the vines from the soil are used. A newer digger, when tractor drawn, lifts and shakes 2 rows of vines at a time leaving them on top of the ground. After they are allowed to wilt, the vines are formed into windows. Machines are used for picking the peanuts from the vines. In some growing areas peanut fields are grazed by hogs which do an excellent job of gleaning the fields.

When grown commercially the Peanut is subject to attack by leaf hoppers, corn earworm and certain soil pests, such as wireworms and grubs of the June bug. Stem rot, sometimes called white mold, wilt or blight is a troublesome fungus in commercial plantations. Caused by *Sclerotinium rolfsi*, it attacks the plant at the soil line, being easily recognized by the white fuzzy growth that spreads along the stems. The fungus overwinters in the soil on organic matter as small resting bodies called sclerotia. With favorable spring weather they germinate and spread rapidly on crop debris. Nuts from stem-rot infected pegs do not cling, remaining in the soil during harvesting. In a severe infection more than half the crop may be lost.

To reduce infection seeds are planted in ridges with a special planter, rather than in furrows. In addition an herbicide is applied to either side of the ridge, and weeding equipment that prevents soil from being thrown

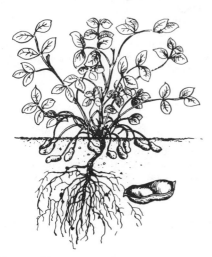

Peanut plant

against the ridge is used. Some peanut growers have found that Dinoseb plus 2, 4, DEP, applied as a post-emergence herbicide, is more effective than a pre-emergence application.

H. GLEASON MATTOON

PEAR. Origin: The Pear, *Pyrus communis*, probably came from western Asia and the eastern part of Europe. It was used for food by the Stone Age man. A few varieties were known by the Greeks as early as 370 B.C., and it was carried westward into Europe by the Romans. As with the Peach and Apple, the Pear also was brought to America by the colonists. Although there are no native American pear species, many varieties were available in this country by the 18th century and in Europe the horticulturists were at work developing new and better varieties. These early pears from Europe, called "butter" pears, were of excellent quality, but a disease called fire blight, caused by the bacterium *Erwinia amylovora*, was killing large limbs and whole trees. It attacked roots, trunk, limbs, flowers, fruit and leaves.

Another kind of Pear, *P. serotina*, commonly called the Sand Pear, grew in eastern Asia and was quite resistant to this disease. Early in the 19th century pears of this type reached the United States by way of Europe. The sand pears have numerous hard sand or grit cells in the flesh and are not equal to the "butter" pears in dessert quality, but were grown where the fire blight disease eliminated the latter. Because of their resistance, the sand pears spread rapidly throughout the eastern U.S.

Pear-producing Areas of the United States

The major pear-producing area includes the West Coast states of Calif., Ore. and Wash. The fire blight disease is less rampant in the warm, dry valleys of these states. Rocky Mountains states are important areas, also, because of the dry climate. In addition, pears are grown in Mich., in the central states and the eastern states from Va. northward, wherever apples are grown. In the humid areas of the U.S., pears are of less commercial importance because the disease is more destructive, but they are adapted to the home garden.

Pear Varieties and Blight Resistance

Soon after the introduction of the sand pears in the U.S. and when their resistance to fire blight became known, there was considerable interest in improving the quality of the Sand Pear. Where the European pear trees and the sand pear trees were planted in the same orchard, many of the young seedling trees were found to be hybrids. The most important of these natural hybrids was named the **'Kieffer'**. This variety was raised from a sand pear seed by Peter Kieffer in Roxborough, Pa., around 1863. It was resistant to blight and soon became widely planted in orchards and home gardens throughout the eastern U.S. The 'Kieffer', which is still available from nurseries, has a better quality and less grit in the flesh than the original sand pears, but is far inferior in dessert quality to the European butter pears.

The fine quality pears that established the early industry in the U.S. are still being grown and are of superb dessert quality. They are grown even though fire blight causes great crop and tree losses in many years. The **'Bartlett'**, best known and most widely planted, originated in England around 1770. Several important varieties originated in France include **'Anjou'**, **'Bosc'**, **'Comice'** and **'Valor'**. **'Anjou'** and **'Bosc'** are second and third to **'Bartlett'** in importance. Belgium contributed **'Flemish Beauty'** and **'Winter Nells'**. One old pear of the species *P. communis* (European type) that originated in the U.S. is **'Seckel'**. This is a small, brownish-yellow pear found as a seedling near Philadelphia about 1800 and this became popular because of its excellent dessert quality and its resistance to fire blight. Another good quality, blight-resistant Pear is **'Maxine'**, originating in Ohio in 1870, also, **'Harrow Delight'**.

Research in breeding has produced many additional varieties since the early 1900's. The N.Y. Agricultural Experiment Station and the USDA have been most active in this work. Varieties from N.Y. are **'Gorham'**, **'Aurora'** and **'Highland'**. Two blight-resistant varieties from the U.S. Department of Agriculture are **'Magness'** and **'Moonglow'** and 2 blight-resistant varieties from Tenn. are **'Morgan'** and **'Carrick'**.

A natural red-skinned mutation of 'Bartlett' called **'Max-Red-Bartlett'** is available with fruits entirely red or streaked with red. A new Bartlett type from Michigan named **'Spartlett'** produces large fruit ripening later than 'Bartlett.'

Pear Culture

It is obvious from the previous discussion that the limiting factor in pear growing is the bacterial disease fire blight. This disease is transferred from tree to tree through the open blossoms by bees. Cankers from previous years' infections ooze at blossom time and bees, attracted to the ooze, carry the bacterium to the open blossoms. During recent years, sprays of antibiotics have been of some help in its control, but nothing has proved entirely satisfactory.

Planting

Pear trees should be planted in a sunny area

of the garden. The soil should be naturally fertile or improved by the addition of peat moss, manures or other organic materials. One- or 2-year-old trees are available from nurseries and both are satisfactory. Planting should be done in early spring in northern areas and either fall or spring in warm southern areas. When planting, be sure to keep the graft union above the soil.

Rootstocks

There is considerable interest in dwarf pear trees for the home garden because they require less space. A smaller tree, of course, is easier to spray, prune, thin and harvest. Pear trees are dwarfed by growing them on a Malling quince 'A' root. Some varieties are not compatible with the quince 'A' root and thus an "interstem" must be used. Incompatibility is often evidenced as a weakness in the bud or graft union. The **'Old Home'** variety is a blight-resistant Pear often used as an interstem between the variety, such as 'Bartlett', and the quince rootstock. This means that the tree has been grafted or budded twice in the nursery. Incompatibility is a problem in some other fruits, as well, and in order to overcome this difficulty, it is necessary to use an interstem that is compatible with both the variety and the rootstock. Another dwarfing rootstock is Quince 'Provence' from France and this has been more compatible than the Quince 'A' with some pear varieties. Dwarf pear trees can be planted about 10 ft. apart in the garden. They may be grown as a free-standing tree or on a trellis and in an espaliered manner. In some cases the pear tree is espaliered on a wall much the same as is done in many European countries. Most of the important varieties, grafted on the dwarfing rootstock, are available from the nurseries.

Pollination

Pear varieties are considered self-unfruitful and therefore cross-pollination should be provided to insure a good crop of fruit. A single variety will not produce consistent crops without cross-pollination and very often it will produce little or no fruit. Most pear varieties are compatible with one another in regard to cross-pollination, but the 'Bartlett'—'Seckel' combination is not satisfactory. If these 2 varieties are planted, a third is needed for cross-pollination. If a single pear tree is growing in the garden, it is possible to provide cross-pollination by placing a bouquet of blossoms during full bloom near the tree to be pollinated. Of course the bouquet must be from a different variety so as to provide the cross-pollination. Usually within 3 or 4 hours on a bright, sunny day, with the temperature about 70° F., bees will accomplish

the cross-pollination and the crop of pears will be set.

Fertilization

Pear trees require less fertilizer and less nitrogen than most other fruit trees and a tree that is growing very vigorously from the use of excessive fertilizer is more susceptible to the fire blight disease than one that is growing more slowly. A pear tree that is producing about 6–12 in. of new terminal growth each year is growing in an ideal condition. If the terminal growth is 2–3 ft. or more, the tree is too vigorous and is more susceptible to fire blight.

A young pear tree in its first and second years of growth generally gains 3 ft. of terminal growth. In its third year and thereafter, the growth is much less and production begins. If the soil is fertile, the young, newly planted tree will not need much fertilizer the first year. After growth begins in the spring, about $\frac{1}{10}$ lb. of actual nitrogen (or 1 lb. of a 10-10-10 mixture) may be applied, either from a nitrogen source such as ammonium nitrate or from a complete garden fertilizer. The amount of nitrogen may be increased by about $\frac{1}{10}$ lb. each year to keep the tree growing as described. Dwarf trees may not need more than about $\frac{1}{4}$ lb. of nitrogen each year. It is much better to have the pear tree a little less vigorous than a little too vigorous. Pear trees grow very well with sod growing beneath the tree and it is not necessary to keep the ground cultivated under them. In fact, it is much better to have a sod cover under the tree to reduce the possibility of an over-vegetative growth condition.

Irrigation

Pear trees can withstand short periods of drought, but during most years one or more prolonged drought periods occur. A good rule of thumb is to water pear trees once every 2 weeks if no rainfall occurs. An excellent method of irrigating a fruit tree is to place a hose near the base and let the water trickle into the soil for several hours. In the arid regions where no rainfall occurs during the growing season, irrigation is a common practice and is well understood to be an essential cultural procedure.

Rodent Control

In most areas rabbits and field mice will attack pear trees during the fall and winter, especially when there is a prolonged snow cover. Field mice, also, are a problem where the ground is covered with snow for an extended period. For the control of both mice and rabbits, it is best to keep free of grass and weeds the soil area immediately around the tree trunk. It is most important that this be done in the fall, but if possible it should be kept clean during the summer also. In addition to the clean area around the tree trunk, a wire guard of $\frac{1}{4}$-in.-mesh hardware cloth around the trunk will aid considerably. This guard should be 18–24 in. tall and it is best to place it a few inches below the soil. There should be about a 1-in. space between the guard and the tree trunk and it should be large enough to permit the edges to overlap and hook together. After the tree grows a few years it may be necessary to place a larger guard on the trunk, although the first 3–4 years are the most critical for rabbit damage. This guard will also protect the trunk against mice; however, mice sometimes damage the roots below the soil without being noticed, so one should check occasionally for mice runs in the sod and, if these are present, the mice should be trapped with an ordinary household mouse trap. Aluminum foil is another material that has been used successfully for protection against rabbits and mice. This can be placed around the trunk in the fall and usually it will last for 1 or 2 winters.

Pruning

Trees must be pruned to produce attractive, high-quality fruit. Moreover, pruning invigorates the plant, prevents overbearing, increases the size of the fruit, and aids in the control of pests. It also results in the formation of a tree having the proper shape, form and size.

Since individual trees vary somewhat and variety habits differ as well, it is difficult to describe or illustrate completely a single pruning procedure that would apply to all forms. The basic framework of the tree is established during the pruning that is done after the growth of the first and second seasons. It is best to prune trees in late autumn after the leaves have fallen, during the winter when the weather is mild, or in early spring before growth starts. Summer pruning is not recommended.

Year-old pear trees will usually arrive from the nursery as straight, unbranched, 4- to 5-ft. whips. Prune these at planting time to a height of about 36 in. At that time also, prune broken or injured roots to a clean cut to reduce the possibility of disease infection. During the first year the tree will produce side branches all along and around the main trunk.

At the end of the first season, remove branches to a height of about 24 in. Also, remove any branches that form a narrow angle with the trunk. Limbs that form about 90° angles with the main trunk are strongest. Angles of less than about 45° are weak. At the top of the tree, remove 1 of any 2 branches that tend to divide the tree into a "V." Retain 1 central leader.

If you plant 2-year-old trees, follow the directions for pruning trees that have completed their first year of growth in the garden. Remove limbs that form weak crotches and retain only the best branches along the main trunk, together with a leading branch that is a continuation of the main trunk. Prune these trees more severely than established 2-year-old trees, removing about half the growth.

After the second season, and until the tree begins to bear fruit, only corrective pruning is needed. Do not prune more than is necessary. Severe pruning will cause long sucker growth in the top of the tree, delay fruiting and make the tree more susceptible to fire blight disease. Moderate, careful pruning results in early fruiting.

After the tree begins to bear, the limbs will bend with the weight of the fruit and the tree will become more open and spreading. Also, the annual growth will be reduced somewhat, so that less pruning will be needed. Bearing trees should not be pruned severely to correct a defective framework. Such corrective pruning should be done during the first 3 years while the limbs are small. After that, thinning out branches to prevent dense growth is usually sufficient.

Most pear trees grow in an upright manner and the desired form is difficult to obtain. Because of this upright growth habit, it is often unwise to train it to a strictly spreading form. Very little pruning of pear trees is necessary after they begin to bear.

If fire blight infects 1 or several small limbs a few weeks after bloom, the leaves on these limbs will turn black. Prune out the infected limb and make the cut at least 1 ft. into apparently healthy tissue. The fire blight disease often is further along in the tissue than is visible from the outside. After each pruning cut, dip or wipe down the shears or saw in alcohol to reduce the possibility of spreading the disease.

Fruit Thinning

Pear trees often produce too many fruits and some must be removed by hand in order to prevent breakage of the tree and also to insure good size and excellent dessert quality. They should be thinned to single fruits when they occur in doubles and triples and, where they are thick on the limb, they should be thinned out to 6–8 in. between each fruit. Thinning may not be necessary every year, but in most years there are certain limbs on the tree that will produce too many fruits and so some thinning is necessary. During the period from petal fall until about 6 weeks after full bloom, many small pears will fall to the ground. If the bloom is very heavy on the tree, many fruits will drop because the tree is unable to supply all these fruits with sufficient water and nutrients. Also, some of the flowers will not have been pollinated and these little fruits will fall soon after blossoming. About 6 weeks after bloom there is a final drop of fruit and, after this, the hand thinning may be done. It is best to complete the hand thinning as soon as possible after this final drop so that the tree may conserve energy to develop the remaining fruit to the best possible size and dessert quality.

Harvesting

The pear is different from most other fruits because it must be harvested in a slightly unripe condition in order to last for any appreciable length of time. If a pear is permitted to ripen on the tree, it will not remain in good condition very long and often it will have a browning or break-down around the core when it is removed from the tree. As the pears begin to show a slight change in color from dark green to lighter green with no definite yellowing, the harvest period is approaching. Usually a few pears will begin to ripen earlier than most of the crop and these can be checked first.

To determine whether harvesting should begin, the pear should be lifted against the curvature of the stem. Most of the pear stems will have a slight curve and where the stem is attached to the spur on the tree there is a slight swelling in the stem. This swelling is called the abscission layer and, if the pear is ready to harvest the stem will separate easily at this swelling. If the spur breaks off from the limb or if the stem breaks at a point between the swelling and the pear, then the pears are not ready to harvest. They should be checked again in a few days, and so on until most fruits separate at the swelling. Then the harvest period has arrived. After 1 or 2 years' experience with a given variety, it is a simple matter to determine the harvest time.

After harvest, the pears will ripen rapidly at room temperature and must be used in order to avoid browning at the core, but even with careful handling and rapid use, some pears will show this browning at the core. In order to avoid this and to have the pears ripen to excellent quality, they should be held in cold storage at a temperature of 31–32° F. for a week or 2. They can be held much longer, of course, but exposure for a short time to the cold temperature is necessary to ripen the fruit and improve its quality. After a week or longer they may be brought out of the cold storage and ripened at room temperature. If no storage at 31–32° F. is available, the fruit can be held in the refrigerator at about 40° F. for a limited period. When brought out of the refrigerator,

they ripen rapidly at temperatures about 70° F. and they will ripen to best quality at about 65–70° F. When ripened at very high temperatures (above 80° F.), the fruit will be of inferior quality.

ERNEST G. CHRIST

Pest Control

It is relatively simple to control the insects and diseases which attack the Pear, by using the new all-purpose fruit tree spray mixtures. These are available in the garden supply stores and are safe to use in the home garden. As with all other fruits, the success of the pest control program depends upon 3 main factors: (1) The use of the proper chemical materials. (2) The timely application of the materials. (3) The thorough coverage of the entire tree with the spray. The main difficulty, as mentioned previously, is in controlling the fire blight disease and since it is such a problem it is best to plant the disease-resistant varieties mentioned previously. Although 'Bartlett' is considered to be the standard of dessert quality, it is also one of the most susceptible to fire blight disease. Therefore, if 'Bartlett' is used in the home garden planting, it is best to include also at least a few of the resistant varieties.

Insect Pests

Codling moth, plum curculio, plant bugs and a blister mite attack pears. For description and control, see APPLE. Pear psylla is the most destructive insect pest of Pear in the East and has now spread to many western areas. It is a jumping plant louse which sucks the sap. The nymphs secrete large amounts of honey dew which attracts ants and other insects. Black sooty mold develops on the honeydew and disfigures all parts of the tree. There are 3 or more generations annually. Timely sprays with insecticide #15 or #37 are effective. Pear thrips damage the blossoms and prevent the development of normal fruit. Spray when the buds are opening in the spring, using insecticide #9 or #15, are recommended. Pear midge, a tiny mosquitolike fly, lays eggs in the blossom and the maggots eat large cavities inside the small pear, which falls. Spraying as for pear thrips is helpful.

Diseases

Fire blight is very destructive to Pear and has limited pear culture in some areas. See APPLE. Pear scab attacks some older varieties, but most of the newer varieties are resistant. See APPLE.

PEARLBERRY, CREEPING = *Gaultheria hispidula*

PEARLBUSH. See EXOCHORDA.

PEARLWORT, CORSICAN = *Sagina subulata*

PEAT. A carbonaceous substance formed by partial decomposition in water of various plants, especially sphagnum; used as a mulch or soil amendment. There are many kinds of peat, most of which are useful as soil amendments but these should not be confused with peat moss. Peats frequently are dug locally and sold by the bushel or the load. They cover a wide range of materials, from decomposed sphagnum moss to humus material merely from the woods. They vary greatly in nutrient materials and especially in their water-retaining properties.

Peat moss (which is derived from sphagnum moss) is the best for retaining water and for providing acids for the growth of ericaceous plants. General peat on the other hand is often good for improving soil structure, especially that of heavy clay soils.

PEAT MOSS. The merits of peat moss are well known. It is probably the best of mulching materials although it is certainly not the least expensive. The term "peat moss" is usually meant to mean partially decayed sphagnum moss. There are many peats (see PEAT) made up variously of all kinds of decayed plant materials, but none of these have the water-holding qualifications of peat moss made up of decayed sphagnum moss. The local peats are undoubtedly less expensive than the baled and dried "peat moss" but seldom will they fulfil the same needs in the garden, especially that of water absorption and retention.

Peat moss has been estimated to hold anywhere from 600%–1200% water when compared on a dry weight basis. It is usually acid in reaction, between 3.6 and 6.8 pH. Peat moss mulches should be applied only 1–2 in. deep. This is usually sufficient to keep most of the weeds in check and to make a nice soil cover to prevent excessive soil evaporation.

Processed peat moss is usually dried and pressed into bales for easy shipping. They are available in different sizes, some containing 4 cu. ft. and weighing 55 lbs., others 6 cu. ft. and weighing about 95 lbs. and others with 7½–8 cu. ft. of materials. To estimate the amount of this pressed and dried material needed as a mulch, a 95-lb. bale of dried and pressed peat moss, broken up and well moistened, will make a 1-in. layer over 300 sq. ft. of space.

The most uniform of the processed peat mosses come from large deposits in Mich., Canada and Europe. The gardener with only a small garden is usually willing to pay premium prices for uniform peat moss devoid of weed seeds.

One word of caution. When completely dry it takes a very long time for it to absorb moisture, the reason why young plants, when planted in almost 100% peat moss, may die in a long drought where plants in the normal soil nearby will not. The small amounts of rain in a dry summer fail to soak through the dry peat moss, although they may soak through the soil. Mixed with a goodly amount of soil, however, it does not present any real hazard.

PECAN = *Carya illinoinensis*

PECTINATE. Comblike.

PEDICEL. The stalk of a flower.

PEDICELLATE. Borne on a pedicel.

PEDICULARIS (pee-dik-yew-LAY-ris)
   canadensis 6"–18" **Zone 3 Canada Wood-betony**
A hairy perennial herb with alternate, finely divided leaves; yellow flowers, often tinged with brown, having a 2-lipped corolla, the upper lip forming a hood, the lower lip having 3 lobes. It grows in dry woods throughout the eastern U.S., extending from southern Canada to Mexico. While it is suitable for the wild garden, it is difficult to cultivate, being somewhat parasitic.

   lanceolata 3' **Zone 6 Swamp Wood-betony**
A perennial herb sometimes planted in rock gardens because of its showy yellow, ¾-in.-long flowers from Aug. to Oct. The leaves are alternate or whorled. Propagated by seed and division. Native from Conn. to Neb.

PEDILANTHUS (pee-dill-ANTH-us)
   tithymaloides 6' **Zone 10 Redbird Slipper-flower**
A peculiar succulent plant from tropical America sometimes used in tropical gardens. The large, thick-branched, zigzag plant stems bear groups of slipper-shaped red and yellow flower bracts, about ¼ in. long, with inconspicuous flowers. The evergreen leaves are variegated white and various shades of green, sometimes with a touch of pink; usually planted in pots to place on the terrace to enhance the tropical effects of the garden or used as a house plant. One should know that the milky juice of this plant is caustic and an irritant. Propagation by cuttings.

PEDIOCACTUS (pee-di-o-KAK-tus)
   simpsonii 6" **Zone 5 Snowball Cactus**
A small globular cactus, native from Kan. to N.Mex. to Wash.; very spiny with 15–20 needle-like spines; flowers pinkish, funnelform, less than an inch long. Not often used as an ornamental.

PEDUNCLE. The stalk of a flower-cluster; also used for the stalk of a solitary flower.

PEDUNCULATE. Borne on a peduncle.

PELARGONIUM (pel-ar-GO-nium). These are the Storksbill, Pelargonium or Geranium of the florist (see GERANIUM for the true Geranium)—a rather large genus of tender South African herbs, shrublike or climbing, with large rounded flower clusters which are brightly colored. For propagation and culture see *P. hortorum*. These are the ideal pot plants for growing indoors and also for using as brilliantly flowered bedding plants out-of-doors. Also excellent for use in window boxes and hanging baskets.

They are divided into 4 general groups—the Show or Lady Washington Pelargonium (*P.*

all of ornamental value. The flowers are produced chiefly at Easter; some of the popular varieties being **'Gardener's Joy'**—pink; **'Easter Greeting'**—red; **'Mme. Loyal'**—pink, white, purple and black; **'Schwaben Maid'**—black blotched and reddish.

echinatum   1½′   Zone 10   Sweetheart Geranium
A so-called "Cactus Geranium" with soft, stem, hooked, soft, thornlike stubbles and gray-

Geranium—different flower and leaf types.

domesticum); the House Geranium (*P. hortorum*), also used for general bedding purposes and sometimes called the Zonal Geranium; the Ivy-leaved Geranium (*P. peltatum*) and the Scented-leaved Geranium which come in more than 50 species and varieties.

capitatum   1′–2′   Zone 10   Rose Scented Pelargonium
With hairy, weak, sometimes sprawling stems, long-stalked, heart-shaped leaves, 1½ in. wide, and rose to rose-purple flowers.

crispum   3′   Zone 10   Finger Bowl Pelargonium
With alternate, rounded, 3-lobed, crinkly margined leaves born in 2 rows on short petioles. They are lemon scented; flowers are pink in 1–3-flowered umbels; the upper 2 petals are a deeper pink than the lower 3.

denticulatum   1′   Zone 10   Skeleton Leaf Pelargonium
With lilac-rose to purple flowers in 1–3-flowered umbels; weak stemmed; leaves with long, linear, deep lobes.

x domesticum   1½′   Zone 10   Lady Washington Geranium
The leaves are 2–4 in. wide and obscurely lobed; the flowers are large and conspicuous, white, pink or red, the upper 2 petals having darker blotches. The umbels have few to many flowers. There are many cultivars of this species,

green lobed leaves which are whitish beneath; single, heart-shaped, white flowers marked with maroon. The 5–7 lobed leaves are 1–1½ in. wide. Native to South Africa.

x fragrans   1′   Zone 10   Fragrant Geranium
A hybrid species (*P. exstipulatum* x *P. odoratissimum*) of a bushy, branching habit with small, rounded, ruffled leaves an inch wide and scented. Flowers whitish with pink veins; 4–8 flowers per cluster.

graveolens   3′   Zone 9   Rose Geranium
A popular garden plant and herb with erect stems, gray-green, heart-shaped to rounded leaves 1–4 in. wide, often palmately lobed, and flowers which are rose colored with a dark purple spot in the middle of the upper petal. Blooms in summer. Native to South Africa.

x hortorum   1′–2′   Zone 10   Common Geranium
This is sometimes called the Zonal Geranium and there are a bewildering number of varieties available, ranging in flower color from red, pink, salmon to white, all having many-flowered umbels. The leaves are 3–5 in. wide.

Propagation

Usually cuttings are about 4 in. long but, if stock is scarce, they can be shorter. When grown in the greenhouse, cuttings may be taken any time during the year except during June and July. They can be allowed to wilt somewhat without injury and, in fact, the drying of the cut end by being exposed to air for 6–12 hours may reduce the loss from damping off, a serious hazard of the cutting bed. Remove the lower leaves and leave at least 3 perfect leaves per cutting. The cuttings usually root in about 4 weeks, but if treated with a root-inducing powder, this time may be reduced. Sand which has been sterilized with steam (to reduce damping off) has proved the best rooting medium. When once inserted, they should be heavily watered at once—then kept somewhat on the dry side, but they should not be allowed to wilt. However, too much water induces damping off.

They should be potted in 2½-in. pots as soon as rooted, although some growers pot them as soon as they are callused—10–14 days after the cuttings have been taken. Others place a newly made cutting in a pot by itself and let it root there.

The soil mixture should be 3 or 4 parts of soil and 1 part of well-rotted manure to which a 4-in. potful of superphosphate has been added to each wheelbarrow of soil mixture. Later they are moved to 4-in. pots, given plenty of room, pinched to produce compactness and maintained at a night temperature of 55° F. if possible.

Complete fertilizer can and should be added to potted plants several times. Excessive spraying of the foliage is not conducive to good, sturdy growth, but rather a weak, soft growth that is highly undesirable. Moisture on the flower head may even cause rot.

There are many varieties, with new ones appearing all the time. Among those generally used are:

Light pink—'Enchantress Fiat', 'Enchantress Supreme'
Salmon—'Fiat', 'Palmiers Salmon Supreme'
Brick Red—'Olympic Red', 'Improved Ricard', 'Polly Red'
Red—'ABC Red', 'Red Fiat', 'Pride of Camden', 'Haase's Scarlet'
Cerise—'Better Times'
White—'Mme. Buckner'

Insect Pests

Mealybugs (see CHRYSANTHEMUM), white fly and aphids infest geraniums. Sprays or aerosols of insecticide #15 control them. Cyclamen mite is an occasional pest. See CYCLAMEN. Termites may tunnel the stems. Use insecticide #15 and kill the termites in nearby wood.

Diseases

The virus diseases, crinkle and mosaic, produce abnormal plants. Use clean cuttings in sterile rooting medium and destroy infected plants. Several rots which infect cuttings are avoided by above precautions. Bacterial leaf spot and botrytis blossom blight develop in cool, damp conditions. In greenhouse, better spacing and careful watering are advised. Experimental sprays of antibiotics have been promising.

Overwatering and high humidity may cause oedema, resulting in small, corky growths on the leaves.

x limoneum 2′ Zone 10 Lemon Pelargonium
With purple and lilac flowers and lemon-scented leaves.

odoratissimum 1½′   Zone 10   Nutmeg Pelargonium
Aromatic leaves an inch wide, white to whitish flowers in 5–10-flowered umbels. The stems are weak and spreading.

peltatum trailing Zone 10 Ivy Geranium
A very popular vinelike or trailing Geranium, used particularly in window boxes and hanging baskets. The leaves are usually glossy, ivy shaped and 5-lobed. If conditions are not too dry they may bloom continually from late winter to early fall. The trailing branches can be up to 4 ft. long. The flowers are white to deep rose, the upper petals with dark markings. The following are only a few of many varieties, but these are supposed to be profuse blooming: **'Charles Monselet'**—red; **'Charles Turner'**—rose pink; **'Comtesse Degrey'**—salmon pink; **'Giant Lavender'**—lavender with red markings; **'Jeanne d'Arc'**—lavender with dark stripes; **'L'Elegante'**—variegated foliage and pink flowers.

quercifolium 4′ Zone 10 Oakleaf Geranium
Somewhat shrubby, free-blooming, with leaves pinnately lobed, having purple veins and shaped somewhat like oak leaves; flowers rosy purple with purple markings on upper petals, in 3–7-flowered clusters. Native to South Africa.

tomentosum 3′–5′ Zone 10 Woolly Pelargonium
With long-stalked, peppermint-scented leaves, densely hairy on both sides and velvety to the touch, 3–5 lobed and 3–4 in. wide. Flowers small and white, in 4–20-flowered clusters. More or less shrubby in habit.

PELLAEA (pell-EE-a)

atropurpurea 1′ Zone 3 Purple Cliff-brake
A small fern found native to North America in rocky areas, with its leathery, tufted fronds a foot long and 6 in. wide. Either pinnate or bipinnate, the pinnae, about 2 in. long and ⅜ in. wide, are set opposite and at right angles to the black-brown tomentose stalks. This can be planted in the fern garden. Propagation by spores and division. See FERNS.

falcata 1½′ Zone 10 Australian Cliff-brake
The leathery fronds of this Australian fern are

3 in. wide and only 1 pinnate, the pinnae being about 2 in. long. It is only for use in the greenhouse and usually is not over 6 in. tall. Propagation by division and spores. See FERNS.

rotundifolia 1′ Zone 10 New Zealand Cliff-brake
A low, tender fern for the greenhouse only. Native to New Zealand. Fronds about 1 ft. long and 1½ in. wide, 1 pinnate, the pinnae rounded and about ¾ in. across. Propagation is by division or spores. See FERNS.

viridis 2′ Zone 10 Green Cliff-brake
A fern for the greenhouse from Africa. The fronds are 2 and 3 pinnate, rather stiff. Propagation by division and spores. See FERNS.

PELLIONIA (pell-i-O-nia)
pulchra creeping Zone 10
A creeping perennial with purple fleshy stems; alternate leaves with the veins black on the upper side of the leaves, purplish on the underside. Native to Indo-China. Often planted in a hanging basket in the greenhouse.

PELTANDRA (pel-TAN-dra)
virginica 12″ Zone 4 Virginia Arrow-arum
A monoecious perennial easily colonized in bog gardens or at the edge of a shallow pool; native to the eastern U.S.; its flower a spathe. The bright green, arrow-shaped leaves are 4–30 in. long and the fruit is green and berrylike. Grown chiefly for its attractive leaves. Propagated by division in the spring. It can become invasive.

PELTATE. Shield shaped; attached to its stalk inside the margin, like the leaf of Nasturtium (*Tropaeolum*).

PELTIPHYLLUM (pel-ti-FILL-um)
peltatum 4′ Zone 5 Umbrella-plant
This perennial herb is a bog plant, formerly termed *Saxifraga peltata*; native to Ore. and Calif. but sometimes planted beside pools or streams in the eastern U.S. Its basal leaves are 2 ft. across, 9–15 lobed, with petioles often 3 ft. long. Flowers are ½ in. across, white to pinkish and numerous, borne in terminal clusters usually in April before the leaves appear. Propagated by division.

PELTOPHORUM (pel-TOFF-or-um)
inerme = *P. pterocarpum*
pterocarpum (*P. inerene*) 50′ Zone 10 Sogabark Peltophorum
Native to Malaya, the large, fernlike, evergreen leaves of this tree are doubly compound. The bright yellow flowers are of somewhat the same shape as those of the closely related Royal Poinciana (*Delonix regia*) and are produced in large triangular clusters. These develop into masses of reddish-brown pods, 2–3 in. long, remaining on the tree a long time.

PENNINERVED. Nerves arising along a central midrib.

PENNISETUM (pen-i-SEE-tum)
setaceum (*ruppelia*) 4′ Zone 7 Fountain grass
A perennial ornamental grass from Abyssinia, with narrow leaves ⅛ in. or less broad, and gracefully arching and curved, bristly fruit heads, sometimes a foot long. These are colored variously rose to copper in certain cultivated forms. Easily propagated, but to keep the colored forms intact these are best propagated by root division and, to survive, the roots should not be subject to freezing. In the North, if seeds are started early enough, this grass might be treated as an annual.

PENNYCRESS. See THLASPI.

PENNYROYAL = *Mentha pulegium*

PENNYROYAL, AMERICAN = *Hedeoma pulegioides*

PENSTEMON (pen-STEE-mon).
Mostly native American wild flowers especially of the Midwest and Rocky Mountain states; herbaceous perennials or shrubs, with opposite or whorled leaves and brightly colored, 2-lipped tubular flowers in terminal racemes during the summer. They do best in full sun, but they need some moisture. Although the following species might be expected to succeed in the northeastern U.S., if one relied on zones of hardiness, actually many do not grow well outside their native habitats. They grow well in a moist atmosphere, preferably in full sun or light shade. The drainage should be good and they should have plenty of water. Usually propagated by seed sown in the late summer, sometimes by cuttings taken in midsummer and occasionally by division of plants in the early spring. There is considerable confusion in identification and nomenclature among these plants at present.

alpinus 1′ Zone 4 Alpine Penstemon
A perennial, with tufts of lanceolate leaves 4 in. long, bearing spikes of purple flowers on stems 10 in. high, blooming in early summer. Native to the Rocky Mountains.

azureus 3′ Zone 8 Azure Penstemon
Flowers blue to violet, 1½ in. wide. Native to Calif.

barbatus 3′–6′ Zones 2–3 Bearlip Penstemon
Native from Utah to Mexico, the flowers are red, an inch wide and very definitely 2-lipped, with the lower lip bearded. The linear leaves are slender and the flowers are borne in thin spires. 'Rose Elf' has been recommended as an excellent trouble-free cultivar, about 2½ ft. tall, with deep rose flowers from June to Aug. It should be planted in the full sun. The var. **torreyi** has larger flowers than the species.

barrettiae 1′ Zone 7 Barrett Penstemon
A perennial with lilac-purple flowers 1½ in.

long; leaves glaucous, thick and leathery, up to 3 in. long. Native to Ore.

caespitosus decumbent   **Zone 3**   **Mat Penstemon**
A small evergreen subshrub, with slender sprawling stems and tiny ovate leaves narrowed at the base. The lilac flowers, ¾ in. long, are borne in racemes in early summer. A fine, mat-like plant, seldom attaining a height of more than 2 in. Native to Wyo. and Colo.

cobaea   **2′**   **Zone 5**   **Cobaea Penstemon**
With about the largest flowers of any of these species (about 2 in. wide), usually purple with lavender and white variations, borne during mid-July on 2-ft.-flower stems; '**Ozark**' is an excellent deep purple. Native from Mo. to Tex.

crandallii 8″ Zones 3–4 Crandall Penstemon
Native to the mountains of Colo., this forms a dense evergreen mat of foliage with bright blue or lilac flowers in June. This withstands drought well but needs good drainage.

cyananthus   **3′**   **Zones 3–4**   **Wasatch Penstemon**
The leaves are ¾–3-in. wide; flowers in dense spikes, bright blue; each flower an inch long. Native to the mountains of Utah, Idaho and Wyo.

davidsonii prostrate   **Zone 6**   **Davidson Penstemon**
With trailing stems and dark green, orbicular leaves, this plant quickly makes a dense mat producing quite large, deep blue to purple flowers, 1½ in. long, in early summer and flowering sporadically throughout the remainder of the season. Native from Calif. to Wash. The var. **menziesii** (formerly *P. menziesii*) is about 6 in. high with leathery, dark, evergreen leaves about ¾ in. long and bears large, trumpet-shaped purple flowers an inch long in May and June. It makes an excellent wall plant.

digitalis   **3″–5″**   **Zone 3**   **White Penstemon**
An erect perennial herb having purplish stems and many basal leaves. The stem leaves are opposite, 4–6 in. long, the bases rounded, the narrowing margins either toothed or entire.The flowers, solitary or several on stalks 1 in. long, are borne in a loose terminal cluster. These are tubular, dilated, 1 in. long, and may be white or pink. The plants are native to the Mississippi Valley, but now extend south to Tex., and north to Quebec. The flowers appear in early summer. It is an attractive plant for the wild garden and may be propagated by seed sown in fall or early spring or by division of the plant in spring.

fruticosus   **3′**   **Zone 4**   **Bush Penstemon**
A shrub or woody herb with inch-long leaves and purple flowers an inch long. Native to Idaho, Wash. and Alberta. The var. **scouleri** is only 10–18 in. high with leaves nearly 2 in. long.

x gloxinioides   **2′**   **Zones 6–7**   **Gloxinia Penstemon**
Hybrid between *P. hartwigii* x *P. cobaea*, this produces wonderful 2-in. flowers with rich red and pink colors throughout the summer. Unfortunately the plants will not withstand hard winters and so might best be transferred to cold frames over winter for protection where necessary. '**Garnet**', '**Ruby King**' and '**Firebird**' are colorful red clones raised in greenhouses or by florists on the West Coast, of course propagated annually by cuttings.

gracilis   **16″**   **Zone 3**   **Slender Penstemon**
Flowers lilac to whitish and ¾ in. long; linear-lanceolate leaves about 3 in. long. Native from Manitoba to N.Mex.

grandiflorus   **3″–4″**   **Zone 3**   **Shell-leaf Penstemon**
A smooth plant with a pale, bluish bloom; the opposite leaves clasp the stem which rises from a small basal rosette. The long-stalked, terminally produced, lavender flowers appear in mid-summer. The dry midwestern prairies are the habitat of this plant which is ideal for sunny gardens. Although a perennial, it is very short-lived and is best cultivated as a biennial, with new plants annually from seed. Native from Ill. to Wyo.

hartwegii   **2½′**   **Zone 9**   **Hartweg Penstemon**
Native to Mexico, with slightly curved, scarlet flowers, each 2 in. long.

heterophyllus   **5′**   **Zone 8**   **Chaparral Penstemon**
Native to Calif.; not hardy in the East; flowers blue to purple, 1¼ in. long, with linear leaves about 1½ in. long.

hirsutus   **1″–3″**   **Zone 3**   **Hairy Beardtongue**
A perennial with hairy stems, opposite, tapering leaves and irregular flowers in a terminal cluster. Each flower has a corolla tube 1 in. long, dilate at the end, and with the upper and lower lips found in this group. It grows in dry, rocky sites from northeastern U.S. to the mid-South and extends to the Midwest. It blooms in June and July. A fine plant for cultivation, it may be propagated easily by seeds, cuttings or by division.

menziesii = *P. davidsonii menziesii*

murrayanus   **3′**   **Zone 6**   **Cutleaf Penstemon**
Native to Ark. and Tenn., with brilliant scarlet flowers and bluish foliage, the leaves up to 4 in. long. This also needs winter protection in areas where winters are very cold.

nitidus   **1′**   **Zone 3**
A small tufted perennial with smooth, narrow leaves, 6 in. long, and bright blue flowers, ¾ in. long, in loose spikes in midsummer. Native from Wyo. to Alberta and Wash.

ovatus   **4′**   **Zone 3**   **Eggleaf Penstemon**
More or less of a biennial; native from Ore. to

British Columbia, but it is only of value for naturalizing. The lavender flowers are small, about ¾ in. long, sometimes with a touch of blue or pink. The autumn color is reddish.

palmeri   3′   Zone 5   Palmer Penstemon
Blooming in June and July with large pink and white flowers on stems 4 ft. long, it is native to Utah, Ariz. and Colo.

procerus tolmiei   9″   Zone 7   Tolmie Penstemon
A tufted perennial with entire, lanceolate leaves and woody roots; flowers reddish, ½ in. long, in dense racemes. Native to Wash.

rupicola   4″   Zone 7   Cliff Penstemon
Decumbent shrub with glaucous leaves, ½ in. long, and rose-crimson flowers 1½ in. long. Native to Wash.

scouleri = *P. fruticosus scouleri*

spectabilis   6′   Zone 7   Showy Penstemon
Another species native to Ariz. and Colo., with rose-purple or lilac flowers about an inch long and leaves up to 3½ in. long.

tolmiei = *P. procerus tolmiei*
torreyi = *P. barbatus torreyi*

unilateralis   2′   Zone 3   Oneside Penstemon
During May and June the bright blue flowers of this species appear on 2-ft. stems, often in 1-sided spikes. The leaves are 4 in. long, the individual flowers but ¾ in. long. Native to Wyo.

PENTAS (pen-TAS)

lanceolata   18″   Zone 10   Egyptian Star-clusters
A compact subshrub, native to tropical Africa and Arabia, used sometimes as a plant in the home greenhouse, with a habit somewhat like that of Bouvardia. The opposite leaves are 1–6 in. long, ⅓ as wide, lanceolate and bright green; the pale purple flowers are borne in large corymbs. There is a white and a rose-flowered variety.

PEONY. See PAEONIA.

PEONY, TREE = *Paeonia suffruticosa*

PEPEROMIA (pep-er-O-mia). Succulent, tropical herbs, often semi-climbing, making excellent house plants. The flowers are minute, bisexual and of no ornamental significance but the slender spikes are certainly noticeable. They need warmth and plenty of moisture. Easily propagated by stem cuttings and leaf cuttings.

Diseases

Root rot is often due to careless overwatering. Corky scab causes corky raised swellings on underside of leaves which resembles oedema.

argyreia (*sandersii*)   **procumbent   Zone 10   Sander's Peperomia**
This plant is stemless with leaves ovate, 5 in. long, often split at the base; stems are dark red and flower spikes 4 in. long. The var. **argyreia** is very popular and has leaves lighter colored

between the veins. This is sometimes listed as the species and *sandersii* a synonym of it.

nummularifolia = *P. rotundifolia*

obtusifolia   prostrate   Zone 10   Oval-leaf Peperomia
A popular pot plant with wrinkled, reddish stems rooting at the joints; alternate fleshy leaves, oblanceolate, 4 in. long and 2½ in. wide, notched at the tip and with a light red margin. Supposedly there is a variegated form of this which florists offer with cream-colored markings on the leaves.

rotundifolia (*P. nummularifolia*)   **procumbent   Zone 10   Coin-leaf Peperomia**
Leaves only about ¼ in. long, orbicular; flower spikes ¾ in. long. The stems root at the nodes.

PEPO. A hard-rinded berry of the Gourd Family such as Pumpkin, Squash, etc.

PEPPER, BLACK = *Piper nigruum*

PEPPER, BUSH RED = *Capsicum annuum*

PEPPER, CELEBES = *Piper ornatum*

PEPPER FAMILY = Piperaceae

PEPPER, GARDEN (*Capsicum annuum*), is of American origin and most probably Central and South America. *Capsicum* is a genus of the Nightshade Family and is closely related to the Tomato, Eggplant, Potato and Tobacco. This crop is widely cultivated in all sections of the U.S.

Varieties

Peppers are divided into 2 major groupings based on pungency. Hot peppers are used primarily as flavorings and in sauces. They include 'Large Red Cherry' and 'Long Red Cayenne', long conical fruits, very hot or pungent. Mild or sweet varieties used for stuffing, flavoring or slicing in salads include many hybrid varieties selected for disease resistance or improved production such as 'Lady Bell', 'Green Boy' and 'Gypsy Hybrid'. Standard varieties include, 'Cubanelle', 'California Wonder' types, 'Pimiento', 'New Ice Hybrid' and 'Gideon Hybrid'.

Culture

Climatic conditions at the time of flower development have a marked effect on fruit set. Periods of high temperature and low humidity as well as temperatures below 55° F. cause blossoms to abort and drop off. A low moisture supply or excessive nitrogen in the fertilizer may cause similar results. Soils, soil preparation and general cultural conditions are similar to those for tomatoes and eggplants. In growing early plants only one transplanting from the seed flat is necessary. In the South seed can be planted out-of-doors in seed rows and the seedlings are then transplanted to their permanent location in the garden. Slightly less fertilizer is used for peppers than for tomatoes, and side dressings with nitrogen should be used only if a period of wet weather has leached out the nitrogen from the complete fertilizer applied at the time of plant setting. Planting distance for most varieties is 18 in. between plants and 24–30 in. between rows.

Peppers are usually harvested when mature in size but still green in color. All of the varieties listed other than Hungarian Wax will turn to a scarlet red in color when fully ripe.

GRANT B. SNYDER

Insect Pests

Garden peppers are infested with the same aphids and flea beetles which attack tomato and are controlled by insecticide #15, #9 or #47. European corn borer and common stalk borer hollow out the stems and are controlled by timely sprays or dusts with insecticide #9 or #37. Pepper maggot which develops from a yellow-striped fly infests the fruit, causing decay. Several white maggots, $\frac{1}{2}$ in. long, may live in each fruit. Dusting or spraying at weekly intervals, beginning when the fruit is $\frac{1}{2}$ in. in dia., with insecticide #21 or #15 to control the flies is suggested. In the South and West, pepper weevil causes buds and small pods to fall and the matured fruits to be misshapen. Spraying or dusting with insecticide #13 or #15 is recommended. Leaf miners are also troublesome in the South and applications of insecticide #13 are advised.

Diseases

Bacterial spot on both leaves and fruit causes defoliation and decay on the fruit. The disease is seed borne and also lives in the soil. Control recommendations include seed disinfection by a soak in fungicide #F followed by protection with fungicide #F or #P, field applications of spray or dust with fungicide #G or #K and rotation. Several leaf spots and blights are destructive in the South where careful destruction of plant refuse, rotation and spraying with fungicide #G are advised. Anthracnose and ripe rot cause decay on fruits. They are controlled by seed treatment and applications of fungicide #G. Tobacco mosaic, cucumber mosaic and curly top are viruses which spot and curl pepper leaves and fruit. They are spread by aphids and leafhoppers which must be controlled and by slight wounds from working around the plants. Tobacco mosaic may be transmitted from smoking tobacco.

Physiological diseases such as blossom end rot and sun scald damage pepper fruits. See TOMATO.

PEPPER-GRASS = *Lepidium virginicum*

PEPPERMINT = *Mentha piperita*

PEPPERMINT-TREE = *Agonis flexuosa*

PEPPERTREE. See SCHINUS.

PEPPERVINE = *Ampelopsis arborea*

PEPPERWEED, GARDEN CRESS = *Lepidium sativum*

PEREGRINA = *Jatropha hastata*

PERENNIAL. Of 3 or more seasons duration.

PERENNIALS. Popularly speaking, these are considered mostly herbaceous plants living in the garden more than 3 years. Actually, bulbs and ferns might be included but usually these are considered in their own categories and, although they are planted in the same garden with herbaceous plants, it is the herbaceous plants that are generally termed "perennials."

There are literally hundreds of perennials from which the gardener can choose, but before this is done it is well to first consider the garden as a whole, what is wanted with perennials, and the problems, if any, connected with growing them. Annuals and biennials create more garden work because they must be sown each year or every other year, either set out singly in the garden or thinned out where the seeds have been sown. Perennials, on the other hand, come up every year, mostly with a minimum amount of attention, and although certain ones create work because they must be divided every so often, or sprayed for insects or diseases, a fine collection of "low maintenance" types can be selected which need no particular care.

Perennials, if properly selected, will bring bloom to the garden from earliest spring until frost in the fall. They supply cut flowers for the home throughout this lengthy season and, when planted together in a border or bed, provide color in the garden a great deal of the time, and most gardeners want to grow them.

They need not be planted in a bed by themselves, but might well be interspersed with bulbs of many kinds, which of course bring the earliest bloom to the garden. Small, low, deciduous and evergreen shrubs also are ideal for including display, form, foliage and even color in the "flower" border when all the bulbs and perennials have died down for the winter. Such a border need not be a hodgepodge of everything but can be intelligently planted to supply interest and color the year around.

Years ago, when large estates were in vogue and it was possible to hire the help to care for them, it was the fad to plant a "blue" garden or a "white" garden in which all the flowers were

1 color. This still can be done but in most gardens where space is a very limiting factor, and garden care is to be restricted to a minimum, the newer concept of planting a little of many things in the so-called "perennial" border seems to be the most popular.

Space can even be found for annuals in such a border, for these bring colorful bloom to the garden in the summer when many perennials and most bulbs are through blooming. There always will be plants that, for some reason or other, fail to live over winter, and if annuals are wanted, there is always space for planting some every spring.

Choosing a Site

The bed or border for perennials might well be in the full sunshine and not in the shade. More plants can be grown in the full sun, but if it must be in a shaded area then only special plants should be selected which will grow and bloom well in the shade. If possible the border should face south, for with this exposure, full sunshine is assured. The border can be anywhere from 6–12 ft. wide, depending on the space available and what is to be grown. The narrow border would not allow space for tall perennials, the reason why the width of 12 ft. or more is often used because this allows for all types of perennials, but many an interesting perennial border is less than 12 ft. wide.

Often the border is not observed from both sides, but has a background of shrubs or trees or fence, either rustic and beautiful of itself, or else covered with vines. In any event the site should be one where high winds do not break the taller plants. Especially should it be done with good soil, and water should be available for use during summer droughts.

Planning

Winter and very early spring are the times when planning is done, for then the seed and nursery catalogues vividly display the many plants available. Supposing the site and dimensions of the bed have been chosen, then comes the extremely interesting time of selecting the species and varieties to be used, As in every garden, personal preferences come first and one should make a list of those plants to be selected for this reason.

Then size, habit, color of flower, time of bloom all enter into the planning. Those who are particularly color conscious must not have varieties growing side by side the flower colors of which clash. If there is a wet spot in the land, special species should be selected for growing there. Spots that are shaded or are known to have dry soil also need special plants selected for them.

The best way to select plants might be to make a list of the species and varieties wanted, their respective heights, color of the flowers and when they bloom. Taller types should be placed at the rear of the border (if it is to be observed from one side only) or in the center (if it is to be observed from both sides) and of course the lowest types should be along the edges. A general plan should be drawn on paper, to make certain all objectives are properly considered.

A large plan, drawn to scale, can be mapped out on paper. Cut-outs can be made, and on each the species or variety, its flower color or height, with the cut-out of sufficient size to include the number of plants wanted. Then these cut-outs can be superimposed on the overall plan, moved about at will, in an effort to visualize the end results. When this is done satisfactorily the final plan is made, showing the names of the plants, the varieties, color and area that each group will properly require. Such planning may be time-consuming but it will enable the gardener to visualize the plant combinations before serious mistakes are made.

Usually it is best to plant 3 or more plants of a kind as a group, the idea being that 1 or 2 might die or be heaved out of the soil during the first winter. A garden might not be very interesting if there were a dozen plants of every species selected, so the number selected should be varied. A few plants (3 or 4) of tall types like the sunflowers or delphiniums, and a dozen or more of the small types like some of the pinks and bellflowers, with possibly 6–8 chrysanthemums, phlox or asters in a group give some idea of numbers for which to plan. These should of course be spaced at different intervals, ranging from 1–4 ft. depending on the mature size of the plant in question.

An excellent book on this subject which might be consulted is "All About the Perennial Garden," by Free, Montague, published by Doubleday & Co., Inc., 1954. Also a later one "Contemporary Perennials" by Roderick W. Cumming and Robert E. Lee, published by the Macmillan Co., in 1960. Suggested plans are given in these books which make initial planning more easy.

Do not forget bulbs which add a great interest early in the spring (see BULBS) and also some of the dwarf woody plants, both deciduous and evergreen, for late fall and winter interest. Some of these which will grow 5–6 ft. tall, like the Japanese Andromeda (*Pieris japonica*); low evergreen barberries or Box, Compact Hinoki False Cypress (*Chamaecyparis obtusa* 'Compacta') and others, are interesting in the perennial border all year long. A very few with yellow or bluish foliage are definitely added attractions. See EVERGREENS, LOW and DWARF.

Seed vs. Plants

Perennials can be started from seed, and there are nurseries selling small seedling plants, but in general, there are so many modern varieties which have been developed for their large or unusually colorful flowers, that it would seem unwise to start with too many seedlings. Many of these good varieties are propagated only asexually, by division of the plants themselves or by root or stem cuttings, and such plants should be bought and planted initially. Seedlings of some of the old-fashioned species might be purchased, but, in general, it is best to start with plants.

Many nurserymen display perennials in long beds or frames in the early spring and a number can be purchased already in flower. In this way, the young gardener who is planting perennials for the first time can actually see the color, size and shape of the flowers at the time they are purchased. It is always possible to increase these plants after 1 or 2 full seasons of growth, usually by simple division.

Preparing the Soil

The better the fertility of the soil at planting time the greater success one will have with the perennial garden. Organic matter might well be worked into the soil before any planting is done. See SOILS. However, it may be inadvisable to make a heavy application of commercial fertilizer at the time of initial planting because this might be too strong for young plants. See FERTILIZERS. It is best to make only a light application at the start, and then to fertilize as needed later in the growing season. A suggested application, after decayed vegetable matter has been thoroughly worked into the soil, would be 2 lbs. of bone meal and 3 lbs. of ground lime per 100 sq. ft.

Planting

The plan drawn out on paper should be carefully adhered to in planting, for on it should be carefully marked the number of plants to be used for each area. With freshly dug plants ready to go in and prepared soil all waiting, this is no time to go back to the references and decide how far apart each set of plants should be spaced. If it is worked out in advance on the plan, then labels can be made in advance with the name and number of the plants decided upon clearly written on the label. The area set aside for each group of plants can be clearly marked on the ground with a stick and the label placed in the center. Then it is simply a matter of spacing the plants in the allotted area. They should be carefully planted in wide holes at exactly the same depth as they were in the nursery or pots. The roots should never be jammed into small holes. Soil should be firmed about them and when the job is completed, the entire planting should be thoroughly watered. If a mulch has been decided upon, this is the time to apply it, not over an inch or two deep, the idea being to reduce weed growth and aid the soil in retaining the moisture provided.

The time to plant depends on the area and the plant. In the North, spring planting of many things is more successful than fall planting, especially if it is done as early in the spring as the ground can be worked properly. Early fall planting is possible in many parts of the country, for in planting in Sept. the roots have many weeks to grow before they become dormant. However, planting perennials late in the fall is not advisable, especially in the North, for the roots will not have sufficient time to "take hold" properly before the ground freezes, and the alternate freezing and thawing of the soil during late winter may be responsible for heaving (which see), that is the actual pushing of the young plants out of the soil.

Many bulbs like narcissus, scillas, crocuses and lilies are best planted in the fall. On the other hand certain fleshy-rooted plants like the oriental poppies and *Gypsophila* species are best planted in the spring.

Fall is the time when many perennials are divided in the garden, a process usually done with a spade to divide large clumps into smaller ones. When moving parts of well-established plants from one part of the garden to another, if done early in the fall, no serious injury should occur. Division can also be done early in the spring if done carefully. However, sometimes it may be difficult to find certain plants before they start growth, and if there are young shoots already growing, one must be extremely careful not to injure them in the dividing operation.

General Culture

Weeding is a necessary operation that must be done in every garden. It may be materially reduced by proper mulching (which see). In our garden we have used many different mulching materials successfully but because it is in the area where the White Pine is native, pine needles have been the cheapest mulch. These are put about the plants, about 2 in. deep in the fall (aiding at that time as winter protection against heaving) and left intact. Some years no additional mulch seems to be needed. Every few years ground limestone is applied to counteract the acid quality of the ever-decomposing pine needles. See LIME. It has worked effectively for 20 years. It must be admitted that undoubtedly some lime-requiring plants may disappear because of this often haphazard method, but still, in raising the water retention of the soil, and in reducing general weed growth it is well worth the effort. Any type of mulch (which does not contain weed seeds) is helpful in this respect.

Watering is sometimes necessary during drought periods but many gardeners might be warned against over-watering. Certainly added water makes the plants grow during drought periods, but when once started it must be continued. See WATERING.

Spraying is sometimes necessary to control insect and disease pests. See PESTS, as well as notes on insect and disease pests under many of the major plant headings. It must be said that some plants are more susceptible to pests than others. The iris borer is most troublesome on Iris and requires special treatment. Sometimes plant lice are absolutely obnoxious on certain plants like lupines. These require special treatment and timely spraying. The other alternative is not to plant those species so affected. There are so many perennials available that the absence of a few beleaguered by specific pests is often not noticed, unless of course they happen to be the prized specimens of the gardener. Then he will have to take the trouble to control such pests.

Staking of lilies, delphiniums and other tall plants is often necessary to prevent undue breakage in summer storms. Bamboo stakes, or metal stakes are available in several sizes and should be used where necessary. See STAKING.

Checking the plants occasionally for pests, and especially checking the garden in general in the early spring to note any heaving or rodent injury to plants during the winter, is necessary. One year we saved several hundred grape-hyacinth bulbs which had been dug by some rodent from all parts of the garden and stored in a pile under an old Juniper for future use. They were replanted without too much loss merely because the problem was noted early in the spring. Many young plants are heaved out of the soil in late winter and if reset early enough they can be saved.

Fertilizing

The best types of fertilizers are organic. See

SOILS, FERTILIZERS. These should be applied as directed on the containers in which they come. A complete fertilizer (5-10-5) might be applied at the rate of 5 lbs. per 100 sq. ft. of flower border after the plants are fully established, preferably in the early spring before growth has started. Occasionally a second and possibly lighter application might be made, especially if the plants have shown a need for it during the previous growing season. However, it is not advisable to make recommendations for all situations, but one should read thoroughly the recommendations that come on the bag, for fertilizers vary greatly in strength and content.

Fall is the time for a general clean-up, cutting off the dead tops of plants and removing the leaves and refuse on the ground (on top of the mulch) to prevent insects and diseases from living over winter in or on such material until the following spring. A few prized specimens may have to be specially protected for the winter, and late fall is the time to do it. When all herbaceous material has died, been cut off at the ground level and removed, it is then that the dwarf woody plants, especially the ever-greens, are appreciated. Some of these have been partially hidden throughout the summer by tall-growing perennials, but at this time they are outstanding in their form and foliage for the entire winter. More of such plants should be used in perennial borders.

The following perennials are only a few of those described in this volume. They are listed here for quick reference, with the height, Hardiness Zone, time of bloom, need for moist or dry soil, value as a cut flower, flower color and common name. Those listed as not needing a moist or dry soil are usually tolerant of both, although they do best of course in a normal soil, neither very moist nor very dry. Those listed with a C have lasting qualities as cut flowers.

There are many other good perennials, and often several to many varieties of those listed. The list should be studied especially for hardiness, height, time of bloom and color of flower when planning the new flower border.

SOME OF THE MORE COMMON PERENNIALS

D = tolerant of or even requiring dry soil; M = tolerant of or even requiring moist to wet soil. In the flower color column: B = blue; O = orange; P = purple; R = red; W = white; Y = yellow.

SCIENTIFIC NAME	HT.	HARDI-NESS ZONE	TIME OF BLOOM	MOIST OR DRY SOIL	CUTT.	FLOWER COLOR	COMMON NAME
Achillea millefolium rosea	6″–2′	2	July–Sept.	D		pink	Pink Yarrow
A. ptarmica	2′	2–3	July–Aug.	D		W	Sneezewort
Aconitum carmichaelii	6′	2–3	Sept.		C	B-W	Azure Monkshood
A. napellus	4′	2–3	July–Aug.		C	B	Aconite Monkshood
Ajuga genevensis	6″–9″	2–3	May–June			B	Geneva Bugle
A. reptans	4″–12″	2–3	May–June			B, W, P	Carpet Bugle

SCIENTIFIC NAME	HT.	HARDI-NESS ZONE	TIME OF BLOOM	MOIST OR DRY SOIL	CUTT.	FLOWER COLOR	COMMON NAME
Amsonia tabernaemontana	3½'	4	May–June			B	Willow Amsonia
Anchusa azurea	3'–5'	3	June–July		C	B	Italian Bugloss
Anemone pulsatilla	1'	5	April			B–R	European Pasqueflower
Anthemis tinctoria	3'	3	July–Aug.	D	C	Y	Golden Marguerite
Aquilegia candensis	1'–2'	2–3	May–July		C	Y–R	American Columbine
Arabis caucasica	4"–10"	6	April–May		C	W	Caucasian Rock-cress
Armeria maritima	6"–12"	3	May–June	D	C	pink	Common Thrift
Artemisia lactiflora	4'–5'	3	Aug.–Oct.		C	W	White Mugwort
A. schmidtiana 'Nana'	4"	2–3	Aug.–Oct.	D		W	Silver-mound Artemesia
A. stelleriana	2½"	2–3	Aug.–Oct.	D		Y	Beach Wormwood
Asclepias tuberosa	3'	3	Aug.–Sept.	D	C	O	Butterfly Milkweed
Aster x frikartii 'Wonder of Stafa'	1½'–2'	4	July–Nov.		C	B	—
A. novae-angliae	3'–5'	2–3	Aug.	M	C	pink-P	New England Aster
A. novi-belgii	3'–5'	2–3	Sept.–Oct.		C	W, pink, B, P	New York Aster
Astilbe x arendsii	2'–3½'	6	June–Aug.	M	C	pink-R	Hybrid Astilbe
A. japonica	2'	5	June	M	C	W	Japanese Astilbe
Aubretia deltoidea	3"–6"	4	April–June			R–P	Purple Rock-cress
Aurinia saxatilis	6"	3	April–May			Y	Golden-tuft
Baptisia australis	3'–4'	2–3	May–June		C	B	Blue Wild Indigo
Brunnera macrophylla	1½'–2'	3	May			B	Heartleaf Brunnera
Caltha palustris	1'–3'	3	April	M		Y	Marsh Marigold
Campanula carpatica	1'	3	July			B	Carpathian Bellflower
C. latifolia	3'	3	July			B	Great Bellflower
C. persicifolia	3'	3	July–Aug.	D	C	B, W	Peach-leaved Bellflower
Centaurea dealbata	2'	3	June–Sept.		C	R–W	Persian Centaurea
C. montana	2'	2–3	May–July			B	Mountain Bluet
Cerastium tomentosum	3"–6"	2–3	June	D	C	W	Snow-in-summer
Chelone lyonii	3'	3	July–Aug.			pink-P	Pink Turtle-head
Chrysanthemum coccineum	1'–3'	2–3	June–July		C	R, W	Painted Daisy
C. maximum	2'–4'	4	June–Oct.		C	W	Shasta Daisy
C. morifolium	2'–5'	5	Aug.–Oct.		C	W, R, pink, Y	Florists' Chrysanthemum
Cimicifuga racemosa	6'–8'	2–3	June–Sept.	M	C	W	Snakeroot
Convallaria majalis	8"	2–3	May–June	D	C	W	Lily-of-the-Valley
Coreopsis auriculata 'Nana'	6"	4	June–Aug.	D	C	Y	Dwarf Eared Coreopsis
C. lanceolata	2'	3	July–Aug.		C	Y	Lance Coreopsis
C. verticillata	2½'	6	July–Aug.		C	Y	Threadleaf Coreopsis
Delphinium cheilanthum	3'–4'	2–3	June–July		C	B–W	Garland Larkspur
D. elatum	4'–6'	2–3	June–July		C	P	Candle Larkspur
Dianthus barbatus	2'	2–3	July–Aug.		C	pink, R, W	Sweet William
D. deltoides	4"–15"	2–3	May, June		C	pink-W	Maiden Pink
D. plumarius	1½'	3	May, June	D	C	pink-W	Grass pink
Dicentra eximia	1'–2'	2–3	July		C	pink	Fringed Bleeding-heart
D. formosa	1'	2–3	May–Sept.		C	pink	Pacific Bleeding-heart
D. spectabilis	2'	2–3	May & June		C	pink	Common Bleeding-heart
Dictamnus albus	3'	2–3	July		C	W & P	Gas Plant
Digitalis purpurea	3'	4	June, July		C	W–P	Foxglove
Doronicum caucasicum	2'	4	May & June		C	Y	Caucasian Leopardsbane
Echinacea purpurea	3½'	3	July & Aug.	D	C	R–P	Purple Echinacea
Echinops ritro	1'–2'	3	July & Aug.	D	C	B	Small Globe-thistle
Epimedium sp.	1'	3	July & Aug.		C	Y–W–P	Bishop's hat
Eupatorium maculatum	6'–10'	2–3	Aug.	M		P	Joe-Pye-Weed
Euphorbia epithymoides	1'	4	July & Aug.	D		Y	Cushion Euphorbia
E. myrsinites	4"		April & May	D		Y	Myrtle Euphorbia
Filipendula vulgaris	3'	3	June, July			W, pink	Meadowsweet
Gaillardia aristata	2'–3'	2–3	July & Aug.	D	C	Y, R	Common Blanketflower
Galium odoratum	8"	4	May–June	M	C	W	Sweet Woodruff
Gypsophila paniculata	3'	2–3	July	D	C	W	Baby's-breath
G. repens rosea	18"	3	June–Aug.	D		pink	Rosy Creeping Gypso-phila
Helenium autumnale	6'	3	July, Aug.	M	C	Y	Common Sneezeweed
Helenium hoopesii	3'	3	May–Sept.	M	C	Y	Orange Sneezeweed
Helianthus tuberosus	12'	4	Aug. & Sept.	M	C	Y	Jerusalem Artichoke
Hemerocallis lilioasphodelus	3'	2–3	June	D		Y	Lemon Daylily
H. fulva	3'	2–3	July–Aug.	D		O–R	Tawny Daylily
Heuchera sanguinea	1'–2'	3	May–Sept.	M	C	R to pink	Coral-bells
Hibiscus moscheutos	3'–6'	5	Aug.–Sept.			Rose	Common Rose Mallow
Hosta ventricosa	3'	3	July–Aug.		C	B	Blue Plantain-lily
Iberis sempervirens	12"	3	April–May			W	Evergreen Candytuft
Iris germanica	24"–36"	4	June			P	German Iris
I. kaempferi	24"	4	June & July	M		W–R–B	Japanese Iris
I. sibirica	2'	3	June		C	P	Siberian Iris
Lavandula angustifolia	3'	5	June	D	C	P	True Lavender
Liatris scariosa	3'–4'	3	Aug.–Sept.		C	W–P	Tall Gayfeather
L. spicata	1'–6'	3	Sept.		C	P	Spike Gayfeather
Linum flavum	2'	5	June–Aug.	D		Y	Golden Flax
L. perenne	2'	4	June–Aug.	D		B	Perennial Flax
Lupinus	1'–8'	3–6	June		C	Y, B, W, pink, P	Lupine
Lychnis chalcedonica	3½'	3	June–July	D		R	Maltese Cross
L. coronaria	3'	2–3	June–July	D		R	Rose Campion
Lythrum salicaria	3'	3	June–Sept.	M	C	R–P	Purple Loosestrife
Macleaya cordata	6'–8'	3	July–Aug.		C	W–pink	Plume-poppy
Mertensia virginica	2'–3'	3	June–July	M		B	Virginia Bluebells
Monarda didyma	3'	4	June–Aug.	M	C	R	Bee-balm
Myosotis scorpioides	12"–20"	3	July–Aug.	M		B	True Forget-me-not

SCIENTIFIC NAME	HT.	HARDI-NESS ZONE	TIME OF BLOOM	MOIST OR DRY SOIL	CUTT.	FLOWER COLOR	COMMON NAME
Oenothera caespitosa	4'	5				pink	Twisted Sundrop
Paeonia officinalis	3'	3	May		C	W–P–R	Common Peony
Papaver orientale	2'–4'	2–3	May–June			W to R	Oriental Poppy
Penstemon barbatus	3'–6'	2–3	June–Aug.		C	R	Bearlip Penstemon
Phlox paniculata	2'–4'	4	June–Sept.			R, W, P	Garden Phlox
P. subulata	6"	2–3	Mar.–May			R–W, pink	Ground Pink
Physalis alkekengi	2'	2–3	Aug.			W (flw) R (fruit)	Chinese-lantern
Physostegia virginiana	4'	2–3	July, Aug.		C	pink	Virginia Lion's-heart
Platycodon grandiflorus	2½'	3	June, July, Sept.	D		W, B	Balloonflower
Primula japonica	2'	5	May	M	C	R, P, W, Y	Japanese Primrose
P. x polyantha	1'	3	May		C	R, P, W, Y	Polyantha Primrose
Ranunculus repens	2'	3	May–Aug.		C	Y	Creeping Buttercup
Rudbeckia hirta	3'	2–3	July, Aug.		C	Y	Black-eyed Susan
Salvia azurea grandiflora	3'–4'	4	Aug.–Sept.			B	Blue Sage
S. pratensis	3'	3	Aug.–Sept.			B, W	Meadow Sage
Scabiosa caucasica	1½'–2½'	2–3	July, Aug.		C	pink to lilac	Caucasian Scabiosa
Sedum spectabile	18"	3	Aug.			rosy pink	Showy Sedum
Stokesia laevis	2'	5	July–Oct.			blue-purplish	Stokesia
Tanacetum vulgare	3'	3	July, Aug.	D		Y	Common Tansy
Thalictrum aquilegifolium	2'–3'	2–3	May & June		C	W & rose	Columbine Meadow-rue
T. rochebrunianum	4'–6'	4	July–Sept.		C	Lavender violet	Lavender-mist
T. speciosissimum rugosum	3'–6'	5			C	Y	Dusty Meadow-rue
Thermopsis caroliniana	5'	3	June, July		C	Y	Carolina Thermopsis
Tradescantia virginica	1'–3'	4	July, Aug.			B, P	Virginia Spiderwort
Trollius europaeus	2'	4	May–Aug.	M	C	Y	Common Globeflower
T. ledebouri	2'	4	June–Aug.	M	C	Y	Ledebour Globeflower
Tunica saxifraga	10"	2–3	July & Aug.			pink–P	Saxifrage Tunicflower
Valeriana officinalis	4'	3	July, Aug.	M	C	W to lavender	Common Valerian
Veronica latifolia	2'	3	May–June			B	Hungarian Speedwell
V. longifolia	2½'	4	Summer		C		
V. spicata	1½'	3	June–Sept.		C	B	Spike Speedwell
Vinca minor	4"	4	Late April			B, W	Periwinkle
Viola cornuta	6"	6	July, Aug.		C	B	Tufted Pansy
V. odorata	8"	6	April, May		C	violet to W	Sweet Violet

PERESKIA (per-ESK-ia)

aculeata   vine Zone 10 Barbados-gooseberry
A tropical, vinelike cactus which can grow 10–20 ft. long with 2 or 3 axillary spines; thick, lanceolate, alternate leaves about 3 in long and white, yellow or pinkish flowers, 1–1¼ in. wide. This is a leaf-bearing cactus propagated by cuttings and native to tropical America. For culture see CACTI AND SUCCULENTS.

PERFECT FLOWER. Having both stamens and pistils; bisexual. See also IMPERFECT FLOWER.

PERIANTH. The floral envelope; commonly used when there is no clear distinction between calyx and corolla; as in the lilies.

PERICARP. The wall of the ripened ovary.

PERILLA (per-ILL-a)

frutescens   18"   annual   Common Perilla
This species is grown especially for its handsome foliage. The opposite leaves, 3–6 in. long, are slightly wrinkled, green on both sides but sometimes marked with reddish brown. The white to reddish flowers are borne in racemes, 3–8 flowers in a raceme.

The variety **crispa** is the most popular variety because of its excellent reddish-brown leaves which have a fine bronzy sheen. This is popular as a bedding plant or just for its colored foliage in the flower border. Native to India and Japan.

Seeds are sown outdoors in mid-April and transplanted at the end of May to where they are to be grown in the garden, preferably in full sun or at best a very light shade. If the variety is a particularly desirable one, cuttings may be taken in the late summer and the plants grown over winter in the greenhouse. The oil from pressed seeds of this plant is widely used in the U.S. as a drying oil for paint.

PERIPLOCA (per-i-PLO-ka)

graeca   twining shrub   Zone 6   Grecian Silkvine
A deciduous twining shrub with opposite leaves, 1½–4 in. long, dark green and glossy; greenish-yellow flowers about an inch across in 8–12-flowered clusters; seed pods in pairs, about 5 in. long. Native to southeastern Europe. The milky sap, if eaten, is poisonous. The leaves remain green late in the fall. Propagated by root division in the spring. **P. sepium** is similar but with smaller leaves and it is more hardy.

PERISTROPHE (per-ISS-tro-fee)

angustifolia = P. hyssopifolia

hyssopifolia   2'   annual   Java Peristophe
Weak stemmed, mostly grown as an annual; leaves 2–3 in. long and lance shaped, tapering at ends; flowers red. Native to India. The var. 'Aureo-variegata' is the one usually grown for its yellow variegated foliage. Native to Java.

speciosa   4'   Zone 10   India Peristrophe
Shrubby, with gray stems; leaves glossy green

and 5 in. long; flowers 2 in. long, twisted and tubular, deeply split, colored purple, blotched crimson, borne 2–3 together. Native to India; propagated by cuttings.

PERIWINKLE. See VINCA, CATHARANTHUS.

PERLITE. A silica derivative, about $\frac{1}{10}$th the weight of sand, now widely being used as an essential in making media for rooting cuttings. It is white and glasslike, and is often mixed with soil or peat moss or some other such material since it has no nutrient qualities whatsoever.

PERNETTYA (originally PERNETTIA) (per-NET-ia)

mucronata 1½′ **Zones 6–7 Chilean Pernettya**
This plant from Chile and Argentina has sometimes been termed the best plant for colorful fruits that is grown in America. Be that as it may, individual plants will not fruit well by themselves for, although the flowers are perfect, several clones or varieties must be grown together to insure cross-pollination and hence fruit production. The lustrous evergreen leaves, ¾ in. long, are excellent, but the bright-colored fruits, varying in color according to variety and each berry ½ in. across, are extremely effective against the evergreen foliage, throughout the fall and winter. If grown in full sun it will remain a neat compact plant, but if grown in the shade it may grow leggy and need corrective pruning. Some of the varieties offered for sale are: **'Alba'**—fruit white; **'Coccinea'**—fruit bright red; **'Lilacina'**—fruit lilac; **'Purpurea'**—fruit violet-purple; **'Rosea'**—fruit pink. Propagation is by seeds, softwood cuttings, layers and rooted suckers.

tasmanica creeping **Zone 7 Tasmanian Pernettya**
This plant is native to Tasmania, but will survive in temperate climates if given protection especially from winter winds. Wiry stems bearing tiny, bright green, pointed leaves, ⅛ in. long, grow to form a mat 3 in. high. The white flowers, growing singly on the plant, are followed by bright red berries.

PERSEA (PER-see-a)

americana 60′ **Zone 10 American Avocado**
The species, sometimes termed Alligator-pear, native to tropical America, is sometimes cultivated as the West Indian Avocado. The branches are many, leaves entire, alternate, 4–8 in. long. The flowers are greenish; the fruit green, pear shaped with 1 large seed. The variety **drymifolia** is the Mexican Avocado and the one so much cultivated in southern Calif. The skin of the fruit of this var. is thin and soft, whereas the skin of the species is thick. See AVOCADO. It is often interesting to grow a house plant out of the seed of this, taken from the fruit as purchased from the grocery store. Merely run a

skewer through the seed (which has been dried a few days) and put in a glass of water so that the skewer rests on the top of the glass and the bottom half of the seed will be in the water, the point of the seed down. When roots have been formed it can be planted in a flower pot and it will be a good house plant.

borbonia 30′–40′ **Zone 7 Red Bay**
An evergreen tree, the alternate 2–4-in. leaves of which are quite good for seasoning soups and savory dishes. It is native from southern Del. to Fla. in swamps. The flowers are not very interesting, but the blue or blue-black fruits, about ½ in. long on red stalks, are of interest against the evergreen foliage in the fall. It is a swamp tree not planted much.

indica 20′ **Zone 9 Madeirabay Persea**
An evergreen tree from the Azores and Canary Islands, with leathery oblong leaves, 4–6 in. long; flowers very small and produced in the leaf axils. Occasionally planted in southern Calif. and Fla. for its foliage.

PERSIMMON. See DIOSPYROS.

PERSIMMON FAMILY = Ebenaceae

PERSISTENT. Remaining attached, not falling off; opposite of deciduous.

PEST CONTROL. See FUNGICIDES, INSECTICIDES.

PEST-FREE PLANTS. Every busy gardener should reduce garden labor by planting as many pest-free plants as possible. It is wasteful of time and garden space to use plants which one knows in advance are continuously susceptible to serious disease and insect pests. Over 1000 attractive, low maintenance (pest-free) plants are listed in "The Saturday Morning Gardener" by Donald Wyman and published by the Macmillan Co. of N.Y. Those interested in using pest-free plants should consult this reference.

PESTICIDES. See INSECTICIDES.

PESTS. See INSECTS, DISEASES, ANIMAL PESTS, INSECTICIDES, FUNGICIDES, etc.

PESTS, ANIMAL. Small animals are often destructive garden pests and several wild species, especially squirrels, rabbits and raccoons, become amazingly well acclimated to suburban conditions.

Chipmunks

Although a welcome asset to garden interest, they eat bulbs and dig tunnels in the garden and lawn especially near walls and stumps. Pesticides such as diazinon dust with or without captan dusted on the bulbs and/or mixed with the soil protects them from destructive insects and diseases as well as from chipmunks and mice. Snap traps and live traps baited with nuts or shelled corn are effective.

Deer

Garden vegetables and shrubbery are often damaged by deer in rural areas. In winter they eat the buds and bark of apple trees. Repellent chemicals, especially carbamates such as z.i.p. and thiram give temporary protection as sprays, but where continued damage occurs only an 8 ft. chain link fence gives protection.

Dogs

In suburban areas, dogs may be both destructive and annoying. Commercial repellents containing pepper and similar offensive material are readily available and helpful. Valuable shrubs often need wire guards supplemented by a few well-placed sharpened points.

Gophers and Ground Squirrels

In the West, tunnels of these animals occasionally extend into gardens where vegetable seeds and plants are destroyed. The standard control is poison bait in the burrows using strychnine on chunks of vegetable, but this violent poison is restricted in many areas and local advice is desirable.

Mice

Field mice and pine mice are universal pests in the garden where they girdle trees and shrubs by eating the bark or roots. Bulbs are also eaten. Winter mulch encourages their activities. In small beds mouse traps can be used effectively. In larger areas a poisoned bait is advised. Mouse poisons are restricted in some states but zinc phosphide dusted on apple or grain as directed and placed in runways is generally approved. A mousing cat is often the only control necessary.

Moles

Although moles primarily eat soil-inhabiting insects and earthworms, they occasionally damage bulbs, and their winding tunnels just beneath the surface can ruin a choice lawn. The elimination of insects and earthworms with insecticides such as #13 as recommended to control Japanese beetle grubs discourages moles. Special choker or harpoon traps are available. Commercial baits usually consisting of poisoned peanuts are the simplest remedies for small infestations.

Rabbits

During the summer rabbits are very destructive to many vegetables, especially lettuce and carrots, and to a few ornamentals. Chemical repellents such as suggested to repel deer have considerable value but should not be used on food crops. The best protection is a fence of chicken wire about 30 in. high and extending 4–6 in. into the ground. In winter rabbits eat the bark with subsequent girdling of fruit trees, deciduous shade trees and shrubs. This injury is most common with heavy snow. Wire guards around the trunk are practical on trees. They should extend about 12 in. above the greatest snow depth. Chicken wire is satisfactory and $\frac{1}{4}$–$\frac{1}{2}$ in.-mesh hardware wire will protect against mice as well as rabbits. Chemical repellents as for deer give temporary protection but often need renewing in midwinter.

Raccoons and Opossums

In the North raccoons and in the South opossums show a strong preference for corn on the cob. They are nocturnal in habit and will ruin a large number of corn ears in one night, showing amazing skill in stripping the husk. They may also damage blackberries, raspberries and strawberries. Fences give no protection and shooting or trapping are the only effective remedies.

Rats

Although not an important garden pest, rats often eat melons, squash and other vegetables. They are most troublesome near an infested dump, barn or storage area. Control at the source with traps or rat poisons is advised but extensive infestations should be handled by a professional exterminator.

Squirrels

Squirrels are both entertaining and destructive. In the garden they damage sweet corn and eat the seeds from small pears and peaches. It is almost impossible to harvest filberts, walnuts or chestnuts in competition with squirrels, and they frequently are annoying and destructive in the attics of buildings. Live traps and shooting are effective control measures.

Woodchucks

These animals have a tremendous appetite for salad vegetables and can ruin a small home garden in a short time. They can be killed in their burrows if all entrances are closed by using phosphorus "bombs" which resemble fire crackers. Shooting or trapping is more practical in some areas. As a last resort fencing as described for rabbit control may be necessary, but the fencing must be deeply imbedded in the ground and topped with barbed wire.

WARREN D. WHITCOMB

PETAL. One of the separate members of the corolla.

PETALOID. Resembling a petal in shape or color.

PETALOSTEMON (pet-al-o-STEE-mon)

candidum   12″–18″   Zone 3   **White Prairie-clover**

The White Prairie Clover has alternate, compound leaves having 7–9 narrow leaflets, the margins of which curl upward when young. The terminal flower head bears tiny white flowers in a tight, oval-shaped cluster. The plant is native to the prairie lands of Canada and the U.S and blooms in midsummer.

purpureum   1′–3′   Zone 4   **Purple Prairie-clover**

A perennial with a straight, glandular-dotted stem, alternate, compound leaves with 5–7 linear leaflets and terminally produced, purple flowers in a tightly clustered, rounded flower head. It is a plant of the dry hillsides of the central states from Mich. to N.Mex. and flowers throughout the summer.

villosum   2′   Zone 4

This shrubby member of the Pea Family is native to the Plains states of the U.S. The finely divided, pubescent leaves grow to form loose mounds of attractive, silvery foliage. The purplish, pubescent flowers, densely borne on short spikes 4 in. long, appear in midsummer. It requires a loose, gravelly alkaline soil in sun.

PETASITES (pet-a-SY-tees)

japonicus   6′   Zone 4   **Japanese Butterbur**

A perennial herb not often planted for ornament except in rocky, poor soils where better plants will not grow. They can easily be propagated by seeds and root division. The rounded leaves are 3–4 ft. across. The whitish-purple flower heads are borne severally at the end of a flower stalk. Excellent for planting at the water edge for striking effects.

PETIOLE. Leaf-stalk.

PETIOLULE. Stalk of a leaflet.

PETREA (PET-rea)

volubilis   vine   Zone 10   **Sandpaper-vine**

A twining vine from tropical America which bears pendant racemes of deep purple flowers, each one having 15–30 flowers. The true flowers are in terminal clusters about 8 in. long. Each raceme is 7–8 in. long. The opposite, evergreen leaves are rough to the touch, giving rise to the common name. It is often considered a substitute for Wisteria in southern Fla. Propagation by cuttings and air layers.

PETROPHYTUM (pet-ROFF-fy-tum)

caespitosum   procumbent   Zone 3   **Tufted Rockmat**

A tiny plant with inch-long leaves forming dense mats, only an inch or two high but growing up to several feet wide. The stems are woody, spreading on or just under the surface of the soil, and the white flowers are densely borne on spikes up to 3 in. long. Native from S.Dak. to Calif. Propagated by seeds and division.

PETRORHAGIA (petro-RAG-ia)

saxifraga (*Tunica saxifraga*)   10″   Zones 2–3   **Tunicflower**

A hardy perennial with flower heads similar to those of *Dianthus* but smaller; tufted in growth habit with linear leaves up to ½ in. long. The flowers are pink to pale purple, ¼ in. wide, and bloom in summer. Native to Europe. There are selections of other colors sometimes available. The double-flowered 'Flore-plena' is more effective as a rock garden plant. Plant in full sun in well-drained soil. Propagated by division or by cuttings from non-flowering shoots any time during the growing season.

PETROSELINUM (pet-ro-sel-LY-num)

crispum = Parsley, which see.

PETUNIA (pet-YEW-nia)

x hybrida   6″–3′   annual   **Garden Petunia**

This is probably a hybrid of 2 species native to Argentina (*P. axillaris* x *violacea*), but the modern petunias available today as a result of much hybridization have flowers far superior in color and size to either of these species. Colors are in all parts of the spectrum and flower size ranges from 2–7 in.

Types

In any seed catalogue one can find a bewildering number of petunia varieties, varying in flower colors and heights. They mostly break down to these general groupings: **Dwarf**—the smallest of all, often under 12 in. high; **Mound**—16 in. high, with flowers 2–2½ in. across, the plants densely leaved and moundlike; **Bedding**—spreading plants 18–24 in. tall; flowers up to 3 in. across; **Giant Ruffled**—1½–2 ft. tall; flowers 5–7 in. across; the largest-flowered group of the lot; F_1 **Grandiflora**—1–2½ ft. tall; flowers fringed or ruffled and 3¼–4 in. across; F_1 **Multiflora**—1–2 ft. tall; flowers with plain edges and 2½ in. across; **Multiflora Doubles**—1–1½ ft. tall; flowers very double, 2½–3 in. across. Other, closely related, may be 4–5 in. across; sometimes called the Giant Fringed.

Culture

Petunia seed is extremely small and the chances are that any "failures" in growing these popular plants can be traced directly to improper seeding practices. Petunias will grow and thrive in almost any soil under almost any conditions, once they are past the tender seedling stage. The large F_1 hybrids are the result of hand pollination, which is costly, and hence is the reason why so few seeds are in each packet. Great care should be taken with sowing all petunia seed, especially these.

For the expensive hybrids (with few seeds) seed had best be sown indoors. Prepare the seed flat well with finely pulverized soil on top. It should be carefully leveled. Sow the petunia seed carefully on top of this, getting good distribution. Sometimes mixing the seed with very fine, dry sand will aid one in getting an equal distribution. Do not cover the seed—it is too small for that—but press it down well, water the flat or pot from below, cover with a glass or piece of polyethylene film to keep it from drying out, and care for it properly (see SEEDS) until the young seedlings are large enough to be transplanted. In fact, they might be transplanted twice before eventually planted outdoors after all danger of frost is over.

When the seedlings are 6 in. high they might be pinched back, that is, the ends might be removed in order to force side shoots and more compact growth all the way around. The bed where they are to be planted should be properly prepared with good compost and manure if available. It is also advisable to mulch the large-flowered types and the double types, to get around the spattering of mud that often mars the heavy flowers as they touch the ground.

As the plants will bloom from July to frost, one should cut back older stems as they become ungainly and in this way tend to rejuvenate the plants during late summer. Cuttings can be taken of the large double-flowered varieties in the late summer, if it is desired to use these as pot plants for winter bloom.

Petunias are excellent for edging, for bedding, for mixing into the general flower border or window box. Personal selection of colors and types is an excellent way of showing personality in any garden.

Insect Pests

Flea beetles eat holes in the leaves. See POTATO. In the greenhouse and hotbeds, the greenhouse orthezia infests Petunia. See LANTANA. White flies become abundant on the underside of the leaves unless killed by insecticide #15 or similar material. Avoid spraying where plants will dry slowly.

Diseases

Mosaic curls or crinkles the leaves. Control insects, use clean seed and plants and avoid growing near Tomato, Potato and other solanaceous plants.

PEYOTE, MESCAL BUTTON = *Lophophora williamsii*

pH. This is a symbol used in expressing acidity or alkalinity, and for gardeners it is used in determining the attributes of soils. Actually it stands for the hydrogen ion concentration of the soil measured by potentiometer or by dyes and judged on a scale from 1–9. Soils registering a pH of 7.0 are neutral, those below that are acid, those above that are alkaline. Most garden plants will grow satisfactorily in soils slightly acid, that is, at a pH of from 6.0 to 6.5. The more acid the soil, i.e., the lower on the pH scale it tests, the fewer plants will grow well.

On the other hand, some plants do much better in a slightly alkaline soil. To change the acidity of a soil to meet the requirements of plants to be grown one can add lime to raise the pH of the soil, or various acid fertilizers to lower the pH of the soil. For detailed information about this see SOILS and FERTILIZERS.

There are simple soil-testing kits available so that the gardener can make his own tests, although these may not be too accurate. These kits come with full directions. Dyes are used which turn color at various degrees of acidity and alkalinity. It is very important that the soil sample be collected properly and be uncontaminated with extraneous material or even by touching with the hands. It is often advisable in making an important test to use several samples of soil and test each one with clean equipment, merely to reassure oneself that the testing is being done properly.

PHACELIA (fass-EE-lia). These are native American herbs, a few of the 100 species of which are used as garden plants. The leaves are alternate, simple or divided and very fleshy. The bell-shaped flowers are not too conspicuous, being white, blue or purple. They are most attractive to bees. They should be given full sun and are best planted in masses for best effect. Seeds of the annual species are sown outdoors in mid-April in a situation where the plants are to grow and thinned to 9 in. apart. Native to Calif.

campanularia 1′ annual **Harebell Phacelia** With blue flowers in crowded clusters. Native to Calif. in desert areas.

ciliata 1½′ annual **Lavender Phacelia** With blue flowers and rough-pubescent leaves.

purshii 4″–12″ Zone 6 **Pursh Phacelia** A somewhat hairy plant, growing as an annual or a perennial, with a stiffly erect habit and alternate, pinnately lobed leaves. The blue flowers are pear shaped, with 5 spreading lobes which are fringed. These are borne in a loose raceme. The plant grows in rich woods from Pa. to Okla. and Wisc. and blooms from April to June.

tanacetifolia 3′ annual **Tansy Phacelia** With pinnatifid leaves and blue to lavender flowers.

viscida   2′   annual   **Sticky Phacelia**
With blue flowers with purple to whitish
centers.

PHAEDRANTHUS = *Distictis*

PHAIUS (FY-us). These epiphytic or terrestrial
orchids are easy to grow in the home greenhouse, not requiring such rigid growing conditions as many of the others. They are very
attractive, with erect flower stems, mostly
brown flowers with white or lavender tips,
blooming during spring and summer. Native to
the Far East and the Philippines. For culture
and propagation see ORCHID.
   flavus   2′   **Zone 10**
With yellow flowers up to 3 in. across, with a
light touch of orange or reddish. There are 2–8
leaves, about 2 ft. long, often spotted with
whitish or pale yellow. Blooms appear during
spring and summer. Native to the Himalayas,
China and Australia.
   tankervilliae   40″   **Zone 10   Nun's Orchid**
This has pseudobulbs and 40-in. leaves; flower
scapes that are up to 4 ft. long, bearing about
18 silvery-white flowers. Each one is about 4 in.
across. The inside of the flower is colored
yellowish brown. Native to the Himalayas,
China and Australia.

PHALAENOPSIS (fal-ee-NOP-sis). A genus of
about 40 species of handsome epiphytic
orchids, some of which have been pointed out
out as the most beautiful of all the orchids;
native to the Far East. They do not have pseudobulbs, but do have thick leathery leaves that are
sometimes mottled; flower clusters in drooping
panicles, usually white or tinted with rose or
purple. Native to Malaya and the Philippines.
There are many fine hybrids better than the
species, among which are **'Chieftain'**, **'Confirma-
tion'**, **'Doris'** (one of the most popular), **'La
Canada'**, **'Pamela'**, **'Psyche'** and **'Winged Victory'**
which is supposed to have the largest flowers of
any species in this genus. For greenhouse culture
and propagation. See ORCHID.
   amabilis   15″   **Zone 10**
Flowers up to 5 in. across, white spotted red and
yellow; leaves 6–15 in. long. The sprays may
have 15–30 flowers each, blooming in winter.
Many varieties—**P. aphrodite** is somewhat
similar. This is the largest-flowered and best of
the *Phalaenopsis* species for ornament.
   stuartiana   12″   **Zone 10**
Flowers 5 in. long, usually white, spotted
reddish brown. Leaves 7–15 in. long and 3–4
in. wide, mottled, purplish underneath. The
sprays may have 15–100 flowers each, blooming
in winter and spring. Native to the Philippines.

PHALARIS (FAL-a-ris)
   arundinacea picta   2′–4′   **Zone 3   Ribbon-grass**

This variety is planted more than the species,
because of the striped white and green leaves,
6–12 in. long and ¾ in. wide; in appearance
somewhat like a short bamboo. It also has

Phalaris arundinacea picta (Ribbon-grass)—an
ornamental striped grass.

grasslike flowers on tall spikes and is native to
Europe and North America. This spreads
rapidly by underground stolons and if it
escapes bounds it can become a vicious pest. It
should be grown only in poor, sterile, dry soils
in the sun for in such places it is retarded
enough to grow dense and thick. In good soils it
grows too tall and becomes lanky. An excellent
poor-soil plant, that can be cut to the ground
several times each year, if need be, to keep it
within bounds.
   canariensis   2′   annual   **Canary-grass**
An ornamental grass native to Europe but
naturalized in North America, with leaves that
are 6 in. long and ¼ in. wide, with ovoid seed
spikes 1½ in. long. The seeds have a shiny
straw-colored covering and seem to be a good
bird food.

PHANERA = *Bauhinia corymbosa*

PHASEOLUS (fass-EE-o-lus)
   coccineus   vine   annual   **Scarlet-runner
                                           Bean**

This is an ornamental bean, climbing by
twining, merely valued for its fast summer

growth and its brilliant scarlet flowers. The fruits are pods a foot long. It is a native to tropical America, is grown as a perennial in the Tropics. There is a white-flowered variety, **albus.** The seeds should be planted outdoors in May where the plants are to grow, after frost. They climb to 15 ft. and should be given poles or some support on which to twine.

limensis = Lima Bean, which see.

lunatus   twining annual   Butter Bean
A twining bean with ovate leaflets to $3\frac{1}{2}''$ long, white or yellowish flowers in loosely open clusters, pods $3\frac{1}{2}''$ long and $\frac{3}{4}''$ wide, native to tropical S. America. Popular in warm countries for its heavy production.

mungo = *Vigna mungo*

vulgaris   twining   annual   Kidney Bean
This is the common garden "pole-bean" with pods like string beans, tall and twining; white to violet-purple flowers which are few and $\frac{1}{4}-\frac{3}{4}$ in. long. The pods are slender, straight or slightly curved; seeds about $\frac{5}{8}$ in. long and colored variously according to variety, white, brown, blue-black or speckled. Probably native to America. See BEANS and VEGETABLE GARDEN.

PHEASANT'S-EYE. See ADONIS.

PHELLODENDRON (fell-o-DEN-dron)
amurense   30′   Zone 3   Amur Corktree
This tree from northern China could be used far more than it is. Primarily a shade tree, with opposite compound leaves, 10–15 in. long, with 5–13 leaflets, it grows into a broad, rounded tree with huge branches, rather open in texture and excellent for allowing electric lines to go through the branching system without too much pruning. The sexes are separate; the small whitish flowers are in panicles in early June and the fruits are round black berries, $\frac{1}{2}$ in. through, in the fall. These are not ornamental, and where possible the staminate tree might be grown for the fruit is rather messy when it drops. The corklike bark, the light shade it gives and its wide-spreading branches are its chief characteristics.

Propagation

Seeds can be sown as soon as ripe or kept dry in airtight containers in a cool place until the following year and then sown. Some are grafted (using species seedlings as understock) and both softwood cuttings and root cuttings root successfully. See GRAFTING, CUTTINGS.

chinense   30′   Zone 5   Chinese Corktree
Chinese tree with opposite compound leaves, each having 7–13 leaflets, turning yellowish in the fall like other species of *Phellodendron*. Sexes separate; fruits are drupes in small grapelike clusters, each fruit about $\frac{1}{3}$ in. or less in dia. As an ornamental it is about as good as

the other more easily obtained species.

PHENOLOGY. The study of climate and the periodic response of plants to it, especially in flowering and fruiting.

PHENOTYPE. The external appearance resulting from the expression of the genotype; often used to denote a specific appearance pattern shared by several to many individuals.

PHILADELPHUS (fill-a-DEL-fus). Mock-orange. There are about 50 species and varieties of Philadelphus being grown in the commercial nurseries of the U.S., so there is a wealth of material from which to select ornamental plants. They all have white flowers, opposite leaves; their fruits are dried capsules and not very interesting, and the autumn color is not especially outstanding—yellow or yellowish. In other words, they are chiefly valued during the short period when they are in bloom; but they are all grown easily in almost any normal soil, and are mostly free from injurious insect and disease pests—reason enough why they have proved popular over the years.

Left: *Philadelphus*
Right: *Deutzia*

Some plants in this group have special merit. *P. coronarius*, for instance, is excellent for planting in dry soil situations. Many of the hybrids have extremely fragrant flowers, and some of the plants, like *P. laxus* and *P.* x *splendens*, have branches which face the ground well all around and make fairly good foliage specimens throughout the length of time they retain their leaves.

On the other hand, the flowers of many of the species are not fragrant, and some plants, like *P. delavayi* and *P.* x *monstrosus* reach heights of 15 ft. or more; they are frequently just too tall and vigorous for the small garden. There are better shrubs of this height with interesting flowers, better autumn color, and fruits in the fall (like some of the viburnums), so, if tall shrubs are desired, it is not the mock-oranges which should have first consideration.

Hybrids

It is particularly noteworthy how many of the mock-oranges originated in the nurseries of Lemoine and Son in Nancy, France. Victor Lemoine, born in 1823, worked in several places while a young man, one of them being the famous estate of Louis Van Houtte in Ghent, Belgium. In 1850, he established his own nursery at Nancy and entered into a long period of plant hybridization. He, and his successors in later years, orignated many of the best deutzias, weigelas, mock-oranges, lilacs and other groups of plants, herbaceous as well as woody. Of the hybrid-mock-oranges in the following list, 17 were originated and introduced by the Lemoines, all between 1894 and 1927.

Because good clones are available, it is probably not advisable to grow *Philadelphus* x *cymosus*, *P.* x *lemoinei* and *P.* x *virginalis* as such, for many plants of these hybrids, especially if grown from seed, are inferior to the named clones which should be grown instead.

As a group, mock-oranges start to bloom by the end of May with *P. schrenkii jackii*, which is first. The majority flower during the first 3 weeks of June, with the peak of bloom about the middle of the month. The last species, *P. incanus*, blooms in the Arnold Arboretum about the last week of June. Some of the newer cultivars like 'Frosty Morn' and 'Minnesota Snowflake' are reported to be hardy to −30° F. (Zone 3), *P. coronarius* and *P. laxus* and 'Mont Blanc' are hardy in Zone 4 and the rest are hardy in Zone 5. There are, of course, other mock-oranges suitable for warmer areas, but of the hardier species and varieties, these are the best ornamentals.

Habit

These shrubs vary considerably in habit and range in height from 4 to 12 ft. 'Avalanche', for instance, has pleasingly arching branches and is only 4 ft. tall. 'Erectus', about the same height, is rigidly upright, which might be desirable in some locations. Others, like *P. inodorus*, *P. laxus*, *P.* x *splendens* and 'Mont Blanc', are

definitely moundlike, making them ideal specimens in many situations.

The habit of several of the *P.* x *virginalis* clones (especially 'Virginal') is not pleasing; they are ruggedly upright and produce few lateral branches at the base. It is usually advisable to use such plants in the rear of the shrub border, with smaller plants in the foreground to hide this somewhat unsightly trait.

Flowers

Fragrance is an important factor, for this is one of the reasons these plants have proved so popular over the years. Some, like *P. indorus* and *P.* x *splendens* are practically scentless. The native *P. microphyllus* is one of the most fragrant, and the reason why the *P.* x *lemoinei* clones (of which it is one parent) are generally so sweetly scented. 'Avalanche', 'Conquête', 'Cole's Glorious', 'Frosty Morn', 'Innocence' and 'Virginal' are among the most fragrant. *P. coronarius* should also be included here, but unfortunately it has too frequently been grown from seed collected from miscellaneous mixed plantings, so that many inferior strains are listed at present. The true, old-fashioned *P. coronarius* is extremely fragrant.

The double-flowered varieties, of course, retain their petals longer than those with single flowers, and so are valued. 'Albâtre', 'Argentine', 'Boule d'Argent', 'Frosty Morn', 'Girandole', 'Glacier', 'Minnesota Snowflake' and 'Virginal' are the best of these. Some, however, are highly variable and when grown under some

Philadelphus 'Albatre' is one of the better double-flowered mock-oranges. (*Photo by Arnold Arboretum, Jamaica Plain, Mass.*)

circumstances may produce many single flowers. Because of variations due to growth conditions, it is difficult to select one variety as the best of this group. The plant that is grown well, with the best soil, light, and water conditions, is usually the one with the best double flowers.

Propagation

Seed can be sown as soon as ripe, or stored dry in airtight containers in a cool place for up to a year and then sown. Older plants can easily be divided by using a sharp spade or even chopping through the center with an axe, best done in the early spring before growth starts. Both softwood and hardwood cuttings (which see) root very easily.

coronarius 9′ Zone 4 **Sweet Mock-orange**
Single flowers, 1½ in. in dia., and very fragrant; this is native to southern Europe. It is this species which has been the most popular in the past, but unfortunately it has been so frequently reproduced by seed that in nurseries it is now badly adulterated by inferior types. The true plant should have very fragrant flowers and it should grow well in dry situations. The variety with yellow foliage is **'Aureus'**.

x cymosus 5′–7′ Zones 5–6 **Cymosus Mock-orange**
A hybrid species (*P. lemoinei* x *P. grandiflorus*), slightly more tender than *P. lemoinei* but with several excellent clones (see hybrid list below) which should be planted instead of the species which is variable.

incanus 9′ Zone 5 **Gray Mock-orange**
Single flowers, 1¾ in. in dia., with only a slight fragrance and native to China. It is one of the last of all mock-oranges to come into bloom usually in late June.

inodorus 9′ Zone 5 **Scentless Mock-orange**
Single flowers, 2 in. in dia., and only slightly fragrant. It is the only Mock-orange with glossy green leaves, making a fine ornamental specimen. The var. **laxus** is 6 ft. tall, has single flowers, 1½ in. in dia., with only slight fragrance. Blooming in early June, this has branches facing the ground on all sides, making a good foliage specimen.

inodorus grandiflorus 9′ Zone 4 **Big Scentless Mock-orange**
A native to the southeastern U.S., this has single flowers 1¾ in. in dia., during mid-June, a good upright habit, but the flowers are not fragrant.

x lemoinei 4′–8′ Zone 5 **Lemoine Mock-orange**
A hybrid (*P. microphyllus* x *P. coronarius*) with leaves smaller than those of *P. coronarius* (about ¾–1¾ in. long) with delicate branching and smaller flowers which are very fragrant. Plants are mostly only 4 ft. tall, a few taller. See hybrids in the list below. Because of the excellent named clones available it is not recommended to plant *P. lemoinei* as such; the clones are much better ornamentals.

microphyllus 4′ Zone 6 **Littleleaf Mock-orange**
Native to N.Mex. and Ariz., this has not proved completely hardy in New England. It is a graceful shrub with small leaves, ½–¾ in. long and ¼–⅓ in. wide, and single white flowers about an inch across in mid-June. The flowers have a pineapplelike fragrance.

x nivalis 6′ Zone 5 **Snowbank Mock-orange**
A hybrid species (*P. pubescens* x *P. coronarius*) probably only of note because its double-flowered var. plenus was one of the parents of the extremely popular *P.* x *virginalis*. Neither *P. nivalis* nor its variety can now compare with the much superior hybrid varieties now available to gardeners. See list below.

pekinensis 6′ Zone 4 **Peking Mock-orange**
A spreading shrub native to northern China and Korea; with small leaves and only slightly fragrant creamy-white flowers; not nearly as good an ornamental as some of the other species.

purpurascens 12′ Zone 5 **Purplecup Mock-orange**
Single flowers, 1½ in. in dia.; each flower with a purple calyx, and very fragrant.

x purpureo-maculatus 'Sirene' 4′ Zone 5
This variety is the hardiest of this hybrid species, which is a cross of *P. lemoinei* and *P. coulteri* made by Victor Lemoine in 1910. The flowers are white, single, 1¼ in. across and bloom in mid-June.

schrenkii jackii 8′ Zone 5 **Jack Mock-orange**
Single flowers, 1 in. in dia., flowering in late May; the first of all the mock-oranges to bloom. It is because of its early flowers that this Mock-orange is recommended.

x splendens 8′ Zone 5
Single flowers, 1½ in. in dia., fragrant, and with bright yellow stamens. Plants are well branched on all sides and make good foliage specimens. Possibly *P. grandiflorus* x *P. gordonianus*.

x virginalis 5′–9′ Zone 5
This is a hybrid group (*P. lemoinei* x *P. nivalus plenus*) originated by Victor Lemoine, from which several clones of merit have been selected, the most commonly available of which is **'Virginal'**. Because it is a hybrid species, named clones (varieties) are definitely the plants to obtain.

Horticultural Varieties

(The species to which they are related are in the parentheses following the name)

'Albâtre' (P. x virginalis) 5′ Zone 5 **Introduced by Lemoine in 1914**
Double flowers, 1¼ in. in dia., slightly fragrant, and of good habit.

'Argentine' (P. x virginalis) 4′ Zone 5 **Introduced by Lemoine in 1914**

Double flowers, 2 in. in dia., sometimes with as many as 32 petals. The flowers are very fragrant.

'Aureus' (P. coronarius)   5′   Zone 4
The foliage first appears colored a bright yellow early in the spring, later turning to almost normal green by midsummer. It originated before 1878.

'Avalanche' (P. x lemoinei)   4′   Zone 5
Introduced by Lemoine in 1896
Single flowers, 1 in. in dia., and one of the most fragrant of all the mock-oranges. It has a pleasing, arching habit.

'Bannière' (P. x cymosus)   7′   Zone 5   Introduced by Lemoine in 1907
Semi-double flowers, 1½–2¼ in. in dia., and fragrant. The bush is rather straggly, but this is the first of these hybrids to bloom.

'Belle Etoile' (P. x lemoinei)   6′   Zones 5–6
Introduced by Lemoine in 1925
Single flowers, 2¼ in. in dia., fragrant and with an arching habit.

'Boule d'Argent' (P. x lemoinei)   5′   Zone 5
Introduced by Lemoine in 1894
Double flowers, 2 in. in dia., and slightly fragrant; an excellent variety.

'Bouquet Blanc' (P. x virginalis)   6′   Zone 5
Introduced by Lemoine in 1903
Single to slightly double flowers, 1 in. in dia., but well distributed over the entire plant. In shape it is well rounded.

'Burford' (P. x virginalis)   9′   Zone 5
Originated in England in 1921
Single to semi-double flowers, 2¼–2½ in. in dia.

'Cole's Glorious' (P. x virginalis x 'Rosace')   6′   Zone 5
Introduced by Cole Nursery Co., Painesville, Ohio, in 1940, this has single flowers, 2 in. in dia., and is very fragrant.

'Conquête' (P. x cymosus)   6′   Zone 5   Introduced by Lemoine in 1903
Flowers single, 2 in. in dia.; one of the very best and most fragrant of all the mock-oranges.

'Erectus' (P. x lemoinei)   4′   Zone 5   Introduced by Lemoine in 1894
Flowers single, 1¼ in. in dia., and very fragrant. This does not grow too well but the habit is definitely erect, and in areas where it is hardy it should prove an interesting plant.

'Fleur de Neige' (P. x lemoinei)   4′   Zone 5
Introduced by Lemoine in 1916
Flowers single, 1½ in. in dia., and very fragrant.

'Frosty Morn'   4′   Zone 3
Originated by Guy D. Bush, Minneapolis, Minn., and patented (#1174) March 10, 1953; it has very fragrant, double flowers and has been noted as withstanding the "coldest Minnesota winters without damage from freezing back." An excellent Mock-orange for cold areas.

'Girandole' (P. x lemoinei)   4′   Zone 5
Introduced by Lemoine in 1916
Flowers double, 1¼ in. in dia., and fragrant.

'Glacier' (P. x virginalis)   5′   Zone 5   Introduced by Lemoine in 1914
Flowers double, 1¼ in. in dia., and fragrant.

'Innocence' (P. x lemoinei)   8′   Zone 5
Introduced by Lemoine in 1927
Flowers single, 1¾ in. in dia., and with 8–10 in a cluster. It is one of the most fragrant of all the mock-oranges.

'Minnesota Snowflake' (P. x virginalis)   6′   Zone 3
Introduced by Guy D. Bush, Minneapolis, Minn., in 1935, and patented (#538) August 11, 1942. It is said to be hardy to −30° F.; flowers double, 1½ in. in dia., with 3–7 flowers in each cluster and fragrant. Clothed with branches well to the ground, it makes an excellent specimen for northern gardens.

'Mont Blanc' (P. x lemoinei)   4′   Zone 4
Introduced by Lemoine in 1896
Flowers single, 1¼ in. in dia., and very fragrant. It is one of the hardier varieties.

'Norma' (P. x cymosus)   6′   Zone 5
Introduced by Lemoine in 1914
Flowers single, 1¾ in. in dia., and fragrant.

'Perle Blanche' (P. x cymosus)   6′   Zone 5
Introduced by Lemoine in 1900
Flowers single, 1½ in. in dia., and one of the most fragrant.

'Virginal' (P. x virginalis)   9′   Zone 5
Introduced by Lemoine 1907
Flowers double, 2 in. in dia., and very fragrant. The one drawback of this variety is that older plants tend to produce few leaves and branches near the base.

PHILESIA (fill-EE-sia)
magellanica   3′   Zone 8   Magellan Box-lily
Belonging to the Lily Family, this low evergreen from southern Chile is handsome for its rosy-red flowers (2 in. long) in the fall. The evergreen alternate leaves are dark green above, whitish beneath and about 1½ in. long and the fruit is a berry. It grows best in peaty soil and a half shady, sheltered position. It can be propagated by cuttings which root very slowly.

PHILLYREA (FIL-li-rea)
angustifolia   9′   Zone 7   Narrowleaf Phillyrea
Evergreen shrub with dense branches; ovate leaves 1–2 in. long; small greenish-white flowers and blue-black fruits (drupes) that are not especially ornamental. Occasionally planted for its evergreen foliage. Native to southern Europe and northern Africa.

decora (P. vilmoriniana)   9′   Zone 6   Lance-leaf Phillyrea
This is the best of the phillyreas for the garden, having dense axillary clusters of small white

flowers, $\frac{1}{4}$ in. long, during April and red to purplish-black drupes in the fall. The leaves are evergreen, lustrous and bronze colored, about $1\frac{1}{2}$ in. long. Formerly this was named *P. vilmoriniana* and it may still be offered by some nurseries under that name. Native to western Asia.

latifolia media   30′   Zone 7   Tree Phillyrea
Similar to *P. angustifolia* but native to southern Europe and Asia Minor.

vilmoriniana = *P. decora*

PHILODENDRON (fill-o-DEN-dron).   These are evergreen vines native to the West Indies and tropical America, belonging to the Arum Family and valued as house and greenhouse display plants because of their interesting leaves. The flowers, when borne, resemble those of the Calla-lily. In the Tropics and in gardens in the far South, they climb trees. The leaves vary considerably, from 3 in. to 3 ft. in length, depending upon the species.

As house plants they need less light than most other plants and do best in a temperature of 60°–72° F. The leaves should be sponged occasionally with soap and water to remove dust and insect pests. They thrive in a moist atmosphere of the greenhouse. It is good to know that they grow best when their roots are somewhat cramped in pots (or tubs), but they should be fed regularly and be provided with rough stakes or supports to which they can cling.

Types of Philodendrons

Propagation is usually simple, by means of cuttings of pieces of stem which have at least 2 joints, placed in sand with bottom heat of 70°–75° F., or even in soil under a bell jar or in a terrarium in a warm room. Some kinds can even be rooted by placing the cuttings in water. Air layering (which see) is another method of starting new plants from a leggy, overgrown vine that has seen its best days. Seeds germinate readily when sown in moist sphagnum moss, but they should not be allowed to dry out after they are fully ripened on the plant. There are over 200 species and many hybrids; the following are the ones most popular at present.

cordatum   climbing   Zone 10   Heartleaf Philodendron
An excellent house plant which can be grown in water or soil, this has oblong leaves, 4–15 in. long and 2–5 in. wide, heart shaped at the base. The spathes are 3 in. long. Native to Brazil. One of the most commonly grown.

x corsinianum   climbing   Zone 10   Redrim Philodendron
With leaves $2\frac{1}{2}$ ft. long and $1\frac{1}{2}$ ft. wide, rather pinnatifid, dark green above, purplish green beneath, with outstanding green veins. The spathe is purplish red, spotted with light green. A hybrid, probably originated in cultivation.

giganteum   climbing   Zone 10   Giantleaf Philodendron
One of the largest-leaved species of this genus, with beautiful, glossy, cordate leaves, 4 ft. long and 2 ft. wide, having pale veins and fleshy petioles. The leaves are split near the base and the long stems sometimes bear whiplike roots. Native to Puerto Rico.

gloriosum   climbing   Zone 10
Leaves 10 in. long, 8 in. wide, reddish on margins and pale green on nerves, with the petioles marked with white. Native to Colombia.

hastatum   climbing   Zone 10
Native to Brazil, with bright green, arrow-shaped leaves. The variety variegatum has leaves beautifully variegated with white.

mamei   non-climbing   Zone 10
Native to Equador, with cordate leaves 10 in. long and 6 in. wide, deep green above and irregularly spotted with silvery white.

panduriforme   climbing   Zone 10   Horsehead Philodendron
A popular species from Brazil, with fiddle-shaped leaves colored a dull, dark green. This makes an excellent house plant. The flower or spathe is yellowish white, rolled inwards.

radiatum   climbing   Zone 10
Often appearing in the trade under the name *P. dubium*, this has deeply lobed, dark green leaves. Native to Guatemala.

scandens scandens   climbing   Zone 10
Leaves small (3 in. long), heart shaped, green

with a silky sheen above, red beneath. The reddish petiole is 3 in. long. Native to Colombia.

selloum   2′   Zone 10
A stemless species bearing long-stalked, deeply lobed or even twice-pinnate leaves of a dark green color. The spathes, when borne, are a foot long and white inside. Native to Paraguay.

squamiferum   climbing   Zone 10
With 5-lobed, glossy leaves of a rich green and leaf stalks that have a furlike covering of long red hairs.

verrucosum   climbing   Zone 10   Warty Philodendron
With heart-shaped, satiny leaves, 8 in. long and 6 in. wide, olive green in color, with nerves sunken and with leaf stalks having conspicuous red hairs. Flowers purplish. Native to Costa Rica and Colombia.

PHLEUM (FLEE-um)

pratense   5′   Zone 3   Timothy
A perennial pasture grass of no garden value, but widely grown for hay. It does not make a good permanent pasture grass. Leaves 12 in. long, $\frac{1}{4}$ in. wide and flowers in columnar terminal spikes 3–6 in. long. Native to Europe and Asia, naturalized in North America.

PHLOX (flox).
A genus of herbs, including annuals and perennials, of the Phlox Family, comprising about 50 species, most of which are native to North America. In habit they differ widely, some being decumbent, while others grow to a height of several feet. The stiff, rather woody stems have lanceolate leaves, either opposite or alternate, and flowers in loose terminal clusters. These have a short tube and a corolla with 5 lobes which untwist to open. The flowers vary in color from white to deep pink, pale lavender or purple and there is generally a distinct eye in the base of the flower lobes. These are good garden plants which do well in well-drained soil and a sunny location. They are easily propagated by seed, cuttings or by division of the roots. The perennials are best grown from cuttings to maintain the true plant, or from root cuttings. Two-inch pieces of the larger roots are planted either in the fall or spring and covered with $\frac{3}{4}$ in. of soil. Many of these will bloom by summer. They should be divided every 3 years.

Insect Pests

Red spider mite (see MITES) is a serious pest of Garden Phlox when it feeds on the under side of leaves and turns them a mottled yellow. They develop rapidly in hot, dry weather and are most abundant in late summer. Spraying with insecticide #31 or #34 gives good control. Phlox plant bug stings and cripples the buds to deform the blossoms. Use insecticide #15.

Diseases

The white, feltlike growth on leaves and stems of powdery mildew in late summer often ruins the perennial Garden Phlox for decoration. Leaves fall progressively from the lower stem upward, but the plant is only slightly damaged. Warm, humid weather favors the disease. Fungicides #V and #M give good control if applied before infection becomes severe. Septoria leaf spot disfigures the leaves. Spraying with fungicide #D or #F is effective.

adsurgens   1′   Zone 8   Periwinkle Phlox
A trailing evergreen perennial from Ore. and not completely hardy in the harsher climate of the northeastern U.S. The leaves, $1\frac{1}{4}$ in. long, are broadly oval and dark green and the salmon-colored flowers, about an inch wide, are clustered on erect stems in spring. It should be grown in acid leaf mold in a moist, shady site. Since flowers are produced on the shoots of the previous season, the plant must not be allowed to winterkill.

x arendsii   2′   Zone 3   Arends Phlox
With lavender to mauve flowers, about 1 in. wide, in loose clusters, this perennial blooms in June and July. These are mostly hybrids between *P. divaricata* and *P. paniculata*, first exhibited in England in 1912 and very floriferous.

bifida   10″   Zone 4   Sand Phlox
Though the stems of this plant are woody, it grows in a tangled mound 10 in. high. The long, narrow, somewhat awl-shaped leaves are a light green and the white to light purple flowers, in loose panicles, bloom in May. The petals are deeply divided in 2; hence the specific name. Cultivate in well-drained, sandy soil in full sun. Native from Mich. to Ark.

carolina   3′–4′   Zone 3   Carolina Phlox
Although native from Ohio southwards, this seems to be hardy much farther north. The slender panicles of white to rose-purple flowers are usually in bloom by late May. The plant does not spread aggressively, as do so many other species of this genus, and the foliage seems to be disease-resistant. Flowering lasts for nearly 6 weeks. Culture is the same as for *P. paniculata*. The excellent white cultivar 'Miss Lingard' is probably a hybrid of this species and is certainly one of the best of all the phlox species and varieties. It is a fine plant for the perennial border. It does not set seeds.

divaricata   8″–12″   Zone 3   Wild Blue Phlox
An excellent ground cover plant, this species with spreading stems and opposite, oblong to ovate leaves has leaflike bracts which surround the base of the loosely clustered, showy, blue

or lavender flowers. These appear from April to June in moist woods and rocky outcrops from New England to the southern and south-central states. The variety **laphamii** comes from the western U.S. and has periwinkle-blue flowers.

drummondii   1½′   annual   **Annual or Drummond Phlox**

Also called Texas-pride, this is the only annual Phlox of all the species used in gardens and it is one of the easiest of garden flowers to grow. If the flowers are kept picked off after they have faded, it will bloom nearly all summer. The upper alternate leaves are ovate to lanceolate, about 3 in. long. The flowers are red, white, pink or purple, with many named varieties being available from seedsmen. Individual flowers are an inch wide, borne in conspicuous terminal umbels. Native to Tex.

The available varieties are from 6–18 in. tall, some densely moundlike in habit, some spreading. The plants can be used in many ways in the flower garden, depending on the habit of the variety, and some are even used in window boxes or in pots in the home.

In ordering seeds, remember that some of the dwarf varieties (6–8 in. high) are ideal for special places in the garden and that some of the new colored varieties like the 'Tetras' have very large flowers, while others like 'Isabellina' are of a soft primrose-buff color that is delightful. 'Apricot' is another. The dwarf compact sorts make fine pot plants. The 'Globe' mixtures are also excellent.

Eaily grown in almost any soil, seed takes over 2 weeks to germinate, but it can be sown indoors or out, as desired. Seedlings are not very easily transplanted.

glaberrima   2′–3′   **Zone 3   Smooth Phlox**

The lanceolate leaves of this species are smooth and shining and the flowers are reddish purple, borne in terminal and axillary clusters. It is found in swamps from Ohio south to Ga. and Tex. and blooms in May and June. Propagation is by division of the plants in spring or by softwood cuttings in summer.

maculata   3′   **Zone 3   Wild Sweet William**

Growing along stream banks and in moist meadows from Quebec to Va., west to Minn. and Mo., this upright perennial has a stem often spotted with purple. The leaves are lanceolate and the flowers, pink, purple or occasionally white, are in loose, showy, terminal clusters 4–10 in. long. It blooms throughout the summer. Excellent for the wild garden; the plant may be increased by division in spring and by softwood cuttings taken in summer.

nivalis   1′   **Zone 7   Trailing Phlox**

This is similar to *P. subulata* in habit and foliage, with flower colors from white to pink and pale purple. Native from Va. to Fla.

ovata   2′   **Zones 2–3   Mountain Phlox**

Underground stems bearing large oval leaves form mats of foliage 3 in. high, from which the flower stems rise to 15 in., bearing flat clusters of dark purple flowers in late May and June. The variety 'Pulchra' has beautiful, dark-veined, fragrant, pink flowers. Cultivate in rich garden soil in sun or semi-shade.

paniculata   2′–4′   **Zone 4   Garden Phlox**

This is the popular Phlox of gardens, native from N.Y. to Ga. and Ark., but in the wild the flowers are usually an unpopular magenta. Various plants from the wild have been selected and crossed so that now a longer list of varieties are offered by commercial growers. These cultivars may have gay blooms from late June to Sept. The flowers range in color according to variety from red to pink and white to purple. Plants, especially of the cultivars, should not be propagated by seed but by cuttings, root cuttings (the commercial method) or division— the easiest method for gardeners. They are easily grown, flower best in full sun, and, to induce more flowering and also to prevent seeding which will result in the growing of inferior varieties, the dead flower clusters should be cut off. Light shade might be best for the blue varieties, the flower colors of which deteriorate quickly in full sun. It is best to divide the clumps every 3–4 years, or the plants deteriorate and become rather shabby. Planting may be done either in spring or fall.

Of the hundreds of varieties, some of the currently popular ones are:

Red flowers: 'Fanal', 'Red Glory', 'Brigadier', 'Leo Schlageter', 'Spitfire'.

Pink flowers: 'Sir John Falstaff', 'Elizabeth Arden', 'Dresden China', 'Windsor'.

Purple flowers: 'Aida', 'Lilac Time', 'Progress', 'San Antonio'.

White flowers: 'Mia Ruys', 'Mary Louise', 'Rembrandt', 'White Admiral'.

x procumbens   1′   **Zone 5   Trailing Phlox**

Probably a hybrid (*P. stolonifera* x *P. subulata*), with procumbent branches; leaves about 2 in. long and flowers a bright purple, about ¾ in. wide, in spring.

stolonifera   5″–12″   **Zones 2–3   Creeping Phlox**

A low, weakly creeping Phlox with few purple-violet flowers about ¾ in. wide, during April and May, native from Pa. to Ga. In woods it will form solid mats of growth; hence it is good as a ground cover in the shade. 'Blue Ridge' and 'Lavender Lady' are 2 of the cultivars.

subulata   6″   **Zones 2–3   Moss-pink, Ground-pink**

This prostrate plant has rather woody stems and stiff, linear leaves. Its matted growth makes it ideal for rock gardens and slopes, especially since it is semi-evergreen. The small clusters of flowers, which may be pink or white in nature, are borne on short flowering branches. The corolla has 5 spreading, cordate lobes. The plant may be found in sandy, open woods in the eastern states from N.Y. to N.Car. and blooms from March through May. It has been widely cultivated and hybridized. Propagation is by layering and by division after blooming. Plants may be started, also, from cuttings taken in late fall and rooted in sand in a cold frame. Many varieties are available. Some of the best are: **'Emerald Cushion'**, lower than the species, **'Chuckles'** and **'Alexander's Surprise'**—these 3 with pink flowers; **'Brilliant'** is nearly red and **'Blue Hills'** and **'Sky Blue'** are blue. Also **'White Delight'** and **atropurpurea** are available.

PHLOX FAMILY = Polimoniaceae

PHOENIX (FEE-nix). These are graceful feather palms from Africa and Asia, including the Date Palm and several others used in ornamental planting. Male and female flowers are on separate plants. Fruit is a fleshy drupe. See PALMS.

canariensis 60′ **Zone 10** **Canary Island Date Palm**
A popular and stately palm with leaves 15–20 ft. long and a trunk up to 3 ft. in dia., considerably enlarged by the bases of the leaf stalks. A single tree may have 100 large leaves which are a good green color and arch gracefully. The clusters of yellowish-red, egg-shaped fruits are frequently pendulous. Native to the Canary Islands.

Date Palm—*Phoenix dactylifera*

dactylifera 100′ **Zone 10** **Date Palm**
This is the true Date of North Africa, widely planted throughout the Tropics. A dense tree with stiff fronds, spiny at the base, the segments 12–18 in. long and bluish green. This has been cultivated for over 4000 years. Male and female flowers are on different trees. Fruits are 1–3 in. long, borne in huge clusters. See DATE.

reclinata 25′ **Zone 10** **Senegal Date Palm**
Next to the true Date, the best palm tree from Africa for ornamental purposes is this Senegal Date Palm. It is used in southern Calif. as a street tree of merit, for it is most graceful in habit and fairly rapid in growth, but the fruits are not edible.

Phoenix rupicola is grown in southern California and southern Florida. (*Photo by Arnold Arboretum, Jamaica Plain, Mass.*)

roebelenii 4′–12′ **Zone 9** **Pigmy Date Palm**
This makes a very graceful tub plant when it is young. The gracefully arching fronds and narrow, folded, dark green pinnae are very feathery. The berrylike fruit is black, about $\frac{1}{2}$ in. through, and borne in foot-long clusters. Often planted in warm areas.

rupicola 20′ **Zone 8** **Cliff Date Palm**
A palm with a graceful trunk devoid of leaf bases, and with graceful arching fronds. The pinnae are 2-ranked, giving a soft texture to the light green foliage. The shining yellow fruits are $\frac{3}{4}$ in. long. Native to India; planted in southern Calif. as an ornamental.

PHORADENDRON (for-a-DEN-dron)
serotinum (*flavescens*) 3′ **Zones 6–7** **American Mistletoe**
There are 2 kinds of mistletoe, one native in Europe and this one native to the southern U.S. The European mistletoe is *Viscum album* and is not used in America, but *Phoradendron flavescens* is commonly seen as a parasite high in trees from N.J. to Fla. The rubbery leaves and translucent berries are familiar objects in Christmas decorations. The seeds germinate on

the trees and of course continue life as parasites. The berries are considered poisonous. It is not a garden plant. There are other kinds of mistletoe in the western part of the U.S.

PHORMIUM (FORM-ium)

colensoi   **7′**   **Zone 9**   **Green Fiber-lily**
A large perennial herb with leaves 5 ft. long and 2½ in. wide; flowers yellow, to 1½ in. long; grown for its foliage and propagated by seeds or division. Native to New Zealand, belonging to the Lily Family. Var. 'Tricolor' has leaves variegated lengthwise with irregular bands of yellow. Propagated by seed and division.

tenax   **15′**   **Zone 9**   **New Zealand Fiber-lily**
Basal leaves 9 ft. long and 5 in. wide, tough and leathery with a red line along the margin. Flowers 2 in. long, dull red. Native to New Zealand. Propagated by seed or division.

PHOSPHATE INSECTICIDES. These are synthetic phosphate compounds containing a sulfur molecule. They are basically nerve poisons and specifically anti-cholinesterase agents which block the normal transmission of nerve impulses. There are many formulations with various degrees of toxicity to warm-blooded animals and all safety precautions on the label should be followed when using them. Among the better known are malathion and diazinon, which are effective for control of many destructive insects and mites and are relatively safe to use. Parathion and guthion are very effective but more toxic. Some insects and mites have developed resistance to these insecticides. New formulae are being developed and tested and many changes in recommendations can be expected. Some organic phosphate insecticides have systemic action. See SYSTEMIC INSECTICIDES.

PHOTINIA (fo-TIN-ia). Alternate-leaved shrubs of the Rose Family; these are excellent ornamental shrubs because of foliage (2 species are evergreen), profuse small white flowers and conspicuous bright red fruits. They are sometimes susceptible to fire blight. *P. serrulata* is probably one of the most popular of ornamental shrubs in the South.

Propagation

Seed should be stratified for 3 months at 40° F., then sown. Layers are sometimes rooted. Grafting, using *Crataegus* and *Cydonia* seedlings as understock, is done commercially. Softwood and hardwood cuttings can be rooted. See STRATIFICATION, LAYERS, GRAFTING, CUTTINGS.

glabra   **10′**   **Zone 7**   **Japanese Photinia**
An evergreen from Japan, with glossy leaves 3 in. long, flower clusters 4 in. across and red fruits in the fall; a plant which seems to be winning some popularity as a landscape plant in the southeastern U.S. at present.

serrulata   **36′**   **Zone 7**   **Chinese Photinia**
The lustrous evergreen leaves of this Chinese plant are its best display. They are about 8 in. long and are a reddish bronze as they first unfurl in the spring. However, it has other assets. The small white flowers are borne in flat heads, sometimes 6 in. wide, in mid-May and the bright red berries, almost ¼ in. in dia., are most effective in the fall and early winter. Well-drained soil and not too much moisture during the summer are conducive to its best growth.

villosa   **15′**   **Zone 4**   **Oriental Photinia**
One of the hardiest of the photinias, this oriental shrub has been used considerably in northern gardens. It is deciduous, bears small white flowers in flat clusters in late May and bears bright red berries in the fall. The autumn color is a fine red-bronze. Unfortunately it is sometimes susceptible to fire blight disease which can be rather serious on certain other rosaceous plants like apples, pears and Cotoneaster.

PHOTOPERIODISM. Plants produce flowers in response to a certain amount of daylight. Long-day plants, mostly those in the temperate region, require 12–16 hours of daylight. Those in the Tropics, with possibly 10 hours daylight, as well as some in the Arctic Regions, are called short-day plants. A short-day plant given longer hours of daylight may not bloom and also a long-day plant given shorter hours of sunshine may not bloom. This most interesting phenomenon is called photoperiodism. Much study has been given this recently so that now commercial growers can get short-day plants to bloom at will merely by shading and withholding the light for certain periods. Likewise, they can force long-day plants into bloom by giving increased light by using fluorescent bulbs. Chrysanthemums are examples of short-day plants and they are now available from the florist in full bloom at almost any time of year, merely because the growers have learned how to shade them properly at the right time of year.

PHOTOSYNTHESIS. The manufacture of carbohydrates within green leaves by energy derived from light, from simple inorganic materials such as oxygen, carbon dioxide and water.

PHRAGMITES (frag-MY-teez)

australis (*maxima*)   **10′–15′**   **Zone 5**
Common Reed
A tall perennial reed grass growing in salty marshes, and once established it is difficult to eliminate. It is a rampant grower, certainly not a plant for the small place but will grow well in marshy areas of either salt or fresh water. It

produces graceful, plumed, fruiting heads that are dried and used in arrangements and is easily propagated by division of rootstalks or by seeds. Native to swamps in North America, Europe and Asia. It is said that young shoots cut from the roots make an excellent pickle.

PHYGELIUS (fy-JEE-lius)

capensis   3'   Zone 7   Cape-fuschia
A small shrub for garden or for use as a pot plant in the greenhouse, belonging to the Figwort Family; opposite leaves, 5-lobed; purple-scarlet, drooping, tubular flowers, each 2 in. long, in panicles 1½ ft. long in summer. Native to South Africa. Propagated by seeds or cuttings taken in the fall.

PHYLA (fy-LA)

nodiflora canescens (*Lippia canescens*)
              creeping   Zone 9   Creeping Lippia
This is grown as a ground cover in southern Calif. often under the name of *Lippia repens*. It has opposite gray leaves, about ¾ in. long, which turn brownish in the winter, blue flowers, the heads about ½ in. across, in spring, summer and fall. Native to South America. It is sometimes grown in hot, dry areas as a substitute for grass, since it forms a flat mat of foliage on the surface of the ground. This is one of the few ground covers used as lawn substitutes which can be walked on. It can be mowed; this to reduce the flowers which attract many bees.

PHYLLITIS (fill-LY-tis)

scolopendrium   1½'   Zone 3   Harts-tongue
                                              Fern
An evergreen rhizomatous fern, native to Europe and parts of North America especially in limestone regions, bearing straight or curved strap-shaped, leathery fronds 1½ ft. long and 3 in. wide. See FERNS.

PHYLLODOCE (fill-LO-do-ce). These are low, evergreen, heathlike plants, mostly native to the extreme North, that are rather difficult to transplant and are only useful as ornamentals in northern rock gardens. They belong to the Heath Family. The bell-shaped flowers are in terminal clusters something like those of Heather. They must be provided with moist, peaty soil in order to survive. Propagated by seeds, cuttings, layers and division.

caerulea   6"   Zone 1   Blue Mountain-heath
Flowers, pink or purple, ⅓ in. long; native from Greenland to N.H., northern Asia and northern Europe.

empetriformis   6"   Zone 5   Red Mountain-
                                              heath
Native from British Columbia to Calif., with rosy-purple flowers.

glanduliflora   1'   Zone 2   Cream Mountain-
                                              heath

Native from Alaska to Calif., with sulfur-yellow flowers.

PHYLLOSTACHYS (fill-OS-tak-is)

bambusoides   70'   Zones 7–8   Japanese
                                          Timber Bamboo
This should only be considered for growth in clumps or groups, and in the right place can be most interesting. It is about the tallest species of Bamboo (from Japan) now growing in the U.S. See BAMBOO.

PHYLLOTAXY. The arrangement of leaves on the stem.

PHYSALIS (FISS-a-lis)

alkekengi   2'   Zones 2–3   Chinese-lantern,
                                    Strawberry Ground-cherry
A perennial ornamental (sometimes grown as an annual) that can become a bad weed where it escapes; native from southeastern Europe to Japan. The long, creeping, underground stems are difficult to eliminate where this plant proves hardy. Leaves alternate and ovate to 3 in. long; flowers white, about ½ in. wide during summer. The fruit, small and cherrylike in outline, is enclosed by a bright red, inflated husk about 2 in. long, from which it gets its common name of Chinese Lantern. Easily propagated by seed and division.

heterophylla   2½'   Zone 3   Clammy Ground-
                                              cherry
A perennial weed native to and widely distributed across eastern, central and northern North America, mostly on gravelly or stony soils. The leaves are alternate, broadly ovate and rounded at the base, somewhat sticky. The flowers are yellow, trumpet-shaped, ¾ in. across, borne singly in the leaf axils on drooping stalks from July to Sept. The fruit, a yellowish berry, is enclosed by a bladderlike husk. It is of no ornamental value.

ixocarpa   4'   annual   Tomatilla Ground-cherry
A Mexican plant used as an ornamental in the South where it can escape and become a weed; with alternate leaves, 3 in. long, bright yellow flowers ¾ in. across, and fruit a purple, inflated, bladderlike body 1 in. long, completely filled with the purple, cherrylike, sticky berry.

subglabrata   5'   Zone 4   Taperleaf Ground-
                                              cherry
A native perennial in North America with erect stems, alternate leaves 4 in. long and oblique at the base; flowers yellow, 1 in. across, from July to Sept.; fruit inflated and bladderlike with the orange-red to purple berry inside, about ¾ in. across. This can become a weed on rich or moist soils.

PHYSARIA (fiss-AR-ia). A small group of tufted plants belonging to the Mustard Family and native to the Rocky Mountains. They grow best on loose limestone soil in full sun.

didymocarpa 6″ Zone 2 Common Twinpod
A plant with trailing stems and broadly oval leaves, 3 in. long, with a soft glistening pubescence and clusters of small yellow flowers. The seeds are encased in rather large, inflated pods. Possibly for use in rock gardens.

PHYSOCARPUS (fy-so-KARP-us). Alternate-leaved deciduous shrubs with small white to pinkish flowers in clusters and small inflated pods for fruits; easily grown on almost any soil but not especially conspicuous as ornamentals. Propagation is by seeds sown as soon as ripe or they can be stored dry in airtight containers in a cool place for up to a year and then sown. Plants can be divided in the early spring, with a sharp spade or even an axe, chopping right through the middle. Softwood and hardwood cuttings (which see) are easy to root. None of these plants are troubled with serious disease or insect pests, hence it is unnecessary to spray them.

intermedius = *Physocarpus opulifolius intermedius*

monogynus 3′ Zone 5 Mountain Ninebark
Native from Wyo. to Tex., this is a neat little shrub of little value except for its rounded habit and the fine texture of its foliage. The alternate leaves are 3–5 lobed and $\frac{1}{2}$–$1\frac{1}{2}$ in. across. The small white flowers are less than $\frac{1}{2}$ in. wide, sometimes pinkish, in few-flowered clusters. Fruits are small dried pods.

opulifolius 9′ Zone 2 Eastern Ninebark
Native from Quebec to Va. and west to Mich., this American shrub is common, rather coarse in texture but growing well and vigorously in most soils. The flowers are small and white or pinkish, in clusters during early June, and the fruits, although dried capsules, are reddish to brown and attractive as they mature in the fall. First they are colorfully reddish, then they change to brown and remain on the plant all winter. The shrub resembles a coarse spirea in all its parts and so can be used at the rear of the shrub border or as a fast-growing "filler."

The variety **'Luteus'** has yellow to yellowish foliage a greater part of the growing season but especially is this yellow color pronounced in the early spring, when it looks from a distance as if it were a mass of yellow flowers. All in all, these are dependable plants but not sufficiently refined to feature in small plantings.

The variety **intermedius** has leaves shallowly lobed, and an inch or 2 long, but the habit is rather ungainly. The variety **'Nanus'** is only about 2 ft. tall, has smaller leaves, is very dense in habit and should be better known for it makes a good hedge plant.

PHYSOSTEGIA (fy-so-STEE-jia)
virginana 4′ Zones 2–3 Virginia Lion's-heart
Sometimes called False Dragonhead, this is a slender perennial with erect stems and opposite, lanceolate and toothed leaves and irregular pink flowers borne in a dense terminal cluster and in axils of the leaves during late summer and for about 6 weeks thereafter. Each corolla tube is about 1 in. long. The plant may be found in moist, slightly acid soil from New England to Minn. and south to the Carolinas and Tex. It is a handsome garden plant, propagated by division of the creeping stolons in spring. There is a white form (**'Summer Snow'**) which is equally attractive and less inclined to spread.

Varieties such as **'Grandiflora'**, growing 5 ft. tall and rather unkempt; **'Vivid'**, only about 2 ft. tall with deep rosy-pink flowers; **'Rosy Spire'** and **'Summer Glow'** have been listed.

PHYTEUMA (fy-TEW-ma). Herbaceous plants, not often used in the garden, with alternate leaves and 5-parted, blue, purplish or white flowers in terminal clusters. Native to Europe and Asia; mostly used in rock gardens where hardy. Easily propagated by seeds and division in spring.

hemisphaericum 6″ Zone 5 Grasstuft Rampion
With tufted growth, blue flowers that sometimes are whitish, 12–15 flowers per head. Native to the Alps Mountains.

orbiculare 2′ Zone (6?) Ballhead Rampion
Leaves ovate, flowers purple, produced in rounded heads. Native to Europe.

scheuchzeri 1$\frac{1}{2}$′ Zone 7 Weakstem Rampion
Leaves oblong to lanceolate; flowers violet-blue in heads an inch wide; native to southern Europe.

sieberi 6″ Zone 6 (?) Apennine Mixedflower
The mounds of small, toothed, lanceolate leaves of this plant are ornamental in spring and early summer; with flower stems 6 in. high surmounted with deep blue flowers arranged in a tight 12–15-flowered ball.

spicatum 4′ Zone 6 (?) Spike Rampion
Leaves ovate to linear; flowers white with greenish tips in thickly flowered spikes. Native to Europe.

PHYTOLACCA (fy-to-LAK-a)
americana 10′–12′ Zone 3 Common Pokeberry
A pernicious garden weed, native throughout the eastern U.S.; the root is poisonous, but children have been poisoned just by eating the black, lustrous berries also. The soft succulent stems grow vigorously and often are cut in the early spring and cooked like asparagus. Care should be taken not to cut any of the root when cutting these young spring shoots. Flowers are borne on erect to nodding racemes. The black berries give a red juice or dye when crushed,

Phytolacca americana—Pokeweed

sometimes used as an ink. It is not necessary to cultivate this as an ornamental with all the other plants available today. Male and female flowers are on the same plant. Propagated by seed or by division.

PHYTOLACCACEAE = The Pokeweed Family

PICEA (PY-see-a). In general, the spruces are not the best of our ornamental trees. Though they are evergreens, few of them mature to perfect specimens; most of them either lose their lower branches or become ragged and sparsely branched at the top. With the exception of *P. pungens*, they are not suited for city planting. It should be pointed out that half of the species discussed here mature at heights of 100 ft. or more; hence they certainly are not trees for the small property. This is a very important point to keep in mind when selecting trees from the following list of recommended trees.

All spruces except the dwarf varieties are rigidly upright, pyramidal, single-trunked trees. They are stiff in outline, many of them having rigidly held horizontal branches produced in whorls and the cones produced are all pendant. Because of their stiff appearance, they are frequently difficult to use in landscape plantings except as prominent specimens. When crowded into mass plantings or when planted in the shade, they quickly lose their lower branches. Most are susceptible to attacks of red spider and the species *P. pungens* is especially susceptible to attacks of the spruce gall aphid. *P. engel-*

mannii, P. glauca, P. pungens and *P. rubens* are all hardy in Zone 2, which means that these are hardy in the coldest parts of the U.S. and all but the coldest parts of Canada. Hence, when extreme winter cold is the factor limiting the use of evergreen trees, these spruces might be the first to be considered.

In slightly warmer areas the pines are often used instead because of their softer foliage texture, and in areas where hemlocks will grow it is these that should be considered before either the pines or the spruces. The Colorado Blue Spruce and its varieties have always been popular and probably always will be, even though they have frequently been misplaced and given too prominent a spot in many gardens.

The Norway Spruce has been used as an ornamental in Europe for over 500 years, but it does much better there than it does in America. It has the characteristic of producing sports either on branches or as seedlings, and over 100 of these have been named, but the nomenclature and identification of these sports have always been hopelessly confused. Most are slow-growing dwarfs; many are certainly similar to one another.

With the exception of a few like *P. omorika*, *P. orientalis* and some of the *P. pungens* varieties, the following spruces are not the best of the ornamental trees available for making beautiful gardens. They are sometimes essential because of their evergreen foliage, the quick growth of certain species, the silvery to bluish foliage color of others, or because of their hardiness. When these conditions can be met by the selection of other trees, the spruces might be overlooked entirely.

Propagation

Seed can be stratified as soon as ripe or stored dry in a cool place in airtight containers for up to a year and then sown. Grafting is done commercially, using *P. abies* or *P. pungens* as understock. Some species, especially the dwarf varieties of *P. abies*, can be rooted from either softwood or hardwood cuttings. See STRATIFICATION, GRAFTING, CUTTINGS.

Insect Pests

Spruce gall aphid on Norway Spruce and Cooley's gall aphid on Blue and White Spruce are common pests on ornamental trees. The pineapple-shaped galls are at the base of twigs on Norway Spruce and at the tip of twigs on Blue Spruce. Infested trees are unsightly and twigs die or grow abnormally. Spraying in early spring with insecticide #44 or #15 or a combination of these to kill the young at the base of the needles is recommended. Oil emulsion sprays temporarily remove the "bloom" from

Blue Spruce. In the northern forests spruce bud worm is a serious pest and may be troublesome on ornamental trees. Needles of new growth are webbed and eaten, which gives the trees a sickly appearance and decreases normal growth. Spraying with insecticide #5 in early summer is advised. Spruce mite is a common and destructive pest of nearly all ornamental evergreens. The tiny spiders (see MITES) discolor the needles and cause them to drop. Dormant sprays of insecticide #44 kill the winter eggs and summer sprays with insecticide #15, #31 or #34 should be used regularly. Sawflies and needle miner are occasional pests requiring sprays of insecticide #15 when the infestation is discovered. In southern Zones bagworms can be troublesome. Hand picking is usually sufficient.

Diseases

Cytosperma canker kills lower and inner branches and causes excessive gumming at the infected area. Fungicides have not given good control and pruning of infected branches and cankered bark during the winter to delay the spread of the disease is suggested. Rusts on the needles are minor pests that seldom need attention.

abies   150′   Zone 2   Norway Spruce
Widely planted, fast-growing when young, this tree from northern Europe does not grow old gracefully. It is often overplanted in America. Other species should be considered as possibilities for good specimen trees, using this species as a cheap, quick-growing "filler" which should be removed before it attains mature height. It is noted for its many sports, over 100 having been listed. The cones are 5–7 in. long.

The following varieties are simply the better-known forms now being grown in America: 'Clanbrassiliana', compact, rounded to flat topped. A 40-year-old plant is 6 ft. tall and 10 ft. in dia.; 'Gregoryana', very dwarf. Seldom over 2 ft. tall; conical to subglobose; 'Conica', a dense, compact cone of foliage, a 31-year-old tree being 25 ft. tall and 12 ft. in dia.; 'Highlandia', a more evenly flat-topped and compact tree than the variety 'Pumila'. A few years ago one plant in the Rochester Parks, Rochester, N.Y., was only 27 in. tall but 6 ft. across; 'Maxwellii', low, spreading, flat-topped, twice as broad as high. A 31-year-old plant is 3 ft. tall and 6 ft. in dia.; 'Microsperma', one of the best pyramidal types, easily propagated by cuttings. A 42-year-old specimen is 15 ft. tall and 15 ft. in dia.; 'Nidiformis', the top is often flat, a 24-year-old specimen being 3 ft. tall and 6 ft. across; 'Parsonsii', dwarf, flat topped, twice as broad as high; often closely resembling

'Gregoryana', but having looser foliage. A 77-year-old specimen is 7 ft. tall and 10 ft. in dia.; 'Procumbens', prostrate form with horizontal branches, a 51-year-old specimen being only 3 ft. tall, yet 15 ft. in dia.; 'Pumila', dwarf, dense, broad, flat topped; almost 3 times as broad as high. May be propagated by cuttings. A 32-year-old specimen is only 1 ft. tall and yet it is 6 ft. in dia. One of the lowest varieties; 'Pygmaea', a very small, dense, conical form about as wide as it is tall; 'Pyramidata', a narrow, slender pyramid; 'Remontii', ovoid to globose or conical form of slow growth, but not unusually small. A 59-year-old specimen is 20 ft. tall and 24 ft. in dia., very dense and compact throughout; 'Repens', low, with procumbent or arching branches. A 23-year-old specimen is 2 ft. tall and 5 ft. across.

asperata   75′   Zone 5   Dragon Spruce
A dense Spruce from China, with the needles remaining on the tree as long as 7 years (the reason it is so dense), somewhat resembling the Norway Spruce in shape. This tree has light green to light bluish needles and is excellent for seashore planting. Cones are 3–5 in. long.

breweriana   120′   Zone 5   Brewer Spruce
With long, whiplike, pendant branches, this tree is recommended only for the cool, high-altitude areas of its native habitat in Ore. and northern Calif. It does not perform well in the East and is rare in cultivation in America. Cones are 2½–5 in. long.

canadensis = *P. glauca*

engelmannii   150′   Zone 2   Engelmann Spruce
A much more desirable tree than the Norway Spruce, this is native to Canada and Ore. and has bluish-green foliage and dense branches. Although, like most other spruces, older trees may lose some of the lower branches, even 25-foot Engelmann spruces may be covered with branches to the ground. Cones are 2–3 in. long. The variety 'Argentea' has silvery-gray leaves and 'Glauca' has bluish to steel-blue leaves.

glauca   90′   Zone 2   White Spruce
This tree, native to southern Canada and the northern U.S., can endure heat and drought better than some others, but it is not so outstanding an ornamental as *P. engelmannii* or *P. omorika*. It is extremely hardy, but, especially in the eastern U.S., many other spruces will make much better ornamentals. In gardens in the eastern part of the country it is decidedly second rate and is frequently sold at "cut rate" prices. Cones are 1½–2 in. long. Some of the varieties are: 'Coerulea', of dense habit and glaucous leaves; 'Conica', the popular Dwarf White Spruce, a compact pyramidal plant found in southwestern Canada in 1904 and widely distributed. Forty-year-old specimens are not much

more than 10 ft. tall, even when grown in good soil; 'Densata', the Black Hills Spruce, is a slow-growing, compact tree with bright to bluish-green foliage and is of value only as a smaller tree. A plant 36 years old is 20 ft. tall.

jezoensis   150′   Zone 4   Yeddo Spruce
This comes from Manchuria and Japan and has scaly bark, flattened needles that are silvery above, green beneath, and cones 2½–3½ in. long. It does not seem to grow well in the eastern U.S. and so might be passed over for better species.

koyamai   60′   Zone 4   Koyama Spruce
A fine, narrow tree, native to Japan, with light green foliage, definitely ascending branches and a pyramidal outline. It lacks the "layered" branching appearance of some of the other spruce species and this makes it better as an ornamental. Cones are 2–4 in. long.

mariana   54′   Zone 2   Black Spruce
This is native across Canada from Labrador to Alaska and down into Wisc. and Mich. It is a forest tree of thin habit and is not an ornamental specimen. Cones ¾–1½ in. long. The young shoots have sometimes been used in making spruce beer. The variety makes a better ornamental.

mariana 'Doumetii'   30′   Zone 2   Doumet Black Spruce
Better than the species for ornamental work because it is a denser, more rounded tree with bluish-green foliage. It may be propagated by cuttings. A 20-year-old tree is 8 ft. tall and 9 ft. wide and very densely cylindrical.

omorika   90′   Zone 4   Serbian Spruce
This might be considered the best of the spruces for ornamental use in eastern U.S. gardens and it comes from southeastern Europe. It is of rather narrow habit, with glossy green needles which are whitish on the under surface and with pendulous branchlets as the tree grows older. The cones are 2–2½ in. long. Some nurserymen propagate plants asexually from the more pendulously branched trees. This is one of the few spruces with needles flat in cross-section like those of a hemlock, and not 4-sided as are those of most other spruces. The variety 'Pendula' has long, slender, pendulous branches.

orientalis   150′   Zone 4   Oriental Spruce
A graceful tree from Asia Minor, with dark green foliage and needles about the smallest of any of the species, generally ⅜ in. long; hence it has fine texture. During severe winters the foliage may tend to burn in the North, making it less hardy than *P. glauca* or *P. pungens*. Cones are 2–3½ in. long. Some varieties are: 'Aurea', leaves bronzy yellow, a fine ornamental; 'Nana', low, broadly pyramidal form; 'Gowdy'. listed as an extremely upright form of very narrow habit. The leaves are small and a rich green.

pungens   100′   Zone 2   Colorado Spruce
A stiffly branched species with whorled branches all in definite planes or layers; the sharp needles, produced at right angles to the twigs, are green to bluish green. It is native to the Rocky Mountain area, but is widely planted across the country. As small trees they are fine, but many older trees lose their lower branches and when this happens they lose much of their effectiveness. If replaced every 20 years, this condition is overcome. For rugged hardiness it is one of the best, but its stiff habit, its susceptibility to the spruce gall aphid pest and the fact that in many areas it has been overplanted in the past, may limit the usefulness of the species. The cones are 3–4 in. long. The following varieties with bluer foliage will probably always be popular: 'Argentea', Silver Colorado Spruce, often sold as Koster's Blue Spruce, but the leaves are silvery white. The true Koster's Blue Spruce is the pendulous-branched form *P. pungens* 'Pendens', not often found in nurseries; 'Bakeri' originated in a batch of seedling *P. pungens* 'Glauca' in Mass. This variety is a deeper blue than that of *P. pungens* 'Argentea' and possibly even a shade more colorful than the Moerheim Spruce. A 32-year-old specimen of Baker's Blue Spruce is only 12 ft. tall and 6 ft. across and rather dense, while a Moerheim Spruce of the same age is 50 ft. tall; 'Caerulea', leaves bluish white—Cerulean Colorado Spruce; 'Hunnewelliana', a slow-growing, densely pyramidal tree, found in a Mass. nursery among a batch of *P. engelmannii* seedlings. A 32-year-old tree is 15 ft. tall by 8 ft. wide; 'Glauca', foliage bluish green, often sold as Koster's Blue Spruce. The color, of course, is not so blue as that of the Moerheim or the Baker's spruces; 'Moerheim', a compact form; the Moerheim Spruce has deeper blue foliage than the other varieties except possibly the Baker's Spruce; 'Pendens', pendulously branched, with the main branches almost horizontal. Leaves bluish white and stiffer than those of Moerheim Spruce, it was originally propagated by the Koster Nurseries of Boskoop, Holland. It is not found very often in the trade and is named Koster Weeping Blue Spruce.

rubens   90′   Zone 2   Red Spruce
This is a forest tree native from Nova Scotia to the mountains of N.Car. It has a pyramidal habit but must be grown in the cool, moist climate of the mountains and it definitely does not grow well in the hot, drier climate of the lower lands of the eastern U.S. Cones are under 2 in. long.

sitchensis   140′   Zone 6   Sitka Spruce
This tree is very ornamental, but can be grown only in a cool, humid climate. It is native from Alaska to Calif. and does not do at all well in

the eastern U.S., but is a prominent timber tree in the moist climate of the Northwest Pacific coastal area. Cones are 3–4 in. long.

smithiana **150′** **Zone 6** **Himalayan Spruce**
A good tree, native to the Himalayas, with broad, pyramidal habit and pendulous branches. Since the young shoots start to grow very early in the season, the tree should not be planted where there is a possibility of late spring frosts. Cones are 5–7 in. long.

torano (*polita*) **90′** **Zone 5** **Tigertail Spruce**
The rigid, spiny needles of this tree and the conspicuous winter buds are its chief marks of identification. The cones are 3–4 in. long. A native to Japan, it is not used much in America, but makes a dignified and interesting pyramidal specimen, nevertheless.

wilsonii **75′** **Zone 5** **Wilson Spruce**
A tree with a good, dense habit and light green foliage; a 50-year-old tree is 20 ft. tall and 20 ft. wide. It is native to China. Cones are $1\frac{1}{2}$–$2\frac{1}{2}$ in. long.

PICKERELWEED = *Pontederia cordata*

PICKERELWEED FAMILY = Pontederiaceae

PIERIS (py-EE-ris). These are alternate-leaved evergreens belonging to the Ericaceae and hence closely related to rhododendrons. There are about 8 species native to North America and eastern Asia, but in America the 2 most prominent in garden plantings are *P. floribunda* and *P. japonica*. The small, waxy white flowers,

A. *Pieris floribunda*
B. *P. japonica*

similar to those of the closely related blueberries, are borne in terminal clusters and are valued because they bloom early in the spring. The fruits are merely dry capsules.

Propagation

Seed can be sown as soon as ripe or stored dry in airtight containers in a cool place for up to a year, then sown. *P. japonica* roots easily from either softwood or hardwood cuttings (which see), but *P. floribunda* roots with difficulty.

Insect Pests

Andromeda lacebug seriously damages the leaves and may infest Azalea. See RHODODENDRON for control and for other insect pests and diseases.

floribunda **6′** **Zone 4** **Mountain Andromeda**
The Mountain Andromeda, the hardiest of the Pieris species and native from Va. to Ga., is a widely used broad-leaved evergreen, valued not only for its foliage but also for the upright pyramidal clusters of small white flowers borne in the very early spring at about the same time that the oriental cherries bloom. The flower

Pieris floribunda—Mountain Andromeda—an excellent broad-leaved evergreen native to the southeastern U.S. (*Photo by Arnold Arboretum, Jamaica Plain, Mass.*)

buds are, of course, conspicuous all winter; hence the plant is an ever-present promise that spring is bound to come, even when the garden is covered with the deepest snows of winter. The leaves are about 1–3 in. long and slightly toothed, and the nodding panicles of white flowers are 2–4 in. long. The variety '**Grandiflora**' is a clone with unusually large flower clusters. It was selected from seed sown in England about 1934 by Messrs. D. Steward and Son, Ltd., Ferndown, Dorset, England.

formosa **12′** **Zone 7** **Himalayan Andromeda**
This species has flower clusters that are 6 in.

long and evergreen leaves about the same length. The variety **'Wakehurst'** differs from the type in that the leaves are relatively short and broad, and are elliptic to oblong, acuminate, finely serrulate, about 2–4 in. long and ¾ in. wide, somewhat clustered at the ends of the shoots. The deep red color of the young foliage sets off the pure, glistening white of the flowers handsomely. The flowers are carried in spreading terminal panicles 5 in. long.

forrestii   6′–10′   Zones 7–8 (?)   Chinese Andromeda

This evergreen species is widely used in Europe where it is hardy, because the young foliage is a brilliant scarlet when it first appears in the spring. The leaves are 2–4½ in. long and ½–1½ in. wide, lustrous above and below. The fragrant white flowers, appearing in April, are borne in pendulous panicles 4–6 in. long. It is not quite so hardy as *P. formosa*. Sometimes called "Flame-of-the-Forest", because of its brilliant scarlet young foliage in early spring. Later, of course, it turns a normal green.

japonica   9′   Zone 5   Japanese Andromeda

This is about the nicest broad-leaved evergreen for ornamental planting in the North. The lustrous, deep green leaves, up to 3½ in. long, the drooping flower clusters about 5 in. long and the dense foliage all combine to make this an excellent ornamental. The flowers appear about mid-April, slightly before those of *P. floribunda*. Young foliage is often a rich bronze in the spring, turning a normal green as it matures. It will grow in the shade, but at least some sunshine is needed to force it into a good display of flowers.

Several clones of this excellent evergreen are beginning to appear in the nursery trade. To date, some of the best are:

'Compacta'—a compact clone about 6 ft. tall, with leaves about one-half the size of those of the species.

'Crispa'—leaves with wavy margins.

'Dorothy Wycoff'—a compact-growing clone with leaves turning a reddish green in the winter. During the winter the flower buds are dark red, turning to dark pink in the spring, while the flowers open a fine, true pink.

'Flamingo'—deep pink flowers, do not fade.

'Pink Bud'—the buds and newly opened flowers are pink.

'Pygmaea'—leaves small, ½–1 in. long.

'Red Mill'—new foliage red.

'Variegata'—leaves with white margins.

'Whitecaps'—this clone has exceptionally long flower clusters and the blooms last for about 6 weeks. The flowers are pure white.

'White Cascade'—perfectly clear white flowers; full flower clusters; flowers stay white for 5 weeks; produces heavy flower set each year.

nana   1′   Zone 1   Kamchatka Pieris

A low, prostrate shrub with leaves usually in whorls of 3 and about ½ in. long. The white flowers are in short terminal racemes. Native to northeastern Asia. Not much used in landscape work.

taiwanensis   6′   Zone 7   Formosa Andromeda

This is a strikingly handsome, broad-leaved evergreen from Formosa, with pure white flowers similar to those of other Pieris, but borne in clusters 6 in. long during the early spring. The glossy evergreen leaves are 3 in. long.

PIGEON-PEA = *Cajanus cajan*

PIGEON-PLUM = *Coccoloba diversifolia*

PIGEON-WINGS = *Clitoria mariana*

PIGGY-BACK PLANT = *Tolmiea menziesii*

PIGNUT = *Carya glabra*

PIGWEED = *Chenopodium album*

PIGWEED, REDROOT = *Amaranthus retroflexus*

PILEA (PILL-ea, also PY-lea)

cadierei   18″   Zone 10   Aluminum Plant

New, only introduced into the U.S. in 1952 from Indo-China, this has small leaves beautifully marked with gray on the upper surface. Excellent for a window garden. Small white flowers on a long stem during the late summer. Easily propagated by cuttings.

involucrata   6″   Zone 10   Panamiga

Sometimes used in terrariums, this little plant from Panama, with erect stems, opposite leaves up to 2 in. long, has minute greenish flowers in many-flowered cymes. The upper leaf surface is greenish brown, below purplish. Forming interesting leaf patterns. Needs plenty of moisture and should be grown in the shade. A delicate little foliage plant for the house.

microphylla   4″–8″   Zone 10   Artillery Plant

A popular house plant for years, native to tropical America and southern Fla., it takes its name from the fact that when the flower buds are moistened they suddenly open, dispersing a cloud of pollen. The fernlike foliage consists of a mass of tiny leaves. The minute reddish flowers in summer are profusely borne but are inconspicuous. Variable, but a most interesting and graceful house plant. Easily propagated by cuttings. Plants require plenty of moisture at all times.

pubescens   6″   Zone 10   Silver Panamiga

A good house plant, fernlike, with opposite leaves 2–3 in. long and velvety light-gray. The flowers are greenish and inconspicuous, borne in a flat cluster. Provide a shaded place with plenty of water. Propagated easily by rooting cuttings in sand.

PILEOSTEGIA (pi-lo-STEE-gia)

viburnoides   clinging vine   Zone 7   Tanglehead
Closely resembling the Climing Hydrangea in
its method of attaching itself to walls, it has
dark, glossy, opposite, leathery, evergreen
leaves, that are entire, oblong to ovate-lanceolate and 3–5 in. long. One of the best evergreen
climbers; seemingly doing best in full shade,
with freely borne small flowers in terminal
clusters during the late summer. Native to
southern China. The flowers are white, somewhat like those of the Climbing Hydrangea.

PILOSE. With long straight hairs.

PIMENTA (pim-EN-ta)

dioica (*officinalis*)   **40′   Zone 10   Allspice**
An aromatic tropical tree from Central America
and Mexico, with leaves 6 in. long, white
flowers about ¼ in. wide and dark brown globose
fruits that are about ¼ in. wide. These are
harvested in July and Aug. but only the green or
unripe berries make the best spice. Allspice has
been used as a very aromatic substitute for
tobacco in the West Indies.

PIMPERNEL. See ANAGALLIS.

PIMPINELLA (pim-pin-ELL-a)

anisum   2′   annual   Anise
A popular herb, native from Greece to Egypt,
and used medicinally as far back as 1500 B.C.
It is a sprawling plant with deeply notched
aromatic leaves and heavy heads of yellowish-
white flowers. The leaves are used for flavoring
foods. The flowers, dried and powdered, are
used to flavor some brands of muscatel and
vermouth. The seeds are used in perfumes,
medicines and soaps and flavor for many
foods. Propagated by seed.

PINACEAE = The Pine, Fir or Spruce Family

PINCUSHION FLOWER = *Scabiosa caucasica*

PINE. See PINUS.

PINEAPPLE (*Ananas comosus*). This New
World plant, a member of the family Bromi-
liaceae, was propagated vegetatively in improved forms by the Central and South
American natives long before the discovery of
the continent by Europeans. Then it was rapidly
spread throughout the world and is now grown
everywhere in the Tropics, to which it is adapted.
In the United States it can be grown only in the
warmest areas of the Fla. peninsula, and in well-
protected garden sites along the southern
Pacific coastal strip. It is a principal crop of
Hawaii, and a minor one in Fla.

The plant is a herbaceous, perennial monocotyledon. It has a short stem or stalk, covered
by the narrow swordlike leaves in a tight spiral;
the stem, at the time of floral differentiation,
bears numerous flowers in a tight spiral just
below the growing point, which continues and
forms a spiral of smaller leaves above the
flowering portion of the stem, known as the
crown. The plant is about 3 ft. tall, and if not
crowded it will spread 4–5 ft. or more with age.

The exact hardiness limits for the Pineapple
are not truly known; in the open it has been
seriously damaged at temperatures of 32° F.,
but under lathe or cover, plants have been
reported to withstand as low as 25° F. for short
periods. However, fruit is injured by a few
hours below 41° F.

Three parts of the plant are commonly used in
propagation. The crown, borne on top of the
fruit; slips, which develop at or near the
flowering stalk, and shoots or suckers, which
develop in the axils of the leaves, or from
below ground. Taken from the mother plant,
usually after the harvest, they are dried for a
week to a month before planting. They are
planted upright in dibbled holes 4 to 6 in. deep.
Slips are usually preferred, then suckers, and
crowns last. An alternative method is to take
the leaves from a stem, cut it into 2 or 3 portions,
burying these in the soil 5 or 6 in. deep.

Planting distance in multiple plantings varies
considerably, but the plants can be grown close
together, as 22 in. x 22 in. in beds of several
rows.

The primary concern in developing quality
fruit of good size is to keep the plant growing
vigorously. Up to 70 or 80 leaves should be
developed before flowering to secure good fruit
size; this can be obtained only with heavy
fertilization. On sandy soils a pound or more of
a 6–6–6 formula applied at 3 or 4 evenly spaced
applications through the year are generally
needed. In addition, extra nitrogen in the winter
and summer is often used. A fertilizer which
contains other elements, such as magnesium
and trace elements, will probably give excellent
results, as pineapples suffer many micro-nutrient
deficiencies.

Foliar feeding is particularly easy with the
Pineapple, for the basal portion of each leaf is
adapted to absorb water and nutrients. A
spray of 1 lb. of urea, 12 oz. of potassium
sulfate, 8 oz. of calcium nitrate and 4 oz. of iron
sulfate, magnesium sulfate, and calgon, plus a
teaspoonful of borax, and a small amount of
copper sulfate per 10 gal. of water sprayed on
the plant at biweekly intervals will satisfy its
mineral needs.

Pineapples are not too particular as to soil,
except that it must be well drained; light sandy
soils are best, but will require greatest fertilization. Watering should be shallow, with mulches
recommended to keep down weed competition
and hold water near the surface of the soil. The

Pineapple does well in full sun if maximum temperatures are not too high; it can also be grown quite satisfactorily in partial shade. It should not be planted exposed to winds, as the heavy fruit and shallow root system make it particularly subject to blowing over.

As the inflorescence appears, the flowers open from the base toward the tip, taking about 20 days to complete. The petals are violet or purplish, and wither after bloom. All pineapples are self-incompatible (will not set seed with their own pollen) so that the fruit on an isolated plant or a field of the same variety develops without seed forming. The edible portion of the fruit is made up of the fused bract, corolla and ovarian portions of the flower, the petals and stamens having dried and dropped, and is a sorosis. If cross-pollinated, hard, bony seeds form in the ovary, deep in the flesh.

The Pineapple may be induced to bloom rather easily by spraying the central growing point with naphthaleneacetic acid (NAA) at about 10 ppm. It seems to be a little more effective if applied during cool weather, and hence might be used as a spring spray to insure fruit development through the best part of the summer. It should not be used unless there are sufficient leaves on the plant to bring the fruit through in best condition and size. Commercially it is used primarily to induce all of the plants to bloom at the same time, so that harvest is simpler. The single flower cluster emerges from the basal rosette of leaves and matures in 15 to 32 months from planting. If, after harvest, the original plant is left in place, flowering occurs annually in the so-called ratoon crops which follow. Ratoon crops have more than a single fruit, but not more than 2 or 3 should be allowed to develop. The plant will exist for many years, although in commercial practice few fields are taken beyond the first or second ratoon crop, because the fruits tend to be smaller and less perfect.

Temperature affects the time of first fruiting to a marked degree. Slips planted in the fall seldom fruit until the second summer following. Crowns will probably take somewhat longer to develop a good plant than slips. Drought and adverse weather during the year may delay the appearance of the inflorescence the next season, or cause it to be smaller than normal. Time from flowering to ripening is lengthened by cool weather. Thus, though fruits usually mature in summer, they may be delayed until exposed to damaging winter temperatures.

There are numerous varieties of Pineapple. 'Cayenne' is the main commercial variety of Hawaii, and is sometimes used in Fla., but 'Red Spanish' and 'Abachi' are preferred there.

The latter has a rich flavor and is yellow fleshed; 'Red Spanish' is more acid and less sweet, with yellowish-white flesh.

Nematodes may devitalize the plant; fumigation of the planting site will be beneficial. Mealybugs, thrips and mites also attack the plant, especially the former. A water spray of malathion will control mealybugs; sulfur dusts most thrips and mites. Control of ants will minimize mealybug attacks.

Weeds are perhaps the greatest enemy of Pineapple. Paper and black polyethylene sheets, or mulches may be used beneficially to keep weeds down in a close-planted bed. Hoeing should be as shallow as possible.

CLARON O. HESSE

PINEAPPLE FAMILY = Bromeliaceae

PINEAPPLE-FLOWER = *Eucomis comosa*

PINEAPPLE GUAVA = *Feijoa sellowiana*

PINEAPPLE-LILY = *Billbergia pyramidalis*

PINE FAMILY = Pinaceae

PINGUICULA (pin-GWIK-yew-la)

vulgaris   6″   Zone 3   Common Butterwort
A small herb with basal entire leaves; violet or purple flowers, $\frac{1}{2}$ in. long and across; ovate leaves $1\frac{1}{2}$ in. long. Native to North America, Europe and Asia, especially in moist places. Linnaeus said of this that it was used by the Laplanders to curdle milk by pouring warm milk fresh from the cow over a strainer on which fresh leaves of *Pinguicula* had been laid. Left for a day or two to stand until it begins to turn sour, this makes a delicious drink.

PINK. See DIANTHUS.

PINK FAMILY = Caryophyllaceae

PINNAE. A term (singular pinna) meaning the primary divisions or leaflets of a pinnate (feather-formed) leaf, especially of a fern frond.

PINNATE. A botanical term meaning feather-formed; that is with leaflets of a compound leaf placed on either side of a central midrib.

PINNATIFID. Cleft or divided in a pinnate way.

PINNULE. Second division of a fern frond, twice compound.

PINUS (PY-nus). The pines constitute the most important group of lumber trees in the world, and as ornamentals they are equally at the top of any list of evergreens. Growing widely about the northern temperate regions of the world, they are represented in North America by many native species and varieties. These, together wth those imported from Europe and the Orient, give the American gardener a glorious collection from which to choose for ornamental plantings.

American nurserymen are offering at least 77 species and varieties. Seventy-two species, 35 varieties and 90 hybrids, with a total of 16,000 trees, are growing in the world's greatest collection of pines at the Institute of Forest Genetics of the U.S. Forest Service in Placerville, Calif.

Pines are mostly trees, but there are a few shrubs among them, growing in soils ranging from good to very poor, from the seashore to the highest timberline. The needles, produced in groups of 2, 3 or 5 and encased in a sheath, will vary in length on almost every tree, but it is fairly well known that a few like *P. banksiana*, *P. aristata* and *P. parviflora* will have needles under 1½ in. long, while others such as *P. canariensis*, *P. caribaea* and *P. patula* will have needles nearly a foot long.

The flowers are unisexual, but both types are borne on the same tree. The cones vary in shape and length and it is these that botanists describe carefully as a final means of properly identifying one species from another. It may take a number of years before a small tree becomes large enough to produce fruits.

The pines may be easily divided into 3 groups, depending upon the number of needles in each cluster or sheath. Additional information is given on the approximate length of the needles and this also frequently aids in their identification, as does information on the color of the bark, the relative hardiness of the species or where they are found to be native. However, there are times when it is extremely difficult, if not impossible, to tell certain species apart (*P. monticola* from *P. strobus*, for one example), especially when only a short twig is available for study.

The following table will be the first step as an aid to identification, but as the identification problems become difficult, one must consult standard botanical texts which give all the details in the differentiation of the species.

The best species for the small garden are *P. aristata*, *P. cembra*, *P. contorta*, *P. koraiensis*, *P. mugo* (possibly *P. nigra*) and *P. peuce*, together with any of the shrubby varieties which appear to have merit for the specific situation. White pines (*P. strobus*) are, of course, widely used even on small properties, but it should be understood that they are not small trees, and when used in cramped situations they must be heavily pruned to keep them within the limits of the property. The Silver White Japanese Pine (*P. parviflora glauca*) is certainly a beautiful tree, but one specimen in the Arnold Arboretum is 60 ft. tall and 60 ft. wide. Pruning a specimen tree such as this to keep it within a 20-foot area would be difficult indeed.

Some pines, such as *P. banksiana* and *P. rigida*, are of merit only for planting in poor soils where better pines or deciduous plants will not grow. Others, like *P. pinaster* and *P. halepensis*, are best used only for planting at the seashore where most evergreens have a difficult time. The Japanese Black Pine (*P. thunbergii*) can be noted as the best evergreen tree of any kind for planting in seashore gardens of the northeastern U.S. Hurricanes and frequent drenchings with salt-water spray fail to retard its normal growth. Even after the worst storms, the foliage of this species is always a fine, dark green color.

Certain species like *P. mugo*, *P. resinosa* and *P. strobus* have produced varieties that are strictly shrubs, of value only in the shrub

NUMBER AND APPROXIMATE LENGTH OF NEEDLES OF RECOMMENDED PINE SPECIES		
5 NEEDLES IN SHEATH	3 NEEDLES IN SHEATH	2 NEEDLES IN SHEATH
P. armandii 4″–8″	P. bungeana 2″–3″	P. banksiana 1″
P. aristata 1″–1½″	P. canariensis 9″–12″	P. caribaea 8″–12″ (some-
P. cembra 2″–5″	P. cembroides 2″	times 3 needles)
P. flexilis 2″–3″	P. jeffreyi 5″–8″	P. contorta 1″–2″
P. koraiensis 2½″–4″	P. palustris 8″–18″	P. densiflora 3″–5″
P. lambertiana 3″–4″	P. patula 12″	P. echinata 3″–5″ (some-
P. monticola 1½–4″	P. ponderosa 5″–11″	times 3 needles)
P. parviflora 1½″–2½″	(sometimes 2 needles)	P. halepensis 2½″–4″
P. peuce 3″–4″	P. radiata 4″–6″	P. mugo ¾″–2″
P. strobus 2″–5″	P. rigida 2″–5″	P. muricata 4″–7″
P. torreyana 8″–12″	P. sabiniana 8″–12″	P. nigra 3″–6½″
P. wallichiana 6″–8″	P. taeda 6″–10″	P. pinaster 5″–9″
		P. pinea 4″–8″
		P. pungens 1″–3″ (some-
		times 3 needles)
		P. resinosa 4″–6″
		P. sylvestris 2″–3″
		P. thunbergii 4″
		P. virginiana 1¼″–3″

border, foundation planting or rock garden. The seeds and inner bark have sometimes been cooked and used as an emergency food.

Pruning pines, especially pruning them in hedges, is not so easy as pruning deciduous hedges. It is best to shear them (in hedge form) when the young shoots are half grown in the late spring or early summer. If the cut is made so that no dormant buds are below the cut, it may be that no new buds or shoots will develop. This bears some study on the gardener's part, as well as requiring experience.

Propagation

The many species of Pine bear seed which vary widely in their germinating performance, some germinating as soon as sown, others having complicated inhibiting conditions. In general, if the exact performance of the seed is not known, the requirements will be met by stratifying the seed for 3 months at 40° F., then sowing. In no

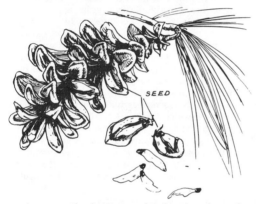

An opened pine cone showing location of seeds and cone scales. Most mature pine cones open in the autumn while still attached to the tree and the seeds are distributed by the wind.

case is this procedure detrimental and it usually results in a more uniform stand of seedlings. The seed may be stored dry in airtight containers and kept in a cool place up to a year or longer before it is treated.

Grafting is usually the standard method by which varieties are asexually propagated, using as understock the same, or closely related, species. See STRATIFICATION, GRAFTING.

Insect Pests

White Pine aphid on the needles and pine bark aphid on the trunk and larger branches are common pests unless controlled by sprays of insecticide #15. Pine needle scale on the needles, especially on Mugo Pine, is con-

trolled with sprays of insecticide #15 when crawlers are hatching in early summer. Larvae of the White Pine weevil, a snout beetle, girdle and kill the leaders of White Pine and Norway Spruce. Spraying with insecticide #9 just before the new growth (candles) starts in spring kills the beetles and cutting and burning the wilted leaders while the grubs are in them decreases later infestations. Trees in shade are infested more often than those in sun. Pales weevil, another snout beetle, gnaws the bark of seedlings and is a serious pest in nurseries and new plantings near freshly cut slash, in which the beetles breed. Small plantings and ornamental trees can be protected by spraying the trunk with insecticide #9. Pine web worms which web needles of Red and White Pine in masses of froth, pine sawflies which eat the needles, pine tube moth which lives in a case among webbed needles and pine spittlebug which lives in a bubble of froth after sucking the sap, are all controlled by timely spraying with insecticide #9. European pine shoot moth is a serious pest of Red and Scotch Pine. It kills the buds and new shoots and causes crooked leaders. The young which hatch in midsummer can be killed by sprays of insecticide #9 when the young start feeding. Two or more applications may be necessary. In the Northeast, Pitch Pine and Red Pine are infected with matsucoccus scale which is difficult to find until yellow needles attract attention. No complete control is known.

Diseases

White Pine blister rust develops cankers on the bark which swell and produce orange spores. Branches, twigs and small trees are killed. It must live on Currant and Gooseberry for part of its life and the elimination of these plants within 300 yds. is advised. Spraying with fungicide #A has been helpful experimentally. Most states in the infected area have quarantines on currants. Needle cast is caused by both fungi and by windburn. The fungus may be killed by spraying with fungicide #D or #F when the needles are about half grown.

aristata 8′–45′ Zone 5 Bristlecone Pine When planted in gardens in the eastern U.S., this tree is a dwarf, growing very slowly, a 16-year-old plant being only 4 ft. tall. It does not conform to any particular form of growth but is picturesque, with short, bluish-green needles closely bunched together, on which are white spots of resin. It is most interesting to note that old trees native to Calif., Colo. and Ariz., dwarfed by age and droughts, have been estimated to be 7100 yrs. old; hence are older than some of the Giant Sequoias of Calif. Needles are

5 in a sheath and 1–2½ in. long. Cones are 1¾–3¾ in. long.

banksiana   75′   Zone 2   Jack Pine
Only of value for planting on loose, dry soils or banks where other evergreens and deciduous plants will fail, especially in northeastern U.S. where it is native. The needles, 2 in a sheath and 1 in. long, turn yellowish over winter and the general habit is very loose and open. It is not recommended as an ornamental of any kind. Cones are 1–2 in. long.

Pinus bungeana—Lace-bark Pine—has interesting exfoliating bark. (*Photo by Arnold Arboretum, Jamaica Plain, Mass.*)

bungeana   75′   Zone 4   Lace-bark Pine
One of the Chinese pines with 3 needles in a sheath, dark green foliage, and often bushy habit of growth with several main trunks; this tree is especially valued for its beautiful bark which exfoliates in irregular plates, exposing the light, creamy-colored, inner bark. It is slow-growing, often weak-wooded, but makes an excellent specimen, often holding its needles for as long as 5 years. Cones 2–3 in. long.

canariensis   80′   Zone 8   Canary Pine
This exotic pine is native to the Canary Islands and is of value only in the far South and southern Calif. Its needles, 3 in each sheath, are 9–12 in. long, making it very picturesque.

Especially does it do well in dry, rocky soils where *P. radiata* will not thrive. Cones are 8–9 in. long.

caribaea   100′   Zone 9   Slash Pine
Although an excellent tree for lumber and for producing turpentine in the area from N.Car. to Fla. where it is native, it is used only occasionally in the southeastern states as an ornamental. The long needles, 2–3 in a sheath and 8–12 in. long, and the loose, open character of the tree give it a rather coarse appearance. Cones are 4–5 in. long.

cembra   75′   Zone 2   Swiss Stone Pine
A tightly pyramidal tree with dense foliage and with needles, 5 in a sheath, from 2½–4½ in. long; native to the Alps of Europe. Unfortunately it is slow-growing, but it is very hardy and is being grown as far north as Dropmore, Manitoba, Canada. The foliage is the same color as that of the native eastern White Pine. An excellent tree for the small property, it has cones 3½ in. long and edible seeds.

cembroides   20′   Zone 7   Mexican Pinyon Pine
Native to Calif., Ariz. and Mexico, there are 2–3 needles per sheath, the needles being about 2 in. long. The seeds have been used as food by the Indians and are still sold in parts of Mexico for that purpose. The egg-shaped cones are 1½–2 in. long, 1½ in. wide, and the seeds are ½ in. long. Not used as an ornamental outside its native habitat.

contorta   30′   Zone 7   Shore Pine
This tree is reported to grow under many different soil and climatic conditions on the West Coast, where it is native from Alaska to Calif., and it has been recommended for use there as an ornamental in far greater quantity than it is being used now. It is adapted equally well to boggy or to dry soils. It has deep, rich green foliage with 2 needles in a sheath, 1–2 in. long, and makes an excellent garden tree. Cones are 3 in. long.

contorta latifolia   75′   Zone 5   Lodge Pole Pine
A hardier and taller-growing variety, this is the most common tree in the general Rocky Mountain area and hence can be used in the Rocky Mountain states as an ornamental where desired. It also has 2 needles in a sheath, 1–2 in. long, and cones 3 in. long.

coulteri   75′   Zone 7   Big Cone Pine, Coulter Pine
A native to Calif., with 2 needles in each sheath, 8–12 in. long, and large cones about 14 in. long and 4 in. through. It is a coarse-looking pine and for this reason it is not used in landscape work, but is frequently seen in the Calif. forests.

densiflora   100′   Zone 4   Japanese Red Pine

With horizontal branches and light bluish-green needles 3–5 in. long, 2 in each sheath, this picturesque tree from Japan is of a definitely flat-topped habit. The bark is orange-red on older branches. Cones 2 in. long. The variety 'Globosa' is dwarf and globose in habit, but of vigorous growth. 'Umbraculifera', the Tanyosho Pine, is low, seldom much over 12 ft. tall, umbrellalike with a flat top. This is popular as a picturesque garden specimen and the reddish color of the older branches adds materially to its exotic effect; 'Oculis-draconis', the Dragon's Eye Pine, has needles, each of which has 2 yellowish bands. Considered simply an oddity.

eldarica   75′ +   Zone 7   Afghan Pine
Introduced into the U.S. in 1960 by the U.S. Dept. of Ag. from southwest Asia, tolerant of hot dry winds and alkaline soil in the southwestern U.S.

excelsa = *P. wallichiana*

flexilis   45′–75′   Zone 2   Limber Pine
Native to western North America, this desirable ornamental pine, often called the Rocky Mountain White Pine, has a tendency to become flat topped as it matures. It grows slowly and individual trees may be 200 years old before the trunk will be 9 in. through. As a perennially small specimen on the small place, it has advantages. The needles are 5 in a sheath, 2–3 in. long, and the cones are 4–6 in. long.

griffithii = *P. wallichiana*

halepensis   60′   Zone 9   Aleppo Pine
Recommended for seashore planting only, where other pines might not do well. It is native to the Mediterranean Region and so is hardy only in the most southerly portions of the U.S. Where better growing conditions are available, better pines should be used. Needles 2 in a sheath, 2½–4 in. long, and cones about 3 in. long.

jeffreyi   120′   Zone 5   Jeffrey Pine
A pyramidal tree with open, bluish-green branches, spreading and even pendant, native to Ore. and Calif., with 3 needles in a sheath, 5–8 in. long, and cinnamon-red to brown bark. The large cones are egg-shaped, 9–12 in. long. Picturesque as a forest tree.

koraiensis   90′   Zone 3   Korean Pine
Because it is slow-growing, this might be considered one of the best pines for small gardens (along with *P. cembra*). It is native to Japan and Korea; is dense, with dark green foliage; the needles, 5 in a sheath, are only 2½–4 in. long. This excellent tree could be used considerably more than it is. Cones are 4–6 in. long.

lambertiana   180′   Zone 5   Sugar Pine
The tallest of the native American pines, native from Ore. to Calif., it is not a tree for the small garden! It is of interest because it bears the largest cones of any of the pines, sometimes 20

Pinus jeffreyi: this one growing in Yosemite National Park is shaped by wind.

in. or more in length. The needles are 5 in a sheath, 3–4 in. long. Although hardy in Boston, Mass., it is probably only of ornamental use on the West Coast. It is narrowly columnar in habit—a tree 60 ft. tall will be 20 ft. wide.

monticola   90′   Zone 5   Western White Pine
Differing from *P. strobus* in being more narrow and symmetrical in habit, this makes a fine ornamental and is native from British Columbia to Calif. In the East, at least, it is doubtful whether it will ever be used much in place of the more readily available *P. strobus*, but it should be kept in mind that it is hardy and might be used where a narrower tree is desired. It

The staminate or pollen-bearing flowers of *Pinus leucodermis.*

makes a beautiful specimen. The needles are 5 in a sheath, 1½–4 in. long, and the cones are 4–9 in. long.

mugo   to 36′   Zone 2   Swiss Mountain Pine
A variable species, native to Europe, with some varieties growing as trees; it is best to propagate these asexually from plants of known characteristics, rather than to grow them from

seeds of indefinite parentage. The species and the varieties are susceptible to often serious infestations of scale, which limit their usefulness, especially as hedges. The needles are 2 in a sheath, $\frac{3}{4}$–2 in. long, and the cones are 2 in. long. Some of the popular varieties are: '**Compacta**'—very dense and globose; **mugo**—Mugho Pine, widely grown, commonly planted shrub. An old plant measured 5 ft. tall and 14 ft.

Pinus mugo is a popular low pine, but is susceptible to infestations of scale. (*Photo by Arnold Arboretum, Jamaica Plain, Mass.*).

across; '**Slavinii**'—a very low dwarf, originating in Rochester, N.Y. The old plant at one time measured 2 ft. tall and 6 ft. across; **rostrata** and **rotundata** are usually small trees.

muricata   45′   Zone 7   Bishop Pine
A handsome tree of regular pyramidal habit, this is used as an ornamental only in Calif. where it is native. Needles 2 in a sheath, 4–7 in. long, and cones 2–4$\frac{1}{2}$ in. long.

nigra   90′   Zone 4   Austrian Pine
A variable species native to Europe, most plants are geographical forms of one kind or another. The species and the variety **nigra** (some prefer to use the name *P. nigra* var. *nigra*) are practically identical and in the trade, in the U.S. at least, they are synonymous. A rapid grower, with stiff, dark green needles 3$\frac{1}{2}$–6$\frac{1}{2}$ in. long, 2 in a sheath; this makes an excellent windbreak or screen, growing well on limestone soils. This is one of the pines that makes a good specimen and also can be used for mass planting. Cones 3 in. long. The variety '**Hornibrookiana**' was found as a witches broom on a tree in Seneca Park, Rochester, N.Y. This grows into a compact, rounded, dwarf evergreen; a 30-year-old plant being only 2 ft. tall and 6 ft. across; '**Pygmaea**'—a very slow-growing, dense bush which, even at 40 years of age, may be only 8 ft. tall; '**Pyramidalis**'—a narrowly pyramidal plant, one in Rochester, N.Y., being 22 ft. tall and only 12 ft. across the base.

palustris   100′   Zone 7   Longleaf Pine
The most interesting characteristic of this pine, native to the southeastern U.S., is that it retains its cones for 15–20 years. The spine-tipped needles are in bundles of 3, 8–18 in. long, and the cones are 3–3$\frac{1}{2}$ in. long and about 2 in. wide at the base. Cut branches of the foliage are used in the North for decoration. A good timber tree, but has little ornamental value.

parviflora   90′   Zone 5   White Japanese Pine
Needing plenty of room for development (1 tree in the Arnold Arboretum is 60 ft. tall and almost as wide), this Japanese tree is an excellent ornamental. The needles are 1$\frac{1}{2}$–2$\frac{1}{2}$ in. long, 5 in a sheath, and often tufted on the long, horizontally spreading branches. Sometimes scions of this are grafted on *P. thunbergii* and as a result the plants grow very slowly, giving opportunity for some to ascribe the varietal name 'Nana' to such plants. A beautiful, wide-spreading tree—about the widest growing of any of these pines, worthy of planting where suitable space is available. The variety '**Glauca**' is even better, for it has silvery-blue foliage. Cones 2–3 in. long.

patula   60′   Zone 9   Jelecote Pine
Of use only in southern Calif. and native to Mexico. The slender, gracefully hanging leaves are 12 in. long, 3 in a sheath, making this a rather striking tree.

peuce   60′   Zone 4   Macedonian, Balkans Pine
This pine from the Balkans is one of the smaller pines for small places, since an 80-year-old tree is 45 ft. tall, yet only 15 ft. across. The branches are produced in whorls, but the foliage is obviously more dense than that of *P. strobus*. The needles are 5 in a sheath, 3–4 in. long, and the cones are 5–8 in. long.

pinaster   90′   Zone 7   Cluster Pine
An attractive tree of rapid growth from the Mediterranean Region, having a pyramidal crown and adapted especially for seashore planting. One of the common names sometimes used for this tree is Maritime Pine. However, the younger the plants used, the better the chances for survival, since it is difficult to transplant. Needles are 2 in a sheath, 5–9 in. long, and the cones are 3$\frac{3}{4}$–7$\frac{3}{4}$ in. long.

pinea   60′   Zone 9   Italian Stone Pine
A picturesque tree from the Mediterranean Region, it is difficult to transplant, is of use only in the very warm parts of the U.S. and has an asymmetrical, umbrellalike head. Sometimes much of the trunk is devoid of branches which are all clustered at the top. The edible seeds are nearly $\frac{1}{2}$ in. long. The tree is much planted in the Mediterranean Region, where the seeds are used for food. The needles are 2 in a sheath, 4–8 in. long, and the cones are 5 in. long.

ponderosa 150′ **Zone 5** **Ponderosa Pine**
A fast-growing tree, forests of which cover large areas in western North America; it is used as an ornamental tree because of its rapid growth and its dark, yellowish-green needles from 5–11 in. in length, with 2 or 3 in a sheath. In the northwestern U.S. this is perhaps the most frequently planted of the long-needled pines, but it is definitely not a tree for the small place, for it can grow up to 200 ft. tall under ideal conditions. Cones 6 in. long. The variety 'Pendula' has drooping to pendulous branches; var. **scopulorum** is smaller in all of its features than the species, is hardier (Zone 4) and has an almost columnar habit. It is often called the Rocky Mountain Ponderosa Pine.

pungens 30′ **Zone 5** **Table Mountain Pine**
Native from N.J. to Tenn. and Ga., this has a very flat-topped habit quite distinct from most other pines and the cones may persist for 10–15 years. The needles are 2 in a bundle, about 1¼–2½ in. long, sharp-pointed, and the cones are 2½–3½ in. long, mostly borne 3 together. Little planted as an ornamental.

radiata 60′ **Zone 7** **Monterey Pine**
Another tree from southern Calif., its use limited largely to seaside plantings in southern Calif. The tree makes a beautiful specimen, with bright green needles 4–6 in. long, 3 needles in a sheath, and is of rapid growth when young. Cones 3–5½ in. long.

resinosa 75′ **Zone 2** **Red Pine**
The Red or Norway Pine is a fine ornamental, native throughout northeastern North America. with a massive head and long, flexible needles, 4–6 in. in length and 2 in a sheath. The reddish bark of the trunk and older branches is the reason for the common name. It is noted for its ability to grow well in poor soils. Cones are 2 in. long.

rigida 75′ **Zone 4** **Pitch Pine**
A scrubby tree native from Canada to Ky., of little ornamental use except on poor, rocky or sandy soils, especially at the seashore. Older trees are picturesque in habit, but this is about all that can be said of them. The varietal name **serotina** has been given to the smaller trees, which may grow only 40–50 ft. tall. Where good soil is available, this species should not be grown. The needles are 3 in a sheath, 2–5 in. long, and the cones are 1½–3 in. long.

sabiniana 50′ **Zone 6** **Digger Pine**
A loose, open-growing pine, native to Calif., with 3 needles in each sheath, 8–12 in. long and cones 6–10 in. long. Not very much used as an ornamental.

strobus 100′–150′ **Zone 3** **Eastern White Pine**
One of the best of the pines for ornamental use, widely native to eastern North America. It withstands the proper kind of shearing, so that young trees may be restrained when necessary. Easily transplanted, beautiful at all seasons and easily grown, this is one of the standard essential landscape plants for the eastern part of the U.S. The needles are 5 in a sheath, 2–5 in. long, and the cones are 4–6 in. long. Varieties: 'Brevifolia' —a slow-growing dwarf with needles scarcely over 1½ in. long, making a dense, globe-shaped bush. A 60-year-old tree is 7 ft. tall and 15 ft. across; 'Fastigiata'—Pyramidal Eastern White Pine, upright in habit; young trees of this variety clearly are fastigiate to pyramidal in habit. The older they grow, the less this habit is evident; 'Nana'—Dwarf Eastern White Pine, a dwarf, rounded to conical bush, suitable for planting in the rock garden; 'Pendula'—the Weeping White Pine, a picturesque tree with pendulous branches. This makes an excellent specimen; 'Umbraculifera'—the Umbrella Eastern White Pine, a compact-growing bush with short leaves, upright branches and a uniformly level top.

sylvestris 75′ **Zone 2** **Scotch Pine**
Over 25 varieties of this widely grown European pine have been named at one time or another. Probably all are not growing in America. Many of these forms are difficult to distinguish from one another on the basis of leaf specimens, but when all are growing in close proximity their differences may be readily seen. The typical Scotch Pine has twisted, bluish-green needles, 2 in a sheath, 2–3 in. long, and a beautiful reddish trunk. It is not dense in habit, but rather picturesque and open. Cones are 2 in. long. Varieties: 'Argentea', the Silver Scotch Pine. Leaves are a pronounced silvery color; 'Fastigiata', the Pyramidal Scotch Pine, columnar and narrow in habit; about the narrowest of any of the pines; 'Nana', Dwarf Scotch Pine, a low, densely rounded bush with short, horizontal or ascending branches; 'Watereri', the Waterer Scotch Pine, a low, densely pyramidal form with steel-blue leaves, almost as high as wide when young.

taeda 90′–165′ **Zone 6** **Loblolly Pine**
Native to the eastern coast of the U.S. from N.J. to Fla. and west to Tex., this has little ornamental value because the leaves, 3 in a bundle, are 6–10 in. long, making even the smallest branches very heavy. However, because of these long leaves, cut branches are often used in floral decorations or in swags at Christmas. The cones are 5 in. long.

thunbergiana 90′ **Zone 4** **Japanese Black Pine**
This is the best evergreen for seaside planting in the northeastern part of the U.S. and it comes from Japan. It grows irregularly, and often grotesquely, and does not seem to do well inland

in gardens where the growing conditions are better than at the seashore. This tree actually grows well within a few feet of the high water mark at the seashore, where it is exposed to occasional drenchings of salt-water spray! The needles are 2 in a sheath, 4 in. long, and the cones are 3 in. long or less.

torreyana **45′** **Zone 8** **Torrey Pine**
A pine native to Calif., open in habit but with spreading and ascending branches. The needles are 5 in a bundle and 8–12 in. long, the cones being 4–6 in. long. It is of merit only in dry situations in southern Calif. where better pines will not grow.

virginiana **45′** **Zone 4** **Virginia, Scrub Pine**
A native of the eastern U.S., this is not used in ornamental planting, being allowed to grow only in poor, dry soils where better pines will not do well. It has an open habit of growth with sparse branching, often with a very wide, stiff top. The needles are 2 in a sheath, 1¼–4 in. long, and the cones are 1½–2½ in. long.

wallichiana **150′** **Zone 5** **Himalayan Pine**
Formerly known as *P. excelsa*, this is a beautiful pine with needles 6–8 in. long, 5 in a sheath, which droop gracefully and are of a soft texture. A tall, wide-spreading tree from the Himalayas, it can be used only where there is plenty of space for proper development. Eventually the branches may need a space 40–50 ft. wide. For specimen use only. Cones 7–12 in. long. Formerly also *P. griffithii*.

PINWHEEL = *Aeonium haworthii*

PIPER (PY-per)
nigrum **climbing** **Zone 10** **Black Pepper**
A trailing plant from the East Indies, valued for its fruits from which black pepper is made. The flower spikes are 3–6 in. long and the fruits, small and globose, ⅛–¼ in. in dia., change color from green to red to black. Black pepper is made from the whole fruit, white pepper from the fruit less its external coat.

ornatum **climber** **Zone 10** **Celebes Pepper**
A climbing Pepper from the Celebes, with ovate-orbicular to peltate, waxy leaves, 3–4 in. long, spotted pink above when young and white when mature. Very attractive with reddish stems and petioles. Often grown in the greenhouse for its handsome foliage. Propagated by seeds or cuttings.

PIPERACEAE = The Pepper Family

PIPSISSEWA. See CHIMAPHILA.

PIQUERIA (py-KWEE-ria)
trinervia **2′** **Zone 10** **Fragrant Piqueria**
A perennial herb native to Mexico and Haiti, with 3-nerved leaves, 3–5-flowered flower heads with white fragrant flowers. Easily propagated by division and by cuttings in the spring, made from the lower part of the plant after the flowers

have been cut off. Usually grown as a pot plant in the home greenhouse and treated as geraniums.

PISTACIA (pis-TAY-shia)
chinensis **50′** **Zone 9** **Chinese Pistache**
Akin somewhat to a sumac, this Chinese plant withstands both heat and drought and it is being used in Fla. as a shade tree. The leaves are compound, with 5–6 pairs of leaflets, and deciduous; the male and female flowers are on separate plants. It is rapid-growing; the foliage colors well in the fall. It is also used as the understock on which the pistachio nut of commerce (*P. vera*) is grafted.

vera **30′** **Zone 9** **Pistachio**
This is the species normally planted in Calif., often grafted on *P. chinensis*. The inch-long fruit is egg-shaped, red and wrinkled and the kernel is the source of Pistachio of commerce. It differs from the Chinese species in that its leaflets are in 1–5 pairs while those of *P. chinensis* are in 5–6 pairs. It should be noted that the sexes are separate and 20 female trees should be planted with about 4 male trees.

PISTIA (PIS-tia)
stratiotes **aquatic plant** **Zone 8** **Water-lettuce**
A floating water plant from South America, making a rosette of leaves sometimes as much as 6 in. across, with long feathery roots; ideal for use in the home aquarium. It has fluted, gray-green leaves, as much as 5 in. long, that are held upright in a graceful pattern above the water surface, and it sends out runners on which new plants grow. Easily propagated by division.

PISTIL. The seed-bearing organ of a flower consisting of ovary, style and stigma.

PISTILLATE. Having a pistil and no stamens; female.

PISUM (PY-sum)
sativum. See PEA, GARDEN.

PITCHER-PLANT = *Nepenthes*, also *Sarracenia*

PITCHER-PLANT, CALIFORNIA = *Darlingtonia californica*

PITCHER-PLANT FAMILY = Sarraceniaceae

PIT HOUSE. For those who can afford a greenhouse, the chances are that a pit house is of little value. Actually, it is a glorified cold frame (which see) sunk into the ground or in the side of a bank so that the sloping glass roof faces the south. The idea is that in such a place, full advantage is taken of the sun's rays in winter to warm the soil and the air inside the pit. In many areas such a place, well built, is one in which sturdy plants can be grown and flowered all winter long. Thus the gardening enthusiast is provided (usually at very little cost) with an outlet for energy throughout the winter months.

It is obvious that if the pit is built against the house or some other building, the temperature in it will probably be higher than if it is set out in the open. Also, to have water available, the pipes must be below the frost line, unless the pit is next to the house foundation. An underground electric cable from the house would be an advantage to provide for light at night, heat for the propagating bed and also for emergency heating if the temperature is likely to fall very low.

The site should certainly be protected from prevailing winter winds. The excavation should be about 6 ft. deep, if possible in the side of a hill so that the glass side of the roof will face south. This is not always possible, but when it is, temperatures in the pit are not likely to go down so frequently to the danger point. The length can be 20 ft. or longer, depending upon the space one is prepared to care for. The width should be enough to allow for a 3-ft. bench on either side of a $2\frac{1}{2}$–3 ft. walk. The benches should be far enough below the glass roof to allow the plants to grow to their proper height. Hence, if the bottom of the glass roof came to within a foot of the ground level, which is about right, the bottom of the bench might be even with the ground level, providing that the slant of the roof is about 45° F. If the slant is less than that, the bottom of the bench should be lower.

The north side of the pit with a peaked roof need not be glass, but can be made of some material insulated to conserve heat. Usually the sides of the pit are made of concrete about 6 in. thick, poured into prepared forms. It should be waterproofed on the outside by painting it with a waterproof paint. It might well be properly insulated on the inside with a layer of styrofoam or other insulating material. Drainage should be allowed for at the base and crushed stone might be used on the ground at the base to allow for better drainage and also to allow ground heat into the structure during the freezing winter months.

The typical, easily available greenhouse sash (3 ft. x 6 ft.) can be used for the roof, with glass panes 16 in. x 24 in., or the standard sash panes of 10 in. x 12 in. These sashes are tightly fitted together so that there is no possibility of an air leak.

Care of such a pit house over winter calls for additional insulation, especially during the colder winter nights. This can be of a second series of greenhouse sash laid over the roof, or of a layer of heavy burlap padding, woven-grass matting or some such material put on in the late afternoon and removed the next morning. This should be done daily if plants are being grown in the pit for flowering purposes.

On the other hand, some pits are merely used for the storage of tender plants over winter. In such cases, it is advisable to keep the air temperature between 28°–34° F. If the plants are evergreen or are dormant (without leaves), they may be stored in the dark for 3–4 months without injury from the lack of light. This allows the using of good, thick, insulating material over the roof which does not need to be taken off and put on again each day. Of course, in such a pit it is necessary to check the plants occasionally, water them if dry, and note whether fungus or any other disease has started. If it has, the pit should be dried out occasionally and the diseased material sprayed promptly.

The gadget-minded gardener can have a field day with a "simple" pit house, by putting in an electric alarm system to warn him of when the temperature drops below a certain point; by installing a few electric heaters which will automatically turn on and off at certain temperatures, etc. Even with these, personal inspection is occasionally necessary to protect the living plant materials from serious attacks of plant fungi.

Consequently a pit can be an inexpensive building in the ground in which tender plants can be over-wintered with minimum attention, or it can be heated by the sun in order to grow (and flower) certain plants throughout the winter. For those who wish to grow plants in the winter and can afford it, a simple greenhouse built against the house is a much better place in which to do it.

Some of the plants which will grow and flower with night temperatures between 35°–45° F. in a sun-heated pit:

Abelia sp.	Abelia
Abutilon hybrids	Abutilon
Acacia	Acacia
Antirrhinum majus	Snapdragon
Bellis perennis	English Daisy
Calceolaria sp.	Calceolaria
Calendula officinalis	Calendula
Camellia japonica	Camellia
Centaurea cyanis	Bachelor's Button
Cheiranthus cheiri	Wallflower

Chrysanthemum morifolium	Florists' Chrysanthemum
Cytisus sp.	Broom
Erica melanthera	Blackeyed Heath
Jasminum sp.	Jasmine
Lathyrus odoratus	Sweet Pea
Lithodora diffusa	Acid–soil Lithodora
Loropetalum chinense	—
Mathiola incana	Stock
Myosotis sylvatica	Forget-me-not
Primula sp.	Primrose
Punica granatum nana	Dwarf Pomegranate
Reseda odorata	Mignonette
Rhododendron sp.	Azalea & Rhododendron, especially Kurume azaleas
Senecio cruentus	Cineraria
Trachymene caerulea	Blue Lace Flower
Viola odorata	Sweet Violet
V. tricolor	Pansy

BULBS, CORMS, ETC.

Crocus sp.	Crocus
Galanthus sp.	Snowdrop
Hyacinthus	Hyacinth
Muscari	Grape Hyacinth
Narcissus sp.	Narcissus
Tulipa	Tulip
Anemone sp.	Anemone
Calochortus sp.	Globe-tulip, Mariposa-lily
Leucocoryne ixioides	Glory-of-the-sun
Oxalis cernua	Buttercup Oxalis
O. rubra	Window Box Oxalis
Ranunculus asiaticus	Persian Buttercup

Of course, the warmer the pit house and the higher the night temperature, the more species and varieties of plants which can be grown therein.

PITTOSPORACEAE = The Tobira Family

PITTOSPORUM (pit-OS-por-um). Evergreen shrubs or small trees, mostly from Australia or New Zealand, but the most popular and one of the hardiest (*P. tobira*) comes from China and Japan. The leaves are alternate; the flowers have 5 petals and are very fragrant. Softwood cuttings root readily. The fruits are many-seeded capsules.

crassifolium   30′   Zone 10   Karo
An evergreen shrub or tree from New Zealand, with lustrous, leathery, obovate leaves about 3 in. long, white tomentose beneath, and with red to purple flowers, $\frac{1}{2}$ in. long, in terminal clusters. The fruit is a tomentose capsule $1\frac{1}{4}$ in. wide.

eugenioides   40′   Zone 10   Tarata Pittosporum
An evergreen from New Zealand, with leaves 2–4 in. long and $\frac{3}{4}$–$1\frac{1}{2}$ in. wide, this is frequently used in sheared hedges. It is oval in shape, sometimes columnar, sometimes pyramidal, but usually open in habit, and is a popular landscape plant in southern Calif.

phillyraeoides   20′   Zone 9   Willow Pittosporum
An evergreen tree with drooping branchlets, linear-lanceolate leaves, 4 in. long, and yellow flowers $\frac{1}{2}$ in. long, either solitary or borne in axillary clusters. The deep yellow fruits are $\frac{1}{2}$ in. long. Native to Australia.

rhombifolium   80′   Zone 10   Diamondleaf Pittosporum
A good tree for parkway planting in the southwestern U.S. where it is hardy and one of the most popular trees in Santa Barbara, Calif. The glossy evergreen leaves of this native Australian plant are 3–4 in. long, and it bears large clusters of bright orange berries in midwinter.

tenuifolium   20′–30′   Zone 8   Tawhiwhi
Evergreen tree with oblong leaves $2\frac{1}{2}$ in. long; flowers dark purple, about $\frac{1}{2}$ in. long, either solitary or in clusters in the leaf axils. Fruits are capsules $\frac{1}{2}$ in. wide. The variety 'Silver Queen' has variegated foliage. Native to New Zealand.

tobira   10′   Zone 8   Japanese Pittosporum
A most serviceable, evergreen hedge plant from China and Japan, this is used a great deal in the southern states and the milder parts of the Pacific Coast. The thick, rubbery, evergreen leaves are up to 4 in. long. The creamy-white

flowers, $\frac{1}{2}$ in. wide, are borne in small terminal clusters during May. These are not very conspicuous, but they are fragrant, reminding one somewhat of orange blossoms. The variety 'Variegata' has leaves with white variegation.

undulatum   30′   Zone 9   Victorian-box
The alternate, shiny, evergreen leaves of this plant are 6 in. long, leathery in texture, and waxy along the margins. The fragrant white flowers appear from May to July, being about $\frac{1}{2}$ in. long in terminal clusters. Native to Australia.

viridiflorum   15′-20′   Zone 10   Cape Pittosporum
Evergreen shrub with lustrous, leathery, obovate leaves 3 in. long; flowers yellowish green and $\frac{1}{4}$ in. long, borne in dense terminal clusters. Fruit a capsule $\frac{1}{4}$ in. wide. Native to South Africa.

PITYROGRAMMA (pit-ty-ro-GRAM-ma)
triangularis   18″   Zone 2   California Goldfern
Fronds 7 in. long, 6 in. wide and deep goldenyellow beneath, sometimes white. A pretty fern. Native from Calif. to Alaska. For culture and propagation see FERNS.

PLACENTA. Part of the ovary which bears the ovules.

PLAGIANTHUS (plaj-i-ANTH-us)
regius (*betulinus*)   **60′   Zone 10   Ribbonwood Twinebark**
A tropical tree from Australia and New Zealand, with alternate simple leaves that are ovatelanceolate, 3 in. long and small; non-showy flowers in 9-in. panicles. Occasionally grown in southern Calif. as an ornamental.

PLANE-TREE. See PLATANUS.

PLANNING A GARDEN. See GARDEN, PLANNING A.

PLANTAGO (plan-TAY-go)
lanceolata   8″   Zone 3   Buckhorn
A perennial weed, mostly in lawns, widespread throughout North America but introduced from Europe and Asia. The leaves are borne in a rosette at the base of the plant, are lanceolate with prominent parallel veins, up to 8 in. or more in length. The flower and fruiting heads are small and triangular, an inch or more in length but borne at the end of a long flower stalk which may be a foot long. This sometimes is considered a biennial for it is not as long-lived as *P. major*. See WEED-CONTROLLING CHEMICALS.

major   6″   Zone 3   Broad-leaved Plantain
A perennial lawn weed, naturalized throughout North America but native to Europe; with broad, ovate, parallel-veined leaves up to 5 in. long and 4 in. wide, sometimes larger in good soils, all clustered at the base. It is reproduced both by seeds and new shoots from the base of the plant. Small flowers are borne on tall narrow spikes, varying in length but sometimes up to 12 in. long, from June to Sept. A pernicious lawn weed. See WEED-CONTROLLING CHEMICALS.

rugelii   8″   Zone 3   Rugel's Plantain
A perennial weed especially in lawns; native to eastern North America; similar in general to *P. major* except that the leaf stalk bases are reddish, not green. See WEED-CONTROLLING CHEMICALS.

PLANTAIN. See PLANTAGO; also BANANA.

PLANTAIN FAMILY, WATER = Alismaceae

PLANTAIN-LILY. See HOSTA.

PLANT DISEASE. See DISEASES, PLANT.

PLANT NAMES. See NOMENCLATURE.

PLANT PATENTS. Over 5000 plants have been "patented" as of this date because of amendments made to the Patent Act in 1930 which now permits plants to be patented if the Patent Office feels that such plants are "new" or "differ" from other plants of the same general kind. A new seedling or sporting branch of an old variety are both deemed possibilities. The Act permits the originator to have the rights of propagation for 17 years. Often the originator will sell these rights to some commercial grower. By far the majority of plants patented have been roses. Usually, premium prices are asked for patented plants. They do not always prove superior to older, long-accepted, popular varieties.

PLANTING. This is a very important garden operation and one should always keep a few essentials in mind. First, one should dig the plants in such a way that as many roots remain attached to the plant as possible and they are not injured in the operation. Second, that they do not dry out during the operation (or afterwards either). Third, that the new place where the plant is to grow is in as good soil as it is possible to supply and that the hole dug to receive the plant is ample and the roots will not be jammed and crushed together in order to squeeze them into a hole too small.

Most plants are moved while dormant and many shrubs and garden perennials are shipped without soil about their roots in a manner perfectly satisfactory providing their roots are not allowed to dry out. This is the reason transplanting is best done in the early spring before growth starts, or in the fall, after growth has been completed and the plants are about to go into a dormant condition. Also the weather is cool in the spring and fall, another excellent reason for planting at this time. In the summer, with plants fully grown, transpiration is high, temperatures are high and many plants just do not recover from the shock of being planted at this time unless special precautions are taken like providing extra shade and moisture. Even then many plants can not be moved satisfactorily. When received they should be opened up immediately, their roots moistened or even soaked in water for an hour or so, and then planted. If this is not possible they should be properly heeled in (which see) and their roots thoroughly covered with moist soil until such time as they can be planted, the sooner the better.

In any planting operation, the tops of the plants should be cut back to compensate for the loss of roots in the digging operation. With seedlings, this is usually not necessary unless they are overgrown, in which case the tops should be cut back. With herbaceous perennials planted in the early spring, the planting is best done before growth starts, hence there are no tops to be considered. If such plants are moved in the fall it is best to do it when the tops are about ready to die, in which case they can be cut back to the ground and then moved. With trees and shrubs it is always advisable to remove about one-third of the linear or branch growth. Failure to do this frequently results in death of many branches or even death of the entire plant. Even evergreens which are "balled and burlaped," i.e., moved with a ball of soil about their roots, should have some of the branches cut off to compensate for roots lost in digging. They will recover faster and make better specimens if this is done.

In reading the description of plants in this volume, it will be noted that some plants are difficult to transplant, and some almost impossible. Some trees and shrubs are in this category also. The commercial grower circumvents this hazard by growing such plants in cans, or baskets and they can be easily set in the soil, but once planted they should not be moved.

Difficult-to-transplant subjects are transported with a ball of soil about the roots, the bigger the ball the more roots in it and hence the better the chances for recovery. Conversely, the smaller the ball, especially evident in some cheaply dug evergreens, the fewer the roots and the greater the chances for dying.

With perennials, especially those moved from one part of the garden to another, dig the plant with as much soil about the roots as possible, plant it immediately without allowing sun or wind to dry the roots while it sits on top of the soil for several hours.

Seedlings from flats in the greenhouse or the cold frame should of course be "hardened off" (which see) before being planted out in the garden. Those grown in individual pots or plant bands always have a better chance of survival because they have soil about their roots and it is undisturbed in the planting operation. Seed-lings that are roughly dug or pulled out of a flat and planted without any soil adhering to the roots, may not survive. Care and patience should be taken in the moving and transplanting of all such small plants no matter what kind of plants they are.

It is much better to plant seedlings on a cloudy cool day, rather than in the middle of a hot sunny day, merely because the plants do not dry out as fast on the cloudy day. If this is impossible, shade herbaceous seedlings after planting and be certain they have plenty of moisture.

Overgrown seedlings, like unusually large tomato plants or zinnias, may be too large to transplant properly. An 18-in. tomato plant, for instance, taken out of a standard flat in which there are 47 other such plants, is just too large to transplant properly, for the roots that can be dug with such a seedling are just not sufficient to support the large top. It will wilt and die before the roots can support it. Some types of seedlings can be pinched back when this overgrown condition occurs but by far the best practice is to transplant the seedlings before they get to this overgrown condition.

On the other hand, do not plant seedlings that are too small, either. Taking the tomato seedling that is only 2 in. high as one example, this is not able to compete in the top inch or so of soil. It will dry out and die quickly merely because it does not have enough roots to maintain the top. Special handling of such small seedlings is necessary, with mulching, shading and frequent watering until they are "established." It only takes 1 or 2 failures in this line for the novice gardener to realize that such small plantlets are tender things and must be grown to a reasonable size in pots or flats before they are set out in the garden to fend for themselves.

It goes almost without saying that the soil where the plants are to go should be carefully prepared, pulverized and dug with organic matter of some kind turned under if possible. See SOILS. No plants should be set out when the soil is powder dry. Transplant just after a rain or after a thorough watering of the soil, but not when it is actually muddy—it should be friable and easily broken up.

The hole should be ample to receive the roots, which should be spread out carefully and not jammed in a ball and forced into a too-small hole. This only creates trouble later, especially with woody plants. It is always a good idea to mulch afterwards if possible (see MULCHES) and to water thoroughly as soon as transplanted, but not in the middle of a very hot, sunny day, rather in the cool of the evening. The young plants should not be allowed to dry out, so care should be given in watering them for the first 2 weeks at least.

In planting trees and shrubs, the principles are all the same. It is always better to plant a dollar shrub in a 2-dollar hole than a 2-dollar shrub in a dollar hole. Ample space for root development is an important prerequisite. Digging the hole at least 18–24 inches deeper than the roots (and wider as well) means that there will be ample room at the base of the hole for overturned sod or well-rotted manure, with a few inches of soil on top and then the shrub or tree set in carefully, the roots spread out, and fine soil firmed well about them.

A depression is left in the surface soil to catch water—an important feature of a well-planted shrub or tree (or even tomato plant for that matter). Then the plant is watered thoroughly and the soil is not allowed to dry out.

One further point should be made, and that is that any damaged or broken roots should be carefully cut off before planting. However, never cut off roots in order to make them conform to a small hole. This is pure folly, for the greater the amount of the roots, the better the plant will recover and grow.

For further information see POTTING, SEED SOWING, TRANSPLANTING.

PLANTS FOR GROWING IN SAND. See SAND, PLANTS FOR GROWING IN.

PLANTS, OLDEST LIVING. There are really 4 plants in the running for this record, living in the Western Hemisphere. Methods of accurately determining the age of such plants are of course subject to question, but here they are for what they are worth:

1. **Pinus aristata**—a tree called 'Grandad' found in the White Mountains of Calif., estimated to be 7100 years old.

2. **Sequoia giganteum**—a Giant Redwood tree named 'General Sherman', 272 ft. high and 32 ft. in dia., estimated at about 4000 years old.

3. **Taxodium mucronatum**—a Mexican Cypress tree at Maria de Tule, Oaxaca, Mexico, 118 ft. tall but a dia. of 36 ft. Variously estimated at between 4000 and 10,000 years old.

4. **Gaylussacia brachycera**—one plant of this Box-huckleberry along the Juniata River in Pa.; this single plant is estimated 1½ miles wide and a rather surprising 13,000 years old.

PLATANUS (PLAT-a-nus). One species (*P. occidentalis*) is native to the eastern U.S., another, *P. racemosa*, to southern Calif., and another *P. orientalis* to southeastern Europe and Asia Minor. All have alternate lobed leaves of coarse texture; ball-like fruits about an inch in dia.; and all have interesting and colorful bark that exfoliates in irregular pieces showing lighter

bark underneath. The hybrid *P. hybrida*, is one of the best street trees for urban areas.

Propagation

If the seed is collected in the autumn it should be stratified for 2 months at 40° F., but if it is collected from the trees in late winter, the seed will germinate as soon as it is sown. Softwood and hardwood cuttings can be rooted. See CUTTINGS.

Insect Pests

Sycamore lace bug is the cause of a white-peppered effect on the upper surface of the leaves. These sucking insects are well controlled by timely sprays soon after the new leaves unfold with insecticide #15. Terrapin scale is common on Sycamore (see MAPLE) and other scales are occasional pests, and it is advisable to keep them under control.

Diseases

Sycamore is a preferred host of anthracnose. Black areas, and dead crisp leaves which resemble frost injury in the spring are the principal symptoms. Cool wet weather favors the disease. Sprays of fungicide #K or #D are effective. Fungicide #M has been used effectively as an eradicant in emergencies.

x acerifolia (*P. hybrida*)   **100′**   **Zone 5 London Plane-tree**

A hybrid between the American *P. occidentalis* and the European *P. orientalis*, this is widely grown. The coarse, palmately veined, lobed leaves are 5–10 in. wide. The widespreading branches and color-exfoliating bark are of interest and the ability to withstand urban growing conditions make this tree the best in this group for city planting. The ball-like fruits, about an inch across, are borne in clusters of 2, rarely 3, whereas those of *P. occidentalis* are usually single and rarely in clusters of 2. This is one of the ways of telling these 2 similar trees apart.

occidentalis   **120′**   **Zone 4**   **Buttonwood, American Plane-tree**

Although native throughout eastern North America, this should not be planted as an ornamental because it is susceptible to a serious canker disease which causes a die-back of the twigs. *P. hybrida* should always be used instead. The Buttonwood has palmately lobed leaves, 3 or 5 lobed, 4–9 in. across, and the ball-like fruits are 1 in. through, usually produced singly, this being the best way of telling it from the hybrid which usually bears its fruits in clusters of 2. The exfoliating bark on this American native is interesting and old trees in the Philadelphia area have been estimated to have been alive in William Penn's time. It has been reported that syrup and sugar have been made from the collected sap and that a fragrant gum exudes from cracks and crevices in the trunk, similar to spruce gum.

orientalis 90′ Zone 6 Oriental Plane-tree Many American nurserymen list this tree but few if any have it, usually mistaking *P. hybrida* for this species. The maplelike, palmately lobed leaves (5–7 lobes) are deeply cut almost to the middle of the leaf and the leaves are 4–8 in. wide. The ball-like fruits, an inch across, are borne 3 in a cluster; those of *P. occidentalis* usually are borne singly and those of *P. hybrida* are usually 2 in a cluster. The London Plane-tree makes the better street tree in the eastern United States.

racemosa 120′ Zone 7 California Plane-tree Native to southern Calif., the ball-like fruits of this are borne 2–7 in a cluster. It also has coarse foliage, like the other species, and is often used in Calif. for its irregular, often gnarled habit of growth, even though it is susceptible to blight.

PLATYCERIUM (plat-i-SEE-rium). These are the staghorn ferns, so unique in humid green-houses or in the Tropics where they are native. They have 2 kinds of fronds; the sterile, less conspicuous ones are thin, rounded or heart shaped at the base, green when young, brown and papery at maturity. It is these rounded flat fronds which cling to the branch or limb or piece of wood on which the fern is growing, eventually enveloping and completely covering it. It is the flat fertile fronds which are from 15 in. to 3 ft. long that are conspicuous, narrow at the base, then growing wider and wider with several ramifications, which are responsible for the name staghorn or elkhorn. These grow on trees in the Tropics. In the greenhouse they need warmth (temperatures not below 55° F. but *P. bifurcatum* will withstand 45° F.) and much humidity. They are attached to a piece of cork, wood or the branch of a tree that is held in an upright position. A mixture of Osmunda fiber, finely sifted sphagnum moss and a little crushed charcoal and decayed leaves is a good mixture. The plants can be wired to the cork or board with the mixture being placed back of it somehow so the base of the plant can be put in it (through a hole in the cork); also they can be attached to flower pots held up at the side of the greenhouse. Or a piece of Redwood, Cypress or Cedar can be held rigidly in a pot with broken crocks and the fern attached to it.

Propagation for most species is by division or the separation of the small plants that form at the base of the plant. These are placed in pots of soil, firmly attached or pegged down on the soil surface. *P. grande*, a species which does not produce small plantlets, must be raised from spores. For this see FERNS.

The most popular species is **P. bifurcatum** with fronds 2–3 ft. long. **P. willinckii** has fronds 2–3 ft. long as does **P. stemaria**, and **P. grande** has fronds 4–6 ft. long.

PLATYCLADUS (plat-y-CLA-dus)
orientalis. This is now the correct scientific name for the old popular *Thuja orientalis*, but it will be a long time before it is widely used.

PLATYCODON (plat-i-KO-don)
grandiflorus 2½′ Zone 3 Balloonflower This fine garden perennial from Eastern Asia belongs to the Campanula Family and is one of the best of garden flowers for the perennial border. It is hardy, blooms well every year and requires no special attention whatsoever. Plants have been known to live in one spot for over 20 years, blooming well annually. They do not spread, flower in late June and often continue until Sept. There are double-flowered varieties, and all seem to grow best in full sun, but for those that are pink, partial shade is also good. Flowers are merely open bells, 2–3 in. across, blue, white or pink ('**Shell Pink**') depending on variety. The Japanese Bellflower (var. **mariesii**) is only 18 in. tall. They are propagated by seeds and careful division only in the spring. In making the cuts through the roots, the cut portions might be dusted with a fungicide to prevent disease entering the roots.

PLATYSTEMON (platy-STE-mon)
californicus 1′ annual Cream Cups In Calif. where this plant is native, one can see large fields covered with the creamy-yellow flowers in the spring. These are about an inch wide and are borne on long stalks. The leaves are linear, about 2 in. long; the fruit is a head of small pods. The var. **crinitus** is sometimes used because the flowers are often splashed with green or pink. It is a member of the Poppy Family and is especially useful for edging. Seeds are sown outdoors in mid-April.

PLEACH. A method of shearing closely planted trees or shrubs into a high wall of foliage. Many kinds of trees have been used, maples, syca-mores, lindens, etc. Because of the time needed in caring for pleached allees, they are but infrequently seen in American gardens, but are frequently observed in Europe.

PLECTRANTHUS (plec-TRAN-thus). These are the spurflowers which include several tropi-cal species ranging in size from 6 in. to 8 ft. They belong to the Mint Family, closely related to the Coleus, are perennial with rounded opposite leaves, and small, bluish, mintlike flowers in many panicles. Sometimes used as house plants in the North. Native to China. Propagated by seeds and cuttings.

oertendahlii trailing **Zone 10** **Spurflower**
Native to Natal, South Africa, this has quickly
become a popular houseplant often used in
hanging baskets. Introduced into Sweden a
few years ago, it has even been called 'Swedish
Ivy.' It needs light, but not too much sunshine;
has terminal, pyramidal clusters of small
bluish-white, two-lipped flowers. There is a
slow-growing variety with white, variegated
leaves. Probably related to a variable group of
plants.

PLEIOSPILOS (ply-o-SPY-los)
  polusii 2″–6″ **Zone 10** **Living Rocks**
South African succulents which look very
similar to the rocks in which they are found
growing. Stemless, with 2–4 leaves; sometimes
divided in the center from which the yellow
flowers emerge. Peculiar oddities of little value
outside of the succulent garden in Zone 10.

PLOWING. This is the age-old method of
turning under the surface crust of the soil
preparatory to planting the next crop. In most
soils east of the Mississippi River plowing is
done with the furrow about 6–8 in. deep. In the
South, it is a little less and in the deep soils of
the Great Plains states about 4–5 in. is sufficient.
The idea is of course to turn under all plant
growth on the soil surface so it rots to form the
much-needed humus, while at the same time
aerating the soil, and then in the final operation
of harrowing, mixing up the soil particles again,
prior to planting.

In areas where the ground freezes in winter,
there is an advantage in leaving plowed soil
untouched over winter, for it allows freezing and
thawing to break up soil particles and also
allows the maximum amount of air to enter the
pore spaces between soil particles. This is good
practice. It also gives the vegetable matter
turned under time in which to rot, preparatory
to forming humus.

It is not always possible, in fact now it is
seldom possible, to plow the average suburban
garden in the old accustomed manner of turning
over furrows. Now, mechanical devices such as
rototillers are used, which "plow" in another
way, that is, they mix up all the surface soil at
once. In fact, although they do not "turn under"
a layer of the soil, the teeth on the revolving
drums of these machines break up the soil and
mix it so effectively that with 1 or 2 times
(sometimes more) over the piece of soil concerned, it is ready for reseeding. However, this
soil also benefits if it is left alone over winter
before it is seeded again.

PLUM. (Also see PRUNUS.) Plums are tree fruits
that are popular with gardeners over a wide
area of the United States. Not all varieties can
be grown in all areas. Plums are grown com-

mercially chiefly in Calif. and the northwest
Pacific states, Ohio and N.Y. In general they
are divided into 3 groups, European Plums (*P.
domestica*) which include the prune plums;
Japanese plums; and native American plums.
These all vary considerably in hardiness and
ability to withstand drought and hot climate.

In general, the European plums are about as
hardy as apples, the Japanese plums are as
hardy as peaches (but some are hardier than the
European varieties); and the American plums
some of which are hardy even in the Great
Plains areas of the central United States and
the prairie provinces of Canada.

One must be extremely careful of the pollination requirements of plums, more so than for
any other fruit, since many are self-sterile and
must have some other variety close by to supply
pollen for fruit development. In the European
group, such popular varieties as 'Stanley',
'Agen', 'Reine Claude', 'Italian Prune', 'California Blue' and 'Yellow Egg', all are self-
fertile. The Japanese and American varieties are
not good pollinizers for the European group.

Damson varieties like 'Shropshire' and
'French' are self-fertile.

European varieties are not good pollinizers
for Japanese varieties. It is always advisable to
have 2 or even 3 varieties of Japanese plums for
cross-pollination purposes.

Most American native plums are self-sterile.
Some of the Japanese-American hybrids are
good pollinizers, such as 'Kaga' and 'South
Dakota 27'. 'Compass' has been recommended
as a good pollinizer for the Sand Cherry-Plum
hybrids.

Culture

One- or 2-year-old trees should be planted
about 20 feet apart. They are similar to apples
in their soil requirements but are more tolerant
of grass than peaches. Mulching is satisfactory
and of course plenty of soil nitrogen is necessary
for good growth. Trees recently planted (1–3
years old) might be given ½ lb. of nitrate of soda
after the first year, and from ½–2 lbs. per tree
up to the fifth year after planting. Then after
that they might receive 2–4 lbs. per tree,
depending on how well they grow. It has been
noted that Italian prune plums sometimes show
a potash deficiency, shown as a curling and
eventual death of the leaves by midsummer.
This is cured by applying manure or fertilizers
high in potash content.

Pruning is not necessarily heavy but usually
merely a light thinning throughout the tree—
enough to eliminate succulent water sprouts and
cure any structural defects in the framework.
Also, one should provide for light and free
circulation of air in the tree. The Japanese

varieties usually grow more vigorously than the others and hence require more pruning.

Plums do not do well in moist or humid climates, nor do they thrive in hot dry climates. Since they vary widely in their growth characteristics, one would do well to check with the local State Experiment Station, on which varieties are recommended for the particular locality in question. This is probably more important with plums than almost any other tree fruit for there are many locations throughout the country where only 2 or 3 special varieties can be grown and no others will provide satisfactory crops.

Plums are susceptible to "June drop," a normal dropping of excess fruits. This may be circumvented somewhat by thinning the fruits before it occurs. In the home garden this is not too difficult when done by hand, but most busy gardeners let nature take its proper course and do not hand-thin. However, it is especially important in the case of the Japanese plums which tend to over-bear markedly. Damson plums, as a rule, are not thinned, but both the Japanese and European varieties will respond to proper thinning by producing larger and better fruits.

Propagation is by budding, using *P. cerasifera* as understock for the European group, *P. persica* or *P. cerasifera* as understock for the Japanese group and *P. americana* or any other native American species as understock for the American group. *P. besseyi*, the native Sand Cherry, has been used to some extent as a dwarfing understock.

Varieties

Among the popular European varieties are:
'Agen'—best type in Calif. for drying and making prunes.

'Arctic'—(Zone 3) probably one of the hardiest of these varieties in this group. Dark purple to black, nearly round, ripening in midseason.

'Bradshaw'—dark purple, one of the last to bloom but ripening in midseason.

DAMSON PLUM—both 'FRENCH' and 'SHROPSHIRE' are included in this group; with small rounded plums, clingstone type, varieties of *P. institia*, at one time called *P. domestica institita*.

'French'—the best of the Damson varieties. 'Shropshire' has more fruits, but they are smaller. One of the best varieties for jam.

'Grand Duke'—bears very large fruit, nearly 2 in. long, purple color.

'Green Gage'—See 'Reine Claude'.

'Italian Prune' (Fellenberg)—purple to black, excellent type for cooking purposes. Widely grown in Ore. and Wash. as a commercial crop, especially for drying.

'Reine Claude'—this originated in France about 1500, but received a great deal of publicity because a gardener, working for the Gage family in England, named it 'Green Gage'. However, he actually obtained it from France where it had been previously named 'Reine Claude'. Many early American gardeners, especially those coming from England, planted it as 'Green Gage', in gardens in the eastern United States. The fruit is rounded and greenish yellow and very sweet. It is still one of the best.

'Shropshire'—a Damson Plum, producing an extremely large number of small fruits, smaller than those of 'French'.

'Stanley'—an excellent home-garden variety originating at the New York State Agricultural Experiment Station and introduced in 1926, with dark blue fruits about 2 in. long. Fine quality and hardy in Zone 4.

'Yellow Egg'—sometimes grown as a small, sweet, yellow plum.

Most of these are hardy in Zones 4 and 5, but 'Arctic' is hardy in Zone 3. Although these have been listed as self-fruitful varieties, it will probably pay to have 2 or more varieties growing together to insure cross-pollination.

JAPANESE VARIETIES: These plums are mostly derived from Chinese species, although the first Japanese varieties were introduced originally to America from Japan about 1870. They are mostly red or yellow, are for fresh fruit only (not cooking) and vary widely as to hardiness. All are self-sterile and so 2 or more varieties should be planted together. Both **'Kaga'** and **'South Dakota 27'** have proved good pollinizers for this group.

'Abundance'—an old variety, imported by Luther Burbank in 1884. The fruit is red and only of fair quality.

'Beauty'—originated by Luther Burbank about 1920. The fruit is red, of the clingstone type, ripening in early to mid-Aug.

'Burbank'—introduced by Luther Burbank in 1887. The fruit is red and the tree tends to bear biennially. One of the most popular varieties of this group in Ore.

'Methley'—originated in South Africa about 1915. The fruit is dull red, becoming purplish, large and conical. A clingstone type of fair quality, ripening early in Aug.

'Santa Rosa'—originated by Luther Burbank about 1907. The fruit is dark purple with red flesh, a clingstone type. It ripens about mid-Aug. in Ore. but a good set of fruit is not always possible.

'Shiro'—originated by Luther Burbank about 1898. The fruit is bright yellow, mild and sweet;

a dependable bearer in Ore., ripening there by mid-Aug.

AMERICAN PLUMS. Several native American plum species like *P. americana*, *P. hortulana* and *P. nigra* have given varieties the fruits of which, although not as good-tasting as the European and Japanese plums, nevertheless are hardier and can be grown in areas where the others can not. Hence, they have some value. *P. americana* has given 'DeSoto' and 'Hawkeye', valued in the northern Mississippi Valley and southern Canada. 'Cheney' is a variety of *P. nigra* grown in eastern Canada.

'Wayland', 'Golden Beauty', and 'Miner' are good jam plums, varieties of *P. hortulana*. *P. munsoniana*, often called the Wild Goose Plum, withstands heat and is used to some extent in the southern Mississippi Valley.

P. besseyi is the Sand Cherry, but has been crossed with various plums, especially at the South Dakota Experiment Station, and has yielded some good "cherry-plum" hybrids. 'Compass', 'Oha', 'Opata' and 'Sapa' are a few.

Other hybrids, chiefly between *P. salicina* and *P. americana*, most of which are red fruited but not as good quality as the European and Japanese plums, are 'Superior', 'Underwood', and 'Monitor', 3 of the best. Others are 'Red-coat', 'Redglow', 'Pipestone' and others. 'Kaga' and 'Surprise' have sometimes been recommended as pollinizers.

Beach Plum (*P. maritima*) which see, is a native bush plum, especially along the eastern coast of North America. It is probably of little value except in gardens near the seacoast. Some of the better varieties are 'Eastham', 'Hancock' and 'Premier'; the fruits of all of these make excellent jams and jellies. They prefer light sandy soil. Fruits are about ⅝ in. across, either red or blue according to variety.

Finally it should be said that in any large orchard planting, provision should be made for keeping bees, at least 1 hive per acre. It has been proved that these aid materially in pollination. The home gardener must rely on other insects to help with the pollinizing of his plums, but certainly he should make certain that he has either self-fruitful varieties, or else the right varieties for cross-pollination. Only in this way is he assured a crop of fruit.

Insect Pests

Plum curculio is often more destructive to plums than to other fruits. See APPLE, PEACH. Egg punctures in the small fruit cause russet scars and malformations at harvest. If the grubs hatch and develop, the fruit falls prematurely. Spraying with insecticide #15 or #9 is effective. Peach borer and shot hole borer may infest Plum and other pests of Peach may be injurious.

Diseases

Black knot is more prevalent on Plum than on other hosts. On a few home trees cutting out the galls is advised. See BLACK KNOT. Brown rot attacks the fruit and bacterial leaf spot occurs on the leaves. See PEACH. Plum pockets which cause the fruit to develop irregular hollow pouches is rare and no control is suggested.

PLUMBAGINACEAE = The Plumbago Family

PLUMBAGO (plum-BAY-go)
auriculata (*capensis*) **climbing shrub Zone 9**
Cape Plumbago

Not a true vine but a shrubby climber, this is common to warm countries and is a native of South Africa. The pale blue flowers, 1 in. in dia., bloom all summer in terminal clusters. The alternate leaves are lance shaped, 2–3 in. long. In some parts of Calif. it flowers continually, and should be allowed to clamber at will in its graceful fashion rather than be restrained artificially. It needs full sun but requires little water.

PLUMBAGO FAMILY = Plumbaginaceae

PLUMCOT. An undesirable hybrid which is a cross between a plum and an apricot, originated by Luther Burbank in 1901, but not used in America any more.

PLUME-FLOWER = *Jacobinia obtusior*

PLUMERIA (ploo-MEE-ria)
obtusa (*emarginata*)   **20′   Zone 10   Blunt-leaved Frangipani**

A tree, native to the West Indies, with slender trunk and only a few spreading branches. The leathery, oblong, alternate leaves are 7–10 in. long and about ½–3 in. wide with rolled margins, and are white-hairy underneath. The white fragrant flowers have a yellow eye and are an inch and more wide. Sometimes planted in southern Fla.

rubra acutifolia   15′   Zone 10   Mexican Frangipani

One of the most popular of all flowers for lei making in Hawaii. Native to tropical America, and since it is closely related to the Periwinkle, the flowers are similar in size and shape. They are very fragrant and last some time after they are cut. They are borne in terminal flat clusters, starting in spring and continuing until winter, and are colored a clear yellow with creamy-white edges of the petals. The species, *P. rubra*, has deep red flowers, but there are numerous hybrids with flowers of different colors. The leaves are 7 in. long and 3 in. wide, narrow, pointed at both ends. Propagation by cuttings at any time of year using any kind of wood.

PLUMOSE. Feathery.

PLUM-YEW. See CEPHALOTAXUS.

POA (PO-a). A genus of over 100 species of temperate and cold-region grasses, a few of which are important lawn grasses. See GRASS, LAWNS. There are actually 5 species that might be mentioned briefly here. One is not tufted (*P. compressa*) but the others are, and one of them, *P. pratensis*, the Kentucky Bluegrass, is the most important and most widely used lawn grass in the central and northern parts of the U.S. All are readily propagated by seed. See LAWNS for the method.

compressa   1'-2'   Zones 2-3   Canada Blue-
                                                   grass, Wire Grass
This is the only one of these 5 species which is not tufted. It is a low, bluish-green grass, with a few wiry blades or culms and long creeping rootstocks; native to Europe and Asia; now widely naturalized as a weed grass or as pasture grass in North America.

nemoralis   1'-3'   Zone 4   Wood Meadowgrass
A tufted grass, able to grow in the shade and sometimes used in lawn mixtures for this purpose. Native to Europe—it is naturalized in Ore. and the northeastern U.S.

palustris   1'-5'   Zone 3   Fowl Meadowgrass
A tufted meadowgrass, little used in lawns but widely native in northern temperate regions.

pratensis   1'-3'   Zone 3   Kentucky Bluegrass
The best of the grasses in this genus for lawns, this is widely used in the northern temperate regions. It is tufted with slender creeping rhizomes and a bluish-green color. See LAWNS, GRASS.

trivialis   1'-3'   Zone 3   Rough Bluegrass
A tufted European grass with creeping rhizomes, sometimes used as a meadow grass in the northern temperate regions. Naturalized throughout the northern U.S. and southern Canada. See LAWNS, GRASS.

POD. A dry dehiscent fruit.

PODALYRIA (po-da-LI-ria)

calyptrata   6'   Zone 8   Fragrant Podalyria
This is a South African evergreen shrub belonging to the Pea Family; with hairy leaves 1-2 in. long and an inch wide. Flowers pealike and pink. The leaves are alternate and about 2 in. long. Propagated by seeds grown chiefly outdoors in the southern states and in southern Calif.

sericea   4'-6'   Zone 8   Satinleaf Podalyria
Similar to the above but covered with soft silvery hairs; flowers purple and leaves lance shaped.

PODOCARPUS (po-do-KAR-pus). These are mostly narrow-leaved evergreens though a few have wider leaves; belonging to the Podocarpus Family, with drupelike fruits, often fleshy and red, somewhat similar to those of yews to which they are closely related. The staminate and pistillate flowers are separate and usually on separate plants (dioecious). They are easily grown and are propagated by cuttings. Young plants are frequently grown in pots for display indoors in the North.

alpinus   15'   Zone 9   Tasmania Podocarpus
An evergreen shrub with needlelike leaves, ½ in. long, pale beneath; fruit red, egg-shaped and ¼ in. through. Native to Australia.

andinus   45'   Zone 9   Andes Podocarpus
Leaves 1¼ in. long, needlelike. Fruit yellowish white and egg-shaped, about an inch long. Native to Chile.

elongatus   70'   Zone 9   Fern Podocarpus
An evergreen tree from western Africa, branches gracefully pendant, densely pinnate, the leaves being 3 in. long, thin and pointed; grown outdoors in southern Calif. but also grown farther north as a tubbed specimen.

macrophyllus   60'   Zone 7   Yew Podocarpus
This evergreen tree has foliage similar to the yews, except that the needles are longer (up to about 3-4 in. long) and wider, and the purplish fleshy fruits are about ½ in. long. The branches are arranged horizontally on the tree and the branchlets are slightly pendulous. It is native to Japan and is a popular plant as a specimen or for shearing from N.Car. south. The variety **maki** is the shrubby or Chinese Podocarpus, which is a shrub or small tree. Both, as young plants, make good tubbed plants for indoor display.

PODOPHYLLUM (po-do-PHYL-lum)

peltatum   2'   Zone 3   Common Mayapple
A perennial spreading by an underground stem, the plant produces a forked branch from which arise 2 kinds of leaves, those which are solitary, with palmately divided lobes, and those which occur in pairs. The nodding flower, 1-2 in. in dia., with 6 spreading white petals and sepals, arises on a short stalk at the fork in the stem. The fruit is an edible yellow berry. The plant grows in rich, moist soil over the eastern half of the U.S. and southern Canada. It spreads rapidly, and so is well suited only to large areas in the wild garden. The roots may be divided in summer. Strangely enough, although the stem and the root are supposed to be poisonous to eat, a luscious marmalade and a drink can be made from the fully ripened fruits.

POGONIA (po-GO-nia)

ophioglossoides   8"-10"   Zone 3   Rose Pogonia
A member of the Orchid Family, this plant has a single oval and pointed basal leaf up to 6 in. long and generally 2 smaller, stalkless leaves on the slender stem which is terminated by a single, rose-pink, nodding, fragrant flower having 1

Podophyllum peltatum—Mayapple

bract beneath it. The petals and sepals are nearly identical and the drooping lip is deeply fringed. It is suitable only for the shady bog garden, being found in swampy areas throughout North America. It blooms in June and July.

POINCIANA, PARADISE = *Caesalpinia gilliesii*

POINCIANA PULCHERRIMA = *Caesalpinia pulcherrima*

POINCIANA, ROYAL = *Delonix regia*

POINSETTIA = *Euphorbia pulcherrima*

POINSETTIA FAMILY = Euphorbiaceae

POISON BAITS. See INSECTICIDES.

POISON-HEMLOCK = *Conium maculatum*

POISON-IVY = *Rhus radicana*

POISON-OAK = *Rhus toxicodendron*

POISON-OAK, PACIFIC = *Rhus diversiloba*

POISONOUS PLANTS. Physicians are frequently besieged with questions about poisonous plants and of course they are the ones to consult for treatment, but frequently they find it necessary to have someone else identify the plants that cause the trouble in the first place. In the book, "Poisonous Plants of the United States and Canada," by John M. Kingsbury (Prentice-Hall, Inc.), over 700 plants that have been known to be poisonous to man or animals are mentioned. Most gardeners know a few poisonous plants. Some of the more common ones are listed below.

Usually, one does not go to the garden and eat miscellaneous foliage. Even youngsters are more attracted to bright-colored fruits than foliage of plants. In the reference works, the term "poisonous" usually means poisonous to man or animals, and many more animals than humans have been poisoned by eating the foliage of plants. One of the prime rules is to avoid any white fruits, both in the northern part of the country and in the Tropics.

The Federal Government has set up a "Pesticide Information Center" in each state, usually in the land-grant college. See STATE EXPERIMENT STATIONS. Also, poison centers have been established about the country, mostly in hospitals where medical aid can be given and where advice on treatment for poisoned individuals can be given to the medical profession and the layman alike. These have been sponsored by a division of the Federal Public Health Service. These centers are the places to call for advice in cases of possible poisoning from insecticides or plants. Their location in each state can be obtained from the Pesticide Information Center in that state.

In the following list are some plants that might be found in or near gardens. The plants under discussion have been divided into 4 groups, those growing in the garden or woods with poisonous fruits, foliage or roots, and also those with poisonous parts commonly used as house plants in the northern United States. Certainly all the poisonous plants are not included. Nor does the absence of a plant from the list mean that its fruit or foliage is not poisonous. Those mentioned here have been known to be poisonous to humans. People with small children, most of whom are experimentally minded, would do well to note these plants and keep small children from them.

Plants in Garden or Woods with Poisonous Fruits

Actea pachypoda   1½′   Zone 3   White Baneberry, Cohosh

An herbaceous perennial native from southeastern Canada to Ga. and Okla., with compound leaves; flowers in small, white, terminal clusters during spring and erect clusters of white berries on red stalks in summer and fall. Frequently seen in the woods in this area. The fruits of this are extremely poisonous. It is often listed incorrectly as *A. alba*. The red fruits of *A. rubra* are also poisonous.

Daphne mezereum   3′   Zone 4   February Daphne

A low shrub, native to Europe but common in American gardens and occasionally naturalized in this area. The small, lilac to rosy-pink flowers are very fragrant, appearing in early April before the leaves, and the scarlet-red berries are borne up and down the stem in June. It is the berries which are most poisonous.

Plate I
1. *Solanum dulcamara*—Deadly Nightshade
2. *Daphne mezereum*—February Daphne
3. *Actea pachypoda*—White baneberry, Cohosh
4. *Phytolocca americana*—Pokeweed

Plate II

1. *Menispermum canadense*—Common Moonseed
2. *Hedera helix* (mature foliage)—English Ivy
3. *Euonymus europaea*—Spindle Tree
4. *Taxus* sp.—Yew species
5. *Phoradendron serotinum*—American Mistletoe

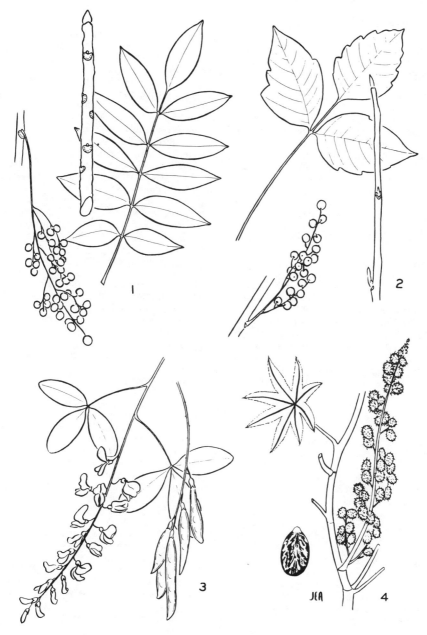

Plate III
1. *Rhux vernix*—Poison Sumac
2. *R. radicans*—Poison Ivy
3. *Laburnum anagyroides*—Golden-chain
4. *Ricinus communis*—Castor-bean

Euonymus europaea 21′ **Zone 3** **Spindle Tree**
This species and probably others in this genus
have proved poisonous in Europe, but no cases
have apparently been reported in North
America. The leaves are opposite and the red
fruit capsules split open and reveal bright,
fleshy, orange-covered seeds inside. This and
other species of Euonymus are popular garden
plants, but it would be wise to prevent children
from eating the fruits which start to color in
early fall.

Hedera helix vine **Zone 5** **English Ivy**
A common house and garden plant, but considered poisonous since the days of Pliny.
However, it is chiefly the berries that would
attract children; blue-black in umbels but
formed in the very late fall on mature vines
with mature foliage. The berries are about ¼ in.
in dia. Apparently no cases of poisoning have
been reported in America but there have been in
Europe.

Laburnum anagyroides 30′ **Zone 5** **Golden-
chain**
This has been considered the second most
poisonous tree in Great Britain (the first is
Taxus baccata, the English Yew). The Golden-
chain is easily recognized for its alternate compound leaves with 3 leaflets and its yellow pealike flowers, borne in pendulous clusters about
6–18 in. long in late May, somewhat similar to
those of Wisteria. The fruit is a pod containing
up to 8 seeds, apparent during summer and fall,
and it is these that are poisonous. Other species
probably have similar poisonous properties.

Menispermum canadense vine **Zone 4**
Common Moonseed
Not very common, but this is a twining vine
native to the eastern United States and a
vicious weed wherever it gets started in a
garden. The leaves are somewhat like those of
English Ivy, and the black berries are ⅓ in.
across, looking something like small grapes in
the fall. The fruits can be severely poisonous.

Phytolacca americana 4′–12′ **Zone 4**
Pokeweed
This common American perennial crops up as
a weed at some time or other in almost every
garden in the northeastern United States. It is
herbaceous, dying down to the ground in the
fall. The root is the most toxic part. The black
berries are attractive and have been used for
making pies, but on the other hand when eaten
raw by humans they may have been responsible
for severe poisoning. The young shoots have
been cooked and eaten like asparagus, especially
if the cooking water is changed. The leaves are
alternate, entire and ovate; the small white or
purplish flowers are borne in terminal racemes
and are bisexual. The fruit is a 10-seeded juicy,
purple berry. All things considered, it would be

advisable to prevent children from eating the
fruits.

Podophyllum peltatum 1½′ **Zone 3** **Mayapple,
Mandrake**
Native in the woods from Quebec to Fla. and
Tex., this is often an interesting wild flower
planted in the wild garden. It has large, peltate,
palmately lobed leaves, solitary, waxy, white
flowers, 2 in. wide, in spring, and yellowish,
fleshy, berrylike fruits 2 in. wide. The root is the
chief poisonous part, but if several of the fruits
are eaten they can cause diarrhea.

Ricinus communis 15′ annual **Castor-bean**
Often called the Castor-oil Plant, this is native
to the Tropics where it can grow into a tree
40 ft. tall, having palmate leaves with 5–11 lobes
as much as 3 ft. wide. The monoecious flowers
are small but are borne in 2-ft. panicles and the
fruit is 1 in. long, covered with soft brown spines.
The seed, looking something like a bean, is
deadly poisonous to humans. Often planted in
New England gardens for the tropical effect of
its foliage.

Robinia pseudoacacia 75′ **Zone 3** **Black
Locust**
A common tree native to the eastern United
States, with alternate compound leaves, entire
leaflets, opposite and in 3–10 pairs; clusters of
white pealike flowers appear in June and fruits
are dry pods. Horses, cattle and sheep have
been poisoned from eating the fruits, suckers or
bark and children have been poisoned by eating
the seeds or inner bark.

Solanum dulcamara vine **Zone 4** **Deadly
Nightshade**
This is a weedy vine apparently widely distributed by birds, with alternate, entire leaves,
sometimes lobed at the base, 1½–4 in. long; the
flowers are violet colored and starlike, produced
in clusters; the fruits are fleshy scarlet berries
about ⅓ in. wide. Flowers are borne from June–
Aug.; fruit from Aug.–Oct. Native to Europe
and North Africa, it is now widely naturalized
in the eastern United States. Cattle, horses and
sheep have been killed from eating the vegetative parts and children have definitely been
poisoned by eating the bright red fruits. It
should always be thoroughly eradicated from
the garden wherever it appears.

Rhus radicans vine **Zone 3** **Poison Ivy**
Sometimes termed *Toxicodendron radicans*, or
Rhus toxicodendron, this is the Poison Ivy so
widely distributed in the Northeast, and leaves,
fruit stems and even smoke from the burning
twigs is extremely toxic, causing a serious skin
rash to many people.

   The compound leaves have 3 leaflets up to
10 in. long, with the margins either entire,
toothed or lobed, and glossy or dull on the
upper surface. The small flowers are greenish

white in the early spring and the berrylike, white, waxy fruits persist into the winter and are borne in erect axillary clusters. Native from British Columbia to Nova Scotia, south to Fla., Tex. and Mexico, it climbs by attaching itself to tree trunks, walls, etc. or rambles over the ground in a dense mass up to 1½ ft. high. It should be given a wide berth by everyone, and certainly children should be warned against collecting the berries.

Rhus vernix   15′   Zone 3   Poison Sumac
Sometimes termed *Toxicodendron vernix* and native from Quebec to Fla., this is a ranging hrub with alternate, pinnately compound leaves, bearing 7–13 leaflets, the leaf margins entire. The small greenish flowers are in pendulous clusters nearly 8 in. long and the white fruits are small. Usually found in swamps and should be given a wide berth at all times because contact with any of the parts causes a serious skin rash to many people.

Taxus sp.   2′–30′   Zones 4–6   Yews
The English Yew (*Taxus baccata*) has been noted as the most poisonous plant in Great Britain. Other Yew species are probably just as poisonous and *T. cuspidata*, the Japanese Yew, and *T. canadensis*, the Canada Yew, are widely planted in New England gardens. The sexes are separate and the pistillate plants are the ones which bear the bright scarlet fruit in the fall. The red flesh covers a hard seed; and although the flesh is not poisonous, the seed is extremely poisonous. Chewing seeds has proven fatal to animals and humans. The foliage is even more toxic and, of course, it is this that proves so poisonous to cattle, sheep and horses.

There are probably more problems with children eating these berries than any other, except possibly Pokeweed. Chewing these seeds and then swallowing can cause serious poisoning.

Wisteria sp.   vines   Zones 4–5   Wisteria
Wisterias are twining vines widely planted for their colorful, pendulous clusters of pealike flowers in late May and June. The pods are 4–6 in. long and flat, containing several seeds, and it is these which have been known to be poisonous to children when eaten. They ripen in the late summer and early fall.

Plants in Garden or Woods with Poisonous Foliage

As noted previously, few humans go to the garden or woods and nibble quantities of foliage indiscriminately. The plants listed here are poisonous mostly to animals, but may prove poisonous to humans also if the foliage is eaten in any quantity.

Aconitum sp.   Aconite, Monkshood
Several species are common garden plants and

the records of poisoning in this country are not common, but it should be remembered that these plants are potentially poisonous.

Cicuta maculata   6′   Zone 3   Water-hemlock
The leaves of this perennial aromatic herb, native from New Brunswick to Fla., are 2–3 times pinnate, 5 in. long and the small white flowers are borne in terminal umbels. It is sometimes used in the wild or bog garden, and is usually found in marshy places. It has caused a great deal of stock losses in the United States. Roots and seeds are the most poisonous parts. Children are sometimes severely poisoned by eating the root.

Conium maculatum   4′–8′   biennial   Poison Hemlock
With large dissected leaves, sometimes 4–5 times (opposite) compound, with a parsniplike root. Small white flowers are borne in umbels and it resembles the Wild Carrot or Queen Anne's Lace (*Daucus carota*), but the stem and leaves of the latter are distinctly hairy. Native to Europe, it has become naturalized in many areas of the United States. Humans and all types of livestock are susceptible to poisoning by this plant, and its poisonous properties have been known since Greek and Roman times. The foliage is sometimes mistaken for Parsley and the seed for Anise.

Datura stramonium   1′–5′   annual   Jimson-weed, Angel's Trumpet
Native to the Tropics but a naturalized garden weed in the northeastern United States, this has ovate leaves 8 in. long, with acute lobes and upright, white to violet-colored, trumpet-shaped flowers 4 in. long. The fruit is prickly and 2 in. wide. All kinds of animals, including ostriches, have been killed from eating the foliage of this plant. Children have been poisoned by eating the seeds or sucking the nectar from the large flowers.

Delphinum sp.   Larkspur
Some of these species are the most important cattle-poisoning plants in our western states. The foliage of most species should be regarded as potentially poisonous.

Digitalis purpurea   4′   biennial   Foxglove
The leaves of this plant are one of the sources for a heart stimulant, digitalis, and if the leaves are ingested in large amounts, they can prove fatal. This is a common garden biennial, sometimes a perennial, with tubular, drooping, purple flowers in the summer, more or less spotted, on a 1-sided spike often 2 ft. long.

Euphorbia cyparrissias   1′   Zone 4   Cypress Spurge
A fast-spreading, linear-leaved perennial with small flowers in many-rayed umbels with the bracts yellowish; this has proved fatal to cattle when ingested in large amounts. It has been

used in the garden as a fast-spreading ground cover.

Ranunculus sp.   **Buttercups**
Foliage eaten in large amounts has poisoned cattle.

Rheum rhabarbarum 1½′–6′ **Zone 2 Rhubarb**
It is interesting to note that the leaves of this common garden food plant are poisonous. The leaf stalks or petioles are commonly eaten, but the leaves when eaten by humans have caused severe poisoning.

Rhus radicans, R. vernix
The foliage of Poison Ivy and Poison Sumac causes serious skin rashes on many people. These plants should be given a wide berth and eradicated immediately as soon as they appear in the garden. See FRUITS.

Sambucus canadensis 12′ **Zone 3 American Elder**
A common shrub native to the eastern United States, with opposite compound leaves, large flat clusters of small white flowers 6–8 in. across in late June, followed by small blue or black berries which have been used in making jams, pies and wines. Eating uncooked berries may produce nausea in humans, and children are reported to have been poisoned by making blow guns from the pithy stems. Apparently such poisoning is neither serious nor common.

Symplocarpus foetidus 3′ **Zone 3 Skunk-cabbage**
The fresh leaves, which are sometimes as much as 3 ft. long and a foot wide, contain a toxic principal which is apparently destroyed when they are dried, heated or boiled. Animals have been poisoned by eating the foliage but one taste of the raw, uncooked acrid leaves is enough to prevent humans from eating more.

House Plants Used as Such in the Northern U.S.A.

Dieffenbachia seguine 6′ **Zone 10 Dumb Cane**
This tropical plant is sometimes used in greenhouses or homes in America as a foliage plant because of its very large, thick, variously spotted leaves. However, it has long been known that to take a bite out of the stalk of this plant causes a throat irritation resulting in the loss of speech for several days or more, and such irritation might cause a swelling of the tongue, and clogging of the windpipe.

Euphorbia pulcherrima 10′ **Zone 9 Poinsettia**
This is the popular greenhouse and house plant familiar to everyone, grown out-of-doors in the South. The milky sap is a skin irritant and the leaves are supposed to be poisonous if eaten.

Lantana camara 4′ **Zone 10 Common Lantana**
A house plant in the North, with opposite leaves and flat axillary clusters of tubular flowers, yellow to pink at first but maturing to orange or bright red. The fruit is greenish blue or black, a fleshy 1-seeded drupe about ¼ in. wide. The foliage has caused considerable livestock poisoning in Fla. and Calif. where the plant is grown out-of-doors, and children have been poisoned by eating the fruit.

Nerium oleander 6′–20′ **Zone 9 Oleander**
A popular garden evergreen in the South and frequently grown in tubs in greenhouses in the North, moved out-of-doors during the summer. It is valued for its evergreen linear leaves and its large clusters of conspicuous pink and white flowers. It has been known as poisonous since classical times.

Philodendron sp. **mostly vines Zone 10**
Many of these species are common house plants. The leaves may contain an irritant principal, and supposedly have been responsible for the death of cats eating the foliage. It would be well to prevent children from eating the leaves.

Phoradendron serotinum 1½′ **Zones 6–7 American Mistletoe**
A common household decorative plant at Christmas with small white berries borne in clusters. This is a parasitic shrub in the South but large quantities of cut branches are shipped north in the fall of every year. Both children and adults have been severely poisoned from eating the fruits. The European Mistletoe, *Viscum album*, is also considered poisonous.

Solanum pseudo-capsicum 4′ **Zone 8 (?) Jerusalem-cherry**
This is a popular greenhouse plant used a great deal at Christmas for the bright red, rounded fruits, ½ in. in dia. and remaining on the plant for a long time. Although no serious experiences with this have been recently documented, the fruits have long been suggested as poisonous. To be safe, it would be wise to prevent children from eating them.

Foliage of other common garden or woods plants such as Rhododendron, Mountain-laurel, Lamb-kill, Chokecherry (*Prunus virginiana*), Indian Poke or False Hellebore (*Veratrum viride*) and *Pieris* species have been poisonous to livestock, especially when eaten in large amounts.

Plants of Garden or Woods with Poisonous Roots and Stems

Arisaema triphyllum	Jack-in-the-pulpit
Colchicum autumnale	Autumn Crocus
Convallaria majalis	Lily-of-the-valley

Dicentra sp.	Bleeding-heart
	Dutchman's Breeches
Gloriosa superba	Glory-lily
Hyacinthus sp.	Hyacinth
Iris sp.	Iris, Flags
Narcissus sp.	Narcissus, Daffodil
Ornithogalum umbellatum	Star-of-Bethlehem
Phytolacca americana	Pokeweed
Podophyllum peltatum	May-apple, Mandrake

POKEBERRY, COMMON = *Phytolacca americana*

POKERPLANT = *Kniphofia uvaria*

POKEWEED FAMILY = Phytolaccaceae

POLEMONIACEAE = The Phlox Family

POLEMONIUM (po-lee-MO-nium). This group of plants is valued for their small, cup-shaped, blue flowers during late spring or early summer and the rather delicate mounds of foliage which look well in the front of the perennial border. They do well in normal soil in either shade or sun; are best planted in the spring. They are propagated by spring-sown seeds, cuttings taken in midsummer or simply by division of the clumps in the late summer.

boreale (*richardsonii*)   9″   **Zone 2   Dwarf Jacob's-ladder**
This species has creeping underground stems. The leaflets are small, oval, 15–21 in number, ¼–½ in. long. There are few blue to purplish flowers about ½ in. wide. Native to Arctic Regions.

caeruleum   15″   Zones 2–3   Jacob's-ladder
With pinnate leaves of up to about 20 leaflets, it is these that are supposed to represent the ladder of which Jacob dreamed. Native to Europe. Stems are erect and the panicles of small blue flowers are in evidence from May to July. 'Blue Pearl' is an excellent cultivar. The variety 'Album' bears white flowers.

carneum   2′   Zone 7 (?)   Salmon Polemonium
Native to the mountains of Calif. and Ore. requiring a moist atmosphere; the flowers are cream colored to pink and are produced in the late spring. Hot sun is not conducive to its best growth.

pauciflorum   1′   Zone 7 (?)   Mexican Polemonium
Native to South America with 12–24 leaflets in each leaf; flowers yellow tinged red, 1½ in. long, often solitary, during July and Aug. If the dead flowers are cut off and seed formation thus prevented, the plant will remain in a healthy condition longer.

pulcherrimum   1′   Zones 2–3   Skunkleaf Polemonium
The leaves have 15–57 oval leaflets; flowers are either violet or light blue with golden-yellow throats in May and June. Native to the mountains of western U.S.

reptans   2′   Zones 2–3   Creeping Polemonium
This weak-stemmed perennial has alternate, compound leaves having 7–9 leaflets and loose, branching, terminal clusters of flowers which are a light blue. The calyx has 5 lobes and is divided halfway down and the short corolla tube is surmounted with 5 lobes. It is a plant ranging in open woods over most of North America, blooming in May. An attractive plant for the wild garden, it may be divided after blooming. The plant self-sows readily.

viscosum   4″   Zone 3   Sticky Polemonium
An attractive small plant growing in mounds of pubescent, glutinous leaves with 30–41 rounded leaflets, ⅛ in. long; clusters of small blue flowers, ¾ in. long, appear in spring, barely overtopping the foliage. A rare plant, native to the Rocky Mountains, doing well in good garden loam in sun or semi-shade.

POLIANTHES (po-li-ANTH-eez)

tuberosa   3½′   Zone 9   Tuberose
A white-flowered popular plant, growing from bulbs or tubers the origin of which is unknown, this has long been a popular garden plant. The leaves are 1½ ft. long and about ½ in. wide, and the waxy, white, fragrant flowers, 2½ in. long, are borne in late summer or early fall, on a tall and prominent spike. The double-flowered form 'Double Pearl' is the most popular. In the North, the tubers or bulbs are planted in early June about an inch deep. In the greenhouse, if potted in Jan. they will bloom beginning in April at temperatures of 75°–80° F. When the foliage has died or if outside before frost, they are lifted, dried and stored at 65°–70° F. until the next season. Easily propagated by offsets.

POLLARD. A severe method of pruning, not often practiced in America but frequently seen in Europe, in which the branches of a tree are cut back almost to the main trunk, every year or so. This results in long, thin branches giving a ball-shaped habit to the tree. Occasionally seen in America years ago, especially when done on the Dwarf Catalpa if it was grafted on an understock of *C. bignonioides*. This results in a densely rounded, ball-shaped mass of twigs and foliage on top of a single trunk. Pollarding is also practiced in Europe on some willows to obtain long, slim twigs for basket-making.

POLLEN. Spores or grains borne in the anther which later produce sperm cells.

POLLINATION. The transfer of pollen from the stamen to the stigma.

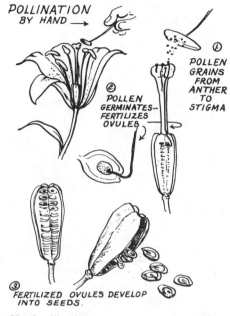

Hand pollination

POLYETHYLENE FILM, AIR LAYERING WITH. See AIR LAYERING.

POLYGALA (po-LIG-gal-a). A large and varied genus including annuals, perennials and sub-shrubs ranging throughout the world. In North America there are about 40 species. The leaves are alternate and lanceolate and the terminally produced flowers are sometimes in dense clusters, generally showy, and of various colors. The calyx has 5 unequal sepals and the petals number 4–5.

calcarea   8″   Zone 5   Lime Polygala
A tiny, evergreen, alpine perennial from Switzerland, growing in mats of leaves barely an inch long and having a profusion of blue flowers in spring. It requires a gritty, alkaline soil in full sun similar to its native moraine habitat.

chamaebuxus   1′   Zone 6   Groundbox Polygala
A small shrub similar to Boxwood, with evergreen leaves an inch long and stems producing yellow flowers, 1 or 2 together, in spring. It requires a shady location with a deep, acid leaf mold and some winter protection. Native to Europe.

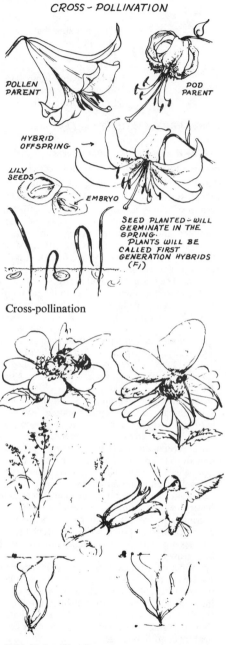

Cross-pollination

Principal pollinating agents:
1. Bees
2. Moths and butterflies
3. Wind
4. Birds
5. Water

cruciata 10″–22″ annual Marsh Milkwort
An erect annual, bearing linear leaves in
whorls of 4 on the square stem terminated by
cylindrical clusters of flowers, each flower
having 2 showy purple or white sepals. The
plant may be found in low, wet, sunny areas
from New England to Ala. and Tex. and blooms
from July to Oct.

x dalmaisiana 3′–6′ Zone 9 Dalmai's
Polygala
The most used of this genus in southern Calif.
with purplish or rosy-red flowers blooming all
the time.

lutea 6″–12″ annual Orange Milkwort
An annual, somewhat tufted plant, with erect,
branching stems and alternate, lanceolate
leaves; the basal leaves ovate-lanceolate. The
oblong flower heads are terminally produced, the
individual flowers ¼ in. long and preserve their
deep yellow color even when dry. The plant
may be found in swamps and woodlands from
Long Island, N.Y. to Fla. and La. and blooms
from May to Oct.

paucifolia 4″–5″ Zone 4 Fringed Milkwort,
Fringed Polygala
An attractive perennial with creeping underground stems. The several ovate leaves and 1–5
flowers are clustered at the end of a short stem.
Each flower, rose-pink or occasionally white,
is up to 1 in. long and is borne on a short stem
and has oval wings and a fringed corolla. It is
native to the moist pine woods of New England,
with its range extending to the higher altitudes
of Ga. Though a beautiful plant for the garden,
it is difficult to cultivate. Stem cuttings may be
taken in summer, but seeds collected in summer
and planted the following spring are generally
more satisfactory.

polygama 4″–15″ Zone 5 Racemed Milk-
wort, Bitter Polygala
A plant generally having several stems rising
from an underground perennial root. The
alternate, broadly lanceolate leaves crowded on
the stem are up to 1 in. long, the lower ones
generally smaller. The irregular, purple,
occasionally white, flowers are borne in a loose
terminal raceme up to 3 in. long. It is a plant of
dry, sandy woods and may be found throughout
the eastern half of the U.S., flowering in June
and July.

ramosa 16″–18″ Zone 6 Pine-barren
Milkwort
An attractive biennial, having a basal rosette of
elliptic leaves and erect stems bearing alternate,
lanceolate leaves and a branched terminal
cluster of greenish-yellow flower heads. These
appear from July to Sept. in the damp evergreen
woods from N.J. to Fla. and Tex.

vayredae 8″ Zone 7 Pyrenees Polygala
A perennial with drooping reflexed leaves and

purplish flowers with a yellow keel in short
axillary racemes. Native to the Pyrenees
Mountains. Resembling *P. chamaebuxus*, but
smaller.

viridescens 16″ annual Purple Milkwort
An annual with alternate, linear leaves and
reddish-purple flower heads, the individual
flowers similar to those of *P. cruciata*. It is
native to wet, acid soil areas from southeastern
Canada to La. and Okla. The flowers appear
in early summer and continue until fall.
Propagation is by seeds sown in fall or early
spring in a cold frame and reset in their permanent location as soon as the small plants can
be handled. Cuttings may be taken in Sept. and
rooted in sand and peat in a cold frame or a
cool greenhouse.

POLYGAMO-DIOECIOUS. A term used to
define a plant that is mostly dioecious but
always having a few flowers of the opposite sex
at flowering time.

POLYGAMOUS. Bearing unisexual and bisexual flowers on the same plant.

POLYGONACEAE = The Buckwheat or
Rhubarb Family

POLYGONATUM (po-lig-o-NA-tum). Members of the Lily Family, these wild flowers grow
from fleshy underground roots. The greenish,
pendant flowers are bell-shaped, about ½ in.
long, produced in May or June, and the shining
fruits mature black or blue in the fall. All are
native to North America and are propagated by
division in fall or spring or by seeds. This
genus is not to be confused with *Smilacina* or
the False Solomon's Seal, which differs in that
the flowers and fruits are gracefully attached
singly or in clusters all along the arching stem,
giving the impression, when it is arching, that
they are all on the underside.

biflorum 2′–3′ Zone 3 Small Solomon's-
seal
This perennial has an arching stem on which are
borne in 2 rows on the upper side of the stem,
the ovate, pointed, sessile, strongly veined
leaves about 4 in. long. The yellowish-white,
tubular flowers hang below the stem in 1–4-
flowered clusters, but generally in pairs. During
May each flower has a bell-shaped corolla about
1 in. long, opening into 6 short, greenish lobes.
Fruits are blue berries. The plant grows in moist,
shady woods in the Atlantic coastal states and
inland to Iowa and Neb. This is a good ground
cover for shady wooded areas of moist soil and
may be propagated by seeds sown in autumn or
by division in spring. *P. canaliculatum* is
similar and found over much the same area.

commutatum 8′ Zone 3 Great Solomon's-
seal
Another coarse native species, with leaves 6 in.

long and 4 in. wide with flowers in a cluster. Too coarse for general garden use.

multiflorum   3′   Zones 2–3   Eurasian Solomon's-seal

This species is native to Europe and Asia, with leaves 3–6 in. long and flowers white to greenish. In Europe this is sometimes called Lady's-seal or David's-harp. This species is often forced as a pot plant in Europe but the native American, *P. biflorum*, is just as good for this purpose.

POLYGONUM (po-LIG-on-um). A genus of many alternate-leaved species of herbs or climbing plants with simple leaves, numerous small flowers (consisting only of a calyx and 5 sepals) in spikes, heads or racemes; some ornamental, some vicious fast-spreading weeds. Most are propagated easily by seeds, some by division. A very few are used for ground covers, but most are not good garden plants.

affine   6″–9″   Zone 3   Himalayan Fleece-flower

A mat-forming perennial which will grow in any normal soil, rather coarse in texture, with leaves 2–4 in. long borne near the base of the plant. The flowers are red, very small, borne in terminal 3-in. spikes in the autumn. It is not a good ground cover except in situations where better, less sturdy plants will not grow. Native to the Himalayas. Propagated by division.

amplexicaule   3′   Zone 6   Mountain Fleece

An herbaceous perennial making a fine border plant because of its conspicuous 6-in. spikes of small rose or white flowers in July. The ovate leaves are 6 in. long; the upper leaves clasp the stem, the lower ones have short stalks. There is a variety **rubrum** with red flowers. Native to the Himalayas.

aubertii   vine   Zone 4   Silver Fleece-vine

A handsome, vigorous-growing, twining vine that may grow as much as 20–30 ft. in a single season. The small white or greenish-white flowers are produced in dense panicles during Aug. when few other woody plants are in bloom. Excellent for planting along a chain link fence and letting the vine take over entirely. Native of western China, its vigor and late blooms are its chief ornamental characteristic.

aviculare   prostrate   annual   Prostrate Knotweed

A flat-growing weed, chiefly in hard ground, native to the northern U.S. and southern Canada. It has slender, much-branched stems, alternate lanceolate leaves about ¾ in. long and bluish-green in color. Small pinkish flowers in axillary clusters are not conspicuous, but it is a bad garden weed. Easily propagated by division.

bistorta   2′   Zone 3   Snakeweed

A perennial, native to northern Europe and Asia, with a dense-flowered spike about 2 in. long, bearing very small pink or white flowers

during the late summer. Not much used as a garden plant in America.

capitatum   3″   Zone 6   Pinkhead Knotweed

A perennial, easily reseeding itself, native to the Himalayas; with pink flower heads ¾ in. across and trailing branches 10 in. long. This is being used as a ground cover in Calif.

convolvulus   vine   annual   Black Bindweed

A twining or prostrate weed, introduced from Europe, now common in the northern U.S. and Canada. The alternate, simple, heart-shaped leaves are about 2½ in. long, and the numerous, small, white flowers are in axillary clusters. It is easily killed by cultivation but if allowed to run rampant can twine about and strangle everything in the garden. Small plants should be pulled out before they have time to bloom and fruit.

cuspidatum   6′–8′   Zone 3   Japanese Fleece-flower

Perennial weed and extremely vigorous spreader, native to Japan but unfortunately escaped cultivation in many parts of northeastern and north central North America. The stems are hollow, often cooked as asparagus stems when they are only a foot high; with jointed stems and alternate leaves that are pointed at the tip but are almost round. It is dioecious; the greenish-white flowers are very small, in axillary panicles, during Aug. and Sept. The roots send up many shoots, and once in good soil it takes years to eradicate. More of a pernicious weed than an ornamental.

cuspidatum compactum   3′   Zone 4   Low Japanese Fleece-flower

Like other members of the genus, this perennial plant can become a vicious weed once it escapes bounds, hence it must be carefully restrained. In poor soils, where definite boundaries do not have to be set, this plant can be expected to increase rapidly by underground shoots, but it dies to the ground in the fall, after the first hard frost. It does best in the full sun. Native to Japan, the oval leaves are 3–6 in. long; the small, greenish-white flowers appear in axillary clusters during the late summer, and the small reddish fruits are most effective in the early fall. Most of the plants in the trade as *P. reynoutria* are actually this taller-growing variety of *P. cuspidatum*. Easily propagated by division.

hydropiper   2′   annual   Smartweed

A native American weed common throughout North America in low poorly drained soils. The leaves are more narrow than those of *P. pensylvanicum*, are peppery to the taste and cause a skin rash on some people. It is distinguished from some of the other *Polygonum* species in that the sepals are covered with dots or glands. The juice of this plant, if inadvertently rubbed in the eyes, causes smarting. This plant is reported to provide a yellow dye.

lapathifolium   2′   annual   Pale Smartweed
A weed common throughout the northern U.S. and on the Pacific Coast, introduced from Europe; with erect or decumbent branched stems, often rooting at the nodes where they touch the soil. The leaves are long and lance shaped, up to 5 in. long. The small pink flowers are in axillary but drooping clusters from July to Sept.

orientale   6′   annual   Prince's-feather
Native to India but introduced as a garden annual about the eastern and southern U.S., this is truly a handsome species because of its pendulous clusters of small pink flowers, the clusters being 3½ in. long, in the autumn. The alternate leaves, up to 10 in. long, are broadly ovate. It is not as pernicious a weed as some of the other members of this genus and really makes a good garden plant. Seeds can be planted in the fall or spring where the plant is to grow and, though it can grow in many soils, moist soils are best.

Polygonum pensylvanicum (Pennsylvania Smartweed)—a common garden weed.

pensylvanicum   2′   annual   Pennsylvania Smartweed
A native weed, common throughout the U.S. and similar in most respects to *P. lapathifolium*, except that the pink flower clusters are held rigidly upright. This is the more widely distributed of the 2 weeds. Both root readily wherever their weak stems touch the soil. Both should be prevented from seeding.

persicaria   2′   annual   Lady's-thumb
A weed native to Europe and naturalized throughout the northern U.S. and southern Canada and similar to *P. pensylvanicum*, but the leaves usually have a triangular dark spot near the middle.

reynoutria   4″–6″   Zone 4   Reynoutria Fleeceflower
The true *P. reynoutria* may not be widely distributed in this country for it is only 4–6 in. tall. *P. cuspidatum compactum*, which grows 3 ft. tall, is often sold as *P. reynoutria*. Similar in flower and fruit, native to Japan; a good ground cover but needs restraint. Easily propagated by division.

sachalinense   12′   Zone 4   Sakhalin Knotweed
Perennial weed from the Orient, similar to *P. cuspidatum* and spreading in the area between Mass. and Md. The oval alternate leaves are 1 ft. long and heart shaped.

scandens   twining   Zone 3   Hedge Bindweed
Perennial native weed, somewhat similar to *P. convolvulus* but it is slightly more coarse.

vacciniifolium   9″   Zone 7   Rose Carpet Knotweed
The red flowers of this species are small, in upright spikes 1½–3 in. long, during Aug. The dark green leaves are only ½ in. long, pointed at both ends. Native to the Himalayas. This also is a vigorous creeper with branches rooting and trailing along the surface of the ground, making a dense mat if in the full sun. It is not coarse in texture but is refined; makes a good ground cover in the South and in some places is evergreen.

POLYPETALOUS. Having separate petals.

POLYPLOID. Plant with a chromosome complement of more than 2 sets of the single or normal number.

POLYPODIACEAE = The Polypody Family

POLYPODIUM (po-li-PO-dium). The genus comprises a very large number of fern species, and botanists working through them are trying to divide them into many separate genera, some of which may be accepted later. They have creeping or running rhizomes. The species that are hardy are good for rock gardens and planting at the bases of rocks. They have simple or compound leaves, and can be propagated either by division or spores. See FERNS.

aureum   3′   Zone 10   Golden Polypody
Sometimes called the Hare's-foot Fern because the rhizomes, which creep along the surface of the soil, are heavily covered with brown, sometimes white scales and is irregular in the way it

grows, about 1 in. through. When one of these hairy rhizomes creeps out over the edge of a pot it looks something like a hare's foot. The blue-green fronds are up to 10 in. wide, deeply cut or pinnatifid but not pinnate.

Native from tropical Fla. through the West Indies to Argentina, it is a very easily grown tropical fern for the greenhouse or conservatory. Because of the interesting rhizomes it is good for hanging baskets, for then, the golden-yellow fruiting bodies on the undersurface of the fronds can be easily seen. The wire baskets are first covered on the inside with sphagnum moss, then a soil mixture of equal parts loam, leaf mold in which is mixed some sand, and the plants then placed in this in such a way that the rhizomes can clamber over the edge of the basket. Propagation is by division of the rhizomes and by spores. See FERNS.

polypodioides   6″–8″   Zone 7   Resurrection Fern
An interesting evergreen fern, it usually is found growing on tree trunks in the moist atmosphere of the subtropics. In dry weather the fronds are rolled up into tight balls, but with added moisture they open up and continue growth. From the southeastern U.S., but of little garden value.

vulgare   10″   Zone 3   Common Polypody
Deeply pinnatifid, this evergreen fern is found in eastern North America with fronds about 2 in. wide. The fronds are leathery. A good fern for the shaded part of the rockery. Since it grows from rhizomes, propagation is easy by simple division. For spore propagation see FERNS.

POLYPODY. See POLYPODIUM.

POLYPODY FAMILY = Polypodiaceae

POLYSCIAS (po-LISS-ias). Sometimes used as greenhouse plants in the North while young, often with colorful evergreen foliage; native to the Tropics of Africa and Asia. They belong to the Aralia Family and by some are classified as *Aralia*. The flowers are inconspicuous. Often used as hedges in the Tropics. Easily grown and propagated by cuttings of hardwood, or root cuttings, or by grafting some of the better forms.

balfouriana   25′   Zones 9–10   Balfour Polyscias
This has leaves spotted with white; usually the leaves have 4 orbicular leaflets, about 4 in. wide, and often heart-shaped at the base. Native to Caledonia. Rare, but it makes an interesting foliage plant in the greenhouse.

fruticosa   8′   Zone 8–9   Ming Aralia
A native of Polynesia, with compound leaves, usually 3 or more leaflets each about 4″ long. There are several varieties noted for fine foliage, but mostly conservatory plants.

guilfoylei   20′   Zones 9–10   Guilfoyle Polyscias
The leaves are once pinnate, the leaflets about 5 in. long and are edged with white, the variety **victoriae** having very finely divided leaves. Native to Polynesia. Many forms, but of use in America chiefly as small potted greenhouse plants.

POLYSTICHUM (po-LISS-tik-um). These Holly Ferns are mostly evergreen, some suitable for the rockery or sheltered fern garden, others for the home greenhouse or for use as pot plants indoors. They are native to all parts of the northern hemisphere, with the fronds varying in length from 1–3 ft. Usually the fronds are twice divided. Most can be propagated by simple division, lifting the clumps in March or April and separating them. If propagation is by spores see FERNS.

acrostichoides   3′   Zone 3   Christmas Fern
This common, evergreen native fern is widely distributed over eastern North America, this being one of the few ferns in this genus with leathery fronds only once divided. They may be up to 5 in. wide, and at maturity are very dark green. They are easily grown in wooded areas with partial shade, but the soil should be kept moist. It is sometimes used as a house plant.

aculeatum   2′   Zone 5   Lobe Holly Fern
A hardy evergreen fern from the Old World with fronds often 6 in. wide, 1 pinnate. One form, **'Proliferum'**, produces buds on the leaves. There are a number of varieties of this fern available from European florists, but apparently they are not popular in America.

braunii   18″–24″   Zone 3   Braun Holly Fern
The frond is twice pinnate and up to 8 in. wide, deep lustrous green and leathery. The rachis is brown, covered with brown scales. It is considered by some to be one of the most handsome of the ferns native to northeastern North America, but it is not evergreen. It should be grown in a cool, moist, partially shaded situation, with plenty of mulch about the rhizomes. The fronds form a ring around the base of the plant.

lonchitis   9″–20″   Zone 3   Mountain Holly Fern
Native to both Europe and North America in high latitudes, this is evergreen, with the leathery fronds about 3 in. wide. It is once pinnate.

munitum   24″–40″   Zone 4   Giant Holly
Native from Alaska to Calif.; the leathery, evergreen fronds are sometimes 10 in. wide at the base.

tsus-simense   1″   Zone 10   Tsus-sima Holly Fern
Because of its small size, this is frequently used in fern dishes. Native to Japan, the fronds are 2

pinnate and 5 in. wide. It makes an excellent house plant, needing a moist, humus-rich soil and some shade. The fronds grow from a crown.

POME. A fleshy fruit like the apple and pear.

POMEGRANATE. The Pomegranate (*Punica granatum*) makes an unusually attractive shrub or small tree for the yard, seldom growing beyond 10–12 ft. high. It is free of pests and diseases in the arid regions where it is best adapted, but the shiny green foliage is likely to be attacked by fungus diseases in the more humid regions of the South and Southeast. Although these diseases have not been studied, neutral copper sprays should effectively protect against most of them.

Pomegranate

The Pomegranate is a deciduous plant, and even in the warmer areas of the Southeast where average winter temperatures are reasonably high it will drop its leaves through the winter period, although new growth may start before all other leaves are off. In areas with a marked winter period, leaf fall occurs in the fall and the trees remain dormant until spring. The species appears to have very little chilling requirement and is therefore vigorous growing even in warm areas. The dormant tree withstands temperatures of 10° to 15° F., and, with protection, can be grown in areas with even lower minimums.

Pomegranates are easily grown from seed, which are pressed out of the surrounding fleshy tissue, and planted shallowly in a prepared seed bed or flat. Seedling plants are almost invariably very inferior in quality, some being extremely acid. Named varieties are recommended. The

Pomegranate is so easily propagated by dormant woody cuttings that any other method of propagation seems unnecessary. Budding, grafting and layering of the simpler kinds can be used if desired. Because they are so universally grown on their own roots from cuttings, no information on rootstocks is available.

The plants may be grown close together in a hedgerow, or as free-standing trees. Standard trees need be no more than 12–16 ft. apart.

Pomegranates tend to sucker very freely, and if the suckers are not removed the plant soon becomes a shrub, usually a dense spiny thicket unless thinned out annually. Except for the removal of suckers and strong watersprouts, pruning consists mostly of thinning out excessively dense growth. A multiple trunk system is easily developed by using 2 or more suckers to develop the top. Two-year or older wood is fruitful and should be retained. Heavy thinning back may be used to keep the plant small.

Pomegranates respond to normal watering practices for yard shrubs; they are somewhat drought-resistant, but best production and appearance results when they do not suffer long drought periods.

Fertilizer requirements are less than for many other fruit plants; if the bright green foliage starts to yellow, light applications of nitrogenous fertilizers are indicated. If the plants become chlorotic, especially in the Southeast, applications of a complete fertilizer with added micronutrients as for citrus (see ORANGE) may prove beneficial.

This plant is adapted to a variety of soils, from heavy to light; only poorly drained areas need to be avoided. It is more tolerant to saline soils than most other fruit trees.

One of its chief attractions as an ornamental is the relatively large, bright orange-red flowers, which bloom in the spring and continue to nearly midsummer. The fruit matures from late July to Sept., depending upon average growing temperatures through the developmental period, and hangs on the trees until winter. As it colors it adds materially to the ornamental value of the plant. Fruits not used should be cut off, as they eventually split, become subject to molds and rots, and are unsightly.

The fruits are normally from 3–4 in. in dia., roughly globose to subglobose in shape, with a persistent tubular calyx. The arils, which are from white to red, the latter being preferred, are encased in the leathery skin. If the calyx end of the fruit is cut off, the skin cut through in 4 or 5 sectors around the fruit, it may be pried open exposing the arils most effectively. The membranous skin separating groups of arils is highly astringent, and should not be eaten.

Few Americans are fond of the fresh fruit, but the expressed juice is used fresh, in cookery, and makes a very delightful jelly.

Two varieties are generally available. 'Wonderful' yields a large fruit, more or less blushed with light red over a straw-colored base. The arils are pinkish red, the seeds small and soft, and the quality very good. 'Ruby' fruits are somewhat smaller, but the fruit is usually fully colored medium red; the arils are bright red, but the seeds are slightly larger and harder, and the flesh more acid.

Non-fruiting ornamental forms with pink, white-frilled, double flowers are available. Also, a very dwarf form, which bears typical but tiny fruits, is offered.

CLARON O. HESSE

POMEGRANATE FAMILY = Punicaceae

PONCIRUS (pon-SY-rus)

trifoliata　　35′　　**Zones** 5–6　　**Hardy-orange**
Commonly grown in the South because it makes a splendid, vigorous and thorny hedge plant, this has been popular ever since it was introduced from China. In fact it has been used as understock on which some commercial orange varieties have been grafted in the past. It withstands shearing very well and has been grown as far north as Boston, Mass. in very protected places, but is not reliably hardy north of Phila. Pa. Its small white flowers, 2 in. across, bloom in late April and they are followed in the fall by fruits which are small, very bitter-tasting but aromatic oranges, 2 in. in dia. The leaves each have 3 leaflets, about 2 in. long.

Propagation

Seed collected in the northern U.S. should be stratified for 3 months at 40° F., then sown. Softwood and hardwood cuttings, which see, can be rooted.

PONTEDERIA (pon-te-DEE-ria)

cordata　　2′–4′　　**Zone** 3　　**Pickerelweed**
An aquatic perennial growing in abundance in shallow fresh water from New England to Fla. and west to Minn. and Okla.; its dark green, heart-shaped leaves are 10 in. long, 6 in. wide. The blue flowers are borne on stout spikes. Each flower is tubular, with a 2-lipped corolla, each divided into 3 lobes. The plant blooms throughout the season. It is a good plant for the water or bog garden and may be propagated by division in the summer while in bloom. Stone should be used to hold the newly reset plants until the roots are established. However, in the right situations it can increase rapidly and become a pest. For controlling it see WEED-CONTROLLING CHEMICALS.

PONTEDERIACEAE = The Pickerelweed Family

POOLS. See WATER GARDENING.

POOLS, CLEANING. When the temperature is high and there is not much living activity in a pool, it frequently becomes covered with a green scum. This can occur on ponds as well. This is usually either an alga or *Azolla caroliniana*, a small fern-leaved plant with leaves about ¾ in. long that multiplies rapidly on the water surface when conditions are just right. Sometimes this can be merely skimmed off.

Copper sulfate can be dissolved in the water at the rate of 2 oz. of the chemical to 10,000 gal. of water. See WEIGHTS AND MEASURES. This is usually not strong enough to harm fish (trout excepted) or plants in the pool, but if there are expensive fish, it might be well to remove them first. The number of gallons in a pool is found by multiplying the area in square feet by the average depth in feet and multiplying by 7½.

Estimate the amount of the chemical needed, place in a cheesecloth bag and trail it back and forth across the pool until the crystals are all dissolved. Unfortunately, Duckweed (*Lemna minor*) can not be killed this way. It must be skimmed off.

POPCORN = *Zea Mays everta*

POPLAR. See POPULUS.

POPPY. See PAPAVER.

POPPY, CELANDINE = *Stylophorum diphyllum*

POPPY-MALLOW. See CALLIRHOE.

POPULUS (POP-yew-lus). The poplars are not valued as ornamental trees, especially in a greater part of the country where many better trees can be grown. Many are native to North America, and in fact the Trembling Aspen (*P. tremuloides*) is the most widely distributed tree on the North American continent, native from Labrador and Alaska to lower Calif. and Mexico. Some 81 species and varieties are listed and described by Rehder in his "Manual of Cultivated Trees and Shrubs," but American nurserymen only list 15. European nurseries, especially those in continental Europe, find poplars more useful and so they list nearly 40.

In general, poplars are fast-growing, weak-wooded trees lacking ornamental flowers and fruits, and in fact some of them have practically no autumn color. At the turn of the century, a few like the Lombardy Poplar and the Carolina Poplar were widely planted—almost over-planted. When disease took its toll on the one, and the roots of the other raised city streets, clogged drains and water pipes, it did not take very long for many cities to pass ordinances against planting them.

It must be admitted that in the hot and dry areas of the Great Plains a few of these, chiefly the cottonwoods, make superior trees, sometimes about the only trees that can be grown. Hence, these have value under those specific trying growing conditions.

Populus alba leaves (left) and *P. alba nivea* leaves (right) showing the white, woolly undersurface of the leaves of this variety. (*Photo by Arnold Arboretum, Jamaica Plain, Mass.*)

As a group many are coarse in texture, having overly large, alternate leaves. Many can be expected to grow 4 ft. a year in good soil, the reason why they sometimes are used in making screens. They are short-lived and definitely susceptible to canker and other diseases which do not make them permanent additions to most gardens. They are voracious feeders, quickly taking the best there is in any garden soil, and some have the disconcerting habit of sending up root suckers when the tree is cut down, unless the stump is properly treated with chemicals. Then too, they have frequently been responsible for clogging drains since their roots easily force their way into such places. The best way to control roots entering the sewer is to allow 5 lbs. of copper sulfate crystals, dissolved in water, go down the drain slowly and to flush no more waste down for several hours. This might be done once a month until free flowage occurs. Then 4 1-lb. applications a year might be enough to keep the roots killed.

Usually the sexes are separate. Female trees produce clusters of small pods which open and discharge a cottonlike fluffy material (even though the tree has not been pollinized), which is a disagreeable addition to a clean, kept garden or terrace. Male trees should be produced as the ornamentals—never the females.

From the lumberman's viewpoint, poplars are excellent as producers of wood for paper pulp, especially pulp used in the manufacture of paper for magazines. Considerable effort has been spent in the past, and now also, in the production of hybrids with increased vigor for fast grow'h.

Crossing poplars is interesting to the geneticist because he can cut male and female branches and take them in the greenhouse in the winter, force them into bloom and seed formation, plant the seed and have a really sizeable 20-ft. seedling all within 2 years time. *Populus* x *generosa* is only one of the hybrid species which has made very vigorous growth and produced some clones of interest to the lumber industry.

The petioles on most poplars are flat, the leaves are easily moved by the wind, especially true in the smaller-leaved species like *P. tremula* and *P. tremuloides*. In Europe, poplars are used as ornamentals considerably more than they are in North America, but American gardeners will do well to overlook most of them except for use in specific areas of the Midwest and Southeast.

Propagation

Seed should be sown as soon as ripe for it quickly loses its viability. Grafting is commonly practiced using *P. grandidentata*, *P. nigra italica* and *P. alba* 'Pyramidalis' as understocks. Some root well from softwood or hardwood cuttings and those that are difficult can be rooted from root cuttings taken in the early spring. See GRAFTING, CUTTING, etc.

Insect Pests

One of the common pests of Poplar and Willow on the home grounds is the poplar curculio, the grub of which tunnels in the twigs and branches causing them to break or leaving conspicuous scars. Cutting out and spraying with insecticide #9 in midsummer is suggested. Cottonwood leaf beetle develops 3 or 4 broods annually. The black grubs skeletonize the leaves. Insecticide #15 is effective. Poplar leaf hopper may become very abundant. Insecticide #15, #13 or #9 is applied where necessary. Poplar is a favorite host of oyster-shell scale. See SYRINGA. Poplar borer and other borers damage older trees. See BORERS. Leaf-eating caterpillars such as tussock moth worms, spiny elm caterpillar, gypsy moth and poplar tentmaker are minor pests that are controlled by sprays of insecticide #9 or #15.

Diseases

European canker causes split bark, dead branches and excessive watersprouts. Lombardy Poplar is most susceptible. Careful pruning and removal of infected trees are recommended but thorough dormant sprays with fungicide #U have been helpful. Rust, scab, leaf curl and anthracnose infect various species but seldom require control.

alba   **90′**   **Zone 3**   **White Poplar**
Needing plenty of room to grow in, this tree from Europe and Siberia does make a "cool" looking tree, especially because of the white undersurface of the leaves. It tends to have a reddish fall color under some conditions, and its whitish-gray bark is also of interest. One of the best of the poplars for large-tree use. Varieties are: 'Nivea'—leaves very white beneath, even better than the species in this respect, and that is why it is called 'Silver Poplar'; 'Pyramidalis'—the Bolleana Poplar is a good substitute for the Lombardy Poplar and is not nearly as susceptible to trunk canker. It is often incorrectly listed as *P. alba bolleana*. This plant was introduced from its native habitat in western Europe between 1875 and 1878; 'Richardii'—the Richard's White Poplar, of ornamental value because the upper surface of the leaf is yellow, lower surface white, a good color combination.

balsamifera (*tacamahaca*)   **90′**   **Zone 2**
Balm-of-Gilead, Balsam Poplar
A very hardy poplar, occasionally planted because the young unfurling foliage in the spring gives off an aroma like Balsam. Leaves are broadly ovate, 2–5 in. long and 1¼–3 in. wide, but sometimes on sucker growth they may reach a foot in length. This is not an important ornamental tree, but should be mentioned. Native from Labrador to Alaska and across the extreme northern U.S.

x berolinensis   **75′**   **Zone 2**   **Berlin Poplar**
A fine poplar hybrid especially for planting in the northwest prairies. It seems to withstand very cold winters and very hot summers and has a desirably narrow habit. However, if not desired for planting in the Midwest it might be overlooked for there certainly are many better ornamental trees in the East.

x canadensis eugenei   **150′**   **Zone 4**   **Carolina Poplar**
Widely planted in the past, this hybrid poplar (*P. deltoides* x *P. nigra*) has an open habit of growth and coarse, glossy leaves, 3–4 in. long. It is not recommended for use; in fact many towns have ordinances against planting it because of its vicious roots which grow into and clog drains and raise the pavement when planted nearby. It is weak wooded and a "dirty" tree, always dropping catkins, twigs or leaves and littering the streets and lawns. Although a vigorous grower, it has no autumn color and nothing to recommend its use except vigorous growth under trying urban conditions. There are better trees for even these situations.

deltoides   **90′**   **Zone 2**   **Eastern Poplar, Cottonwood**
Often planted for its rapid growth, but only of value in the Midwest where other trees are unable to withstand the high temperatures and long droughts of summer. It is native from Quebec to Tex. The variety **virginiana** is supposed to be the typical form in the northern part of its range and **missouriensis** is the southern form. Where other trees can be grown the Cottonwood should be overlooked entirely. It is definitely not a tree for the small place.

fremontii   **90′**   **Zone 7**   **Fremont Cottonwood**
A poplar native to Calif. and Ariz., this has widespreading branches and a loose, open habit. The texture is coarse and it is only used for planting in dry, alkaline soils in the southwestern part of the country where it is difficult to get any trees to grow.

grandidentata   **60′**   **Zone 3**   **Large-toothed Aspen**
Largely a tree of the woods in eastern North America—there is little merit in planting this tree in the garden. *P. tremuloides* would be better because of its smaller leaves and finer texture. The leaves are 3–4 in. long and the tree has an open habit of growth, being weak-wooded like all other poplars.

lasiocarpa   **60′**   **Zone 5**   **Chinese Poplar**
Conspicuous with bright green leaves 6–10 in. long, with red midrib and petiole, this tree from China is one of the better poplars, but still not a tree to use in preference to oaks and maples. In many situations it would be considered of coarse texture.

maximowiczii   **90′**   **Zone 4**   **Japanese Poplar**
A fast-growing, large tree from Japan, with dull green, rather coarse, thick leaves and grayish bark; this is the first of the poplars to produce leaves in the spring. Like most others it is susceptible to canker and breaks easily in wind, snow and ice storms.

nigra 'Italica'   **90′**   **Zone 2**   **Lombardy Poplar**
This is a short-lived, fastigiate tree, overplanted in the last 50 years but a common tree in America for nearly 2 centuries. It frequently acquires a canker as it matures, leaving the top dead. It grows rapidly and now, since there are other columnar trees that are more permanent, should only be used as a quick-growing temporary screen which should be removed while the plants are still young and before canker sets in. It is often extremely difficult for the amateur gardener to refrain from planting trees such as this. They are always attractively advertised by some unscrupulous growers. Admittedly it does grow fast, making a good screen, but in the long run proves very unsatisfactory, because eventually the top gets cankerous.

simonii   **50′**   **Zone 2**   **Simon Poplar**
Handsome, with bright green leaves and vigorous growth, from northern China. The leaves are 2–5 in. long and may taper to a point at both ends. Old trees have bark which is almost white. The variety 'Fastigiata' is not as

narrow as the Lombardy Poplar, but dense in growth. We have found that the trunk is susceptible to winter sunscald, even though it is listed as hardy in Zone 2.

tremula erecta   50′   Zone 2
An excellent, narrowly fastigiate tree, found in the forests of Sweden about 1926. It should be tried more generally in America for it may supplant the canker-ridden Lombardy Poplar.

tremuloides   90′   Zone 1   Quaking Aspen
This tree is native from coast to coast across North America and is probably the most widely distributed tree on the continent. The leaves are comparatively small (1–3 in. long) and because of the flat petiole most poplars have, they are in continual motion even in the slightest breeze. The bark is greenish white and the autumn color is a gorgeous yellow. It is one of the first trees to sprout up after a forest fire and, like all poplars, grows vigorously. Planted in groups or clumps it shows off better than if planted singly. Easily broken by storms.

PORANA (po-RAY-na)
paniculata   vine   Zone 10   Porana Vine
Native to India and Malaya, this high-climbing vine is covered with small, white, fragrant flowers ⅓ in. across, borne in huge terminal clusters during autumn and winter, something akin to miniature morning-glories. The alternate, evergreen leaves are heart-shaped, 6 in. long, and gray-green in color. It is at its best about Christmas. Since it grows vigorously it might be pruned back after flowering.

PORTIA-TREE = *Thespesia populnea*

PORTULACA (por-tew-LAY-ka)
grandiflora   8″   annual   Common Portulaca
There are many bright-flowered variants of this Brazil native; a common garden annual with white, pink, yellow, red and purple flowers, both single and double up to an inch across. The fleshy stems and small fleshy leaves up to an inch long, the bright terminal flowers all are well known. The flowers open in the full sun, close at night, hence plantings should be made in full sun, preferably in light sandy soil that can be slightly dry. Seed can be sown in May where plants are to grow. It is very fine, hence should be raked in only lightly. Thin out seedlings to about 6 in. apart. Excellent for edging, or in the rock garden, or planting around the base of some tree trunk to brighten up the little area where grass may not grow because the soil is too dry.

oleracea   prostrate   annual   Purslane
Probably the worst weed troubling all gardeners throughout the U.S. and Canada. It was introduced to Mass. from Europe, as early as 1672 but now it is a recurring weed everywhere. It has fleshy stems and leaves, and hence is able to store water so that it survives during drought periods, or even when it is hoed out of the ground and left on the surface of the soil, roots form again after the first shower. Then too, the seeds have to remain viable in the soil for many years and then germinate when plowed up to the surface. Leaves are opposite, obovate or wedge-shaped, to 1½ in. long; the much-branched stems thick and succulent, rooting whenever they touch the soil. The small yellow flowers are axillary, open only in the sun. It should be destroyed while in the seedling stage as mature plants produce prodigious amounts of minute seed. For eradication see WEED-CONTROLLING CHEMICALS.

PORTULACACEAE = The Purslane Family

PORTULACARIA (por-tew-lak-KAY-ria)
afra   12′   Zone 10   Elephant Bush
A South African plant used in the greenhouse in America but can be grown out-of-doors in the warmer part of Calif. Sometimes grown as fodder. With softwood, opposite, obovate leaves that are fleshy and ½ in. long and pink flowers about ₁₂ in. across, borne in clusters. Actually a succulent shrub, but it makes an attractive greenhouse plant; belonging to the Purslane Family. It should be given the same care as cacti (which see) and is easily propagated at any time of year by cuttings.

POSSUM HAW = *Ilex decidua*

POTATO (*Solanum tuberosum*). The Potato is the world's leading vegetable crop. As a food, it is one of the cheapest sources of carbohydrates plus appreciable amounts of vitamins and minerals. Its culture is practically world-wide.

The Potato is a native of South America and, while it was cultivated by the ancient Incas, its general culture as a food crop did not become important until late in the 17th century. The Potato is a member of the Nightshade Family which also includes Tomato, Pepper, Eggplant, Tobacco, Petunia and a number of other common flowers and weeds.

The potato is a succulent, non-woody, annual plant which, under favorable conditions, blossoms and develops underground tubers. There is, however, little or no relationship between the abundance of flowers and subsequent development of seedballs and the formation, growth and yield of tubers.

The Potato is a cool-season crop, but is only moderately tolerant to frost. When days are hot and long as in midsummer the material manufactured by the leaves is used in the normal process of producing vegetative growth. Under cooler conditions, 60° F.–65° F., and shorter days vegetative growth is reduced and the surplus food manufactured by the plant is moved in the form of soluble sugars down through the stems to the underground stolons. Here the sugar is changed to starch and the cells of the stolons divide and enlarge to form the storage tuber of the potato plant. The best potato regions are in those areas which have a temperate climate and an abundant rainfall. Me., N.Y., and the Great Lakes region, the mountain states of Id. and Colo., and in winter, Calif., Tex., and Fla.

Soils and Fertilizers

Most garden soils are suitable for potatoes. Tubers produced on light, sandy, loam soils generally have a more desirable shape and a brighter skin color than those grown on the heavier clay-type soils. The potato plant is very sensitive to drainage and aeration and, therefore, it is essential that the soil be well drained and thoroughly prepared by plowing or spading prior to planting. It is usually recommended that potatoes be grown in a soil having a pH of 5.0 to 6.0 in order to control potato scab.

The soil must have an abundance of plant food. Well-rotted stable manure, if available, can be used at the rate of 5–7 bu. per 100 ft. of row. Fresh manure should be avoided unless it is applied and worked into the soil in the fall. If no manure is used, 35–40 lbs. of a 5-10-10 commercial fertilizer should be used per 1000 sq. ft., one-half of which is broadcast prior to planting and the other half applied at the time of planting in bands 2–3 in. to the side and slightly below the seed piece.

Planting

Potatoes are propagated by cutting up an ordinary potato tuber, allowing 1–2 "eyes" (really buds of the underground stem) to each piece. Cut the pieces so that each will weigh from 1½–2 oz. It is essential that only certified, disease-free tubers purchased from a reliable dealer be used in order to prevent many diseases which are carried over on the tubers.

Cut seed pieces should be cured to encourage rapid suberization or callusing of the cut surface. They will do this naturally if placed in a cool (50–65° F.), dry place for 2–3 days. For treatment of seed before planting see DISEASES below.

Make the trenches about 5 in. deep and put a piece of cut potato tuber every 8–12 in. in the row and space the rows from 24–36 in. apart. Cover the seed piece thoroughly and allow 2–3 weeks to sprout above ground. Plan on about 7–8 lbs. of tubers to plant 100-ft. row.

The date for planting is important. Early varieties should be planted at least 10 days or 2 weeks before the date of the last killing frost in your location. Late varieties should be planted a few weeks later.

Cultivation

This operation should be often enough and just deep enough to control weeds. During cultivation, as the plants reach a height of 6–8 in., the soil is thrown up against the plants to form ridges of 4–6 in. in height. Hilling covers weeds in the row with soil and provides additional protection against greening of the tubers as a result of exposure to light.

Varieties

There are a large number of varieties that vary in maturity, color of tuber, quality and resistance to disease. For pink varieties recommended sorts are 'Red Pontiac' and 'Red La Soda'. For white varieties, common sorts are 'Irish Cobbler', 'Chippewa', 'Kennebeck', 'Russet Burbank', 'Sebago', 'Katahdin', 'Superior', 'Belrus', 'Green Mountain', 'Cayuga', and 'Cherokee'.

Harvesting

When the tops have withered and died down the potatoes may be dug. The early varieties can be left in the ground for a short period, several weeks, after they are ready to dig if the weather is not too hot or wet. The late varieties are quite safe to leave in the ground for 3–4 weeks after the tops have died down.

After digging, the potatoes should be dried enough to remove the soil moisture and loose soil (2–3 hours is sufficient), before placing in storage. During the first week of storage the temperature should range from 50° to 60° F. with a relative humidity of 85% to permit proper curing. The temperature is then dropped to 40–45° F. in order to prevent sprouting of the tubers after their rest period.

Sprouting may also be prevented by using various chemicals such as Mena and Maleic Hydrazide. These materials may be purchased from dealers and directions for their use are on the containers.

Potato storage should be dark because tubers exposed to light will develop a green color and take on a semi-bitter taste.

Diseases

The Potato is subject to many fungus, bacterial and virus diseases. Only a few of the more important and common can be noted here. Early blight: leaves show small, irregular, dark brown areas which enlarge by concentric rings to damage and reduce foliage. It is a fungus carried over in the soil. Late blight appears first as water-soaked areas in leaves, resulting in dark irregular areas on leaves and stems; has a moldlike growth on the underside of the leaf, most serious in cool, moist weather. Fungus is carried over in tubers. For both early and late blight use only certified seed, spray every 7–10 days with Bordeaux mixture or use a dust containing copper or maneb. The varieties 'Sebago' and 'Kennebec' are resistant to late blight. Verticillium wilt shows up in yellow leaves, wilted appearance of plant, brown rings inside stems and tubers. Fungi live over in tubers and in the soil. Do not grow potatoes in infected soil, use certified seed. The varieties 'Houma' and 'Ontario' have some resistance. Common scab is recognized by rough corky lesions on the tubers, which affect appearance of the potato but not its eating quality. Fungus lives over in the soil and is most active in a soil with a pH of 5.5 to 7.0. Plant certified seed, treat seed pieces with Semesan. See FUNGICIDES. Do not use lime, wood ashes or fresh manure, select resistant varieties such as 'Cherokee', 'Cayuga' or 'Ontario'. Black leg, a bacterial disease causing severely stunted plants having brown or black rotted areas at the base of the stem. Tubers show darkened areas which develop into a soft rot. The disease is carried over in tubers and control lies in using certified seed and treating the cut seed pieces with corrosive sublimate or semesan. See FUNGICIDES. Mosaic and leaf roll are 2 common virus diseases that are carried in the tubers and are spread by aphids. Both cause a stunted growth with nettled green and curled leaves. Use certified seed, control aphids (see below) and plant resistant varieties such as 'Chippewa', 'Katahdin', 'Kennebec' or 'Sebago'.

Insects

Colorado potato beetle, Adults: yellow, black striped, $\frac{3}{8}$ in. long. Larva, soft-bodied, brick red, hump-backed, $\frac{3}{8}$ in. long. To control apply Sevin, Guthion or methoxychlor repeatedly. Flea beetles are dark brown or black and $\frac{3}{16}-\frac{1}{8}$ in. long. Control with the above. Leafhoppers, small wedge-shaped insects which feed on leaves causing them to curl upward and turn yellow. Control by dusting at 6–10-day intervals with Guthion or 5% malathion. Aphids, tiny, green to black, soft-bodied sucking insects cause curled distorted leaves and stunted plants; spread virus diseases. Control with a 4% malathion dust or dimethoate spray. Wireworms are $\frac{1}{2}-1\frac{1}{2}$ in. long. They puncture and tunnel into tubers. Control, spray #13 as a broadcast application prior to planting and this should prove satisfactory.

GRANT B. SNYDER

POTATO-BEAN, AMERICAN = *Apios americana*

POTATO, SWEET (also see *Ipomoea batatus*). The Sweet Potato is a staple food crop especially in the South, and should not be confused with the Yam (*Dioscorea* sp.) which is something else, but unfortunately the common name has been used incorrectly for the true Sweet Potato. The Sweet Potato can be grown from southern N.J. and southern Ill. southward on a commercial scale, but the areas with long hot summers (Zones 8, 9, 10) are usually the best growing areas. However, the home gardener in the northern part of the country can sometimes grow a few hills just for the fun of it, if the plants are set out after the middle of June and the roots are not subjected to frost of any kind.

These are vines, growing luxuriantly on the surface of the soil, with alternate, triangular to heart-shaped leaves, often deeply lobed according to variety. They seldom bear flowers except in the area about Key West and the most tropical parts of Tex. The tubers are brown colored, often with yellow or orange mixed in, are oval in shape and a hill of 6–8 well filled-out tubers is considered normal.

They grow best on warm sandy soils with plenty of available moisture, but not wet. They do not grow well on dry or muck soils. In fact,

A live Sweet Potato can grow into an interesting house plant. The suckers are rooted in water and finally planted in the garden.

if too much fertilizer is provided, their growth may all go to tops and not to the roots where most of the nourishment should be stored. Some commercial growers do not fertilize growing plants just for the reason they do not wish to force too much top growth.

The Sweet Potato is propagated by rooting the numerous shoots which grow from the tuber. In fact, if a live tuber can be obtained from the grocery store, it can be placed with its lower half in water and numerous shoots will develop. These can be cut off and rooted in water, and eventually set out in the garden in the North, preferably about June 15th, and it may well be that a few tubers will be produced by the end of the summer. However, apparently most sweet potatoes now are treated with some chemical which prevents sprouting. Rooted sprouts can always be purchased from garden supply houses in the South.

When commercially grown, these rooted cuttings are set out in the field in rows 2½–5 ft. apart, depending on variety, and 15–20 in. apart in the row. The should be given as long a period in the ground as possible, and when dug, preferably just before frost, should not be left out on top of the soil overnight as they are very susceptible to the slightest frost. Curing them, after harvest, should be done with extreme care, often done in a curing room where an even temperature of 85–90° F. can be kept night and day for about a 10-day period. After this time the temperature is gradually lowered, but it should not be allowed to drop below 45° F.

Some of the varieties are 'Big Stem Jersey', 'Yellow Jersey', 'Red Jersey', 'Yellow Belmont' and 'Pumpkin'. In Calif. 'Prolific' and 'Priestly' are also grown.

POTATO-TREE = *Solanum macranthum*

POT-BOUND. A term used to signify a potted plant which has been allowed to grow in its pot too long, so that the pot is full of too many roots. The plant should have either been repotted into a larger container, or, if it is to remain in the same pot, some of the roots should be removed. Woody plants when pot-bound, especially those with long tap roots, frequently never recover from intertwining roots, which, if cut off, will enlarge and eventually strangle each other, resulting in the death of the plant. See GIRDLING ROOTS.

POTENTILLA (po-ten-TILL-a). The cinquefoils are a widespread genus of annuals, of herbs and woody plants, many native to the Arctic regions of the northern hemisphere. They belong to the Rose Family and hence have single, 5-petalled flowers, usually yellow, white or shades of red. The alternate leaves are digitately compound with 3–5 leaflets. Only a few are of ornamental

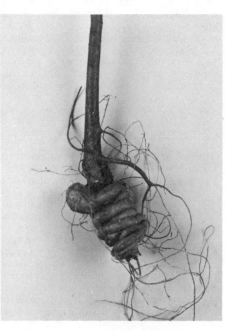

Pot-bound plant caused by winding roots that are too long and forcing the plant to grow in pot that is too small. This tree will probably eventually die, for as the roots enlarge it will strangle itself. (*Photo by Arnold Arboretum, Jamaica Plain, Mass.*)

value and of these *P. fruticosa* and *P. tridentata* are most significant. They are rugged, hardy plants, needing practically no attention once they are established.

Propagation

Seed should not be allowed to dry out before it is sown. Softwood and hardwood cuttings root easily, especially during Sept. and Oct. Most of the herbaceous species are easily divided. See CUTTINGS.

alba   10″   Zone 5   White Cinquefoil
This beautiful little plant from central Europe has palmate leaves which are covered with soft white hairs on the underside and white flowers, blooming in loose sprays on stalks 10 in. high in May and June. It is a low and in habit mounded.

argentea   1½′   Zone 4   Silvery Cinquefoil
A native to southern Europe but naturalized as a perennial weed in the northeastern and north central U.S. The alternate leaves are palmately compound with 5 leaflets, densely white tomentose on the undersurface. The sulfur-yellow

flowers are produced from June to Aug. in many-flowered clusters. It is especially common in limestone regions.

atrosanguinea 1½′ **Zone 5 Himalayan Cinquefoil**
A plant having silky-tomentose, tripartite leaves with toothed margins; growing in mounds and bearing sprays of bright red flowers on stalks 18 in. high. Native to the Himalayan Mountains.

canadensis creeping Zone 3 Oldfield Cinquefoil
A common weed of the fields and roadsides from Nova Scotia to the Carolinas, west to Ohio, this low-growing plant spreads by creeping runners. The pinnately compound leaves have 5, toothed leaflets which are white on the underside and yellow flowers ¾ in. wide, with 5 petals in June.

cinerea 2″–4″ **Zone 3 Rusty Cinquefoil**
Leaves palmately divided, leaflets oblong and toothed, thick and hairy. Flowers pale yellow. Native to the Alps Mountains.

flabellifolia 1′ **Zone 3 Fanleaf Cinquefoil**
A small, mounding plant from the Rockies. This has 3-parted leaves and bright yellow flowers in sprays, on stalks 12 in. high. It blooms in May.

fragiformis (*emarginata*) 5″–8″ **Zone 2 Strawberry Cinquefoil**
A perennial from Siberia and the Aleutian Islands, with hairy, 3-parted leaves or leaflets ½–2 in. long. Flowers yellow, ¾ in. dia., in a few clusters appearing in July and Aug. Of little ornamental value.

fruticosa 4′ **Zone 2 Bush Cinquefoil**
The Bush Cinquefoil is one of the few woody plants native over both northern hemispheres. It can be found as a low mat of dense woody growth on top of the Olympic Mountains in Wash. or high up in the Himalayas, and as 3-ft. shrubs in Mich., as well as in Great Britain, Europe and China. Because of its wide habitat, there are many varieties being grown in various parts of the world, but all are considered as low shrubs under 4 ft. in height and make truly excellent garden specimens.

Not only are these plants valued from the standpoint of their height, but also they are in that admirable class which does not have any serious insect or disease troubles. The entire group is of interest for several months in the summertime when few woody shrubs produce blooms, for their small, bright yellow or white flowers begin to appear in July and are in evidence throughout the summer and well into the fall. Several varieties have originated in English gardens, some have been introduced from far off China and the Himalayan region and some are growing right here in America. Unfortunately many varieties have been named,

new ones appearing periodically, and unquestionably many have become mixed in the trade and in botanical gardens.

It is incorrect to claim that these are outstanding ornamental plants. They are not in the same ornamental class with the Rose, or the azaleas, but they are of value because of their interest in the summer, their dense habit of growth, and their lack of persistent insect and disease pests. Plantsmen are usually anxious to grow these shrubs and trees which require no care, and the varieties of this species are certainly in this category. One plant has been growing in the Arnold Arboretum for 65 years, and never has required any spraying.

Some of these varieties have been described in horticultural literature, but usually only 1 or 2 varieties are mentioned at one time. At least 35 varieties have been named.

All are not sufficiently different to warrant growing them in landscape plantings, for some are so similar that it is impossible for the gardener to tell them apart unless they are observed growing side by side.

These are sun-loving plants which will not grow well in shaded situations. In order to flower profusely they must have a situation in the full sun. They seem to grow in any normal soil. Poor dry soil situations will result in slower, less vigorous growth, for they do not require large amounts of moisture. The leaves are small and compound, usually with 3–7 leaflets; the single flowers, having 5 petals, are about ¾ in. in dia., some varieties having white flowers but most being creamy white to deep yellow. The fruits are dried capsules which unfortunately can remain on the plant several years and so give it a rather untidy appearance. This can be alleviated by light pruning in the fall after the flowering period is over.

The potentillas are not susceptible to severe insect or disease pests. This species is easily propagated by seeds, and the varieties are easily propagated by softwood cuttings. As noted previously, these are not conspicuous landscape plants, but their small size, dense habit, length of bloom, hardiness and ease of cultivation make them of increasing interest in small gardens where summer interest is desired.

Varieties

x 'Beanii'—flowers white, originating before 1910 and formerly termed var. *leucantha*. It is reportedly a hybrid betweeen *P. fruticosa* 'Friedrichsenii' and *dahurica*;

'Beesii'—flowers yellow; leaves white, hairy above and below giving them a strictly silvery hue. Similar to 'Albicans' but differs in that the upper surfaces of the leaves are more hairy than the under-leaf surfaces;

dahurica—flowers white; native of northern China and Siberia; differing from some of the other varieties by being less than 1½ ft. tall. Although it was introduced into cultivation over a century ago (1822) it is still very rare;

'Farreri'—flowers deep yellow; leaves very small, the individual leaflets being less than ⅓ in. in length, making them the smallest of any of the varieties here mentioned. This was first collected by Reginald Farrer in Tibet in 1920 at an altitude of 8000 ft. The variety 'Purdomii', also coming from Tibet, has flowers that are a lighter yellow. One plant about 20 years old, is only 2 ft. high and 3 ft. across, making it one of the truly dwarf forms. It is similar to *parvifolia*, except it is slightly lower in height. (Syn. 'Gold Drop');

'Firedance'—about 2 ft. tall with beautiful flowers that are yellow on the edges and red in the center;

'Friedrichsenii'—flowers creamy white to pale yellow; one of the more vigorous-growing forms, originating in the famous Spaeth Nurseries in Germany about 1895. One plant, about 53 years old, is 4½ ft. high and 6 ft. across;

'Goldcup'—flowers a deep golden yellow;

'Grandiflora'—flowers bright yellow and up to 1⅜ in. in dia., with leaves about the largest of any of the varieties here listed. In England this is supposed to be the most vigorous and tallest of all, sometimes reaching a height of 6 ft.;

'Katherine Dykes'—flowers pale yellow; foliage silvery green in color. This plant originated as a chance seedling in an English garden prior to 1946. It is of value for its silvery foliage, although the variety 'Beesii' is better;

'Mandshurica'—flowers white; leaves with densely whitish pubescence on upper and lower surfaces and slightly smaller than the leaves of either 'Veitchii' or dahurica. The habit is lower than that of 'Friedrichsenii';

'Micrandra'—flowers bright yellow; shrub of a lower spreading habit than the species;

'Mount Everest'—flowers 1¼ in. dia., a vigorous tall-growing shrub. The calyx quickly falls off after the flowers fade, and does not remain to be unsightly (as happens in most of the other varieties);

'Ochroleuca'—flowers creamy white; foliage light green; plant originated in the Spaeth Nurseries in Germany prior to 1902;

parvifolia—flowers deep yellow; leaves small and less than ⅓ in. long, although not so small as those of 'Farreri'. The leaflets are either 5 or 7 in number, and the plant habit, the flowers and flower color are similar to 'Farreri', although it is slightly taller;

'Princess'—2½ ft. tall, flowers from May into summer colored pink, but if in dry soil or during dry weather the flowers may be white. A good plant for partial shade;

'Purdomii'—flowers pale yellow; leaflets usually less than ⅓ in. long but slightly larger than those of 'Farreri'. This plant was "reluctantly" named by Rehder in 1922, for at the time he admitted that it differed only slightly from some of the other forms. A batch of seed from a plant sown a few years ago resulted in seedlings of a surprisingly uniform habit and flower color. This plant today is one of the densest and best rounded of all the varieties;

'Red Ace'—18–30 in. tall, flowers 1 in. dia. and colored vermilion red. Plant Pat. #4226;

'Snowflake'—flowers white, 1 in. dia. and semi-double, the only clone of all these with this characteristic;

'Tangerine'—with orange flowers but only if grown in partial shade. In full sun they are yellow;

'Veitchii'—flowers white; being the best of all the varieties for white flowers. This was introduced by E. H. Wilson from Hupeh Province in China during 1900, from an elevation of approximately 6000 ft.;

'Vilmoriniana'—flowers pale yellow to creamy white and a native of the northern British Isles. The foliage is silvery tomentose, somewhat similar to that of 'Katherine Dykes', although the leaves of the latter are smaller.

The differences noted above among the varieties can be considered minute. After all, with the exception of 3 or 4 dwarf varieties, the remainder have approximately the same habit. For those who are not particular whether the flowers are white, creamy white, or yellow, they need not be particular concerning the variety of *P. fruticosa* they obtain—any available variety would probably be satisfactory. For those plantsmen who are more particular, the following suggestions might prove helpful:

The Best of the Potentilla fruticosa *Varieties for Landscape Planting*

For dwarf habit	*dahurica*
Most vigorous	'Grandiflora' or 'Friedrichsenii'
For silvery foliage	'Beesii', 'Katherine Dykes' or 'Vilmoriniana'
For smallest leaves	'Farreri'
For pale yellow flowers	'Ochroleuca' or 'Purdomii'
For bright yellow flowers	'Farreri', 'Grandiflora' or 'Parvifolia'
For white flowers	'Veitchii'

nepalensis 2′ **Zone 5** **Nepal Cinquefoil**
A vigorous perennial, native to the Himalayas,

with 5-parted leaves up to a foot long. The showy, rosy-red flowers are an inch wide, borne in clusters on long stalks and appearing during the summer. It is this species which has given rise to several red-flowered hybrids. The var. **willmottiae** is dwarf and profusely flowered with magenta-rose flowers.

nevadensis   prostrate   Zone 7   Spanish Cinquefoil
The silky-tomentose, palmate leaves of this tiny prostrate or tufted plant have 5 lobes and, like the leaves, the stems are also covered with silky hairs. Loose sprays of yellow flowers, on stems 3–4 in. tall, are borne in May. Native to Spain, it requires gravelly lime soil and full sun.

nitida   1″   Zone 4   Snowline Cinquefoil
Native to the high Alps, this is a low, mat-forming perennial with rose, rarely white, solitary flowers about an inch wide. The foliage is silky hairy.

norvegica   1½′   annual   Snowy Cinquefoil
Sometimes a biennial, native to North America and widespread throughout the northern states and Canada. The alternate leaves are trifoliate and silky hairy. The small flowers are yellow, produced in clusters from July to Oct.

palustris   1′–2′   Zone 3   Marsh Cinquefoil
From the creeping stems of this species arise erect branches with pinnately compound leaves, having 5–7 toothed leaflets. The flower has a dark red calyx with 5 lobes extending beyond the 5 petals. The plant grows in swamps and bogs from Canada to Pa., west to Calif. and blooms from June through Aug.

pyrenaica   1′   Zone 6 (?)   Pyrenees Cinquefoil
Leaves palmately divided, leaflets ¾ in. long; flowers are golden yellow and about an inch wide in racemelike clusters. Native to the Pyrenees Mountains.

recta   2½′   Zone 3   Sulfur Cinquefoil
A troublesome weed in limestone regions, it was introduced from Europe and has become naturalized in the northeastern U.S. Leaves are alternate with 5–9 palmately arranged hairy leaflets. The pale yellow flowers are numerous, about ¾ in. wide, and produced from June to Aug.

simplex   3′   Zone 3   Barren-strawberry
Often prostrate, with branches and stems running on the surface of the ground, native to eastern North America, and a weed in dry, gravelly fields. Alternate leaves are palmately 5 parted into toothed leaflets. The yellow flowers are ½ in. wide and appear during May and June.

x tonguei   (*tormentillo-formosa*)   8″   Zone 6   Tormentilla Cinquefoil
Sometimes listed as *P. tongei*, this is a hybrid having dark green, 3- to 5-parted leaves growing in mounds 4 in. high; annual; training stems to

2 ft. in length and pale yellow flowers with red centers which bloom from July to Sept. This is excellent as a wall plant.

tridentata   2″–12″   Zone 2   Wineleaf Cinquefoil, Three-toothed Cinquefoil
An herbaceous perennial which is actually ever-green in many areas, this is native from Greenland to Ga. It can be planted in dry soil in the full sun and still be expected to grow, even to expand. The white flowers are not conspicuous, being only ¼ in. wide and similar to those of small strawberries. The dark green, lustrous, compound leaves have 3 leaflets palmately arranged, ½–1 in. long. It does best in acid soils and is frequently found growing in the rocky outcrops of the higher mountains along the eastern seaboard. As an ornamental it does very well if the situation is to its liking.

verna—A Linnean species now considered ambiguous—plants referred to *P. crantzii* and *P. tabermontani*.

villosa   1′   Zone 2   Hairy Cinquefoil
With a few yellow flowers an inch wide, this perennial is native to Alaska and Siberia. The leaves are 3 parted, coarsely toothed, silky above and white tomentose beneath. Of little ornamental value.

POTERIUM

sanguisorba (*Sanguisorba minor*)   2′   Zone 3   Salad Burnet
A perennial herb, sometimes a weed, native to Europe and Asia, common in the northeastern states and southeastern Canada. The alternate, compound, edible leaves are numerous and bunched at the base of the plant, with few on the stem. There are 7–19 pinnately arranged leaflets, each one ¾ in. long. The greenish flowers are small in dense heads, about ½ in. long, during June and July. Frequently found in dry, gravelly fields or pastures. The leaf is sometimes used in salads, vinegar and iced drinks. Propagated by seeds and division of the plant.

POT-MARIGOLD = *Calendula officinalis*

POTS. There are many kinds of pots on the market, and gardeners using pots in the hotbed or greenhouse would do well to experiment a little and find the ones most suitable. The old-fashioned clay pots are still good. There are cheaper ones available, made of heavy paper, pressed wood, pressed peat, pressed peat and manure, etc., all temporary, only for potting transplants for a few weeks when pot and plant are planted out together. This may save work, as well as time in growing plants to maturity.

Pots are round or square; the latter make better use of the available space when set closely together on the greenhouse bench or in the hotbed. Plastic pots are used a great deal but

Pots

Potting

plants or seedlings but might not be screened for large plants.

If the pots are old they should be thoroughly cleaned; if new they should be soaked in water before being used. Drainage material of broken clay pots or gravel should be placed in the bottom inch of the pot, then a small amount of soil. The plant is carefully placed on this in such a way that, when it is fully planted in the pot, the top roots will be covered by at least a half-inch of soil, and the top of the soil will be an inch below the top of the pot.

they do have some disadvantages over the old clay pots, although they may look better on the greenhouse bench. Pots usually come in 2¼ in., 2½ in. and then every half-inch size up to 10 in., but the temporary pots are only in sizes of 4 in. or less.

POTTING. Everyone who grows plants indoors encounters the problem of potting plants at some time or other. It can be a very simple process or a highly complex one if one is going to follow the excellent recommendations for mixtures for container-grown plants suggested by the University of California (See Manual 23, Div. of Ag. Sciences, Univ. of Calif. "The U.C. System for Producing Healthy Container-grown Plants," edited by Kenneth F. Baker, Sept. 1957). Most gardeners, however, are content with having a normal potting mixture that is suitable for most plants and this is what will be discussed here.

Clean pots of a suitable size are essential. Clay pots seem to be preferred for maximum growth but many like the colored plastic pots as well. A soil mixture should be decided on and the following is merely one of many, but it meets many situations:

  2 parts loam
  1 part leaf mold or peat
  1 part coarse sand
  1 lb. bone meal per bushel of the above mixture.

This is all thoroughly mixed together by shovelling from one pile to another several times. The loam might be screened for small

If the plant is to be taken from a flat, it should have around the roots as much soil as possible. If it is to come from another pot, it should be removed by turning the pot upside down, placing a hand over the soil and tapping the rim solidly on some substantial object. The roots should be examined, for sometimes a potted plant does not grow well because the soil is too wet, too dry, or the roots are being eaten or it is just "pot-bound." This condition is shown by the soil being full of roots and, of course, it is evident at first glance by the roots being thick on the outside of the potted soil ball.

In cases of "pot-bound" roots, it may be only necessary to open the ball of roots up a bit with a stick and repot in a larger pot. On the other hand, if the "pot-bound" condition has gone to the extent where the leaves are turning yellow and falling off, then a third of the roots might be cut off (not pulled off but cleanly cut with a pair of sharp shears) then repotted.

One should guard against the tendency to place a plant in a larger pot than is necessary. In fact, some plants that are not pot-bound and are not growing well may be helped if they are put in a smaller pot. We are inclined to give plants too much room in their pots. It is interesting to note that many plants fail to bloom until they become pot-bound. It takes considerable judgment to decide when to repot and when not to repot. In any event, it should never be done when the soil is dry. Water the plants the day before they are to be repotted.

When the plant is placed in the pot, the roots should be slightly opened and spread out, not jammed in a pot that is much too small. The soil should be put in a bit at a time, firmed around the roots on all sides either with the fingers or a rounded planting stick, especially made for the purpose. All plants should be thoroughly watered immediately after potting.

One should try not to repot during the time the plant is actively growing.

Plants are repotted for many reasons. If they are small and actively growing into larger sizes, they may need repotting twice a year. On the other hand, large plants like fuschias, once they have grown sufficiently large for a large pot or tub, may not need repotting for 5–10 years, providing they receive sufficient added nourishment occasionally in the form of fertilizer.

House plants are of so many kinds and sizes, and their requirements are so diversified it is difficult to make any generalization. The busy home owner with a varied group of house plants might well decide to mix one potting mixture for the lot, repotting them at the same time they are taken from the house in June and placed in a shady protected spot over the summer. In June each plant can be gingerly knocked out of its pot, its roots inspected and either repotted or let alone as circumstances warrant. Usually, in such a situation, the desire is to keep them in the same sized pots; hence it may be that some of their roots may have to be cut off, possibly the tops may require thinning a bit; then they are set out and have all summer to recover and start growth. They would presumably be taken back into the house in good condition in the early fall before the first frost.

POWDERPUFF-REDHEAD = *Calliandra haematocephala*

POWDERY MILDEW. These are true mildews which live entirely on the plant surface and obtain nourishment through tiny suckers which penetrate the outer cells. The name describes the white feltlike coating on the infected parts of the plant. They thrive in low moisture conditions and are most prevalent in foggy areas and in late summer when dew is prevalent. Apples, pears and quince develop powdery foliage. Rose, peach and apricot develop crippled leaves and scarred fruits. Phlox mildew also attacks aster, chrysanthemum, dahlia and zinnia as well as cucumbers, melons and summer squash and a closely related species infects Crape Myrtle. Lilac foliage is often completely discolored by lilac powdery mildew which also develops on blueberry, euonymus and privet. Fortunately these plants suffer no serious damage. Sulfur dust or spray and Karathane are very effective fungicides for control of powdery mildew.

PRAIRIE-CLOVER. See PETALOSTEMON.

PRAIRIE-GENTIAN, RUSSELL = *Eustoma grandiflorum*

PRAYER PLANT—*Maranta leuconeura*

PRICKING OFF. A horticultural term used when transplanting extremely small seedlings which are so small they can not easily be moved with the fingers alone. One must take the tip of a pen knife or wooden label and lift the young seedlings gently from the seed pan and place them carefully in a slight hole in the soil of the flat where they are to be planted.

PRICKLE. Spinelike outgrowth from bark or epidermis.

PRICKLE-POPPY. See ARGEMONE.

PRICKLY-ASH = *Zanthoxylum americanum*

PRICKLY-PEAR. See OPUNTIA.

PRICKLY-THRIFT. See ACANTHOLIMON.

PRIDE-OF-CALIFORNIA = *Lathyrus splendens*

PRIMROSE. See PRIMULA.

PRIMROSE, EVENING-. See OENOTHERA.

PRIMROSE, EVENING-, FAMILY = Onagraceae

PRIMROSE FAMILY = Primulaceae

PRIMULA (PRIM-yew-la). There are nearly 400 species of Primula, many native to the North Temperate Zone. They are popular perennial herbs, mostly low in stature, noted for their vivid flowers of almost every color. They do well in partial shade, and many of the unusual Himalayan species do much better in the moist atmosphere of England, Scotland and Ireland than they do in the U.S., especially in those areas where summer droughts are common. Since it is not the easiest thing in the world to provide for such a moist atmosphere in many American gardens, our efforts in growing *Primula* species should be limited to those species which are less exacting as to their requirements.

All primroses should be provided with fertile soil containing plenty of humus and also should have plenty of water, especially during drought periods. The Pacific Northwest coastal area provides excellent growing conditions, certainly much better than many inland regions of the U.S.

These plants adapt themselves well to massing—1 or 2 plants by themselves do not make a good display. Some gardeners like to use them as border plants and when they bloom in April and May they are colorful indeed. Planting them in masses along shaded brooks is an excellent way to use them to good advantage, or possibly under the outspreading branches of Dogwood or Redbud. One should not plant them in dense shade, for in such a situation they probably will not flower well.

They should be divided when necessary, about every 3–4 years. Sowing the seeds as soon as ripe is probably the best way to propagate them in large numbers, but division of plants is a simple way for the amateur. If seed has been stored dry until spring, a few days of alternate freezing and thawing in an ice-cube tray of the refrigerator is an excellent means of overcoming certain dormancy problems prior to sowing. For those species grown in the greenhouse as pot plants (chiefly *P. sinensis* and *P. malacoides*), the seed should be sown in Jan. or Feb. in order to provide plants of flowering size for Christmas.

Insect Pests

In the greenhouse, white fly is a frequent pest and spraying with insecticide #15 or fumigating with insecticide #27 or #12 is necessary. Garden slugs eat the leaves and flowers at night. Use insecticide #43.

Diseases

Fungus leaf spot produces gray blotches with yellow borders. Fungicide #D or #F is effective. Bacterial leaf spots have yellow centers. Destroy infected plants or try experimental spraying with fungicide #B. Root rots kill plants and can be prevented by growing clean plants in sterilized soil. Nematodes produce nodules or swellings on the roots. See NEMATODES.

auricula 8″ Zones 2–3 Auricula Primrose
Flowers of many colors, about an inch wide, native to the Alps of Europe. This has been hybridized with other species so that there are several forms from which to choose, some with slightly fragrant flowers which have centers of colors contrasting to those of the outer petals; borne in many-flowered umbels in spring. The leaves, about 4 in. long, make an evergreen rosette at the base of the plants. Some winter protection is advisable to prevent heaving of the shallow-rooted plants in winter.

beesiana 2′ Zone 6 (?) Bees Primrose
Flowers rose-lilac with a yellow eye, about ¾ in. wide, borne on a flower stalk in whorls, each flower above the other, during summer. The oblong leaves are narrowed to a winged petiole. Native to China.

x bullesiana 2′ Zone 6 (?) Bulles Primrose
A group of hybrids (*P. beesiana* x *P. bulleyana*) noted for their cream, orange, purple, pink or crimson-colored flowers in summer.

bulleyana 2½′ Zone 6 (?) Bulleys Primrose
Deep yellow flowers about an inch wide, borne in whorls one above the other on the stalk in summer. The leaves are narrowed to winged petioles. Native to China.

burmanica 2′ Zone 6 (?) Burman Primrose
Reddish-purple flowers with an orange eye, ½ in. wide, borne one above the other in 16-flowered umbels. The oblanceolate leaves are up to a foot long, with narrowed leaf blades forming winged petioles. Native to Burma.

capitata 1½′ Zone 6 (?) Purplehead Primrose
Upright perennial with lance-shaped basal leaves, 3–5 in. long, and grayish underneath. Lavender flowers are produced in April and May, many in a rounded head on a single stalk. Native to the Himalayas.

chionantha 1½′ Zone 5 Snowblossom Primrose
Leaves lance shaped, oblong, 7–10 in. long. Fragrant white flowers 1 in. wide in many-flowered umbels or clusters, several on one stem, during May and June. Native to China. Should be planted in a shaded place with plenty of moisture.

clusiana 7″ Zone 5 Clusius Primrose
Native to the Alps, with ovate, glossy leaves 3½ in. long; flowers rose to lilac, 1 in. wide, in 2–6-flowered umbels. A dainty rock garden plant.

cortusoides 1′ Zones 2–3 Cortusa Primrose
With heart-shaped basal leaves, 2–4 in. long, slightly lobed. Flowers rose colored, ¾ in. wide, in loose, many-flowered umbels during May and June. Native to western Siberia.

denticulata 10″ Zones 4–5 Himalayan Primrose
The rounded flower heads have individual flowers ½ in. wide, colored lilac, violet or white, appearing in the spring before the foliage. The flower stalks are about 10 in. high. The white-flowered form will breed true from seed. Native to the Himalayas.

elatior 8″ Zone 5 Oxlip Primrose
This has flowers slightly larger than the common Cowslip Primrose. The wrinkled leaves are 3 in. long; the flowers are yellow, an inch wide and

borne in many-flowered umbels in the spring. It is one of the parents of the popular *P. polyantha* group. Native to Europe.

florindae   4′   Zone 5   Tibetan Primrose
The sulfur-yellow flowers may be only ½ in. wide, but they are often produced on 3-ft. stalks with umbels bearing 30–40 flowers. It grows best in moist soil; blooms in late July and Aug. The ovate leaves are about 8 in. long, but have foot-long reddish petioles which add to the general interest of the plant. Native to the Himalayas of Tibet; hence probably does best in situations where the atmosphere is moist.

frondosa   5″   Zone 6 (?)   Balkan Primrose
Native to the Balkans, with oblong leaves an inch long and rosy-lilac flowers ½ in. wide, in many-flowered umbels.

helodoxa   2′   Zone 7   Amber Primrose
Flowers dark yellow, in several umbels one above the other on the flower stalk, blooming in summer. Native to China.

✗ **iaponica   2′   Zone 5   Japanese Primrose**
One of the very popular species, especially in the group which has superimposed whorls of flowers on the flower stalk. This requires shade and moisture to succeed properly. The rose, purple or white flowers are 1 in. and wider and are produced in several superimposed whorls on the flower stalk during May to July. Native to Japan.

juliae   3″   Zone 5   Julia Primrose
A fine dwarf primrose with rose, red or crimson-purple flowers an inch wide, on stalks 2 in. long during April and May which, if massed, makes a carpet of color. The small, wrinkled leaves form somewhat rounded tufts. Tolerant of light droughts. Native to the Caucasus. Several varieties and many hybrids are offered by European sources.

x kewensis   1½′   Zone 9   Kew Primrose
A hybrid (*P. floribunda* x *P. verticillata*) with 8-in., narrow leaves, bright yellow and fragrant flowers, ¾ in. wide, borne in umbels one above the other on a flower stalk. Apparently a species for the greenhouse alone, flowering during winter and spring.

littoniana = *P. vialii*

malacoides   1½′   Zone 8   Fairy Primrose
Lilac to rose-colored flowers, ½ in. wide, in many-flowered umbels, one above the other, in winter and spring in the greenhouse. Although the leaves may be only 3 in. long, the petioles may be 7 in. long. Native to China. Many varieties are being grown in Europe. This is a very popular species.

marginata   5″   Zone 5   Silveredge Primrose
Leaves silver margined, 4 in. long; flowers violet-rose, up to an inch wide in spring, borne in 2–20-flowered umbels. Native to the Alps Mountains.

mistassinica   6″   Zone 3   Dwarf Canadian Primrose
A perennial herb with spatulate to obovate basal leaves, somewhat toothed, blunt, and tapering at the base; sessile or nearly so. The flower stalk rises from the basal rosette and is crowned with 2–8 pink to pale blue flowers which may have a yellow eye. Each flower has a 5-lobed corolla. It is excellent for northern rock gardens, being a northern or alpine plant native to moist, rocky woodlands from New England to N.Y. and southern Canada east of the Rockies.

obconica   1′   Zone 8   Top Primrose
Flowers lilac to pink, 1 in. wide, in many-flowered umbels. A plant for the greenhouse, blooming in winter. Leaves 4 in. long, hairy, causing a skin irritation to some people handling them and so earning another common name, Poison Primrose. Native to China. Many varieties have been named.

parryi   1′   Zone 4   Parry Primrose
With heart-shaped leaves 8 in. long, narrowing to a winged petiole; flowers purple with yellow eye about an inch wide, borne in many-flowered umbels during the summer. Native to the Rocky Mountains.

x polyantha   1′   Zone 3   Polyantha Primrose
This is the largest and most popular hybrid group of primroses (*P. veris*, *P. elatior* and *P. vulgaris* intercrossed). An old-time favorite with varieties of many colors and containing most of the types which most gardeners consider to represent the genus. Pastel-colored forms and dwarf forms are among them, some of the flowers being 1½ in. and more in dia. The variety '**Marie Crousse**' is one of the double-flowered forms. New ones are constantly being offered. Because of their hybrid nature, they must be propagated asexually if a specific color is to be maintained. Blooming in May, they are the easiest of all the primroses to grow.

polyneura (*P. veitchii*)   1′   Zone 6 (?)   Veitch Primrose
Leaves rounded, 4 in. long, and silvery beneath; flowers rose colored, in many-flowered umbels, possibly superimposed. Native to China.

x pubescens   8″   Zone 4
A hybrid group (*P. auricula* x *P. hirsuta*) with rosy-crimson flowers with white centers.

pulverulenta   3′   Zone 5   Silverdust Primrose
Purple flowers with an orange eye, in tiered whorls on silvery stalks 2½ ft. tall, appear in early summer, but there are strains and hybrids of other colors, as well. The leaves are up to 16 in. long; flowers are an inch wide. Native to China. These can be grown in the bog garden.

secundiflora   8″   Zone 5   Sideflower Primrose
Oblong leaves, about 3 in. long, are narrowed at the base to winged petioles. Flowers are deep

violet, $\frac{3}{4}$ in. wide, in several umbels, one above the other, on 1 stalk. Native to China.

sieboldii 9″ Zone 4 Siebold Primrose
This Japanese species withstands more sun than most other species and so is valued for this reason. The leaves, 4 in. long, are lobed or scalloped and can disappear during summer. Flowers are white, rose or purple, $1\frac{1}{2}$ in. wide, and appear in late May and June. The white forms are outstanding. For use in bog gardens.

sikkimensis 2′ Zone 6 Sikkim Primrose
Wrinkled leaves, oblong, 5 in. long and with sharp teeth; flowers yellow, an inch wide, in many-flowered umbels during May and June. Native to the Himalayas. For bog gardens.

sinensis 8″ Zone 8 (?) Chinese Primrose
Flowers of many colors, $1\frac{1}{2}$ in. wide, in many-flowered umbels. A plant for the greenhouse blooming from Jan. to April. Native to China. The variety **stellata**, the Star Primrose, has star-shaped flowers.

spectabilis 4″ Zone 5 Showy Primrose
With stiff, lustrous leaves, 4 in. long and oblong; flowers rosy purple, an inch wide, in 2–7-flowered umbels. Native to the Alps Mountains.

veitchii = *P. polyneura*

veris 8″ Zone 5 Cowslip Primrose
Native to England and Europe where it is colorfully elegant in the fields and along the roadsides everywhere during May. Flowers yellow with an orange eye, fragrant, and produced in nodding umbels in spring. One variant has one corolla superimposed in another, the "hose-in-hose" type seen in azaleas. However, in gardens, the more spectacular *P. polyantha* type is usually preferred.

vialii (*P. littoniana***) 2′ Zone 8 (?) Littons Primrose**
With fragrant, violet-blue flowers, $\frac{1}{3}$ in. wide, in dense 5-in. spikes. Leaves broadly lanceolate, 8 in. long. Native to China.

viscosa 8″ Zone 5 Clammy Primrose
Rank-smelling leaves, 7 in. long, rather oval in shape; fragrant flowers rosy lilac, $\frac{1}{2}$ in. wide, in many-flowered umbels in late spring. Native to the Alps and Pyrenees Mountains.

vulgaris 6″–9″ Zone 5 English Primrose
Native to Europe, with flowers yellow to purple or blue, $1\frac{1}{2}$ in. wide, solitary, on long stems. Blooming in spring. Many color forms are listed. A good plant for the rock garden.

wulfeniana 2″ Zone 5 Wulfen Primrose
A tufted perennial from the Alps Mountains with 2-in., glossy, lanceolate leaves and rose-colored flowers with white throats, 1 in. wide, in 1–3 flowered umbels. Native to the Alps.

PRIMULACEAE = The Primrose Family

PRINCE'S-FEATHER. See POLYGONUM.

PRINCE'S-PLUME, DESERT = *Stanleya pinnata*

PRINCESS-FEATHER = Amaranthus hybridus

PRINSEPIA (prin-SEE-pia)

sinensis 10′ Zone 4 Cherry Prinsepia
From Manchuria. The small leaves appear very early in the spring, making it about the first of all the woody plants to show green foliage. The small, light yellow flowers appear in April and make a display, even though they are not as prominent as those of Forsythia. In late summer, the red, fleshy, cherrylike fruits appear and these are very attractive to the birds. It is not troubled with important insect or disease pests. As a sheared hedge it is excellent, serving as a barrier because of its stiff and profuse thorns. The alternate leaves are 2–3 in. long. It is very easily propagated by seed, sowing the seed as soon as it is ripe in Aug. Softwood cuttings (which see) can be rooted.

uniflora 4′ Zone 5 Hedge Prinsepia
A very thorny, deciduous shrub with long, gray, upright branches, very dense; with alternate leaves, 1–2½ in. long, and dark, purplish-red, globular fruits in the late summer, about $\frac{1}{2}$ in. in dia. Native to China and rare in cultivation.

PRITCHARDIA (pritch-AR-dia)

pacifica 30′ Zone 10 Fiji Island Fan Palm
With many short-stalked fan fronds forming a large head, this is one of the most beautiful palms of the South Pacific Area. The leaves are 4 ft. wide, bright green and deeply pleated, younger ones have a brownish-white covering of minute hairs. The yellowish-brown fragrant flowers in a 3-ft. spadix are followed by shiny blue-black fruits about $\frac{1}{2}$ in. wide. Native to Fiji and Samoa but widely distributed in the Tropics.

PRIVET. See LIGUSTRUM.

PROBOSCIDEA (pro-bo-SCI-dea)

louisianica (*jussieui***) sprawling annual Common Devil's-claws**
Often called the Unicorn-plant, this is a curiously fruited annual native to the southeastern U.S. The alternate rounded leaves are 7–10 in. wide and heart shaped at the base. The funnel-shaped flowers are yellowish purple and $1\frac{1}{2}$ in. long, borne in few-flowered clusters. The unique fruit is a curved, beaked capsule about 6 in. long, which splits when it is dried into 2 clawlike, curved ends, about 3 in. long. The green fruits are often used for pickling.

PROCUMBENT. Trailing on the ground.

PROPAGATION. Practicing the art of plant propagation is fascinating to many people and can become a most interesting and rewarding hobby. One should understand the rudiments of plant growth, that the leaves manufacture the foods used by the plant in growth; that the raw materials are supplied by the roots as well as the leaves, for it is these which absorb various gases and a certain amount of moisture from the air. Also one should understand that these foods and raw materials are sent up and down the stem, and are stored in the stem and the roots over winter for future use. One should realize that most plants in the temperate regions of the world have a rest period during which there is little active growth, clearly defined in the northern temperate regions of the world by the leaflessness of deciduous plants in the winter and the dormancy of all plants during winter cold.

One should also understand that hardy trees, shrubs and perennials, living out-of-doors, have active growing periods in the spring and this tapers off as summer approaches and is usually governed by moisture, heat and the amount of light available. These and other factors all vary with different plants and vary in different regions of the country, so that the best time to propagate plants varies with the area, the season and the kind of plant.

Plants grown under controlled conditions like English Ivy, Rex Begonia, Mother-of-Millions (indoors) can frequently be propagated almost any time. Then too, seeds can be sown any time after they have passed through their dormancy period.

Left: Cutting of half-matured wood or soft-wood cutting.
Right: Cutting of mature dormant wood or hardwood cutting.

Division of Hemerocallis plant

Most plants reproduce their own kind in nature by seeds, but here there are many variations. Ornamental horticulture is built around the growing and using of many ornamental plants which will not "come true" from seeds, and must be propagated asexually. This is extremely important to know and to keep in mind. The Yellow-leaved Barberry, the Weeping

Ash, the Columnar Maple and the dwarf forms of the Norway Spruce are only a few of the varieties or clones which, if seed of them is sown, will not produce their kind. They will produce instead the species to which they are related, not the variety. There are a few exceptions to this of course, but in general clones must be asexually propagated. Hence, we do not rely on seed for propagating these, but on asexual means, i.e., cutting, grafting, budding, layering, division, etc.

Raising plants from seed is interesting in itself, but propagating plants by asexual means is fascinating, for, in so doing, one reproduces the mother plant and is assured the offspring will have all the characteristics of the parent. Planting seeds of the beautiful *Lilium* 'Red Knight' may result in a very mixed batch of seedlings, but propagating it from bud scales or bulblets assures one that each one of the new plants will be identical with the parent and have the same flower color, size and shape.

The gardener then comes to the point where he must decide on the method he will choose to propagate his plants. If he is interested in the Tree of Heaven (*Ailanthus altissima*) sowing seeds is the easiest approach, for this does not root readily from cuttings and need not be grafted since it is a species and is known to "come true" from seed. The same is true of the common

Norway Maple. However, if he has a Weeping European Beech and wishes to propagate it, he must know that grafting is the currently accepted method used. Seedlings will not all be identical with the parent, cuttings are difficult to root, but grafting done at the right time in the right way results in plants identical with the parent.

Most of these methods of propagating plants require special techniques and facilities. Sowing carrot seeds in the garden is the easiest method, but breaking the complicated dormancy of cotoneaster seed prior to sowing takes a knowledge of just how to go about assuring germination. Grafting requires the proper understock ready in the greenhouse in Feb. or March. Budding takes a knowledge of special techniques and requires the proper understock of the right age and size ready in the nursery at just the right time in the summer. Propagation by cuttings takes a special knowledge of timing the making of the cuttings and having the proper place to put them—greenhouse bench with bottom heat or electric hotbed with bottom heat.

Methods to select for propagating most of the plants mentioned in this volume are usually discussed under the generic names. The general description of procedures to follow for the propagation of many annuals, perennials and woody plants will be found under seeds, cuttings, grafting, budding, layering, etc. Also under electric hotbed will be described the way to build such a unit and the many ways in which it can be utilized.

Propagation for bulbs, corms, tubers, etc. is as follows:

Bulbs

Some plants are easily propagated by small bulbs, formed either at the base of the parent bulb as in Narcissus, along the lower stem as in a few lilies; in small "bulbils" or "bulblets" produced in the axil of the leaf as in some lilies; in heads at the end of the long flowering stem as in certain ornamental onions. All such small bulbs are allowed to grow as long as they will attached to the parent but carefully removed by early fall and planted in prepared soil in flats or in the ground. A hyacinth bulb can be gouged out at the base, or cut slightly in order to promote the formation of numerous small bulbs.

Lily bulbs can be carefully partially dug, just after flowering, and a few scales removed and placed in a polyethylene bag with moist (not wet) vermiculite. However, they should first be dusted with Arasan or some other fungicide to prevent disease from entering the scales. The bag is tied tightly, placed at the back of the kitchen shelf for a few weeks and new bulblets will be formed at the base of each scale,

together with roots. These can be inspected carefully from time to time, and when the roots are an inch long and the first leaf is developing, then each scale is carefully planted in prepared soil in a furrow, deep enough to let the tip of the scale come just above the soil when the roots are covered. They should be spaced about 6 in. apart in the row, and left for 2 years if possible.

Plants that can be increased by bulbs are:
> Chionodoxa (Glory-of-the-Snow)
> Erythronium (Trout-lily)
> Fritillaria (Guinea Hen Flower)
> Galanthus (Snow Drop)
> Hyacinthus (Hyacinth)
> Iris (bulbous)
> Lilium (Lily)
> Muscari (Grape-hyacinth)
> Narcissus (Daffodil)
> Scilla (Squill)
> Tulipa (Tulip)
> and other tender bulb types.

Corms

Crocus, Freesia, Gladiolus, Colchicum (Autumn Crocus) are examples of corms—or solid stem structures. When these are dug, about 2 months after flowering, the small new corms can be seen and separated from the parents. These (and the parent corms as well) are dusted with a good fungicide to counteract disease, and then they are stored in a cool place (about 40° F.) where they will not dry out, until planting time.

Tubers

These are short parts of an underground stem, full of reserve food materials. The Potato and Jerusalem Artichoke (*Helianthus tuberosus*) are 2 examples and these of course are propagated either by planting the tubers themselves, or cutting them up in sections, making certain that an "eye" or very small growing point is in each section cut off from the main tuber.

There are many so-called tuberous-rooted plants like the Sweet Potato, Dahlia, Bleeding Heart (*Dicentra*), Wind Flower (*Anemone*), Winter Aconite (*Eranthis*) and Tuberous Rooted Begonia. These only have growing points at that end of the root which was closest to the main plant. Hence care must be taken in noting the end of these when planted. This can be clearly demonstrated in the kitchen. Take a Sweet Potato which is alive and has not been killed by gas treatment, stick a skewer through it and place the lower $\frac{3}{4}$ of it in a glass of water. If the top (i.e., the end which was closest to the main plant) is out of water, and the long tapering root is in the water, sprouting occurs. If it is reversed, the tuber may die. However, in propagating sweet potatoes, the vigorous young shoots from such a root growing in water can themselves be taken and rooted in water, later to be planted out in the vegetable garden and each planted as a single plant.

Division

Many perennials and shrubs can be propagated merely by dividing them—cutting them apart with a spade or pulling them apart after the plant has been dug. This, of course, is the simplest and easiest method of propagation and should not be overlooked when the plant is such that it can be handled in this way. Some perennials in this category are peonies, *Hosta, Geum, Dictamus, Platycodon, Lupinus,* etc. Shrubs like Spirea, Mock-orange, Coral Berry, Honeysuckle and False Spirea are in this group.

PROPAGATION, BUDDING. See BUDDING.

PROPAGATION, GRAFTING. See GRAFTING.

PROPAGATION, LAYERING. See LAYERING.

PROPHET-FLOWER = *Arnebia echioides*

PROSOPIS (pro-so-pis)

    glandulosa glandulosa   50′   Zone 8   Honey Mesquite
A tough-wooded, slow-growing, deciduous tree of the southwestern U.S. this is drought-resistant but will not withstand temperatures much below zero. The yellowish-orange flowers are borne in racemes and they are most attractive to bees.

PROTECTING PLANTS. See WINTER PROTECTION.

PROTHALLUS. One of the stages in the reproduction of ferns. Usually a flat, leaflike organ on the ground bearing the sexual organs. See FERNS.

PROTOPLASM. The semifluid, viscous, translucent colloid which is the essential matter in all animal and plant cells.

PRUNE. Prunes are the dried fruits of certain varieties of the European Plum (*Prunus domestica*) which are especially valued for drying because of their high sugar content. Prunes are grown in the U.S. almost solely on the Pacific Coast, where growers can make good use of long periods of hot sunny weather for the drying process.

Prune plums are usually picked mechanically, i.e., the trees are shaken and the fruit picked up from the ground. They are dipped in hot water or a lye solution (1 lb. of lye to 20 gal. of water) and set out on wooden trays in the hot sun for from 4–5 days to 2 weeks, after which time they are usually dried sufficiently in the sun so that trays can be stacked one on top of the other

and the air drying process continued until they reach the desired leathery consistency of prunes. Then they are stored in a cool place, preferably in airtight containers, until used. See PLUM for information on culture.

PRUNELLA (pru-NELL-a)

    grandiflora   1′   Zone 5   Bigflower Self-heal
Of questionable worth in the rock garden, this creeping plant from the Mint Family forms a mat of large, oval, evergreen leaves an inch long, and in midsummer sends up 12-in. stems bearing spikes of purple labiate flowers about an inch long. There are several color forms, 'Alba', 'Rubra', 'Rosea' and 'Carminea', and the plants are easily grown from seed or by division and in ordinary garden soil, but they probably would not be grown if better plants were available. Native to Europe.

    vulgaris   2′   Zone 3   Common Self-heal
A perennial weed, native to North America and widespread throughout the continent. The opposite leaves are ovate to 4 in. long, either toothed or entire; the 4-angled stems are pubescent; purple or violet flowers, borne from June to Sept., are $\frac{1}{2}$ in. long and are borne in cylindrical terminal heads, an inch or two long. It is frequently a low weed in lawns, and, being a perennial, it should be removed wherever it occurs for the often-prostrate branches root readily wherever they touch the soil.

PRUNING. Artificial removal of twigs or branches from trees, shrubs, etc.

PRUNING, LORETTE. This is a system of pruning developed by M. Lorette, Professor at the Practical School of Agriculture at Wagonville in northern France, published in 1925. It involves a complicated procedure of summer pruning, more concerned in the growing of espaliers and dwarf fruits than anything else. The average American gardener might do well to forget it, since, even though it be practiced carefully, summer droughts and early fall freezes and other weather complications can create havoc with the end results. The system seems to work very well in northern France where large numbers of flowers are produced on espaliered fruit trees as a result.

Essentially the Lorette system of pruning is employed on cordons, single and double, U palmettes and winged pyramids of espalier fruit trees, with the objective of reducing vegetative growth and increasing flower-bud formation and fruit production. It is usually applied to apples and pears and apparently works very well in northern France where climatic and growth conditions seem to be geared to its general effectiveness.

There is no winter pruning. In the early

spring the terminal growth of the branches is cut back when the lateral growth is about 2 in. long. About $\frac{1}{4}$ of the previous season's growth is removed, sometimes even $\frac{1}{2}$. Also superfluous shoots are removed so that fruiting laterals are about 3–4 in. apart. All this seems to check terminal growth and aids in the production of adventitious buds on the short lateral stubs.

Extremely strong growth of tips can be removed during the season. Lateral shoots are severely cut back when they are 12 in. long and about the diameter of a lead pencil, usually about the last of June for pears and the middle to the last of June for apples. They are cut back to about $\frac{3}{8}$ in., usually leaving 1 or 2 small leaves only. Buds will be formed on these short stubs, many of which will be flowering buds.

A month later, any other shoots that have reached a foot in length are similarly cut back to $\frac{3}{8}$ in. This is also repeated in still another month.

There are numerous modifications. For instance, any weak shoots that will not form fruit buds are tied downwards with their tip down. Sometimes they are slit longitudinally with a knife between the third and fourth leaf. This often tends to produce fruit buds at the base of the bent branch.

For special details on the ramifications of this intricate and very specialized system see "Dwarfed Fruit Trees" by H. B. Tukey, Macmillan, 1964.

PRUNING ORNAMENTAL SHRUBS AND TREES. A little knowledge of what to prune and how to do it goes a very long way in assisting plants to grow into well-balanced specimens which prove an asset in any garden. Conversely, the indiscriminate hacking of shrubs and trees at definite heights is the quickest means by which otherwise beautiful plantings are made unsightly.

When pruning is contemplated it might be well to pause a few moments and carefully consider why it is to be done, for many a tree or shrub can grow to be a perfect specimen with no pruning whatsoever. In other words, there are times when contemplated pruning will be found to be totally unnecessary.

As far as the growth of the plant is concerned, pruning can be done almost any time except in the early summer, but if done then, the new growth may not have sufficient time to mature before winter and killing may result. However, as far as our interest in the ornamental qualities of plants is concerned, shrubs are divided into two groups, those that bloom in the early spring, like Daphne, Forsythia and Lilac, which might be pruned after they flower in order to obtain the full benefit of their flower in the current year; and secondly, plants which bloom on the current year's wood, like Hydrangea and

Rose of Sharon, which can be pruned in the late winter or early spring and still be expected to bloom the same year. Trees are usually pruned in the late winter and early spring (with the exception of those that "bleed" profusely, like the Birch, Maple, and Yellow-wood), for at this time, before the leaves appear, it is much easier to see which branches should be removed and also it gives the tree the entire spring and summer to form new growth. However, they may be pruned any time, except the "bleeders" as noted above.

What to Prune

1. Dead, broken or diseased branches.
2. Broken roots and one-third of the branches at transplanting time. Some roots are always cut when a plant is dug. A good general rule is to remove about one-third of the total linear branch length when the plant is moved, by thinning out weak or damaged branches and correcting structural defects. This compensates for the loss of roots which have been cut in the transplanting operation, and always results in more vigorous plants at the end of the first year. This is hard for the home owner to do, since the new plant looks smaller than the original specimen purchased from the nursery, but it is always better for the plant in the end. When plants are to be moved from their native place in the woods, it is advisable to root prune (merely forcing a spade into the ground in a wide circle about the plant) one year in advance, to force the production of many roots close to the base so the transplanting operation will be easier. Nursery-grown plants are usually root pruned periodically.
3. Young trees should be pruned early. Timely corrective pruning saves trouble later. If the tree is one that normally has a single trunk, see that only 1 straight trunk develops and cut out any others that try to grow. Occasionally several branches grow out from the trunk at the same place and these will always make weak crotches. All but one should be removed. A Dogwood can grow with many leaders from the base. Unless most of these are removed at once, the plant will be a bush (and a poor one, at that) and never a fine tree. Sometimes young shrubs should be "headed back" a bit to force them to grow more branches from the base. A Forsythia, for instance, with just one leader would never become an interesting shrub. In other words, by knowing how the tree or shrub should have developed by maturity, one may help it in early life by selecting the proper leaders and removing the others, if necessary.
4. Correct structural defects. Never allow 2 equally vigorous leaders to develop on exactly

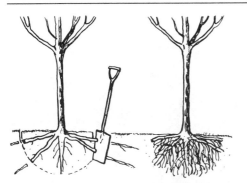

Root pruning a young tree growing in one place for several years results in many fibrous roots a year later and makes transplanting them much easier.

opposite sides of the same trunk. This will always be a "weak" crotch, susceptible to splitting as the tree grows older. It may spoil the symmetry of the entire tree when this happens.

5. Cut suckers from the bases of grafted or budded plants. Many plants used in gardens, such as roses, crab apples, lilacs and fruit trees, are either grafted or budded on another kind of understock. Usually this graft or bud is never more than a foot or so from the ground. Hence, all suckers developing below this point should be removed as soon as they are observed, for if allowed to develop, they will not only spoil the symmetry of the plant and sap the strength of the variety wanted, but will develop into an entirely different and usually undesirable plant. Excellent examples are often seen of this in roses which have been grafted on understock of *Rosa multiflora*. This species is extremely vigorous and if a few shoots are allowed to grow from the understock, it may not be long before this unwanted part of the plant completely smothers the rose variety which was budded or grafted on it. Frequently, when 2 kinds of blossoms or leaves are seen on 1 plant this is the reason. Cut out understock suckers as soon as they develop.

6. Rejuvenate old shrubs. A mock-orange, privet, lilac, spirea, or many another shrub may grow too tall and become open and ungainly at the base. Most shrubs can be rejuvenated in one of two ways: Either by cutting the entire shrub to 6 in. above the ground in the early spring and allowing it to develop as a new plant; or by thinning out the old wood, cutting some of the older branches off near the ground and allowing new ones to form, then repeating the process with a few more of the older branches the second and third years. Lilacs are often

treated thus, for in this way they produce a few blooms each year of the change, while when they are cut to the ground they do not bloom for 2 or 3 years. Forsythia, as an example, when cut to the ground late in the winter of one year, can bloom with a few flowers the next. The second year it should be covered with bloom.

7. Hedges, screens and windbreaks. These should be pruned with the objective of increasing their density, for if a twig is cut back a few inches, it frequently sends out more than one new shoot to take the place of the one removed. This growth habit of plants can be utilized to force them to grow more densely.

8. Certain limbs for utility purposes. The lower limbs of street trees, or limbs that interfere with a certain view, walk, window or wire, must sometimes be removed.

Sycamore trees severely pruned in France. This is not a good way to grow trees in America. (*Photo by Arnold Arboretum, Jamaica Plain, Mass.*)

9. Girdling root. Close observation of the base of poorly growing trees often discloses a girdling root; that is, a root partly on the surface of the soil or just beneath, which is growing in such a way as to choke or constrict the trunk of the tree or a larger root. Such girdling roots can do real harm and usually should be cut as near as possible to the trunk of the tree, or at least at the point where they are doing the damage.

These, then, are the reasons for pruning. Be certain the reason for pruning is understood before it is done, for it is always a dwarfing process, and there are some plants that never need it. Study the situation and have a good reason for all pruning.

How to Prune

1. Make all cuts clean with sharp tools.
2. Never leave any stubs. A short stub may

never heal over and is always a source for infection. Make all cuts back to a bud, branch or main trunk. The removal of a large limb should be done in 3 cuts. First, an undercut is made by sawing up one-fourth or one-third through the limb, about a foot from the trunk of the tree. Then the uppercut is started 1–2 in. beyond the first cut away from the trunk on the top of the branch and sawed down until the limb falls. As the 2 cuts near each other and the limb begins to sag, its weight will break the wood at the center and the limb will jump clear without stripping and tearing the bark down the tree trunk. Finally the stump is removed by a cut flush with the trunk of the tree.

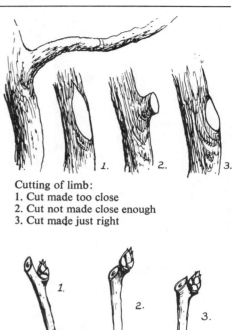

Cutting of limb:
1. Cut made too close
2. Cut not made close enough
3. Cut made just right

Left: Wrong way to clean wounds on tree trunks. Callus will not form properly at top and bottom.
Right: Correct way to clean wounds. Eventual callus formation is shown at bottom.

3. Paint all cuts over 1–2 in. in dia. with a protective paint.

4. Disinfect tools after each cut on diseased plants. A satisfactory disinfectant to have for this purpose is alcohol, which should be kept in a suitable can.

5. Shrub rejuvenation. Thin out the older branches over a period of a few years or cut the shrub to within a few inches of the ground in late winter or early spring. The obvious exception to this would be weak-growing shrubs or those which have been budded or grafted. Never cut any shrub off at a horizontal line

1. Tip pruned off too far above a bud
2. Cut made too close to the bud
3. Cut made just right

several feet above the ground. This is an outmoded practice and always results in unsightly, artificial-looking specimens. Thin out here and there, cut one branch back hard and another not nearly so much and thin out from the base simultaneously. In this way, an old plant can be reduced in size, still look natural and will produce new growth at different levels from the ground on up to the top.

6. Shear hedges wider at the base than at the top. Both evergreen and deciduous hedges should be sheared in such a way that they are wider at the base than at the top, thus allowing the important lower branches plenty of room, light and air. If the hedge is pruned narrower at the base than at the top, the lower branches will often die from lack of light. Once these lower branches die on an evergreen hedge, it is practically impossible to force any new ones to grow in the same place. Deciduous hedges, on the other hand, are mostly vigorous-growing plants, and when they become open at the base, the entire hedge can be cut to within a few inches of the ground and form a new hedge in a few years' time.

7. Pruning rhododendrons. Pruning ever-green rhododendrons is possible if it is done properly. In the more humid climate of the British Isles, rhododendrons are frequently sheared into hedges or "rejuvenated" by cutting

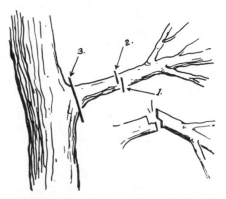

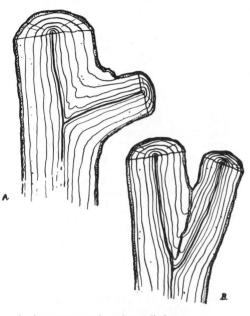

A. A strong crotch resists splitting.
B. A very weak crotch splits easily. The line between the trunk and side branch is not strongly made wood, but actually a strip of bark—making the crotch an easily-broken one.

Removing a branch to prevent stripping the bark from a tree:
1. First cut halfway through underside of branch—a foot or so from the trunk.
2. Second cut is on upper side, an inch or so towards trunk from undercut. Branch will break away without stripping bark.
3. Stub is carefully removed with no bark stripping.

them to within a few inches of the ground—in the same manner that we use to rejuvenate privet or forsythia. However, in the drier climate of the United States, rhododendrons cannot be safely treated in this way.

In the first place, the pruning should be done early in spring so that the plant can have as long a growing season as possible to send out new shoots.

Second, the cut should be made so that there are always either a few buds, dormant or

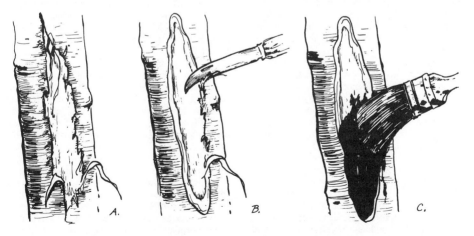

Repairing a jagged wound by making all edges straight and painting the wound at top and bottom. Paint the entire wound with some good asphalt wound paint.

growing, below the cut. An examination of rhododendron stems will show that there are old stems which have no shoots or dormant buds for quite some distance from the ground. If the pruning cut is made on such a branch, it might die back to the ground. If all the branches were similar (without dormant buds or shoots at the base) and they were all cut off, the plant might die as a result of the pruning.

If the last year's growth of a rhododendron branch is examined carefully, it will be noticed that there is a part of the branch (between the leaves and the node where the growth started) where there are no buds. If the cut is made in this part of the stem, it will die back to the last node for below that node are dormant buds on the previous year's growth. If the cut is made just above 1 or 2 leaves, the stem will not die, but the buds in the axils of those leaves will start to grow.

It must be admitted that many rhododendrons will grow too tall as they mature, and the bending stems may be susceptible to damage from high winds or from heavy ice and snow accumulation. So, a little pruning is definitely in order to keep the plant in a good shape and to remove older branches when they grow out of proportion. Done early in the spring, making certain that buds or shoots are just below the cut, pruning will result in more vigorous and better shaped plants which should give better blooms than older, more spindly specimens.

Pruning need not be difficult. It is important, however, that one understands exactly why the contemplated pruning is necessary and can visualize the probable results. Even yews can be heavily pruned and old plants rejuvenated by the expert gardener who has previously studied what to do, and when to do it.

Certain it is that time and effort can be saved if one carefully considers all these factors before adopting a policy of indiscriminate pruning.

PRUNUS (PROO-nus). This group of alternate-leaved, deciduous and evergreen shrubs and trees is probably as diversified as any group of ornamental woody plants, ranging in size from those used as ground covers to 90-ft. trees. A large proportion of them are grown for their fruits—cherries, peaches, apricots, plums, prunes, nectarines and almonds. Each of these groups is written up separately under the common name. Every nurseryman grows some of them, but in recent years their troubles seem to have been increasing. In fact, fruit growers in Calif. have spent considerable time and money recently in trying to obtain virus-free stocks.

The virus problem has become so serious and the testing process to guard against it so time-consuming (it takes several years to test or "index" them for virus) that the U.S. Department of Agriculture has virtually closed the door to the importation of *Prunus* from abroad. The scale and insect pests common on *Prunus* are more easily discernible troubles with which most growers are familiar, but the increasing seriousness of the virus problem is one with which every grower will soon need to concern himself.

There are some 200 species of *Prunus* and probably many more varieties—a great many have little ornamental value when compared with some of the best in the following list. Over 150 species and ornamental varieties are being grown by the nurserymen of America. In 1959 Professor George Cochran of Utah State College found by mail survey that over 600 different *Prunus* species, varieties and hybrids were being grown in the various collections and arboretums of the U.S. and Canada.

One group of ornamentals might be used as an example of what has been done with these plants. The ornamental flowering peaches (not the commercial varieties) have been valued for some time and over 75 have been named. About a third of this number are currently being grown by the nurserymen of the country. Some of these double-flowered varieties are certainly conspicuous in flower, but at best the trees are short-lived and the culture needed to keep them in good growing condition is unknown to most gardeners. The varieties offered now are not the same ones grown 10 years ago and undoubtedly others will be offered 10 years hence. In other words, new varieties are continually being accepted and older ones discarded.

On the other hand, sturdy trees like the Sargent Cherry and the Black or Rum Cherry (*P. serotina*) are always good trees to have and are usually as reliable as any of the *Prunus* species or varieties which can be obtained. Many of the shrubby types are familiar like *P. triloba* and the Beach Plum (*P. maritima*), but the latter is of little ornamental value except in sandy seaside soils where other plants will not grow.

A goodly number of *Prunus* shrubs and some of the small trees have little to offer to the general landscape picture. Single flowers, sparse fruits, or fruits that are difficult to see, being black in color, and little autumn color do not make them valued landscape specimens, especially when combined with the pest problems which accompany most *Prunus*.

It should be noted that certain of the *Prunus* species (*P. avium, P. caroliniana, P. pensylvanica, P. serotina* and *P. virginiana*) have been known to be poisonous to cattle if the leaves are eaten in great quantities when they are in a wilted condition, such as would occur in a drought when all of the range grass is gone and the animals browse the leaves of the trees. The bark of some Prunus species produces a brownish-yellow dye.

The oriental cherries, of course, are important ornamental assets, but many are short-lived and the single-flowered forms do not retain their attractiveness so long as the double-flowered varieties. Many of the native cherries, although having some merit as bird food, are not good ornamentals.

Asia has played a major role in supplying the northern temperate regions with cherries and many individuals have studied these plants and written about them. Charles S. Sargent and E. H. Wilson, both of the Arnold Arboretum, studied the cherries of Asia and introduced many to America. Wilson's "Cherries of Japan," written in 1916, is still a classic on the subject. Paul Russell of the U.S. Department of Agriculture wrote a very informative booklet, "The Oriental Flowering Cherries," (U.S.D.A. Circular 313, March 1934), and Collingwood Ingram of England in 1948 wrote "Ornamental Cherries," (Charles Scribner's Sons). All these are helpful if one wishes to delve deeper into the study of this popular but confusing group.

Propagation

Seeds may be stratified as soon as ripe or kept dry in a cool place in airtight containers for up to a year, and then stratified for 4 months at 40° F. Grafting or budding is commonly practiced, using closely related species as understock. Softwood cuttings of many kinds root readily. See STRATIFICATION, GRAFTING, BUDDING, CUTTINGS.

Insects and Diseases

See ALMOND, APRICOT, CHERRY, NECTARINE, PEACH, PLUM, PRUNE.

americana   50′   Zone 3   American Plum
This native American tree is found over the eastern half of North America but is not often planted primarily as an ornamental. The profuse white flowers, about an inch in dia., do make a display when they open before the willowlike leaves appear in the spring. The fruits also are an inch in dia., usually red but sometimes yellowish.

amygdalus = *P. dulcis dulcis*

armeniaca   30′   Zone 5   Apricot
The flowers are single, an inch in dia., white or pinkish and appear in late April or earlier, for this is one of the first of the genus to flower after *P. davidiana*. The autumn color of the foliage is sometimes a good red. It is this tree, native to western Asia, which is cultivated for its fruits on the Pacific Coast from Calif. to Ore. Two ornamental varieties are: 'Ansu'—the flowers of this old-fashioned variety are a flushed pink; and 'Charles Abraham'—this is popular at

present in Calif. It has deep red flower buds and double, deep pink flowers. It was imported from China and named after the San Francisco nurseryman who imported it. It remains in bloom longer than other varieties. Also see APRICOT.

avium   60′   Zone 3   Mazzard Cherry
The common Mazzard Cherry is native to Europe and has been planted for centuries there, as well as in America, for its fruits. American nurserymen also use it as an understock on which to graft other cherries and undoubtedly there are seedlings of this species growing over wide areas of the U.S. However, everything considered, it does not make an outstanding ornamental specimen because the flowers are single and white, lasting only a few days, and then it has little ornamental value for the rest of the year.

The Double Mazzard Cherry 'Plena' is valuable because of its double white flowers, $1\frac{1}{2}$ in. in dia., with as many as 30 petals. It blooms in early May (before most of the double-flowered oriental cherries) and, because they are double, the flowers remain effective a week or 10 days. Because of its hardiness it can be used in areas where the double-flowered oriental cherries are not hardy. This variety has been known and grown for at least $2\frac{1}{2}$ centuries.

besseyi   7′   Zone 3   Western Sand Cherry
Although this is grown in the Midwest chiefly for its sweet fruits, it does make a good white-flowered ornamental. However, it does not flower and fruit so well in the East as it does throughout its native habitat from Manitoba to Kan. The fruits are black and about $\frac{1}{2}$ in. wide. Professor N. E. Hansen of Brookings, S.Dak., was much interested in this species and grew seedlings for 14 generations, selecting better and better forms for fruiting purposes. The Hansen Bush Cherry grown in the Midwest today is the result of this work of selection.

x blireiana   24′   Zone 5   Blireiana Plum
The 2 ornamental characteristics of this tree are its double, light pink flowers (opening after the apricots and before the peaches) which are 1 in. in dia., and its foliage which opens with a rich copper color and retains this color well into the summer. Unfortunately, considerable pruning is necessary to keep the plant in a good growing condition. Since the purplish-red fruits are about the same color as the leaves, they are not very noticeable. It originated in France in 1895 as a cross between *P. cerasifera* 'Atropurpurea' and *P. mume*.

campanulata   24′   Zone 7   Taiwan Cherry
In southern Calif. this beautiful tree from Japan and Formosa bears its rose-colored blossoms very early in the spring or late in the winter. Supposedly it withstands high temperatures and

dry air. The luxurious green leaves are 1½ in. long and the fruits are red.

caroliniana   20′–40′   Zone 8   Carolina Cherry-laurel
This is a variable plant but serviceable in gardens throughout the southeastern U.S., where it is native, and in southern Calif., chiefly for its evergreen leaves which are 2–4 in. long. The very small, white flowers and shiny black fruits are not effective, but because the plant withstands shearing it is used as a hedge as well as a specimen plant. 'Compacta' is a form being offered in Calif. for its more compact habit of growth.

cerasifera   24′   Zone 3   Myrobalan Plum
This tree from southeastern Asia has been widely used as stock on which apricots and other plums have been grafted. The leaves are thin, oval, 1½–2 in. long, and the flowers are white, 2–3 per cluster and about ¾ in. wide, blooming in late April. The twigs are sometimes thorny. Ornamentally it is better known for its varieties, some of which are: 'Atropurpurea'—often called the Pissard Plum; this reddish-purple form was introduced into France from Persia in 1880 through the efforts of a Mr. Pissard, gardener to the Shah. The flowers are light pink, ¾ in. in dia., not lasting long enough to be truly effective for more than a few days. The reddish-purple foliage color, however, is retained throughout the summer. The purple fruits are about an inch in dia. and are edible. The leaf color is best developed in the full sun, not in the shade, and the plant is used a great deal in the hot, dry areas of the Midwest; 'Hollywood'—unique, since the foliage first appears green as it opens, then turns a deep purple; 'Nigra'—the foliage color of this clone is very dark purple, slightly darker than that of 'Atropurpurea', and is retained throughout the summer. The flowers are single, pink, ⅝ in. wide. It is called the **Black Myrobalan Plum;** 'Pendula'—branches of this are pendulous. It is being grown in Calif.; 'Thunder-cloud'—first offered in Ore. in 1937. It is reputed to be about the best of these varieties for retaining its deep purple foliage color during the summer; 'Vesuvius'—leaves are large and deep purple, one of the most colored of these varieties. It seldom blooms, but this is no defect since the pink bloom of these purple-leaved varieties is ineffective, to say the least. It is interesting to note that this was a Luther Burbank introduction before 1929.

cerasus   30′   Zone 3   Sour Cherry
The single white flowers of this Sour Cherry are ¾–1 in. in dia. and bloom in early May. The tree is native to western Asia and southeastern Europe and was probably brought to America in colonial times. The sour red fruits are widely familiar and the leaves are about 2–3½ in. long. Of course there are many commercial varieties of this tree, but the best one for ornamental use is 'Rhexii', because of its double flowers and its extreme hardiness. It can be used farther north than any other double-flowered cherry except *P. avium* 'Plena'.

x cistena   7′   Zone 2   Purple-leaved Sand Cherry
The flowers of this are white, sometimes pink, and the small fruits are a blackish purple. Its chief ornamental feature is its red-purple leaves, the color of which is retained all summer long. It is especially of value in the gardens of the Midwest, originating in Brookings, S.Dak., about 1909, as one of Prof. N. E. Hansen's selections. It is a cross between *P. pumila* and *P. cerasifera* 'Atropurpurea'.

conradinae 'Semiplena'   30′   Zone 6   Double Conradina Cherry
The fragrant, white to pale pink, semi-double flowers are 1 in. in dia., and of course remain effective longer than those of the single-flowered species. It is valued in England for its very early flowers, which sometimes appear in early March, and probably came from Central China.

davidiana   30′   Zone 3   David Peach
A tree from China, sometimes planted because of its very early, light pink flowers, 1 in. wide, often borne in late March. There is a variety 'Rubra', with red flowers and alba with pure white flowers. The leaves are 2½–5 in. long and the small apricot fruit is 1½ in. long. It is the first species of this genus to bloom in the spring.

domestica   30′   Zone 4   Garden Plum
A small tree native to Europe and western Asia, with single white flowers in late spring, bearing red or yellow plums. Not planted as an ornamental, but there have been many varieties selected and bred for their fruits. See PLUM.

dulcis dulcis (*Prunus amygdalus*)   24′   Zone 6   Almond
Blooming in Feb. or March, the flowers of this tree from western Asia are pink and white, 1–2 in. in dia. Except for the early blooming qualities, the flowering peaches might be chosen instead, since they have been developed into more outstanding ornamentals with more conspicuous flowers. The variety 'Albo-plena' has double white flowers; 'Nana' is a dwarf compact form being grown in Calif.; 'Pendula' has pendulous branches; and 'Roseo-plena' bears double pink flowers.

fruticosa   3′   Zone 3   Ground Cherry
Cultivated for over 3 centuries, this is a densely branched and mounded shrub which is frequently grafted high on *P. avium* (in Europe) to present a moplike plant. The flowers are white and ¾ in. in dia. It is recommended here chiefly because of its hardiness and not necessarily for

its ornamental qualifications. In warmer zones, better shrubs may be grown. Native to Europe and Siberia.

glandulosa 'Alboplena'   4′   Zone 6   White Dwarf Flowering Almond
Both this and its pink double-flowered variety **'Sinensis'** are much appreciated, dwarf flowering shrubs, very beautiful when in full bloom; with foot-long branches covered with very double flowers, about 1–1½ in. in dia. Both *P. glandulosa* and **'Sinensis'** apparently are not reliably hardy in Zone 5. They are frequently used in Europe for forcing in the greenhouse. The pink variety is frequently listed incorrectly as *P. glandulosa rosea plena.*

x 'Hally Jolivette'   10′   Zone 5
A hybrid (*P. subhirtella* x *P. yedoensis* crossed back on *P. subhirtella*), this has pink buds and double white flowers 1¼ in wide, opening in early May before the leaves appear. The flowers open consecutively over a 10- to 20-day period, making it a valuable ornamental. The branches are fine and densely produced, so that it grows into a dense, rounded mass of foliage.

x hillieri 'Spire'   25′   Zone 5
This originated in the Hillier Nurseries, Winchester, England, about 1940, as a cross between *P. incisa* and *P. sargentii*. The flowers appear early, before the leaves, and are single and a soft pink. Supposedly the autumn color is a good red, this trait being retained from one of its parents, *P. sargentii*. It is a neat pyramidal tree which, when it is 25 ft. tall, is only 8 ft. wide. Unfortunately, it is not yet readily available in America.

hortulana   30′   Zone 5   Hortulan Plum
A native tree in the central U.S., this has been cultivated for its fruits which are red or yellow plums about an inch wide. The flowers are white, about ½ in. wide, and the leaves are 3–4½ in. long. Seldom planted for ornament.

ilicifolia   8′–12′   Zone 8   California or Holly-leaf Cherry
The dark, evergreen, hollylike leaves of this Calif. shrub are 2 in. long. It requires little moisture and is very slow in growth, but where it is properly established it will do better than many other shrubs. It is grown only in Calif. and then only where soil conditions are suitable. The white flowers are about ½ in. wide, borne in short racemes, and the dark red to nearly black fruits are about ½ in. wide.

incisa   6′–30′   Zone 5   Fuji Cherry
The Fuji Cherry from Japan is often reported as blooming very early in the year. It is very shrubby in habit, usually covered with delicate, pale pink to white flowers, but it is none too popular because the flowers remain on the plant for only a very short time. The leaves are

1½–2 in. long and the fruit is small and purple-black.

japonica   4½′   Zone 2   Chinese Bush Cherry
A low, hardy shrub bearing bright red cherries in the late summer; this white- to pink-flowering species might have some use in the colder parts of the U.S. where other better ornamental shrubs are not flower-bud hardy. It is native to Central China and is similar to *P. glandulosa.*

laurocerasus   18′   Zones 6–7   Cherry-laurel
This popular European plant has proved to be one of the most serviceable of shrubs in the southern U.S., both as a specimen and for use as sheared hedges and windbreaks, where it can be left unsheared for long periods. The lustrous

Prunus laurocerasus schipkaensis is about the hardiest evergreen variety of this species and is hardy as far north as Boston, Mass. (*Photo by Arnold Arboretum, Jamaica Plain, Mass.*)

evergreen leaves are 4–6 in. long. The racemes of small white flowers, 2–5 in. long, in late spring, followed in late summer by purple to black cherries, ½ in. wide, are slightly effective, but it is the glossy evergreen foliage which makes the plant truly useful. It has been in America since colonial times and although several varieties are listed in Europe, most differ little from the species. Popular varieties are: **'Rotundifolia'**, reputed to be a bushy form and because of this it is perhaps the best clone for making hedges; **schipkaensis,** the Schipka Cherry-laurel, is the hardiest of some 20 varieties and can be grown out-of-doors in a protected place in the vicinity of Boston, Mass. (Zone 5). It has smaller leaves than the species and seldom exceeds 9 ft. in height; **'Zabeliana'**, with even smaller leaves than the Schipka Cherry-laurel and with horizontal branches, so that the plant grows into a spreading shrub 4–5 ft. tall and twice as broad. It is apparently just about as hardy as the Schipka Cherry-laurel.

lusitanica   6′–60′   Zone 7   Portugal Cherry-laurel

An evergreen tree from Spain and Portugal with glossy leaves 5 in. long; this serviceable tree has many uses in the South where it can be grown as a tree or restrained as a shrub.

lyonii   25′   Zone 8   Catalina Cherry
Formerly termed *P. integrifolia*, the Catalina Cherry is used only in southern Calif. where it is native to a few islands off the coast. It is a bushy evergreen tree with small flowers in axillary racemes and small, red to dark purple fruits, but its glossy evergreen leaves, 2–4 in. long, are its chief asset.

maackii   45′   Zone 2   Amur Chokecherry
The excellent brownish-yellow bark of this tree peels off in thin strips like that of the White Birch. It is one of the hardiest of the cherries, native to Korea and Manchuria, and certainly should be used more than it is, especially in the colder areas of the U.S. and southern Canada. The flowers are white, less than $\frac{1}{2}$ in. wide, and borne in racemes 2–3 in. long, followed by small black fruits.

mahaleb   30′   Zone 5   Mahaleb Cherry
This tree, native to Europe and western Asia, has been widely used as the understock on which cherry varieties are grafted. Because of the aromatic wood, the branches have been used in the manufacture of pipestems. The small white, very fragrant flowers, 6–10 in a cluster, are followed by black fruits about $\frac{1}{4}$ in. in dia.

maritima   6′   Zone 3   Beach Plum
This shrub and its better varieties make invaluable plants for seashore gardens in the eastern and northeastern U.S. where it is native, but they have little value as ornamentals in refined gardens further inland, where better soils make it possible to grow a wider variety of shrubs. The alternate leaves are $1\frac{1}{2}$–$2\frac{1}{2}$ in. long and the blue or red fruits or plums are round and $\frac{5}{8}$ in. wide. This species has been the subject of some selective study during the past 15 years and several excellent varieties with larger fruits and with red fruits are now available. Some of the better varieties are 'Eastham', 'Hancock' and 'Premier'. The fruits are used in making jams and jellies but the plants are valued for little else. In a light, sandy, acid soil, especially that found in seashore communities, these plants grow into dense, rounded bushes, producing their fruits in the late summer.

maximowiczii   48′   Zone 4   Miyama Cherry
The brilliant scarlet autumn color of this Korean tree makes it one of the few cherries with 2 seasons of ornamental interest. The flowers are yellowish white, about $\frac{1}{2}$ in. wide, followed by small red or black fruits.

mume   30′   Zone 6   Japanese Apricot
The flowers of this species, native to China and Japan, are light pink, very prolific and very fragrant, appearing before the leaves in early May, and the yellow or greenish, edible fruits are about 1 in. in dia. These flowering apricots are somewhat similar to the flowering peaches, but are less hardy. There are many unnamed varieties in the nurseries, but the more popular ones are: 'Albo-plena', white double flowers; 'Alphandii', double pink flowers; 'Dawn', large, double, shell-pink flowers, one of the late-blooming varieties; 'Rosemary Clarke', fragrant white flowers, each having a red calyx; it was named by W. B. Clarke, San Jose, Calif., in 1938.

nipponica   18′   Zone 5   Nippon Cherry
This is another "two season" cherry, with white to pale pink flowers in the spring and excellent yellow and orange foliage in the fall. The fruits are black. The small size, dense, bushy habit and good flowers of this Japanese tree make it of value in small gardens.

padus   45′   Zone 3   European Bird Cherry
The European Bird Cherry is superior to our native *P. virginiana* as an ornamental because the small, fragrant, white flowers are larger and are borne in 3- to 6-in. drooping racemes during early May and because the small black cherries, $\frac{1}{4}$ in. in dia., are also larger. The foliage is better, also, and apparently it is less susceptible to attacks from the tent caterpillars. Particularly is this plant conspicuous as one of the first trees to produce leaves in the spring. Some of the varieties are: 'Commutata', the earliest variety in producing leaves in the spring; the flowers are $\frac{1}{2}$ in. in dia. and in some years it may bloom several weeks before the others; 'Plena', the Double European Bird Cherry, is one of the best of these varieties because, with double flowers, it is effective for a considerably longer period than trees with single flowers; 'Spaethii', this Bigflower European Bird Cherry is one of the best.

pensylvanica   30′–40′   Zone 2   Pin Cherry
This Cherry, native to eastern and central North America, is only for wooded areas where its small, bright red fruits, $\frac{1}{4}$ in. in dia., make good bird food. It is short-lived and is not a desirable tree for specimen planting. The leaves are 3–$5\frac{1}{2}$ in. long and the white flowers, $\frac{1}{4}$ in. wide, are about 2–5 in a cluster. The autumn foliage color is a good red. This is one of the first "nurse" trees to appear after certain hardwood forests are cut over.

persica   24′   Zone 5   Peach
In general, peaches have single pink flowers, 1–$1\frac{1}{2}$ in. wide, blooming before the leaves appear in late April, and red and yellow fruits 2–3 in. wide. The species is native to China and has been grown in America, in one form or another, since colonial times. The Peach is not considered a good ornamental because of the many disease

and insect pests infesting it (see PEACH), as well as the required pruning needed to keep it in good growing condition. Consequently the public is not very familiar with some of the large-flowered ornamental varieties, though there have been nearly 75 of these named in recent years, a third of them being offered for sale by nurserymen today. It is a changing list—those varieties grown 10 or 15 years ago, for the most part, have been replaced by other varieties and those grown today may be unpopular in the future.

The ornamental peaches are best in those areas along the East and West Coasts where commercial peach production is a major operation. Of some 25 being grown commercially today, many with flowers 2½ or more inches wide, the following seem to be the most popular: **'Double White'**, the flowers are double and pure white; **'Early Double Red'**, double red flowers appearing before the other varieties; **'Helen Borchers'**, originated and selected by the W. B. Clarke Nursery, San Jose, Calif., in 1936. Valued because of clear pink flowers 2½ in. in dia. It keeps well; **'Iceberg'**, introduced by W. B. Clarke in 1939. The flowers are white and it blooms very early; **'Late Double Red'**, a late double red-flowering variety; **'Peppermint Stick'** another of W. B. Clarke's introductions (1933) and valued because of the flowers which are double white, mottled with pink stripes. This is similar to, if not identical with, **'Versicolor'**, introduced by the German nursery of Spaeth in 1889; **'Royal Redleaf'**, with reddish leaves. There are probably others in the trade with reddish leaves, also. The leaves first appear a brilliant dark red, later turn a bronze green; **'Weeping Double Pink'**, pendulous branches and double pink flowers; **'Weeping Double Red'**, pendulous branches and double red flowers.

pissardi = *P. cerasifera* 'Atropurpurea'

pumila   7′   **Zone 2**   **Sand Cherry**
A very hardy, shrubby bush, often prostrate, native to the area from N.Y. to Ill.; leaves 1–2 in. long, flowers white, 2–4 in a cluster, and lustrous black fruits, ⅜ in. wide, scarcely edible. It can be used as a ground cover, but other plants are usually much better.

sargentii   75′   **Zone 4**   **Sargent Cherry**
The Sargent Cherry was introduced into America from Japan in 1890 and since that time has proved to be one of the hardiest of the oriental cherry trees. The flowers are a deep pink, 1¼ in. wide, and the brilliant scarlet autumn foliage constitutes a second reason why this excellent, widespreading tree is valued for specimen planting. The fruits are small black cherries, generally hidden by the foliage. The variety **'Columnaris'** is a columnar form, but this will grow wider as the tree grows older.

It has all the fine qualities of the Sargent Cherry except that it is columnar in habit.

serotina   90′   **Zone 3**   **Black or Rum Cherry**
For ornamental work, this is the best of the cherry trees native to eastern and central North America. Its graceful, lustrous, peachlike leaves, its tendency to produce gracefully drooping branches and its dense branching habit, as well as its profuse bloom and attractiveness to birds when in fruit, make it a fine tree. Unfortunately, it is too often overlooked in favor of exotic trees that frequently are inferior. The small white flowers are produced in gracefully drooping racemes in late May and the small cherries are colorfully effective while they are red, though at maturity they turn black. They have been used in sauces, pies, jams and jellies. The tent caterpillar selects this tree, together with **P. virginiana**, in which to build its conspicuous nests. The variety **pendula** has fully pendulous branches, a truly graceful form.

serrula   30′   **Zone 5**
Although the single white flowers and the foliage of this tree from western China are not outstanding, it is the best of all cherries when judged for its bark. The brilliant, lustrous, red color of the smooth bark makes the tree of great interest throughout the year. Unfortunately it is difficult to find in American nurseries, although it is a very popular garden tree in Europe.

serrulata   20′–25′   **Zones 5–6**   **Oriental Cherry**
This is the most mixed-up group of cherries in the entire genus. Over 120 varieties have been named; many have been cultivated in Japan for centuries, and well over 50 are being grown and offered for sale in the U.S. In general, they are small trees under 25 ft. in height, with single or double, white or pink flowers, 3–5 in a cluster, blooming before the leaves appear during early to mid-May. The leaves are long and narrow, 2¼–5½ in. long. The hardiest varieties are supposed to be **'Kwanzan'**, **'Fugenzo'** and **'Shiro-fugen'**. The ones listed are not the only *P. serrulata* varieties that should be grown, but they have proved themselves to be among the best. Others may well be just as good: **'Amanogawa'**—the only truly fastigiate Oriental Cherry worth growing; seldom over 20 ft. tall and with semi-double, light pink flowers; **'Fugenzo'**—sometimes known as **'James H. Veitch'** or **'Kofugen'**—has double rosy-pink flowers, often 2½ in. wide, fading to a lighter pink when they open. It blooms with 'Kwanzan'; **'Kwanzan'**—the correct name for this variety is **'Sekiyama'**, but the name 'Kwanzan' has been used so much and so long in American nurseries that it will be difficult to drop. This has double (30 petals), deep pink, pendulous flowers, borne on a small tree which, when it is young, is decidedly

Prunus serrulata 'Amanogawa' is a very columnar-growing Japanese cherry. (*Photo by Arnold Arboretum, Jamaica Plain, Mass.*)

upright in habit. As it grows older it becomes more rounded in general outline. The foliage, first appearing with the flowers, is a copper-bronze color and greatly augments the appearance of the tree at this time. As the leaves mature, they turn green; **'Sekiyama'**—this is the correct name for 'Kwanzan', which name has been so long used that it is doubtful if it will be dropped now; **'Shirofugen'**, often called **'White Goddess'**, this has double pink flowers, up to 2½ in. in dia., which quickly fade to white as the flowers mature. The young foliage, like that of 'Kwanzan', is bronze, turning to green by the time it is fully mature; **'Shirotae'**—there is no double white cherry with as many petals as 'Kwanzan', but this is considered the finest double or semi-double white of all the oriental cherries. Its name means "snow white" and the flowers are fragrant. The petals (about 12) are slightly ruffled at the edges, giving a pleasing appearance; **'Shogetsu'**—flowers pale pink, often with a white center, either semi-double or double, and with about 30 petals; **'Sieboldii'**—this double, pink-flowered cherry has been considered as a species, but recently has been placed as a variety of *P. serrulata*, and so it is considered here. The flowers are about 1¼ in. in dia. and appear in early May at the same time as

other double-flowered forms of *P. serrulata*. Certainly it is as hardy as 'Kwanzan'; **'Ukon'**—the pendulous, semi-double flowers are a very pale yellow. The young foliage of this tree is also bronze as the leaves begin to unfurl, and at the time of bloom this forms a very beautiful color combination.

spinosa   12′   Zone 4   Sloe, Blackthorn
This shrub is not used much in the U.S., but is very popular in Europe where it is native, especially because of its profuse white blooms early in the spring. It is seen in Europe mostly in the hedgerows or where poor soils predominate. The small white flowers are about ½ in. wide and the shiny black fruits, ½ in. wide, have some slight ornamental merit. It is a spiny shrub of dense growth and hence it makes fine hedges. Other species undoubtedly take its place in America, but it does have potential value on poor soils. The variety **'Plena'** is even better, with double flowers, and the variety **'Purpurea'** has pink flowers, fewer spines and foliage which is a bronzy red throughout the season.

subhirtella   30′   Zone 5   Higan Cherry
This is a bushy, early-flowering but short-lived Cherry from Japan. In late April it is covered with single, light pink blossoms, about 1½ in. in dia. The leaves are small, giving the tree a fine texture. Fruits are small black cherries ripening in the early summer. These are not effective because they are hidden by the leaves. There are some excellent clones of this species that are most popular: **'Autumnalis'**, the semi-double pink flowers of this autumn-flowering cherry are ¾ in. in dia. and during a warm fall some of the flowers may bloom. On the other hand, if the weather is cold, none may bloom until the following spring. It is one of the best of this species because, by reason of its semi-double flowers, it remains effective for a longer period of time; **'Pendula'**, the most popular variety of the Higan Cherry, with gracefully pendulous branches and single, pale pink flowers. It was first introduced to American gardens from Japan about 1862; **'Yae-shidare-higan'**, many nurseries incorrectly list this plant as *P. subhirtella* 'Pendula Plena'. The tree has pendulous branches and the small pink flowers are double —hence it is effective longer than *P. subhirtella* 'Pendula'. When seedlings of the Weeping Higan Cherry are planted, variations do occur among the seedlings and this accounts for many of the names occasionally appearing that are given to describe these variations. The 3 varieties here mentioned are the most important.

tenella   4½′   Zone 2   Russian Almond
This hardy shrub grows from southeastern Europe to eastern Siberia and has value as an ornamental plant in the colder parts of North America. The single flowers are rosy red, ¾ in.

wide, appearing in midspring, and the narrow leaves are 1–3 in. long. The variety **alba** has white flowers, and **'Gessleriana'** has good, deep red flowers nearly 1 in. wide.

tomentosa   9′   Zone 2   Manchu Cherry
The Manchu or Nanking Cherry from China and Japan is another extremely hardy shrub which is used as a specimen or as a flowering hedge, since it can be sheared on occasion. The single, small, white flowers appear with those of other oriental cherries in late April. The bright red, edible fruits, about ½ in. in dia., are an ornamental asset in June and July. Many have been grown from seed in America and some selections have been made with better fruiting habits than others. The variety **'Leucocarpa'** has white fruits.

triloba   15′   Zone 5   Flowering Almond
The small, pink, roselike flowers, 1 in. in dia., make an excellent display when fully open. These double flowers, appearing before the leaves, have made this plant one of the most popular of shrubs—frequently listed in nursrey catalogues as *P. triloba* plena. The leaves show slight indications of 3 points at the tip, the reason it was named *triloba*. When not in flower, it has little else to recommend it. It is native to China.

virginiana   30′   Zone 2   Choke Cherry
Native from Newfoundland to N. Car. and Mo., this is commonly found everywhere in eastern North America as a weed plant. The birds are responsible for distributing the seeds. Flowers are small and white, in dense racemes 3–6 in. long, and the lustrous black fruits are about ⅓ in. wide, ripening in early summer. Several varieties have been found and named, but one called **'Shubert'** is of particular interest because the leaves appear green at first, changing in early June to a dark, reddish purple and remaining so until fall. The fruits have been used in making wine, sauces, pies, jams and jellies.

yedoensis   48′   Zone 5   Yoshino Cherry
This Japanese tree has single, white to pink, slightly fragrant flowers, 1–1½ in. in dia. It is this species which constitutes the greater number of trees about the Tidal Basin in Washington, D.C., where about 900 were planted in 1912. It grows rapidly, tends to be flat topped and, like most cherries, is short-lived. The variety **'Akebono'** was selected in 1920, named and introduced about 1925 by W. B. Clarke & Co., San Jose, Calif., as a tree with flowers a softer pink than those of the species. The synonym, under which some nurseries list it, is 'Daybreak'.

PSEUDERANTHEMUM (soo-der-ANTH-em-um)

reticulatum   6′   Zone 10   Yellowvein Eranthemum

This plant is valued more for its foliage than its flowers. It is planted in gardens in Hawaii, is of southern Polynesian origin, and has leaves (especially the younger ones) that are yellowish green and the veins are clearly marked in yellow. They are 6–10 in. long. The small flowers, about 1½ in. wide, are borne in small, loose, terminal spikes and are white, marked with purple dots.

PSEUDOBULB. A term used in describing orchids, referring to the thickened, bulblike stems which are borne above ground and usually from which the leaves grow.

PSEUDOLARIX (soo-do-LAY-rix)

amabilis (kaempferi)   120′   Zone 5   Golden Larch
Broadly pyramidal with widespreading branches, the Golden Larch is the best of the larch group, a native of eastern China. Actually a "false larch" because of the peculiar cones it bears, this was originally brought from China by Robert Fortune about 1850 who found the tree grown as an ornamental pot plant, and later he found the tree itself being grown in a monastery garden. One tree in the Arnold Arboretum, 70 years old, is 45 ft. high and 51 ft. across, with

Pseudolarix amabilis—the Golden Larch—is rare in America. It is deciduous and bears very interesting cones which completely shatter and fall in the autumn. (*Photo by Arnold Arboretum, Jamaica Plain, Mass.*)

spreading horizontal branches, rather widely spaced apart. The needlelike leaves (it is a conifer but drops all its leaves in the fall like the larches) are $1\frac{1}{2}$–$2\frac{1}{2}$ in. long, making them the longest of any of the larch group. In the fall the foliage turns a bright yellow color, adding to its effectiveness. Cones are borne erect on the upper side of the branches and shatter out completely in late Oct. It has not been susceptible to the insect and disease pests commonly troubling most larch trees.

Propagation

Seeds will germinate without pretreatment, but if they are given 2 months stratification at 40° F., this will unify germination.

kaempferi = *P. amabilis*

PSEUDOPHOENIX (soo-do-FEE-nix)
　**sargentii　10′–25′　Zone 10　Buccaneer Palm,
　　　　　　　　　　　　　Hog-cabbage Palm**
Native to the West Indies and on a few Fla. Keys, this is a slow-growing tree with a smooth, light gray, ringed trunk often bulging near the middle. The gray-green leaves are feather shaped, borne at the top of the trunk and up to 7 ft. long and 3 ft. wide. The yellow flowers are borne in branched clusters 3 ft. long. Fruits are orange-red, round or 2–3 lobed and up to $\frac{3}{4}$ in. wide; used by early settlers in southern Fla. to fatten hogs. The terminal bud is edible. The sap used to be used for making an alcoholic drink. It grows well in sandy soils but is not as ornamental as several other palms.

PSEUDOSASA. See BAMBOO.

PSEUDOTSUGA (soo-do-SUGA)
　**menziesii　200′　Zones 4–6　Pacific Coast
　　　　　　　　　　　　　　　Douglas-fir**
Unfortunately, the specific name of this plant has been changed in recent years from *douglasii* to *taxifolia* and now to *menziesii*, so that undoubtedly all of these names are still in use. They refer to an excellent ornamental evergreen, almost as beautiful and serviceable as one or the other of our native eastern hemlocks. Growers should be very careful as to where their stock originated, since the hardiness of the Douglas-fir varies considerably. Those native on the Pacific Coast are hardy only in Zone 6, and so have restricted use in the eastern U.S. This is the form that grows quickly, reaches 200 ft. in height and is one of the most valuable timber trees of the Pacific Coast.

The slower-growing form, which should be termed the variety **glauca**, is native to the Rocky Mountains and is perfectly hardy in Zone 4. Unfortunately, it is not deeply rooted and can be blown over by high winds. Also, some

varieties as they reach 40–50 ft. in height have rather widespreading branches which are easily broken in high winds.

As a rapidly growing, pyramidal, evergreen specimen, it is one of the best. It holds its needles well when cut; hence it makes a fine Christmas tree. It is easily distinguished from other narrow-leaved evergreens because of its soft needles, peculiar pendulous cones and long, pointed, terminal end buds which have many scales.

Some of the varieties are:
　'Compacta Viridis'—Zone 4—with compact, conical growth.

Pseudotsuga menziesii—the Douglas-fir—is one of the best ornamental narrow-leaved evergreens. (*Photo by Arnold Arboretum, Jamaica Plain, Mass.*)

　'Fastigiata'—Zone 6—fastigiate habit.
　glauca—Zone 4—the hardier Rocky Mountain form which has several variants to be noted in this listing as hardy in Zone 4. This form is slower in growth than that of the Pacific Coast, is denser and has bluish-green needles.
　'Glauca Pendula'—Zone 4—the pendulous-branched hardier form.
　'Pendula'—Zone 6—the pendulous-branched form of the Pacific Coast type.
　'Viridis'—Zone 6—the Pacific Coast type, not so hardy as that native to the Rocky Mountains.

Propagation

Seed may be stratified as soon as ripe for 2 months at 40° F., or they may be stored dry in a cool place in airtight containers up to a year and probably longer, and then stratified and sown. Varieties are grafted on seedlings of the species. See STRATIFICATION, GRAFTING.

Insect Pests

Douglas-fir pitch moth is a destructive borer

Pseudotsuga menziesii—Douglas-fir cone

which is dug out when it infests ornamental trees. Black-headed budworm cripples the buds and is often serious on Western Hemlock. Spraying with insecticide #9 or #37 is done. Zimmerman pine moth mines the cambium on the top branches, causing "spike top," and is primarily a forest pest. Hemlock looper, fir tussock moth and tiger moth are leaf-eating insects which may require control especially where Douglas-fir is grown for Christmas trees. Several aphids disfigure the buds and needles and Douglas-fir is the alternate host for the Cooley gall aphid on Blue Spruce. See PICEA. Pine needle scale (see PINUS), black pine leaf scale and a soft scale are controlled with dormant sprays of insecticide #44.

Diseases

See ABIES.

PSIDIUM (SID-ium)

guajava   30′   Zone 10   Common Guava
Many clones have come from this species, native to tropical America and grown under cultivation for a long time. The true species has a crooked trunk branching near the ground. The dull, light green, opposite and simple leaves have side veins impressed in the blade. The fragrant white flowers are $\frac{1}{2}$–1 in. wide, and the fruits are about the size and color of a lemon. It is much used in jellies and preserves and also, with bark and leaves, used in native medicines. Propagated by seeds and shield or patch budding. For culture see GUAVA.

littorale longipes (*cattleianum*)   **25′   Zone 9**
Strawberry Guava, Brazilian Guava
A dense shrub with obovate, leathery, alternate leaves 2–3 in. long; flowers white an inch wide, with many stamens and purplish-red berrylike fruits, $1\frac{1}{2}$ in. across, tasting like strawberries. Native to Brazil. Grown in southern Fla. for its edible fruits which are made into excellent jellies and preserves. This plant can grow wherever oranges do. Propagated by cuttings or shield or patch budding.

PSORALEA (so-RAY-lee-a). A genus of the Pea Family, mostly from the warm climates. They may be annuals, biennials or perennials, generally having glandular dots, and with the compound leaves, pealike flowers and fruiting pods characteristic to this family. The flowers are often fragrant.

argophylla $1\frac{1}{2}′$ Zones 3–4   Silverleaf Scurf-
pea
The palmately lobed, compound leaves of this plant have 3–5 leaflets and are covered with silky, silvery-white hairs which contrast well with the blue, pealike flowers borne in the axils of the upper leaves. The plant is native to the dry waste areas of the central states and blooms in June and July.

bituminosa $1\frac{1}{2}′$ Zone 9   Arabian Scurf-pea
A perennial, native to Arabia, with compound leaves, 3 leaflets, and purple flowers in dense heads during spring and early summer. It gives the impression of a large, mounded clover plant. This is able to withstand droughts which cause the plant to go into a dormant period, but it quickly starts growth again when the rains come. This has been recommended as a ground cover in parts of southern Calif. for its ability to withstand burning.

esculenta $1\frac{1}{2}′$ Zone 3   Common Breadroot
The fleshy perennial root of this plant was used by the early settlers as a source of food. The compound leaves have 5 leaflets and the blue flowers are borne in dense spikes. These appear in May and June. It is a plant of the high ground from Tex. to Manitoba and west to the Rocky Mountains. The roots are used in as many ways as potatoes.

onobrychis   3′   Zone 5   Sainfoin
Compound leaves with 3 leaflets distinguish this perennial species. The blue flowers form dense spikes up to 4 in. long on flower stalks rising from the axils of the leaves. The seed pods are leathery and wrinkled. Growing along the river banks in rich woods soil, the plants may be found from Ohio to Va., west to Ill. and Mo. It flowers throughout the summer. An attractive plant for the wild garden; the young seedlings may be reset in spring or seeds may be planted in spring.

PTELEA (TEE-lee-a)

trifoliata 24′ Zone 4 Common Hoptree
Practically a weed shrub or tree, with aromatic, alternate, compound leaves of 3 leaflets, each about 2½–4 in. long, inconspicuous flowers and fruit a broadly winged, 2-seeded samara, something like a large elm seed. The bark and leaves are strongly aromatic when bruised. Easily propagated by seeds or cuttings. The leaves turn yellow in the fall and **'Aurea'** has golden-yellow leaves most of the growing season. The fruits have been used in the past as a substitute for HOPS in making yeast or in brewing.

Propagation

Seeds may be stratified as soon as ripe for 3 months at 40° F., or they may be stored dry in a cool place up to a year in airtight containers and then stratified and sown. Layers are rooted and grafting is practiced using seedlings of *P. trifoliata* as understock. See STRATIFICATION and GRAFTING.

PTERETIS STRUTHIOPTERIS = *Matteuccia struthiopteris*

PTERIDIUM (ter-ID-ium)

aquilinum 4′ Zone 3 Bracken
A fern widely native to North America, with fronds which may be as much as 3 ft. wide, and long, running rootstocks underground which may be up to 9 ft. long. Chiefly infesting sterile or gravelly soils; sometimes used as a background for its foliage in the rockery or garden. This fern is poisonous to livestock when eaten. The young shoots have been used in making yellow-green dyes. For propagation see FERNS.

PTERIS (TER-is). A large group of ferns, some of which make excellent pot plants and are very popular for this purpose. Fronds are from a few inches to several feet long, usually characterized by long, narrow, ribbonlike segments. Both *P. cretica* and *P. tremula* and their varieties make fine pot plants, but must not be allowed to dry out or be too near radiators which are a source of drying heat, and when indoors for long periods can be freshened up if placed outdoors in the rain for a few hours. They are propagated by pulling them gently apart at potting time or dividing them by cutting through them with a sharp knife. For propagation by spores see FERNS.

cretica 6″–12″ Zone 10 Stove Fern
Found in tropical regions and in central Fla., the fronds usually have 1 long pinna and then 2–5 opposite, sessile pairs of pinnae, each one slightly ribbonlike but they may be branched at the tip. Varities would include **'Albo-lineata'** which has the broad pinnae with a central whitish band; **'Mayii'** and **'Wimsettii'** both with interesting crested fronds. The variety

'Wilsonii' is one of the best for its widely crested frond tips. Many other varieties are in the trade.

ensiformis 15″–20″ Zone 10 Sword Brake
Similar to *P. multifida* and common in the trade, this is native to Polynesia and India. It is most noted for its variety **'Victoriae'** which has fronds variegated with white. The fronds are once compound and of 2 kinds, the fertile fronds being shorter than the sterile ones.

multifida (*P. serrulata*) **3″–12″ Zone 8 Spider Brake**
Native to China and Japan, the frond of this has a terminal pinna and 5–6 pairs of lateral ones, the lower ones frequently much forked and divided, giving rise to many variations that are ornamental.

quadriaurita 'Argyraea' 18″ Zone 10 Silver Brake
This tropical cultivar is the one chiefly grown for ornament because the fronds are light green to blue-green, with a central band of silvery white, nearly half as wide as they are long. At least once compound and sometimes twice, the pinnae or pinnules are deeply cut. Although it propagates easily from spores (see FERNS), in order to retain its good variegated foliage it should be separated or divided. This is an excellent fern for growing under fluorescent light (14 hours per day).

serrulata = *P. multifida*

tremula 2′–4′ Zone 10 Trembling Brake
The fronds of this New Zealand fern are 1 pinnate at the tip but 2–3 pinnate below, with yellow-green foliage. The larger sizes of this fern are used in tubs as major decorations at weddings, but smaller plants are used in the home and greenhouse. They should be syringed with water frequently. It grows fast and makes a good decorative plant. Propagation is by separation or division. See FERNS.

PTEROCARYA (ter-o-KAY-ria)

fraxinifolia 90′ Zone 5 Caucasian Wing-nut
Although rare in America and unimportant, this can be considered interesting because of its fruits which are oblong, winged, 1-seeded nutlets borne in racemes 8–14 in. long. Its habitat is China. Its alternate compound leaves, 8–24 in. long, are made up of 11–23 leaflets, each 3–4 in. long. The male and female flowering catkins are both on the same tree, sometimes being 12–20 in. long in early spring. The more tender species **P. stenoptera** also makes fast growth and is used on poor soils in Calif. as a substitute for *Ailanthus altissima*. It is closely related to *Carya* and *Juglans*, requiring moist soil.

Propagation

Seeds may be stratified as soon as ripe for 3

months at 40° F., or they may be stored dry in a cool place for a while in airtight containers, then stratified and sown. Layers root, also suckers are produced freely, and digging these up with roots attached is about as easy a way as any to propagate a few plants.

PTEROCEPHALUS (ter-o-SEFF-al-us). Native to the Mediterranean Area, this small group of herbaceous plants is named for the fruiting head which has the appearance of being feathered. It belongs to the Teasel Family.

parnassii   3″–4″   Zone 6   Teasel Winghead
Lyre-shaped leaves, cut in feather form and covered with a gray pubescence, form a spreading mat on which soft pink flowers in tight heads bloom in spring and summer. It is a fine plant for the rock wall, requiring deep, well-drained limestone soil and full sun. Propagation is by cuttings or divisions. Native to Greece.

PTEROSTYRAX (ter-OS-ty-rax)
hispidus   45′   Zone 5   Fragrant Epaulette-tree
The creamy-white, fragrant flowers of this Japanese tree are borne in pendulous panicles, 4½–9 in. long, during June. The slender branches form an open head and the foliage is also open and coarse. The leaves are alternate and 5–7 in. long. The fruit is a 10-ribbed drupe.

Propagation

Seed may be stratified as soon as ripe for 3 months at 40° F., or it may be stored dry in a cool place up to a year, in airtight containers, then stratified and sown. Softwood cuttings (which see) can be rooted.

PTYCHOSPERMA (ty-ko-SPER-ma)
elegans   20′   Zone 10   Solitaire Palm
A feather palm from Australia, the leaves are sparsely borne in a terminal crown. Leaves are 3–5 ft. long with segments 18–24 in. long and 1½–2 in. wide, bright green. The white fragrant flowers are on a cluster about 20 in. long and the red fruits are about ¾ in. long. Frequently used as an ornamental palm in southern Fla.

PUBERULENT, PUBERULOUS. Minutely pubescent.

PUBESCENT. Covered with hairs, particularly if short and soft.

PUDDLING. Not much practiced any more because it is a time-consuming, troublesome job. The main idea is to coat all the roots of a tree or shrub to be transplanted with a fine coating of moist mud. A large half-barrel or tub is half filled with a heavy mixture of clayey soil and water, the plant roots are stirred in this and come out moist, with mud all over them. This of course is an aid in keeping the fine feeding roots from drying out during the transplanting operation, but, when such an operation is

necessary, the new methods of spraying waxes or other synthetic materials on the roots are much easier.

PUERARIA (PEW-ra)
lobata (*P. thunbergiana*)   vine   75′   Zone 6
                                              Kudzu-vine
This is the fastest growing of all the woody vines which are being grown at present in the temperate parts of the U.S., sometimes producing stems 60 ft. long in a single season. It climbs by twining but does it in a lazy sort of way, the shoots winding around the supports only a few times where other vines like the Bittersweet would twine around many times. Native to China and Japan, the violet-purple, beanlike flowers borne in July are mostly hidden by the dense leaves. These are compound and consist of 3 leaflets somewhat similar to those of the garden bean though slightly larger. In the mid-South, it can escape cultivation and when it once does this it increases so fast it becomes a pernicious pest. The fleshy roots can be cut into pieces, crushed and washed, and starch settles out which, dried, is a food sometimes used in Japan.

Propagation

By seeds, layers and division.

thunbergiana = *P. lobata*

PULMONARIA (pul-mo-NAY-ria)

angustifolia   6″–12″   Zones 2–3   Cowslip
                                          Lungwort
The alternate leaves of this European perennial are entirely green and the small, blue, trumpet-shaped flowers are produced in the early spring. In England, it is propagated by seed sown in late summer or by division at the same time. They need plenty of water especially after transplanting.

officinalis   1′   Zones 2–3   Common Lungwort
A perennial herb, with light green, alternate leaves, irregularly splotched with white, and with red funnel-form flowers which gradually turn purple. Native to Europe. Easily grown and propagated by division.

saccharata   6″–18″   Zones 2–3   Bethlehem-
                                         sage
A perennial native to Europe, with white-spotted, alternate leaves that are acuminate or pointed at both ends. Flowers vary from white to blue or reddish violet. The var. 'Mrs. Moon' has proved popular because of its large pink flower buds and showy gentian-blue flowers. They prefer shade.

PUMPKIN. See SQUASH.

PUNCTATE. With translucent or colored dots or depressions

PUNICA (PEW-nik-a)

granatum **15′** **Zones 7–8** **Pomegranate**
The Pomegranate, from southeastern Europe and across Asia to the Himalayas, has long been grown for its fleshy, deep yellow fruits, about 2½ in. through. The shrub itself is a popular garden plant in the South because the flowers are scarlet and over an inch wide, blooming throughout May and June, although varieties with white or yellow, single or double flowers are available. It is a deciduous plant, not an evergreen. Also see POMEGRANATE.

PUNICACEAE = The Pomegranate Family

PURPLE FUNNEL-VINE = *Arrabidaea magnifica*

PURSHIA (PER-sha)

tridentata **4′–6′** **Zone 5** **Antelope-brush**
This member of the Rose Family has alternate, silver-colored leaves which are only ¼–⅝ in. long and 3-toothed at the end. The solitary yellow flowers are not showy—only ½ in. wide. Native to the dry parts of the Rocky Mountain Region from Ore. to Calif. Only of value in planting dry areas.

PURSLANE = *Portulaca oleacea*

PURSLANE FAMILY = Portulacaceae

PUSCHKINIA (push-KIN-ia)

scilloides **1′** **Zone 4** **Striped Squill**
A spring-blooming bulbous herb, not an especially valued ornamental, with leaves a foot long and an inch wide, bluish-striped flowers, ½ in. long, in a raceme at the end of a single stalk in April. Native to Asia Minor. Closely related to *Scilla* and the culture is the same. The bulbs should be planted 4 in. deep. Easily propagated by offsets. The variety **libanotica** has larger flowers.

Purslane—*Portulaca oleracea*

PUSSY-EARS = *Cyanotis somaliensis*

PUSSY-TOES. See ANTENNARIA.

PUTTYROOT = *Aplectrum hyemale*

PUYA (PEW-ya)

alpestris **2′** **Zone 8**
An herb for dry areas of the Southwest with spiny-margined leaves 2 ft. long, in a dense rosette at the base, light gray-green, ½–1 in. wide and silver-gray beneath. The metallic blue flowers, 1½ in. long, bear orange-colored anthers, and appear in many-branched clusters. Native to Chile.

PYCNOSTACHYS (pik-NOSS-tak-is)

dawei **4′–6′** **Zone 10**
A loosely branched, pyramidal perennial with opposite, narrow, lanceolate, slender-pointed leaves and cobalt-blue flowers, about ¾ in. long, in short spikes up to 5 in. long. Native to tropical Africa. Sometimes grown in the home greenhouse for its flowers.

PYRACANTHA (py-ra-KAN-tha). There are over 30 species and varieties of Pyracantha being grown by U.S. nurserymen. The genus belongs to the Rose Family and all species have alternate leaves and are valued for their brightly colored berries which are either red, reddish orange or yellow. All are susceptible to fire blight. Scab disease is sometimes prevalent, also, causing the fruit to turn black. This can be controlled by spraying with Ferbam at first when the buds break open and then twice at 10-day intervals.

In general, it should be said that many of these spiny shrubs are still too new to be properly evaluated, but all those mentioned here are being grown commercially and sold on a regional basis. In flower, their flat clusters of small white flowers are conspicuous and in fruit, of course, they are excellent. As everyone knows, they are easily espaliered and provide some of the best possible subjects for this purpose. It has been noted that the true species are rarely found in gardens; they hybridize easily and since nurserymen have been growing them from seed, new hybrids are being selected all the time. It is hoped that sometime these can be properly evaluated.

Propagation

Seeds may be stratified as soon as ripe or stored in airtight containers in a cool place for up to a year and then stratified for 3 months at 40° F. Grafting is commonly practiced, using either *Pyracantha*, *Crataegus* or *Cotoneaster* for understock. Both softwood and hardwood cuttings root readily. See STRATIFICATION, GRAFTING, CUTTINGS.

Insect Pests

Rose leaf roller eats and rolls the leaves, giving the plants a scorched appearance. Infestation by the active, yellowish-green, black-headed worms occurs soon after bloom. Insecticide #37 is effective. Lace bugs mottle the leaves. See RHODODENDRON. Lace bugs are annoying pests. See CRATAEGUS.

Diseases

Fire blight (see PEAR) blackens the leaves and kills the twigs. Scale (see APPLE) makes dark spots on the leaves and berries and leaf spots are minor pests. See CRATAEGUS.

angustifolia 12′ Zone 7 **Narrowleaf Firethorn**
Valued because it often retains its bright orange to brick-red fruits until early spring. The narrow leaves are $\frac{1}{2}$–2 in. long; the small white flowers are borne in umbels up to $1\frac{1}{2}$ in. wide and the small, brightly colored berries are about $\frac{1}{4}$ in. in dia. Native to southwestern China. It sometimes is prostrate rather than upright in growth like the others.

atalantioides 18′ Zone 6 **Gibbs Firethorn**
The Gibbs Firethorn has the largest leaves of any species—3 in. long. It is one of the tallest in this genus, but its red fruits are slightly smaller than those of *P. coccinea*. It is native to southeastern China.

coccinea 6′ Zone 6 **Scarlet Firethorn**
This and its variety 'Lalandei' are the most widely grown. Perhaps no other woody plant is so vividly colorful as the species when it is covered with bright red berries in the fall. Native from Italy to western Asia. This is deciduous in the North, evergreen in the South, with leaves $1\frac{1}{2}$ in. long.

Varieties

'**Aurea**'—with yellow fruits.
'**Lalandei**'—Zone 5—probably the most widely grown of all, and among the hardiest. '**Monrovia**', with its orange-red berries, is only slightly less hardy; '**Sensation**', with orange fruits, is definitely hardy only up to Zone 6, but '**Thornless**' with its red fruits should be as hardy as 'Lalandei'. '**Rutgers**'—no spraying needed.

pauciflora—this has orange-colored fruits, but is not so hardy as the other *P. coccinea* varieties.

'**Kasan**'—Zone 5—This has orange-red fruits and is proving to be one of the 3 hardiest of all the *Pyracantha* varieties. (The others are supposed to be 'Lalandei' and 'Thornless'.) 'Kasan' was first introduced into the U.S. from Europe in 1951. Fruits are a bright orange-red.

'**Fiery Cascade**'; '**Mohave**'; '**Teton**' are new varieties worthy of trials.

crenato-serrata = *P. fortuneana*

crenulata 10′ Zones 6–7 **Nepal Firethorn**
The most popular variety of this species is the variety '**Rogersiana**'. The lustrous, bright green leaves of this variety are small, about $\frac{1}{2}$–$1\frac{1}{2}$ in. long, and hence give a fine texture to the plant. The fruits are an excellent red-orange, $\frac{1}{4}$ in. wide, and they are borne in great profusion. Some forms of this species produce yellow fruits. This form, native to western China, is hardier and more ornamental than the species.

fortuneana (*P. crenato-serrata*) 9′ Zone 7 **Chinese Firethorn**
Usually an evergreen, this is closely related to *P. atalantioides*, but is more spiny and less pubescent. It is supposed to hold its red fruits all winter long and well into the spring. Two clones, '**Graberi**' and '**Rosedale**', have been selected for good growth.

koidzumi 10′ Zone 8 **Formosa Firethorn**
This is the least hardy of the *Pyracantha* species and varieties mentioned here, but it is probably grown in the southeastern U.S. more than any other species. It is just barely able to withstand winters in Washington, D.C. The fruit is orange-red and clonal selections have been made. Among these are '**San Jose**' which is widespreading, '**Santa Cruz**' which is prostrate and '**Victory**' which has very dark red berries. Native to Japan.

PYRENE. A seedlike nutlet or stone of a small drupe.

PYRETHRUM. See CHRYSANTHEMUM COCCINEUM.

PYRETHRUM INSECTICIDES. An extract from the achene of *Chrysanthemum* sp. contains insecticidal components called Pyrethrum I and II, which represent an insecticide which has a low order of toxicity to warm-blooded animals, is not hazardous to apply and leaves no harmful residues on food crops. A synthetic form of Cinerin I called Allethrin is also available. Dusts usually are prepared with 0.5–1% pyrethrins, and sprays containing a synergist such as piperonyl butoxide have 0.025–0.25% pyrethrum. Most formulations are used for control of flies and aphids. Aerosol preparations are convenient for home use.

PYRIFORM. Pear-shaped.

PYROLA (py-RO-la). Woodland plants native to northern Temperate Zone. They have rounded, shiny leaves growing in low mats and produce waxy white, pink or light purple flowers, on stems 4–10 in. high, in late summer. They require acid leaf mold and dense shade.

elliptica 8″–10″ Zone 3 **Waxflower Pyrola**
A perennial of the Heath Family, having a spreading rootstalk and rounded basal leaves borne on leafstalks longer than the leaf blades. The nodding, fragrant, greenish-white flowers

are borne in a terminal raceme. Each flower has a 5-lobed calyx and 5 petals with margins which curve inward and an up-curved pistil extending beyond the corolla. The plant is native to the shady, acid-soil woodlands of southern Canada to Pa., and N.Mex. and blooms in June, July and Aug. Although attractive for the wild garden, it is difficult to cultivate and seeds do not germinate readily. Division of the rootstalks can sometimes be accomplished successfully, planting in sand and peat in a shaded coldframe.

rotundifolia   20″   Zone 4   European Pyrola
Very similar to *P. elliptica*, it differs chiefly in having more leaves in the basal cluster, flowers which are more white occasionally tinged with pink, and a flower stalk several inches taller. Its range reaches from New England to N.Car. and west to Minn. and Ind.

PYROSTEGIA (py-ro-STEE-jia)
ignea = *P. venusta*
venusta (*P. ignea*)   **vine   Zone 10   Orange-trumpet**
A high evergreen growing from Brazil; planted in tropical gardens for its brilliant orange, trumpet-shaped flowers, 3 in. long and borne in loose clusters of many flowers and usually 4 petals, although sometimes the fourth petal is split in the middle. Four stamens appear at the end of the corolla and it blooms for 2–3 weeks in midwinter, sometimes bearing a few flowers in the summer. Propagated by layers and cuttings. Leaves are lustrous and compound with 2–3 leaflets; the tendrils cling to stone and wood. The fruit is a 12-in. pod.

PYRULARIA (pi-ru-LA-ria)
pubera   6′   Zone 6   Allegheny Oil-nut
A parasitic shrub growing on the roots of deciduous trees. It is shrubby in habit, with small, greenish flowers. It is native to the southeastern states from Pa., to Ala.; not a plant for the garden.

PYRUS (PY-rus). The pears are not outstanding ornamental trees. When they are planted in orchards and home gardens for their fruits, they must be persistently cared for, since most of them, unfortunately, are very susceptible to fire blight disease. This is probably the greatest scourge in the growing of this particular fruit. Other pests trouble these trees, also.

P. calleryana and *P. ussuriensis* are the least susceptible to the blight, and recently a cultivar of one of these species has been tried successfully for street tree work. *P. salicifolia* is suggested because it has a graceful habit and interesting foliage, but it can be severely cut back by fire blight disease. Everyone is familiar with pear trees as they flower in early spring, and they are beautiful. On the whole, however, the problems in keeping them in good growing condition are many and difficult, and not worth taking the time nor the trouble to master. Fruit growers in certain areas of the country may find it profitable to battle these problems on a large scale and, of course, many experiment stations have long-range studies dealing with them.

Propagation

Seeds may be stratified as soon as ripe for 3 months at 40° F., or they may be stored dry in airtight containers in a cool place for up to a year and probably longer and then stratified and sown. Grafting and budding is the most common procedure, using *P. communis* as understock. See GRAFTING, STRATIFICATION. For culture of economic types, see PEAR.

calleryana   30′   Zone 5   Callery Pear
This is the least susceptible to fire blight of the species in this genus. Consequently, and for this reason alone, it has earned a place in fruit-breeding programs. The white flowers appear in early May and the small fruits have no economic value, since they are only about ½ in. long. However, the foliage turns a red to glossy scarlet in the fall, giving this Chinese tree 2 seasons of ornamental value.

calleryana 'Bradford'. This tree has been selected from seedlings grown from seed collected by Frank Meyer in China in 1918 and grown at the U.S. Department of Agriculture Plant Introduction Station at Glenn Dale, Md. It was named in honor of F. C. Bradford, former director of the station. This vigorous tree does not have spines and the original tree, now 45 years old, is about 50 ft. tall with a spread of about 30 ft.

calleryana 'Whitehouse'. Narrow columnar habit, an excellent new tree for street tree planting, with pure white flowers and shining scarlet autumn color. This is another introduction by the U.S. Dept. of Agriculture, and probably better than **'Bradford'** because of its narrow habit.

communis   45′   Zone 4   Common Pear
The Pear, native to Europe and western Asia, and has long been in America. There are many trees in commercial pear orchards throughout the country which are propagated on this as the understock. It has escaped cultivation in many places. One can recognize it by its clusters of white flowers in the early spring before the leaves appear, sometimes by the thorns it bears or the vigorous young shoots, and certainly by its glossy, deep red, autumn color. The leaves are somewhat lustrous and about 1–3 in. long. The typical fruit is pear shaped, but only about 2 in. long, although some of its varieties have fruits much larger than that.

kawakamii   30′   Zone 9   Evergreen Pear
This Japanese evergreen tree is proving popular
in southern Calif. The glossy evergreen leaves
are acute at both ends. The flowers are white
and fragrant and the fruits are about $\frac{1}{3}$ in. wide.
The growth is unruly, and the limbs and
branches are very limber, but it can be pruned
to make good espaliers.

salicifolia   24′   Zone 4   Willowleaf Pear
This species from southeastern Europe and
western Asia is susceptible to fire blight, but if
this disease is not a serious hazard, it has merit
as an ornamental because of its graceful, willowlike leaves which are covered with a silvery-
gray tomentum when they first appear and for
several weeks thereafter. The fruits, about $1\frac{1}{4}$ in.
long and nearly as wide, have no value. Even
more ornamental is the variety 'Pendula' with
gracefully drooping branches; not much seen
in America but used a good deal in European
gardens.

ussuriensis   50′   Zone 4   Ussurian Pear
Chiefly of merit for its vigorous, dense growth,

good foliage and glossy scarlet autumn color,
this is the hardiest of all pears and comes from
northeastern Asia. It is also, with *P. calleryana*,
the least susceptible to fire blight. The fruits are
only 1–$1\frac{1}{2}$ in. long and worthless in this country,
although some clones are cultivated for their
fruit in Korea, Manchuria and northern China.
One of its best ornamental characteristics is the
fact that the flower buds sometimes have a faint
tinge of pink—unusual among pears.

PYXIDANTHERA (pix-id-anth-EE-ra)
barbulata   2″   Zone 6   Flowering Moss
A creeping evergreen perennial resembling a
moss, having narrow, wedge-shaped leaves and
growing with a matted habit. The solitary white
flowers, borne in profusion on the short
branchlets, have a corolla of 5 spreading petals
which are united at the base. The plant may be
found in the sandy pine forests from N.J. south
to S.Car. and blooms in spring.

PYXIE FAMILY = Diapensiaceae

Q

QUACK GRASS = *Agropyron repens*

QUAKER LADIES = *Hedyotis caerulea*

QUAMOCLIT = *Ipomoea*

QUARANTINES, PLANT. In response to a growing need to protect the United States from the depredations of plant pests which were entering this country with nursery stock imports, Congress passed the Plant Quarantine Act in 1912.

This act made it unlawful for any person to import nursery stock without a permit issued by the Secretary of Agriculture. It further empowered him to regulate the entry of all plants and plant products in order to prevent the introduction into the United States of any plant disease or injurious insect new to, or not widely prevalent within, this country. On June 1, 1919, under the authority of the Plant Quarantine Act of 1912, and upon completion of the required public hearing, Nursery Stock, Plant, and Seed Quarantine No. 37 went into effect. From 1912 to that time some 20 restrictive orders and quarantines had regulated the importation of nursery stock in a piecemeal fashion.

Through the years, Quarantine 37 has been revised from time to time to counter each new risk of introducing a harmful plant pest into the United States. In order to accomplish this purpose and exert a minimum restraint on the importations of plants and plant products, Quarantine 37 has necessarily become complex.

Certain species of plants may be admissible from one area of the world but prohibited from another. Seeds of a given plant may be enterable but the plant itself or vegetative parts thereof may not be imported. In other cases, the reverse is true. There are sound biological reasons for these restrictions. Some plants may not be imported from certain areas of the world in one form or another. The prohibitions are updated when destructive diseases and insects are reported in new areas.

At the present time (1986) the following plants are prohibited entry from the countries listed to everyone except the U.S. Department of Agriculture.

PROHIBITED PLANT EXCEPT SEEDS UNLESS SPECIFICALLY MENTIONED	FOREIGN COUNTRIES FROM WHICH PROHIBITED
Abies	All except Canada
Acacia	Australia and Oceania
Acer	Bulgaria, E. and W. Germany, Great Britain, Japan
Actinidia	Japan and Taiwan
Adonidia	All
Aesculus	Czechoslovakia, E. and W. Germany, France, Great Britain, Japan
Allagoptera arenaeia	All
Althaea	Africa, India
Areca, Arenga, Arikuryroba	All
Articles listed in 319-37-2b	All except Canada
Berberis (with some exceptions) and seed	All
Borassus, Caryota	All
Cedrus	Europe
Chaenomeles (some)	All
Chrysanthemum	Argentina, Brazil, Europe (except Great Britain), South Africa and all countries located in part or entirely between 90 and 180 East Longitude
Chrysidocarpua	All
Cocus nucifera (and seed) with certain exceptions	All except Jamaica with certain exceptions
Cocus, Corypha, Cydonia	All
Datura	Columbia
Dictyosperma, Elaeis, Erianthus	All

900

Eucalyptus	Argentina, Europe, Sri Lanka, Uruguay
Euonymus	E. and W. Germany
Fragaria	Australia, Austria, Czechoslovakia, France, Great Britain, Ireland, Italy, Japan, Lebanon, The Netherlands, New Zealand, Russia, Switzerland
Fraxinus	Europe
Gaussia	All
Gladiolus	Africa, Italy, Malta, Portugal
Gossypium	All
Hibiscus	Africa, India, Nigeria, Trinidad and Tobago
Howeia	All
Hydrangea	Japan
Ipomoea	All except Canada
Jasminum	Belgium, E. and W. Germany, Great Britain
Juniperus	Austria, Europe, Romania
Larix	Europe
Latania	All
Lens	South America
Ligustrum	E. and W. Germany
Livistona	All
Mahoberberis and seed, with exceptions	All
Malus not meeting certain conditions	All
Mangifera seed	All except North and South America
Manihot	All except Canada
Mascarena	All
Morus	China, India, Japan, Russia
Nannorrhops, Oryza	All
Persea and seed	Central and South America, Mexico
Philadelphus	Europe
Phoenix	All
Picea	Europe, Japan, Siberia
Pinus, 2- or 3-leaved	Europe, Japan
Populus	Europe
Pritchardia	All
Prunus (most with a few exceptions)	All
Pseudotsuga	Europe
Pyrus	All
Quercus	Japan
Ribes nigrum	Austria, British Columbia, Europe, New Zealand
Rosa	Austria, Italy, New Zealand
Salix	East and West Germany, Great Britain, The Netherlands
Seeds of all kinds with pulp	All except Canada
Solanum (tuber bearing species only)	All except Canada
Sorbus	Australia, China, East and West Germany, Japan, New Zealand, Oceania, Philippines
Syringa	Europe
Trachycarpus	All
Ulmus and seeds	Europe
Vitis	All except Canada
Zizania, Veitchia	All

For approved sources, write to Permit Unit, Plant Protection and Quarantine Programs (PPQ), Animal and Plant Health Inspection Service, Room 638, Federal Building, Hyattsville, Maryland 20782.

The permit requirement of Quarantine 37 enables the Department of Agriculture to inform prospective importers of the prohibitions, special restrictions, and entry requirements for admissible material. Permits are required for importations of plants or plant products from all countries except Canada. Only a few types of plant material require a permit from Canada. Import permits are granted only to persons or firms resident in the United States and only upon receipt of written application from them. In addition to the name and address of the applicant, requests for permits should include the following:

1. Country of origin of plant material. If Canada, give the city and province; if Mexico give the state.

2. Quantity and names of plants. Botanical or well-known common names should be given and the form of the material e.g. seeds, bulbs, plants, cuttings, etc., should be indicated. This information is required in order to determine the entry status of each item.

3. The means of importation. Indicate whether shipment will be by air mail, air parcel post, air cargo, air freight, surface mail, freight (motor, rail, or water), or as accompanied baggage.

4. United States port or ports of arrival. Entry is limited to certain ports depending upon the type of material. If the material is enterable at the port named in the application and the usual trade routes will take it to that gateway, the requested port will be given on the permit.

5. Approximate date of arrival of shipment.

6. Whether or not other importations are contemplated within the next 2 years.

While any written request containing the foregoing information is acceptable, a regular application (PQ form 587) is available for this purpose. Copies of this form may be obtained at any P.P.Q. office or from the Permit Unit, Plant Quarantine Division, U.S. Department of Agriculture, Hyattsville, Md. 20782.

Propagative plant material falls into 3 general categories: (1) prohibited, (2) enterable under permit subject to growing in postentry quarantine, and (3) enterable under permit but not subject to any special restrictions. The last category encompasses by far the largest number of plants. Prohibited material may be imported only by the Department of Agriculture itself and then only if it is needed for experimental purposes or to introduce new varieties of horticultural value.

Plants entered subject to postentry quarantine requirements must be grown in detention, usually for 2 growing seasons, on land controlled by the importer. Throughout this period plants must be segregated from domestic material, plainly identified and available for inspection during any reasonable daylight hour. No distribution may be made of such plant material or the increase therefrom while it is in detention. Plants in postentry quarantine are subject to whatever remedial measures, including destruction, that the inspector may determine necessary to prevent the dissemination of a plant pest. Any United States resident who possesses a suitable growing site may obtain a permit to import plants which are subject to the postentry restrictions and state approval. Plant quarantine entry requirements for propagating material imported from countries other than Canada are summarized in Plant Protection and Quarantine Circular Q.37-2 which is quoted below. Most plant material from Canada is accorded a freer movement than materials from other countries because the United States Department of Agriculture works closely with its Canadian counterpart and has a firsthand knowledge of the plant pests in that country.

Plant importation is sufficiently important to many people and of sufficient interest to others, to reproduce here the "Responsibilities of Plant Importers" word for word as issued by the Plant Protection and Quarantine Animal and Plant Health Inspection Service of the U.S. Dept. of Agriculture.

Responsibilities of Plant Importers

"1. To avoid delay in the clearance of importations of plant propagating material importers have four important responsibilities to assume. Failure to assume all of these may result in loss or deterioration of material.

"These responsibilities are:

(a) To obtain, before placing orders, an import permit or to make certain that an existing permit provides for the entry of the desired material. If in doubt, obtain written assurance from the Plant Protection and Quarantine Program, Federal Bldg., Room 638, Hyattsville, Md. 20782.

(b) To transmit appropriate instructions to the foreign shipper. Please read carefully #2 below and 3, 4.

(c) To make advance arrangements for meeting all Customs requirements. See #13.

(d) To supply labor, materials, etc., through broker or agent, when necessary. See #16.

What the Foreign Shipper Must be Told

"2. The permittee should instruct the foreign shipper concerning the freedom from soil requirement; the use of approved packing materials; the woody seedling prohibition, the size-age limitations, the defoliation requirement, when necessary; the need for labeling, invoicing, and certification; and the means by which shipment is to be made. Information on these requirements appears in #3 to 13 which follow.

"3. FREEDOM FROM SOIL. All plant material must be free from sand, soil, and earth. Leaf-mold and other decayed vegetable molds are considered as soil. Plants arriving in or contaminated with sand, soil or earth may be refused entry.

"4. PACKING MATERIAL. (a) Only approved packing material should be used. Leaves, forest litter, woods moss and any similar material taken from or out of the ground and dried grasses, weeds, hays, and straws are not approved. Among the commonly used packing materials which are approved are peat moss, sphagnum, pulp-free coconut or other vegetable fibers (excluding sugar cane and cotton) osmunda fiber, excelsior (woodwool), shavings, sawdust, ground cork, buckwheat hulls, and vermiculite. Willow withes should not be used to tie bundles. (b) Nursery stock that has been wrapped, coated, dipped, sprayed or otherwise packaged in plastic, wax or other impermeable material which renders adequate inspection and treatment unreasonably difficult or impracticable may be refused entry if the objectionable condition is not corrected by the importer.

"5. SIZE-AGE LIMITATIONS. (a) Only plants no more than two years of age when grown from cuttings or seeds or having no more than one year's growth after severance from the parent plant when produced by layers, or having no more than two years' growth from the bud or graft are admissible except that for rhododendron (including azalea) or other genera or species of similar slow growth habit, an additional year is allowed. The size-age limitations do not apply to natural dwarfed or miniature forms of woody plants not exceeding 12 inches in height from the soil line nor to artificially dwarfed forms of the character popular in parts of the Orient. (b) Cactus cuttings may not be more than 6 inches in diameter and 4 feet in length. (c) Cacti, cycads, yuccas, dracaena, and other plants (other than cuttings) whose growth habits simulate the woody character of trees and shrubs may not be more than 18″ in height. (d) Stem cuttings, such as dracaena or yucca (without lvs. roots, sprouts or branches) (other than cactus cuttings) may not be more than 4 inches in diameter and 6 feet in length. (e) Herbaceous perennials, such as bleeding heart, which are usually imported in the form of root crowns or clumps, may not be more than 4 inches in diameter.

"6. DEFOLIATION. Certain material from several subtropical and tropical sources must be defoliated prior to shipment or treated on arrival. Full details on this requirement are contained in another circular, a copy of which is automatically furnished to the permittee.

"7. LABELING. All material must be plainly and legibly labeled as to genus, species, and variety. Lack of labeling delays handling; hence, it is important that plants or bundles of plants be labeled, preferably with scientific names. If the latter are not available a well-known English common name may suffice.

"8. INVOICES. The copies of invoices required for plant quarantine clearance are in addition to those required by Customs, the broker, and the importer. (It really is important to have these items all in order so that the plants will not be held up and forced to dry out.) In addition a packing list must accompany each container of material or a copy of the invoice must be enclosed within container No. 1. For importations by mail: One copy of the invoice must be enclosed within the parcel or within one of the parcels in the event of a lot shipment.

"9. CERTIFICATION. Quarantine No. 37 requires that material be appropriately certified by the proper phytopathological official of the country of origin. For cargo importations: A copy of the certificate must be attached to the outside of each container and the original certificate must be submitted (to the U.S. Customs Agent) when Customs entry is made. For importations by mail: A copy of the certificate must be attached to the outside of each parcel, and the original certificate must be enclosed within the parcel or within one of the parcels in the event of a lot shipment.

"10. MEDIUM OF IMPORTATION. The importer may import material by any medium he wishes and should instruct the foreign shipper as to the means by which shipment is to be made. Mail shipments, whether by letter mail, parcel post, air parcel post, or other classes of mail do not require a bonded carrier to get the material to an inspection station. This does not apply to importations made by other mediums. Air express and air freight should not be confused with air mail and air parcel post.

"11. MAIL SHIPMENTS. (a) There are several kinds of mail service as mentioned in the preceding paragraph. Not all countries offer air parcel post; moreover, the character of air parcel post service may vary with the country. From some countries air parcel post moves by air only to the United States port of first arrival and thence by surface transportation to destination; other countries provide air movement to final destination; still other countries provide both types of air parcel post service leaving the shipper to select the type desired. Information on air parcel post can best be obtained from the foreign shipper or at your local post office. Letter-rate air mail, sometimes used for seeds, valuable cuttings, etc. when air parcel post is not available, carries material through to destination by air. Shipments sent letter-rate air mail or first class mail should be marked "This parcel may be opened for inspection." Importers who plan importing by air will find that when air parcel post is not available there will be times when even letter-rate air mail is as economical as air express in view of the savings of Customs brokerage and bonded carrier fees, (b) Regardless of the address on the green-and-yellow mailing label, the plant materials will be cleared at the first U.S. port of arrival which has an inspection station. Ports with inspection stations are NY (JFK International Airport and Hoboken, NJ); Miami, FL; New Orleans, LA; Brownsville, Laredo and El Paso, TX; Nogales, AZ; San Diego (San Ysidro), Los Angeles (Inglewood), and San Francisco, CA; Seattle, WA; Honolulu, HI; and San Juan, P.R. (c) After Plant Protection and Quarantine (PPQ) clearance at an inspection, mail shipments are returned to the mails and go to destination under the original postage. If the value of the shipment is less than $250, Customs duty is collected at the post office of destination. If valued $250 or more, the shipment goes to the Customs port closest to the destination post office where the importer must either make the formal entry directly or employ a customs broker or agent. The importer is notified by Customs of the arrival of the shipment and the port at which entry must be made. (d) *Addressing mail shipments.* When shipments are to be imported by mail the permittee should request a green-and-yellow label for each parcel involved. For mail shipments it is especially important that the permittee's name, address, telephone number, and permit number, be enclosed in each parcel. Green-and-yellow labels are to be used only for mail importations.

"12. SHIPMENTS OTHER THAN BY MAIL. (a) Importations arriving by means other than mail require a Customs entry regardless of value and must move in bond to an inspection station. The importer or his agent must make arrangements for this and for delivery to final destination. (b) Addressing other than mail shipments. Each case, box or other container of a shipment shall be clearly and plainly marked to show the general nature and quantity of the contents and the country where grown, bear distinguishing marks, be individually numbered, and be addressed in the following way:

"Collector of Customs............................
(name of port where material is authorized to clear quarantine)
For delivery to Plant Quarantine Inspection Station.
For account of..............Permit No.........
(name and address of permittee)
From ....
(name and address of foreign shipper)

"13. MEETING CUSTOMS REQUIREMENTS. (a) Numerous delays resulting in loss or deteriora-

tion of material occur because importers fail to make arrangements in advance for a Customs broker or other agent to attend to Customs formalities in connection with freight, air freight, express or air express consignments. Such shipments are in Customs custody at plant quarantine inspection stations and, unless under an I.T. entry, cannot go forward until all Customs requirements have been completed. Plant Quarantine Inspectors are without authority to act as or render the services of a customs broker. Government employees cannot employ a Customs broker on behalf of an importer nor should they be requested to recommend one. (b) All arrangements with the Customs broker or other agent should be made well in advance of importation. He will need to know the expected time of arrival and the vessel, train or plane on which the material is expected to arrive; and should be supplied with invoices, other necessary documents, the importer's permit number, instructions on forwarding the importation, and the type of Customs entry to be made. The broker is in a position to arrange, on the importer's behalf, for bonded transportation to the inspection station and supply labor and materials if needed. The inexperienced importer will do well to consult his Customs broker or agent ahead of time and ascertain what is expected of him (the importer). (c) There are three kinds of Customs entries normally used for plant material imported other than through the mails. They are as follows:

"1. Informal Entry. This type of entry may sometimes be employed to advantage when the port of arrival is the same as the authorized port of plant quarantine clearance and the shipment is valued at less than $250. The duty must be paid in cash or certified check to a Customs inspector at the port of entry (pier, airport, etc.). At times an informal entry, if allowable, may not be practical or convenient for the broker or agent.

"2. Duty Paid Entry. Here payment of duty is guaranteed by the broker's bond or is paid at the custom house. When the port of arrival is not the same as the authorized port of plant quarantine clearance the shipment must move under a Customs Special Manifest to the port of plant quarantine clearance.

"3. I.T. (In-Transit) Entry. Under this type, the broker or agent (or carrier acting as such) merely makes the entry and arranges for handling at the inspection station and for movement onward towards destination. At the Customs port nearest to destination the services of a Customs broker are again necessary to make a consumption type entry, an Informal or Duty Paid, and to pay the duty before the shipment can be delivered. The "double" service makes this a more costly type of entry.

"Paragraph 11 explains customs procedures governing mail importations.

"14. BAGGAGE ENTRIES. The importation of most plant material (except certain bulbs and flower seeds) by baggage may prove more costly than entry by mail because it may be necessary to arrange for a bonded carrier to transport the material to the nearest inspection station. Upon completion of the plant quarantine handling someone will also have to care for the forwarding of the material to final destination and the costs attending such forwarding. For those reasons travelers in foreign countries may wish to consider mailing plants to the United States whenever possible, thereby avoiding the inconvenience of having to make arrangements for bonded cartage to an inspection station and forwarding to final destination and eliminating the charges for such transportation. Inspection stations are generally open from 8.30 a.m. to 5.00 p.m., Monday through Friday, except on Federal holidays.

"15. PORTS OF QUARANTINE CLEARANCE. Material may be offered for plant quarantine clearance at New York, N.Y. (including N.Y. International Airport and Hoboken, N.J.); Miami, Florida; New Orleans, Lousiana; Brownsville, and Laredo, Texas; San Francisco, and Los Angeles, California; and Seattle, Washington, for mainland destinations and at Honolulu and San Juan respectively for destinations in Hawaii and in Puerto Rico and the Virgin Islands. If your permit does not provide for handling of the importation at the logical point of plant quarantine clearance, application should be made to have it revised. When doing so, bear in mind that uninspected and untreated material may not move long distances overland for inspection and treatment but must be inspected and treated at the authorized point at or nearest the port of arrival. For example, South American material arriving by air usually clears at Miami. The same material coming by water would enter New York and clear at Hoboken. Asiatic material coming via the Suez Canal, and African material by water usually clear at Hoboken. Most Mexican material clears at Laredo and Brownsville. Trans-Pacific material clears at San Francisco, Los Angeles, or Seattle depending upon the time and method of dispatch from origin. See #14 for hours during which inspection stations are open.

"16. LABOR, SUPPLIES, ETC. Labor is usually required for the handling of shipments imported other than by mail. It is needed to unpack and repack material, to load the containers into and out of the fumigation chambers, and to move the containers into and out of the inspection station. Labor costs vary with the size of the shipment and the amount of work that may be involved. Customs brokers can readily arrange for labor. Supplies such as lumber, material for reconditioning, etc., may or may not be necessary depending upon the condition of the shipment.

"17. TREATMENTS. It is the purpose of the Plant Quarantine Act to protect the United States against introductions of plant pests and that purpose must receive first consideration. To protect his country and himself against pest introductions, the importer should emphasize to the shipper the necessity of sending clean, healthy material. Treatments which are given as a condition of entry are those which, in the light of present knowledge, are deemed most effective for the pest concerned and least likely to cause injury to the plants involved. In those exceptional cases where injury might result from treatments given, the importer must regard this as the price of protecting himself and other plant growers against pest introductions. All treatments are given entirely at the risk of the importer. In most cases of alleged fumigation injury which have been investigated, the plant material reached the inspection station in a deteriorating condition because of too much or too little moisture, inadequate ventilation, or other adverse factors encountered in transportation. When the plants reach the inspection stations the injury done to plants as a result of such adverse factors has not always run its course and the injury which subsequently develops is often erroneously attributed to fumigation. It is important that vigorous, healthy plants be shipped and that they be packed properly.

The interstate movement of plants from certain areas is regulated by one or more federal domestic plant quarantines, postal regulations, and various state requirements.

Notes on the latest restrictions are available and quickly sent on request. Special information on quarantines about bulbs, seeds, artificially dwarfed trees from Japan, how to import plant propagation material under Quarantine 37 restrictions, suggestions for the packing and shipping of plant material, all are available in special leaflet form.

The best and most authoritative information on these regulations is from the Plant Protection and Quarantine APHIS, U.S. Dept. of Agriculture, Hyattsville, Md., 20782. That office publishes résumés, by states, of state nursery stock and quarantine regulations. It also supervises the enforcement of federal domestic plant quarantines.

QUEEN-ANNE'S-LACE = *Daucus carota*

QUEEN-OF-THE-MEADOW = *Filipendula ulmaria*

QUEEN-OF-THE-NIGHT = *Selenicereus macdonaldiae*

QUEEN-OF-THE-PRAIRIE = See FILIPENDULA RUBRA.

QUEENSLAND NUT = *Macadamia ternifolia*

QUERCUS (KWER-kus). The oaks constitute one of the most important groups of trees in the world, both as timber trees and as ornamentals. They are native throughout the northern temperate regions of the world and in tropical Asia, being just as important in Europe and in certain parts of Asia as they are in North America. In general, they are large trees, the alternate-leaved foliage of many being rather large and coarse. The best examples of small leaves (and of the finest foliage texture, as well), might be *Q. phellos*, *Q. palustris*, *Q. ilex* and *Q. libani*.

There are only 5 in the following list which have mature heights under 60 ft. These are *Q. acutissima*, *Q. glandulifera*, *Q. engleriana*, *Q. liaotungensis* and *Q. libani*. Of these, the first 2 mature at about 45 ft. and the others at about 30 ft. This is one of the reasons these smaller trees, not grown widely in America at the present time, are recommended for trial.

There are 7 of the recommended oaks with evergreen leaves and of course these are for growing only in the South. They are *Q. agrifolia*,

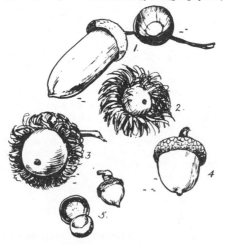

Acorns—*Quercus*:
1. English oak—*Q. robur*
2. Daimyo Oak—*Q. dentata*
3. Mossycup Oak—*Q. macrocarpa*
4. Red Oak—*Q. borealis*
5. Pin Oak—*Q. palustris*

Q. chrysolepsis, *Q. engleriana*, *Q. ilex*, *Q. suber*, *Q. virginiana* and *Q. wislizenii*.

Those species native to America are especially noted for their excellent red autumn color, although all do not necessarily turn red in the fall. For instance, *Q. imbricaria* turns a rich yellow-bronze. Those native to Europe, like many other European plants, usually have no special autumn color, the leaves sometimes dropping before turning brown.

The oaks are noted as being long-lived and

Quercus—15 species of oak:
Top row: *Quercus velutina, robur, variabilis, rubra maxima, marilandica*
Middle row: *Quercus glandulifera, imbricaris, macrocarpa, palustris, bicolor*
Bottom row: *Quercus alba, prinus, arkansana, coccinea, dentata*
(*Photo by Arnold Arboretum, Jamaica Plain, Mass.*)

growing to a great size. The following measurements are from records kept by the American Forestry Association which has listed "400 Big Tree Champions" growing in the U.S.

All in all, there are many excellent ornamental trees among the oaks, and plantsmen would do well to choose from the following list those trees which will grow well under local conditions. It is perhaps of interest that the Indians are said to have dried the acorns, ground them and made breadstuffs from the flour, and of course the acorns have been fed to hogs.

Propagation

Do not allow the seeds to dry out and if they are sown out-of-doors in the fall for their overwinter dormancy period, take steps to protect them from rodents. See SEEDS. Oaks belonging to the White Oak group should have seeds sown as soon as ripe; those belonging to the Black Oak group should have seeds stratified at 40° F. for 3 months (or over winter out-of-doors) and then sown. Also oaks are grafted on understocks of close affinity. See GRAFTING, STRATIFICATION.

	TRUNK CIRCUMFERENCE AT 4½ FT.	CROWN SPREAD	TOTAL HEIGHT
Quercus alba	27'8"	165'	95'
Q. agrifolia	38'	123'	88'
Q. bicolor	16'11"	112'	90'
Q. rubra maxima	23'3"	100'	86'
Q. chrysolepis	36'3"	130'	60'
Q. imbricaria	9'7"	72'	61'
Q. laurifolia	14'3"	69'	77'
Q. palustris	18'2"	—	—
Q. macrocarpa	21'4"	114'	143'
Q. montana	19'1"	111'	82'
Q. phellos	20'	106'	118'
Q. prinus	30'3"	—	110'
Q. velutina	19'6"	136'	90'
Q. virginiana	35'	168'	78'

Insect Pests

Oak is a preferred host of the gypsy moth which may defoliate the tree in about 2 weeks. Two or 3 annual defoliations kill many trees. Brown hairy egg masses are laid on bark or nearby and are killed by painting with creosote. The large, striped, hairy caterpillars feed in early summer. The dirty white female moths with black angular lines on wings have a heavy brown body and cannot fly. Spraying with insecticide #9 or #15 is necessary to prevent defoliation. Canker worms in the spring and orange-striped oak worm in late summer are important leaf eaters. Several gall insects make conspicuous galls such as oak-apple, wool sewer and oak bullet gall on the leaves. Gouty oak gall wasp forms rough, lumpy galls on the twigs and branches on Scarlet and Red Oak and are very unsightly. Infested twigs should be cut promptly. Other gall insects and leaf miners seldom require control. Small twigs with leaves on the ground in midsummer may have been infested by the oak twig pruner, which tunnels in the twig causing it to break, especially from wind. The worm is in the fallen twig which should be promptly burned. The pit-making oak scale, so named because it lives in a depression in the bark, is especially injurious to White Oak. Dormant sprays of insecticide #44 have been used effectively.

Diseases

Oak wilt is a serious disease of black and red oaks especially in the Middle West. Infected leaves turn black and curl upward and the tree dies. The disease is spread by root grafts and insects. Infected trees should be destroyed and Oak should not be replanted nearby. Anthracnose curls the leaves of White Oak inward and spots the leaves of Black and Red Oak along margins and veins. Spraying with fungicides #G, #D, or #F control this and other leaf spots. Shoe string root rot often causes the death of weakened trees. The inside of loose bark is covered with black stringlike threads. It commonly lives on dead stumps and roots in the woods. Small ornamental trees have been treated with fungicide #M according to directions.

acuta 20'-40' Zone 7 Japanese Evergreen Oak
Often a shrubby evergreen, native to Japan, with stout, leathery leaves that are oval in general outline, the upper surface a dark glossy green. The leaves have blunt points but are rounded at the base and are 2½-5½ in. long. Not a very important ornamental tree and especially not good for growing on limestone soils.

acutissima 45' Zone 6 Sawtooth Oak
The Sawtooth Oak is an excellent, wide-spreading tree with glossy foliage resembling that of the Chestnut. The tree usually grows as broad as it does high, hence plenty of space should be allowed for its full development. The bark produces a fine dye. Native to China, Korea, Japan.

agrifolia 90' Zone 9 California Live Oak
This round-headed, evergreen tree with holly-like foliage is chiefly of value as an ornamental in the hills and valleys of the Calif. coast where it is native.

alba 90' Zone 4 White Oak
The broad, round head, spreading branches and purplish-red autumn color of this tree make it an excellent specimen in the open. Slow in growth, its open-branching system usually makes the passage of electric wires through the tree a simple matter. Native to the eastern U.S.

bicolor 60' Zone 3 Swamp White Oak

This species is similar to *Q. alba*, but has coarser leaves. It does well in moist to wet soils and is native to eastern and central North America.

borealis = *Q. rubra*

canariensis   90′   Zone 7   Canary Oak
A handsome deciduous tree with leaves which frequently remain on the tree until Christmas, this has not been widely used in America, but its good performance in Europe would seem to recommend its trial here. It is native to Spain and North Africa.

cerris   90′   Zone 6   Turkey Oak
This broadly pyramidal tree from southern Europe and western Asia has fine texture, the leaves ranging in length from 2 to 4 in. It is one of the faster growing oaks, but in this country does not do well north of southern New England. In the Washington, D.C., area it is an excellent street tree.

chrysolepis 60′ Zone 7 Canyon Live Oak
An evergreen oak, among the most beautiful of those native to Calif., this has a widespreading head and branches which are often pendulous.

coccinea   75′   Zone 4   Scarlet Oak
This lustrous-leaved tree, more open in habit than either the Pin or the Red Oak, has been planted profusely. The autumn color is a brilliant scarlet. Unfortunately, it is difficult to transplant and in the Midwest the Shumard Oak is taking its place for this reason. It is more open in habit than is *Q. rubra*. Native to eastern and central U.S.

dentata   75′   Zone 5   Daimyo Oak
One of the Asiatic oaks (native to Japan, Korea and northern China) and not easy to find in American nurseries; with rounded head and leaves that are 4–8 in. long and sometimes even 12 in. long and up to 8 in. wide. Hence it is coarse in texture and not outstanding as an ornamental when compared with some of the much better native American oaks.

engleriana   30′   Zone 7   Engler's Oak
Because of its small size and evergreen foliage, this might be worthy of trial wherever larger evergreen oaks thrive. The leathery leaves are 3 to 7 in. long. Native to central and west China.

falcata 75′ Zone 5 Spanish Oak, Southern Red Oak
The branches of this tree form an open, round-topped head with dark green, deeply cut leaves. The autumn color is dull orange to brown. Because it is a native, it has been used to some extent in landscape work. Native from N.J. to Fla. and Mo.

garryana 90′ Zone 6 Oregon White Oak
This round-headed tree with ascending branches is native to the Pacific Coast area of the U.S. and is the most important oak for timber purposes on the Pacific Coast. As an ornamental it does well on dry gravelly soils within its native habitat. The foliage is similar in size and shape to that of *Q. alba*.

glandulifera 45′ Zone 5 Glandbearing Oak
A small, shapely tree, native to Japan, Korea and China, with open-branching habit and lustrous green leaves which retain their color until late fall.

ilex   60′   Zone 9   Holly or Holm Oak
Round-headed, with broad, spreading branches, this evergreen oak has been popular for centuries in southern Europe where it is native. The small, often hollylike leaves, although varying somewhat in size, are generally $1\frac{1}{2}$ to 3 in. long and the tree takes shearing well. It does best in areas near the seashore where there is a high degree of atmospheric moisture.

ilicifolia   9′–21′   Zone 5   Scrub Oak
Not an ornamental, usually a shrub in very poor soils where practically little else will grow native from Me. to Va. and Ky. Leaves are 2–5 in. long, 2–5–7 lobed, the lobes pointed and bristle tipped (like Red Oak) and almost a felty pubescence underneath. The autumn color is yellowish to red.

imbricaria   75′   Zone 5   Shingle Oak
A round-topped, rather open tree when mature, but nicely pyramidal while young, this excellent deciduous tree native to the central U.S. is not grown much at present. It is one of the very best of the oaks. Its lustrous leaves are similar in shape to those of Mountain-laurel, although somewhat longer, and have a russet fall color. The Shingle Oak makes an excellent windbreak and can be sheared to grow as a clipped hedge. There are many excellent reasons why it should be used much more in landscape work than it is at present.

kelloggii 90′ Zone 7 California Black Oak
This is a dense round-headed tree with stoutly spreading branches and with leaves similar to those of the Red Oak. This long-lived tree is used only on the Pacific Coast where it is native and where it does well in dry, sandy or gravelly soils.

laurifolia   60′   Zone 7   Laurel Oak
The semi-evergreen, lustrous leaves of this species are mostly entire, 2 to $5\frac{1}{2}$ in. long, with some slightly lobed. It is often used as a street tree in the southeastern U.S. The variety 'Darlington' is sometimes listed as being more dense and compact and as retaining its leaves longer than the species. Native from Va. to Fla. and La.

liaotungensis 30′ Zone 5
Closely related to *Q. mongolica*, this tree has foliage somewhat similar to that of *Q. robur*. A 50-year-old specimen in the Arnold Arboretum

is only about 30 ft. tall, but has a nicely arched habit, with branches facing the ground on all sides. It is native to northeastern Asia.

libani   30′   Zone 5   Lebanon Oak
The leaves of this handsome, deciduous or half-evergreen tree from Syria and Asia Minor are long, narrow, regularly toothed, about 2 to 4 in. in length and look from a distance like those of a willow. This and *Q. phellos* have the smallest leaves of any of the oaks growing in the Arnold Arboretum. *Q. libani* is used extensively in England and does well there.

lyrata   90′   Zone 5   Overcup Oak
This is a round-headed tree with large lyre-shaped leaves, 3–8 in. long, with 3–4 pairs of obtuse acutish lobes, the 2 lower pairs being much smaller and often triangular and separated from the upper pair by wide sinuses, the terminal lobe usually 3-lobed. Often white tomentose beneath. The acorn is about an inch high and is usually nearly entirely enclosed by the cup. Branches are often pendulous. Native from N.J. to Fla. and Tex.

macrocarpa   75′–100′   Zone 2   Bur Oak
This is a majestic member of the White Oak group, possibly not planted as much as *Q. alba* but nevertheless native over the central and eastern half of North America. Sometimes termed Mossycup Oak because of the irregular fringed cup of the fruit. The acorn itself is an inch and more high. The tree grows with a tall trunk and leaves 4–10 in. long, rather obovate, but with 2–3 pairs of lobes, turning reddish in the fall. Usually with a broad head. Very hardy and large, not a tree for the small place.

montana = *Q. prinus*

nigra   75′   Zone 6   Water Oak
A conical to round-topped tree with small leaves 2 to 6 in. long, similar to *Q. velutina*. It is easily transplanted and is frequently used in the South on moist to wet sites. Native from Del. to Fla.

palustris   75′   Zone 4   Pin Oak
One of the most beautiful of the oaks, this tree has a definitely dense and pyramidal habit, with low or drooping branches. Widely used as a specimen because of its graceful habit and brilliant red autumn color; when used in street tree plantings it should be placed far enough from the curb to prevent the drooping branches from obstructing traffic. It is at its best with the branches touching the ground on all sides, and is found native to central and mideastern U.S.

phellos   50′   Zone 5   Willow Oak
The Willow Oak is an excellent specimen or street tree, having slender branches. It has a fine texture, with leaves 2–5½ in. long, pointed at both ends like those of a willow and turning a dull yellow in the autumn. It is native to the eastern seacoast and Gulf states.

prinus   90′   Zone 4   Chestnut Oak
Although this tree has a compact, round top and better foliage than *Q. muhlenbergii*, it does not have especially outstanding autumn color, even in the eastern U.S. where it is native. It is useful in dry, rocky soils where better oaks will not grow well.

robur   75′–150′   Zone 5   English Oak
A member of the White Oak group, this European tree has an open, broad head with a short trunk and leaves 2 to 4 in. long and up to 2¼ in. wide, with no autumn color. It is widely planted in Europe, but is not entirely satisfactory in the U.S. as far north as Boston, where cold winters often seriously injure the plant. This fact was noted by Professor C. S. Sargent many years ago and certainly it has been true during the past 25 years also. However, it is long-lived in England, for there are some trees now living in Windsor Great Park which Sir Eric Savill estimates are over 1000 years old. If the young foliage is eaten exclusively by cattle, especially in the spring, it causes poisoning. Some of the varietes are: 'Fastigiata'—the Pyramidal English Oak, definitely upright and columnar in habit; has a shape similar to that of a Lombardy Poplar. Nearly 80% of the seedlings retain the upright habit of the parent tree; 'Asplenifolia'—this is called the Fern-leaved Oak and has a fine texture with deeply lobed leaves; 'Atropurpurea'—this tree is purported to have dark purple leaves, although such specimens appear to be very rare in America. The tree in the Arnold Arboretum has faintly purplish-green leaves, the color differing only slightly from that of the species; 'Concordia'—this is the Golden English Oak, a weak grower, sometimes scorching badly in very hot sun. The leaves are a bright yellow, especially in the early spring. An excellent specimen of this formerly grew near Highland Park in Rochester, N.Y., but small plants tried on several occasions in the Arnold Arboretum have invariably succumbed to winter killing and heavy sun scorch; 'Pendula' —this is a form reported to have pendulous branches. It appears to be rare in the U.S. Since plants of this variety apparently vary considerably, it is likely that the poorer clones would have little value as ornamentals.

rubra   75′   Zone 3   Red Oak
This tree is commonly grown throughout much of the U.S., where it is hardy and it is native to northeastern and central North America. This tree for a long time was termed *Q. rubra*, then the name was changed to *Q. borealis*, now it has been changed back again to *Q. rubra*. Trees in the southern part of its range are the var. **rubra** (*Q. rubra rubra*) and those in the northeastern U.S. are *Q. rubra* **maxima**. It can be transplanted easily and is one of the fastest-growing of the

oaks. In shape it is pyramidal when young, generally becoming rounded with age, and has excellent red autumn color. The variety **maxima** is practically identical, for ornamental purposes at least, differing slightly from the species in that it has larger fruit and a slightly wider range. It is noted as being one of the fastest-growing of the oaks, especially good for street and avenue planting.

shumardii   120′   Zone 5   Shumard Oak
Throughout its native habitat in the central and southern U.S., this tree makes a good substitute for the Scarlet Oak, which it resembles in many ways.

suber   60′   Zone 7   Cork Oak
Usually an evergreen, round-headed tree with massive branches, this plant requires full sun

The true cork tree is an oak—*Quercus suber*—native to southern Europe and northern Africa. (*Photo by Arnold Arboretum, Jamaica Plain, Mass.*)

and semi-arid soil conditions in areas where the winter temperatures never drop below zero Fahrenheit. This tree is the source of cork for commerce and many are being planted experimentally in the southern U.S. It is native to southern Europe and northern Africa.

variabilis   75′   Zone 5   Oriental Oak
The foliage of this Asiatic tree is dull green in color and of a size and shape resembling that of *Castanea crenata*. The interesting bark, only about ½ in. thick, is corky and very ornamental, showing off especially well in winter.

velutina   100′–150′   Zone 4   Black Oak
One of the largest of the northern American oaks, this tree has lobed, lustrous green leaves which turn red in the fall. There is usually a deep tap root, making larger trees difficult to transplant. It is not a good tree for the small place, but has excellent red autumn color and is native to the eastern and central U.S. Quercitron, an extract made from the powdered inner bark of Black Oak, is used for dye (buff, gold, orange).

virginiana   60′   Zone 7   Live Oak
A tree with massive trunk and branches, the spread of which is twice that of the height; this is evergreen in the far South and deciduous in the northern limits of its habitat, which is the southeastern U.S. It is widely used in the South, both as a specimen and as an avenue tree.

wislizenii   70′   Zone 7   Interior Live Oak
The Interior Live Oak of Calif. and N.Mex. is another evergreen oak with glossy leaves and slow growth. It is of use ornamentally only near the valleys of the southern Calif. coastal region where it is native.

QUILLAJA (kwill-AY-ja)
saponaria   60′   Zone 10   Soapbark-tree
This is native to Chile, with shining, alternate, evergreen leaves, ⅔ in. long, and white unisexual flowers, ½ in. in dia., in the spring. The bark has been used in Chile by the natives to make soap.

QUINCE. The scientific name of this popular fruit is *Cydonia oblonga,* which see. It is a tree about 24 ft. tall, beginning to bear its fragrant, pear-shaped fruit when 4–5 years old. Two plants are all that are necessary to keep the home gardener plentifully supplied with fruit—all he will use, plus supplying gifts of many to his friends. The variety 'Orange' is the most popular, but 'Champion', 'Pineapple' and 'Smyrna' are grown to a lesser extent, producing green fruits that just begin to turn orange in the fall at about the time of frost. In fact, the fruits can withstand a few light frosts and might well be left on the tree until these occur, if they do not ripen before. Quince is self-fruitful, so actually one need have only one tree to obtain good fruiting.

Commercially, quince seedlings or layers are used as the understock on which the variety is grafted. They will grow on a wide variety of soils, but probably not much farther north than Zone 5 (or possibly Zone 4), since they can be injured by severe cold in winter. They might be fertilized generally like pears or apples.

Insect Pests

The fruit is very susceptible to oriental fruit moth infestation, especially in late summer and early fall when nearly all unprotected fruit has many small tunnels through the flesh. Spray with insecticide #37 until about 10 days before harvest. See PEACH. In some areas quince curculio damages the fruit severely by laying eggs from which small, legless grubs hatch and tunnel through the flesh. Spraying with insecticide #9 or #13 in midsummer reduces the infestation. Apple aphids and lace bugs are controlled by sprays of insecticide #15.

Diseases

The cedar-quince stem rusts live during part of their development on Quince, causing orange swollen galls on the twigs and large circular orange-colored areas on the fruit. Spraying at blossom time with fungicide #D effective. See JUNIPERUS and RUSTS. Black spot infects the leaves and causes sunken black spots on the fruit. Spraying with fungicide #D in early summer is advised.

Other than this, quinces need little attention, little pruning. They bear well annually, sometimes too well, and a little fruit thinning proves beneficial.

The fruit ripens in the fall, in Sept. or Oct., and it can be stored in a cool place for several months. Because of the way it grows, producing flowers on the ends of the current year's spur shoots, it takes some time to produce the flowers in the spring; hence it is not so susceptible to injury from frosts as are apples and peaches.

In general, quinces are about as susceptible to fire blight as pear trees. Propagation is mostly by budding on quince seedlings, or by budding on quince layers.

For the "Japanese" Quince, or the Oriental Quince, see CHAENOMELES. Incidentally, the fruits of Chaenomeles can also be used for making jams, preserves and jellies.

QUINCE, JAPANESE, ORIENTAL. See CHAENOMELES.

QUISQUALIS (kwis-KWAY-lis)
indica   vine   Zone 10   Rangoon-creeper
A fast-growing vine with opposite, simple, oblong leaves 3–5 in. long. The showy, fragrant flowers are white, changing to pink and red, in conspicuous, drooping, terminal clusters and are evident throughout the summer. The fruit is a leathery 5-angled capsule about an inch long. Propagated by softwood cuttings.

R

RABBITBRUSH, GREENPLUME = *Chryso-thamnus nauceosus graveolens*

RACE. A permanent variety or group of individuals whose distinguishing characters are constant and are reproduced true to type from seed.

RACEME. A simple inflorescence of stalked flowers on a more or less elongated axis.

RACEMOSE. In racemes or resembling a raceme.

RACHIS. An axis bearing flowers or leaflets.

RADIATE. Spreading from a common center.

RADISH (*Raphanus sativus*). This is the easiest of all vegetables to raise and includes all of the varieties commonly grown in America. *R. sativus longipinnatus* or Chinese Radish develops a much larger, firmer-fleshed root, requiring a longer-growing season and is usually cooked. It is also known as a winter radish and is widely grown in the Orient, but of little importance in the United States.

Varieties

There are a large number of varieties of the common radish offered by seedsmen. They vary in color: white, scarlet, red, and yellow; in size and shape, round, ovate, long and cylindrical, and in maturity, 20–60 or more days. Varieties that are suggested for the home gardener are 'French Breakfast', 'Cherry Belle', 'Comet', 'White Icicle', 'Champion', 'Scarlet Globe', 'Sparkle' and 'White Chinese' and perhaps 'Round Black Spanish' as winter radishes.

Culture

The common radish seed will germinate in 4–5 days and, if grown properly, will be ready to harvest in 25–40 days depending on the variety planted. Rapid growth is essential to develop juicy, crisp roots and, therefore, a rich, sandy loam soil of fine tilth is very important. See soil preparation under VEGETABLE GARDEN. The seed is sown in drills $\frac{1}{2}$ in. deep and spaced 12–15 in. apart. Succession plantings should be made every 10 days during the early spring and again starting in Aug. Radishes grown during midsummer produce woody and pithy roots very rapidly. Because of the short maturity period, radishes work in well as an intercrop.

Insects

Root maggot is the only serious pest of Radish. For control see CABBAGE.

GRANT B. SNYDER

RADISH, CHINESE = *Raphanus sativus longipinnatus*. See RADISH.

RADISH, WILD = *Raphanus raphanistrum*

RAFFIA. This is a product of a palm, much used in horticulture. The leaf of the palm **Raphia farinifera** (Madagascar) is split into thin strips and, when moistened, these are used in all sorts of tying operations. Plastic materials are replacing it somewhat, but it is still widely used.

RAGGED ROBIN = *Lychnis flos-cuculi*

RAGWEED. See AMBROSIA.

RAINFALL. The amount of rain falling in an area, and especially the time of year it falls, is the most important single factor governing garden making. The U.S. is such a large area that it is impossible to give much specific information on this subject without getting involved in a lengthy discussion and many statistics. There are large areas of the U.S. where the normal rainfall is sufficient, coming at the proper time during the growing season so that many plants can be grown. Because the country is so large and has mountain ranges and is bordered by 3 oceans, rainfall varies from 3 in. or less in parts of Ariz. to over 60 in. on the coast of Wash. In fact, only 300 miles away from this heavy rainfall, the average can be under 10 in. In Puerto Rico the rainfall on the east coast is only 26 in., while a short 20 miles away in the mountains it is 180 in. With such a wide variation in such a comparatively small area, it is obvious that a general discussion of rainfall will not prove helpful to individual gardeners spread all over the country from coast to coast.

Rainfall information is a matter which has been studied by the U.S. Weather Bureau since it was established in 1891. For specific details, one should contact the local weather bureau station which has all available records. Even with a study of these records, one is often at a loss, for the vagaries of the weather keep us constantly guessing. For instance, in New England, with a normal average of about 43 in. over the years, the last 3 have been punctuated with serious summer droughts, one being so severe that there was only half the normal rainfall, yet a few hundred miles west of this area, gardeners experienced the heaviest rainfall in years.

Although at present there is little that can be done about increasing the rainfall, one should be cognizant of the fact that it varies greatly throughout the country, and if one contemplates moving to an entirely new area, gardening may be practiced there on an entirely different scale because of a difference in the all-important rainfall. Information on this from the U.S. Weather Bureau, discussion with gardeners in the new area, as well as personal observation should be sufficient to give one an idea concerning what may (or may not) be grown in the new area.

RAIN-LILY. See COOPERIA.

RAIN-OF-GOLD = *Galphimia glauca*

RAINTREE, BRAZIL = *Brunfelsia calycina*

RAISIN. Raisins or dried grapes are a staple food in many parts of the world. Production amounts to about 600,000 tons annually. Of this Calif. produces 39%; Greece 20%; Australia 13%; Turkey 12%; Iran 8% and other countries smaller amounts to make up the total. About 95% of the raisins produced in Calif. come from the 'Thompson Seedless' clone. Others are various muscat and currant types.

Essentially raisin production is the growing of a uniformly ripened variety of grape, drying them in the sun under several sets of conditions (for slightly varying end products), storing them and then packaging them for distribution and selling.

The grapes are carefully and uniformly grown so that when they are ripe they will be uniform. They are picked, placed in slat-bottom trays, one bunch deep, and set out in the sun for drying. This must be done in an area where there is full (and strong) sunshine during late summer and early fall, and no rain. Rain can spoil the product if it falls at the wrong time. With 10 days in the tray, those on top start to turn brown and the tray contents are turned upside down for another 10–11 days (in the case of 'Thompson Seedless' variety).

Then they are dipped in a .02% solution of caustic soda at 200–212° F. for 2–3 seconds, thoroughly washed with fresh water and spread out to dry again in the full sun for 3–4 days. The dipping in caustic soda produces the numerous small cracks in the skin that are so desirable. After this drying the trays are stacked a week in the open, then taken to the storing shed where they are cleaned, stored a while and finally packed.

In this entire process the fresh grapes lose about 90–95% of their original water content.

There are variations in this method but in general this is the way raisins are produced from grapes in Calif.

RAISINTREE, JAPANESE = *Hovenia dulcis*

RAMONDA (ray-MON-da)

myconi (*pyrenaica*)   3″   Zone 5   Rosette-mullein

A small, rosette-leaved perennial, with hairy leaves, deeply toothed, and purple flowers borne in few-flowered clusters; sometimes grown in rock gardens. Native to the Pyrenees Mountains. Propagated by seed or division.

RAMONTCHI = *Flacourtia indica*

RAMPION. See PHYTEUMA.

RANGOON-CREEPER = *Quisqualis indica*

RANUNCULACEAE = The Buttercup Family

RANUNCULUS (ra-NUN-kew-lus). The buttercups are a large group of north temperate herbs, some fibrous rooted, some with tubers, with simple or compound leaves often lobed or divided. Generally the flowers are yellow, but in the newer varieties of *R. asiaticus*, the species so widely grown by florists, the flowers are yellow, orange, red, pink or white. Most of the ones listed here are generally hardy (except *R. asiaticus*) and are perennial, propagated by seed or division.

aconitifolius   2′–3′   Zone 5   Aconite Buttercup

A European species, native of moist soils, with handsome, glossy green leaves similar to those of the Aconite and producing loose sprays of small white flowers. The variety **flore-pleno** has double white flowers.

acris   2′–3′   Zone 3   Tall Buttercup

A European species with an open, weedy habit, this plant is naturalized in the moist meadows and along the roadsides from New England to Va., extending inland to Ill. and Minn. The alternate, compound leaves have 5 leaflets which are toothed and lobed. The cuplike flowers, terminally borne, and in few-flowered clusters, are bright golden yellow with 5 heart-shaped petals and numerous stamens. The flowers bloom throughout the season, but principally in midsummer.

amplexicaulis   1′   Zone 5   Yelloweye Buttercup

An excellent white buttercup for the rock garden, native to the Pyrenees Mountains of Europe, with 2–3 flowers about an inch in dia. The gray-green, lance-shaped leaves clasp the stem near the base. It quickly grows into a strong clump, easily divided in the spring. It can also be propagated by seed sown in the fall as soon as ripe and left in their pot in the cold frame for a full year.

asiaticus   1½′   Zone 8   Persian Buttercup

A tuberous-rooted species often grown by the

florist, it produces flowers 1–4 in. wide. There are many varieties, some with double flowers, yellow, orange, red, pink and white. Easily propagated by division or by seeds, and grown the same way as anemones (which see). Native to southeastern Europe and southwestern Asia and sometimes called the Turban or Persian Buttercup. It is advisable, when the plant is past flowering and the leaves have turned yellow, to lift the tuberous roots and allow them to dry, hanging them up in a paper bag until between Nov. and Feb., when they can be planted again in the greenhouse. The tubers are peculiarly clawlike and, in planting, these should be placed down. It is left out in gardens out-of-doors only in frost-free areas, but may be planted in other gardens after danger of frost is over in the spring and, of course, lifted again before the fall frosts. For plants grown in the greenhouse, the temperature should be cool, with night temperatures 45°–50° F. and day temperatures only 10° higher.

bulbosus   12″   Zone 4   Bulbous Buttercup
Another European species, this hairy-stemmed plant rises from a bulblike corm. The compound leaves have 3 lobes which are deeply divided and the golden-yellow flowers have 5, 6 or 7 petals. Its habitat are the fields and meadows of the Atlantic coastal states, where it has become a common weed, from New England to Ala. A pretty garden plant if kept under control; it may be propagated by self-sown seed or by division of the corms in late autumn. There is also a double-flowered form.

crenatus   4″   Zone 5   Crenatus Buttercup
A dainty white buttercup of early spring, having small tufts of wavy, slightly toothed leaves and flowers 1 in. wide. Native to Europe.

creticus   2″   Zone 5   Crete Buttercup
Native to Crete, a very small perennial with rounded leaves up to 4 in. wide. Flowers golden yellow.

ficaria   6″ or less   Zone 5   Lesser-celandine
A European plant which has escaped in the northeastern U.S. in waste places and open woodlands. Flowers yellow, an inch wide, with up to a dozen petals during April and early May. The stems are decumbent and it usually grows flat on the surface of the ground. Leaves are cordate-ovate, about 2 in. long and glossy. The only disadvantage of this as a ground cover is that the foliage entirely disappears during early summer.

geraniifolius   6″   Zone 5   Mountain Buttercup
A low perennial from Europe with creeping rootstocks, suitable for display in the rockery. The bright yellow flowers are about 1 in. wide and are usually solitary.

gramineus   1′   Zone 6   Grassy Buttercup
With grasslike leaves, yellow flowers 1 in. wide,

in clusters of 1–7. Native to Europe.

lyallii   4′   Zone 8   Lyall Buttercup
Flowers white to pale yellowish white, 2–3 in. wide. Native to New Zealand.

montanus   6″   Zone 5   Mountain Buttercup
With creeping rootstocks and small, 3–5-parted leaves which are longitudinally lobed, this small, matlike European plant with attractve foliage sends up single yellow flowers an inch wide in spring. Native to the mountains of Europe.

repens   2′   Zone 3   Creeping Buttercup
The leaves are 3 parted, mostly borne near the base of the ground, the lower leaves with long petioles so that when the flowers are not evident the plant is only about 6 in. high. It is supposedly a native of Europe, but it has become a weed in the U.S. The flowers are bright yellow, single, $\frac{3}{4}$ in. wide, cup-shaped and appear from May to Aug. The double-flowered variety 'Pleniflorus' has good flowers. Both species and variety make nice ground covers in sunny situations. The fast-growing runners may extend 2 ft. or more each season, rooting repeatedly at the joints. Propagation is by division.

septentrionalis   2′   Zone 3   Swamp Buttercup
A native perennial, growing in moist woods and meadows from Canada south to Ga. and west to Neb. Thick, fibrous roots nourish the hollow stems of the plant which tend to become reclining after the plant has flowered. The leaves are 3-lobed, each lobe being long and narrow. The bright yellow flowers are 1 in. or more wide and bloom from April to Aug.

RAOULIA (ray-OO-lia)
australis   Prostrate   Zone 8 (?)   Silvermat Raoulia
Prostrate ground cover from New Zealand. Lvs. white or yellowish tomentose, pale yellow fls. The small alternate leaves are only $\frac{1}{8}$″ long.

RAPE = *Brassica napus*   3′   Zone 8
Grown extensively in India, Japan and Europe for its oily seeds supplying the colza or rape oil of commerce. Little grown in the U.S. except as a cover crop. Flowers yellow.

RAPHANUS (RAFF-ay-nus)
raphanistrum   3½′   annual   Wild Radish
A common garden weed and in grain fields in the northeastern and central states, in Canada and in the Pacific Northwest. Introduced from Europe. It has a long fleshy tap root, alternate lyre-shaped leaves with more or less regular, rounded lobes. The flowers have 4 yellow to white petals, about ¼ in. across, produced from July to Sept. and the fruits are in linear pods.

sativus   3½′   annual   Radish
This is the garden Radish which has sometimes

escaped and is found as a weed in the Pacific Coast states. Introduced from Europe. The var. **longipinnatus** is called the Chinese Radish, with leaves 1–2 ft. long bearing 8–12 leaflets, and long hard roots, usually cooked. It is little grown in America. Also see RADISH.

RAPHE. A botanical term meaning a seamlike union of the 2 lateral halves or part of an organ, often with a ridge or furrow.

RAPHIA (RAFF-ia)
farinifera (*ruffia*)   65′   **Zone 10   Raffia**
A feather palm with sturdy trunk 25–30 ft. this has erect leaves that may be as much as 40–50 ft. long, the individual leaflets being 5 ft. long. When split these leaflets furnish the well-known raffia so often used in horticultural practices. Native to Madagascar.

RAPHIDOPHYLLUM (ra-fid-o-FILL-um)
hystrix   6′   Zone 8   Needle Palm
This is native to the southeastern U.S. from S. Car. to Fla. It is low and shrubby, making a fine rounded specimen 10 ft. across. The common name is given because of the small, black, needlelike spines which protrude from the trunk. The trunk is short but densely packed with palmate shiny leaves, 3–4 ft. long, which make a rounded specimen.

RAPHIOLEPIS (raf-i-OLL-ep-is)
indica   5′   Zone 8   India Raphiolepis
This has alternate, leathery, shining leaves about 3 in. long and bluntly toothed; with pinkish flowers, about ½ in. across, in loose racemes. Native to southern China. The var. **rosea** has flowers a darker pink.

umbellata   6′   Zone 7   Yeddo-Hawthorn
The dark, leathery, evergreen leaves of this southern Japanese plant are up to 3 in. long. The fragrant white flowers are produced in dense upright panicles during late May, and the bluish-black berries, ⅜ in. across, are effective during the fall and winter. A handsome Japanese shrub, it can be grown in either full sun or partial shade and appears to be fairly drought resistant.

RASPBERRY. (Also see RUBUS). These shrubs are among the hardiest of the bush fruits and are perfectly at home in the northern United States and southern Canada. The canes are biennial, as in blackberries, that is, they normally are produced one year, fruit the second year and then die and should be removed in the annual thorough pruning that these shrubs require to keep them in good bearing condition. The new shoots either appear at the base of the plant or as suckers a foot or so removed from the plant.

There are 2 types of red raspberries, those that only fruit once a year, and those some-times termed "ever-bearing" that fruit early in the season (July), have a few weeks rest, and then fruit again in Sept. or until frost. After growing both types, I must admit to liking the "ever-bearing" group better, for in a good growing season it does seem that we have fresh fruit from early summer to frost, with a break of about 2 weeks. However, some gardeners may not care for raspberries this much or may be away from home in early summer. It also must be admitted that fruits of the "ever-bearing" types may not be quite as large or sweet as the others. So, one has a decision to make concerning the type to plant.

Pruning the "ever-bearing" group is a little different because the same canes that bear in early summer bear again in the early fall. After fruiting in the fall, the fruiting canes can be removed, together with weak canes. This pruning can also be done in the winter or early spring.

Training

Because of the method of sending up miscellaneous suckers, often at some distance from the original plant, raspberries, like blackberries, might best be restrained in the home garden to a strip about a foot wide. Shoots coming up outside this should be relentlessly removed. This can easily be done merely with the mechanical rotovator, but hoeing them out is the simpler method.

Raspberry canes grow 5–6 ft. tall (or more) and, when heavily laden with fruit, they bend over to the ground, are hard to pick and even more difficult to pass by (without injury) when mechanical garden equipment is used for cultivation and weeding. Consequently, it is best to give them some support. This of course can be done by tying each cane to a horizontal wire, but this takes too much work. Much better is to erect a series of strong posts (metal pipes for permanence) 30 ft. apart and then 2 sets of wires, one about 2 ft. above the ground, the other about 3½ ft. above the ground. Each set of 2 wires would be held 12–18 in. apart by a series of crosspieces. These 4 wires, then, are the area within which all the canes grow and are held upright in place. There is no tying of individual canes, no work except seeing to it that all canes are kept within the limits set by these wires. There are other methods, but this works well and, if made of sturdy materials, needs no attention for years.

As noted, pruning is done after fruiting in the late summer, for the 1-crop varieties, or in the fall, winter or early spring for the 2-crop or "ever-bearing" varieties. Canes left may have the tops snipped off at about 4½ to 6 ft. high, depending on variety.

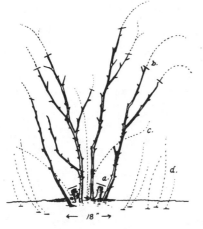

Raspberry Pruning:
A. Two-year-old canes are removed entirely.
B. Topping one-year-old canes slightly.
C. Remove weak canes.
D. Remove unwanted suckers.

The Black Raspberry (or Blackcap) and the Purple Raspberry are treated in the same manner, except that the shoots tend to be long and trailing and the ends might well be cut off when they have reached their proper manageable height (5–6 ft.) which forces lateral growth, especially desirable since these plants only produce 3–12 canes per plant and can get top heavy if the canes are cut off much higher. This heading back should be done as soon as the growth reaches this height.

Propagation is simply by dividing the plants, digging up rooted suckers, or using a sharp spade through the center of a plant from which many canes have developed. The blackcaps are reproduced by tip layering, merely selecting a long arching shoot, placing the tip firmly in the ground with just the end showing. This is done in late summer and by the following spring this should be rooted.

Planting can be done in either the fall or the spring, but other things being equal, early spring is probably best. When properly planted (about 30–48 in. apart in the row for the raspberries and 3–6 ft. apart for the blackcaps) the canes are cut back to about 6 in.

Varieties

RED RASPBERRIES—single crop
'Bristol'—an excellent home garden variety introduced by the N.Y. Agricultural Experiment Station a few years ago.
'Canby'—a thornless variety, originated in Ore. in 1961. Vigorous, high-yielding, and being grown on the Pacific Coast.

'Jewel'—large, glossy black, not susceptible to serious disease.
'Latham'—a popular variety in the past, widely grown, but susceptible to mosaic and disease.
'Milton'—often not susceptible to mosaic, well worthy of trial.
'Newburgh'—one of the best home garden varieties, originated in N.Y., but grown widely throughout the country.
'Summer'—originated in Wash. in 1956, vigorous and productive on the West Coast, but plants are susceptible to mildew.
'Taylor'—heavy yields are produced, almost as hardy as 'Latham'.
'Willamette'—the leading variety grown in Ore. today, where it originated in 1942.
RED RASPBERRIES—2-crop varieties
'Indian Summer'—originated in N.Y., vigorous grower but yields are not high.
'September'—also of N.Y. origin and superior in most respects to 'Indian Summer'.
BLACKCAP RASPBERRIES
'Munger'—this is the variety mostly grown in Ore.
'Plum Farmer', 'Black Pearl', 'Jewel', 'Maples'—all are grown in the East and are nearly immune to disease.
PURPLE RASPBERRIES
'Sodus'—relatively free from mosaic and should replace the older variety 'Columbian'.
'Marion'—well worth testing. Also 'Brandywine' and 'Royalty'.
The varieties of raspberries are being augmented all the time by various state experiment stations. It is always best before selecting a variety for the home garden to consult the local state experiment station for the most up-to-date varietal recommendations for the area in question.

Insect Pests

Raspberry cane borer, red-necked cane borers and raspberry cane maggot all puncture and girdle the tips of canes and cause them to wilt. Spraying just before bloom with insecticide #9 usually combined with fungicide #D prevents much injury, but careful pruning of wilted shoots is also necessary. Raspberry fruit worm is a beetle which eats holes in the first leaves and lays eggs in the blossoms. Small grubs feed in the developing berry. Spraying as above is recommended. Japanese beetle is attracted to Raspberry and spray or dust of insecticide #15 or #28, together with hand-picking, should prevent significant loss. Red spider mites often reach the peak of abundance during harvest and a miticide spray such as insecticide #34, just before the fruit forms and after harvest, is advisable.

Diseases

Mosaic resulting from infection by several viruses is the most destructive disease. Discolored, twisted, curled, abnormal leaves are the principle symptoms. Planting the more resistant varieties and careful removal of infected or suspicious plants is the only protection. Infected soil should be avoided for new plantings and any aphids promptly sprayed with insecticide #15. Leaf curl and streak are treated in the same way. Anthracnose may weaken or kill canes following the development of gray spots on the bark. Careful pruning and thinning of weak canes and application of a general spray schedule usually checks the disease. Cane blight and spur blight produce gray or purple blotches on bark which may kill the cane or the fruit spur. A dormant spray of fungicide #N or a general schedule is advised. A white powdery growth on the wilted tips of new canes indicates powdery mildew.

SPRAY SCHEDULE

1. When first leaves open—insecticides #15 and #9 and fungicide #D
2. Just before blossom—insecticides #15 and #9 and fungicide #D
3. Soon after harvest—insecticides #15 and fungicide #D
4. Early September—insecticides #15 and #9 and fungicide #D

RATIBIDA (rati-BID-a) (*Lepachys*)
    columnifera   1′–3′   Zone 3   Prairie Cone-flower

A hairy, branching, perennial plant of the Composite Family, having alternate leaves divided into 7–9 linear lobes and solitary flower heads terminating the flower stalks. These flower heads have blunt-toothed, yellow, ray flowers and a conical disk of grayish flowers. It is native to the Plains states from Canada to Mexico and blooms throughout the summer. The plant is sometimes transplanted to the wild garden and it will thrive in any good garden soil. Propagation is by seed. There is a variety **pulcherrima** with brownish-purple rays and a double-flowered form.

    pinnata   4′   Zone 3   Gray-headed Cone-flower

A slender hairy perennial with alternate, pinnately compound leaves having 3–5 leaflets and flower heads of drooping, blunt-toothed yellow ray flowers and grayish disk flowers in an oblong disk. It is native to dry soils from N.Y. to Minn. and southwards to Fla. and Tex., and blooms throughout the summer. It is propagated by seed.

RATOON. A stalk or sprout of a plant which has come up from the base of a perennial plant

the second year, such as a sprout of sugar cane or cotton which comes up from the base of the old plant after the first year's growth.

RATTLEBOX. See LUDWIGIA.

RATTLE BROME = *Bromus brizaeformis*

RATTLESNAKE-PLANTAIN. See GOODYEARA.

RAVENALA (ray-ven-AY-la)
    madagascariensis   30′   Zone 10   Madagascar Traveler's Tree

This striking and unusual tree, closely related to the Banana, is used in subtropical areas for its picturesque habit. The common name comes from the fact that it stores a palatable, watery fluid at the base of the leaves which can be used in lieu of water by the weary traveler. Native to Madagascar, this palm has huge leaves, sometimes 15–30 ft. long, arranged like a large fan.

RAY. A botanical term used to denote the margin portion of a composite flower head. Ray flowers of *Viburnum opulus* are those on the outside margin of the flat composite cluster. See DISC or DISK flowers.

REBUTIA (reb-BEW-tia). Globular, spiny cacti similar to *Lobivia* species, native to South America; usually only a few inches high, bearing yellow or red flowers. Of little ornamental value except in the cactus gardens of the southwestern U.S.

RECEPTACLE. The more or less expanded portion of an axis which bears the organs of a flower or the collected flowers of a head.

RECURVED. Curved downward or backward.

REDBUD. See CERCIS.

RED-CEDAR. See JUNIPERUS.

RED-RIBBONS = *Clarkia concinna*

RED-ROOT = *Lachnanthes carolina*

RED-SILK-COTTON-TREE = *Bombax malabaricum*

REDTOP = *Agrostis alba*. See GRASS, LAWNS.

REGIONAL GARDENING. See GARDENING, REGIONAL.

REDWOOD = *Sequoia sempervirens*

REED, COMMON = *Phragmites australis*

REED, GIANT = *Arundo donax*

REFLEXED. Abruptly turned downward.

RENANTHERA (ree-nan-THEE-ra). About 20 species of Indo-Malayan epiphetic orchids, not of too much horticultural interest but the following species have been recommended. For culture and propagation see ORCHID.

    coccinea   2′–6′   Zone 10

With 25–60 orange-scarlet flowers per raceme, each 3–4 in. across, blooming during spring and summer. A sparsely branched plant needing full sun.

imschootiana 8"–36" **Zone 10**
With 10–30 dark red flowers per raceme, each 2–2½ in. across, blooming during the spring and summer. Dwarf and producing profuse blooms, making a fine (although rare) specimen.

storiei 2½'–7' **Zone 10**
With 25–75 orange-red flowers per cluster during the winter and spring; this will grow and bloom with half shade but prefers full sun all the time.

RENIFORM. Kidney shaped.

RESEDA (ree-SEE-da)

odorata   decumbent   annual   Common Mignonette
An excellent old-fashioned flower for the flower garden, particularly valued for its very fragrant blossoms all summer long. These are small, borne on inconspicuous small spikes, whitish, red or yellowish. Varieties may be obtained in the separate colors and there are dwarf vars. as well. Native to Africa. It is grown either in the greenhouse or the flower garden and is excellent for cutting to be used in bouquets. It does not transplant easily, hence the seed should be sown in the garden (or the greenhouse) in the spot where the plants are to grow, preferably a cool, moderately moist and partially shaded one. The plants should be thinned to a foot apart.

RESEDACEAE = The Mignonette Family

RETARDING. The partial withholding of some growth-requisite such as light, water, fertilizer or even root space, in order that the plant will not grow as rapidly as it normally might.

RETICULATE. In the form of a network; net-veined.

RETINOSPORA = *Chamaecyparis*

RETUSE. Slightly notched at the rounded apex.

REVOLUTE. Rolled backward.

REGISTRATION OF PLANT NAMES. A concerted effort is being made by all botanical and horticultural organizations throughout the world to bring order to the naming of new cultivars (clones or cultivated varieties) of plants. An International Code of Nomenclature for Cultivated Plants was originally drawn up by a special committee representing international and botanical interests and the first edition was published in 1953. Since then, it has been the responsibility of a special commission of the International Union of Biological Sciences.

Many organizations and individuals, both in America and in Europe, are working on national and international registration lists, these to comprise names of all cultivars published in accordance with the Rules of Nomenclature. It is hoped that in the years to come, this Code and the registration lists which are prepared and published under the authority of the International Horticultural Congresses will be the foundation governing the naming of all new cultivated varieties of plants. All those who are about to name new cultivated plants are urged to obtain a copy of the Code from the American Horticultural Society, Inc., Mount Vernon, Va. 22121, and to obtain proper registration blanks from the Registration Authority concerned.

The American Horticultural Society is responsible for assigning genera or groups to organizations which would serve as national registrars. Many have been assigned, but for further information write the secretary of the American Horticultural Society.

Obviously this is an ever-changing list of authorities with names and addresses of those responsible changing from time to time. At present (1986) there are over 200 genera assigned, some of the most important of which are:

Acacia
Achimenes
Acidanthera
Allium
Alstroemeria
Amaryllidaceae
Amaryllis
Amelanchier
Andromeda
Anemone
Begonia
Billbergia
Bloomeria
Bougainvillea
Brodiaea
Bromeliaceae
Bruckenthalia
Brunsvigia
Bulbocodium
Buxus
Calla
Callistephus
Calluna
Calochortus
Camassia
Camellia
Canistrum
Canna
Caprosma
Carissa
Chaenomeles
Chionodoxa
Chrysanthemum
Clematis
Clivia
Colchicum
Columnea
Conifers

Cornus
Corydalis
Cotoneaster
X Crinodonna
Crinum
Crocosmia
Crocus
Cryptanthus
Cyclamen
Daboecia
Dahlia
Delphinium
Dianthus
Endymion
Episcia
Eranthis
Eremurus
Erica
Escallonia
Eucomis
Fagus
Forsythia
Freesia
Fritillaria
Fuchsia
Galanthus
Galtonia
Gesneriaceae
Gleditsia
Gloriosa
Gloxinia
Guzmania
Hebe
Hedera
Hemerocallis
Herbertia
Hibiscus
Hosta
Hyacinthella
Hyacinthus
Hydrangea
Hymenocallis
Ilex
Iris
Ismene
Lachenalia
Lagerstroemia
Lantana
Leptospermum
Leucodendron
Leucojum
Leucospermum
Lilium
Lycoris
Magnolia
Malus
Mango
Montbretia
Muscari
Narcissus

Nerine
Orchidaceae
Ornithogalum
Orothamnus
Oxalis
Pancratium
Pelargonium
Penstemon
Petunia
Philadelphus
Pieris
Pittosporum
Plumeria
Populus
Protea
Pyracantha
Ranunculus
Rhododendron
Rosa
Saintpaulia
Scilla
Scilla campanulata & nutans
Sempervivum
Serruria
Sinningia
Sparaxis
Sternbergia
Streptocarpus
Syringa
Tagetes
Tigridia
Tillandsia
Triteleia
Tritonia
Tulipa
Ulmus
Vallota
Viburnum
Vriesea
Weigela
Zantedeschia
Zephyranthes
Zigadenus

REHMANNIA (ree-MANN-ia)
    elata   3′   Zone 10   Beverly-bells Rehmannia
A perennial herb from central China, grown in
the cool greenhouse for its large, showy, rosy-
red flowers which have a yellow throat spotted
purple, somewhat similar to those of Foxgloves.
The sticky-hairy, alternate leaves are irregularly
lobed and borne in a rosette at the base of the
plant. Propagated by softwood cuttings or
seeds producing blooming plants in 2 years.
Var. **tricolor** has purple flowers which mature
to violet-rose with a whitish throat. Sometimes
planted outdoors in southern Calif.

REINWARDTIA (ryn-WARD-tia)
    indica   4′   Zone 8   Indian Yellow-flax
A bushy, shrubby plant with gold cup-shaped

flowers, 1–2 in. wide, doing best if pinched back to keep it compact. The alternate, elliptic leaves have a sharp tip at the end. Native to eastern India and sometimes mistaken for *Linum flavum* or Golden Flax.

RHAMNACEAE = The Buckthorn Family

RHAMNUS (RAM-nus). There are very few species in this large genus of shrubs and trees that have any value as landscape plants. They are deciduous or evergreen; the leaves are normally alternate, but occasionally opposite. They grow well in normal soil; their fruits are small berries, mostly black at maturity, and some are easily distributed by the birds, sometimes so much so as to become pests. *R. frangula* and *R. cathartica* are in this category.

Propagation

Seed may be stratified as soon as ripe for 3 months at 40° F., then sown; or they can be stored dry in airtight containers in a cool place for up to a year and then stratified and sown. Various *Rhamnus* species and varieties are grafted, using their own roots as understock, or they may be rooted by softwood cuttings, which see.

alaternus   15′   Zone 7   Italian Buckthorn
The small flowers of this evergreen shrub are borne in short racemes during March and April, and the black berries appear during the summer. Native to the Mediterranean Region, its flowers are polygamo-dioecious and the foliage is lustrous.

californica   15′   Zone 7   Coffee-berry
Evergreen shrub, native to Calif. and Ore.; leaves 1–4 in. long, with small, inconspicuous flowers and red to black berries in Aug. and Sept., about ⅓ in. wide. A new selection, 'Sea View', has been made of this species, not much over 4 ft. tall and recommended for planting on banks. The flowers are most attractive to bees.

caroliniana   30′   Zone 5   Indian-cherry
A shrub or small tree with fruits in the early fall changing from red to black and sweet to the taste, with foliage turning yellow at the same time that the fruit ripens. Native throughout much of the eastern U.S. from N.Y. southward and west to Neb. and Tex.

cathartica   18′   Zone 2   Common Buckthorn
Native to Europe and Asia, this plant has escaped cultivation in the eastern U.S. It grows vigorously, is easily identified from other shrubs because the short branchlets are often tipped with a sharp thorn and, like the other buckthorns, the alternate leaves have parallel veins. Male and female flowers have been noted to be

Rhamnus cathartica (Buckthorn)—showing fruits and thorns.

on separate plants and the fruits are small black berries. It is hardy throughout the colder parts of the U.S. and has been used in clipped hedges, especially in poor soils where better plants will not grow. It is certainly not good enough to be used as a specimen plant.

davurica   30′   Zone 2   Dahurian Buckthorn
Extremely hardy, this Buckthorn from the colder parts of northeastern Asia is a vigorous grower with lustrous foliage and shiny black berries, ¼ in. in dia., in the fall. It is similar to *R. cathartica*.

frangula   18′   Zone 2   Alder Buckthorn
This is the most ornamental of the buckthorns, but, like the others, can be quickly spread by seeds. The dark, lustrous green foliage of this deciduous plant is especially meritorious and makes a fine impression in the garden. It is native to Europe, western Asia and North Africa. The dense habit, rapid growth and ¼-in.-wide fruits that turn from green to red to black before they are eaten by the birds are of special importance, since they appear while the shrub is still bearing most of its small white flowers, which continue throughout the summer. This has been grown in America since colonial times and certainly must be naturalized in some places.

Two varieties of importance are:

'Asplenifolia'—an unusual cut-leaved variety of very fine texture;

'Columnaris'—probably the best of all the few columnar shrubs available at present; this is sometimes called "Tallhedge" and was patented in 1955 by the Cole Nursery Company of Painesville, Ohio. As a hedge it needs no shearing on the sides, but merely a quick shearing on the top once every other year or so to keep it properly restrained.

purshiana   45′   Zone 6   Cascara Buckthorn
A West Coast Buckthorn, in use there for the same general purposes that *R. caroliniana* is used in the southeastern U.S. The flowers are very small and the fruits are purplish-black berries.

RHAPIS species   18′   Zone 9   Lady Palms
R. humilies is a fan palm reaching 9–18 ft., each leaf having 10–20 leaf segments. **R. excelsa** is smaller growing, only about 5 ft. tall, and each leaf bearing 5–8 broad leaflets, somewhat similar to those of bamboos like the *Sasa palmata*. Both species do well in shade and make good ornamental specimens. They grow in clumps, something few palms do. These grow well in southern Fla., southern Calif. and Hawaii.

RHEUM (REE-um)
rhabarbarum (*rhaponticum*)   2½′   Zone 3
                                    Garden Rhubarb
A native to Siberia, this deep-rooted, perennial herb is in almost every vegetable garden, and with a minimum amount of attention lasts indefinitely. The leaf blades may be 18 in. across, on long, succulent, acid-tasting stalks, as much as 2½ ft. long. The flowering stalks are up to 6 ft. tall, with small greenish-white or reddish flowers. Although the leaf stalks are edible, the leaf blades are poisonous to man and animals and cases have been reported of death to man and swine from eating them. See RHUBARB.

RHEXIA (REX-ia). A group of attractive North American perennial herbs which are bog plants with showy petals. The fruit is a dry, 4-valved capsule.

lutea   6″–10″   Zone 8   Yellow Meadow-beauty
A hairy perennial with opposite, elliptic, sessile leaves and bearing flowers in loosely branched, terminal clusters on short, branching stems in the upper leaf axils. Each flower has a bulbous, 4-lobed calyx and 4 petals, with the pistil and 8 stamens projecting down over the lower petal. It is an attractive plant, although limited to use in southern bog gardens. It may be found in swamps from N.Car. to Fla. and La., and blooms throughout the spring and summer.

mariana   1′–2′   Zone 4   Maryland Meadow-
                                    beauty
Growing somewhat taller than *R. lutea*, this species has opposite, oblong-linear leaves on a hairy stem and pale purple flowers about 1 in.

wide. It, too, grows in swamps and wetlands, extending northward to Mass. and west to Ky. It flowers throughout the summer.

virginica   9″–15″   Zone 3   Common Meadow-
                                    beauty
This perennial species has square, nearly smooth stems and ovate to lanceolate leaves. The purple flowers, in few-flowered clusters, are 1½ in. wide and very handsome. It is native to the swamplands from southeastern Canada to Ga. and Mo., and blooms from July to Sept. Propagation is by division of the plants in spring.

RHIZOME. An underground stem, often enlarged by food storage.

RHIZOPHORA (ry-ZOFF-ora)
mangle   40′–80′   Zone 10   American Man-
                                    grove
Native to southern Fla., the West Indies, Central and South America, this tree grows at the edge of salt water and in brackish swamps. This plant bears thick, leathery, opposite leaves and the seeds start to germinate on the tree before the fruits drop. When they do fall, they become buried in the mud and start growth at once. Stilt roots grow from the branches to the ground beneath and in this way the trees form impenetrable tangles. The trees do protect shorelines from erosion, and so are valued.

RHODODENDRON (ro-do-DEN-dron). Over 4000 species, varieties and hybrids of this versatile genus have been catalogued as being grown in America. They come from all parts of the world. Some have been cultivated for a century or more, while others have come from comparatively recent exploration in the southern and southeastern sections of Asia. About 30 species are native to North America.

Botanically, azaleas are classified as rhododendrons (for differences, see AZALEA) and will be so treated here. Because all of these do better in a cool, moist climate with plenty of moisture in the atmosphere, and because they need acid soil and soil moisture as well, they cannot be grown in all parts of the U.S. It has become evident that the area around Seattle, Wash., is ideal for these plants, and more species and varieties are proving hardy there than in any other area of North America.

It is difficult, if not impossible, to grow rhododendrons in a large part of the central U.S. where neither soil, climate nor moisture conditions are conducive to their good growth.

Most of the azaleas are deciduous, although a few are evergreen. They are to be differentiated from rhododendrons in that they have 5 stamens (rhododendrons have 10 or more). Of course, they have been hybridized and there are literally hundreds of clones valued for their bright-colored flowers. The main hybrid groups are

"Exbury," "Gable," "Ghent," "Glenn Dale," "Indian," "Kaempferi," "Knapp Hill," "Kurume," and "Mollis."

For detailed information about all azaleas, see Galle, Fred, "Azaleas," Timber Press, P.O. Box 1632, Beaverton, OR 97075.

The leathery-leaved evergreen rhododendrons are valued landscape plants wherever growing conditions are suitable. In the urban areas of the northeastern U.S., only those species and hybrids hardy in Zones 4, 5 and 6 can be grown, but in the warmer parts of the South and especially in the moist areas of the Pacific Northwest, many of the tender species are being tried. For detailed information concerning all the species and varieties of the evergreen rhododendrons, see Leach, David G., "Rhododendrons of the World," Charles Scribner's Sons, New York, N.Y.

Culture

Rhododendrons and azaleas must be grown in cool, moist, acid soil that is not exposed for long periods to the hot summer sun. They will not do well in sandy or gravelly soil that dries out quickly and often. Rather, they like a soil with plenty of humus or decaying organic matter, for this not only supplies food for the roots, but it aids materially in keeping the soil moist. The feeding roots of these plants are very close to the surface and because of this they are very susceptible to heat and drought. To forestall this, a good rhododendron soil must contain plenty of humus.

The soil, of course, must be acid, of a pH between 4.5 and 6.5. If the garden contains alkaline soil, spots may be made acid with special preparation, but it is not really worth the effort specially to prepare the soil to make it acid—and then keep it acid indefinitely. It is much easier to give up growing azaleas and rhododendrons and concentrate on other plants that will grow without special soil preparation.

A mulch is always excellent—it keeps the ground cool and moist throughout the summer. Materials such as pine needles, peat moss or oak leaves are ideal, for they produce an acid reaction in the soil as they disintegrate. There are many other suitable mulches which might be used, but whatever the material, it should be about 2–3 in. deep, no deeper. It need not be removed in the spring, but may be left on permanently, if not too deep. As it decomposes, more mulch may be added every other year or so. One should refrain from using maple or elm leaves, for these do not produce an acid soil reaction when they decompose and the maple leaves pack down so tightly that they may be a deterrent to good growth.

Because rhododendrons require moist soil,

they should be watered thoroughly at least once every other week during droughts. Like all evergreens, they should not be allowed to go into the winter in dry soil, so just before the ground freezes they should be given plenty of water to make certain that they have sufficient before the winter when their roots can obtain no more.

Picking off the dead flower clusters as soon as they fade is a good practice, though not absolutely necessary. The theory is that it prevents

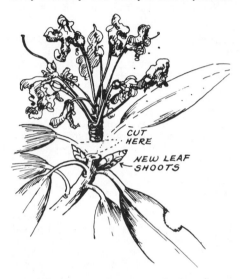

Rhododendron—Removing dead flower clusters to prevent seed formation·

the plant from wasting nutrients in seed production. Rather, the nutrients should be used for the formation of flower buds for the next year.

Most evergreen rhododendrons and many of the azaleas grow better if they have some shade, especially in the hot summer months. They also show less foliage windburn if planted in a situation where they are not repeatedly exposed to high winter winds. In fact, young plants might even be protected over winter the first year or so with a screen of evergreen boughs or burlap.

Pruning is not so easy in America as it is in certain humid areas of Europe where rhododendrons are sometimes clipped as a hedge, or cut to the ground when too robust, with the expectation that they will quickly grow back into good form. Here in America, with its dry, hot summers, one must be careful to prune early in the spring so that the plant will have plenty of time to send out new shoots before the fall. Also, one should always be certain to cut back to a bud or small shoot, and not to cut off large branches with no buds or shoots below the cut, and expect them to produce new buds, like a Privet or a Forsythia. This they will not do. So, they can be pruned if it is done intelligently and if some obvious growing points are left below the pruning cut.

Pruning azaleas is simple. Merely cut back or cut out the older branches at the base of the plant as needed. Many an azalea never needs pruning, but when one does, the chances are that if this older wood is at least partially removed, the younger branches will soon grow vigorously and the plant will be quickly rejuvenated.

Fertilizers are needed occasionally. Well-rotted manure is satisfactory. Then one may use the commercial fertilizers which leave an acid reaction in the soil. Ammonium sulfate is often suggested, but one should be extremely careful not to apply too much, for this quickly kills plant tissue if applied over-generously.

Finally, one planting suggestion might be remembered. Both azaleas and rhododendrons are frequently used in foundation plantings and the buildings may be of brick and mortar or plain stucco, with a large amount of exposed cement. Rain, splashing continually on such surfaces, dissolves a certain amount of lime from these materials and frequently it is not long before the ericaceous plants in such a planting begin to weaken and die, due, of course, to the fact that the soil is becoming more and more alkaline. When this is the case, steps should be taken to reacidify the soil by adding the proper amount of aluminum sulfate. The state experiment station, or a soil analyst, can suggest the proper amount, after making a simple pH test of the soil involved.

Rhododendrons and azaleas are always moved with a ball of soil about the roots, for, as has been previously mentioned, the feeding roots are close to the surface and as many roots as possible should be left unharmed in the moving operation.

The surest way to have good rhododendrons and azaleas is to plant them in the proper soil at the start, mulch them well and water them during droughts. A yearly application of the proper fertilizer sometimes helps, and sometimes is not at all necessary.

Propagation

Seed can be sown as soon as ripe, or can be stored dry in an airtight container in a cool place for up to a year before being sown. Grafting of the evergreen types has been done in the past, using *R. ponticum* as the understock, but most growers today either grow their species from seed collected from pure stands, or root softwood or hardwood cuttings. Advances in plant propagation have proceeded to a point where grafting is no longer a necessary practice. Rhododendrons (the evergreen, broad-leaved species), with few exceptions, root easily if cuttings are taken any time after the new growth shows firmness. In the Boston, Mass., area, suitable timing would be from July into midwinter. Deciduous azaleas propagate well from softwood cuttings taken early in the growing season. Evergreen azaleas can be rooted throughout the summer. See CUTTINGS.

Since it has been noted that the Ghent azaleas may be difficult to root from cuttings, the following notes by Roger Coggeshall, former Propagator at the Arnold Arboretum, regarding proper techniques in this respect, may be of interest.

Rooting Ghent Azaleas under Polyethylene Plastic

The cuttings are rooted under wire frames covered with plastic. The frames are constructed of turkey wire, No. 9 gauge, with 2 in. × 4 in. squares. The wire is bent to allow a 10-in. distance from the surface of the medium to the inside top of the wire. Frames are 4 ft. long, with the width determined by the width of the bench used.

A mixture of one-third sand, one-third peat and one-third ground Styrofoam has proved to be the best rooting medium. The cuttings not only root more heavily but also produce a uniform root system. The type of peat used in this combination is optional.

This rooting mixture is heated by a lead-covered cable, thermostatically controlled. The thermostat is set to turn on the current at 72° F., but only at night, since in the daytime there is sufficient heat beneath the polyethylene plastic. The everyday temperature outside the greenhouse is high and the heat builds up accordingly. On many days the median temperature is 85° to 95° F., a factor which aids in the successful rooting of Ghent azaleas.

After the cuttings have been placed in the medium, they are flooded with water and the frames are placed over them. The medium is never pounded. After this, the ends and sides of the frames are covered completely with sheets of 2-mil. polyethylene plastic. This same type of structure can be used equally well over flats of cuttings. Whatever kind of structure is used, the plastic must be completely sealed.

TIMING. Before the introduction of polyethylene plastic, it was necessary to wait until the new growth had set a terminal bud and had begun to harden off before the cutting material could be collected, because the softer, more succulent cuttings would wilt. Now, however, by use of polyethylene covers to maintain conditions of high relative humidity, it is possible to collect the cutting material from soft, succulent growth.

Prior to the use of polyethylene plastic covers, cuttings of Ghent azaleas were not collected until late July or early Aug., when growth had matured to a point at which it could be kept from wilting under open-bench conditions. This was accomplished by shading the cuttings with newspaper or cheesecloth and syringing them manually at least once every hour. The procedure, however, did not give good results.

Now it is possible to collect the cutting material in late May or early June. Collected at this time, the cuttings not only root faster, but also root more heavily, because of the soft growth used. Once the cuttings are rooted, every attempt is made to stimulate new vegetative growth. This helps in the successful overwintering of Ghent azaleas and can be accomplished successfully by using artificial lights.

ARTIFICIAL LIGHTS. After the potting operation, the azaleas are placed on an open bench under a single row of 100-watt incandescent lights. The lights are spaced 2 ft. apart in the row and 15 in. above the level of the bench; the benches themselves are 32 in. wide. The lights are operated in the following manner:

At 5 p.m. the lights are turned on and left on all night until 8 a.m. One can eliminate the overlap of artificial light and normal daylight by using a time clock. The plants are kept under the row of lights for approximately 2 months. During this period, the terminal buds break dormancy and produce 2 to 8 in. of new growth. This new growth is then hardened off, and the cuttings are overwintered in a cold pit, where the temperature is 35° to 40° F.

CUTTING PROCEDURE. The cutting material is collected in late May or early June, whenever the new growth is 2 or 3 in. long—long enough to make a cutting. Cuttings are placed immediately in polyethylene plastic bags, which contain a small quantity of moistened sphagnum, and stored in a refrigerator at 40° F. until they are used, sometimes 5–7 days.

One prepares the cuttings for rooting by stripping the leaves from the bottom inch and making a fresh cut at the basal end. Once the basal end has been recut, the cutting is dipped first into water and then into the hormone powder, Hormodin No. 3. Whether or not wounding is advisable depends upon the condition of the cutting material. When soft, succulent material is used, the value of wounding is questionable. However, when firmer cutting material is collected in July and Aug., a wound is definitely beneficial.

Once treated with Hormodin No. 3, the cuttings are placed in the sand, peat and Styrofoam medium, where they take from 2 to 3

months to root. When rooted, they are potted into 2½-in. standard pots and placed on a bench under artificial lights. In conclusion:

1. The asexual propagation of Ghent azaleas is definitely feasible when polyethylene plastic is used.
2. The use of artificial lights is a necessity if these varieties are to be overwintered successfully in commercial quantities.
3. The use of a wound on soft, succulent cuttings is not necessary.
4. A medium of sand, peat and Styrofoam, mixed in thirds by volume, produces a more uniform root system than a half-and-half mixture of sand and peat alone.

ROGER COGGESHALL

Azalea Insect Pests

Azalea bark scale, a small scale with white woolly covering, clusters in the axils of the branches and weakens the plants where numerous. Applications of insecticide #15 in midsummer are used. Azalea lace bug, a black and white sucking insect, on the underside of leaves often is abundant on the evergreen varieties of Azalea. Infested leaves show a mottled discoloration on the upper side. There are 3 or more generations annually. Sprays of insecticide #9 are effective and good control of the first generation usually eliminates later treatments. Azalea leaf miner causes yellow leaves which fall prematurely. Use insecticide #15 when necessary.

Azalea Diseases

Flower spot, a fungus which spots and completely collapses the flowers, spreads rapidly under favorable conditions, so that the flowers of a large planting may be destroyed in a few days. Hand picking the infected flowers and renewing mulch annually help to reduce infection. Spraying with fungicide #F has been effective in experiments. See Rhododendron for other diseases. Mushroom root-rot fungus lives in the soil and planting in infected soil should be avoided.

Rhododendron Insect Pests

Rhododendron borer, the larva of a clearwing moth, kills or weakens many branches of older plants. Cut and destroy infected branches as soon as observed. When the moths are active in early summer, spraying with insecticide #9 is recommended. Rhododendron lace bug is similar to azalea lace bug in development and control. See AZALEA. Azalea bark scale also lives on rhododendrons. See AZALEA. Some wasps bite holes in the leaves of Rhododendron and chew them to make paperlike nests, but no control is suggested.

Rhododendron Diseases

Rhododendron wilt, caused by a fungus attacking the roots and lower stem, is a serious disease of young plants, particularly hybrids. Destroy infected plants and adjust soil and general growing conditions. Die back in the form of watersoaked areas on leaves and cankers on wood may kill branches or the entire plant. Cut and burn infected branches and spray with fungicide #D, #K or #G. At least 7 different fungi may cause leaf spots which are controlled by timely sprays of fungicide #D. Bud blast or bud blight prevents blooms from opening normally. Picking and burning infected blooms and resulting seed pods is advised.

Species and Varieties

albrechtii **4½′** **Zone 5** **Albrecht Azalea**
Not yet commonly grown, this is native to Japan, with uniform, unique, red to rose flowers, 2 in. in dia., blooming in mid-May. Autumn color is yellow, with deciduous leaves 3–5 in. long. This should be grown much more than it is, for the unique soft color is uniform and good.

ambiguum **10′** **Zone 7**
The flowers of this Chinese evergreen rhododendron are lemon-yellow spotted with green, about 1½ in. across, appearing in May, and are not very outstanding. The leaves are 1½–3 in. long and the whole plant is neat and compact.

anthopogon **2′** **Zone 7** **Sulfur Rhododendron**
An evergreen from the Himalayan mountains, with sulfur-yellow flowers, ¾ in. across, and evergreen leaves, rusty scaly beneath, that are ¾–1½ in long. Not particularly ornamental.

arborescens **9′** **Zone 4** **Sweet Azalea**
An unusually fragrant, deciduous azalea with white flowers in mid-June, this is native from Pa. to Ga., chiefly in the mountains. The deciduous leaves are 1 in. long and bright green, turning a dark, glossy red in the fall. **'Rubescens'** has flowers tinged a purplish pink and is rarely found, but is well worth cultivating.

arboreum **50′** **Zone 7** **Tree Rhododendron**
One of the most vividly colored of all the evergreen rhododendrons, this has been much used in hybridizing, and has imparted the beautiful scarlet of its flowers to many of its hardier hybrids. The flowers are 1½–2 in. across, borne in trusses 5½ in. across, and containing 12–20 flowers in a truss. These appear in April. The leaves are usually 4–8 in. long and 1–2½ in. wide. Native to the Himalayas.

atlanticum **1½′** **Zone 6** **Coast Azalea**
One of the very few azaleas that are stoloniferous; used to some extent in naturalistic plantings for its very fragrant, white flowers which are flushed crimson, 1½ in. across, and which appear in late May. The deciduous leaves are 1–2½ in. long. Native from Del. to S.Car.

augustinii **15′** **Zone 6** **Augustine Rhododendron**
Usually this rhododendron, with flowers varying from lavender-rose to blue, is seen in cultivation growing at a height under 10 ft. The flowers are 1½–2 in. across, in clusters of 3, blooming in May. The evergreen leaves are 1–3 in. long and the plant often has a leggy habit. Not a very ornamental shrub, it is native to China and roots easily from cuttings.

auriculatum **15′** **Zone 6** **Earleaf Rhododendron**
Blooming in July and Aug., this Chinese rhododendron has fragrant, white to pinkish flowers, 2½–4 in. across, in 7–15-flowered umbels. The leaves are 5–12 in. long and evergreen. The plant will grow in the shade, but needs considerable atmospheric moisture to do its best.

auritum **5′** **Zone 8**
Native to Tibet, this plant has inch-long flowers, creamy white to yellow or occasionally the white flowers are tinged with pink, with 4–7 flowers in each truss. Foliage is evergreen.

baileyi **6′** **Zone 7**
The reddish-purple flowers of this evergreen rhododendron appear in May; they are about ½ in. long, with 5–18 flowers in each truss. The leaves are 1¼–2½ in. long and are rust colored on the under side. Native to Tibet.

barbatum **30′** **Zone 7** **Giantblood Rhododendron**
The flowers of this Himalayan rhododendron are 1 in. long and crimson to scarlet or blood red, in small trusses 4 in. wide, and appear in March or April. The dull, evergreen leaves are 4–10 in. long. Apparently this plant is difficult to grow.

caeruleum **5′** **Zone 6**
Native to China, having 3 or 4 white to rose-lavender flowers in each truss. Each flower is ¾ in. long and the evergreen leaves are 1¼ in. long.

calendulaceum **9′ rarely 15′** **Zone 5** **Flame Azalea**
The most showy of the native American azaleas, this has yellow, orange and reddish-orange flowers in early June, after the leaves are fully developed. It has the unique property of retaining its colorful flowers in good condition in the full sun for nearly 2 full weeks. Native from Pa. to Ga. and greatly appreciated by visitors to the Great Smoky Mountains when the flowers bloom in mid-June, this is an excellent species for landscape work. The deciduous leaves are 1½–3½ in. long. Plants with yellow flowers have the varietal name **croceum**; those with orange to scarlet flowers, **aurantiacum**. Many excellent clones have this species as one of the parents.

**calophytum   36′   Zone 6   Bigleaf Rhododen-
dron**
This blooms in March and April, having white
to rose flowers 2–2½ in. dia., and evergreen
leaves 8–12 in. long. Native to China, it requires
plenty of shade and moisture, but is valued
especially for its very early bloom.

**calostrotum   1′   Zone 6   Purple-elf Rhodo-
dendron**
Native to Burma, with reddish-purple flowers,
1½ in. across, appearing in May and evergreen
leaves about an inch long and half as wide.

**campanulatum   15′   Zone 5   Bellflower
Rhododendron**
A rhododendron with white, pink or purplish-
blue flowers, about 2 in. across, bell-shaped, in
a compact truss, blooming in April, and with
evergreen leaves 3–5½ in. long. Native to the
Himalayas. The foliage of this is excellent,
making a fine ornamental specimen, but the
flowers are not especially outstanding.

**campylocarpum   4′–12′   Zone 6   Honeybell
Rhododendron**
A small, rounded, evergreen bush, native to the
Himalayas, with clear, canary-yellow, slightly
fragrant flowers, 1½ in. long and 2 in. wide,
blooming in June. There are not many yellow-
flowering rhododendrons, so this is often a
valued specimen.

canadense   3′   Zone 2   Rhodora
This deciduous plant, native to swampy areas of
Canada and New England, has rose-purple
flowers before the leaves appear in mid-May.
There is a variety **'Albiflorum'** with white
flowers. Leaves are 1–2 in. long. The flowers do
not make the show of many other azaleas, but
in naturalistic plantings or in bogs where they
grow well they show off to excellent advantage.

**carolinianum   6′   Zone 5   Carolina Rhodo-
dendron**
An evergreen, this is excellent for its pale, rosy-
purple flowers in mid-May. The leaves, about
3 in. long, are brownish on the under side.
Native to N.Car. Compact in habit, generally
rounded in outline. One of the first rhododendrons to "roll" its leaves when the temperature
approaches 20° F., this is a natural method of
protecting its leaves, but detracts somewhat
from its appearance. The variety **'Album'** has
white flowers. An excellent and serviceable
rhododendron, one of the very best and most
popular.

**catawbiense   6′ rarely to 18′   Zone 4   Catawba
Rhododendron**
Native from Va. to Ga., this evergreen with
leaves 2½–5 in. long is native throughout the
Great Smoky Mountains. The flowers are a
poor color, lilac-purple, spotted olive-green on
the inside of the corolla, but the variety **album**
has white flowers, 2¼ in. wide, with yellow

The habitat of *Rhododendron catawbiense* is in
the Great Smoky Mountains. Here they cover
the mountain side at Craggy Gardens, North
Carolina. (*Photo by Arnold Arboretum, Jamaica
Plain, Mass.*)

markings. 'Compactum' is a dense, rounded,
compact form. Many hybrids are available,
having the excellent foliage of this species but
better flowers. Some of the better clones are:

FLOWER COLOR
'Albert'—white to pastel lilac
'Album Grandiflorum'—white
'Amphion'—fuchsia-purple
'Arno'—double flowers, purplish
'Atrosanguineum'—spiraea red
'Charles Dickens'—red
'Everestianum'—rosy lilac
'Henrietta Sargent'—Persian rose
'Kettledrum'—magenta
'Lady Armstrong'—purplish pink
'Mrs. C. S. Sargent'—Persian rose
'Present Lincoln'—amaranth rose
'Purpureum Elegans'—violet
'Purpureum Grandiflorum'—purple
'Roseum Elegans'—fuchsia-purple
'Wellesleyanum'—white, tinged pink

**caucasicum   2′   Zone 6   Caucasian Rhodo-
dendron**
Native to the Caucasus Mountains, this has
evergreen leaves 2–4 in. long, rusty colored
beneath, and white to yellowish flowers, 1½ in.
long and as much across, with wavy margins,
blooming during May. It is not very often used
as a cultivated ornamental specimen.

ciliatum   6′   Zone 7   Fringed Rhododendron
White to rose-colored, bell-shaped flowers,
1½–2 in. across, in March or April; with evergreen leaves 1½–4 in. long. Native to the mountains of Sikkim.

**cinnabarinum   15′   Zone 6   Cinnabar Rhodo-
dendron**
With funnel-formed flowers, 2¾ in. long and
1¼ in. across, red, orange, yellow, pink and
purple, but usually brick-red; blooming in May;

doing very well in England. The evergreen leaves are $3\frac{1}{2}$ in. long and $1\frac{3}{4}$ in. across. Native to the mountains of Sikkim.

crassum   15′   Zone 8   Sweetbay Rhododendron
A sweet-scented, tender, evergreen, Chinese rhododendron, blooming in June, with white flowers $2\frac{1}{4}$–$3\frac{1}{2}$ in. long and 4 in. across. The black-green, glossy, evergreen leaves are $2\frac{1}{4}$–6 in. long.

davidsonianum   10′   Zone 7   Davidson Rhododendron
An evergreen shrub with white, pink or rose flowers, 1–$1\frac{1}{2}$ in across, during April and May, the leaves being 1–$2\frac{1}{2}$ in. long. It does not do very well in the eastern U.S., but is fine in Great Britain. Native to China.

decorum   18′   Zone 5   Sweetshell Rhododendron
This shrub has white to pink flowers in early June and evergreen leaves 2–6 in. long. The fragrant, waxy flowers are excellent, but it should be given light shade and some protection within the northern limits of its hardiness range. It is popular with gardeners wherever it can be grown. It is native to western China.

diaprepes   15′–25′   Zone 7
A fine evergreen rhododendron from southwestern Yunnan Province in China, this has white to pale rose flowers in June and July. They are up to 4 in. long and 5 in. across, slightly fragrant. The leaves are 7–12 in. long and $2\frac{3}{4}$ in. wide.

discolor   15′   Zone 6   Mandarin Rhododendron
A fragrant, Chinese, evergreen rhododendron, with white to pale pink flowers in June and leaves up to 8 in. long. One of its important features is its late bloom, making it a popular specimen plant.

drumonium   2′   Zone 6   Woodelf Rhododendron
Native to Yunnan Province in China, with mauve to magenta flowers, $\frac{1}{2}$ in. across in April, and evergreen leaves less than $\frac{1}{3}$ in. long.

edgeworthii   8′–10′   Zone 9   Edgeworth Rhododendron
Another evergreen rhododendron from the Himalayan Mountains of Sikkim, this very tender species blooms in April and May; with white to pink, very fragrant flowers, 3–4 in. long and $4\frac{1}{2}$ in. across, but having only 2–3 flowers in a cluster. It grows into a straggling bush with evergreen leaves, $1\frac{1}{2}$–$4\frac{1}{2}$ in. long, that have a felty covering of pubescence underneath. In planting, the gardener should place several specimens close together as a means of overcoming this straggling habit.

Exbury Hybrids. See Knapp Hill and Exbury Hybrids.

fargesii   10′   Zone 6   Pere Farges Rhododendron
An excellent, Chinese, evergreen shrub with white, pink or rose flowers, $1\frac{1}{2}$ in. across, which blooms floriferously in early April. This may grow as far north as Cape Cod, Mass., and is one of the rhododendrons that should have the dead flowers removed; otherwise it will injure itself with excessive seed production. The leaves are 2–3 in. long. It is an excellent foliage plant.

ferrugineum   4′   Zone 4   Rock Rhododendron
Native to the southern European Alps, this has evergreen leaves, 1–$1\frac{1}{2}$ in. long, and rose-crimson to white flowers that are only $\frac{3}{4}$ in. across, appearing in June. It tends to be rather open at the base and needs correctional pruning to overcome this. Not especially popular in America because of the extra attention it requires to keep it looking well.

fictolacteum   25′   Zone 6   Corrietree Rhododendron
A shapely evergreen tree form from China, this has white to ivory or rose flowers in April and May, the flowers 7- to 8-lobed, $1\frac{1}{2}$ in. long and $2\frac{1}{2}$ in. across, spotted and blotched with deep crimson. The evergreen leaves are 5–12 in. long and 2–5 in wide, with a colorful orange tomentum underneath; hence it has considerable value as a foliage plant in the garden.

flavidum   3′   Zones 6–7   Amberbloom Rhododendron
A low shrub, having light green, scaly leaves, about $\frac{1}{2}$ in. long, and clusters of small, pale yellow flowers in spring. Native to China. There are only 3–6 flowers per cluster, each flower about $\frac{3}{4}$ in. wide.

flavum = *R. luteum*

floccigerum   6′   Zone 6   Tuft-wool Rhododendron
A Chinese evergreen rhododendron from Yunnan Province, blooming in March or April, with crimson, rose or yellow flowers in loose, 4–7-flowered trusses, each flower about $1\frac{1}{4}$ in. long. The leaves at first are woolly-tomentose beneath, but as they mature this disappears and they are glaucous.

fortunei   12′   Zone 6   Fortune Rhododendron
An evergreen rhododendron from eastern China, with leaves 4–8 in. long and rosy lilac or blush, fragrant flowers in late May. The individual flowers are as much as $3\frac{1}{2}$ in. across and some of the hybrids have flowers as much as 5 in. across. Many are being grown now from Boston, Mass., southward along the East Coast and in the Northwest Pacific area, also. Among the better hybrids of this species are:

FLOWER COLOR
'Ben Moseley'—pink
'Duke of York'—mauve, $3\frac{1}{2}$ in. dia.
'Ernest Gill'—rose-carmine

'Essex Scarlet'—deep crimson
'Luscombei'—rose-pink
'Scintillation'—pink
'Sunset'—pale yellow, shaded pink
'Wissahickon'—bright red

GABLE HYBRID AZALEAS. Joseph B. Gable of Stewartstown, Pa., crossed some azaleas, mostly *R. yedoense poukhanense* and *R. obtusum kaempferi*, and obtained some hardy evergreen clones, many fairly hardy in Zone 5 but not completely evergreen that far north. Most have flowers 1½–2¼ in. across, predominantly of purple or purplish shades. Some of the varieties are:

FLOWER COLOR

'Big Joe'—reddish violet, 2½ in. dia.
'Caroline Gable'—red, 1¾ in. dia.
'Chinook'—orange-red, 2 in. dia.
'Herbert'—reddish violet, hose in hose, 1¾ in. dia.
'Kathleen'—clear pink
'La Première'—violet-red, very double, 1¾ in. dia.
'Mary Dalton'—orange-red, hose in hose, 1½ in. dia.
'Old Faithful'—reddish violet, 2¼ in. dia.
'Rosebud'—violet-red, double, 1¾ in. dia.
'Springtime'—violet-red, 1¾ in. dia.
'Stewartstonian'—clear red
'Viola'—reddish violet, 2¾ in. dia.

x gandavense 6'–10' Zone 4 Ghent Azalea
This hybrid group includes many deciduous azaleas of mixed parentage, some of which are hardy as far north as central Me. They have white, pink or red single or double flowers in late May, according to variety. They are of hybrid origin (*R. flavum* x *R. mortieri*). A bright-colored ornamental group, some of the better varieties are:

SINGLE FLOWERS

'Altaclarensis'—orange-yellow
'Beauté Celeste'—scarlet
'Bijou des Amateurs'—light pink
'Charlemagne'—coral to orange
'Coccinea Speciosa'—red
'Comte de Flandres'—carmine
'Cymodece'—light pink
'Flamboyant'—orange
'Furst Camille von Rohan'—white to yellowish
'General Trauff'—rose, shaded orange
'Gloria Mundi'—fire red
'Heureuse Surprise'—white, shaded rose
'Irene Koster'—light pink
'Nancy Waterer'—yellow
'Pallas'—brilliant reddish orange
'Pucelle'—rose
'Unique'—bronze

DOUBLE FLOWERS

'Bijou de Gentbrugge'—white, flushed pink
'Graf von Meran'—rose, white center

'Narcissiflora'—sulfur yellow
'Raphael de Smet'—white, flushed pink
'Souvenir du President Carnot'—orange and brick-red.

giganteum 80' Zone 9 Giant Rhododendron
This is the tallest of all the evergreen rhododendrons and it takes many years before the plant produces its first flowers. Furthermore, it is hardy only in the very warmest parts of the U.S. It is not a plant for the small garden! The flowers are funnel-shaped, deep crimson, 2½ in. long and borne in trusses of 20–25, blooming between Jan. and March.

GLENN DALE HYBRID AZALEAS. Mr. B. Y. Morrison, formerly of the U.S. Department of Agriculture and first director of the National Arboretum in Washington, D.C., made many crosses in an attempt to obtain better azaleas for the Mid-Atlantic states. Nearly 500 varieties were selected and named (from 70,000 seedlings) at Glenn Dale, Md. Many species and varieties were used as parents, including the Indian hybrid azaleas, the Kaempferi hybrids, *R. mucronatum* and *R. yedoense poukhanense*. Some of the resulting clones have flowers as large as 4½ in. wide. The habits of those selected vary widely, ranging from low, mounded types to tall types. Many bloom from mid-May to early June, but there are varieties among this large group which bloom from mid-April to mid-June. Most of the varieties are not hardy much north of Washington, D.C., but a few can be grown as far north as Boston, Mass. A few varieties are:

FLOWER COLOR

'Bacchante'—red with purple dots, 3 in. dia.
'Bayou'—white with occasional scarlet stripes, 2½ in. dia.
'Blushing Maid'—pink, 2½ in. dia.
'Campfire'—brilliant purple, 1½ in. dia.
'Green Mist'—white with greenish blotch, 2½ in. dia.
'Marjorie'—rose, 3 in. dia.
'Pink Ice'—double, mallow purple, 3 in. dia.
'Rosalie'—brilliant pink, 3 in. dia.
'Souvenir'—hose in hose, salmon pink, 1¼ in. dia.
'Vanity'—deep rose pink, 1¾ in. dia.
'Whitehouse'—white, 3¾ in. dia.
'Yeoman'—white, striped red, 2½ in. dia.

grande 30' Zone 8 Silvery Rhododendron
A Himalyan species, beautiful in its native habitat but very tender in America, having flowers 2–2½ in. long, white or cream with purple blotches. The evergreen leaves are 5½–15 in. long, 3–5 in. wide, and usually silvery tomentose on the under side. The truss is about 7 in. across with 25 flowers. Extremely popular in the warmer parts of Great Britain because of the large flower trusses.

griersonianum 8′ Zone 8 Grierson Rhododendron

With scarlet flowers, 2½–3 in. long and 3–4 in. across, blooming in June. Native to China, with evergreen leaves 3½–7 in. long and 1–2 in. wide, this is considered one of the better ornamental rhododendrons in England, but because it is tender, the areas where it can be grown in America are limited.

griffithianum 20′ Zone 8 Griffith Rhododendron

This has served as a parent for many valuable hybrids. It blooms in May, with white to pink, slightly fragrant, 5-lobed blossoms, 1½–2½ in. long and as much as 4½–6 in. across, with the edges often frilled. The evergreen leaves are 4–12 in. long and 1½–4 in. wide. Some consider these blossoms the best of all the rhododendrons. If it can be grown, it should have a sheltered situation with partial shade. It is native to the Himalayan mountains.

haematodes 4′–10′ Zone 7 Royalblood Rhododendron

A scarlet-flowering rhododendron from China, this has bell-shaped flowers, 1½–2 in. long and 2 in. across, in 6–8-flowered clusters during May. The dark evergreen leaves are 1½–2 in. long, lustrous above but covered with a beautiful reddish-brown tomentum underneath. A very popular garden species where it proves hardy.

hippophaeoides 3′ Zone 6 Sea Buckthorn Rhododendron

The common name is given this plant because it does resemble Sea Buckthorn at a distance, the evergreen leaves being pale green and only an inch long. The flowers are 1 in. across, varying in color from light blue to pale rose, and are borne in terminal trusses about 1½ in. across, appearing in April. It needs plenty of moisture, almost a boggy situation, in order to do well. It is native to China.

hirsutum 3′ Zone 4 Garland Rhododendron

Native to the mountains of Europe, this is one of the few evergreen rhododendrons which can grow in limestone soils. The leaves are about an inch long, ½ in. wide, slightly scaly beneath. The small flowers, about ½–¾ in. across, are rosy pink to rosy scarlet, produced in terminal clusters in June. Not especially outstanding except for its ability to grow in limestone soils.

impeditum 18″ Zone 4 Cloudland Rhododendron

A good rock garden plant, with blue flowers ⅔ in. across, appearing in April and May, and small evergreen leaves less than ½ in. long; native to China. It is easily cultivated and is compact in habit, but does not do well where there are hot, dry summers. Plenty of atmospheric moisture seems to be what it needs.

INDIAN HYBRID AZALEAS Zones 7–8

The large-flowered azaleas commonly grown in greenhouses in the North are at their best outdoors in the famous gardens of the Deep South. Both single- and double-flowered varieties are available, ranging in shades from white to rose, with many variegated forms, the flowers being from 1½–3 in. in dia. They are derived from a single species but are the result of crossbreeding a number of different species including *R. simsii*, *R. pulchrum*, *R. mucronatum* and others. Years ago this heterogenous mixture became known as the Indian azaleas, although *R. indicum* probably has had little to do with their ancestry and they certainly are not native to India. Some of the better varieties of this mixed evergreen group are:

FLOWER COLOR

'Alice'—deep rose, double
'Apollo'—vermillion red, semidouble
'Charles Pynaert'—salmon, bordered white, double
'Diamond'—white, blotched crimson
'Emil Leibig'—pink
'Fielder's White'—pure white, 2¼ in. dia.
'Flambeau'—crimson
'Fred Saunders'—salmon pink, double
'Mme. L. Van Houtte'—scarlet rose, bordered white
'Niobe'—white, double
'Professor Wolters'—pink with darker blotch
'Vervaeneana' — rose-salmon, variegated, double, 2¼ in. dia.

indicum 6′ Zone 6 Indica Azalea

An evergreen azalea species from Japan, with red to scarlet flowers, 2–3 in. across in late June, and leaves about 1½ in. long. It should not be confused with the so-called Indian hybrid azaleas which actually have little of this species in them, but more of *R. simsii*, *R. pulchrum* and *R. mucronatum*. 'Balasaminaeflorum' is a dwarf, double-flowered, salmon-red variety. Some varieties that have been used for forcing as house plants in the North are 'Lambertus C. Bobbink', bright velvety red; 'Paul Schame', double, salmon-pink; 'Jean Haerens', very double and rose-carmine; 'Niobe', large double white.

japonicum 6′ Zone 5 Japanese Azalea

A very hardy, deciduous azalea from Japan, with orange-red or salmon-red to brick-red flowers, 2–3 in. across, in late May. These have an obnoxious odor. The leaves are 1½–4 in. long. Valued because of its hardiness, it is often used in hybridizing work, but it should not be planted in large masses near the house because of the unpleasant odor of the flowers.

keiskei 8′ Zone 5 Keisk Rhododendron

Valued in the northern U.S. because it is the only hardy, yellow-flowered, evergreen rhododendron, this plant, native to Japan, has a rather straggly habit. The flowers are mimosa yellow, 1¾ in. wide, appearing in mid-May, and the leaves are up to 2¼ in. long.

KNAP HILL AND EXBURY HYBRID AZALEAS. These contain many gorgeous azaleas with brilliant colors, the flowers being 2–3 in. across, mostly single. Some have as many as 18–30 flowers in a single cluster. Colors range from white through cream, pink and orange to red. They originated in England in 1870, and many of the more recent hybrids originated on the English estate of Lionel de Rothschild. They were chiefly from *R. molle, R. occidentale* and *R. arborescens* crosses and are hardy in Zones 5 and 6. A few striking ones are:

FLOWER COLOR
'Brazil'—reddish orange
'Daybreak'—orange-yellow
'Debutante'—rose-pink
'Exbury White'—white
'Fireglow'—orange-vermillion
'Gibraltar'—orange
'Glowing Embers'—reddish orange
'Gold Dust'—deep yellow
'Hiawatha'—bright red
'Pink Ruffles'—pink
'Rocket'—apricot
'Satan'—scarlet
'Sun Chariot'—yellow, flowers 3½ in dia.

keleticum   6″   Zones 6–7   Lhasa Rhododendron

An interesting and useful rhododendron, since it has a prostrate habit. The small acuminate leaves are only ½ in. long, have a hairy margin and the funnel-form flowers, about an inch wide, are crimson with strong purple markings. This is an unusually beautiful rock garden plant where hardy. Native to Tibet.

x kosterianum   5′   Zone 5   Mollis Hybrid Azaleas

A cross between *R. mollis* and *R. japonicum,* the flowers of these deciduous clones range in color from yellow to red, in many combinations, blooming in late May. These are not so hardy as the Ghent azaleas. A few of the better varieties are:

FLOWER COLOR
'C. B. Van Nes'—fire red
'Comte de Gomer'—soft red
'Comte de Papadopoli'—rose, shaded orange
'Comtesse de Kerchove'—pale pink or orange
'Consul Ceresole'—porcelain rose, 3½ in. dia.
'Hugo Koster'—poppy red
'Otto Lilienthal'—ivory white
'Phidias'—light pink and yellow
'Snowdrift'—white

KURUME HYBRID AZALEAS. (Zones 6–7.) Most of these hybrid azaleas can be traced to the various forms of *R. obtusum.* As a group they are hardier than Indian azaleas, with smaller flowers, smaller leaves and a more compact habit. Some forms can be grown out-of-doors as far north as Long Island. Well over 50 varieties are available from American nurseries, many of them grown as greenhouse pot plants. Northern gardeners should not try to grow them in the garden, since with only a few exceptions they are not reliably hardy north of Zone 7. These flowers may be single or double, depending on the variety, usually delicate pink to bright scarlet, and about ¾–1½ in. wide. Most withstand clipping well. A few of the more popular varieties are:

FLOWER COLOR
'Bridesmaid'—salmon
'Coral Bells'—flowers hose in hose, red, 1⅛ in. dia.
'Debutante'—red, 1½ in dia.
'Hinodegiri'—red, 1½ in. dia., one of the most popular
'Lavender Queen'—reddish violet, 1¼ in. dia.
'Peach Blow'—carmine, 1¼ in. dia.
'Morning Glow'—rose, hose in hose, 1 in. dia.
'Salmon Beauty'—red, hose in hose, 1¾ in. dia.
'Yayegiri'—orange-red, hose in hose, 1½ in. dia.

x laetevirens   4′   Zone 4   Wilson Rhododendron

An evergreen hybrid (*R. carolinianum* x *R. ferrugineum*) with pink to purplish flowers, 1 in. wide, appearing in early June, and light green leaves 3½ in. long; this is a small, neat plant for the foundation planting or for a partly shaded spot in the rock garden. A good species, it should be used more.

lapponicum   1½′   Zone 2   Lapland Rhododendron

A prostrate evergreen shrub, native to the mountains of northern North America, Europe and Asia, with very small, purple, bell-shaped flowers ½ in. wide, appearing in June, and leaves only ¾ in. long. It has fine texture and does not grow well in areas with hot summers. Otherwise, it is a splendid plant for the rock garden or the front of the ericaceous border.

leucaspis   2′   Zone 7   Whiteshield Rhododendron

Native to Tibet, this little evergreen rhododendron has white flowers, 1¼ in. long and 2 in. wide, appearing in March and April. The leaves are 1½–2½ in. long. This is a fine, bushy, dwarf ornamental suitable for the Pacific Coast, though it needs protection from late frosts in order to be dependable.

x 'Loderi'   Zone 7

Actually, this is a large group of evergreen hybrids (*R. griffithianum* x *R. fortunei*) originated in 1901. A few of the popular clones are **'Loderi King George'**, blush white and fragrant;

'**Loderi Pink Diamond**', fragrant pink; '**Loderi Sir Joseph Hooker**', deep shell pink.

lutescens 15′ Zone 7 Canary Rhododendron
An evergreen rhododendron, native to China, having fragrant flowers, 1½ in. long, pale yellow spotted with green. The leaves are 1–3 in. long. Since the habit is loose and open, it should be planted as a thick mass of plants, possibly in partial shade. Roots easily from cuttings, and because it blooms so early in the spring, the flowers may be injured by late frosts.

macrophyllum 9′ Zone 6 California Rhododendron
An evergreen from the Pacific Coast, with pale rose to purplish flowers in early June and with leaves up to 8 in. long. It is the western counterpart of *R. catawbiense*, and on the mountains and in the gardens along the Pacific Coast it is a commonly appreciated evergreen plant.

maddenii 9′ Zone 9 Madden Rhododendron
Native to Sikkim, the plant has very fragrant, white flowers, 1¾ in. long, in summer. An evergreen, it is easy to grow and has ornamental interest throughout the year.

maximum 12′–36′ Zone 3 Rosebay Rhododendron
Perhaps the hardiest of the large evergreen rhododendrons, this has leaves 5–10 in. long and small rose-colored or purple-pink flowers in late June, after much of the current year's growth has been made; hence the flowers are frequently hidden. It should be given semi-shade, for it is found in rather open woods in eastern North America. Used not so much for its flowers as for its evergreen foliage in background plantings. Varieties **album** (with white flowers) and **purpureum** (with flowers deep pink to purple).

metternichii 8′ Zone 6 Metternich Rhododendron
The true *R. metternichii* is a fine plant, rarely found in cultivation, having bell-shaped, white to pale pink, 7-lobed flowers, about 3 in. wide, with 12–14 flowers in each truss, the flowers appearing in May. The evergreen leaves are 4–6 in. long. Native to Japan.

micranthum 5′ Zone 3 Manchurian Rhododendron
The evergreen leaves are only ¾–1¾ in. long, and the small white flowers, appearing in June, are produced in many flowered terminal clusters 2 in. across. From a distance the flowering formation has been likened to that of a spirea. Native to Korea and Manchuria, it is not one of the most ornamental rhododendrons.

minus 15′ Zone 4 Piedmont Rhododendron
Native to the southeastern U.S., this is somewhat similar to *R. carolinianum*, with rose to white flowers, 1½ in. across, in June and evergreen leaves 2½–4 in. long. This species, however, is taller and more vigorous than *R. carolinianum*

and hence is not so well adapted to foundation planting.

x morelianum 7′ Zone 6 Ponticataw Rhododendron
A hybrid evergreen species (*R. catawbiense* x *R. ponticum*) with lilac-violet flowers. Two clones would be '**Everestianum**' with rosy-lilac flowers and '**Fastusosum Plenum**' with mauve, partially double flowers. Both of these are popular plants.

moupinense 4′ Zone 7 Moupin Rhododendron
The white, sometimes pinkish, fragrant flowers are about 1½ in. wide and the evergreen leaves are 1–2 in. long. A native to China, it blooms very early in Feb. or March and so it is sometimes injured by freezes. It should be given some shade and protected where possible from late frosts.

mucronatum 6′ rarely 9′ Zone 5 Snow Azalea
An evergreen or half-evergreen azalea from Japan, with fragrant white flowers 2 in. wide and leaves, 1–2½ in. long, of a poor, grayish-green color. It is the hardiest of the white-flowered evergreen azaleas. Its dense habit of growth is important in making it useful. Several varieties are available: '**Amethystinum**' with pale lilac-purple flowers; '**Narcissiflora**' with double white flowers and '**Plenum**' with double, rose-purple flowers.

mucronulatum 6′ Zone 4 Korean Rhododendron
Actually a deciduous rhododendron, from north China, Manchuria, Korea and Japan, with pale, rosy-purple flowers in mid-April. The leaves, appearing after the flowers, are 1–3 in. long and turn a yellow to bronzy crimson in the fall. Because it blooms so early, it might well be planted with a northern exposure to protect it from late freezes which may kill its blossoms. A good variety is '**Cornell Pink**', with flowers a soft pink without any of the purple shades which appear in the flowers of the species.

x myrtifolium 4′ Zone 5 Myrtle Rhododendron
A very nice hybrid (*R. minus* x *R. hirsutum*), with light rosy-pink flowers, about 1 in. wide, and elliptic evergreen leaves, 1–2 in. long, which are densely produced. An excellent low shrub for foundation planting, though it is not readily available from commercial growers.

neriiflorum 6′–12′ Zone 7 Oleander Rhododendron
The scarlet to rose flowers of this popular rhododendron are about 2 in. wide and 1½ in. long, produced in 5-in. wide clusters of 6–12 flowers. The evergreen leaves are about 2–4 in. long and glaucous white beneath. Native to China, it is a good garden species because even

small plants produce a profusion of blossoms in April. Though the species is good, there are many hybrids which are even better.

obtusum 3′ **Zone 6** **Hiryu Azalea**
The species itself is not a prominent ornamental, but is valued for its many extremely ornamental varieties and hybrids. Half-evergreen to evergreen leaves are ½–1 in. long and the flowers, varying considerably from orange-red to bright red, bloom in mid-May. Some varieties are: 'Amoenum', flowers double, rich magenta. A very popular and widely grown form; x **arnoldianum**, flowers single, pink, 1½ in. wide, hardy in Zone 4, a hybrid between 'Amoena' and *kaempferi*; 'Hinodegiri', flowers single, rose colored, 1⅝ in. wide, frequently used as a clipped hedge and widely planted in Zones 6 and 7; **kaempferi**, flowers rose colored, 2⅝ in. wide, hardy in Zone 5. The so-called Kaempferi hybrids originated in Holland about 1920 as crosses between *R. obtusum kaempferi* and some other clones possibly related to the Kurume azaleas. They are hardy in Zone 6. Plants are tall, blooming with *R. obtusum kaempferi* in mid-May, with flowers 1½–2½ in. wide, before the leaves appear. A few of the varieties are:

FLOWER COLOR
'Carmen'—red, 2½ in. dia.
'Cleopatra'—red, 2½ in. dia.
'Fedora'—violet-red, 2 in. dia.
'Norma'—violet-red, 2½ in. dia.
'Othello'—red, 2 in. dia.
'Zampa'—violet-red, 2¼ in. dia.

occidentale 9′ **Zones 6–7** **Western Azalea**
A handsome native of the Pacific Coast, with white or pinkish flowers, 1½–2 in. wide, during late May. The deciduous leaves are 1–3½ long, turning scarlet and yellow in the fall. Unfortunately it does not grow well in the eastern U.S.

orbiculare 10′ **Zone 6** **Globe Rhododendron**
A Chinese rhododendron with round leaves, 2–4 in. wide, and a perfectly rounded form. The rose-colored flowers are 1½ in. wide, borne in late April and May. This is a neat evergreen rhododendron which makes a fine specimen, but it needs some shelter and plenty of space, since a 6-ft. plant may be 13 ft. wide.

oreotrephes 8′ **Zone 6** **Oread Rhododendron**
A valued evergreen rhododendron from China, mauve to rosey-red flowers, 2¼ in. wide, blooming in May, and comparatively small, gray-green leaves 1½–3 in. long. This is a good garden plant because of its fine texture and graceful habit.

'**P.J.M. Hybrids**' (*R. dauricum sempervirens* x
        R. carolinianum) 6′ **Zone 5**
The flowers of these hybrids are a vivid lavender pink and extremely profuse, literally covering the plant in late April. The plants produce little

seed, which is one of the reasons why they bloom so heavily each year. The evergreen leaves are like those of *R. carolinianum* in size and shape. These turn a rich purple in the fall. Fine plants for early garden display. One of the earliest rhododendrons to bloom in New England, these are usually grown as a mixed group of clones, but '**Victor**' is the earliest clone to bloom, '**Regal**' blooms next, followed by '**Elite**'.

pemakoense 6″–2′ **Zone 6** **Pemako Rhododendron**
One of the nicest of all the dwarf evergreen rhododendrons, this spreads by suckers and underground runners and makes an excellent rock garden plant. Native to Tibet. The scaly evergreen leaves are ½–1¼ in. long and about ¼ in. wide. The small, silvery-lilac flowers appearing in April are about 1¾ in. wide.

periclymenoides (*nudiflorum*) 6′ **Zone 3** **Pinxterbloom**
Native from Mass. and Ohio to N.Car. and called Wild Honeysuckle, this deciduous Azalea has white to light pink, slightly fragrant flowers, 1½ in. wide, in late May. *R. prinophyllum* is similar, but flowers are a deeper pink.

polylepis 12′ **Zone 6** **Batang Rhododendron**
The purplish-magenta to dark purple flowers of this Chinese species are 1 in. wide, blooming in April. Because of the flower color, this evergreen species is not popular.

ponticum 15′ **Zone 6** **Ponticum Rhododendron**
Native to Asia Minor, Spain and Portugal, this densely branched plant has become naturalized in the British Isles where it grows luxuriantly and is frequently heavily pruned to form hedges. Blooming in June, with purplish-pink flowers 1½–2 in. wide; it has evergreen leaves which are narrow and pointed at both ends, about 2½–5 in. long. It has been widely used as understock on which better rhododendrons are grafted merely because it grows so vigorously. The pointed and glossy leaves are easily distinguished from those of *R. catawbiense* hybrids.

x praecox 10′ **Zone 6** **Winter Rhododendron**
With evergreen or half-evergreen leaves 1–2 in. long, a lustrous dark green above and scaly below; the few, bright rosy-purple flowers are less than an inch wide. It is a hybrid (*R. dauricum* x *R. ciliatum*), but is not outstanding as an ornamental.

praevernum 15′ **Zone 6** **February Rhododendron**
The white to rose-colored, bell-shaped flowers of this compact Chinese species are 2 in. wide and are produced from late Feb. to early April. The evergreen leaves are 3½–10 in. long.

prinophyllum (*roseum*) 9′ **Zone 3** **Roseshell Azalea**
Similar mostly to *R. periclymenoides* except

that the fragrant flowers are bright pink and 2 in. wide. The deciduous leaves are 1–3 in. long, and it is native to northeastern North America. A better plant than *R. periclymenoides*.

prunifolium   8'   Zone 7   Plumleaf Azalea
Native to Ga. and Ala., this has crimson flowers in July—about the last of the azaleas to bloom. The deciduous leaves are 1–5 in. long. An excellent ornamental; some plants are hardy in certain protected spots as far north as Boston, Mass.

pubescens   6'   Zone 6
A Chinese evergreen species with white to rose-colored flowers, $\frac{1}{2}$–$\frac{3}{4}$ in. wide, in April. Not a very dense shrub.

racemosum   2'–6'   Zone 5   Mayflower
**   Rhododendron**
The evergreen leaves of this western Chinese plant are about $1\frac{1}{2}$ in. long or less. The flowers are only $\frac{3}{4}$ in. wide, in few-flowered clusters, colored a light pink in mid-May. It is an excellent plant for mass plantings or for the rock garden.

radicans   6"   Zone 6   Rockmantle Rhodo-
**   dendron**
A prostrate evergreen shrub, native to Tibet, with purple flowers $\frac{3}{4}$ in. long in May. Attractive for the rock garden.

riparium = *R. calostrotum*

rubiginosum   25'   Zone 7   Rusty Rhododendron
One of the few evergreen rhododendrons reportedly tolerating limestone soils, this is native to China, with pink to mauve flowers, $1\frac{1}{4}$ in. wide, in late April and early May. The aromatic leaves are $1\frac{1}{2}$–3 in. long and densely red-brown, scaly beneath. A desirable and floriferous evergreen species.

rupicola   2'   Zone 5
A rare Chinese evergreen rhododendron with purplish-crimson, funnel-shaped flowers, $\frac{1}{2}$ in. long, in April or May. Apparently able to grow in limestone soils.

russatum   2'–4'   Zone 5 (?)   Royal Alp
**   Rhododendron**
Blue-purple flowers in April are about 1 in. wide and number 5–10 to the truss. Leaves about $\frac{3}{4}$–$1\frac{1}{4}$ in. long. Native to China. This is a very floriferous, dwarf, evergreen shrub, but needs alpine conditions, with plenty of cool summer temperatures and atmospheric moisture, to do best.

x rutherfordianum   6'   Zone 7
These are hybrids mostly developed by Bobbink and Atkins at Rutherford, N.J., in the 1920's. They have been developed from *R. mucronatum* and some of the Indian azaleas, and the plants are mostly tender evergreens, probably hardy at Washington, D.C., and doing well in San Francisco, Calif. Flowers are single, semi-double

or double, some fragrant, ranging in color from red to purple to white. About 30 named clones have been introduced, among them being:
  'Alaska'—flowers single, white
  'Crimson Glory'—flowers semi-double, violet-red
  'Rose Queen'—flowers double, $2\frac{1}{2}$ in. wide, rose, with creamy-white throat
  'Salmon Glow'—flowers hose in hose, rose colored

schlippenbachii   15'   Zone 4   Royal Azalea
One of the very best deciduous azaleas, with pale pink blossoms 3 in. wide during mid-May and leaves, 2–4 in. long, which turn yellow, orange and crimson in the fall. It is native to Korea, Manchuria and Japan; a valued plant for any garden with acid soil.

simsii   6'   Zone 7   Sims Azalea
Evergreen or half-evergreen azalea, with rose-red to crimson flowers, $1\frac{1}{2}$–2 in. wide, 2–6 flowers being in each truss, in May. The leaves are 1–2 in. long. Native to China and Formosa; there are many garden forms.

smirnowii   6'–18'   Zone 4   Smirnow Rhodo-
**   dendron**
An evergreen rhododendron with leaves 3–6 in. long which are covered with a thick, felty tomentum underneath—an excellent deterrent to the lace-winged flies which frequently infest

Rhododendron smirnowii—Smirnow Rhododendron—bears pink flowers in June. (*Photo by Arnold Aboretum, Jamaica Plain, Mass.*)

most other rhododendrons. The flowers vary from white to rosy red, most plants having lavender-pink flowers. Native to the Caucasus.

souliei   12'   Zone 6 (?)   Soulie Rhododendron
A species from Tibet and China, with white to rose-colored flowers, 1–$1\frac{1}{2}$ in. long and 3 in. wide, with 6–8 flowers in each truss. The evergreen leaves, often almost heart shaped, are $1\frac{1}{4}$–$3\frac{1}{2}$ in. long.

sutchuenense 25′ Zone 6 Szechwan Rhododendron
A popular evergreen where hardy because of its large, pale rosy-lilac flowers, 2–3½ in. wide, blooming between Feb. and April, and its large and handsome leaves, 9 in. long. It should be grown in a protected place with some shade. Native to China. However, because it blooms so early, it should be grown only in areas not susceptible to frosts after April.

tephropeplum 3′–6′ Zone 7 Ashrobe Rhododendron
A white or pink-flowering evergreen with flowers 1¼ in. wide, having 4–6 flowers in each cluster during April or May. The leaves are 1¼–5 in. long. Native to Tibet and Burma, it is noted to bloom well when only a foot tall and apparently has the ability to grow in limestone soils.

thomsonii 20′ Zone 6 Thomson Rhododendron
A lanky evergreen rhododendron from Nepal, with blue-green leaves 1½–3 in. long; this has blood-red flowers, 2–2½ in. wide, in April. Of value only on the West Coast. It is unfortunate that there are many clones of this species which are only mediocre ornamentals.

triflorum 10′ Zone 6 Triflorum Rhododendron
An evergreen from the Himalayan Mountains, with pale yellow, fragrant flowers, 1½ in. wide, and with only 2–3 flowers in each cluster. Although it is available in a few Pacific Coast nurseries, it is not especially ornamental.

ungneri 20′ Zone 5 Ungern Rhododendron
Evergreen, with leaves 3–6 in. long, and pale white to rose-colored flowers, 1½–2 in. wide, in large, 6-in. trusses. Native to the Caucasus.

vaseyi 6′–9′ Zone 4 Pinkshell Azalea
Native to N.Car., this deciduous azalea is perfectly hardy in New England. It is valued for its light rose flowers in mid-May (before the leaves appear), the light red autumn color of its foliage and its ability to withstand growing in moist soil situations. The leaves are 2–5 in. long. The variety **album** has white flowers. One of the very best of the native American azaleas.

virgatum 6′ Zone 9 Willowtwig Rhododendron
This is an evergreen, with pale mauve or shell-pink flowers 1 in. wide. Native to Sikkim and very tender.

viscosum 9′ rarely 15′ Zone 3 Swamp Azalea
A very fragrant, native, white-flowering, deciduous azalea, blooming in early July after all the leaves have been fully developed; this is found, especially in moist soils, from Me. to S.Car. The leaves are 1–2½ in. long and turn orange to bronze in the fall. The variety

rhodanthum is rare, but should be grown, whenever it can be obtained, for its bright pink flowers.

wallichii 9′ Zone 7 Wallich Rhododendron
Native to Sikkim, with lilac flowers 1¾ in. long. It is sometimes regarded as a variety of *R. campanulatum*. It is evergreen.

wardii 10′–25′ Zone 7 Ward Rhododendron
This has been pointed out as the best yellow-flowered rhododendron for general garden use. The glossy, dark green leaves are 1¼–4¾ in. long and ¾–2½ in. wide, and the flowers, produced in May, are 2½ in. wide. It is native to China. Unfortunately, good forms of this rhododendron are still very hard to find.

williamsianum 5′ Zone 7 Williams Rhododendron
Native to western China, this rhododendron has pink flowers about 2 in. wide, blooming in April, and heart-shaped leaves, ½–1½ in. long, bronze colored when first opened in the spring and slightly bluish when mature. It has horizontal branches which form a flattened, almost prostrate bush and is a very desirable plant where it is hardy. Easily propagated from cuttings.

yedoense 5′ Zone 5 Yodogawa Azalea
The double flowers of this species are purple, appearing in mid-May. Even the deciduous leaves, which are 1–3 in. long, turn purplish in the fall. It is native to Korea and Japan. The single-flowered variety **poukhanense** has flowers 1⅞ in. wide and is hardy in Zone 4, being hardier than the species. It flowers freely even when quite small.

yunnanense 10′ Zone 7 Yunnan Rhododendron
Rather leggy in habit, this species has white, lavender or pink flowers 1½ in. wide, appearing in late May, and evergreen or partially deciduous leaves 1½–3 in. long. It is valued for its profuse bloom which sometimes nearly hides the leaves.

RHODORA CANADENSE = *Rhododendron canadense*

RHODOTYPUS (ro-DO-tip-us)
scandens 6′ Zone 5 Jetbead
With white flowers, 2 in. across, consisting of 4 petals and shiny, black, hard fruits remaining on the plant all winter, the Jetbead is often used in foreground plantings. A native of Japan and China; it used to be very popular about 50 years ago but now there are many plants which make better landscape specimens. It is comparatively low, faces the ground well and can be used as one of the general-purpose shrubs which usually can be worked into any shrub border.

Propagation

Seed may be stratified as soon as ripe or stored dry in an airtight container in a cool place and stratified the following year, first for 3 months at room temperatures, then for 3 months at 40° F. Softwood and hardwood cuttings can both be easily rooted. See STRATIFICATION, CUTTINGS.

RHOEO (REE-o)
  discolor = *R. spathacea*
  spathacea (*R. discolor*) **8″ Zone 10 Three-men-in-a-boat, Oyster Rhoeo**
Popular names for this perennial herb and greenhouse plant include "Moses-on-a-raft," "Purple-leaved Spiderwort," etc. It is a perennial herb from the West Indies; has become naturalized in southern Fla.; has stems 8 in. long with leaves up to a foot long and 3 in. wide, purple underneath, dark green above. The white flowers borne in umbels are nearly hidden by 2 boat-shaped bracts. The variety **vittatus** which is frequently grown bears leaves that are purple both above and below, and striped longitudinally with pale yellow.

RHOICISSUS (ro-e-CISS-us)
  capensis climbing Zone 9 Evergreen Treebine
A vigorous climbing vine with forked tendrils, simple leaves, 4–8 in. wide, and 3 veined, rusty colored beneath. Tuberous rooted—native to South Africa and popular in southern Calif.

RHUBARB (*Rheum rhabarbarum*). Rhubarb is native to eastern Asia. In the U.S. it is a popular herbaceous, very hardy perennial which is grown in nearly all home gardens. Like Asparagus it must be located in the garden plot so that normal annual garden work does not disturb the plant. A few plants, 5–10, at the side of the garden will supply all that a family can use fresh, canned or frozen.

Rhubarb thrives best in regions having cool, moist summers and winters cold enough to freeze the ground to a depth of several inches. It is not adapted to most sections of the South.

Varieties

'Victoria' is a vigorous-growing variety that produces very large stalks of a somewhat green color. 'Mac Donald' and 'Valentine' are generally preferred because of the deep red color to the stalks. Other names listed by seedsmen include 'Ruby' and 'Strawberry', both of which have red stalks but are generally less vigorous. 'Linneas' is also an old standard variety.

Soil Preparation

Any deep, well-drained, fertile soil is suitable for Rhubarb. The method of soil preparation outlined for Asparagus is suitable for Rhubarb.

See ASPARAGUS. The use of a good application of manure, however, is even more important for Rhubarb than is the case for Asparagus. Rhubarb has a deeper, more fleshy root system than Asparagus.

Planting and Season Care

A piece of root containing a strong bud, under favorable conditions, will produce a strong plant in 1 year. Old plants may be divided in the fall or early Spring into 4–8 parts for use in starting a new bed. Spring planting is preferred.

The root "steckling" or a single section of a divided clump is placed at the bottom of a trench 8–10 in. deep and covered with soil to a depth of 3–4 in. As soon as the young stalks appear the soil is again pulled in to fill the trench or hill.

Rhubarb is sometimes grown in the cellar for winter use.

After the first year top dress each plant in the spring with a forkful of manure. If manure is not available apply 1 lb. of a complete fertilizer (5-8-7 or 5-10-5) around each hill. Rhubarb is a gross feeder and is not readily over-fertilized.

Remove seed stalks as soon as they appear. No stem should be harvested until the second year. From the third year on the leaf stalks may be pulled when they reach a proper size for approximately 4 weeks. Use only the leaf stalk, not the leaf itself.

Forcing

Dig up a few plants in the fall, place in a protected spot where they will not dry out but where they will freeze. After freezing for several weeks, place the roots in a box in the cellar, cover the crowns with several inches of soil or sand and apply just enough water to keep the soil or sand moist. A temperature of 50°–65° F. is ideal. Light is not necessary and actually stalks develop more color in the dark.

Roots that have been forced should not be reset into the garden.

Rhubarb is not generally injured by insects or diseases.

GRANT B. SNYDER

Editor's Note: The leaves of this common garden food plant are poisonous. The leaf stalks or petioles only are commonly eaten, but the leaves, when eaten by humans, have caused severe poisoning.

RHUBARB FAMILY = Polygonaceae

RHUS (RUSS). The sumacs are coarse-growing, suckering shrubs not at all suited for the small garden. They have alternate, compound leaves and are best used for naturalizing where there is plenty of space, especially on poor, sandy soils in sunny situations. They are mostly shrubs or small trees of special value for their orange to scarlet autumn color. The flowers are unisexual, but there are plants with both types of flowers and it is these plants which should be propagated.

The shrubby sumacs are weak-wooded, breaking up easily in heavy snow and ice storms. The flowers are small and yellowish, usually borne in pyramidal clusters that are not especially prominent except for the Chinese Sumac which has the largest flower clusters. Most species flower during the summer, but the low Fragrant Sumac (*R. aromatica*) bears small yellow flowers in the spring before the leaves appear.

The fruits of the common shrubby species are small, reddish, and borne in tight upright clusters that often remain on the plants all winter. The fruits of the poisonous species are white berries, while those of the Fragrant Sumac are small red berries borne in early summer.

All do well in poor, dry soils. In fact, this is usually the only place they are used, for in better soils, better plants are usually selected. However, the Smooth, Staghorn and Shining Sumacs are all very much a part of the roadside picture in the eastern U.S. and because of this, they should not be discarded altogether.

The best for fine texture are the cut-leaved forms of *R. glabra* and *R. typhina*. The best for all-round foliage throughout the growing seasons is *R. copallina*, because it has glossy green leaves superior to those of any of the other species.

Although the greenish-yellow flower clusters of *R. glabra* and *R. typhina* are obvious in the early summer, it is the foliage colors of all these in the fall that make them outstanding. When planted in the shade, or in very good soil, the autumn color is not nearly so colorful as when the plants are placed in poor, dry soil in a sunny situation.

As for the native poisonous sumacs, there are 5, namely *R. diversiloba*, *R. radicans* and its variety *rydbergii*; *R. toxicodendron*; and *R. vernix*. All have whitish or whitish to yellowish fruits. All have brilliant orange to scarlet autumn color. The Pacific Poison-oak (*R. diversiloba*) is the western representative, native from British Columbia to Calif., and is similar in appearance to the Poison-ivy (*R. radicans*) of the eastern U.S. The others are native in the eastern or middle U.S. *R. vernix*, the Poison Sumac, is the only one with leaves having more than 3 leaflets, usually 7–15, and is a shrub or small tree up to 20 ft. tall, growing in swampy or damp areas in the eastern and midwestern U.S.

The most common is *R. radicans*, the common Poison-ivy, which is a scrambling or climbing vine with 3 leaflets. Its variety *rydbergii* is shrubby and is less than 3 ft. tall. The Poison-oak (*R. toxicodendron*), native chiefly in the southeastern U.S., is another plant the leaves of which have 3 leaflets, but it seldom grows over 2 ft. tall. All should be avoided and eliminated wherever possible.

Propagation

Do not allow the seeds to dry out, but stratify as soon as ripe for 5 months at greenhouse temperatures, then for 3 months at 40° F., then sow. If germination fails to take place then, provide a second cold period after several months have elapsed. Some species, like *R. aromatica*, can be divided or rooted from softwood cuttings. Other species can be rooted from root cuttings taken in early spring. See STRATIFICATION, CUTTINGS, etc.

aromatica   3′   Zone 3   Fragrant Sumac
This was formerly termed *R. canadensis* and is widespread over eastern North America. The leaves have 3 leaflets. First it is conspicuous when its small yellow flowers appear in the spring before the leaves. In early summer the fruits turn red, and in the fall the brilliant scarlet to orange color of the foliage makes it an outstanding ornamental. Especially is it good for planting on low, sunny, dry banks where it can be easily cut with a brush scythe if for any reason it grows too irregularly. It is an excellent plant for borders along the roads. *R. trilobata* is very similar, with smaller flowers and more upright in growth. It is found mostly in the western part of the U.S.

canadensis = *R. aromatica*

chinensis   24′   Zone 5   Chinese Sumac
Some have considered this one of the best

sumacs in bloom, for the flowers appear in large pyramidal heads late in the summer. It is native to China and Japan and the leaves have 7–13 leaflets. The bark and leaf galls are used for making dyes.

copallina   30'   Zone 4   Shining Sumac
This native of the eastern U.S. is the best of the sumacs for ornamental planting because the foliage is a lustrous dark green, a color far more interesting than that of the foliage of any other sumac. This and *R. chinensis* are the only 2 species with a rachis along the midrib. In *R. copallina*, however, the 9–21 leaflets of each compound leaf are entire, with just a few teeth near the apex of each leaflet. The leaflets of the Chinese Sumac (7–15 leaflets per leaf) are coarsely serrate, and they are not a lustrous green. The Shining Sumac is native over a wide part of the eastern U.S. and merits being planted wherever growth conditions (i.e. dry soil and plenty of sunlight) are conducive to good growth. Although it can grow to be 30 ft. tall, it is usually seen, both in gardens and in its native habitat, as a shrub under 8 ft. tall. It is one of the prominent fall-colored plants along the lower half of the Blue Ridge Parkway leading into the Great Smoky Mountains of N.Car.

diversiloba   6'   Zone 6   Pacific Poison-oak
A poisonous species native from British Columbia to Calif. This is similar to *R. radicans* of the eastern U.S., but is more shrubby. The leaves have 3 leaflets.

glabra   9'–15'   Zone 2   Smooth Sumac
A common plant native to the eastern U.S., used on poor ground; it is not a plant for small places. For those who like to see fruits on all sumacs, it must be remembered that some plants are entirely fruitless because they are staminate. The young stems and under surface of the leaves of this species are a glaucous green, which is an aid in its identification. One point in its favor is that mature plants are lower than those of the more vigorous Staghorn Sumac. The cut-leaved variety 'Laciniata' is sometimes used because of the extremely fine foliage texture. The leaves are frequently doubly pinnate and it is similar, as far as general landscape effect goes, to *R. typhina* 'Dissecta'. All these have excellent scarlet autumn color and the leaves, shoots, bark and roots, as well as the fuzzy red "berries" of Sumac have been used in making yellowish-tan or gray dyes.

integrifolia   25'–30'   Zone 9   Sour-berry
An evergreen shrub with simple leaves, not used much outside its native habitat in southern Calif.

laurina   12'   Zone 9   Laurel Sumac
A native to southern Calif. with evergreen leaves, but of little ornamental value outside its native habitat.

ovata   10'–20'   Zone 9   Sugarbush
This is native to the desert regions of the southwestern U.S., has evergreen leaves 1–3 in. long, but is not used much outside its native habitat.

radicans   shrubby vine   Zone 3   Poison-ivy
Poisonous and native to the eastern U.S., this is found everywhere, along roads, scrambling over walls or up trees, at the seashore within reach of salt-water spray and in the best of gardens. The alternate leaves have 3 leaflets and

Poison-ivy—*Rhus radicans*

the fruits are white berries. The autumn color is a vivid orange to scarlet, but the plant is very poisonous to the touch and should be eradicated with proper chemical sprays wherever it appears.

The variety **rydbergii** is shrubby and is less than 3 ft. tall, but it is just as poisonous as the species.

toxicodendron   2'   Zone 5   Poison-oak
This poisonous plant is native chiefly to the southeastern U.S. but, unlike some of the others, it seldom grows over 2 ft. tall and the 3 leaflets on each leaf are 3–7 lobed.

typhina   50'   Zone 3   Staghorn Sumac
The Staghorn Sumac is the largest of our sumacs, native to the eastern U.S., but like all of this group, it breaks up easily in snow and ice storms. The extremely pubescent, young twigs are the reason for its common name. It should be used only on poor, dry soil and is always best when planted in clumps. Like the

other species, this has vivid scarlet autumn color and is a common sight along the roadsides of the eastern U.S. The variety 'Dissecta' has leaflets pinnately dissected, giving a finer texture than variety 'Laciniata'. A well-grown plant of this variety is certainly beautiful as long as it does not break up in snow, wind or ice storms.

verniciflua 60′ Zone 5 Japanese Lacquer-tree
A tree with alternate, compound leaves having 7–15 leaflets, each about 3–8 in. long; small yellowish-white flowers in drooping panicles, 6–10 in. long, during June and July and bright red, drooping fruit clusters. In China and Japan, where it is native, it is planted in quantity because it yields the famous varnish or lacquer of Japan and the oil extracted from the fruits is used in candle-making. Contact with this species frequently produces severe inflammation and blistering of the skin.

vernix 21′ Zone 4 Poison Sumac
The leaves of this poisonous plant have 7–13 leaflets which turn orange to scarlet in autumn. This plant also has light yellowish-gray berries in the fall and is most poisonous to the touch. It is native to the eastern part of North America. Contact with Poison Sumac frequently produces severe inflammation and blistering of the skin.

RHYNCHELYTRUM (rin-chel-E-trum)
repens (*Tricholaena rosea*) 4′ **annual Ruby Grass**
An ornamental grass usually grown as an annual, with leaves ¼ in. wide and fruiting panicles 10 in. long, colored pink to reddish, and attractive for this reason. Native to South Africa. Propagated by seeds. Considered a colorful ornamental grass.

RIB. A primary or prominent vein in the leaf.

RIBBON-GRASS = *Phalaris arundinacea picta*

RIBES (RY-beez). These are the currants and gooseberries (which see) so popular in home gardens years ago but now mostly out of style for 2 reasons. They are time-consuming to pick and to prepare as food, and also most have been forbidden to be grown in certain areas where the White Pine is native because they are the alternate hosts of the serious disease white pine blister rust. They are alternate-leaved deciduous shrubs, some slightly thorny and some dioecious. The fruits are small in the currants, about ¼ in. in dia., and larger in the gooseberries, about ½ in., and are borne in clusters. The flowers are small, yellow to yellowish in most species but red in *R. sanguineum*. Few are mentioned here because it just is not worth while growing them.

Propagation

Seeds should be stratified for 3 months at 40° F., then sown. If they fail to germinate after 3 months, they should be given a second 3 months cold treatment. Some *Ribes* plants are easily divided. Softwood and hardwood cuttings (which see) are good ways of forming new plants. See BUDDING, GRAFTING, STRATIFICATION.

alpinum 7½′ Zone 2 Alpine Currant
The Alpine Currant, native to Europe, is one of the neatest of the *Ribes* for garden use. Usually it is not seen in gardens over 3–4 ft. tall. The leaves are small, 1–2 in. long; the staminate and pistillate flowers are on different plants and the staminate form is supposed to be immune to the black stem rust of wheat. The fruits are scarlet-red berries. Like all species of this genus, the leaves appear very early in the season, and because of its bushy growth it has been used in making hedges.

grossularia = *R. uva-crispa*
nigrum 6′ Zone 4 European Black Currant
This is a European plant which has escaped cultivation and become naturalized in the eastern and northeastern U.S., where it was probably brought to America by the earliest settlers because of its edible black fruits. However, it acts as an alternate host of the white pine blister rust and as such is energetically eradicated by plant quarantine state and federal agencies wherever it is found growing in areas where White Pine is native.

odoratum 6′ Zone 4 Clove Currant
This is susceptible to the stem rust of wheat but it is an old-fashioned favorite, native from Minn. to Tex. east of the Rocky Mountains, and had been used a lot before restrictions were passed about its continued growth. The yellow and fragrant flowers appear in small clusters in May; the fruits are black berries (here again male flowers are on one plant, female on another) and the autumn color is a rich and glossy scarlet.

sanguineum 12′ Zone 5 Winter Currant
In Europe there are a dozen varieties of this red-flowering currant, but the best is 'King Edward VII' because of its strikingly red flowers and good growth. The flowers appear in mid-May before the leaves have fully developed and the fruits are merely bluish-black berries, the staminate flowers being all on one plant and the pistillate flowers being on another. The species is a native of the Pacific Coast, but unfortunately this species also is susceptible to the black stem rust of wheat, and should not be grown in wheat-producing areas.

uva-crispa (*R. grossularia*) 3′ **Zone 4 English Gooseberry**
This is the famous English Gooseberry, even

now widely planted in Great Britain in small home gardens. See GOOSEBERRIES. It bears spines $\frac{1}{2}$ in. long, small greenish flowers and red or yellow berries that are often covered with bristles. Not much planted in American gardens at present.

RICCIA (RISS-ia)

fluitans   aquatic liverwort   Zone 7   Common Riccia

A liverwort, floating on water, sometimes in large masses; only of value as an interesting oddity floating on the surface of the home aquarium. It has no stems, nor leaves, nor fruit. It is one of the most valuable of water plants to the breeder of aquarium fishes for it is firm enough to catch the spawn of the surface egg-layers and young fish can hide under it. It is native to ponds in the central and southern Atlantic states. Easily propagated by division.

RICE = *Oryza sativa*

RICE-PAPER-TREE = *Tetrapanax papyriferum*

RICE, WILD = *Zizania aquatica*

RICHARDIA = *Zantedeschia*

RICINUS (RISS-in-us)

communis   15′   annual   Castor-bean

A vigorous-growing annual which can grow to a 40 ft. tree in the Tropics, with large, palmately lobed leaves, 5–11 lobes, up to 3 ft. across; flowers monoecious, in panicles 2 ft. long; fruit 1 in. long covered with soft spines. Native to Africa. All parts of the plant, but particularly the beans, are poisonous to humans, cattle, horses, sheep, pigs and poultry. Several varieties available in the trade: '**Borboniensis arboreus**', with red stems and glaucous leaves; '**Cambodgensis**', with very dark foliage and stems; '**Sanguineus**', with red leaves; '**Gibsonii**', smaller with metallic-colored leaves. Seeds may be started indoors in April or outdoors after frost. The plants should be at least 4 ft. apart and are best planted in the full sun.

RIVINA (riv-Y-na)

humilis   3′   Zone 9   Rougeplant

An alternate-leaved herb of the American Tropics, with small bisexual white or rosy flowers in many-flowered racemes. Leaves are ovate, about 4 in. wide. Most ornamental are the red, berrylike fruits, sometimes yellow or orange, about the size of peas. When well-grown pot plants are in fruit, the 3-in. racemes may have 12–24 fruits each. Easily propagated by seeds or cuttings and needing little attention as a greenhouse pot plant. If the soil in the pots is allowed to become dry, the berries will drop.

ROBINIA (ro-BIN-ia). Members of the *Robinia* clan are legumes and have pendulous clusters of small pealike flowers in wisterialike clusters, alternate compound leaves and usually thorns.

Sixteen species and a variety of *R. pseudoacacia* have pink to rosy-colored flowers, which when they bloom are colorful indeed. American nurserymen are growing only a half dozen of these pink-flowered trees and shrubs, undoubtedly because they have little ornamental interest when the plants are not in flower.

None have interesting autumn color; the fruits are merely dry pods. The genus as a whole is frequently susceptible to attacks from several stem and branch borers and to leaf miners as well. The borer problem may not be serious in all areas, but where it is, locusts should be planted with discretion. Most of the 25 or more varieties of *R. pseudoacacia* which have been named have little more to offer as ornamentals than the species.

Propagation

Seeds may be processed as soon as ripe or stored dry in airtight containers in a cool place up to a year and then processed. Because of the very hard seed coat, the seed had best be soaked in water at 90° F. overnight or treated for a short period with concentrated sulfuric acid.

Grafting and budding are done using *R. pseudoacacia* as understock, and root cuttings root well if taken in spring. See SEED, GRAFTING, BUDDING, CUTTINGS.

Insect Pests

Many trees and groves of Black Locust have been ruined by the locust borer. Large scars in the bark, crooked branches and exit holes of the beetle are characteristic. Control measures have not been developed but spraying in late summer when beetles are active with insecticide #9 should be helpful. Putnam scale attacks Black Locust. See SCALE INSECTS. Locust leaf miner makes large blotch mines where the orange-colored larva lives for 3 or 4 weeks. Sprays of insecticide #15 are effective.

On small trees the main trunk and branches show distinct swelling caused by the locust twig borer. The reddish-yellow borer emerges through a conspicuous exit hole in the gall. Cutting and burning the infested twigs while the borer is in them is suggested.

Diseases

No important diseases are recognized.

hispida   3′   Zone 5   Rose-acacia

A low shrubby type with beautiful pendulous clusters of rosy-pink flowers, similar in shape to those of Wisteria; suitable for planting on banks of poor soil. It increases rapidly by underground suckers and often can become a vicious pest. However, in poor soils where little else will grow, it has its uses. The bright red bristles on young stems and fruits is an added attraction. It is native from Va. to Ga. The variety **macrophylla** has perhaps the most beautiful flowers of any in this genus. They are a deep rose color, with both flowers and leaves larger than those of the species. The bristles on the young growth are mostly lacking but, in flower, this low shrub is outstanding.

x 'Idaho'   40'   Zone 4
This is a hybrid with a mixed-up parentage. It is in the trade under several misleading names. Although treelike, it is not a variety of *R. pseudoacacia* nor *R. luxurians*. The flowers are a dark reddish purple, the darkest of any. It is being grown by several nurseries, especially in the Midwest where it has earned a reputation in withstanding some of the trying growing conditions in certain parts of Kan. and Colo.

leucantha   1½'   Zone 4
This is a rare, low, stoloniferous shrub native to Ga., having 3-in. clusters of pure white flowers. First discovered in 1926 and not named until 1945. This species might well be grown more where it proves hardy.

x margaretta   12'   Zone 6
A possible hybrid of *R. pseudoacacia* x *hispida*, this has very light pink flowers in clusters up to 6 in. long, and is native to S.Car.

x 'Monument', another pink-flowered hybrid now offered by some nurseries; growing 10–12 ft. tall, but with flower clusters only about 4 in. long.

pseudoacacia   75'   Zone 3   Black Locust
A tree native from Pa. to Mo. and Ga., valued chiefly for its pendulous clusters of fragrant white flowers. It is upright and very open in habit and might even be termed picturesque. It is very susceptible to attacks of trunk and twig borers and, in the summer, to attacks of leaf miner which, in eastern New England at least, can make whole plantings brown and disreputable-looking unless they are properly sprayed at the right time. The bark of the young shoots is poisonous when eaten, but the flowers have been fried and eaten. Some varieties are:—

'Bessoniana'—somewhat similar to *R. pseudoacacia* 'Umbraculifera' but less dense;

'Burgundy'—with good, dark pink flowers;

'Decaisneana'—flowers light rose;

'Erecta'—of columnar habit;

'Semperflorens'—blooms intermittently throughout the summer;

'Umbraculifera'—with many branches forming a dense, rounded, almost globelike head. Sometimes grafted high on *R. pseudoacacia* but usually resulting in a very poor tree which readily breaks up from borer attacks or from snow and ice in the winter.

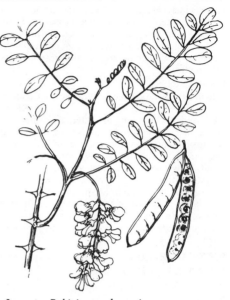

Locust—*Robinia pseudoacacia*

x slavinii (*R. kelseyi* x *pseudoacacia*)   **15'**
Zone 4
With light pink flowers and more of them than either parent.

viscosa   36'   Zone 3   Clammy Locust
Not a popular ornamental tree, this native from N.Car. to Ala. has viscous glands along the twigs and leaf petioles. The bark of young shoots is poisonous when eaten. The alternate compound leaves have 13–25 leaflets, each 1–1½ in. long, and the pink, pealike flowers are borne in 6–16-flowered racemes, 2–3½ in. long, during June.

ROCHEA (RO-kea)
coccinea   2'   Zone 9
A succulent perennial with brilliant scarlet flowers. The leaves, 1½ in. long, are pointed and closely set on a fleshy stem and are red beneath but green above. The tubular, fragrant flowers are 2 in. wide and are borne in clusters. Native to South Africa. Sometimes used as a ground cover in southern Calif. and indoors as an interesting pot plant in the North.

ROCK-CRESS. See ARABIS.

ROCK-CRESS, PURPLE = *Aubrieta deltoidea*

ROCKET. See HESPERIS.

ROCKET, DAME'S = *Hesperis matronalis*

ROCKET-SALAD = *Eruca vesicaria*

ROCKET, YELLOW = *Barbarea vulgaris*

ROCK GARDEN. Growing plants in rock gardens has long been practiced as a form of gardening. When it was introduced to the United States from England in the 1920's, it soon became a craze. Those early rock gardens were developed in the English tradition, with emphasis on the beauty of composition of both rocks and plants, but after a while many of these man-made gardens became an ugly conglomeration of rocks and stones. Soon, they were overdone, followed by a decline, but after World War II, a fresh approach was introduced in the Japanese style, with stress on openness and simplicity.

A rock garden may be defined as an outcropping of rocks—natural or devised—where alpine plants from the mountainous regions of the world are grown. Usually it is on a slope, and although the plants chosen generally come from rocky places, usually at high elevations, many are simply low-growing perennials, annuals, bulbs, and shrubs that fit into the category.

Many gardeners are fortunate in having natural rock gardens, where their choice treasures are brought in and arranged in an artistic manner. In other instances, they are constructed with rocks—and boulders—that have been hauled in. This requires great skill, and the best are the the result of the skillful execution of outstanding landscape architects and plantsmen. Unless well done, a rock garden can be an eyesore, nothing more than a mere pile of rocks among which plants are set and often allowed to grow rampant.

The natural rock garden is characterized by light, poor, gravelly, well-drained soil. In the constructed garden, this kind of soil is essential. It provides the kind of medium in which most of these plants survive. A heavy soil in winter becomes water logged. By remaining too damp, plants tend to rot, especially where winter rains are heavy. A too-rich soil promotes lush, soft growth that likewise is inclined to become winter-killed.

The artificial rock garden should be constructed with the proper growing conditions in order to display plants that generally cannot be grown elsewhere. It is intended for alpine plants, which are found growing wild on mountains between the tree line and the lower limits of snow. The rocks not only show off the plants to best advantage, but perform other important functions. They help to keep the soil cool and to conduct moisture to the plant roots. Excessive moisture through evaporation is prevented, and the soil is held by them in place. Even when all these conditions are provided, the rock garden may not fare well, but for another reason. It has to do with the length of the growing season, usually varying with that of the natural habitat of the plants. That is why the careful selection

of plants is of great importance.

The well-designed rock garden, especially if large, will be represented by many different kinds of topographical areas. It may have a rocky hillside and a steep slope. It may display a low plain, a hidden valley, a bog, a brook or stream, and a quiet pool, as commonly found in nature. At some point, it may even possess a high and windy mountain peak where few plants grow.

In extensive stretches, larger, bolder plants may be used. The smaller the rock garden, the smaller the plants should be. Most rock plants are under a foot in height when full grown, but dwarf shrubs, may be up to 3 feet. Although alpine and rock plants are usually selected, others qualify if their size and height are right. They may be mat-forming or spreading and may come from meadows, woods, prairies or bogs. Many that are typical rock plants are often grown in borders with other flowers, among them Arabis, Aubrieta, Gold-dust, Cerastium, Hardy Candytuft, Dwarf Iris, Ground Phlox, Trillium, and Epimedium. To these can be added a wide variety of small bulbs and low annuals, like Sweet Alyssum, Lobelia and dwarf French marigolds.

The classical rock garden, with its need for hand and knee labor by skilled gardeners, has become a thing of the past. It was intended to copy nature and to display many interesting and unusual plants, some of them rare. Today's rock gardens have changed to meet the needs of the times. Simplicity and ease of maintenance is the keynote. Yet there are many lovely compositions that have resulted from this new concept which have combined the best and most practical elements of the British and the Japanese, the 2 styles that have helped to mold the contemporary rock garden of today.

As with other forms of gardening, certain basic principles apply—scale, proportion, balance and good design, which includes a pleasing arrangement of the various parts into an harmonious whole. Most of all, it is originality and imagination that count.

Location

The site of the rock garden is of prime importance. If there is a natural outcropping of rocks, such as found in New England, the Appalachians, the Rockies and other mountainous areas of the country, then select it, since there is nothing more beautiful than an arrangement of rocks placed in position by the forces of nature.

Most home owners, however, are not fortunate enough to possess such a setup. If an artificial rock garden is to be constructed, then look for a bank or a slope. Even at that, it can be built on level ground, although it takes far greater ingenuity to make it look as if it has always been there. Some of the great rock gardens of the world, often found in botanic gardens, are made, and are so artfully executed that they have every feeling of being natural.

A rock and wall garden combined. (*Photo by Arnold Arboretum, Jamaica Plain, Mass.*)

When choosing the location, look for a spot that receives abundant sunshine, away from the shade of large trees which cut out the sunlight and rob plants of precious nourishment and needed moisture. When dealing with a slope, this is not always possible, but sometimes, there is a choice. Keep away from artificial surroundings, since a rock garden is essentially a casual, informal type of garden expression that should harmonize with its immediate surroundings. Avoid as backgrounds high, austere walls, porches or the façades of houses, driveways and sidewalks, and a strictly formal garden, with clipped hedges and plants arranged in geometric patterns.

Exposure should also be taken into consideration. Rock garden and alpine plants are sun loving, although this does not mean full exposure to the all-day sun. In some instances, specially if the slope faces south, this can be harmful in the case of winter sun and winds. One that faces east is considered ideal, but northeast, west and northwest are also excellent. When dealing with alpines from high mountain tops, north exposure, open to the sky, without any interference from trees, is recommended. This is because these small plants are covered, in their native haunts, by a thick blanket of snow all winter, and are not exposed to the sun or biting winds.

Southern exposures, particularly in the case of more rampant plants such as Ground Phlox, Aubrieta, Arabis, Gold-dust, and Dwarf Iris, are not to be neglected altogether. Many outstanding rock garden specialists have thriving plants in such locations, but they know the needs of the various kinds in order to keep them in top shape. In some cases, it may mean some form of winter protection. These gardeners avoid plants that require shade during the hottest part of the day, or find cool, shady nooks for them in crevices of large rocks or boulders. On south-facing slopes, small trees that cast light or limited shade, as birches, crabapples, and flowering dogwoods, are planted to cut out the intensity of the baking sun.

In any case, allow for full sun for at least part of the day. Yet charming rock gardens can be established on natural outcroppings where large trees, too precious to cut down, exist on the property. In such instances, the rock garden will not be gay and colorful in spring and early summer, but it can impart simple charm and a feeling of coolness with hostas, Lily-of-the-valley, epimediums, *Ajuga*, trilliums, Bloodroot, yellow lady's slippers, ferns, and low yews and azaleas. In summer, bits of color can be added with *Coleus*, Patient Plant, tuberous begonias, Madagascar Periwinkle, fancy-leaved caladiums, Thunbergii. In early spring, before trees don their leaves, miniature bulbs and species daffodils and tulips will unfold their pretty flowers.

Design

Before starting to build, whether you will plant around existing rocks or start from the beginning, make sketches on paper. A rock garden, like any other type of garden, is based on principles of design. If it is large, it will need paths and walks, or at least stepping stones, and the paths should be of a winding, informal nature. Straight, rigid lines are not appropriate. Paths not only make delightful wandering, but make it possible to reach the plants in order to care for them. Unless comprised of stones, they should be covered with natural material, like pine needles, tanbark, shredded tree bark, or stone chips or pebbles. Be certain that these paths blend in with the surrounding plants.

If working with a steep slope, it will be necessary to make several terraces to hold back the soil. Areas can be leveled off every 2 or 3 feet before rocks are arranged on them. in many cases, this can add to the appeal of the rock garden, adding interest because of the level variations.

It is also well to jot down on paper the positions of several plants. At this point, it is advisable to get to know their growth habits. Some, like Arabis and Ajuga, are aggressive by nature, so try to place them between large rocks where their spreading nature can be checked. On the other hand, trailers, like Gold-dust or Ground Phlox, can be allowed to trail over the sides of rocks where they present a glorious sight when in full flower. Less vigorous kinds, like small alpines, should be placed in narrow crevices where they will not be overpowered.

When designing the rock garden, avoid pockets where water collects, since good drainage is essential for success. Secure rocks well by placing them deeply. Any that are loose can cause damage when accidentally walked on. Look for rocks that are native to the region, since they fit into the setting better. Weathered rock of any kind is good, but obtain stones that are irregular and asymmetrical and dark in coloring. Rounded stones are bad because they do not look natural.

Select rocks of different sizes, but avoid the use of too many. A rock garden is not a collection of rocks, but a collection of plants arranged around carefully selected and placed rocks and stones. Few types of gardening are more easy to overdo than this. A mountain of rocks presents a jarring note that not even a healthy grouping of flowering plants can ameliorate.

Soil

In a way, soil and construction go hand in hand. If soil is not the right kind, it can be specially prepared to meet the needs of the plants. In the case of existing rocks, poor soil will have to be scooped out and replaced with the proper mixture.

Most rock garden plants are not fussy about soil, and will grow in almost any kind, provided there is good drainage. Some plants require an acid soil, others prefer one that is alkaline. Yet most thrive in soil that ranges between pH6 and pH8. A thin, porous one is best, more so in sections of the country where rainfall is heavy.

Where droughts prevail during the growing season, the soil should be heavier and more moisture-retentive to meet the needs of plants. In this case, it should be prepared beforehand with humus. Other aids consist of using mulches of fine gravel or stone chips to hold in the moisture. These will also help to prevent weeds from taking over.

A simple preparation consists of equal parts soil, coarse sand, and peat moss, leaf mold or compost. Another combines equal parts loam, leaf mold, peat moss, sand and fine gravel. Since most rock garden plants are lime-loving, add agricultural lime. Unless soil is very acid, a heavy sprinkling will do. Bone meal or super phosphate, slow-acting phosphoric fertilizers, can be added at the recommended amounts. Some rock plants do not need it, but others like Dianthus, campanulas and daphnes appreciate it.

If scooping out soil in pockets and between crevices in natural rock outcroppings, dig to a depth of about a foot, where this is possible. Place a layer of stones, pebbles, or pieces of broken bricks at the bottom. Then add a layer of coarse sand or gravel before placing the soil on top. Wash each layer with the hose to make it settle firmly and eliminate air pockets.

Construction

Constructing the rock garden is not the easiest task. It is advisable to do considerable reading beforehand and, where possible, employ the services of a qualified landscape architect. In either instance, observe and study rock formations in nature. The idea is not to copy them, but to receive inspiration and understand how they comprise a harmonious whole. Small rock can be lifted easily, but with larger ones you will need suitable tools. One or two crowbars will be among the handiest.

If proceeding on your own, first bring together the rocks to be used. Unless you have mastered your design so it is clearly in your mind, keep the plan sketched on a piece of paper close at hand.

Start to work at the lowest point. After placing a layer of drainage material at the bottom, add about ¾ of the prepared soil in that particular spot, leaving the rest to spread around the rocks when in their final position. Generally speaking, keep the largest rocks for the base. In some instances, existing soil will have to be removed to make room for these boulders. Place them on their broadest bases, making certain they are secure. When completed, more than half of each rock should be under the surface of the ground. Arrange each so it leans toward the soil in order to catch rain water. Most of the rocks will have to be concentrated in steep places to hold back the soil. Use fewer where the grade is less abrupt, and allow for large levels where quantities of vigorous rock plants will be permitted to spill over the sides. Here and there small rocks can be used to give the impression that they have tumbled down. The key of the successful rock garden is to make it look as natural as possible, rather than man-made.

Before setting each rock in its permanent position, stand back to see how it looks. Turn it around a few times, and you will discover that, what was previously the bottom, may well be the top. At this stage, it is easier to make changes.

When completed, and before you start to plant, let the rock garden rest for a few days. Up to this point, you have been too close to it and need to get away from it. You will have the opportunity to stand back and see the rock garden from several different angles at various times of the day, under divergent condition of sunlight and shadows. Strive for unity, harmony, and balance, and try to capture the rhythm and the feeling of a natural ledge, the kind you have often admired in nature.

Planting

Planting the rock garden requires a special kind of skill. First, become acquainted with the different kinds of plants. Some are shy, others are vigorous. Some are very hardy, others will need winter protection. It is important to know the forms and growth habits of each, as they vary to include the prostrate, rounded, spreading and upright forms.

The famous rock garden at Kew, England. (*Photo by Arnold Arboretum, Jamaica Plain, Mass.*)

As a beginner, start with some of the easier kinds, but this does not imply a limited variety. In fact, much of the interest in the rock garden stems from its varied number of plants. As you become familiar with these easy kinds, bring in the more difficult. They call for more specialized attention, but they offer keener pleasure.

A harmonious composition between rocks and plants is the aim of every rock garden, be it large or small. In a way, it is no different from other forms of gardening. Colors of many rock garden plants and alpines are bright and vivid— magentas, rose-pinks, golden yellows, orange-reds. Yet this does not mean they cannot be brought together into a harmonious unit. Where colors tend to clash if placed side by side, break them up through the use of white, the "peacemaker." Also in the unobstructed sunshine, where rock gardens are located, bright colors go together more easily, as is often seen in tropical gardens.

Early spring is a good time to plant, but better still is late summer or early fall when most rock plants are dormant. In spring, they are making rapid growth to come into bloom. If dealing

with pot grown plants, as is often the case nowadays, you can do the work any time during the growing season, if water is available. Set out plants when soil is moist and crumbly. Avoid a very wet soil, which tends to cake and pack the roots, cutting down on the air supply.

When planting, firm the soil around the roots. You will have to take special precaution to get rid of air between rock crevices. Work slowly, ramming the soil as you proceed. Where space permits, use 3 or more specimens of the same kind in order to produce a broad splash of foliage and color. In small crevices and nooks use small alpines. They look more endearing, and are protected from vociferous neighbors by surrounding rocks. Dwarf types, as saxifrages, primulas, aubrietas, and small achilleas, can be spaced 6–8 in. apart. More spreading thymes, cerastiums and Ground Phlox will need at least a foot.

Always strive for informality in the rock garden. A formal rock garden does not exist in nature. Plant singly or in clumps, but never in rows. Allow an occasional plant to stray here and there. Tuck one in a sheltered crevice, another in a narrow opening between stones. Always permit some to cascade, for they impart a special charm. Bring together beguiling foliage textures and patterns, not so difficult if you put your imagination to play.

Maintenance

On the whole, the rock garden requires little care, no hoeing or cultivating and very little weeding, once weeds are pulled up and thick mulches are applied. A minimum of feeding is needed, since a too-rich diet will promote lush growth that tends to rot or winterkill.

Even so, like any other form of gardening, general upkeep must be practiced if the rock garden is to look its best. It can quickly become an eyesore.

In the early spring, after winter covers are removed, gradually, according to the dictates of the weather, check plants to see if they need to be firmed back. Winter thawing and heaving will loosen them, but with the hands or feet this is easily done when soil is moist, but not wet. Some plants may require replanting if they have been pushed out of the soil too much.

A light scattering of a high phosphoric fertilizer, such as 5–10–5, can be spread on the surface of the soil and scratched in with a weeder where this is permissible, if it does not interfere with plant roots. Better still, topdress the rock garden, using a mixture of 3 parts garden soil, 1 part leaf mold or peat moss, and 1 part coarse sand. To this add a 6-in. pot of bone meal to each wheelbarrow of prepared soil.

In spring, you will want to check each plant

carefully to see how it is doing. There may be dead growth in need of removal. Some large plants, not pruned the previous summer, may need cutting back, but do this carefully in order not to cut down on the display of bloom. If some plants have died, remove them and replace with others. Large specimens can be divided, but it is better to wait until after flowering is past and plants go into their semi-dormant period.

In established rock gardens, plants in crevices may appear weak. Most likely they have exhausted the soil, so lift them and provide a fresh mixture, well fortified with organic matter and some fertilizer. Their revival will be amazing. If these are to be separated, retain the outer shoots, which are the most vigorous.

Many rock plants are drought-resistant, but during prolonged dry periods they will need deep watering. Allow the sprinkler to run for a long time or use watering wands or soakers that permit the water to ooze out slowly. If watering is too quick much of the water will roll away and be of little aid to the rock garden.

Through the summer months, some hand weeding will be needed. For this, a dandelion weeder is excellent or use a long-handle cultivator with 2 prongs. A well-designed and built rock garden is one that enables the gardener to reach any part without stepping on plants. Paths, walks, and large, flat rock surfaces make this possible.

Trim back rampant growers in late summer, such kinds as Gold Alyssum and Arabis. Some plants can be sheared, but try to keep this uneven. If each plant is clipped into a neat, rounded mound, it will look unnatural. Allow some to trail over rocks or the ground provided they do not infringe on their less aggressive neighbors. To keep up appearances, keep removing dead flower heads and stalks as much as possible. This will also prevent seed formation (except where wanted), which can be exhausting to plants.

In Aug. or early Sept., lift, divide, and replant pieces of those in need of it. Give fresh soil mixtures and mulch with gravel or another material, the kind you are in habit of using. Extra plants may be given to friends and neighbors or planted in the garden in out of the way places. They may come in handy later on.

Winter Mulches

Strangely enough, in spite of their extreme hardiness, many rock garden and alpine plants require some form of a mulch to protect them during the winter. Where they grow naturally on mountain slopes and tops, they are covered most of the winter by a thick blanket of snow, which provides perfect insulation against wind and sun. The greatest winter enemy of rock plants is the possibility of building up excessive moisture, and it is dampness, if it persists, that causes foliage to mat and rot. Alternate thawing and heaving present another problem, and this is eliminated by a thick, airy blanket in winter. Where snowfall is heavy and lasts all winter, this is less apt to occur, and mulching is not so necessary.

There are some plants with foliage that mat which do not require a mulch, of which Arabis is an outstanding example. Those that die to the ground, like Fringed Bleeding Heart and Epimedium, come through the best, but those with woolly, mat-forming rosettes should not be overlooked.

A good mulch is light, airy and attractive. It should not hold too much moisture or tend to decay. Evergreen branches, like unused Christmas trees or branches of White Pine or other native evergreens (more readily available) are highly recommended because they allow air to pass through. At the same time, they are good looking.

Salt or marsh hay and straw are equally good. They are easily worked in among the stones or small shrubs. Cranberry branches will do the same job. If you are going to use leaves, cut branches of Oak with the leaves attached, they make a desirable winter cover, but keep away from maple, which flatten when wet and cause plants to smother. The time to apply these covers is in early winter after the ground has frozen. Remove gradually in the early spring after the snow has melted, when the frost is out of the ground, and when temperatures will stay above freezing.

Some of the more unusual and difficult-to-grow plants that are subject to injury or killing from excessive dampness will require a collar of stone chips. It will lift leaves above the ground, in the case of evergreen or nearly evergreen kinds, and aid in drawing the moisture away from the crowns. With some, a mixture of peat moss, sand, and stone chips may be worked in the soil around the tops. In the late fall, after the first freeze, a small alpine often tends to be lifted out of the ground a few inches. Press back with the foot or a stick or trowel and then mulch. The most prized plants may even have to be lifted and placed in the cold frame for the winter.

The Wall Garden

The wall garden can be a charming addition to any garden. More difficult to build than the rock garden, it presents a mood and character of its own. The major advantage is that it enables the owner of a small place to grow rock garden and alpine plants. It can also form the boundary of the sunken garden. In this case, it should rarely be more than 3 ft. high.

Sometimes a low, dry wall, with stones that are loosely set, can be effective as is this one in the Director's personal garden in Kew Gardens, England. (*Photo by Arnold Arboretum, Jamaica Plain, Mass.*)

The wall garden is more difficult to construct than the rock garden, but the same principles of design are involved. In it are grown small plants that abound in crevices and on cliffs, some that are tufted, some that droop, some that cling. The early spring is the best time to build and plant the wall garden, followed by Sept., which allows enough time for roots to become firmly established before the ground freezes.

A wall garden is usually placed in front of a bank to hold back the soil behind it. To do this properly, it should be solidly built, able to withstand the pressure exerted by freezing soil behind it. Properly made, it can be as much as 12 or 15 ft. high.

As with the rock garden, the largest rocks should be used at the bottom, followed by smaller at the top. Since no mortar will be used, it is the weight of the stones, one on top of the other, that will keep the wall firm and make it last for years. It is preferable to use local stone, although exotic kinds can be brought in. The kind of stone to be used will depend, in the end, on the desired effect and the overall surroundings.

The wall garden inclines backward, so that it is lower at the back than in the front. Each individual stone also tilts backward toward the bank. This way the bank is held more firmly in position and the sloping angle permits rain to seep through the crevices to reach the roots of the plants as they stretch out to the soil beyond.

When gathering stones, avoid those that are rounded, and select those that are flat and narrow. The largest, that will form the foundation, need not be below the frost line, but they should be secured firmly. Place them in a sloping position, that is toward the soil, about 10 in. deep, which is sufficient to provide a firm hold and prevent them from moving after heavy rains or cold winter weather. The width of the base should be about one-third of the height of the wall.

A tall wall makes an effective background for a display of vines. (*Photo by Arnold Arboretum, Jamaica Plain, Mass.*)

The larger the wall, the larger should be the stones. First place a row of the heaviest at the base, each leaning backward. Then add a few inches of soil, and it is well to use the specially prepared mixture recommended for rock gardens. Always place about 6 in. of this soil in back of each rock or stone. Pack it in firmly to avoid air pockets, which dry out quickly and usually result in poor growth.

The next layer of rocks will require careful placement. Do not rest a rock on top of another but between two, so that its weight is borne by the rocks and not the soil. Continue in this

A dry wall garden that is effectively planted can be of continuing interest. (*Photo by Arnold Aroboretum, Jamuica Plain, Mass.*)

manner all the way to the top. Always place each rock in a horizontal position. When completed, the weight will be carried by the rocks, and there will be no vertical crevices in the dry wall.

The ideal way to plant is as you go along. After the rocks are laid and 2 or 3 in. of soil is placed over them, rest plants in position and spread out the roots, covering them with 2 or 3 in. of the soil preparation. Plant 1 layer at a time, and be certain to tamp the soil carefully.

In many instances, it is not possible to plant as you build. When the construction is completed, scoop out 1 or 2 trowelfuls of soil from a crevice, insert the roots of the plant, and replace as much of the soil as possible, pressing it firmly. Use smaller plants than you would by the other method, but also be prepared to expect some losses. Water and keep moist until plants are established.

Seeds can be sown in the wall garden in the spring. Mix the seed with moist sandy loam and press into the openings and crevices. A small piece of moss placed on the soil will help to prevent excessive drying out.

Kinds of Plants

Plants for rock gardens consist mainly of low-growing perennials, along with dwarf kinds of annuals that are grown to introduce color during the summer months. Hardiness varies with the section of the country, but for the most part rock and alpine plants are tough, able to withstand considerable winter cold. Small shrubs, usually under 2 ft. high, fit well into the picture, and are planted to add height, color in the case of flowering kinds, green from evergreens in winter, and picturesqueness of form and branching habit. In very large rock gardens some that grow as much as 3 ft. tall are worthy of consideration.

The following are a few of the most suitable, easy to grow, and readily available that the beginning gardener can use. Local nurseries offer a wide variety, and these can be chosen on the basis of appeal. There are, for example, many kinds of low-growing azaleas, but because their hardiness varies, they are best purchased from nearby nurseries.

Arctostaphylos uva-ursi (Bearberry)—trailing evergreen, with small glossy leaves, that turn purplish in winter. Good in poor, sandy soil and hot places. Small white-pink flowers followed by red fruits. Very hardy.

Berberis wilsoniae (Wilson Barberry)—a low, spreading, almost prostrate barberry, with small, spiny, pale green leaves that turn bright red in autumn.

Cotoneaster horizontalis (Rock Spray Cotoneaster)—flat shrub that spreads in horizontal manner, with small, shiny leaves and red berries

in the fall. *C. microphylla* (Small-leaved Cotoneaster), an evergreen, has the smallest leaves of all. Both these cotoneasters form dense mounds.

Daphne cneorum (Rose Daphne)—sprawling evergreen, with small, narrow leaves, and clusters of tiny pink flowers known for their sweet scent. Give full sun, good drainage, and an alkaline soil. Tops require protection from winter wind and sun in exposed places in cold regions.

Erica carnea (Spring Heath)—a low, spreading evergreen, with fine, needlelike foliage and small rosy-pink flowers in early spring. Give sun and light, acid soil. There is a white variety, as well as many improved hybrids for the collector.

Ilex crenata 'Convexa' (Convex-leaved Japanese Holly) one of the larger-growing shrubs in this category, recommended for large rock gardens. With pruning, its size can be controlled. It has small, rounded, glossy, dark green leaves. It is evergreen, as are 2 dwarf, compact forms, *I. crenata* 'Helleri' (Heller Holly) and 'Kingsville' which is extremely slow growing.

Juniperus chinensis sargentii (Sargent Juniper)—a low trailer, 6–12 in. high, with upright branchlets. It has silvery-gray leaves, and forms an excellent ground cover where space permits. *J. communis depressa* (Prostrate Juniper), also low growing and spreading, grows to a foot. Its soft green foliage turns bronzy in winter. *J. horizontalis* (Creeping Juniper), mat forming, has steel-blue needles. One of its better known forms is 'Waukegan'.

Leiophyllum buxifolium (Box Sand-myrtle)—a dwarf evergreen, with small, glossy leaves and clusters of white flowers in May. Recommended for sandy, highly acid soils.

Leucothos fontanesiana (*L. catesbaei*) (Drooping Leucothoe)—a large broad-leaved evergreen that will give emphasis to large rock gardens or outcroppings. Long, shiny leaves become purplish red with cold weather in winter. Small white flowers in drooping clusters appear in spring. Will do well in shade.

Paxistima canbyi (Canby Pachistima)—a dense evergreen, with tiny leaves and small dark red flowers. Will form a soft carpet if given space. For acid soil in partial shade. Grows a foot high.

Picea glauca 'Conica' (Dwarf Alberta Spruce)—extremely slow growing, dense, conical evergreen that will impart accent and focal point to the rock garden. Requires full sun.

Potentilla fruticosa (Shrubby Cinquefoil)—small, dense, deciduous shrub, with small leaves and pale yellow flowers that appear constantly from June to frost. For poor soil in sunny places.

Spiraea bumalda 'Anthony Waterer'—an upright shrub, about 2 ft. tall, with showy flat clusters of bright crimson flowers in early summer. Will add needed color in sunny sections of larger rock gardens.

Taxus cuspidata 'Nana' (Dwarf Japanese Yew)—low, spreading, dense Yew, with dark green needles that remain lustrous all year-round. It grows in an irregular manner, in sun or shade.

The list of rock garden plants is so extensive that the beginner will want to start out with some of the easiest, as well as more readily procurable. Later, after making a study of rarer kinds, a few new ones can be added each year. The following, however, represent an interesting collection that will make a colorful and dependable start.

Achillea tomentosa—a yarrow, with soft, feathery, woolly leaves and clusters of yellow flowers on 8-in. stalks. Give full sun and poor soil. Variety 'Moonlight' has light yellow flower heads.

Alyssum alpestre—a creeper, with rough gray leaves and clusters of yellow flowers. The vigorous *A. saxatile*, known as Basket-of-Gold, is a sprawling plant, with gray leaves and masses of dazzling yellow blossoms. *A. saxatile citrinum* is a soft yellow form.

Anemone pulsatilla—this is the intriguing European Pasque-flower, admired for its purple cup-shaped flowers, with their striking yellow stamens, that appear in early spring. Its finely cut leaves are woolly.

Aquilegia canadensis—good in partial shade is the Wild Columbine, with its quaint red and yellow flowers on hanging stems. It will grow in rock crevices. *A. chrysantha*, another native, has soft yellow blossoms with long spurs that continue to appear over a long period of time. It, too, is excellent in light shade.

Arabis caucasica—one of the common, early spring-flowering rock plants that forms dense mats of pure white flowers. There is a double form that is superior because it lasts much longer.

Armeria maritima—this charming rock plant grows abundantly along the cliffs in Cornwall, England, the reason it is called sea thrift. It forms dense tufts of green, and produces heads of bright rose flowers. It is ideal for edging or to grow in openings in pavements.

Aubrieta—there are many varieties of this low-growing perennial that forms carpets of bright pink, lavender, or violet in early spring. Grow it on banks or along the tops of walls, where it will receive the excellent drainage it needs.

Calluna vulgaris—there are many forms of Heather, an evergreen with fine leaves and masses of small pink, red, purple or white flowers. Give an acid soil, with plenty of sand and peat added. Shear in early spring.

Campanula carpatica—a low-growing Canterbury Bell, 1 ft. tall, with wiry stems of purple or white flowers. It is easy to grow in sun or light shade, and is available in several attractive hybrids. *C. portenschlagiana* is a dwarf species 4–5 in. tall, with violet-blue flowers. It grows with ease.

Cerastium tomentosum—another popular rock plant, vigorous and spreading, forming large mats of gray leaves and sheets of white flowers. Cut back after flowering to keep in check.

Dianthus deltoides—this is the Maiden Pink of England, a dainty perennial, with tiny glossy leaves and clusters of small, deep pink flowers. More common is *D. plumarius*, the Scotch Pink that is an old favorite. Blue-gray leaves are enlivened with fragrant, toothed, pink flowers in June. There are many handsome hybrids. Give full sun and a well-drained soil.

Dicentra eximia—a summer-flowering Bleeding Heart, with soft, finely cut leaves and hanging clusters of rose-pink flowers. It thrives in shade. There is a white form for contrast.

Epimedium macranthum—the common name of this low perennial is Barrenwort. Heart-shaped leaves appear on wiry stems. There are several variations of this favorite that are good ground covers in the shade.

Eranthis hyemalis—Winter Aconite is the common name of this small bulb that in every early spring unfolds golden-cupped flowers on 3 in. stems. The round buds are enveloped by feathery ruffs. The leaves disappear after the seed ripens.

Gentiana septemfida—an easy Gentian that is happy in moist, well-drained soil in sun or part shade. Clear blue flowers appear in summer. Available are many forms and hybrids.

Gypsophila repens—a Baby's-breath that trails and grows only 6 in. tall. Mounds of silvery-gray leaves are enlivened by sprays of small, pink or white flowers.

Heuchera—Coral-bells, good in shade, is appreciated for its airy sprays of small pink, rose, or white flowers. Rounded, scalloped leaves form neat rosettes. There are several hybrids, and all do well in sun or light shade, provided they have moisture.

Iberis sempervirens—Hardy Candytuft is one of the most striking of rock garden plants, even when planted in borders. Large plants become sheets of purest white in May. Hybrids include 'Little Gem' with narrow leaves, and 'Snowflake', medium in height. All are best in full sun.

Iris cristata—this dwarf spring-flowering

Iris, only 6 in. tall, produces soft blue and white flowers. Creeping plants appreciate light shade. A white form is choice. *I. tectorum*, the Roof Iris of Japan, grows to 8 in. and has broader leaves and crested lavender or white flowers. Good drainage is important.

Lavandula sp.—Lavender is cherished for the pungent fragrance of the leaves and the spikes of lavender flowers. A small shrub, with gray leaves, it is best in a warm, sunny location in poor soil. It comes in pink, blue and white.

Leontopodium alpinum—this is the famed Edelweiss of Switzerland, an easy alpine, with flowers, composed of bracts, that look like woolly stars, gray or white, and requires sun.

Mitchella repens—the native Partridge-berry is an evergreen, trailing ground cover, with small, glossy leaves and white flowers followed by bright red berries.

Phlox divaricata—Blue Phlox is the common name for this favorite that brightens rock gardens and borders where tulips and pansies are grown. A creeping plant attaining 1 ft., it has narrow leaves and clusters of pale blue flowers. Sun or shade suit it. *P. stolonifera* is another species that is prostrate. Its glossy, rounded leaves provide a perfect foil for the lavender flowers. It needs a rich, peaty soil. *P. subulata* is the proverbial Moss or Ground Phlox, with its needle evergreen leaves and dense masses of magenta, pink, rose, light blue, lavender, or white flowers. Use it to cover a sandy bank.

Primula denticulata—a charming Primrose that forms rosettes of bright green leaves and rounded flower clusters, lavender in color, in spring. These may be up to 10 in. in height. Colors also include rose, red, lavender, purple and white. Provide a moist soil and high shade. *P. polyantha* is the Common Primrose that produces flower clusters in many colors. Give moisture at all times and keep out of the hot sun.

Saponaria ocymoides—a trailing plant that develops mats of leafy stems and quantities of pink flowers. Use it to drape over rocks. It requires good drainage.

Sedum acre—a crawling plant that hugs the ground with its stems of bright green leaves that root as they go along. Yellow flowers last a long time. It can become a weed unless checked. Grow it in crevices on steps. *S. album*, also spreading, has fleshy stems and round leaves. White flowers appear in midsummer. It is recommended for hot, sunny banks. Trailing is *S. spurium*, with its flat leaves and pinkish flowers. Variety 'Dragon's Blood' has reddish leaves and deep red blossoms.

Shortia galacifolia—this bears the picturesque name of Oconee Bells. An American native, it is a creeper, with rounded leaves and small, white,

bell flowers in spring. It needs a peaty soil and part shade.

Silene acaulis—a winsome plant that grows in dense clumps of small, pointed leaves. Cushion Pink is the common name of this plant that unfolds solitary pink flowers for a period of several weeks.

Teucrium chamaedrys—this member of the Mint Family, known as Germander, is a small shrub, to a foot, with rounded glossy leaves. It is often grown as a hedge because it withstands trimming.

Thalictrum kiusianum—a Meadow-rue from Japan, 3–4 in. tall, that spreads by stolons so that it takes over among rocks. Dainty, feathery, pink-lavender flowers are covered by stamens.

Thymus serpyllum—this is the Mother-of-thyme, a sprawling, mat-forming plant with tiny leaves and white to purple flowers on upright stems. Grow it in full sun. *T. vulgaris* is the common Thyme, robust and spreading. It has small fragrant leaves and lavender flowers.

Tiarella cordifolia—the Foam-flower of our woods has deeply lobed, maplelike leaves and spikes of feathery white flowers. It forms a neat ground cover in shade.

Veronica incana—a low Veronica, characterized by light gray leaves and 8-in. spikes of purple-violet flowers in late spring. Give it good drainage. *V. repens*, a creeper an inch or two high, sports smooth, glossy leaves and pale blue flowers, forming a perfect ground cover where a dense mat is needed. Or grow it between stepping stones. It is best in a moist soil in part shade.

Violas and *violets*—there are several kinds of both, all excellent for rock gardens. Violas, short-lived perennials, resemble small pansies, but are available in several solid colors, including purple, blue, apricot, yellow and white. Violets, with heart-shaped leaves, may be blue, purple, pink or white. They flower in spring and grow luxuriantly in shade with plenty of moisture. The leaves remain attractive all summer long.

Books on the subject of constructing, planting, and maintaining a rock garden are of tremendous help. One of these, a large paperback, called "How to Plan, Establish and Maintain Rock Gardens," is published by Sunset Magazine, Menlo Park, Calif., and abounds in pictures. "All About Rock Gardens and Plants" by Walter A. Kolaga, published by Doubleday & Co., N.J. (1966) is excellent, with many fine plants and their cultural needs described.

Enthusiasts will want to become members of the large and active National Rock Garden Society by writing to the American Rock Garden Society. (See SOCIETIES).

GEORGE TALOUMIS

ROCKMAT, TUFTED = *Petrophytum caespitosum*

ROCK-PURSLANE. See CALANDRINIA.

ROCK-ROSE. See CISTUS.

ROCK-ROSE FAMILY = Cistaceae

ROCKSPRAY. See COTONEASTER.

RODGER'S-FLOWER. See RODGERSIA.

RODGERSIA (ro-JER-sia)

  podophylla   5′   Zones 5–6   Bronzeleaf
                                   Rodger's-flower
An herbaceous perennial needing winter protection in the North, valued for its metalbronze colored foliage during the summer. The finger-shaped, 5-lobed leaves are 10 in. long and 6 in. wide, light green at first but later turning to the desirable bronze color. The flowers are small, yellowish white, in foot-long spraylike panicles. Native to China. This is the most popular species but should be planted in a peaty soil and be given plenty of moisture. Not a plant for a dry situation. Easily propagated by division.

  tabularis   3′   Zones 5–6   Shieldleaf Rodger's-
                                  flower
With alternate, peltate or rounded, long-petioled leaves, 3 in. wide, these have many short lobes or large teeth. The flowers are small and white in many small panicles. Native to China. Easily propagated by division.

RODRIGUEZIA (rod-ree-GAY-zia). A group of 30 or more epiphytic, pseudobulbous orchid species, native to tropical America, with usually showy flowers, in a many-flowered raceme. For greenhouse culture only, in which the winter temperatures do not go below 60° F. Propagation is usually by division. For culture see ORCHID.

ROGUE. In horticulture this term is used for a plant, differing from the rest of the seedling population, usually an undesirable type. It is "rogued out" or removed from the field.

ROHDEA (RO-dea)   japonica   2′   Zone 9
                                         Omoto Nippon-lily
A good perennial with many varieties, valued especially as a house plant or in the garden in the South for its long-lasting foliage. The flowers are inconspicuous. Leaves are borne in a rosette at the base of the plant. They are oblanceolate, thick, leathery, arching, 2 ft. long and 3 in. wide. The fruit is a large berry with red pulp. Native to China and Japan where it is frequenty grown for its colorful, variegated-leaved varieties. It belongs to the Lily Family.

ROLLING. An operation most used in the garden during the preparation of a lawn, either to make the ground smooth and level after winter, or to press the newly-distributed grass seed into the soil after it has been raked. Metal rollers are available which can be filled with water, to supply weight. These are good because the amount of weight needed is not the same for every operation. Rolling the lawn after the winter heaving (see HEAVING) of grass plants is of course a good practice to get them properly reestablished in the soil. It is done while there is still plenty of moisture left in the soil and it responds to the rolling operation. When vrye dry and hard, rolling may do little good. Combined with this operation is the seeding and raking of bare spots in the lawn, then rolling the whole area. Usually, other parts of the garden soil can be levelled better by proper harrowing and raking, rather than by rolling.

RONDELETIA (ron-del-LEE-shia)

  cordata   5′–7′   Zone 9   Heartleaf Rondeletia
A handsome evergreen shrub with opposite leaves, 3–5 in. long. The pink to rose-red flowers are ¼ in. wide, the throat yellow. Native to Guatemala. Easily propagated by softwood cuttings.

ROOF GARDEN. Although the history of roof gardening goes back to the Hanging Gardens of Babylon, it was not until the advent of the modern high rise apartment building that this peculiarly urban field of gardening came into its own. Today, in spite of the many problems that beset them, thousands of roof-gardeners have discovered that an upstairs garden can help to make urban living very tolerable, whether on spacious penthouses or on tiny balcony terraces.

A realistic approach, and an understanding of the difficulties that must be faced are prime requisites for a successful roof garden. Since the roof gardener starts with nothing but a bare floor his first concern is something to hold the growing medium. The containers may range from standard-size window boxes to built-in masonry beds. The former, being only 6 or 7 in. deep, play a limited role in roof-garden landscaping, because few plants will winter over in them—which means that they must be replanted each spring in the traditional fashion. The nearest thing to natural growing conditions and natural landscaping is achieved by the use of masonry-retaining walls, 18–24 in. high. Such raised beds have the greatest potentials of all, but are usually practical only on the terraces of cooperative penthouse apartments. The great majority of roof gardeners depend on terrace-boxes and tubs to contain the soil and supply garden frame-work.

Terrace boxes may be anywhere from 10 to 18 in. deep and wide—4- or 5-ft. lengths are most practical. The best all-round material is wood, especially for the build-it-yourself gardener. Redwood and cedar are best, but fir and pine serve very well if treated with a preservative. Those who want a classic look may prefer concrete, or the modern look of reinforced fiberglass. Both offer excellent durability and insulation but at a higher cost.

Perhaps "planter" is a better word to use than tub, for in this category is included not only the tubs and barrels but wooden cubes, concrete urns, fiberglass cylinders, large terra cotta pots etc. Fine accent effects are possible when the container that will bring out the best in a plant is chosen or a plant to show off the container at its best.

Whatever type of planters or beds are used, the soil-mix that fills them must be of the highest quality. Suggested mixtures per cu. ft. are as follows:

GENERAL PURPOSE	ALKALINE pH	ACID pH
25 lbs. topsoil	35 lbs. topsoil	20 lbs. topsoil
2 qts. humus	2 qts. humus	2 qts. humus
1 qt. peat moss	2 qts. perlite	4 qts. peat moss
1 qt. perlite	2 handfuls lime	2 qts. perlite
1 handful bone meal	1 handful bone meal	1 handful dried cow manure
1 tbsp. 5–10–5	1 tbsp. 5–10–5	1 small handful sulfur

Preparing such soil mixtures is a tedious chore, but one that pays handsome dividends for years to come. To an even greater extent than in a conventional garden, soil is the key to success. When unimproved soil is dumped into roof-garden planters it becomes muddy when wet and rock-hard when dry—and since it requires frequent watering, there is an excessive leaching-out of nutrients. After a couple of seasons of this, very few plants will survive.

Although some leaching is inevitable it can be kept to a minimum by proper attention to drainage. An inch or so of drainage material should line the bottom of the planter. Shards or clinkers seem to work out best, especially the former, which can be placed over drainage holes with the concave side down. If a layer of sphagnum moss or fiberglass is then laid over the drainage material the result is a slow, steady drain-off of moisture, with a minimum of leaching. "Outside" drainage is provided simply by raising all planters an inch or two off the floor. Masonry beds must have built-in "weep-holes" every few feet.

A year-round surface mulch is of great benefit to roof-grown plants. Mulching helps to keep roots cool and moist under the blistering heat that roof-garden plants must withstand in midsummer. In winter it keeps the soil evenly cold and prevents heaving, which can otherwise be disastrous in narrow planters.

Although space does not permit a detailed discussion here of landscape construction in the roof garden, mention should be made of fencing and overhead protection. Before doing any planting, it is important to erect some sort of windbreak if none exists—for high winds can seriously damage many plants, especially when newly planted, and the higher the floor, the higher the winds will be. An awning, arbor or lathe house is almost a necessity, to filter the full glare of the sun. A small pool fitted with a circulating pump can also help to beat the heat, and provide a perfect setting for plants as well.

Trees

Planted in large containers or masonry beds with a soil depth of 18–36 in., small trees can be grown for a good many years. For best results choose nursery-grown, balled and burlapped specimens not over 6 or 7 ft. tall. Those with compact growth habits and good tolerance for wind and smog are of course preferred. Recommended small trees include Honey-locust (*Gleditsia triacanthos*), Russian-olive (*Eleagnus angustifolia*), Hawthorn (*Crataegus*), Cornelian Cherry (*Cornus mas*), crab apples, and Silk Tree (*Albizia julibrissin*). Good shade trees for a spacious terrace include London Plane (*Platanus acerifolia*), Littleleaf European Linden (*Tilia cordata*) and Ginkgo (*G. biloba*). For a quick accent display Weeping Willow (*Salix babylonica* or *S. vitellina*) can be tub-grown if watered faithfully. Another fast grower, Lombardy Poplar (*Populus nigra* 'Italica') can be useful as a screen.

Evergreens

Conifers for roof planting should be tightly balled or container-grown specimens. Can-grown plants are a particular boon because they are easy to transport, easy to fit into narrow planters, and easy to transplant with a minimum of shock. Those most adaptable to roof gardens are the ones that thrive, in nature, on windswept hills. Pines, especially Japanese Black Pine (*Pinus thunbergii*), head the list—followed by Spruce (*Picea*), Red-cedar (*Juniperus virginiana*). Yew (*Taxus*) does well with the aid of an adequate windbreak. For roof rockeries Dwarf Mugo Pine (*P. mugo mugo*) and the prostrate junipers are excellent.

Most broad-leaved evergreens need considerable shelter to do well in a roof garden. Heath (*Erica*) and Heather (*Calluna vulgaris*), however, can be used to good advantage in exposed positions if protected by evergreen boughs in winter. Andromeda (*Pieris*) is remarkably tolerant of roof conditions, and other good bets are Japanese Holly (*Ilex crenata*) and American Holly (*I. opaca*). Rhododendrons and azaleas need considerable pampering, and are most at home in a protected masonry bed. English Ivy (*Hedera helix*) is a dependable evergreen vine if given winter protection, but for a hot southern exposure Winter Creeper (*Euonymus fortunei* "Vegetus") is better suited. Special attention to the soil mixture is needed for all roof-garden evergreens (see suggested acid mixture above) and a year-round mulch is indispensable.

Shrubs

Almost any deciduous shrub can thrive in a roof garden if given a foot or more of soil depth, as in a terrace box or 16–18 in. tub. Some of the best choices are Abelia, Winged Euonymus (*E. alatus*), Butterfly Bush (*Buddleia*), Flowering Almond (*Prunus triloba*), Forsythia, bush honeysuckles, Weigela. Privet can provide a living windbreak, but will choke out other plants.

Vines

Most hardy vines are easily grown on the roof garden. Tried and true are grapes, Boston Ivy, honeysuckles, Silverlace Vine (*Polygonum aubertii*) and wisterias. Where possible these vines should, like privet, be grown in separate containers to prevent their roots from crowding out other plants.

Roses

The most tolerant roses are climbers, floribundas, and polyanthas, all of which do well in 12–18 in. of good soil depth if mulching and winter protection are adequate. Miniature roses are fine for window box culture if wintered indoors. Container-grown plants are better able to cope with the conditions than bare-root ones, and spring planting is best. Filtered shade is usually needed if exposure is south or west.

Perennials

Quite logically, those perennials that originally grew in the open fields (like the daisies), or on dry slopes (like the sedums), are among the best choices for roof gardens. The list includes Evergreen Candytuft (*Iberis*), Creeping Charlie (*Lysimachia nummularia*), chrysanthemums, Dianthus, Gaillardia, Showy Stonecrop (*Sedum spectabile*), Moss Pink (*Phlox subulata*), creeping sedums, Creeping Thyme, Yarrow (*Achillea*) and Yucca, as well as most perennial herbs. Soil heaving is a serious menace where volume of soil is so small, which means that a winter mulch for perennials takes on added importance. Spring planting is usually best.

Summer Bulbs

Roof gardeners who find that in such small planting areas perennials do not provide long enough blooming seasons can easily fill in gaps by interplanting with summer bulbs. There is one to suit almost any situation. Tuberoses, dwarf gladioli, or dwarf hybrid dahlias are made to order for terrace boxes. Cannas are effective in tubs, and climbing Gloriosa-lily is a showy, low-growing vine for trellis or arbor. Under the arbor is the best place for caladiums. Even for window boxes there are small bulbs like Oxalis or Zephyr-lily.

Spring Bulbs

A perfect time to improve used-up soil and plant spring-flowering bulbs is when dead annuals are removed in the fall. A spectacular, early season color display is possible, even in shallow planters, in which small bulbs can be grown. Preference logically should lean toward early-flowering, low-growing types, but any spring bulb will thrive in a roof garden when plenty of sun and good drainage are easily available. Unless they have masonry beds, most roof gardeners find that the most realistic cultural approach is to plant new bulbs each year.

Annuals

Recommended annuals for the foreground include Alyssum, Annual Candytuft, Ivy Geranium, Balcony Petunia, Portulaca, Lantana and Verbena. For the middle ground: Chinese Forget-me-not (*Cynoglossum*), Coreopsis, Ice Plant (*Mesembryanthemum*), French Marigold, California Poppy, Snapdragon and Dwarf Zinnia. For the background: African Marigold, Cleome, Tithonia and Giant Zinnia. Among annual vines Black-eyed Susan Vine (Thunbergia) and Cardinal Climber are outstanding for boxes. Morning Glory pays off best if interplanted with Moon-flower, since the latter contributes better foliage and evening bloom. Castor Bean is useful where a quick-growing specimen plant is needed for a tub. Cherry tomatoes and many other small vegetables are often grown in boxes with good results. For those who want to be adventurous and get away from the standard bedding plants a small cold frame is a very worthwhile investment.

Maintenance

Faithful watering is the most important

single factor in roof-garden maintenance. In summer heat the transpiration of moisture becomes extreme, and, since there are no underground reserves, drying out can cause serious losses. Rain can never be completely depended upon, since the foliage may deflect most of it from the soil itself. Sprinkling, except to wash soot and dust from the leaves, does more harm than good, for light watering brings the roots to the surface. The soil, therefore, must be given a deep and thorough soaking, with a water bubbler or soaker-hose rather than a nozzle. Watering must be started early in the season and continued late.

With frequent watering comes an inevitable leaching out of nutrients, so fertilizer boosters in liquid form take on special significance during the growing season.

Insect pests and diseases pose a comparatively minor problem in 'such limited areas. Spot spraying with aerosol bombs is usually all that is needed, if a vigilant lookout is maintained to catch trouble before it gets out of hand. The chief menace is from spider-mites, which thrive under hot dry roof conditions. On the other hand Japanese beetles, which breed in sod, are seldom seen.

As mentioned above, good winter protection as well as mulching is of prime importance in roof-garden maintenance. In protected lower-floor terraces an anti-dessicant spray may suffice for evergreens, but 20 stories up a protective screening of evergreen boughs is called for. Mounding soil around roses is usually impractical, but collars filled with a perlite peat mixture work out very well.

For further information on roof gardens see Yang, Linda, 'The Terrace Gardener's Handbook," Doubleday.

PHILIP E. TRUEX

ROMNEYA (ROM-ney-a)
  coulteri   8'   Zone 9   Matilija-poppy
A perennial herb, native to southern Calif. and Mexico. Plants produce large, single, fragrant, white flowers, 6 in. wide, something like a large poppy, for it belongs to the Poppy Family. There are 3 sepals and 6 petals. It is difficult to transplant and is propagated by suckers and seeds, but seedlings take several years before they bloom. The pinnately cut leaves are 4 in. long and very thin.

ROOT. A true root is the part of the plant that gathers most of the food of the plant from the soil or in some cases from the air. The roots act as a storehouse for the plant food after it is manufactured.

ROOT PRUNE. A horticultural term used to denote the pruning of roots. Every time any

Rooting in water

sizeable plant is dug a certain proportion of its roots are cut off in the digging operation and this is a root pruning in itself. Nurserymen, who grow woody plants for sale, periodically prune the roots of the plants in the nursery often by pulling long U-shaped steel blades down the nursery row under the plants, thus cutting all the roots but still leaving the plants in place. Then the cut roots produce many new ones close to the base of the plant, thus making it much easier to transplant with a much better chance of survival.

A tree growing in the woods any length of time may develop very long roots running 15–25 ft. or more away from the plant. These are sufficient because of many-branched side roots, to support the tree, but if one were to investigate the area in a 3-ft. radius about the trunk of that tree one would undoubtedly find very few of the small feeding roots so essential to gathering nourishment for the tree. These would probably be at quite some distance from the trunk, branching off the long main roots. As a consequence, if the tree were to be balled and moved, a major part of the necessary feeding roots would be cut off in the balling operation and the tree might easily die when it is transplanted. This is the reason that the nurseryman root prunes nursery plants, to force them to grow a large number of small feeding roots near the base of the plant which could be moved in the balling operation and insure growth after transplanting.

To make it possible to safely dig trees or shrubs in the woods, such trees should be root pruned a year or so before they are moved. This is done merely by forcing a sharp spade into the soil around the plant in a circle slightly smaller than the size of the contemplated ball, thus cutting all the roots to a depth of a foot or more. Or a trench can be dug slightly deeper than this, all the lateral roots cut, the soil returned to the trench and the plant left for a year to form new roots. The operation can be done in the very early spring and, if the plant does not suffer too much, it might be moved late in the fall.

Another way of accomplishing the same thing is to cut the roots all on one side in the spring, then on the other side the following spring, moving it that fall.

Bonsai plants (which see) are root pruned as a dwarfing measure, taken out of their pots every few years, and the longer roots pruned off at the ends.

Root pruning is also used to force a vigorous-growing fruit tree, Wisteria vine or Flowering Dogwood into bloom, merely as a dwarfing process. Using a spade to cut the roots in a circle about the plant early in the spring, as explained above, is all that is sometimes necessary to force a tree, shrub or vine into bloom the following year.

ROOTSTOCK. The root or "stock" on which the scion or bud of some different plant is grafted or budded.

ROSA (RO-sa). The rose species and botanical varieties are not appreciated in America nearly so much as they are in Europe. Only about 50 are offered by a very few U.S. nurseries, though nearly 150 are offered by European nurseries. Approximately 50 million rose bushes are sold in the U.S. annually, but very few of these are the species—most are the "modern" rose hybrids.

It is known that roses, in some form or other, have been on the North American continent for 32 million years—truly a long time and undoubtedly much mutation and segregation has occurred during that period. It is of interest to note that the majority of "modern" roses now so popular in American gardens are chiefly derived from 2 or more of the following species: *R. chinensis, R. damascena, R. foetida, R. moschata, R. multiflora, R. odorata, R. rugosa* and *R. wichuraiana*. These are all Asiatic in origin, showing that American and European species have contributed little. However, many of these species are themselves of value for certain distinctive uses in the garden, even though they rarely bloom more than once a season.

Many of the rose species are far more hardy than the hybrids so commonly grown. Gardeners who live in the northern U.S. and Canada might do well to remember this, for it means less need for winter protection. Also, the species are less susceptible to insect and disease troubles, which means less dusting, spraying and pruning. It is such plants which take less care that should be grown more in order to take a good deal of the drudgery out of garden maintenance.

Some of the rose species are valuable in the landscape because they can be appreciated for more than one season of the year. The Virginia Rose, for instance, is of interest during every season of the year. In late spring and early summer the light pink flowers appear; all through the summer it has shining green leaves; in the fall it has red fruits and a beautiful orange autumn color, and in the winter the red twigs and fruits remain to give bright color all season long. Such plants as these, which have interest for more than one season, should be grown more, regardless of whether they are roses or dogwoods. All roses have alternate, pinnately compound leaves and most species have thorns. The petals are pleasant to nibble and sometimes they are prepared as a salad, or are candied. The pulpy fruits of a few species have been used for making jellies rich in Vitamin C.

Propagation

There are so many rose species that it is reasonable to expect a wide variation in the germination of seeds of the different species. In general, however, seeds might well be stratified for 3 months at 40° F. and then sown. If they fail to germinate after a period of 3 months, give them another 3-month cold treatment.

Roses are budded or grafted, but of the roses grown commercially, the greater proportion are budded. *R. multiflora* is usually used as understock for outdoor types and *R. noisettiana* 'Manettii' is often used for greenhouse plants. Many can be rooted by softwood or hardwood cuttings and, for the home gardener, this certainly is the easiest method. See STRATIFICATION, BUDDING, GRAFTING, CUTTINGS.

For Insect and Disease Pests see following article.

x alba   6'   **Zone 4**   **Cottage Rose**
With white or blush-pink fragrant flowers, more or less double, 2–3 in. across and red fruits in the fall. The plant is a hybrid (*R. corymbifera* x *R. gallica*), but its variety **'Incarnata'** is better than the species. This blooms in mid-June when all the pink- and red-flowering roses are at their height of bloom, and the orange to scarlet fruits, ¾ in. long, are very effective from Aug. to Nov.

amblyotis   5'   **Zone 2**   **Kamchatka Rose**
The flowers are red, single and 2 in. across, native to Kamchatka. It is recommended especially for gardens in the colder parts of the

country where many of the other roses will not survive the winter. There are only 3 other wild roses in this list which have proved hardy in Zone 2. These are *R. blanda*, *R. rubrifolia* and *R. rugosa*.

arkansana 1¼′ **Zone 4 Arkansas Rose**
Native to Ark., this small rose with pale single, pink flowers, 1½ in. wide, blooms in June and July. It is an excellent native rock garden plant.

x arnoldiana 5′ **Zone 4 Arnold Rose**
A semi-double red rose of vivid coloring, the flowers are 2 in. across and similar to those of *R. rugosa*, but of a much more vivid shade. It is a hybrid of *R. rugosa* x *R. borboniana*.

banksiae 18′ (by climbing) **Zone 7 Banks Rose**
The flowers of this beautiful, tender, Chinese rose are white to yellow, about 1 in. wide, and are slightly fragrant. The plant is an indifferent climber. Some excellent varieties have been named, such as '**Alba-plena**', with double white, very fragrant flowers; '**Lutea**', with double yellow, scentless flowers and '**Lutescens**', with single yellow flowers.

blanda 6′ **Zone 2 Meadow Rose**
Few roses withstand the cold climate of the northern U.S. and Canada as does this native and so it is listed here. With single pink flowers up to 2½ in. across, there is nothing truly outstanding about it except that it is one of the 4 species in this list withstanding Zone 2 growing conditions.

californica 9′ **Zone 5 California Rose**
A native rose of the West Coast, this has some merit in the area about its native habitat. The single pink flowers, about 1½ in. across, are borne in clusters of a dozen or more.

canina 9′ **Zone 3 Dog Rose**
A rose with single, white to pink flowers, up to 2 in. across, and bright scarlet fruits, ¾ in. long, but otherwise of little ornamental value. It grows vigorously and is often used as stock for budding. Native to Europe, it is widespread there and is said to be naturalized in certain places in the U.S. In Europe several varieties have been named, but as yet they have not proved to be of much value in America.

carolina 3′ **Zone 4 Carolina Rose**
Since this rose with single red flowers and effectively colored red fruits is native to a large part of the eastern U.S., it is included in this list. It increases by underground stems and is good for bordering the edges of thickets. The foliage is not so glossy as that of *R. virginiana*. The variety **alba** has white flowers.

centifolia 6′ **Zone 5 Cabbage Rose**
The "Rose of a Hundred Petals" from the East Caucasus has been popular in America since colonial times and in Europe for centuries before that. It is being grown for its many varieties and for its historical significance. The pink flowers of the species are 2½ in. across and are very double and very fragrant. The Dutch painters often used it as a subject for their canvasses. The variety '**Muscosa**' has double rose flowers, the sepals and pedicels being covered with a mosslike growth, giving rise to the common name "Moss" Rose. This is another of the old-fashioned varieties which have been popular for centuries and which have many descendants.

chinensis 3′ **Zone 7 China Rose**
Native to China, upright in habit, with single, crimson to pink to white flowers, about 2 in. across. It is not a good ornamental type itself, but has been used as one of the parents of many of the horticultural varieties used today. The variety '**Minima**' (*R. roulettii*) is not over 10 in. tall, with single or double, red, pink or almost white flowers 1 in. across and, with *R. multiflora*, is the forerunner of our popular diminutive "Baby Ramblers" of today. The variety **semperflorens**, the Crimson China Rose, has leaflets stained with purple and flowers either crimson or deep pink, blooming until fall.

damascena 6′ **Zone 4 Damask Rose**
The Damask Rose from Asia Minor has large clusters of pale pink to red flowers that are 2½–3½ in. wide and very fragrant. This is the rose that early European hybridists started with and crossed in so many ways, and it was probably grown in England by the early Romans. From an historic standpoint alone, this is a most interesting rose to have in the garden. The variety '**Versicolor**' is the historic York and Lancaster Rose, with partially double flowers that are white striped and blotched with pink. Some flowers on the plant may be mostly pink, some mostly white, while others may be both pink and white; '**Trigentipetala**' has semi-double red flowers and is one of the most important roses from which "attar of roses" is extracted in European countries.

dumalis froebelii 9′ **Zone 4 Froebel Rose**
The creamy-white flowers, 2½ in. across, are single, but the red fruits are very effective in the early fall. One of its distinct advantages is that the flowers are always profusely produced. This is native to Europe and western Asia.

eglanteria 6′ **Zone 4 Sweet Brier**
Sometimes a single pink rose is of value and this one from Europe might be one because of its beautiful orange to scarlet fruits in the fall. In Europe it is found chiefly in hedgerows, both clipped and unclipped, with *R. canina*, because it has a very dense habit of growth. The foliage is sweet-scented, another factor adding to its popularity, especially in England. The variety '**Duplex**' has double pink flowers.

foetida 9′ **Zone 4 Austrian Brier**

The deep yellow, single flowers, 2–3 in. across, have an unpleasant odor (hence the name), but at a distance they are attractive. It has been a popular favorite in gardens for 3 to 4 centuries and is native to western Asia. The varieties of this species are especially popular: 'Bicolor', with single, coppery-red flowers, is the popular Austrian Copper Brier. There is no other rose in this group of "wild" roses of the world with such a vivid, coppery tone. Not a strong grower, it is nevertheless frequently used for its bloom in the garden; 'Persiana', popularly called the Persian Yellow Rose, has double flowers slightly smaller than those of the Austrian Brier, but the abundance of yellow petals make up for their lack in size.

gallica   4′   Zone 5   French Rose
Cultivated in Europe for centuries and native to southern Europe and western Asia this single-flowered, brick-red rose is one of the half dozen lowest in habit of these species roses and has been used in hybridizing for centuries, the hybrid perpetuals being descended from it. The flowers are up to $2\frac{1}{2}$ in. across. There is a variety 'Versicolor' with semi-double flowers that are striped white and red which is sometimes mistaken for the true York and Lancaster Rose, and 'Officinalis', the Apothecary Rose or Double French Rose, has double pink to red flowers and is also in the group of "old-fashioned" favorites of past centuries.

x harisonii 6′ Zone 4 Harison's Yellow Rose
The prominent, double, yellow flowers are 2 in. in dia., and the shrub has been a garden favorite in America and elsewhere since 1830 when it originated in N.Y. as a hybrid.(R. foetida x R. spinosissima). Harison's Yellow Rose is really not one of the wild roses of the world since it originated in cultivation, but it is used generally with the other species roses and so is considered as a valued addition to this group. The fruit is nearly black and is not ornamental.

helenae   15′   Zone 5   Helen Rose
The white flowers of this rose from central China are slightly larger than those of R. multiflora and are produced in profuse clusters. It may need as much as 15 ft. in which to grow and it will produce a dense mass of stems, so it is definitely not a rose for the small garden. The fruit is a dull orange.

hugonis   7′   Zone 5   Father Hugo Rose
Yellow roses are ncne too numerous among the species, but this one from central China is certainly one of the best, with single, canary-yellow flowers, 2 in. across. It blooms in late May, together with the other early-flowering yellow roses such as R. primula, R. ecae and R. xanthina. The fruits are dark scarlet to blackish red.

laevigata   15′   Zone 7   Cherokee Rose
All who are familiar with fragrant plants of the South are well acquainted with this white-flowered, fragrant rose, native to China. The plant, with single flowers often 3 in. across, has proved so popular and so well adapted to southern U.S. that it has become naturalized in many places from Ga. to Tex.

x l'heritieranea 12′ Zone 4 Boursault Rose
The flowers are double to semi-double and light to dark purple. It is an interesting hybrid (R. pendulina x R. chinensis), but not one for the small garden.

x 'Max Graf'   3′–4′   Zone 5
This is probably a R. rugosa x R. wichuraiana hybrid originating in 1919, and it is attractive all season with profuse single, bright pink flowers, somewhat like those of R. rugosa in size and shape, and glossy foliage. Though slightly bushy, it is also trailing in habit and years ago was a popular ground cover.

moschata nastarana   6′   Zone 6   Persian Musk Rose
Hardier and with a sturdier habit of growth than the species, this Persian Musk Rose has single flowers over 2 in. in dia. The shrub itself grows or almost climbs vigorously and this variety is mentioned here in preference to the species merely because it is hardier and more vigorous, with larger and more profuse flowers.

moyesii   9′   Zone 5   Moyes Rose
A native to western China, this rose has blood-red single flowers, $2\frac{1}{2}$ in. across, during mid-June. The flowers are small when compared with some of those of the hybrids, but the color is unique. The deep orange-red fruits are $2\frac{1}{2}$ in. long. Since the species varies considerably when grown from seed, it might be wise to propagate asexually from one of several named seedlings available. 'Geranium' is one of the better cultivars available, for this has excellent blood-red flowers.

multiflora   10′   Zone 5   Japanese Rose
Unfortunately this rose from Japan is being overplanted in America today and can well become one of our most vicious, woody weeds. Being a rank grower, it is definitely not a hedge plant for the small place. In the ᵣorthern parts of this country, although the canes may grow 10 ft. or more, the plant may be severely injured by winter cold, and unless considerable effort is spent on time-consuming pruning, it can become unsightly. As an understock on which to graft other roses, it has advantages. Even as a single shrub it has merit, but when used in large numbers, it may prove trouble-some. Its dense, arching habit of growth, myriads of small white flowers during mid-June and small, bright red fruits about $\frac{1}{4}$ in. in dia., often remaining effective all winter, are the chief ornamental characters, good in them-

selves, certainly, but nurserymen can grow the plant so easily and quickly in many areas of this country that they have overemphasized these good characteristics. Though not well suited to the small garden, this rose might well be used where plenty of space is available. It is one of the parents of the modern rambler rose. Some varieties are: **cathayensis**, similar to the species but with pale pink flowers; **'Inermis'**, without thorns. An excellent plant to use as understock for it makes the budding operation much easier; **'Platyphylla'**, with double, deep pink flowers, this is called the Seven Sisters Rose, the name arising from the fact that frequently with 7 flowers in a cluster, the shade of each flower may vary slightly from the others. It does not make a sturdy bush and dies out rather easily.

nitida   2′   **Zone 3**   **Shining Rose**
Although of the wild roses this is about the smallest in stature, the single rosy-red flowers are 2 in. across. The fruit is less than ½ in. wide. Its outstanding ornamental characters are its brilliantly colored flowers, its small size and the very glossy leaves which usually turn bright red in the autumn. It is found native from Newfoundland to Conn.

odorata   15′   **Zone 7**   **Tea Rose**
The flowers of this tender rose are pink, double, and 2½–3 in. wide. In the South it is either ever-green or semi-evergreen, depending upon the situation. It has been long cultivated in the gardens of India and China, where it is native, and is considered one of the parents of the hybrid tea roses. The common name comes from the fact that the flowers give off a delicious fragrance, reminding one of tea.

omeiensis   12′   **Zone 6**   **Omei Rose**
The pear-shaped red fruits on yellow fruit stalks seem to be the chief claim to fame of this small, single, white-flowered rose, only 1–1½ in. across, together with its conspicuously large red prickles. It is native to western China. Vars.: **chrysocarpa**—since there are not many yellow-fruited rose species, this might be one to use, but at present it is not available in America. It is called the Goldfruit Omei Rose; **pteracantha** —a variety of the above with even larger, red prickles all along the vigorous canes. These remain in evidence throughout the winter. This plant is known as the Wingthorn Omei Rose.

palustris   6′   **Zone 4**   **Swamp Rose**
Native over a wide area of the eastern U.S., this has single rose-colored flowers about 2 in. across and red fruits effective in the fall. It is not superior to *R. virginiana* in most situations, but it does grow readily in moist or wet soils.

pendulina   3′   **Zone 5**   **Alpine Rose**
With single rose-colored flowers about 2 in. across, this rose from southern Europe is of

interest principally because of its large, inch-long nodding, red fruits which remain on the plant late into the fall.

primula   8′   **Zone 5**   **Primrose Rose**
Light yellow, single flowers, about 1½ in. across, are profusely borne on this plant at the start of the season. Indeed, it is the first rose to bloom in the collection of over 100 species and botanical varieties growing in the Arnold Arbor-etum. A canker sometimes infests Father Hugo's Rose and then this Primrose Rose proves a likely substitute, for apparently it is not troubled with the disease. The fruits are small and red and not particularly effective, so if it is not to be planted for its very early yellow flowers, it might be eliminated from this list. It is native to China.

x pteragonis 'Redwing'. An ornamentally important hybrid (*R. omeiensis pteracantha* x *R. hugonis*) both for the flowers, 1½ in. wide and a rich yellow, and for its brilliant red thorns, especially on young shoots. These thorns are so large that they are actually a hazard in the garden and, unless this plant can be placed out of the way of people or animals, it might best be omitted. It is doubtful whether many nursery-men will want to expose their personnel to the dangers of handling it!

x (rambler roses). See following article.

roulettii = *R. chinensis* 'Minima'

roxburghii   7′   **Zone 5**   **Roxburgh Rose**
The Roxburgh Rose, native to China and Japan, is a bold-growing shrub with shredding bark on older stems which proves to be quite an orna-mental characteristic throughout the winter. Although the flowers are single, and singly borne, they are 2½ in. across, pink at the edges fading to white in the center. The large, unusual fruits, 1½–3 in. long, are red and covered with conspicuous prickles, which make them highly ornamental. The variety **plena** has double flowers, but is practically impossible to find in America.

rubrifolia   6′   **Zone 2**   **Redleaf Rose**
One of the hardiest of roses, this is also valued for its reddish foliage which may add desirable color to an otherwise monotonously green shrub border, though the few single (1½ in. across) red flowers are not among the best in this group of species roses. It is native to central Europe.

rugosa   6′   **Zone 2**   **Rugosa Rose**
The "Sea Tomato" of Japan (also China and Korea, as well) is undoubtedly one of the most popular of the species roses and is especially good for seashore plantings where it can with-stand salt-water spray without serious injury. This is another of the hardiest of the roses and both single and double, white- or red-flowered varieties are available. Since the individual flowers can be as much as 3½ in. in dia. and the

brick-red fruits are nearly an inch in dia., this is one of the larger flowering roses of this group. The autumn foliage is a gorgeous orange. There are many varieties, some being: **'Alba'**, flowers single and white; **'Albo-plena'**, flowers double and white; **'Plena'**, flowers double and reddish; **'Rosea'**, flowers single and deep pink.

setigera   15'   Zone 4   Prairie Rose
Late-blooming roses among the species are none too numerous and this one from central North America blooms in early July. It needs plenty of room to spread out, forming a thicket with shoots 12–15 ft. long. The single, rose-colored flowers are 2 in. across, the fruit is red and the autumn color is reddish.

spinosissima   3'   Zone 4   Scotch Rose
More widely distributed over the temperate regions of the world than any other rose species and the only one native to Ireland, this is low, dense and moundlike in habit and blooms profusely. The variation in flower color and doubleness of its varieties are among its several assets. The flowers are single, pink, white or yellow and 1–2 in. across; the fruit is black or dark brown and is not ornamental. Some of the better varieties are: **'Alba Plena'**, about 3 ft. tall. One of the excellent Scotch Roses, this has very double white flowers about 3 in. in dia.; **'Altaica'**, 6 ft. tall. The creamy-white flowers of the Altai Scotch Rose are 3 in. in dia. and the plant is more vigorous than most Scotch roses. It is native to Siberia; **'Fulgens'**, 3 ft. tall. The flowers are double, $2\frac{1}{2}$ in. in dia. and a bright rose color; **'Lutea'**, 3 ft. tall. The flowers of the Yellow Scotch Rose are a bright buttercup yellow, 2 in. in dia., and the plant is easier to grow than *R. foetida* 'Persiana'; **'Lutea Plena'**, flowers double, mimosa yellow. All are old-fashioned favorites.

villosa (*pomifera*)   6'   Zone 5   Apple Rose
With single, 2-in., pink flowers; probably only of value for its very large red fruits which are up to $1\frac{1}{2}$ in. long and 1 in. wide. These fruits are among the largest of those borne by the wild roses. It is native to Europe and western Asia.

virginiana (*R. lucida*)   6'   Zone 3   Virginia Rose
Although this is a lowly native and widely distributed in the eastern U.S., it can be used in landscape planting and is easily kept only 3 ft. tall by proper pruning. The flowers are single and pink, 2–3 in. wide, the fruits are bright red, $\frac{1}{2}$ in. across, and the autumn color is an excellent red and orange, while the twigs are bright red in winter. Added to these sterling qualities is the fact that it can spread very fast by underground stems. In fact, it can be cut to the ground in the early spring and may be expected to grow 3 ft. tall and even bloom a little that same year. A double-flowered variety has been

named **'Plena'**, but it is not commonly grown, nor is it easily available. Another, **lamprophylla**, is an excellent variety of the Virginia Rose, only 3 ft. tall and with glossy leaves, both of which characteristics make it a good landscape specimen. It is called the Glossy Virginia Rose.

wichuraiana   procumbent   Zone 5   Memorial Rose
The Memorial Rose from China, Korea and Japan was originally introduced into North America in 1891 by the Arnold Arboretum and has been a very popular plant for banks and slopes ever since. The small white flowers, 2 in. across, appear in the late summer, making it the last of all the species roses to bloom. The glossy green foliage is often semi-evergreen, and the plant grows vigorously flat on the ground, making dense, thick mats of foliage. It is the only species that is truly procumbent and makes an excellent ground cover, especially on banks, rooting wherever the stems touch moist ground. The fruits are reddish, but they are not particularly ornamental.

xanthina   9'   Zone 5   Manchu Rose
The sulfur-yellow flowers, $1\frac{1}{2}$–2 in. in dia., are semi-double; otherwise it is similar to *R. hugonis*. This is native to China and Korea.

Popular Hybrids

For as many years as man has enjoyed gardening, roses have maintained a prominence unequaled by any other flower. They have, in fact, existed much longer than modern records can substantiate. Geologists tell us that the rose is several million years old. Fossil evidence from Mont. and Ore., dating the rose back 32 million years, establishes its existence on earth prior to man. Furthermore, it seems to have been the first cultivated flower.

Although the rose has been used extensively, inspiring art, poetry, music, literature and fashion, its established dignity in all cultural fields has never been lost. Throughout history, and today more than ever, it merits the title "the Queen of Flowers" originally bestowed on it by the Greek poetess Sappho.

One might reasonably assume that aside from an inherent symbolism the popularity of roses is due for the most part to the ease with which they are grown. While, in fact, good roses may be produced with a minimal effort, there are numerous merits contributing to this universal appeal.

Botanically classified as a shrub, roses vary greatly in plant types and habit of growth. Roses blend easily into the landscape pattern for almost any need. Whether a border planting, ground cover, a climbing or trailing plant, a potted plant for the patio or terrace, or a miniature for the window box, there are roses to meet the needs of every gardener.

Variety of color, flower form, fragrance, plant size and habit, lend to the widespread appeal of roses. With proper care, a favorite rose bush may be expected to remain in the garden many years; a long and profitable return on a small investment. While a vast number of roses are now being grown throughout the world, the prevalent, but false theory that they are difficult to grow has undoubtedly limited their use in many gardens. Although the culture of roses may be more specialized than some other plants, any gardener willing to adhere to a basic schedule of procedures can expect rewards that will greatly offset the efforts.

Selecting Roses for the Home Garden

Time is well spent researching the performance of any rose variety to be introduced into the garden for the first time. Guard against illusions from striking photographs in the many nursery catalogs available today. It is well to see how the rose has done in national tests as well as in your own area. Most roses perform equally well in all sections, but there may be certain environmental factors to influence your decision. The American Rose Society conducts an annual survey of its members to determine the performance of new varieties in each locale. Ratings based on a scale of 10 points with compiled remarks are published each year in the "American Rose Annual" The Society also prints annually a leaflet called "A Guide for Buying Roses," giving ratings and other pertinent information on all rose varieties on the American market. This guide is valuable to anyone interested in roses and may be obtained free by writing the American Rose Society, P.O. Box 30,000, Shreveport, La. 71130.

The most dependable of the new varieties introduced each year are the All-American Rose Selection winners. Roses earning this distinction are identified with an AARS tag. They are designated by a non-profit organization of commercial rose-growing firms known as All-America Rose Selections, Inc. AARS maintains test gardens throughout the United States and the varieties designated as AARS winners have competed and proven themselves superior in all sections of the country.

A few of these official All-America Rose Selection test gardens are as follows:

Armstrong Nurseries, Inc. 1265 S. Palmetto St., Ontario, Calif.

Elizabeth Park Rose Garden, Hartford, Conn.

University of Southwestern Louisiana, Lafayette, La.

International Rose Test Gardens, Washing-ton Park, Portland, Ore.

Woodward Park, Tulsa, Okla.

Bobbink & Atkins, Freehold, N.J.

Cornell University Garden, Ithaca, N.Y.

Jackson & Perkins Co., Experimental Nursery, Tustin, Calif.

Ohio State University, Columbus 10, Ohio

The Pennsylvania State Univ., University Park, Pa. 16802

Mo. Botanical Garden, St. Louis, Mo. 63110

Whitnall Park, Boerner Botanical Gardens, Hales Corners, Wisc. 53130

Once varieties have been selected for the garden, it is important to purchase plants of superior quality. It seldom pays to "bargain hunt" for roses. A slightly higher price will be repaid by plant vigor and performance. It is better to economize by purchasing older varieties that have become accepted as the "standbys." These are usually less expensive than the newer introductions yet their continuous popularity is proof that they are good performers. It is usually preferable to purchase bare-root roses as opposed to plants that have been packaged or potted. Packaged plants are fine when purchased from a dealer who has taken care to store them under proper moisture and temperature conditions. Potted plants are gaining in popularity with nurseries and garden centers. It is important that containers used for potted roses be large enough to allow freedom of root growth.

Before making a selection of roses for the home garden, one must first be familiar with the types of classes of roses and the characteristics of each. This section will briefly define today's popular types and list varieties of each type that have proven themselves in the gardens of prominent rosarians throughout the United States.

HYBRID TEAS. Hybrid teas are the most popular grouping of rose varieties grown today. For the last 50 years, hybrid teas have dominated the rose market in both greenhouses and garden roses. Through cross-breeding, hybridizers have successfully produced a combination of favorable characteristics seen individually in many of the older roses. The hybrid tea class is a result of interbreeding the Tea Rose with the hybrid perpetual. They are available in almost every desirable color, with most varieties possessing a degree of pleasing fragrance.

Hybrid tea roses are of bush form, with large flowers borne singly or in small clusters on a stem. Flowers vary from single blooms with one row of petals to double blooms with many rows. Generally speaking the plants are hardy, but some winter protection is needed in the colder regions. They are not immune to disease, but with modern chemical controls prevention is relatively easy. Hybrid teas are characteristically repeat bloomers and with minimum care will provide an array of color all season.

The following varieties have earned the highest ratings of the American Rose Society:

1. 'Peace', yellow blend
2. 'First Prize', pink blend
3. 'Tropicana', orange-red
4. 'Tiffany', pink blend
5. 'Granada', yellow-red blend
6. 'Mister Lincoln', dark red
7. 'Century Two', medium pink
8. 'Garden Party', white
9. 'Fragrant Cloud', orange-red
10. 'Swarthmore', pink blend
11. 'Miss All-American Beauty', medium pink
12. 'Chicago Peace', pink blend
13. 'Chrysler Imperial', dark red
14. 'Confidence', pink blend
15. 'Pascali', white
16. 'Oregold', golden yellow
17. 'Perfume Delight', medium pink
18. 'Medallion', apricot blend
19. 'Golden Girl', yellow
20. 'Eclipse', yellow

FLORIBUNDAS. Floribundas came into being through crossing Polyantha with hybrid tea varieties. They are used extensively for decorative purposes in the garden. Flowers are borne in clusters of varying sizes. Most varieties produce well-formed flowers usually smaller than hybrid teas, although the trend in recent years has been toward larger flowers and modern hybridizers predict for the future floribunda varieties with flower size equal to the Hybrid Tea.

Floribundas are usually low-growing, bushy plants producing a continuous mass of bloom. They are likely to be more hardy and resistant to disease than hybrid teas.

1. 'Europeana', dark red
2. 'Little Darling', yellow blend
3. 'Iceberg', white
4. 'Gene Boerner', medium pink
5. 'Ivory Fashion', white
6. 'Redgold', yellow blend
7. 'Apricot Nectar', apricot blend
8. 'Angel Face', mauve
9. 'Faberge', pink blend
10. 'Betty Prior', medium pink
11. 'Eutin', dark red
12. 'Circus', yellow blend
13. 'Sparten', orange-red
14. 'Saratoga', white
15. 'Fashion', pink blend
16. 'Sarabande', orange-red

17. 'Orangeade', orange-red
18. 'Rose Parade', pink blend
19. 'Fire King', orange-red

GRANDIFLORAS. In recent years the grandiflora class has developed through the continuous crossing of hybrid teas and floribundas. The Grandiflora is an intermediate class and in some cases closely resembles the dominant parent. A true variety produces large hybrid tea-type blooms usually 1 to a stem, but in a clusterlike formation. Plants tend to be as vigorous as either parent. Hardiness is about the same as with hybrid teas.

1. 'Queen Elizabeth', medium pink
2. 'Pink Parfait', pink blend
3. 'Camelot', medium pink
4. 'Montezuma', orange-red
5. 'Olè', orange-red
6. 'Comanche', orange-red
7. 'Aquarius', pink blend
8. 'John S. Armstrong', dark red
9. 'Sonia', pink blend
10. 'Mount Shasta', white

CLIMBING ROSES. While no rose is a true climber having natural means for gripping or holding onto supports, many varieties produce long shoots or canes which can be trained over fences, trellises or other structures. A rose garden is usually incomplete without a background of climbers.

Climbers have a wide variation of characteristics comprising habits of many classes. Some bloom only once in the spring, some have recurrent bloom, while others are described as everblooming although the bloom may be sparse at times. There are climbers with clusters of small flowers and others with large hybrid tea-type blooms; the latter known as large-flowered climbers. The large-flowered climbers are most popular today.

1. 'Don Juan', dark red
2. 'New Dawn', light pink
3. 'Improved Blaze', medium red
4. 'Blossomtime', medium pink
5. 'Golden Showers', medium yellow
6. 'Joseph's Coat', red blend
7. 'Rhonda', medium pink
8. 'White Dawn', white
9. 'Red Fountain', red
10. 'Royal Sunset', apricot blend

MINIATURE ROSES. In the past decade miniature roses have earned a prominent status with rose lovers. The miniature description applies not only to stature, which usually ranges in height from 3 in. to a little more than a foot, but also to buds, stems and foliage that are equally dwarf.

Available in a host of colors, miniatures are usually winter-hardy outdoors and may be expected to produce continuous bloom for many seasons. They are also grown indoors as potted plants and may be transferred to the garden during the summer months.

1. **'Baby Darling'***, orange-pink
2. **'Beauty Secret',** medium red
3. **'Chipper',** light pink
4. **'Cinderella'***, white
5. **'Mary Marshall'**, orange-pink
6. **'Pixie Rose'***, deep pink
7. **'Scarlet Gem'***, orange-red
8. **'Starina'**, orange-red
9. **'Toy Clown'**, red blend
10. **'Hi Ho'** (climber), deep pink

* suitable for growing in pots

SHRUB ROSES. There are a number of roses that do not fit well into any of the groups previously described. All have bushy shrublike form although differing greatly in origin. Shrub roses are usually vigorous, hardy, resistant to insects and diseases and well adapted for general landscape use.

1. **'Sea Foam'**, white
2. **'The Fairy'**, light pink
3. **'Frau Karl Druschki'**, white
4. **'Parkdirector Riggers'**, dark red
5. **'Sarah Van Fleet'**, medium pink
6. **'Sparrieshoop'**, light pink
7. **'Harison's Yellow'**, bright yellow
8. **'Paul Neyron'**, medium pink
9. **'Pink Grootendorst'**, medium pink
10. **'Therese Bugnet'**, medium pink

TREE ROSES OR STANDARDS. Tree roses are not a type or class, but a novelty form derived primarily from the bush roses and some of the climbers. Tree roses are developed by budding a rose variety onto a tall, sturdy trunk. The trunk is often budded onto another rootstock.

Arranging the Rose Garden

The variety of types and habits of roses allows for their use to satisfy almost any landscape need. Although cultural requirements may determine the location of beds, the possibilities are limited only by the gardener's imagination. Before laying out the rose garden, thought should be given to the specific purpose it will serve and the role that will be played by the roses in the over-all landscape scheme.

Roses are often given a prominent location in the garden, serving as the main attraction or focal point. It is possible, however, to blend them into the complete plan and use them to form a background or in some other way to complement other garden features.

Roses are usually more attractive when displayed for mass effect. A practical and striking arrangement of exhibition or cutting varieties is a narrow bed with varieties grouped together. This allows for a massive color effect and provides room for movement in caring for the plants. If a mixture of varieties is used in a single bed, some consideration should be given to blending of colors. If plants of varying heights are used together, the taller plants should be placed in the background.

For striking garden displays nothing is more effective than a hedge or foundation planting of floribundas. If separate beds for hybrid teas are not included in the garden, they may blend comfortably into the arrangement of floribundas and provide flowers for cutting. Miniatures may add an interesting and colorful border for arrangements of other plantings or garden features. Tree roses are always conversation pieces in the garden and may be used to break the monotony of continuous lines.

Roses are equally satisfying in formal or informal landscape schemes. There is always a place for climbers on fences and existing structures. Many gardeners provide structures for the dual purpose of displaying the climbing varieties as well as providing background for other plantings or screening undesirable sights. An arched trellis covered with flowering climbers provides an inviting entrance to the garden.

Culture

SITE. Roses should be planted in a location receiving 6–8 hours of sunlight a day. The ideal site is a southern exposure offering morning sunlight which aids in discouraging disease and late afternoon shade which helps retain color of the blooms and protects them from excessive heat during the hot summer days. A level or slightly sloping area providing free circulation of air as well as some wind protection is most desirable. Roses should be planted away from trees and other plant materials. Even if shading is not a problem, competition for soil moisture and nutrients as well as exposure to insects and diseases makes such locations undesirable.

SOIL. The type of soil available for the planting is not usually as vital as the care given the soil that is selected. Almost any well-drained soil that will grow other plants will grow good roses. It is important that the soil have ample drainage to prevent the roses from standing in water for a long period of time. Should the selected site have insufficient drainage, it may be necessary to elevate the beds or install tile to move the water away.

Since roses are likely to remain in the same location for many years, the soil should be thoroughly prepared before the planting is established. Proper preparation should be made several weeks in advance of planting. The soil should be removed to a depth of 2 ft. and organic material thoroughly mixed with the topsoil before it is replaced in the beds.

Roses do best in a slightly acid soil but are known to be tolerant of some variation from the ideal. The pH range of soil for roses should be from 5.5 to 7.0. If the soil tends to be highly acid the condition may be improved by adding ground limestone. Soils of a highly alkaline nature may often be corrected by incorporating forms of sulfur. Soil conditions vary greatly in all areas and no rose garden should be started without the information provided from a soil test. Testing services are available in all areas either through nurseries or garden centers, commercial laboratories, private testers, or the state agricultural extension service or experiment station. Information obtained from the soil test and the recommendations received should be followed explicitly.

PLANTING. Roses planted in either the spring or fall can be expected to give good results. Except in the colder regions where the ground freezes in early Oct., fall planting provides an opportunity for an early start of growth in the spring. If roses are to be planted in the spring, they should be put in as early as possible.

When plants arrive from the nursery, they should be put into the ground immediately. If, for some reason, planting must be delayed for a short time or should the roses arrive in a dry, shriveled condition, they may be temporarily buried in a loose moist soil until they can be planted.

Although most roses are shipped properly pruned for planting, it is still wise to prune the tops back to 10–12 in., remove all dead or damaged wood, and clip the root tips an inch or less to insure that they are alive and promote rapid new growth.

The hole for each plant should be large enough for the roots to sit freely without crowding and deep enough for proper location of the bud union, (the point where the understock was budded. See UNDERSTOCK and BUDDING). A good plant will require a hole at least 12 in. deep and 18 in. across. In no case should the root system of the plant be crowded into a hole. If the roots cannot be placed into the hole freely, the hole should be made larger. The bud union is planted even with or slightly

below the soil level except in extremely cold areas where it should be buried to 2 in. for protection from severe freezes. Before setting the plant into the hole, a cone-shaped mound of loose topsoil should be piled at the bottom of the hole. The plant should then be placed on top of the mound and the roots allowed to lie freely in a downward position. Cover the roots with a shallow layer of loose topsoil and pack to eliminate air pockets. Fill the remainder of the hole with loose soil, pack again, then fill with water and allow to drain. It is also a good practice to build a mound of soil high enough to cover the stems of the plant for protection from wind and cold weather until growth begins. As soon as the plant shows the first signs of growth, the mound must be removed.

MULCHING. Once spring growth has begun, the soil mound removed from around the plants, and the roses have received their first feeding, the beds should be covered with a mulching material. A good mulch will retain moisture, keep the soil cool in summer and help to retain temperature balance in the winter. It will prevent the growth of weeds, add to the organic content of the soil and provide an attractive setting for the plants. In addition to eliminating the hard work of controlling weeds by hand or with gardening tools, the mulch is more desirable since manual cultivation may damage the shallow roots of the bushes. Many different materials are used for mulching (which see). Since there are numerous good mulches, many of them available as by-products, such as cocoa hulls, cottonseed hulls, sawdust, ground hardwood bark and ground corncobs, it is best to select one that is easily obtainable. Most mulches will produce the same effects providing they allow for movement of air and moisture and do not compete for soil nutrients. Many mulches will, however, absorb nitrogen which will eventually need to be replaced with additional fertilizer. An even covering of mulching material 2–3 in. deep is sufficient and will eventually decay and add to the humus content of the soil.

FEEDING. There are many theories as to the proper fertilization of roses. The beginner, confused by numerous recommendations of commercial firms and amateur rosarians, is more apt to damage his bushes by overfeeding than by failing to provide the necessary nutrients. If the soil test has indicated a good balance of nutrients, 3 light applications of general fertilizer each season is adequate. There is no substitute for following the manufacturer's recommendations for the proper amount of fertilizer to apply. The first feeding should be done after the roses have shown 2–3 in. of growth in the spring, the second immediately following the June cycle of bloom, and the third about 6 weeks later. Fertilization later in the fall should be avoided as it will produce tender new growth making the entire plant more susceptible to winter injury. There are a number of gardeners who rely solely on organic fertilizers and grow excellent roses. There is much to be said for organic gardening and the best answer is a compromise using chemical fertilizers periodically for immediate needs and organic fertilizers such as well-rotted cow manure to provide a constant nutritive environment.

WATERING. Roses are known to be thirsty plants and when water is not provided by nature, the beds should be thoroughly soaked every week to 10 days. Frequent, light watering should be avoided as the roots will be drawn toward the surface of the soil. A soaker-type watering system is recommended. If an overhead system is used, watering should be done early enough in the day to allow the bushes to dry before sundown. When plants are allowed to remain moist overnight, they are more susceptible to disease.

Rose Pests

The amount of discussion and publicity given to insect and disease pests of roses has shaped a relatively small problem into an untrue perspective, conveying the idea that to control rose pests one must possess an extensive knowledge and collection of chemicals, a variety of apparatus for applying sprays and dusts, and be willing to fight a constant battle throughout the growing season. Fortunately, rose growers soon discover that these ideas are not only exaggerated, but for the most part are false. In reality, pests are controlled with little difficulty and it is not uncommon for one all-purpose pesticide, applied in either spray or dust form, to keep the garden free of insects and diseases.

A preference factor exists in deciding whether to spray or dust. Spraying is usually preferred by growers having a large number of bushes to protect. Spraying can be depended upon to give the best coverage of all parts of the rose bush. However, for a small number of plants a ready-mixed dust can be applied faster and without going to the trouble of mixing pesticides. Dusting must be done when there is little or no air movement if ample coverage is to be obtained. Under normal conditions a regular schedule of spraying or dusting every week or 10 days will give effective control of insects and diseases.

The proverbial "ounce of prevention" theory applies to the control of all insects and disease that may invade the rose garden. The gardener need only be aware of the pests to which roses are likely susceptible and schedule a preventive control program to assure immunity to the common rose enemies. It is true, however, that without such precautions the full potential of the rose garden will be limited.

While numerous insects and diseases are known to cause trouble with roses, only a few are commonly found, and control measures for these important few will normally give protection from the others. Listed below are the most important diseases and insects of roses with brief descriptions and control recommendations. Recent federal regulations controlling the distribution of certain pesticides make it difficult to offer widespread recommendations. It is advisable to check with your agricultural extension agent or local garden center to determine the effective controls that are legally distributed in your area. The user must always follow the recommendations of the manufacturer.

Diseases and Insect Pests

BLACKSPOT—circular black areas in varying sizes on the leaf which will eventually turn yellow and drop. Preventive control is possible with many fungicides including Mancozeb, Folpet, Benlate, and Daconil.

MILDEW—a white or grayish powdery growth causing shrivelling of leaves. Mild occurrences controlled with Folpet, sulfur or copper. Actidione PM and Benlate have proven to give best control for serious outbreaks, although the newer Pipron is showing equal effectiveness in areas where it has been used.

CANKER (several kinds)—dark spots on the cane after which all growth above the canker dies. Infected area should be removed. Same fungicides as are recommended for blackspot.

RUST—bright orange spots on underside of leaves. Problem is greatest on the West Coast and is now spreading. Same fungicide recommendation as for blackspot.

APHIDS—small, soft, green or brown, sucking insects which insert a pointed mouth part into the tender growth of young shoots and later on flower buds. Control—Malathion, Sevin or one of the systemics.

LEAFHOPPERS—adults are small, greenish-white, sucking insects about $\frac{1}{8}$ in. long. In the nymph stage they suck plant juices from the underside of the leaves. Sevin, Malathion or a systemic.

THRIPS—tiny insects feeding on tender parts of the flower causing it to turn brown around the edges of the petal. Flower may ball and fail to open. Heavy seasonal infestations require frequent applications of Cygon, Vapona or

Malathion. Systemics have also been used successfully.

JAPANESE BEETLES—bright metallic-green beetles with coppery-brown wing covers, about $\frac{3}{8}$ in. long. Most common in Middle Atlantic states but spreading to other regions. Sevin is the best insecticide for adults. When done as a community project grubs may be biologically controlled with milky spore disease.

ROSE BUGS AND ROSE CHAFERS—best controlled with Malathion.

SPIDER MITE—tiny red insects that can be seen by the naked eye when placed against a white background. Damage is done by sucking juices from the underside of rose leaves. Controlled with miticides such as Kelthane, pentac, Tedion.

ROSE SLUGS OR SAWFLIES—most active in early spring. They resemble tiny slugs in the larval stage. Controlled with Sevin or Malathion.

Winter Protection

Roses are surprisingly hardy in the colder climates, particularly those that go into the winter in a strong and vigorous condition. Yet, in regions where the temperature drops to 15° F. and below some protection is needed for the bush types. The severe temperatures alone cannot be blamed for winter injury as most damage is a result of warm periods followed by a sudden drop in temperature. Protection should be applied to help maintain a constant temperature. Many theories and products are applied to the task of protecting the roses in the winter. In recent years, there have been a number of commercial products designed to give protection, each having some merit under certain conditions. There is no set method that is foolproof under all conditions. The location and exposure of the roses are factors in determining the amount of protection needed. Naturally, the average low winter temperatures for the area should be considered.

While there is no one best means of protection, a mound of soil covering each plant is a tried and proven method practiced widely in all areas. The soil should be mounded around the plants after the first hard killing frost. Exposure of the plants to frost and moderately cold temperatures will allow for some natural hardening and prevent severe shock to tender canes when the first cold spell arrives. The height of the mound will vary with the nature of the winters and the desires of the grower. However, the amount of wood saved is directly proportional to the size of the mound of soil. Since the piled-up soil is for protective purposes only, it does not have to be the best topsoil and may be obtained from any available source. The task of uncovering and removing soil in the spring

may be reduced, however, if rich topsoil has been used that may be left in the beds. A mound of ground corncobs, compost or other organic material used for protection may also remain in the beds when the plants are uncovered in the spring. The mounds should be removed in early spring before new growth begins. If left until the buds begin to swell, considerable damage may be done to new growth.

Tree roses are likely to need protection in all the northern areas. By digging out one side of the root system, the plant can be laid over and covered with soil. In mild areas ample protection may be provided by wrapping the top and trunk with burlap or heavy paper.

Climbers tend to be hardier than the bush roses and many times receive ample protection due to location of the supporting structure. If additional protection is needed they may be laid on the ground and covered with soil.

Pruning

Pruning is important as it affects the quality and appearance of the rose bush and the blooms it produces. Pruning is done to shape the plant, remove dead and infected canes, and promote vigorous growth which will produce large numbers of good quality blooms.

For modern hybrid teas, floribundas and grandifloras, pruning is best done in early spring, just as the plant breaks dormancy. Rather than prune the long canes in the fall before the plant begins to die back, it is preferable to tie the canes together and stake them to prevent wind whipping. Then wait until spring to see how much wood has been lost.

The first step in pruning is to remove all diseased, dead or undesirable wood. Next, the plants should be properly shaped, provided enough healthy wood is available to allow for shaping. This will not likely be the case in the colder northern climates.

The height to which the rose normally grows and the height desired will help determine how much wood to remove from the plant, although in the colder areas there may not be a choice as the plant may be killed back to the ground or protective covering. Fortunately, roses can withstand this treatment and vigorous new canes will come back each year.

Pruning should be done with very sharp tools that will give a clean, slanting cut. The wood should be removed to $\frac{1}{4}$ in. above an outside bud. It is always necessary to cut back to good healthy wood. Many times a green cane is deceiving as the inside tissue may be discolored and diseased. The cross-section of a healthy cane shows no signs of discoloration. Clean cuts usually heal quickly and without damage to the cane. A protective coating of grafting wax or a commercial wound compound is advisable for the larger cuts.

Climbing roses are pruned according to class. Ramblers blooming only in the spring are pruned as soon as they have flowered. The old wood which has just flowered should be removed to make room for new growth which will flower the following season.

Large-flowering climbers are pruned lightly in the spring, removing diseased and dead wood. Occasionally a few of the older canes are shortened or removed to promote new growth.

Tree roses are pruned primarily for shape and balance. Pruning is usually more severe than for other types in order to keep the top from becoming too large and unbalanced. Weak canes, diseased and dead wood should be removed and the strong healthy canes cut back to 8–12 in. above the union.

Pruning for rose shows—Rosarians who become experienced at exhibiting usually become quite adept in pruning the canes at the best time for producing a peak crop of blooms for the rose show. The exact number of days for pruning for shows varies with the variety as well as season and locality, but usually ranges from 39 to 53 days. The new exhibitor should seek the advice of one of the American Rose Society's Consulting Rosarians or an experienced exhibitor in his area. With a little experimentation and record-keeping, an individual can determine the best time for each variety in his own garden.

Cutting Flowers

The chores involved in growing roses should not be considered alone without remembering the rewards to be expected. Once the gardener has his roses established and begins to give them proper care, he should be prepared for "rose fever" to set in. It seldom takes more than the first few blooms on the dining-room table to wipe out memories of any hard work that might have been done. After the flowering has begun it is not long until the rose gardener becomes the envy of his neighborhood. There will be a natural inclination to cut blooms for the home, for the neighbors, and for every special occasion. Care should be taken, however, that the cutting of blooms is not so extensive as to damage the plants. First-year plants in particular should be allowed to grow and produce blooms without continuous and severe cutting. Blooms should be removed in moderation from healthy plants until they are well established and producing vigorous growth. Then they can be cut in abundance without damaging the bush.

Exhibiting

After attaining success in growing beautiful roses many rose growers find a new world of challenge and fantasy by exhibiting their blooms in competition at rose shows. The hobby of exhibiting roses has spread rapidly, and there are now some 350 affiliate organizations of the American Rose Society sponsoring and staging at least one rose show each season. There are also 18 American Rose Society district shows and 2 national rose shows, in which every skill and technique is employed by amateur rose growers in an effort to exhibit perfect specimen blooms in a natural state of beauty. To produce exhibition blooms the gardener must give the utmost care and attention to his roses throughout the year. The most perfect hybrid tea specimen will have a long, straight stem, lush foliage arranged to complement the bloom and abundant petals arranged symmetrically around a high center. Exhibition hybrid teas are at their best stage for showing when one-half or two-thirds open. The first step toward exhibiting hybrid teas is the selection of varieties having exhibition qualities. The 10 exhibition-type hybrid teas to win most frequently the coveted "Queen of the Show" award in recent years are 'Royal Highness', 'Peace', 'Christian Dior', 'Chrysler Imperial', 'Crimson Glory', 'Granada', 'Garden Party', 'Tropicana', 'Confidence' and 'Tiffany'. The American Rose Society rules require all hybrid teas to be exhibited without side buds. Side buds must be removed when they are very young and tender. Buds allowed to grow to more than $\frac{1}{2}$ in. not only subject the rose to judging penalties, but also use up food and nutrients that should be going into the exhibition bloom.

Other types of roses such as floribundas, polyanthas and climbers are exhibited "naturally grown" for mass effect and are not disbudded. Grandifloras may be exhibited disbudded like the hybrid teas or naturally grown with side buds. Classes for grandifloras will likely vary with different show schedules.

The American Rose Society point scoring system for judging roses is as follows:

Color	25
Form	25
Substance	20
Stem and foliage	20
Size	10

All approved American Rose Society shows are conducted according to specified standards and judged by ARS Accredited Judges. Similar judging standards and show procedures are taught and practiced throughout the U.S.A.

Expanded Rose Interests

Many accomplished rosarians delve into specialized fields to expand to the fullest their rose interest. The art and skill of making rose arrangements are often intriguing for both the ladies and men alike. Rose arrangements provide an opportunity for expressing originality of thought and feeling through floral design. In addition to a magnificent display of beauty for all occasions, arrangements are often exhibited and judged in competition at rose shows.

There is also an increased interest in the production of new plants by propagation and hybridization. Both ventures require much skill and patience, but many gardeners are proud to display a new plant which they have developed by propagation or a new variety through their own breeding efforts. A number of rose shows now have classes for seedlings developed by amateur hybridizers.

The American Rose Society

A basic prerequisite of continued success and enjoyment with roses is membership in the American Rose Society. The Society, through its publications, provides a flow of up-to-date information on all aspects of roses.

The Society's publications include the American Rose Annual, a 250-page, bound book with many beautiful color plates of the new varieties. The annual gives extensive coverage of all subjects on roses, ranging from the light and humorous to technical research reports. American Rose Society members also receive a 32-page monthly magazine that provides "how to" information and a broad scope of interesting articles on roses. Monthly features include a section of rose news from each of the Society's 18 geographic districts, a calendar of rose events that are scheduled throughout the country, and a monthly listing of the new rose varieties that are registered through the International Rose Registration Authority. The Society also maintains for its members an extensive lending library, containing more than 1000 volumes on roses and related horticultural subjects.

O. KEISTER EVANS, JR.

For specialized reading, the American Rose Society suggests "A Botanical History of Roses" by John Lindley; "Meilland: A Life in Roses" by A. Meilland; "Old Roses" by Ethelyn Emery Keays; "The Rose Manual" by Robert Buist; "History of the Rose" by Roy E. Shepherd; "How to Grow Roses" by Sunset Magazine; "Modern Roses 8" by the American Rose Society; "Prince's Manual of Roses" by William Robert Prince; "Roses, a Popular Guide" by Mark Mattock; "Shrub Roses of Today" by Graham Thomas; "The Book of Roses" by Catherine Core; all available from the American Rose Society, P.O. Box 30,000, Shreveport, LA 71130.

ROSACEAE = The Rose Family

ROSARY-PEA = *Abrus precatorius*

ROSARY PLANT = *Ceropegia woodii*

ROSE, ROSE PESTS. See ROSA.

ROSE-ACADIA = *Robinia hispida*

ROSE-APPLE = *Syzygium jambos*

ROSE FAMILY = Rosaceae

ROSE-GENTIAN. See SABATIA.

ROSEMALLOW. See HIBISCUS, ABELMOSCHUS.

ROSEMARY = *Rosmarinus officinalis*

ROSEMARY, BOG = *Andromeda polifolia*

ROSE-OF-VENEZUELA = *Brownea grandiceps*

ROSEROOT = *Sedum rosea*

ROSETTE. A cluster of leaves or other organs in a compact circular arrangement.

ROSETTE-MULLEIN = *Ramonda myconi*

ROSINWEED. See SILPHIUM.

ROSMARINUS (rose-ma-RY-nus)

officinalis	6'	Zone 6	Rosemary

This common herb or subshrub has been used in gardens for centuries, especially because the leaves and stems have a lasting aromatic fragrance. The violet-blue, rarely white flowers are borne in upright spikes during the winter or early spring. The lustrous, gray-green, evergreen foliage is definitely aromatic and the plant is native to southern Europe and Asia Minor, probably coming to America with the earliest settlers. The lance-shaped leaves are narrow, about an inch long. Honey made from Rosemary blossoms is supposed to be very tasty and a fragrant oil has been extracted from the plant. As an herb it is used for many culinary purposes. The variety **'Lockwood de Forest'** has lighter brighter foliage and bluer flowers. It is popular in Calif.

The variety **humilis** is a low-growing, more or less prostrate, type with the shoots sprawling over the ground and not erect, as are those of the species.

The var. **'Prostratus'** is a variety sometimes found listed and used as a ground cover especially in Calif., but it is considerably less hardy than *R. officinalis humilus*, and has been termed by some botanists *R. lavendulaceus*. It is probably only hardy in Zone 8, but where it can be grown it makes a nice ground cover.

ROTENONE. An insecticidal compound extracted from the roots of *Derris elliptica* (derris) and *Lonchocarpus* sp. which has good insecticidal activity. It is also a fish poison but relatively safe to animals. Action is slow and it deteriorates rapidly. New supplies should be secured each season. Rotenone-copper dust has been a standard pesticide mixture for use on vegetables. The usual concentration in dusts is 0.75 to 1%.

ROTOTILLER. Rototillers or rotary hoes are excellent garden machines, and save the home gardener a great deal of back-breaking work. They are power driven, usually with rubber tires, the main part being a rotary power-driven shaft on which are tines or long curved teeth that dig into the soil as the machine moves forward. The depth at which these teeth operate can be regulated, depending on the condition of the soil. However, by going over a piece several times one can pulverize the soil (or a grass sod) to a depth of at least 6 in., and prepare a piece of rough ground for seed sowing in an hour's time.

As a machine for cultivating in the garden it is ideal, for when the teeth are allowed to go only 1 in. deep, the machine moves faster and the surface of the soil is quickly broken up or "hoed" and the weeds of course cut off or dug out in the operation.

There are other motorized garden "cultivators" advertised to do many garden operations, but one would do well to investigate a rototiller type before investing money in other machines.

ROTS. Diseases causing rots indicate decay which may be wet, slimy, mushy or dry. Many rots occur on fruits, vegetables and bulbs in storage and others on growing plants, especially the roots. Both bacteria and fungi cause rots while physiological conditions often cause breakdown which is followed by pathological rots. Most storage rots develop from infection in the field or from contamination on containers in the storage. See APPLE. Apple bitter rot infects the nearly mature fruit in the warmer fruit-growing areas and severe infection produces mummied fruit. A mummy disease also infects blueberries. Brown rot of stone fruits is well known wherever they are grown. See PEACH. Black rot of grapes rots berries in the cluster. See GRAPE. Red stele on roots of strawberries reduces the crop and kills plants. See STRAWBERRY. Phytophthora fungus infects Calla rhizomes and causes root and stem rot (collar rot) on fruit and nut trees. Mushroom root rot, which is recognized by the mushroom-like clumps at the base of infected trees, attack many trees especially Oak in the West and citrus in the South. Calla root rot, lily fusarium rot and gray rot of tulip are common bulb rots. Crown rot, sometimes called mustard seed fungus because of the resemblance of the reproductive bodies, is serious in the South on carrots, onions, Iris, Phlox and many other plants. Cotton stem rot decays the stems of Peony, Dahlia, Snapdragon and many others. Trunks and large branches of many trees become infected with heartwood or sapwood rots, which produce bracket fungi which extend from the infected wounds. Blossom end rot of tomatoes is physiological. See TOMATO. Fruit and stem rots can be controlled by spraying with fungicides, tree rots are cut out, and root rots must be combatted by destruction of infected plants, sanitation, soil sterilization and rotation.

ROUGEPLANT = *Rivina humulus*

ROWAN, MORAVIAN = *Sorbus aucuparia edulis*

ROYSTONEA (roy-STO-nea)

regia   70′   Zone 10   Royal Palm

This native of Cuba and southern Fla. is the most graceful of the palms planted in the southeastern U.S. The lower leaves droop, the central leaves are upright and 15 ft. long but they always sway gracefully in every breeze. The trunk is swollen slightly in the center but then tapers gracefully above and below, and its male and female flowers are separate but are in the same cluster. For culture see PALMS.

RUBBER-PLANT, INDIA = *Ficus elastica*

RUBBER-TREE, HARDY = *Eucommia ulmoides*

RUBBERVINE, PALAY = *Cryptostegia grandiflora*

RUBIA (ROO-bia)

tinctorum   4′   Zone 6   Common Madder

An herb, native to southern Europe and Asia, with leaves in whorls of 4–8 and red fruits which eventually turn black; of little garden value except that its red fleshy roots, when ground, yield a red dye.

RUBIACEAE = The Madder or Coffee Family

RUBUS (ROO-bus). The raspberries, blackberries, etc., are frequently considered to be a mixed-up group of thorny, alternate-leaved shrubs belonging to the Rose Family. There are approximately 400 species in the northern temperate zone. The leaves are simple, lobed or more usually compound. The fruits are red or black. In the case of the Raspberry the fruit separates from the receptacle; in the case of the Blackberry, receptacle and fruit remain together and both are eaten.

The plants in this genus are not used much as ornamentals but supply fruits of considerable economic importance. For information about these, their culture, pests and diseases, see BLACKBERRY, RASPBERRY, etc.

Propagation

Seed of *Rubus* species is usually doubly dormant, which means that it should be stratified, placed at warm room temperatures for 3 months, then placed at 40° F. for 3 months and sown. Layers are usually profusely borne and can easily be dug up from many species and varieties. Division of plants is simple and easy, being done in the early spring while the plants are still dormant. Softwood cuttings, hardwood cuttings and root cuttings (which see) all root easily. There is no difficulty in propagating *Rubus*!

allegheniensis   10′   Zone 3   Blackberry
An erect, arching plant with vicious hooked thorns and prickles; leaflets 3–5, white flowers and sweet black berries. This plant spreads rapidly, and in good soil can become a serious pest. Native from Nova Scotia to Mo. For culture, see BLACKBERRY.

deliciosus   9′   Zone 5   Boulder Raspberry
Native to Colo., this is a gracefully arching shrub bearing white flowers, about 2 in. wide, mostly solitary. The fruit is not palatable, but the plant is occasionally grown for ornament.

flagellaris   prostrate   Zone 3   Northern Dewberry
A prostrate perennial, with runners 6 ft. long, weak recurved prickles, leaflets 3–5. Fruit is black, about the size of a thimble. A few forms are occasionally cultivated for their large fruit, but otherwise the plant has little value. Native from Me. to Minn., south to Va.

hispidus   prostrate   Zone 3   Swamp Dewberry
A half-evergreen plant with prostrate runners sometimes 5 ft. long. Native throughout eastern North America. Occasionally it is grown as a ground cover in moist or shaded places. The leaflets are 3, rarely 5; flowers are white and borne in few-flowered clusters; the fruit is purple.

idaeus   6′   Zone 3   European Raspberry
Not very much grown in America, but native to northern Europe and Asia as well as North America. The stems are finely tomentose when young, sometimes with a few prickles, leaflets 3–5, flowers small and white in short racemes and the fruit is a red raspberry. This is one of the parents of many modern raspberry varieties. See RASPBERRY.

illecebrosus   3′   Zone 5   Strawberry-raspberry
Almost herbaceous, with 5–7 leaflets that are long and pointed and 3–4 in. long, this has white flowers, 1½ in. wide, and large scarlet fruit that are sometimes cooked. Blooming is from July to Sept. The plant is native to Japan.

laciniatus   3′   Zone 5   Cutleaf Blackberry
With long, arching, often procumbent stems and vicious prickles; leaflets usually 5 and pinnately lobed. The flowers are pinkish white, borne in June and July, and the fruit is a sweet blackberry about ½ in. long. Native to Europe, but escaped in parts of the U.S.

x loganobaccus   vinelike   Zone 8   Loganberry
A hybrid with *R. idaeus* as one of the parents, somewhat vinelike in habit and cultivated only in the the Pacific Northwest where growing conditions are just right. The fruit is about 1¼ in.

long, acid and red, and cannot be kept very long. See BLACKBERRY for culture.

occidentalis   9′   Zone 3   Blackcap Raspberry
With glaucous, prickly, often purplish stems and black raspberries for fruits, this is native throughout eastern North America. The white flowers are about ½ in. wide and the fruit is delicious. For culture see RASPBERRY.

odoratus   9′   Zone 3   Flowering Raspberry
This is probably the best of the raspberries as an ornamental, for the fragrant purple flowers are 2 in. wide and the 5-lobed leaves are 4–12 in. wide. The plant blooms from June to Aug. The fruit is red, but not tasty, and the branches have practically no prickles. It makes a nice shrub for the shaded spot. Native from Nova Scotia to Ga.

parviflorus   6′   Zone 3   Western Thimbleberry
Native from Ontario to N.Mex. and Alaska, this has small 3- to 5-lobed leaves, white single flowers, 1–2 in. wide, in dense clusters and red fruit ¾ in. wide. The fruits are edible and have been used in making preserves and jellies.

phoenicolasius   9′   Zone 5   Wineberry
One of the ornamental members of this genus because of the numerous and colorful red-brown hairs covering the stems. It is gracefully arching in habit; the leaflets are usually 3, purplish veined and white tomentose beneath. The flowers are small, white to pinkish in clusters, and the edible fruits are small and bright red. Native to China and Japan. In good soil this can increase rapidly and form an impenetrable mass of branches.

x tridel 'Benenden'   10′   Zone 6 (?)
A comparatively new plant raised by Captain Collingwood Ingram in England about 1950 (*R. trilobus* x *R. deliciosus*), this will probably have a better record in flower than either parent. The flowers are single, white, 2 in. wide and bloom in May. The northern limits of its hardiness have not yet been determined. It was given Plant Patent #1589 in 1957.

trivialis   prostrate   Zone 6   Southern Dewberry
A half-evergreen prostrate plant with 3–5 leaflets and prickly stems; solitary white flowers about ½ in. wide, and small, black, sweet-tasting berries about ½ in. long; native from Va. to Tex. Sometimes cultivated in the South for its fruit.

RUDBECKIA (rood-BEK-ia). A group of North American plants including annual, biennial and perennial species of the Composite Family, generally having alternate, simple or compound leaves, sometimes deeply lobed. Flower heads terminal or axillary, the ray flowers generally yellow, the disk flowers sometimes brown or black. The fruit is dry, 1 celled and 1 seeded. These are of easy culture and are frequently used in perennial gardens. Seed may be sown in early spring in a cold frame and the seedlings transplanted when large enough to handle. Plants may be divided in March or April. It is of note that some of the new clones are far superior to the old-fashioned, often weedy types.

fulgida   10′–12′   Zone 4   Showy Coneflower
A plant similar to *R. laciniata*, although less hairy; the leaves have long petioles. It is native to the woodlands of eastern U.S. and flowers in late summer. There is a clone named 'Goldstrum' which may belong to this species, only 2½ ft. tall with excellent deep yellow flowers 3–4 in. across. It is sometimes listed as *R. sullivantii* 'Goldstrum'.

hirta   3′   annual or biennial   Black-eyed Susan
An annual or biennial with rough, hairy stems and leaves, the basal leaves ovate, twice as long as broad, the upper leaves narrow and sessile. The deep yellow flower heads, 2–3 in. wide, are borne on terminal or axillary stalks. The disk flowers are dark brown, the disk cone shaped. This plant ranges from western Mass. to Ill., south to Ga. and Ala. A biennial (*R. serotina*), closely resembling this perennial species, has a wider range in the eastern states. It should be remembered that this is not a permanent garden plant, being annual or biennial and at best only a short-lived perennial.

hirta pulcherrima (*bicolor*)   2′   annual   Thimble-flower
With lance-shaped leaves about 2 in. long; yellow flowers, with the ray florets often purplish black at the base. Native from Ga. to Ark. and Tex.

laciniata   12′   Zone 3   Cutleaf Coneflower
A familiar perennial at the edges of moist woods and in the weedy flower beds of abandoned farm houses in the East, the lower leaves of this rough, hairy plant are deeply lobed into 3–7 segments, while the upper ones are ovate. The flower heads have a green conical receptacle rising from the center of the flower head which has tubular disk flowers, giving it a bristly appearance. It is a familiar component of the vegetation in moist woods from Quebec to Fla., west to Mont. and Ariz. and flowers from July to Sept. The var. **hortensia** is the very popular Golden Glow, with double yellow flowers, which has been widely used in ornamental plantings during the past century. 'Golden Globe' is a new clone only 4–5 ft. tall but can spread rapidly and invade other parts of the flower garden.

maxima   9′   Zone 7   Great Coneflower
Native to the southern U.S., blooming in July and Aug., this perennial has yellow flower heads 5–6 in. across, the disk florets being brownish. The oval grayish-green leaves are nearly a foot long.

nitida   4′   Zone 3
Leaves 6 in. long; the flowers with bright yellow rays and the central disk about 2 in. high. Native from Ga. to Tex.

subtomentosa   6′   Zone 5   Sweet Coneflower
All parts of this perennial seem to be covered with grayish hairs. The leaves are often 3 lobed and 5 in. long. The ray florets are yellow, disk flowers are dark brown, the flower heads being about 3 in. across. Native from Ill. to Tex.

triloba   5′   biennial   Brown-eyed Susan
This should be mentioned for, together with *R. serotina* and *R. hirta*, these are the common "Black-eyed Susan" species native throughout much of the eastern and middle U.S. *R. triloba* is native from N.J. to Ga. and La.; with deep yellow or almost orange flower heads, 2½ in. across, the center disk flowers being brown to black-purple.

RUE = *Ruta graveolens*

RUELLIA (roo-ELL-ia)
ciliosa   1′–2½′   Zone 6   Ruellia
A hairy perennial herb belonging to the Acanthus Family. The erect stem bears opposite, lanceolate leaves and axillary clusters of lavender or light blue flowers having a calyx with 5 elongated segments and a corolla with 5 spreading lobes. It is native to the sandy woods from N.J. to Fla. and west to Mich. and Kan. and blooms in July and Aug. The plant is an attractive addition to the wild garden. Plants may be divided in spring or seeds may be sown in spring.

RUFOUS. Reddish brown.

RUGOSE. Wrinkled.

RUMEX (ROO-mex)
acetosa   3′   Zone 3   Garden Sorrel
A perennial weed, native to Europe and Asia but naturalized in the North Atlantic States and southern Canada; with alternate, simple, entire leaves that are arrow-shaped and up to 5 in. long. Flowers dioecious, small, in terminal panicles. This used to be grown for greens in the old-fashioned kitchen garden. L. H. Bailey notes that the variety 'Large Belleville' is the one usually grown in the garden.

acetosella   1′   Zone 3   Sheep Sorrel
A perennial weed with long creeping roots just under the surface of the soil, common throughout the U.S. and Canada, native to Europe and Asia; leaves alternate, arrow-shaped, about 2 in. long. The dioecious flowers are small, on terminal panicles from May to Sept. and seed is profusely produced. It usually appears in acid

Sheep Sorrel (*Rumex acetosella*)—a common garden weed.

soils, but can withstand neutral to slightly alkaline soils. Because of its running roots it is a particularly obnoxious weed. For control see WEED-CONTROLLING CHEMICALS.

crispus   3′   **Zone 3**   **Curly Dock**
A perennial weed with a very deep tap root, common across the continent but native to Europe; this has long, curly, alternate leaves and small flowers in whorls crowded on a tall spike. The buckwheatlike fruits turn brown and remain conspicuous all winter.

obtusifolius   4′   **Zone 3**   **Bitter Dock**
A perennial weed, with alternate, oblong, lanceolate leaves up to 14 in. long; widespread throughout the U.S. and Canada but native to Europe and Asia. A rank weed wherever it occurs, the buckwheatlike brown seeds remain conspicuous on the flower stalk all winter. The roots are used to prepare a dark yellow dye.

patientia   6′   **Zone 5**   **Patience-dock**
A perennial, native to Europe, naturalized in North America; of little importance in the garden but occasionally grown for its early basal leaves used in salads. It has a strong tap root, long-petioled lanceolate leaves, a foot long with wavy margins; small flowers on a spike often 2 ft. long.

RUNCINATE. Coarsely saw-toothed or cut, the pointed teeth turned toward the base of the leaf; as in the Dandelion.

RUNNER. A slender and prostrate branch, rooting at the end or at the joint.

RUNNING-PINE = *Lycopodium clavatum*

RUSCUS (RUS-kus)
aculeatus   1½′–4′   **Zone 7**   **Butcher's Broom**
A stiff, low, evergreen shrub with leathery, pointed leaves about 1½ in. long, native of the southern and western parts of Europe. Branches of this shrub are cut, dried and dyed different colors, especially red, and used in floral decorations. It does need an occasional thinning to do well, and notably survives in hot sun, dry soil and shade as well. Although the bright red berries are ½ in. across (male and female flowers are on different plants) and are effective in winter, it is chiefly thought of as a foliage plant.

RUSH, SPIRAL = *Juncus effusus spiralis*

RUSSELIA (russ-EE-lia)
equisetiformis   8′   **Zone 10**
A shrub, usually with leafless, drooping, green branches, native to Mexico and Central America. The bright red flowers are slender, tubular, 1 in. long, in sprays. Sometimes grown in southern Fla. Easily propagated by cuttings in the spring and occasionally used as a pot plant in the North.

RUSSIAN-OLIVE = *Elaeagnus angustifolius*

RUST. A plant disease causing rusty or orange-colored areas on leaves and fruit. Many rust diseases confine their infection to specific plants. Common rust diseases infect Hollyhock, Snapdragon, Carnation, Asparagus and Bean. Several rusts have alternate hosts and must live a part of their life on other plants, such as wheat rust on Barberry, white pine blister rust on plants of Currant Family (see RIBES) and apple rust on Juniper. The least important of the 2 hosts should be destroyed, and extensive campaigns to destroy gooseberries and currants in the White Pine areas, barberries in the Wheat areas and junipers in the apple-growing areas of Va. have been conducted. Timely applications of ferbam or thiram give good control.

RUTA (ROO-ta)
graveolens   3′   **Zone 4**   **Common Rue**
Hardy perennial with woody base, native to southern Europe, with evergreen, alternate, twice-compound, fragrant leaves. The flowers are a poor yellow, ½ in. across, blooming in July and fruit is a 4–5-lobed capsule. Propagated by division. The leaves have been known to cause dermatitis in susceptible people, but they have also been used for medicinal and culinary purposes.

RUTABAGA (*Brassica napa napobrassica*). The Rutabaga is used like the Turnip, but varies in type of foliage, root character, and maturity.

See TURNIP. It is commonly found on our markets in late fall and winter and is a questionable crop to include in the small home garden.

Varieties

The more popular yellow-fleshed varieties are **'American Purple Top'** and **'Long Island Improved'**. **'Macombre'** is a very sweet, white-fleshed sort very adaptable to home garden use.

The Rutabaga is a cool-season crop and is best adapted for culture in the northern states. The soil and fertilizer requirements are similar to that for turnips. See TURNIP. The seed should be planted from June 15–July 1 in rows 24–30 in. apart and the plants in the row spaced at 6–8 in. Shallow, frequent cultivation is necessary to control weeds and to conserve soil moisture.

The roots should be allowed to reach full maturity before they are pulled, usually in late Sept. and Oct., in order to be sweet and of peak quality. For storage, the tap root and crown is trimmed with a knife and then placed in a pit or storage cellar having a low temperature, 35°–40° F., a high relative humidity, 90–95%, or conditions similar to that recommended for other root crops.

Most commercial rutabagas are waxed just prior to shipment to the market in a hot paraffin diluted with resin, beeswax or mineral oil to reduce shrinkage and shrivelling during the marketing period. This is not recommended for home garden storage.

Insects and Diseases

Insects and diseases are similar to those of Cabbage and Turnip. In addition, roots grown in a soil deficient in boron may develop a serious tissue breakdown known as brown heart or water core. Control lies in adding several oz. of borax to the complete fertilizer, or spraying the plants with a solution of borax in Aug. when the roots are making their most rapid growth.

GRANT B. SNYDER

RUTACEAE = The Rue or Citrus Family

RYANIA. An alkaloid insecticide obtained from the roots and stems of **Ryania speciosa**. It has both contact- and stomach-poisoning action to insects and is relatively safe to mammals. The principal uses have been for control of corn borer and codling moth.

RYE. Annual or perennial grasses under the scientific name of *Secale cereale*, these grow to 5 ft. tall and of course are one of the major agricultural grains of America, but it is not planted for ornament. The color is bluish green and the leaves are $\frac{1}{2}$ in. wide. The long awned spikes are crowded with seeds and are up to 6 in. long. The seed is $\frac{1}{3}$ in. long. This grain is used in making bread and rye whiskey. This is a cultigen or a plant supposedly originating in cultivation and of course this particular one has been cultivated for many centuries. Winter Rye is a form of this species planted in the early fall, used as a green manure.

RYE, BLUE WILD = *Elymus glaucus*

RYE-GRASS. See LOLIUM.

S

SABADILLA. An alkaloid which has insecticidal activity. When ground the powder is combined with lime or pyrophyllite to make a dust, and kerosene extracts are emulsified for spraying. It is less toxic than rotenone and is generally used for the same purpose. Supplies are limited.

SABAL (SAY-bal)

    minor   **3′–4′**   **Zone 9**   **Dwarf Palmetto**
A stemless palm, with vigorous-growing fan-shaped leaves, native to the extreme south-eastern U.S., adapted to being grown in swampy land. This and *S. palmetto* are 2 of the few palms native in the U.S. outside typically tropical regions.

    palmetto   **90′**   **Zone 8**   **Palmetto**
A palm native from N.Car. to Fla., this provides the dried leaves that are cut and distributed so widely in religious services on Palm Sunday. The fanlike leaves are 5–6 ft. long and 7–8 ft. across, partially divided into long, narrow segments. The Seminole Indians used the trunk for making houses, the fiber for twine, the leaves for thatching and the young buds for cooking and eating. Thus prepared they taste like cabbage but if the bud is taken the palm dies. It is one of the hardiest palms.

SABATIA (sa-BAY-shia). A genus of the Gentian Family, having 15 species of annual or biennial herbs native to North America. These have simple, opposite leaves and a corolla of 4–1 segments, with anthers which are conspicuously coiled. These plants are not widely grown, probably because they are usually biennials. They are chiefly for the swamps or brackish marshes in the wild garden, and do not provide large masses of color. Seeds are usually sown in May.

    angularis   **1½′**   **Zone 6**   **Square-stem Rose-gentian**
The square stems of this branching biennial attest to its relation to the gentians. From a rosette of oval leaves the stem rises, clothed with opposite, ovate, clasping leaves and bearing branched flower stalks, each terminated by a solitary pink flower having a calyx with elongated segments, a corolla with a short tube and 5 narrowly oblong lobes. The corolla has a greenish, star-shaped eye, 5 curled anthers and a green, 2-pronged style. It is native to the coastal salt marshes from southern New England to Fla. and blooms from July to Sept.

    campestris   **15″**   **Zone 5**   **Prairie Rose-gentian**
With 4-angled stems and alternate branching; leaves only an inch long; this bears lilac-colored flowers and is native from Mo. to Tex.

    dodecandra   **2′**   **Zone 6**   **Marsh Rose-gentian**
Another attractive plant capable of growing in brackish marshes, this species has opposite, sessile, lanceolate or linear leaves and pale pink to white flowers which untwist to open. Each corolla has 10–12 lobes marked with several red streaks at the base, giving the eye a distinctive appearance. The plant is native to the salt marshes from southern New England to Tex. and blooms in July.

    stellaris   **5″–20″**   **Zone 6**   **Salt-marsh Rose-gentian**
A colorful herbaceous plant of the salt marshes of the East Coast and La.; the stems are somewhat 4-angled near the base, the linear leaves are opposite and the flowers, up to 1 in. wide, terminate the stem. Each corolla has 4–7 deep pink or white, spreading lobes and the starlike eye is edged with red.

SACCATE. Sac shaped.

SACCHARUM (SAK-ka-rum)

    officinarum   **15′**   **Zone 9**   **Sugar Cane**
A tall grass, similar to Corn except that flowering and fruiting panicles are terminal. The stems are almost woody but, when crushed, yield a juice rich in sugar. It has been cultivated for centuries but usually needs a warmer climate than that of the continental U.S., although some strains are grown in La. and Fla. The ground and dried cane (after the juice has been crushed out) makes an excellent mulching material and can be baled and shipped north economically because of its light weight.

SAFFLOWER = *Carthamus tinctorius*

SAFFRON, MEADOW = *Colchicum autumnale*

SAFFRON, SPRING MEADOW = *Bulbocodium vernum*

SAGE. See SALVIA.

SAGEBRUSH. See ARTEMISIA.

SAGINA (sa-JY-na)

    subulata   **4″**   **Zone 4**   **Corsican Pearlwort**
This mosslike evergreen perennial is especially suitable for shady situations and is excellent for planting in between stepping stones or as a mass in small spots where it can create a dense mat. It is similar to *Arenaria* species except that the leaves of the Pearlwort are mostly shorter. Native to Europe, the small white flowers on

short stalks are produced in July and Aug. and are often so profuse that the foliage is covered by them. The evergreen leaves are only ¼ in. long and are produced so close together that a dense mat of foliage is formed. The plant is easily reproduced by division. The variety **aurea**, with leaves a yellowish color, is not especially ornamental.

SAGITTARIA (saj-it-TAY-ria). The members of this genus are aquatic perennials with tuberous root-stalks. Underwater leaves are ribbonlike, the floating leaves are generally oval, and the leaves growing above the water are shaped like an arrowhead. The flowers are borne in whorls on leafless stalks. In some species the flowers are perfect; in others, the male flowers, with 3 greenish-white sepals and 3 white stamens, are borne on the stalk above the female flowers which have numerous pistils and no petals. These plants are excellent for ponds, large aquariums or bog gardens, but care must be taken to keep them free of aphis and to keep the plants within bounds. They are easily propagated by seeds sown in flats of rich soil and plunged in shallow water, reset when the plants are large enough to be handled and then later placed permanently. The roots may be divided during the summer. There are at least 3 species used in aquaria, all with linear leaves. **S. graminea** has leaves 2 ft. long, native from Newfoundland to Tex.; **S. subulata subulata**, the Beach Arrowhead, has leaves 6–12 in. long, is native to Europe and Siberia, but it is long-lived in the home aquarium. **S. subulata**, or the Awlleaf Arrowhead, differs from the other 2 in having narrower and thicker leaves; they are straighter and of a darker green color and are only 5–10 in. long. It makes an excellent ornamental grass for the aquarium, native from N.Y. to Fla.

latifolia   4′   Zone 4   **Common Arrowhead** This plant has arrow-shaped leaves with extremely acute, basal lobes. The white flowers are 1½ in. wide. The edible roots were a starch staple for the Indians of the Northwest. It is native throughout North America and blooms from July to Sept.

sagittifolia 'Florepleno'   4′   Zone 5   **Double Oldworld Arrowhead** This double-flowered variety is the one usually grown, not the species. An aquatic or marsh plant with double white flowers an inch wide, with the petals spotted purple at the base. Underground edible tubers are produced. The leaves are arrow shaped. Native to Eurasia.

SAGITTATE. Shaped like an arrowhead, the basal lobes directed downward.

SAGO PALM FAMILY = Cycadaceae

SAINFOIN = *Psoralea onobrychis*

ST.-BERNARD-LILY = *Anthericum liliago*

ST.-BRUNO-LILY = *Paradisea liliastrum*

ST.-JOHN'S-WORT. See HYPERICUM.

ST.-JOHN'S-WORT FAMILY = Hypericaceae

SAINTPAULIA. Among house plants, the African Violet continues to be the most popular with indoor gardeners across the country. This is a distinction it has long held, and will doubtless continue to do so, in view of the fact that it has so much in its favor.

African violets, which are not violets at all but members of the genus *Saintpaulia*, to which gloxinias are related, are basically easy-to-grow house plants. Most of all, they are flowering plants, in bloom all year round. To flower, they do not require sunlight, which is rare among flowering plants that are grown indoors.

The merits of this favorite are numerous. They are small plants, and require little space. Narrow windowsills suit them well, and because of their ability to thrive on low amounts of light, they can be placed on tables, shelves and brackets.

African violets grow well under average room temperatures, which are warm, and unsuited to many other kinds of plants. They tolerate the dry atmospheres of homes in winter. They propagate and hybridize easily; they come in a wide variety of colors and forms, single and double, and they reach flowering size relatively quickly. For the plant enthusiast who lives in a city apartment—or even in one room—they are ideal.

It is not surprising that this universal appeal has resulted in an active African Violet Society, as well as several regional clubs throughout the country. They are all active, and many hold shows that are always well attended. The national society has thousands of members, and publishes a diverting magazine. Those who are devotees will profit from *The African Violet Book* by Helen Van Pelt Wilson, Hawthorne, N.Y., 1970, one of the most outstanding on the subject.

On the other hand, African violets can be temperamental and fail to flourish and bloom. They resent over-watering and too much moisture at their crown, which causes rotting. Insufficient watering results in wilting and poor growth. Using cold water causes yellowish spots to appear on the velvety leaves, and a fertilizer that is high in nitrogen means lush foliage, with with few or no blooms. Like other plants, they have their problems—aphids, mealybugs, cyclamen mites, and chlorosis. If there is the slightest presence of cooking gas, blossoms will drop.

Important in the life of any African violet plant is proper soil mixture. Many formulas are given, and African violet soil preparations are available from florists and at garden centers. Since this is a plant that is native to moist, humus woods of East Africa, plenty of organic matter is essential. This kind of soil is also recommended for ferns, begonias, and other plants with fine, fibrous root systems.

A good combination consists of equal thirds garden loam, leaf mold or peat moss, and sand, plus bone meal or superphosphate at the rate of 1 teaspoon to each quart of preparation. Another can be made up of 1 part good garden loam, 1 sand, 2 leaf mold or peat moss, and $\frac{1}{2}$ dried manure. Or combine 4 parts loam, 4 leaf mold or peat moss, 2 sand, 1 dried manure, plus the usual bone meal or superphosphate.

Available are several kinds of African violet foods, all excellent if used according to directions. A regular complete chemical fertilizer can also be used every 2 weeks as 5–10–5, or one high in phosphorus, as 4–12–4. Avoid feeding plants with liquid fertilizer when soil is dry, as leaves will turn yellow. Saintpaulias have a natural rest period after flowering. When blooms begin to get smaller, let up on the feeding to encourage rest.

There is considerable controversy as to how to water. Some advocate watering from the bottom, but others advocate watering from the top. In either case, use room temperature or lukewarm faucet water, as cold water causes chilling and possible injury to these tropical plants. If watering from the top, keep water close to the rim and away from the crown. African violets have succulent leaves, which tend to rot with over-watering or in periods of extended cloudy or rainy weather.

Much has been written about the hazards of wetting the foliage. Leaves will not be harmed if leaves are sprinkled with warm water and plants are allowed to dry in a shady place. If placed in sun, spots on the foliage will result. Chilling water will do the same, even if plants are allowed to dry out away from the sun. When giving a lukewarm bath, be sure plants are on the dry side. An already wet soil may result in rotting.

Soft, light sunshine, in the early or late part of the day will produce compact plants, full of flowers. During the winter, southern exposures are satisfactory, but as the sunlight becomes stronger, move the plants to less sunny windows or provide some kind of screening. Venetian blinds will regulate the amount of sunlight, and thin curtains will cut down on its intensity. In the greenhouse, shading is required. Plants flower in north windows, but less profusely. Many people grow them under fluorescent lights in basements or other rooms of the house.

New plants come easily from leaf cuttings. Use leaves taken from the middle of the plant, since the outer leaves tend to rot because they are too hard. They can be rooted in trays of vermiculite or in dark bottles with water, adding charcoal to keep the water sweet. When roots develop in 14–21 days, plant in $2\frac{1}{4}$-in. pots. Many prefer plastic pots, because they hold moisture longer. When the adolescent plants develop their second set of leaves, move them to $2\frac{1}{2}$-in. containers. After their first flowering, they can be shifted to 3-in. pots, where they should remain. Single-crown plants are preferred—when more than one crown develops, divide and repot.

Saintpaulia. African Violet leaves can sometimes be rooted in water; then the new plants are potted.

To keep plants well rounded, turn pots around periodically. Dust that collects on the hairy leaves can be removed with a soft camel's-hair brush. Showers from time to time will also keep the foliage clean and lustrous. During the long periods of cloudy weather, plants will perk up if placed under lamps for a few hours after darkness sets in.

In summer, plants will benefit from a vacation outdoors. Do not place outside until all danger of frost is past. African violets, being of tropical origin, are very tender. Keep them in sheltered places, as porches or secluded corners on terraces, where driving rains or strong winds will not injure them. They will need shade, and a good place for plants is under large shrubs. Plunge pots in the ground up to their rims, but not over. Feed regularly every 2 weeks and bring indoors early, just after Labor Day in the northern portions of the country.

Different flower types of the African Violet (*Saintpaulia*).

Common pests, such as aphids, mealybugs, red spider and cyclamen mites are easily controlled with aerosol bombs. These are manufactured especially for African violets. Always read all the directions carefully before using. Often, instructions indicate that the can should be held 12–18 in. away and that short, quick 1-second bursts be applied. With regular spraying when ailments appear, and by sterilizing soil in the oven at 200° for an hour before planting, there will be no problem with pests. Systemic insecticide #21 can be tried experimentally and aerosols are a supplement to regular spraying with insecticide #15. Hot water treatment (see MITES) may be necessary on heavily infected plants.

A common difficulty is induced by stem or petiole rot. This is not a disease, but is caused when the stems of the outer leaves touch the rims of pots and rot. This happens more frequently with clay pots. This can be avoided with wick-watering types of pots or by placing Scotch tape on the rims of pots. A cardboard dipped in paraffin can be placed as a collar around each plant. The problem is also eliminated if glazed containers are used.

There are so many varieties of African violets that one hardly knows where to begin when it comes to collecting. The best rule to follow is to select what is the most appealing. Doubles last longer, so are generally preferred. They do not present the problem of petal dropping.

Some varieties chosen by hobbyists as top favorites include:

'White Pride', white; 'Wedgewood', 'Winter Magic', and 'Charm Song', blue; 'Pride of Rochester', pink; and 'Doll Dance', white and lavender, all doubles.

Others that are outstanding are: 'Green Dawn', pink with green edge; 'Wintry Rose', deep rose with white edge; 'Blue Boy', deep violet-blue; 'Blue Girl', rich violet-blue; 'Amethyst', lavender-blue; 'Orchid Beauty', pale lavender-pink; 'Gorgeous', orchid rose; 'Redhead', red-violet; and 'White Lady'.

GEORGE TALOUMIS

SAKAKI = *Cleyera japonica*

SALAL = *Gautheria shallon*

SALICACEAE = The Willow Family

SALICORNIA (sal-ik-KORN-ia)

europaea 2′ **annual** **Marshfire Glasswort** Not of much horticultural interest; its leaves are reduced to scales and turn a brilliant red in the fall. Flower spikes are 3 in. long. Native to Europe, Asia, North America. Usually found growing erect in salty marshes.

SALIX (SAY-lix). The willows are a large group of deciduous plants which include trees, shrubs and even ground covers, all of which have proved difficult to identify ever since the days of Linnaeus. The sexes are separate, the simple leaves are alternate, the wood is brittle and cracks easily, and the plants are susceptible to attacks, often severe, from several disease and insect pests. They are valued because, of the pendulous trees, they are the most graceful. A few of the shrubby types are used in ornamental plantings because of their early spring catkins. One or 2 have colored twigs which are of ornamental interest, especially during the winter, if the plants have been grown well. The fruits are capsules, most of which break open in the early spring and loose their cottony masses of minute seeds, somewhat similar to those of the Milkweed, which are blown away by the slightest breeze. Some are mere ground covers, hardy into Zone 1 in the far North, but of little interest elsewhere except in rockeries or in poor soils in the northern parts of U.S. and Canada. Some are noted for their ability to grow in wet soil, while others appear to be more at home in the poor, dry soils of the northern U.S.

Though the willows have been planted to some extent in America, they have been used for centuries in the Low Countries, being planted on banks of moist soil to keep the soil in place, or in low, wet spots where it seems that pests are not so rampant as in comparable areas in America. Also, they are used for making baskets and weaving mats in many European countries.

The weeping willows are considerably mixed

up in the trade. There are at least 6 willows that can be considered "weepers" and, of these, the most commonly mentioned is the Babylon Weeping Willow, *S. babylonica*. This species is hardy only in the lower third of the U.S. The hardiest of the weeping willow group is the Golden Weeping Willow (*S. alba* 'Tristis'), now often incorrectly listed as *S. vitellina pendula*. Of those remaining, 1 is a native of China (*S. matsudana* 'Pendula') and probably not much distributed in this country, and the other 3 are hybrids, each having *S. babylonica* as one of its parents. It is this affinity which causes the confusion in identification.

The least pendulous of these *S. babylonica* hybrids is *S. sepulcralis*, formerly incorrectly listed as *S. salamoni*. Because it is none too pendulous, it is not in the following recommended list. Some nurserymen are still growing it under the name of Solomon Weeping Willow. The Thurlow Weeping Willow (*S. elegantissima*) and the Wisconsin Weeping Willow (*S. blanda*) are both grown and recommended, but the latter is probably the less desirable, since the branchlets of mature specimens are not so long as those of the Thurlow Weeping Willow.

The 3 most pendulous are *S. babylonica*, *S. alba* 'Tristis' and *S. elegantissima*, and these can be easily distinguished, one from the other, by the following simple key. *S. matsudana* 'Pendula' is probably not grown very much in America and *S. sepulcralis* is the least pendulous. The Wisconsin Weeping Willow (*S. blanda*) is a very popular one because of its good growth and lustrous leaves, even though its branchlets are not so long as those of the Thurlow Weeping Willow.

To assist in the identification of the 4 weeping willows commonly found in the trade, the following key is offered, although, like other keys dealing only in visible vegetative characters, it should never be thought of as infallible.

1. One-year-old twigs definitely yellow and pendulous; very little, if any, red on upper side of young twigs; young leaves hairy above and below. *S. alba* 'Tristis'.
2. Young twigs yellowish green and reddish on upper side; leaves less than ⅜ in. in width and glabrous; branchlets very pendulous—1-year rooted cuttings grow almost prostrate on the ground; petiole ⅜ in. *S. babylonica*.
3. Twigs distinctly green; growth much more upright; leaves ⅝–⅞ in. in width and glabrous; (a) Leaves lustrous above, 1-year twigs reddish to brown. *S. blanda.* (b) Leaves not lustrous above, 1-year twigs green. *S. elegantissima.*

There are 3 willows which are being grown primarily for their male flower catkins; namely, *S. discolor, S. caprea* and *S. gracilistyla*. The first is a native of swampy lands in the eastern U.S. and will grow up to 20 ft. tall. The second, often called "French Pussy Willow," is the one which responds so well to heavy pruning; if well fertilized it will grow vigorously and will produce the long spikes of catkins much used in the florist trade at Easter time. The third is the smallest (6–10 ft.) and perhaps the prettiest in flower because the male catkins have a decidedly pinkish tinge which, when combined with the bright yellow stamens, makes quite a picture. The male catkins of all 3 species are about 1¼ in. long.

Willows grown for their general habit of growth, other than the weeping willows already mentioned, are *S. matsudana* 'Tortuosa', with its uniquely contorted branches, and 3 dwarf willows: *S. purpurea gracilis*, densely rounded and globe shaped; *S. tristis*, only 1½ ft. tall and making good cover on bankings of poor, dry soil; and *S. repens*, also only 1½ ft. tall, for moist, poor soil.

Willows with colorful twigs are *S. alba* 'Chermesina', with bright red twigs, and the more vigorous the plant, the more colorful the twigs; *S. alba* 'Vitellina', with yellow twigs; and *S. purpurea*, with purplish twigs. The latter certainly is not so colorful as the other 2 but, because of the dense, shrubby growth, the plant is used considerably to form thickets.

Others of value chiefly for their foliage are *S. elaeagnos*, with gray, feathery foliage; *S. pentandra*, a tree with excellent, lustrous, dark green leaves; and *S. lanata*, about 4 ft. tall, one of the handsomest of the dwarf willows, having silvery foliage.

Propagation

Seed must be sown immediately when it is ripe, for its viability is quickly lost. Both softwood and hardwood cuttings root readily. See CUTTINGS.

Insect Pests

Willows are very susceptible to insect injury and approximately 120 different insects have been observed to feed on the various species. The most important are: Imported willow leaf beetle which is about ¼ in. long and of a dark metallic blue. The grubs are bluish black and resemble small alligators. Beetles and grubs eat holes or skeletonize the leaves. Two or more generations develop annually. On Basket Willow the poplar and willow leaf beetle, with irregular black marking on yellow wing covers, has a similar life history. Both are controlled with insecticide #9. Laurel Willow and other species are defoliated and disfigured by the beetles and grubs of the willow flea weevil which kills the tips of new shoots and feeds on the under side of leaves. Later the grubs mine the leaves, giving the infected trees a scorched appearance. Spraying with insecticide #9 controls the beetles and #15 or #9, the grubs in the mines. Poplar and willow curculio (see POPULUS) is a serious pest of Pussy Willow. Gypsy moth (see QUERCUS) and fall webworm (see JUGLANS) attack Willow. Several sawfly larvae girdle the new shoots and devour the leaves. Timely spraying with insecticide #9 or #15 controls them. Aphids, especially a purplish species, clustered on the twigs in the fall, are harmful. Insecticide #15 is effective. Galls on the tips of branches resembling small pine cones are caused by a gall midge. They are more curious than harmful. Among 7 species of scale insects on Willow, oystershell scale is commonest. Dormant sprays of insecticide #44 or fungicide #L or #N are effective, but sprays in early summer when young are hatching with insecticide #15 or #13 also may be necessary.

Diseases

Willow blight and willow scab blacken and shrivel the leaves and twigs. Blight is active in the spring and scab in late summer. On valuable trees, spraying with fungicide #D, #F or #K, starting when leaves are half grown and repeated 2 or 3 times, gives protection. Small, black, sunken cankers in the bark will kill weak trees. Pruning is the only helpful treatment. Orange blisters on the under side of leaves caused by rust and black raised swellings on the leaves caused by tar spot are minor diseases. Crown gall on the lower trunk and roots (see CROWN GALL) is harmful in nurseries and on small trees, but is seldom important on large trees.

alba   75′   Zone 2   **White Willow**
One of the best of the upright willows for ornamental planting, this is native to Europe, northern Africa and western Asia. It is loose and open in habit and, if an upright willow must be used, this is a good selection for planting in moist soil. Some of the varieties in use now are: 'Chermisina', the Redstem Willow, with younger branchlets colored a bright red—outstanding on younger plants in winter. As the tree matures the over-all color is not so pronounced. Practices leading to the forcing of vigorous young branches result in good color; var. **sericea**, with grayish leaves; 'Tristis', the Golden Weeping Willow, often incorrectly listed as *S. vitellina pendula*, is the weeping willow with yellow branchlets. A good tree, one of the hardiest of its group, it is at its best when kept in a vigorous growing condition by pruning and fertilizing; 'Vitellina', the Yellowstem Willow, has branchlets which are yellow when young, of interest where the variety 'Tristis' is not desired.

babylonica   30′–50′   Zone 6   **Babylon Weeping Willow**
A tree at first thought to be native to Babylon, but later found in China, undoubtedly reaching the Middle East in early times along the old caravan routes. This is the best, but the least hardy, of the weeping willows, with long, gracefully pendulous branches. When propagated from cuttings, it can be easily distinguished in the nursery row for the first year or two, since it lies completely prostrate on the ground before forming a main leader.

x blanda   40′   Zone 4   **Wisconsin or Niobe Weeping Willow**
Originating as a hybrid (*S. babylonica* x *S. fragilis*) before 1830, this is one of several hybrid weeping willows, and is probably less desirable than another plant of the same cross, *S.* x *elegantissima*, because at maturity its pendulous branches are only half as long as those of the Thurlow Weeping Willow. Whether the term "Niobe" is a synonym has been a matter for much discussion for the past 50 years.

caprea   27′   Zone 4   **Goat Willow**
Sometimes called "French" Pussy Willow, but nevertheless native to Europe and northern Asia, this is really a tree, but of little ornamental value except for its early spring catkins, the male flowers being the better, and about 1½ in. long. Often forced into long shoot growth by cutting to the ground every few years, followed with heavy applications of fertilizer, this is the Pussy Willow sold in the florist shops in early spring.

discolor   20′   Zone 2   **Pussy Willow**
A native shrub throughout eastern North America, hardier than *S. caprea* and hence easier to grow in the North.

elaeagnos   45′   Zone 4   **Elaeagnus Willow**
The grayish, feathery foliage is of interest and it turns yellow in the fall, but it would seem that if this characteristic were desired, it would be better to plant the true *Elaeagnus angustifolius*, which is free of most insect and disease pests. *Salix elaeagnos* is native to southern Europe.

x elegantissima   40′   Zone 4   **Thurlow Weeping Willow**
Originally introduced about 1860, this hybrid (*S. babylonica* x *S. fragilis*) is the best substitute for the Babylon Weeping Willow in the North. The Wisconsin Weeping Willow has more lustrous leaves, but the pendulous branches of this Thurlow Weeping Willow are considerably longer. Both probably have the same parents.

gracilistyla   6′–10′   Zone 5   **Rose-gold Pussy Willow**
An interesting shrub of the pussy willow type from Japan and Manchuria; of interest for its comparatively low growth (when compared with the 20 ft. of *S. discolor* and the 27 ft. of

S. caprea), and also for the fact that the male catkins, 1¼ in. long, have a certain amount of reddish color, giving rise to the common name appropriately coined only a few years ago by a nurseryman with a large number of plants for sale.

lucida   20′   Zone 2   Shining Willow
Native from Newfoundland to Neb., with glossy leaves 3–5 in. long and closely resembling *S. pentandra*, which is more in use at present.

matsudana 'Tortuosa' 30′ Zone 4 Corkscrew
or Contorted Willow
Best grown as a vigorous shrub with many branches from the base; valued for its twisted or contorted branches, unique among woody plants. As a tree with a single trunk, it is not an interesting specimen, for the slower growth of the branches, often well above eye level, does not have the interest of a lower-growing shrub under 10 ft. in height. It is native to China. The species, native to China and Korea, is not a good ornamental and is not used in planting.

pentandra   60′   Zone 4   Laurel Willow
A European tree with lustrous, dark green leaves, similar in size and shape to those of Mountain-laurel. Although a beautiful specimen, if kept properly sprayed, it is a mistake to make large plantings of any willows along the highways, since neglected trees can become the haven of insects that will quickly mar the foliage and make the trees look most disreputable.

purpurea   9′   Zone 4   Purple Osier
Not a valuable garden shrub, but useful in making a dense nondescript mass of foliage and twigs in moist soils where other plants might not grow. Otherwise of little ornamental value. Native to Europe and Asia. The variety **'Gracilis'**, often listed as "Purpurea Nana," or "Purpurea Dwarf," is a very slender-branching plant with very narrow leaves. Probably of little use except as a contrast to the more vigorously growing species.

repens rosmarinifolia 3′ Zone 4 Rosemary
Creeping Willow
This low, very narrow-leaved willow is an excellent one for poor, moist soils or for the rock garden. It often has prostrate stems and leaves only ½–1½ in. long. Native to Europe and Asia.

reticulata 5″–6″ Zone 1 Neatleaf Willow
A spreading dwarf shrub, growing extensively in Alaska and northern Canada. The dark green, netted leaves are ½ in. long, and the colorful reddish-magenta catkins appear very early in the spring. This is sometimes planted in the rock garden.

sachalinense 'Sekko' 30′ Zone 4 Japanese
Fan-tail Willow
This Japanese plant is of interest only as a unique specimen in the garden. It is mostly shrubby, with peculiarly twisted and contorted branchlets which are used sometimes in flower arrangements. The stems are often abnormally flattened and twisted into curious shapes. It is usually grown as a shrub, under 10 ft. in height.

tristis 1½′–3′ Zone 2 Dwarf Gray Willow
A poor-soil shrub only, with leaves whitish underneath, giving the foliage an over-all gray effect. Although widely native over the eastern half of the U.S. and even doing well in seashore plantings, it is extremely difficult to find this willow listed, currently, in commercial nursery catalogues.

uva-ursi   2″   Zone 1   Bearberry Willow
A creeping, matlike willow with glossy, bright green leaves that are whitish on the under surface. The small catkins produced in early spring are a soft red and are held close to the twigs. Native from Labrador to Alaska and sometimes planted in the rock garden.

SALPIGLOSSIS (sal-pi-GLOSS-is)
sinuata   2½′   annual   Painted-tongue
A member of the Nightshade Family, this species comes from Chile. It has funnel-shaped, vari-colored flowers, about 2½ in. wide, and is long-blooming in summer. The colors range from lavender to crimson-yellow and rose with various colors on the flower veins. Many fine colored hybrids have been developed and make splendid garden plants. Leaves are alternate, entire, with the fruit a capsule. The **Emperor** strain is one of the best, and is available either as a mixture or in separate colors. It is best to plant the seeds indoors in March and set the pots out after frost or to sow seeds in mid-April in the beds where they are to grow since they do not transplant easily. Seedlings should be thinned out about a foot apart. With a situation in fertile soil, in full sun, these should bloom throughout the summer and early fall until killed by frost. They also are good as cut flowers and may be perennial in a warm climate.

SALSIFY (*Tragopogon porrifolius*) is also known as oyster plant. It is a hardy biennial belonging to the Composite Family with leaves that are very narrow, resembling those of Leek, but smaller. While of minor importance it is tasty, having a very delicious flavor. For closely related plants see Black Salsify (see SCORZONERA) and Spanish Salsify. See SCOLYMUS.

Salsify is an all-season crop and needs a longer growing season than parsnips to produce its long, tapering, white root. It is comparatively hardy and seed should be sown as early as possible in the spring. Sow in drills 12–15 in. apart and thin the seedlings to 1½–2 in. in the row.

The soil should be of a deep, 10–12 in.,

sandy loam. In heavier soils liberal applications of well-rotted manure or compost should be used to open the soil structure. The plant is a rich feeder and responds well to manure and commercial fertilizer. See PARSNIP. Plants may be harvested as needed in the fall or left in the ground all winter if mulched. See MULCH. If the winters are too severe, the roots may be dug and stored. The best variety is 'Sandwich Island'.

GRANT B. SNYDER

SALSOLA (SAL-so-la)

pestifer   2′   annual   Common Russian Thistle, Saltwort

A weed from Europe and Asia, often seen along seashores in eastern North America. The alternate leaves are ¾ in. long, grayish, stiff and spiny tipped. The small solitary flowers are not ornamental. Late in the season the plant hardens, breaks off at the base and is blown about by the wind in large balled clusters.

SALTBUSH, FAT-HEN = *Atriplex patula*

SALT-TREE = *Halimodendron halodendron*

SALTWORT = *Salsola pestifer*

SALVIA (SAL-via). Belonging to the Mint Family, there are many species of this genus which make fine garden plants both as annuals and as perennials. The leaves are opposite, the flowers are in whorls with 2 to many flowers per cluster. The stems, like those of so many mints, are usually square. Perennial species are propagated by seeds, division and cuttings and the annual sorts by seeds sown indoors in Feb. and March, and the seedlings are planted out in the full sun after all danger of frost is past.

azurea   3′–4′   Zone 4   Blue Sage
Blue flowers appear in Aug. and Sept. in whorls, and even the leaves are faintly blue on the under surface. Native from S. Car. to Tex. White-flowering forms are not very outstanding.

azurea grandiflora   4′   Zone 5   Pitcher's Sage
The blue or white flowers are an inch long and are borne in dense racemes and many-flowered whorls. Blooms in Aug. and Sept. Native to the midwestern U.S. Unfortunately the flower stalks tend to flop over and hence this does not make a good display.

elegans (*rutilans*)   2′–3′   Zone 9   Pineapple Sage
A popular herb, flowers scarlet, about an inch long, listed in many herbals for its fragrant, aromatic foliage. This is shrubby, with pineapple-scented leaves and scarlet flowers in the summer. It can live out-of-doors over winter only where there is no winter frost.

farinacea   2′   annual, perennial   Mealycup Sage
Grown in the North as an annual and in the South as a perennial, this has shrubby stems, lanceolate leaves and violet-blue tubular flowers in lengthy racemes. **'Blue Bedder'** is an excellent

∟ also 'Victoria'

one for bedding purposes. The leaves are up to 8 in. long; the flowers are ½ in. long, a deep blue with a white spot, and are borne in racemes 8 in. long. Native to Tex.

greggii   3′   Zone 7   Autumn Sage
A beautiful woody species with red to purple-red flowers, 1 in. long in 4-in. clusters, during the fall; leaves about ¾ in. long. Native of Tex. and Mexico. The variety **alba** has white flowers. Both are extremely drought-resistant.

lyrata   1′–2′   Lyre-leaved Sage
A member of the Mint Family, this perennial has the square stems, aromatic foliage and labiate flowers characteristic of that family. The opposite leaves are sessile or nearly so, oval to elliptic, about 6 in. long, with unevenly serrated margins, the lower leaves larger and lyre shaped. The lavender flowers are borne in whorls of 6 at the upper end of the stalk. Each corolla has a straight upper lobe and a curving lower lip with a large middle lobe. The plant is native to the eastern U.S. from Conn. to Fla., west to Mo., Okla. and Tex. This is an excellent plant for the wild garden and may be treated as an annual in the North, with seeds sown in spring or fall. Cuttings may be taken in summer.

officinalis   subshrub   Zone 3   Garden Sage
A popular garden herb with white, woolly, wrinkled leaves, 2 in. long; flowers white, blue or purple, ¾ in. long, in terminal spikes. Native to the Mediterranean Region. Varieties have different colored flowers; **albiflora**—white; **rubriflora**—red; and **tricolor** has multicolored leaves with yellowish veins. The foliage has many culinary uses. Easily propagated by either seed or cuttings.

patens   2½′   annual, perennial   Gentian Salvia
Grown in the North as an annual and in the South as a perennial, this native of Mexico has blue flowers 2 in. long and arrow-shaped leaves covered with sticky hairs.

pratensis   3′   Zone 3   Meadow Sage
A European tuberous-rooted perennial, bearing racemes of bright blue flowers in whorled racemes during the summer. The flowers are about an inch long.

sclarea   3′   biennial   Clary, Clary Sage
A popular herb which will seed itself continually if allowed to produce seeds; the leaves are 9 in. long; flowers are whitish blue, up to an inch long, in whorled panicles and the bracts are white and rose. The flowers are used in medicines for eye diseases. Seeds and foliage are used in various medicines. Easily propagated by seeds. Native to southern Europe.

splendens   3′–8′   annual, perennial   Scarlet Sage
The most commonly used species which, in warm climates, becomes almost shrubby and can grow up to 8 ft. high. When planted as an

annual, as it usually is, it seldom grows over 3 ft. tall (or less) before it is killed by frost. The leaves are 3½ in. long, ovalish; the flowers are scarlet, 1½ in. long, whorled, in racemes held rigidly upright. Native to Brazil. It has been so popular that several varieties have been introduced, some that are dwarf and only about 10 in. long. Seeds of another, **'St. John's Fire'**, produces plants that are unusually compact and uniform in size. The **Welwyn Hybrids** are plants with pink, salmon or buff flowers. All are generously used for bedding purposes and, once they start blooming, they continue until killed by frost.

x superba   3′   Zone 5
This hybrid (*S. sylvestris* is one parent) bears violet-purple flowers with red bracts from mid-June until late Aug. 'Purple Glory' is one of the best of the most recent introductions.

viridis (*horminum*) 1½′ **annual Joseph Sage**
With oblong leaves and showy purple bracts ½ in. long in racemes; the color in this plant is long-lasting, which is the reason it is sometimes used in the garden. Native to the Mediterranean Region.

SALVINIA (sal-VIN-ia)
rotundifolia aquatic plant Zone 10 Salvinia
This is a floating water plant imported from Brazil and does extremely well in the home aquarium. The leaves are round, about ¾ in. across, and the upper surface of the leaves are covered with vertical hairs. It multiplies rapidly and can be easily propagated by simple division.

SAMANEA (sam-an-EE-a)
saman   50′   Zone 10   Raintree Saman
A tree from tropical America, given its common name probably because its leaflets fold up at night time and at the onset of rainy weather. Member of the Pea Family, with a flat top; leaves 2 or 3 times compound; in habit sometimes 100 ft. wide. Each leaflet about 2 in. wide. Yellow flowers in ball-like clusters, somewhat similar to those of acacias, and red stamens 3 times the length of the corolla. Fruit, a pod 6–8 in. long. Native to the islands of the Caribbean, among other places, blooming from March to Sept. Sometimes grown for the 8-in. long pods as cattle fodder. Easily propagated by seed.

SAMARA. An indehiscent winged fruit. See KEY.

SAMBUCUS (sam-BEW-kus). Deciduous shrubs with opposite compound leaves, fast growth and coarse texture. The flowers are very small but produced in large flat clusters, 5 and 10 in. across, in the late spring followed by small fleshy berries, black or red, from which wine and preserves have been made from time immemorial. Some of the elders with yellow foliage are the best of these yellow-colored foliage plants we have. They are fast and vigorous in growth, for 3 years after the seed is sown plants 8–10 ft. tall can result. They are usually not plants for the small garden.

Propagation

Seed germination is variable but usually stratification for 3 months at 40° F. is sufficient to satisfy the dormancy requirements. Plants can be divided easily in the early spring while still dormant. Softwood, hardwood and root cuttings (which see) all root easily if properly handled. One should use only asexual means of propagation if the named varieties are to be increased. Seeds would yield plants like the species.

caerulea   45′   Zone 5   Blueberry Elder
Native to the Pacific Coast of the U.S. and Canada, this tree or shrub is popular within its native habitat because of the whitish-blue appearance of the blue-black fruit clusters and also because of its vigorous growth. When cut back hard it can grow 3–12 ft. in one year. The small flowers are yellowish white in large flat clusters, 7 in. across, during late June and of course the fruit colors during the late summer. The leaves have 5–7 leaflets.

canadensis   12′   Zone 3   American Elder
The American Elder probably grows from border to border halfway across the U.S. It is not a plant for the small garden but is best used in moist soils and on the borders of woodlands. It has large (6–8 in.) flat clusters of small white flowers in June and blue to black small berries in the late summer. Jellies, preserves and wines are made from the ripened fruits and, of course, they are most attractive to the birds. Some strains have been selected with larger fruits than others, and 'Adams' is one of these clones, selected by William W. Adams of Union Springs, N.Y., for its vigor and large fruits. However, none of these are plants for the small garden, but rather for areas where there is plenty of space. Fresh leaves, flowers, bark and young buds, and roots contain a bitter alkaloid—producing small amounts of prussic acid, causing fatal results if eaten by cattle and sheep. Poisoning in children has been ascribed to chewing or sucking the elderberry bark. Vars.: 'Acutiloba'—the leaflets are very deeply divided and hence this has a finer foliage texture than the coarser-leaved species; 'Aurea'—fruits red and foliage yellow. This actually has a fine yellow-colored foliage throughout the entire summer, if it is grown in good soil in the full sun. Usually the plants with yellow foliage are not good landscape subjects but this is one of the few exceptions for it does grow vigorously and looks well all season; 'Maxima'—the flowers

and fruit clusters of this variety are up to 13 in. in dia.

nigra   30′   Zone 5   European Elder
Cultivated since ancient times in Europe for the fruits, this species is native to Europe, northern Africa and western Asia. There are 3–7 leaflets in each leaf, the yellowish-white flowers are in clusters or cymes 5–8 in. across, and the fruits are lustrous black berries. There are many varieties of this grown in Europe; especially is the variety **'Aurea'** popular, because of its golden-yellow leaves, but none of these are grown much in America.

pubens   12′–24′   Zone 4   Scarlet Elder
Not quite as hardy as the American Elder, but widely native, this blooms in mid-May with yellowish-white flowers in 5-in. pyramidal clusters, followed by red fruits at about the time *S. candensis* is in flower. This species is particularly prevalent in the moist atmosphere of the mountains in the eastern U.S. It is not as easily grown in the coastal areas that are hotter and drier. The variety **'Dissecta'** has leaflets that are deeply cut.

racemosa vars.   12′   Zone 4   European Red Elder
This vigorous shrub is popular in the gardens of Europe where it is native and from there to western Asia. The small flowers are yellowish white, borne in large clusters during early May, and the red berries are most effective during the summer. There are many varieties in Europe but since they are somewhat similar to those of our native *S. canadensis* they are not grown much in America. There are 5–7 leaflets in each leaf. Vars: **'Flavescens'**—yellow fruits with a red cheek; **'Plumosa-aurea'**—golden-yellow leaves with deeply toothed leaflets.

SANCHEZIA (san-CHEE-zia)
nobilis   5′   Zone 9
A tropical shrub with large opposite leaves, a foot long, and bright yellow, tubular flowers, 2 in. long, with bright red bracts, usually borne in spikes. Propagated by cuttings. Native to Ecuador.

SAND. Sand is used a great deal in horticultural activities. Its addition to heavy soils makes them more porous; it is frequently added to potting mixtures to make them more porous, and clear "sharp" sand is used in rooting cuttings. "Sharp" means that when it is rubbed between the thumb and forefinger it is harsh to the touch. Some sands have very fine grains and are "soft" when rubbed similarly. These do not have as much air spaces between the grains and hence are not desirable in rooting mixtures.

All sand in potting mixtures or in propagation should be washed and clean, free of impurities. If seashore sand is used, it should be thoroughly washed, spread out and exposed to rain for several weeks. Sometimes this is too fine for horticultural use.

Sandy soils are good growing media unless they are very sandy, in which case they dry out too rapidly and do not have enough humus material for good plant growth. In this case, cover crops of Rye, Vetch, Buckwheat, etc., should be grown and plowed in to improve them. See SOILS.

SANDBOX-TREE = *Hura crepitans*

SANDBUR = *Cenchrus pauciflorus*

SANDMYRTLE, BOX = *Leiophyllum buxifolium*

SANDPAPER-VINE = *Petrea volubilis*

SAND, PLANTS FOR GROWING IN. There are some places, especially in seashore gardens (which see), where plantings must be made in almost pure sand. Of course the more humus incorporated into the sand (like peat moss, decayed vegetable matter and well-rotted manure) the better. However, the following plants are candidates for planting in the sand or sandy soils where nothing else seems to grow properly. Also see SEASHORE GARDEN.

SCIENTIFIC NAME	HEIGHT	ZONE	COMMON NAME
Abronia sp.	10″	5–8	Sand-verbena
Acacia farnesiana	10′	8	Sweet Acacia
Ammophila arenaria	4′	4	European Beach Grass
A. breviligulata	7′–8′	3	American Beach Grass
Arctospaphylos uva-ursi	ground cover	2	Bearberry
Artemesia sp.	4″–5′	3–5	Wormwood
Atriplex sp.	4′–6′	annual	Saltbush
Baccharis sp.	1′–12′	4–7	Groundsell-bush
Cocos nucifera	80′	10	Coconut
Elymus arenarius	8′	perennial	European Dune Grass
Eriophyllum lanatum	9″–18″	5	Woolly Eriophyllum
Juniperus conferta	1′	5	Shore Juniper
Lathyrus littoralis	decumbent	8	Beach Pea

SCIENTIFIC NAME	HEIGHT	ZONE	COMMON NAME
Leptospermum laevigatum	25′	9	Australian Tea-tree
Limonium sinuatum	2′	biennial	Notch-leaf Sea-lavender
Myrica pensylvanica	9′	2	Bayberry
Opuntia sp.	prostrate 12′	4–10	Prickly-pear
Prunus maritima	6′	3	Beach Plum
Robinia hispida	3′	5	Rose-acacia
Rosa rugosa	6′	2	Rugosa Rose
Sabal palmetto	90′	8	Palmetto
Sanvitalia procumbens	6″	annual	Trailing Sanvitalia
Solidago sp.	10″–6′	3–5	Goldenrod
Tamarix sp.	4′–30′	2–8	Tamarisk
Uniola paniculata	2′–5′	7	Sea-oats

SAND-VERBENA. See ABRONIA.

SANDWORT, LARCHLEAF = *Arenaria lancifolia*

SANDWORT, SEABEACH = *Arenaria peploides*

SANGUINARIA (sang-gwin-AY-ria)
  canadensis   3″–6″   Zone 3   Bloodroot
A lovely, perennial, spring flower of the Poppy Family, the sap, the rhizomous root and the stems of which are red. In early spring the tightly rolled, basal leaf is pushed up through the soil. The general outline of the leaf is rounded, with an irregular margin and deeply cut, wavy lobes. As it unfolds it reveals the flower bud, terminally borne on a leafless stalk. Each flower has 2 sepals which fall away quickly, 8–12 waxy white sepals and numerous stamens. There is a double-flowered form **'Multiplex'** which is even hardier and more beautiful. The flowers bloom from March to May in the woods over most of southern Canada and eastern U.S. to Kan. It is an interesting plant for the wild garden, preferring rich, slightly acid woods soil. It self-sows readily and may be divided in spring or fall. The sap of this plant contains a bitter-tasting toxic alkaloid which affects the heart, nervous system and muscles. In some cases it has caused death. The Indians used the red sap as a dye and war paint.

SANGUISORBA (sang-gwi-SOR-ba)
  canadensis   4′–5′   Zone 3   American Burnet
A handsome perennial of the Rose Family, native to the wet meadows and swamps from Labrador to Ga. and west to the Mississippi River. Pinnately compound, basal leaves, with 7–12-toothed, ovate leaflets and progressively smaller stem leaves, grow luxuriantly, above which rise the flower stalks with a dense terminal spike of tiny flowers which may be either male, female or perfect. These have a 4-lobed calyx, no corolla and, in the male flowers, a mass of long white stamens. Since this plant flowers in the fall, it is an important addition to the wet, acid-soil wild garden. It may be propagated by division in the spring or by seed collected in fall and sown at any time.

minor = *Poterium sanguisorba*
  officinalis   5′   Zone 4   Burnet
A popular herb from Europe and Asia but naturalized in North America. Flowers are about 1 in. across, dark purple and in spathes. Leaves are alternate, pinnately compound with 7–13 leaflets. Propagated by seeds. The tender young leaves have been eaten in salad and crushed leaves have been used to garnish and flavor drinks.

SANSEVIERIA (san-sev-EE-ria). Herbaceous tropical plants with stiff, upright, narrow leaves; long grown as house plants, especially *S. trifasciata laurentii*, which has the leaf margin longitudinally striped with yellow. They bear stiff, erect, leathery, straplike dark green leaves a foot or so long and pointed at the tip and several inches wide. Some are streaked with yellow or white. These plants thrive with less sunlight than most other house plants and should not be given much water, especially when they are dormant. This is important, for a common mistake is to over-water. Propagation is by division or root cuttings; most, except *S. trifasciata laurentii*, can be propagated by sections of the leaf placed as cuttings in a moist rooting medium. *S. thyrsiflora* and *S. trifasciata* are undoubtedly mixed in America and Europe as well.

  hyacinthoides   1½′   Zone 10   Sweet Sansevieria
This species and *S. trifasciata* are seriously mixed in this country and abroad as well. Both have transverse bands of light green or yellowish color on their leaves; both are rhizomatous; both bear fragrant greenish-white flowers. This species sends up a rosette of 20 stiff, fairy narrow leaves, channeled angularly. *S. trifasciata* supposedly sends up only 6–8 leaves from a single rhizome. Both are good house plants; both

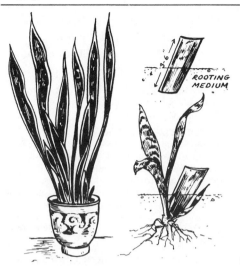

Sansevieria and rooted cutting.

undoubtedly offered interchangeably in the trade. Native to South Africa.

parva   1½'   Zone 10
The leaves are 18 in. long, several inches wide, variegated, recurved and spreading and very concave, borne in a dense rosette. Flowers are in foot-long racemes, pinkish white inside, darker outside. Native to East Africa.

trifasciata   1'–4'   Zone 10   Snake Sansevieria
This creeps by rhizomes ½–1 in. thick. The leaves are stiffly erect and deep green, with transverse sections of lighter green. The fragrant flowers are pale greenish, scattered in groups of 2–3 on a loose raceme, with fruits bright orange, ⅓ in. across. The var. **laurentii** is the most popular of the group with longitudinal stripes of golden yellow. Native to tropical Africa. This blooms at unpredictable times. There are other variegated clones in the trade, one an interesting dwarf named **'Haknii'** which is a sport of *laurentii* found in New Orleans in 1939, sometimes called 'Birdsnest' because of its small, vaselike, rosette form of broad, spirally arranged leaves. It suckers freely.

zeylanica   2½'   Zone 10   Ceylon Sansevieria
Sometimes called Bow String Hemp, the leaves sometimes have white markings or transverse bands of dark green, are deeply channeled and the margins are red lined. Flowers greenish white, 1¼ in. long, on a foot-long raceme. Native to Ceylon. This is sometimes confused with *S. trifasciata*, but is more graceful, with leaves ending in a long circular tip.

SANTOLINA (san-to-LY-na)
chamaecyparissus   1½'–2'   Zones 6–7
                                        Lavender-cotton

A half shrubby evergreen with alternate, aromatic, silvery-gray, woolly leaves, ½–¾ in. long. Native to southern Europe; chiefly used as a ground cover on poor, sandy or gravelly soils. It should be given a stiff pruning annually, preferably after flowering, to prevent untidy, over-vigorous growth. The yellow flowers are produced in many-flowered heads, ½–¾ in. across, during July and Aug. As an herb the stem is sometimes used in the household as a moth repellant, also to produce an oil for perfume.

virens   15"   Zone 7   Green Lavender-cotton
A spreading perennial herb with narrow, linear, green leaves, about 2 in. long but only 1/16 in. wide, with solitary yellow flower heads, ⅝ in. across. Native to the Mediterranean Region. Suitable for edging. Propagated by cuttings in the spring from plants wintered over in a cold frame.

SANVITALIA (san-vit-TAY-lia)
procumbens   6"   annual   Trailing Sanvitalia
With opposite, nearly entire, leaves about an inch long and little yellow flower heads with purple centers, this is an excellent trailing plant which might well be more widely used. The flower heads are about ¾ in. across. Native to Mexico. Excellent for edging, for on the top of a sunny wall it will bloom throughout the summer until killed by frost. It should be planted in the full sun. Easily grown from seeds sown in March indoors or in May outdoors. Members of the Composite Family. The var. **'Flore-pleno'** with double flowers is the one usually planted.

SAPINDACEAE = The Soapberry Family

SAPINDUS (sap-IND-us)
drummondii   45'   Zone 5   Western Soapberry
Native from Mo. to Mexico, this has alternate compound leaves with 8–18 leaflets, 1½–3 in. long; small yellowish-white flowers in panicles 6–10 in. long during June. The fruits are globular, about ½ in. across, yellow at first, finally black. Some individuals have developed dermatitis from handling the fruits. Not especially ornamental; the Indians were supposed to have made a soap from the berries.

SAPIUM (SAY-pium)
sebiferum   40'   Zone 9   Chinese Tallow-tree
This tree from China and Japan has the general ornamental aspects of a poplar, with alternate, lustrous, light green leaves, 1–3 in. long, the stalks of which are red. The fruit is a capsule about ½ in. wide and the milk-white seeds adhere to the central part of the capsule long after it is open. The Chinese use the milky coating about the seeds for making candles and soap. It is remarkably free of pests and is adaptable for planting in a wide variation of soils.

SAPODILLA FAMILY = Sapotaceae

SAPONARIA (sap-o-NAY-ria). This is a group of annuals or perennial herbs of about 50 different species belonging to the Pink Family, mostly native to the Mediterranean area. With opposite, simple leaves, the bright, colorful flowers are either pink or white. The genus is called *Saponaria* because the bruised leaves or stems of some species have been used in making soap. They are useful in the border or the rock garden. Propagation is by seeds sown in the early spring, or by division in the early fall or early spring. Cuttings of vigorous shoots can also be taken in Aug. or Sept.

caespitosa *6″* **Zone 6 Pyrenees Soapwort** A delightful, little, evergreen perennial from the Pyrenees, well suited to rock walls or crevices in gravelly or sandy limestone soil. The thick, succulent leaves, an inch high, form cushions of foliage which in many are dotted with large pink flowers having inflated calyxes.

calabrica *9″* **annual Calabrian Soapwort** Excellent for the rock garden or the front of a flower border, this sticky-leaved annual is valued for its solitary, pale, rose-colored flowers, about $\frac{1}{2}$ in. across, borne in little panicles in the leaf axils during the spring. Native to Italy and Greece. There is a white-flowered var. **(alba)** and one with good scarlet flowers, 'Scarlet Queen'. Easily grown from seed sown indoors in March and then planted outdoors after the frost.

ocymoides *9″* **Zone 2 Rock Soapwort** A trailing, many-branched perennial, this will grow in any good soil in full sun. It is native to southern and central Europe. The leaves are less than 1 in. long; the bright pink flowers, each with 5 petals, appear in loose sprays from May to Aug. It should be cut back severely after flowering to keep it neat and compact. This is one of the European wild flowers seen in great masses along the railways in the Alps Mountains of Switzerland. Easily propagated by division and seed; it is a popular garden plant.

officinalis *2′–3′* **Zones 2–3 Bouncing Bet** This is a European perennial which has become naturalized throughout the eastern U.S. The strong, straight, seldom branching stems are jointed at the axils of the opposite, ovate leaves, which have strong longitudinal veins and wavy margins. The pale pink flowers are borne in axillary and terminal clusters. Each flower has a 5-pointed calyx and 5 widespreading petals having a cordate margin; they bloom throughout the summer, more especially at night. They are an interesting addition to the wild garden and increase by underground stolons. Propagation is by division in spring, seed sown in the spring, cuttings taken in summer or clumps may be transplanted. 'Rosea Plena'—double fls.

vaccaria = *Vaccaria pyramidata*

SAPOTA ACHRAS = *Achras zapota*

SAPOTACEAE = The Sapodilla Family

SAPOTE, WHITE = *Casimiroa edulis*

SAPROPHYTE. A plant which lives on humus in the soil, or dead or decaying organic materials, i.e., most mushrooms.

SARCOBATUS (sar-ko-BAT-us)
vermiculatus *10′* **Zone 4 Black Greasewood** Native to western North America in alkaline soil regions. Leaves alternate, fleshy and linear, $1\frac{1}{2}$ in. long, with whitish branches, spiny; flowers either monoecious or dioecious. The wood is hard, yellow and about its only use is for fuel. Not a valued ornamental. The foliage is poisonous to sheep and cattle if a large amount is eaten in a short time.

SARCOCOCCA (sar-ko-KOK-a). Only two species of this small group of Asiatic shrubs are mentioned here. They are evergreen, belong to the Box Family, and are closely related except that these have alternate and longer leaves, while those of box are opposite. The flowers are small and inconspicuous, the male and female flowers being separate but on the same plant. The fruit is a drupe, fleshy and dark red. Their culture is the same as for box, which see.

hookeriana *6′* **Zones 5–7 Himalayan Sarcococca** A handsome evergreen shrub with lustrous and leathery, alternate leaves, 1–3 in. long, from the Himalayas. The fragrant flowers are white and small in short, 4-flowered, axillary racemes, with pistillate and staminate flowers being borne in the same raceme in midspring. The fruits are black berries, $\frac{1}{4}$ in. across. The variety **humilis** is hardier (Zone 5) and lower, only about 1–3 ft. hence can be used for a ground cover.

ruscifolia *6′* **Zone 7 Fragrant Sarcococca** An evergreen shrub with lustrous evergreen leaves, $1\frac{1}{4}$–2 in. long, and fragrant, white, unisexual flowers in 4-flowered axillary racemes. The fruits are dark scarlet, $\frac{1}{4}$ in. across. It is native to China. **S. saligna** is being used a little but it differs from these other 2 species little except that it has purple fruits.

SARITAEA (sari-TEE-a)
magnifica (*Bignonia magnifica*) **vine Zone 10 Purple Funnelvine** Native to Columbia, this vine has purple flowers of the size and shape of members of the genus *Bignonia*. These flowers are 3 in. long and appear throughout the year. Each leaf is made up of 2 leaflets 4 in. long. Climbing by the use of tendrils, this is a popular vine in Hawaii. Fruit is a capsule.

SARRACENIA (sar-rass-EE-nia). An insectivorous genus of herbaceous perennials of North America. Both tender and hardy species grow only in bogs on wet, sandy peat or sphagnum moss. Spreading by the underground stolons, the plants have tubular or pitcherlike leaves, with a lid, in which insects are trapped, being attracted by nectar. The nodding flowers rise on leafless stalks and may be yellow, reddish or purplish in color, The calyx, having 5 sepals, may be colored; the stamens are numerous and the pistil has a flaring stigma.

flava   3′   Zone 7   Trumpet Pitcher-plant
The leaves of this species are upright, tubular, red veined and fluted, with a lid which bends over the leaf opening. The drooping flowers have 5 spreading, greenish-yellow sepals, 5 yellow petals, 3 times the length of the sepals and which narrow at the base and are marked with strong longitudinal veins. Within the petals is a conspicuous green pistil. A very interesting plant for the bog garden. Native from Va. to Fla.

purpurea   12″–18″   Zone 3   Common Pitcher-plant
The red-veined basal leaves of this plant are tubular, swollen in the center, with a wide longitudinal wing and a 2-lobed, upright lid. The insects drowned in the water collected in these pitchers supply food for the larvae of a fly which aids in the cross-pollination of the solitary flowers on the leafless stalks. Each

Sassafras leaves

flower has 5 reddish sepals and 5 red, incurved petals surrounding the umbrellalike stigma. Native to eastern North America.

SARRACENIACEAE = The Pitcher-plant Family

SARSPARILLA. See ARALIA.

SASA. See BAMBOO.

SASSAFRAS (SASS-a-fras)
albidum   60′   Zone 4   Sassafras
Widely distributed in the eastern U.S., this tree is noted for its irregularly, often mitten-shaped leaves, 4–6 in. long, and the aromatic odor of leaves and twigs when crushed. It is sparsely branched, the branches being very short, hard to move, but survives in the poorest of gravelly soils. The autumn color is a rich red and orange and the inconspicuous male and female and sometimes perfect flowers may be on different trees or the same tree. The fruits are bluish berries, less than ½ in. across, on long, bright red fruit stalks. The oil of sassafras is distilled from the roots and the bark, and it was from these that sassafras tea was made by the early settlers.

Propagation

Do not let the seed dry out but stratify as soon as ripe for 3 months at 40° F. Root cuttings also prove satisfactory, taken in the early spring. See CUTTINGS, STRATIFICATION.

Insect Pests

Sassafras stem borer tunnels in the pith of the stem and discharges quantities of frass through small holes. The trees are more often disfigured than killed. In the Northeast the gypsy moth (see OAK) eats the leaves and makes the tree unsightly. Sassafras is one of the favorite hosts of Japanese beetle.
officinale = *S. albidum*
varifolium = *S. albidum*

SATINFLOWER = *Godetia grandiflora*

SATSUMA, ORANGE. See ORANGE.

SATUREJA (also spelled Satureia) (sat-yew-REE-jia)
These low-growing aromatic herbs belong to the Mint Family and they are similar to mints. They have opposite leaves, small, white, pink or purplish flowers, borne in whorls, and axillary or terminal racemes; they are of easy culture and have long been grown for flavoring foods. Mostly native to Europe they are either annuals or perennials, and are easily propagated by seed, division of plants or by softwood cuttings.
calamintha = *Calamintha nepeta*
douglasii   2″   Zone 4   Yerba Buena
A perennial, sometimes with trailing stems, with white or purplish flowers. Western U.S.

glabella   2′   **Zone 6**
A completely prostrate, matlike perennial with
thin stems and with dark green leaves appressed
to the ground. The sprays of small purple
flowers are borne on stems 3 in. high. This
Savory, which has a strong aromatic scent when
the leaves are bruised, is native from Ky. to
Ark.

hortensis   18″   **annual   Summer Savory**
A popular annual herb, with bushy stems that
tend to fall over. The opposite leaves are 1½ in.
long and narrow, and the small fragrant flowers
are pink to purplish, borne in loose whorls and
spikes. The leaves are used in flavoring various
foods. Native to Europe, naturalized in the
eastern U.S. Propagated by seed.

montana   15″   **Zone 5   Winter Savory**
A popular herb but shrubby and perennial, with
weak stems. Otherwise, similar to *S. hortensis*
but the flowers can be darker, from pinkish
white to a good purple. The opposite leaves and
tender tips are used in flavoring foods. Native
to Europe. Propagated by seeds and division as
well as softwood cuttings.

vulgaris = *Clinopodium vulgare*

SAUROMATUM (saw-ROM-at-um)

guttatum   2′   **Zone 7   Monarch-of-the-East**
A peculiar perennial herb growing from a corm-
like underground tuber; of little ornamental
value but sometimes planted for curiosity. The
2–4-in. long scape can be produced from the
tube even though it is not planted in soil, if it is
3 in. in dia. or more. The long-tailed spathe is
dull purple, yellowish spotted and 1–2 ft. long.
Native to the Himalayas and Africa, but can be
wintered over outside as far north as New York
City if the tuber is planted 6 in. deep and
mulched over winter.

SAUSAGE-TREE = *Kigelia pinnata*

SAVORY. See SATUREJA, CALAMINTHA, CLINO-
PODIUM.

SAWBRIER = *Smilax bona-nox*

SAXIFRAGA (SAX-iff-rag-a). This genus con-
tains nearly 300 species of small annual, biennial
or perennial herbs, most of which are native to
the temperate regions of America and Europe.
Many make excellent rock garden plants and
one (*S. stolonifera*, but popularly termed *S.
sarmentosa*) makes one of the best and most
rugged of pot plants for the home. They vary in
habit from mosslike plants to thick-leaved
succulents. Flowers are of various shades of
pink, red, yellow, white or purple. Nearly all
like rocky limestone soil and do best if in a
partially shaded situation. They are easily
propagated by seeds, division of plants, rootstock, runners or bulblets.

aizoon = *S. paniculata*

x andrewsii   6″   **Zone 3   Andrews Saxifrage**
One of the parents of this hybrid species is *S.
paniculata*. Flowers are white with red markings.

x apiculata   3½″   **Zone 6**
Small, matlike plants with tiny, linear leaves
and deep yellow flowers blooming in April.
The variety **alba,** with white flowers, has foliage
of a somewhat lighter hue.

x boeckeleri   1″   **Zone 6**
A so-called Kabchia hybrid, which means that
the secondary shoots remain attached to the
perennial rhizome; this forms inch-high tufts of
silvery-green rosettes, about 1 in. in dia., which
bear yellow flowers tinged with red on 3-in.
stems in spring.

burserana   4″   **Zone 6   Bursar Saxifrage**
A Kabchia hybrid growing in tufts and having
small, pointed, silvery-gray leaves and white
flowers in April. The white flowers of the
variety **major** have red stems; variety **crenata**
has frilled white flowers, while the flowers of the
variety **sulphurea** are light yellow.

caespitosa   6″   **Zone 2**
A dwarf perennial native to northern North
America, with a tufted habit of growth and
leaves only about ½ in. long. White flowers
appear in the spring, ½ in. wide, produced in
loose clusters. Suitable for the rock garden.

callosa (*S. lingulata*)   1′   **Zone 6   Tongue
                                             Saxifrage**
Native to the Pyrenees, the leaves of this plant
are somewhat linear, 3 in. long, and the white
flowers are ⅓ in. wide. There are also several
varieties of this species having silvery foliage,
rose-red flowers, or flowers larger than those of
the species.

cochlearis   9″   **Zone 6   Snail Saxifrage**
A small herbaceous plant with rosettes of silvery-
gray, spatulate leaves an inch long and flower
stems 10 in. tall, bearing large white flowers,
¾ in. in dia., in May. Native to the Alps Mountains.

cortusifolia   1¼′   **Zone 7**
A very attractive, tender saxifrage from the
woodlands of Japan, having rosettes 3–4 in.
wide of shiny green, long-petioled leaves which
are fleshy and have rounded lobes. The rosettes
send out runners which form new plants and
produce a matlike growth. The irregular white
flowers, having 2 lower petals larger than the 2
upper ones, are produced in a loose spray on a
tall, swaying stem. It requires a shady situation
and an acid leaf mold.

cotyledon   2′ **Zone 6 (?) Jungfrau Saxifrage**
Long, widely spatulate, pubescent leaves, in
rosettes 4 in. wide, send up tall, slender flower
stems crowned with delicate sprays of fragrant
white flowers veined in red. Native to the mountains of Europe.

crustata 1′ Zone 6 **Salzburg Saxifrage**
Small, narrow, lime-encrusted leaves grow in closely formed rosettes. From these, the flower stems rise to a height of 12 in., with white flowers having a touch of purple at the base of each petal. Native to Tyrol.

cuneifolia 1′ Zone 6 **Wedgeleaf Saxifrage**
The smooth, leathery leaves of this European woodland succulent are dark green, 1¼ in. long, and grow closely together in rosettes. In May the flower stems rise to 10 in., displaying sprays of tiny white flowers ¼ in. wide. Cultivate in good, slightly acid garden soil in shade or semi-shade.

decipiens = *S. rosacea*

x geum 1′ Zone 3 **Kidneyleaf Saxifrage**
A plant having broad rosettes of rather large, rounded, leathery leaves, 1 in. long, and having a shiny, dark green surface. From these rosettes, sprays of tiny white flowers, ¼ in. wide, on slender stems 3 or 4 in. high, appear in May. Native to Europe and eastern Canada.

grisebachii 8″ Zone 6 **Grisebach Saxifrage**
Short, tufted, pubescent leaves with an abruptly acute tip from closely growing rosettes less than half an inch wide. From these arise in early spring stems bearing dark red flowers, ⅙ in. or less wide. Native to the Mediterranean Region.

x haagii 3″ Zone 6 **Haag Saxifrage**
A delightful mat-forming hybrid, with trailing stems clothed with extremely narrow, bright green leaves and sunshine-yellow flowers in April.

x irvingii 1′ Zone 6 **Irving Saxifrage (Kabchia)**
A freely flowering hybrid with extremely narrow, grayish leaves in tight clusters, giving it the appearance of a pincushion. The nodding pink flowers, on red stems, appear in March and April. This is one of the prettiest and easiest to grow of these hybrids.

juniperifolia sancta 2″ Zone 6 **Sacred Saxifrage**
This easily grown saxifrage has bright, emerald green, prickly leaves ⅓ in. long, with trailing stems that form a mat and a mass of deep yellow to orange flowers, ⅓ in. wide, in early April. Native to the Mediterranean Region.

longifolia 2′ Zone 6 **Longleaf Saxifrage**
A succulent with rosettes of long, narrow, silvery-green leaves, having heavily encrusted and reflexed margins. In May, flower stems 2–3 ft. high bear open, airy sprays of white flowers in many-flowered panicles. Native to the Pyrenees Mountains.

x macnabiana 18″ Zone 6 **MacNab Saxifrage**
S. callosa is one of the parents of this hybrid, which has basal leaves 2–3 in. long in a rosette at the base of the plant and white flowers spotted purple in the summer. For the rock garden.

marginata 3″ Zone 7 **Hornrim Saxifrage**
Tiny, compact cushions of silvery cartilaginous leaves with silky marginal hairs and black flower stems, on which are clustered small white flowers, ½ in. wide, in late spring and summer characterize this plant native to southern Italy.

micranthidifolia 3′ **biennial Lettuce Saxifrage**
Flowers white in small panicles; leaves 1 ft. long. Native from Pa. to Ga. and Tenn.

moschata 5″ Zone 6 **Musk Saxifrage**
Mounds of linear leaves, so small as to have the appearance of moss, on trailing stems. The flowers are white or a pale, creamy yellow. Many hybrids and cultivars have arisen from this species and *S. rosacea*. Native to Europe.

paniculata (*S. aizoon*) 20″ Zone 2 **Aizoon Saxifrage**
Native to the Arctic regions of America, Europe and Asia, this has leaves 1½ in. long in a rosette at the base of the plant. Flowers are pale yellow marked with purple, ½ in. wide, blooming in the summer. Fine plants for the rock garden. There are several excellent varieties being grown, including: **'Alba'**, with white flowers; **'Atropurpurea'**, with rose-purple flowers'; **'Balcana'**, flowers white with red spots; **'Baldensis'**, with ash-gray leaves that are short and thick; **'Brevifolia'** and **'California'**, both with white flowers; **'Churchillii'**, with gray leaves in stiff rosettes; **'Cristata'**, with narrow silvery leaves and cream-colored flowers; **'Densa'**, rosettes small and compact; **'Flavescens'**, with lemon-yellow flowers; **'Hainoldii'**, flowers rose colored; **'Lutea'**, with yellow flowers; **'Notata'**, leaves with a silver margin; **'Paradoxa'**, bluish leaves white flowers.

x paulinae 2″ Zone 7 **Paulina Saxifrage**
A very small, prickly cushion plant with silvery leaves and pale yellow flowers on stems 2 in. high. Blooming occurs in late March and April.

pensylvanica 3′ **biennial Pennsylvania Saxifrage**
This has a thick rhizome, basal leaves about a foot long and greenish flowers about ¼ in. wide. Native Me. to Va.

rosacea (*S. decipiens*) 1′ Zone 6 **Ivyleaf Saxifrage**
A low, tufted, perennial plant with obovate-cuneate leaves having 3–5 linear lobes. Flowers white, ½ in. wide, blooming in the spring. Native to Europe. There are several varicolored varieties available.

sancta = *S. juniperifolia sancta*

sarmentosa = *S. stolonifera*

stolonifera (*S. sarmentosa*) 2′ Zone 5 **Strawberry Saxifrage**
Often called Mother-of-thousands or Strawberry Geranium, this is one of the best of house plants, easily grown if kept moist and of con-

siderable interest because of its rounded leaves, up to 4 in. wide, reddish on the under surface, veined with white above, its long runners with small plantlets attached and also because of its delicate, small, white flowers in upright spikes; each flower about an inch wide with 2 petals longer than the others. Excellent for hanging baskets or for growing in pots in the house. Easily propagated by simply rooting the small plantlets formed on the numerous runners.

tennesseensis   1′   Zone 7
This plant is native to the cliffs and rock faces of the southeastern U.S. It grows in flat rosettes of light green, leathery leaves, 5 in. long, which are oval in outline and unevenly toothed. Flower stems 6 to 6⅙ in. high are crowned with an openly branched spray of small, creamy flowers in spring. Cultivate in a loamy limestone leaf mold in sun or shade.

trifurcata   8″   Zone 6   Threefork Saxifrage
Evergreen mats are formed of bright green, shiny leaves standing stiffly erect. These leaves are divided into 3 prongs, like a stag's horn. Creamy-white flowers, ¾ in. wide, are borne in spring. Native to the Pyrenees Mountains.

umbrosa   1′   Zone 7   Londonpride Saxifrage
Much grown in England, this European species grows funnel-form rosettes of large, long-petioled leaves, becoming tumbling mounds 6 in. high. Small pink or white flowers, on 6-in. stems, bloom in spring. The plant of variety 'Primuloides' is smaller, but the deep pink flowers are larger than those of the species.

virginiensis   4″–12″   Zone 3   Virginia Saxi-frage
The name "saxifrage" means "rock-breaker," an allusion to the persistent way in which the roots of these plants burrow into rocky hillsides and among crevices of stone. The toothed, ovate leaves, narrowing at the base to a margined petiole, grow in a basal rosette, often with the outer leaves pressed closely to the ground. The hairy flower stalk bears a branched terminal cluster of starlike flowers which may be white or greenish in color. A variety of *S. virginiensis* bears a flower with stamens but without petals. The plant grows on wet or dry rocks and gravelly soil, in either sun or shade, from southern Canada to Ga. It is an excellent plant for the alpine or rock garden and may be propagated by seed sown at any time or by division of the plants in spring.

SAXIFRAGE. See SAXIFRAGA.

SCAB. Scale diseases produce corky or warty lesions on the fruit or leaves of infected plants. Apple scab (see APPLE) is the most serious disease of that fruit in many areas. Peach scab attacks all related fruits and requires regular fungicide treatments to control it. Citrus scab spots and distorts the fruit and foliage of most citrus species except Sweet Orange. Spraying of spring growth is advised. Pear scab resembles apple scab but most of the desirable varieties are resistant. Potato scab (see POTATO) thrives only in alkaline soil. Gladiolus scab produces watersoaked spots on the corms and is controlled by dips of mercury compounds or Arasan. Violets and pansies develop scabby lesions on the leaves and stems from violet scab. Where spraying or dusting is practical, applications of fungicides give control. See FUNGICIDES.

SCABIOSA (skab-i-O-sa). Although the common name is Scabious, the chances are most people will continue to call this plant by its generic name, not its true common name. Be that as it may, these are excellent garden annuals and perennials, belonging to the Teasel Family. They have opposite leaves, flower heads like small circular pincushions and they grow and flower freely. They are propagated by seed and division.

atropurpurea   3′   annual   Sweet Scabious
There are many forms of this valued summer-blooming garden plant from southern Europe. Typically the flowers are dark purple, rose or white in heads 2 in. across. The basal leaves are lyre shaped and the stem leaves are finely cut and lobed. Seed mixtures or seeds of separate colors are available. They are excellent for massing in the garden and are excellent for cutting purposes.

Seeds may be sown indoors in March or outdoors in mid-April, being set out in the garden in late May about a foot apart.

caucasica   1½′–2½′   Zones 2–3   Caucasian Scabious
A hardy perennial making an excellent garden plant, especially good for cut flowers. It grows well in the moist atmosphere of the Pacific Northwest but in hot dry situations it has problems. The flowers are usually blue, the heads flat and about 3 in. across, with a tufted rounded center to the flower from which the name Pincushion Flower is obtained. It blooms in July and Aug. It is unfortunate that named selections increase slowly but American nurseries list many varieties, the seed of which can be sown and expected to produce plants fairly true to name. Native to the Caucasus.

columbaria   1′–2½′   Zones 2–3   Dove Scabious
A perennial or biennial with flowers about 1½ in. across, colored a clear pink or lilac and shaped like a ball, rather than flat. Blooms appear in July and Aug. Native to Europe and western Asia.

fischeri   2½′   Zones 2–3   Fischer's Scabious

A perennial with many-branched stems, flowers bluish purple in heads up to 2½ in. across. Native to Dahuria. This is not nearly as good a garden plant as *S. caucasica*.

graminifolia 1½′ **Zone 6 Grassleaf Scabious**
A perennial with silvery-gray grassy foliage and soft violet-pink flowers. It has a creeping root-stock. Native to Europe.

lucida 1′–2′ **Zone 5**
A perennial with rose-lilac flowers suitable for the rock garden. Native to Europe.

ochroleuca 1′–2½′ **Zone 5 Cream Scabious**
A perennial or biennial with small globes of yellow flowers about an inch wide from June to Sept. Native to Europe and western Asia.

SCABIOUS. See SCABIOSA. However, most people will continue to call these, popularly, Scabiosas.

SCABROUS. Rough to the touch.

SCALD. Injury from exposure to bright sunlight is called scale or sun scald. On fruits and vegetables, especially tomatoes and sweet peppers, the skin is burned to a dirty white or brown color. On trees, especially Beech, Sugar Maple and other species with thin bark, the removal of branches and leaves exposes the bark to unnaturally bright sun and the bark is scalded. Apple trees suffer bark scald from sun reflected off the snow in winter. Scald on apples in storage is a recognized physiological disease due to lack of ventilation to diffuse the natural gas of fruit maturity.

SCALE. A minute leaf or bract, usually appressed or dry.

SCALE INSECTS. Scale insects feed by sucking the sap through a long flexible beak. The young may hatch from eggs or be born alive. Crawlers have 6 legs and crawl or are carried to new feeding areas. They are very prolific and may produce several annual generations. All male scales develop 1 pair of wings when adult. Scale insects are attacked by many beneficial parasitic and predatory insects which keep them in check in many areas. They are divided into armored scales, soft scales and mealybugs. Armored scales are protected by a stiff waxy covering which they secrete and enlarge as they grow but it is free from their body. After a female scale has settled it does not move. The most destructive, armored scales are San Jose scale, oyster shell scale and scurfy scale on deciduous trees; pine needle scale and juniper scale on evergreens; Fla. red scale, purple scale and dictyosperm scale on citrus; and euonymous scale and ivy scale on vines. Soft scales have a cottony or feltlike deposit in the back but no free covering. Some species move slightly in the young stages. The best known soft scales are

Oyster shell scale—many times larger than life size.

terrapin scale, European fruit lecanium, cottony maple scale and liriodendron scale on deciduous trees; the black scale and the hemispherical scale on citrus and the soft brown scale on many plants in the South and in greenhouses. Mealybugs move about freely for most of their life but often live in colonies. Their bodies are covered with long waxy threads. Citrus mealybug, long tailed mealybug, coconut mealybug, pineapple mealybug and cottony cushion scale are destructive pests in the warmer areas. Greenhouse orthezia and many of the above species infest greenhouse grown plants and the taxus mealybug is destructive in cooler areas.

The standard control measures are spraying with Superior type oil emulsion at dormant strength on dormant plants in the North and at summer strength in the South. Crawlers are easily killed by insecticide #15 or #13 and timely applications when the crawlers are active are very effective. Mealybugs are controlled also by insecticides #15 and #13.

WARREN D. WHITCOMB

SCANDENT. Climbing.

SCAPE. A leafless stalk arising from the ground. It may bear scales or bracts or one to many flowers. The flower stalk of an Iris is a scape.

SCARBOROUGH-LILY = *Vallota speciosa*

SCARLET-BUSH = *Hemelia erecta*

SCARLET-RUNNER BEAN = *Phaseolus coccineus*

SCHEFFLERA (sheff-LEE-ra)
actinophylla = *Brassaia actinophylla*. Still widely grown under the name of Schefflera.

An evergreen shrub or tree with few lateral branches; native to Australia and used in America as a popular house plant. The long-stemmed leaves have 6–8 glossy leaflets, each 6–8 in. long, spreading out like an umbrella. The small, fleshy, dark red flowers are borne closely on small branches (from which comes the name Octopus-tree). These flower clusters are only produced after a plant is at least 10 years old. Mentioned under the name of *Schefflera* here because it is widely grown under this name. To be botanically correct it should be *Brassaia actinophylla*.

SCHINUS (SKY-nus)

molle   **40'**   **Zone 9**   **California Peppertree**
An excellent tree for planting along the highways and used for this purpose in Calif. It is native to Peru. The feather-shaped, alternate, evergreen, compound leaves are 9 in. long. The sexes are separate, so if the red ¼-in. berries in the fall are wanted, and they persist most of the winter, then plants of both sexes should be planted. It seems to thrive on poor soils, has widespreading branches and a rounded top, but it is susceptible to a black scale and is banned near orange orchards in some sections for this reason. It has a bad reputation for dropping litter on well-kept lawns; otherwise it is a fine tree.

terebinthifolius   **40'**   **Zones 9–10**   **Brazil Peppertree**
Native to Brazil, this is used chiefly in Fla. as a lawn and avenue tree and is often locally called Christmas-berry Tree, since its small, bright red fruits are conspicuous in midwinter. Growing very rapidly in dry areas, it also is an alternate-leaved tree, the attractive, evergreen, compound leaves being 4–8 in. long, with 5–9 leaflets. Even in Hawaii the berries are used for Christmas decorations. The small greenish-yellow flowers are mostly inconspicuous. It is propagated by seeds and by cuttings of the better fruiting clones.

SCHISANDRA (also, incorrectly, SCHIZANDRA) (sky-ZAN-dra)

chinensis   **vine**   **Zone 4**   **Chinese Magnolia-vine**
A weak-growing, twining, deciduous vine, with alternate leaves and sexes separate. It is not much planted in the U.S. and its chief value is its clusters of red fruits in the fall, about the size of those of the American Bittersweet. The leaves are 3–4 in. long; the flowers are white to pink, about ½ in. wide and none too conspicuous, in short clusters. Only of value ornamentally for its fruits in the early fall and then one must be certain to plant both sexes in order to insure the fruiting of the female plant. Native to China. Propagation is easiest by layers but also by

division, hardwood and softwood cuttings.
propinqua   **twining vine**   **Zone 8**   **Himalayan Magnolia-vine**
An evergreen vine, native to the Himalayas, noted for its orange flowers, ¾ in. across, in the summer. The sexes are separate and the red fruits only appear on the pistillate plants.

SCHIVERECKIA (shiv-er-REK-ia)

bornmuelleri = *S. doerifleri*
doerifleri (*S. bornmuelleri*)   **2½'**   **Zone 6**
This is an evergreen member of the Mustard Family and grows in small mounds. It has soft, gray-green, entire leaves in rosettes, about ⅓ in. long, and sprays of small white flowers on 6-in. stalks in spring. It does best in well-drained garden soil in full sun. Native to Asia Minor.

SCHIZANTHUS (sky-ZAN-thus)

pinnatus   **4'**   **annual**   **Butterfly-flower**
This member of the Nightshade Family is mostly a plant for the greenhouse but can be used in the open garden in the milder parts of the U.S. It is excellent as a pot plant on the terrace, or for cutting. The leaves are alternately finely cut and fernlike. The flowers are profusely borne, in showy, many-flowered terminal clusters, each flower being 1½ in. across, purplish to yellowish, with considerable variation among the seedlings. The shape of the peculiar flowers is the reason for its common name. To get plants to flower in the garden, seeds must be sown in Feb., but if sown in the greenhouse in the autumn, they will flower by spring. Native to Chile.

SCHIZOBASOPSIS = *Bowiea*

SCHIZOPETALON (sky-zo-PET-al-on)

walkeri   **30″**   **annual**
A very delicate annual from Chile, valued for its white, fringed and very fragrant flowers, but little known in America. Its fragrance at night is outstanding. Flowers are in long racemes through the summer. Leaves are alternate, 4–5 in. long. Seeds may be sown indoors in March or outdoors in early May, with the seedlings eventually about a foot apart.

SCHIZOPHRAGMA (sky-zo-FRAG-ma)

hydrangeoides   **clinging vine**   **Zone 5**   **Japanese Hydrangea-vine**
This vine has been confused with *Hydrangea anomala petiolaris*, which is actually the better of the two as an ornamental. Both climb by attaching rootlike holdfasts to the means of support, but *S. hydrangeoides* has dull leaves with wider teeth along the margin and the sterile flower has a solitary sepal which the Hydrangea does not have. Both are native of Japan.

Propagation

Seeds can be sown as soon as ripe, or stored

dry in airtight containers in a cool place and sown later. Layers and softwood cuttings (which see) are easily rooted.

SCHIZOSTYLIS (sky-ZOS-til-is)

coccinea **2′** **Zone 9** **Crimson-flag**
With fleshy roots and grasslike leaves, native to South Africa, this is a popular greenhouse plant, also grown for cut flowers. Actually a member of the Iris Family. The flowers are deep crimson, 2 in. wide and 1 in. long. The roots can be planted outdoors in the spring after all danger of frost; the plant carefully lifted and potted in the fall (before frost) and taken into the greenhouse where it will bloom from Oct. to Dec. After flowering the roots can be stored until used again in the late spring. Not a very popular plant for the home gardener. Propagated by division; sometimes termed Kafir-lily, a name appropriately used for *Clivia* species.

SCHLUMBERGERA (shlum-BERG-era)

truncata **18″** **Zone 10** **Christmas Cactus**
A common house plant easily grown; leafless with flat jointed stems, branching considerably, the individual segments being about an inch long and half that wide. The scarlet (or white) flowers are produced in terminal clusters $2\frac{1}{2}$–$3\frac{1}{2}$ in. wide. The pear-shaped fruits are about $\frac{3}{4}$ in. across and red. Good for potted houseplants and especially in hanging baskets; blooming at Christmas. Often called the Crab Cactus. It requires more water than most other cacti and is easily rooted from cuttings.

Many people have their own way of handling this temperamental plant, and if one is having current success do not change the procedure. During the summer, it can be placed out-of-doors in a shaded spot but should be brought indoors before the first frost. It is kept on the dry side until about Christmas when it blooms and it should be given normal amounts of water. After it is through and before growth starts in the spring, it should be kept on the dry side again, but not so dry that the foliage withers up. When growth starts again, give it more water and then set out-of-doors for over summer again. Many people do not have success with this plant merely because they give it plenty of water all the time. (See drawing, p. 1221.)

SCHOMBURGKIA (shom-BURK-ia).
A genus of about 10 species of South American orchids, somewhat difficult to grow in the home greenhouse. For culture and propagation see ORCHID.

SCIADOPITYS (sy-a-DOP-it-is)

verticillata **120′** **Zone 5** **Umbrella-pine**
This is one of the best evergreens for specimen planting in the eastern U.S. and should be grown far more than it is. Native to Japan, it bears its dark green needles (3–5 in. long) in whorls of 20–30 about the twigs and they remain on the tree 2–3 years before dropping. It is densely pyramidal in outline with branches facing the ground, and has no serious pests. It grows slowly at first and there is not too much seed available in America yet, but it is very well worth growing. Cut branches, placed in water indoors, keep in perfect condition for weeks. An excellent plant especially for specimen use.

Propagation

Seed does not take pre-treatment but germination does not take place for several months. They can be stored dry in airtight containers in a cool place up to a year before sown. Hardwood cuttings root if taken during the winter, or if taken in the early spring before growth starts. See CUTTINGS.

SCILLA (SILL-a).
Excellent, early spring-flowering bulbs for naturalizing because of their small size (mostly 6 in. although some species grow to 20 in.) the azure-blue color of their flowers, the earliness of bloom (April), their hardiness and the thoroughness with which they repropagate themselves when the growing conditions are right. Easily propagated by offsets and seeds. There are over a dozen species offered by European nurseries, but in America the following 6 species are the only ones planted and of these *S. sibirica* is the most popular. Native to Southern Europe and southwestern Asia.

bifolia **6″** **Zone 4** **Twinleaf Squill**
The star-shaped blue flowers appear in 3–8-flowered racemes at the end of a short stalk in early spring. There are white and pink-flowered varieties. Native to southern Europe and southwestern Asia.

campanulata = *Endymion hispanicus*
hispanica = *Endymion hispanicus*
litardierei **18″** **Zone 5** **Meadow Squill**
The flowers are very small, pale blue, but are borne in 12–30-flowered racemes. Leaves are linear. Native to Europe. Not as good an ornamental as some of the others.

non-scripta = *Endymion non-scriptus*
nutans = *Endymion non-scriptus*
pictus **climbing** **Zone 10** **Painted Ivy-arum**
A climbing vine from the Solomon Islands; leaves only 6 in. long and 3 in. wide, spotted dark green above. The var. **argyraeus** has cordate leaves and the spots are silvery white.

scilloides **1′** **Zone 5** **Chinese Squill**
A small, bulbous plant from China. The grasslike leaves grow to maturity in the fall, dying away the following summer before the deep pink flowers appear in Aug. The flowers, in dense spikes, are on stalks 12 in. high. The petals are edged with green.

siberica 6″ **Zones** 2–3 **Siberian Squill**
A splendid bulb for naturalizing, with deep blue, wheel-shaped flowers, ½ in. across, each spike about 3 in. long and usually nodding. If the ground is slightly moist, these quickly reseed themselves and produce a beautiful blue blanket of flowers in the early spring. If the blanket of bulbs is worthy, an application of well-rotted manure occasionally produces increased bloom. Several varieties (including a white-flowered one) are available.

SCION. A slip or shoot used for grafting. See GRAFT.

SCIRPUS
acutus 9′ **Zone** 4 **Tall Bulrush**
Of use only in the water or bog garden, with grasslike leaves reduced to basal sheaths and spikelets either solitary or in clusters of 2–7. Native to North America. Propagated by seeds or division and suckers.
lacustris tabernaemontani 2′ **Zone** 5
The leaves are reduced to 1–2 sheaths and the spikelets are terminal. It is only of value in the water or bog garden. Native to Europe. Propagated by seeds, suckers and division.

SCLERANTHUS (scler-AN-thus)
annuus 4″ **annual** **Knawel**
A persistent weed introduced from Europe. Naturalized in the eastern half of North America with small, threadlike, opposite leaves. The flowers are small, green, often hidden by the densely branched inflorescence at the end of the branchlets, blooming from May to Oct. It produces many seeds that remain viable in the soil for many years. It is not one of the most conspicuous weeds, but is usually present in eastern gardens. In dry soils it can form rounded, matlike clumps 1 ft. in dia. For control see WEED-CONTROLLING CHEMICALS.

SCLEROLEPIS (scler-o-LEP-is)
uniflora 12″ **Zone** 6 **Sclerolepis**
This plant is an attractive member of the Composite Family with a creeping underground stem and erect, flowering branches clothed with short, linear leaves in whorls of 4–6. The buttonlike, terminal flower cluster is composed of tubular blue flowers. Each corolla is campanulate, with 5 slightly spreading lobes. Two curving stamens extend beyond the corolla. The plant may be found in scattered locations along the shores of ponds and swamps in the eastern coastal states and flowers throughout the summer and well into the fall.

SCORCH. A term applied to injury to leaves due to lack of sufficient water, excessive transpiration or injury to the water-conducting system of the plant. Maple leafscorch is a typical example. On conifers scorch is similar to tip burn of needles. On broadleaf evergreens brown areas in the leaves may develop when drying. Winds cause excess transpiration while the roots are in frozen soil.

SCORZONERA (skor-zo-NEE-ra)
hispanica 3′ **Zone** 6 (?) **Black Salsify**
A perennial herb belonging to the Composite Family. The long, fleshy tap root has a black skin; the leaves, alternate, grasslike, are oblong and linear; the flowering heads are yellow and 2 in. long. It is not an important root vegetable but can be eaten and the foliage can be used in salads. It is usually raised as an annual or biennial. Native to Europe.

SCOURING-RUSH = *Equisetum hyemale*

SCREE. A term sometimes used in describing the type of bed for a rock garden—usually a bed of crushed rocks, possibly as much as 2 ft. thick, on which is a few inches of soil. This makes possibly speedy drainage, so watering must be carefully provided.

SCREENS. (Also see HEDGES, WINDBREAKS.) The screening of junkyards, gravel pits and dumps is an important activity recently given great impetus nationally. This is the very thing for which many a civic-minded group has been fighting during the past decade. It would not be amiss to take a hard look at some of our town dumps, and state-owned gravel pits also, with the idea of planting trees and shrubs to screen them from public view.

Public-spirited groups could well be active in planting, for it would add materially to the appearance of the countryside, especially as viewed by the passing motorist. Along the major highways around any large city's perimeter, several dumps, which are conspicuously unshielded, come to mind. This is a condition too often repeated in many communities throughout the country.

The sites of these depositories have undoubtedly been selected because the land is poor. Also, it is impractical to expect that, if a highly ornamental planting were made in such places, it would be maintained. The realistic approach is to admit that these areas are necessary, that they cannot be moved at this point, and that no individual or group will give the time or money to mow lawns, or care for extensive flower beds and ornate plantings, year in and year out.

However, there might be those interested enough to make an initial planting of rugged, fast-growing trees and shrubs; that is, plants which, once established, have a good record for taking care of themselves without much additional attention. True, such plants might not be the best ornamentals available, but the chances are that the soil would not be the best either.

These plants should be given the best possible attention at planting time, with good soil, water and mulching. It is particularly necessary that the plants be checked and watered during the first 2 years of the planting, even periodically, where needed. Arrangements and funds for doing this should be the responsibility of the planning organization and funds should be provided for this at the start of the project. Many a good, well-conceived planting has failed because this was not done at the start.

Of the plants suggested in the following lists, the fastest-growing trees are the poplars, willow, elms and the Douglas-fir, in that order. Of the shrubs, the fastest growing are the Forsythia,

Japanese Tree Lilac, Sweet Mock-orange and Japanese Rose. In addition, and probably the fastest growing of all the shrubs suggested here for making a quick screen, is the new *Rhamnus frangula* 'Columnaris', the Tallhedge Buckthorn. Using plants 2–3 ft. high, a 12-ft. hedge can result in 5 years in good soil. Plants should be placed 3–4 ft. apart to make a solid screen. They bear berries (red, turning black) throughout the summer and are most attractive to birds. The ability of this plant to grow well and fast, its freedom from serious pests, its narrow and very dense habit (not much over 4 ft. wide), its glossy foliage, and the ease with which it is transplanted, all combine to make it an ideal, quick-growing screen, well suited to shield dumps and gravel pits from the public eye.

SCREENING TREES FOR DRY, SANDY SOILS

* = Evergreen; E = Easy to move; B = Must be moved carefully with a ball of soil.

		HEIGHT	HARDINESS ZONE	
Acer negundo	Box-elder	60′	2	E
Ailanthus altissima	Tree-of-heaven	60′	4	E
Betula populifolia	Gray Birch	30′	3–4	B
Fraxinus pennsylvanica lanceolata	Green Ash	60′	2	E
Maclura pomifera	Osage-orange	60′	5	
*Pinus banksiana	Jack Pine	75′	2	B
Populus alba	White Poplar	90′	3	E
Sassafras albidum	Sassafras	60′	4	B
Sophora japonica	Japanese Pagoda Tree	75′	4	
Ulmus pumila	Siberian Elm	75′	4	E

SCREENING SHRUBS FOR DRY AND SANDY SOILS

		HEIGHT	HARDINESS ZONE	
Acer ginnala	Amur Maple	20′	2	
Berberis thunbergii	Japanese Barberry	7′	4	E
Caragana arborescens	Siberian Pea-tree	18′	2	E
Comptonia peregrina	Sweet Fern	4′	2	B
Elaeagnus angustifolia	Russian Olive	20′	2	B
Hamamelis virginiana	Common Witch-hazel	15′	4	E
*Juniperus communis	Common Juniper	3′–30′	2	B
*J. virginiana	Red-cedar	10′–90′	2	B
Kolkwitzia amabilis	Beauty-bush	10′	4	E
Ligustrum amurense	Amur Privet	15′	3	E
Lycium halimifolium	Common Matrimony-vine	5′	4	E
Myrica pensylvanica	Bayberry	9′	2	B
Physocarpus opulifolius	Eastern Ninebark	9′	2	E
Prunus maritima	Beach Plum	6′	3	B
Rhamnus frangula	Alder Buckthorn	18′	2	E
Rhus aromatica	Fragrant Sumac	3′	3	
R. copallina	Shining Sumac	30′	4	B
R. glabra	Smooth Sumac	9′–15′	2	B
R. typhina	Staghorn Sumac	30′	3	B
Rosa rugosa	Rugosa Rose	6′	2	E
Viburnum lentago	Nannyberry	30′	2	

SCREENING TREES FOR NORMAL SOILS

		HEIGHT	ZONE	
Acer platanoides	Norway Maple	90′	3	E
Catalpa speciosa	Northern Catalpa	90′	4	E
Cercidiphyllum japonicum	Katsura Tree	60′–100′	4	
*Juniperus chinensis	Chinese Juniper	60′	4	B
Morus alba	White Mulberry	45′	4	
*Picea abies	Norway Spruce	150′	2	B
*P. pungens	Colorado Spruce	100′	2	B
*Pinus resinosa	Red Pine	75′	2	B
*P. strobus	Eastern White Pine	100′–150′	3	B
Populus nigra 'Italica'	Lombardy Poplar	90′	2	E
*Pseudotsuga menziesii	Douglas-fir	100′–300′	4–6	B
Quercus rubra maxima	Red Oak	75′	3	
Q. palustris	Pin Oak	75′	4	
Salix alba 'Tristis'	Golden Weeping Willow	75′	2	E
S. babylonica	Babylon Weeping Willow	30′	6	E
S. x blanda	Wisconsin or Niobe Weeping Willow	40′	4	E
S. x elegantissima	Thurlow Weeping Willow	40′	4	E
*Thuja occidentalis	American Arborvitae	60′	2	B
Tilia cordata	Little-leaf Linden	90′	3	
*Tsuga canadensis	Canada Hemlock	90′	3	B
Ulmus parvifolia	Chinese Elm	50′	5	
Viburnum prunifolium	Blackhaw	15′	3	B
V. sieboldii	Siebold Viburnum	30′	4	B

SCREENING SHRUBS FOR NORMAL SOILS

Cornus mas	Cornelian Cherry	24′	4	E
Forsythia x intermedia	Border Forsythia	9′	5	E
Lonicera maackii podocarpa	Amur Honeysuckle var.	15′	4	E
Philadelphus coronarius	Sweet Mock-orange	9′	4	E
Rhamnus frangula 'Columnaris'	Tallhedge Buckthorn	12′	2	E
Rosa multiflora	Japanese Rose	10′	5	B
R. setigera	Prairie Rose	15′	4	E
Spiraea x vanhouttei	Vanhoutte Spiraea	6′	4	E
Syringa amurensis japonica	Japanese Tree Lilac	30′	4	E
S. x chinensis	Chinese Lilac	15′	5	E
S. josikaea	Hungarian Lilac	12′	2	E
S. x prestoniae	Preston Lilac	9′	2	E
S. vulgaris	Common Lilac	20′	3	E
Taxus cuspidata	Japanese Yew	50′	4	B

SCREW-PINE. See PANDANUS.

SCREW-PINE FAMILY = Pandanaceae

SCROPHULARIA (skroff-yew-LAY-ria)
   lanceolata   8′   Zone 4   Lanceleaf Figwort
A perennial with flowers green to purple in early summer; leaves lanceolate to ovate; native from Vt. to Ore. south to Va. and Okla. Not often a weed, nor is it outstanding enough to be planted in the garden.
   marilandica   10′   Zone 4   Maryland Figwort
A perennial with flowers a dull, greenish purple and only ⅓ in. long, blooming in midsummer; leaves about 5 in. long. Not often a weed, nor is it outstanding enough to be planted in the garden. Native from Me. to Ga.

SCROPHULARIACEAE = The Figwort, Snapdragon or Foxglove Family

SCUFFLE HOE. See DUTCH HOE.

SCURF-PEA. See PSORALEA.

SCUTELLARIA (skew-tel-AY-ria). Species of this genus of annual or perennial herbs may be found throughout the world, but they center chiefly in the temperate zones. They are members of the Mint Family and have the characteristic opposite leaves and labiate flowers which are generally blue, violet, red or yellow. The 2-celled fruit splits into 4 nutlets at maturity. Most species are weedy, although a few are sometimes cultivated. They germinate readily from seed sown on sand in a cool greenhouse, the seedlings being reset outside as soon as they may be handled. The roots may be divided in early spring.

galericulata   1'–3'   Zone 3   Marsh Skullcap
The leaves of this perennial are opposite, ovate, with a slightly serrate margin and cordate base and leaves are sessile, or nearly so. The blue flowers, about 1 in. long, have an upper lip shaped like a hood and a light blue or whitish lower lip which is flaring and fluted. It frequents the wet, gravelly shores and moist meadows from Alaska to Calif. and Ariz. and Newfoundland to Del. and blooms throughout the summer.

integrifolia   6″–18″   Zone 5   Hyssop Skullcap
This species, having much the same range as *S. galericulata*, has very narrow leaves and solitary blue flowers on stalks arising from the upper leaf axils. It is native to the eastern coastal states, but may be found also from Ohio to Tenn. It blooms in June and July. It is a handsome plant for the moist wild garden and may be propagated from cuttings taken in early summer, by division in early spring or by self-sown seed.

laterifolia   6″–2'   Zone 3   Blue Skullcap
This species spreads by underground stems. The flowers, borne in axillary and terminal 1-sided racemes, are up to ½ in. long and may shade from blue to nearly white. It may be found in wet meadows over much of Canada and the U.S. and blooms throughout the summer.

serrata   2'   Zone 5   Showy Skullcap
Having bright green, ovate leaves and deep blue flowers, 1–1¼ in. long, this species deserves its name of Showy Skullcap. It is excellent as a plant for the moist, semi-shaded wild garden with slightly acid soil and blooms in late spring. It is easily propagated as indicated for *S. integrifolia*. Native from N.Y. to Tenn.

SEA-BUCKTHORN, COMMON = *Hippophae rhamnoides*

SEA-FIG = *Carpobrotus chilensis*

SEA-GRAPE = *Coccoloba uvifera*

SEA-HOLLY. See ERYNGIUM.

SEA-KALE = *Crambe maritima*

SEA-LAVENDER. See LIMONIUM, CONIOLIMON.

SEA-OATS = *Uniola paniculata*

SEA-ONION = *Urginea maritima*

SEA-POPPY = *Glaucium corniculatum*

SEASHORE GARDEN. Many plants will grow in seashore gardens providing there is good soil with plenty of humus, and there is protection from continuous high winds and salt spray. Admittedly, it is not always possible to protect plants from these hazards, hence it is advisable to seek out those plants which apparently withstand seashore conditions better than others. Bayberry (*Myrica pensylvanica*) as well as the Rugosa Rose and the Sea Buckthorn (*Hippophae rhamnoides*) grow within reach of salt-water spray and so are among the best of plants for seashore gardens. Since we do not want to confine ourselves to a few plants, the first thing is to make the soil as rich as possible.

Sandy soil loses water rapidly and hence plants attempting to grow in it dry out quickly. It is the humus in soils which aids in the retention of water (see SOILS, HUMUS, COMPOST, etc.) and the more of this which can be worked into sandy seashore soils, the more kinds of plants can be grown. Peat moss, compost, decayed manure or leaves, even the mixing-in of good clay soil—all these are helpful in order to obtain a soil which will retain water longer than the normal sandy soil of the seashore and of course be better for the plants. Also, mulch as many of the plants and beds as possible to conserve soil moisture (see MULCHES) for this is one of the best means of aiding good plant growth in sandy soils.

One can not make a good garden in sandy soil by the addition of inorganic fertilizers alone, although these must be applied more frequently to sandy soils, for they leach out faster. One should study the soil available, possibly have an analysis made by the state experiment station, note what grows in the local area, and then make the soil more productive by the addition of organic matter in some form.

Shelter from the continuous winds is also necessary. Plants standing out in the open wind all the time transpire rapidly, and lose great amounts of water regardless of how good the soil is. Reducing water loss in the garden by giving shelter from the prevailing winds and salt spray is also essential in order to grow a large variety of plants. This type of shelter is given by erecting board fences, by planting windbreaks and screens of especially rugged and resistant shrubs and trees, as well as by taking advantage of every possible dune or rise of ground which would aid in this respect.

If it is necessary to start with almost pure sand, the first thing is to build up a sand dune and get a vegetative cover on the sand to prevent its blowing. A trip to Cape Hatteras in N.Car. will provide an excellent demonstration of the way this is done on a wild wind-swept shore.

First, it is necessary to prevent the sand from blowing along the shore line and, in order to accomplish this, dunes must be built up to the proper height. This is accomplished by placing 2 rows of picket fencing (the popular snow fence with the wooden pickets held in place by wires) at about 40 ft. apart, parallel to the shore line or at right angles to the prevailing wind. These stop the sand from blowing and a dune is built up on the same principle that makes this same fencing so effective in stopping blowing snow.

When the dune is sufficiently high, then it is planted to the native American Beach Grass (*Ammophila breviligulata*) which spreads vigorously by underground stems. This grows up and down the eastern seacoast and can be collected, separated into very small clumps and planted in a staggered fashion at 18-in. intervals. This is about the best and fastest-growing grass available for the purpose, but others which have been used are Broom Sedge (*Andropogon virginicus*); Seacoast Bluestem (*A. littoralis*); Sea Oats (*Uniola paniculata*); Veld Grass (*Ehrlarta amarum*); Volga Wild Rye (*Elymus gigantea*); Weeping Lovegrass (*Eragrostis curvula*) and on the northwest Pacific Coast the European Beach Grass (*Ammophila arenaria*).

A seashore garden with a wall to protect the flowers from high winds off the ocean. (*Photo by Arnold Arboretum, Jamaica Plain, Mass.*)

The roots of the American Beach Grass are set 8 in. deep, any time between Oct. 1st and April 30th. They should be fertilized heavily with about 400 lbs., of 10-10-10 fertilizer (per acre) in April and the same amount again in July, in order to get the grass off to a good start. Water well after fertilizing and follow through as necessary until the grass is well established. This is the first step in preventing blown sand from spoiling an area for planting. In fact, as is clearly seen in the Cape Hatteras National Seashore Recreational Area of N.Car., it is the first step in making roads possible, for unless the sand is controlled it is impossible to make any kind of a permanent road.

The next step is of course to improve the soil by adding organic matter, then to erect windbreaks so that plants other than the beach grasses can be grown. When these things have been done properly and all existing dunes and

existing vegetation have been utilized as windbreaks, gardens can be made within a few hundred feet of the shore line.

One other problem can harass gardeners on low-lying land at the seashore, and that is caused by salt water flooding the garden or lawn in times of severe storms. Seldom does such temporary flooding cause serious permanent injury to the soil, but of course it depends on how long the water remains and how much of it there is.

Lawns

Heavy rain, before salt-water flooding, is a blessing because the soil becomes saturated with rain water and hence takes up less of the salt water when it comes. If the soil is dry when salt-water flooding occurs, damage can be greater. In any event, there are many cases where the lawn grass foliage or the grass roots, or both are killed by the flooding.

Standard practice for renovating immersed lawns (after the salt water has completely drained away) is to apply ground limestone at the rate of 20–50 lbs. per 1000 sq. ft. and thoroughly water the areas after the limestone is applied. If the grass roots are not killed, new growth appears the following spring. If the grass roots are killed, the soil is dug up and reseeded according to standard lawn practices. See LAWNS. Bent grasses and Kentucky Blue Grass are easily killed, while the omnipresent Crab Grass eventually reappears even after being submerged 24 hrs. or more.

Trees and Shrubs

Since soil conditions vary considerably, as well as the length of time of submersion in salt water, it is difficult to make broad statements concerning plants "resistant" to salt-water immersion. However, the roots and sometimes the tops of the following plants were submerged for at least 24 hrs. after one of the coastal hurricanes along the New England coast a few years ago, and when observed one year later were recovering nicely. Although injured, they were sending out vigorous suckers from the base of or from large stems, or the tops were sending out new shoots. It should be noted, however, that the soil was saturated with rain water before the flooding occurred. If it had not been, considerably more injury might have occurred.

Acer pseudoplatanus
Aesculus hippocastanum
Ailanthus altissima
Aronia arbutifolia
Calluna vulgaris
Campsis radicans
Catalpa speciosa

Clematis paniculata
Clethra alnifolia
Comptonia asplenifolia
Corylus americana
Cryptomeria japonica
Hibiscus syriacus
Ilex glabra
Juniperus chinensis 'Pfitzeriana'
J. virginiana
J. virginiana glauca
Ligustrum amurense
L. ovalifolium
Malus sylvestris
Myrica pensylvanica
Nyssa sylvatica
Parthenocissus tricuspidata
Populus grandidentata
Picea canadensis
P. pungens 'Kosteri'
Pinus sylvestris
P. thunbergii
Prunus maritima
P. serotina
P. virginiana
Pyrus communis
Quercus alba
Rhododendron viscosum
Rhus aromatica
R. copallina
R. glabra
R. toxicodendron
R. typhina
R. vernix
Robinia pseudoacacia
Rosa (Ramblers)
R. rugosa
R. virginiana
R. wichuraiana
Salix alba
Sambucus canadensis
Smilax glauca
Spiraea prunifolia
Tamarix parviflora
Tilia cordata
Ulmus pumila
Vaccinium corymbosum
Viburnum dentatum
Vitis labrusca
Wisteria sinensis

Spray Injury

Any plant subjected to continuous salt-water spray is obviously at a disadvantage. A few survive, but most will not. If a large amount of salt-water spray is deposited on tender foliage that has not properly matured (i.e. during late spring) damage will be greater than if the foliage is mature. Usually high wind storms occur in the late summer or early fall. The first thing to do after such a storm is to spray the plants thoroughly and forcibly with much fresh water to wash off as much salt as possible.

The following plants were subjected to heavy salt-water spray (during one of the hurricanes along the eastern seaboard) during early Sept., and were either uninjured or not injured seriously. The injury was worse on the evergreens than it was on the deciduous trees and shrubs which were due to drop their leaves normally in another few weeks.

Acer platanoides
A. pseudoplatanus
Actinida arguta
Ailanthus altissima
Amelanchier canadensis
Arctostaphylos uva-ursi
Baccharis halimifolia
Cedrus atlantica glauca
Cephalanthus occidentalis
Chamaecyparis pisifera plumosa
Chamaecyparis pisifera squarrosa
    (damaged somewhat)
Clethra alnifolia
Crataegus crus-galli
Cytisus scoparius
Elaeagnus angustifolia
E. longipes
Fagus sylvatica
Forsythia species
Hippophae rhamnoides
Hydrangea macrophylla (H. hortensis)
Ilex glabra
I. opaca
Juniperus communis
J. communis depressa
J. excelsa stricta
J. horizontalis
J. virginiana
J. virginiana glauca
Kalmia angustifolia
Ligustrum amurense
Lonicera japonica 'Halliana'
L. morrowii
L. tatarica
Malus sylvestris
Myrica pensylvanica (M. carolinensis)
Parthenocissus tricuspidata
Physocarpus opulifolius
Picea abies
P. asperata
P. canadensis
P. glauca
P. orientalis
P. pungens 'Kosteri'
Pieries japonica
Pinus mugo mughus (varied responses
    on different soils)
P. nigra
P. thunbergii
Populus alba

Prunus maritima
Pyrus communis
Quercus marilandica
Rhamnus cathartica
Rhus copallina
R. glabra
R. toxicodendron
R. typhina
Robinia pseudoacacia
Rosa (ramblers)
R. blanda
R. humilis
R. nitida
R. rugosa
R. virginiana
R. wichuraiana
Salix humilis
Sambucus canadensis
Spiraea species
Syringa vulgaris (if submerged, it was killed)

Tamarix parviflora
Taxus species and vars. (even took submergence for 2–3 days in some instances though they did not respond as well as Pfitzer's Juniper)
Tilia americana
T. cordata
T. vulgaris
Thuja occidentalis vars.
Ulmus pumila
Vaccinium corymbosum
Viburnum cassinoides
V. dentatum
Wisteria sinensis

Plants for Seashore Gardens

All things considered, the following plants are offered as suggestions for planting in gardens near the seashore. It is these which gardeners might consider first before they try others.

SCIENTIFIC NAME	HEIGHT	ZONE	COMMON NAME
	TREES		
Acacia sp.	10'–50'	8–10	Acacia sp.
Acer platanoides	90'	3	Norway Maple
A. pseudoplatanus	90'	5	Sycamore Maple
Aesculus hippocastanum	75'	3	Horse-chestnut
Ailanthus altissima	60'	4	Tree-of-heaven
Arbutus unedo	10'–30'	8	Strawberry-tree
Betula pendula	60'	2	European Birch
Casuarina sp.	30'–70'	10	Beefwood
Chamaecyparis pisifera	150'	3	Sawara False Cypress
Chilopsis linearis	30'	7	Desert-willow
Cocos nucifera	80'	10	Coconut
Crataegus crus-galli	36'	4	Cockspur Thorn
C. monogyna	30'	4	Single-seed Hawthorn
Cryptomeria japonica	150'	5	Cryptomeria
Cupressus macrocarpa	75'	7	Monterey Cypress
Eucalyptus sp.	15'–300'	9	Eucalyptus
Fraxinus velutina	45'	7	Velvet Ash
Gleditsia triacanthos	135'	4	Common Honeylocust
Hippophae rhamnoides	30'	3	Sea-buckthorn
Ilex opaca	45'	5	American Holly
Lagunaria patersonii	50'	9	Paterson Sugar-plum Tree
Magnolia grandiflora	90'	7	Southern Magnolia
Maytenus boaria	35'	9	Chile Mayten Tree
Melaleuca leucadendron	40'	10	Cajeput-tree
Nyssa sylvatica	90'	4	Black Tupelo
Olea europaea	25'	9	Common Olive
Picea asperata	75'	5	Dragon Spruce
P. pungens	100'	2	Colorado Spruce
P. sitchensis	140'	6	Sitka Spruce
Pinus contorta	30'	7	Shore Pine
P. halepensis	60'	9	Aleppo Pine
P. mugo	to 36'	2	Swiss Mountain Pine
P. muricata	45'	7	Bishop Pine
P. nigra	90'	4	Austrian Pine
P. pinaster	90'	7	Cluster Pine

SCIENTIFIC NAME	HEIGHT	ZONE	COMMON NAME
P. radiata	60'	7	Monterey Pine
P. rigida	75'	4	Pitch Pine
P. sylvestris	75'	2	Scotch Pine
P. thunbergii	90'	4	Japanese Black Pine
Populus alba	90'	3	White Poplar
Prunus serotina	90'	3	Black or Rum Cherry
Quercus alba	90'	4	White Oak
Q. ilex	60'	9	Holly Oak
Q. marilandica	30'	6	Black Jack Oak
Q. virginiana	60'	7	Live Oak
Robinia pseudoacacia	75'	3	Black Locust
Roystonea regia	70'	10	Royal Palm
Sabal palmetto	90'	8	Palmetto
Schinus sp.	40'	9–10	Peppertrees
Thuja occidentalis	3'–60'	2	American Arborvitae
T. orientalis	50'	6	Oriental Arborvitae
Tilia cordata	90'	3	Littleleaf Linden
Ulmus parvifolia	50'	5	Chinese Elm
U. pumila	75'	4	Siberian Elm
Umbellularia californica	75'	7	California-laurel
Watingtonia robusta	90'	10	Mexican Washington Palm

SHRUBS

SCIENTIFIC NAME	HEIGHT	ZONE	COMMON NAME
Abelia grandiflora	5'	5	Glossy Abelia
Arctostaphylos hookeri	2'	8	Hooker Manzanita
A. uva-ursi	Ground cover	2	Bearberry
Aronia arbutifolia	9'	5	Red Chokeberry
Atriplex sp.	4'	5–7	Saltbush
Aucuba japonica	15'	7	Japanese Aucuba
Aurinia saxatilis	6"	3	Golden-tuft
Baccharis halimifolia	12'	4	Groundsel-bush
Berberis thunbergii	7'	5	Japanese Barberry
Buddleia sp.	2'–30'	5–10	Buddleia
Callistemon lanceolatus	30'	9	Lemon Bottlebrush
Calluna vulgaris	18"	4	Heather
Camellia japonica	45'	7	Common Camellia
Carissa grandiflora	18'	9	Natal-plum
Ceanothus sp.	3'/20'	4–9	Ceanothus
Celastrus sp.	Vine	4	Bittersweets
Chaenomeles sp.	3'–6'	4	Flowering Quince
Choisya ternata	9'	7	Mexican-orange
Clematis sp.	Vines	3–7	Clematis
Clethra alnifolia	9'	3	Summersweet
Coccoloba uvifera	40'	10	Sea-grape
Comptonia peregrina	4'	2	Sweet Fern
Cordyline sp.	6'–40'	10	Dracena
Cornus sericea (stolonifera)	7'	2	Red Osier Dogwood
Cotoneaster sp.	1'–18'	4–7	Cotoneasters
Cytisus sp.	1'–9'	5–6	Brooms
Elaeagnus sp.	9'–20'	2–7	Elaeagnus
Empetrum nigrum	10"	2	Crow-berry
Erica carnea	1'	5	Spring Heath
Escallonia sp.	3'–15'	8	Escallonia
Euonymus japonicus	15'	8	Evergreen Euonymus
Fuchsia sp.	3'–5'	5–10	Fuschias
Halimodendron halodendron	6'	2	Salt-tree

SCIENTIFIC NAME	HEIGHT	ZONE	COMMON NAME
Hibiscus syriacus	15'	5	Shrub Althea
Hydrangea anomala petiolaris	Vine	4	Climbing Hydrangea
H. macrophylla	12'	5–6	House Hydrangea
Hyssopus officinalis	1½'	5	Hyssop
Iberis sempervirens	12"	3	Evergreen Candytuft
Ilex glabra	9'	3	Inkberry
Juniperus sp.	1'–90'	2–5	Junipers
Lavandula officinalis	3'	5	Lavender
Leiophyllum buxifolium	18"	5	Box Sandmyrtle
Leucothoe sp.	3'–6'	4–6	Leucothoe
Ligustrum amurense	15'	3	Amur Privet
L. ovalifolium	15'	5	California Privet
Lonicera sp.	3'–15'	2–7	Honeysuckles
Lupinus arboreus	8'	8	Tree Lupine
Lycium sp.	5'	4	Matrimony-vine
Myrica pensylvanica	9'	2	Bayberry
Myrtus communis	5'–10'	8–9	Myrtle
Nerium oleander	20'	7–8	Oleander
Olearia haasti	9'	8	New Zealand Daisy-bush
Pachysandra terminalis	Ground cover	5	Pachysandra
Parthenocissus quinquefolia	Vine	3	Virginia Creeper
Pieris floribunda	6'	4	Mountain Andromeda
Pittosporum tobira	10'	8	Japanese Pittosporum
P. undulatum	15'–20'	10	Cape Pittosporum
Polygonum aubertii	Vine	4	Silver Fleece-vine
Potentilla sp.	4'	2	Cinquefoils
Prunus maritima	6'	3	Beach Plum
P. spinosa	12'	4	Sloe
Raphiolepis umbellata	6'	7	Yeddo-hawthorn
Rhamnus sp.	9'–30'	2	Buckthorns
Rhus sp.	3'–30'	2–5	Sumacs
Romneya coulteri	8'	9	Matilija-poppy
Rosa—Many sp.	6'–15'	3–7	Roses
R. rugosa	6'	2	Rugosa Rose
R. wichuraiana	2'	5	Memorial Rose
Rosmarinus officinalis	6'	6	Rosemary
Ruscus aculeatus	1¼'–4'	7	Butcher's-broom
Salix repens	3'	4	Creeping Willow
Sambucus canadensis	12'	3	American Elder
Santolina chamaecyparissus	1½'–2'	6–7	Lavender-cotton
Schizophragma hydrangeoides	Vine	5	Japanese Hydrangea-vine
Senecio sp.	12"–2½'	4–9	Groundsel
Severinia buxifolia	6'	8	Chinese Box-orange
Shepherdia canadensis	7'	2	Russet Buffalo-berry
Skimmia sp.	1½'–4'	7	Skimmia
Smilax sp.	Vine	4–7	Catbriers
Spartium junceum	10'	7	Spanish Broom
Spiraea sp.	1'–12'	4–6	Spireas
Suaeda fruticosa	3'	6	Shrubby Goosefoot
Syringa vulgaris	20'	3	Common Lilac
Tamarix sp.	15'	2–8	Tamarix
Taxus cuspidata	50'	4	Japanese Yew
Thymus serpyllum	Ground cover	3	Thyme, Mother-of-Thyme
Trachelospermum jasminoides	Vine	9	Chinese Star-jasmine
Ulex europaeus	3'–5'	6	Common Gorse
Vaccinium corymbosum	6'–12'	3	Highbush Blueberry
V. vitis-idaea	Ground cover	2	Mountain Cranberry

SCIENTIFIC NAME	HEIGHT	ZONE	COMMON NAME
Veronica prostrata	8″	5	Harebell Speedwell
Viburnum cassinoides	6′	3	Withe-rod
V. dentatum	15′	2	Arrow-wood
V. tinus	10′–20′	7–8	Laurustinus
Vinca minor	Ground cover	4	Periwinkle
Wisteria sinensis	Vine	5	Chinese Wisteria
Yucca sp.	3′	4	Yuccas
	PERENNIALS		
Achillea tomentosa	6″–12″	2	Woolly Yarrow
Ajuga sp.	4″–12″	4	Bugleweed
Althaea rosea	9′	Annual or biennial	Hollyhock
Anchusa azurea	3′–5′	3	Italian Bugloss
Aquilegia sp.	1′–3′	3	Columbines
Arabis sp.	2″–10″	4–6	Rock cress
Armeria maritima	6″–12″	3	Common Thrift
Artemesia stelleriana	2½′	2	Dusty Miller
Asclepias tuberosa	3′	4	Butterfly Milkweed
Astilbe sp.	2′–3½′	5–6	False Spirea
Baptisia australis	3′–4′	2–3	Blue Wild Indigo
Chrysanthemum sp.	1′–4′	3–10	Chrysanthemum
Cichorium intybus	3′–6′	3	Common Chicory
Cimicifuga sp.	4′–8′	2–3	Snakeroots
Delphinium sp.	1′–6′	3–8	Delphiniums
Dianthus sp.	4″–15″	2–5	Pinks
Dicentra spectabilis	2′	2–3	Bleeding Heart
Digitalis sp.	3′	4–6	Foxgloves
Doronicum caucasicum	2′–5′	5	Leopard's-bane
Echinops sp.	1′–12′	2–3	Globe Thistles
Erigeron sp.	4″–30′	Annual or 2–9	Fleabanes
Eryngium amethystinum	1½′	2–3	Amethyst Eryngium
E. maritimum	1′	5	Sea-holly
Festuca ovina glauca	5′	4	Blue fescue
Gaillardia sp.	2′	Annual	Gaillardias
Gladiolus sp.	2′–6′	7–9	Gladiolus
Gypsophila sp.	4″–3′	3–7	Baby's-breath
Helianthemum sp.	1′	5–6	Sun-rose
Hemerocallis sp.	1½′–6′	3–7	Daylilies
Heuchera sanguinea	12′	3	Coral-bells
Hibiscus moscheutos	3′–6′	5	Rose Mallow
Hosta sp.	1′–3′	3	Plantain-lilies
Iberis sempervirens	6″	2–3	Evergreen Candytuft
Kniphofia sp.	1′–4′	7	Torch-lily
Lathyrus littoralis	Decumbent	8	Beach Pea
Lilium sperbum	6′–10′	5	Turk's-cap Lily
Limonium sp.	2½′	3–9	Sea Lavenders
Liriope spicata	8″–12″	4	Creeping Lily-turf
Lychnis coronaria	3′	2–3	Rose Campion
Lythrum salicaria	3′	2–3	Purple Loosestrife
Monarda didyma	3′	3	Bee-balm
Ophiopogon japonicus	6″–15″	7	Dwarf Lily-turf
Paeonia sp.	3′–5′	2–5	Peonies
Papaver orientale	2′–4′	2–3	Oriental Poppy
Phlox sp.	1½′–4′	3–8	Phlox

SCIENTIFIC NAME	HEIGHT	ZONE	COMMON NAME

PERENNIALS

SCIENTIFIC NAME	HEIGHT	ZONE	COMMON NAME
Phormium tenax	7′–15′	9	Fiber-lily
Physostegia virginiana	4′	2–3	Virginia Lion'sheart
Sedum sp.	2″–3′	3–7	Stonecrop
Sempervirum tectorum	1′	4	Hen-and-chicken
Solidago sp.	1′–4′	3	Goldenrods
Stachys olympica (*S. lanata*)	1′–1½′	4	Lamb's-ears
Viola cornuta	6″	2–3	Tufted Pansy

ANNUALS

SCIENTIFIC NAME	HEIGHT	ZONE	COMMON NAME
Ageratum houstonianum	6″–18″	Annual	Ageratum
Calendula officinalis	1′–2′	Annual	Pot-marigold
Centaurea cyanus	2½′	Annual	Cornflower
Clarkia sp.	1½′–3′	Annual	Clarkia
Cleome sp.	1′–3′	Annual	Spiderflower
Cobaea scandens	Vine	Annual or 9	Cup-and-Saucer Vine
Coleus sp.	6″–3′	Annual or perennial	Coleus
Coreopsis sp.	6″–9″	Annual	Coreopsis
Cosmos sp.	10′	Annual	Cosmos
Delphinium sp.	1′–4′	3–6	Larkspur
Dianthus—annual sp.	3″–2′	3–8	Pinks
Dolichos lablab	Vine	Annual	Hyacinth-bean
Eschscholtzia californica	2′	Annual	California-poppy
Euphorbia marginata	2′	Annual	Snow-on-the-Mountain
Gaillardia sp.	2′	Annual	Gaillardia
Glaucium corniculatum	1½′	Annual	Sea-poppy
Godetia sp.	1′–3′	Annual	Godetia
Gypsophila (Annual sp.)	6″–3′	Annual	Gypsophila
Helianthus sp.	6′–7′	Annual	Sunflower
Helichrysum bracteatum	3′	Annual	Straw-flower
Ipomoea sp.	Vine	Annuals	Morning-glories
Lathyrus odoratus	Vine	Annual	Sweet Pea
Lobularia maritima	1′	Annual	Sweet Alyssum
Nemesia sp.	1′–2′	Annual	Nemesia
Nicotiana sp.	1½′–20′	Annual or 9	Tobacco
Nigella damascena	1½′–2′	Annual	Love-in-a-mist
Papaver—Annual sp.	2′	Annual	Poppy
Petunia sp.	6″–3′	Annual	Petunia
Phaseolus coccineus	Vine	Annual	Scarlet-runner Bean
Portulaca sp.	8″	Annual	Portulaca
Reseda odorata	Decumbent	Annual	Mignonette
Salpiglossis sinuata	2½′	Annual	Painted-tongue
Salvia sp.	1′–3′	Annual	Sage
Scabiosa sp.	1′–3′	Annual	Scabious
Tagetes sp.	1′–3′	Annual	Marigolds
Thunbergia alata	Vine	Annual	Clockvine
Tithonia rotundifolia	3′–6′	Annual	Tithonia
Tropaeolum sp.	1′–4′ or vine	Annual or perennial	Nasturtium
Verbena tenera (V. pulchella)	2″	Annual or perennial	Sand Verbena
Zinnia sp.	18″–3′	Annual	Zinnia

SEA-URCHIN = *Hakea laurina*

SEABASTIANA sp. Jumping Bean. Tropical members of the Euphorbia Family, the fruits of which are curious because when put in a warm place they jump around, action caused by the movements of a larva inside the bean.

SECALE (seek-KAY-le)
  cereale = Rye, which see.

SECHIUM (SEE-kium)
  edule   **climbing**   **Zone 8**   **Chayote**
A tropical vine, climbing by attaching its tendrils to the means of support; grown for its edible fruits which are 3–4 in. long, pear shaped, furrowed, green or white, fleshy and enclosing a single seed. It belongs to the Gourd Family. The fruits are boiled like squash and a well-grown plant will produce 50–100 fruits a year. The alternate triangular leaves are 7–10 in. long and the female and male flowers are separate, but on the same plant. The staminate flowers are in a raceme and the pistillate flowers are 1 or 2 in the leaf axils. It is often called "vegetable pear" and is widely grown throughout the Tropics where it is perennial and where its tubers can grow large. These are also edible. It must have high temperatures and a long growing season, hence is not often grown in the North. Native to the American Tropics.

SECURINEGA (sec-ur-in-EE-ga)
  suffruticosa   **6′**   **Zone 5**
A weedy deciduous shrub with alternate leaves, native to northeastern Asia; of little ornamental value in flower, fruit or autumn color. Seldom planted.

Propagation

Seed may be sown as soon as ripe or stored dry in airtight containers in a cool place up to a year and then sown. Hardwood cuttings (which see) can be rooted.

SEDGE = *Carex*

SEDGE FAMILY = Cyperaceae

SEDGE, FRASER = *Cymophyllis fraseri*

SEDGE, MORROW'S = *Carex morrowii*

SEDGE, NUT = *Cyperus esculentus*

SEDUM (SEE-dum). Stonecrop. This is a group of over 350 species of low succulent plants, mostly suited for the rockery, but a few can be used in the perennial border. Some are weedy and spread rapidly, others are evergreen and ideally suited for display on rock walls or rock ledges. With the correct selection of species, one can have them in bloom from May to Oct. The flowers range in color from white, yellow, pink and red to purple. They can be easily divided at almost any time of year and cuttings or broken stem pieces root readily. It is advisable in using sedums to know their particular characteristics so that they can be planted in the proper areas for best display. Most of them are good plants for poor, stony soil in the hot sun, or in rock crevices or between stepping stones or on the partially paved terrace. Only about 3, namely *S. sieboldii*, *S. spectabile* and *S. spurium*, are worthwhile in the flower border. Most of the others are not.

Propagation

Seeds germinate readily when sown. However, the simplest method of propagation is merely to divide the plants, although softwood and hardwood cuttings can be easily rooted when necessary.

  acre   **2″**   **Zone 3**   **Goldmoss Stonecrop**
Creeping, mat-forming, with the smallest leaves of any of the more commonly used sedums, this comes from Europe and Asia, and has small, pointed, light green, slightly succulent, alternate, evergreen leaves, about $\frac{3}{16}$ in. long. The bright yellow flowers, $\frac{1}{2}$ in. across, appear in late May and June. This Sedum is a vigorous grower and can become a weed in the garden if not restrained. Even small pieces of it, broken off by raking or weeding, take root quickly when lying on the soil surface. It is excellent for planting between stepping stones. Easily propagated by division and cuttings. A few varieties are of interest, such as **'Majus'** with larger leaves and flowers, **'Aureus'** with the tips of the shoots bright yellow; **'Elegans'**, somewhat similar except that the shoot tips are silver colored and not yellow; **'Minus'** which is diminutive in all its parts and is seldom over $\frac{1}{2}$ in. high.

  adolphi   **6″**   **Zone 6**   **Adolph Sedum**
Native to Mexico, this has fleshy inch-long leaves colored yellow-green to bronze. A perennial evergreen with broadly lanceolate, slightly curved leaves, $1\frac{1}{2}$ in. long, and small white flowers blooming in March and April.

  aizoon   **15″**   **Zone 3**   **Aizoon Stonecrop**
Native from Siberia to Japan, this has alternate leaves up to 3 in. long, large knotty rootstocks and long tuberous roots. The flowers are yellow to orange in summer, about $\frac{1}{2}$ in. across, and the flower cluster is about 2–3 in. wide. The tops die to the ground in the fall.

  album   **8″**   **Zone 3**   **Worm-grass**
A common, creeping, evergreen Sedum, often misnamed, native to Europe and Siberia. It grows into large mats of stems and foliage with flat white flower panicles 1–2 in. across. The variety **'Chloroticum'** has vivid green leaves and many pure white flowers, making it a fine garden plant. The var. **'Murale'** has purplish foliage and

pinkish flowers and is an especially popular garden plant among the sedums.

allantoides   1′   Zone 7
With gray-green foliage covered with a waxy bloom; flowers greenish white during June and July. Native to Mexico.

anglicum   2″   Zone 3   English Sedum
A creeping evergreen from western Europe with white flowers up to ½ in. across during the summer. The leaves are only about ¼ in. long.

brevifolium   2″   Zone 5   Shortleaf Stone-
crop
Creeping evergreen with white flowers ¼ in. wide in summer. The leaves are borne in 4 rows and are only ⅛ in. long. Native to the Mediterranean Region. Difficult to locate in U.S.

caeruleum   3″–9″   annual   Blue Stonecrop
This is the only annual Sedum worth growing; and also the only one bearing blue flowers in summer. It should be planted in poor, light soil with full sun, where stems and leaves eventually turn bright red, contrasting well with the blue flowers. It may self-seed. Native to southern Europe and northern Africa.

cauticolum   3″   Zone 3
Similar to *S. sieboldii*, it has rosy-red flowers and blooms 2 weeks earlier in the summer. Native to the mountains of Japan, and excellent for planting in wall gardens or among rocks because of its creeping tendencies. Apparently this species is one of the few which will exist in moist soils.

crassipes   6″–12″   Zone 6
With linear to lanceolate leaves about ¾″ long, this is an erect perennial with small yellowish-white to greenish flowers, blooming in the early summer and sometimes a second time. The flowers are about ½″ wide and are crowded together in a flat-topped cluster that is 1½″ wide. Native to the Himalayas and China.

dasyphyllum   2″   Zone 4   Leafy Stonecrop
An evergreen with opposite gray-green leaves, about ⅛ in. long, and heads of pinkish flowers in June. Excellent for the rock garden or for odd rock crevices, especially for the wall garden. Easily propagated by pieces or cuttings often taking root wherever they are broken off. Native to Europe and northern Africa.

ewersii   1′   Zone 4   Ewers Stonecrop
With opposite leaves about ¾ in. long; purplish-pink flowers ½ in. across in Aug. and Sept. Native to the Himalayas, easy to grow and with a var. **homophyllum** that is only 2–3 in. tall. Somewhat like a smaller *S. spectabile* which is common in gardens.

gracile   3″   Zones 5–6
An excellent evergreen for the rock garden, it will provide year-round color where the winters are mild. The small, linear leaves, growing close

together on the stem, form a dense cover. In winter, this foliage turns a bronzy green. The flowers are white dotted red and appear in great profusion on tiny stems only an inch high in May. Native to the Caucasus.

guatemalense This procumbent species has been mixed up in the trade for some time. The authors of *Hortus III* now note that it is not in cultivation in America and that the name has been misapplied for plants of x *Sedum rubrotinctum*, which see.

gypsicolum   6″   Zone 7
A plant from Spain, this is not entirely winter hardy in northern gardens. The thick, prostrate stems are covered sparsely with large, round, light green leaves which have red markings on them and are ¼ in. long. The flowers are white and are borne in clusters in July.

kamtschaticum   (*S. middendorffianum*)   1′
Zone 3   Kamschatca Sedum
A beautiful, little, mounded plant from Manchuria, with trailing or decumbent stems and tiny, alternate, dark green linear leaves. The flowers, which are both sparse and infrequent, are yellow, ⅝ in. wide, bloom in the summer, and quite attractive. The stems of the current season keep their leaves, which turn bronze at the approach of winter, while the older stems die. This is an excellent wall plant, though quite rare. The var. **floriferum** has stems more decumbent than those of the species and the pale green leaves are narrow. Flowers appear in early May. The var. '**Variegatum**' has pale green leaves variegated with yellow, pink and red. The var. '**Ellacombianum**' is often grown with wavy leaf margins and bright yellow flowers.

lineare   6″   Zone 7
This Japanese evergreen plant requires winter protection when grown in the northern U.S. Closely growing, upright stems are clothed with long, pale green, cylindrical leaves 1 in. long and bear clusters of yellow 5-petalled flowers, each ½ in. wide, in summer. The var. **variegata** has leaves with a white margin.

lydium   3″–6″   Zone 3   Lydian Stonecrop
From Asia Minor, this charming little Sedum is used especially in rock gardens, in wall gardens or in the crevices between stepping stones. The foliage is evergreen and, in the full sun, the whole plant is tinged red occasionally. The white flowers are ¼ in. across, produced in heads and blooming during the early summer. Native to Asia Minor.

maximum   3′   annual   Great Stonecrop
Large opposite leaves, usually 3 in. long, and greenish-white flowers ⅜ in. across during Aug. Native to Europe and southwestern Asia.

middendorffianum = *S. kamtschaticum*

moranense   3″–4″   Zone 7   Moran Stonecrop
Evergreen with wiry red stems; leaves triangular,

⅛ in. long and only half as wide; flowers white, ½ in. wide, tinged red on back. Native to southern Mexico.

morganianum trailing **Zone 10** **Burro-tail Stonecrop**
A tender sedum, excellent for the hanging basket indoors because of its pendulous stems which may be 2–3 ft. long, clothed with whitish-green, almost cylindrical, uncurved, succulent leaves about an inch long. The red flowers are borne in a terminal cluster. Native to Mexico.

nevii 4″ **Zone 4**
This is a beautiful little mountain plant native to Va. It has small, silvery, alternate leaves about ½ in. long, touched with pink, and grows in tightly mounded rosettes. The small white flowers, appearing in June, have conspicuous rosy anthers. It is an excellent plant for a garden spot with acid soil, in partial shade.

oaxacanum creeping **Zone 6** **Oaxaca Stonecrop**
A low creeping evergreen from Mexico, with alternate leaves, ¼ in. long, and yellow flowers in 1–4-flowered clusters. Native to Mexico.

oreganum 6″ **Zone 4** **Oregon Stonecrop**
Native to western North America, attractive, green-tinged red leaves, which in a hot situation will turn completely red. The flowers are yellow, fading to light pink.

pachyphyllum 1′ **Zone 9**
A small, slightly shrubby, succulent, evergreen perennial with cylindrical jelly-bean-shaped leaves, 1½ in. long, curved upwards, light green to glaucous with red tips; flowers bright yellow, ½ in. wide, in 2- in. clusters. Native to Mexico; used as a ground cover where hardy.

populifolium 1½′ **Zone 3** **Poplar Sedum**
A small Siberian shrub with stiff, woody stems and fleshy, dark green, alternate, deciduous leaves, about ¾ in. long, forming an open rounded plant. The clusters of 5-petalled, white to pink flowers appear in June, each one of which is ⅜ in. across.

pruinatum = *S. rupestre*

purdyi 4″ **Zone 8** **Purdy Sedum**
Although native to the mountains of Calif., this plant is quite rare. It has thick, wide leaves formed in rosettes and spreads by prostrate red stolons, which form new rosettes at their tips. It produces clusters of white flowers in spring and grows in acid soil in partial shade.

rosea 18″ **Zone 2** **Roseroot**
When the roots of this plant are dried they smell like rose water, hence the common name. It is widely native from Greenland to Europe, Asia, Japan and North America to N.Mex. The heads of flowers are greenish yellow to reddish purple, with individual flowers being ¼ in. across; the leaves are 2 in. long.

rubrotinctum 6″ **Zone 9** **Christmas-cheer**
One of the best sedums, vigorous in growth and will crowd out weak species; with small club-shaped leaves turning coppery red in the sun. The flowers are yellow—good for massing where hardy.

rupestre 6″ **Zone 7**
This is an attractive evergreen, excellent for the rock garden in mild climates since it is of interest throughout the year. It grows with quickly spreading stems clothed with linear leaves of a very pronounced bluish green. These turn a deep purple in fall and remain so throughout the winter. The clusters of pale yellow flowers, on stems 15 in. high, bloom in early summer. Native to Portugal.

sarmentosum 6″ **Zone 3** **Stringy Stonecrop**
A prostrate plant from northern China and Japan, with prostrate stems up to 1 ft. long, rooting at the tip. It is good as a ground cover only in sunny places. The bright yellow flowers, ⅝ in. across, are borne in July and the evergreen leaves, borne in groups of 3, are 1 in. long. Easily propagated by division and cuttings.

sediforme 2′ **Zone 9**
An alternate-leaved succulent, native to the Mediterranean Region, with lanceolate leaves to 1½ in. long and greenish-white flowers, ½ in. wide, in summer. Used for massing.

sexangulare 3″ **Zones 2–3** **Hexagon Stonecrop**
Similar to *S. acre* but more neat in appearance and the flowers are a deeper yellow and appear in July. Native to Europe. Actually a creeping evergreen with leaves in 6 spiral rows, each leaf about ¼ in. long.

sieboldii 6″–9″ **Zones 2–3** **Siebold Stonecrop**
From Japan, this popular Stonecrop blooms in Aug., continues until Oct. with pink flowers. It is mostly decumbent with leaves produced in whorls of 3, each leaf being nearly round and 1 in. long. There is a form with variegated (yellow-blotched) leaves.

spathulifolium 3″–4″ **Zone 5**
With evergreen, bluish-green leaves often tinged red, spoon shaped and 1 in. long. Flowers are yellow, ½ in. across, in leafy blot clusters during May and June. The beautiful var. **'Purpureum'** has larger, purple-colored leaves and is considered by many to be the best of all the stonecrops for ornamental planting. Native to western North America.

spectabile 18″ **Zone 3** **Showy Sedum**
This is the showiest of all the sedums, with large fleshy leaves 3 in. long, gray-green in color. It does not spread much but is easily propagated by division. The flat flower clusters, 3–4 in. across, are composed of many rosy-pink flowers appearing from Aug. until frost. It will grow equally well in full sun or light shade.

'**Brilliant**' is the best and most popular cultivar with raspberry-carmine flowers. '**Carmen**' and '**Meteor**' are other deep pink-flowered forms. The white-flowering varieties are not as attractive simply because the flowers are not pure white. Native to Japan.

spurium   6″   Zone 3   Two-row Stonecrop
A creeping perennial, forming dense mats of stems and foliage, making a fine ground cover. In some places in New England, many of the opposite leaves are deciduous but the ones near the end of the stems remain on and turn red, giving the plant an interesting color over winter. The flowers are pink to white, ½ in. across, in 2-in. clusters from mid-July to early Aug. It is native to the Caucasus area of Asia Minor. Easily propagated by division, cuttings and seed.

Of many sedums, this one has proved the best in the ground cover experiments at the Arnold Arboretum in Boston. It is not exactly evergreen, but does keep its leaves a long time and looks well at any time of year. Added to this is the fact that the stems appear reddish all winter long.

stahlii   8″   Zone 6   Stahl Stonecrop
Evergreen, opposite leaves, ½ in. across, and yellow flowers the same size during summer and fall. Native to Mexico.

subulatum   8″   Zone 6
An evergreen, mounded perennial with succulent, decumbent stems and small, blue-gray leaves which are linear and cylindrical, sharply acute at the tip. It has clusters of rather unattractive, white flowers on stems 12 in. high. Native to Asia Minor.

tatarinowii   4″   Zone 6 (?)
Another rare Sedum from China, with arching stems, narrow leaves deeply lobed at the apex and white to pink flowers.

ternatum   6″   Zone 4   Mountain Stonecrop
Although most species of sedum are found in arid areas of the world, this evergreen is at home along the streams and on damp slopes from N.Y. to Ga., and west to the Great Lakes. It is a prostrate perennial, spreading by underground stolons. From the center of a rosette of fleshy, ovate to cordate leaves, a flowering stalk extends along the ground. On the stem are a few ovate, succulent leaves in whorls of 3. The bluish-white flowers, in a loose, somewhat one-sided cluster, clothe the upper part of the stalk and appear in early summer. It is a good rock garden plant readily transplanted and self-sows freely.

treleasii   1′   Zone 9
A sprawling evergreen sedum from Mexico, with very fleshy, crowded, alternate leaves, 1¼ in. long, and curving upwards. The bright yellow flowers are ½ in. wide in globe-shaped clusters 1½ in. in dia.

SEED. The ripened ovule consisting of the embryo and its integuments.

SEEDS. Plants producing seeds are divided into 2 main groups, those called the gymnosperms producing naked seeds (like those of the conifers, hemlocks, pines, spruces, etc.) and the true flowering plants (angiosperms) which have seeds produced in an ovary such as apples, beans, milkweeds. Both types of seeds, when properly sown and germinated, produce plants similar to the parent from which the seeds were taken unless cross-fertilization has taken place. See HYBRIDS, FERTILIZATION, etc. Seeds are handled in many different ways (see SEEDS OF WOODY PLANTS) in order to obtain proper germination and many can be stored for surprisingly long periods and still be viable.

Distribution

Seeds are distributed in nature by various means:

1. WIND. Many seeds like those of catalpas, maples, milkweeds, and poplars are so formed that they are easily blown by the wind, sometimes considerable distances, until they finally come to rest on the soil where some eventually germinate.

2. WATER. The Coconut is the outstanding example of seed distributed great distances by water. Many other seeds are taken short distances by brooks and streams, but the Coconut has reached places thousands of miles away and is now a habitant of most of the tropical regions of the world, at least along the seacoasts.

3. ANIMALS. Animals and man distribute many. Oaks, walnuts, filberts and many another nut are distributed by the busy squirrels and other rodents. Fruits like apples and cherries are eaten by animals and man and the seeds thus distributed.

4. BIRDS. Even more fruits are distributed by birds than by animals. Junipers, honeysuckles, maples, crab apples and a thousand and one other things are eaten by the birds, the seed passed through their digestive tracts and eventually eliminated at places some distance removed from where they were eaten.

5. FORCE. Certain plants like the witch-hazels and boxwoods open their fruiting capsules with such a force that the fruits are actually thrown for distances of several to many feet.

6. ATTACHMENT. Cockle burrs and similar fruits have hooked barbs that enable the fruits to cling to passing objects (animals or man) and these of course are distributed in this fashion.

Longevity

The longevity of seeds, especially those of many ornamental plants, has not been given an exhaustive study. However, it varies greatly from poplar seeds which must be sown during the first few days after they ripen on the tree, to those of Lotus which have been known to have been kept 1000 years and then germinated when the proper conditions of heat and moisture were provided. Many annual flower seeds keep their viability 2–3 years if stored under normal conditions. Many vegetable seeds can be kept up to 10 years (beets, Cucumber, Radish). Some of the cereals can be kept 2–15 years. Some weed seeds, stored in tightly closed bottles in the soil, like Smart Weed, Moth Mullein and Evening Primrose, have germinated 50 years after they were produced on the plant.

VIABILITY OF CERTAIN VEGETABLE SEEDS

	YEARS VIABLE
Asparagus	4–8
Beans	3–8
Beets	3–10
Broccoli	5–10
Cabbage	3–4
Carrots	4–9
Celery	8–10
Corn	2–4
Cucumber	4–10
Eggplant	6–10
Lettuce	5–9
Melons	5–9
Okra	5–10
Onion	2–4
Parsley	2–6
Parsnip	2–4
Peas	2–7
Pepper	4–13
Pumpkin	6–8
Radish	3–10
Spinach	5–7
Turnip	3–9
Squash	4–5
Tomato	4–13
Turnip	5–10

VIABILITY OF CERTAIN OTHER SEEDS

	YEARS VIABLE
Anise	3–5
Aster	1–13
Bee Balm	4–7
Dandelion	2–5
Gourds	6–10
Marjoram	3–5
Nasturtium	5–8
Purslane	7–10
Rosemary	4
Tansy	2–4
Thyme	3–5

The length of time these seeds remain viable depends on the variety, but mostly on the conditions under which the seed was grown and under which it is stored. Placing seed in stoppered bottles in a cool cellar is far more conducive to a long period in which they are viable than storing them in the hot sun on an open shelf.

A seed germinates after absorbing moisture in a suitable warm temperature. Most flower and vegetable seeds can be germinated as soon as they are thoroughly ripe but many of the seeds of woody plants (which see) can not because of various dormancy problems which must be broken in one way or another. See PROPAGATION. Flower and vegetable seeds which have been packaged by reliable firms, have the % anticipated germination stamped on the outside of the package. This is an extremely valuable bit of information for every gardener. It shows that the seed company has given this serious consideration usually by testing. Years ago, seeds were often sold by unscrupulous dealers, in which old seed with low germination potential was mixed with fresh seed, but no % germination was given on the package. The end result was extremely low germination. Today, reliable companies stamp the germination potential on the packet.

This can be checked by the gardener. Take a soup dish, moisten a paper towel, count out 100 seeds of those to be tested, place another moist towel (not wet) on top and another inverted soup dish or pan on top. Put this in a warm place, examine every few days and keep the paper moist but not wet, and shortly one can count the number of seeds which germinate. This is the percentage of germinating seeds.

Seed Structure

In elementary botany one learned that a seed consists of an embryonic plant having a primary root (radicle) and primary shoot (plumule). These are attached to 2 seed leaves or cotyledons in the case of some plants (dicotyledons) or 1 seed leaf (in the case of monocotyledons). All this is covered with a seed coat or testa, and at the end (or side) of the seed is a scar (hilum) showing where the seed was attached to the fruit. Near this scar is a very small hole (micropyle) and it is through this that the root first grows when germination starts.

Seeds vary in size from those of the double coconut (*Ladoicea maldivica*) which may weigh 50 lbs. each, down to the extremely fine rhododendron seed, 1 lb. of which may contain 5 million seeds.

Collecting seeds is a hobby with many gardeners. They should be carefully recorded as they are collected, with the name of the plant, location and date collected. They should be dried properly before being stored, or cleaned if the fruits are fleshy. See SEEDS OF WOODY PLANTS, PROPAGATION, etc. The seeds of most garden flowers and vegetables can be stored dry, but those of woody plants will have to be handled in a variety of ways on account of dormancy problems.

It has been noted that with some of the trees, especially the conifers, large amounts of seed are not produced every year. In fact, some times only every other year, every third year or even every tenth year. This is probably because, when a large crop is produced, the stored foods in the plant are exhausted in the production of the crop and it takes several years to be replenished. Hence, when those interested in collecting cones note that it is a "good" year, i.e., many cones are produced on many species and varieties, enough cones and seed should be collected that year to last several years, until the next "good" season comes along.

Weather may have a great deal to do with good crops and poor crops of seed. We know, for instance, that holly species bloom mostly in early June. Years when the weather is bright and warm, the fruit production is excellent, for bees, which do the pollinizing, and wind are both active during such periods. On the other hand, when early June weather is cold (below 57° F.) and rainy, bees are not active and fertilization does not take place as well as it should, then there is poor fruit production. The same is true in commercial fruit production. So, in nature, possibly for a combination of reasons, there are years when trees have many fruits and others when they have few fruits.

Usually it does not pay to collect the seeds of annual flowers and vegetables for these are offered so cheaply that it is easier to buy them. Also, one should continually keep in mind the fact that cross-pollination can occur in the garden and some seeds may actually be hybrids and so will not produce plants identical with the parent. Take gourds for one example. Like most cucurbits, these have staminate and pistillate flowers both on the same plant but when pumpkins or squash are near, insects can carry the pollen from one plant to the other, resulting in seed that will grow plants neither pure squash nor pure gourds.

SEED DORMANCY. The easiest seeds to use (for the gardener) are those of vegetables and the annual flowers. These seeds are usually ready to sow as soon as they are ripe and thoroughly dried. On the other hand, most of them can be kept dry in a cool place for a year or more then sown and expected to germinate with a minimum loss of germination. The longevity of seed is also of importance to the gardener who has seed left over after planting his flowers and vegetables. Stored in a tightly closed container in a cool place, most of the commonly grown annual and vegetable seeds are almost as good the second year as they were the first, but if stored in a hot room, open to the air, viability may depreciate rapidly.

Some of the seed growers mark their seed packets with the tested % of germination, an excellent procedure for them and especially for their customers. Unscrupulous dealers can mix old seed with new (resulting in a lower germination count) and not include the % germination on the package. It pays to buy the best seed possible, from a reliable concern.

The seeds of woody plants are divided into several groups according to the way they germinate. There are those which germinate as soon after ripe as they are sown. These require no dormancy period and would include among many:

Alnus	Diervilla	Leucothoe
Azaleas	Enkianthus	Phellodendron
Betula	Erica	Philadelphus
Buddleia	Evodia	Pieris
Catalpa	Hydrangea	Potentilla
Cercidiphyllum	Hypericum	Rhododendron
Clethra	Kalmia	Spiraea
Deutzia	Kolkwitzia	Weigela

Such seed can be collected when it is ripe, stored in a cool dry place until one is ready to sow it the following spring or it can be sown at once.

Seeds Requiring a Dormant Period

Many woody plants have seeds which require a dormant period before they will germinate. This may be on account of an impermeable seed coat, or conditions within the seed itself, or a combination of the two. To overcome this dormancy the seed must be exposed to cold for a definite amount of time; or it may be that they should be exposed first to warm temperature for a definite period, then to cold for a definite period before they will germinate.

The dormancy of these seeds and the treatments suggested to break the dormancy have been worked out for many plants. Years ago, such seed was planted out-of-doors in the fall. The winter cold would satisfy the cold-period prerequisites for some but there were those which would not germinate until the second year after sowing. It was these that had the complicated "double dormancy" period. Much information is available now on the proper treatment of such seeds, making it possible to bring about much better and faster germination.

Simple Dormancy

The old-fashioned method of treating seeds with simple dormancy was to "stratify" them, that is, place in a box 4 in. deep a layer of moist soil or peat moss, then a thin layer of seed, then another layer of moist soil or peat moss and so on until the box was filled. This was then placed out-of-doors over winter or placed in a cool cellar where it was kept moist and observed from time to time, and when the seed started to germinate, it was taken out of the boxes and sown in flats in the greenhouse.

Now, after years of experimentation, we know that the best temperature for this stratification period is about 40° F. or about the temperature in the family refrigerator. We also know the time required in most cases.

With polyethylene plastic bags available, there are easier ways of stratifying seeds than this layer by layer method mentioned above. The procedure would be something like this:

Collect and clean the seed, store it dry until the correct time to stratify it. This time would be worked out knowing the length of cold required and taking into consideration the time that the germinating seeds could be handled. If the stratification time is 3 months at 40° F. and the seed was to be sown out-of-doors June 1, then the time of stratification would be March 1. On the other hand, if the germinating seeds could be sown any time in the greenhouse stratification time would be any time after the ripened seed has been cleaned and dried.

Using the polyethylene bags, the seed is mixed with moistened sand, peat moss, sphagnum moss or a mixture of half sand and peat moss, or vermiculite placed in the bag, which is tightly tied and then placed at a temperature of 40° F. for the required length of time. This mixture must not be soggy and wet but merely dampened or moist. The seeds can be examined through the polyethylene film. When the prescribed time is up or the seeds are germinating, then they can merely be sown in flats, on top of the prepared soil-mixture medium and seeds together, soil sprinkled on top and the flats placed on the greenhouse bench for complete germination, or the seeds sown in drills out-of-doors if danger from frost is over.

Woody plant seeds in this group with simple dormancy and the approximate time they are stratified at 41° F. are:

	APPROX. STRATIFICATION TIME IN MONTHS
Abies sp. (Fir)	2–3
Acer sp. (Maple) most kinds	3
Aesculus sp. (Horsechestnut)	4
Berberis sp. (Barberry)	2–3
Betula sp. (Birch)	2–3
Campsis sp. (Trumpet Creeper)	2
Carpinus sp. (Hornbeam)	3–4
Carya sp. (Hickory)	3–4
Cedrus sp. (Cedar)	1–2
Celastrus (Bittersweet)	3
Chamaecyparis sp. (False Cypress)	2
Clematis sp. (Virgin's Bower)	3
Cornus florida (Flowering Dogwood)	3
C. kousa (Japanese Dogwood)	3
Fagus sp. (Beech)	3
Fraxinus sp. (Ash)	2–3
Ligustrum sp. (Privet)	3
Liquidambar sp. (Sweetgum)	3
Magnolia sp.	3–4
Malus sp. (Apple)	1–3
Nyssa sp. (Tupelo)	3
Picea sp. (Spruce) most species	1–3

	APPROX. STRATIFICATION TIME IN MONTHS
Pine (most species)	2
Prunus sp. (cherries, etc.)	3–4
Pseudolarix (Golden Larch)	1
Pyrus sp. (Pear)	3
Ribes sp. (Currant and Gooseberry)	3
Sorbus sp. (Mountain-ash) most kinds	3
Syringa sp. (Lilac)	2–3
Thuja sp. (Arborvitae)	2
Tsuga sp. (Hemlock)	3
Vitis sp. (Grape)	3

These recommendations cover most species in the general list. In the maples and mountain ashes, for example, there are some species that will not respond to this treatment.

Double Dormancy

Chionanthus, Cotoneaster, Crataegus, Davidia, Hamamelis, Halesia, Ilex, Juniperus, Rhus, Taxus and Viburnum among others.

These are seeds which if sown in the fall when ripe may take 2 years to germinate. This lengthy period is shortened by the following procedure:

The seed is collected, cleaned and dried, then mixed with a moistened medium (not wet) like sand, peat moss, sphagnum or a mixture of sand and peat moss, placed in a polyethylene bag which is tied tightly and placed in a warm place (65°–85° F.) such as the back of a kitchen shelf for a period of 4–6 months. Then it is taken and put in the refrigerator at about 40° F. for 3 months, then sown.

Seed Coat Dormancy

Recommendations as suggestions for seed treatment cover many of the North Temperate Zone species in the genera listed. However, those involved with seed germination realize that seed age, methods of storage and source of origin can greatly affect germinational behavior.

One should not generalize when considering seed dormancies, for species can differ widely within the same genus. To find entirely different, germinational behavior between seeds from different sources within the same species is not uncommon. Seeds of *Ilex opaca* selections from northern parts of the plants' range, are characterized by conditions which, despite pre-treatment, may result in partial germination one year and further germination each year several successive years. *I. opaca* 'East Palatka', however, from the southern part of the range, has no inhibiting conditions and will germinate without pre-treatment.

To obtain prompt germination of seeds characterized only by seed coat dormancy, rapid means of effecting the entry of water is necessary. Some plants with seeds in this category are:

Albizia	Genista	Robinia
Caragana	Gleditsia	Sophora
Cladrastis	Gymnocladus	Wisteria
Cytisus	Laburnum	

Several procedures are used to overcome this seed coat dormancy:

MECHANICAL TREATMENT. Large seeds, in small quantities, can be perforated with a knife, file or any tool that performs the job. Seeds large enough to hold between the fingers can be easily prepared for the entry of water by scraping them along the uppermost edge of a 3-cornered file placed on a bench. Several strokes are usually sufficient to cut through the seed coat if the file is sharp. Seeds too small to hold or those handled in volume, can be treated by mechanical scarification, or one of the methods next described.

HOT WATER TREATMENT. Treatment with hot water involves placing the seeds in a container and pouring water heated to a temperature of about 190° F. over them. The seeds are then left in the water overnight. In amount, the water should be at least 5 or 6 times the volume of the seeds, and this is important, as too small a quantity can cool before it has the desired effect. On being moved from the water, the seeds are sown at once, without being allowed to dry out. A second, but less effective method, is to sow the seeds and pour boiling water over the seed-pan or seed-flat.

CONCENTRATED SULPHURIC ACID TREATMENT. Some seeds with coats not responsive to hot water treatment can quickly be germinated after a more drastic measure—immersion in concentrated sulfuric acid (H_2SO_4). This highly corrosive substance, when employed for this purpose, accomplishes in hours, or portions thereof, a process that could require months or years if the seed were not treated.

When dealing with small amounts of seeds, sulfuric acid treatment consists of placing the dry seeds in a glass container and carefully pouring acid over them until they are covered. Sulfuric acid is a viscous substance of high surface tension which acts superficially on seed coats without penetration. The length of treatment varies greatly depending upon the subject, the objective being to corrode away sufficient seed coat to permit the entry of water without exposing the interior to destruction by the acid. Observations can be made during treatment by removing a few seeds, rinsing them and examining the seed coat to see how much of it has been eaten away. When treating large batches it is advisable to run a few trial lots to determine proper timing before processing the main bulk. An important point which must be considered when using sulfuric acid is the effect of temperature. Higher temperatures accelerate the rate of action while lower temperatures retard it. Acid treatments at the Arnold Arboretum are usually performed in the winter when room temperature is maintained at approximately 70° F.

On completion of the treatment, seeds are placed in a sieve and washed thoroughly in running water for several minutes to remove all of the acid. Then, they are ready for the next step, which involves either immediate sowing or cold stratification. We do not employ a neutralizer after the use of acid and have never noticed detrimental effects for not having done so. Precautions to be taken when handling sulfuric acid cannot be overemphasized, for it should be handled with the greatest respect.

STRATIFICATION. At the Arnold Arboretum our pretreatment of seeds requiring periods of stratification is done by using polyethylene plastic bags. Polyethylene film has the property of being air permeable yet vapor proof, with the result that oxygen is available to the contents by diffusion. The stratifying medium to be used is dampened; the emphasis here is on the word dampened for too wet a medium could exclude sufficient oxygen. In proportion, the medium should not exceed 2 or 3 times the volume of seed. (This too is stressed as at planting time the seeds are not separated from the medium but the entire content of the bag is sown). The seeds are distributed throughout the medium and placed in the bag which is then twisted at the mouth and made vapor tight with a rubber budding band, using much the same technique employed to bind a graft union. A properly sealed bag, providing it has no flaws, will not require attention during pre-treatment no matter how long this period might be.

Bags of seeds needing pre-treatment by cold are placed in a refrigerator, set at about 40° F.

for the required time. Those needing 2 stages of pre-treatment to overcome double-dormancy are placed on a greenhouse bench to undergo warm stratification; after this is done, they are transferred to the refrigerator to fulfill the cold requirement.

This method of handling seeds has a number of distinct advantages for the amateur. No attention is needed during treatment periods, making it care-free; and the possibility of human misjudgment or neglect are eliminated, making it dependable. Seeds treated in the conventional manner, if kept under wet soggy conditions or if permitted to dry out through human error, can, through such mistreatment, pass into new dormancies or perish. The transparent bag has the advantage that visual inspection can be made to reveal any activity that occurs within. For example, when dealing with materials such as *Davidia*, *Chionanthus* and many of the viburnums which have epicotyl, or shoot-bud dormancy, the extent of radicle development can be easily observed in this way.

ALFRED J. FORDHAM

Longevity

The longevity of ornamental woody plant seeds has not been given exhaustive study. The United States Department of Agriculture reviewed the literature on this subject in its "Woody Plant Seed Manual" Misc. Pub. No. 654, issued June, 1948, and for detailed information the reader is directed to this publication and its excellent bibliography.

The longevity of seeds depends on the kind of seed, where and how it is grown and matured, the conditions under which it is stored, etc.—all variable factors. Poplar seeds lose their viability very fast and must be sown within a few weeks of ripening—willow seeds are viable even a shorter time. Experimentation has shown that many annual garden flower seeds are viable under normal conditions for 2–3 years and many 4–5 years. Many vegetable seeds are good up to 10 years (beets, Cucumber, Radish), many of the cereals from 2–15 years, and certain weed seeds like Smartweed, Moth Mullein and Evening Primrose germinate after having been stored in inverted bottles in the soil 50 years. The recent classic example of Lotus seeds which have proved to be 1000 years old and germinated is the extreme.

Experiments in dormancy and the keeping qualities of seeds have shown that longevity usually increases with a drop in the temperature of the stored seeds, so that now it is generally believed that temperatures of 32°–41° F. are ideal for seed storage, especially when the moisture content of the seeds can be maintained uniformly. Many commercial nurseries have mechanical refrigeration equipment now which can be easily regulated and such equipment is proving almost a necessity in the storage of woody ornamental plant seeds.

Suffice it to say that although some woody plant seeds can be satisfactorily stored for a year or two in open containers at room temperatures, by far the greater proportion can be kept longer if stored in airtight containers at temperatures between 32°–41° F.

Germination Data

Most annuals and perennials will germinate in 2–14 days if temperature and moisture are at an optimum. Those that may take slightly longer under normal conditions are:

Abronia	14–20
Adonis	14–20
Alonsoa	14–20
Anagallis	15–30
Anchusa	10–20
Angelica	30–60
Argemone	15–20
Campanula	14–21
Cardiospermum	14–40
Convolvulus	5–28
Cuphea	20–30
Datura	15–21
Delphinium	15–20
Dimorphotheca	15–21
Eccremocarpus	20–35
Euphorbia	20
Gaillardia	15–20
Gazania	15–25
Glaucium	14–20
Humulus	15–30
Lavatera	10–20
Limonium	15–21
Linaria	14–20
Oenothera	15–30
Papaver	10–20
Penstemon	14–21
Phacelia	14–20
Portulaca	14–20
Ricinus	14–21
Rudbeckia	14–21
Salvia	14–21
Scabiosa	14–20
Sedum	14–20
Silene	14–20
Thunbergia	10–20
Tithonia	15–20

For days to germinate for vegetable seeds see VEGETABLE GARDEN. Woody plant seeds vary widely in the number of days it takes them to germinate, mostly depending on dormancy factors. See factors. See SEED DORMANCY.

SEED SELECTIONS, ALL AMERICA = See ALL AMERICA SEED SELECTIONS.

SEED, SOWING. Anyone can push a bean in a pot of soil and expect it to sprout within a few days. Not all seed sowing is this easy. First the seed must be viable or living and able to germinate when sufficient moisture and heat are provided. Secondly, if it is in the group of those complicated by dormancy problems, these must first be satisfied before it germinates. See SEED DORMANCY. Providing the seed is ready to germinate then moisture and warmth must be provided before this takes place.

Medium

Many quick-germinating seeds like peas and beans can be germinated between 2 pieces of moist paper towels covered top and bottom by ordinary dinner plates. Lily seeds can be mixed with moist (not wet) vermicule, placed in a tightly closed, polyethylene bag and put up on the kitchen shelf, and be expected to germinate in a few weeks. However, what is usually needed is a medium in which the seeds will not only germinate but will continue to grow—namely soil. Sowing seed in pots or flats in the greenhouse is a simple operation. Good loam is sifted very fine, placed in a flat or pot provided with good drainage, the seed is sown in rows (or drills) or broadcast, then covered with soil and watered. A piece of glass (or polyethylene film) is placed over the flat or pot and in turn this is covered with newspaper until the seed germinates, when both the shade and the glass are gradually removed but definitely not taken away in one sudden swoop. With many seeds this is all that is necessary.

There are variations of this needed sometimes. To prevent damping off of the seedlings (which see) the soil might best be sterilized before seed sowing. See SOIL STERILIZATION.

If one has a pressure cooker, sowing seed in quart oil cans is most interesting. They are obtained gratis from the gas station, one end removed and holes punched in the other and thoroughly cleaned. Then they are filled ¾ full with gravel or crushed stone, 2 in. of the finely sifted soil mixture placed on top of the stone and firmed down, the soil moistened and then the cans placed in the pressure cooker. An inch of water is placed in the bottom of the cooker, and the temperature regulated for 180° for 30 minutes. The cans are removed, cooled, all watered from the bottom, then drained, the seed sown and then the cans covered with glass or polyethylene. If the seed is not sown too thick, little damping off will occur. Thus one has the advantage of being able to grow several things in easily movable containers and of growing them up to the time the seedlings are ready for their first transplanting.

Then, too, seeds vary as to size; some are

extremely fine like those of azaleas and rhododendrons, and some are large like those of squash and pumpkins. All are not placed in the soil at the same depth. A general rule is to plant the seed at a depth equal to the size of the seed, not always a practical thing to do because of the extremely small sizes of some seeds.

Soil used can be any one of several mixtures but in general 2 parts good loam, 1 part peat, 1 part coarse sand; and add to each bushel of this 1½ oz. of superphosphate and ¾ oz. of ground limestone. For ericacious seedlings, which do not need limestone, use 3 parts peat or leaf mold, 1 part good loam and 1 part coarse sand. These should be mixed thoroughly, and if kept in a pile or can for future use, do not let them dry out but slightly moisten them occasionally.

Sowing Seed Indoors

In sowing extremely fine seed like that of azaleas and rhododendrons, it is advisable to rub dried sphagnum moss over a screen about the size of normal window screening and let this be about ⅛ in. deep on top of the prepared soil. Then sow the fine seed in this (after the whole flat or pot has been watered from the base); do not cover the seed but do cover the flat or pot with glass or polyethylene so the finely grated moss will not dry out.

Sowing fine seed.

Small seed like tomato, cabbage or pansy seed can be broadcast on the soil surface after it has been firmed down with a short strip of wood, and watered from the bottom, then soil or finely grated sphagnum moss or a mixture can be gently scattered on top of the seed, to a depth of about ⅛ in. Then it is covered preparatory for germination.

In watering a pot or flat from the bottom one merely places it in a container filled with water

to a level such that it just barely comes to the top of the flat or pot. When the soil is thoroughly wet the flat or pot is removed and the excess water drains out. This is frequently done the day before seeding to prevent seeds from floating around if water comes up this far.

Larger seed may be scattered and covered with soil, or actually sown in rows made by impressing the edge of a wooden label ¼–⅜ in. in the soil, then covering the seed with soil. Seed should not be sown too thick. In the first place it is hard to separate the roots of the individual seedlings after germination when it comes time for transplanting and secondly, if the seedlings are too close together there is a much greater danger of the damping-off disease (which see) taking its toll as soon as they have germinated.

The best way of actually sowing most seeds (except the large ones like nasturtium and squash) is right from the packet. Open up one end and gently tap the packet so that the seeds gradually slide out over the end flap. In this way, amounts can be easily controlled. But always guard against the tendency to sow the seeds thickly, for this only creates trouble and one ends up with far fewer seedlings than if seeds had been thinly scattered in the first place.

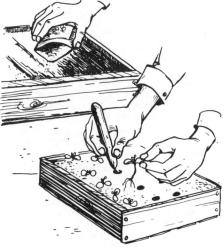

Sowing seed and transplanting small seedlings into flats.

Larger seed like nasturtium or squash can merely be pressed down in the soil and covered about ¼ in. deep. Such seeds should be at least an inch or more apart. Since both these are difficult to transplant they are often sown 4 to a 4- or 5-in. pot, and then the whole soil mass planted intact as a unit when it finally comes time to plant them in the garden. In this way their roots are not disturbed.

Sowing Seed Outdoors

Vegetable and flower seeds sown in the vegetable garden are usually sown in drills, made with a hoe for the larger seeds like beans, corn, squash and pumpkins, or with the hoe handle or some similar implement for smaller seeds like those of lettuce and carrots. In any event the soil must be level and very finely pulverized, for if there are large lumps of soil, rocks or stones present, there is not the close contact necessary between soil and seed. Even though the seed may germinate, the seedlings will quickly die if the soil is in coarse lumps. Many gardeners have trouble with such fine seed and when it fails to come up the seed is blamed and not the procedure which is really at fault.

The planting of seeds in rows requires that one uses a line to make the rows straight. Also one should have a knowledge of temperatures, often more popularly expressed in terms of date. "Plant as soon as the soil can be prepared in the spring," a suggestion often used for planting peas, indicates that these seeds will germinate and grow with low soil temperatures. Corn, on the other hand, is a hot weather crop and will not germinate so early. Such seed may even rot if planted in a soil too cold for its germination. So, one should carefully review the instructions on the seed package and not sow some seeds too early.

Sowing fine seed like that of lettuce and carrot and many flower seeds, requires special attention, or they just will not germinate properly. As already explained, they must not be sown too deep, and the soil must be very finely pulverized so that it comes in contact with the seed. The soil must not be allowed to dry out, and this may require daily sprinklings. Just imagine a line of recently germinated, fine seed in the upper ¼ in. of soil, when that crust dries out completely for lack of water. The seed just does not have any chance at all. Frequent sprinkling, or a very thin mulching or even covering rare and valuable seed with shading material, all helps to get it started properly. Such precautions are well worth the effort. To help in this, one should know the approximate number of days it takes certain seeds to germinate after being planted in the open soil. See VEGETABLE GARDEN.

Some seed like corn, squash, pumpkin, cucumber, melon, etc., are planted in "hills," or groups of 5–7 seeds. When this is done the individual seeds are spaced in a group about 3 in. apart. In the case of cucumbers these hills are 3–4 ft. apart. The seed is merely planted in a circular area and covered with the proper

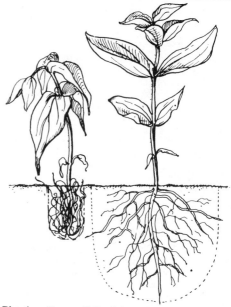

Planting. Even a Calendula or Zinnia (which has opposite leaves) should be planted in a large hole with roots carefully spaced and not jammed in a hole that is too small.

amount of soil. After germination the seedlings are usually reduced to 3 or 4 per hill depending on the crop. Too many left in such a small area would mean that root competition would be too great for any to develop properly. It is difficult for the novice gardener to remove sturdy seedlings in these instances but it is absolutely necessary if good crops are to be obtained One always plants a few more seeds in each hill than is required but one should never neglect to reduce the number of proper seedlings afterward.

In all seed-sowing operations out-of-doors, fine soil is raked over the sown seed to the proper depth, then slightly firmed with rake or hoe. Seeding should never take place in wet soil, for in working such soil it can be pressed too heavily and then it may dry into a hard, bricklike crust, not conducive to good seed germination.

Be certain the rows are marked so that one knows what is planted and where. There is always the possibility that seed may not germinate for one reason or another and it is essential to know what seed was used and where it was planted if it becomes necessary to resow.

SEEDS OF WOODY PLANTS—Collecting, Cleaning, Shipping. The studies of seeds of plants, their collection, care and requirements for germination, has been an intriguing one over the years. Much work has been done, mostly with the seeds of cereals, annuals and trees used for reforestation. Textbooks on forestry have much detailed information concerning forest tree seeds, but the seeds of many woody ornamental plants have not been studied as thoroughly as many a commercial grower would wish.

Collecting

Seeds should not be collected until they are ripe, for in many cases seeds collected prematurely do not germinate. Any collector who has had experience in this field knows that there are various methods of determining the ripeness of the fruit—the shrivelling of the pod or the cord connecting the seed to the pod in the legumes, the color or softness of the pulp of the fruit of *Malus*, *Viburnum* and *Cotoneaster*, and close examination of the cones of coniferous trees, sometimes even tested by determining the specific gravity of the unopened cones.

Seeds should be collected wherever possible from pure stands. There are many groups of plants which cross-pollinate easily, and when seed is collected from arboretums or other closely planted collections of many species, there is ample opportunity for hybridization. This is also true in nature, so that in order to insure good seed, collect it either in pure stands or from isolated specimens.

One very important fact to keep in mind is that the seed of many a variety, botanical as well as horticultural, may not "come true to name." There are some cases, admittedly, in which the variety will yield a surprising percentage of the seedlings true to name. Such is the case with *Quercus robur* 'Fastigiata'. But the rule in most cases is that the seed of the variety

yields seedlings similar to the species.

The actual date on which seed ripens in one locality may vary from year to year in the same way and for the same reasons as do the blooming dates of plants and the autumn color. Often one makes a special effort to collect seed of a certain plant only to find, on coming to the plant, that all the seed has fallen on the ground or been eaten by the birds and rodents, or has been partially destroyed by weevils. The seeds of witch-hazels, in particular, must be collected before the capsules open, for at that time they are actually thrown considerable distances by the explosive opening of the capsule. Certain plants like *Chionanthus virginicus*, with fleshy fruits, may appear ripe one day and be gone the next, merely because a flock of birds has taken them all from the plant in a few hours' time.

There are many plants which retain their fruits for a long time in the fall, and far into the winter, and these may be collected over a long period. Many of the seeds collected on the dates in the following list will need to be cleaned and dried, preferably in the greenhouse. Then there is an after-ripening period, or a period of dormancy, for many seeds so that frequently it is months from the time the seed is collected before it is ready for planting. However, when seed is to be obtained for special purposes, it is best to collect it as soon as it is ripe, instead of waiting and taking the chance of its disappearing. The following list of dates on whch seed collections have been made in the Arnold Arboretum in Boston, Mass., can be considerably more flexible than the single date entry would lead one to believe. All these dates should be coordinated with the fruit ripening dates in the locality where the list is to be used, and collecting dates for many more can be inserted as they become known.

WOODY PLANT SEED COLLECTION DATES
(Plants arranged chronologically)

May 5

Ulmus americana	U. pumila

May 15

Populus tremuloides	Salix sp.

May 30

Acer rubrum	Lonicera fragrantissima
A. saccharinum	L. standishii
Elaeagnus multiflorus	

June 15

Daphne mezereum	Prunus alba
Populus abla	

June 20

Amelanchier oblongifolia	P. subhirtella
Cornus alba	P. tomentosa
Prunus sargentii	Viburnum farreri

June 30

Lonicera morrowii

Prunus cerasus

July 5

Amelanchier spicata
Cornus seriea
Lonicera bella
L. chrysantha
L. maximowiczii

L. tatarica
L. xylosteum
Mahonia aquifolium
Nemopanthus mucronatus

July 20

Morus sp.
Rosa hugonis
R. roxburghii

R. spinosissima
Vaccinium vitis-idaea
Viburnum plicatum

July 30

Amelanchier amabilis
A. sanguinea
Populus maximowiczii

Rosa ecae
Vaccinium corymbosum

August 5

Prinsepia sp.
Prunus japonica
P. glandulosa
P. maritima

Rhamnus frangula
Rhus typhina
Ribes odoratum
Rosa harisonii
R. primula

August 15

Acer ginnala
Ceanothus pallidus roseus
Cedrus libani stenocoma
Cornus racemosa
Crataegus arnoldiana
Cytisus nigricans

C. purpureus
Gaylussacia sp.
Ostrya virginiana
Shepherdia argentea
Viburnum sieboldii

August 20

Betula papyrifera
Carpinus sp.
Kolkwitzia amabilis
Prunus cerasifera

Spiraea veitchii
Viburnum alnifolium
V. lantana

August 30

Caragana maximowicziana
Cornus mas
C. kousa
Cotinus coggygria
Cotoneaster racemiflora
Laburnum sp.

Rosa carolina
R. pendulina
Sambucus canadensis
Syringa amurensis
Viburnum trilobum

September 5

Acer negundo
Cladrastis sp.
Cornus glabrata
Crataegus punctata

Potentilla fruticosa
Rhus copallina
Rosa rugosa
Zanthoxylum americanum

September 15

Acer griseum
A. pensylvanicum
Aesculus sp.
Akebia quinata
Aronia melanocarpa
Betula lenta
B. lutea
B. pendula
B. populifolia
Chionanthus sp.
Clethra alnifolia
Deutzia sp.

Evodia daniellii
Lindera benzoin
Paeonia suffruticosa
Philadelphus virginalis
Rosa alba
R. blanda
R. coriifolia
R. rubrifolia
R. willmottiae
Sassafras sp.
Schisandra chinensis
Viburnum wrightii

September 20

Acer platanoides
A. saccharum
Aralia spinosa
Corylopsis sp.
Cotoneaster adpressus
C. melanocarpus
C. moupinensis
Fagus sp.

Halesia sp.
Ilex yunnanensis
Kalopanax pictus
Nyssa sylvatica
Pieris sp.
Quercus sp.
Viburnum dilatatum

September 30

Actinidia arguta
Ailanthus altissima
Cercis canadensis
Clerodendron trichotomum
Cornus sanguinea

Exochorda sp.
Koelreuteria paniculata
Pinus sp.
Symplocos paniculata

October 5

Ampelopsis sp.
Berberis bretschneideri
Cornus florida
Cotoneaster foveolata
Fothergilla sp.
Hamamelis sp.
Larix sp.
Magnolia acuminata
M. soulangiana
M. stellata
Robinia sp.

Solanum dulcamara
Sorbaronia jackii
Sorbus sp.
Vaccinium oldhamii
Viburnum betulifolium
V. carlesii
V. cassinoides
V. dentatum
V. ovatifolium
V. prunifolium

October 10

Acanthopanax sp.
Aronia sp.
Celastrus sp.
Cotoneaster acutifolius
C. dielsianus
C. divaricatus
C. lucidus

C. zabelii
Enkianthus sp.
Hydrangea anomala petiolaris
Pseudotsuga menziesii
Symphoricarpos sp.
Taxus sp.
Tsuga sp.

October 15

Abies sp.
Berberis gilgiana
Caragana arborescens
Castanea mollissima
Celtis occidentalis
Chaenomeles sp.
Clematis paniculata
Corylus americana
C. avellana
C. cornuta
Davidia involucrata
Euonymus alata
E. americana
E. bungeana
E. fortunei 'Vegeta'
E. obovata
Fraxinus sp.
Ginkgo biloba

Hicoria sp.
Ilex verticillata
Juglans sp.
Juniperus sp.
Leucothoe fontanesiana
Liriodendron sp.
Picea sp.
Rhododendron many sp.
Rosa canina
R. eglanteria
R. helenae
Stewartia sp.
Thuja occidentalis
Tilia sp.
Ulmus parvifolia
Viburnum acerifolium
V. setigerum
Vitis sp.

October 20

Albizia julibrissin rosea
Alnus glutinosa
Berberis vulgaris
Buddleia sp.
Cercidiphyllum japonicum

Malus baccata
M. toringoides
Oxydendrum arboreum
Phellodendron sp.
Photinia villosa

Crataegus laevigata   Physocarpus sp.
Lycium sp.   Viburnum lentago

October 30

Berberis koreana   Kalmia latifolia
Cotoneaster horizontalis   Ligustrum sp.
C. tomentosus   Malus, many sp.
Gleditsia sp.   Pseudolarix amabilis
Gymnocladus dioica   Rosa virginiana
Hippophae rhamnoides   Viburnum burkwoodii
Ilex opaca   Wisteria sp.

November 5

Baccharis halimifolia   Paulownia tomentosa
Callicarpa sp.   Rhodotypos scandens
Cotoneaster multiflorus   Viburnum lobophyllum
Elaeagnus angustifolius   V. opulus
Myrica pensylvanica   V. sargentii

November 15

Berberis thunbergii   L. korolkowii
Cotoneaster affinis   L. maackii
Elaeagnus umbellata   Pyracantha coccinea
Franklinia alatamaha   Rosa setigera
Lonicera henryi   R. wichuraiana

November 20

Crataegus lavallei   C. prunifolia
C. nitida   Rosa multiflora

November 30

Cotoneaster rugosa   Crataegus phaenopyrum
C. salicifolia   Ilex glabra

SEED COLLECTION DATES
(Plants arranged alphabetically)

Abies sp.	Oct. 15	Caragana maximowicziana	Aug. 30
Acanthopanax sp.	Oct. 10	Carpinus sp.	Aug. 20
Acer ginnala	Aug. 15	Castanea mollissima	Oct. 15
A. griseum	Sept. 15	Ceanothus pallidus roseus	Aug. 15
A. negundo	Sept. 5	Cedrus libani stenocoma	Aug. 15
A. platanoides	Sept. 20	Celastrus sp.	Oct. 10
A. saccharum	Sept. 20	Cercidiphyllum japonicum	Oct. 20
Aesculus sp.	Sept. 15	Chaenomeles sp.	Oct. 16
Akebia quinata	Sept. 15	Chionanthus sp.	Sept. 15
Albizia julibrissin rosea	Oct. 20	Cornus alba	June 20
Alnus glutinosa	Oct. 20	C. amomum	Aug. 30
Amelanchier amabilis	July 30	C. florida	Oct. 5
A. oblongifolia	June 20	C. glabrata	Sept. 5
A. sanguinea	July 30	C. kousa	Aug. 30
A. spicata	July 5	C. mas	Aug. 15
Ampelopsis sp.	Oct. 5	C. racemosa	Aug. 15
Aralia spinosa	Sept. 20	C. sanguinea	Sept. 30
Aronia sp.	Oct. 10	C. sericea	July 5
A. melanocarpa	Sept. 15	Cotinus coggygria	Aug. 30
A. prunifolia	Oct. 10	Cotoneaster acutifolius	Oct. 10
Berberis bretschneideri	Oct. 5	C. adpressus	Sept. 20
B. gilgiana	Oct. 15	C. affinis	Nov. 15
B. koreana	Oct. 30	C. dielsianus	Oct. 10
B. thunbergii	Nov. 10	C. divaricatus	Oct. 10
B. vulgaris	Oct. 20	C. foveolatus	Oct. 5
Betula papyrifera	Aug. 20	C. horizontalis	Oct. 30
Buddleia sp.	Oct. 20	C. lucidus	Oct. 10
Callicarpa sp.	Nov. 5	C. melanocarpus	Sept. 20

C. moupinensis	Sept. 20	Lycium sp.	Oct. 20
C. multiflorus	Nov. 5	Magnolia acuminata	Oct. 5
C. racemiflorus	Aug. 30	M. soulangiana	Oct. 5
C. rugosus	Nov. 30	M. stellata	Oct. 5
C. salicifolius	Nov. 30	Mahonia aquifolium	July 5
C. tomentosus	Oct. 30	Malus baccata	Oct. 20
C. zabelii	Oct. 10	M. robusta	Oct. 30
Crataegus arnoldiana	Aug. 15	M. toringoides	Oct. 20
C. lavallei	Nov. 20	M. many sp.	Oct. 25
C. nitida	Nov. 20	Morus sp.	July 25
C. oxyacantha	Oct. 20	Myrica pensylvanica	Nov. 5
C. phaenopyrum	Nov. 30	Nemopanthus mucronatus	July 5
C. prunifolia	Nov. 20	Nyssa sylvatica	Sept. 20
C. punctata	Sept. 5	Oxydendrum arboreum	Oct. 22
Cytisus nigricans	Aug. 15	Philadelphus virginalis	Sept. 10
C. purpureus	Aug. 15	Photinia villosa	Oct. 20
Daphne mezereum	June 15	Physocarpus sp.	Oct. 20
Elaeagnus multiflora	July 5	Picea sp.	Oct. 15
E. umbellata	Nov. 15	Pieris sp.	Sept. 20
Euonymus alata	Oct. 15	Pinus sp.	Sept. 25
E. americana	Oct. 15	Prinsepia sp.	Aug. 5
E. bungeana	Oct. 15	Prunus canescens	June 15
E. fortunei 'Vegeta'	Oct. 15	P. cerasus	June 30
E. obovata	Oct. 15	P. cersaifera	Aug. 20
Evodia daniellii	Sept. 15	P. glandulosa	Aug. 10
Fagus sp.	Sept. 20	P. japonica	Aug. 5
Fothergilla sp.	Oct. 5	P. maritima	Aug. 8
Gaylussacia sp.	Aug. 15	P. sargentii	June 20
Ginkgo biloba	Oct. 15	P. subhirtella	June 20
Halesia sp.	Sept. 20	P. tomentosa	June 20
Hamamelis sp.	Oct. 5	Pseudolarix amabilis	Oct. 30
Hicoria sp.	Oct. 15	Pseudotsuga menziesii	Oct. 10
Hippophae rhamnoides	Oct. 30	Pyracantha coccinea	Nov. 15
Hydrangea anomala		Quercus sp.	Sept. 10–20
petiolaris	Oct. 10	Rhamnus frangula	Aug. 5
Ilex glabra	Nov. 30	Rhododendron many sp.	Oct. 15
I. laevigata	Sept. 20	Rhodotypos scandens	Nov. 5
I. opaca	Oct. 30	Rhus copallina	Sept. 5
I. verticillata	Oct. 15	R. typhina	Aug. 5
I. yunnanensis	Sept. 20	Ribes odoratum	Aug. 5
Juglans sp.	Oct. 15	Robinia sp.	Oct. 5
Juniperus sp.	Oct. 15	Rosa acicularis	Sept. 15
Kalopanax pictus	Sept. 20	R. agrestis	July 20
Kolkwitzia amabilis	Aug. 20	R. amblyotis	Aug. 5
Laburnum sp.	Aug. 20	R. blanda	Sept. 15
Leucothoe fontanesiana	Oct. 15	R. canina	Oct. 15
Ligustrum sp.	Oct. 30	R. carolina	Aug. 30
Lindera benzoin	Sept. 15	R. coriifolia	Sept. 15
Lonicera altmannii	July 5	R. ecae	July 30
L. bella	July 5	R. eglanteria	Oct. 15
L. chrysantha	July 5	R. harisonii	Aug. 5
L. fragrantissima	May 30	R. helenae	Oct. 15
L. henryi	Nov. 15	R. hugonis	July 20
L. korolkowii	Nov. 15	R. multiflora	Nov. 20
L. maackii	Nov. 15	R. pendulina	Aug. 30
L. maximowiczii	July 5	R. primula	Aug. 5
L. morrowii	June 30	R. roxburghii	July 20
L. standishii	May 30	R. rubrifolia	Sept. 15
L. tatarica	July 5	R. rugosa	Sept. 5
L. xylosteum	July 5	R. setigera	Nov. 15

R. spinosissima	July 20	Viburnum acerifolium	Oct. 15
R. virginiana	Oct. 30	V. alnifolium	Aug. 20
R. wichuraiana	Nov. 15	V. betulifolium	Oct. 5
R. willmottiae	Sept. 15	V. burkwoodii	Oct. 30
Sambucus canadensis	Aug. 30	V. carlesii	Oct. 5
Schisandra chinensis	Sept. 15	V. cassinoides	Oct. 5
Solanum dulcamara	Oct. 5	V. dentatum	Oct. 5
Sorbaronia jackii	Oct. 5	V. dilatatum	Sept. 20
Sorbus sp.	Oct. 5	V. farreri	June 20
Spiraea veitchii	Aug. 20	V. lantana	Aug. 20
Stewartia sp.	Oct. 15	V. lentago	Oct. 20
Symphoricarpos sp.	Oct. 10	V. lobophyllum	Nov. 5
Symplocos paniculata	Sept. 30	V. opulus	Nov. 5
Syringa amurensis	Aug. 30	V. ovatifolium	Oct. 5
Taxus sp.	Oct. 10	V. plicatum	July 15
Thuja occidentalis	Oct. 15	V. prunifolium	Oct. 5
Tilia sp.	Oct. 15	V. sargentii	Nov. 5
Tsuga sp.	Oct. 10	V. setigerum	Oct. 15
Ulmus americana	May 5	V. sieboldii	Aug. 15
U. parvifolia	Oct. 15	V. trilobum	Aug. 30
U. pumila	May 5	V. wrightii	Sept. 15
Vaccinium corymbosum	July 30	Wisteria sp.	Oct. 30
V. oldhamii	Oct. 5	Zanthoxylum americanum	Sept. 5
V. vitis-idaea	July 20		

Cleaning Seeds

Most seeds must be cleaned before they are sown. The fruits of rosaceous plants, viburnums, magnolias, dogwoods and many other fruits with pulp about the seeds, must be cleaned before the seed is shipped or even before it is stored in large quantities, for the rotting pulp quickly heats and in many cases the high temperatures will kill the embryos. Even elm seed must be dried before it is shipped. This seed is frequently picked while it is still slightly green on the tree, or picked up from the ground while it is damp, and if stored or shipped in large quantities before it is thoroughly dry, it may heat and be completely killed on arrival.

On the other hand, many of the seeds produced in dry capsules, like those of the ericaceous plants, spireas, mock oranges, etc., can be merely sun-dried and then shipped.

There are many ingenious methods for cleaning seeds, some of them worked out on the spur of the moment. Cones from evergreen and cone-bearing deciduous trees must be dried and in many cases have hot air applied to them in order for the cones to open and allow the seeds to fall out. For a few cones, this is easily accomplished in the hot sun or on the greenhouse bench, with the cones on screens so that the seed will fall into a receptacle below. For large quantities of cones, the foresters have invented several types of drying kilns.

Conifer seeds and others such as maple and ash, can be shipped with the wings on, but should be dewinged before they are sown. This can be accomplished in several ways, but for small amounts the best method is by hand rubbing; or, secondly, by lightly rubbing the seeds over a screen. Too much pressure can injure the seeds, so care must be taken in this operation. Screening and even fanning of the resultant mixture are means of separating chaff from seed.

Some of the larger seed can be handled by regular farm machinery. Hulls of the Black Walnut, for instance, can be removed by running the fruits through the corn sheller. Various fruits can be run through threshing equipment in order to produce clean seed.

Finally, the pulpy seeds are usually cleaned by macerating them and soaking them in water during which process the pulp and poor seeds usually float to the surface and can be removed, while the viable seeds sink and can be dried later for storage and shipping. Acorns have been "cleaned" by the water method, since the cups and weeviled acorns float and the viable acorns sink to the bottom. Naturally, the amount of seed to be cleaned governs the method chosen.

For small amounts of seed the Waring Blendor is most serviceable. This has been used by several institutions (and possibly similar blenders have been used, as well). One should remove the metal blade of this electrically operated, household machine and substitute one cut from the casing of an automobile tire. This is a small piece of rubber $1\frac{1}{2}$ in. square held horizontally on the revolving axis of the machine. The standard whirling metal blade which comes with the machine will quickly scarify and injure the seeds of many plants and hence should not be used. Even with the rubber blade, the fruits should be completely ripe so that the flesh is easily macerated (or else it should be partly macerated in advance by hand) and the seed put in for no longer than 2 minutes, together with an ample supply of water. The length of time depends on the kind of seed, its degree of softness and the amount of seed. None larger than the fruits of *Prunus americana* or *P. hortulana* should be used. Obviously, only small amounts of seed can be handled in this fashion, but undoubtedly larger equipment could be made if necessary. This method has proved a timely and quick one for cleaning small amounts of pulpy seed.

Many seeds are sun-dried after the cleaning process and then sown, stratified or stored, but if one wants to be certain no disease gets into the seed, a simple treatment with some disinfectant, such as washing in a 5–10% solution of potassium permanganate might be well worth the effort. To kill weevils and worms and other insects, the seeds may be dusted with rotenone, available in most countries. With acorns, carbon bisulfide has been used to kill the weevils. A small amount is placed in a large covered container and the acorns left in long enough to kill the weevils. Naturally the amount of the chemical used depends on the size of the container and the amount of seed to be disinfected. The use of this chemical may not prove suitable for all kinds of seeds.

Shipping Seeds

When seeds must be sent long distances, great care should be taken in their packing and the means by which they are shipped. Every seed collector should know something about the seeds he is sending, how they should be cleaned, and which ones should be shipped as soon as collected. This last point is a very important one. Unfortunately many institutions shipping seeds from abroad, and many a botanical collector as well, consider that all seeds can be handled alike; that is, that they can be stripped from the plants in the fall, cleaned within a month or so and held possibly for 6 months until all the seeds are ready for shipment at one time or until weather conditions are such that the collector can take the time to ship them.

It will be noted from the following lists that some seeds cannot be allowed to dry out, but should be shipped immediately after they are collected. Certain seeds such as those of *Populus*, *Salix*, *Magnolia* and *Ulmus*, should always be shipped promptly by air since they will remain viable for only a very short time,

even under ideal conditions. Willow seeds may remain viable only a few days.

Seeds of *Cytisus*, *Robinia* and *Quercus* are susceptible to attacks of weevils or other insects and if the period of shipment is long and slow, it may well be that the seed will be worthless on arrival. Such seeds should be treated with some material to kill such pests. Carbon bisulfide gas has been used satisfactorily with acorns, but the amount used depends on the size of the closed container in which the fumigating is to be done, the amount of seed and even the kind of seed. One excellent suggestion is that such seeds may be dusted with rotenone when they are placed in the packet, the amount of dust used being equivalent to ¼ the bulk of the seeds.

Any seeds that might be unusually susceptible as disease carriers might be treated with a mild disinfectant, such as a 5–10% solution of potassium permanganate, then dried and bagged for shipment.

Before the days of air transportation, moist sawdust or moist peat moss could not be used if the shipping period were to be lengthy or the temperatures en route likely to be high, for the seeds would either germinate or the high temperatures would cause the packing materials to heat and kill the seeds. To avoid these difficulties, seeds were shipped in charcoal which, being inert, would not heat or harbor fungi, but would absorb a certain amount of moisture and so provide a sufficiently moist atmosphere in the package to prevent the seeds from drying out.

Today, polyethylene bags can be used to excellent advantage. Cuttings, scions, budwood and plants wrapped in this material are sent to many parts of the world. The polyethylene film is impermeable to water vapor, but not to gaseous vapors. Bags made of polyethylene should be tightly sealed, and may contain several paper packets of seeds and a very small amount of moistened moss to keep the small amount of air in the bags slightly humid, for those seeds which should not dry out. Another method for shipping such seeds as acorns or chestnuts would be to dip them in paraffin.

The plant quarantine laws of the United States prohibit the entry of certain seeds into this country. None can be sent in with moist pulp about them. In the northern part of the United States, the more important woody plants the seeds of which are prohibited are *Berberis* species, *Ribes nigrum* and bamboos and their relatives. These same quarantine laws approve only certain packing materials, such as peat moss, sphagnum, excelsior, wood shavings, sawdust, ground cork, buckwheat hulls, expanded vermiculite and charcoal.

Prohibited packing materials are soil, sand, leaves, forest litter, woods moss, hay, straw, etc.—anything taken from direct contact with the soil. Seeds packed in such materials will be prohibited entry.

Seeds of woody plants collected in foreign countries and destined for recipients in the United States must be accompanied by a permit. The Bureau of Entomology and Plant Quarantine of the U.S. Department of Agriculture issues such permits to individuals and institutions upon application. A number is given the applicant and this number appears on a standard green and yellow tag bearing the address of the quarantine station (Hoboken, N.J., Miami, Fla., Laredo, Tex., or San Francisco, Calif.). This required tag is the only address appearing on the outside of the package, other than the collector's name and address in the upper left-hand corner. See QUARANTINES.

The following 3 lists do not contain all those woody plants commonly grown from seed, but they should serve as a guide to collectors to indicate how certain seeds should be handled and how rapidly they should be shipped. Special emphasis should be placed on list "A" as the "perishable" group. List "B" includes those which can be sown or stratified at once or dried and used later. List "C" contains those which can be kept in a dry condition, some of them for periods longer than 1 year.

The procedure in shipping seeds should therefore be:

1. Clean all seeds thoroughly and at once, taking special precautions not to allow pulpy or wet seeds to "heat" before cleaning.
2. Prevent certain seeds from drying out— List "A"—by proper packaging.
3. Properly dry the remainder.
4. Fumigate or in other ways treat for insects or disease pests if necessary.
5. Label all seed packets completely.
6. Ship as soon as picked (and by air) those in List "A."
7. Send the remainder of the shipment as soon as possible, keeping the seeds dry and away from contamination with insect and disease pests.

A. SEEDS WHICH SHOULD NOT BE ALLOWED TO DRY OUT IN SHIPPING

These should be shipped immediately as soon as ripe. They should be sent great distances only by air and should be sown as soon as received. Special precautions should be taken in packaging these for shipment so that they will not dry out en route; otherwise they may be worthless on arrival at their destination. Some will remain viable only a few days (*Salix*); others a few weeks to 6 months (*Cedrus*).

Acer	Davidia	Populus
Aesculus	Diospyros	Potentilla
Alnus	Fagus	Quercus
Amelanchier	Franklinia	Rhus
Ampelopsis	Halesia	Salix
Aralia	Juglans	Sassafras
Asimina	Liriodendron	Shepherdia
Carpinus	Lindera	Sophora
Carya	Liquidambar	Spiraea
Castanea	Lycium	Staphylea
Cedrus	Magnolia	Stewartia
Cercidiphyllum	Mahonia	Styrax
Chamaecyparis	Myrica	Ulmus
lawsoniana	Nandina	Zelkova
Clerodendrum	Nyssa	
Cryptomeria	Ostrya	

B. SEEDS WHICH MAY BE SOWN OR STRATIFIED AS SOON AS RIPE OR
DRIED AND SOWN THE FOLLOWING SPRING

These need not necessarily be shipped quickly by air, but may be sown or stratified as soon as received from the collectors.

Berberis	Celtis	Cotoneaster
Betula	Chaenomeles	Crataegus
Buxus	Chionanthus	Elaeagnus
Caragana	Cladrastis	Exochorda
Celastrus	Cornus	Ginkgo

Gleditsia	Lonicera	Rhodotypos
Hippophae	Malus	Robinia
Ilex	Phellodendron	Taxus
Juniperus	Prunus	Viburnum
Ligustrum	Pyracantha	

C. SEEDS WHICH MAY BE STORED DRY AND SOWN WITHIN THE YEAR

These may be stored and shipped dry, and may be held dry on receipt from collectors. Naturally all seed should be shipped as soon as reasonably possible by the collector, but this group may be held the longest and does not deteriorate so rapidly in shipment as seeds in List "A."

Actinidia	Euonymus	Platanus
Akebia	Evodia	Pseudotsuga
Ailanthus	Fraxinus	Pyrus
Albizia	Hibiscus	Rhododendron
Amorpha	Kalmia	Ribes
Aronia	Koelreuteria	Robinia
Atriplex	Laburnum	Rosa
Callicarpa	Lagerstroemia	Sciadopitys
Calycanthus	Larix	Sophora
Caryopteris	Leucothoe	Sorbus
Catalpa	Libocedrus	Symphoricarpos
Cercis	Metasequoia	Syringa
Chamaecyparis	Morus	Taxodium
Cupressus	Paulownia	Thuja
Cytisus	Philadelphus	Tsuga
Elaeagnus	Physocarpus	Vaccinium
Deutzia	Picea	Vitex
Diervilla	Pinus	Wisteria

To give an idea of the tremendous number of seeds in a pound, the following statistics are given, taken from the U.S. Department of Agriculture Miscellaneous Publication 654.

AVERAGE NUMBER OF CLEANED SEEDS PER POUND

Abies balsamea	59,800
A. concolor	15,100
Acer platanoides	2600
A. rubrum	22,800
A. saccharum	6100
Aesculus hippocastanum	109
Alnus incana	666,000
Amelanchier alnifolia	82,000
Amorpha canescens	296,000
Aronia arbutifolia	256,000
Berberis thunbergii	27,000
Betula papyrifera	1,380,000
Carya ovata	100
Cedrus deodara	3600
Chaemaecyparis lawsoniana	210,000
Clematis vitalba	320,000
Cocos nucifera	1
Cornus florida	4500
C. serica	18,700
Corylus avellana	480
Cotoneaster horizontalis	64,000
Cupressus macrocarpa	66,000

Elaeagnus angustifolius	5200
Euonymus europaeus	10,900
Fagus grandifolia	1600
Fraxinus americana	10,000
Ilex opaca	27,000
I. verticillata	92,000
Juglans nigra	40
J. regia	40
Juniperus virginiana	43,200
Larix decidua	77,000
Ligustrum vulgare	20,000
Liquidambar styraciflua	82,000
Liriodendron tulipifera	14,000
Lonicera tatarica	142,000
Magnolia grandiflora	5800
Malus baccata	66,000
Morus alba	235,000
Myrica cerifera	56,000
Nyssa sylvatica	3300
Ostrya virginiana	30,000
Oxydendrum arboreum	5,500,000
Parthenocissus quinquefolia	18,000
Picea abies	64,000
P. glauca	240,000
Pinus resinosa	52,000
P. strobus	27,000
Platanus occidentalis	204,000
Populus tremuloides	3,600,000
Prunus avium	2600

P. virginiana	5800
Pseudotsuga menziesii	42,000
Pyrus communis	15,000
Quercus alba	150
Q. macrocarpa	75
Q. virginiana	390
Rhamnus frangula	19,000
Rhododendron catawbiense	5,000,000
Rhus glabra	68,600
Ribes aureum	217,000
Robinia pseudoacacia	24,000
Rosa blanda	44,000
Rubus occidentalis	334,000
Sambucus canadensis	232,000
Sassafras albidum	5000
Sequoia sempervirens	122,000
Shepherdia argentea	41,000
Sorbus aucuparia	130,000
Symphoricarpos orbiculatus	144,000
Syringa vulgaris	90,000
Taxodium distichum	4800
Taxus canadensis	21,000
Thuja occidentalis	346,000
Tilia americana	5000
Tsuga canadensis	187,000
Ulmus americana	68,000
Viburnum trilobum	13,200
Vitis riparia	15,200
Zizyphus jujuba	750

SELAGINELLA (sel-aj-in-ELL-a)

pallescens 1′ Zone 10 Emmel Selaginella

A mosslike, lacey, almost fernlike, branching, flowerless herb with scalelike leaves; grown in the greenhouse for its interesting foliage. Easily propagated by spores or cuttings in the early spring in moist, shaded situations where the temperature is at least 70° F. Native to tropical America. It needs high humidity in which to grow properly.

SELECTION. This refers to the selecting of seedlings, usually hybrid seedlings, with the main object of picking out plants that have better or more desirable characteristics than others in the same seed lot. This has become a large-scale experimental operation, where thousands of seedlings are grown with only a few selected for further study, the remainder discarded. With annual plants this is often the means by which new varieties are obtained. With woody plants, which take a longer time to flower and fruit and which take more space, it is a costly operation. When a woody plant is "selected" it is propagated asexually so that all the characteristics of the progeny will be identical to those of the parent. Many of our best ornamental annual herbaceous and woody plants as well as chance seedlings, have arisen in the nursery row among hundreds of others, or in nature, and have been spotted by some keen-eyed individual because they are different and more desirable than the majority of the others. The earnest gardener will continually be on the watch for variants in his garden, be they large or small, and if any worthwhile variants are found he will take steps to propagate them, preferably asexually, wherever that is possible.

SELENICEREUS (see-lee-ni-SEE-reus)

macdonaldiae climbing Zone 10 Queen-of-the-night, Lady-of-the-night

A night-blooming cactus, very showy, with flowers reddish yellow on the outside, 10–14 in. long, the numerous petals white, not fragrant. The ribbed stems have some aerial roots aiding in the climbing habits of this species. Spines small and few. Often grown as a house plant. Native to Uruguay and Argentina. For culture see CACTI and SUCCULENTS.

SELF-FERTILE. The pollen of the flowers of a single plant will fertilize the pistils of the flowers of that plant.

SELF-HEAL = *Prunella vulgaris*

SELF-STERILE. The pollen of the flowers of a single plant will not fertilize the pistils of the flowers of that plant. In other words, pollen from another plant of a different clone is necessary, or cross-fertilization is required.

SEMESAN. A mercuric fungicide, which see.

SEMIARUNDINARIA species. See BAMBOO.

SEMIDOUBLE. Partly changed into a double flower with the inner stamens perfect and the outer stamens petallike.

SEMPERVIVUM (sem-per-VY-vum). Succulent herbs from the Old World, mostly the Alps, the houseleeks are excellent garden plants, the ones mentioned here being hardy in the North, but still others are tender. They grow in small rosettes of succulent leaves and multiply by the simple process of forming new plants about the base of the old. They can be grown in full sun, in hot dry situations and are ideal far planting in rock gardens, in or on rock walls where they really need very little soil in which to thrive. The name *Sempervivum* means live forever, and in Central Europe it has been a superstition for many years that if a Houseleek is planted on the roof of a house neither lightning nor fire will harm it.

The flowers are greenish, yellow and red, sometimes not outstanding at all, but it is the foliage and its sturdy ability to last the winters, that makes these plants valuable. Some are used for house plants. When this is done, they should be potted up in the fall, but left outdoors or in a cold pit until Jan. before being brought inside to give them a needed dormant rest period in the cold. Houseleeks, especially *S. tectorum*, can grow so tightly together in a dense mass of small rosettes that they can be even used as a ground cover for a small garden area. There is one in our ground-cover demonstration plot that has been a tight mass of rosettes for 10 years, never sprayed or fertilized but always in good appearance throughout the entire year.

Propagation is very easy, merely by taking the small rosettes about the base of the old plant and potting them separately. Also seed can be sown in early spring or summer. Excellent plants of very easy culture, suitable for planting about almost any kind of rock that may appear in the garden.

arachnoideum   **4″**   **Zone 5**   **Spiderweb Houseleek**
Rosettes of succulent foliage, ¾ in. across, and leaves connected by light cobweblike strands; flowers bright red, 1 in. across, in few-flowered panicles. The flowers are more ornamental than those of any other Houseleek. Native to mountains of southern Europe.

arenarium   **9″**   **Zone 5**
Globular rosettes of foliage with the small succulent leaves reddish brown on the back; flowers ½ in. long, pale yellow, tinted reddish on the outside. Native to the eastern Alps.

braunii = *S. montanum braunii*

calcareum = *S. tectorum calcareum*

x fauconnetti (*arachnoideum* x *tectorum*   **8″**   **Zone 5**
Rosettes of foliage 1½ in. across; leaves tinged with red and purple and about ¾ in. long; flowers bright red, 1 in. wide. Native to eastern France in the Jura Mountains.

x fimbriatum   **10″**   **Zone 5**
Rosettes of foliage 1½ in. across, oblanceolate succulent leaves tipped with hairs, the other ones red; flowers an inch across, bright red. Considered a hybrid of *S. arachnoideum*. Native to the eastern Alps and the Pyrenees.

globiferum   **1′**   **Zone 5**
Usually considered as a variety of *S. montanum*, with rosettes 3 in. across; flowers pale yellow and an inch wide. Native to Russia. An attractive Houseleek.

mettenianum = *S. tectorum*

montanum   **6″**   **Zone 5**
One of the most common of the houseleeks seen in the Alps and common in gardens. Rosettes of foliage 1¾ in. across; leaves dark green, covered with dense hairs. Flowers bluish purple in hairy panicles 2 in. across. The var. **braunii** is 9 in. high, bears rosettes of foliage 2 in. wide and dull yellow flowers 1 in. wide in panicles 4 in. wide.

ruthenicum   **1′**   **Zone 5**
Rosettes of foliage to 1½ in. across; leaves obovate and pubescent; flowers pale yellow, an inch across, with purple filaments. Native to Eastern Europe.

soboliferum   **9″**   **Zone 5**
Rosettes of foliage 1½ in. across; leaves obovate to 1 in. long, with the outer ones tinged brown; flowers pale yellow in panicles 4 in. across. Native to Austria.

tectorum   **1′**   **Zone 4**   **Hen-and-chickens**
The most commonly grown in American gardens, listed as more hardy than the other

Sempervivum tectorum. The popular Hen-and-chickens makes an interesting specimen, ground cover, or pot plant for the house. (*Photo by Arnold Arboretum, Jamaica Plain, Mass.*)

species only because it is known to be growing in colder areas in America. The sturdy rosettes of grayish leaves are 3–4 in. across; flowers are pink, up to an inch across in ft.-high hairy stalks. Sometimes called Old-man-and-old-woman or the Common Houseleek; often brought into the house over winter as a house plant. Native to Europe and Asia. Many varieties are listed in catalogues. The var. **calcareum** has glaucous leaves tipped with red-brown; flowers pale red, ¾ in. wide on 3–4 panicles.

SENECIO (sen-EE-sio). This genus of the Daisy Family contains a large number of widely varying herbs, shrubs or small trees, sometimes fleshy, with either alternate or basal leaves and single or clustered flowers of the daisy type. Some of the herbaceous kinds are grown for garden display, some are rank weeds, but all can be easily grown. The annuals are grown by seed, and the perennial types, either by seed, stem or root cuttings or division.

articulatus 2′ **Zone 10 Candleplant** A succulent plant from Africa with swollen, fleshy branches covered with a waxy bloom, leaves deeply lobed and white flower heads about ½ in. wide in long stalked corymbs. Sometimes used as a house plant.

aureus 1′–2′ **Zone 4 Golden Groundsel** Although most of the composites flower in summer, this, as well as *S. obovatus*, flower in the spring from April to May or June. It is a smooth-stemmed perennial with toothed, orbicular leaves and deeply lobed, ovate to lanceolate stem leaves. The deep yellow flower heads are in a branched terminal cluster, each being 1–1½ in. wide and composed of 8–10 notched ray flowers and finely lobed disk flowers. It is a swamp-loving plant native to North America and is excellent for the bog garden. The plant may be divided in spring.

cineraria 2½′ **Zone 6 Silver Groundsel** Native to the Mediterranean Region, this is sometimes popularly called Dusty Miller, but this name should be kept only for *Centaurea cineraria*. The Silver Groundsel is a perennial but can be grown as an annual. The leaves are deeply cut into blunt parts and are white woolly. The yellow flower heads are ½ in. across and bloom from late spring to fall. An interesting garden plant because of its gray foliage; it prefers full sun. The var. **aureo-marginatus** bears leaves with a yellow to orange border. Seeds can be sown indoors in March and the seedlings set out after frost a foot apart.

cruentus 18″ **Zone 9** The Cineraria of the florists shops is supposed to have originated with this Canary Island species, probably by hybridizing with other *Senecio* species. This one has large cordate-ovate leaves, short woolly stems and purple-red flowers. For information and culture of the popular hybrids see CINERARIA.

jacobaea 4′ **Zone 4 Ragwort Groundsel** Biennial or perennial, with stem leaves sessile, flowers yellow in heads ½ in. across. Native to Europe, naturalized in New England. Cattle have been poisoned by eating this plant.

macroglossus 'Variegatum' vine **Zone 10 Variegated Wax Vine** Waxy, variegated leaves, similar in size and shape to those of English ivy, vigorous-growing house plant. Older vines have small, yellow, 2½″ wide flowers. Roots easily. An excellent

house plant in the North.

mikanioides twining **Zone 9 German-ivy** An old-fashioned house plant, native to South Africa, and easily rooted, from cuttings placed in water or moist sand. The thin alternate leaves, shaped like those of the English Ivy, with 4 or 5 lobes, are yellow-green and the flowers are yellow, small and daisylike. It climbs by twining and as a house plant does best with a cool winter temperature of about 50° F.

obovatus 12″–18″ **Zone 4 Squaw-weed** Similar to *S. aureus*, although somewhat rare, this species has a rosette of perennial, obovate, basal leaves and stem leaves more nearly lyre shaped. It is a plant of dry, rocky outcrops from New England to Mich. and southward to Fla. It may be divided in spring.

pulcher 2′–4′ **Zone 6 Showy Groundsel** An erect-growing, vigorous perennial from Uruguay and Argentina, not often grown in U.S. and difficult to find in nurseries. The stems have a white cobweb appearance, not very leafy but the leaves are oblong-lanceolate, 4–10 in. long. The flower heads are 2–3 in. across, with the rays red-purple and the central disk yellow.

vira-vira 2′ **Zone 9 Argentine Groundsel** Somewhat woody but it can be grown in the North as an annual. This is native to Argentina and is valued like *S. cineraria* for its gray foliage. The leaves are more finely divided than those of *S. cineraria*. In the South it can be grown from cuttings, in the North, when used as an annual, from seed. This has been used in planting window boxes because of its valued gray foliage.

vulgaris 1½′ **annual Groundsel** A weed, introduced from Europe, now widely naturalized throughout the northern U.S. and Canada, with alternate, lyre-shaped, lobed leaves with bristles on the margin, flowers in heads or clusters about ½ in. across. The disk flowers are yellow but since there are no ray flowers it is not outstanding in flower. The seeds have threadlike appendages similar to those of the Milkweed and are easily blown by the wind.

SENNA. See CASSIA.

SENSITIVE-PLANT = *Mimosa pudica*

SEPAL. A division of the calyx.

SEPTUM. A partition.

SEQUOIA (see-KWOY-a)
gigantea = *Sequoiadendron giganteum*
sempervirens 365′ **Zone 7 Redwood** The Redwood is native in southern Ore. and Calif. The small evergreen needles about 1 in. long and 2-ranked, somewhat like those of hemlocks. The tree grows open and straight with a massive trunk which may measure 75–85 ft. in circumference and the small cones are up to 1 in. long. The bark is very thick and the

wood red, solid and long lasting. These are the tallest trees in North America, some being over 300 ft. tall. This species does not grow well in the eastern U.S. but it makes a beautiful park tree where it has plenty of room in which to grow. Sometimes called "Coast Redwood" because of the extensive forests of this tree along the Pacific Coast of Calif. For propagation see SEQUOIADENDRON. Redwood burls, bought as souvenirs, if placed in a dish of water in a warm room will frequently send up many shoots, although they may not root or will root but with great difficulty.

SEQUOIADENDRON (se-kwoy-a-DEN-dron)
giganteum   300′   Zone 6   Giant Sequoia
Native only in small areas of Calif., this species does not grow as high as *Sequoia sempervirens*

Sequoiadendron giganteum: The Giant Redwood of California. (*Photo by Arnold Arboretum, Jamaica Plain, Mass.*)

but it will grow larger in trunk size. The 'General Sherman' tree in Sequoia National Park is 37 ft. in dia. at the base and still 17 ft. in dia. 120 ft. above the ground. Trees of this species are estimated to be 3000 years old, older than most other living trees in North America except some *Pinus aristata* specimens. This Giant Sequoia is also hardier than *Sequoia sempervirens* and makes a more interesting ornamental when it is small. The evergreen scalelike needles are about

½ in. long and the cones are 2–3 in. long. This is not a tree for the small garden!

Propagation

Seeds should be stratified for 2 months at 40° F., then sown. Shoots which appear on burls can be propagated as cuttings, although if left on the burls, the burls may not root.

SERENOA (ser-en-O-a)
repens   3′   Zone 8   Saw Palmetto
The hardiest of the palms, native in N.Car., widely distributed over large areas in the South, westward to Tex. and Ark. It is mostly prostrate or has creeping branches and, when unmolested, grows into great masses of foliage.

SERISSA (ser-ISS-a)
foetida variegata   2′   Zone 7   Yellow-rim
A small shrub from southeastern Asia, with small, opposite, ovate leaves about ½ in. across with yellow margins; mentioned merely because it has been recommended as a colorful pot plant or dish-garden plant grown in the greenhouse. The white funnel-shaped flowers are only ½ in. long. Propagated by softwood cuttings.

SERRATE. Having teeth pointed forward.

SERRULATE. Serrate with fine teeth.

SERVICEBERRY. See AMELANCHIER.

SESAME = *Sesamum indicum*

SESAMUM (SES-am-um)
indicum   2′   annual   Sesame
An oriental herb from China, India and Turkey, known for centuries, with soft, fuzzy, dark green leaves, square stems and creamy-white to lavender flowers, similar to those of the Foxglove, about an inch long and borne close to the stem. The Romans used the seed, ground, as a paste for use on bread. It is a prized food in the Orient, and used in America in baked goods and confectionery. The seeds are about ⅛ in. long. Easily grown from seed, the plant does well in areas with long, hot summers.

SESBANIA (ses-BAY-nia)
exaltata   12′   annual   Hemp Sesbania
A native weed of the central U.S. and southward, and is sometimes grown as a cover crop for improving the soil, especially in Calif. The alternate compound leaves have 30–70 leaflets, each about 1 in. long; the flowers are yellow, about ½ in. across, and pealike; pods are flat and 7–9 in. long. It is a member of the Pea Family, the reason it is used as a green manure crop.

SESSILE. Without any stalk.

SETACEOUS. Bristlelike.

SETARIA (see-TAY-ria)
italica   5′   annual   Foxtail Millet
A grass, probably originating in cultivation, not

known in the wild, grown for forage or hay; with rough grasslike leaves about ¾ in. wide; flowering cluster of seeds 2–10 in. long. Several varieties vary in the color of the grains, i.e., black, reddish orange or yellow.

verticillata   4′   annual   Bristly Foxtail
A weed grass, introduced from Europe, common on waste ground in the Midwest, with long, terminal, dense, yellow seed heads up to 8 in. long.

viridis   4′   annual   Green Foxtail
A weed grass similar to *S. verticillata*, but with seed heads slightly pointed and green, not yellow.

SETOSE. Beset with bristles.

SEVENLEAF CREEPER = *Parthenocissus heptaphylla*

SEVERINIA (sev-er-IN-ia)
buxifolia   6′   Zone 8   Chinese Box-orange
An unusually spiny plant for use in hedges in Zone 8 areas, this comes from China and Formosa and has small white flowers in the spring and round, black, pea-sized berries in the fall. The leaves are rounded and somewhat like those of Box, about an inch long, but there is a small spine on each side of the bud, making this a plant which can be used in barrier hedges.

SEVIN. An insecticide, which see.

SEWAGE SLUDGE. An organic fertilizer containing about 6% nitrogen and 2.5% phosphoric acid. Actually it is dry, processed sewage and the contents varies. A widely advertised form goes under the trade name of Milorganite. See SOILS.

SEXES SEPARATE. See DIOECIOUS PLANTS.

SHADBLOW. See AMELANCHIER.

SHADE, PLANTS FOR. There is often the need to select plants which will grow and look well in the shade. There are all degrees of shade; light shade caused by high branches of an open-growing tree, dense shade caused by a grove of evergreen trees, and intermittent shade caused by a building or trees interrupting continual direct sunlight on a certain garden spot.

Shade caused by trees or tall shrubs brings another growing hazard—that of root competition. A Norway Maple or Beech with low branches creates much dense shade. If it were only this some plants could be selected to grow underneath them. However, their numerous feeding roots are very near the surface of the soil and there are many times when it is practically impossible to grow anything in the shade of such trees. Rather than to be continually disappointed with a series of trials, it is far better to place flagstones or crushed stone under the tree if the bare ground is unsightly.

Also the deeper the shade, the fewer the plants which can be selected to grow in such situations. Soil in the shade should be very well prepared (see SOILS, SOIL MIXTURES, SOIL OPERATIONS) prior to setting out plants in order to provide the best growing conditions possible. Occasionally it may even be necessary to remove encroaching tree roots in order to provide a better growing medium. Usually such roots have a way of growing back into the area unless they are periodically cut or a concrete wall is sunk several feet deep around the area in question.

Most plants grow better in full sunlight than they will in shade, but there are some which require some shade in order to grow well. There are others which will endure shade better than most, and both kinds will be found in the following list:

TREES WITHSTANDING SHADE

SCIENTIFIC NAME	HEIGHT	ZONE	COMMON NAME
Acer circinatum	25′	5	Vine Maple
A. pensylvanicum	36′	3	Striped Maple
A. spicatum	25′	2	Mountain Maple
• Amelanchier sp.	25′–60′	4	Serviceberries
، Cercis canadensis	36′	4	Eastern Redbud
Cornus florida	40′	4	Flowering Dogwood
. Ilex sp.	24′–70′	5–7	Hollies
Podocarpus macrophyllus	70′	7	Yew Podocarpus
Prunus pensylvanica	36′	2	Pin Cherry
• Rhododendron maximum	12′–36′	3	Rosebay Rhododendron
Thuja occidentalis	60′	2	American Arborvitae
، Tsuga sp.	90′	4–5	Hemlocks

SHRUBS WITHSTANDING SHADE

Abelia sp.	5′	5–8	Abelias
Acanthopanax sieboldianus	9′	4	Five-leaved Aralia
Alnus sp.	9′–60′	2	Alders

SCIENTIFIC NAME	HEIGHT	ZONE	COMMON NAME
Amelanchier sp.	6'–25'	4	Serviceberries
Ardisia crispa	1'	9	Coral Ardisia
Aronia sp.	1½'–9'	4	Chokeberries
Aucuba japonica	15'	7	Japanese Aucuba
Azara microphylla	12'–18'	8	Boxleaf Azara
Berberis sp.	2'–10'	5–7	Barberries
Brunfeldsia sp.	3'	10	Raintree
Calycanthus floridus	9'	4	Carolina Allspice
Camellia japonica	8'–45'	7	Common Camellia
C. sinensis	30'	9	Tea
Cercis chinensis	40'	6	Chinese Judas-tree
Chamaecyparis obtusa vars.	2'–15'	3	Hinoki Cypress vars.
Chimonanthus praecox	8'	7	Wintersweet
Chionanthus virginicus	30'	4	Fringetree
Clethra alnifolia	9'	3	Summersweet
Colutea arborescens	12'	5	Bladder-senna
Comptonia peregrina	4'	2	Sweet Fern
Cornus sp.	1½'–24'	2–8	Dogwoods
Corylopsis sp.	10'–18'	5–7	Winter-hazels
Corylus sp.	15'–30'	3–4	Hazels
Cotoneaster salicifolius floccosus	15'	5	
Daphne mezereum	3'	4	February Daphne
D. odora	4'–6'	7	Winter Daphne
Diervilla sessilifolia	4½'	4	Southern Bush-honeysuckle
Euonymus japonicus	15'	8	Evergreen Euonymus
Fatsia japonica	15'	7	Fatsia
Fothergilla sp.	3'–9'	5	Fothergillas
Fuchsia magellanica	3'	5–6	Magellan Fuchsia
Gaultheria shallon	5'	5	Salal, Shallon
Gaylussacia brachycera	18"	5	Box-huckleberry
Hamamelis sp.	10'–30'	4–5	Witch-hazels
Hardenbergia comptoniana	Vine	9	Compton Coral-pea
Hydrangea macrophylla	12'	5–6	House Hydrangea
H. quercifolia	6'	5	Oak-leaved Hydrangea
Hypericum sp.	1'–6'	4–7	St.-John's-wort
Ilex sp.	9'–30'	3–6	Hollies
Illicium floridanum	9'	7	Florida Anise Tree
Jacobina sp.	2'–5'	10	Plume-flower
Kalmia sp.	3'–30'	2–4	Mountain-laurels
Laurus nobilis	30'	7	Sweet Bay, Laurel
Leucothoe fontanesiana	6'	4	Drooping Leucothoe
Ligustrum sp.	6'–30'	3–7	Privets
Lindera benzoin	15'	4	Spice Bush
Lonicera sp.	3'–15'	2–7	Honeysuckles
Lycium halimifolium	5'	4	Common Matrimony-vine
Magnolia virginiana	6'–60'	5	Sweet Bay
Mahonia sp.	10"–12'	5–6	Mahonias, Holly-grapes
Michelia figo	15'	7–8	Banana-shrub
Myrica sp.	9'–36'	2–6	Bayberry, Wax-Myrtle
Nandina domestica	8'	7	Nandina
Osmanthus fragrans	30'	8–9	Sweet Osmanthus
Pachysandra terminalis	Ground cover	5	Japanese Spurge
Paxistima canbyi	12"	5	Canby Pachistima
Philesia magellanica	3'	8	Magellan Box-lily
Phillyrea latifolia	30'	7	
Photinia sp.	15'–36'	4–7	Photinias
Pieris sp.	6'–12'	4–7	Andromedas
Pittosporum tobira	10'	8	Japanese Pittosporum

SCIENTIFIC NAME	HEIGHT	ZONE	COMMON NAME
Pyracantha sp.	6'–18'	6–7	Firethorns
Raphiolepis umbellata	6'	7	Yeddo-Hawthorn
Rhamnus sp.	6'–30'	2	Buckthorns
• Rhododendron sp.	4½'–36'	2–7	Azaleas, Rhododendrons
Rhodotypos scandens	6'	5	Jetbead
Rubus odoratus	9'	3	Flowering Raspberry
Ruscus aculeatus	1½'–4'	7	Butcher's Broom
Sabal minor	3'–4'	9	Dwarf Palmetto
Sambucus carulea	45'	5	Blueberry Elder
S. pubens	12'–24'	4	Scarlet Elder
Sarcococca ruscifolia	6'	7	Sarcococcas
Sasa palmata	5'–8'	5–6	Bamboo
Severinia buxifolia	6'	8	Chinese Box-orange
Skimmia japonica	4'	7	Japanese Skimmia
Stachyurus praecox	12'	6	
Symphoricarpos sp.	3'–6'	2–5	Coralberry
Taxus sp.	3'–60'	2–6	Yews
Thuja sp.	3'–60'	2–6	Arborvitaes
Torreya sp.	40'–70'	7	Torreya
Tsuga canadensis vars.	2'–10'	4	Common Hemlock varieties
Vaccinium sp.	8"–27'	2–7	Blueberries
Viburnum sp.	3'–12'	2–7	Viburnums
Vinca minor	4"	4	Periwinkle
Xanthorhiza simplicissima	2'	4	Yellow-root
Zamia integrifolia	1½'	9	Coontie
Zenobia pulverulenta	6'	5	Dusty Zenobia

	PERENNIALS FOR SHADE		
• Aconitum sp.	5'	2–4	Monkshood
Aegopodium podograria	6"–14"	3	Goutweed
• Ajuga sp.	4"–12"	4	Bugleweed
Anchusa azurea	3'–5'	3	Italian Bugloss
• Anemone sp.	6"–18"	3–8	Anemones
• Aquilegia sp.	1'–3'	2–3	Columbines
• Aruncus sylvester	5'–7'	2–3	Sylvan Goats-beard
• Asperula odorata	8"	2–3	Sweet Woodruff
• Aster sp.	1'–3'	2–3	Asters
• Astilbe sp.	2'–3½'	5–6	Astilbe
• Baptisia australis	3'–4'	2–3	Blue Wild Indigo
Begonia sp.	1'–8'	6–10	Begonias
Billbergia nutans	1½'	10	Blue Rim Airbrom
Brunnera macrophylla	1½'–2'	3	Heartleaf Brunnera
Campanula rapunculoides	3'	2–3	Creeping Bellflower
C. rotundifolia	1'–2'	2–3	Bluebell-of-Scotland
Cleone glabra	3'	3	White Turtle-head
• Cimicifuga racemosa	6'–8'	2–3	Snakeroot
Cineraria cruenta	1'–3'	10	Cineraria
• Convallaria majalis	8"	2	Lily-of-the-valley
• Corydalis sp.	8"–18"	3	Corydalis
Dicentra eximia	1'–2'	2–3	Fringed Bleeding-heart
• D. spectabilis	2'	2–3	Common Bleeding-heart
Dictamnus albus	3'	2–3	Gasplant
• Dodecatheon meadia	6"–20"	3	Common Shooting Star
Doronicum caucasicum	2'–5'	5	Leopardbane
• Epimedium sp.	9"	3	Epimediums
• Eupatorium maculatum	6'–10'	2–3	Joe-Pye-weed

SCIENTIFIC NAME	HEIGHT	ZONE	COMMON NAME
• Ferns—many	3"–5'	3–10	Ferns
Filipendula ulmaria	6'	2–3	Queen-of-the-meadow
Galax urceolata	6"–12"	3	Galax
• Galium mollugo	3'	3	White Bedstraw
• Geranium sanguineum	12"	3	Blood-red Geranium
• Hemerocallis sp.	1½'–6'	3–7	Daylilies
• Heuchera sanguinea	12"	3	Coral-bells
Hibiscus moscheutos	3'–6'	5	Common Rose Mallow
• Hosta sp.	1'–3'	3	Plantain-lilies
Hypericum sp.	1'–6'	2–6	St.-John's-wort
• Iberis sempervirens	12"	2–3	Evergreen Candytuft
Impatiens wallerana (*I. sultani*)	2½'	Annual, perennial	Garden Balsam
Lathyrus latifolius	9'	3	Perennial Pea Vine
• Ligularia clivorum	3'–4'	5	Bigleaf Golden-ray
• Lobelia cardinalis	2'–3'	2	Cardinal-flower
Lychnis chalcedonica	2'–3'	2–3	Maltese Cross
Lythrum salicaria	3'	2–3	Purple Loosestrife
Meconopsis sp.	1½'–6'	6–7	Blue-poppy
• Mertensia virginica	2'–5'	2–3	Virginia Bluebells
• Monarda didyma	3'	3	Bee-balm
• Myosotis sp.	6"–3'	2–3	Forget-me-nots
Oenothera missouriensis	1'	2–3	Ozark Sundrops
Oxalis sp.	3"–12"	3–9	Oxalis
Pachysandra terminalis	Ground cover	5	Pachysandra
• Phlox—certain sp.	5"–4'	3–8	
Physostegia virginiana	4'	2–3	Virginia Lion's-heart
• Platycodon grandiflorum	2½'	2–3	Balloonflower
Polemonium sp.	4"–2'	2–7	Polemoniums
Poterium sanguisorba	2'	3	Salad Burnet
• Primula sp.	3"–2'	2–8	Primrose
• Pulmonaria sp.	1'	2–6	Lungworts
Rudbeckia, several sp.	2'–12'	2–3	Coneflowers
Saintpaulia ionantha	6"	10	African-violet
Saponaria officinalis	2'–3'	2–3	Bouncing Bet
Saxifraga stolonifera (*S. sarmentosa*)	2'	7	Strawberry Saxifrage
Sedum sp.	2"–3'	2–7	Stonecrop
Sinningia speciosa	10"	10	Common Gloxinia
• Solidago caesia	1'–3'	4	Wreath Goldenrod
Tanacetum vulgare	3'	2–3	Common Tansy
• Thalictrum dipterocarpum	2'–7'	4	Yunnan Meadow-rue
• Tradescantia virginiana	1'–3'	4	Virginia Spiderwort
• Trillium sp.	12"–18"	3–6	Trilliums
• Trollius sp.	2'	3–5	Globeflowers
Valeriana officinalis	4'	5	Common Valerian
Veronica prostrata	8"	5	Harebell Speedwell
Vinca major	Trailing	7	Big Periwinkle
• Viola sp.	6"–12"	2–3	Violets
VINES WITHSTANDING SHADE			
Akebia quinata	Vine	4	Fiveleaf Akebia
Ampelopsis sp.	Vine	4–7	Ampelopsis
Asparagus plumosus	Vine	8	Fern Asparagus
Celastrus sp.	Vine	2–4	Bittersweets
Euonymus fortunei vars.	Vine	5	Wintercreeper
Hedera helix	Vine	5	English Ivy
Hydrangea anomala petiolaris	Vine	4	Climbing Hydrangea

SCIENTIFIC NAME	HEIGHT	ZONE	COMMON NAME
Lapageria rosea	Vine	10	Red Chile-bells
Lonicera japonica 'Halliana'	Vine	4	Hall's Honeysuckle
L. sempervirens	Vine	3	Trumpet Honeysuckle
Parthenocissus quinquefolia	Vine	3	Virginia Creeper
Philodendron sp.	Vine	10	Philodendrons
Pueraria lobata	Vine	6	Kudzu Vine
Smilax sp.	Vine	4-7	Greenbriers
Trachelospermum jasminoides	Vine	9	Star Jasmine
Vitis sp.	Vine	4-7	Grapes

ANNUALS FOR SHADE

SCIENTIFIC NAME	HEIGHT	COMMON NAME
Ageratum houstonianum	6″-18″	Ageratum
Bellis perennis	6″	English Daisy
Clarkia sp.	2′-3′	Clarkia
Digitalis purpurea	2′-4′ (Biennial)	Foxglove
Impatiens balsamina	2½′	Garden Balsam
Lobularia maritima	1′	Sweet Alyssum
Lunaria annua	3′	Honesty
Matricaria recutita	2′	German Camomile
Mimulus cupreus	8″	Chilean Monkey-flower
Myosotis sylvatica	9″-24″	Woodland Forget-me-not
Nicotiana alata	1½′-4′	Winged Tobacco
Nigella damascena	1′-2′	Love-in-a-mist
Reseda odorata	6″	Mignonette
Rudbeckia bicolor	2′	Thimbleflower
Salpiglossis sinuata	2½′	Painted-tongue
Torenia fournieri	12″	Blue Torenia
Viola sp.	6″-12″	Violets

SHADE TREE FERTILIZING. See SOILS, FERTILIZERS.

SHALLON = *Gaultheria shallon*

SHALLOT (*Allium ascalonicum*). A perennial plant which seldom produces seed, but the bulb when planted divides into a number of cloves or small bulblets which remain attached at the bottom. It is sometimes grown for the dry bulbs but usually for the young plants which are used as green onions. Shallot is grown by planting the small bulbs in the same manner as onion sets and their subsequent care and cultivation is the same. See ONIONS. It is an important crop in sections of the South where it is grown as a green or bunching onion for the northern markets.

GRANT B. SNYDER

SHALLU = *Sorghum vulgare roxburghii*

SHAMROCK. Several plants have been given this name, but the most common is White Clover, *Trifolium repens*. Others are *Medicago lupulina* and Wood Sorrel (*Oxalis*).

SHAMROCK-PEA = *Parochetus communis*

SHEATH. A tubular envelope, as the lower part of the leaf in grasses.

SHEEPBURR. See ACAENA.

SHEEP-LAUREL = *Kalmia angustifolia*

SHELLFLOWER. See ALPINIA.

SHELTERBELT. See WINDBREAK.

SHEPHERDIA (shep-HER-dia)
argentea   18′   Zone 2   Buffalo-berry Much taller growing than *S. canadensis*, also this has silvery foliage, and is native over the same area. This has small red fruits that are sour but edible. In fact, early settlers used these a great deal for making jellies. It can be successfully sheared to form a very nice hedge. The berries, when sweetened, were considered a delicacy by the Indians.
canadensis   7′   Zone 2   Russet Buffalo-berry This plant is dioecious, that is, male and female flowers are on different plants and they both should be present to assure fruiting. A native of central and northern North America; the gray-green to silver foliage and small red berries in large clusters, during the early summer, are the 2 very important reasons the plant is used in

landscape work. It is well suited for dry, alkaline soils especially in the Midwest and Prairie States, in places where better shrubs will not grow. In good, fertile soils, better plants might be used.

Propagation

Do not let the seeds dry out but stratify as soon as ripe for 3 months at 41° F., then sow. Since the sexes are separate in this genus, known sexes are sometimes grafted on seedlings or *Elaeagnus* understock has been used. Root cuttings have proved successful. See STRATIFICATION, CUTTINGS, GRAFTING, etc.

SHEPHERD'S PURSE = *Capsella bursa-pastoris*

SHIBATAEA sp. See BAMBOO.

SHIELD FERNS. See DRYOPTERIS.

SHOOTING-STAR. See DODECATHEON.

SHORTIA (SHORT-ia)

galacifolia 8″ **Zone** 4 **Oconee-bells**
A delightful ground cover or subject for the moist rockery. It should be given a situation in the shade, often complete shade, in a rich, moist soil with plenty of organic matter. Also, in the North, a light covering of oak leaves might be given it over winter. In just the correct conditions it has been known to survive for 25 years or more in a garden where winter temperatures reached −40° F. It is a native American plant found growing in N.Car. and S.Car. When in bloom there is no plant more dainty and beautiful in this size group. The evergreen leaves are 1–5 in. across and are tinged with bronze in the winter. They all arise from the base of the plant in a rosette. The nodding, white, bell-shaped flowers fade to a delicate pink. They are 1 in. across on upright stalks, with the corolla deeply 5 lobed, borne in May and June. It is propagated by division.

uniflora 8″ **Zone** 4 **Nippon-bells**
Similar to *S. galacifolia* except that the leaves are more heart shaped and the leaf margins more wavy. Native to Japan.

SHOWER-TREE, GOLDEN. See CASSIA.

SHRIMP-PLANT = *Justicia guttata*

SHRUB. A woody plant branched from the base.

SHRUB ALTHEA = *Hibiscus syriacus*

SHRUBS FOR AT LEAST TWO SEASONS OF BEAUTY. Many gardeners fail to realize that there are literally several thousand shrubs that are being grown in various parts of the northern United States. Certainly all are not of the best! There must be some basis on which these plants can be judged in which the better ones might be easily selected. One basis on which such shrubs can be selected is the number of seasons during which they are of real ornamental value.

Take for instance the yews or *Ilex crenata* 'Convexa' or many of the evergreen rhododendrons—these plants are of interest every season of the year because of their evergreen foliage. On the other hand, some of the forsythias, deutzias, spireas and lilacs are only of special interest during the 2-week period that they are in bloom. They have no interesting autumn color, they have no bright colored fruits, they have nothing particularly meritorious for winter display. Of course such plants will always be needed in many gardens, but the important point to emphasize is that in the small garden, where space is at a premium, plants might well be used that have ornamental interest more than one season during the year.

The viburnums are excellent examples of plants in this group. These plants have conspicuous flowers in the spring, many of them have bright-colored fruits in the fall, some of them lasting all winter long, and most have a rich red to purple-red autumn color. Surely such plants merit first consideration on the small property. A suggested list of some of these good plants is given here together with some specific information as to why they are included.

1. Flowers	4. Autumn coloration
2. Fruit	5. General form
3. Summer foliage	6. Winter twig or bark
7. Winter foliage	

The numbers refer to the reasons why these shrubs are valued for ornamental use:

Abelia grandiflora	1, 3
Acer palmatum varieties	3, 4, 5
Amelanchier grandiflora	1, 4, 6
Berberis species	1, 2, 4, and some 7
Chionanthus virginicus	1, 2, 4
Cornus alba sibirica	1, 4, 6
C. mas	1, 2, 4, 5
Cotinus coggygria purpureus	2, 4
Cotoneaster dammeri	2, 7
C. horizontalis	1, 2, 5, 7
C. microphyllus	1, 2, 7
C. salicifolius floccosus	2, 7
Cytisus praecox	1, 6
C. scoparius	1, 6
Daphne species	1, 2
Enkianthus species	1, 4
Euonymus alata 'Compactus'	4, 5
E. fortunei 'Vegetus'	2, 3, 5, 7
Fothergilla species	1, 4
Hamamelis species	1, 4
Hydrangea anomala petiolaris	1, 3, 5, 6
Ilex cornuta	2, 3, 7
I. crenata	2, 3, 7

I. yunnanensis	2, 3, 7
Kalmia latifolia	1, 3, 7
Kolkwitzia amabilis	1, 2, 6
Leucothoe fontanesiana	1, 3, 4, 7
Ligustrum obtusifolium	
'Regelianum'	1, 2, 3, 5
Lonicera amoena	
'Arnoldiana'	1, 2, 5
L. bella	1, 2
L. fragrantissima	1, 2, 3, 7
L. korolkowii floribunda	1, 2, 3
L. maackii	1, 2
L. tatarica	1, 2
Magnolia stellata	1, 2, 3, 4
M. virginiana	1, 2, 3
Mahonia species	1, 2, 3, 4, 7
Malus sargentii	1, 2, 5
Philadelphus floridus	1, 5
P. grandiflorus	1, 5
P. laxus	1, 5
P. splendens	1, 5
P. virginalis 'Bouquet Blanc'	1, 5
Pieris species	1, 3, 5, 7
Prinsepia sinensis	1, 2, 5
Prunus tomentosa	1, 2
Rhododendron	
carolinianum	1, 7
R. catawbiense	1, 7
R. fortunei	1, 7
R. schlippenbachii	1, 4
R. vaseyi	1, 4
Rosa helenae	1, 2, 5
R. multiflora	1, 2, 5
R. roxburghii	1, 5, 7
R. rugosa	1, 2, 4
Spiraea prunifolia 'Plena'	1, 4
Taxus baccata	2, 3, 5, 7
T. cuspidata	2, 3, 5, 7
T. media	2, 3, 5, 7
Vaccinium corymbosum	1, 2, 4, 6
Viburnum cassinoides	1, 2, 4
V. dilatatum	1, 2, 4
V. japonicum	1, 2, 3, 7
V. lentago	1, 2, 3, 4
V. opulus	1, 2, 3, 4
V. prunifolium	1, 2, 3, 4, 5
V. rufidulum	1, 2, 3, 4
V. sargentii 'Flavum'	1, 2, 3, 4
V. sieboldii	1, 2, 3, 4, 5
V. plicatum 'Mariesii'	1, 2, 3, 4, 5
V. trilobum	1, 2, 3, 4

SIBERIAN-LILY = *Ixiolirion tataricum*

SICANA (sic-ANA)

   odorifera   vine   Zones 9-10   Casa-banana
A tropical vine, member of the Cucumber Family, climbing by tendrils, planted only in the warmest parts of the South. It will grow stems 40 ft. long and may not die out completely in areas where there is no frost, otherwise it is grown as an annual. A very long growing season is essential, the reason why it will not flower and fruit in the North. The flowers are yellowish, both male and female flowers being on the same vine. Fruits are edible, orange-crimson and cylindrical, about 15-24 in. long, and are very fragrant. Also see GOURDS.

SIDALCEA (sy-DAL-sea)
   candida   3′   Zones 5-6   White Checker-mallow
A perennial native to the Rocky Mountain area; the upper leaves 5-7 parted; white flowers, ¾ in. long, produced in racemes looking somewhat like miniature hollyhocks. These give the vertical effect in the garden, are not weedy and make fine border plants blooming in July and Aug. Easily cultivated and propagated by seeds or division
   malviflora   2′   Zone 8   Foothill Checker-mallow
A perennial from Calif. with erect or decumbent branches and rose flowers, 1¼ in. across, in many-flowered racemes. Some of the excellent named cultivars are **'Rosy Gem'**, **'Pink Beauty'**, **'Rose Queen'** and **'Pompadour'**.

SILENE (sy-LEE-ne). A very large genus of the Pink Family with species distributed throughout the world, it includes both hardy and tender plants, which may be annual, biennial or perennial. The habit may be erect, tufted or matted, occasionally with hairy, sticky stems. The leaves are opposite and entire, and the flowers solitary or in clusters, generally red, white or shades of pink. The toothed, tubular calyx encloses the corolla of 5 petals. Stamens number 10. The fruit is a dry capsule.

   A number of species of this genus are good plants from the perennial border or the rock garden. Easily started from seed sown ⅛ in. deep where the plants are desired, perennial species may also be started from seed sown in a cold frame in spring and transplanted when large enough to be handled. Plants may be divided in early spring and cuttings taken in July. These plants should not be moved often, but will respond to annual top dressings of good soil and manure.
   acaulis   2″   Zone 5   Moss Campion
Native to both Europe and North America, this is a tufted, mosslike, little plant with linear leaves ½ in. long; reddish-purple flowers, ½ in. across, from May to Aug. A good plant for the rock garden.
   alba (*Lychnis alba*)   **2′   Zone 3   Evening Campion**
A deeply-rooted biennial or perennial weed naturalized in the eastern, northwestern and Pacific Northwest states, as well as in Canada. The sticky-hairy stems, opposite, oval, stem leaves and fragrant, 1-in.-wide white or pink

flowers opening in the evening from June to Aug. are indicative. There is usually a cluster or rosette of much longer leaves at the base of the plant. Each flower has a large bulblike calyx below the petals which are 5 in number and 2-lobed. It is interesting to note that male and female flowers grow on separate plants.

armeria   12″–18″   annual   **Sweet William Catchfly**

This is a European annual which has escaped from the gardens in the eastern states to become naturalized wild flowers in sunny areas throughout much of the eastern U.S. The smooth, slender stem is erect and bears opposite, ovate, sessile leaves and a flat-topped terminal cluster of deep pink flowers which bloom from June to Oct. An attractive and dainty annual for the wild garden; it is well to collect seed in the fall and sow it in the spring to insure the continuance of the plant.

caroliniana   4″–9″   Zone 5   **Wild-pinks**

This densely tufted, short-lived perennial shows its relation to *Dianthus*, in its smooth, jointed stem and its narrow, opposite, bluish-green leaves. The white to deep pink flowers, up to 1 in. wide, are borne in loose terminal clusters. Each flower has 5 petals which are wedge shaped and toothed. It is a plant of the dry, sandy woods throughout most of the eastern states and blooms in early summer.

dioica (*Lychnis dioica*)   2′   Zone 5   **Red Campion**

A hairy, coarse perennial with usually red flowers an inch long in loose clusters opening in the morning during summer. Native to Europe, but naturalized in the eastern U.S.

noctiflora   2′   annual   **Night-flowering Catchfly**

A weed common in eastern N.Car. and on the northwest Pacific Coast but native to Europe; with erect stems covered with sticky hairs; opposite, lanceolate, entire leaves. The small flowers are pink or nearly white, have 5 2-lobed petals and open at night from June to Sept.

pendula   10″   annual   **Drooping Catchfly**

Native to the Mediterranean Region, the flowers of this species are ½ in. wide, flesh colored, borne in loose axillary clusters. The plant is slightly pendulous. There is a dense and compact form available (**'Compacta'**) as well as one with deep pink flowers (**rosea**).

quadrifida   6″   Zone 5   **Alpine Catchfly**

An attractive small perennial from the European Alps, with linear leaves on creeping stems which spread slowly, forming mats. Dainty white flowers in open clusters on stems 6 in. high bloom all summer.

The var. **'Flore-pleno'** is double and resembles its relative, the Carnation. Native to the mountains of Europe.

schafta   6″   Zone 4   **Schafta Campion**

An attractive, easily cultivated alpine from the Caucasus of Europe, with light green leaves in dense tufts and a profusion of pink flowers, 1 or 2 on a stem, in Aug. and Sept. Suitable for the edge of the border.

stellata   2′–3′   Zone 5   **Starry Campion**

A handsome, erect plant with smooth stems and strongly veined, lanceolate, sessile leaves with wavy margins, arranged on the stem in whorls of 4. The flowers, in a loose terminal spike, and with an occasional flower stalk rising from the axil of an upper whorl of leaves, are pale pink, about 1 in. wide, wedge-shaped, and with toothed margins. It is a plant of dry, sunny locations of the eastern states and flowers in spring and early summer.

virginica   2′   Zone 3   **Fire-pink Catchfly**

A perennial with opposite, narrowly lanceolate leaves and bright scarlet flowers in a loose terminal cluster. The calyx, about 1 in. long, is toothed and the 5 petals are notched. It is a plant of open, sandy woods from Ontario to Ala., and blooms in spring and early summer. Ideal for the wild garden, it may be propagated by seed sown in early spring or by cuttings taken in summer.

The leaves of the **wherryi** variety are not glutinous. Native from Ohio to Ala.

vulgaris   12″–18″   Zone 4   **Bladder Campion**

This plant, having a smooth, branching stem and narrow, clasping, opposite leaves, bears its loose clusters of nodding flowers at the upper joints of the stem. Of no particular ornamental value, the chief characteristic is the large, green, inflated calyx, from which the 5 small white petals and the stamens extend. A native to Europe, it is now a common roadside plant from New England to Kan. and blooms throughout the summer.

vulgaris maritima   1′   Zone 4   **Sea Campion**

A plant with trailing stems and leaves that are covered with a soft bloom. The white flowers, about ¾ in. across, have notched petals and an inflated calyx and bloom throughout the summer. Var. **'Plena'** is completely prostrate, with fleshy bluish leaves and double flowers 1¼ in. wide.

SILK-COTTON TREE = *Ceiba pentandra*

SILK-COTTON TREE FAMILY = Bombacaceae

SILK-TASSEL. See GARRYA.

SILK-TASSEL FAMILY = Garryaceae

SILKTREE = *Albizia julibrissin*

SILK-WORM TREE = *Cudrania tricuspidata*

SILPHIUM (SIL-fium). Hardy perennial herbs of the Composite Family, numbering about 25 species, all native to North America. Of rank growth, they have large, coarse leaves which may be alternate, opposite or in whorls, sometimes surrounding the stem and forming a cup which holds water. The flower heads, usually yellow, have numerous notched ray flowers and comparatively few tubular disk flowers. Of some limited use in the wild or bog gardens; the roots may be divided in fall or early spring, or seed may be sown shallowly in good garden soil.

laciniatum 8′–10′ Zone 5 Compass-plant
A tall, coarse, rough-stemmed perennial with large, alternate, pinnately lobed leaves. The basal leaves, held vertically, often point north-and-south, giving the plant its common name. The flowers are large and showy, about 4 in. wide. It grows on the prairies of the Midwest and Southwest, showing a preference for regions with a deep subsoil. The plant blooms from mid- to late summer. Propagation is best done by seed, for the root is too large to be easily divided. Native from Ohio to Tex.

perfoliatum 4′–8′ Zone 4 Cup Rosinweed
The opposite, ovate leaves of this perennial are joined at the base to form a cup around the stem and in this structure rainwater is sometimes caught and held. The branching flower stalks, arising from leafy bracts, bear yellow flower heads 2–3 in. wide. These bloom from July to Sept. in the rich lowlands from the Great Lakes to Ga. and Ala., but the plant has also been naturalized in New England. It has rather coarse texture for use in flower gardens since the leaves are 6–12 in. long.

Silphium terebinthinaceum—Dock Rosinweed. *(Photo by Arnold Arboretum, Jamaica Plain, Mass.)*

terebinthinaceum 7′–8′ Zone 4 Dock Rosin-weed
The smooth, slender stem of this perennial gives the plant a cultivated appearance which is belied by the toothed, ovate to cordate leaves, 12–24 in. long. The flower heads, in loosely branching clusters, appear in late summer and autumn on the prairie lands of the Midwest.

SILVERBELL. See HALESIA.

SILVERBERRY = *Elaeagnus commutatus*

SILVER-CROWN = *Cotyledon undulata*

SILVER-DOLLAR = *Crassula arborescens*

SILVER DOLLAR TREE = *Eucalyptus cinerea*

SILVER MOUND = *Artemisia schmidtiana nana*

SILVERROD = *Solidago canadensis*

SILVER-TORCH = *Cleistocactus straussii*

SILVERTREE = *Tabebuia argentea*

SILVER VEIN CREEPER = *Parthenocissus henryana*

SILVERVINE = *Actinidia polygama*

SILVERVINE FAMILY = Dilleniaceae

SILYBUM (SILL-i-bum)
marianum 4′ annual or biennial Blessed Milk-thistle
These are thistlelike herbs with spiny-toothed leaves having white spots on the upper surface, the leaves being glossy and 2½ ft. long. The rose-purple flower heads (it belongs in the Composite Family) are 2½ in. wide. Native to the Mediterranean Region and naturalized in Calif. Propagation is easy by seed.

SINARUNDINARIA species. See BAMBOO.

SINNINGIA (sin-IN-jia)
speciosa 10″ Zone 10 Common Gloxinia
This and the African Violet are the 2 most popular members of the Gesneria Family. The Gloxinia is a plant for the greenhouse or the home with large, trumpet-shaped flowers, 3 in. long and often 5 in. wide, available with flowers red, purple, blue, white and pastel colors, both single and double. Native to Brazil. Chiefly grown in a warm, moist greenhouse and should be kept out of the strong sun. After blooming the tubers should be stored at 45° F. until Feb., when they are started again and can bloom in 6 months. Gloxinias for winter bloom can be started 6 months before the bloom is wanted and grown under fluorescent lights (which see), greatly improving the bloom.

Gloxinias are nearly stemless herbs forced by the florist and greatly appreciated as house plants. The velvety soft leaves are opposite and have long petioles.

Seeds usually come in mixtures and are sown in the greenhouse in spring. Also leaf cuttings can be grown and in fact a leaf has been known to produce a tuber when merely placed in a glass of water!

In planting the tuber in a 4- or 5-in. flower pot, it should only have ½ in. of soil on top. The soil mixture might well be garden soil and peat moss, half and half. When the young leaves emerge do not wet them but water from the bottom. Fertilize monthly with 1 teaspoonful of a complete fertilizer (such as 12-12-12) in a gallon of water.

SINUATE. With the outlines of the margin strongly wavy.

SINUS. The recess between lobes, as in the leaves of some oaks.

SIPHONOSMANTHUS = *Osmanthus delavayi*

SISAL-HEMP = *Agave sisalana*

SISYRINCHIUM (sis-i-RINK-ium). These are the so-called blue-eyed grasses, members of the Iris Family, with very narrow, grasslike leaves and small blue or yellow flowers in umbels. They are easily grown in any border and are propagated by seed or division.

angustifolium   6″-10″   Zone 3   Common Blue-eyed Grass
A member of the Iris Family, this dainty, grasslike, tufted plant bears upright, bluish-green, linear leaves and leaflike stems terminating in 1–4 small, blue, starlike flowers having 6 notched perianth segments. Each flower lasts only a few hours. The fruit is in a tiny, round, 3-celled capsule. It is a spring-flowering plant, native to southern Canada and throughout much of the United States, requiring wet soil and full sun. A charming plant for the wild garden, it may be propagated by division of the plants in spring or fall, or by seeds sown late in winter.

birameum   1½′   Zone 6
Flowers of this plant are dark blue with yellow eyes and are borne on short, grasslike stems. Native to Wash.

douglasii   1′   Zone 4   Douglas Blue-eyed Grass
Flowers a beautiful magenta, ¾ in. wide. Native from British Columbia to Calif.

idahoense   1½′   Zone 3   Idaho Blue-eyed Grass
Deep blue flowers each with a yellow eye, about ¾ in. long, borne on glaucous foliage. Native from British Columbia to Ore. and Wyo.

mucronatum   1′   Zone 5
This species grows in dense tufts, each narrow leaf being winged, and it bears many pale blue flowers. Var. **alba** has white flowers. An excellent native plant for the well-drained, sunny rock garden having acid soil. Native from Mass. to Va. and Mich.

SIUM (SY-um)
sisarum   3′   Zone 5   Skirret
An old-fashioned, aromatic, perennial herb, native to eastern Asia, used for its tuberous roots which can be boiled and eaten like a vegetable. The white flowers are borne in umbels and it grows best in alkaline soils. The leaves are pinnately compound. The roots can

either be dug and stored in the winter or left in the ground. Propagated by seed and division.

suave   5′-6′   Zone 4   Hemlock Water-parsnip
A perennial herb frequenting the marshes and wet meadows of the U.S. and having smooth, hollow stems; deeply lobed, pinnately compound leaves; the leaflets 7–17, linear to lanceolate, 2–5 in. long, sharply pointed at apex, the margins finely toothed. The flower stalks bear pinnately compound leaves with 3–5 narrowly lanceolate leaflets with finely toothed margins, and have a petiole which clasps the stem. The small white flowers are borne in compact, much-branched, compound umbels and appear from July to Oct.

SKIMMIA (SKIM-ia)
japonica   4′   Zone 7   Japanese Skimmia
This very popular Japanese plant is of merit for its flowers, its fruits and its bright, evergreen, alternate leaves (about 3–5 in. long) as well as its fairly rounded habit. Male and female flowers are on different plants and both should be present to assure fruit production but the fragrant, white, male flowers are interesting in themselves. The bright red berries are about ⅓ in. thick and the evergreen leaves are about 5 in. long. These are handsome evergreens, especially if grown in partial shade and not the full sun. Since the sexes are separate, both male and female plants should be used to insure fruiting.

reevesiana   1½′   Zone 7   Reeves Skimmia
Probably even more desirable to some gardeners than *S. japonica*, this evergreen is lower growing and has the added advantage of having perfect flowers, which of course means that every plant bears fruits. It is a native of China, with rather dull, evergreen leaves, 4 in. long, and compact growth. A fine plant for the small garden.

SKIRRET = *Sium sisarum*

SKULLCAP. See SCUTELLARIA.

SKUNK-CABBAGE = *Symplocarpus foetidus*

SKUNK-CABBAGE,   YELLOW = *Lysichitum americanum*

SKYROCKET = *Ipomopsis aggregata*

SLIMEFLUX. The name of an exudation from the trunk of trees which oozes out of a wound but does not harden like pitch or gum. The cause is not understood. It often occurs on American Elm at wounds or split crotches. Oozing may continue for several months and delays or prevents the normal healing of the wound but does not otherwise appear to harm the tree. Correction of any abnormal or unhealthy condition of the tree is the only suggestion.

SLIMEMOLD. This is a group of fungi which feed primarily on decayed organic matter rather than living plants. Irregular, white, slimy patches on the lawn are easily broken by raking or watering. One notable exception is clubroot of Cabbage (see CABBAGE) which causes swollen misshapen roots and stunts the plants.

SLIP. A softwood cutting removed from the mother plant; applied also to similar parts cut off.

SLIPPERFLOWER, REDBIRD = *Pedilanthus tithymaloides*

SLOE = *Prunus spinosa*

SLOTHTREE = *Cecropia palmata*

SLUGS. Slugs, which are snails without a shell, are related to oysters and clams. Garden slugs feed by eating or rasping the leaves of many plants. They are active at night and are usually found in cool, damp places. During the day they hide under stones, boards and plant refuse. Eggs are laid in rotted wood and decaying leaves. The slimy trails which they leave are very objectionable. Lime and salt are repellents and may kill them by dehydration. Salt is also toxic to plants and must be used with caution. Several things used in home-made baits are now banned. The best suggestion is to buy something at the garden center that is advertised as a control. Baits are most effective when spread at dusk and they lose effectiveness when dry or washed by heavy rain or other water. Metaldehyde is also available in sprays and dusts but may injure orchids. A jar lid, set in soil at ground level, filled with beer, sometimes traps them.

SMARTWEED. See POLYGONUM.

SMILACINA (smy-lass-Y-na). Native North American wild flowers, the small greenish-white flowers are borne in terminal racemes on long, curving, alternate-leaved stems up to 3 ft. long. Fruits are bright-colored red berries in the fall. For use only in woodlands for naturalizing. Easily propagated by division and seeds.

racemosa 2′–3′ Zone 3 False Solomon's-seal, Wild Spikenard
A stout perennial of the Lily Family, with arching branches and alternate, ovate leaves having strong longitudinal veins. The small white flowers are in a pyramidal-shaped terminal cluster and are followed by small, whitish berries which turn red in autumn. It is a plant of the moist, somewhat acid woods of southern Canada and the northeastern U.S. reaching inland as far as Mich. It is ideal for the shady wild garden and may be propagated by division of the plant in spring or by sowing seed in fall.

stellata 10′–12′ Zone 3 Starry Solomon's-seal
Similar to *S. racemosa* in its arching habit, this species has leaves sometimes ovate but generally narrowly lanceolate, and sessile. In flowers and fruit it resembles *S. racemosa*. Native to North America and Europe.

trifolia 5″–6″ Zone 3 Labrador Solomon's-seal
This dainty bog plant has 3 alternate, sessile leaves and a small terminal cluster of tiny white flowers. The red berries in fall add to its usefulness as a plant for the bog garden. Native to North America and Siberia.

SMILAX (SMY-lax). These are often thorny vines which climb by tendrils, a pair at the base of each leaf. They are evergreen or deciduous, with fairly inconspicuous male and female flowers on different plants, the female plants bearing red or blue-black berries. The florists "smilax" often turns out to be *Asparagus asparagoides*. Smilax species can become impenetrable thickets, so one should think twice before using them in the garden. Propagation is chiefly by division of plant clumps or else by root cuttings.

bona-nox vine Zone 6 Sawbrier
The roots of this are in the form of tubers which are edible and have been dried and ground into a flour used for breadstuffs. It is a prickly, twining, alternate-leaved, partially evergreen climber, with leaves that are 3-lobed to triangular sometimes, 4½ in. long, spiny on the margins and midrib below. The fruit is a black berry. Native from N.J. to Tex.

glauca vine Zone 5 Catbrier
Partially evergreen; native from Mass. to Tex.; with alternate leaves 2–3 in. long, stems squarish, sometimes with prickles, sometimes without, and fruit an inconspicuous blue-black berry. The roots and sometimes the new shoots are said to have been eaten by the Indians. It does grow in dry soil and can form impenetrable masses.

herbacea vine Zone 4 Carrionflower
A deciduous vine of little merit. Native from New Brunswick to Okla. The roots and young shoots are said to have been eaten sometimes by the Indians.

laurifolia vine Zone 7 Laurel Greenbrier
An alternate-leaved, evergreen, climbing vine, native from southern N.J. to Fla. and Tex. The stems are very prickly; leaves up to 5 in. long and wedge shaped at the base; the fruit a black 1-seeded berry, taking usually 2 years to mature. Not an ornamental, but the Indians have been known to eat the young shoots.

megalantha twining vine 18′ Zone 7 Coral Greenbrier
A handsome climbing vine from China, with excellent, lustrous, alternate, evergreen leaves, 9 in. long and 6 in. wide, with scattered spines, brilliant coral-red fruits, borne in umbels 2 in. in dia. The sexes are separate so both male and

female plants should be present to insure fruiting. Even without the fruit the handsome foliage of this vine makes it a fine ornamental.

rotundifolia twining vine 30′ Zone 4 Common Greenbrier, Horsebrier
Native to eastern North America, this is often a pest where it grows in thick impenetrable masses because it is very vigorous and tenacious even on poor soils. The leaves are alternate, 2–4½ in. long, and the fruits are bluish-black berries on the female plants. It is a pest because it sends out long underground shoots that appear at quite some distance from the main plant. The stems are green. The very thorny stems are particularly hazardous in the woods.

SMITHIANTHA (smith-i-AN-tha). Often termed *Naegelia*, these are tropical American, herbaceous, tuberous-rooted perennials, with opposite leaves that are heart shaped and velvety; often cultivated as pot plants in greenhouses and propagated easiest by seeds, tubers or offsets. Native to Mexico.

cinnabarina 1½′–2′ Zone 10 Temple-bells
Flowers are 1½ in. long, bright red, bell-like, creamy colored in the throat, borne on a red central stalk. Growing from rhizomes or tubers, the leaves are thickish with soft red or purple hairs.

zebrina 3′ Zone 10 Purple Gesneria
Densely pubescent and much like the preceding, with densely hairy leaves; the veins marked with purple, red or dark brown. Flowers are red with yellow spots.

SMOKETREE. See COTINUS.

SMUT. A fungus which is so named because it produces conspicuous masses of black spores. To the gardener corn smut and onion smut are the best examples. It is not controlled in the field with fungicides but seed treatment is advised. A few plants can be protected by promptly cutting and burning the gray leathery "boils" on corn and by pulling infected onions.

SNAILSEED. See COCCULUS.

SNAKEROOT, WHITE = *Eupatorium rugosum*

SNAKEROOT = *Cimifuga racemosa*

SNAKEROOT, VIRGINIA = *Aristolochia serpentaria*

SNAKEWEED = *Polygonum bistorta*

SNAPDRAGON. See ANTIRRHINUM.

SNAPDRAGON, SMALL = *Chaenorrhinum minus*

SNAPWEED. See IMPATIENS.

SNEEZEWEED. See HELENIUM.

SNEEZEWORT = *Achillea ptarmica*

SNOWBALL, CHINESE = *Viburnum macrocephalum*

SNOWBALL, EUROPEAN = *Viburnum opulus* 'Roseum'

SNOWBALL, FRAGRANT = *Viburnum x carlecephalum*

SNOWBALL, JAPANESE = *Viburnum plicatum*

SNOWBALL, MEXICAN = *Echeveria elegans*

SNOWBELL. See STYRAX.

SNOWBERRY = *Symphoricarpos rivularis*

SNOWBERRY, CREEPING = *Gaultheria hispidula*

SNOWCUP = *Anoda cristata*

SNOWDROP. See GALANTHUS.

SNOWDROP-TREE = *Halesia diptera*

SNOWFLAKE. See LEUCOJUM.

SNOW-IN-SUMMER = *Cerastium tomentosum*

SNOW-ON-THE-MOUNTAIN = *Euphorbia marginata*

SNOW-WREATH = *Neviusia alabamensis*

SOAPBARK-TREE = *Quillaja saponaria*

SOAPBERRY = *Sapindus drummondii*

SOAPBERRY FAMILY = Sapindaceae

SOAP-PLANT = *Chlorogalum pomeridianum*

SOAPWEED = *Yucca glauca*

SOAPWORT. See SAPONARIA.

SOCIETIES. (Horticultural and Plant Name). North America is very fortunate in having many horticultural organizations. An individual can become a member of a general horticultural organization like the American Horticultural Society and receive its general quarterly magazine, and also if his special interests are in roses, the American Rose Society and receive its monthly publication. Some of these organizations are well established with permanent offices, paid secretaries and publications of long standing. Others are maintained by a group of volunteer enthusiasts dedicated to the organization and writing its publications for the length of time they remain in office. Because of the temporary terms of the officers of some of these, the "headquarters" address may be changed every few years.

Because of this, only those addresses will be given in the following lists which are more or less permanent. The current address of the others can be obtained in the *Directory of American Horticulture* of the American Horticultural Society. Most of the "Plant Name" societies produce their own publications, some of which are far superior and more informative than others. The following list is certainly not complete but is sufficient so that an individual new to gardening can obtain some idea about where and how he can contact others with some of his same interests.

American Horticultural Society, Inc.
    Mount Vernon, Va. 22121
American Orchid Society, Inc. (1948)
    Botanical Museum of Harvard University, Cambridge, Mass. 02138
American Rose Society (Inc. 1921)
    P.O. Box 30,000, Shreveport, La. 71130
California Horticultural Society (Inc. 1938)
    California Academy of Sciences, (Golden Gate Park), San Francisco, Calif.
Garden Club of America (Inc. 1923)
    598 Madison Ave., New York, N.Y. 10022
International Shade Tree Conference
    Box 71-5 Lincoln Square, Urbana, Ill. 61801
Massachusetts Horticultural Society (Inc. 1829)
    300 Massachusetts Avenue, Boston, Mass. 02115
Men's Garden Clubs of America
Michigan Horticultural Society
    302 Horticulture Building M.S.U., East Lansing, Mich. 48824
Minnesota Horticultural Society
    161 Alderman Hall, Univ. of Minnesota, St. Paul, Minn. 55108
National Council of State Garden Clubs, Inc.
    4401 Magnolia Avenue, St. Louis, Mo. 63110
The Horticultural Society of New York, Inc.
    128 W. 58th St., New York, N.Y. 10019
Pennsylvania Horticultural Society
    325 Walnut Street, Philadelphia, Pa. 19106
Worcester County Horticultural Society
    30 Elm Street, Worcester, Mass.
African Violet Society of America, Inc. (1947)
American Association of Botanical Gardens and Arboretums
American Begonia Society (Inc. 1940)
American Camellia Society (Inc. 1946)
American Carnation Society (Inc. 1902)
American Daffodil Society (Inc. 1954)
American Dahlia Society (Inc. 1915)
American Fern Society, Inc.
American Fuchsia Society (Inc. 1929)
American Gesneria Society (Inc. 1952)
American Gloxinia Society (Inc. 1953)
American Hemerocallis Society (Inc. 1955)
American Hibiscus Society (Inc. 1950)
American Iris Society (Inc. 1920)
American Peony Society (Inc. 1904)
American Rhododendron Society (Inc. 1945)
American Rock Garden Society (Inc. 1934)
Bromeliad Society (Inc. 1953)
Cactus and Succulent Society of America (Inc. 1929)
Chicago Horticultural Society (Inc. 1890)
Connecticut Horticultural Society (Est. 1887)

Florida State Horticultural Society
Gourd Society of America, Inc. (1942)
Herb Society of America (Est. 1933; Inc. 1935)
Holly Society of America (Inc. 1947)
Indiana Horticultural Society (Inc. 1861)
International Geranium Society
Long Island Horticultural Society (Inc. 1934)
Men's Garden Clubs of America (Inc. 1932)
National Gladiolus Society (Inc. 1949)
Nebraska Horticultural Society (Inc. 1954)
New Hampshire Horticulture Society (Est. 1893)
New Jersey State Horticultural Society (Inc. 1875)
North American Lily Society (Inc. 1947)
North Dakota State Horticultural Society
Northern Nut Growers Association (Inc. 1923)
Ohio State Horticultural Society (Inc. 1846)
Oregon State Horticultural Society (Inc. 1909)
Palm Society (Inc. 1957)
Rhode Island Horticultural Society (Inc. 1854)
Society for Louisiana Irises (Inc. 1942)
South Dakota State Horticultural Society
Southern California Horticultural Institute (Inc. 1937)
Tennessee State Horticultural Society (Inc. 1919)
The American Forestry Association
The Garden Club of Virginia
Virginia State Horticultural Society (Inc. 1900)
Washington State Horticultural Association (Inc. 1947)
West Virginiana State Horticultural Society (Inc. 1913)
Woman's National Farm and Garden Association, Inc.

SODIUM SELENATE. This is a commercial formation of selenium, a highly poisonous chemical, which was used as a systemic insecticide for control of aphids, spider mites and thrips infesting greenhouse flowers. Edible plants growing in treated soil several years after treatment may acquire a harmful amount of selenium. It is now replaced by systemic formations of organic phosphate insecticides.

SOFT SCALE. A term which refers to a group of scale insects without a waxy covering (armored scales) so that their soft body is exposed to insecticide applications. They are either naked or covered with cottony, woolly, waxy or felt-like growth. Some of the destructive pests of this group are soft brown scale on greenhouse plants, cottony maple scale on Maple and other trees, European fruit lecanium on fruit and shade trees and the terrapin scale on shade trees. See SCALE INSECTS for control.

SOFTWOOD. A term used in connection with

woods, meaning any that are light and easily worked, like those of coniferous trees. The term is also used in horticulture as softwood cuttings, meaning a piece of soft, succulent, easily bent, plant growth that has not fully matured. Hardwood cuttings are those usually for dormant twigs in which the growth has fully matured and is not easily bent. See CUTTINGS.

SOIL MIXTURES. There are many different kinds of soil mixtures, some better than others for special kinds of plants. In general, a good mixture for growing seeds and cuttings as well (after they are rooted) would be:

2 parts, good loam
1 part peat
1 part sand
1½ oz. of superphosphate per bushel of above
mixture
¾ oz. ground limestone
If ericaceous plants are to be grown:
1 part loam (without lime)
3 parts peat or leaf mold
1 part clean sand

If the soil is to be used for potting rooted cuttings it is not so important to have it sterilized, but it would be good insurance against failure. If seeds are to be sown, it might well be sterilized. See SOIL STERILIZATION. The mixture would have been thoroughly screened beforehand. It is placed in the pots or flats, leveled, gently pressed down, and the seed sown either broadcast or in drills.

The general rule for the depth at which seed is sown is usually to sow at a depth equal to the size of the seed. In some cases (lettuce seed is an excellent example) there should not be much soil above the seed. Gardeners who have sown lettuce seeds an inch or more deep have wondered why it did not come up. Sowing such seeds in flats is safer than sowing it in the garden row, for in flats the small amount of soil placed on top can be properly gauged. Also, by placing a glass pane, with shade like a newspaper, over the flat, moisture can be controlled until germination takes place, when the shade and the glass are removed.

Sometimes, instead of placing soil over fine seed, one can grate a little moist sphagnum moss through a sieve. When larger seeds are used they should be carefully spaced. Sowing many seeds closely together is not only wasteful of seed, but it will give the damping-off fungus an opportunity to get started as soon as the seed comes up. Spread it thin.

Watering seed, especially fine seed, after it is first sown is very important too. It might well be done from the bottom at first, allowing the flat or the pan to stand in a pan of water with the level just a fraction of an inch below the soil surface after the flat is in. Capillary attraction will be responsible for the water eventually reaching the soil surface. If the fine seeds are watered by hose or watering-can from the top, they will be spread all over and be forced out of place.

Watering well at the time of planting, and placing the glass or polyethylene film over the top, might be sufficient so that additional watering would not be necessary for several days to a week. Never overwater, just apply enough to keep the soil moist but not wet.

When the seed starts to germinate, one should be even more careful with the water, for it is then that the damping-off fungus can do the most damage. Good precautions to take against this have already been mentioned, namely, do not sow the seed too thick, and do not water too much. If the fungus does get started, dust the seedlings immediately with a good fungicide like Semesan, preferably removing the seedlings affected with the soil about them.

When the seedlings have developed a leaf or two they should be transplanted to the pot or flat in which they are to grow until they go out permanently into the garden. The soil mixture could well be the same as has been already described. Tomatoes might be put into 3-in. pots, or 24–40 to the standard flat. It is important that the seedlings be given sufficient space in the flat, for if planted too close, they get spindly and unsuitable for planting in the garden.

Sowing seeds directly in the garden should be done with care. The seed bed should be raked level and all the large lumps of soil should be broken, especially if fine seed is to be sown. The rows made should be straight and deep enough but not too deep for the seed. Once distributed, the soil should be carefully raked over the seed and gently firmed. Watering at this time often proves helpful, especially if the soil is dry. The larger the seed, the more space should be given. Bean plants, for instance, are best about 6 in. apart as growing plants, but since one can never depend on 100% germination in the open ground, the individual seeds might be placed 3 in. apart and, if they all come up, they can be thinned to the proper distance. The same is true of other garden seeds—sow intelligently, but once the seeds are up, thin out so the seedlings allowed to remain will have plenty of space in which to develop.

SOIL OPERATIONS. These are simple and practically known to everyone. Plowing or digging is simply the turning over the soil preparatory to planting. Plowing is usually done to a depth of 6–8 in. in soils east of the Mississippi River. In the South, it is a little less and in the deep soils of the Great Plains about 4–5 in. is sufficient. In areas where the ground freezes in winter, soil that is plowed in the fall might best be left as is until spring when it is harrowed and prepared for planting. Leaving it thus over winter allows it to become properly weathered, opened up or "aired" by successive freezing and thawing so that it will be in a proper rejuvenated condition in the spring.

In the spring it is harrowed, either by disk or spring-tooth harrow depending on the kind of soil (heavier soils are disk harrowed, light sandy soils in certain areas break up properly merely with the use of a spring-tooth harrow). Sometimes a leveling process is necessary with a spike-toothed harrow. In small garden operations this is all frequently accomplished with the use of one machine, the rototiller. If the soil is not dug sufficiently deep with one time through, it is rototilled again, but the better machines are so efficient that, when properly used, they leave the soil all ready for sowing. The advantage of these machines is of course that they can easily prepare short narrow strips of soil as well as larger ones.

Simply to make certain the soil is perfectly level for seeding, or to remove stones and debris, it is carefully raked just preparatory to seeding or planting.

Cultivation may consist of several operations. The objective has a twofold purpose, to keep the weeds from growing and to keep a dust mulch on the soil surface, therefore reducing the evaporation of capillary water from the soil. Various machines, large and small, have been devised for this purpose. The gardener who is mechanically minded will have a field day in selecting the right tool or machine. The 3-pronged hoe or push cultivator with adjustable teeth are both satisfactory, but the hard-working gardener will undoubtedly sell himself the idea that he deserves a machine that does the same thing.

When cultivating it is well to remember that the roots of the plants should not be molested. In the vegetable garden, for instance, this means that cultivating close to the row of plants while they are young is satisfactory, but as they mature the machine should be kept away from them. Also, it is not necessary—in fact it is harmful—to cultivate the soil more than an inch in depth, especially as the plants mature, for deep cultivation can injure the spreading roots. Especially is this true in times of drought.

In order to save time and labor, we keep our vegetable garden free of weeds until July 15th after which we let everything grow. The vegetables are far enough along to grow in spite of weeds after that, and the fine crop of weeds which develop after that date we choose to look on as a "cover crop" to be turned under as a green manure in the fall. This attitude, right or wrong, does save labor and still the vegetables are produced nevertheless.

Cultivation need not be undertaken after every rain. In fact, the energetic gardener should guard against cultivating too often—it is not necessary. One must keep the weeds under control and keep the surface soil crust broken, for in doing this the soil is opened up and is more receptive to the lightest shower.

Hoeing is the simple act of cutting off the weeds and breaking up the soil crust, usually between or around plants where mechanical cultivators can not reach. There is a knack to it. The weeds should be cut but the soil should not be scraped away from the plant in so doing for it should be left in place, with the weeds removed. Hoeing should never be done more than $\frac{1}{2}$–1 in. deep. It takes some practice to perform this century-old act properly. Tall weeds might best be pulled and raked out to prevent their rooting in the next shower. Common sense should dictate that hoeing weeds just before a shower is a waste of time, unless they are raked off. If they are lying on the soil surface, a heavy shower can stir up the soil just enough to re-plant a good proportion of them. It is best to pick a time when the sun is out bright and hot and will kill the small weeds that are hoed out and left on the soil surface.

Rolling is done chiefly to level off a piece of ground like a lawn, or to press back grass plants into the soil which have been heaved out during the winter. It is also done as the final operating in sowing grass seed on a new lawn. In some areas it is done merely to break up the clods of soil in a plowed field.

"Heaving" is the pushing out of the soil of small, shallow-rooted plants as a result of the alternate freezing and thawing action in the soil. This takes place during the early winter and especially in the early spring, and can be serious to many young plants. Heaving must be corrected as soon as possible by replanting the young plants before their roots dry out too much. Such young plantings should be carefully inspected periodically in the spring, just for the purpose of noting heaved plants in time.

Top-dressing is a term generally accepted for the application of fertilizer, compost, manure or other soil amendment to the surface of the soil. Almost anything put on lawns is understood to be "top-dressing," but the term applies to materials applied to other parts of the garden as well.

Digging the soil, or turning over by hand, is a simple enough operation but to the uninitiated it is the act of turning soil upside down, or a plowing by hand. Turning it upside down is to ensure getting all weeds and surface plants underneath a layer of soil so they will rot and form valuable humus material.

Draining the soil is the act of digging ditches in the soil or placing tile drains underneath soil to remove water from wet spots or from hard-pan areas, that will not drain through the soil normally. For details see DRAINING.

Caution should be exercised in undertaking all these soil operations, not to work the soil when it is wet. This can do more harm than good. In walking on or working machines on wet soil, the air is pushed out of the spaces between the soil particles and the soil does not have the ability, by itself, to open up those air spaces again. When it dries, it often takes on a hard, cementlike character and plants have a most difficult time growing in it. The only way this situation can be overcome, once it happens, is to harrow the soil, cultivating it over a period of time, breaking it up into fine particles so the proper amount of air is allowed in once again. Do not work wet soil, but wait until it has dried out into a friable, mealy condition. Take a handful of soil and squeeze it—if water runs out and it turns a slimy muddy mass, it is too wet. If after squeezing it the soil still breaks up properly, it is friable and proper for working.

This warning about compacting wet soil is most important (and too often overlooked) in planting a shrub or tree. Everyone knows about firming the soil thoroughly about the roots, but that soil should be friable and mealy, not wet. If it is wet, stamping it about the roots is an excellent way of killing the plant. In other words, if the soil is right, firm it well about the roots, then water it and let it remain untouched after watering. Never water the soil and then stamp it in.

SOILS. Soil is the highly complex material which covers the earth's crust. It results from centuries of erosion, the grinding action of glaciers, wind and water on the surface rocks. It has been augmented by the complex action of many micro-organisms which have lived and continue to live in it, as well as the numerous materials which have been added to it as a result of de-caying plant and animal growth. A few general statements can be made about it so that the gardener can better understand how it can be modified both physically and chemically when necessary for his various needs.

Roughly speaking, soils are of 3 kinds, sandy soils, clay soils and loams. Sandy soils are those with a predominance of sand and thus do not retain or absorb much moisture. Very clayey soils are "heavy" with extremely fine soil particles and do not allow for much drainage. It is these clay soils that become sticky or gummy when they are wet and then when dry become hard and solid, with a concretelike consistency. It is the clay soils that do not hold much air, whereas the sandy soils have many air spaces and do not hold much water.

The third type of soil are the loams which actually are mixtures of sand and clay soils together. When these also have a sufficient amount of humus material, they are the best for gardening purposes.

The United States Department of Agriculture uses a system of dividing soils into the 3 classifications depending on the proportions of sand, silt or clay they contain. Soils containing 35% or more of sand are sandy soils and these in turn are divided into several groups depending on the amount and size of the sand particles. Soils with 30% or more of clay particles are the clayey soils and these also are further divided into groups depending on the amount of cay and silt in each. Loams are soils that have evenly divided amounts of sand, silt and clay.

The differences between silt, clay and sand particles in soils are measured according to the following scale in millimeters (1 millimeter = .039 in.).

	DIA. IN MILLIMETERS
Clay	below. 002
Silt	.002–.05
Very fine sand	.05–.10
Fine sand	.10–.25
Medium sand	.25–.50
Coarse sand	.50–1.0
Very coarse sand	1.0–2.0
Pebbles and stone	above 2.0

It is obvious that soil must hold moisture so that plant roots can absorb it continuously for proper growth. Soil must also hold air, usually in about equal amounts with the water. Finally, and this is the advantage of having some sandy soil in a good loam, soil must be able to drain surplus water, for if it did not do this, plant roots would actually be killed by drowning.

Organic matter plays a very important part in the soil. Good garden soil does not result from a mixture of sand and clay alone, it must have humus or decayed organic matter in addition and this is added to the soil by de-composed animal or plant material. It is highly complex, teeming with various kinds of organisms which result in continuing chemical reactions. Organic matter does 3 things in the soil as it decomposes:

1. Certain chemicals are made available for absorbtion by plant roots.
2. Humus is added to the soil structure, and this is essential for its water-holding capacity as well as its fertilizing value as it decomposes!
3. It affords food for bacteria in the soil which

in turn release chemicals that might otherwise be unavailable to the plants.

Humus added to the soil makes it open and porous. It absorbs and holds moisture as well as the various chemicals that are in solution in that water and are in a condition available to plants. Because it is light and porous it allows for free drainage of surplus water, a very important characteristic of a good soil. Humus does not pack in clods like a heavy clay, but makes a soil that is "mealy" and easily broken up. It aids in the soil warming up early in the spring and makes it friable and easily worked. So much for the physical condition of soils.

The food in the soil needed by plants is made up of a number of things. First, there must be oxygen, carbon and hydrogen, all of which come from the air and the water available in the soil.

Then there must be other elements such as magnesium, calcium, iron and sulfur but most soils have enough of these (except calcium) and usually they do not have to be added except in rare circumstances. Then, too, there are essential trace elements like boron, zinc and molybdenum (sometimes magnesium is included here), but these are present in most soils. They are sometimes added in extremely small amounts to commercial fertilizers, especially since it has been shown that in some areas both boron and magnesium are deficient in some soils.

The most important elements which are heavily drawn upon by every plant crop are nitrogen, phosphorus and potassium. Of the 3, the nitrogen is the element most used by plants in growth and usually the first one to become deficient in the soil. Most "complete" fertilizers contain all 3 (N, P, K) and the percentage of each in the fertilizer must be noted on the bag. Hence a 10–10–10 fertilizer has 10% nitrogen, 10% phosphoric acid and 10% potash. Several combinations such as 5–10–10; 4–8–4; 10–10–10; 8–16–16; 10–6–4; 8–6–2 and others are usually available from garden supply stores; each one, supposedly, is of particular value for a particular purpose. As noted above, other trace elements are also added to "play it safe" and include everything that might be needed. As every gardener knows there are plants which respond remarkably to just an application of nitrogen in the form of sodium nitrate, especially true since nitrogen is usually the first element that needs replenishing.

Important also is the type of chemical which goes to make up the "complete" fertilizer. For instance, nitrogen can be in the form of sodium nitrate or in the form of dried slaughter-house products. In the first instance, the source is inorganic, in the second, organic. These 2 materials do not release the nitrogen at the same rate; that coming from the inorganic material is available to the plant as soon as it is in solution and the organic material is released slowly over a period of time. The nitrogen from the inorganic chemical could be leached out of the soil quickly by heavy rains before it has been used by the plant, but that from the organic material could not be so quickly leached out. Also, organic fertilizers add humus to the soil, an extremely important point.

It should be stressed that both organic and inorganic fertilizers are important. In combination they are probably better than either one alone. The inorganic fertilizer is excellent for becoming quickly available, the organic for its ability to be more slowly available and eventually to add humus to the soil. One should not get the idea that perfect soil for growing vegetables may be had merely by adding inorganic materials year in and year out. Such procedures would be better than adding no material whatsoever, but best would be to add organic as well as inorganic fertilizers.

Acid vs. Alakaline Soils

Soils differ widely, sometimes in the same field. This can be seen during any airplane trip over the country where there are spots in the grain fields where the plants are yellowish green and not the lush green they are in the rest of the field. In other words, they vary within small areas, in general makeup, both physical and chemical, as well as in acidity.

The acidity or alkalinity of a soil is measured in terms of pH—a scale is used with 1 to 6.9 being acid in decreasing amounts; 7.0 is neither acid nor alkaline but neutral; and soil from 7.1 to 9 is alkaline in increasing amounts. Most plants will grow in slightly acid soil, but a few require alkaline soil. In areas of normal to heavy rainfall (in the U.S. up to 50 in. per year) the soils are usually acid to neutral but in areas where the soils have been made from limestone rock, they are of course alkaline.

In the far west and in desert areas, where rainfall is low, the salts in the soil are not leached out by heavy rainfall but remain near the surface, thus making the soil alkaline. The less the rainfall, the more alkaline the soil. There are some plants, like rhododendrons and azaleas, which require acid soil in which to grow and there are means of changing or controlling the acidity or alkalinity of the soil as will be mentioned later.

Subsoil

This is that part of the soil underneath the surface soil. It has been there hundreds of years and has not been disturbed except in making excavations for buildings and roads, etc. The farmer "tills" the upper 8–10 in. and the sub-soil continues to go unmolested. Surface soils may vary from a few inches deep in rocky New England to several feet in depth in the rich areas of the grasslands in the Midwest. Subsoils are of 2 types—either porous or non-porous. The latter is the difficult-to-handle "hardpan" situation where water will not drain through it but collects and, by so doing, forces out the necessary air between the soil particles and actually drowns the plant roots that reach it.

The farmers years ago recognized this fact in planting many an orchard where the subsoil was hardpan, circumventing the situation by setting off a stick of dynamite in each situation where a tree was to be planted, thus breaking the hard-pan and allowing surplus water to drain through. Gardeners now must usually take steps to lay drains to carry off the water in soils that have this type of subsoil.

If the surface soil is only 3–5 in. deep, it is advisable to plow up an inch or so of subsoil occasionally and mix it with the surface soil, the idea being of course to get a deeper soil in which to grow plants. When this is done, increased fertilizers and cover crops are certainly in order to increase the soil's productivity. Plants differ regarding the depth of soil needed for their feeding roots, a fine turf needing a few inches while 80% of a tree's feeding roots are in the upper 18 in. of soil. It goes without saying that a fertile loam 10 in. deep will produce better plants than a soil 4 in. deep.

There may be situations where a tree is to be planted or a vegetable garden made, where the "hardpan" type of subsoil simply has to be drained first, for, if planted without draining, standing water could kill the plants. Regular tile drains are carefully laid 8–12 in. below the surface in such a way as to drain the water away from the proposed area. The newer type composition drains are longer, easier to lay and have perforations their full length. Crushed stone or coarse gravel, filled in around these pipes aids in draining the water.

If the soil is too porous and all the water quickly drains from it without any being absorb-ed for plant use, then humus must be added. Peat moss, barnyard manure, garden compost are all good examples of organic material. Turning under "green manures," that is, fast-growing grasses like Rye, Oats, or other plants like Buckwheat, Clover or Vetch, is also an excellent method of introducing organic material into the soil. These "green manures" are allowed to grow vigorously and just before they mature and while still in succulent green growth they are plowed under to decompose in the soil.

Special Soil Types

There are clay and/or sandy soils every-where and when these are mixed together with humus they form the desirable loams that are the most productive for the gardener's use.

There are also peat soils, usually bog areas where plants have been lushly growing and dying for centuries. These by themselves are not productive. One of the hardest lessons I have ever learned was when I bought many truck loads of "soil" taken from a road excavation made from a diverted river bed. The soil looked rich and black but later proved to be so sterile it would not even grow weeds! It just did not have the required plant nutrients—the appear-ance alone of a soil is not enough to prove its worth.

Peats vary greatly, depending on the material from which they are made. A sphagnum peat is the result of decaying sphagnum moss, but a sedge peat, resulting from decaying mosses of several types, has characteristics quite different from those of a sphagnum peat. The uses to which local peats can best be put in the garden should be carefully checked with the local state experiment station, for they definitely are not all the same.

Muck soils are those in dried-up bog lands where there has not been time enough (or plants enough) for peat to form. These are often used for growing certain vegetable crops on a commercial scale, but the local state experi-ment station should be consulted for the best methods of utilizing these soils.

Adobe or gumbo soils in the far west and southwest areas are highly alkaline soils, which may have enough plant nutrients for good growth but they are not in solution because of insufficient rainfall. These also need special treatment in order to prove productive.

Improving the Soil

Soils must be properly maintained and kept up or poor productivity results. Humus is continually being used up, and therefore it must be replaced. The so-called marginal farm land we hear about is usually soil that is only a few inches deep, which has been farmed re-peatedly without the proper replacements of humus or chemicals. There are special problems with special soils but, by and large, the normal soils of this country can be "improved" in the following way:

1. Study the soil available and how plants grow in it. Look at other soils in the area and see how plants grow. Is it too sandy or does it have too much clay? Does water drain too fast and the soil dry out too quickly, or is there a "hardpan" that needs proper draining?

2. Add an inch or so of clay soil to the surface and work it in if it is too sandy or if too clayey add an inch or two of sandy soil and work that in, and together with added lime and humus good growth might well result. The local county agent or the local state experiment station can give invaluable assistance here. Actually it saves much time, trouble and expense to have a soil analysis made by the experiment station. If you know the past history of the soil, whether it has been farmed, or used as a garden or is converted woodland soil, these facts should be given when submitting the soil for analysis. Also one should state what kind of plants are contemplated to be grown on the soil in question, i.e., a lawn, vegetable garden, perennials or just trees and shrubs. Add gypsum to a heavy clay or waterlogged soil as a soil conditioner.

3. Add manure or humus to the soil—cow or horse manure, 2–3 in. deep plowed under is excellent. If this is decomposed (not fresh) it is the quickest way of improving soil texture as well as giving immediately usable plant foods. Hen and sheep manures are stronger and should be applied lightly or else mixed with compost, leaves or straw when they are added.

Animal manures are difficult to obtain now so that the next best things to use are the "green manures" and peat moss. Peat moss is the more expensive but is immediately effective as humus as soon as it is mixed with the soil. Green manures are less expensive, the only cost is for the seed and sowing, but it may take 6 months or a year before they have grown, been plowed under, and started to decay sufficiently to become effective as humus. Peat moss, applied over an area at a rate of about 100 lbs. per 1000 sq. ft., should be effective as humus when worked well into the soil.

Green manures would include quick growing succulent crops like Rape, Italian Rye, Buckwheat, cow peas, Winter Rye and the vetches. The type of material used varies in different sections of the United States and the time of year they are to be sown. Some good gardeners in the northeastern United States just dislike to see their vegetable garden land idle. In the fall they plant Winter Rye, after first applying a quick-acting fertilizer to force the Rye into fast growth, and then in the spring, when the Rye is about 9 in. tall, it is plowed under. Of course the cow peas, clovers and vetches, being legumes, add additional nitrogen to the soil. It has been shown that even a very thin and barren soil has been converted into a rich, productive one by growing and turning under 3 successive crops of Winter Rye.

Usually when green manure crops are sown with the intention of plowing them under to add additional humus to the soil, they are sown at rates with 25–50% more seed than normally, merely to produce as much green foliage as possible. Consequently, the following rates are suggested, with the rate per acre being the normal recommendation for the crop, and the rate per 1000 sq. ft. being the rate recommended to gardeners for cover crops:

COVER CROPS—RECOMMENDED RATES FOR SOWING SEED

MATERIAL	FIELD RATE LB/ACRE	COVER CROP RATE LBS/1000 SQ. FT. FOR GARDENS
Perennial Rye	40–50	1–2 lb.
Rye Grass	40–50	2–3 lb.
Buckwheat	35–60	2–3 lb.
Cow Peas	75–120	3–4 lb.
Vetch—Hairy	25–40	$\frac{3}{4}$–$1\frac{1}{2}$ lb.
V. Crown	25–40	$\frac{3}{4}$–$1\frac{1}{2}$ lb.
V. common	40–80	—
Crimson Clover	15–20	1 lb.
Lespedeza—Annual	30–40	1–$1\frac{1}{2}$ lb.
L. serecia	30–40	$\frac{3}{4}$–$1\frac{1}{2}$ lb.
Soybeans	100–150	3–5 lb.
Millet	20–25	1 lb.
Rape	4–6	2–5 oz.
Sudan Grass	30–40	1–$1\frac{1}{2}$ lb.

Also garden compost can be added to the soil as a soil amendment or as a garden mulch. More gardeners should become interested in making their own compost and use it to turn back additional humus into the soil. For method of making see COMPOST.

Chemical (Inorganic) Fertilizers

The above discussion has been concerned chiefly with the physical makeup of the garden soil and methods of improvement. The chemical makeup is just as important. It has already been pointed out that nitrogen, phosphorus and potassium are the most important elements in any soil and the ones which are depleted or used up first. These must be added from time to time in order to have optimum plant growth.

Nitrogen, the most important (and usually the first to become deficient), is used by the plant in making lush growth and dark green leaves. It is applied to the soil in organic fertilizers such as manure, tankage and cottonseed meal. Today's gardeners, probably because of excessive advertising, mostly look to inorganic fertilizers for adding nitrogen, such as sodium nitrate and ammonium nitrate. These have 5–20% nitrogen which is quickly available to the plants as soon as it is in solution. Effects of adding nitrate of soda to the vegetable garden (if it is watered in thoroughly) can be seen within 2 or 3 days. Urea (an organic fertilizer) in some of its new forms, is also available, the nitrogen in this being released much more slowly over a longer period. These fertilizers are highly effective but should be applied in exact quantities as they can burn foliage very quickly. Also, too heavy an application, short of burning, can cause over-succulent growth, which is not desirable.

Phosphorus, supplied by superphosphate (20% P) or triplephosphate (45% P) promotes root growth, tuber development, flower and seed production. This is one of the best chemicals to use in trying to force otherwise vigorous lilacs and wisterias into flower. Merely by digging a 12-in. ditch around the recalcitrant plants in question and mixing superphosphate with the soil so removed and then replacing it, some plants can be brought back into bloom the following year.

Potassium is the third element needed to be frequently replenished in soils, for although it may be present in sufficient quantities in most soils it is not present in the right form for absorption by the roots unless there is a large amount of humus present. Potash (the oxide of potassium) is usually applied as sulfate or muriate of potash. Wood ashes contain potash in ample amounts. It is potassium that is needed to make strong stems and vigorous-growing roots.

"Complete" fertilizers contain all 3 of these materials in varying quantities and from various sources. The law requires that the materials making up the fertilizer be clearly printed on the bag. So, there are available all sorts of "mixtures," a 5–10–5 (5% nitrogen, 10% phosphoric acid 5% potash) having only half as much nitrogen, phosphoric acid and potash as a 10–20–10, per 100 lbs. Hence, one would apply the 10–20–10 fertilizer at only one-half the rate of a 5–10–5 in order to apply the same amount of nitrogen, phosphoric acid and potash

to the soil. Obviously cost enters into these calculations as a very important item.

The average gardener usually does not have time to study the specific assets of individual fertilizers for specific crops. It can become a complicated affair. Nor does he wish to make his own fertilizer mixtures. He is perfectly content to use some of the complete fertilizers available today, in amounts generally recommended. Many of these if used properly are perfectly satisfactory. For those who wish more information the following fertilizers are available in some areas:

Dried Blood (12–14% N) is of course organic and immediately available. It leaves an acid reaction.

Hoof and Horn Meal (12–14% N) organic but slowly available with traces of other elements.

Tankage (6–11% N) organic; leaves alkaline reaction.

Fish Meal (8–10% N; 4.5–9% P; 2–3% K) organic; many brands.

Guano (10–14% N; 8–10% P; 2–4% K) organic; usually very strong and should be used with care.

Sewage Sludge (6% N; 2.5% P) organic; dried processed sewage; analysis varies.

Nitrate of Soda (15.5–16% N) inorganic; burns foliage if it drops on moistened leaves; should be used with extreme care as too heavy an application kills plant tissues. Leaves an alkaline reaction.

Calcium Nitrate (15.5–16% N) inorganic; readily available; leaves alkaline reaction.

Ammonium sulfate (20.6% N) inorganic; readily available; should be used with caution as too heavy an application quickly kills succulent plants.

Urea (46% N) organic; rapidly available; highly concentrated, should be used with care.

Urea-form fertilizers release nitrogen slowly over a long period, should only be used in quantities recommended by the manufacturer; highly concentrated.

Fertilizers used for applying phosphoric acid alone would include superphosphate (one of the best), triplephosphate, basic slag, bone meal (raw bone meal contains 20–24% phosphoric acid, acting slowly, while steamed bone meal acts more quickly).

Fertilizers used for applying potash alone would include Kainite (14% K) but care should be taken in its application; muriate of potash (50–60% K) slow in availability; and wood ashes. It will be found that various of these materials, in varying amounts are used in the preparation of "complete" fertilizers.

Soil Tests

The all-important problem is what fertilizer

to use and how much. This varies with the soils, the past history of fertilizing on the soil in question, the locality and the kinds of plants that are intended to be grown. In the case of acid-soil plants like azaleas, rhododendrons and blueberries, it depends on the soil acidity, also. Before the advent of the automobile, the simplest of all fertilizers was manure. One could hardly go wrong on this, using it on all soils for all crops. It added chemical nutrients as well as humus. No other fertilizer was needed.

Now, with manure unavailable in many areas, the problem of what to use and the rate of application is all important. For those in a hurry, the complete fertilizers can be applied (a 5–10–5) at the rate of 15–20 lbs. per 1000 sq. ft., and this may be satisfactory. For the individual who is particular and wants to have the best possible medium in which to grow his plants, he might well have a soil analysis made, to receive exact answers to his questions.

In taking soil samples, one should take 5–10 samples from the plot that is to be planted and mix them up together, using about a pint of the final mixture sealed in a can or plastic bag and properly labeled to be sent to the local state experiment station. Each sample should be a piece of soil, a few square inches in area but about 6–8 in. deep. These are all mixed together in a pail from which the final sample is taken.

The reason for multiple sampling is that 1 sample might not tell the composite story of the soil. As has been previously shown, soils do vary considerably sometimes within a hundred feet or less. Also, the one spot chosen for a single sample might just be where a pile of fertilizer had been dropped the year before, or where the children's aquarium had been dumped several years previously leaving an unusually high percentage of sand.

It is helpful to the individual making the analysis if he can know when the soil was limed or fertilized previously, what is or was growing on it and what is intended to be grown. Drainage problems, if any, should be noted. The report should be returned with recommendations of procedures and fertilizer applications to bring the soil into optimum productivity.

One should also differentiate between a soil analysis and a simple pH determination (for growing acid-soil plants). Soil pH can vary greatly; near the foundation of a brick building it will be more alkaline because of water continually splashing on the mortar, washing out the lime and carrying it to the soil. In pine woods, it will be more acid because of the decaying pine needles which leave an acid reaction. In either case, it is most helpful to take soil samples properly and obtain the specific recommendations for needed soil amendments from the state experiment station.

Acid Soils

Sometimes soils are very acid and in order to give plants a better medium in which to grow the pH must be raised. The growing of cover crops and plowing them into the soil raises the pH slightly and at the same time is excellent because humus is added. Also the pH may be raised by applying ground limestone in amounts suggested by the local state experiment station after an acidity test has been made. The following table shows the approximate amount of ground limestone needed to raise the pH of a 7-in. layer of soil from pH 4.5 to pH 5.5 per 1000 sq. ft.

Sands and sandy loams	15–45 lbs.
Loams	40–60 lbs.
Silt loams	60–80 lbs.
Clay loams	80–100 lbs.

The great variation in amounts is caused by the different soil structures of the different soils and the different areas where they occur. It is much better to apply a portion of the estimated amount at first, work it into the soil and let it remain for a few months or a year and test it again to ascertain how much more should be added. It is best not to change the pH more than 1 pH unit by one application of ground limestone at one time. Dolomitic limestone is by far the best type of lime to use in any garden because it contains magnesium which is frequently deficient in many soils. It is also only very slowly soluble in neutral or alkaline soils, hence less caustic than burned or slaked lime. Usually an application of lime will remain effective for 4–5 years.

On the other hand, soil acidity may have to be increased, especially if ericaceous plants like azaleas, rhododendrons and blueberries are to be planted. Two materials are used for this purpose, aluminum sulfate and finely powdered sulfur. Powdered sulfur is preferred, even though it is slower-acting, because it takes nearly 6 times as much aluminum sulfate as powdered sulfur to accomplish the same acidifying results. Also, aluminum accumulating in the soil can become very toxic to plant growth. Finally sulfur is cheaper than aluminum sulfate. It takes between 1.2 and 3.5 lbs. of powdered sulfur per 100 sq. ft. to bring an 8-in. layer of soil down from a pH of 7.0 to 5.5, or between .8 and 2.4 lbs. to bring it down from a pH of 6.5 to 5.5. It should be worked thoroughly into the soil, well moistened and allowed to stand (without planting) for at least 2–6 weeks, then again tested, corrected if necessary and planted.

Then too, mulches should be used that leave an acid reaction, like pine needles and peat moss. Fertilizers should be used that are known to leave an acid reaction. These things help to stabilize the soil at the lower pH and aid in keeping it there.

Alkaline and saline soils present special problems and best recommendations for procedures would be obtained from the nearest state experiment station. Many such soils are in arid regions of little rainfall, where irrigation is necessary to leach out some of the accumulated salts and thus make the land productive. Gypsum (calcium sulfate) with 19.5–21% calcium and 16–18% sulfur is frequently used on alkaline soils for the calcium is readily available.

For additional information, see *An Introduction to Soils and Plant Growth* by Roy L. Donahue, Prentice Hall, Inc., Englewood Cliffs, N.J. 3rd Ed. 1971

SOIL STERILIZATION. Soil-borne diseases such as damping-off, nematodes and soil-infesting insects such as symphylids are eliminated or controlled by sterilizing the soil. In addition to volatile chemicals (see FUMIGATION) chemical drenches such as VC-13 and Mylone can be used effectively. Heat is the most practical soil sterilant. In greenhouses, the heating plant is usually used to supply steam or hot water. Effective temperatures are 180° F. for 30 minutes to destroy plant diseases and 130° F. for 25 minutes to kill insects and related animals. The effective temperature must be maintained at the depth in the soil at which the plant roots grow. A small amount of soil for houseplants can be sterilized in the kitchen stove by the same temperature and exposure which will bake a potato.

SOIL TESTS. See SOILS.

SOLANDRA (so-LAN-dra)

guttata   vine   Zone 10   Goldcup Chalice-vine

A Mexican vine, frequently planted in Hawaii and southern Fla., this has outstanding yellow, cup-shaped flowers, about 9 in. long. The color and brownish markings are similar to the color of bananas. Very fragrant flowers open in Jan. and for 2–3 months thereafter and the round red berries are 2½ in. across. The evergreen leaves are 6 in. long. Propagated by layers.

SOLANUM (so-LAY-num). Belonging to the Potato Family, this genus, widely distributed but largely tropical, includes over 1000 species. Some, such as the Potato, are important food plants and others bear fruits which are deadly poisonous and the wilted leaves of many species are poisonous. The alternate leaves may be lobed or entire and the flowers, borne at or near the axils in 1- to 4-flowered clusters, have a 5-lobed calyx and a star-shaped or bell-shaped, 5-lobed corolla.

aculeatissimum   2'   Zone 10   Soda-apple Nightshade

A perennial shrubby plant, native to the Tropics, with spiny stems and leaves which are 5–7 lobed and about 4 in. long. The white flowers are an inch across in few-flowered cymes; the fruit is rounded, orange-colored globe about 2 in. across. Easily grown from seed in the greenhouse or out-of-doors in the far South, and valued for its bright colored fruits which are dried for ornamental use.

capsicastrum   2'   Zone 10   False Jerusalem-cherry

Native to Brazil, this is similar to the Jerusalem-cherry. The foliage is grayish, the stems are hairy, and the fruits do not remain on as long as do those of the true Jerusalem-cherry. Fruits are scarlet to orange-red, ½ in. across, but it is definitely no substitute for the other plant.

carolinense   2'   Zone 3   Carolina Horse-nettle

A pernicious perennial weed, native to North America and widely distributed. The stems have many, sharp, yellow spines and so do the leaf stalks as well as the underside of the midrib of the leaf. The flowers are purplish or white, in loose racemes, resembling those of the Potato, and the fruit is a yellowish smooth berry. The alternate leaves are shaped like white oak leaves and are nearly the same size. It is a most troublesome pest with very deep roots. *S. rostratum* is somewhat similar and is a common pest throughout western Canada.

crispum   15'   Zone 8

A small shrub from Chile and Peru, with hairy leaves 2–4 in. long and light purple flowers, each about ¾ in. across, borne in Aug. in large wide clusters. The fruit is round and globe shaped, pale yellow and ¼ in. across. Occasionally grown as an ornamental in mild climates for its ornamental flowers and fruits.

dulcamara   climbing Vine   Zone 4   Bitter Nightshade

Native to Europe and northern Africa and western Asia, this twining vine has unfortunately become naturalized in North America. It is a vicious pest, cropping up everywhere. The violet flowers are borne in clusters; the brilliant scarlet fruits are about ⅜ in. long and are very conspicuous against the green alternate leaves in late summer. Both leaves and berries and new shoots are very poisonous when eaten, hence the plant should not be near children or grazing animals. It is spread by birds and can become a vicious weed, especially because of its vigorous-growing, invading roots. It is often called bittersweet in Europe but in America this name should be reserved for *Celastrus* species.

giganteum 25′ Zone 9 Giant Nightshade
Sometimes called "African Holly" in Calif., because of its stem prickles. The leaves are 6–8 in. long, silky white underneath. The showy, blue to violet flowers are only ½ in. wide but are in profuse clusters. The red fruits are ¼ in. in dia. Native to India.

integrifolium 3′ Zone 10 Ethiopian Eggplant
Native to Africa, this plant is very spiny, with large leaves, 8 in. long; white flowers, ¾ in. across, with few to a cluster, and red or yellow rounded fruits, 2 in. across. It is very ornamental and can be grown in the same way as *S. aculeatissimum*.

jasminoides 20′ Zone 9 Jasmine Nightshade
A shrubby, climbing plant from Brazil, without leaf or stem prickles; leaves 3 in. long and the star-shaped flowers, 1 in. across, are white, tinged blue, borne in large trusses during the late summer and autumn. It is a vigorous grower. The var. **grandiflorum** bears larger flowers than the species and **variegatum** bears variegated leaves.

macranthum 6′ Zone 10 Potatotree
The 2-in. flowers of this spiny tropical shrub from Brazil are bright blue, star-shaped, set off with bright yellow stamens in the center. The flower fades to almost white in the spring. Fruits are small yellow berries but are not always produced. The leaves, about 1 ft. long, have irregular lobes and the midribs and sometimes the branches have small hooked thorns. Occasionally planted in Hawaii.

melongena esculentum 2′–4′ Annual Eggplant
A vegetable from tropical Africa mostly grown in the U.S. as an annual, with angled or lobed leaves 10–15 in. long, violet-purple flowers, 2 in. across, and usually purple but sometimes white or yellow fruits 6–10 in. long. The var. **serpentinum** is the Snake Eggplant with almost cylindrical fruit 1 in. in dia. and 1 ft. long. The var. **depressum**, the Dwarf Eggplant, is smaller in all its parts.

nigrum 3′–4′ annual Common Nightshade
Another European annual species, now common in fields and along roadsides in the Atlantic coastal states. This plant has alternate, ovate leaves and flowers in small clusters on short, stout, leafy stalks appearing near the tips of the branches, similar to those of the Potato. Each flower has a 5-lobed calyx and a corolla of 5 white, reflexed segments. The fruits are round, dull black berries. The plant blooms throughout the summer.

pseudocapsicum 4′ Zone 9 Jerusalem-cherry
A very popular pot plant grown or offered for sale by most florists because of its profuse, orange-red, cherrylike fruits which are about ½ in. in dia., and remain on the plant in good

Jerusalem-cherry—Solanum pseudocapsicum.

condition for months. Especially raised in the greenhouse to be in good condition at Christmas time. Flowers are small and white, the leaves are oblong and may be up to 4 in. long. Propagated by sowing seeds in Feb. or March. They will start to fruit that fall. If, after the fruits have dropped after the first of the year, they are heavily cut back, shaken free of soil and re-potted, they can be used for producing larger plants that second fall. Cuttings are easily rooted.

rantonnetii 6′ Zone 9 Paraguay Night-shade
Considered by some as the most handsome of the shrubby species of this genus because of its beautiful, dark lavender flowers, each one of which is 1 in. across, and they are borne in clusters during an extended period in the summer. The red fruits are heart shaped and drooping. Native to Paraguay and Argentina.

seaforthianum climber Zone 10 Brazilian Nightshade
Leaves about 8 in. long with 3-pinnate, un-equal leaflets; this slightly woody climber produces numerous drooping clusters of flowers that are purple, star-shaped and have conspicuous yellow anthers. The vivid red berries, ⅓ in. wide, are sought by the birds. Native to tropical America.

tuberosum 2′ grown as annual Potato
The common Potato has been derived from species native to South America and is now grown throughout the temperate regions of the world. There are many varieties. A weak-growing, compound-leaved, herbaceous plant grown for its edible tubers. Flowers (and fruits which are globe-shaped, yellowish or greenish and about ¾ in. in dia.) may or may not be produced but it is the large starchy tubers which are of such great economic importance. For culture see POTATO.

wendlandii **climbing** **Zone 10** **Costa Rican Nightshade**
Shrubby but climbing, this has prickly, pinnately compound, glossy leaves and is a handsome climbing plant for the greenhouse if the temperature does not go below 45° F. The pale blue flowers are 2½ in. across, borne in rather large pendulous clusters. Easily propagated by softwood cuttings. Native to Costa Rica and a popular outdoor plant in the gardens of southern Fla.

SOLDANELLA (sol-dan-ELL-a). These are low-growing perennial herbs belonging to the Primrose Family, native to the high mountains of Europe. They must be provided with a rocky habitat, in shaded places with moist soil, or they will not survive. They have the reputation of being extremely difficult to grow properly. Propagation is by division just after flowering, and seeds sown as soon as ripe. They have thick, rounded, leathery leaves and pretty, bell-shaped or funnel-shaped, deeply fringed flowers. In the Alps they bloom right after the snow has melted, often pushing up their flowers right through the snow.

alpina **6″** **Zone 4** **Glacier Alpenclock**
One of the daintiest of this group, with small, lavender-fringed flowers marked inside with reddish lines, borne on 3-in. stems. The leaves are rounded, 1½ in. wide; flowers are pale blue, ½ in. long, in 1–3-flowered umbels in May.

minima **1″** **Zone 4** **Least Alpenclock**
This is the smallest of the 4 species and the small, bell-like flowers are usually single borne. The leaves are round; the flowers white with a few violet-colored lines inside.

montana **15″** **Zone 4** **Greater Alpenclock**
The most handsome of this group, with large, rounded, somewhat leathery leaves 2½ in. wide, and violet-lilac-colored flowers, borne 5–6 on a 6–9-in. stem. These are spread widely open, ¾ in. wide, and appear from May to July.

pusilla **6″** **Zone 4** **Little Alpenclock**
Mostly it looks similar to *S. minima* but is larger, with flowers borne singly or 2 on a stem, and not widely open but tube shaped, colored pale lavender to white. They are fringed but not as much as those of other species.

SOLEIROLIA (sol-e-ROLL-ia)
soleirolii (*Helxine soleirolii*) **3″** **Zone 10** **Baby's-tears**
A common creeping house plant sometimes merely growing over a porous stone kept moist in a saucer of water and often growing at will under the greenhouse bench where it is moist and cool, this is almost a weed in some greenhouses; native to Corsica and Sardinia where it makes dense mats. It will not withstand frost.

The leaves are orbicular about ¼ in. wide. The minute flowers have no ornamental value. It grows best in partial shade but must have plenty of moisture. Easily propagated merely by placing the stems in moist sand.

SOLIDAGO (sol-i-DAY-go). The goldenrods form an important part of the late summer wild flower display of North America. They are members of a genus with over 125 species having an erect, somewhat woody, seldom branching stem, simple, alternate leaves, either toothed or entire, and flower heads in a wide variety of terminal clusters, these frequently being 1-sided. The tiny flower heads, generally yellow, but in one instance white, have perfect disk flowers and pistillate ray flowers. Although these individual flower heads may be only ¼-in. wide, they are borne so profusely in frequently compound clusters as to be one of the showiest of the late summer wild flowers. They spread rapidly and self-sow readily and so are difficult to keep within bounds in the wild garden. Most are common throughout southern Canada and eastern U.S. Many people are allergic to the pollen causing hay fever. The flowering heads are often used in making a yellow dye. Easily propagated by seeds (they bloom the second year after sowing) or by division.

bicolor **1′–3′** **Zone 3** **Silver Goldenrod, Silverrod**
The alternate leaves of this perennial or biennial species are without toothed margins and the ray flowers are white, the small clusters of flower heads arranged in a terminal panicle and in the axils of the upper leaves. Although found less frequently than the yellow-flowered species, it ranges from Southeastern Canada to Ga. and west to the Mississippi River. It flowers from July to Oct.

caesia **1′–3′** **Zone 4** **Wreath Goldenrod**
This species is characterized by purplish, unbranched stems, toothed, lanceolate leaves which are sessile, and small, axillary clusters of golden flower heads. It prefers rich, woodsy sites and extends throughout eastern U.S., flowering in late summer.

canadensis **1′–4′** **Zone 3** **Canada Goldenrod**
The narrowly lanceolate leaves of this plant may reach 5 in. in length and the yellow flower heads are compactly arranged in a branching, 1-sided, terminal panicle. It is an extremely showy plant of the fields and meadows throughout southern Canada and the U.S. and blooms in late summer and autumn.

cutleri **3″–12″** **Zone 4** **Cutler Goldenrod**
A tiny evergreen Goldenrod from the mountain tops of N.Y. Its leaves, growing in clusters, are 4 in. high and it flowers in midsummer.

flexicaulis **2′–3′** **Zone 4** **Zigzag Goldenrod**

The broadly ovate leaves of this Goldenrod are finely toothed and taper to a slender point. These are arranged alternately on a stem which grows in a zigzag fashion, especially toward the upper end where short flower stalks bear the loosely clustered yellow flower heads. The branch terminates with a short, leafy flower cluster. Its range extends from New England to N.Dak., and south to S.Car. It blooms from midsummer to autumn.

graminifolia   2′–4′   **Zone** 3   **Grass-leaved Goldenrod**
The narrow, grasslike leaves give this plant its name. The fragrant yellow flower heads are borne in a relatively sparse, flat-topped, branching cluster. It is found in open, sunny sites over most of southern Canada and the eastern half of U.S., and flowers from July to Oct.

juncea   2′–4′   **Zone** 3   **Plume Goldenrod**
This plant has narrowly oval, toothed, basal leaves and small, lanceolate leaves ascending the smooth stem. The gracefully branching and arching yellow flower cluster is arranged on the upper side of the stem. Native from New Brunswick to N.Car. and Mo.

nemoralis   2′   **Zone** 3   **Dyersweed Goldenrod**
A plant for dry sandy banks with terminal clusters of yellow flowers, in 1-sided, spreading or recurved racemes; Nova Scotia to Tex.

odora   4′   **Zone** 3   **Sweet Goldenrod**
Native from Nova Scotia to Fla. and Tex., this has yellow flowers in 1-sided racemes but rather large clusters, and 4-in. long lanceolate leaves that are a ise scented. The leaves have been used in mak g a tea.

puberula   2′–3′   **Zone** 3   **Downy Goldenrod**
An erect, slender, unbranching plant with a purplish stem and small, lanceolate leaves, 1½–3 in. long. The showy terminal panicle of flowers heads is lengthened by the clusters of flower heads rising on short stalks at the axils of the upper leaves, resulting in a graceful and pleasing transition from leaves to flowers. A plant preferring dry, sandy soil and blooming from July to Oct. Native throughout eastern North America.

rugosa   8′   **Zone** 3   **Wrinkled Goldenrod**
Native from Newfoundland to Fla. and Tex., this has oval 4 in. leaves and yellow flowers in 1-sided but large racemes.

sempervirens   2′–5′   **Zone** 4   **Seaside Goldenrod**
A hardy plant, withstanding even the gales and salt spray of the Atlantic salt marshes; the rather thick leaves are narrowly lanceolate with slender tips, closely alternating on the stem, the lower leaves clasping the stem. The flower heads are borne in a 1-sided panicle, the lower flower heads arising on axillary stalks. Flowers persist into late fall. Native throughout eastern North America.

shortii   4′   **Zone** 6   **Short's Goldenrod**
With leaves about 4 in. long and toothed; yellow flowers in large 1-sided clusters in summer. Native to central U.S.

speciosa   3′–6′   **Zone** 5   **Noble Goldenrod**
Among the handsomest of the goldenrods, this has narrowly lanceolate leaves, the margins entire, and a showy, branched, slightly arching, terminal panicle. It is found in open woods and prairies from Mass. to Ark., and blooms from Aug. to Oct.

virgaurea   10″–3′   **Zone** 4   **European Goldenrod**
A vigorous perennial with obovate leaves 7 in. long; yellow flowers in dense clusters up to 10 in. long. Native to Europe but not much used in America.

x SOLIDASTER (sol-i-DAS-ter)
luteus   2½′   **Zone** 5   **Hybrid Goldenrod**
Actually a bigeneric hybrid (*Aster* sp. x. *Solidago* sp.), this has lanceolate leaves, 4 in. long, and daisylike, golden-yellow flowers in midsummer. Cultural methods are the same as for Aster.

SOLOMON'S-SEAL. See POLYGONATUM.

SOLOMON'S-SEAL, FALSE. See SMILACINA.

SONCHUS (SON-kus)
arvensis   5′   **Zone** 3   **Field Sow-thistle**
A perennial weed with a long underground root which can send up numerous shoots, widespread throughout the northern U.S. and southern Canada but native to Europe. Leaves are alternate, similar in shape and size to those of Dandelion, with bristles on the margin. The yellow flower heads are 1½ in. across and bloom from June to Sept. on long stalks. These should be kept from seeding by mowing.

oleraceus   2′–6′   **annual**   **Sow-thistle**
Native to Europe, but a common weed throughout North America although not as bad as *S. arvensis*, but it should be kept from seeding by mowing. The yellow flower heads and the leaves are similar to those of *S. arvensis* but produced in loose panicles. For control see WEED-CONTROLLING CHEMICALS.

SOOTY MOLD. This fungus is not a plant parasite. It lives on the sweet honey dew secreted by some sucking insects, especially aphids, psyllas and some scale insects. See HONEY DEW. When plants are infested with these insects, the honey dew falls on all lower parts of the tree and the plants beneath it. Black sooty mold develops on the honey dew giving a sooty appearance to the plants. Sooty mold may prevent normal growth by interfering with the natural functions of the stomata. Pear trees badly infested with pear psylla and subsequent honey dew and sooty mold have failed to bloom because of abnormal development of the blossom buds. Control of insects is the only prevention.

SOPHORA (SOFF-or-a)

davidii   7′   Zone 5   Vetch Sophora
Sometimes termed *S. vicifolia*, this deciduous shrub has 13–19 leaflets in the leaf, each leaflet being about ½ in. long. The bluish-violet to whitish, pealike flowers appear in June but the fruit is merely a dried pod. It is a graceful shrub, from western China, the chief merit of which is to grow and thrive in poor sandy soils in dry situations. Its graceful habit and vetchlike foliage give it a feathery appearance in the garden.

japonica   75′   Zone 4   Japanese Pagoda Tree
It is the last of the taller trees to bloom (late Aug.) and so is naturally a popular tree wherever it can be used. The leaves are alternate and compound.

Its ability to withstand city growing conditions is another point in its favor. Although rather large for a street tree, it is excellent in city parks. Specimens in the Arnold Arboretum have been growing since 1891 and still are in fairly good condition, and 1 specimen in England was known to have been nearly 200 years old.

The fruits are pealike pods which turn brown and may hang on the tree a greater part of the winter. It does lack autumn color and it is true that the tree may not bear flowers until it is over 25 years old. These flowers do not fade on the tree but drop off while they are still fresh. However, its round-headed habit, its profuse flowers, especially when it gets older, and its lack of insect and disease pests all point to making it an excellent and most serviceable ornamental.

The variety 'Pendula', when grafted high on a young seedling of the species, develops into a densely rounded, globe-shaped head with pendulous branches and old specimens do flower.

Propagation

Do not allow the seed to dry out. As soon as it is thoroughly ripe soak it in hot water (at 190° F.) overnight or for one hour in concentrated sulfuric acid, then thoroughly wash and sow. Varieties are grafted on seedlings of the same species. Softwood cuttings have also proved successful. See GRAFTING.

secundiflora   35′   Zone 8   Mescal-bean
Evergreen shrub, native to Tex., N.Mex. and Mexico; alternate compound leaves 4–6 in. long, 7–9 leaflets; flowers violet-blue, 1 in. long and very fragrant, borne in racemes 2–3 in.

long; fruit a dried pod 1–7 in. long. It is used in ornamental plantings but the leaves and seeds are said to be poisonous.

tetraptera   40′   Zone 9   New Zealand Sophora
It is interesting to note that this is native both to Chile and New Zealand, for it is one of the most conspicuous flowering trees grown in the subtropical U.S. The flowers are golden yellow and pealike, borne in racemes 4–8 in. long during May. The leaves are evergreen to semideciduous, alternate, pinnately compound, 1½–4½ in. long. The fruits are peculiar 4-winged pods about 7 in. long.

SOPHRONITIS (so-fro-NY-tis). This is a small genus of very attractive orchids which are said to bloom one year from seed. *S. coccinea* is particularly outstanding because it bears brilliant scarlet flowers, 1½–3 in. across. It is variable in habit, grows from pseudobulbs, and has great value to the hybridist who uses it in crosses with *Cattleya* and *Laelia* species as well as others. Native to Brazil. For culture and propagation see ORCHID.

SORBARIA (sor-BAY-ria). These are deciduous shrubs having alternate compound leaves with 13–23 leaflets and large, pyramidal, creamy-white flower clusters, 4–12 in. long, in the summer. They have no autumn color, no interesting fruits and are coarse in texture because of their large leaves. None are valued landscape plants and most are not for the small garden but rather for the public park where they can be observed from a distance and grown in clumps valued chiefly for their large summer-blooming spires of creamy-white flowers.

Propagation

Seed may be sown as soon as ripe or stored dry in airtight containers in a cool place for up to a year, then sown. Plants may be divided by cutting through them with a sharp spade in the early spring before growth has started. Softwood, hardwood, and root cuttings (which see) all can be rooted if taken at the proper time.

aitchisonii   9′   Zone 6   Kashmir False Spirea
This is offered by only 3 nurseries in the U.S. but might be tried by others. It is somewhat similar to *S. sorbifolia*, although taller, and has very bright green leaves which contrast favorably with the bright red color of the young branchlets. Because of its height, there is probably no place for this in the small garden.

arborea   18′   Zone 5
Native to central and western China, the leaves have 13–17 leaflets and the loose-branching flower clusters are a foot long. Too tall for normal garden use.

sorbifolia   6′   Zone 2   Ural False Spirea

The most popular of the false spireas, this is available from many nurseries. It is chiefly valued for its 10-in. pyramidal clusters of small white flowers during late July, at a time when few woody plants bloom. The leaves are pinnately compound, with 13–23 leaflets, coarse in texture and do not have a prominent autumn color. The shrub spreads easily by suckers and so is adapted to being grown in clumps. It is one of the first plants to produce leaves in the spring and, if observed from a distance when in bloom, its arching branches with heavy terminal flower clusters do make an interesting picture. However, it is doubtful if it has sufficient merit to plant in the small garden.

tomentosa 18′   Zone 5   Lindley False Spirea
Native to the Himalayas, this has 15–21 leaflets in the compound leaf and the flower clusters are 8–12 in. long and 6–8 in. broad.

x SORBARONIA (SORB-aron-ia). A bigeneric hybrid (*Sorbus* x *Aronia*) but of little ornamental value and not worth considering here.

SORBUS (SOR-bus). Mountain-ash. These trees are native throughout the northern temperate regions of the world. Perhaps the most commonly planted in America is the European *S. aucuparia*, which has been popular here since colonial times and grows vigorously. There are several native American species that are just as good and might be used a great deal more. Some of the white-fruiting Asiatic types present variation in the fall and the most recent introduction, a plant under the name at present of *S. cashmiriana*, shows promise of being one of the most ornamental of all. All have alternate leaves; some species have simple or lobed leaves and many have pinnately compound leaves.

The greatest drawback in general is their susceptibility to borer attacks in the base of the trunk, especially the flat-headed apple tree borer which can be a serious pest and actually girdle small trees if it is not eradicated in time.

Concerning the ornamental qualifications of Sorbus, they have profuse clusters of small white flowers in the late spring, followed by clusters of bright-colored red or orange or yellow berries in the fall. Most have yellow to reddish autumn color in addition. They are symmetrical trees, weak wooded but fast growing, and their alternate compound leaves (some have simple leaves) add to their general effectiveness.

Looking them over more carefully, the Korean Mountain-ash (*S. alnifolia*) and the new Cashmir Mountain-ash (*S. cashmiriana*) have about the largest individual flowers of any, between ¾–1 in. in dia. In fact, the latter has flower buds tinged a pale pink and the flowers open tinged blush pink, making them outstanding when observed closely.

S. hybrida, *S. folgneri* and *S. aria* species have leaves that are white tomentose underneath, so much so as to be of considerable ornamental value. Some of the varieties are of fastigiate habit, and while the tree is young and under about 20′ high, such plants make excellent specimens. Older plants, however, will crack and break up, so that these fastigiate forms should be considered for only short service.

Fruits of the different species vary in size and color between red, orange and yellow. Some have fruits that are slightly brownish and these are not recommended for ornamental use. The fruit of several species is palatable and edible and the berries have been dried and ground into a flour, or used in making preserves or acid drinks. However, the foliage of many will turn a rich yellow to orange and reddish and this makes them stand out as excellent specimens in the fall.

Finally, the Korean Mountain-ash should be singled out again because of its gray bark, similar to that of the European Beech. Such a bark is of considerable interest all winter long.

In Europe, the mountain-ashes are used considerably more than they are in America. Several species are widely native and others have been used to make jellies and preserves for centuries. One Dutch nurseryman has recently named 25 hybrids, giving each a very colorful name, and is merchandising these widely in Europe and America. All in all, the Mountain-ash is not one of our best ornamental trees. Certainly its disease and insect pests are sufficiently numerous to prevent it from being used widely as a street tree. However, as an ornamental here and there, especially for fall display when it can be grown in the full sun where it does best, and not in partial shade, then it will add a colorful spot of interest to almost any planting.

Propagation

Seed stratified for 3 months at 40° F. and then sown will usually germinate. However, if it is sown after that cold period and fails to germinate after about 3–4 months, then give it another 3 months cold period. Grafting and budding is practiced commercially, using understocks of Sorbus species of close affinity to that from which scions are taken. See STRATIFICATION, BUDDING, GRAFTING.

Insect Pests

The greenish-yellow larvae of the mountain-ash sawfly may defoliate large branches. Spraying in midsummer with insecticide #5 or #37 prevents serious damage. Lilac borer infests Mountain-ash. See LILAC. Several scale insects that also infest Apple may be injurious. See APPLE.

Diseases

Fireblight, black rot and rust are pests. See APPLE.

alnifolia 60′ Zone 5 Korean Mountain-ash
This Korean native might easily be considered the best of the Sorbus. The flowers are profuse; individual flowers being as much as 1 in. in dia., making these the largest single flowers in the Sorbus group. The excellent scarlet to orange fruits are $\frac{1}{3}$–$\frac{1}{2}$ in. long, borne in large flat or rounded clusters, and the autumn color is orange to scarlet. The leaves are simple —not compound. The smooth, dark gray bark gives much the same effect as bark of the European Beech and the whole tree is vigorous and pyramidal to oval in general outline. Apparently not as susceptible to borers as are most of the other species.

americana 30′ Zone 2 American Mountain-ash
Small, sometimes shrubby, with bright red fruit, this is a native of northeastern North America. The taller, more vigorous European Mountain-ash is used more in America and can usually be distinguished from its American counterparts because its winter buds are densely white pubescent while those of the American Mountain-ash are glabrous or only slightly pubescent. *S. decora* is often considered the better of these 2 natives.

aria 45′ Zone 5 White Beam Mountain-ash
A common native tree in Europe and in England where it does very well on limestone soils. The scarlet-red berries, $\frac{1}{3}$–$\frac{1}{2}$ in. long, are specked with brownish dots, ripen in the fall but are quickly eaten by the birds as soon as they are ripe. It is especially desirable (but not in areas with considerable smoke, soot or dust in the atmosphere) because of the white, pubescent undersurface of the leaves, giving them a delightful contrasting color. The 2 varieties most used are: '**Aurea**', the Yellow White Beam, usually considered the best of the yellow-leaved Sorbus varieties. The name *chrysophylla* is synonymous. However, any yellow-leaved plant is often difficult to use properly in landscape planting. The second var. '**Majestica**,' the Majestic White Beam, is very popular in England, not in America. The red fruits are as much as $\frac{3}{8}$ in. in dia. The undersurface of the simple leaves (which are as much as 7 in. long) is covered with a white pubescence which adds much to the ornamental character of the tree. This is considered to be the most conspicuous variety of this species, sometimes incorrectly termed *decaisneana*, which is a synonym. Excellent for

growing in alkaline soils but does well in acid soils also. If the leaves and fruits of this variety are considered too large, then the species might well be substituted for it.

The European Mountain-ash has orange-red fruits in the fall.

aucuparia 45′ Zone 2 European Mountain-ash
Called the Rowan Tree, this has been a popular ornamental in America since colonial times when it was introduced from its native habitat in Europe, and is definitely a taller tree than its American relative, *S. americana*. It has even become naturalized in Alaska! With large clusters of bright red fruits, $\frac{1}{4}$ in. in dia., and reddish autumn color, it has been widely planted in America for a century. Some varieties are: '**Asplenifolia**'—a graceful tree with double serrate leaflets; **beissneri**—a graceful variety with pinnately lobed leaflets, leaf petioles and branchlets bright red; **edulis**—the fruit is larger than that of the species. In Europe where it is native in Czechoslovakia, the fruits are even used in making preserves. Sometimes called the Moravian Rowan; '**Fastigiata**'—with narrow, upright habit. Sometimes listed as *erecta*; '**Pendula**'—with pendulous branches called Weeping European Mountain-ash; **xanthocarpa**—with yellow fruits.

cashmiriana 40′ Zone 4 Kashmir Mountain-ash
This tree is being grown in England under this name, although some consider it merely a variety of *S. tianshanica*. However, the Kashmir Mountain-ash, a native to the Himalayas, is hardier. The flower buds are blush pink; the flowers open tinged pink, the only one in our

collection with such beautiful flowers, each one of which is $\frac{3}{4}$ in. in dia. The fruits are large, $\frac{3}{8}$ in. dia., colored white with a pink tinge on pink or red fruit stalks, making the plants most ornamental. A vigorous tree, well worthy of trial wherever mountain-ash trees are grown.

decora **30′** **Zone 2** **Showy Mountain-ash**
One of the best of the native Sorbus species from northeastern North America, with larger fruits ($\frac{1}{2}$ in.) than the native *S. americana*. It is a shrubby tree, but the large, bright red berries, make it an excellent ornamental for the colder parts of the country.

discolor **30′** **Zone 5** **Snowberry Mountain-ash**
The white fruits, $\frac{3}{8}$ in. in dia., of this Chinese tree have been variously described by reliable botanists as "yellow" or "pink." The fruits on the Arnold Arboretum trees have always been white, and even though they may vary in color they make a most colorful display in the fall of the year.

folgneri **24′** **Zone 5** **Folgner Mountain-ash**
Because it is a tree, but still smaller than most others in this group, this plant from central China should be noted as a desirable type. The fruits are red, about $\frac{1}{2}$ in. long, the leaves are dark green above and white woolly beneath, making a good color contrast. It may be that red spider and lace fly, which can infest Sorbus foliage, do not do much injury to this species because of this woolly pubescence.

x hybrida 'Fastigiata' **36′** **Zone 4**
This is a hybrid of *S. aucuparia* x *S. intermedia* with a narrow fastgiate habit. The fruit is red, about $\frac{1}{2}$ in. in dia. The leaves are usually compound, sometimes being only pinnately lobed or cut nearly to the midrib. The species is found wild in central Europe.

x hybrida 'Gibbsii'—similar to the species except that the fruit is a beautiful coral red and might be used in place of the variable hybrid species to produce more uniform plants.

sargentiana **30′** **Zone 6** **Sargent Mountain-ash**
The pinnately compound leaves of this Chinese tree are 8–12 in. long. The white flowers are borne on woolly flower stalks and the rounded, scarlet fruits are about $\frac{1}{4}$ in. in dia. The large leaves and woolly-stalked flower clusters are its chief claims to fame. The young shoots also are white woolly at first.

tianshanica **15′** **Zone 5**
This shrub or small tree from Turkestan is listed here merely because of its potential use in small gardens. The flowers are nearly $\frac{3}{4}$ in. in dia.— with those of *S. alnifolia* and *S. cashmiriana* about the largest of the *Sorbus* group. Each fruit cluster is 3–5 in. across. The bright red

fruits, $\frac{1}{2}$ in. across, and the dark green, lustrous leaves make this small plant useful in certain restricted areas.

vilmorinii **18′** **Zone 5** **Vilmorin Mountain-ash**
Often a shrub, about as wide as high, with bright red fruits, $\frac{1}{4}$ in. in dia., that may turn to nearly white as they mature. The leaves are neatly divided and among the smallest in the mountain-ash group, being only 3–5$\frac{1}{2}$ in. long, but they may have up to 31 small leaflets, each one slightly under an inch in length. It is native to China.

SORGHUM (SOR-gum)
bicolor (*vulgare*) **12′** **annual** **Sorghum**
An economic crop, probably native to Africa, with many varieties grown in the U.S. A coarse-growing grass with stems which sometimes yield a sweet syrup when crushed. Another form is the Broom-corn. Others are used for forage and fodder. On a commercial scale most will be found growing in Zone 7 or in even warmer parts of the U.S. Vars: **caffrorum**, called Kafir, is taller than the species but does not produce any syrup. Grown for the white, red or black, edible grains it produces but it is more of a millet than a corn; **caudatum**, called Feterita, this is only 6–14 ft. high, producing a white, yellow or red, nutritious grain; **drummondii**, Chicken-corn popularly called, but again, more of a millet than corn. The popular name comes from the fact that the orange-yellow grain heads can be 12–16 in. long; **durra**, called Durra and used centuries ago by the Egyptians as a cereal grain. Not much grown in America; **roxburghii**, called Shallu, this is a grain grown in India but not often seen in the U.S. It grows about 12 ft. tall with a waxy stem; **saccharatum**, sometimes called Sorgho or Sweet Sorghum or even Sugar Sorghum because of the sweet sap that can be crushed from it; commercially a sweet syrup. Leaves can be used for stock feeding but it does not produce edible grain. The height is about 6–17 ft.; **sudanense**, Sudan-grass, an annual similar to *S. halepense* but usually only grown in the southern U.S. for it can only be grown in warmer areas. Native to Africa; **technicum**, called Broom-corn because it is from the stiff branches of the large-flowered, tufted and slightly twisted fruiting heads that the common brooms are made. The branches may be 12–30 in. long, depending on variety.

halepense **3′–6′** **Zone 7** **Johnson-grass**
Although native to the Mediterranean Region this has become naturalized in the South and is a serious weed in many areas. It has strong creeping rootstocks, leaves up to 2 ft. long and 1 in. wide. See GRASS. For control see WEED-CONTROLLING CHEMICALS.

SOROSIS. A collective fruit formed by the union

of several to many flowers with their axis a flesh or pulpy mass as in the Breadfruit, Mulberry, Pineapple.

SORREL. See RUMEX.

SORRELTREE = *Oxydendrum arboreum*

SORUS. A cluster of fruit dots of ferns.

SOTOL, TEXAS = *Dasylirion texanum*

SOUR-BERRY = *Rhus integrifolia*

SOUR-GRASS. See OXALIS.

SOURSOP, MOUNTAIN = *Annona montana*

SOURWOOD = *Oxydendrum arboreum*

SOUTHERN-PLUME = *Elliottia racemosa*

SOUTHERNWOOD = *Artemisia abrotanum*

SOWING SEED. See SEED, SOWING.

SOW-THISTLE. See SONCHUS.

SOYBEAN = *Glycine max*

Soybean plant

SPADIX. A spike with a fleshy axis.

SPANISH-BAYONET = *Yucca aloifolia*

SPANISH-DAGGER = *Yucca aloifolia*

SPANISH-LIME = *Melicocca bijuga*

SPANISH-MOSS = *Tillandsia usneoides*

SPARAXIS (spar-AX-is)
 grandiflora   1′   Zone 10   Wand-flower
A perennial herb from South Africa growing from a corm; belonging to the Iris Family; with narrow, basal leaves and yellow or purple flowers, an inch or more long, borne in short spikes, blooming in the spring.

SPARMANNIA (spar-MAN-ia)
 africana   20′   Zone 9   African-hemp
Resembling a miniature linden tree in habit, with large-lobed, light green leaves, 5–7 angled, 9 in. long, heart shaped at the base, white hairy above and below. The white flowers have yellow filaments. It grows rapidly with many trunks. Native to South Africa.

SPARTIUM (SPAR-tium)
 junceum   10′   Zone 7   Spanish Broom
This bright yellow-flowering broom is native to the Canary Islands and in the area about the Mediterranean Sea. The flowers are very fragrant, appearing in the summer and the foliage is bluish green. Like the *Cytisus* species it is very hard to transplant properly and is best brought to the garden and planted from pots. It does well in hot dry situations, but needs considerable pruning to keep it neat.

SPATHE. A large bract enclosing the inflorescence; like the "hood" in Jack-in-the-pulpit.

SPATHIPHYLLUM (spath-i-FILL-um)
 floribundum   2½′   Zone 10
A tropical perennial herb from Columbia, sometimes used as a house or greenhouse plant, with leaves 6 in. long and 2½ in. wide, one half of the blade larger than the other. Greenish flowers are borne in a spathe 2½ in. long. Not grown very often.

SPATHODEA (spath-O-dea)
 campanulata   70′   Zone 10   African Tuliptree,
 Bell Flambeau-tree
Native to tropical Africa, with large, compound, evergreen leaves up to 18 in. long; the interesting feature of this tree is that some of its fiery red flowers seem to be in bloom at all times of year, but it is at its best in late winter. The clusters are large with many buds in the center and only a few flowers on the perimeter in bloom at one time. The flowers have 5 irregular lobes, tinged with yellow on the edge and the rest of the petals are yellowish, tinged with fiery red. Fruit is a long pod, 8–24 in. long, which splits open and exposes the winged, shining, flaky seed masses inside. Propagated by cuttings.

SPATHULATE. Gradually narrowed from a rounded summit.

SPATTERDOCK = *Nuphar advenum*

SPEARMINT = *Mentha spicata*

SPECIES. A natural botanical unit; composed of individuals which exhibit characters distinguishing them from all other units within a genus, still not differing from one another beyond the limits of a recognizable and intergraded pattern of variation.

SPECULARIA   PERFOLIATA = *Legousia speculum-veneris*

SPEEDWELL. See VERONICA.

SPERGULA (sper-GU-la)

arvensis   1½′   **annual**   **Corn Spurry**
A weed in grain fields and gardens especially on
sandy or gravelly soils in the Pacific Northwest,
but widely distributed in North America.
Introduced from Europe. Stems are jointed and
at each joint there is a whorl of threadlike leaves
about 1 in. long. In the past it was used in
Europe as a forage crop. Flowers are small and
white, borne in very loose, open-branched,
terminal clusters. It is easily controlled by
cultivation.

SPHAERACEA (sfee-RAY-cea)

coccinea (*Malvastrum coccineum*) 12″ **Zone 5**
Prairie Mallow
A perennial of the Rocky Mountains with thin,
reclining stems and feathery silvery foliage. The
red flowers are about an inch wide, the shade of
terra cotta. It spreads by means of shoots
springing from the deep, rather woody roots.
Propagated by seed and division.

SPHAGNUM. There are several mosses called
sphagnum, which grow in bogs and are valued
especially in horticultural procedures such as
propagation, seed sowing and the shipment of
plants. They are also valued by the florist for
their ability to retain large amounts of moisture.
They are usually grayish in color, light and
fluffy, often very acid and are available from
florists supply houses, dried by the bale or bag.
Shredded dried sphagnum moss is often used in
preparing the medium for sowing fine seeds (like
those of Azalea and Rhododendron).

SPICE. These are plant products with a little
more zest to them than most of the common
herbs. Most of them are from plants native to
the Tropics, most in fact from the general area
of southern Asia and the East Indies. The Arabs
were the first to merchandize these tropical
products. Even today, the only major spice
coming to Americans from the western hemisphere is Allspice. The rest are brought from
East Indies. These spices are all briefly described
in their proper alphabetical listing in this
volume. Some of the most important are:
Allspice—*Pimenta dioica*; Cassia—*Cinnamomum cassia*; Chili Powder—*Capsicum frutescens*
var.; Cinnamon—*Cinnamomum zeylanicum*;
Cloves—*Syzygium aromaticum*; Ginger—*Zingiber officinale*; Nutmeg—*Myristica fragrans*;
Paprika—*Capsicum frutescens* var; Pepper,
Black—*Piper nigrum*; Pepper, Cayenne—*Capsicum frutescens* var.; Pepper, Red—*Capsicum
frutescens longum*; Pepper, White—*Piper nigrum*;
Saffron—*Crocus sativum*; Sage, Pineapple—
Salvia rutilans; Tumeric—*Curcuma longa*.

SPICEBUSH = *Lindera benzoin*

SPIDERFLOWER. See CLEOME.

SPIDER-LILY. See HYMENOCALLIS.

SPIDER PLANT = *Chlorophytum commosum*

SPIDERWORT OR DAYFLOWER FAMILY
= Commenlinaceae

SPIDERWORT, VIRGINIA = *Tradescantia virginiana*

SPIGELIA (spy-JEE-lia)

marilandica 1′–2′ **Zone 8 Pinkroot Spigelia**
A perennial, hardy in the southern U.S. It is an
erect plant with thin-textured, opposite, ovate
to lanceolate leaves and bearing a 1-sided
terminal cluster of trumpet-shaped flowers. Each
flower is 2 in. long and has a 5-lobed calyx and
a reddish-pink, 5-lobed corolla and a yellow
throat. It is native to N.Car., Fla. and Tex. and
blooms in summer.

SPIKE. A simple inflorescence with the flowers
sessile or nearly so on a common axis.

SPIKE-HEATH = *Bruckenthalia spiculifolia*

SPINACH (*Spinacia oleracea*) is the most
important pot herb or green grown in the U.S.
It is included in most home garden plantings.
Spinach is rich in vitamin A and high in
ascorbic acid, riboflavin plus some thiamine. It
is also rich in iron and calcium.

Spinach thrives best during relatively cool
weather and will withstand temperatures in the
low 30's F. It is what we know as a short-day
plant and, consequently, when grown during
the long light and high temperatures of summer,
develops a seed stalk very quickly. In the North
it is therefore grown as a spring and fall crop
and during late fall, winter and early spring in
the South.

Varieties

There are many varieties listed by seedsmen;
some of which have curly, crinkled or savoyed
leaves, while others are a lighter green with flat
leaves. Good standard varieties for the home
garden include '**Dark Green Bloomsdale**',
'**America**', '**Melody**', '**Blight Resistant Savoy**',
and '**American Savoy**', resistant to yellows and
downy mildew.

Culture

The lighter sandy and silt loam soils are
preferred. Spinach is sensitive to both an alkaline and an acid soil. Soils having a pH range
of 6.0–7.0 are excellent (see LIME). Soil preparation should be thorough. Apply 20–30 lbs. of a
5-10-10 fertilizer per 1000 sq. ft. prior to
planting and then side dress with several pounds
of nitrate of soda when the plants have a leaf
spread of 2–3 in. Plant 1 oz. of seed per 100 ft.
row and space the rows 12–15 in. apart. Plant
only as much as can be used in 4–6 days and
make 3–4 sowings at weekly intervals. The last

planting should not mature later than mid-June or July 1. Fall plantings should start about Aug. 1. Cultivation should be shallow and only sufficient to control weeds.

Spinach can be harvested as soon as 5–6 leaves have fully developed by cutting the top root just below the lowest leaves.

Diseases and Insects

Spinach blight or yellows, is a virus disease spread by aphids. Affected plants show a yellowing of the leaves and stunted, twisted plant growth. Control aphids and use resistant varieties such as 'Virginia Blight Resistant'. This disease is most common in the fall and winter plantings. Blue mold is a disease showing yellow spots on the upper surface of the leaf and downy purple or blue mold on the underside. It is most prevalent during cool, high-humid weather. No specific control except good drainage, weed control and crowding of plants. Aphids, green soft-bodied insects usually most common in warmer weather, controlled with nicotine sulfate or a 5% malathion dust. Be sure the spray material covers the underside of leaf.

New Zealand Spinach, *Tetragonia expansa*, is not a true Spinach. The plants are much branched, spreading from 2½–4 ft. across and 1–2 ft. in height. The leaves are thick, dark green and are used in the same manner as true Spinach. The seeds are enclosed in a hard, rough pod.

New Zealand Spinach thrives in hot weather and, therefore, is an excellent substitute for ordinary Spinach for summer culture.

The seed germinates slowly and, therefore, may be treated for several hours in hot water prior to sowing. Some gardeners prefer to start the plants in a hotbed and then transplant them into the garden when 2–3 in. tall. Normal planting distance is 3 ft. between rows and about 2 ft. in the row. Actually, only 5–6 plants are sufficient for the average family. Cultural practices are similar to those for ordinary Spinach.

Harvesting

The tips of the branches 2–4 in. long are cut off. New shoots will develop so that a continuing supply will be available throughout the entire season. Good growth is essentail to develop soft, succulent and tender growing points.

GRANT B. SNYDER

SPINACH, NEW ZEALAND (*Tetragonia tetragonioides*). A prostrate, succulent annual, grown as a vegetable, native to Japan, Australia, New Zealand and South America, especially for its tender young stems and leaves which are cooked and eaten like Spinach. Plants are taller, more vigorous and more tough than Spinach but it makes a good substitute for growing in hot weather. Leaves are alternate, flowers few, small and without petals, leaves ovate, often triangular, up to 5 in. long.

SPINACIA (spy-NAY-sia)

oleracea = Spinach, which see.

SPINDLE-TREE = *Euonymus europaeus*

SPINE. A sharp-pointed woody outgrowth from the stem.

SPIRAEA (spy-REE-a). As a group, these are not a very important part of the garden picture. They are alternate-leaved, deciduous shrubs with either white or pink flowers in the late spring. Easily grown and easily propagated, they have few cultural problems. A few have been extremely popular and at least one may have been overplanted in the past. There are several native to North America. *S. latifolia* is the hardiest of all (Zone 2) and grows about 4 ft. tall with white to pink flowers in pyramidal spikes, but it is planted only in the coldest regions (if at all), where other plants are not hardy.

It should be noted that the generic name is spelled *Spiraea* and the common name Spirea. All have alternate leaves, usually toothed or slightly lobed, and fibrous roots, and the individual flowers of most are only about ¼ in. (more or less) across, but they are borne in profuse numbers and arranged in flat or globular clusters, or in pyramidal spikes, and are either white, pink or red.

S. tomentosa, the native Hardhack Spirea of the eastern U.S., is a weedy, 3-ft. high shrub with poor foliage, possibly looking well in old cow pastures where it is native, but suited for little else than in naturalistic plantings. It is listed by only a few U.S. nurseries.

The majority are hardy in either Zone 4 or 5. Other than those already mentioned, it is highly probable that most spireas would suffer winter injury and hence require much renewal pruning if tried in colder areas, although there may be a few exceptions. They will grow in sun or shade, and some can be clipped for hedges. They are easily transplanted and will grow in almost any kind of soil.

As a group they are valued chiefly for their flowers. None has ornamental fruits. Only a few like *S. prunifolia* and *S. thunbergii* may have autumn color worth mentioning.

Concerning the time of bloom, they are listed below in groups as they bloom in the vicinity of Boston, Mass.

EARLY MAY	JUNE	EARLY TO
thunbergii	brachybotrys	MID-JULY
MID-MAY	decumbens	albiflora
arguta	margaritae	bumalda
multiflora	nipponica	canescens
prunifolia	superba	japonica
LATE MAY	trichocarpa	JULY–AUGUST
cantoniensis	veitchii	bullata
vanhouttei	wilsonii	

Most growers know that spireas can be divided into 2 groups for pruning purposes. Those that bloom on the previous year's growth (i.e., the early-flowering ones) should be pruned before they flower. In fact, if this is done in the very early spring it is one way to increase the size of the flower clusters of such species as *S. bumalda*, *S. japonica* and *S. margaritae*. Other species blooming on the current year's growth are *S. albiflora*, *S. bullata* and *S. canescens*. (All the others in the following list bloom on the previous year's growth.)

As a group, the spireas are thought of as having small, creamy-white flowers in flat clusters of pyramidal spikes. Mention must be made of 4 species with pink flowers (*S. brachybotrys*, *S. bullata*, *S. margaritae* and *S. superba*) and 2 species with deep pink and almost red flowers—*S. bulmalda* and *S. japonica*.

'Anthony Waterer' is perhaps the most popular of all low, red-flowered spireas, but *S. bumalda* 'Crispa' has flowers practically the same color and much better foliage. Both are about 2 ft. tall, while the *S. japonica* varieties are about twice that height. These are undoubtedly mixed up or misnamed in the trade. The variety with the darkest red flowers of all the spireas is *S. japonica* 'Atrosanguinea'. The variety 'Ruberrima' has lighter colored flowers, but they are still an excellent deep pink.

Finally, mention should be made of height and habit. The lowest of the spireas are *S. japnica alpina* (less than a foot tall), *S. decumbens* and *S. bullata* which are 12 in. and 15 in. tall respectively—suitable only for planting in limited situations. *S. albiflora* is only 18 in. high and the *S. bumalda* varieties about 2 ft. The tallest of the recommended spireas is *S. veitchii* —about 12 ft. high. There must be a lot of planting room available to put in such a plant requiring an area of at least 225 square feet, where better shrubs such as viburnums or rhododendrons would give much longer ornamental interest.

It must be admitted that species like *S. arguta* and *S. vanhouttei* have a gracefully arching habit which is difficult to improve upon, especially when the branches are covered with flowers.

Spireas are easily propagated by cuttings, grow fast and so make salable plants in a short time. They have no serious insect or disease pests, can be harshly pruned and recover quickly, and so have been used as cheap landscape "fillers" in many situations. As they mature they frequently require renewal pruning. The discerning plantsman will not grow many spireas, and the more valuable the garden space available, the fewer the spireas that should be considered for it.

Propagation

Do not allow the seed to dry out before sowing. It should be sown as soon as ripe. Most plants can be easily divided with a sharp spade. Softwood and hardwood cuttings root easily for most species. See CUTTINGS.

Insect Pests

Spirea leafroller webs and rolls the leaves of *S. vanhouttei* and disfigures the bushes. Cut off the nests and spray with insecticide #9 or #37 in midsummer. Several species of aphids infest certain species and are controlled by sprays of insecticide #15. A special scale insect is known to infest *S. thunbergii*. It is a white, mealy, soft scale which is found in the crotches of twigs and branches. Thorough forceful spraying with insecticide #15 is advised in early summer and repeated in late summer when the young are hatching.

Diseases

Fireblight is an occasional pest. See PEAR. Powdery mildew develops on the leaves in shady damp locations. Use fungicide #V or #M. Clusters of small, fibrous roots near the soil may be caused by the hairy root disease. Nursery plants showing this condition should not be planted.

albiflora 1½′ **Zone 4 Japanese White Spirea** This Japanese species is in many nurseries as *S. japonica alba* which is actually a synonym. It is a fine, July-blooming, low, white spirea with flowers in rounded or flat clusters which can be used to excellent advantage with the taller, pink to red-flowering *S. japnica*. It is also good in combination with *S. bumalda*.

x arguta 5′–6′ **Zone 4 Garland Spirea** Originating before 1884 as a hybrid of *S. thunbergii* x *multiflora*, this is the most free-flowering of the early spireas blooming in mid-May. The white flowers are borne in small, flat clusters on arching branches, making it excellent for specimen planting.

x billiardii 6′ **Zone 4 Billiard Spirea** Often desirable for planting in masses on banks, since it quickly increases by underground stems forming a dense mass of growth. It is a hybrid (*S. douglasii* x *S. salicifolia*) with bright rose flowers in pyramidal spikes about 4–8 in. long. The variety 'Triumphans' is the best of several clones of this hybrid species, for the pyramidal clusters are 8 in. tall and 4 in. across at the base, often appearing from mid-July to Sept.

x billiardii 'Macrothyrsa' 5′ **Zone 4** The bright pink flowers in dense panicles during the summer and the horizontal spreading branches of this hybrid species (*S. douglasii* x *S. latifolia*) give it interest, especially in the summer.

x brachybotrys   8′   Zone 4
One of the best of the taller summer-blooming spireas, with small, bright pink flowers in panicles 1½–3 in. long. It is a hybrid of *S. canescens* x *douglasii* and blooms in late June.

bullata   15″   Zone 5
Flowers deep rosy pink, appearing in July and Aug.—valued only as a dwarf shrub. It is native to Japan.

x bumalda 'Anthony Waterer'   2′   Zone 5
For 70 years the variety 'Anthony Waterer' has been taken to be the sole variety of this hybrid species (*S. japonica* x *S. albiflora*). It is unfortunate that it has sometimes been propagated by seed, for since it is of hybrid origin, the resulting seedlings have varied considerably in height and flower color. The true variety should be propagated asexually by cuttings or division. The flowers, appearing in late June, are rose-red and the clusters may be as much as 6 in. across, but the color is not so dark as that of the true *S. japonica* 'Atrosanguinea'. The young foliage is tinged with pink when it first appears. A new variety from Japan, 'Alpina', is an excellent mounded dwarf with light pink flowers in late June. It is much less than a foot tall.

canescens   6′–10′   Zone 7   Hoary Spirea
Blooming in July, with clusters of white flowers, 2 in. in dia., borne on the upper side of gracefully arching branches; this is a native of the Himalayas.

cantoniensis   3′   Zone 6   Reeve's Spirea
Sometimes incorrectly termed *S. reevesiana*, this is often considered an even better ornamental than the very popular *S. vanhouttei*, although the latter is more hardy. In parts of Calif. it keeps its foliage a greater part of the year. The small, rounded, white flower clusters are only 1–2 in. across and appear in late May. It is native to China and Japan.

decumbens   1′   Zone 5
Of special interest for rockeries, this low southern European plant has white flowers but at present is rarely found in America.

japonica   4½′   Zone 5   Japanese Spirea
A handsome Japanese Spirea, but its height limits its use in favor of the lower *S. bumalda* varieties. However, the flowers are pale to deep pink, sometimes white, appearing in flat clusters during mid-June. Other varieties: 'Atrosanguinea', the Mikado Spirea, has the deepest red flowers of any Spirea, the flat flower clusters often being 4–5 in. across; **ovalifolia**—flowers white; **'Ruberrima'**—flowers deep pink; **'Alpina'**—flowers red are 10 in. tall.

latifolia   4′   Zone 2   Meadowsweet
Native from Newfoundland to N.Car., this is a common plant in the fields of eastern U.S. The flowers are white or slightly pinkish, are borne in broadly pyramidal clusters and bloom from June to Aug. It is one of the hardiest of all spireas, but not a particularly good subject for the garden.

x margaritae   4′   Zone 4   Margarita Spirea
With flat clusters of rosy-pink flowers in late June. If the plant is thinned out in the late winter and the few remaining shoots cut back to about 1 ft., it should be covered with blooms by late June, the blooms being from 3–6 in. in dia. It may bloom a second or even a third time during the summer and is a hybrid of *S. japonica* x *S. superba*.

x multiflora   5′   Zone 4   Snow Garland Spirea
An excellent hybrid (*S. crenata* x *S. hypericifolia*) originating before 1884, with long, slightly arched branches covered with small white flower clusters in May. This does very well indeed in the Dakotas, apparently better than in New England. Sometimes incorrectly listed as *S. multiflora arguta*.

nipponica rotundifolia   7′   Zone 4   Big Nippon Spirea
With bluish-green foliage, this Japanese shrub is rather stiff and not so graceful as others. The small clusters of white flowers are numerous, appearing in late May. It has larger leaves and flowers than the species and is better than the species for landscape planting.

prunifolia   9′   Zone 4   Bridalwreath
The small, double, white, button-sized flowers in mid-May are this plant's popular feature. It is also one of the very few spireas which has red to orange autumn color in the fall. The single-flowered variety, **simpliciflora**, does not make nearly so good an ornamental. There is no such variety as "plena" or "floreplena". This double-flowered plant was the first to be found by botanists in the Orient (1843) and was given the specific name *prunifolia*. When the single-flowered form was found later, it was given the varietal name **simplicissima** and is inferior to the species as an ornamental plant. Usually the sequence is just reversed.

x superba   3′   Zone 4   Striped Spirea
Only valued because of its late June flowers (light rose) in flat clusters and its low height. It is a hybrid of *S. albiflora* x *S. corymbosa*.

thunbergii   5′   Zone 4   Thunberg Spirea
Bearing single white flowers in early May, this is usually the first of the spireas to bloom. It is native to Japan and China. The leaves are small and pointed, the plant is graceful and finely branched and the foliage may turn orange in the fall under some conditions. However, it does better in the Middle Atlantic States and

the South than in New England, where it tends to be killed back somewhat by winter cold or by late spring frosts which injure the early blossoms.

tomentosa   4′   **Zone 3**   **Hardhack**
Native throughout the eastern half of the U.S. and part of southeastern Canada, this can be listed as a common wild flower in open fields. The flowers are deep rose to rose-purple in narrow panicles 3–8 in. long, appearing from July to Sept. There is a white-flowered variety (**alba**) occasionally seen, but neither this nor the species are very desirable plants for the garden.

trichocarpa   6′   **Zone 5**   **Korean Spirea**
Somewhat similar to *S. nipponica* and its varieties but with larger flower clusters than *S. vanhouttei* and blooming shortly afterwards. It is native to Korea.

x vanhouttei   6′   **Zone 4**   **Vanhoutte Spirea**
Originating before 1868, this has become the most popular of all the spireas and is a hybrid, *S. cantoniensis* x *S. trilobata*. It blooms in late May and has an excellent arching habit, one of its best assets. The flowers are borne in flat clusters and the growth is dense and vigorous, making it possible to use this as an informal flowering hedge or as a sheared hedge.

veitchii   12′   **Zone 5**   **Veitch Spirea**
The tallest of the spireas, this is native to central and western China. Flat white flower clusters about 2 in. in dia. bloom during mid-June.

wilsonii   7′   **Zone 5**   **Wilson Spirea**
In general this looks like *S. vanhouttei* but blooms slightly later—in early June. It is native to central and western China, and makes a fine arching specimen for garden use.

SPIRANTHES (spy-RANTH-ees)

cernua   6″–18″   **Nodding Ladies'-tresses**
A member of the Orchid Family, native to the damp woods and moist meadows from Nova Scotia to Fla. and extending beyond the Mississippi River. The narrow, pointed leaves, with strong longitudinal veins, grow in a basal cluster. Small, alternate, leaflike bracts ascend the rather thick flower stalk to the base of the flower spike on which the small, white, irregular flowers are arranged in a spiral around the stalk. The flowers appear in late summer and autumn.

SPIREA. See SPIRAEA. The common name is Spirea for the botanical genus *Spiraea*.

SPITTLE INSECTS. A group of sucking insects called frog hoppers in the adult stage. As nymphs they suck more sap than they can digest and the excess is mixed with air in a mass of froth or spittle in which they live. They are only mildly destructive. They may be so abundant in meadow grass that the grass is literally wet with the spittle over a large area.

Many garden perennials are infested. One species, the pine spittle bug, is a serious pest of Scotch Pine. Control with insecticides is quite simple since the spittle retains the insecticide leaving the insect enclosed in a poisonous bath. Insecticides #9 and #15 are suggested. Dusts are as effective as sprays.

SPLEENWORT. See ASPLENIUM.

SPONDIAS (SPON-dias)

cytherea   60′   **Zone 10**   **Ambarella**
A tree common throughout tropical America, with compound leaves containing 11–23 oval leaflets, 3–4 in. long, and purple-green flowers. The egg-shaped fruits are 1–4½ in. long and are yellow and plumlike. They have a tart pineapple flavor, making excellent preserves.

mombin   60′   **Zone 10**   **Hog-plum**
Cultivated occasionally in southern Florida and popular throughout tropical America, with compound leaves of 7–17 leaflets, purplish green flowers and egg shaped fruit 1–1½″ long. with a sweetish to slightly acid taste, ripening during the late summer. Native in the general tropical regions. The fruit is a drupe. Easily propagated by seeds.

SPORANGIUM. A spore case.

SPORE. A simple reproductive body, usually a single detached cell. Usually used when discussing the reproduction of ferns, fungi and mosses.

SPORT. A shoot usually arising from a single bud, different in character from the typical growth of the plant that produced it. The difference is usually in a single character, as a branch with double flowers, on a plant producing all single flowers. Sports must be propagated asexually to retain their variation.

SPOTTED EVERGREEN = *Aglaonema costatum*

SPRAYING AND DUSTING EQUIPMENT.

Sprays and dusts are most effective when applied as a thin but complete coating on the plant. Over-spraying as indicated by substantial drip or runoff and overdusting to apply a heavy coating are wasteful, expensive and may cause plant injury or create a hazard to wild and domestic animals.

Choice of equipment depends both on the area to be treated and the inclinations of the operator. Spraying is usually less expensive in material and equipment but requires more time and labor, especially in preparing the proper mixture. It gives more complete coverage and longer-lasting protection. Dust is easily and quickly applied and most formulations are prepared and are secured ready for use. The materials are more expensive and cannot be effectively and safely applied in wind. On most small garden plants the dust should be blown onto the ground so that it will "bounce" and cover the underside of leaves and fruit as well as the top side. Experiments have shown that pest control on low-growing vegetables, flowers and shrubs is equally effective from regular timely applications of both dust and spray. When plants such as tomatoes are full grown they may require twice as much spray or dust as when they are small.

Spraying equipment for all types of application is available. Large concentrate sprayers which deliver the spray from a bank of nozzles with an air blast from a rapidly rotating fan are commonly used in orchards. A high-pressure, high-volume sprayer with a "fire hose" type nozzle is used for spraying tall shade trees. Mist blowers which dilute the pesticide in air instead of water by discharging a small stream of it into a strong current of air are used in spraying trees and the same principle is used in airplanes. All of these treatments are adjusted to apply a given amount of pesticide per acre which is governed by the speed at which the sprayer travels as well as the concentration of the mixture. Low-gallonage, low-pressure sprayers are now used in field and vegetable crops. Small power sprayers mounted on a "wheelbarrow" chassis are convenient for estate gardens and grounds. Hand-operated force pumps mounted in a "garbage can on a wheelbarrow frame" will hold about 15 gal. of spray conveniently. Other hand sprayers are the 1½ to 3½ gal. compressed-air sprayer with a shoulder strap and hand sprayers holding 1 pint to 2 quarts. A recent innovation which has attracted much favorable attention is the hose sprayer which sucks the pesticide from a small container into the stream of water and dilutes it in a satisfactory proportion.

Dusting equipment also ranges from the power duster to the hand bellows. Power dusters mounted on light trailers or the back of trucks use a rapidly revolving fan to blow the dust. Airplanes depend on the slip stream from the plane. Large orchards, vegetable and forage fields and forest areas frequently use this equipment. However, drift of pesticide dust to areas beyond the planned target has caused some criticism. Small power dusters to be carried on the back are available. Typical hand dusters are the rotary type operated by turning a crank and the plunger type with a plunger in a cylinder providing the force to blow the dust. These are most satisfactory for the small garden. A bellows-type hand duster is now outmoded. Like all mechanical equipment it must be given the proper care to operate smoothly. Power equipment should be handled according

to the manufacturer's directions. Hand equipment should be lubricated as needed and stored to prevent rusting and drying. Excess pesticide should never be left in the sprayer or duster from operation to operation and especially during the winter.

WARREN D. WHITCOMB

SPREADER. A substance added to pesticides to spread the active ingredient over the plant in a uniform film rather than in drops. It is particularly desirable when spraying leaves with a smooth or waxy surface such as Carnation, Onion or Rhododendron. Soaps, casein, household detergents and special chemicals such as sulfonated alcohols are most commonly used. Commercial formulations usually have a spreader incorporated in them in the proper amount for average use. Spreaders may also refer to wheeled carts for applying fertilizer, lime, dusts and granules in measured quantities. They are especially made for applying these materials to lawns and to garden plots before planting in predetermined amounts.

SPREKELIA (sprek-EE-lia)

| formosissima | 1½' | Zone 9 | Aztec-lily, Jacobean-lily |

A Mexican bulbous herb mostly for the greenhouse, of the Amaryllis Family. The flowers, 1 to a stalk, are reddish to bright crimson, to 4 in. long, blooming in April. The 3 upper petals differ from the lower reflexed petals in that they are erect. Leaves are straplike. Cultivation is similar to that of the Amaryllis. Easily propagated by offsets. If grown outdoors it blooms in the summer.

SPRING BEAUTY. See CLAYTONIA.

SPRING BEAUTY, VIRGINIA = *Claytonia virginica*

SPRING GARDEN. See GARDEN, SPRING.

SPRUCE. See PICEA.

SPRUCE FAMILY = Pinaceae

SPUR. Any projecting appendage of a flower, looking like a spur but hollow as in the flower of a Delphinium. Also, used to denote a short lateral branch with nodes close together, like the spurs on apple trees which bear the flowers and fruits.

SPURGE. See EUPHORIBA, PACHYSANDRA.

SPURGE or the **POINSETTIA FAMILY** = Euphorbiaceae

SPURRY, CORN = *Spergula arvensis*

SQUASH AND PUMPKINS. These 2 crops are grouped together because their culture is similar and also because of the confusion in nomenclature. Both belong to the genus *Cucurbita* which for our purpose is divided into 3 species, *C. maxina*, *C. moschata* and *C. pepo*. Each of these species contain varieties listed as squash and as pumpkins. See CUCURBITA for description and classification.

It is probable that squash and pumpkins are of American origin. While neither of these crops are highly important on the commercial market, both are common in many home gardens. Generally, the bush types are grown because the running vine varieties require too much space, about 50–100 sq. ft. per hill. Bush types will do well with 9–16 sq. ft. per hill.

Varieties

Many varieties, including an increasing number of hybrids, are listed in seed catalogues but only a few are of much importance in the home garden. The summer squash, those sorts

Squash—several kinds that are popular among home gardeners.

that are bushy in habit of growth, mature in 50–60 days; the rind of the fruit is soft and tender. These include types of **'Prolific Straight-neck'**, **'Seneca Butterbar'**, **'Early Prolie'**, **'Hybrid Cocozelle'**, **'Patty Pan'** and **'Zucchini'**. These are all classified as *C. pepo*. Fall and winter varieties have running vines 8–10 ft. plus, require 90–125 days to develop a hard rind at maturity. If space permits the inclusion of fall squash, suggested varieties include **'Table Queen'** or **'Acorn'** (*C. pepo*), **'Butternut'** (*C. moschata*) and **'Buttercup'** (*C. maxima*). The winter types, 110–125 days, include Blue and Green **'Hubbard'** and **'Delicious'** (*C. maxima*). All of these varieties can be held in storage for two to four months. Varieties normally classified as pumpkins include **'Small Sugar'** and **'Connecticut Field'** (*C. pepo*), and **'Large Cheese'** (*C. moschata*). All of these have long vines to 10 ft. plus and require from 100–125 days to maturity.

Culture

All squash and pumpkins are frost-tender, and grow best during the heat of summer in soils that are warm and have a high water-holding capacity. The plants have very extensive root systems and respond to thorough soil preparation and the application of 25–35 lbs. of a 5–10–10 fertilizer per 1000 sq. ft.

Planting distances vary widely, but the bush types are usually planted in hills 3 ft. × 3 ft. or 4 ft. × 4 ft. and the vine types from 8 ft. × 8 ft. to 12 ft. × 12 ft. apart. Five to 6 seeds are planted per hill and then later thinned to 3 plants. If earliness is a factor plants may be started in hotbeds in plant bands or berry baskets, 3–4 weeks prior to replanting in the open garden. Do not disturb the soil around the roots of such transplants in replanting.

Home gardeners frequently are confused because many flowers do not set fruit. Squash and pumpkins, as do most cucurbits, bear separate male and female flowers on the same vine. The ratio may vary but only the female flowers bear fruit. Pollination is carried on by insects.

Cultivation should be shallow and sufficient to control the weeds. Hand weeding may be necessary after the vines begin to develop.

Harvesting

Summer squash of all types should be havested when the fruits are immature and the rinds are soft. Winter squash on the other hand should be left on the vines until the fruit is fully matured, the rind is hard and tough. If the fruit is to be stored, the fruits should be cut from the vine with 2–3 in. of the fruit stem remaining attached to the fruit. In storage the squash and pumpkins should be exposed to a temperature of 75° to 80° F. for 1 to 2 weeks to thoroughly harden the shell. The temperature should then be reduced to 50° F. plus a low relative humidity, 20–35%, for optimum storage conditions.

GRANT B. SNYDER

Insect Pests

Squash borer, the larva of a clear wing moth, tunnels in the stems of most varieties. 'Butter-nut' and other varieties of the species *moschata* are resistant. The large white worms make holes in the stems and deposit frass nearby. The vines wilt. Dusting or spraying at the base of the stems 3 or 4 times at weekly intervals with insecticide #9 or #28 will kill the young worms before they enter the stems. Squash-bug is dark brown and about ½ in. long. The over-wintered adults suck the sap from young plants and kill them. In midsummer the gray young bugs feed on new growth. Spraying or dusting with insecticide #15 when the bugs are first seen gives control. In mid- and late summer the melon aphid is often so abundant that sprays or dusts of insecticides #15 and #37 prevent serious damage. Striped cucumber beetle may spread wilt (see CUCUMBER); white fly, melon worm and pickle worm are occasional pests. Squash beetle, which resembles the Mexican bean beetle, is troublesome in the Middle West in midsummer; use #28 or #37.

Diseases

Powdery mildew is especially troublesome on summer squash late in the season. See CUCUMBER for this and other diseases. Storage rots are reduced by storing at 45°–50° F. and at humidity below 75%. Only squash without bruises should be stored. Attics are the most favorable part of house. Pre-storage dipping in fungicide #G—2 lbs. per 100 gals. of water has reduced spoilage from black rot on 'Butternut' squash.

SQUAW-WEED = *Senecio obovatus*

SQUILL. See SCILLA, ENDYMION.

SQUILL, STRIPED = *Puschkinia scilloides*

SQUIRREL-CORN = *Dicentra canadensis*

STACHYS (STA-chys). The 3 species mentioned here are opposite-leaved perennials, with small, white or violet flowers borne in profuse whorls arranged on terminal spikes. These are Old World species making excellent "fillers" in the flower border. Easily grown in almost any garden soil; they are propagated by seeds sown in early spring or by division in early fall or early spring.

byzantina (*olympica*) 1′–1½′ Zone 4 **Lamb's-ears, Woolly Betony**
The leaves of this are soft and woolly, shaped somewhat like a lamb's ear. The pink to purplish flowers are not outstanding but they continue to bloom from July to frost on stalks a foot high. The plant is usually placed for foliage accent. Native to the Caucasus. The flowering stems are sometimes cut back to the ground and the grayish foliage is left for contrast with normal green foliage. Easily propagated by division and seed.

grandiflora 1′ Zones 2–3 **Big Betony**
The deep purple flowers of this hardy perennial from Asia Minor appear in whorls, 10–20 flowers in each, on a stalk sometimes 18 in. tall. The flowers are a violet color, and the tube is about an inch long. Sometimes offered as *Betonica grandiflora*.

officinalis 3′ Zone 4 **Common Betony**
Rather hairy leaves; purple flowers about ½ in. long are produced in July and Aug. Grows best on hot, dry soils. Native to Europe and Asia Minor.

STACHYURUS (stak-i-YEW-rus)
praecox 12′ **Zone 6**
An interesting Japanese plant, this produces small, yellow, bell-shaped flowers, ½ in. long, in racemes 2–3 in. long during March before the leaves appear, but they come so early that late freezes can injure them. Hence it is best grown in an area where there are no late spring freezes. The leaves are semi-evergreen up to 5½ in. long; the winter twigs are red and the plant does well if provided with a peaty soil and some leaf mold.

STAGGERBRUSH = *Lyonia mariana*

STAKING. Annual and perennial plants sometimes send up such long flower stalks or produce such heavy flower heads that they must be staked in order to show off well. Trees frequently need proper staking for the first several years after transplanting, otherwise they might be blown over by heavy wind storms. After their roots have grown a few years and they have become thoroughly anchored, then the stakes or guy wires can be removed.

Staking individual plants like delphiniums, lilies and dahlias is simple. One should know the approximate height of the staking required and the strength needed. For instance, bamboo stakes can be anywhere from ¼ in. to ¾ in. in dia., wooden stakes from ½ to 1½ in. and wire stakes of varied thicknesses. The main objective should be to give the right kind of support but the stakes should not be prominent and certainly should not reach above the plants. Bamboo stakes can be bought painted green and these are not conspicuous. Wooden stakes are pointed at one end, thus making them easy to force into the ground.

Branches of Birch or Cherry are frequently used, for these are sturdy and twiggy and, if pointed at one end, are easily forced into the ground and make a fine scaffold on which tall growing annuals or perennials (like Delphinium) can gain sufficient support. Such supports as these are usually placed when the plants are only half grown, so the stalks can grow up through the branches as they mature.

Where there is a group of plants requiring staking, 3 or 4 stakes can be placed on the outside of the group and a string also on the outside, connecting all stakes, thus keeping the foliage together in one mass and preventing stalks from flopping over as they often will.

A line of raspberry bushes can be "staked" by placing uprights of pipe or wood at 10–12 ft intervals on either side, then stringing 2 lengths of wire the full length of the planting on either side, one at about 18 in. high and the other at 36–40 in. In this way the branches are kept

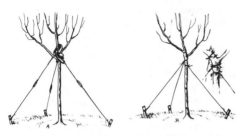

Bracing and staking a newly planted tree: (left) Right Way; (right) Wrong Way. (Note that the wires around the tree are not covered.)

Staking plants must be done in such a way that the tie does not bind or choke the living stem.

confined and will not flop over as they will without the supports.

Staking young trees is often necessary until their roots have become thoroughly anchored. The taller the tree, the more important it is, for wind can easily blow over such trees. Almost any newly planted tree, 10–12 ft. tall or taller, should be staked as part of the planting operation. Usually 3 heavy wires are placed about the trunk, each one looped through a length of hose so it will not injure the trunk and with a

large enough loop so that it will not constrict it in any way. Each wire is firmly attached to a sturdy stake in the ground; preferably the wire is marked with a small piece of cloth so it will not be walked into unknowingly. The wires about the trunk should be checked every few months to make certain they are not binding or injuring the trunk in any way. Once the roots are thoroughly anchored, in 2 or 3 years, the wires can be removed. The smaller the tree, the sooner this can be done.

STAMEN. The pollen-bearing male organ of a flower.

STAMINATE. Having stamens and no pistil; male.

STANDARD. A term variously used in horticulture to denote a plant that stands upright with a single stalk; also used in botanical descriptions to describe the prominent parts making up the flowers of the Pea Family. The flower consists of a standard or large petal at the top, wings or the 2 lateral parts of petals and a keel which consists of the 2 anterior united petals.

STANHOPEA (stan-HO-pea). This genus consists of about 50 species of tropical American orchids with 3–8-in. flowers, 1–7 in a stalk, colored yellow and fragrant, blooming in the summer or fall. The flowers of **S. tigrina** are 7 in. wide in 2–4 flowered racemes, yellow marked with purplish-blue and blooming from Aug. to Nov. Native to Mexico. **S. wardii** has 6–10 orange-yellow flowers in each hanging raceme which can be up to 16 in. long. They are usually spotted with purple and bloom from July to Sept. These of course are only grown in the moist greenhouse. For culture and propagation see ORCHID.

STANLEYA = (STAN-lee-a)
pinnata   5′   Zone 3   Desert Prince's-plume
A perennial herb, native to western North America from S.Dak. to N.Mex. and Calif., belonging to the Mustard Family; with lobed or pinnately divided leaves; golden-yellow flowers an inch wide in spikes; with fruit a pod. Easily cultivated and propagated by seeds or division.

STAPELIA (stap-EE-lia). Leafless, cactuslike plants, with thick, fleshy, 4-angled stems and large, grotesque, wheel- or bell-shaped flowers barred with dull colors and with an offensive odor; native to South Africa. Because of the odor, these have little ornamental value, with a few exceptions.
gigantea   9″   Zone 10   Giant Stapelia
Flowers brown-purple, hairy; 11 in. wide, in midsummer.
grandiflora   1′   Zone 10
Flowers dark purple-brown with no markings;

6 in. wide and usually 1–3 borne at the base of the stem.

hirsuta   1′   Zone 10   Shaggy Stapelia
Flowers dark purple-brown, crossed with lines of cream or purple; with pale purplish leaves, 5 in. wide, 1–3 at the base of the stem.

variegata   6″   Zone 10   Variegated Stapelia
Flowers greenish yellow with dark purple-brown spots; 3 in. wide, 1–3 borne at the base of the stem. Several varieties have flowers ranging from crimson-brown to almost black.

STAPHYLEA (staf-ill-EE-a)
bumalda   6′   Zone 4   Bumalda Bladdernut
The bladdernuts in general are weedy shrubs not used much in America as ornamentals. This comes from Japan, with opposite compound leaves of 3 leaflets, each 1½–2½ in. long. Flowers are whitish, not very conspicuous, and the conspicuous, yellowish, bladderlike fruits are 1 in. across. The best that can be said for this plant is that it makes a vigorous but nondescript filler in the shrub border.

Propagation

Do not let the seed dry out before stratification, 3 months in the warm greenhouse followed by 3 months at 40° F. Softwood and hardwood cuttings both can be easily rooted. These shrubs can sometimes be divided with a sharp spade. See STRATIFICATION, CUTTINGS.

STAR-ANISE = *Illicium anisatum*

STARCACTUS. See ASTROPHYTUM.

STARCH. The first food manufactured in the leaves of plants by the action of chlorophyll, together with sunlight, water, various gases and various nutrients from the soil and air. This is sometimes changed to sugars or merely translocated to the roots as starch where it is stored, as in the potato.

STAR-CLUSTERS, EGYPTIAN = *Pentas lanceolata*

STARFLOWER = *Trientalis borealis*

STARGLORY, CRIMSON = *Mina lobata*
STARGLORY, SCARLET = *Ipomoea coccinea*

STAR-GRASS = *Hypoxis hirsuta*

STAR-GRASS, WHITETUBE = *Aletris farinosa*

STAR-JASMINE, CHINESE = *Trachelospermum jasminoides*

STAR-JASMINE, YELLOW = *Trachelospermum asiaticum*

STAR-LILY = *Leucocrinum montanum*

STAR-OF-BETHLEHEM. See ORNITHOGALUM.

STAR-OF-PERSIA = *Allium christophii*

STAR-OF-TEXAS = *Xanthisma texanum*

STAR-OF-THE-DESERT = *Amberboa maroccana*

STARTER SOLUTION. There are several "starter solutions" on the market now which have merit when applied as directed on the package to newly set-out plants or seedlings. These aid the young plants in getting quickly established and in making new roots rapidly.

START-THISTLE, EUROPEAN = *Centaurea maculosa*

STATE FLOWERS, have been officially designated as such by the legislatures of most states: in Miss., N.Y., R.I. and Wisc. they have been chosen by vote of school children.

Alabama: Goldenrod (*Solidago serotina*)
Alaska: Forget-me-not (*Myosotis alpestris*)
Arizona: Saguaro Cactus (*Carnegiea gigantea*)
Arkansas: Apple Blossom (*Malus sylvestris*)
California: California-poppy (*Eschscholzia californica*)
Colorado: Columbine (*Aquilegia caerulea*)
Connecticut: Mountain-laurel (*Kalmia latifolia*)
Delaware: Peach Blossom (*Prunus persica*)
District of Columbia: American Beauty Rose
Florida: Orange Blossom (*Citrus sinensis*)
Georgia: Cherokee Rose (*Rosa laevigata*)
Hawaii: Hibiscus or Pua Aloa (*Hibiscus rosa-sinensis*)
Idaho: Mock Orange (*Philadelphus lewisii*)
Illinois: Native Violet (*Viola*)
Indiana: Zinnia (*Zinnia elegans*)
Iowa: Wild Rose (*Rosa suffulta*)
Kansas: Sunflower (*Helianthus annuus*)
Kentucky: Goldenrod (*Solidago serotina*)
Louisiana: Magnolia (*Magnolia grandiflora*)
Maine: Pine Cone and Tassel (*Pinus strobus*)
Maryland: Black-eyed-Susan (*Rudbeckia hirta*)
Massachusetts: Trailing Arbutus (*Epigaea repens*)
Michigan: Apple Blossom (*Malus sylvestris*)
Minnesota: Showy Lady's-slipper (*Cypripedium reginae*)
Mississippi: Magnolia (*Magnolia grandiflora*)
Missouri: Red Haw (*Crataegus mollis*)
Montana: Bitterroot (*Lewisia rediviva*)
Nebraska: Goldenrod (*Solidago serotina*)
Nevada: Sagebrush (*Artemisia tridentata*)
New Hampshire: Purple Lilac (*Syringa vulgaris*)
New Jersey: Violet (*Viola*)
New Mexico: Yucca (*Yucca*)
New York: Wild Rose (*Rosa*)
North Carolina: Flowering Dogwood (*Cornus florida*)
North Dakota: Wild Prairie Rose (*Rosa arkansana*)
Ohio: Scarlet Carnation (*Dianthus caryophyllus*)
Oklahoma: Mistletoe (*Phoradendron flavescens*)
Oregon: Oregon Grape (*Mahonia aquifolium*)

Pennsylvania: Mountain-laurel (*Kalmia latifolia*)

Rhode Island: Violet (*Viola*)

South Carolina: Yellow Jessamine (*Gelsemium sempervirens*)

South Dakota: Pasque Flower (*Anemone patens*)

Tennessee: Iris (*Iris*)

Texas: Bluebonnet (*Lupinus subcarnosus*)

Utah: Sego Lily (*Calochortus nuttallii*)

Vermont: Red Clover (*Trifolium pratense*)

Virginia: Flowering Dogwood (*Cornus florida*)

Washington: Rhododendron (*Rhododendron macrophyllum*)

West Virginia: Rhododendron (*Rhododendron maximum*)

Wisconsin: Violet (*Viola*)

Wyoming: Indian Paintbrush (*Castilleja lineariaefolia*)

STATE TREES—The following trees have been selected by acts of the state legislatures as the various "official" trees of each state, or by some interested state-wide organization that has deemed it advisable to list a tree as sufficiently important to suggest one for this list. For example, Iowa has listed "oak" instead of one species; though several are of value in the state, it was decided not to single out one species alone. It is interesting to note that the Sugar Maple has been popular enough to be selected by 5 different states, the Tulip Tree by 4, and the Cottonwood (*Populus deltoides*) by 3 states. This list easily represents a cross-section of the native trees valued across the continent.

Alabama—Southern Pine—a compromise bill was passed to include under this general heading 3 native and valued pines—namely, Slash Pine (*P. caribaea*), Longleaf Pine (*P. palustris*), and Loblolly Pine (*P. taeda*)

Alaska—Sitka Spruce (*Picea stichensis*) 1962

Arizona—Palo Verde (*Circidium* sp.)

Arkansas—"Pine"

California—Redwood (*Sequoia sempervirens*)

Colorado—Colorado Blue Spruce (*Picea pungens glauca*)

Connecticut—White Oak (*Quercus alba*)

Delaware—American Holly (*Ilex opaca*)

District of Columbia—Scarlet Oak (*Quercus coccinea*)

Florida—Cabbage Palmetto (*Sabal palmetto*) 1953

Georgia—Live Oak (*Quercus virginiana*)

Hawaii—Kuki or Candlenut (*Aleurites molucana*) 1959

Idaho—Western White Pine (*Pinus monticola*)

Illinois—"Native Oak"

Indiana—Tulip Tree, Tulip or Yellow Poplar (*Liriodendron tulipifera*)

Iowa—"Oak" (*Quercus* sp.) 1958

Kansas—Cottonwood (*Populus deltoides* or *P. balsamifera*)

Kentucky—Tulip Tree, Tulip or Yellow Poplar (*Liriodendron tulipifera*)—unofficial

Louisiana—Bald Cypress (*Taxodium distichum*)

Maine—White Pine (*Pinus strobus*)

Maryland—White Oak (*Quercus alba*)

Massachusetts—American Elm (*Ulmus americana*)

Michigan—Eastern White Pine (*Pinus strobus*)

Minnesota—Red Pine (*Pinus resinosa*)

Mississippi—Southern Magnolia (*Magnolia grandiflora*)

Missouri—Flowering Dogwood (*Cornus florida*) 1955

Montana—Western Yellow Pine (*Pinus ponderosa*)

Nebraska—American Elm (*Ulmus americana*)

Nevada—Singleleaf Pine (*Pinus cembroides monophylla*)

New Hampshire—Canoe Birch (*Betula papyrifera*)

New Jersey—Red Oak (*Quercus rubra*)

New Mexico—Pinyon or Nut Pine (*Pinus edulis*)

New York—Sugar Maple (*Acer saccharum*)—unofficial

North Carolina—Pine sp.

North Dakota—American Elm (*Ulmus americana*)

Ohio—Ohio Buckeye (*Aesculus glabra*) 1953

Oklahoma—Redbud (*Cercis canadensis*)

Oregon—Douglas-fir (*Pseudotsuga menziesii*)

Pennsylvania—Canada Hemlock (*Tsuga canadensis*)

Rhode Island—Red Maple (*Acer rubrum*)

South Carolina—Cabbage Palmetto (*Sabal palmetto*)

South Dakota—Black Hills Spruce (*Picea glauca* 'Densata')

Tennessee—Tulip Tree or Tulip Poplar (*Liriodendron tulipifera*)

Texas—Pecan (*Carya illinoensis*, formerly *C. pecan*)

Utah—Colorado Blue Spruce (*Picea pungens glauca*)

Vermont—Sugar Maple (*Acer saccharum*)

Virginia—Flowering Dogwood (*Cornus florida*)

Washington—Western Hemlock (*Tsuga heterophylla*) 1947

West Virginia—Sugar Maple (*Acer saccharum*)

Wisconsin—Sugar Maple (*Acer saccharum*) 1955

Wyoming—Plains Cottonwood (*Populus sargentii*)

STATICE. This is an old-fashioned name for some of the *Limonium* species, but it has been used also for *Armeria* species. It might be well to drop the often-confusing common name Statice and use the common name Sea-lavender for *Limonium* species.

STATUES, VASES. See GARDEN FIXTURES.

STAUNTONIA (stawn-TO-nia)
   hexaphylla **vine** **Zone 7** **Japanese Staunton**
                              Vine
An evergreen woody vine from Japan and
China; with alternate compound leaves, 3–7
palmately arranged leaflets, each oval leaflet
about 3–4 in. long. Male and female flowers are
separate but are on the same plant, white,
fragrant, violet tinted and about ¾ in. across,
borne in small clusters in the leaf axils. The
vine can grow 40 ft. high. The fruit is a berry.
Propagated by softwood cuttings.

STAUNTON VINE, JAPANESE = *Stauntonia*
hexaphylla

STECTORUM (stec-TOR-um)
   glaucum **1′** **Zone 5**
Rosettes of foliage 3 in. across; oblanceolate
leaves, brownish spotted at tips; flowers an
inch long and red, borne in 2–3-in. panicles.
Native to Central Europe.

STEIRONEMA = *Lysimachia*

STELLARIA (stel-AY-ria). The chickweeds
always seem to be in every garden. There are
about 120 species distributed around the world,
both annuals and perennials. The most common
one in our gardens is *S. media*, a native of
Europe but now widely distributed throughout
America and always one of the weeds first
appearing in many a garden. They have small
white flowers, the seeds have great viability and
are easily distributed by both birds and wind,
quickly germinating where they fall. The flowers
are small, white and inconspicuous, blooming,
it seems, almost throughout the entire growing
season.
   holostea **2′** **Zone 6** **Stitchwort**
A perennial, native in Eurasia but now naturalized in North America. Showy white flowers.
   media **12″** **annual** **Chickweed**
Now a common weed naturalized in all the
temperate regions of the world, originally native
to Europe. The stems are often decumbent and
grow rapidly in the fall. The rounded, opposite
leaves can be 2½ in. long but are usually less,
and the white starlike flowers are ½ in. across,
borne in terminal leafy clusters. Since it roots
readily along its stems and produces flowers
(and seeds) from March to Dec., it is an
omnipresent garden pest throughout North
America. For control see WEED-CONTROLLING
CHEMICALS.
   pubera **12″** **Zone 6** **Great Chickweed**
Although members of the Pink Family,
species of *Stellaria* are small and inconspicuous
but among the largest is *S. pubera*, having a
much branched, 4-angled stem and slightly
hairy, opposite, lanceolate leaves. The flowers
are borne in clusters accompanied with leafy

bracts. Each flower has a calyx of 5 segments
and 5 bluish-white, deeply forked petals. The
plant prefers rich soil in partly shaded sites from
N.J. to Ala. and blooms in spring.

STELLATE. Star shaped; where several similar
parts spread out from a common center, like a
star.

STEM. The axis or axes of a plant arising from
its root.

STENANTHIUM (sten-ANTH-ium)
   gramineum robustum **5′** **Zone 6** **Feather-**
                                   fleece
A native American wild flower found from Pa.
to S.Car. and Mo., with leaves a foot long and
¾ in. wide; flowers greenish or white, ⅓ in. wide,
but borne in panicles sometimes 2 ft. long and
more. Best used in the wild garden.

STENOCARPUS (sten-o-KARP-us)
   sinuatus **50′** **Zone 10** **Tall Firewheel-tree**
A tropical tree with alternate, leathery, shiny,
oaklike leaves. The bright red flowers, shaped
like a wheel, are up to 4 in. in dia., and have
yellow stamens but they have a disagreeable
odor especially at night. Native to New South
Wales.

STENOLOBIUM STANS = *Tecoma stans*

STENOTAPHRUM (sten-o-TAFF-rum)
   secundatum **1′** **Zones 7–8** **St. Augustine**
                                  Grass
A creeping, stoloniferous grass with leaves 6 in.
long, ⅓ in. wide, native from S.Car. to Tex. and
tropical America. Widely planted for lawns in
the South. The var. **variegatum** with leaves
striped white is sometimes used in hanging
baskets. Also see GRASS LAWNS.

STEPHANANDRA (steff-an-AND-ra)
   incisa **7′** **Zone 5** **Cutleaf Stephanandra**
The Cutleaf Stephanandra, native to Japan
and Korea, has not proved a very popular
garden plant, although its small leaves are very
finely cut and hence the plant has a fine texture.
A reddish-purple to red autumn color adds to its
usefulness. Much better is the variety ‘Crispa’
which originated in a Denmark nursery about
1930, for it is much lower in size, being 1½–3 ft.
tall, and is very dense. It should make a fine
low hedge, requiring practically no clipping
whatsoever. The flower clusters are 2 in. long,
loose, greenish white and rather insignificant.

Propagation

The easiest method is to divide the clumps,
usually in the spring before growth has started.
Somtimes many of the branches actually strike
root where they touch moist soil. Also softwood
cuttings (which see) root readily and easily.

STEPHANOTIS (steff-an-O-tis)

floribunda   vine   **Zone 10**   Madagascar
                                Stephanotis

A twining, opposite-leaved, woody vine from Madagascar; the flowers of this are pure white, 1–2 in. long and narrowly tubular, with 6–8 flowers in each cluster. They are borne from April to Oct. and are often used in making leis in Hawaii. The leaves are opposite, slightly indented at the tip and 4 in. long.

STEPS. Steps in the garden are made of many materials but in order to be safe and sound they should have at least a foot of well firmed gravel or crushed stone beneath them. A good dimension for garden steps is a 12-in. tread with a 6-in. riser; sometimes they are even slightly wider and if so the riser might be reduced to 5 in.

Steps are made of brick, stepping stones, heavy stones, concrete and railroad ties. Where possible each step should overlap the one below it by an inch or so. To build concrete steps one would first put in the cinder or crushed stone base, then build the wooden form into which the concrete is poured, and this of course should be reinforced with rods or wire (see CONCRETE) depending on the size and extent of the steps. Stepping stones, when used as steps, are best set in concrete. Railroad ties make excellent steps and give a rustic appearance much appreciated in the garden. Brick steps are frequently used but in each case the material used to construct the steps should conform to other materials used in the garden. Bricks, if used in steps, are best set in concrete. See CONCRETE.

STERCULIA (ster-KEW-lia)

discolor = *Brachychiton discolor*

diversifolia = *Brachychiton populneum*

foetida   60′   **Zone 10**   Hazel Sterculia
An alternate-leaved, palmately compound tree of the Old World Tropics; with 5–9 lanceolate leaflets each 6 in. long; red to purplish, odoriferous flowers; fruits, red pods 4 in. long, include 5 carpels, the inside colored bright red and holding black seeds. Propagated by seeds and hardwood cuttings. Only grown in extreme southern Fla.

STERCULIACEAE = The Chocolate Family

STERILE. Barren; not fertile.

STERNBERGIA (stern-BER-gia)

lutea   1′   **Zone 7(?)**   **Fall-daffodil**
This member of the Amaryllis Family is a bulbous plant which is found wild in Israel and is known as the "Lily-of-the-Field" of Biblical times. It grows in dry rocky areas, bears shining yellow flowers, 1½ in. long, and straplike leaves a foot long and ¾ in. wide, in autumn. The bulbs should be planted 4–5 in. deep. In cold regions the bulbs can be lifted every fall, cleaned, dried and stored for spring planting. One of the best bulbs for sunny hot dry situations.

STEWARTIA (stew-ART-ia). There are only 7 species and 1 variety of these shrubs or trees that are grown in the U.S. today. They all have conspicuous, perfect, white flowers borne singly in early summer, usually in July, and alternate leaves. Since there are few summer-blooming woody plants, these are definitely valued. Apparently all 7 species are available from some American nurseries, 2 being American natives and the others natives of China, Japan or Korea.

The stewartias are valued not only for their camellialike white summer flowers, but also for their colorful flaking bark, somewhat similar to, but much more colorful than, that of the sycamore tree. They have alternate leaves, 1½–5 in. long, and the autumn color is purplish to a vivid orange-red. Fruits are rather woody capsules of little ornamental value. These plants do best in soils devoid of lime, but need plenty of rich humus material and plenty of moisture.

Unfortunately they are difficult to transplant. It is recommended that they be container-grown and, if they must be moved, that it be done with a large ball of soil about the roots. However, it is best to plant them in their permanent location direct from container if at all possible, in a permanently sheltered, yet sunny, location where they will grow best. They should be considered specimen trees—1 in a garden is plenty, especially when given a prominently featured space so that its summer flowers and beautiful autumn color will be displayed at their best. Then, too, their beautiful bark is an outstanding feature throughout the entire year and especially in the winter when the surrounding deciduous foliage has disappeared.

Propagation

Do not let the seed dry out before stratifying for 5 months at normal greenhouse temperatures, then 3 months at 40° F., then plant. Layers and softwood cuttings are also used. See STRATIFICATION, LAYERS, CUTTINGS.

koreana   45′   **Zone 5**   Korean Stewartia
Closely related to *S. pseudo-camellia*, this tree from Korea is considered by some to be a variety of it. In general habit it is smaller, but has larger flowers—up to 3 in. in dia.—and not so definitely cup shaped as in *S. pseudo-camellia*, but they are just as prominent and have a wavy margin which lends interest to them. The leaves turn orange to orange-red in the fall and the exfoliating bark is as beautiful throughout the year as it is on the other species.

malacodendron 18′ Zone 7 Virginia Stewartia
This species, native from Va. to La., is only for the South, where its large, 4-in. flowers and shrublike habit may have some merit. In this size range (18 ft.) there are undoubtedly many other shrubs just as suitable and far easier to grow.

monadelpha 75′ Zone 6 Tall Stewartia
Native to Japan, this is the least ornamental of this genus because of its comparatively small, white flowers, 1–1½ in. wide, in early summer. The leaves are 1½–3 in. long.

ovata 15′ Zone 5 Mountain Stewartia
This species with its cup-shaped white flowers has the largest leaves of any Stewartia, they being 2½–5 in. long. It is native from N.Car. to Fla.

ovata grandiflora 15′ Zone 5 Showy Stewartia
Although this is native to Ga., it can be used in gardens as far north as southern New England. It is one of the prettiest of the stewartias because each large white flower, 4 in. wide, has a ring of very beautiful, purple stamens in the center. Like the other stewartias, these flowers bloom in early July. The autumn foliage color is orange to scarlet and on branches and trunk the older bark flakes off in irregular patches so that there are interesting light and dark areas, similar to, but more colorful than, those of the Sycamore.

pseudocamellia 60′ Zone 5 Japanese Stewartia
The flowers of this species from Japan are about 2½ in. in dia., white and similar in size to that of the Camellia. The flaking bark is more colorful than that of the other stewartias, being red and peeling off in large plates. Other features are a purplish autumn color and a pyramidal habit.

sinensis 30′ Zone 6 Chinese Stewartia
The fragrant, white, cup-shaped flowers (about 2 in. in dia.) are the only outstanding characteristic of this species which E. H. Wilson introduced from China in 1901. It is not so hardy as other species.

STITCHWORT = *Stellaria holostea*

STIGMA. The part of the pistil that receives the pollen.

STINKING-CEDAR = *Torreya taxifolia*

STIPA (STY-pa)
pennata 3′ Zone 5 European Feather Grass
A perennial, ornamental grass, native to Europe and Asia, with narrow leaves, and graceful, long, narrow and feathery fruiting stalks, sometimes a foot long. See ORNAMENTAL GRASS.

STIPE. The stalk of a pistil, also the stalk or petiole of a fern frond.

STIPULE, The appendage at the base of the petiole, usually 1 on each side.

STOCK. A horticultural term used to denote the rooted portion of a plant to which a graft has been applied. This can either be a stem or a root. Sometimes referred to as the understock when speaking of the plant as a whole. It also is used to denote the rhizome or crown from which roots grow. A third meaning is a race of plants or a collection from which plants can be drawn for any purpose.

STOCK. See MATTHIOLA.

STOKESIA (sto-KEE-sia)
laevis 1′–2′ Zone 5 Stokesia
This herbaceous perennial is the only species of this genus grown in gardens today but a very popular one, native from S.Car. to Fla. and La. A member of the Composite Family, it has alternate leaves 2–8 in. long, solitary flower heads, blue or purplish blue, 3–4 in. across, from July to Oct. Propagated by seeds and division. A valued plant and one easily grown.

STOLON. A slender stem above or below ground which produces a new plant at its tip.

STOLONIFEROUS. Bearing stolons.

STOMA (plural stomata) or **STOMATE.** A "breathing" pore in the epidermis of the leaf leading into an intercellular space.

STONECRESS. See AETHIONEMA.

STONECROP. See SEDUM.

STONECROP FAMILY = Crassulaceae

STOOL. A clump of roots or rootstalk that may be used in propagation; also an established low plant from which layers are taken.

STORAGE. The majority of suburban gardeners today do not wish to be bothered with special cellars or pits for storing their root crops over winter. Fresh carrots, for example, can now be purchased for so little at the grocery store that the individual who raised them in his vegetable garden in the summer, just does not want to be bothered with storing his own produce over winter. He enjoys what he raises when he uses it right out of the garden, and that is the end of it. The same with beets, parsnips, cabbage and the rest of the common vegetable crops.

A few words in general about storage should be offered. The crops should not be allowed to dry out, the reason they are stored in a cool cellar, without a furnace. An earthen floor is especially good. The temperature for storage should be just a bit above freezing—hence the old cellar suggestion. Years ago pits were dug in the garden, lined with hay or leaves, filled with vegetables, covered over with more hay and leaves and then soil on top of that. State experiment stations still have available bulletins on the construction of such pits.

The modern cellar is usually not a good place for vegetable or fruit storage for it is usually too warm. The open garage is not a good place because temperatures inside, when the doors are left open, will go below freezing in the winter. The cellar of an unused building, especially if it has an earthen floor, might be ideal. Provide a wire enclosure (to protect the vegetables from rodents), place the root crops in boxes and mix with soil; place the apples in boxes and cover with polyethylene film, if necessary, to keep them from drying out, and this sort of storage might be found worth while.

If not, obtain a special bulletin from the state experiment station on the subject and build a pit for the purpose in the garden. Most suburbanites will not want to be bothered, and those who live in the country frequently have an old cellar hole handy which serves admirably.

STORAX FAMILY = Styracaceae

STRAIN. A group of plants differing from the race to which it belongs by no apparent morphological characters, but by some enhanced or improved growth characteristics; as heavier yield in fruit; resistance to disease, etc.

STRANVAESIA (stran-VEE-sia)

davidiana 24' Zone 7 Chinese Stranvaesia
A fine evergreen from West China, this is used a great deal in southern Calif., the leaves being $2\frac{1}{2}$–$4\frac{1}{2}$ in. long and colored purple and bronze. The small white flowers are borne in terminal clusters, 4 in. wide, during June and the scarlet fruits, about $\frac{1}{4}$ in. wide, are at their best about Christmas. One should know that it is widespreading and vigorous in habit, needing plenty of space in which to grow.

Propagation

Seed should be stratified for 3 months at 40° F. just prior to sowing. Hardwood cuttings can be rooted. See STRATIFICATION, CUTTINGS.

STRATIFICATION. A process used in the propagation of woody plants by which dormancy of seed is quickly overcome. This entails the thorough cleaning of the mature seed and freeing it from all pulp of any kind (see SEED, SEED DORMANCY, etc.), drying for a few hours or a few days, then mixing with slightly moistened sand, peat moss or a mixture of both. This mixture is then put in a polyethylene bag, the top tied tightly shut. In general, a cold treatment of from 1–4 months is required, depending on the kind of seed, at about 40° F.—the approximate temperature of the home refrigerator (not the freezing unit). Then medium and seed are sown as a unit.

In some cases of double dormancy, depending on the seed species, a warm period is required first of 3–5 months, at normal room temperatures. After this, the bags are placed in the cold unit for 3 months at 40° F. At no time is it necessary to open the bags but one can easily inspect the condition of the seed through the transparent polyethylene film. For further information see SEED DORMANCY.

STRAWBERRY. Origin. There are many species of strawberries and they are native to most of the temperate regions of the world. The large-fruited berries that are grown today in the U.S. have come from the union of species found in North and South America. Wild strawberries were found over much of Europe as early as the year 70 B.C. The European species produce fruit of good quality and were especially notable for their aroma, but the fruit was small and the production was light. When the colonists landed in America they were amazed at the vigor, fruitfulness and size of the native American strawberry plants. This is the species *Fragaria virginiana*. Another American species, *F. chiloensis*, is found along the Pacific Coast from Alaska to Calif. and along the coast of Chile. The cultivated strawberry that is grown today is a hybrid of these 2 American species.

The American Strawberry, *F. virginiana*, was taken to France in the early 1600's and from France it was taken to other European countries and to England. This proved to be much more productive than the native European strawberries and so it was cultivated in the gardens in Europe. In the early 1700's some strawberry plants of the species *F. chiloensis* were taken from Chile, South America, to France and later to England. These plants bore fruit as large as walnuts and were superior to those found in North America. It is quite probable that the European gardener planted both the Chilean and the North American strawberries in the same garden and as a result, the seedling plants were hybrids of *F. virginiana* and *F. chiloensis*. These plants were selected for vigor, large fruits and productiveness and returned to America from Europe to become the basis of the commercial Strawberry cultured in the U.S. By 1825, strawberry growing was well established in the U.S. in home gardens and also in commercial fields. In 1838 the first variety, called 'Hovey', was developed in Mass. by a fruit grower named Charles M. Hovey. It is reported that in N.J. in 1875 the 'Hilton' strawberry variety grew to a size of 9 in. in circumference.

Areas in the United States

Strawberries are grown to some extent in every state in the Union. The large areas of production are in Fla., La., Tenn., Ark., Ore., Calif., N.C., Md., Del. and N.J.

Research Breeding

The varieties grown today are a result of breeding by private growers, the federal experiment stations and various state agricultural experiment stations. Strawberry breeding began in N.Y. at the Geneva Station as early as 1889. Breeding work began in Alaska in 1905 and in Calif. and N.J. in the late 1920's. Many other states began breeding programs after 1930.

Many varieties are adapted to a wide area, but specific varieties must be grown in the southern areas of the country, while others are best adapted to more northern areas. Varieties grown in Fla. and southern Calif., for example, are not suitable for more northerly areas. Since strawberry varieties do not have so wide an adaptation as many other fruits, it is recommended that the home gardener consult his agricultural college for those varieties recommended for his area. In Fla. the main variety is **'Florida Ninety'** which was developed at the Florida Experiment Station. This is also an important variety in Mexico. In southern Calif. the varieties **'Lassen'** and **'Shasta'** are especially adapted. 'Shasta' is grown also in Ore. and Wash. The variety **'Headliner'** is grown in La. and is not adapted to central and northern states. Varieties such as **'Catskill'**, **'Sparkle'**, **'Midland'**, **'Guardian'**, **'Redcoat'** and **'Robinson'** are not adapted to the most southern areas, but do well in the middle east and central part of the country. All important varieties are self-fruitful, so there is no cross-pollination problem.

Climatic conditions influence the Strawberry perhaps more than other fruit plants. In Fla., for example, the old **'Missionary'** variety and the newer **'Florida Ninety'** begin ripening fruit after Dec. 1 and continue until after June 1. In this same section of the country the variety **'Klondike'** will begin to bear fruit in Feb. and will continue until June. A similar situation occurs in southern Calif. where the production begins in early March and continues until fall. In the more northerly areas of the country a shorter fruiting period occurs. Fruit ripens for about a month for any given variety and under high temperatures it may last for only 3 weeks.

Everbearing Strawberries

The so-called Everbearing Strawberry is one that produces a crop in the spring and another in late summer and until frost occurs. Everbearing varieties have the ability to make fruit buds during the early summer after the spring crop is done and thus are able to produce the late summer and fall crops. The single-crop varieties develop fruit buds in late summer and early fall for the next spring crop. There are several good everbearing varieties and additional ones are being developed constantly. Since the everbearing strawberries have originated in the northern states, they succeed best in these areas, but they can be grown in southern states at the higher, cooler elevations. The everbearing strawberries have one advantage over the ordinary kind since they are able to produce a second series of blossoms if the spring blossoms are killed by frost. A small- to medium-sized crop is produced in the spring and then the plants go into a short rest period during which they produce more fruit buds, begin blossoming again in July and produce a fairly good crop during Aug., Sept. and Oct. or until the first frost.

Strawberry runner

The culture of the Everbearing Strawberry differs somewhat from the ordinary single-crop variety. Since they produce very few runner plants, they can be set in 3- or 4-row beds with plants spaced 1 ft. apart in each direction. There should be a space of at least 2 ft. between the beds. All of the blossoms should be removed as they are produced on the newly set plants until about July 15. Removing these first blossoms permits the plants to grow vigorously and a larger fall crop is produced from blossoms which appear during the late summer. The soil should be kept weed-free and if sawdust is available it can be used as a mulch. Peat moss, wood chips and pine needles are also excellent mulches. All runners should be removed as they appear throughout the life of the plantings and, of course, watering is extremely important. In areas where the summers are extremely hot and dry the everbearing varieties will not do well.

The "climbing" Strawberry is an everbearing type and is often trained to a trellis. It does not have the ability to attach itself to a trellis since it does not have tendrils like a grape plant and it does not grow well in areas where summer temperatures are high for prolonged periods. The general culture described for the ever-bearing plants is applicable to the "climbing" types.

Culture

The culture of the ordinary strawberry varieties that produce 1 crop differs somewhat throughout the country, but in general the practices are much the same.

Planting

Early spring planting has always been recommended for strawberries and still is where fresh plants are used. During recent years, however, cold storage plants have become available and these can be planted later in the spring and even in early summer. Storage plants are held at 30° F. in a dormant condition in polyethylene bags and remain in excellent condition as late as early summer.

Fresh-dug strawberry plants can be planted in the home garden in late summer, but some special care is required. Watering is extremely important during this time of the year and the soil must not be permitted to dry out. Plants are not generally available from nurseries in late Aug., so one must use plants from the garden. An excellent method for obtaining good plants is to place flower pots or cans in the soil beneath runner plants during June and July and let them root in the pot or can. These "potted" plants will grow large and can be cut loose from the mother plant and removed to the new location with more success than bare root plants. Strawberries require full sunshine to grow well and produce a good crop. They will not tolerate a shady location.

Do not plant strawberry plants where tomatoes, peppers, potatoes, eggplants or okra grew the previous year. It is best to wait several years before planting in such an area in the garden, since a soil-borne disease called verticillium wilt often attacks these vegetables and also is damaging to the Strawberry.

In setting out the strawberry plant it is extremely important that the roots be spread out in the soil and not jammed into a small hole. Unless the roots are spread out the plants will not grow satisfactorily. The crown of the plant should be kept above the soil level. In most areas a fertilizer solution is used at planting time and this is a good practice. There are many so-called starter solutions available for the planting of strawberries and vegetable plants. The varieties grown in northern areas of the country produce many runner plants, while those grown in Fla. and southern Calif., such as the everbearing varieties, produce few runner

plants. Those that produce few runner plants may be planted in double-row beds with the plants about a foot apart in both directions. The few runner plants should be removed during the growing season, or a few may be left to develop into fruit-producing plants. Those varieties that produce many runners, and these include most varieties, are best grown in a single plant row with plants spaced about $2\frac{1}{2}$ ft. apart in the row.

Blossom Removal

Soon after plants are established and growing they will produce blossoms. These should be removed so that the plant will grow vigorously and produce runner plants. If fruit is permitted to grow and ripen on the newly set plant, the growth of the plant is retarded and runner plants are produced later in the season. Late-formed runner plants are not so productive as early-formed ones.

Runner Thinning

As the runners begin to grow from the mother plant, they should be spaced around the mother plant similar to the spokes in a wheel. It is best that each runner plant be 3–4 in. apart from every other runner plant. After a sufficient number of runner plants have been placed and the row is filled with plants to a width of 2–3 ft., the additional runner plants should be removed and destroyed. This system is called the matted row, in comparison with the single-plant bed.

Use Healthy Plants

There has been considerable effort by the U.S. Department of Agriculture and the state agricultural experiment stations to develop strawberry varieties that are essentially free from virus diseases. Until the early 1950's, most strawberry plants throughout the country were heavily infected with a complex of virus diseases which caused the plants to grow in a weakened condition. As a result, the production was much less than it is today. A concerted effort to rid the plants of the virus diseases was begun about 1950, when it was determined that this was a serious and widespread problem, and research workers were successful in producing the so-called virus-free plant stock that is available today from most nurseries. Virus-free plants produce 3–4 times as many berries as the older, virus-infected plants. For example, the 'Catskill' variety, when infected, was producing a total of about 1 qt. of berries for each plant and all of its runner plants. If 25 plants were set in the garden, these original plants and the resulting runner plants would produce a total of 25 qts. Today this same variety, now virus-free, will produce 3–4 qts. where 1 grew before.

Fertilization

The strawberry plant is shallow rooted and must be fertilized during the growing season to keep it vigorous. Plants should be well fertilized before Sept., prior to the period of fruit-bud initiation. During the second year when the fruit crop is developing, the plants also require some nitrogen, especially on the sandy soils. One must be careful not to use excessive amounts of fertilizer in the spring of the fruiting year, because this can result in heavy foliage, fruit rot and soft berries of poor dessert quality.

The strawberry plant suffers greatly from lack of water, especially during the blossoming and fruit-developing period. Thorough watering should be done at least once a week during this period if no rainfall occurs. On sandy soils, watering may be necessary every 5 days during hot, dry periods. In the arid regions, irrigation is a common procedure.

Weed Control

Hand-hoeing and hand-weeding are very necessary in strawberry planting. Weeds rob the strawberry plants of moisture and nutrients and prevent them from becoming large and vigorous. There are available some excellent chemical weed-control materials for the Strawberry, but in general the home garden plantings are best weeded without the use of chemicals. It is difficult to apply the chemical at the proper rate without the necessary equipment and there is the danger of doing damage to adjacent vegetable or flower plants.

Plastic materials are excellent for weed control for everbearing varieties and those that do not produce many runners. These materials are used in Fla. and Calif. The plastic sheets are placed on the soil and plants are set in the soil through a hole made in the plastic. This material can be used also on varieties that produce many runners, but holes must be made through the plastic to allow the runner plants to root in the soil.

Mulching

In the northern areas where the soil freezes, it is best to cover the strawberry bed with a mulch of straw, salt hay, pine needles or wood chips unless plastic is used. The mulch should be applied in the early winter, preferably after the ground has frozen for the first time. Sufficient mulch should be applied so that the plants are just barely visible through the mulch. This prevents the soil from freezing and thawing and heaving of the plants. It also protects them from cold, drying winds when there is no snow cover.

When growth begins in the spring, the mulching material should be carefully removed from over the plants and left in place between the plants. This mulch on the ground helps to keep the berries clean as they ripen, conserves the moisture in the soil and is an excellent means for controlling weeds.

Harvesting

Strawberries ripen rapidly during hot weather and it is best to pick over the plantings each

Polyethylene covers bring these strawberries into bearing several weeks before those in the open. (*Photo by Arnold Arboretum, Jamaica Plain, Mass.*)

morning while they are cool. Berries may be harvested when they are fully red or when about 25% of the surface is white or light pink. A berry that has about 25% white will ripen to fully red within a day and it will be of good flavor. By picking berries before they are fully red or completely ripe, one will avoid rot and decay. This method of harvesting is especially helpful especially if several rainy days occur during the ripening period, since there will be fewer berries to become overripe or decayed during the rain when harvesting is not possible.

ERNEST G. CHRIST

Pest Control

In most areas there are at least a few insects and diseases that attack the Strawberry and it is advisable to consult the state agricultural experiment station to learn what spray or dusting materials are best suited for the control of these insects and diseases. However, the following are a few that might give trouble.

White grubs in soil recently in sod often eat the roots. Injury is prevented by growing a different crop for 1 year and by treating the soil with insecticide #15. See JAPANESE BEETLE. Strawberry root weevils are universal strawberry pests, but are most injurious in the West. The larvae eat the roots and the beetles cause minor damage to the leaves. Chemical soil treatment as above is helpful, but control of adult weevils is also necessary. Dusts or sprays of insecticide #9 before bloom and after harvest is advised. Recently methoxychlor and Sevin have been found helpful as prebloom applications as either dusts or sprays.

Strawberry weevil lays eggs in the bud and partially bites off the stem of the blossom, sometimes reducing the crop 50%. It is most serious on varieties with perfect flowers. Spray in spring as for root weevils. Strawberry crown borer is a snout beetle which, as grubs, eats the roots and crown of strawberry plants. This pest has discouraged growing strawberries in parts of the Midwest. Set only clean plants and spray with insecticide #9 or #46 twice before bloom and twice after harvest. Strawberry leafroller webs the leaflets and heavy infestations prevent normal ripening of the berries. Pre-blossom sprays as for crown borer are helpful. Insecticides #37 and #28 are suggested after the berries form.

White fly and aphids may require the use of insecticide #15. Spittle bugs enclosed in a mass of froth are easily killed with insecticide #15 or #28. In the South mole crickets burrow in soil around plants. Use same treatment as for root weevils. Cyclamen mite cripples the buds in the crown and spreads to the runners. A drenching spray with insecticide #13 has prevented serious injury, and plants for setting may be disinfected by soaking in hot water at 110° F. for 20 minutes. Red spider mites can be troublesome. Use insecticide #31 or #34 before bloom and after harvest.

Diseases

Gray mold rot is the cause of most fruit decay. Infection may start in the blossom, green fruit or flower stalk, but is most destructive to the berries which rest on the ground. Thinning of plants to allow normal drying after rain is helpful and spraying with fungicide #W at 7-day intervals after fruit is set gives control. During transportation and marketing, berries may be infected with a white, cottony growth called "whiskers" or "leak." To prevent it, pack only firm berries without bruises and hold at 35–30° F. as much as possible. The sunken, tan-colored spots on berries which follow tan rot infection and a hard rot on one side of the berry are both troublesome in the South. The control for gray mold is also effective against these rots.

The most serious root disease is red stele which is identified by a red center in an infected root. Diseased plants are stunted, wilt in dry weather and produce worthless fruit, if any. To avoid this trouble, plant only certified, disease-free plants and rotate beds where possible. Black root, which is not identified with a specific

disease, permits a few stunted live roots among many dead black roots. The same treatment as for red stele is suggested. Strawberry leaf spot on the leaves weakens the plant and decreases yield. Spraying or dusting during wet weather with fungicide #W or #D keeps it in check if resistant varieties are not available. Nematodes cause "dwarf" or "crimp" which describes the appearance of infested plants and leaves. To control, set clean plants and sterilize the soil with Nemagon or other recommended chemicals. Verticillium wilt, which also thrives on Tomato, Potato, Pepper and other plants, is very destructive to an infected bed. Set clean plants in uninfected soil and sterilize the soil in infected beds. See SOIL STERILIZATION.

STRAWBERRY, AMERICAN = *Fragaria vesca americana*

STRAWBERRY-BUSH = *Euonymus americana*

STRAWBERRY CACTUS = *Ferocactus setispinus*

STRAWBERRY CORN = *Zea mays everta*

STRAWBERRY JAR. This is a potting container made with a large opening at the top and numerous pocketlike openings around the sides. Suitable drainage material is placed in the

Strawberry jar planted with sedums.

bottom of the jar, then it is filled with a suitable soil mixture. Ornamental strawberries, sedums or other plants are planted in the pockets as well as in the top of the jar.

STRAWBERRY-RASPBERRY = *Rubus illeceborosus*

STRAWBERRY-SHRUB FAMILY = Calycanthaceae

STRAWBERRY-TREE = *Arbutus unedo*

STRAW-FLOWER = *Helichrysum bracteatum*

STRELITZIA (strel-ITS-ia)
   nicolai   25′   Zone 10   White Bird-of-Paradise
A tree from South Africa and, like other species of this genus, a member of the Banana Family. The leaves are 4 ft. long and 2 ft. wide, like those of a Banana, and borne in the shape of a fan. The flowers have 3 white petals and a blue "tongue" which is up to 15 in. long. Propagation by seeds or division.
   reginae   3′   Zone 10   Queen's Bird-of-Paradise
An extremely popular, trunkless plant from South Africa, with an orange and blue flower spike consisting of about 6 flowers in a sheath, each flower with 3 pointed petals and another arrowlike, part blue, about 8 in. long. These flowers are borne on a long stalk that make them very conspicuous. The bananalike evergreen leaves are 1½ ft. long, 6 in. wide; in young leaves the midrib is red. Grown in greenhouses and conservatories in the North but outdoors in southern Fla. and southern Calif. and especially in the gardens of Hawaii. Propagation by seeds or division.

STREPTOCARPUS (strep-to-KARP-us)
   x hybridus   1′–2′   Zone 10   Hybrid Cape-primrose
A complex group of showy hybrids are included under this name, all of them blooming profusely with trumpetlike flowers ranging in color from white to reddish to blue and violet. The leaves are 6–12 in. long, usually with wavy margins, and 6–8 2-in. flowers are borne in each flower cluster. The parents are natives to South Africa. Suitable for the cool greenhouse and propagated by seeds sown in Feb. or March, leaf cuttings and division.

STREPTOPUS (STREP-top-us)
   roseus   1′–3′   Zone 3   Rosy Twisted-stalk
A member of the Lily Family with a perennial, branching rootstalk. The plant much resembles the Solomon's-seal, with its arching stems and alternate, ovate leaves, but the stems of *S. roseus* are branched and twisted, with 1, occasionally 2, purple or pink, bell-shaped flowers hanging from the leaf axils. These flowers appear in early summer, followed by round red berries. Its range extends from southern Labrador to Ga., in the South, Mich. to the west. Propagation is by division in early spring or by seed, cleaned and sown as soon as ripe. A similar species, **S. amplexifolius** var. **americanus**, has greenish-white flowers and extends throughout Canada and the upper portion of the U.S.

STREPTOSOLEN (strep-to-SO-len)
   jamesonii   6′–8′ (climbing)   Zone 10   Orange Streptosolen
A member of the Potato Family, with trumpet-shaped orange flowers in terminal panicles; the individual flowers borne in June are 1½ in. long and as much wide, with 5 lobes. The evergreen leaves are oval, about 1½ in. long. Propagated by cuttings and used chiefly as a popular pot plant in the home greenhouse.

STRIATE. Marked with fine longitudinal lines.

STRIGOSE. Beset with appressed straight and stiff hairs.

STRIKE. To emit roots as from a cutting.

STROBILANTHES (stro-bil-ANTH-eez)
   dyeranus   3′   Zone 10   Burma Conehead
A beautiful herbaceous shrub with opposite leaves 8 in. long, colored purple and silver above, purple beneath. Flowers violet, 1¼ in. long, produced in spikes. Native to Burma. Propagated by cuttings. A fine greenhouse plant in the North, and valued in the garden outdoors where hardy.
   isophyllus   3′   Zone 10   Bedding Conehead
A shrub with opposite, lustrous, willowlike leaves 4 in. long; flowers lavender or blue and white, 1 in. long in axillary clusters. Native to India.

STROBILE. An inflorescence marked by imbricated bracts or scales; as in the pine cone.

STRUCTURES. See GARDEN FIXTURES.

STYLE. A stalk between the ovary and stigma.

STYLOPHORUM (sty-LOFF-or-um)
   diphyllum   1½′   Zone 4   Celandine Poppy
The Celandine Poppy is an attractive perennial with a thick root which sends up a flower stalk bearing a cluster of 2–15 deep yellow flowers and 2 deeply lobed leaves. The flowers, 1½–2 in. wide and having 4 petals, appear in spring in the states adjacent to, and south of, the Great Lakes. It is an excellent plant for the wild garden and self-sows readily. The roots may be divided in spring or cuttings taken of the roots in summer.

STRYRACACEAE = The Storax Family.

STYRAX (STY-rax). This comprises a group of beautiful trees which are not well known to American gardeners. The leaves are deciduous and alternate. The white flowers are usually produced in pendulous racemes. Care should be taken with the plants while young, especially in giving them the proper amount of winter protection. Also, they are not the easiest things in the world to transplant and the smaller the size at transplanting time, the better the chances for the plant's survival.

Propagation

Do not let the seed dry out before stratification, first for 5 months at greenhouse temperatures, then 3 months at 40° F. Layers and softwood cuttings also root. See STRATIFICATION, LAYERS, CUTTINGS.

hemsleyana   30′   Zone 7   Hemsley Snowbell
This is a handsome tree in bloom, native to China and rare in America. The flower stalks are 4–6 in. long and the individual flowers are about 1 in. in dia. Like all the members of this genus, the flowers are slightly bell shaped. The leaves are sometimes as much as 5½ in. long.

japonicus   30′   Zone 5   Japanese Snowbell
This is the most popular and best known of the snowbells, native to China and Japan, but it could be more widely grown as a specimen. It is excellent when in full bloom in June, with the small, bell-like, white flowers profusely arranged on the under side of the branches. It has no serious insect or disease pests, and this alone makes it a valued ornamental.

obassia   30′   Zone 6   Fragrant Snowbell
The handsome flowers of this Japanese species are partly hidden by the large leaves which are broadly oval, 3–8 in. long and often as broad. The fragrant white flowers appear in June and are borne on terminal racemes 6–8 in. long. This tree has been killed completely both in the Arnold Arboretum in Boston and at Rochester, N.Y., by winter cold. It has been noted in England that this should be grown in fairly moist soil, for it grows with difficulty in dry soils.

shiraiana   20′   Zone 6   Strigila Snowbell
A distinctly handsome species, but very rare in America. It might be tried if and when it becomes available. Even in its native Japan it is rare. The white flowers bloom in June on racemes 8–10 in. long. The leaves are about the size and shape of those of the Japanese Witch-hazel.

wilsonii   9′   Zone 7   Chinese Snowbell
One of the interesting characteristics of this species from western China is the fact that it blooms well when only a few inches high. It is dense in habit, and the nodding white flowers, each one about ¾ in. in dia., are borne in groups of 1–4 in the leaf axils and at the end of short lateral twigs in June. This is also rare in America but, because of its unusual character (as a shrub), might be tried where it proves to be hardy.

SUAEDA (SWAY-da)
fruticosa . 3′   Zone 6   Shrubby Goosefoot
This small deciduous shrub is only of value for planting in brackish situations or where salt-water spray will touch the foliage. It is found on the West Coast from Alberta to southern Calif. as well as in Europe, Asia and Africa. The lustrous black fruits, as well as semi-evergreen foliage and its ability to grow very near salt water where many other plants will not, are its only meager claims for garden use.

SUBSHRUB. An undershrub or small shrub which may have partially herbaceous stems.

SUBSOIL. See SOILS.

SUBULATE. Awl shaped.

SUCCULENT. Fleshy; juicy.

SUCCULENTS. This is a horticultural term used to denote those plants with large succulent leaves, many of which are desert plants or certainly inhabitants of dry areas and store water in their leaves. The numerous cactus species are examples but others would be species of *Echeveria, Sempervivum, Sedum, Aloe, Agave* and many others. See CACTI AND SUCCULENTS.

SUCKER. A shoot arising from the roots or beneath the surface of the ground.

Suckers growing up from the base of a tree should be removed.

SUDAN-GRASS = *Sorghum vulgare sudanese*

SUFFRUTESCENT. Slightly woody; woody at the base.

SUFFRUTICOSE. Perennial plant with only the lower part of the stem and of the branches woody and persistent.

SUGAR-APPLE = *Annona squamosa*

SUGAR BEET = a selected form of *Beta vulgaris.*

SUGARBUSH = *Rhus ovata*

SUGAR CANE = *Saccharum officinarum*

SUGARPLUM TREE, PATERSON = *Lagunaria patersonii*

SULFATE OF POTASH. A fertilizer containing 48.5% potash, readily available and used at the rate of ½–1 oz. per sq. yard.

SULFUR-FLOWER = *Eriogonum umbellatum*

SUMAC. See RHUS.

SUMAC or MANGO FAMILY = Anacardi-aceae

SUMMER CYPRESS = *Kochia scoparia*

SUMMER-HYACINTH = *Galtonia candicans*

SUMMERSWEET = *Clethra alnifolia*

SUNDEW. See DROSERA.

SUNDIALS. See GARDEN FIXTURES.

SUNDROPS. See OENOTHERA.

SUNFLOWER. See HELIANTHUS.

SUNRAY. See HELIPTERUM.

SUN-ROSE. See HELIANTHEMUM.

SUPERPHOSPHATE. A fertilizer containing 16–18% phosphoric acid, and can be used at the rate of 1–2 oz. per sq. yard. Double superphosphate is twice as concentrated and should only be used at $\frac{1}{2}$ oz. per sq. yard.

SUPPLEJACK. See BERCHEMIA.

SURINAM-CHERRY = *Eugenia uniflora*

SUTURE. A line of splitting.

SWAG. See CHRISTMAS DECORATIONS.

SWAINSONIA. This is a genus of over 50 species of herbs and subshrubs native to Australia and New Zealand. Only one species, *S. galegifolia*, has much economic value in America. Called Swan Flower, it is grown in greenhouses for its red flowers, about $\frac{3}{4}''$ long, and its ability to bloom throughout the year. Cuttings.

SWALLOW-WORT, BLACK = *Cynanchum nigrum*

SWAMP-PINK = *Helonias bullata*

SWEDISH IVY = *Plectranthus oertendaklii*

SWEET BAY = *Magnolia virginiana* (*M. glauca*)

SWEETBELLS = *Leucothoe racemosa*

SWEET BRIER = *Rosa eglanteria*

SWEET CICELEY = *Myrrhis odorata*

SWEET CLOCK-VINE = *Thunbergia fragrans*

SWEET CORN. See CORN, SWEET.

SWEETFERN = *Comptonia peregrina*

SWEET FLAG = *Acorus calamus*

SWEETGALE = *Myrica gale*

SWEET-GUM = *Liquidambar styraciflua*

SWEETLEAF, ASIATIC = *Symplocos paniculata*

SWEET PEA = *Lathyrus odoratus*

SWEET-PINESAP = *Monotropis odorata*

SWEET-POTATO = *Ipomoea batatas*

SWEET-SHADE = *Hymenosporum flavum*

SWEETSHRUB. See CALYCANTHUS.

SWEETSPIRE, VIRGINIA = *Itea virginica*

SWEET SULTAN = *Centaurea moschata*

SWEET VETCH. See HEDYSARUM.

SWEET WILLIAM = *Dianthus barbatus*

SWEET WILLIAM, WILD = *Phlox maculata*

SWEET WOODRUFF = *Galium odoratum*

SWIETENIA (swy-TEE-nia)

mahogani	75′	Zone 10	West Indies Mahogany

A well-known, hard-wood, evergreen tree grown in the Tropics, actually one of several kinds given the popular name Mahogany. This species has opposite, leathery, compound leaves with 4–8 leaflets arranged pinnately. The inconspicuous flowers are borne in whitish clusters. The 5-valved fruits are woody capsules, 3–4 in. long, with winged seeds 2 in. long. The wood is valued for making many things and the tree itself is sometimes planted as an ornamental tree.

SWIMMING POOLS. See GARDEN FIXTURES.

SWISS CHARD (*Beta vulgaris cicla*). Chard or Swiss Chard is a foliage beet which has been developed for its large fleshy leafstalk. It is an excellent pot herb for summer use in that it is well adapted to hot weather. The leaves are prepared for the table like spinach, while the leafstalks are frequently cooked and served like asparagus.

Varieties

There are only a few varieties of Swiss Chard. The most important are '**Lucullus**', '**Large Ribbed White**' and '**Fordhook Giant**'. All of these varieties are somewhat similar in growth and productivity with large leaves and light to dark green leafstalks. '**Rhubarb Chard**' has dark green leaf blades but bright crimson leafstalks.

Culture

Chard is planted and cultivated the same as the Garden Beet. See BEETS. The rows are spaced from 15–18 in. apart and the plants thinned when 2–4 in. high to 6–8 in. in the row. The plants removed in thinning may be used as greens.

A planting made in the spring will produce greens throughout the season.

Harvesting

The usual method of harvesting is to cut off the outer leaves 1–2 in. from the ground while they are still tender. Care should be taken not to injure the remaining leaves or the bud.

Insects and Disease

Insects and disease problems are the same as for the Garden Beet. See BEETS.

GRANT B. SNYDER

SWORD PLANT. See ECHINODORUS.

SYAGRUS WEDDELLIANA = *Microcoelum weddellianum*

SYMPHORICARPOS (sim-for-ik-KAR-pos). A group of much-branched, opposite-leaved shrubs of little interest for their small inconspicuous flowers, but of considerable interest for their brightly colored, fleshy berries, closely allied to the honeysuckles.

Propagation

Seeds are difficult to germinate and should not be considered as a method of propagation unless there is a specific reason for doing so, since cuttings—softwood, hardwood and root—are so readily rooted. See CUTTINGS. Plants can easily be divided and rooted suckers and sometimes layers can easily be separated from the parent plant. If seed must be sown, a suggested treatment is to stratify it for 5 months at warm temperatures, then 4 months at 40° F., then sow. See STRATIFICATION.

Insect Pests

Large brown or purplish caterpillars with a horn at the rear are the larvae of the snowberry clear wing moth which eat the leaves. Use insecticide #9 or #15 in early summer and in late summer if a second generation develops. Aphids and San Jose scale may be troublesome. See INSECT PESTS.

Diseases

Two types of anthracnose infect Snowberry. On the fruit, cinnamon-colored spots appear and the berries are mummied. On the leaves, purple or black spots cause partial defoliation. Spraying with fungicide #D or #G controls both types.

x chenaultii 3′ **Zone 4 Chenault Coralberry**
A hybrid (*S. microphyllus* x *S. orbiculatus*), this produces handsome fruits slightly larger and pinker than those of the common Indian Currant. The fruits also differ from those of the Indian Currant in that they are white on the side hidden from direct sunlight, while those of the Indian Currant are pink all over. This is a splendid low plant and is valued in the fall.

The variety 'Hancock' is a low, widespreading ground cover; a 12-year-old plant being only 2 ft. tall, but 12 ft. wide, originating in the nurseries of Leslie Hancock, Cooksville, Ontario, Canada, about 1940.

x doorenbosii
This is a hybrid (*S. albus laevigatus* x *S. chenaultii*) originating in The Hague several years ago. The variety 'Mother of Pearl' is one of the best clones, with whitish fruits tinted a very pale pink. Other clones are 'Magic Berry' and 'White Hedge'.

orbiculatus 3′-6′ **Zone 2 Indian Currant, Coralberry**
In the southeastern and south central U.S. this popular native shrub is frequently found in the wild. Popular because it is easily grown; it has practically no pests. It is excellent for bank planting, where it can be let alone and its suckers readily increase, making it an excellent plant for holding soil that otherwise might be washed away. The very small, densely produced, yellowish flowers are rather inconspicuous, but the purplish-red corallike berries are most effective throughout the fall and far into the winter. The variety **leucocarpus** bears white to whitish fruits.

rivularis (*albus laevigatus*) 6′ **Zone 3 Snowberry**
The Snowberry is found growing over a part of southern Canada and a large part of the northern U.S. The variety **laevigatus** is the most popular because it is taller than the species, has larger leaves and larger fruits, as well. The very small, pinkish flowers are produced in small terminal spikes about mid-June, and the conspicuous white berries, sometimes ⅝ in. wide, develop in the fall before the leaves drop and these give the plant its real value, since there are not many shrubs with ornamental white fruits. The branches of this plant are often seen bending to the ground because they are so heavily laden with berries. These fruits should remain plump and conspicuous for several weeks, but sometimes they are attacked by a disease and quickly turn brown. Where this occurs frequently, these plants might well not be grown.

SYMPHYANDRA (sim-fi-AND-ra)
hoffmannii 2′ **Zone 4**
A hairy perennial with obovate, toothed, alternate leaves up to 7 in. long; flowers white, bell-shaped, ½ in. long, ½ in. wide, drooping, in leafy panicles during July. These somewhat resemble *Campanula* species. Native to Yugoslavia.

wanneri 6″ **Zone 7**
Very similar to *Campanula* species, and a member of the Campanula Family, this perennial has clumps of hairy lanceolate leaves with toothed margins. The blue-violet flowers, like nodding bells 1¼ in. long, appear in late spring. It does well in good, well-drained garden soil in sun or partial shade and may be propagated by seed or by division. Native to southeastern Europe.

SYMPHYTUM (SIM-fit-um)
caucasicum 3′ **Zone 3 Blue Comfrey**
More ornamental than *S. officinale*, producing many pink and blue flowers during June, July and early Aug., especially if the dead flowers are removed. Native to the Caucasus.

officinale 3′ **Zone 3 Comfrey**
Introduced from Europe as a medicinal herb, this has escaped and become a weed in the

eastern part of North America especially on moist, rich, limestone soils. It is a perennial, with alternate leaves that are oblong, up to 8 in. long, and covered with prickly hairs. Flowers are yellowish white to pink and purplish, about $\frac{1}{2}$ in. long, produced from June to Aug. in nodding racemelike clusters. This is occasionally planted in the flower border but is rather coarse and not a good ornamental.

SYMPLOCARPUS (sim-plo-KARP-us)
foetidus   1′–3′   **Zone 3**   **Skunk-cabbage**
One must search early in spring to find the inconspicuous skunk-cabbage flower, for it often raises its hood above the patches of snow that rim the swamps of New England although it is quite as much at home in Ga., extending its range to the Mississippi River. A member of the Arum Family, the rounded, green or brown-spotted spathe, 6–12 in. high, shields the clublike spadex, appearing before the leaves. As the

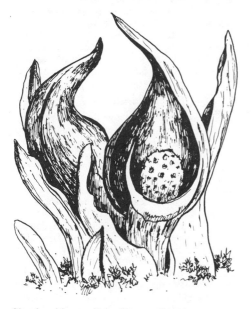

Skunk-cabbage—*Symplocarpus foetidus*

flower fades, the large leaves appear. If crushed or broken, the leaves and flowers emit an unpleasant odor. It is an interesting specimen for the bog garden, if only for its optimistic approach towards the chilling damp of early spring. Not to be confused with the Yellow Skunk-cabbage (*Lysichitum americanum*) of the Pacific Northwest.

SYMPLOCOS (SIM-plo-kos)
paniculata   35′   **Zone 5**   **Asiatic Sweetleaf**
Where space is available for growing large,

unique plants, this native to China and Japan might be tried. Its fruits are bright blue berries, about $\frac{1}{4}$ in. in dia., borne in Oct. of a color not seen in the fruits of any other hardy woody plant. The white fragrant flowers are produced in small clusters during late May. The fruits do not remain on the plant long when fully ripe, and even the flowers fade quickly. Because of these short periods of interest, other plants might be sought which remain effective longer. The alternate, deciduous leaves are 1½–3 in. long.

Propagation

Seed germinates erratically regardless of how it is treated but the best method is to stratify it for 3 months at 40° F. before sowing. Softwood cuttings can be rooted. See STRATIFICATION, CUTTINGS.

SYNCARP. A fleshy aggregate fruit.

SYRINGA (si-RING-ga). Lilacs have changed greatly since the Common Lilac (*S. vulgaris*) was brought to this country by early settlers probably before 1700. Seventy years later the first hybrid Lilac was produced but still there were only purple and white flowers. Since that time, 2 dozen species have been introduced into America and well over 500 varieties.

At this time 530 different lilacs are growing in the collection of the Arnold Arboretum. So, in 2½ centuries of planting gardens in America, the number of varieties of Lilac has jumped from 2 to over 500.

Flowers are larger, more fragrant, deeper in color as well as more diversified, with many double-flowered varieties available. This gives the modern gardener real opportunity to select plants of different color, habit and time of bloom. Lilacs start to bloom in early May and continue to late June, although the greatest number are in full bloom about the third week in May.

Attempts have been made to select the 100 best lilacs, judged by their performance over many years and in many situations throughout the U.S. and Canada. When this list was compiled a few years ago, it was found that at least 75 of the current 100 best were introduced by Lemoine Nursery of Nancy, France.

It takes time for a Lilac or any woody plant to be grown widely enough to become popular. This is one of the reasons why the Lemoine varieties still head the list and this also is the reason for the popular assumption that good lilacs are French hybrids. Some are good but there are many others, originated in other countries, that are just as good.

Our modern lilacs can now be classed in 7 or 8 color groups. One of the most outstanding in the blue to bluish grouping is 'President

Lincoln', developed by the late John Dunbar of Rochester, N.Y., in 1924. At the head of the list of deep purple lilacs would be 'Ludwig Spaeth', bred by the famous German nursery of Spaeth about 1883, and 'Mrs. W. E. Marshall' produced on the Havemeyer Estate on Long Island, N.Y., in 1924. The best of the pinks would include 'Lucie Baltet' and 'Katherine Havemeyer', while top-ranking whites are 'Vestal', 'Ellen Willmott' and 'Mont Blanc'.

The popular group of late-flowering lilacs originated by Miss Isabella Preston at Ottawa, Canada, and named the Preston Hybrids in her honor, have considerable red and pink in the flowers. They bloom a week or so after the Common Lilac and are extremely hardy. The variety 'Isabella' is one of the best.

The last of all the lilacs to bloom is the Japanese Tree Lilac (*S. amurensis japonica*) which is really a tree, with cherrylike bark. Its large terminal flower clusters of creamy white appear in mid-June.

Not all of our modern lilacs are upright shrubs. Low and mounded, almost twice as broad as it is high is *S. microphylla* 'Superba', originated in the Chenault Nurseries in France in 1934 and brought to this country by the Arnold Arboretum in 1939. The flowers are deep pink, opening at the same time as those of the Common Lilac.

The only Lilac to have any color at all in the fall is also the earliest of the lilacs to bloom, the Broadleaf or Early Lilac (*S. oblata dilatata*). This has red leaves in the fall, and if planted with several other lilacs, is a very worthwhile plant for this reason. It is difficult to get some people to realize that there is a Lilac with more fragrance than any other. A study of large lilac collections has proved it time and again. *S. pubescens*, which goes under the inappropriate name of Hairy Lilac, is the plant that might be used in every small lilac collection, even if planted at the rear inconspicuously, to give more fragrance to the group.

Individual plants differ as to the number of flowers they bear, depending on the age of the plants and the soil conditions, but the floriferous little Persian Lilac or the Chinese Lilac have long been recommended as being best suited for cutting purposes, because of the profusely borne, small flower clusters. There are white and pink varieties of both now in the trade.

Sometimes lilacs fail to bloom well. Perfect blooms are normally expected only every other year, for this is the habit of many woody plants. However, several things can be done to obtain better blooming annually:

1. Don't starve lilacs. Apply fertilizer and occasionally limestone.

2. Cut out a majority of the suckers at the base of the plant. Leave enough to supply renewal flowering branches as older ones are removed. Leave only healthy and sturdy branches.

3. Remove dead flower clusters, thus preventing seed formation. If this is done as soon as the blossoms have faded, fine, but if you wait for several weeks, removal of the seed clusters after they have formed probably does little to aid flowering.

4. Often the plant is growing too fast and vigorously—all its effort is being put into growing vegetative shoots. If this seems to be the case, reduce the fertilizer and root prune the plant in the spring just after flowering. Also a ditch might be dug about 12–18 in. deep all around the plant and an application of superphosphate made to the soil before it is returned to the ditch. This has been known to aid in producing flowers the following year.

The lilac story continues year by year. During the last few years a widely advertised "yellow" Lilac was introduced which at first seemed merely a creamy white. This variety, now called 'Primrose', is certainly not a dark yellow but has possibilities, certainly distinguishable from white.

Pruning

Pruning the Lilac is not always easy, since each bush often presents a different problem. In any event, it is usually best to prune after they have flowered, for lilacs bloom on last year's wood, and any pruning done in the early spring will necessarily mean that just so many flower buds are being taken off with each twig or branch. It is always a good plan, if you are interested in the best display of flowers possible, to cut off all the old, faded flowers and so prevent any seed formation. This takes time. It is important enough so that in large collections like those in the Arnold Arboretum and the Rochester Parks, the officials spend considerable time and money in getting this job thoroughly done as soon as the flowers have gone past their prime. For, if the flowers remain on the plants, seeds form, and much plant nourishment goes into their formation when it might otherwise be going to form more growth and flower buds for the next year.

Dead or diseased wood should always be cut out whenever it appears. It may be necessary sometimes to take a few branches out of the center of the plant to give those remaining more light and air. Then, too, old plants may be too high so that their flowers are far above the eye level and can not be enjoyed as much as if they were lower. Here would be a case for drastically cutting down the larger limbs, either all at once or, better, a few each year, in order to force the plant to branch out lower at the base. This sounds rather drastic and it certainly will not look good for a year or two, but it is the only way of getting such old "leggy" plants back into scale again.

One should always be careful with grafted hybrid lilacs, to keep them from suckering from the underground parts which may be either the Common Lilac or Privet. All such suckers should be removed as soon as they appear, for if allowed to grow, they may soon outgrow the plant itself. The Common Lilac is a very strong grower and, if given half a chance, suckers very freely. That is why there are old hedgerows of this plant often as broad as they are high. To preserve the beauty of the hybrids, be sure to cut out the suckers on grafted plants as they appear.

Propagation

Since asexual propagation is the usual means selected for all but a few species, seeds are not often sown. However, they should be stratified for 2 months at 40° F. before sowing. Softwood cuttings are frequently used, but here timing is most critical. Cuttings are best taken during a period ranging from just before flowering to shortly afterwards, while the plants are still in active growth.

Lilacs may be grafted (or budded) using California Privet as understock. When planted out, the grafts should, be set deep in the ground in order to induce the scion to produce its own roots. It is highly desirable that lilacs be on their own roots and this procedure will lead to own-root material. See STRATIFICATION, GRAFTING, BUDDING, CUTTINGS.

Insect Pests

Lilac borer, the larva of a clearwing moth, causes the death of many branches in old well-established clumps. Depressions in the bark may show the location of a tunnel. Infested branches should be cut and burned. Spraying with insecticide #9 just before bloom will kill the moths and newly hatched worms. Lilac is a favorite host of oyster shell scale. Spraying before buds swell with dormant strength of insecticide #44 followed by 2 or 3 applications of insecticide #15 or #13 when young are hatching, about 2 weeks after bloom, is recommended. See APPLE.

Diseases

Powdery mildew in late summer may turn all leaves a dirty white color. It is more unsightly than destructive. See POWDERY MILDEW. Both bacteria and fungi produce twig blight which blackens the leaves and may kill new shoots. Cut off and burn infected shoots. Spraying with fungicide #B or #G may be helpful.

x chinensis   15′   Zone 5   Chinese Lilac
Supposedly this was the first hybrid Lilac on record (*S. laciniata* x *S. vulgaris*), having originated in the Botanic Garden at Rouen, France, about 1777. The leaves in size are half-way between those of the Persian Lilac (*S. persica*) and the Common Lilac (*S. vulgaris*) and the same can be said for the habit of the plant. Although it can grow 15 ft. tall it is usually seen about 6 ft. high. Flowers are a purple-lilac color, in small clusters during late May. The variety 'Alba' has white flowers and 'Saugeana' has very good, lilac-red flowers.

x henryi 'Lutece'   10′   Zone 2
This is one of the late-blooming lilacs, the flowers coming in early June after all the Common Lilac hybrids have faded. The flowers are a pale violet-pink. It is a hybrid, (*S. villosa* x *S. josikaea*) and blooms with *S. villosa* which of course has creamy-white flowers. Neither are as ornamental in flower as are some of the excellent *S. vulgaris* hybrids.

x josiflexa 'Guinevere'   9′   Zone 3
This is included here because it is one of the very best of the later blooming sorts, a cross between *S. josikaea* and *S. reflexa*, with orchid-purple flowers, originated by Miss Isabella Preston (Ottawa, Canada) in 1920. Although the flower clusters are somewhat loose, the color does not fade even if the plant grows in the full sun.

josikaea   12′   Zone 2   Hungarian Lilac
The glossy green foliage of this native Hungarian Lilac and its ability to withstand shearing are its 2 prominent assets. The lilac-violet flowers in early June are slightly less handsome than those of *S. villosa* for which it is frequently mistaken when not in flower, but the leaves are definitely more glossy.

laciniata   6′   Zone 5   Cutleaf Lilac
Formerly called *S. persica laciniata*, this species is now considered to be a native of Turkestan and China. The small, pale lilac flowers are distributed all along the branches and bloom in late May. The leaves are deeply lobed, giving the plant an unusually delicate and feathery appearance. Sometimes shoots 3 ft. long are literally covered with pale lilac flowers.

meyeri   6′   Zone 5   Meyer's Lilac
F. H. Meyer of the U.S. Department of Agriculture was given the credit for introducing this Lilac from northern China in 1908. It is comparatively dwarf and compact in habit, has violet-purple flowers in panicles 4 in. long and 2 in. wide and is highly regarded as a fine ornamental.

microphylla   6′   Zone 5   Littleleaf Lilac

Native to China, this is perhaps best known for its recently introduced variety '**Superba**' to America from the nurseries of R. Chenault, in France, in 1939. It blooms at the same time as *S. vulgaris* varieties and has single, deep pink flowers. The flower buds are actually reddish. The plant is dense, twice as broad as high. An 18-year-old plant in the Arnold Arboretum is about 7 ft. high but 14 ft. across. The leaves are about the same size and shape as those of *Lonicera tatarica*. All in all, flowers and habit are somewhat unusual for a Lilac. It should be widely planted.

oblata dilatata   12′   **Zone 3**   **Korean Early Lilac**

Coming from Korea in 1917, this is the earliest of all the lilacs in flower—usually in early May. The pinkish flowers, in large loose clusters, appear before the leaves are fully open, and *S. oblata* is the only lilac species to have reddish autumn color, usually pretty good. Some of the better hybrids of *S. oblata* or one of its several varieties are: '**Alice Eastwood**'—double flowers, magenta color; '**Assessippi**'—single flowers, pinkish mauve; '**Blue Hyacinth**', single flowers, bluish; '**Esther Staley**', single flowers, magenta; '**Necker**', single flowers, pink; '**Pocahontas**', single flowers, reddish purple. All of these bloom early, a week before most of the *S. vulgaris* varieties.

patula (*velutina*)   9′   **Zone 3**   **Manchurian Lilac**

A very hardy species with lilac flowers in upright panicles 2½–8 in. long, native to China and Korea. The leaves are 2–2½ in. long. Not especially outstanding as an ornamental.

x persica   6′   **Zone 5**   **Persian Lilac**

This is now considered to be a hybrid between the little known *S. afghanica* from Persia and *S. x laciniata* described above. It is very popular and is one of the smallest of the lilacs; with pale lilac flowers in late May, the clusters often covering the branches. The leaves are only 2½ in. long while those of *S. vulgaris* are 2–6 in. long. It is especially valued for its low height and profuse flowers.

potanini   9′   **Zone 5**   **Potanin Lilac**

Pinkish flowers in clusters 4–8 in. long, this is native to western China and blooms in mid-May with the large group of Common Lilac varieties. It is graceful in habit and is distinguished from the other lilacs by its pink flowers.

x prestoniae varieties   9′   **Zone 2**   **Preston Lilac**

These hybrids were first selected before 1925 by Miss Isabella Preston, Horticulturist of the Canadian Experiment Station, Ottawa, Canada. Then F. L. Skinner of Dropmore, Manitoba, Canada, made some additional crosses, all these being mostly *S. villosa* x *S. reflexa* hybrids.

They have pink to deep pink flowers, in large clusters, blooming from early to mid-June, about 2 weeks after the many Common Lilac varieties have faded. These plants are sturdy, dense and upright in habit with the leaves as large as those of *S. villosa*. They are not particularly fragrant, but they are a fine group for making specimens, or windbreaks or late-flowering hedges. Of a large group, the best varieties are probably the following: '**Isabella**'—largest pyramidal flower clusters, pink; '**Audrey**'—dense clusters, 7 in. × 6 in., phlox-purple; '**Handel**'—tight clusters, 5 in. × 3 in., buds amaranth rose, fading to white; '**Donald Wyman**'—deepest pink to almost reddish flowers with buds and flowers the same color.

reflexa   12′   **Zone 5**   **Nodding Lilac**

A graceful Lilac when in flower because of the nodding or pendulous cylindrical clusters of pink flowers, that are as much as 4–9 in. long. The leaves are ovate-oblong, about 3–6 in. long. Native to China. Strangely enough this Lilac is used far more in the Scandinavian countries than it is in America.

reticulata (*amurensis japonica*)   30′   **Zone 4**   **Japanese Tree Lilac**

A tree, with large, pyramidal, creamy-white flower clusters that are almost ill smelling, and cherrylike bark. Blooming in mid-June, it is one of the last species to produce flowers. The variety **japonica** from Japan differs slightly from the species in being more treelike in habit, taller and slightly later to flower.

x swegiflexa   9′   **Zone 5**   **Swegiflexa lilac**

The deep red flower buds of this hybrid (*S. sweginzowii* x *reflexa*) and the fragrant pink flowers which follow should make this plant popular when it is better known and more widely distributed. It originated in 1934 in the Hesse Nurseries of western Germany and has performed well in the U.S., blooming in late May and early June

villosa   9′   **Zone 2**   **Late Lilac**

One of the hardiest of all lilacs, with rosy-lilac to white flowers blooming in early June just after the majority of the Common Lilac varieties have faded. It is dense and upright in growth, making a dense screen. The leaves are elliptic to oblong, 2–7 in. long, and the flowers are always borne profusely. It is a native of northern China.

vulgaris   20′   **Zone 3**   **Common Lilac**

Although no Lilac is native to North America, this one from southeastern Europe was brought over by the earliest settlers and has probaby become naturalized in several places. Certainly it has been commonly used in garden plantings in the eastern U.S. for over 3 centuries. The lilac-colored fragrant flowers (and its white-flowering variety **alba**) are known to all. It is dense, vigorous growing, suckering readily, sometimes far more than it should. The heart-shaped leaves and profuse fragrant flowers in mid-May are admired everywhere. Over 400 varieties are being grown in American botanical gardens;

the many beautiful varieties of *S. vulgaris*, they are found lacking in color, fragrance and size; but when the *S. vulgaris* varieties are not in flower for comparison, these species and their comparatively few varieties are of interest and

SINGLE	DOUBLE
WHITE	
'Jan Van Tol'	'Edith Cavell'
'Marie Legray'	'Ellen Willmott'
'Mme. Florent Stepman'	'Jeanne d'Arc'
'Mont Blanc'	'Mme. Casimir Perier'
	'Mme. Lemoine'
YELLOWISH TO WHITE	
'Primrose'	
VIOLET	
'Cavour'	'Marechal Lannes'
'DeMiribel'	'Violetta'
BLUE TO BLUISH	
'Ambassadeur'	'Ami Schott'
'Decaisne'	'Olivier De Serres'
'Firmament'	'President Grevy'
'President Lincoln'	
LILAC	
'Christophe Colomb'	'Alphonse Lavellee'
'Jacques Caliot'	'Leon Gambetta'
	'President Carnot'
	'Victor Lemoine'
PINK TO PINKISH	
'Lucie Baltet'	'Belle de Nancy'
'Macrostachya'	'Katherine Havemeyer'
	'Marc Micheli'
	'Mme. Antoine Buckner'
	'Waldeck-Rosseau'
MAGENTA	
'Capitaine Baltet'	'Charles Joly'
'Charles X'	'Mrs. Edward Harding'
'Congo'	'Paul Thirion'
'Mme. F. Morel'	'President Poincaré'
'Reamur'	
'Rhum Von Horstenstein'	
PURPLE	
'Ludwig Spaeth'	'Adelaide Dunbar'
'Monge'	'Anne Tighe'
'Mrs. W. E. Marshall'	'DeSaussure'
'Night'	'Paul Hariot'

many of them are similar. Of these the best and most popular would certainly be in the following list of 52 varieties, 37 of which originated in the famous Lemoine Nurseries in France.

Lilacs in their Order of Bloom

There can be at least 5 full weeks of lilac blooms by selection of the right species and varieties. The most popular of the lilacs, the *S. vulgaris* varieties, bloom only during a 10-day period in late May.

When some of the species are compared with

contain several plants well worth including in many garden plantings. It should be noted here that the excellent survey "Lilacs for America," published in October 1953, is available from most of the major arboretums of the United States. This was an intensive study of all lilacs grown now in America, notes on color and origin together with actual sources where each variety is being grown and where each variety can be purchased.

Lilacs are here listed according to the times at which they start to bloom in Zone 5. Frequently they may remain in bloom sufficiently long so that they can be used ornamentally with lilacs in another group. Thus, *S. chinensis* and *S. persica* come into bloom after the *S. vulgaris* varieties have reached their peak, but still can

when the flower buds are injured by severe winters. The leaves are rarely disfigured by the mildew so evident on the Common Lilac in late summer. The variety *dilatata* is perhaps the

LILAC SEQUENCE OF BLOOM (in Zone 5)

GROUP 1

BLOOMING ABOUT MAY 10	COMMON NAME
S. hyacinthiflora	Hyacinth Lilac
S. oblata and varieties	Early Lilac
S. pinnatifolia	Pinnate Lilac

GROUP 2

BLOOMING ABOUT MAY 20	
S. chinensis and varieties	Chinese Lilac
S. julianae	Juliana Lilac
S. laciniata	Cutleaf Lilac
S. meyeri	Meyer Lilac
S. microphylla	Littleleaf Lilac
S. patula	Manchurian Lilac
S. persica	Persian Lilac
S. potanini	Potanin Lilac
S. pubescens	Hairy Lilac
S. vulgaris and varieties	Common Lilac

GROUP 3

BLOOMING ABOUT JUNE 5	
S. emodi	Himalayan Lilac
S. henryi and varieties	Henry Lilac
S. josikaea and varieties	Hungarian Lilac
S. komarowii	Komarof Lilac
S. prestoniae and varieties	Preston Lilac
S. reflexa	Nodding Lilac
S. swegiflexa	Swegiflexa Lilac
S. sweginzowii	Chengtu Lilac
S. tomentella	Felty Lilac
S. villosa	Late Lilac
S. wolfii	Wolf's Lilac
S. yunnanensis	Yunnan Lilac

GROUP 4

BLOOMING ABOUT JUNE 15	
S. pekinensis	Pekin Lilac
S. reticulata	Japanese Tree Lilac

be used at the same time effectively. As is the case with the sequence of bloom of other ornamental trees and shrubs, weather conditions may alter the dates.

Not all the lilacs listed are of outstanding ornamental value, and not all are available in the trade in this country. It may be of value if a few in each group are pointed out as being good ornamental additions to garden plantings.

GROUP 1. The Early Lilac, *S. oblata*, comes from northern China and is valued because it is the first of all the lilacs to bloom and also because it is the only Lilac with a red to orange autumn color. Unfortunately, there are times

best because of its large lilac-pink flower clusters.

There are several varieties of *S. hyacinthiflora*, chiefly originated in France as a result of Victor Lemoine's hybridization at Nancy, France, and are of an intermediate lavender color. The varieties Turgot and Necker are probably the most prominent of the group. However, all the varieties of *S. hyacinthiflora* can be used for ornamental planting since they bloom slightly in advance of *S. vulgaris* and as a rule form larger-growing and more vigorous shrubs. *S. pinnatifolia* is the least ornamental of any lilac here listed.

GROUP 2. The better varieties selected as a result of the Lilac Survey of 1953, are listed mostly according to their popularity by the individuals who judged them. There are well over 400 varieties of the Common Lilac being grown in America today.

This group of lilacs begins to bloom at the time the Common Lilac varieties are at their best. Both the Chinese and the Persian lilacs are valued for their lower habit of growth and for the larger number of blooms produced every year. Frequently the varieties of the Common Lilac tend to bloom well one year but have comparatively few blossoms the year following. These 2 species, however, bloom profusely every year and so are particularly good for cutting purposes. Of the Chinese Lilac varieties, 'Saugeana' is possibly the best because of its deep pink flowers. The Cutleaf Lilac (*laciniata*) is also of value because of the feathery texture of its small lobed leaves. The Hairy Lilac (*S. pubescens*) is important because it is considered to be the most fragrant of all the lilacs, but the flowers are not as beautiful as those of the Chinese or Persian Lilac, or, in fact, those of most of the Common Lilac varieties.

GROUP 3. Probably the best known of the varieties of *S. henryi* is 'Lutece', noted for its large, pale purple flower clusters which are not fragrant. This variety and the others in Group 3 are important for they bloom at a time when all the flowers of *S. vulgaris* varieties have faded. The variety 'Lutece' grows vigorously and is available from many nurseries.

The Late Lilac, *S. villosa*, is common in gardens, and justly so, because of its many creamy-white flower clusters and good dense habit of growth.

Two hybrids are well worth growing, both being the result of Miss Isabella Preston's work at Ottawa, Canada. *S. prestoniae*, named by Mrs. McKelvey in honor of Miss Preston, is a group of hybrids, the flowers of which contain a great deal of pink. Most of the lilacs blooming in early June have white flowers, but, because the pink-flowering *S. reflexa* is one parent, *S. prestoniae* varieties are predominantly pink. This whole group is very important because the plants retain the vigorous-growing qualities of *S. villosa* and some of the good color of *S. reflexa*. *S. reflexa* has not proved a good shrub in some areas though the individual flowers are very beautiful; but Miss Preston's hybrids are well worth growing in the United States. The second hybrid group has been named *S. swegiflexa*. Large plants clearly show that nurserymen in the United States would do well to grow at least a few of these varieties for their late flowers.

GROUP 4. The last of the lilacs is the largest growing of all—the Japanese Tree Lilac. This was formerly considered to be a separate species (and is listed by most nurserymen as *S. japonica*), but it is now considered to be a variety of *S. amurensis*. It forms a single trunk and has very conspicuous, large, creamy-white flower clusters in mid-June. The bark is distinctly ornamental for it is very similar to that of *Prunus avium*. Where it is given sufficient space in which to expand, it develops into the most prominent of all lilacs.

SYZYGIUM (si-ZYG-ium)

aromaticum   30′   **Zone 10**   **Clove Tree**
This tree, native to the Molucca Islands, produces the cloves of commerce which are the small, dried flower buds. The tree bears its first flowers when about 7 years old and may continue to do so after that for 100 years. Not much cultivated in the U.S.

jambos (*Eugenia jambos*)   30′   **Zone 10**
                                              Rose-apple
Narrow, pointed, simple leaves 6–8 in. long with fluffy flowers 2 in. across made up of masses of greenish-white stamens in the spring, appearing at the terminals of the branches. The fruit is globular, rose-colored, and edible, often being used to make jam. Native to tropical Asia.

malaccense (*Eugenia malaccensis*)   50′
                              Zone 10   **Malay-apple**
This tree from India and Malaya has red flowers with many red stamens which grow directly from the trunk and main branches during winter and spring. The red petals are short, not nearly as prominent as the stamens. Fruit looks like a small red apple, but has no special flavor.

paniculatum (*Eugenia paniculata*) 40′ **Zone 9**
                                    Brush-cherry Eugenia
Widely planted in Calif. and Fla., this is probably the most popular species. It is native to Australia and the evergreen leaves are 2–3 in. long, dense and glossy, tinged with red when young. The flowers are white, $\frac{1}{2}$ in. across with conspicuous stamens, borne in small terminal clusters during a good part of the year. The fruits are rose-purple berries, about $\frac{3}{4}$ in. across and edible. The var. **australis** is more bushy in habit and is popular for shearing into topiary objects.

T

TABEBUIA (tab-bee-BEW-ia). Timber trees of the American Tropics but also of increasing importance as ornamental trees in the Tropics. They belong to the Trumpetcreeper Family, have compound or simple evergreen leaves and bright-colored, trumpet-shaped flowers in terminal racemes during the winter. Fruits are long, narrow pods. Propagation is by seeds, cuttings and air layers.

argentea   25′   Zone 10   Silvertree
The golden-yellow flowers, $2\frac{1}{2}$ in. long, borne in clusters, are tube shaped and each has 5 crepelike lobes. The leaves have 5–7 leaflets, each about 6 in. long. The bark is light gray. The light wood is used considerably for interior decorating, in fact, so much so that the tree is becoming scarce in Central America and Paraguay where it is native.

pallida   35′–60′   Zone 10   Pink Tecoma-tree
A small evergreen tree (sometimes deciduous) native to tropical America; valued for its petunialike pink blossoms which bloom erratically throughout the year. The base of the corolla is white and $2\frac{1}{2}$–3 in. long. The leaves are digitately compound with 3–5 leaflets, 4–6 in. long, silvery-scaly on both upper and lower surfaces. Frequently seen in Hawaiian gardens as well as in those on the islands of the Caribbean. Propagated by seeds, air layers and grafting.

serratifolia   10′   Zone 10   Yellow Tecoma-tree
Similar to *T. pallida* except the flowers are a pure golden yellow. The leaves are opposite, compound, with 5 stalked leaflets of unequal size radiating from a 5–6-in. petiole. The larger leaflets are about 6 in. long. Often seen in gardens of the Caribbean Islands since the flowers are frequently seen when the leaves have dropped. The crown is large and wide-spreading and trunks are measured from 4–7 ft. in circumference. The wood of the Pink Tecoma-tree, when used for construction, does not last nearly as long as that of the Yellow Tecoma-tree; for few woods are better for construction purposes. Propagated by seeds.

TAGETES (ta-JEE-tees). The modern garden marigolds are mostly derived from the 4 species mentioned below. All are native to Mexico even though many are called French or African Marigolds. The tallest species (*T. erecta*) is often used at the back of the flower border because of its height; *T. tenuifolia pumila* or its derivatives are the ones chiefly used for their small size in edging; and *T. patula*, the French Marigold and

its derivatives make up the bulk of the varieties available and popular today.

Marigold seeds germinate in 3–4 days and grow rapidly, so if they are started indoors for outdoor planting it should only be about 3–4 weeks before the day they can be set out in the garden, after all frosts to which they are most susceptible. Otherwise, with a longer period in the greenhouse they will get very "leggy" and difficult to use.

All make good cut flowers but the foliage rots very quickly in water, especially that of the African Marigold, so, when used with stems in deep water, cut off the leaves first.

The commercial seedsmen have been energetically hybridizing marigolds. The Marigold as a garden flower has been grown in gardens for over 400 years, but now delightful hybrids are available, with colors varying from all the shades of red and orange to yellow.

The suggestion here in making selections of marigolds for the garden is to study the catalogue descriptions carefully and make certain ones of the desired height are selected. There are nice varieties, lemon yellow only, others mostly red or a combination of yellow and red. They should be planted in the full sun for, unlike many garden flowers, their blooms are best in the hot sun of midsummer. All can be counted on to produce flowers throughout the entire summer and with zinnias they are about the easiest garden annuals that can be grown. The flower heads have been used to produce a yellow buff dye.

Insect Pests

Aphids, leaf hoppers (see CALISTEPHUS) and tarnished plant bug (see CELERY) frequently infest marigolds.

Diseases

Yellows virus causing malformed or discolored flowers and witch's-broom growth of leaves infects Marigold. It is spread by leaf hoppers which must be controlled. Stem rot and fusarium wilt have no satisfactory control with pesticides. Destroy infected plants promptly.

erecta   3′   annual   African Marigold
With large, solitary, yellow to orange flower heads up to 4 in. across, this is perhaps the largest flowered and the tallest of the marigolds. Leaves pinnately divided. It is not native to Africa. It must be relegated to the back of the border because of its size, but once it starts to

bear flowers in the late summer it will continue to do so until frost. Many varieties are available.

lucida   1½′   **annual**   **Sweet Marigold**
Leaves not divided, finely toothed; flower heads ½ in. across with 2–3 layers of rays, yellow to orange, in dense terminal clusters. This is not found in gardens very often.

patula   1½′   **annual**   **French Marigold**
A very popular garden species with solitary flower heads, 1½ in. across, several layers of rays, yellow with red markings. Many varieties.

tenuifolia   2′   **annual**   **Striped Marigold**
With the smallest flower heads of the 3 most popular species, only an inch across; leaves are finely incised; flower rays few and colored yellow. The var. **pumila** is a dwarf, 1 ft. or less in height. It is this variety which mostly represents this species in gardens. Many varieties available.

TAHOKA-DAISY = *Machaeranthera tanaceti-folia*

TALINUM (ta-LY-num). Small plants of the Purslane Family with fleshy foliage and many, small, bright flowers which may be yellow, pink or red and bloom for most of the late spring and summer. They need sandy, well-drained soil and full sun and the plants self-sow readily.

calycinum   4″   **Zone 6**   **Rockpink Fame-flower**
A perennial, with cylindrical leaves 2 in. long and fire-red flowers an inch wide in erect terminal clusters blooming from June to Oct., the flowers opening only on sunny days and only after midday. Native to the western plains of the U.S. Sometimes grown as a pot plant or in the flower border.

paniculatum (*patens*)   2′   **Zone 10**   **Panicled Flameflower**
A perennial, fleshy herb, related to but not like Portulaca, with opposite leaves about 2 in. long and small carmine-colored flowers borne in cymes. Native to the West Indies and South America. The var. 'Variegatum' is the form usually seen used as a pot plant because its leaves are marked with white or pink. As a pot plant it can survive much heat and drought.

teretifolium   1′   **Zone 6**   **Quill Flameflower**
Similar to *T. calycinum*, but with smaller flowers and a somewhat larger habit. Native from Pa. to Ga.

TALLOW TREE, CHINESE = *Sapium sebi-ferum*

TAMARACK = *Larix laricina*

TAMARICACEAE = The Tamarisk Family

TAMARIND = *Tamarindus indica*

TAMARINDUS (tam-ar-IND-us)

indica   80′   **Zone 10**   **Tamarind**
A picturesque evergreen tree of tropical Africa, valued as an ornamental and also for its brown, 8-in. long, fleshy pods which are eaten in various forms or used for medicinal purposes. A member of the Pea Family, with alternate, feathery, pinnately compound leaves, the leaflets about ¾ in. long. The pale yellow flowers are an inch wide and borne in few-flowered racemes. Propagated by seeds and shield-budding. This tree requires plenty of water.

TAMARISK. See TAMARIX.

TAMARISK, FALSE = *Myricaria germanica*

TAMARISK FAMILY = Tamaricaceae

TAMARIX (TAM-ar-ix). Shrubs or small trees from the Old World, often at home near the seashore or where the soil is subjected to salt-water spray occasionally. The feathery foliage is made up of minute scalelike leaves and the light, fluffy, pink flowers are what is most valued ornamentally in these plants. They are easily rooted from cuttings. In fact, one author tells of making hedges of 1 species in the south of England merely by cutting canes a yard or so long, sharpening one end and then driving them into the soil in a line where the hedge is desired. It is not quite that easy in the U.S., but we can note that, given a little care in the rooting medium, they will come readily from either softwood or hardwood cuttings. Seed may be sown as soon as ripe or stored dry in airtight containers in a cool place for up to a year and then sown.

As a rule, these are excellent plants for the seashore or for sandy gardens in the Southwest. Their foliage has a texture quite different from that of most other woody plants because of the fine foliage. At first glance it might look as if the plants were leafless, but the fine, scalelike leaves are very closely appressed to the stems and branches. In fact, some of the very fine branchlets are dropped in the fall along with the leaves. Because of their pliable branches, they sway gracefully in every breeze, another good reason why they are adapted to seashore planting.

africana   10′   **Zone 7**   **African Tamarisk**
Although this is listed by many American nurserymen, it has been noted time and agan that this species is probably not in cultivation and that the plants offered under this name are usually *T. parviflora*.

aphylla   30′   **Zone 8**   **Athel Tamarisk**
Only of value for growing in desert and alkali soil regions of southwestern North America where it is planted as a windbreak. Native to western Asia. The small, scalelike, sheathing leaves give this the appearance of a Casuarina but of course the feathery flowers are pink, borne in terminal panicles.

chinensis 15′ Zones 7–8 **Chinese Tamarisk**
A shrub or small tree that is grown in the southwestern U.S. but can become very weedy in appearance and can invade good soil areas. The small pink flowers are in tight clusters, 1″–2″ long. Native to China.

gallica 30′ Zone 5 **French Tamarisk**
This is supposedly native to the west coast of France, flowering in the late summer and early autumn. The small pink flowers are in racemes up to 2 in. long.

hispida 4′ Zone 6 **Kashgar Tamarisk**
All Tamarix species have small leaves somewhat similar to those of the heaths, making the texture very feathery. This one, from the region of the Caspian Sea, has been found in deserts, proof that it will grow in dry soil. The flowers are small, bright pink, very fluffy in general appearance and appear during Aug. and Sept. This might be considered the best for small gardens because it does not have to be kept pruned so much as the others, but because it blooms on the current year's growth it can be pruned in very early spring before growth starts and still be expected to flower the same season.

parviflora 15′ Zone 4 **Small-flowered Tamarisk**
This Tamarisk, from southeastern Europe, has small pink flowers like *T. hispida* and the others but they bloom in mid-May on the previous year's growth. Because of this the plant should be pruned after it flowers, and it does have to be pruned considerably to keep it from becoming a most ungainly specimen. It, too, does well in dry soils and has been used in seashore plantings. Pink flowers, small heathlike foliage and general habit are all similar to those of other Tamarix species.

ramosissima (*pentandra*) 15′ Zone 2 **Five Stamen Tamarisk**
The hardiest *Tamarix* species, from southeastern Europe, it can be grown and expected to flower well in New England gardens, but it must be heavily pruned in order to be kept within a reasonable height. The small pink and feathery flowers are borne on the current year's growth, hence pruning can be done in early spring while the plant is dormant. It has the same type of flowers and foliage texture as *T. hispida* and also does well in seashore gardens.

TANACETUM (tan-ass-EE-tum)
vulgare 3′ Zone 3 **Common Tansy**
A European perennial that has escaped cultivation in the eastern U.S. and is commonly seen as a weed everywhere. The foliage is strong scented, the leaves alternate and very much divided. The flowers are ¼–½ in. round, yellow and buttonlike, in flat-topped clusters during the

summer. The var. **crispum** has leaves that are even more divided. If eaten, the leaves and stems are poisonous to man and animals. In Me. occasionally Tansy-cheese is made by steeping the herb and pouring the extract into milk before the curds are made. In England cakes and puddings with Tansy as the "bitter herb" are used during Lent.

TANAKAEA (tan-a-KAY-ea)
radicans 2″ Zone 6 (?)
An attractive, shade-loving, stoloniferous perennial from the mountains of Japan; this grows in tufts, having thick, leathery leaves and greenish-white, minute flowers which are without petals. It increases by long runners, thus becoming matlike in its habit of growth. It does best in acid leaf mold.

TANBARK OAK = *Lithocarpus densiflorus*

TANGELO. A hybrid citrus fruit, originating in 1897 from crossing a Tangerine ('Dancy') with a Grapefruit ('Bowen'). The hybrid is rather thin skinned, slightly pear shaped, with a pulp colored like that of an orange. It is a good tasting fruit but does not keep as well as does the orange. For culture see ORANGE.

TANGERINE. This is a variety of the King Orange, *Citrus nobilis*, the scientific name being **C. nobilis deliciosa**. The fruits are 2–3 in. in dia., are rounded, but with a flat and depressed top and bottom, and the skin is readily loosened from the pulp and is peeled off much easier than that of an orange. For culture see ORANGE.

TANKAGE. An organic fertilizer containing 6–11% nitrogen, usually leaving an alkaline soil reaction. Recommended for use at the rate of 2 oz. per sq. yard. See SOILS.

TANSY = *Tanacetum vulgare*

TAP ROOT. The main root (of a Dandelion, Hickory, etc.) which usually grows straight down. Tap roots are unusually long, and if it is trees that have them such trees are often very difficult to move unless the tap root is periodically severed and the tree is thus forced to send out many lateral roots. Tap-rooted trees are best root pruned a year or so in advance of moving to encourage many lateral roots. The sudden cutting of the main tap root of a tree can prove fatal quickly.

TARAKTOGENUS = *Hydnocarpus*

TARAXACUM (ta-RAX-ak-um)
officinale 10″ Zone 3 **Dandelion**
A perennial weed in most parts of the world, probably originally native to Europe. The bitter-tasting leaves are up to 10 in. long, deeply and pinnately cut or toothed, forming a rosette at the ground level below which is a long sturdy tap root. Hollow stems bear the bright yellow flower heads up to 1½ in. across, and the seeds

are provided with silky hairs and are easily wind blown. A pernicious lawn weed with milky juice. Dandelions are sometimes grown in the garden as edible greens. They are easily raised from seed and if the foliage is hidden from the sun when they are about ¾ grown it will turn white and not be quite so bitter. If collected early in the spring before they are fully grown the leaves are not so bitter. For control see WEED-CONTROLLING CHEMICALS.

TARO = *Colocasia esculenta*

TARRAGON = *Artemisia dracunculus*

TARWEED. See MADIA.

TASSEL-FLOWER = *Emilia javanica*

TAWHIWHI = *Pittosporum tenuifolium*

TAXACEAE = The Yew Family

TAXODIUM (tax-O-dium)

   ascendens = *T. distichum nutans*

   distichum distichum   150′   Zone 4   **Common Bald Cypress**

A common, deciduous tree, native of swampy areas in the southeastern and south central U.S., with small needlelike leaves about ¾ in. long arranged in 2 ranks along the twigs, and cones about 1 in. across. This is the tree that produces the unique "knees," rootlike protuberances of soft, spongy wood above the ground that may be up to 10 ft. high, probably aiding in supplying air to the roots which are frequently covered with water. It is not a tree for the small place, nor is it a good shade tree, but in parks or on large estates, a grove beside a stream or pond is distinctive. The wood is excellent for use in greenhouse benches and the like since it does not rot for long periods, even in standing water. *T. ascendens*, now termed **T. distichum nutans,** is similar but not much planted. It is more narrow in habit and less handsome in general. **T. mucronatum** is the famous Montezuma Cypress of Mexico, differing from *T. distichum* in that the needles are more persistent and shorter. It is only hardy in southern Calif.

Propagation

Seed may be stratified for 2 months at 40° F. before sowing. Plants can be grafted, using as understock the species. See GRAFTING, STRATIFICATION. Also hardwood cuttings (which see) can be rooted.

TAXON (pl. TAXA). A general term applied to any taxonomic element, population, or group regardless of its level of classification.

TAXONOMY. The science of classification and arrangement of living organisms according to relationships.

TAXUS (TAX-us). The yews are excellent ornamental plants and are widely grown from

Taxus baccata 'Repandens'—the hardiest of the English Yew varieties. (*Photo by Arnold Arboretum, Jamaica Plain, Mass.*)

Taxus baccata. This is at least 100 years old and was photographed on a rainy day in Northern Ireland.

coast to coast. The English Yew (*T. baccata*) is not as hardy as is its Japanese relative, *T. cuspidata.* These species easily hybridize and the resulting forms frequently have the good foliage of the English species but some of the rugged hardiness of the Japanese species. Sometimes, much of the tenderness of *T. baccata* is passed along to the offspring seedling hybrids, and the winter begins to take its toll among these. Undoubtedly, there are some forms of Taxus being grown under 2 or 3 different names. There are over 120 different yews being offered at present by American nurserymen.

All yews are narrow-leaved evergreens, the needles being about an inch long, spirally arranged and often 2-ranked along the green 1-year twigs. The fruits are fleshy red berries about the size of a pea, open at one end showing the single hard seed inside. The seeds are often poisonous, and sometimes the foliage is poisonous when eaten by livestock. Yews in general are excellent, serviceable plants, grow-

Taxus baccata 'Fastigiata'. The superbly beautiful Irish Yew growing in Dublin, Ireland.

ing well in normal soils, surviving a shady situation but growing well also in full sun. They are easily sheared and make fine hedges and subjects for topiary work. One staminate plant is sufficient for each 6–8 pistillate plants.

The English Yew has been a popular plant for centuries, and because it has been grown for so long over such a wide area, there are a large number of varieties which have been named. Not all are mentioned here—in fact, it is highly probable that some of the very old-fashioned forms have been lost to cultivation.

The Japanese Yew, on the other hand, was first introduced into America about 1850 and not nearly as many varieties of it are known. The Chinese Yew is not used as an ornamental in America, and the Western Yew (*T. brevifolia*) is not a very good plant in most areas in America. The Canada Yew (*T. canadensis*) is good mostly for shaded situations. When the first cross of the English and Japanese yews was noted in 1900, the new hybrid *T. media* was highly considered. Since that time many others have been introduced, some under the right name of *T. media*, and undoubtedly others merely being considered varieties of *T. cuspidata*.

The forms or habits of growth of the many hybrids vary considerably from the dwarf, almost prostrate, form, through the rounded and globed shaped, vase shaped, narrowly columnar, to the tree forms of the true *T. cuspidata* and *T. baccata*. In this time of small homes and small gardens, it is the smaller, more dwarf types that have merit.

The sexes are separate, all pistillate or fruiting flowers being on one plant and all staminate or male flowers on another plant and both should be present in the near vicinity to insure fruiting. The presence of fruit in the fall of the year denotes the pistillate forms, and the presence of numerous, rounded, staminate flower buds of the male is almost a sure sign that the plants having them will not fruit. If for some reason a pistillate plant has not fruited the current year, its sex can still be noted in the fall by its small, but pointed (not globular), flower buds. Sometimes a plant has been known to produce a few pistillate flowers when before it has always produced staminate flowers. And the reverse

English Yew is carefully sheared in this garden at Bodnant, Wales, as a background for an outdoor stage. (*Photo by Arnold Arboretum, Jamaica Plain, Mass.*)

Taxus baccata aurea is trained and sheared into figures sitting in chairs in Hever Castle, England. (*Photo by Arnold Arboretum, Jamaica Plain, Mass.*)

may also be true. It is of interest to know that there are at least nearly 30 male clones being sold by the nurseries in North America at the present time.

Propagation

Seeds may be stratified as soon as ripe or stored dry in airtight containers in a cool place up to a year and then stratified. The seed should be stratified for 5 months at room (warm) temperatures and then 3 months at 40° F., then sown. See STRATIFICATION. If, after several months they still do not germinate, then they should be given another 3 months cold

Taxus baccata sheared **annually**. These in Kells, Ireland, are about 400 years old. (*Photo by Arnold Arboretum, Jamaica Plain, Mass.*)

period. Cuttings (either softwood or hardwood) of most varieties of Japanese yews root freely, while those of English yews may be difficult, taking a year or more to produce roots. Those difficult may be grafted on seedlings or forms that root readily. See STRATIFICATION, CUTTINGS, GRAFTING.

Insect Pests

Black vine weevil, which is also one of the strawberry root weevils, is a destructive pest of Yew. The brown snout beetles feed on leaves and bark and the grubs eat the roots. Weak and dying branches often occur before the cause is identified. Treating the soil with insecticide #15 (see JAPANESE BEETLE) is helpful but not adequate. Spraying in early summer with insecticide #13 or #15 to kill the weevils is effective. Taxus mealybug clustered at the axils of the branches are easily killed by thorough spraying with insecticide #15. The soft scales, Pulvinaria scale and Fletcher scale disfigure the needles, weaken the plants and secrete honeydew which turns black with sooty mold. Spraying with insecticide #15 in early summer where young are hatching is advised.

Diseases

Rhizoctonia root rot kills the roots causing wilted and dead branches. Soaking the soil with fungicide #D will discourage the spread of the disease. Yews prefer alkaline soil and do not thrive when growing among vigorous Rhododendron, Azalea and most evergreens.

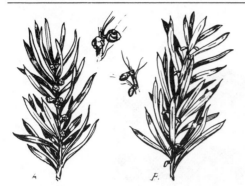

Taxus sp.: A. Male flower buds. B. Female flower buds.

baccata   60′   Zone 6   English Yew
There are many varieties of the English Yew which is native throughout Europe and of course this is the only species used in European gardens. The forms vary considerably both as to foliage color, texture, as well as the general form of the plants. Some varieties are almost prostrate shrubs, others are towering trees 60 ft. and more in height. In America the English Yew and its varieties are used from Long Island southward. *T. baccata* 'Repandens' has proved to be the hardiest of all the English varieties, perfectly hardy in Zone 5. Some varieties are:

'Adpressa'—originating in England about 1828; this is a distinct Yew with a rounded bushlike habit, no main leader and small, blunt, evenly arranged leaves only about half the size of those of the species. It is a fruiting plant; eventually becomes a widespreading bush. A 20-year-old plant is only 6 ft. tall and 3 ft. across; 'Aurea'—the leaves of this pistillate variety are yellow on the margins and the tips but they turn green the second year. The color is most pronounced on the undersurfaces of the leaves. This variety has erect and ascending branches and a 30-year-old specimen in the parks of Rochester, N.Y., was 8 ft. high and more than 15 ft. across; 'Dovastoniana'—this is the Westfelton Yew, originally raised about 1777 by Mr. John Dovaston of Westfelton, near Shrewsbury, England. It is one of the very handsome forms of the English Yew, making an erect tree with horizontal branches and pendulous branchlets. It is said that the original tree, a male, eventually produced 1 fruiting branch. In 1876 the original tree measured 34 ft. high, with a trunk 7½ ft. in circumference and 72 ft. in circumference of the branches; 'Elegantissima'—a handsome male clone; this is a widespreading bush with branches more or less horizontal, and leaves striped a pale yellow,

later becoming whitish; 'Fastigiata'—the Irish Yew, sometimes termed in England *T. baccata stricta*, is one of the most popular of all English Yew varieties. Two plants were found near Florence, Ireland, about 1780, both of which were pistillate. All branches are upright, with the needles spread spirally about the twigs. The entire habit and outline is one of rugged upright character and dark green foliage. Well-grown old plants of the Irish Yew make striking specimens; 'Fastigiata Aurea'—sometimes termed the Golden Irish Yew, this is a conspicuous golden-leaved variety with the leaves especially yellow on the undersurface. It originated before 1908 and is of course similar in general habit to the Irish Yew; 'Lutea'—a golden-yellow fruited form; this is similar to the species in every way except for the color of the fruit. Apparently this was first discovered near Glasnevin, Ireland, about 1817; 'Pendula'—a popular tree form, this male clone has an erect habit and horizontal branches. The branchlets are long, graceful and pendulous and the leaves are a glaucous green; 'Repandens'—the hardiest of the *T. baccata* varieties and a low, flat-topped shrub with the tips of the branchlets pendulous. This is a fruiting form, hardy in Zone 5; 'Semperaurea'—the young shoots and needles of this variety are yellow and the color is supposedly retained, in the milder climate of England, throughout the second year. Hence, it differs from most other yellow-colored forms, the needles of which turn green after the first growing season; 'Washingtonii'—a popular variety; this is noted for its yellow foliage and widespreading habit without a particular leader. A few years ago there were specimens of this in the Rochester, N.Y., parks that were 15 ft. tall and about 14 ft. wide.

brevifolia   45′   Zone 6   Pacific Yew
This tree, native from British Columbia to Calif., is rarely used as a cultivated specimen. The plant usually offered in nurseries under this name is *T. cuspidata nana*. The wood, bark, leaves and seeds of this are poisonous.

canadensis   3′–6′   Zone 2   Canada Yew
This is the hardiest of the yews, but it is not the handsomest. It withstands shade much better than other species, but does not fruit as well, nor is its foliage as good a dark green as that of other species. Plants of this species are frequently monoecious and the foliage can turn brownish in the winter, especially if growing in direct sunlight. Native to eastern North America from Newfoundland to Va. and Iowa. The variety 'Stricta' has stiff upright branches and was discovered by Richard M. Wyman in a block of *T. canadensis* at Framingham, Mass., in 1929. It makes a good hedge plant; the plants of this clone bear fruits and a 20-year-

old plant at the Secrest Arboretum is only 4 ft. high yet 16 ft. in dia.

cuspidata   50′   Zone 4   Japanese Yew
This is the Yew commonly planted in the northern U.S.; not as hardy as the Canada Yew but certainly hardier than the English Yew and native to Japan and Korea. The Japanese Yew, strictly speaking, is a single-trunked tree, but when grown from seed many variations occur and of course many clones and varieties have been named. Among them are the following: **'Aurescens'**—the Hall estate of Bristol, R.I., is credited with first having this variety in America, probably considerably before 1923. It is a dwarf variety with shoots tinged yellow a greater part of the season. A 20-year-old male plant was 1 ft. high and 3 ft. across; **capitata**— *T. cuspidata* is actually a tree with 1 or several trunks. This name of "capitata" has been used for the tree form and it has no botanical standing. However, it must be included here for so many nurserymen still use it, even though improperly. The plants grown under this name are excellent specimens, both male and female; stiffly upright and pyramidal trees that grow rapidly. Unfortunately the chances are the name will be continued in use for a long, long time regardless of what is said about it; **'Densa'**—50-year-old specimens in the Arnold Arboretum are only 4 ft. tall, yet 20 ft. across. It is usually a pistillate plant with short side branchlets, very dense and widespreading branches—one of the very best of the yews without question. This clone is lower in height of growth than is *T. cuspidata* 'Nana' and, because of this, these 2 plants are usually very easy to tell apart; **expansa**—the true *T. cuspidata* is a tree with an upright trunk, but this variety is vase shaped with an open center. Twenty-year-old plants are 10 ft. high and 10 ft. across; **'Jeffrey's Pyramidal'**—this is listed as a dark green-leaved Yew, one of the heaviest-fruiting forms. It is definitely pyramidal in habit: **'Nana'**—40-year-old plants of this are 10 ft. tall and 20 ft. across. It is mostly female, the shoots are dense and compact. It, too, is one of the very best varieties—slightly taller than *T. cuspidata* 'Densa'; **'Prostrata'**—undoubtedly there must be several plants with this name. It is low and spreading, pistillate, and most important of all, it is reported to maintain its good green color when *T. media* 'Densiformis' will have its foliage burned by winter cold; **'Thayerae'**— several seedings were given this name in 1930 grown from the seed of 1 plant in South Lancaster, Mass. The plants are dense, flat topped, twice as wide as tall and pistillate, and under rules of the International Code of Nomenclature for Cultivated Plants, because of their uniformity they can be considered

together as a cultivar. The branches are almost horizontal; the centers of the plants are not open but are filled with foliage. Twenty-five-year-old plants are 8 ft. tall and 16 ft. in dia.

x media   40′   Zone 4   Intermediate Yew
Mr. T. D. Hatfield, Supt. of the Hunnewell Estate in Wellesley, Mass., first made this cross in 1900 between *T. cuspidata* and *T. baccata*. Usually the plants are broadly pyramidal, frequently with a central leader. The hardy qualities of the Japanese Yew and the ornamental qualities of the English Yew, combined in the hybrid species, have resulted in many excellent plants. Varieties: **'Adams'**—a male clone, and a good upright tree type, 10–25 ft. tall; **'Berryhill'**—this too is an excellent female clone, a 20-year-old plant being 5 ft. tall and 9 ft. across, looking somewhat similar to *T. cuspidata* 'Nana'; **'Brownii'**—although a male, this has a fine, dense, rounded habit, 1 plant being 9 ft. tall and 12 ft. across; **'Densiformis'**—many nurserymen list this name, whether or not they have the real plant. Apparently it is a male clone, rather dense and rounded in habit with many, short, lateral branches; **'Halloran'**—a slow-growing, compact but rounded, female type, this has short, stocky, lateral branches. A 20-year-old plant at the Secrest Arboretum is 7 ft. tall and 6 ft. across; **'Hatfieldii'**—Mr. T. D. Hatfield, former Supt. of the famous Hunnewell Estate in Wellesley, Mass., originated this long-time favorite. Plants of this clone are male, pyramidal, with dense upright branches. Twenty-year-old plants are 12 ft. high and 10 ft. across; **'Hicksii'**—one of the long-time favorites and the first one of this hybrid species to be upright in habit. It is similar in form to the Irish Yew except that it is hardier and usually has several main stems from the base. Most of the plants under this name are pistillate. It is usually 2 or 3 times as tall as it is wide; **'Kelseyi'**—sometimes called the Kelsey Berrybush Yew, this is supposed to fruit when 4 or 5 years old. It was named after F. W. Kelsey of New York City about 1915. A 20-year-old plant at the Secrest Arboretum is 12 ft. tall and 9 ft. across; **'Moon'**—a narrow, upright, female type, sometimes known as Moon's Pyramidal, it still has a somewhat rounded outline; **'Natorp'**—an excellent female yew; this is twice as broad as it is high and looks similar to *T. cuspidata* 'Nana' except that it is more flat on top. One plant was 4 ft. tall and 9 ft. across; **ovata**—a female clone with needles somewhat shorter than those of either *T. cuspidata* or *T. baccata*. It is deep green, apparently not harmed by temperatures of −20° F. The plant is upright in general habit, dense, and two-thirds as wide as it is tall; **'Stovekenii'**—another good columnar form;

this is a male. It was found by Alexander Stoveken, Supt. of A. N. Pierson Nurseries, Cromwell, Conn., prior to 1938, a 20-year-old specimen being 12 ft. tall and 6 ft. across; **'Vermeulen'**—an excellent, slow-growing, compact, rounded, pistillate type; a 20-year-old plant of this is 8 ft. tall and 9 ft. across; **'Wardii'** —this is one of the widest as well as the flattest, spreading yew forms, a 20-year-old fruiting plant being 6 ft. tall and 19 ft. across. It is very dense in habit.

TEA = *Camellia sinensis*

TEA FAMILY = Theaceae

TEA, NEW JERSEY = *Ceanothus americanus*

TEASEL = *Dipsacus sylvestris*

TEASEL FAMILY = Dipsaceae

TECOMA (te-CO-ma)
   stans (*Stenolobium stans*)   **20′**   **Zones 9–10**
                                      Yellow-bells
A popular tropical member of the Bignonia Family, bearing racemes of bright yellow, funnel-shaped flowers and opposite, pinnately compound leaves with 5–13 leaflets. Native from Fla. to South America. The fruit is a narrow pod 6–8 in. long. Easy to grow; propagated by seeds.

TECOMARIA (tee-ko-MAY-ria)
   capensis   **sprawling shrub**   **Zone 9**   **Cape-**
                                  honeysuckle
Native to South Africa, with brilliant orange, trumpet-shaped flowers, each about 2 in. long, borne in loose heads. The compound evergreen leaves are opposite, with 7–9 leaflets each ¾–2 in. long. The fruits are small pods 2 in. long and ¼ in. wide. Grows well in sandy soil, and is often used as a hedge. There are other varieties, 1 with yellow flowers and 1 with variegated leaves. Propagation by cuttings or seeds and layers.

TECOMA-TREE. See TABEBUIA.

TEFF = *Eragrostis tef*

TELLIMA (tel-LY-ma)
   grandiflora **1′–2′** **Zone 4** **Alaska Fringecup**
A hairy herb, similar to *Mitella* species, native from Alaska to Calif., with cordate, lobed leaves 4 in. wide. The nodding flowers turn from greenish to pinkish to red, the petals pinnately cut. Sometimes grown in the shaded wild garden in areas throughout its habitat.

TENDRIL. A coiling threadlike organ by which a vine grasps an object for support.

TEPHROSIA (teff-RO-sia)
   virginiana **1′–2′** **Zone 7** **Virginia Tephrosia**
An upright perennial of the Pea Family, having silky white hairs on the stems and underside of the leaves. These are compound, with 17–29 oblong leaflets. The pealike flowers, ¾ in. long and growing in compact terminal clusters, have

a rounded yellow petal, and reddish or purplish, lateral petals and keel. The slender, silky seed-pod is 1–2 in. long. This plant grows in dry, sandy soils in southeastern U.S. to Tex. It is an attractive plant for the wild garden and may be propagated by division of the rather woody root in spring or by sowing seed either in spring or in fall.

TERETE. Circular in cross-section.

TERMINALIA (ter-min-AY-lia)
   catappa **80′**   **Zone 10**   **Tropical-almond**
A tropical deciduous tree from Malaya, valued for its wood, for its edible nuts and often planted as an ornamental. The leaves are 9 in. long, glossy green, turning beautiful shades of yellow, red and purple twice each year before the new leaves are produced. The white flowers are inconspicuous, and the almondlike fruits have oil-bearing kernels and are of excellent flavor. The branches are horizontal. Widely used in the Tropics as a street tree, especially in sand at the seashore for it is resistant to salt-water spray and is able to thrive within a few feet of the shore line.

TERMITES. Any wood in contact with the ground is subject to attack by termites or white ants. Plants with woody stems such as Tomato and Chrysanthemum may also be damaged, especially when grown near an established infestation. In the garden wooden stakes, fence posts, cold frames, tool sheds, summer houses and tree stumps are susceptible. Dusts of insecticide #3 mixed in the soil give control in planting. This insecticide is also recommended around posts and stumps. Infestations in permanent buildings should be handled by a professional exterminator. Termites are most troublesome in the warmer areas.

TERNATE. In threes.

TERRACES. See GARDEN FIXTURES.

TERRARIUM. This is a tightly closed glass (or plastic) case, usually with a moveable glass top, for the growth and display of small plants. When it is properly planted it requires very little attention. Growing plants give off a certain amount of water vapor through their leaves, and this, together with what may evaporate from the soil, condenses on the inside of the glass and is returned to the soil as water. This is of course taken up by the plant roots again and used in the process of photosynthesis. This process does not continue indefinitely without the addition of a small amount of water, but it can go on some time, perhaps weeks at a time, if conditions are just right.

In the first place, there must not be too much water at the start. The soil should be moist, not wet. Dead leaves should be removed, whenever they appear, to decrease the possibility of disease. Because the terrarium is enclosed by glass, the humidity inside is considerably greater than that in the room, hence molds can appear and take a quick toll of plant life unless the case is thoroughly ventilated as soon as they appear. The case should not be placed in direct sunlight for lengthy periods but rather in indirect sunlight or even under fluorescent light for 12–16 hours per day.

When the terrarium is "watered" the water might best be added as a fine foliage spray, not a thorough soaking of the soil. Once light, moisture and temperature have become properly distributed, the terrarium needs little attention.

These cases are usually discarded fish aquaria which have developed minor leaks but which are perfectly satisfactory for terrarium purposes. They can also be made at home with a wood or metal frame, and a top which can be opened on occasion for partial ventilation. An inch of gravel is placed in the bottom and about 2 in. of good potting soil on top, but it might well be arranged with an undulating surface for creating interest and variation in planting.

Terrarium

The terrarium can also be used as the place where sick plants are placed to recuperate (because of the higher atmospheric moisture).

Beauty is created by placing miniature plants in scale, planting in such a way as to create interesting scenes because of plant placement, form, shape or color of the plants selected. It is like planting an aquarium or a garden—there must be a main display of plants, a background, vistas and interesting combinations, and the ingenuity of the individual is tested to the utmost in making these miniature planting combinations.

Two types of plantings can be made, a desert planting with dry soil plants, or a normal planting with plants requiring more moisture. It is folly to try to mix the two, for cacti and succulents simply will not survive under the moist conditions needed to grow ferns and other woodland natives.

If the desert planting is to be made, the bottom of the terrarium should have 2 in. of sand with a minimum of topsoil. Cacti and various types of small succulents would be used, but the temperature should be on the warm side, with plenty of sunlight.

If the room in which the terrarium is to be used is cool, all kinds of woodland plants could be included, such as small ferns, mosses, Heptica, Rattlesnake Plantain, Partridge-berry, Moneywort, Pipsissewa, *Saxifraga sarmentosa*, Wintergreen, violets, and small tree seedlings of junipers, hollies, spruces, hemlocks, pines and and other similar materials. However, it should be remembered that such plants may not survive long in good condition if the temperature is 70°F. or over. Temperatures 5–10°F. less than this are more suitable.

In warm rooms (temperatures 75°F.) some tropical plants might be used such as African violets, begonias, crotons, Chinese evergreens, dracenas, peperomias, Baby's Tears, Creeping Fig and small tropical ferns.

Overwatering is one of the commonest mistakes in terrarium care and must be guarded against at all times.

TESTA. The outer seed-coat.

TETRA. Greek prefix meaning 4; tetragonal (4-angled); tetragynous (with 4 pistils or styles); tetramerous (with its parts or sets in 4's); tetrandrous (with 4 stamens).

TETRAGONIA TETRAGONIOIDES = New Zealand Spinach, which see.

TETRAPANAX (tet-ra-PAY-nax)

papyriferus   14′   Zone 10   Rice-paper-tree
This is the small tree, native to Formosa, that supplies the well-known rice paper of the Orient. The leaves are large, a foot wide, lobed and deep green above, silvery below and when young are covered with a white felty pubescence. The rice paper is pared from the pith of this plant.

TEUCRIUM (TEW-krium). Perennial, somewhat woody, herbs of the Mint Family grown chiefly for their fragrance or for ornament, but many of the over 150 species are rather weedy in appearance. The leaves, generally covered with a gray pubescence, are opposite, ovate to lanceolate, and becoming bractlike near the dense terminal spikes of tiny, labiate flowers which are arranged in a whorl on the flower stalk. Often grown in the wild garden, the plants may be divided in spring or may be propagated from seed.

Propagation

By seed which can be sown as soon as ripe, division of plants and softwood cuttings.

canadense 3′ Zones 7–8 American Germander
Erect, pubescent stems and thin, sharply-toothed and pointed, ovate to lanceolate leaves, 1–4 in. long, characterize this species. The flowers are pink to purple and appear from July to Sept. The plant may be found in moist woods over the southern states and west to Tex.

chamaedrys 10″ Zone 5 Chamaedrys
Germander
This is a low, dense, shrubby, little plant from central and southern Europe, popular because of its low height and because of the fact that it can be sheared for edging purposes. There is a variety **prostratum** that is supposed to be even lower in size. The small purple or rose flowers are about ¾ in. long in upright spikes during the summer. It makes a neat plant, as a ground cover (which can be clipped), for edging along a border or walk, or as an interesting summer-blooming plant in front of an evergreen border.

TEXAS-PLUME = *Ipomopsis rubra*

TEXAS-PRIDE = *Phlox drummondii*

THALIA (THAY-lia)

dealbata 6′ Zone 7 Water-canna
An aquatic perennial plant, native from S.Car. to Tex., growing in marshes or shallow pools. It is a white, powdery, stemless herb with basal leathery leaves 20 in. long and 10 in. wide on long petioles, but the small violet flowers are produced on a 10-ft. stalk. Propagated by division and, if to be grown in a pool, it should first be planted in a pot of good soil and then the pot submerged in the water.

THALICTRUM (thal-IK-trum). These species have light airy foliage and flowers which are interesting because they have no petals, but are conspicuous because of colored sepals and stamens. Since they are tall they are for the rear of the border. They are accustomed to growing in light shade but need good rich soil with plenty of moisture. They can be planted in either the fall or the spring and might be divided every fourth or fifth year. Also seed can be sown in the fall as soon as it is ripe.

alpinum 1′ Zone 2 Alpine Meadow-rue

A delicate Arctic plant, 12 in. tall with much-divided, compound, light green leaves having a fernlike appearance and yellow flowers.

aquilegifolium 2′–3′ Zone 5 Columbine
Meadow-rue
These, native to Europe and Asia, flower in May and June with small lilac-purple blossoms in loose clusters of countless small umbels. White- and rose-flowered vars. are available. The gray-green foliage is almost similar to that of Columbine.

dioicum 1′–2′ Zone 4 Early Meadow-rue
A dainty plant with compound leaves having unevenly numbered, rounded and lobed leaflets, separated from one another by branching petioles as long as, or longer than, the length of the leaflets, giving the leaves a delicate, feathery appearance. The nodding flowers grow in a loose panicle 12 in. or more in length. Male and female flowers occur on separate plants. The flowers have brownish sepals, no petals and greenish-yellow stamens extending below the sepals. The plant is an attractive component of low, wet meadows and stream banks in eastern U.S. and Canada, west to Kan., and blooms in early summer. It may be transplanted, divided in spring or propagated by seed sown in summer.

dipterocarpum 2′–7′ Zone 4 Yunnan
Meadow-rue
Found by E. H. Wilson in western China, this produces large sprays of lavender flowers with yellow stamens in Aug.; the last of the meadow-rues to bloom. Flowers are polygamous.

glaucum = *T. speciosissimum*

kiusianum 2″–5″ Zone 5
An extremely low plant with purplish leaves, pink-lilac sepals and very blue stamens. If in very good soil it might be used as a small ground cover. It is stoloniferous and native to Japan.

minus 1′–1½′ Zones 2–3 Low Meadow-rue
With fernlike leaves (often listed as *T. adianti-folium*). The poor greenish-yellow flowers in June and early July are not outstanding. It could be massed under shrubbery or on moist banks for best effects. Native to Europe.

polygamum 8′ Zone 3 Tall Meadow-rue
A perennial suited only to the wild garden because of its size; found throughout eastern North America. This has many branches, compound leaves, the leaflets of which are roundish and 3 lobed. The small, numerous, white flowers are produced in early summer in large terminal clusters, with the stamens and sepals being of about equal length, and of course in this genus there are no petals. Not very often used as a garden plant because of its height.

rochebrunianum 4′–6′ Zone 4 Lavender-
mist
This is noted as being superior in every way to *T. dipterocarpum*. Large masses of lavender-

violet blossoms are borne with yellow stamens from mid-July to early Sept. It is probably the best ornamental species in this genus. Japan.

rugosum = *T. speciosissimum*
speciosissimum (*T. rugosum, T. glaucum*)
    3′–6′   **Zone 5**   **Dusty Meadow-rue**
Native to southern Europe, popular in the trade under its synonym *T. glaucum*, this bears blue-gray leaves that are excellent for use with cut flowers. It should be planted for this characteristic alone. The soft yellow flowers are slightly fragrant. The leaves are 2 and 3 times pinnate and the flowers are bisexual.

venulosum 1½′ **Zone 2** **Veiny Meadow-rue**
Coming from the Rocky Mountains, this plant forms mounds of stiff stems clothed with much divided, bluish-green leaves and bearing a widely branched stalk of pale green flowers. The plant prefers a dry soil and full sun. Native from Manitoba to Utah.

THALLUS. A flat leaflike organ; in ferns it is the entire plant at one time in its development which shows no differentiation to stem or leaf.

THEA = *Camellia*

THEACEAE = The Tea Family.

THELESPERMA (thel-es-PERM-a)
burridgeanum 1½′ **annual** **Burridge Green-thread**
Somewhat like Coreopsis, with the alternate and opposite leaves divided into threadlike lobes. The flowers are red-brown to deep orange, the rays having a yellow margin, and the heads are 1½ in. wide. This belongs to the Composite Family. Easily grown in the garden.

THELYPTERIS
hexagonoptera (*Dryopteris hexagonoptera*) 18″
    Zone 3   **Broad Beech Fern**
The pinnate fronds of this North American fern rise from a creeping rootstock. They grow in shady situations in acid soil and may be propagated from sections of the rootstock. Native from Quebec to Fla.
noveboracensis (*Dryopteris noveboracensis*)
    1′–2′   **Zone 2**   **New York Fern**
Native to eastern North America, this has pale yellowish-green fronds, once pinnate, 3–6 in. with the lower pinnae gradually smaller and smaller than the middle ones, the smallest being at the bottom of the frond. It should be in slightly acid soil, can be grown in full sun and spreads rapidly by creeping rhizomes. The fronds are killed by the first fall frost. Usually found in the woods in very moist situations.
palustris (*Dryopteris thelypteris*)   2½′
    Zone 4   **Marsh Fern**
With a creeping rootstock and 1-pinnate fronds 2½ ft. long and 6 in. wide, chiefly seen in marshes in the northern U.S. and Canada, as well as in Europe and Asia.

THEOBROMA (theo-BRO-ma)
cacao 25′ **Zone 10** **Cacao, Chocolate-tree**
Widely cultivated throughout the Tropics as the source of chocolate or cocoa. It is native to American Tropics; has alternate, evergreen, leathery leaves, 8–12 in. long. The flowers are yellowish, often borne right on the main trunk of the tree; the woody fruits are colored red to brown, are ribbed and about a foot long, with seeds about an inch wide from which chocolate is obtained. Propagated by seed.

THERMOPSIS (therm-OP-sis)
caroliniana 5′ **Zone 3** **Carolina Thermopsis**
A member of the Pea Family, with erect racemes, 8–12 in. long, of yellow pealike flowers, during June and July; native from N.Car. to Ga. The leaves are alternate and compound, with 3 leaflets. Plants are of easy culture, having deep roots, and are propagated by spring division or by seeds, but it should be remembered that the seed does not remain viable long. Hence sow the seed in late summer.
montana 2′ **Zone 3** **Mountain Thermopsis**
This is a lower edition of *T. caroliniana*, good for a garden where space is limited. The racemes of yellow flowers are not as dense and only about 8 in. long. Native to the western Rocky Mountains, blooming during June and July.
rhombifolia 1′ **Zone 3** **Prairie Thermopsis**
Native from Saskatchewan to Colo., this is even smaller than the other 2 species; good for rock gardens and it can self-sow itself. Its yellow flowers also appear during June and July.

THESPESIA (thes-PEE-sia)
populnea 30′–50′ **Zone 10** **Portia-tree**
This tree has the general aspect of a Poplar. Native to tropical parts of the Orient, this tree has heart-shaped, alternate, evergreen leaves, 4 in. long, and small, yellow, bell-shaped flowers similar in shape to those of the *Hibiscus*. The wood of this tree has been used to make food bowls by the early Hawaiians because it is almost free of flavor. Often planted by the seashore in Fla. and Calif.; blooming in late spring or early summer. Propagated by cuttings and layers.

THEVETIA (thev-EE-shia)
peruviana 25′ **Zone 10** **Yellow-oleander**
The leaves are 3–6 in. long and less than ½ in. wide, similar to those of the Oleander. Flowers are bright yellow, trumpet shaped, about 3 in. long and sweetly fragrant; can be seen on the tree at most times of year. The fruit is a brown to black nut. Native to tropical America.

THIMBLEBERRY, WESTERN = *Rubus parviflorus*

THIMBLEFLOWER = *Rudbeckia hirta pulcherrima*

THISTLE. See CIRSIUM.

THISTLE, ASTER, DAISY or GOLDENROD FAMILY = Compositae

THISTLE, COMMON RUSSIAN = *Salsola pestifer*

THISTLE-FLAX, RUSSIAN = *Linum salsoloides*

THLASPI (thl-AS-pi)

alpestre 1′ **Zone 6 (?) Alpine Pennycress**
An alpine forming mats to 12 in. high; the glossy foliage is arranged in rosettes from which clusters of flowers, white tinted with red, rise on stalks blooming in April and May. Native to the mountains of Europe.

arvense 18″ **annual Field Pennycress**
A weed, native to Europe but troublesome in the prairie provinces of Canada and the northwestern U.S. The leaves are alternate, oblong shaped, simple, toothed and nearly clasp the stem. Flowers are white in racemes during May and June and the fruits are flat pods about ⅜ in. across. The young leaves are sometimes used in salads.

rotundifolium 8″ **Zone 6 Roundleaf Pennycress**
The cushions of thick, rounded leaves, forming a matlike growth, increase in area by stolons that slowly extend the plant's width. The pale lilac flowers are clustered up and down the stalks which rise above the foliage. Native to the mountains of southern Europe.

THORN, COCKSPUR = *Crataegus crus-galli*

THOROUGHWORT. See EUPATORIUM.

THREE-MEN-IN-A-BOAT = *Rhoeo spathacea* (*R. discolor*)

THRIFT. See ARMERIA.

THRIPS. For control see ROSE PESTS, p. 963.

THROATWORT, COMMON = *Trachelium caeruleum*

THRYALLIS = *Galphimia*

THUJA. The arborvitaes have long been staple plants in many American gardens. Easily rooted and quickly grown, they make salable plants in a short time. Because of this popularity among the growers, it is no wonder that at least 50 varieties are being offered at the present time, while in various parts of this country and in Europe over 150 varieties are being grown. Both the native White-cedar or American Arborvitae (*T. occidentalis*) and its Oriental counterpart (*T. orientalis*) have produced many varieties. All arborvitaes have evergreen, scalelike leaves arranged in flat sprays and small dried capsules as fruits. They are easily propagated by cuttings.

The American Arborvitae is native throughout the northern half of eastern North America, especially in moist soil areas and in the mountains

where the atmospheric moisture is high, so it is no wonder that the early settlers began using it as an ornamental. In fact, they even made a tea from boiling the twigs and chips of wood. Introduced into Europe from America in the 16th century, it has been assiduously grown by European nurserymen and they, too, have selected many new forms. Well over 150 of these have been named and new ones are still appearing.

Most *T. occidentalis* varieties are not really evergreen—they turn brown in the late fall and remain so all through the winter. This characteristic may not hold true in all areas where they are grown, but it is certainly true in the North where winters are cold.

Secondarily, they must be grown in areas with a good deal of atmospheric as well as soil moisture; otherwise they do not look well. In areas with hot summers and long droughts they quickly indicate their lack of adaptability by showing dead branches here and there. In dry areas, serious infestations of red spider can ruin plants.

In addition, many varieties of this plant do not grow old gracefully. Their habit of growth is such that wind, snow, ice or decay may break one of the several main branches or trunks at the base, creating such a hole in the general form of the plant that often it can never properly grow back into a good ornamental specimen again.

Most of the *T. occidentalis* varities are not nearly so popular now as they were 50 or 75 years ago. With the introduction of many excellent exotic trees and shrubs from the Orient and from Europe since the turn of the century, these arborvitaes have gradually taken a back seat as truly "old-fashioned" ornamentals, although some growers still carry the older varieties, many of which are known to be second-rate evergreens today. It would seem, then, that the *T. occidentalis* group, at least, is a group of mixed-up, often old-fashioned, second-rate ornamentals, for which there is still some demand.

Thuja occidentalis *Propagation*

Seed is occasionally used (stratified for 2 months at 40° F.), but mostly plants are propagated asexually by either softwood or hardwood cuttings which root easily at various times throughout the year. See CUTTINGS.

Insect Pests

Arborvitae leaf miner worms tunnel the leaves, causing semi-transparent mines which may join to include branchlets. Heavy infestations give the plant a scorched appearance. Spraying with insecticide #13 or #15 in early summer gives control. Arborvitae weevil and other root weevils (see TAXUS) eat cup-shaped holes in the leaf margins and the grubs seriously damage the roots. Spraying in late spring with insecticide #9 is advised. Juniper scale and lecanium scale live on arborvitae. See JUNIPERUS for control. Spruce mite is often a serious pest. See PICEA. Insecticide #31 or #34 can be added to spray for the above pests for practical control, or used alone as needed.

Diseases

Juniper blight occurs on arborvitae and may be serious on nursery plants in wet weather. Frequent spraying with fungicide #D is advised. Winter injury is often confused with disease infections. Mulching to conserve moisture or a loose wrap of burlap around individual shrubs in exposed locations will help prevent winter injury from excessive loss of moisture from the foliage.

occidentalis 60′ Zone 2 American Arborvitae

This tree and its varieties are used from the Canadian provinces down to southern Pa. From that point southward to Fla. and Tex., the Oriental Arborvitae is commonly grown. This is also very popular on the Pacific Coast from Calif. to Wash. There are few ornamental varieties of the Western Arborvitae (*T. plicata*). The *T. occidentalis* varieties are as follows:

'Booth Globe', not necessarily globe shaped but low and compact with large leaves, reportedly developing into a flat-topped globe, broader than tall; 'Compacta', also called Parson's Compact Arborvitae, it was named about 1850. In 1955 1 plant was 5½ ft. tall by 3 ft. wide and in 1960 the same plant was 6 ft. by 5 ft., pyramidal and dense; 'Compacta Erecta', selected and named by Westminser (Md.) Nurseries in 1947, this is a semi-dwarf pyramidal plant. A 7-year-old plant was 47 in. tall; 'Douglas Pyramidal', a dense, pyramidal form, probably named about 1855; this is one of the best of the narrow pyramidal group. It is tall and grows vigorously; 'Fastigiata', branches are short, narrowly upright, probably growing to about 25 ft. tall; 'Globosa', years ago this was called 'Tom Thumb' but is now dignified with the name of Globe Arborvitae. A 22-year-old plant is 5 ft. tall and 7 ft. wide, still globose and dense, making a good specimen. In 1933 it was 4 ft. by 4 ft.; 'Hetz Midget', selected by Fairview Nursery Company (Fairview, Pa.) in the early 1930's, this has extremely slow growth. The habit is globe shaped and 10-year-old plants are scarcely 12–15 in. tall; 'Hovey', another low, globose form named about 1859; a 58-year-old plant is 5 ft. high and 10 ft. wide.

Because of its age, it is no longer globose but mostly flat on top. Certainly it can be classed with the slower-growing arborvitaes; 'Little Champion', selected and introduced in 1956; this is reported to be extremely hardy and one of the finest of the globes; 'Lutea', often termed the 'George Peabody' Arborvitae of years ago; this is one of the best of the colored-foliage forms. It originated in Geneva, N.Y., before 1873, grows tall and pyramidal, and is one of the very few of the many color forms of the American Arborvitae to keep its good color throughout the full growing season into the fall; 'Pumila', named many years ago and called "Little Gem," but as the plants have shown a tendency to grow larger, the term "Little Gem" has been dropped. An 80-year-old plant is now a rounded pyramid, 10 ft. tall and 12 ft. wide at the base, but still very dense. Still, young plants are very low and broad, often twice as broad as high, and make excellent ornamentals; 'Rheingold', first listed by Hesse Nurseries in Germany in 1910; this is cone shaped with bright yellow foliage, both juvenile and mature. It usually turns bronze in winter; 'Robusta', the Ware Arborvitae, originally raised by Thomas Ware, Coventry, England, about 1850, grows into a low, dense pyramid of blue-green foliage. A plant 35 years old is 5 ft. tall. This is one of the hardiest forms and one of the last to discolor from winter burning; 'Rosenthal', a 50-year-old plant is still only 7 ft. tall, evidence that this variety grows slowly, but it is very dense and, of course, pyramidal in habit; 'Sherman', a sport of the Ware Arborvitae, originating about 1920. Pyramidal in growth, the claim has been made that this is more winter-hardy than 'Robusta', especially in areas of the north central United States, 'Umbraculifera', with flat top; an 11-year-old plant is 4 ft. by 4 ft., dense and rounded. It was named before 1891 and has been frequently termed "globe-shaped," which it is, while young; 'Woodward', named in 1871; this is a densely globose form which has a tendency to spread out with age. A 72-year-old plant is 8 ft. tall and 18 ft. wide, but still dense and globose. This is a popular variety.

orientalis 50′ Zone 6 Oriental Arborvitae

With the large home-building programs in Fla., southern Calif. and other mild parts of the U.S., the more recently available varieties of *T. orientalis** have become most popular. Generally these are not hardy in the upper half of the U.S., but are widely popular in the South.

*It is most unfortunate that this name *T. orientalis* has been recently changed to *Platycladus orientalis*. Since it will be some time before the name *Platycladus* will be in general use, the old name is used here, but those who wish to be meticulously correct should take note of the change.

Above: Fruits of *Thuja occidentalis*.
Below: Fruits of *T. orientalis*.

The species itself is a tree up to 50 ft. tall, native in northern China and Korea, but the densely branching, shrubby forms often have their branches all carefully arranged in vertical planes. Then also, the dry, capsulelike fruits have small curved "horns" while those of the American Arborvitae do not have such "horns."

Outstanding among the Oriental shrubby forms are those with yellow or blue foliage, both types widely popular, and because they are usually grown in areas lacking severe winter cold, they may well hold their foliage color throughout the entire year. Some of the recommended varieties are: **'Aurea'**, said to be one of the most popular forms in Japanese gardens; globose, low, compact, yellow foliage in the spring and keeping this color most of the summer. The foliage is dense but arranged in vertical planes; **'Baker'**, pale green foliage; used especially in hot, dry situations; **'Berckmann's'**, grows to about 5 ft. and retains its attractive golden-yellow foliage a greater part of the time. Sometimes incorrectly listed as *T. orientalis aurea nana*; **'Beverly Hills'**, often termed 'Beverlyensis'; one of the most popular types on the Pacific Coast; columnar to pyramidal with tips of branchlets golden yellow, often throughout the year; **'Blue Spire'**, sometimes listed as *howardii* or 'Howard's Blue Spire', this originated in one of the Howard's Nurseries, Austin, Tex. Pyramidal in habit and foliage bluish; **'Bonita'**, bright green foliage, slow in growth, rounded or conelike in general habit; leaves have some yellow at tips. Grows to about 3 ft. high; **'Elegantissima'**, a low columnar form, bright yellow foliage in the spring turning to yellowish green by summer. Attains a height of 12–15 ft.; **'Globosa'**, of globose shape; **'Rochester'**, original plants were selected by the former B. H. Slavin of the Rochester Parks, Rochester, N.Y. These were trees similar to the species, but were hardier than other *T. orientalis* clones and hardy in Rochester, N.Y. Apparently they are also hardy at Ames, Iowa; **sieboldii**, globe shaped to conical; compact, low and popular in southern states; sometimes listed as *T. orientalis compacta*.

plicata   180′   Zone 5   Giant Arborvitae
This is native from northern Calif. to Alaska. It will grow to 180 ft. in height and is, of course, a most imporant source of lumber. It has been found that there are really 2 strains as far as hardiness is concerned. Plants grown on the Pacific Coast yield seedlings hardy only in Zone 6, while seed collected from the high mountains of Mont. and Utah yield seedlings hardy in Zone 5. Actually, this is about the best of the tree arborvitaes for ornamental use, chiefly because of its lustrous green foliage which does not turn brown in the winter, as does that of most *T. occidentalis* varieties.

Several varieties of this species have been named, chiefly in Europe, and until they have been given thorough trials in the eastern U.S. we will not know the northern limits of their hardiness; i.e., whether they will be hardy only up to Zone 6 or whether they can be grown successfully in Zone 5.

However, the hardy strain of the species makes an excellent, vigorous, fast-growing, pyramidal tree—one of the best, if not the best, of all the arborvitaes for ornamental use. The lustrous, dark green leaves turn a delightful bronze in the fall, maintaining that color throughout the entire winter.

standishii   40′   Zone 5   Japanese Arborvitae
A native to Japan, this is handsome and more spreading in habit than other American species. The foliage does not turn brown in the winter, as does that of *T. occidentalis*, but it is not so ornamental as the foliage of *T. plicata*.

THUJOPSIS (thew-YOP-sis)
dolobrata   45′   Zone 6   Hiba False Arborvitae
This evergreen from Japan is somewhat similar to arborvitae but the lustrous scalelike leaves are larger. In good soil with plenty of moisture it develops into a beautiful dense tree but of no particular merit in preference to the arborvitae.

THUNBERGIA (thun-BER-ja)
alata   Vine   annual   Clockvine
This is a tender perennial vine, not very strong

in the North where it is grown as an outdoor annual, more vigorous in the South. The opposite leaves are triangular to ovate, 3 in. long. The flowers are white to orange-yellow with purple throats, $1\frac{1}{2}$ in. wide, blooming throughout the summer. They are funnel shaped, solitary and borne in the leaf axils. The var. 'Bakeri' has pure white flowers, but 'Alba' is better because the white flowers have a dark center. The var. 'Aurantiaca' is the one with good orange-yellow flowers. Seeds are sown indoors in March, or outdoors in May, and given a place in the full sun or semi-shade where they can be watered during dry spells. It is native to tropical America, and in the South is used to cover trellises and porches.

erecta   6'   Zone 10   Bush Thunbergia
A shrub from West Africa frequently planted in the Tropics, this is valued for its rich, purple and white, tubular flowers, similar in size and shape to those of morning-glories. The flower is 2 in. long and 2 in. across and is produced singly in the leaf axil. The leaves are opposite, small, 2–3 in. long, pointed at both ends.

fragrans   vine   Zone 10   Sweet Clockvine
An evergreen vine from India, with white fragrant flowers (sometimes not very fragrant) about the size and shape of those of Periwinkle. The stem is square, and the leaves are opposite, slightly lobed.

grandiflora   vine   Zone 8   Bengal Clockvine
Another evergreen vine from India, with blue or white tubular flowers, nearly 3 in. long, that are borne in long pendulous clusters which can be 2–3 ft. long. The individual flowers are about 3 in. across, and although the plants bloom off and on throughout the year, they are covered with blossoms in midspring. This is frequently planted in the gardens of Fla., southern Calif. and Hawaii.

laurifolia   vine   Zone 10   Laurel-leaved Thunbergia
A native twining vine of India, planted in gardens in Hawaii for its purple to light blue, tubular flowers which are 3 in. across. The inside throat of each flower is yellow. There are those who consider it the most beautiful vine in the world. The leaves are 5 in. long and have 3 main nerves originating at the base.

THYME. See THYMUS.

THYMELAEACEAE = The Mezereon Family

THYMUS (TI-mus). These are low, aromatic creepers, mostly evergreen or nearly so, belonging to the Mint Family, some of them making excellent ground covers. The flowers are small, 2-lipped, with only a few flowers in each cluster. They are propagated most easily by division of plant clumps and also by seed.

herba-barona   2"   Zone 4   Caraway Thyme
A trailing plant with long stems, having small, dark green leaves and densely covered, wide clusters of tiny purple flowers in midsummer. The plant forms a thick mat and gives off the odor of caraway when the leaves are bruised. Native to Corsica.

lanicaulis = *thracicus*

nitidus   8"   Zone 5   Sicily Thyme
A plant with rather stiff stems growing in a rounded mound and having pale, grayish, shining leaves. It bears short stalks of tiny violet flowers in late spring. The leaves of this plant are used in poultry seasoning. Native to Sicily.

serpyllum   Ground cover   Zone 3   Mother-of-thyme
An excellent, low, evergreen ground cover, native to Europe, western Asia and northern Africa, that has been a very popular garden plant in America since colonial times. The rosy-purple flowers in small terminal heads appear during late May and continue until Sept. The extremely small, opposite leaves, less than $\frac{1}{4}$–$\frac{1}{2}$ in. long, are aromatic, and the plant is variable itself for there are several forms or varieties available. Its best use is in the rockery or between the stones in a walk where the plants are allowed to grow slowly over rocks and they will not be crowded out by more vigorous-growing plants. Of the varieties, **albus** has white flowers, **coccineus** has bright red flowers; **roseus** has pink flowers; **lanuginosus** has excellent gray-pubescent leaves for which it gets the very good name Woolly Mother-of-thyme.

thracicus   4"   Zone 3   Wooly-stem Thyme
A thyme native to the Balkans, with rose-pink flowers in rounded heads during June; leaves about $\frac{1}{4}$ in. long, opposite, and the stems are white woolly. It is definitely not as low nor as versatile a ground cover as *T. serpyllum* and its many varieties.

vulgaris   ground cover   Zone 5   Common Thyme
A popular low plant for the rock garden or to border walks or to plant between stepping stones in places where weeds and other plants will not encroach on it. This plant is widely valued for its aromatic flowers and foliage, which have been used for flavoring foods since colonial times. A native to southern Europe, its small, lilac to purplish flowers are borne in small upright spikes during late May. The small, evergreen, aromatic leaves are $\frac{1}{2}$ in. long.

TIARELLA (ty-a-RELL-a)

cordifolia   6"–12"   Zone 3   Allegheny Foam-flower
From a perennial root this plant sends up on long, slender, downy petioles the basal leaves, also downy, which are broadly ovate to orbicular, unevenly toothed, 5–7 lobed, either blunt or

Tiarella cordifolia. (Photo by Arnold Arboretum, Jamaica Plain, Mass.)

pointed at the apex, and strongly veined. The white flowers are borne on an unbranched flower stalk, forming a terminal raceme 1–4 in. long. Each flower has a white, 5-lobed calyx and 5 oblong petals, sometimes slightly toothed, and 10 stamens with reddish-yellow anthers. The plant is native to the rich, moist woods throughout much of eastern Canada and the U.S. to the Carolinas and Tenn., extending west to Mich., and blooms from April to July. It is an excellent plant for the shady wild garden with slightly acid soil and may be propagated by division or by seeds sown in late summer. It makes a fine ground cover in partial shade.

TIBOUCHINA (tib-book-KY-na)

urvilleana (*semidecandra*) 10′ **Zone 9**
Brazilian Glorybush
With red flower buds and conspicuous, velvety, purple flowers, 3–5 in. across, each with 5 petals. The interesting evergreen leaves are opposite, 2–4 in. long, have parallel veins and are thickly covered with silky hairs giving a silver sheen. Older leaves turn red before they drop, thus adding to the conspicuous color of this plant. This is a rampant sprawling shrub valued especially for its flaring purple flowers which bloom during summer. Propagated by cuttings.

TICK-CLOVER, CANADA = *Desmodium canadense*

TICKSEED = *Coreopsis grandiflora*

TIDY-TIPS, SHOWY = *Layia platyglossa*

TIGER-FLOWER = *Tigridia pavonia*

TIGER'S-CLAW = *Erythrina variegata orientalis*

TIGER'S-JAW = *Faucaria tigrina*

TIGRIDIA (ty-GRID-ia)

pavonia 1½′ **Zone 6** **Tiger-flower**
A cormous plant from Mexico, valued for its large, colorful, irislike flowers in the summer; colored various shades of yellow, orange and

purple, usually very spotted. They are 3–5 in. across. The corms are often eaten by certain Mexican Indians for their high starch content. Fruit is a capsule. Several varieties are on the market. Culture is similar to that of Gladiolus, for it is tender and the corm must be lifted, dried and stored over winter in all but the warmest parts of the country. Propagation is by division.

TILIA (TIL-ia). This is an important group of shade trees, both as specimens and as street and avenue trees, chiefly of value for their foliage. They are used especially for shearing into tall hedges in formal gardens of Europe, but little of this is seen in America. All lindens have alternate leaves, somewhat heart shaped in outline.

Plantsmen should know that the American species, and most of the Asiatic as well, are not nearly such good tree specimens as are some of the European species. The American trees, like *T. americana*, are too large leaved and hence are coarse in texture when compared with the smaller-leaved European types. Also, the American types (especially *T. americana*) and to some extent the Asiatic types, do not look well in the late summer. Their leaves turn brownish very early. The European lindens, on the other hand, retain their leaves in a good green condition until late autumn and sometimes turn yellow before they drop.

A word should be said about the common Linden, *T. europaea* or *T. vulgaris*. Years ago this was widely planted in Europe and Britain, but it is not so good an ornamental as some of the other species. It should not be recommended. Mature trees are continually throwing up suckers at the base which must be cut off and it seems to be the species most susceptible to severe infestations of plant lice.

Two of the smaller Asiatic lindens (*T. chinensis* and *T. mongolica*) might be tried experimentally because of their smaller heights (45 and 50 ft. respectively). These are rare in America, and are not even needed if larger trees will suffice, or if the slow-growing *T. cordata* would be adaptable for the particular situation.

As for the rest of the recommended types, they vary in habit, some being fastigiate, some narrowly pyramidal but more are densely pyramidal in habit—a form by which a member of this genus can usually be told at great distances.

The flowers are extremely fragrant and are borne in the greatest profusion at the end of June. They are most attractive to bees and honey made from them is excellent.

Wood of the Linden is used for drawing boards or sounding boards on pianos. Many

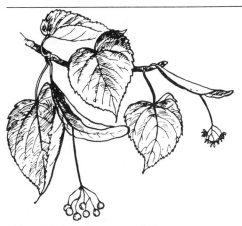

Tilia or Linden—flowers and fruits.

centuries ago, the inner fiber was used for making paper, and even today in parts of Europe the "bast" fibers are used in making mats, coarse cloth and occasionally shoes.

The leaves have been collected (in Europe) and fed (dry or fresh) to cattle. Linden oil distilled from the flowers is used in perfumes. In the past, Americans have planted the native species (*T. americana*, *T. heterophylla*, *T. caroliniana*, *T. floridana*, *T. neglecta* and *T. monticola*), but with the excellent performance of the European species and their hybrids and the long-lasting qualities of their foliage, the native American species have been relegated to the background as far as ornamental purposes are concerned.

Propagation

Seed should be stratified for 5 months at warm temperatures, then 4 months at 40° F., then sown. If they fail to germinate after a few months, give them another 3-month cold treatment.

Budding and especially grafting are commonly practiced commercially, using species as the understocks for their particular varieties. See STRATIFICATION, BUDDING, GRAFTING.

Insect Pests

Linden borer is a serious pest of young trees, often causing the trunk and limbs to break because of large cavities. The olive-green beetles, about ¾ in. long with long antennae and 4 black spots near the center of the wing covers, are active in late summer and fall. Spraying at this time with insecticide #9 gives protection. Mulberry white fly may become abundant on Linden and require sprays of insecticide #15. Linden is also a favorite host of the oyster shell scale. See APPLE and LILAC. Japanese beetle attacks Linden. See JAPANESE BEETLE. Elm span worm and white marked tussock moth worms may become epidemic and require emergency spraying with insecticide #9.

Diseases

Among several leaf diseases, anthracnose is the most destructive. Browning of the leaves inward from the margin is characteristic. Spraying with fungicide #D or #F when buds break and when leaves are about half grown is suggested.

americana   120′   Zone 2   American Linden, Basswood
Native from Canada to Va. and Tex., this is a common tree in the woodlands of the eastern U.S. The alternate leaves are 4–8 in. long and coarse. The small, fragrant flowers are none too conspicuous and appear in late June. During the late summer the leaves turn brown much earlier than those of the European species. Because of this, as well as its large leaves and coarse texture, it is not much used as an ornamental. The variety **'Fastigiata'** has an upright and columnar habit. The sap of the American Linden has been collected and boiled down to make sugar. The fruits and flowers have been ground together to make a paste the taste of which resembles chocolate. The dried flowers have been used as a substitute for tea—indications of the importance of this tree in the lives of the early settlers.

cordata   90′   Zone 3   Littleleaf Linden
The leaves of this European Linden are only 1½–3 in. long, giving the tree an excellent texture. It grows in a tightly pyramidal outline, has a reputation for slow growth, and makes an excellent specimen for street and avenue planting especially in the city. It is usually seen only half as high in cultivation as it is in its native habitat, and without question it is one of the best of this group. Some of the varieties of this species are:

'Greenspire', originating before 1955 (Plant Patent #2086), grows with a straight trunk and radially produced branches; excellent for street tree planting;

'Pyramidalis', with a widely pyramidal habit;

'Handsworth', 1-year twigs are a beautiful, light, yellow-green. Small trees of this are outstanding in the winter;

'Swedish Upright', a narrow form originating in the Arnold Arboretum. A 58-year-old specimen was 35 ft. tall, with a dia. of branch spread of only 12 ft. A narrowly upright tree, growing slowly, with especially short side branches.

x euchlora   60′   Zone 4   Crimean Linden
The leaves of this hybrid (*T. cordata* x *T. dasystyla*) are a bright, glossy green and about 2–4 in. long. The branches are only slightly pendulous. It is one of the best lindens, growing vigorously and making an excellent shade tree. The variety **'Redmond'**, a tightly pyramidal tree good for growing in many situations, has met with much popularity in the Midwest.

x europaea (*T. vulgaris*)   120′   Zone 3
                                         European Linden
A tree no longer recommended for ornamental planting because of its profuse suckering habit, causing considerable work to keep the suckers under control, and also because it seems to be the linden species most susceptible to serious infestations of plant lice. *T. euchlora* should be used instead.

mongolica   30′   Zone 4   Mongolian Linden
The leaves of this Chinese tree are $1\frac{1}{2}$–3 in. long, making it a very graceful tree meriting continued trial in ornamental planting.

petiolaris   75′   Zone 5   Pendent Silver Linden
A beautiful Linden from southeastern Europe and western Asia, this has slightly pendulous branchlets and leaves 2–$4\frac{1}{2}$ in. long on long petioles that make it possible for the leaves to flutter in the slightest breeze. This closely resembles *T. tomentosa* but is more graceful, and the under surface of the leaves is less downy.

platyphyllos   120′   Zone 3   Big-leaf Linden
This has the largest leaves (2–5 in.) of any of the European lindens and so might be considered slightly coarse in texture, though it is a much better ornamental tree than *T. europaea* (*vulgaris*). Varieties:
   'Aurea', with young twigs and branches yellow;
   'Fastigiata', narrowly pyramidal in growth and called the Columnar Bigleaf Linden;
   'Laciniata', a considerably smaller tree than the species with irregularly lobed leaves;
   'Rubra', with young twigs red.

tomentosa   90′   Zone 5   Silver Linden
So named because of the dense white pubescence on the under surface of the leaves that give the whole tree a whitish appearance especially when there is a slight breeze. Possibly not a tree for planting in areas where there is much smoke or dust in the air, since minute particles will adhere to the undersurface of the leaves. In the open, however, it makes an excellent specimen. It is native to southeastern Europe and western Asia.

vulgaris = *T. europaea*

TILIACEAE = The Linden or Jute Family

TILLANDSIA (til-LAND-sia). These are epiphytic bromeliads occasionally used as house plants. They need light, heat and moisture in which to develop properly but can do this wired to a board or rafter in the greenhouse if a little peat is cupped around the roots. With thin, grayish, narrow leaves, there are over 400 species.

fasciculata   18″   Zone 10   Quill-leaf Tillandsia
Gray-green leaves, narrow, stiff, 18 in. long. Flowers blue on a spike 4–6 in. long, appearing from imbricated bracts tinged red. Native to southern Fla. and central America.

lindenii   12″   Zone 10   Linden's Tillandsia
The leaves are in a basal rosette, 12 in. long and $\frac{3}{4}$ in. wide. Bluish-purple flowers are borne in large spikes appearing from carmine-colored bracts on the imbricated flower stalk. Native to Ecuador and Peru.

usneoides   hanging   Zone 8   Spanish-moss
An epiphytic herb seen hanging in the trees of the South, usually where there is plenty of atmospheric moisture, with strands sometimes as much as 20 ft. long. Gray, delicate leaves narrow to 3 in. long; flowers small and yellow. Those with greenhouses in the North sometimes keep it alive and growing from the rafters of the moist greenhouse. Native to the southern U.S. and tropical America.

TIMOTHY = *Phleum pratense*

TI PLANT = *Cordyline terminalis*

TIPUANA (tip-yew-AY-na)

tipu   30′   Zone 10   Common Tiputree
This is a beautiful, South American, evergreen tree, 30–100 ft. tall, with small pinnate leaves, 11–21 leaflets, each $1\frac{1}{2}$ in. long and notched at the tip. The prominent, golden-yellow, butterflylike flowers are produced in large terminal panicles lasting for weeks, and the pod (it is a member of the Pea Family) is winged and $2\frac{1}{2}$ in. long. It is a source of rosewood.

TIPUTREE, COMMON = *Tipuana tipu*

TITHONIA (ty-THO-nia)

rotundifolia   3′–6′   annual   Tithonia
Not a true Sunflower but a member of the Composite Family (as are all the sunflowers), this is a tall-growing, vigorous annual from Mexico valued for its orange-yellow flower heads that are 3 in. across. The leaves are alternate, coarse, 6 in. long and sometimes 3 lobed. There is a variety **'Torch'** which is good because it is only 4 ft. tall. Rather than sunflowers, these flowers remind one of single-flowered dahlias. Because of their vigor and coarseness, they are best used as background plants for summer bloom. Seeds should be started indoors in March in individual pots that are eventually set out in the full sun after frost.

TOADFLAX. See LINARIA.

TOAD-LILY. See TRICYRTIS.

TOADSTOOL. A popular term used for various fungi with umbrellalike structures above ground. As generally used it includes all such fungi, but sometimes only the poisonous ones are meant, the term mushroom being used to include the edible sorts.

TOBACCO. This is *Nicotiana tabacum* and is grown on a commercial scale in parts of Conn., Pa., and from Va. southward. There is even an area in southern Canada where the plants are cultivated. There are of course many varieties, the leaves varying in texture and used for different kinds of tobacco. Since it is a tropical plant, seedlings are started in the greenhouse and set out in areas where the high summer temperatures are conducive to its growing well. Tobacco grown in Conn. is mostly for wrapping cigars—a very fine type of tobacco which is grown under large cloth houses that give partial shade and raise the humidity about the plants so the leaves will develop perfectly. This results in a thinner, smooth, small-veined and larger leaf which is most desirable for wrapping cigars. Ky. grows much pipe tobacco; Va. and the Carolinas specialize in growing cigarette tobacco.

TOBIRA FAMILY = Pittosporaceae

TOLMIEA (TOLL-me-a)

menziesii   2′   Zone 7   Piggy-back Plant
Closely related to *Tiarella* of the eastern U.S., this is native from Alaska to Calif. and makes a perfect house pot plant because of its interesting habit of forming new plantlets in the base of the heart-shaped or lobed leaf blade at the end of the petiole. These can be planted any time and new plants started. The flowers of this differ from those of *Tiarella* in having only 2 or 3 stamens. Those of *Tiarella* have 10 stamens. The small greenish-white flowers are not outstanding but are borne on spikes 8–15 in. long. If grown outdoors it needs moist soil and shade. An excellent house plant requiring little care. This is sometimes called "Mother-of-thousands", a common name which should be kept for *Saxifraga stolonifera*.

TOLPIS (TOL-pis)

barbata   1′   annual
An annual herb from the Mediterranean Region, with lanceolate leaves containing milky juice. The yellow composite flower heads are not over $\frac{1}{2}$ in. wide and are not especially showy if it were not for the threadlike bracts underneath. The flowers appear from midsummer to frost. Seeds can be sown outdoors in the full sun in May and thinned to 6 in. apart.

TOMATO (*Lycopersicum esculentum* var. *commune*). The Tomato is one of the most popular vegetables grown in the United States. It ranks second only to potatoes in economic value. Its fruit is high in food value, vitamins and minerals and is served raw in salads, baked, stewed, fried and made into soup, conserves, pickles, catsup and a variety of sauces.

The Tomato is native to Central and South America. While its culture is ancient it has only reached its present prominence since the mid-19th century.

Types and Varieties

Most authorities recognize 2 distinct species, *L. esculentum* which includes the common, potato-leaved, cherry and pear types and *L. pimpinellifolium* or the Currant Tomato.

Seed companies list a large number of so-called varieties which may vary in days to maturity, habit of growth, shape and color of fruit and disease resistance. Hybrid sorts are becoming most important. Suggested varieties are **'Early Hybrid'**, **'Valiant'**, **'Delicious'**, **'Roma'**, **'Marglobe'**, **'Big Boy'**, plus **'Jubilee'** (orange-yellow fruit) and **'Red Cherry'** as one of the best small fruit sorts used for paste. Check seed catalogues for other sorts of excellent quality. Many other varieties are available that are good to use in various parts of the country.

Climatic Requirements

The Tomato is a warm-season plant, frost tender, and most varieties require at least $3\frac{1}{2}$ months to produce a full crop. A number of factors may affect fruit set such as faulty nutrition, injury from disease or insects and weather conditions. Temperature is very important in that temperatures below 55° F. and above 95° F. reduce fertilization of the flower. A period of rainy or cloudy weather will have a similar effect. Fruit set of the first and second clusters of plants set out fairly early in the spring can be materially increased by the use of chemicals sprayed onto the flowers. These come under a number of trade names such as "Sureset" and are available at most trade outlets, seed houses or garden centers.

Soils and Fertilizers

The Tomato will grow in a variety of soils provided such soils are warm, have a high water-holding capacity, contain a readily available supply of plant food and test a pH of 5.5 to 6.5. In general, the loam soils are preferred. Soil preparation resulting in a deep friable condition is important for the development of a strong root system.

Tomatoes will respond to an application of well-rotted manure if it is available. In most cases, it is advisable to apply 30–40 lbs. of a 5–10–10 fertilizer broadcast per 1000 sq. ft. just prior to planting. This is then supplemented by side dressings of nitrate of soda, 2–3 oz. per plant, at 2–3-week intervals if the plant growth is weak and lacks vigor. Side dressing is applied in fairly wide bands around the plant and then cultivated into the top 2 in. of soil. In many cases an application of ½ cupful of a starter solution (see VEGETABLE GARDEN) applied at the time the plants are set out in the garden is beneficial.

Plant Growing

Under most conditions tomato plants are started in greenhouses or hotbeds some 6–8 weeks prior to planting out-of-doors. Plant seeds in flats or boxes where the temperature is approximately 70° F. Use fine, medium-rich soil (see VEGETABLE GARDEN), sowing seed in drills ¼ in. deep and 2 in. apart. When the seedlings are 2–2½ in. high, replant at 2 in. × 2 in. intervals and allow to grow until 4–5 in. tall. At this stage the plants should again be replanted to a spacing of 4 in. × 4 in. Plant bands, clay or plastic pots, berry baskets or tin cans can be used for this last transplanting. A day temperature of 70°–75° F. and a night temperature of 60°–65° F. is ideal. Apply enough water to maintain a moist soil.

Outdoor Planting

Tomato plants should not be planted outdoors until all danger of frost is past and the soil has become reasonably warm. The spacing will vary because of variety and method of culture. Plants that are not trained or pruned are planted 3 ft. × 3 ft. or 3 ft. × 4 ft. for such varieties as Fireball or Victor and 4 ft. × 4 ft. for the larger plants of the main crop varieties. Where space is a limiting factor it may be advisable to stake or trellis the plants. In each case, all lateral or side shoots are pinched out as they develop so as to restrict the plant to 1 main stem. In staking, a 5–6-ft. stake is driven into the soil 1½–2 ft. next to each plant. As the plant develops the stem is loosely tied to the stake with jute twine, twistems or ordinary strips of cloth. In trellis culture a post is placed at each end of the row. A heavy wire is then stretched from the top and bottom of these posts. Jute twine is tied to the bottom and top wires at each plant and the plant is twirled around the string as it develops. Planting distances for staked and trellised plants are 15–18 in. in the row and rows spaced at 3–4 ft. Self-topping or determinate varieties should not be staked.

Cultivation

Normal shallow cultivation is necessary to control weeds. Mulches of various types are also recommended to control weeds and to conserve moisture. Strawy manure free from weed seeds or marsh hay or black plastic are excellent materials. See MULCH.

Harvesting

Top quality is only obtained if the fruits are left on the vine until they are red-ripe but still firm. In the fall if green tomatoes still remain on the plant at frost time, if they are from ¾ to fully matured in size they can be picked and stored for up to 3–4 weeks at a temperature of 50° F., a fairly high humidity and preferably in the dark. To ripen stored fruit place on the kitchen window sill at a temperature of 70° F. or higher for from 3–5 days.

GRANT B. SNYDER

Insect Pests

Cutworms cut stems of transplants. See CUTWORMS. Flea beetles which eat holes in leaves which permit entrance of disease are controlled by sprays or dusts of insecticide #37 or #9 usually combined with fungicide #E. An application just before transplants are set and 2 or 3 times at weekly intervals is usually necessary. Aphids deform new growth and spread disease. Use insecticide #15. Larger voracious horn worms can be hand-picked or sprayed with insecticide #37 or #4. Tomato fruit worm, which is also the corn ear-worm, eats holes in the fruit. Sprays of insecticide #9 or #4 are suggested. European corn borer, stalk borer and Colorado potato beetle are occasional pests. See POTATO. Red spider mite is controlled with insecticide #34 or #36.

Diseases

Early blight and late blight are most destructive. Early blight starts about the time the first fruits begin to ripen and may cause defoliation. Late blight starts in late summer and infects both fruit and foliage. Sprays or dusts of fungicide #E or #G at weekly intervals are recommended. Shiny dark spots on both green and ripe fruit indicate anthracnose which is checked by the above fungicides. Fusarium wilt causes yellow and dead leaves on the lower part of the plant and decreases the size and quality of the fruit. No fungicides are effective. Grow resistant varieties where fusarium has occurred. Mosaic-infected plants are weak and unproductive. Destroy infected plants as soon as they are observed and control aphids. Blossom-end rot is not caused by disease. It is produced by uneven water supply and acid soil. See ACID SOIL. Apply ground limestone to give pH 6.0–6.5 acidity and mulch to help maintain adequate moisture. Rolling of older leaves especially on staked tomatoes is due to hot sun and excess transpiration. It is not controllable except by temporary shading.

TOMATO, CURRANT = *Lycopersicum pimpinellifolium*

TOMENTOSE. Dense woolly pubescence.

TOMENTUM. Dense covering of matted hairs.

TONGUELEAF = *Glottiphyllum longum*

TOOLS. Little can be said here about the tools one should have in the garden for this depends on the individual, the soil and the extent of gardening activities. Certainly they should be of the best, sturdy and made of durable materials. A fork, spade, rake, several trowels and hoes of different sizes and shapes are essential. A 100-ft. line for making straight rows is good to have. Mechanical tools are available in many sizes and makes, but here the individual is on his own to select the right machine for the jobs he has to do. Rototillers, lawn mowers, etc., all should be inspected carefully, remembering that the more machines one has the more space they take to store and the more time it takes to keep them in proper running condition.

TOON, CHINESE = *Cedrela sinensis*

TOOTHWORT. See DENTARIA.

TOP-DRESSING. This is fertilizer, compost, peat moss, manure or other soil additive applied to the soil surface. The term usually is applied to lawn operations because it is obvious such materials, applied to the grass, can not be cultivated into the soil. However, the term is also used with similar applications to vegetables and flowers but sometimes the wording is "top dressed and then worked into the soil." See LAWNS.

TOPIARY. This is the art of shaping plants, by careful pruning or shearing, into various forms or objects. It is almost a lost art in America, but it was practiced in ancient Rome. Today, there are a few estates which still have topiary objects of interest, but in England one finds more examples of this art than any other place in the modern world. The orientals have their Bonsai (see BONSAI) and this is rapidly increasing in popularity in America, but topiary objects take so much continual care and special pruning that few Americans have the time or wish to spend the money to have others take the time to keep such objects in good condition.

Geometric objects are the easiest to formulate. Pyramids, globes and cones—these and many others dreamed up by imaginative gardeners have been used. The ones causing the most interest are the figures, horses, giraffes, foxes, human figures and their caricatures. Even more elaborate figures have been created such as ships, various objects depicting hunting with horsemen and guns, all in one general group. It is not the easiest thing to clip a plant into the form of a dog so that all of it is in good proportion, and even the caricatures that are attempted must be in good proportion, or the time and effort is wasted. One does have to be somewhat of an artist and sculptor to visualize the right shapes desired, and certainly one needs to know the growth habits of plants to force them into the desired forms.

The plants used for topiary objects vary with the location of the garden. Evergreens are usually best, for the object is there at its best during all times of the year. Deciduous plants like privets have been used, but they do not look well during the winter months when the leaves have dropped. Also, the evergreen privets do grow very fast and require more clipping than do slower-growing evergreens.

Boxwood (*Buxus sempervirens*) is at the top of the list of plant materials used to form topiary objects. Yew comes next, both the Japanese (*Taxus cuspidata*) and the English (*T. baccata*). Since there are many varieties of these 2 species, some flat and prostrate, others tall and columnar, still others wide and spreading, one should give some thought to selecting the right variety which would be most suitable for the object desired. It would be difficult to formulate a peacock from the Columnar Japanese Yew, and the same Columnar Yew would grow too fast to form a small chow dog. On the other hand, a giraffe of sizeable proportions might best be shown if one started with 4 of the Columnar Yew, 1 eventually for each leg, and then, by training and tying branches to a wire form, eventually one might be able to grow the rest of the object. Certainly *T. baccata* 'Repandens' would never grow into a form suitable for a giraffe.

Arborvitae species (*Thuja*) have been used and surely there are enough varieties of these for many different objects. In the South and on the Pacific Coast, Incense Cedar has been used together with Myrtle, Eugenia and Pittosporum. The hemlocks are good subjects but these should be used only in gardens where they have sufficient moisture to grow well. There is nothing so disconcerting as training and shearing a plant for years to get it into the desired shape, only to have an important branch die at the wrong time. Rosemary (*Rosmarinus officinalis*) has long been used for smaller topiary objects.

Large-leaved plants are to be shunned for this purpose, for although they may take the shearing satisfactorily, they may be too coarse in texture to show the figure to good advantage. Small-leaved plants are best, for these can be sheared repeatedly to good advantage.

When object and plant have been selected, then the means by which the shearing is done or the branches tied or staked have to be carefully studied. Many times branches must be tied to a wired frame that has been bent into the desired form. In tying such branches, care should be taken to use tying materials (not wire) that will not cut into the bark and constrict growth or break the branch. Even loosely tied, rubber-coated, electric wire is better than copper wire only, but such ties made should be examined periodically so that they can be loosened before they injure the branches.

Sometimes it may be advisable to mold the entire object out of chicken wire or wire mesh cloth of $\frac{1}{4}$–$\frac{1}{2}$-in. mesh and tie the branches to this model. It is of course essential to have a well-proportioned skeleton frame to start with. Clipping can be done any time except during the fall for, if done then, it might be that tender, young growth would be exposed and be injured during the winter, or that young growth would be forced which would not have sufficient time to mature before winter cold begins.

One suggestion has been made concerning small objects which merits consideration. A small dog, for instance, can be molded out of wire mesh and packed solid with sphagnum moss. This is kept moist all the time and a small clinging vine like a small-leaved variety of *Hedera helix* or *Euonymus fortunei* trained to grow over and around the object. When it is completely covered, then it is clipped and kept clipped.

TORCH-LILY, GALPIN = *Kniphofia galpinii*

TORENIA (to-REN-ia)

fournieri   12″   annual   Blue Torenia
With 2-lipped tubular flowers of pale violet and yellow borne in short racemes, this blooms from late summer until frost. The opposite leaves are 2 in. long, borne on a 4-angled stem. Shade and cool weather suit it best. Since it blooms late it can be used to follow pansies. Also it can be potted and brought indoors for late fall and winter bloom. Native to China.

TORREYA (to-REE-a)

californica   60′   Zone 7   California-nutmeg
Similar to the Japanese *T. nucifera*, this evergreen is native to Calif. and also forms a pyramidal to rounded tree at maturity. The leaves of this native species are $1\frac{1}{2}$–$2\frac{1}{4}$ in. long while those of *T. nucifera* are only $\frac{3}{4}$–$1\frac{1}{4}$ in. long but the leaves of both have a strong aromatic odor when crushed.

nucifera   75′   Zone 5   Japanese Torreya
Very similar to yews in habit and leaf, this is also a native of Japan, the hardiest of the 3 species. The needlelike evergreen leaves are $\frac{3}{4}$–$1\frac{1}{4}$ in. long but the fruits are larger than those of Yew, being $1\frac{1}{4}$ in. long with green, faintly tinged purple flesh covering a large seed. Like the

yews, these species are all dioecious. *T. nucifera* grows into an excellent pyramidal or ovoid evergreen specimen. Propagated by seed which should be stratified for 3 months at 40° F. then sown. Also hardwood cuttings can be rooted.

taxifolia   45′   Zone 8   Stinking-cedar
An evergreen tree, the foliage of which has an objectionable odor when it is crushed. This is a member of the Yew Family, with small, stiffly pointed, yewlike leaves. Like others of this family, the flowers are not ornamental and male and female flowers are on separate plants. The branches are in whorls; the fruits are purple, egg-shaped drupes and about $1\frac{1}{4}$ in. long. Native to Fla.

TOWNSENDIA (town-SEN-dia)

exscapa   2″   Zone 3   Stemless Townsendia
This is a stemless little Daisy belonging to the Composite Family, from the western half of the U.S. The pale gray, linear leaves grow in a tuft 1 in. high, and in late spring the plant bears short-stemmed white daisies 2 in. wide, having narrow, pink, ray flowers which are framed in the foliage. This needs well-drained lime soil and full sun. Native from Alberta to Ariz.

TOYON = *Heteromeles arbutifolia*

TRACHELIUM (tra-KEEL-ium)

caeruleum   3′   Zone 8   Common Throatwort
Sometimes grown as a pot plant in northern greenhouses, or outdoors as an herbaceous perennial in the warm South; this has alternate, toothed and simple leaves about 3 in. long, and large decorative panicles of lavender-blue flowers $\frac{1}{4}$–$\frac{1}{2}$ in. long. Native to southern Europe. Propagated by seeds and cuttings. If the seed is sown in a greenhouse in April, the seedlings will flower out-of-doors in late summer and fall.

TRACHELOSPERMUM (trak-ee-lo-SPERM-um)

asiaticum   twining vine   Zones 7–8   Yellow Star-jasmine
Native to Japan and Korea, this vine has fragrant, yellowish-white flowers from April to July. The evergreen leaves are 3 in. long, and the fragrant flowers have twisted petals somewhat the shape of a pin wheel. The young growth is a ruddy bronze.

jasminoides   twining vine   Zone 9   Chinese Star-jasmine
A Chinese evergreen vine, this also has fragrant white flowers in small clusters, 1 in. across, from April to July. It is a popular, twining, evergreen vine for the far South and should be planted in the moist cool shade. The extreme fragrance of its blossoms is one of its best attributes, but it is also rapid in growth and makes a thick screen. This plant has been

popular for so long in the South that it is sometimes referred to as the Confederate Jasmine.

TRACHYCARPUS (trak-i-KARP-us)

fortunei   15′–35′   Zone 8   Windmill Palm
With fan-shaped leaves 3 ft. or more across, these are considered hardy for palms; some have endured winter temperatures of 10° F. but when grown in extremely hot places they do not make good ornamental specimens. It is widely used as a tub plant and as a street tree. Native to China.

TRACHYMENE (trak-KIM-ee-nee)

coerulea   2′   annual   Blue Laceflower
With compound leaves composed of 3-lobed leaflets; blue summer flowers on long stems in showy umbels up to 3 in. across. Something remindful of a blue Queen Anne's Lace. It makes a fine cut flower. Seeds may be sown outdoors in May, in the cutting garden, and the seedlings thinned to a foot apart. Native to Australia.

TRADESCANTIA (trad-ess-KAN-tia)

fluminensis   prostrate   Zone 8   Wandering Jew
A common, house and greenhouse, prostrate plant, able to grow satisfactorily under the most trying of conditions and well known everywhere; this is a trailing plant frequently used in hanging baskets and window boxes because of its graceful habit. The oval leaves are 2–2½ in. long and pointed at both ends. The white flowers have 3 petals and 3 sepals. One variety (**variegata**) has leaves with white stripes. Easily propagated by cuttings or division. See also ZEBRINA PENDULA. Native to South America but now naturalized at many places in the U.S.

virginiana   1′–3′   Zone 4   Virginia Spiderwort
A plant of the Spiderwort Family and resembling its relative the Dayflower (*Commelina communis*), this is a larger plant with showier flowers. The alternate, grasslike leaves may be 12 in. long, ½–1 in. wide, often channeled down the middle. These sheathe the stem, giving it a jointed appearance. The deep blue, purple or rarely white flowers arise in few-flowered axillary clusters. Each flower, ½–3 in. wide, has 3 small sepals, 3 equal, obovate petals and 6 stamens and each is in bloom for only a few hours, generally in the morning. They bloom successively until all of the buds have flowered. It is a plant of the rich woods of the mideastern and central states but has been cultivated widely in the Northeast, as well. It blooms in July and Aug. Although it has long been in use in northern gardens, it is best used where its straggly foliage will not detract from the general appearance after the plant has bloomed. Propagation may be by self-sown seed, by division of the plant in spring or by cuttings taken in summer.

Several forms of this species are available with white or even pink flowers and some with a dwarf, compact habit. (*x andersoniana*)

TRAGOPOGON (trag-o-PO-gon)

pratensis   3′   Zone 3   Meadow Salsify
A biennial weed naturalized throughout eastern North America but introduced from Europe, with grasslike leaves and golden-yellow flower heads about 2 in. across during June and July. The root and young stems and bases of the lower leaves are also used as a cooked vegetable.

porrifolius   4′   Biennial   Salsify
This tap-rooted biennial has roots a foot long that are edible and taste something like oysters. The leaves are grasslike and the purple flowers are borne in heads 4 in. wide blooming in May and June. It belongs to the Composite Family, with flowers opening in the morning and closing at noon. Native to southern Europe and naturalized in North America. Propagated by seeds sown out-of-doors in the garden. Also see SALSIFY.

TRANSPIRATION. The physiological process by which water is given off by the leaves through the stomata, situated usually in both the lower and upper side of the leaf. Water loss through the stomata is high when temperatures are high and when winds blow across the leaves. Water loss is low when temperatures are low and there is no wind activity. Transpiration can be reduced by shading plants and also by protecting them from high winds.

TRANSPLANTING. Most ornamental garden plants are transplanted at some time in their life history. One should keep in mind several things in undertaking this operation regardless of whether it is seedlings or trees that are being moved:

1. The smaller the plants, the easier the operation and usually the quicker the recovery.

2. The more soil about the roots, the better it is for the plants. For instance, in transplanting tomato plants from the flat to the vegetable garden, the plant that is moved carefully with as much soil as possible about the roots, is the one that quickly recovers. The one from which all soil has been removed about the roots, is the one that immediately wilts and can even die if it is large and is not watered. On the other hand, many woody plants can withstand shipment without soil about their roots, when they are dormant, but most plants can not be transplanted when they are in leaf unless there is an undisturbed mass of soil about the roots, and even then it may be difficult to transplant them without subsequent wilting and possible dying.

3. Roots are living plant parts and must not be allowed to dry out in transplanting. Keep them moist by covering them, or syringing them

and always make the time they are out of the ground as short as possible. Do not allow them to be exposed to sun or wind.

4. In digging, cut as few roots as possible. These supply nourishment and water to the tops, and when some are removed there are not enough roots to supply the top as it was previously growing. When small seedlings an inch or so in height are moved, chances are that most of the roots are dug also. When 18-in. seedlings and trees and shrubs are moved, some of the roots are cut off in the digging operation and this must be compensated for by pinching back (in the case of tall overgrown flower seedlings) or pruning off, in the case of trees and shrubs, a certain amount of top growth.

5. In transplanting trees and shrubs it is a good rule to cut off ⅓ of the linear growth of the plant. This is easy with some shrubs, but one finds it difficult to remove branch growth from the perfectly symmetrical, high-priced evergreen that looks perfectly at home where it has just been planted. Experiments have definitely shown, however, that this rule should be a rigid one and always adhered to in order to assure quick and permanent recovery of the plant concerned. This point can not be stressed enough. The shrub or tree unpruned at transplanting time may look satisfactory at the start but soon starts to languish, showing poor foliage, poor growth and a dead branch or two. It may take years to recover, if it ever does recover. The plant rigidly pruned at transplanting time gets off to a good start because it has sufficient roots to support the amount of growth left on the top. This same rule is also to be followed in transplanting herbaceous perennials, although these are usually transplanted just before or immediately after the dormant period and so the tops are usually cut to the ground in the process. For further details see PLANTING.

TRAPA (TRAY-pa)

natans aquatic Zone 5 Water-chestnut
An aquatic herb from eastern Asia, naturalized in some of the streams of the eastern U.S. The peculiar horned fruits, 2 in. across, are often found floating in some streams and ponds, and are differently shaped from any other nut or fruit found in this country. The fruits have been used to make flour in China, and they are also candied much as a true chestnut. Leaves are opposite; the submerged ones are pinnatifid and the floating ones are clustered, rhombic-orbicular. Small white flowers are borne among the leaves. Propagation is by seeds, but they should not be allowed to dry out if they are to remain viable.

TRAVELER'S JOY = *Clematis vitalba*

TRAVELER'S TREE, MADAGASCAR =

Ravenala madagascariensis

TREE. A woody plant with 1 main stem, and at least 12–15 ft. tall.

TREEBINE. See CISSUS.

TREEBINE, EVERGREEN = *Rhoicissus capensis*

TREE-FILLING. See TREE SURGERY.

TREE HEIGHT, MEASURING. This can be done accurately with tape, string and ladders, but a reasonable approximation can be made in the following simple method:

Take a ruler, walk away from the tree to be measured to a distance where, holding the ruler upright at arm's length, you can sight the top and bottom of the tree at points on the ruler.

Then the distance between top and bottom of the tree is noted in inches on the ruler, also the distance from the eye to the ruler. Also the distance in inches from the spot where the sighting was done to the base of the tree in inches.

Then multiply (in inches) the measurement on the ruler by the distance (in inches) to the base of the tree and divide this by the distance (in inches) from the eye to the ruler. This gives the approximate height of the tree in inches.

TREE-MALLOW = *Lavatera trimestris*

TREE-OF-HEAVEN = *Ailanthus altissima*

TREE RINGS. The living tissue of most plants (the cambium) is immediately under the bark and this is the part of the tree which enlarges. Buds and twig tips have living tissue that increases in length, forms flowers, leaves, fruits etc., but once the twig has elongated the living tissue left in it only increases laterally. This is the reason that a nail or cut in a tree trunk never reaches a different height than that at which it was originally placed.

Growth in trunks then is lateral only, and can be noted in cross-section, when a trunk or limb

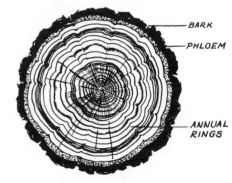

Cross-section of a tree trunk.

is cut, by annual rings, only 1 of which is made each year. These can be counted, when a tree is cut down, and give the accurate age of the tree.

It is interesting to note that these are not all the same size. Near the outside of the trunk they often are close together, indicating that the tree was maturing and manufacturing less and less wood as it grew older. Also, the rings are usually widest apart at the center, indicating that the young seedling grew at first at a very fast rate.

Sometimes a study of tree rings in very old trees shows that in some years with good rains the tree grew fast (wide distances between the rings) and during years of drought they grew very little (with small spaces between the rings). Much has been learned about weather and growing conditions of the past in some areas by studying these tree rings of very old trees.

TREE-TOMATO = *Cyphomandra betacea*

TREES, FASTIGIATE. Frequently one needs to plant a fastigiate tree in the garden for some very special purpose. These may be difficult to find in small, local nurseries, but of the 60 or more being grown in the Arnold Arboretum in Jamaica Plain, Mass. at least 40 of them are available from some nursery in America. Of course it is possible by continual shearing, to make a columnar mass of foliage out of almost any tree, but the older and larger the tree becomes, the more difficult and time-consuming is the task of shearing. It is far better to obtain the normally fastigiate tree, the one that naturally grows with a narrow, upright habit, and there are enough of these to supply any reasonable need.

In the first place, fastigiate trees are used as accents in front of buildings especially where there is little space between the building foundation and the sidewalk. There may well be a limit to the height at which such trees are useful, for in crammed quarters one usually does not need a tree much higher than the building itself.

Then there is the need for placing a narrow, upright, accent point at some place on the home grounds. We seldom use Lombardy poplars now, but they were very much in demand at the turn of the century.

Windbreaks and screens can easily be formed in a narrow strip by the use of fastigiate trees. In fact, this is probably their most popular use. Not all the varieties mentioned in this article will grow as fast as the Lombardy Poplar but such trees do not take up much space on a narrow city lot and can be very important assets, especially for screening purposes.

If the windbreak or screen is needed only up to a certain height, such trees are easily controlled merely by cutting off the tops every year or so. It is not difficult to "top" them and the home owner can easily perform the operation, using a step ladder and pole shears.

Fastigiate trees differ materially in their respective habits and in the way in which they grow over the years. Some, like the maples, will retain their narrow habit throughout their normal life span. Others, such as the narrow varieties of *Malus*, *Cornus* and *Sorbus*, will not. As youthful trees they are excellent, but as columnar specimens, they fail miserably when mature. The simple fact is that as the upright branches grow longer and longer, and the trees bear heavier and heavier crops of fruits, the branches are bent, sometimes almost to the horizontal. There comes a time when these branches will not spring back to the upright position after the fruits have fallen, and so these trees will eventually tend to take on the normal, widespreading habits of the species.

There are at least 6 maples in this narrow

Street tree planting of *Acer plantaoides* 'Globosum'. These are budded or grafted high on the understock to form roundheaded, single-trunked trees. (*Photo by Arnold Arboretum, Jamaica Plain, Mass.*)

group and all of them are good. The narrowest is probably *Acer sacchrum* 'Temple's Upright' which has a single central leader. The 69-year-old tree in the Arnold Arboretum is approximately 75 ft. tall and only 15 ft. in dia. of branch spread. A younger plant propagated from this tree is 40 ft. tall and only 1 ft. in dia.! This is so narrow that it is really a freak and has little ornamental value. The 'Newton Sentry' Maple is slightly wider in branch spread than the 'Temple's Upright', but it has several main upright branches and no main trunk. *A. platanoides* 'Erectum' is another narrow clone, narrower than *A. platanoides* 'Columnare'. The oldest specimen we have of *A. rubrum* 'Columnare' is about the widest of all these narrow maples and is still a narrow tree for its size.

Two of the narrowest of these fastigiate trees are probably *Populus tremula* 'Erecta' and *Koelreuteria paniculata* 'Fastigiata'. The former was brought to America by the Arnold Arboretum in 1939 from the Botanic Garden of Goteborg, Sweden. Now approximately 18 ft. tall, it is only 2 ft. wide, but, being a Poplar, it is undoubtedly susceptible to several disease and insect troubles and thus cannot be counted on for permanence. The same is true of the other fastigiate poplars, which are vigorous growers but which may succumb to an assortment of troubles.

K. paniculata 'Fastigiata' was introduced to America from the Royal Botanic Garden at Kew, England, by the Arnold Arboretum in 1941. Our original tree eventually died, but younger trees show a very narrow habit which, in a climate milder than Boston's might make this tree a respectable addition to the "very narrow" group.

The Sentry Gingko is another excellent tree, columnar to narrowly pyramidal in habit, without any serious insect or disease problems. There appear to be several clones about the country which might be carefully investigated with the idea of selecting the most narrow of the male types. Although a few are being grown, it woud seem advisable to give these more prominence and for the commercial growers to give more information concerning the heights and widths of the original plants from which scions were taken.

The 2 narrow hawthorns are interesting and different. *Crataegus monogyna* 'Stricta' is a slow growing, densely oval mass of twigs and leaves which may be considered to be in this narrow group. *C. phaenopyrum* 'Fastigiatum' on the other hand is faster growing, with several main branches, mostly from the base of the tree. It originated before 1930 in Durand-Eastman Park of Rochester, N.Y., but I think it will eventually be in the group with branches bent down to the horizontal from bearing fruits or from the weight of snow and ice, by the time it reaches maturity.

The upright variety of the European Beech, and its corresponding variety of the English Oak, are really 2 of a kind—excellent upright trees which may grow to a ripe old age and retain their columnar habit. It is interesting to note that, in our experience, at least, 80% of the seedlings of *Quercus robur* 'Fastigiata' will result in trees which have the desirable fastigiate habit.

The columnar forms of the Tulip-tree (*Liriodendron tulipifera*) and the Sargent Cherry (*Prunus sargentii*) are excellent as young trees but, unless they have some corrective pruning along the way, may spread wider and wider as they reach maturity.

All littleleaf European lindens seem to grow better under trying conditions than most other trees. In 1906 Alfred Rehder, of the Arnold Arboretum, sent scions from a narrow tree he observed in Sweden. One of these, now nearly 40 ft. tall, has a dia. of branch spread of 12 ft. Most important is the fact that this tree has a central leader with lateral branches borne at right angles to the trunk and more or less regularly produced. The lower branches become pendulous, dipping gracefully toward the ground. This was named *Tilia cordata* 'Swedish Upright' by the Arnold Arboretum in Sept., 1963, and is an excellent tree, especially for city conditions.

There are several elms, all vigorous growers, among which the columnar clones will retain their columnar habit for many years. 'Augustine' and 'Moline' have been 2 popular favorites among the clones of *Ulmus americana*, and *U. carpinifolia* 'Sarniensis' is an Old World favorite which has performed well wherever it has been used in America.

The *Betula* and *Carpinus* varieties ar- disappointing. As young plants they are excellent, filled with dense foliage on upright branches. branches. But in the varieties with long upright branches originating near the base of the tree, these also tend to grow heavier with age. A young *Betula pendula* 'Fastigiata' was an excellent, tightly columnar specimen for its first 17 years, but then the tips of the branches became so long and heavy with foliage that they began to spread, reaching for the horizontal position and eventually spoiling the outline of the tree.

Cornus florida 'Fastigiata' is another tree in this same category. Young trees of this clone are nicely upright and narrow, with their major branches coming from the base of the tree, but the original specimen in the Arnold Arboretum was as wide as it was tall (25 ft.) when it was 25 years old, and so could not longer be considered fastigiate in habit.

Of the evergreens with columnar habits, the narrowest is probably the upright variety of the Italian Cypress (*Cupressus sempervirens* 'Stricta'). Hardy only from Zone 7 southward, trees of this can be 25 ft. or more in height, but only a few feet in branch spread. This is the tree so popular in formal gardens of the Mediterranean area. The California Incense-cedar is another narrowly pyramidal, almost columnar tree which has been used considerably in West Coast gardens. It is hardier and taller than the Italian Cypress, but is used chiefly on the West Coast or in the East where the climate is mild and the humidity high.

A narrow evergreen which should not be overlooked is *Pinus sylvestris* 'Fastigiata'. Trees of this at least 20 ft. tall are only 4 ft. across at the base, with a narrow pyramidal form tapering to a point at the top. These make truly excellent ornamental specimens and are perfectly hardy in the northern United States. There is a fastigiate form of the White Pine (*P. strobus* 'Fastigiata') which starts out as a columnar tree, but as it matures, the branches spread more and more. Old trees may have branches so widely spreading that they approach the dia. of the species.

There are several varieties of the Lawson False Cypress which are narrow in habit, such as 'Allumii', 'Erecta' and 'Fletcheri'. These will probably not reach the great heights of the species (120 ft.), but are popular garden plants in the areas where they prove hardy. They just barely exist as far north as Boston, Mass., where sometimes, in very severe winters, they are badly injured.

Finally, the junipers and the arborvitaes include several cultivars in this narrow group, but most of the tree types in these 2 genera tend to be narrowly pyramidal in habit. The Irish Yew (*Taxus baccata* 'Stricta') is a wonderful example of an upright tree, but can hardly be termed columnar at maturity. Old plants indeed are upright in growth, but may be as much as one-third as wide as they are high.

The following list of fastigiate trees is of interest because the measurements were made on trees growing in the Arnold Arboretum. It does not include all the narrow trees grown here, although most of those commonly seen in gardens are included in this list. It goes without saying that trees of the same clones might grow larger (or smaller) in other situations. The heights listed are merely estimates, and the column for "Possible Mature Heights" is the listing for the heights of the species given in Alfred Rehder's "Manual of Cultivated Trees and Shrubs." Many of these fastigiate clones would never reach these heights, if for no other reason than that they might break up before attaining them. However, the figures do have some value as an indication of how these trees perform over the years.

(Note: All trees with ages listed are growing currently in the Arnold Arboretum.)

	HEIGHT (EST.)	DIA. OF BRANCH SPREAD	AGE	EST. POSSIBLE MATURE HEIGHT
Acer platanoides 'Columnare'	30'	16'	39	90'
A. platanoides 'Erectum'	35'	19'	34	90'
A. pseudoplatanus 'Erectum'				90'
A. rubrum 'Columnare'	90'	25'	64	120'
A. saccharum 'Newton Sentry'	75'	20'	42	120'
A. saccharum 'Temple's Upright'	75'	15'	69	120'
Betula pendula 'Fastigiata'	32'	10'	20	60'
Carpinus caroliniana 'Pyramidalis'	18'	6'	21	36'
C. betulus 'Columnaris'	30'	12'	30	60'
C. betulus 'Fastigiata'	30'	30'	42	60'
Cercidiphyllum japonicum (one trunk)	40'	15'	18	75'
Cornus florida 'Fastigiata'	25'	25'	25	25'
Crataegus monogyna 'Stricta'	6'	4'	13	30'
C. phaenopyrum 'Fastigiata'	10'	4'	15	30'
Fagus sylvatica 'Fastigiata'	60'	20'	50	90'
Ginkgo biloba 'Fastigiata'	60'	15'		120'
Koelreuteria paniculata 'Fastigiata'	9'	2'	5	50'
Liriodendron tulipiferum 'Fastigiatum'	75'	30'	65	150'
Malus baccata 'Columnaris'	12'	15'	10	50'
M. prunifolia 'Fastigiata'	10'	6'	11	20'
M. robusta 'Erecta'	10'	6'	11	40'
M. 'Van Eseltine'	8'	4'	13	25'
Populus alba 'Pyramidalis'	40'	12'		90'
P. nigra 'Italica'	40'	9'		90'
P. simonii 'Fastigiata'	25'	20'	14	50'
P. tremula 'Erecta'	18'	3'	25	75'
Prunus sargentii 'Columnaris'	15'	10'	29	75'
P. serrulata 'Amanogawa'	15'	4'	15	20'
Quercus robur 'Fastigiata'	25'	10'	33	75'
Robinia pseudoacacia 'Erecta'	18'	12'	13	50'

	HEIGHT (EST.)	DIA. OF BRANCH SPREAD	AGE	EST. POSSIBLE MATURE HEIGHT
Sorbus aucuparia 'Fastigiata'	25′	15′	13	45′
Taxodium ascendens	30′	9′	58	75′
T. distichum	30′	12′	30	150′
Tilia americana 'Fastigiata'	16′	3′	12	120′
T. cordata 'Swedish Upright'	35′	12′	58	90′
T. platyphyllos 'Fastigiata'	7′	3′	10	120′
T. tomentosa 'Erecta'	6′	3′	6	90′
Ulmus americana 'Ascendens'				120′
U. americana 'Augustine'	30′	15′	15	120′
U. americana 'Columnaris'	80′	25′	41	120′
U. americana 'Fiorei'	15′	1½′	6?	120′
U. americana 'Lake City'	80′	30′	33	120′
U. americana 'Moline'	40′	30′	37	120′
U. americana 'Princeton'	40′	30′	29	120′
U. carpinifolia 'Dampieri'	30′	20′	56	90′
U. carpinifolia 'Sarniensis'	75′	25′	61	90′
U. glabra 'Exoniensis'	7′	3′	13	120′
U. procera 'Viminalis'	12′	4′	13	120′
EVERGREEN TREES				
Chamaecyparis lawsoniana	24′	8′	65	120′
C. lawsoniana 'Allumii'	6′	4′	11	120′
C. lawsoniana 'Erecta'	20′	8′	24	120′
C. lawsoniana 'Fletcheri'	12′	6′	—	?
C. obtusa 'Erecta'				120′
Cupressus sempervirens 'Stricta'	25′	3′		75′
Juniperus chinensis 'Columnaris'	8′	4′		60′
J. chinensis 'Mas'	30′	12′	45	60′
J. chinensis 'Pyramidalis'	6′	4′	15	60′
J. virginiana 'Pyramidalis'	30′	10′	62	90′
J. virginiana 'Schottii'	20′	12′	63	90′
Libocedrus decurrens	60′	25′	65	135′
Picea abies 'Columnaris'				150′
Pinus cembra	15′	8′	45	75′
P. strobus 'Fastigiata'	60′	30′	67	100′
P. sylvestris 'Fastigiata'	20′	4′		75′
Pseudotsuga menziesii 'Fastigiata'	6′	3′	12	120′
Taxus baccata 'Stricta'	30′	12′		60′
Thuja occidentalis 'Douglasii Pyramidalis'	9′	6′	12	60′
T. occidentalis 'Fastigiata'				60′
T. plicata 'Fastigiata'				150′
Tsuga canadensis 'Kingsville'	18′	3½′		90′

TREES, HIGHWAY AND STREET PLANT-INGS. Planting the highways of our country has become a very specialized science. Undoubtedly, many who drive along them have personal ideas of how trees should be planted but it is the landscape engineer who has studied such plantings for many years, and he knows the many complex problems involved. He also knows how to properly evaluate them. The more permanent the planting that he can make, the better it is, not only for the taxpayer and the highway but also for the drivers along the highway. When one considers that the magnificent Live Oak of the South will outlast anything along or in any highway that man can build including the roadbeds and the bridges, one can understand that the proper selection of the right trees and the proper placing of them along the highway is an extremely important task.

Experience has shown that it is usually advisable to use trees that are native to the vicinity of the highway because these will merge much better with the surrounding open country. Also, trees with definite shapes like the Blue Spruce and the firs are not advisable in many instances, particularly where they are not native, because they stand out in the landscape and are too conspicuous. People who drive at the fast speeds now allowed on most major highways should not have their attention diverted by specific shapes along the road such as these trees have. Taking this idea a little further, some of the exotic, colorful, flowering and fruiting trees are not assets in many highway plantings because these too are conspicuous especially when they are in flower. They tend to divert the driver's attention from his main objective. It has also been found that vandals will stop along the highway, sometimes at dangerous places, in order to cut or break the branches of flowering or fruiting specimens. This is hard on the trees concerned and also creates a serious hazard along the road.

Trees are no longer spaced regularly along the open highways, as everyone knows. Rather they are placed in informal groups at irregular intervals anywhere from 75 to 300 ft. apart so that if 1 tree dies or must be removed, it does not spoil the continuity of the planting. However, for parkways in the suburbs where the driving may be much slower than on the highways of the open country, there are occasions when the spacing of trees is more or less at regular intervals. It has been found from sad experience that if the trees are close to the highway, accidents occur much more frequently and trees are broken off here and there along the road, materially spoiling the continuity of the regularly planted parkway.

In modern times it is essential to think of the future when planting trees. So many times a road is planned to be a 2-lane or a 4-lane road, then, after a few years, increasing traffic makes it necessary to widen the road. Hence, if trees have been planted very close to the original highway they would all have to be removed when the time came to widen the lanes. As a result, it is best to consider the future widening of highways and plan for that in planting. This of course means that trees are planted at some distance from the highway edge. They should be used to frame pictures in the landscape, to augment what nature has already provided and in some cases to hide objectionable views or objects. The highway engineer knows that sometimes they are used to define the highway from a distance at curves so that the motorist is warned beforehand that he is approaching a curve.

Of course trees along the highway should not be planted underneath existing utility wires or where they create problems with plowing snow. There are many areas along highways which are beautiful if left open, without any tree planting. Distant views of lakes, streams, native woodlands, need not be hidden from view. In fact some of the new toll roads about the country have no funds left for tree planting after the

road is built and if the proper trees and groups of trees have been removed, the resulting picture is one of a normal countryside, unadorned with trees especially brought in. In planting trees, the landscape engineer should indulge all the tricks of his trade in order to prevent monotonous or conspicuous plantings and thus aid the motorist in keeping awake and alert at the wheel.

When it becomes necessary to plant a stretch of highway, the one who is making the selection of trees should have before him the list of those trees native in the area. This does not mean that only these trees should be planted but it does mean that if trees not native to the area are to be selected, they should be such types that will blend in easily and well with those that are native to the area and are seen in large numbers along the highway. Sturdy, wooded, long-lived trees which have a low maintenance cost should be selected. Those trees that are known to be disease-resistant and insect-free should have the best chance of growing in the area and take the least amount of care after they have once become established. Future maintenance costs should definitely be kept in mind at the time of planting. It is folly to plant a highway with disease-prone trees which will need constant spraying and care if they are to grow. Most of the cherry trees and other members of the *Prunus* genus are in this class and such should be omitted chiefly because they are so susceptible to attacks from various insects and disease pests. If they are not cared for, it is not long before they become most unsightly along any highway.

Nut trees certainly should not be used in highway planting, for their fruits create hazards and the same thing can be said with a number of the trees that we think of as good ornamentals—as an example, the oriental crab apples. These are outstanding in the spring when they flower but their fruits can create hazards as they fall on the highway and even when the plants are in flower they are so colorful and so conspicuous that they can be a hazard to drivers. These have been used to line many an urban parkway but in such instances the speeds of driving are slower and the type of planting verges on park planting rather than highway planting.

Street Tree Planting

The average home owner knows much more about the street trees planted in his town or city for he is close enough to them to examine them from season to season. In many a suburban town there is a committee of laymen, appointed or elected to be responsible for overseeing the planting and care of the town's trees. There are many excellent trees which grow well in the suburbs, but selecting trees for the built-up urban areas is most difficult because the growing conditions are extremely difficult. There is not enough room for proper root development, and in many situations there is not enough open soil area about the base of the tree for the roots to absorb sufficient air and moisture. Most difficult are the poisonous gases prevalent as a result of automobile exhausts and the numerous chimney exhausts of gas, smoke and dirt.

Although designers of large buildings frequently include trees in the final building plan as a living source of beauty to help set off the architectural features of the building, the roots of such trees often have to cope with heating pipes—even in midwinter—and cramped growing space that makes even mere existence extremely difficult.

The absolute minimum of an open soil area about the trunk at the base of the tree is a square 8 ft. on a side and 12 ft. would be much better. Sometimes pedestrian traffic over such an area is so great that when the soil is wet it is stamped down to such an extent that when it dries out it is almost like concrete. In such situations, iron gratings can be put over the soil to prevent this heavy pounding when it is wet. Suffice it to say, however, that only the most sturdy and pest-resistant types of trees should be selected for planting in the centers of our larger cities.

Planting trees along suburban streets is much easier for there are many more trees from which to select. However, space is still often at a premium. In the horse and buggy days, street trees were often planted abutting the curbstone but with automotive transportation what it is today, much more room must be given drivers to travel these streets, for a skidding accident can be serious not only to the traffic but also to the trees themselves. Many trees fail to recover from such accidents if the bark has been stripped more than halfway around the trunk.

Ideally, the street tree planting of a suburban area should be planned when the entire area is laid out for subdivision lots. There should be a strip of ground between the sidewalk and the property line on which trees are planted and it should be a minimum of 7 to 8 ft. wide or even wider. There might also be an open strip of grass between the sidewalk and the curbstone in which no trees are planted. There are problems caused by such a planting but it does allow for normal development of good trees. It places the trees away from the electric service lines, pipes and sewers that are frequently placed at the edge of the street paving. It is a decided advantage to have trees as far away from such pipes as possible for, when such areas are opened up, the tree roots are always in the way and are usually mercilessly cut. The property owner can take care of this grass strip and the town can be responsible for the care of the trees that are planted in it but it does create a definite situation for cooperation between the town and the private property owner. It is a good system however to keep in mind when new areas are being laid out for streets and building lots.

Another arrangement has been worked out in older suburban areas where houses have been set back considerably from the street but where the private property line abuts the curb. In such areas the town plants the trees on private property well back from the curb area. This, of course, creates several obvious complications. It would require special town ordinances governing the care and removal of such trees. It would also require the major cooperation and enthusiasm of the original property owners along a certain street. Once the system is agreed upon and approved, it is seldom that purchasers of such property already planted with street trees would seriously object.

It is obvious that such planting has many good points also, especially from the standpoint of the health of the trees. They are situated in good, open soil, away from the hazards of traffic; their major roots would be away from the destructive ditchdigging operations frequently encountered and the property owners as a rule would take pride in their general good health. It is of course an ideal plan for which many towns would like to strive and it is of note that some towns already have such plants and they seem to be working satisfactorily.

Of course there are many areas where neither one of these tree planting plans could prove satisfactory and trees must be planted between the sidewalk and the curb. If such is the case, no tree should ever be planted closer than $3\frac{1}{2}$ ft. from the curb and the farther away it is, the better off both to passing traffic and to the survival of the tree. The ideal width of this strip of grass between the street curb and the sidewalk would be about 12 ft. and the tree would not be centered in it but would be planted closer to the sidewalk than it would to the curb.

The distance apart that street trees should be planted of course depends upon the species and variety. They should not be planted exactly opposite each other on either side of the street but rather they should be alternated as this will give more room, light and air for proper growth. Usually they should be planted at least 75 ft. apart except in rare instances where small tree species have been decided upon. Planting closer together for an immediate display only creates costly care later and often requires the removal of some trees later. It is much better to plant fewer trees at the beginning of a street tree planting program and take care of them properly, than to plant a large number and then have to take care of them at cut-rate prices.

The size of the tree at planting time is important and, in general, one should keep in mind that the smaller the tree, the easier it is to transplant and the quicker it will start into vigorous growth. Trees that are 12 to 15 ft. tall and 3–4 in. in trunk dia. are frequently used in planting streets but it is a well-known fact that those which are planted 7 to 8 ft. tall get off to a quicker start and within a few years will overtake the taller trees in growth. Also, when smaller trees are used at the start, it is possible to spend more money on obtaining the right kind of soil or mulching material for each plant and also to spend the time necessary to water the trees well after they have been planted. No street tree planting should be started without complete plans for watering the trees the first few years. A recent street tree planting in a large city started off with much fanfare in the local newspapers and over $50,000 was spent in buying and planting trees. However, heavy droughts came during the first year, no money was available for watering the trees and, as a result, the effort was almost a complete failure. No planting program should be initiated unless full care in mulching, fertilizing, and watering can be given the trees the first few years.

Should all the tree species or varieties on 1 street be the same? This is a troublesome question to be solved by local groups in their own ways but there are advantages in having several different kinds of trees planted along 1 street. In the first case, we have all learned that streets lined with 1 species like the American Elm can be seriously hurt when a specific disease strikes that 1 tree. With several different species of trees along the street there always will be a few in good condition even though

disease may strike 1 of the species. Also with a varied planting, interest is increased. Some might be chosen for their bloom or for their interesting autumn color and this makes a planting in front of suburban homes most interesting.

Such an informal planting has merit in that 1 or 2 trees can be missing without seriously breaking the continuity, as it would if there were a formal planting of all 1 species. Because of the different habits of the trees, replacements are easier to make. In the uniform, single-species type of planting, replacements should be of the same species of similar size, not always possible to do.

There are some towns which have a policy of planting certain small streets with 1 species only. The street tree commissioners might decide what this should be, or hold a meeting of property holders on that street and have a majority vote for the variety wanted. In this way, valued cooperation is obtained with the property holders who should have an interest in the planting. One group might select oriental crab apples, another group might select the Little-leaf Linden (*Tilia cordata*) and still another the Sargent Cherry (*Prunus sargentii*). Short suburban streets lined with such ornamental trees would have considerable interest at different times of year. An intelligent, street-tree commission with certain standard policies and a willingness to help property holders with tree selections could easily mold an interesting over-all tree planting program in the town that could make the town beautiful at all times of year.

The following suggested small trees, might be used along small suburban streets. For other suggestions, especially for wider streets, see "Trees for American Gardens" by Donald Wyman, published by the Macmillan Company, 1965.

SCIENTIFIC NAME	HEIGHT (IN FT.)	ZONE	COMMON NAME
Acer argutum	35	5	
A. buergerianum	20	6	Trident Maple
A. campestre	25	5–6	Hedge Maple
A. capillipes	30	5	
A. carpinifolium	30	5	Hornbeam Maple
A. ginnala	20	2	Amur Maple
A. glabrum	24	5	Rocky Mountain Maple
A. monspessulanum	25	5	Montpelier Maple
A. nikoense	25	5	Nikko Maple
A. platanoides 'Globosum'	20	3	
A. saccharum 'Globosum'	20	3	
A. tataricum	30	4	Tatarian Maple
A. tschonoskii	20	5	Tschonoski Maple
Carpinus betulus 'Globosa'	25	5	Globe European Hornbeam

SCIENTIFIC NAME	HEIGHT (IN FT.)	ZONE	COMMON NAME
C. caroliniana	35	2	American Hornbeam
C. japonica	45	4	Japanese Hornbeam
C. orientalis	25	5	Oriental Hornbeam
Chionanthus virginicus	30	4	Fringetree
Cornus florida	40	4	Flowering Dogwood
C. kousa	20	5	Japanese Dogwood
C. mas	24	4	Cornelian Cherry
Crataegus arnoldiana	30	4	Arnold Hawthorn
C. coccinioides	20	5	Kansas Hawthorn
C. crus-galli	35	4	Cockspur Thorn
C. lavallei	20	4	Lavalle Hawthorn
C. mollis	30	4	Downy Hawthorn
C. monogyna	30	4	Single-seed Hawthorn
C. monogyna inermis	20	4	Thornless Single-seed Hawthorn
C. monogyna 'Stricta'	20	4	
C. nitida	30	4	Glossy Hawthorn
C. phaenopyrum	30	4	Washington Hawthorn
C. pruinosa	20	4	Frosted Hawthorn
C. succulenta	15	3	Fleshy Hawthorn
C. 'Toba'	15	3	
Evodia daniellii	35	5	Korean Evodia
Fraxinus holotricha	35	5	
F. mariesii	24	7	Maries' Ash
F. uhdei	30	9	Shamel Ash
F. velutina glabra	20–45	7	Modesto Ash
Halesia carolina	30	5	Carolina Silverbell
Koelreuteria paniculata	30	5	Golden-rain Tree
Ligustrum lucidum	30	7	Glossy Privet
Malus baccata 'Columnaris'	40	2	
M. halliana parkmannii	15	5	Parkman Crab Apple
M. hupehensis	24	4	Tea Crab Apple
M. 'Marshall Oyama'	25	5	
M. 'Radiant'	30	4	
M. scheideckeri	20	4	Scheidecker Crab Apple
M. 'Van Eseltine'	20	4	
M. zumi calocarpa	25	5	Redbud Crab Apple
Maytenus boaria	35	9	Chile Mayten Tree
Prunus serrulata 'Kwanzan'	20	5	
Pyrus calleryana 'Bradford'	30	4	
Quercus libani	30	5	Lebanon Oak
Q. phellos	50	5	Willow Oak
Robinia x 'Idaho'	40	3–4	
Styrax japonicus	30	5	Japanese Snowbell
Syringa reticulata	30	4	Japanese Tree Lilac
Viburnum prunifolium	15	3	Blackhaw
V. rufidulum	30	5	Southern Blackhaw
V. sieboldii	30	4	Siebold Viburnum

TREES, STATE. See STATE TREES.

TREE SURGERY. Occasionally trees need some attention to keep them in a sturdy growing condition. Pruning (see PRUNING) is a means whereby limbs are removed for one reason or another but sometimes a tree needs more than the removal of a few limbs. A weak crotch may be spotted that needs bracing; a frost crack may show or a split may have developed which is badly in need of screw bolts to keep it from getting progressively worse. A cavity may have a great deal of rotten wood in it, or a girdling root may actually be choking the tree to death. These problems are a few which need attention when they are spotted, and come under the general heading of "Tree Surgery," for lack of a better name.

Weak crotches do exist on trees and where

they have not been properly cared for (by pruning off part) it may be necessary to strengthen the crotch either with steel screws, rods or cables, depending on the size and weight of the limbs concerned. Special galvanized screw bolts and rods can be purchased for this purpose. If there is little tension on the crotch and the limbs are small, a simple screw bolt is sufficient. They are available in different sizes. A hole is bored through the first limb, large enough to permit the screw and in the second limb slightly smaller so the screw can take effect. Care should be taken to make the hole such that the end of the screw will be about 1 in. under the bark. The outside hole is countersunk so the screw head will be flush with the bark. When it is screwed tightly in place it is daubed with asphaltum paint to prevent the entry of disease spores.

For larger branches, bolts are used with a head at one end and a diamond washer and nut at the other, both ends countersunk so that when they are screwed tightly together and the unused end of the bolt beyond the nut is sawed off flush with the bark, the cambium tissue will have an opportunity to grow over the ends and cover them. Both ends are coated with an asphalt paint to finish the job properly.

One should not apply too much pressure to screwing on the final nut, for it is only necessary to give additional strength to such a crotch, not to be the sole means by which the crotch is held together.

Long rods can be used for the purpose, up to 3–4 ft. long. These would have countersunk holes in the limbs at both ends of the rod for diamond-shaped washers and nuts. The asphaltum painting of the rods and the cutting of one end flush with the trunk would be done in the same manner as with the screw. Here, also, one should remember that branches must be allowed to sway in the wind somewhat; they should not be held rigid. Screwing such rods too tightly, i.e., by taking too much weight on the rod itself, can result in limb breakage.

For distances over 5 ft. long galvanized steel cables are used. Eye bolts are attached to the limbs and the cables securely attached. A $\frac{1}{4}$-in. cable is deemed sufficient for limbs up to 6 in. through, while a $\frac{5}{16}$-in. cable is strong enough for limbs 10 in. through. The placement of such cables should be such that they do not rub either limbs or other cables. They should not be pulled too tightly but should allow some leeway for the limbs to sway in the wind. These also should be painted, preferably with asphaltum paint, and since limbs do grow, the cables should be inspected every few years, slack taken up if necessary and painted to prevent rust. In much of the work with strengthening crotches,

the limbs in question are pulled together slightly with rope, block and tackle, so that the weight of the limbs is temporarily taken from the places where the screws, rods or cables are being placed.

Splits occur in trunks as the result of lightning and wind storms, as well as by the action of winter cold in the form of frost cracks (which see). These splits in the trunk should certainly be painted with an antiseptic asphaltum tree paint as soon as they are noted. They may occur for quite some distance up and down the trunk. Screw bolts are usually used to repair them, applied in the same way as for crotches.

The objective here is to hold the 2 edges of the trunk tightly together, thus allowing the cambium tissue ample opportunity to form new growth to repair the split. The screws might be 1 ft. apart, alternating from the right side and from the left side throughout the length of the split. Rods can be used with nuts at both ends, but screws are better and make a neater-looking job where they can be used.

Cavities are also problems. Usually this is a job for professionals. If the cavity is too large and the tree is severely weakened, the chances are it should be removed, for cleaning cavities properly is a very expensive process. If the cavity is to be cleaned the main objective is to clean out, with chisel or gouge, all the dead, rotten and diseased wood, and then to paint the wood remaining with an antiseptic tree paint. It is most advisable, in cutting out the rotten wood, to leave the cavity in such a way that water will drain out. This is usually done in the form of a small trough or drain pipe sticking out 6 in. beyond the side of the trunk so the drip will not stain the trunk itself. So often this drain material from wounds contains sugary tree sap, and if it drips down on the trunk, many disease spores grow in it and insects are attracted to it carrying more disease spores. It should not be allowed to occur, and the proper placing of a drain is the way to prevent this happening. Standing water in a tree trunk is the quickest possible way of encouraging further disease and rot.

Years ago, cavities were filled with wood, rubber or cement. Now the tendency is to leave them open since the filling is no insurance that disease will not continue to rot away the inner wood, and filling seldom strengthens the tree. It may be advisable to place rods through the trunk to strengthen it at the place of the cavity. Filling of course makes the trunk look better, and if the opening is not too large, provides a base over which cambium tissue can make succeeding layers of tissue which eventually might cover the opening over a period of years.

Cavities are the result of improper pruning

and improper care. They should not be allowed to happen in the first place. They will not if the following things are done:

1. Remove all dead and broken limbs as soon as they appear.
2. Make all pruning cuts in a clean manner, flush with the trunk. See PRUNING.
3. Leave no short stubs.
4. Paint all wounds over 1 in. dia. with an antiseptic tree paint, preferably an asphaltum paint.
5. Inspect painted wounds annually and repaint when necessary.
6. Properly clean and paint all injuries to the bark as soon as they occur. See PRUNING.

Girdling roots frequently cause serious injury, if not death, to certain trees that apparently are in good health. This results from roots being jammed in a hole at planting time, or in a pot so that they are twisted around each other or the main trunk. Both the trunk and the roots expand or become wider in dia. as they grow. If a long root has been wrapped around the basal part of the trunk at planting time, it increases in size, as does the trunk, until the time comes when it is actually restricting (by choking) the upward and downward movements of nutrients in the trunk. It can do this as effectively as a tight wire about the trunk.

To prevent this, lay out properly all the roots in an ample hole at planting time. If a root does girdle, cut it off, cleanly as one would a branch, and paint the wound. When a girdling root is suspected, carefully pull away the soil at the base of the trunk to inspect the general way in which the main roots grow away from the trunk. When the root is found, merely cut it, paint the wound and replace the soil.

For further information on pruning or tree surgery, see Christopher, Everett P. "The Pruning Manual," The Macmillan Company, 1954.

TREE WOUND PAINT. See PRUNING. An asphaltum tree paint for covering fresh wounds on trees is best. This is lasting, is black, and does not injure the living cambium tissue. Creosote should never be used as it is most harmful to living tissue. Actually, white or red lead paints are not injurious to the growing cells but both these are too conspicuous for general use. T. H. Everett of the New York Botanical Garden has recommended the following mixture which is most suitable and can be mixed at home.

Mix a small amount ($\frac{1}{2}$ cup) of white lead with an equal amount of powdered sulfur and add enough lamp black to make the mixture black. Stir in enough linseed oil so the mixture has the consistency of paint, and then merely paint this on the tree wounds with a paint brush. The results are truly excellent.

Other paints are frequently found available at the garden centers in pressure cans. Most of these are perfectly satisfactory and make the paint very easy to apply. Tree wounds or cut branch ends over $\frac{1}{2}''$ wide should be painted in order to prevent disease infection.

TREFOIL, BIRD-FOOT = *Lotus corniculatus*

TRELLIS. See GARDEN FIXTURES.

TREVESIA (trev-EE-sia)

palmata 20′ Zone 10 Himalayan Trevesia
A tropical evergreen shrub, with variable, palmately 5–9-lobed leaves, thin, leathery, glossy green but covered with silvery dots, especially in young leaves. Native to China.

TRICHOCEREUS (tri-co-CEER-eus)

pachanoi 18′ Zone 10
A branched cactus native to Ecuador, with 6–8 ribs; few spines; white flowers that are reddish brown outside, 10 in. long, night blooming and very fragrant. For culture see CACTI AND SUCCULENTS.

spachianus 3′ Zone 9 White Torch Cactus
A branched cactus with nocturnal, funnelform, fragrant, white flowers about 8 in. long. Upright and usually branching at the base, it bears branches parallel to the main stem. The branches have 10–15 ribs and 8–10 spines in each cluster. Native to Argentina. For culture see CACTI AND SUCCULENTS.

TRICHODIADEMA (tric-o-dia-DEM-a)

densum 3″ Zone 10
Closely allied to *Mesembryanthemum*, these are small succulents from South Africa, with cylindrical-shaped leaves, $\frac{3}{4}$ in. long and $\frac{1}{8}$ in. thick, tipped with long white hairs; solitary, short-stalked, violet-red flowers 2 in. across, that are daisylike in general outline. Often used as a good house plant. For culture see CACTI AND SUCCULENTS.

TRICHOLAENA ROSEA = *Rhynchelytrum repens*

TRICHOPILIA (try-ko-PILL-ia). This genus contains 25 species of beautiful epiphytic orchids, native to the warmer parts of America. One which is offered commercially, **T. torilis,** has twisted yellowish flowers about $2\frac{1}{2}$ in. long, sometimes creamy white spotted with pale rose. It blooms in the greenhouse Feb.–June and from Sept.–Dec. For culture and propagation see ORCHID.

TRICHOSANTHES (try-ko-SAN-thees)

anguina climbing annual Edible Snake Gourd
A climbing annual with tendrils; member of the Gourd Family; monoecious, with triangular to ovate, alternate leaves about 9 in. wide, sometimes with 3 shallow lobes. The pistillate flowers are white and single; the staminate are usually in short racemes. The fruit is a long, often

twisted, cylindrical gourd 1–6 ft. long. In India, where it is native, the fruits are eaten but in America they are usually grown as ornamentals. The vine should be supported on a trellis to yield the best fruit. This needs a very long, hot, growing season to mature properly and gardens in the North do not have just these conditions.

TRICHOSTEMA (try-ko-STEE-ma)
  dichotomum 6″–20″ annual Forked Blue-curls
A small, slender, erect and much-branching annual with minutely pubescent stems and opposite, narrowly lanceolate leaves 1–3 in. long, becoming smaller as they ascend the stem. The small, blue, pinkish, or rarely white, flowers are borne in few-flowered, spreading clusters at the tips of the branches. Each has an irregular calyx with 5 lobes, the 3 upper ones longer and more united. The corolla is 2-lipped, with curving blue stamens protruding from the upper lip and extending well beyond the corolla. The lower lip is declined, with a whitish, spotted throat. In the autumn after the leaves have fallen, the stems turn a deep red. The plant may cover large areas of sandy fields or roadsides from Ontario to Fla., west to Tex. and Mo., and blooms from July to Oct.

TRICYRTIS (try-SER-tis). Perennial herbs with short spreading rootstocks, belonging to the Lily Family; with alternate leaves and small lilylike flowers, either in clusters or singly in the axils of the leaves. Flowers wide but funnel shaped, spotted and colored yellow, white or purplish. Seldom used as garden plants in the North but occasionally as greenhouse potted plants. Easily propagated by division. They should not be left out-of-doors over winter in the North. Otherwise the culture is similar to that for lilies. The roots may be gradually dried in the fall and stored over winter.
  flava 1′ Zones 7–8 (?) Yellow Toad-lily
Flowers yellow in racemes, not spotted. Native to Japan.
  hirta 3′ Zone 5 Hairy Toad-lily
Leaves to 6 in. long, hairy; flowers whitish, spotted with purple and black, 1 in. long, 6–15 together in leaf axils. Native to Japan. Blooms in late Sept. or Oct.
  macropoda 3′ Zone 5 Speckled Toad-lily
Leaves 5 in. long; flowers pale purple, ¾ in. long, in terminal clusters. Native to China and Japan. Blooms in June and July.

TRIENTALIS (try-en-TAY-lis)
  borealis 6″–9″ Zone 3 American Starflower
A dainty perennial herb with a creeping underground stolon which sends up an erect, slender unbranched stem bearing a whorl of 5–9 narrowly lanceolate leaves. The 1–2 flowers, generally white but occasionally pink, arise on hairlike stalks from the center of the whorl of leaves. Each flower has a calyx of 5–9 sepals, 5–9 widespreading, ovate petals and 5–9 stamens. The plant is widely distributed in the moist, acid woodlands of the northeastern U.S. and southeastern Canada and blooms from May to Aug. Although it cannot withstand the strong midday sun, the plant is ideal for the shady wild garden and may be propagated by seed sown, when ripe, on loose, moist leaf mold. Where plentiful, the plants may be divided and transplanted.

TRIFOLIUM (try-FO-lium). A large genus of the Pea Family having species throughout the temperate regions of the world and valuable as forage plants, bee plants and as green manure when plowed into the soil. Seeds of certain species also occur in lawn seed. The compound leaves generally have 3 rounded, stalkless leaflets and dense, rounded or oval flower heads, consisting of tiny, pink, white or yellow flowers which are pealike in structure, although somewhat elongated. Propagation is by seed.
  agrarium 2′–3′ annual Yellow Clover
A European annual which has become a naturalized wild plant over much of southeastern Canda and the U.S. It is distinguished by its sparsely branching habit and the oval, yellow flower heads of rather crisp flowers. It blooms throughout the summer.
  arvense 10″–12″ annual Rabbit's-foot Clover
This rather small and delicate annual species has a branched, hairy stem and an oval flower head which appears grayish in color because of the silky calyx which extends beyond the corolla of each flower. It can survive in dry, sunny, sandy soil where few other plants could live.
  hybridum 2′ Zone 3 Alsike Clover
A perennial Clover with pink flowers in globular heads. Native to Europe and naturalized in the U.S. An important fodder plant and one often used for soil improvement.
  incarnatum 3′ annual Crimson Clover
With bright red flowers ½ in. long from May to July. Native to Europe but occasionally escaped to roadsides in New England.
  pratense 2′–3′ Zone 3 Red Clover
A European biennial or perennial species with a branched stem considerably stouter than that of *T. hybridum*. The compound leaf has a white marking midway of the 3 leaflets and the bracts at the bases of the leaf stems and flower stalks are larger. The deep pink, globular flower heads are somewhat hairy, due to the calyx hairs which extend beyond the corolla. It grows over much of North America and blooms throughout the summer. It is not generally cultivated because of its rather straggly growth habit.
  repens Creeping Zone 3 White Clover
This is the native (or European) creeping Clover

so often used in lawn seed mixtures, but it can become a difficult weed in gardens because it adheres so closely to the soil and roots all along its creeping stems. The leaves are trifoliate, like all clovers, and are long stalked. The flowers are white and very fragrant, and the plants form dense mats of growth. This plant is claimed to be the true "shamrock" of Ireland. The var. **purpureum** usually has 4 leaflets that are a purplish color and it makes a most interesting rock garden plant, especially if it is planted at the edge of the rockery where visitors can easily see that it has 4 leaflets. For control or eradication see WEED-CONTROLLING CHEMICALS.

TRIGONELLA (try-go-NELL-a)

foenum-graecum 2′ annual Fenugreek
An herb, native to the south of France, blooming from June to Aug. with small white flowers. This has 3-foliate alternate leaves. It was once used in medicine. The ground seeds have a maple flavor and are sometimes used in confectionery. The fruits look like elongated string beans, but the plant is of little value ornamentally.

TRILISA (TRIL-i-sa)

odoratissima 3′ Zone 8 Carolina-vanilla
A perennial herb; alternate leaves entire or toothed up to 10 in. long, giving an odor of vanilla when bruised. Native from N.Car. to Fla. Belonging to the Composite Family, the flowers are rose-purple in the autumn. A good plant for the flower border and propagated by seeds or division in spring.

TRILLIUM (TRILL-ium). A genus of the Lily Family with some 30 species in North America and Asia. The plants have thick rootstalks and fleshy stems enclosed at the base with sheathing leaves. A whorl of 3 ovate leaves crown the stem and from the center of this leaf-cluster the white, pink or greenish flowers arise. Each flower has a calyx of 3 sepals and 3 spreading petals arranged alternately. Stamens number 6. Fruit is a 3-celled berry. Propagation is by seeds. Best grown in good rich soil and partial shade. Excellent wild flowers for the wooded areas.

cernuum 6″–18″ Zone 3 Nodding Wake-robin, Nodding Trillium
This species, with pale green leaves and nodding, single, fragrant, white or pinkish flowers 1 in. wide, has leaves with a wavy margin and somewhat recurved. The fruit is a deep reddish-purple berry. The plant is native to the rich, peaty soils from Newfoundland to Wisc., but extends south to Pa. and blooms in June. It may be propagated by seed, which may be cleaned and sown when ripe, or by division of the root in late fall.

erectum 10″–12″ Zone 4 Purple Trillium
This rather common Trillium has large leaves,

5–7 in. long, and solitary, arching flowers, each having 3 brownish sepals equal in length to the 3 deep red petals, 6 stamens, a 3-angled pistil and an unpleasant odor. The fruit is an oval red berry. It is native to moist woods of the eastern U.S. and blooms in spring. Occasionally this plant has yellow or white flowers which do not have a disagreeable odor. Propagation is generally by division, since the species is rather plentiful, but seedlings may be transplanted or seeds may be sown as for *T. cernuum.*

grandiflorum 12″–14″ Zone 4 Snow Trillium
One of the handsomest of the trilliums, this species has more rounded, sessile leaves, narrowly pointed, and solitary white flowers, becoming a faint pink as the flower ages. The calyx of 3 short, green sepals is alternate to the corolla of 3 wide petals which overlap at the base. The fruit is a blue-black berry. The plant frequents the moist, rich woods and shady ravines throughout eastern and northern U.S. and blooms from April to June. It is an excellent plant for the wild garden and it may be transplanted from wild clumps or the cleaned seed may be sown as soon as ripe. **plenum**—rare doubled flowered form.

nivale 4″–5″ Zone 6 Dwarf Trillium
This tiny species has oblong, rather blunt-pointed, sessile leaves, a pale green, cuplike calyx of 3 sepals and 3 oblong, white petals with a blunt apex. It is among the first of the spring flowers, appearing sometimes in March in the woods from Pa. to Ky. west to Minn. It is an excellent species for the rock garden and may be propagated as for *T. cernuum.*

ovatum 1½′ Zone 8 Pacific Trillium
A white-flowered perennial with the flowers 2 in. wide fading to rose, native to the Pacific Coast from British Columbia to Calif. There are 3 leaves in a whorl, each about 6 in. long on the top of a stem.

recurvatum 12″ Zone 5 Prairie Trillium
A thick stem supports the 3 widely ovate leaves of this species and rather dwarfs the solitary, stalkless flower. The 3 narrowly lanceolate sepals are strongly reflexed and the 3 strongly keeled, narrowly ovate, deep red petals are held erect in the center of the whorl of leaves. The plant is native to the Plains States and blooms in the spring.

sessile 1′ Zone 6 Toad Trillium
Although not beautiful, this species is interesting because of the mottled, brown, sessile leaves and dark red or yellow flowers which are held erect. It is a plant of the moist, neutral or slightly acid woods of Pa., extending southwest to Mo. and Ark. It is easily transplanted to the shady wild garden and is best moved when dormant.

undulatum 16″–18″ Zone 3 Painted Trillium
One of the most beautiful of the North Ameri-

can species, this Trillium has tall, reddish stems and dark green, lanceolate leaves with wavy margins and short petioles. The solitary flowers, rising on a stalk ½–1 in. long, have a calyx with 3 tapering sepals and 3 white petals with fluted margins and with the base of the petals handsomely splashed with crimson. The flowers appear in spring and early summer and are followed by the bright red, oval berries. This is a northern species, ranging over much of Canada and into the U.S. as far as the Carolinas in the East and the area around the Great Lakes in the Midwest. Cultivation is difficult since it requires peaty, strongly acid soil and much moisture. Propagate as for *T. cernuum*.

vaseyi   **2'**   **Zones 6–7**   **Sweet Trillium**
A lovely, rare plant, native to the woodlands of Tenn., this has fragrant, deep magenta flowers, 6 in. wide, borne on stems 18 in. high. Suitable only for shady gardens with deep, moist, acid soil.

TRIOSTEUM (try-OS-teum)
perfoliatum   **4'**   **Zone 5**   **Common Horse-gentian**
A weedy perennial herb with opposite, entire sessile leaves 9 in. long and usually connate at the base; flowers are purplish and ¾ in. long; fruit is a yellow, leathery drupe. Native from Mass. to Ky. and Kan. Not especially ornamental. Easily propagated by division.

TRIPLEUROSPERMUM
tchihatchewii (*Matricaria tchihatchewii*) **6"–12"**
Zone 3   **Turfing-daisy**
A member of the Composite Family, sometimes used as a lawn substitute in dry, hot areas, especially where grass has difficulty in growing properly. The leaves are finely cut, the flowers are small white daisies an inch or less across. It will withstand mowing and can be maintained about 2 in. high. Native to Asia Minor.

TRIPLOID. Having 3 sets of chromosomes, i.e., 3 times the normal number.

TRIPTERYGIUM (trip-ter-RIJ-ium)
regelii **shrub or vine** **8'** **Zone 4** **Tripterygium**
A scrambling deciduous plant, this can be trained to grow either as a shrub or as a vine. Its small white flowers are produced in large pyramidal clusters 8–10 in. long during the summer. Coarse in texture; native to Korea, Manchuria and Japan; it is a unique plant as vines go, but does need some training and additional support if it is to be grown as a vine and not a shrub.

Propagation

Seed should be stratified for 3 months at 40° F., or it can be stored dry in airtight containers in a cool place for up to a year, then stratified. Both softwood and hardwood cuttings will root.

TRISTANIA (tris-TAY-nia)
conferta   **60'**   **Zone 10**   **Brisbane-box**
An interesting evergreen tree from Australia, with reddish-brown bark and leathery leaves 3–6 in. long, alternate or whorled. It is cultivated only in the warmest parts of Calif., chiefly for its white flowers that are ¾ in. across and produced in small clusters. Propagated by seeds and softwood cuttings.

TRITICUM (TRIT-i-cum)
aestivum   **4'**   **annual**   **Wheat**
Next to Rice, this is the most important agricultural grain in the world. It has been developed over the centuries, probably originally from plants somewhere in Asia, although it is not now known to be native to any place in the world. It is a grass (like Barley and Oats) and bears a fruiting head about 4 in. long. Its leaves are up to 16 in. long and about ½ in. wide. Many varieties and strains have been developed over the years for growing in specific areas or for specific purposes. However, it is not a plant grown as a garden ornamental.

TRITONIA (try-TO-nia). These are South African plants belonging to the Iris Family, valued for their summer flowers and closely related to freesias. The leaves are sword shaped; the flowers are pink, yellow, red or white in spikes, the individual flowers being about 2 in. wide. Plants are 3–4 ft. tall and are often used as pot plants for late spring display. As the leaves begin to yellow and die, water should be gradually withheld from them until growth starts again. Propagation is simply by division or seeds. These are sometimes confused with montbretias which are correctly *Crocosmia aurea* x *C. pottsii*, the latter sometimes being incorrectly termed *Tritonia pottsii*.

crocata   **3'–4'**   **Zone 6**   **Saffron Tritonia**
With small, yellow to orange-red flowers, 2 in. wide, in few-flowered and 1-sided clusters. It is not planted nearly as much as some of the closely related *Crocosmia* hybrids. Several varieties are listed including '**Orange King**', flowers orange; **coccinea**, flowers scarlet; **purpurea**, flowers purple and **sanguinea** with blood-red flowers.

pottsii = *Crocosmia pottsii*

TROCHODENDRON (trok-o-DEN-dron)
aralioides   **60'**   **Zone 7**   **Wheel-stamen Tree**
An evergreen tree from Japan and Korea, sometimes planted in the U.S. with long, wavy-toothed, lanceolate, alternate or clustered leaves 6 in. long, lustrous above; bright green flowers ½ in. wide in 3-inch racemes; conspicuous not because of petals but because of stamens and borne in June. The fruit is a pod, 5–10 clustered together. Closely related to Magnolia.

TROLLIUS (TROL-ius). Herbs belonging to the

Buttercup Family, valued especially for their bright yellow, globe-shaped flowers in the spring. They grow chiefly in swampy places and have thick fibrous roots. Propagated chiefly by seeds and division.

asiaticus **2′** **Zone 3** **Siberian Globeflower**
With orange globe-shaped flowers, 2 in. across, made up of 10 sepals and shorter petals. Leaves finely lobed and deeply cut, dark green. Native to Siberia. Blooms in May and June.

europaeus **2′** **Zone 4** **Common Globeflower**
Flowers lemon yellow, 2 in. across, with 10–15 colored sepals and shorter petals. Native to Europe. Blooms from May to Aug. This species is widely planted in gardens.

laxus **2′** **Zone 5** **American Globeflower**
A perennial wild flower having rather weak, branched stems; the lower leaves long stalked, the upper ones short stalked or sessile. The leaves are 3–5 in. wide, with deeply divided, wedge-shaped lobes. The leaves increase markedly in size after the plant has flowered. The solitary flowers, borne on short, terminal stalks, have 5–7 yellow, spreading sepals, 15 or more very inconspicuous petals, and numerous stamens. The fruit is a collection of small pods. This is a somewhat rare plant of isolated areas in the northeastern U.S. and blooms in early spring. It is easily cultivated, preferring a moist, semi-shaded location, and may be propagated by division of the rootstalk in spring or fall or by seed shallowly planted in a shady bed in spring or fall and transplanted when large enough to handle.

ledebouri **2′** **Zone 3** **Ledebour Globeflower**
Flowers yellow with only 5 sepals, 10–15 shorter petals. Native to Siberia. Blooms from June to Aug.

pumilus **1′** **Zone 5** **Dwarf Globeflower**
With yellow flowers an inch wide, this mountain perennial from the high Himalayas bears flowers with 5–6 spreading sepals and 8–10 petals.

TROPAEOLUM (tro-PEE-o-lum). Nasturtium. This group of perennials or annuals is native to South America from Mexico to Peru. They are alternate-leaved vines or low annuals, noted for their brilliant, yellow to orange to red, funnel-shaped, spurred flowers in the summer. They are easily grown from seeds outdoors in April or May. Some of the truly double-flowered forms are propagated by cuttings.

Insect Pests

Black aphids thickly clustered on the stem and underside of leaves are a common pest. Careful spraying with insecticide #15 is recommended. Serpentine leaf miner and other leaf miners disfigure the leaves but seldom require control. If necessary insecticide #15 is suggested.

Diseases

A wilt disease which also lives on Tomato, Potato, Eggplant, Pepper and related plants attacks Nasturtium causing wilted, yellow leaves. Plant in new or sterilized soil and avoid rotation with other host plants.

majus **1′–4′** **annual** **Common Nasturtium**
There are dwarf and vine varieties of this species, with single or semi-double or double funnel-shaped flowers 2½ in. wide, each with a long spur, some very fragrant; leaves are round, 2 in. across, on long petioles. Colors range from pure yellow through rich orange to red. Some of the truly double-flowered forms must be grown from cuttings since they produce no seed. All should be grown in a sunny situation. The climbing of the vines is done, not so much by twining stems which are rather thick and succulent, but by twisting leaf stalks.

Once they start to bloom they will continue until frost and form a very colorful group, subject only on occasion to infestations of plant lice which can be quickly brought under control by spraying with Black Leaf 40, if applied promptly.

The bitter taste of stem and leaves has resulted in the common name Nasturtium, which is actually the generic name of the native Watercress, *Nasturtium officinale*. Stems and leaves have been used in salads and green seeds in pickling. 'Golden Gleam' and 'Scarlet Gleam' are excellent varieties as well as the Gleam hybrids. They are best grown in sandy soil that does not have too much manure and leaf mold; otherwise these valued annuals have few requirements. The only thing is to be certain of the right variety selected to suit the situation, i.e., dwarf or climbing. Sometimes the dwarf varieties in the foreground with the climbing plants at the rear make an excellent combination. Seed should be sown in place and thinned or, if started early in the greenhouse, sown in pots to be set out later, since nasturtiums are not readily transplanted with bare roots.

peltophorum **climbing** **annual** **Shield Nasturtium**
With long-spurred, large, orange flowers; leaves round.

peregrinum **climbing** **annual** **Canary Nasturtium**
Leaves round, divided into 3 deep lobes; flowers light yellow, 1 in. across, with a long green spur. Supposedly this is a fast climber quickly reaching a height of 6–10 ft. making a good screen.

polyphyllum **climbing** **Zone 7** **Wreath Nasturtium**
Gray-blue leaves, round, deeply divided into 7–9 lobes; flowers yellow with some red, about

1 in. in dia. This has an edible tuberous root, and many pale yellow to orange flowers. Propagated either by seeds or division of the tuberous root.

speciosum vine Zone 9 Vermilion Nasturtium
A difficult plant to grow in most parts of the U.S., although it is being cultivated in the Pacific Northwest. It will climb to about 15 ft. and produces brilliant scarlet flowers. The fruits are dull red capsules but inside are turquoise-blue seeds the size of peas.

tricolor vine Zone 8 Cornucopia Nasturtium
A tuberous-rooted perennial, growing 6–10 ft. tall, with funnel-shaped flowers, orange, red, yellow, purplish black to green colored. It also forms tubers and is propagated by seeds, cuttings or division of the tubers. The leaves are divided into 6 leaflets.

tuberosum climbing Zone 8 Tuber Nasturtium
With large edible tubers, flowers only $\frac{3}{4}$ in. long, yellow with a long red spur. Leaves rounded with 5 lobes. It grows 6–10 ft. tall.

TROPICAL-ALMOND = *Terminalia catappa*

TROUT-LILY. See ERYTHRONIUM.

TRUFFLES. The fruiting bodies of a fungus of the genus *Tuber*, a member of the Ascomycetes, the most important species being *T. aestivum*, considered by many an outstanding delicacy among mushrooms. They grow entirely under the soil surface, sometimes 12 in. below the surface. They are tuberlike, fleshy, fruiting bodies, 1–4 in. across, bluish black when moist but brown when dry, and covered with hard, ribbed and furrowed warts. They have a pleasant odor but since they grow beneath the surface they are difficult to find except for those who have had experience looking for them. France is probably the only country exporting them, but they are found in England, Italy and other European countries. Usually they grow in soil at the edge of woodlands, especially near groups of evergreen oaks (*Quercus ilex* and *Q. coccifera*) as well as near beeches (*Fagus sylvatica*).

In the past, animals have been trained to hunt for them. In France, small dogs or poodles have been used, and even pigs. Where abundant, men who have hunted them for some time can detect the faint odor and find them satisfactorily. Truffles have not proved easy to cultivate artificially and are not grown in America.

TRUMPETCREEPER. See CAMPSIS.

TRUMPETCREEPER FAMILY = Bignoniaceae

TRUMPETVINE. See CAMPSIS.

TRUMPETVINE, BLOOD = *Distictis buccinatorius*

TRUNCATE. The end nearly straight across; as the apex of the leaf in the Tulip-tree.

TRUSS. A compact flower cluster at the top of a stem, often used in connection with describing the clusters of flowers borne by rhododendrons.

TSUGA (TSOO-ga). Hemlocks are about the most graceful of the coniferous, narrow-leaved, evergreen trees growing in North America. They do well where there is plenty of atmospheric moisture and good rainfall. They do not grow well where hot, dry, summer droughts are the rule rather than the exception. Two species (*T. canadensis* and *T. caroliniana*) are natives in the mountains of the eastern U.S., and 2 other species (*T. mertensiana* and *T. heterophylla*) are natives in the high moist mountain areas of the Pacific Coast. Incidentally neither of these species grows well in the East. Two other species (*T. diversifolia* and *T. sieboldii*) come from Japan and do well in America. Although there are a few other species, these are the main ones.

All of these are dark, pyramidal evergreens with small needles about $\frac{3}{4}$ in. long. They all are shallow rooted, can be easily transplanted with a ball of soil about their roots, and all can be sheared, easily making excellent clipped hedges. The Canada Hemlock has the most variants, over 40 having been named, while the others have few if any. The Canada Hemlock holds its needles 3–4 years, the Carolina Hemlock holds them a year longer. The very dense Japanese Hemlock (*T. diversifolia*) holds its needles nearly 8 years, the reason why it always has such a nice dense appearance.

The Carolina Hemlock seems to be the best for growing in city conditions, for the others need more moisture both in the atmosphere and in the soil. The cones on all these species are small, pendulous and about 1–1$\frac{1}{2}$ in. long.

Propagation

Seed should be stratified for 3 months at 40° F. and then sown, or it may be stored dry in airtight containers in a cool place up to a year or possibly longer, then stratified. The many varieties of *T. canadensis* are propagated asexually either by grafting on seedlings of the species as understock or by softwood or hardwood cuttings (which see).

Insect Pests

Spruce mite is often more destructive to Hemlock than to other evergreens. See SPRUCE. Hemlock scale causes heavy needle drop when abundant. Use insecticide #15 in midsummer. Black vine weevil and smaller strawberry root weevil feed on the roots in the grub stage and may wilt or kill ornamental trees. Treat soil around roots with insecticide #3. Hemlock looper which has defoliated and killed many acres of forest trees is occasionally found on ornamental trees. Spray with insecticide #5 or #37.

Diseases

Three rust diseases which also live on azalea rhododendron, hydrangea and poplar form orange pustules on the needles. If a rust is prevalent, remove any host plants nearby and spray in early summer with fungicide #D. Botrytis tip blight may kill new shoots in cool damp weather. No control is suggested.

canadensis 90′ Zone 4 Canada Hemlock The most commonly planted of the hemlocks, popular over a wide area and native to the eastern U.S. Trees 200 and even 500 years old have been known. It is easily sheared into hedges, and makes an extremely graceful, evergreen hedge of value in almost any situation except city conditions. However, because of its graceful drooping branches it makes a perfect specimen. There are over 40 variants of this species known, probably because the tree is native over such a wide area and has been closely observed by many people for more than a century. Like some of the spruce species, the inner bark has been used as an emergency food and the young shoot tips have been used to make beer and tea.

Some of the varieties are: **'Bradshaw'**—originated at Kingsville Nurseries, Kingsville, Md., making a perfect pyramid of growth, dense and wide base; **'Fremdii'**—a dense specimen at 30 ft., found in Rye, N.Y. in 1887. Densely pyramidal; **globosa**—dense and rounded, as broad as high; named in 1887; **'Kingsville'**—narrow fastigiate clone; an 18 ft. tree is

The Sargent Weeping Hemlock is a variety of the native Canada Hemlock. (*Photo by Arnold Arboretum, Jamaica Plain, Mass.*)

only 3½ ft. wide at base; **'Macrophylla'**—originating in France before 1891 with leaves slightly longer and wider than the type; **'Pendula'**—named the Sargent Hemlock, this is the most popular variety of all. Twice as broad as high, flat topped with pendulous side branches, originally found near Beacon, N.Y., before 1870. Easily propagated by cuttings—a very graceful specimen; **'Pomfret'**—faster growing than 'Fremdii', but dense and pyramidal in habit; **'Taxifolia'**—yewlike foliage; selected in Vt. about 1928; **'Westonigra'**—introduced by Weston Nurseries, Hopkinton, Mass., about 1948, for its very dark green foliage.

caroliniana 75′ Zone 4 Carolina Hemlock Practically unknown to American gardens a century ago when it was first "discovered" growing in the mountains of the southeastern U.S. Now, having proved itself about as hardy as the Canada Hemlock it makes a perfect, ornamental, evergreen specimen. Some consider it slightly more tolerant of city conditions than the Canada Hemlock. Certainly the whorled arrangements of the needles on the twigs give it a softer character.

diversifolia 90′ Zone 5 Japanese Hemlock An excellent, dense, rounded Hemlock, doing very well in the eastern U.S. and native to Japan. One of the reasons it appears so dense is the fact that it retains its evergreen needles 8–10 years, while those of some of the other species fall off at the end of 4 years; those of *T. caroliniana* drop off after about 5 yrs. This Japanese Hemlock has a rounded, almost clipped look which makes it a neat ornamental. This and the Siebold Hemlock differ from the other hemlocks in that their needles are notched. The 1-year branchlets of the Japanese Hemlock are pubescent while those of *T. sieboldii* are glabrous.

heterophylla 200′ Zone 6 Western Hemlock The tallest of the hemlocks, this species makes rapid growth but does not do well in the eastern U.S., because it needs the moist atmosphere of the mountain slopes, where it is native from Alaska to Calif. It has short, pendulous side branches, makes a narrow tree, of use as an ornamental only in its limited habitat.

mertensiana 100′ Zone 6 Mountain Hemlock Very little used outside its native habitat (the mountains from Alaska to Calif.), the leaves of this Hemlock are unique in that they have stomata on both the upper and lower surfaces. It is a beautiful evergreen but requires cool, moist atmospheric conditions, usually available in the higher altitudes of the mountains.

sieboldii 90′ Zone 5 Siebold Hemlock An excellent ornamental tree from Japan, with dark, glossy green leaves and dense pyramidal habit. The cones are ¾–1 in. long and egg shaped.

TUBER. A thickened portion of a subterranean stem or branch, provided with eyes (buds) on the sides.

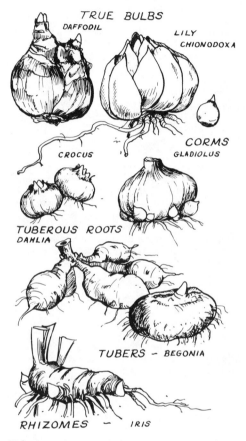

Tubers

TUBERCLE. A small tuber, also applied to nodule (which see); small pealike bodies on the roots of legumes which contain helpful bacteria having the power to draw nitrogen from the air and put it in the soil.

TUBEROSE = *Polianthes tuberosa*

TUBEROUS. Bearing or producing tubers.

TULBAGHIA (tul-BAG-ia). South African herbs growing from corms grown in the greenhouse or outdoors in southern Calif. *T. violacea* the Violet Tulbaghia, is the most popular species at present, growing 2½ ft. tall with linear leaves, bright, violet-colored, urn-

shaped flowers ¾ in. long in 8–16 flowered umbels. The leaves are 8–12 in. long. In Calif. this blooms from June to Sept. It should be planted in the full sun. **T. fragrans** produces fragrant pinkish-lavender flowers.

TULIP. See TULIPA.

TULIPA (TEW-lip-a). Tulips are very popular bulbous plants, mostly native to southern and southwestern Europe and the Near East but at least one comes from Siberia and another from Asia. As far as American gardening is concerned they are divided into 2 general groups— the "botanicals" or species native throughout southern Europe and Asia; and the more popular modern hybrids, of which there are hundreds of varieties in practically all colors except true blue, most of which are descended

Tulips: A. Darwin.
        B. Cottage.
        C. Parrot.
        D. Double.
        E. Multiflowered.
        F. Species.
        G. Species.

from *T. gesneriana* and *T. suaveolens*. More recently other species like *T. kaufmanniana* are being used in hybridization.

Some tulips are grown commercially in America, especially in the vicinity of Holland, Mich., but by far the largest number of tulip bulbs sold in America are imported from the Netherlands. Anyone who has ever seen the tulip fields near Lisse and Haarlem in the Netherlands will realize the tremendous numbers produced annually.

Tulips bloom in the spring but the bulbs have the disappointing habit of lasting only a year or so and then either disappearing or just failing to bloom. Standard recommendations are to replant with new bulbs each year, especially if the planting is an important one from the standpoint of massing or design.

Tulips usually produce a single cup-shaped flower, although a few species produce 2–5. The leaves are usually basal, but in a few species there are a few stem leaves as well. They are planted for their colorful spring bloom, for use as subjects for early forcing in pots in the greenhouse, and also for the interest created by certain species, especially the dwarf ones, when used as accent points in the rock garden. They are best propagated by offsets or the separation of the new small bulbs from the parent. When these are grown by themselves for 2 years they will be large enough to bloom.

Culture

Tulips should be provided with rich soil, preferably with a goodly amount of compost worked in. Manure should not touch the bulbs. Otherwise, they can be grown in many soils over large areas of the country. In the far South, they must be given a cold treatment of several weeks at 40° F. before they are planted in the fall. All tulips should be planted in the fall with about 4 in. of soil on top of them. If massed, they should be about 8–9 in. apart. In colder parts of the country it is advisable to mulch the plantings after the first freeze to aid in protecting them over winter. As has already been pointed out, it has been found best to renew plantings each year.

In some areas, rodents will eat the bulbs and, to protect them, small clumps might well be planted in wire baskets, using small-mesh wire screening for the purpose. They should be planted in the full sun on well-drained soil. They are not so well suited for naturalizing, as are the more permanent narcissus, but rather are used in clumps and formal beds.

Sometimes it might be well to lift the bulbs in the early summer after the foliage has died, dry them and store them in a cool place until fall planting time. Indoors, they can be used as greenhouse plants, planting them in pots from Sept. to Nov. They require 10–12 weeks in a cool, moist and dark situation before the pots can be brought out on the greenhouse bench. (They do not force easily in the unregulated temperature conditions of the normal home, and failures can be expected if such forcing is attempted.) In the greenhouse, where temperature and moist conditions are regulated, tulips can be forced into bloom in 3–4 weeks from the time they are brought in from the cool cellar if they are the Early Single or Double varieties. Darwins, Breeders, and Cottage tulips take 6–9 weeks from the time they are brought in. Hence, by proper selection of varieties and timing (i.e., bringing pots in at 10-day intervals) tulips can be had in bloom in the greenhouse for many weeks in the winter.

Insect Pests

Tulip bulb aphid feeds on the bulb scales and causes crippled leaves and deformed flowers. Before bulbs are planted, any infested bulbs should be dusted with insecticide #15 or treated as for bulb fly. See NARCISSUS. Tulip leaf aphid clusters on the leaves is controlled by spraying or by dusting as above. Bulb flies occasionally infest tulips. See NARCISSUS.

Disease Pests

Botrytis blight infects all parts of the plant. Water-soaked twisted lesions on the leaves and dry wrinkled spots on the bud are characteristic. Planting only clean bulbs, soil sterilization and prompt destruction of infected plants and plant debris are advised. Frequent spraying with fungicide #D starting when first leaves appear may check the disease but not eliminate it. Gray bulb rot has somewhat similar symptoms and similar precautions are suggested. Breaking or abnormal streaks in the petals may be due to a virus which is transmitted by aphid. See above. Topple or the collapse of flower stalks with no visible injury is believed due to calcium deficiency in the soil. Add limestone to bring soil acidity to pH 6.0–6.5 before planting. See ACID SOIL.

acuminata 12″–18″ **Zone 4** **Turkish Tulip** Flowers long and pointed, yellow with red lines; midspring; native to Turkey.

australis 12″–18″ **Zone 4** **Southern Tulip** Flowers, yellow, reddish outside, bud nodding. Midspring; native to France and Algeria.

batalinii 6″ **Zone 4** **Batalin Tulip** Flowers pale yellow. Early spring; native to western Asia.

biflora **Zone 4** **Two-flower Tulip** Two small, pale yellow flowers, whitish inside and purplish outside. Early spring. The var. **turkestanica** has 4-5 slightly larger flowers.

chrysantha   6″   **Zone 6**   **Golden Tulip**
A tiny tulip having yellow flowers with the outside of the petals tinted red, and blooming in April. Native to Asia Minor.

clusiana   12″-18″   **Zone 4**   **Clusius Tulip**
Small, fragrant, white to yellowish flowers with pink on the outside. Flowering in midspring and a delightful and colorful as well as very popular little tulip. Native from Portugal to Persia.

var. stellata   12″-18″   **Zone 4**   **Starry Tulip**

dasystemon   6″   **Zone 4**   **Kuenlun Tulip**
Usually several flowers, yellow with petals edged white and greenish on back. Native to Turkestan.

didieri   12″-18″   **Zone 4**   **Didier Tulip**
Flowers large and bright red, the ends of the flower segments slightly reflexed. Midspring. Native to Southern Europe.

eichleri   12″   **Zone 4**   **Eichler Tulip**
Flowers large, deep red, blue-black at base; leaves broad and long pointed. Native to southwestern Asia.

fosterana   12″   **Zone 4**   **Foster Tulip**
Flowers large, very crimson, darker at base. Native to Turkestan.

gesnerana   18″-24″   **Zone 4**   **Common Tulip**
Most of our modern garden tulips are related to this species which has broad leaves, flowers now red, yellow and many varying colors. Native to Armenia and Persia.

greigii   12″   **Zone 4**   **Greig Tulip**
Flowers orange-scarlet with dark blotch in base. Leaves are broad and dark green. Early spring. Native to Turkestan.

hageri   6″   **Zone 4**   **Hager Tulip**
Flowers red or yellow, often 2, with darker base; early spring. Leaves narrow and acute. Native to Greece.

humilis   5″   **Zone 4**   **Ground Tulip**
Flowers small, pale purplish, yellow in base and reddish to green outside. Leaves are linear. Native to Persia.

kaufmanniana   5″-10″   **Zone 4**   **Waterlily Tulip**
One of the very good ornamental species and very popular. Flowers are large and open, creamy white and light yellow with yellow center and red streaks. Early spring; native to Turkestan.

kolpakowskiana   6″   **Zones 2-3**   **Kolpak Tulip**
Flowers yellow but sometimes reddish or purplish outside; leaves are narrow and pointed. Early spring; native to Turkestan.

linifolia   10″   **Zone 4**   **Slimleaf Tulip**

Flowers red with bluish base. Leaves are grass-like. Early spring; native to Bokhara.

marjolettii   18″-24″   **Zone 4**   **Marjolett Tulip**
Flowers yellow with broad purple-margined segments. Leaves are narrow. Midspring; native to Savoy.

orphanidea   12″   **Zone 4**   **Spartan Tulip**
Flowers yellow, nearly 2 in. long and starlike; leaves narrow and long. Early spring. Native to Greece.

patens   9″   **Zone 4**   **Persian Tulip**
Flowers 1-3, fragrant, whitish or yellowish; leaves narrow and curved. Midspring. Native to Siberia.

praestans   12″-18″   **Zone 4**   **Leather-bulb Tulip**
Flowers light red; leaves broad and short pointed. Early spring. Native to Bokhara.

primulina   12″   **Zone 4**   **Primrose Tulip**
Flowers fragrant, pale yellow. Native to Algeria.

saxatilis   12″-18″   **Zone 4**   **Cliff Tulip**
Flowers fragrant, usually 2, mauve with yellow base. Midspring; native to Crete.

suaveolens   4″-8″   **Zone 4**   **Duc Van Tol Tulip**
Flowers fragrant, vivid yellow. Very early spring. Native to southern Europe. One of the very oldest tulips in cultivation.

sylvestris   9″-18″   **Zone 4**   **Florentine Tulip**
Flowers bright yellow, occasionally 2, fragrant; leaves narrow. Late spring. Native to Europe.

'Viridiflora'   24″   **Zone 4**
Flowers large, light green with yellowish or whitish edges; leaves large and broad. Late spring. Apparently known only in cultivation.

Classification

Tulips have been grouped in the following classes:

    I Duc Van Tol; 6 in.
   II Single Early; 9-16 in.
  III Double Early; 9-16 in.
  IV Mendel; 16-26 in. (resembling Darwins, blooming 2 weeks earlier)
   V Triumph; 16-26 in. (resembling Darwins, slightly earlier than Mendels)
  VI Cottage; all tulips not in other classes
 VII Dutch Breeders; flowers oval or cupped, brown, purple, red or bronze; base white or yellow generally stained green or blue
VIII English Breeders; flowers forming $\frac{1}{3}$-$\frac{1}{2}$ of a hollow ball when expanded
  IX Darwin; lower part of flower usually rectangular in outline.
   X Broken Dutch Breeders; Dutch Breeders with color feathered or striped
  XI Broken English Breeders; English Breeders with color feathered or striped
 XII Rembrandt; Darwin tulips with color feathered or striped

XIII Broken Cottage tulips; Cottage tulips with color feathered or striped

XIV Parrot; varieties with slashes and fringed petals

XV Late Doubles

XVI Species and first crosses between species.

Classes I, VIII, X, XI, XIII are little planted in America at the present time. Dutch Breeders (VII) are usually found in catalogues simply listed as Breeders, and Lily-flowered tulips, correctly a part of Class VI, are frequently listed by themselves.

A "broken" tulip is one in which the flower color is streaked with variegation and sometimes the leaves are also variegated with pale green stripes and some mottling. Centuries ago, this was highly prized in tulips, but not today. It is usually caused by a virus disease which can spread to otherwise sound bulbs either by aphids or by grafting a piece of a diseased bulb into an otherwise sound one.

Tulips were first brought to Holland over 350 years ago and probably came to America with the earliest settlers. Today, literally hundreds of varieties are available. All bloom in the spring, all are best fall-planted. There are many with double flowers.

SINGLE EARLY TULIPS. This group is best planted alone or used for forcing indoors, since they are not as tall as the ones that bloom later. The earliness of bloom is their most outstanding characteristic, for these bloom at the same time as *Primula polyantha*. A few characteristic varieties would be 'DeWet', golden-orange; 'Ibis', pink; 'Prince of Austria', orange-scarlet; 'White Hawk', white; 'Yellow Prince', canary yellow.

DOUBLE EARLY TULIPS. These double-flowered varieties last a few days longer than the above, but otherwise they are used in the same ways. Examples would be 'Dante', blood red; 'Electra', carmine-pink; 'Orange Nassau', orange-yellow; 'Schoonoord', white; 'Vuurbaak', orange-scarlet.

MENDEL TULIPS. These bloom 2 weeks or less before the Darwin tulips but later than the Early tulips. Examples would be 'Athleet', white; 'Hildegarda', deep red; 'Pink Gem', white edged pink; 'Scarlet Admiral', scarlet with a black base.

TRIUMPH TULIPS. Vigorous-growing, robust tulips, proving very popular for forcing as well as cutting because of their strong stems. They bloom between the Single Early group, and the Darwins. Examples are 'Bruno Walter', golden-brown tinged purple; 'Johanna', salmon pink; 'Kansas', white; 'Paris', orange-red and yellow; 'Red Giant', bright red. In general these apparently lack the yellow colors of varieties in some of the other groups.

COTTAGE TULIPS. The name comes from the fact that many of these varieties are long-time favorites in the cottage gardens of Great Britain. They bloom in May and have many excellent yellow varieties. The Lily-flowered tulips belong here, so called because the flower segments are pointed and reflexed, not rounded as are the other Cottage tulips. 'Captain Fryatt', ruby violet; 'Ellen Willmott', white; 'Marcellina', salmon pink; 'Yellow Marvel', excellent yellow; are a few examples of this excellent lily-flowered group.

DUTCH BREEDER TULIPS. Although they are listed in most catalogues as "Breeders" they resemble the Darwin tulips except that in color range these are confined to purples, bronze, copper and dull reds. Good examples would be 'Bacchus', violet; 'Dom Pedro', brown; 'Indian Chief', red-brown; 'Louis XIV', violet and bronze.

DARWIN TULIPS. The rich colors of this group make it one of the most popular of all the tulips. Squarish flowers, vigorous sturdy stems make these excellent for any purpose. Examples are 'Bleu Aimable', lavender; 'Charles Needham', brilliant red; 'Glacier', white; 'Golden Age', deep yellow; 'La Tulipe Noire', maroon-black; 'Pride of Haarlem' carmine-rose; 'Niphetos', deep cream; 'William Copeland', mauve-lilac.

REMBRANDT TULIPS. These have variegated-colored flowers, being Darwin tulips that are infected with virus, many of them extremely beautiful in their striping or feathered colors. A few are 'American Flag'; 'Clara'; 'Kathleen'; 'Madame de Pompadour'; 'Refinement'. It is these Rembrandt tulips that are frequently depicted in old Dutch paintings.

PARROT TULIPS. With large, shaggy flowers, the edges of the flower segments being cut and feathered and the flower itself usually widely opened and not cup shaped. These are interesting as specimens but are little used for massing. They range greatly in color. Best appreciated indoors as cut flowers. Examples would be 'Black Parrot', maroon-black; 'Fantasy', pink and green; 'Orange Favorite', orange and green; 'Texas Gold', golden yellow.

LATE DOUBLE TULIPS. Sometimes listed as "Peony-flowered tulips," these are sturdy double-flowered varieties that last well in the garden and as cut flowers. They might well be planted in a spot protected from the wind for the flowers are heavy and are easily blown over. Examples would be 'Golden Lion', golden yellow; 'Clara Carder', clear pink; 'Mount Tacoma', white; 'Uncle Tom', deep wine-red.

SPECIES TULIPS. Sometimes listed as the "Botanical tulips"—these are the wild species and some of their hybrids. These are excellent as individual specimens in the rockery and some like *T. clusiana*, *T. kaufmanniana*, and *T. fosteriana* are also used for massing. It should be noted that bulbs of *T. kaufmanniana* are more "permanent" in the garden than any other tulip species, coming up annually for years. A most delightful tulip species, well worth growing. The species tulips are also valued because, by selecting the right ones, the blooming period will extend over a 6-week period.

TULIP POPPY = *Papaver glaucum*

TULIP-POPPY, MEXICAN = *Hunnemannia fumariaefolia*

TULIP-TREE = *Liriodendron tulipifera*

TUMBLEWEED = *Amaranthus albus*

TUNG-OIL-TREE = *Aleurites fordii*

TUNICA SAXIFRAGA = *Petrorhagia saxifraga*

TUNICFLOWER = *Petrorhagia saxifraga*

TUPELO. See NYSSA.

TURBAN BUTTERCUP = *Ranunculus asiatica*

TURBINATE. Top shaped; inversely conical.

TURF. This is the solid, dense mat of closely clipped foliage and roots represented in a good grass lawn. Although grass forms the most common turf, other plants are included in the term. When used as a verb it means the using of squares or rolls of this grass material, usually 2–3 in. thick, which includes the foliage, roots and soil about the roots, to make or "lay" a new lawn area.

The laying of turf is the fastest way of making a new lawn or repairing an old one. Many a golf course has its own turf-growing area, where fine grasses are grown, fertilized and mowed, primarily to be dug and used in repairing worn out turf on parts of the course. Also an industry has been built around the idea, where turf is grown on a large-scale basis and dug by machine, sold by the truck load. When machine-dug the rolls are about 12 in. wide and 3–5 ft. long, so that they are not too heavy for a man to handle, rolled up with the grass on the inside. It is absolutely essential that these sods or rolls do not dry out, for the roots are exposed to the atmosphere and hot sun or high, winds can quickly reduce the moisture in them. Also, if left rolled up for more than 2 days, the grass will turn yellow. Hence sods or turf should be quickly used as soon as they are cut.

The soil where the turf is to be planted should be graded and prepared in the same way as that for lawns (which see). Allowances should be made for depth, since the turf is about 2–3 in. thick and hence raises the level of the prepared soil by just that much.

Turf should be laid with the pieces as closely together as possible. Under no condition should spaces be left between them. If such spaces exist after the sod is tightly laid together, fill them in with good soil. Then roll the entire turfed area with a heavy roller or tamp down if necessary. Then water thoroughly. If the sods are laid on a steep bank, it might be advisable to peg them in place with sticks, to prevent them being washed down in a heavy rain. See LAWNS.

TURFING-DAISY = *Tripleurospermum tchihatchewii*

TURGID. Swollen as a result of internal water pressure.

TURKEY CORN = *Dicentra canadensis*

TURKEY OAK = *Quercus cerris*

TURKISH HAZEL = *Corylus colurna*

TURK'S-CAP LILY = See LILIUM.

TURMERIC = *Curcuma longa*

TURNIP (*Brassica rapa*). The true Turnip and the Rutabaga (Swede Turnip) are frequently listed in the trade under the common name of turnip. Actually, the Turnip has little or no neck, the leaves and petioles are hairy and coarse and the root texture is quite coarse. The Rutabaga *B. napobrassica*, on the other hand, has a distinct crown or neck, leaves that are smooth and covered with a bluish bloom. The roots are larger than Turnip, finer texture and take longer to mature. See RUTABAGA for culture.

Varieties

'White Milan' and **'White Flat Dutch'** are early flat sorts (40–45 days) popular in the south as are also **'Seven Top'** and **'Shogrin'** grown only for greens. **'Purple Top White Globe'**, **'Just Right Hybrid'** and **'Snowball'** are popular white-fleshed varieties; **'Aberdeen'**, later maturing and yellow fleshed.

Culture

Turnips will thrive on all types of soil that are properly prepared by the application of 20–30 bu. of well-rotted animal manure or approximately 40 lbs. of a 5–8–7 or 5–10–5 commercial fertilizer per 1000 sq. ft. The use of organic matter, rotted manure or compost is advisable for both very light sandy soils or the heavier clay loams

The seed is sown where the crop is to mature in drills 15 in. apart where hand cultivation is practiced. After the plants become established they are thinned to a 3–5-in. spacing. The varieties, **'Seven Top'** and **'Shogrin'** are not thinned. Since turnips are a cool-season crop the seed is planted early in the spring and in late summer in the North and during the fall and winter in the South.

The varieties 'Purple Top White Globe' and 'Aberdeen Yellow' may be harvested in the fall and stored for several months.

Diseases and Insects

Turnips are subject to most of the same diseases and insects common to Cabbage. Club root and black root are the most serious diseases and aphids, root maggot and flea beetles the most common insect pests. See CABBAGE for control.

GRANT B. SNYDER

TURTLE-HEAD. See CHELONE.

TUSSILAGO (tuss-i-LAY-go)

farfara **12"** **Zone 3** **Coltsfoot**
A perennial, sending up flowering stalks from the ground before the leaves appear in early spring. The rootstocks spread rapidly underground. The bright yellow flowers appear in daisylike heads on foot-long stalks with a few scaly bracts. It belongs to the Composite Family. Flower heads are $\frac{1}{2}-\frac{3}{4}$ in. across, often in March or April. The leaves are basal, heart shaped at the base and lobed with a toothed margin 7 in. across, with the undersurface white felty. It can be grown on dry banks but also can grow out of limits or become a weed difficult to control because of vigorous rootstalks. The leaves have a way of drying and disappearing by early summer. Propagated by division. The leaf and flower are sometimes used in cough medicines.

TWAYBLADE. See LIPARIS.

TWINEBARK, RIBBONWOOD = *Plagianthus betulinus*

TWINFLOWER = *Linnaea borealis*

TWINLEAF = *Jeffersonia diphylla*

TWINPOD, COMMON = *Physaria didymocarpa*

TWINSPUR = *Diascia barberae*

TWISTED-STALK, ROSY = *Streptopus roseus*

TYPE. The specimen with which the scientific name of a taxon is always associated; the type along with other related specimens is used in describing the taxon.

TYPHA (TY-fa)

angustifolia **4'** **Zone 3** **Narrowleaf Cattail**
Similar to the Common Cattail except slightly smaller; leaves only $\frac{1}{2}$ in. wide, and the staminate and pistillate flowers are separated but on the same flowering stalk. Fruiting stalks narrower. Native over the same area as well as South America. Both species spread rapidly but only grow in marshy places.

latifolia **4'-6'** **Zone 3** **Common Cattail**
Surely everyone in the U.S. is familiar with the Cattail and no swamp is complete without its tall, swordlike leaves which are about an inch wide, which in rich muck will sometimes attain a height of 8 ft. or more, and the brown, clublike inflorescence on which the Red-wing Blackbird likes to perch and which he also uses to line his nest. The flowers of this plant are imperfect, the male flowers being carried on the erect flower stalk above the mass of tiny, brown, pistillate flowers which form the familiar "club," 6–8 in. long, often collected for dried arrangements. When the seeds are ripe these fuzzy brown flowers act as parachutes for the wind-dispersed seeds. An interesting plant for the bog garden, it should be kept in bounds. Propagation is by division of the creeping rootstalk in spring or summer. Native throughout North America, Europe and Asia.

minima **1'-2$\frac{1}{2}$'** **Zone 8 (?)** **Dwarf Cattail**
This is a tender Cattail, the smallest of the 3 species, and can be used in heated pools or planted in tubs that are moved from outside pools to greenhouses for over-wintering. The leaves of sterile stems are very narrow, only about $\frac{1}{12}$ in. wide. The female spike is rusty brown, ovate or shortly cylindrical and the male flowers are either separated from or in with the female flowers. Native to the Caucasus, Europe and Eastern Asia.

U

UGLI. A tropical fruit originating in Jamaica. Possibly a hybrid between grapefruit and mandarin, rather unattractive but ships well and is juicy; slightly acid, with leathery thick orange-colored skin. May not prove popular. Fruit about the size of a small grapefruit.

ULEX (YEW-lex)

europaeus 3′–5′ Zone 6 Common Gorse
A weedy, extremely spiny, densely branched, deciduous shrub, usually covered with bright yellow, pealike flowers in the spring and a few are produced off and on at other times of year. It is native throughout central and western Europe and has become naturalized in the Middle Atlantic states and on Vancouver Island. It has little value as a garden plant except it might be used on dry banks. The double-flowered variety **'Plenus'** is interesting.

ULMACEAE = The Elm Family

ULMUS (ULL-mus). These are all alternate-leaved deciduous trees, more or less susceptible to the rather serious Dutch Elm disease as well as some other diseases and insect pests. No tree has the desirable vase-shaped form of the American Elm. The flowers are inconspicuous, appearing before the leaves (except those on *U. parvifolia* which are borne in the fall) and in fact many of the fruits which are actually samaras ripen also while the leaves are still enlarging.

Because the elms are susceptible to so many problems, especially the Dutch Elm disease, it might be advisable to consider a wide variety of other trees first, before deciding on elms.

Propagation

Do not let the seed dry out but sow as soon as ripe. Most species ripen seeds early in the spring but *U. parviflora* and *U. serotina* ripen their seeds in the fall. Grafting and budding on to elm understock of close affinity is the usual commercial practice. Sometimes softwood cuttings are rooted. See GRAFTING, BUDDING, etc.

Insect Pests

Elm leaf beetle which skeletonizes the leaves, canker worms, gypsy moth caterpillars and tussock moth larva and spiny elm caterpillars which defoliate branches are all controlled by timely sprays of insecticide #37 or #42. DDT encouraged the infestation of aphids and mites and insecticide #15 or #34 are added to the above or applied separately when needed.

Weakened trees are infested with the elm borer which may be checked in the beetle stage by sprays for leaf-eating insects or in their tunnels. See BORERS. Several scale insects, especially the European elm scale, are combatted by a dormant spray of insecticide #44 or by #15 applied when the crawlers are active in June. European elm bark beetle and American bark beetle spread Dutch Elm disease by eating the bark at the axil of twigs in the spring. They breed under the bark of weakened trees. Dormant spraying preferably by commercial or municipal operators using a pesticide usually aids in controlling the beetle and this is one of the major ways of controlling the fast spread of this disease. Elm cockscomb gall, a curious deformity of the leaves as the name implies, is caused by an aphid and is more interesting than destructive.

Diseases

Dutch Elm disease, the cause of many dead elm trees in the northeastern states and spreading, is first indicated by yellow leaves (flags) which are followed by the death of twigs and branches. It is spread by bark beetles as described above and the only control is directed at the bark beetles. American Elm is very susceptible but some of the other species have shown a degree of resistance. The disease is positively identified only by culture. Careful pruning of all broken branches and any suspected limbs may prolong the tree's life.

Phloem necrosis, caused by an uncontrollable virus, has killed many elm trees in the Mississippi Valley and is spreading. The American Elm is very susceptible. The virus is spread by leaf hoppers and control of them by a regular schedule of sprays with insecticide #15 or #9 is the only suggested treatment. Black spot also causes yellow leaves but is checked by spraying with fungicides #D and #F.

americana 120′ Zone 2 American Elm
This is the best of the elms as an ornamental tree native to the central and eastern part of North America. The leaves are about 3–5 in. long, doubly serrate, usually uneven at the base. Its prime character is the vase-shaped habit which no other tree has to this extent. Autumn color is yellow. Of the many varieties grown some of the more common ones are: **'Ascendens'**—ascending habit, Ascending American Elm; **'Augustine'**—columnar habit;

originating at Normal, Ill., about 1922. It grows rapidly, the original tree being 80 ft. tall when only 25 years old; **'Columnaris'**—widely columnar in habit, Columnar American Elm; **'Lake City'**—upright habit; a 28-year-old plant was 50 ft. tall and 25 ft. across; **'Moline'**—narrow in habit but with a bad reputation of splitting in ice storms and requiring cabling; **'Pendula'**—with pendulous branches but generally vase-shaped habit; **'Princeton'**—selected in 1922 because of larger leathery leaves and vigorous growth. Mature trees are vase shaped; young trees are upright.

campestris = *U. procera*

carpinifolia   90′   Zone 4   Smooth-leaved Elm

A variable tree with many forms, native to Europe and western Asia. Usually it has a single trunk with slender branches forming a pyramidal head. The varieties should be propagated asexually, and are:

'Bea Schwarz'—a selection made in Holland because of its resistance to the Dutch Elm disease. Other than its resistance to the disease it has little ornamental value since it does not have a distinctive vase shape; **'Christine Buisman'**—a selection made in Holland, introduced into the U.S. in 1939. Valued only because of its resistance to the Dutch Elm disease. With rounded habit, it has little to offer in ornamental planting; **'Koopmannii'**—

Ulmus glabra 'Pendula' grafted about 8 ft. high. (*Photo by Arnold Arboretum, Jamaica Plain, Mass.*)

with upright oval head, dense branches, the only Elm with this habit. A 57-year-old plant is 30 ft. tall and 15 ft. in dia.; **'Pendula'**—with gracefully pendulous branches; **'Sarniensis'**—narrowly upright and columnar in habit; **'Umbraculifera'**—if grafted high on its understock this develops a densely globose head.

glabra   120′   Zone 4   Scotch or Wych Elm

Growing in America since it was introduced in colonial times, this is native to Europe and western Asia. It is rather open with a wide-spreading habit; with coarse foliage (the leaves being 3–6 in. long) but the elm leaf beetle will riddle the leaves of this tree before they will touch the leaves of other species. Two very popular varieties have been used: **'Camperdownii'**—rounded head with pendulous branches when grafted high on an understock, called Camperdown Elm; **'Pendula'**—with a flat-topped head, main branches horizontal then pendulous at the ends, when grafted high on an understock. Called the Table Top Elm.

parvifolia   50′   Zone 5   Chinese Elm

This tree would be a fine ornamental if it were not for its susceptibility to the Dutch Elm disease. The leaves are small, only 1–2 in. long, and turn a reddish color in the fall. The tree forms a round top and the older bark is mottled, often exfoliating in irregular patches, exposing lighter bark beneath. The flowers appear in the fall (not in the spring when most of the other elms produce flowers before the leaves appear). It is native to China, Korea and Japan. The variety **'Pendens'** has leaves evergreen at least in southern Calif., where it is planted a great deal and sometimes listed as *U. parvifolia sempervirens*.

procera   120′   Zone 5   English Elm

Another species native to England and western Europe, this was formerly termed *U. campestris* and was planted in America even in colonial times. It has an oval or oblong head, is widespreading and can grow to great size, but when compared with the habit of *U. americana* it is really uninteresting.

pumila   75′   Zone 4   Siberian Elm

Native to eastern Siberia and northern China, this is a fast-growing tree, widely publicized as the "Chinese Elm". The small leaves are $\frac{3}{4}$–$2\frac{3}{4}$ in. long and it forms a rather open head. However, it can withstand shearing and hence is used in clipped windbreaks or screens and has special merit in the dry areas of the Midwest or on dry banks where better trees will not grow. In the eastern U.S. this should not be considered a good ornamental specimen for there are many others which are better, but in the drought areas of the Midwest it has its uses. The variety **'Pendula'** has pendulous branches. There are other named seedlings and hybrids of this species which are supposed to have better ornamental qualities than the species.

rubra   60'   Zone 3   Slippery Elm
Native from Quebec to Fla. and west to the Dakotas and Tex., this is a coarse, ungainly tree, not of value for ornamental planting. The large leaves are 4–8 in. long and rough and the twigs when bruised have a characteristic odor. It was formerly called *U. fulva*.

thomasii   90'   Zone 2   Rock Elm
An extremely hardy species, native from Quebec to Tenn., and Neb.; this is not an ornamental tree.

UMBEL. An inflorescence with pedicles or branches arising at the same point and of nearly equal length.

UMBELLIFERA = The Carrot, Celery or Parsnip Family.

UMBELLULARIA (um-bell-yew-LAY-ria)
californica   75'   Zone 7   California-laurel
An evergreen, native to Calif. and Ore., with lustrous, green, alternate leaves, 2–5 in. long, that are aromatic when crushed. It is a handsome, dense, round-headed tree, used on the West Coast as a street or park tree and as a garden specimen. The flowers are yellowish green in clusters and the fruit is a fleshy, egg-shaped, yellowish-green drupe about 1 in. long.

UMBRELLA-PINE = *Sciadopitys verticillata*

UMBRELLA-PLANT = *Peltiphyllum peltatum*

UNDULATE. Wavy surface or margin.

UNI. In compound words meaning 1.

UNICORN-PLANT = *Proboscidea jussieui*

UNIOLA LATIFOLIA = *Chasmanthium latifolium*
paniculata   2'–5'   Zone 6   Sea-oats
A grass native to the southeastern U.S. which increases by creeping rhizomes; used for controlling sand-dune erosion within its hardiness limits.

UNISEXUAL. Of 1 sex, either staminate or pistillate.

URCEOLATE. Urn shaped.

UREA. An organic fertilizer containing 46% nitrogen, much of which is readily available. This should be used with great care as it is highly concentrated. See SOILS.

UREA-FORM FERTILIZERS. Highly concentrated, organic fertilizers which release nitrogen slowly over a long period of time and should only be used in amounts recommended by the manufacturers. See SOILS.

URGINEA (er-JIN-ea)
maritima   3'   Zone 9   Sea-onion
A popular, old-fashioned house plant, growing from a large bulb 4–6 in. through and partially above ground; 10–20 fleshy and glaucous strap-shaped leaves about 12–18 in. long, wide above the middle. The whitish flowers, about $\frac{1}{2}$ in. long, are borne on a stalk 1–3 ft. long. Native to Syria and South Africa. The bulbs are often collected for their medicinal properties. Closely related to *Scilla*.

URSINIA (er-SIN-ea)
anthemoides   1$\frac{1}{2}$'   annual   Dill-leaf Ursinia
A South African herb with daisylike, yellow, solitary flower heads, with the rays purplish on the underside. The flowers are 2 in. across on long stalks. The leaves are alternate, deeply cut into lobes. This is also grown in the cool greenhouse. For the garden, sow seeds indoors in March or outdoors in May. Set out in garden in full sun after frost.

pulchra = anthemoides

URTICA (ur-TI-ca)
dioica   4'   Zone 3   Stinging Nettle
A perennial weed, widely naturalized in North America, but introduced from Europe. These are plants with opposite leaves, up to 5 in. long and 3 in. wide and covered with minute, but very stinging hairs. The rootstocks creep readily in the soil and aid materially in the spread of the plant. Flowers are small, greenish, rather inconspicuous and often dioecious but borne in axillary clusters. The upper parts of the plant have been chopped up to yield a greenish-yellow dye. See WEED-CONTROLLING CHEMICALS.

USDA. The U.S. Department of Agriculture is an agency of the Federal Government, created in 1862 and directed by law to acquire and diffuse useful information on agricultural subjects in the most general and comprehensive sense. The Secretary of Agriculture is responsible for the administration of the numerous functions and authorities assigned to the Department by law, and for advising the President of the United States on Federal policy and programs affecting agriculture.

The 17 operating agencies of the Department are divided into 6 major groups: Agricultural Economics, International Affairs, Commodity Programs, Marketing and Consumer Services, Rural Development and Conservation, Research and Education. USDA has about 87,000 full-time employees, of whom about 75,000 are located at about 15,000 duty stations. Approximately 4900 of these are full-time professional scientists. Other large groups of employees work with the Department, including 21,000 employees of the State extension services and 20,000 attached to state agricultural experiment stations. The states have about 9600 scientific personnel, some of whom are engaged part time in research and part time in teaching and extension work at land-grant colleges.

The U.S. Department of Agriculture works in close cooperation with the state agricultural experiment stations, and administers the Federal grant funds made available by Congress, which are matched by state funds. The state experiment stations are responsible for scientific operations and research at more than 500 centers, and the USDA carries on research at about 225 field locations, including Federal field stations and laboratories and the state experiment stations at which USDA undertakes cooperative work.

The Agricultural Research Service (ARS) conducts a diversified national research effort to provide farmers with better ways to grow and market their products, and consumers with an abundant and varied supply of food and fiber. In the international area, the agency assists foreign countries with both agricultural knowledge and improved agricultural products.

The ARS program concentrates on six major research goals: increasing farm production efficiency; reducing the cost of marketing agricultural products and developing new and improved products and processes; improving the environment and developing effective use of natural resources; reducing food-related health hazards and improving family living; providing new knowledge of human requirements for nutrients to maintain good health as well as sources of these nutrients in food; and developing foreign agriculture and markets.

The work done in the area of farm production efficiency is of direct interest to farm and suburban gardeners. The research objectives include: the discovery, development, testing and production of crops and livestock with improved genetic, physiological, and nutritional yield characteristics; the worldwide collection and preservation of valuable germplasm stocks; the protection of plants and animals from environmental stress factors; and the development of improved and effective insect, weed, and disease controls, including safe pesticidal and alternative methods of pest control.

Other research objectives include the development of improved machinery and equipment; development of improved energy-efficient systems of production; translation of new technologies into effective management practices; and the creation of new or improved systems to increase farm productivity.

Publications on the work of the Agricultural Research Service can be obtained from the Publications Branch, Information Division, ARS, Hyattsville, Md. 20782, or from USDA's Office of Communication, Washington, D.C. 20250.

The Plant Protection and Quarantine Program (PPQ), part of the Animal and Plant Health Inspection Service, is responsible for protecting U.S. gardens and crops against destructive plant insects and diseases. To accomplish this, PPQ conducts programs to (1) keep out foreign items that could harbor plant pests and (2) control or eradicate outbreaks of both foreign and native destructive pests—usually with the cooperation of affected states. A booklet, "Travelers' Tips", gives information on what food, plant and animal products are permitted into the U.S. from a foreign country. For this and other free PPQ publications, write to: APHIS Information Division, PPQ, USDA, Federal Building, Hyattsville, MD 20782.

The Extension Service—the educational arm of the department—cooperates with state and county extension workers throughout the country to help people solve their farm, garden, home and community problems. The county extension agent has information and publications on the research work of USDA, state land-grant universities, and state experiment stations. The county agent is often a reliable source of gardening information because of familiarity with local conditions and problems. County agents' offices are often located in county courthouses, and are listed under county governments in local telephone directories.

UTRICULARIA (yew-trik-yew-LAY-ria)

cornuta 5″–7″ Zone 3 Horned Bladderwort
Growing at the edge of bogs or small bodies of water, *U. cornuta* has creeping stems and small, hairylike leaves about ¾ in. long which are borne at or beneath the surface of the bog. The leafless flower stalk bears a few-flowered raceme of irregular yellow flowers having an upward-curving horn. It has no horticultural value except as an aquarium plant. Propagated by seeds and winter buds. The plant is native from Canada to Tex.

purpurea 5″–7″ Zone 3 Purple Bladderwort
Similar to *U. cornuta*, this species grows in ponds and streams. The submerged stems bear much-divided, threadlike, floating leaves, at the tips of which are tiny bladders which trap small insects. The purple flowers, similar in size and shape to *U. cornuta*, bloom in summer. The plant is native to eastern North America from Canada to Fla. and La., and sometimes becomes a nuisance in ponds and waterways.

vulgaris 5″–7″ Zone 3 Common Bladderwort
A perennial native to the bogs of North America, sometimes used as an aquarium plant and can grow in the water. The leaves are about ¾ in. long and are equipped with bladders for catching insects, floating on top of the water surface. The irregular yellow flowers, ½ in. long,

are borne in few-flowered clusters, 5–7 in. above the water. Propagated by seeds.

UVULARIA (yew-vew-LAY-ria). A North American perennial genus of the Lily Family, having a creeping rootstalk, alternate, sessile leaves which sometimes clasp the stem and drooping, bell-shaped flowers having 3 colored sepals and 3 petals. Flowers appear in spring. The plants do best in light, peaty soil and partial shade. They may be divided in early spring or late fall; seeds may be sown in autumn.

grandiflora 12″–18″ **Zone 3 Big Merrybells**
The bending stems of this plant are circled by the leaf bases and the drooping, lemon-yellow flowers are 1 in. or more in length. They bloom from April to June in the woods from Quebec to N.Dak. and from Ga. to Okla.

perfoliata 12″–20″ **Zone 4 Wood Merrybells**
This species has a forking stem and sparse leaves, the bases of which circle the stem. The terminally borne flowers are solitary or few in number, drooping and bell shaped. They flower in early summer in woods over eastern U.S.

sessilifolia 12″ **Zone 4 Little Merrybells**
Widely known as Wild Oats, the slender, upright stem bears oblong, tapering leaves, smooth on the upper surface and with fine white hairs on the undersurface, and 1 or several drooping, creamy-yellow flowers having 6 segments. These inconspicuous flowers may be found along roadsides or in open, moist woods over much of eastern U.S., blooming in spring and early summer. The young shoots have been cooked as for Asparagus.

V

VACCINIUM. The blueberries are widely distributed over the Northern Hemisphere from the Arctic Circle to high mountains in the Tropics. As ornamentals there are only a few which are of much value and these chiefly as foliage plants, especially for their brilliant scarlet autumn color. Fruits of some varieties are important

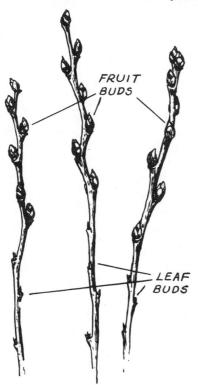

Vaccinium or Blueberry twigs

economically, and within the last few decades considerable interest has been given, first to selecting the better fruiting forms from the wild, then to improving the size and quality of these fruits by breeding. All blueberries require acid soil; most need plenty of moisture if they are to grow well; all have alternate leaves and most have vivid autumn color.

The fruits do attract birds, the reason why many are interested in growing them in the garden and why others do not choose to do so. It has been pointed out that most of the blueberry varieties are self-pollinating, so that it is not absolutely essential to grow several varieties for good pollination. On the other hand, it may help.

Propagation

Seed usually has no dormancy, hence it may be sown at any time. Some of the lower-growing species may be propagated merely by dividing the plants with a sharp spade early in the spring before growth has started. Both softwood and hardwood cuttings (which see) can be rooted.

Insect Pests

Blueberries are infested by 15 or more insects which are destructive in some areas. Among those attacking cultivated blueberries are blueberry maggot, a close relative of the apple maggot, infesting the berries in the northern areas during June and July. The white maggots eat the inside of the berry. Spraying or dusting with insecticide #15 while the flies are active gives control. A few bushes in the home garden may be protected from the flies and other insects as well as from birds by a tent of cloth or wire screen. Cranberry fruit worm, cherry fruit worm and plum curculio (see APPLE) attack the fruit soon after the blossoms fall and require regular spraying with insecticide #9 to prevent serious losses. A leafhopper which spreads the stunt disease virus is controlled by the same treatment. Cranberry weevil eats into the buds and may reduce the yield 50%. Clean cultivation and spraying when buds swell with insecticide #15 are recommended. Blueberry bud mite may be serious in southern areas where sprays of 2% summer oil (insecticide #45) after harvest are advised. Stem gall is unsightly and galls should be cut.

Diseases

Stunt, a virus causing dwarfed growth and small berries, is serious wherever blueberries are grown. Infected plants cannot be cured and must be destroyed. Spread is prevented by complete control of the leafhopper. Mummy berry develops from a fungus which blights blossoms and new shoots before infecting the berries. After reaching nearly full size the infected berries turn brown and dry. Prompt removal of wilted shoots and cultivation under the bushes is recommended since spraying with fungicide #D is only partially effective. Stem canker, causing swellings and cracks on stems, is destructive in the South. Planting only resistant varieties is advised. Double spot leaf disease causing defoliation is serious in the South. Two small spots within a larger spot identify this disease. Spraying with fungicide #K has been effective. In the Northwest botrytis tip blight has killed the entire annual growth on some bushes. No control is known.

angustifolium   8″   Zone 2   Lowbush Blueberry

This is the common Lowbush Blueberry found wild over much of the northeastern U.S. and southeastern Canada. It used to be called *V. angustifolium laevifolium* but after considerable study of the American blueberries in their natural habitat, Dr. W. H. Camp decided a few years ago that this name was actually a synonym of *V. angustifolium*, as is the older name *V. pensylvanicum*. It is this species that is grown commercially in Me. in large fields, often burned over every third year or so to keep the plants stocky and weed-free. This plant makes a ground cover in acid soils, is widely distributed in the woodlands or in sunny situations, and of course, like other blueberries, the foliage turns a vivid scarlet in the fall. Sometimes individual plants are found in a stand of *V. angustifolium* which are twice the size in habit and have larger fruits. These are the tetraploid, *V. lamarckii*. For information on culture see BLUEBERRY.

arboreum   27′   Zone 7   Farkleberry
Because it is evergreen and a small tree with lustrous green leaves, this plant is sometimes grown as an ornamental in the southeastern part of the U.S. where it is native.

ashei   4′–18′   Zone 7   Rabbiteye Blueberry
The Rabbiteye Blueberry, native to the southeastern U.S., sometimes deciduous and sometimes evergreen, is one cultivated in the Deep South instead of *V. corymbosum*. It is very susceptible to injury by fire, and was first grown commercially in Fla. in 1898. For information on culture see BLUEBERRY. Some varieties which have been selected primarily for the southeastern U.S. are:

'Callaway', originated at Tifton, Ga., by the U.S. Department of Agriculture in 1943 and introduced in 1949. The fruit is large;

'Clara', originated in Ga. and introduced in the 1930's.

'Garden Blue', selected in 1944 in Raleigh, N.Car., by the N.Car. Agricultural Experiment Station and introduced in 1958. It ripens in mid-June;

'Homebell', originated in Beltsville, Md., by the U.S. Department of Agriculture and the Ga. Experiment Station. The original cross was made in 1940 and the variety was introduced in 1955;

'Menditoo', selected in 1944 in Raleigh, N.Car., by the N.Car. Agricultural Experiment Station and introduced in 1958;

'Myers', originated in Ga. and introduced in the 1930's;

'Suwanee', originated along the old Suwanee River in Ga. and introduced in the 1930's. This is not so good as 'Clara', and might be overlooked;

'Tifblue', originated by the Ga. Experiment Station and the U.S. Department of Agriculture in 1945 and introduced in 1955.

bracteatum   4′   Zone 7   Oriental Blueberry
The red fruits and evergreen leaves of this oriental shrub from China and Japan give to it ornamental characteristics which might have value. The leaves are 1–2½ in. long and the flower clusters are 1–2 in. long.

corymbosum   6′–12′   Zone 3   Highbush Blueberry
The Highbush Blueberry is undoubtedly the most important of the blueberry clan, economically as well as ornamentally, and is native throughout the eastern U.S. Its tall vigorous growth, profuse fruit production and brilliant autumn color, combined with the ease with which it can be grown, make it a very popular plant. Then too, the fact that most varieties are self-pollinated and need no other pollen for fruit production make it a popular, small-garden fruit plant as well.

Over 50 years ago, Dr. F. V. Coville of the U.S. Department of Agriculture started what became an extensive program of selecting from the wild good-fruiting clones and hybridizing them. Miss Elizabeth White of Whitesbog, N.J., cooperated in this effort, along with many other individuals, as well as staff members in some state experiment stations. Some 40 or more clones of the Highbush Blueberry have been named and today the production of blueberries as a commercial fruit crop is a very important one in the East, as well as in Mich. and the Pacific Northwest. The value of the total crop (from so-called "cultivated" plants) amounts to well over 10 million dollars. The crop picked from wild plants might amount to two-thirds as much.

The season of fruiting lasts about 2 months, and the most important of the varieties are listed according to the season in which they ripen.

Very early

'Earliblue'   'Wolcott'
'Weymouth'

Early

'Bluecrop'	'Murphy'
'Cabot'	'Pacific'
'Collins'	'Rancocas'

Midseason (1 week after Cabot)

'Berkeley'	'Gem'
'Blueray'	'Ivanhoe'
'Concord'	'Pioneer'
'Dixi'	'Stanley'

Late (2 weeks after Cabot)

'Atlantic'	'Pemberton'
'Burlington'	'Rubel'
'Herbert'	'Sam'
'Jersey'	'Scammel'
'Katherine'	

Very late

'Coville'	'Wareham'

It may be difficult to determine which among these many varieties should be grown, either commercially or in the small garden fruit lot. The best information on this subject is always from the nearest state experiment station. In Mass., the State Experiment Station recommends the following:

'Earliblue', 'Collins', 'Blueray', 'Bluecrop', 'Berkeley', 'Pemberton', 'Herbert', 'Jersey', 'Coville', for commercial growing as well as for home gardens.

For information on culture and varieties see BLUEBERRY.

crassifolium procumbent Zone 7 Creeping Blueberry
Somewhat similar to *V. vitis-idaea*, this procumbent woody plant has some use as an evergreen ground cover in acid soils within its hardiness range. It is native from N.Car. to Ga. The fruits are merely black.

delavayi 1'–3' Zone 7 Delavay Blueberry
This Blueberry from western China makes a neat little evergreen for the small garden and is especially valued for its boxlike leaves. The fruits are reddish.

hirsutum 5' Zone 5 Hairy Blueberry
In moist, partially shaded soils this spreads rapidly by underground suckers and hence can be used as a ground cover in acid soils. The fruits are black. Native from Tenn. to Ga.

macrocarpon creeping Zone 2 Cranberry
Everyone is familiar with the Cranberry, native to bogs throughout eastern and northeastern North America, and grown commercially in carefully maintained bogs for its red fruits which, in a few states, are highly important commercial products. As an ornamental it has little value unless it is planted in a bog. For information on culture, see CRANBERRY.

ovatum 10' Zone 7 Box Blueberry
This lustrous-leaved evergreen is used chiefly for its foliage. Native to the northwest Pacific Coast, its small boxlike leaves, 1¼ in. long, are highly valued by florists and cut branches are a common commodity in the florist industry throughout America.

pallidum 3' Zone 3 Dryland Blueberry
A good Blueberry for planting in dry-soil situations, this is native to the eastern U.S. The autumn color is of course scarlet, but otherwise it can be overlooked in ornamental plantings.

pensylvanicum = *V. angustifolium*

praestans 2' Zone 3 Cherry Blueberry
Although rare in America, this Japanese plant might have possibilities in northern gardens because of its low, creeping habit, somewhat similar to that of *Gaultheria procumbens*. It is deciduous and the fruit is bright red.

stamineum 2' Zone 5 Common Deerberry
Widely native throughout the eastern U.S., this is sometimes used because its white, bell-shaped flowers, produced in clusters, are among the prettiest and most conspicuous of all the blueberries, the individual flowers sometimes being ½ in. wide.

vitis-idaea minus creeping Zone 2 Mountain Cranberry
This is a native evergreen (northern U.S. and Canada), never over 4–8 in. high if that, creeping over the soil mostly in moist situations. It is difficult to get it established in gardens, but where the situation is just right, with acid and moist soil, it is valued especially when its diminutive white flowers are in bloom and when its red fruits ripen in the early fall.

It is of interest to note that *V. vitis-idaea* is chiefly a native of Europe and northern Asia, found occasionally only mixed in with the far more common variety **minus** in America. The leaves of the species are up to 1¼ in. long, while those of the variety **minus** are only up to ¾ in. long. Those of the variety **majus** are larger than either one. It is the common variety **minus** which is chiefly found growing wild in America and which makes the better, lower, matlike planting.

VAGINATE. Sheathed or surrounded by a sheath.

VALERIAN. See VALERIANA for the true Valerian.

VALERIAN, RED = *Centranthus ruber*

VALERIANA (val-ee-ri-AY-na)

arizonica 6" Zone 6 Arizona Valerian
A rare plant from the hot, dry sands of Ariz. It forms a low mat, with creeping rootstock and oval-shaped leaves and clusters of whitish to pink flowers, each ½ in. long, which bloom in June. It is fine for the rock garden, requiring a sweet soil and full sun.

officinalis 4' Zone 3 Common Valerian
A garden herb with fragrant, bisexual, whitish to pinkish or lavender flowers in loose clusters,

forming a flat head with an odor something like Heliotrope; blooming during July and early Aug. Leaves are opposite, and divided into 7–10 pairs of lance-shaped segments. They sometimes are used to flavor tobacco and the rhizome is used as a sedative. Native to Europe and Asia, naturalized in North America. Easily propagated by seed and division. In the well-tended perennial garden, the weedy character can be objectionable.

VALERIANELLA (val-ee-ri-an-ELL-a)
   locusta   1′   annual   European Corn-salad
With opposite oblong leaves, 3 in. long, either toothed or entire and light blue flowers in a flat-topped flower cluster. The fruits are 3 celled but 2 of these are always empty. This is a native to Europe where it is used as a spring salad. Sow the seed out-of-doors after frost, thin to 6 in. apart and the crop should be ready in 6–8 weeks. Successive sowings are also suggested about 2 weeks apart.

VALLISNERIA (val-liss-NEE-ria)
   spiralis   aquatic plant   Zone 8   Eel-grass
This is native to Europe and southern Asia and is the grass so much used in aquaria because the leaves are from 6 in. to 6 ft. long (depending on the temperature of the water and growing conditions in general), and $\frac{1}{12}$–$\frac{1}{3}$ in. wide. The "Italian type" is probably the one in the trade not hardy in the waters of central and northern U.S. The native **V. americana** is not a good water plant for the aquaria.

VALLOTA (val-LO-ta)
   speciosa   3′   Zone 10   Scarborough-lily
A bulbous plant, sometimes forced in the greenhouse and used as a pot plant indoors, with straplike leaves 2 ft. long and an inch wide; scarlet, funnelform flowers, 3 in. across, in terminal umbels at the end of a 3-ft. stem, blooming in the summer and autumn. During the rest period, the roots should be kept moist. This belongs to the Amaryllis Family and is native to southern Africa.

VALVATE. Opening by valves; meeting by the edges without overlapping as leaves or petals in the bud.

VALVERIANACEAE = The Valverian Family

VALVERIAN FAMILY = Valverianaceae

VANCOUVERIA (van-koo-VEE-ria)
   hexandra   1¼′   Zone 5   American Barrenwort
This plant comes from the Pacific Coast forests where it can be found as a ground cover under some of the giant coastal redwoods. It is a relative of the barberries as well as the epimediums, doing best only in shaded situations where there is an abundance of moisture. It dies to the ground in winter. If the soil is sandy,

peat moss or compost might well be added to it for the better growth of this plant. The feathery, delicate leaves are $\frac{1}{2}$–$1\frac{1}{2}$ in. long. The white flowers have 6 petals, each $\frac{1}{2}$ in. long, in panicles of 6–45 during May and June. Easily propagated by division.

   planipetala   7″–12″   Zone 6
Native to northern Ore. and Calif., this plant is being used as a ground cover in Calif. The evergreen leaves are 2–3 times ternate, sometimes with 5 leaflets, each up to $2\frac{1}{4}$ in. long and as wide, but usually smaller. The flowers are white or lavender tinged, about $\frac{3}{10}$ in. long in a many-flowered panicle; blooming in May and June.

VANDA (VAN-da). The latest hobby among owners of home greenhouses is the growing of the Vanda orchids, native to southern Asia and the islands of the South Pacific. These are beautiful epiphytic plants with small flowers in long graceful racemes; individual flowers varying from 1–$6\frac{1}{2}$ in., almost every color but predominantly lavender-blue and yellow-brown. Flowers are usually flat but often the petals are twisted or reflexed. Most are climbing vines that start growth in the ground and then develop into complete epiphytes up in the trees. They vary in height from a few inches to 7–10 ft. The roots are large and fleshy, many developing into aerial feeders. Many hybrids are beginning to appear and because of the great popularity of these flowers now, many more will undoubtedly appear in the future. For culture and propagation see ORCHID.

   coerulea   2′–3′   Zone 10
Flowers 7–20 in a raceme each up to 5 in. across, pale blue color. Native to Burma. A very beautiful orchid; the only one of this sky-blue color, but a little difficult to grow.

   dearei   2′–5′   Zone 10
Flowers 4–8 on a raceme, each 3–4 in. across, yellow and with a fragrance like lemons. Can bloom any time throughout the year. Native to the Sunda Isles.

   luzonica   1′–5′   Zone 10
Flowers 8–15 on a raceme, each $2\frac{1}{2}$–4 in. across, cream colored with reddish spots at the tips of sepals and petals with the capability of blooming any time. Rare and very beautiful. Native to the Philippines.

   merrillii   1′–4′   Zone 10
Flowers 8–15 on a raceme, each $1\frac{1}{2}$ in. across, colored dark red on yellow; petals reflexed; blooming in the summer and autumn. Native to the Philippines.

   sanderana   7″–30″   Zone 10
Flowers 6–15 on a raceme, each 4–6 in. across, light yellowish to pink with reddish veins, flat and round. Considered by many as the best of the Vanda orchids and very popular. There are many varieties but they do grow rather slowly,

blooming from July to Dec. Native to the Philippines.

spathulata   1½'–6'   **Zone 10**
Few flowers to a raceme, each 1½ in. across, bright yellow and appearing almost any time. A rare Orchid, requiring some shade on the lower leaves but sun on the top in order to flower. Native to India and Ceylon.

teres   1'–5'   **Zone 10**
With 2–10 flowers per raceme, each 2–4 in. across and colored dark lavender, blooming in spring or summer. A slender plant, not too vigorous. Native to Burma.

tricolor   1'–10'   **Zone 10**
With 6–12 fragrant flowers per raceme, each 3–4 in. across and mostly cream colored with brown spots and lavender-colored edge to petals, slightly reflexed and twisted and capable of blooming any time. A strong grower that can withstand full sun. Native to Java.

VANILLA (van-ILL-a)
planifolia   **vine**   **Zone 10**   **Common Vanilla**
This is the Orchid, the dried fruit of which produces the vanilla of commerce, much of which now is made synthetically. It is a loosely climbing vine, sometimes reaching a length of 300 ft.; with green flowers, 2 in. across, in many-flowered racemes and the 3-angled fruits about 6–9 in. long. Native to tropical America. There is a form (**variegata**) with leaves variegated with white. For culture and propagation see ORCHID.

VARIEGATED. Having marks, stripes or blotches of some color other than the basic ground-color, in plants which are green.

VARIETY (as a botanical unit). A subdivision of the species composed of individuals differing from other members of the species in certain minor characters which are usually perpetuated through generations by seed. However, as used in this book the general term variety also includes clone, which see.

VASCULAR. With vessels or ducts.

VASES. See GARDEN FIXTURES.

VEGETABLE. According to L. H. Bailey, a vegetable is "In horticultural usage, an edible herbaceous plant or part thereof that is commonly used for culinary purposes." In common usage the fruits of the Tomato, Cucumber, Squash, etc. are considered as vegetables, grown with other vegetables in the home garden, although of course each one is a seed-bearing organ and hence, under strict usage of the language, might be considered a fruit.

VEGETABLE GARDEN. A kitchen garden can be a definite asset to any family that has land available and an interest in working with plants. With proper planning it can be a very satisfying addition to the home plantings. It can

provide recreation and a relaxing change from the normal work-a-day responsibilities. There is a definite satisfaction in the growing and harvesting of garden-fresh produce plus the additional value that fresh vegetables have in the diet as sources of essential minerals and vitamins. This garden can also be of real economic value in helping to reduce the family food bill at the retail food store.

The size of the garden will depend on many factors but basically it should not require more time in its care than can readily be given by the members of the family. Its operation should be an enjoyable pastime and not a menial task.

A small vegetable garden with a polyethylene cover for forcing early plants. (*Photo by Arnold Arboretum, Jamaica Plain, Mass.*)

A garden of 5000 sq. ft. which is well planned and cared for should supply an adequate supply of a variety of fresh vegetables for an average family, and perhaps leave a surplus for the home freezer.

Planning the Garden

It is very desirable to make a definite plan of the garden on a piece of paper well in advance of the growing season. Such a plan should list the crops to be grown, where each should be located, their spacing and the dates of seeding or the setting of plants. This information will provide an orderly basis for the various operations during the entire year and an accurate check listing of the various materials, supplies, and tools that will be needed such as seeds, plants, fertilizers, spray and dust materials, etc.

In planning the garden there are several basic considerations. The amount of daily or weekly time that can readily be allotted to the care of the garden. The likes and dislikes of the family need to be checked in selecting the kinds and varieties of vegetables. The type and condition of the soil will not only modify the kind of vegetable that will flourish, but also modify the time needed for good gardening care. Climatic conditions and length of frost-free growing periods must also be considered in selecting the crops to be grown.

The small plot (1500–3000 sq. ft.) should contain only a few kinds to be used as fresh or green vegetables such as tomatoes, snap beans, carrots, Cabbage, Chard, Spinach, Radish and Lettuce. These normally provide the greater value and yield in food units for the time and care necessary in their production. In larger gardens it may be desirable to include sweet corn, peppers, peas, cucumbers, squash, turnips, parsnips and even a few hills of Asparagus and Rhubarb. On a basis of yield per sq. ft. and cost, it is questionable to include winter squash and potatoes in the average home garden.

In planning the cropping program, plant small amounts at frequent intervals in order that the supply of well-matured produce will be enough for immediate needs. For example, 4 or 5 plantings of 15 ft. of beans is preferable to planting 100 ft. at one time. A spread in maturity will provide better eating and less spoilage.

The proper arrangement of crops requires good judgment and consideration of the number of days to maturity and spacing needed to permit sufficient room for the full development of each plant.

Making the rows run according to the compass is of questionable importance in the average garden. In general planning, the following points should be given consideration:

1. Perennial crops such as Rhubarb and Asparagus that will remain in 1 place for several years should be planted at one end or one side of the garden, so that they will not interfere with plowing and cultivation.

2. Tall crops and those that spread out such as sweet corn, pole beans, staked tomatoes, cucumbers and squash should be planted toward one side of the garden.

3. Many quick-growing crops such as Radish, Lettuce and Spinach can be planted between rows of slower-growing crops such as Celery, tomatoes, or even sweet corn. This is known as companion cropping.

4. As soon as each crop is harvested the plan should indicate another crop that can be planted and matured before the end of the growing season. Early Lettuce may be followed by beans, Spinach by Celery, peas by late Cabbage. This is known as successive cropping.

Quantity of Seed and Number of Plants

Check the Table which lists the quantity of seed or the number of plants required for 100-ft. row, average planting distances, days to maturity and hardiness for the various crops as a guide in the development of a plan of operation.

PLANTING TABLE FOR VEGETABLES
(Hardy = will stand a few degrees of frost; Tender = foliage will be killed by any degrees of frost; Half Hardy = in between those extremes)

KIND OF VEGETABLE	REQUIREMENTS FOR 100 FEET OF ROW		PLANTING DISTANCE IN INCHES		APPROX. NO. OF DAYS PLANTING SEED TO		HARDY HALF HARDY TENDER
	SEED	PLANTS	ROWS	PLANTS	GERMINATION	HARVEST	
Asparagus	1 oz.	75 roots	42–48	15–20	10–15	3 yr.	H
Beans, Bush Snap	1 lb.		24–30	2–4	4–8	40–65	T
Pole Snap	½ lb.		30–36	Hills 24	4–8	60–75	T
Bush Lima	1 lb.		24–30	4–6	4–8	60–75	T
Pole Lima	½ lb.		30–36	Hills 24	4–8	75–100	T
Beets	2 oz.		12–15	2–3	6–10	40–65	H
Broccoli		75	24–30	15–20	4–8	60–100	HH
Cabbage		75	24–36	15–24	4–8	60–90	H
Chinese Cabbage	¼ oz.		18–24	8–10	4–8	70–90	H
Carrots	½ oz.		12–15	2–3	10–15	65–100	H
Cauliflower		75	24–30	15–20	4–8	60–100	HH
Celery		200	24–30	6	12–20	100–140	HH
Chard, Swiss	2 oz.		12–15	4–8	6–10	40–65	H
Corn, Sweet	¼ lb.		30–36	Hills 24	6–8	65–100	T
Cucumber	½ oz.		48	8–10	6–10	55–70	T
Eggplant		50	30–36	24–30	10–15	100–120	T
Endive	½ oz.		12–15	10–12	10–12	60–90	H
Kale	¼ oz.		20–24	12–18	4–8	55–65	H
Kohlrabi	¼ oz.		12–15	3–4	4–8	55–70	HH

PLANTING TABLE FOR VEGETABLES

KIND OF VEGETABLE	REQUIREMENTS FOR 100 FEET OF ROW		PLANTING DISTANCE IN INCHES		APPROX. NO. OF DAYS PLANTING SEED TO		HARDY —HALF HARDY
	SEED	PLANTS	ROWS	PLANTS	GERMINATION	HARVEST	TENDER
Lettuce Head	¼ oz.	100–125	15	9–15	4–8	75–90	HH
Cos	¼ oz.		15	8–10	4–8	60–80	HH
Heat	¼ oz.		12–15	2–4	4–8	30–60	HH
Mustard	¼ oz.		12–15	2–4	4–8	35–45	H
Muskmelon	½ oz.		48–60	Hills 48	6–10	75–110	T
Onion Plants		400	12–15	3–4		100	HH
Sets		2 lb. Small	12–15	3–4		60–80	HH
Seed	1 oz.		12–15	3–4	6–12	100–110	HH
Parsnip	½ oz.		12–18	2–3	12–20	95–110	H
Peas Dwarf	1 lb.		24–30	1–2	8–10	55–70	H
Tall	1 lb.		36	1–2	8–10	70–75	H
Peppers		75	18–30	15–18	6–10	60–75	T
Potatoes	6–10 lbs.		24–36	8–10	8–12	90–120	T
Pumpkin	1 oz.		72	Hills 60	4–8	80–100	T
Radish	1 oz.		6–12	1–2	4–8	25–30	HH
Rhubarb		35	36	24		2 yrs.	H
Rutabaga	¼ oz.		18–24	6–8	4–8	80–100	H
Spinach	1 oz.		10–15	1–2	6–10	40–50	H
Squash							
Bush	½ oz.		36–48	36	4–8	50–60	T
Vine (Winter)	½ oz.		84–96	Hills 72–84	4–8	85–120	T
Tomatoes							
Not Staked		35–40	36–48	24–36	6–10	70–90	T
Staked		75	36	12–18	6–10	65–90	T
Turnip	¼ oz.		12–15	3–4	4–8	60–80	H
Watermelon	1 oz.		48–60	Hills 48	6–10	70–100	T

The data of the above table are to be used primarily as a general guide.

The garden plan should also include a general work program, noting for each month the basic things that need to be done. This will serve as a check in having seeds, plants, supplies and materials available prior to the time that they will actually be needed.

Suggested Varieties of Vegetables

With many kinds of vegetables there are a number of very excellent varieties which may vary in days to maturity, resistance to disease, size of plant, fruit or pod and even color as well as eating quality. The selection of the right variety for a particular purpose means a thorough and careful study of at least several catalogues of reputable seed companies. It may also be advisable to check with the extension service of the state university for a listing of recommended varieties.

During the past decade many of the old, so-called standard varieties have been replaced by hybrids in an effort to provide more vigorous growth, higher yields and better quality. This is particularly true with sweet corn, tomatoes and cucumbers.

The following listing is simply a suggested guide of some of the more common kinds and varieties of vegetables:

Asparagus—Mary Washington

Beans—Green Bush, Tendergreen, Contender, Harvester

Wax Bush, Surecrop, Pencil Pod Wax, Pole, Kentucky Wonder types, Blue Lake, Romano

Bush Lima—Fordhook 242, Henderson Bush (small seeded)

Pole Lima—King of the Garden, Burpee's Best, Sieva or Carolina

Shell—French Horticultural

Beets—Crosby or Wonder types, Detroit Dark Red, Red Ball

Broccoli—Green Sprouting, De Cicco, Calabrese, Green Comet Hybrid

Brussels Sprouts—Catskill, Jade

Cabbage, Green—Jersey Wakefield, Golden Acre, Copenhagen, Danish Ballhead type

Red—Red Acre
Savoy—Chieftan
Chinese Cabbage—Michihli
Carrots—Chantenay, Gold Pak, Long Imperator, Nantes Half Long
Cauliflower—Snowball types
Celery—Golden Self Blanching, Pascal, Utah
Cucumber Pickling—National Pickling, Ohio MR 17
Slicing—Marketmore 70, Burpee Hybrid
Eggplant—Black Beauty, Black Magic
Endive—Green Curled, Broad Leaved Batavian
Kale—Blue Curled, Siberian
Kohlrabi—Early Purple Vienna, Early White Vienna
Lettuce Crisphead—Pennlake, Great Lakes
Butterhead—Bibb, White Boston
Loose Leaf—Salad Bowl, Grand Rapids, Ruby Red, Green Ice
Cos—White Paris Cos
Leek—American Flag
Mustard—Green Wave, Giant Curled
Muskmelon—Cantaloupe—Hearts of Gold, Hales, Maineyrock Hybrid
Standard—Delicious, Harper Hybrid
Winter—Honey Dew, Cranshaw
Okra—Perkins Mammoth Long Green, Early Dwarf
Onions, Bunching—Japanese Green, Long White
Mature Bulbs—Ebenezer (sets) Yellow and Red Globe types, Bermuda types, Sweet Spanish types, White Portugal (pickling)
Parsnip—Hollow Crown, Guernsey, Model
Peas, Dwarf—Little Marvel, Laxtonian, Alaska
Tall—Freezonian, Alderman, Imp. Telephone
Edible Pod—Oregon Sugar, Sugar Snap
Peppers, Mild—California Wonder, World Beauty, Ruby King, Pimiento; Hot—Hungarian Wax, Long Red Cayenne
Pumpkin—Small Sugar, Mammoth, Cushaw, Winter Luxury
Radish—Scarlet Globe, Cherry Belle, White Icicle, White Chinese (winter type)
Rhubarb—McDonald, Victoria
Rutabaga—American Purple Top
Spinach—Dark Green Bloomsdale, American Savoy, Nobel, New Zealand
Squash, Summer—Early Prolific Straightneck, Caserta, Zucchini, Bush Scallop
Fall and Winter—Table Queen, Buttercup, Butternut, Blue Hubbard
Sweet Corn—Each seed company lists many varieties, therefore it is difficult to suggest varieties available in all sections such as North Star, Sugar and Gold, Butter and Sugar, Golden Cross Bantam, Jubilee, Iochief, and the standard variety Golden Bantam
Swiss Chard—Fordhook Giant, Rhubarb

Tomatoes—Early Hybrid, Marglobe, Valiant, Morton Hybrid, Rutgers, Big Boy, Supersonic, Ponderosa (pink), Jubilee (orange), San Marzano (Italian)
Turnip—Purple Top White Globe, Early Snowball
Watermelon—Klondike, New Hampshire Midget

Soil Preparation

It is seldom that the land available for the kitchen garden is entirely satisfactory for optimum plant growth. It may be of a "fill" type with only a shallow coating of good loam, a heavy clay with poor drainage, a very light, sandy soil having excessive drainage, or carry a heavy sod made up largely of quack grass and weeds. Each of these conditions will need a different treatment in developing a basic soil of a proper acidity, fertility and water holding capacity. See SOILS.

The preparation of the soil is an important and sometimes difficult job. No amount of care will result in a satisfactory crop in a so-called poor soil. The ultimate aim in building a good soil base is one having a high fertility, test slightly acid, contain a good supply of organic matter, be well drained and, of course, free from weeds. Proper root development for most vegetable crops will require a good loam topsoil of at least 8 to 10 in.

Heavy soils such as those containing a high percentage of clay can be improved by the addition of humus-forming materials such as animal manures, peat, compost or, in large gardens where conditions permit, the use of cover crops and green manures. The same materials will improve the texture and water-holding capacity of the lighter sandy-type soils.

All organic materials should be applied before spading or plowing the garden so that they may be thoroughly incorporated into the top 6 to 8 in. of soil.

Proper soil preparation prior to planting will help to keep it mellow during the entire growing season, make more food available, improve air drainage and promote a deeper rooting of plants. A small garden of say 25 ft. × 50 ft. is usually spaded by hand and then smoothed with a stout iron rake. In large plots plowing and harrowing by machine is a distinct labor saver. A rototiller will do a very excellent job. These machines are for hire by many garden supply stores, landscape gardeners and nurserymen.

In plowing or spading turn the soil over to a depth of at least 6 in., but care should be taken not to dig up more than an inch of subsoil in any one year.

Soil Fertility

Animal manures are preferred when available because they supply both humus and plant food. Their value will vary depending on amount of litter, age and exposure to the air. Fresh cow or horse manure will vary with the rate of application from 20–50 bu. per 1000 sq. ft., depending on the general type and fertility of the soil. The same rates hold for dry cow or sheep manure. Poultry manure, because of its higher fertility value, should not be used in quantities of more than 10 to 20 bu. per 1000 sq. ft.

Peat of any kind can be used to build up the organic content of the soil. These materials contain little plant food and tend to be acid and, therefore, limestone should be applied at the rate of 10 lb. per cu. yd. or 5 lb. per bale before the peat is worked into the soil.

Compost made from leaves, grass clippings or garden refuse will make very desirable artificial manure and an excellent source of humus. In general, it is advisable to apply 5 to 10 lbs. of a nitrogen fertilizer per 1000 sq. ft. where a raw compost is used in order to feed the bacteria that cause proper decomposition.

In addition to the soil-improving crops, it is advisable to use a complete commercial fertilizer as a supplement and more readily available plant nutrient. Where a good application of cow or horse manure has been used apply 30 to 40 lbs. of a 5-10-5 or a 5-10-10 fertilizer per 1000 sq. ft. If no mannure was used increase the commercial fertilizer application to 40 or 50 lb. per 1000 sq. ft. An analysis of 5-10-5 represents the percentage of available nitrogen, phosphorus and potash.

The most satisfactory method of applying fertilizer is to broadcast it over the soil after spading or plowing and then work it into the top 2 to 3 in. by raking or with a harrow. Again a rotary tractor does an excellent job in a small or large garden in preparing an ideal seed bed.

In soils having a relatively low, fertility level it may be advisable to apply some of the fertilizer in the row in addition to the broadcast application. The proper placement is at the side of the seed or plant, not on top or below. Make a furrow 2 to 3 in. deep and spaced 2 in. on each side of the row. If the overall application of commercial fertilizer is 40 to 50 lb. per 1000 sq. ft., one-half may be broadcast and the other half applied in the row. This means approximately 5 oz. per 10 ft. of row when the rows are 18 in. apart and 10 oz. per 10 ft. where the row spacing is 3 ft. Two level tablespoonsfuls equal 1 oz. of fertilizer.

Where transplants are used a "starter solution" may be used with good results. This is a water solution of a fertilizer applied at the rate of ½ cupful to the transplant at the time of planting. Starter solutions consist of readily soluble chemicals such as ammonium phosphate potassium nitrate, urea, etc. Various mixtures are available at garden supply centers.

Most vegetables do best in a soil that is slightly acid (pH 6.0–6.5). Lime is used to correct soil acidity, but garden soils should not be limed unless they have been tested to show whether or not lime is needed. Tests will also indicate the amount of limestone that should be applied. A good rule-of-thumb practice is to apply 50 lb. of ground limestone or 35 lb. of hydrated lime per 1000 sq. ft. every 3 or 5 years. Wood ashes are also a good substitute for lime but should be used at the rate of 3 times the quantity of limestone.

During the growing season it is frequently advisable to top dress (fertilize) certain of the crops, such as sweet corn, tomatoes, peppers, late cabbage, etc. to provide an extra boost to plant growth. Use a complete fertilizer broadcast between the rows at the rate of about 10–15 lb. per 1000 sq. ft., and then rake or cultivate it into the topsoil. This practice is also recommended where 2 or 3 crops are grown on the same area or after a prolonged rainy spell which can result in a definite depletion of nitrogen. Under this latter situation the use of a straight nitrogen fertilizer such as nitrate of soda or sulfate of ammonia might be used at the rate of 5 lb. for 1000 sq. ft.

Tools and Equipment

Relatively few tools are needed for the average garden. A spade, digging fork, iron rake (14 to 16 teeth), 1 or 2 narrow-bladed hand hoes, several trowels, a 3- or 4-pronged hand weeder, a wheelbarrow or garden cart, a hose and sprinkler, and a garden line are basic tools. A wheel hoe or a hand cultivator with different attachments (teeth, shovels and blades) will save much hand labor. Also, as basic equipment, hand dusters or sprayers are recommended for the small garden and the knapsack or small power types for the larger projects.

There are a number of small, rototiller-type tractors on the market which can be effectively used in even the smaller gardens. These machines can save much time and labor in not only preparing the seedbed, but also in cultivating the garden during the cropping season.

Growing Plants for Transplanting

Early plants may be started in window-boxes, hotbeds, cold frames or greenhouses. This is done either to obtain a crop earlier than is possible by direct seeding in the garden, or to properly mature certain crops that require a long frost-free period to develop a full crop.

Growing early plants successfully requires a good soil, a reasonably uniform temperature and soil moisture and at least 6 to 7 hours of normal daylight.

SOIL. An ideal soil is loose and friable with a pH 6.0 to 6.8, holds moisture yet is not wet, and it should not cake or crust. There are a number of soil mixtures that are satisfactory, but the following formula has given very good results:

For seeding soil, 2 parts of a sandy loam, 1 part fine peat moss and 1 part sand. Add 2 oz. of superphosphate and 2 oz. of ground limestone per bu. of soil. Mix thoroughly.

For transplanting and potting soils, 7 parts of sandy loam, 3 parts peat moss, 2 parts sand. Add 2 oz. of a 5-10-5 fertilizer and 2 oz. of ground limestone per bu. of soil and mix thoroughly.

CONTAINERS. Shallow wooden boxes are preferred, but any container that will hold soil to a depth of at least 2-3 in. may be used. A number of plastic-type trays are available at most garden centres, hardware stores or from seed companies.

In sowing the seed, plant only a few inches of row for each kind. This will provide a fairly large number of seedlings. Sow the seed in rows spaced a few inches apart and at a depth of $\frac{1}{8}$ to $\frac{1}{4}$ in. depending on the size of the seed. Cover the seed with soil, press the soil firmly with a flat board and then water.

In watering use a fine spray to prevent washing the seeds out. Too much water may cause "damping off" of the seedlings and a soil that is too dry will prevent germination. During the germination period a pane of glass, a piece of cardboard or a sheet of cellophane placed over the seed flat will prevent rapid drying of the top layer of soil. These covers should be removed as soon as the seeds germinate.

An ideal temperature for normal germination of most vegetable seed is 70° to 80° F.

As soon as the seedlings have developed their first true leaves, they should be carefully removed from the seed flat and transplanted into containers filled with the potting soil mixture. Transplants are usually spaced from $1\frac{1}{2}$ to 3 or even 4 in. apart. For example, Celery is spaced at 1 to $1\frac{1}{2}$ in. and tomatoes 3 in. × 3 in. or 4 in. × 4 in. apart. The use of plant bands is recommended for Celery, Cabbage, Broccoli and Lettuce and where space permits use clay, plastic or peat pots for Eggplant, Pepper, Tomato, melons, cucumbers and squash. Beets and onions are not transplanted before planting into the garden.

Transplants must have as much direct sunlight as possible. Subdued light causes long, spindly, weak plants. Artificial light, either incandescent or fluorescent, may be used to supplement daylight.

Do not water until the surface of the soil starts to dry. Growing temperatures should be between 60°–65° F. at night to 75° or 85° F. in the daytime.

It is not possible to specify actual dates at which seed should be planted to start early plants. In general, the time allowed in weeks from the date of seeding to transplanting into the garden plot is approximately 4 to 5 for melons, squash and cucumbers, 6 to 7 for beets, Broccoli, Cabbage, Cauliflower, and Lettuce, 7 to 8 for onions, 8 to 10 for Eggplant, Pepper and Tomato.

Hardy plants (see pages 1146-47) may be planted into the garden 2 to 3 weeks prior to the average date of the last killing frost, half hardy about the date of the average last frost and for tender plants the delay should be 10 days to 2 weeks after possibility of a frost.

Planting and Care of the Garden

The time for planting seeds and setting plants in the garden depends largely on the last date of frost in the spring and the first killing frost in the fall. Some crops must be planted early to avoid hot weather, others thrive best in warm weather. Some plants are frost hardy and others are very readily injured by temperatures in the lower thirties. (See pages 1146-47 for hardiness rating.)

Hardy crops can be planted as soon as the frost is out of the ground. The seedlings and plants will stand temperatures as low as 28° F. Half hardy crops will withstand short exposures of temperatures in the low 30° F. range.

Tender crops are killed or severely injured by temperatures below 40° F. and, therefore, are not planted until the weather has settled and danger of a frost or freeze has past.

Plants that are injured by low temperatures can be started indoors. See TRANSPLANTING. The use of some sort of plant protector may also serve to allow early planting of tender crops. These may consist of small wooden boxes with a glass top, small baskets, and a variety of plastic caps, cones or tents that are available at garden supply centers. These are especially recommended for early plantings of such crops as summer squash, melons, tomatoes or even sweet corn if planted in hills.

A fine, well-pulverized seedbed is very important and, therefore, the preparation of the soil is the first operation of the garden planting program. Follow the garden plan for planting dates and spacing of rows and plants in the row. Sow the seed at a proper depth, 2 to 3 times the diameter of the seed, and not too thick. A seed sower can be used in the larger

COLD-HARDY CROPS FOR EARLY SPRING PLANTING		COLD-TENDER OR HEAT-HARDY CROPS FOR LATE SPRING OR EARLY SUMMER PLANTING	
VERY HARDY, PLANT 4–6 WEEKS BEFORE FROST-FREE DATE	HARDY, PLANT 2–4 WEEKS BEFORE FROST-FREE DATE	NOT COLD-HARDY PLANT ON FROST-FREE DATE	REQUIRE HOT WEATHER PLANT 1–2 WEEKS AFTER FROST-FREE DATE
Broccoli	Beets	Snap Beans	Beans, All
Cabbage	Carrots	Celery	Eggplant
Dandelion	Cauliflower	Okra	Pepper
Kale	Chard	Sweet Corn	Cucumber
Lettuce	Leek	Squash	Melons
Onions	Mustard	Soybeans	Sweet Potato
Potato	Parsnip	Tomato	
Peas	Radish		
Spinach			
Turnip			

garden but hand seedage is preferable for short rows and plantings in the smaller garden. Moisture is very important for proper seed germination. If the soil is dry, it will help to water after the seed is planted. A wet soil will cake, be cold and retard germination.

Garden care involves many operations which will vary for different crops. There are, however, several practices that are general in nature.

CULTIVATION. Vegetables cannot compete with weeds. Cultivation should start as soon as the seeds have germinated and the transplants have started to grow. The best time to control weeds is before they have become well established for they can then be destroyed by shallow cultivation. Vegetable plants are shallow rooted and therefore, deep cultivation by hand cultivators, wheel hoes or hand hoes can cause considerable plant damage by destroying the root systems close to the soil surface.

If time is a factor in proper garden care it might be well to consider the use of mulches to control weeds and to conserve soil moisture. The mulch should be applied as soon as the plants are well established. Mulch materials commonly used are strawy manure, hay, grass clippings, salt hay, peat moss, and sheets of black plastic. See MULCHING.

The successful use of herbicides for weed control in vegetable crops is influenced by several factors such as soil, temperature, moisture and the activity of the chemical. Most of the chemicals involved are selective, meaning that they can be safely used on only 1 or 2 crops. In commercial plantations this is no problem, but it can be a very serious problem in the home garden and, therefore, herbicides are not recommended for use in the kitchen garden.

WATER. Vegetables must have a steady supply of water to produce a normal crop of good quality. In arid or semi-arid regions irrigation is essential as a definite planned practice during the entire growing season. In humid regions it may be necessary to apply water at infrequent intervals during the summer months. When water is applied the amount should be equivalent to 1 in. of rainfall (approximately 900 gals. for a 30 ft. × 50 ft. garden) or enough to soak to a depth of several inches. Sprinkling the soil surface will tend to bring the feeder roots into the topsoil and therefore expose them to variable soil moisture resulting in slow or checked growth of the plant. The use of a good overhead sprinkler is advisable in preference to a hand-held nozzle sprinkler. (For details covering cultural practices for the various vegetables see the special crop article.)

SUCCESSION CROPPING. Succession cropping means planting several successive crops on the same piece of land in the same year. This practice permits the utmost utilization of the garden area. Examples of succession cropping might be early Lettuce followed by snap beans, or a later planting of beets or carrots, early peas by a second planting of sweet corn, Spinach followed by Cabbage or Broccoli.

In the warmer regions 3 or even 4 crops can be grown on the same land in 1 season.

INTERCROPPING. Intercropping or companion cropping is practiced when 2 or more crops are grown on the same land at the same time.

In planning for intercropping the gardener should consider the time each crop is to be planted, the time each crop will mature and the space needed by each at various stages of growth. Small, quick-growing crops can be planted with larger, late-maturing crops.

Two rows of beans may be grown between 2 rows of squash, a single row of beets between 2 rows of Celery, Radish between rows of onions or early Cabbage.

Both succession and intercropping practices will require careful planning at the time the garden plan is prepared in the spring if the gardener hopes to make the maximum use of the land that is available for the vegetable garden.

HARVESTING. Planting in the home garden should be so planned that each crop may be harvested at its proper stage of maturity, when it has reached its full nutritive value and its best and most satisfying eating quality. The harvest period in most areas of the country start with Asparagus, dandelion greens, Rhubarb and then carries through with a variety of products until the late frosts destroy Kale, Cabbage and the various root crops. A well-planned garden provides an abundance of good eating products.

Some crops have a very short period of peak maturity. Peas and sweet corn deteriorate very rapidly and have a harvest period of only a few days. This means several or more successive plantings, each containing just enough to provide peak quality for 3 to 5 days. On the other hand, certain other crops have a long period during which a quality product may be harvested. Beets, carrots, green and red peppers, and onions are good examples. Then we have those crops of an intermediate category which will have a peak maturity period of from 1 to several weeks such as Lettuce, Spinach, tomatoes, broccoli, beans, etc.

The length of time that most vegetables remain in an edible condition depends on weather conditions. High temperatures hasten maturity and cause such crops as Spinach and Lettuce to shoot to seed rapidly. Peak quality of sweet corn is a matter of 1 or 2 days in summer and 5 to 6 days in the cooler fall weather. A dry period followed by rains may cause cabbage to split, tomatoes to crack.

GRANT B. SNYDER

VEGETABLE-OYSTER = *Tragopogon porrifolius*

VEGETABLE-SPONGE. See LUFFA.

VEINS. The small ribs or branches of the framework of leaves.

VELTHEIMIA (vel-TY-mia)
  viridifolia   1′   **Zone 9**
A bulbous perennial, with straplike leaves 3 in. wide; with showy, terminal, pendulous flowers borne on a spike. The flowers are about 1½ in. long, 25–30 on a spike and are colored red or yellow with greenish tips appearing in late winter. Native to South Africa. Little cultivated in America except in Calif. Belonging to the Lily Family; propagated by offsets.

VELUTINOUS. Velvety.

VELVETLEAF = *Abutilon theophrasti*

VELVETPLANT, JAVA = *Gynura aurantiaca*

VENATION. Arrangement of veins.

VENIDIUM (ven-ID-ium)
  fastuosum 18″ annual Monarch Namaqualand-daisy
A South African member of the Composite Family; the alternate leaves are lyre shaped, very fuzzy at first. Flowers are daisylike, bright orange, with a dark purple-brown base, up to 4 in. across. They should not be given too much water. Seeds can be sown indoors in March or outdoors in May. Plant out in well-drained soil in the full sun.

VENTRAL. Relating to the inner surface or part of an organ; the part nearer the axis.

VENTRICOSE. Swelling unequally, or inflated on 1 side.

VENUS FLYTRAP = *Dionaea muscipula*

VENUS LOOKING-GLASS = *Legousia speculum-veneris*

VERATRUM (vee-RAY-trum)
  viride 2′–4′ Zone 3 American False Hellebore
Hardy, perennial leaves about 1 ft. long and very broad, yellowish-green flowers 1 in. wide, in terminal clusters sometimes 2 ft. long, in July. Native to North America especially in swampy woodland areas. Sheep and chickens sometimes die from eating the green tops or the seeds. In the spring it is sometimes mistakenly thought of as Skunk Cabbage which it is not. V. californicum is somewhat similar, found chiefly in Colo., Wyo., northern Calif. and Ore. Because of their poisonous character they are not grown in gardens.

VERBASCUM (ver-BAS-kum)
  blattaria 3′–4′ Zone 3 Moth Mullein
A common roadside biennial over much of North America, this plant of Europe and Asia has an erect, unbranched stem and alternate, lanceolate leaves about 2½ in. long with a serrate margin. At the base of the stem the leaves are 2½ in. long and diminish in size as they ascend the stem, becoming bractlike at the tip. The loosely clustered flowers form a terminal spire, each flower arising from the axil of a bractlike leaf, and they appear from June to Sept. Each flower, 1 in. wide, has a corolla of 5 slightly irregular petals which are yellow or pink in bud, opening to white, the petals remaining pink on the outside. This is an attractive plant for the wild garden and should be propagated by seed.
  chaixii 3′ Zone 5 Chaix Mullein
With leaves 6 in. long, white tomentose; flowers yellow or a tall spike with purple, woolly stamens. Native to southern Europe.
  olympicum 5′ Zone 6 Olympic Mullein
With entire leaves 6 in. long, white tomentose; flowers an inch long and yellow on a tall spike with many flowers. Native to Greece.
  phoeniceum 5′ Zone 6 Purple Mullein

Flowers purple or red on a simple slender raceme with purple woolly stamens. Leaves are glabrous above, pubescent beneath and toothed. Native to southeastern Europe, Asia.

thapsus   4'-5'   Zone 3   Flannel Mullein
A European biennial weed widely naturalized in the pasture lands of the U.S., it is so woolly textured as to have a surface like rather coarse velveteen. Rising from a rosette of lanceolate leaves 12-14 in. long, having round-toothed margins and narrowing towards the base, with a strong central rib, the rather thick, erect, unbranched flower stalk is clothed with alternate, clasping leaves. Above the several leafy bracts, which are strongly keeled and have wavy margins, the crowded, yellow flower cluster arises. Each flower has a widespreading, 5-lobed, slightly uneven corolla and 5 unequal stamens. The plant blooms throughout the summer. It is not a particularly attractive garden plant since the gray-green foliage becomes very dusty in dry weather. The leaf has been used in various medicines for asthma and pulmonary diseases.

VERBENA (ver-BEE-na). A genus of the Verbena Family with 70 species native to America. These may be annual or perennial, tender or hardy. Leaves of most species are opposite and lobed or toothed. Flowers small, in terminal clusters, spiked or rounded. The tubular calyx has 5 sharply pointed lobes, the corolla has 5 rounded lobes. Stamens are 4, occurring in pairs. Flowers may be white, lavender, rose or purple. Many are useful garden plants; some are grown as house plants. Propagated by seeds or cuttings.

Insect Pests

The large yellowish caterpillar with long hairs which feeds on the leaves of Verbena is the yellow woolly bear. The caterpillars are most active in late summer. They can be hand picked or controlled with insecticide #37. Verbena leaf miner makes blisterlike mines in the leaves. Insecticide #15 controls them when necessary. Verbena budworm is a borer in new shoots causing them to wither. Hand picking or spraying as for woolly bear is suggested.

Diseases

Powdery mildew is often a greenhouse pest and infects outdoor plants late in summer. Use fungicide #V or #M.

bipinnatifida   3"   Zone 3   Dakota Verbena
This hardy plant, native to the northern Midwest states, has dark green, deeply lobed leaves on prostrate stems and forms a thick mat of foliage. The light purple flowers, about ½ in. wide, bloom throughout the growing season. Propagation is by seeds or cuttings.

canadensis   6"   annual   Rose Verbena
Although many verbenas have stiff, upright stems, this recumbent species merely lifts up its head of deep rose to magenta flowers. The plant is native to the southern U.S., extending from Va. to Fla. and reaching from Colo. into Mexico. Perennial in the South.

hastata   4'-6'   Zone 3   Blue Verbena
This species, treated as either an annual or perennial, is characterized by a stiffly erect habit, square, rough-hairy stems, opposite, lanceolate and toothed leaves, the lower ones sometimes 3-lobed at the base, and slender spikes of purple, pink or white sessile flowers. The plants are widely distributed over North America growing alongside streams and lakes, and bloom in late summer.

hortensis = *V. hybrida*

x hybrida (*V. hortensis*)   8"-18"   annual
                                  Garden Verbena
One of the most popular and common of all garden annual flowers. The lance-shaped, opposite leaves of this are 2-4 in. long, bluntly toothed. The flowers are borne in terminal, broad, flat, compact clusters, 2-3 in. across, colored pink, red, yellowish, white and purple. The stems are frequently decumbent. There are many varieties available and new ones are frequently being added to seed lists. They make excellent edging plants for the border or the rock garden and bloom continually throughout the summer and fall until killed by frost. Before this happens, plants can be brought indoors for winter bloom. Seeds should be sown indoors in Feb. or March, transplanted at least once, and set out in the garden after frost. Cuttings of desired varieties can easily be rooted and kept indoors for planting the next year.

laciniata   decumbent   annual   Moss Verbena
Often grown as a perennial in warm climates; decumbent and with branches rooting where they touch the ground. The leaves are deeply 3 parted; flowers short in rounded heads. Native to Argentina and Chile.

**peruviana   prostrate   annual   Peruvian
                                      Verbena**
Native to South America, this is a prostrate annual, rooting frequently along the stems. The leaves are 1-2 in. long; the scarlet to crimson flowers are borne on an upright spike. This makes a fine ground cover.

pulchella = *V. tenera*

rigida   1'-2'   Zone 8
This perennial has tuberous roots, creeping stems at the base and oblong leaves 2-4 in. long. Flowers purplish to sky blue, ¼ in. across. Native to southern Brazil and Argentina but naturalized from N.Car. to Fla. It will flower 4 months after the seed is sown.

stricta   3'   annual   Woolly Verbena

Since this plant is covered with down, it has a soft, gray-green appearance. Of upright habit, the leaves are ovate to elliptic and unevenly toothed. The slender flower spikes, to 6 in. long, bear tiny purple flowers crowded around the stalk. Native to the Plains States west of the Great Lakes, the plant blooms from June to Sept. Treated as either annual or perennial.

tenera (*V. pulchella*) **20″   annual or perennial**
Sand Verbena
A perennial in the South, often grown as an annual, this has deeply lobed, hairy, opposite leaves and terminal flat clusters of lilac flowers. Plant seeds outdoors in April in full sun. Native to South America and supposedly widely naturalized in the U.S.

VERBENACEAE = The Vervain or Verbena Family

VERBENA, LEMON = *Aloysia triphylla*

VERBESINA (ver-bes-SY-na)
encelioides   3′   annual   Golden Crown-beard
A member of the Composite Family, with alternate, triangular, ovate, grayish, hairy leaves 4 in. long and solitary heads of golden-yellow flowers with an orange disk, 2 in. across. Native from Fla. to Mexico.

VERMICULITE. A micalike mineral much lighter than sand and useful as a mulch.

VERNATION. The arrangement of leaves in the bud.

VERNONIA (ver-NO-nia)
altissima   7′   Zone 4   Tall Ironweed
Having a branched flower head with branches rising from the axils of the upper leaves, this plant has purple flowers (it belongs to the Composite Family) and grows from N.Y. to Mich. and over most of the southern U.S. It is a handsome plant for the large wild garden and may be propagated by self-sown seed, by division in the early spring or by cuttings taken in early summer.

noveboracensis   3′–6′   Zone 5   New York
Ironweed
A plant of the Composite Family with a rather woody, erect stem, occasionally branching near the summit, with alternate, narrowly linear leaves with slightly irregular margins and a strong central vein, the stem and central vein streaked with red. The flower heads, in a loose, leafy, terminal cluster, are composed of an involucre of brownish bracts with extended tips and a cluster of purple tubular flowers with 5-lobed corollas and stamens extending beyond the corollas. It is a common plant of low, moist ground from New England to Mo. and Ohio and blooms from Aug. to Oct. A handsome plant despite its rather coarse appearance. Propagate as for *V. altissima*.

VERONICA (ver-ON-ik-a). Some of the taller and more conspicuously flowered species are excellent additions to the summer border because of their tall spikes of blue flowers, a color frequently lacking in the border in mid-summer. Some of the lower species are used as ground covers or in front of the perennial border. Seeds can be sown in late spring, cuttings made in summer, but division of plants in the fall or the spring is the easiest method of propagation.

allionii   4″   Zone 4   Allioni Speedwell
A mat-forming perennial plant for the rock garden, with stems creeping over the ground surface and rooting at the joints. The leathery leaves are about ¼ in. long. The flowers, appearing in summer, are purple, small, and in dense spikes about 2 in. long. Native to the Alps.

amplexicaulis = *Hebe amplexicaulis*
andersonii = *Hebe andersonii*
armena   4″   Zone 4
An attractive, tufted, evergreen plant with deeply lobed, pale green, pubescent leaves which are pinnate, the small leaflets about ¼ in. long, borne on long, trailing stems and in early summer bearing bright blue flowers arranged in a loose terminal spike. Native to Armenia.

arvensis   1′   annual   Corn Speedwell
A weed, possibly native throughout the U.S. and southern Canada, with mostly opposite leaves about ⅜ in. wide, lanceolate to entire. The small, bright blue flowers are borne in terminal racemes from April to Aug. in the axils of the upper leaves which are frequently sessile and alternate.

austriaca   2′   Zone 6 (?)   Austrian Speedwell
Perennial with large blue flowers ½ in. wide in long racemes. The leaves are deeply cut. Native to Europe and Asia Minor.

chamaedrys   1′   Zone 3   Germander Speed-
well
A practically evergreen, European plant which makes a good ground cover because of its compact habit and creeping rootstock. The opposite leaves are ½–1½ in. long during May and June. It has escaped cultivation and become a weed in some places.

cupressoides = *Hebe cupressoides*
filiformis   2″   Zone 3   Creeping Veronica
A perennial creeping weed, native to Europe and Asia, but now escaping cultivation and becoming a serious pest in lawns of the north-eastern U.S. and southern Canada. The opposite, rounded leaves are about ¼ in. wide, crenate on the margin, and the stems root all along their length, thus forming dense mats of growth. The pale blue, 4-petalled flowers are ⅓ in. wide or less, borne singly in the leaf axils during early summer.

fruiticans 6″ Zone 5 **Rock Speedwell**
A shrubby, very branched perennial with oblong, opposite leaves ½ in. long and blue flowers in short racemes from July to Sept. Native to Europe, especially in the Alps Mountains. Easily propagated by seeds and division. Suitable for the rock garden.

fruticulosa 4″–6″ Zone 3
A woody perennial herb native to Europe as well as to Greenland, with oblong leaves ½ in. long and with small, blue, sometimes pale pink flowers. Propagated by division in fall or spring. Suitable for the rock garden.

gentianoides 2′ Zone 4 **Gentian Speedwell**
A perennial with leaves 2–3 in. long; blue flowers ½ in. wide in loose, showy, terminal clusters during summer. Native to southeastern Europe and Asia Minor. It is a good rock garden plant.

hulkeana = *Hebe hulkeana*

incana 2′ Zone 3 **Woolly Speedwell**
A very popular and easily obtained garden perennial with white woolly stems and porcelain-blue flowers in June and July. The cultivar **'Rosea'** is especially popular because of the flushed pink color of its flowers. The leaves are up to 3 in. long and the flower spikes up to 6 in. long. Native to northern Asia and a fine edging plant. It is valued for its grayish leaves and slender terminal spikes of flowers from mid-June to late July.

latifolia 2′ Zone 3 **Hungarian Speedwell**
This perennial, native to Europe, is a nice garden plant because of its blue to reddish flowers in panicled racemes during May and June. The leaves are linear, ½–¾ in. long, and opposite. The variety **prostrata**, about 8 in. tall, makes an excellent ground cover. Propagated easily by division.

longifolia (*V. maritima*) 2½′ Zone 4
This was a popular perennial in the old-fashioned perennial garden, but now is superseded by new varieties and hybrids. The flowers are small, lilac-blue, borne in pyramidal spikes during the summer. It is probably one of the best of these species for garden use.

The variety **subsessilis** has striking royal-blue flower spikes in late July and is called the Clump Veronica because it grows into a beautiful clump 2 ft. wide. Many garden varieties are probably hybrids (*V. longifolia* x *V. spicata*) and they begin to flower in June and continue in flower much of the summer. Most of these should have good drainage or they will succumb during the winter.

'Blue Champion' has medium blue flowers from July 1 to Sept. 1. **'Icicle'** is excellent for its 2-ft. clumps of gray foliage and provides 3 months of bloom—an excellent plant. **'Sunny Border Blue'** is a stocky, 18–24 in. plant with good flowers during July and Aug. **'Blue Spires'** is another good clone.

maritima = *V. longifolia*

officinalis 1′ Zone 3 **Drug Speedwell, Gypsy-weed**
Possibly a little lower in habit than the Germander Speedwell, this is an excellent ground cover because of its creeping branches. The opposite, practically evergreen leaves are 2 in. long and the pale blue flowers, about ¼ in. wide, are borne in racemes or small spikes, usually axillary. It is native to Europe, Asia and North America. As a ground cover it rarely requires any attention. Easily propagated by division. Used in the manufacture of vermouth. The leaves have been used as a substitute for tea, as well.

pectinata prostrate Zones 2–3 **Comb Speedwell**
A prostrate perennial with deep blue, white-eyed flowers produced in profuse racemes during May and June. The leaves, about ½ in. long, are white, pubescent, toothed and often cut. Native to Asia Minor. Often used in the rock garden. There is a variety **(rosea)** with rose-pink flowers.

prostrata (*V. rupestris*) 8″ Zone 5 **Harebell Speedwell**
Sometimes considered a form of *V. latifolia*, this is a tufted perennial native to Europe, with gray-hairy often prostrate stems; oblong to linear leaves ½–¾ in. long. The pale blue flowers are ⅓ in. long, borne in axillary spikes.

repens 4″ Zone 5 **Creeping Speedwell**
Native to Corsica and Spain, this is a prostrate, mat-forming plant good for covering bare spots of soil, doing best in the full sun in soil that is on the moist side. The opposite, mosslike leaves are only ½ in. long, but are lustrous. The rose to bluish flowers are ¼ in. wide and appear in May in few-flowered terminal racemes. Easily propagated by division.

rupestris = *V. prostrata*

saturejoides 3″ Zones 2–3
Somewhat similar to *V. fruticans*; mat-forming in the rockery; blooming in very early spring with dark blue flowers on spikes 2 in. long. Leaves are about ⅓ in. long. Easily propagated by division in either the fall or spring. Native to Yugoslavia.

serpyllifolia 1′ Zone 3 **Thyme-leaved Speedwell**
A native perennial weed; opposite, ovate leaves about ½ in. long, toothed or entire; flowers pale blue, ⅓ in. wide, in terminal racemes from April to Oct. The stems are creeping and prostrate, thus forming dense mats of foliage. This weed is at its worst in lawns, but in gardens is easily controlled by clean cultivation.

speciosa = *Hebe speciosa*

spicata   1½'   Zone 3   **Spike Speedwell**
Widely grown in American gardens, although
native to northern Europe and Asia; popular
because of its neat-appearing, lance-shaped
leaves about 2 in. long and its blue or pink
flowers borne in dense racemes from late June
to early Aug. Several cultivars are available,
including 'Nana'—a very dense form; 'Bar-
carolle'—with deep rose-colored flowers,
probably a hybrid of *V. spicata*; 'Icicle'—
produces 2-ft. clumps with gray-green leaves,
blooming from June to Sept.; an excellent
garden specimen. Many more varieties or
hybrids of this popular species are available.
   spuria   2'   Zones 2–3   **Bastard Speedwell**
A perennial, native to southeastern Europe
and southern Asia, with inch-long linear leaves
and racemes of blue flowers. A variety called
'Royal Blue' has veen noted as a good one.
   traversii = *Hebe traversii*

VERONICASTRUM (veron-i-CAS-trum)
   virginicum   5'–6'   Zone 3   **Culver's-root**
A plant often found listed under several
botanical names, one of which is *Veronica
virginiana*, indicating its close relationship to that
genus. An erect perennial with oblong to
lanceolate leaves, borne in whorls or pairs, and
a branching, terminal flower cluster up to 9 in.
long. The flowers are white, each flower
having a tubular corolla with 4 rounded lobes,
the style and stamens extending beyond the
corolla and the clusters being up to 9 in. long.
It is a good background plant for the wild
garden and will do well in sun or partial shade.
Its range extends from Ontario and Manitoba
south to Ga. and La. It does best in moderately
acid soil and may be propagated by division in
spring, by cuttings in summer or by seeds sown
spring or fall.

VERRUCOSE. Covered with wartlike elevations.

VERSATILE. Relating to an anther attached
near the middle and moving freely on its
support.

VERTICILLATE. Disposed in a whorl.

VERVAIN FAMILY = Verbenaceae

VESICARIA (ves-sik-KAY-ria)
   utriculata   18"   Zone 5   **Bladder-pod**
A member of the Mustard Family from central
Europe, with alternate leaves crowded near the
base of the stems; yellow flowers in racemes.
Native to the Mediterranean Region. Some
botanists classify it as *Alyssoides utriculata*.

VETCH. See VICIA.

VETCH, CROWN = *Coronilla varia*

VETCHLING, SPRING = *Lathyrus vernus*

VETIVERIA (vet-i-VEER-ia)
   zizanioides   8'   Zone 8   **Khuskhus Vetiver**
A tropical perennial grass from the East Indies,
occasionally naturalized in the South. In the
East Indies the roots have been used for
centuries for perfumes and medicines. The
thick aromatic rootstocks are readily divided in
propagation. The leaves are 3 ft. long and ⅓ in.
wide, the margins roughly serrate. Flowers are
borne in 2's, in foot-long spikes.

VIABILITY OF SEED. Seeds vary greatly in the
length of time they retain their viability or the
ability to germinate. This may vary from a few
days in *Populus* to hundreds of years in *Nelumbo*.
For a discussion of this topic see SEED, SEED
DORMANCY, SEEDS OF WOODY PLANTS.

VIBURNUM (vy-BER-num). The viburnums
are shrubs, though a few could be considered
small trees, with opposite leaves and clusters of
small white flowers followed by fleshy, berrylike fruits. These are either red, yellow, blue or
black, depending upon the species or variety,
but the red- and yellow-fruiting forms are
among the most colorful. These shrubs are
vigorous growers and, though troubled with a
few insects, they are well worth having in the
garden for their spring flowers, good foliage,
interesting forms and colored fruits which
attract the birds, as well as for their fair autumn
color. Few of them need attention once they
are properly established in good soil. The
fruits of certain viburnums, such as *V. prunifolium* and *V. trilobum*, are edible and have
been used in making jellies and preserves.

Types of Flowers

The viburnums bear 3 general types of flowers.
One group has flowers consisting of flat
clusters several inches in dia., made up of
hundreds of small, perfect, usually creamy-
white flowers. Another group, called the snowballs, has rounded clusters of sterile flowers
which do not bear fruits. Finally, there is the
group of plants with flat clusters of fertile
flowers having large, sterile or ray flowers at the
perimeter.
   The viburnums usually flower well every year,
although they may not bear heavy crops of
fruit annually. Good fruiting requires that wind
and insects must be operating at the time the
pollen is ripe; if during this period the weather is
cold or rainy, with little wind, little pollination
occurs and hence fruiting will be sparse. The
gardener usually loses sight of this fact by the
time fall comes, when the fruits are then conspicuously absent.
   Some species (*V. dilatatum* is certainly one)
should be planted in groups of several seed-
grown plants to insure proper cross-pollination

Viburnums—Three types of flower clusters:
Upper: Snowball type—all sterile flowers, no fruits.
Middle: Sterile flowers on outside of cluster, fertile flowers in center.
Lower: All fertile flowers, eventually bearing fruits.

and hence good fruiting. In many cases of isolated specimen plants, poor fruiting may be traced to lack of sufficient pollen of the right type. Undoubtedly there is a certain amount of cross-pollination among the species, but certain ones are not good pollinizers. Until more is known about this subject, it is best to plant several seed-grown plants together, or at least on the same property.

Four of the earlier-blooming viburnums should be considered together, since they compete for prime space in the early spring garden. *V. carlesii* is the old-fashioned favorite, hard to displace since it is so fragrant—it is the most fragrant of the 4—and so many people have come to like it. However, the fact remains that this is frequently susceptible to a disease which can kill mature plants quickly, even after many years of healthy growth.

V. burkwoodii originated in the nursery of Burkwood and Skipworth, Kingston-on-Thames, England, in 1924, as a hybrid (*V. carlesii* x *V. utile*). The flowers are fragrant,

though less so than those of *V. carlesii*, and the leaves are smaller and glossier. In certain parts of Calif. it is proving to be evergreen, but in the area of Boston, Mass., it is entirely deciduous and perfectly hardy. The habit of growth is somewhat open, not dense and compact.

V. juddii originated at the Arnold Arboretum in 1920 as a hybrid (*V. carlesii* x *V. bitchiuense*) and is proving to be popular, having better foliage than *V. carlesii*, though not quite such fragrant flowers, and being more dense in habit than *V. bitchiuense*.

V. carlcephalum originated in the nursery of Burkwood and Skipworth in 1932 and is in sufficient demand in the U.S. to have been patented here. It is a cross between *V. carlesii* and the Chinese Snowball, *V. macrocephalum*, which is not reliably hardy in New England. However, this hybrid is apparently hardy and makes a very dense shrub with foliage quite similar to that of *V. carlesii*. The flower clusters are rounded, often up to 5 in. in dia., and somewhat fragrant. The flower buds are pinkish, but the flowers are pure white. So far as we have seen, none of these 3 last-mentioned species has proved susceptible to the graft blight diseases; thus any one of them, especially *V. carlcephalum*, might be selected as an early-flowering substitute for *V. carlesii*.

At least 3 viburnums have flat clusters of perfect flowers which are borne profusely and make quite a display each year. They are *V. dilatatum*, *V. lentago* and *V. sieboldii*. Others, like *V. dentatum*, are also meritorious, but none surpasses those mentioned.

In the group bearing flat clusters of fertile flowers surrounded with large, sterile ray flowers might be listed *V. opulus*, *V. sargentii*, *V. trilobum* and *V. plicatum* varieties *tomentosum*, *mariesii* and 'Roseum'. All of these are good for other reasons, as well as for their flowers.

V. plicatum 'Roseum' has sterile flowers on the outside of the cluster. These flowers are white when first opened, but under certain soil or climatic conditions they gradually turn a deep and very conspicuous pink. This color may vary in intensity (on the same plant), probably depending upon changing soil or climatic conditions. Thus it may not be reliably pink every blooming season.

There are only 3 snowballs: The largest, the Chinese Snowball, *V. macrocephalum*, is reliable hardy only up to Zone 6 or sometimes to Zone 5. The European Snowball, *V. opulus* 'Roseum', frequently becomes so infested with plant lice that it is not worth the effort of growing. The least hardy—but the best—the Japanese Snowball, *V. plicatum* (formerly *V. tomentosum sterile*), is the only one worth growing in the North.

Order of Bloom

This is the sequence in which the viburnum species bloom in the Arnold Arboretum, Jamaica Plain, Mass.:

Early to Mid-April
Viburnum farreri (fragrans)
Early May
Viburnum buddleifolium
V. alnifolium
V. burejaeticum
V. furcatum
V. rhytidophylloides
V. schensianum
Mid-May
Viburnum bitchiuense
V. burkwoodii
V. carlesii
V. juddii
V. lantana
V. veitchii
Late May
Viburnum betulifolium
V. bracteatum
V. carlcephalum
V. erosum
V. lentago
V. macrocephalum
V. opulus
V. opulus 'Roseum'
V. orientale

Late May (cont.)
Viburnum plicatum (*tomentosum sterile*)
V. plicatum 'Mariesii'
V. plicatum tomentosum
V. rafinesquianum
V. rhytidophyllum
V. rufidulum
V. sargentii
V. setigerum 'Aurantiacum'
V. sieboldii
V. trilobum
V. urceolatum
V. wrightii
Early June
Viburnum cassinoides
V. dentatum
V. dilatatum
V. hupehense
V. lobophyllum
V. prunifolium
V. ovatifolium
Mid-June
Viburnum acerifolium
V. bracteatum
V. molle
V. pubescens

Viburnums for Fruits

There are 3 yellow-fruited forms, *V. opulus* 'Xanthocarpum', *V. sargentii* 'Flavum' and *V. dilatatum* 'Xanthocarpum'. All are good, the first 2 being somewhat similar in size of fruit clusters and individual fruits and, in fact, in the general habit of the shrubs themselves. *V. dilatatum* 'Xanthocarpum' has smaller fruits but much larger, flatter clusters.

Red-fruiting forms include *V. lantanoides*, *V. dilatatum*, *V. opulus* and its variety 'Compactum', *V. sieboldii*, *V. trilobum* and its variety 'Compactum', and *V. wrightii* and its variety 'Hessei'. One other species, *V. setigerum* 'Aurantiacum', has been considerably mentioned in the past for its orange fruit. However, it does not make a good specimen plant, being very open and leggy at the base. True, the fruits are colorful for the short period in which they are conspicuous, but it does not seem advisable to recommend the plant because of its poor growth habit.

Really blue fruits are borne by the Arrow-wood, *V. dentatum*.

The black-fruited species are *V. acerifolium* and *V. lantana*. There are others like *V. sieboldii*, *V. plicatum* varieties and *V. veitchii* in which the fruits are black at maturity, but in ripening they go through a stage when they are red and at that

time are most interesting. Truly black fruits cannot be seen from a distance, but red fruits are conspicuous, so we value the fruits of these species particularly during the ripening period. With *V. sieboldii* and some of the others, the fruits are usually red for some time, but as soon as they turn black, and sometimes just before that, they are taken by the birds.

Finally, there is a group with fruits a blue-black at maturity that, while ripening, go through a most colorful change from green to yellow to red to blue-black—sometimes with all of these colors apparent in one cluster at the same time. These species include *V. cassinoides*, *V. lentago*, *V. prunifolium* and *V. rufidulum*; all of them are excellent.

The early-flowering species—*V. burkwoodii*, *V. carlcephalum*, *V. carlesii*, *V. juddii* and *V. rhytidophylloides*—do not appear to fruit so well as some of the others. This may be due to inclement weather at the time the pollen is ripe, or the lack of other pollinizing plants in the near vicinity. Also, since these fruits are black they are usually well hidden under the new growth and because they ripen so early in the summer, when few other plants have ripened fruits, the birds eat them before they are noticed. In any event, these are not recommended primarily for their fruits.

Viburnums for Shade

V. acerifolium, V. lantanoides (*V. alnifolium*) and *V. cassinoides* are the best for shaded situations; in fact, the first 2 must have a cool, moist, shaded situation or they cannot be grown at all.

Viburnums for Foliage

Siebold Viburnum (*V. sieboldii*) is the best of all for foliage alone. Its large, dark green, deeply rugose leaves appear in clusters on the branches so that there are open spaces without foliage, lending a most pleasing aspect to the plant as a whole. Then, the long leaves of *V. rhytidophylloides* (formerly *V. lantanaphyllum*) are also good, possibly the 'Willow Wood Seedling' being the best clone of this hybrid species. The Wayfaring Tree, *V. lantana*, is not grown much any more, but its variety *rugosum* is a very good form, with rugose, slightly glossy, dark green leaves that have none of the light green of the species. Other viburnums also have handsome foliage, but the above-mentioned might be considered the best for this purpose.

Viburnums for Habit

Some viburnums may be grown with a single trunk and eventually will grow into small trees up to 30 ft. tall. These include *V. lentago, V. prunifolium* (which incidentally, is about the best for a vivid scarlet autumn color), *V. rufidulum* and *V. sieboldii*. One variety, *V. sieboldii reticulatum*, is supposed to be lower in habit. Of the low forms, the lowest is *V. opulus* 'Nanum', seldom exceeding 2 ft. in height, though it may grow 5 ft. wide. Normally it does not flower. There are also dwarf forms of *V. farreri* (*fragrans*) which make low, compact plants. Shrubs attaining 5–6 ft. include *V. opulus* 'Compactum' and *V. trilobum* 'Compactum'.

In discussing the habit of viburnums, the varieties of *V. plicatum* certainly should be mentioned, for 'Mariesii,' 'Lanarth' and 'Roseum' have horizontal branching habits, bearing their flat clusters of flowers and fruits on the upper side of each branch, making the plants conspicuous among other shrubs in the landscape planting.

Propagation

Viburnum seeds need not be processed at once, but may be stored dry in a cool place in airtight containers for up to a year and then may be stratified. Species vary, but in general, stratify seeds for 5 months at warm temperatures and then 3 months at 40° F. During the warm stratification of many temperate-zone species, roots will appear. When this condition becomes general throughout the lot of seeds, the cold treatment may be started.

Viburnums are propagated also by division, layers, and by softwood or hardwood cuttings which see.

Insect Pests

Snowball aphid is a perennial pest of Viburnum, especially of *V. opulus* 'Roseum'. Curled, stunted leaves in the spring badly disfigure the plants. Dormant sprays of fungicide #L or #N kill the overwintering eggs and insecticide #15 is effective against those aphids not protected by the curled leaves.

Diseases

Powdery mildew attacks Viburnum. Sprays or dusts of fungicide #V or #M control it. Leaf spot is more difficult to control. Pruning the infected branches followed by sprays of fungicide #B are suggested.

acerifolium 6' Zone 3 Mapleleaf Viburnum
With black fruit and purplish autumn color, this is a native of the woodlands of the northeastern U.S. and is of value only for planting in shaded areas; other viburnums are much better in full sun.

alnifolium (*V. lantanoides*) 12' Zone 3 Hobblebush
The red fruits which turn black at maturity and the early bloom of this shrub, with its conspicuous sterile flowers on the outside of the flat cluster, are of no value except in cool, moist woodlands, for it will not grow in dry, sunny situations. The fresh fruit is edible and is used for making jellies. It is native to the woodlands especially of the mountainous areas of the northeastern U.S.

betulifolium 12' Zone 5 Birchleaf Viburnum
Native to China, with flat cymes of perfect flowers and bearing red fruits in the fall. Attractive, but no better as an ornamental than many of the other viburnums.

x burkwoodii 6' Zone 5 Burkwood Viburnum
Originated in the nursery of Burkwood and Skipworth, Kingston-on-Thames, England, in 1924, this is a hybrid of *V. carlesii* x *V. utile*. It is semi-evergreen in England and is proving to be evergreen in certain parts of Calif. The flowers are very fragrant and it can be considered an improvement over *V. carlesii*, even in New England, although its smaller, glossier leaves are not completely evergreen there. The **'Park Farm Hybrid'** form is an English cultivar which is supposed to have a more spreading habit with slightly larger flower clusters, but it does not perform in New England so well as the species.

x carlcephalum 9' Zone 5 Fragrant Snowball

A most interesting hybrid (*V. carlesii* x *V. macrocephalum*) with rounded, fragrant flower heads up to 5 in. dia., raised in 1932 at the Burkwood and Skipworth Nursery in England. The foliage has a sheen, making it better in this respect than the foliage of *V. carlesii*. Certainly it is one of the best of the viburnums, although admittedly not so fragrant as *V. carlesii*.

carlesii   5′   Zone 4   Fragrant Viburnum
This old-fashioned favorite from Korea is fast

Viburnum carlcephalum bears large, fragrant, white flower clusters in May. (*Photo by Arnold Arboretum, Jamaica Plain, Mass.*)

being replaced by *V. burkwoodii*, *V. carlcephalum* and *V. juddii*, for it is often subject to a graft blight disease as it grows older. The flowers have a pinkish tinge and appear very early in the spring before the leaves. Because of its sweet fragrance, it will be a hard plant to eliminate from any list, but the fact should be noted that, in the long run, other species may be considered to be of more enduring ornamental value. The fruit is blue-black and appears very early in the summer. The variety **'Compacta'** is much lower in maximum height and blooms well.

cassinoides   6′   Zone 2   Withe-rod
This shrub is native to the northeastern U.S. especially in moist woodlands and has red-black fruits and red autumn foliage, always with a dependable display of both in the fall. The fruits go through an interesting color change from green to yellowish to red to black, sometimes with all colors in the same cluster at once. This plant lends itself well to massing, either in wooded areas or in full sun.

davidii   3′   Zone 7   David Viburnum
Light blue fruits in Sept. to Oct. or later and dark, evergreen, leathery leaves which are deeply rugose—a handsome foliage specimen for the South, and native to China.

dentatum   15′   Zone 2   Arrowwood
The blue fruits of this shrub, as well as its glossy, reddish, autumn color and vigorous growth, with many shoots from the base, are its

best qualities. It is native throughout the eastern U.S. and is not for specimen use, but is a generally serviceable foliage plant since it grows well in almost any kind of soil and can be used as a quick-growing "filler," especially in mass plantings.

dilatatum   9′   Zone 5   Linden Viburnum
The handsome and profuse red fruits, russet-red autumn foliage and dense habit make this shrub from eastern Asia one of the best viburnums for fall display. Fruiting has been found to be much better when several seedlings are grown together. Flower clusters are often 5 in. in dia. The variety **'Xanthocarpum'** bears yellow fruits.

farreri (*V. fragrans*)   9′   Zone 6   Fragrant Viburnum
The first Viburnum to bloom in the North, this native to northern China has not proved to be satisfactory in the Boston area because severe winter cold, or late freezes, will kill or mar the flowers buds that normally open in early April. It may have more merit in warmer areas like southern Pa. or eastern Va. It can be classed as an interesting shrub, but not one that will prove highly satisfactory in all situations. It is of value chiefly for its very fragrant, early spring flowers, the clusters being only $1\frac{1}{2}$–2 in. wide, and is very popular in England. There is a white-flowered variety **'Album'** and a dwarf variety **'Nanum'**.

fragrans = *V. farreri*

grandiflorum   6′   Zone 7
Fruits blackish purple; flowers in Feb. and March, white to pale blush rose and fragrant. Closely allied to *V. fragrans*, but the flowers are larger, being 2–3 in. dia., and the plant is less hardy.

henryi   9′   Zone 7   Henry Viburnum
An evergreen from Central China, with leaves up to 5 in. long and with red to black fruits; of special interest because its flower and fruit clusters are slightly pyramidal in nature, 4 in. high and about as wide.

ichangense   6′   Zone 6   Ichang Viburnum
Not a prominent ornamental. Leaves deciduous, 1–$2\frac{1}{2}$ in. long, white flowers in small clusters $1\frac{1}{2}$ in. wide, and red fruit. Native to central and western China. Rarely used in planting.

japonicum   6′   Zone 7   Japanese Viburnum
This Japanese shrub has lustrous evergreen leaves 6 in. long, fragrant flowers and red fruits in the fall.

x juddii   8′   Zone 5   Judd Viburnum
The fragrant flowers and reddish-black fruits of this hybrid (*V. carlesii* x *V. bitchuense*) are outstanding. The plant originated in 1920 in the Arnold Arboretum and is of more bushy and spreading habit than *V. bitchuense* and hence a better ornamental. It also has better foliage than *V. carlesii*, but the flowers are not so fragrant.

lantana rugosum 15′ Zone 3 Rugose Wayfaring Tree

The species, with its black, raisinlike fruits and gray-green leaves, is not nearly so popular as it use to be, even though it is noted as being one of the few viburnums for dry-soil situations. It is native to Europe and western Asia. This variety seems to have larger, darker green leaves; hence the plant looks better than the species and the variety 'Lee's' eventually may prove to be even better. These are recommended in preference to the old-fashioned *V. lantana*.

lentago 30′ Zone 2 Nannyberry

Each year the large, flat clusters of small flowers are profusely borne on this shrub and make it very conspicuous in the spring. The fruits go through a colorful change from green to yellowish to red to blue; sometimes the 4 colors show simultaneously on the same cluster. The glossy foliage turns purplish red in the fall. This useful background or screen plant of the eastern U.S. can be grown as a shrub or tree with a single trunk, either as a specimen or on the edge of the woods.

lobophyllum 15′ Zone 5

The fruit of this shrub from central and western China is bright red and, although it is not borne very profusely while the plant is young, it is one of the best at maturity. This species is very similar in ornamental qualities to *V. betulifolium* but is more easily grown, the reason it is recommended in preference to the other species.

macrocephalum 12′ Zone 6 Chinese Snowball

The largest of the snowballs, with clusters of sterile white flowers 6 in. in dia. Sometimes it is semi-evergreen in the South. The variety keteleeri is the wild form of the Chinese Snowball with only the marginal flowers being sterile, but it is still a handsome bush for the South and is slightly hardier than the species.

nudum 15′ Zone 6 Smooth Withe-rod

Closely akin to *V. cassinoides* and also a native of the eastern U.S., this is more adapatable to the South where it is native. The fruits are blue-black and the leaves are lustrous, turning red in the fall.

odoratissimum 10′ Zone 9 Sweet Viburnum

This is an excellent Viburnum for southern gardens because of the glossy evergreen leaves that may be 6 in. long. In fact, it is often considered to have foliage as handsome as that of rhododendrons. In deep, moist soil it may grow into a pyramidal tree 20 ft. tall. Native to India and Japan, the small, white, fragrant flowers are born in pyramidal clusters 3–6 in. tall. The berries are red to black.

opulus 12′ Zone 3 European Cranberry-bush

The European Cranberry-bush from Europe is one of the most common of all exotic garden shrubs, having bright red fruits and red fall foliage. It has been a popular plant in the U.S. for a long time, even though the fruit has an unpleasant odor. The marginal flowers in the flat cluster are large and sterile. It is similar to *V. trilobum*, but its fruits are too tart to make preserves. It has been too popular too long to discard, yet there is no reason why the native *V. trilobum* or one of its many clones would not prove just as ornamental in gardens. There are several varieties of this now being grown in America: 'Compactum', a form that flowers and fruits well, making a desirable plant for the small place where the species would be too tall. This variety grows 5–6 ft. tall; 'Nanum', a low, dense dwarf that seldom flowers and is only 1–3 ft. tall; 'Roseum', which is the snowball type, with all sterile flowers and is called European Snowball. Although it is hardier than *V. plicatum*, it is very susceptible to serious disfiguring infestations of plant lice and, because of this, might be overlooked for planting in many areas; 'Xanthocarpum', identical with the species except that it has bright yellow fruits.

plicatum 9′ Zone 4 Japanese Snowball

This is the familiar Japanese Snowball with white sterile flowers in round, ball-like clusters 2–3 in. wide, appearing in late May. This has been cultivated for centuries in China and Japan, and of course bears no fruits. It is most unfortunate that this species name has had to be changed once again. At first it was *V. tomentosum plicatum*, then *V. tomentosum sterile* and now is *V. plicatum*. In any event, it is a most desirable shrub, not so hardy as the European Snowball, but far less susceptible to infestations of plant lice. All the varieties have a flat, horizontal branching habit with the flowers borne on the upper side of the branches. The fruiting varieties are especially desirable, with the fruits held upright and rigidly displayed on the upper side of the branches. The best varieties are: 'Mariesii', inner flowers fertile, surrounded by a ring of sterile flowers. This is the best fruiting form, with red fruits on red fruit stalks; the fruit eventually turns black; tomentosum, still called by many simply *V. tomentosum*, this Doublefile Viburnum is a very serviceable plant and is widely grown. The flat flower clusters have a ring of sterile flowers around the outside. The small, fertile flowers in the center bear fruits which are red before they turn black in the fall. This, like the other varieties of *V. plicatum*, has the very desirable habit of horizontal branching and sometimes it becomes as broad as it is tall. Although this is more widely distributed, the variety 'Mariesii' is the better ornamental; 'Roseum', the sterile flowers open white and gradually deepen to pink, a color which may be more pronounced in some years and in some situations than in others; 'Lanarth', with an unusually wide-spreading habit. 'Shasta'—with larger flowers.

prunifolium   15′   Zone 3   Black Haw
Another Viburnum from the eastern U.S., this has autumn color of a shining red, white flowers in flat clusters and blue-black fruits. This plant is frequently grown as a small tree. It can be used as a substitute for hawthorns because of its habit of growth and it is not susceptible to all of the pests which trouble hawthorns. The fruits, often being as much as $\frac{1}{2}$ in. long, have been used for preserves since colonial times. It certainly is one of the best large viburnums for ornamental use in the North.

x rhytidophylloides   18′   Zone 5
This hybrid of *V. lantana* x *V. rhytidophyllum* may well take the place of the old-fashioned *V. lantana* because of its better foliage. The leaves are 4–7 in. long and the few fruits are reddish. Actually, this is not planted for its flowers and fruits, but for its good foliage.

rhytidophyllum   9′   Zone 5   Leatherleaf Viburnum
Not a plant for the open, windy place, the long (3–7 in.), handsome, crinkled leaves of this large Viburnum make it an excellent specimen, evergreen in the warmer South but semi-evergreen and fairly hardy as far north as Boston. The red to black fruits are outstanding. It is native to central and western China.

rufidulum   30′   Zones 5–6   Southern Black Haw
This southern counterpart of *V. prunifolium* is native to the southeastern U.S., but is hardy as far north as Boston. The autumn color is a rich red, the fruits are dark blue and the leaves are an excellent, lustrous, dark green. All in all, it is one of the best of the larger viburnums. Fine specimens live over winter in Zone 5, but in the North *V. prunifolium* is more reliably hardy.

sargentii   12′   Zone 4   Sargent Cranberry-bush
This shrub is similar to *V. opulus*, but it is native to northeastern Asia. The large, flat, white flower clusters are ringed with sterile flowers. The shrub bears red fruits and has a reddish autumn color. The leaves are lobed and slightly longer than those of *V. opulus*, sometimes being over 5 in. wide, but otherwise are similar in ornamental characteristics to both *V. opulus* and *V. trilobum*. Actually, this species is best known for its yellow-fruited variety 'Flavum'. This variety is similar to *V. opulus* 'Xanthocarpum' except that it may be slightly

more colorful and more vigorous. Seed sown of 'Flavum' results in seedlings that segregate into red and yellow fruiting forms. Yellow-fruited forms will have yellowish petioles the first year.

setigerum   12′   Zone 5   Tea Viburnum
The Tea Viburnum is native to central and western China. The leaves, 3–5 in. long, are ovate to oblong and the fertile flowers are borne in small, flat clusters. The fruits are red. This species is perhaps best known for its orange-fruiting variety 'Aurantiacum', the only Viburnum with distinctly orange berries.

sieboldii   30′   Zone 4   Siebold Viburnum
Easily one of the very best of the viburnums, this one from Japan has dark, wrinkled but lustrous leaves about 2½–5 in. long, a vigorous, upright, treelike habit and slightly rounded clusters of fertile white flowers. The fruits, at first bright red, at maturity turn black and fall,

Viburnum sieboldii is a tall-growing shrub, but one of the best ornamental viburnums in flower and fruit as well as in foliage. (*Photo by Arnold Arboretum, Jamaica Plain, Mass.*)

but the red fruit stalks remain on the plant for several weeks after the fruits have fallen, thereby giving the plant a reddish color. As a large specimen plant, it might be considered best of the viburnums for the northern U.S.

suspensum   6′   Zone 9   Sandankwa Viburnum
Flowers white, tinged pink, fragrant; fruits red; this Japanese plant with glossy evergreen leaves, 2–5 in. long, does well when planted in shade, but it has the reputation of not flowering freely.

tinus   10′–20′   Zones 7–8   Laurestinus Viburnum
This is considered an indispensable shrub in many southern gardens and comes from the

Mediterranean Region of Europe. Several varieties are available; the fruits are metallic blue and the glossy leaves are small ($1\frac{1}{2}$–4 in. long) and evergreen. It can be used as a clipped hedge and will thrive in the shade, but flowers better in the sun. The variety **'Lucidum'** is probably the best of several, with flower clusters larger than the species, but it is more tender.

trilobum 12′ Zone 2 American Cranberry-bush
Similar to *V. opulus* in both ornamental and botanical characteristics, this is native to the northern U.S. and southern Canada. It may well be that these 2 species are considerably mixed in the trade. The fruit of the native species is red, starting to turn color in late July and remaining on the plant a greater part of the winter. The fruits are edible and various clones like **'Wentworth'**, **'Hahs'** and **'Andrews'** have been selected for their large and excellent-tasting fruits which have been used in preserves for years. This species seems to do best only in the North and does not prove satisfactory as far south as Va. The variety **'Compatcum'** is a very good one for the smaller garden, since it is considerably lower in size and very compact in habit, flowering and fruiting very well indeed. It has been used as a hedge.

veitchii 6′ Zone 5 Veitch Viburnum
The Veitch Viburnum from central China has red to black fruits and is one of the best of the *V. lantana* group; more rounded in outline and not nearly so upright as *V. lantana*, but nevertheless very dense.

wrightii 9′ Zone 5 Wright Viburnum
Native to Japan, this has red fruits $\frac{1}{3}$ in. long and it is these that give it outstanding character in the fall. It is closely related to *V. dilatatum*.

VICIA (VISS-ia). A group of mostly American annuals or perennials of the Pea Family comprising about 15 species, of which many climb by means of tendrils. The leaves are compound, with 1–12 pairs of ovate leaflets, and have 2 stipules at the base of the petiole and 1–3 tendrils at the tip. The blue, violet or yellowish, pealike flowers are generally in axillary racemes. The fruit is a flat pod. Most can become vicious pests in the garden.

americana 3′ Zone 3 American Vetch
A perennial species, with leaves having 4–9 pairs of leaflets and purple flowers. It is a plant of low, wet meadows and of the coastlines from southern Canada and Alaska throughout much of the U.S. and blooms in early summer.

angustifolia climbing annual Narrow-leaved Vetch
A weed introduced from Europe but widely distributed throughout North America, with alternate compound leaves, each one ending in a tendril, and 2–5 pairs of leaflets. Flowers are pealike, purplish, 2 in the axil of a leaf and the fruits are black pods 3 in. long.

caroliniana vine Zone 5 Carolina Vetch
The compound leaves have 6–12 pairs of leaflets and open, axillary racemes of dainty, blue or violet flowers. It is a well-known component of the fields and meadows over much of eastern U.S. and blooms in summer.

cracca 6′ Zone 3 Cow Vetch
A climbing perennial plant with stems extending 6 ft. and with compound, sometimes silky-haired leaves having 8–12 pairs of narrowly lanceolate leaflets. The pealike purple flowers are in 1-sided axillary racemes and bloom throughout the summer. The plant is native to North America and Eurasia and the Plains States of the U.S. It may be propagated by self-sown seed or by division of the root.

faba 2′–6′ annual Broad bean
Probably native to North Africa and southwestern Asia, this is the bean which has been grown for centuries for food for man and animals; also called Windsor Bean, Horse Bean and English Bean. It is very leafy with compound leaves (3 leaflets) usually alternate; with white flowers having a purplish blotch in the leaf axils (1 to several) and the bean a thick, flat pod 2–4 in. long at least $\frac{1}{2}$ in. wide and in some varieties up to a foot long with the individual seeds about an inch across. It is these that are edible and have been popular in Europe for centuries. They are being grown in America also.

sativa 3′ annual Common Vetch
Sometimes a biennial weed with a slightly climbing habit; with alternate compound leaves ending in tendrils and 3–7 pairs of leaflets. The pealike flowers are purplish, usually borne 2 together in a leaf axil. Fruits are pods 3 in. long. This is grown for forage and as a green manure.

villosa climbing annual Hairy Vetch
Sometimes biennial, a weed naturalized in North America but native to Europe. The alternate compound leaves end in tendrils and are composed of 5–10 pairs of leaflets. The flowers are violet-blue, pealike, in long racemes, usually 1-sided. Fruits are pods 1 in. long.

VICTORIA (vik-TO-ria). These belong to the Water-lily Family and are known for their huge leaves, slightly turned up at the edge. Small children have been seated on the larger leaves without sinking. The fragrant flowers are 6–18 in. across, opening in late afternoon and remaining open until the second day, changing from white to pink or red as they mature. They usually are grown in glass houses in the North, where the water is heated and, if grown outdoors, the water must be warmed (by heating pipes) at least until early summer. For cultivation and propagation see WATER GARDENING.

amazonica (*regia*) **aquatic Zone 10 Amazon
Water-platter**
Native to the Amazon River, with leaves 5–6 ft. across, purplish red underneath; with flowers white to pink, 12 in. across and opening at dusk on 2 successive nights.

**cruziana aquatic Zone 10 Giant Water-
platter**
Native to Paraguay with leaves 5–6 ft. across, the upturned margins 5–6 in. high and violet-blue underneath. Flowers are fragrant, white to pink, 12 in. across and opening at dusk on 2 successive nights. Commonly grown in America.

regia. The water lily has been widely misnamed, here and abroad, in the past. Undoubtedly it is *V. amazonica* which has been widely grown and photographed so much, often with a child sitting on the tremendous platterlike leaves. Some of the material in the United States may be *V. cruziana*, a similar species. In any event, the name *V. regia* should be dropped at present.

VICTORIAN-BOX = *Pittosporum undulatum*

VICTORY-PLANT = *Cheiridopsis candidissima*

VIGNA (VIG-na)
mungo (*Phaseolus mungo*)   **1'–3'   annual
Mungo Bean**
A spreading annual, growing about 3 ft. wide; not much grown in the U.S. but grown in India for food where it is probably native. Not ornamental. Flowers yellow, ¼ in. or less long; pods about 2 in. long; seeds mostly black with a square end.

unguiculata   2'   annual   Common Cow-pea
Vinelike herbs blonging to the Pea Family, with alternate 3-foliate leaves; yellowish-white to purplish pealike flowers; pods 8–12 in. long. Very susceptible to frost; grown best in the South because of the long growing season. Sometimes called Black-eyed Pea. Used for fodder, cover cropping and the fruits for human consumption. Probably native to Asia.

VILLOUS. Bearing long and soft, usually curved or curly hairs.

VINCA (VIN-ka). These are prostrate, creeping vines that do not twine or twist or climb by adhering to anything, but merely creep along the ground, rooting at many places along their stems. They are opposite leaved, mostly evergreen and are not long-extended vines, that is, when they are used in window boxes, for which they are very well suited, they are pendant for only 1½–2 ft. Their flowers are funnel-form, about 1–2 in. across, colored white, blue, pink or red depending on variety or species, and their leaves are pointed, 1–2 in. long. They are easily propagated by division, layers, cuttings, seeds.

**major   ground cover or trailing vine   Zone 7
Big Periwinkle**
Widely grown as an ornamental greenhouse pot-plant in the North, and in gardens outdoors in the South. This is native to southern Europe and western Asia. The bright blue, funnel-shaped flowers borne in mid-May are about 1–2 in. across. The variety **variegata** has leaves variegated with creamy white and is most popular for growing in window boxes, or in the South as a conspicuous ground cover.

**minor   ground cover   Zone 4   Periwinkle,
Myrtle**
A very popular, evergreen ground cover, this grows well in the sun or the shade; has dark lustrous leaves about 2 in. long and lilac-blue flowers ¾ in. across, during late April. It is native to Europe and western Asia, but has escaped cultivation in many places in the eastern U.S., especially because it has been a popular plant in American gardens since colonial times. It increases rapidly in all but the poorest soils. It is easily reproduced by division, for the stems running on top of the ground easily root at many places. Vars.: **'Alba'**—flowers white; **'Atropurpurea'**—flowers purple; **'Bowles Variety'**—flowers light blue; plant grows vigorously but tends to grow more in clumps than do the other varieties; **'Multiplex'**—flowers purple and double; **'Variegata'**—flowers blue, leaves variegated with rich yellow.

rosea = *Catharanthus roseus*

VINE. A plant which trails over the ground or climbs either by twining or by attaching certain appendages to the means of support like a wire, trellis, wall, tree trunk, etc.

VINES. There are many kinds of vines from which the discerning gardener can choose. Essentially they are of 3 types: Those that climb by twining, those that climb by attaching

The English Ivy—a vine—trained over posts and crosspiece to simulate a fence. This, of course, can only be effectively done in areas where it is completely hardy in the winter. (*Photo by Arnold Arboretum, Jamaica Plain, Mass.*)

tendrils or leaf stalks (*Clematis*) to the means of support, and those that cling by attaching small disks or rootlike hold-fasts to the wall. The first 2 groups need a trellis, fence or wire as a means of support. The third group usually needs nothing but a wall surface or tree trunk. Obviously one should not select twining vines or those which climb by means of tendrils to grow on a flat surface and expect them to adhere to it. Also, one should not plant clinging vines on a wire fence or wire. The vines in the following list are segregated as to the means by which they climb.

It is inadvisable to plant a clinging vine on a wooden surface like the boards of a clapboard house for they can ruin the wood and of course must be removed when the house is painted. Usually such vines are used on a brick, stone or concrete surface. If an old clinging vine must be removed from a brick wall for repointing the brick wall, it is difficult to put it back without cutting it to the ground and allowing it to grow up again with vigorous young growth. There are various types of hooks and screws which can be obtained to put in the wall to keep the vines in place, and these might very well be investigated when needed.

When rapid-growing vines are wanted to cover some objectionable object, a few which might be first considered are:

The following list of vines includes those that are most popular at present.

Cl. = Climbs by clinging
Tend. = Climbs by means of attaching tendrils to a means of support
Tw. = Climbs by twining
Ann. = An annual plant
D = With deciduous foliage
Ev. = With evergreen foliage
Per. = A perennial, usually with the top dying to the ground in winter, but sprouting from the roots the following spring

SCIENTIFIC NAME	CLIMBS BY	FOLIAGE	HARDINESS ZONE	COMMON NAME
Actinidia sp.	Tw.	D	4–7	Actinidia
Akebia sp.	Tw.	D	4	Akebia
Ampelopsis sp.	Tend.	D	4–7	Ampelopsis
Anredera cordifolia	Tend.	Ev.	9	Madeira-vine
Antignon leptopus	Tend.	Ev.	9	Coralvine
Aristolochia durior	Tw.	D	4	Dutchman's-pipe
Asparagus plumosus	Tw.	Per.	8	Fern Asparagus
Bauhinia corymbosa	Tend.	Ev.	10	Phanera
Bignonia capreolata	Cl.	Ev.	6	Cross-vine
Bougainvillea spectabilis	Tw.	Ev.	10	Brazil Bougainvillea
Campsis radicans	Cl.	D	4–7	Trumpetcreeper
Cardiospermum halicacabum	Tend.	Ann.		Balloon-vine
Celastrus sp.	Tw.	D	2–4	Bittersweet
Cissus incisa	Tend.	Ev.	8	Marine-ivy
Clematis sp.	Leaf stalks	D	4–7	Clematis
Clerodendrum thompsoniae	Tw.	Ev.	9	Bleedingheart Glorybower
Cobaea scandens	Tend.	Per.	9	Cup and Saucer Vine
Cocculus carolinus	Tw.	D, Ev.	6	Carolina Snailseed
Convolvulus arvensis	Tw.	D	3	European Glorybind
Cryptostegia grandiflora	Tw.	Ev.	10	Palay Rubbervine
Dioscorea batatas	Tw.	Ev.	10	Cinnamon-vine
Distictis buccinatorius	Cl.	Ev.	9	Blood Trumpetvine
D. lactiflora	Tend.	Ev.	9	
Dolichos lablab	Tw.	Ann., Per.	10	Hyacinth-bean
Euonymus fortunei vars	Cl.	Ev.	5	Wintercreeper
Ficus pumila	Cl.	Ev.	9	Creeping Fig
Gelsemium sempervirens	Tw.	Ev.	7	Carolina Jessamine
Hedera sp.	Cl.	Ev.	5–7	Ivy
Hoya carnosa	Tw.	Ev.	10	Common Waxplant
Humulus japonicus	Tw.	Ann.		Japanese Hop
Hydrangea anomala petiolaris	Cl.	D	4	Climbing Hydrangea

SCIENTIFIC NAME	CLIMBS BY	FOLIAGE	HARDINESS ZONE	COMMON NAME
Ipomoea aculeatum	Tw.	Ann.		Moonflower
I. purpurea	Tw.	Ann.		Common Morning-glory
I. quamoclit	Tw.	Ann.		Cypress Vine
Kadsura japonica	Tw.	Ev.	7	Scarlet Kadsura
Lagenaria siceraria	Tend.	Ann.		Calabash Gourd
Lathyrus odoratus	Tend.	Ann.		Sweet Pea
Lonicera sp.	Tw.	D	3–9	Honeysuckle
Luffa sp.	Tend.	Ann.		Dishcloth Gourd
Macfadyena unguis-cati	Cl.	Ev.	8	Cat-claw Vine
Mandevilla suaveolens	Tw.	Ev.	9	Chilean Jasmine
Menispermum sp.	Tw.	Per.	4	Moonseed
Momordica balsamina	Tend.	Ann.		Balsam-apple
M. charantia	Tend.	Ann.		Balsam-pear
Muehlenbeckia complexa	Tw.	Ev.	5	Wire Vine
Parthenocissus sp.	Cl.	D	3–8	Creeper
Passiflora sp.	Tend.	Ev.	7–8	Passion-flower
Phaseolus coccineus	Tw.	Ann., Per.	8	Scarlet Runner Bean
Philodendron sp.	Cl.	Ev.	10	Philodendron
Pileostegia viburnoides	Cl.	Ev.	7	—
Polygonum aubertii	Tw.	D	4	Silver Fleece Vine
Pueraria lobata	Tw.	D	6	Kudzu-vine
Pyrostegia venusta	Cl.	Ev.	10	Orange-trumpet
Schisandra propinqua	Tw.	D	8	Himalayan Magnolia-vine
Senecio confusus	Tw.	Ev.	9	Mexican Fire-vine
S. macroglossus 'Variegatus'	Tw.	Ev.	10	Variegated Wax Vine
Smilax glauca	Tend.	D, Ev.	5	Catbrier
Solanum jasminoides	Tw.	Ev.	9	Potato-vine
Stauntonia hexaphylla	Tw.	Ev.	7	Japanese Staunton Vine
Tecomaria capensis	Tw.	Ev.	9	Cape-honeysuckle
Thunbergia alata	Tw.	Ann.		Clockvine
T. grandiflora	Tw.	Ev.	8	Bengal Clockvine
Trachelospermum sp.	Tw.	Ev.	7–9	Star-jasmine
Tropaeolum majus	Tend.	Ann.		Nasturtium
Vitis sp.	Tend.	D	2–6	Grape
Wisteria sp.	Tw.	D	4–6	Wisteria

VIOLA (VY-o-la). This is a large genus of the Violet Family which includes annual and perennial species. These are distributed throughout the temperate regions of the world. Many species are low-growing, tufted plants with basal or stem leaves, generally heart shaped, blunt toothed, and frequently with 2 types of flowers. The showy, solitary, infertile spring flowers of some species have a calyx of 5 sepals and a corolla of 5 petals, with 2 unlike pairs of petals and a spur on the lower petal. The inconspicuous fertile flowers of these same species are present in the summer, never open, are self-fertile and generally bury themselves into the ground. The pods are 3 celled and many seeded. All are good garden plants and may be propagated from seed, transplanted from the wild, or the clumps may be divided. While responding to rich garden soil, the plants will do well under most situations.

Insect Pests

Blue-black worms which eat the leaves at night are the larvae of the Violet sawfly. Although there is only 1 generation annually the worms may be active throughout the summer. Insecticides #9, #37, and #15 are effective. Violet gall midge which rolls and twists the opening leaves is often a greenhouse pest. Frequent sprays or aerosols of insecticide #15 when the flies are active should be effective. Slugs frequently eat the leaves. Use insecticide #38.

Diseases

Anthracnose causing large dead spots on the leaves is often destructive to outdoor violets. Root rot is also an occasional pest. Both diseases require sanitation and soil sterilization to eradicate them but sprays of fungicide #G or

#D may keep them in check. See PANSY for other diseases.

blanda   2″   **Zone** 3   **Sweet White Violet**
A dainty white-flowered Violet, very low with tiny fragrant flowers. It makes an excellent ground cover in moist, shaded places. Native from Quebec. to Ga., westward.

canadensis   12″   **Zone** 3   **Canada Violet**
Growing in tufts, this perennial has fragrant white flowers with a yellow eye, tinged purple on the outside. These plants are native to the northern half of the U.S. and southern Canada, also in the mountains of the South and West. They do best in a shaded garden soil.

conspersa   6″   **Zone** 3   **American Dog Violet**
Clumps of small, heart-shaped leaves and profuse violet flowers striped with deep purple blooming in spring make this especially desirable for rock garden cultivation. Native from Quebec to Minn. and Ga.

cornuta   6″   **Zone** 6   **Horned Violet, Tufted Pansy**
A perennial which can be grown as an annual, with flowers smaller than those of regular pansies, but some good strains have been developed like 'Chantryland' (apricot); 'Yellow Perfection'; 'Jersey Gem' (purple), a very popular one. The species is native to Spain. These all make excellent border or bedding plants. Seed sown indoors in Jan. should produce flowers after the plants are set out in April. Also, seed can be sown in frames in late Aug., the young plants protected from severe cold in the winter and planted out in April in the same manner as pansies.

fimbriatula   6″   **Zone** 3   **Fringed Violet**
Ovate leaves, sometimes with deeply incised lobes at the base, characterize this perennial species. The violet-colored flowers, $\frac{1}{2}$ in. wide, are striated with dark blue lines and rise from the base on slender stalks. The plant grows over the northern areas of the U.S., extending south to Ga., and blooms from April to May.

jooi   3″–4″   **Zone** 3
A Violet with pinkish-lilac fragrant flowers making a compact plant, blooming in May with a few flowers in the fall. Flowers $\frac{3}{4}$ in. wide; leaves ovate to oblong. Native to southeastern Europe.

lanceolata   6″   **Zone** 3   **Lance-leaved Violet**
True to its name, this perennial has narrowly lanceolate leaves with slightly scalloped edges and a blunt-pointed apex. The flowers are white, striated with blue, and may be found in spring or early summer in the bogs and wet meadows throughout the northeastern U.S. This species puts forth runners which may be propagated by layering.

nuttallii   10″   **Zone** 3   **Nuttall Violet**
A Violet with bright yellow flowers and clumps of long, narrow leaves. It prefers a rather dry soil in semi-shade and blooms in early summer. Native from Manitoba to Ariz.

occidentalis   6″   **Zone** 3   **Siskiyou Violet**
Similar to *V. lanceolata*, this species has slightly larger flowers.

odorata   8″   **Zone** 6   **Sweet Violet**
The fragrant Violet used by florists, with colors ranging from deep violet or white to the rare rose shades. 'Parma' is a double-flowered variety. Sometimes they are grown in gardens blooming from mid-April through May. 'Double Russian' is a small, double-flowered, purple variety; 'Royal Robe' is dark purple with 8-in. stems and is very fragrant. The Sweet Violet is tufted, forming long runners. Native to Europe, Asia, and Africa.

palmata   5″–8″   **Zone** 5   **Early Blue Violet, Palmate Violet**
The ovate leaves of this species are deeply and unevenly lobed and blunt toothed. The pale blue flowers, 1 in. wide, rise on a stem marked by 2 stipules midway up its length. The plant is found in rich woods in eastern U.S. and blooms from April to June.

pedata   5″–6″   **Zone** 4   **Birdfoot Violet**
The erect leaves of this perennial are palmately divided into 5 deeply lobed segments. The deep blue flowers, 1 in. wide, borne singly on slender stalks, rise just above the leaves. The upper petals are generally somewhat darker in color than the lower. A very beautiful flower frequenting open, sunny sites in the eastern U.S. to Minn., extending south to Fla. It blooms from early March to June.

pedatifida   6″   **Zone** 7   **Prairie Violet**
With clumps of palmately divided leaves, the lobes divided in linear segments. The violet-colored flowers on long stems appear in May. Native to Calif.

primulifolia   10″   **Zone** 3   **Primrose Violet**
A moisture-loving Violet with long, oval leaves and white flowers, having prominent purple veins. It blooms in spring and is native from New Brunswick to Fla.

pubescens   8″–12″   **Zones** 2–3   **Downy Yellow Violet**
Taller than some of the other species with most of the leaves near the top of the plant, this produces yellow flowers in the axils of the branched stems. It is found in slightly shaded places in the woods of the eastern U.S. and west to Iowa and blooms during April and May. It is easily reproduced by seeds and runners.

rotundifolia   6″   **Zone** 3   **Roundleaf Violet**
This has pale golden flowers early in the season and the plants form flat mats, making good ground covers in the middle of the summer. It grows in rich woodlands, bears rounded leaves

which lay flat on the soil surface, but must be grown in a cool climate. It does not perform well in hot sunny situations. Native from Me. to Ga.

rupestris   **3″**   **Zones 2–3**   **Sand Violet**
A perennial with small, ovate leaves having a moundlike growth and bearing pale violet-colored flowers in profusion all summer. The var. **rosea** has rosy-pink flowers. Native from Quebec to Mass., west to Alaska.

sagittata   **6″**   **Zone 5**   **Arrowleaf Violet**
This Violet, with bright, violet to purple flowers, has arrow-shaped leaves which are long and tapering. Native from Mass. to Ga.

sororia (*papilionaceae*)   **6″–8″**   **Zone 4**
Butterfly Violet
The most common of the violets in the northeastern U.S.; the petioles of the cordate leaves rise directly from the small, fleshy root, as do the stalks of the deep blue flowers. Sometimes the petals are slightly curled or twisted. This plant makes an interesting ground cover for a semi-shaded location, since it self-sows readily. The var. **priceana** has a white flower heavily striated and tinted with blue. Preferring richer soil than the species, it may be found throughout the eastern U.S. and west to Ark., and Wyo. It blooms in spring.

striata   **6″–12″**   **Zone 4**   **Striped Violet**
This species has long-stalked, cordate leaves and generally 2–3 leafy flower stalks, the leaves and flowers rising from the small, green, bristly-toothed stipules. The solitary, short-stalked flowers are white, sparsely striated with blue, the center tinged with rose. It is native to the woods and fields of the Mid-Atlantic states, extending west to Wisc., and blooms from April to June.

tricolor   **6″–12″**   **Zone 4**   **Johnny-jump-up**
A short-lived European perennial which has been naturalized in some areas in eastern U.S.; the plant has a square stem and a rather decumbent habit. The lower leaves are orbicular, the upper ones alternate, ovate to lanceolate, the margins scalloped or toothed, the apex blunt pointed. The stipules are large and deeply lobed. The solitary flowers are blue, yellow or white, and the petals overlap.

walteri   **6″**   **Zone 8**   **Walter Violet**
An evergreen plant needing dense shade with light green, pubescent leaves mottled dark green and purple and forming a low mat. The dark purple flowers, borne on short stems, bloom in early spring. Native from S.Car. to Fla. and Texas.

x wittrockiana   **6″–12″**   **Annual or biennial**
Common Pansy
These are the true pansies of which there are innumerable varieties. Some gardeners prefer to plant all 1 color in a bed or border, others like the variety in a widely mixed population. There are many different strains, some with large flowers, some with small. These too can be treated as annuals or biennials (see *V. cornuta* for culture) but the largest blooms usually are produced by plants in rich soil with plenty of humus and manure. It usually does not pay to save seed for it soon reverts or produces inferior plants. Also, keeping the flowers picked and preventing seed formation results in longer bloom. Heavy cutting when the plants become "leggy" may also help to keep them neat and contained. They do best with some light shade, not out in the hottest sun.

Insect Pests

Cutworms and garden slugs may be troublesome. See CUTWORMS. Insecticide #43 is specific for slug control. Violet sawfly also skeletonizes and eats holes in Pansy. The worms are bluish black, smooth and about $\frac{1}{2}$ in. long. Insecticide #15 or #9 controls them.

Diseases

Root rot, crown rot and wilt may develop where pansies grow for several years. Soil sterilization and rotation are advised. Anthracnose and scab are prevented by sprays of fungicide #G and powdery mildew is controlled with fungicide #M or #V.

VIRGIN ISLANDS, ORNAMENTAL PLANTS OF. Many tourists going to the Virgin Islands for the first time are overwhelmed with the diverse flora of the Tropics. Names gradually are associated with the correct plants after a few days' visit, and one frequently cultivates an interest in learning more about these plants.

The following list contains only a few of the more common ornamental plants one normally sees in the gardens or beside the roads. It is not practical to list all the palms, succulents and other small plants used. This short list of the most conspicuous plants may prove helpful to the person visiting there for the first time. Each one of the plants mentioned is briefly described in this book in the general alphabetical index.

SCIENTIFIC NAME	HEIGHT	ZONE	COMMON NAME
Acalypha hispida	8′–15′	10	Chenille Copperleaf
A. wilkesiana	10′	10	Painted Copperleaf
Allamanda cathartica williamsii	40′	10	Williams Allamanda
Aloe vera	3′	10	Barbados Aloe

SCIENTIFIC NAME	HEIGHT	ZONE	COMMON NAME
Aloysia triphylla	10′	8	Lemon Verbena
Alpinia purpurata	8′	10	Red Shellflower
A. speciosa	12′	10	Shellflower
Amaryllis belladonna	2′	9	Belladonna-lily
Amomum cardamon	8′	10	Cardamon Amomum
Anthurium andraeanum	2′	10	Flamingo Anthurium
Antigonon leptopus	Vine	9	Coralvine
Araucaria bidwillii	80′–150′	10	Bunya-bunya
Aristolochia elegans	Vine	9	Calico Dutchman's-pipe
Arrabidaea magnifica	Vine	10	
Artocarpus communis	40′	10	Breadfruit
Bambusa vulgaris	80′	10	Common Bamboo
Bauhinia variegata	20′	10	Orchid-tree
Beaumontia grandiflora	Vine	10	Easter Herald's Trumpet
Billbergia pyramidalis	3′	10	Pineapple-lily
Bombax malabaricum	100′	10	Red-silk-cotton Tree
Bougainvillea glabra	Vine	10	Lesser Bougainvillea
Brassaia actinophylla	40′	10	Octopus-tree
Brugmansia candida	20′	10	Angel's-trumpet
Brunfelsia americana	6′–8′	10	Lady-of-the-night
Caesalpinia pulcherrima	15′	10	Barbados Flower-fence
Calliandra californica	4′	10	California Calliandra
Callistemon citrinus	30′	9	Lemon Bottlebrush
Cananga odorata	80′	10	Ylang Ylang
Canna generalis	2′–8′	9	Canna
Carica papaya	25′	10	Papaya
Carissa grandiflora	18′	9	Natal-plum
Caryota mitis	25′	10	Tufted Fishtail Palm
Cassia sp.	3′–30′	6–9	Senna
Castanospermum australe	60′	10	Moreton Bay Chestnut
Casuarina equisetifolia	70′	9	Horsetail Beefwood
Cecropia peltata	36′–60′	10	Trumpet-tree
Ceiba pentandra	120′	10	Kapok
Cestrum nocturnum	12′	10	Nightblooming Cestrum
Citrus sp.	4′–30′	8–10	Orange, Lemon, Grapefruit, etc.
Clerodendrum sp.	20′	6	Glorybowers
Clitorea ternatea	Vine	10	Butterfly-pea
Clusia rosea	40′	10	Copey Clusia
Cocos nucifera	80′	10	Coconut
Cochlospermum vitifolium	20′	10	Buttercup-tree
Codiaeum variegatum	6′–10′	10	Crotons
Costus speciosus	10′	10	Crepe or Malay-ginger
Couroupita guianensis	100′	10	Cannon-ball-tree
Crinum sp.	18″–5′	7–9	Crinums
Cryptostegia grandiflora	Vine	10	Palay Rubbervine
Cyathea arborescens	20′–40′	10	Tree Fern
Delonix regia	40′	10	Royal Poinciana
Dombeya wallichii	30′	10	Scarlet Dombeya
Duranta repens	18′	10	Golden Dewdrop
Eranthemum nervosum	6′	9	Blue Eranthemum
Erythrina sp.	4′–25′	8–10	Coral-bean
Eucharis grandiflora	18″	9	Amazon-lily
Euphorbia pulcherrima	12′	9	Poinsettia
Gliricidia sepium	25′	10	Madre-de-Cocao
Gloriosa rothschildiana	Vine	10	Rothschild Gloriosa-lily
Hedychium coronarium	7′	10	Common Ginger-lily
Heliconia bihai	18′	10	Wild Plantain
Hemerocallis fulva	6′	4	Tawny Daylily

SCIENTIFIC NAME	HEIGHT	ZONE	COMMON NAME
Hibiscus rosa-sinensis	30′	9	Chinese Hibiscus
H. schizopetalus	12′	10	Fringed Hibiscus
Hoya carnosa	Vine	10	Common Waxplant
Hylocereus undatus	25′	10	Night-blooming Cereus
Ipomea horsfalliae	Vine	10	Horsfall Morning-glory
Ixora coccinea	15′	10	Flame-of-the-woods
Jacaranda mimosifolia	50′	10	Sharpleaf Jacaranda
Jatropha curcas	15′	10	Barbados Nut
J. hastata	5′	10	Peregrina Nettlespurge
Justicia guttata (*Beloperone guttata*)	8″–8′	9	Shrimp-plant
Kalanchoe sp.	1′–5′	10	Kalanchoe
Kigelia pinnata	30′	10	Sausage-tree
Koelreuteria elegans	20′–40′	9	Chinese Flame-tree
Lagerstroemia indica	21′	7	Crape-myrtle
L. speciosa	60′	10	Queen Crape-myrtle
Lantana montevidensis	2′	10	Trailing Lantana
Merremia tuberosa (*Ipomea tuberosa*)	Vine	10	Wood-rose
Murraya paniculata	12′	10	Orange Jessamine
Musa paradisiaca	15′–20′	10	Common Banana
Neomarica northiana	3′	9–10	Apostle-plant
Nerium oleander	20′	7–8	Oleander
Parkinsonia aculeata	30′	9	Jerusalem-thorn
Pedilanthus tithymaloides	6′	10	Slipperflower
Peltophorum inerme	50′	10	Sogabark Peltophorum
Pentas lanceolata	18″	10	Egyptian Star-clusters
Petrea volubilis	Vine	10	Sandpaper-Vine
Plumbago capensis	Climbing shrub	9	Cape Plumbago
Plumeria acutifolia	15′	10	Mexican Frangipani
P. emarginata	20′	10	Blunt-leaved Frangipani
Porana paniculata	Vine	10	Porana Vine
Psidium guajava	30′	10	Common Guava
Punica granatum	15′	7–8	Pomegranate
Pyrostegia venusta (*P. ignea*)	Vine	10	Orange-trumpet
Quisqualis indica	Vine	10	Rangoon-creeper
Ravenala madagascariensis	30′	10	Travellers' Palm
Ricinus communis	15′	10	Castor-bean
Roystonea regia	70′	10	Royal Palm
Russelia equisetiformis	8′	10	
Solandra guttata	Vine	10	Goldcup Chalice-vine
Spathodea campanulata	70′	10	Bell Flambeau-tree
Stapelia gigantea	9″	10	Giant Stapelia
Stephanotis floribunda	Vine	10	Madagascar Stephanotis
Strelitzia reginae	3′	10	Queens Bird-of-Paradise
Tecomaria capensis	Sprawling shrub	9	Cape-honeysuckle
Thevetia nereifolia	25′	10	Yellow-oleander
Thunbergia erecta	6′	10	Bush Thunbergia
T. grandiflora	Vine	8	Bengal Clockvine
Vinca rosea	2′	10	Madagascar Periwinkle
Yucca aloifolia	10′–25′	8	Spanish-dagger
Zephyranthes rosea	1′	10	Cuban Zephyr-lily
Zingiber officinale	3′	10	Common Ginger

VIOLET. See VIOLA.

VIRGINIA CREEPER = *Parthenocissus quinquefolia*

VIRGINIA-STOCK = *Malcomia maritima*

VIRGIN'S BOWER = *Clematis virginiana*

VIRUS. Virus diseases are microscopic organisms which cause mottling, deformed, stunted or other abnormal growth. The appearance of infected plants has suggested such names as yellows, mosaic, stunt, false blossom, leaf curl, dwarf, streak, ring spot, leafroll, curly top and spotted wilt. Infections on Peach are called X disease and phony peach disease. Viruses are commonly spread by sucking insects. Certified virus-free strawberries are available and resistant strains of plants are being developed and tested.

VISCID. Glutinous; sticky.

Viscum album, the European Mistletoe, is a parasite and here it is growing on the trunk of a poplar tree. (*Photo by Arnold Arboretum, Jamaica Plain, Mass.*)

VISCUM (VISS-cum)
  album 6″–12″ Zone 7 European Mistletoe
This is a parasite, living in Europe on many kinds of trees including Apple, Poplar and Maple. It is this which has been written about so much in Old World literature, but the plant

does not grow in America. The native mistletoe is *Phoradendron flavescens*, which see.

VISTA. A long view. In landscape planning usually taken to mean a long, unobstructed view usually framed or lined on either side with tall trees. Vistas are most essential to any good garden design so one can see and appreciate distance.

VITEX (VY-tex)
  agnus-castus 9′ Zones 6–7 Chaste-tree
The Chaste-tree, a native of southern Europe and western Asia, has gray aromatic foliage but of a coarser texture than V. negundo 'Heterophylla'; the flowers are more prominent and they bloom from July to Sept., being small and fragrant, lilac or pale violet. The plant frequently dies to the ground during cold winters, but since it blooms in mid-Aug. it blooms on the current year's growth, so it could be cut back to the ground in the very early spring. It is not necessarily a desirable plant in the garden unless the late summer flower or gray foliage are wanted. The variety **'Alba'** has white flowers and **'Rosea'** has pink flowers.

Propagation

Seed should be stratified for 3 months at 40° F., then sown. Plants may be layered. Both softwood and hardwood cuttings may be rooted.
  negundo heterophylla 15′ Zone 5 Cutleaved Chaste-tree
Slightly more hardy than *V. agnus-castus*, this also blooms in mid-Aug. with lilac or lavender, small flowers in loose clusters and has gray aromatic foliage of a very fine texture. It is native to northern China and Korea, and is like the other species in most respects, requiring hard pruning to keep it in good form. Not an especially desirable plant except for its feathery gray foliage and small summer flowers; it has been long known under the name of *V. negundo incisa*.

VITIS (VY-tis). Deciduous alternate-leaved vines which climb by attaching their tendrils to the means of support. The flowers are unisexual or polygamous and are inconspicuous, and the fruits are large or small grapes, depending on the species, black, blue, red or yellow.

A few species like *V. coignetiae* have qualities valued in landscape work, but most of the species have little ornamental value. The brown bark on older vines is shredding, leaves are alternate, and tendrils are either branched or unbranched depending on the species. Flowers are small and inconspicuous. For information concerning culture see GRAPE.

Propagation

Seeds should be stratified for 3 months at

40° F. before sowing. Shoots are easily layered and sometimes can be dug up as natural layers. Both softwood and hardwood cuttings may be rooted also. Grapes are often grafted commercially, the common species being used for understock. See STRATIFICATION, LAYERS, CUTTINGS, GRAFTING, GRAPE.

Many grapes are propagated by cuttings which may be made in early spring, a cutting consisting of 1 bud and an inch or so of stem of the previous year's growth above and below the bud. A slanting cut is made on the stem below the bud, just about reaching it. If the cutting is placed in a pot of sandy soil (the bud uncovered but just at surface) and the pot given some bottom heat, the cutting will root shortly. Cuttings of *V. coignetiae* are very difficult, if not impossible, to root and so this species is best grown by seed.

amurensis   vine   Zone 4   Amur Grape
Native to Manchuria, this is a vigorous vine with black grapes and leaves that are usually 3 to 5 lobed, 5–10 in. wide, turning a crimson to purplish color in the fall.

californica   vine   Zone 7   California Grape
Native to Ore. and Calif., this has leaves 3–5 in. wide and little to recommend it for ornamental planting except that the leaves turn red in the fall. The glaucous-white, rather dry grapes are pleasant tasting. For culture see GRAPE.

coignetiae   vine   Zone 5   Gloryvine
A handsome vine from Japan, probably the fastest growing of all the grapes, with leaves 4–10 in. wide and shoots sometimes growing as long as 50 ft. in 1 season. The autumn color is red. For a rapid-growing screen it is ideal, since an established plant will cover 1000 sq. ft. of trellis in a few years. Practically the best of the grapes for ornamental use.

labrusca   vine   Zone 5   Fox Grape
A rampant grower native from New England to Ga., this is one of the parents of most of the American grapes now in cultivation. The fruits are purple-black, sometimes red-brown or amber-green. The leaves are 3–6½ in. wide. For culture see GRAPE.

labruscana = *Vitis labrusca*
riparia   vine   Zone 2   Riverbank Grape
A high-climbing vine native to the eastern half of North America. Its staminate flowers are fragrant but not sufficiently prominent to be effective ornamentally. The leaves are usually

3 lobed, about 3–7 in. wide and a light bright green. For culture see GRAPE.

rotundifolia   vine   Zone 5   Muscadine Bullace Grape
A strong climbing vine native from Del. to Fla. and west to Kan. and Mexico, from which several varieties of grapes have been selected especially for growing in the South. The leaves are rounded, broadly ovate, and the small, dull purple fruits are less than an inch in dia. Autumn color is a splendid yellow. For culture see GRAPE.

vinifera   vine   Zone 6   Vine Grape
Probably native to the Caucasus but cultivated for centuries, it is from this species that the best wine grapes in the world have been selected. The varieties are grown commercially chiefly in Calif. The fruits vary in size, form and color according to variety. Leaves are nearly round, 3½–6 in. wide, heart shaped at the base. For culture see GRAPE.

vulpina   vine   Zone 5   Frost Grape
Native in eastern North America, this is a high climber, with broadly ovate leaves, usually not lobed, lustrous above. The fruits are dull black, ¼ in. or less in dia., edible after frost. For culture see GRAPE.

VITTADINIA (vit-a-DIN-ia)
australis   1′   Zone 8 (?)   Australian Vittadinia
A perennial herb with thick rootstocks, alternate leaves about ½ in. long, spatulate or linear, simple or toothed; the flowers are white; the heads are borne singly and at the ends of the branches. Native to Australia and New Zealand. Propagated by seeds and division. A member of the Composite Family.

VRIESEA (VREE-sia)
carinata   10″   Zone 10   Lobster-claws
With pale green, sword-shaped leaves 7–8 in. long and ⅔ in. wide; the yellow flowers borne in spikes with spreading yellow bracts, deep red at the base. Native to Brazil. These are epiphytic plants, members of the Pineapple Family.

hieroglyphica   1½′   Zone 10   Hieroglyphic Vriesia
A large epiphytic plant with a rosette of broad leaves 1½ ft. long and 2½ in. wide, yellow-green but marked with cross bands colored dark green above and purplish brown beneath; the flowers 2 in. long, yellow and borne in a tall spike. Native to Brazil. Members of the Pineapple Family.

W

WAHOO = *Euonymus americana*

WAKE-ROBIN, NODDING = *Trillium cernuum*

WALDSTEINIA (wald-STY-nia)

    fragarioides   4″   **Zone 4**   **Barren-strawberry**
This is an inedible relative of the Strawberry with a similar habit of growth. Leaves alternate, 3 foliate and glossy green and evergreen, each leaflet 1–2 in. long. Flowers are yellow with 5 petals, ½ in. across, and borne in 3–8-flowered clusters during May and June. It is native to southern Canada, and the northern and eastern U.S. It has a stout, creeping rootstock and makes a flat-growing ground cover, especially in sunny situations on poor, dry soils.

WALLFLOWER. See ERYSIMUM.

WALLFLOWER, COMMON = *Cheiranthus cheiri*

WALLS AND WALL GARDENING. See ROCK GARDENS.

WALNUT. All walnut species (*Juglans*) flower before the expansion of the leaves. Conspicuous catkins of male (staminate) flowers and small female (pistillate) flowers appear at the same time on the tree. They are followed by seed in the form of edible nuts enclosed in an outer husk. The husk, leaves and sap contain a dye which stains many things with which it comes in contact.

Most walnut species require a growing season of at least 150 days. No species will stand a hard freeze after growth has started in the spring. Such late freezes do not kill the tree, but they destroy new growth and the potential nut crop. Winter cold is also a factor in nut tree hardiness.

Walnuts are raised from seeds which are stratified during the winter to prevent drying out. A wire screen is placed over the flat or box containing the buried nuts to prevent invasion by vermin. For reforesting purposes seeds are sown where they are to grow. If seedlings are to be moved they should be root pruned frequently to increase fibrous root growth.

Named varieties and hybrids of both Black Walnut and Persian Walnut are grafted or budded on seedling stock. Usually Persian Walnut nursery trees are propagated either by whip graft on a year-old seedling or by patch budding in late summer. The understock often employed is California Black Walnut, *J. hindsii*, although recent trend is toward using Persian Walnut seedlings which appear to be immune to a problem disease on the West Coast, known as crown rot. It is not uncommon to top work well-grown seedling walnuts, both Persian and Black, to named varieties. Often this will produce a higher yield sooner than results from planting 1-year-old grafts.

Trees may be planted in the fall after leaf drop or in early spring. Guard the roots against exposure to sun and drying winds and set the trees at the same depth they stood before, using compost or humus loam for back filling. Do not fertilize during the planting process, but assure the transplanted tree of ample moisture during the growing season.

Young walnuts are pruned to establish a leader and to shape the tree. Because walnut trees are apt to bleed freely when branches are removed during the dormant season, it is wise to prune them in late spring or early summer.

Like other fruit trees walnuts respond to fertilization and to other good cultural practices. A healthy well-grown tree results from optimum soil conditions such as a light deep loam containing available plant food and moisture.

From the time walnuts are first planted, they will benefit if given proper attention. This includes, in addition to a deep fertile soil, little or no competition from weeds. Prevent weed growth by keeping a thick mulch under the branch spread. Any one of several materials is suitable to use as a mulch. Be governed by cost and availability.

Those who operate a walnut orchard find that fertilizing with a complete fertilizer such as a 10-6-4 every year produces adequate growth and a steadily increasing yield of nuts. The first year after planting a Black Walnut orchard only ½ lb. of fertilizer is applied per tree, with the amount gradually increased each year as the branch spread and bole diameter increase. Rarely zinc deficiency occurs, usually evidenced late in the season by small yellowish leaves, the edges of which curl upward. A zinc sulfate application is normally an effective correction.

The Black Walnut, *J. nigra*, grows naturally in rich bottom lands in the eastern half of the country. It has interest for cabinet makers and other wood users, because of the fine graining and the high polish the wood will take. With widening interest in the Black Walnut as a nut crop tree, the variableness of the nuts has engaged the attention of plantsmen especially interested in its nut-producing potential. It is a valuable forest tree in the hardwood forests east of the Mississippi River, occasionally reaching 100 ft. in height in rich bottom lands. Grown unrestricted, it is a broad, round-headed tree with heavy branches and a thick bole.

The belief exists that the foliage and roots of Black Walnut contain a chemical named juglone which is harmful to many plant species, such as Alfalfa and Tomato. Death or poor growth of these species when growing under the branch spread is attributed to this chemical.

The Black Walnut becomes a large, broad tree when growing in a deep loam. On upland slopes it will also thrive if suitable soil and adequate moisture are available. Variableness in the size of the nuts, thickness of the shell and tree yield are responsible for many selections. Some of those named have as much as 35% kernel. Many varieties contain at least 20% kernel. Seedlings often have less than 15%.

One of the earliest to be named and still one of the best for all but the northern limits of the species is the 'Thomas', selected by Joseph W. Thomas about 1880. The shell cracks easily, while the kernel can often be removed in 2 parts. In more recent times many other selections have been made, among them 'Ohio' which in the tidewater area of Md. yields handsomely. Others well regarded are 'Stambaugh', 'Sparrow', 'Ten Eyck', 'Huber', 'Elmer Myers', 'Mintle', 'Snyder' and 'Stabler'. 'Deming Purple' has foliage of unusual color. 'Vanderslooth' and 'Victoria' are selections made because of their resistance to the annoying anthracnose leaf spot. A distinguishing characteristic of Black Walnut kernels is that they retain their distinctive flavor after cooking.

Pests

A limited number of insect enemies are sufficiently troublesome to require control. The Black Walnut caterpillar which appears in midsummer is sometimes plentiful enough to defoliate a tree. Since these caterpillars feed gregariously and travel from the leaves to the trunk to cast their skins, it is possible to collect them while they are within reach of the trunk. If a spray is used an arsenical is preferred.

Fall webworm, another defoliator which appears in late June, may also be controlled by spraying with arsenate of lead. The Persian Walnut, especially on the West Coast, is attacked by a codling moth. This may be controlled when the spray is applied for fall webworm.

Aphids and lacebugs are occasionally troublesome in a walnut orchard because they cause early defoliation which prevents filling of the nuts. Check with the county agricultural agent for recommended control chemicals.

The walnut bunch disease was first reported on Japanese Walnut. This witches broom-type growth has appeared with possibly increasing frequency on Japanese Walnut, Heartnut, Black Walnut, Persian Walnut, the hickories and the Pecan. Although much research has been projected, little is still known of the cause of bunch disease and nothing about control. Fortunately it seldom appears on nut trees grown as lawn specimens.

The Persian Walnut, *J. regia*, is a stately tree native to eastern Europe and Asia Minor, and now grown successfully in many parts of North America including Canada. It becomes round headed, 80 or more feet in height and produces nuts which are generally known as English Walnuts. Based on yield, size of nut and ease of cracking many varieties have been named. It is grown commercially chiefly in the West Coast states and in Vancouver, Canada. A few varieties have been grown successfully in the eastern half of the country.

Great interest was aroused in the thirties by a large shipment of *J. regia* nuts collected in the Carpathian Mountain area of Poland by the Rev. P. C. Crath, That part of Poland is noted for its severe winters and generally rugged climate. Seedlings grown from these nuts have varied in form and yield, but generally they have proved more suitable for the northeastern and north central states. Many varieties have been named and are now being reproduced vegetatively. Among the better known varieties of the Persian Walnut grown east of the Mississippi are 'Hansen', 'Colby', 'Broadview', 'Somers', 'Greenhaven', 'Gratiot', 'McDermid' and 'McKinster'.

In commercial orchards of Persian Walnut on the West Coast a few different varieties are grown, notably 'Eureka', 'Farquette', 'Mayette', 'Placentia', 'Hartley', 'Spurgeon', and 'Blackmer'. These all produce nuts that are thin shelled with a thin web between the 2 halves of the kernel. This is easily removed.

In addition to the trees selected for fruit yield or other nut characteristics, a few cultivars distinctive in form are available from nurseries. Among them are *J. regia laciniata* which has leaves much more fernlike in form; also *J. regia pendula* which has a weeping outline, and *J. regia praeparturiens* of shrubby habit. The last produces thin-shelled nuts at an early age.

H. GLEASON MATTOON

WALNUT OR HICKORY FAMILY = Juglandaceae

WALNUT, JAPANESE. *Juglans sieboldiana* is distinctly ornamental with compound leaves up to 3 ft. long, the leaflets of which vary from 9 to 17. They are oblong in shape and minutely toothed. Nuts round or egg-shaped are borne as early as 4 years from seed, appearing in fascinating, long, pendulous bunches. A rank-growing tree, it is suitable for the large property, which can provide ample room for its development. It is a voracious feeder, the roots often ranging twice as far as the branches. The feathery stigma of the female flower is red.

From the standpoint of nut production, the variety **cordiformis**, known as the Heartnut, is more often planted. The heart-shaped shell on this sport or mutation is thin, while the kernel slips out of it with ease. In other respects there appears little difference between the species and this natural mutation. Both are hardy in the northern states. Heartnut selections have been made and named, a few of which are readily available from nurserymen. Probably 'Lancaster', 'Bates', 'Ritchie' and 'Fodermaier' are most popular.

H. GLEASON MATTOON

WAMPEE, CHINESE = *Clausena lansium*

WANDERING JEW = *Tradescantia fluminensis*, also *Zebrina pendula*

WAND-FLOWER = *Sparaxis grandiflora*

WASHINGTONIA (wash-ing-TO-nia)

filifera 60′–80′ Zone 8 California Fan Palm
This is supposed to be the only palm native to the western U.S., a fan palm, often growing with its old dead leaves as a "skirt" reaching to the ground, but many prefer to remove the dead leaves because they are considered unsightly and are a fire hazard. The fan-shaped leaves have 50–70 segments deeply cut, $\frac{1}{2}$–$\frac{2}{3}$ the distance to the leaf base. The stout leaf stalks are 3–5 ft. long and have broad hooked spines. Easily propagated by seeds which germinate readily. For culture see PALMS.

robusta 90′ Zone 10 Mexican Fan Palm
This with its fan-shaped leaves is native to Mexico. The foliage is only at the top of a long trunk, and is coarse in texture. The trunk is frequently covered with a dense, fibrous mass and through this remain the old spiny leaf stalks. It makes an impressive street tree in the warmer parts of Calif. but because of the dead leaves remaining on the trunk it is easily set on fire unless these are cut up to 10 ft. high. For culture see PALMS.

WATER-ARUM = *Calla palustris*

WATER-CANNA = *Thalia dealbata*

WATER-CHESTNUT = *Trapa natans*

WATER-CHESTNUT, CHINESE = *Eleocharis dulcis*

WATER-CLOVER = *Marsilea drummondii*

WATERCRESS = *Nasturtium officinale*

WATER-FERN = *Ceratopteris pteridoides*

WATER GARDENING. Water gardening whether on a large or small scale is one of the most enjoyable, fascinating and (once the initial construction and landscaping is completed) trouble-free forms of ornamental horticulture.

The attractiveness of a water garden extends over a long season. Few garden plants can compare with tropical water-lilies by providing a succession of flowers from June onwards until cut back by frost. These gardens lend themselves superbly to artificial illumination. Both the night-flowering water-lilies and the Giant Water Platter (*Victoria cruziana*) open their flowers at dusk, to provide a nocturnal display.

The most important consideration before planting and construction of the garden is the site. Full sunlight is essential for successful development of nearly all the aquatic plants. If the garden is shaded, growth becomes etiolated, and less floriferous. Trees growing in the near vicinity of a pool are undesirable as the leaves tend to accumulate in the pool, releasing harmful products as they decay under water. In wind-swept locations, a windbreak of the American Arborvitae or Canadian Hemlock planted at a suitable distance on the north side will prevent damage to the more tender plants, and also assist in extending the display season.

The source of water should be relatively free of salinity as well as industrial and municipal wastes. Where fish are desired the water should be able to sustain a flora for the small organisms which serve as fish foods; and to have an optimum dissolved oxygen content of 4%.

Pool Design

The design of the pool may vary from the formal or traditional with a rectangular or circular shape to the informal or more natural form. For the smaller gardens a simple pattern is advocated, being less complicated to build and maintain. This type of pool is more likely to blend with the landscaping of a smaller garden. Eighteen to 24 in. is an ideal depth. To accommodate shallow water and certain moisture-loving bog plants, cement blocks or large stones can be placed under the plant containers in order to bring them up to the correct depth of water (2–4 in.).

Pool Construction

The best material for pool construction is concrete—preferably reinforced—poured into wooden forms. The site selected should be excavated to the necessary depth and outline. Provision for drainage should be made as this will facilitate periodic cleaning. The drain can be run to low ground or sump built nearby. Galvanized iron pipe 2–3 in. in dia. is excellent, fitted with brass couplings, and a threaded plug. Extra refinements can be installed in order to maintain pool cleanliness, including a small pump to insure slow circulation—plus a filter to remove algae and other debris. The sides and floor should be 6 in. thick, built on a 6-in. base of crushed stone. The mixture should consist of 1 part cement, 2 parts clean sand and 3 parts aggregate gravel ($\frac{3}{16}$–$\frac{3}{4}$ in. being satisfactory). This can be obtained ready mixed from a local contractor. For reinforcement, either rods or mesh can be utilized, paying extra attention to the corners—where a double thickness should be used. The forms should be wiped over with old motor oil to prevent binding as the concrete sets. The bottom is poured first, progressing to the sides—filling and tamping the wall forms especially at the corners in order to achieve a thorough bonding. Before the forms are removed, and ornamental stone work or rock construction carried out around the edge, be sure the concrete has set.

Pool showing concrete construction and water-lily boxes.

Puddled pools, with curved sides (no steeper than 45°) can be constructed. They may not possess the permanence of a pool built with forms, but are less expensive and not so much trouble to build. They allow one to build a pool to almost any shape with a minimum of complications. After excavations are completed and provision made for drainage, the floor and sides are covered with a 3–4 in. layer of gravel or crushed stone which is then consolidated. Reinforced rod or mesh is then placed over this layer. Six inches of concrete is then poured over the floor and sides, insuring that the reinforcing is raised evenly to work the con-

crete around it. The final smoothing can be carried out as the concrete commences to set. Burlap can be placed over the pool, and kept moist for a week or so in order to prevent the concrete from drying out too rapidly.

Freshly poured concrete will release a considerable amount of calcium, which subsequently causes the water in the pool to be too alkaline for both plants and fish. The pool can either be painted with one of the water-proofing compounds, or better still given an artificial "curing" or maturation treatment. This consists of several fillings and flushings—followed by a thorough scrubbing with a 25% solution of vinegar—then drained and refilled for planting.

Prefabricated Pools

Prefabricated pools mainly of fibreglass composition have become increasingly popular. They are obtainable in a wide variety of shapes and sizes, are extremely durable, and long lasting. All that is necessary is to excavate the depression to fit the pool, place in position, level and firm. Some of the more elaborate fibreglass pools are obtainable in 2 depths—to accommodate a variety of plant material. Heavy-duty polyethylene can also be used, its disadvantage being its limited length of life compared with the other types of pools. The excavated area is smoothed, all stones removed —then covered with a layer of sand. Then cover with a double thickness of the plastic film, allowing an over-lap of at least 6 in. on all sides. This can be covered with soil or better still with stones. Even the smallest garden can feature an aquatic display—wooden or metal tubs, half barrels, even kettles, can be used to provide a focal point of beauty, when planted with the smaller varieties of water plants.

Bog Gardens

A companion bog garden can enhance the pool, and provide a site to grow an extensive range of unusual plants such as the giant-leaved *Gunnera manicata*, bog primulas, certain native orchids and insectivorous plants, to name just a few. A bog garden does not have to be waterlogged. All that is necessary is to allow the roots access to water at all times. Making an artificial bog garden is considerably less complicated than building the pool. The area selected adjacent to the pool is excavated to a depth of 12–15 in. The base can either be lined with heavy-duty polyethylene and lightly perforated or flat tiles. These are placed over-lapping to prevent too rapid drainage. The area is then filled with a mixture of 2 parts field soil, and 1 part coarse peat. An ideal arrangement is to provide a slow trickle of water from the pool to the bog, insuring a uniformly moist condition.

Natural Pools

Many natural pools or ponds can be utilized to create water gardens. Some of the drawbacks include aquatic weeds which can offer severe competition; varying water levels; muskrats; and stagnation. A stream can be dammed and an area excavated to provide deeper, reasonably still water conditions. Spring-fed pools are often not practical for the tropical water-lilies, due to cool water temperature. Natural pools provide the gardener with maximum scope as regards landscaping the area around the pool, emphasis being to blend the pool with the surroundings, and to create as naturalistic an effect as possible.

A water-lily pool as the center of a garden. (*Photo by Arnold Arboretum, Jamaica Plain, Mass.*)

In states where severe frosts occur some form of winter protection for artificial pools is necessary. Logs or any floating object will take care of the effects of alternate freezing and thawing. For large pools expansion joints every 15 to 20 ft. will greatly reduce the danger of frost damage. Provided the crowns and roots of hardy water-lilies, lotus and other hardy plants are below the frost line, they will winter over satisfactorily.

Planting Water-lilies and General Maintenance

Water-lilies, since they are the showiest and most important plants in a water garden, deserve primary consideration. Planting in containers, either stationary or movable, is advisable for nearly all types of pools. Being able to move the tubs or boxes is an added advantage. The size of the containers is largely governed by the size of the pool and will, of course, influence the eventual size and vigor of each plant.

Tropical water-lilies should have a planter no smaller than 24 in. in dia. by 12 in. deep. The pygmy types may be grown in clay pots as small as 10 in. across. Soil structure and nutrition are as important for water-lilies as for any container-grown plant. The mixture for planting should consist of 5 parts fibrous loam (the type termed field soil by the agronomist) and 1 part partially rotted cow manure (the dried commercial form is quite satisfactory). Leaf soil and silt should be avoided. Peat, although an excellent soil conditioner, tends to cause bulging of the container's contents, due to its spongelike qualities. Perlite, too, is undesirable as it floats, causing unsightliness. To each bushel of mixture should be added 8 oz. of a well-balanced, preferably slow-acting fertilizer.

After filling the container with the soil mixture to within 2 in. of the rim it should be topped off with a 1-in. layer of clean sand. This will prevent any organic matter from floating in the pool. Hardy water-lilies may be planted from April to May. For the tropicals, the water temperature is the limiting factor, a minimum of 70° F. being necessary. If the water is too cool, tropical water-lilies tend to lose their floating leaves and become dormant for a few weeks. They are slow to recover from this check. In the southern states they may be planted around mid-May and in the northern states from the first of June on, depending of course upon the weather. Only 1 Water-lily should be planted in each container, otherwise the radial symmetry of the leaf pattern is lost. Avoid overcrowding reflections, and always leave sufficient room for development.

Water-lilies should be spaced 3 to 5 ft. apart depending upon the variety. For a large pool a scale plan will be of great assistance to obtain balance and color harmony. The water level above the crown of the plant should be about 9–12 in. Often after planting under water the leaves are submerged, but they rapidly extend their petioles to attain a surface floating position within 24 hours. Strong plants commence to flower within a week or two, and will continue flowering until the advent of cold weather, throughout the summer months. Yellowing leaves, faded flowers and seed pods should be removed weekly. Water-lilies, especially the tropicals, are good indicator plants and exhibit hunger signs readily. Supplemental feeding can be carried out by using the soluble fertilizer tablets. These are pushed down among the feeder roots. Such feeding at the rate of 2 oz. for each plant can be carried out every 14 days once the water-lilies are well established.

PATRICK A. NUTT

WATER-HAWTHORN, LACE = *Aponogeton madagascariensis*

WATER-HEMLOCK,   SPOTTED = *Cicuta maculata*

WATER-HYACINTH,   COMMON = *Eichhornia crassipes*

WATERING. One should have a thorough knowledge of soil structure (see COMPOST, SOIL, SOIL WATER) to understand properly the application of additional water to the soil as an aid to plant growth. Millions of gallons of water are uselessly wasted throughout the country in "watering" the garden improperly at the wrong time. In times of normal rainfall this may not be important but in times of drought it can become critical. Soils differ in their capacity for retaining water, but the soil with the larger amount of humus retains more than a sandy soil without humus.

It has been estimated that 1 in. of rain water will keep a soil moist for 5–15 days depending on the temperature of the air and the type of soil. One gallon of water per minute, applied to 1000 sq. ft. of soil surface, must continue $10\frac{1}{2}$ hours to equal 1 in. of water added to the soil. In times of drought it is essential to check the soil and see whether it is moist or has dried out and is in need of additional water.

Plants vary in their water requirements. Those with large, succulent leaves need more water than others. Some, like onions, for instance, do not need as much water as carrots. Most garden vegetables and flowers are shallow rooted and have their feeding roots in the upper few inches of soil. Trees, on the other hand, have 80% of their feeding roots in the upper 18 in. of soil. The age of the plants is important also, for a group of vegetables half grown, but in the midst of vigorous growth, needs more water than a similar group which has matured.

One can note the condition of the foliage to watch for wilting, another indication that water has become deficient. In the very early spring when the leaves of plants are not fully matured, they may wilt in the morning or at noon when the temperature is very high, merely because they are too young and succulent to withstand excessive evaporation without such wilting. During the cool of the evening, they would quickly become turgid again. On cloudy days the same plants would not wilt. An examination of the soil around such plants would probably show the soil to be sufficiently moist, hence the wilting in such cases is caused on very young succulent foliage by excessively high temperatures.

It is much better to give a thorough soil soaking, rather than a light sprinkling. Actually the light sprinkling can prove harmful! In times of water deficiency when just a little water is applied to the soil surface, it may only moisten the upper inch of an otherwise dry soil, thus bringing out young rootlets which, in order to be kept alive, will have to be continually moistened by such light sprinklings. It is readily seen that it is much better to moisten the soil deeply, aiding the deeper roots in their normal growth, rather than water in such a way as to produce new rootlets in the upper inch of soil—an area always critical in times of drought.

The amount of water applied should be estimated and checked properly. If it is desired to have water penetrate to 4 in. then check the soil by digging to see when this occurs. At the same time, have a pan under the sprinkler to see how much water is applied to reach a certain depth; then the next time watering is done, one knows that if the water is a certain depth in the pan, then it has penetrated to proper depth in the soil.

Watering by "soil soakers," or porous hoses, is often an excellent procedure either along the rows in a vegetable garden where water might be useless in between the rows or in circles around trees and shrubs. Watering the lawn with sprinklers is common but, even here, one good soil soaking does more good than several light "sprinkles." Also, allowing water to run out of the hose slowly and soak into the ground about a plant slowly is better than forcefully spraying it over the ground and having it run off in all directions.

The time at which water is applied to the garden is important. The best time is in the cool of the evening when the soil has the rest of the night to absorb it, when the leaves can be moistened and also absorb water without it rapidly evaporating.

The worst time for watering the garden is at high noon of a hot sunny day. In the first place, water on the foliage can act like a lens and concentrate the sun's rays so that the foliage can actually be burned. Secondly, with the high temperature, loss by evaporation is very rapid. Only a proportion of the water applied at noon would benefit the plant, whereas, in the cool of the evening, all of it would benefit the plant. Then, too, watering on a very windy day is conducive to excessive water loss by immediate evaporation.

Finally, one should not overlook the possibility of providing an underground water system with outlets conveniently located at various parts of the garden. With the modern plastic piping now available the installation of such a system is not nearly as expensive as it used to be with the conventional metal piping.

The same principles govern the watering of pot plants indoors although the tendency here is to over-water. No general recommendation can be given for "how often" to water, since plant requirements are different, room temperatures are different, older plants that are pot bound can require more water than smaller plants. In general, one should examine the soil and water "when needed"; one thorough watering is better than several lighter ones. It is not long before one becomes accustomed to watering the plants growing under one set of conditions according to a definite schedule. Water should not be allowed to stand in the base of pots, but all excess water should drain out completely.

WATERLEAF. See HYDROPHYLLUM.

WATERLEAF FAMILY = Hydrophyllaceae

WATER-LETTUCE = *Pistia stratiotes*

WATER-LILIES. In order to break up the straight lines and flat surfaces of a water garden various aquatic plants can be judiciously added. These will provide height, variation of leaf form and texture, in order to achieve a balanced and aesthetic effect. Floating aquatics too are useful to provide interesting leaf patterns and provide shelter for fish. Oxygenating plants are important to maintain the correct balance of desirable organisms in the pool itself. The margins and surrounding of informal and natural pools can also be planted with clumps of bamboos, ornamental grasses, and perennial plants such as astilbes, the very showy hardy lobelias and a host of other plants adapted to blend with the water garden. A number of the more interesting and exotic aquatic plants are not hardy, requir-

Nelumbo lutea—The native American Lotus

ing either overwintering in a greenhouse or replacement each year. Most of them are easily propagated by division during the fall.

Propagation of Water-lilies—Hardy Varieties

Nearly all of the hardy water-lilies, including the pygmy types, can be propagated by division. Unless the pools are drained annually this will be only necessary every 2 or 3 years for container-grown plants. Hardy lilies can also be stored in a cool cellar when the pools have to be drained for the winter. Where the more vigorous varieties are naturalized in large lakes they are best left undisturbed for many years.

The rootstocks of the hardy water-lilies vary in shape. The *Nymphaea odorata* and *N. tuberosa* varieties possess fleshy, horizontal rhizomes, often branching and bearing buds. These can be divided with a sharp knife—each division having at least 1 strong bud. The new plant is replanted horizontally. The *N. marliacea* hybrids and pygmy types are distinguished by a thickly clustered, fleshy rootstock. These are slightly more difficult to divide—the new offsets being replanted vertically. The younger terminal portions of both these types of water-lilies develop into more floriferous and vigorous plants; the older woody portions, being relatively unproductive, are best discarded. To insure anchorage when replanting, several stones can be placed around the crowns of the new divisions.

Tropical Varieties

Tropical *Nymphaea* species are best treated as annuals and replaced each year, unless one has facilities to propagate and overwinter them. In sheltered, frost-free locations in southern Calif. and Fla. many of the tropical varieties will over winter safely. The most reliable method of propagating this group is by growing a number of plants of each variety separately, preferably in a greenhouse in tanks. These plants are grown in 3–4-in. pots, where they can form small tubers about the size and shape of a hickory nut and then become dormant.

They are stored over winter in mason jars—containing slightly moist sand at a temperature of 50° F. The following spring, they are planted deeply in small pots and placed in shallow tanks in the greenhouse where the water temperature should be kept around 70°–75° F. They will send up stoloniferous growths which should be carefully removed witn the forefinger and thumb when they possess about 3 floating leaves. They should be removed at the junction of the stem and tuber and planted in 4-in. pots, the soil mixture consisting of 3 parts loam and 1 part sand. These plants will develop a tuber identical to the parent tuber, which can be used for growing display plants or for further propagation.

A healthy tuber can produce a succession of these growths before becoming exhausted. A number of the tropical Nymphaeas are viviparous and produce "piggy backs" on the parent leaf. Some varieties even produce flowers while attached to the mother plant. This characteristic is influenced by the latitude and climate—more varieties being viviparous in the South, and less in the eastern and northern states. The young plantlet develops in the center of the leaf between the sinuses, then sends out adventitious roots. They are severed from the leaf—the surplus trimmed and planted in small pots where they will eventually produce a tuber and become dormant. After lifting the flowering plants in the fall, tubers about the size of a walnut can usually be found around the base of the rootstock. These can be removed, dusted with a fungicide and grown in small pots. They should produce small plants within a few weeks. These should be grown under the daylight type of fluorescent lamps in heated tanks or aquariums, as they do not winter as well as tubers produced by the other 2 methods.

Propagation by Seed

Propagation by seed is only resorted to in order to raise new varieties, and to perpetuate certain rare species that are difficult to propagate by vegetative methods. Few gardeners have sufficient room to flower hybrid seedlings in order to evaluate them. The pistillate or seed-bearing flower should be selected the day prior to opening, the flower of a Nymphaea being most receptive on the first day of opening. The staminate parent is selected one day earlier, as the anthers are dehiscent on the second day of opening. They are both kept closed by using strong rubber bands around the petals. This is looped around the base of the bud to prevent it slipping off.

The pistillate or seed-bearing flower should be emasculated the day before pollination. Use great care when removing the anthers which not to injure the bases of the stamens which would result in the loss of nectar from the stigmatic cup. After emasculation the flower should be closed and banded securely.

The next day, preferably before noon, one can commence pollination. The first step is to obtain the anthers from the staminate flower. The flower is unbanded and, using the finger and thumb, the sepals and petals are folded back in order to reach the stamens. The anthers which bear the pollen are removed with tweezers and placed in a phial. Next remove the band from the pistillate flower, fold back the sepals and petals exposing the stigmatic cup, which if receptive should be filled with nectar. Drop at least half a dozen anthers into the cup and with the aid of the blunt end of the tweezers slightly agitate the anthers in the nectar. By doing so one reproduces the action of the pollinating insect in its struggle to escape. The flower is now banded again—covered with cheesecloth and tied to a stake, this tie being removed the following day. This will allow the flower to descend into the water where the seed pod should develop if the pollination is successful. A pollination label should be attached to the stake as a record. After each pollination, dip the tweezers in a phial of alcohol to prevent contamination of unwanted pollen.

When the seed pod is ripe, in about 3 weeks, it will rise to the surface of the water. The pod should be removed from the cheesecloth bag when ready to burst and placed in a receptacle of water. The fleshy portions plus the decaying floral parts will soon disintegrate, the seeds being covered with a gelatinous aril, and will float for a day or so. When they sink to the bottom, the contents should be screened to remove the pulp. The seeds should not be left in water for longer than a week, otherwise premature germination may take place.

The seed when dry should be sown in a mixture of 2 parts finely sieved loam and 1 part fine sand, (steam sterilized). Use a shallow pan with a little roughage over the drainage hole. The pans should be filled to within $\frac{1}{4}$ in. of the top and the seeds sown evenly, then covered with a very light layer of fine sand. They are then immersed in the propagating tank and left with the top inch out of the water for a few days to thoroughly soak the seed. This prevents seeds from floating and loss. After this, they may be fully immersed, the temperature of the water being maintained at 70°–75° F. Once the first floating leaves have developed, the plants may be potted up singly in small pots and kept at the same temperature, in full sunlight.

The Giant Water-platters

Victoria amazonica *and* V. cruziana

These 2 giant, aquatic plants are spectacular subjects for large pools. They produce leaves 5–6 ft. with upturned leaf margins. The underside of the leaf has a very prominent, honeycomblike network of veins which trap air, giving the leaf sufficient buoyancy to support considerable weight if it is evenly distributed.

V. amazonica is indigenous to the Amazon River basin, while the species found farther south in Paraguay, Bolivia and Argentina was named *V. cruziana* after General Santa Cruz.

Numerous unsuccessful attempts were made to introduce *V. amazonica* into cultivation, after its discovery in 1801, but it was not until 1849 that this was finally accomplished. Joseph Paxton, the gardener and general factotum for the Duke of Devonshire, produced a vigorous plant in a specially built greenhouse. This remarkable aquatic was introduced into the U.S.A. in 1851, Caleb Cope of Philadelphia being the first to have a plant in his garden.

V. amazonica is the larger of the 2 species, but due to its hardiness *V cruziana* is more adaptable to outdoor culture, particularly in the northern states. The F$_1$ hybrid cv. 'Longwood' combines the adaptability of *V. cruziana*, and the large leaves of *V. amazonica*, besides possessing a marked degree of hybrid vigor.

The 2 species can be readily distinguished even in the seedling stage. The undersides of the leaves of *V. cruziana* are of a violet-blue color, those of *V. amazonica* are purplish red. The upturned leaf margins of *V. cruziana* commence to form much earlier and are higher in the mature plant. The sepals of *V. cruziana* have spines only at their bases, whereas those of *V. amazonica* bear spines to the tip. The spines of the latter are longer and more needlelike. The seed too is distinct; that of *V. cruziana* being globose with a prominent raphe, while the seed of *V. amazonica* is elliptic-globose with a rather indistinct raphe. Although a perennial in its native habitat, it is best grown as an annual in the United States.

The seeds should be sown about March 1st, depending upon the locality, at about twice their depth in shallow pans and are spaced about 1 in. apart. The soil mixture should consist of 1 part screened loam and 1 part sand (both steam sterilized). The pans are then submerged in tanks with the water level from 2–3 in. above the rims of the pans. The water temperature should be kept around 70°–75° F. for *V. cruziana*, 85°–90° F. for *V. amazonica*. Germination takes from 3 to 4 weeks. *V. cruziana* does not germinate evenly, some seeds taking up to 8 weeks. The light intensity is a most important factor; if dull cloudy weather is experienced, germination will be delayed. A long needle-shaped shoot appears first—followed by a pair of hastate-shaped submerged leaves. When the seedlings possess 2 floating leaves they should be potted up singly into 3-in. pots, using a mixture of 3 parts loam and 1 part sand. They should be kept growing actively—repotting them when necessary to a 5-in. and then 8-in. pan, using a slightly richer mixture each time they are repotted. This will take care of the plant's needs until they are planted outdoors.

The soil preparation is important, for *Victoria* species are gross feeders and respond to generous treatment. An ideal mixture consists of 4 parts field soil and 1 part partially rotted cow manure. Six ounces of a well-balanced fertilizer should be mixed with each bushel of mixture when filling the plant containers, which should be boxes generous in size in order to accommodate the giant plants. The soil contents should be covered with a 1-in. layer of sand.

Victoria species should not be planted out-of-doors until the water temperature is around 75° F.; for *V. amazonica* a minimum of 80° F. is necessary. If the young plants are checked at this stage they are slow to recover. The depth of water should be from 12–14 in. above the crown of the plant.

Once the young *Victoria* species are established they grow prodigiously, the new leaves rapidly increasing in size. In order to keep the leaves in place and to prevent damage in periods of high wind they are best anchored. Strong wire hoops placed over the leaf blades and pushed down into the soil are suitable for this purpose. A well-developed plant will support from 8 to 10 leaves.

Both species commence to flower the beginning of Aug. The flower opens at dusk for 2 successive nights. On the first night it is white, incurved and very fragrant; on the second night the deep pink or crimson, innermost petals appear, the flower becoming completely reflexed as it changes color. A well-grown plant can produce upwards of 35 12-in. flowers in a single season.

During late July, Aug. and Sept., supplemental feeding of the Victorias can be carried out to keep the plants growing as vigorously as possible. Fertilizer can be placed in a cheesecloth bag and pushed down into the soil, 3 ft. or so from the crown of the plant, 12 oz. being given to each plant in 3 separate bags every 14 to 21 days. One of the readily soluble 20–20–20 fertilizers is most satisfactory for this purpose.

Victoria species will usually set seed, especially if more than 1 plant is growing in the near vicinity. To guarantee seed for the following year, the flowers should be hand-pollinated. Victorias are protogynous so the pollen should be obtained from the anthers of a second-night flower and lightly distributed over the stigmatic surface, in the bottom of the first-night flower, using a small camel's-hair brush. Pollen can also be kept refrigerated for 96 hours at 45° F. If fertilization has taken place, the seed pod will commence to swell rapidly within 10 to 14 days. The pod should be covered with a cheesecloth bag. When the pods are fully developed, taking 4 to 5 weeks, they will dehisce, releasing the seeds which are covered with a gelatinous aril. The seed pods should be placed in containers of water, which should be changed frequently to eliminate all the products of the putrefication of the arils.

The ripening period for *Victoria* seed is most important since seed will not germinate unless fully ripened. The results of experiments at Missouri Botanical Garden have shown that the ripening period can be reduced and better germination obtained by storing the seed in containers of moist sand kept at 60° F. for 8 weeks. For *V. amazonica* 70° F. has been found more satisfactory. When the seeds are removed from the containers, the seed coats will have attained a dark brownish-black color, usually associated with full ripeness. After ripening, the seeds can be cleaned and refrigerated in jars of water at 50° F. until sowing time.

Lotus

The lotus species are remarkably handsome, aquatic plants, well worthy of a place in the larger pools. There are 2 species, the native *Nelumbo lutea* and the East Indian *N. nucifera*. Unlike *Nymphaea* species the *Nelumbo* species differ fundamentally by possessing large peltate leaves—growing several feet out of the water. The flowers are also borne on long stems and are large and showy. They open on 3 successive days. When the petals fall the spongy receptacle develops into a rather attractive seed pod, often containing seeds in the large, flat, curious carpels. When fully formed, they are prized for dried arrangements.

There are many cultivated varieties. The *Nelumbo* species are vigorous-growing plants, and require rich soil and sufficient room in order to develop satisfactorily. They are propagated by division of the banana-shaped tubers. This is best done in late spring, taking care not to injure the tender growing points of the tubers which are brittle. The tubers should be planted 2 in. beneath the soil, barely covering the growing tips—the water depth being 6 in. The tubers develop a long creeping rootstock often 10–15 ft. in a single season with new tubers at intervals.

As long as the roots are well below the frost line they are perfectly hardy. They can also be propagated by seed, the hard-coated seeds needing scarification before sowing.

Pests and Diseases of the Water Garden

Aquatics, by comparison with other garden plants, have few pests. If a reasonable biological balance can be maintained, the problems will be minimized. Fish are most beneficial, for many injurious insects can be washed with a hose into the pool where they will be consumed. Water snails of the scavenger type are also desirable. They consume and break down organic matter that otherwise would be unsightly. There are several varieties of water snails that feed on living plant material, any one of which would be suitable for this purpose.

Where more drastic control measures are needed, the water gardener will have to resort to chemicals selected and used with discrimination. One group of insecticides that should never be used in the water garden are the chlorinated hydrocarbons (DDT, Chlordane etc.). These are all extremely toxic to many forms of aquatic life, fish, beneficial insects and amphibians, besides possessing long residual effects in the water.

The most persistent pest of aquatic plants is the brownish-black aphid (*Ropalosiphum nymphaeae*). This pest, like all aphids, reproduces very fast and should be controlled before becoming well established. Malathion in emulsified form is very effective in controlling the water-lily aphid.

Two types of beetles can be troublesome to water-lilies. The Japanese beetle can cause severe damage to the flowers of Nymphaeas in bad years of infestation. The leaf-eating beetle (*Galerucella nymphaeae*) is a pest in a number of states. The bluish-black larvae about ⅜ in. long can cause considerable damage to the foliage of water-lilies. Sevin applied as a liquid is very effective against these 2 beetles.

Caterpillars of the *Noctuid* moths can be destructive during the latter part of the season. The night-flying moths lay eggs on the leaves which hatch into black and yellow or brownish-grey larvae. They are particularly found at the upturned leaf margins of the Victorias—where damage is most noticeable. The larvae of the Delta or sometimes known as the Brown China Marks Moth (*Hydrocampa propialis*) can also be a nuisance. The clear-colored caterpillars feed on the leaves of Nymphaeas and other aquatic plants. They will eventually spread over the pool by floating on detached sections of the decaying leaves if not controlled. Sevin or Malathion can be used for control of both these caterpillars.

During the early part of the season water-lilies are attacked by the larvae of one of the midges (*Chironomus modestus*). These tiny, almost translucent larvae will tunnel into the undersides of the leaves. One of the methyl-carbamate insecticides used for mosquito control will combat this pest.

The *Nelumbo* species are sometimes attacked by 2 pests—the European corn borer and the leaf roller. Sevin is an effective control for these 2 pests, if applied at the first sign of damage. Once colonized, their natural method of feeding causes them to be difficult to eradicate. The larvae of caddis flies (*Trichoptera*) which can be quite destructive are controlled by fish.

Nymphaeas are sometimes attacked in very hot humid weather by a fungal disease leaf spot (*Cercosporae* sp.). This disease is usually established under stagnant, overcrowded conditions. Removal of infested leaves and general cleanliness is important. Folpet is an effective fungicide but coverage is difficult on water-lily leaves as they are coated with a waxy covering. Spraying in bright sunlight can cause severe leaf scorch. Care should also be taken not to allow excess spray to drift into the pools containing fish. The tubers of tropical *Nymphaea* sp. can be attacked by a fungal storage rot. A most effective, preventive control for this is to dip the tubers in a thick solution of equal parts of Captan and Thiram, then dry before storage. Seedling *Nymphaea* and *Victoria* species and varieties can be infected with a fungus soon after germination. The symptoms are very similar to damping off. Hygiene is the only method of preventing this fungus which can be very destructive. All the ingredients in the soil mixture should be sterilized before use, and the water should be uncontaminated. The seeds can be disinfected in a 10% solution of Chlorox and then dried before sowing.

Algae can be an unsightly problem, especially during the early part of the season before the pool surface becomes shaded. Two chemicals give reasonably effective control, their disadvantage being rather short residual effect. Potassium permanganate 1 oz. to 100 gallons of water or copper sulfate at 1 part per million. Care should be taken to check the tolerance of the fish in the pools for the copper sulfate is toxic to a number of the more exotic species. Copper sulfate can also cause severe leaf scorch to *Victoria* and to a lesser degree to a number of the tropical *Nymphaea* species and varieties.

Classification of Water-lilies (*Nymphaea*)

Generally speaking the popular term water-lily includes species from 3 genera, *Nymphaea*, *Nuphar* and *Victoria*. Actually the genus *Nymphaea* contains the true Water-lily species; *Nuphar* contains the so-called Pond-lilies or Spatterdock of the eastern U.S. and the genus *Victoria* contains the huge-leaved Water-platters.

Nymphaea species are usually divided into the hardy water-lilies that will be hardy over winter in northern pools (if the roots are below the ice level) and the tropical water-lilies which can not live out-of-doors over winter in the North but need warm water to survive. Flowers of hardy types usually float on the water surface while those of tropical varieties are held on stems slightly above the water level. Actually some of the best types of both groups are hybrids. Many were originated by George Pring of the

Missouri Botanical Garden. Here are some of the most important species:

Hardy Water-lilies (*Nymphaea*)

N. alba—the European White Water-lily with leaves 12 in. across and reddish when young; white flowers 4–5 in. across opening during the day.

N. odorata—Fragrant Water-lily, widely native in the eastern U.S. with leaves 10 in. across; fragrant white flowers 3–5 in. across, opening during the day. The variety **gigantea** has larger flowers.

N. tetragona—Pygmy Water-lily, native to eastern Asia and North America from Idaho to Ontario, with leaves 3–4 in. across and yellow beneath; white flowers $1\frac{1}{2}$–$2\frac{1}{2}$ in. across opening during the day.

N. tuberosa—Magnolia Water-lily, native to North America; white flowers 4–9 in. across with no fragrance, opening during the day; tubers 1–3 in. long.

Tropical Water-lilies (*Nymphaea*)

N. caerulea—The Blue Lotus of Egypt—not very showy but blooming freely with leaves 12–16 in. wide and light blue flowers 3–6 in. wide with a dull white center, showing 14–20 petals. Native to northern and central Africa.

N. capensis—Cape Water-lily with leaves 12–16 in. across; flowers sky blue, 6–8 in. across, opening during the day and native to South Africa. The variety *zanzabariensis* has smaller leaves but larger, very deep blue flowers 6–12 in. across.

N. gigantea—Australian Water-lily, native to Australia, has blue flowers 6 in. across and opens during the day.

N. lotus—Egyptian Lotus, native to Egypt, with leaves 12–20 in. across, dark green above, brownish underneath; flowers are white shaded pink or red, 5–10 in. across, opening on 4 successive nights and remaining open each morning until noon.

N. stellata—Blue Lotus of India, one of the finest of the blue-flowering types with the flowers opening during the day.

Victoria *Species* (*Water-platters*)

V. amazonica—Amazon Water-platter, native to the Amazon River, with leaves 5–6 ft. across and purplish red underneath; with 12-in. white to pink flowers opening at dusk on 2 successive nights.

V. cruziana—Giant Water-platter, native to Paraguay, with leaves 5–6 ft. across and violet-blue underneath with white to pink, fragrant, 12-in. flowers opening at dusk on 2 successive nights.

V. regia—This is actually *V. amazonica*. Some

of the material in the U.S. as *V. regia* may be *V. cruziana*. The popular one is certainly *V. amazonica*.

Nuphar—*Pond-lilies or Spatterdocks*

N. advenum—Spatterdock or Cow-lily, native in ponds and streams throughout the eastern U.S., with leaves up to 12 in. across; flowers yellow, globular, 2½ in. in dia. held above the water and not at all like those of typical water-lilies. (There are other American, European and Japanese species but *N. advenum* is the most important).

The development of the modern Water-lily has been primarily through collection of species that had been previously isolated geographically the combining of their respective good qualities by cross-hybridization, and selection of the most desirable progeny. One disadvantage of the showy tropical varieties for small pools, their large size, has been overcome. A number of these floriferous varieties are now adaptable for home pools. The following varieties, many of them hybrids, are listed according to the color and size of their flowers.

Recommended Varieties

TROPICAL DAY FLOWERING
(with color and size of flowers)

BLUE AND VIOLET

'Bagdad'—light violet—medium size—leaves viviparous and heavily mottled

'Bob Trickett'—pale violet—large size (10–12 in.)

'Director George T. Moore'—strong violet—medium size (5–6 in.)—compact habit

'Judge Hitchcock'—strong violet—large size (8–9 in.)

Nymphaea x daubenninna—very pale lilac—small—viviparous—adaptable

'Midnight'—strong violet—medium size (6–8 in.)—compact growth

'Pamela'—purplish blue—large size (10–12 in.)—mottled leaves

'Panama Pacific'—light purple—medium size —compact (viviparous)

PINK

'Afterglow'—yellowish pink—medium size (8–9 in.)

'American Beauty'—deep reddish pink—flowers are medium size (6–8 in.)

'Evelyn Randig'—deep reddish purple— —medium large (8–9 in.)—leaves heavily mottled

'General Pershing'—purplish pink—large size (9–10 in.)

'Peach Blow'—purplish pink—moderate size —viviparous habit

'Persian Lilac'—strong purplish pink— large size (8–9 in.)

'Pink Platter'—very pale purple—large size (10–12 in.)—viviparous habit

'Shell Pink'—light purplish pink—medium to large (9–10 in.)

YELLOW

'Aviator Pring'—brilliant greenish yellow— large size (9–10 in.)—viviparous habit

'St. Louis'—pale yellow—large size (10 in.)

'St. Louis Gold'—brilliant—greenish yellow —small to medium flowers (6–7 in.)— compact habit

WHITE

N. gigantea alba—flowers large (9–10 in.)— peony shaped, held up well above water

'Mrs. George H. Pring'—large, up to 12 in.

'Isabelle Pring'—large (9–10 in.)—viviparous habit

TROPICAL NIGHT FLOWERING

RED

'B. C. Berry'—strong purplish red—medium size (6–8 in.)

'H. C. Haarstick'—purplish red—large (10–12 in.)

PINK

'Emily Grant Hutchins'—large purplish pink (9–10 in.)

'James Gurney'—deep purplish pink (10–12 in.)

'Mrs. George C. Hitchcock'—strong purplish pink (10–12 in.)

WHITE

'Missouri'—flowers very large, up to 13 in.

HARDY VARIETIES

YELLOW

'Cromatella'—compact—brilliant yellow— medium size

'Helvola'—brilliant yellow—pygmy variety— flowers (1–2 in.)

'Sunrise'—brilliant yellow—large flowers (5–6 in.)

PINK

'Joanne Pring'—purplish pink, pygmy variety —(1–2 in.)

'Pink Opal'—medium size

'Pink Sensation'—compact—medium size (3–4 in.)

'Rose Arey'—deep purplish pink—medium size (3–4 in.)

RED

'Attraction'—strong purplish red—large flowers (5–6 in.)

'Escarboucle'—red—medium size (2–3 in.)

'James Drydon'—red

SUNSET SHADES

'Comanche'—yellow-red—medium large size (4–5 in.)

'Paul Harriot'—yellow-red—small compact (2–3 in.)

WHITE

'Gonnere'—double compact (3–4 in.)

N. odorata—fragrant (2–3 in.)

N. tuberosa 'Nichardsoni'—vigorous habit

N. tetragona—pygmy variety—tiny flowers (1–1½ in.)

N. candida—compact

AQUATIC PLANTS

Acorus calamus—3 ft—hardy—Sweet Flag

A. gramneus—8–12 in.—hardy

Aponogeton distachyus—floating—tender—Cape Pond Weed

Colocasia esculenta—3 ft.—attractive foliage—tender—Taro

C. antiquorum—18–24 in.—tender—Elephant's-ear

Cyperus alternifolius—2½ ft.—tender—Umbrella Flatsedge

C. papyrus—5 ft.—tender—Egyptian Paper Plant

Eichornia crassipes—floating—shallow water—tender—Water Hyacinth

Hydrocleys nymphoides—floating leaves—tender—Water Poppy

Jussiaea longifolia—2½ ft.—tender—Brazilian Water Primrose

Nymphoides peltatum—shallow water—hardy—floating habit—Floating Heart

Pistia stratiopes—floating—shallow water—tender—Water-lettuce

Pontederia cordata—2 ft.—hardy—Pickerel-weed

Sagittaria sagittifolia 'Florepleno'—2 ft.—hardy—Arrow-head

Thalia dealbata—3½ ft.—hardy—Powdered Thalia

Typha angustifolia—3–4 ft.—hardy—Slender Cattail

T. minima—12–18 in.—tender—Dwarf Cattail

OXYGENATING PLANTS

Vallisneria spiralis	Eel Grass
Ludwigia mulerttii	False Loose-strife
Anacharis canadensis	Elodea
Myriophyllum proserpinacoides	Chile Parrotfeather
Cabomba caroliniana	Carolina Fanwort

LOTUS

Nelumbo nucifera—pink	East Indian Lotus
N. lutea—yellow	American Lotus

N. nucifera 'Roseum Plenum'—deep pink

N nucifera 'Album Striatum'—white—red edged

PATRICK A. NUTT

WATER-LILY. See NYMPHAEA, VICTORIA, NUPHAR and WATER GARDENING.

WATER-LILY FAMILY = Nymphaeaceae

WATERMELON, *Citrullus lanatus*, and a member of the Gourd Family which includes most of our important vine crops. It is probably native to Africa although it was grown by the Indians in America as early as 1629. (Some botanists now call this *C. lanatus*.)

The Watermelon is frost-tender, requires a long growing season and, therefore, is more important in the southern region than in the northern states. When grown in northern sections, early-maturing varieties must be used and/or the plants started in hotbeds or, if seeded in the garden, the young plants are covered with various types of plant protectors.

This is a questionable crop for the average home garden because of the space required for the relatively few fruits produced per hill or plant.

Varieties

In regions with a short growing season the smaller, early-maturing varieties such as **'New Hampshire Midget'**, **'Sugar Baby'**, **'Fordhook Hybrid'**. The larger, later-maturing sorts include **'Dixie Queen'**, **'Sweet Meat'**, **'Sweet Favorite'**, **'Klondike'** and **'Seedless Hybrid'**, without seeds.

The Citron or Preserving Melon, *C. vulgaris* var. *citroides*, is not edible, but the rind is used for the making of conserves and sweet pickle.

The culture of Watermelon is similar to that of muskmelons. See MELONS. Plant seed after all danger of frost is past and the soil is thoroughly warm. Place 6–8 seeds in groups with 2–3 in. between seeds and the groups 6–8 ft. apart each way. Cover the seeds with 1 in. soil and when plants are well established thin each group to 2 or 3 plants.

The fruits should remain on the vine until fully mature. It is difficult to determine when a watermelon is fully mature and, therefore, many methods are used to indicate peak maturity and quality. The immature green fruit gives off a metallic ring when thumped and a more muffled, a deader sound, when mature.

Insects and diseases are the same as for melons and cucumbers. See MELONS.

GRANT B. SNYDER

WATER-PARSNIP, HEMLOCK = *Sium suave*

WATER-PLANTAIN = *Alisma plantago-aquatica*

WATER-PLATTER. See VICTORIA.

WATER-POPPY = *Hydrocleys nymphoides*

WATER-PRIMROSE. See LUDWIGIA.

WATER-SHIELD, SCHREBER = *Brasenia schreberi*

WATER-SNOWFLAKE = *Nymphoides indica*

WATERWEED, CANADA = *Anacharis canadensis*

WATER-WILLOW = *Decodon verticillatus*

WATSONIA (wat-SO-nia). Bulbous plants of the Iris Family from South Africa with sword-shaped leaves; cultivated as Gladiolus; often grown in Calif.

coccinea 1′ **Zone 8 Scarlet Bugle-lily**
With scarlet flowers in the summer, the tube is 2 in. long.

iridifolia 4′ **Zone 8 Irisleaf Bugle-lily**
With pink flowers, 3 in. long. blooming in the summer. The var. o'brienii has white flowers.

meriana 4′ **Zone 8 Meriana Bugle-lily**
With bright rose flowers, the tube curved and 2 in. long, borne in spikes with 12–20 flowers in each spike, blooming in the summer.

pyramidata 3′-6′ **Zone 8 Rosy Bugle-lily**
With rose-red flowers, the tube flaring, blooming in the summer.

WATTLE. See ACACIA.

WAX-MYRTLE, SOUTHERN = *Myrica cerifera*

WAX PLANT, COMMON = *Hoya carnosa*

WAX VINE = *Senecio macroglossus* 'Variegatus'

WAYFARING TREE = *Viburnum lantana*

WEDELIA TRILOBATA Ground cover / Zone 10

A popular, creeping, easily rooting ground cover native to Florida and tropical America. Used especially in Hawaii. Flowers bright yellow to yellow-orange.

WEED-CONTROLLING CHEMICALS in the Garden. Herbicides to control unwanted plants are one of the latest developments available to gardeners. Before World War II, only a few chemicals such as table salt, dinitro, oils and sodium chlorate were available. Since that time, a large number of products have been offered for sale, and an even larger number have been tested by industrial and university laboratories. These chemicals have helped to reduce the estimated 4-billion-dollar loss caused by weeds each year.

Herbicides are widely used in commercial agriculture where large acreages are planted to a single crop but are little used in home gardens. There are several reasons for this situation. First, most gardens contain a wide variety of plant materials which have different tolerances to herbicides. Second, few herbicides come in small packages. Third, directions for use in small areas have not been available. These directions are provided in Table V. The one exception to the lack of use of herbicides in the home garden has been in the lawn area. A lawn represents a comparatively large area of one type of plant, and thus resembles commercial agriculture. Small packages of lawn herbicides and directions for their use are widely available.

Herbicides are classified into several groups: soil sterilants, pre-emergence herbicides, post-emergence herbicides and soil fumigants. Soil sterilants are used around railroad right-of-ways, industrial sites and other locations where vegetation can be unsightly or constitute a fire hazard. These chemicals are sometimes applied before a blacktop driveway is laid around a home to prevent the growth of some of the perennial weeds. Some of the chemicals used as soil sterilants at rates of 10 lbs. or more per acre are widely used selective herbicides at 4 lbs. or less per acre. These include Atrazine, Karmex and Simazine, and others.

Pre-emergence herbicides must be applied before the weed seeds germinate, preventing the growth of the weeds. In addition to the area being weed free, there must be soil moisture for this type of herbicide to be effective. Some of these herbicides must be incorporated into the soil surface to be effective.

Post-emergence herbicides are applied after the weeds have appeared. This type of herbicide usually must be applied as a directed spray so that the crop foliage is not contacted. The action of oil, dinitro and other contact herbicides causes a rapid discoloring or killing of the foliage. Hormone-type sprays kill the weeds in a slower but effective manner by disrupting the metabolism of the plants after its absorption by the leaves and stems.

If open ground is to be developed into a garden, the use of a soil fumigant such as Methyl Bromide, Vapam or VPM, or Vorlex should be considered. This is the one time when all major soil pests can be eliminated with a single treatment. There are several restrictions on the use of these chemicals, such as cost of the chemical of approximately 1 dollar per 100 sq. ft., danger to the applicator, danger to roots of plants which may be growing into the treated area, or difficulty of application, since these materials work best injected into the soil or under a plastic cover. Soil fumigants are only effective if the soil temperature is about 55° F. and with no undecomposed organic matter in the soil. The soil should be worked into a seed bed condition and be moist, but not saturated, at the time of application for the treatment to be effective. A time interval of between 7 and 21 days must elapse between application and planting so that the chemical may dissipate. This time period depends on the chemical used and the weather conditions following treatment. A longer time is needed when cool, wet conditions prevail than when it is hot and dry.

A soil fumigant that is easier to apply is Basamid-Granular. When tilled into the soil at 9–13 oz. per 100 sq. feet or 3–5 oz. per cubic yard, it controls germinating weed seeds, soil diseases and nematodes. The amount of time before this soil can be used for planting varies with the 4 inch soil temperature. Above 65° F. (18° C) it takes 10–12 days while it takes more than 30 days at 43–47° F. (6–8° C).

Fumigation may slow down nitrification (the conversion to nitrates from ammonia by bacterial action). Some ammonia-sensitive plants may show injury if calcium or sodium nitrate is not added to the soil. Fall fumigation for spring planting will avoid this problem.

In all cases when using an herbicide, the manufacturer's directions should be followed. State experiment station and extension service recommendations can be of value to select those treatments which have been most effective in your area. Soil type, weeds present, amount of soil moisture, season of the year and possibly other conditions all make a difference in the effectiveness of an herbicide. Many weed species are resistant to certain herbicides. Because of this, an alternation or a combination of herbicides has been used in many cases.

Weed Control in the Lawn

Lawn areas have been the target for most home chemical weed-control projects to date. Control of broadleaved weeds, such as Dandelion and Plantain, has been relatively easy with 2,4-D herbicides. Crabgrass has been controlled by disodium methyl arsonate, Dacthal and other compounds.

We could conclude that weeds in lawns are no longer a problem because there are chemical means to control them. However, chemical control is only one of many factors in the proper maintenance of a good lawn. Adequate fertilizer and water as well as proper mowing height and frequency for the particular grass species are perhaps more important in the maintenance of a weed-free lawn.

Aluminum strip to prevent grass from encroaching on walk.

As many common weeds such as Dandelion and Plantain have been satisfactorily controlled, other weeds have been noted as being problems. These problem weeds include Annual Blue Grass, clovers and Veronica. There are controls for these weeds available but these control measures may cause other problems. Dacthal will prevent the growth of Annual Blue Grass but it may damage existing stands of Bentgrass. It is possible to sow desirable turf grasses within a year of a Dacthal application, if necessary.

Betasan has a longer residual life than Dacthal and is less affected by soil type and soil cover. It does not seem to damage established stands of desirable turf grasses, but should be used only where the desirable turf makes up the majority of the stand. This caution is necessary since it is not possible to establish new grass seedlings for an extended period.

Dicamba or Banvel D has been very effective on many of the harder-to-kill species of broadleaved weeds, including the clovers. Considerable caution must be used with this chemical since it can damage ornamental plants both by spray drift and soil absorption. This damage (distorted leaves) has not caused plant losses where Dicamba was used at rates higher than suggested for clover control. The plants will outgrow the symptoms if the spray was not applied directly to them. Sometimes it may be necessary to tolerate some damage to eliminate some difficult weed.

Veronica is the major remaining broadleaved pest for which there is no really successful control. Endothal is effective but is so dangerous to turf grasses that it should be avoided unless expert care is available.

Table I gives the suggested treatments for various problem lawn weeds.

Weed Control in Ornamental Plantings

Several herbicides with long residual properties have been found useful in nurseries and plantings containing woody ornamental plants, since these plantings are not changed frequently. With many of these chemicals, 1 application in the fall will prevent weed development until the following May. During this period it is often difficult to kill weeds by mechanical means since conditions are too cool and moist for the weeds to dry out after they are disturbed by cultivation.

Mulching with various organic materials such as sawdust, barkdust, leaves, ground cobs, cocoa bean shells and other products is an effective way to control many annual weeds in the home garden. Generally, mulches do not stop most perennial weeds and they tend to tie up or deactivate many herbicides. Casoron seems to be one of the herbicides least affected by mulches. If a mulching program has been followed, it may be necessary to rely on herbicides which kill by foliage absorption. Roundup, when used as a directed spray with repeated application, will control many problem weeds such as Quackgrass, Horsetail Rush and Canada Thistle.

The herbicides and amounts to use in ornamental plantings are given in Table II.

Weed Control in Fruit Plantings

Weed control in fruit plantings is complicated by the problem of achieving satisfactory control without having a residue of the herbicide in the fruit. This is possible to do if the manufacturer's directions as to the amounts to use, method of application and time of applications are followed carefully. Many of the same herbicides used on ornamental plantings are also used on fruit plants.

Oils (rarely used in ornamentals) are used to kill existing weeds around fruit trees, with care being used not to contact the trunk of the tree. Repeated applications need to be made since there is no residual control with the types of oils which can be safely used.

With the exception of the oils, most herbicide applications are made after harvest in the fall or before bloom in the spring.

The herbicides and the amounts to use in different fruit crops are shown in Table III.

Weed Control in Vegetable Crops

This is the most difficult area in the home garden in which to use herbicides. Many of the plants remain in the soil only a short time, so that long residual herbicides cannot be used. A very wide variety of plants are grown which have different susceptibilities and tolerances to herbicides, so that there are as many different herbicides used as there are varieties grown. Finally, and perhaps most important, one should avoid leaving a residue of the herbicide in the edible portion of the plant.

Herbicides and instructions for their use in vegetable crops are given in Table IV.

Amounts to Use in the Garden
(Editor's Note)

As the author of this article states, the herbicide trade apparently is listing the application amounts of herbicides in pounds or gallons of active ingredients per acre. The gardener should take special note of this for if he uses tables and recommendations made up this way, serious and damaging mistakes can be made if he figures amounts of application on any other basis. For instance, in Table III it is noted that the herbicide Simazine is recommended for controlling weeds in blackberries, used at the rate of 4 lbs. active ingredient per acre. In Table V Simazine is noted as an 80% wettable powder. Hence the amount of the actual product to apply per acre is figured thus: 4.0 lbs. divided by 0.8 (80%) = 5 lbs. of the actual product to be used. This, of course, would be dissolved in a sufficient quantity of water so that it could be spread evenly over the entire area concerned. To find the amount for 100 sq. ft., one observes in Table V that if 1 lb. active ingredient of Simazine is applied to 1 acre, the amount for 100 sq. ft. is 1.25 grams, or $\frac{3}{4}$ of a teaspoonful. Since the recommendation for blackberries is for 5 lbs. per acre, the amount for 100 sq. ft. of blackberries would be 1.25 grams × 5 = 6.25 grams, dissolved, of course, in a sufficient amount of water to cover evenly the area involved.

One proceeds similarly with the emulsifiable concentrates. Note that 3–6 lbs. of Eptam is recommended for use in controlling weeds in beans (Table IV). In Table V one sees that Eptam is listed as an emulsifiable concentrate. It is listed 6EC which simply means that 6 lbs. of active ingredient of the herbicide are in 1 gal. of the concentrate. Hence when 3–6 lbs. of the Eptam (active ingredient) are recommended for an acre of beans, it means 2 qts. to 1 gal. of 6 EC Eptam concentrate, mixed, of course, in sufficient water to cover the area evenly. For 100 sq. ft. of beans it would be (from Table V) 1.5 ml. of the concentrate, mixed in sufficient water to cover the area evenly.

This does seem complicated to the gardener. However, it is just as well that these amounts be treated with mathematical exactitude for even the smallest mistake in application could result in a serious loss of plants.

Many gardeners will not want to bother with these herbicides simply because their use on small plots requires such careful planning and application. The products and their contents, and hence their application rates, may very well be changed from year to year, so that these recommendations suggested here should not be taken as final. The home gardener should obtain the latest information on herbicides from his local state experiment station, and should read and follow in every case the directions for application which are printed on the package.

TABLE I. TURFGRASS CHEMICAL WEED CONTROL SUGGESTIONS
Application Code: A—Before seed germination
B—After seed germination
C—During active growth
D—Fall or Spring
E—Any time

WEED	CHEMICAL	AMT. OF ACTIVE INGREDIENT/A*	APPLICA- TION TIME	CAUTION
Common broadleaved weeds (dandelions, plantains, and mustards)	2,4D Amine	1 lb. or follow label instruction	D	Grass at least 60 days old. Avoid spray drift
Clovers	2,4D Amine		D	Same as 2,4-D Amine. Repeat monthly applications as needed.
	Banvel D	$\frac{1}{4}$–$\frac{1}{2}$ lb.	D	Dangerous to shrub and tree roots.
	MCPP	1–1$\frac{1}{2}$ lbs.	D	
Chickweeds	Banvel D	$\frac{1}{2}$ lb.	C,D	Dangerous to shrub and tree roots
	MCPP	1–1$\frac{1}{2}$ lbs.	C,D	
Speedwell (Veronica sp.)	Endothal	1 lb.	C,D	Bentgrass and fescue may be damaged
English Lawn Daisy	Banvel D	$\frac{1}{2}$–1 lb.	C	Dangerous to shrub and tree roots
Yarrow	Trimel or 2,4D	1 lb.	E	
	Banvel D	$\frac{1}{2}$ lb.	C	Dangerous to shrub and tree roots
Moss and Pearlwort	Ferrous Ammonium Sulfate	400 lbs.	C	Apply to moist foliage. Temporary grass discoloration. Rust stains sidewalks and driveways
Sheep Sorrel	Banvel D	$\frac{1}{4}$ lb.	C	Dangerous to shrub and tree roots
Knotweed	2,4-D	1 lb.	B	Sensitivity to 2-4D decreases rapidly with plant size increase
	Banvel D	$\frac{1}{4}$–$\frac{1}{2}$ lb.	C	Dangerous to shrub and tree roots
Annual Bluegrass	Betasan	15 lbs.	A,D	Just prior to rapid seed germination. Emerging Turfgrass seedlings damaged for 2–3 months
Crabgrass	Metallic Arsenates, Calcium Arsenate, or others	Follow directions on container	A	Residual pre-emergent control

* A = Amount of active ingredient given per acre.

WEED	CHEMICAL	AMT. OF ACTIVE INGREDIENT/A*	APPLICA- TION TIME	CAUTION
	Ronstar	2 lbs.	A	
	Balan	1.5–3 lbs.	A	Do not use on Bentgrass.
	Disodium methyl Arsonate	Follow directions on container	B,C	Two or more applications at weekly intervals needed. Do not use when soil is dry. Tip burn on Bluegrass. Bentgrass may be damaged.
	Dachtal	10 lbs.	A	
	Tuperstan	12 lbs.	A	

TABLE II. ORNAMENTAL PLANT CHEMICAL WEED CONTROL SUGGESTIONS
Application Code: A—Before planting
B—Before crop emerges
C—After transplanting
D—Applied to established plants

CROP	CHEMICAL	AMT. OF ACTIVE INGREDIENT/A*	APPLICA- TION TIME	CAUTION
All Crops (soil fumigation)	Methyl Bromide	400 lbs. (1 lb./ 100 sq. ft.)	A	Poisonous gas used under plastic cover. Soil temperature above 50° F. 1 week before planting
	Vapam	400 gal. (1 qt./ 100 sq. ft.)	A	Must be incorporated or watered into soil immediately. Soil temperature above 50° F. 2–4 weeks before planting
	Basamid-Granular	250–350 lbs. (5–8 lbs./100 sq. ft.)	A	Mix into upper soil layer 6–8 weeks before planting. Keep soil moist
Bulbs	Furloe 20+G	2 lbs.	B	Fall application
	Diphenamid	4–6 lbs.	B	Weed-free soil
	Simazine	1 lb.	D	Weed-free soil, needs soil surface moisture
Christmas Trees	Atrazine	2–4 lbs.	D	Directed spray. Oct. through March
	Kerb	1–3 lbs.	D	For perennial grass control apply Oct. to March
	Simazine	2–4 lbs.	C,D	Weed-free soil. Soil must be settled around transplants
General Ornamentals	Roundup	2–3 lbs.	A,D	Kills perennial grasses by absorption. Do not contact desirable plants
	Atrazine	1 lb.	D	Weed-free soil. Directed spray

* A = Amount of active ingredient given per acre.

CROP	CHEMICAL	AMT. OF ACTIVE INGREDIENT/A*	APPLICA-TION TIME	CAUTION
	Atrazine	4 lbs.	D	Grass control in pine and fir
	Casoron	3–5 lbs.	D	Weed-free soil. Incorporate for best results
	Casoron	4–8 lbs.	D	For perennial grass control use the granular formulation
	CIPC	4–8 lbs.	D	Weed-free soil. Best in cool weather
	Diphenamid	4–6 lbs.	C,D	Weed-free soil. May be cultivated
	Devrinol	4–6 lbs.	C,D	Weed-free soil, needs soil surface moisture
	Dacthal	9–12 lbs.	C,D	Weed-free soil
	Ronstar	2–4 lbs.	C,D	Weed-free soil, needs soil surface moisture
	Simazine	1–3 lbs.	D	Weed-free soil, needs soil surface moisture
	Treflan	½–1 lb.	A,C,D	Incorporate after application
	Kerb	1–3 lbs.	D	For perennial grass control apply Oct.–March

TABLE III. FRUIT CROP CHEMICAL WEED CONTROL SUGGESTIONS

Key:
A — Before planting
B — Immediately after planting
C — Spring when crop growing
D — Within 2 weeks after harvest
E — Oct. or Nov.; repeat April
F — Late fall or early spring crop dormant
G — Fall, crop dormant, weeds active
H — Winter (Jan. to March)
I — After cultivation in spring

CROP	CHEMICAL	AMT. OF ACTIVE INGREDIENT/A*	APPLICA-TION TIME	CAUTION
Apricot	Dalaphon	8.5 lbs.	C	Grass control—not more than 2 applications per year
	Simazine	0.8–1.6 lbs.	F	Non-bearing trees—do not use on light soil
	Devrinol	4 lbs.	G	
Apple	Diuron	3.2 lbs.	F	Treat only small area around tree. Do not use under dwarf trees
	Simazine	2–4 lbs.	F	Treat only small area around tree. Do not use under dwarf trees
	Surflan	2–6 lbs.	F	
	2,4-D Amine or Acid	1 lb.	C	Do not contact leaves, fruit or stem of tree. Broadleaved weeds
	Dalapon	8.5 lbs.	C	Grass control—not more than 2 applications per year
	Casoron	4–6 lbs.	F	
Blackberries	Simazine	1.6 lbs.	C	Does not control established weeds; can be used in new plantings
	Diuron	1.6–2.4 lbs.	H	After vines trained. Planting must be at least 6 months old

*A = Amount of active ingredient given per acre.

CROP	CHEMICAL	AMT. OF ACTIVE INGREDIENT/A*	APPLICA- TION TIME	CAUTION
	Casoron	4 lbs.	H	Use on established plantings only
	Simazine	4.0 lbs.	H	Reduce rate to 1.6 lbs. after good weed control established
	Devrinol	4.0 lbs.	F	Weed-free soil, needs soil surface moisture
Blueberries	Simazine	1.6 lbs.	C	Does not control established weeds; can be used in new plantings
	Casoron	6 lbs.	H	For perennial weeds in plantings over one year old
	Diuron	1.6 lbs.	E	Avoid spraying foliage. Do not use within 6 months of planting
	Simazine	4.0 lbs.	H	Do not use within 6 months of planting
	Simazine	2.0 lbs.	E	Suggest alternating between Diuron and Simazine
	CIPC	12.0 lbs.	F	Will control some perennial weeds
	Casoron	3–6 lbs.	F	For perennial weeds in plantings over one year old
	CIPC	6–8 lbs.	F	Avoid getting spray on plantings
Citrus	Simazine	2–4 lbs.	E	Use on trees established one or more years
Cranberries	CIPC	12.0 lbs	F	Wash spray off vines. Bog should be 3 years old
	Casoron	4.0 lbs.	F	Do not apply after blooming begins
	Simazine	4.0 lbs.	G	Post harvest on established bogs
	Dalapon	10 lbs.	G	After harvest for grass control
Gooseberries	Diuron	2.4 lbs.	H	Avoid getting spray on plants
	Diuron	1.6 lbs.	E	Avoid getting spray on plants
	Surplan	2–6 lbs.	F	
Grapes (at least 3 years old)	Diuron	3.2 lbs	I	Soil surface moisture necessary
	Devrinol	4 lbs.	F	Rainfall or irrigation necessary
	Simazine	2.4 lbs.	F	Soil surface moisture necessary
	Surplan	2–6 lbs.	E	Soil surface moisture necessary
Non-Bearing Orchard Crops	Simazine	0.8–1.6 lbs.	F	Do not use on light soils; do not use on basin-irrigated trees

*A = Amount of active ingredient given per acre.

CROP	CHEMICAL	AMT. OF ACTIVE INGREDIENT/A*	APPLICA-TION TIME	CAUTION
Peach	Casoron	4–6 lbs.	F	Incorporate immediately
	Devrinol	4 lbs.	F	Rainfall or irrigation necessary for activation
	Dalapon	8.5 lbs.	C	Do not use more than 2 times in one season
	Simazine	2–4 lbs.	F	Use only on established trees
Pear	Diuron	3.2 lbs.	F	Spray only area necessary to remove rodent cover. Do not use on dwarf trees
	Simazine	2–4 lbs.	F	Use only on established trees
	2,4-D Acid or Amine	1.0 lb.	C	Do not contact leaves, fruit or stems of trees. For broad-leaf weed control
	Dalapon	8.5 lbs.	C	Grass control—not more than 2 applications a year
Plum and Prunes	Dalapon	8.5 lbs.	C	Grass control—not more than 2 applications a year
	Simazine	3.2 lbs.	F	Use on trees established one year or more
Raspberries (new plantings)	Simazine	1.6 lbs.	C	Soil surface moisture necessary
Raspberries (old plantings)	Diuron	2.4 lbs.	H	Later sprays cause crop damage
	Diuron	1.6 lbs.	E	Avoid contacting plants
	Simazine	4 lbs.	H	Planting at least 6 months old
	Simazine	2 lbs.	E	Soil surface moisture necessary
Raspberries	Surplan	2–4 lbs.	F	Before weed emergence
Strawberries (new plantings)	Dacthal	9 lbs.	B	Do not apply after bloom
	Diphenamid	4 lbs.	B	Soil surface moisture necessary any time except 60 days before harvest. Requires irrigation
Strawberries (established plantings)	Teneoran Amine	1 lb.	D	Date of application critical because of possible injury to fruit buds
	Simazine	1.0 lbs.	D & G	Soil should be weed free at time of application
Walnuts	Simazine	2–4 lbs.	F	Trees established one year or more
	Casoron	4–6 lbs.	F	Incorporate in warm climates
	Teneoran	4 lbs.	F	Not closer to harvest than 60 days
	Diphenamid	4–6 lbs.	F	Not closer to harvest than 60 days

*A = Amount of active ingredient given per acre.

TABLE IV. VEGETABLE CROP CHEMICAL WEED CONTROL SUGGESTIONS

Application Code: A — Before planting
                       B — Immediately after planting seed
                       C — Before crop emerges
                       D — At emergence of crop
                       E — After crop emerges
                       F — After transplanting
                       G — During dormant season

CROP	CHEMICAL	AMT. OF ACTIVE INGREDIENT/A*	APPLICATION TIME	CAUTION
artichokes	Simazine	4 lbs.	G	Weed-free soil
Asparagus (seed bed)	Amiben	3 lbs.	C	
	Stoddard Solvent Oil	50 gal.	E	Use on cool, cloudy day
Asparagus	Monuron or Simazine	1.6 lbs. light soil; 3.2 lbs. heavy soil	G	Do not cultivate
	Devrinol	3 lbs.	C–G	Weed-free soil
	Monuron or Simazine	1.5 lbs.	C	Only one application per season
Beans	Roundup	1–5 lbs.	A–C	Lower rates for annuals
	Treflan	½–1 lb.	A	Incorporate within 8 hours
	Eptam	3–6 lbs.	A	For grass control. Do not use on lima beans
	Dacthal	9 lbs.	B	Annual grasses
Beans, Lima only	Amiben	3 lbs.	B–C	Do not feed plant parts to livestock
Beets	Table salt	200 lbs.	E	After beets have 2–3 leaves. Best on hot, humid day
	Stoddard Solvent Oil	60–80 gal.	C	Best on cool, cloudy day. Use 1–2 days before beets emerge
	Pyramin RB	3–4 lbs.	C–E	Best on moist soil
	Eptam	2 lbs.	A	Annual grass control
Broccoli, Brussels Sprouts, Cabbage, and Cauliflower	Betasan	4 lbs. / 5–6 lbs.	B / A,B	Incorporate physically or by irrigation
	Dacthal	9 lbs.	F	Immediately after transplanting
Cantaloupes, Cucumbers, and Watermelons	Alanap	4 lbs.	B	Follow application with irrigation
Carrots, Celery (seed bed), Dill, Parsley, and Parsnips	Stoddard Solvent Oil	60–80 gal.	E	Spray parsley when weeds appear. Spray others after 3-leaf stage but weeds small. Best on cool, cloudy day. Do not spray wet plants
Corn	Atrazine	1 lb.	A,B,C,D,E	Follow with light irrigation. Only one application
	2,4-D Amine	0.5–0.75 lb.	E	Spray only once
	Eptam	2–3 lbs.	A	Plant corn shallow
Leaf crops: spinach, kale	Furloe	1–2 lbs.		Cool weather mostly below 60° F. Irrigate after application
	Bladex	1.2–4 lbs.	C–E	Do not use on sandy soil

*A = Amount of active ingredient given per acre.

CROP	CHEMICAL	AMT. OF ACTIVE INGREDIENT/A*	APPLICA- TION TIME	CAUTION
Leaf crops collards, Hanover salad	CIPC	1 lb.	B	Mostly below 60° F. Irri- gate after application
Turnip Greens, Mustard	Dacthal	9 lbs.	B–F	Irrigate after application
Beet Greens	Treflan	$\frac{1}{2}$–$\frac{3}{4}$ lb.	A	Incorporate
Lettuce	Betasan	5–6 lbs.	A,B	Primarily grass control
	Kerb	1–2 lbs.	A–B	Incorporate after appli- cation
	IPC	6 lbs.	A,B,C,E	Lettuce should have 4 leaves for E
Onions	CIPC	8 lbs.	C,D,E	Warm weather, mostly above 60° F.
	CIPC	6 lbs.	C,D,E	Cool weather, mostly below 60° F.
	Dacthal	9 lbs.	B	Irrigate after spraying
Peas	Dinitro Amine	3–6 lbs.	B	Spray only once
Peppers	Diphenamid	3–5 lbs.	B,F	Low rate on light soils. Do not plant other food crops for 6 months
	Devrinol	1–2 lbs.	A	Incorporate 1–2 inches deep
Potatoes	Eptam	3–6 lbs.	A	Incorporate
Squash, Summer	Alanap	4 lbs.	B	Follow with irrigation
Squash and pumpkins	Amiben	3 lbs.	B	
Sweet Potatoes	Vegiben	2–3 lbs.	F	Do not use treated plants for feed
	Diphenamid	6 lbs.	F	Do not plant other food crops for 6 months
	Eptam	2–3 lbs.	A	Incorporate
Tomatoes	Diphenamid	4–6 lbs.	B or F	Lower rate on light soils. Do not plant other food crops for 6 months
	Dacthal	9 lbs.	F	3–5 days or 4 weeks after transplanting. Irrigate after application
	Treflan	$\frac{1}{2}$–1 lb.	A	Incorporate

*A = Amount of active ingredient given per acre.

TABLE V. AMOUNTS OF HERBICIDES TO USE FOR AN AREA OF 100 SQUARE FEET

EC = Emulsifiable concentrate
G = Granular
W = Wettable powder
ml. = 1/1000th of a liter, which equals 1.0567 liquid quarts

g = About 1/28th of an ounce
c = cups
T = tablespoons
t = teaspoons

CHEMICAL AND FORMULATION		POUNDS OR GALLONS PER ACRE ACTIVE INGREDIENT	GRAMS OR ML. OF PRODUCT PER 100 SQ. FT.	TABLE AND TEASPOONS OF PRODUCT PER 100 SQ. FT.
Alanap	2EC	4	17.4 ml	$3\frac{1}{2}$ t
Atrazine	80W	1	1.25 g.	$\frac{3}{8}$ t

* See manufacturer's directions.

CHEMICAL AND FORMULATION	POUNDS OR GALLONS PER ACRE ACTIVE INGREDIENT		GRAMS OR ML. OF PRODUCT PER 100 SQ. FT.	TABLE AND TEASPOONS OF PRODUCT PER 100 SQ. FT.
Balan	2.5G	1	41.5 g.	3 T + 1½ t
Banvel D	4EC	½	4.7 ml.	1 t
Basamid-Granular		354	338.6 g. or 13 oz.	
Betasan	4EC	15	140.8 ml.	½ c + 1 T + 1 t
Casoron	50W	1	2.1 g.	1 t
Casoron	4G	1	25 g.	1 T + ¾ t
CIPC	4EC	1	2.2 ml.	½ t
Dacthal	75W	3	4.0 g.	1½ t
Dalapon	85W	8.5	10.0 g.	1 T + 1½ t
Devrinol	50W	1	2.1 g.	1½ t
Dinitro amine	5EC	1.5	3.3 ml.	¾ t
Enide	50W	1	2.0 g.	1¼ t
Enide	90W	1	1.25 g.	¾ t
Diuron	80W	1.6	2.0 g.	¾ t
Endothal	2EC	1	4.3 ml.	1 t
Eptam	6EC	1	1.5 ml.	¼ t
Ferrous ammonium sulphate		400	400 g. or 14 oz.	
IPC	2EC	6	26 ml.	1 T + 2 t + ¼ t
Kerb	50W	1	2.1 g.	1¼ t
MCPP*		1		
Methyl bromide		400	1 lb. can	1 lb. can
Ornamental Herbicide II		100	104.1 g.	½ c + 2 t
Pyramin RW	75.5W	1	2.1 g.	1 t
Ronstar	26	1	52.1 g.	5 T + 1½ t
Ronstar	50W	1	2.1 g.	1¼ t
Roundup	4EC	1	2.2 ml.	½ t
Rout	16	100	104.1 g.	½ c + 2 T + ½ t
Simazine	80W	1	1.25 g.	¾ t
Solan*				
Stoddard Solvent		10 gal.	86.9 ml.	¼ c + 3¼ t
Surflan	75W	1	1.4 g.	1 t
Table salt				
Tenoran	50W	1	2.1 g.	1¾ t
Treflan	4 EC	1	2.2 ml.	½ t
2,4-D Amine*		1		
Vapam		100 gal.	1 qt.	1 qt.
Vegiben	2EC	1	4.3 ml.	¾ t

* See manufacturer's directions.

ROBERT L. TICKNOR

WEEDS. A weed is often considered to be any plant growing where it is not wanted. Some plants, because of their tenacity or deep roots or running rootstalks or the way their profuse seeds are distributed, are vigorous intruders on garden space and seem difficult to keep out of the lawn or garden permanently. Most grasses would be in this category, but a few like Quack Grass, Johnson Grass and Crab Grass are worse than others.

As for reproducing themselves, all weeds do this profusely and usually their seeds remain viable for several years regardless of the winter cold. The extremely minute seeds of Purslane, for instance, are smaller than the size of a pin head, yet when they are plowed under they can remain viable in the soil for many years and germinate only when they are brought to the surface again by plowing. Then air, warmth and moisture are just right for germinating.

It has been noted that 1 well-grown plant of Purslane (*Portulaca oleracea*) can produce 193,213 seeds in 1 season; Tumbleweed (*Amaranthus alba*) can produce 180,220 and 1 plant of Wild Lettuce (*Lactuca scariola*) can produce 32,700 seeds in 1 year. As for retaining their viability, 88% of Purslane seed stored dry for 5 years will germinate, 28% stored in soil will germinate after 5 years. Ninety-four per cent of the seed of Great Burdock (*Arctium lappa*) stored dry for 5 years will germinate and if stored in soil 5 years, 54% will germinate. Broadleaved Dock—93% of the seed will germinate after being stored dry 5 years and 38% will germinate after being stored in soil 5 years. In fact, some weeds retain their viability 10, 20 or even 40 years after having been buried in soil.

In addtion to bearing profuse seeds of lengthy viability, there are those weeds with very deep tap roots. These may be pulled or broken off and the roots left in the soil are sufficient to form new plants.

Then there are those with vigorous, fast-growing, underground rootstocks, which frequently are able to send up new shoots at many places throughout their length. Hoe these up, or break them off and roots remaining in the soil are sufficient to grow new plants. Worse still, harrow them, and one merely cuts them up and distributes potential plants about a field. Canada Thistle is one of the very worst offenders in this category and a vicious spreader like this must be completely dug out or killed with chemicals. In the garden, the Japanese Fleeceflower (*Polygonum cuspidatum*) or its dwarf variety being sold in the trade as *P.*

reynoutria, are similar vicious spreaders that are impossible to permanently eradicate without the greatest effort in digging them out.

Also, there are weeds which send out numerous runners over the surface of the soil and these root throughout their length, forming many new plants. So it is seen that weeds are persistent growers, increase rapidly by one or several means, and are able to withstand much winter cold.

In this book some 250 common weeds are mentioned and of course there are many more. Other than grasses, and almost all grasses are weeds in some areas, some of the most persistent of the weeds are in the following list. Those marked as annuals, should be kept from seeding —the easiest way to control them. Those not listed as annuals all live over winter in Zone 3, hence can be weeds in almost any part of the U.S. and southern Canada, as far as winter cold is concerned. Two exceptions are *Lonicera japonica* 'Halliana' and *Phylotacca americana*, which might be listed in Zones 4–5.

The weeds marked "T" in the following list have a deep-seated tap root and are often difficult to eliminate except by careful and deep digging or with chemicals. Those marked "R" have vigorous-growing, underground stems or rootstocks capable of sending up new plants at many places, or they may have fast-growing runners or procumbent stems on the soil surface, both capable of rooting and sending up new plants.

THE MOST PERSISTENT WEEDS

Barren-strawberry	R		3′	Potentilla simplex
Beggar's-tick, Devil's		Annual	3′	Bidens frondosa
Bindweed, Black		Annual	Vine	Polygonum convolvulus
Bindweed	T		Vine	Convolvulus arvensis
Bindweed, Hedge	T		Vine	C. sepium
Black-eyed Susan			3′	Rudbeckia hirta
Buckhorn			8″	Plantago lanceolata
Burdock, Great	T	Biennial	9′	Arctium lappa
Buttercup, Creeping	R		2″	Ranunculus repens
Buttercup, Tall			3′	R. acris
Carrot, Wild	T		3′	Daucus carota
Cat's-ear	T		1′	Hypochoeris radicata
Chickory	T		6′	Cichorium intybus
Chickweed		Annual	12″	Stellaria media
Chickweed, Mouse-ear	R		6″	Cerastium vulgatum
Cinquefoil, Oldfield	R		4″	Potentilla canadensis
Cinquefoil, Sulfur	R		2½′	P. recta
Clover, White Sweet			10′	Melilotus alba
Cocklebur		Annual	3′	Xanthium sp.
Cranesbill, Small Flowered	R	Annual	Prostrate	Geranium pusillum
Daisy, Oxeye	R		2′	Chrysanthemum leucanthemum pinnatifidum
Dandelion	T		10″	Taraxacum officinale
Devil's Paint-brush	R		20″	Hieracium aurantiacum
Dewberry	R		Trailing	Rubus flagellaris

Dock, Broad-leaved	T	4′	Rumex obtusifolius
Dock, Curly	T	3′	R. crispus
Field Chickweed		8″	Cerastium arvense
Fleeceflower, Japanese	R	8′	Polygonum cuspidatum
Garlic, Field		10″	Allium vineale
Grass, Crab	Annual	2′	Digitaria sp.
Grass, Quack	R	3′	Agropyron repens
Ground-ivy	R	3″	Glechoma hederacea
Hawkweed, Orange	R	20″	Hieracium aurantiacum
Hawkweed, Mouse-ear	R	1′	H. pilosella
Honeysuckle, Hall's—Zone 4	R	Vine	Lonicera japonica 'Halliana'
Horse Nettle, Carolina	T	2′	Solanum carolinense
Knawel	Annual	4″	Scleranthus annuus
Knotweed, Prostrate	Annual	Prostrate	Polygonum aviculare
Lady's Thumb, Spotted	Annual	2′	P. persicaria
Lamb's Quarters	Annual	10′	Chenopodium album
Lettuce, Prickly	Annual	5′	Lactuca scariola
Mallow, Round-leaved	Annual	Procumbent	Malva rotundifolia
Mayweed	Annual	2′	Anthemis cotula
Milkweed, Common	R	5′	Asclepias syriaca
Mustard, Wild	Annual	3′	Brassica kaber pinnatifida
Nettle, Stinging	R	4′	Urtica dioica
Nightshade, Bitter	R	Vine	Solanum dulcamara
Oats, Wild	Annual	4′	Avena fatua
Oxalis, European Yellow		6″	Oxalis europaea
Parsnip, Wild	T	5′	Pastinaca sativa
Pepper-grass	Annual	2′	Lepidium virginicum
Pepperweed Whitetop	R	2½′	Cardaria draba
Pigweed	Annual	10′	Chenopodium album
Pigweed, Redroot	Annual	10′	Amaranthus retroflexus
Plaintain, Broad-leaved	R	6″	Plantago major
Poison Ivy	R	Vine	Rhus radicans
Pokeberry, Common—Zone 4	T	12′	Phytolacca americanum
Purslane	Annual	Prostrate	Portulaca oleracea
Purse, Shepherd's	Annual	3′	Capsella bursa-pastoris
Radish, Wild	Annual	3½′	Raphanus raphanistrum
Ragweed	Annual	3′	Ambrosia artemisiifolia
Sage, Western	R	3′	Artemisia ludoviciana
Sandbur		1′	Cenchrus pauciflora
Self-heal, Common	R	2′	Prunella vulgaris
Shepherd's Purse	Annual	3′	Capsella bursa-pastoris
Smartweed	Annual	2′	Polygonum hydropiper
Smartweed, Pennsylvania	Annual	2′	P. pensylvanicum
Sorrel, Garden		3′	Rumex acetosa
Sorrel, Sheep	R	1′	R. acetosella
Sow-thistle, Field	R	5′	Sonchus arvensis
St. John's-wort	R	2′	Hypericum perforatum
Speedwell, Drug	R	1′	Veronica officinalis
Spurge, Spotted	Annual	3′	Euphorbia maculata
Spurry, Corn	Annual	1½′	Spergula arvensis
Swallow-wort	T	Vine	Cynanchum nigrum
Tansy	R	3′	Tanacetum vulgare
Thistle, Canada	R	4′	Circium arvense
Velvet-leaf	Annual	5′	Abutilon theophrasti
Veronica, Creeping	R	2″	Veronica filiformis
Vetch, Wild	R	5′	Vicia cracca
Wheat-grass, Bluestem		3′	Agropyron smithii

A good reference with 225 drawings of the more common weeds, an excellent means of identification is: Montgomery, F. H., "Weeds of the Northern United States and Canada," Frederick Warne & Co., New York, 1964.

WEIGELA (wy-GEE-la). The weigelas constitute a group of once-popular, opposite-leaved, deciduous, flowering shrubs which are now, on the whole, outmoded. Although American nurserymen are offering 44 varieties there is still little room for these shrubs in the small garden. A study of their flowers shows that far too many are markedly similar in their general landscape characteristics. They all have opposite leaves and may be divided into about 8 different color groups. However, from the standpoint of landscape use, that is, the effectiveness of these plants in blossom at a distance, the general divisions for these flowers are yellow, white, red and pink. The last group (pink) is by far the largest for there are many varieties with pink and white flowers or flowers that open white and gradually fade, that belong here.

The species are native to Eastern Asia. The first one brought to England from China by Robert Fortune in 1845 was *W. florida*. Since that time, other species and varieties have been found in eastern Asia and, from the large number of named clones that have been grown since, it is obvious that various individuals have made new crosses over the years and named many resulting seedlings.

The earliest varieties come into bloom during mid-May with the Common Lilac; other varieties come into bloom during the following 4 weeks. The weigelas as a whole are practically pest-free but require continual pruning because of winter die-back. This, and the fact that they lack interesting fruits, as well as the similarity of the general flower color of many varieties, points to the fact that only about a dozen are really worth growing.

Weigelas are grown for their bright flowers. There is one yellow-flowered Weigela and of course several native species which actually belong to the genus *Diervilla*. The remainder have flowers that range from pure white through various shades of pink to deep red, with various combinations of pinks, red and white in the same flower or in the same cluster. It is this changeable coloring that makes so many varieties similar. As an example, *Weigela florida alba* produces flowers that are at first white, but gradually fade to pink, and this trait of the flowers changing color is reproduced in many of the varieties, so that at one stage of flowering or another, there is the time when many of them appear similar. There are a few varieties that produce flowers of clear, pure colors such as 'Stelzneri' a moderate purplish pink; 'Vanicekii' and 'Bristol Ruby' which are both dark red; and 'Candida' which, up to now, has the best pure white flowers that do not fade pink. *W. middendorffiana* is the only true Weigela with yellow flowers.

There are a few varieties with colored foliage, for which they are valued for use in certain restricted circumstances. *W. florida* 'Variegata' and its lower growing form 'Variegata Nana', both have leaves that are edged with pale yellow. These are the cleanest and about the best plants with variegated foliage that one can use. The variety 'Looymansii Aurea' is an old-fashioned type with leaves that are a soft yellow throughout the spring and summer. Others have recommended that this is best grown in the partial shade, which is an indication that in the full sun the foliage might be "burned." Hence its uses are restricted.

Another, *W. florida* 'Foliis Purpuriis' has foliage that is purplish green, quite marked. This is a compact, slow-growing plant that does not exceed 4 ft. in height at 20 years of age. Most are approximately 6–9 ft. tall at maturity. The tallest is *W. coraeensis* which eventually grows 12 ft. high, and the lowest is *W. florida* 'Variegata Nana' which is about 3 ft. tall. Other varieties of compact growth, although about 4–5 ft. tall, are *W. florida* 'Foliis Purpuriis', *W. florida* 'Variegata' and possibly W. 'Looymansii Aurea'.

The hardiest are *W. florida venusta* and *W. middendorffiana* (Zone 4), all others being hardy through most winters in Zone 5, except *W. hortensis* which is only hardy in Zone 6. This species has entered into the parentage of several hybrids such as 'Deboisii', 'Dame Blanche' and 'Mont Blanc', so that one can reasonably look for more tenderness in such varieties.

Some of the better varieties are:

'Candida'—about the only one with pure white flowers which do not fade to pink.

'Conquerant'—an early blooming variety introduced by Lemoine that has rose-colored flowers about the largest of any, 2 in. in dia.

'Dame Blanche'—a mid-season blooming variety with flowers on the same branch that may be either white or pink. These open white but gradually fade pink, giving the 2-tone effect which to some is pleasing. A Lemoine introduction.

'Eva Supreme'—dwarf, compact and flowers a bright shining red.

'Floreal'—flowers a moderate purplish pink; do not fade as much as those of some other varieties. Early blooming.

'Richesse'—an early blooming variety with flowers uniformly pale pink.

'Seduction'—an early blooming Lemoine hybrid; very floriferous, with flowers about the darkest red of any variety.

'Styriaca'—very floriferous; moderate purplish-pink flowers, best color of any in its group.

'Vanicekii'—one of the best and hardiest of

the red-flowered varieties. The color is similar to that of 'Bristol Ruby' but it is a hardier plant. Discovered by V. A. Vanicek of Newport, R.I., many years ago but he never thought enough of it to grow in much quantity. Eventually some cuttings were sent and propagated in Holland under the name 'Newport Red'. More recently "introduced" as a new variety 'Cardinal Red'. Again grown in Ala. under the name 'Rhode Island Red'. All these are identical and should be termed 'Vanicekii', an excellent, hardy, red-flowering variety.

Propagation

The seed has no particular dormancy requirements, hence may be sown any time. With all the horticultural varieties asexual propagation by softwood and hardwood cuttings is the normal procedure. See CUTTINGS.

florida   9′   **Zone 5**   **Old-fashioned Weigela**
This species is native to Korea and northern China. The flowers are rosy pink, like a funnel, 1 in. long, with rounded and spreading flower lobes appearing in late May and June. The leaves are 2–4 in. long and opposite like all the members of this genus. Some varieties of this species are: **'Foliis Purpuriis'**—purplish-green foliage, pink flowers, dwarf habit about 4 ft. tall; **'Variegata'** —flowers deep rose, leaves edged pale yellow, compact habit and about 4 ft. tall; **'Variegata Nana'**—smallest of all the weigelas, seldom over 5 ft. tall with variegated foliage; **venusta**— the hardiest (with **W. middendorfiana**) Zone 4, graceful in habit with pale, uniformly purplish-pink flowers. This could well exemplify the best of the *W. florida* forms.

middendorffiana   4′   **Zone 4**   **Middendorff Weigela**
This shrub is not seen much in America but it is the only Weigela with sulfur-yellow flowers during late May and June. The flowers are only about $\frac{1}{4}$–$\frac{3}{8}$ in. in dia., in terminal clusters 2 in. by 2 in. It is native to northern China and Japan and, though rare in America, it is very well thought of in England. It does best in a cool, moist situation.

WEIGHTS AND MEASURES. The following are a few of the many weights and measures with which a gardener is confronted when applying pesticide or fertilizer or merely when measuring his garden to determine the amount of seed he must apply.

DRY MEASURE

1 gram = 1 cubic centimeter of water or 1/28 ounce
6 tablespoonfuls = approx. 1 ounce
16 drams = 1 ounce
1 ounce = 28.35 grams
16 ounces = 1 pound

1 pound = 453.6 grams
2 pints = 1 quart
8 quarts = 1 peck
4 pecks = 1 bushel or 2150 cubic inches
2000 pounds = 1 ton
2240 pounds = 1 long ton

LIQUID MEASURE

3 teaspoonfuls = 1 tablespoonful
2 tablespoonfuls = $\frac{1}{8}$ cup or 1 fluid ounce
8 tablespoonfuls = $\frac{1}{2}$ cup or $\frac{1}{4}$ pint
1 cup = $\frac{1}{2}$ pint or 8 fluid ounces (or 2 gills)
2 cups = 1 pint or 16 fluid ounces
2 pints = 1 quart
1 liter = 1.0567 quarts
1 quart = 0.946 liters
4 quarts = 1 gallon or 3.785 liters or 231 cubic inches
1 gallon of water weighs 8.34 pounds
6 gallons = 1 cubic foot
$31\frac{1}{2}$ gallons = 1 barrel
2 barrels = 1 hogshead (all measurements made in level containers)

MEASUREMENT

1 inch = 2.54 centimeters or 25.4 millimeters
1 foot = 12 inches or 30.48 centimeters
1 yard = 3 feet or 36 inches or 0.914 meters
1 meter = 3.28 feet or 39.37 inches
1 kilometer = 100 meters or 3280.83 feet or 0.621 miles
1 rod = $16\frac{1}{2}$ feet
40 rods = 1 furlong
1 mile = 320 rods or 1760 yards or 5280 feet or 8 furlongs
1 acre = 43,560 square feet or 160 square rods or 0.4 hectare
1 acre = a plot of 217.8 feet by 200 feet
1 hectare = 2.471 acres or 10,000 square meters

TEMPERATURE

To change figures in Centigrade to Fahrenheit, multiply by 9/5 and add 32
To change figures in Fahrenheit to Centigrade subtract 32 then multiply by 5/9

WOOD MEASURE

16 cubic feet = 1 cord foot
8 cord feet = 1 cord

WELSH-POPPY = *Meconopsis cambrica*

WET SOIL PLANTS. It is usually advisable to drain wet spots in the garden (see DRAINING) particularly where water stands for any length of time. The roots of most plants (except true aquatics, see WATER GARDENING) require a certain amount of air in the soil and if this is not present, the plants die. However, some plants withstand a certain amount of excess moisture in the soil, and the following plants can withstand more moisture in the soil than most others. If there are wet spots in the garden that can not be drained, plants from the following list might be considered for planting therein.

| SCIENTIFIC NAME | TREES FOR WET SOILS | | COMMON NAME |
	HEIGHT	ZONE	
Acer rubrum	120'	3	Red or Swamp Maple
Alnus sp.	45'–75'	2–5	Alders
Calocedrus decurrens	135'	5	California Incense-cedar
Eucalyptus leucoxylon	50'–60'	9	White Ironbark
Ilex sp.	24'–70'	5–7	Hollies
Larix laricina	60'	1	Eastern Larch
Liquidambar styraciflua	125'	5	Sweet-gum
Magnolia virginiana	60'	5	Sweet Bay Magnolia
Melaleuca leucadendra	40'	10	Cajeput-tree
Nyssa sylvatica	90'	4	Black Tupelo
Salix sp.	3'–50'	2–6	Willows
Taxodium distichum	150'	4	Common Bald Cypress
Thuja occidentalis	60'	2	American Arborvitae

	SHRUBS FOR WET SOILS		
Alnus sp.	9'–20'	2	Alders
Amelanchier sp.	10'–25'	3–5	Service-berries
Andromeda sp.	1'	2	Andromedas
Aronia arbutifolia	9'	5	Red Chokeberry
Calluna vulgaris	18"	4	Heather
Cephalanthus occidentalis	15'	4	Buttonbush
Chamaedaphne calyculata	4'	2	Leatherleaf
Clethra alnifolia	9'	3	Summersweet
Cornus sericea (C. stolonifera)	7'	2	Red Osier Dogwood
Dirca palustris	6'	4	Leatherwood
Enkianthus sp.	15'–30'	4–5	Enkianthus
Gaultheria shallon	1½'	5	Salal
Gaylussacia brachycera	18"	5	Box-huckleberry
Hippophae rhamnoides	30'	3	Sea-buckthorn
Ilex cassine	36'	7	Dahoon
I. glabra	9'–21'	3	Inkberry
I. verticillata	9'	3	Winterberry
Kalmia sp.	1'–30'	2–4	Lambkill, Mountain-laurel
Ledum groenlandicum	3'	2	Labrador-tea
Leiophyllum buxifolium	18"	5	Box Sandmyrtle
Leucothoe fontanesiana	6'	4	Drooping Leucothoe
Lindera benzoin	15'	4	Spice bush
Lyonia mariana	6'	5	Staggerbush
Lysimachia clethroides	2'–3'	3	Japanese Loosestrife
Myrica sp.	3'–9'	2–6	Bayberry, Wax-myrtle
Rhododendron arborescens	9'	4	Sweet Azalea
R. canadense	3'	2	Rhodora
R. periclymenoides	6'	3	Pinxterbloom
R. maximum	12'–36'	3	Rosebay Rhododendron
R. vaseyi	6'–9'	4	Pinkshell Azalea
R. viscosum	9' rarely 15'	3	Swamp Azalea
Rosa palustris	6'	4	Swamp Rose
Sabal minor	3'–4'	9	Dwarf Palmetta
Salix caprea	27'	4	Goat Willow
S. discolor	20'	2	Pussy Willow
S. purpurea	9'	4	Purple Osier
Sambucus canadensis	12'	3	American Elder
Spiraea tomentosa	4'	4	Hardhack
Thuja occidentalis vars.	2'–20'	2	American Arborvitae
Vaccinium corymbosum	6'–12'	3	Highbush Blueberry
V. macrocarpum	Creeping	2	Cranberry

(Herbaceous! perennial!) → *[handwritten note pointing to Lysimachia clethroides]*

SCIENTIFIC NAME	HEIGHT	ZONE	COMMON NAME
Viburnum cassinoides	6′	3	Withe-rod
Zamia integrifolia	1½′	9	Coontie
Zenobia pulverulenta	6′	5	Dusty Zenobia

HERBACEOUS PERENNIALS FOR WET SOILS

SCIENTIFIC NAME	HEIGHT	ZONE	COMMON NAME
Acorus calamus	2′	3	Sweet Flag
Alisma plantago-aquatica	2′–3′	5	Water-plantain
Althea officinalis	3′–6′	5	Marshmallow
Arethusa bulbosa	5″–10″	3	Arethusa
Arisaemia sp.	12″–18″	4	Dragonroot
Arundo donax	6′–20′	6	Giant Reed
Asclepias incarnata	5′	3	Swamp Milkweed
sh. Asperula odorata	8″	2–3	Sweet Woodruff
Aster lateriflorus	4′–5′	3	Calico Aster
A. novae-angliae	3′–5′	2–3	New England Aster
sh Astilbe sp.	2′	5–6	Astilbe
Calla palustris	8″–12″	2	Water-arum
Caltha palustris	1′–3′	3	Marsh Marigold
Calopogon pulchellus	12″–15″	3	Grass Pink Orchid
Camassia leichtlinii	2′	5	Leichtlin Camas
Canna flaccida	5′	7	Golden Canna
Chelone obliqua	2′–3′	6	Rose Turtlehead
Cimicifuga racemosa	6′–8′	2–3	Snakeroot
Coptis trifolia	6″	3	Alaska Goldthread
Cyperus—some species	3′–8′	3–10	Sedges
Darlingtonia californica	3′	7	California Pitcher-plant
Dionoea muscipula	8″–12″	8	Venus Flytrap
Drosera sp.	6″–8″	3	Sundew
Eichornia sp.	Aquatic Plant	8	Water-hyacinth
Epilobium hirsutum	4′	3	Hairy Willow-weed
Erica carnea	1′	5	Spring Heath
Eupatorium maculatum	6′–10′	2–3	Joe-Pye-weed
Ferns, Many kinds	6″–6′	2–7	Ferns
Gentiana crinita	1′–2′	Biennial	Fringed Gentian
Geum rivale	3′	3	Water Avens
Gratiola aurea	1′	3	Golden Hedge Hyssop
Habenaria sp.	1′–4′	3–7	Fringed Orchid
Helenium autumnale	6′	3	Common Sneezeweed
Helianthus tuberosa	12′	4	Jerusalem Artichoke
Hibiscus moscheutos	3′–6′	5	Common Rose Mallow
Houstonia caerulea	3″–6″	3	Common Bluets
Hydrophyllum virginicum	1′–2′	3	Virginia Waterleaf
Hymenocallis occidentalis	2′	5	Inland Spider-lily
Iris—several species	2′	3–4	Iris
Juncus effusus spiralis	4′	3	Spiral Rush
Jussiaea repens	Creeping	7	Creeping Water-primrose
Lathyrus palustris	2′–3′	4	Marsh Pea
Lilium canadense	2′–5′	3	Canada Lily
L. superbum	6′–10′	5	Turkscap Lily
Liparis liliifolia	6″	4	Lily Twayblade
Lobelia cardinalis	2′–3′	2	Cardinal-flower
L. siphiltica	1′–3′	5	Big Blue Lobelia
Lysichitum camtschatcense	1′–2½′	6	
Lysimachia clethroides	2′–3′	3	Japanese Loosestrife
Lythrum salicaria	3′	2–3	Purple Loosestrife
Mentha pulegium	Prostrate	7	Pennyroyal
Menyanthes trifoliata	Creeping	3	Common Bogbean

SCIENTIFIC NAME	HEIGHT	ZONE	COMMON NAME
Monarda didyma	3′	3	Bee-balm
Myosotis scorpioides	12″–20″	3	True Forget-me-not
Peltandra virginica	12″	4	Virginia Arrow-arum
Primula japonica	2′	5	Japanese Primrose
Ranunculus—several sp.	6″–4′	3–6	Buttercups
Sagittaria latifolia	4′	4	Common Arrowhead
Sarracenia—several sp.	12″–3′	3–7	Pitcher-plant
Saxifraga pennsylvanica	3′	Biennial 3	Pennsylvania Saxifrage
Senecio aureus	1′–2′	4	Golden Groundsel
Smilacina trifolia	15″	3	Labrador Solomon's-seal
Symplocarpus foetidus	10′–12′	4	Skunk-cabbage
Thalia dealbata	6′	7	Water-canna
Trollius sp.	1′–2′	3–5	Globeflower
Typha sp.	1′–6′	3–8	Cattails
Valeriana officinalis	4′	5	Common Valerian
Veratrum viride	2′–4′	3	American False Hellebore
Viola—several species	6″–8″	2–6	Violets

WHEAT = *Triticum aestivum*

WHEAT-GRASS, BLUESTEM = *Agropyron smithii*

WHEEL-STAMEN TREE = *Trochodendron aralioides*

WHISPERING-BELLS, YELLOW = *Emmenanthe penduliflora*

WHITE-CEDAR = *Chamaecyparis thyoides*

WHITE FORSYTHIA. = See ABELIOPHYLLUM.

WHITE POPINAC = *Leucaena glauca*

WHITETOP, PEPPERWEED = *Cardaria draba*

WHITLOWGRASS = *Draba aizoides*

WHORL. The arrangement of 3 or more like organs in a circle around the axis.

WHORLFLOWER = *Morina longifolia*

WILD-PLANTAIN = *Heliconia bihai*

WILLOW. See SALIX.

WILLOW FAMILY = Salicaceae

WILLOWLEAF-OXEYE = *Buphthalmum salicifolium*

WILLOW-MYRTLE = *Agonis flexuosa*

WILT. In addition to lack of soil moisture and excess transpiration which cause wilting, there are several fungi and bacteria which produce this condition. Verticillium wilt is almost universal and infects many perennial plants including elm, maple, strawberries, raspberries, tomato, eggplant, chrysanthemum, rose and fruit trees. It lives in the soil and infects the roots and water-conducting cells of the plant causing wilting of foliage. Fungicidal sprays are ineffective and removal, sanitation, soil sterilization and rotation are suggested.

Fusarium wilt is also common and species of this fungus attack China Aster, Cabbage and related plants, Carnation, Celery, Gladiolus, peas, Sweet Potato and Tomato. Seed treatment, soil disinfection and rotation are the recommended controls. Bacterial disease causing wilt occurs on Carnation, Sweet Corn (Stewart's disease), cucurbits (see these plants); cephalosporium (Dothiorella) wilt or die back of elms causes wilted, yellow foliage and dead twigs. It can be identified only by culture. Prune the infected branches.

WINDBREAK. In the eastern United States the term "windbreak" is usually applied to a single or double line of trees planted to break the force of prevailing winds during some particular season. Houses or gardens built near the seashore must often be protected from high winds off the ocean. Greenhouses are frequently protected from high winter winds, for this greatly reduces expensive heating bills. Then, too, a house built on a hill or in an exposed situation can often be effectively protected from high winds by planting a simple windbreak. If properly spaced and sufficiently tall, such a windbreak should aid materially in cutting the fuel bill during the winter. In such situations, the windbreak would be a very simple thing, merely a single or double line of trees of sufficient height, planted over a length sufficient to protect the area in question.

In the Great Plains area of the West, the term "shelterbelt" has been used instead of windbreak, for in this region such a barrier must be more than just an obstruction to the wind. Tree plantings are often necessary to keep snow from objectionable drifting and to prevent the wind erosion of soil and the drifting of windblown soil about the home grounds. A shelterbelt planting includes several lines of different kinds of trees and shrubs, interplanted in such a way as to offer considerable resistance to the prevailing winds, winter and summer.

Shelterbelts are used not only for the protection of buildings, but also for the protection of crops as well. In the East, almost any dense-growing tree or shrub can be used in the wind-break planting. However, in the Great Plains area of the West there are only a comparatively few of the most hardy types of plants which are able to survive the bitter cold winters and the extreme heat and drought of the summers. Many different types of plants have been tried at one time or another, but there are only a comparatively few types which have successfully with-stood the severe droughts of the past few years. Such plants are Boxelder, Chinese Elm, Choke-berry, and others with little ornamental value have been found to withstand the extremely trying, climatic conditions of the Great Plains; consequently only a few types can be recommended for use in shelterbelts.

The exact spot where the windbreak should be located with reference to the house or garden naturally depends on the height of the wind-break, its length, and the velocity of the wind. No definite recommendations can be given except to suggest that if the windbreak is to be of real service, it usually should be located between 20 and 75 ft. from the house and planted so that the prevailing winds will hit it broadside. If, after it has reached sufficient height, it does not give satisfactory protection, its length can be increased thus increasing the depth of the protected area. When there is a question concerning its location usually the closer it is to the house, the better the protection.

In windbreaks, as in shelterbelts, the planting is fairly close, the idea being to grow a leafy barrier of sufficient density to decrease the velocity of the wind. In shelterbelts the suggested planting distances are 2 by 2, 4 by 8, and 6 by 12, depending on the type of plant material used. However, with the dense columnar-growing trees available it is not necessary to plant less than 5 ft. for a normal windbreak, particularly on small properties. With shelter-belt plantings it is different, for the number of plants from which to choose is greatly limited. In this case, the plants should be chosen primarily for their ability to withstand the severe climatic conditions rather than for their density.

A cross-section of a typical shelterbelt planting would show the taller trees in the center, the smaller trees on either side, and a low planting of some good dense hedge shrubs to taper the planting well down to the ground. It is essential to make these low plantings as dense as possible to prevent wind from creeping through. It is often customary to use evergreens on the outside in order to give protection both winter and summer.

The area protected by such a shelterbelt varies considerably. If the wind does not shift, but hits such a planting squarely, the protected area will be triangular in general outline. It is readily seen that the longer the line of trees, the deeper the area protected.

In certain sections of the northwestern U.S. and southern Canada landowners have found it advisable to include in their shelterbelt planting a snow trap to catch the snow and prevent it from drifting into places where it would be undesirable. This type of planting is of value only in areas with a heavy snowfall and with prevailing high winds in the winter.

The following is a list of a few plants which can be used in shelterbelt planting in the Mid-west. There are other plants of course, selected for special areas, but these suggested here have been widely used and might be studied first in making selections:

Acer negundo	Boxelder
Amelanchier alnifolia	Saskatoon
Caragana arborescens	Siberian Pea-tree
Celtis occidentalis	Hackberry
Elaeagnus angustifolia	Russian-olive
E. argentea	Silverberry
Fraxinus pensylvanica lanceolata	Green Ash
Gleditsia triacanthos	Common Honeylocust
Juniperus scopulorum	Colorado Juniper
J. virginiana	Redcedar
Lonicera tatarica	Tatarian Honeysuckle
Picea glauca	White Spruce
P. pungens	Colorado Spruce
Pinus ponderosa	Western Yellow Pine
Populus species	Poplars
Prunus americana	American Plum
P. virginiana	Common Chokeberry
Pseudotsuga menziesii	Douglas-fir

Quercus macrocarpa	Mossycup Oak
Salix alba	White Willow
S. pentandra	Laurel Willow
Syringa species *	Lilacs
Ulmus pumila	Dwarf Asiatic Elm

WINDFLOWER = *Anemonella thalictroides*

WINDOW BOX. The growing of plants in boxes on the balcony or on the windowsill is not only a source of pleasure but at the same time a worthy contribution to the beautification of a city or town.

The procedure itself is rather simple but, to be fully successful and to achieve long-lasting displays, certain governing principles must be heeded. The most important of these principles is that plant culture in boxes is a distinct type of gardening, very different from gardening in the open ground. Not only are the plants confined, which means that the space available for the spread of their roots is limited but they also are much more exposed.

Most serious is the exposure of the roots of the plants, which in the soil of the garden are well sheltered. In the box, only the outer wall protects them from the heat of the sun, and overheating of the soil, which easily happens on a hot summer day, is the most common cause of failure with window boxes. For this reason, metal boxes are undesirable because they are much more likely to overheat than wooden ones. That a dark-colored box is warmer than a light-colored one is equally evident. This must be carefully considered, especially in regions with ample sunshine and hot summers.

The keen root competition between the plants, caused by their confinement in a box, results in rapid exhaustion of the nutrients contained in the limited amounts of available soil. Under such conditions, annual summer flowers quickly go to seed and die. To prevent this, judicious feeding with a complete fertilizer is absolutely essential; quite contrary to garden culture, where most annuals thrive best in a lean soil and, when given additional fertilizer, are likely to become too leafy, producing few or no flowers.

The ornamental effects, which one may achieve with window boxes, are also entirely different from those in the garden and, because of the small number of plants involved, leaf texture becomes almost as important in the effect of a composition as flower color. There is no doubt that the careful planning of a flower-box display is as much worth while as the planning of the layout of a garden.

Observation of the details outlined below will not only bring greater satisfaction but will also save labor.

Size of the Box

No matter what length of railing or sill is to be ornamented with flowers, it is undesirable to construct very long boxes which are awkward to handle. Boxes should never be made so small that the plants can not develop properly and dry out. The opportunity for an attractive arrangement must also be considered in the size of the box. The following dimensions have been found most generally satisfactory:

3 to 4 ft. long, 8 to 10 or 11 in. wide (inside) on top, 6 to 8 in. wide at the bottom, and 7 to 8 in. deep.

Such reasonably short boxes will not only be lighter but also more stable than longer ones and can, of course, be lined up to any desired length. For special effects they may also be planted alternately or in groups with different, though harmonizing or contrasting plants. A greater depth of the box is unnecessary and even undesirable. An upper width of 7 to 8 in. will accommodate 2 rows of plants; 10 or 11 in. will provide space for 3 rows, permitting a more elaborate display. Greater width again is undesirable because proper watering then becomes more difficult, the outer rows drying out more quickly than those in the middle. In addition, it is evident that the wider the box is the less stable it is.

Construction of the Box

Wood, presswood or laminated wood is still the best of all possible materials for the construction of a window box. Not only is wood most easily workable, so that the box can be made at home by anybody who can handle tools, but it also has considerable insulating properties, much desired as protection from overheating by the sun. To take full advantage of this insulation, the boards should be about 1 in. thick. Thinner boards are undesirable also because they are likely to warp badly. After being cut to size, the boards should be fastened together with brass screws, not with nails because nails will pull out and the box falls apart, when the soil in the box is watered. For the safe placing of the screws it is advisable to drill holes for them before they are inserted.

The bottom board must be provided with drainage holes which should be about $\frac{1}{2}$ in. in dia. and may be spaced 6 to 9 in. apart, preferably in 2 alternating rows. If the box is not suspended but is to stand on the floor of the balcony or on a sill, its bottom must be slightly raised by means of $\frac{1}{2}$ to 1 in.-thick strips of wood, nailed along the short sides of the box. Otherwise, drainage will be blocked.

Painting of the Box

The finished box must be painted, not only for appearance but also to preserve the wood. Both the outside and the inside must be painted, which is advisable also because painting the boards on 1 side only is likely to cause warping. Actually, the inside, being most exposed to rotting, needs the painting most. A quick-drying paint is most suitable and after the paint is dry the inside surfaces should be wiped with a moist cloth to remove all paint residues before the soil is filled in.

The most generally recommendable color for a window box is cream which readily blends with all other colors and sets them off to best advantage. Dead white is much less desirable and green which is most frequently chosen is the least desirable of all colors because it clashes with the varying shades of green of the plants. It has already been pointed out that a light color should be chosen in preference to a dark one.

Boxes suspended from a balcony rail or placed on a windowsill must be securely fastened.

Soil and Drainage

The bottom of the box must be covered with a $1\frac{1}{2}$–2-in. layer of drainage material to prevent the drainage holes from clogging and the soil from being washed out. The most desirable material for this purpose is one which is porous, such as potsherds, weathered hard-coal cinders, or broken up brick. Such a material will not only allow surplus water to pass through but will absorb some of it, as well as some of the washed-out soil nutrients, holding them in reserve where the plant roots can find them when needed. If no such material is available, gravel ($\frac{1}{4}$ to $\frac{1}{2}$ in. size) may be used but since gravel is non-absorbent, it is advisable to cover it with a 1-in. layer of sphagnum moss (not peat moss) as a separation between gravel and soil.

The soil for a window box should be reasonably rich, especially in nutrients which become available gradually, yet must be of such consistency that it does not pack down tight when watered.

A good mixture is the following:
   3 parts garden soil (and/or leaf mold),
   1 part granulated peat moss
   $\frac{1}{2}$ part sharp builder's sand
To each bushel of this mixture should be added 1 3-in. flower potful of bonemeal and half that amount of dehydrated sheep manure. All these ingredients must be thoroughly mixed and moderately moistened before they are placed in the box.

It is distinctly advisable to use fresh soil every year. Watering must be adjusted to the weather but should always be so thorough that the water runs out at the bottom. On hot, windy days, this may be required in the morning as well as in the evening. At other times, twice or only once a week may be sufficient. Light watering, only on the top, can actually be harmful.

Feeding

Four to 6 weeks after planting of the box a complete fertilizer should be applied once a week (1 level teaspoonful dissolved in 1 gal. of water, not stronger). Without such feeding, the plants will not develop to their fullest potentiality and will not last out the season.

The Self-watering Window box

By applying the principles of hydroponics, a window box can be constructed which may be left unattended for 4 or 5 days and which never drips. Such a box has a double bottom, and the lower compartment contains a tin tray, holding a fertilizer solution. Glass-wool wicks take this solution into the upper compartment which is filled with vermiculite instead of soil. The plants are inserted with all the soil which adheres to their roots. Such a box is highly satisfactory and all kinds of plants thrive equally well in it. The only critical points are that the fertilizer used must be very complete and that the solution must never be stronger than 1 level teaspoonful to 1 gal. of water. Otherwise, salt accumulation will cause stunting of the plants and few if any flowers will be produced. Directions for the construction of such a box are included in the book mentioned below.

Selections of Plants

The choice of suitable plants is extraordinarily wide and easily permits a year to year change of the display for a whole lifetime. Naturally though, one must select plants which are adapted not only to the exposure (full sun, partial shade or shade) but also to the climatic zone in which the window box gardener lives.

The following climatic zones may be distinguished:

   I. Northern temperate zone, with an average frost-free growing period of $4\frac{1}{2}$ months (end of May to end of Sept. or early Oct.)
   II. Intermediate Zone, where winter temperatures drop rarely below $+25°$ F.

III. Subtropical Zone, where winter frosts are rare and very light. A few suggestions of effective displays are:

ZONE I. Sunny exposure: Petunias in red, white, with a hanging variety in front.

or: Dwarf Scarlet Sage (*Salvia splendens*), with Dwarf Orange Snapdragon and with purple (not white) Sweet Alyssum in front.

Partial shade: *Begonia semperflorens* (red, white, pink) with hanging blue Lobelia in front.

or: Red and white geraniums (*Pelargonium*) with hanging *Nepeta hederacea variegata*.

No winter display is possible in Zone I.

ZONE II. This Zone is distinguished mainly by the fact that window boxes need not remain empty during winter. Dwarf evergreens with long, fruiting, red-berried *Nandina domestica* between them will make a pleasing winter display.

During summer, long-flowering Floribunda roses may be displayed in the boxes in this Zone and with light covering may be left in place all winter.

Special precautions should be taken here, as well as in Zone III, against overheating of the box, which should receive an outer lining of a presswood board, with the space between the boards filled with peat moss. The surface between the plants may be covered with washed pebbles.

ZONE III. The long-growing season in this Zone invites the use of some of the long-flowering South-African composites, such as: African Daisy, (*Arctotis*), white or purplish; Swan River Daisy (*Brachycome*), blue, rose or white; Cape Marigold (*Dimorphotheca*), orange; and Gazania, white, yellow, orange or scarlet. All of these are sun loving.

In partial shade one may use fuchsias or gerberas in many colors. In shade the long-flowering achimenes can be highly recommended, as well as other Gesneriads, such as *Sinningia* (Gloxinia) and *Smithiantha* (Temple-bells). All of these require wind shelter as well as shade.

For more detailed information—Teuscher, H., "Window-Box Gardening," The Macmillan Company, 1956.

HENRY TEUSCHER

WINEBERRY = *Rubus phoenicolasius*

WINEBERRY, NEW ZEALAND = *Aristotelia racemosa*

WING. Any membranous expansion.

WINGED-PEA. *Lotus tetragonolobus*

WINGHEAD, TEASEL = *Pterocephalus parnassii*

WING-NUT, CAUCASIAN = *Pterocarya fraxinifolia*

WINGS. In botanical descriptions this is often used to describe one of the prominent parts making up the flowers of members of the Pea Family. The flower consists of a standard or large petal at the top, wings or the 2 lateral parts or petals, and a keel which is the 2 anterior united petals.

WINTERBERRY = *Ilex verticillata*

WINTERCREEPER = *Euonymus fortunei*

WINTER-CRESS. See BARBAREA.

WINTERGREEN = *Gaultheria procumbens*

WINTERGREEN, ONE-FLOWERED = *Moneses uniflora*

WINTERGREEN, OREGON = *Gaultheria ovatifolia*

WINTER-HAZEL. See CORYLOPSIS.

WINTERING PLANTS IN THE HOTBED. It is presupposed that all the plants in the hotbed have been thoroughly hardened off. When real cold weather comes, the sashes are put on the frames, but they should be raised a few inches so that the temperature under them will not be raised extremely high on warm, sunny days. When the ground freezes, then the sash can be closed and shaded with lath or evergreen boughs, the idea again being to prevent exposing the plants to extremes in temperature.

One of the most important things is to see to it that the plants in the frames have sufficient moisture. With the sash on, the soil will not freeze underneath as soon as it will outside the frame, hence water must be applied until the soil freezes in the frame itself.

The covering should be left on the hotbed until March or such time as it is evident the plants outside are soon to start into growth. It would seem inadvisable to turn on the electricity at this time to force early growth, for it would be much better to let the plants come along with those outside the frame. However, if early growth is allowed in the frame, one should take all precautions against allowing low temperatures inside the frame to kill the young foliage.

WINTERKILL. The death of plants or plant parts occurring in the winter. This may be due to several single causes such as low temperatures, sudden extreme drops in temperature, high winds, etc. Or it may be due to a combination of them.

WINTER PROTECTION. In the northern parts of the United States, some plants in exposed situations can be brought through the winter in better condition if they are given some kind of winter protection. This is not to keep them warm, which is impossible, but is to protect them from 4 things:

1. Excessive winds, which dry out the foliage of evergreen plants.

2. Excessive sun or heat, especially on warm days in Jan. and Feb. when the ground is still frozen.

3. The alternate thawing and freezing of the soil in early spring, which is especially hazardous to ground covers and small plants that have been recently planted. This causes "heaving" or actually pushes some of these small plants out of the ground and exposes their roots to drying out and subsequent death.

4. Actual protection against heavy snow, especially to protect foundation plantings from heavy snow sliding off roofs.

All leaves lose water or transpire, through their leaves. In the fall the deciduous plants drop their leaves as they stop growth and this materially reduces transpiration. Evergreens, however, retain their leaves throughout the winter and therefore continue to lose water through them. This water loss is greater when winds are high and when the sun is bright and warm. The roots continue to absorb soil moisture as long as it is available, but if it is not available, either because of a serious drought or because it is frozen, then trouble starts. Water continues to be given off through the leaves and when no more is taken up by the roots to compensate for that lost through the leaves, some is taken from the actual living cells. When too much is lost this way, the cells die, with the resultant browning or death of the evergreen foliage.

Therefore, most winter protection is aimed at reducing water loss from the foliage. It is obvious that if certain broad-leaved evergreens

An evergreen that is "balled and burlaped."

like evergreen rhododendrons, Mountain-laurel or some of the hollies, are planted in a situation where there are consistently high winds during winter, excessively high winter transpiration can result. Also, if such plants are planted in a situation exposed to full winter sun, transpiration on warm winter days can be excessive, and those plants so exposed to wind and full winter sun may have an exceedingly difficult time coming through the winter without injury.

These are the reasons such plants should be placed in protected spots, shielded from wind and partially shaded. When this is not possible, some means of winter protection is in order.

Another type of injury sometimes occurs in the North on the trunks of young trees, especially those recently transplanted from protected places to situations exposed to full sun. This often occurs on fruit trees and is called "sun scald" occurring when in winter the warm sun on the southwestern side of the tree warms the trunk so that it may be well above freezing just before sunset. Then there may be a sudden drop in temperature immediately after sunset of some 20°–30° F. This is enough to cause the killing of some cells on the trunk and larger limbs of thin-barked young trees.

Sun scald is sometimes prevented by wrapping the trunks of recently transplanted, thin-barked trees (Sycamore, Yellow-wood, Beech, etc.) with burlap. Rolls of this about 4 in. wide are available and it is merely wrapped about the trunk, spirally, at transplanting time and left on over the first winter.

"Heaving" young plants out of the soil by the alternate freezing and thawing of the soil in

Wrapping the trunk of a recently planted tree to prevent sun scald of the trunk the first winter.

early spring, or even in the winter during warm days when there is no snow cover, is reduced by mulching. See MULCHING. Pine boughs (not hemlock or fir because the needles of these may not remain on cut branches throughout the winter) pine needles, peat moss, leaves, almost anything 3–4 in. deep, keeps the soil from freezing later in the fall and keeps it frozen longer in the spring. Mulching material to prevent heaving might be best applied after the ground freezes in the fall, and is removed in the spring after the ground has permanently thawed.

These are various ways of reducing the loss of water from the foliage of evergreen plants in the winter. The easiest is to tie evergreen boughs over them, with the butts of the branches thoroughly imbedded in the soil, and the boughs tied just enough to prevent them being moved by heavy winds or snows. Here also, pine boughs retain their needles longer in the winter than do those of hemlock, spruce or fir.

Burlap screens can be erected about the problem evergreens, to give light shade and wind protection. They are usually left open at the top and a foot above the ground for air circulation which is important. Wrapping plants tightly in burlap is not so good merely because there is not proper air circulation. Wrapping plants in polyethylene films can compound the danger of possible injury because of the extremely high heat under such a film when the sun is shining.

Sometimes board shelters are built. These are more cumbersome but are effective over prized evergreens in the foundation planting when they are susceptible to breakage from heavy snow sliding off the roof. One should remember here also, the objective is not to board them up in a light boxlike affair, but to stop snow breakage and usually to leave the sides open to light and air.

Small tender plants, or those recently transplanted that take several years of growth before they are fully established, can be aided in coming through the first few winters by placing 4 stakes about the plant, wrapping burlap on the outside of the stakes to the top of the plant and filling in lightly with oak leaves. Some leaves like those of maple, pack tightly together and this is not desirable. Air circulation is essential and it can usually occur through oak leaves which do not pack but remain loose and fluffy.

New sprays are being offered for reducing transpiration loss from evergreen leaves. There seems to be a difference of opinion about the lasting effectiveness of some of these. The ideal preparation would be one that could be sprayed on the foliage late in the fall reducing water loss from the leaves, but would not injure them in

Winter protection. Merely wrapping a wide tape around an evergreen in the fall is frequently enough protection to save it from breaking up in the winter from the weight of ice and snow.

any way, would not be noticeable but would be an effective cover all winter, wearing off in the spring.

In addition the following suggestions might be made, and certainly these would bring others to mind as well.

1. Prized bulbs, usually planted in the fall, might be planted in wire mesh baskets to prevent attacks from rodents. After observing gray squirrels confiscating many of my small but prized lily bulbs last fall, I can speak with much feeling on the subject.

2. If a light mulch of salt hay or similar material is used as winter protection, placing some brush on top prevents it being blown away by winter winds.

3. Mounding up soil around the base of some winter-tender woody plants aids in preventing these being killed out completely, so that shoots will sprout from them the following spring.

4. Straw mats or rolls are available, excellent covering for rolling over the electric hotbed to aid in keeping plants alive over winter.

5. Tying some plants together with cord (upright junipers, arborvitaes and yews) aids in preventing ice and snow from bending the branches apart and breaking them.

6. Knock heavy snow off breakable branches as soon as it appears and before it has been transformed to ice. Once it freezes, little can be done to prevent breakage.

WINTER-PURSLANE = *Montia perfoliata*

WINTERSWEET = *Chimonanthus praecox*

WIREVINE = *Muehlenbeckia complexa*

WISTERIA (wis-TEE-ria). These lovely twining vines are widely used as ornamentals in the gardens of this country, and those who have travelled in Japan will long remember the striking specimens as they are grown there. They are without doubt among the best of our ornamental vines. They have alternate, pinnately compound leaves and all climb by twining. All vines should bloom, some just will not—at least it may take them 10–15 years to produce their first flowers. It is inadvisable to grow plants from seed. They had best be propagated asexually from plants known to flower early. Grafted plants of one variety, *W.* 'Issai' are known to flower when very young, often at 3 years. But all too frequently valued specimens of other varieties do not bloom for a long time. Then the standard recommendations are to root prune, to prune the vigorous-growing young shoots, and sometimes to give a feeding of superphosphate. These things have been known to help plants bloom, but sometimes even these do not seem to help. The old standard recommendations of top and root pruning, and feeding with superphosphate are best to follow.

There is even a controversy on which soils seem best—that is, in aiding flower production. Planted in a light sandy soil, the plants may grow less vigorously, but tend to produce flowers sooner than when grown in a rich soil where vegetative growth is pronounced. However, E. H. Wilson, who studied this group thoroughly in Japan, made the observation that the larger, better-flowering vines were those frequently planted by ponds where they had an unlimited water supply.

There are about 9 species of wisterias in North America and eastern Asia. The Chinese (*W. sinensis*) and Japanese (*W. floribunda*) wisterias, have far outstripped the others in popular acclaim, at least in northern gardens, because of their profuse bloom, their large flower clusters and their varieties of varying colors and fragrance. Varieties are available with flower clusters from 6–48 in. in length, pink, white, varying shades of lilac, single or double flowers, some very fragrant. The double-flowered varieties make poor ornamentals because their bloom is erratic and the double flowers quickly decay in wet weather. *W. frutescens*, native on the East Coast from Va. to Fla. and Tex., is not a strong vine. *W.*

macrostachya is perfectly hardy, but blooms late, after the leaves are developed so the blooms are considerably hidden by the foliage. *W. venusta* has poor flowers when compared with its 2 Asiatic relatives. *W. formosa* might be considered even a better ornamental than *W. sinensis* because it is deliciously fragrant.

The longest flower cluster measured in the collection at the Arboretum was one 36 in. long, but E. H. Wilson has measured them up to 64 in. long on well-grown specimens in Japan. Soil, moisture, and general culture all enter into the picture as far as length of bloom is concerned. The point is that there are some varieties which, if given optimum growing conditions, will produce flower clusters 3–4 ft. long in this country.

The genus was named in honor of Dr. Caspar Wistar (1761–1818), Professor of Anatomy at the University of Pennsylvania. The first species named was *W. frutescens*, a native of the southeastern U.S. from Va. to Fla. and Tex. About the same time seeds of *W. sinensis* were first sent to England where they were grown and it was not long before some reached this country. The Japanese Wisteria (*W. floribunda*) was first sent to the old Parson's Nursery at Flushing, L.I., by Dr. George R. Hall, whom we have to thank for several of our very best ornamentals. This was done in 1862. *W. formosa* was named from a plant growing on the Sargent Estate in Brookline, Mass., about 1905. *W. floribunda* 'Violacea Plena' first flowered in the garden of Francis Parkman of Jamaica Plain, Mass., before 1875. The original *W. floribunda* 'Rosea', in this country at least, was probably that found in a garden owned by a Japanese years ago in Calif. The entire place was bought by the late Mr. Henry S. Huntington of San Marion, Calif., primarily to preserve this beautiful vine. If seeds are sown of *W. sinensis*, the resulting plants will not vary much, but seedlings of *W. floribunda* (formerly *W. multijuga*) vary considerably, both as to flower color and cluster size.

Some plants like the huge "Rosecraft" Wisteria at Point Loma, Calif., or the excellent plant so carefully tended for many years by Miss Mary P. Barnes of Hingham, Mass., or the huge *W. sinensis* growing in the little town of Sierra Madre, Calif., have created wide interest because of tremendous size and profuse bloom. These have grown to such proportions that they cover hundreds of square feet, and undoubtedly have been propagated. Some may have been given varietal names. So, today, there are many wisterias in this country. Only the better varieties should be grown.

"Tree" or "standard" wisterias are merely vines which have been staked rigidly upright and then the tops heavily pruned for years, thus forcing the stem to grow in trunklike proportions. In the South, wisteria vines are allowed to ramble into the tops of the tallest trees, but it should always be kept in mind that they are twining vines and can kill trees and shrubs on which they climb by strangulation.

In certain parts of China, the natives consider the flowers of *W. sinensis* quite a delicacy. The flowers are collected when in full bloom and shipped to areas of wealth where they bring premium prices. They are steamed and eaten. Flowers of the more fragrant Japanese species are not so valued, for in these the flower odor is very strong and is a continual reminder that they are flowers after all!

The Chinese Wisteria is not quite as hardy as the Japanese (*W. floribunda*). During very cold winters, the flower buds of both may be killed. Some gardeners in the northern states and southern Canada like wisterias so much that they are willing to take the pains of laying the vines on the ground each fall and covering them with soil to protect the flower buds from too low temperatures. This is a considerable effort, since the main stem of the Wisteria becomes very woody and more or less rigid as it grows older, making the vine much more difficult to handle in this way than rambler roses.

It is of considerable interest to note that the wisterias can be sharply divided into 2 groups by the way they twine. Some vines climb by twining from left to right, others twine by climbing from right to left. The 2 named species, *frutescens* and *macrostachya*, and the Chinese Wisteria, *sinensis*, twine by climbing from left to right. The other 3 species (*floribunda, formosa, venusta*) all twine by climbing from right to left. As one looks at a plant which is naturally growing around some upright object, if it starts on the lower left side of the rigid object and grows or twines upward towards the right side, it belongs to one group; if the reverse is true, then the other.

This is most helpful, not only in training the vine properly, but also in identifying it. Of all the Japanese varieties checked on this subject, several plants of each, none showed any variation from twining by climbing from right to left.

Since most wisterias in northern gardens at least are either varieties of *W. sinensis* or *W. floribunda*, distinguishing characteristics between them are needed. The following points might be helpful:

	W. sinensis	W. floribunda
Length of flower clusters	6–12 in.	8–48 in.
Fragrance of flowers	not fragrant	fragrant
Leaflets	7–13, large	13–19, small
Autumn color	none	yellow
Time flowers appear	before leaves appear	with the leaves
Twines by climbing from	left to right	right to left

The following key is offered merely as a help in identification. It is always best to consult a standard botanical reference with complete keys when positive identification is necessary. It should be pointed out that the native wisterias (*W. frutescens* and *W. macrostachya*) and *W.* venusta do not appear often in northern gardens as they are not among the better ornamental types. *W. formosa* may appear, for it is a hybrid and a very beautiful one. The flowers appear similar to its Chinese parent, the fragrance and twining are similar to its Japanese parent.

Wisteria *Species*

Vine twines by climbing from left to right	
Flower clusters 2–5 in. long	*W. frutescens*
Flower clusters 6–14 in. long	
Leaflets usually about 9	*W. macrostachya*
Leaflets 7–13	*W. sinensis*
Vine twines by climbing from right to left	
Flower clusters 4–6 in. long	*W. venusta*
Flower clusters 8–48 in. long	
Leaflets 13 to 19, flowers open progressively downwards	*W. floribunda*
Leaflets 7–15, flowers open all together	*W. formosa*

Order of Bloom

The wisterias bloom throughout a 4 to 5-week period, starting with *W. venusta*, the earliest, and ending with *W. macrostachya*, which blooms after the other have all faded. In fact, it blooms after the leaves are out so that they frequently hide the pale bluish blossoms. *W. frutescens* has not been recorded, but it probably blooms after *W. macrostachya*.

Early—May 6–13—*W. venusta* and vars.
Midseason—May 13–20— *W. floribunda macrobotrys*
                              W. formosa
                              W. sinensis and vars.
Late—May 20–25   *W. floribunda* and vars.
Very Late—June 1–6   *W. macrostachya*

Best for Fragrance

The varieties noted for their delicious fragrance belong mostly to the species *W. floribunda* or its hybrid, *W. formosa*. The true Chinese Wisteria has no fragrance, but it may well be that there are many vines passing in gardens as *W. sinensis* that are actually hybrids (i.e., *W. formosa*). *W. venusta* is only slightly fragrant. The best of all the varieties for fragrance might be: *W. floribunda* 'Kuchi Beni'; *W. floribunda* 'Longissima alba'; *W. floribunda* 'Macrobotrys'; *W. floribunda* 'Naga Noda'; *W. floribunda* 'Rosea'; *W. formosa*; *W. sinensis* 'Jako' (possibly a hybrid).

Wisteria floribunda alba grown as a self-sustaining specimen. (*Photo by Arnold Arboretum, Jamaica Plain, Mass.*)

The length of the clusters varies with the species, variety and growing conditions. *W. frutescens* has the shortest clusters, about 2–5 in. long, thus eliminating it as a desirable ornamental. *W. floribunda* has the longest, some of its varieties having clusters 36 in. long. E. H. Wilson measured clusters of *W. floribunda* 'Macrobotrys' in Japan as much as 64 in. long, grown under ideal conditions. This was a huge vine growing on a bamboo trellis covering one-sixth of an acre. However, this length of cluster can also vary on the individual plant.

Propagation

Although seeds can be sown and germinated if treated previously by the hot water method (see SEEDS), wisterias are usually grafted, layered or grown from softwood or hardwood cuttings, chiefly because these asexual methods are necessary so that the exact flower color will be reproduced. Root cuttings also have been used but even here it may be that the original plant was grafted and, if propagating by root cuttings is used, one will not propagate the desired plant but actually its inferior flowering understock. See SEEDS, CUTTINGS, etc.

floribunda **twining vine** **Zone 4** **Japanese Wisteria**
The hardiest of the wisterias, native to Japan, with alternate compound leaves, 13–19 leaflets in each leaf. The flowers are usually fragrant, open in late May after those of *W. sinensis*, are borne in clusters 8–20 in. long and open progressively from the base towards the tip, not all at once as do those of *W. sinensis*. The standards of the flowers are whitish, the keel and wings cobalt-violet. They have a moderate fragrance. Many varieties have been grown by the Japanese and some of them are: **alba**—flowers white, moderate fragrance and dense cluster; **'Beni fugi'**—flowers light reddish violet to violet, fragrance fair; **'Geisha'**—flowers violet to bluish violet, fragrance moderate; **'Kuchi Beni'**—flowers pinkish white giving a slightly faded appearance, fragrant; **'Longissima'**—flowers reddish violet to violet. Some nurserymen have given this name to selected seedlings so plants of this name are probably mixed; **'Longissima Alba'**—flowers white, good fragrance; **'Macrobotrys'**—flowers reddish violet to violet, fragrance excellent; supposedly this is the variety with the longest flower clusters for they have been measured up to 36 in. long in America and up to 64 in. long when grown in Japan under ideal conditions; **'Naga Noda'**—flowers reddish violet to violet; fragrance excellent; **'Rosea'**—flowers light pink, excellent fragrance; **'Shiro Noda'**—listed as having racemes 24–30 in. long; flowers white, moderate fragrance.

x formosa **twining vine** **Zone 5** **Formosa Wisteria**
This is a hybrid (*W. floribunda* x *W. sinensis*) originating about 1905. The flowers are violet to bluish violet, opening all together during late May and are very fragrant. The clusters are about 12 in. long. It may well be that many of the so-called Chinese wisterias in gardens today are actually this hybrid.

frutescens **twining vine** **Zone 5** **American Wisteria**
This has lilac-purple flowers in clusters 2–4½ in. long. It is native from Va. to Fla. and Tex.,

blooming in June. It is not one of the better ornamental vines.

japonica twining vine Zone 7 **Nippon Wisteria**
The white flowers of this Japanese species are borne in clusters 6–12 in. long but they are less showy than those of *W. macrostachya*. The leaflets in each leaf are 9–13.

macrostachya twining vine Zone 5 **Kentucky Wisteria**
A native of the Mo., Tenn., Tex. area, the flowers of this Wisteria are lilac purple with the clusters being about 10 in. long and appearing in early June, after the leaves have opened. Its only merit is the fact that it blooms late, after most of the other species in mid- to late June.

sinensis twining vine Zone 5 **Chinese Wisteria**
This (or the Formosa Wisteria) is the most popular and widely planted at present in America. The flowers are blue-violet, slightly fragrant, and borne in 7–12-in. clusters during late May, usually a week before those of *W. floribunda*, but they remain in bloom long enough so both species can be seen in bloom together. The variety '**Alba**' has white flowers and '**Jako**' in the trade is probably a selected form of 'Alba' that is extremely fragrant. Both are excellent varieties.

venusta twining vine Zone 5 **Silky Wisteria**
The flower clusters of this species are only 3 in. long and are thin and open, having little fragrance, making it a poor ornamental. This has been cultivated in Japan, but is not much used in America.

WITCHES BROOM. This is a dense bushy growth frequently seen on woody plants, especially Blueberry, Cherry, Spruce, Pine, Fir, Hackberry, caused by a parasitic fungus and mite. They do no damage to the tree except they do make the common Hackberry (*Celtis occidentalis*) unsightly. In the case of the evergreens, when they are reproduced by cutting or grafting, the same bushlike dwarf character of the growth is retained. The Norway Spruce (*Picea abies*) has probably produced more of these growths, judging from the number of dwarf varieties being grown today, than any other single species. There is always a possibility that, with asexual propagation (cuttings or grafts) good ornamental dwarf specimens can be obtained from many of these growths.

WITCH-HAZEL. See HAMAMELIS.

WITCH-HAZEL FAMILY = Hamamelidaceae

WITHE-ROD = *Viburnum cassinoides*

WOADWAXEN. See GENISTA.

WOLFBERRY, CHINESE = *Lycium chinense*

WOMANS-TONGUE-TREE = *Albizia lebbek*

WOOD ASH. Often "put on the garden" when it is available, this contains 5–25% potash, 2% phosphoric acid and 30–35% lime, but it varies depending on the kind of wood burned. Hardwoods make the best kind of ash for soil improvement. It may be used at the rate of 4–5 oz. per sq. yard, but it should not be soaked with water or left out in the open before use since this takes out much of the potash. Hence it can be used to raise the soil acidity.

Coal ashes, on the other hand, are not beneficial to plants and should not be used as a soil amendment.

WOOD-BETONY = *Pedicularis canadensis*

WOODBINE, CHINESE = *Lonicera tragophylla*

WOOD-MINT = *Blephilia ciliata*

WOOD-NYMPH = *Moneses uniflora*

WOOD-ROSE = *Merremia tuberosa*

WOODRUFF. See ASPERULA, GALIUM.

WOODSIA (WOOD-sia)
alpina 5" Zones 2–3
A small fern, native to the Northern Temperate Zone and growing in tufts, generally preferring a shady spot in moist woodlands with acid soil.

ilvensis 3"–6" Zone 3 **Rusty Woodsia**
An excellent fern for the rock garden. The small fronds are only an inch wide, 1–2 pinnate and a gray-green color. Sometimes known as the Rusty Cliff Fern because of its rusty color on the undersurface at maturity. It does need some moisture, for with long periods of dry weather the fronds merely dry up and new ones do not grow again until moisture is provided. Native to northeastern North America. For culture and propagation see FERNS.

obtusa 12"–16" Zone 3 **Common Woodsia**
Larger than Rusty Woodsia but native to the same general area of northeastern North America, this has fronds which can be up to 4 in. wide and are 2 pinnate. The color is gray-green. It is easy to grow and is often used in the rock garden. For culture and propagation see FERNS.

WOOD-SORREL. See OXALIS.

WOOD-SORREL FAMILY = Oxalidaceae

WOODWARDIA (wood-WAR-dia)
areolata 2' Zone 4 **Narrow-leaved Chain Fern**
Native to the eastern U.S., this inhabits bogs, swamps and marshy places in acid soils. The foliage is glossy and dark green, the sterile fronds are deeply lobed at the end but toward the middle they are pinnate. The fertile fronds have much more narrow pinnae although the fronds themselves are larger. It spreads rapidly from a creeping rhizome, sending up fronds at intervals

throughout its length and, in an established planting, making dense mats of rhizomes and clumps of fronds. The name Chain Fern comes from the fact that the sporangia on the underside of the fronds are so arranged that they look like 2 lines of chain links. Propagated by division. For spore propagation see FERNS.

virginica 3′–4′ **Zone 4 Virginia Chain Fern** Somewhat similar to *W. areolata*, but fronds longer. This also is a vigorous spreader in swampy, acid soil. For propagation see FERNS. Native to eastern North America.

WOOLLY. Clothed with long and entangled soft hairs.

WORMSEED, AMERICAN = *Chenopodium ambrosioides*

WORMWOOD. See ARTEMISIA.

WREATH. See CHRISTMAS DECORATIONS.

WULFENIA (wulf-EE-nia)

carinthiaca 9″ **Zone 5 Corinthian Wulfenia** A low herbaceous perennial grown in the rock garden, with oblong leaves 8 in. long and racemelike clusters of blue, tubular, 4-lobed flowers, each about ⅓ in. long on stalks 2 ft. tall. Native to Greece. Propagated by division and seeds.

WYETHIA (wy-ETH-ia)

angustifolia 2′ **Zone 9 Narrowleaf Wyethia** An herb native to Calif., with alternate, usually entire, lanceolate leaves up to a foot long or longer; the flower heads are yellow with the rays 2 in. long. This belongs to the Composite Family. Not often used in the garden.

X

XANTHISMA (zan-THIS-ma)

texanum   1′–3′   **annual**   **Star-of-Texas**
With yellow, composite, daisylike flower heads,
2 in. across, with bloom starting about midsummer. The alternate gray-green leaves are
linear and about 2½ in. long. A fine bedding
plant, good for cutting purposes, which is one
of the last of the fall-flowering garden annuals to
be killed by frost. Seed should be sown indoors
in March and the seedlings set out a foot apart
in late May.

XANTHIUM (ZAN-thium) sp.   3′   **annual**
                                        Cocklebur
Several species of this noxious weed, both native
and introduced, are growing throughout the
U.S. and southern Canada. The alternate leaves
have long petioles, are triangular or heart
shaped and coarsely toothed and bristly. The
flowers are rather inconspicuous, the heads are
unisexual and the fruits are inch-long burrs that
will stick to any clothing or fur that touches
them. They should be cut and kept from fruiting.
For control, see WEED-CONTROLLING CHEMICALS.

XANTHOCERAS (zan-THOS-ee-ras)

sorbifolium   20′   **Zone 5**   **Shinyleaf Yellow-
                                         horn**
Little known but occasionally seen, this native
of North China has shiny, pinnately compound
leaves with 9–17 leaflets each up to 2 in. long,
lustrous and dark green. The small white flowers
are produced in wisterialike racemes 10 in. long
during late May and the green burrs as fruits
are somewhat similar to those of the horse-
chestnuts. An unusual plant, usually a shrub
and difficult to transplant, but does well in
shaded, damp places.

XANTHORHIZA (zan-tho-RY-za)

simplicissima   2′   **Zone 4**   **Yellow-root**
A native ground cover frequently found from
N.Y. to Fla. It grows into a dense mass of
foliage and increases rapidly by underground
stolons. The beauty of this as a ground cover
is that it keeps a regular uniform height of 2 ft.
It is only of value for its foliage which turns a
good yellow to reddish orange in the fall, since
the small purplish flowers, appearing before the
leaves, are none too conspicuous. The bark and
root of this plant are yellow.

Propagation

Very easily accomplished merely by dividing

the plants in the early spring before growth
starts.

XANTHOSOMA (zan-tho-SO-ma)

atrovirens   5′   **Zone 10**   **Darkleaf Malanga**
Tropical herbs with thick tuberous rhizomes,
arrow-shaped leaves 3 ft. long, 2 ft. wide, dark
green above, gray-green below and borne on
petioles 2 ft. long. Native to South America and
the West Indies. Flowers are spathes. Grown
in the Tropics for their edible roots and in
greenhouses for their colorful leaves.

lindenii   3′   **Zone 10**   **Linden's Malanga**
Native to Colombia, sometimes grown as a
greenhouse plant for its handsome white-veined
foliage, the arrow-shaped leaves of which are
about a foot long and half as wide. The white
spathe is 6 in. long. It is not as showy a plant
as Caladium but makes a much better house
plant. Difficult to propagate by offsets; hard to
find but still worth looking for as a house plant.
Usually grown in a warm greenhouse with
winter temperatures no less than 55° F.

sagittifolium   6′   **Zone 10**   **Yautia Malanga**
This has a 3-ft. trunk, and arrow-shaped leaves
3 ft. long and almost as wide, with petioles 3 ft.
or longer. Spathes are greenish and about 9 in.
long. Also grown in the Tropics for its edible
roots. Native to South America.

violaceum   2′   **Zone 10**   **Primrose Malanga**
This also grows from an edible rhizome eaten
in the West Indies in place of Taro. Arrow-
shaped leaves 2 ft. long, 1½ ft. wide, green with
nerves colored purplish and purplish petioles
2½ ft. long. The spathes are yellowish white and
a foot long. Native to South America, and the
West Indies.

XERANTHEMUM (zee-RAN-them-um)

annuum   3′   **annual**   **Immortelle**
This is another of the "everlasting" flowers,
making fine garden flowers for cutting, as well
as for drying for use in dried arrangements. It
is a member of the Composite Family with
white, purple, violet or rose flower heads 1½ in.
across, 1 variety (**perligulosum**) with double
flowers. The white-tomentose leaves are 1–2 in.
long. Native to the Mediterranean Region.
Seeds are sown indoors in March or outdoors
in May in the full sun.

XEROPHYLLUM (zee-ro-FILL-um)

asphodeloides   5′   **Zone 6**   **Turkey-beard**
This is native from N.J. to Fla., with leaves 1½ ft.
long, $\frac{1}{12}$ in. wide and 6 in. racemes of flowers;

sometimes planted in the wild garden where it is hardy. A grasslike member of the Lily Family.

tenax   5′   Zone 5   Elkgrass, Beargrass
A grasslike member of the Lily Family, the leaves of which are used by the west coast Indians in weaving baskets. The creamy-white flowers bearing purple stamens are borne in summer in 20-in. racemes on 5-ft. stems. Native from British Columbia to Calif. Sometimes planted as a graceful addition to the flower border in the area where it is native.

XEROPHYTE. A plant adapted to withstand long periods of drought, like a cactus, or species of *Crassula*, *Sedum* or *Sempervivum*. These are usually plants of desert areas.

XYLOSMA (xy-LOS-ma)
congestum (*X. senticosa*)   **low shrub   Zone 8**
                                      Shiny Xylosma
A low, tropical, evergreen shrub with alternate, simple leaves with axillary spines; the leaves are ¾ in. long. The unisexular flowers, borne 5–7 in a raceme, are not conspicuous. Native to southern China.

senticosa = *X. congestum*

XYRIS (ZYR-is)
caroliniana   15″–18″   Zone 4   Carolina Yellow-
                                              eyed Grass
A tufted, grasslike plant with linear leaves 5–12 in. long and flowering stalks rising above the leaves. These are crowned with an oval flower head having overlapping bracts. The yellow flowers are borne on short peduncles emerging from the axils of the bracts. Each flower is ¼ in. wide, and has a 3-lobed corolla, 3 stamens and a 3-parted style. This is a bog plant native to the coastal areas from Me. to Fla. and La. and blooms from June to Aug.

flexuosa   18″   Zone 4   Twisted Yellow-eyed
                                      Grass
Strongly resembling *X. caroliniana*, the flower stalks of this plant are bulbous at the base. It is to be found over the same range.

Y

YAM. See DIOSCOREA.

YAM FAMILY = Dioscoreaceae

YARROW. See ACHILLEA.

YATE TREE = *Eucalyptus cornuta*

YAUPON = *Ilex vomitoria*

YEDDO-HAWTHORN = *Raphiolepsis umbellata*

YELLOW-BELLS = *Tecoma stans*

YELLOW ARCHANGEL = *Lamium galeobdolon*

YELLOW-EYED GRASS. See XYRIS.

YELLOW-FLAX, INDIAN = *Reinwardtia indica*

YELLOWHORN, SHINYLEAF = *Xanthoceras sorbifolium*

YELLOW-OLEANDER = *Thevetia peruviana*

YELLOW-RIM = *Serissa foetida variegata*

YELLOW-WOOD, AMERICAN = *Cladrastis lutea*

YERBA BUENA = *Satureja douglasii*

YERBA SANTA = *Eriodictyon trichocalyx*

YEW. See TAXUS.

YEW FAMILY = Taxaceae

YLANG YLANG = *Cananga odorata*

YOUNGBERRY. See BLACKBERRY.

YOUPON = *Ilex vomitoria*

YUCCA (YUK-ka). These members of the Lily Family are native to the semi-desert areas of Mexico, the Southwest, Fla. and the Atlantic coastal areas as far north as R.I. Although some are treelike, most species have no stem, being comprised of succulent, swordlike, basal leaves terminating in a strong, sharp point and an upright flowering stalk, having a panicle of waxy, white, drooping flowers with 6 petals or sepals and 6 stamens. These flowers may be fragrant at night. The plants are highly ornamental and the smaller species are frequently used in the perennial garden where the soil is sandy and not moist in winter.

Propagation

By separating the well-rooted offshoots from the base of the plant; also by root cuttings.

Insect Pests

Black aphids in large colonies clustered on the flower stalks of Adam's Needle ruin the blossoms. A single spray of insecticide #15 eliminates them.

Diseases

Leaf spot on leaves is checked by cutting and burning the infected leaves. Spraying with fungicide #D or #K is effective when justified.

aloifolia   10′–25′   Zone 8   Spanish-bayonet, Spanish-dagger
Native to the southern U.S. and Mexico, this produces a tall, sometimes branched trunk with stiff, pointed leaves 2½ ft. long and 2 in. wide. The waxy white flowers may be 4 in. wide and are produced in a cluster 2 ft. long, flowering late in the summer.

brevifolia   30′   Zone 7   Joshuatree
Grown only in hot dry desert areas, native to the southwestern U.S., these huge yuccas, with trunks sometimes 15 ft. long and toothed leaves 9 in. long, grow in peculiar and interesting shapes. The flowers are greenish white, 2 in. long and are produced in foot-long panicles.

filamentosa   3′   Zone 4   Adam's needle
This is the most popular species by far, probably because it is hardy in the northern U.S. as well as in the southern parts of the country. The creamy-white, pendulous flowers are 2–3 in., across, borne in spikes 1–3 ft. tall about mid-July. The long lance-shaped leaves are an inch or so wide and 2½ ft. long, are stiffly upright, rigid and evergreen, making them conspicuous wherever they are grown. Propagation is made easy by simply cutting or separating some of the numerous suckers from the mother plant, and establishing them in fertile soil by themselves. A variegated leaf form is now available. Some botanists term this species *Y. smalliana*.

glauca   3′   Zones 2–3   Soapweed
The Soapweed has a short, prostrate stem and a cluster of leaves nearly 3 ft. long, thready along the whitish margin. The flower stalk is borne upright and the greenish-white flowers are 2 in. wide. Native to the Southwest, it extends north to Ia. and S.Dak. and is one of the hardiest of the yuccas.

gloriosa   8′   Zone 7   Mound-lily Yucca
In N.Car., the northern edge of its range, this plant generally has no trunk, but in Fla. it has a short trunk. The leaves are 2½ ft. long and 2 in. wide, having a strong, sharp point and a smooth margin. The large flowers, nearly 4 in. wide, are greenish white but occasionally reddish.

Z

ZAMIA (ZYA-mia)

floridana   **3′–4′**   **Zone 9**   **Coontie**
A member of the Cycad Family, usually with an underground woody trunk and a crown of evergreen leaves, each one made up of 14–20 mostly opposite leaflets which are rolled on the margin, blunt at the tip and slightly arched. This was used by the Indians to make soap. The female cones are 5–6 in. long. Native to southern Fla. Propagated by seed, offsets or division, if there is more than 1 crown.

integrifolia   **1¼′**   **Zone 9**
A near relative of the palms, this is a member of the Cycad Family and is an evergreen native of the West Indies, with beautiful, fernlike, dark green leaves, consisting of 14–32 narrow leaflets. It grows well both in sun and shade in poor or wet soil, and is chiefly used in Fla. gardens or those bordering the Gulf of Mexico. This is the species which is supposed to have been used by the Seminole Indians to make arrowroot an important food for them.

ZANTEDESCHIA (zan-tee-DESH-ia).
This is a South African genus of several species, the callas, noted for their large conspicuous flower spathes (white, yellow or pink) and their arrow-shaped leaves. They are members of the Arum Family and are only hardy out-of-doors in the warmest parts of southern Fla. and southern Calif., but a few are being planted outdoors in the Pacific Northwest, in protected areas, and are surviving. If the plants are to flower outdoors in the North, they are started indoors in March or April, planted outside after frosts are over and lifted and dried indoors before fall frosts. They grow from rhizomatous root stalks, planted with just the growing tip of the root protruding above the soil. In most of the U.S. they are cool greenhouse plants but requiring plenty of moisture. The roots are planted in Sept. in 5- or 6-in. pots, using a soil mixture of 2 parts loam and 1 part well-rotted manure.

After they have bloomed and the leaves begin turning yellow, water can be withheld and, when dried out, the pots can be stored on their sides under the greenhouse bench until re-potting time in Sept. Or, if it is easier, the plants can be set out-of-doors in the garden, in the shade, after danger of frost is over and lifted in Sept. for repotting. Mostly propagated by offsets except *Z. elliottiana* which is propagated by seed.

Insect Pests

Aphids on underside of leaves require careful spraying with insecticide #15 to keep them in check. Yellow bear caterpillars with long yellowish hairs feed rapidly in late summer. A few may be handpicked but insecticides #13 or #15 are effective.

Diseases

Root rot which causes yellow leaves and complete rotting of the feeder roots is often very destructive. Old rhizomes (see ROOTSTOCK) must be cleaned of rot and dried. Dormant rhizomes may be soaked in a seed disinfectant such as ethyl mercury chloride or in water heated to 122° F. for 1 hour. Slimy soft rot is controlled by the same treatment. Spotted wilt virus causes yellowish-white streaks and flecks in the leaves. Destroy all infected plants and control thrips which spread the disease by spraying with insecticide #15 or #13.

aethiopica   **3′**   **Zone 10**   **Common Calla**
This is the commonly grown, white-flowered species with arrow-shaped leaves 1½ ft. long and 10 in. wide. The flower (spathes) are 10 in. long. The variety **'Godfreyana'** is smaller and is supposed to be a more profuse bloomer.

albomaculata   **2′**   **Zone 10**   **Spotted Calla**
The leaves of this are spotted with white; the spathes are 5 in. long and creamy white, purplish in the throat.

elliottiana   **2¼′**   **Zone 10**   **Golden Calla**
Leaves to 10 in. long and 6 in. wide, bright green, translucent dots in them. Flowers are yellow, 6 in. long.

rehmannii   **1′**   **Zone 10**   **Red or Pink Calla**
Leaves narrow with white spots; spathe 3–4 in. long, colored red or pink.

ZANTHOXYLUM (zan-THOX-ill-um)

americanum   **24′**   **Zone 3**   **Prickly-ash**
An American shrub or small tree, native from Quebec to Neb. and Va., the young branches having thorns or prickles; leaves opposite, compound with 5–11 leaflets 1–2 in. long. The male and female flowers are inconspicuous, either on separate plants or the same and the small black fruits, ⅓ in. long, are not ornamental. This is not a shrub planted for ornamental characters but is seen occasionally in wooded areas.

Propagation

Seed may be stratified for 3 months at warm temperatures, followed by 4 months at 40° F., then sown. Root cuttings root readily.

clava-herculis   **30′–50′**   **Zone 6**
Sometimes a tree, sometimes a lower shrub, with trunk and branches prickly, compound leaves a foot long with 5–19 leaflets each 2″ long. Native from Va. to Fla. and Tex.

ZAUSCHNERIA (zaush-NEAR-ia)

californica   **2½′**   **Zone 9**   **California-fuschia**
An erect or decumbent shrub with alternate lanceolate leaves up to 1¼ in. long; useful as a wall cover. Flowers are scarlet and fuschialike in racemes, blooming late in the season. Easily propagated by division, cuttings or seeds. It is said to be very drought-resistant, and is particularly valued for this trait.

ZEA (ZEE-a)

mays   **2′–12′**   **annual**   **Corn**
This is one of the 3 most valuable food plants of the world and probably is native to Mexico. It has been used in many forms for many centuries and of course is grown all over the world especially in the temperate regions. Corn is actually a grass with the male flowers, the "tassels", at the top of the plant and the female flowers lower down on the stalk which eventually form the "ears." The long threadlike styles of these female flowers constitute the "corn silk" familiar to everyone. The species, Z. mays, is the common Field Corn, and several varieties of it are widely grown both for ornament and for food. For culture see CORN.

The species is the common Field Corn which is vigorous, tall-growing and does not contain as much sugar as the Sweet Corn (Z. mays rugosa).

Recently great strides have been made in producing hybrid corn with greatly increased vigor which materially increases the yield per acre. This is produced on a large scale by planting several rows of the female parent (and the immature tassels of these are removed before they mature) interspersed with several rows of the male parent. The resulting seed on the female parent stalks is the hybrid corn so much in demand by farmers in the Midwest because of greater yields.

The variety **everta** is the Popcorn of commerce, a corn with smaller ears and pointed seeds which explode when heated; var. **indenta** is the Dent Corn, not much grown; **indurata** is the Flint Corn with very small, hard ears; **japonica** is a good ornamental grass because the leaves are striped with white, yellow or pink; a fine plant for flower arrangers and colorful in the garden; **rugosa** is the Sweet Corn or Sugar Corn which is so highly valued as a garden plant. Also 'Strawberry Corn' is a variety, with red kerneled

strawberry-shaped cobs about 1½ in. long—an excellent ornamental. For its culture see CORN.

For those who grow "Indian Corn," the colored forms of Z. Mays, one should remember that to obtain the vari-colored kernels (white, yellow, red, black) on a single ear it is well to take pollen tassels from several stalks and hand pollinate the pistillate ears merely by rubbing the tassels over the receptive stigmas on the long silky-hairlike styles. This insures a pollen mixture which is necessary to obtain the vari-colored ears.

ZEBRINA (zee-BRY-na)

pendula   **decumbent**   **Zone 9**   **Wandering Jew**
Often confused with *Tradescantia fluminensis*, but this species has white flowers and green leaves striped with white or yellow according to variety, whereas Z. pendula bears purple flowers, and the upper sides of the leaves have a metallic appearance, the underside of the leaves are purple. This vine and the *Tradescantia* are among the toughest of house plants and extremely easy to grow. They can be rooted in water—even grown for a while in water, and both are excellent in hanging baskets. When *Zebrina* shoots get about 2 ft. long, it is time to either cut some back a bit or to cut off a few 4-in. shoots, root them in sand or water and eventually use them to replace the older planting. The variety 'Quadricolor' is one of the most colorful, with leaves striped green, red and white. Native to Mexico. The genus *Commelina* contains plants somewhat similar but they are vicious weeds and are never used as house plants since the interesting foliage colors and graceful decumbent growing habit is lacking.

ZELKOVA (zel-KO-va)

carpinifolia   **75′**   **Zone 6**   **Elm Zelkova**
Slow-growing and long-lived, this tree from the Caucasus may prove as good as Z. serrata as an elm substitute. It is dense in branching, seldom has much of a main trunk, and the alternate leaves are 1–2 in. long, turning red in the fall. The flowers are small and practically inconspicuous, appearing at the time the leaves expand in the spring. The fruit is a 2-edged drupe about ⅛ in. wide. The bark peels off in irregular flakes.

serrata   **90′**   **Zone 5**   **Japanese Zelkova**
A Japanese tree and elm relative, this is perhaps the most resistant species to the Dutch Elm disease, and so is valued as a specimen and street tree and also as understock on which are grafted some of the so-called "resistant" varieties of elms. The alternate leaves are 2–5 in. long and turn yellow to russet in the fall. It might be accepted as the best substitute for the Elm even though its habit is rounded and its trunk is

Zelkova serrata. Often recommended as a substitute for the American Elm. (*Photo by Arnold Arboretum, Jamaica Plain, Mass.*)

short with many ascending branches. The variety **'Village Green'** is a good substitute for the American Elm, with slightly arching branches. It is highly resistant to the Dutch elm disease. **'Green Vase'** (Plant Patent #5080) is also good.

Propagation

Do not allow seeds to dry out but sow when they are thoroughly ripened. Varieties are grafted on the species. Sometimes half-ripened wood yields cuttings that root. See GRAFTING, CUTTINGS.

ZENOBIA (zee-NO-bia)
pulverulenta   6'   Zone 5   Dusty Zenobia
The Dusty Zenobia is an overlooked native American plant from the southeastern U.S. Closely related to the blueberries, it has white, bell-shaped flowers, ½ in. across, on slender nodding flower stalks in mid-June. The foliage is a beautiful gray to gray-green and it turns a fine red color in the fall. Doing well in sandy, acid soil, it is used chiefly for its fine gray-green foliage, especially as a contrast with normally green-leaved shrubs. Also, it faces the ground well and can be used as a specimen plant which, if pruned occasionally and kept from growing too tall, stays in a well-rounded

mass of foliage and has gracefully upright, arching stems.

Propagation

Easily propagated by layers or division of plants in the early spring before growth starts. Also softwood cuttings can be rooted. See LAYERS, CUTTINGS.

ZEPHYRANTHES (zef-fy-RANTH-eez). Bulbous herbs, belonging to the Amaryllis Family, sometimes night-blooming, with fragrant, single, white flowers, grasslike leaves, native to Tex. and Mexico. Sometimes used for naturalizing and chiefly valued for their flowers blooming in the summer. In Va. and other areas north of their native habitat, they might best be lifted in the fall and stored in a cool cellar over winter.

atamasco   3"   Zones 7–8   Zephyr-lily
This grows in moist meadows and at the edge of woods from Va. to Ala., and Miss. The slender, shiny, grasslike leaves, 12 in. long, are bright green and persist after flowering. The upright, solitary flowers, white, occasionally tinged with purple, are borne on stalks 10–12 in. long. Each flower has a funnel-shaped corolla with 6 segments. A very attractive plant, it may be used to advantage in colonies, much as crocuses are used, but only in those areas where the ground does not freeze deeply. Seeds may be sown in April in leafy soil and the bulbs may be divided in early summer.

candida   1'   Zone 9   Autumn Zephyr-lily
Leaves linear, flowers white, sometimes tinged rose, 2 in. wide, appearing in summer or early fall. Native to South America.

drummondii   10"   Zone 7 Evening Star, Rain-lily
Gray-green linear leaves, flowers white tinged red on the outside, and 6 in. long with the tube about 5 in. long.

grandiflora   1'   Zone 9   Rose Pink Zephyr-lily
Flowers rose to pink, 4 in. wide, blooming in spring or summer, native to Mexico and Guatemala. Popular among gardeners because of its large flowers.

longifolia   6"   Zone 8   Copper Zephyr-lily
Flowers bright yellow and copper colored outside, about 1 in. wide. Native to western Tex. and Mexico.

pedunculata   8"   Zone 7   Red Tinge Rain-lily
Glaucous green leaves, slightly twisted, flowers white tinged red outside, up to 3 in. long and tube about 1½ in. long.

rosea   1'   Zone 10   Cuban Zephyr-lily
Similar to *Z. grandiflora* but the leaves are broader, the flowers smaller and they do not bloom until fall. Not as conspicuous in flower. Native to Cuba.

traubii   10"   Zone 7   Traub Rain-lily
Flowers white and starlike, tinted pink on the outside.

ZEPHYR FLOWERS, AUTUMN = *Zephryan-thes candida*
ZEPHYR-LILY. See ZEPHYRANTHES.
ZIGADENUS (zy-GAD-ee-nus)
   elegans 1′–3′ Zone 3 Mountain Deathcamus
A bulbous grass of the Lily Family of no ornamental value, native from Alaska to Ariz. The leaves are grasslike, grayish and flowers are greenish or yellowish white in terminal panicles. Mostly found in moist soil situations. Bulb poisonous if eaten.
   glaucus 1′–2′ Zone 4 White Deathcamus
This member of the Lily Family has a stem 1–2 ft. long, with grasslike leaves arising from the lower portion of it. An open cluster of creamy-white flowers crown the stem, and these open in late summer or early fall. The plant is native to the Great Lakes region and extends eastward from Quebec to Va., growing principally on limestone soil. Bulb poisonous if eaten.
   nuttallii 6″–18″ Zone 7 Nuttall Deathcamus
Native from Tenn. to Tex., this perennial herb has leaves up to 1½ ft. long and ½ in. wide; with flowers ½ in. wide, greenish white, in panicles, during June. Propagated by division or seeds, bulbs poisonous and sometimes cattle are poisoned by eating the foliage.
   paniculatus 2′ Zone 4 Foothill Deathcamus
Similar to *Z. nuttallii* but more stout. Native from Mont. to N.Mex. Bulb poisonous, if eaten.

ZINGIBER (ZIN-jib-er)
   officinale 3′ Zone 10 Common Ginger
A plant native to the East Indies, the rhizome of which is the ginger of commerce. The "coated" ginger is the rhizome with the rind still on and the "scraped" ginger is the rhizome with the rind scraped off. This is a very beautiful, tropical plant, the flowers developing into a conelike cluster with overlapping bracts, each bract enclosing 1–3 blossoms. It takes 10 months to a year for the plant to mature sufficiently to be dug. Easily propagated by division of the rhizomes. Not to be confused with the genus *Asarum* which contains several ornamental species popularly called "Wild Ginger."

ZINGIBERACEAE = The Ginger Family

ZINNIA (ZIN-nia). At least 3 species native to Mexico, and many garden varieties make popular garden annuals for summer bloom with flower heads almost any color except blue and green. Plants range in size from the dwarf varieties, less than a foot high, to tall plants over 3 ft. high. Flowers range in size from 1–4½ in. depending on the variety. This group is one of the easiest of all garden annuals to grow. Seed germinates quickly in 4–5 days and should be planted indoors only about 3–4 weeks before they are set out. If sown outdoors, sow just as

soon as all danger of frost is over. They can be easily transplanted and should be thinned according to variety and height in order to allow each plant plenty of room to develop properly. Pinching, to produce busy plants, is not as essential as with many other garden annuals, especially if the first flowers are picked. One has a wealth of varieties and colors from which to choose, for with "Dahlia-flowered", "Cactus-flowered Giant", "Super-giant", "Fantasy", "Liliput", "Tom Thumb" and "Persian Carpet" strains there are many available. It is suggested that the gardener study his seed catalogue carefully to select those types and colors which he wishes to grow. Many are available and usually are colorfully illustrated in every seed catalogue.

Insect Pests

   Stalk borer (see DAHLIA) occasionally tunnels the stems and kills the plant above the burrow. Cutting out and killing the borer is usually sufficient. Japanese beetle feeds on Zinnia. See ROSE. Tarnished plant bug stings the buds and cripples the growth. Insecticide #15 or #9 is effective.

Diseases

   In late summer powdery mildew produces white feltlike patches on the leaves which disfigure the plants. Fungicide #M or #V in weekly applications gives control.
   angustifolia 1′ annual Narrowleaf Zinnia
Leaves linear to lanceolate, flower heads 2 in. across and golden yellow, profusely produced; each ray flower has a margin of orange. The plant is densely branched. A popular garden annual, easily grown, profuse flowering and native to Mexico.
   elegans 3′ annual Common Zinnia
Sometimes called "Youth and Old Age," this is the Common Zinnia with hairy leaves, flower heads up to 4½ in. across and almost every color except blue and green. The habit of all the varieties is fairly stiff. Many horticultural varieties, shapes and colors.
   grandiflora 8″ Zone 4 Rocky Mountain Zinnia
A small perennial from the Rockies, with clumps of stiff stems and narrow, hairy leaves. The yellow flowers are similar to the Daisy, but with age the ray flowers turn white while the disk flowers turn red. It requires a loose gravelly soil in full sun. Native from Colo. to Tex.

ZIZANIA (zy-ZAY-nia)
   aquatica 7′–10′ annual Annual Wild Rice
A marsh grass cultivated in eastern North America for its grain and its beautiful stalks which are used for ornamentation. Also, it is

excellent as bird food. The flowering panicle is nearly 2 ft. long and the awns of some of the grains are nearly 3 in. long. Seed should be planted in mud at the bottom of shallow pools (where the water is 3 in. to 3 ft. deep.) or marshes, not in sand.

ZIZIA (ZIZ-ia)

aurea 1′–3′ **Zone 3** **Golden Zizia**

A perennial of damp, shady woods and marshy meadows from Canada to Tex., this erect member of the Parsley Family has compound leaves with irregularly lobed, toothed leaflets and a compound umbel of tiny yellow flowers, each having 5 petals. These appear during the summer. Although rather weedy, it may be used effectively in the moist wild garden. Propagation is by seed sown when ripe or by division of the plants in the spring.

ZIZYPHUS (ZY-ziff-us)

jujuba 30′ **Zone 7** **Common Jujube, Chinese-date**

The Common Jujube of southern Europe and Asia is not especially ornamental but it has been found to withstand heat, drought and alkaline soils in the southwestern U.S. It is cultivated for the edible fruits in the Mediterranean Area. These fruits are datelike, up to 1 in. long, and dark red to black. The leaves are mostly 3-nerved from the base and 1–2 in. long. There are many varieties grown in the Orient.

Although the species is self-fertile the growing of 2 or more varieties in the same location results in better fruit. In America, 'Tusoa', 'Li' and 'Ling' are the most popular varieties. Each bears fruits up to 2 in. across. While the pulp is still solid the fruits may be eaten raw. When fully ripe the fruits are candied, made into butter or mince meat.

As an ornamental tree it has glossy green leaves, is of small size and it is apparently free from serious insect and disease troubles. It has been known to withstand a short temperature drop down to +22° F.

ZONES OF HARDINESS. See HARDINESS.

ZOYSIA (ZOY-sia). Three species of perennial creeping grasses, with specially selected cultivars, that are being used in the South as substitutes for regular grasses in making lawns. **Z. japonica**, native to China and Japan, with leaves ⅛ in. wide and 1–3 in. long; **Z. matrella** from Korea, often called Manila-grass, with leaves 1/12 in. wide and 3 in. long from southern Asia and the East Indies; and **Z. tenuifolia**, the Mascarene-grass, similar to Z. matrella but even finer foliage, actually creeping from the Mascarene Islands. This makes a flat turf and is being used in Calif. but apprently not elsewhere. For details of how these grasses are used see LAWNS, GRASS.

Christmas cactus—Formerly *Zygocactus truncatus*, now *Schlumbergera truncata*

ZYGOCACTUS TRUNCATUS = *Schlumbergera truncata*

ZYGOPETALUM (zy-go-PET-al-um). One of several orchid genera which are being restudied by various botanists and often split up into several other genera. One such study limits this genus to about 20 species of pseudobulbous epiphytes from tropical America, producing rather large flowers in loose racemes. **Z. mackayi** from Brazil produces leaves up to 20 in. long with yellow-greenish fragrant flowers spotted with brown-purple, up to 3 in. across, blooming in the warm greenhouse from Nov. to June. Usually propagated by division. For culture see ORCHID.

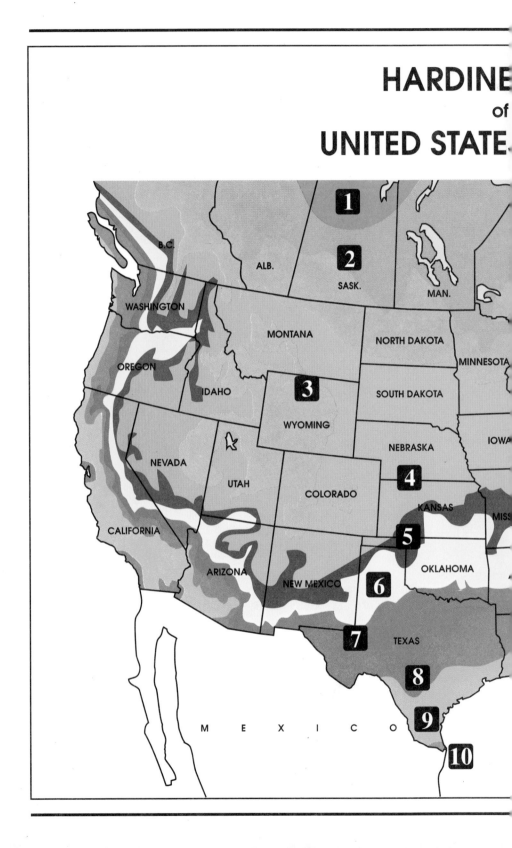